Administration of Government Contracts

Fourth Edition

Wolters Kluwer
Law & Business

Administration of Government Contracts

Fourth Edition

John Cibinic, Jr.
Ralph C. Nash, Jr.
James F. Nagle

The George Washington University
WASHINGTON DC
NATIONAL LAW CENTER

GOVERNMENT CONTRACTS PROGRAM

Printed in the United States of America.

Product No. 0-4750-200
ISBN No. 0-8080-1435-8

PREFACE TO THE FOURTH EDITION

In 1960 the National Law Center of the George Washington University decided to establish a special program devoted to research and teaching in the field of government procurement. We named it the Government Contracts Program and began to teach a series of continuing education courses and to publish in the field. In the early years, we devoted our attention to publishing a casebook on the law, *Federal Procurement Law*, and a series of monographs. The university was highly supportive in establishing two tenured positions on the law faculty devoted to work in the field of government procurement. John Cibinic and I were fortunate to hold those positions for 30 years, enabling us to accomplish the work that we have done.

By 1980 it was clear that our publications were being used by many businesspeople as well as lawyers and that our courses were being heavily attended by contracting officers and corporate contract managers. To assist these people in performing their jobs, we embarked on a project to publish a series of textbooks in the field. *Administration of Government Contracts*, published in 1981, was the first in this series. After the enactment of the Competition in Contracting Act and the publication of the Federal Procurement Regulation in 1984, it became clear that a revision was necessary. Hence, the second edition of *Administration of Government Contracts* was published in 1985. After the enactment of the Federal Acquisition Streamlining Act in 1994 we published a third edition of *Administration of Government Contracts*, in 1995. Now that 10 more years have passed, it is time for a fourth edition.

This fourth edition adds the relevant court and board decisions during the past decade as well as the statutory and regulatory changes that occurred in that period. The organization is essentially the same as the third edition because there has been little change in the basic principles that govern the performance of government contracts. We continue to follow the practice of including a large number of subheadings to distinguish among the numerous detailed issues that are at the heart of contract administration. We recommend that users of the book become familiar with the detailed table of contents as a means of seeing the fundamental logic of each chapter and finding the specific problem area about which information is needed. The subject index can also be used to find a specific topic. Detailed familiarity with the book provides a ready source of research into many, if not most, issues that arise in the various areas of contract administration.

This book complements our other textbooks in the field. *Formation of Governments Contracts* (3d ed. 1998) covers the elements of the government contracting process up to the signing of the basic contract. *Cost Reimbursement Contracting* (3d ed. 2004) covers the many issues that arise in that unique form of contracting. That book deals with cost reimbursement contracting cradle to grave. *Competitive Negotiation: The Source Selection Process* (2d ed. 1999) deals with the competitive negotiation in great detail. Our three-volume *Intellectual Property in Government Contracts* (5th ed. 2004) covers the many elements of the government's treatment of patents, technical data, and computer software in the procurement process.

I welcome a new author, James F. Nagle, to this edition. Jim is a successful attorney and teacher of government contracts. He also is a graduate of the George Washington University Law School with both master's and doctoral degrees. His research has been a substantial asset in ensuring that relevant decisions have been included in the book.

I am sad to report that John Cibinic died on August 1, 2005, just as our editing of the book was being completed. John and I worked together for almost 45 years, co-teaching many courses and co-authoring our books. His analytical ability and writing skill played a major role in making the book what it is. Very few people have the opportunity, as I have had, to exchange ideas and discuss issues with a person of John's competence. He will be sorely missed as we continue to update our books in this field.

Washington, DC
February 2006

Ralph C. Nash Jr.

ABOUT THE AUTHORS

Ralph C. Nash, Jr. is a widely recognized author and lecturer in the Government contracts field. He taught at the George Washington University Law School from 1960 to 1993, retiring to become Professor Emeritus. In 1960, he founded the University's Government Contracts Program and served as its Director from 1960 to 1966 and from 1979 to 1984. In addition to teaching, he does consulting work for government agencies, private corporations, and law firms. He is a member of the Public Contract Section of the American Bar Association, is a member of the Procurement Round Table, and is a Fellow and serves on the Board of Advisors of the National Contract Management Association. He was a member of the DOD Advisory Panel on Streamlining and Codifying Acquisition Laws (Section 800 Panel). Professor Nash is the author of *Government Contract Changes* and the coauthor of several texts, including *Formation of Government Contracts*, *Administration of Government Contracts*, *Competitive Negotiation: The Source Selection Process*, *Construction Contracting*, *Patents and Technical Data*, and *The Government Contracts Reference Book*. He received an A.B. from Princeton University and a J.D. from George Washington University.

John Cibinic, Jr. was Professor Emeritus at The George Washington University Law School where he taught from 1963 to 1993. From 1966 to 1974, he was Director of the Government Contracts Program. A respected spokesman in the field of government contracts, Professor Cibinic conducted seminars and conferences on government contracts for professionals in government and corporations, and for lawyers. He also served as a consultant to government agencies, private corporations, and law firms. He was vice-chairman of the Cost and Pricing Committee of the Public Contract Section of the American Bar Association. Professor Cibinic coauthored several books, including *Formation of Government Contracts*, *Administration of Government Contracts*, *Competitive Negotiation: The Source Selection Process*, and *Construction Contracting*. He received an A.B. from the University of Pittsburgh and a J.D. from George Washington University. Together, with Professor Ralph Nash he coauthored the *Nash & Cibinic Report*, a monthly newsletter.

James F. Nagle, a Partner in Seattle's Oles Morrison Rinker & Baker LLP, received his Bachelor's degree from Georgetown University School of Foreign Service, his J.D. from Rutgers, and his LL.M. and S.J.D. in government contracts from the National Law Center, George Washington University. Mr. Nagle has written five books on federal contracting, *Federal Procurement Regulations: Policy, Practice and Procedures* (American Bar Association Press, 1987); *How to Review a Federal Contract and Research Federal Contract Law, Second Edition* (ABA Press, 2000); *Federal Construction Contracting* (Wiley Law Publications, 1992); *The History of Government Contracting, Second Edition* (CCH Incorporated, 1999), and Whelan and Nagle, *Cases and Materials on Federal Government Contracts* (Foundation Press). He has also co-authored and co-edited *Washington Building Contracts and Construction Law* (Aspen Publishers, 1994). Besides being a contributing author to eight other books, his over 80 articles, on subjects as diverse as protests, changes, terminations, claims, and the Federal Acquisition Regulation, have appeared in such publications as *The Public Contract Law Journal*, *Military Law Review*, *NCMA Journal*, and *Contract Management*.

SUMMARY TABLE OF CONTENTS

Chapter 1—Contract Administration Personnel 1

Chapter 2—Contract Interpretation 155

Chapter 3—Risk Allocation 245

Chapter 4—Changes 379

Chapter 5—Differing Site Conditions 483

Chapter 6—Delays 537

Chapter 7—Government Property 611

Chapter 8—Pricing of Adjustments 659

Chapter 9—Inspection, Acceptance, and Warranties 775

Chapter 10—Default Termination, Damages, and Liquidated Damages 883

Chapter 11—Termination for Convenience 1049

Chapter 12—Payment and Discharge 1125

Chapter 13—Disputes 1231

CONTENTS

Chapter 1
CONTRACT ADMINISTRATION AND PERSONNEL 1

I. NATURE AND PURPOSE OF CONTRACT ADMINISTRATION. . . . 1
A. Nature of Contract Administration 2
1. Working Relationship. 3
a. Cooperation and Good Faith 3
b. Mutual Confidence and Respect 6
2. Timely Identification and Resolution of Problems. 8
a. Problem Identification 8
b. Problem Resolution 9
3. Partnering 10
B. Protection of Public Interest 11
1. Consideration Required 12
2. Competitors' Complaints 13

II. CONTRACT ADMINISTRATION RULES AND THEIR SOURCES . . 16
A. Legislative Branch 16
1. Appropriations and Authorizations. 16
2. Procurement Legislation. 17
3. Oversight Function 17
4. Government Accountability Office. 17
B. Executive Branch 18
1. Procurement Regulations 18
2. Legal Effect of Regulations 19
3. Publication 22
C. Judicial and Quasi-Judicial Decisions. 23
D. Effect of Statutes and Regulations
with the Force and Effect of Law 24
1. Contract Avoidance 24
2. Exclusion or Inclusion of Clause 26
3. Government Bound. 27
E. Deviations and Waivers. 28
1. Deviations from Regulations 28
2. Waiver of Statutory Requirements 29

III. AUTHORITY OF GOVERNMENT AND CONTRACTOR PERSONNEL . . 30
A. Government Personnel 31
1. Actual Authority Required 31
2. Delegation of Authority 33
a. Designated Contracting Officers 35
b. Authorized Representatives. 38

(1) Formally Designated Representatives 39
(2) Other Representatives 41
3. Dealing with Personnel Lacking Specifically Delegated Contractual Authority 43
a. Implied Authority 43
b. Ratification 46
(1) Authority to Ratify 46
(2) Authority to Perform or Authorize Acts Being Ratified 48
(3) Knowledge of Unauthorized Acts 49
(4) Adoption of Unauthorized Acts 51
(5) Ratification and Quantum Meruit 52
c. Knowledge Imputed to Authorized Personnel 53
(1) Technical Representatives 54
(2) Inspectors 56
(3) Administrative and Clerical Personnel 57
(4) Auditors 57
B. Contractor Personnel 58
1. Delegation 58
2. Apparent Authority 58
3. Ratification and Estoppel 59

IV. GOVERNMENT BOUND BY CONDUCT OF ITS AUTHORIZED AGENTS 60
A. Finality 60
1. Sources of Finality 61
2. Authority Required 63
3. Government Bound by Prejudicial Decisions 63
B. Estoppel 65
1. Government Not Estopped by Unauthorized Actions 67
2. Sovereign Capacity Exception 68
3. Knowledge of Facts 69
4. Reliance 69
5. Injury 70
6. Waiver 70
7. Estoppel Improperly Used 71

V. SUITS AGAINST GOVERNMENT EMPLOYEES 72

VI. STANDARDS OF CONDUCT 76
A. Sanctions 76
1. Forfeiture and Cancellation 76
2. Debarment 78
3. Suspension or Dismissal of Government Employees 81
B. Improper Influence of Government Decisions 82

1. Bribery 82
a. Thing of Value 83
b. Corrupt Intent 84
c. Public Official 85
2. Gratuities 85
a. Thing of Value 86
b. Purpose of Gratuity 88
c. Contract Termination 90
3. Conduct of Former Employees 91
a. General Restrictions 91
(1) Particular Matter 92
(2) Personal and Substantial Participation 92
(3) Representation 93
(4) Types of Employment or Contracting Permitted 94
b. Additional Statutory Restrictions 95
4. Conduct of Current Employees 98
a. General Restrictions 98
(1) Extent of Financial Interest 98
(2) Employment Discussions 100
b. Procurement Integrity Restrictions 102
c. Biased Decision Making 105
d. Contracting with Government Employees 105
5. Anti-Kickback Act 107
6. Covenant Against Contingent Fees 108
C. Honesty in Dealing 110
1. Statutory Requirements 110
a. False Claims 111
(1) Civil Fraud 111
(a) Specific Intent 112
(b) Definition of "Claim" 114
(c) Materiality 116
(d) Qui Tam 116
(2) Criminal Fraud 120
(a) Specific Intent 120
(b) Definition of "Claim" 121
(c) Materiality 121
b. False Statements 122
(1) Definition of Statement 122
(2) Knowingly and Willfully 123
(3) Materiality 125
c. Truth in Negotiations 125
(1) Mandatory Submission Requirement 126
(2) Exceptions to Submission Requirement 127
(a) Adequate Price Competition 128

(b) Prices Set by Law or Regulation 128
(c) Commercial Items 129
(3) Definition of Cost or Pricing Data 130
(4) Insignificant Data 132
(5) Submission Techniques 133
(6) Currency of the Data 136
(7) Explaining the Significance of the Data. 137
(8) Subcontractor Data. 138
d. Contract Disputes Act of 1978 139
e. 10 U.S.C. § 2410 Certification 141
2. Types of Illegal Conduct 142
a. Product Substitution 142
b. Mischarging/Accounting Fraud. 143
c. Fraudulent Pricing 144
(1) Fraudulent Data 145
(2) Inaccurate Estimates. 146
(3) Buying-In 147
d. Equitable Adjustment Claims 147
D. Obtaining Information Improperly 148
1. Disclosure of Confidential Information 148
2. Disclosure of and Obtaining Bid or Proposal Information or Source Selection Information. 148
3. Information about Competitors. 152
E. Conspiracy 153

Chapter 2
CONTRACT INTERPRETATION. 155

I. BASIC OBJECTIVE OF INTERPRETATION 157

II. DEFINITION OF TERMS 159
A. Definitions in the Document 159
B. Dictionary or Common Usage Definitions 159
1. Dictionary Definitions 160
2. Common Usage 161
3. Limitations on Dictionary and Common Usage Definitions . . . 163
C. Technical Terms 163
1. Trade Usage 163
2. Government Forms and Regulations 165

III. ANALYSIS OF LANGUAGE OF CONTRACT DOCUMENTS 167
A. Plain Meaning 168
B. Read the Writings as a Whole. 169
1. Interpret to Avoid Rendering Terms Meaningless 170

2. Interpret to Avoid Conflict . . . 172
3. Interpret to Fulfill Principal Purpose of the Parties . . . 174
C. Order of Precedence . . . 176
1. Order of Precedence Clauses . . . 176
2. Common Law Order of Precedence Rule . . . 179
D. Enumerated Items . . . 180

IV. EXTRINSIC EVIDENCE . . . 183
A. Discussions and Concurrent Actions . . . 184
1. Requests for Clarification . . . 184
2. Pre-Bid and Pre-Proposal Conferences . . . 187
3. Pre-Dispute Interpretations . . . 189
4. Pre-Dispute Actions Evidencing Interpretation . . . 190
5. Pre-Dispute Interpretations Made Known to Other Party . . . 194
6. Limitations on the Use of Discussions and Concurrent Actions . . . 196
a. Authority . . . 196
b. Post-Dispute Conduct and Discussions Excluded . . . 198
c. Parol Evidence Rule . . . 199
(1) Integrated Agreements . . . 200
(2) Complete or Partial Integration . . . 201
(3) Contradiction versus Resolution of Ambiguities . . . 206
(4) Establishing an Ambiguity . . . 207
B. Prior Course of Dealing . . . 210
1. Interpretation . . . 211
a. Actual Knowledge Required . . . 212
b. Application to Changed Language . . . 214
2. Waiver of Legal Rights . . . 215
C. Custom and Trade Usage . . . 218
1. Interpreting Vague Language . . . 218
2. Ambiguous Language Not Required . . . 220
3. Clear Language Superior to Trade Custom . . . 221
4. Proof of Trade Practice . . . 224
5. Supplying Missing Terms . . . 226

V. POST-INTERPRETATION AMBIGUITIES . . . 226
A. Finding Ambiguous Terms . . . 227
B. Interpretation Against the Drafter . . . 228
1. Reasonable Interpretation . . . 229
2. Identifiable Drafter . . . 231
3. Reliance . . . 233
C. Duty to Seek Clarification . . . 235
1. Establishing a Patent Ambiguity . . . 237
2. Government Obligation to Inform Bidders of Ambiguity . . . 242
3. Failure to Respond to Inquiry . . . 242

Chapter 3
RISK ALLOCATION 245

I. GOVERNMENT PROMISES (WARRANTIES) OF FUTURE EVENTS OR CONDITIONS 246
A. Availability of Work Site 247
B. Means of Access to Site 250
C. Availability of Utilities 253
D. Issuance of Notice to Proceed 254

II. INCORRECT STATEMENTS AND NONDISCLOSURES 255
A. Incorrect Statements 256
1. Factual Statements 256
2. Laws and Regulations 257
3. Estimates 258
B. Nondisclosures 261
1. Government Knowledge of Vital Information 262
a. Vital Information 263
b. Government Knowledge 264
2. Contractor Knowledge or Reason to Know 266
a. Actual Knowledge 266
b. Reason to Know 267
3. Government Knowledge or Reason to Know of Contractor Ignorance 270

III. IMPLIED WARRANTY OF SPECIFICATIONS 272
A. Basis of Government Responsibility 273
B. Scope of the Warranty 275
1. Type of Specification Language 276
a. Design Specifications 279
b. Performance Specifications 285
2. Specified Alternatives 286
3. Commercial Availability 287
4. Degree of Accuracy Required 289
C. Causation and Reliance 290
1. Contract Formation 290
a. Actual Knowledge 291
b. Reason to Know 292
2. Performance 294
a. Actual Use 294
b. Use with Knowledge of Defects 296
c. Cause of Problem 296

IV. IMPLIED DUTY OF GOOD FAITH AND FAIR DEALING 296
A. Breach by the Government 298

1. Duty to Cooperate and Not Hinder Performance 299
a. Active Interference 299
b. Lack of Cooperation 302
c. Abuse of Discretion. 306
2. Improper Contract Administration 308
3. Lack of Good Faith in Negotiating Modifications 310
4. Lack of Good Faith in Changing Requirements. 311
B. Breach by the Contractor 312
1. Deliberate Inaction in Asserting a Claim 313
2. Lack of Diligence 313

V. IMPRACTICABILITY OF PERFORMANCE AND MISTAKE 314
A. Impracticability. 314
1. Competence of Contractor 315
2. Unforeseen Technological Problems 317
3. Incurrence of Increased Costs. 320
B. Mistake 322
1. Mutual Mistake. 322
a. Mutual Mistake as to a Basic Assumption 322
(1) Basic Assumption. 323
(2) Mutuality 326
(3) Material Effect 328
(4) Assumption of Risk 328
b. Mutual Mistake in Integration. 329
2. Unilateral Mistake 330
a. Type of Mistake. 330
(1) Business Judgment. 331
(2) Misreading Specifications 331
(3) Clerical or Arithmetical Errors. 333
b. Knowledge of Error and Verification 334
(1) Knowledge or Reason to Know 335
(2) Adequacy of Verification Request 338
3. Unconscionability. 339
4. Remedies. 341
a. Reformation. 341
(1) Mutual Mistake of Basic Assumption 341
(2) Unilateral Mistakes 342
b. Rescission 343

VI. GOVERNMENT DEFENSES 344
A. Disclaimer and Exculpatory Clauses 344
1. Public Policy. 345
2. Interpretation. 346
3. Clear Disclaimers 348
4. Misleading Statements and Nondisclosure. 349

5. Effect of Exculpatory/Disclaimer Clauses on Other Clauses . . . 351
6. Commonly Used Exculpatory/Disclaimer Clauses . . . 352
a. Omissions and Misdescriptions Clause . . . 352
b. Production Drawing Changes Clause . . . 354
c. Preproduction Evaluation of Technical Data Clause . . . 355
d. Verification Clause . . . 356
e. Shop Drawings Clause . . . 357
f. Coordination Clause . . . 358
B. Duty of Coordination . . . 359
1. Omissions of Information . . . 359
2. Defective Drawings or Specifications . . . 360
C. Sovereign Acts Doctrine . . . 361
1. Public and General Acts . . . 362
2. Contractual Acts . . . 365
3. Implementation of a Sovereign Act . . . 365
4. Impact of Contract Language . . . 367

VII. PROPORTIONAL RISK ALLOCATION . . . 369
A. Joint Fault . . . 370
B. Joint Negligence . . . 372
C. Improper Default Terminations . . . 373
D. Concurrent Delays . . . 375

Chapter 4
CHANGES . . . 379

I. PURPOSE AND COVERAGE OF THE CHANGES CLAUSE . . . 380
A. Purposes Served . . . 380
B. Coverage . . . 381
1. Meaning of "Within the General Scope" . . . 382
a. Disputes Between Contractor and Government . . . 382
(1) Nature of Work . . . 382
(2) Cost and Disruption . . . 384
b. Third-Party Protests . . . 385
2. Descriptive Words . . . 389
a. The Contract Work . . . 390
b. Terms and Conditions . . . 391
c. Changes in Quantity . . . 392
d. Changes in Time of Performance . . . 393
e. Method or Manner of Performance . . . 394
f. Government-Furnished Property . . . 395
g. Place of Delivery . . . 396
C. Contractor's Acceptance of Change . . . 396

II. FORMAL CHANGE ORDERS 396
A. Contractor-Originated Changes 397
B. Government-Originated Changes 399
C. Unilateral versus Bilateral Change Orders 401
1. Policy 401
2. Modifying Language in Unilateral Change Orders 402
3. Clause Permitting Only Bilateral Change Orders. 404
D. Procedure for Ordering Changes. 405
1. Requirement for Written Change Order 405
2. Standard Form 30 408
3. Obtaining Proposal for Downward Adjustment 409

III. VALUE ENGINEERING 409
A. Standard Clauses. 410
1. Types of Savings. 410
a. Acquisition Savings. 410
(1) Instant Contract Savings. 412
(2) Concurrent Contract Savings 412
(3) Future Contract Savings. 413
b. Collateral Savings 414
2. Uses of the Value Engineering Clause 415
a. Supply and Service Contracts 416
b. Construction Contracts 416
c. Architect/Engineer Contracts 417
B. Interpretation. 417
1. Liberal versus Literal Interpretation 417
2. Applicability of the Value Engineering Clause 418
3. Origination of the Proposed Change. 419
4. Origination by Two Contractors. 420
5. Finality of Contracting Officer Decisions. 421
6. Identification of Proposals Not Required 422
7. Acceptance of Proposals. 423
8. Finality of Contract Modification 425
C. Government Use of Data. 425
D. Unsolicited Value Engineering Proposals. 426

IV. CONSTRUCTIVE CHANGES. 426
A. Basic Theory 427
1. Continuing Vitality of the Doctrine 427
2. Elements of the Doctrine 428
3. Government Claims for Price Decreases 429
B. Types of Constructive Changes 430
1. Disagreements Over Contract Requirements 431
a. Work That Could Have Been Ordered as a Change. . . . 432
(1) Direct Government Orders. 433
(2) Government Suggestions 434

(3) Government Interpretation of Specifications . . . 435
(4) Government Rejection of a Method Permitted by the Contract. 436
(5) "Orders" of Authorized Representatives 437
b. Work Outside the Changes Clause 438
(1) Unauthorized Government Disclosure of Technical Data 438
(2) Improper Exercise of Options 439
(3) Improper Withholding of Progress Payments. . . 440
(4) Government Action Leading the Contractor to Increase Employee Wages 440
(5) Government-Ordered Change in Accounting System 441
2. Defective Specifications and Misleading Information 441
a. Defective Specifications 442
b. Undisclosed or Incorrect Information 443
3. Acceleration. 445
a. Elements of Constructive Acceleration. 446
(1) Excusable Delay. 447
(2) Knowledge of the Contracting Officer 447
(3) Orders to Accelerate. 448
(a) Direct Orders 449
(b) Requests to Accelerate 451
(c) Threats to Terminate for Default 451
(d) Government Pressure to Complete on Schedule 451
(e) Refusal to Grant Time Extensions Plus Liquidated Damages. 452
(f) Refusal to Grant Time Extension and Insistence That Contractor Meet Original Schedule. 453
(g) Failure to Grant Time Extension 453
(h) Delays in Granting Extensions. 454
(i) Denial of Request for Time Extension . . . 456
(4) Causation 456
b. Acceleration to Mitigate Delay 456
c. Post-Constructive Acceleration Time Extensions. . . . 457
d. Acceleration Orders Where There Are Both Excusable and Nonexcusable Delays 457
e. Recovery Not Dependent on Contractor's Recoupment of Lost Time. 458
4. Hindrance or Failure to Cooperate 458
a. Direct Order. 460
b. Actions and Inactions 460
(1) Overzealous Inspection 461
(2) Failure to Provide Assistance. 461

(3) Inaction or Silence 462
(4) Unreasonable Conduct 464
(5) Other Actions 465
c. Abuse of Discretion 465
C. Procedures for Resolving Constructive Changes 466
1. The Contractor's Obligations 466
a. Loss of Control of Work 467
b. Informing the Contracting Officer 468
2. Government Resolution of Problem 470

V. CONTRACTUAL NOTICE REQUIREMENTS 471
A. Assertion of Right to Equitable Adjustment on Ordered Changes 472
1. Contractor Claims 472
2. Government Claims 474
B. Constructive Changes Claims 475
1. Applicability of 30-Day Notice Requirement 475
2. Construction Contract Notice Requirement 476
3. Notification of Changes Clause 478
4. Accelerations 480
5. Military Shipbuilding Contracts 480

Chapter 5
DIFFERING SITE CONDITIONS 483

I. GENERAL RULES GOVERNING APPLICATION OF THE CLAUSE 484
A. Condition Must Predate Contract 485
B. Force Creating Conditions 485
1. Weather and Acts of God 486
2. Man-Made Conditions 487
3. Interaction of Site Conditions and Weather or Other Causes 488
C. Physical Conditions 489
D. "At the Site" 490
E. Differing Materially 491
F. Burden of Proof 492

II. UNIQUE ASPECTS OF THE TWO CATEGORIES OF CONDITIONS 494
A. Category I Conditions 494
1. Contract Documents 495
2. Indications 497
a. Express Indications 498
b. Implied Indications 499
3. Reasonably Unforeseeable 501

4. Reasonable Interpretation 502
5. Reliance 505
a. No Reasonable Reliance 506
b. Reasonable Reliance 508
6. Costs Attributable to Condition 508
B. Category II Conditions 508
1. Unknown Condition 509
2. Unforeseeable Condition 510
3. Unusual Condition 512

III. BREACH OF CONTRACT CLAIMS RELATED TO DIFFERING SITE CONDITIONS 514
A. Misrepresentation and Category I Conditions 515
B. Government Nondisclosure and Category II Conditions 515

IV. INVESTIGATION OF DATA and INSPECTION OF SITE 516
A. Investigation of Data 517
1. Contract Documents 517
2. Data Not in Contract 518
3. Information Known to Competitors 518
4. Reasonableness of Investigation 519
B. Inspection of Site 521
1. Category I Conditions 522
2. Category II Conditions 523
C. Failure to Investigate 524
1. Prevention by Government 526
2. Impossibility 526

V. NOTICE 527
A. Nature of Notice 527
B. Actual or Constructive Government Notice 527
C. No Prejudice 528

VI. PROCEDURE 529
A. Contractor's Duty to Proceed 529
B. Government's Procedure 529

VII. EXCULPATORY CLAUSES 530
A. General Exculpatory Clauses 530
B. Specific Exculpatory Clauses 531
C. Relation to Representation 531

VIII. VARIATION IN ESTIMATED QUANTITIES 532
A. Absent a Variation in Quantity Clause 533

B. Impact of Variation in Quantity Clause . . . 534
C. Interpretation of Variation in Quantity Clause . . . 535

Chapter 6
DELAYS . . . 537

I. EXCUSABLE DELAYS . . . 537
A. General Requirements . . . 539
1. "Beyond the Control" of the Contractor . . . 539
2. Without Contractor's Fault or Negligence . . . 542
3. Foreseeability . . . 543
B. Causes of Delay . . . 545
1. Enumerated Causes of Delay . . . 545
a. Strikes . . . 545
b. Weather . . . 546
(1) Unusually Severe . . . 547
(2) Impact of the Weather . . . 548
c. Government Acts . . . 551
(1) Contractual Acts . . . 551
(2) Sovereign Acts . . . 553
d. Subcontractor and Supplier Delays . . . 555
(1) Subcontractors Designated by the Government . . . 555
(2) Obtainable from Another Source . . . 557
(3) Firms Classified as Subcontractors . . . 558
e. Floods . . . 558
f. Fires . . . 559
g. Epidemics . . . 559
h. Freight Embargoes . . . 559
i. Acts of God . . . 559
2. Non-Enumerated Causes of Delay . . . 560
a. Financial Difficulties . . . 561
b. Lack of Facilities and Equipment . . . 563
c. Lack of Materials . . . 564
d. Lack of Know-How . . . 565
e. Labor Problems . . . 566
C. Time Extensions . . . 567
1. Causation . . . 568
2. Concurrent Delays . . . 568
3. Delay of Overall Completion Required . . . 570
4. Measuring Time Extensions . . . 572
5. Burden of Proof . . . 574
6. Notice and Schedule Extension . . . 575

II. COMPENSABLE DELAYS . . . 576
A. No Applicable Clause . . . 577
B. Ordered Suspensions . . . 578
C. Constructive Suspensions . . . 579
1. Delays Not Attributable to Government Fault . . . 579
2. Delay in Issuance of Notice to Proceed . . . 581
3. Delays in Availability of Site . . . 582
4. Delay Because of Interference with Contractor's Work . . . 585
5. Government Delays of Approvals . . . 586
6. Delay in Providing Funding . . . 588
7. Delay in Inspection of the Work . . . 589
8. Delay in Issuance of Changes . . . 589
9. Miscellaneous Acts of the Government . . . 591
D. Reasonableness of Delays . . . 591
1. Unreasonable Delays . . . 592
2. Reasonable Delays . . . 593
3. Measuring the Amount of Delay . . . 594
4. Burden of Proving Unreasonableness . . . 595
5. Proving the Delay . . . 596
E. Limitations on Recovery . . . 599
1. Sovereign Acts . . . 599
2. Concurrent Delays . . . 601
3. Notice Requirement . . . 604
F. Applicability of Delay Clauses . . . 605
1. Other Clauses Granting Relief for Delays . . . 605
2. Completion Within Contract Schedule . . . 607
3. Delays Preceding Award . . . 610

Chapter 7
GOVERNMENT PROPERTY . . . 611

I. OBTAINING PROPERTY FOR CONTRACT PERFORMANCE . . . 612
A. Materials, Components, and Supplies . . . 612
B. Special Tooling and Special Test Equipment . . . 615
1. Special Tooling . . . 615
2. Special Test Equipment . . . 617
3. Accounting Rules . . . 619
C. Facilities . . . 620
D. Special Rules for Government Production and Research Property . . . 623
1. Use on Government Work . . . 624
2. Use on Non-Government Work . . . 627
E. Progress Payments Inventory . . . 628

II. GOVERNMENT OBLIGATIONS WHEN IT FURNISHES PROPERTY 630
A. Interpretation Principles 630
B. Late or Not Delivered GFP 631
C. Suitable for Intended Use 633
1. Intended Use 634
2. Suitability 636
3. Cause of Contractor's Injury 638
D. Notice Requirements 639
E. Disclaimers 641
1. Government Property Furnished "As Is" 641
2. Government-Furnished Property Disclaimer Clause 643
F. Contractor Inspection 645

III. CONTRACTOR OBLIGATIONS 646
A. Control of Property 646
B. Risk of Loss 648
1. Clauses Covering Risk of Loss 648
2. Bailment Rules 654
3. Subcontractor Risk of Loss 654
4. Risk of Loss for Incomplete Work 654
5. Faulty Government-Furnished Design Specifications 655
C. Disposal of Government Property 656

Chapter 8
PRICING OF ADJUSTMENTS 659

I. BASIC PRINCIPLES 660
A. Price Adjustments Under Contract Clauses 661
1. Basic Pricing Formula 661
a. Pricing the Deleted Work 662
(1) Deductive Changes 663
(2) Exceptions to General Rule 665
(a) Complete Deletion of a Severable Item 666
(b) Ambiguous Specifications 667
(c) Special Contracting Agreements 667
(d) Deletion of Minor Items 668
(e) Waiver of Buy American Act 668
b. Pricing the Added Work 669
2. Cost Impact on Contractor 669
a. Incurrence of Costs 670
b. Value Measures 672
c. Allowable Costs 673
3. Subcontract Problems 675

a. Claims by Subcontractors in Contractor's Name 676
b. Lack of Equitable Adjustment Clause............. 677
B. Damages 678
1. Similarity to Equitable Adjustment 678
2. Methods of Computing Damages.................... 680
a. Expectancy Damages.......................... 680
b. Reliance Damages 683
c. Restitutionary Damages...................... 683
C. Quantum Meruit 685
1. Value Standard 685
2. Value Measured by Contractor's Costs............ 686

II. PROOF OF ADJUSTMENT............................ 686
A. Burden of Proof................................. 687
1. Causation 688
2. Reasonableness of Amount........................ 689
B. Methods of Proof................................ 691
1. Actual Cost Data................................ 691
2. Estimates....................................... 695
a. Vague Estimates 695
b. Expert Testimony 696
c. Statistical Techniques 698
C. Total Cost Method............................... 699
1. Not Favored 699
2. Safeguards for Use 700
a. Other Methods of Proof Not Available 700
b. Realistic Contract Price.................... 701
c. Reasonableness of Actual Costs 702
d. Contractor Not Responsible for Increases.... 703
3. Modified Total Cost Method...................... 703
D. Jury Verdict.................................... 704
1. Conditions for Use 704
2. Purposes Served 706
a. Resolving Conflicting Evidence 706
b. Evidence Not Available...................... 707
c. Adjusting for Lack of Proof of Causation.... 708
3. Techniques Used................................. 709
a. Computing a "Round" Number.................. 709
b. Awarding an Amount Based on the Government Estimate 709
c. Making an Independent Calculation 710
d. Awarding a Percentage of the Total Extra Costs Incurred................ 711

III. IMPACT AND DELAY 711
A. Theory of Recovery 711
1. Delays Preceding a Change 712
2. Delays Resulting from a Change or Differing Site Condition 712
B. Impact on Other Work 716
C. Consequential Damages 719
D. Unabsorbed Overhead 720
E. Idle Labor and Equipment 726
1. Labor 726
2. Contractor-Owned Equipment 727
3. Rented Equipment 730
F. Loss of Efficiency 730
G. Escalation of Labor Rates and Material Prices 733
H. Miscellaneous Costs 733

IV. OVERHEAD AND PROFIT 734
A. Overhead 734
B. Profit 735
1. Intermingled Changes and Suspensions 736
2. Deductive Changes 737
3. Breach of Contract Claims 738
4. Amount of Profit 739
5. Construction Contract Clauses 741
6. Cost-Plus-Percentage-of-Cost Relationship 744

V. GOVERNMENT CLAIMS FOR DEFECTIVE PRICING 745
A. When the Government Is Entitled to a Reduction 747
B. Government Reliance on the Defective Data 747
C. Computing the Price Reduction 749
D. Offset 750
E. Defective Subcontractor Data 752
F. Interest and Penalties 753

VI. COSTS OF PREPARING AND FINANCING ADJUSTMENTS 754
A. Preparation and Negotiation Costs 754
1. Distinction Between Claim Prosecution and Contract Administration 755
2. Costs Covered 759
3. Recovery by Small Contractors 760
a. Eligibility Requirements 760
b. Prevailing Parties 761
c. Substantially Justified 764
d. Amount Recovered 766

B. Costs of Financing Adjustments 769
1. Interest on Claims 769
2. Interest on Borrowings 772
a. Recovery When Cost Principles Not Applicable 772
b. Recovery When Cost Principles Applicable 773

Chapter 9
INSPECTION, ACCEPTANCE, AND WARRANTIES 775

I. INSPECTION 776
A. Government Inspection 776
1. Type of Inspection or Test 778
a. Contractually Specified Test 779
b. Use of Unspecified Tests 780
(1) Increased Costs 781
(2) Notice 782
c. Subjective Standards 783
d. Tests Imposing Higher Standards 783
e. Inspection Standards Established by Conduct 784
2. Place of Inspection 786
3. Time of Inspection 787
a. Inspection During the Work 787
b. Acceptance Inspection 788
c. Time of Inspection Affecting Validity 788
4. Number of Inspections 788
5. Manner of Inspection 789
6. Government Inspection Not for Contractor Benefit 790
a. No Waiver on Acceptance From Inspection 791
b. Basis for Government Liability 792
7. Reinspection 794
B. Contractor Inspection 795
1. General Inspection Clauses 795
2. Higher-Level Quality Control Requirement 798
3. Specified Tests 801
C. Cost of Inspection 803
1. Contractor Duty to Facilitate Government Inspection 803
2. Cost of Tearing Out Completed Work 805
D. Special Inspection Techniques and Issues 806
1. Inspection by Sampling 806
a. Contractually Specified Sampling 806
b. Sampling Not Specified 808
2. First Article Testing 809
3. Safety Inspections 811

a. Responsibility for Safety Inspections 811
b. Government Liability for Negligence 812

II. REJECTION, ACCEPTANCE, AND REMEDIES FOR DEFECTS . . . 814
A. Rejection 815
1. Rejection Standards 815
a. Strict Compliance 815
b. Nature of Specifications 816
(1) Specifications Not Suited to Strict Compliance 817
(2) Brand Name or Equal Specifications 817
(3) Brand Name and Proprietary Specifications 818
c. Limitations on Strict Compliance 821
(1) Construction Contracts 821
(2) First Articles 823
2. Proving Noncompliance 825
3. Notice of Rejection 827
a. Content 827
b. Time 829
4. Previous Action Limiting Rejection 831
B. Acceptance 833
1. Authority to Accept 833
2. Time and Place of Acceptance 834
3. Methods of Acceptance 835
a. Formal Acceptance 835
b. Implied Acceptance 837
(1) Late Rejection 837
(2) Government Acts Inconsistent with Contractor Ownership 838
c. Payment Alone Not Acceptance 839
d. Acceptance for a Limited Purpose 840
e. Use and Possession Under Construction Contracts . . . 841
f. Conditional Acceptance 842
C. Remedies 843
1. Contractor Correction 843
2. Government Correction 845
3. Price Reduction 846

III. POST-ACCEPTANCE RIGHTS 848
A. Latent Defects, Fraud, and Gross Mistakes 850
1. Latent Defects 850
a. Known Defects 851
b. Reliance on Contractor Testing or Assurances 851
c. Nature of the Specification 852

d. Ease of Government Inspection . . . 852
e. Past Experience . . . 854
2. Fraud . . . 854
3. Gross Mistake Amounting to Fraud . . . 855
a. Nature of Misrepresentation . . . 856
b. Reliance . . . 857
c. Injury . . . 858
4. Effect of Contractor Certification . . . 858
5. Notice and Proof of Defects . . . 861
a. Proof of Defect . . . 861
b. Notice of Defect . . . 862
6. Government Rights After Retraction of Acceptance . . . 863
B. Warranties . . . 866
1. Scope of Warranty Clauses . . . 869
2. Specification Provisions and Implied Warranties . . . 871
3. Notice and Burden of Proof . . . 873
a. Government Notice of Nonconformance . . . 873
b. Government's Burden of Proof . . . 874
4. Remedies Under Warranty Clauses . . . 876
C. Cumulative Remedies . . . 880

Chapter 10
DEFAULT TERMINATION, DAMAGES, AND LIQUIDATED DAMAGES . . . 883

I. CONSEQUENCES OF DEFAULT TERMINATION . . . 883
A. Impact on Contractor . . . 883
B. Impact on Government . . . 886
C. Fixed-Price Supply Termination Inventory . . . 886

II. RIGHT TO TERMINATE . . . 888
A. Grounds for Termination . . . 889
1. Failure to Perform or Deliver . . . 889
a. Slight Delays in Performance . . . 889
b. Timely Delivery of Defective Supplies . . . 893
(1) Timely Tender . . . 893
(2) Reasonable Belief That The Goods Conform . . . 894
(3) Defects Minor in Nature and Readily Correctable . . . 895
(4) The Cure Period . . . 897
c. Limitations on Termination of All Work . . . 898
(1) Accepted Work . . . 898
(2) Substantial Completion . . . 899
(A) Construction Contracts . . . 899
(B) Service Contracts . . . 902

(3) Severability . . . 904
(4) Installment Contracts Excepted . . . 905
d. Preproduction Items . . . 906
2. Progress Failures . . . 908
a. Basic Principle . . . 908
b. Evaluating Progress Failures . . . 909
(1) The "Impossible" Test . . . 909
(2) The "No Reasonable Likelihood" Test . . . 909
(3) Failure to Comply with the Contract Quality and Other Requirements . . . 910
c. Proof of Endangered Performance . . . 911
d. Construction Contracts . . . 913
3. Failure to Comply with Other Provisions . . . 915
a. Scope of Right . . . 915
b. Application of Rule . . . 916
4. Failure to Proceed . . . 918
a. Notification to Proceed . . . 921
b. Scope and Nature of Obligation . . . 922
c. Exceptions to the Duty to Proceed . . . 924
(1) Government Material Breach . . . 924
(2) Impractical to Proceed . . . 927
(3) Lack of Clear Direction . . . 930
5. Anticipatory Repudiation . . . 932
a. Timing of the Remedy . . . 932
b. Evidence Considered . . . 933
c. Examples of Anticipatory Repudiation . . . 934
(1) Express Refusal to Perform . . . 934
(2) Failure to Give Adequate Assurances . . . 935
(3) Express Statement of Inability to Perform . . . 937
(4) Actions Indicating Inability to Perform . . . 939
d. Retraction of Repudiation . . . 939
6. Subcontractor Termination . . . 940
B. Waiver of the Right to Terminate . . . 940
1. The Basic Concept . . . 941
a. Construction Contracts . . . 942
b. Waiver Prior to a Due Date . . . 944
2. Reasonable Forbearance . . . 945
3. Government Election to Continue Performance . . . 946
a. Unreasonable Delay . . . 946
b. Acts of the Government . . . 946
4. Contractor Reliance . . . 948
5. Reservation of Right to Terminate After Completion Date . . . 951
6. Reestablishment of the Right to Terminate After Waiver . . . 952

III. THE TERMINATION DECISION . . . 955
A. Discretionary Function . . . 956
1. Person Exercising Discretion . . . 958
2. Factors to Be Considered . . . 960
a. FAR Factors . . . 960
b. Other Relevant Considerations . . . 962
c. Alternatives . . . 963
(1) Convenience Termination . . . 963
(2) Negotiating a Schedule Extension . . . 964
3. Improper Decision Making . . . 965
a. Informational Deficiencies . . . 966
b. Improper Motive . . . 967
c. Other Objectionable Conduct by the Government . . . 969
B. Reconsideration of Default Termination . . . 969

IV. TERMINATION PROCEDURES . . . 970
A. Delinquency Notices . . . 970
1. Cure Notices . . . 970
a. Circumstances for Use . . . 971
b. Form of Cure Notice . . . 972
c. Effect of Denial of Cure Period . . . 973
d. Adequate Assurances . . . 974
2. The Show Cause Notice . . . 976
B. Termination Notice . . . 978

V. EXCESS COSTS OF REPROCUREMENT . . . 981
A. The Fulford Doctrine . . . 982
B. Reasonableness of Government Action . . . 986
1. Similarity . . . 987
a. Changes Reducing Cost of Work . . . 988
b. Test for Determining Similarity . . . 989
c. Changes in Inspection and Testing . . . 992
d. Changes in Terms and Conditions . . . 993
e. Changes in Method of Procurement . . . 994
2. Effect of Relaxed Specifications That Contractor Could Have Met . . . 995
3. Variations in Quantity Reprocured . . . 996
4. Mitigation . . . 997
a. Lack of Negotiation or Price Analysis . . . 998
b. Lack of Competition . . . 1000
c. Soliciting Original Bidders . . . 1003
d. Delayed Award of Reprocurement Contract . . . 1004
e. Effect of Failure to Mitigate . . . 1006
f. Refusal to Deal with Original Contractor . . . 1009

C. The Reprocurement Contract 1013
1. Intent to Reprocure 1013
2. Proof of Cost Incurrence........ 1015
3. Poor Administration of Reprocurement Contract........ 1016
4. Use of Government Personnel 1017
D. Computation of Excess Costs 1019
1. Price Adjustments Under Defaulted Contract 1019
2. Adjustments in Reprocurement Contract Costs 1020
3. Time Period Covered 1021
E. Right to Other Damages 1021
F. Administrative Requirements for Reprocurement 1023

VI. LIQUIDATED DAMAGES 1024
A. General Policy........ 1025
B. Enforceability of Liquidated Damages Clause 1027
1. Reasonableness of the Forecast 1028
a. Time of the Forecast 1028
b. Accuracy of Measurement of Forecast Damages ... 1030
(1) Proportional Application 1031
(2) Fixed Daily Rates........ 1031
(3) Inclusion of Administrative Expenses 1033
(4) Maximum Assessment 1034
(5) Use of Standard Formulae 1034
2. Difficulty of Accurate Estimation........ 1036
C. Relief from Liquidated Damages 1036
1. Excusable Delays 1036
2. Substantial Completion........ 1039
D. Relationship with Default Termination........ 1041
1. Concurrent Running of Liquidated Damages and Excess Costs of Reprocurement........ 1041
2. Effect of Waiver 1043
E. Computation of Time Covered by Liquidated Damages 1043
F. Government Right to Actual Damages........ 1044
1. Damages Covered by the Clause 1044
2. Damages Outside the Clause 1046
G. Remission of Liquidated Damages........ 1046

Chapter 11
TERMINATION FOR CONVENIENCE 1049

I. BACKGROUND........ 1049

II. THE RIGHT TO TERMINATE 1050
A. Termination Clauses 1050

B. Exercising the Right to Terminate 1053
1. The Decision to Terminate 1053
a. "The Government's Interest" 1053
b. Special Situations 1055
c. Terminations in Support of Competition 1055
2. Limitations on the Right to Terminate 1057
a. The Kalvar Test—Government Bad Faith or Abuse of Discretion 1058
b. The Torncello Test—No Change in Circumstances . . . 1062
c. The Krygoski Test—No Intention to Fulfill Promise . . . 1066
d. Violation of Paramount Government Policies 1068
C. Partial Terminations 1068
D. Procedural Requirements 1069
1. Notice of Termination 1069
2. Termination for Default versus Termination for Convenience 1070
E. Finality of Termination for Convenience 1070
F. Deletion of Work Through Termination for Convenience, Changes, or Other Clauses 1071

III. CONSTRUCTIVE TERMINATION 1073
A. Wrongful Default Terminations 1074
B. Government's Failure to Perform Under an Indefinite Delivery Contract 1075
C. Cancellation of Award 1076

IV. TERMINATION SETTLEMENTS 1076
A. Procedures 1077
1. Obligations of the Parties 1077
2. Basis for Settlement Proposals 1080
3. Time of Submission of Proposals 1082
4. Imperfect Proposals 1083
5. Terminations for Convenience Settlement Proposals Under a Termination for Default 1084
6. Negotiation of Final Settlement 1084
7. Unilateral Determination 1086
8. Appeal of Convenience Terminations 1087
B. Nature and Amount of Settlements 1089
1. Basic Principles 1089
2. Recoverable Costs 1090
a. Common Items 1094
b. Costs Continuing After Termination 1096
c. Initial Costs 1098
d. Loss of Value of Assets 1101
e. Rental Costs 1103

f. Subcontract Claims 1104
g. Termination Inventory 1108
3. Settlement Expenses 1109
4. Overhead, Profit, and Loss Contracts 1114
a. Post-Termination Overhead 1114
b. Profit or Loss Adjustment 1115
(1) Profit 1115
(2) Loss Adjustment 1118
5. Variable Quantity Contracts and Cost Limitation Clauses . . . 1120
6. Partial Termination 1122
C. Short Form Termination Settlements 1123

Chapter 12
PAYMENT AND DISCHARGE 1125

I. TYPES OF PAYMENT 1125
A. Payment of the Price 1125
1. Partial Payments 1128
2. Billing Prices 1129
B. Progress Payments 1130
1. Progress Payments Based on Costs 1130
2. Progress Payments Based on Percentage of Completion. . . . 1131
3. Performance Based Payments 1133
C. Other Financing Techniques 1134
1. Advance Payments 1135
2. Commercial Item Financing 1136
3. Provisional Payments 1137

II. PAYMENT PROCEDURES 1139
A. Documentation and Authority 1140
1. Invoices and Vouchers 1140
2. Documentation of Acceptance 1143
3. Assignment of Payment 1144
4. Payment Authority 1146
5. Overpayments 1147
6. Discounts 1148
B. Electronic Payment 1149
C. Time for Payment of the Price 1151
1. Other Than Simplified Acquisitions 1151
2. Fast Payment 1153
D. Progress Payment Procedures 1155
1. Cost-Based Progress Payments 1155
a. Time for Payment 1155
b. Delays in Payment 1155

c. Suspension or Reduction of Progress Payments 1156
d. Liquidation of Progress Payments................ 1159
2. Construction Progress Payments 1160
a. Time for Payment 1160
b. Certification.................................... 1161
c. Subcontract Payments 1162
d. Retainage.. 1164
E. Payment Under Incrementally Funded Contracts............ 1166
F. Withholding.. 1166
1. Government Right to Withhold 1167
2. Limitations on Withholding 1168
3. Discretionary Actions............................... 1170

III. SETOFF.. 1171
A. Right to Setoff.. 1172
B. Limitations on Setoff.................................. 1173
1. Rights to Payment Assigned to Financing Institutions.... 1173
2. Performance-Bond Surety 1174
3. Separate Debts of Partners or Joint Venturers 1175
4. Bid Deposits 1175

IV. DEBT COLLECTION PROCEDURES 1175
A. FAR Debt Collection Procedures 1175
1. Debt Determination 1176
2. Negotiation and Demand 1176
3. Deferment Agreement 1178
4. Contracting Officer Decision 1179
5. Withholding or Setoff............................... 1179
B. The Debt Collection Act................................ 1181
C. The Contract Disputes Act 1182

V. REMEDIES... 1183
A. Contractor Remedies for Delayed Payment 1183
1. Interest 1184
a. Prompt Payment Act............................... 1184
(1) Coverage..................................... 1185
(2) Interest Penalty.............................. 1187
(3) Procedures 1188
b. The Contract Disputes Act 1189
(1) Time of Accrual of Interest 1189
(2) Rate of Interest.............................. 1190
(3) Delay in Payment............................. 1191
(4) Conversion into a Claim...................... 1191
(5) Settlement................................... 1192
(6) Government Claims 1194

2. Injunctions and Other Remedies . . . 1195
B. Government Remedies for Overpayment and Improper Claims . . . 1196
1. Interest on Overpayments . . . 1196
a. Statutory Requirement . . . 1197
b. Contract Clause . . . 1198
2. Fraudulent Claims for Payment . . . 1199
a. Civil Fraud . . . 1199
b. Criminal Fraud . . . 1201

VI. DISCHARGE . . . 1202
A. Final Payment . . . 1202
1. Delay in Contract Closeout . . . 1202
2. Legal Effect of Final Payment . . . 1203
a. The Contractor's Release of Claims . . . 1203
b. Effect of Release . . . 1204
c. Government Claims . . . 1207
d. Clauses Barring Claims After Final Payment . . . 1208
B. Mutual Agreement and Rescission . . . 1209
C. Contract Modifications . . . 1210
1. Accord and Satisfaction . . . 1210
2. Modifications Without Specific Release Language . . . 1212
3. Modifications with Release Language . . . 1214
D. General Releases . . . 1219
E. Techniques for Avoiding Releases . . . 1222
1. Lack of Consideration . . . 1222
2. Mistake . . . 1223
3. Economic Duress . . . 1225
4. Fraud and Misrepresentation . . . 1228
5. Lack of Authority . . . 1229

Chapter 13
DISPUTES . . . 1231

I. COVERAGE OF DISPUTES PROCESS . . . 1232
A. Claims Relating to the Contract . . . 1236
1. Remedy Granting Clauses . . . 1237
2. Breach of Contract Claims . . . 1237
3. Mistakes Alleged After Award . . . 1238
B. Government–Contractor Controversies Not Subject to Disputes Process . . . 1238
1. Independent Torts . . . 1238
2. Fraud . . . 1240
3. Penalties or Forfeitures Administered by Other Agencies . . . 1244

4. Contract Award Controversies and Mistakes Alleged Prior to Award. 1246
5. Violation of Statutory or Constitutional Rights 1247
C. Subcontractor Controversies 1247
1. Direct Subcontractor Claims. 1248
2. Indirect (Sponsored) Subcontractor Claims 1250

II. ASSERTION OF CLAIMS. 1252
A. Nonroutine Requests for Price Adjustment. 1253
1. Distinguishing Routine and Non-Routine Requests for Payment. 1253
2. Routine Request Converted Into Claim 1254
3. REA Submissions Converted Into a Claim 1255
4. Convenience Termination Settlement Proposals 1255
5. Continued Negotiations 1257
B. Nonmonetary Claims versus Declaratory Relief. 1257
C. Assertion of Contractor Claim 1260
1. Party Entitled to Assert Claim 1260
a. Dissolved Contractors 1260
b. Separate Entities 1261
(1) Assignees 1261
(2) Sureties. 1262
(3) Merged Contractors 1263
(4) Agents of a Contractor 1263
2. Claim Content. 1264
3. Request for Sum Certain. 1266
4. Request for Contracting Officer Decision. 1267
5. Submittal to the Contracting Officer. 1269
6. Certification 1270
a. Threshold. 1272
b. Significance of Defective Certification or Absence of Certification 1273
(1) Correctable Defective Certifications 1273
(2) Intentional or Negligent Disregard. 1275
(3) Absence of Certificate 1275
(4) Certification by Combination. 1276
c. Revision of Claim 1276
d. Claims Not Involving Quantum 1278
e. Authorized Signature. 1278
7. Conversion into a Claim. 1279
D. Assertion of Government Claims 1280
E. Time for Submittal 1284

III. CONTRACTING OFFICER'S ROLE 1286
A. Negotiated Settlement. 1286
1. Policy Favoring Settlement. 1287

2. Settlement Authority . . . 1288
a. Negotiation after Issuance of Final Decision . . . 1290
b. Settlement During Litigation . . . 1291
B. Final Decision of the Contracting Officer . . . 1292
1. Time for Issuance of Decision . . . 1294
2. Failure to Issue a Timely Decision . . . 1297
a. An Order to Issue a Decision . . . 1297
b. Appeal of "Deemed Denied" Decisions . . . 1298
3. Form and Content of Decision . . . 1300
a. Written Decision . . . 1301
b. Notification . . . 1301
c. Responsive to the Claim . . . 1304
d. Reasons for the Decision . . . 1305
e. Decision in Wrong Form May Bind the Government . . . 1305
4. Quality of the Decisional Process . . . 1306
a. Replacement of Contracting Officer . . . 1306
b. Advice from Other Officials . . . 1307
c. Orders of Superior . . . 1309
d. Review of Decisions . . . 1310
e. Unbiased and Impartial Decision . . . 1310

IV. LITIGATION OF DISPUTES ACT CLAIMS . . . 1311
A. The Decision to Appeal or Bring Suit . . . 1311
B. Choice of Forums . . . 1313
1. Election of Forum Binding . . . 1313
2. Fragmentation and Consolidation of Claims . . . 1314
3. Bankrupt Contractors . . . 1315
C. Timely Appeal or Suit . . . 1315
1. Receipt of Decision . . . 1316
2. Date of Appeal or Suit . . . 1319
a. Boards of Contract Appeals . . . 1319
b. Court of Federal Claims . . . 1322
D. Organization and Function of Forums . . . 1322
1. Boards of Contract Appeals . . . 1322
2. Court of Federal Claims . . . 1324
3. Court of Appeals for the Federal Circuit . . . 1325
a. Review of Board Decisions . . . 1325
b. Review of Court of Federal Claims Decisions . . . 1327

Appendix—Standard FAR Clauses . . . 1329
Acronyms and Abbreviations . . . 1397
Subject Index . . . 1401

CHAPTER 1

CONTRACT ADMINISTRATION AND PERSONNEL

This book is largely concerned with the legal rights of the parties to enforce contractual obligations and the techniques for making contract adjustments and resolving claims. Since contract administration involves many different subject areas, each with a unique set of rules and procedures, most of the chapters focus on specific contract provisions. By contrast, this chapter deals with several matters that pervade all contract administration activity. The first section analyzes the nature and purpose of contract administration. The next section considers the sources and significance of contract administration rules. The following three sections deal with issues concerning the authority of government and contractor personnel, the extent to which the government is bound by activities of authorized personnel, and the limitations on personal suits against government personnel. The final section addresses the various types of inappropriate contract administration activity.

I. NATURE AND PURPOSE OF CONTRACT ADMINISTRATION

As used in this book, *contract administration* includes all relationships between the government and the contractor that arise out of contract performance. It encompasses all dealings between the parties from the time the contract is awarded until the work has been completed and accepted, payment has been made, and disputes have been resolved. As such, contract administration constitutes a large part of the activity in the government contracting process. See FAR 42.302 for a detailed list of contract administration functions.

The broad goals of contract administration are to ensure that the government obtains the needed work on time and at the level of quality called for by the contract and that the contractor receives proper compensation. This will often involve *ensuring that both parties fulfill their contractual obligations*. However, in many contracts, adjustments must be made when the assumptions on which the contracts were based are not borne out. As circumstances change, it is often necessary to change contract requirements. Thus, a large part of contract administration activity is devoted to *adapting to changing circumstances*. This may require changing contract specifications when they do not reflect the current needs of the user or terminating the contract when the goods or services are no longer required. In other cases, it may be necessary to change contractors when the contractor is unable to perform. In numerous instances, contract administration will consist of resolving a contractor's difficulties when the government cannot carry out its part of the bargain or has failed to meet one of its contractual obligations. Similarly, the government may find it necessary to assist the contractor when it encounters difficulties in meeting the contract requirements. In all of these efforts, the goal is to obtain goods and services needed by the government in the most efficient and effective manner. While the legal rights and duties of the parties sometimes determine the proper course of action, more often than not the exercise of skill and business judgment is required. The parties must consider legally appropriate actions and determine the most effective course of action. Further, since government contracts involve public funds, the public interest must always be considered.

A. Nature of Contract Administration

The specific nature and extent of contract administration activity varies from contract to contract. It can range from extensive government involvement in the contractor's activities to almost complete disengagement. Factors influencing the degree of contract administration include the nature of the work, the type of contract, and the experience and attitudes of the personnel involved. For example, contracts for off-the-shelf goods will involve relatively little effort, while firm fixed-price contracts for construction, manufacture of complex equipment, or the performance of unique services require a great deal of contract administration activity. This is also true for most cost-reimbursement contracts. However, the nature of contract administration under cost-reimbursement contracts is significantly different from that under fixed-price contracts. The broader scope of work, the reduced risks assumed by the contractor, and the significantly different method of payment result in many unique administrative problems and legal issues. This book deals primarily with the administration of fixed-price contracts. For in-depth coverage of cost-reimbursement contracts, see Cibinic and Nash, *Cost-Reimbursement Contracting* (3d ed. 2004).

Because the rules of contract administration are derived from statutes and regulations as well as from judicial and quasi-judicial decisions, the analysis of these rules is necessarily legalistic. This is appropriate when determining the outer limits of permissible activity of the parties concerned. However, the great majority of contract administration actions involve the identification and resolution of problems before they escalate into legal controversies. This requires that the parties establish an appropriate working relationship and solve problems as they arise and before they escalate.

Properly conducted postaward, prework meetings can be a substantial aid in reaching this goal. FAR Subpart 42.5 deals with postaward orientation. FAR 42.501 states the benefits to be achieved by such orientation:

> (a) A postaward orientation aids both Government and contractor personnel to (1) achieve a clear and mutual understanding of all contract requirements, and (2) identify and resolve potential problems. However, it is not a substitute for the contractor's fully understanding the work requirements at the time offers are

submitted, nor is it to be used to alter the final agreement arrived at in any negotiations leading to contract award.

(b) Postaward orientation is encouraged to assist small business, small disadvantaged, women-owned, veteran-owned, HUBZone, and service-disabled veteran-owned small business concerns (see Part 19).

(c) While cognizant Government or contractor personnel may request the contracting officer to arrange for orientation, it is up to the contracting officer to decide whether a postaward orientation in any form is necessary.

(d) Maximum benefits will be realized when orientation is conducted promptly after award.

1. Working Relationship

One of the most important but difficult tasks in contract administration is to develop a proper working relationship. Cooperation between the parties is essential if the work is to be successfully performed, and yet the parties can be, in a very real sense, adversaries. The government often attempts to obtain performance within the contract price, while the contractor attempts to maximize profits either by doing the minimum acceptable work or by attempting to obtain price increases. Such efforts can be seen as adversarial or as a means of cooperatively carrying out the contract. These goals can be achieved cooperatively if the contractor's employees understand that the government is entitled to receive the promised performance, and the government employees understand that the contractor is entitled to price adjustments under a number of the standard clauses. The key to good contract administration is the establishment of such an arm's-length but cooperative relationship.

a. Cooperation and Good Faith

Cooperation during contract administration is not only mandated by common sense, but is a legal requirement. The government's rights to insist upon strict compliance with contract requirements and to enforce all contractor obligations do not relieve the government from its duty to cooperate with the contractor in the performance of the work. Similarly, the contractor is obligated to work to meet the government's expectations.

Lack of cooperation is a frequent cause of disputes. See, for example, *Ingalls Shipbuilding Div., Litton Sys., Inc.*, ASBCA 17717, 76-1 BCA ¶ 11,851, in which the board stated at 56,718:

> While [the contractor] had the responsibility to deliver the three nuclear submarines by the dates spelled out in the contract, the Government undertook the responsibility to acquire the hull steel with which construction of the three submarines necessarily began. Under such circumstances, the parties should have

> been partners in the undertaking, working toward the common goal of having the submarines delivered by the specified dates. Instead, when the Government was unable to discharge its responsibility for delivering the hull steel in keeping with [the contractor's] requirements, it displayed an arm's-length attitude that was unsuited to the contractual arrangement that existed between the parties.

One element of the proper cooperative attitude on the part of the government is even-handed treatment of all contractors. Although this does not require identical treatment, conduct toward other contractors is relevant to demonstrating lack of cooperation. See *G.W. Galloway Co.*, ASBCA 16656, 73-2 BCA ¶ 10,270, *recons. denied*, 74-1 BCA ¶ 10,521, in which the board observed at 48,500-01:

> [The contractor] has no legal cause for complaint because it was subject to a higher level of inspection than were prior producers such as Allison. The Government has a right to insist upon strict compliance with the specifications and had the right to impose the level of inspection (e.g. 100% in-process independent inspection) deemed appropriate to achieve its goal. The fact that a prior producer was not subjected to the same close scrutiny does not, in-and-of-itself, afford [the contractor] grounds for relief. [It] must still show, as it has done, that the inspection practices at its own facilities were improper and beyond the scope of the governing contractual provisions. Acknowledgment of this basic principle, however, does not mean that the Board thinks the contrast in inspection levels imposed upon the two contractors is irrelevant. The contrast tends to show that [the contractor] was not afforded the degree of cooperation and assistance by DCAS [Defense Contract Administration Service] normally afforded most other Government contractors. Specifications dealing with pin hardness and clevis forgings, which the Government has come to concede were, in effect, erroneous or impossible to meet, were, nevertheless, strictly applied to [the contractor's] work, but apparently ignored, or overlooked, on prior contracts. Riveting requirements are another example. Protestations of tooling difficulties were given no credence by DCAS and requests for assistance to alleviate the problems were largely ignored by both DCAS and MECOM [Mobility Equipment Command]. Time consuming requests for deviation or waiver were insisted upon in cases where the drawings were concededly erroneous. Lack of cooperation by responsible Government activities involved in the procurement added to the burden, delay, and difficulties encountered by [the contractor] for other causes.

Contractors are also expected to work cooperatively with the government during contract performance. For an example of extremely uncooperative behavior leading to a default termination, see *Lucille Holden*, AGBCA 81-208-1, 84-1 BCA ¶ 17,066. In that case, the contractor was verbally abusive to government employees, including the use of obscene language and cursing. See also *Robert Earl Lanier*, PSBCA 3143, 94-2 BCA ¶ 26,693, where a contractor was terminated for default for sexually harassing female government employees.

To encourage cooperative behavior by contractors, agencies are required to evaluate the performance upon the completion of all contracts over $100,000, FAR 42.1502(a). Among other factors, these evaluations are to consider "the contractor's history of reasonable and cooperative behavior and commitment to customer satisfaction; and generally, the contractors business-like concern for the interest of the customer," FAR 42.1501. These evaluations are used as a "past performance" element in the source selection process for best value procurements, FAR 15.305(a)(2), and commercial item procurements, FAR 12.206. They can also come into play in the selection of recipients of task and delivery orders in multiple-award task and delivery order contracts, FAR 16.505(b)(1)(iii)(A)(1). Such evaluation of cooperative behavior in the source selection process is proper, *RMS Indus.*, Comp. Gen. Dec. B-247229, 92-1 CPD ¶ 451. It is also proper to downgrade a competitor for uncooperative behavior in a simplified acquisition, *John Blood*, Comp. Gen. Dec. B-290593, 2002 CPD ¶ 151 (missing meetings, hanging up on a teleconference, and generally "unprofessional" and "adversarial" behavior).

There is also a general legal rule requiring contracting parties to exhibit good faith in their dealings. Both §1-203 of the *Uniform Commercial Code* (U.C.C.) and §205 of *Restatement, Second, Contracts* impose an obligation of good faith in the *performance* and *enforcement* of the contract. The comments to the *Restatement* contain the following guidance:

> a. *Meaning of "good faith"* . . . . The phrase "good faith" is used in a variety of contexts, and its meaning varies somewhat with the context. Good faith performance or enforcement of a contract emphasizes faithfulness to an agreed common purpose and consistency with the justified expectations of the other party; it excludes a variety of types of conduct characterized as involving "bad faith" because they violate community standards of decency, fairness or reasonableness.
>
> . . .
>
> d. *Good faith performance.* Subterfuges and evasions violate the obligation of good faith in performance even though the actor believes his conduct to be justified. But the obligation goes further: bad faith may be overt or may consist of inaction, and fair dealing may require more than honesty. A complete catalogue of types of bad faith is impossible, but the following types are among those which have been recognized in judicial decisions: evasion of the spirit of the bargain, lack of diligence and slacking off, willful rendering of imperfect performance, abuse of a power to specify terms, and interference with or failure to cooperate in the other party's performance.
>
> e. *Good faith in enforcement.* The obligation of good faith and fair dealing extends to the assertion, settlement and litigation of contract claims and defenses. . . . The obligation is violated by dishonest conduct such as conjuring up a pretended dispute, asserting an interpretation contrary to one's own understanding, or falsification of facts. It also extends to dealing which is candid but unfair, such as taking advantage of the necessitous circumstances of the other party to extort a modification of a contract for the sale of goods without legitimate commercial reason. . . . Other types of violation have been recognized in judicial decisions: harassing demands for assurances of performance, rejection of performance for

> unstated reasons, willful failure to mitigate damages, and abuse of a power to determine compliance or to terminate the contract. . . .

It has been held that "[t]he need for mutual fair dealing is no less required in contracts to which the government is a party, than in any other commercial arrangement," *Maxim Corp. v. United States*, 847 F.2d 1549 (Fed. Cir. 1988).

Cases enforcing good faith requirements against the government include *Malone v. United States*, 849 F.2d 1441 (Fed. Cir. 1988), in which the court converted a default termination into a termination for the convenience of the government because the government had failed to act in good faith in responding to the contractor's legitimate inquiries about the required quality of the work. Similarly, in *Abcon Assocs., Inc. v. United States*, 49 Fed. Cl. 678 (2001), the court found a lack of good faith in the government's improper assessment of liquidated damages, which severely impacted the contractor's ability to perform, and in *Nash Janitorial Serv., Inc.*, GSBCA 6390, 84-1 BCA ¶ 17,135, *recons. denied*, 84-2 BCA ¶ 17,355, the board found a lack of good faith in the government's failure to respond to constructive change claims, failure to coordinate the work with the building occupants, and coercive tactics in negotiating a contract modification. See also *Apex Int'l Mgmt. Servs., Inc.*, ASBCA 38087, 94-2 BCA ¶ 26,842, *recons. denied*, 94-2 BCA ¶ 26,852, in which the board found that government employees exhibited "hostility" and "contempt" toward the contractor by refusing to supply keys to vehicles, storage areas, and equipment, "even maliciously throwing them on a roof or in trash dumpsters," "removing telephones and tearing out telephone wiring and air conditioning equipment."

Contractors have also been found to have failed to act in good faith. For example, failure to assert a mistake claim in a timely manner has been held to exhibit a lack of good faith and fair dealing, *All-American Poly Corp.*, GSBCA 7104, 84-3 BCA ¶ 17,682 (assertion after completion of contract), and *J.C. Mfg., Inc.*, ASBCA 34399, 87-3 BCA ¶ 20,137 (assertion 15 months after it was aware of the claim). See Chapter 3 for an in-depth discussion of the government's duty to cooperate.

b. Mutual Confidence and Respect

Good contract administration also depends on the development of mutual confidence and respect between government and contractor officials. Unfortunately, personality conflicts and temper tantrums occasionally preclude the amicable settlement of legitimate controversies, *Maintenance Eng'rs*, ASBCA 23131, 81-2 BCA ¶ 15,168, and can even lead to violence, *Mann Constr. Co.*, AGBCA 76-111-4, 81-1 BCA ¶ 15,087 (personality conflicts led to a fist fight). See *Donohoe Constr. Co.*, ASBCA 47310, 98-2 BCA ¶ 30,076, in which the government was held liable when its quality control manager unreasonably harassed the contractor to "get even" for complaints to his superior.

Some cases illustrate the extreme antagonism that can arise during the contract administration process. For example, in *Murdock Constr. Co.*, IBCA 1050-12-74, 77-2 BCA ¶ 12,728, the board found that the government project supervisor acted inappropriately by introducing himself as an S.O.B. at the preconstruction conference and stating "that before the job was completed [the contractor] would wish he had bid this job at 25 percent more money." Similarly, in *G.W. Galloway Co.*, ASBCA 17436, 77-2 BCA ¶ 12,640, the board was critical of the administration of the contract, stating at 61,297:

> Given this background, Edgewood Arsenal's reaction to [the contractor's] production difficulties is not comprehensible. Key Arsenal personnel, including the original contracting officer, commenced their contractual relationship with [the contractor] in an atmosphere of apprehension and with a suspicion that [the contractor] was "buying into" the contract in the expectation of recouping its supposed losses on change orders. The record offers no support for the validity of these suspicions, but the Arsenal staff, nevertheless, constantly recommended close surveillance and monitoring of [the contractor's] production efforts. Close surveillance and inspection was ordered from the outset and continued throughout the life of the contract. [The contractor's] production efforts were often subjected to what [it] justifiably characterizes as "nit-picking" and its normal managerial functions and prerogatives were sometimes invaded by the Arsenal and DCAS. Conversely, on a number of occasions when [the contractor] earnestly sought the Arsenal's assistance and cooperation on Arsenal-created problems it was not forthcoming.

See *Fire Security Sys., Inc.*, VABCA 5559, 02-2 BCA ¶ 31,977, for a case where the contractor's conduct led to contract administration difficulties. The board described that conduct as follows at 158,012:

> In many of the letters to the VA, [the contractor] had referred to COTR Atchley as a "human DDT" (with DDT as an acronym for Delays, Disruption & Trauma). On several occasions, he also applied the term to Mr. Donald Birchler, one of the members of the VA's A/E design team. Often the letters were tinged with sarcasm, once referring to statements by the CO as "more likely to be the product of prozac than prose." In another letter, the CO was likened to "the Empress of India, Queen Victoria, Ruler of the Raj, talking to a delegation of Hindu untouchables in India, circa 1876." The preceding was intended to describe the CO's attitude toward [the contractor] during a substantive meeting concerning several issues impacting progress toward completion that was held between representatives of the VA and the Contractor on January 5, 1995. The confrontational tone of these letters and others was consistent throughout Contract performance.

Although the first goal of good contract administration is to avoid this type of destructive relationship, if it does occur, the personnel exhibiting this confrontational attitude should be removed from the contract administration process. For example, in *Ben Levine Timber*, AGBCA 92-124-1, 94-1 BCA ¶ 26,342, the contractor and the contracting officer resolved the problem by agreeing to have higher level officials—the contractor's representative and the Forest Service Timber Sale Officer—conduct the day-to-day activities of administering the contract.

2. Timely Identification and Resolution of Problems

Even the best of working relationships will not yield good contract administration unless the parties properly document contract events, timely identify problems, and work out mutually agreeable solutions. The lack of effective communication can lead to disputes, as indicated by the board in *Eyring Research Inst.*, IBCA 1169-10-77, 82-2 BCA ¶ 15,887, at 78,787:

> It is apparent that the dispute here was the inevitable result of a general lack of communication and coordination among the various scientists and contract administrators employed by both the prime and subcontractors. The otherwise good contract performance was denigrated by inattention to detail with respect to the administrative requirements of Government contracting.

a. Problem Identification

When either party identifies a problem during contract performance, the other party should be informed immediately. Early communication regarding problems is especially important when a contractor believes that the government is the cause of the problem. In such cases, the contractor will probably be entitled to additional compensation under one of the standard clauses, and the government should be entitled to minimize the amount of such compensation by devising the most cost-effective solution to the problem. Failure to tell the government about the problem deprives it of this opportunity.

The need for such early identification of problems led the courts and the appeals boards to devise a special legal rule in this regard. In 1965 the Court of Claims recognized that the government was prejudiced by lack of notice of defective specifications and announced a rule denying a contractor compensation for costs that might have been avoided if the contractor had given timely notice, *Kings Elecs. Co. v. United States*, 169 Ct. Cl. 433, 341 F.2d 632 (1965). This rule has been followed in cases of contractor failure to give notice of an alleged government misrepresentation, *Ling-Temco-Vought, Inc. v. United States*, 201 Ct. Cl. 135, 475 F.2d 630 (1973); of failure to cooperate, *Cameo Bronze, Inc.*, GSBCA 3646, 73-2 BCA ¶ 10,135, *recons. denied*, 73-2 BCA ¶ 10,365; of defective government-furnished materials, *J.S. Alberici Constr. Co. & Martin K. Eby Constr. Co., a joint venture,* ENGBCA 6178, 98-2 BCA ¶ 29,875; and of alleged impossibility of performance, *SMC Info. Sys., Inc. v. General Servs. Admin.*, GSBCA 9371, 93-1 BCA ¶ 25,485 and *Sanders Assocs., Inc.*, ASBCA 17550, 74-1 BCA ¶ 10,536, *recons. denied*, 76-1 BCA ¶ 11,632. The rule continues to be applied in defective specification situations, *Precision Specialties, Inc.*, ASBCA 48717, 96-1 BCA ¶ 28,054 (lack of notice until finding solution precludes recovery of costs prior to giving notice), and *JGB Enters., Inc.*, ASBCA 49493, 96-2 BCA ¶ 28,498 (lack of notice precludes recovery of costs of correcting defective specifications). In *Axel Elecs., Inc.*, ASBCA 18990, 76-1

BCA ¶ 11,667, the board explained that in such a situation the contractor should give notice to allow "the Government to protect itself and to have the choice of electing alternatives in the event the Government finds merit in the claim."

b. Problem Resolution

Prompt problem identification is of little use if the problem is not resolved in a manner that is clear to both parties. Memoranda to file, oral understandings, and memoranda or side agreements not incorporated into the contract should be avoided. Failure to promptly and properly resolve problems often leads to litigation. See *Colorado Dental Serv.*, ASBCA 24666, 82-2 BCA ¶ 15,836, stating at 78,500:

> During the first three years of contract performance, the parties were in frequent contact and as problems arose, they were discussed. Problems giving rise to the instant disputes were discussed in general terms without a clear understanding of varied perceptions and conduct of personnel of both parties directly involved with the contracts. . . . For the most part, during the first three years, both parties administered the contracts oblivious to the contract provisions which are now the center of this dispute and oblivious to the impact of those provisions to the performance of the contract and the accounting of costs and funds. . . .

Untimely resolution of problems by the government can result in contractor recovery on a claim. See, for example, *Essex Electro Eng'rs, Inc.*, ASBCA 49915, 02-1 BCA ¶ 31,714 (contractor awarded price adjustment when agency did not respond in a timely manner to a request for changes to the specifications necessary to permit performance); *Turbine Aviation*, ASBCA 51323, 98-2 BCA ¶ 29,945 (default termination converted to convenience termination because government did not provide missing technical information in a timely manner).

The government is primarily responsible for resolution of performance problems that are a result of defective specifications or government actions, *Hardrives, Inc.*, IBCA 2319, 94-1 BCA ¶ 26,267. Thus, it is improper to request that the contractor devise a solution and to defer action until the solution is proposed, *Pilcher, Livingston & Wallace*, ASBCA 13391, 70-1 BCA ¶ 8331. See also *Hughes-Groesch Constr. Corp.*, VABCA 5448, 00-1 BCA ¶ 30,912, finding that the government acted improperly in requiring a construction contractor to perform redesign work rather than to obtain the redesign from the cognizant architect/engineer.

To ensure a timely response to contract administration problems identified by small business contractors, Section 2353 of the Federal Acquisition Streamlining Act of 1994, Pub. L. No. 103-355, requires that a provision be included in the FAR that contracting officers "make every reasonable effort to respond in writing within 30 days to any written request . . . relating to the administration of a contract from a small business concern." If the contracting officer is unable to respond within the 30-day period, the contracting officer must send "written notification of a specific date by which [it] expects to respond." This is implemented in FAR 42.1601. Although not mandated by the statute, this rule is equally applicable to large companies.

When the government has determined the best solution to a problem that is its responsibility, the parties must continue to cooperate to ensure that the contractor can be compensated for any extra costs that it will incur. This will require the contractor to submit a well-documented proposal for a price adjustment, the government to promptly analyze the proposal, and both parties to negotiate a fair amount of compensation. Thereafter, the government must promptly issue a contract modification that can be used as the basis of payment for any extra work that has been performed. In many, if not most, of the litigated cases identified and discussed in this book, the parties failed to carry out these steps in a timely manner—with the result that litigation was necessary to enable the contractor to obtain the compensation it merited.

In some instances, the most cooperative identification of problems and attempts to resolve those problems will not completely avoid the necessity for litigation. However, good contract administration can greatly facilitate the litigation in such cases. See, for example, *P.J. Dick, Inc.*, VABCA 5597, 01-2 BCA ¶ 31,647, *award revised*, 01-2 BCA ¶ 31,732, in which the parties negotiated the direct costs of hundreds of changes but could not agree on the impact costs. However, the parties stipulated a pricing formula and presented the board with a critical path schedule that had been updated throughout contract performance. The board commented that this was a "unique situation" that was "in sharp contrast to the usual problems we encounter in dealing with CPMs." The superior contract administration on this case enabled the board to fully resolve relatively complex claims in slightly more than two years.

3. Partnering

In the early 1990s, the Corps of Engineers initiated an innovative program called "partnering" in an effort to improve the working relationships of contracting parties. Partnering is designed to create a positive, disputes-prevention atmosphere during contract administration, U.S. Army Corps of Engineers, Partnering (IWR Pamphlet 91-ADR-P-4). In this pamphlet, the Corps set forth the following objectives of partnering:

> Partnering is the creation of an owner-contractor relationship that promotes achievement of mutually beneficial goals. It involves an agreement in principle to share the risks involved in completing the project, and to establish and promote a nurturing partnership environment. Partnering is not a contractual agreement, however, nor does it create any legally enforceable rights or duties. Rather, Partnering seeks to create a new cooperative attitude in completing government contracts. To create this attitude, each party must seek to understand the goals, objectives, and needs of the other—their "win" situation—and seek ways that these objectives can overlap.

Partnering encourages contracting parties to recognize common interests and to establish trust at the beginning of a project. One of the major goals of partnering is to resolve all disputes by negotiation rather than by litigation. Thus, the parties explicitly agree to forego adversarial relationships to the greatest extent possible.

An important element in Corps of Engineers partnering is a partnership workshop. See U.S. Army Corps of Engineers, Partnering (IWR Pamphlet 91-ADR-P-4), which states:

> The Partnership workshop helps participants establish open communications, develop a team spirit, set long range Partnering goals for the project, and gain commitment to the implementation plan. A combination of group activities, lectures, and experiential learning exercises has been effective in helping groups reach these goals in the workshop setting.
>
> Suggestions for a successful Partnering workshop include conducting the workshop as soon as possible after contract award; scheduling the workshop for several days since new working relationships take time to develop; using a location away from the office or project site to allow participants the chance to get away from their daily duties and concentrate on Partnering.

For current information on Corps of Engineers partnering efforts, see the Associated General Contractors/Corps of Engineers website at http://www.partneringbestpractice.org.

Other agencies have also adopted partnering procedures. See the Army Material Command Guide, *Partnering for Success: A Blueprint for Promoting Government-Industry Communication and Teamwork* (http://www.amc.army.mil/amc/command_counsel/partnering.html) and the Navy's *Industry-Government Partnering Resources Guide.*

B. Protection of Public Interest

In pursuing a goal of flexible contract administration to obtain the goods and services needed by the government, contracting officers and other government officials must be constantly aware of their obligation to protect the public interest. In administering government contracts, much attention is devoted to the public's interest in maintaining the integrity of the competitive system. This requires that the contracting officer take no actions during contract administration that would give the contractor an advantage that would not have been received by other competitors and grant no additional compensation that is not called for by contract clauses or other legal obligations of the government. The contracting officer's responsibilities are set forth in FAR 1.602-2, as follows:

> Contracting officers are responsible for ensuring performance of all necessary actions for effective contracting, ensuring compliance with the terms of the contract,

and safeguarding the interests of the United States in its contractual relationships. In order to perform these responsibilities, contracting officers should be allowed wide latitude to exercise business judgment. Contracting officers shall—

> (a) Ensure that the requirements of 1.602-1(b) have been met, and that sufficient funds are available for obligation;
>
> (b) Ensure that contractors receive impartial, fair, and equitable treatment; and
>
> (c) Request and consider the advice of specialists in audit, law, engineering, transportation, and other fields, as appropriate.

FAR 3.501-2 deals with buy-ins, which is the submission of a below-cost bid or proposal, with the offeror expecting to increase the contract amount through change orders or to receive follow-on contracts at artificially high prices, *K & P, Inc.*, Comp. Gen. Dec. B-219608, 85-2 CPD ¶ 121. FAR 3.501-2 specifically admonishes contracting officers to take appropriate action during contract administration to ensure that buying-in losses are not recovered through change orders or follow-on contracts.

1. Consideration Required

When it is necessary to deviate from the contract specifications or to permit the contractor to perform less work than called for by the contract, the integrity of the procurement system is maintained by obtaining consideration for the reduction in the contractor's obligation. See FAR 46.407(f), providing guidance on actions required when accepting nonconforming work:

> When supplies or services are accepted with critical or major nonconformances as authorized in paragraph (c) of this section, the contracting officer must modify the contract to provide for an equitable price reduction or other consideration. In the case of conditional acceptance, amounts withheld from payments generally should be at least sufficient to cover the estimated cost and related profit to correct deficiencies and complete unfinished work. The contracting officer must document in the contract file the basis for the amounts withheld. For services, the contracting officer can consider identifying the value of the individual work requirements or tasks (subdivisions) that may be subject to price or fee reduction. This value may be used to determine an equitable adjustment for nonconforming services. However, when supplies or services involving minor nonconformances are accepted, the contract need not be modified unless it appears that the savings to the contractor in fabricating the nonconforming supplies or performing the nonconforming services will exceed the cost to the Government of processing the modification.

The requirement for the government to receive consideration has sometimes been stated as a legal rule that no government official may "dispose of the rights and property of the United States" unless authorized by legislation, *Royal Indem. Co. v.*

United States, 313 U.S. 289 (1941). Thus, contract modifications will be overturned if the government obtains no benefit whatsoever, *Medica, S.A.*, ENGBCA PCC 142, 00-2 BCA ¶ 30,966; *H.Z. & Co.*, ASBCA 29572, 85-2 BCA ¶ 17,979; *A.O. Smith Corp.*, ASBCA 16788, 72-2 BCA ¶ 9688. Similarly, payments made without any basis in the contract provisions will be returned to the government, *Fansteel Metallurgical Corp. v. United States*, 145 Ct. Cl. 496, 172 F. Supp. 268 (1959); *Heritage Reporting Corp.*, ASBCA 51755, 99-2 BCA ¶ 30,474. This rule does not preclude the contracting officer from altering the contract requirements or settling claims as long as the government receives some benefit in the transaction. That benefit can include the contractor's release of an invalid claim so long as the contractor's position is not "beyond any color of a claim of right," *American Air Filter Co.*, ASBCA 14794, 72-1 BCA ¶ 9219. In *Institutional & Envtl. Mgmt., Inc.*, ASBCA 32924, 90-3 BCA ¶ 23,118, the board refused to enforce an agreement because it did "not consider [the contractor's] asserted interpretation as having any color of a claim of right." In such cases, the boards have made it clear that they will not overturn a contracting officer's contract modification merely because it is alleged that a bad bargain was made, *Airmotive Eng'g Corp.*, ASBCA 15235, 71-2 BCA ¶ 8988. See *Raytheon Co.*, ASBCA 51652, 03-2 BCA ¶ 32,337, in which the board refused to overturn a termination settlement that did not apply a loss adjustment because the Termination Contracting Officer had the authority to determine that he could not apportion the loss between the contractor and the agency.

The same principle applies to modifications where the contractor argues that it received no consideration. See, for example, *Lawrence W. Metzger*, ENGBCA 6426, 00-1 BCA ¶ 30,689, in which the board rejected the contractor's argument that a modification ending the contract was invalid because the government gave up its "colorable legal right to terminate" in exchange for the contractor's promise to not claim any further right to perform the work.

2. *Competitors' Complaints*

Unsuccessful competitors for a contract often feel that they have a right to insist on the contract being performed according to its terms. Complaints to contracting officers sometimes result in satisfactory resolution of the problem. However, competitors do not have standing to litigate poor contract administration unless it is related to a contract award protest, *M. Steinthal & Co. v. Seamans*, 455 F.2d 1289 (D.C. Cir. 1971). In *Gull Airborne Instruments, Inc. v. Weinberger*, 694 F.2d 838 (D.C. Cir. 1982), the court held that an unsuccessful competitor did not have the right to challenge the contracting officer's alleged "maladministration" of a contract, stating at 842-43:

> Unlike the regulations governing the award of contracts, see *Merriam v. Kunzig*, 476 F.2d at 1242, the regulations governing termination of contracts for default are not designed to foster competition or to protect unsuccessful bidders from illegal injury to their economic interests. The default regulations, see 32 C.F.R.

> §§ 8-600 to 8-602 (1981), are intended to protect the government against injury from the contractor's inability to perform the contract and the contracting party from the government's premature or unjustified cancellation. As a result, Gull must rely on its protest against the original award of the contract to CAS, not its subsequent administration, to establish that the government has illegally injured its economic interests.

See also *Cray Research, Inc. v. Department of the Navy*, 556 F. Supp. 201 (D.D.C. 1982), denying a competitor's right to sue to prevent substitution of a product since the substitution was not considered "such a 'cardinal change'. . . as to constitute, in effect, a completely new sole source procurement in violation of the competitive bid process." The cardinal change doctrine prevents government agencies from circumventing the competitive process by adopting modifications outside of the general scope of a contract. The basic standard, as applied in *Cray*, is whether the modified contract calls for essentially the same performance as that required by the contract when originally awarded, such that the modification does not materially change the field of competition, *Air-A-Plane Corp. v. United States*, 408 F.2d 1030 (Ct. Cl. 1969).

The Government Accountability Office (GAO) has also refused to consider matters of contract administration not involving bid protests. See, for example, *Lockheed Martin Fairchild Sys.*, Comp. Gen. Dec. B-275034, 97-1 CPD ¶ 28 (allegation that contractor was not complying with subcontracting limitation clause); *Parmatic Filter Corp.*, Comp. Gen. Dec. B-210138, 83-1 CPD ¶ 187 (allegation that contractor was not satisfactorily performing); *Pacific Horizons, Inc.*, Comp. Gen. Dec. B-204888, 82-2 CPD ¶ 32 (allegation that agency was not following specifications in approving work); and *Armidir, Ltd.*, Comp. Gen. Dec. B-204075, 82-2 CPD ¶ 188 (allegation that contractor was improperly allowed to substitute technician). In a unique case, the GAO followed this reasoning in refusing to address a protester's allegation that conducting a competition for follow-on work breached its contract because it was a requirements contract, *Hawker Eternacell, Inc.*, Comp. Gen. Dec. B-283586, 99-2 CPD ¶ 96. See also *Jones, Russotto & Walker*, Comp. Gen. Dec. B-283288.2, 99-2 CPD ¶ 111, refusing to rule on the issue of whether the agency should have exercised an option rather than conduct a new procurement because the decision to exercise an option is a matter of contract administration.

By contrast, protests claiming that the competitive procurement rules have been violated by awarding work to a contractor that should have been treated as a new procurement are regularly heard. See, for example, *AT&T Communications, Inc. v. WilTel, Inc.*, 1 F.3d 1201 (Fed. Cir. 1993), where competitors alleged that contractor proposals for improvements to the services, features, or other requirements of the contract allowed for modifications that were outside the scope of the original procurement and required new bid procedures. The GAO will review contract changes to determine whether they are outside the scope of the competition. See *Webcraft Packaging Div. of Beatrice Foods Co.*, Comp. Gen. Dec. B-194087, 79-2 CPD ¶ 120 (change in the paper quality was a material alteration because more companies would have been in the field of competition with a lesser grade of paper); *Memorex Corp.*, 61 Comp. Gen. 42 (B-200722), 81-2 CPD ¶ 334 (major specification changes and conversion from outright purchase to lease to ownership resulted in a cardinal change); *CPT Corp.*, Comp. Gen. Dec. B-211464, 84-1 CPD ¶ 606 (adding three years of work and additional types of equipment was outside the scope of the original competition); *Avtron Mfg., Inc.*, Comp. Gen. Dec. B-229972, 88-1 CPD ¶ 458 (change to the performance specifications in the purchase description for aircraft generator test stands would materially alter the terms of the original contract and change the field of competition); *MCI Communications Corp.*, Comp. Gen. Dec. B-276659.2, 97-2 CPD ¶ 90 (adding a service that was intrinsically different from services in initial contract is outside scope); and *Sprint Communications Co.*, Comp. Gen. Dec. B-278407.2, 98-1 CPD ¶ 60 (adding services not included in original work statement outside scope).

Task orders under indefinite-delivery, indefinite-quantity contracts may be issued without competition as long as the task order is within the general scope of the contract, *Astronautics Corp. of Am.*, 70 Comp. Gen. 554 (B-242782), 91-1 CPD ¶ 531. There, the GAO stated that protesters are precluded from contesting the issuance of a task order on the ground that the statement of work in the contract was too broad, reasoning at 557:

> Since the delivery order falls within the scope of the existing engineering services contract, there is no basis to require a separately-competed procurement as urged by the protester. *See Stanford Telecommunications, Inc.*, B-241449, Dec. 10, 1990, 90-2 CPD ¶ 475.
>
> Here, the basic contract appears to encompass an extremely broad spectrum of items and services, which prompted the protester to hypothesize that DOD could use the contract routinely to obtain a wide range of electronic items without meaningful competition. While on the limited record presented in this case we could not resolve the question, we recognize that where an agency conducts a procurement for a total package or for broadly aggregated needs without a legitimate basis for bundling its requirements rather than breaking them out, competition is inhibited in derogation of the mandate for "full and open competition" under the Competition in Contracting Act of 1984, 10 U.S.C. § 2304(a)(1)(A) (1988). *See LaBarge Products, Inc.*, B-232201, Nov. 23, 1988, 88-2 CPD ¶ 510; *Pacific Sky Supply, Inc.*, B-228049, Nov. 23, 1987, 87-2 CPD ¶ 504; *Systems, Terminals & Communications Corp.*, B-218170, May 21, 1985, 85-1 CPD ¶ 578. However, as the protester also acknowledges, the [Commerce Business Daily] synopsis indicated the broad range of services which could be acquired. [The protester] did not timely protest the scope of the procurement in 1988. To the extent that [the protester] is now protesting the scope of the requirements under the basic contract, the protest is untimely.

Whether a task order is within the general scope of the contract will be determined on a case-by-case basis. See *Information Ventures, Inc.*, Comp. Gen. Dec. B-240458, 90-2 CPD ¶ 414 (tasks logically related to the overall purpose of agreement); *Liebert Corp.*, Comp. Gen. Dec. B-232234.5, 91-1 CPD ¶ 413 (work within the general scope of the contract but quantity beyond maximum scope); and *Symetrics Indus., Inc.*, Comp. Gen. Dec. B-289606, 2002 CPD ¶ 65 (retrofitting modems within scope of contract calling for maintenance of modems). See, however, *Dynamac Corp.*, Comp. Gen. Dec. B-252800, 93-2 CPD ¶ 37, finding that an order for support of a computerized information system was not within the general scope of the contract because the original solicitation did not adequately advise offerors of the potential for this type of order. It has also been held that a task order may be protested on the grounds that it is for work that was required to be set aside for small business, *N&N Travel & Tours, Inc.*, Comp. Gen. Dec. B-285164.2, 2000 CPD ¶ 146.

II. CONTRACT ADMINISTRATION RULES AND THEIR SOURCES

The administration of contracts between private parties is generally limited only by the good faith enforcement of contract rights. However, when the government is one of the contracting parties, contract administration is also governed by a great number of rules emanating from statutes, regulations, and decisions. These rules affect the rights and duties of both parties. They also determine the types of actions of government personnel that will be binding upon the government. Knowledge of these rules is essential in determining the scope of the contractual bargain between the government and the contractor. All three branches of the government have a role in formulating these contract administration rules.

A. Legislative Branch

The Constitution is silent on the power to contract but does vest the spending power in the legislative branch of the government. Article I, Section 9, Clause 7 states:

> No Money shall be drawn from the Treasury, but in Consequence of Appropriations made by Law; and a regular Statement and Account of the Receipts and Expenditures of all public Money shall be published from time to time.

Thus, *through control of the spending power*, the legislative branch of the government has significant control of the contracting process. This control has been manifested in a number of different ways.

1. Appropriations and Authorizations

The cornerstone of Congress's budgetary control over executive agency contracting is the Anti-Deficiency Act, 31 U.S.C. § 1341, which prohibits government employees from obligating the government in excess or in advance of an amount available in an appropriation. Since a contract is an obligation, this Act prohibits contracts in advance of appropriations. Congress appropriates money to agencies in a two-step process. First, it passes an act authorizing the activity (authorization act), then it passes an act appropriating funds (appropriation act). In addition to providing funds to support procurement, both of these types of statutes often contain general provisions affecting contract administration.

2. Procurement Legislation

The two principal procedural statutes affecting federal contracting activity are the Armed Services Procurement Act of 1947, 10 U.S.C. §§ 2302-2314, and the Federal Property & Administrative Services Act of 1949, 41 U.S.C. §§ 251-260. Additional procedures are contained in the Office of Federal Procurement Policy Act of 1974, 41 U.S.C. §§ 403-437. Although these statutes provide detailed requirements for the awarding of contracts, they provide little guidance on matters of contract administration. Thus, there is no comprehensive statutory coverage of the contract administration process.

In the last two decades, however, Congress has regularly enacted other legislation addressing specific areas of the contract administration process. The most pervasive legislation in this regard is the Contract Disputes Act of 1978, Pub. L. No. 95-563, 41 U.S.C. § 601 et seq., which prescribes detailed procedures for resolving disputes relating to government contracts. The balance of this book will identify other specific statutory provisions as applicable to the subject matter covered.

3. Oversight Function

Congressional oversight of general procurement matters is principally carried out in the Senate by the Governmental Affairs and Small Business Committees and in the House of Representatives by the Government Reform and Small Business Committees. However, each committee of Congress with authority over the programs of a procuring agency, such as the Senate and House Armed Services Committees, monitors the procurement practices of that agency, and the Appropriations Committees are quite active in reviewing selective procurement policies. Although only a few binding procurement rules are enacted into statute as a result of the oversight process, agencies normally give great respect to the views of these committees when formulating contract administration policies.

4. Government Accountability Office

The GAO is a part of the legislative branch of the government, with a large staff that monitors the work of the executive branch. Although it has taken on broad responsibilities in adjudicating disputes arising out of the award of government contracts, it has played a relatively limited role in matters bearing on the day-to-day contract administration—primarily because of the U.S. Supreme Court's conclusion that the GAO lacks authority to decide matters that fall within the ambit of the disputes process, *S & E Contractors, Inc. v. United States*, 406 U.S. 1 (1972); *Bradley Mechanical Contracting, Inc.*, 53 Comp. Gen. 829 (B-180726), 74-1 CPD ¶ 229. Nevertheless, the GAO can affect certain aspects of contract administration through its authority to approve or disapprove payments by government officials, 31 U.S.C. § 3526, and through exercise of its audit and supervisory authority under 31 U.S.C. §§ 712 and 3521, 10 U.S.C. § 2313(c), and 41 U.S.C. § 254d(c). Thus, in cases where the agency's authority is uncertain or questionable, the government or a contractor can seek an advance decision from the GAO before taking significant contract action, such as recognizing or paying a claim. If the matter does not fall within the disputes procedure, the GAO will respond with a decision that will be binding on the GAO but not upon the contractor. See *Greene County Planning Bd. v. Federal Power Comm'n*, 559 F.2d 1227 (2d Cir. 1976), *cert. denied*, 434 U.S. 1086 (1978), stating at 1239:

> 31 U.S.C. § 74 [3529] permits the head of an executive department, in his discretion, to apply to the Comptroller General for a commitment in advance that the General Accounting Office will not question the validity of a specific disbursement in passing upon the account of that department. A commitment given in response to such a request operates as a form of estoppel against subsequent challenge by the GAO. It is not, however, a binding legal opinion, but one which may be contested in the courts. *United States ex rel. Brookfield Construction Co. v. Stewart*, 234 F. Supp. 94, 100 (D.D.C.), *aff'd*, 119 U.S. App. D.C. 254, 339 F.2d 753 (1964). It is for the courts to determine the intent of Congress as expressed in its legislative enactments. In making this determination, as we do in this case, we interfere in no way with the authority of the Comptroller General to approve or disapprove disbursements made by executive agencies. We simply hold that the Federal Power Commission has no statutory authority to make the disbursements in question. Cf. *Miguel v. McCarl*, 291 U.S. 442, 78 L. Ed. 901, 54 S. Ct. 465 (1934) (footnote omitted).

These GAO decisions, although not legally binding, are sometimes cited as authority for actions taken in contract administration.

B. Executive Branch

Rules affecting contract administration are promulgated in a number of different regulations. Executive orders issued by the president, Office of Management and Budget (OMB) circulars, and Office of Federal Procurement Policy (OFPP) policy letters address matters having broad application throughout the executive branch. Another type of regulation impacting contract administration is one issued by an agency having the responsibility of overseeing a specific government program or policy. For example, the Department of Labor has issued regulations under the Service Contract Act, 41 U.S.C. §§ 351-58 (29 C.F.R. pt. 8) and Executive Order 11246 (29 C.F.R. pt. 60).

1. Procurement Regulations

The principal sources of guidance in administration of contracts are the procurement regulations issued by the procuring agencies. Since April 1, 1984, the Federal

Acquisition Regulation (FAR) has been applicable throughout the executive branch of the government. It is published in Title 48, Chapter 1 of the Code of Federal Regulations (C.F.R.) and was promulgated pursuant to Executive Order 12352, March 17, 1982, by the Secretary of Defense and the Administrators of the General Services Administration (GSA) and the National Aeronautics and Space Administration (NASA). It replaced the Defense Acquisition Regulation (DAR), the NASA Procurement Regulation (NASAPR), and the Federal Procurement Regulations (FPR) as the top-level regulation under the Armed Services Procurement Act of 1947, 10 U.S.C. § 2302 et seq., and the Federal Property & Administrative Services Act of 1949, 41 U.S.C. § 252 et seq. Guidance on the FAR is contained in 41 U.S.C. § 421.

The FAR is implemented by FAR supplements issued by each major agency with significant procurement responsibilities. These supplements may only contain "(A) regulations essential to implement Government-wide policies and procedures within the agency, and (B) additional policies and procedures required to satisfy the specific and unique needs of the agency," 41 U.S.C. § 421(c)(2). In many agencies there are also additional supplements issued by organizations within the agency. For example, in the Department of Defense (DoD), there is a DoD FAR Supplement (DFARS) supplemented by a number of agencies, including the Navy (NARSUP), the Air Force (AFFARS), and the Army (AFARS). While the FAR and its first-tier supplement are published in the *Federal Register*, the lower-tier supplements in the various agencies may not be. A contractor can request the Administrator of OFPP to review any supplementary regulation to ensure that it is consistent with the FAR, 41 U.S.C. § 421(c)(4).

2. Legal Effect of Regulations

The legal status of regulations published by the executive branch depends on the authority under which they are promulgated. Procurement regulations are authorized by the two procurement statutes. FAR 1.103 contains the following citation of authority for its publication:

> (a) The development of the FAR System is in accordance with the requirements of the Office of Federal Procurement Policy Act of 1974 (Pub. L. 93-400), as amended by Pub. L. 96-83.
>
> (b) The FAR is prepared, issued, and maintained, and the FAR System is prescribed, jointly by the Secretary of Defense, the Administrator of General Services, and the Administrator, National Aeronautics and Space Administration, under their several statutory authorities.

The Office of Federal Procurement Policy (OFPP) Act, Pub. L. No. 98-191, grants significant regulatory authority to the Administrator at 41 U.S.C. § 405:

> Authority and Functions of the Administrator

> (a) Development of procurement policy; leadership. The Administrator shall provide overall direction of procurement policy and leadership in the development of procurement systems of the executive agencies. To the extent that the Administrator considers appropriate, in carrying out the policies and functions set forth in this Act, and with due regard for applicable laws and the program activities of the executive agencies, the Administrator may prescribe Government-wide procurement policies. These policies shall be implemented in a single Government-wide procurement regulation called the Federal Acquisition Regulation and shall be followed by executive agencies in the procurement of—
>
> (1) property other than real property in being;
>
> (2) services, including research and development; and
>
> (3) construction, alteration, repair, or maintenance of real property.

This leadership function is carried out by having the Administrator serve as chairperson of the FAR Council, which maintains and supplements the FAR. The OFPP Act also authorizes OFPP to issue government-wide regulations if DoD, NASA, and GSA fail to agree on necessary FAR provisions, 41 U.S.C. § 405(b). In addition, the Director of OMB is authorized to deny the promulgation of or to rescind procurement regulations, 41 U.S.C. § 405(f). These powers of the Administrator of OFPP and the Director of OMB have not been utilized in any significant manner, and the FAR continues to be promulgated under the statutory powers of DoD, GSA, and NASA.

Regulations will have the force and effect of law only if authorized by Congress, *Chrysler Corp. v. Brown*, 441 U.S. 281 (1979). However, there is disagreement as to the nature and extent of the required congressional authorization. *G.L. Christian & Assocs. v. United States*, 160 Ct. Cl. 1, 312 F.2d 418, *reh'g denied*, 160 Ct. Cl. 58, 320 F.2d 345, *cert. denied*, 375 U.S. 954 (1963), is the leading case for the proposition that procurement regulations may have the force and effect of law. In finding that a procurement regulation that mandated inclusion of a Termination for Convenience of the Government clause in defense contracts had the force and effect of law even though there was no specific statutory authority for such provision, the court looked to the general authority of the agency to issue procurement regulations and then considered the importance of the government policy. More recently, the focus has been on connecting the regulatory provision with the statutory authority rather than on the importance of the policy. In *Liberty Mut. Ins. Co. v. Friedman*, 639 F.2d 164 (4th Cir. 1981), the court considered whether the Labor Department had the statutory authority to issue a regulation stating that an insurance provider was a subcontractor subject to the equal employment requirements of Executive Order 11246. The court stated at 169:

> A congressional grant of legislative authority need not be specific in order to sustain the validity of regulations promulgated pursuant to the grant, but a court must "reasonably be able to conclude that the grant of authority contemplates

> the regulations issued." [*Chrysler Corp. v. Brown*, 441 U.S. 281] at 308, 99 S. Ct. at 1721. Our examination of the possible statutory sources of congressional authorization for Executive Order 11,246 convinces us that none of the statutes reasonably contemplates that Liberty, as a provider of workers' compensation insurance to government contractors, may be required to comply with Executive Order 11,246. We conclude therefore that none of the cited statutes authorize the action taken by [the Labor Department].

The court went on to hold that the delegation of general procurement power by Congress to the executive by the Federal Property & Administrative Services Act, 40 U.S.C. § 101 et seq., would support regulations not specifically authorized only to the extent that they were adopted to further the congressional purpose of achieving an "economical and efficient system" of procurement. The court rejected "the proposition that equal employment goals themselves, reflecting important national policies, validate the use of procurement power," disagreeing with *United States v. New Orleans Pub. Serv., Inc.*, 553 F.2d 459 (5th Cir. 1977), *vacated and remanded on other grounds*, 436 U.S. 942 (1978), to the extent that it so held. In *Matter of Gary Aircraft Corp.*, 698 F.2d 775 (5th Cir. 1983), the court held that prior to the Contract Disputes Act of 1978, the Disputes clause mandated by the regulations did not have the force and effect of law because the clause was not specifically authorized by the Armed Services Procurement Act. However, the court reasoned that the clause was an important mechanism for resolving disputes and that a bankruptcy court should defer to the appeals board in initially determining the rights of the parties in the contract. In finding that the clause did not have the force and effect of law, the court did not discuss the general authority of the Secretary of Defense to promulgate regulations contained in 10 U.S.C. § 2202. There was also no discussion of the efficiency and economy nexus found necessary in the *Liberty Mutual* case. Arguably, the Disputes clause, with its remedial provisions, would satisfy this requirement. In *AFL-CIO v. Kahn*, 618 F.2d 784 (D.C. Cir.), *cert. denied*, 443 U.S. 915 (1979), the court upheld the requirement for government contractors to certify compliance with "voluntary" wage and price guidelines under Executive Order 12092. It found that the Executive Order's predominant objective of containing procurement costs furnished the required nexus with the Procurement Act's criteria of efficiency and economy. Accord, *UAW-Labor Employment & Training Corp. v. Chao*, 325 F.3d 360 (D.C. Cir. 2003), holding that Executive Order 13201, requiring employers to notify employees that they could work without joining a union, had the required nexus to the Procurement Act's goal of promoting an economical and efficient procurement system.

Most regulations that have a direct impact on the procurement process have the force and effect of law. Thus, contractors are bound by such regulations. See, for example, *Hawpe Constr. Co. v. United States*, 46 Fed. Cl. 571 (2000), *aff'd*, 10 Fed. Appx. 957 (Fed. Cir. 2001) (Small Business Administration change to an SIC Code provision published in the *Federal Register*); *ECC Int'l Corp. v. United States*, 43 Fed. Cl. 359 (1999) (Air Force FAR Supplement barring the use of an Economic

Price Adjustment clause without approval of higher authority); *Melrose Assocs., L.P. v. United States*, 43 Fed. Cl. 124 (1999) (agency regulation limiting the authority of local contracting officers); and *New America Shipbuilders, Inc. v. United States*, 871 F.2d 1077 (Fed. Cir. 1989) (Small Business Administration regulation limited the delegated authority to approve business development expense grants to $350,000).

3. Publication

In order for a regulation to have the force and effect of law, the contractor must have actual or constructive notice of the regulation. Constructive notice occurs when regulations have been published in the *Federal Register, Federal Crop Ins. Corp. v. Merrill*, 332 U.S. 380 (1947). The Freedom of Information Act (FOIA), 5 U.S.C. § 552(a)(1), follows this rule that a person can be bound by both actual and constructive notice, stating:

> Except to the extent that a person has actual and timely notice of the terms thereof, a person may not in any manner . . . be adversely affected by a matter required to be published in the Federal Register and not so published.

FOIA also provides that "substantive rules" must be published in the *Federal Register*; however, according to § 552(a)(2) "administrative staff manuals and instructions to staff that affect a member of the public" need only be made available for public inspection or copies be offered for sale.

In order to have a binding effect, procurement regulations must be published in the *Federal Register* in accordance with 41 U.S.C. § 418b:

> [N]o procurement policy, regulation, procedure, or form (including amendments or modifications thereto) relating to the expenditure of appropriated funds that has (1) a significant effect beyond the internal operating procedures of the agency issuing the procurement policy, regulation, procedure or form, or (2) a significant cost or administrative impact on contractors or offerors, may take effect until 60 days after the procurement policy, regulation, procedure, or form is published for public comment in the Federal Register pursuant to subsection (b) of this section.

This permits public comment on proposed regulations prior to their taking effect. Generally, at the time of issuance of the final regulation the agency will provide responses to the public comments. Waiver of this publication requirement is permitted in specified circumstances, 41 U.S.C. § 418b(d).

Actual notice of unpublished regulations has been established in several ways. In *Planning Research Corp.*, 55 Comp. Gen. 911 (B-184926), 76-1 CPD ¶ 202, the contractor was held to have notice of the contents of an agency manual that was incorporated in the contract by reference. See also *Timber Access Indus. Co. v. United States*, 213 Ct. Cl. 648, 553 F.2d 1250 (1977), in which a contractor was held to have had actual and timely notice of regulations contained in an unpublished Forest Service manual and was bound by the terms of the manual. The court stated at 656:

> The record clearly shows that [the contractor] had knowledge of the . . . Manual. During the course of negotiations preceding the contract modification, [the contractor] in fact quoted part of the Manual to the Forest Service. In addition, the contract itself invites the contractor to search out the meaning of [the term]. . . . Just slight inquiry would have brought forth the information . . . .

C. Judicial and Quasi-Judicial Decisions

Although statutes and agency regulations supply broad guidelines for administering government contracts, they provide little or no guidance for many aspects of day-to-day contract administration. As a result, contractors and government officials must frequently look to decided cases to interpret contract provisions and ascertain appropriate courses of conduct in administering contract performance. Decisional guidance is supplied by both judicial and quasi-judicial forums.

Prior to 1982, the Court of Claims, pursuant to the Tucker Act, 28 U.S.C. § 1491, had been the court most extensively involved in government contract administration matters. Under this statute, the court had exclusive jurisdiction over contract cases against the government exceeding $10,000 and had sole jurisdiction of all contract cases covered by the Contract Disputes Act of 1978, 41 U.S.C. § 601 et seq. Review of decisions of the Court of Claims could only be obtained through a petition for certiorari to the Supreme Court, 28 U.S.C. § 1255, and in recent years the Court has generally refused to grant certiorari in procurement law cases. Thus, the Court of Claims effectively served as the court of last resort in the litigation of procurement matters. The Federal Courts Improvement Act of 1982, Pub. L. No. 97-164, abolished the Court of Claims, effective October 1, 1982, and in its place substituted the United States Claims Court and the Court of Appeals for the Federal Circuit. The Federal Courts Administration Act of 1992, Pub. L. No. 102-572, effective October 29, 1992, changed the name of the Claims Court to the United States Court of Federal Claims. The Court of Federal Claims holds trials and renders decisions on contractor claims, whereas the Court of Appeals for the Federal Circuit hears appeals from both the Court of Federal Claims and boards of contract appeals.

Perhaps the most important sources of decisional guidance on contract administration matters are the boards of contract appeals. Although these boards are actually within the contracting agencies, they are required to function in a quasi-judicial capacity as independent boards rendering decisions on contract disputes. There are currently 10 principal agency boards. The boards are more involved in contract administration matters as a result of the Contract Disputes Act of 1978, which expands the authority of the boards by authorizing them to decide all disputes relative to a contract, 41 U.S.C. § 607(d). For many years they have provided detailed commentary on the rights of the contracting parties during performance as they have resolved the numerous controversies that have arisen during administration of government contracts. A detailed discussion of the jurisdictions and roles of courts and boards of contract appeals is contained in Chapter 13.

D. Effect of Statutes and Regulations with the Force and Effect of Law

When the procedures used to enter into or administer a contract or its terms and conditions do not comply with a statute or a regulation with the force and effect of law, a variety of consequences may follow. In some cases, the government may be permitted to avoid the contract. In other instances, the contract may be rewritten to add a mandatory clause or exclude a prohibited clause. Finally, the contractor may require the government to abide by mandatory procedures that benefit the contractor.

1. Contract Avoidance

The government has the right to avoid a contract that is made in violation of a statute or a regulation with the force and effect of law. Such contracts have been variously described as void ab initio, *Trilon Educ. Corp. v. United States*, 217 Ct. Cl. 266, 578 F.2d 1356 (1978); invalid, *Prestex, Inc. v. United States*, 162 Ct. Cl. 620, 320 F.2d 367 (1963); or illegal, *Alabama Rural Fire Ins. Co. v. United States*, 215 Ct. Cl. 442, 572 F.2d 727 (1978). Government avoidance is limited to clear violations of statutes or regulations, *John Reiner & Co. v. United States*, 163 Ct. Cl. 381, 325 F.2d 438 (1963), *cert. denied*, 377 U.S. 931 (1964). In *Reiner*, the court held that an improper cancellation should be treated as a termination for the convenience of the government, stating that the "binding stamp of nullity" should only be imposed when the illegality is "plain." See also *United States v. Amdahl Corp.*, 786 F.2d 387 (Fed. Cir. 1986), where the contracting officer's failure to comply with statutory requirements in making an award rendered the contract null and void. While the government may avoid contracts tainted by fraud, kickbacks, conflicts of interest, or bribery, the government must exercise its right of avoidance in a timely manner or it will be forfeited, *Godley v. United States*, 26 Cl. Ct. 1075 (1992), *vacated and remanded*, 5 F.3d 1473 (Fed. Cir. 1993).

Following avoidance, the contractor will be denied compensation if the illegality involved criminal activity by the contractor, *K & R Eng'g Co. v. United States*, 222 Ct. Cl. 340, 616 F.2d 469 (1980) (contractor not entitled to payments due for completed work on contracts involving a violation of the conflict of interest statute, 18 U.S.C. § 208, and government entitled to recover amounts already paid) or if the illegality should have been apparent to the contractor and the government received no benefit, *Toyo Menka Kaisha, Ltd. v. United States*, 220 Ct. Cl. 210, 597 F.2d 1371 (1979). See also *Prestex, Inc. v. United States*, 162 Ct. Cl. 620, 320 F.2d 367 (1963) (Government permitted to reject a shipment of supplies that conformed to the contract but not to the invitation for bids).

Where no criminal activity was involved *and* the government received a benefit, recovery has been permitted, *New York Mail & Newspaper Transp. Co. v. United States*, 139 Ct. Cl. 751, 154 F. Supp. 271, *cert. denied*, 355 U.S. 904 (1957) (even though the contract was null and void for violating the advertising statute, the contractor was entitled to recover for the value of services rendered to the date of avoidance, not limited to quantum meruit). In *United States v. Amdahl Corp.*, 786 F.2d 387 (Fed. Cir. 1986), the court stated at 393:

> [I]n many circumstances it would violate good conscience to impose upon the contractor *all* economic loss from having entered an illegal contract. Where a benefit has been conferred by the contractor on the government in the form of goods or services, which it accepted, a contractor may recover at least on a *quantum valebant* or *quantum meruit* basis for the value of the conforming goods or services received by the government prior to the rescission of the contract for invalidity. The contractor is not compensated *under* the contract, but rather under an implied-in-fact contract. [Footnote omitted.]

See also *Urban Data Sys., Inc. v. United States*, 699 F.2d 1147 (Fed. Cir. 1983), granting recovery of the reasonable value of work on a cost-plus-percentage-of-cost contract barred by statute. In that case, the court held that only the price term was invalid, not any other part of the agreement. Similarly, in *Beta Sys., Inc. v. United States*, 838 F.2d 1179, 1185-86 (Fed. Cir. 1988), the court allowed reformation of the contract price term to correct a regulatory violation, and in *Fluor Enters., Inc. v. United States*, 64 Fed. Cl. 461 (2005), the court found the contractor entitled to recover the reasonable value of the services rendered when the agency had not complied with the statute limiting the fees of architect/engineers. In *Maintenance Serv. & Sales Corp.*, 70 Comp. Gen. 664 (B-242019) (1991), the GAO permitted recovery of the contract price even though the contracting officer's warrant had expired, one delivery order was under a fictitious GSA Federal Supply Schedule number, orders were issued without competition, and the work was funded with annual appropriations but not completed until after the expiration date of those appropriations. The GAO stated at 665-66:

> A contract should not be treated as void, even if improperly awarded, unless the illegality of the award is plain or palpable. *See John Reiner & Co. v. United States*, 325 F.2d 438, 440 (Ct. Cl. 1963), *cert. denied*, 377 U.S. 931 (1964); *Memorex Corp.*, B-213430.2, Oct. 23, 1984, 84-2 CPD ¶ 446. An award is plainly or palpably illegal if the award was made contrary to statutory or regulatory requirements because of some action or statement by the contractor, or if the contractor was on direct notice that the procedures followed were unlawful. 52 Comp. Gen. 215, 218-219 (1972). Here, there is no indication in the record that the impropriety was due to some action or statement by the contractor or that the contractor was on notice that the contracting officer failed to obtain competition. Under these circumstances, we are unable to conclude that the award of delivery order No. 0028 was plainly or palpably illegal and therefore void. Consequently, the contractor may recover under the terms of that contract. Interest on the amount due may be recovered as provided for under the Prompt Payment Act, 31 U.S.C. §§ 3901-3906 (1988).

2. *Exclusion or Inclusion of Clause*

Another major effect of a statute or a regulation with the force and effect of law is the impact on the contract language. Thus, if a clause is required to be included in the contract and it "is sufficiently ingrained in public procurement policy," the contract will be read to include it even though it is not physically incorporated in the document, *G.L. Christian & Assocs. v. United States*, 160 Ct. Cl. 1, 312 F.2d 418, *reh'g denied*, 160 Ct. Cl. 58, 320 F.2d 345, *cert. denied*, 375 U.S. 954 (1963) (Termination for Convenience of the Government clause); *Maintenance Eng'rs, Inc.*, VABCA 5350, 99-2 BCA ¶ 30,513 (Default clause); *University of Cal., San Francisco*, VABCA 4661, 97-1 BCA ¶ 28,642 (Price Reduction for Defective Cost or Pricing Data clause); *S.J. Amoroso Constr. Co. v. United States*, 12 F.3d 1072 (Fed. Cir. 1993) (Buy American Act clause); *General Eng'g & Mach. Works v. O'Keefe*, 991 F.2d 775 (Fed. Cir. 1993) (Time and Material Payments clause); *Balimoy Mfg. Co.*, ASBCA 43768, 93-1 BCA ¶ 25,437 (First Article Approval clause); *Santa Fe-Andover Oil Co.*, ASBCA 35256, 88-2 BCA ¶ 20,607 (Disputes clause); *Dayron Corp.*, ASBCA 24919, 84-1 BCA ¶ 17,213 (Government Property clause); *Spectrum Am. Contractors*, ASBCA 33039, 87-2 BCA ¶ 19,864 (Disputes Concerning Labor Standards clause); *Centel Communications Co.*, GSBCA 8218, 89-1 BCA ¶ 21,225 (price adjustment for fixed-price multiyear service contracts clause). Similarly, if a certain clause is prohibited, it will be read out of the contract even though it is physically present, *Johnson Mgmt. Group CFC, Inc. v. Martinez*, 308 F.3d 1245 (Fed. Cir. 2002) (special clause waiving security for advance payments); *Charles Beseler Co.*, ASBCA 22669, 78-2 BCA ¶ 13,483 (Value Engineering clause).

If a clause does not implement a procurement policy that is "significant" or "deeply engrained," it will not be incorporated in the contract, *Lambrecht & Sons, Inc.*, ASBCA 49515, 97-2 BCA ¶ 29,105 (Variations in Estimated Quantities clause); *Computing Application Software Tech., Inc.*, ASBCA 47554, 96-1 BCA ¶ 28,204 (National Aeronautics & Space Administration Liability for Government Property Furnished for Repair and Services clause). See also *Ace-Federal Reporters, Inc. v. Barram*, 226 F.3d 1329 (Fed. Cir. 2002), holding that regulations governing the Federal Supply Schedules stating that agencies could buy services even though they were mandatory users were not applicable to the contract because they did not meet this test.

In applying the "Christian Doctrine," the court or board will carefully scrutinize the regulation to ensure that the clause is mandatory. If not, it will not be incorporated. See *IBI Sec. Serv., Inc. v. United States*, 19 Cl. Ct. 106 (1989), *aff'd without op.*, 918 F.2d 188 (Fed. Cir. 1990), refusing to include a price adjustment clause because the regulations were not clear as to whether the clause was mandatory. See also *Professional Servs. Unified, Inc.*, ASBCA 48883, 96-1 BCA ¶ 28,073 (Federal, State and Local Taxes clause calling for equitable adjustments not applicable to competitive procurements), and *Shawn K. Christensen*, AGBCA 95-188-R, 95-2 BCA ¶ 27,724 (Differing Site Conditions clause not a required clause for service contracts).

3. *Government Bound*

Initially, these rules involving statutes and regulations were used only for the benefit of the government. Subsequently, however, regulations have been applied to benefit contractors. In *Fletcher v. United States*, 183 Ct. Cl. 1, 392 F.2d 266 (1968), the court held that regulations intended to define or state the rights of a class of persons are presumptively intended for the benefit of those persons. Such regulations can be asserted by a contractor to its benefit, *Moran Bros., Inc. v. United States*, 171 Ct. Cl. 245, 346 F.2d 590 (1965) (AEC procurement regulation that permitted appeals within 60 days had the effect of law, and appeal was timely even though it exceeded the 30-day limit included in the contract); 47 Comp. Gen. 457 (B-162272) (1968) (mandatory government liability for insurance premiums read into the contract); *Bethlehem Steel Corp. v. United States*, 191 Ct. Cl. 141, 423 F.2d 300 (1970) (regulation prescribing technique for determining the profit applied for the benefit of contractors); *Chris Berg, Inc. v. United States*, 192 Ct. Cl. 176, 426 F.2d 314 (1970) (procurement regulation giving contractors the right to correct clerical mistakes in bids binding on the government).

Significant doubt about the ability of a contractor to take advantage of statutes that make contracts illegal was created by the decisions in *American Tel. & Tel. Co. v. United States*. In the initial round of litigation, the courts held that a firm fixed price contract was void because it violated § 8118 of the Defense Appropriations Act of 1987, 101 Stat. 1329 (1987), prohibiting such contracts without Secretarial approval, 32 Fed. Cl. 672 (1995), *aff'd,* 124 F.3d 1471 (Fed. Cir. 1997), *vacated and withdrawn*, 136 F.3d 793 (Fed. Cir. 1998). However, the Federal Circuit ruled that since the contract was fully performed, the only remedy for the contractor was replevin of the weapon system—denying monetary recovery or reformation. Subsequently, the Federal Circuit decided en banc that the statutory violation did not make the contract void, 177 F.3d. 1368 (1999). On remand, the Court of Federal Claims dismissed the contractor's claim for reformation because the regulations gave the agency discretion to negotiate a firm fixed-price contract and the contractor had willingly agreed to such a contract, 48 Fed. Cl. (2000), *aff'd*, 307 F.3d 1374 (Fed. Cir. 2002), *cert. denied*, 540 U.S. 937 (2003). The crux of the court's reasoning was that a statute requiring internal approvals prior to the use of fixed-price contracts was not enacted for the benefit of contractors but rather as a means of congressional policing of contracting agencies. See also *Northrop Grumman Corp. v. United States*, 47 Fed. Cl. 20 (2000), finding a fixed-price incentive contract illegal because it violated subsequent statutes limiting the use of fixed-price type contracts but denying any remedy such as reformation, and *Gould, Inc. v. United States*, 66 Fed. Cl. 253 (2005), holding that the multiyear contracting statute, 10 U.S.C. § 2306(h), requiring findings prior to the use of such a contract, gave the contractor no rights because it was not enacted for the benefit of contractors.

E. Deviations and Waivers

The existence of procurement regulations and statutes that have wide-reaching effects necessarily gives rise to instances when their application will not be in the best interest of the government. This section addresses the authority and procedures for deviating from regulations and waiving statutory requirements.

1. Deviations from Regulations

Authority and procedures for obtaining deviations from the regulations in the interest of providing flexibility in the procurement system are contained in FAR 1.402, which states:

> Unless precluded by law, executive order, or regulation, deviations from the FAR may be granted as specified in this subpart when necessary to meet the specific needs and requirements of each agency. The development and testing of new techniques and methods of acquisition should not be stifled simply because such action would require a FAR deviation. The fact that deviation authority is required should not, of itself, deter agencies in their development and testing of new techniques and acquisition methods.

Regulatory deviations are granted within each agency, FAR 1.403-.404. The authority to approve deviations varies according to the agency and whether the deviation is requested for an individual contract or for more than one contract or contractor. See, for example, DFARS Subpart 1.4. No similar deviation procedure exists for other executive branch regulations such as executive orders, OMB circulars, and OFPP policy letters.

Deviations are not valid unless they are granted strictly in accordance with the regulations. In *G.L. Christian & Assocs. v. United States*, 160 Ct. Cl. 1, 312 F.2d 418, *reh'g denied*, 160 Ct. Cl. 58, 320 F.2d 345, *cert. denied*, 375 U.S. 954 (1963), the court refused to find that a deviation was approved in the absence of a specific request for a deviation addressed to the official with deviation authority, stating on rehearing, at 70:

> The Armed Services Procurement Regulations contemplated a specific mechanism for receiving permission to deviate from required forms or articles. There is no proof, or offer to prove, that this mechanism was used. It is said, however, that the general agreement of the Assistant Secretary of Defense (Properties and Installations) with the Federal Housing Commissioner upon a number of forms, including a form of housing contract, constituted sufficient permission to eliminate the termination-for-convenience clause. Here, too, there is lacking any proof that this particular Assistant Secretary was empowered to approve alterations in articles mandatorily required by the [regulation]. More importantly, we are not persuaded that a conscious decision was made, at the appropriate level in the Defense Department, to eliminate the required termination article and thus to sub-

ject the Government to the full common-law measures of damages (including unearned profits).

See also *McDonnell Douglas Corp. v. United States*, 229 Ct. Cl. 323, 670 F.2d 156 (1982), holding that deviation from the precise wording of a prescribed clause without obtaining approval pursuant to the regulations was beyond the authority of the contracting officer; and *Johnson Mgmt. Group CFC, Inc. v. Martinez*, 308 F.3d 1245 (Fed. Cir. 2002), holding that the contracting officer had no authority to add language to a required clause without obtaining a proper deviation. In *Whittaker Corp.*, ASBCA 18422, 81-1 BCA ¶ 15,055, the board refused to find that a deviation was required when, after award of the contract, the contracting officer entered into a modification that gave a board of contract appeals jurisdiction over a claim specifically excluded from its jurisdiction by a mandatory contract clause. The board noted that the government received consideration for the modification and that the "granting of such a waiver was well within the ambit of the contracting officer's authority to administer the contract." The impact of the board's decision is that, absent an approved deviation, the contracting officer had no authority to modify or exclude the clause when the contract was formed, but could do so during contract administration.

Class deviations that have a significant impact on contractors do not take effect until notice of their issuance is published in the *Federal Register*, *La Gloria Oil & Gas Co. v. United States*, 56 Fed. Cl. 211 (2003); *Tesoro Haw. Corp. v. United States*, 58 Fed. Cl. 65 (2003), *rev'd on other grounds*, 405 F.3d 1339 (Fed. Cir. 2005). This publication requirement is not contained in the FAR but is found in 41 U.S.C. § 418b(a). In holding that class deviations fell within this statute, the court reasoned that they were modifications of a regulation since they permitted deviation from the FAR.

2. Waiver of Statutory Requirements

Government officials do not have the authority to waive statutory requirements in the absence of a specific statutory provision granting such authority, *Sam Gray Enters. v. United States*, 43 Fed. Cl. 596 (1999), *aff'd*, 250 F.3d 755 (Fed. Cir. 2000) (requirements of Anti-Deficiency Act); *M-R-S Mfg. Co. v. United States*, 203 Ct. Cl. 551, 492 F.2d 835 (1974) (requirements of the Truth in Negotiations Act not waivable by the contracting officer); *Harry L. Lowe & Assocs.*, 53 Comp. Gen. 620 (B-178307), 74-1 CPD ¶ 96 (requirement for a valid ICC operating authority for interstate motor transportation services cannot be waived by a government agency). However, Congress has provided such authority in a significant number of statutes. For example, see 41 U.S.C. § 10a (authorizes heads of agencies to waive the requirements of the Buy American Act upon determination that the cost of compliance is unreasonable or application is inconsistent with the public interest); 40 U.S.C. § 3133(c) (authorizes contracting officers to waive Miller Act bond requirements with respect to cost-type contracts for construction of public buildings and procurement of certain material and supplies for the Army, Navy, Air Force, and Coast Guard); 40 U.S.C. § 501(a)(2) (authorizes the Secretary of Defense to exempt DoD from certain procurement methods and policies prescribed by GSA unless the president directs otherwise); 41 U.S.C. § 40 (authorizes the Secretary of Labor to provide exemptions from wage and hour requirements of the Walsh-Healey Act and authorizes the president to suspend certain sections of the Act upon judgment that such action would be in the public interest); 40 U.S.C. § 3706 (authorizes the Secretary of Labor to provide exemptions from the Contract Work Hours Standards Act); 41 U.S.C. § 353(b) (authorizes the Secretary of Labor to provide exemptions from the Service Contract Act of 1965); 40 U.S.C. § 3147 (authorizes the president to suspend the provisions of the Davis-Bacon Act in the event of a national emergency); 46 U.S.C. App. § 1241(b) (authorizes the president or the Secretary of Defense to temporarily waive requirements of the Cargo Preference Act upon declaration that an emergency exists justifying such action); and 10 U.S.C. § 2306a(b)(2), 41 U.S.C. § 254A(b)(2) (authorizes agency heads to waive requirement for cost or pricing data in exceptional cases).

A judicially forged exception to the requirement for specific statutory authority for a government official to waive a statute has been applied to the Anti-Assignment Act, 41 U.S.C. § 15. The statute states that any prohibited assignment "shall cause the annulment of the contract." In *Tuftco Corp. v. United States*, 222 Ct. Cl. 277, 614 F.2d 740 (1980), the court held that a contracting officer possessed the necessary authority to waive the statute. This seemingly controverts not only conventional concepts of sources of authority but also the specific policies inherent in the Act.

III. AUTHORITY OF GOVERNMENT AND CONTRACTOR PERSONNEL

Contract administration involves thousands of government and contractor representatives performing various functions, including

- Technical supervision and direction;
- Production surveillance;
- Inspection and acceptance;
- Change order issuance and negotiation;
- Default or convenience termination issuance and settlement;
- Price analysis and negotiation; and
- Claims review, settlement, and disposition.

See FAR 42.302 for a more detailed listing of contract administration functions. Both the government and the contractor conduct contract administration functions through officers or employees, who typically are delegated varying degrees of authority and responsibility. The numerous parties and organizations involved in contract administration often make it difficult to determine the exact authority of an officer or employee. Thus, legal problems are frequently encountered—most often when the government refuses to recognize a contractor's alleged rights on the grounds that the contractor has dealt with an unauthorized employee of the government. Contractors occasionally raise the same defenses, but with much less success. The first section below considers the legal principles relevant to determining the authority of government personnel, the consequences of dealing with unauthorized personnel, and the effect of notice of limitations on authority. The second section examines a number of the same principles as applied to contractor personnel.

A. Government Personnel

The fundamental rule is that the government is not bound by unauthorized acts of its officers or agents, *Wilber Nat'l Bank v. United States*, 294 U.S. 120 (1935). The government has taken advantage of this rule by allocating the major grant of contractual authority to *a special and limited class of employees* called *contracting officers*. Contracting officers have the sole authority to legally bind the government to contracts and contract modifications. However, in many instances they are involved in a relatively small portion of the day-to-day contract administration activities. Thus, during performance of a contract the contractor will usually deal primarily with government personnel bearing titles such as project manager, technical director, engineer, inspector, contracting officer's representative, procurement specialist, contract administrator, and attorney. A contractor will have formal communications, but usually significantly less direct contact, with contracting officers. In many cases, persons who are not contracting officers may be delegated authority to perform specific functions even though the general grant of contractual authority is made only to contracting officers, FAR 1.601. In addition, the authority of contracting officers may range from full authority regardless of nature and size of transaction (plenary authority) to authority to perform only a limited class of contractual activities described by type and dollar amount. This fragmentation of authority in the contract administration process has created difficult legal problems.

1. *Actual Authority Required*

In private agency law, an employer will be legally bound by acts of an employee under the theory of *apparent authority* if the employer has permitted the employee to assume authority or has held the employee out as possessing authority. See *Restatement (Second) of Agency* § 8. Recognizing the importance of effective government control over the conduct of its agents, the courts and boards have rejected the apparent authority rule, holding that *actual authority* is required to bind the government. See *Federal Crop Ins. Corp. v. Merrill*, 332 U.S. 380 (1947), in which the Court stated at 384:

> Whatever the form in which the Government functions, anyone entering into an arrangement with the Government takes the risk of having accurately ascertained that he who purports to act for the Government stays within the bounds of his

> authority. The scope of this authority may be explicitly defined by Congress or be limited by delegated legislation, properly exercised through the rule-making power. And this is so even though, as here, the agent himself may have been unaware of the limitations upon his authority. See, e.g., *Utah Power & Light Co. v. United States*, 243 U.S. 389, 409 (1916); *United States v. Stewart*, 311 U.S. 60 (1940).

For cases in which government employees with apparent authority were found to have no actual authority, see *Starflight Boats v. United States*, 48 Fed. Cl. 592 (2001) (Deputy Chief of Procurement had no authority to order contractor to assist in investigation); *Jascourt v. United States*, 207 Ct. Cl. 955, *cert. denied*, 423 U.S. 1032 (1975) (government not bound by the actions of the Deputy Assistant Secretary of Labor for Labor Relations, or the Director of the Division of Public Employees, since neither official had the authority to enter into a contract); *Housing Corp. of Am. v. United States*, 199 Ct. Cl. 705, 468 F.2d 922 (1972) (HUD Secretary's unauthorized signature would not bind government as a third party responsible for costly changes); *Byrne Org., Inc. v. United States,* 152 Ct. Cl. 578, 287 F.2d 582 (1961) (letters of intent issued by director and chief administrative officer of the National Capital Sesquicentennial Commission not binding on the government); and *Gordon Woodroffe Corp. v. United States*, 122 Ct. Cl. 723, 104 F. Supp. 984 (1952) (special assistant to State Department Coordinator for aid to Greece and Turkey had no authority to purchase equipment).

The fact that an official appears to be a superior of a contracting officer does not establish the authority of that official. See *Inter-Tribal Council of Nev., Inc.*, IBCA 1234-12-78, 83-1 BCA ¶ 16,433, stating at 81,745-46:

> The facts that the Assistant Area Director for Education was the "boss" for Area education matters . . . that the CO sought his approval for a contract budget modification . . . and that he was named as the "contact person" for negotiations for an upcoming contract . . . are irrelevant in this context. The best that can be said about them is that they are probative of the fact and conclusion that the Assistant Area Director had *apparent* authority here, which we have already noted is insufficient authority for [the contractor's] reliance under the *Federal Crop Insurance* rule. The reason for excepting the government from the rule of apparent authority generally applicable to private contracts has been oft-stated as grounded in the difference between protecting the public treasury, a public right or a public interest on the one hand, and protecting private concerns on the other. *Federal Crop Insurance Corp. v. Merrill, supra* at 385, and *Utah Power & Light Co. v. United States*, 243 U.S. 389, 37 S. Ct. 387, 391 (1916). Also, the Government practice of specifically designating only one person, the CO, as having exclusive actual authority for dealing with the administration of a contract avoids the chaos and lack of protection for those Government interests which would result if a contractor were allowed to rely on the authority of any one of dozens or potentially hundreds of Government "agents" who might have some relationship with the contract. See *Dresser Industries, Inc. v. United States*, [596 F.2d 1231, 1237 (5th Cir. 1979)].

See also *Henry Burge & Alvin White*, PSBCA 2431, 89-3 BCA ¶ 21,910, in which a project manager was held to have no authority to relax the specifications. Compare

Zoubi v. United States, 25 Cl. Ct. 581 (1992), in which an acting program director was held to have authority to contract for services because he was responsible for obtaining such services and had obtained them in the past.

Within contracting offices, personnel with official-sounding titles such as contract specialists, negotiators, and administrators work for contracting officers and handle the day-to-day contracting activity of the government, but such personnel generally do not have authority to order additional work or to commit the government by virtue of their position. Contractors are expected to recognize this lack of authority. In *General Elec. Co.*, ASBCA 11990, 67-1 BCA ¶ 6377, *rev'd on other grounds*, 188 Ct. Cl. 620, 412 F.2d 1215 (1969), the board stated at 29,525-26:

> [The contract specialist's] only function was to serve as contact point between the Government and [the contractor]. He can be considered little more than a messenger. There is no evidence that he was delegated any power to bind the Government; on the contrary the testimony establishes that he was delegated no authority to bind the Government. No authority to bind the Government for additional funds by demanding the report notwithstanding the funding situation can be implied from [his] position.

See also *Precision Standard, Inc.*, ASBCA 41375, 96-2 BCA ¶ 28,461 (government not bound by alleged waiver of delivery schedule by contract administrator), and *Mil Spec Contractors, Inc. v. United States*, 835 F.2d 865 (Fed. Cir. 1987) (government not bound by alleged oral agreement by contract negotiator). In *Kahaluu Constr. Co.*, ASBCA 33248, 90-2 BCA ¶ 22,663, the government argued that a binding agreement had been reached on a Board on Changes Report signed by a contractor's representative and government members of the board. However, the ASBCA found that neither the government members nor the contractor's representatives had authority to bind their respective parties.

2. Delegation of Authority

The contracting authority in each agency flows from the head of the agency to contracting officers. See FAR 1.601(a), stating:

> [A]uthority and responsibility to contract for authorized supplies and services are vested in the agency head. The agency head may establish contracting activities and delegate to heads of such contracting activities broad authority to manage the agency's contracting functions. Contracts may be entered into and signed on behalf of the Government only by contracting officers. In some agencies, a relatively small number of high level officials are designated contracting officers solely by virtue of their positions. Contracting officers below the level of a head of a contracting activity shall be selected and appointed under 1.603.

This regulation recognizes two types of officials with contracting officer authority. At the upper level of the agency, in secretarial positions or as head of a contracting activity, officials have contracting authority "by virtue of their positions." These officials are not required to meet the qualification requirements for appointment and generally do not act as contracting officers except on special matters. Yet they have full authority to act as contracting officers. Below these officials are the *designated contracting officers*, appointed in accordance with the regulations discussed below.

Each agency is authorized to delegate contracting officer authority in accordance with its own procedures. See FAR 1.603-1, stating:

> Subsection 414(4) of title 41, United States Code, requires agency heads to establish and maintain a procurement career management program and a system for the selection, appointment, and termination of appointment of contracting officers. Agency heads or their designees may select and appoint contracting officers and terminate their appointments. These selections and appointments shall be consistent with Office of Federal Procurement Policy's (OFPP) standards for skill-based training in performing contracting and purchasing duties as published in OFPP Policy Letter No. 92-3, Procurement Professionalism Program Policy—Training for Contracting Personnel, June 24, 1992.

Thus, contracting officers may be granted authority to appoint subsidiary contracting officers or other representatives. FAR 1.602-1(a) requires clear instructions in the appointment document, as follows:

> Contracting officers may bind the Government only to the extent of the authority delegated to them. Contracting officers shall receive from the appointing authority (see 1.603-1) clear instructions in writing regarding the limits of their authority. Information on the limits of contracting officers' authority shall be readily available to the public and agency personnel.

The term "contracting officer" is used to describe those individuals with the authority to execute contractual documents that bind the government and to sign determinations and findings and other internal documents. FAR 2.101 contains the following definition:

> "Contracting Officer" means a person with the authority to enter into, administer, and/or terminate contracts and make related determinations and findings. The term includes certain authorized representatives of the contracting officer acting within the limits of their authority as delegated by the contracting officer. "Administrative contracting officer (ACO)" refers to a contracting officer who is administering contracts. "Termination contracting officer (TCO)" refers to a contracting officer who is settling terminated contracts. A single contracting officer may be responsible for duties in any or all of these areas. Reference in this regulation (48 CFR Chapter 1) to administrative contracting officer or termination contracting officer does not—
>
> > (a) require that a duty be performed at a particular office or activity; or

> (b) restrict in any way a contracting officer in the performance of any duty properly assigned.

The first sentence of this FAR definition refers to the official who has been designated as a "contracting officer." However, the second sentence creates confusion by stating that *the term includes* any authorized representative of the contracting officer. This considerably broader definition of contracting officer is also included in the standard definitions clause in FAR 52.202-1.

The inclusion of "authorized representatives" within the definition of contracting officer is misleading because formally designated contracting officers will normally have a much broader grant of authority than authorized representatives. In addition, not all representatives are appointed in the same manner or with the same degree of authority. The following discussion explores the method of appointment and stated scope of authority of three categories of government employees—designated contracting officers, contracting officers' representatives, and other employees with contractual duties.

a. Designated Contracting Officers

FAR Subpart 1.6 calls for the appointment of designated contracting officers *by name* using the Certificate of Appointment, Standard Form 1402. In addition, each agency is required to establish a system that ensures that each designated contracting officer is fully qualified by experience and training. The following guidance for selection criteria is given in FAR 1.603-2:

> In selecting contracting officers, the appointing official shall consider the complexity and dollar value of the acquisitions to be assigned and the candidate's experience, training, education, business acumen, judgment, character, and reputation. Examples of selection criteria include—
>
> (a) Experience in Government contracting and administration, commercial purchasing, or related fields;
>
> (b) Education or special training in business administration, law, accounting, engineering, or related fields;
>
> (c) Knowledge of acquisition policies and procedures including this and other applicable regulations;
>
> (d) Specialized knowledge in the particular assigned field of contracting; and
>
> (e) Satisfactory completion of acquisition training courses.

An OFPP Memorandum on Government-Wide Guidance on Contract Administration (1991) provides that a contracting officer's postaward responsibilities include:

(1) *Monitoring for contract compliance.* The contracting officer must rely on the COTR and the project officer for an alert when encountering problems with contract compliance. A problem that frequently surfaces in contract administration is that the COTR or the project officer does not alert the contracting officer to potential problems early enough because they hope that they can straighten things out. It is important that these problems be brought to the attention of the contracting officer as soon as they occur or are noticed.

(2) *Enforcing contract provisions.* It is the contracting officer's duty to enforce the contract as written or amended. If contract provisions are not enforced, the government frequently suffers a loss of time or product quality with concomitant costs.

(3) *Issuing timely performance and payment approvals.* Issuing approvals required by the contract so that work proceeds on a timely basis and the contractor receives payments. The contracting officer is the government official with the authority to approve contract performance so that progress payments or other authorized expenditure of funds flowing to the contractor are made.

(4) *Modifying the contract as necessary.* As contract work proceeds, modifications or changes to a contract may become necessary. After the technical issues of these proposed changes are resolved, it is the contracting officer who has the legal authority to execute contract changes on behalf of the government. Unless they result from equitable adjustments, or failures on the part of the government, contract extensions should not be granted without additional consideration to the government.

(5) *Acting to close out the contract.* When the contract performance is completed, it is the contracting officer's responsibility to close out the contract. FAR SUBPART 42.1 provides guidance on establishment of indirect cost rates and contract close out. Agencies are encouraged to focus on close out issues and reduce backlogs. For contracts in which funds have been obligated but not expended, savings accrue to the government by closing out these contracts and re-depositing the funds in the Treasury.

In each agency there are one or more contracting officers with plenary authority. Even these contracting officers, however, may be subject to internal regulations governing how that authority is exercised, and the contractor is responsible for being aware of any regulations made known to it through publication or otherwise, *Federal Crop Ins. Corp. v. Merrill*, 332 U.S. 380 (1947). In *Porter v. United States*, 204 Ct. Cl. 355, 496 F.2d 583 (1974), *cert. denied*, 420 U.S. 1004 (1975), published regulations delegated authority to the high commissioner and the Director of the Office of Territories to contract for shipping services "on behalf of the Trust Territory of the Pacific Islands." The contractor was deemed to have notice that these officials were acting for the Trust Territory government and had no authority to bind the United States. In contrast, the contractor is not responsible for limitations in unpublished regulations. See *NI Indus., Inc. v. United States*, 841 F.2d 1104 (Fed. Cir. 1988) (contractor not bound by limitations on authority in unpublished regulation); *New England Tank Indus. of N.H., Inc.*, ASBCA 26474, 88-1 BCA ¶ 20,395, *vacated and remanded on other grounds*, 861 F.2d 685 (Fed. Cir. 1988) (government bound to modification signed by contracting officer even though unpublished regulation prohibited agreement); and *A-1 Garbage Disposal & Trash Serv.*, ASBCA 30623, 89-1 BCA ¶ 21,323 (contractor not bound by unpublished regulation of Small Business Administration). See also *Devil's Lake Sioux Tribe*, IBCA 1953, 88-1 BCA ¶ 20,320, in which the board held that the contractor was not bound by a published regulation that was so vague and ambiguous that it could not be understood by a typical contractor. However, if the contractor is aware of the unpublished regulation, it will be bound by the limitations contained therein. See *D.M. Summers, Inc.*, VABCA 2570, 89-3 BCA ¶ 22,123 (contractor could not recover for lost work because it had actual knowledge of changes in internal agency regulations that reduced the requirements of the contract).

Authority to administer contracts may be delegated to designated administrative contracting officers (ACOs) not located at the procuring office. Contracting officers who award contracts usually retain authority to administer them, regardless of any delegation to an ACO, and are frequently referred to as procuring contracting officers (PCOs). There may be additional specialized contracting officers with limited scopes of authority, such as terminating contracting officers (TCOs) and corporate administrative contracting officers (CACOs). This allocation of authority is widely used within the Department of Defense. Outside the Department of Defense, the designation of contracting officers in field offices has been relatively uncommon. Field functions are typically handled through representatives of the contracting officer.

FAR 1.603-3 requires that limitations on authority must be included in the certificate of appointment of each contracting officer, and that contractors are responsible for ascertaining the limits of authority of contracting officers. See, for example, *Atlantic, Gulf & Pac. Co. of Manila, Inc.*, ASBCA 13533, 72-1 BCA ¶ 9415 (termination settlement not binding because TCO acted beyond authority); *Strick Corp.*, ASBCA 15921, 73-2 BCA ¶ 10,077 (modification not binding because ACO had no authority to sign it); and *OAO Corp. v. United States*, 17 Cl. Ct. 91 (1989) (government not bound by handshake of contracting officer when approval of higher authority required; however, court did find an implied-in-fact contract). However, such limitations on authority will not control if they are neither published nor communicated to the contractor. See *Texas Instruments, Inc. v. United States*, 922 F.2d 810 (Fed. Cir. 1990) (government bound by ACO signature on agreement even though internal regulations required internal approvals).

There is also a difference in the way contracting officer authority is distributed relative to construction and supply and service contracts. In construction contracts, the contractor can generally expect to be informed of a single named individual who has authority to bind the government. There is usually no designation of administrative contracting officers—the field functions relating to the day-to-day administration of the contract are performed through contracting officers' representatives. In supply and service contracts, there is usually no designation of a single person to serve as contracting officer. Thus, any employee of the agency who has been properly designated a contracting officer may act on any contract of the agency provided that he or she is acting within the limits of this authority. This procedure gives the agency much greater internal operating flexibility, but it creates difficulties for contractors in ascertaining the authority of the person with whom they are dealing.

Further, particularly in supply and service contracts, there may be various tiers of contracting officers with decreasing amounts of authority given to each succeeding lower tier. At the top may be the contracting officer who signed the contract and has full ("plenary") authority within the agency. Below may be a contracting officer with authority to sign contracts and changes up to $500,000 in value, and another step down may be a contracting officer with authority to sign changes up to $25,000. The contractor must know this internal structure and be aware of the personnel and organizational changes that occur within the agency in order to determine whether a particular employee has authority at any given time. Since, as a general rule, no notice is given to contractors of such personnel or organizational changes, this task is a difficult one for the contractor who does not deal with the agency regularly.

Contractors must ascertain the monetary limitations on the authority of subsidiary contracting officers. See *Comspace Corp.*, DOTCAB 3095, 98-2 BCA ¶ 30,037 (delivery order not binding because it was in excess of $25,000 authority of contracting officer who signed it); *Edwards v. United States*, 22 Cl. Ct. 411 (1991) (government not bound when contracting officer agreed to modification above dollar limitation for agreements without approval of higher authority); and *Danac, Inc.*, ASBCA 30227, 90-3 BCA ¶ 23,246 (government would not have been bound by a settlement agreement above dollar limitation in contract, without approval of higher authority as provided for in contracting officer's warrant).

b. Authorized Representatives

A considerable degree of confusion surrounds the term "authorized representative." One source of the confusion is the regulatory definition of contracting officer, set forth above, which defines the term to include the authorized representative of the contracting officer acting within the limits of the delegated authority, FAR 2.101. However, authorized representatives traditionally have *a much narrower scope of authority* than those specifically appointed as contracting officers. Further confusion results from the varying methods used by contracting officers to appoint representatives—with some representatives being formally designated as contracting officers' representatives (CORs) and other representatives merely being assigned functions to be performed in the procurement process without specific use of the term "authorized representative" in their selection or appointment. For this reason, these two types of representatives are discussed separately.

(1) Formally Designated Representatives

There are a number of formally designated representatives who act on behalf of the government during contract administration. Depending upon the agency involved, these representatives have titles such as contracting officer representative (COR), contracting officer technical representative (COTR), Government Technical Representative (GTR), or Government Technical Evaluator (GTE). Although their responsibilities vary, an OFPP memorandum, Government-Wide Guidance on Contract Administration (1991) states that the principal responsibilities of COTRs are as follows:

> (1) *Inspecting and accepting or rejecting work performed under the contract.* It is important that the COTR alerts the contracting officer immediately when it is discovered that the contractor is not performing adequately. Since the COTR is most often a member of the project office, the COTR should not assume the role of advising the contractor on how to resolve deficiencies in performance or to presume that given enough time the contractor will take corrective actions.
>
> (2) *Representing the government in technical phases of the work.* The COTR is responsible for the technical administration of the contract and will advise the contractor on all technical matters relating to the contract. The COTR will also interpret technical directives having a bearing on the contractor's performance.

For guidance on best practices in contract administration for COTRs, see *A Guide to Best Practices for Contract Administration* (OFPP October 1994).

There is no guidance in the FAR as to the method of appointing these representatives except for the statement in the definition. Thus, one must look to the subsidiary regulations in each agency to determine the method of appointment. Generally such regulations provide that appointment will be in writing, either by a separate letter or by designation in the contract, and that each contractor affected should receive notice of the appointment. The OFPP's Government-Wide Guidance on Contract Administration indicates that a separate designation must be issued for each contract. The OFPP memorandum also states that "[t]he delegated responsibilities of the COTR shall not be redelegated to others. A COTR cannot inherit authority of another COTR who previously held that position." Authority delegated to representatives is always much narrower than that possessed by the contracting officer. See, for example, Department of Interior Regulation DIAR 1401.670 (http://www.doi.gov/pam/1401.html#670), containing appointment procedures but stating the following limitations:

> 1401.670-5 Limitations.
>
> Each appointment of a COR made by the CO shall clearly state that the representative is not authorized under any circumstances to—

> 1. award, agree to, or execute any contract, contract modification, or notice of intent;
>
> 2. obligate, in any way, the payment of money by the Government;
>
> 3. make a final decision on any contract matter which is subject to the clause at FAR 52.233-1, Disputes; or
>
> (d) terminate, for any cause, the contractor's right to proceed.

The Department of Defense uses the following standard clause in DFARS 252.201-7000 to alert its contractors that CORs may be appointed:

> (a) Definition. Contracting officer's representative means an individual designated in accordance with subsection 201.602-2 of the Defense Federal Acquisition Regulation Supplement and authorized in writing by the contracting officer to perform specific technical and administrative functions.
>
> (b) If the Contracting Officer designates a contracting officer's representative (COR), the Contractor will receive a copy of the written designation. It will specify the extent of the COR's authority to act on behalf of the contracting officer. The COR is not authorized to make any commitments or changes that will affect price, quality, quantity, delivery, or any other term or condition of the contract.

Limitations on authority of CORs or COTRs that have been communicated to the contractor are binding on the contractor. See, for example, *Elter S.A.*, ASBCA 52349, 01-2 BCA ¶ 31,547 (government's construction representatives clearly had no authority to order changes); *California Consulting Eng'rs*, ASBCA 50355, 98-2 BCA ¶ 29,995 (COR had no authority to order extra work); *Niko Contracting Co. v. United States*, 39 Fed. Cl. 795 (1997) (COTR had no authority to promise that modification could be reopened); *Toloff Constr.*, AGBCA 95-227-3, 96-1 BCA ¶ 28,156 (COR had no authority to order extra work); *David W.E. Cabell*, VABCA 3402, 93-2 BCA ¶ 25,598 (COR has no authority to interpret an unambiguous contract in a manner that leads to additional compensation); *HTC Indus., Inc.*, ASBCA 40562, 93-1 BCA ¶ 25,560, *recons. denied*, 93-2 BCA ¶ 25,701, *aff'd*, 22 F.3d 1103 (Fed. Cir. 1994) (COTR had no authority to order contractor to continue performance while he sought additional funding in view of the specific language in the contract); *Construction Equip. Lease Co. v. United States*, 26 Cl. Ct. 341 (1992) (COR Technical Project Officer had no authority to change contract in face of explicit language in appointment letter); *Essen Mall Props. v. United States*, 21 Cl. Ct. 430 (1990) (project manager acting as authorized representative had no authority to bind government agency to contract); and *Carothers & Carothers Co.*, ENGBCA 4015, 88-3 BCA ¶ 21,162 (COR had no authority to issue major change). The proper course of action when receiving an order for extra or changed work from such an employee is to demand that the order be issued by the contracting officer, *Adventure Group, Inc.*, ASBCA 50188, 97-2 BCA ¶ 29,081 (contractor compensated for delay due to government refusal to resolve the need for extra work ordered by contract administrator).

On the other hand, the government will be bound by the actions of a COR or COTR acting within the scope of his or her authority even if additional work is called for. See *Hudson Contracting, Inc.*, ASBCA 41023, 94-1 BCA ¶ 26,466 (making government property available to contractor within authority of COR); *Diversified Marine Tech, Inc.*, DOTCAB 2455, 93-2 BCA ¶ 25,720 (granting permission to perform work within scope of COR's delegation when, as the government representative at the site, he was the most logical person to act); *MJW Enters., Inc.*, ENGBCA 5813, 93-1 BCA ¶ 25,405 (interpretation of vague specification within scope of COR's authority); and *Farr Bros., Inc.*, ASBCA 42658, 92-2 BCA ¶ 24,991 (COR had authority to order work suspension).

(2) Other Representatives

The vast majority of personnel involved in the contract administration process are designated neither as contracting officers nor contracting officers' representatives. Many of these personnel are organizationally separate specialists, such as attorneys, auditors, or engineers, from whom the contracting officer is required to request advice, FAR 1.602-2(c). These same personnel may receive information from contractors and may, in the course of their duties, participate in discussions or negotiations. Thus, their role may be seen as independent government representatives or as informally recognized representatives of the contracting officer. Other government personnel, such as inspectors or procurement specialists, often are assigned responsibilities in the contract administration process without formal designation as contracting officers' representatives. The regulations in this area do not clearly delineate the authority of these personnel and generally do not require specific written designation as contracting officers' representatives.

The absence of formal delegation as a "representative" has not prevented the courts and boards of contract appeals from finding that these personnel are authorized representatives of the contracting officer. See, for example, *H. Landau & Co. v. United States*, 886 F.2d 322 (Fed. Cir. 1989) (employees with contract administration authority held to bind the government when they stated that government would guarantee payment for materials); *Zoubi v. United States*, 25 Cl. Ct. 581 (1992) (program director had authority to enter into a contract for interpreter services because his job carried with it an implied authorization to obtain all necessary personnel); *Walter Straga*, ASBCA 26134, 83-2 BCA ¶ 16,611 (project manager considered by board to be proper official to respond to technical inquiries and was a representative of the contracting officer); and *Contractors Equip. Rental Co.*, ASBCA 13052, 70-1 BCA ¶ 8183 (statement by contracting officer that official was "the man to satisfy" and deferral to him for equipment needs held "tantamount to a delegation de facto" as contracting officer's authorized representative).

When a contractor is expressly informed of limitations on the authority of these representatives, the contractor is generally unable to recover for unauthorized acts. Such notifications are often contained in letters to contractors or in contract clauses. One standard clause containing such an express statement is the Inspection of Construction clause in FAR 52.246-12, which states:

> (d) The presence or absence of a Government inspector does not relieve the Contractor from any contractual requirement, nor is the inspector authorized to change any term or condition of the specification without the Contracting Officer's written authorization.

For cases denying relief based on this language, see *DeKonty Corp.*, ASBCA 32140, 89-2 BCA ¶ 21,586; *Commercial Contractors, Inc.*, ASBCA 30675, 88-3 BCA ¶ 20,877; and *Allen's of Fla., Inc.*, ASBCA 14656, 71-1 BCA ¶ 8646. For a rare case in which the government was held liable in the face of this clause, see *Townsco Contracting Co.*, ASBCA 13742, 71-2 BCA ¶ 8962, where a government inspector gave the contractor faulty direction.

> Similar language in other contract provisions has been used to deny relief to contractors. See, for example, *Woodcraft Corp. v. United States*, 146 Ct. Cl. 101, 173 F. Supp. 613 (1959), in which the court held that the contractor was not entitled to compensation for performing additional work called for by a government inspector where the contract contained a clause advising the contractor that "[t]he Inspector has no authority to advise or direct a contractor to use a particular method of production"; *Jerry Dodds*, ASBCA 51682, 02-1 BCA ¶ 31,844, where two agency clauses warned the contractor that only the contracting officer had authority to change the contract; *Gavosto Assocs., Inc.*, PSBCA 4058, 01-1 BCA ¶ 31,389, where an agency clause and a warning at the pre-construction meeting informed the contractor of limitations on authority; *King Fisher Co. v. United States*, 51 Fed. Cl. 94 (2001), where an agency clause required contracting officer approval of changes; *Twigg Corp. v. General Servs. Admin.*, GSBCA 14064, 98-1 BCA ¶ 29,452, where a clause warned the contractor that only the contracting officer could order extra work; *Crow & Sutton Assocs.*, ASBCA 44392, 93-1 BCA ¶ 25,503, where the contract contained two agency clauses warning that inspectors had no authority to order changes; and *Inez Kaiser & Assocs., Inc.*, ASBCA 22212, 88-2 BCA ¶ 20,732, where the contract stated that only the contracting officer could order changes.

Letters limiting the authority of representatives generally have the same result. See *Franchi Realty Trust v. General Servs. Admin.*, GSBCA 11149, 92-3 BCA ¶ 25,180, and *F.H. Antrim Constr. Co.*, IBCA 882-12-70, 71-2 BCA ¶ 8983. Similarly, a notice on the minutes of project meetings of technical personnel stating that only "no-cost" changes could be approved by such personnel precluded recovery, *Metric Constructors, Inc.*, ASBCA 49374, 96-2 BCA ¶ 28,418, and the contractor's acknowledgment that it had been told that an inspector had no authority precluded recovery, *AAA Eng'g & Drafting, Inc.*, ASBCA 44605, 96-1 BCA ¶ 28,182.

3. Dealing with Personnel Lacking Specifically Delegated Contractual Authority

As previously indicated, the vast majority of government personnel with whom a contractor deals do not possess the authority to act as contracting officers. However, this does not mean that dealings with such unauthorized personnel are without legal significance. This section considers the major theories used to bind the government when the contractor has dealt with personnel who do not have explicit authority to bind the government. The first of these theories is implied authority, where no authority has been specifically granted. The second is contracting officer ratification of the unauthorized act or statement. The third is imputation of knowledge of unauthorized representatives to contracting officers.

a. Implied Authority

Although apparent authority will not be sufficient to bind the government, the courts and boards have frequently granted contractors relief on the basis of "implied authority." The implied authority cases primarily involve determining what delegations would mean under a reasonable person standard. Thus, precise written delegations leave little room for implication of authority, while broad general delegations provide a greater opportunity for finding implied authority, *DOT Sys., Inc.*, DOTCAB 1208, 82-2 BCA ¶ 15,817. Most of the cases finding implied authority have involved delegations by contracting officers to project managers, engineers, inspectors, and other personnel involved in contract administration. Although the principle of implied authority is not necessarily inapplicable to designated contracting officers, the nature of the Certificate of Appointment and pertinent regulations leave relatively little room for its application, *Strick Corp.*, ASBCA 15921, 73-2 BCA ¶ 10,077. The Court of Federal Claims explained the concept of implied authority in *Aero-Abre, Inc.v. United States*, 39 Fed. Cl. 654 (1997), as follows, at 657:

> In order to find implied actual authority, a court must conclude that the government intended to grant such authority but failed to do so explicitly due to some oversight or that such authority inheres in a particular position. See, e.g., *Cruz-Pagan v. United States*, 35 Fed. Cl. 59, 62-63 (1996) ("the doctrine of implied actual authority . . . serves to fill in the gap when an agency reasonably must have intended certain representatives to possess contracting authority but failed expressly to grant that authority"). Actual authority to bind the government has not been implied when a regulation, a contract, or a letter to the contractor expressly states that the employee does not have actual authority. See *Cruz-Pagan*, 35 Fed. Cl. at 62-63; *Construction Equip. Lease Co. v. United States*, 26 Cl. Ct. 341, 346-47 (1992); *Essen Mall Properties v. United States*, 21 Cl. Ct. 430, 444-45 (1990).

To find implied authority, there must have been some authority delegated. See *California Sand & Gravel, Inc. v. United States*, 22 Cl. Ct. 19 (1990), *aff'd*, 937 F.2d 624 (Fed. Cir. 1991), where the Claims Court stated at 27:

> [A] person with some limited actual authority impliedly may have broader authority. However, a person with no actual authority may not gain actual authority though the court-made rule of implied actual authority. Specifically, the court may not substitute itself unconditionally for the executive agency in granting authority to an unauthorized person. The most the court can do is interpret the limited authority of an authorized person in a broader manner than ordinarily would be the case.

The courts have, however, found that government employees with no authority to act in the contracting process have authority to bind the government in an emergency situation, *Philadelphia Suburban Corp. v. United States*, 217 Ct. Cl. 705 (1978) (firefighting foam to put out ship fire); *Halvorson v. United States*, 126 F. Supp. 898 (E.D. Wash. 1954) (equipment to deal with blizzard); *Sigma Constr. Co.*, ASBCA 37040, 91-2 BCA ¶ 23,926 (small alterations to ensure that concrete cured properly). However, this means of overcoming the lack of authority has been construed narrowly. See *City of El Centro v. United States*, 922 F.2d 816 (Fed. Cir. 1990), *cert. denied*, 501 U.S. 1230 (1991), in which the court found no emergency when border patrol agents agreed to pay for hospital services for illegal aliens injured in a high-speed chase, and *Gardiner v. Virgin Islands Water & Power Authority*, 145 F.3d 635 (3d Cir. 1998), in which the court refused to find an emergency where the contractor had provided services for 10 weeks following the occurrence of a hurricane.

Authority to bind the government is generally implied when such authority is considered to be "an integral part of the duties assigned" to a government employee, *H. Landau & Co. v. United States*, 886 F.2d 322 (Fed. Cir. 1989). In *DOT Sys., Inc.*, DOTCAB 1208, 82-2 BCA ¶ 15,817, the board stated at 78,386:

> However, as we point out below, the fact that the COTR had neither actual nor apparent authority to bind the Government does not necessarily preclude the granting of relief under the circumstances as here exist. Rather, such authority may be implied when considered an integral part of specific duties assigned to a government employee, *Urban Pathfinders, Inc.*, ASBCA No. 23134, 79-1 BCA ¶ 13,709; *Contractors Equipment Rental Co.*, ASBCA No. 13052, 70-1 BCA ¶ 8183. In view of the specific duties assigned to the COTR, and the circumstances surrounding his directives regarding the arrangement of the exhibits, we find the COTR was clothed with the requisite implied authority to bind the government to a constructive change under the terms of the contract.

See also *Jordan & Nobles Constr. Co.*, GSBCA 8349, 91-1 BCA ¶ 23,659, in which implied delegation of authority was found. The board noted at 118,511:

> [The government] argues that the on-site representative lacked authority to make a change to the contract. The authority of officials subordinate to the contracting officer is derived from the facts of each case, based on the words of the contract and the conduct of the parties during the contract administration. *Stephenson Assoc., Inc.*, GSBCA Nos. 6573, 6815, 86-3 BCA ¶ 19,017 at 96,325-26. Here, by the admission of the contracting officer, the on-site representative had the author-

ity to determine whether supplies met contract requirements and to direct [the contractor's] work under the contract.

Similarly, inspectors with authority to accept or reject the work have been held to bind the government when they ordered minor adjustment to the work, *Construction Foresite, Inc.*, ASBCA 42350, 93-1 BCA ¶ 25,515; improperly rejected the work, *Donohoe Constr. Co.*, ASBCA 47310, 98-2 BCA ¶ 30,076, and *Gonzales Custom Painting, Inc.*, ASBCA 39527, 90-3 BCA ¶ 22,950; misidentified defects causing extra work, *Dan Rice Constr. Co.*, ASBCA 52160, 04-1 BCA ¶ 32,595; insisted on performance beyond the contract requirements, *A & D Fire Protection, Inc.*, ASBCA 53103, 02-2 BCA ¶ 32,053; ordered extra work in the course of contract administration, *Gricoski Detective Agency*, GSBCA 8901 (7823), 90-3 BCA ¶ 23,131; or prescribed additional testing procedures, *Switlik Parachute Co., Inc.*, ASBCA 17920, 74-2 BCA ¶ 10,970. See also *Kumin Assocs., Inc.*, LBCA 94-BCA-3, 98-2 BCA ¶ 30,007 (authorized representative and project manager had implied authority to change work because contracting officer relied on them); *Urban Pathfinders, Inc.*, ASBCA 23134, 79-1 BCA ¶ 13,709 (project officer with authority to certify vouchers, receive progress reports, perform inspections, and accept work had the implied authority to issue a change order where immediate action was required); *Tasker Indus., Inc.*, DOTCAB 71-22, 75-2 BCA ¶ 11,372 (authority to issue engineering interpretations or to reject end product, erroneously exercised, amounted to constructive change even though contractor was on notice that representative was not authorized to order any changes); *WRB Corp. v. United States*, 183 Ct. Cl. 409 (1968) (authority to inspect, reject, and require replacement implied authority to order constructive change); and *Cameo Curtains, Inc.*, ASBCA 3574, 58-2 BCA ¶ 2051 (inspector authorized to reject work had implied authority to change work through improper rejection).

It has been held that a contractor is not obligated to appeal to the contracting officer if a representative with such implied authority erroneously construes the contract, *WRB Corp. v. United States*, 183 Ct. Cl. 409 (1968). However, prudent contract administration demands that contractors bring to the attention of the contracting officer any interpretation or instruction issued by an official who lacks formal contracting authority, rather than rely on the implied authority doctrine, and there are numerous cases denying relief because of lack of notification of the contracting officer. See *Singer Co., Librascope Div. v. United States*, 215 Ct. Cl. 281, 568 F.2d 695 (1977), denying a constructive change claim based on interpretations issued by a technical coordinating group where the contractor was aware that the group lacked formal contracting officer authority but failed to bring the interpretations to the attention of the contracting officer. See also *MC II Generator & Elec.*, ASBCA 53389, 04-1 BCA ¶ 32,569 (project manager had no authority to order change); *Northrop Grumman Corp. v. United States*, 47 Fed. Cl. 20 (2000) ("field marines" had no authority to constructively change contract); *John C. Grimberg Co.*, ASBCA 51693, 99-2 BCA ¶ 30,572 (trial counsel had no authority to settle claim); *Safeco Credit & Fraley Assocs., Inc. v. United States*, 44 Fed. Cl. 406 (1999) (Assistant Resident Officer in Charge of Construction had no authority to bind the government); *Contel of Cal., Inc. v. United States*, 37 Fed. Cl. 68 (1996) (technical personnel had no authority to approve extra work); *J.S. Alberici Constr. Co.*, GSBCA 10977, 91-3 BCA ¶ 24,204 (architect had no authority to order corrections of defective work); *RMTC Sys.*, AGBCA 88-198-1, 91-2 BCA ¶ 23,873 (shipment before purchase order in response to an unauthorized request did not form a contract); and *United Food Servs., Inc. v. United States*, 19 Cl. Ct. 539 (1990), *aff'd without opinion*, 928 F.2d 411 (Fed. Cir. 1991) (mess sergeant had no authority to order extra work). Such action is particularly necessary when the contract contains a clause informing the contractor of the limited authority of government personnel, *Brand S Roofing*, ASBCA 24688, 82-1 BCA ¶ 15,513 (Designation of Technical Representative clause); *W. W. Wilkinson, Inc.*, ASBCA 23031, 80-2 BCA ¶ 14,749 (Government Inspectors clause).

b. Ratification

Ratification is the adoption of an unauthorized act resulting in the act being given effect as if originally authorized, *Restatement (Second) of Agency* § 82. In government contracting, representatives' unauthorized actions may subsequently be ratified by those with authority to bind the government. If the ratifying government official has actual or constructive knowledge of a representative's unauthorized act and expressly or impliedly adopts the act, ratification will be found, *Williams v. United States*, 130 Ct. Cl. 435, 127 F. Supp. 617, *cert. denied*, 349 U.S. 938 (1955). See also *Moran Bros. Co. v. United States*, 39 Ct. Cl. 486 (1904) ("[I]f upon a full knowledge of the facts, the superior officer ratifies and confirms the action of his subordinate, is not that in law equivalent to an express authority in the subordinate at the time he ordered the performance of the labor?").

(1) Authority to Ratify

In general, the authority to ratify has been considered an integral part of an agent's authority without the need for specific statutory or regulatory coverage. For many years, the procurement regulations contained no specific ratification provisions. However, the government has been bound on the basis of ratifications without reference to regulatory authorities, *DBA Sys., Inc.*, NASABCA 481-5, 82-1 BCA ¶ 15,468; *Norwood Precision Prods.*, ASBCA 24083, 80-1 BCA ¶ 14,405; *Michael Guth*, ASBCA 22663, 80-2 BCA ¶ 14,572.

In the 1970s and 1980s, agency regulations began to provide for ratification of unauthorized acts and to specify how such ratifications should be handled. Finally, in 1988, the following government-wide guidance was added to FAR 1.602-3:

> (b) *Policy*. (1) Agencies should take positive action to preclude, to the maximum extent possible, the need for ratification actions. Although procedures are provided in this section for use in those cases where the ratification of an unauthorized commitment is necessary, these procedures may not be used in a manner that encourages such commitments being made by government personnel.

(2) Subject to the limitations in paragraph (c) of this subsection, the head of the contracting activity, unless a higher level official is designated by the agency, may ratify an unauthorized commitment.

(3) The ratification authority in subparagraph (b)(2) of this subsection may be delegated in accordance with agency procedures, but in no case shall the authority be delegated below the level of chief of the contracting office.

(4) Agencies should process unauthorized commitments using the ratification authority of this subsection instead of referring such actions to the General Accounting Office for resolution. (See 1.602-3(d).)

(5) Unauthorized commitments that would involve claims subject to resolution under the Contract Disputes Act of 1978 should be processed in accordance with Subpart 33.2, Disputes and Appeals.

(c) *Limitations*. The authority in subparagraph (b)(2) of this subsection may be exercised only when—

(1) Supplies or services have been provided to and accepted by the Government, or the Government otherwise has obtained or will obtain a benefit resulting from performance of the unauthorized commitment;

(2) The ratifying official has the authority to enter into a contractual commitment;

(3) The resulting contract would otherwise have been proper if made by an appropriate contracting officer;

(4) The contracting officer reviewing the unauthorized commitment determines the price to be fair and reasonable;

(5) The contracting officer recommends payment and legal counsel concurs in the recommendation, unless agency procedures expressly do not require such concurrence;

(6) Funds are available and were available at the time the unauthorized commitment was made; and

(7) The ratification is in accordance with any other limitations prescribed under agency procedures.

(d) *Nonratifiable commitments*. Cases that are not ratifiable under this subsection may be subject to resolution as recommended by the General Accounting Office under its claim procedure (GAO Policy and Procedures Manual for Guidance of Federal Agencies, Title 4, Chapter 2), or as authorized by FAR Part 50. Legal advice should be obtained in these cases.

Although these procedures are quite explicit, they have not prevented findings of express ratification, *Tri-West Contractors, Inc.*, AGBCA 95-200-1, 97-1 BCA ¶ 28,662, or implied ratification, *Reliable Disposal Co., Inc.*, ASBCA 40100, 91-2 BCA ¶ 23,895. See also *Kumin Assocs., Inc.*, LBCA 94-BCA-3, 98-2 BCA ¶ 30,007, in which the contracting officer's review of changed drawings was found to show implied ratification, and *Tripod Inc.*, ASBCA 25104, 89-1 BCA ¶ 21,305, where the contracting officer's knowledge of the contractor's complaints and review of inspection reports evidenced implicit ratification. For a similar ruling under prior regulations, see *Driftwood of Ala.*, GSBCA 5429, 81-2 BCA ¶ 15,169. Compare *Fish & Wildlife Serv.*, Comp. Gen. Dec. B-208730, 83-1 CPD ¶ 75, in which ratification regulations were specifically invoked to support a finding of ratification.

Boards and courts do not possess the authority to ratify. They may only determine whether a ratification has occurred. They have recommended, however, that ratification authority be liberally exercised in cases where an injustice would result if the government did not become bound. See *Globe Indem. Co. v. United States*, 102 Ct. Cl. 21 (1944), *cert. denied*, 324 U.S. 852 (1945), in which the court stated at 38:

> The head of the department, or his duly authorized agent, of course, could have ratified these unauthorized acts, and in our opinion should have done so, since the work was necessary and for [the government's] benefit, but he did not do so, and we are powerless to do it for him.
>
> From this case two lessons are to be drawn: (1) contracting officers and heads of departments should exercise the great powers conferred on them by these contracts to do equity; they should not feel under obligation to take advantage of technicalities, where to do so would defeat justice; (2) contractors must study their contracts and insist on compliance with their terms; before relying on any promise they should ascertain that it is made by a person having authority to make it.

(2) Authority to Perform or Authorize Acts Being Ratified

The ratifying official must have the power to perform or authorize the unauthorized act. See 22 Comp. Gen. 1083 (B-33769) (1943). Thus, an official lacking the authority to enter into contracts cannot ratify an agreement, *Western Contract Furnishers*, PSBCA 317, 76-2 BCA ¶ 12,216; *Consortium Venture Corp. v. United States*, 5 Cl. Ct. 47 (1984). Similarly, illegal actions cannot be ratified because officials lack the authority to enter into illegal agreements. In *Trio Mach. Works, Inc.*, NASABCA 480-6, 82-1 BCA ¶ 15,465, *recons. denied*, 82-2 BCA ¶ 15,968, an alleged agreement between the contractor and a representative—in which the contractor, for keeping a modification under a certain dollar amount, was to receive preferred treatment in future contract awards—was illegal and beyond the contracting officer's ratification authority. Similarly, where an agency purchased spark plugs on a sole source basis in violation of statutes requiring formal advertising, the Assistant Secretary of War could not subsequently ratify the transaction by classifying the spark plugs as an experimental item subject to negotiated procurement, 15 Comp. Gen. 618 (B-66806) (1936).

Proper authority to ratify was found in *Romac, Inc.*, ASBCA 41150, 91-2 BCA ¶ 23,918 (officer in charge of construction could order additional work); *Mil-Pak Co.*, GSBCA 5849, 83-1 BCA ¶ 16,482 (contracting officer had authority to issue a change order); *W. Southard Jones, Inc.*, ASBCA 6321, 61-2 BCA ¶ 3182 (contracting officer had authority to alter contract); and *Fish & Wildlife Serv.*, Comp. Gen. Dec. B-208730, 83-1 CPD ¶ 75 (Acting Director of Fish and Wildlife Service had authority to issue a split procurement).

Under these rules, ratification normally requires action or inaction by a specific individual having the requisite authority to ratify the previously unauthorized act. However, some cases have found ratification without identifying such a specific individual (characterizing this as "institutional ratification"). In *Silverman v. United States*, 230 Ct. Cl. 701, 679 F.2d 865 (1982), the court found that the agency ratified the agreement by accepting the benefits flowing from the unauthorized official's promise. See also *Rapp v. United States*, 2 Cl. Ct. 694 (1983), in which the court found ratification where a government auctioneer's authority to extend the winning bidder's period of payment was in dispute: "[I]f any question remains as to the auctioneer's authority, it is rendered moot by the Customs Service's ratification of the announcement." Compare *City of El Centro v. United States*, 922 F.2d 816 (Fed. Cir. 1990), *cert. denied*, 501 U.S. 1230 (1991), in which the Federal Circuit reversed a decision of the Claims Court (16 Cl. Ct. 500 (1989)) finding institutional ratification. This decision appeared to indicate that institutional ratification was no longer a viable doctrine. See also *Choe-Kelly, Inc.*, ASBCA 43481, 94-1 BCA ¶ 26,431, refusing to apply the institutional ratification logic. See, however, *Janowsky v. United States*, 133 F.3d 888 (Fed. Cir. 1998), remanding a case to the Court of Federal Claims to determine if institutional ratification had occurred. See also *Digicon Corp. v. United States*, 56 Fed. Cl. 425 (2003) (denying motion for summary judgment because facts indicated that institutional ratification had occurred); *Perri v. United States*, 53 Fed. Cl. 381 (2002) (denying claim of institutional ratification because there was evidence of promise that could be ratified); *Hawkins & Powers Aviation, Inc. v. United States*, 46 Fed. Cl. 238 (2000) (denying institutional ratification claim because government received no benefit); and *Dolmatch Group, Ltd. v. United States*, 40 Fed. Cl. 431 (1998) (denying motion for summary judgment because plaintiff might be able to prove institutional ratification).

(3) Knowledge of Unauthorized Acts

A prerequisite to ratification is the ratifying official's knowledge, either actual or constructive, of the facts affecting the unauthorized action. In *United States v. Beebe*, 180 U.S. 343 (1901), the Court stated at 354:

> Where an agent has acted without authority and it is claimed that the principal has thereafter ratified his act, such ratification can only be based upon a full knowledge of all the facts upon which the unauthorized action was taken. This is as true

> in the case of the government as in that of an individual. Knowledge is necessary in any event. Story on Agency, 9th ed. sec. 239, notes 1 and 2. If there be want of it, though such want arises from the neglect of the principal, no ratification can be based upon any act of his. Knowledge of the facts is the essential element of ratification, and must be shown or such facts proved that its existence is a necessary inference from them.

See *California Sand & Gravel, Inc. v. United States*, 22 Cl. Ct. 19 (1990), *aff'd*, 937 F.2d 624 (Fed. Cir. 1991), holding that there could be no ratification without full knowledge of all facts pertinent to the unauthorized commitment; *Durocher Dock & Dredge, Inc.*, ENGBCA 5768, 91-3 BCA ¶ 24,145, in which ratification was denied because the contracting officer, as the only official with authority to ratify, had no knowledge of the events; and *Tymshare*, PSBCA 206, 76-2 BCA ¶ 12,218, in which there was no ratification of an unauthorized representative's agreement because the authorized official neither knew nor should have known of the unauthorized agreement.

The ratifying official may obtain actual knowledge from various sources, *Mick DeWall Constr.*, PSBCA 2580, 91-1 BCA ¶ 23,510 (contracting officer received notice in claim that COR had agreed to modification); *Globe Constr. Co.*, GSBCA 2197, 67-2 BCA ¶ 6478 (contracting officer received notice of prior actions from his representative and through the contractor's formal claim for additional compensation); *Brown Constr. Co.*, ASBCA 22648, 79-1 BCA ¶ 13,745 (contracting officer participated in a pre-construction conference where a representative stated that construction policy required a contract change).

A ratifying official may also gain knowledge constructively. Constructive notice was found in *Williams v. United States*, 130 Ct. Cl. 435, 127 F. Supp. 617, *cert. denied*, 349 U.S. 938 (1955), where an unauthorized Air Force officer and the contractor agreed that the contractor could use the Air Force's asphalt plant in return for seal coating the base's roads. The base contracting officer was held to have constructive knowledge of the agreement because the roads were wholly within the base where he was located.

Imputed knowledge from representatives may also serve as constructive knowledge of a ratifying official. See, for example, *W. Southard Jones, Inc.*, ASBCA 6321, 61-2 BCA ¶ 3182, where base technical personnel knew that the contractor's performance did not conform to contract drawings. This knowledge was imputed to the contracting officer, who frequently met with the base engineer and discussed projects at the base. When the relationship between two persons creates a presumption that one would have informed the other of certain events, the boards may impute the knowledge of one to the other, *Leiden Corp.*, ASBCA 26136, 83-2 BCA ¶ 16,612, *recons. denied*, 84-1 BCA ¶ 16,947. See also *Southwestern Sheet Metal Works, Inc.*, ASBCA 22748, 79-1 BCA ¶ 13,744, *recons. denied*, 79-2 BCA ¶ 13,949, in which the board held that the inspectors functioned as the contracting officer's eyes and ears; hence, the contracting officer had actual or constructive knowledge of the inspector's directive changing contract terms, where the inspector lacked authority to issue such a change.

(4) Adoption of Unauthorized Acts

The contractor must show that an authorized official has adopted the unauthorized conduct, either expressly, by conduct, or by silence. In *DBA Sys., Inc.*, NASABCA 481-5, 82-1 BCA ¶ 15,468, ratification did not occur because the contracting officer "consistently and expressly disavowed the purported funding agreement and likewise did nothing which, by implication, could be reasonably interpreted as his concurrence with [his representative's] belief that the overrun should be funded." See also *Prestex, Inc. v. United States*, 162 Ct. Cl. 620, 320 F.2d 367 (1963) (upon learning of deviations from specifications, the government repudiated the contract, never having accepted or used the product, so that no ratification of deviations existed).

An express adoption of an unauthorized act clearly establishes ratification, *Globe Constr. Co.*, GSBCA 2197, 67-2 BCA ¶ 6478 (contracting officer stated that his subordinate's prior action had been done within his authority); *Fish & Wildlife Serv.*, Comp. Gen. Dec. B-208730, 83-1 CPD ¶ 75 (authorized official signed a document expressing his intent to ratify the unauthorized act).

An authorized official's adoption of an unauthorized act may result from conduct, *T.W. Cole*, PSBCA 3076, 92-3 BCA ¶ 25,091 (acceptance of work with knowledge of order to modify it); *Henry Burge & Alvin White*, PSBCA 2431, 89-3 BCA ¶ 21,910 (acceptance of work with knowledge of modification); *Norwood Precision Prods.*, ASBCA 24083, 80-1 BCA ¶ 14,405 (payment for products accepted after a default termination indicated the official's adoption of the inspector's unauthorized acceptance); *Mil-Pak Co.*, GSBCA 5849, 83-1 BCA ¶ 16,482 (contracting officer ratified a change order by unilaterally fixing the amount of the equitable adjustment). But see *Metcalf & Assocs.*, GSBCA 3190, 72-2 BCA ¶ 9516, in which the board held that a contracting officer's award of compensation to a contractor for certain changes directed by unauthorized representatives did not constitute a ratification but was an attempt at settlement not binding on the government.

Silence or inaction may also constitute adoption by an authorized official. See *KRW, Inc.*, DOTCAB 2572, 94-1 BCA ¶ 26,435 (contracting officer acquiesced in alteration of work product); *HFS, Inc.*, ASBCA 43748, 92-3 BCA ¶ 25,198 (contracting officer took no action on letter describing the order for extra work); *Gricoski Detective Agency*, GSBCA 8901, 90-3 BCA ¶ 23,131 (total inaction after letter was sent to contracting officer describing an order to change the method of performance); *Lox Equip. Co.*, ASBCA 8985, 1964 BCA ¶ 4463 (failure of contracting officer to take effective action to correct the situation adopted his inspector's directives); *Michael Guth*, ASBCA 22663, 80-2 BCA ¶ 14,572 (contracting officer affirmed by not questioning a manager's interpretation of liability provisions); *Brown Constr.*

Co., ASBCA 22648, 79-1 BCA ¶ 13,745 (contracting officer silent when unauthorized official prohibited the use of contract-designated plywood); and *Triangle Elec. Mfg. Co.*, ASBCA 15995, 74-2 BCA ¶ 10,783 (contracting officer's silence regarding representatives' interpretation was conduct amounting to consent to the performance of such duties). Compare *SAE Americon*, PSBCA 3866, 00-1 BCA ¶ 30,867, in which no ratification by silence was found where the COR promptly notified the contractor that a construction technique was not required after finding out about the purported direction to use the technique. See also *Harbert/Lummus Agrifuels Projects v. United States*, 142 F.3d 1429 (Fed. Cir. 1998), *cert. denied*, 525 U.S. 1177 (1999), finding no ratification when a contracting officer was present when an unauthorized official made an oral promise to the contractor but did not object or warn the contractor. The court reasoned at 1433-34:

> In our case, the trial court merely found that the CO was present when the Deputy Director made the offer and was silent after the offer was made. There was no finding that the CO even heard the statement. This is not sufficient evidence to support a finding of actual knowledge by the CO of the offer. In addition, the facts as found by the trial court do not support imputing to the CO constructive knowledge of the unilateral contract. The mere fact that Harbert/Lummus continued performing its construction activities would not have put the CO on notice of the existence of a new, unilateral contract because Harbert/Lummus had been performing its construction activities before the offer by the Deputy Director in accordance with its construction contract with Agrifuels. In the absence of either actual or constructive knowledge of the unilateral contract, the CO's silence cannot be a ratification of the unilateral contract.

Acquiescence has been premised on the ratifying official's constructive notice coupled with silence. See *Williams v. United States*, 130 Ct. Cl. 435, 127 F. Supp. 617, *cert. denied*, 349 U.S. 938 (1955); *W. Southard Jones, Inc.*, ASBCA 6321, 61-2 BCA ¶ 3182; and *Southwestern Sheet Metal Works, Inc.*, ASBCA 22748, 79-1 BCA ¶ 13,744, *recons. denied*, 79-2 BCA ¶ 13,949.

(5) Ratification and Quantum Meruit

The GAO has often held that ratification by authorized officials is required before it will approve payment to persons conferring a benefit on the government. In discussing recovery under quantum meruit or quantum valebant theories, the GAO in *Acme, Inc.*, Comp. Gen. Dec. B-182584, 74-2 CPD ¶ 310, stated:

> Before a right to payment under such basis may be recognized it must be shown that the Government has received a benefit, and that the unauthorized goods or services were expressly or impliedly ratified by authorized contracting officials.

Further, ratification is not permissible if the original action was improper. See *Checker Van Lines*, Comp. Gen. Dec. B-206542, 82-2 CPD ¶ 219, *recons. denied*, 84-2 CPD ¶ 253 (obligation of funds beyond a 180-day period was statutorily prohibited; therefore, ratification could not support the requisite implied-in-fact contract for recovery); and Comp. Gen. Dec. B-164087, July 1, 1968, *Unpub.* (no basis for quantum meruit recovery where the authorized contracting officials were not aware of the Project Director's action and immediate action was taken to curtail such activity when it became known). In *Dan J. Carney, Controller*, Comp. Gen. Dec. B-259926, Mar. 31, 1995, *Unpub.*, the GAO advised the agency that it could properly ratify an agreement for services even though the contractor had been paid for the services before the ratification. The GAO has also found implied ratifications. See *Equal Employment Opportunity Comm'n*, Comp. Gen. Dec. B-207492, 82-2 CPD ¶ 112 (failure of authorized representatives to curtail contractor's activities constituted adoption); *INTASA, Inc.*, Comp. Gen. Dec. B-180876, 74-1 CPD ¶ 148 (unauthorized notice to proceed affirmed by intention to formalize a contract and recommendation for payment); *Mathews Furniture Co.*, Comp. Gen. Dec. B-195123, 79-2 CPD ¶ 131 (acquiescence by an authorized official determined from his negotiations seeking a settlement); and *Defense Mapping Agency*, Comp. Gen. Dec. B-183915, 75-2 CPD ¶ 15 (recommendation for payment).

Ratification has been found even after the authorized contracting officer refused to adopt the unauthorized act. In *Acme, Inc.*, Comp. Gen. Dec. B-182584, 74-2 CPD ¶ 310, an officer exceeded his authority by soliciting informal quotations. The authorized contracting officer found that the work was necessary, the government benefited, and the contractor performed in good faith at a reasonable price, but the contracting officer refused to ratify the procurement. However, payment was recommended by the Director of Fiscal Management. The GAO inferred an implied ratification from the contracting officer's determination that the work performed was in the best interest of the government and the Director's recommendation for payment. Similarly, authorized contracting officers refused to ratify an unauthorized order for a contractor to conduct training sessions in *Singer Co.*, Comp. Gen. Dec. B-183878, 75-1 CPD ¶ 406, "primarily because the officials had no basis to determine if the price was reasonable." Implied ratification was inferred from the issuance of a contract for a subsequent identical training session to be conducted by the contractor. See *Maintenance Serv. & Sales Corp.*, 70 Comp. Gen. 664 (B-242019) (1991), where the contracting officer refused to ratify and took no action, but the GAO granted relief under quantum meruit. A similar result was arrived at in *Mohawk Data Science Corp.*, 69 Comp. Gen. 13 (B-232357) (1989), and *Hocking Int'l Chem. Corp.*, 66 Comp. Gen. 351 (B-225842) (1987).

c. *Knowledge Imputed to Authorized Personnel*

In many cases, it is important to determine whether the contracting officer or other authorized representative has knowledge of certain facts. Such knowledge may be important because the contract requires that information be furnished to the authorized person or that notice be given of events such as delays or constructive changes. In other situations, the legal significance of statements or acts of an authorized person depends on whether the person was in possession of specific knowledge.

The authorized person is held to have knowledge under the common law concept that a principal is charged with knowledge that an agent has a duty to deliver to the principal, *Restatement (Second) of Agency* § 272. In applying this rule to government contracts, the courts and boards have imputed knowledge to contracting officers and other authorized persons when the nature of the relationship between the authorized person and the representative establishes a presumption that the authorized person would be informed. Thus, knowledge of a claim based on nondisclosure of information by the government was imputed in *Cryo-Sonics, Inc.*, ASBCA 11483, 66-2 BCA ¶ 5890 (information known to a government engineer was imputed to the government negotiators). See also *J.A. Jones Constr. Co. v. United States*, 182 Ct. Cl. 615, 390 F.2d 886 (1968). In most cases involving imputed knowledge, the unauthorized representative possesses actual knowledge. In *Xplo Corp.*, DOTCAB 1250, 86-2 BCA ¶ 18,863, the board noted at 95,110:

> The COTR, as the Contracting Officer's authorized representative, had a duty to communicate [the contractor's] notice of problems to the Contracting Officer and therefore knowledge of [those problems] will be imputed to the Contracting Officer.

See also *KRW, Inc.*, DOTCAB 2572, 94-1 BCA ¶ 26,435, in which the board not only imputed notice to a COTR to the contracting officer but further stated that upon receipt of notice it is incumbent upon the contracting officer to make some response, and *Sociometrics, Inc.*, ASBCA 51620, 00-1 BCA ¶ 30,620, in which the board imputed knowledge that the contractor was performing work even though an option had not been exercised because the COR was the "eyes and ears" of the contracting officer.

Two cases have held a contracting officer to have imputed knowledge although only constructive knowledge on the part of the representatives was demonstrated, *W. Southard Jones, Inc.*, ASBCA 6321, 61-2 BCA ¶ 3182, and *Inet Power*, NASABCA 566-23, 68-1 BCA ¶ 7020.

Constructive notice to a representative has been expressly rejected in cases involving cost or pricing data. Because of the contractor's affirmative duty to submit such data, knowledge would not be imputed to the government if auditors lack actual knowledge. See *Sylvania Elec. Prods., Inc.*, ASBCA 13622, 70-2 BCA ¶ 8387, *aff'd*, 202 Ct. Cl. 16 (1973) (auditors did not cross-check data and therefore failed to uncover a materials cost error; absent auditors' actual knowledge, the contracting officer was not charged with knowledge), and *Libby Welding Co., Inc.*, ASBCA 15084, 73-1 BCA ¶ 9859 (contractor listed costs twice on bill that auditors overlooked and imputation held improper).

(1) Technical Representatives

Knowledge of information related to technical details of performance is imputed to the authorized person when such knowledge is in the possession of the government's technical representatives, *U.S. Fed. Eng'g & Mfg., Inc.*, ASBCA 19909, 75-2 BCA ¶ 11,578 (government project engineer was "not only the person responsible for inspection and acceptance of the job but was also the most significant contact the contractor had with the Government"). Finding that the contracting officer was uninformed both of the required additional work and of the fact that it was to be performed, the board stated at 55,298-99:

> The fact that the contracting officer did not have actual knowledge of the additions to be made to the device does not insulate the Government from the consequences that actual knowledge would impose. His various representatives are his eyes and ears (if not his voice) and their knowledge is treated for all intents and purposes as his.

See also *Glenda R. Whitaker*, PSBCA 3443, 94-2 BCA ¶ 26,643 (knowledge of contractor's protests, having been communicated to those authorized by the contracting officer to administer the contract, may be imputed to the contracting officer); *Powers Regulator Co.*, GSBCA 4668, 80-2 BCA ¶ 14,463 (the presumption that the representative would inform the contracting officer arose from the complex technical issues that required the contracting officer's reliance on the representative's technical expertise); *Carl J. Bonidie, Inc.*, ASBCA 25769, 82-2 BCA ¶ 15,818 (Changes clause notice requirement was satisfied by knowledge of base civil engineer, whose recommendations apparently determined the contracting officer's contractual decisions); *Piland Corp.*, ASBCA 22560, 78-2 BCA ¶ 13,227, *recons. denied*, 78-2 BCA ¶ 13,503 (knowledge was imputed to the contracting officer in order to satisfy the Suspension of Work clause notice requirements); *Burn Constr. Co.*, IBCA 1042-9-74, 78-2 BCA ¶ 13,405 (government engineer lacked authority to make changes, but knowledge imputed because he was charged with administering the contract); *Singleton Contracting Corp.*, IBCA 1413-12-80, 81-2 BCA ¶ 15,269 (COTR's knowledge of potential claim imputed to contracting officer); *W. Southard Jones, Inc.*, ASBCA 6321, 61-2 BCA ¶ 3182 (knowledge imputed upon presumption that the base engineer and contracting officer met not infrequently about projects); and *Walter Straga*, ASBCA 26134, 83-2 BCA ¶ 16,611 (project manager's knowledge that the contractor's interpretation of the drawings differed from his own imputed to contracting officer).

Not all information possessed by a representative will be imputed. The information may not be the type that technical representatives would be presumed to convey to a contracting officer. In *A.L. Constr. Co.*, NASABCA 178-1, 78-2 BCA ¶ 13,284, a project engineer who was not authorized to change the contract had actual knowledge of the contractor's installation of vents. Since it was unclear at the time of the extra performance that a claim would result, the board found that the project engineer's failure to object to the contractor's installation of the vents was not a constructive order to proceed by an unauthorized representative, and the knowledge of the contractor's actions did not constitute constructive notice to the contracting officer. See also *Donat Gerg Haustechnik*, ASBCA 41197, 97-2 BCA ¶ 29,272, refusing to impute technical person's knowledge of nonconforming work. In addition, in *Franchi Realty Trust v. General Servs. Admin.*, GSBCA 11149, 92-3 BCA ¶ 25,180, a directive by a Drug Enforcement Administration (DEA) representative concerning the construction of new DEA offices was not imputed to the contracting officer. The board stated at 125,483-84:

> Of course, the actions of the DEA employee might be found to be binding if there was a showing that a "responsible officer" (authorized contracting officer) "knew or should have known of the situation" such that knowledge of the DEA employees could be imputed to the contracting officer so as to bind the Government. . . . [H]owever, there simply is no basis to find that a contracting officer knew or had reason to know [of the situation]. . . . Under the circumstances, we can find neither actual nor implied notice of the subject change.

In *United States v. Hanna Nickel Smelting Co.*, 253 F. Supp. 784 (D. Ore. 1966), *aff'd on other grounds*, 400 F.2d 944 (9th Cir. 1968), an engineer was instructed to maintain surveillance of purchase orders and paid vouchers to assure that funds were charged against the proper account. Finding knowledge of the contractor's accounting system imputable through others, the court made no determination of the engineer's duties, noting at 794:

> Whether [the engineer's] duties can be interpreted to include meaningful reporting on the Company's accounting practices, since he was not a trained accountant, is not free from doubt.

(2) Inspectors

Information pertinent to an inspector's duties has been imputed to the contracting officer, *Polan Indus., Inc.*, ASBCA 3996, 58-2 BCA ¶ 1982. In *Tasker Indus., Inc.*, DOTCAB 71-22, 75-2 BCA ¶ 11,372, the board stated at 54,139:

> When a Contracting Officer licenses technical personnel, such as engineers or inspectors, to give guidance or instructions about specification problems to contractors the Government is liable for the consequences of the guidance given.

See also *Hartford Accident & Indem. Co.*, IBCA 1139-1-77, 77-2 BCA ¶ 12,604 (field inspector was the representative of the government on the job); *Raby Hillside Drilling, Inc.*, AGBCA 75-101, 78-1 BCA ¶ 13,026 (knowledge of inspectors who daily administer a contract on the site must be imputed to the contracting officer); *Peters Mach. Co.*, ASBCA 21857, 78-1 BCA ¶ 12,865, *recons. denied*, 79-1 BCA ¶ 13,649 (knowledge of inspector of deviation imputed to the contracting officer); and *Gresham & Co. v. United States*, 200 Ct. Cl. 97, 470 F.2d 542 (1972) (contracting officer could not reject nonconforming items because his Quality Assurance Representatives had known of the deviations). See also *Hudson Contracting, Inc.*, ASBCA 41023, 94-1 BCA ¶ 26,466, in which the board upheld a government inspector's oral agreement for the furnishing of government property in return for the contractor providing equipment and an operator for unrelated government work. The contracting officer had allowed the project manager to exercise broad authority in administering the contract. The board found that the project manager thus had the authority to provide the government property involved. The board found that while the project manager must have known of the inspector's agreement, knowledge of the agreement would be imputed to him "in any event by virtue of [his] supervision of the inspector . . . [and his] extensive day-to-day involvement in the progress of the contract."

Not all relationships between contracting officers and inspectors are sufficiently close to raise the presumption that the contracting officer would be informed of relevant facts. In *Canadian Commercial Corp.*, ASBCA 17187, 76-2 BCA ¶ 12,145, *recons. denied*, 77-2 BCA ¶ 12,758, an inspector's knowledge of design defects was not imputable to the contracting officer because close contact between the resident Canadian inspector and the government's contract administration or technical personnel was not established. Further, the contractor knew the inspector lacked authority to make design changes and that such changes were within the contracting officer's discretion. The presumption that the inspector would act as the contracting officer's informant was held improper.

(3) Administrative and Clerical Personnel

Whether knowledge possessed by administrative and clerical personnel will be imputed to authorized representatives depends on the nature of the relationship. In *Precision Prods.*, ASBCA 25280, 82-2 BCA ¶ 15,981, government representatives responsible for administering the contract were the eyes and ears of the contracting officer, so their knowledge was imputed to the contracting officer. Similarly, in *KRW, Inc.*, DOTCAB 2572, 94-1 BCA ¶ 26,435, the knowledge of a contract administrator was imputed to the contracting officer because the contractor had been directed to send reports to the contract administrator. However, the relationship between an airman, who knew of the contractor's causes of delay, and the contracting officer was not sufficient to establish a presumption that the information would be reported, *M.J. Newsom*, ASBCA 9799, 1964 BCA ¶ 4444. The board noted that the airman's status with respect to the contracting officer remains undetermined.

(4) Auditors

Since audit information is to be conveyed to the contracting officer, information related to the audit function will be imputed. In *Chrysler Corp.*, ASBCA 17259, 75-1 BCA ¶ 11,236, *recons. denied*, 76-1 BCA ¶ 11,665, Army Audit Agency knowledge of the contractor's accrual account and the manner in which it operated was imputed to the contracting officer. Similarly, in *E-Systems, Inc.*, ASBCA 18877, 76-1 BCA ¶ 11,797, where the DCAA was aware of the contractor's pooling and allocation of material costs, this information was imputed to the contracting officer.

See also *United States v. Hanna Nickel Smelting Co.*, 253 F. Supp. 784 (D. Ore. 1966), *aff'd on other grounds*, 400 F.2d 944 (9th Cir. 1968) (contractor's accounting practices regarding allocation of capital items known by auditors), and *Western Elec. Co.*, ASBCA 21294, 79-1 BCA ¶ 13,550.

B. Contractor Personnel

In contrast to the special rules pertaining to government representatives, general principles of agency law apply to contractor's representatives. There is considerably less litigation in this area.

1. Delegation

Authority may be expressly or impliedly delegated to a contractor's representatives. When a corporation is involved, the plenary authority to transact all the ordinary business of the corporation within its charter powers is vested in the board of directors. Express delegation of authority to others is normally contained in resolutions of the board of directors, which are often furnished to the government agencies with whom the corporate contractor does business.

2. Apparent Authority

The major difference between the legal rules applicable to government representatives and those applicable to contractor representatives is that a contractor may be bound by a representative possessing apparent authority. See *American Anchor & Chain Corp. v. United States*, 166 Ct. Cl. 1, 331 F.2d 860 (1964), in which the court stated at 4:

> Although the Federal Government still stands on the stricter requirements of actual authority for its own agents (see, e.g., *Federal Crop Ins. Corp. v. Merrill*, 332 U.S. 380 (1947)), the agents of Government contractors are governed by the usual rules.

See also *Kaco Contracting Co.*, ASBCA 44937, 01-2 BCA ¶ 31,584, and *Western Box-O-Matic Corp.*, GSBCA 3562, 73-1 BCA ¶ 9968, in which it was held that the government was entitled to rely on the apparent authority of the contractor's plant manager to interpret contract language. In *Menches Tool & Die, Inc.*, ASBCA 21469, 78-1 BCA ¶ 13,167, the board rejected the contractor's arguments that it had never authorized its attorney to make certain statements:"The Government has the right to assume an agent has actual or apparent authority to bind his principal."

However, if government employees know or should know that a contractor representative does not have contracting authority, that representative will not be found to have apparent authority. See, for example, *Tectonics Asia Architects & Eng'rs, Inc.*, ASBCA 17067, 75-2 BCA ¶ 11,456, in which the board stated at 54,567:

> It is also clear from the record that Mr. a'Becket was not an officer of the corporation and this fact should have been known to AID contracting personnel since he always signed correspondence and invoices as "contract administrator," acted in that capacity and did not represent himself as a corporate officer. There is nothing in the record to indicate that AID was ever notified that Mr. a'Becket had contracting authority. His participation in negotiations for Amendment No. 1, together with [the contractor's] vice-president Mr. Anderson, did not clothe him with apparent or implied authority on which AID personnel could have been [relying.] The authorities cited in [the government's] brief (*American Anchor & Chain Corporation v. United States* [9 CCF ¶ 72,578], 166 Ct. Cl. 1 (1964) and *Video Engineering Company, Inc.*, DOT CAB No. 72-5, 72-1 BCA ¶ 9432) involve distinctly different factual situations and thus do not support the proposition that Mr. a'Becket had apparent authority to act for the corporation and bind it contractually.

See also *Peter Bauwens Bauunternehmung GmbH & Co. KG*, ASBCA 44679, 98-1 BCA ¶ 29,551 (contractor not bound by agreements of its project manager because government "knew or had reason to know" that he had no contracting authority); *Piracci Corp.*, GSBCA 6007, 82-2 BCA ¶ 16,047 (contractor not bound by a settlement negotiated by attorney when government negotiator had no reason to believe that attorney had authority to settle a claim); *Ray Wilson Co.*, ASBCA 17084, 75-1 BCA ¶ 11,066 (government was not justified in inferring that a second-tier subcontractor's employees had authority to bind the contractor); Comp. Gen. Dec. B-171802, March 2, 1971, *Unpub.* (contractor not bound by the actions of its employees who had no real, implied, or apparent authority); *Colorado Sec. Agency, Inc.*, GSBCA 5650, 84-1 BCA ¶ 16,940 (contractor not bound because contracting officer knew contractor's employee had no authority); and *Kahaluu Constr. Co.*, ASBCA 33248, 90-2 BCA ¶ 22,663 (proposed settlement agreement approved by an agent of a contractor and an agent of the government, both without authority, was not an offer to settle).

3. Ratification and Estoppel

Even though the government deals with an unauthorized representative, the contractor will be bound if the action is ratified by an authorized official. In *Tectonics Asia Architects & Eng'rs, Inc.*, ASBCA 17067, 75-2 BCA ¶ 11,456, the contractor was held bound by an unauthorized amendment when it had continued performance for two and a half months with full knowledge of the terms of the amendment.

The principles of estoppel are also similarly applicable to the contractor. In *Ampex Corp.*, GSBCA 5913, 82-1 BCA ¶ 15,738, *recons. denied*, 82-2 BCA ¶ 15,858, the board held that the contractor was estopped to deny an agreement where a contractor's representative had informed the government that the contractor had agreed to accept the agreement. The board found that the representative did not have authority to make the agreement but did have the authority to convey information to the government, stating at 77,861:

> Granted, [the contractor's representative] was not an agent of the company authorized to bind it contractually. We have already indicated that we do not consider that to be the point in dispute. Rather, the issue is whether [the representative] had the authority to tell the Government that [the contractor] had agreed to be bound. If she had that authority, then [the contractor] is bound by her representation:
>
>> Except as to statements with relation to the agent's authority, in actions brought upon a contract or to rescind a contract, a disclosed or partially disclosed principal is responsible for unauthorized representations made incidental to it, if the contract is otherwise authorized and if true representations as to the same subject matter are within the authority or the apparent authority of the agent, unless the other party thereto has notice that the representations are untrue or unauthorized.
>
> *Restatement (Second) of Agency* (1958), § 162.

See also *Detroit Diesel Allison Div., Gen. Motors Corp.*, ASBCA 20199, 77-1 BCA ¶ 12,414, in which the contractor was estopped to deny applicability of long-standing accounting practice. Compare *CRF v. United States*, 224 Ct. Cl. 312, 624 F.2d 1054 (1980), stating that the contractor was not estopped to deny the validity of a contract awarded in a manner contrary to the regulations. In *Piracci Corp.*, GSBCA 6007, 82-2 BCA ¶ 16,047, the board held that the contractor was not estopped on the basis, among others, that there was no justifiable reliance by the government.

IV. GOVERNMENT BOUND BY CONDUCT OF ITS AUTHORIZED AGENTS

Since the government can act only through its agents and employees, it is clear that it will be bound when authorized agents carry out their duties properly. However, government personnel cannot be expected to act only in ways favorable to the United States. Whether resulting from mistakes, negligence, or poor judgment, their statements, acts, or omissions are sometimes contrary to the government's best interests. This may become evident from later reflection or subsequent events, or it may be determined by the agents' advisors, superiors, or successors. In such cases, attempts may be made to avoid the consequences by repudiating or countermanding the agents' acts. Two major concepts are invoked to prevent the government from disowning authorized agents' acts or agreements—thereby making them binding on the government. The first concept is finality; the second is estoppel.

A. Finality

The actions of a government employee acting within the scope of his or her employment are the actions of the government itself, and, as with any contracting party, once the government has taken the final step toward committing a contractual act, it is bound by it. Thus, the focus of analysis in this area is on the action of the government employee that contains the elements of finality in the contracting process.

1. Sources of Finality

It appears that finality of contractual acts may attach as a result of either the application of a provision of the contract that is interpreted as defining when finality attaches or the operation of a legal rule. The most direct example of a contract clause providing for finality is the Disputes clause, which makes decisions of contracting officers final. The government was held bound by such decisions in *Bell Helicopter Co.*, ASBCA 17776, 74-1 BCA ¶ 10,411. Another such clause is the Inspection clause, which states that government acceptance of work will be final, with certain exceptions. In *McQuagge v. United States*, 197 F. Supp. 460 (W.D. La. 1961), the contracting officer had issued a certificate of final acceptance despite the knowledge of the government that the concrete used in airport taxiways did not measure up to the specifications. The court found the acceptance final and conclusive, stating at 468:

> In a case such as this, the government can only act through those to whom it has delegated authority to make decisions. It was within the discretion of the Contracting Officers to determine whether the work was acceptable to the government, and final acceptance by such officers was subject to being opened or questioned only upon evidence of collusion, fraud, or obvious error.

See also *Mil-Spec Contractors, Inc. v. United States*, 835 F.2d 865 (Fed. Cir. 1987); *S.E.R., Jobs for Progress, Inc. v. United States*, 759 F.2d 1 (Fed. Cir. 1985); *Walsky Constr. Co.*, ASBCA 19875, 77-1 BCA ¶ 12,388; *Conrad Weihnacht Constr., Inc.*, ASBCA 20767, 76-2 BCA ¶ 11,963; and *Genuine Motor Parts of Pa., Inc.*, ASBCA 19063, 76-1 BCA ¶ 11,860. Another clause that has been interpreted as creating finality is the Allowable Cost, Fixed Fee, and Payment clause. See *Chrysler Corp.*, ASBCA 17259, 75-1 BCA ¶ 11,236, *recons. denied*, 76-1 BCA ¶ 11,665, holding that this clause should be interpreted to bar the government from contesting payments after final payment on the contract has been made. In *Bell Aircraft Corp. v. United States*, 120 Ct. Cl. 398, 100 F. Supp. 661 (1951), the court held that approval and payment of invoices under a cost-reimbursement contract was binding on the government at the time the payment was made. The same result was reached in *United States v. Mason & Hanger Co.*, 260 U.S. 323 (1922), and *Leeds & Northrup Co. v. United States*, 101 F. Supp. 999 (E.D. Pa. 1951). Finality was also found when a contracting officer made a decision to fund an overrun under the Limitation of Cost clause, *General Elec. Co. v. United States*, 188 Ct. Cl. 620, 412 F.2d 1215 (1969), and where an award fee official determined the award fee under an Award Fee clause, *URS Consultants, Inc.*, IBCA 4285-2000, 02-1 BCA ¶ 31,812. Neither the Allowable Cost, Fixed Fee, and Payment clause, the Limitation of Cost clause, nor the Award Fee clause contains explicit language stating that decisions or actions of the contracting officer will be final, yet the courts and boards have interpreted the clauses to have this effect. Compare *Litton Sys., Inc. Guidance & Control Sys. Div.*, ASBCA 45400, 94-2 BCA ¶ 26,895, holding that an administrative contracting officer's determination that the contractor was not in compliance with Cost Accounting Standards 405 and 410 was not entitled to finality because no contract clause provided that such decisions would be final. See also *ENCORP Int'l, Inc.*, ASBCA 49474, 99-1 BCA ¶ 30,254, finding an agreement of a contracting officer to release Miller Act bonds not entitled to finality because it was in violation of an important public policy.

Two cases have found an internal decision of a contracting officer to be final even though it was not communicated to the contractor. In *General Electric*, the court found a decision to be final because the contracting officer had signed an internal memorandum stating that an overrun would be funded. The same result was reached in *Texas Instruments, Inc. v. United States*, 922 F.2d 810 (Fed. Cir. 1990), where an ACO had signed a price negotiation memorandum (PNM) agreeing to a negotiated settlement of a claim. The court found that this was a final decision, stating at 813-14:

> Under *General Electric*, the law presumes that when an ACO acquainted with the underlying facts signs an internal document, such as the PNM, that she has decided to express a definite opinion on the merits of the claim in the absence of contrary testimony or evidence. Such contrary evidence or testimony is lacking here.

These cases indicate that the government will be bound during contract administration by the doctrine of finality whenever an authorized employee signs a document or takes an action that is properly construed as resolving the issue at hand.

The clearest example of a legal rule creating finality is the binding effect on the government of the acceptance of an offer. See *United States v. Purcell Envelope Co.*, 249 U.S. 313 (1919), in which the Court held that the government was bound when the Postmaster General accepted the offer of a company in a formally advertised procurement. Similarly, the government will be bound if an authorized official enters into a contract modification adjusting the price after a change has been ordered, *Liberty Coat Co.*, ASBCA 4119, 57-2 BCA ¶ 1576. See also *Airmotive Eng'g Corp.*, ASBCA 15235, 71-2 BCA ¶ 8988, in which the board held that the government was bound when a contracting officer entered into a contract amendment modifying the price to reflect the adoption of a value engineering proposal.

A variety of other actions and determinations by government officials may also be final and binding on the government. For example, a determination by a contracting officer that the contractor's labor cost estimating technique was not defective was final and binding on the government and could not be revoked or overruled by his successor, *Bell Helicopter Co.*, ASBCA 17776, 74-1 BCA ¶ 10,411. In *Southern, Waldrip & Harvick Co. v. United States*, 167 Ct. Cl. 488, 334 F.2d 245 (1964), the court held that the Chief of Engineers could not overrule a finding of the contracting officer that a telegraphic bid modification had been timely received. The instructions to bidders had stated that a determination of timeliness of modifications would rest with the contracting officer. These instructions constituted an agreement between the government and the contractor and left the Chief of Engineers without authority to independently determine timeliness.

2. Authority Required

For the action to be binding and final, the government employee must be acting within his or her authority. See *Trevco Eng'g & Sales*, VABCA 1021, 73-2 BCA ¶ 10,096, in which the board found that an inspector had not been delegated the authority to make final acceptance. See also Comp. Gen. Dec. B-170360, Apr. 6, 1971, *Unpub.*, stating that an award by a contracting officer to the second low bidder could be overruled by his superiors, since the contracting officer had no authority to make a valid award to anyone but the low responsible bidder, and 35 Comp. Gen. 63 (B-120714) (1955), stating that no finality attaches to payment contrary to the cost plus percentage of cost prohibition. Acts of unauthorized representatives that are ratified by an authorized official are also accorded finality, *Tucker & Assocs. Contracting, Inc.*, IBCA 1468-6-81, 83-1 BCA ¶ 16,140.

3. Government Bound by Prejudicial Decisions

The government is bound by the acts of its authorized representatives, even if their decisions are erroneous. In *Liberty Coat Co.*, ASBCA 4119, 57-2 BCA ¶ 1576, the contracting officer issued findings and determinations that certain changes reduced the contractor's costs, and adjusted the contract price accordingly. A successor contracting officer issued new determinations and findings on the same changes and greatly increased the reductions in price. In ruling for the contractor that the original contracting officer's decision was binding, the board stated at 5671-72:

> The Government makes no allegation of mutual mistake and, while admitting that it has no other evidence of fraud or collusion, argues that we are required to draw such an inference from the gross disparity between the equitable adjustments agreed to by the original contracting officer and the "correct and equitable adjustment for the deviation[s]" as found by the successor contracting officer. Assuming, for the purposes of decision on [the contractor's] motion, the validity of the successor contracting officer's determination of "correct and equitable" price adjustments, in the absence of even a scintilla of other evidence of fraud and collusion, we think the proper inference is that, relying on erroneous advice of his price analysts, the original contracting officer made a bad bargain. We are not aware of any authorities, nor has counsel invited our attention to any, holding that an agreement is vitiated by this fact alone.
>
> The Government seeks to distinguish these cases from our prior holdings on the ground that in their determination the Board did not consider its present argument that the original contracting officer acted "outside the bounds of his author-

> ity" in agreeing to allegedly grossly inadequate price adjustments. Under the terms of the standard "Changes" article of these contracts, and procurement regulations, the contracting officer had clear authority to make changes in the specifications of the contracts. Upon doing so he was specifically charged with the responsibility of determining whether the change caused "an increase or decrease in the cost of * * * this contract * * *, and, upon such a determination, the clause continues, an equitable adjustment shall be made in the contract price * * * and the contract shall be modified in writing accordingly." The Government's argument, reduced to its lowest common denominator, is that while the contracting officer had authority to make a good bargain, he had no authority to make a bad one. We are unable to accept such an argument. It confuses the contracting officer's authority to act with the judgment displayed by him in performing the act. It seeks to measure authority by the results obtained upon its exercise. Counsel has not cited, and we have been unable to find, any cases supporting this method of measuring authority.

See also *Chrysler Corp.*, ASBCA 17259, 75-1 BCA ¶ 11,236, *recons. denied*, 76-1 BCA ¶ 11,665. While it cannot be said that the government authorizes its agents to make mistakes or to commit torts, it is liable for the agent's action if it is within the scope of his or her authority. See *Cooke v. United States*, 91 U.S. (1 Otto) 389 (1875), in which the Court stated at 398:

> Laches is not imputable to the government, in its character as sovereign, by those subject to its dominion. Still a government may suffer loss through the negligence of its officers. If it comes down from its position of sovereignty, and enters the domain of commerce, it submits itself to the same laws that govern individuals there. Thus, if it becomes the holder of a bill of exchange, it must use the same diligence to charge the drawers and indorsers that is required of individuals; and, if it fails in this, its claim upon the parties is lost. Generally, in respect to all the commercial business of the government, if an officer specially charged with the performance of any duty, and authorized to represent the government in that behalf, neglects that duty, and loss ensues, the government must bear the consequences of his neglect. But this cannot happen until the officer specially charged with the duty, if there be one, has acted, or ought to have acted. As the government can only act through its officers, it may select for its work whomsoever it will; but it must have some representative authorized to act in all the emergencies of its commercial transactions. If it fails in this, it fails in the performance of its own duties, and must be charged with the consequences that follow such omissions in the commercial world. [Citations omitted.]

See also *URS Consultants, Inc.*, IBCA 4285-2000, 02-1 BCA 31,812 (government bound by allegedly mistaken award computations made by award official and contracting officer in CPAF contract); *Honeywell Fed. Sys., Inc.*, ASBCA 39974, 92-2 BCA ¶ 24,966 (government bound by contracting officer determination that cost or pricing data not required because contractor met commercial item exemption); *Sterling Millwrights, Inc. v. United States*, 26 Cl. Ct. 49 (1992) (government bound where contracting officer made progress payments with full knowledge of costs included therein); *Summit Contractors*, AGBCA 81-252-1, 86-1 BCA ¶ 18,632 (government bound by contract modification favorable to contractor); and *United States v. Hadden*, 192 F.2d 327 (6th Cir. 1951) (government could not recover mistaken payments made to contractor's creditors). Of course, the government will not be bound by a bad decision of an employee without authority, *Winn-Senter Constr. Co. v. United States*, 110 Ct. Cl. 34, 75 F. Supp. 255 (1948) (absent special circumstances, government agent has no authority to order contractor to increase wages and agree to government reimbursement).

B. Estoppel

Estoppel is a concept that prohibits a party from escaping liability for statements, actions, or inactions if they have been relied on by the other party. It has traditionally been thought that two prerequisites exist for estopping the government: (1) the government's representative must have been acting within the scope of his or her authority, and (2) the government must be acting in its proprietary capacity rather than its sovereign capacity, *United States v. Georgia-Pacific Co.*, 421 F.2d 92 (9th Cir. 1970). The Supreme Court has altered the focus of the first prerequisite to the requirement that the act of the government must be one that is not barred by statute or published regulation, *OPM v. Richmond*, 496 U.S. 414, *reh'g denied*, 497 U.S. 1046 (1990). Once these threshold requirements are met, the court in *Burnside-Ott Aviation Training Ctr., Inc. v. United States*, 985 F.2d 1574 (Fed. Cir. 1993), appeared to hold that the normal common law rules of estoppel apply. The court stated at 1581:

> The Claims Court improperly relied on *Richmond* to conclude that Burnside-Ott's equitable estoppel claim is barred as a matter of law. In particular, the Claims Court erred in concluding that *Richmond* stands for the proposition that equitable estoppel will not lie against the government for any monetary claim. The *Richmond* holding is not so broad. *Richmond* is limited to "claim(s) for the payment of money from the Public Treasury *contrary to a statutory appropriation*." 496 U.S. at 424 (emphasis added). Indeed, because the Supreme Court's analysis in *Richmond* is based entirely on the Appropriations Clause of the Constitution, Article 1, Section 9, Clause 7, which provides that No Money shall be drawn from the Treasury, but in Consequence of Appropriations made by Law, its holding must be limited to claims of entitlement contrary to statutory appropriations.
>
> Burnside-Ott's assertion of a right to payment of money from the Public Treasury, however, is not based upon a statutory entitlement. Burnside-Ott's assertion is instead based upon its contract with the Navy. Nor does Burnside-Ott claim entitlement contrary to statutory eligibility criteria, as did Richmond. Thus, neither the holding nor analysis in *Richmond* is applicable in this case, and Burnside-Ott's equitable estoppel claim is not barred as a matter of law because of *Richmond*. Equitable estoppel may or may not apply in this case depending on facts yet to be established.

The elements of estoppel were detailed in *Emeco Indus., Inc. v. United States*, 202 Ct. Cl. 1006, 485 F.2d 652 (1973), as follows: "(1) The party to be estopped must know the facts; (2) he must intend that his conduct shall be acted on or must so act that the party asserting the estoppel has a right to believe it is so intended; (3) the latter must be ignorant of the true facts; and (4) he must rely on the former's conduct to his injury."

In two recent cases, the Federal Circuit has stated that the contractor must prove an additional element—affirmative misconduct—in order to use estoppel against the government, *United Pac. Ins. Co. v. Roche*, 401 F.3d 1362 (Fed. Cir. 2005); *Rumsfeld v. United Techs. Corp.*, 315 F.3d 1361 (Fed. Cir. 2004). In *United Pacific* the court stated, at 1366:

> Although the application of equitable estoppel against the government is not entirely foreclosed, the Supreme Court has qualified that "the Government may not be estopped on the same terms as any other litigant." *Heckler v. Cmty. Health Servs.*, 467 U.S. 51, 60, 81 L. Ed. 2d 42, 104 S. Ct. 2218 (1984). Our own precedent dictates "that if equitable estoppel is available at all against the government some form of affirmative misconduct must be shown in addition to the traditional requirements of estoppel." *Zacharin v. United States*, 213 F.3d 1366, 1371 (Fed. Cir. 2000).

This rule has been followed in *General Elec. Co. v. United States*, 60 Fed. Cl. 782 (2004), and *Kearfott Guidance & Navigation Corp.*, ASBCA 49271, 04-2 BCA ¶ 32,757. However, there is no explicit statement in any of the Supreme Court decisions indicating that affirmative misconduct is always a required element of a claim of estoppel against the government. It is clear that estoppel will not be permitted if a government employee's conduct violates a statute or mandatory regulation. See *INS v. Hibi*, 414 U.S. 5 (1973); *Schweiker v. Hansen*, 450 U.S. 785 (1981); and *INS v. Miranda*, 459 U.S. 14 (1982).

When the official is acting within the scope of delegated authority and the actions are not prohibited by statute or regulation, estoppel has been found even though the action is based on a mistaken interpretation of the government's obligations, *USA Petroleum Corp. v. United States*, 821 F.2d 622 (Fed. Cir. 1987); *Portmann v. United States*, 674 F.2d 1155 (7th Cir. 1982); *Broad Ave. Laundry & Tailoring v. United States*, 231 Ct. Cl. 1, 681 F.2d 746 (1982). Note, however, that *Broad Avenue Laundry* is questionable precedent since the contracting officer's statement was contrary to a published regulation. In *Kozak Micro Sys., Inc.*, GSBCA 10519, 91-1 BCA ¶ 23,342, *recons. denied*, 91-1 BCA ¶ 23,593, the board stated that, where government representatives acting within their scope of authority make statements to contractors that result in factual interpretations that are not consistent with the contract or its provisions, and the recipients of these statements can prove the elements of estoppel, the government cannot act contrary to its representations. See also *Dynamic Concepts, Inc.*, ASBCA 44738, 93-2 BCA ¶ 25,689, in which the government was estopped where the contracting officer paid invoices exceeding the contract ceiling and the contractor continued performance in reliance on such conduct.

In one case, the government was estopped because of affirmative misconduct of government employees. See *New England Tank Indus. of N.H., Inc.*, ASBCA 26474,

88-1 BCA ¶ 20,395, *vacated and remanded on other grounds*, 861 F.2d 685 (Fed. Cir. 1988), where the government was barred from exercising contract options because of concealment and misrepresentation of facts in the negotiation of the contract.

Estoppel accomplishes the same result as finality, and because of this the two concepts are often confused. However, there are two important differences between finality and estoppel. Estoppel requires detrimental reliance by the party who seeks to invoke it, while reliance is not an element of finality. The other difference is that the statement or action leading to finality is by its very nature contractually binding upon the government through the operation of legal principles such as offer and acceptance, acceptance of goods, etc. The government is held bound by estoppel, however, because it would be unfair not to do so even though the statement, action, or inaction would not be contractually binding. Thus, the government has been estopped through its course of conduct as well as through its verbal representations. See *Peninsular ChemResearch, Inc.*, ASBCA 14384, 71-2 BCA ¶ 9066 (government required to accept results of accounting method it previously approved by implication), and *Litton Sys., Inc. v. United States*, 196 Ct. Cl. 133, 449 F.2d 392 (1971) (government's knowledge, acquiescence, and approval of contractor's accounting system precluded retroactive disallowance of cost).

1. Government Not Estopped by Unauthorized Actions

The government will not be estopped by the unauthorized actions of representatives, *United States v. Georgia-Pacific Co.*, 421 F.2d 92 (9th Cir. 1970). Frequently, the lack of authority results from the action being contrary to statutory requirements. In such cases, courts will construe authority narrowly, *Schweiker v. Hansen*, 450 U.S. 785 (1981) (all courts have a duty to observe conditions defined by Congress for charging the public treasury); *OPM v. Richmond*, 496 U.S. 414, *reh'g denied*, 497 U.S. 1046 (1990) (government cannot be bound by payment contravening explicit statutory limitation). Similarly, in *Singer Co., Librascope Div.*, ASBCA 17604, 75-2 BCA ¶ 11,401, *aff'd*, 217 Ct. Cl. 225, 576 F.2d 905 (1978), the contractor submitted cost or pricing data that the government representative knew was not current. Since the government official had no authority to waive the requirements of the Truth in Negotiations Act, 10 U.S.C. § 2306a, the government could not be estopped from obtaining a price reduction. The board stated at 54,288:

> In the appeal before us, no Government representative had authority to waive the statutory requirement of disclosure of accurate, complete and current data. We need not further discuss the application of estoppel since it fails at a threshold question. We note parenthetically that a far different case would exist had [the contractor] fully disclosed its data in relation to its proposal and the Government then, for whatever reason, failed to make use of the data in the negotiation process. *Muncie Gear Works, Inc.*, ASBCA No. 18184, decided 26 June 1975 [75-2 BCA ¶ 11,380]; *Levinson Steel Co.*, ASBCA No. 16520, 73-2 BCA ¶ 10,116.

The same rule applies when the employee is acting contrary to delegated authority, *Atlantic Gulf & Pac. Co. of Manila v. United States*, 207 Ct. Cl. 995 (1975) (no estoppel to disavow settlement agreement negotiated without required advance approval).

Other cases finding no estoppel because of lack of authority include *Seaboard Lumber Co. v. United States*, 45 Fed. Cl. 404 (1999) (Forest Service supervisor lacked authority to agree to cancel contract); *Grigor E. Atonian v. Gen. Servs. Admin.*, GSBCA 12765, 95-1 BCA ¶ 27,444 (non-contracting officer had no authority to state that claim would be paid); *Essen Mall Props. v. United States*, 21 Cl. Ct. 430 (1990) (Postal Service negotiator lacked implied actual authority to bind Postal Service); *Lance Dickinson & Co.*, ASBCA 36408, 89-3 BCA ¶ 22,198, *recons. denied*, 90-1 BCA ¶ 22,511 (no implied contract where contractor knew that government employee lacked authority to contract); *Aetna Cas. & Sur. Co. v. United States*, 208 Ct. Cl. 515, 526 F.2d 1127 (1975), *cert. denied*, 425 U.S. 973 (1976) (government not estopped from recovering illegal payment); *California-Pacific Utils. Co. v. United States*, 194 Ct. Cl. 703 (1971) (no authority to include indemnity provision in contract); *Fansteel Metallurgical Corp. v. United States*, 145 Ct. Cl. 496, 172 F. Supp. 268 (1959) (unauthorized overpayment does not bind government); and *Carroll Beaver*, Comp. Gen. Dec. B-184130, 75-2 CPD ¶ 14 (Government not bound to rental exceeding maximum authorized). See *Toyo Menka Kaisha, Ltd. v. United States*, 220 Ct. Cl. 210, 597 F.2d 1371 (1979), in which the court held that the government was not estopped to deny the validity of a contract since the contracting officer was not authorized to make an award on a bid that was nonresponsive. The GAO has consistently held that, even with a contractor's detrimental reliance in formulating its bid, "erroneous advice or contract actions of Government officials do not estop an agency from rejecting a nonresponsive bid when required to do so by law," *International Waste Indus.*, Comp. Gen. Dec. B-210500.2, 83-1 CPD ¶ 652. See also *International Med. Indus., Inc.*, Comp. Gen. Dec. B-208235, 82-2 CPD ¶ 386.

In *Urban Data Sys., Inc. v. United States*, 699 F.2d 1147 (Fed. Cir. 1983), a small business contract contained a cost-plus-a-percentage-of-cost pricing clause at the government's insistence. Because agents lack the authority to compensate contractors under such a clause, the government was not estopped to deny its validity. Urban was entitled to compensation, however, under quantum valebant.

2. *Sovereign Capacity Exception*

It has been stated that the government will not be estopped from performing sovereign acts, *United States v. Georgia-Pacific Co.*, 421 F.2d 92 (9th Cir. 1970). In *United States v. Lazy FC Ranch*, 481 F.2d 985 (9th Cir. 1973), the court considered both the questions of lack of authority and actions within the government's sovereign capacity. Citing *Georgia-Pacific, Moser v. United States*, 341 U.S. 41 (1951), *Brandt v. Hickel*, 427 F.2d 53 (9th Cir. 1970), and *Schuster v. C.I.R.*, 312 F.2d 311 (9th Cir. 1962), the court stated at 989:

> The *Moser-Brandt-Schuster* line of cases establish the proposition that estoppel is available as a defense against the government if the government's wrongful conduct threatens to work a serious injustice and if the public's interest would not be unduly damaged by the imposition of estoppel. *Gestuvo v. District Dir. of I.N.S.*, 337 F. Supp. 1093 (C.D. Cal. 1971). This proposition is true even if the government is acting in a capacity that has traditionally been described as sovereign (as distinguished from proprietary) although we may be more reluctant to estop the government when it is acting in this capacity. See *Georgia-Pacific, supra.*

This case rejects the "sovereign capacity" exception and also appears to reject the rule that the government is not estopped by unauthorized acts. However, the court found that the agency's published regulations arguably permitted the action taken by the government's representatives. The Supreme Court has not ruled on whether estoppel lies against the government when the government acted in its sovereign capacity. In *Schweiker v. Hansen*, 450 U.S. 785 (1981), the Court referred to *Lazy FC Ranch* in a footnote at 789:

> We need not consider the correctness of these cases. We do think that they are easily distinguishable from the type of situation presented in this case and the line of cases we rely upon above.

3 Knowledge of Facts

To estop the government, the contractor must prove that the government did not reveal facts that it knew and the contractor did not know. See *Henry H. Norman v. General Servs. Admin.*, GSBCA 15070, 02-2 BCA ¶ 32,042, denying recovery because, although the contractor did not know all of the detailed facts in the possession of the government with regard to the possibility of injury because of an insecure government building, it was aware of many of these facts. See also *Western Aviation Maint., Inc. v. General Servs. Admin.*, GSBCA 14165, 00-2 BCA ¶ 31,123 (parties had equal but incomplete knowledge of the facts); *Davis Group, Inc.*, ASBCA 48431, 95-2 BCA ¶ 27,702 (contractor knew the contents of a contract clause).

4. Reliance

Reasonable reliance by the contractor is essential to estoppel, *California-Pacific Utils. Co. v. United States*, 194 Ct. Cl. 703 (1971). In that case, the court held that the contractor could not claim reliance on an alleged agreement to include an indemnification clause in a permit when it had notice that the government official who allegedly agreed to include the clause did not have authority to do so. See also *Brenda R. Ronhaar*, AGBCA 98-147-1, 00-1 BCA ¶ 30,591 (reliance on opinion that options would be exercised unreasonable); *Robertshaw Control Sys. Div. v. Department of the Army*, GSBCA 12714-P, 94-2 BCA ¶ 26,713 (reliance on government lawyer's opinion on legal rule unreasonable); *State St. Mgmt. Corp. v. General Servs. Admin.*, GSBCA 12374, 94-1 BCA ¶ 26,500 (unreasonable to rely on statement of future intention); *C Constr. Co.*, ASBCA 41706, 94-1 BCA ¶ 26,263 (unreasonable to rely on inadvertent specification deviation approved by architect/engineer); *Turner Constr. Co. v. General Servs. Admin.*, GSBCA 11361, 92-3 BCA ¶ 25,115 (unreasonable to rely on contracting officer's interpretation of standard contract clause); *Meridan Inc.*, PSBCA 2203, 89-2 BCA ¶ 21,648 (reliance must be on government conduct or statements); *Diamond v. Fed. Emergency Mgmt. Agency*, 689 F. Supp 163 (E.D.N.Y. 1988) (reliance in contradiction of policy provision was unreasonable); *Rockwell Int'l Corp.*, ASBCA 20304, 76-2 BCA ¶ 12,131 (no reliance since contractor changed its accounting system before government acted); *Codex Corp.*, ASBCA 17983, 75-2 BCA ¶ 11,554, *remanded on other grounds*, 226 Ct. Cl. 693 (1981) (costs were incurred before action by contracting officer); and *Baifield Indus., Div. of A-T-O, Inc.*, ASBCA 19025, 75-1 BCA ¶ 11,245 (no indication that contractor would have altered actions if government had made demand earlier). In *Mountain Plains & Econ. Dev. Program, Inc.*, ASBCA 21714, 78-1 BCA ¶ 13,083, the government was not estopped to deny the reasonableness of payments under employment contracts where the contractor never relied on the contracting officer's concurrence in the validity of the proposed payments.

5. Injury

Injury is essential to estoppel. The contractor must establish that its reliance has placed it in a worse position than it would have been in otherwise, *Chula Vista City Sch. Dist. v. Bennett*, 824 F.2d 1573 (Fed. Cir. 1987), *cert. denied*, 484 U.S. 1042 (1988). See also *Okaw Indus., Inc.*, ASBCA 17863, 75-1 BCA ¶ 11,321, *recons. denied*, 75-2 BCA ¶ 11,571 (no injury to contractor from disallowance of settlement); *Simmonds Precision Prods., Inc.*, ASBCA 18110, 74-1 BCA ¶ 10,472 (government not estopped from assessing liquidated damages after two years absent proof of prejudice from delay); and *General Dynamics Corp.*, ASBCA 13868, 69-2 BCA ¶ 8044 (contractor not deprived of recovery of allocable costs by retroactive change of accounting system).

6. Waiver

Closely related to and sometimes used interchangeably with estoppel is the concept of waiver. See *American Nat'l Bank & Trust Co. of Chicago v. United States*, 23 Cl. Ct. 542 (1991); *Branch Banking & Trust Co. v. United States*, 120 Ct. Cl. 72, 98 F. Supp. 757, *cert. denied*, 342 U.S. 893 (1951); and Comp. Gen. Dec. B-174410, June 30, 1972, *Unpub*. Similar to estoppel, the government will be bound by a waiver if the contractor relies on it to its detriment, *De Vito v. United States*, 188 Ct. Cl. 979, 413 F.2d 1147 (1969). However, a waiver may be retracted if it is not supported by consideration or if the contractor has not relied on the waiver to its detriment, *Tri-West Contractors, Inc.*, AGBCA 95-200-1, 97-1 BCA ¶ 28,662; *Mark Dunning Indus.*, ASBCA 29599, 86-1 BCA ¶ 18,521.

The term "waiver" is frequently used in connection with the government's failure to promptly terminate a delinquent contractor when that contractor has relied on the government's failure to terminate by continuing performance or preparation for performance with the government's knowledge and express or implied consent. In such cases, the government will have waived its right to terminate the contractor for default. In *Freeway Ford Truck Sales, Inc. v. General Servs. Admin.*, GSBCA 10662, 93-3 BCA ¶ 26,019, a default termination was held to be improper despite the contractor's late delivery. The board found that the government had waived its right to terminate by allowing the contractor to continue with production. In *Marci Enters., Inc. v. United States*, GSBCA 12197, 94-1 BCA ¶ 26,563, the board held that the government improperly terminated the contract, stating that the government had waived the delivery date by telling the contractor to delay the shipment for inspection and by continuing to encourage the contractor to correct the deficiencies. See also *Vista Scientific Corp.*, ASBCA 25974, 87-1 BCA ¶ 19,603 (government waived completion date by encouraging and participating in contractor's efforts to fulfill contract after due date), and *S.T. Research Corp.*, ASBCA 39600, 92-2 BCA ¶ 24,838 (government waived right to terminate where the contracting officer told the contractor to continue and proposed a new delivery schedule). See Chapter 10 for a complete discussion of this type of waiver.

The term "waiver" is also used when the government permits the contractor to deviate from contract requirements, *Gresham & Co. v. United States*, 200 Ct. Cl. 97, 470 F.2d 542 (1972). In these cases, the elements of estoppel are used to determine if the government is liable. See *Houston Helicopters, Inc.*, IBCA 3196, 96-1 BCA ¶ 28,172, where the government waived a requirement that led the contractor to purchase unacceptable equipment; *Walsky Constr. Co.*, ASBCA 36940, 90-2 BCA ¶ 22,934, where the government waived a specification requirement, which induced the contractor to perform unacceptable work; and *General Motors Corp., Delco Radio Div.*, ASBCA 15807, 72-1 BCA ¶ 9405, where the government was held to have waived the reliability requirement by knowingly authorizing the contractor to proceed with production despite nonconformity with reliability criteria.

7. Estoppel Improperly Used

In numerous cases involving finality of action, the boards and courts have unnecessarily used the term *estoppel* in holding that the government is bound. This, of course, has led to a degree of confusion because it has been the operation of the legal principle involved (acceptance of offer or goods, interpretation of contract, etc.) rather than the doctrine of equitable estoppel that has bound the government. See *H & M Moving, Inc. v. United States*, 204 Ct. Cl. 696, 499 F.2d 660 (1974) (ambiguous term construed in contractor's favor); *Emeco Indus., Inc. v. United States*,

202 Ct. Cl. 1006, 485 F.2d 652 (1973) (implied-in-fact contract existed based on government's actions); *Dana Corp. v. United States*, 200 Ct. Cl. 200, 470 F.2d 1032 (1972) (contractor's offer accepted); *Gresham & Co. v. United States*, 200 Ct. Cl. 97, 470 F.2d 542 (1972) (ambiguous term construed in contractor's favor based on similar interpretation by government representative); *Manloading & Mgmt. Assocs., Inc. v. United States*, 198 Ct. Cl. 628, 461 F.2d 1299 (1972) (oral agreement at bidder's conference not precluded by parol evidence rule); *Mercury Mach. & Mfg. Co.*, ASBCA 20068, 76-1 BCA ¶ 11,809; *Fink Sanitary Serv., Inc.*, 53 Comp. Gen. 502 (B-179040), 74-1 CPD ¶ 36; and *Unidynamics/St. Louis, Inc.*, ASBCA 17592, 73-2 BCA ¶ 10,360.

A good example of the confusion that exists in the use of the term estoppel is *Lockheed Shipbuilding & Constr. Co.*, ASBCA 18460, 75-1 BCA ¶ 11,246, *recons. denied*, 75-2 BCA ¶ 11,566. This controversial case involved broad multicontract, multiservice negotiations between Deputy Secretary of Defense Packard and the contractor whereby an overall settlement plan was negotiated. Pursuant to these negotiations, the contractor agreed to assume a fixed loss of $2 million under its C-5A contracts with the Air Force and to accept a $62 million settlement on its Navy contracts. The board held that Deputy Secretary Packard had impliedly assured the contractor that the $62 million settlement would be approved by higher authorities in the Navy, as required by regulations. Although the overall agreement between Deputy Secretary Packard and the contractor appeared to have all the elements of an enforceable contract, the board used the doctrine of estoppel to hold that the Navy higher authorities could not refuse to approve the $62 million settlement.

V. SUITS AGAINST GOVERNMENT EMPLOYEES

Suits against government officers, employees, or agents are usually of two types. First is the suit, almost always for monetary damages, that seeks to obtain relief directly from the officer, employee, or agent. The second seeks relief from the government by a suit against the employee, officer, or agent in his or her official capacity. Such suits usually seek some form of injunctive relief.

Both types of litigation may be subject to some form of immunity defense. Suits against the individual personally will invariably be challenged on the ground that the employee is entitled to the personal immunity that attaches to public employees. In suits against the officer or employee in his or her official capacity, the government may move for dismissal if it has not waived its sovereign immunity from such suits.

Traditionally, government employees were *immune from personal suit* when acting within the scope of their authority. The courts have recognized the necessity of protecting the freedom of federal officers and employees to exercise the discretion that is required for the proper execution of their duties by prohibiting suits against such employees in their personal capacity. In *Ove Gustavsson Contracting Co. v. Floete*, 299 F.2d 655 (2d Cir. 1962), *cert. denied*, 374 U.S. 827 (1963), a contractor brought suit against federal employees in their private capacities, seeking damages for alleged intentional and malicious falsification of progress reports filed with the government. Affirming the district court's grant of summary judgment for the government employees, the court stated at 658:

> [O]fficials of the federal Government are not personally liable for alleged torts based upon acts, done within the scope of their duties, which necessarily involved the exercise of a judgment or discretion which public policy requires be made without fear of personal liability.

This type of immunity has been referred to as absolute immunity.

When the government officer or employee is charged with violating a person's *constitutional rights*, a qualified immunity rather than an absolute immunity will be invoked. In *Scheuer v. Rhodes*, 416 U.S. 232 (1974), involving a suit under 42 U.S.C. § 1983 against the governor of Ohio and other high state officials, the Court ruled that state officials could claim only a qualified immunity. Thus, they would be immune only to the extent that the acts were within the scope of their duties, that they were done with a good faith belief that they were correct, and that such belief was reasonable in light of the facts as they existed at the time of the acts.

The U.S. Supreme Court extended this rule to federal government employees in *Butz v. Economou*, 438 U.S. 478 (1978), when violations of constitutional rights were alleged. Absolute immunity for constitutional violations was held to apply only to "those exceptional situations where it is demonstrated that absolute immunity is essential for the conduct of the public business." Subsequently, the Court has indicated that absolute immunity for constitutional violations is to be accorded to legislators and judges in their legislative and judicial capacities, respectively; prosecutors and similar officials of executive agencies; and executive officers engaged in adjudicative functions. Other federal officials who seek absolute exemption from personal liability for unconstitutional conduct must bear the burden of showing that public policy requires an exemption of that scope based on their functions, not merely their positions. See *Harlow v. Fitzgerald*, 457 U.S. 800 (1982).

In *Harlow*, senior presidential aides and advisors were charged with violating Fitzgerald's constitutional and statutory rights. The Court held that absolute immunity is not "an incident of the office of every presidential subordinate based in the White House." However, an official would be entitled to absolute immunity for constitutional violations by showing (1) "that the responsibilities of his office embraced a function so sensitive as to require a total shield from liability," and (2) "that he was discharging the protected function when performing the act for which liability is asserted." With respect to qualified immunity, the Court stated that it would not apply if the official "*knew or reasonably should have known* that the action he took within his sphere of official responsibility would violate the constitutional rights of the [plaintiff], *or* if he took the action with *malicious intention* to cause a deprivation of constitutional rights or other injury," further stating "that government officials performing discretionary functions generally are shielded from liability for civil damages insofar as their conduct does not violate clearly established statutory or constitutional rights of which a reasonable person would have known." The judge is to determine the threshold question of whether a clearly established law existed at the time of the action of which the government employee knew or should have known.

The Supreme Court placed another limitation on absolute immunity in *Westfall v. Ervin*, 484 U.S. 292 (1988). There, the Court ruled that absolute immunity would be granted only if the act was discretionary in nature. Thus, not all acts of high-level officials would necessarily be eligible for absolute immunity. The Court also described the following policy reasons as supporting such immunity, at 295-96:

> The purpose of such official immunity is not to protect an erring official, but to insulate the decisionmaking process from the harassment of prospective litigation. The provision of immunity rests on the view that the threat of liability will make federal officials unduly timid in carrying out their official duties, and that effective government will be promoted if officials are freed of the costs of vexatious and often frivolous damages suits. . . . This Court always has recognized, however, that official immunity comes at a great cost. An injured party with an otherwise meritorious tort claim is denied compensation simply because he had the misfortune to be injured by a federal official. Moreover, absolute immunity contravenes the basic tenet that individuals be held accountable for their wrongful conduct. We therefore have held that absolute immunity for federal officials is justified only when "the contributions of immunity to effective government in particular contexts outweighs the perhaps recurring harm to individual citizens." *Doe v. McMillan*, [412 U.S. 306, 320 (1973)].

In response to the Court's decision in *Westfall*, Congress enacted the Federal Employees Liability Reform and Tort Compensation Act of 1988, Pub. L. No. 100-694, which contained the following statement:

> It is the purpose of this Act to protect Federal employees from personal liability for common law torts committed within the scope of their employment, while providing persons injured by the common law torts with an appropriate remedy against the United States.

To achieve this purpose, the Act amended the Federal Torts Claims Act, 28 U.S.C. § 1346(b) and § 2671 et seq., to restore the immunity that the Supreme Court had taken away in *Westfall*. The Act restored absolute immunity for suits for money damages when common law torts are alleged and did not make the immunity dependent upon the discretionary nature of the employee's duties. In such cases, only the government may be sued. See 28 U.S.C. § 2679(b).

As a result, government employees have absolute immunity from suits for monetary compensation unless such suit is based on (1) an act totally outside of the scope of their employment, or (2) an act that deprives a person of his or her constitutional rights and the employee is not a member of the class of employees that has absolute immunity. The Supreme Court has held that this immunity applies even "when an FTCA exception precludes recovery against the Government," *United States v. Smith*, 499 U.S. 160 (1991).

Under 28 U.S.C. § 2679(d) the Attorney General is required to make a determination as to whether the act was accomplished within the scope of employment. A certification that the employee was acting within the scope of employment has two effects: (1) the government is substituted as the defendant, and (2) the case is removed to federal district court if it has been filed in a state court. The certification is reviewable by the district court with regard to the substitution of the government as the proper party but is conclusive as to removal from a state court, *Gutierrez de Martinez v. Lamagno*, 515 U.S. 417 (1995). This can lead to the anomalous result that, if a court finds the certification incorrect, the government employee becomes the defendant but the case remains in federal district court, *Garcia v. United States*, 88 F.3d 318 (5th Cir. 1996); *Ross v. Bryan*, 309 F.3d 830 (4th Cir. 2002). In *Aversa v. United States*, 99 F.3d 1200 (1st Cir. 1996), the court held that while federal law "does determine whether a person is a federal employee and the nature and contours of his or her federal responsibilities . . . state law governs whether the person was acting within the scope of that employment and those responsibilities." A good summary of the standards that are applied to determine whether actions are within the scope of employment is contained in *Davric Maine Corp. v. U.S. Postal Serv.*, 238 F.3d 58 (1st Cir. 2001), at 66:

> Under Maine law an employee's actions are within the scope of employment if they are of the kind that he is employed to perform, they occur within authorized time and space limits, and they are actuated by a purpose to serve the employee's master. See Restatement (Second) of Agency § 228, at 504 (1958), cited in *Bergeron [v. Henderson]*, 47 F. Supp. 2d [61 (D. Me. 1999)] at 65. Under the Restatement (Second), an action may be within the scope of employment although "forbidden, or done in a forbidden manner," see Restatement (Second) §230, or even "consciously criminal or tortious," see *id.* § 231. Actions "relating to work" and "done in the workplace during working hours" are typically within the scope. See id. §§ 229, 233, 234. Whether the motivation of the employee is to serve the master's interest or his or her own private purposes is often an important element in this determination. See id. §§ 228, 235-236; see also *Lyons [v. Brown]*, 158 F.3d [650 (1st Cir. 1998)]at 609. Where seemingly work-related acts taken by the federal employee are done with a private purpose on the employee's part to retaliate or discriminate against the plaintiff, they may fall outside the scope of employment under Maine law; where the acts were done in good faith to serve the employer's interest, even if the federal employee's judgment was mistaken, then the conduct is likely within the scope of employment. See *Lyons,* 158 F.3d at 610.

Several situations have been held to be outside of the scope of employment, making the employee personally liable for his or her conduct. See *Ross v. Bryan*, 309 F.3d

830 (4th Cir. 2002) (an automobile accident while commuting to work—Virginia law); *Borneman v. United States*, 213 F.3d 819 (4th Cir. 2000) (intentional tort such as assault and battery during work frequently, but not always, outside of scope of employment—North Carolina law); and *Mackey v. Milam*, 154 F.3d 648 (6th Cir. 1998) (sexual harassment outside scope of employment if done by employee with no control over plaintiff but within scope of employment if done by supervisor or other person with control over plaintiff—Ohio law). Compare *Taboas v. Mlynczak*, 149 F.3d 576 (7th Cir. 1998), where allegedly malicious and vindictive complaints lodged against a fellow employee were found to be within the scope of employment under Illinois law. Accord, *McLachlan v. Bell*, 261 F.3d 908 (9th Cir. 2001) (California law). It is also held that individuals performing work for the government are not employees for these purposes if they qualify as independent contractors, *Rodriguez v. Sarabyn*, 129 F.3d 760 (5th Cir. 1997).

VI. STANDARDS OF CONDUCT

In order to maintain public confidence in the federal procurement process, government and contractor employees must follow exemplary standards of conduct. There are numerous statutory and regulatory provisions giving guidance on the standards that are expected to be followed and prescribing stringent penalties for noncompliance. This section discusses these standards in three broad categories—those dealing with *improper influence* on government decisions, those requiring *honesty in dealing* with the government, and those dealing with *improper obtaining or disclosure of information* related to the procurement process. The focus of the material is on the nature of the conduct that is proscribed. A general discussion of the types of sanctions imposed for improper conduct is followed by a discussion of the various types of activities.

A. Sanctions

Each statute prohibiting a certain type of conduct contains its own sanction or penalty. Since most of these sanctions involve straightforward criminal or civil fines or imprisonment, this section does not discuss the precise way that these penalties have been interpreted and enforced. Rather, the focus is on the broader sanctions covered by other statutes or the common law that courts have held are available to the government. In many, if not most, cases, these broader sanctions are a more serious threat to government contractors than the criminal or civil sanctions contained in the specific statutes covering the prohibited conduct.

1. *Forfeiture and Cancellation*

The first of these general sanctions is forfeiture. This sanction can lead to the loss of all rights under the contract. The Supreme Court has held that the government can cancel a contract and need not pay for work done or benefit conferred if it is tainted with illegal conduct, *United States v. Mississippi Valley Generating Co.*, 364 U.S. 520 (1961) (conflict of interest); *Pan American Petroleum & Transp. Co. v. United States*, 273 U.S. 456 (1927) (bribery). The Court of Claims went even further and held that the government can recover the full amount paid on a completed contract that is subsequently found to have been tainted with illegal conduct, *K & R Eng'g Co. v. United States*, 222 Ct. Cl. 340, 616 F.2d 469 (1980) (bribery and conflict of interest). See also *Bureau of Land Mgmt.: Payment of Pocatello Field Office Photocopying Costs*, Comp. Gen. Dec. B-290901, 2003 CPD ¶ 2, holding that the contract was void and unenforceable because it violated 44 U.S.C. § 501 requiring agencies to obtain all printing services through the Government Printing Office; and *Schuepferling GmbH & Co., KG*, ASBCA 45567, 98-2 BCA ¶ 29,828, holding that it was proper to refuse to pay for work on 22 fully performed delivery orders because the contractor had bribed the contracting specialist at the inception of the contract. While it has been held that a contract containing a contingent fee arrangement is void and unenforceable, *Quinn v. Gulf & Western Corp.*, 644 F.2d 89 (2d Cir. 1981); *LeJohn Mfg. Co. v. Webb*, 222 F.2d 48 (D.C. Cir. 1955), the government may not cancel a contract for breach of the covenant where it knew of the arrangement during prolonged negotiations and the arrangement had many indicia of a bona fide covenant, *Companhia Atlantica De Desenvolvimento E Exploracao De Minas v. United States*, 148 Ct. Cl. 71, *cert. denied*, 364 U.S. 862 (1960). The fact that Congress may have specifically provided for other statutory civil sanctions, *United States v. Acme Process Equip. Co.*, 385 U.S. 138 (1966) (violation of Anti-Kickback Act, 41 U.S.C. § 51); or criminal sanctions, *Horton J. Brown v. United States*, 207 Ct. Cl. 768, 524 F.2d 693 (1975) (violation of False Statement Act, 18 U.S.C. § 1001) does not deprive the United States of the right to cancel such contracts tainted with illegal conduct. However, the question has been raised concerning which officials in the government are authorized to cancel contracts and the nature of the activity that would entitle the government to cancel. In *Medico Indus., Inc.*, ASBCA 22141, 80-2 BCA ¶ 14,498, *recons. denied*, 80-2 BCA ¶ 14,665, *motion to suspend hearings granted*, 81-1 BCA ¶ 14,983, it was held that the contracting officer was not authorized to cancel a contract because of improper conduct by a former government employee. The board distinguished *Mississippi Valley Generating Co.* on the grounds that it involved the more serious violation of action by a public official having simultaneous conflicting interests. The board also questioned whether improper conduct of a former government employee was a sufficiently serious violation to allow the government to cancel. Following the board's suspension of the hearing, the government sued in U.S. District Court for a declaratory judgment that the contract cancellation was authorized. The district court granted the contractor's motion to dismiss for lack of jurisdiction, and in *United States v. Medico Indus., Inc.*, 685 F.2d 230 (7th Cir. 1982), the circuit court reversed, holding that the board of contract appeals did not have jurisdiction under the Disputes clause to determine whether 18 U.S.C. § 207(a) was violated, and remanded the matter to the district court for disposition. Contrast *Four-Phase Sys., Inc.*, ASBCA 27487, 84-1 BCA ¶ 17,122, suggesting that the Contract Disputes Act gives jurisdiction to the appeals boards over a government affirmative defense of cancellation for a violation of 18 U.S.C. § 208. 18 U.S.C. § 218 provides for cancellation by the president or, under regulations prescribed by him, the head of any department or agency if there has been a final conviction for offenses involving bribery, gratuities, and conflicts of interest during and after government employment. Executive Order 12448, 48 Fed. Reg. 51281 (1983), delegates the authority to exercise this power to heads of executive agencies and provides that implementing regulations should contain specified procedural protections. FAR 3.705 sets forth the procedures for exercising this authority.

28 U.S.C. § 2514 also provides for the forfeiture of fraudulent claims. This statute calls for forfeiture of any claim presented to the Court of Federal Claims if there is fraud in the presentation of the claim or in the performance of the contract to which the claim is related, *UMC Elecs. Co. v. United States*, 43 Fed. Cl. 776, 790 (1999), *aff'd*, 249 F.3d 1337 (Fed. Cir. 2001); *First Fed. Sav. Bank of Hegewisch v. United States*, 52 Fed. Cl. 774 (2002). To obtain forfeiture under this statute, the government must prove its fraud claim by clear and convincing evidence. *Glendale Fed. Bank, FSB v. United States*, 239 F.3d 1374, 1379 (Fed. Cir. 2001); *Commercial Contractors, Inc. v. United States*, 154 F.3d 1357, 1362 (Fed. Cir. 1998). See also *O'Brien Gear & Mach. Co. v. United States*, 219 Ct. Cl. 187, 591 F.2d 666 (1979), forfeiting a renegotiation claim against the government because it was tainted with fraud.

The boards of contract appeals cannot use 28 U.S.C. § 2514 to forfeit claims, *DEL Mfg. Co.*, ASBCA 43801, 94-3 BCA ¶ 27239, and are precluded by 41 U.S.C. § 605(a) from litigating the issue of fraud, *Simko Constr., Inc. v. United States*, 852 F.2d 540 (Fed. Cir. 1988). However, if a court has found that the contractor has committed fraud during the performance of the contract, the board will follow this determination and dismiss the case, *Beech Gap, Inc.*, ENGBCA 5585, 95-2 BCA ¶ 27879, *aff'd*, 86 F.3d 1177 (Fed. Cir. 1996), or award the government any amount that has been paid to the contractor as a result of the fraud, *Medica, S.A.*, ENGBCA PCC 142, 00-2 BCA ¶ 30,966. Furthermore, a board's granting of an appeal finding a claim valid is not binding if the government later obtains a court ruling of fraud, *J.E.T.S., Inc. v. United States*, 838 F.2d 1196 (Fed. Cir. 1988), *cert. denied*, 486 U.S. 1057 (1988).

2. Debarment

The second broad sanction is debarment of the contractor or its employees from taking any government contracts for a stated period of time. FAR 9.406-2 states:

> The debarring official may debar—
>
> (a) A contractor for a conviction of or civil judgment for—
>
> (1) Commission of fraud or a criminal offense in connection with—
>
> (i) Obtaining;
>
> (ii) Attempting to obtain; or

(iii) Performing a public contract or subcontract.

(2) Violation of Federal or State antitrust statutes relating to the submission of offers;

(3) Commission of embezzlement, theft, forgery, bribery, falsification or destruction of records, making false statements, tax evasion, or receiving stolen property;

(4) Intentionally affixing a label bearing a "Made in America" inscription (or any inscription having the same meaning) to a product sold in or shipped to the United States or its outlying areas, when the product was not made in the United States (see section 202 of the Defense Production Act (Public .Law 102-558)); or

(5) Commission of any other offense indicating a lack of business integrity or business honesty that seriously and directly affects the present responsibility of a Government contractor or subcontractor.

(b)(1) A contractor, based upon a preponderance of the evidence, for—

(i) Violation of the terms of a Government contract or subcontract so serious as to justify debarment, such as—

(A) Willful failure to perform in accordance with the terms of one or more contracts; or

(B) A history of failure to perform, or of unsatisfactory performance of, one or more contracts.

(ii) Violations of the Drug-Free Workplace Act of 1988 (Pub. L. 100-690), as indicated by—

(A) Failure to comply with the requirements of the clause at 52.223-6, Drug-Free Workplace; or

(B) Such a number of contractor employees convicted of violations of criminal drug statutes occurring in the workplace as to indicate that the contractor has failed to make a good faith effort to provide a drug-free workplace (see 23.504).

(iii) Intentionally affixing a label bearing a "Made in America" inscription (or any inscription having the same meaning) to a product sold in or shipped to the United States or its outlying areas, when the product was not made in the United States (see Section 202 of the Defense Production Act (Public Law 102-558)).

(iv) Commission of an unfair trade practice as defined in 9.403 (see Section 201 of the Defense Production Act (Pub. L. 102-558)).

(2) A contractor, based on a determination by the Secretary of Homeland Security or the Attorney General of the United States, that the contractor is not in compliance with Immigration and Nationality Act employment provisions (see Executive Order 12989, as amended by Executive Order 13286). Such determination is not reviewable in the debarment proceedings.

(c) A contractor or subcontractor based on any other cause of so serious or compelling a nature that it affects the present responsibility of the contractor or subcontractor.

Debarment precludes contracts with any agency of the federal government for a period up to three years, FAR 9.406-4. However, some debarments last considerably longer. See, for example, *Roderick Nielson*, HUDBCA 99-C-107-D6, 99-2 BCA ¶ 30,569, where, over the opposition of the government, the board terminated a debarment that had been in effect for 10 years.

Debarment of a company has been sustained for submitting false claims, *Dowling Group v. Williams*, Civ. 82-1775 (D.D.C. 1982); for bribery and collusive bidding, *Robinson v. Cheney*, 876 F.2d 152 (D.C. Cir. 1989); and for bribery, *Atlantic Chem. Co.*, GSBCA 5822-D, 80-2 BCA ¶ 14,801. Debarment of an officer of a company was also sustained when the company bribed government officials, *Taylor v. Marsh*, Civ. 81-2643 (D.D.C. 1982). For a rare case in which the agency refused to debar a company and the court ordered the prior temporary action of suspension to be voided ab initio, see *Leon Sloan, Sr. & Jimmy Lee Furby v. Department of Hous. & Urban Devel.*, 231 F.3d 10 (D.C. Cir. 2000). See also *Lion Raisins, Inc. v. United States*, 51 Fed. Cl. 238 (2001), in which the court found a debarment to be an abuse of discretion because the agency had awarded five contracts between the time it found out about the acts that allegedly indicated a lack of integrity and when it issued the suspension order; and *Dantran, Inc., v. Department of Labor*, 171 F.3d 58 (1st Cir. 1999), in which the court overturned a debarment for improper wage payments because there was substantial evidence that the contractor had complied with agency procedures. See Cibinic and Nash, *Formation of Government Contracts* ch. 4 (3d ed. 1998) for a more complete discussion of debarment and suspension of contractors.

Debarment is a particularly harsh sanction because when an agency *proposes* to debar a contractor, it is immediately placed on the List of Parties Excluded from Federal Procurement and Nonprocurement Programs, FAR 9.404(a)(1), and may not receive contract awards or solicitations thereafter, FAR 9.405(a). See *IMCO, Inc. v. United States*, 97 F.3d 1422 (Fed. Cir. 1996), sustaining the dismissal of a protest where the agency deprived the Small Business Administration of the opportunity to issue a certificate of competency by proposing to debar the offeror. See also *Aardvark Keith Moving, Inc.*, Comp. Gen. Dec. B-290565, 2002 CPD ¶ 134, denying a protest that the agency declared the protester ineligible because it was affiliated with a company that had been proposed for debarment five years earlier.

Debarment can be imposed simultaneously with civil or criminal penalties for the improper conduct. See *United States v. Glymph*, 96 F.3d 722 (4th Cir. 1996), holding that conviction for criminal fraud was proper because the prior debarment was not punitive but remedial—thus precluding any defense of double jeopardy. Accord, *United States v. Hatfield*, 108 F.3d 67 (4th Cir. 1997). See also *Hudson v. United States*, 522 U.S. 93 (1997), finding no double jeopardy in a criminal prosecution following a settlement that included a civil fine and an agreement to refrain from participation in government programs without written authorization from the agency.

3. Suspension or Dismissal of Government Employees

A third broad sanction is suspension or dismissal of a government employee who has violated the standards of conduct. Such actions must be taken in accordance with 5 U.S.C. § 7513, which permits appeal by the employee to the Merit System Protection Board. See 5 C.F.R. pt. 1200. Dismissal of an employee was upheld in *Womer v. Hampton*, 496 F.2d 99 (5th Cir. 1974), where a government inspector had taken payments from a contractor and did not give a satisfactory explanation for the payments. Dismissal was also sustained in *Polcover v. Secretary of Treasury*, 477 F.2d 1223 (D.C. Cir. 1973), on the basis that the employee accepted a bribe even though he was later acquitted in a criminal prosecution. The court held that the evidence was sufficient to meet a preponderance of the evidence test in the dismissal proceeding even though it failed to meet the beyond a reasonable doubt test of the criminal action. The Court of Claims repeatedly held that agencies had broad discretion in selecting administrative sanctions for acceptance of bribes and gratuities. In *Jones v. United States*, 223 Ct. Cl. 138, 617 F.2d 233 (1980), the court upheld a decision of the Civil Service Commission Appeals Review Board sustaining the dismissal of a Department of Agriculture meat inspector who had accepted a single bottle of whiskey from a meat packer. In *Parker v. United States*, 224 Ct. Cl. 618 (1980), the court rejected the contention that dismissal of an employee who had accepted meals and entertainment valued at more than $3,000 from a contractor constituted an abuse of agency discretion. In *Lane v. United States*, 225 Ct. Cl. 209, 633 F.2d 1384 (1980), the court upheld the dismissal of IRS auditors who had accepted a whole series of free meals from a firm being audited. See also *Baker v. Department of Health & Human Servs.*, 912 F.2d 1448 (Fed. Cir. 1990), sustaining dismissal of an employee who accepted a lunch during which he disclosed internal agency information; and *Monahan v. United States*, 173 Ct. Cl. 734, 354 F.2d 306 (1965), sustaining the dismissal of a procuring agency employee for permitting a contractor to pay for hotel rooms and for accepting loans from three contractors.

Dismissal of an employee was also upheld for falsification of records, which was a violation of 18 U.S.C. § 1001, *Santornino v. Department of Veterans Affairs*, 45 F.3d 442 (Fed. Cir. 1994) (affirming ruling of administrative law judge in unpublished opinion). See also *Pararas-Carayannis v. Department of Commerce*, 9 F.3d 955 (Fed.

Cir. 1993), upholding an indefinite suspension without pay for laundering money for escort/prostitution operations, in violation of 18 U.S.C. § 1956(a)(3). See also *Brook v. Corrado*, 999 F.2d 523 (Fed. Cir. 1993) (dismissal for possession of cocaine with intent to distribute it); *Stanek v. Department of Transp.*, 805 F.2d 1572 (Fed. Cir. 1986) (dismissal for solicitation of loan from company that might have benefitted from employee's research); *Kumferman v. Department of Navy*, 785 F.2d 286 (Fed. Cir. 1986) (dismissal for theft of government property); and *Brewer v. United States Postal Serv.*, 227 Ct. Cl. 276, 647 F.2d 1093 (1981), *cert. denied*, 454 U.S. 1144 (1982) (dismissal of an employee with 27 years of service for falsifying time cards). Compare *Miguel v. Department of Army*, 727 F.2d 1081 (Fed. Cir. 1984), reversing an agency decision to dismiss an employee with 24 years of service for stealing two bars of soap.

B. Improper Influence of Government Decisions

One of the most serious threats to the integrity of the procurement process is the possibility of conduct by contractors that will improperly influence the decisions of contracting officers and other government employees. To protect against this threat, there are a number of very strict criminal statutes.

1. Bribery

18 U.S.C. § 201(b) makes it a criminal offense to offer or give a bribe to a government official or for a government official to solicit or receive a bribe. The crimes are defined as follows:

> (b) Whoever—
>
> (1) directly or indirectly, corruptly gives, offers or promises anything of value to any public official or person who has been selected to be a public official, or offers or promises any public official or any person who has been selected to be a public official to give anything of value to any other person or entity, with intent—
>
> (A) to influence any official act; or
>
> (B) to influence such public official or person who has been selected to be a public official to commit or aid in committing, or collude in, or allow, any fraud, or make opportunity for the commission of any fraud, on the United States; or
>
> (C) to induce such public official or such person who has been selected to be a public official to do or omit to do any act in violation of the lawful duty of such official or person;
>
> (2) being a public official or person selected to be a public official, directly or indirectly, corruptly demands, seeks, receives, accepts, or agrees to re-

ceive or accept anything of value personally or for any other person or entity, in return for:

(A) being influenced in the performance of any official act; or

(B) being influenced to commit or aid in committing, or to collude in, or allow, any fraud, or make opportunity for the commission of any fraud, on the United States; or

(C) being induced to do or omit to do any act in violation of the official duty of such official or person.

a. *Thing of Value*

To constitute bribery, the statute requires that something "of value" be given, offered, promised, solicited, or received. Courts have adopted an expansive reading of the value requirement for both bribery and gratuities. Most cases involving bribery under the statute understandably concern cash payments, *United States v. Kinter*, 235 F.3d 192 (8th Cir. 2000), *cert. denied*, 532 U.S. 937 (2001) (cash payment to technical employee advising contracting officer during source selection); *United States v. Hollingshead*, 672 F.2d 751 (9th Cir. 1982) (cash payment to employee of Federal Reserve Bank); *United States v. Myers*, 635 F.2d 932 (2d Cir.), *cert. denied*, 449 U.S. 956 (1980) (cash paid by undercover agents to members of Congress); *United States v. Johnson*, 621 F.2d 1073 (10th Cir. 1980) (cash payment offered to FAA procurement official); *United States v. Strand*, 574 F.2d 993 (9th Cir. 1978) (cash payment by undercover agent to summer border guard); *United States v. Arroyo*, 581 F.2d 649 (7th Cir. 1978), *cert. denied*, 439 U.S. 1069 (1979) (cash payments to Small Business Administration loan officers from loan applicant); *United States v. Brasco*, 516 F.2d 816 (2d Cir.), *cert. denied*, 423 U.S. 860 (1975) (cash payments to Post Office officials to obtain contracts); *United States v. Deutsch*, 475 F.2d 55 (5th Cir. 1973) (cash payments to Post Office employees to obtain stolen credit cards); *United States v. Rosner*, 485 F.2d 1213 (2d Cir. 1973), *cert. denied*, 417 U.S. 950 (1974) (cash payments by lawyer to undercover agent to obtain secret grand jury minutes); *United States v. Jacobs*, 431 F.2d 754 (2d Cir. 1970), *cert. denied*, 402 U.S. 950 (1971) (cash payment to IRS auditor). However, a variety of other benefits have also been considered as value by courts in relation to bribery charges, *United States v. McDade*, 28 F.3d 283 (3d Cir. 1994), *cert. denied*, 514 U.S. 1003 (1995) (travel expenses); *United States v. Harary*, 457 F.2d 471 (2d Cir. 1972) (prostitutes and cameras); *United States v. Ellenbogen*, 365 F.2d 982 (2d Cir. 1966), *cert. denied*, 386 U.S. 923 (1967) (an automobile). It is not necessary for the government to establish the exact value of a bribe, since the express language of 18 U.S.C. § 201(b)(1) defines the offense as giving anything of value to a public official, *United States v. Rasco*, 853 F.2d 501 (7th Cir.), *post-conviction proceedings*, 697 F. Supp. 343 (N.D. Ill.), *cert. denied*, 488 U.S. 959 (1988).

b. Corrupt Intent

To establish a violation of the provision, a specific "corrupt" intent on the part of the giver or receiver of the bribe must be proved. The requisite intent is proved by showing a quid pro quo—an expectation of a favorable official act in return for the bribe. In *United States v. Strand*, 574 F.2d 993 (9th Cir. 1978), in which a U.S. Customs Service official was found to have violated this provision by soliciting and accepting an $800 payment in return for allowing drugs to be smuggled through a border checkpoint, the court discussed the intent required under 18 U.S.C. § 201(c) (now § 201(b)(2)(c)) at 995:

> To be guilty under § 201(c)(3), Strand must have "corruptly" accepted the $800 from the Customs agent for himself or some other person in return for knowingly violating his official duty. The requisite "corrupt" intent has been defined as "incorporating a concept of the bribe being the prime mover or producer of the official act." *United States v. Brewster*, 165 U.S. App. D.C. 1, 21, 506 F.2d 62, 82 (1974). It is this element of quid pro quo that distinguishes the heightened criminal intent requisite under the bribery sections of the statute from the simple mens rea required for violation of the gratuity sections.

In proving the exchange or quid pro quo element, the accompanying intent to influence some identifiable public act must be shown. In *United States v. Heffler*, 402 F.2d 924 (3d Cir. 1968), a government technical employee was convicted for having solicited a bribe in return for an offer to influence an award even though he was not the awarding officer. The nexus between solicitation and intent was found in the employee's purported ability to indirectly affect the award, his offer to do so, and the specificity of the act to be performed. Similarly, in *United States v. Arroyo*, 581 F.2d 649 (7th Cir. 1978), *cert. denied*, 439 U.S. 1069 (1979), an SBA loan officer was convicted of accepting a bribe even though the loan had already been consummated, because the loan officer had told the borrower that the loan had not yet been finalized. In *United States v. Pommerening*, 500 F.2d 92 (10th Cir.), *cert. denied*, 419 U.S. 1088 (1974), loan applicants were convicted of bribery for giving an SBA official a $5,000 automobile in exchange for expediting a $200,000 loan application to finance their car dealership.

The number of reported cases involving government procurement officials and contractors is relatively small. The typical case involves payments made in the hope of influencing contract awards. In *United States v. Johnson*, 621 F.2d 1073 (10th Cir. 1980), the court found the requisite indicia of an expected quid pro quo where the contractor, who had given a $10,000 check to a government procurement agent, credited it on its books to government contracts it expected to win. *United States v. Iaconetti*, 540 F.2d 574 (2d Cir.), *cert. denied*, 429 U.S. 1041 (1976), involved a GSA inspector who was assigned to conduct a preaward survey of a contractor and was convicted of soliciting a bribe for offering to ensure the favorable treatment of the contractor by the upper echelon of GSA in exchange for 1 percent of the contract price.

Corrupt intent can be found even though some of the payments are for services rendered. For example, in *United States v. Biaggi*, 909 F.2d 662 (2d Cir. 1990), the court found corrupt intent in payments made by a contractor to a law firm that had rendered services because part of the payment was for "services" demanded by a congressman who was "of counsel" to the firm.

c. Public Official

The statute prohibits payments to "public officials," defined by 18 U.S.C. § 201(a) as a

> Member of Congress, Delegate, or Resident Commissioner, either before or after such official has qualified, or an officer or employee or person acting for or on behalf of the United States or any department, agency or branch of Government thereof, including the District of Columbia, in any official function under or by authority of any such department, agency, or branch of Government, or a juror.
>
> . . .

The class of public officials is an expansive one, consisting of federal prison administrators, *United States v. Alessio*, 528 F.2d 1079 (9th Cir.), *cert. denied*, 426 U.S. 948 (1976); IRS agents, *United States v. Johnson*, 647 F.2d 815 (8th Cir. 1981); congressional aides, *United States v. Carson*, 464 F.2d 424 (2d Cir. 1972), *cert. denied*, 409 U.S. 949 (1972); *United States v. Dixon*, 658 F.2d 181 (3d Cir. 1981); and a contracting officers' representative, *K & R Eng'g Co. v. United States*, 222 Ct. Cl. 340, 616 F.2d 469 (1980). Generally, persons in a position of public trust with regard to government funds are classified as public officials even though they are not directly employed by the federal government. See *United States v. Kenney*, 185 F.3d 1217 (11th Cir. 1999) (government contractor); *United States v. Hang*, 75 F.3d 1275 (8th Cir. 1996) (employee of local housing authority); *United States v. Strissel*, 920 F.2d 1162 (4th Cir. 1990) (director of local housing authority); *United States v. Velazquez*, 847 F.2d 140 (4th Cir. 1988) (county jailer where jail housed federal as well as state prisoners, county jailers supervised federal inmates, and jail was subject to inspections by federal prison authorities); *United States v. Kirby*, 587 F.2d 876 (7th Cir. 1978) (privately employed grain inspector licensed by the Department of Agriculture); *United States v. Griffin*, 401 F. Supp. 1222 (S.D. Ind. 1975), *aff'd without opinion,* 541 F.2d 284 (7th Cir. 1976) (privately employed broker under a HUD contract). Compare *United States v. Loschiavo*, 531 F.2d 659 (2d Cir. 1976) (Model Cities program administrator was not acting on behalf of federal government by suggesting leasing arrangement with one who bribed administrator).

2. Gratuities

18 U.S.C. § 201(c) makes it a crime to offer or give a gratuity to a government official or for a government official to solicit or receive a gratuity. The crimes are defined as follows:

(c) Whoever—

(1) otherwise than as provided by law for the proper discharge of official duty—

(A) directly or indirectly gives, offers, or promises anything of value to any public official, former public official, or person selected to be a public official, for or because of any official act performed or to be performed by such public official, former public official, or person selected to be a public official; or

(B) being a public official, former public official, or person selected to be a public official, otherwise than as provided by law for the proper discharge of official duty, directly or indirectly demands, seeks, receives, accepts, or agrees to receive or accept anything of value personally for or because of any official act performed or to be performed by such official or person.

This statute is implemented by Executive Order 12674, 54 Fed. Reg. 15159 (1989), as modified by Executive Order 12731, 55 Fed. Reg. 42547 (1990), and by the regulations at 5 C.F.R. § 2635, which provide a uniform set of rules for all executive branch employees.

a. *Thing of Value*

A variety of benefits have been deemed to constitute value in relation to gratuities, including cash, meat, liquor, and clothing, *United States v. Romano*, 583 F.2d 1 (1st Cir. 1978); paid vacations, *United States v. Hartley*, 678 F.2d 961 (11th Cir. 1982); loans and promise of future employment, *United States v. Gorman*, 807 F.2d 1299 (6th Cir. 1986), *cert. denied*, 484 U.S. 815 (1987). In *Gorman*, the court noted that the term "thing of value" should be broadly construed and not limited to gratuities as that term is commonly understood. In determining what constitutes a thing of value, the court placed the focus on the subjective value the receiver of the gratuity attached to the items received. See *United States v. McDade*, 827 F. Supp. 1153 (E.D. Pa. 1993), *aff'd*, 28 F.3d 283 (3d Cir. 1994), where a United States congressman charged with accepting illegal gratuities argued that many of the gifts allegedly received, such as a golf jacket, a golf bag, and a golf umbrella, had only nominal value and were thus not things of value under the gratuities statute. He cited *Gorman* to support the proposition that the term "anything of value" should be construed as meaning substantial value. The court could find nothing in *Gorman* to support this argument and denied the congressman's motion to dismiss the indictment. The court noted that even the smallest of the items allegedly received was objectively valuable enough under the gratuities statute, and that the items may have also had additional subjective value to the congressman. As an example, the court noted that the golf jacket was a green jacket similar to the one awarded each year to the winner of the Masters Golf Tournament and thus presumably covetable by a golf buff.

The federal standards of conduct in 5 C.F.R. § 2635 contain extensive guidance on gifts to federal employees. 5 C.F.R. § 2635.203 provides the following definition of the term "gift":

> *Gift* includes any gratuity, favor, discount, entertainment, hospitality, loan, forbearance, or other item having monetary value. It includes services as well as gifts of training, transportation, local travel, lodgings, and meals, whether provided in-kind, by purchase of a ticket, payment in advance, or reimbursement after the expenses has been incurred.

This regulation contains nine exceptions to this definition, as follows:

1. Modest items of food and refreshments, such as soft drinks, coffee and donuts, offered other than as part of a meal;

2. Greeting cards and items with little intrinsic value, such as plaques, certificates and trophies, which are intended solely for presentation;

3. Loans from banks and other financial institutions on terms generally available to the public;

4. Opportunities and benefits, including favorable rates and commercial discounts, available to the public or to a class consisting of all Government employees or all uniformed military personnel, whether or not restricted on the basis of geographic considerations;

5. Rewards and prizes given to competitors in contests or events, including random drawings, open to the public unless the employee's entry into the contest or event is required as part of his official duties;

6. Pension and other benefits resulting from continued participation in an employee welfare and benefits plan maintained by a former employer;

7. Anything which is paid for by the Government or secured by the Government under Government contract;

8. Any gift accepted by the Government under specific statutory authority, including:

   (i) Travel, subsistence, and related expenses accepted by an agency under the authority of 31 U.S.C. 1353 in connection with an employee's attendance at a meeting or similar function relating to his official duties which takes place away from his duty station. The agency's acceptance must be in accordance with the implementing regulations at 41 CFR part 304-1; and

   (ii) Other gifts provided in-kind which have been accepted by an agency under its agency gift acceptance statute; or

9. Anything for which market value is paid by the employee.

5 C.F.R. § 2635.204 contains detailed guidance on a number of additional exceptions that pertain to special situations. See, for example, 5 C.F.R. § 2635.204(a), which permits employees to accept unsolicited gifts with a value of $20 or less and an aggregate annual value of $50 per giver; 5 C.F.R. § 2635.204(b), which permits acceptance of gifts based on a personal relationship; 5 C.F.R. § 2635.204(d), which permits the acceptance of awards and honorary degrees with a value of no more than $200; 5 C.F.R. § 2635.204(f), which permits acceptance of gifts in connection with political activities; 5 C.F.R. § 2635.204(g), which permits acceptance of free attendance for speakers and panelists at public meetings; and 5 C.F.R. § 2635.204(h), which permits acceptance of food and refreshments at social events where the invitation has been issued by other than a prohibited source. This regulation contains detailed guidance on these exceptions, including numerous specific examples of their application.

Even though acceptance of a gift may be permitted by one of the described exceptions, the regulations note at 5 C.F.R. § 2635.204 that "it is never inappropriate and frequently prudent for an employee to decline a gift offered by a prohibited source or because of his official position." In addition, 5 C.F.R. § 2635.202(c) contains the following broad restrictive guidance:

> Notwithstanding any exception provided in this subpart . . . an employee shall not:
>
> (1) Accept a gift in return for being influenced in the performance of an official act:
>
> (2) Solicit or coerce the offering of a gift;
>
> (3) Accept gifts from the same or different sources on a basis so frequent that a reasonable person would be led to believe that the employee is using his public office for private gain;
>
> (4) Accept a gift in violation of any statute. . . .
>
> (5) Accept vendor promotional training contrary to applicable regulations, policies or guidance relating to the procurement of supplies and services for the Government, except pursuant to § 2635.204(l).

This would appear to make it inappropriate for a government employee to accept any gift from a contractor if the employee has official duties with regard to the contract. See 5 C.F.R. § 3601.103 for supplemental guidance provided for Department of Defense employees.

b. Purpose of Gratuity

The gratuity must be linked to a *specific* act that the official has performed or is expected to perform, *United States v. Sun-Diamond Growers of Cal.*, 526 U.S. 398 (1999). In reaching this conclusion, the Court held that the statute did not intend to make it a crime to give gifts to employees merely because they held high positions in the government. See also *United States v. Arthur*, 544 F.2d 730 (4th Cir. 1976), stating that a gift given to create goodwill was not a gratuity. In earlier cases, some circuits had construed the statute more broadly. See, for example, *United States v. Campbell*, 684 F.2d 141 (D.C. Cir. 1982), concluding that a gift offered or solicited merely to "generally influence" an official was sufficient to satisfy the "for or because of" element of the statute. See also *United States v. Evans*, 572 F.2d 455 (5th Cir.), *cert. denied*, 439 U.S. 870 (1978), stating at 480:

> The purpose of these statutes is to reach any situation in which the judgment of a government agent might be clouded because of payments or gifts made to him by reason of his position "otherwise than as provided by law for the proper discharge of official duty." Even if corruption is not intended by either the donor or the donee, there is still a tendency in such a situation to provide conscious or unconscious preferential treatment of the donor by the donee, or the inefficient management of public affairs. These statutes, like the predecessor legislation, are a congressional effort to eliminate the temptation inherent in such a situation.

In *United States v. Niederberger*, 580 F.2d 63 (3d Cir. 1978), where an IRS employee violated this statute by accepting five golfing trips, the court discussed the different degrees of intent required for establishing violations of the bribery and gratuity sections, at 68:

> It is clear, then, that § 201(c)(1) [now § 201(b)(1)] requires as one of its elements a quid pro quo. In fact, we find this to be the primary distinction between subsections (c)(1) and (g) [now § 201(c)]. Support for this view is found in *United States v. Brewster*, 165 U.S. App. D.C. 1, 506 F.2d 62 (1974), where the court, analyzing the differences between subsections (c)(1) and (g), held that "[t]he bribery section [(c)(1)] makes necessary an explicit *quid pro quo* which need not exist if only an illegal gratuity is involved." *Id.*, at 11. [Footnote citing other cases omitted.]
>
> Thus, we find it unnecessary for the Government to allege in an indictment charging a § 201(g) offense that a gratuity received by a public official was, in any way, generated by some specific, identifiable act performed or to be performed by the official. A quid pro quo is simply foreign to the elements of a subsection (g) offense. . . .

In *United States v. Bishton*, 463 F.2d 887 (D.C. Cir. 1972), a supervisor was convicted under this section for soliciting a $400 gift from an employee for whom the supervisor had previously obtained a promotion. In *United States v. Evans*, 572 F.2d 455 (5th Cir. 1978), acceptance of a $500 gratuity by an official who had previously accepted an offer of government employment but had not commenced work was sufficient to establish a violation of this section.

Since a gratuity need only be paid "for or because of any official act" (18 U.S.C. § 201(c)), and no quid pro quo need be proved, it may be difficult to discern whether the alleged payment was made out of friendship or other disinterested motive. While it is clear that *corrupt* intent need not be shown, the government must at least demonstrate *some* nexus between the giving or receiving of the thing of value and the employee's official position. In *United States v. Standefer*, 610 F.2d 1076 (3d Cir. 1979), *aff'd*, 447 U.S. 10 (1980), sufficient evidence of intent was found despite a corporate officer's assertion that certain vacation trips to Florida given to an IRS employee were motivated by disinterested friendship, because no evidence was offered that similar gifts were given either prior or subsequent to the recipient's employment in the government, and a subordinate of the corporate officer characterized the relationship as a business friendship. However, many of the reported cases actually involve facts reflecting an expectation of a quid pro quo, perhaps reflecting a prosecutorial reluctance to impose bribery sanctions in cases involving small payments. For example, in *United States v. Mosley*, 659 F.2d 812 (7th Cir. 1981), an Illinois state official, whose salary was entirely paid by the federal government under the CETA program, was convicted of violating 18 U.S.C. § 201(g) (now § 201(c)(1)(B)) for soliciting $50 payments from applicants for CETA jobs in exchange for favorable referral to CETA hiring agencies. In *United States v. Kirby*, 587 F.2d 876 (7th Cir. 1978), the defendants were convicted of conspiring to violate 18 U.S.C. § 201(f) (now § 201(c)(1)(A)) by making payments to grain inspectors in exchange for false certifications that inspected grain was of a higher quality than it actually was.

c. Contract Termination

10 U.S.C. § 2207 requires that all Department of Defense contracts over the simplified acquisition threshold contain a clause giving the government the right to terminate the contract if gratuities have been offered or paid. The standard clause used for this purpose is the Gratuities clause in FAR 52.203-3. FAR 3.202 requires this clause to be used by all agencies. However, it is not applicable to contracts for personal services and contracts between the military departments or defense agencies and foreign governments that do not obligate Department of Defense funds, FAR 3.202. In addition to the right to terminate the contract, the clause gives agencies the right to damages for breach of contract and gives the Department of Defense the right to exemplary damages from three to ten times the "cost incurred by the contractor in giving [the] gratuities."

Several cases indicate that contractors can be subjected to severe penalties for bribery or gratuities under this clause. See, for example, *Erwin Pfister General-Bauuntemehmen*, ASBCA 43980, 02-1 BCA ¶ 31,431, where the government terminated the contracts, refused to pay for work performed, refused to pay for claimed extra work, and assessed substantial exemplary damages. The board denied the contractor's appeal to recover the payments owed on the contract on the basis of the contractor's conviction for bribing a contract specialist. The same result was reached in *Andreas Boehm Malergrossbetrieb*, ASBCA 44017, 01-1 BCA ¶ 31,354; *Schneider Haustechnik GmbH*, ASBCA 43969, 01-1 BCA ¶ 31,264; and *Schuep-*

ferling GmbH & Co., KG, ASBCA 45567, 98-2 BCA ¶ 29,828. In these cases, the board rejected the argument that the government had ratified the contracts by allowing performance to continue after it learned of the bribes.

3. Conduct of Former Employees

The government has sought to prevent former government employees and military officers from making unfair use of their prior positions and affiliations. At the same time, the government recognizes the legitimate interest and rights of former employees to seek employment and to enter into business ventures. Thus, activity that seeks to influence government action or that would undermine confidence in the fairness of government proceedings is prohibited, but former government employees and military officers retain a great amount of freedom to pursue legally permissible activity.

a. General Restrictions

18 U.S.C. § 207 restricts "officers and employees" in the following circumstances:

1. A former employee is prohibited for life from representing anyone else before the government on a particular matter the employee handled personally and substantially while a government official.

2. A former employee is prohibited for two years from representing a party on a particular matter that had been under the employee's official responsibility during the last year of the employee's government service.

3. A former employee is prohibited for one year from assisting others in trade or treaty negotiations in which the employee had been personally and substantially engaged during the employee's final year of government service.

4. A former senior level employee is prohibited for one year from making any communication or appearance before the employee's former agency regardless of prior involvement in the matter.

5. A former "very senior level" employee is prohibited for one year from contacting employees of the executive branch of the government.

6. A former senior level employee is prohibited for one year from representing any foreign entity before the government.

Criminal prosecutions under this statute are rare, and a violation will not make invoices on a contract false claims, *United States ex rel. Siewick v. Jamieson Science & Eng'g, Inc.*, 214 F.3d 1372 (D.C. Cir. 2000). However, alleged violations of this statute are frequently raised in contesting the validity of contracts. The most egregious conduct falling within this provision is hiring government employees who have worked on the procurement before the award has been made. A contracting officer's disqualification of an offeror for such conduct was sustained in *NKF Eng'g, Inc., v. United States*, 805 F.2d 372 (Fed. Cir. 1986). In that case, a former Navy civilian employee, who had participated substantially in the procurement process on a particular RFP, left federal employment to take a job with one of the offerors before the contract was awarded. That offeror subsequently submitted a price revision that was 33 percent lower than its earlier offer. The court upheld the disqualification of the offeror on the basis of an appearance of impropriety, even though the offeror claimed that it had carefully isolated the former government employee from its preparation of the final offer. The court agreed that the potential for an unfair competitive advantage so tainted the procurement process that the integrity of the process had been damaged.

(1) Particular Matter

Violations of the first two restrictions require participation in a particular matter that was in the agency during the official's employment. 5 C.F.R. § 2637.201(c)(1) states that "[s]uch a matter typically involves a specific proceeding affecting the legal rights of the parties or an isolatable transaction . . . between identifiable parties." Excluded is formulation of general policy, rulemaking, and legislation. For a violation to occur, the subsequent representation must concern the same matter in which the employee participated during employment, 5 C.F.R. § 2637.201(c)(4). In *CACI, Inc.-Fed. v. United States*, 1 Cl. Ct. 352, *rev'd*, 719 F.2d 1567 (Fed. Cir. 1983), the Justice Department issued an RFP for ADPE services for the Information Systems Support Group (ISSG) of the department. Before award was made, an offeror who had provided these services for some time alleged that a conflict existed in that a vice president of a competitor had previously served as chief of the ISSG. In issuing an injunction barring award, the court merely found that the employee was involved in the same particular matter while working for the government, a criterion that satisfies either § 207(a) or § 207(b). The Federal Circuit reversed, holding that a follow-on service contract did not cover the same particular matter as the prior contract since the nature of the services had evolved and they were broader than those on the earlier contract. The court appears to have read the statute narrowly in arriving at this conclusion. Contrast the *CACI* decision with *United States v. Medico Indus., Inc.*, 784 F.2d 840 (7th Cir. 1986), holding that a contract amendment adding a large quantity of units to an existing contract was sufficiently related to the original contract to be the same particular matter.

(2) Personal and Substantial Participation

Violation of the first restriction occurs only when there has been a personal and substantial participation in the matter during employment. 5 C.F.R. § 2637.201(d)(1) states:

> Basic requirements. The restrictions of section 207(a) apply only to those matters in which a former Government employee had "personal and substantial participation," exercised "through decision, approval, disapproval, recommendation, the rendering of advice, investigation or otherwise." To participate "personally" means directly, and includes the participation of a subordinate when actually directed by the former Government employee in the matter. "Substantially" means that the employee's involvement must be of significance to the matter, or form a basis for a reasonable appearance of such significance. It requires more than official responsibility, knowledge, perfunctory involvement, or involvement on an administrative or peripheral issue. A finding of substantiality should be based not only on the effort devoted to a matter, but on the importance of the effort. While a series of peripheral involvements may be insubstantial, the single act of approving or participation in a critical step may be substantial.

Review of a proposed notice of income tax deficiency and recommendation for its issuance constituted personal and substantial participation, *United States v. Nasser*, 476 F.2d 1111 (7th Cir. 1973). Preparing a memorandum and answering a legal question were also held to be such participation. Review of a patent application was held to be sufficient involvement in *Kearney & Trecker Corp. v. Giddings & Lewis, Inc.*, 452 F.2d 579 (7th Cir. 1971), *cert. denied*, 405 U.S. 1066 (1972).

(3) Representation

The basic prohibition in 18 U.S.C. § 207(a)(1) is against representational activities carried out "with the intent to influence." "Representation" may occur in the course of formal or informal appearances and in written or oral communications. In 5 C.F.R. § 2637.201(b), representation is defined as "acting as agent or attorney, or other representative in an appearance, or communication with intent to influence." 5 C.F.R. § 2637.201(b)(2) makes it clear that such representation can be by any former employee:

> The statutory prohibition covers any other former employee, including managerial and technical personnel, who represents another person in an appearance or, by other communication, attempts to influence the Government concerning a particular matter in which he or she was involved. For example, a former technical employee may not act as a manufacturer's promotional or contract representative to the Government on a particular matter in which he or she participated. Nor could such employee appear as an expert witness against the Government in connection with such a matter.

5 C.F.R. § 2637.201(b)(3) provides guidance on "appearances" and "communications":

> An appearance occurs when an individual is physically present before the United States in either a formal or informal setting or conveys material to the United States in connection with a formal proceeding or application. A communication is broader than an appearance and includes, for example, correspondence, or telephone calls.

5 C.F.R. § 2637.201(b)(5) contains the following example:

> Example 1: A Government employee, who participated in writing the specifications of a contract awarded to Q Company for the design of certain education testing programs, joins Q Company and does work under the contract. She is asked to accompany a company vice-president to a meeting to state the results of a series of trial tests, and does so. No violation occurs when she provides the information to her former agency. During the meeting a dispute arises as to some terms of the contract, and she is called upon to support Q Company's position. She may not do so. If she had reason to believe that the contractual dispute would be a subject of the meeting, she should not have attended.

See *Robert E. Derecktor of R.I., Inc. v. United States*, 762 F. Supp. 1019 (D.R.I. 1991), in which the court, interpreting the predecessor to § 207(a), held that a former employee's delivery of a bid package to his former agency did not constitute an appearance within the meaning of this restriction and that the employee did not deliver the bid with the intent to influence. See, however, *United States v. Coleman*, 805 F.2d 474 (3d Cir. 1986), where a former employee's presence at a meeting related to tax cases, which had been within the employee's supervisory responsibility before retiring, was found to constitute representation within the meaning of this restriction.

18 U.S.C. § 207(j)(5) permits communications solely for the purpose of furnishing scientific or technological information to the agency. See *J. L. Assocs., Inc.*, Comp. Gen. Dec. B-201331.2, 82-1 CPD ¶ 99, in which this exception was applied by the Air Force to a briefing by a retired military officer concerning the same activity that he had commanded. The briefing concerned the contractor's experience on similar work with other agencies and occurred before issuance of an RFP.

Under a predecessor statute, participation in the preparation of a claim for reimbursement was held not to violate the statute since it did not amount to prosecution of a claim, *Acme Process Equip. Co. v. United States*, 171 Ct. Cl. 324, 347 F.2d 509 (1965), *rev'd on other grounds*, 385 U.S. 138 (1966).

(4) Types of Employment or Contracting Permitted

Absent a violation of the specific provisions of 18 U.S.C. § 207, there is no general prohibition against employment of a former government employee by a contractor. 5 C.F.R. § 2637.101(c)(5) provides:

> (5) The provisions of 18 U.S.C. § 207 do not, however, bar any former Government employee, regardless of rank, from employment with any private or public employer after Government service. Nor do they effectively bar employment even on a particular matter in which the former Government employee had major official involvement except in certain circumstances involving persons engaged in professional advocacy. Former Government employees may be fully active in high-level supervisory positions

> whether or not the work is funded by the United States and includes matter in which the employee was involved while employed by the Government. The statutory provisions are not intended to discourage the movement of skilled professionals in Government, to and from positions in industry, research institutions, law and accounting firms, universities and other major sources of expertise. Such a flow of skills can promote efficiency and communication between the Government and private activities, and it is essential to the success of many Government programs. Instead, only certain acts which are detrimental to public confidence in the Government are prohibited.

See *Bray Studios, Inc.*, Comp. Gen. Dec. B-207723, 82-2 CPD ¶ 373 (former agency employee now president of contractor and working in same area); *Culp/Wesner/Culp*, Comp. Gen. Dec. B-212318, 84-1 CPD ¶ 17 (former agency employee in charge of preparing solicitation subsequently awarded subcontract); *Medical Dev. Int'l*, Comp. Gen. Dec. B-281484.2, 99-1 CPD ¶ 68 (former employee who will serve as associate director of company and had policy position in agency); and *Perini/Jones, Joint Venture*, Comp. Gen. Dec. B-285906, 2002 CPD ¶ 68 (former employee who will serve as company's project manager was in the procuring agency at time proposals were submitted and evaluated).

Neither is there any general prohibition against entering into contracts with former government employees, *Sterling Med. Assocs.*, 62 Comp. Gen. 230 (B-209493), 83-1 CPD ¶ 215 (former employee of Veterans Administration awarded contract by the Department of the Navy); *Edward R. Jereb*, 60 Comp. Gen. 298 (B-200092), 81-1 CPD ¶ 178 (restriction prohibiting award of services contract to former agency employees held invalid); *Western Eng'g & Sales Co.*, Comp. Gen. Dec. B-205464, 82-2 CPD ¶ 277 (former employee awarded contract by agency based on proposal submitted after employment terminated). See, however, *Aviation Enters., Inc. v. Orr*, 29 CCF & 82,053 (D.D.C. 1981), *vacated*, 716 F.2d 1403 (D.C. Cir. 1983), in which a contract award to a company owned by a former military officer was enjoined because of a conflict of interest, without reference to the statute.

b. Additional Statutory Restrictions

In addition to the government-wide post-employment restrictions imposed by 18 U.S.C. § 207, there are special, broad post-employment restrictions in the Procurement Integrity Act, 41 U.S.C. § 423(d), applicable only to procurement personnel. This act was amended and simplified in Section 4304 of the Clinger-Cohen Act of 1996, Pub. L. No. 104-106, to state:

> (d) *Prohibition on former official's acceptance of compensation from contractor.* (1) A former official of a Federal agency may not accept compensation from a contractor as an employee, officer, director, or consultant of the contractor within a period of one year after such former official—
>
>> (A) served, at the time of selection of the contractor or the award of a contract to that contractor, as the procuring contracting officer, the source

selection authority, a member of the source selection evaluation board, or the chief of a financial or technical evaluation team in a procurement in which that contractor was selected for award of a contract in excess of $ 10,000,000;

(B) served as the program manager, deputy program manager, or administrative contracting officer for a contract in excess of $ 10,000,000 awarded to that contractor; or

(C) personally made for the Federal agency—

(i) a decision to award a contract, subcontract, modification of a contract or subcontract, or a task order or delivery order in excess of $ 10,000,000 to that contractor;

(ii) a decision to establish overhead or other rates applicable to a contract or contracts for that contractor that are valued in excess of $ 10,000,000;

(iii) a decision to approve issuance of a contract payment or payments in excess of $ 10,000,000 to that contractor; or

(iv) a decision to pay or settle a claim in excess of $ 10,000,000 with that contractor.

(2) Nothing in paragraph (1) may be construed to prohibit a former official of a Federal agency from accepting compensation from any division or affiliate of a contractor that does not produce the same or similar products or services as the entity of the contractor that is responsible for the contract referred to in subparagraph (A), (B), or (C) of such paragraph.

FAR 3.104-3 contains guidance on this employment prohibition, including detailed guidance on the calculation of the one-year period during which employment is prohibited. This regulation also states that the statute does not prohibit employment by a division or affiliate of a contractor that does not produce the same or similar products or services as the division with which the official previously had contact.

41 U.S.C. § 423(d)(5) requires the issuance of regulations permitting officials or former officials to request advisory opinions from agency ethics officials to determine whether they are subject to these provisions. This is implemented in FAR 3.104-6, which provides in paragraph (d)(3):

If the requester is advised in a written opinion by the agency ethics official that the requester may accept compensation from a particular contractor, and accepts such compensation in good faith reliance on that advisory opinion, then neither the requester nor the contractor will be found to have knowingly violated subsection 27(d) of the Act. If the requester or the contractor has actual knowledge or reason to believe that the opinion is based upon fraudulent, misleading, or otherwise incorrect information, their reliance upon the opinion will not be deemed to be in good faith.

41 U.S.C. § 423(g) provides that these restrictions may not serve as the basis for protests. See, however, *PRC, Inc.*, Comp. Gen. Dec. B-274698.2, 97-1 CPD ¶ 115, *recons. denied*, 97-2 CPD ¶ 10, in which the GAO found no impropriety in the employment of the former commanding officer of the procuring agency who had obtained an opinion that he was not a procurement official under this statute even though he concurred in the acquisition plan and appointed the source selection official. The GAO's inquiry was whether the contractor had obtained an unfair competitive advantage, not whether there was a violation of the statute.

These provisions replaced prior restrictions in 41 U.S.C. § 423(f) that did not prohibit employment but prohibited procurement officials for two years from participating in negotiations or in contract performance as employees of a contractor or a significant subcontractor. Under this statute, the GAO held that its enforcement was primarily a matter for the procuring agency and the Department of Justice—with the result that protests would determine only "whether any action of the former government employee may have resulted in prejudice for, or on behalf of, the awardee," *Central Tex. Coll.*, 71 Comp. Gen. 164 (B-245233.4), 92-1 CPD ¶ 121. See also *FHC Options, Inc.*, Comp. Gen. Dec. B-246793.3, 92-1 CPD ¶ 366, denying a protest based on the employment of a former government employee by the awardee's subcontractor because, although the former employee had assisted in the initial development of the performance work statement and the source selection plan for the solicitation, he had left the government before the RFP was issued, was not involved in the preparation of the awardee's proposal, and would not be involved in performing the contract.

There were also special post-employment restrictions in 10 U.S.C. § 2397b applicable to defense officials who had performed a procurement function. These provisions were repealed by § 4304(b)(1) of the Clinger-Cohen Act of 1996.

Formerly, a retired military officer was subject to two additional restrictions under 37 U.S.C. § 801 and 18 U.S.C. § 281. The Federal Acquisition Streamlining Act of 1994, Pub. L. No. 103-355, repealed 37 U.S.C. § 801. Under the provisions of that statute, a retired regular officer could not be paid from any appropriation for three years after retirement if the former officer was selling for himself or herself or for others or was contracting or negotiating to sell supplies or war materials to the DoD, the Coast Guard, NASA, or the Public Health Service. Section 4304(b)(3) of the Clinger-Cohen Act of 1996 repealed 18 U.S.C. § 281. That statute made it unlawful for a period of two years after retirement for a former military officer to be compensated for representing any person in the sale of goods or services to the military service from which the officer retired.

Section 4304(b)(6) of the Clinger-Cohen Act of 1996 also repealed 42 U.S.C. § 7216, prohibiting the Department of Energy from using employees of energy concerns in departmental matters involving that concern for a period of one year after employment. In *TRW Envtl. Safety Sys., Inc. v. United States*, 18 Cl. Ct. 33 (1989), award to an offeror was permanently enjoined when the court found a violation of that statute. In that case, an ex-employee of a competitor had participated in drafting the statement of work and was appointed chairman of the source evaluation board within the one-year period.

4. Conduct of Current Employees

There are numerous statutes and regulations circumscribing the activities of government employees. See, for example, 18 U.S.C. § 203 (limitation on receiving payment from others for official activity); 18 U.S.C. § 205 (prohibition against acting as an agent or attorney for a party before the government); and 18 U.S.C. § 209 (prohibition against receiving compensation from other than the United States for official duties). This section discusses the two major statutes applicable to government contracting. It also discusses administrative restrictions on contracting with organizations owned or controlled by government employees.

a. General Restrictions

Officers and employees of the government with a financial interest in an organization are prohibited from participating personally and substantially in any matter concerning that organization and the government, 18 U.S.C. § 208. This provision was intended to expand the proscriptions against employee participation with the private sector beyond the prior § 434, which merely prohibited certain "transactions of business."

(1) Extent of Financial Interest

The Standards of Ethical Conduct contained in 5 C.F.R. § 2635 Subpart D provide detailed guidance implementing this statutory proscription. See 5 C.F.R. § 2635.403(c) for the following definition of "financial interest":

> (1) Except as provided in paragraph (c)(2) of this section, the term financial interest is limited to financial interests that are owned by the employee or by the employee's spouse or minor children. However, the term is not limited to only those financial interests that would be disqualifying under 18 U.S.C. § 208(a) and § 2635.402. The term includes any current or contingent ownership, equity, or security interest in real or personal property or a business and may include an indebtedness or compensated employment relationship. It thus includes, for example, interests in the nature of stocks, bonds, partnership interests, fee and leasehold interests, mineral and other property rights, deeds of trust, and liens, and extends to any right to purchase or acquire any such interest, such as a stock option or commodity future. It does not include a future interest created by someone other than the employee, his spouse or dependent child or any right as a beneficiary of an estate that has not been settled. [Examples omitted]

(2) The term financial interest includes service, with or without compensation, as an officer, director, trustee, general partner or employee of any person, including a nonprofit entity, whose financial interests are imputed to the employee under § 2635.402(b)(2)(iii) or (iv).

The Ethics in Government Act of 1978, 5 U.S.C. App. § 201 et seq., further requires the public disclosure of financial information by all political appointees and all civil service employees of GS-16 and above.

A financial interest is present if it is more than insubstantial, remote, or inconsequential. In 83 OGE 1 (1983), the Office of Government Ethics ruled that vested rights in a private corporation's pension plan constituted a financial interest. In another ruling, dated August 17, 1979, the Office ruled that leaves of absence or re-employment rights with a former employer were financial interests in that company.

Case law indicates that a statutory violation occurs when the employee has both a financial stake in the outcome of the transaction and a sufficient contact with the transaction. It seems clear that the threshold is quite low for both elements. In *United States v. Mississippi Valley Generating Co.*, 364 U.S. 520 (1961), the Court gave an expansive reading to the term "transacting business" in prior § 434 and found a violation of the statute where the employee's financial stake consisted of the potential business he had generated for another employer and where his contact with the transaction involved him in preliminary contract negotiations on behalf of both parties. In that case, a temporary employee of the Bureau of the Budget who served at the request of the Bureau Chief without pay also served as an officer of a bank. An offeror on an RFP for construction of a power plant negotiated the early stages of the contract with the temporary employee and also asked him to inquire into financing with bank officials. The temporary employee was not involved in the final contract negotiations but confidentially suggested revisions to the offeror's second proposal. Regarding the employee's financial stake, the Court held that positive corruption is not a prerequisite for violation of the conflicts statute and stated at 550: "[T]he statute is more concerned with what might have happened than with what actually happened." See also *Smith v. United States*, 305 F.2d 197 (9th Cir. 1962), in which the court found a violation of § 434 even though the transaction consisted merely of an employee's failure to circumscribe the activities of subordinates who were involved in a conflict.

Although current § 208 is much broader in scope than was § 434, the cases decided under this section do not appear to have given it as strict an interpretation as was given to the prior statute. See *United States v. Ponnapula*, 246 F.3d 576 (6th Cir. 2001), finding no conflict where a person acting for the Small Business Administration in the sale of foreclosed property took a $5,000 retainer for future employment from the buyer but had no substantial participation in the transaction because her actions with regard to the sale were only ministerial; *Cexec, Inc. v. Department of Energy*, GSBCA 12909-P, 95-1 BCA ¶ 27,380, finding no conflict when an employee, whose wife had a financial interest in the winning contractor, had only peripheral contact with the procurement; and *United States v. Tierney*, 947 F.2d 854 (8th Cir. 1991), finding no conflict because the fact that the prosecutor's husband was representing the defendant's insurance company was too remote a connection. See also *Grassetti v. Weinberger*, 408 F. Supp. 142 (N.D. Cal. 1976), in which a grant applicant who had been denied a grant by the National Cancer Institute claimed a conflict of interest because the evaluation team consisted of members from institutions competing for research grants. The court denied the claim, stating that, although a conflict would arise where team members participated in a decision as to whether to award themselves a grant, the denial of a grant to another applicant was too remote to create a conflict—even though it would leave more money for their organizations.

The cases that have enforced § 208 have generally dealt with considerably greater financial interests and contacts than those in *Mississippi Valley* or *Smith*. See, for example, *United States v. Bouchey*, 860 F. Supp. 890 (D.D.C. 1994) (alleged participation by government employee in conspiracy to pay inflated consulting fees); *K & R Eng'g Co. v. United States*, 222 Ct. Cl. 340, 616 F.2d 469 (1980) (chief of a branch of the Corps of Engineers took kickbacks and profits from contracts awarded by his office to a particular contractor after giving contractor advance notice of the IFB and of the maximum amount the Corps would pay); *United States v. Conlon*, 628 F.2d 150 (D.C. Cir. 1980) (indictment under § 208 was reinstated where it was shown that the Director of the Bureau of Engraving, who was also President of the American Bank Note Development Corp. (ABNC), participated in decision making regarding replacement of a Bureau signature system with one developed by ABNC); *United States v. Irons*, 640 F.2d 872 (7th Cir. 1981) (program officer for HEW recommended to a contracting officer that an IFB be sent to a company he established for the purpose of receiving the IFB); and *United Tel. Co. of the Northwest*, GSBCA 10031-P, 89-3 BCA ¶ 22,108 (offeror disqualified because its subcontractor had used a government employee participating in the procurement as a consultant during the competition).

A potential violation of § 208 is grounds for rejection of an offer. See *NKF Eng'g, Inc. v. United States,* 805 F.2d 372 (Fed. Cir. 1986), agreeing that it was proper to reject an offer from a company that had hired a member of the source selection board after the initial evaluation and prior to the submission of the best and final offer. The court agree that there was an appearance of impropriety even though the offeror claimed that the employee had been carefully prevented from contacting members of the company who were working on the procurement.

(2) Employment Discussions

Conducting employment negotiations has also been held to be a conflict of interest under 18 U.S.C. § 208. Employment discussions are considered a financial interest by the Standards of Ethical Conduct, 5 C.F.R. § 2635.603. The following definition of "seeking employment" is found at 5 C.F.R. § 2635.603(b):

An employee is seeking employment once he has begun seeking employment within the meaning of paragraph (b)(1) of this section and until he is no longer seeking employment within the meaning of paragraph (b)(2) of this section.

(1) An employee has begun seeking employment if he has directly or indirectly:

(i) Engaged in negotiations for employment with any person. For these purposes, as for 18 U.S.C. § 208(a), the term negotiations means discussion or communication with another person, or such person's agent or intermediary, mutually conducted with a view toward reaching an agreement regarding possible employment with that person. The term is not limited to discussions of specific terms and conditions of employment in a specific position;

(ii) Made an unsolicited communication to any person, or such person's agent or intermediary, regarding possible employment with that person. However, the employee has not begun seeking employment if that communication was:

(A) For the sole purpose of requesting a job application; or

(B) For the purpose of submitting a resume or other employment proposal to a person affected by the performance or nonperformance of the employee's duties only as part of an industry or other discrete class. The employee will be considered to have begun seeking employment upon receipt of any response indicating an interest in employment discussions; or

(iii) Made a response other than rejection to an unsolicited communication from any person, or such person's agent or intermediary, regarding possible employment with that person.

(2) An employee is no longer seeking employment when:

(i) The employee or the prospective employer rejects the possibility of employment and all discussions of possible employment have terminated; or

(ii) Two months have transpired after the employee's dispatch of an unsolicited resume or employment proposal, provided the employee has received no indication of interest in employment discussions from the prospective employer.

(3) For purposes of this definition, a response that defers discussions until the foreseeable future does not constitute rejection of an unsolicited employment overture, proposal, or resume nor rejection of a prospective employment possibility.

Negotiations for employment were found in *United States v. Schaltenbrand*, 930 F.2d 1554 (11th Cir. 1991), *cert. denied*, 502 U.S. 1005 (1991), where an Air Force reserve officer approached a prospective employer, filled out an application, came for an interview, discussed his qualifications, and indicated a willingness to meet company officials, even though neither side made any formal offer until after he was finished with the project; *United States v. Lord*, 710 F. Supp. 615 (E.D.Va. 1989), *aff'd*, 902 F.2d 1567 (4th Cir. 1990), where a government program manager discussed employment with a contractor; *United States v. Gorman*, 807 F.2d 1299 (6th Cir. 1986), *cert. denied*, 484 U.S. 815 (1987), where the government employee had an initial conversation with a company and gave them a list of conditions for employment. The Principal Deputy Assistant Secretary of the Air Force for Acquisition also pled guilty to a violation of § 208 when she met with an officer of a company to discuss future employment at the same time she was negotiating a major contract with that company. See *Lockheed Martin Aeronautics Co.*, Comp. Gen. Dec. B-295401, 2005 CPD ¶ 41, for a description of this plea agreement. Compare *Air Line Pilots Ass'n, Int'l v. Department of Transportation*, 899 F.2d 1230 (D.C. Cir. 1990), in which no conflict was found where the Secretary of Transportation made a regulatory ruling at the time he was negotiating for employment with a law firm. The court based its conclusion on the fact that the law firm was not representing any of the parties to the regulatory ruling.

It is clear that terminating an immediate employment discussion will not result in rejection of an offer of employment if the discussion is only deferred. See *Express One Int'l, Inc. v. United States Postal Serv.*, 814 F. Supp. 93 (D.D.C. 1992), in which the court enjoined award of a contract because the employee of a consultant of the procuring agency had told the winning offeror "he would not be available for a personal meeting or to discuss a position until [after award of the contract]."

Violations of § 208 are valid grounds for rejecting an offer. In *AT&T Communications, Inc.*, GSBCA 9252-P, 88-2 BCA ¶ 20,805, an offeror was disqualified after receiving information from a government employee with whom it had discussed employment. Compare *Chemonics Int'l Consulting Div.*, 63 Comp. Gen. 14 (B-210426), 83-2 CPD ¶ 426, holding that it was improper to withhold award from a firm that had offered employment to a government employee who had attended subsequent negotiations, and *CACI, Inc.-Fed. v. United States*, 719 F.2d 1567 (Fed. Cir. 1983), finding no violation of § 208 when negotiations with a government employee occurred 16 months after an employment discussion had occurred. In *Four-Phase Sys., Inc.*, ASBCA 26794, 86-2 BCA ¶ 18,924, a violation of § 208 was found where employment negotiations occurred during the negotiation of a change order. As a result, the board held that the violation of § 208 was a valid defense to a breach of contract claim based on the change order.

b. Procurement Integrity Restrictions

Additional restrictions on employment contacts or discussions are contained in 41 U.S.C. § 423(c). This statute, as amended by the Clinger-Cohen Act of 1996, provides:

(c) *Actions required of procurement officers when contacted by offerors regarding non-Federal employment.* (1) If an agency official who is participating personally and substantially in a Federal agency procurement for a contract in excess of the simplified acquisition threshold contacts or is contacted by a person who is a bidder or offeror in that Federal agency procurement regarding possible non-Federal employment for that official, the official shall—

(A) promptly report the contact in writing to the official's supervisor and to the designated agency ethics official (or designee) of the agency in which the official is employed; and

(B) (i) reject the possibility of non-Federal employment; or

(ii) disqualify himself or herself from further personal and substantial participation in that Federal agency procurement until such time as the agency has authorized the official to resume participation in such procurement, in accordance with the requirements of section 208 of Title 18, United States Code, and applicable agency regulations on the grounds that—

(I) the person is no longer a bidder or offeror in that Federal agency procurement; or

(II) all discussions with the bidder or offeror regarding possible non-Federal employment have terminated without an agreement or arrangement for employment.

The new Act provides for completely different procedures than those in the former Act. It is implemented in FAR 3.104-3(c)(2) which defines a "contact" as "any of the actions included as 'seeking employment' in 5 CFR 2635.603(b)" as well as "unsolicited communications from offerors regarding possible employment." FAR 3.104-5(a) also warns that contacts by "agents or other intermediaries" of an offeror may fall within these procedures. The first step in the new procedures is an immediate reporting requirement when an agency official receives an employment contract, FAR 3.104-3(c)(1). This report must be submitted to the official's supervisor and the agency ethics official. The second step is for the official to either "reject the possibility of non-Federal employment" or disqualify himself or herself from further participation in the procurement. Under the new Act, the disqualification decision appears to be in the sole discretion of the official, while under the former Act recusal was a decision of the agency. FAR 3.104-5(b) contains the following additional reporting requirements:

(b) *Disqualification notice.* In addition to submitting the contact report required by 3.104-3(c)(1), an agency official who must disqualify himself or herself pursuant to 3.104-3(c)(1)(ii) must promptly submit written notice of disqualification from further participation in the procurement to the contracting officer, the source selection authority if other than the contracting officer, and the agency official's immediate supervisor. As a minimum, the notice must—

(1) Identify the procurement;

(2) Describe the nature of the agency official's participation in the procurement and specify the approximate dates or time period of participation; and

(3) Identify the offeror and describe its interest in the procurement.

After disqualification, FAR 3.104-5(c) places the decision on reinstatement of the official in the sole discretion of the agency as follows:

> (c) *Resumption of participation in a procurement.* (1) The official must remain disqualified until such time as the agency, at its sole and exclusive discretion, authorizes the official to resume participation in the procurement in accordance with 3.104-3(c)(1)(ii).
>
> (2) After the conditions of 3.104-3(c)(1)(ii)(A) or (B) have been met, the head of the contracting activity (HCA), after consultation with the agency ethics official, may authorize the disqualified official to resume participation in the procurement, or may determine that an additional disqualification period is necessary to protect the integrity of the procurement process. In determining the disqualification period, the HCA must consider any factors that create an appearance that the disqualified official acted without complete impartiality in the procurement. The HCA's reinstatement decision should be in writing.
>
> (3) Government officer or employee must also comply with the provisions of 18 U.S.C. 208 and 5 CFR part 2635 regarding any resumed participation in a procurement matter. Government officer or employee may not be reinstated to participate in a procurement matter affecting the financial interest of someone with whom the individual is seeking employment, unless the individual receives—
>
> (i) A waiver pursuant to 18 U.S.C. 208(b)(1) or (b)(3); or
>
> (ii) An authorization in accordance with the requirements of subpart F of 5 CFR part 2635.

The new Act also narrows the scope of these restrictions. First, the rule only applies to contracts over the simplified acquisition threshold of $100,000. Second, the rule applies only to a "Federal agency procurement," which excludes sole source contracts and contract modifications. Note, however, that entertaining employment discussions or negotiations during such transactions would be a violation of 18 U.S.C. § 208 and 5 C.F.R. § 2635.603(b). A third narrowing is that the new Act restricts only bidders and offerors from making contacts with officials regarding future employment, while the former Act restricted "any entity that is, or is reasonably likely to become, a competitor for or recipient of a contract or subcontract."

c. *Biased Decision Making*

One result of improper influence on government officials can be biased decision making. This occurred in at least two instances when the Principal Deputy Assistant Secretary for Acquisition of the Air Force admitted favoring one company over others during the source selection process. As a result, two protests were granted several years after the award of the contracts calling for the agency to reopen a long-term contract to competition for the work that could be separated from the work that had already been accomplished. See *Lockheed Martin Aeronautics Co.*, Comp. Gen. Dec. B-295401, 2005 CPD ¶ 41, and *Lockheed Martin Corp.*, Comp. Gen. Dec. B-295402, 2005 CPD ¶ 24. These decisions contain a detailed analysis of the specific actions taken by the biased Air Force official to direct the award to the company that she favored.

d. *Contracting with Government Employees*

Government employees who do not fall within the proscriptions of 18 U.S.C. § 208 because they are not involved in the procurement process are nevertheless restricted from entering into contracts with any agency of the government. FAR 3.601(a) states:

> Except as specified in 3.602, a contracting officer shall not knowingly award a contract to a Government employee or to a business concern or other organization owned or substantially owned or controlled by one or more Government employees. This policy is intended to avoid any conflict of interest that might arise between the employees' interests and their Government duties, and to avoid the appearance of favoritism or preferential treatment by the Government toward its employees.

Valiant Sec. Agency, Comp. Gen. Dec. B-205087, 81-2 CPD ¶ 367, *recons. denied*, 81-2 CPD ¶ 501, explains this policy as follows:

> Contracts between the Government and its employees are not expressly prohibited by statute except where the employee acts for both the Government and the contractor in a particular transaction or where the service to be rendered is such as could be required of the contractor in his capacity as a Government employee. 18 U.S.C. § 208 (1976); *Hugh Maher*, B-187841, March 31, 1977, 77-1 CPD ¶ 204. However, it has long been recognized that such contracts are undesirable because among other reasons they invite criticism as to alleged favoritism and possible fraud and that they should be authorized only in exceptional cases where the Government cannot reasonably be otherwise supplied. 27 Comp. Gen. 735 (1948); *Capital Aero, Inc.*, B-183833, September 30, 1975, 75-2 CPD ¶ 201; *Burgos & Associates, Inc.*, 59 Comp. Gen. 273 (1980), 80-1 CPD ¶ 155. The fact that a service would be more expensive if not obtained from an employee of the Government does not by itself provide support for a determination that the service cannot reasonably be obtained from other sources. 55 Comp. Gen. 681 (1976).

The sole exception to this prohibition is in FAR 3.602, which requires a determination by a high-level official that there is a "most compelling reason" to enter into a contract with a former government employee, such as when the government's needs cannot otherwise reasonably be met. The contracting officer has discretion in determining whether this exemption applies. Compare the *Valiant* case with *International Alliance of Sports Officials*, Comp. Gen. Dec. B-210172, 83-2 CPD ¶ 328, sustaining a contracting officer's decision to award a contract at approximately $223,000 in contrast to the next low offer of $275,000.

Substantial ownership or control is determined by the facts of each individual case. Mere employment by a government contractor is not prohibited by this restriction. See *National Serv. Corp.*, Comp. Gen. Dec. B-205629, 82-2 CPD ¶ 76 (no substantial ownership or control when government employee gave up partnership and became part-time bookkeeper), and *H H & K Builders, Inc.*, Comp. Gen. Dec. B-238095, 90-1 CPD ¶ 219 (sole owner's husband was government employee, but sufficient separation of ownership). Compare *Electronics West, Inc.*, Comp. Gen. Dec. B-209720, 83-2 CPD ¶ 127 (change in title from President to Treasurer did not prevent disqualification). An agency does not have to establish with certainty that an employee has a substantially controlling interest but rather needs only to have a reason to believe that the government employee has such control, *Gurley's Inc.*, Comp. Gen. Dec. B-253852, 93-2 CPD ¶ 123. See *Elogene Thurman*, Comp. Gen. Dec. B-206325, 82-1 CPD ¶ 487 (award to wife of government employee improper when husband in fact ran the business); *American Truss & Mfg. Corp.*, Comp. Gen. Dec. B-205962, 82-1 CPD ¶ 477 (award improper where government employee owned 50 percent of stock and wife owned balance); *Marc Indus.*, Comp. Gen. Dec. B-246528, 92-1 CPD ¶ 273 (substantial control found where government employee represented the firm in pre-work conferences under prior contracts with the agency, served as the contact for any complaints about contract performance, and, based on his involvement with the firm, was disciplined for violating his agency's conflict of interest regulations); and *KSR, Inc.*, Comp. Gen. Dec. B-250160, 93-1 CPD ¶ 37 (substantial control found where government employee was president and was one of five owners). The restriction does not apply when a contractor employee has a similar conflict with a subcontractor, *Science Pump Corp.*, Comp. Gen. Dec. B-255737, 94-1 CPD ¶ 246.

Some agencies have further restrictions on contracting with members of a former government employee's family. See, for example, *Joann Flora*, Comp. Gen. Dec. B-212776, 83-2 CPD ¶ 520 (regulations prohibiting contract with immediate member of the household of agency employee barred contract with unmarried party living as spouse), and *Heidi Holley*, Comp. Gen. Dec. B-211746, 83-2 CPD ¶ 241 (regulations stating that contracts should generally not be awarded to members of an agency employee's family and requiring close scrutiny barred award to spouse of agency employee required to supervise contract).

If the contracting officer inadvertently makes an award to a company owned or controlled by a government employee, the GAO will not disturb the award absent an indication of favoritism or other impropriety, *Sterling Med. Assocs.*, 62 Comp. Gen. 230 (B-209493), 83-1 CPD ¶ 215; *Biosystems Analysis, Inc.*, Comp. Gen. Dec. B-198846, 80-2 CPD ¶ 149. In both cases, the employee worked for an agency other than the one awarding the contract.

5. Anti-Kickback Act

Contractors and subcontractors are prohibited from soliciting, accepting, or attempting to accept any kickbacks from their subcontractors by the Anti-Kickback Act of 1986, 41 U.S.C. §§ 51-58. The Act contains a broad definition of the term "kickback," as follows:

> The term "kickback" means any money, fee, commission, credit, gift, gratuity, thing of value, or compensation of any kind which is provided, directly or indirectly, to any prime contractor, prime contractor employee, subcontractor, or subcontractor employee for the purpose of improperly obtaining or rewarding favorable treatment in connection with a prime contract or in connection with a subcontract relating to a prime contract.

The purpose of this statute is to prevent payments that impede the competitive process. The typical kickback is paid to a purchasing agent of a contractor or subcontractor to obtain the award of a subcontract without having to participate in a fair competition. The purchasing agent, in turn, takes some action that distorts the competition The presumption is that the government eventually pays the amount of the kickback in higher prices, and the Act permits the procuring agency to reduce the price by the amount of the kickback. The Act also contains criminal and civil sanctions.

The Act is implemented in FAR 3.502, and the Anti-Kickback Procedures clause is at FAR 52.203-7. This clause requires the contractor to have internal procedures to detect and prevent kickbacks. It also requires the prompt reporting of kickbacks and cooperation with government agencies in the investigation of kickbacks. The clause is not required for contracts under $100,000 or contracts for the acquisition of commercial items, § 4104 (civilian agency acquisitions) and § 8301 (armed services acquisitions) of the Federal Acquisition Streamlining Act of 1994, Pub. L. No. 103-355. However, such procurements are still subject to the Act.

There has been very little significant litigation under this Act. However, see *Morse Diesel Int'l, Inc. v. United States*, 66 Fed. Cl. 788 (2005), finding a violation of the Act when the contractor's surety bond broker paid 50 percent of its commissions to the contractor in exchange for the right to be its exclusive broker. See also *Aalco Forwarding, Inc.*, Comp. Gen. Dec. B-277241.8, 97-2 CPD ¶ 110, holding that payment of commissions or rebates from tariff rates from carriers to brokers under government contract were not per se violations of the Act, and *United States v. Guthrie*, 64 F.3d 1510 (10th Cir. 1995), holding that contractors can be required to pay restitution for violations of the Act.

There was considerable litigation under a prior Act that was narrower in scope. There the courts required proof of specific intent and construed the value and intent elements of the kickback prohibition, following the cases on bribery, *Howard v. United States*, 345 F.2d 126 (1st Cir.), *cert. denied*, 382 U.S. 838 (1965). In addition, it was held that the government was not precluded from suing under both this Act and the False Claims Act, *United States v. General Dynamics Corp.*, 19 F.3d 770 (2d Cir. 1994).

6. Covenant Against Contingent Fees

The government has a long-standing policy against the payment of contingent fees. This policy developed because of the government's concern that contingent fee arrangements expose government agencies to corrupting influences. It also reflects the government's recognition that such agreements could allow for the payment of exorbitant fees by contractors, leading to higher costs for the government, thereby resulting in an unnecessary waste of public funds. See *Quinn v. Gulf & Western Corp.*, 644 F.2d 89 (2d Cir. 1981). Thus, a clause is required in negotiated contracts by statute, 10 U.S.C. § 2306(b) and 41 U.S.C. § 254(a), and in sealed bid procurements by regulation, FAR 3.404. As provided by the Federal Acquisition Streamlining Act, the requirement does not apply to contracts at or below the simplified acquisition threshold of $100,000 (§ 4102(b) and § 8204(b), civilian agency and armed services, respectively) or to a contract for the acquisition of commercial items (§ 4103(c) and § 8105(a), civilian agency and armed services, respectively). The clause to be used is contained in FAR 52.203-5:

> COVENANT AGAINST CONTINGENT FEES (APR 1984)
>
> (a) The Contractor warrants that no person or agency has been employed or retained to solicit or obtain this contract upon an agreement or understanding for a contingent fee, except a bona fide employee or agency. For breach or violation of this warranty, the Government shall have the right to annul this contract without liability or, in its discretion, to deduct from the contract price or consideration, or otherwise recover, the full amount of the contingent fee.
>
> (b) "Bona fide agency," as used in this clause, means an established commercial or selling agency, maintained by a contractor for the purpose of securing business, that neither exerts nor proposes to exert improper influence to solicit or obtain Government contracts nor holds itself out as being able to obtain any Government contract or contracts through improper influence.
>
> "Bona fide employee," as used in this clause, means a person, employed by a contractor and subject to the contractor's supervision and control as to time, place, and manner of performance, who neither exerts nor proposes to exert improper influence to solicit or obtain Government contracts nor holds out as being able to obtain any Government contract or contracts though improper influence.

"Contingent fee," as used in this clause, means any commission, percentage, brokerage, or other fee that is contingent upon the success that a person or concern has in securing a Government contract.

"Improper influence," as used in this clause, means any influence that induces or tends to induce a Government employee or officer to give consideration or to act regarding a Government contract on any basis other than the merits of the matter.

The covenant does not prohibit the payment of all contingent fees—only those made for the purpose of obtaining a contract. In *Browne v. R & R Eng'g Co.*, 264 F.2d 219 (3d Cir. 1959), the court held that contingent fee services in connection with a proposed contract that did not involve any dealings with officials responsible for the award of contracts were not prohibited. The GAO has followed this ruling. See *Holmes & Narver Servs., Inc.*, 70 Comp. Gen. 424 (B-242240), 91-1 CPD ¶ 373, where an incumbent contractor offered to sell access to its employees and competitively useful contract information to potential offerors, who agreed to purchase inventory and equipment at set prices if they won the contract. The GAO held that this was not a prohibited contingent fee arrangement because the payment would not be made for the purpose of soliciting or obtaining the contract at issue and the arrangement did not involve any dealings with government officials. See also *Kasler Elec. Co.*, DOTCAB 1425, 84-2 BCA ¶ 17,374, where a payment to a nonemployee estimator was contingent on award of the contract. The board held that the arrangement did not violate the covenant, since the estimator's function was to price out a bid and not to solicit a government contract.

In addition, the covenant does not apply to a bona fide employee or bona fide agency. See *Acme Process Equip. Co. v. United States*, 171 Ct. Cl. 251, 347 F.2d 538 (1965), setting forth factors to be considered in determining whether the recipient of a contingent fee falls within this "bona fide" rule. The FAR contains no guidance on this issue. However, an earlier version of the FAR contained the following factors at FAR 3.408-2(c):

(1) The fee should not be inequitable or exorbitant when compared to the services performed or to customary fees for similar services related to commercial business.

(2) The agency should have adequate knowledge of the contractor's products and business, as well as other qualifications necessary to sell the products or services on their merits.

(3) The contractor and the agency should have a continuing relationship or, in newly established relationships, should contemplate future continuity.

(4) The agency should be an established concern that has existed for a considerable period, or be a newly established going concern likely to continue in the future. The business of the agency should be conducted in the agency name and characterized by the customary indicia of the conduct of regular business.

(5) While an agency that confines its selling activities to Government contracts is not disqualified, the fact that an agency represents the contractor in Government and commercial sales should receive favorable consideration.

Established sales arrangements that are not confined to sales to the government do not violate the covenant, *Puma Indus. Consulting, Inc. v. Daal Assocs., Inc.*, 808 F.2d 982 (2d Cir. 1987). In *General Sales Agency*, Comp. Gen. Dec. B-24133.2, 92-1 CPD ¶ 544, a newly established arrangement with a sales organization for a 7½ percent contingent fee was held proper because the parties anticipated that the arrangement would be long-standing and no improper influence had been exerted to obtain the contract. See also *Howard Johnson Lodge*, Comp. Gen. Dec. B-244302.2, 92-1 CPD ¶ 305, in which a 10 percent contingent fee was held proper because there was "no hint" of improper influence in the arrangement. Similarly, in *Convention Mktg. Servs.*, Comp. Gen. Dec. B-245660.3, 92-1 CPD ¶ 144, no violation was found where contractors had entered into contingent fee arrangements with sales agents to assist in the acquisition and preparation of contracts, but they had exerted no improper influence to solicit or obtain the contracts. The GAO stated that "[t]he fact that an agent's fee is contingent upon the contractor receiving the contract award is insufficient to bring a fee arrangement under the contingent fee prohibition; rather, the regulation contemplates a specific demonstration that an agent is retained for the express purpose of contacting Government officials." See *Wickes Indus., Inc.*, ASBCA 17376, 75-1 BCA ¶ 11,180, for a decision in which the government was not allowed to cancel a contract where a contingency arrangement was bona fide considering the factors set forth in the DAR. See also Comp. Gen. Dec. B-157815, Jan. 21, 1966, *Unpub.*

The bona fide employee exemption focuses on the nature of the arrangement between the agent and the contractor. In *Quinn v. Gulf & Western Corp.*, 644 F.2d 89 (2d Cir. 1981), a contract was held to be unenforceable because the contingent fee arrangement between the turbine blade manufacturer and the owner of the consulting firm, who was also a special government employee, failed to satisfy the bona fide employee criterion.

C. Honesty in Dealing

One of the most important requirements of the public contracting process is that contractors and subcontractors be honest in their dealings with governmental agencies and contractors. This section reviews this requirement by first discussing the applicable statutes and then considering the major types of conduct that have been found to violate this requirement.

1. Statutory Requirements

In federal contracting, the requirement for honesty and disclosure of facts is supported by a number of criminal and civil statutes imposing a variety of penalties on contractors and others who do not comply with the minimum standards of disclosure and honesty.

a. *False Claims*

The fundamental federal statute with the goal of promoting honesty in dealing is the False Claims Act. This Act was originally enacted in 1863 to prevent fraud and is now divided into a civil provision in 31 U.S.C. § 3729 and a criminal provision in 18 U.S.C. § 287.

(1) Civil Fraud

For many years this provision was set forth in 31 U.S.C. § 231. In 1982 it was codified in 31 U.S.C. § 3729 and amended by the False Claims Amendments Act of 1986 to read as follows:

(a) Liability for certain acts. Any person who—

> (1) knowingly presents, or causes to be presented, to an officer or employee of the United States Government or a member of the Armed Forces of the United States a false or fraudulent claim for payment or approval;
>
> (2) knowingly makes, uses, or causes to be made or used, a false record or statement to get a false or fraudulent claim paid or approved by the Government;
>
> (3) conspires to defraud the Government by getting a false or fraudulent claim allowed or paid;
>
> (4) has possession, custody, or control of property or money used, or to be used, by the Government and, intending to defraud the Government or willfully to conceal the property, delivers, or causes to be delivered, less property than the amount for which the person receives a certificate or receipt;
>
> (5) authorized to make or deliver a document certifying receipt of property used, or to be used, by the Government and, intending to defraud the Government, makes or delivers the receipt without completely knowing that the information on the receipt is true;
>
> (6) knowingly buys, or receives as a pledge of an obligation or debt, public property from an officer or employee of the Government, or a member of the Armed Forces, who lawfully may not sell or pledge the property; or
>
> (7) knowingly makes, uses, or causes to be made or used, a false record or statement to conceal, avoid, or decrease an obligation to pay or transmit money or property to the Government, is liable to the United States

> Government for a civil penalty of not less than $5,000 and not more than $10,000, plus 3 times the amount of damages which the Government sustains because of the act of that person, except if the court finds that—
>
> > (A) the person committing the violation of this subsection furnished officials of the United States responsible for investigating false claims violations with all information known to such person about the violation within 30 days after the date on which the defendant first obtained the information;
> >
> > (B) such person fully cooperated with any Government investigation of such violation; and
> >
> > (C) at the time such person furnished the United States with the information about the violation, no criminal prosecution, civil action, or administrative action had commenced under this title with respect to such violation, and the person did not have actual knowledge of the existence of an investigation into such violation;
>
> the court may assess not less than 2 times the amount of damages which the Government sustains because of the act of the person. A person violating this subsection shall also be liable to the United States Government for the costs of a civil action brought to recover any such penalty or damages.

In *Hughes Aircraft Co. v. Schumer*, 520 U.S. 939 (1997), the Court held that the 1986 amendment does not apply to actions that took place prior to its enactment.

(A) Specific Intent

Under the Act, as amended in 1986, the government can establish liability without showing that the contractor had a specific intent to defraud as long as the act is committed knowingly. "Knowing," which was not defined in the original Act, is now defined as (1) actual knowledge of the information, (2) deliberate ignorance of the truth or falsity of the information, or (3) reckless disregard of the truth or falsity of the information. Further, the Act specifically states that "no proof of specific intent to defraud is required." See *United States v. TDC Mgmt. Corp.*, 24 F.3d 292 (D.C. Cir. 1994), stating at 298:

> To prevail under the False Claims Act, the government must prove either that TDC actually knew it had omitted material information from its monthly progress reports or that it recklessly disregarded or deliberately ignored that possibility. The government need not prove that TDC intended to deceive the government by omitting such information.

Reckless disregard has been called the "loosest" of the three standards, *United States ex rel. Siewick v. Jamieson Science & Eng'g, Inc.*, 214 F.3d 1372 (D.C. Cir.

2000). Thus, failure to review Medicare claims prepared by others has been held to be reckless disregard, *United States v. Krizek*, 111 F.3d 934 (D.C. Cir. 1997). Similarly, filing an equitable adjustment claim for "actual costs" when estimates are used is reckless disregard, *UMC Elecs. Co. v. United States*, 43 Fed. Cl. 776 (1999). However, failing to consult a lawyer prior to submitting a claim for payment is not reckless disregard, *United States ex rel. Quirk v. Madonna Towers, Inc.*, 278 F.3d 765 (8th Cir. 2002). Reckless disregard does not extend to simple negligence or mistakes, *United States v. United Tech. Corp.*, 51 F. Supp. 2d 167 (D. Conn. 1999) (no liability for honest mistake); *Wang ex rel. United States v. FMC Corp.*, 975 F.2d 1412 (9th Cir. 1992) (engineering miscalculations and lack of engineering insight no more than innocent mistake); *First Interstate Bank v. United States*, 27 Fed. Cl. 348 (1992) (mere negligence by bank would not satisfy requirement of "knowing").

Since what constitutes the offense is not an intent to deceive but a knowing presentation of a claim that is either "fraudulent" or simply "false," the fact that a germane government official knew of a claim's falsity may not be a defense, *Hagood v. Sonoma County Water Agency*, 929 F.2d 1416 (9th Cir. 1991) (government officials condoned contractor's inaccurate cost allocation, violating federal water supply law). However, the government's knowledge may be relevant in proving that the defendant did not submit a claim with "deliberate ignorance" or "reckless disregard" of the "truth or falsity of the information." For example, in *Chemray Coatings Corp. v. United States*, 29 Fed. Cl. 278 (1993), the court held that the government's knowledge of the condition of paint pigment contaminated by fire debris, for which the contractor received payment under a termination for convenience settlement, was relevant to the determination of False Claims Act liability, stating at 284:

> GSA's knowledge of the contents of the drums is relevant for purposes of section 3729(a). Intent to deceive need not be proved under the Act. . . . What must be proved is that the contractor knowingly presented a false or fraudulent claim. . . . If GSA officials knew that the drums referred to in the termination for convenience settlement contained debris and [the contractor] did not know that its representation of the contents was false, [the contractor] is not guilty of "knowingly" making a false or fraudulent statement to the Government.

Similarly, in *United States ex rel. Durcholz v. FKW, Inc.*, 189 F.3d 542 (7th Cir. 1999), the court held that the government's approval of the particulars of a claim demonstrated that the claim was not "knowingly" false, and in *United States ex rel. Lamers v. City of Green Bay*, 168 F.3d 1013 (7th Cir. 1999), the court held that discussions of a method of using grant funds with city officials showed lack of knowing falsehood. See also *United States ex rel. Becker v. Westinghouse Savannah River Co.*, 305 F.3d 284 (4th Cir. 2002), finding no false claim where the company changed its accounts to reflect a pending change in congressional appropriations at the request of the government agency. The court found that although the company may have "negligently disregarded" whether Congress had approved the change, this did not meet the scienter requirement of the Act.

Generally, proof that a statement or action was in accord with a reasonable interpretation of the contract or regulation will be sufficient to demonstrate a lack of intent. See *United States ex rel. Lamers v. City of Green Bay*, 168 F.3d 1013 (7th Cir. 1998) (even though the City's interpretation of regulations was questionable, a review of all of the facts indicated that it did not intend to defraud the government); *United States ex rel. Hochman v. Nackman*, 145 F.3d 1069 (9th Cir. 1998) (good faith interpretation of contract indicates lack of intent); *United States ex rel. Lindenthal v. General Dynamics Corp.*, 61 F.3d 1402 (9th Cir. 1995) (parties' interpretation of ambiguous specification indicated lack of intent). Contrast *United States ex rel. Oliver v. Parsons Co.*, 195 F.3d 457 (9th Cir. 1999), in which the court held that the question of reasonableness of the interpretation of a regulation was not dispositive but that the district court should address the question of intent directly. The result of this reasoning could be that a false claim could be found because the contractor's interpretation was not made in good faith but with the intent to defraud the government. Accord, *United States ex rel. Minn. Ass'n of Nurse Anesthetists v. Allina Health Sys. Corp.*, 276 F.3d 1032 (8th Cir. 2002) (submitting a bill based on a reasonable interpretation of an ambiguous regulation is a false claim if the submitter knows that the government interprets the regulation differently). See also *United States v. Rule Indus., Inc.*, 878 F.2d 535 (1st Cir. 1989), in which the court affirmed a jury determination that the contractor had defrauded the government by following its interpretation of the ambiguous Buy American Act.

(b) Definition of "Claim"

A "claim" for purposes of the False Claims Act is any demand upon the government for the payment of money or the transfer of property, *United States v. Tieger*, 234 F.2d 589 (3d Cir.), *cert. denied*, 352 U.S. 941 (1956). In *Tieger*, the court found no claim where the defendant had fraudulently induced the government to guarantee loans but no demand for satisfaction of the guarantee had been made against the government. Similarly, no claim was found in *United States ex rel. Butler v. Hughes Helicopters, Inc.*, 71 F.3d 321 (9th Cir. 1995), finding no false claim when the contractor submitted a DD 250 "material Inspection and Receiving Report." See also *United States v. Farina*, 153 F. Supp. 819 (D.N.J. 1957), where a bidder had conspired with a government employee to submit a lower bid after the bids had been opened. While the court recognized that such conduct subverted the competitive bidding process, it found no claim because no contract had been awarded and hence no request for payment was made. But any request for payment will constitute a claim. See *United States ex rel. Marcus v. Hess*, 317 U.S. 537 (1943), finding a claim where the contractor submitted a payment voucher on a contract obtained through collusive bidding. The Court held that the Act covered all claims grounded in fraud. See also *Bly-Magee v. California*, 236 F.3d 1014 (9th Cir. 2001), finding a claim when the defendant allegedly defrauded the state on a federal program where overpayments to a state would not revert to the United States Treasury but would be distributed to other states.

The demand for payment need not be based on an existing contractual relationship since the Act encompasses all fraudulent attempts to cause the government to pay out a sum of money, *United States v. Neifert-White Co.*, 390 U.S. 228 (1968) (false application to Federal Commodity Credit Corp. for loan held to be claim). The Act has been held to apply to a subcontractor's failure to comply with specifications, *United States ex rel. Varljen v. Cleveland Gear Co.*, 250 F.3d 426 (6th Cir. 2001); a knowing misrepresentation about the need for and cost of using a subcontractor, *Harrison v. Westinghouse Savannah River Co.*, 176 F.3d 776 (4th Cir. 1999); endorsement and deposit of government checks known to have been issued by mistake, *United States v. McLeod*, 721 F.2d 282 (9th Cir. 1983); repeated inclusion of rejected items in shipments, *United States v. Milton Marks Corp.*, 240 F.2d 838 (3d Cir. 1957); fraudulently submitted Medicare claim forms by health care providers, *United States v. Lorenzo*, 768 F. Supp. 1127 (E.D. Pa. 1991); cashing fraudulently obtained social security checks, *United States v. Fowler*, 282 F. Supp. 1 (E.D.N.Y. 1968); submission of false payroll reports, *United States v. Greenberg*, 237 F. Supp. 439 (S.D.N.Y. 1965); and endorsement and deposit of government checks known to have been issued by mistake, *Scolnick v. United States*, 331 F.2d 598 (1st Cir. 1964).

Some courts have held that a demand for payment can be false if the contractor submitting the invoice is not in compliance with contract requirements at the time of submission. Thus, some courts have held that there is an "implied certification of compliance in such situations." See *United States ex rel. Augustine v. Century Health Servs., Inc.*, 289 F.3d 409 (6th Cir. 2002) (implied certification that contractor would continue to be in compliance with regulations after submission of cost report); *Shaw v. AAA Eng'g & Drafting, Inc.*, 213 F.3d 519 (10th Cir. 2000) (implied certification that contractor was in compliance with environmental requirements of contract); *BMY-Combat Sys. Div. of Harsco Corp. v. United States*, 38 Fed. Cl. 109 (1997) (invoices of contractor impliedly but falsely represented contractual compliance, which was "critical to defendant's decision to pay"); *United States ex rel. Pogue v. American Healthcorp, Inc.*, 914 F. Supp. 1507 (M.D. Tenn. 1996) (by submitting Medicare claims defendants implicitly certified compliance with the statutes, rules, and regulations governing the Medicare program); *Ab-Tech Constr., Inc. v. United States*, 31 Fed. Cl. 429 (1994), *aff'd,* 57 F.3d 1084 (Fed. Cir. 1995) ("payment vouchers represented an implied certification by Ab-Tech of its continuing adherence to the requirements for participation in the [minority-owned business] program"). Not all courts have agreed with this theory, holding that there can be a false claim of this nature only when a certification is an express condition of payment of the claim. See *Mikes v. Straus*, 274 F.3d 687 (2d Cir. 2001); *United States ex rel. Siewick v. Jamieson Science & Eng'g, Inc.*, 214 F.3d 1372 (D.C. Cir. 2000); *Harrison v. Westinghouse Savannah River Co.*, 176 F.3d 776 (4th Cir. 1999); *United States ex rel. Thompson v. Columbia/HCA Healthcare Corp.*, 125 F.3d 899 (5th Cir. 1997); *United States ex rel. Hopper v. Anton,* 91 F.3d 1261 (9th Cir.1996); and *United States ex rel. Joslin v. Cmty. Home Health of Md., Inc.*, 984 F. Supp. 374 (D. Md. 1997).

"Reverse false claims" also fall under the Act, 31 U.S.C. § 3729(a)(7). These are actions taken to prevent the government from making a claim against the contractor or obtaining the full amount owed by a contractor. For example, in *United States v. Pemco Aeroplex, Inc.*, 195 F.3d 1234 (11th Cir. 1999), a false claim was found where the contractor identified valuable and usable inventory as scrap and bought it at a very low price. See also *United States v. Eilberg*, 507 F. Supp. 267 (E.D. Pa. 1980), in which the court found a false claim when a former congressman submitted a false certification intended to prevent the government from demanding reimbursement of funds previously paid. See also *United States v. Raymond & Whitcomb Co.*, 53 F. Supp. 2d 436 (S.D.N.Y. 1999) (claims include false statement intended to conceal obligation to government). Compare *American Textile Mfrs. Inst., Inc. v. The Limited, Inc.*, 190 F.3d 729 (6th Cir. 1999), holding that false statements made to avoid payment of fines were not reverse false claims because the obligation to the government must exist before the false statement is made, and *United States v. Q Int'l Courier, Inc.*, 131 F.3d 770 (8th Cir. 1997), finding no reverse false claim because there was no "existing, specific legal duty in the nature of a debt" owed to the government.

(c) Materiality

Although the Act is silent on the issue, some courts have held that liability only attaches if the false claim is material. False claims have been held to be material only if they are "an essential, important, or pertinent part of the claim," *Tyger Constr. Co. v. United States*, 28 Fed. Cl. 35 (1993). In that case, the court held the contractor's legal arguments in a Contract Disputes Act claim were not false claims because they were opinions, not facts and hence did not have a tendency to influence a decision maker in the government. See *United States ex rel. Berge v. Board of Trs.*, 104 F.3d 1453 (4th Cir. 1997), holding that minor misstatements on a grant application did not influence the decision to award the grant. See also *United States v. Intervest Corp.*, 67 F. Supp. 2d 637 (S.D. Miss. 1999), holding that false statements about the condition of property did not influence the decision to pay invoices for the property (based on testimony of a government employee that she would know the true condition when she authorized payment).

(d) Qui Tam

Any person may bring a civil action (termed "qui tam") under the Act "for the person and the United States," and the action is "brought in the name of the United States," 31 U.S.C. § 3730(b). The qui tam plaintiff (termed "the relator") files a civil complaint. The complaint is sealed while the government decides whether to take over the case. If the government intervenes, it bears primary responsibility for prosecuting the action, 31 U.S.C. § 3730(c)(1). If the government elects not to proceed with the action, the person who initiated the action has the right to conduct the action, 31 U.S.C. § 3730(c)(3). In either case, the elements of the action are the same as discussed above.

Qui tam actions are barred if they are based on a "public disclosure" of the fraudulent activity unless the relator is an "original source" of the information on which the fraud allegations are based, 31 U.S.C. § 3730(e). This limitation on qui tam suits has generated a substantial amount of litigation peripheral to the actual proof of the fraud.

Public disclosure occurs when the allegations upon which the qui tam suit is based are affirmatively disclosed to the public, *United States ex rel. Ramseyer v. Century Healthcare Corp.*, 90 F.3d 1514 (10th Cir. 1996). In that case, the court held that a relator whose allegations were similar to findings made in a routine state audit report did not base her suit on publicly disclosed information because the report remained in government files and was never released to the public. Similarly, in *United States ex rel. Newsham v. Lockheed Missiles & Space Co.*, 190 F.3d 963 (9th Cir. 1999), there was no public disclosure when the relator alleged continuing violations of conduct that, unknown to her, had been previously disclosed. Compare *United States ex rel. Fine v. MK-Ferguson Co.*, 99 F.3d 1538 (10th Cir. 1996), in which the court held that a qui tam suit filed by a former government auditor was barred under § 3730(e). The court found that the complaint was substantially identical to a government audit report that had been sent to a state without any restriction on dissemination. Similarly, in *United States ex rel. Fine v. Advanced Sciences, Inc.*, 99 F.3d 1000 (10th Cir. 1996), the court held that a qui tam suit filed by a former government auditor was barred because the action was substantially identical to a memorandum, which contained allegations and transactions set out in a government audit, that the relator had given to his representative in an unrelated age discrimination case. The court found that the memorandum was made public when it was disclosed to an American Association of Retired Persons representative. In *United States ex rel. Doe v. John Doe Corp.*, 960 F.2d 318 (2d Cir. 1992), the court held that a public disclosure occurred when federal investigators executing a search warrant informed employees of their investigation into fraudulent overcharging. Information that has been furnished to a requester under the Freedom of Information Act (FOIA) will be considered publicly disclosed, *United States ex rel. Mistick PBT v. Housing Auth. of Pittsburgh*, 186 F.3d 376 (3d Cir. 1999). There is one unreported decision holding that information obtainable through FOIA is publicly disclosed even though it has not yet been furnished, *United States ex rel. Branhan v. Mercy Health Sys.*, No. 98-3127 (6th Cir. 1999). But see *United States ex rel. Schumer v. Hughes Aircraft Co.*, 63 F.3d 1512 (9th Cir. 1995), in which the court held that information cannot be deemed to be publicly disclosed if it is only theoretically available through the FOIA. Some courts have held that information made available through discovery is also considered to be publicly disclosed even if the material has not been filed with the court, *United States ex rel. Stinson v. Prudential Ins. Co.*, 944 F.2d 1149 (3d Cir. 1991); *United States ex rel. Kreindler & Kreindler v. United Tech. Corp.*, 985 F.2d 1148 (2d Cir. 1993). Other courts have held that discovery material is considered publicly disclosed only when actually filed and not subject to protective order, *United States ex rel. Springfield Terminal Ry. Co. v. Quinn*, 14 F.3d 645 (D.C. Cir. 1994); *United States & Mathews v. Bank of Farmington*, 166 F.3d

853 (7th Cir. 1999); *United States ex rel. Ramseyer v. Century Healthcare Corp.*, 90 F.3d 1514 (10th Cir. 1996).

If public disclosure is found, the suit will not be barred unless it is based on the disclosed information. Most courts hold that this is determined by comparing the allegations to the disclosed information. Using this test, a suit can be found to be based on disclosed information even if the relator did not learn of the allegations from the disclosure. Thus, in *United States ex rel. Fine v. MK-Ferguson Co.*, 99 F.3d 1538 (10th Cir. 1996), the court examined whether a qui tam complaint was based upon a publicly disclosed audit report. The court held that "based upon" means "supported by" and the inquiry is "whether the relator's complaint is 'substantially identical' to the allegations contained in the public disclosure." The court compared the audit report with the complaint and found substantial identity and thus barred the action. See also *United States ex rel. Mistick PBT v. Housing Auth. of Pittsburgh*, 186 F.3d 376 (3d Cir. 1999) (public disclosure contained essential elements of complaint); *United States ex rel. Biddle v. Board of Trs.*, 161 F.3d 533 (9th Cir. 1998), *cert. denied*, 526 U.S. 1066 (1999) (irrelevant if source of knowledge is different from public disclosure if allegations are the same); *United States ex rel. McKenzie v. BellSouth Tel., Inc.*. 123 F.3d 935 (6th Cir. 1997), *cert. denied*, 522 U.S. 1077 (1998) (suit partially based upon the allegations brought in other suits). The Second Circuit has held that "based upon" should be defined as "the same as," *United States ex rel. Doe v. John Doe Corp.*, 960 F.2d 318 (2d Cir. 1992). Other circuits interpret the phrase "based upon" to mean "derived from." See *United States ex rel. Siller v. Becton Dickinson & Co.*, 21 F.3d 1339 (4th Cir.), *cert. denied*, 513 U.S. 928 (1994), in which the court stated that the "derived from" definition would grant jurisdiction when the relator's suit would not be "based upon" public disclosures of which the relator had no knowledge. In this case, the relator learned of the overcharging through an independent source and thus the court held that the information was not based upon public disclosures. When the facts show that the relator used the disclosed information, it will be barred under either test. See, for example, *United States ex rel. Fine v. Advanced Sciences, Inc.*, 99 F.3d 1000 (10th Cir. 1996), in which the court found that the plaintiff's qui tam complaint was "based upon" a memorandum that had been publicly disclosed because he admitted that the costs specified in the memorandum provided the basis for the allegations in his complaint and his knowledge about the practices of Advanced Sciences came in part from the work papers of the memorandum.

If the relator is the original source of the information, public disclosure will not be a bar to the suit. To be considered an original source a plaintiff must have direct and independent knowledge of the allegations in the qui tam suit and voluntarily provide the information to the government before filing the suit, 31 U.S.C. § 3730(e)(4). In *United States ex rel. Barth v. Ridgedale Elec., Inc.*, 44 F.3d 699 (8th Cir. 1995), the court stated at 703:

> "Independent knowledge" has been consistently defined as knowledge that is not dependent on public disclosure. See, e.g., *United States ex rel. Stinson, Lyons, Gerlin & Bustamante, P.A. v. Prudential Ins. Co.*, 944 F.2d 1149, 1160 (3d Cir. 1991).

In *United States ex rel. Devlin, Sidicane, & Kodman v. State of Cal.*, 84 F.3d 358 (9th Cir. 1996), the court held that the relators could not meet the original source test because, while they were a source for a news article, they had learned of the fraud from an employee of the defendant and did not have sufficient firsthand information to satisfy the direct knowledge prong of the original source test. In *United States ex rel. Fine v. MK-Ferguson Co.*, 99 F.3d 1538 (10th Cir. 1996), the court held that the plaintiff did not have direct and independent knowledge because the plaintiff did not discover the alleged fraud but rather was the supervisor to whom the auditors reported the fraud. See also *Seal 1 v. Seal A*, 255 F.3d 1154 (9th Cir. 2001), holding that the relator of information against one contractor was not an original source for the information as it was used against another contractor because he did not play a sufficient role with regard to the second contractor. Government contracts attorneys who learned of the information during a bid protest are not original sources, *United States ex rel. Grayson & Hodges v. Advanced Mgmt. Tech., Inc.*, 221 F.3d 580 (4th Cir. 2000). Compare *United States ex rel. Minn. Ass'n of Nurse Anesthetists v. Allina Health Sys. Corp.*, 276 F.3d 1032 (8th Cir. 2002), holding that an association can be an original source because its members had direct knowledge of the alleged fraud. A person who is obligated as part of his or her job to investigate and report fraud will not be considered an original source, *United States ex rel. LeBlanc v. Raytheon Co.*, 913 F.2d 17 (1st Cir. 1990) (quality assurance specialist); *United States ex rel. Fine v. Chevron U.S.A., Inc.*, 72 F.3d 740 (9th Cir. 1995), *cert. denied*, 517 U.S. 1233 (1996) (Inspector General auditor); *United States ex rel. Biddle v. Board of Trs.*, 161 F.3d 533 (9th Cir. 1998), *cert. denied*, 526 U.S. 1066 (1999) (administrative contracting officer). But see *Hagood v. Sonoma County Water Agency*, 81 F.3d 1465 (9th Cir. 1996), in which a government attorney was held to be an original source because his job did not entail exposing fraud. The D.C. Circuit adds an element to the original source test by requiring that, to qualify as an original source, a relator must have direct and independent knowledge of the information on which the publicly disclosed allegations are based and must have voluntarily provided that information to the government before the public disclosure occurred, *United States ex rel. Findley v. FPC-Boron Employees' Club*, 105 F.3d 675 (D.C. Cir. 1997).

Once a qui tam suit has been filed, no other person can file a "parasitic" suit based on the same facts. See 31 U.S.C. § 3730(b)(5), providing that "when a person brings a [qui tam action], no person other than the Government may intervene or bring a related action based on the facts underlying the pending action." See *United States ex rel. Prawer & Co. v. Fleet Bank*, 24 F.3d 320 (1st Cir. 1994), holding that a suit against a different defendant was not parasitic because the defendant could not have been brought into the prior suit. Compare *United States ex rel. Lujan v. Hughes Aircraft Co.*, 243 F.3d 1181 (9th Cir. 2001), holding that this provision barred a claim even though the plaintiff had added a few facts to the previously filed suit.

Relators are given a share of the government's monetary recovery and are granted whistleblower protection. The amount depends on whether the government elects to proceed with the action. 31 U.S.C. § 3730(d) provides that if the government proceeds with an action, the relator will receive at least 15 percent but not more than 25 percent of the proceeds, "depending upon the extent to which the person substantially contributed to the prosecution of the action." However, the relator is permitted to receive no more than 10 percent of the recovery if the action is based primarily on disclosures of specific information, allegations, or transactions in a criminal, civil, or administrative hearing; in a congressional, administrative, or government (General) Accounting Office report, hearing, audit, or investigation; or from the news media. If the government does not take over the case, the relator receives not less than 25 percent nor more than 30 percent of the proceeds. In either case, the relator receives an amount for reasonable expenses plus reasonable attorneys' fees and costs.

There is a disagreement over whether the government has the right to challenge a settlement in a case in which it chose not to intervene. In *United States ex rel. Killingsworth v. Northrop Corp.*, 25 F.3d 715 (9th Cir. 1994), the court held that the government had no right to challenge the settlement agreed to between the relator and the defendant. In *Searcy, Trustee for Bankruptcy Estate of C&P Bus. World Inc. v. Philips Elecs. N. Am. Corp.*, 117 F.3d 154 (5th Cir. 1997), the court took the opposite position, allowing the government to enter the case to contest the settlement. See also *United States v. Health Possibilities, P.S.C.*, 207 F.3d 335 (6th Cir. 2000), barring a settlement without the written consent of the Attorney General. See *Riley v. St. Luke's Episcopal Hosp.*, 252 F.3d 749 (5th Cir. 2001), for a full discussion of the powers of the federal government after it chooses not to intervene in a qui tam suit.

(2) Criminal Fraud

As amended by the False Claims Amendments Act of 1986, 18 U.S.C. § 287 provides:

> Whoever makes or presents to any person or officer in the civil, military, or naval service of the United States, or to any department or agency thereof, any claim upon or against the United States, or any department or agency thereof, knowing such claim to be false, fictitious, or fraudulent, shall be imprisoned not more than five years and shall be subject to a fine in the amount provided in this title.

The same issues have arisen under this provision as those discussed with regard to civil fraud.

(a) Specific Intent

The courts have held that proof of specific intent to defraud the government is not necessary to prove criminal intent. Acting with "knowledge that the claim is false or fictitious is sufficient," *United States v. Maher*, 582 F.2d 842 (4th Cir.), *cert. denied*, 439 U.S. 1115 (1978); *United States v. Precision Med. Labs., Inc.*, 593 F.2d 434 (2d Cir. 1978); *United States v. Milton*, 602 F.2d 231 (9th Cir. 1979). See also *United States v. Catton*, 89 F.3d 387 (7th Cir.1996) (willfulness need not be charged); *Giuliano v. Everything Yogurt, Inc.*, 819 F. Supp. 240 (E.D.N.Y. 1993) (dishonesty, recklessness, deceptiveness, and deliberate disregard satisfied the intent requirement for fraud); and *United States v. Irwin*, 654 F.2d 671 (10th Cir. 1981) (comparing the language of the False Statements Act—which includes the term "willfully"—and concluding that the False Claims Act intentionally excludes the question of the state of mind of the claimant). Deliberate ignorance has been found sufficient to prove intent, *United States v. Wallace*, 40 F. Supp. 2d 131 (E.D.N.Y. 1999). However, no intent to defraud the government was found when a claim was submitted to the government of the Virgin Islands without knowledge that federal funds were involved, *United States v. Gumbs*, 283 F.3d 128 (3d Cir. 2002). In contrast, an intent to defraud has been found when the defendant presented a claim to a state knowing that a federal program was involved, *United States v. Beasley*, 550 F.2d 261 (5th Cir.), *cert. denied*, 434 U.S. 863 (1977). See also *United States v. Prigmore*, 243 F.3d 1 (1st Cir. 2001), holding that a defendant charged with violating a regulation is entitled to an interpretation of that regulation that is "most congenial to their case theory and yet also objectively reasonable."

(b) Definition of "Claim"

The courts have followed the rule used in the Civil False Claims Act that a criminal false claim can occur only if there is a request for the payment of money or the transfer of property. However, a valid request for payment will be a false claim if it is made under a contract obtained by fraudulent means, *United States v. Winchester*, 407 F. Supp. 261 (D. Del. 1975). Presenting a voucher for payment knowing that the goods had not been properly inspected and accepted was also held to be a false claim, *United States v. U.S. Cartridge Co.*, 198 F.2d 456 (8th Cir. 1952), *cert. denied*, 345 U.S. 910 (1953).

The Act encompasses claims submitted indirectly to the government. For example, a claim submitted to a contractor processing Medicare claims for the government was held to be a false claim, *United States v. Precision Med. Labs., Inc.*, 593 F.2d 434 (2d Cir. 1978). Similarly, in *United States v. Beasley*, 550 F.2d 261 (5th Cir.), *cert. denied*, 434 U.S. 863 (1977), the court held that a claim submitted to the state of Louisiana for housing units never constructed was a claim against the federal government since federal funds were to be used for the payments.

(c) Materiality

The courts disagree on whether proof of materiality of the claim is an element of this criminal offense. The majority of the circuits have held that a conviction is proper without proof of materiality of the claim, *United States v. Logan*, 250 F.3d 350 (6th Cir.), *cert. denied*, 534 U.S. 895 (2001); *United States v. Upton*, 91 F.3d 677 (5th Cir. 1996); *United States v. Taylor*, 66 F.3d 254 (9th Cir. 1995); *United*

States v. Parsons, 967 F.2d 452 (10th Cir. 1992); *United States v. Elkin*, 731 F.2d 1005 (2d Cir. 1984), *overruled on other grounds by United States v. Ali*, 68 F.3d 1468 (2d Cir. 1995). However, two circuits have held that materiality is a necessary element of the offense, *United States v. Wells*, 63 F.3d 745 (8th Cir. 1995), *vacated on other grounds*, 519 U.S. 482 (1997); *United States v. Snider*, 502 F.2d 645 (4th Cir. 1974). See also *United States v. Foster*, 229 F.3d 1196 (5th Cir. 2000), in which the court stated that its view of *Neder v. United States*, 527 U.S. 1 (1999), was that the Supreme Court is now requiring a jury instruction that it must find materiality.

b. False Statements

The False Statements Act, 18 U.S.C. § 1001 provides:

> (a) Except as otherwise provided in this section, whoever, in any matter within the jurisdiction of the executive, legislative, or judicial branch of the Government of the United States knowingly and willfully -
>
> > (1) falsifies, conceals or covers up by any trick, scheme, or device a material fact;
> >
> > (2) makes any materially false, fictitious or fraudulent statements or representation; or
> >
> > (3) makes or uses any false writing or document knowing the same to contain any materially false, fictitious or fraudulent statement or entry;
>
> shall be fined under this title or imprisoned not more than 5 years, or both.

The key elements of the conduct prohibited by this statute are "knowingly and willfully" making a false "statement." Courts added the requirement that the statement be material prior to its inclusion in the statute, *United States v. Gafyczk*, 847 F.2d 685 (11th Cir. 1988); *United States v. Godwin*, 566 F.2d 975 (5th Cir. 1978); *United States v. Rose*, 570 F.2d 1358 (9th Cir. 1978).

(1) Definition of "Statement"

The scope of the False Statements Act is considerably broader than that of the False Claims Act. It has been held that the Act covers all false statements that might support fraudulent claims or might pervert or corrupt the authorized functions of a government agency to which the statement was made, *United States v. Bedore*, 455 F.2d 1109 (9th Cir. 1972). The statement need not be on a government form if it affects the government, *United States v. Heuer*, 4 F.3d 723 (9th Cir.1993), *cert. denied*, 510 U.S. 1164 (1994) (bill of lading). The Act covers oral as well as written statements and unsworn as well as sworn statements, *United States v. Massey*, 550 F.2d 300 (5th Cir. 1977), as well as "private discussions" between members of the executive and legislative branches of the government, *United States v. Poindexter*, 951 F.2d 369 (D.C. Cir. 1991). It also covers the omission of information on a certified statement when the information should have been included, *United States v. Irwin*, 654 F.2d 671 (10th Cir. 1981). In *United States v. Johnson*, 937 F.2d 392 (8th Cir. 1991), the court stated at 395:

> It is generally recognized that section 1001 creates two distinct offenses with different elements: (1) concealing material facts from a federal agency by trick, scheme, or device; (2) making false or fraudulent statements of material facts to a federal agency. See *United States v. Mayberry*, 913 F.2d 719, 722 n.7 (9th Cir. 1990); *United States v. St. Michael's Credit Union*, 880 F.2d 579, 590 (1st Cir. 1989).

The transferring of acceptance stamps from goods that had been accepted to goods that had not been inspected was held to be a false statement, *United States v. Steiner Plastics Mfg. Co.*, 231 F.2d 149 (2d Cir. 1956). Statements made during settlement negotiations were also found to be false statements, *New York v. Sokol*, 113 F.3d 303 (2d Cir. 1997). False statements were also found to be made by an employee of a contractor who included false information on a security questionnaire, *United States v. Dale*, 991 F.2d 819 (D.C. Cir. 1993); *Pitts v. United States*, 263 F.2d 353 (9th Cir.), *cert. denied*, 360 U.S. 935 (1959); and by an applicant for employment with a defense contractor who included false statements on the employment application, *United States v. Giarraputo*, 140 F. Supp. 831 (E.D.N.Y. 1956). False statements have also been found to have been made by government employees when they included false entries on documents during the transaction of government business, *United States v. Leviton*, 193 F.2d 848 (2d Cir. 1951), *cert. denied*, 343 U.S. 946 (1952); *United States v. Eisenmann*, 396 F.2d 565 (2d Cir. 1968). The question of the authority of the agency to seek or obtain the statement is not relevant if the false statement influences the agency, *United States v. Arcadipane*, 41 F.3d 1 (1st Cir. 1994).

The Act applies to matters that involve a government agency's activity even though the false statement is not made to the government, *Ebeling v. United States*, 248 F.2d 429 (8th Cir.), *cert. denied sub nom. Emerling v. United States*, 355 U.S. 907 (1957) (false invoices submitted by subcontractor to contractor under price redeterminable contract); *United States v. Huber*, 603 F.2d 387 (2d Cir. 1979), *cert. denied*, 445 U.S. 927 (1980) (false statements made to hospitals receiving money under Federal programs). See also *United States v. Popow*, 821 F.2d 483 (8th Cir. 1987) (false identification presented to customs inspector is a matter concerning INS), and *United States v. Herring*, 916 F.2d 1543 (11th Cir. 1990) (Georgia Department of Labor involves activity of United States Department of Labor).

(2) Knowingly and Willfully

To fall within the scope of the Act, the statement must have been made with the intent to deceive, but the government need not prove an intent to defraud, *United*

States v. Lichenstein, 610 F.2d 1272 (5th Cir. 1980); *United States v. Leo*, 941 F.2d 181 (3d Cir. 1991). One court stated that the knowing and willful intent requirement was met when the government proved that the defendant knew that the false statement was necessary for the fraudulent scheme to succeed, *United States v. Beck*, 615 F.2d 441 (7th Cir. 1980). See also *United States v. Cutaia*, 511 F. Supp. 619 (E.D.N.Y. 1981), in which criminal intent was found when the defendant was advised of the government's requirements and deliberately gave answers to avoid compliance. However, there can be no intent to deceive unless the statement is false at the time it is made, *United States v. McCarrick*, 294 F.3d 1286 (11th Cir. 2002) (alleged wrongdoing occurred after document was signed).

An honest misinterpretation on government forms precludes conviction under the Act, *United States v. Weatherspoon*, 581 F.2d 595 (7th Cir. 1978), but reckless disregard of the truthfulness of the statement and a conscious effort to avoid learning the truth will be deemed to be a knowing and willful false statement, *United States v. Evans*, 559 F.2d 244 (5th Cir. 1977), *cert. denied*, 434 U.S. 1015 (1978). See also *United States v. Puente*, 982 F.2d 156 (5th Cir.), *cert. denied*, 508 U.S. 962 (1993), holding that it was reckless disregard to sign a government form certifying that the offeror had never been convicted of a felony without reading it.

Generally proof that the contractor followed a reasonable interpretation of an ambiguous regulation or contract is sufficient to demonstrate that there was no intent to make a false statement. See *United States v. Whiteside*, 285 F.3d 1345 (11th Cir. 2002), holding that an ambiguous regulation prevented a finding of the requisite intent. The court stated at 1351-52:

> In a case where the truth or falsity of a statement centers on an interpretive question of law, the government bears the burden of proving beyond a reasonable doubt that the defendant's statement is not true under a reasonable interpretation of the law. *United States v. Migliaccio*, 34 F.3d 1517, 1525 (10th Cir. 1994) (holding that the government bears the burden to negate any reasonable interpretations that would make the defendant's statement correct); *United States v. Johnson*, 937 F.2d 392, 399 (8th Cir. 1991) (holding that one cannot be guilty of a false statement beyond a reasonable doubt when his statement is a reasonable construction); *United States v. Race*, 632 F.2d 1114, 1120 (4th Cir. 1980) (same); *United States v. Anderson*, 579 F.2d 455, 460 (8th Cir. 1978) (same); see also *United States v. Calhoon*, 97 F.3d 518, 526 (11th Cir. 1996) (noting that even though the Medicare regulations were clear regarding the royalty fees paid to a related party, the government failed to establish as a matter of *fact* that the fees claimed were actually in excess of what was clearly allowed under the regulations, and thus, had "failed to sustain its burden to prove the claim false by virtue of the nonreimbursable nature of the interest").

However, if the court finds the contractor's interpretation unreasonable, intent to defraud the government will be found, *United.States v. White*, 765 F.2d 1469 (11th Cir. 1985) (rule not applicable because contractor's interpretation unreasonable);

United States v. Dale, 991 F.2d 819 (D.C. Cir. 1993) (rule not applicable because defendant's interpretation "far too restrictive"). In addition, one circuit has held that the argument of ambiguity will not prevail if there is sufficient evidence that the contractor knew that the government had a contrary interpretation, *United States v. Carrier*, 654 F.2d 559 (9th Cir. 1981).

It has been held that the maker of the false statement can be convicted even if he or she does not know that the federal government is involved in the transaction, *United States v. Baker*, 626 F.2d 512 (5th Cir. 1980); *United States v. Wright*, 988 F.2d 1036 (10th Cir. 1993).

(3) Materiality

Although the Act did not originally mention materiality, the courts are in general agreement that a statement must be material to fall within the scope of the Act, *United States v. Ali*, 68 F.3d 1468, *amended on denial of reh'g*, 86 F.3d 275 (2d Cir. 1996); *Gonzales v. United States*, 286 F.2d 118 (10th Cir. 1960), *cert. denied*, 365 U.S. 878 (1961). The test of materiality is whether a statement has a natural tendency to influence, or is capable of influencing, the actions of a federal agency, *Kungys v. United States*, 485 U.S. 759 (1988); *United States v. Gaudin*, 515 U.S. 506 (1995). There is no need to prove either reliance by the government, *United States v. Hicks*, 619 F.2d 752 (8th Cir. 1980), or actual pecuniary loss by the government, *United States v. Lichenstein*, 610 F.2d 1272 (5th Cir. 1980). Thus, a criminal false statement can occur even if the government employee hearing the statement knows that it is false at the time, *United States v. Goldfine*, 538 F.2d 815 (9th Cir. 1976) (statements made during administrative "compliance investigation"); *United States v. LeMaster*, 54 F.3d 1224 (6th Cir. 1995) (statements to FBI agency during investigation). In *United States v. Coastal Contracting & Eng'g Co.*, 174 F. Supp. 474 (D. Md. 1959), a contractor knowingly submitted fictitious statements in connection with a change order proposal. They were not relied on by the government negotiator because he thought the prices were entirely out of line. Nevertheless, the contractor violated the Act because the misstatements were material and were calculated to induce reliance and action.

Materiality in a false statement is a question of fact to be decided by the jury, *United States v. Gaudin*, 515 U.S. 506 (1995). Prior to *Gaudin* there were numerous decisions holding that materiality was a question of law.

c. *Truth in Negotiations*

The Truth in Negotiations Act (TINA) was added to the Armed Services Procurement Act in 1962 to improve the government's ability to negotiate contracts and contract modifications by ensuring that the government has the same factual data as the contractor at the time of price negotiations. The Act does this by requiring the submission of cost or pricing data. The requirement was added to the Federal Property and Administrative Services Act in 1985. The Federal Acquisition Streamlining Act of 1994 amended these statutes to contain the same requirements in 10 U.S.C. § 2306a and 41 U.S.C. § 254b (previously § 254(d)). These statutes now require the submission of cost or pricing data on all negotiated contracts over $550,000 but prohibit obtaining such data when one of four exceptions applies. FAR Subpart 15.4 gives guidance on the procedures when obtaining data is mandatory.

These statutes contain elaborate guidance on the contractual price adjustments available to the government if a contractor fails to comply with their requirements. The computation of such adjustments is discussed in Chapter 8.

(1) Mandatory Submission Requirement

10 U.S.C. § 2306a(a) and 41 U.S.C. § 254b(a) contain mandatory requirements for the submission of cost or pricing data. These requirements are implemented in FAR 15.403-4 as follows:

> (a)(1) The contracting officer must obtain cost or pricing data only if the contracting officer concludes that none of the exceptions in 15.403-1(b) applies. However, if the contracting officer has sufficient information available to determine price reasonableness, then the contracting officer should consider requesting a waiver under the exception at 15.403-1(b)(4). The threshold for obtaining cost or pricing data is $ 550,000. Unless an exception applies, cost or pricing data are required before accomplishing any of the following actions expected to exceed the current threshold or, for existing contracts, the threshold specified in the contract:
>
> > (i) The award of any negotiated contract (except for undefinitized actions such as letter contracts).
> >
> > (ii) The award of a subcontract at any tier, if the contractor and each higher-tier subcontractor were required to submit cost or pricing data (but see waivers at 15.403-1(c)(4)).
> >
> > (iii) The modification of any sealed bid or negotiated contract (whether or not cost or pricing data were initially required) or any subcontract covered by paragraph (a)(1)(ii) of this subsection. Price adjustment amounts must consider both increases and decreases (e.g., a $ 200,000 modification resulting from a reduction of $ 400,000 and an increase of $ 200,000 is a pricing adjustment exceeding $ 550,000). This requirement does not apply when unrelated and separately priced changes for which cost or pricing data would not otherwise be required are included for administrative convenience in the same modification. Negotiated final pricing actions (such as termination settlements and total final price agreements for fixed-price incentive and redeterminable contracts) are contract modifications requiring cost or pricing data if—

(A) The total final price agreement for such settlements or agreements exceeds the pertinent threshold set forth at paragraph (a)(1) of this subsection; or

(B) The partial termination settlement plus the estimate to complete the continued portion of the contract exceeds the pertinent threshold set forth at paragraph (a)(1) of this subsection (see 49.105(c)(15)).

Although these provisions are written as a requirement for the government to obtain these data, they have been interpreted as mandatory submission requirements. Thus, contractors are liable for nonsubmission because contracting officers have no authority to waive the requirements. See *M-R-S Mfg. Co. v. United States*, 203 Ct. Cl. 551, 492 F.2d 835 (1974); *Conrac Corp. v. United States*, 214 Ct. Cl. 561, 558 F.2d 994 (1977); *Southwest Marine, Inc.*, DOTCAB 1577J, 95-2 BCA ¶ 27760; and *Numax Elec., Inc.*, ASBCA 29186, 85-3 BCA ¶ 18,396. However, waiver of the requirement is permitted by the Head of the Contracting Activity, as prescribed in FAR 15.403-1(c) as follows:

(4) *Waivers*. The head of the contracting activity (HCA) may, without power of delegation, waive the requirement for submission of cost or pricing data in exceptional cases. The authorization for the waiver and the supporting rationale shall be in writing. The HCA may consider waiving the requirement if the price can be determined to be fair and reasonable without submission of cost or pricing data. For example, if cost or pricing data were furnished on previous production buys and the contracting officer determines such data are sufficient, when combined with updated information, a waiver may be granted. If the HCA has waived the requirement for submission of cost or pricing data, the contractor or higher-tier subcontractor to whom the waiver relates shall be considered as having been required to provide cost or pricing data. Consequently, award of any lower-tier subcontract expected to exceed the cost or pricing data threshold requires the submission of cost or pricing data unless—

(i) An exception otherwise applies to the subcontract; or

(ii) The waiver specifically includes the subcontract and the rationale supporting the waiver for that subcontract.

(2) Exceptions to Submission Requirement

Aside from a situation in which a waiver has been obtained, there are three situations in which cost or pricing data are not required. These situations were called exceptions in the original statute but were denominated *prohibitions* in the 1994 amendments to the Acts.

(A) Adequate Price Competition

FAR 15.403-1(c) defines the scope of this exception as follows:

(1) *Adequate price competition.* A price is based on adequate price competition if—

(i) Two or more responsible offerors, competing independently, submit priced offers that satisfy the Government's expressed requirement and if—

(A) Award will be made to the offeror whose proposal represents the best value (see 2.101) where price is a substantial factor in source selection; and

(B) There is no finding that the price of the otherwise successful offeror is unreasonable. Any finding that the price is unreasonable must be supported by a statement of the facts and approved at a level above the contracting officer;

(ii) There was a reasonable expectation, based on market research or other assessment, that two or more responsible offerors, competing independently, would submit priced offers in response to the solicitation's expressed requirement, even though only one offer is received from a responsible offeror and if—

(A) Based on the offer received, the contracting officer can reasonably conclude that the offer was submitted with the expectation of competition, e.g., circumstances indicate that --

(1) The offeror believed that at least one other offeror was capable of submitting a meaningful offer; and

(2) The offeror had no reason to believe that other potential offerors did not intend to submit an offer; and

(B) The determination that the proposed price is based on adequate price competition, is reasonable, and is approved at a level above the contracting officer; or

(iii) Price analysis clearly demonstrates that the proposed price is reasonable in comparison with current or recent prices for the same or similar items, adjusted to reflect changes in market conditions, economic conditions, quantities, or terms and conditions under contracts that resulted from adequate price competition.

(B) Prices Set by Law or Regulation

FAR 15.403-1(c) defines the scope of this exception as follows:

> (2) *Prices set by law or regulation*. Pronouncements in the form of periodic rulings, reviews, or similar actions of a governmental body, or embodied in the laws, are sufficient to set a price.

(c) Commercial Items

FAR 15.403-1(c) defines the scope of this exception as follows:

> (3) *Commercial items*. (i) Any acquisition for an item that meets the commercial item definition in 2.101, or any modification, as defined in paragraph (3)(i) or (ii) of that definition, that does not change the item from a commercial item to a noncommercial item, is exempt from the requirement for cost or pricing data. If the contracting officer determines that an item claimed to be commercial is, in fact, not commercial and that no other exception or waiver applies, the contracting officer must require submission of cost or pricing data.
>
> (ii) Any acquisition for noncommercial supplies or services treated as commercial items at 12.102(f)(1), except sole source contracts greater than $ 15,000,000, is exempt from the requirements for cost or pricing data (41 U.S.C. 428(a)).

This exception was narrowed by § 818 of the FY 2005 National Defense Authorization Act, Pub. L. No. 108-375, amended at 10 U.S.C. § 2306a(b) to include the following provision.

> (3) *Noncommercial modifications of commercial items*.—(A) The exception in paragraph (1)(B) does not apply to cost or pricing data on noncommercial modifications of a commercial item that are expected to cost, in the aggregate, more than $500,000 or 5 percent of the total price of the contract, whichever is greater.
>
> > (B) In this paragraph, the term "noncommercial modification", with respect to a commercial item, means a modification of such item that is not a modification described in section 4(12)(C)(i) of the Office of Federal Procurement Policy Act (41 U.S.C. 403(12)(C)(I)).
> >
> > (C) Nothing in subparagraph (A) shall be construed—
> >
> > > (i) to limit the applicability of the exception in subparagraph (A) or (C) of paragraph (1) to cost or pricing data on a noncommercial modification of a commercial item; or
> > >
> > > (ii) to require the submission of cost or pricing data on any aspect of an acquisition of a commercial item other than the cost and pricing of noncommercial modifications of such item.

A decision by a contracting officer that no data are required because an item is commercial is binding on the government even if it is incorrect, *Honeywell Fed. Sys., Inc.*, ASBCA 39974, 92-2 BCA ¶ 24,966. In *Honeywell*, the board ruled that the determination of commerciality is a judgmental decision of the contracting officer, which is binding even in the face of poor judgment.

(3) Definition of Cost or Pricing Data

The regulations contain a comprehensive definition of cost or pricing data emphasizing that the data are factual in nature; however, some of the illustrations in the regulations are less than clear. See FAR 2.101, which states:

> "Cost or pricing data" (10 U.S.C. 2306a(h)(1) and 41 U.S.C. 254b) means all facts that, as of the date of price agreement or, if applicable, an earlier date agreed upon between the parties that is as close as practicable to the date of agreement on price, prudent buyers and sellers would reasonably expect to affect price negotiations significantly. Cost or pricing data are data requiring certification in accordance with 15.406-2. Cost or pricing data are factual, not judgmental, and are verifiable. While they do not indicate the accuracy of the prospective contractor's judgment about estimated future costs or projections, they do include the data forming the basis for that judgment. Cost or pricing data are more than historical accounting data; they are all the facts that can be reasonably expected to contribute to the soundness of estimates of future costs and to the validity of determinations of costs already incurred. They also include such factors as—
>
> (1) Vendor quotations;
>
> (2) Nonrecurring costs;
>
> (3) Information on changes in production methods and in production or purchasing volume;
>
> (4) Data supporting projections of business prospects and objectives and related operations costs;
>
> (5) Unit-cost trends such as those associated with labor efficiency;
>
> (6) Make-or-buy decisions;
>
> (7) Estimated resources to attain business goals; and
>
> (8) Information on management decisions that could have a significant bearing on costs.

10 U.S.C. § 2306a(i)(1) and 41 U.S.C. § 254b(i)(l) contain a much shorter definition, which was derived from the FAR definition. It is difficult to arrive at a precise distinction between factual data and judgmental information. Clearly, recorded costs are factual; therefore, they are classified as cost or pricing data. The term thus includes actual labor rates, *Boeing Co.*, ASBCA 32753, 90-1 BCA ¶ 22,270, *recons. denied*, 90-1 BCA ¶ 22,426; *Kaiser Aerospace & Elecs. Corp.*, ASBCA 32098, 90-1

BCA ¶ 22,489, *recons. denied*, 90-2 BCA ¶ 22,695; labor hours, *Grumman Aerospace Corp.*, ASBCA 35188, 90-2 BCA ¶ 22,842; and indirect costs, *Norris Indus., Inc.*, ASBCA 15442, 74-1 BCA ¶ 10,482. Information in the offeror's purchasing department relating to the prices of materials is also clearly factual. Thus, the term includes purchase orders, *Grumman Aerospace Corp.*, ASBCA 35188, 90-2 BCA ¶ 22,842, and vendor quotations, *Cutler-Hammer, Inc. v. United States*, 189 Ct. Cl. 76, 416 F.2d 1306 (1969). The fact that a contractor had an unopened bid for materials to be used on the contract was also held to be cost or pricing data, *Aerojet Solid Propulsion Co. v. White*, 291 F.3d 1328 (Fed. Cir. 2002). Although the bids were not due to be opened until after the close of price negotiations, the court reasoned that the fact of their receipt was significant information. See also *Lockheed Martin Corp.*, ASBCA 50566, 02-2 BCA ¶ 31,907, holding that engineering advances that permitted the contractor to perform the work in a more efficient manner than proposed were cost or pricing data.

Accounting information on the costs of prior work on different projects may also be cost or pricing data if it is sufficiently relevant to be usable in the analysis of proposed costs. Thus, it has been held that prices paid for similar items are cost or pricing data, *Hardie-Tynes Mfg. Co.*, ASBCA 20717, 76-2 BCA ¶ 12,121. See *PCA Health Plans of Tex., Inc. v. LaChance*, 191 F.3d 1353 (Fed. Cir. 1999); and *Qualmed Plans for Health of N.M., Inc. v. United States*, 267 F.3d 1319 (Fed. Cir. 2001), holding that submission of data on dissimilar work was defective cost or pricing data. In these cases, the contractors had based their medical charge rates on the costs incurred with dissimilar organizations to the organizations being covered under the contract.

Estimating systems that contain a mixture of factual data and judgmental information constitute cost or pricing data, *Texas Instruments, Inc.*, ASBCA 23678, 87-3 BCA ¶ 20,195. In that case, the board concluded that a computer-generated report containing an estimate of the costs of future work was cost or pricing data. The cost estimate was derived from actual cost data, then manipulated using complex estimating formulas. Similarly, in *Black River Ltd. P'ship*, ASBCA 46790, 97-2 BCA ¶ 29,077, the board held that a computer pricing model used to compute the "internal rate of return" of a capital investment was cost or pricing data. See also *Lambert Eng'g Co.*, ASBCA 13338, 69-1 BCA ¶ 7663, holding that labor-hour estimates derived from actual information were cost or pricing data even though they were not technically actual cost data, and *United Techs. Corp.*, ASBCA 51410, 04-1 BCA ¶ 32,556, holding that internal documents showing how the costs were used to calculate the proposed price were cost or pricing data. Compare *Litton Sys., Inc.*, ASBCA 36509, 92-2 BCA ¶ 24,842, in which an estimating system that contained standard labor hours for parts based on estimates of industrial engineers was held not to be cost or pricing data. The board reached this conclusion because the system was not "mixed fact and judgment" but pure judgment in that "no two industrial engineers . . . would estimate either the task or the frequency of the task the same."

The best and final offer submitted by a contractor is not cost or pricing data because it is "not a set of facts" but rather "a mistake of judgments as to how best to accomplish work at a price," *United Techs. Corp.*, ASBCA 51410, 04-1 BCA ¶ 32,556.

A contractor's analysis of a subcontractor's estimate is cost or pricing data if it contains facts as well as judgment. See *Aerojet-Gen. Corp.*, ASBCA 12264, 69-1 BCA ¶ 7664, *modified on recons.*, 70-1 BCA ¶ 8140, in which the board held that the underlying factual data in an internal company report analyzing a subcontractor's pricing proposal were cost or pricing data. See also *Grumman Aerospace Corp.*, ASBCA 27476, 86-3 BCA ¶ 19,091, holding that an internal company report analyzing a subcontractor's proposal was cost or pricing data because it was the most readily available document and contained some factual data. The same result was reached in *McDonnell Douglas Helicopter Sys.*, ASBCA 50447, 00-2 BCA ¶ 31,082. See also *McDonnell Aircraft Co.*, ASBCA 44504, 97-1 BCA ¶ 28,977, 03-1 BCA ¶ 32,154, holding that a major subcontractor's "preliminary cost analysis" of a sub-subcontractor was cost or pricing data.

Management decisions affecting future costs are cost or pricing data if they (1) have a substantial relationship to a cost element and (2) are made by an official with authority to approve the action under consideration, *Lockheed Corp.*, ASBCA 36420, 95-2 BCA ¶ 27,722. In *Lockheed* the board found that a decision to bargain for reduced labor rates was not cost or pricing data because, at the time of the close of price negotiations, it had not been approved by top management. In *Motorola, Inc.*, ASBCA 48841, 96-2 BCA ¶ 28,465, *aff'd*, 125 F.3d 1470 (Fed. Cir. 1997), the board held that a corporate "Policy and Procedure" memorandum stating that the facilities capital cost of money was not to be included in its general and administrative expenses was a management decision that constituted cost or pricing data because the memorandum was a "verifiable fact." See also *McDonnell Douglas Corp.*, ASBCA 44637, 95-2 BCA ¶ 27,858, concluding that proposed changes to the contractor's cost accounting system were cost or pricing data, and *Millipore Corp.*, GSBCA 9453, 91-1 BCA ¶ 23,345, holding that a decision to change the company's discount policy constituted cost or pricing data. In contrast, in *Aerojet Ordnance Tenn.*, ASBCA 36089, 95-2 BCA ¶ 27,922, a decision by the general manager of the contractor to proceed "with all possible haste" to close a waste disposal pond was held not to be "a meaningful management decision" because the pond could not be closed until the state approved the action and, thus, the cost consequences of the "decision" could not be ascertained.

(4) Insignificant Data

In a few cases, contractors have escaped liability for nonsubmission of cost or pricing data by demonstrating that prudent buyers and sellers would not have viewed their data as having a significant effect on pricing. For example, in *Plessey Indus., Inc.*, ASBCA 16720, 74-1 BCA ¶ 10,603, it was found that a rejected vendor quotation was insignificant, and in *Boeing Military Airplane Co.*, ASBCA 33168, 87-2 BCA ¶ 19,714, it was held that incurred labor hours at the beginning of the contract were the type of information that prudent buyers and sellers would not have used in the pricing process. See also *Alliant Techsystems, Inc.*, ASBCA 47626, 00-2 BCA ¶ 31,042, in which the board followed this reasoning with regard to a contractor's undisclosed purchasing strategy that would combine purchases on two contracts. The board held that this was not significant data because the contractor had disclosed other data as to vendor prices that yielded lower prices than the purchasing strategy. The opposite conclusion was reached in *GKS, Inc.*, ASBCA 47692, 00-1 BCA ¶ 30,914, where the contractor had failed to disclose vendor quotations because they could not be verified for accuracy before the time of negotiations with the government. The board cited a number of cases holding that if there is any doubt as to the relevance of the data, they must be disclosed. See also *Loral Aerospace Corp.*, ASBCA 48250, 00-1 BCA ¶ 30,835, denying a motion for summary judgment because undisclosed data on labor hours incurred on the most recent contract might well have been data that a prudent buyer would consider to be significant. Similarly, in *McDonnell Douglas Helicopter Sys.*, ASBCA 50447, 99-1 BCA ¶ 30,271, the board held that vendor quotations on parts that the contractor intended to manufacture were data that a buyer might consider significant.

Old information once used as cost or pricing data would no longer be significant. For example, contractors have labor-rate and overhead rate information dating back many years. However, only data relating to recent years are useful in estimating future costs. Reasonable buyers and sellers might disagree about how many years' information is significant for this purpose, but all would agree that old information is of little use.

(5) Submission Techniques

FAR 15.408 provides that there are two techniques for the submission of cost or pricing data—*physical submission* and *specific identification*: See the following guidance in Table 15-2—Instructions for Submitting Cost/Price Proposals When Cost or Pricing Data Are Required:

> **Note 1**: There is a clear distinction between submitting cost or pricing data and merely making available books, records, and other documents without identification. The requirement for submission of cost or pricing data is met when all accurate cost or pricing data reasonably available to the offeror have been submitted, either actually or by specific identification, to the Contracting Officer or an authorized representative. As later information comes into your possession, it should be submitted promptly to the Contracting Officer in a manner that clearly shows how the information relates to the offeror's price proposal. The requirement for submission of cost or pricing data continues up to the time of agreement on price, or an earlier date agreed upon between the parties if applicable.

The instructions also contain two nonstatutory submission requirements:

> B. In submitting your proposal, you must include an index, appropriately referenced, of all the cost or pricing data and information accompanying or identified in the proposal. In addition, you must annotate any future additions and/or revisions, up to the date of agreement on price, or an earlier date agreed upon by the parties, on a supplemental index.
>
> C. As part of the specific information required, you must submit, with your proposal, cost or pricing data (that is, data that are verifiable and factual and otherwise as defined at FAR 2.101). You must clearly identify on your cover sheet that cost or pricing data are included as part of the proposal. In addition, you must submit with your proposal any information reasonably required to explain your estimating process, including—
>
> > (1) The judgmental factors applied and the mathematical or other methods used in the estimate, including those used in projecting from known data; and
> >
> > (2) The nature and amount of any contingencies included in the proposed price.

The boards and courts have analyzed the adequacy of the submission by ascertaining whether the disclosure of the information was "meaningful." See *Aerojet Ordnance Tenn.*, ASBCA 36089, 95-2 BCA ¶ 27,922, stating at 139,437:

> Disclosure is not confined to a formal, written submission. Instead, the contractor's disclosure obligation is fulfilled if the Government obtains the data in question in some other manner or had knowledge. However, the disclosure must be meaningful, regardless of the form it takes. "If the Truth in Negotiations Act is to have any force and effect then the Government must be clearly and fully informed. This can only be achieved by complete disclosure of the item or items in question." *Sylvania Electric Products, Inc. v. United States*, 479 F.2d 1342, 1348 (Ct. Cl. 1973). A determination of whether a data disclosure was meaningful depends on the application of a "rule of reason" to the circumstances of each case to determine whether the data was conveyed to the Government in a reasonably meaningful fashion. *Plessey Industries*, ASBCA No. 16720, 74-1 BCA ¶ 10,603; *Whittaker Corp.*, ASBCA No. 17267, 74-2 BCA ¶ 10,938; *Hughes Aircraft Co.*, ASBCA No. 30144, 90-2 BCA ¶ 22,847. Or, in other words, has the Government established that the data was not provided in a "useable, understandable format" to a proper Government representative? *Litton Systems*, [ASBCA 36509, 92-2 BCA ¶ 24842]. See also *Motorola, Inc.*, ASBCA No. 41528, 94-2 BCA ¶ 26,596; *EDO Corp.*, ASBCA No. 41448, 93-3 BCA ¶ 26,135; *Grumman Aerospace Corp.*, ASBCA No. 27476, 86-3 BCA ¶ 19,091; *Boeing Co.*, ASBCA No. 33881, 92-1 BCA ¶ 24,414, *summarily aff'd on reconsid.* 19 August 1991 (unpublished).

Although the specific identification requirements are somewhat cryptic, merely making the data available is insufficient. Thus, giving an agency representative complete access to all contractor data does not meet the submission requirement, *Aerojet-Gen. Corp.*, ASBCA 12873, 69-1 BCA ¶ 7585 (government plant representative); *Mc-*

Donnell Douglas Corp., ASBCA 12786, 69-2 BCA ¶ 7897 (government auditor); *Grumman Aerospace Corp.*, ASBCA 35188, 90-2 BCA ¶ 22,842 (contractor with complete access to subcontractor data). See also *McDonnell Douglas Corp.*, ASBCA 44637, 95-2 BCA ¶ 27,858 (informing Principal Administrative Contracting Officer of prospective change to accounting system not adequate disclosure with relation to negotiation of specific contract that had just been concluded); *Motorola, Inc. v. West*, 125 F.3d 1470 (Fed. Cir. 1997) ("mere deposit of books and records [with DCAA auditor] does not meet the requirement for identifying cost information"); *Hughes Aircraft Co.*, ASBCA 46321, 97-1 BCA ¶ 28,972 (making ledgers available to DCAA auditor is not sufficient identification of the data to fulfill submission requirement); *McDonnell Douglas Helicopter Sys.*, ASBCA 50447, 99-1 BCA ¶ 30,271 (providing access to data that were difficult to use was insufficient to meet disclosure requirement); and *GKS, Inc.*, ASBCA 47692, 00-1 BCA ¶ 30,914 (CO's knowledge of subcontractor's price on separate contract was not sufficient identification of data). In addition, inadequate submissions have been found when field personnel could not have been expected to bring the data to the attention of the contracting officer. See, for example, *McDonnell Douglas Helicopter Sys.*, ASBCA 50447, 00-2 BCA ¶ 31,082 (availability of purchasing information to government field pricing personnel after submission of field pricing reports to contracting officer was not adequate disclosure because those people were not further involved in negotiations), and *McDonnell Douglas Helicopter Sys.*, ASBCA 50341, 99-2 BCA ¶ 30,546 (inadequate submission when offeror's subcontractor submitted the data to its resident DCAA auditor who was not "focal point" for receipt of data to be used in negotiations of the prime contract).

If, however, the government pricing personnel have actual knowledge of the data, the submission requirement is satisfied, *Texas Instruments, Inc.*, ASBCA 23678, 87-3 BCA ¶ 20,195; *Boeing Co.*, ASBCA 32753, 90-1 BCA ¶ 22,270, *recons. denied*, 90-1 BCA ¶ 22,426. See also *Alliant Techsystems*, ASBCA 47626, 00-2 BCA ¶ 31,042 (disclosure of prices on another contract to DCAA auditor who passed information on to contracting officer); *Motorola, Inc.*, ASBCA 48841, 96-2 BCA ¶ 28,465, *aff'd*, 125 F.3d 1470 (Fed. Cir. 1997) (subcontractor general and administrative expenses data submitted to cognizant DCAA auditor); *Motorola, Inc.*, ASBCA 41528, 94-2 BCA ¶ 26,596 (subcontractor indirect cost rate data submitted to cognizant DCAA auditor); and *Boeing Co.*, ASBCA 32753, 90-1 BCA ¶ 22,270 (pricing rates negotiated with government plant representative and noted to contracting officer), *recons. denied*, 90-1 BCA ¶ 22,426. Submission of indirect cost information to the cognizant DCAA auditor has also been found to be an adequate submission when that auditor is responsible for establishing indirect cost rates, *Litton Sys., Inc.*, ASBCA 34435, 93-2 BCA ¶ 25,707, in which the board rejected the government's argument that the submission was inadequate because the auditor was not participating directly in the negotiations—finding that the parties had a long-standing practice of indirect cost rates being determined between the contractor and the DCAA auditor.

(6) Currency of the Data

Contractors certify that the cost or pricing data are "current" at the date that "price negotiations were concluded and price agreement was reached," and the parties are encouraged to agree on "closing or cutoff dates" when appropriate for classes of data, FAR 15.406-2(c). The best way to carry out this policy is for the contracting officer and the offeror to agree on the closing dates for various types of data at the conclusion of the negotiation and to attach this agreement to the certificate.

In order to comply with the currency requirement, the offeror must continually update cost and pricing data until the price is agreed upon, and this requirement may not be waived by a government employee, *Singer Co. v. United States*, 217 Ct. Cl. 225, 576 F.2d 905 (1978). If there is not enough time to compile the data in a usable form, the requirement can arguably be met by submitting raw data as they exist in the contractor's records, *Conrac Corp. v. United States*, 214 Ct. Cl. 561, 558 F.2d 994 (1977); *Lambert Eng'g Co.*, ASBCA 13338, 69-1 BCA ¶ 7663.

The permissable lag time for the transmission of cost or pricing data within the corporate structure has been difficult to determine. In *Sylvania Elec. Prods., Inc. v. United States*, 202 Ct. Cl. 16, 479 F.2d 1342 (1973), the Court of Claims established a strict rule that the data must be current at the time of the price negotiation. The contractor in this case argued that a lower price quotation, which it received from one of its suppliers one week before price negotiations, could not be furnished since it took approximately 30 days for such information to get from the company's purchasing office to its contract negotiators. The court held that the data were required, as this information could have been telephoned to the negotiators. This decision raises the question as to whether any period of time is permitted for processing the information through a company. An earlier board decision allowed such lag time, *American Bosch Arma Corp.*, ASBCA 10305, 65-2 BCA ¶ 5280, 66-2 BCA ¶ 5747, and a later case permitted substantial lag time in a situation where the contracting officer concurred in the nonsubmission of current data, *LTV Electrosystems, Inc.*, ASBCA 16802, 73-1 BCA ¶ 9957, *recons. denied*, 74-1 BCA ¶ 10,380. However, it is clear from the language in *Sylvania* that the court will not tolerate a lag time of any significant length. See, however, *Boeing Co.*, ASBCA 20875, 85-3 BCA ¶ 18,351, in which the board permitted a three-week lag in the preparation of labor-cost data since this was the period required by the contractor's accounting system. With that limitation, cost or pricing data must be updated so that they meet the currency requirement. See, for example, *Hughes Aircraft Co.*, ASBCA 46321, 97-1 BCA ¶ 28,972, where this requirement was not met because vendor quotations received before the agreement on price were not disclosed.

The update requirement includes subcontractor data that are required by FAR 15.404-3(c) to be submitted to the government because of the size of the subcontract, *Martin Marietta Corp.*, ASBCA 43223, 96-2 BCA ¶ 28,270. In *Arral Indus.*,

Inc., ASBCA 41493, 96-1 BCA ¶ 28,030, the board rejected the contractor's argument that price agreement had been reached on a date several weeks earlier than the date on the Certificate of Current Cost or Pricing Data because the government contract specialist involved on the earlier date did not have the authority to agree on the price. As a result, the board found the contractor failed to update a vendor price. See also *Martin Marietta Corp.*, ASBCA 48223, 98-1 BCA ¶ 29,592, in which the board rejected the contractor's argument that no updated subcontractor data were required because the subcontract was firmly priced a number of months before the contractor's Certificate. The board found that there were continuing negotiations between the contractor and the subcontractor, which required that the data be updated.

(7) Explaining the Significance of the Data

In a number of cases, it has been held that the submission of cost or pricing data without an explanation of their significance is a failure to meet the statutory requirement. Thus, a contractor must make efforts to tell the government pricing personnel, in instances where a connection is not readily apparent, how the data are relevant to the cost estimate. This obligation occurs in two distinct situations—when the data are complex or unusual in nature, and when data are resubmitted to update previously submitted data.

The complexity of the data is determined on a case-by-case basis. For example, in *Grumman Aerospace Corp.*, ASBCA 35188, 90-2 BCA ¶ 22,842, the contractor had not explained the significance of labor-hour data submitted to the government in computerized form. The board determined that the relevance of the data was not readily apparent to the government pricing personnel and that the contractor failed to meet the submission requirement when it did not explain the data. In contrast, in *Boeing Co.*, ASBCA 32753, 90-1 BCA ¶ 22,270, *recons. denied*, 90-1 BCA ¶ 22,426, it was found that the contractor met the submission requirement when it submitted raw data on labor rates without explanation. The board found that the government personnel were fully capable of using the data in a raw form and that, therefore, no further explanation of the data was required.

This rule requiring explanation of the data also applies if the data contain information that is unusual in nature. For example, in the *Grumman* case, the contractor submitted information on an interdivisional order but did not disclose that the price of the order included profit. The board ruled that this nondisclosure was a failure to meet the submission requirement because the contractor knew that the inclusion of profit in such orders was generally against government policy.

The rule also applies in cases where the contractor updates prior data. For example, in *Singer Co. v. United States*, 217 Ct. Cl. 225, 576 F.2d 905 (1978), the court held that the mailing to government field pricing personnel and auditors of monthly reports that cited labor hours incurred by the offeror did not meet the submission requirement. The court was critical of the offeror's failure to identify specifically how this information related to the cost estimate. Similarly, cost or pricing data that are related to other procurements do not meet the submission requirement if the offeror has not connected the data to the contract at hand, *Sylvania Elec. Prods., Inc. v. United States*, 202 Ct. Cl. 16, 479 F.2d 1342 (1973).

(8) Subcontractor Data

Since the Truth in Negotiations Act applies to subcontractors as well as contractors, subcontractors are required to submit cost or pricing data to their contractors or higher tier subcontractors when the statutory exceptions do not apply. Contractors and higher tier subcontractors are required to "[c]onduct appropriate cost or price analysis to establish the reasonableness of proposed subcontract prices" and the "[i]nclude the results of these analysis in the price proposal," FAR 15.404-3(b). This can lead to the anomalous situation, when the contractor or higher tier subcontractor does not obtain cost or pricing data until after it has negotiated its price with the government or contractor respectively, of giving the contractor or higher tier subcontractor a right to a price adjustment for defective data, but leaving the government or the contractor no such remedy.

In order to avoid this result, FAR 15.404-3(c) requires contractors and higher tier subcontractors to submit certain subcontractor cost or pricing data to the government as part of their submission:

> (c) Any contractor or subcontractor that is required to submit cost or pricing data also shall obtain and analyze cost or pricing data before awarding any subcontract, purchase order, or modification expected to exceed the cost or pricing data threshold, unless an exception in 15.403-1(b) applies to that action.
>
>> (1) The contractor shall submit, or cause to be submitted by the subcontractor(s), cost or pricing data to the Government for subcontracts that are the lower of either—
>>
>>> (i) $ 10,000,000 or more; or
>>>
>>> (ii) Both more than the pertinent cost or pricing data threshold and more than 10 percent of the prime contractor's proposed price, unless the contracting officer believes such submission is unnecessary.
>>
>> (2) The contracting officer may require the contractor or subcontractor to submit to the Government (or cause submission of) subcontractor cost or pricing data below the thresholds in paragraph (c)(1) of this subsection that the contracting officer considers necessary for adequately pricing the prime contract.

> (3) Subcontractor cost or pricing data shall be submitted in the format provided in Table 15-2 of 15.408 or the alternate format specified in the solicitation.
>
> (4) Subcontractor cost or pricing data shall be current, accurate, and complete as of the date of price agreement, or, if applicable, an earlier date agreed upon by the parties and specified on the contractor's Certificate of Current Cost or Pricing Data. The contractor shall update subcontractor's data, as appropriate, during source selection and negotiations.
>
> (5) If there is more than one prospective subcontractor for any given work, the contractor need only submit to the Government cost or pricing data for the prospective subcontractor most likely to receive the award.

When the contractor has submitted such subcontractor cost or pricing data with its data, it is liable for defects in the data, *Lockheed Aircraft Corp. v. United States*, 193 Ct. Cl. 86, 432 F.2d 801 (1970). In that case, the court held the contractor liable even though the subcontractor data had been submitted directly to the government, not to the contractor. The court reasoned that the contractor's liability was dictated by the contract clause requiring price reductions. See also *McDonnell Aircraft Co.*, ASBCA 44504, 97-1 BCA ¶ 28,977, holding a contractor liable for not furnishing updated subcontractor information on a lower tier subcontractor. In a later decision, *McDonnell Aircraft Co.*, ASBCA 44504, 03-1 BCA ¶ 32,154, the board rejected the contractor's argument that this rule should not apply because the subcontractor data applied only to a prospective subcontractor, not an actual subcontractor.

d. Contract Disputes Act of 1978

The Contract Disputes Act of 1978, 41 U.S.C. § 605(c)(1), provides that each claim over $100,000 must be certified with regard to four specific elements:

> For claims of more than $100,000, the contractor shall certify that the claim is made in good faith, that the supporting data are complete and accurate to the best of his knowledge and belief, that the amount requested accurately reflects the contract adjustment for which the contractor believes the government is liable, and that the certifier is duly authorized to certify the claim on behalf of the contractor.

Neither the statutes nor regulations specifically require the submission of supporting data. All that is expressly required is that the contractor certify that "supporting data" are accurate and complete. Although a certification that the data are "complete" could be interpreted as a requirement for submission, there has been disagreement over whether the contractor is affirmatively required to submit data. See *Joseph P. Mentor*, GSBCA 6757, 85-1 BCA ¶ 17,887, in which the board held that the certification was not intended to force contractors to submit evidence in support of their claims, but was merely an "honesty" requirement designed to discourage inflated claims. However, the scope of the certification of data is broad. See *LaBarge Elecs.*,

ASBCA 44401, 93-2 BCA ¶ 25,617, holding that supporting data for a claim cannot be limited to data concerning the amount but must also include data in support of entitlement. See also *Triasco Corp.*, ASBCA 42465, 91-2 BCA ¶ 23,969, stating that this certification covers "all supporting data." See Chapter 13 for an in-depth discussion of the certification requirements under the Contract Disputes Act.

The Contract Disputes Act contains sanctions for the misrepresentation of facts when submitting a claim. 41 U.S.C. § 604 provides:

> If a contractor is unable to support any part of his claim and it is determined that such inability is attributable to misrepresentation of fact or fraud on the part of the contractor, he shall be liable to the Government for an amount equal to such unsupported part of the claim in addition to all costs to the Government attributable to the cost of reviewing said part of his claim. Liability under this subsection shall be determined within six years of the commission of such misrepresentation of fact or fraud.

The Act contains no definition of fraud. However, 41 U.S.C. § 601(7) defines "misrepresentation of fact" as follows:

> [T]he term "misrepresentation of fact" means a false statement of substantive fact, or any conduct which leads to a belief of a substantive fact material to proper understanding of the matter in hand, made with intent to deceive or mislead.

It is not possible to enforce this section in litigation before the appeals boards under the Contract Disputes Act because of the following language in 41 U.S.C. § 605(a):

> Each claim by a contractor against the government relating to a contract and each claim by the government against a contractor relating to a contract shall be submitted within 6 years after the accrual of the claim. The preceding sentence does not apply to a claim by the government against a contractor that is based on a claim by the contractor involving fraud. . . . The authority of this subsection shall not extend to a claim or dispute for penalties or forfeitures prescribed by statute or regulation which another Federal agency is specifically authorized to administer, settle or determine.

Based on this language, the boards of contract appeals have refused to rule on a counterclaim for the penalty prescribed in § 604, *Comada Corp.*, ASBCA 26613, 83-2 BCA ¶ 16,681 ("actions to enforce the Government's rights under [Section 604] would be solely the responsibility of the Department of Justice and would be instituted by the United States in a court of competent jurisdiction"), or on a defense that the claim was fraudulent, *Schmalz Constr., Ltd.*, AGBCA 86-207-1, 91-3 BCA ¶ 24,183 ("[I]t is sufficient for the Board to determine whether statements in a claim are correct or incorrect. The Board does not need to determine whether incorrect statements were made knowingly or with an intent to deceive."). Thus, the remedy in the boards of contract appeals for claims that have been found in another proceeding to be "tainted by fraud" is dismissal of the claim, *Beech Gap, Inc.*, ENGBCA 5585, 95-2 BCA ¶ 27,879, *aff'd* 86 F.3d 1177 (Fed. Cir. 1997); *P.H. Mech. Corp. v. General Servs. Admin.*, GSBCA 10567, 94-2 BCA ¶ 26,785. Following this view that the appeals boards have no jurisdiction over claims involving § 604, a board has also refused to hear a contractor's claim that the contracting officer improperly assessed the penalty prescribed in that section, *Warren Beaves*, DOTCAB 1324, 83-1 BCA ¶ 16,232.

Counterclaims for the § 604 penalty can be asserted in the Court of Federal Claims in the same manner that all fraud counterclaims are asserted in that court without a prior decision of the contracting officer, *Simko Constr., Inc. v. United States*, 852 F.2d 540 (Fed. Cir. 1988). Such counterclaims are generally asserted along with counterclaims under the False Claims Act and the False Statements Act, *UMC Elecs. Co. v. United States*, 43 Fed. Cl. 776 (1999); *Crane Helicopter Servs., Inc. v. United States*, 45 Fed. Cl. 410 (1999); *Commercial Contractors, Inc. v. United States*, 154 F.3d 1357 (Fed. Cir. 1998); *Chemray Coatings Corp. v. United States*, 29 Fed. Cl. 278 (1993); *Tyger Constr. Co. v. United States*, 28 Fed. Cl. 35 (1993). See *JANA, Inc. v. United States,* 34 Fed. Cl. 447 (1995), in which the court held that the government's counterclaim alleging fraud under the CDA was timely because the Act's six-year statute of limitations for fraud could begin to run no earlier than the submission of the contractor's certified claim, regardless of when the conduct rendering the contractor's false claim allegedly occurred.

e. 10 U.S.C. § 2410 Certification

Another statute dealing with certifying supporting data for requests for equitable adjustment and requests for relief under Pub. L. No. 85-804 on DoD contracts is 10 U.S.C. § 2410. This statute was amended by the Federal Acquisition Streamlining Act to make it clear that the provision applies only to requests for equitable adjustment or for relief under Pub. L. No. 85-804. As amended, 10 U.S.C. § 2410 establishes the following certification requirement:

> (a) Certification Requirement.—A request for equitable adjustment to contract terms or request for relief under Public Law 85-804 (50 U.S.C. 1431 et seq.) that exceeds the simplified acquisition threshold may not be paid unless a person authorized to certify the request on behalf of the contractor certifies, at the time the request is submitted, that—
>
>> (1) the request is made in good faith, and
>>
>> (2) the supporting data are accurate and complete to the best of that person's knowledge and belief.

Note that this statute also does not contain a clear requirement for the submission of data. The Federal Acquisition Streamlining Act also repealed the DoD-unique claim certification requirement contained in 10 U.S.C. § 2410e, thus leaving the Contract Disputes Act claim certification as the single government-wide standard.

2. Types of Illegal Conduct

In the 1980s and 1990s government contractors were heavily investigated and prosecuted for failure to deal openly and honestly with the federal government. The major types of conduct that have led to such accusations of criminality are covered in this subsection.

a. Product Substitution

Product substitution generally refers to attempts by the contractor to deliver to the government a product that does not conform to the contract requirements. Such substitution can occur by mismarking products, deviating from specifications, and other types of conduct that may indicate an intention to deceive the government in the performance of the contract. Such conduct may subject contractors to criminal or civil sanctions under the False Claims Act. See, for example, *BMY-Combat Sys. Div. of Harsco Corp. v. United States*, 38 Fed. Cl. 109 (1997), finding false claims when the contractor knowingly failed to fully inspect military equipment. The court also voided final acceptance of the equipment and held the contractor liable for breach of contract. See also *Varljen v. Cleveland Gear Co.*, 250 F.3d 426 (6th Cir. 2001) (false claim when subcontractor changed manufacturing process without approval after qualifying item); *United States ex rel. Roby v. Boeing Co.*, 100 F. Supp. 2d 619 (S.D. Ohio 2000) (false claim to knowingly furnish helicopter transmission gears known to be defective); *United States v. Hangar One, Inc.*, 563 F.2d 1155 (5th Cir. 1977) (false claim to rig inspection system to omit required inspections and deliver rejected items); and *Imperial Meat Co. v. United States*, 316 F.2d 435 (10th Cir.), *cert. denied*, 375 U.S. 820 (1963) (false claim when contractor substituted an inferior grade of meat on a DoD contract). In *United States v. National Wholesalers*, 236 F.2d 944 (9th Cir. 1956), *cert. denied*, 353 U.S. 930 (1957), the contractor indicated to the government that it would supply brand name regulators, but instead manufactured the regulators itself and attached false brand name labels before delivery. The court found the contractor liable for a false claim even though the regulators were in fact equal. See also *United States v. Aerodex, Inc.*, 469 F.2d 1003 (5th Cir. 1972), in which the court found a false claim when the contractor knowingly substituted aircraft bearings that differed from the contract specifications, even though there was no proof that they were inferior. Other statutes used to prosecute product substitution include the False Statements Act, 18 U.S.C. § 1001; the conspiracy statutes, 18 U.S.C. § 286 and § 371; the mail and wire fraud statutes, 18 U.S.C. § 1341 and § 1343; and the Racketeer Influenced and Corrupt Organizations Act, 18 U.S.C. §§ 1961-1968.

Product substitution with an intent to defraud has also led to the loss of disputes cases in the boards of contract appeals. For example, in *D & H Constr. Co.*, ASBCA 37482, 89-3 BCA ¶ 22,070, the contractor's substitution of refrigerators with counterfeited certification labels rose to the level of fraud and voided final acceptance. Similarly, a default termination will be sustained if the contractor has fraudulently performed defective work, *Beech Gap, Inc.*, ENGBCA 5585, 95-2 BCA ¶ 27,879, *aff'd*, 86 F.3d 1177 (Fed. Cir. 1997).

When a contractor does not deliver goods that conform precisely to contract requirements, there may not be an intent to defraud, but the government still has contract remedies. Thus, it may obtain a price reduction equivalent to the amount of costs saved plus overhead and profit, *Santa Fe Engr's, Inc.*, ASBCA 44906, 93-1 BCA ¶ 25,298 (substitution of less expensive door); *Arnold M. Diamond, Inc.*, ASBCA 38974, 92-2 BCA ¶ 24,869 (use of fewer expansion joints than called for by specifications); *J.S. Alberici Constr. Co.*, GSBCA 10630, 92-1 BCA ¶ 24,392 (substitution of less expensive doors); *Bruce Andersen Co.*, ASBCA 29412, 89-2 BCA ¶ 21,872 (omission of work called for by contract). Even if the substitute is equal to that specified in the contract, acceptance may harm the procurement system, which is based on all competitors offering to furnish only the product called for in the contract. Allowing offerors to substitute products according to their own judgment would defeat the concept of bidding on an equal basis. See *Ideal Rest. Supply Co.*, VACAB 570, 67-1 BCA ¶ 6237, in which the board found that the government was justified in rejecting equivalent supplies that did not meet contract specifications and noted that allowing the contractor to substitute aluminum for nickel alloy and stainless steel in steam kettle parts could have a negative effect on the competitive bidding process. Similarly, in *J.L. Malone & Assocs.*, VABCA 2335, 88-3 BCA ¶ 20,894, *aff'd*, 879 F.2d 841 (Fed. Cir. 1989), the government rejected a contractor's substitution of a technically equivalent computer in the installation of a fire alarm system. The board stated that the preservation of the integrity of the competitive procurement system was more important than any benefits that could derive even from replacing the specified computer with a more advanced one at no extra cost to the government.

b. Mischarging/Accounting Fraud

Mischarging is the term used to describe a particular type of fraud involving the accounting treatment of costs by contractors. Mischarging is the false description and the improper charging of costs to a government contract. The contractual remedy for mischarging is the disallowance of the costs, including all costs incurred because of the mischarging. See FAR 31.205-15, which provides:

> (b) Costs incurred in connection with, or related to, the mischarging of costs on Government contracts are unallowable when the costs are caused by, or result from, alteration or destruction of records, or other false or improper charging or recording of costs. Such costs include those incurred to measure or otherwise determine the magnitude of the improper charging, and costs incurred to remedy or correct the mischarging, such as costs to rescreen and reconstruct records.

Mischarging can arise in several instances, including improper allocation of costs and charging of expressly unallowable costs to a contract. If a contractor includes an "expressly unallowable" cost in a proposal to settle indirect costs, the agency must assess a penalty against the contractor, in addition to disallowance of the cost, in the amount of the cost claimed plus interest on those costs, 10 U.S.C. § 2324(b); 41 U.S.C. § 256(b). These sections also provide that the penalty will be double the amount of the claimed cost if it has been "determined to be unallowable in the case of such contractor before the submission of such proposal."

Mischarging is also subject to criminal and civil sanctions under the False Claims Act as well as other criminal sanctions. For example, in *United States v. McGunnigal*, 151 F.2d 162 (1st Cir.), *cert. denied*, 326 U.S. 776 (1945), a criminal conspiracy was found between welders and counters who manufactured and constructed ships under a cost-reimbursement contract, resulting in inflated payroll costs. See *United States v. Maher*, 582 F.2d 842 (4th Cir. 1978), *cert. denied*, 439 U.S. 1115 (1979), where false claims requesting payments under a time-and-materials contract were submitted. The accountant involved was instructed to inflate labor hours on monthly billings, prepare new time sheets that conformed to the changes, trace over employees' signatures on the new time sheets, and destroy the originals. See also *United States v. Newport News Shipbuilding, Inc.*, 276 F. Supp. 2d 539 (E.D. Va. 2003) (charging costs of designing commercial ships to IR&D); *United States ex rel. Newsham v. Lockheed Missile & Space Co.*, 190 F.3d 963 (9th Cir. 1999) (allegedly billing costs of unproductive labor and time workers spent on personal projects); *Jana, Inc. v. United States*, 41 Fed. Cl. 735 (1998) (altering time cards); *United States ex rel. Mayman v. Martin Marietta Corp.*, 894 F. Supp. 218 (D.C. Md. 1995) (proposing low costs for work with intention of charging costs of performance to IR&D); *Young-Montenay, Inc. v. United States*, 15 F.3d 1040 (Fed. Cir. 1994) (altering subcontractor invoice in order to inflate progress payment); *United States v. TDC Mgmt. Corp.*, 24 F.3d 292 (D.C. Cir. 1994) (omission of information from cost reports); *United States v. Sperry Corp.*, Civ. 89-2472 (E.D.N.Y. 1991) (contractor employees falsely filled out time cards indicating work on one contract when the work was properly chargeable to other jobs); and *United States v. Lagerbusch*, 361 F.2d 449 (3d Cir. 1966) (false representations in invoices submitted to cost-type contractor). See also *United States v. Richmond*, 700 F.2d 1183 (8th Cir. 1983). For an in-depth analysis of other mischarging cases, see Graham, "*Mischarging: A Contract Dispute or a Criminal Fraud*?" 15 Pub. Cont. L.J. 208 (1985).

c. *Fraudulent Pricing*

As discussed previously, the Truth in Negotiations Act requires that before price negotiations for negotiated contracts, government contractors must disclose the facts relevant to those negotiations and certify that the facts are accurate, complete, and current. However, the failure to submit complete, current, and accurate cost or pricing data has been treated as fraud in only a few cases. There are two types of defective pricing situations that are often treated as instances of fraud—the falsification of cost or pricing data and the submission of inaccurate estimates.

(1) Fraudulent Data

For many years, *United States v. Foster Wheeler Corp.*, 447 F.2d 100 (2d Cir. 1971), which affirmed a district court decision that the contractor had committed civil fraud by submitting defective cost or pricing data, was the only reported decision in this area. More recently, in *UMC Elecs. Co. v. United States*, 43 Fed. Cl. 776 (1999), fraud was found when the contractor submitted full cost or pricing data to support its claim but listed its "actual costs" by summarizing its purchase order prices even though there were several instances where subcontractors and suppliers had not invoiced for work at those prices. The court found that the contractor knew full well the difference between actual costs and estimates because it had made the difference clear in prior submissions of cost or pricing data. The court therefore found that the inclusion by the contractor of uninvoiced costs in its statement of "actual costs" was a fraudulent statement. Similarly, in *United States v. Leo*, 941 F.2d 181 (3d Cir.1991), fraud was found when a contractor's negotiator affirmatively stated that its estimate of subcontract prices would be difficult to attain when it had knowingly failed to provide the government with subcontract prices that had been substantially reduced, and in *United States v. Pimental & Duroyd Mfg. Co.*, 810 F.2d 366 (2d Cir. 1987), fraud was found when the contractor obtained quotations from eight vendors but submitted only the highest quote to the contracting officer while buying at the low price. See also *United States v. Poarch*, 878 F.2d 1355 (11th Cir. 1989), in which the circuit court affirmed the conviction of a defense firm's contracts administrator for conspiracy to defraud the United States and for criminal false statements. Fraud was found when an administrator (1) told an employee to charge time to a wrong account in order to build up labor hours and (2) omitted current labor-hour data from the submission of cost or pricing data that had been required by the contracting officer. A number of fraud cases in this area involve the creation and submission of false data by the contractor. See *United States v. Barnette*, 800 F.2d 1558 (11th Cir. 1986), *cert. denied*, 480 U.S. 935 (1987), where the contractor created false payroll records and false invoices from bogus vendors to inflate its proposed contract prices, and *United States v. Busher*, 817 F.2d 1409 (9th Cir. 1987), where the contractor falsified data relating to performance of work by subcontractors.

Cases litigating the issue of whether the government should obtain a price reduction for defective pricing appear to be easily distinguishable from those involving prosecution for civil or criminal fraud. Price reduction cases largely deal with technical interpretations of the submission requirement. In most instances, the contractor has made major submissions but has omitted some discrete data. The fraud cases generally involve either falsification of data or a scheme to obtain a higher price. Thus, if a contractor makes a serious effort to disclose the cost or pricing data used in preparing its proposal, it is probably not in jeopardy of being charged with fraud. However, a contractor that adopts practices that permit regular nondisclosure of such data is taking an unreasonable business risk. If the government concludes that higher prices are being obtained through the use of such practices, a charge of fraud is likely.

(2) Inaccurate Estimates

In a few cases, contractors have been held liable for submitting egregiously inaccurate estimates. In the original case of this type, *United States ex rel. Taxpayers Against Fraud v. Singer Co.*, 889 F.2d 1327 (4th Cir. 1989), the fraud was found in not submitting the contractor's "best estimates" as certified on the Standard Form 1411, as follows:

> This proposal is submitted in response to the RFP, contract, modification, etc. in Item 1 and reflects our best estimates and/or actual costs aqs of this data and conforms with the instructions in FAR 15.804-6(b)(2). . . .

Similarly, in *United States v. Sperry Corp.*, Civ. 89-2472 (E.D.N.Y. 1991), the government alleged that the contractor submitted a low estimate on the original contract, and after buying in, submitted high estimates on the follow-on contracts for which the contractor was the sole source. Subsequently, in *United States v. Bicoastal Corp.*, Cr. No. 92-CR-261 (N.D.N.Y. 1992), a contractor pleaded guilty to charges arising from the submission of inflated, fraudulent labor estimates on negotiated sole-source contracts for flight simulators. The contractor had submitted cost estimates that included amounts allocated for fictitious jobs and personnel that purported to be necessary costs. The contractor certified that each cost estimate was its best estimate, while it routinely concealed a lower estimate. The Standard Form 1411 has been removed from the FAR, but Table 15-2—Instructions for Submitting Cost/Price Proposals When Cost or Pricing Data Are Required, FAR 15.408, contains the following required statement (removing the word "best") on such proposals:

> This proposal reflects our estimates and/or actual costs as of this data and conforms with the instructions in FAR 15.403-5(b)(1) and Table 15-2. . . .

This removes the issue of whether the estimate submitted was the "best" estimate but does not affect the question of whether the estimate was fraudulently compiled.

Other fraud cases also involve the submission of estimates of a contract's cost of performance when the contractor is aware that the estimate does not reflect its anticipated allowable costs. See *United States v. White*, 765 F.2d 1469 (11th Cir. 1985), where the contractor submitted an estimate of the cost of fully performed work under change orders that was far higher than the actual costs that had been incurred and recorded in its accounting data. The court held that the contractor had represented to the government that its estimate reflected actual costs. See also *Harrison v. Westinghouse Savannah River Co.*, 176 F.3d 776 (4th Cir. 1999) (false claim to misstate the scope and length of work to be subcontracted in order to obtain government approval to subcontract), and *United States v. General Dynamics Corp.*, 19

F.3d 770 (2d Cir. 1994) (false claim to include kickbacks paid to subcontractor in cost estimates submitted to the government).

(3) Buying-In

Submitting a low price in order to obtain additional compensation during contract performance or through obtaining follow-on contracts is not per se fraudulent, *United States ex rel. Bettis v. Odebrecht Contractors of Cal., Inc.*, 297 F. Supp. 2d 272 (D.D.C. 2004), *aff'd*, 393 F.3d 1321 (D.C. Cir. 2005). After concluding that contracting at a low price could not be equated with falsely claiming money to which the contractor was not entitled, the district court reasoned at 281:

> The fact that a deflated bid alone cannot suffice to impose liability under the FCA is not, however, cured by merely adding a claim that defendant sought monies above and beyond the bid price. Such a proposition completely ignores the reality of government contracting where it is common for a contract that was bid at one price to ultimately cost far more. For instance, as previously noted, in a unit-price contract, such as [this] contract, the final price will necessarily be different if the actual quantities of materials turn out to be greater than the government's original quantity estimates. Further, as plaintiff concedes..., it is perfectly acceptable for the government to modify the scope of work or to change the design specifications. Alternatively, the final price can be increased if the government's representations about the nature of the project turn out to be inaccurate. Since there are a myriad of legitimate adjustments that can increase a contract price beyond the bid price, it necessarily follows that plaintiff cannot rest only on proof of a fraudulently induced contract by means of a low bid and an attempt by the bidder to obtain monies in excess of the bid price. Rather, there must be a claim "for money to which...[the contractor] is not legitimately entitled."

d. Equitable Adjustment Claims

Making false statements or allegations in equitable adjustment claims has also been found to be fraudulent. For example, in *United States ex rel. Wilkins v. North Am. Constr. Corp.*, 101 F. Supp. 2d 500 (S.D. Tex. 2000), the court found a proper allegation of fraud when the contractor based a differing site conditions claim on allegedly defective information that had been provided by the government when it had considerable indications that the government information was accurate. In *Commercial Contractors, Inc. v. United States*, 154 F.3d 1357 (Fed. Cir. 1998), the court also found fraud in the substantive allegations in a differing site condition claim. Similarly, in *P.H. Mech. Corp. v. General Servs. Admin.*, GSBCA 10567, 94-2 BCA ¶ 26,785, fraud was found where a contractor falsified receipts, invoices, and records supporting an equitable adjustment claim. See also *Shaw v. AAA Eng'g & Drafting, Inc.*, 213 F.3d 519 (10th Cir. 2000), where the contractor falsely inflated numbers on official work orders used to support an equitable adjustment claim. In *AAA Eng'g & Drafting, Inc.*, ASBCA 47940, 01-1 BCA ¶ 31,256, the board denied a subsequent equitable adjustment claim based on this court decision.

D. Obtaining Information Improperly

There are several sanctions for improperly disclosing or obtaining information related to the procurement process. 18 U.S.C. § 1905 imposes criminal sanctions on any government employee who discloses trade secrets and other proprietary data obtained from any person or organization. The procurement integrity provisions of the Office of Procurement Policy Act of 1989, 41 U.S.C. § 423, prohibit any person from disclosing "contractor bid or proposal information" or "source selection information" before contract award, 41 U.S.C. § 423(a). There may also be improper conduct involved in obtaining information about a competitor.

1. Disclosure of Confidential Information

18 U.S.C. § 1905 provides:

> Whoever, being an officer or employee of the United States or of any department or agency thereof, any person acting on behalf of the Office of Federal Housing Enterprise Oversight, or agent of the Department of Justice as defined in the Antitrust Civil Process Act (15 U.S.C. 1311-1314), or being an employee of a private sector organization who is or was assigned to an agency under Chapter 37 of title 5, publishes, divulges, discloses, or makes known in any manner or to any extent not authorized by law any information coming to him in the course of his employment or official duties or by reason of any examination or investigation made by, or return, report or record made to or filed with, such department or agency or officer or employee thereof, which information concerns or relates to the trade secrets, processes, operations, style of work, or apparatus, or to the identity, confidential statistical data, amount or source of any income, profits, losses, or expenditures of any person, firm, partnership, corporation, or association; or permits any income return or copy thereof or any book containing any abstract or particulars thereof to be seen or examined by any person except as provided by law; shall be fined under this title, or imprisoned not more than one year, or both; and shall be removed from office or employment.

The conviction of a government employee under 18 U.S.C. § 1905 for improper disclosure of information was affirmed in *United States v. Wallington*, 889 F.2d 573 (5th Cir. 1989). The court held that the Act was not overly broad to constitute a valid criminal statute.

2. Disclosure of and Obtaining Bid or Proposal Information or Source Selection Information

The Clinger-Cohen Act of 1996 amended the Procurement Integrity Act, 41 U.S.C. § 423, to streamline the provisions on disclosure of and obtaining information. The amended Act contains two provisions relating to such transmission of information. 41 U.S.C. § 423(a) prohibits a "person" from knowingly disclosing "contractor bid or proposal information" or "source selection information" before award of a contract. The "person" covered is defined in 41 U.S.C. § 423(a)(2) as anyone who

> (A) is a present or former official of the United States, or a person who is acting or has acted for or on behalf of, or who is advising or has advised the United States with respect to, a Federal agency procurement; and
>
> (B) by virtue of that office, employment, or relationship has or had access to contractor bid or proposal information or source selection information.

The term "official" is defined in 41 U.S.C. § 423(f)(7) as (1) an officer as defined in 5 U.S.C. § 2104, (2) an employee as defined in 5 U.S.C. § 2105, and (3) a member of the uniformed forces as defined in 5 U.S.C. § 2101(3). FAR 3.104-3 adds to this the category of "special Government employees" as defined in 18 U.S.C. § 202. This statute provides a new test for what persons are covered by this paragraph of the Act. They are persons who have either "acted" or "advised" regarding a federal agency procurement and have obtained information through that contact with the procurement. Neither the statute nor the implementation of this part of the Act in FAR 3.104-4 contains any guidance on the meaning of the terms "acted" or "advised," with the apparent effect that this rule applies to persons who have acted or advised no matter how small their contact with the procurement. This would seem to apply this part of the Act to virtually anyone who obtained information in the course of participating in the procurement, unless he or she was a total bystander who obtained information in the course of observing the procurement.

The second prohibition is in 41 U.S.C. § 423(b), prohibiting a "person" from knowingly obtaining "contractor bid or proposal information" or "source selection information" before award of a contract to which the information pertains. The Act contains no definition of the "persons" covered by this paragraph, with the result that it appears to apply to any contractor, other business entity, or individual who obtains information even if that person is not participating in the procurement. It also seems to apply the prohibition without regard to the source of the information, with the result that it could arguably be a violation to obtain the information from a newspaper reporter or some other person not connected with the procurement. The only narrowing of the rule is that it is no longer a violation of the Act to solicit information if the information is not obtained.

The Act applies only to a "federal agency procurement," and this term is defined in 41 U.S.C. § 423(f)(4) to mean only acquisitions using competitive procedures. This is an important reduction from the coverage of the prior Act because officials who have participated in sole source procurements or contract modifications are not covered by the new Act. However, the implementation of this provision of the Act in FAR 3.104-4 applies these rules without regard to this statutory limitation, as follows:

> (a) Except as specifically provided for in this subsection, no person or other entity may disclose contractor bid or proposal information or source selection informa-

> tion to any person other than a person authorized, in accordance with applicable agency regulations or procedures, by the head of the agency or the contracting officer to receive such information.

(b) Contractor bid or proposal information and source selection information must be protected from unauthorized disclosure in accordance with 14.401, 15.207, applicable law, and agency regulations.

This broadening of the prohibition beyond the scope of the Procurement Integrity Act reflects the fact that 18 U.S.C. § 1905 is a blanket prohibition on disclosure of proprietary information.

The two types of information protected from disclosure are defined in 41 U.S.C. § 423(f) as follows:

> (1) The term "contractor bid or proposal information" means any of the following information submitted to a Federal agency as part of or in connection with a bid or proposal to enter into a Federal agency procurement contract, if that information has not been previously made available to the public or disclosed publicly:
>
> > (A) Cost or pricing data (as defined by section 2306a(h) of title 10, United States Code, with respect to procurements subject to that section, and section 304A(h) of the Federal Property and Administrative Services Act of 1949 (41 U.S.C. 254b(h)), with respect to procurements subject to that section).
> >
> > (B) Indirect costs and direct labor rates.
> >
> > (C) Proprietary information about manufacturing processes, operations, or techniques marked by the contractor in accordance with applicable law or regulation.
> >
> > (D) Information marked by the contractor as "contractor bid or proposal information", in accordance with applicable law or regulation.
>
> (2) The term "source selection information" means any of the following information prepared for use by a Federal agency for the purpose of evaluating a bid or proposal to enter into a Federal agency procurement contract, if that information has not been previously made available to the public or disclosed publicly:
>
> > (A) Bid prices submitted in response to a Federal agency solicitation for sealed bids, or lists of those bid prices before public bid opening.
> >
> > (B) Proposed costs or prices submitted in response to a Federal agency solicitation, or lists of those proposed costs or prices.
> >
> > (C) Source selection plans.

(D) Technical evaluation plans.

(E) Technical evaluations of proposals.

(F) Cost or price evaluations of proposals.

(G) Competitive range determinations that identify proposals that have a reasonable chance of being selected for award of a contract.

(H) Rankings of bids, proposals, or competitors.

(I) The reports and evaluations of source selection panels, boards, or advisory councils.

(J) Other information marked as "source selection information" based on a case-by-case determination by the head of the agency, his designee, or the contracting officer that its disclosure would jeopardize the integrity or successful completion of the Federal agency procurement to which the information relates.

41 U.S.C. §423 contains a number of "savings provisions," as follows:

(h) *Savings Provisions.*—This section does not—

(1) restrict the disclosure of information to, or its receipt by, any person or class of persons authorized, in accordance with applicable agency regulations or procedures, to receive that information;

(2) restrict a contractor from disclosing its own bid or proposal information or the recipient from receiving that information;

(3) restrict the disclosure or receipt of information relating to a Federal agency procurement after it has been canceled by the Federal agency before contract award unless the Federal agency plans to resume the procurement;

(4) prohibit individual meetings between a Federal agency official and an offeror or potential offeror for, or a recipient of, a contract or subcontract under a Federal agency procurement, provided that unauthorized disclosure or receipt of contractor bid or proposal information or source selection information does not occur;

(5) authorize the withholding of information from, nor restrict its receipt by, Congress, a committee or subcommittee of Congress, the Comptroller General, a Federal agency, or an inspector general of a Federal agency;

(6) authorize the withholding of information from, nor restrict its receipt by, the Comptroller General of the United States in the course of a protest against the award or proposed award of a Federal agency procurement contract; or

> (7) limit the applicability of any requirements, sanctions, contract penalties, and remedies established under any other law or regulation.

These provisions are implemented at FAR 3.104-4(e) and (f). It seems clear that these rules should not prevent open communication between contracting agencies and potential offerors regarding the work to be procured and the procurement strategy before solicitations are issued as long as specific finalized source selection plans and technical evaluation plans are not revealed. It also places no limitations on obtaining information during litigation. See *Pikes Peak Family Hous., LLC v. United States*, 40 Fed Cl 673 (1998), permitting normal discovery in an award protest citing paragraph (7) above providing for discovery in a court proceeding as a "remedy" covered by the saving provisions of the Act.

There are severe penalties for violations of these provisions. See 41 U.S.C. § 423(e), which states:

> (1) *Criminal penalties*. Whoever engages in conduct constituting a violation of subsection (a) or (b) for the purpose of either—
>
> > (A) exchanging the information covered by such subsection for anything of value, or
> >
> > (B) obtaining or giving anyone a competitive advantage in the award of a Federal agency procurement contract, shall be imprisoned for not more than 5 years or fined as provided under title 18, United States Code, or both.
>
> (2) *Civil penalties*. The Attorney General may bring a civil action in an appropriate United States district court against any person who engages in conduct constituting a violation of subsection (a), (b), (c), or (d) of this section. Upon proof of such conduct by a preponderance of the evidence, the person is subject to a civil penalty. An individual who engages in such conduct is subject to a civil penalty of not more than $ 50,000 for each violation plus twice the amount of compensation which the individual received or offered for the prohibited conduct. An organization that engages in such conduct is subject to a civil penalty of not more than $ 500,000 for each violation plus twice the amount of compensation which the organization received or offered for the prohibited conduct.

3. Information about Competitors

The techniques for gaining information about competitors are diverse and may or may not be proper. These techniques range from the benign, such as reading a competitor's sales brochure, to the potentially criminal, such as business espionage. In *Compliance Corp. v. United States*, 22 Cl. Ct. 193 (1990), *aff'd*, 960 F.2d 157 (Fed. Cir. 1992), the offeror approached employees of the incumbent contractor, who was competing for a follow-on services contract, to obtain detailed information on how the incumbent contractor was performing the work and to discover the contents of the incumbent's proposal for the follow-on work. Upon learning of this conduct, the contracting officer disqualified the offeror, and the GAO sustained this action, *Compliance Corp.*, Comp. Gen. Dec. B-239252, 90-2 CPD ¶ 126, *recons. denied*, B-239252.3, 90-2 CPD ¶ 435. The Claims Court agreed with this decision, stating at 204:

> The court finds actual or attempted "industrial espionage" to be outside the realm of normal business practices, and the contracting officer is entitled to disqualify those who engage in such conduct, not only to protect the integrity of the contracting process, but also to deter others from similar conduct.

Both the GAO and the GSBCA have disqualified companies that have improperly obtained information during the procurement process. In *Computer Tech. Assocs., Inc.*, Comp. Gen. Dec. B-288622, 2001 CPD ¶ 187, the GAO agreed that a competitor should be disqualified when it obtained and read e-mail transcripts of its competitors' oral presentations. The decision cites the Procurement Integrity Act provisions barring such conduct. Similarly, in *Litton Sys., Inc.*, 68 Comp. Gen. 422 (B-234060), 89-1 CPD ¶ 450, *recons. denied*, 68 Comp. Gen. 677 (B-234060.2), 89-2 CPD ¶ 228, the GAO disqualified an offeror that had obtained source selection information through a marketing consultant. See also *AT&T Communications, Inc.*, GSBCA 9252-P, 88-2 BCA ¶ 20,805, in which the board disqualified an offeror that had been given the competitive range prices by a government employee.

E. Conspiracy

It is a crime for two or more persons to agree to (1) commit any offense against the United States, 18 U.S.C. § 371, or (2) defraud the United States, 18 U.S.C. § 286, if any of the persons perform an act to effect the conspiracy. The unlawful object of a conspiracy could be the violation of any civil or criminal statute, *United States v. Feola*, 420 U.S. 671 (1975). A conspiracy to commit bribery is clearly included, and conspiracies involving gratuities or conflicts of interest also fall within 18 U.S.C. § 371, *United States v. Razete*, 199 F.2d 44 (6th Cir.), *cert. denied*, 344 U.S. 904 (1952). However, it is not necessary for the agreed-upon action to be a violation of statute. An agreement to defraud the United States in any manner would qualify. It is not necessary that the government lose money or property as a result of the fraud. All that is required is that "[the government's] legitimate official action and purpose shall be defeated by misrepresentation, chicane or . . . overreaching," *Hammerschmidt v. United States*, 265 U.S. 182 (1924).

An agreement to give preferential treatment to an offeror for a government contract is prohibited, Executive Order 12674, § 101(h) as modified by Executive Order 12731; 5 C.F.R. § 2635.101(b)(8). In proving the existence of such an agreement, the government is not required to establish a formal express agreement but can show a tacit understanding between the parties, *United States v. Paramount Pictures, Inc.*, 334 U.S. 131 (1948). This understanding can be proved by circumstantial evidence, *Hamling v. United States*, 418 U.S. 87 (1974); *Glasser v. United States*, 315 U.S. 60 (1942).

CHAPTER 2

CONTRACT INTERPRETATION

Numerous government contract performance problems and controversies stem from disagreements about the precise scope of the bargain between the government and the contractor . The complexity of government projects, the formality of the procedures used in contract formation, and the lengthy contract documents and specifications that are often present in federal procurement provide fertile ground for contract interpretation controversies. Resolution of these disputes will determine the amount or quality of work to be performed, the price to be paid, or the party who bears the responsibility for various events that may occur. Thus, an understanding of the rules and procedures used in the interpretation process is essential for resolving controversies and disagreements. It is also essential for parties to appreciate the significance of communications and acts that transpire during contract formation and performance and their relationship to the words in the contract document. Moreover, actions under a contract or a series of contracts and the interpretation of such contracts may impact obligations under future contracts.

Contract interpretation is the process of determining what the parties agreed to in their bargain, *Restatement, Second, Contracts* § 200. This process involves determining the meaning of words, supplying missing terms and filling in gaps, resolving ambiguities, and sometimes ruling that parties are bound to perform in a manner that appears to be contrary to the words of the contractual document. Courts and boards follow no predetermined, well-defined analytical framework when giving a contract meaning through the interpretive process. One cardinal rule, however, is to seek to ascertain a single interpretation of the contract that reflects the parties' intent. This is generally done by using an objective standard to give a contract its legally enforceable meaning.

Courts and boards seek this correct interpretation of a contract by looking to two sources of information that, when examined under various rules of interpretation, are intended to ensure that contract language is not given a distorted meaning: (1) the language in the contract documents and (2) evidence extrinsic to the contract documents, pertaining to facts and circumstances surrounding contract formation and performance.

When analysis of intent-determinative information fails to compel an interpretation, courts and boards will find that the contract language is ambiguous and will invoke other secondary methods to resolve interpretation issues. At this level, they will invoke rules calling for interpretation of the document against the drafter and imposing a duty to seek clarification on the contractor. These rules allocate risks of contractual ambiguities by resolving disputes in favor of the party least responsible for the ambiguity. For these secondary rules to be used, the party must have relied on the asserted interpretation, *Edward Marden Corp. v. United States*, 803 F.2d 701 (Fed. Cir. 1986).

This process of interpretation is fluid rather than rigid. Hence, courts and boards can and do begin the interpretive process at any of the above steps. If a clear interpretation is found, analysis ends; otherwise, a circuitous evaluation of the other factors may ensue.

The ultimate determination of what meaning is to be ascribed to the contract is a matter of law. However, questions of fact often must be dealt with in arriving at an interpretation. The relationship of questions of fact and law in the interpretation process was discussed in *Darwin Constr. Co. v. United States*, 31 Fed. Cl. 453 (1994), as follows at 456:

> Although contract interpretation is generally a question of law, questions of fact can arise as part of the analysis. What is most reasonable in a given set of circumstances is an issue of fact. *D & S Universal Mining Co. v. United States*, 4 Cl. Ct. 94, 97 (1983). Moreover, the existence of industry or trade practice is a question of fact, *John McShain, Inc., v. United States*, 199 Ct. Cl. 364, 370, 462 F.2d 489 (1972), evidence of which may always *explain* or *define*, as distinguished from *vary* or *contradict*, contract language. *W.G. Cornell Co. v. United States*, 179 Ct. Cl. 651, 670, 376 F.2d 299 (1967) (emphasis in original).

If there are no material questions of fact to be resolved, the interpretation can be resolved without an evidentiary hearing. See *Crown Laundry & Dry Cleaners, Inc. v. United States*, 29 Fed. Cl. 506 (1993), setting out the standards for disposition of an interpretation issue through summary judgment, stating at 515:

> Pure contract interpretation is a question of law which may be resolved by summary judgment. *P.J. Maffei Bldg. Wrecking Corp. v. United States*, 732 F.2d 913, 916 (Fed. Cir. 1984); *H.B. Zachry Co. v. United States*, 28 Fed. Cl. 77, 80 (1993). But, the question of interpretation of language, the conduct, and the intent of the parties, *i.e.*, the question of what is the meaning that should be given by a court to the words of a contract, may sometimes involve questions of material fact and not present a pure question of law. *Beta Systems, Inc. v. United States*, 838 F.2d 1179, 1183 (Fed. Cir. 1988); *Bayou Land & Marine Contractors, Inc. v. United States*, 23 Cl. Ct. 764, 771 (1991). When necessary to best interpret the contract, the court should examine the materials the parties have submitted pursuant to RCFC 56(c) and 56(d). Should a genuine issue of material fact be presented, summary judgment would be inappropriate. In this case, though, the question of whether this contract was for requirements or indefinite quantities does not involve any factual disputes that are material to interpreting the contract, see *H.B. Zachry Co.*, 28 Fed. Cl. at 80, thus summary judgment may be used to resolve this question. Further, determination of the type of contract the parties entered into is generally a matter of law. *Maintenance Engineers, Inc. v. United States*, 749 F.2d 724, 726 n. 3 (Fed. Cir. 1984).

The distinction between questions of fact and law in resolving interpretation disputes is also relevant to the appellate treatment of interpretation decisions. On appeal from a Court of Federal Claims or board of contract appeals decision, factual questions are reviewed for clear error, whereas the contract interpretation based thereon is reviewed de novo on appeal, *C. Sanchez & Son, Inc. v. United States*, 6 F.3d 1539 (Fed. Cir. 1993). See also *Maxwell Dynamometer Co. v. United States*, 181 Ct. Cl. 607, 386 F.2d 855 (1967); *Teledyne Lewisburg v. United States*, 699 F.2d 1336 (Fed. Cir. 1983); and *A & K Plumbing & Mech., Inc. v. United States*, 1 Cl. Ct. 716 (1983). However, the Court of Appeals for the Federal Circuit has acknowledged that the Armed Services Board of Contract Appeals has considerable experience and expertise in interpreting government contracts, and its interpretation is given "careful consideration and great respect," *Community Heating & Plumbing Co. v. Kelso*, 987 F.2d 1575 (Fed. Cir. 1993); *Grumman Data Sys. Corp. v. Dalton*, 88 F.3d 990 (Fed. Cir. 1996).

I. BASIC OBJECTIVE OF INTERPRETATION

The basic objective of contract interpretation is to determine the intent of the parties. See *Restatement, Second, Contracts* § 201; *Hegeman-Harris & Co. v. United States*, 194 Ct. Cl. 574, 440 F.2d 1009 (1971) ("[t]he cardinal rule of contract interpretation is to carry out the intent of parties"); *Firestone Tire & Rubber Co. v. United States*, 195 Ct. Cl. 21, 444 F.2d 547 (1971) ("It has been a fundamental precept of common law that the intention of the parties to a contract controls its interpretation."); *R.G. Robbins & Co. v. United States*, 4 Cl. Ct. 91 (1983) ("It is a fundamental principle, a 'bedrock of contractual analysis,' that the intention of the parties to a contract controls its interpretation," citing *Firestone*); and *Alvin, Ltd. v. United States Postal Serv.*, 816 F.2d 1562 (Fed. Cir. 1987) ("In the case of contracts, the avowed purpose and primary function of the court is the ascertainment of the intention of the parties," citing 4 Williston, *A Treatise on the Law of Contracts*, § 601 (3d ed. 1961)). See also *General Elec. Co.*, ASBCA 24913, 83-1 BCA ¶ 16,130 (the meaning that is relevant is that which was intended at the time the contract was made, "not some meaning propounded by a party at some later occasion").

Since it is rarely possible to discern what was in the minds of the parties, courts and boards seek intent by using a so-called objective test. This recognizes that uncommunicated intentions are not relevant to the interpretation process. In *Corbetta Constr. Co. v. United States*, 198 Ct. Cl. 712, 461 F.2d 1330 (1972), the court explained that "'the crucial question is what the [contractor] would have understood as a reasonable construction contractor,' not what a drafter of the contract terms subjectively intended," citing *Norcoast Constructors, Inc. v. United States*, 196 Ct. Cl. 1, 448 F. 2d 1400 (1971); *Firestone Tire & Rubber Co. v. United States*, 195 Ct. Cl. 21, 444 F. 2d 547 (1971); and *L. Rosenman Corp. v. United States*, 182 Ct. Cl. 586, 390 F.2d 711 (1986). Similarly, in *Oxnard v. United States*, 851 F.2d 344 (Fed. Cir. 1988), the court held that, if the subjective intent of one of the parties is contrary to the reasonable and unambiguous text of the written contract, there is no basis for reformation. Thus, a subjective, unexpressed intent will be given no weight unless it coincides with an objective manifestation of intent. See *Hughes Communications Galaxy, Inc. v. United States*, 26 Cl. Ct. 123 (1992), *rev'd on other grounds*, 998 F.2d 953 (Fed. Cir. 1993) (evidence of subjective intent not relevant); *Pacificorp Capital, Inc. v. United States*, 25 Cl. Ct. 707 (1992), *aff'd*, 988 F.2d 130 (Fed. Cir. 1993) (evidence of subjective intent insufficient to bind the other contracting party); and *Hoffman Constr. Co.*, VABCA 3676, 93-3 BCA ¶ 26,110 (intent of drafter of specification not relevant). The Federal Circuit in *L.S.S. Leasing Corp. v. United States*, 695 F.2d 1359 (Fed. Cir. 1982), reiterated this position as it quoted from *Hotchkiss v. National City Bank of N.Y.*, 200 F. 287, 293 (S.D.N.Y. 1911), *aff'd*, 201 F. 664 (2d Cir. 1912), *aff'd*, 231 U.S. 50 (1913), at 1364:

> A contract has, strictly speaking, nothing to do with the personal, or individual intent, of the parties. A contract is an obligation attached by the mere force of law to certain acts of the parties, usually words, which ordinarily accompany and represent a known intent. If, however, it were proved by twenty bishops that either party, when he used the words, intended something else than the usual meaning which the law imposes upon them, he would still be held, unless there were some mutual mistake or something else of the sort. Of course, if it appear[s] by other words, or acts, of the parties, that they attribute a peculiar meaning to such words as they use in the contract, that meaning will prevail, but only by virtue of the other words, and not because of their unexpressed intent.

Thus, courts and boards interpret a contract in the way it would be interpreted by a reasonably intelligent person familiar with all the facts and circumstances surrounding contract formation. See *Hol-Gar Mfg. Corp. v. United States*, 169 Ct. Cl. 384, 351 F.2d 972 (1965), stating at 388 that "the language of a contract must be given that meaning that would be derived from the contract by a reasonably intelligent person acquainted with the contemporaneous circumstances." Under this approach, parties are held to appropriate standards of knowledge and experience. See *Adrian L. Roberson*, ASBCA 6248, 61-1 BCA ¶ 2857, stating at 14,915:

> We must seek to put ourselves in the position of [the contractor] at the time he bid on the contract, i.e., we must seek the meaning that would be attached to the language by a reasonably intelligent bidder in the position of [the contractor], who would be expected to have the technical and trade knowledge of his industry and to know how to read and interpret technical engineering specifications and perform construction work in accordance with such specifications.

See also *Metric Constructors, Inc. v. National Aeronautics & Space Admin.*, 169 F.3d 747 (Fed. Cir. 1999), reiterating the rule that the contract must be given the meaning that a reasonably intelligent person acquainted with the contemporaneous circumstances would derive. In *Turner Constr. Co. v. United States*, 367 F.3d 1319 (Fed. Cir. 2004), the court stated at 1321:

> The parties are charged with knowledge of law and fact appropriate to the subject matter, and reasonable professional competence in reading and writing contracts is presumed. See *Lockheed Martin IR Imaging Sys., Inc. v. West*, 108 F.3d 319, 322 (Fed. Cir. 1997).

II. DEFINITION OF TERMS

Terms and symbols contained in contract documents must be given some meaning in the interpretive process. There are, generally, three sources used by the courts and boards to define these terms and symbols. First, they will apply any definitions that the parties have incorporated into the contract documents. Absent definitions contained in the writings, dictionaries or common usage will provide the definitions unless the circumstances indicate that the parties used a technical term or word of art. These latter two sources of definitions are described in *Restatement, Second, Contracts* § 202(3), which states:

> Unless a different intention is manifested,
>
> > (a) where language has a generally prevailing meaning, it is interpreted in accordance with that meaning;
> >
> > (b) technical terms and words of art are given their technical meaning when used in a transaction within their technical field.

A. Definitions in the Document

Contract documents often contain definitions. These definitions may be included in standard clauses or in provisions specifically drafted for the contract. See, for example, *Reflectone, Inc. v. Dalton*, 60 F.3d 1572 (Fed. Cir. 1995) (interpreting the term "claim" in the FAR 52.233-1 Disputes clause), and *Sears Petroleum & Transport Corp.*, ASBCA 41401, 94-1 BCA ¶ 26,414, *recons. denied*, 94-2 BCA ¶ 26,631 (interpreting the date of delivery defined in the special provisions of the contract as the date and time the vessel begins to discharge). Since the use of definitions in the documents gives effect to the parties' intentions, it is improper to apply a dictionary definition in place of one contained in the contract documents, *Fry Communications, Inc. v. United States*, 22 Cl. Ct. 497 (1991). However, the mere inclusion of a definition in the documents does not resolve all definitional problems. The words in the definition must be defined.

B. Dictionary or Common Usage Definitions

A number of different phrases have been used to characterize these sources of definitions. The *Restatement* uses the term "generally prevailing meaning." However, that term is used infrequently in government contract cases. The most commonly used descriptions in government contract cases are "plain language," *Hunt Constr.*

Group v. United States, 281 F.3d 1369 (Fed. Cir. 2002), and *McAbee Constr., Inc. v. United States*, 97 F.3d 1431 (Fed. Cir. 1996); "plain meaning," *C. Sanchez & Son, Inc. v. United States*, 6 F.3d 1539 (Fed. Cir. 1993); or "plain and ordinary meaning," *Alaska Lumber & Pulp Co. v. Madigan*, 2 F.3d 389 (Fed. Cir. 1993).

1. Dictionary Definitions

In a number of cases the courts and boards have, on the basis of dictionary definitions, arrived at the meaning of words. See, for example, *NISH v. Cohen*, 217 F.3d 197 (4th Cir. 2001), in which the court used *Webster's* to determine the meaning of "cafeteria" in a dispute over whether a mess hall was a vending facility. Similarly, in *Plano Builders Corp. v. United States*, 40 Fed. Cl. 635 (1998), the court used *Webster's* to determine whether consulting fees were incurred "in connection with" the prosecution of a claim. The dictionary defined the term "connection" as "an association or relationship." See also *Rumsfeld v. United Tech. Corp.*, 315 F.3d 1361 (Fed. Cir. 2003) (dictionaries, the Federal Acquisition Regulation, and the *Uniform Commercial Code* used to define the word "cost" in dispute over proper accounting treatment of collaboration agreements with suppliers of engine parts); *General Constr. Co.*, DOTBCA 4137, 03-1 BCA ¶ 32,102 (dictionary used to determine that a facsimile of an invoice is not an "original" invoice); *Taisei Rotec Corp.*, ASBCA 50669, 02-1 BCA ¶ 31,739 (dictionary used to determine that no "force majeure" caused damage because term covered only forces that could not be avoided by the exercise of due care); *M.A. Mortenson Co.*, ASBCA 53062, 01-2 BCA ¶ 31,573 (dictionary used to determine that government was required to give contractor an electronic version of original drawings because a "copy" was a duplicate of the original); *Elter S.A.*, ASBCA 52491, 01-2 BCA ¶ 31,435 (dictionary used to determine that "repair" included the "notion of replacement"); *Young Enters., Inc.*, VABCA 6480, 01-1 BCA ¶ 31,384 (two dictionaries used to determine meaning of "blend" in dispute over whether roof tiles blended with existing roofs); *Sundstrand Corp.*, ASBCA 51572, 01-1 BCA ¶ 31,167 (two dictionaries used to determine that requirement for "security" backing up installment payments could include the contractor's good financial condition as well as collateral); *TRW, Inc.*, ASBCA 51003, 00-2 BCA ¶ 30,992 (two dictionaries used to determine that "delivery" in the context of earning profit on a convenience termination means the transfer of actual or constructive possession or control); *Kinetic Builders, Inc.*, ASBCA 51012, 98-2 BCA ¶ 29,899 (dictionary used to determine meaning of "exposed" in painting contract requiring painting of exposed surfaces); *Blake Constr. Co.*, DOTBCA 3059, 98-2 BCA ¶ 29,850 (dictionary used to determine meaning of "ceiling" in requirement that electrical conduit be concealed); *Rockwell Int'l Corp.*, ASBCA 41095, 95-1 BCA ¶ 27,459 (dictionary used to determine meaning of "clear cut" in case alleging mistake in computer computation of prices); *Ralph Larsen & Son, Inc. v. United States*, 17 Cl. Ct. 39 (1989) (dictionary used to determine meaning of "embed" in ruling that conduit placed in or on top of drainage gravel with cement poured over it is not embedded conduit, but rather below "slab-on-grade"); and *Frank A. Kennedy, Inc.*,

NASABCA 773-9, 75-1 BCA ¶ 11,019 (dictionary used to determine meaning of "sand" in claim for equitable adjustment because government furnished material that contained stones and other debris).

Dictionary definitions are rejected when they are not useful or there is better evidence to determine the meaning of a term. See *Ingalls Shipbuilding, Inc. v. Dalton*, 119 F.3d 972 (Fed. Cir. 1997), finding the dictionary definition of "penalty" not helpful because it had many possible meanings. See also *Northrop Grumman Corp. v. Goldin*, 136 F.3d 1479 (Fed. Cir. 1998), in which the court refused to use the dictionary definition of "i.e." because the contracting officer testified that she thought the term meant "for example"; *Ed A. Wilson, Inc. v. General Servs. Admin.*, 126 F.3d 1406 (Fed. Cir. 1997), in which the court rejected a dictionary definition of "incurred" as meaning an amount paid or liable for and held that the Equal Access to Justice Act permitted compensation for fees paid by an insurer as long as they were for litigation on behalf of a small company; and *Carter Indus., Inc.*, DOTBCA 2995, 98-1 BCA ¶ 29,625, in which the board rejected the meaning of "action" in *Black's Law Dictionary* as meaning only a suit brought in a court as being too narrow because disputes before appeals boards were also litigation. In *Libertatia Assocs., Inc. v. United States*, 46 Fed. Cl. 702 (2000), the court consulted a dictionary to determine the meaning of the court test of "well-nigh irrefragable proof" to show that the government official acted in bad faith. It concluded that the *American Heritage Dictionary of the English Language* definition of "irrefragable" as "impossible to refute or controvert; indisputable" was a far too stringent standard of proof and that the term must mean "evidence of some specific intent to injure" the contractor.

In appears that any recognized dictionary will suffice, *David W.E. Cabell*, VABCA 3402, 93-2 BCA ¶ 25,598 (*American Heritage Dictionary of the English Language* (1969) used for definition of "linear feet"), and *Charles Mace Constr. Co.*, ASBCA 29331, 85-2 BCA ¶ 18,006 (*Webster's Third New International Dictionary* cited in determining that "ducting" includes plenums but excludes hoods).

2. Common Usage

In a number of cases, the courts and boards have determined the meaning of words based on their own understanding, without reference to dictionaries or other evidence. See, for example, *Barseback Kraft AB & Empresa Nacional del Uranio, S.A. v. United States*, 121 F.3d 1475 (1997), in which the court held that the plain meaning of contract provisions that the "charges to be paid to DOE" for enrichment services will "be determined in accordance with established DOE pricing policy" which was "any policy established by DOE that is applicable to prices or charges in effect at the time of performance of any services under this contract" gave the government the right to contract out the enrichment work and permitted the contractor to alter the pricing policy to add a significant profit to the prices. See also *McAbee Constr., Inc. v. United States*, 97 F.3d 1431 (Fed. Cir. 1996), in which the court reversed the Court of Federal Claims because it had used extrinsic evidence to determine the meaning of an easement to place waste on the plaintiff's land. The court reasoned at 1435:

> The language of the easement expressly permitted the Corps to deposit fill and waste on McAbee's land, and to perform any other work on the tract as long as it was "necessary and incident" to the project. There is nothing ambiguous about this. The terms are not susceptible of more than one reasonable interpretation. Nowhere in the contract did the parties agree that the Corps was only permitted to dump a specified amount of waste on McAbee's land. Nor did they agree that upon termination of the easement the Corps was required to return the property at a specified elevation. The only possible limitation on the amount of waste that the Corps could deposit was its character or source, not its amount or height. Consequently, the trial court's conclusion that the absence of a height restriction created an ambiguity is incorrect.

Similarly, in *A-Transport Northwest Co. v. United States*, 36 F.3d 1576 (Fed. Cir. 1994), the government had the right to terminate a contract for transportation services from a third party's warehouse to various government installations upon the occurrence of changing supply missions or requirements. The court held that the plain and ordinary meaning of the phrase included the decision by the third party to move the location of its warehouse. In *Gustafson P'ship*, GSBCA 6701-COM, 84-1 BCA ¶ 17,086, the contractor read the phrase "[t]he Government may terminate this lease at any time (after eight months) with 60 days' notice in writing to the Lessor" to mean that prior to eight months into the lease term the government was prohibited from initiating a termination. The board rejected this interpretation, stating at 85,065:

> We find the termination provision to be unambiguous. Its specific words are clear, unremarkable, everyday, short, common English words, none of which are individually or collectively susceptible to other than their everyday meaning. Let us parse the termination provision. The government may terminate this lease—when? At any time after eight months. That much seems unalterably set in concrete. The second phrase, with 60 days' notice in writing to the Lessor, modifies the first. Clearly the notice, if that word is to have any meaning, must precede the termination by sixty days.

There are some decisions in which the court finds a plain meaning when its own opinion indicates that there is ambiguity in the language. See, for example, *HRE, Inc. v. United States*, 142 F.3d 1274 (Fed. Cir. 1998), in which the court ruled against the contractor based on its view of the plain meaning of the contract language and, at the same time, criticized the government for including ambiguous language in the contract. See also *SCM Corp. v. United States*, 230 Ct. Cl. 199, 675 F.2d 280 (1982), in which some judges found one clear meaning to the contract language and a dissenting judge found a different clear meaning. The logic of such a finding of a plain meaning was challenged in *Norflor Constr. Co.*, ASBCA 31577, 89-1 BCA ¶ 21,265, in which three judges found that the plain meaning of the contract was the meaning asserted by the government and two judges found that the contractor's interpretation was reasonable. On motion for reconsideration, 90-1 BCA ¶ 22,277, the board denied reconsideration, stating: "The mere fact of disagreement, whether by individual judges, or the parties, or anyone else, over the reasonableness of Norflor's interpretation, does not prove the existence of an ambiguity in the contract."

3. Limitations on Dictionary and Common Usage Definitions

Neither dictionary nor common usage definitions should be used if the contract terms indicate that another meaning is intended. See *Metric Constructors, Inc. v. National Aeronautics & Space Admin.*, 169 F.3d 747 (Fed. Cir. 1999), in which the court reversed a board decision ruling against the contractor based on plain meaning, stating at 752, "to interpret disputed contract terms, 'the context and intention [of the contracting parties] are more meaningful than the dictionary definition,'" quoting *Rice v. United States*, 192 Ct. Cl. 903, 908, 428 F.2d 1311, 1314 (1970). This rule was followed in *Corman v. United States*, 26 Cl. Ct. 1011 (1992), finding the meaning of "prorate" in the context of the contract rather than by using a dictionary definition. See also *P.R. Burke Corp. v. United States*, 47 Fed. Cl. 340 (2000), stating: "This court prefers to use the context in which the contract language appears and the intent of the parties, rather than general dictionary definitions, to provide plain meaning to contract terms," citing *Fry Communications, Inc. v. United States*, 22 Cl. Ct. 497, 505 (1991). Accord, *Transportes Especiales De Automoviles, S.A.*, ASBCA 40658, 91-1 BCA ¶ 23,292 (board found the government's proffered dictionary definition of "reimburse" to be strained in relation to the terms and context of the contract).

C. Technical Terms

When words have a clear or well-defined special meaning in the trade or industry involved in the contract, the courts will defer to that technical meaning. The technical meaning may either supply the definition of the term or establish an ambiguity by providing support for an alternative to the ordinary meaning of the term. See *Western States Constr. Co. v. United States*, 26 Cl. Ct. 818 (1992), for a discussion of these principles. However, in order to qualify, there must be sufficient evidence of the technical usage. In *John E. Day Assocs., Inc.*, ASBCA 43758, 94-1 BCA ¶ 26,337, the board held that there was insufficient evidence of a trade usage to overcome the dictionary definition of "existing."

There are two broad sources of technical terms and words of art: (1) the technical language of various industries and trades and (2) the technical language of government forms.

1. Trade Usage

Evidence of trade usage is frequently used to resolve an interpretation dispute. See *Restatement, Second, Contracts* § 202, stating that technical terms and words of art are given their technical meaning when used in a transaction within their technical field unless a different intention is manifested. See also *Jimenez, Inc.*, VABCA 6351, 02-2 BCA ¶ 32,019, stating that "[e]vidence of trade practice is superior to evidence of common usage in interpreting language relating to work done by a particular trade," citing *Bodell Constr. Co.*, ASBCA 38355, 92-1 BCA ¶ 24,433. In *MPE Business Forms, Inc. v. United States*, 44 Fed. Cl. 421 (1999), the court held that a printing contractor reasonably relied on the industry meaning of "copy" when the government changed the solicitation language from "set" to "copy" to prescribe the units for which the contractor was to be paid. In *William Clairmont, Inc.*, ASBCA 15447, 73-1 BCA ¶ 9927, the board granted the contractor's claim for additional compensation for removing boulders during performance of an excavation contract. The fixed-price contract provided for separate pay for the removal of solid rock. The board found that according to trade usage in the area of performance the term solid rock included boulders .5 cubic yard and larger. In *Blinderman Constr. Co.*, ASBCA 20333, 76-1 BCA ¶ 11,807, the contractor sought additional compensation for welding the inside as well as the outside sections of joints in pieces of C-shaped channel. All welding was to be done according to the standards of the American Institute of Steel Construction (AISC) and the American Welding Society (AWS), which were incorporated into the contract by reference. At issue was the proper interpretation of the weld-all-around symbol that was part of the schematic instructions for welding the C-shaped channel. The board rejected the contractor's claim, stating at 56,376:

> Both parties are in agreement that the symbol used in this contract has been taken from the publication of the American Welding Society and represents established trade usage in structural building design . . .
>
> * * *
>
> We find no ambiguity in applying the meaning of this symbol as it is employed in the simple detail sketch appearing on this Government drawing. The AWS publication clearly sets forth the distinction between the use of the primary symbol with the weld designation, and the addition of the supplementary weld-all-around symbol intended for use in lieu of multiple arrows to indicate that the particular welding operation shall be performed completely around a joint. This meaning is explicit on that score in both text and illustration in the AWS and AISC publications. . . . In summary, the phrase employed by the Government's expert witness properly and succinctly expresses the meaning of the symbol used in this drawing: Weld all around until you meet yourself.

In *American Trans-Coil Corp.*, ASBCA 27037, 85-1 BCA ¶ 17,864, the board found "with increasing phase lead" to be technical words with clear meaning. The board ruled that the problem was that the contractor either did not understand or misinterpreted the phrase. See also *Astro-Space Lab., Inc.*, NASABCA 1168-19, 70-1 BCA ¶ 8107 (defining "tensile yield strength"), and *M.S.I. Corp.*, ASBCA 10125, 65-1 BCA ¶ 4579 (defining "attic spaces").

Usage in an area of the law can also supply the meaning of a term. See *Greenwood Assocs. v. Perry*, 399 F.3d 1317 (Fed. Cir. 2005), holding that the term "taxes paid for" a designated year had a well-understood meaning in tax law. Compare *Rumsfeld v. United Techs. Corp.*, 315 F.3d 1361 (Fed. Cir. 2003), in which the Federal Circuit rejected evidence of usage in the accounting profession. In that case the Armed Services Board of Contract Appeals had heard evidence from six accounting and economic experts concerning the meaning of "cost" in generally accepted accounting principles and had ruled that the Cost Accounting Standards did not require the contractor to treat an amount it paid for engine parts under "collaboration agreements" as incurred costs, *United Techs. Corp., Pratt & Whitney*, ASBCA 47416, 01-2 BCA ¶ 31,592. The Federal Circuit reversed, ruling that the expert testimony was "irrelevant" at 1369:

> The views of the self-proclaimed CAS experts, including professors of economics and accounting, a former employee of the CAS Board, and a government contracts accounting consultant, as to the proper interpretation of those regulations is simply irrelevant to our interpretive task; such evidence should not be received, much less considered, by the Board on the interpretive issue. That interpretive issue is to be approached like other legal issues—based on briefing and argument by the affected parties.

See also *United States v. Lachman*, 387 F.3d 42 (1st Cir. 2004), holding that evidence of the "common legal meaning" of the term, of statements of agency officials at meetings, and of usage in other agency publications was not sufficient proof that there was a technical meaning of the term "specially designed" sufficient to overcome the plain meaning of the term as derived from dictionaries and an evaluation of the legislative intent in enacting the export control laws.

2. Government Forms and Regulations

It has frequently been held that special terms used in the field of government contracts will be given their special meanings. In *General Builders Supply Co. v. United States*, 187 Ct. Cl. 477, 409 F.2d 246 (1969), the court stated at 482:

> The concept of an equitable adjustment has had a long history in federal procurement, going back for about fifty years. . . . First used in the standard changes and changed conditions articles, the term has been taken over for other clauses, such as the suspension of work and Government-furnished property provisions. . . . The consistent practice appears to have been that an equitable adjustment, as that phrase is used in these articles, can cover an allowance for profit on work actually done, but does not encompass unearned but anticipated profits. . . . This is far from an unnatural interpretation since, in these clauses, the equitable adjustment is usually tied by express words to an increase or decrease in the contractor's costs.

The [contractor], which impliedly concedes that this has been the practice under the other clauses, maintains that a different reading for equitably adjusted is proper in the newer "default" article. The contention is that the "changes," "changed conditions," and similar clauses dealt with a different problem, and the interpretation which was appropriate in that context does not fit as well into the present situation. There are, we think, two related answers to that argument. One is that "equitable adjustment" has become a term of art (in federal contracts) with a commonly understood meaning in the aspect involved in this case . . . and that accepted content should be followed unless there are very strong counter-balancing reasons. Such a counterweight might be a marked alteration in context, but if the change is not significant and drastic it should not be sufficient to alter the established meaning of this specialized term. Here, the change in context—even if one accepts [the contractor's] point that the context does in fact differ—is moderate, rather than severe. A concept hitherto applied to an ongoing agreement is now to be applied to one which is at its end, without any future. That change in context does not seem any greater than the transfer of the concept of an "equitable adjustment" from the "changes" article to the clause controlling Government-furnished property or allowing an award for "suspension of work."

While it is not clear that the FAR is always contractually binding on contractors, its definitions have been used in the contract interpretation process. Numerous definitions are contained in FAR 2.101, and there are other definitions in other parts of the FAR. See *Rumsfeld v. United Techs. Corp.*, 315 F.3d 1361 (Fed. Cir. 2003) (using the definition of "material costs" in FAR 31.205-26); *UMC Elecs. Co. v. United States*, 249 F.3d 1337 (Fed. Cir. 2001) (using the definition of "actual costs" in FAR 31.001); and *Alliant Techsystems, Inc. v. United States*, 178 F.3d 1260 (Fed. Cir. 1999) (using the definition of "option" in FAR 17.201). Care must be used in relying on the definitions in FAR 2.101 because they tend to be general in nature. See *Craft Mach. Works, Inc. v. United States*, 926 F.2d 1110 (Fed. Cir. 1991), rejecting use of the FAR 2.101 definition of "supplies" because this part of the FAR "sets out broadly the scope of what 'supplies' can mean within the regulations, but does not presume to explain the term's meaning within any particular contract." The current guidance of the scope of these FAR 2.101 definitions states:

> (a) A word or a term, defined in this section, has the same meaning throughout this regulation (48 CFR chapter 1), unless—
>
>> (1) The context in which the word or term is used clearly requires a different meaning; or
>>
>> (2) Another FAR part, subpart, or section provides a different definition for the particular part or portion of the part.
>
> (b) If a word or term that is defined in this section is defined differently in another part, subpart, or section of this regulation (48 CFR chapter 1, the definition in—
>
>> (1) This section includes a cross-reference to the other definitions; and

> (2) That part, subpart, or section applies to the word or term when used in that part, subpart, or section.

Evidence of government trade usage will be rejected if it does not comport with widespread usage of the term. See, for example, *Security Ins. Co. of Hartford*, ASBCA 51759, 02-2 BCA ¶ 31,973, in which the board rejected evidence that progress payments made for construction materials stored off of the site were to be made only when they were supported by paid invoices for the materials. The board concluded that inclusion of this requirement in internal regulations and training manuals was not sufficient evidence of trade usage when the contractor had no way of knowing of such unpublished materials.

III. ANALYSIS OF LANGUAGE OF CONTRACT DOCUMENTS

The written contract document is the primary evidence of the parties' agreement in virtually all cases involving government contract interpretation controversies. A thorough analysis of the provisions actually included in the contract as well as those that are incorporated by reference is therefore essential to resolve the issues properly. If a plain meaning is not evident, analysis should proceed as described in *M.A. Mortenson Co. v. United States*, 29 Fed. Cl. 82 (1993), at 96:

> When interpreting the language of a contract, a court must give reasonable meaning to all parts of the contract and not render portions of the contract meaningless. *Fortec Constructors v. United States*, 760 F.2d 1288, 1292 (Fed. Cir. 1985); *United States v. Johnson Controls, Inc.*, 713 F.2d 1541, 1555 (Fed. Cir. 1983). Otherwise stated, in ascertaining the intentions of the parties, the contract should be construed in its entirety "so as to harmonize and give meaning to all its provisions." *Thanet Corp. v. United States*, 219 Ct. Cl. 75, 82, 591 F.2d 629, 633 (1979); *ITT Arctic Services, Inc. v. United States*, 207 Ct. Cl. 743, 751-52, 524 F.2d 680 (1975); accord *Firestone Tire & Rubber Co. v. United States*, 195 Ct. Cl. 21, 30, 444 F.2d 547, 551 (1971). The language of a contract, moreover, must be given the meaning that would be derived from the contract by" a reasonably intelligent person acquainted with the contemporaneous circumstances." *Hol-Gar Mfg. Corp. v. United States*, 169 Ct. Cl. 384, 388, 351 F.2d 972, 975 (1965).

In analyzing the contract language, the contractor should not make inferences from government modifications of the solicitation. See *Program & Constr. Mgmt. Group v. General Servs. Admin.*, 246 F.3d 1363 (Fed. Cir. 2001), where the contractor had inferred that there was no requirement to keep a cafeteria open during contract performance because the government had deleted that requirement from the solicitation. The court held that other language in the contract required that the cafeteria remain in operation during performance.

This section discusses these rules along with other criteria that are examined to ascertain meaning.

A. Plain Meaning

In a series of recent decisions, the Federal Circuit has indicated that the paramount means of interpreting a contract will be to look for the "plain meaning" of the contract's language. See *Coast Fed. Bank, FSB v. United States*, 323 F.3d 1035 (Fed. Cir. 2003), in which the court, in an en banc decision, rejected the use of extrinsic evidence, stating at 1040-41:

> When the contractual language is unambiguous on its face, our inquiry ends and the plain language of the Agreement controls.

In this case the court found that the language of the contract had a plain meaning even though it was very complex and confusing. Both the Court of Federal Claims (48 Fed. Cl. 402 (2000)) and the original panel of the Federal Circuit (309 F.3d 1353 (Fed. Cir. 2002)) had found it necessary to resort to extrinsic evidence to determine the correct interpretation of the contract language, but the full court rejected the use of such evidence.

This rejection of the use of extrinsic evidence in favor of finding "plain meaning" from the words of the contract alone appears to be in conflict with the guidance in *Restatement, Second, Contracts* § 202. See the following comments to that section:

> *b. Circumstances.* The meaning of words and other symbols commonly depends on their context; the meaning of other conduct is even more dependent on the circumstances. In interpreting the words and conduct of the parties to a contract, a court seeks to put itself in the position they occupied at the time the contract was made. When the parties have adopted a writing as a final expression of their agreement, interpretation is directed to the meaning of that writing in the light of the circumstances. See §§ 209, 212. The circumstances for this purpose include the entire situation, as it appeared to the parties, and in appropriate cases may include facts known to one party of which the other had reason to know. See § 201.
>
> *g. Course of performance.* The parties to an agreement know best what they meant, and their action under it is often the strongest evidence of their meaning. But such "practical construction" is not conclusive of meaning. Conduct must be weighed in the light of the terms of the agreement and their possible meanings. Where it is unreasonable to interpret the contract in accordance with the course of performance, the conduct of the parties may be evidence of an agreed modification or of a waiver by one party. See Uniform Commercial Code § 2-208. Or there may be simply a mistake which should be corrected. The rule of Subsection (4) does not apply to action on a single occasion or to action of one party only; in such cases the conduct of a party may be evidence against him that he had knowledge or reason to know of the other party's meaning, but self-serving conduct is not entitled to weight.

Earlier cases had enunciated the court's desire to rely on the bare contract language whenever possible. See *McAbee Constr., Inc. v. United States*, 97 F.3d 1431 (Fed. Cir. 1996), stating at 1435:

> We begin [the process of interpretation] with the plain language. *Foley Co. v. United States*, 11 F.3d 1032, 1034 (Fed. Cir. 1993); see also *C. Sanchez and Son, Inc. v. United States*, 6 F.3d 1539, 1543 (Fed. Cir. 1993) ("A contract is read in accordance with its express terms and the plain meaning thereof."). We must interpret the contract in a manner that gives meaning to all of its provisions and makes sense. *Hughes Communications Galaxy, Inc. v. United States*, 998 F.2d 953, 958 (Fed. Cir. 1993). Thus, if the "provisions are clear and unambiguous, they must be given their plain and ordinary meaning," *Alaska Lumber & Pulp Co. v. Madigan*, 2 F.3d 389, 392 (Fed. Cir. 1993), and the court may not resort to extrinsic evidence to interpret them. *Interwest Constr.*, 29 F.3d 611 at 615 ("Extrinsic evidence . . . should not be used to introduce an ambiguity where none exists."); *Beta Sys., Inc. v. United States*, 838 F.2d 1179, 1183 (Fed. Cir. 1988) ("Extrinsic evidence will not be received to change the terms of a contract that is clear on its face."). To permit otherwise would cast "a long shadow of uncertainty over all transactions" and contracts. *Trident Ctr. v. Connecticut Gen. Life Ins. Co.*, 847 F.2d 564, 569 (9th Cir. 1988) (criticizing the California approach, which does not follow the traditional principle that extrinsic evidence is inadmissible to interpret, vary, or add to the terms of an unambiguous integrated instrument).

See also *HRE, Inc. v. United States*, 142 F.3d 1274 (Fed. Cir. 1998), stating at 1276:

> [The contractor's] construction of the contract violates the well-settled rule that when the provisions of a contract are clear, "the court may not resort to extrinsic evidence to interpret them." *McAbee Constr., Inc. v. United States*, 97 F.3d 1431, 1435 (Fed. Cir. 1996). "Outside evidence may not be brought in to create an ambiguity where the language is clear." *City of Tacoma v. United States*, 31 F.3d 1130, 1134 (Fed. Cir. 1994).

For a critique of this rule, see Johnson, *Interpreting Government Contracts: Plain Meaning Precludes Extrinsic Evidence and Controls at the Federal Circuit,* 34 Pub. Ct. L. J. 635 (2005).

B. Read the Writings as a Whole

One basic common law rule for interpretation of contract documents is that a writing is interpreted as a whole, and all writings that are part of the same transaction are interpreted together, *Restatement, Second, Contracts* § 202(2). When a contract is set forth in writing, it is the entire writing that embodies the agreement of the parties, not individual sections or clauses. Since language derives its meaning largely from the context in which it appears, an attempt to interpret a word, term, or clause independent of the remainder of the contract document may distort its meaning and thus not accurately reflect the intent of the parties. See *NVT Techs., Inc. v. United States*, 370 F.3d 1153 (Fed. Cir. 2004), stating at 1159:

> Contract interpretation begins with the language of the written agreement. *Foley Co. v. United States*, 11 F.3d 1032, 1034 (Fed. Cir. 1993). When interpreting the

> contract, the document must be considered as a whole and interpreted so as to harmonize and give reasonable meaning to all of its parts. *McAbee Constr., Inc. v. United States*, 97 F.3d 1431, 1434-35 (Fed. Cir. 1996). An interpretation that gives meaning to all parts of the contract is to be preferred over one that leaves a portion of the contract useless, inexplicable, void, or superfluous. *Gould, Inc. v. United States*, 935 F.2d 1271, 1274 (Fed. Cir. 1991).

This rule requires that offerors analyze all of the documents and all of the portions of each document to ascertain what the contract requires. For example, in *H.B. Zachry Co. v. United States*, 28 Fed. Cl. 77 (1993), *aff'd without opinion*, 17 F.3d 1443 (Fed. Cir. 1994), the contractor was required to furnish galvanized steel for a roof deck even though the materials section of the specifications did not specify galvanized steel because another portion of the specifications required that the deck be formed of galvanized steel. In many cases where the general "read the contract as a whole" rule is invoked, the boards and courts also rely on two related principles of interpretation: (1) parts of a contract must be read together and harmonized if at all possible, and (2) preference is given to an interpretation that gives effect to all terms and leaves no provision meaningless. See *Hughes Communications Galaxy, Inc. v. United States*, 26 Cl. Ct. 123 (1992), *rev'd on other grounds*, 998 F.2d 953 (Fed. Cir. 1993), in which the court read two clauses incorporating government policies in a manner that gave meaning to all of the policies covered by the clauses.

1. Interpret to Avoid Rendering Terms Meaningless

An interpretation will generally be rejected if it leaves portions of the contract language meaningless, useless, ineffective, or superfluous. See *Restatement, Second, Contracts* § 203(a). In *Alliant Techsystems, Inc. v. United States*, 178 F.3d 1260 (Fed. Cir. 1999), the court rejected the government's assertion that it had no jurisdiction to decide on the proper interpretation of an option until after the work was performed because that would render meaningless the definition of "claim" in the Disputes clause as including "interpretation of the contract terms." Similarly, in *Energy Capital Corp. v. United States*, 47 Fed. Cl. 382 (2000), the court rejected the contractor's argument that its lost profits should be calculated on work beyond $200 million because that would ignore the $200 million ceiling on the work covered by the contract. See also *Fortec Constructors v. United States*, 760 F.2d 1288 (Fed. Cir. 1985), in which the court rejected the contractor's assertion that the Corps of Engineers' on-site Quality Assurance Representative had accepted work by observing it without objection during construction because it would render meaningless the statement in the Inspection clause that no inspection or test by the government shall be construed as constituting or implying acceptance. In *Hunkin Conkey Constr. Co. v. United States*, 198 Ct. Cl. 638, 461 F.2d 1270 (1972), the court rejected the contractor's contention that the Changes clause precluded the government from awarding a separate contract for performance of this work, concluding that to adopt that interpretation of the Changes clause would render meaningless another clause in the contract that authorized the government to award other contracts for additional work. In *Freeman Elec. Constr. Co.*, DOTCAB 74-23, 75-1 BCA ¶ 11,184, the General Provisions of the contract contained two clauses numbered "57"—one entitled Listing of Employment Openings and the other Layout of Work. The Index of General Provisions, however, showed only the Listing of Employment Openings clause. The contractor did not check the individual clauses and, as a result, did not provide for layout work in its successful bid. The contractor first learned of the Layout of Work clause when the contracting officer denied its claim for survey work. The board denied the contractor's appeal, stating at 53,265:

> While the bid documents display a deplorable lack of care on the Government's part in putting the bid package together, there is no question that the bid package contained the Layout of Work clause and that the clause became part of the contract as awarded. Appellant's shortcut of merely checking the index and not the whole bid package may be an understandable concession to the shortness of human life. However, it furnishes no basis for reading the clause out of the contract, as appellant would have us do. The clause is in the contract, and a contract must be read as a whole. It would be a perversion of normal rules of contract construction to say that the failure to list the clause in the index completely negates the clause. All parts of the contract must be read together to establish its meaning.

In *Bay Ship & Yacht Co.*, DOTBCA 2913, 96-1 BCA ¶ 28,236, the contract required the contractor to remove asbestos encountered in the specified work at no additional charge to the government regardless of whether it was identified in the specification and also required the contractor to determine for itself whether the specific work required asbestos removal. The court determined that together these provisions covered only asbestos that the contractor could have anticipated at the time of bidding. See also *Hill Bros. Constr.*, ENGBCA 5673, 90-1 BCA ¶ 22,630, where the construction of haul roads was covered in a lump sum portion of the contract, and clearing, grubbing, and stripping was to be done on a unit price basis. The court rejected the government's argument that clearing, grubbing, and stripping of the area necessary for haul roads did not fall within the unit price payment provision. In *D.W.S. Inc.*, ASBCA 29743, 93-1 BCA ¶ 25,404, the contractor argued that the Quality Assurance Evaluator (QAE) did not have the authority to alter work orders under the contract because one provision of the contract stated the QAE's role was to be responsible for checking contractor performance. However, other provisions in the contract provided that the QAE was a representative of both the contracting officer and the training and audiovisual support officer, both of whom had broad authority under the contract. The board rejected the contractor's interpretation, acknowledging that it was correct if viewed alone, but holding that the provision could not be read in isolation, which would make the other related provisions ineffective. Similarly, in *Granite Constr. Co. v. United States*, 962 F.2d 998 (Fed. Cir. 1992), *cert. denied*, 506 U.S. 1048 (1993), the contract required the contractor to tender conforming waterstop materials and also required the government to periodically test the materials prior to installation. However, Special Provision 38 precluded the contractor from disclaiming liability to the government for installing nonconforming waterstop materials. Reading the contract as a whole, the court held that the special provision did not relieve the government of all liability for failure to inspect the materials because to do so would render meaningless the provision that required the government to test all waterstop materials. See also *Southwest Marine, Inc.*, ASBCA 53561, 02-1 BCA ¶ 31,834 (rejecting contractor's interpretation because it would "render superfluous" a number of drawings and a specification provision); *Phillips Grading & Constr., Inc.*, ENGBCA 6440, 00-2 BCA ¶ 31,026 (rejecting contractor's interpretation of meeting fill requirements because it did not incorporate all of the contract approval requirements); and *Raytheon Co. v. United States*, 2 Cl. Ct. 763 (1983) (rejecting contractor's interpretation that the "last originally scheduled" date meant the last revised date because that would render the word "originally" meaningless).

Contracts that include work that is normally subcontracted are generally to be read as a whole to relieve the government of any obligation to coordinate when writing specifications that separate work among trades. Thus, if work is included in one part of the specifications, it is the obligation of the contractor to coordinate that work among the trades. See *Caddell Constr.*, VABCA 3509, 93-3 BCA ¶ 26,114, where, under a construction contract, the ductwork drawings showed only some of the smoke dampers. Other smoke dampers were indicated on the contract drawings. After relying on the ductwork drawings alone, the subcontractor asserted that it was required to furnish only the dampers indicated in the ductwork drawings. However, the board held that all the smoke dampers were clearly required even though they were not all shown on the ductwork drawings, stating at 129,796:

> A contractor who limits a part of his bidding estimate to one part of the contract documents, ignoring the provisions of other contract documents, is still charged with the knowledge of what is required by all of the contract documents read as a whole, and will be responsible for assuring that all of the requirements of the entire contract are met.

The same result was arrived at in *W.B. Meridith II, Inc.*, ASBCA 53590, 03-1 BCA ¶ 32,166 (electrical work on architectural drawings); *M.A. Mortenson Co.*, ASBCA 50383, 00-2 BCA ¶ 30,936 (structural work on architectural drawings); *Hensel Phelps Constr. Co.*, ASBCA 49716, 00-2 BCA ¶ 31,092 (finishing work not on room finish schedule but on other drawings); *R.A. Burch Constr. Co.*, ASBCA 39017, 90-1 BCA ¶ 22,599 (rejecting the contractor's theory that each bid or quotation from a potential subcontractor is to be treated as a separate entity and as having come directly from the government); *G.W. Murphy Constr. Co.*, DOTBCA 2053, 91-1 BCA ¶ 23,431 (insulation work scattered through architectural and structural drawings); and *M.C. Dean Elec. Contracting, Inc.*, ASBCA 38132, 90-1 BCA ¶ 22,314, *recons. denied*, 90-2 BCA ¶ 22,711 (electrical work on general drawings).

2. *Interpret to Avoid Conflict*

When the documents are read as a whole, the provisions should, if possible, be interpreted so as to be in harmony with each other. In *Unicon Mgmt. Corp. v. United*

States, 179 Ct. Cl. 534, 375 F.2d 804 (1967), the government pointed to certain drawings that referred to a metal plate and contended that the contractor had been required to install a sheet of steel between the concrete base and the tile floor. The contractor contended that the specifications discussed only the installation of the concrete base and that the conflict between the specifications and drawings should be resolved by following the specifications. The court held for the government, finding no conflict between the drawings and the specifications even though the work was not discussed in both documents, stating at 537-38:

> [Contractor] seems to insist that, if the specification can be read as conflicting with the drawings, that reading must be adopted even though a more harmonious interpretation is also reasonably available. The rule, however, which the courts have always preferred is, where possible, to interpret the provisions of a contract as coordinate not contradictory. See *Thompson Ramo Woolridge, Inc. v. United States*, 175 Ct. Cl. 527, 536, 361 F.2d 222, 228 (1966). Contractors, too, have long been on notice that in reading contract documents they should seek to find concord, rather than discord, if they properly can.

In *Roy McGinnis & Co.*, ASBCA 50053, 97-1 BCA ¶ 28,727, *rev'd*, 135 F.3d 778 (Fed. Cir. 1998), the board found a conflict in the contract provisions stating that the contractor would "provide" all items but that the government would furnish some items. The court reversed, holding that the word "provide" sometimes included government-furnished items—thus harmonizing the contract provisions. See also *Montana Ref. Co.*, ASBCA 50515, 00-1 BCA ¶ 30,694, holding that the guaranteed minimum in an indefinite-delivery, indefinite-quantity contract could be harmonized with the Termination for Convenience clause of the contract. Similarly, in *Massachusetts Bay Trans. Auth. v. United States*, 129 F.3d 1226 (Fed. Cir. 1997), the court reversed the lower court's ruling that a disclaimer of liability for defective drawings furnished by the government overrode other clauses in the contract. The court held that all of the clauses could be harmonized to permit suit against the government if it did not carry out all of its contract obligations that were included in the contract to protect the authority from claims by its contractor for defective drawings.

This rule is often stated as one that attempts to give a reasonable meaning to all of the contract language. See *Ace Constr. Co. v. United States*, 185 Ct. Cl. 487, 401 F.2d 816 (1968), stating at 495, "preference is given to an interpretation of a contract which accords reasonable meaning to each of its provisions." Thus, the court or board will look for an interpretation that avoids finding contract language ambiguous. In *Coker Corp.*, GSBCA 6918, 84-1 BCA ¶ 17,007, the contractor was required to remove existing tiles and carpeting before installing new covering. Although two clauses in the contract specifically mentioned the removal and other clauses required the contractor to furnish all work necessary for performance, the contractor argued that the selective demolition provision implied that removal was not required. However, the board rejected this argument, stating at 84,707 that "[the contractor] simply created the ambiguity that it complains of by failing to consider all provisions of the contract as a whole." Reading the specifications as a whole, the court in *BCM Corp. v. United States*, 2 Cl. Ct. 602 (1983), found that one clause, which explicitly referred to the removal of existing feeders as well as to their replacement, resolved any potential confusion that might otherwise have been present. The court in *Wunschel & Small, Inc. v. United States*, 1 Cl. Ct. 485 (1982), *aff'd*, 714 F.2d 161 (Fed. Cir. 1983), read two clauses together and found that the contract evinced a single intent of the parties. In *Lane Constr. Corp.*, ENGBCA 5880, 93-1 BCA ¶ 25,448, the contractor alleged that it was entitled to reimbursement for payments it made for discretionary performance bonds covering subcontractor default under a contract line item containing a "not to exceed" amount for performance and payment bonds. The board denied the appeal, holding that, reading the contract as a whole, the line item only applied to bonds required under the Miller Act. See also *Intercontinental Mfg. Co.*, ASBCA 48506, 03-1 BCA ¶ 32,131 (finding harmonious interpretation of technical specifications); *P.R. Burke Corp. v. United States*, 47 Fed. Cl. 340 (2000) (finding requirement that "the plant shall remain in operation during the entire construction period" precluded interpretation that vital parts of the plant could be temporarily shut down); *Northrop Grumman Corp. v. United States*, 41 Fed. Cl. 645 (1998) (Incentive Fee clause and Changes clause in cost-plus-incentive fee contract read together to permit reduction in target cost and target fee for work not performed); *System Sales Corp.*, ASBCA 50615, 97-2 BCA ¶ 29,280 (interpreting a schedule clause stating: "Liquidated damages shall be in the sum of $200" to fill in the *daily* rate of damages in standard Liquidated Damages clause); *Pioneer Enters., Inc.*, ASBCA 43803, 93-1 BCA ¶ 25,395 (reading a contract amendment and the specification harmoniously to hold that the contract terms were not ambiguous); *Big Chief Drilling Co. v. United States*, 26 Cl. Ct. 1276 (1992) (holding that, when a specification paragraph was read in its entirety, its language was not susceptible to differing interpretations); and *Mason v. United States*, 222 Ct. Cl. 436, 615 F.2d 1343 (1980) (accepting the government's interpretation, which was compatible with other clauses when read harmoniously, instead of the contractor's interpretation, which rendered the Guaranteed Minimum Quantity clause superfluous).

3. Interpret to Fulfill Principal Purpose of the Parties

Apparent gaps or omissions may be resolved through application of the interpretation as a whole rule in conjunction with the rule requiring great weight to be accorded to the principal purpose of the parties. See *Restatement, Second, Contracts* § 202(1), stating "words and other conduct are interpreted in the light of all the circumstances, and if the principal purpose of the parties is ascertainable, it is given great weight." This rule was cited in *United States v. Winstar Corp.*, 518 U.S. 839 (1996), to affirm the lower court's holding that contracts with savings and loan institutions were based on existing regulations. It was also used in *ITT Defense Communications Div.*, ASBCA 44791, 98-1 BCA ¶ 29,590, to interpret a repricing clause pertaining to situations where the government did not order all of the option quantities. The board looked to the purpose of the clause to reduce pricing risks in order to induce the contractor to submit the lowest possible unit prices. In *J.W. Bateson Co.*, VACAB 676, 68-1 BCA ¶ 6829, the contractor was held liable for installation of ice water lines not shown on the drawings because the plans and specifications required installation of a complete, ready for operation system.

Government specifications often contain provisions that call for the contractor to furnish and install complete systems. In addition, construction contracts frequently contain an omissions and misdescriptions provision (paragraph (d) of the Contract Drawings and Specifications clause in DFARS 252.236-7001) that requires the contractor to do all work "manifestly necessary to carry out the intent of the drawings and specifications" even though it is omitted or misdescribed in some of the documents. Similarly, the Specifications and Drawings for Construction clause in FAR 52.236-21 provides:

> Anything mentioned in the specifications and not shown on the drawings, or shown on the drawings and not mentioned in the specifications, shall be of like effect as if shown or mentioned in both.

See *P.R. Contractors, Inc.*, ASBCA 52937,02-2 BCA ¶ 31,941, denying a claim for extra work that was necessary to perform work required by the contract. See also *Wilco Constr., Inc.*, ASBCA 53683,02-2 BCA ¶ 31,942 (contractor required to do work called for by specifications but not in drawings), and *Elter S.A.*, ASBCA 52791, 02-1 BCA ¶ 31,672 (contractor required to wire electrical equipment to provide a building "complete and ready for use").

In *Daniel H. Foster*, ASBCA 21965, 78-2 BCA ¶ 13,541, *recons. denied*, 79-2 BCA ¶ 14,161, the contractor asserted that the contract did not require it to remove the existing pipe on the first floor of the north wing because one section of the contract implied that other workers would do so. However, many other sections of the contract stated that the contractor would remove all pipe. The board found that the contract documents, read together, indicated that the purpose of the contract was to obtain all work necessary for the replacement of a complete system. Compare *United Dominion Indus.*, ASBCA 43338, 92-2 BCA ¶ 24,911, where the government ordered the contractor to upgrade the lockset cylinders from Schlage to Medeco, contrary to the written specifications. The government asserted that its specification for a Medeco cylinder in lockset number 35 was also intended for lockset numbers 1-34. The board recognized that the government may have intended that all the cylinders be Medeco, yet held that this purpose was not evident from the contract terms and that the subjective, unwritten intent could not bind the contractor. See also *B.D. Click Co. v. United States*, 222 Ct. Cl. 290, 614 F.2d 748 (1980) (requiring the contractor to install inside and outside connections of the sprinkler system, even though the contract drawings referred only to the outside connections), and *Andrews & Parrish Co.*, ASBCA 27251, 84-1 BCA ¶ 16,933 (reading the contract as a whole to demonstrate that, although all the drawings did not show complete rib roofing, complete rib roofing was clearly intended by the contract).

C. Order of Precedence

Government contract documents are long and complex, containing many clauses that are drafted independently of each other. Consequently, it is frequently impossible to arrive at an interpretation that gives a reasonable effect to all parts of a contract document. Such conflicts may be resolved by use of interpretation rules establishing an order of precedence. *Restatement, Second, Contracts* § 203 states:

> (c) specific terms and exact terms are given greater weight than general language;
>
> (d) separately negotiated or added terms are given greater weight than standardized terms or other terms not separately negotiated.

However, the government almost always inserts an Order of Precedence clause in its contracts that varies from this common law logic.

For an Order of Precedence clause to be applied, there must be a conflict between the provisions in question, *Amelco, Inc.*, ASBCA 50826, 99-2 BCA ¶ 30,549; *Stewart/Tampke, J.V.*, ASBCA 29607, 87-2 BCA ¶ 19,687. One of the most common areas of misunderstanding by contractors is where one document is silent on a matter that is covered by another document. Since mere silence in either the specifications or the drawings does not constitute a conflict between them, order of precedence rules are not used to deal with silence in one contract document but only to resolve direct conflicts between the contract documents, *Edward R. Marden Corp. v. United States*, 803 F.2d 701 (Fed. Cir. 1986).

Neither are order of precedence clauses usable to resolve alleged discrepancies between performance specification requirements and specific design requirements, *Apollo Sheet Metal, Inc. v. United States*, 44 Fed. Cl. 210 (1999). In that case, the court reasoned that the general discretion given by a performance specification was limited by specific design requirements included in the contract.

1. Order of Precedence Clauses

The basic Order of Precedence clauses used in sealed bid and negotiated procurements, in FAR 52.214-29 and FAR 52.215-8, respectively, provide:

> Any inconsistency in this solicitation shall be resolved by giving precedence in the following order: (a) the Schedule (excluding the specifications); (b) representations and other instructions; (c) contract clauses; (d) other documents, exhibits, and attachments; and (e) the specifications.

See *Cessna Aircraft Co. v. Dalton*, 126 F.3d 1442 (Fed. Cir. 1997), giving a schedule provision precedence over a clause in the General Provisions. See also *Manuel Bros., Inc. v. United States*, 55 Fed. Cl. 8 (2002), holding that statements of the contracting officer at a pre-bid conference are not the type of "representations and instructions" covered by the clause because they were not incorporated into the contract.

In construction contracts, this clause is supplemented by the following portion of FAR 52.236-21, Specifications and Drawings for Construction clause:

> (a) The Contractor shall keep on the work site a copy of the drawings and specifications and shall at all times give the Contracting Officer access thereto. Anything mentioned in the specifications and not shown on the drawings, or shown on the drawings and not mentioned in the specifications, shall be of like effect as if shown or mentioned in both. In case of difference between drawings and specifications, the specifications shall govern. In case of discrepancy in the figures, in the drawings, or in the specifications, the matter shall be promptly submitted to the Contracting Officer, who shall promptly make a determination in writing. Any adjustment by the Contractor without such a determination shall be at its own risk and expense. The Contracting Officer shall furnish from time to time such detailed drawings and other information as considered necessary, unless otherwise provided.

These FAR clauses may also be supplemented by agency clauses. See, for example, General Services Acquisition Regulation (GSAR) 552.236-77 (construction), Department of Education Acquisition Regulation (EDAR) 3452.215-33 (negotiated contracts), and Veterans Administration Acquisition Regulation (VAAR) 852.236-71 (construction). When both the FAR 52.214-29 and FAR 52.236-21 clauses are included in a construction contract, the latter clause governs because it is mandatory for such contracts, *Interstate Gen. Gov't Contractors, Inc. v. United States*, 40 Fed. Cl. 585 (1998); *Hickman Mech., Inc.*, ASBCA 46492, 94-2 BCA ¶ 26,914.

Construction contracts may also contain provisions stating that large-scale drawings control over small-scale drawings. See the Contract Drawings, Maps, and Specifications clause in DFARS 252.236-7001, stating:

> (c) In general—
>
> > (1) Large scale drawings shall govern small scale drawings; and
> >
> > (2) The Contractor shall follow figures marked on drawings in preference to scale measurements.

In *R.B. Hazard, Inc.*, ASBCA 41295, 93-2 BCA ¶ 25,577, the board held that the above DFARS 252.236-7001 clause was not a true order of precedence clause because of its inclusion of the phrase "in general." In *Rexach-HRH Constr. Corp.*, VACAB 721, 68-1 BCA ¶ 6924, under a previous version of the clause, which read that large-scale drawings would supersede the small-scale drawings, the contractor was held entitled to perform to the less rigorous large-scale drawings as opposed to the small-scale drawings.

Order of precedence clauses have the advantage of permitting a relatively mechanical resolution of a conflict without the necessity of attempting to determine which of the conflicting provisions was intended. There is, however, no assurance that the decision reached as a result of their application will reflect the intent of the parties. As stated by the board in *John A. Volpe Constr. Co.*, VACAB 638, 68-1 BCA ¶ 6857, at 31,705-06:

> Where conflict between the specifications and drawings exists under such conditions, the rights and obligations of the parties under a contract containing Clause 2 of Standard Form 23-A [the Order of Precedence clause] are not to be governed by inferences that may be drawn as to which of the conflicting provisions was correct and which was in error. The reason is that Clause 2, which is a special provision obviously designed for such a situation, takes over to express the contractual intent by specifically providing which of the two conflicting requirements shall take precedence and be effective as stating the contract obligation assumed by the parties. The parties have in their contract agreed, by a clause binding on both of them, that in such a situation the specification shall govern. Operation of the clause may appear to be arbitrary, for it resolves the conflict and fixes the contract requirement without regard to which of the conflicting provisions was correct, but it does not discriminate in favor of either party and it is not unreasonable as a practical solution to the problem of conflicting requirements that could otherwise exist in the written contract. It has been consistently recognized as a legally valid and fully effective agreement by the parties as to how their contract is to be interpreted.

Order of precedence clauses have been used to require the contractor to furnish work required by the specifications even though the drawings called for a lower level of work. See *Cadell Constr. Co.*, DOTBCA 2967, 96-2 BCA ¶ 28,549 (specification required higher quality pipe than drawing); *Kerr Contracting Corp.*, ASBCA 44783, 93-2 BCA ¶ 25,674 (contract drawings stated that the transformer was government-furnished equipment although the contract specifications stated that the contractor was to provide the transformer); *American Line Builders, Inc.*, 26 Cl. Ct. 1155 (1992) (requiring contractor to adhere to the specifications and to supply all hardware specified therein); and *Electrical Contracting Corp. of Guam*, ASBCA 34337, 90-3 BCA ¶ 23,003 (requiring contractor to provide higher quantity required by specifications as compared to drawings). However, if the specifications and drawings can be given a reasonable interpretation that avoids a conflict, the clause will not apply, *J. Kokolakis Contracting, Inc. v. General Servs. Admin.*, GSBCA 15648, 02-1 BCA ¶ 31,711. See, for example, *A.R. Mack Constr. Co.*, ASBCA 49526, 97-1 BCA ¶ 28,742, in which the board refused to use the order of precedence clause because the specific drawing requirements merely amplified the general specification requirements.

Contractors are entitled to follow an order of precedence clause even though the conflict between the drawings and specifications is seen at the time of bidding. See *Hensel Phelps Constr. Co. v. United States*, 886 F.2d 1296 (Fed. Cir. 1989), in which the court held that it was not necessary for the contractor to seek clarification in such a situation, stating at 1298:

> Contractors should, as a general rule, be entitled to rely on the order of precedence clause and not be required to seek clarification of a putative inconsistency between the specifications and drawings. The order of precedence clause itself resolves that inconsistency. It is, after all, the government that is the author of this contract clause, as well as the specifications and drawings.

See also *McGhee Constr., Inc.*, ASBCA 45175, 93-3 BCA ¶ 26,154, where after award, the government discovered that some of the specification requirements were incorrect but correctly shown on the drawings while others were correct on the specifications but incorrect on the drawings. The board denied the government's motion for summary judgment based on the contractor's allegation that in each case it had used the correct figures. Thus, the board stated at 130,022:

> [The contractor] would not have overreached the Government by not notifying the contracting officer prior to award of the conflict. The Government would have received the benefit of the correct figure already, and equitable principles would not allow the Government to benefit again by a reduction in the contract price for the reduction in quantity for removal of inner asbestos sealant.

Thus, contractors have been successful in using order of precedence clauses to their advantage. See, for example, *Shah Constr. Co.*, ASBCA 50411, 01-1 BCA ¶ 31,330, where the contractor properly resolved a conflict by using the specification requirement. See also *Hills Materials Co.*, ASBCA 42410, 92-1 BCA ¶ 24,636, *rev'd on other grounds*, 982 F.2d 514 (Fed. Cir. 1992) (proper to use lower quantities in the specifications than in drawings for bid preparation), and *W.R. Johnson, Inc.*, ASBCA 40251, 91-3 BCA ¶ 24,172 (proper to follow lesser specification requirement for explosion-proof motors).

2. Common Law Order of Precedence Rule

The common law order of precedence rule is used in government contracts when a specific order of precedence clause is not applicable. This would ordinarily occur where the conflict is between two terms within the same document. However, in such cases the matter may be handled as an ambiguity, *Edward R. Marden Corp. v. United States*, 803 F.2d 701 (Fed. Cir. 1986). The general rule of common law is that specific provisions will prevail over general provisions and that written or typed provisions will prevail over general provisions, *Restatement, Second, Contracts* § 203(c) and (d).

A specific provision was held to apply over a general provision in *Hughes Communications Galaxy, Inc. v. United States*, 26 Cl. Ct. 123 (1992), *rev'd on other grounds*, 998 F.2d 953 (Fed. Cir. 1993). There it was held that a contract clause incorporating a specific government policy was to be given effect even though a more general clause stated that the contract was subject to several other government policies. See also *Abraham v. Rockwell Int'l Corp.*, 326 F.3d 1242 (Fed. Cir. 2003), in which a specifically drafted clause was held to prevail over a general clause, and *Hills Materials Co. v. Donald B. Rice*, 982 F.2d 514 (Fed. Cir. 1992), in which the Accident Prevention clause in FAR 52.236-13 was held to govern over the Permits and Responsibilities clause in FAR 52.236-7 because it contained a more specific statement on the issue in the case. Compare *Walashek Indus. & Marine, Inc.*, ASBCA 52166, 00-1 BCA ¶ 30,728, where this order of precedence was not applicable because neither of the conflicting specification provisions was found to be specific or general.

The general rule of common law does not apply where a specific provision conflicts with a standard government contract clause that is required by statute or regulation. See, for example, *Hydracon Corp.*, ENGBCA 3462, 75-2 BCA ¶ 11,489, in which the board stated at 54,812-13:

> The two versions of the "Variations in Estimated Quantities" clause which the Government included in this contract are in conflict and cannot be reconciled. The version contained in the standard, printed General Provisions speaks of variations of a pay item of the contract, whereas the version included as a special provision attempts to limit the clause to variations of a part of the pay item.
>
> It is an established canon that standard clauses for Government contracts, which are required by law and by regulations having the effect of law, cannot be contradicted by other specially drafted provisions so that they are, in effect, written out of the contract or subordinated to such special provisions. *Thompson Ramo Wooldridge, Inc. v. U.S.*, 175 Ct. Cl. 527, 536, 361 F.2d 222. Consequently, it is the Board's determination that SP-30 is without force or effect in this contract and that the Variations in Estimated Quantities clause of the standard General Provisions applies, as written, to the whole of bid items 1 and 1A.

D. Enumerated Items

Government contracts frequently contain provisions that incorporate lists of things covered or excluded. Such lists may be included in work statements or standard contract clauses. The determination of whether the lists are exclusive or merely illustrative depends on whether words of qualification such as "included," "including but not limited to," and "for example," precede the list.

If there are no words of qualification, the contractor may reasonably assume, absent other contract provisions to the contrary, that those items not listed are not included. In *Henry J. Korpi*, ASBCA 6948, 61-1 BCA ¶ 3030, the contractor agreed to demolish and remove a building. The issue was whether it was entitled to remove a buried fuel tank that the government argued was not a part of nor intended to be sold with the building. The board pointed to a provision of the contract that enumerated items that were not to be damaged during demolition. Since the purpose of including this list was to protect the property that was not to be removed, and because the fuel tank was not included, the board held that the contractor was justified in removing it, stating at 15,710:

> [The contractor] was cautioned not to damage water, sewer, and electrical lines leading to the building. The insertion of these provisions, obviously, was intended to apprise bidders that those items were to remain and were not be to damaged. Nothing is said concerning the materials which were to be removed, for, as is also apparent, the Government had no interest in them other than that they be removed without damage to the remaining facilities. The contract does not indicate that precaution was to be taken not to damage the fuel tank and the pipe leading to the building. The failure to do so, particularly in view of the specific reference made to other items, we believe, would lead reasonably intelligent persons to conclude that the fuel tank was to be removed.

See also *Tripod, Inc.*, ASBCA 25104, 89-1 BCA ¶ 21,305, holding that cleaning work not specified in the list of cleaning tasks was not required. Compare *Coastal Dry Dock & Repair Corp.*, ASBCA 31894, 87-1 BCA ¶ 19,618, in which the board held that a short enumeration was too small and isolated to exclude other work.

When words of qualification are inserted, items not listed are covered by the clause if they are similar in kind and character to those listed. This has been referred to as the rule of *ejusdem generis*. In a number of cases, this rule has been used to exclude items of coverage. In *Carnegie Steel Co. v. United States*, 240 U.S. 156 (1916), the Court held that technical difficulties in performing the work were not "of the same kind" as the excusable delays enumerated in the contract because such difficulties were not "extraneous" to the contractor's fundamental undertakings. Similarly, in *North Star Alaska Housing Corp.*, 30 Fed. Cl. 259 (1993), the contractor claimed that a list C of water, sewer, gas, electric current, oil, or other form of power, fuel, or utility was not all-inclusive and was open to incorporate other unenumerated utilities, specifically, refuse collection. In denying the contractor's claim, the court stated that "an item . . . included on a list will be qualified and limited to the words which it is associated." Thus, refuse collection did not logically flow from the list. However, in *Kato Corp.*, ASBCA 51513, 02-1 BCA ¶ 31,669, the board refused to apply the rule when the general words were all-encompassing, stating at 156,497:

> Assuming, arguendo, handling contaminated soil is work of a different character than the listed items, the general phrase, "all work defined in the contract documents," precedes the specific list and is linked to the list by the word "including." We think the rule is inapplicable. Cf. *Cooper Distributing Co., Inc. v. Amana Refrigeration, Inc.*, 63 F.3d 262, 280 (3d Cir. 1995). Moreover, ejusdem generis "is subject to the contrary agreement of the parties . . . [and] will not preclude the inclusion of things not of the same class or kind when it appears the parties so intended." 11 Samuel Willistro & Richard A. Lord, *A Treatise on the Law of Contracts*, § 32.10, 451-53 (4th ed. 1999). We believe the only reasonable interpretation is that the parties intended the base bid to include measures arising from soil contamination.

In *C.W. Roberts Constr. Co.*, ASBCA 12348, 68-1 BCA ¶ 6819, the issue was whether a prefinished sheetrock ceiling covered with printed paper was painted within the meaning of the specification definition:

> The term "paint" as used herein includes emulsions, enamels, paints, stains, varnishes, sealers, cement-latex filler, and other coatings, whether used as prime, intermediate, or finish coats.

The board held that paper applied to sheetrock was of a different kind than paint, holding at 31,510:

> [T]he term "paint" is defined as including a number of products that are used as prime, intermediate or finish coats. The listed group of products appear to be liquids in their normal state as distinguished from gases or solids. Moreover, . . . the products in this group appear in each instance, under normal practice, to be applied as a coating by a brush, roller, or a spraying device.
>
> The printed paper surface of the sheetrock, on the other hand, is in its normal state a solid, not a liquid. The Government has argued, without contradiction, that the printed paper is not applied to the sheetrock surface by any of the means normally employed to apply the products listed by name in the definition of "paint" . . . . Consequently, it is unreasonable that the term "other coatings," which is linked with the preceding list of products that are used to define the term "paint" . . . should be read to include a printed paper surface.
>
> Words, like men, are known by the company they keep. . . . The meaning of a doubtful word may be ascertained by the reference to the meaning of words with which it is associated. . . . Within th[is] context, the term "other coatings" cannot reasonably include a printed paper surface because, in two significant respects, it differs from the products connected with the term "paint."

See *C. Sanchez & Son, Inc. v. United States*, 6 F.3d 1539 (Fed. Cir. 1993) (trencher was not within a class of "crawler and rubber-tire tractors such as [an enumerated list] . . . and other self-propelled construction equipment such as [an enumerated list]"); *Kimmins Contracting Corp.*, ASBCA 43800, 94-2 BCA ¶ 26,608 (contractor was not required to sandblast process piping when the contract called for sandblasting of structural and support steel items because the piping was not within that class); and *Long Elevator & Machine Co.*, VABCA 2246, 90-2 BCA ¶ 22,637 (the term "springs," "guides," "seals," etc. was held to invoke the rule of *ejusdem generis*—with the result that an electrical switch was found not to be in the class of mechanical parts).

For a case holding that unlisted items are similar in kind and character and therefore covered by the clause, see *Ken Rogge Lumber Co.*, AGBCA 84-145-3, 84-2 BCA ¶ 17,381. There, the contractor alleged that the contract allocated the risk of loss for theft of timber to the government. The government contended that the causes for risk of loss did not specifically include theft. In holding for the contractor, the board stated at 86,594:

> The causes listed in Clause B8.12 include "fire, wind, flood, insects disease, or similar causes." Presumably, under the Forest Service's theory, which limits the

> application of the clause to natural casualties, losses due to such causes as volcanic eruption, drought or meteorite impact would be included, whereas losses due to theft would not be since theft is not a natural cause. In accordance with the well established rule of interpretation, *ejusdem generis*, the phrase in B8.12, "or similar causes" must be limited to the same type of cause. See, for example, *C.W. Roberts Construction Co.*, ASBCA No. 12348, 68-1 BCA ¶ 6819; *Austin v. United States*, [9 CCF ¶ 72,019], 161 Ct. Cl. 76, 314 F.2d 518, *cert. denied*, 375 U.S. 83 (1963). The question we must answer here is what is or is not a similar cause. In this case because of the other terms and conditions of the clause, we must also construe the clause as a whole.
>
> First, we note that fire, one of the listed causes in B8.12, may result from both natural and man-made causes. Therefore, the causes listed in B8.12 are obviously not limited to "natural causes" as the Forest Service alleges. It is also apparent that logging operations could block a stream and cause a flood that results in a loss of timber. While flood is listed as a cause in B8.12, recovery for timber loss due to flood would not be automatic because of the operation of the last sentence of B8.12. This sentence provides that B8.12 should not be construed to relieve either party of liability for negligence. We conclude that this latter provision is the key to interpreting the clause as a whole. That is, liability follows title for losses resulting from natural and man-made causes, except where the loss is caused by the negligence of one of the parties. Therefore, it follows that theft is a covered cause in B8.12, so long as such theft does not arise from [the contractor's] fault or negligence, *Louisiana-Pacific*, [AGBCA 81-141-3, 81-2 BCA ¶ 15,280]

See also *Buse Timber & Sales, Inc.*, AGBCA 90-168-1, 94-1 BCA ¶ 26,456, finding that vandalism was a similar cause within the provision for fire, flood, insects, disease, or similar cause.

IV. EXTRINSIC EVIDENCE

Facts and circumstances surrounding the formation and performance of the contract are used by courts and boards to determine the intent of the parties. Reliance on this kind of evidence is necessary to ensure that the interpretation is based on a knowledge of all the facts and circumstances that could have a bearing on the parties' intent. See *Max Drill, Inc. v. United States*, 192 Ct. Cl. 608, 620, 427 F.2d 1233, 1240 (1970), stating that the practical interpretation of a contract, as shown by the words or conduct of the parties before the controversy, is given, "great, if not controlling weight," in interpreting the contract. Compare *Beta Sys., Inc. v. United States*, 838 F.2d 1179 (Fed. Cir. 1988), calling for a limitation on the use of extrinsic evidence by stating at 1183, "The general rule is that extrinsic evidence will not be received to change the terms of a contract that is clear on its face." Accord *McAbee Constr., Inc. v. United States*, 97 F. 3d 1431 (Fed. Cir 1996); *Fluor Daniel, Inc. v. Regents of the Univ. of Cal.*, EBCA C-9909296, 02-2 BCA ¶ 32,017.

Three types of evidence of surrounding circumstances frequently are used to assist in resolution of contract interpretation controversies: (1) discussions and concurrent actions, (2) prior course of dealing between the parties, and (3) custom and trade usage. This section gives detailed consideration to these three kinds of extrinsic evidence. However, other extrinsic evidence, such as the economic conditions prevailing in a particular locality and the financial condition of the contractor, may also be used to assist in resolution of interpretation controversies.

A. Discussions and Concurrent Actions

Evidence of the parties' discussions and actions is frequently found persuasive in discerning their intent. For example, evidence of discussions and conduct occurring prior to the submission of bids or proposals may serve as proof that the parties have agreed as to the meaning of particular terms. Such pre-bid or pre-proposal evidence may also indicate that one party should be held to the other party's interpretation that was made known to it. Furthermore, evidence of discussions or conduct occurring after contract award but prior to controversy may indicate the reasonableness of one party's interpretation.

This section first discusses the various settings in which this evidence is generated and then considers various limitations on its use. The principal limitation discussed is the parol evidence rule, which is frequently invoked when one of the parties seeks to introduce evidence of discussion or agreement for the purposes of either contradicting the apparently clear meaning of a disputed term or adding terms to an allegedly complete agreement.

1. Requests for Clarification

During contract formation or early in the performance of a contract, either the contractor or the government may become aware of an apparent ambiguity or that the other party's interpretation differs from its own. In these circumstances, it is common for one party to specifically request the other party to clarify its interpretation of the terms in question. The solicitation provision in FAR 52.214-6 contains procedures to be followed by bidders and government officials in dealing with requests for clarification submitted in the pre-bid stage of a sealed bid procurement:

> EXPLANATION TO PROSPECTIVE BIDDERS
>
> Any prospective bidder desiring an explanation or interpretation of the solicitation, drawings, specifications, etc., must request it in writing soon enough to allow a reply to reach all prospective bidders before the submission of their bids. Oral explanations or instructions given before the award of a contract will not be binding. Any information given a prospective bidder concerning a solicitation will be furnished promptly to all other prospective bidders as an amendment to the solicitation, if that information is necessary in submitting bids or if the lack of it would be prejudicial to other prospective bidders.

Prior to 1998, FAR 52.215-14 contained an almost identical solicitation provision to be used in negotiated procurements. This was removed from the FAR by Federal Acquisition Circular 97-2, 62 Fed. Reg. 51,224, Sept. 30, 1997.

The purpose of these clauses has been construed as being to ensure that relevant information be afforded equally to prospective offerors, *Manloading & Mgmt. Assocs., Inc. v. United States*, 198 Ct. Cl. 628, 461 F.2d 1299 (1972); *Centel Business Sys.*, VABCA 2079, 86-3 BCA ¶ 19,120.

Oral explanation or instruction given to a contractor before award will not change the clear terms of the contract. Whether or not a clause was applicable, the parol evidence rule would have excluded it. See *Green Thumb Lawn Maint.*, ENGBCA 6249, 98-1 BCA ¶ 29,688 (alleged oral statements inconsistent with "unambiguous contract requirements"); *Structural Finishing, Inc.*, ASBCA 26647, 84-2 BCA ¶ 17,303 (alleged oral concurrence made by a government representative would have been totally ineffective since the interpretation was inconsistent with the plain, unambiguous provisions of the solicitation); *Hoedad's, Inc.*, AGBCA 76-168-4, 83-1 BCA ¶ 16,288 (government representative's oral interpretation of a clause could not be relied on since the clause was clear and unambiguous and thus the representative's inconsistent interpretation constituted a change to the solicitation, which required a written amendment); *Rogers Helicopters, Inc.*, AGBCA 75-147, 77-2 BCA ¶ 12,562 (no ambiguity existed; any oral understanding would have varied or modified the written contract); and *Ralph Rosedale*, AGBCA 441, 77-1 BCA ¶ 12,344 (contractor attempt to vary terms of tree planting contract by a government representative's preaward oral agreement to provide flagging was inappropriate because of clause). In *Sipco Servs. & Marine, Inc. v. United States*, 41 Fed. Cl. 196 (1998), the government was precluded from enforcing an interpretation given at a pre-bid conference because it conflicted with a reasonable interpretation of the specifications. See also *Manuel Bros., Inc. v. United States*, 55 Fed. Cl. 8 (2002), holding that the government was not bound by an oral statement of the contracting officer at a pre-bid conference even though it furnished information about subsoil conditions that was missing from the solicitation.

A contractor is, however, permitted to rely on an oral clarification if the clarification simply confirms the contractor's interpretation and does not in any way modify the written solicitation. See *Max Drill, Inc. v. United States*, 192 Ct. Cl. 608, 427 F.2d 1233 (1970), in which the court held that the contractor was reasonable in relying on statements made by a representative of the contracting agency who gave reassurances during a pre-bid inspection that the prospective contractor's interpretation of the specifications was in line with what the contract called for. The court explained its position in footnote 6 at 625:

> [The Explanation to Prospective Bidders] provision means that the government is not to be estopped by such oral explanations or instructions which conflict with or depart from the specifications or the contract. The provision does not mean

> that the bidder cannot take into account, in determining what the specifications reasonably call for, the statements made by a knowledgeable government official, who is representing the contracting officer, which appear to be in conformity with the plans, specifications, and contract.

Similarly, in *Unidynamics/St. Louis, Inc.*, ASBCA 17592, 73-2 BCA ¶ 10,360, the board used oral pre-bid confirmations made by a government survey team as evidence that the contractor's own interpretation had been reasonable. The board stated at 48,934:

> For the purposes of this appeal we treat them not as modifications of the IFB but as evidence which may be considered in evaluating the reasonableness of [the contractor's] interpretation of an ambiguous specification and determining the meaning of the written contract.

See also *Sharon F. Graves*, PSBCA 3399, 94-2 BCA ¶ 26,788 (government bound by oral clarification of conflicting terms); *Pioneer Drilling Co.*, AGBCA 439, 76-2 BCA ¶ 12,028 (contractor was led to believe by contracting officer's representative that the two sides were in such complete accord that there was no need for a written request for clarification); and *DeRalco, Inc.*, ASBCA 20630, 76-2 BCA ¶ 11,971 (subcontractor's interpretation accepted after it made an unproductive inquiry to the proper contact point and was advised to bid the painting requirements as it understood them). Compare *Structural Finishing, Inc.*, ASBCA 26647, 84-2 BCA ¶ 17,303 (board held that the government representative "never agreed with [contractor's] interpretation or gave [it] any reasonable basis for having so concluded"). See also *Plano Bridge & Culvert*, ASBCA 35497, 90-3 BCA ¶ 23,224, in which the board held that the government had waived the requirement for written requests for clarification by orally discussing the issue several times.

The government's interpretation will prevail when requests for clarification are not timely made. In *Klingensmith, Inc. v. United States*, 205 Ct. Cl. 651, 505 F.2d 1257 (1974), the court held that the government could not be deemed to have acquiesced in the contractor's interpretation made known to it only three hours before bid opening since the contractor untimely sought clarification under the Explanation to Prospective Bidders clause. See also *Mid Eastern Builders, Inc.*, ASBCA 33845, 90-1 BCA ¶ 22,361, in which the board held that a clarification request submitted three hours before bid opening was too late. Compare *Wright Assocs., Inc.*, ASBCA 22492, 79-2 BCA ¶ 14,102, *recons. denied*, 80-1 BCA ¶ 14,253, upholding the contractor's interpretation where it presented sufficient evidence establishing that no meaningful response would have been made within the last 10 days of the bidding period.

If an offeror makes a diligent attempt to obtain clarification of an ambiguity under the clause and obtains no formal response from the government, its interpretation has prevailed. In *Sipco Servs. & Marine, Inc. v. United States*, 41 Fed. Cl. 196 (1998), the government's interpretation was rejected because it failed to clear up a defective specification after the issue was raised in a pre-bid conference. See also *Plano Bridge & Culvert*, ASBCA 35497, 90-3 BCA ¶ 23,224 (several discussions with government employees without obtaining clear guidance), and *BMY, Div. of Harsco Corp.*, ASBCA 36805, 93-2 BCA ¶ 25,684, *recons. denied*, 94-2 BCA ¶ 26,725 (request for clarification before bidding unanswered and reassertion of interpretation, in response to a request for verification of bid price, not acknowledged). However, a single request for clarification with no follow-up has been held to be insufficient to permit the contractor's interpretation to prevail, *Community Heating & Plumbing Co. v. Kelso*, 987 F.2d 1575 (Fed. Cir. 1993) (failure to submit a second request for clarification after receiving nonresponsive answer to first request); *Delcon Constr. Corp. v. United States*, 27 Fed. Cl. 634 (1993) (failure to follow up by seeking written clarification from contracting officer). See *Hydro Group, Inc. v. United States*, 17 Cl. Ct. 668 (1989), in which several attempts to obtain clarification were held sufficient to require a trial on the issue of whether the offeror had been diligent.

2. Pre-Bid and Pre-Proposal Conferences

Contract interpretations are also given at pre-bid or pre-proposal conferences. In *Sylvania Elec. Prods., Inc. v. United States*, 198 Ct. Cl. 106, 458 F.2d 994 (1972), the court held that an oral agreement reached at a pre-bid conference, to the effect that certain government-furnished property would be compatible with the contractor's equipment, served as a binding expression of the government's intent. The court stated at 131:

> To hold that the writing signed following such a conference as here took place negates the oral agreement reached at the conference would be reckless of the reputation of the procurement system in which bidders' conferences are an integral part. Meetings between Government procurement officers and prospective bidders would become a sham. Questions would be useless, for answers would be without force, and the amounts of the bids received would soon show the results. Respect for the answer is required by the respect given the Government's procurement process.

Accord, *Sharpe Refrigeration, Inc. v. United States*, 30 Fed. Cl. 735 (1994); *Macke Co. v. United States*, 199 Ct. Cl. 552, 467 F.2d 1323 (1972). See also *Goss Fire Protection, Inc.*, DOTBCA 2782, 97-1 BCA ¶ 28,853, holding that a contractor was entitled to rely on pre-bid conference statements that were recorded and distributed to the bidders. Similarly, in *Pettijohn Eng'g Co.*, IBCA 1346-4-80, 83-2 BCA ¶ 16,559, after a storm necessitated the reconstruction of the work constructed under a contract, the board held the government bound to pre-proposal conference statements made by a government official regarding risk allocation for such an event, stating at 82,357:

> Such statements of authorized Government officials made at a prebid conference, attended by prospective bidders, can and should be taken into account in ascertaining the parties' intentions and joint understanding of the contract requirements. The *Macke Co. v. United States*, 199 Ct. Cl. 552 (1972). In the instant case, the

> above dialogue represents an agreement by the parties with respect to the question of risk of loss, that prospective bidders were entitled to rely upon even though such statements were oral representations made before award of the contract.

Compare *Sipco Servs. & Marine v. United States*, 41 Fed. Cl. 196 (1998), holding that statements at a pre-bid conference could not enlarge contract requirements. See also *White Sands Constr., Inc.*, ASBCA 51875, 02-2 BCA ¶ 31,858, holding that the government was not bound by statements at a pre-proposal conference regarding the amount of anticipated work to be awarded in an IDIQ contract because attendees were warned that such statements did not alter the terms of the contract.

Contractors have also been bound by statements made at pre-bid or pre-proposal conferences. See *Swede Constr. Corp.*, PSBCA 4099, 98-2 BCA ¶ 30,082, holding the contractor bound by additional information given in a pre-bid conference as to times when work was permitted. See also *DRC Corp. v. Department of Commerce*, GSBCA 14919-COM, 00-1 BCA ¶ 30,649, binding the contractor to supplementary information provided at a pre-bid conference. In *Goss Fire Protection, Inc.*, DOTBCA 2783, 97-1 BCA ¶ 28,854, the board held the contractor bound by information given out at the pre-bid conference and included in its minutes even though the contractor did not attend the conference. The information supplemented very vague specification provisions as to the contractor's access to a prison where the work was performed.

The government has in certain cases attempted to avoid responsibility for representations made at pre-bid conferences by relying on the Explanation to Prospective Bidders clause. In *Manloading & Mgmt. Assocs., Inc. v. United States*, 198 Ct. Cl. 628, 461 F.2d 1299 (1972), the court found that the clause did not apply to oral explanations made during a pre-bid conference, stating at 634:

> [The clause] appears to negate the Government's liability. However, when considered in context we think that this language also does not apply to [the Government official's] statements. Rather, we think that the clause should be construed in accordance with its obvious purpose, which is to ensure that relevant information be afforded equally to prospective offerors. The clause speaks of requests made individually by a prospective bidder and provides that any explanation given him must be furnished to all other bidders. Thus, we do not believe it was designed to apply to a prebid conference where typically all of the prospective bidders are present and oral questions and answers are expected and encouraged.

This reasoning was followed in *M.G.C. Co.*, DOTCAB 1553, 86-1 BCA ¶ 18,571, and *Morrison-Knudsen Co.*, ASBCA 16483, 72-2 BCA ¶ 9733. Compare the questionable decision in *Fairchild Indus., Inc.*, ASBCA 16302, 74-1 BCA ¶ 10,567, in which the board held that the government was not bound by the government's interpretation offered at a pre-proposal conference since the Request for Proposal contained a provision stating that oral discussions would not be used at any later date in the interpretation of any provision of the final contract.

In *Centel Bus. Sys.*, VABCA 2079, 86-3 BCA ¶ 19,120, the board held in favor of the contractor's interpretation, based on statements made in a pre-proposal conference, despite the lack of corroborative testimony from other contractors present at the meeting. Though the board indicated that such additional evidence would have been helpful, they refused to draw any negative inferences from this failure since they recognized the difficulties involved in obtaining favorable testimony from one's competitors.

In *Romac, Inc.*, DOTBCA 4028, 01-2 BCA ¶ 31,552, the contractor was granted an equitable adjustment for work that was not clearly required by the contract but was stated to be required in the pre-bid conference because it had not attended the conference and the government had not made the minutes of the conference available to nonattendees.

3. Pre-Dispute Interpretations

If one of the parties can demonstrate that the other party's interpretation of the contract language matched its own at some time prior to the dispute, that is strong evidence that the interpretation is reasonable. See *Blinderman Constr. Co. v. United States*, 695 F.2d 552 (Fed. Cir. 1982), stating at 558:

> It is a familiar principle of contract law that the parties' contemporaneous construction of an agreement, before it has become the subject of a dispute, is entitled to great weight in its interpretation.

In *Boeing Co.*, ASBCA 37579, 90-3 BCA ¶ 23,202, the director of contracts of an agency issued a modification purporting to exercise an option based on his interpretation of the option clause in the contract. The board rejected this interpretation on evidence that the contracting officer originally assigned to the contract had refused to exercise the option because it had expired. The board stated that this pre-dispute interpretation was more persuasive. Similarly, in *Sundstrand Corp.*, ASBCA 51572, 01-1 BCA ¶ 31,167, the board held the government bound to an interpretation of the contracting officer prior to obtaining legal advice to the contrary. See also *P.J. Dick, Inc. v. Principi*, 324 F.3d 1364 (Fed. Cir. 2003) (government bound to its interpretation of stipulation prior to litigation); *B.R. Servs., Inc.*, ASBCA 47673, 99-2 BCA ¶ 30,397 (contractor bound to interpretation in estimating cost of work); *Saul Subsidiary II Ltd. P'ship v. Barram*, 189 F.3d 1324 (Fed. Cir. 1999) (contractor bound to parties' prior interpretation of method of compensating contractor for added work); *Omni Corp. v. United States*, 41 Fed. Cl. 585 (1998) (government bound to contractor's interpretation when it acquiesced to that interpretation during the early stages of performance); *United States v. Human Res. Mgmt., Inc.*, 745 F.2d 642 (Fed. Cir. 1984) (contractor bound by parties' interpretation during negotiations that there was a ceiling on reimbursement of overhead costs); *Metzger Towing*, ENGBCA 5862, 94-2 BCA ¶ 26,651 (memo from pre-dispute meeting of both parties detailing agreement of work schedule held as best evidence of interpretation); *Head, Inc.*, ASBCA

39824, 92-1 BCA ¶ 24,755 (contractor bound by its interpretation during bidding and early performance); and *Sperry Corp. v. United States*, 845 F.2d 965 (Fed. Cir. 1988), *cert. denied*, 488 U.S. 986 (1988) (contractor bound to the government's interpretation because it had followed that interpretation in a progress report and an interoffice memorandum).

Evidence from prior contracts has also been held to support a contemporaneous interpretation. See *Albert Ginsberg v. Richard G. Austin*, 968 F.2d 1198 (Fed. Cir. 1992), in which the court ruled for the contractor because its interpretation was the same as the interpretation in an agency handbook and on prior contracts. Similarly, in *Harrison W. Corp.*, ENGBCA 5652, 93-1 BCA ¶ 25,231, the board accepted the contractor's interpretation because it was the same as the interpretation followed by the government on prior contracts.

If the government has previously attempted to formally clarify an apparent ambiguity, it may be held to that interpretation. In *Algernon Blair, Inc.*, GSBCA 7089, 84-2 BCA ¶ 17,450, the board held that the government's pre-dispute interpretation was "identical to [the contractor's] current position" where the government had previously agreed that the installation of certain meters was not required by the contract and had even originated a pre-dispute change order to clarify any apparent ambiguity.

Pre-dispute interpretations of a party will not be used against that party when the evidence is unclear. See *Westinghouse Elec. Co. v. United States*, 41 Fed. Cl. 229 (1998), in which the board declined to bind the government to an interpretation that the contractor argued was stated in its documents because the language was vague. In *Hof Constr., Inc.*, GSBCA 8354-R, 92-1 BCA ¶ 24,669, the board rejected the government's claim that a subcontractor should be held bound by an interpretation in its second shop drawing submittal. The board found different earlier interpretations of the subcontractor and held that the evidence was too unclear to use for this purpose. See also *Blough v. United States*, 17 Cl. Ct. 186 (1989), in which the court refused to rely on a pre-dispute letter because it was not written by an attorney, and noted that the government had also made pre-dispute interpretations contrary to its position in the litigation.

4. Pre-Dispute Actions Evidencing Interpretation

In many instances the parties may evidence their intent through their actions even though they never discuss a specific problem of contract interpretation. Generally, the courts and boards will give great weight to the interpretation indicated by the parties through their actions during formation or performance and prior to dispute. This is in accordance with the common law rule. See, for example, *Restatement, Second, Contracts* § 202(4):

> Where an agreement involves repeated occasions for performance by either party with knowledge of the nature of the performance and opportunity for objection

> to it by the other, any course of performance accepted or acquiesced in without objection is given great weight in the interpretation of the agreement.

The Court of Claims discussed this rule in *Macke Co. v. United States*, 199 Ct. Cl. 552, 467 F.2d 1323 (1972), stating at 556:

> In this inquiry, the greatest help comes, not from the bare text of the original contract, but from external indications of the parties' joint understanding, contemporaneously and later, of what the contract imported. The case is an excellent specimen of the truism that how the parties act under the arrangement, before the advent of controversy, is often more revealing than the dry language of the written agreement by itself. We are, of course, entirely justified in relying on this material to discover the parties' underlying intention.

See *Blinderman Constr. Co. v. United States*, 695 F.2d 552 (Fed. Cir. 1982), where the government was held bound by the contractor's interpretation because its project manager had acted in accordance with this interpretation in the early stages of the contract. Similarly, in *Julius Goldman's Egg City v. United States*, 697 F.2d 1051 (Fed. Cir. 1983), *cert. denied*, 464 U. S. 814 (1983), the court rejected the contractor's restrictive interpretation of the phrase "poultry premises," noting at 1058 that the contractor's pre-dispute actions were inconsistent with this interpretation:

> Moreover, the [contractor] when ordered, proceeded to clean and disinfect its entire premises without protest. A principle of contract interpretation is that the contract must be interpreted in accordance with the parties' understanding as shown by their conduct before the controversy.

See also *WDC West Carthage Assocs. v. United States*, 324 F.3d 1359 (Fed. Cir. 2003) (government made initial payments in accordance with contractor's interpretation); *T&M Distribs., Inc.*, ASBCA 51279, 01-2 BCA ¶ 31,442 (government didn't assert interpretation until dispute arose); *C.S. McCrossan Constr., Inc.*, ASBCA 49647, 99-1 BCA ¶ 30,661 (contractor acceded to government technique for measuring a pay item for half of contract performance); *JTL, Inc.*, ENGBCA 6323, 98-2 BCA ¶ 29,873 (contractor treated delays as its own fault during contract performance); *J.A. Jones Constr. Co.*, ENGBCA 6252, 97-1 BCA ¶ 28,918 (contractor identified government delays as not on critical path during CPM updates); *Midland Maint., Inc.*, ENGBCA 6087, 96-2 BCA ¶ 28,301 (contractor performed in accordance with government interpretation for a year); *Crown Laundry & Dry Cleaners, Inc. v. United States*, 29 Fed. Cl. 506 (1993) (government administered contract for significant time in accordance with contractor's interpretation); *Baggett Transp. Co. v. United States*, 969 F.2d 1028 (Fed. Cir. 1992) (contractor submitted bills in accordance with the government's interpretation); and *Drytech, Inc.*, ASBCA 41152, 92-2 BCA ¶ 24,809 (contractor performed for over two years without complaining that it was performing work outside the scope of the contract). Compare *Washington Constr. Co.* ENGBCA 5318, 89-3 BCA ¶ 22,077, where the contractor's assertion that an on-site representative allowed overexcavation was not supported by daily

Quality Control Reports and Daily Logs of Construction; and *Coastal Dry Dock & Repair Corp.*, ASBCA 31894, 87-1 BCA ¶ 19,618, where the contractor was not bound to the performance of its workforce because they had not studied the specifications with care and had not participated in bidding the job. See *Metric Constructors, Inc.*, ASBCA 48852, 98-1 BCA ¶ 29,384, in which the board ruled that a contractor's conduct in negotiating a price reduction based on the government's interpretation had indicated that it agreed with that interpretation, but the Federal Circuit in *Metric Constructors, Inc. v. National Aeronautics & Space Admin.*, 169 F.3d 747 (Fed. Cir. 1999), reversed, finding that accepting the other party's position in a negotiation did not necessarily indicate agreement with that position.

The actions of government employees prior to the dispute have also been held to be persuasive evidence of a reasonable interpretation of the contract. In *Sentell Bros., Inc.*, DOTBCA 1824, 89-3 BCA ¶ 21,904, the government's project engineer observed the contractor testing a cleaning method in accordance with its interpretation of the specifications and made no objection to this method. The board held that this constituted a contemporaneous interpretation of the contract, which was persuasive evidence for the contractor's interpretation. Similarly, in *White Buffalo Constr.*, IBCA 2166, 91-1 BCA ¶ 23,540, the government's interpretation was rejected because the government inspector had observed the contractor performing in accordance with its own interpretation and had not objected. See also *Do-Well Mach. Shop, Inc.*, ASBCA 35867, 92-2 BCA ¶ 24,843 (government inspector's acceptance of first article embodying contractor's interpretation); *J.S. Alberici Constr. Co.*, GSBCA 10961, 91-3 BCA ¶ 24,068 (government issuance of modification based on contractor's interpretation); *South Carolina Pub. Serv. Auth.*, ENGBCA 5564, 91-2 BCA ¶ 23,760 (contractor's interpretation incorporated in prior contract amendment); and *Pinay Flooring Prods., Inc.*, GSBCA 9286, 91-2 BCA ¶ 23,682 (government's initial acceptance of contractor's improper testing method).

Even if pre-dispute actions are later determined to be a mistake, such actions may be persuasive evidence of a party's interpretation. In *Alvin, Ltd. v. United States Postal Serv.*, 816 F.2d 1562 (Fed. Cir. 1987), the court held that the Postal Service had to continue paying the special assessment taxes on leased land even though such payment was not explicitly required under the terms of the contract. The court reasoned that, by paying the special assessments in the early years of the lease, the Postal Service had acknowledged that the intent of the contract was that it pay such costs. Therefore, even though the Postal Service could reasonably claim that paying the special assessments was a mistake under the terms of the contract, the court held it to its pre-dispute actions. A mistaken interpretation will also be upheld if it is accepted by the other party for a significant period of time during performance of the contract. In *Bates Lumber Co.*, AGBCA 81-242-1, 88-2 BCA ¶ 20,707, the board rejected the contractor's claim for reimbursement of overcharges because it had accepted the government's method of calculation for at least 18 years prior to the controversy. In *John Jennings, Jr.*, GSBCA 7520, 87-2 BCA ¶ 19,824, the board held that the contractor was not responsible for supplying and administering feedwater chemicals for a cooling system since the government had been performing this task, without protest, for eight years prior to the controversy, and even if it had been mistaken, its pre-dispute actions demonstrated a contemporaneous interpretation similar to the contractor's. However, evidence of a pre-dispute interpretation that is not in accord with the plain language of the contract must be compelling. Thus, in *Underground Constr. Co. v. United States*, 16 Cl. Ct. 60 (1988), the court rejected the contractor's claim that the government had agreed with its interpretation that the contract did not require it to pay for electricity. The pre-dispute activity that the contractor pointed to was the government's failure to immediately bill it for the electrical services. Since the contractor could give no reason why it should have been billed immediately, the court held that such a brief period of time could not form the basis of a pre-dispute interpretation.

Actions taken during the contract formation process may evidence the reasonableness of the contractor's subsequent interpretation. In *Diamond AH, Inc.*, ENG-BCA 4304, 82-2 BCA ¶ 16,066, the board rejected the contractor's otherwise reasonable interpretation that it was not responsible for dewatering wells, since the contractor had included a significant contingency in its bid for varying water flow and had, during performance, dewatered the wells without hesitation or instruction. Though a careful analysis of the contract might have supported the contractor's interpretation, the board doubted that such a simplistic interpretation represented either party's intent. The board stated at 79,702-03:

> We are troubled by the fact that we, as lawyers, had to make a very careful analysis of the specifications—and this in the light of a discrete question presented for after-the-fact resolution—to reach this conclusion. We recognize that contractors did jobs within restricted time periods, without careful legal analysis, prospectively, and without the benefit of specific problems necessarily in mind. This could incline us toward the reasonableness of [the contractor's] asserted, more simplistic, reading of the specification focusing on the one sentence.
>
> However, we conclude from [the contractor's] actions that it probably did not understand the specifications in quite so simplistic a manner as it now contends.

When one party attempts to change the requirements of the contract before a dispute arises, the courts and boards often take this as evidence of that party's original interpretation of the contract. In *Cascade Pac. Int'l*, GSBCA 6287, 83-1 BCA ¶ 16,501, the board noted that the contractor offered, and the government accepted, money for a decrease in the testing requirements called for in the contract. In holding against the contractor, the board stated at 82,005:

> We do not suppose that [the contractor] made those offers with an eleemosynary intent, and can only conclude by their conduct that the parties agreed that a flex test would be performed for production items.

5. *Pre-Dispute Interpretations Made Known to Other Party*

Where one of the contracting parties, either expressly or by its actions, clearly makes known to the other party its interpretation of the contract or a particular term, and the other party remains silent or does not object, that interpretation will be binding on the parties. This is true whether the interpretation is made known prior to award or during performance. The rule applies with particular force, however, where the interpretation and acquiescence take place before the contract is executed, *Restatement, Second, Contracts* §2 01(2) and § 202(4). See *E.I. Du Pont De Nemours & Co. v. United States*, 24 Cl. Ct. 635 (1991), *aff'd*, 980 F.2d 1440 (Fed. Cir. 1992), in which the government was held bound by the contractor's interpretation of words in a contract modification when it signed the modification after repeated discussions indicating the contractor's meaning. In *Newman Constr. Co. v. United States*, 48 Fed. Cl. 231 (2000), the parties negotiated a contract modification reserving the contractor's right to claim additional costs. The court rejected the contractor's assertion that the language of the reservation permitted the recovery of overhead because the contractor knew that the government's interpretation of that language was that it barred such costs. See also *Ship Analytics Int'l, Inc.*, ASBCA 50914, 01-1 BCA ¶ 31,253 (government bound by contractor's interpretation in letter preceding the signing of the contract); *Shah Constr. Co.*, ASBCA 50044, 00-1 BCA ¶ 30,667 (contractor bound by government interpretation stated at pre-bid conference); *Freightliner Corp.*, ASBCA 42982, 98-2 BCA ¶ 30,026 (contractor bound by government interpretation explained in pre-contract communication); *United Tech. Corp.*, ASBCA 46880, 97-1 BCA ¶ 28,818 (government bound by contractor's interpretation discussed with several government officials prior to signing of contract); *ABC Health Care*, VABCA 3462, 93-2 BCA ¶ 25,672 (government bound by rate of compensation that contractor intended to charge when it signed contract knowing of contractor's intention); *Arkel Int'l, Inc.*, ASBCA 37469, 89-3 BCA ¶ 21,965 (contractor bound by government interpretation where contracting officer had notified all offerors of interpretation prior to submission of proposals); and *MJW Enters., Inc.*, ENGBCA 5813, 93-1 BCA ¶ 25,405 (contractor bound by government interpretation when contracting officer's representative told contractor of it both before and after award). Compare *BMY, Div. of Harsco Corp.*, ASBCA 36805, 93-2 BCA ¶ 25,684, *recons. denied*, 94-2 BCA ¶ 26,725, where, in a sealed bid procurement, the board did not hold the contractor to the government's interpretation because the contractor had made the ambiguity known before the bid and no agreement had been reached.

Contractors have been bound by the government's pre-dispute interpretation made known to them in the course of prior disputes. In *Perry & Wallis, Inc. v. United States*, 192 Ct. Cl. 310, 427 F.2d 722 (1970), the contractor argued that its subcontractor's overhead and profit should be included in its actual necessary costs for purposes of determining the amount of an equitable adjustment under its fixed-price contract with the National Park Service. The Department of Interior Board of Contract Appeals had previously rejected such claims in three cases construing substantially similar contracts, including one in which the present contractor was involved as a subcontractor. The court held the contractor bound by its knowledge of the government's interpretations, stating at 314-15:

> We take note of three prior cases decided by the IBCA which reach this same conclusion. These are *Samkal Mines, Inc.*, IBCA No. 582-8-66, 66-2 BCA ¶ 6010; *Seal & Co.*, IBCA No. 181, 61-1 BCA ¶ 2887; and *Irvin Prickett & Sons*, IBCA No. 203, 60-2 BCA ¶ 2747. Although these decisions are not those of a court, we refer to them to show the interpretation of the IBCA of contract terms identical to and similar to those in the instant case.
>
> * * *
>
> We are especially cognizant and take note of the fact that in *Seal* the Department of Interior was, as here, the agency of the government involved and [the contractor] was the subcontractor of the complaining contractor in the case.
>
> * * *
>
> It is clear that the [contractor], by reason of its experience in the *Seal* case, knew or had reason to know the meaning intended by the identical agency of the government in the contract clause involved here. In any event, it was put on inquiry by such experience to investigate such intended meaning. Notwithstanding its duty in this regard, it did not make any inquiry nor assert any protest nor claim any different meaning before it made its bid and signed the contract. Under these circumstances, we conclude that [the contractor] acquiesced in and is bound by the meaning of the clause as intended by the government.

Contractors have also been held bound by government interpretations published in agency policy letters, *Sun Shipbuilding & Dry Dock Co. v. United States*, 183 Ct. Cl. 358, 393 F.2d 807 (1968), and *Lykes-Youngstown Corp. v. United States*, 190 Ct. Cl. 348, 420 F.2d 735, *cert. denied*, 400 U.S. 865 (1970); in the *Federal Register* as part of the process of promulgating the regulation, *PCA Health Plans of Texas, Inc.*, ASBCA 48711, 98-2 BCA ¶ 29,900; and in prior contracts with the same contractor, *RJS Constructors, Inc.*, ENGBCA 5956, 93-2 BCA ¶ 25,673.

In a sealed bid procurement, contractors will not be held bound by unreasonable interpretations known to them at the time of bidding. See *CRF v. United States*, 224 Ct. Cl. 312, 624 F.2d 1054 (1980), in which the court refused to hold the contractor to the government's interpretation, first stated after the contractor verified its bid, even though the contractor acquiesced in this interpretation. The court stated at 325-26:

> [W]e are not dealing with an ambiguous contract provision, or with a reasonable interpretation placed upon such a provision by one party during the precontract

> negotiations and acquiescence (express or implied) by the other party, or with a negotiated contract. Instead, we are dealing with an unreasonable and arbitrary interpretation of the competitively bid terms by the contracting officer, contrary to the governing statute and regulations. The pertinent bid and contractual documents could not have stated more plainly than they did that the Navy Department was soliciting bids on, and the parties were entering into a contract for, the furnishing of eight first-article samples and 362 production quality radio transmitters, with the eight first-article samples to be refurbished to production-quality and furnished as part of the 362 production units.
>
> We emphasize strongly that our position in this case rests on the undeniable element here that the contracting officer's demand was plainly contrary to the terms of the invitation for competitive bids, was unreasonable, and without any support in the bid documents. That being so, he had no authority to make a contract embodying his own plainly mistaken views and the agreement reached should be interpreted, if possible, within the confines of the only lawful contract that could be made. [The government's] contrary position would give contracting officers, in competitive bid situations, carte blanche to evade the controlling legislation and regulations by forcing low bidders, on pain of cancellation of the entire IFB, to agree to wholly arbitrary and illegal demands outside the contracting officer's authority to impose.

6. Limitations on the Use of Discussions and Concurrent Actions

Although the boards and courts are generally quite willing to consider evidence of discussions and actions of the parties that demonstrate the interpretation of contract language, there are three limitations on such evidence. First, the government employee in question must be acting within the scope of his or her authority. Second, post-dispute conduct or discussions are generally excluded. Third, such discussions or actions must not contradict the written language of the contract. This third limitation is called the parol evidence rule.

a. Authority

One limitation on the use of discussion and conduct evidence in the interpretive process concerns the authority of government officials who provide clarification or acquiesce in the contractor's interpretation. The government is not bound by officials' unauthorized statements or conduct.

This rule is most likely to be enforced in the situation where the contractor obtains an interpretation or clarification from a government official. Such interpretation will have little weight if the official has no authority. For example, in *Van Stafford*, AGBCA 77-133, 79-2 BCA ¶ 13,979, the government was not bound by a clarification request on the meaning of an ambiguous price term given by an administrative government official, who was not authorized by the contracting officer to act as his representative. See also *Masterclean, Inc.*, VABCA 3818, 96-2 BCA ¶ 28,298, holding that a project architect had no authority to "amend the substance of the bid package." In some instances, however, the court or board may impute the actions of the unauthorized person who provided the interpretation or clarification to the contracting officer. In *Unidynamics/St. Louis, Inc.*, ASBCA 17592, 73-2 BCA ¶ 10,360, the IFB to furnish and install elevators included drawings insufficiently detailed to show whether the openings left in the elevator shafts would be large enough to accommodate the installation of factory-assembled cabs. Wishing to bid on the basis of preassembled cabs, the contractor sought clarification of this point but did not receive a clear answer. The contractor reasonably interpreted the government's answer to mean that use of preassembled cabs would be feasible. Subsequently, the government's preaward survey team assured the contractor that the necessary openings would be available. The board found that the government was bound by this interpretation, stating at 48,933:

> While the IFB did not require a submission of design information and installation description for approval until after award, [the contractor] at a conference with the preaward survey team provided this information to [the Government] and was assured that the necessary elevator openings would be available at dates of installation. This preaward interpretation confirmed [the contractor's] understanding that the contract specification permitted the use of preassembled cabs as a design choice and that the interface between the work of the elevator contractor and building contractor at the elevator shaft openings was the Government's responsibility to arrange. The contracting officer's representatives were sent to the preaward survey to determine on his behalf appellant's ability to manufacture the elevator cabs to the Government's specifications and to meet the project's installation requirements. Their knowledge and understanding of [the contractor's] interpretation of the IFB as to design choice and work interface of the elevator shaft openings at installation time is imputed to the contracting officer. See *Gresham & Co. v. United States*, [200 Ct. Cl. 97], 470 F.2d 542 at pp. 555-556 (1972). Such preaward clarifications of ambiguities in the specification establish a mutual understanding of the requirements of the contract as of the date of execution.

However, communications will not be imputed to the contracting officer in the absence of evidence of a meaningful connection between the government official giving the information and the contracting officer, *Unitec, Inc.*, ASBCA 22025, 79-2 BCA ¶ 13,923.

Even though a government official may lack authority to supply a binding interpretation, his or her statements or actions can be highly persuasive evidence of the reasonableness of the contractor's interpretation, *Kraus v. United States*, 177 Ct. Cl. 108, 366 F.2d 975 (1966). This is particularly the case where the government employee is an expert in the matter under consideration or is employed in that area. For example, in *Max Drill, Inc. v. United States*, 192 Ct. Cl. 608, 427 F.2d 1233 (1970), the contractor sought additional compensation for having been required to paint wooden sashes beneath aluminum storm windows where the contract for repair and painting of dormitories required that all exterior painted surfaces be painted. Prior to bidding, the contracting officer's technical representative, who had prepared the IFB, had informed the contractor that the contract did not require painting of interior wooden sashes. The court held for the contractor, stating at 624-25:

> There is merit, as a general proposition, to [the government's] contention that the Government will not be bound by unauthorized interpretation of its ordinary employees. It has long been held that a subordinate Government employee cannot render contract interpretations binding on the parties, *Commercial Metals Co. v. United States*, 176 Ct. Cl. 343, 350-51 (1966). A person negotiating with an officer or agent of the Government must inform himself regarding the authority of such individual, since an officer of the Government cannot bind the Government with respect to matters beyond the limit of his authority, *Wilber Nat'l Bank v. United States*, 294 U.S. 120, 123-24 (1935); *Miami Metropolitan Bldg. Corp. v. United States*, 180 Ct. Cl. 503, 514 (1967).
>
> But it is not necessary to believe that Lt. Paynic had the authority to render binding contract interpretations in order to find for [the contractor] here. Nor is it suggested that Lt. Paynic had the authority to issue major change orders in the contract, for no change was made by him. Indeed, the only change made in this case was that initiated by the Government's unilateral reversal of the contractor's (and Paynic's) interpretation of the contract and specifications. However, it would be inane to believe that he was at the site for no real purpose. *Cf. General Casualty Co. v. United States*, 130 Ct. Cl. 520, 533, 127 F. Supp. 805, 812-13, *cert. denied*, 349 U.S. 938 (1955). [The contractor's] estimator acted reasonably in discussing the matter with Lt. Paynic at the . . . jobsite, and in believing, after the conversation between him and the Technical Representative, that [the contractor] had correctly interpreted the invitation for bids. The statements of the Technical Representative cannot be completely disavowed and repudiated on the ground that he was without authority to speak for the contracting officer. *General Casualty Co., supra*. When an official of the contracting agency is not the contracting officer, but has been sent by the contracting officer for the express purpose of giving guidance in connection with the contract, the contractor is justified in relying on his representations.

b. Post-Dispute Conduct and Discussions Excluded

A second limitation on the use of evidence of conduct or discussions in the interpretive process is that such action or discussions must have occurred prior to the time of the dispute. *Dynamics Corp. v. United States*, 182 Ct. Cl. 62, 389 F.2d 424 (1968), concerned correspondence written after the dispute had arisen. Discussing the rule concerning interpretation of the contract as shown by conduct of the parties, the court stated at 73:

> [T]he significant point here is that the correspondence referred to was written after the dispute arose. It is well settled that the practical interpretation of a contract, as shown by the conduct of the parties, is of great weight in interpreting the contract. *General Warehouse Two, Inc. v. United States*, 181 Ct. Cl. 180, 187, 389 F.2d

> 1016, 1020 (1967), and cases cited; *Universal Match Corp. v. United States*, 161 Ct. Cl. 418, 422 (1963), and cases cited. However this rule only applies to conduct during performance, and * * * prior to the time when the contract becomes subject to controversy, * * *. *Union Paving Co. v. United States*, 126 Ct. Cl. 478, 489, 115 F. Supp. 179 [185] (1953). Only the action of the parties before a controversy arises is highly relevant in determining what the parties intended. *Northbridge Electronics, Inc. v. United States*, 175 Ct. Cl. 426, 438 n.8 (1966).

See also *Puerto Rico Dep't of Labor & Human Res. v. United States*, 49 Fed. Cl. 24 (2001), in which the court refused to consider government funding action occurring after the dispute arose; *General Dynamics Corp. v. United States*, 47 Fed. Cl. 514 (2000), in which the court refused to consider a declaration of the contracting officer prepared after the dispute arose; and *Tilley Constructors & Eng'rs, Inc. v. United States*, 15 Cl. Ct. 559 (1988), in which the court refused to consider the content of a government letter written after the dispute had arisen.

This limitation applies primarily to interpretations of a party favorable to its litigation position. Such interpretations are of little weight because they appear to be self-serving. A post-dispute interpretation favorable to the other party would not appear to be within this rule. See *Mick DeWall Constr.*, PSBCA 2580, 91-1 BCA ¶ 23,510, in which such an interpretation by the government was found to be dispositive against the government. Curiously, on reconsideration at 91-3 BCA ¶ 24,180, the board ruled for the government on the ground that the post-dispute interpretation of the government was contrary to the clear meaning of the contract clause.

c. Parol Evidence Rule

A contracting party sometimes seeks to prohibit the consideration of extrinsic evidence in the interpretive process by invoking the parol evidence rule. *Restatement, Second, Contracts* § 213 renders inoperative prior written or oral agreements that contradict an integrated agreement. Thus, in the absence of fraud, duress, mutual mistake, or something of the kind, the parol evidence rule will preclude a party from presenting such prior agreements to prove that the words of a contract have a meaning contrary to their clear meaning. The rule does not preclude parol evidence from being introduced to interpret the words of a contract. See *Restatement, Second, Contracts* § 215, comment b., stating:

> b. *Interpretation and contradiction.* An earlier agreement may help the interpretation of a later one, but it may not contradict a binding later integrated agreement. Whether there is a contradiction depends . . . on whether the two are consistent or inconsistent. This is a question which often cannot be determined from the face of the writing; the writing must first be applied to its subject matter and placed in context. The question is then decided by the court as part of the question of interpretation.

The parol evidence rule has been a problematic rule with considerable disagreement on its scope and application. At the present time, it is of limited effect in preventing the use of extrinsic evidence in government contract controversies because it has no application when the sole issue is interpretation of ambiguous language. Evidence of prior and contemporaneous actions and discussions may be used to resolve an ambiguity, add consistent terms to certain (i.e., partially integrated) agreements, or show whether and to what extent the agreement is integrated. However, the rule bars the admission of evidence to contradict language in an integrated contract or to add language to a completely integrated agreement. This section first considers the issues concerning integration. It then considers the use of parol evidence to resolve ambiguities and to establish an ambiguity.

It is occasionally stated that the parol evidence rule bars the admission of evidence of subjective intent of one of the parties, *Pacificorp Capital, Inc. v. United States*, 25 Cl. Ct. 707 (1992), *aff'd without op.*, 988 F.2d 130 (Fed. Cir. 1993); *Hughes Communications Galaxy, Inc. v. United States*, 26 Cl. Ct. 123 (1992), *rev'd on other grounds*, 998 F.2d 953 (Fed. Cir. 1993). This chapter treats the issue of the use of evidence of subjective intent as a separate element of the contract interpretation process. See the discussion at the beginning of the chapter.

(1) Integrated Agreements

Since virtually all government contract interpretation cases involve a written contract, courts and boards initially face the question of whether the contract document constitutes an integrated agreement. See *Gresham Sand & Gravel Co.*, GSBCA 6858, 84-1 BCA ¶ 17,019, *aff'd*, 776 F.2d 1061 (Fed. Cir. 1985). *Restatement, Second, Contracts* § 209 states:

> (1) An integrated agreement is a writing or writings constituting a final expression of one or more terms of an agreement.
>
> (2) Whether there is an integrated agreement is to be determined by the court as a question preliminary to determination of a question of interpretation or to application of the parol evidence rule.
>
> (3) Where the parties reduce an agreement to a writing which in view of its completeness and specificity reasonably appears to be a complete agreement, it is taken to be an integrated agreement unless it is established by other evidence that the writing did not constitute a final expression.

Typically, government contracts and solicitations that initiate the procurement consist of four parts: (1) the schedule (Sections A through H); (2) contract clauses (Section I); (3) a list of documents, exhibits, and other attachments (Section J); and (4) representations (Section K) and instructions (Sections L and M). See FAR 14.201-1 (sealed bidding) and FAR 15.204-1 (negotiation), implementing a uniform contract format with certain exceptions, such as construction and shipbuilding contracts. The schedule contains a description of and the requirements for performance of the specific contract. Within the contract clauses section are included clauses required by law or regulation and other clauses, including those incorporated by reference. In this section are boilerplate clauses of government contracts, such as the Changes, Disputes, and Default clauses. The list of attachments is a listing of the appended documents, exhibits, and other attachments, and the title, date, and number of pages for each. The representations and instructions section includes solicitation provisions requiring representations, certifications, or the submission of other information by offerors or quoters; information and instructions useful in proposal or quotation preparation; as well as the significant evaluation factors and the relative importance each is to be given. The resulting agreement consists of Sections A through K (Sections L and M are not part of the contract), FAR 14.201-1(c), FAR 15.204-1(b). Such contracts are integrated agreements.

Even when the uniform contract format is not used, the contract documents used in federal procurement are generally fairly specific and relatively complete, representing a final expression of the agreements. When integration is in dispute, parol evidence is admissible to establish whether or not a writing has been adopted as an integrated agreement or which of several writings was intended to constitute a final expression of the terms of agreement. *Restatement, Second, Contracts* § 214(a) expressly makes admissible "[a]greements and negotiations prior to or contemporaneous with the adoption of a writing" in order to establish that an agreement is or is not integrated. This rule was followed in *David Nassif Assocs. v. United States*, 214 Ct. Cl. 407,. 557 F.2d 249 (1977). See also *Massachusetts Bay Trans. Auth. v. United States*, 129 F.3d 1229 (Fed. Cir. 1997) (pre-modification letters used to determine that modification was not a fully integrated agreement); *National Park Concessions, Inc.*, IBCA 2995, 94-3 BCA ¶ 27,104 (parol evidence used to determine that two agreements were complementary rather than later agreement being fully integrated); *Design & Prod., Inc. v. United States*, 18 Cl. Ct. 168 (1989) (admitting a large amount of parol evidence to determine the extent of integration); *Triple A South*, ASBCA 35824, 90-1 BCA ¶ 22,567 (admitting parol evidence to determine whether the parties intended that an agreement be integrated); and *Schiffahrt & Kohlen-Agentur*, ASBCA 10219, 65-2 BCA ¶ 50381 (receiving evidence on the question of "which writing had been assented to as the complete integration of the contract"). Parol evidence was also admitted in the course of finding a complete integration in *W&F Bldg. Maint. Co. v. United States*, 56 Fed. Cl. 62 (2003), and *McAbee Constr., Inc. v. United States*, 97 F.3d 1431 (Fed. Cir. 1996).

(2) Complete or Partial Integration

An integrated agreement adopted by the parties as a complete and exclusive statement of the terms of the agreement is completely integrated, *Restatement, Second, Contracts* § 210. However, an agreement is not completely integrated if the writing omits a consistent additional agreed term (a) that is agreed to for separate consideration, or (b) such a term as in the circumstances might naturally be omitted from the writing, *Restatement, Second, Contracts* § 216. This distinction is significant because inconsistent prior agreements are discharged by either partially or completely integrated agreements, whereas a completely integrated agreement also discharges all prior agreements to the extent that they are within its scope, *Restatement, Second, Contracts* § 213(2), and excludes evidence of consistent additional terms, *Restatement, Second, Contracts* § 216. Note, however, that parol evidence may be used to establish whether or not an agreement is completely or partially integrated, *Restatement, Second, Contracts* § 214(b).

The scope and complexity of problems encountered throughout the performance of a government contract ordinarily involve contingencies not expressly provided for under the terms of the agreement. Resolution of such problems often requires information outside the contract documents. Thus, the written contract in many instances cannot be characterized as the complete and exclusive agreement of the parties, and therefore should be considered to be partially integrated. This is particularly so for contract modifications and other agreements that are entered into during contract performance.

In *Sylvania Elec. Prods., Inc. v. United States*, 198 Ct. Cl. 106, 458 F.2d 994 (1972), the contractor sought to recover costs of performing certain work necessitated when government-furnished property proved incompatible with the contractor's equipment. The contractor attempted to rely on statements made by a government official in a pre-bid conference that the government-furnished property would in fact be compatible with the contractor's equipment. The court rejected the government's contention that evidence of these statements was precluded under the parol evidence rule, stating at 128-31:

> Parol or extrinsic evidence must be admissible on the issue of the extent to which a written agreement is integrated, for as has been said, the writing cannot prove its own integration, 3 *Corbin, Contracts*, *supra*, § 582; see also 9 *Wigmore, Evidence*, §§ 2400(5), 2470 (1940). Accordingly, any relevant evidence is admissible on whether the parties intended their written agreement to be a complete and exclusive statement of all the terms of their agreement. *Restatement, Contracts*, *supra*, comment (a); see also 3 *Corbin, Contracts*, *supra*, §§ 581, 582, 588.
>
> Application to the facts of the foregoing principles raises two closely related questions for decision by the court. One is whether the oral graft to the specifications by the evidence of the bidders' conference is contradictory of or consistent with the written agreement. If it is inconsistent, the parol evidence rule would bar it, even if the written agreement is only partially integrated. The second question is whether all the circumstances were such as show an intention by the parties that any oral agreement should not survive the written execution of the contract or, in other words, an intention that the formal written agreement should not only be their final, but also their exclusive agreement on all subjects. Such an exclusive

agreement would be a completely integrated one, excluding not only the inconsistent prior understanding, if any there had been, referred to by the Board, but any prior oral understanding with respect to appliques or signaling characteristics, one of the subjects of the written agreement.

* * *

[I]n the instant case, the sequence of events, in which written specifications came first and were followed by an oral interchange, and the nature of the meeting at which the interchange took place, goes far to confirm both that the oral term is not contradictory of the written specification and that the formally executed written agreement was not intended to supersede the oral agreement. The bidders' conference, here, was no ordinary pre-formal-execution meeting of ordinary parties of the first and second parts. Leading electronic concerns had been asked by the Air Force to demonstrate their technical proficiency to perform a multimillion-dollar contract for a national defense communications system of a new and complex type. Uncertainties in the written specifications might, unless dispelled, lead to contingencies, variations in the prices bid, and consequent extra costs to the Government or, worse, defective performance of work of importance to the national security. Accordingly, the prospective bidders were invited to send their representatives to a meeting where they were encouraged to ask questions of Air Force representatives present, qualified and authorized to explain to those gathered the meaning of the specifications, to fill in any gaps in the specifications and eliminate any uncertainties in the minds of bidders. The contracting officer, the senior buyer, and the technically knowledgeable officers were there, each responsible for questions in his own field. The obvious gap in the specifications as to appliques led to an inevitable question at the conference, and the answer filled in the specifications.

The second of the dispositive questions set out above, as to the intent of the parties, may now also be answered in favor of the [contractor]. Since the words spoken at the bidders' conference were intended as an addition to the specifications, to resolve an open question and doubt in the minds of the bidders, it could not have been intended that those words should be wiped from the record by the formal execution of the contract. Quite the contrary.

To hold that the writing signed following such a conference as here took place negates the oral agreement reached at the conference would be reckless of the reputation of the procurement system in which the bidders' conferences are an integral part. Meetings between Government procurement officers and prospective bidders would become a sham. Questions would be useless, for answers would be without force, and the amounts of the bids received would soon show the results. Respect for the answer is required by the respect given the Government's procurement process.

It is therefore concluded that the written agreement here was not so completely integrated as to bar consideration of an oral agreement at the bidders' conference that the signaling characteristics of the Government-furnished equipment would in fact be compatible with the characteristics of plaintiff's equipment, if such an

> agreement is found to have been made. Neither the rules governing integrated agreements nor the parol evidence rule would in the circumstances prevent the enforcement of such an agreement.

In *Pan Arctic Corp.*, ASBCA 20133, 77-1 BCA ¶ 12,514, the board found that a written contract for construction of a hydrant refueling station on a remote island was not completely integrated and did not supersede a previous oral agreement that the contract would be performed concurrently with the installation of a diesel-powered generator on the same island. During negotiations the contractor had agreed to lower its price for the refueling station because it expected to use men and equipment already on the island during slack time in the generator work. The board relied heavily on *Sylvania*, stating at 60,668-69:

> We think *Sylvania* is controlling in the instant case. Actually, the facts in this case are stronger for the finding of a collateral oral agreement than were the facts in *Sylvania*. Here the written contract was completely silent as to the concurrent performance upon which the parties had agreed. Such agreement could not and did not contradict the terms of that supplementary agreement. The evidence is also completely persuasive that the parties did not contemplate that the written agreement was intended to constitute the exclusive agreement of the parties. Stated otherwise, the agreement that the Worthington generator project and the hydrant refueling project would be performed concurrently was not submerged into the written hydrant refueling project contract for that written contract was not intended to be the exclusive agreement of the parties on all subjects.

In *Florida East Coast Ry. Co. v. United States*, 228 Ct. Cl. 647, 660 F.2d 474 (1981), the court adopted the trial judge's opinion, 29 CCF ¶ 81,927, which discussed in detail integration and parol evidence. A memorandum of agreement involved FEC's construction and operation of a railroad spur system and the rates for transportation over it. The judge found a partial integration based on various factors. First, as a memorandum of agreement, the very title indicated that it was not the final word. "The body of the document merely sets forth the 'substance' of their understanding concerning their 'cooperative arrangement,' while numerous details are left unspecified." Second, "[t]he preexisting negotiations, on the other hand, clearly demonstrate the details of the respective undertakings of the parties." Furthermore, the memorandum "suggests only a partial integration because it references additional agreements to be entered into by and between the parties. Because the document was not fully integrated, the contractor was not barred from introducing evidence of additional terms consistent with those set forth in the document, or evidence tending to clarify ambiguities and uncertainties in the writings." See also *ED.Zueblin, A.G. v. United States*, 44 Fed. Cl. 228 (1999) (negotiation memorandum admissible because settlement agreement not an "independent, fully integrated agreement"); *D&R Mach. Co.*, ASBCA 50730, 98-1 BCA ¶ 29,462 (evidence of discussion with judge admissible because subsequent district court settlement agreement not "an integrated agreement"); *United Tech. Corp.*, ASBCA 46880, 97-1 BCA ¶ 28,818 (evidence of prior negotiations admissible because government "failed to establish that there was a completely integrated or even a partially integrated agreement" with respect to the contract language in dispute); and *Pettijohn Eng'g Co.*, IBCA 1346-4-80, 83-2 BCA ¶ 16,559 (construction contract deemed partially integrated where it did not specifically address risk allocation for loss or damage to the work, and at the pre-proposal conference an authorized government official described risks that would be assumed by the government).

A court rarely finds that a government contract is fully integrated, but the inclusion of an integration clause can lead to this result. See *McAbee Constr., Inc. v. United States*, 97 F.3d 1431 (Fed. Cir. 1996), in which the court found a contract fully integrated relying on two contract clauses stating that no other terms were to be included. See also *Rumsfeld v. Freedom N.Y., Inc.*, 329 F.3d 1320 (Fed. Cir. 2003), *cert. denied*, 541 U.S. 987 (2004), in which the court found that a contract modification was fully integrated based on an integration clause, stating at 1328:

> We have recognized the importance of integration clauses in determining whether a contract is completely integrated. In *McAbee*, we emphasized that, although they are not dispositive, integration clauses create a "strong presumption that a contract [is], as it purports to be, a fully-integrated agreement." 97 F.3d at 1434. One attempting to add terms to a contract with an integration clause "carries an extremely heavy burden in overcoming this attestation to the document's finality and completeness." *Id.* See also *Campbell v. United States,* 228 Ct. Cl. 661, 661 F.2d 209, 218 (Ct. Cl. 1981) (Where a contract includes an integration clause, "it is a fair bet that the parties agreed to no more than they said.").
>
> Where, as here, the parties are both commercial entities or the government, integration clauses are given particularly great weight. As the Second Circuit has stated, "the presumption of completeness is particularly strong where sophisticated parties have conducted extensive negotiations prior to entering into the agreement." *Telecom Int'l Am., Ltd. v. AT&T Corp.*, 280 F.3d 175, 191 (2d Cir. 2000). See also *Binks Mfg. Co. v. Nat'l Presto Industries, Inc.*, 709 F.2d 1109, 1116 (7th Cir. 1982).

See also *Barron Bancshares, Inc. v. Masterson*, 366 F.3d 1360 (Fed. Cir. 2004), finding the government bound by an integration clause. In *Gemini Elecs., Inc. v. United States*, 65 Fed. Cl. 55 (2005), the court cited *Freedom N.Y.* for the proposition that "an integration clause 'conclusively establishes that the integration is total unless (a) the document is obviously incomplete or (b) the merger clause was included as a result of fraud or mistake or any other reason to set aside the contract.'" In *W&F Bldg. Maint. Co. v. United States*, 56 Fed. Cl. 62 (2003), the court found a modification fully integrated based on language stating that it was the "full and final release . . .of claims" but still considered parol evidence to determine the extent of integration.

A few other cases have concluded that agreements are completely integrated, but the cases generally have been decided on additional grounds as well as the exclusion of parol evidence. See *Starflight Boats v. United States*, 48 Fed. Cl. 592 (2001) (court rejected evidence of prior secret oral agreement because contractor did not make an effort to incorporate it in written modifications); *Nicholson v. United States*, 29 Fed. Cl. 180 (1993) (court rejected addition of term to contract because of plain meaning of integrated contract and no evidence of agreement to added term was proffered); *California Sand & Gravel, Inc. v. United States*, 22 Cl. Ct. 19 (1990), *aff'd*, 937 F.2d 624 (Fed. Cir. 1991) (court rejected the addition of terms to contract but determined that proffered oral agreements were made by unauthorized officials); and *Gresham Sand & Gravel Co.*, GSBCA 6858, 84-1 BCA ¶ 17,019, *aff'd*, 776 F.2d 1061 (Fed. Cir. 1985) (supplemental agreement adding space in a building to existing lease deemed completely integrated based on review of all contemporaneous evidence presented by parties).

(3) Contradiction versus Resolution of Ambiguities

The parol evidence rule prohibits the introduction of extrinsic evidence to contradict terms of an integrated agreement, *Restatement, Second, Contracts* § 215. This rule reflects recognition that the parties may agree to final terms differing substantially from those sought during negotiations. However, this rule is tempered by the rule that parol evidence is admissible to resolve an ambiguity, *Restatement, Second, Contracts* § 214(c). In *Sylvania Elec. Prods., Inc. v. United States*, 198 Ct. Cl. 106, 458 F.2d 994 (1972), the court stated at 126:

> The function of the parol evidence rule, a rule of substantive law misnamed a rule of evidence, is the prevention of the variance of integrated agreements, usually written, by inconsistent contemporaneous or prior terms, usually oral. . . . Interpretation, however, must precede awareness of variance. And meaning can usually be given to a writing only on consideration of all circumstances, including the prior negotiations between the parties. The parol evidence rule is therefore no bar to the use of the oral statements of the parties during negotiations, in aid of the interpretations of ambiguous or uncertain clauses in written agreements. . . . Expressions of the parties during negotiations for the contract are thus a frequent source for interpretation of its text . . . (citations omitted).

Thus, the court or board may, using the general rules of contract interpretation, declare that no ambiguity exists and therefore exclude extrinsic evidence, or it may find an ambiguity and then accept parol evidence to resolve it.

When it is determined that the parol evidence contradicts the language of an integrated agreement, the evidence is excluded. See, for example, *United States v. Triple A Mach. Shop, Inc.*, 857 F.2d 579 (9th Cir. 1988), in which an alleged oral agreement was excluded because it directly contradicted the subsequent written agreement. Similarly, in *Computer Network Sys., Inc. v. General Servs. Admin.*, GSBCA 11368, 93-3 BCA ¶ 26,233, terms from the prior contracts for the work were excluded because they were in conflict with the terms of the current contract. See also *TRW, Inc.*, ASBCA 51003, 00-2 BCA ¶ 30,992 (contractor barred from using evidence of its personnel's understanding of agreement that contradicted clear meaning of agreement); *Bart Assocs., Inc.*, EBCA C-9406176, 97-2 BCA ¶ 29,206 (modification contradicted previous contract amendment); and *Gould, Inc.*, ASBCA 16869, 75-2 BCA ¶ 11,534 (government barred from using evidence of the proposed design on which the contractor based its cost and pricing data to prove that contractor agreed to do that work because specification was clear on work to be done).

There are numerous cases admitting parol evidence to aid in interpreting ambiguous contract language. See, for example, *Coast-to-Coast Fin. Corp. v. United States*, 52 Fed. Cl. 352 (2002) (pre-contract negotiations admitted to interpret contract language); *Northrop Grumman Corp. v. United States*, 50 Fed. Cl. 443 (2001) (contractor's bid documents used to interpret ambiguous term); *DRC Corp. v. Department of Commerce*, GSBCA 14919-COM, 00-1 BCA ¶ 30,649 (pre-bid conference statements admitted to interpret vague phasing of work requirement); *Perry-McCall Constr., Inc. v. United States*, 46 Fed. Cl. 664 (2000) (parol evidence admitted to interpret two "full" releases); *Cray Research, Inc. v. United States*, 41 Fed. Cl. 427 (1998) ("extrinsic" evidence needed to interpret ambiguous modification); *Aerojet-Gen. Corp.*, ASBCA 47206, 97-1 BCA ¶ 28,887 (deposition testimony and complaint in court used to interpret memorandum agreement); *KMS Fusion, Inc. v. United States*, 36 Fed. Cl. 68 (1996) (extensive evidence of negotiation used to determine meaning of ambiguous modification); *Cessna Aircraft Co.*, ASBCA 48118, 95-1 BCA ¶ 27,560, *rev'd on other grounds*, 98 F.3d 1298 (Fed. Cir. 1996) (pre-award interchanges with government personnel admitted to interpret contract); *Northwest Marine, Inc.*, ASBCA 43502, 94-1 BCA ¶ 26,521 (pre-bid questions and answers used to interpret specifications); *Hemphill Contracting Co.*, ENGBCA 5698, 94-1 BCA ¶ 26,491 (evidence of negotiations used to determine scope of contract work); *Service Eng'g. Co.*, ASBCA 40272, 92-3 BCA ¶ 25,106 (discussion at pre-bid conference used to interpret contract); and *Towne Realty, Inc. v. United States*, 1 Cl. Ct. 264 (1982) (court admitted parol evidence as an aid to interpretation).

(4) Establishing an Ambiguity

There are different views on the admissibility of parol evidence to establish the ambiguity of an apparently unambiguous term. An extremely limited interpretation of the rule excludes extrinsic evidence if no ambiguity exists and permits such evidence only if the integrated agreement is ambiguous on its face. In *Butz Eng'g Corp. v. United States*, 204 Ct. Cl. 561, 499 F.2d 619 (1974), the contractor was awarded one of two contracts for Phase I design for modernization of a post office facility. It was contemplated that one of the two contractors would be awarded a contract for Phase II fabrication and installation. The government subsequently decided not to award to either contractor, and neither design was used in the modernization. The contractor sued for anticipated profits, contending that the government had assured it that the it would be given the Phase II work. The court denied the claim, stating at 578-79:

> The contract's "schedule of work" recites the contractor's objective of both developing designs for the Morgan Station, and fabricating and installing the proposed modernization system. It then goes on to describe in detail both phases of projected work. In paragraph C of the Additional Provisions, however, the parties agree:
>
>> Although the Schedule of Work is written for two phases, this contract, as executed, is for work to be performed under Phase I only. Within 30 days after completion of the Phase I work, the parties may at the option of the United States Postal Service enter into negotiations for the performance of the Phase II work.
>
> It would be difficult to imagine a more direct statement by the parties as to the scope of their agreement, and [the contractor] is bound by it.
>
> [The contractor] asserts the contract as a whole is ambiguous and must be interpreted in the light of the parties' alleged prior understanding that [the government] would be contractually bound to allow the party with the superior modernization design to proceed with Phase II. This contention, however, flies in the face of the parol evidence rule, by which all negotiations prior and contemporary to the writing of a contract are considered merged in, and cannot amend or add to, the written terms of the document, *Brawley v. United States*, 96 U.S. (6 Otto) 168, 173-74 (1878); *Baggett Transportation Co. v. United States*, 162 Ct. Cl. 570, 577, 319 F.2d 864, 868 (1963). Because the written terms here in question are on their face unambiguous, no legitimate purpose exists for introducing evidence of such prior negotiations and understandings.

The same result was reached in *Gustafson P'ship*, GSBCA 6701-COM, 84-1 BCA ¶ 17,086, where to establish the meaning of the Termination clause reading "[t]he Government may terminate this lease at any time after eight months with 60 days' notice in writing to the Lessor," the contractor wanted to introduce evidence that the government leasing agent assured it that the lease, in essence, would last at least 10 months. The representative claimed never to have made such statements and that he had always viewed the clause as permitting termination after eight months if notice had been given 60 days earlier. The board found no ambiguity and therefore excluded such evidence, stating at 85,065:

> We find the termination provision to be unambiguous. Its specific words are clear, unremarkable, everyday, short, common English words, none of which are individually or collectively susceptible to other than their everyday meaning. Let us parse the termination provision. The Government may terminate this lease—when? "At any time after eight months." That much seems unalterably set in concrete. The second phrase, "with 60 days' notice in writing to the Lessor," modifies the first. Clearly the "notice," if that word is to have any meaning, must precede the termination by sixty days.

* * *

> The lease contract appears to be a complete and final expression of the terms of the parties' agreement, and thus we may take it as an integrated agreement. . . . Our interpretation is to be addressed to the writing adopted by the parties. Restatement, Second, Contracts § 212(1) (1979). The words of that writing are clear, and we need not resolve the conflict in the evidence extrinsic to the writing since that evidence cannot be used to vary the unambiguous words of that agreement.

See also *HRE, Inc. v. United States*, 142 F.3d 1274 (Fed. Cir. 1998), rejecting trade usage evidence because there was no ambiguity on the face of the contract. At the same time, the court criticized the government for writing a contract that "is hardly a model of clarity" and suggested that the government should "review its provisions to make them more comprehensible and avoid ambiguity for the benefit of contractors."

Another way of stating this version of the rule is that parol evidence cannot be used "to create an ambiguity," *Fluor Daniel, Inc. v. Regents of the Univ. of Cal.*, EBCA C-9909296, 02-2 BCA ¶ 32,017. Other cases merely reject parol evidence because the contract language is clear, *Smelser v. United States*, 53 Fed. Cl. 530 (2002) (language "unambiguous"); *Gutz v. United States*, 45 Fed. Cl. 291 (1999) (language "clear and unambiguous"); *GTE Gov't Sys. Corp.*, ASBCA 44080, 96-2 BCA ¶ 28,342 (language "unambiguous").

This ambiguity on its face rule should be contrasted with the view that a word cannot be considered to be unambiguous until some meaning is attributed to the word. Recognizing that the parties to a contract are free to adopt whatever meaning they wish for the terms they use, the boards and courts admit parol evidence to establish whether an ambiguity exists. As the Court of Claims stated in *Blackburn v. United States*, 126 Ct. Cl. 874, 116 F. Supp. 584 (1953), at 877:

> The language inserted in the contract [(The prices quoted in this bid are subject to any increase or decrease as affected by the O.P.A.).] is by no means so clear, if language ever is so clear, as to make inadmissible evidence as to what the parties to the contract intended it to mean. That intention, if it is mutual, is the essence of any contract, and the parties to it are privileged to use whatever form of shorthand, code, trade, ungrammatical, or other expression they may hit upon. They may make trouble for themselves and for a court by their unorthodox expression, but they do not forfeit their rights.

Judge Frank gave the following analysis of the rule in his concurring opinion in *United States v. Lennox Metal Mfg. Co.*, 225 F.2d 302 (2d Cir. 1955), at 310-13:

> Even if a word in a written agreement is not ambiguous on its face, the better authorities hold that its context, its "environment," must be taken into account in deciding what the parties mutually had in mind when they used that verbal symbol.
>
> The problem of interpreting a contract is, of course, that of understanding the communication between the parties. Like many communication problems in non-legal fields, it is frequently none too easy of solution. Judge Learned Hand has sagely warned that, in attempting a solution, it is "one of the surest indexes of a mature and developed jurisprudence not to make a fortress out of the dictionary . . . ."
>
> * * *
>
> In 1932, it was observed in *Hurst v. W.J. Lake & Co.*, 141 Or. 306, 16 P.2d 627, 629, 89 A.L.R. 1222 that "the language of the dictionaries is not the only language spoken in America." Corbin, in 1951 said, "There is no dictionary on earth . . . that can record all the usages of words or other symbols . . . . There is no law requiring the contractors to express themselves in `good English.' . . . On the contrary, the law requires the court to put itself as nearly as possible, in the position of the parties, with their knowledge and their ignorance, with their language and their usage. It is the meaning . . . of the parties, thus determined, that must be given legal effect."
>
> Accordingly, it is regarded by many authorities as a fallacy that, in interpreting contractual language, a court may not consider the surrounding circumstances unless the language is patently ambiguous. Any such rule, like all rules of interpretation, must be taken as a guide, not a dictator. The text should always be read in its context. Indeed, text and context necessarily merge to some extent, just as an individual's "inner environment" includes the air in his lungs.
>
> * * *
>
> To shut out the light furnished by the parties themselves—to read their words not as they meant them but as they appear when denuded of that meaning—is to decide an unreal, fictitious, hypothetical case. To reject the insights derived from their previous negotiations, which reveal their actual purposes, is to create a narrow rule of relevance which artificializes the facts. Doubtless on that account, even those courts which still say ambiguity is a necessary condition of considering such extrinsic evidence are quick to find such ambiguity, on slight grounds, when the extrinsic evidence is convincing. (Footnotes omitted)

B. Prior Course of Dealing

Evidence of prior course of dealing between the parties is an important type of extrinsic evidence used in the interpretive process to establish the meaning of ambiguous language. A prior course of dealing may also be used to demonstrate that an explicit requirement of the contract is not binding because that requirement was not enforced in the past. This application of prior course of dealing differs from interpretation in that it is based on legal theories of waiver and estoppel. Thus, prior dealings relating to interpretation evince intent, whereas prior conduct constituting a waiver defines the bargain itself.

The following material initially considers the use of evidence of prior dealings in the interpretive process, then discusses the use of such information as it relates to waiver. Courts and boards may discuss both uses of evidence of prior conduct under the general rubric of interpretation. However, it is more difficult to establish the formal elements of waiver and estoppel than to apply prior conduct evidence for interpretive purposes. Only a limited class of government employees has the specific authority to change contractual requirements, while the prior conduct of a broader class may be useful in establishing intent. Furthermore, a course of conduct must generally occur repeatedly to establish waiver or estoppel, while a more limited number of occurrences may be used for intent-determinative purposes, although the more frequent the occurrence, the greater the persuasiveness.

1. Interpretation

Where the parties to an interpretation dispute have interpreted, either expressly or by their actions, the provisions of a similar, previously performed contract in a certain manner, they will be presumed to have intended the same meaning for those provisions in the disputed contract. This presumption is rebuttable by clear evidence that the parties have changed their intent or are in disagreement at the time they enter into the disputed contract. See, for example, *Aviation Contractors Employees, Inc. v. United States*, 945 F.2d 1568 (Fed. Cir. 1991), holding a contractor bound to the government's interpretation of an option pricing provision because the government had followed that interpretation in their previous contract. In *Benning Aviation Corp.*, ASBCA 19850, 75-2 BCA ¶ 11,355, the board held that a contract to furnish flight instruction and clerical services to a military flight club required the contractor to provide a Chief Flight Instructor (C.F.I.). Although the contract did not expressly require a C.F.I., the contractor had provided a C.F.I. under a prior identical contract, and this action took precedence over its undisclosed intention not to be bound to furnish a C.F.I. under the current contract. See also *T&M Distrib., Inc.*, ASBCA 51405, 00-1 BCA ¶ 30,677 (government bound by ordering pattern on seven prior contracts); *Cresswell v. United States*, 146 Ct. Cl. 119, 173 F. Supp. 805 (1959) (with billing and delivery under an asbestos supply contract in dispute, where the contractor had accepted the government's interpretation under the first 19 lots delivered under the given contract and had similarly acted under an identical contract, the court found that the contractor failed to support its contrary interpretation); and *Dynaport Elecs., Inc.*, ASBCA 17895, 73-2 BCA ¶ 10,324 (both by the interpretation of a controlling earlier contract and by delivery of the first 12 units under the instant contract, the contractor had acquiesced in the government's interpretation of specifications). In *Holt Hauling & Warehousing Sys., Inc.*, ASBCA 19136, 76-2 BCA ¶ 12,185, the contractor was obligated, under two separate contracts, to load and unload automobiles belonging to military personnel from ocean carriers. During performance of the contracts, a dispute arose concerning who was obligated to pay for gate charge services. The board found that, as to the first contract, government actions that precluded the contractor from collecting gate charges from the carriers amounted to a constructive change entitling the contractor to additional compensation. The board, however, denied the contractor's claim on the second contract, stating at 58,679:

> The situation under the second contract is significantly different. At the time of negotiation of that contract both parties were aware of the gate charge problem and it was specifically discussed. The contract was entered into with the understanding that the Government would not pay gate charges and that the [contractor] would take no action to frustrate the movement of cargo through its terminal. With regard to the second contract, we conclude that the [contractor] gave up any right it had to collect gate charges from the Government as a part of the consideration for award of that contract.

Evidence of prior course of dealing must be clear to demonstrate the other party's agreement with the interpretation. Thus, in *Underground Constr. Co. v. United States*, 16 Cl. Ct. 60 (1988), the court held that inaction by the government in not asserting a claim until the completion of contract performance was not sufficiently clear to constitute a prior course of dealing.

a. Actual Knowledge Required

The reasoning underlying the prior course of dealing rule requires that both parties have had actual knowledge of the prior course of dealing and of its significance to the contract. Clearly, it would be unreasonable to find that a party had agreed to a term of which it was not aware. See *Sperry Flight Sys. Div. of Sperry Rand Corp. v. United States*, 212 Ct. Cl. 329, 548 F. 2d 915 (1977), stating at 342:

> [A] course of dealing can supply an enforceable term to a contract (or may even supplement or qualify that contract) provided that the conduct which identifies that course of dealing can reasonably be construed as indicative of the parties' intentions—a reflection of their joint or *common* understanding.

See also *Transco Contracting Co.*, ASBCA 25315, 82-1 BCA ¶ 15,516, stating at 76,973:

> The reasoning underlying the prior course of dealing rule requires that both parties have an actual knowledge of the prior course of dealing and of its significance to the contract.

Thus, in *J.W. Bateson Co.*, ASBCA 26617, 83-2 BCA ¶ 16,682, prior conduct involving other projects did not demonstrate an interpretation of the current contract because there was no evidence that government representatives concerned with the contract were aware of the conduct on other contracts where the contractor's interpretation was accepted. Similarly, in *Lake State Mfg. Corp.*, ASBCA 17286, 73-2 BCA ¶ 10,190, *recons. denied*, 74-1 BCA ¶ 10,462, the board held that the contractor was not entitled to receive government-furnished fabric of exactly the same size and texture as it had received under prior contracts because no "responsible representatives of the Government knew or relied upon" that past conduct. In *U.S. Flag & Signal Co.*, ASBCA 27049, 83-1 BCA ¶ 16,196, the contractor failed to establish the existence of a prior course of dealing because it had had no prior dealings with the contracting agency. The board noted at 80,468 that as "courts have pointed out . . . the Government is not a monolithic body where the activities of the separate agencies or departments are involved." Similarly, in *Romala Corp. v. United States*, 20 Cl. Ct. 435 (1990), *aff'd*, 927 F.2d 1219 (Fed. Cir. 1991), prior dealings with other offices in the agency were rejected because they were of insufficient similarity and repetitiveness. See also *Wheatley Assocs.*, ASBCA 24846, 83-1 BCA ¶ 16,306, *recons. denied*, 83-2 BCA ¶ 16,604 (prior course of dealing inapplicable where different agencies (Army and Navy) have no meaningful connection).

Similarly, a contractor normally cannot always rely on a prior course of dealing to which it was not a party. See *Southwest Welding & Mfg. Co.*, 206 Ct. Cl. 857 (1975), in which the court held that a contractor who observed an apparent specification deviation being permitted by the government by inspecting similar items produced by another contractor, but who did not know the reason for the deviation, could not rely on the alleged prior course of dealing. In *Atlas Fabricators, Inc.*, ASBCA 17556, 75-2 BCA ¶ 11,350, the contractor purchased equipment to make practice bombs for the government. The equipment was designed for use in accordance with several changes that had been granted under a previous contract. The government, however, refused to grant any deviations from the present contract, and the contractor sought an equitable adjustment. The board denied the claim, stating at 54,078-79:

> The Government had good and sufficient reasons for each of the drawing requirements and was reluctant to depart from them. It had no duty to do so. Its duty to cooperate with its contractors so as not to hinder or make more onerous their performance does not extend to a duty to make the work easier. *Banks Constr. Co. v. United States*, 176 Ct. Cl. 1302, 364 F.2d 357 (1966). And the mere fact that certain deviations to drawing or specification requirements were allowed to another, prior contractor did not require that the same deviations be granted to the appellant. *Southwest Welding & Manufacturing Company v. United States*, [206 Ct. Cl. 857 (1975)]; *McDowell & Rapp Construction Company*, ASBCA 17287, 73-1 BCA ¶ 9834.

See also *All Star/SAB Pac., J.V.*, ASBCA 50856, 99-1 BCA ¶ 30,214 (no proof that contractor relied on prior course of dealing with other contractors in preparing its bid), and *Optimal Data Corp.*, NASABCA 381-2, 85-1 BCA ¶ 17,760 (belief that prior contractors had interpreted contract certain way insufficient proof of prior course of dealing).

The opposite result has been reached when the contractor gained direct knowledge of the prior course of dealing. For example, in *Hamilton Enters.*, ASBCA 21951, 78-2 BCA ¶ 13,242, the board ruled that the contractor was reasonable in construing ambiguous contract terms to limit the scope of work based on site visits and the contemporaneous construction placed on similar language by the government and the immediately prior contractor. Similarly, in *Hydromatics, Inc.*, ASBCA 12094, 69-2 BCA ¶ 7962, the board refused to give the government a credit for a testing requirement that had been deleted from the present contract. Despite the fact that the requirement had been present in prior contracts, in which Hydromatics was either a contractor or subcontractor, testing was never required absent a change order. The board noted at 37,005:

> It is a familiar principle that the practical interpretation by the parties of the contract clauses has great weight in determining the contractual intent. *Ace Construction Company, etc. v. United States*, 185 Ct. Cl. 487; *Centre Manufacturing Company, Inc. v. United States*, 183 Ct. Cl. 115; *Dittmore-Freimuth Corp. v. United States*, 182 Ct. Cl. 507; *General Warehouse Two, Inc. v. United States*, 181 Ct. Cl. 180; *Merritt-Chapman & Scott Corporation v. United States*, 178 Ct. Cl. 883. While the parties were not identical in this case the facts show the ambiguity and the reasonableness of [the contractor's] interpretation.

Similarly, in *Wheatley Assocs.*, ASBCA 24760, 83-2 BCA ¶ 16,760, the board noted at 83,333:

> [The] rule has been extended to subcontractors who have relied in submitting their bids to prime contractors on the Government's repeated and consistent practice of failing to enforce an otherwise explicit contract provision in prior contracts with other firms where they were the subcontractors. *King-Hunter, Inc.*, [ASBCA 22376, 78-2 BCA ¶ 13,426].

Recovery, however, was denied because the contractor and subcontractor failed to establish reasonable good faith reliance on government actions under prior contracts.

b. Application to Changed Language

Use of prior conduct is more problematic when the government has changed the language in a succeeding contract. See *Troise v. United States*, 21 Cl. Ct. 48 (1990), holding that the contractor was not entitled to rely on the government's continued acceptance of deviating products when the contract was altered to remove language giving the contractor the discretion to deviate from the specifications. See also *Coastal Dry Dock & Repair Corp.*, ASBCA 31894, 87-1 BCA ¶ 19,618 (prior practice not indicative of intent on current contract because terms were different); *L.B. Samford, Inc.*, DOTCAB 1457, 85-2 BCA ¶ 18,081 (course of dealing on prior contract not usable when terms of contract "differed significantly" from current contract), and *Jansen v. United States*, 170 Ct. Cl. 346, 344 F.2d 363 (1965) (contractor not entitled to rely on the interpretation on prior contracts when the government made "clear and significant" changes to the specifications).

Parties may be bound by their interpretation of prior contracts even though the language of the disputed contract has been altered. In *Watson Elec. Constr. Co.*, GSBCA 4260, 76-1 BCA ¶ 11,912, the board held that an electrical contractor was entitled to an equitable adjustment for furnishing lamps on a construction project. The prior contracts had contained a standard specification stating that the contractor would not supply lamps unless specifically required by the project specifications. Although this standard provision was not included in the disputed contract, the board found that the contractor was reasonable in relying on its prior experience that lamps were not a standard electrical contract requirement and thus were not its responsibility.

A prior course of dealing may also clarify the parties' intent by demonstrating the rationale for an alteration of their agreement. In such cases, prior course of dealing provides a valuable interpretive aid even though it is clear that the obligations of the parties have changed. See *Engineered Sys., Inc.*, ASBCA 20919, 76-2 BCA ¶ 12,098, *recons. denied*, 77-2 BCA ¶ 12,630, in which the board held that the contractor reasonably interpreted vague language that incorporated a new policy from its prior contracts as altering its obligation to pay for its employees' use of officers' quarters and officers' and NCO clubs. The board reasoned that there was little reason for the new contract language unless the government intended to change this element of the policy.

2. Waiver of Legal Rights

Beyond its use in the interpretive process to establish intent, prior course of dealing may also amount to a waiver. This can occur when a government official with authority and knowledge of the essentials of performance makes a decision by action or inaction under a similar prior contract that permits the contractor to perform at variance with an explicit requirement. If reasonable contractor reliance is shown, the government cannot argue that those previously waived terms found in the present contract are obligatory. The rule, with its limitations, was expressed by the board in *Wheatley Assocs.*, ASBCA 24760, 83-2 BCA ¶ 16,760, at 83,333:

> A prior course of dealing between contractual parties can extinguish an otherwise explicit contract requirement. See, e.g., *Gresham & Company, Inc. v. United States*, 200 Ct. Cl. 97, 470 F.2d 542 (1972); *King-Hunter, Inc.*, ASBCA No. 22376, 78-2 BCA ¶ 13,426. However, the granting of a few isolated occasional waivers of an explicit contract requirement will not establish such a course of dealing to estop the contracting officer from enforcing that requirement. *Doyle Shirt Manufacturing Corp. v. United States*, 199 Ct. Cl. 150, 462 F.2d 1150 (1972).

In *Gresham & Co. v. United States*, 200 Ct. Cl. 97, 470 F.2d 542 (1972), the court found that the contractor was reasonable in assuming that an express contract requirement for automatic detergent dispensers had been waived from a series of contracts for single-tank dishwashing machines. The court based its finding in large part on the fact that the government had accepted dishwashers without dispensers under the first 21 contracts before insisting that they be installed under the subsequent 15. See also *L.W. Foster Sportswear Co. v. United States*, 186 Ct. Cl. 499, 405 F.2d 1285 (1969), where the contractor properly relied on a course of dealing under at least five prior contracts, identical or very closely similar to the given contract, in concluding that it would be permitted to deviate from precise contract specifications in order to produce acceptable flying jackets for the Navy. Compare *Davis Group, Inc.*, ASBCA 48431, 95-2 BCA ¶ 27,702 (no waiver when government paid two invoices for material on site); *Kvaas Constr. Co.*, ASBCA 45965, 94-1 BCA ¶ 26,513 (no waiver by the approval of a specification deviation on four prior contracts); and *Western States Constr. Co.*, ASBCA 37611, 92-1 BCA ¶ 24,418 (no waiver by a course of dealing on two prior contracts, one with another contractor). In *Walsky Constr. Co.*, ASBCA 36940, 90-2 BCA ¶ 22,934, the board found a waiver when the contracting officer permitted the contractor to seal coat a road when the temperature was below the specified minimum. The board reasoned that it would be inequitable to require the contractor to reperform the work at its own expense even though the waiver had occurred only on the contract being performed. See also *Caddell Constr. Co.*, DOTBCA 2967, 96-2 BCA ¶ 28,549, in which the board denied a motion for summary judgment because the contractor had submitted proof that the government had permitted performance not in compliance with the contract and that entitled it to prove sufficient government acquiescence to constitute a waiver. Summary judgment on the waiver issue was also denied in *Products Eng'g. Corp. v. General Servs. Admin.*, GSBCA 12503, 96-2 BCA ¶ 28,305.

The more exact the contract language, the more convincing the evidence of a prior course of dealing must be to controvert that language and establish waiver. For example, see *Doyle Shirt Mfg. Corp. v. United States*, 199 Ct. Cl. 150, 462 F.2d 1150 (1972), where the contract called for khaki military shirts that were required to pass a shade evaluation by the government's laboratory. Although a portion of the first material lot submitted by the contractor did not come within the required shade tolerances, the government issued a shade waiver in exchange for a reduction in contract price. The contractor manufactured additional shirts and subsequently requested waivers. Because the material in these shirts was found to vary significantly more than the first lot, the government refused to grant a waiver. The court rejected the contractor's argument that the government was bound by its prior acceptance, stating at 158:

> We do not believe that the *Foster* case is controlling here because of the following findings by the Board which are supported by substantial evidence. *Rice v. United States*, 192 Ct. Cl. 903, 909, 428 F.2d 1311, 1314-1315 (1970); *Koppers Co. v. United States*, 186 Ct. Cl. 142, 147-151, 405 F.2d 554, 558-559 (1968). First, [the contractor] knew at the time this contract was awarded on January 16, 1968, of only three waivers that had been granted for shade 2111 deficiencies. Second, [the

> government] did not have any consistent practice of granting waivers in every case. Third, [the contractor] was aware that waivers would not be granted when deficiencies affected serviceability or appearance. As stated above, Shirt Lots 3 and 4 were defective to a significantly greater degree than Shirt Lot 1 because the former lots' shade defects fell into Category 3. If, instead, they had been in Category 4, [the contractor] might have a stronger argument. Even then, however, [the contractor] would still be faced with the fact that the Government did not always grant waivers, and it warned [the contractor] when it granted the waiver for Shirt Lot 1 that it "[did] not waive its rights to reject future quantities of supplies containing the same or other nonconformities * * * ." We therefore agree with the Board that [the government] was not estopped from refusing to grant waivers for Shirt Lots 3 and 4.

See *Parris v. General Servs. Admin.*, GSBCA 15512, 01-2 BCA ¶ 31,629, in which the board relied on a "no waiver" provision in the contract to deny the contractor's claim that the government had waived a requirement that tax adjustment documentation be submitted within 60 days. The government had waived the initial noncompliance but refused to waive subsequent noncompliances. Compare *4J2R1C Ltd. P'ship v. General Servs. Admin.*, GSBCA 15584, 02-1 BCA ¶ 31,742, finding a waiver of the same requirement when the contract did not contain the "no waiver" provision and the government had waived the requirement seven times.

Reliance is an essential element of waiver. See *General Sec. Servs. Corp. v. General Servs. Admin.*, GSBCA 11381, 92-2 BCA ¶ 24,897, in which the board rejected the contractor's waiver argument because, although the government had approved a specification deviation on six prior contracts, the contractor did not indicate in negotiations that it was relying on this waiver. Similarly, in *Snowbird Indus., Inc.*, ASBCA 33027, 89-3 BCA ¶ 22,065, no waiver was found where the contractor did not know, at the time of bidding, that the government had waived a specification requirement on 30 prior contracts. See also *M.E.S., Inc.*, PSBCA 4553, 01-2 BCA ¶ 31,580 (no reliance on single payment for damages for which contractor was responsible).

The distinctions between the intent-determinative and waiver-based uses of prior conduct are often blurred by courts and boards as they broadly discuss prior dealings with interpretive language. For example, in *Huber, Hunt & Nichols, Inc.*, VACAB 1200, 77-1 BCA ¶ 12,500, *recons. denied*, 77-2 BCA ¶ 12,689, the contractor sought additional compensation for costs incurred in complying with an express contract requirement that the control equipment for humidity control systems be tested and balanced by an independent firm. The same requirement had been included in prior contracts but had been waived, and the contractor had been allowed to use the installing subcontractor to perform the testing and balancing. The board noted at 60,574:

> It is recognized that practices and interpretations arising under prior contracts may be used as a basis for the interpretation by the same parties of a later contract containing similar provisions.

> The Board finds that the Government's acquiescence in the [contractor's] interpretation of prior contracts having identical or similar specifications constituted a course of conduct which supports the [contractor's] interpretation of the contract here involved.
>
> No further authority need be cited for the proposition that where a Government agency responsible for the administration of contracts has followed a definite practice of interpretation for a long period of time, it will not be permitted suddenly to change its interpretation to the detriment of an individual who has acted in reliance of the Government's practice. When the two contracts were executed with Cotton on June 1, 1974, Johnson was entitled to assume, in accordance with past practice, that it would be permitted to perform the testing and balancing on the subject project.

Thus, the contractor prevailed, either because past government practice waived its right to compliance with the contract provision or because the past dealings reflected the intent of the parties. See also *General Time Corp.*, ASBCA 21211, 79-1 BCA ¶ 13,611, *recons. denied*, 85-1 BCA ¶ 17,842, in which the board discussed both interpretation cases and waiver cases in finding that the contractor was bound by acceptance criteria that had been followed by both parties over many years.

C. Custom and Trade Usage

Government contracts are interpreted in light of the involved industry's custom and trade usage. See *Restatement, Second, Contracts* § 222, which states:

> (1) A usage of trade is a usage having such regularity of observance in a place, vocation, or trade as to justify an expectation that it will be observed with respect to a particular agreement. It may include a system of rules regularly observed even though particular rules are changed from time to time.
>
> * * *
>
> (3) Unless otherwise agreed, a usage of trade in the vocation or trade in which the parties are engaged or a usage of trade of which they know or have reason to know gives meaning to or supplements or qualifies their agreement.

1. *Interpreting Vague Language*

When the contract contains vague language, evidence of custom and trade usage will be a primary means of interpreting that language. In *W.G. Cornell Co. v. United States*, 179 Ct. Cl. 651, 376 F.2d 299 (1967), the contract specified a certain rigid insulation. The contractor argued that it should be allowed to use a particular flexible insulation on the basis of an established trade practice and a provision in the contract permitting the use of other equally suitable material. The court agreed with the government that custom and usage may not vary or contradict plain language, but held for the contractor, stating at 670-71:

> The decisions of the Boards below are replete with declarations of the general rule that evidence of trade usage may not vary or contradict plain contract language. While that rule is correctly stated, it is not applicable or controlling here because a close analysis of the administrative opinions discloses that only one provision of the contract was examined and taken into consideration. Moreover, evidence of trade usage and custom may always *explain* or *define*, as distinguished from *vary* or *contradict*, contract language. That is the status of the controversy before us. Assuming, *arguendo*, that the only ordinary meaning which could be placed upon the words "other equally suitable material" would exclude flexible insulation, evidence of trade usage still must be taken into consideration, since it supplies a meaning to that phrase which is not disclosed from a casual reading thereof. Even in the absence of ambiguity, contract language must be given that meaning which would be derived from the contract by a reasonably intelligent person acquainted with the contemporaneous circumstances." [Citation omitted]
>
> * * *
>
> In summary, whether or not the contract specifications are considered ambiguous, evidence of trade usage, custom and practice should have been considered at the administrative level. Since this was not done, legal error was committed.

There are numerous cases in which evidence of trade custom and usage has been used to interpret vague language. See *Grunley Constr. Co.*, ENGBCA 6327, 99-1 BCA ¶ 30,138, where trade practice was used to determine that "light grey/white" indicated that either light grey or white granite is an acceptable material. See also *Hensel Phelps Constr. Co. v. General Servs. Admin.*, GSBCA 14744, 01-1 BCA ¶ 31,249 (evidence that vibration isolation had never been required on plumbing systems accepted as showing that the vibration requirement only applied to the HVAC system); *Atlas Railroad Constr. Co.*, ENGBCA 5972, 94-3 BCA ¶ 26,997 (evidence that "lateral" test in railroad work was applying pressure in perpendicular manner); *Hoffman Constr. Co.*, DOTBCA 2150, 93-2 BCA ¶ 25,803 (contractor reasonably used standard industry practice of installing conduit in the topping slab to interpret vague specifications of method to be used for installing conduit); *Domgaard Assocs. v. General Servs. Admin.*, GSBCA 11421, 93-3 BCA ¶ 25,955 (requirement for uniform lighting is equivalent to an average lighting level according to the general understanding in the relevant industry); and *Gracon Corp.*, IBCA 2271, 89-1 BCA ¶ 21,232 (despite requirement for contractor to coordinate components of hoist system, government was not relieved from liability on a claim for defective specifications where government had design responsibility and it was industry custom not to fragment that responsibility). Compare *Nielsen-Dillingham Builders J.V. v. United States*, 43 Fed. Cl. 5 (1999), in which the court held that evidence of trade practice "should not play a dispositive role" to resolve an ambiguity created by clearly conflicting contract requirements.

Evidence of trade practice is superior to evidence of common usage in interpreting language relating to work done by a particular trade. See *Bodell Constr. Co.*,

ASBCA 38355, 92-1 BCA ¶ 24,433, where the contract called for a smooth form finish for concrete surfaces exposed to public view. The board used a definition of the term stated in a standard specification of the American Concrete Institute to reject the contractor's argument that the proper interpretation should be based on a dictionary definition of public. Compare *John E. Day Assocs., Inc.*, ASBCA 43758, 94-1 BCA ¶ 26,337 (common usage of word "existing" used because no evidence for a special trade usage of the word was presented); *DWS, Inc.*, ASBCA 29743, 93-1 BCA ¶ 25,404 (no evidence of an industry practice to support assertion that "diazo copies" means only paper copies).

2. Ambiguous Language Not Required

Evidence of a trade usage may be considered even though the language in the contract is superficially unambiguous. This rule was discussed by the Court of Claims in *Gholson, Byars & Holmes Constr. Co. v. United States*, 173 Ct. Cl. 374, 351 F.2d 987 (1965), at 395:

> The Board's failure to consider the evidence of trade practice and custom on the basis of absence of ambiguity was in error. For the principle is now established in this court (and almost every other court) that in order that the intention of the parties may prevail, the language of a contract is to be given effect according to its trade meaning notwithstanding that in its ordinary meaning it is unambiguous. That is to say that trade usage or custom may show that language which appears on its face to be perfectly clear and unambiguous has, in fact, a meaning different from its ordinary meaning.

See also *J.A. Jones Constr.*, VABCA 5414, 99-1 BCA ¶ 30,380 (trade practice used to ascertain reasonable meaning of concrete specification); *Gaffny Corp.*, ASBCA 37639, 94-1 BCA ¶ 26,522 (trade practice gives meaning to specifications in contract regarding installation standards for ceramic tile); and *Riley Stoker Corp.*, ASBCA 37019, 92-3 BCA ¶ 25,143 (trade practice used to determine meaning of seemingly clear term). But see *R.B. Wright Constr. Co. v. United States*, 919 F.2d 1569 (Fed. Cir. 1990), in which the court rejected the contractor's attempt to prove an ambiguity by trade usage that one coat of paint was proper, because the contract clearly called for three coats of paint. In *Western States Constr. Co. v. United States*, 26 Cl. Ct. 818 (1992), the court discussed many of the court cases rejecting evidence of trade usage to prove ambiguity and found that they were fully reconcilable with the rule set forth in the *Gholson, Byars & Holmes* case. The court stated at 824:

> In the court's view, the guiding principle is that the contract controls the work to be done and cannot be trumped by a trade practice, regardless of how prevalent. This is the import of cases such as *R.B. Wright Constr. Co.*, 919 F.2d at 1572 . . . . If the contract calls for three coats of paint, . . . then the fact that industry practice only calls for one coat is irrelevant. . . . There is not question in that circumstance what the phrase "three coats" means. From the contractor's perspective it is only too clear. The term "three" has no special meaning in the construction business.

> If, however, in the context of a particular contract a term has a special meaning within an industry, the contractor is permitted to introduce evidence to establish that meaning. The government is accountable, as drafter, for using a term that has a particular, specialized meaning to the anticipated reader. As the court wrote in *Hurst v. W.J. Lake Co.*, 141 Or. 306, 16 P.2d 627 (1932), "[o]ne cannot understand accurately the language of such sciences and trades without knowing the peculiar meaning attached to the words which they use. It is said that a court in construing the language of the parties must put itself into the shoes of the parties. That alone will not suffice; it must adopt their vernacular." *Hurst*, 16 P.2d at 629.
>
> Trade practice and custom can thus be used to support a contention that a certain contract provision was legitimately interpreted in a way different than a layman's reading. However, the evidence would only be accepted because a contractor, in the industry targeted by the solicitation, made a colorable showing that it relied on a competing interpretation of words and not just on the fact that things are not customarily done in the manner called for by the contract. As a result, there would thus be present the ambiguity necessary to resort to trade custom and usage.

See *ArBee Corp.*, ASBCA 38446, 91-1 BCA ¶ 23,297, in which the board denied a government motion for summary judgment because the contractor showed that the trade practice of not painting an assembly unless specified was different from the seemingly clear contract language that required painting of parts.

3. Clear Language Superior to Trade Custom

Although evidence of custom and trade usage is widely used in the interpretation process, it must be recognized that the government is free to require performance in excess of or below the level or standard normally accepted in a trade. In order to preserve this right, the courts and boards have held that evidence of trade practice or custom cannot overrule unambiguous contract provisions. See *WRB Corp. v. United States*, 183 Ct. Cl. 409 (1968), in which the court stated at 436:

> Although the evidence in the record indicates that masonite is the usual and customary material that is used for doors on paint-grade cabinets, and that a masonite cabinet door has equal utility to a cabinet door made of wood, the pertinent contract specification in this case plainly required that the cabinet doors be made of plywood or solid stock. This was the Government's prerogative, and it was a provision to which the [contractor] had agreed when it entered into the contract with the Government. A trade practice in the building industry of using masonite doors on paint grade cabinets cannot properly be permitted to overcome an unambiguous contract provision.

A contractor's argument that trade practice permitted it not to meet certain lumber specifications of a construction contract and to later settle with a downward price adjustment was rejected in *S.S. Silberblatt, Inc. v. United States*, 193 Ct. Cl. 269, 433 F.2d 1314 (1970). The court stated at 288, "Trade practice in the building industry cannot override an unambiguous contract provision." See *All Star/SAB Pac.,*

J.V., ASBCA 50856, 98-2 BCA ¶ 29,958 (clear language in price adjustment clause precludes use of evidence of trade custom and trade practice); *Craft Mach. Works, Inc. v. United States*, 20 Cl. Ct. 355, *rev'd*, 926 F.2d 1110 (Fed. Cir. 1991) (contract documents and regulations speak clearly as to what the parties intended the term "supplies" to mean; this case differs from cases typically calling for insight into trade practices); *Ralph Larsen & Son, Inc. v. United States*, 17 Cl. Ct. 39 (1989) (evidence of trade practice precluded when contract indicated a clear meaning of requirement for embedded conduit); *Lomas & Nettleton Co. v. United States*, 1 Cl. Ct. 641 (1982) (Seller's Guide incorporated in contract clearly required execution and return of forms as condition precedent to binding contract, such that trade practice to the contrary, which treated oral commitments as binding, was unavailing); *Sears Petroleum & Transp. Corp.*, ASBCA 41401, 94-1 BCA ¶ 26,414 (trade practice not pertinent where contract is unambiguous as to date of delivery); *Tomahawk Constr. Co.*, ASBCA 41717, 93-3 BCA ¶ 26,219 (although there was a trade practice that cast iron soil pipe is not wrapped, there is nothing to prevent the government from specifying a requirement that exceeds or departs from the trade custom or practice; thus, contractor required to wrap pipe because contract unambiguously required it); *MK-Ferguson Co.*, ASBCA 42436, 93-2 BCA ¶ 25,751 (trade practice or custom does not overrule unambiguous contract provision requiring use of a revised safety manual); *RJS Constructors*, ENGBCA 5956, 93-2 BCA ¶ 25,673 (trade practice that a standard product meant one with no special features would not override unambiguous contract term specifically requiring cranes to be complete with all appurtenances); and *F.E. Constructors*, ASBCA 23458, 82-2 BCA ¶ 15,825 (clear and unambiguous contract drawings and language override trade usage). See also *Santa Fe Eng'rs, Inc.*, ASBCA 25173, 82-1 BCA ¶ 15,489 (drawings and specifications unambiguously required use of certain insulation in roofing, contrary to trade practice; "[i]ndustry practice cannot take precedence over clear and unambiguous contract language"); *Bruce Kinney*, AGBCA 81-258-1, 83-1 BCA ¶ 16,506 ("Pilot-in-Command is a term of art in the aviation transport industry [which] must be given the meaning and interpretation described by a regulation of general applicability [the C.F.R.]"); and *Zinser-Furby, Inc.*, ASBCA 26301, 82-2 BCA ¶ 16,080 (specifications clearly and unambiguously required the use of two types of flanges in the functioning system; "[i]t makes no legal difference that such a mating was not normally done if a requirement for it was clearly called out, which was the case").

In some cases, the court or board has rejected contrary evidence of trade custom and usage because it has arrived at a clear meaning of the contract language through analysis. See, for example, *Blake Constr. Co. v. United States*, 25 Cl. Ct. 177 (1992), *rev'd*, 987 F.2d 743 (Fed. Cir. 1993), *cert. denied*, 510 U.S. 963 (1993), where the contract provided diagrammatic drawings of electrical lines to be installed in a building, showing the lines running through the corridor ceilings and requiring coordination with other trades. The Claims Court held that a contract change had occurred when, to accommodate necessary coordination with other trades, the government permitted location of numerous electrical lines outside the corridors but would not permit their installation in an underground duct. The court reasoned that the specification was a performance specification and that the trade usage was that the best practice was to install electrical lines in underground conduits. The Federal Circuit reversed, holding that the proper interpretation of the contract precluded underground installation because of the requirement for overhead installation and that evidence of trade usage was irrelevant. Similarly, in *George Hyman Constr. Co. v. United States*, 832 F.2d 574 (Fed. Cir. 1987), the court held that evidence of trade practice was not relevant to interpret the meaning of the term "heavy duty auger" when the correct meaning could be determined by an analysis of all of the contract provisions. See also *Hunt Constr. Group v. United States*, 281 F.3d 1369 (Fed. Cir. 2002) (trade practice evidence cannot be used to override clear meaning of Federal, State, and Local Taxes clause); *Jowett, Inc. v. United States*, 234 F.3d 1365 (2000) (requirement to insulate all "supply ducts; return air ducts [and] . . . plenums" clearly overrides trade practice); *Pete Vicari Gen. Contractor, Inc. v. United States*, 51 Fed. Cl. 161 (2001) (language requiring monitoring of fill until "additional settlement is expected to be less than ½ inch" is clear and not subject to modification by trade practice); *Hoffman Constr. Co. v. United States*, 40 Fed. Cl. 184 (1998) (clear specification requirements to insulate ducts cannot be overcome by evidence of trade practice); *M.A. Mortenson Co.*, ASBCA 49917, 97-1 BCA ¶ 28,682, *recons. denied*, 97-1 BCA ¶ 28,886 (specification giving government right to reject masonry with chips or cracks that detracted from its appearance plus lack of inclusion of industry standard overrides evidence of trade practice that small cracks were permissible); and *J.W. Bateson Co.*, ASBCA 19043, 75-2 BCA ¶ 11,410 (government had expressly modified trade usage when several of the contract work sheet notes specifically called for bronze-colored glass even though the contract specifications called for polished glass, which according to trade usage indicated clear glass). In *HRE, Inc. v. United States*, 142 F.3d 1274 (Fed. Cir. 1998), the court rejected evidence of trade usage because of clear language while, at the same time, it criticized the government for writing a specification containing ambiguous language.

In *Metric Constructors, Inc. v. National Aeronautics & Space Admin.*, 169 F.3d 747 (Fed. Cir. 1999), the court attempted to explain the "seemingly divergent" cases in which trade practice is used to overcome "clear" language and where it is rejected because the language is clear, stating at 752:

> These two lines of cases, however, only seem to diverge. In practice, they are both consistent with contract interpretation doctrines and practices. The United States Court of Federal Claims recognized those unifying principles in *Western States Construction Co. v. United States*, 26 Cl. Ct. 818 (1992). In that case, the trial court considered the meaning of a contract term requiring wrapping of underground "metallic pipe" with protective tape. The contractor introduced evidence showing that, in the industry, "cast iron soil pipe," although technically "metallic pipe," was not wrapped with protective tape. The Court of Federal Claims, aptly reconciling the two seemingly conflicting lines of cases of this court and its predecessor, consulted trade practice and custom to determine whether wrapping of cast iron soil pipe was consistent with the contract and thus whether an ambiguity arose at all. See *id.* at 826. This *Western States* analysis correctly applies the law of contract interpretation.

> This court adheres to the principle that "the language of a contract must be given that meaning that would be derived from the contract by a reasonably intelligent person acquainted with the contemporaneous circumstances." *Hol-Gar Mfg. Corp. v. United States*, 169 Ct. Cl. 384, 351 F.2d 972, 975 (Ct. Cl. 1965). Thus, to interpret disputed contract terms, "the context and intention [of the contracting parties] are more meaningful than the dictionary definition." *Rice v. United States*, 192 Ct. Cl. 903, 428 F.2d 1311, 1314 (Ct. Cl. 1970); see also *Western States*, 26 Cl. Ct. at 825; *Corman v. United States*, 26 Cl. Ct. 1011, 1015 (1992). Trade practice and custom illuminate the context for the parties' contract negotiations and agreements. Before an interpreting court can conclusively declare a contract ambiguous or unambiguous, it must consult the context in which the parties exchanged promises. Excluding evidence of trade practice and custom because the contract terms are "unambiguous" on their face ignores the reality of the context in which the parties contracted. That context may well reveal that the terms of the contract are not, and never were, clear on their face. On the other hand, that context may well reveal that contract terms are, and have consistently been, unambiguous.

Thus, where the government fails to unambiguously or expressly modify an accepted trade custom or practice, the contractor that performs in accordance with trade custom will generally prevail. See *John McShain, Inc. v. United States*, 199 Ct. Cl. 364, 462 F.2d 489 (1972) (no express language negating trade practice of including concrete floor fill in design of tee members), and *Tecon-Green (JV)*, ENGBCA 2667, 67-1 BCA ¶ 6147 (where specifications did not clearly direct a specific method, contractor was justified in using accepted industry practice). See also *Everett Plywood Corp. v. United States*, 206 Ct. Cl. 244, 512 F.2d 1082 (1975) (Forest Service bound to follow its established practice of extending the time for contract performance absent contract language to the contrary); *Marvin Eng'g Co.*, ASBCA 25460, 82-2 BCA ¶ 16,021 (Air Force decided prior to award that it would not accept out-of-round holes, acceptable under trade usage and custom; however, failure to express such intent in drawings or elsewhere in the contract resulted in trade usage being determinative); and *Exposaic Indus., Inc.*, GSBCA 5218, 80-2 BCA ¶ 14,764 (government liable for equitable adjustment where it did not succeed in drafting a specification that imposed a requirement on the contractor to furnish steel hangers and braces in contradiction of trade practice).

4. Proof of Trade Practice

The party seeking to take advantage of an alleged trade practice must present substantial evidence that the practice is clear and well recognized, *W. G. Cornell Co. v. United States*, 179 Ct. Cl. 651, 376 F.2d 299 (1967). See also *RJS Constructors, Inc.*, ENGBCA 5956, 93-2 BCA ¶ 25,673 (party asserting a trade practice bears the burden of proving, by the preponderance of the evidence, the existence of the trade practice), and *Davho Co.*, VACAB 1004, 73-1 BCA ¶ 9848 ("use of trade practice or custom as an aid to interpretation must be predicated upon proof that the alleged trade practice or custom has become established to the extent it can be recognized as such"). Trade practice must be "well-defined, widespread, long-standing, and well-recognized," *Jake Sweeney Auto Leasing, Inc.*, PSBCA 3069, 93-2 BCA ¶ 25,601. Thus, testimony or assertions of the contractor have been held to be insufficient proof of a trade practice. See *Roxco, Ltd.*, ENGBCA 6435, 00-1 BCA ¶ 30,687 (testimony of company employees insufficient to prove trade practice); *Gulf Coast Trailing Co.*, ENGBCA 5795, 94-2 BCA ¶ 26,921 (statement reiterating allegation in claim letter as to existence of trade practice not sufficient to establish prima facie case); *Southwest Marine, Inc.*, DOTCAB 1497, 93-3 BCA ¶ 26,170 (proof must rest on more than bare assertions of trade practice); *River Equip. Co.*, ENGBCA 5934, 93-2 BCA ¶ 25,804 (mere allegations do not meet the burden of proof required of the party asserting the existence of a trade practice); *Westmac, Inc.*, AGBCA 85-511-1, 91-2 BCA ¶ 23,925 (testimony of contractor held insufficient proof of a trade practice); and *Turner Constr. Co.*, ASBCA 25602, 86-2 BCA ¶ 18,966 (testimony of contractor's employees insufficient to prove trade practice). Similarly, conflicting testimony of the parties' experts has led to the conclusion that there was insufficient evidence to establish a trade practice, *Dominion Eng'g Works*, ENGBCA 6140, 97-1 BCA ¶ 28,638. Testimony of a single supplier has also been rejected as adequate proof of a trade practice, *Bruce-Anderson Co.*, ASBCA 29460, 88-3 BCA ¶ 20,998. See also *Sinclair Oil Corp.*, EBCA 416-8-88, 90-1 BCA ¶ 22,462, *recons. denied*, 90-2 BCA ¶ 22,827, in which the board found inadequate proof of a trade practice because the contractor presented the testimony of only one expert witness and there was conflicting testimony. In *Peters v. United States*, 694 F.2d 687 (Fed. Cir. 1982), a large-scale logging contractor claimed that the established practice in the region was to permit changes in logging methods by letter agreement without increased rates. The court found no such practice, since the few changes by letter agreement in the region primarily involved small-scale loggers and were not for substantial cost changes. See also *Rough & Ready Timber Co. v. United States*, 707 F.2d 1353 (Fed. Cir. 1983), where the contractor argued that the Forest Service manual's provisions and the Forest Service's actions under prior contracts established a custom or trade practice for granting time extensions on timber sale contracts. The court held that the evidence failed to establish a custom or trade practice contrary to the Forest Service's actions, which were permitted under the clauses construed as a whole.

The relevant trade usage may be national in scope or it may vary from community to community within a single state, *William Clairmont, Inc.*, ASBCA 15447, 73-1 BCA ¶ 9927. Under U.C.C. § 1-205(5), the trade practice of the place where any part of performance is to occur shall be used in interpreting the agreement as to that part of the performance. See, for example, *T. Brown Constructors, Inc.*, DOTBCA 1986, 95-2 BCA ¶ 27,870 (New Mexico trade practice used for federal work without detailed specification requirement), and *Slattery Assocs., Inc.*, ENGBCA 3650, 78-1 BCA ¶ 13,095 (contractor not entitled to rely on New York City trade practice when work was to be performed in the District of Columbia).

One method of establishing trade practice is to introduce contemporaneous interpretations of other bidders on the disputed contract. See *Eagle Paving*, AGBCA 75-156, 78-1 BCA ¶ 13,107, where a contractor's interpretation was supported by affidavits from other bidders stating that they had similarly interpreted the specifications as permitting a dry batching method of transporting concrete to the job site. Compare *Maecon, Inc.*, ASBCA 20104, 76-2 BCA ¶ 11,961, where a contractor was not entitled to additional compensation for constructing housing for comminutors since all other bidders, except one, had concluded that the housing was required as a basic item.

For a case in which the government was unable to prove an agency practice, see *Andersen Constr. Co. & Krow Constr., Inc.*, IBCA 2347, 90-3 BCA ¶ 23,135. There the board interpreted the contract in accordance with trade practice and rejected the government's contention that there was a contrary agency practice. It stated that, even if there was such a practice, the contractor was not bound because it had no knowledge of such a practice.

5. *Supplying Missing Terms*

Evidence of trade practice or custom provides an important interpretive aid where the contract specifications are silent on the precise scope of the work or method of performance. In such cases, the court or board will normally use trade custom and usage to fill in the missing term. In *Industrial Research Assocs., Inc.*, DCCAB WB-5, 68-1 BCA ¶ 7069, the specification called for a particular size wire cable but was silent on whether the cable should be shielded or unshielded. Relying on the *Restatement of Contracts* § 248(2), the board held that the specifications should be interpreted in accordance with trade usage and that the standard in the industry was unshielded cable. See also *Stoeckert v. United States*, 183 Ct. Cl. 152, 391 F.2d 639 (1968).

Supplying missing terms is a common use of evidence of trade custom and usage. See *Riley Stoker Corp.*, ASBCA 37019, 92-3 BCA ¶ 25,143 (responsibility for providing boiler operators during start-up of boilers installed by contractor); *US West Info. Sys., Inc.*, GSBCA 9028, 90-2 BCA ¶ 22,746 (responsibility for identifying and marking existing cable in contract for installing new telephone cables); and *Devonshire West Realty Trust*, GSBCA 9650, 90-2 BCA ¶ 22,875 (responsibility for wiring phone outlets required to be installed by landlord).

V. POST-INTERPRETATION AMBIGUITIES

In many cases the court or board, after exhausting the interpretation process outlined in the preceding sections, will find that an ambiguity still exists. See, for example, *Salem Eng'g & Constr. Corp. v. United States*, 2 Cl. Ct. 803 (1983), and *Blount Bros. Constr. Co. v. United States*, 171 Ct. Cl. 478, 346 F.2d 962 (1965). At this stage, the ambiguity is generally resolved by using one of two risk allocation principles: (1) the rule of *contra proferentem,* which adopts the interpretation that favors the nondrafting party, or (2) the pre-contract clarification rule, which denies adoption of a contractor's interpretation when it has failed to request clarification of an ambiguity of which it knew or should have known. It should be noted that the court or board that applies these rules is no longer seeking to discern the parties' intent but rather to fairly determine responsibility for ambiguous language. This section examines these principles.

If *contra proferentem* cannot be applied and there is no duty to seek clarification because no obvious (patent) ambiguity existed, these risk allocation rules will not resolve the dispute. In that case, the contract will be interpreted as it would probably be understood by reasonable men standing in the parties' shoes at the time of contracting, *Deloro Smelting & Ref. Co. v. United States*, 161 Ct. Cl. 489, 317 F.2d 382 (1963). Or, as stated in *Tulelake Irrigation Dist. v. United States*, 169 Ct. Cl. 782, 342 F.2d 447 (1965), at 793, "[i]t follows that, since no general canon of interpretation provides a ready solution, we are to determine what method of computation is the most reasonable, in the light of the language of the contract and the circumstances of its creation."

A. Finding Ambiguous Terms

An ambiguity exists when there are two reasonable interpretations of contract language. The determination of ambiguity is generally made after each party to the litigation has offered the evidence supporting its interpretation of the contract. See *Metric Constructors, Inc. v. National Aeronautics & Space Admin.*, 169 F.3d 747 (Fed. Cir. 1999), stating at 751:

> When a contract is susceptible to more than one reasonable interpretation, it contains an ambiguity. See *Hills Materials Co. v. Rice*, 982 F.2d 514, 516 (Fed. Cir. 1992). To show an ambiguity it is not enough that the parties differ in their respective interpretations of a contract term. See *Community Heating & Plumbing Co. v. Kelso,* 987 F.2d 1575, 1578 (Fed. Cir. 1993). Rather, both interpretations must fall within a "zone of reasonableness." See *WPC Enters., Inc. v. United States*, 163 Ct. Cl. 1, 323 F.2d 874, 876 (Ct. Cl. 1964).

See also *C. Sanchez & Son, Inc. v. United States*, 6 F.3d 1539 (Fed. Cir. 1993), in which the court remanded a case to the Claims Court because it had granted summary judgment without hearing the facts supporting the contractor's interpretation of the contract language. The court stated at 1544-45:

> We conclude that the Claims Court incorrectly described the contract as unambiguous. A contract term is unambiguous if there is only one reasonable interpretation. Although a disagreement as to the meaning of a contract term does not of itself render the term ambiguous, *Blake Constr. Co. v. United States*, 220 Ct. Cl. 56, 597 F.2d 1357, 1359 n. 16, if more than one meaning is reasonably consistent with the contract language it can not be deemed unambiguous. *Edward R. Marden Corp. v. United States*, 803 F.2d 701, 705 (Fed. Cir. 1986); *Hills Materials Co. v. Rice*, 982 F.2d 514, 516 (Fed. Cir. 1982). The record shows a genuine factual dispute as to how the Safety Manual listing would reasonably be read by engineers and experts in the field.

The key to determining ambiguity is thus a detailed analysis of each party's proffered interpretation. In making this analysis, the courts and boards ignore the fact that the parties are in disagreement as to the meaning of the contract language and consider each interpretation in light of the interpretation rules discussed in this chapter. See, for example, *Bloomington Hosp. v. United States*, 29 Fed. Cl. 286 (1993), and *Kiewit/Tulsa-Houston v. United States*, 25 Cl. Ct. 110, *aff'd*, 981 F.2d 531 (Fed. Cir. 1992).

The fact that the judges hearing the case disagree about the meaning of the contract language does not necessarily demonstrate that there is an ambiguity. See *SCM Corp. v. United States*, 230 Ct. Cl. 199, 675 F.2d 280 (1982), in which the majority of the court found that the contract language had a single clear meaning, while a dissenting judge found a different clear meaning. The judges appeared to agree that there was no ambiguity in these circumstances. The same result was reached in *Norflor Constr. Corp.*, ASBCA 31577, 89-1 BCA ¶ 21,265, *recons. denied*, 90-1 BCA ¶ 22,277, where three judges found the contractor's interpretation unreasonable and two dissenting judges found it reasonable. On motion for reconsideration, the board rejected the contractor's argument that this disagreement among the judges proved that the language was ambiguous. For similar cases, see *Midwest Found. Corp.*, ENGBCA 5762, 93-1 BCA ¶ 25,380, and *Brantley Constr. Co.*, ASBCA 40002, 92-2 BCA ¶ 24,792.

B. Interpretation Against the Drafter

Unless the nondrafting party knew or should have known of an ambiguity, the risk of ambiguities in contract language is generally allocated to the party responsible for drafting the contract document. See *Sofarelli Assocs., Inc. v. United States*, 1 Cl. Ct. 241 (1982), and *B.B. Andersen Constr. Co. v. United States*, 1 Cl. Ct. 169 (1983). *Restatement, Second, Contracts* § 206 provides:

> In choosing among the reasonable meanings of a promise or agreement or a term thereof, that meaning is generally preferred which operates against the party who supplies the words or from whom a writing otherwise proceeds.

A basic rationale for *contra proferentem* was stated in *Peter Kiewit Sons' Co. v. United States*, 109 Ct. Cl. 390 (1947), at 418:

> Where the Government draws specifications which are fairly susceptible of a certain construction and the contractor actually and reasonably so construes them, justice and equity require that construction be adopted. Where one of the parties to a contract draws the document and uses therein language which is susceptible of more than one meaning, and the intention of the parties does not otherwise appear, that meaning will be given the document which is more favorable to the party who did not draw it. This rule is especially applicable to Government contracts where the contractor has nothing to say as to its provisions.

The court in *Gorn Corp. v. United States*, 191 Ct. Cl. 560, 424 F.2d 588 (1970), noted at 566:

> A contractor should not be required to wade through a maze of numbers, catalogues, cross-reference tables and other data resembling cross-word puzzles in order to find out what the government requires in an invitation for bids. This is especially true where, as in this case, the requirements of the government could have been clearly specified by the use of a half dozen ordinary words and figures. There would have been nothing complicated in a plain and simple statement by the government in the invitation for bids that it required "115 volt alternating current switches." If this had been done, this lawsuit could have been avoided.

See also *Sturm v. United States*, 190 Ct. Cl. 691, 421 F.2d 723 (1970), stating at 697:

> [*Contra proferentem*] puts the risk of ambiguity, lack of clarity, and absence of proper warning on the drafting party which could have forestalled the controversy; it pushes the drafters toward improving contractual forms; and it saves contractors from hidden traps not of their own making.

1. Reasonable Interpretation

Contra proferentem is a means of choosing among conflicting, reasonable, actual interpretations. Thus, each party must show that its interpretation falls within the zone of reasonableness before the rule will be applied against the drafter. See *WPC Enters., Inc. v. United States*, 163 Ct. Cl. 1, 323 F.2d 874 (1963), in which the court stated at 5-6:

> This summary of the opposing contentions is enough to show that no sure guide to the solution of the problem can be found within the four corners of the contractual documents. As with so many other agreements, there is something for each party and no ready answer can be drawn from the texts alone. Both [the contractor's] and [the government's] interpretations lie within the zone of reasonableness; neither appears to rest on an obvious error in drafting, a gross discrepancy, or an inadvertent but glaring gap; the arguments, rather, are quite closely in balance. It is precisely to this type of contract that this court has applied the rule that if some substantive provision of a government-drawn agreement is fairly susceptible of a certain construction and the contractor actually and reasonably so construes it, in the course of bidding or performance, that is the interpretation which will be adopted—unless the parties' intention is otherwise affirmatively revealed.

In *Folk Constr. Co. v. United States*, 2 Cl. Ct. 681 (1983), contract clauses did not explicitly or by clear implication prohibit the contractor's interpretation. Hence, the documents were strictly construed against the government [drafter]. When the government refused to deliver books to the highest bidder at a public auction, claiming the auctioneer acted outside the scope of his authority, the court in *Rapp v. United States*, 2 Cl. Ct. 694 (1983), stated at 698:

> Where, as here, a public announcement is involved, its terms must be construed as they would have been understood by a member of the public. The court concludes that those attending the auction would not have perceived the fine distinction pressed here by the government but would have read paragraph 6 of the Conditions of Sale as authorizing the auctioneer to make the announcement permitting delayed payment.

The reasonableness of a contractor's proffered interpretation may be proved by showing that other bidders adopted the same interpretation, *Eagle Paving*, AGBCA 75-156, 78-1 BCA ¶ 13,107 (affidavits from two other bidders), and *Watson Elec. Constr. Co.*, GSBCA 4260, 76-1 BCA ¶ 11,912 (testimony of three other bidders); or disproved by other bidders' contrary interpretation, *Community Heating & Plumbing Co. v. Kelso*, 987 F.2d 1575 (Fed. Cir. 1993); *Daniel H. Foster, Jr.*, ASBCA 21965, 78-2 BCA ¶ 13,541, *recons. denied*, 79-2 BCA ¶ 14,161 (no bidders on mechanical portion of the contract other than the contractor interpreted the contract as did the contractor); *Byrd Tractor, Inc.*, Comp. Gen. Dec. B-212449, 83-2 CPD ¶ 677 (seven bidders, including the four low bidders, offered general purpose tractors, not industrial, as the contractor contended the IFB required).

Government interpretations that are patently unfair have been rejected as unreasonable. See *Souter Constr. Co.*, ENGBCA 5701, 93-3 BCA ¶ 26,175, rejecting a government interpretation because it placed an unforeseen risk on the contractor. The government had argued that the contract required the contractor to continue working for an unlimited distance depending on the circumstances. The board rejected this interpretation, stating that such a requirement would be unconscionable. Similarly, in *M.A. Mortenson Co.*, ASBCA 39978, 93-3 BCA ¶ 26,189, the board rejected the government's proffered interpretation that estimated quantities in a design/build contract were not to be used in computing the prices of the construction. The board viewed this interpretation as unreasonable because it would require the contractor to assume a large risk with no reasonable way of including it in its price. See also *Meridith Constr. Co.*, ASBCA 41736, 93-2 BCA ¶ 25,864, in which the board found that a government interpretation was unreasonable because it called for work at the job site to remove surface imperfections on steel when the government had elected to delete the part of the standard specification calling for the steel fabricator to remove such imperfections. The board concluded that, since the government had elected to save the substantial costs of removing the imperfections in the fabrication process, it would be patently unfair to interpret other specifications as calling for such work.

The nondrafting party's interpretation need not be preferable but only within the zone of reasonableness, *City Elec., Inc.*, ASBCA 24565, 82-2 BCA ¶ 16,057. Hence, even though the drafter's interpretation is more reasonable than the nondrafting party's, the latter prevails. See *Swinerton & Walberg Co.*, ASBCA 18925, 75-1 BCA ¶ 11,052, in which the board stated at 52,592:

> In truth we believe that [the government's] interpretation is the best and preferred one but that is not the test. If there are two reasonable interpretations, as we have found that there were here, [the contractor's] interpretation will be accepted and the contract construed against the drafter.

This rule has been followed in *Big Chief Drilling Co. v. United States*, 26 Cl. Ct. 1276 (1992), and *Holmes & Narver Servs., Inc./Morrison-Knudsen Co., A Joint Venture*, ASBCA 42871, 93-1 BCA ¶ 25,467. See *Beta Constr. Co. v. United States*, 39 Fed. Cl. 722 (1997), *rev'd*, 185 F.3d 884 (Fed. Cir. 1999), in which the trial court found that there was a latent ambiguity but that the contractor's interpretation was not reasonable. The Federal Circuit reversed, agreeing that the ambiguity was latent and finding the contractor's interpretation reasonable.

2. *Identifiable Drafter*

Another requirement for application of *contra proferentem* is an identifiable drafter (to be distinguished from a mere scrivener) of the disputed contract or bid language. In any case, before interpreting a contract *contra proferentem,* it must be clear to the court that the form of expression in words was actually chosen by one party rather than the other, 3 *Corbin on Contracts* § 559 at 266 (1960). In government contracts cases, the method of procurement used is a major factor in determining the drafter. The regulations governing sealed bidding in effect require the government to draft the contract document. Thus, in the absence of contrary evidence, the courts and boards generally assume, without discussion, that the government is responsible for the language in sealed bid contracts.

Because of the government-contractor interactions possible in negotiated procurement, a more detailed analysis is required to determine which party was the drafter of a negotiated contract. In certain cases, the government is clearly the drafter of ambiguous provisions such that there is no substantive difference between the negotiation process and sealed bidding. See, for example, *J.W. Bateson Co. v. United States*, 196 Ct. Cl. 531, 450 F.2d 896 (1971) (government drafted specifications incorporated into negotiated amendment), and *B.F. Goodrich Co. v. United States*, 185 Ct. Cl. 14, 398 F.2d 843 (1968) (government drafted Value Engineering clause used in negotiated contract interpreted against the government regarding contractor's proposed variations under the clause).

Contra proferentem will generally be inapplicable where there have been extensive negotiations between the parties. In *Deloro Smelting & Ref. Co. v. United States*, 161 Ct. Cl. 489, 317 F.2d 382 (1963), when the contractor failed to meet the established delivery schedule, a dispute arose as to whether date of delivery in the escalation clause referred to the date of actual delivery or the scheduled date of delivery. The court found the language ambiguous but refused to attribute it to either party. The court stated at 495:

> In its pertinent articles, this was not a standard-form agreement but an ad hoc arrangement negotiated by the parties for a special situation. The record contains no enlightening information on comparable escalation or adjustment provisions. We cannot charge the [government] with any ambiguities since [the contractor] appears to have initially proposed the terms which are now disputed; but there was also considerable negotiation and [the contractor] does not seem to be so much the author that it should bear, on that account, the brunt of uncertainties.

See also *Cray Research, Inc. v. United States*, 44 Fed. Cl. 327 (1999), holding that the rule of *contra proferentem* was not applicable even though a government employee drafted a modification because the terms of the modification were negotiated. Similarly, in *Tulelake Irrigation Dist. v. United States*, 169 Ct. Cl. 782, 342 F.2d 447 (1965), the court refused to construe the language of an interagency contract drafted completely by the government against the government because it was incorporated into a negotiated contract, which could have been modified at the time of the negotiation. The same result will occur in a situation where each party had contributed ambiguous language to the contract under dispute, *Randallstown Plaza Assocs. v. United States*, 13 Cl. Ct. 703 (1987).

In a limited number of cases, *contra proferentem* has been applied against the contractor. This normally occurs where a communication from the contractor proposing a modification or additional terms is accepted by the government and incorporated into the contract unchanged. See *Canadian Commercial Corp. v. United States*, 202 Ct. Cl. 65 (1973) (contractor-drafted clause regarding proprietary rights of tendered information was reasonably interpreted by the government to be inapplicable to contractor-submitted drawings, such that government interpretation prevailed), and *S.S. Mullen, Inc.*, ASBCA 8808, 1964 BCA ¶ 4449 (contractor-submitted contract modification regarding tower demolition was accepted by the government and ambiguous portions were construed against the contractor, whose interpretation was deemed unreasonable in light of its experience and knowledge). See also *Thanet Corp. v. United States*, 219 Ct. Cl. 75, 591 F.2d 629 (1979), where the original offer was drafted and submitted to the government by the contractor. In such cases, the government must meet the additional requirements of seeking clarification and reliance, discussed below, *Barry L. Miller Eng'g, Inc.*, ASBCA 20554, 75-2 BCA ¶ 11,567; *Sanders Int'l Ventures, Ltd.*, ASBCA 38504, 91-3 BCA ¶ 24,295.

Contra proferentem was first applied against the government and then against the contractor in *Eugene Iovine, Inc.*, DOTCAB 1188, 83-1 BCA ¶ 16,206, *vacated for lack of certification*, 727 F.2d 1120 (Fed. Cir. 1983). Under a contract to replace underground feeder cables, specifications were ambiguous regarding contractor requirements during the replacement period. In this respect *contra proferentem* applied against the government, as stated at 80,523:

> It is beyond question that it is the obligation of an owner who is preparing and issuing a specification for construction to clearly state both what work the successful contractor is to perform and, if the owner elects to prescribe or proscribe any of several possible approaches, to clearly state how it is to be performed.

However, noting a possible contractor mistake, the government sought clarification-verification from the contractor, which responded, "[w]e shall provide what you want in accordance with the plans and specifications." The board applied the *contra proferentem* rule against the contractor for its ambiguous reply, which, the board found, the government reasonably concluded implied compliance with the government-enunciated interpretation.

Contra proferentem has been cited by GAO in holding that construing the bid against the bidder would permit the acceptance of what appeared to be an ambiguous bid, Comp. Gen. Dec. B-161336, June 23, 1967, *Unpub.*; 39 Comp. Gen. 546 (B-141786) (1960). The GAO found in both of these cases that the resulting interpretation was actually the same as the bidder's. Contrast *Kerite Co.*, Comp. Gen. Dec. B-212206, 83-2 CPD ¶ 198, which noted that an ambiguous bid must be rejected as nonresponsive. The common law rule that a party's interpretation will not be accepted if that party, prior to contract formation, knew or had reason to know that the other party attached a different meaning to the contract, would appear to preclude the government from knowingly awarding a contract on the basis of an ambiguous bid and then attempting to impose its interpretation on the contractor. See *Restatement, Second, Contracts* §§ 200, 201. The GAO has noted that in negotiated procurements, as a basis for contract award, *contra proferentem* is not to be applied against the offeror to clarify an ambiguous offer. A contrary rule would thwart the ambiguity-clarifying purpose of oral or written discussions, *PRC Info. Sciences Co.*, 56 Comp. Gen. 768 (B-188305), 77-2 CPD ¶ 11.

3. Reliance

The nondrafting party seeking to have its interpretation prevail through application of *contra proferentem* must demonstrate that it relied on its interpretation during preparation of its offer, *T. Brown Constructors, Inc. v. Pena*, 132 F.3d 724 (Fed. Cir. 1997). See *Randolph Eng'g Co. v. United States*, 176 Ct. Cl. 872, 367 F.2d 425 (1966) (the contractor's interpretation of a government-drawn agreement will be adopted if the contractor actually and reasonably relied on that interpretation when it entered into the contract); and *Nash Janitorial Serv., Inc.*, GSBCA 7338, 88-2 BCA ¶ 20,809 (an essential element of success on a contract interpretation question is proof of contractor reliance on its interpretation at the time it entered into the contract). This requirement is apparently intended to prevent the contractor from taking advantage of a latent ambiguity discovered after a dispute arises. The rule applies only when the contractor seeks to have the case resolved by interpretation against the drafter of the disputed language. Thus, if the contractor can show that its interpretation is the only reasonable interpretation, it has no need of demonstrating that it relied on that interpretation at the time of bidding, *Meridith Constr. Co.*, ASBCA 41736, 93-2 BCA ¶ 25,864.

Reliance during performance will not satisfy the requirement, *Fruin-Colnon Corp. v. United States*, 912 F.2d 1426 (Fed. Cir. 1990). In that case, the court denied a claim submitted on behalf of a subcontractor that had begun performance in accordance with a reasonable interpretation but could not demonstrate that it had bid the contract following the interpretation. The court declined to follow prior cases that had stated that reliance during performance would be sufficient to meet the requirement. Among these cases are *Framlau Corp. v. United States*, 215 Ct. Cl. 185, 568 F.2d 687 (1977), and *Winfield Mfg. Co.*, ASBCA 20482, 78-2 BCA ¶ 13,487. In some cases, this rule has resulted in a very unfair result. See, for example, *Lear Siegler Mgmt. Servs. Corp. v. United States*, 867 F.2d 600 (Fed. Cir. 1989), where the contractor apparently bid the job based on its prior performance of similar work for the agency without making a detailed estimate of the costs of performance. The court held that the contractor could not recover on the basis of its reasonable interpretation of an ambiguous specification drafted by the government because its interpretation was arrived at during performance. The contractor was therefore required to perform in accordance with the government's interpretation at a cost significantly in excess of the amount it had bid for the work. See also *Santa Fe Eng'rs, Inc.*, ASBCA 32448, 89-3 BCA ¶ 22,024, where the contractor lost its claim for lack of reliance when it had bid nothing for the work (believing that no work was required). The board held that this interpretation was unreasonable and that the later interpretation arrived at during performance failed for lack of reliance. The contractor was therefore required to perform to the government's higher-priced interpretation.

Reliance must be proved by clear, affirmative evidence, *Craft Mach. Works, Inc. v. United States*, 20 Cl. Ct. 355 (1990), *rev'd on other grounds*, 926 F.2d 1110 (Fed. Cir. 1991). Thus, contractors that present no evidence of reliance automatically lose their claims, *Moreland Corp.*, VABCA 5409, 00-1 BCA ¶ 30,640; *Santa Fe Eng'rs, Inc.*, ASBCA 24720, 92-2 BCA ¶ 24,996; *D.E.W., Inc.*, ASBCA 35172, 92-1 BCA ¶ 24,548, *recons. denied*, 93-1 BCA ¶ 25,526. Generally, reliance is difficult to prove without submission of the bid documents showing that the bid price was calculated using the proffered interpretation, *MCSD Constr. Co.*, ASBCA 37226, 91-2 BCA ¶ 23,986; *M.A. Mortenson Co.*, ASBCA 37115, 89-1 BCA ¶ 21,330. However, an affidavit of the person preparing the bid has been accepted as satisfactory proof of reliance, *Ogden Allied Servs. Corp.*, ASBCA 40823, 91-1 BCA ¶ 23,455. Compare *Malloy Constr. Co.*, ASBCA 25055, 82-2 BCA ¶ 16,104, in which the board rejected testimony on reliance without documentary evidence to support it. In earlier cases, the proof requirement was less stringent. See *Quiller Constr. Co.*, ASBCA 22556, 80-1 BCA ¶ 14,427, in which the board held that reliance did not have to be proved by establishing a specific amount included in the bid, stating at 71,127:

> The rule requiring contractor reliance . . . on its interpretation of a disputed term does not require a mathematical link between that interpretation and a particular amount in the bid. See *Dale Ingram, Inc. v. United States*, 201 Ct. Cl. 56, 72, 475 F.2d 1177, 1185 (1973), and cases cited therein. There are many factors which go into bidding decisions which cannot be shown to have affected the bid by any specific amount, but which nevertheless may influence the contractor as to either the total amount bid, bidding strategy or the decision to submit a bid.

When the work under dispute is being performed by a subcontractor, the contractor must prove reliance of both itself and its subcontractor. See *Froeschle Sons, Inc. v. United States*, 891 F.2d 270 (Fed. Cir. 1989), in which the court accepted proof that the subcontractor had bid based on its proffered interpretation and the contractor had used the subcontractor's bid in preparing its bid. For cases in which reliance was not proved because the contractor could not show that the subcontractor followed the proffered interpretation in its bid, see *L.D. Docsa Assocs., Inc.*, ASBCA 45267, 93-3 BCA ¶ 26,066, and *J.W. Bateson Co.*, VABCA 3460, 93-2 BCA ¶ 25,819. For cases in which the contractor proved reliance by the subcontractor but lost because it could not prove that it used the subcontractor's bid in preparing its bid, see *Intermax, Ltd.*, ASBCA 41828, 93-2 BCA ¶ 25,699, and *R.B. Hazard, Inc.*, ASBCA 41295, 93-2 BCA ¶ 25,577. Two cases seem to impose an even more stringent rule that the contractor must prove that both it and its subcontractor relied on the proffered interpretation during the preparation of the bid, *J.W. Bateson Co.*, VABCA 3482, 93-3 BCA ¶ 26,115; *Brantley Constr. Co.*, ASBCA 43828, 93-1 BCA ¶ 25,370. This would appear to be beyond the level of proof required by the Federal Circuit.

C. Duty to Seek Clarification

Even though a nondrafting party may otherwise be able to establish the reasonableness of its interpretation, *contra proferentem* will not be applied if the nondrafting party fails before bidding to seek clarification of an ambiguity of which it *was or should have* been aware. By failing to inquire, the contractor forfeits the opportunity to rely on its unilateral, uninformed interpretation and bears the risk of misinterpretation, *Triax Pac., Inc. v. West*, 130 F.3d 1469 (Fed. Cir. 1997); *Nielsen-Dillingham Builders, J.V. v. United States*, 43 Fed. Cl. 5 (1999). The Court of Claims explained this rule in *S.O.G. of Ark. v. United States*, 212 Ct. Cl. 125, 546 F.2d 367 (1976), at 131:

> The rule that a contractor, before bidding, should attempt to have the Government resolve a patent ambiguity in the contract's terms is a major device of preventive hygiene; it is designed to avoid just such post-award disputes as this by encouraging contractors to seek clarification before anyone is legally bound. The rule is the counterpart of the canon in government procurement that an ambiguous contract, *where the ambiguity is not open or glaring*, is read against the Government (if it is the author). See *Sturm v. United States*, 190 Ct. Cl. 691, 697, 421 F.2d 723, 727 (1970). Both rules have their place and their function. In addition to its role in obviating unnecessary disputes, the patent-ambiguity principle advances the goal of informed bidding and works toward putting all the bidders on an equal plane of understanding so that the bids are more likely to be truly comparable. Conversely, the principle also tends to deter a bidder, who knows (or should know) of a serious problem in interpretation, from consciously taking the award with a lower bid (based on the less costly reading) with the expectation that he will then be able to cry "change" or "extra" if the procuring officials take the other view after the contract is made (emphasis added).

The Court of Claims described the situations to which this rule applies as those where there is an obvious error in drafting, a gross discrepancy, or an inadvertent but glaring gap, *WPC Enters., Inc. v. United States*, 163 Ct. Cl. 1, 323 F.2d 874 (1963). See *Blount Bros. Constr. Co. v. United States*, 171 Ct. Cl. 478, 346 F.2d 962 (1965), stating at 496-97:

> [C]ontractors are businessmen, and in the business of bidding on Government contracts they are usually pressed for time and are consciously seeking to underbid a number of competitors. Consequently, they estimate only on those costs which they feel the contract terms will permit the Government to insist upon in the way of performance. They are obligated to bring to the Government's attention major discrepancies or errors which they detect in the specifications or drawings, or else fail to do so at their peril. But they are not expected to exercise clairvoyance in spotting hidden ambiguities in the bid documents, and they are protected if they innocently construe in their own favor an ambiguity equally susceptible to another construction, for as in *Peter Kiewit Sons' Co. v. United States*, 109 Ct. Cl. 390, 418 (1947), the basic precept is that ambiguities in contracts drawn by the Government are construed against the drafter. In the case before us the ambiguity was subtle, not blatant; the contractor was genuinely misled and not deliberately seeking to profit from a recognized error by the Government.

Thus, minor ambiguities not foreseen by the contractor at the time of bidding are not within the rule.

Actual failure to recognize an obvious ambiguity does not excuse the contractor from its duty to seek clarification. See, for example, *J.A. Jones Constr. Co. v. United States*, 184 Ct. Cl. 1, 395 F.2d 783 (1968), where the contractor noted discrepancies in specifications only immediately before it commenced performance. However, the duty to inquire arose because the discrepancies were present from the start of solicitation and of a type of which the contractor should have been aware. See also *Chris Berg, Inc. v. United States*, 197 Ct. Cl. 503, 455 F.2d 1037 (1972), in which the court enunciated the rule at 515: "We need not go on to establish if [the contractor] actually knew of the obvious conflict, since it is not the actual knowledge of the contractor, but the obviousness of the discrepancy which imposes the duty of inquiry."

There is no duty to seek clarification when an amendment conflicts with the original solicitation and the contractor follows the language of the amendment, *Gibson Hart Co.*, VABCA 2847, 89-2 BCA ¶ 21,830. The board found that it was reasonable to assume that the later guidance in the amendment was controlling.

In one case, the Court of Claims stated that the duty to request clarification is the overriding consideration in the contract interpretation process. Thus, in contrast to the description of the process in this chapter, the court described consideration of this issue as the first step in the process. See *Newsom v. United States*, 230 Ct. Cl. 301, 676 F.2d 647 (1982), stating at 304:

> First, the court must ask whether the ambiguity was patent. This is not a simple yes-no proposition but involves placing the contractual language at a point along a spectrum: Is it so glaring as to raise a duty to inquire? Only if the court decides that the ambiguity was not patent does it reach the question whether a [contractor's] interpretation was reasonable. The existence of a patent ambiguity in itself raises the duty of inquiry, regardless of the reasonableness vel non of the contractor's interpretation. It is crucial to bear in mind this analytical framework. The court may not consider the reasonableness of the contractor's interpretation, if at all, until it has determined that a patent ambiguity did not exist.

This reasoning has been followed by a number of judges in the courts and boards. See, for example, *PCL Constr. Servs., Inc. v. United States*, 47 Fed. Cl. 745 (2000); *ITT Fed. Servs. Corp. v. United States*, 45 Fed. Cl. 174 (1999); *W. B. Meredith II, Inc.*, ASBCA 53590, 03-1 BCA ¶ 32,166; *Sociotechnical Research Applications, Inc.*, IBCA 3969-98, 01-1 BCA ¶ 31,235; and *Lockheed Martin Tactical Def. Sys., Inc.*, ASBCA 46797, 00-2 BCA ¶ 30,919.

1. Establishing a Patent Ambiguity

The determination of whether an ambiguity is patent (or obvious) is made on a case-by-case basis because it is dependent on an analysis of the specific facts of each contractual situation. *Interstate Gen. Gov't Contractors v. Stone*, 980 F.2d 1433 (Fed. Cir. 1992); *H.B. Zachry Co. v. United States*, 28 Fed. Cl. 77 (1993), *aff'd without opinion*, 17 F.3d 1443 (Fed. Cir. 1994). See *Max Drill, Inc. v. United States*, 192 Ct. Cl. 608, 427 F.2d 1233 (1970), stating at 626: "What constitutes the type of omission sufficient to put [a contractor] under obligation to make inquiries cannot be defined generally, but on an ad hoc basis of looking to what a reasonable man would find to be patent and glaring."

Thus, interpretations arrived at following complex after-the-fact analyses will not be persuasive. See *Gorn Corp. v. United States*, 191 Ct. Cl. 560, 424 F.2d 588 (1970), stating at 566:

> We suspect that the Government attorneys themselves used hindsight and devoted many hours of Monday morning quarterbacking to come up with their circuitous cross-checking solutions.

The board in *Transco Contracting Co.*, ASBCA 25315, 82-1 BCA ¶ 15,516, noted at 76,974 that the most critical factor in deciding cases regarding the duty to inquire is the degree of scrutiny reasonably required of a bidder in order to perceive the discrepancy between contract provisions or omissions in the solicitation documents. Generally, the court or board will consider the question from the same objective point of view used to consider questions of interpretation. See, for example, *Blount Bros. Constr. Co. v. United States*, 171 Ct. Cl. 478, 346 F.2d 962 (1965), in which the court stated at 496-97:

> [C]ontractors are businessmen, and in the business of bidding on Government contracts they are usually pressed for time and are consciously seeking to underbid a number of competitors. Consequently, they estimate only on those costs which they feel the contract terms will permit the Government to insist upon in the way of performance. They are obligated to bring to the Government's attention major discrepancies or errors which they detect in the specifications or drawings, or else fail to do so at their peril. But they are not expected to exercise clairvoyance in spotting hidden ambiguities in the bid documents, and they are protected if they innocently construe in their own favor an ambiguity equally susceptible to another construction . . .

Elements to consider when determining if ambiguities create a duty to inquire were set forth in *George Hyman Constr. Co.*, ENGBCA 4653, 83-1 BCA ¶ 16,283, at 80,899:

> (1) The knowledge of the contractor with respect to the possibility of multiple interpretations of the ambiguity; (2) whether the contractor was a knowledgeable bidder; (3) whether the ambiguity was subtle or insignificant; and (4) whether the contractor acted without trying to resolve the ambiguity.

Thus, under a subway station construction contract, the absence of the typical requirement for certain precast concrete panels, combined with the apparent requirement for some form of panel, where no additional information existed for the contractor to conclude that a panel different from that generally used was required, indicated a patent ambiguity.

In determining whether ambiguities were obvious during bidding, boards and courts may simply view the elements of the bid package and contracts bearing on the dispute to determine that a reasonable bidder would have seen the ambiguity. See *P.R. Burke Corp. v. United States*, 277 F.3d 1346 (Fed. Cir. 2002) (contractor's interpretation was inconsistent with conspicuous contract provision); *Hunt Constr. Group v. United States*, 281 F.3d 1369 (Fed. Cir. 2002) (court finds three relatively obscure clauses on state and local taxes unambiguous); *Lee Lewis Constr., Inc. v. United States*, 54 Fed. Cl. 88 (2002) (no ambiguity after reading the "plain and ordinary" meaning of contract language); *Pete Vicari Gen. Contractor, Inc. v. United States*, 51 Fed. Cl. 161 (2001) (no ambiguity because no facial inconsistency in contract language); *GPA-I, LP v. United States*, 46 Fed. Cl. 762 (2000) (contractor's interpretation unreasonable because it doesn't use all words of contract); *Nielsen-Dillingham Builders, J.V. v. United States*, 43 Fed. Cl. 5 (1999) (facially inconsistent provisions result in patent ambiguity); *Triax Pacific, Inc. v. West*, 130 F.3d 1469 (Fed. Cir. 1997) (conflict in specification requirements "immediately apparent"); *Conner Bros. Constr. Co.*, VABCA 2519, 95-2 BCA ¶ 27,910, *aff'd*, 113 F.3d 1256 (Fed. Cir. 1997) (clear conflict between drawings and specifications); *Emerald Isle Elec., Inc. v. United States*, 28 Fed. Cl. 71 (1993) (obvious inconsistencies in contract language); *Newsom v. United States*, 230 Ct. Cl. 301, 676 F.2d 647 (1982) (two parts of the contract said very different things); *Sturm Craft Co.*, ASBCA 37856, 90-1 BCA ¶ 22,620 (clear conflict between drawing legend and accompanying note);

Coastate Assocs., VABCA 1701, 83-1 BCA ¶ 16,314 (omission of exterior ducts from contract drawings was patently obvious); *Pettinaro Constr. Co.*, DOTCAB 1257, 83-1 BCA ¶ 16,536 (any inconsistency was apparent upon review of a single IFB amendment, and was in fact so obvious that the supplier admitted to being confused); *Bromley Contracting Co.*, HUDBCA 81-624-C30, 83-1 BCA ¶ 16,466 (contractor's bid package was missing one page, which included a description of installation procedures for repairs as well as a drawing illustrating the placement and shape of certain repair work; this absence rendered the contract all but meaningless, such that a patent ambiguity existed); *Blake Constr. Co.*, ENGBCA 4594, 83-2 BCA ¶ 16,632 (whether finish contractor of subway construction contract was responsible for installing emergency exit stairs was patently ambiguous when drawings and notations were considered); *Walsky Constr. Co.*, ASBCA 27099, 83-2 BCA ¶ 16,771 (contractor assumed risk by not inquiring into meaning of sash screen where it had no prior knowledge of the term and the term's meaning according to the standard industry definitions was not compatible with other portions of the specifications); and *Assurance Co.*, ASBCA 25254, 83-2 BCA ¶ 16,908 (phrase "[e]xisting sinks may or may not be replaced" held to be patently ambiguous since drawing notations clearly called for replacement). In one case, the court found no patent ambiguity even though the contractor's interpretation was so disadvantageous to the government that it was highly unlikely that the government intended that interpretation, *HPI/GSA-3C, LLC v. Perry*, 364 F.3d 1327 (Fed. Cir. 2004).

It is not uncommon for judges to perform a detailed analysis of the contract documents and come to a different conclusion as to whether the ambiguity is latent or patent. See *Dalton v. Cessna Aircraft Co.*, 98 F.3d 1298 (Fed. Cir. 1996), reversing a board decision finding the contractor's interpretation correct because the contractor should have seen that its interpretation created a patent ambiguity. A dissenting judge criticized the decision for finding an ambiguity based on the government's "litigation-induced" interpretation that conflicted with the actions of the government during contract performance. See also *Jowett v. United States*, No. 98-641C (Fed. Cl. 2000), *rev'd*, 29 Fed. Appx. 584 (Fed. Cir. 2002), in which the trial judge found that an ambiguity was latent but the Federal Circuit reversed, holding that the ambiguity was patent, and *Hoffman Constr. Co. of Or. v. United States*, 40 Fed. Cl. 184 (1998), *rev'd*, 178 F.3d 1313 (Fed. Cir. 1999), in which the trial judge found a patent ambiguity but the Federal Circuit reversed, finding that there was no ambiguity because the contractor's interpretation was correct. Similarly, in *A.S. McGaughan Co. v. General Servs. Admin.*, GSBCA 13367, 96-1 BCA ¶ 28,261, *rev'd*, 113 F.3d 1256 (Fed. Cir. 1997), the court reversed a board judge's finding that an ambiguity was patent, holding that the contractor could not have reasonably seen the government's "strained" but reasonable interpretation. The court interpreted a drawing requirement labeled "suggested" and "for design intent only" as giving the contractor flexibility in meeting the requirement.

Boards and courts have used objective criteria in determining obviousness, with none to receive controlling weight but each to be a possible factor. Often noted is the ratio of the contractor-sought recovery to the total contract price. When the ratio is low, the interpretive problem may be found to be of the type that could escape notice during the estimating period, *L.B. Samford, Inc.*, ASBCA 19138, 76-1 BCA ¶ 11,684. In *Gelco Builders v. United States*, 177 Ct. Cl. 1025, 369 F.2d 992 (1966), a duty to seek clarification was found in a $2.2 million contract when the contractor sought to delete $385,000 of work without any regard to what meaning was then to be given to the sentence. In *Transco Contracting Co.*, ASBCA 25315, 82-1 BCA ¶ 15,516, the omission of a clause that had a significant cost and control impact on project performance triggered the duty to inquire. The interpretation involved a $277,000 claim under a $2.7 million contract. In *Mountain Home Contractors v. United States*, 192 Ct. Cl. 16, 425 F.2d 1260 (1970), the court found no duty to inquire when the claim was $19,764 on a contract price of $4,918,600, noting that "[a]lthough this is certainly not the sole determinative factor in leading us to our conclusion, it is illustrative of the overall unimportance of this one item, which is less than half of one percent of the total contract price." In *NAB-Lord Assocs.*, PSBCA 190, 78-1 BCA ¶ 12,976, the board found that, given the difference between the magnitude of the electrical subcontract price ($12.8 million) and the contractor's claim for circuit breakers ($56,000), the ambiguity was insignificant. See, however, *Gall Landau Young Constr. Co.*, ASBCA 21549, 77-1 BCA ¶ 12,515, which stated that the insignificance of the contractor's claim ($5,883) in comparison to the contract price ($1,086,000) was not determinative where, from examining the specifications and drawings together, it was clear that there was an obvious omission in the specifications about which the contractor had a duty to seek clarification.

A second objective factor is the conduct of all of the bidders on the contract during the bidding period. See *Gaston & Assocs., Inc. v. United States*, 27 Fed. Cl. 243 (1992) (only one of seven bidders requested clarification, and government did not amend solicitation in response to request); *L.B. Samford, Inc.*, ASBCA 19138, 76-1 BCA ¶ 11,684 (seven firms bid on the procurement with no protest or inquiry concerning the interpretive problem in dispute); *Tennessee Valley Serv. Co.*, ASBCA 22822, 79-1 BCA ¶ 13,579 (no other bidder requested clarification); and *W.M. Schlosser Co.*, VABCA 1802, 83-2 BCA ¶ 16,630 (government offered no testimony to indicate other bidders interpreted contract differently from contractor or that other bidders made preaward inquiry).

When the price-ratio factor and the other-bidders factor are in conflict, the other-bidders factor has been considered more persuasive. See *Stroh Corp. v. General Servs. Admin.*, GSBCA 11029, 93-2 BCA ¶ 25,841 (latent ambiguity where other bidders did not seek clarification of language that ultimately led to a claim of $151,734 on a $676,000 contract), and *Texas Painter Craft, Inc.*, ASBCA 34520, 91-1 BCA ¶ 23,304 (latent ambiguity where three bidders did not seek clarification on claim constituting 7 percent of the contract price). Of course, when both factors are in the contractor's favor, there is a high likelihood that the ambiguity will be held to be latent, *Robert L. Guyler*, ASBCA 20371, 76-1 BCA ¶ 11,690 (five of six bidders failed to discover a conflict that existed in the solicitation, and the added costs of $20,197 were small compared to a total contract price of $2,995,675); *Wick Constr. Co.*, ASBCA 35378, 89-1 BCA ¶ 21,239 (no bidder requested clarification and claim was for less than 1 percent of contract price).

Another factor that is considered is the failure of government personnel to discover the ambiguity. See *Carl Garris & Son, Inc. v. United States*, 918 F.2d 187 (Fed. Cir. 1990), *rev'g*, ASBCA 36614, 90-2 BCA ¶ 22,655, holding that an ambiguity was latent because the architect and the contracting officer perceived no ambiguity and a request for clarification from another bidder was answered with a statement that it should read the contract. Similarly in *Robert L. Guyler Co.*, ASBCA 20371, 76-1 BCA ¶ 11,690, the failure of government engineers to discover the problem when reviewing specifications drawn by an independent firm was held to demonstrate that the ambiguity was latent. See also *Foothill Eng'g*, IBCA 3119-A, 94-2 BCA ¶ 26,732, suggesting that the government should be held to a stringent test when it alleges that ambiguities are patent even though it did not identify them in drafting the contract.

Other objective factors that have been considered include the importance of the disputed work to the entire contract requirements, *L.B. Samford, Inc.*, ASBCA 19138, 76-1 BCA ¶ 11,684; that several credible witnesses arrived at differing reasonable interpretations, *J.W. Bateson Co.*, VABCA 3460, 93-2 BCA ¶ 25,819; and that the contractor did not gain anything of consequence as a result of its interpretation, *Kraus v. United States*, 177 Ct. Cl. 108, 366 F.2d 975 (1966). In *Kraus*, the contract contained ambiguous specifications regarding strap length. However, no evidence demonstrated that the contractor would have materially gained from its interpretation, which led to the production of shorter straps, where the contractor received its material from a supplier and had the government inspector approve the strap length. In *Whalen & Co.*, IBCA 1034-5-74, 75-2 BCA ¶ 11,377, the board considered the fact that the contract had been awarded on a small business set-aside, stating at 54,152, "[w]e think the Government's contention requires more sophistication than can reasonably be required of small business concerns for which this project was set aside."

If the ambiguity is actually known to the contractor at the time of bidding, it will be held to be patent no matter how small, *James A. Mann, Inc. v. United States*, 210 Ct. Cl. 104, 535 F.2d 51 (1976). See *General Elevator Co.*, VABCA 3666, 93-2 BCA ¶ 25,685 (contractor bid based on interpretation in conflict with government answer at pre-bid conference); *Tom Shaw, Inc.*, DOTBCA 2109, 90-2 BCA ¶ 22,861 (contractor included ambiguity on list of potential problems); *A.F. Lusi Constr., Inc.*, VABCA 2693, 90-2 BCA ¶ 22,826 (testimony indicated contractor knew of ambiguity); *Ranco Constr., Inc.*, ASBCA 39050, 90-1 BCA ¶ 22,614 (contractor prepared bid following one interpretation and then revised bid to use other interpretation); and *Solar Turbines Int'l v. United States*, 3 Cl. Ct. 489 (1983) (contractor's trial brief admitted the contractor was actually aware of a significant ambiguity).

2. Government Obligation to Inform Bidders of Ambiguity

An exception to the duty to seek clarification occurs when one of the bidders requests clarification of an ambiguity and the government does not clear up the ambiguity and fails to inform other bidders that it is present in the bid documents. This exception relieves all of the other bidders of the duty to seek clarification. See *Peter Kiewit Sons' Co.*, ASBCA 17709, 74-2 BCA ¶ 10,975, stating at 52,530:

> The Government created an ambiguity for which it was responsible, but the appellant failed in its duty to inquire. The ambiguity was, however, called to the attention of the Government prior to the bid opening. This placed upon it a duty to clarify the ambiguity, which it failed to do. In these circumstances the onus of the original ambiguity still rests upon the Government.

The same result was arrived at in *Metcalf Constr. Co. v. United States*, 53 Fed. Cl. 617 (2002), and *Price/CIRI Constr., J.V.*, ASBCA 37002, 89-3 BCA ¶ 22,059. In *Hunt Constr. Group, Inc. v. United States*, 281 F.3d 1369 (Fed. Cir. 2002), the court accepted this rule but held that it did not apply because, in the facts of that case, there was no ambiguity.

3. Failure to Respond to Inquiry

The government often includes clauses in the bidding documents requiring that requests for clarification or interpretation be submitted not less than a specified number of days before bid opening. The failure to make inquiry within such period may defeat the contractor's claim. See Section IV.A, discussing pre-bid requests for clarification or information. However, the time limits established by the government can operate to excuse the contractor from seeking clarification of a discrepancy of which it had actual knowledge. In *Wright Assocs., Inc.*, ASBCA 22492, 79-2 BCA ¶ 14,102, *recons. denied*, 80-1 BCA ¶ 14,253, the board stated at 69,379:

> We have found that appellant made no such inquiry and, normally such failure to do so would result in a holding that it assumed the risks resulting from its interpretation. However, the well-established rule imposing upon bidders the duty to make inquiry when confronted with a patent ambiguity pre-supposes that such inquiry will yield a response that will clarify the Government's intent. *Peter Kiewit Sons' Company*, ASBCA No. 17709, 74-1 BCA ¶ 10,430, *clarified on recon.*, 74-1 BCA ¶ 10,488. In the instant appeal we have probative evidence, and have found thereon, that if appellant had inquired within five to ten days prior to bid opening, or later, it probably would have been told to submit its bid in accordance with its own interpretation.
>
> * * *
>
> In our opinion it is immaterial that contractors were allowed 30 days in which to prepare bids or that the IFB provided that inquiries must be received no later

> than 10 days prior to bid opening. The realities of bidding are that contractors may become aware of discrepancies in plans and specifications shortly before bid opening. If the Government is not prepared to provide meaningful responses to last minute requests for clarification, or to extend the bid opening date, it must accept the consequences.
>
> Hence, the contractor's lack of inquiry regarding the manner of ceramic tile installation was excused when evidence established that no meaningful response would have been made to a last minute request for clarification when contractor became aware of the ambiguity through its tile subcontractor, who had learned of the contract within 10 days prior to bid opening.

It has been very difficult for contractors to demonstrate that requests for clarification would not have been answered. See *S. Head Painting Contractor, Inc.*, ASBCA 26249, 82-2 BCA ¶ 15,886, in which the board stated, "We will not weaken the beneficial effect of this rule by allowing exceptions based on speculation as to what the Government would or would not have done if timely notice had been given." Thus, in *NBM Constr. Co.*, ASBCA 37095, 89-3 BCA ¶ 22,252, the board held that the government's failure to answer a question at the preconstruction conference did not indicate that it would not have addressed a pre-bid inquiry. Similarly, the fact that the government gave no answer in eight months to a request for clarification submitted during contract performance was not accepted as proof that it would not have responded to a pre-bid request, *Wilder Constr. Co.*, ASBCA 37686, 89-3 BCA ¶ 22,196. See *Jennings & Churella Eng'rs & Contractors*, DOTBCA 1820, 88-2 BCA ¶ 20,670, stating that there is a presumption that the contracting officer will answer a pre-bid inquiry in a timely manner.

If a contractor's inquiry is not resolved by the government, it may be required to inquire further. See *Community Heating & Plumbing Co. v. Kelso*, 987 F.2d 1575 (Fed. Cir. 1993), stating at 1580:

> [I]t is not enough under the duty to inquire that a contractor merely make an initial inquiry. *Beacon Constr. Co. v. United States*, 161 Ct. Cl. 1, 314 F.2d 501, 504 (Ct. Cl. 1963) (holding that duty to inquire requires the contractor to call attention to obvious contract omissions and make certain they were deliberate). Also instructive on this point is *Construction Service Co.*, ASBCA No. 4998, 59-1 BCA (CCH) ¶ 2077 at 8838, where a contractor requested clarification of a contract but received an addendum which did not alleviate the confusion. The board found that the duty to inquire had not been met. "If after receiving the addendum, the intended meaning was still not clear to appellant, it should have requested a further clarification." Id. at 8846-47.

CHAPTER 3

RISK ALLOCATION

Unanticipated events that occur during contract performance may substantially increase the cost of or time for completion or make performance impossible. Similar difficulties may be caused by matters inherent in the performance of the work that are not recognized until difficulties are encountered or substantial cost increases become apparent. The risks of such events or circumstances are allocated either by the parties through contractual language or by courts or boards during dispute resolution. This entire process is generally referred to as risk allocation. See Nash, *Risk Allocation in Government Contracts,* 34 Geo. Wash. L. Rev. 693 (1966).

In government contracts numerous risk allocation techniques are utilized. Risks are broadly allocated by the selection of the pricing arrangement reflected in the contract type. Thus, under cost-reimbursement contracts the government accepts the risks of increased costs, delays, and nonperformance, while under firm-fixed-price contracts the contractor bears the majority of these risks. Within these contract types, risks are specifically allocated by contract clauses. Standard clauses expressly provide for time extensions or price adjustments if various conditions differ from those expected or represented. Examples include the Changes, Differing Site Conditions, Suspension of Work, and Default clauses, which are discussed in detail in later chapters. Special clauses explicitly covering other events or circumstances are also frequently included in contracts.

This chapter discusses the common law methods of risk allocation and their application to government contracts. These risk allocation techniques may provide for a remedy in the absence of any contract clause or serve as the basis for invoking contract clauses granting remedies such as constructive changes and constructive suspensions of work. In either case, the fundamental rules of risk allocation stem from these common law principles. The first section discusses situations in which the contractor seeks recovery based on an express government promise regarding future events or conditions. The second section covers situations in which a contractor alleges that increased costs are compensable because the government misled it by incorrect statements or failure to disclose facts or knowledge. Considered next are instances where the contractor claims that the risks belong to the government under theories of implied warranties or implied duties. The fourth section covers the implied duty of good faith and fair dealing. The fifth section discusses the circumstances under which impracticability of performance or mistake can cause risks to be shifted. The sixth section examines defenses commonly raised by the government—exculpatory clauses and the sovereign acts doctrine. The chapter concludes with a discussion of the circumstances under which losses may be apportioned between the parties, resulting in a sharing of risks.

I. GOVERNMENT PROMISES (WARRANTIES) OF FUTURE EVENTS OR CONDITIONS

Events outside the control of either the government or the contractor frequently increase the cost of performance. Normally, in fixed-price contracts the contractor bears the cost impact of such events but is entitled to time extensions under the excusable delays provisions. Contractors have attempted to recover these costs even though the event occurred without government fault. However, courts have been reluctant to grant recovery in such cases absent relatively express language in the contract allocating the risk to the government. If the language is considered sufficiently definite to induce reliance, then it is termed an "express warranty." Otherwise the contractor will not recover.

There are no precise rules to differentiate assertions that amount to a warranty from those that do not. Since contract language frequently does not contain the words "promises," "warrants," "guarantees," or similar explicit terms, the contractor generally has a difficult burden to show that such language amounts to a warranty. In cases involving the question of when a work site will be available to a contractor, the burden on the contractor is very great. By contrast, in cases involving the means by which the contractor can gain access to the work site, the finding of such a warranty is fairly routine.

Although most of the warranty cases deal with issues related to construction sites, the warranty rationale has on occasion been extended to other types of situations. See *Swinerton & Belvoir*, ASBCA 24022, 81-1 BCA ¶ 15,156, where permission was required to import temporary alien workers into Guam for a construction contract, and the Clearance for Aliens clause stated at 74,983:

> Bidders are advised that clearance for aliens may require up to 90 days before issuance of any resultant authority for individual entry.

The board read this as a warranty, noting at 74,987-88:

> Nevertheless, the government is liable for whatever damages may have been caused by reason of actual clearance times exceeding the 90 day maximum represented in the Clearance clause, notwithstanding that sovereign acts and acts of third parties were involved.
>
> * * *
>
> The Clearance clause in S & B's contracts was a representation of fact on which S & B reasonably relied when it bid on and entered into those contracts.

Compare *AT&T Communications, Inc. v. Perry*, 296 F.3d 1307 (Fed. Cir. 2002), holding that a government statement that "the potential target revenue shares" resulting from a recompetition of a telephone service contract would be 76 percent and 24 percent was not a guarantee that the winning contractor would receive 76 percent of the revenue. See also *HK Sys., Inc.*, PSBCA 3712, 97-2 BCA ¶ 29,079, holding that the specification requirement that a mechanization system be designed to seismic zone 4 standards was not a representation that horizontal bedrock accelerations at the site would not exceed 4g.

A. Availability of Work Site

It has been very difficult for a contractor to prove a warranty that the work site will be available at a given date because the government's ability to furnish the site is commonly recognized as being subject to numerous variables. In *H.E. Crook Co. v. United States*, 270 U.S. 4 (1926), the contractor was to furnish and install a heating system in buildings that were under construction by another contractor at the time of award. The contract contained a specific date for the completion of construction of the building, stating that it was "[t]he approximate contract date of completion." The Court stated at 6:

> When such a situation [of dependency] was displayed by the contract it was not to be expected that the Government should bind itself to a fixed time for the work to come to an end, and there is not a word in the instrument by which it did so, unless an undertaking contrary to what seems to us the implication is implied.

The contractor was similarly dependent on another contractor's performance in *United States v. Rice*, 317 U.S. 61 (1942), where differing site conditions delayed the other contractor's performance, which in turn delayed the contractor's commencement of its work. The Court found no promise regarding when the work site would be available to the contractor. It noted at 64-65:

> We do not think the terms of the contract bound the Government to have the contemplated structure ready for respondent at a fixed time. Provisions of the contract showed that the dates were tentative and subject to modification by the Government. The contractor was absolved from payment of prescribed liquidated damages for delay, if it resulted from a number of causes, including "acts of Government" and "unusually severe weather." The Government reserved the right to make changes which might interrupt the work, and even to suspend any portion of the construction if it were deemed necessary. [The contractor] was required to adjust its work to that of the general contractor, so that delay by the general contractor would necessarily delay [the contractor's] work. Under these circumstances it seems appropriate to repeat what was said in the Crook case. . . . Decisions of this Court prior to the Crook case also make it clear that contracts such as this do not bind the Government to have the property ready for work by a contractor at a particular time. *Wells Bros. Co. v. United States*, 254 U.S. 83 [(1920)]; *Chouteau v. United States*, [95 U.S. 61 (1877)]; cf. *United States v. Smith*, 94 U.S. 214 [(1876)].

See also *United States v. Howard P. Foley Co.*, 329 U.S. 64 (1946), where government delay in preparation of runways delayed their becoming available to the contractor. The Court denied that the government's actions, which precluded completion in accordance with the contract schedule, demonstrated a breach of warranty, stating at 66:

> In no single word, clause, or sentence in the contract does the Government expressly covenant to make the runways available to [contractor] at any particular time.

Accord, *Ryco Constr., Inc. v. United States*, 55 Fed. Cl. 184 (2002) ("contract timeline" not a warranty).

In *Gilbane Bldg. Co. v. United States*, 166 Ct. Cl. 347, 333 F.2d 867 (1964), the contract contained a more explicit statement than in the prior cases—stating that "the work under another contract will be completed and the site available to commence the work under this contract on November 22, 1954." The contractor could not commence work on that date because the predecessor contractor's completion of work had been delayed by hurricanes. The court found no warranty, reasoning at 351-52:

> These are not words of warranty. The [government] represented that the site would be available at a specified time, but it did not guarantee that it would be. Other provisions of the contract and specifications show that it was expected that it might not be.

Based on these precedents, the finding of a warranty of site availability is highly unlikely. See *Fort Sill Assoc. v. United States*, 183 Ct. Cl. 301 (1968) (delays caused by other contractor not compensable absent an express warranty); *Paccon, Inc. v. United States*, 185 Ct. Cl. 24, 399 F.2d 162 (1968) (no warranty from preaward assurance of government representative that other contractor's performance would be scheduled to accommodate contractor); *Koppers/Clough v. United States*, 201 Ct. Cl. 344 (1973) (no warranty from ambiguous, inconclusive, or general discussions or contract provisions); *Star Communications, Inc.*, ASBCA 8049, 1962 BCA ¶ 3538 (no warranty when completion date of other contractor included in contract); *Industrial Maint. Servs., Inc.*, ASBCA 15176, 71-1 BCA ¶ 8793 (no warranty found in the estimates and forecasts of when another contractor should be finished with its work); and *P&L Inv. Corp.*, HUDBCA 79-408-C29, 83-1 BCA ¶ 16,285 (warranty not inferred lightly from general representations).

In contrast to the above cases, in which no warranty of site availability was found in the face of relatively explicit contract language, a few cases have found such a warranty to exist. Significant factors in these cases are the importance of the site and the critical nature of the limited period for performing the work. See *Dravo Corp.*, ENGBCA 3800, 79-1 BCA ¶ 13,575 (importance of disposal site to project and that disposal operations be completed by specific date); *Perini, Horn, Morrison-Knudsen (JV)*, ENGBCA 4821, 87-1 BCA ¶ 19,545 (specific outage times in contract held to be warranty because contractor could not be expected to mobilize and demobilize for each passing train); and *American Int'l Contractors, Inc./Capitol Indus., Constr. Groups, Inc., A Joint Venture*, ASBCA 39544, 95-2 BCA ¶ 27,920 (access to borrow areas integral to contract schedule). A promise to make housing units available at a specific date was also enforced when the government had complete control of the units, *Carousel Dev., Inc.*, ASBCA 50719, 01-1 BCA ¶ 31,262. Compare *ECOS Mgmt. Criteria, Inc.*, VABCA 2058, 86-2 BCA ¶ 18,885 (no warranty when delays in gaining access to secured areas were forewarned and were minimal in nature); *Lane Constr. Corp.*, ENGBCA 4231, 88-2 BCA ¶ 20,769 (no warranty when sniper fire related to a labor dispute forced the contractor to abandon the site sporadically and hire private security, because contractor was warned of labor problems and there was no express warranty of a peaceful labor situation); *Durocher Dock & Dredge, Inc.*, ENGBCA 5768, 91-3 BCA ¶ 24,145 (no warranty of site availability when the local sheriff, in a search for missing persons, temporarily restricted access to the site, as neither contracting party was at fault for the delay); and *Oman—Fischbach Int'l, a Joint Venture,* ASBCA 44195, 00-2 BCA ¶ 31,022, *aff'd*, 276 F.3d 1380 (Fed. Cir. 2002) (no warranty when access to a disposal site was restricted by action of the Portuguese armed forces).

The cases involving site availability have been more prone to find a warranty when the contract contained a Suspension of Work clause. For example, in *Merritt-Chapman & Scott Corp. v. United States*, 194 Ct. Cl. 461, 439 F.2d 185 (1971), the court held the government liable under the Suspension of Work clause for nonavailability of the site based on contract language stating that the site would be available "about 1 December 1955." Similarly, in *Blinderman Constr. Co. v. United States*, 695 F.2d 552 (Fed. Cir. 1982), the contractor was delayed in obtaining access to apartments where the work was to be done, and the Navy project manager was unable to assist in obtaining timely access. Although the contract contained no express warranty of site availability, the court found that there was "an implied obligation to provide such access so that the contractor could complete the contract within the time required by its terms." In *Renel Constr. Co.*, GSBCA 5175, 80-2 BCA ¶ 14,811, an implied warranty of site availability was found from the issuance of a notice to proceed, the government-approved construction schedule, and a provision requiring completion of work at a specified time. See also *American Int'l Contractors, Inc./Capitol Indus., Constr. Groups, Inc., A Joint Venture*, ASBCA 39544, 95-2 BCA ¶ 27,920 (designation of work site made government liable for providing it when needed); *Henderson, Inc.*, DOTBCA 2500, 94-2 BCA ¶ 26,728 (provision in contract prohibiting the contractor working during certain period held to be a warranty that contractor could work during nonprohibited period resulting in suspension of work); and *G & S Constr., Inc.*, ASBCA 28677, 86-1 BCA ¶ 18,740, 86-2 BCA ¶ 18,791 (clause requiring that the contractor obtain security clearances before beginning work held to be warranty that the government would process the applications in a timely manner or make the site available in some other way). In *Raytheon STX Corp. v. Department of Commerce*, GSBCA 14296-COM, 00-1 BCA ¶ 30,632, the board granted relief for a government shutdown on the basis that the cost-reimbursement contract containing a government Delay of Work clause indicated that the government had promised to pay the contractor's costs during the period that it could not work on the government site.

Erickson Air Crane Co., EBCA 50-6-79, 83-1 BCA ¶ 16,145, *aff'd*, 731 F.2d 810 (Fed. Cir. 1984), appears to have confused the warranty of site availability with the warranty of access to the site. There, relief was granted for government breach of warranty under a contract to construct transmitter lines. The board stated at 80,207-08:

> The Government specified in the contract that the right-of-way over McCabe and Chimney Rock property would be available on January 31, 1976. In turn, [the contractor], and [its subcontractor], had a right to rely on that specification in scheduling its work at the site. The Government also was aware that McCabe consistently objected to the Government's attempts to secure a right-of-way over his property and had actually evicted the Government's survey crew in early May.
>
> [The contractor] was not advised of the prior McCabe incident nor did it have reason to believe that it would encounter problems of access to the area. The fact that it was the act of a third party that caused the contractor to move from the property does not relieve the Government of liability because the Government, in its contract, unconditionally provided that the right-of-way would be available by January 31, 1976. *Dale Construction Co. v. United States Seaboard Surety Co.*, 168 Ct. Cl. 692 (1964); *D&L Construction Co. and Associates v. U.S.*, 402 F.2d 990 (1968), 185 Ct. Cl. 736.

This decision appears to be questionable. The government's liability in *Dale Construction* was based on a breach of the implied duty not to hinder the contractor in performance, while *D&L Construction* involved the more liberal access to site cases.

B. Means of Access to Site

Courts and boards frequently find warranties in contract provisions stating that a specific access route will be available during performance. In most of these cases alternate means of access are unavailable or are much more costly. In *Gerhardt F. Meyne Co. v. United States*, 110 Ct. Cl. 527, 76 F. Supp. 811 (1948), a specification stated at 541:

> Entrance for trucks shall be at South Gate of reservation, over Walker Avenue, Highwood, Illinois, via Patten Road to site.

When military authorities closed Patten Road, the contractor was required to construct and maintain a temporary road. The court equated the specification with a warranty and a concomitant government promise to compensate the contractor if the road was not available. The court stated at 549-50:

> The specifications clearly contemplated the use of Patten Road and other paved roads. . . . This was a representation that such roads were available and [the con-

> tractor's] bid was, of course, based upon it. This promise was not carried out and [the contractor] is entitled to recover whatever extra expense to which it was put as a result.

Similarly, in *D & L Constr. Co. v. United States*, 185 Ct. Cl. 736, 402 F.2d 990 (1968), a warranty was found in the contract documents and a contracting officer's letter to the contractor stating that the government "will provide suitable access and means of ingress and egress to and from the subject project." Compare *Premier Elec. Constr. Co. v. United States*, 473 F.2d 1372 (7th Cir. 1973), refusing to follow this logic. There, the court refused to apply the warranty rationale where an early thaw made an access road "an impassable sea of mud." The court found no warranty although the language was similar to that in the *Meyne* case. It distinguished the cases on the questionable ground that the problem was caused by a force of nature rather than a sovereign act as in *Meyne*.

The various boards of contract appeals generally follow *Meyne* and *D & L* rather than *Premier Electric*. For instance, in *Carl W. Linder Co.*, ENGBCA 3526, 78-1 BCA ¶ 13,114, when a town restricted the contractor's use of roads, thereby making the access gate unavailable, the contractor was entitled to relief for breach of warranty. The board, critical of the *Premier Electric* rationale, elaborated at 64,098:

> Of course, the warranty relied upon must be expressly stated in the contract documents, [*U.S. v.*] *Howard P. Foley*, [329 U.S. 64 (1946)]. It cannot be established by taking portions of the drawings and specifications out of context and placing them side by side to form a peg on which to hang government liability, *Lenry, Inc. and William P. Bergan, Inc.*, 156 Ct. Cl. 46 (1962). Such is not the case here where both the specifications and the drawings clearly direct that the 15th Street gate is to be the point of access for construction access, especially trucks.

See also *Mountain Fir Lumber Co.*, Comp. Gen. Dec. B-186534, 76-2 CPD ¶ 150 (timber sale contract clause authorizing the use of a certain road amounted to a warranty, since the Forest Service had determined the Elliot Creek Road to be the least expensive hauling route and had based its appraisal value of the timber on use of that road); *Swinging Hoedads*, AGBCA 77-212, 79-1 BCA ¶ 13,859 (warranty where maps depicted spur roads available for contractor's use, but barriers made the roads unusable); *J.W. Bateson Co.*, GSBCA 4687, 80-2 BCA ¶ 14,608 (warranty that street would remain open during construction was found where site plans, included in the contract, and a contract amendment indicated the availability of the street, and contractor inquiries to the government and the appropriate District of Columbia personnel bolstered contractor's belief that a warranty was present); *Varaburn, Ltd.*, ASBCA 22177, 82-1 BCA ¶ 15,744 (warranty found in a provision specifying when the access road, which was under construction by another contractor, was required to be completed); *Bechtel Envtl., Inc.*, ENGBCA 6137, 97-1 BCA ¶ 28,640 (government responsibility to obtain easements a warranty that they would be obtained in time to commence work); *R.W. Jones Constr., Inc.*, IBCA 3656-96, 99-1 BCA ¶ 30,268 (government liable for not providing a key to work site but requiring contractor to obtain access from third party); and *Commercial Contractors Equip., Inc.*, ASBCA 52930, 03-2 BCA ¶ 32,381 (government liable for obtaining access to site from third party).

Some cases have refused to find a warranty because the language of the contract was imprecise. See *Oman-Fischbach Int'l, a Joint Venture*, ASBCA 44195, 00-2 BCA ¶ 31,022, *aff'd*, 276 F.3d 1380 (Fed. Cir. 2002), in which no warranty was found when a foreign government opened the gates to a base for only a limited period each day. The board reasoned that there was no explicit promise of site availability and that the government does not normally warrant that other governments will act in a certain way. The board relied on *Lenry, Inc. v. United States*, 156 Ct. Cl. 46, 297 F.2d 550 (1962), which found no contract language that would constitute a warranty that city streets would be available after a flood had made them unusable. See also *T. Brown Constructors, Inc.*, DOTBCA 1986, 95-2 BCA ¶ 27,820, *rev'd on other grounds*, 132 F.3d 724 (Fed. Cir. 1997), finding no representation that a "project-length detour" would be available for a road construction project.

The site access warranty has been extended to the means of access within the work site. In *Robert R. Marquis, Inc.*, ASBCA 38438, 92-1 BCA ¶ 24,692, the board held that the contractor had the right to expect the use of an elevator in a construction contract because the contract did not bar its use. The government argued that the elevator, once used, would not be new, as required by specifications. The board, looking to the common practice of the industry, held that the failure of the government to supply the elevator with power during construction caused inefficiencies for which the contractor should recover. Compare *Aydin Corp.*, EBCA 355-5-86, 89-3 BCA ¶ 22,044, in which it was found that the contract language, which provided for access through a wall for equipment too large for the freight elevator, was not a warranty of elevator availability. The board stated at 110,900:

> To go from the mere mention of elevator dimensions to a guarantee of access to the elevators requires a gargantuan leap well beyond the limits of established contractual construction.

See also *Marks Movers & Storage, Inc. v. General Servs. Admin.*, GSBCA 13191, 96-2 BCA ¶ 28,597, denying relief for lack of access to elevators because the contract disclaimed government liability for delays caused by the contractor's failure to make arrangements with the building management, and *Construction Foresight, Inc.*, ASBCA 42350, 93-1 BCA ¶ 25,515, denying relief when one freight elevator broke down.

Warranties are often not found when the contractor had notice of the potential for delay by an outside party or element. In *Harry Claterbos Co. (JV)*, ENGBCA 5009, 89-3 BCA ¶ 21,973, no warranty was found in a contract for clean-up work on Mount St. Helens when the contract had warned that the contractor should anticipate the loss of the access road for 10 percent of the work period due to volcanic activity and excavation. In *Summit Contractors, Inc. v. United States*, 23 Cl. Ct. 333 (1991), the contract language advised the logging company of the access roads and related that "delays up to two hours should be expected for log hauling" because of other contractors using the roads in the "normal operating season" for logging operations. This language was held to be a disclaimer of liability and a warning of possible difficulties, not a warranty of the availability of the access roads.

C. Availability of Utilities

The government often warrants the availability of utilities in contract specifications or standard clauses. FAR 36.514 requires use of the Availability and Use of Utility Services clause in FAR 52.236-14 in fixed-price construction contracts when the contracting officer determines that (1) the existing utility system is adequate for the needs of the government and the contractor, and (2) furnishing it is in the government's interest. The clause states:

> (a) The Government shall make all reasonably required amounts of utilities available to the Contractor from existing outlets and supplies, as specified in the contract. . . .
>
> (b) The Contractor, at its expense and in a workmanlike manner, satisfactory to the Contracting Officer, shall install and maintain all necessary temporary connections and distribution lines, and all meters required to measure the amount of each utility use for the purpose of determining charges. . . .

This clause is read as a warranty that utilities dealt with in the contract documents will be available to the contractor. In *Hull-Hazard, Inc.*, ASBCA 34645, 90-3 BCA ¶ 23,173, the board looked at the intent of the contracting parties to determine whether telephone service should be considered a warranted utility under the contract specifications. The board found that the government's failure to inform the contractor of nearby, accessible telephone lines and its provision of telephone service during the contract performance indicated that both parties expected the government to furnish the telephone service as a utility. Because the government had admitted that the service was unreliable and caused interruptions in work, the contractor was held entitled to an equitable adjustment. Similarly, in *Mit-Con, Inc.*, ASBCA 42916, 92-1 BCA ¶ 24,539, the government was found to have promised to supply gas service, because the contract specified other utilities for which the contractor would be responsible but remained silent regarding gas service, and the contract drawings showed an existing gas line. In *Engineering Tech. Consultants, S.A.*, ASBCA 44912, 93-1 BCA ¶ 25,556, *recons. denied*, 93-2 BCA ¶ 25,732, the government argued that there was not adequate electricity for the contractor at the school that it had contracted to renovate, and therefore the government could not be expected to provide it. Relying on the instructions in FAR 36.514 that the contracting officer was to determine that there were adequate utilities before including the Availability and Use of Utility Services clause, the board stated at 127,289:

> While the Government obviously cannot provide [the contractor] with electrical power that it does not have, that does not immunize the Government from contract liability for contract language which suggests to the contrary.

The board also rejected the government's contention that the request of the contractor for power for its standard welding equipment was unreasonable when the contract called for a considerable amount of welding work.

The boards limit the warranty of utilities strictly to the language of the clause or contract specifications. In *Techno Eng'g & Constr., Ltd.*, ASBCA 32938, 88-1 BCA ¶ 20,351, for instance, the board held that the contract language warranted access only to "existing" utilities and that the government lived up to its warranty by making its portable generator available to the contractor. As the contractor could not prove that it had been denied access to any other utilities that existed, the claim was denied. See also *Marcus Thomas & Co.*, ASBCA 37539, 90-1 BCA ¶ 22,531, in which no warranty was found where the government reasonably construed the contract terms to include a job telephone as a temporary utility for which the contractor was responsible and otherwise made a good faith effort to provide telephone access to the contractor.

When the delay caused by a lack of utility service is very minor, the boards have denied contractor claims for adjustment and extensions. In *Sauer, Inc.*, ASBCA 37205, 90-2 BCA ¶ 22,784, the board held that a 20-minute power outage of warranted utilities would not constitute enough of a delay to be considered unreasonable under the Suspension of Work clause. In *Skyline Painting, Inc.*, ENGBCA 5810, 93-3 BCA ¶ 26,041, the board held that four brief power outages and a delay in determining which cords were needed to do the job did not represent an inadequate supply of utilities by the government. The board stated at 129,459:

> [The contractor] has presented no evidence demonstrating how these otherwise innocuous-in-duration delays palpably affected performance. In view of the *de minimis* character of the delays and the failure of the record to fix the cause of the delays on the Government, this aspect of the appeal fails.

D. Issuance of Notice to Proceed

An express warranty regarding the time of issuance of a notice to proceed was found in *Abbett Elec. Corp. v. United States*, 142 Ct. Cl. 609, 162 F. Supp. 772 (1958). The specification provided:

> [N]otice to proceed for the work under Schedule No. 2 will be issued at the discretion of the contracting officer any time within two hundred and forty (240) calendar days for the work under Part I, and two hundred and seventy-five (275) calendar days, for the work under Part II, after date of award of the contract.

The court found that such an express statement about the time a notice to proceed will be issued constituted the type of warranty for which relief is available. See also *A. S. Schulman Elec. Co. v. United States*, 145 Ct. Cl. 399 (1959). Most notice to proceed cases will be adjudicated under the Suspension of Work clause, which provides adjustments for unreasonable delay without the necessity for finding a warranty. See *M. E. Brown*, ASBCA 40043, 91-1 BCA ¶ 23,293, in which the government was held to have unreasonably delayed issuance of the notice to proceed, due to difficulties with the removal of asbestos from the site, until the contract was terminated for convenience; the contractor prevailed under the Suspension of Work clause. In *Manis Drilling*, IBCA 2658, 93-3 BCA ¶ 25,931, the government was held not to have unreasonably delayed the issuance of the notice to proceed because the solicitation stated that such notice would be issued after the submission of bonds, which the contractor was late in submitting. See also *Marine Constr. & Dredging, Inc.*, ASBCA 38412, 90-1 BCA ¶ 22,573, in which government delay of issuance of notice to proceed for six months was held to be reasonable because the delay was based on the government's understanding that dredging was permitted only during a certain time of year, and *American Eagle Indus., Inc.*, IBCA 3507-95, 97-2 BCA ¶ 29,261, in which the government was held not liable for subcontractor costs incurred after the government had told the contractor not to incur costs during the delay.

Early award will not overcome the government's obligation to issue the notice to proceed in a timely fashion. See *Bechtel Envtl., Inc.*, ENGBCA 6137, 97-1 BCA ¶ 28,640, in which the board stated at 143,024-25:

> These arguments ignore the facts and the practicalities of scheduling the job in a dynamic environment. Regardless of whether the actual award date could have been 40 days later, the fact is that it occurred on July 12, 1989. Once the contract was awarded, Bechtel was entitled to assume that the Government would proceed in accordance with its terms. Concomitantly, the contractor was required to plan the job based on the contractually-based assumption that the NTP would be issued within 20 days after submission of the requisite bonds and insurance. The critical planning date was July 12. In this regard, it is of little consequence whether Bechtel's pre-bid schedule was reasonable or unreasonable prior to award of the contract. Once the contract was awarded early, Bechtel's pre-bid expectations concerning early commencement of the job became the reality. Although the contractor may have been fortunate that its assumptions proved correct, it also was responsible for quickly mobilizing for the job after issuance of the NTP so as not to lose time.

II. INCORRECT STATEMENTS AND NONDISCLOSURES

The government is liable if it misleads the contractor by making incorrect statements or failing to disclose information that it possesses. This is to be distinguished from those situations discussed in the previous section in which the characteristic element was a promise concerning events to occur in the future.

Situations involving misstatements or nondisclosures are often referred to as "misrepresentations." However, this term is also used to refer solely to affirmative misstatements. This section divides the discussion between incorrect statements and nondisclosures without regard to the usage of the term "misrepresentation" in the decisions.

A. Incorrect Statements

The government may be held liable if its statements to the contractor are not correct. It is not necessary for contractor recovery that there be an intent to deceive, *Womack v. United States*, 182 Ct. Cl. 399, 389 F.2d 793 (1968), or bad faith, *Summit Timber Co. v. United States*, 230 Ct. Cl. 434, 677 F.2d 852 (1982) (erroneous representation not rendered innocuous simply because it was due to mere negligence or inadvertence). Contractors are not ordinarily required to conduct investigations to determine whether the government's statements are correct, *Hollerbach v. United States*, 233 U.S. 165 (1914). However, the contractor may not recover damages incurred when it cannot prove that it relied on a misrepresentation, *AT&T Communications, Inc. v. Perry*, 296 F.3d 1307 (Fed. Cir. 2002); *Whittaker Elec. Sys. v. Dalton*, 124 F.3d 1443 (Fed. Cir. 1997), or when it knows it has been misled, *Ling-Temco-Vought, Inc. v. United States*, 201 Ct. Cl. 135, 475 F.2d 630 (1973). In some cases, contractors recover for misrepresentation by having the contract reformed to reflect the contract prices that would have been agreed to but for the misrepresentation, *Defense Sys. Co.*, ASBCA 50918, 01-1 BCA ¶ 31,152. The following discussion deals with the types of government statements that justify contractor reliance.

1. Factual Statements

The government is most clearly liable when it makes a misstatement of fact. The primary sources of such statements are the specifications, bidding documents, and contract provisions. Liability for certain factual misstatements may be dealt with expressly within the contract. For example, statements relating to latent or subsurface physical conditions at the site are generally dealt with under the Differing Site Conditions clause, *Tobin Quarries, Inc. v. United States*, 114 Ct. Cl. 286, 84 F. Supp. 1021 (1949). See Chapter 5. Absent express provisions, the government's liability is based on an implied warranty that the information furnished is correct.

The government has been found liable for a wide variety of factual misstatements. See, for example, *Raytheon Co.*, ASBCA 50166, 01-1 BCA ¶ 31,245, *remanded on other grounds*, 305 F.3d 1354 (Fed. Cir. 2002) (item being procured was a "build-to-print" product); *Environmental Safety Consultants, Inc.*, ASBCA 47498, 00-1 BCA ¶ 30,826 (material in pond was "liquid waste"); *D.F.K. Enter., Inc. v. United States*, 45 Fed. Cl. 280 (1999) (wind conditions at construction site); *T. Brown Constructors, Inc. v. Peña*, 132 F.3d 724 (Fed. Cir. 1997) (specific test data on amount of clay in quarry); *Marty's Maid & Janitorial Serv. v. General Servs. Admin.*, GSBCA 10614, 93-1 BCA ¶ 25,284, *aff'd*, 11 F.3d 1070 (Fed. Cir. 1993) (prior contractor had fully complied with the contract specifications); *PK Contractors, Inc.*, ENGBCA 4901, 92-1 BCA ¶ 24,583 (inaccurate statement of water levels of river); *Wayne L. Grist, Inc.*, ENGBCA 5503, 90-2 BCA ¶ 22,915 (inaccurate cross-section diagram of alluvial sands); *Teledyne Lewisburg v. United States*, 699 F.2d 1336 (Fed. Cir. 1983) (government-furnished drawings were current and that model conformed to drawings); *Summit Timber Co. v. United States*, 230 Ct. Cl. 434, 677 F.2d 852 (1982) (boundary not marked as represented in contract documents); *Kolar, Inc. v. United States*, 227 Ct. Cl. 445, 650 F.2d 256 (1981) (condition of items sold by government); *Maurice Mandel, Inc. v. United States*, 424 F.2d 1252 (8th Cir. 1970) (air conditioning needs of proposed building); *Chris Berg, Inc. v. United States*, 186 Ct. Cl. 389, 404 F.2d 364 (1968) (expected weather conditions); *Railroad Waterproofing Corp. v. United States*, 133 Ct. Cl. 911 (1956) (incorrect measurements in drawings); *Arcole Midwest Corp. v. United States*, 125 Ct. Cl. 818, 113 F. Supp. 278 (1953) (statement that power company had stated power could be made available at work site misleading when government gave power company underestimated usage data); *Potashnick v. United States*, 123 Ct. Cl. 197 (1952) (core boring data); *Myers v. United States*, 120 Ct. Cl. 126 (1951) (misstatement as to preparatory work done by government); and *Dunbar & Sullivan Dredging Co. v. United States*, 65 Ct. Cl. 567 (1928) (specifications indicated that sand and clay would be found even though government engineers had reason to know otherwise).

The government may also be liable for incorrect information given to offerors in the contract formation process even though the information is not contained in the bidding documents, *Lear Siegler, Inc.*, ASBCA 16079, 73-1 BCA ¶ 10,004 (contractor reasonably relied on the government's representation concerning the availability of a certain item, because the contractor could not be expected to go to the supplier of the item, who was a competitor for the instant contract); *Snyder-Lynch Motors Inc. v. United States*, 154 Ct. Cl. 476, 292 F.2d 907 (1961) (pricing information given to contractor during negotiations was incorrect). However, the Court of Federal Claims will not take jurisdiction of a misrepresentation claim unless it is connected to a contract provision, *Gonzalez Elec. & General Contractor, Inc. v. United States*, 55 Fed. Cl. 447 (2002); *Dakota Tribal Indus. v. United States*, 34 Fed. Cl. 295 (1995). Compare *Schweiger Constr. Co. v. United States*, 49 Fed. Cl. 188 (2001), finding "a sufficient nexus between [the alleged misrepresentation] and the government's contractual obligations."

2. Laws and Regulations

The government may also be liable if it misinforms the contractor about the laws applicable to the contract. For instance, in *Blackhawk Hotels Co.*, ASBCA 13333, 68-2 BCA ¶ 7265, government liability was found when the contracting officer advised all prospective bidders that "[y]ou are hereby notified that the Service Contract Act of 1965 [SCA] . . . does not apply to this procurement." Relying on this information, the contractor prepared its bid. After award the Department of Labor advised that the SCA was applicable, and the contractor was required to pay higher wages than it anticipated. Compare *T.L. Roof & Assocs. Constr. Co. v. United States*, 28 Fed. Cl. 572 (1993), in which the court stated that, as a general rule, courts are reluctant to reform a contract when there has been a misrepresentation as to the legal rules governing the situation.

Similarly, the government has been held liable for its representations regarding applicable taxes. See Comp. Gen. Dec. B-153472, Dec. 2, 1965, *Unpub.*, where a representation that the contractor would not have to pay sales taxes was discerned from the Final Appraisal and Eligibility sheets, which included a schedule of costs and fees to be included in the total bid price. On this schedule was a line marked "sales taxes (where applicable)," with a blank in which the government marked an "X" instead of inserting an amount. This was deemed to be notice from the government that sales taxes were not applicable and as such were not to be included in the bids. See also *Sena Constr. Co.*, IBCA 3761, 98-2 BCA ¶ 29,891 (contracting officer stated government was exempt from tax); Comp. Gen. Dec. B-169959, Aug. 3, 1970, *Unpub.* (although the misrepresentation was innocent and inadvertent, the government was liable for a statement that a particular state tax was not applicable to the work advertised); *Rust Eng'g Co.*, Comp. Gen. Dec. B-180071, 74-1 CPD ¶ 101 (government representative's statement at a pre-bid meeting that contractor would be exempt from paying state sales and use taxes was misrepresentation); and Comp. Gen. Dec. B-159066, May 6, 1966 and Feb. 13, 1969, *Unpub.* (government liable for statement that Michigan use taxes were not applicable to the work). Compare *Visicon, Inc.*, ASBCA 51706, 02-2 BCA ¶ 31,887, denying a misrepresentation claim because it was unreasonable for the contractor to rely on a statement of a government employee without contracting officer authority that state taxes did not apply to the project, and *Foley Co. v. United States*, 36 Fed. Cl. 788 (1996), denying the claim because the contractor should not have relied on an oral statement that the project was exempt from state taxes—even though the contractor called the telephone number provided in the IFB when information was needed.

Different types of solicitations may put different responsibilities regarding knowledge of applicable laws on the contracting parties. In *Edwards v. United States*, 19 Cl. Ct. 663 (1990), the court held that it was the contractor's responsibility to ascertain the local zoning laws and regulations in a contract to build a post office on land owned by the contractor. The court reasoned that providing the site carried with it the obligation of ascertaining local zoning requirements.

3. Estimates

The government often furnishes offerors with estimates of the amount of work anticipated or other matters that are important in preparing the offer. Such estimates are not statements of fact. However, by furnishing the estimates to offerors, the government may be held to have made implied representations concerning estimating methods or factors considered in arriving at the estimate. While most estimate cases are based on these factual aspects of the estimates, the courts and boards sometimes hold the government to have impliedly warranted the reasonable accuracy of estimates. The theory of warranty of reasonable accuracy should be distinguished from representations concerning the preparation of the estimates, since the accuracy warranty does not necessarily involve existing facts.

The government is liable for misleading estimates if it does not use due care in gathering relevant information and using that information in the estimating process. See *Womack v. United States*, 182 Ct. Cl. 399, 389 F.2d 793 (1968), in which the court stated, at 412-13:

> An estimate as to a material matter in a bidding invitation is an expedient. Ordinarily it is only used where there is a recognized need for guidance to bidders on a particular point but specific information is not reasonably available, *H.L. Yoh Co. v. United States*, 153 Ct. Cl. 104, 105, 288 F.2d 493, 494 (1961). Intrinsically, the estimate that is made in such circumstances must be the product of such relevant underlying information as is available to the author of the invitation. If the bidder were not entitled to so regard it, its inclusion in the invitation would be surplusage at best or deception at worst. Assuming that the bidder acts reasonably, he is entitled to rely on Government estimates as representing honest and informed conclusions. *Snyder-Lynch Motors, Inc. v. United States*, 154 Ct. Cl. 476, 479, 292 F.2d 907, 909-10 (1961). In short, in promulgating an estimate for bidding-invitation purposes, the Government is not required to be clairvoyant but it is obliged to base that estimate on all relevant information that is reasonably available to it.

See also *Chemical Tech., Inc. v. United States*, 227 Ct. Cl. 120, 645 F.2d 934 (1981) (estimate negligently prepared because government did not take into account all relevant factual data); *Skip Kirchdorfer, Inc. v. United States*, 14 Cl. Ct. 594 (1988) (government negligently estimated that the job required a daily average of 29.68 service calls but the contractor found an average of 77.99 service calls per day); *Steelcare, Inc.*, GSBCA 5491, 81-1 BCA ¶ 15,143 (government negligent in failing to adequately investigate amount of work to be done); *Atlantic Garages, Inc.*, GSBCA 5891, 82-1 BCA ¶ 15,479 (government negligent in failing to use all available information and in using faulty estimating method); *LBM, Inc.*, ASBCA 39606, 91-2 BCA ¶ 24,016 (government did not consider the rate of increase in the historical data in formulating the estimate of necessary service calls to heating and air units on a naval base); *Management & Training Corp. v. General Servs. Admin.*, GSBCA 11182, 93-2 BCA ¶ 25,814 (government liable for not including a chilled-water component in its estimate of costs to be used as base for utility rate increases over life of contract); *Datalect Computer Servs., Ltd. v. United States*, 40 Fed. Cl. 28 (1997), *rev'd on other grounds*, 215 F.3d 1344 (Fed. Cir. 1999), *cert. denied*, 529 U.S. 1037 (2000) (estimate of requirements not updated for new information); *Fairfax Opportunities Unlimited, Inc.*, AGBCA 96-178-1, 98-1 BCA ¶ 29,556 (government used prior year quantities when it had later data indicating that they were not accurate); *J.A. Jones Mgmt. Servs., Inc.*, ASBCA 46793, 99-1 BCA ¶ 30,303 (lack of due care in preparing workload estimate); *Griffin Servs., Inc. v. Gen-*

eral Servs. Admin., GSBCA 14507, 00-2 BCA ¶ 30,988 (estimate of maintenance services double in-house estimate); *Hi-Shear Tech. Corp. v. United States*, 53 Fed. Cl. 420 (2002), *aff'd*, 356 F.3d 1372 (Fed. Cir. 2004) (government estimate of requirements not based on known information); *S.P.L. Spare Parts Logistics, Inc.*, ASBCA 51118, 02-2 BCA ¶ 31,982 (government liable for estimate of requirements not taking policy changes into account); and *Applied Cos., Inc.* ASBCA 50749, 01-1 BCA ¶ 31,325, *recons. denied*, 01-2 BCA ¶ 31,430, *aff'd*, 325 F.3d 1328 (Fed. Cir. 2003) (negligent estimate of requirements). The government has also been found liable for an inaccurate estimate absent a finding of fault on the theory that there was a warranty of reasonable accuracy, *Everett Plywood & Door Corp. v. United States*, 190 Ct. Cl. 80, 419 F.2d 425 (1969). See also *Cedar Lumber, Inc. v. United States*, 5 Cl. Ct. 539 (1984).

If the estimate is reasonably accurate and based on the available data, the government will be found to have exercised due care, *Timber Investors, Inc. v. United States*, 218 Ct. Cl. 408, 587 F.2d 472 (1978). In *Medart, Inc. v. Austin*, 967 F.2d 579 (Fed. Cir. 1992), the court held that the government followed the GSA's reasonable estimate procedures and was under no obligation to do more, stating at 582:

> The government *may* go beyond the requirements of the regulations, of course. And it might be well advised to do so if it wants to secure the best prices and avoid contractors raising their bids to cover the uncertainties. But we are in no position to impose such a requirement either in this case or as a general proposition in the face of the regulations promulgated by competent authority.

See also *Anthony G. Bamonte*, AGBCA 77-154, 78-2 BCA ¶ 13,508 (good faith effort resulting in a reasonably accurate estimate); *Broken Lance Enters., Inc.*, ASBCA 22588, 78-2 BCA ¶ 13,433 (estimates prepared with considerable care by knowledgeable persons); *Mattatuck Mfg. Co.*, GSBCA 4847, 80-1 BCA ¶ 14,349 (estimates derived from sophisticated computer system); *Systems & Elecs., Inc.*, ASBCA 41113, 97-1 BCA ¶ 28,671 (government must only consider "all relevant information reasonably available" not perform research to arrive at accurate estimate); *American Marine Decking Servs., Inc.*, ASBCA 44440, 97-1 BCA ¶ 28,821 (estimate based on prior year quantity); and *Centurion Elec. Serv.*, ASBCA 51596, 03-1 BCA ¶ 32,097 (estimate using prior year quantity satisfactory even though requirements declined precipitously).

There is no warranty of the reasonableness of estimates in indefinite-delivery, indefinite-quantity contracts. See *Travel Centre v. Barram*, 236 F.3d 1316 (Fed. Cir. 2001), stating at 1319:

> Regardless of the accuracy of the estimates delineated in the solicitation, based on the language of the solicitation for the IDIQ contract, Travel Centre could not have had a reasonable expectation that any of the government's needs beyond the minimum contract price would necessarily be satisfied under this contract.

See also *C.F.S. Air Cargo, Inc.*, ASBCA 40694, 91-2 BCA ¶ 23,985, *aff'd*, 972 F.2d 1353 (Fed. Cir. 1992), in which the board held that indefinite-quantity contracts were specifically designed so that, with the contracted-for maximum and minimum numbers, the government could require and purchase as much of a product as it needed. As such, requiring the government to ascertain and then honor a reasonable estimate of orders negates the very flexibility for which the parties contracted. See also *Scientific Mgmt. Assocs., Inc.*, ASBCA 50956, 00-1 BCA ¶ 30,828 (summary judgment granted because negligence of estimate not a material issue), and *DynCorp*, ASBCA 38862, 91-2 BCA ¶ 24,044 (board refused to examine the reasonableness of an estimate in a Navy supply contract of indefinite quantity).

B. Nondisclosures

Government liability for nondisclosure of information is based on an implied duty to disclose information that is vital for the preparation of estimates or for contract performance. This implied duty has been found to be consistent with the implied warranty of specifications, *Granite Constr. Co. v. United States*, 24 Cl. Ct. 735 (1991); *United States v. Atlantic Dredging Co.*, 253 U.S. 1 (1920), or the duty of good faith and fair dealing, *Northrop Grumman Corp. v. United States*, 63 Fed. Cl. 12 (2004); *Southern California Edison v. United States*, 58 Fed. Cl. 313 (2003). However, most cases treat it as a separate duty which is similar to the duty not to misrepresent the facts during the formation of a contract. See also Dygert, *Implied Warranties in Government Contracts,* 53 Mil. L. Rev. 39 (1971).

In *Helene Curtis Indus., Inc. v. United States*, 160 Ct. Cl. 437, 312 F.2d 774 (1963), the leading case on nondisclosure, the contractor had unsuccessfully used a method of manufacturing a chemical only to learn, subsequently, that the government agency knew of a successful method. The court stated at 444:

> [T]he circumstances here gave rise to a duty to share information. The disinfectant was novel and had never been mass-produced; the Government had sponsored the research and knew much more about the product than the bidders did or could; it knew, in particular, that the main ingredient, chlormelamine, was a recent invention, uncertain in reaction, and requiring extreme care in handling; it also knew that the more costly process of grinding would be necessary to meet the requirements of the specification, but that in their understandable ignorance the bidders would consider simple mixing adequate; and the urgency for disinfectant was such that potential contractors could not expend much time learning about it before bidding. In this situation the Government, possessing vital information which it was aware the bidders needed but would not have, could not properly let them flounder on their own. Although it is not a fiduciary toward its contractors, the Government—where the balance of knowledge is so clearly on its side—can no more betray a contractor into a ruinous course of action by silence than by the written or spoken word.

Subsequent cases have used the term "superior knowledge" to describe this obligation of the government. See, for example, *Hercules, Inc. v. United States*, 516 U.S. 417 (1996), and *McDonnell Douglas Corp. v. United States*, 323 F.3d 1006 (Fed. Cir. 2003).

In *J.A. Jones Constr. Co. v. United States*, 182 Ct. Cl. 615, 390 F.2d 886 (1968), the court summarized the elements for a claim of superior knowledge, finding liability when

(1) the government had knowledge of facts,

(2) the contractor neither knew nor should have known the facts, and

(3) the government should have been aware of the contractor's ignorance.

Later cases have stressed the necessity for the information in question to be vital to the efficient performance of the contract and for the nondisclosure of the information to somehow have misled the contractor. In *GAF Corp. v. United States*, 932 F.2d 947 (Fed. Cir. 1991), *cert. denied*, 502 U.S. 1071 (1992), the court stated at 949:

> To show a breach under the superior knowledge doctrine, a contractor claiming a breach by non-disclosure must produce specific evidence that (1) it undertook to perform without vital knowledge of a fact that affects performance costs or direction, (2) the government was aware the contractor had no knowledge of and had no reason to obtain such information, (3) any contract specification supplied misled the contractor, or did not put it on notice to inquire, and (4) the government failed to provide the relevant information.

If the government has disclosed the information orally, it will not be found to be an effective disclosure unless it was "heard, and understood, actually or apparently," *Petrochem Servs., Inc. v. United States*, 837 F.2d 1076 (Fed. Cir. 1988).

The duty to disclose applies even if the information is highly classified, *McDonnell Douglas Corp. v. United States*, 27 Fed. Cl. 204 (1992). In that case, the court concluded that the government could have revealed the presence of the information even if it could not have disclosed the precise information because of security concerns. Such disclosure would have warned the contractor that it was facing greater risks in performing the contract. See, however, *McDonnell Douglas Corp. v. United States*, 323 F.3d 1006 (Fed. Cir. 2003), holding that the government could prevent the contractor from using superior knowledge as a defense to a default termination by declaring the information too highly classified to permit its disclosure in litigation.

1. Government Knowledge of Vital Information

To meet the first element of a superior knowledge claim, the contractor must show that the government had knowledge of information that was vital to permit successful performance of the contract.

a. *Vital Information*

The term "vital information" refers to the type of information that would have an impact on the contractor's estimates or performance. The duty of disclosure applies to specific information that impacts the cost of the work. In *Bradley Constr., Inc. v. United States*, 30 Fed. Cl. 507 (1994), the court held that the duty applied to a $13,500 utility fee on a $4 million contract. The court rejected the government's argument that the rule applying the duty to "vital" information should be construed to limit its application to only information that had a substantial impact on the cost of performance.

Information is "vital" if it would permit the contractor to prepare a more accurate estimate of the cost of performance. See *Kloke Transfer*, ASBCA 39602, 91-3 BCA ¶ 24,356, finding that knowledge that contents of boxes required complete assembly was vital information because assembly resulted in a significant increase in labor. See also *Ogden-HCI Servs.*, ASBCA 32169, 93-3 BCA ¶ 26,141, finding prior sales data vital for a contractor competing for a contract to run a Morale, Welfare and Recreation facility. In *C. M. Moore Div., K.S.H., Inc.*, PSBCA 1131, 85-2 BCA ¶ 18,110, *recons. denied*, 86-1 BCA ¶ 18,573, *aff'd*, 818 F.2d 874 (Fed. Cir. 1987), the board found information vital when the agency knew about the ineffectiveness of a process the contractor intended to use. The board's subsequent decision limiting the contractor's recovery, PSBCA 2208, 90-3 BCA ¶ 23,174, was reversed, 940 F.2d 678 (Fed. Cir. 1991). Compare *Randolph & Co.*, ASBCA 52953, 03-1 BCA ¶ 32,080 (soil information not vital when other information was sufficient); *Franklin Pavkov Constr. Co.*, ASBCA 50828, 00-2 BCA ¶ 31,100 (prior design specification not vital when contract contained performance specification giving contractor flexibility in choosing method of performance); *Dailco Corp.*, ASBCA 50191, 00-2 BCA ¶ 31,048 (undisclosed government report did not contain information on problem encountered by contractor); *Aspen Helicopters, Inc. v. Department of Commerce*, GSBCA 13258-COM, 99-2 BCA ¶ 30,581 (plan not to exercise options not vital to contractor bidding to lease aircraft for two months with two one-year options); *Moore Overseas Constr. Co.*, ENGBCA PCC-125, 98-1 BCA ¶ 29,682 (sketches of buried structures not vital because they contained no indication of the specific location of the structures); and *Hardwick Bros. Co. v. United States*, 36 Fed. Cl. 347 (1996) (contours of construction site not vital because contractor did not use contours in bid package). See also *Solar Turbines, Inc. v. United States*, 26 Cl. Ct. 1249 (1992), *aff'd*, 114 F.3d 1206 (Fed. Cir. 1997), holding that the agency's plans for future procurement of the devices being designed under the contract were not the type of knowledge covered by the doctrine.

It has been held that the duty to disclose does not cover information regarding the methodologies used by prior contractors when the contractor is responsible for determining the method of performance. See *Intercontinental Mfg. Co. v. United States*, 4 Cl. Ct. 591 (1984), stating at 599:

> [W]ith an end-product specification such as is here involved, an imposition upon the Government of a duty of disclosure regarding manufacturing processes and techniques, accomplishes, in practical terms, a reallocation of the performance risks normally shouldered by the fixed-price contractor. Caution demands, therefore, that before such a shift in contractual obligations be enforced, the record substantiate that the performance difficulties likely to be encountered exceed a rightfully expected level of skill and competence in the industry.
>
> In the demonstration of this point, the experience of other contractors is, of course, a relevant consideration. But proof that relies only upon a cataloging of those experiences is not enough. Since we are litigating this case and not some other, it is incumbent upon the aggrieved contractor to explain why, in this procurement, it would have been beyond its properly expected skills and abilities to have foreseen the manufacturing problems that were encountered and the solutions they demanded. To recognize a duty of disclosure on any lesser basis—to require it, for example, simply because claims arose in past procurements—would carry with it the real possibility of obliging the Government to assume the duty of informing the contractor about what it ought to know on its own. To put it another way, adherence to [the contractor's] basis for disclosure runs the distinct risk of elevating substandard performance into an industry norm.

On the other hand, the government has been held liable for not disclosing to small business contractors the fact that prior contractors had difficulties in performing the work, *Johnson Elecs., Inc.*, ASBCA 9366, 65-1 BCA ¶ 4628; *Riverport Indus., Inc.*, ASBCA 30888, 87-2 BCA ¶ 19,876. Compare *General Dynamics Corp.*, ASBCA 13001, 71-2 BCA ¶ 9141, refusing to follow this logic when the contractor was a large company that should have known of the procurement history. See also *Granite Constr. Co. v. United States*, 24 Cl. Ct. 735 (1991), denying relief for claimed nondisclosure of construction difficulties on prior contracts. The court stated at 753 that the government is not a guarantor against poor judgment with respect to methodologies selected by the contractor. In *Woerner Eng'g, Inc.*, ASBCA 52248, 03-1 BCA ¶ 32,196, the board denied a claim because the government had only "general knowledge" about past difficulties and "did not control the manufacturing processes selected and technical choices made by contractors" to perform the contract. Similarly, in *La Belle Indus., Inc.*, ASBCA 49307, 98-2 BCA ¶ 29,774, the board denied the claim of a small contractor because it was presumably able to ascertain the necessary manufacturing processes, having obtained a Certificate of Competency from the Small Business Administration. The board reached this conclusion even though a preaward survey had reported that the contractor did not have the competence to perform the work.

b. Government Knowledge

The contractor must also show that the government possessed the undisclosed information. See *Oceanic Steamship Co. v. United States*, 218 Ct. Cl. 87, 586 F.2d 774 (1978) (knowledge of anticipated rate increases); *Program Res., Inc.*, AS-

BCA 21656, 78-1 BCA ¶ 12,867 (contractor failed to establish that government had knowledge of labor unrest on predecessor contract); *COVCO Hawaii Corp.*, ASBCA 26901, 83-2 BCA ¶ 16,554 (search of government records failed to show surface or subsurface conditions of the site before or after excavation of the pool); *Wilner Constr. Co.*, ASBCA 25719, 83-2 BCA ¶ 16,886 (contractor failed to establish that the government had knowledge that only a sole supplier existed); *P.J. Maffei Bldg. Wrecking Corp. v. United States*, 732 F.2d 913 (Fed. Cir. 1984) (contractor failed to prove that the government possessed better information than that supplied); *Ilbau Constr., Inc.*, ENGBCA 5465, 92-1 BCA ¶ 24,476 (unsubstantiated rumors and anecdotes that the government had heard regarding a previous and similar job could not be considered vital knowledge; the previous contractor had never filed a claim and had been found responsible for all performance problems); *SMC Info. Sys., Inc. v. General Servs. Admin.*, GSBCA 9371, 93-1 BCA ¶ 25,485 (government had no specific knowledge of difficulties in the providing of automatic data processing services; it had informed the contractor of information it would have to retrieve regarding the past difficulties encountered by the prototype designer); *CTA, Inc. v. United States*, 44 Fed. Cl. 684 (1999) (government did not know extent of work requiring specific skill levels); and *Staffco Constr., Inc.*, ASBCA 51764, 02-2 BCA ¶ 31,905 (no "responsible Government official" knew half-scale drawings had been sent to contractor).

Knowledge of one government agency will not be attributed to another government agency absent some meaningful connection between the agencies. In *S.T.G. Constr. Co. v. United States*, 157 Ct. Cl. 409 (1962), the court stated at 416-17:

> To attribute knowledge to one agency of information contained in the files of another governmental department is absurd, in light of the vast number of federal departments, bureaus, and agencies, and the tons of papers contained in the files of each.

See also *Bateson-Stolte, Inc. v. United States*, 158 Ct. Cl. 455, 305 F.2d 386 (1962) (no reason for the Corps of Engineers to know of the Atomic Energy Commission's building plans); *Bethlehem Corp. v. United States*, 199 Ct. Cl. 247, 462 F.2d 1400 (1972) (the fact that there were humidity experts in National Bureau of Standards who would have anticipated technical difficulties was immaterial; there was no showing that laboratory or purchasing office in the Department of Army involved in preparing specifications knew of difficulties that the contractor might experience); *Unitec, Inc.*, ASBCA 22025, 79-2 BCA ¶ 13,923 (board refused to impute knowledge of information in the possession of the Corps of Engineers to procurement personnel on an Air Force base, finding no meaningful connection between Air Force and Corps personnel); *L'Enfant Plaza Props., Inc. v. United States*, 227 Ct. Cl. 1, 645 F.2d 886 (1981) (District of Columbia Redevelopment Land Agency not charged with constructive knowledge of GSA activities, since they were independent entities with minimal connections); *Hawaiian Dredging & Constr. Co.*, ASBCA 25594, 84-2 BCA ¶ 17,290 (Navy found not to have imputed superior knowledge of Department of Labor plans to change regulations regarding foreign employment on Guam because there was no relationship between the two agencies regarding the contract), and *Ryco Constr., Inc. v. United States*, 55 Fed. Cl. 184 (2002) (report of Fish & Wildlife Service of the Department of Interior not within knowledge of Forest Service in Department of Agriculture).

A meaningful connection was found between the Department of the Air Force and the Army Corps of Engineers in *J.A. Jones Constr. Co. v. United States*, 182 Ct. Cl. 615, 390 F.2d 886 (1968), because the Corps was acting as the construction agency for the Air Force on the project involved. In *Cryo-Sonics, Inc.*, ASBCA 11483, 66-2 BCA ¶ 5890, knowledge was imputed from one Air Force command to another Air Force command because the contractor's proposal referred to a report and identified an engineer in the other command. Thus, the procuring command was charged with the knowledge possessed by that engineer. The board stated, however, that it would not automatically impute knowledge from one Air Force command to another absent some meaningful connection.

2. Contractor Knowledge or Reason to Know

The government will not be held liable for nondisclosure of information if it can show that the contractor had actual knowledge of the information or had reason to know of the information.

a. Actual Knowledge

In a number of cases, the government has been able to show that the contractor had actual knowledge of the information, *National Radio Co.*, ASBCA 14707, 72-2 BCA ¶ 9486 (contractor's research prior to award demonstrated that it was "fully acquainted with the facts"); *Jet Power, Inc.*, ASBCA 21559, 83-1 BCA ¶ 16,516 (government nondisclosure of information related to overhaul of armored personnel vehicles harmless where contractor obtained vital knowledge from other sources); *Haas & Haynie Corp.*, GSBCA 5530, 84-2 BCA ¶ 17,446 (government not liable for not disclosing since the information was independently obtained by contractor); *Wayne Constr.*, ENGBCA 4942, 91-1 BCA ¶ 23,535 (no nondisclosure was found where government, though not specifically using the words "glacial till," accurately described the conditions in the harbor that the contractor was required to dredge and excavate); *Ilbau Constr., Inc.*, ENGBCA 5465, 92-1 BCA ¶ 24,476 (information was in the geologic and geotechnic drawings provided by the government); *Caddell Constr. Co.*, ASBCA 43776, 93-3 BCA ¶ 26,001 (contractor knew information from work on prior contract); *Defense Sys. Co.*, ASBCA 50918, 00-2 BCA ¶ 30,991 (contractor had done extensive investigation of problems); and *Vermaas Constr.*, PSBCA 4582, 02-2 BCA ¶ 31,877 (bid package informed bidders of availability of geotechnical report).

b. Reason to Know

Absent proof of actual knowledge, the government can avoid liability for nondisclosure by showing that the contractor should have known the information. For example, the nondisclosure of information that is general knowledge will not make the government liable. See *Johnnie Quinn Painting & Decorating*, ASBCA 22735, 79-1 BCA ¶ 13,797 (knowledge that the work would be difficult was not solely the government's); *Max Jordan Bauunternehmung*, ASBCA 23055, 82-1 BCA ¶ 15,685 (list of qualified interior coating contractors was in public domain); *R.M. Crum Constr. Co.*, IBCA 1627-10-82, 83-2 BCA ¶ 16,597 (fact that "Kleen-Strip" would be an effective paint remover could be determined from general brochures); and *Robin C. Uhde*, AGBCA 90-117-1, 91-1 BCA ¶ 23,604 (weather at site). The fact that the government's general knowledge in the area is more extensive than the contractor's is not material so long as the information is reasonably available elsewhere, *Bermite Div. of Whittaker Corp.*, ASBCA 19211, 77-2 BCA ¶ 12,675; *La Pointe Indus., Inc.*, ASBCA 20291, 78-2 BCA ¶ 13,444; *Continental Rubber Works*, ASBCA 22447, 80-2 BCA ¶ 14,754 (government knowledge of difficulties of prior suppliers of signals was not held exclusively by the government and was reasonably available from other sources). In *Drillers, Inc.*, EBCA 358-5-86, 90-3 BCA ¶ 23,056, the board rejected the argument that, because the government's knowledge of the corrosive levels of hydrogen sulfide in the area where the contractor would be drilling was more extensive than the contractor's, it was superior knowledge per se. The board stated at 115,747:

> Superior knowledge is a much narrower concept than [the contractor] alleges. Superior knowledge does not mean that the Government knows more about a subject than does a particular contractor. Rather it means that the Government knows some fact that is not known or otherwise available to the industry concerned.

Information known in a particular industry is considered knowledge that a contractor could or should know and can therefore rarely be found to be undisclosed superior knowledge, *Industrial Elecs. Hardware Corp.*, ASBCA 10201, 68-1 BCA ¶ 6760, *recons. denied*, 68-2 BCA ¶ 7174 (information was considered generally available in trade circles, as other companies were shown to have manufactured the product); *H.N. Bailey & Assocs. v. United States*, 196 Ct. Cl. 166, 449 F.2d 376 (1971) (metallurgical and technical data that were well known in the industry and thoroughly discussed in textbooks); *B.F. Goodrich Co.*, ASBCA 19960, 76-2 BCA ¶ 12,105 (contractor failed to establish that government possessed information regarding polyurethane-based coated fabrics that was not reasonably available in the industry); *Prestex, Inc.*, ASBCA 21284, 81-1 BCA ¶ 14,882, *recons. denied*, 81-2 BCA ¶ 15,397 (method of fabrication of balloon cloth obtained from the industry and equally available to the contractor); *Granite Constr. Co. v. United States*, 24 Cl. Ct. 735 (1991) (contractor had experience in the field of concrete drilling and should have known that drilling into concrete dam with no knowledge of the amount of aggregate rock within was risky and experimental); *Hill Aviation Logistics*, ASBCA

40817, 93-1 BCA ¶ 25,274 (properties of specified materials to be used in manufacturing contract); *Cosmechem Co. v. General Servs. Admin.*, GSBCA 12147, 93-3 BCA ¶ 26,057 (method of manufacturing commercial product).

A contractor's general knowledge about an area or field will not bar recovery if it can demonstrate that the government failed to disclose specific information not available to the industry. In *Jack L. Olsen, Inc.*, AGBCA 87-345-1, 93-2 BCA ¶ 25,767, *rev'd in part, remanded in part*, 26 F.3d 141 (Fed. Cir. 1994), the contractor on a construction contract was aware that the area of Minnesota in which it was working did not contain many quality sources of "borrow," or fill, from which roads could be built, yet it recovered for nondisclosure by the government of a specific "Materials Report" giving precise information on the quality of the designated borrow areas. In *Sanders Constr. Co.*, IBCA 2309, 90-1 BCA ¶ 22,412, though the contractor was aware that a certain amount of sediment builds up behind dams of the type on which it was contracted to work, the government had an obligation to disclose information revealing unusual levels of sediment in the reservoir. The time when information was generally available may have a bearing on whether the contractor should have known of it. For example, in *Sanders*, the board rejected the government's argument that a local lawsuit and scandal that was common knowledge in the area 10 years earlier was general knowledge that the contractor should have known.

The government often succeeds in arguing that the contractor should have known the information in dispute by showing that it was reasonably available from other sources, *General Maint. & Eng'g Co.*, ASBCA 14691, 71-2 BCA ¶ 9124 (the condition of bridging materials could have been learned through site inspection); *Atlas Constr. Co.*, PSBCA 267, 76-2 BCA ¶ 12,217 (contractor had full access to Water District charges and merely had to request the information); *L.G. Everist, Inc. v. United States*, 231 Ct. Cl. 1013 (1982), *cert. denied*, 461 U.S. 957 (1983) (knowledge of quantity of acceptable rock in a quarry was equally available to both parties); *Young Enters., Inc.*, ASBCA 34138, 89-3 BCA ¶ 22,061 (contractor could easily have researched the pricing and availability of a sole source component of the contract); *Drillers, Inc.*, EBCA 358-5-86, 90-3 BCA ¶ 23,056 (information was in report available in the agency's library); *JEM Dev. Corp.*, ASBCA 42644, 92-1 BCA ¶ 24,451 (contractor could have located the sandblasting material needed for the contract performance by calling some companies listed in the Yellow Pages); *MC Info. Sys., Inc. v. General Servs. Admin.*, GSBCA 9371, 93-1 BCA ¶ 25,485 (information on prior performance difficulties available from historical data on the project, and contractor had been told that it would be working on a prototype system); *Southwood Builders, Inc.*, ASBCA 43489, 93-3 BCA ¶ 26,072 (fact that named product was proprietary could have been obtained by contacting supplier); *J.A. Jones Constr. Co.*, ASBCA 43344, 96-2 BCA ¶ 28,517 (knowledge of budget history of program available from congressional sources); *Reflectone, Inc.*, ASBCA 42363, 98-2 BCA ¶ 29,869 (contractor made no inquiry about difficulties to its subcontractor that had prior experience with product).

The contractor is expected to have such knowledge as a reasonable investigation of the bidding documents or work site would reveal, *Klingensmith v. United States*, 703 F.2d 583 (Fed. Cir. 1982). See also *Key, Inc.*, IBCA 690-23-57, 68-2 BCA ¶ 7385, *recons. denied*, 69-1 BCA ¶ 7447 (contractor did not make a reasonable site investigation); *Kirk L. Whitcombe*, AGBCA 77-184, 79-1 BCA ¶ 13,734 (when the government suggested that the contractor use an alternate route for performance, noting that such use had to be cleared with the owner, the board held that the government was not under a duty to disclose that the city had control over the road as well, because the contractor was responsible for making the appropriate inquiries); *Wayne Constr.*, ENGBCA 4942, 91-1 BCA ¶ 23,535 (visual inspection of quarry would have alerted the contractor to the fractured state of the rock); *Bradley Constr., Inc. v. United States*, 30 Fed. Cl. 507 (1994) (information obtainable from official named in solicitation); *Gonzalez Elec. & General Contractors, Inc. v. United States*, 55 Fed. Cl. 447 (2003) (site investigation would have revealed traffic at site); and *Sherman R. Smoot Corp.*, ASBCA 52173, 03-1 BCA ¶ 32,212 (thorough site investigation would have revealed pealing paint).

The size and sophistication of the contractor may also have a bearing on whether the contractor should be charged with reason to know. See *Tyroc Constr. Corp.*, EBCA 210-3-82, 84-2 BCA ¶ 17,308, in which the board noted that the size of a business is a relevant factor when determining what information a contractor should be able to obtain on its own. It stated at 86,261:

> In a situation involving a small business set-aside-project under Section 8(a), it is especially important for the Government to reveal the information it possesses that would bear on the conditions of performance.
>
> * * *
>
> Under the circumstances of a Section 8(a) negotiation, it would not seem reasonable to require [the contractor] to conduct its own engineering investigation in order to ascertain the accuracy or completeness of the METC estimates supplied to [the contractor].

In *Numax Elecs., Inc.*, ASBCA 29080, 90-1 BCA ¶ 22,280, the government was held liable for failing to reveal to a small contractor that no prior contractor had manufactured the product without deviations from the specifications. In *Johnson Elecs., Inc.*, ASBCA 9366, 65-1 BCA ¶ 4628, award of a manufacturing contract was made on the basis of a small business set-aside. Relief was granted where the government failed to disclose that major electronics companies had been unable to meet all of the specifications. The *Johnson* case was distinguished in *General Dynamics Corp.*, ASBCA 13001, 71-2 BCA ¶ 9161, based on the size of the contractor. The board held that a large, sophisticated firm should have known the difficulties of the job. See also *Northrop Grumman Corp. v. United States*, 47 Fed. Cl. 20 (2000), denying that the government had superior knowledge as to the amount of development work necessary to perform the contract, and stating at 52:

> When a sophisticated contractor's concept is adjudged technically competent and that contractor projects an air of competency with regard to what was required for performance, the Government cannot be held accountable for constructive knowledge of a lack of information about the nature of the contract.

3. Government Knowledge or Reason to Know of Contractor Ignorance

The government will not be held liable for nondisclosure unless it is found to have knowledge or reason to know of the contractor's ignorance of the information. In *Hardeman-Monier-Hutcherson v. United States*, 198 Ct. Cl. 472, 458 F.2d 1364 (1972), the government was liable for knowledge of contractor ignorance of weather and sea conditions at the site when the contractor expressly requested the information from the government. See also *Jack L. Olsen, Inc.*, AGBCA 87-345-1, 93-2 BCA ¶ 25,767, *rev'd in part, remanded in part*, 26 F.3d 141 (Fed. Cir. 1994), where the contractor's request for information from the government regarding the availability of sources for hauling in landfill put the government on notice of the contractor's ignorance.

Contractor ignorance of certain information can sometimes be made evident to the government by the contractor's misunderstanding of bids, proposals, or contract documents. In *Wackenhut Corp.*, IBCA 2311, 91-1 BCA ¶ 23,318, it was clear from the bids as well as requests for information that the contractor was ignorant of the character and costliness of the work. In *Sanders Constr. Co.*, IBCA 2309, 90-1 BCA ¶ 22,412, the contractor's proposal indicated that it expected less sediment in a reservoir than government information revealed was present.

In some cases government reason to know of contractor ignorance can be readily established because the government has control of the information and has restricted its release. See *J.A. Jones Constr. Co. v. United States*, 182 Ct. Cl. 615, 390 F.2d 886 (1968), where the information in question was "classified and released even to other federal agencies only on a 'piecemeal need-to-know basis.'" Thus, there was no way for a private business to know the information. See also *McDonnell Douglas Corp. v. United States*, 27 Fed. Cl. 204 (1992) (Navy was found to know of contractor ignorance because it refused to release information regarding an A-12 Stealth fighter on national security grounds).

The government is generally entitled to assume that the contractor has acquainted itself with the difficulties involved in performing the work, *Intercontinental Mfg. Co. v. United States*, 4 Cl. Ct. 591 (1984). Thus, it has been held that the government is not obligated to furnish bidders with generalized information concerning difficulties encountered by prior contractors, *Granite Constr. Co. v. United States*, 24 Cl. Ct. 735 (1991). See also *Piasecki Aircraft Corp. v. United States*, 229 Ct. Cl. 208,

667 F.2d 50 (1981), *aff'g*, ASBCA 18783, 78-1 BCA ¶ 12,886, where the contractor claimed that the government failed to disclose that the product had not been successfully prototyped, that prior contractors for similar products encountered various difficulties, and that at the time of award the government was unaware of any banner material conforming to the performance requirements. Relief was denied on the ground that the government was relying on the bidder's expertise regarding banner fabrication and that the government had either disclosed its relevant knowledge or information was available in the industry. In *American Ship Bldg. Co. v. United States*, 228 Ct. Cl. 220, 654 F.2d 75 (1981), the court reasoned that the government, when not asked about prior contracts, reasonably concluded that the contractor had obtained the information somewhere else.

The government is not obligated to investigate to determine if the contractor has knowledge of facts that are generally known in its industry. Thus, there is no government obligation to ascertain the state of a contractor's knowledge of the hazards connected with products made of asbestos, *GAF Corp. v. United States*, 932 F.2d 947 (Fed. Cir. 1991), *cert. denied*, 502 U.S. 1071 (1992); *Lopez v. A.C.&S., Inc.*, 858 F.2d 712 (Fed. Cir. 1988).

Where the information is specific and the contractor likely would not be able to obtain it, the government will be assumed to have reason to know of the contractor's ignorance. For example, in *Lear Siegler, Inc.*, ASBCA 22235, 81-2 BCA ¶ 15,372, *recons. denied*, 82-2 BCA ¶ 15,832, the government was liable for not disclosing specific problems experienced by prior producers. Some cases have held that the government should assume contractor ignorance of information that prior manufacturers of the same item had found it necessary to modify a certain component that was called for by the specifications, *G.W. Galloway Co.*, ASBCA 17436, 77-2 BCA ¶ 12,640; *Federal Elec. Corp.*, ASBCA 13030, 69-2 BCA ¶ 7792. It has also been assumed that the contractor did not have information that only the specified item in a brand name or equal solicitation would meet the government specifications, *Elrich Constr. Co.*, GSBCA 3657, 73-2 BCA ¶ 10,187. Compare *Young Enters., Inc.*, ASBCA 34138, 89-3 BCA ¶ 22,061, denying recovery in the same situation because the contractor could have learned that only the brand name item could meet the requirements by checking other sources before bidding. Information that modification of existing products would be required has also been assumed to be outside the scope of contractor knowledge, *Joseph Penner*, GSBCA 4647, 80-2 BCA ¶ 14,604; *F.F. Slocomb Corp.*, ASBCA 16715, 73-2 BCA ¶ 10,209. Knowledge that specifications are defective has been found not to be reasonably expected of the contractor, *E.J.T. Constr. Co.*, ASBCA 22795, 83-2 BCA ¶ 16,712; *Bromley Contracting Co.*, HUDBCA 75-8, 77-1 BCA ¶ 12,232. See also *Power City Elec., Inc.*, IBCA 950-1-72, 74-1 BCA ¶ 10,376 (condition of access roads to the work site found too specific for contractor to be acquainted with).

Information regarding subsurface conditions is often considered knowledge that the government should assume the contractor is unaware of, *Levering & Garrigues*

Co. v. United States, 73 Ct. Cl. 566 (1932) (government found liable for nondisclosure of a sunken sea wall). See also *Potashnick v. United States*, 123 Ct. Cl. 197 (1952) (contractor not expected to know of government misuse of core boring data in specifications and drawings); *JB & C Co.*, IBCA 1020-2-74, 77-2 BCA ¶ 12,782, *recons. denied*, 78-1 BCA ¶ 13,025 (contractor ignorant of subsurface water migration); *Pacific Western Constr., Inc.*, DOTCAB 1084, 82-2 BCA ¶ 16,045, *recons. denied*, 83-1 BCA ¶ 16,337 (only government reasonably held to have knowledge that prior contractors had encountered amounts of clay); *Flores Drilling & Pump Co.*, AGBCA 82-204-3, 83-1 BCA ¶ 16,200, *recons. denied*, 83-1 BCA ¶ 16,336 (government knowledge about the probable nature of the material and the formation to be encountered assumed unknown by contractor); and *Sanders Constr. Co.*, IBCA 2309, 90-1 BCA ¶ 22,412 (unusual amount of sediment at bottom of full reservoir was not apparent to contractor on site examination).

III. IMPLIED WARRANTY OF SPECIFICATIONS

Government specifications may describe the work in extensive detail, may simply require an end result, or may contain any combination of these two techniques. Traditionally, the government has included significant amounts of detail in its specifications, for a number of reasons, including obtaining standardization, avoiding duplication of costs of design, ensuring fair competition, creating a firm baseline for measuring contractor performance, and ensuring contractor performance. Whatever the reason, the government will generally be liable for extra costs incurred by the contractor if the details that it specifies create problems that the contractor could not reasonably have foreseen. The legal theory used in such cases is the implied warranty of specifications, which allocates the risk to the government when the specifications it furnishes are not suitable for their intended purpose, *United States v. Spearin*, 248 U.S. 132 (1918). The warranty does not extend to third-party claims against the contractor. See *Hercules, Inc. v. United States*, 516 U.S. 417 (1996), in which the court stated at 425:

> Neither the warranty nor *Spearin* extends that far. When the Government provides specifications directing how a contract is to be performed, the Government warrants that the contractor will be able to perform the contract satisfactorily if it follows the specifications. The specifications will not frustrate performance or make it impossible. It is quite logical to infer from the circumstance of one party providing specifications for performance that that party warrants the capability of performance. But this circumstance alone does not support a further inference that would extend the warranty beyond performance to third-party claims against the contractor. In this case, for example, it would be strange to conclude that the United States, understanding the herbicide's military use, actually contemplated a warranty that would extend to sums a manufacturer paid to a third party to settle claims such as are involved in the present action. It seems more likely that the Government would avoid such an obligation, because reimbursement through contract would provide a contractor with what is denied to it through tort law.

The analysis of implied warranty in this section begins with a discussion of the theory upon which the warranty is based. The next subsections address the type of specification language from which an implied warranty will be construed and the extent of the warranty. The section concludes with an examination of the roles of causation and reasonable reliance in fixing responsibility.

A. Basis of Government Responsibility

It was thought at one time that government liability for defective specifications was based on "superior knowledge" or expertise. Now it is clear that this liability is based on the fact that the government has undertaken the responsibility by preparing or supplying the specifications that will be used in preparing estimates and performing the work. See *Consolidated Diesel Elec. Corp.*, ASBCA 10486, 67-2 BCA ¶ 6669, stating at 30,951-52:

> The Government's implied warranty of the adequacy of its specifications is based on its responsibility for the specifications rather than any presumed superior knowledge in the sense of greater expertise. When one of the parties to a contract undertakes to prepare the specifications, that party is responsible for the correctness, adequacy and feasibility of the specifications, and the other party is under no obligation to check and verify the work product of the party who assumed responsibility for the preparation of the specifications, even though he may be as much or more of an expert than the party who prepared the specifications.
>
> * * *
>
> It is a misapplication of the superior knowledge concept when the implied warranty of the adequacy of the specifications is made to depend on whether the Government or a particular contractor has greater knowledge, experience and expertise in the technical field to which the specifications relate. The Government cannot be relieved from its responsibility for the proper preparation of the advertised specifications on the ground that the successful bidder is more of an expert on the item involved than is the Government.

See also *Greenbrier Indus. Inc.*, ASBCA 22121, 81-1 BCA ¶ 14,982, *recons. denied*, 81-1 BCA ¶ 15,057, where a contractor was to produce chemical protective suits in accordance with government design specifications, which called for the use of charcoal-impregnated foam rubber lining. During the first mass production of the article, workers coming in contact with the lining suffered numerous and various health problems, which caused the contractor great difficulty. The board noted at 74,135:

> Since each side appears to be an innocent party, the law of warranty permits the [contractor] to have recourse against the Government as author of the specifications, the root cause of the [contractor's] production problems.

This implied warranty attaches to government-furnished specifications even though the government does not actually prepare the specifications. Thus, the government is liable when it obtains the specifications from another contractor, as it often does, and provides them to the contractor. See *North Am. Philips Co. v. United States*, 175 Ct. Cl. 71, 358 F.2d 980 (1966), in which the court stated that "the [government] being the procurer and supplier of the drawings must bear the responsibility," and *Radionics, Inc.*, ASBCA 22727, 81-1 BCA ¶ 15,011, where the government's adoption of the drawings made it irrelevant that a third party had originally authored them. The government has also been held responsible when it has adopted specifications prepared by the contractor on a prior development contract, *United Techs. Corp. v. United States*, 27 Fed. Cl. 393 (1992), *recons. denied*, 31 Fed. Cl. 698 (1994); *Boeing Military Airplane Co.*, ASBCA 33674, 92-1 BCA ¶ 24,470; *General Elec. Co.*, ASBCA 36005, 91-3 BCA ¶ 24,353; *Temco Aircraft Corp.*, ASBCA 6541, 61-2 BCA ¶ 3211. See also *Tranco Indus., Inc.*, ASBCA 22379, 78-2 BCA ¶ 13,307, *recons. denied*, 78-2 BCA ¶ 13,522, in which the government was held liable for detailed requirements that it adopted from the contractor's value engineering proposal that was withdrawn before being accepted. However, the government is not liable if the contractor enters into a contract to construct a ship before it has completed the design of the ship, *Peterson Builders, Inc. v. United States*, 37 Fed. Cl. 407 (1997), *aff'd*, 155 F.3d 566 (Fed. Cir. 1998).

Since government liability is based on its adoption and promulgation of the specification, it is not liable if the contractor voluntarily participates substantially in the process of drafting the specification. See *Johns-Manville Corp. v. United States*, 13 Cl. Ct. 72 (1987), *vacated for lack of jurisdiction*, 855 F.2d 1571 (Fed. Cir. 1988), in which the court stated at 119-20:

> [For the warranty to apply it must be determined] that the design specifications [were] devised and drafted by the Government. Because of the often extensive interplay between contractors and the Government during the development, modification, and purchase of products, it must be determined whether design specifications are truly the Government's own, or whether the contractor has assisted in their drafting and provided such expertise as to negate the Government's implied warranty, because the Government specifications, in effect, endorse the contractor's product or input.
>
> * * *
>
> In *Austin Co. v. United States*, 161 Ct. Cl. 76, 314 F.2d 518, *cert. denied*, 375 U.S. 830 (1963), the contractor's implied warranty claim failed because its proposed technical modifications were incorporated into the Government's specifications. The contractor's voluntary preparation of the specifications for what was essentially a new product indicated to the court that the contractor had assumed the risk of impossibility of performance, and the court found no implied warranty by the Government. In *Bethlehem Steel Corp. v. United States*, 199 Ct. Cl. 247, 462 F.2d 1400 (1972) (per curiam), the court also denied a warranty of specifications claim. Although the Government had drafted the specifications for an environmental test chamber, it did so in reliance on extensive information provided by the contractor and with the con-

tractor's full knowledge that the Government was relying on its expertise. The court held that the contractor had assumed the risk of non-performance.

For this rule to apply, the contractor must have significant involvement in drafting the defective specification. Thus, mere participation in panel discussions during the drafting process will not shift the risk to the contractor, *Haehn Mgmt. Co. v. United States*, 15 Cl. Ct. 50, *aff'd*, 878 F.2d 1445 (Fed. Cir. 1989). Similarly, no assumption of risk by the contractor was found when the government amended a specification using a contractor's suggestion that had been submitted in a value engineering proposal but withdrawn before the government acted on it, *Tranco Indus., Inc.*, ASBCA 22379, 78-2 BCA ¶ 13,307, *recons. denied*, 78-2 BCA ¶ 13,522.

Although performance to defective government specifications may in some cases be literally impossible, a finding of impossibility of performance or commercial impracticability is not an element of the implied warranty of specifications. See *Dynalectron Corp.*, ASBCA 11766, 69-1 BCA ¶ 7595, in which the board recognized the confusion created by characterizing such cases under the doctrine of impossibility of performance, stating at 35,275:

> To the extent that the contract drawings specified the dimensions, weight and configuration of the antennas, the specifications of the subject contract were design specifications. If compliance with those requirements failed to produce the electrical performance characteristics of WCLG-3B, then the specifications were deficient. . . . There is no necessity in this case for a leap into the complicated, turbulent and esoteric seas of "impossibility." As a matter of grammar, when deficient specifications preclude fabrication of an item, it may be said that performance is "impossible." But that is not the set of circumstances which create the legal doctrine of impossibility of performance, as we understand it.

When defective specifications are encountered, the contractor is entitled to recover the increased expenditures caused by the defect, even though they may be relatively minor in amount, *Sierra Blanca, Inc.*, ASBCA 32161, 90-2 BCA ¶ 22,846; *Virginia Elecs. Co.*, ASBCA 18778, 77-1 BCA ¶ 12,393, *aff'd*, 221 Ct. Cl. 962 (1979); *R.C. Hedreen Co.*, ASBCA 20599, 77-1 BCA ¶ 12,328. However, the contractor must prove that it incurred additional costs in order to recover. See *Franklin Pavkov Constr. Co. v. Roche*, 279 F.3d 989 (Fed. Cir. 2002), denying recovery when the contractor was furnished obsolete drawings that required more work than the amount actually performed. The court reasoned that there had been no cost impact from the defective drawings.

B. Scope of the Warranty

Implied warranties of specifications generally arise out of provisions dealing with the details of the work. There is no implied warranty if the specification provides only for the attainment of end results. This section first analyzes the type of language that will be construed as providing details and the nature of the details provided. Next, it considers two special applications of the implied warranty of specifications—specified alternatives and commercial availability. It concludes with a discussion of the degree of accuracy required of government specifications.

1. Type of Specification Language

Specifications detailing the method or manner of the contractor's performance are often categorized as design specifications. These are contrasted with performance specifications, which leave to the contractor's discretion the details of performance. This distinction between the types of specifications was discussed in *Monitor Plastics Co.*, ASBCA 14447, 72-2 BCA ¶ 9626 at 44,971:

> Because of the characteristics of the specifications involved in the instant contract, we deem it essential to discuss and apply our definition of the three basic types of specifications. There are DESIGN specifications which set forth precise measurements, tolerances, materials, in process and finished product tests, quality control, inspection requirements, and other specific information. Under this type specification, the Government is responsible for design and related omissions, errors, and deficiencies in the specifications and drawings. PERFORMANCE specifications set forth operational characteristics desired for the item. In such specifications design, measurements and other specific details are not stated nor considered important so long as the performance requirement is met. Where an item is purchased by a performance specification, the contractor accepts general responsibility for design, engineering, and achievement of the stated performance requirements. The contractor has general discretion and election as to detail but the work is subject to the Government's reserved right of final inspection and approval or rejection. PURCHASE DESCRIPTIONS are specifications which designate a particular manufacturer's model, part number, or product. The description may be modified by the phrase "or equal." Under this specification if the contractor furnishes, or uses in fabrication, the specified brand name or an acceptable and approved or equal, the responsibility for proper performance generally falls upon the Government. We state "generally" because the Government's responsibility is conditioned upon the correct use of the product by the contractor. If the contractor elects to manufacture an equal product in-house, it is his responsibility to assure that the product is equal to the specified brand named product.
>
> Specification problems become more complex when a specification is a composite of two or all three of these types. When there is a composite it is necessary to test each portion of the specification, insofar as responsibility is concerned. *Aerodex, Inc.*, ASBCA No. 7121 [1962 BCA ¶ 3492]; *Dynalectron Corporation-Pacific Division*, ASBCA Nos. 11766 & 12271, 69-1 BCA ¶ 7595; *A.C. Hoyle Company*, [ASBCA 15363, 71-2 BCA ¶ 9137].

In *J.L. Simmons Co. v. United States*, 188 Ct. Cl. 684, 412 F.2d 1360 (1969), the court elaborated on the design-performance specification distinction at 689:

> The specifications, which were prepared by the [government], are a classic example of "design" specifications, and not "performance" specifications. In other words, in these specifications, the [government] set forth in precise detail the

> materials to be employed and the manner in which the work was to be performed, and [the contractor] was not privileged to deviate therefrom, but was required to follow them as one would a road map. In contrast, typical "performance" type specifications set forth an objective or standard to be achieved, and the successful bidder is expected to exercise his ingenuity in achieving that objective or standard of performance, selecting the means and assuming a corresponding responsibility for that selection.

In *Big Chief Drilling Co. v. United States*, 26 Cl. Ct. 1276 (1992), the court confirmed the distinction, stating at 1294:

> Design specifications set forth in detail the materials to be employed and the manner in which the work is to be performed, and the contractor is "required to follow them as one would a road map." *J.L. Simmons Co. v. United States*, 188 Ct. Cl. 684, 689, 412 F.2d 1360, 1362 (1969). Whereas, performance specifications simply set forth an objective or end result to be achieved, and the contractor may select the means of accomplishing the task. *Id.* at 689, 412 F.2d at 1362.

Since most government specifications contain both design and performance requirements, it is usually necessary to determine which requirement caused the contractor's difficulties, *Aleutian Constructors v. United States*, 24 Cl. Ct. 372 (1991). Thus, even though a specification contains many details of performance, recovery will be denied if the contractor's problems are in an area in which the contractor has discretion to formulate its own method of performance such that it is responsible for successful contract completion. See, e.g., *Engineering Tech. Consultants, S.A.*, ASBCA 43600, 92-3 BCA ¶ 25,133, *recons. denied*, 93-1 BCA ¶ 25,507 (general drawings of roofing flashing considered only schematic in nature and not detailed enough to be considered design specifications); *Continental Rubber Works*, ASBCA 22447, 80-2 BCA ¶ 14,754 (suggested formulations for manufacture of hose did not shift risks to the government where the specification was of the performance and not design variety); *Flinchbaugh Prods. Corp.*, ASBCA 19851, 78-2 BCA ¶ 13,375 (detailed drawings and specifications, but method of fitting aluminum sleeve to body not specified); *Sarkisian Bros., Inc.*, PSBCA 408, 78-1 BCA ¶ 13,076 (specifications contained only minimum design requirements such as type of material and minimum thickness, with contractor responsible for design and fabrication of load plates on vehicle lifts of postal facility); and *Piasecki Aircraft Corp.*, ASBCA 18783, 78-1 BCA ¶ 12,886, *aff'd*, 229 Ct. Cl. 208, 667 F.2d 50 (1981) (contract silent on type of materials and method of fabrication of tow targets).

In determining whether design requirements or performance requirements are controlling, the courts and boards frequently look to the overall contractual scheme to determine if the contractor reasonably relied on the specification in preparing its offer. The key element in such analysis is the ability of the contractor to analyze the problem during the contract formation process, when it has only limited time and resources. Thus, in *M.A. Mortenson Co.*, ASBCA 39978, 93-3 BCA ¶ 26,189, the board found that the government was liable for the estimated quantities of material indicated in conceptual design drawings even though the contract to be awarded was a design/build contract under which the contractor had the responsibility for completing the design and preparing the construction drawings. The board reasoned that the contractor had no choice but to rely on the conceptual drawings in preparing a firm price for the construction aspect of the work. See also *J.E. Dunn Constr. Co.*, GSBCA 14477, 00-1 BCA ¶ 30,806, holding the government liable for curtain wall design even though the contract contained a number of performance requirements. In contrast, see *Wilco Constr., Inc.*, ASBCA 53683, 02-2 BCA ¶ 31,942, relieving the government of liability when the contract required the contractor to move 21,500 books but the specifications called for moving all books; *PCL Constr. Servs., Inc. v. United States*, 47 Fed. Cl. 745 (2000), relieving the government of liability because the contract stated "that the design package conveyed only the 'design and engineering intent' for the project, and that the design drawings would be supplemented and detailed as necessary to construct the final product"; and *Bailey & Son Constr. Co.*, ASBCA 38435, 90-1 BCA ¶ 22,419, relieving the government of liability for detailed requirements because the solicitation required offerors to make design calculations to ensure the integrity of the building to be constructed.

Broad contract language attempting to overcome the implied warranty is generally unsuccessful. See *Al Johnson Constr. Co. v. United States*, 854 F.2d 467 (Fed. Cir 1988), stating at 468:

> The implied warranty is not overcome by the customary self-protective clauses the government inserts in its contracts, as in *Spearin* itself, requiring the contractor to examine the site, to check the plans, and to assume responsibility for the work, including its safekeeping, until completion and acceptance.

See *White v. Edsall Constr. Co.*, 296 F.3d 1081 (Fed. Cir. 2002) (government liable for poor design even when contractor was required to "verify" details of design); *Essex Electro Engrs., Inc.*, ASBCA 49915, 99-1 BCA ¶ 30,229, *rev'd on other grounds*, 224 F.3d 1283 (Fed. Cir. 2000) (government liable for defective drawings even though contract required contractor to identify incorrect drawings); *Geo-Con, Inc.*, ENGBCA 5749, 94-1 BCA ¶ 26,359 (government liable for defective mixing formula even though contract stated it might require some adjustments); *Robert & Son Constr.*, VABCA 3552, 93-3 BCA ¶ 26,113 (requirement for verification of accuracy of detailed drawings did not relieve government of liability for inaccuracies); and *Gracon Corp.*, IBCA 2271, 89-1 BCA ¶ 21,232 (requirement to coordinate parts of system did not relieve government of liability for defects). Compare *J.S. Alberici Constr. Co.*, GSBCA 10427, 92-1 BCA ¶ 24,393 (requirement for verification of dimensions during site visit relieved government of liability for inaccuracies).

The nature of the specification may override a general contract requirement. Thus, in *Parsons of Cal.*, ASBCA 20867, 82-1 BCA ¶ 15,659, the detailed specifications in the contract were found to have placed the liability for defects on the government even though the solicitation required the contractor to design, manufacture, test, and deliver the hospital. Similarly, in *Toombs & Co. v. United States*, 4 Cl. Ct.

535, 547 (1984), the contractor's responsibility for detailed design in preparing shop drawings was found not to have "overcome the detailed requirements of the contract documents and the control in fact exercised by the [government's] consultants."

The government sometimes attempts to convert a design specification to a performance specification by including language obligating the contractor to install or construct a complete job. While such provisions may be held to require the contractor to furnish relatively minor items not specifically mentioned in the drawings and specifications, *Highland Constr. Corp.*, CGBCA T-222, 67-1 BCA ¶ 6094 (door hinges and lock in hangar construction), they do not relieve the government from liability for errors in the specifications, *Leslie-Elliott Constructors, Inc.*, ASBCA 20507, 77-1 BCA ¶ 12,354. Similarly, the mere addition of a statement to a design specification to the effect that the item being manufactured must work properly will not place the responsibility on the contractor. See *Harrison Western/Franki-Denys, Inc.*, ENGBCA 5523, 92-1 BCA ¶ 24,582, in which the government's argument that the contractor was working under a performance specification was rejected by the board because the specifications contained substantial and detailed criteria of design intent. See also *R.E.D.M. Corp. v. United States*, 192 Ct. Cl. 891, 428 F.2d 1304 (1970), in which the court stated at 901-02:

> Manifestly, these were so-called "design" drawings and specifications by which the contractor was given detailed instructions respecting the fabrication of each of the many components of the total fuze [sic] assembly. The mere addition of a brief narrative admonition that the completed article had to arm properly did not transform the fundamental character of the drawings and specifications into the so-called "performance" type, under which the contractor is simply told to achieve a given result and essentially left to his own devices as to how to do so.

Although in general performance requirements in specifications give the contractor discretion to determine how to accomplish the job, the amount of discretion must be determined by reading the contract as a whole. See *Blake Constr. Co. v. United States*, 987 F.2d 743 (Fed. Cir. 1993), in which the court rejected the contractor's argument that the electric conduit schematic drawings were merely performance requirements giving it full discretion to locate the conduits in the most desirable location. The court reasoned that, although the drawings did not impose detailed requirements, they could not be reasonably interpreted as permitting the contractor to locate the conduits in an area completely different from that indicated on the drawings.

a. Design Specifications

There are many types of design specifications. The clearest examples are where the government requires or advises that a contractor follow a given design or blueprint during production, use specific material, or incorporate specific processes into its performance. However, performance-type statements can also be design specifications if they leave the contractor no discretion during performance. See *Johns-*

Manville Corp. v. United States, 13 Cl. Ct. 72 (1987), *vacated for lack of jurisdiction*, 855 F.2d 1571 (Fed. Cir. 1988), stating at 131:

> When a specification includes a compositional requirement, that portion is a design specification because it tells the manufacturer which materials must be used, *USA Petroleum Corp.*, 821 F.2d at 622; *J.L. Simmons Co.*, 188 Ct. Cl. at 689, 412 F.2d at 1362. When a specification includes a requirement that the product conform to certain standards for density, tensile strength, or ability to withstand vibration, for example, the distinction between design and performance specifications becomes more clouded. The categorization of such requirements must depend on the circumstances attendant to manufacturing the product or products covered by the particular specification, if the distinction between design and performance specifications is to have any theoretical integrity. At the crux of this distinction is the degree to which the contractor or manufacturer is free "to exercise his ingenuity in achieving that objective or standard of performance, [and] selecting the means" to do so, *J.L. Simmons Co., id.* When the contractor is left no discretion or choice in the materials to be used, the specification (or portion of it) is design-type. The specification is no less a design specification when, although a particular material or composition is not expressly required, it is apparent that only one material or a certain composition will enable the product to meet the performance standards expressed in the specification.

The government is most clearly liable for defective specifications when it designates a particular type of material or component to be used. See *Jimenez, Inc.*, LBCA 2001-BCA-2, 02-2 BCA ¶ 31,981 (specified flashing could not be soldered without damaging paint); *M.A. Mortenson Co. v. United States*, 40 Fed. Cl. 389 (1998), *aff'd*, 250 F.3d 762 (Fed. Cir. 2000) (specified pipe did not meet performance requirements); *C.L. Fairley Constr. Co.*, ASBCA 32581, 90-2 BCA ¶ 22,665, *recons. denied*, 90-3 BCA ¶ 23,005 (specified asphalt did not reach appropriate compaction levels for airport runway); *T.H. Taylor, Inc.*, ASBCA 26494, 82-2 BCA ¶ 15,877 (more than minor modifications necessary to make transformers comply with performance requirements where contract permitted only use of commercial transformers); *Parsons of Cal.*, ASBCA 20867, 82-1 BCA ¶ 15,659 (specified weather stripping adhesive did not work); *Greenbrier Indus. Inc.*, ASBCA 22121, 81-1 BCA ¶ 14,982, *recons. denied*, 81-1 BCA ¶ 15,057 (use of charcoal-impregnated foam rubber lining in chemical protective suits caused health problems for contractor's employees); *R.C. Hedreen Co.*, ASBCA 20599, 77-1 BCA ¶ 12,328 (specified pipe was incompatible with the testing standard such that it could not pass the requisite tests); and *Valley Asphalt Corp.*, ASBCA 17595, 74-2 BCA ¶ 10,680 (tack coat applied according to specification did not properly cure). See also *J.S. Alberici Constr. Co.*, ENGBCA 4800, 90-1 BCA ¶ 22,320 (piling structure specified in contract was inadequate for cofferdam installation job, because the method was unstable in the strong river current); *Santa Fe Eng'rs, Inc.*, ASBCA 21450, 77-1 BCA ¶ 12,403 (government-specified conductors and panelboards were incompatible); *Leslie-Elliott Constructors, Inc.*, ASBCA 20507, 77-1 BCA ¶ 12,354 (government design of three-pipe sprinkler system was defective since it did not meet performance requirements); *J.D. Hedin Constr. Co. v. United States*, 171 Ct. Cl. 70, 347 F.2d 235 (1965); and *J.L. Simmons Co. v. United States*, 188 Ct. Cl. 684, 412 F.2d 1360 (1969) (contracts to construct hospital facilities contained similar detailed specifications requiring concrete piles to be thin-shelled, which proved to be inadequate since they could not be properly driven).

Specifications that set forth required dimensions are defective if the item built to the dimensions is not usable as specified. In *Harrison Western/Franki-Denys, Inc.*, ENGBCA 5523, 92-1 BCA ¶ 24,582, for example, the design specification for the size of a gasket needed in the construction of a subway tunnel was found defective because neither the basic gasket profile nor the alternate plan contained dimensions proper for the job. In *Monmouth Fund, Inc.*, ASBCA 20158, 77-1 BCA ¶ 12,305, the government was liable where the plan dimensions of an air conditioning duct were such that the ceiling height specified was unattainable. Similarly, when the government sets forth dimension tolerances for components of a product, the implied warranty permits the contractor to use the full tolerance on each component. See *Sterling Millwrights, Inc. v. United States*, 26 Cl. Ct. 49 (1992) (incorrect dimensions of steel structure); *MRC Corp.*, PSBCA 1083, 84-1 BCA ¶ 17,013 (government found liable when the full use of dimension tolerances in ball bearings resulted in a failure of the rotating parts of a postal depository to function properly); *R.E.D.M. Corp. v. United States*, 192 Ct. Cl. 891, 428 F.2d 1304 (1970) (contract drawings were defective in giving too broad a range of leaf-metal thickness for the proper arming of fuse assemblies); and *Ithaca Gun Co. v. United States*, 176 Ct. Cl. 437 (1966) (contractor recovered its increased costs attributable to components that did not satisfactorily mate when manufactured within permissible dimension tolerances). However, in *Chaparral Indus., Inc.*, ASBCA 34396, 91-2 BCA ¶ 23,813, *aff'd*, 975 F.2d 870 (Fed. Cir. 1992), the board gave no relief to a contractor who met the contractually specified dimensions in cutting foam cushions but found that they would not fit into missile containers. The board found that the defect was caused by swelling resulting when the cushions were delivered in Denver, and reasoned that the contractor was liable because it had chosen to manufacture the cushions at sea level and thus had added an unforeseen element, the altitude fluctuation, to the contract performance method.

Design specifications depicting a method of performance or the particular processes a contractor is to follow are also warranted. In *Ordnance Research, Inc. v. United States*, 221 Ct. Cl. 641, 609 F.2d 462 (1979), the court permitted the contractor to recover increased costs caused by explosions during production of fire bombs when the contractor followed specifications that described in detail the materials and the manufacturing processes to be used. See also *Apollo Sheet Metal, Inc. v. United States*, 44 Fed. Cl. 210 (1999) (drawings described precise size of excavation for specified size of pipe); *Sipco Servs. & Marine, Inc. v. United States*, 41 Fed. Cl. 196 (1998) (specifications required removal of paint in inaccessible area); *Ball, Ball & Brosamer, Inc.*, IBCA 2841, 97-2 BCA ¶ 29,072 (specifications prescribed an aggregate source that had unsuitable material); *Hobbs Constr. & Dev., Inc.*, ASBCA

34890, 91-2 BCA ¶ 23,755 (detailed requirements for pouring concrete); *Maecon, Inc.*, ASBCA 31081, 89-2 BCA ¶ 21,855 (detailed procedures for pouring concrete); *Real Fresh, Inc.*, ASBCA 27274, 84-2 BCA ¶ 17,414 (specifications set forth the requisite sterilization temperatures); and *Turner Constr. Co.*, GSBCA 3549, 74-2 BCA ¶ 10,934, *recons. denied*, 75-1 BCA ¶ 11,106 (government-specified soldering method led to excessive leakage).

Similarly, the government is liable if specified equipment cannot be successfully used in performing the contract. See *Maitland Bros. Co.*, ASBCA 23849, 83-1 BCA ¶ 16,434 (use of the D-8 type crawler led to inefficiencies and decreased productivity); *Evergreen Eng'g, Inc.*, IBCA 994-5-73, 78-2 BCA ¶ 13,226 (use of traveling cement mixers with designated materials led to unexpected difficulty and costs); and *Telecommunications Servs., Inc.*, VACAB 1185, 77-2 BCA ¶ 12,847 (required camera incompatible for use with designated operating microscope). In *Wilson Constr., Inc.*, AGBCA 89-178-1, 92-2 BCA ¶ 24,798, however, the board held that the terms in the specifications mandating the chipping of cleared timber and brush into mulch were general and did not provide a warranty that the contractor's use of one wood chipper would be satisfactory to complete the job on time or that its use would be free of difficulties.

Liability has also been placed on the government when a specified test causes unexpected problems. See *Transtechnology Corp. v. United States*, 22 Cl. Ct. 349 (1990) (test procedures cracked flares being tested), and *Astro Dynamics, Inc.*, ASBCA 28320, 83-2 BCA ¶ 16,900 (contractually required hydrostatic pressure test deformed booster tubes being produced). See also *Technical Ordnance, Inc.*, ASBCA 48086, 95-2 BCA ¶ 27,744, in which the government was held liable where the product failed the tests after the contractor had built both the product and the test chamber in accordance with detailed specifications. In *Fox Constr., Inc. v. General Servs. Admin.*, GSBCA 11543, 93-3 BCA ¶ 26,193, however, the board found no government liability when the contractor's use of water to test the tubing in an air conditioning unit, as required by the specifications, resulted in the damaging of the tubes when residue water froze in the winter weather and split the tubing. The board held that the test procedure was not the actual cause of the damage, but that the contractor's inappropriate timing of the tests was to blame.

The government also assumes the risk if its detailed specifications require performance contradictory to local codes or ordinances. In *Castle Constr. Co.*, ASBCA 28509, 84-1 BCA ¶ 17,045, the specifications were defective because they required the contractor to construct a sewer line with more fixtures than were permitted under the local plumbing codes. In *Huber, Hunt & Nichols, Inc.*, GSBCA 4311, 75-2 BCA ¶ 11,457, the government was held liable when its detailed drawings of drain lines and a ventilation system conflicted with local codes. Compare *Edwards v. United States*, 19 Cl. Ct. 663 (1990), where the contract specifications for the building of a post office by the contractor called for curb dimensions in violation of local zoning ordinances, but no government liability was found because the contractor, in the open advertising procurement program, was responsible for the choice of the location of the building and, thus, for investigation of and compliance with local regulations.

Specifications may be defective if they are unusually difficult to use. See *John McShain, Inc. v. United States*, 188 Ct. Cl. 830, 412 F.2d 1281 (1969), where the specifications were defective because the drawings were illegible, blurred, and not properly coordinated with one another. The contractor's assumptions that it could readily obtain readable drawings and that addenda drawings corrected errors of the original drawings were held to be reasonable. The government has also been held liable when it provided microfilm drawings of poor quality, *Thompson Ramo Wooldridge, Inc. v. United States*, 175 Ct. Cl. 527, 361 F.2d 222 (1966); *Teledyne Lewisburg v. United States*, 699 F.2d 1336 (Fed. Cir. 1983). Specifications are not considered defective, however, if the difficulty in using them arises from the contractor's duty to coordinate multiple drawings or plans. In *Caddell Constr. Co.*, VABCA 3509, 93-3 BCA ¶ 26,114, unclear contract drawings could be coordinated and cross-referenced to accurately reveal the location of smoke dampers and were therefore not found to contain insufficient or unusable specifications.

The implied warranty of specifications is applicable if the government designates certain materials or procedures that are incompatible with the level of production expressed in the contract, or made evident by the length of the performance period or other indicia. In *La Crosse Garment Mfg. Co. v. United States*, 193 Ct. Cl. 168, 432 F.2d 1377 (1970), defects in the design portions of the specifications for the manufacture of gas mask carriers made mass production at the contemplated level of production impossible. In granting relief, the court stated at 180-81:

> "Mass production" is a variable; there are countless degrees between laborious production of units, one at a time, and their rapid flow on an assembly line. Cf. *Natus Corp. v. United States*, 178 Ct. Cl. 1, 11, 371 F.2d 450, 457 (1967). The conclusion that mass production was possible did not foreclose [the contractor's] rights.
>
> * * *
>
> Performance may become unsatisfactory and costs may increase, in varying degrees, by reason of defects in the drawings which cause difficulties, interruptions, slowdowns and delays which interfere with mass production without making it impossible. The measure for determination of damages is therefore the degree of interference with satisfactory performance.

See also *R.E.D.M. Corp. v. United States*, 192 Ct. Cl. 891, 428 F.2d 1304 (1970), where the contractor experienced a 20 percent reject rate when it manufactured the parts using the full tolerance specified in the contract. The court held that the fact that the specifications yield some acceptable finished articles does not mean that they may not be defective. See also *Hill Aviation Logistics*, ASBCA 40817, 93-1 BCA ¶ 25,274, where specified heat-treating procedures were found defective because they precluded production of "acceptable units on a consistent mass-production basis," and *Amertex Enters., Ltd. v. United States*, No. 90-684 C, 41 CCF ¶ 77,047 (1995), *aff'd*, 108 F.3d 1392 (Fed. Cir. 1997), *cert. denied*, 522 U.S. 1075 (1998), where defective and incomplete specifications precluded the contemplated mass production of clothing items. In *Switlik Parachute Co.*, ASBCA 15560, 73-1 BCA ¶ 9865, the government specified that a particular size of thread be utilized for stitching rucksacks. Sewing machines could be run at only 40 to 70 percent of their anticipated speed because of unforeseen problems with the thread. The board stated at 46,135:

> [W]hen the Government specifies a particular component, such as the size B polyester thread, for a contract item that is to be mass produced, it impliedly warrants that that component must be suitable for use on the high speed machines, run at their rated capacity, which are used to accomplish the mass production. Accordingly, we conclude that [the contractor] is entitled to recover on this claim for breach of the implied warranty.

In *Transtechnology Corp. v. United States*, 22 Cl. Ct. 349 (1990), the court held that a technical data package was defective because it contained insufficient information to permit mass production on a contract where all other indications were that such production was possible. Other cases have indicated, however, that a contractor is responsible for determining that detailed information is not included in a technical data package, *Northwest Marine, Inc.*, ASBCA 43502, 94-1 BCA ¶ 26,521, *recons. denied*, 94-2 BCA ¶ 26,798; *Service Eng'g Co.*, ASBCA 40272, 92-3 BCA ¶ 25,106; *Bachan Aerospace Corp.*, ASBCA 34786, 88-3 BCA ¶ 20,867.

In *Natus Corp. v. United States*, 178 Ct. Cl. 1, 371 F.2d 450 (1967), the court indicated that recovery for inability to mass-produce an item must be based on commercial impracticability. *Whittaker Corp.*, ASBCA 14191, 79-1 BCA ¶ 13,805, is one of the few cases to discuss this standard of difficulty. There, recovery was granted for unsuccessful attempts to mass-produce batteries that were commercially impossible to so produce under an advertised mass-production contract. More often recovery for inability to mass-produce an item is granted under the implied warranty rationale. See *Baifield Indus., Div. of A-T-O, Inc.*, ASBCA 18057, 77-1 BCA ¶ 12,348, in which the board stated at 59,728:

> [The contractor] did not assume the risk that manufacture of the units on a production-line basis using the new Government-provided option might not be commercially possible. This was an implied warranty made by the Government when it included the optional method in its RFP package. *Hol-Gar Mfg. Corp. v. United States*, [11 CCF ¶ 80,438], 175 Ct. Cl. 518, 360 F.2d 634 (1966).

Relief was denied, however, because the contractor's difficulties arose under the performance portion of the specification and the contractor failed to show that production was not possible within the government-furnished design aspects of the specifications.

The contractor has the burden of proof that the detailed requirements of the specifications are defective. However, the actions of the government during performance of the contract may demonstrate such defects. For example, in *Big Chief Drilling Co. v. United States*, 26 Cl. Ct. 1276 (1992), the court found a defective drilling specification when the government refused to permit relaxation of the specification on the first well but granted a blanket deviation on subsequent wells. Similarly, in *McNally Indus., Inc.*, ASBCA 43027, 93-3 BCA ¶ 26,130, the government's issuance of changes to correct design errors was held to prove that the original specifications were defective. In *J.S. Alberici Constr. Co.*, ENGBCA 4800, 90-1 BCA ¶ 22,320, the contracting officer's refusal of the contractor's recommendation, when difficulties had arisen, of an alternate method of pile driving on the cofferdam installation contract was held to establish that the recommended method was not within the performance parameters of the contract specifications.

b. Performance Specifications

Performance specifications detail the performance characteristics of the end product and are distinguished from design specifications, which dictate contractor performance. The government is not liable for a contractor's increased costs in achieving the performance requirements unless such a specification embodies requirements objectively impossible or commercially impracticable to attain. In *Intercontinental Mfg. Co. v. United States*, 4 Cl. Ct. 591 (1984), in discussing performance specifications, the court stated at 595:

> [A] case for defective specifications could exist only if performance had proven impossible, either actually or from a standpoint of commercial impracticability (i.e., commercial senselessness). Short of these extremes, however, the risks of unanticipated performance costs remained upon the contractor's shoulders alone.

Performance specifications are found when they give the contractor discretion in achieving the end result called for by the contract. See *Aleutian Constructors v. United States*, 24 Cl. Ct. 372 (1991), in which a roofing specification was found to be a performance specification because it gave the contractor considerable latitude in designing the roof; *Southwest Marine, Inc.*, DOTBCA 1661, 93-3 BCA ¶ 26,168, finding a performance specification where the method of installing sleeves on a shaft was left up to the contractor; and *Engineering Tech. Consultants, S.A.*, ASBCA 43600, 92-3 BCA ¶ 25,133, *recons. denied*, 93-1 BCA ¶ 25,507, in which a specification for the installation of flashing on a roof was held to be a performance specification because the contractor was responsible for the method, location, and direction of the flashing. In *American Ship Bldg. Co. v. United States*, 228 Ct. Cl. 220, 654 F.2d 75 (1981), the court held that the contract delivery schedule was a performance requirement and that the government did not warrant that the work could be done by the scheduled dates.

The fact that the government specifies a minimum requirement for some detail of performance does not transform a performance specification into a design specification. Therefore, it is generally held that such provisions oblige the contractor to select proper items while there is no warranty that items meeting the minimum requirements will perform properly, *Ahern Painting Contractors, Inc.*, DOTCAB 67-7, 68-1 BCA ¶ 6949 (provision that surfaces be at minimum temperature of 45 E F when painted was not warranty that satisfactory result would be obtained at that temperature); *Inlet Co.*, ASBCA 9095, 1964 BCA ¶ 4093 (no warranty that government specified minimum of not less than 14-gauge steel would meet performance requirement); *Williams & Dunlap, Gen. Contractors*, ASBCA 6145, 1963 BCA ¶ 3834 (government specification requiring a minimum of 4½ sacks of cement per cubic yard did not entitle contractor to recover when it had to use five sacks to pass performance tests).

2. Specified Alternatives

The implied warranty of specifications extends to each specified alternate method of performance. Thus, if the contractor selects from among alternatives in the specifications, the government will be liable if the alternative does not accomplish the desired results. See *Southern Paving Corp.*, AGBCA 74-103, 77-2 BCA ¶ 12,813, in which the board stated at 62,363:

> Even assuming that the diversion method selected by [the contractor] had been offered by the Government as an alternate method of performance under the contract, it is recognized by the boards that there is an implied warranty that each of the alternatives offered will accomplish the desired results, and the contractor should be able to recover extra expenses resulting from failure of the method selected, barring the fault or negligence of the contractor or a finding that he knew or should have known that the method was impracticable. (citations omitted)

In *S & M-Traylor Bros.*, ENGBCA 3852, 78-2 BCA ¶ 13,495, the government had contractually provided two alternate means to produce curved columnar beams. The board noted at 66,054:

> [The "assumption of risk" doctrine] has no place in the case of an owner-generated design, where the contractor's only discretion is to choose between two specified procedures. Nor do we agree that a clause which, on its face, appears to enlarge the contractor's range of alternatives, can be construed as a warning that the specified alternative may be infeasible. The rule is exactly the opposite; by providing two methods of performance the contract implies that either will achieve the desired result.

See also *SPS Mech. Co.*, ASBCA 48643, 01-1 BCA ¶ 31,318 (contractor chose one of a number of "preapproved" systems that created performance problems); *C.T. Builders*, ASBCA 51615, 99-1 BCA ¶ 30,319 (contractor chose one of several specified products); *Bart Assocs.*, EBCA C-9211144, 96-2 BCA ¶ 28,479 (contractor chose one of two specified insulators); *Harrison Western/Franki-Denys, Inc.*, ENGBCA 5523, 92-1 BCA ¶ 24,582 (the contractor, having found the contract specification's principal design for a subway tunnel gasket to be defective, relied on an equally defective alternative design in the specification and therefore could not complete the job); *Baifield Indus., Div. of A-T-O, Inc.*, ASBCA 18057, 77-1 BCA ¶ 12,348 (contractor had a right to rely on a new government-provided optional method of performance); *Detweiler Bros., Inc.*, ASBCA 17897, 74-2 BCA ¶ 10,858 (contract specifying use of fibrous cellulose insulation, but giving contractor option to use urethane foam insulation, impliedly warranted that use of the latter could satisfy performance); and *E.W. Bliss Co.*, ASBCA 11297, 68-2 BCA ¶ 7090 (the very fact that the government included an alternate design in the drawings and specifications impliedly warranted its suitability). Contrast *Campeau Tool & Die Co.*, ASBCA 18436, 76-1 BCA ¶ 11,653, *aff'd*, 223 Ct. Cl. 743, 650 F.2d 287 (1980), finding no warranty where specifications authorized the use of a variety of starting materials for the production of nozzle bodies, and drawings indicated a range of steels that could be utilized in production and also set forth final mechanical properties regarding yield strength and elongation of the metal. See also *Fru-Con Constr. Corp. v. United States*, 42 Fed. Cl. 94 (1998), finding no warranty where the alternate methods are performance specifications giving "significant latitude or discretion."

When the specifications provide alternate materials, there is no implied warranty that each will permit a highly efficient method of performance. See *Lionsgate Corp.*, ENGBCA 5391, 91-1 BCA ¶ 23,368, in which recovery was denied when the contractor selected the lowest cost material, with the result that it incurred higher labor costs to complete the work.

3. Commercial Availability

There is ordinarily no implied warranty that specified material will be commercially available. See *Franklin E. Penny Co. v. United States*, 207 Ct. Cl. 842, 524 F.2d 668 (1975), stating at 853-54:

> Where the Government issues a contract drawing upon which are listed the names of Government-approved sources of supply, one could readily accept the proposition that such a listing constitutes a representation, i.e., a warranty by the Government, that the listed suppliers have the ability to do the work contemplated by the contract. Indeed, the common sense of the situation could tolerate no less a construction of such contract statements. But it is quite another matter to say, as [the contractor] also does, that in addition to guaranteeing the abilities of the listed manufacturers to perform, the Government is also warranting their willingness to do so and within the time period contemplated by the contract.
>
> * * *
>
> Fairly construed, the language that was used in the contract drawing promises only that those named can do the job; not that they will.

See also *Pioneer Enters., Inc.*, ASBCA 43739, 93-1 BCA ¶ 25,395 (no warranty of commercial availability because, although the contractor had trouble obtaining needed precast concrete, several companies could have supplied it), and *Toyad Corp.*, ASBCA 26785, 85-3 BCA ¶ 18,354 (no general warranty of commercial availability, but only specific cases stating exceptions to general rule).

The same rule applies to sole source suppliers, *Interstate Coatings, Inc. v. United States*, 7 Cl. Ct. 259 (1985); *DeLaval Turbine, Inc.*, ASBCA 21797, 78-2 BCA ¶ 13,521; *Therm-Air Mfg. Co.*, ASBCA 17128, 74-2 BCA ¶ 10,652; *Datametrics, Inc.*, ASBCA 16086, 74-2 BCA ¶ 10,742. These cases generally reason that the contractor is responsible because it could have checked with the vendors in the process of preparing its offer. See also *Alabama Dry Dock & Shipbuilding Corp.*, ASBCA 39215, 90-2 BCA ¶ 22,855, in which the government was not liable when the sole source supplier delivered defective items and later corrected the defect. The board reasoned that the implied warranty was that the supplier could manufacture a conforming item, not that it would do so. Contrast *Ballenger Corp.*, DOTCAB 74-32, 84-1 BCA ¶ 16,973, *modified on other grounds*, 84-2 BCA ¶ 17,277, where there was an implied warranty of commercial availability with sole source subcontractors.

Similarly, in *WRB Corp. v. United States*, 183 Ct. Cl. 409 (1968), and *James Walford Constr. Co.*, GSBCA 6498, 83-1 BCA ¶ 16,277, no warranty of commercial availability was found to cover generically described products or products of listed manufacturers. See also *ACS Constr. Co.*, ASBCA 33832, 87-3 BCA ¶ 20,138, *aff'd*, 848 F.2d 1245 (Fed. Cir. 1988) (no warranty found because the responsibility to determine the availability of a type of concrete mix from suppliers was that of the contractor prior to bidding); *Callison Constr. Co.*, AGBCA 88-309-1, 92-3 BCA ¶ 25,071 (no warranty that a product could be obtained locally); *Tri Indus.*, ASBCA 47880, 99-2 BCA ¶ 30,529 (no warranty specific parts were available); and *W.G. Yates & Sons Constr. Co. v. United States*, 53 Fed. Cl. 83 (2002) (no warranty that product was still being manufactured). In contrast, when the government specifies a product by name, it impliedly warrants that it was in fact manufactured at one time and existed at least at the time the specifications were prepared, *Parker's Mech. Constructors, Inc.*, ASBCA 29020, 84-2 BCA ¶ 17,427. See also *Omega Constr. Co.*, ASBCA 22705, 78-2 BCA ¶ 13,425, in which a warranty was found because the sole source supplier was out of business at the time of award.

By contrast, where the specifications require the use of a "standard product," the contractor is entitled to an implied warranty of commercial availability of an item meeting the detailed specifications in the contract, *J.W. Bateson Co.*, ASBCA 19823, 76-2 BCA ¶ 12,032, *recons. denied*, 77-1 BCA ¶ 12,275 (nurse call system); *Thurmont Constr. Co.*, ASBCA 13417, 69-1 BCA ¶ 7602 (security vault doors). Similarly, in *Blackhawk Heating & Plumbing Co.*, GSBCA 2432, 75-1 BCA ¶ 11,261, *recons. denied*, 76-1 BCA ¶ 11,649, the board found a warranty of commercial availability when the specifications called for items that had been in successful commercial use for at least one year. The government may also have a duty to disclose its knowledge of the lack of commercially availability, *Aerodex, Inc. v. United States*, 189 Ct. Cl. 344, 417 F.2d 1361 (1969); *Haas & Haynie Corp.*, GSBCA 5530, 84-2 BCA ¶ 17,446.

There is ordinarily no implied warranty that unspecified equal products are available, *M.S.I. Corp.*, IBCA 554-4-66, 68-1 BCA ¶ 6983 (the board noted at 32,291 that "the contract provisions respecting substitutes are not representations regarding the EXISTENCE of acceptable substitutes"). However, where the government has special knowledge concerning the items, a limited implied warranty may be found. See *Aerodex, Inc. v. United States*, 189 Ct. Cl. 344, 417 F.2d 1361 (1969), where the government developed an item under a research and development contract and then issued an invitation for the item or its "approved equal." The court stated at 354:

> [I]t is the obligation of the Government to ascertain and assure to bidders the commercial availability of the component from its manufacturer before it employs it as a purchase description or, failing that, to provide bidders with a sufficient description of the physical specifications and performance characteristics so that it may be duplicated by the bidders either by in-house fabrication or by purchase from suppliers.

The lack of a commercially available equal product may enable the contractor to substitute a nonconforming product, *Ocean Elec. Corp.*, NASABCA 371-8, 73-2 BCA ¶ 10,335. There, the absence of a commercially available equal product meeting the salient characteristics prompted the board to conclude that a commercially available item not meeting the salient characteristics was equal.

4. Degree of Accuracy Required

There is no requirement that the specifications be completely accurate. In *John McShain, Inc. v. United States*, 188 Ct. Cl. 830, 412 F.2d 1281 (1969), the court stated at 833: "Although Government-furnished plans need not be perfect, they must be adequate for the task or 'reasonably accurate.'" See also *Centex Bateson Constr. Co.*, VABCA 4613, 99-1 BCA ¶ 30,153, holding that "minor clarifications" and "normally expected contractor coordination of details" were not changes due to defective specifications, and *Hardwick Bros. Co. II v. United States*, 36 Fed. Cl. 347 (1996), *aff'd*, 168 F.3d 1322 (Fed. Cir. 1998), holding that in spite of minor errors, "on balance, the Plans were adequate." The nature of the work determines the required degree of accuracy and detail, *Anthony P. Miller, Inc. v. United States*, 191 Ct. Cl. 292, 422 F.2d 1344 (1970) (grade elevations on drawings off by an average of .24 feet were defective since the contractor was required to supply extra fill); *Datronics Eng'rs, Inc. v. United States*, 190 Ct. Cl. 196, 418 F.2d 1371 (1969) (specifications were drawn to a scale of 1 inch, 200 feet; drawings that showed no cable within 5 feet of antenna pole were not defective, although cable was within this area). In *J.W. Bateson Co.*, VACAB 1148, 79-1 BCA ¶ 13,573, the board recognized these principles, stating at 66,492:

> A design, when it is brought to fruition under field conditions, can never be perfect and the contractor has assumed a basic but limited obligation to adjust it to actual conditions. The experience and ingenuity of the contractor, which lead to the ability to resolve discrepancies and adapt the design to actuality, are part of the consideration the Government receives under the contract agreement.
>
> In other cases, we have held that discrepancies in contract documents were errors resulting in entitlement of the contractor to an equitable adjustment to the extent that they had resulted in financial damage to him. Many factors must be considered and the facts in the cases are never the same. A primary consideration is the nature of the error, but the magnitude of the cost impact and the number of conflicts are certainly relevant factors.

C. Causation and Reliance

The contractor's recovery under the implied warranty of specifications is dependent on proof that the defective specifications caused the performance difficulties and that the contractor reasonably relied on the specifications. These factors are determined by analyzing the information available to the contractor and the contractor's activities during the contract formation and performance periods.

1. Contract Formation

Contractor claims based on breach of implied warranty of specifications will not be successful if the contractor had actual or constructive knowledge of the defects prior to award. See *L.W. Foster Sportswear Co. v. United States*, 186 Ct. Cl. 499, 405 F.2d 1285 (1969), in which the court cited a line of cases granting the contractor recovery for defective specifications and then stated at 508:

> However, we have consistently held that "an experienced contractor cannot rely on government-prepared specifications where, on the basis of the government furnished data, he knows or should have known that the prepared specifications could not produce the desired result for * * * 'he has no right to make a useless thing and charge the customer for it.' *R.M Hollingshead Corp. v. United States*, 124 Ct. Cl. 681, 683, 111 F. Supp. 285, 286 (1953)." *J.D. Hedin Constr. Co. v. United States*, [171 Ct. Cl. 70, 347 F.2d 241 (1965)].
>
> * * *
>
> The rationale of these two lines of cases is that the contractor can rely upon the Government's representations as to how a desired product should and can be made, unless he ought to know better. In the latter situation, he cannot argue that he has been misled or that he had any right to make his bid on the basis of the specifications which he knew (or should have realized) were not correct. The rule is parallel to the ordinary defense to a suit for misrepresentation that the plaintiff did not, or had no right to, rely upon the challenged statement.

In *Foster*, the knowledge of the contractor was derived from work performed on a prior contract using the same specification, and the court granted relief on the first contract but denied it on the second contract. Failure to rely on the specifications in preparation of the bid will also preclude relief, *T.H. Taylor, Inc.*, ASBCA 26494, 82-2 BCA ¶ 15,877.

a. Actual Knowledge

A contractor's actual preaward knowledge of defects in specifications prevents the contractor from recovering any of its increased costs allegedly resulting from those defects. In *S. Head Painting Contractor, Inc.*, ASBCA 26249, 82-1 BCA ¶ 15,629, *recons. denied*, 82-2 BCA ¶ 15,886, the board stated at 77,204:

> Defects in specifications of which a contractor has actual knowledge prior to bidding must be brought to the Contracting Officer's attention before the opening of bids, or the contractor will be deemed to have assumed the risk. *Allied Contractor Inc. v. United States*, 180 Ct. Cl. 1057, 1062-64, 381 F.2d 995, 998-1000 (1967).

In *Wickham Contracting Co. v. United States*, 212 Ct. Cl. 318, 546 F.2d 395 (1976), the government avoided liability by advising the contractor of the defective nature of the specifications before award.

A contractor cannot recover for defective specifications on a follow-on contract. See *R.E.D.M. Corp. v. United States*, 192 Ct. Cl. 891, 428 F.2d 1304 (1970), in which the contractor recovered under the first contract while seeking to comply with specifications containing erroneous data but was refused recovery under a follow-on contract. The court reasoned that when it entered that contract, "it could not reasonably assume that the specifications and drawings were adequate" even though the exact cause of the problem had not been disclosed. In *Robins Maint., Inc. v. United States*, 265 F.3d 1254 (Fed. Cir. 2001), the court denied recovery to a follow-on contractor even though it had brought a defective estimate of the amount of work to the attention of the contracting officer but had been told to bid the job as described in the solicitation. See also *Price/CIRI Constr., J.V.*, ASBCA 37001, 89-2 BCA ¶ 21,697 (contractor was aware of the existence of drains omitted from contract drawings because of a reference to them in other pre-bid documents); *McQuiston Assocs.*, ASBCA 24676, 83-1 BCA ¶ 16,187, *recons. denied*, 83-2 BCA ¶ 16,602 (because of contractor's involvement in similar earlier procurements, it knew about problems that could result from the specifications); *Joseph Kaplan, Inc.*, ASBCA 26120, 82-1 BCA ¶ 15,503, *recons. denied*, 82-1 BCA ¶ 15,690 (contractor had affirmative duty to inquire after it learned that actual site conditions differed from those represented in the specifications); *Johnson Controls, Inc. v. United States*, 229 Ct. Cl. 445, 671 F.2d 1312 (1982) (contractor knew of defects in specifications before entering into contract); and *Wunderlich Contracting Co. v. United States*, 173 Ct. Cl. 180, 351 F.2d 956 (1965) (statement in IFB that specifications contained defects). Compare *J.S. Alberici Constr. Co.*, ENGBCA 4800, 90-1 BCA ¶ 22,320, in which the fact that a master pile method of driving sheet steel was well known in the industry as the only effective piling method in the construction of cofferdams was not found to be sufficient to show that the contractor knew before bidding that the government's specified method was defective.

b. Reason to Know

Since proof of actual contractor knowledge is very rare, most of the controversy in this area deals with the question of whether the contractor had reason to know of the defects at the time of bid submission or verification. If the existence of the defect is obvious from a review of the bid package, the contractor will be denied relief. In *Allied Contractors, Inc. v. United States*, 180 Ct. Cl. 1057, 381 F.2d 995 (1967), the court denied relief, stating at 1062-63:

> It is not necessary to determine the dispute between the parties as to whether the design of the walls was in fact improper or as to the technically correct interpretation of the Structural Note concerning hydrostatic pressure. For even assuming, *arguendo*, the correctness of [the contractor's] contentions in these respects, the errors of which [the contractor] complains were so obvious that the conclusion is compelled that [the contractor] either knew of them or certainly should have recognized them as such.

See also *Bayou Land & Marine Contractors, Inc. v. United States*, 23 Cl. Ct. 764 (1991) (contractor had all the necessary information in the contract drawings regarding low-water points to know that divers would be needed for work on a wharf dock).

This rule is limited to obvious errors, because the contractor is not normally under a duty to conduct an independent investigation of government drawings and specifications to determine if they contain defects, *E.L. Hamm & Assocs., Inc. v. England*, 379 F.3d 1334 (Fed. Cir. 2004); *John McShain, Inc. v. United States*, 188 Ct. Cl. 830, 412 F.2d 1281 (1969). The limited extent of the contractor's responsibility was recognized in *Seven Sciences, Inc.*, ASBCA 21079, 77-2 BCA ¶ 12,730, in which the board stated at 61,878:

> The design defects and missing information which [the contractor] reported to the Government after award were based upon [the contractor's] detailed scrutiny of, first, the 40 drawing package and, later, the 66 drawing package. As indicated by the many decisions issued by the Court of Claims and the boards of contract appeals discussing the pre-award duty to inquire, there is no precise formula for determining whether pre-award inquiry was reasonably warranted. See, *Pathman Construction Company*, ASBCA No. 13911, 70-2 BCA ¶ 8557. It follows from the Government's warranty of the adequacy of its design that [the contractor] was not obliged to undertake time consuming and expensive checking of the Government's drawings prior to bidding to assure that they accurately and completely provided the information needed to fabricate operable battery chargers, *Ithaca Gun Company, Inc. v. United States*, 176 Ct. Cl. 437 (1966). We are unable to

> conclude that the design deficiencies and insufficient parts descriptions which [the contractor] reported after award were so patent or glaring that [it] reasonably should have been prompted to inquire concerning them prior to award.

See also *J.A. Jones Constr. Co.*, ENGBCA 6164, 95-1 BCA ¶ 27,482 (contractor reasonably assumed that all cable was listed in a cable schedule furnished by the government); *Vern W. Johnson & Sons, Inc.*, ENGBCA 5554, 90-1 BCA ¶ 22,571, *recons. denied*, 90-2 BCA ¶ 22,914 (no duty to find error that was not obvious); and *Bechtel Nat'l, Inc.*, ASBCA 30917, 89-1 BCA ¶ 21,325, *aff'd*, 887 F.2d 1095 (Fed. Cir. 1989) (no duty to find minor error).

The nature of the error, the dollar value of the error and the procurement, the degree of analysis necessary to determine that an error has been made, and the available bidding time are examples of the factors that will be examined by the boards and courts in determining whether the contractor should have known of the error. The standards are similar to, but not as stringent as, those applied to determine if an ambiguity is patent, as discussed in Chapter 2. In *Mechaneer, Inc.*, DOTCAB 1201, 82-2 BCA ¶ 15,831, a contract containing two related drawings with the same scale indicated that the ductwork described in the first drawing had dimensions half as large as those in the continuation second drawing. The contractor constructed a duct one-half the appropriate size and sought to recover its increased costs resulting from the error. Applying the standard of what a reasonable and prudent bidder should have detected, the board held that the contractor should have been on notice of the obvious discrepancy, and thus, by failing to inquire about the error, the contractor assumed the risks that would normally be the government's for supplying defective specifications. In using the reasonable and prudent bidder standard, the board expressly refused to apply the standard of what an architect should have discovered in its examination of the bid information. See also *Commercial Prods. & Eng'g Co.*, ASBCA 40392, 96-2 BCA ¶ 28,411 (contractor should have seen different metal thicknesses in drawings and bill of materials); *Bayou Land & Marine Contractors, Inc. v. United States*, 23 Cl. Ct. 764 (1991) (any disparity in documentation of water depth and statements by government agents could have been resolved with minimum inquiry); *William Maloney*, AGBCA 81-105-1, 82-1 BCA ¶ 15,529 (contractor's failure to visit a site and failure to establish that the visit would not have disclosed the actual conditions precluded recovery); *Bromley Contracting Co. v. United States*, 72-1 BCA ¶ 9252 (obvious error to rely on dimensions after drawings were photographically reduced to half-size); and *Johnnie Quinn Painting & Decorating*, ASBCA 22735, 79-1 BCA ¶ 13,797 (contractor should have known that specified method of paint removal would not in and of itself be adequate for type of paint contractor should have expected to encounter).

The mere fact that the defects could have been discovered will not prevent recovery if it is found that the contractor acted reasonably. In *Johnson Controls, Inc.*, VACAB 1197, 79-1 BCA ¶ 13,763, *rev'd*, 80-1 BCA ¶ 14,212, *aff'd in part, rev'd in part*, 229 Ct. Cl. 445, 671 F.2d 1312 (1982), the bid package furnished by the government contained two sets of drawings. The board held that the contractor acted reasonably in consulting only one set of drawings since there was no indication that there were discrepancies between the sets. Similarly, in *Parsons of Cal.*, ASBCA 20867, 82-1 BCA ¶ 15,659, the fact that the contractor had found minor deficiencies in the drawings did not establish that it should have known of the massive number of drawing problems it encountered after award. In *J.D. Hedin Constr. Co. v. United States*, 171 Ct. Cl. 70, 347 F.2d 235 (1965), the court ruled that the contractor was not responsible for conducting an independent subsurface investigation because the 43-day period between the issuance of IFBs and bid opening was an insufficient time to make such investigation.

A voluntary examination of the drawings and specifications before bidding does not deprive the contractor of the right to use the implied warranty, unless it obtained actual knowledge of errors. See *Thompson Ramo Wooldridge, Inc. v. United States*, 175 Ct. Cl. 527, 361 F.2d 222 (1966), in which the court stated at 541:

> Lastly, we hold that Thompson Ramo's pre-bid examination of the microfilm did not render the contract warranty inoperative (through waiver or estoppel) or prevent the [contractor] from invoking it as a basis of recovery. It has not been proven, in the first place, that this examination provided actual knowledge of the microfilm's inferior capacity for making prints. The contrary seems more probable, for, after the contract was executed, the [contractor] promptly shipped the microfilm out to have prints made, apparently on the assumption that it was in condition good enough to produce usable prints. A fair inference is that the inspection revealed nothing to warn [the contractor] that the [government's] representations might be erroneous as to print-making. Secondly, the contract did not require the [contractor] to inspect. It could have relied exclusively on the warranty without taking any additional steps, but it undertook on its own to view the film. This extra caution should not deprive it of the right to rely on the warranty which it would ordinarily enjoy, unless there is a clear affirmative showing that the inspection revealed actual knowledge of the critical facts.

2. Performance

A contractor will not recover under the theory of implied warranty of specifications if it does not adhere to the specifications, if it uses specifications after having learned of their deficiencies, or if its increased costs are not caused by the defective specifications.

a. Actual Use

Actual use of the defective specifications is a prerequisite to recovery of increased performance costs. In *Gulf & Western Precision Eng'g Co. v. United States*, 211 Ct. Cl. 207, 543 F.2d 125 (1976), a contractor that substituted its own design in producing prototype warheads in place of the government advisory specifications was not entitled to recovery when the prototypes failed to meet performance requirements, even though it was later proved that the government's advisory specifications were defective. The court reasoned that the contractor assumed the risk of increased costs by adopting its cheaper method, and, further, that by doing so, the defective specifications did not, in fact, cause the contractor to incur additional costs. See also *McElroy Mach. & Mfg. Co.*, ASBCA 46477, 99-1 BCA ¶ 30,185 (contractor altered the design without notifying government); *James Reeves Contractor, Inc.*, ASBCA 44065, 95-2 BCA ¶ 27,718 (contractor used a new product that the supplier had substituted for the specified product); *Ball, Ball, & Brosamer, Inc.*, IBCA 2103-N, 93-1 BCA ¶ 25,287 (contractor did not follow specified procedures for mixing sealing compound); *Sundex, Ltd.*, ASBCA 43354, 92-3 BCA ¶ 25,047, *recons. denied*, 93-1 BCA ¶ 15,629 (contractor did not use a primer approved by specifications and therefore could not recover for problems encountered in painting contract); *Middlesex Contractors & Riggers, Inc.*, ASBCA 35068, 89-3 BCA ¶ 21,958 (contractor used alternate method of performance after recognizing that specified method was defective); *Atlantic Elec. Co.*, GSBCA 6053, 83-2 BCA ¶ 16,738 (contractor failed to establish that different installation methods did not cause problem); *S. Head Painting Contractor, Inc.*, ASBCA 26249, 82-2 BCA ¶ 15,886 (contractor failed to use a specified finish coat); and *T.H. Taylor, Inc.*, ASBCA 26494, 82-2 BCA ¶ 15,877 (the defect did not cause harm because the government altered the specification before performance).

This rule does not apply if the alternate method of performance is contained in the government specification. In *Hawaiian Bitumuls & Paving v. United States*, 26 Cl. Ct. 1234 (1992), the contract called for one method, but the contractor requested permission to use an alternate method in the same specification. The court held that the contractor could still recover under the government's implied warranty because it did not create its own specification or assist in developing any contract specification.

If the contractor can show that the defective work was not due to its failure to strictly adhere to the specifications but rather was caused by defects in the specifications, it is not precluded from recovery, *Maecon, Inc.*, ASBCA 31081, 89-2 BCA ¶ 21,855 (defective specifications and not the contractor's deviations from the specifications were shown to have caused the cracking of concrete). In an unusual case, a contractor that did not use a defective specification was excused from liability because the work accomplished was at least as good as it would have been had the specification been strictly followed, *Robert Whalen Co.*, ASBCA 19720, 78-1 BCA ¶ 13,087.

If a contractor defectively performs the work, it cannot assert a claim for a defective specification. See *Tyger Constr. Co. v. United States*, 31 Fed. Cl. 177 (1994), in which full recovery was denied because the contractor's supplier used very poor manufacturing techniques. The court stated at 227:

> Although the court has found the design specifications to be defective, plaintiff still may not recover if it cannot prove that it complied with the specifications. The implied warranty attached to design specifications only applies if the contractor complies with the specifications. *Al Johnson Constr. v. United States*, 854 F.2d 467, 469 (Fed. Cir. 1988).

b. Use with Knowledge of Defects

The contractor's unilateral decision to perform the work with knowledge of specification defects may preclude recovery. In *Delphi Indus., Inc.*, AGBCA 76-160-4, 84-1 BCA ¶ 17,053, the board noted at 84,907:

> Even if the errors had not been patent, and were not discovered until after award as was the case here, when [the contractor] commenced fabrication and became aware of such dimensional errors and other alleged deficiencies, an inquiry of the Contracting Officer prior to the fabrication would have enabled him to avoid "the costs of erroneous interpretation, including protracted litigation."

In *Hunter Ditch Lining, An Ariz. Gen. P'ship*, AGBCA 87-391-1, 91-2 BCA ¶ 23,673, the contractor's superintendent knew of an error in the government's property staking yet built a road accordingly, without notifying the government agency. The board held that the contractor was therefore not entitled to recover for correction of the error. Similarly, in *Ordnance Research, Inc. v. United States*, 221 Ct. Cl. 641, 609 F.2d 462 (1979), the contractor was denied recovery because it did not follow the government's prescribed method of avoiding the problems caused by the defective specifications.

c. Cause of Problem

Recovery for defective specifications requires proof that the specifications caused increased costs, *Santa Fe Eng'rs, Inc.*, ASBCA 25549, 82-2 BCA ¶ 15,982. See also *Pioneer Enters., Inc.*, ASBCA 43739, 93-1 BCA ¶ 25,395 (contractor's difficulty with concrete joint specification not proven to be cause of contract performance delay); *Chaparral Indus., Inc.*, ASBCA 34396, 91-2 BCA 23,813, *aff'd*, 975 F.2d 870 (Fed. Cir. 1992) (contractor's shipping practice, not the government's design specifications, caused problem with final product); *Brantley Constr. Co.*, ASBCA 27604, 84-3 BCA ¶ 17,532 (contractor failed to show that alleged design error was the most probable cause of its problems); *Baifield Indus., Div. of A-T-O, Inc. v. United States*, 706 F.2d 320 (Fed. Cir. 1983) (contractor problems were due to defective equipment and lack of technical expertise, not defective specifications); *Meyer-Weddle Co.*, GSBCA 5736, 81-1 BCA ¶ 14,952 (contractor's attempt to recover for defective specifications failed where it did not establish causation and impact); and *Felton Constr. Co.*, AGBCA 406-9, 81-1 BCA ¶ 14,932, *recons. denied*, 81-2 BCA ¶ 15,371 (contractor's problems stemmed from inadequate or defective equipment, experience, and knowledge).

IV. IMPLIED DUTY OF GOOD FAITH AND FAIR DEALING

The implied duty of good faith and fair dealing is increasingly being used in government contract decisions. U.C.C.§ 1-203 contains the first clear enunciation of the duty:

> Every contract or duty within this Act imposes an obligation of good faith in its performance or enforcement.

Good faith is defined in U.C.C. § 1-201(19) to mean "honesty in fact in the conduct or transaction concerned." This duty of good faith is also included in the *Restatement, Second, Contracts* § 205, where the same rule is stated:

> Every contract imposes upon each party a duty of good faith and fair dealing in its performance and its enforcement.

The comments to the *Restatement* section give guidance on some of the ways in which the duty has been applied. Comment c. notes that, while this section does not apply to the formation of a new contract, mainly because there are other rules that apply to this area, it is applicable to the negotiation of modifications to a contract. Comment d. discusses some of the ways in which the duty has been applied to performance of contracts:

> Subterfuges and evasions violate the obligation of good faith in performance even though the actor believes his conduct to be justified. But the obligation goes further; bad faith may be overt or may consist of inaction, and fair dealing may require more than honesty. A complete catalogue of types of bad faith is impossible, but the following types are among those which have been recognized in judicial decisions: evasion of the spirit of the bargain, lack of diligence and slacking off, willful rendering of imperfect performance, abuse of a power to specify terms, and interference with or failure to cooperate in the other party's performance.

Comment e. provides similar guidance in the enforcement area:

> The obligation of good faith and fair dealing extends to the assertion, settlement and litigation of contract claims and defenses. . . . The obligation is violated by dishonest conduct such as taking advantage of the necessitous circumstances of the other party to extort a modification of a contract for the sale of goods without legitimate commercial reason. . . . Other types of violation have been recognized in judicial decisions: harassing demands for assurances of performance, rejection of performance for unstated reasons, willful failure to mitigate damages, and abuse of a power to determine compliance or to terminate the contract.

The duty has also been incorporated into the rules on economic duress. Section 175(1) of the *Restatement* states:

> If a party's manifestation of assent is induced by an improper threat by the other party that leaves the victim no reasonable alternative, the contract is voidable by the victim.

Section 176(1) states:

> A threat is improper if . . . (d) the threat is a breach of the duty of good faith and fair dealing under a contract with the recipient.

The guidance in the *Restatement* contains a variety of examples of conduct that violates the duty of good faith and fair dealing. Most government contract decisions that have discussed the duty of good faith and fair dealing have dealt with the duty to cooperate. This duty has been recognized as part of the government procurement process for well over a hundred years, *United States v. Smith*, 94 U.S. 214 (1876), and has played a regular part in the resolution of government contract disputes. The duty is stated in two forms: (1) a duty not to act in a way that will hinder performance, and (2) a duty to cooperate by taking affirmative action. Other types of breaches of good faith asserted by contractors against the government are improper administration of a contract and lack of good faith in negotiating modifications of a contract. The government has used breach of the duty of good faith as a defense when a contractor has been deliberately slow in asserting a claim or has exhibited a lack of diligence in performance. However, nothing precludes the government from claiming a breach offensively against the contractor. In some cases, a breach of a general obligation of good faith is alleged, and in others, several types of breach of good faith are claimed. These cases have been classified into the above-stated categories for the purposes of this chapter.

A. Breach by the Government

In most cases of a breach of the duty of good faith and fair dealing, the contractor asserts the breach against the government. The contractor either asserts the breach offensively, seeking a price adjustment, or defensively, as an excuse for default.

One issue that a contractor must address when it alleges that a government official did not act in good faith is whether it must overcome a presumption of good faith. In a case alleging bad faith, the court ruled that the contractor must submit "clear and convincing evidence" to overcome this presumption, *Am-Pro Protective Agency, Inc. v. United States*, 281 F.3d 1234 (Fed. Cir. 2002). This "clear and convincing evidence" standard has been adopted in some cases: *Boston Edison Co. v. United States*, 64 Fed. Cl. 167 (2005) (clear evidence of the government's breach of its contractual obligations met the standard); *J. Cooper & Assocs. v. United States*, 53 Fed. Cl. 8 (2002) (speculation as to why government did not issue further work orders did not meet the standard). See also *Tecom, Inc. v. United States*, 66 Fed. Cl. 736 (2005), concluding that there is no presumption of good faith when the contractor claims breach of the implied duties to cooperate and not to hinder performance. See *H & S Mfg., Inc. v. United States*, 66 Fed. Cl. 301 (2005), summarizing this view at 310:

> Implicit in every contract are the duties of good faith and fair dealing between the parties. *Centex Corp. v. United States*, 395 F.3d 1283, 1304 (Fed. Cir. 2005). As an aspect of these duties, "every contract . . . imposes an implied obligation 'that neither party will do anything that will hinder or delay the other party in performance of the contract.'" *Essex Electro Eng'rs v. Danzig*, 224 F.3d 1283, 1291

> (Fed. Cir. 2000) (quoting *Luria Bros. v. United States*, 369 F.2d 701, 708, 177 Ct. Cl. 676 (Ct. Cl. 1966)). Such covenants require each party "not to interfere with the other party's performance and not to act so as to destroy the reasonable expectations of the other party regarding the fruits of the contract." *Centex Corp.*, 395 F.3d at 1304. These duties apply equally to the Government and private parties.

Determinations of whether the duty of good faith and the duty not to hinder performance have been breached are based on similar considerations. Generally, a failure to cooperate with the other party in the performance of a contract serves as a breach of that contract because a failure to cooperate violates the duty of good faith. See *Malone v. United States*, 849 F.2d 1441, 1445 (Fed. Cir. 1988). Notably, however, a showing of "bad faith" or "bad intent" is not required to demonstrate a breach of this implied duty. *Abcon Assocs. v. United States*, 49 Fed. Cl. 678, 688 (2001). Instead, the *Restatement, Second, Contracts* § 205 is instructive: "Subterfuges and evasions violate the obligation of good faith in performance even though the actor believes his conduct to be justified." Comparatively, the duty not to hinder is breached when the government commits "actions that unreasonably cause delay or hindrance to contract performance," *C. Sanchez & Son, Inc. v. United States*, 6 F.3d 1539, 1542 (Fed. Cir. 1993). As such, a government official cannot "willfully or negligently interfere with the contractor in the performance of his contract[,]" *Peter Kiewit Sons' Co. v. United States,* 151 F. Supp. 726, 731, 138 Ct. Cl. 668 (Ct. Cl. 1957).

1. Duty to Cooperate and Not Hinder Performance

A contractor's performance is often affected by the government's action or inaction. The government may actively interfere with the contractor, thereby making performance more costly or difficult. If the government's interference is justified, there is no government liability. However, if the government's action is wrongful, it will be held to have breached its implied duty not to hinder or interfere with the contractor's performance. When some government action is essential for the contractor to perform, the government will be held liable if it wrongfully fails or refuses to take the action. In such cases, the government is said to have breached its implied duty to cooperate. These implied duties are a part of every government contract, *George A. Fuller Co. v. United States*, 108 Ct. Cl. 70, 69 F. Supp. 409 (1947). Most of the recent cases decided under this theory grant relief under the doctrines of constructive change or constructive suspension of work. See Chapters 4 and 6, respectively.

a. Active Interference

Unjustified government interference resulting in a breach of the implied duty not to hinder or interfere can occur in various ways during performance, including restricting the manner of performance, *Heritage Cos.*, VABCA 3004, 91-1 BCA ¶ 23,482; directing the contractor to perform in a specific way, *Murdock Constr. Co.*, IBCA 1050-12-74, 77-2 BCA ¶ 12,728; taking action that damages the work site, *Volentine & Littleton, Contractors v. United States*, 144 Ct. Cl. 723, 169 F. Supp.

263 (1959); *John M. Bragg*, ASBCA 9515, 65-2 BCA ¶ 5050; *C.M. Lowther, Jr.*, ASBCA 38407, 91-3 BCA ¶ 24,296; disrupting performance, *Nichols Dynamics Inc.*, ASBCA 17949, 75-2 BCA ¶ 11,556; *Evergreen Helicopters, Inc.*, IBCA 1388-8-80, 81-2 BCA ¶ 15,286; *Gramercy Contractors, Inc.*, GSBCA 6495, 83-2 BCA ¶ 16,825; removing the contractor's project manager, *Harvey C. Jones, Inc.*, IBCA 2070, 90-2 BCA ¶ 22,762, *recons. denied*, 91-1 BCA ¶ 23,388; denying access to the work site, *Hector Rivera Ruiz*, PSBCA 1756, 88-3 BCA ¶ 20,829; confiscating paperwork relating to the contract, *R&B Bewachungsgesellschaft GmbH*, ASBCA 42220, 91-3 BCA ¶ 24,310; rejecting work without a reason, ordering a novel test, and refusing to pay for the test after work passed, *Centric/Jones Constructors*, IBCA 3139, 94-1 BCA ¶ 26,404; and impeding the contractor's opportunity to render services and reap profits, *S&S Equip.*, ASBCA 36681, 89-1 BCA ¶ 21,469. In a major case, the government was found to have actively interfered with performance of a Foreign Military Sales contract by undermining a coproduction agreement between the contractor and two foreign governments, *Lockheed Martin Tactical Aircraft Sys.*, ASBCA 49530, 00-1 BCA ¶ 30,852.

Interference with contract performance appears to occur most frequently in the inspection process. Thus, such interference has been found when there was overzealous inspection, *Adams v. United States*, 175 Ct. Cl. 288, 358 F.2d 986 (1966); *WRB Corp. v. United States*, 183 Ct. Cl. 409 (1968); *SMS Data Prods. Group, Inc. v. United States*, 17 Cl. Ct. 1 (1989); *J.R. Cheshier Janitorial*, ENGBCA 5487, 91-3 BCA ¶ 24,351; the imposition of multiple punchlists, *H.G. Reynolds Co.*, ASBCA 42351, 93-2 BCA ¶ 25,797; and inspection of the work by incompetent inspectors, *Harvey C. Jones, Inc.*, IBCA 2070, 90-2 BCA ¶ 22,762, *recons. denied*, 91-1 BCA ¶ 23,388; *Hull-Hazard, Inc.*, ASBCA 34645, 90-3 BCA ¶ 23,173. Compare *H & S Mfg., Inc. v. United States*, 66 Fed. Cl. 301 (2005), finding "thorough" inspections not overzealous where inspectors attempted to assist contractor, and *Engineering Tech. Consultants, S.A.*, ASBCA 45065, 95-2 BCA ¶ 27,804, finding no breach of the duty by a "very stringent inspector" who was thorough but had no "malicious intent" toward the contractor.

Breach of the duty not to interfere with performance has also been used to permit recovery for government action occurring prior to contract performance and resulting in interference, *Lewis-Nicholson, Inc. v. United States*, 213 Ct. Cl. 192, 550 F.2d 26 (1977) (inadequate advance planning and staking errors); *J.G. Watts Constr. Co. v. United States*, 174 Ct. Cl. 1, 355 F.2d 573 (1966) (excessive number of staking errors by the government). See *Herbert Lumber Co.*, IBCA 3974-98, 99-2 BCA ¶ 30,461, finding breach of the duty when the government awarded a contract knowing that a third party was seeking an injunction to bar performance on environmental grounds and immediately suspended performance for three years.

The contractor will not be permitted to recover for the government's breach of the duty not to hinder performance if no damages result from the breach. See, for example, *Summit Contractors, Inc. v. United States*, 23 Cl. Ct. 333 (1991) (government permitting another contractor to perform road construction hampered, but did not prevent, the contractor's performance), and *J.R. Cheshier Janitorial*, ENGBCA 5487, 91-3 BCA ¶ 24,351 (government interruption to advise employees of proper procedure did not increase costs). In *Mega Constr. Co. v. United States*, 29 Cl. Ct. 396 (1993), the court went so far as to state that not only must the contractor prove delay damages from the government's breach, but the delays must affect activities on the critical path—thus requiring proof of delay to the entire project. The court held that, although the government withheld consultant reports, the contractor could not recover because it did not prove critical path delays.

It is a good defense to a claim of breach of the duty not to hinder performance to demonstrate that the government conduct was permitted by a contract provision or a legal requirement. For example, in *J.A. Ross & Co. v. United States*, 126 Ct. Cl. 323, 115 F. Supp. 187 (1953), a contractor was not able to recover where increased costs resulted from delays due to the government's exercise of its contractual right to order changes. In *Mann Constr. Co.*, EBCA 362-6-86, 88-3 BCA ¶ 21,014, the contractor's claim failed because the government's action was found not to be wrongful. The court stated that the government protest of the small business status of the contractor was not an interference because the contracting officer was obligated to protest the status to protect the interests of the United States. In *Truesdale Constr. Co.*, ASBCA 36645, 89-1 BCA ¶ 21,483, it was proper to remove the contractor's superintendent when a contract clause permitted such removal if the work was not being supervised in a competent manner. In *Lionsgate Corp.*, ENGBCA 5425, 90-2 BCA ¶ 22,730, it was held proper to refuse to permit a manner of performance that would have created a safety hazard.

It is also a good defense to the duty not to hinder the contractor to demonstrate that the government had no knowledge that its act was impacting the contractor. For example, in *United States v. Beuttas*, 324 U.S. 768 (1945), the government awarded a subsequent construction contract in the same general area at higher labor rates, with the result that the initial contractor, who had delayed in starting work, had to pay higher labor rates than anticipated. The Court held that there was no breach of implied duty by the government because it had not caused the initial contractor's delay in starting and had no reason to know that the award of the second contract at a higher minimum wage rate would precipitate a labor dispute causing higher wage rates for the initial contractor. See also *Piasecki Aircraft Corp. v. United States*, 229 Ct. Cl. 208, 667 F.2d 50 (1981), where the government purchased material that the contractor urgently needed. The government was held not to have breached its implied duty because there was nothing in the record to indicate that the contractor had told the government that it intended to use the material or that the government knew it was depriving the contractor of the opportunity to use the material. In contrast, see *Peter Kiewit Sons' Co. v. United States*, 138 Ct. Cl. 668, 151 F. Supp. 726 (1957), in which the contractor was excused from performance since the government issued a contract with a particular supplier even though it was aware that the contractor was having difficulty obtaining goods from that supplier. Similarly, in *United States v.*

Peck, 102 U.S. 64 (1880), wrongful conduct was established when the government hired another contractor to cut hay based on its belief that the first contractor could not perform. The contractor was thus prevented from fulfilling its contract because the hay was the same that the parties had anticipated would be cut and was the only hay the contractor could have procured within hundreds of miles.

b. Lack of Cooperation

Failure to cooperate will be found when the government's conduct during contract performance is unreasonable. Such unreasonable conduct occurs in a number of ways, which include failing to respond to a contractor's requests for information and delays in inspection, *Hardie-Tynes Mfg. Co.*, ASBCA 20582, 76-2 BCA ¶ 11,972; *Oak Cliff Realty, Inc.*, VABCA 3232, 91-1 BCA ¶ 23,481; approving a contractor's proposed schedule of progress and billings knowing that "funds of this magnitude would not be appropriated because not requested," *S.A. Healy Co. v. United States*, 216 Ct. Cl. 172, 576 F.2d 299 (1978); failing to issue timely orders, *Raytheon Serv. Co.*, GSBCA 5695, 81-1 BCA ¶ 15,002; untimely furnishing of models needed for performance, *George A. Fuller Co. v. United States*, 108 Ct. Cl. 70, 69 F. Supp. 409 (1947); late deliveries of materials and delayed acceptance of contractor's products, *Kehm Corp. v. United States*, 119 Ct. Cl. 454, 93 F. Supp. 620 (1950); untimely delivery of information on government-furnished property, *Ballenger Corp.*, DOT-CAB 74-32, 84-1 BCA ¶ 16,973, *recons. denied*, 84-2 BCA ¶ 17,277; failure to issue a sufficient number of security clearances, *Old Dominion Sec.*, ASBCA 40062, 91-3 BCA ¶ 24,173, *recons. denied*, 92-1 BCA ¶ 24,374; failing to provide plans and drawings when necessary, *Cedar Lumber, Inc. v. United States*, 5 Cl. Ct. 539 (1984); failing to permit on-site mixing of concrete, *Century Concrete Servs., Inc.*, ASBCA 48137, 97-1 BCA ¶ 28,889; failing to issue a timely notice to proceed, *Abbett Elec. Corp. v. United States*, 142 Ct. Cl. 609, 162 F. Supp. 772 (1958); interpreting the contract so it was impossible to perform timely, *Triax Co.*, ASBCA 33899, 88-3 BCA ¶ 20,830; failing to review technical shop drawings, *Sterling Millwrights, Inc. v. United States*, 26 Cl. Ct. 49 (1992); and misleading the contractor through evasive conduct, *Malone v. United States*, 849 F.2d 1441 (Fed. Cir. 1988).

Failure to cooperate has also been found in the contract award process. See *Blackstone Consulting, Inc. v. United States*, 65 Fed. Cl. 463 (2005), where the contracting officer settled a contract award controversy involving the improper disclosure of proprietary data by agreeing to require the winning contractor to subcontract work through a given date. The court found that the government's delay in awarding the contract was a breach of its duty to cooperate but that the breach was excused because repeated protests made it impossible for the government to cooperate in the manner expected.

One of the most common situations in which the government is found to have failed to cooperate is when it fails to help in the solution of a problem that has arisen during contract performance. This has occurred when the contractor encounters problems with the contract specifications, *Hardrives, Inc.*, IBCA 2319, 94-1 BCA ¶ 26,267; encounters differing site conditions, *Kahaluu Constr. Co.*, ASBCA 31187, 89-1 BCA ¶ 21,308, *recons. denied*, 89-1 BCA ¶ 21,525; has difficulties in dealing with changes ordered by the government, *Pittsburgh-Des Moines Corp.*, EBCA 314-3-84, 89-2 BCA ¶ 21,739; encounters damage to the work site during performance, *James Lowe, Inc.*, ASBCA 42026, 92-2 BCA ¶ 24,835, *recons. denied*, 93-1 BCA ¶ 25,516; needs assistance in dealing with an adjoining property owner, *R.W. Jones Constr., Inc.*, IBCA 3656, 99-1 BCA ¶ 30,268; or has to perform work that conflicts with work of another contractor, *Robert R. Marquis, Inc.*, ASBCA 38438, 92-1 BCA ¶ 24,692. In this situation, the duty of cooperation arises even if the government action is not contemplated at the time of award of the contract. For example, in *CRF v. United States*, 224 Ct. Cl. 312, 624 F.2d 1054 (1980), the contractor terminated a subcontractor for nonperformance and requested the government's assistance in obtaining the subcontractor's work-in-process inventory from the subcontractor's trustee in bankruptcy. The refusal of the contracting officer, on the grounds that this was the sole responsibility of the contractor, was held to be a failure of cooperation. Similarly, in *Better Health Ambulance Servs.*, VABCA 5475, 01-1 BCA ¶ 31,345, lack of cooperation was found when the agency failed to follow state procedures not included in the contract that would have allowed the contractor to staff ambulances with paramedics. There is no obligation to provide assistance when the contractor could have readily resolved the problem, *Moore Mill & Lumber Co.*, AGBCA 87-172-1, 90-3 BCA ¶ 23,111 (no duty to provide information that is readily available); *John S. Vayanos Contracting Co.*, PSBCA 2317, 89-1 BCA ¶ 21,494 (no duty to assist in obtaining local permit). Neither is there any such duty where the problem is under the control of the contractor, *Blaze Constr. Co.*, IBCA 2863, 91-3 BCA ¶ 24,071 (no duty to make subcontractor perform); *Ecoflo, Inc.*, HUDBCA 96-B-135-C17, 97-1 BCA ¶ 28,730 (contractor caused problem), or where the contractor is not sufficiently specific about its needs for assistance, *PBI Elec. Corp. v. United States*, 17 Cl. Ct. 128 (1989).

Another common situation in which there is a failure of cooperation is where the government is unable to make the site of the work available to the contractor to permit timely completion of the work, *L.L. Hall Constr. Co. v. United States*, 177 Ct. Cl. 870, 379 F.2d 559 (1966), or fails to provide access to the work site in the manner anticipated when the offer was prepared, *Blinderman Constr. Co. v. United States*, 695 F.2d 552 (Fed. Cir. 1982). In some cases, when the government has warranted the site availability, liability will be found even when the government is not responsible for its unavailability, *Singleton Contracting Corp.*, GSBCA 9614, 90-3 BCA ¶ 23,125, *recons. denied*, 91-1 BCA ¶ 23,344; *Carl W. Linder Co.*, ENGBCA 3526, 78-1 BCA ¶ 13,114. Cases in this category include a failure to provide roads necessary to perform the work efficiently, *Ferguson Mgmt. Co.*, AGBCA 83-207-3, 83-2 BCA ¶ 16,819; failure to provide adequate roads, *Southern Paving Co.*, AGBCA 74-103, 77-2 BCA ¶ 12,813; failure to keep the work area clear, *Elrich Constr. Co.*, GSBCA 5241, 80-1 BCA ¶ 14,197; and failure to vacate an area to be painted, *Morin Indus., Inc.*, ASBCA 33611, 87-2 BCA ¶ 19,856.

Failure to cooperate has also been found when the government does not take steps to prevent interference by another contractor. The obligation to prevent such interference is most often found in the following construction contract clause in FAR 52.236-8:

> OTHER CONTRACTS (APR 1984)
>
> The Government may undertake or award other contracts for additional work at or near the site of the work under this contract. The Contractor shall fully cooperate with the other contractors and with Government employees and shall carefully adapt scheduling and performing the work under this contract to accommodate the additional work, heeding any direction that may be provided by the Contracting Officer. The Contractor shall not commit or permit any act that will interfere with the performance of work by any other contractor or by Government employees.

If the government does not make a good faith effort to make an interfering contractor comply with this clause, a failure to cooperate will be found, *Toombs & Co.*, ASBCA 34590, 91-1 BCA ¶ 23,403 (failure of other contractor to meet contract schedule); *Harvey C. Jones, Inc.*, IBCA 2070, 90-2 BCA ¶ 22,762, *recons. denied*, 91-1 BCA ¶ 23,388 (failure of other contractor to coordinate work in same area); *Jacobson & Co.*, GSBCA 5605, 80-2 BCA ¶ 14,521 (installation by other contractor of work that did not comply with specifications); *Hensel Phelps Constr. Co.*, ENGBCA 3719, 77-2 BCA ¶ 12,853. A failure of cooperation in these circumstances has also been found when the contract contained no clause like the "Other Contractors" clause, *Steve P. Rados, Inc.*, AGBCA 77-130-4, 82-1 BCA ¶ 15,624; *American Int'l Constructors, Inc.*, ENGBCA 3633, 77-2 BCA ¶ 12,606. In the *Rados* case, the board reasoned that the other contractor had a common law duty to cooperate—which the government should have made a good faith effort to enforce. See also *Sauer, Inc. v. Danzig*, 224 F.3d 1340 (Fed. Cir. 2000), remanding a case to the appeals board to determine if a compensable delay was caused by another contractor on the site. On remand, *Sauer, Inc.*, ASBCA 39605, 01-2 BCA ¶ 31,525, the board appeared to hold that the contractor had reasonably relied on the other contractor completing on schedule but denied the claim for failure to prove damages. The boards have sometimes found warranties of site availability when the government implicitly assumes management responsibilities by dividing the work among a number of contractors. In *Singleton Contracting Corp.*, GSBCA 9614, 90-3 BCA ¶ 23,125, *recons. denied*, 91-1 BCA ¶ 23,344, the board found that the contract specifically stated that the contractor's phase of the work could be started no later than May 15, yet the government did not make the site available until November 16. The board stated at 116,107:

> [The government] is responsible for properly supervising progress on phased construction projects, and for compensating efficient contractors for delays caused by their inefficient predecessors. Any cause of action which the Government may have against the latter firms is a separate matter. *Pierce Associates, Inc.*, GSBCA no. 4163, 77-2 BCA ¶ 12,746, *aff'd on recons.*, 78-1 BCA ¶ 13,078.

If the government makes a good faith effort to obtain performance by the other contractor but fails, it will not be liable, *Development, Mgmt. Consultants, Inc.*, HUDBCA 79-405-C28, 85-3 BCA ¶ 18,338; *General Ry. Signal Co.*, ENGBCA 4250, 85-2 BCA ¶ 17,959.

The government's breach of its implied duty to cooperate is determined by the reasonableness of its actions under the circumstances. If the conduct of the government is determined to be reasonable, the contractor cannot recover. In *Ben C. Gerwick, Inc. v. United States*, 152 Ct. Cl. 69, 285 F.2d 432 (1961), the contractor was not entitled to relief where delayed availability of the work site was caused by another government contractor, since the government was not at fault. The officer in charge did all he could reasonably do to hasten the predecessor contractor's performance. See also *Asheville Contracting Co.*, DOTCAB 74-6, 76-2 BCA ¶ 12,027, *recons. denied*, 78-1 BCA ¶ 12,971 (government acted reasonably to get the other contract completed timely); *Tolis Cain Corp.*, DOTCAB 72-2, 76-2 BCA ¶ 11,954 (no government fault or negligence where government had no notice of any problems prior to shutdown and promptly had services restored after they were terminated); *Sun Oil Co. v. United States*, 215 Ct. Cl. 716, 572 F.2d 786 (1978) (contractor failed to establish that government acted unreasonably in delaying approval); and *Zinco Gen. Contractor, Inc.*, GSBCA 6182, 82-2 BCA ¶ 15,917 (government acted reasonably promptly in first rejecting contractor's proposal and then negotiating a modification after reviving the proposal). In *PBI Elec. Corp. v. United States*, 17 Cl. Ct. 128 (1989), the contractor claimed that the government breached its duty to cooperate by failing to provide helpful information. The court, however, determined that the government had given a reasonable response in saying it did not consider the information necessary. See also *John McCabe*, ASBCA 36958, 90-2 BCA ¶ 22,785, in which the board decided that the government was reasonable in failing to assign additional work to an indefinite-quantity contractor because of mediocre performance of the work originally assigned. Similarly, in *Mann Constr. Co.*, EBCA 362-6-86, 88-3 BCA ¶ 21,014, the board found no breach of the duty to cooperate since the contracting officer reasonably protested the small business status of the contractor without a lengthy delay. In *John S. Vayanos Contracting Co.*, PSBCA 2317, 89-1 BCA ¶ 21,494, the board found that the government's failure to answer an inquiry about an alternate source of water was not a breach of good faith because there was no evidence that the contractor would have performed timely even if the government had provided a timely response.

Even if the contractor does prove a breach of the duty to cooperate by the government, it will not recover if no damages are shown. For example, in *Commerce Int'l Co. v. United States*, 167 Ct. Cl. 529, 338 F.2d 81 (1964), no recovery was granted because the contractor could not prove damages from a government delay in furnishing materials where there were concurrent delays that were the responsibility of the contractor. See also *Toombs & Co.*, ASBCA 34590, 91-1 BCA ¶ 23,403, where, even though the government breached its duty of cooperation by failing to ensure a more timely performance by other contractors, there was no substantial delay and therefore no recovery.

In a few instances, the court has used diligence, instead of reasonableness, to determine if the government breached its duty to cooperate. In *Summit Contractors, Inc. v. United States*, 23 Cl. Ct. 333 (1991), the government was found to have acted diligently, although unsuccessfully, to avoid delays in the availability of the work site, and therefore did not breach its implied duty of cooperation. See also *United States v. Howard P. Foley Co.*, 329 U.S. 64 (1946), in which the court said that since the government "worked with great, if not unusual, diligence" in making the work site available, it did not breach its duty of good faith.

The government is not subject to an increased standard under the implied duty to cooperate when dealing with small or disadvantaged businesses. In *Blaze Constr. Co.*, IBCA 2863, 91-3 BCA ¶ 24,071, the contractor claimed that, because it was Indian, the government had heightened duties. The board stated that not only did the government not owe a greater contractual duty to a small business contractor, but in this case the government did not breach the duty to cooperate at all, since it was not the government's responsibility to assist the contractor in obtaining a construction yard and sand pit from a subcontractor. See also *Monoko, Inc.*, ASBCA 46283, 94-1 BCA ¶ 26,570, in which the board considered a small contractor's claim that the government had pursued a Machiavellian plan in administering the contract but found that normal procedures had been followed. Similarly, in *Smith v. United States*, 34 Fed. Cl. 313 (1995), the court found that somewhat inept handling of the contract by the government agency did not rise to the level of lack of good faith because it was a simple supply contract awarded through sealed bidding. The court commented at 321:

> The policies behind the small business and woman-owned business programs is to provide an opportunity to participate in government procurements. The government is not expected to be a guarantor of success.

c. *Abuse of Discretion*

Government contracts contain a number of clauses stating that the contractor may follow a certain course of action upon obtaining the approval of the contracting officer. The government's duty of cooperation under these clauses is to exercise discretion fairly in granting such approvals. In effect, this requires that approval be granted unless there is a valid government interest served in disapproving the contractor's request. Thus, unreasonable denials of approvals or delays in giving approvals called for by the contract are breaches of the duty of cooperation. See *Hoel-Steffen Constr. Co. v. United States*, 231 Ct. Cl. 128, 684 F.2d 843 (1982) (unreasonable denial of approval to substitute subcontractor); *Liles Constr. Co. v. United States*, 197 Ct. Cl. 164, 455 F.2d 527 (1972) (unreasonable disapproval of use of subcontractor); *Richerson Constr., Inc. v. General Servs. Admin.*, GSBCA 11161, 93-1 BCA ¶ 25,239 (unreasonable direction to use another subcontractor); *Vogt Bros. Mfg. Co. v. United States*, 160 Ct. Cl. 687 (1963) (unreasonable delay in review and approval of shop drawings); *Unidynamics/St. Louis, Inc.*, ASBCA 17592, 73-2 BCA ¶ 10,360 (unreasonable disapproval of shop drawings); *Sterling Millwrights, Inc. v. United States*, 26 Cl. Ct. 49 (1992) (incompetent management of shop drawing process); and *Albert C. Rondinelli*, ASBCA 9900, 65-1 BCA ¶ 4674 (unreasonable disapproval of alternate method of performance). But see *Dawson Constr. Co.*, VABCA 1967, 88-1 BCA ¶ 20,335, in which the board found no evidence that the government improperly rejected a contractor proposal since the contractor did not comply with all requirements, and *White & McNeil Excavating, Inc.*, IBCA 2448, 92-1 BCA ¶ 24,534, *appeal after remand*, IBCA 1992, 93-1 BCA 25,286, in which the government's denial of an alternate quarry source was found to be reasonable and not a breach of cooperation since there already was an approved source.

The most common place where abuse of discretion in granting approvals has been found is with regard to brand name or equal provisions. FAR 10.004(b) requires that equal products be permitted when the government specifies an item by brand name, unless authority is obtained for a sole source procurement. This policy is implemented in the construction contract Material and Workmanship clause in FAR 52.236-5, which states:

> (a) The Contractor may, at its option, use any equipment, material, article, or process that, in the judgment of the Contracting Officer, is equal to that named in the specifications, unless otherwise specifically provided in this contract.

Under this clause, disapproval of a functionally equivalent item is an abuse of discretion, *Jack Stone Co. v. United States*, 170 Ct. Cl. 281, 344 F.2d 370 (1965); *W.G. Cornell Co. v. United States*, 179 Ct. Cl. 651, 376 F.2d 299 (1967). This rule has also been applied to the situation where the brand name is not stated in the contract but the specifications are written around a specific product, *William R. Sherwin v. United States*, 193 Ct. Cl. 962, 436 F.2d 992 (1971); *D.E.W., Inc.*, ASBCA 36698, 89-1 BCA ¶ 21,312. The government cannot disapprove a proposed equal because it does not meet unstated government requirements, *Manning Elec. & Repair Co. v. United States*, 22 Cl. Ct. 240 (1991); *Page Constr. Co.*, AGBCA 92-191-1, 93-3 BCA ¶ 26,060. Furthermore, functional equivalency does not permit disapproval for not meeting a minor requirement of the specification, *Eslin Co.*, AGBCA 90-222-1, 93-1 BCA ¶ 25,321. In *Plandel, Inc.*, HUDBCA 92-7171-C1, 93-3 BCA ¶ 26,103, the board stated at 129,761:

> The term "or equal" in the specification does not mean that the substituted product has to be identical to the specified one. The alternate item must meet the quality aspects of the specification and must be the functional equivalent of the specified product. It need not match it in every detail.

Valid disapprovals have been found when the proposed equal was not functionally equivalent, *Centex Constr. Co.*, ASBCA 32874, 89-1 BCA ¶ 21,431, and when it did not contain comparable warranties to the brand name item, *C.E. Wylie Constr. Co.*, ASBCA 26545, 85-1 BCA ¶ 17,933. Proposed substituted materials in buildings have also been properly disapproved when they did not have the same appearance as the brand name item, *Hammond Constr. Inc.*, NASABCA 06-0290, 93-1 BCA ¶ 25,288, or when they were not aesthetically equal, *Centex Constr. Co.*, VABCA 1630, 85-3 BCA ¶ 18,391.

Abuse of discretion has been found when the contracting officer demanded a contract price reduction in return for granting approval of a substitute item, *Consolidated Diesel Elec. Co. v. United States*, 209 Ct. Cl. 521, 533 F.2d 556 (1976). It has also been held to be an abuse of discretion to disapprove a proposed equal item without giving any reason for the disapproval, *Bruce-Andersen Co.*, ASBCA 29411, 88-3 BCA ¶ 21,135.

2. *Improper Contract Administration*

The duty of good faith and fair dealing has been cited in cases against the government for its actions during contract administration. In *Mutual Maint. Co.*, GSBCA 7492, 85-2 BCA ¶ 17,944, the government improperly administered the contract by failing to promptly issue a forward-priced change order. In *Nash Janitorial Serv., Inc.*, GSBCA 6390, 84-1 BCA ¶ 17,135, *recons. denied*, 84-2 BCA ¶ 17,355, the contracting officer breached the duty by not acting promptly on claims for constructive changes and a request for a change that would make the work more efficient, and by not coordinating properly with the agency occupying the building that the contractor was cleaning. Compare *Martin-Copeland Co.*, ASBCA 26551, 83-2 BCA ¶ 16,752, in which the board did not find a breach of good faith by the government when it refused to change a contract to permit the use of a cheaper material when conditions changed and the price of the material had risen drastically. The board stated that the government was entitled to strict compliance with the specifications of the contract.

A breach of the duty of good faith was found in *Orange Cove Irrigation Dist. v. United States*, 28 Fed. Cl. 790 (1993), where the agency set an unreasonably tight deadline for the performance of delinquent work under the contract. The court stated at 800-01:

> Every contract, including those in which the Government is a party, contains an implied covenant of good faith and fair dealing. *Hughes Communications Galaxy, Inc. v. United States*, 26 Cl. Ct. 123, 140 (1992); *Solar Turbines, Inc. v. United States*, 23 Cl. Ct. 142, 156 (1991). When one party has the authority to exercise discretion to determine an essential term of a contract, as here, the covenant of good faith and fair dealing requires that the exercise of that discretion be reasonable. See, e.g., *Boone v. Kerr-McGee Oil Indus.*, 217 F.2d 63, 65 (10th Cir. 1954). This requires that what is done "be done honestly to effectuate the object and purpose the parties had in mind in providing for the exercise of such power." *Id.* Moreover, although the parties to a contract are normally bound by the terms thereof, it is well settled that a contractual provision that produces an egregious, unfair, or unreasonable result will not be enforced. *Forest Envtl. Servs. Co. v. United States*, 5 Cl. Ct. 774, 777 (1984).

A potential breach of the duty of good faith was found in *Solar Turbines, Inc. v. United States*, 23 Cl. Ct. 142 (1991), where the contractor alleged that the contracting agency had embarked on a strategy to induce the contractor to request termination of a contract—with the effect of ending a program. The agency allegedly had opted for this strategy because congressional committees were in favor of the program and the agency did not want to confront them. The strategy entailed actions to cause the contractor to spend significant sums that could not be recovered because of a ceiling price in the contract. See also *Hubbard v. United States*, 52 Fed. Cl. 192 (2002), finding a breach of the duty of good faith and fair dealing when the government took a number of actions that precluded a concessionaire contractor from earning the profits it had forecast. Similarly, in *Odebrecht Contractors of Cal., Inc.*, ENGBCA 6372, 00-2 BCA ¶ 30,999, breach of the duty was found when the agency awarded a contract permitting use of wells knowing that a local water authority would not permit such use, did not tell the contractor of this problem until after it had rehabilitated the wells, and did not work to obtain the authority's permission to use the wells. See also *Celeron Gathering Corp. v. United States*, 34 Fed. Cl. 745 (1996), finding breach when the government did not give the contractor "an accurate, non-evasive assessment" of problems it was having in performing its part of the contract, and *Keno & Sons Constr. Co.*, ENGBCA 5837, 95-2 BCA ¶ 27,687, finding breach when the government did not disclose its reasons for rejecting a contractor's proposed method of performance.

Improper default terminations by the government have sometimes been deemed breaches of good faith. In *Kahaluu Constr. Co.*, ASBCA 31187, 89-1 BCA ¶ 21,308, *recons. denied*, 89-1 BCA ¶ 21,525, the government failed to give directions to the contractor to proceed with performance. In *Drain-A-Way Sys., Inc.*, GSBCA 7022, 84-1 BCA ¶ 16,929, the government did not tell the contractor how to properly contest termination. The board used very broad language in stating at 84,216:

> Where the motive for an act, or a failure to act, violates generally accepted notions of fair-dealing, decency, or reasonableness, the bare legality of the act does not excuse its wrongfulness. . . . And where actions taken by Government officials are improper on their face, a mirror image of the presumption of regularity arises. That is, it is to be presumed that an action taken by Government officials that on its face appears irregular was taken for an improper motive. *United States v. Roses, Inc.*, 706 F.2d 1563, 1567 (Fed. Cir. 1983) (Nicols, J.). Here, the termination notice . . . was manifestly improper because it did not tell [the contractor] how to contest that termination, and the Federal Procurement Regulations required that it do so. We must presume that the contracting officer's failure to tell [the contractor] how to contest the contract termination resulted from an improper motive.

Thus, the contractor was able to recover its $19 filing fee, since it was induced to file a suit in the wrong forum. In *Malone v. United States*, 849 F.2d 1441 (Fed. Cir. 1988), the court also stated that the default termination was improper. There, it was the contracting officer's evasiveness about whether the model for the contract had been approved that created the breach of good faith. Since the contracting officer was not clear on whether the exemplar was accepted, it could not default the contractor for refusing to reperform the work after performing most of it according to the specifications of the model. See also *Apex Int'l Mgmt. Servs., Inc.*, ASBCA 38087, 94-2 BCA ¶ 26,852, finding a default termination improper because government employees had exhibited bad faith in intentionally obstructing the performance of the contractor, and *Libertatia Assocs. v. United States*, 46 Fed. Cl. 702 (2000), finding lack of good faith in default terminating a contract because the action was motivated by an intent to harm the contractor.

3. Lack of Good Faith in Negotiating Modifications

The implied duty of good faith and fair dealing has been used against the government in several cases regarding the bargaining process. In *6800 Corp.*, GSBCA 5880, 83-2 BCA ¶ 16,581, the board explained the meaning of the duty of good faith in the context of bargaining, at 82,449:

> All that is required is honest bargaining. . . . Good faith bargaining does not require the reciprocation of concessions, . . . nor does it impose an inexorable ratchet, binding negotiators to previous, unaccepted proposals. . . . A lack of good faith bargaining may not be found merely because a party attempts to secure that which the other party deems unacceptable; it may rather be found only from conduct showing an intent not to enter into an agreement of any nature.

In *6800 Corp.*, the board found that the government did not breach its duty of good faith and fair dealing by failing to reveal the length of the renewal term or rental rate it would offer in its negotiation for a new lease because it was an honest bargaining technique. Similarly, in *Robert L. Merwin & Co.*, GSBCA 6621, 83-2 BCA ¶ 16,745, *recons. denied*, 83-2 BCA ¶ 16,859, the court denied the contractor's argument. The government tried to modify the contract price of a lease to reflect higher electricity rates, which it was responsible for paying. This was held to be a good faith negotiation technique, even though the modification was unacceptable to the contractor, which did not want its rent to increase.

The government has been found to have breached its duty of good faith and fair dealing in cases where it has taken advantage of its superior bargaining position. For example, in *Mann Constr.*, EBCA 379-9-86, 87-2 BCA ¶ 19,770, the contracting officer allowed the contractor to substitute smaller rock in a construction contract provided that the contract price was reduced by $9,000. In fact, the substitution did not save costs, and the board held that the government unfairly made demands on the contractor to reduce the price where the contractor was unable to negotiate. See also *Isadore & Miriam Klein*, GSBCA 6614, 84-2 BCA ¶ 17,273, where the government said it was forbidden to pay a higher rental price when it knew or should have known that was not true. The board found that the government breached its duty of good faith and fair dealing.

When the government uses coercion or threats to force the contractor to agree to terms without any alternative, the government is not negotiating in good faith and therefore is in breach. Courts have described such economic duress as included in breaches of good faith. See, for example, *David Nassif Assocs. v. United States*, 226 Ct. Cl. 372, 644 F.2d 4 (1981), stating at 385:

> To render an agreement voidable on grounds of duress it must be shown that the party's manifestation of assent was induced by an improper threat which left the recipient with no reasonable alternative save to agree. . . . Such forms of economic duress . . . include threats that would breach a duty of good faith and fair dealing under a contract as well as threats which, though lawful in themselves, are enhanced in their effectiveness in inducing assent to unfair terms because they exploit prior unfair dealing on the part of the party making the threat.

See also *Rumsfeld v. Freedom N.Y., Inc.*, 329 F.3d 1320 (Fed. Cir. 2003), *cert. denied*, 541 U.S. 987 (2004), finding a lack of good faith when the government withheld progress payments in order to force the contractor to sign a disadvantageous modification. In *Environmental Tectonics Corp.*, ASBCA 23374, 86-1 BCA ¶ 18,649, the board decided that economic duress was not proven because the acts of stopping progress payments until a modification including a liquidated damages provision was accepted did not violate notions of fair dealing. It was just hard bargaining in the interest of the government. Similar results occurred where contract modifications were not found to be the result of economic duress because they were negotiated in good faith, *H.A. Ekelin & Assocs.*, ASBCA 31694, 88-3 BCA ¶ 21,033, *recons. denied*, 89-1 BCA ¶ 21,309; *Aerospatiale Helicopter Corp.*, DOT-BCA 1962, 89-2 BCA ¶ 21,706.

Failure to negotiate in good faith was also found in *Systems Mgmt. Am. Corp.*, ASBCA 45704, 00-2 BCA ¶ 31,112, where the agency refused to issue a contract modification definitizing option ceiling prices as required by the contract. The board rejected the excuse that a former employee of the small business contractor had pleaded guilty to participating in a kickback, reasoning that the government could have definitized the prices and protected its interests by not exercising the options until the kickback issue had been resolved.

4. *Lack of Good Faith in Changing Requirements*

When the government does not have firm requirements, it frequently enters into requirements contracts providing an estimate of its requirements and promising to order its requirements under the contract. See FAR 16.503. Under such contracts it is not liable to the contractor for changed requirements unless such changes are based on a lack of good faith. See *Technical Assistance Int'l, Inc. v. United States*, 150 F.3d 1369 (Fed. Cir. 1998), finding no breach of the duty of good faith when an agency's requirements were reduced significantly because the agency made major changes in the way it was performing its work. The court stated at 1373:

> [T]he only limitation upon the government's ability to vary its requirements under a requirements contract is that it must do so in good faith. Our holding is in accord with numerous decisions from other courts. See, e.g., *HML Corp. v. General Foods Corp.*, 365 F.2d 77, 81 (3d Cir. 1966) ("the buyer in a requirements contract is required merely to exercise good faith in determining his requirements and the seller assumes the risk of all good faith variations in the buyer's requirements"); *Oregon Plywood Sales Corp.*, 246 F.2d at 470-71; *Southwest Natural Gas Co. v. Oklahoma Portland Cement Co.*, 102 F.2d 630, 632-33 (10th Cir. 1939); *In re United Cigar Stores Co. of Am.*, 72 F.2d at 675 ("There are many decisions to the effect that the obligation on the part of a buyer in a requirements contract to continue to have requirements without substantial variance is not to be implied more strictly than to impose upon him the obligation to act in good faith."); see also Note, Requirements Contracts, "More or Less," Under the Uniform Commercial Code, 33 Rutgers L. Rev. 105, 120 (1980) (noting that at least with respect to decreases in requirements, "almost every court has stated that good faith constitutes the sole limitation" on the buyer). That rule has the benefit of simplicity, and it enables the government to take full advantage of the flexibility for which it has bargained.
>
> * * *
>
> The party alleging a breach of contract bears the burden of proving the breach. See *Perry v. Department of the Army*, 992 F.2d 1575, 1577 (Fed. Cir. 1993). Thus, in a requirements contract case in which the seller alleges that the buyer breached the contract by reducing its requirements, the burden of proof is on the seller to prove that the buyer acted in bad faith, for example, by reducing its requirements solely in order to avoid its obligations under the contract. In the absence of such a showing, the buyer will be presumed to have varied its requirements for valid business reasons, i.e., to have acted in good faith, and will not be liable for the change in requirements.

This burden of proving bad faith will make it difficult to recover for breaches of the duty of good faith in changing requirements. See, for example, *Workrite Uniform Co. v. General Servs. Admin.*, GSBCA 14839, 99-2 BCA ¶ 30,455, finding no bad faith when the government did not inform the contractor of continuing requirements during the period when the parties were resolving specification problems and then placed large orders in the months following resolution of the problems. Compare *Adams Mfg. Co.*, GSBCA 5747, 82-1 BCA ¶ 15,740, finding a breach when the government violated its own regulations in placing a moratorium on ordering under a requirements contract. See also *Rowe, Inc. v. General Servs. Admin.* GSBCA 15217, 03-1 BCA ¶ 32,162, recognizing that a diversion of work to another contract would be a breach of the duty of good faith, but finding that the work ordered from another contractor was not within the scope of the contractor's requirements contract.

B. Breach by the Contractor

The government may also assert a breach of the implied duty of good faith against the contractor. So far, though, the government has alleged a breach only as a defense to a contractor's claim. However, there is nothing to prevent the government from bringing a claim against a contractor offensively, if the contractor has caused damages to the government due to a breach of good faith.

1. Deliberate Inaction in Asserting a Claim

Sometimes when a contractor waits an unreasonable length of time to notify the government of a mistake, the delay has been considered a breach of good faith. In *All-Am. Poly Corp.*, GSBCA 7104, 84-2 BCA ¶ 17,682, the contractor did not notify the government of the mistake in the bid until the contract was completed, even though it discovered the mistake when it received the award. The board stated that "[a] party whose deliberate inaction precludes rescission as a remedy for a unilateral mistake has breached its implied duty of good faith and fair dealing." The same result was reached in *J.C. Mfg., Inc.*, ASBCA 34399, 87-3 BCA ¶ 20,137 (contractor waited 15 months after discovery of the mistake in the bid to file claim for reformation), and *Turner-MAK (JV)*, ASBCA 37711, 96-1 BCA ¶ 28,208 (contractor waited almost three years to file claim).

No breach of the duty of good faith and fair dealing will be found if the time waited was not unreasonable or if the government should have known, even before notification, that the proposal was in error. See *Aguila Corp.*, EBCA C-9102103, 91-3 BCA ¶ 24,276, where the government was not able to prove that the contractor waited an unreasonable time to assert its claim that it was forced under economic duress to agree to a repayment provision. Similarly, in *Chemtronics, Inc.*, ASBCA 30883, 88-2 BCA ¶ 20,534, the government failed to prove that the contractor's delay in asserting its claim for mistaken bid was not in good faith even though the contractor delayed 15 months after discovery. The board denied the allegation that the contractor was acting in bad faith because it found that the government should have known that the proposal was in error prior to the award.

A board has also accepted the government's argument that the duty of fair dealing requires a contractor that knew or should have known about an excusable cause of delay prior to entering into an extension of the contract delivery date to "raise that cause of delay prior to signing the extension," *Empire Energy Mgmt. Sys., Inc.*, ASBCA 46741, 03-1 BCA ¶ 32,079.

2. Lack of Diligence

The government will sometimes assert as a defense the contractor's lack of diligence in the performance of the contract. For example, in *John S. Vayanos Contracting Co.*, PSBCA 2317, 89-1 BCA ¶ 21,494, the contractor asserted a breach of the duty of cooperation because the government failed to answer an inquiry about an alternate source of water and did not assist in obtaining construction permits. The government countered, and the board ruled that, if the contractor had been more diligent, it would have obtained the information it needed on water and permits, and therefore the contractor, not the government, breached the duty of good faith and fair dealing. In *J.B.L. Constr. Co.*, VABCA 1799, 86-1 BCA ¶ 18,529, the government contended that the delays in the performance were due to the contractor's failure to work diligently, not to a delay in the approval of materials. The court decided that the delays were due to the fault of both parties, and therefore neither party could recover.

V. IMPRACTICABILITY OF PERFORMANCE AND MISTAKE

Contractors can also obtain relief on government contracts under the doctrines of impracticability of performance and mistake. These legal theories are different from those discussed previously in that they are not premised on government breach or government fault. Instead, the contractor is relieved from its agreement to perform because performance is found to be greatly different from what was expected. Although closely related, impracticability and mistake have been analytically and historically treated as separate bases for relief, and so they are separately treated here. See, however, *SMC Info. Sys., Inc. v. General Servs. Admin.*, GSBCA 9371, 93-1 BCA ¶ 25,485, in which the board concluded that "'impossibility' is a sub-set of the longstanding common-law doctrine of mutual mistake."

A. Impracticability

The doctrine of impracticability originated in the concept of impossibility of performance where some supervening event such as destruction of a building or death of the performing party made performance literally impossible. As the law in this area developed, it was recognized that there were also cases in which performance, although possible, was commercially senseless. The modern trend is to subsume all cases under this theory under the term "impracticability," U.C.C. § 2-615; *Restatement, Second, Contracts* §§ 261-72.

The use of the doctrine of impracticability in government contract law has been limited mainly to instances of "existing" impracticability, which is based on facts in existence at the time the contract was made, rather than "supervening" impracticability, where impracticability results from events occurring after contract formation. This reflects the traditional government contract law approach, which treats supervening impracticability under excusable delay provisions. The *Restatement* reflects the fact that both types of impracticability are included in the doctrine, while U.C.C. § 2-615 appears mainly to cover supervening impracticability by requiring the occurrence of a contingency as the event leading to impracticability. See *RNJ Interstate Corp. v. United States*, 181 F.3d 1329 (Fed. Cir.), *cert. denied*, 528 U.S. 967 (1999), for a rare case where the contractor asserted a claim for work done on a building prior to destruction of the building by fire. The court denied the claim because contract language placed the risk on the contractor until the work was accepted.

Relief can be obtained under the doctrine of impracticability when the contractor can demonstrate that performance is substantially more difficult or expensive than foreseen by the parties and that it has not assumed the risk of this difficulty or expense. The tests for impracticability have been stated in a variety of ways. In *Transatlantic Fin. Corp. v. United States*, 363 F.2d 312 (D.C. Cir. 1966), the court stated at 315-16:

> When the issue is raised, the court is asked to construct a condition of performance based on the changed circumstances, a process which involves at least three reasonably definable steps. First, a contingency—something unexpected—must have occurred. Second, the risk of the unexpected occurrence must not have been allocated either by agreement or by custom. Finally, occurrence of the contingency must have rendered performance commercially impracticable.

Restatement, Second, Contracts § 266(1) formulates the rule for existing impracticability as follows:

> Where, at the time a contract is made, a party's performance under it is impracticable without his fault because of a fact of which he has no reason to know and the non-existence of which is a basic assumption on which the contract is made, no duty to render that performance arises, unless the language or circumstances indicate the contrary.

All of these elements of impracticability are intertwined in the analysis of specific cases. The following material discusses the cases in this area in terms of the problem encountered by the contractor rather than by the legal elements of the analysis. The first section covers those situations in which the difficulty results from a lack of competence on the part of the contractor. The second section deals with those cases in which unforeseen technological problems would have made the work more difficult for any contractor. The third section concludes with a discussion of those instances where the contractor has incurred greatly increased costs in contract performance.

1. Competence of Contractor

When a contractor can demonstrate that it encountered significant difficulties in performing the contract, the initial inquiry deals with the cause of those difficulties. The contractor must show that performance was objectively impracticable because all other contractors would have encountered the same difficulties. See *ASC Sys. Corp.*, DOTCAB 73-37, 78-1 BCA ¶ 13,119, *aff'd*, 223 Ct. Cl. 672 (1980), in which the board stated at 64,134:

> Performance impossibility must be established on an objective basis, not subjectively. That is, the contractor may not rely solely upon his own inability to accomplish the specified task; he must also negate the possibility of performance by others, whether those be other makers of the item or other component parts used in making the item. *Koppers Co. v. U.S.*, 186 Ct. Cl. 142 (1968); *General Instrument Corp.*, DOTCAB 67-9C, 72-1 BCA ¶ 9389. Here the availability of a suitable alternative vidicon and the possibility of performance by others leaves a significant gap in the [contractor's] proof.

Inherent in this analysis is the reasoning that the contractor assumes the risk that it is as competent as other contractors in its field of work.

The government frequently demonstrates that the problem was caused by the contractor's lack of competence by submitting proof that other contractors successfully performed. See, for example, *Flight Refueling, Inc.*, ASBCA 46846, 97-2 BCA ¶ 29,000 (other contractor developing a prototype delivered a compliant product); *GLR Constructors, Inc.*, ENGBCA 6128, 96-1 BCA ¶ 28,218 (other contractors met painting requirement); *MM-Wave Tech., Inc.*, ASBCA 41606, 93-1 BCA ¶ 25,272 (reprocurement contractor completed work following same specification); *PRB Uniforms, Inc.*, ASBCA 21504, 80-2 BCA ¶ 14,602, *aff'd on other grounds*, 706 F.2d 319 (Fed. Cir. 1983) (another contractor performed the work using ingenuity, determination, foresight, and diligence); *Prestex, Inc.*, ASBCA 21284, 81-1 BCA ¶ 14,882, *recons. denied*, 81-2 BCA ¶ 15,397 (several other contractors had performed on earlier contracts); *Continental Rubber Works*, ASBCA 22447, 80-2 BCA ¶ 14,754 (other manufacturers "successfully produced [the] hose in substantial quantities and in accordance with the exact same specifications"); *Remco Hydraulics, Inc.*, ASBCA 17077, 74-2 BCA ¶ 10,732 (other manufacturer successfully produced the contract item under identical specifications); and *F.K. James & Assocs.*, ASBCA 10410, 65-2 BCA ¶ 5051 (other producers furnished the required fluorescent lights). The government has also shown the contractor's lack of competence by proving that it completed the work readily with its own forces, *Tarzan Constr., Inc.*, ENGBCA 5552, 91-2 BCA ¶ 23,887.

The government can also prove lack of competence by showing that the contractor did not perform the contract in an effective manner. See *Oak Adec, Inc. v. United States*, 24 Cl. Ct. 502 (1991), in which the court rejected the contractor's argument that affirmative evidence of its incompetence was irrelevant to a determination of impracticability. The court stated that the contractor could recover on the basis of impracticability only if both (1) it performed with competence, and (2) other contractors could not perform. Thus, in *J.A. Maurer, Inc. v. United States*, 202 Ct. Cl. 813, 485 F.2d 588 (1973), the contractor's claim failed when the government demonstrated that technical and business mistakes were the main cause of its difficulties. In *Crouse-Hinds Sepco Corp.*, DOTCAB 1027, 83-1 BCA ¶ 16,136, *aff'd*, 714 F.2d 161 (Fed. Cir. 1983), the contractor's impracticability claim failed even though it incurred costs of $732,500 in performing a $399,331 contract because the government proved that many of the costs were attributable to the contractor's inexperience and negligence. Similarly, in *Boozer, Wharton & Ziegler, Inc.*, ASBCA 24529, 81-1 BCA ¶ 14,910, the board concluded that the lack of profitability on the contract was due solely to the contractor's pre-bid failure to ascertain a patently obvious requirement. See also *X-Tyal Int'l Corp. v. United States*, 229 Ct. Cl. 827 (1982), in which the court concluded that if the contractor had acted prudently by obtaining firm commitments for materials at the time of award, its prospective loss on the contract would have been limited to $20,000, and *Gene Peters*, PSBCA 999, 83-2 BCA ¶ 16,694, in which the board gave no relief where the contractor had entered into a long-term lease at a very low rental without regard to the possibility that costs of maintenance would increase.

Conversely, the contractor can often prove its competence by proving that other contractors also failed to produce the intended results using the same or similar specifications. See *Dynalectron Corp. v. United States*, 207 Ct. Cl. 349, 518 F.2d 594 (1975) (after termination the government could find no other manufacturer who could perform and changed its specifications); *Ace Elecs. Assocs., Inc.*, ASBCA 10711, 66-2 BCA ¶ 5750 (three successive contractors with identical contracts were unable to perform within the required time, and the record did not show that anyone had succeeded); and *L&O Research & Dev. Corp.*, ASBCA 3060, 57-2 BCA ¶ 1514 (impracticability not negated because the successful contractor performed under materially different contracts).

2. Unforeseen Technological Problems

The most common cases in which contractors recover on the grounds of impracticability of performance are those where the contractor encounters serious technological problems that were unforeseen by the parties at the time of contracting. A number of cases involve manufacturing contracts where it is clear from the nature of the contract that neither party contemplated that a large amount of research and development work would be necessary to meet the specifications. For example, in *Foster Wheeler Corp. v. United States*, 206 Ct. Cl. 533, 513 F.2d 588 (1975), the court found that the performance was impracticable in a contract to manufacture and deliver a product in 13 months because meeting the specification requirement would have required an extensive research and development effort taking from 19 to 24 months. The court concluded that the contractor had not assumed the risk because the government had equal, if not superior, knowledge of the technology when it wrote the specification. Similarly, in *Dynalectron Corp. v. United States*, 207 Ct. Cl. 349, 518 F.2d 594 (1975), the work was found to be impracticable because no contractor could manufacture certain antennas within the specified tolerances without significant waivers of the specification requirements. The court found no assumption of risk by the contractor because there had been no overt acceptance of the risk that the specifications were overly demanding. See also *Whittaker Corp.*, ASBCA 14191, 79-1 BCA ¶ 13,805, where the contractor failed to successfully perform a sealed bid contract to manufacture a large number of products. The board found that neither party contemplated the research and development effort that would have been necessary to perform and that the contractor had not assumed the risk because the government had more expertise than the contractor. In *Numax Elecs., Inc.*, ASBCA 29080, 90-1 BCA ¶ 22,280, impracticability was found when a small business contractor could not mass-produce an item without a significant research and development effort. The board found that the government had assumed the risk because of its superior expertise. In *Scope Elecs., Inc.*, ASBCA 20359, 77-1 BCA ¶ 12,404, *recons. denied*, 77-2 BCA ¶ 12,586, the board arrived at similar results with an initial manufacturing contract in which the contractor was to demonstrate that an item could be mass-produced. The board concluded that meeting certain new requirements was impracticable where both parties appeared to have equal knowledge and expertise.

In these cases it is frequently performance requirements in the specifications that cannot be met. See, for example, *Hol-Gar Mfg. Corp. v. United States*, 175 Ct. Cl. 518, 360 F.2d 634 (1966), where generator sets manufactured within the dimensional tolerances were to be capable of operating 23 hours per day for a period of 6 months (4,000 operating hours) with only normal maintenance and without major overhaul. Impracticability was found when no engine of the specified design could meet these performance requirements. See also *Owen-Corning Fiberglass Corp. & Polytron Co. v. United States*, 190 Ct. Cl. 211, 419 F.2d 439 (1969), where the contract for insulation installation in underground shafts contained design specifications regarding the insulation material to be used; the process of installation; and performance requirements specifying density, stress, and elasticity properties of the insulation. When the government strictly interpreted these properties so as to make the contract impossible to perform as written and interpreted, the contractor recovered its costs incurred while attempting to meet the requirements of the government-drawn specifications. Similarly, in *Defense Sys. Corp. & Hi-Shear Tech. Corp.*, ASBCA 42939, 95-2 BCA ¶ 27,721, a "zero defect" testing requirement was found to be impracticable.

There are a few cases in this category where impracticability has been found on construction contracts. See *Guy F. Atkinson Co.*, ENGBCA 4771, 88-2 BCA ¶ 20,714, holding that a required moisture content in aggregate was impossible to attain and granting an equitable adjustment when the government refused to relax the requirement. Similarly, impracticability has been found when a material called for by the specifications is unavailable, *Blount Bros. Corp. v. United States*, 872 F.2d 1003 (Fed. Cir. 1989); *Granite Constr. Co.*, ENGBCA 4172, 89-2 BCA ¶ 21,683. In these cases, the responsibility appears to be placed on the government, to a considerable extent, because it was slow in relaxing the specification.

There are a variety of circumstances that give rise to the conclusion that the contractor has assumed the risk of overcoming technological problems. For example, where a contractor proposes to perform according to its own specifications, it assumes the risk that those specifications will produce satisfactory results, *Austin Co. v. United States*, 161 Ct. Cl. 76, 314 F.2d 518, *cert. denied*, 375 U.S. 830 (1963). See also *Wallace C. Boldt, Gen. Contractor, Inc.*, ASBCA 24862, 83-2 BCA ¶ 16,765 (although it was quite difficult and dangerous to erect a panel in one piece at the given stage of construction, the contractor could not establish commercial impracticability because it determined the sequence of work on the project, and at least one method and order of construction would have safely permitted erection of the panel in one piece). Likewise, where the contractor possesses superior expertise in the field of endeavor, the government is entitled to rely on the contractor's representation that performance is possible, and the contractor assumes the risk that it was in error, *Bethlehem Corp. v. United States*, 199 Ct. Cl. 247, 462 F.2d 1400 (1972). See *Reflectone, Inc.*, ASBCA 42363, 98-2 BCA ¶ 29,869, finding an assumption of the risk when the contractor proposed a new technical solution to meet the government performance specification and had the technical expertise to determine the extent of risk in performing under a fixed-price incentive contract. The contractor may also assume the risk by entering into the contract when it knows of the difficulties to be encountered in performance, *Whittaker Corp.*, ASBCA 14191, 79-1 BCA ¶ 13,805, or by insisting that the contract be on a fixed-price basis knowing that research and development work is contemplated, *Aerosonic Instrument Corp.*, ASBCA 4129, 59-1 BCA ¶ 2115. Finally, a contractor, in proposing to extend the state of the art, assumes the risk that such may ultimately prove impossible, *J.A. Maurer, Inc. v. United States*, 202 Ct. Cl. 813, 485 F.2d 588 (1973). See also *Moreland Corp. v. Principi*, 259 F.3d 1377 (Fed. Cir. 2001), rejecting a claim based on the assertion that it was impossible to provide only the number of square feet of floor space and comply with the contractually specified floor plans. The court reasoned that the offeror assumed the risk of this situation since it was to design the building.

A contractor will not succeed on a claim of impracticability if it does not follow the technique called for by the specifications. See *Gulf & Western Precision Eng'g Co. v. United States*, 211 Ct. Cl. 207, 543 F.2d 125 (1976), in which the court found assumption of risk when the contractor proposed to meet a performance requirement by substituting its own specification for government non-binding advisory specifications. The dissent noted that the decision ignored the fact that the performance requirement itself was stipulated to by the parties and found by the board to be impossible of attainment. See also *Chronometrics, Inc.*, NASABCA 185-2, 90-3 BCA ¶ 22,992, *recons. denied*, 91-1 BCA ¶ 23,479, in which recovery was denied when the contractor used a technique different from that in its proposal. The board found that there was no proof that the proposed technique would not have met the contract requirements. Similarly, in *Oconto Elec., Inc.*, ASBCA 40421, 93-3 BCA ¶ 26,162, the contractor's claim was denied because it had substituted material for that called for by the specification. The board held that it would not find impracticability in such circumstances unless the contractor permitted the government to test the specified material to determine if it could be practicably used.

In order to recover for impracticability, the contractor must demonstrate that it diligently attempted to perform the contract. See *Jennie-O Foods, Inc. v. United States*, 217 Ct. Cl. 314, 580 F.2d 400 (1978), in which the court stated that the contractor must establish that it explored and exhausted alternatives before concluding performance was commercially senseless and impracticable. In *Koppers Co. v. United States*, 186 Ct. Cl. 142, 405 F.2d 554 (1968), relief was denied for lack of a diligent effort to perform where the contractor had stopped work after expending $48,000 on a $60,000 contract. See also *Crown Welding, Inc.*, ASBCA 36107, 89-1 BCA ¶ 21,332, finding no proof of impracticability where the contractor stopped work before expending half of the contract funds.

In two-step sealed bidding, the contractor performs in accordance with its own design specifications, submitted in step one to meet the government's performance requirements. However, it may still be granted relief if the government-furnished performance requirements prove to be impracticable, *Kinn Elecs. Corp.*, ASBCA 13526, 69-2 BCA ¶ 8061; *Conrad, Inc.*, ASBCA 14239, 71-2 BCA ¶ 9163. In these cases, the board found that the contractors had not assumed the risk that the performance requirements could not be met merely by submitting their designs in response to the solicitation.

3. *Incurrence of Increased Costs*

In a number of cases in which a contractor has alleged impracticability of performance, there appears to be no serious technological problem but merely the encountering of higher-than-anticipated costs to perform the work. In such cases the courts and boards impose stringent standards for relief. The basic test is whether the costs of performing the work are so much greater than anticipated as to render performance commercially senseless. In *Ocean Salvage, Inc.*, ENGBCA 3485, 76-1 BCA ¶ 11,905, practical impossibility occurred when an 800-ton crane costing more than double the contract price was required to remove a sunken barge that the parties had assumed could be removed by only a 50-ton crane. The board reasoned that this new undertaking was "wholly beyond the control and ability of the [contractor] to perform." Similarly, impracticability was found in *GAI Consultants, Inc.*, ENGBCA 6030, 95-2 BCA ¶ 27,620, where excavation in the winter would have required "commercially unacceptable costs and time input far beyond that contemplated in the contract," and *Soletanche Rodio Nicholson (JV)*, ENGBCA 5796, 94-1 BCA ¶ 26,472, where excavation using the specified methods would have cost many times the contract price. See also *SMC Info. Sys., Inc. v. General Servs. Admin.*, GSBCA 9371, 93-1 BCA ¶ 25,485, finding impracticability when the contractor expended more than four times the contract price attempting to accomplish the work, but refusing to grant relief because the contractor had not given the government notice of its difficulties. Compare *Gene Peters*, PSBCA 999, 83-2 BCA ¶ 16,694, where the rental rate in a long-term lease to the government appeared to be approximately 15 percent of the fair market value, but the board gave no relief on the grounds that the contractor had assumed the risk in entering into such an arrangement.

Increases in contract price that are not substantial will not support recovery. For example, in *Transatlantic Fin. Corp. v. United States*, 363 F.2d 312 (D.C. Cir. 1966), the court ruled that a 14 percent increase in price for a supervening event that made performance more costly was not sufficient to constitute impracticability. In this case, the court cited two British cases holding that 50 percent and 100 percent increases in costs were not large enough to meet the impracticability test. In *Raytheon Co.*, ASBCA 50166, 01-1 BCA ¶ 31,245, *aff'd*, 305 F.3d 1354 (Fed. Cir. 2002), the board held that a 57 percent increase in price would not support an impracticability claim, while in *Naughton Energy, Inc.*, ASBCA 33044, 88-2 BCA ¶ 20,800, the board held that the contractor had assumed the risk when its price increased 59 percent. Similarly, in *Jalaprathan Cement Co.*, ASBCA 21248, 79-2 BCA ¶ 13,927, the board refused to find impracticability in a case where the contractor lost $208,408.59 on a fixed-price contract of $639,993.08. In that case, the board analyzed the situation not only in terms of the loss on the contract but also the loss on the total business of the contractor and found that the impact was not so crippling as to constitute impracticability. It relied on two cases in which the courts had used similar total-impact logic, *Eastern Airlines, Inc. v. Gulf Oil Corp.*, 415 F. Supp. 429 (S.D. Fla. 1975) and *United States v. Wegematic Corp.*, 360 F.2d 674 (2d Cir. 1966). See also *J. Filiberto Sanitation, Inc.*, VABCA 2696, 88-3 BCA ¶ 21,160, granting no relief where one element of performance became far more costly although the entire contract price did not increase excessively.

A "willing buyer" test has been used to determine whether the contractor's costs of performance are so excessive as to constitute commercial senselessness. In *Brazier Lumber Co.*, ASBCA 18601, 76-2 BCA ¶ 12,207, the board stated at 58,774:

> This Board has stated that it is economically impracticable to supply an item when the costs which would be incurred in doing so would be so great that buyers could not be found who would be willing to pay a price consisting of such costs plus a reasonable profit. *Cavite Lumber & Hardware Co.*, ASBCA No. 18579, 74-1 BCA ¶ 10,435; *Firestone Industrial Rubber Products Co. and GoCorp., Inc.*, ASBCA Nos. 16650 and 17938, 74-1 BCA ¶ 10,516; *Industrial Electronics Hardware Corp.*, ASBCA Nos. 10201 and 11364, 68-2 BCA ¶ 7174. The evidence in the instant appeal does not conform to this definition, however, as it appears that an active market did exist, during the performance periods of the subject contracts, for the sale and purchase of the needed lumber. Except for one line item the prices ultimately paid by respondent for the repurchased lumber exceeded those which prevailed on the delivery dates contained in appellant's contracts.

See also *Read Plastics, Inc.*, GSBCA 4159-R, 77-2 BCA ¶ 12,609, *modified on recons.*, 77-2 BCA ¶ 12,859, noting that impracticability "require[s] a showing that no buyers existed which were willing to pay a price consisting of the costs of production plus a reasonable profit" and denying recovery where the "availability of both producers and purchasers for the defaulted items [had] been conclusively established" by the award of two separate reprocurement contracts.

The contractor has been held to have assumed the risk of unavailability and price fluctuation of necessary materials and components in the absence of special circumstances, *Jennie-O Foods, Inc. v. United States*, 217 Ct. Cl. 314, 580 F.2d 400 (1978) (alternate sources of turkeys were available but untapped by contractor, whose turkey suppliers were experiencing disease problems); *Brazier Lumber Co.*, ASBCA 18601, 76-2 BCA ¶ 12,207 (lumber price increases of between 130 and 155 percent after award but before actual purchase date were deemed normal business risks that contractor assumed); *Southern Dredging Co.*, ENGBCA 5843, 92-2 BCA ¶ 24,886 (price increase of oil because of war in Middle East a risk that contractor assumed); *Seaboard Lumber Co. v. United States*, 308 F.3d 1283 (Fed. Cir. 2002) (changed market conditions reducing price of lumber made contract unprofitable but not "objectively impossible," and contractor assumes such market risks).

B. Mistake

Restatement, Second, Contracts § 151 contains a simple definition of mistake: "A mistake is a belief that is not in accord with the facts." Contractors frequently discover after award that they were mistaken about the degree or type of effort required to perform the contract. As a result they seek either an adjustment in contract price or to be excused from their obligation to perform. If the government participated in the mistake, relief is sought under the theory of mutual mistake. If not, relief must be predicated on the theory that the government knew or had reason to know of the contractor's unilateral mistake. The procedures for processing mistakes discovered after award on seal bid contracts are outlined in FAR 14.407-4. In rare cases where relief would not be granted on mistake theory, contractors have been relieved from their obligations on the ground that it would be unconscionable for the government to contractually bind the contractor who made a mistake. This section discusses the criteria used to determine whether relief should be granted. It also considers the appropriate relief to be granted.

1. Mutual Mistake

There are essentially two types of mutual mistake that have been recognized as providing a basis for contract relief: mutual mistake as to a basic assumption on which the contract is based and mutual mistake in integration.

a. Mutual Mistake as to a Basic Assumption

In government contracts, relief for a mutual mistake of a basic assumption is granted when the court or board determines that the parties would have altered the agreement had they known the correct information at the time of contract formation. The cases generally follow the common law rule. Thus, obtaining relief requires a showing that (1) both the contractor and the government had at the time of contract formation made a mistake as to (2) a basic assumption on which the contract was based, which had (3) a material effect on performance, (4) provided that the contractor did not assume the risk of that mistake, *Restatement, Second, Contracts* § 152.

The landmark case involving all of these elements is *National Presto Indus., Inc. v. United States*, 167 Ct. Cl. 749, 338 F.2d 99 (1964), *cert. denied*, 380 U.S. 962 (1965). The contractor had agreed to undertake production of 105 mm shells by using a new experimental production method that did not call for the use of turning and grinding equipment. The government had initiated the idea of using this approach, which had been the subject of considerable preaward discussion. The court granted relief to the contractor when it turned out that the shells could not be produced without using turning equipment. It found that the parties had "reasonably labored, for most of the contract period, under a mutual mistake as to a most material set of facts." The basic assumption as to which the parties had been mistaken related to the feasibility of producing the shells without turning procedures, while the mutuality of this mistaken assumption was established primarily by the extensive pre-contract discussions between the parties. In reaching this conclusion, the court emphasized that the undertaking was a joint enterprise and that the government was interested just as much in the perfection of the new process as it was in the end product. As to allocation of risk, the court pointed out that nothing in the contract or the parties' dealings indicated that the contractor assumed the full risk of the mistake even though the contract was fixed-price and the contractor was claiming a loss of only approximately $750,000 on a $15 million contract.

(1) Basic Assumption

To be a basic assumption, a matter must be a significant part of the bargaining process. In *National Presto*, this was established by the discussions in negotiations, which demonstrated that a major portion of the contract was to be the demonstration of a new method of production. A mutual mistake in basic assumption was found in *Air Compressor Prods., Inc.*, ASBCA 40015, 91-2 BCA ¶ 23,957 (inquiries and discussions concerning the nature of the product); *Management & Training Corp. v. General Servs. Admin.*, GSBCA 11182, 93-2 BCA ¶ 25,814 (parties intended to include utility costs in the agreement); and *Richlin Sec. Serv. Co.*, DOTBCA 3034, 98-1 BCA ¶ 29,651, *aff'd*, 155 F.3d 566 (Fed. Cir. 1998) (parties assumed type of labor specified in solicitation—implementing Service Contract Act).

A corollary to the necessity for the matter to be considered by the parties is that the facts on which the alleged assumption is based must be knowable at the time the contract was formed, *Atlas Corp. v. United States*, 895 F.2d 745 (Fed. Cir. 1990), *cert. denied*, 498 U.S. 811 (1990). In *Atlas*, the court rejected the contractor's contention that there had been a mutual mistake when the parties entered into a contract for uranium production not realizing that by-products of the work produced serious hazards. The court stated at 750-51:

> In the cases where courts have reformed a contract, the parties recognize the existence of a fact about which they could negotiate, they mutually form a belief concerning that fact, but their belief is erroneous. In those cases, the court may reform the contract to bring the parties' agreement in accord with the true state of the facts.

For example, in *National Presto*, . . . the Court of Claims granted reformation of a contract to permit reimbursement for the cost of an additional step in a process of manufacturing artillery shells. Before the parties entered into the contract, they discussed whether an additional step was needed in which excess metal was shaved from the shells. Their contract did not include provision for the equipment for this additional step, but during the performance of the contract, it was determined that the additional step was in fact necessary. The [contractor] was required to obtain additional equipment. The court permitted reformation of the contract. Although the parties did not know of the need for the additional equipment, . . . they clearly recognized that the equipment might be needed. They recognized the existence of a fact on which they could reach agreement, and they formed an erroneous belief concerning that fact. Therefore, there was a mutual mistake.

Similarly, in *R.M. Hollingshead Corp. v. United States*, 124 Ct. Cl. 681, 111 F. Supp. 285 (1953), the [contractor] agreed to sell DDT in metal containers to the government under a contract which required the chemical to be a clear, stable liquid. When the DDT subsequently turned cloudy, the government refused payment. The Court of Claims denied the government's motion to dismiss, stating that when the parties entered into the contract, neither knew that it was impossible to store DDT in metal containers without a resulting loss of clear color. The clear color requirement was part of the government's specifications, and the parties considered that fact when contracting. Their erroneous belief concerning that fact was their mistake.

Other cases in which courts have permitted reformation of contracts similarly show that the parties held an erroneous belief concerning a fact whose existence the parties recognized and about which they could reach agreement. See, e.g., *Southwest Welding & Mfg. Co. v. United States*, 179 Ct. Cl. 39, 373 F.2d 982 (1967) (the parties mistakenly believed the price of steel was lower than it actually was); *Walsh v. United States*, 121 Ct. Cl. 546, 102 F. Supp. 589 (1952) (the parties erroneously believed the minimum wage rate was a certain amount, even though it had increased earlier); *Aluminum Co. of America v. Essex Group, Inc.*, 499 F. Supp. 53 (W.D. Pa. 1980) (the parties erroneously believed that the Wholesale Price Index would accurately represent non-labor production costs for the purpose of a contractual escalation clause). See also *Bowen-McLaughlin-York Co. v. United States*, 813 F.2d 1221 (Fed. Cir. 1987) (reformation permitted where the parties erroneously omitted certain price items that were in existence and could have been included in the contract). *Macke Co. v. United States*, 199 Ct. Cl. 552, 467 F.2d 1323 (1972), does not show a different rule. The opinion in that case does not indicate whether a mistake was made by the parties. Rather, the court interpreted or reformed the contract to conform to the parties' practical construction. *Id.* at 1328.

[Contractors] argue that the Claims Court's distinction between "knowable" and "unknowable" facts has no bearing on whether a [contractor] has properly stated a claim for relief by reformation. The [contractors] cite *Aluminum Co. of America* in which the district court observed "[t]he law of mistake has not distinguished between facts which are unknown but presently knowable, and facts which presently exist but are unknowable. Relief has been granted for mistakes of both

> kinds." 499 F. Supp. at 64 (citations omitted). It is true that even though the outcome of a fact is unknowable, the parties can make a mistake concerning that fact. But where the existence of a fact is unknowable, the parties cannot have a belief concerning that fact, and they cannot make a mistake about it.

The same result was reached in *Dairyland Power Coop. v. United States*, 16 F.3d 1197 (Fed. Cir. 1994), in which the court found no mutual mistake as to the future availability of a certain industry when the government plant was bought by the contractor under a contract option to buy. The court stated that mistake law did not cover predictions or judgments regarding events to occur in the future. See also *Reflectone, Inc.*, ASBCA 42363, 98-2 BCA ¶ 29,869 (contractor's belief that proposed design would be simple, low cost, and state of the art and would use off-the-shelf hardware and software were predictions or judgments about future events rather than existing, verifiable facts); *John T. Jones Constr. Co.*, ASBCA 48303, 98-2 BCA ¶ 29,892 (parties' beliefs about performance method were not mistaken facts existing at the time of entering into modification but were judgments about future events); and *Southern Dredging Co.*, ENGBCA 5843, 92-2 BCA ¶ 24,886 (no mistake in the alleged basic assumption that fuel prices in the Middle East would remain stable during the performance of the contract because these were forecasts of future events).

It has been difficult for contractors to establish that a matter is a basic assumption. For example, in *Evans Reamer & Mach. Co. v. United States*, 181 Ct. Cl. 539, 386 F.2d 873 (1967), *cert. denied*, 390 U.S. 982 (1968), a set-aside contractor agreed to supply products for $76.036 per unit, in part based on the belief that the non-set-aside contractor was to receive the same amount. Although the non-set-aside contractor later received extraordinary relief, increasing its unit recovery to $87.9391, no mutual mistake was found where there was no indication that, had the contracting officer been able to forecast this increase, it would have negotiated a higher price with Evans. Similarly, in *Pauley Petroleum, Inc. v. United States*, 219 Ct. Cl. 24, 591 F.2d 1308, *cert. denied*, 444 U.S. 898 (1979), the contractor failed to prove that availability of necessary insurance coverage was a basic assumption of an oil exploration and production lease. See also *Lindsay v. United States*, 41 Fed. Cl. 388 (1998) (mailbox count not basic assumption in contract for postal delivery); *Westinghouse Elec. Corp. v. United States*, 41 Fed. Cl. 229 (1998) (expected sole-source status after award of contract not basic assumption); *Reflectone, Inc.*, ASBCA 42363, 98-2 BCA ¶ 29,869 (no evidence that government employees assumed that contractor's proposed technical solution was simple and workable without extensive technical effort); *Knieper v. United States*, 38 Fed. Cl. 128 (1997) (belief that well water would be available on purchased property not basic assumption); *Cobra, S.A.*, ASBCA 28146, 84-3 BCA ¶ 17,535 (nothing to show a belief that the peseta would remain a stable currency and that, had fluctuation been foreseen, escalation provisions would have been included); *Space Age Eng'g, Inc.*, ASBCA 25761, 83-2 BCA ¶ 16,607 (subject was addressed by neither the contract nor the parties prior to award); and *Diplomatic Painting & Bldg. Servs. Co. v. General Servs. Admin.*,

GSBCA 12031, 94-1 BCA ¶ 26,502 (no evidence of consideration of consequences of a reduction in Service Contract Act wage rates).

(2) Mutuality

Relief requires a showing that both parties made the same mistake at the time of contracting. In *McNamara Constr. of Manitoba, Ltd. v. United States*, 206 Ct. Cl. 1, 509 F.2d 1166 (1975), a contractor performing a fixed-price contract sought to recover for increased labor costs resulting from strikes, delays, and harassment by its workers and their union. The court rejected the contractor's attempt to rely on the mutual mistake rule of *National Presto*. This conclusion was based primarily on its finding that no assumption of labor harmony had been made a basis of the bargain, thereby demonstrating a lack of mutuality of mistake. The failure to demonstrate that both parties made the same mistake was the basis for denying relief in *Natus Corp. v. United States*, 178 Ct. Cl. 1, 371 F.2d 450 (1967), and *Olin Mathieson Chem. Corp. v. United States*, 179 Ct. Cl. 368 (1967). In *Natus*, a contractor engaged in production of steel airplane landing mats sought to recover additional costs incurred when the production method it initially selected proved unworkable. The court denied relief under a theory of mutual mistake, distinguishing *National Presto* at 13-14:

> The linchpin of our decision in that case is to be found in the Government's active participation in the precontract negotiations wherein the parties mutually agreed to the exclusion of certain equipment later found to be indispensable to satisfactory production. The expenses which [the contractor] sustained, attributable directly to the unanticipated problems resulting from the absence of the necessary turning equipment, were relieved, in part, through our application of the mutual mistake concept. And in reaching that result, we noted that [the contractor's] commitment to a fixed-price contract strongly suggested that it had assumed all the uncovered risks inherent in its promised performance—this obstacle being overcome only because a review of the parties' dealings as a whole convincingly demonstrated the mutual contemplation and error respecting the need for turning equipment or the time in which such need would become known.
>
> * * *
>
> Apart from the fact that the landing mat was a new product, we find nothing in the present factual pattern which would support our finding that the mistake made here was a mutual one. As pointed out, [the contractor's] decision to use a rolling machine was wholly unilateral—the Government at no time expressing any views as to how production should proceed. Furthermore, the question as to what quantity should or could be produced was left entirely to the contractor's judgment. Under these circumstances, we find that [the contractor's] acceptance of a fixed-price contract forecloses any possibility of expense allocation along the lines of mutual mistake.

In *Olin Mathieson*, the court rejected the contractor's attempt to rely on *National Presto*, finding that there was no proof that the parties had contracted on the basis of a mutual assumption that extra work under a fixed-price contract was required.

See *Quality Elec. Serv.*, ASBCA 25811, 81-2 BCA ¶ 15,380, in which the board noted that a mutual mistake is an unconscious ignorance by both parties to a contract of a fact material to such contract, or an erroneous belief by both such parties in the present existence of a thing material to such contract. See also *Martin-Copeland Co.*, ASBCA 26551, 83-2 BCA ¶ 16,752, in which the court noted at 83,299, "[T]hese assumptions may well have been in the back of [the contractor's] mind when the contract was entered into, but to say that the Government entertained the same assumptions, or agreed to be bound by them, stretches credulity beyond the breaking point."

Contractors have been able to prove mutuality by demonstrating that the government knew of the mistaken fact at the time of contract formation. For example, in *Tempo, Inc.*, ASBCA 7403, 91-1 BCA ¶ 23,298, a government memorandum showed that both parties had assumed that certain work would not be required. Similarly, in *Management & Training Corp. v. General Servs. Admin.*, GSBCA 11182, 93-2 BCA ¶ 25,814, proof that the parties had communicated about the mistake during discussions in a negotiated procurement sufficiently established a mutual mistake claim. The board also found mutual mistake where the government incorporated into a contract a letter from the contractor containing a mistake, *Air Compressor Prods., Inc.*, ASBCA 40015, 91-2 BCA ¶ 23,957. However, the mere acceptance by the government of an erroneous estimate of the contractor will not constitute sufficient proof of mutuality, *Ocean Tech., Ltd.*, IBCA 2651, 91-2 BCA ¶ 23,797, *aff'd*, 954 F.2d 733 (Fed. Cir. 1992); *Southwest Marine, Inc.*, ASBCA 34058, 91-1 BCA ¶ 23,323; *EDC/MTI (JV)*, ENGBCA 5631, 90-2 BCA ¶ 22,669.

It has generally been difficult to prove that the contracting officer's execution of the contract was based on the same assumptions as those of the contractor. See, for example, *Servicios Profesionales de Mantenimiento, S.A.*, ASBCA 52631, 03-2 BCA ¶ 32,276 (no mutual ignorance of amount of cleaning work when contractor "knew the buildings well"); *Westfed Holdings, Inc. v. United States*, 52 Fed. Cl. 135 (2002) (parties' different views of contract interpretation not mutual mistake of fact); *Rich Macauley*, AGBCA 2000-155-3, 01-1 BCA ¶ 31,350 (fact that unauthorized agents of government shared contractor's belief immaterial since contracting officers testified that they did not); *Minuteman Aviation, Inc.*, AGBCA 99-115-1, 00-1 BCA ¶ 30,831 (no evidence that government shared in contractor's mistaken judgment on equipment to be used or was even aware that the equipment contractor intended to employ or rate it used in calculating its bid); *EFG Assocs., Inc.*, ASBCA 49356, 00-1 BCA ¶ 30,638 (no mutual mistake based on failure to include subcontractor overhead and profit since contracting officer knew at all times that they were not included); *Heritage Healthcare Servs., Inc.*, VABCA 5603, 99-1 BCA ¶ 30,209 (government denied "ever having the conversation on which" contractor claimed to rely for establishing mutuality); *Bath Iron Works Corp.*, ASBCA 44618, 96-2 BCA ¶ 28,475, *aff'd*, 113 F.3d 1256 (Fed. Cir. 1997) (no proof that government shared contractor's belief, and no mistake as to an existing fact, but an error in judging the complexity of constructing the ships); and *Peterson Builders, Inc. v. United States*,

34 Fed. Cl. 182 (1995), *aff'd*, 155 F.3d 566 (Fed. Cir. 1998) (no proof that government shared in belief that the design was "substantially complete).

(3) Material Effect

Although recovery also requires that the mistake have a material effect, this requirement has not been a significant factor in government contracts litigation. The *National Presto* decision indicates that it simply means that, because of the mistake, performance or risks were more than insignificantly altered. For a more restrictive view, see *MPT Enters.*, ASBCA 25339, 83-2 BCA ¶ 16,761, *recons. denied*, 84-1 BCA ¶ 17,169, in which, relying on *Restatement, Second, Contracts* § 152, the board held that the resulting imbalance in the agreed exchange must be so severe that the contractor cannot fairly be required to carry it out. Such a material effect was established where the contractor signed an amendment creating liability under the mistaken belief that such liability already existed.

(4) Assumption of Risk

If the contractor has assumed the specific risks at issue, the mutual mistake argument will fail. In *Flippin Materials Co. v. United States*, 160 Ct. Cl. 357, 312 F.2d 408 (1963), the court noted, at 368, that "a mutual mistake as to a fact or factor, even a material one, will not support relief if the contract puts the risk of such a mistake on the party asking reformation . . . or normally if the other party, though made aware of the correct facts, would not have agreed at the outset to the change now sought." Normally, the contractor will be held to have assumed the risk of mistakes relating directly to the effort involved in performing the contract. See *McNamara Constr. of Manitoba, Ltd. v. United States*, 206 Ct. Cl. 1, 509 F.2d 1166 (1975), in which the court denied monetary relief for multiple harassing strikes on the theory that the excusable delay provisions of the contract granting time extensions constituted the parties' full bargain as to such events. See also *Patty Precision Prods. Co.*, ASBCA 24458, 83-1 BCA ¶ 16,261, stating that "[t]he risk of having a proper work force is simply one of several risks accepted by a contractor when it undertakes to perform under a fixed price contract." In *Olin Mathieson Chem. Corp. v. United States*, 179 Ct. Cl. 368 (1967), the court found that the government relied on the expertise of the contractor and concluded that the contractor, therefore, "voluntarily assumed the risk of shouldering the entire expense under the supply contract—whatever it might be." In *Emerald Maint., Inc. v. United States*, 925 F.2d 1425 (Fed. Cir. 1991), the court found that the contractor had assumed the risk of a mutual mistake as to the local labor practices because of the Site Investigation & Conditions Affecting the Work clause, which made the contractor responsible for investigating conditions at the site of the work. See also *PACCAR, Inc.*, ASBCA 27978, 89-2 BCA ¶ 21,696 (contractor's obligation to comply with Cost Accounting Standards resulted in its assumption of the risk of mistake concerning cost accounting practice); *DK's Precision Machining & Mfg.*, ASBCA 39616, 90-2 BCA ¶ 22,830 (risk of price increases on contractor in view of the state of the economy); *Bescast, Inc.*, ASBCA 38149, 90-3 BCA ¶ 23,244 (risk of inability to reverse engineer product on contractor because government believed task was risky); *Blaze Constr. Co.*, IBCA 2863, 91-3 BCA ¶ 24,071 (risk of sacred Indian land placed on contractor by Permits and Responsibilities and Tribal Taxes, Requirements and/or Restrictions clauses); *Charles E. Irons*, ENGBCA 6318, 00-2 BCA ¶ 30,965 (contractor assumed risk of excavating and handling moist borrow since there were no "explicit promises" in contract with respect to moisture); *NAVCOM Def. Elecs., Inc.*, ASBCA 50767, 01-2 BCA ¶ 31,546 (performance-type specification put the risk on contractor and no proof that government had knowledge of contractor's proposed design); *Pratt v. United States*, 50 Fed. Cl. 469 (2001) ("as is" clause placed risk on contractor); and *Humlen v. United States*, 49 Fed. Cl. 497 (2001) (contractor bears risk of mistake in dealing with unauthorized agent). Compare *Beta Sys., Inc. v. United States*, 838 F.2d 1179 (Fed. Cir. 1988), in which the court found no assumption of risk by the contractor when the parties included an Economic Price Adjustment clause in the contract that contained an index that did not track the material used to perform the contract. The court relied on language in the procurement regulations, which required the contracting officer to use an accurate index, as demonstrating that there was no intent for the contractor to bear the risk of an inaccurate index.

b. Mutual Mistake in Integration

A mistake in integration occurs when the written contract document fails to express the actual agreement of the parties, *Restatement, Second, Contracts* § 155. The key factor in mistake in integration cases is proof of the actual agreement of the parties. This proof may be established from contemporaneous documents or the parties' actions after award, *Sutcliffe Storage & Warehouse Co. v. United States*, 125 Ct. Cl. 297, 112 F. Supp. 590 (1953) (1½ years of performance varying from the document established actual agreement); *Walsh v. United States*, 121 Ct. Cl. 546, 102 F. Supp. 589 (1952) (contract between same parties one week later furnished proof of actual agreement); *Gresham Sand & Gravel Co.*, GSBCA 6858, 84-1 BCA ¶ 17,019 (actual agreement established from cover letter sending government amendment); *Transportes Especiales de Automoviles, S.A.*, ASBCA 43851, 93-2 BCA ¶ 25,745 (omitted details from Economic Price Adjustment clause determined from negotiation documents).

Some cases relying on mistake in integration theory contain elements of mutual mistake of a basic assumption. For example, in *Southwest Welding & Mfg. Co. v. United States*, 179 Ct. Cl. 39, 373 F.2d 982 (1967), the contractor sought relief where the parties' written agreement reflected their assumption that the contractor's cost of steel per 100 lbs. would be $7.53, when the actual cost was $7.98 per 100 lbs. The court found that the intent of the parties was that the contractor would recover its actual costs and held that an adjustment in contract price was appropriate since the written contract failed to express accurately that intention. This case was followed in *Bowen-McLaughlin-York Co. v. United States*, 813 F.2d 1221 (Fed. Cir. 1987), where the parties omitted certain escalation costs from the incurred costs that were used in the conversion of a letter contract to a fixed-price contract. The court concluded that the intent of the parties had been that the fixed price include all incurred costs. In *Poirier & McLane Corp. v. United States*, 128 Ct. Cl. 117, 120 F. Supp. 209 (1954), the court granted relief where the contract reflected the parties' mistaken assumption that the prevailing wage rate for unskilled laborers for purposes of the Davis-Bacon Act was 85 cents but the prevailing wage as determined by the Secretary was actually $1.00. See also *Lea Co.*, GSBCA 5697, 81-2 BCA ¶ 15,208, where the contractor's version of an agreement was established from the unreasonableness of terms in the document and a letter from a mortgage broker.

2. Unilateral Mistake

A contractor's unilateral mistake may be grounds for relief in cases where, at the time of formation, the government should have known of the contractor's mistake. The criteria for obtaining reformation of the contract to correct the mistake under a theory of unilateral mistake are that (1) a mistake in fact occurred prior to contract award; (2) the mistake amounts to a clear-cut clerical or mathematical error or a misreading of the specifications and not a judgmental error; (3) prior to award, the government knew or should have known that a mistake had been made and, therefore, should have requested bid verification; (4) the government did not request bid verification or its request for bid verification was inadequate; and (5) proof of the intended bid is established, *McClure Elec. Constructors, Inc. v. Dalton*, 132 F.3d 709 (Fed. Cir. 1997). If the contractor is requesting rescission of the contract on the basis of a unilateral mistake, the fifth requirement is not applicable. If these predicates are not established, the contractor's sole basis for relief for unilateral mistake is unconscionability.

Contractor negligence is not a bar to relief in these cases. See *Ruggiero v. United States*, 190 Ct. Cl. 327, 420 F.2d 709 (1970), in which the court pointed out that in most cases where relief was granted the bidders were "guilty of egregious blunders." Further, these principles have been applied to negotiated contracts as well as to sealed bids, 48 Comp. Gen. 672 (B-165573) (1969); 45 Comp. Gen. 305 (B-157254) (1965).

a. Type of Mistake

In granting relief for unilateral mistake, courts distinguish between ministerial errors and judgmental errors. In *Ruggiero v. United States*, 190 Ct. Cl. 327, 420 F.2d 709 (1970), the court stated at 1157:

> The mistake . . . must be . . . a clear cut clerical or arithmetical error, or a misreading of specifications, and the authorities cited do not extend to mistakes of judgment.

(1) Business Judgment

Contractors make numerous business judgments in the contracting process. They must assess the complexity of the task, decide whether to submit bids or proposals, and determine the amount of effort required to perform the work. If their judgments in these areas prove to be mistaken, affirmative monetary relief will not be granted on the theory of unilateral mistake. However, if the government knew or should have known of the error, the contractor may be relieved of liability for excess costs of reprocurement, *United States v. Hamilton Enters., Inc.*, 711 F.2d 1038 (Fed. Cir. 1983) (underestimation of required labor hours was a judgmental error, but the government did not properly notify the contractor of the possibility of an error). As the Federal Circuit described in *Liebherr Crane Corp. v. United States*, 810 F.2d 1153 (Fed. Cir. 1987), where the contractor "undertakes a conscious gamble with known risks and thereby assumed the risk of its deliberative choice," unilateral mistake will not be found. For example, in *Aydin Corp. v. United States*, 229 Ct. Cl. 309, 669 F.2d 681 (1982), the court refused to provide relief for errors concerning the nature and costs of materials necessary to perform the work, concluding that these were mere errors in judgment. See *American Ship Bldg. Co. v. United States*, 228 Ct. Cl. 220, 654 F.2d 75 (1981), denying relief where the contractor committed an error in judgment in not fully assessing the difficulty of the work, and *Trio Mach. Works, Inc.*, NASABCA 480-6, 82-1 BCA ¶ 15,465, *recons. denied*, 82-2 BCA ¶ 15,968, *aff'd*, 714 F.2d 161 (Fed. Cir. 1983), denying relief where the contractor committed an error in judgment with respect to the availability of tool parts that caused a substantial reduction in the planned use of the contractor's numerically controlled machinery. See also *RQ Constr., Inc.*, ASBCA 52376, 01-2 BCA ¶ 31,627 (neither contractor nor subcontractor made an effort to determine cost of underpriced work); *EFG Assocs.,Inc.*, ASBCA 49356, 99-1 BCA ¶ 30,638 (contractor chose pricing formula without adequate analysis or checking with subcontractors); *Kitco, Inc.*, ASBCA 45347, 93-3 BCA ¶ 26,153 ($208 per kit offer on an aircraft supply contract found to be an error in judgment); *Fan, Inc.*, GSBCA 7836, 91-1 BCA ¶ 23,364, *recons. denied*, 91-2 BCA ¶ 23,768 (experience of contractor precluded reformation claim where the contractor employed its in-house estimate of the number of air handling devices needed to construct a building as required in the solicitation); *Sciaba Constr. Corp.*, VABCA 2611, 89-3 BCA ¶ 22,031 (contractor's failure to secure pricing information for a potential supplier precluded its claim for equitable adjustment); and *Tri-States Serv. Co.*, ASBCA 31139, 90-3 BCA ¶ 23,059 (contractor made a business judgment when it failed to examine the government's in-house estimates of manning levels).

(2) Misreading Specifications

Misreading of specifications is not considered to be a mistake in business judgment when it involves the quantity or nature of the work rather than the effort required to perform the work. In *Liebherr Crane Corp. v. United States*, 810 F.2d 1153 (Fed. Cir. 1987), the court described the distinction between a business judgment and the misreading of specifications at 1157:

> [This mistake] cannot be said to have resulted from a misreading of specifications. To the contrary, Liebherr's errant bid clearly resulted from [its president's] gross negligence in failing to read and consider the specifications thoroughly. The distinction is critical. If a contractor fails to interpret correctly various elements of the specifications, he has "misread" the specifications. If a misreading produces a mistake in bid, it may, in appropriate circumstances, furnish a basis for reformation. The price may be reformed, provided the contractor can provide clear and convincing evidence of what his bid would have been but for the error. Such relief does not extend, however, to mistakes in judgment on the part of the contractor or its representative. *Ruggiero v. United States*, 420 F.2d 709, 190 Ct. Cl. 327 (1970).

The Federal Circuit ultimately concluded that this highly experienced contractor had made an error in business judgment by reading only four of the 98 pages of specifications and assuming that its standard crane would be sufficient to complete the job. Thus, the mistake did not result from a misinterpretation of the specifications (which would be recoverable) but did result from a miscalculation of the effort needed to comply with the specifications (which is not recoverable). See also *Giesler v. United States*, 232 F.3d 864 (Fed. Cir. 2000), holding that *failure to read* the specifications cannot be classified as a misreading of the specifications. By contrast, see *Walter Straga*, ASBCA 26134, 83-2 BCA ¶ 16,611, where the contractor based its estimate on an unreasonable but mistaken interpretation of the specifications. The board granted relief, finding no exercise of business judgment involved in misreading the specifications as to the quantity of items covered. Similarly, in *BCM Corp. v. United States*, 2 Cl. Ct. 602 (1983), a contractor who unreasonably misinterpreted the contract specification received an equitable adjustment because a mistake in judgment had not occurred. When determining its bid price, the contractor failed to include a particular, identifiable portion of work and had not underestimated the work it thought was included. See *Faulkner Corp.*, VABCA 2998, 90-1 BCA ¶ 22,507, where the contractor interpreted the amended specifications as deleting a requirement to build a new canteen storage area. Given the conflicting aspects of the specifications, the board found this mistake to involve the nature of the work rather than the effort needed to perform the contract and allowed reformation. See also *Minnesota Well Drillers*, ASBCA 26097, 82-1 BCA ¶ 15,539, where the contractor failed to take into account revised specifications describing the harder material through which the contractor would drill. The board commented at 77,045:

> [Contractor's] stupidity in bidding without reading the revised specifications does not forfeit relief because such foolishness or a variation thereof is common to most bidders who err in bidding and such conduct is of diminished importance in deciding whether to reform a contract. *Chris Berg, Inc. v. United States*, 192 Ct. Cl. 176, 426 F.2d 314 (1970).

This rule on misreading of specifications does not apply when the specification is properly interpreted and the contractor makes a deliberate choice to use a cheaper, nonconforming material, *Ralph Larsen & Son, Inc. v. United States*, 17 Cl. Ct. 39 (1989); *Technology Chem., Inc.*, ASBCA 26304, 82-2 BCA ¶ 15,927.

(3) Clerical or Arithmetical Errors

Clerical or arithmetical errors are the most common types of unilateral mistakes for which relief is granted. See, for example, *Bromley Contracting Co. v. United States*, 794 F.2d 669 (Fed. Cir. 1986) (labor cost for one element of work omitted from bid); *Allen L. Bender, Inc.*, LBCA 80-BCA-103, 81-2 BCA ¶ 15,435 (cost of several items omitted from recap sheets); *McCarty Corp. v. United States*, 204 Ct. Cl. 768, 499 F.2d 633 (1974) (numbers transposed on bid document); *Columbia Pac. Constr. Co.*, Comp. Gen. Dec. B-207313, 82-1 CPD ¶ 436 (contractor divided rather than multiplied in making metric conversion); *PK Contractors, Inc.*, Comp. Gen. Dec. B-205482, 82-1 CPD ¶ 368 (error in pagination resulted in failure to include estimated costs on one page of estimating sheets); *Carl Garis & Son, Inc.*, 89-1 BCA ¶ 21,399 (failure of contractor to double the cost of electrical work in its bid); *Government Micro Res., Inc. v. Department of the Treasury*, GSBCA 12364-TD, 94-2 BCA ¶ 26,680 (contractor's unintentional reversal of discount and cost rates while preparing its offer); and *Paragon Energy Corp. v. United States*, 227 Ct. Cl. 176, 645 F.2d 966 (1981) (omission of one element of cost estimates).

In *Rockwell Int'l Corp.*, ASBCA 41095, 95-1 BCA ¶ 27,459, *recons. denied*, 95-2 BCA ¶ 27,897, the board denied relief for a mathematical mistake that occurred when the contractor used the wrong algorithm because it was not "clear cut." See *Holmes & Narver Constructors, Inc.*, ASBCA 52429, 02-1 BCA ¶ 31,849, applying this requirement that the mistake be clear cut in denying a motion for summary judgment.

In some cases, the issue of whether there is a clerical or arithmetical error or a mistake in judgment is a close one. See, for example, *Ruggiero v. United States*, 190 Ct. Cl. 327, 420 F.2d 709 (1970), in which the court concluded that failure to include an all or none stipulation in a multiple-item contract was a clerical mistake because the price of one item made no commercial sense without the other items. See also *JAL Constr., Inc.*, AGBCA 80-117-3, 81-1 BCA ¶ 14,850, in which an omission of work in a subcontractor's estimate due to a misunderstanding between the contractor and the subcontractor was held to be a clerical error. Compare *Structural Concepts, Inc.*, ASBCA 48933, 98-1 BCA ¶ 29,486, *recons. denied*, 98-2 BCA ¶ 29,743, in which omission of work from a subcontractor's estimate was not a clerical error because it was unexplained, and *Transco Contracting Co.*, ASBCA 47289, 96-1 BCA ¶ 28,090, in which omission of work from a subcontractor's estimate was not a clerical error but was a mistake in judgment not to obtain quotes from suppliers of the subcontractor. See also *Montgomery Ross Fisher, Inc. & H.A. Lewis, Inc. (JV)*,

VABCA 3696, 94-1 BCA ¶ 26,527, in which the board held that the acceptance of an ultimately unfavorable settlement agreement amounted to a business judgment rather than a clerical error.

b. Knowledge of Error and Verification

The rationale underlying relief for unilateral mistakes is that it would be unfair for the government to hold a contractor to a bargain when circumstances indicate that the government should have discerned the mistake and called it to the attention of the offeror. If the government appropriately notifies the offeror of a possible mistake or the offeror alleges a mistake, the offeror can attempt to withdraw or modify the offer or can elect to stand by the offer as originally submitted.

If the government fails to notify the offeror of a suspected mistake, it may be subject to claims for price adjustment, or the contractor may use a claimed mistake as a basis for avoiding performance obligations. To avoid these problems, the regulations impose verification requirements on the contracting officer. FAR 14.407-1 provides the following guidance for sealed bidding:

> After the opening of bids, contracting officers shall examine all bids for mistakes. In cases of apparent mistakes and in cases where the contracting officer has reason to believe that a mistake may have been made, the contracting officer shall request from the bidder a verification of the bid, calling attention to the suspected mistake. If the bidder alleges a mistake, the matter shall be processed in accordance with this section 14.407. Such actions shall be taken before award.

Prior to 1998, this rule was also applicable to negotiated procurements. However, FAR 15.607(c) and FAR 15.610(c)(4), containing this requirement, were deleted from the FAR at that time, with the result that the current regulation now contains no explicit verification requirements. See *Griffy's Landscape Maint., LLC v. United States*, 46 Fed. Cl. 257 (2000), holding under the new FAR that a contracting officer was obligated to verify a potential mistake when the offeror omitted requirement information on insurance coverage from its proposal. Compare *C.W. Over & Sons, Inc. v. United States*, 54 Fed. Cl. 514 (2002), criticizing the decision to the extent that it "is not limited to clerical errors." See also *Comspace Corp.*, DOTBCA 4034, 99-2 BCA ¶ 30,473, finding an inadequate verification in a negotiated procurement conducted under the pre-1998 FAR and holding that the opportunity to submit a best and final offer was not a substitute for a proper verification request.

The detailed procedures for withdrawal or modification are part of the award process and are dealt with in Cibinic and Nash, *Formation of Government Contracts* (3d ed. 1998). This section deals with the issues involved when a contractor seeks relief after award. The first subsection discusses the circumstances under which the government obtains actual knowledge of a mistake or is held to have reason to know. The second subsection deals with the adequacy of the verification process.

(1) Knowledge or Reason to Know

There are relatively few litigated cases in which the government actually knows of an error and awards without adequate verification. One example is *Walter Straga*, ASBCA 26134, 83-2 BCA ¶ 16,611, where the government project manager's actual knowledge of the contractor's error was imputed to the contracting officer. Moreover, the same result will occur where the government rejects a bid without requesting verification because it has a strong reason for believing that a mistake has been made, *RMTC Sys., Inc. v. Department of the Navy*, GSBCA 12164-P, 93-2 BCA ¶ 25,725.

In determining whether the government should have known of the mistake, the initial question is the scope of the government's examination. In *Giesler v. United States*, 232 F.3d 864 (Fed. Cir. 2000), the court held that the verification duty applies "only in instances where the alleged error was contained in a contractor's original bid, not in other subsequently submitted papers." Thus, the government was not obligated to take into account information obtained in a preaward survey that indicated that the contractor's bid was not based on the contract specifications.

The general test of whether the contracting officer should have known of a mistake is whether a reasonable person, knowing all the facts and circumstances, would have suspected a mistake. See *Chernick v. United States*, 178 Ct. Cl. 498, 372 F.2d 492 (1967), in which the court stated at 504:

> In *Wender Presses, Inc. v. United States*, 170 Ct. Cl. 483, 343 F.2d 961 (1965), are collected and collated a number of leading cases on mistakes in bids. Insofar as the legal principles stated in *Wender Presses, Inc., supra*, and the cases cited therein are applicable to the factual situation in the instant case, plaintiffs may recover only if defendant's responsible officials knew or should have known of the mistake at the time the bid was accepted. The test of what an official in charge of accepting bids should have known must be that of reasonableness, i.e., whether under the facts and circumstances of the case there were any factors which reasonably "should" have raised the presumption of error in the mind of the contracting officer; among such factors are obvious wide range of bids, and gross disparity between the price bid and the value of the article which was the subject of the bid.

The circumstances that can put the contracting officer on notice are more specifically detailed in *BCM Corp. v. United States*, 2 Cl. Ct. 602 (1983), at 610:

> An oft-cited article, Doke, Mistakes in Government Contracts—Error Detection Duty of Contracting Officer, 18 S.W.L.J. 1 (1964) ("Doke"), delineates these general categories: (1) facially apparent errors, such as multiplication errors made when computing unit prices into total price; (2) disparity in prices among the bids; (3) disparity between the bid and the private government estimate; (4) disparity between the bid and the cost of prior procurements of the same item; (5) disparity

> between the bid price, and, if the contracting officer knows it, the market value for the goods. Doke at 16-26. BCM's bid was 82 percent of the Government's estimate and, like those of LD/S and Tunnel, was out of line with the other bids.

These rules are not applied mechanically. Thus, the government will properly be charged with knowledge only after a full consideration of all the circumstances, *Darwin Constr. Co.*, GSBCA 6590, 84-1 BCA ¶ 17,230, *recons. denied*, 84-2 BCA ¶ 17,356; *Felix Endzweig, GmbH*, ASBCA 33985, 89-1 BCA ¶ 21,468.

The most common situation putting the contracting officer on notice of a possible error is a disparity between a favorable bid and the bids of others or the government estimate. See *Figgie Int'l, Inc.*, ASBCA 27541, 83-1 BCA ¶ 16,421, where the contractor's failure to include costs for packaging should have been noted by the contracting officer because other responsive bids were from 43 to 82 percent higher than the contractor's bid, and the contractor had not significantly increased its price from that of a prior contract with significantly less costly packaging requirements. Similarly, in *Faulkner Corp.*, VABCA 2998, 90-1 BCA ¶ 22,507, the board found that the contracting officer had constructive knowledge of a mistake in a bid submitted in a small business set-aside procurement despite the fact that the bid was lower than the government in-house estimate. The low bid was 20 percent lower than the next two low bids, and the government solicitation materials were conflicting at times and could have been confusing to bidders. Accordingly, the board sustained the contractor's request for an equitable adjustment. See also *George A. Harris Enters., Inc.*, GSBCA 9888, 90-1 BCA ¶ 22,405, where a 24 percent differential between the low and next low bid should have put the contracting officer on notice of a potential error. The GAO has found constructive notice when there was a significant variation from the average of all other bids (127 percent higher) or from the next low bidder (59 percent higher), *American Food Serv. Equip. Co.*, Comp. Gen. Dec. B-181878, 74-2 CPD ¶ 83; a variation of more than 21 percent from the government estimate, *Murphy Elevator Co.*, Comp. Gen. Dec. B-180607, 74-1 CPD ¶ 164; a disparity between the mistaken bid, the only other bid, and the prior year's contract price, *Ace Window Cleaning Co.*, Comp. Gen. Dec. B-183380, 75-1 CPD ¶ 379; or a variation from the general pattern of prior bids and market prices, *Calumet Y Farm Store*, Comp. Gen. Dec. B-181284, 74-2 CPD ¶ 11. In *Murphy*, the GAO held the contracting officer had constructive notice of error when the only bid received amounted to $7,949 as compared to the government's $10,214 estimate for the work. See also *James R. Sloss*, Comp. Gen. Dec. B-180402, 74-1 CPD ¶ 53, stating:

> To rule otherwise would permit Government estimates to be rationalized away at any time a contractor made a substantial error, especially in a sole bidder situation, merely by evolving a possible hypothesis which might explain a lower bid. 48 Comp. Gen. 672, 676 (1969).

Constructive knowledge will not be found if the government can successfully explain the reasoning that led to a decision not to request verification. See *Aydin Corp.*

v. United States, 229 Ct. Cl. 309, 669 F.2d 681 (1982), in which the court found no constructive knowledge in an expedited negotiated procurement where the only two proposals were $2,866,808 and $3,989,790. The government was able to persuade the court of a lack of constructive notice because its analysis of cost differences in the proposals explained some of the disparity and the government's cost estimate was very close to the low proposal. While these factors, standing alone, might be sufficient to justify the failure to verify the price, the government's own documents appeared to demonstrate that the contracting officer indeed suspected mistake and intended to verify the price, but did not do so. See also *Singleton Contracting Co.*, ASBCA 26862, 82-2 BCA ¶ 15,994, *aff'd*, 723 F.2d 68 (Fed. Cir. 1983), where, although the contractor's bid, the only other bid, and the government estimate were $123,460, $247,000, and $98,000, respectively, the variations did not place the contracting officer on notice of a mistake because (1) the contracting officer reasonably believed the high bid contained errors; (2) the contractor "enjoyed a reputation of skill, integrity and competency in bidding and contracting"; and (3) there was reason to believe that the government estimate was adequate, although low, with the contractor's bid "exactly 'on target.'" See also *Hankins Constr. v. United States*, 838 F.2d 1194 (Fed. Cir. 1988) (bid below government estimate but close to other bidders and bidder ignored subcontractor's claim of mistake prior to award); *Bromley Contracting Co. v. United States*, 794 F.2d 669 (Fed. Cir. 1986) (government estimate, although itself containing errors, was 10 percent lower than bid containing mistake); *Aerospace Components, Inc.*, ASBCA 28606, 84-3 BCA ¶ 17,536 (no reason for contracting officer to have known of contractor's alleged unilateral mistake in bid where the next three low offerors were only 3 percent, 13.4 percent, and 18.8 percent higher than contractor's bid); *P. J. Valves, Inc.*, ASBCA 39398, 91-3 BCA ¶ 24,251 (relief denied where low bid was 13 percent lower than next low bid); *CESICA S.p.a.*, ASBCA 42021, 92-2 BCA ¶ 24,964 (12 percent disparity not enough to imply constructive notice, especially where the low bid exceeded the government's in-house estimate); *Diamond Shamrock Ref. & Mktg. Co.*, ASBCA 43729, 92-3 BCA ¶ 25,132 (rejecting the contractor's argument for constructive notice of a mistake when its gasoline supply bid was only $.02 per gallon less than the bid reference price); *Mid-South Metals, Inc.*, ASBCA 44241, 93-2 BCA ¶ 25,675 (40 percent disparity not sufficient for constructive notice where wide range of prices is to be expected as in surplus property sales); *Construction Admin. Servs., Inc.*, ENGBCA 6033, 93-3 BCA ¶ 26,091 ($14,000 mistake on a $209,000 bid that was only 8 percent lower than the next lowest bid and 12 percent lower than the government estimate did not impute notice of mistake); and *Walsh Constr. Co.*, ASBCA 52952, 02-2 BCA ¶ 32,024, *aff'd*, 80 Fed. Appx. 679 (Fed. Cir. 2003) (significant disparity in bid line-item prices but total bid prices indicated no significant disparity).

It has been held that a contracting officer has no reason to know of a possible mistake if the bidder attends the bid opening, sees the disparity in the bids, and raises no question as to whether its bid includes a mistake, *Packard Constr. Corp.*, ASBCA 45996, 94-1 BCA ¶ 26,512, *aff'd*, 39 F.3d 1197 (Fed. Cir. 1994); *GOECO*, ASBCA 46573, 96-2 BCA ¶ 28,412.

(2) Adequacy of Verification Request

A contracting officer who suspects a mistake must "call attention to the suspected mistake" by requesting a bid verification, FAR 14.407-1. In negotiated procurements, suspected mistakes may be addressed during evaluation of proposals, FAR 15.306(a) and (b), but there is no requirement for verification. If verification is requested in negotiated procurement, prices of other offerors cannot be disclosed, *Rex Sys., Inc.*, ASBCA 45297, 93-3 BCA ¶ 26,155 (instruction by contracting officer to the offeror that it should review all elements of its offer found sufficient).

The adequacy of a verification request will turn on an assessment of the reasonableness of the contracting officer's disclosure. Thus, if the request would alert a reasonable bidder of the possibility of a mistake, it will be sufficient. See *McClure Elec. Constructors, Inc. v. Dalton*, 132 F.3d 709 (Fed. Cir. 1997) (request for verification with attached Abstract of Bids but with no statement that an error was suspected), and *Klinger Constr., Inc.*, ASBCA 41006, 91-3 BCA ¶ 24,218 (request to review worksheets, confirm bid price, and waive claims for mistakes with statement that the bidder's submission as a whole was substantially lower than the next lowest bid). A verification will not be found reasonable if the contracting officer merely requests the contractor to confirm that no mistake has been made. A contracting officer on notice of a possible mistake must also disclose the particular reasons that led to the suspicion, FAR 14.407-3(g)(1). Absent such a disclosure, the request is inadequate, *United States v. Metro Novelty Mfg. Co.*, 125 F. Supp. 713 (S.D.N.Y. 1954). See *United States v. Hamilton Enters., Inc.*, 711 F.2d 1038 (Fed. Cir. 1983) (contractor not informed of large variation in labor hours between its bid and government estimate, 1,941 and 6,402 hours, respectively); *BCM Corp. v. United States*, 2 Cl. Ct. 602 (1983) (contractor, third low bidder, was told neither of the 18 percent variation between its bid price and the government estimate nor that the contracting officer was on notice of a possible misinterpretation of the solicitation); *BDF Tesa Corp.*, GSBCA 8307, 89-3 BCA ¶ 21,925 (finding inadequate a verification that stated the low bid was unusually low without providing the price disparity or indicating that a mistake was suspected); *Steve Nanna, Inc.*, DOTCAB 1343, 83-2 BCA ¶ 16,692 (verification request should have disclosed variations between contractor's bid, the next low bid, and the government estimate—$75,926.40, $98,440, and $100,033, respectively); *J. Robert Dowie & Co.*, ASBCA 25922, 82-2 BCA ¶ 15,876 (verification did not put bidder on notice of actual suspected mistake); and *Walter Straga*, ASBCA 26134, 83-2 BCA ¶ 16,611 (verification identifying price disparity inadequate where government knew exact nature of error).

Adequate verification was found in *Structural Finishing, Inc.*, ASBCA 26647, 84-2 BCA ¶ 17,303 (government called contractor's attention to substantial disparity in bid prices); *Aerospace Am., Inc.*, ENGBCA 3515, 77-1 BCA ¶ 12,523 (contractor was told that, on three schedules, its prices were 37 percent, 31 percent, and 32 percent lower than the next low bidder and 18 percent, 17 percent, and 14 percent below the government estimate on the three schedules); *Tri-States Serv. Co.*, ASBCA 31139, 90-3 BCA ¶ 23,059 (verification found adequate despite the contractor's argument that the verification should have noted that the staffing levels cited in the solicitation provided for recommended staffing rather than the government's actual in-house staffing levels); and *DWS, Inc.*, ASBCA 29743, 93-1 BCA ¶ 25,404 (verification adequate despite its omission of price disparity information because bid opening was held in public and the contractor could easily have obtained this information by attending).

Inadequate verification alone will not justify reformation if the mistake is one of business judgment, *United States v. Hamilton Enters., Inc.*, 711 F.2d 1038 (Fed. Cir. 1983). The contracting officer had informed the bidder that its bid had achieved low bid status but failed to say that its estimate of labor hours was substantially lower than the government's estimate. However, because the underestimation of labor hours was considered to be a mistake in business judgment, reformation was denied, but the contractor was relieved from liability for excess costs of reprocurement. Accord, *Sealtite Corp.*, ASBCA 25805, 84-1 BCA ¶ 17,144.

3. Unconscionability

If the contractor's mistake results in a contract that is grossly imbalanced, relief may be granted on the theory of unconscionability even if the contractor had verified the bid after appropriate request for verification, 53 Comp. Gen. 187 (B-178795) (1973) (acceptance of $10.00 unit price was unconscionable when other bids were $38.00 and $39.54 per unit); *Yankee Eng'g Co.*, Comp. Gen. Dec. B-180573, 74-1 CPD ¶ 333 (award at $199,669 unconscionable where price was $106,000 lower than the next lowest bid and $137,000 lower than the government's estimate).

The rationale of the unconscionability cases has been that to enforce the contract would permit the government to get something for nothing. In subsequent cases, the GAO has been reluctant to make a finding of gross disparity even though the price disparities appeared equally large. In *Porta-Kamp Mfg. Co.*, 54 Comp. Gen. 545 (B-180679), 74-2 CPD ¶ 393, the contractor submitted a bid that was 37 percent lower than the next lowest bid and 60 percent lower than the third lowest bid. The three bids were as follows: Porta-Kamp $719,563, Atlantic Mobile $1,136,902, and Trans-World $1,670,848. The contractor verified its bid following a government telephone request for verification. The GAO refused relief on the basis of unconscionability, distinguishing *Yankee Engineering* on the grounds that in this case there was no indication following verification that the government was getting something for nothing. Similarly, in *Omni Research, Inc.*, Comp. Gen. Dec. B-186301, 77-1 CPD ¶ 10, the contract price was $6.40 per test sample, while the next lowest proposed price was $13.59 per test sample. The GAO held that high cost of contract performance or economic hardship will not, in and of itself, justify a claim for unconscionability, and that an essential element of unconscionability is government awareness that it was taking advantage of the contractor. Such element was not apparent in *Omni* because (1) the government had no knowledge of essential facts unknown to the contractor; (2) the contractor verified the bid twice before award, (3) there was no mathematical, clerical, or typographical mistake; and (4) the government acted reasonably in deferring to the contractor's seemingly superior knowledge of its own capabilities, facilities, and proposed testing techniques. In *Contract Servs. Co.*, Comp. Gen. Dec. B-225651, 87-1 CPD ¶ 521, the protester's bid (the low one) was for $5,643,144.50, while the next lowest bid and the government's performance estimate were $8,851,336 and $9,754,615, respectively. The government notified the bidder that its bid was so much lower than the others and the government's estimate that a mistake in bid was likely. After a review of its bid, the protester responded that no mistake had been made, but the procuring agency rejected its bid anyway because "it is so far out of line with all the other bids . . . that acceptance would be [unconscionable] to [the protester] and to the other bona fide bidders." The GAO sustained the ensuing protest and, in so doing, distinguished *Yankee Engineering* and other cases that found unconscionability by stating that, in each of those cases, evidence existed in the record that the contractor had made a mistake in bid. Here, however, there was no such evidence that the government would be getting something for nothing. See also *Carrier Corp. v. United States*, 6 Cl. Ct. 169 (1984), in which the court held that a mistake resulting in a bid of approximately one-half the intended bid was not unconscionable because it was not extreme.

Unconscionability has also been used as a basis for relief in cases where the bid verification was not properly accomplished and there was a disparity in only one element of the contract price, *Samuel R. Clarke*, ASBCA 24306, 82-1 BCA ¶ 15,627 (unconscionability existed despite contractor's verification following general request, which did not reveal government estimate, when contract price of $99,949.50 included only $6,500 for a segment of the work that the government had estimated to cost $34,190); *J. Robert Dowie & Co.*, ASBCA 25922, 82-2 BCA ¶ 15,876 (unconscionability found when verification was inadequate and government knew that sole source subcontractor could not meet delivery requirements and would submit prices 150 percent higher than the prices used in the bid). Compare *Tri-States Serv. Co.*, ASBCA 31139, 90-3 BCA ¶ 23,059 (contractor had assumed the risk of mistake when it confirmed its bid without an adequate investigation, and a claim of unconscionability was precluded). Disparity in bid prices standing alone, however, is not sufficient to establish a cognizable claim of unconscionability, *W.B. & A., Inc.*, ASBCA 32524, 89-2 BCA ¶ 21,736 (58 percent difference between bid price and government estimate does not impute knowledge to the government that it is getting something for nothing); *Fan, Inc.*, GSBCA 7836, 91-1 BCA ¶ 23,364, *recons. denied*, 91-2 BCA ¶ 23,768 (rejecting an unconscionability argument where a 10 percent price disparity caused the contractor to lose money on the contract because there was no evidence of the government's bad faith or that it took unfair advantage of the negotiation process); *Turner-MAK (JV)*, ASBCA 37711, 96-1 BCA ¶ 28,208 (price 65 percent of next low offer); *Rockwell Int'l Corp.*, ASBCA 41095, 97-1 BCA ¶ 28,726 (alleged $18 million mistake only 4.3 percent of total contract price).

4. Remedies

The remedies available for mistake are to adjust the price of the contract (usually referred to as "reformation") or to excuse the contractor from its obligation to perform (often called "rescission" or "avoidance"). See FAR 14.406(b). This section discusses the factors to be considered when determining the relief to be granted.

a. Reformation

Traditionally, reformation was not available unless the actual agreement of the parties could be shown. This generally limited its use to mistake in integration cases because, in mistake in basic assumption cases and unilateral mistake cases, frequently there is no agreement of the parties, only a mistake. However, in government contract cases, price adjustments have been granted for basic assumption and unilateral mistake cases, and this has generally been referred to as "reformation." The theory underlying this use of reformation is apparently that the contracting parties would have agreed to the corrected price. In *Lea Co.*, GSBCA 5697, 81-2 BCA ¶ 15,208, the board summarized the requirements for such reformation at 75,306-07:

> The party seeking reformation by reason of mistake must establish: (a) that it intended to be bound, at the time or times antecedent to, or contemporaneous with, the transaction in dispute, by the version it seeks, *Burnett Elecs. Lab., Inc. [v. United States*, 202 Ct. Cl. 463, at 472-73, 479 F.2d 1329, at 1334 (1973)]; (b) that the party against whom reformation is sought would have been willing, at times antecedent to, or contemporaneous with, the transaction in dispute, to agree to the writing as it is sought to be reformed, *ITT Arctic Servs., Inc. [v. United States*, 207 Ct. Cl. 743, at 768, 524 F.2d 680, at 693 (1975)]; and (c) that the writing to be reformed does not put the risk of the mistake upon the party seeking reformation. *McNamara Constr. of Manitoba, Ltd. [v. United States*, 206 Ct. Cl. 1, at 6, 509 F.2d 1166, at 1168-69 (1975)].

See also *Bromley Contracting Co. v. United States*, 219 Ct. Cl. 517, 596 F.2d 448 (1979), and *Pacific Coast Molybdenum Co.*, AGBCA 84-162-1, 89-2 BCA ¶ 21,755.

(1) Mutual Mistake of Basic Assumption

Obtaining reformation in mutual mistake of basic assumption cases is difficult because of a lack of evidence as to whether the parties would have agreed to a different price. In *National Presto Indus., Inc. v. United States*, 167 Ct. Cl. 749, 338 F.2d 99 (1964), *cert. denied*, 380 U.S. 962 (1965), the Court of Claims stated that reformation will be available in the absence of such evidence, only if the government has received a benefit from the extra work and would have been willing to share a portion of the additional expense if it had been aware of the true facts at the time of the contract. In *Hannelore Brown*, ASBCA 23492, 83-1 BCA ¶ 16,305, the board noted a shifting court view regarding mutual mistake, declaring at 81,055:

> We perceive a common thread in the Court of Claims cases which have granted relief because of a mutual mistake as to an antecedent material fact. That thread has been the belief of the Court of Claims that had the parties not been ignorant of the true facts they would have agreed to write the contract as the Court found that it should have been written. In other words, the Court rewrote the contract to say what it (the Court) concluded the parties would have had it say.

The board denied reformation because there was evidence that the parties would not have agreed absent the mistake.

Reformation was granted in *Louisiana-Pac, Corp.*, AGBCA 80-163-3, 81-1 BCA ¶ 14,928 (mutual mistake arising from the contractor's reliance on the Forest Service's clerical error in listing excavation quantities, where both parties assumed the given estimate was correct), and *LDG Timber Enters., Inc.*, AGBCA 89-126-1, 92-3 BCA ¶ 25,070, *recons. denied*, 93-1 BCA ¶ 25,319 (mutual mistake arising out of a change in the utilization standards to be applied in a timber contract where, unbeknownst to either of the parties, the change was unintentionally added to the base rate rather than the bid rate). Contrast *Olin Mathieson Chem. Corp. v. United States*, 179 Ct. Cl. 368 (1967), rejecting the contractor's contention that it was entitled to an upward adjustment in contract price when performance of one government contract interfered with performance of another, stating that there was no basis here in the parties' negotiations or in the transaction as a whole for saying that the Air Force would have been willing to bear any part of the extra expense had it known all the facts at the outset. In *SMC Info. Sys., Inc. v. General Servs. Admin.*, GSBCA 9371, 93-1 BCA ¶ 25,485, the board denied relief for a mistake because the government had received no benefit from the work that the contractor had done.

(2) Unilateral Mistakes

For reformation in unilateral mistake cases, the intended bid must be proved by clear and convincing evidence, *Chris Berg, Inc. v. United States*, 192 Ct. Cl. 176, 426 F.2d 314 (1970). However, this does not require that the contractor prove the exact amount of the intended bid. In *Chris Berg*, the fact that the bidder had rounded its total bid downward did not foreclose relief when the contractor proved the amount of cost omitted from this bid. The court held that a relatively narrow range of uncertainty was not inconsistent with the clear and convincing evidence standard. In *Bromley Contracting Co. v. United States*, 219 Ct. Cl. 517, 596 F.2d 448 (1979), the court followed this logic and granted reformation by taking as the intended bid the lowest of three possible amounts within a narrow range. In another case involving the same contractor, the board reformed the contract by adding a fair price for an omitted item even though the contractor did not appear to prove the intended bid, *Bromley Contracting Co.*, HUDBCA 81-624-C30, 84-2 BCA ¶ 17,493.

In unilateral mistake cases, reformation will not be granted for an amount greater than that which would have been accepted by the contracting officer at the time of award. Thus, in sealed bid contracting, the adjusted price is limited to the amount of the next most favorable bid, *BCM Corp. v. United States*, 2 Cl. Ct. 602 (1983). See *Yankee Eng'g Co.*, Comp. Gen. Dec. B-180573, 74-1 CPD ¶ 333, holding that this rule applied to the next most favorable responsible bidder. In *Chernick v. United States*, 178 Ct. Cl. 498, 372 F.2d 492 (1967), reformation was limited to an amount that the government might have agreed to in negotiation. Compare *George A. Harris Enters.*, GSBCA 9888, 90-1 BCA ¶ 22,405, in which the board allowed a 20 percent markup in price for profit and overhead as part of the contract reformation.

A similar general rule is applied in the negotiated procurement context. See *Taylor & Sons Equip. Co.*, ASBCA 34675, 89-2 BCA ¶ 21,584, where both parties conceded that a unilateral mistake had been made and that the price for the parts already purchased by the government was to be reformed. However, the board limited this reformation price to that of the next low offer because to do otherwise would be to fashion a contract that the parties did not intend and would be beyond the authority of the contracting officer. Accordingly, the board denied the contractor's claim for greater relief.

b. Rescission

Rescission would appear to be appropriate only in cases where reformation would not be available. In *Rash v. United States*, 175 Ct. Cl. 797, 360 F.2d 940 (1966), the court stated that "the Government was under an obligation to grant the [contractor's] request for rescission" because the government would have been unable to perform the contract as reformed. Thus, where the contractor cannot prove the intended bid by clear and convincing evidence, rescission may still be an appropriate remedy, *Institutional & Envtl. Mgmt., Inc.*, ASBCA 32924, 90-3 BCA ¶ 23,118 (citing *Restatement, Second, Contracts* § 152). A form of rescission excusing excess costs of reprocurement has also been granted where the government failed to adequately request verification but reformation was not available because the mistake was one of judgment, *United States v. Hamilton Enters., Inc.*, 711 F.2d 1038 (Fed. Cir. 1983); *Sealtite Corp.*, ASBCA 25805, 84-1 BCA ¶ 17,144.

A remedy in the nature of rescission has been used to excuse contractors from the consequences of default terminations. See *PAVCO, Inc.*, ASBCA 23783, 80-1 BCA ¶ 14,407 (contract rescinded where, prior to contract award, the government should have known of contractor's mistake); *B.L. Parker*, ENGBCA 3501, 75-1 BCA ¶ 11,012 (contractor's request that the contract be rescinded was improperly denied and excess costs could not be assessed against the contractor); *MKB Mfg. Corp.*, 59 Comp. Gen. 195 (B-193552), 80-1 CPD ¶ 34 (inadequate verification precludes binding contract); and *Don Simpson*, IBCA 2058, 86-2 BCA ¶ 18,768 (default termination found improper and contract rescinded because the contracting officer should have requested verification of the contractor's bid, which was 40 percent less than the next lowest bid and 50 percent less than the government estimate).

In *Chris Berg, Inc. v. United States*, 192 Ct. Cl. 176, 426 F.2d 314 (1970), the Court of Claims suggested that rescission may not be available on mistake in bid cases where the government desires performance and can establish an intended bid below the next low bidder. However, the government cannot limit the contractor to rescission if there has been a significant amount of performance and reformation is possible, *Chernick v. United States*, 178 Ct. Cl. 498, 372 F.2d 492 (1967). The board followed this logic in *Government Micro Res., Inc. v. Department of the Treasury*, GSBCA 12364-TD, 94-2 BCA ¶ 26,680, in which it expressed concern that, while all the other requisites for unilateral mistake were satisfied, neither rescission (because the contractor had completed performance) nor reformation (because the intended bid was impossible to decipher as the mistake affected the entire negotiation process) could provide a sufficient remedy. The board awarded the contractor restitution on a quantum valebant basis. Thus, the government was ordered to provide the contractor the reasonable value of the goods that it had been furnished by the contractor under the mistaken assumption. Rescission is not considered the proper remedy, however, in cases where a mistake relates only to the parties' written expression of intent—that is, a mistake in integration, *Higgs v. United States*, 212 Ct. Cl. 146, 546 F.2d 373 (1976). The logic of this rule is that rescission in such circumstances is an unnecessary violation of the actual intent of the parties.

VI. GOVERNMENT DEFENSES

There are three major defenses that the government frequently asserts to avoid bearing risks that would otherwise be allocated to it. One of these defenses utilizes contract language warning the contractor of potential problems or otherwise seeking to impose the risks of these problems on the contractor. Such clauses are generally called "exculpatory" or "disclaimer" clauses. Another defense is called the duty of coordination. This so-called duty requires the contractor to review all the drawings and specifications to ensure that there is no misplaced or omitted information. The third defense, known as the defense of sovereign acts, immunizes the government from liability for public and general acts that affect the contractor.

A. Disclaimer and Exculpatory Clauses

Clauses that warn the contractor of potential problems are not generally disfavored by the courts. However, clauses that seek to relieve the government from liability for its fault are closely scrutinized and may not be fully enforced, depending on the facts and circumstances of each case. One of the first considerations is whether the use of the exculpatory clause violates public policy. If it does, it will not be enforced. If it does not, the clause will then be subjected to other tests to determine its impact on the contractual relationship. This section considers the various techniques courts and boards use to analyze such clauses.

1. Public Policy

The use of an exculpatory clause is not generally against public policy even though the bargain is harsh on the contractor, *Rixon Elecs. Inc. v. United States*, 210 Ct. Cl. 309, 536 F.2d 1345 (1976). In *Rixon*, the court stated at 320-21:

> As regards the alleged wrong by the Government that sets up the contractor to be victimized by a coerced release, the invitation to an inexperienced contractor to entangle itself in this briar bush may be deemed morally reprehensible. But it cannot and is not denied that the law allows the Government to do it, if it disclaims any warranty by clear and unambiguous language. Any more effort to deter this contractor from its losing deal would probably have generated accusations that they were trying to preserve the sole source's monopoly. So the question boils down to this: is the disclaimer clear enough, alone or as aided by the warning to check the bid? You can engage a contractor to make snowmen in August, if you spell it out clearly, you are not warranting there will be any subfreezing weather in that month.
>
> * * *
>
> It appears that the main reason for the [contractor's] then parlous economic conditions was its pig-headed resolve to take the contract despite provisions in the invitation amply sufficient to alert it, and despite express warnings that it was going to lose money. The alleged wrong by the Government was either non-existent, or at most a secondary cause. This is what the Board found, it appears with support of substantial evidence.

See also *Irvin Indus. Inc.*, ASBCA 20208, 76-2 BCA ¶ 12,181, in which the board found that a clause in the contract that gave the government the right without liability to substitute cloth up to two inches narrower than that called for in the contract was not unconscionable. The contractor was aware of the deviation clause and therefore should have been prepared for such changes to the contract.

It is not against public policy to insert clauses that insulate the government from liability for simple negligence, *Wood v. United States*, 258 U.S. 120 (1922). In *United States v. Croft-Mullins Elec. Co.*, 333 F.2d 772 (5th Cir. 1964), *cert. denied*, 379 U.S. 968 (1965), the court stated at 778, n. 11:

> We know of no general rule that parties to a contract dealing at arms length may not agree that one should save another harmless from simple negligence. As this court said in *Philippine Air Lines v. Texas Engineering & Mfg. Co.*, 5 Cir., [sic] 181 F.2d 923, 925, such a provision is "no more against public policy . . . than an indemnity clause in an insurance policy would be."

Exculpatory language that would relieve the government from liability for willful misconduct is against public policy, *Ozark Dam Constructors v. United States*, 130 Ct. Cl. 354, 127 F. Supp. 187 (1955). In *Ozark*, the court held that the government could not avoid liability for failing to deliver cement to the contractor as promised, solely on the basis of an exculpatory clause. The clause stated that "[t]he Government will not be liable for any expense or delay caused the contractor by delayed deliveries except as provided under Article 9 [the Delays-Damages clause] of the contract." The court considered such exculpatory language to be contrary to public policy because the government could easily have taken action to have the cement delivered, and its failing to do so was almost willful neglect. This logic may apply to any clause that absolves the government of liability for its own breaches of contract. See *Freedman v. United States*, 162 Ct. Cl. 390, 320 F.2d 359 (1963), stating that contract provisions that immunize the government from damages due to its own breach should not cover serious breaches or willful defaults causing a significant loss to the contractor. See also *McGaughan Co.*, PSBCA 2074, 90-1 BCA ¶ 22,411, in which the contractor was allowed to recover despite a contract clause that provided for no damages for government-caused delays. Finding that the government could have provided access to the work site by reasonable means yet chose not to do so, the board stated that the government was in effect preventing the contractor from performing its obligations under the contract. Similarly, in *Hoel-Steffen Constr. Co. v. United States*, 231 Ct. Cl. 128, 684 F.2d 843 (1982), where the contract clause relieved the government from liability for refusing to allow substitutions of subcontractors, the contracting officer's refusal to approve the substitution of a subcontractor was held to be arbitrary and capricious, or so grossly erroneous as to imply bad faith and, therefore, was against public policy. See also *G.W. Galloway Co.*, ASBCA 16656, 73-2 BCA ¶ 10,270, *recons. denied*, 74-1 BCA ¶ 10,521, in which the government's failure to disclose the condition of the tools was seen as being against public policy. In *G. D'Alesio S.A.S.*, ASBCA 31149, 86-1 BCA ¶ 18,732, the government's failure to deliver oil, as required by the contract, caused a significant loss to the contractor. The contract contained a clause limiting the government's liability, but the board reasoned at 94,261 that "[t]o read the [liability] clause in that unlimited fashion—excusing all damages for any type of breach—would come close to (if not reach) the pit of voidness; the Government would in effect promise nothing although the other party would supposedly be bound." The board concluded that provisions immunizing the government from its own breach or negligence should not cover serious breaches, especially willful defaults. Compare *Service Eng'g Co.*, ASBCA 40272, 92-3 BCA ¶ 25,106, in which it was held that a clause making the contractor responsible for "interferences not shown on the guidance plans" was not unconscionable because the interferences were minor.

2. Interpretation

Exculpatory clauses are narrowly construed because they are drafted by the government and shift to the contractor risks that would otherwise be borne by the government. Thus, exculpatory clauses may be interpreted to hold that a contractor did not assume specific risks. See *White v. Edsall Constr. Co.*, 296 F.3d 1081 (Fed. Cir. 2002), stating at 1085:

> [G]eneral disclaimers requiring the contractor to check plans and determine project requirements do not overcome the implied warranty, and thus do not shift the

> risk of design flaws to contractors who follow the specifications. [*United States v. Spearin*, 248 U.S. 132 (1918)] at 137; see also *Al Johnson Constr. Co. v. United States*, 854 F.2d 467, 468 (Fed. Cir. 1988) ("The implied warranty is not overcome by the customary self-protective clauses the government inserts in its contracts . . . ."). Only express and specific disclaimers suffice to overcome the implied warranty that accompanies design specifications. Absent such disclaimers, the contractor is entitled to any additional costs reasonably incurred to produce a satisfactory result.

Based on this reasoning, the court held that a clause requiring the contractor to "verify" the accuracy of the design did not overcome the government's implied warranty of the drawings and specifications.

Thus, clauses with vague or general language will frequently not be enforced. See, for example, *Bethlehem Steel Corp.*, ASBCA 13341, 72-1 BCA ¶ 9186, where the contract contained a Changes clause as well as a special provision requiring the contractor to make necessary changes due to inadequate specifications. The board stated that the clause would not preclude a price adjustment because the special clause lacked clear and unmistakable language to impose such a requirement. See *Marshall Associated Contractors, Inc. & Columbia Excavating, Inc. (JV)*, IBCA 1901, 01-1 BCA ¶ 31,248 (clause making contractor responsible for conclusions drawn from data on underground conditions did not relieve government of liability for inaccurate data); *Enviroserve, Inc.*, DOTBCA 3012, 97-1 BCA ¶ 28,644 (clause calling for a request for clarification if offeror found discrepancies in plans or specifications did not relieve the government from liability for highly inaccurate estimate of area of roof); *Turner Constr. Co.*, ASBCA 25447, 90-2 BCA ¶ 22,649 (clause calling for design review prior to establishing maximum price did not preclude claim for defective specifications because review was necessarily perfunctory); *Department of Natural Res. & Conservation v. United States*, 1 Cl. Ct. 727 (1983) (exculpatory language lacked clear, express, direct, and unambiguous language, and, therefore, did not limit the government's liability); *Radionics Inc.*, ASBCA 22727, 81-1 BCA ¶ 15,011 (disclaimer clause was ambiguous and failed to clearly state an intent to exculpate the government from liability for defective drawings); and *Christy Corp. v. United States*, 198 Ct. Cl. 986 (1972) (when clauses are inconsistent with each other and cannot be read together, the exculpatory clause must give way).

When the contractor is aware of a disclaimer clause and also has knowledge of problems in the contract, such as defects in the specifications, it will not be able to recover. See *Service Eng'g Co.*, ASBCA 40272, 92-3 BCA ¶ 25,106, where the contractor's questions regarding ambiguities in the contract were clarified at a meeting for bidders. The board upheld a disclaimer of implied warranties, stating at 125,186 that "words spoken at a bidders conference can add to and answer unresolved questions in the specifications." See also *Loral Aerospace Corp.*, ASBCA 46373, 97-2 BCA ¶ 29,128, enforcing a Preproduction and Production Evaluation Requirements clause against the company that had designed the product and knew that the technical data package was not in a condition to permit mass production.

In construction contracts the government requires shop drawings containing the details of elements of the work, and it disclaims any responsibility for errors when it approves these drawings. See the Specifications and Drawings for Construction clause in FAR 52.236-21, stating in ¶ (e):

> Approval by the Contracting Officer shall not relieve the Contractor from responsibility for any errors or omissions in such drawings, nor from responsibility for complying with the requirements of this contract, except with respect to variations described and approved in accordance with (f) below.

In *Toombs & Co. v. United States*, 4 Cl. Ct. 535 (1984), the court rejected the government's argument that this clause exculpated the government from liability for defective specifications.

3. Clear Disclaimers

If an exculpatory clause is not against public policy and is clearly worded to indicate to the contractor that the government does not expressly or impliedly warrant the accuracy or usefulness of information or material that it furnishes, it will be enforced. Such enforcement is most readily granted when the exculpatory language gives the contractor specific information on the inferior condition of the drawings, *Wunderlich Contracting Co. v. United States*, 173 Ct. Cl. 180, 351 F.2d 956 (1965). In that situation, the contractor is expected to include a contingency in its offer to cover the potential defects, and the court or board will place the risks on the contractor.

Clear general exculpatory language is also enforced in most instances. See *Massachusetts Bay Transp. Auth. v. United States*, 21 Cl. Ct. 252 (1990), enforcing an exculpatory clause stating: "[The agency] makes no warranties, express or implied, concerning the Project Design Documents." See *Commercial Constr. Corp.*, ASBCA 24087, 80-1 BCA ¶ 14,312, in which the board noted at 70,532:

> [The contractor assumes the risk of performance] in situations where the Government properly uses exculpatory language or disclaimers in its specifications and drawings. Generally speaking, such exculpatory language should be enforced according to its terms unless enforcement was not contemplated by the parties when the contract was entered into, or unless enforcement would be unreasonable under the circumstances, or unless it would be inconsistent with some other significant contract provisions.

In *P.J. Maffei Bldg. Wrecking Corp. v. United States*, 3 Cl. Ct. 482 (1983), *aff'd*, 732 F.2d 913 (Fed. Cir. 1984), the contractor maintained that the government was liable for improperly identifying contract drawings as depicting existing conditions in a demolition contract. The court held for the government because the exculpatory provisions put the contractor on notice that the government was not implying representations concerning the drawings. The court stated at 487:

> The contract language in question—"some drawings of some of the existing conditions"—was a representation that came replete with caveats. Literally in the same paragraph (one could almost say "in the same breath") that the Government advised of the drawings, it went on to say that neither their "quantity, quality, completeness, accuracy and availability" was being guaranteed. In assessing a claim of misrepresentation, such warnings may not be disregarded for "[w]hether a statement is false depends on the meaning of the words in all the circumstances, including what may fairly be inferred from them." *Restatement, Second, Contracts* § 159 comment a (1979); *Flippin Materials Company v. United States*, 160 Ct. Cl. 357, 364 n. 7, 312 F.2d 408, 413 n. 7 (1963).

See also *PRB Uniforms, Inc. v. United States*, 706 F.2d 319 (Fed. Cir. 1983) (clauses stating that government did not expressly or impliedly warrant the adequacy of the technical data package precluded recovery), and *M. Bianchi*, ASBCA 26362, 90-1 BCA ¶ 22,369 (government not liable due to the exculpatory clause). In *John Massman Contracting Co. v. United States*, 23 Cl. Ct. 24 (1991), the court held that a Site Investigation clause requiring bidders to beware of hazards that might arise from weather conditions precluded recovery for delays caused by such conditions. In *Johnston Elec. & Constr. Co.*, DOTCAB 78-11, 78-2 BCA ¶ 13,520, where a clause stated that any changes of layout due to variations in apparatus configuration must be accomplished at no additional costs to the government, the board held that the clause was clear enough to preclude an equitable adjustment but not a time extension.

4. *Misleading Statements and Nondisclosure*

Where the government makes an express statement that turns out to be incorrect, the contractor may recover even though an exculpatory clause is included in the contract. In *Dunbar & Sullivan Dredging Co. v. United States*, 65 Ct. Cl. 567 (1928), the contractor was able to recover, despite an exculpatory provision, for increased costs resulting from false statements made by government agents concerning the type of material that was to be encountered in a river-dredging contract. The court held that these statements were made knowingly by the government or were equal to gross and inexcusable error. In *Mighty Mouse Fish Co.*, ASBCA 25381, 82-1 BCA ¶ 15,763, *recons. denied*, 83-2 BCA ¶ 16,550, the government entered into an agreement with a contractor to sell an air caisson drydock and expressly warranted that the caisson weighed 1,250 tons. The caisson, in fact, weighed only 230 tons, and the board stated at 78,009 that "because of the peculiar circumstances surrounding the sale, [the contractor] was entitled to rely on the warranty; [and] that it did rely and was damaged." As a result, the warranty disclaimer clause was not enforced. In *Simpson Constr. Co.*, VABCA 3176, 91-1 BCA ¶ 23,630, the board found a misrepresentation when the contract indicated that the wallboard height was 14'-0"+/- but it actually ranged from 15'-3" to 17'-6". The board rejected the government's argument that the "+/-" symbol following the measurements warned the contractor of the differences in the actual wallboard height. The board held that the "+/-" could reasonably be found to refer only to inches, not feet. See also *A. Mansour Vahdat*, GSBCA 5916, 81-2 BCA ¶ 15,199 ("As Is" clause did not negate the express warranty found in the description of the car), and *Barstow Truck Parts & Equip. Co. v. United States*, 5 Cl. Ct. 224 (1984) ("As Is" sale did not bar contractor's claim where a Guaranteed Description clause served as an express warranty from the government). In *Ball, Ball & Brosamer, Inc.*, IBCA 2841, 97-2 BCA ¶ 29,072, the board refused to enforce a broad exculpatory clause disclaiming the accuracy of borrow pit data when the contractor based its bid on a convenient pit that was described in the solicitation as containing clean material.

Exculpatory provisions will not be enforced where the government fails to disclose to the contractor specific information that it possesses. In *Transdyne Corp.*, ASBCA 13198, 70-2 BCA ¶ 8365, a provision in the contract disclaiming any government representations as to the accuracy of the specifications was not enforced to relieve the government from liability for nondisclosure of information. As a result, a default termination of a contract was converted to a termination for convenience. The board stated at 38,903-04:

> The Government relies on the disclaimer clause in the contract as having placed the risk of non-performance resulting from defects in the drawings and the model upon [the contractor]. This clause might be construed as relieving the Government of the burden of furnishing [the contractor] with a perfect set of drawings or a model which, at the time of delivery to [the contractor], had been demonstrated to comply fully with the performance specifications. However, we cannot regard the disclaimer as relieving the Government of its duty to convey to [the contractor] its specialized knowledge of the manner in which the development contractor rectified performance defects in the IF amplifier of the equipment with which appellant's equipment was required to be interchangeable. We find that the Government's failure to disclose this information rendered [the contractor's] inability to fabricate acceptable preproduction models to be beyond its control and without its fault or negligence within the meaning of the "Default" clause.

See also *Raytheon Co.*, ASBCA 50166, 01-1 BCA ¶ 31,245, *aff'd in part & remanded on other grounds*, 305 F.3d 1354 (Fed. Cir. 2002), refusing to enforce the Preproduction and Production Evaluation Requirements clause because the government misrepresented the sufficiency of the drawing for mass production. Similarly, in *Federal Elec. Corp.*, ASBCA 13030, 69-2 BCA ¶ 7792, the board refused to give effect to broad exculpatory language where the government failed to advise the contractor of its superior knowledge as to the necessity of making adjustments in the specifications in order to complete the contract work. See also *Boland Mach. & Mfg. Co.*, ASBCA 13664, 70-2 BCA ¶ 8556, where an "As Is" clause was ineffective to disclaim liability for the cost of removing mud and foreign matter from the pipes of a ship. The board stated that the government was under a duty to disclose the possible incompleteness of the work performed by the previous contractor. However, in *John Massman Contracting Co. v. United States*, 23 Cl. Ct. 24 (1991), the court indicated that there is no duty to disclose if there is an error or defect that would be obvious to the contractor.

5. Effect of Exculpatory/Disclaimer Clauses on Other Clauses

A broad exculpatory clause will not be given its literal effect if the impact would be to negate other contract clauses and if a meaning can be devised that will harmonize the two clauses. In *Morrison-Knudsen Co. v. United States*, 184 Ct. Cl. 661, 397 F.2d 826 (1968), the court refused to enforce a clause that would have precluded the contractor's recovery for failure of a government-designated borrow pit to contain sufficient material, stating at 666:

> With respect to the first claim (based on the relocation of the borrow pits), the court stresses . . . the inclusion in this contract of the mandatory standard Changes article with its broad and general reach. We have repeatedly indicated that, where that (or a comparable) clause is contained in a contract, the court will construe the agreement, to the extent it is fairly possible to do so, so as not to eliminate the standard article or deprive it of most of its ordinary coverage. *United Contractors v. United States*, 177 Ct. Cl. 151, 165-66, 368 F.2d 585, 598 (1968); *Thompson Ramo Wooldridge, Inc. v. United States*, 175 Ct. Cl. 527, 536, 361 F.2d 222, 228 (1966). The [government] says that here it attempted to "cast" the whole risk of borrow pit location on the contractor, but if that was its purpose it should have sought permission to delete the mandatory Changes article or to substitute a more limited form of the clause. So long as the Changes article in its normal form is included in a contract, the court is justified in reading the specifications, if reasonably possible, to harmonize and not conflict with that standard clause.

See also *C.H. Leavell & Co. v. United States*, 208 Ct. Cl. 776, 530 F.2d 878 (1976), in which the court interpreted a disclaimer of liability for failure to fund the contract as only precluding recovery of damages for breach of contract and permitting a recovery under the Suspension of Work clause. This rule has been applied most frequently with disclaimers that overlap the Differing Site Conditions clause. See the discussion in Chapter 5.

If the exculpatory provision's purpose in overcoming the other clause is clear and precise, then it will protect the government from liability. In *Gunther & Shirley Co.*, ENGBCA 3691, 78-2 BCA ¶ 13,454, the board refused to adopt the logic of *Leavell*, stating at 65,756-57:

> With due respect to the Court of Claims, it is this Board's judgment that it is hardly possible to devise language which more clearly and more specifically allocated the risk of a shortage of funds to the contractor alone than that contained in the Funds Available for Payment clause.

* * *

> Thus, these decisions hold that if a contractor is damaged on account of delays in payments due to lack of funds under a contract containing both a Funds Available for Payment clause and a Suspension clause, that contractor's claim has been converted from one for breach of contract to one for equitable adjustment under the Suspension clause.
>
> Consequently, to say that the disclaimer in the Funds Available for Payment clause bars breach of contract actions for delayed payments due to lack of funds, but not claims for equitable adjustments under the Suspension clause, when both clauses are present, means essentially that the disclaimer bars nothing.

6. Commonly Used Exculpatory/Disclaimer Clauses

Government agencies have used a variety of clauses in an attempt to shift to contractors risks associated with defects or omissions in government-supplied specifications, drawings, and technical data.

a. Omissions and Misdescriptions Clause

A clause commonly used by the Department of Defense in construction contracts was the Omissions and Misdescriptions clause. This clause is now incorporated as ¶ (d) of the Contract Drawings and Specifications clause in DFARS 252.236-7001:

> Omissions from the drawings or specifications or the misdescription of details of work which are manifestly necessary to carry out the intent of the drawings and specifications, or which are customarily performed, shall not relieve the contractor from performing such omitted or misdescribed details of the work, but they shall be performed as if fully and correctly set forth and described in the drawings and specifications.

This clause has been interpreted to be a partial disclaimer of government liability covering details of the work that are obviously missing. See *W. B. Meredith II, Inc.*, ASBCA 53590, 03-1 BCA ¶ 32,166, stating that the clause covers "patent" but not "latent" defects in the drawings. In *Jefferson Constr. Corp.*, ASBCA 23732, 79-2 BCA ¶ 14,186, the board held that a contractor was required to furnish motor starters that had been omitted from the contract specifications, stating at 69,835:

> In the language of the "Omissions and Misdescriptions" clause, furnishing the motors was a "manifestly necessary" detail of the work, required to "carry out the intent" of the contract, that is, to construct a medical clinic "complete and ready for use." As such, [the contractor] was obligated to perform even if this aspect of the work was described inadequately.
>
> We are in accord with the Comptroller General's conclusion that the "Omissions and Misdescriptions" clause represents a reasonable allocation of risk between

> the Government and a contractor and is not unduly burdensome on either party. It is designed, in our view, to cover "details" of the work only, not major portions thereof, that may be (inadvertently or otherwise) omitted from a contract's requirements. Here [the contractor] was put on notice that it was to provide the Government with a completed facility. It was further put on notice that it was to furnish and install a key "detail" of that facility. If an omission then caused a discrepancy to arise, "reading the contract as a whole, as one must, the omission was not obscure or subtle but obvious," and a duty to inquire logically arose. *J.A. Jones Const. Co. v. U.S.*, 184 Ct. Cl. 1 (1968).

See also *EZ Constr. Co.*, ASBCA 25441, 83-1 BCA ¶ 16,468, in which the contractor was required to install tile around the valve handle in dormitory showers being repaired under the contract. The board stated that this was a detail of the work necessary to carry out the intent of the contract. Similarly, in *Pike Paschen Joint Venture III*, ASBCA 37353, 89-1 BCA ¶ 21,429, the contractor was required to install omitted electric wiring that was necessary to permit operation of a laboratory being constructed under the contract. See also *P.R. Contractors, Inc.*, ASBCA 52937, 02-2 BCA ¶ 31,941 (turn-arounds for levee construction); *Elter S.A.*, ASBCA 52791, 02-1 BCA ¶ 31,672 (electrical connections for equipment); *M. A. Mortenson Co.*, ASBCA 50383, 00-2 BCA ¶ 30,936 (structural support for elevator guide rails); *David Boland, Inc.*, ASBCA 48715, 97-2 BCA ¶ 29,166 (electrical wiring); *Blake Constr. Co.*, ASBCA 36300, 90-3 BCA ¶ 23,077 (missing details for cabinet work); and *Robert McMullan & Son, Inc.*, ASBCA 34425, 90-2 BCA ¶ 22,779 (missing electrical raceways). See *EM Sys., Inc.*, ASBCA 51782, 01-2 BCA ¶ 31,586, in which the board commented that it had found no case using this clause to require the performance of tests omitted from the contract specifications but denied the contractor's claim because the tests that had been required were "reasonably standard" tests necessary to ensure that the work met the contract requirements.

This clause has limited application. See *M.A. Mortenson Co.*, ASBCA 50716, 99-1 BCA ¶ 30,270, stating at 149,692:

> [A] contractor has the duty under the "Omissions and Misdescriptions" provision to furnish missing details of the work "manifestly" necessary to carry out the intent of the specifications when (i) such omitted detail is obvious, see, *Hogan Const., Inc.*, ASBCA No. 37241, 94-1 BCA ¶ 26,541 at 132,101; *Blinderman Const. Co., Inc.*, ASBCA No. 35589, 91-1 BCA ¶ 23,457 at 117,679; *Jefferson Const. Corp.*, ASBCA No. 23732, 79-2 BCA ¶ 14,186 at 69,835; (ii) the contractor had actual or constructive knowledge of the omission when bidding, see, *Basic Const. Co.*, ASBCA No. 20585, 76-2 BCA ¶ 12,142; or (iii) it is customary to provide the omitted work, see, *Allen L. Bender, Inc.*, ASBCA No. 46243, 94-2 BCA ¶ 26,916.

See also *Monterey Mech. Co.*, ASBCA 51450, 01-1 BCA ¶ 31,380, stating that the clause "does not address undisclosed subsurface site conditions," citing *Gebr. Kittelberger GmbH & Co.*, ASBCA 36596, 89-1 BCA ¶ 21,306.

If the work to be completed is more than mere details, the contractor will be able to recover for its additional costs. See *Price/CIRI Constr. (JV)*, ASBCA 36988, 89-3 BCA ¶ 22,146 (removal and reattachment of electrical equipment); *Stallings & McCorvey, Inc.*, ASBCA 25125, 81-1 BCA ¶ 15,094 (failure in government design of doors not a mere omission of a detail of work when it required additional work to correct defect); *NAB-Lord Assocs.*, PSBCA 687, 81-1 BCA ¶ 15,033 (omitted thermostats in renovation contract); *Strauss Constr. Co.*, ASBCA 22791, 79-1 BCA ¶ 13,578 (government's failure to expressly state its requirement for a dry chemical fire-extinguishing system was an omission of more than a detail); and *Kuk Dong Constr. Co.*, ENGBCA 5069, 87-1 BCA ¶ 19,574 (omission of radiological equipment that was not manifestly necessary to carry out the specifications' intentions).

b. Production Drawing Changes Clause

Another clause aimed at reducing the government's liability for defective specifications and data is the Production Drawing Changes clause. This clause requires a contractor to review drawings for discrepancies or inaccuracies prior to the start of work and states that the government is not liable for costs relating to subsequently discovered deficiencies that should have been discovered during that process. In *Coditron Corp.*, ASBCA 18129, 76-1 BCA ¶ 11,818, the contract clause stated at 56,432:

> The contractor agrees to thoroughly check the furnished Government drawings and utilize same in the manufacture of the item they cover and the contractor agrees to revise the drawings as directed by the Contracting Officer. Inaccuracies, incompleteness, errors, etc. of the drawings will be resolved by consultation with the [Government] BEFORE proceeding with production. The Government will not be responsible for damages or extra costs resulting from an inadequate check of the drawings or revisions to the drawings. If, because of the above action, there results a change in the contract requirements, the contractor and the Government will negotiate an equitable adjustment in contract price.
>
> The contractor agrees to furnish the Contracting Officer a complete statement detailing his operations in the checking of the Government drawings. Any discrepancies which might arise between the drawings and the model will be resolved in consultation with the Contracting Officer, or addressee for this requirement set forth under Shipping Instructions of the contract.

The board held that the contractor was not entitled to an equitable adjustment for costs resulting from defects in the contract specifications because the defects could have been discovered through a reasonably thorough check of the drawings. The board stated at 56,437:

> The duty imposed on the contractor by the Production Drawing Changes clause distinguishes this case from the cases cited by [the contractor] in its brief with respect to the implied warranty by the Government that its specifications and drawings are correct. That clause does not absolve the Government from liability

> for drawing errors which cannot be detected by a reasonably thorough check of the drawings before proceeding to assemble the units. However, that clause is a warning that the contractor must review the drawings with reasonable thoroughness and detect and resolve discrepancies before incurring assembly costs.

In contrast, in *Sentinel Elecs., Inc.*, ASBCA 24207, 85-3 BCA ¶ 18,464, the contractor was held entitled to recover the costs incurred in working to defective drawings but not the costs of checking the drawings to find the defects. The board reasoned that such recovery was in accordance with the terms of the clause.

c. *Preproduction Evaluation of Technical Data Clause*

The government has sometimes sought to minimize its liability for defective technical data supplied to its contractors through the inclusion of a Preproduction Evaluation of Technical Data clause. This clause requires the contractor to undertake a review of the government-furnished data prior to beginning performance to discover any defects or omissions in those data. The clause purports to charge the contractor with the responsibility of identifying and correcting discrepancies, errors, or deficiencies in design or technical data that preclude practical manufacture or assembly or obtainment of required performance. It was used as a defense against claims for the same immature technical data package in *Loral Aerospace Corp.*, ASBCA 46373, 97-2 BCA ¶ 29,128, and *Raytheon Co.*, ASBCA 50166, 01-1 BCA ¶ 31,245, *aff'd in part and remanded on other grounds*, 305 F.3d 1354 (Fed. Cir. 2002). It was held to be a valid defense in *Loral,* where the contractor was the designer of the system and knew that the data package had not been proven for mass production. In contrast, in *Raytheon* the clause did not bar recovery of the cost of correcting the data package to make it suitable for mass production because the contractor had no knowledge of this situation and government policies called for use of the clause only when the data package had been fully validated. However, the contractor did not recover the full costs of working to the defective data package. See 305 F.3d 1354 (Fed. Cir. 2002) and 03-2 BCA ¶ 32,359.

Other cases have enforced the clause. In *Defense Sys. Co.*, ASBCA 50918, 00-2 BCA ¶ 30,991, *recons. granted in part*, 01-1 BCA ¶ 31,152, the board denied a claim by the contractor that the government knew that the data package was defective—based partially on the fact that the contractor had "a passing familiarity" with the product described in the data package through work on prior contracts and work in the evaluation phase of a parallel contract containing the clause. In *Kasel Mfg. Co.*, ASBCA 26975, 89-1 BCA ¶ 21,464, the contractor was denied compensation for a change required when a major part became difficult to obtain from the vendor. The board reasoned that this type of change was covered by the clause. See also *Dynamic Corp. of Am.*, 48 Comp. Gen. 750 (B-165953) (1969), in which the contractor argued that it should have been able to rely on the adequacy of the government-furnished specifications. The GAO ruled that the inclusion of the preproduction data clause put the contractor on notice of the possible inadequacies in the specifications. Hence, the contractor bore the responsibility to make the necessary corrections. In *Applied Cos.*, ASBCA 45470, 94-3 BCA ¶ 27,198, the board denied a contractor's motion for summary judgment because there were disputed facts as to whether the data package was defective and whether the clause covered the specific defect alleged by the contractor. Thus the clause, at a minimum, will be construed to make contractors responsible for errors or omissions that could have been discovered through a reasonably thorough review of the data at the beginning of contract performance, and it can be assumed that this review will have to be considerably more extensive than the review required before preparing an offer. The clause, however, does not relieve the government from liability for delays in responding to contractor-proposed changes. See the discussion in *Therm-Air Mfg. Co.*, ASBCA 15842, 74-2 BCA ¶ 10,818, in which the board held that the contractor could recover for unreasonable delays by the government in responding to proposed changes.

d. Verification Clause

Construction contracts frequently contain a clause requiring verification of specifications and drawings associated with the project. When the clause is specific in its requirements and the verifications can be made by the contractor without undue hardship, it will be enforced, and the government will not be liable for any additional costs claimed by the contractor. In *Commercial Constr. Corp.*, ASBCA 24087, 80-1 BCA ¶ 14,312, the exculpatory language in the contract drawings stated at 70,531 that "[t]he contractor shall verify all dimensions shown with certified shop drawings of equipment purchased. If purchased equipment requires different foundations, pits or trenches, the contractor shall provide proper foundations, bolts, pits, or trenches at no additional cost." The specifications also contained similar language, while another clause stated that it was the contractor's responsibility to make all necessary corrections in the contract. The contractor was held liable for the increased costs related to its installation of additional anchor bolts. In *Wiggins Elec. Co.*, DOTCAB 1102, 80-2 BCA ¶ 14,758, a clause required the contractor to verify all window dimensions. The board stated at 72,854 that the "notes and provisions adequately warn of the possible defects and require a verification which would uncover such defects." In *J.S. Alberici Constr. Co.*, GSBCA 10427, 92-1 BCA ¶ 24,393, the contractor was denied reimbursement for additional costs. The board concluded at 121,807:

> [B]y expressly calling for verification of the stated dimension by reference to the existing structure, all of the drawings do nothing more than indicate that the real dimension will be that which is found to exist upon actual measurement of the existing structure—nothing more, nothing less.
>
> The specifications and the drawings contained in the solicitation were clear as to how the contractor was to proceed. A dimension, such as that stated in the three drawings for the depth or width of the dock, was to be verified through on-site

> inspection for purposes of preparing a proper estimate. . . . [The Contractor] obviously failed to do this.

If the clause requires blanket verification and the specifications contain latent defects, it will not be enforced. See *Bromley Contracting Co.*, ASBCA 14884, 72-1 BCA ¶ 9252, in which a provision requiring the contractor to verify all dimensions and conditions prior to submission of a bid was narrowly construed to not shift risks. The government was not relieved from liability because the bidders could not be expected to discover hidden or subtle defects. See also *Robert & Son Constr.*, VABCA 3552, 93-3 BCA ¶ 26,113, where the government had furnished faulty information and sought to deny responsibility based on exculpatory language in the agreement that directed the contractor to verify the information. The board found for the contractor, stating at 129,791:

> [W]e have concluded that a proper balancing of responsibilities in a particular situation depends on the degree and juxtaposition of several considerations. Verification requirements that are quite detailed and specific as to particular elements of work are more likely to protect the Government than will broad, general clauses. This usually arises in cases involving fitting new work into existing spaces. For example, in *Imac Company*, ASBCA No. 36298, 90-2 BCA ¶ 22,840, a contractor's claim for additional costs of installing wall recessed medicine cabinets was denied where the cabinets were ordered without measurements having been taken where the dimensions in the contract were stated to be approximate and were immediately followed by the wording, "Contractor shall verify."

e. Shop Drawings Clause

The shop drawings provision provides that contracting officer approval of shop drawings furnished by the contractor does not bind the government to any deviations from the contract specifications and that the contractor must still perform in accordance with those specifications. However, if the drawings contain clear variations from the specifications, the government will be bound by approval. See the Specifications and Drawings for Construction clause, FAR 52.236-21, which provides in part:

> (d) Shop drawings means drawings, submitted to the Government by the Contractor, subcontractor, or any lower tier subcontractor pursuant to a construction contract, showing in detail (1) the proposed fabrication and assembly of structural elements and (2) the installation (i.e., form, fit, and attachment details) of materials or equipment. It includes drawings, diagrams, layouts, schematics, descriptive literature, illustrations, schedules, performance and test data, and similar materials furnished by the contractor to explain in detail specific portions of the work required by the contract. The Government may duplicate, use, and disclose in any manner and for any purpose shop drawings delivered under this contract.
>
> (e) If this contract requires shop drawings, the Contractor shall coordinate all such drawings, and review them for accuracy, completeness, and compliance

> with contract requirements and shall indicate its approval thereon as evidence of such coordination and review. Shop drawings submitted to the Contracting Officer without evidence of the Contractor's approval may be returned for resubmission. The Contracting Officer will indicate an approval or disapproval of the shop drawings and if not approved as submitted shall indicate the Government's reasons therefor. Any work done before such approval shall be at the Contractor's risk. Approval by the Contracting Officer shall not relieve the Contractor from responsibility for any errors or omissions in such drawings, nor from responsibility for complying with the requirements of this contract, except with respect to variations described and approved in accordance with (f) below.
>
> (f) If shop drawings show variations from the contract requirements, the Contractor shall describe such variations in writing, separate from the drawings, at the time of submission. If the Contracting Officer approves any such variation, the Contracting Officer shall issue an appropriate contract modification, except that, if the variation is minor or does not involve a change in price or in time of performance, a modification need not be issued.

This clause is generally enforced in accordance with its terms. See *Structural Painting Corp.*, ASBCA 36813, 89-2 BCA ¶ 21,605, *recons. denied*, 89-3 BCA ¶ 21,978, in which the government's approval of shop drawings did not relieve the contractor from its responsibilities for the accuracy of the drawings. The board stated at 108,771 that "the contract clearly placed responsibility for accurate shop drawings on the [contractor]. The Government cannot be held responsible for [the contractor's] own errors and misplaced assumptions." See also *Joseph Co.*, ENGBCA 5887, 92-3 BCA ¶ 25,075 (government not bound by rejection of shop drawing); *Price/CIRI Constr., J.V.*, ASBCA 37001, 89-2 BCA ¶ 21,697 (government not bound by approval of an incomplete shop drawing); and *Westerchil Constr. Co.*, ASBCA 35191, 88-2 BCA ¶ 20,528 (government not bound by erroneous approval of shop drawings).

The government was bound by a clear variation from the specifications in *EM Sys., Inc.*, ASBCA 51782, 01-2 BCA ¶ 31,586. The board concluded that the shop drawing submittal notice made the government aware of the variation. Compare *R.P. Richards, Inc.*, ASBCA 52465, 01-2 BCA ¶ 31,548, in which the government was not bound when it approved a shop drawing without noticing that it varied from the specifications but the variation was not clear. See also *A. D. Roe Co.*, ASBCA 46920, 95-1 BCA 27,591, holding that the government was not bound by approval of a variation from the specifications before the shop drawings were formally submitted for approval.

f. Coordination Clause

The inclusion of a coordination clause is to ensure that the contractor is aware of its duty to coordinate drawings and specifications with its subcontractors and to ensure that all work contracted for is done. In *Bruce-Andersen Co.*, ASBCA 29559, 87-1 BCA ¶ 19,470, the contract included a general provision that the board found clearly required the contractor to coordinate the electrical work with the other contract work. The board, quoting from *Santa Fe Eng'rs*, ASBCA 24467, 80-2 BCA ¶ 14,763, stated at 98,394-95:

> [A]s long as the prime contract as a whole identifies the specified work with reasonable clarity, the Government is not liable for the consequences of omitted information in provisions labeled as applicable to a particular trade, which is supplied by another provision in the instrument of which the prime . . . is reasonably on notice. Where the prime contract is clear . . . the prime contractor is responsible for informing its subcontractors of obligations applicable to their work even if not all of the provisions applicable to the work of a particular subcontractor appear in the sections of most concern to that subcontractor. The Government engaged the prime contractor, and relies on the prime contractor to coordinate the work among itself and its subcontractors so all that is required is performed. . . . Selective reliance on particular provisions, disregarding others applicable to the same work, is inconsistent with well established principles of contract interpretation.

See also *P.J. Dick Contracting, Inc.*, VABCA 3177-82, 92-2 BCA ¶ 24,827, *recons. denied*, 93-1 BCA ¶ 25,263, in which the contractor was relieved of liability for defective drawings for ductwork but was held responsible for failing to coordinate plumbing drawings that were so general that they required analysis. These cases appear to follow the same reasoning that would be followed absent a clause. See the discussion below.

B. Duty of Coordination

When a contractor makes a claim, the government often defends itself by asserting that the contractor failed to carry out its "duty of coordination." This "duty" describes the contractor's need to review the drawing packages for the various trades on a construction project to ensure that each contains the information necessary for the specialty subcontractors to include all required work in their bids. This places the risk on the contractor to detect instances in which the designer of the project has failed to check the drawings and specifications to determine that each package contains all relevant information. The defense works very effectively in cases of omissions of information from some of the drawings or specifications, but not in cases where the drawings or specifications are defective.

1. *Omissions of Information*

All of the recent cases involving omissions of information have been decided in favor of the government. In *Shumate Constructors, Inc.*, VABCA 2772, 90-3 BCA ¶ 22,946, a pipe with asbestos insulation was listed on a demolition drawing but not on an asbestos abatement drawing. The board held at 115,195 that the "[contractor] bears the risk of its failure to coordinate drawings among its subcontractors." In *R.A. Burch Constr. Co.*, ASBCA 39017, 90-1 BCA ¶ 22,599, the requirement for a minor amount of electrical work to be performed was omitted from electrical drawings but was included on mechanical drawings. The board held that it was the contractor's responsibility to coordinate its subcontractors' bids, stating at 113,396:

> We have carefully, and at length, considered [the contractor's] arguments as to the practicalities of the bidding situation. What [the contractor], in essence, asks us to stamp with our imprimatur is the theory that each bid or quotation from a potential subcontractor is to be treated as a separate entity and as having gone directly to the Government from the potential subcontractor with the general contractor acting solely as a conduit through which the bids passed on their journey. Such a theory has not in the past and will not now receive our approval.

See also *David Boland, Inc.*, ASBCA 51259, 01-2 BCA ¶ 31,423 (need for plenum-rated cable on mechanical drawings but not on communications drawings); *Caddell Constr. Co.*, VABCA 3509, 93-3 BCA ¶ 26,114 (smoke dampers on control drawings but not on ductwork drawings); *M.C. Dean Elec. Contracting, Inc.*, ASBCA 38132, 90-1 BCA ¶ 22,314, *recons. denied*, 90-2 BCA ¶ 22,711 (electrical work not specified on an electrical drawing but included on a general drawing); and *Price/CIRI Constr., J.V.*, ASBCA 36999, 89-3 BCA ¶ 22,010 (electrical work omitted from electrical drawings but listed on architectural drawings). In *Dawson Constr. Co.*, VABCA 1967, 88-1 BCA ¶ 20,335, the contractor was denied compensation for additional costs incurred during the installation of a fire alarm system. The board stated at 102,833 that "the mere omission of a device from an electrical drawing which is shown on another drawing does not excuse . . . [the contractor] from its general contractual duty to coordinate the requirements among its various subcontractors."

These cases indicate that the duty of coordination will make contractors liable for omissions, no matter how small the problem. Whether or not the omission is obvious appears not to be part of the decision.

2. Defective Drawings or Specifications

When there is a discrepancy between the drawing and specification packages, the contractor has no duty to coordinate because no amount of coordination could cure the defect. For example, in *Blake Constr. Co.*, ASBCA 36303, 90-3 BCA ¶ 23,076, the mechanical drawings called for certain heaters, but the architectural drawings called for a hole that was too small to accommodate the heaters. The board held that the duty of coordination did not apply in such cases because the coordination would not have solved the problem of a design defect. In *Hoffman Constr. Co.*, DOTBCA 2150, 93-2 BCA ¶ 25,803, the board stated that "the Government cannot rely upon the duty of a contractor to coordinate the work of its subcontractors and suppliers to escape liability for unsuitable dimensions and tolerances contained in its plans and specifications." Similarly, in *Century Constr. Co.*, ASBCA 31702, 89-1 BCA ¶ 21,333, the board held that there was a design defect; hence, no amount of coordinating could have cured the defect. See also *M.C. Hodom Constr. Co.*, GSBCA 8532, 88-3 BCA ¶ 20,903, in which the board compensated the contractor for rerouting ductwork when the space designated for it was insufficient. In *Dawson Constr. Co.*, VABCA 2202, 87-1 BCA ¶ 19,502, a contractor was granted an equitable adjustment because of discrepancies in the drawings. The board stated at 98,577:

> We conclude that the error on [the] Drawings . . . was not obvious to the Contractor at the time it reviewed the drawings for bid purposes. Nor is the Board persuaded that mislocation of several small light fixtures in a contract costing more than $7 million constituted an obvious error that should have put the contractor on notice.
>
> When a Government drawing is found to be defective, requiring a redesign of a system, a contractor's duty to coordinate does not exculpate the Government from liability.

A contractor must fully coordinate the drawings and specifications to find omissions but has no obligation to find conflicts within those drawings and specifications unless the defects were patent or obvious. The test is whether a reasonable contractor, under like circumstances, would have been aware of the defect.

C. Sovereign Acts Doctrine

The government may avoid liability for actions that are considered to be sovereign acts. This is based on the theory that government contractors should not benefit more than private contractors when the government passes a statute or takes other action affecting the public. This reasoning was explained in *Deming v. United States*, 1 Ct. Cl. 190 (1865), where one statute imposed additional duties on the contract articles included in the rations and another increased the cost of the articles. In denying the contractor's claims for recovery of its increased costs, the court stated at 191:

> A contract between the government and a private party cannot be *specially* affected by the enactment of a *general* law. The statute bears upon it as it bears upon all similar contracts between citizens, and affects it in no other way. In form, the claimant brings this action against the United States for imposing new conditions upon his contract; in fact he brings it for exercising their sovereign right of enacting laws. But the government entering into a contract stands not in the attitude of the government exercising its sovereign power of providing laws for the welfare of the State. The United States as a contractor are not responsible for the United States as a lawgiver. Were this action brought against a private citizen, against a body corporate, against a foreign government, it could not possibly be sustained. In this court the United States can be held to no greater liability than other contractors in other courts.

This reasoning was expanded upon in *Jones v. United States*, 1 Ct. Cl. 383 (1865), in which the contractor, who performed a survey, sought recovery for obstructions and hindrances caused by the government's withdrawal of troops in the area. The court noted at 384-85:

The two characters which the government possesses as a contractor and as a sovereign cannot be thus fused; nor can the United States while sued in the one character be made liable in damages for their acts done in the other. Whatever acts the government may do, be they legislative or executive, so long as they be public and general, cannot be deemed specially to alter, modify, obstruct or violate the particular contracts into which it enters with private persons. The laws of taxes and imposts affect preexistent executory contracts between individuals, and affect those made with the government, but only to the same extent and in the same way. In this court the United States appear simply as contractors; and they are to be held liable only within the same limits that any other defendant would be in any other court. Though their sovereign acts performed for the general good may work injury to some private contractors, such parties gain nothing by having the United States as their defendants. Wherever the public and private acts of the government seem to commingle, a citizen or corporate body must by supposition be substituted in its place, and then the question be determined whether the action will lie against the supposed defendant. If the enactment of a law imposing duties will enable the claimant to increase the stipulated price of the goods he has sold to a citizen, then it will when the United States are defendants, but not otherwise. If the removal of troops from a district liable to invasion will give the claimant damages for unforeseen expenses, when the other party is a corporate body, then it will when the United States form the other party, but not otherwise. This distinction between the public acts and private contracts of the government—not always strictly insisted on in the earlier days of this court—frequently misapprehended in public bodies, and constantly lost sight of by suitors who come before us, we now desire to make so broad and distinct that hereafter the two cannot be confounded; and we repeat, as a principle applicable to all cases, that the United States as a contractor cannot be held liable directly or indirectly for the public acts of the United States as a sovereign.

1. Public and General Acts

In judging whether a government act constitutes a sovereign act, the courts and boards frequently focus on whether the government act is directed at only the contractor or affects the public generally. In *Amino Bros. Co. v. United States*, 178 Ct. Cl. 515, 372 F.2d 485, *cert. denied*, 389 U.S. 846 (1967), it was necessary for the contractor to construct a water crossing in order to perform its work on a flood control project. The water crossing was washed out twice. The first washout was caused by natural runoff, and the second was caused when the U.S. Army Corps of Engineers released water from the Kanopolis flood control dam, which was located 88 miles upstream. The waters were released in conformance with the Reservoir Regulation Manual of the United States Army Corps of Engineers for the Kanopolis dam. The Court of Claims held that the sovereign acts doctrine precluded recovery, stating at 525:

> We hold that the [government] in releasing the water from the Kanopolis Dam which caused the second washout of [the contractor's] crossing was acting in its sovereign capacity and that its action in so doing, affected the public generally and was not directed solely toward the [contractor]. It has long been held that the United States as a contractor cannot be held liable directly or indirectly for public acts of the United States as a sovereign. *Horowitz v. United States*, 267 U.S. 458 (1925).

Similarly, in *Air Terminal Servs., Inc. v. United States*, 165 Ct. Cl. 525, 330 F.2d 974, *cert. denied*, 379 U.S. 829 (1964), the court found a sovereign act where the government reduced a concessionaire's income by using its public powers to provide alternate facilities to the concession. For other instances in which contractor relief was barred because increased contractor costs resulted from a sovereign act, see *Glasgow Assocs. v. United States*, 203 Ct. Cl. 532, 495 F.2d 765 (1974) (FHA interest rate increase and DoD implementation in Capehart contracts); *American Int'l Constructors, Inc.*, ENGBCA 3633, 77-2 BCA ¶ 12,606 (directive to use specified stevedoring company uniformly applied to all vessels unloading at given port); *Wunderlich Contracting Co. v. United States*, 173 Ct. Cl. 180, 351 F.2d 956 (1965) (government's awarding of other contracts, which allegedly diverted the workforce and caused contractor to incur additional expenses to maintain an adequate labor force); *Horowitz v. United States*, 267 U.S. 458 (1925) (Railroad Administration embargo delaying silk shipment); *Anthony P. Miller, Inc. v. United States*, 161 Ct. Cl. 455, *cert. denied*, 375 U.S. 879 (1963) (government's raising of interest rates); *Hills Materials Co.*, ASBCA 42410, 92-1 BCA ¶ 24,636, *rev'd and remanded on other grounds*, 982 F.2d 514 (Fed. Cir. 1992) (new excavation safety standard issued by Occupational Safety & Health Administration); *Inter-Mountain Photogrammetry, Inc.*, AGBCA 90-125-1, 91-2 BCA ¶ 23,941 (Department of Transportation denial of operating permit); *Mergentime Corp.*, ENGBCA 5765, 92-2 BCA ¶ 25,007 (delay ordered by Secret Service to facilitate presidential visit); *Holmes & Narver Servs., Inc.*, ASBCA 38867, 90-3 BCA ¶ 23,198 (congressional creation of new national holiday); and *Broadmoor Corp.*, ASBCA 37028, 89-1 BCA ¶ 21,441 (banning of pesticide by Environmental Protection Agency).

If an act that is sovereign in nature is motivated by a desire to avoid contractual liability, the sovereign act defense will not apply. See *Winstar Corp. v. United States*, 518 U.S. 839 (1996), holding that a statute prohibiting certain accounting treatment of bank assets was not a sovereign act. The government argued that its contracts promising such treatment were impossible to perform after the statute was passed and it was thereby not liable for breach of contract. The plurality opinion of the Court rejected this argument because the object of the statute was "self-relief," reasoning at 896-98:

> If the Government is to be treated like other contractors, some line has to be drawn in situations like the one before us between regulatory legislation that is relatively free of Government self-interest and therefore cognizable for the purpose of a legal impossibility defense and, on the other hand, statutes tainted by a governmental object of self-relief. Such an object is not necessarily inconsistent with a public purpose, of course, and when we speak of governmental "self-interest," we simply mean to identify instances in which the Government seeks to shift the costs of meeting its legitimate public responsibilities to private parties. Cf. *Armstrong v. United States*, 364 U.S. at 49 (The Government may not "force some people alone to bear public burdens which . . . should be borne by the public as a whole"). Hence, while the Government might legitimately conclude that a given contractual commitment was no longer in the public interest, a govern-

> ment seeking relief from such commitments through legislation would obviously not be in a position comparable to that of the private contractor who willy-nilly was barred by law from performance. There would be, then, good reason in such circumstance to find the regulatory and contractual characters of the Government fused together, in *Horowitz's* terms, so that the Government should not have the benefit of the defense.
>
> *Horowitz's* criterion of "public and general act" thus reflects the traditional "rule of law" assumption that generality in the terms by which the use of power is authorized will tend to guard against its misuse to burden or benefit the few unjustifiably. See, e. g., *Hurtado v. California*, 110 U.S. 516, 535-536, 28 L. Ed. 232, 4 S. Ct. 111 (1884) ("Law . . . must be not a special rule for a particular person or a particular case, but . . . 'the general law . . .' so 'that every citizen shall hold his life, liberty, property and immunities under the protection of the general rules which govern society'") (citation omitted). n43 Hence, governmental action will not be held against the Government for purposes of the impossibility defense so long as the action's impact upon public contracts is, as in *Horowitz*, merely incidental to the accomplishment of a broader governmental objective. See *O'Neill v. United States*, 231 Ct. Cl. 823, 826 (1982) (noting that the sovereign acts doctrine recognizes that "the Government's actions, otherwise legal, will occasionally incidentally impair the performance of contracts"). The greater the Government's self-interest, however, the more suspect becomes the claim that its private contracting partners ought to bear the financial burden of the Government's own improvidence, and where a substantial part of the impact of the Government's action rendering performance impossible falls on its own contractual obligations, the defense will be unavailable. Cf. *Sun Oil Co. v. United States*, 215 Ct. Cl. 716, 768, 572 F.2d 786, 817 (1978) (rejecting sovereign acts defense where the Secretary of the Interior's actions were "'directed principally and primarily at plaintiffs' contractual right'"). [Footnotes omitted]

See also *Conoco, Inc. v. United States*, 35 Fed. Cl. 309 (1996), *rev'd on other grounds*, 177 F.3d 1331 (Fed. Cir 1999), *rev'd on other grounds*, 530 U.S. 604 (2000), rejecting the sovereign act defense where a statute was directly aimed at oil leases of the type held by the company. Similarly, in *General Dynamics Corp. v. United States*, 47 Fed. Cl. 514 (2000), the government's retroactive application of a statutory cap on allowable executive compensation costs was held to be a sovereign act aimed at a class of contractors. In *R&B Bewachungsgesellschaft mbH*, ASBCA 42213, 91-3 BCA ¶ 24,310, the board held that the defense was not applicable to a claim for the disruptive impact of a criminal investigation that was instigated by contracting officials and resulted in no criminal charges being filed. Similarly, in *California Meat Co.*, AGBCA 76-152, 80-2 BCA ¶ 14,607, the defense was rejected where the government's withdrawal of inspection and grading services "for valid regulatory program reasons," directly affected the contractor. Compare *Yankee Atomic Elec. Co. v. United States*, 112 F.3d 1569 (Fed. Cir. 1997), *cert. denied*, 524 U.S. 951 (1998), holding that a statutory "special assessment" against users of uranium enrichment services was a sovereign act because it was not directed only at contractors that had previously bought such services from the government but at all companies buying such services in the future. The court stated at 1575-76:

> The reach of the Act . . . makes clear that Congress was not focused on a retroactive increase in the price of the Government's prior contractual agreements. Rather than targeting those utility companies that had prior contracts with the Government, the Act targets whichever utility eventually used and benefited from the DOE's enrichment services. Congress's main purpose was to spread the costs of a problem that it realized only after the contracts had been performed.

2. Contractual Acts

Acts that are not public and general in nature will not be considered sovereign acts that relieve the government of liability. In *Sun Oil Co. v. United States*, 215 Ct. Cl. 716, 572 F.2d 786 (1978), the court found that the actions by the Secretary of the Interior in denying offshore oil permits did not constitute sovereign acts since they "were not actions of public and general applicability, but were actions directed principally and primarily at plaintiff's contractual right to install a platform on Tract 401 and to extract oil and gas therefrom." See also *Volentine & Littleton Contractors v. United States*, 144 Ct. Cl. 723, 169 F. Supp. 263 (1959) (closing of floodgates to permit another contractor to work constituted breach of an upstream contract), and *John M. Bragg*, ASBCA 9515, 65-2 BCA ¶ 5050 (government's digging of ditches to protect other work from flooding not a sovereign act). In *E.C. Ottinger v. United States*, 116 Ct. Cl. 282, 88 F. Supp. 881 (1950), work was to be performed in a critical labor area, which meant that labor had to be furnished through the War Manpower Commission. Ruling, without a valid basis, that a labor dispute existed with a contractor, the Commission refused to refer workmen to the contractor. The court found that, by assuming control over the manpower in the area, the government was obligated to treat the contractor equitably. In refusing to invoke the sovereign act doctrine, the court stated at 285:

> We think that when agents of the Government, without justification in statute, executive order, administrative discretion or otherwise, engage in conduct which is a violation of an express or implied provision of a Government contract, the mantle of sovereignty does not give the Government immunity from suit. It needs no such immunity in order to be able to go on governing wisely and as circumstances require without being hampered by its outstanding contracts. We think that to treat every act of a Government agent, done in the name of the Government, as an act of sovereignty within the meaning of the doctrine here under discussion would be retreat, without reason, from the purpose of the statute permitting citizens to sue the United States for breach of contract.

3. Implementation of a Sovereign Act

In many cases, the contracting agency is required to take steps to implement the sovereign act. If it does not do so in a reasonable manner, it will be liable for the resulting costs. The government's implied duty of cooperation requires it to work with the contractor to implement the sovereign act with the least disturbance of the contract. See *Miller v. United States*, 135 Ct. Cl. 1, 140 F. Supp. 789 (1956). In *Freedman v. United States*, 162 Ct. Cl. 390, 320 F.2d 359 (1963), the Air Force canceled a contract for the sale of tanks located in England when the U.S. State Department, based on foreign policy concerns, would not ask the British government for an export permit. The Court of Claims held the cancellation improper, stating at 401-02:

> Once it is recognized that the Government had assumed the obligation to deliver the tanks to the rail-head at Dunkirk, the breach becomes plain—as defendant admits. The duty to ship and deliver necessarily encompassed the subsidiary duty to obtain an export license for plaintiff or to by-pass that requirement by shipping the material as the Federal Government's own. Without that secondary obligation, the primary promise would have no meaning; and the defendant was surely in a better position to fulfill its agreement by obtaining the permit (or a waiver) than plaintiff, a private American purchaser. Similarly, the defendant, having bound itself to deliver abroad, could not refuse to take the necessary steps because the State Department felt that it was inopportune to ask the British Government for an export permit. The doctrine of "public and general" "sovereign acts", laid down in *Horowitz v. United States*, 267 U.S. 458 (1925), does not relieve the Government from liability where it has specially undertaken to perform the very act from which it later seeks to be excused. See *The Sunswick Corp. v. United States*, 109 Ct. Cl. 772, 798, 75 F. Supp. 221, 228 (1948), *cert. denied*, 334 U.S. 827; cf. *Stebel v. United States*, 108 Ct. Cl. 35, 44-45, 69 F. Supp. 221, 222-23 (1947); *Miller v. United States*, 135 Ct. Cl. 1, 140 F. Supp. 789 (1956); *Metal Exports, Inc. v. United States*, 137 Ct. Cl. 258, 146 F. Supp. 951 (1957). In any event, it is clear that the Air Force refused to adopt the other feasible method of exporting the tanks—shipping them as property of the United States for which no license would be required—simply because the British Government would not pay for that type of transportation. There was no conceivable foreign policy obstacle to following that course, only a pecuniary drawback. The existence of this court is proof enough that the desire to save money is a poor reason to break an outstanding promise. Cf. *Lynch v. United States*, 292 U.S. 571, 580 (1934). [Footnotes omitted]

See also *Weaver Constr. Co.*, DOTBCA 2034, 91-2 BCA ¶ 23,800, holding that the government is obligated to implement sovereign acts in the least restrictive or least costly manner, and *M.D. Funk*, ASBCA 20287, 76-2 BCA ¶ 12,120, holding that the contractor could recover the costs resulting from the government's unreasonable delay in responding to its request for priority assistance in obtaining controlled materials even though sovereign acts were involved in controlling availability of materials and lifting of government price controls. In *Borderland Spraying Serv.*, AGBCA 90-180-1, 93-3 BCA ¶ 26,214, the government suspended the contract until it could obtain an environmental impact statement. The board indicated that if the suspension was more costly than a termination would have been, the contractor might have had a basis for recovery. However, because the contractor never proved that it suffered any damages such as storage or standby costs, its appeal was denied.

4. *Impact of Contract Language*

Although contracting officers may not make an agreement precluding the government from exercising its sovereign duties, it is permissible for contracts to contain provisions entitling the contractor to a price adjustment if sovereign acts increase the costs of performance. In *Gerhardt F. Meyne Co. v. United States*, 110 Ct. Cl. 527, 76 F. Supp. 811 (1948), the court noted at 550:

> [The government] cannot enter into a binding agreement that it will not exercise a sovereign power, but it can say, if it does, it will pay you the amount by which your costs are increased thereby. *United States v. Bostwick*, 94 U.S. 53, 69; *Sunswick Corp. v. United States*, 109 C. Cls. 772, *certiorari denied.*

See *Orlando Helicopter Airways, Inc. v. Widnall*, 51 F.3d 258 (Fed. Cir. 1995), recognizing this principle but finding no contract provision giving the contractor a right to a price increase under the firm-fixed-price contract. See also *Pacific Architects & Eng'rs, Inc.*, ASBCA 21168, 79-2 BCA ¶ 14,019, *recons. denied*, 79-2 BCA ¶ 14,174 (permitting recovery where the contract specified sovereign acts for which a price adjustment would be negotiated), and *M.D. Funk*, ASBCA 20287, 76-2 BCA ¶ 12,120, *recons. denied*, 77-1 BCA ¶ 12,241 (government contracted to be liable for the consequences of suspension of work resulting from sovereign act regarding priority designations of controlled material, but the lifting of price controls was an independent sovereign act). In *Landes Oil Co.*, ASBCA 22101, 78-1 BCA ¶ 12,910, *recons. denied*, 78-2 BCA ¶ 13,275, the government's deregulation of unleaded gasoline prices was a sovereign act for which a price increase was granted under the Economic Price Adjustment clause.

In a cost-type contract, the costs of a sovereign act should be recoverable without any contract clause granting recovery unless the costs are expressly unallowable. See *Raytheon STX Corp. v. Department of Commerce*, GSBCA 14296-COM, 00-1 BCA ¶ 30,632, holding that the cost of a government shutdown was an allowable cost even though it was a sovereign act. See also *DynCorp,* ASBCA 49714, 97-2 BCA ¶ 29,233, rejecting the government's argument that the sovereign acts doctrine prohibited the contractor from recovering costs incurred as a result of an investigation of acts by the contractor's employees.

The contractual promise to reimburse the contractor for a sovereign act can be implied as well as express. See *Old Dominion Sec.*, ASBCA 40062, 91-3 BCA ¶ 24,173, *recons. denied*, 92-1 BCA ¶ 24,374, in which the board held that failure to issue a sufficient number of security clearances overcame a sovereign act because the contract requirement for a certain number of security guards contained an implied promise that security clearances would be issued. Compare *Bared Int'l Co.*, ASBCA 30048, 88-1 BCA ¶ 20,378, in which a sovereign act was found when the Navy changed its messing rate for enlisted personnel. No implied promise was found even though the contract permitted contractor personnel to eat at Navy messes "at current rates, presently $4.90/man per day."

If the contracting officer uses a contract clause to implement a policy that originates in a sovereign act, the act may be held to be contractual. In *Empire Gas Eng'g Co.*, ASBCA 7190, 1962 BCA ¶ 3323, in finding that the act was not sovereign, the board relied heavily on the fact that the contracting officer issued a suspension order. In that case the contractor was working at a Strategic Air Command base under a contract awarded by the U.S. Army Corps of Engineers, the construction agency for the Air Force. On July 15, 1958, the base was put on alert as a result of the international crisis in Lebanon. The next day the contracting officer directed the contractor to stop work and then confirmed this direction by a letter dated July 21, 1958, which stated that it was necessary to restrict operations and that any cutting of pavement was strictly prohibited until further notice. The board found that the contractor was entitled to an adjustment under the Suspension of Work clause, holding that the suspension order constituted an act of the government in its contractual capacity. The board distinguished the order suspending the work, which was issued by the contracting officer, from the reason for the suspension. The board questioned the use of the public and general test, and stated at 17,128:

> In determining what would have been the effect of the Government act if a private party were substituted for the Government as the other party to the contract, we must not lose sight of the terms of the contract itself. If the contract contains express or implied provisions protecting the contractor against the consequences of certain acts of the government, such contract provisions must be given effect.

The bases for holding the government liable were stated at 17,128:

> The contract contemplated performance while the base was being operated in a state of normal peacetime readiness, and a state of alert was not anticipated by the terms of the contract. The fact that the suspension of work order was in writing addressed to the contractor by name, referring to the contract by number, and signed by the contracting officer as contracting officer is almost exclusive proof that such order was (1) an act of the Government in its contractual capacity and (2) issued in exercise of the Government's right to suspend the work under the Suspension of Work clause.

The same reasoning was applied in *Federal Elec. Corp.*, ASBCA 20490, 76-2 BCA ¶ 12,035, where the contractor's work in an airport control tower was suspended during state visits of the Shah of Iran and the King of Jordan. The board held that the suspension was a contractual act for which the contractor was entitled to compensation under the government Delay of Work clause. See also *Inman & Assocs., Inc.*, ASBCA 37869, 91-3 BCA ¶ 24,048, where the contractor incurred extra costs in complying with an order of the contracting officer to keep trailers on the site. The board found that this was a contractual change order even though the order had been issued at the request of the Environmental Protection Agency to facilitate the investigation of an environmental problem. Compare *Goodfellow Bros., Inc.*, AGBCA 75-140, 77-1 BCA ¶ 12,336, where the U.S. Forest Service District Ranger had issued a fire closure order under published Forest Service regulations and refused to issue a permit to the contractor to work in the forest during the fire closure. The contracting officer then issued a Suspension of Work order to the contractor. The board denied compensation, finding that the suspension was a sovereign act, and stated at 59,641:

> We do not believe that the suspension of work order issued by the Contracting Officer for the purpose of stopping the running of contract time converts the fire closure sovereign act into a contractual act. To the extent that *Empire Gas Engineering Co.*, ASBCA No. 7190, 1962 BCA ¶ 3323, may be construed to mean that a contracting officer's action, absent a contractual agreement to compensate for a sovereign act, makes such act compensable, we do not agree.

This reasoning was followed in *Lloyd H. Kessler, Inc.*, AGBCA 88-170-3, 91-2 BCA ¶ 23,802, and *Carter Constr. Co.*, ENGBCA 5495, 90-1 BCA ¶ 22,521.

VII. PROPORTIONAL RISK ALLOCATION

The courts and boards have used proportional risk allocation when traditional techniques of placing the entire risk on one of the parties do not lead to fair results. Most of the cases have awarded the contractor a percentage of its increased cost on the theory that the government and the contractor should share responsibility for the problems encountered. The decision that responsibility should be shared may be based on (1) joint fault or (2) joint negligence. The trend toward proportional risk allocation appears to have had its genesis in the Court of Claims decision in *National Presto Indus., Inc. v. United States*, 167 Ct. Cl. 749, 338 F.2d 99 (1964), *cert. denied*, 380 U.S. 962 (1965), in which the court reformed the contract, based on the parties' mutual mistake as to the feasibility of using a manufacturing method, and divided the increased cost equally between the parties. The court stated at 768-69:

> [I]t is unsatisfactory to tell a party who did not, either in terms or by fair implication, assume a certain heavy risk that he alone must bear it simply because of the happenstance that it fell to his lot . . . . To do justice here we need go no further than formulate and apply a rule for cases of mutual mistake in which the contract, properly construed, allocates the specific risk to neither party C and the side from whom relief is sought received a benefit from the extra work of the type it contemplated obtaining from the contract, and would have been willing, if it had known the true facts from the beginning, to bear a substantial part of the additional expenses. Cf. *Virginia Engr. Co. v. United States*, 101 Ct. Cl. 516, 532-33 (1944).
>
> * * *
>
> For such a case it is equitable to reform the contract so that each side bears a share of the unexpected costs, instead of permitting the whole loss to remain with the party on whom it chanced to light. In contract suits courts have generally seemed loath to divide damages, but in this class of case we see no objection other than tradition. Reformation, as the child of equity, can mold its relief to attain any fair result within the broadest perimeter of the charter the

> parties have established for themselves. Where that arrangement has allocated the risk to neither side, a judicial division is fair and equitable. The division can follow from the special circumstances if there are any; in their absence an equal split would fit the basic postulate that the contract has assigned the risk to neither party.

See also *Big Star Testing Co.*, GSBCA 5793, 81-2 BCA ¶ 15,335, *recons. denied*, 82-1 BCA ¶ 15,635, where neither party was at fault and the additional costs of performance were shared by the parties. The board stated at 75,941:

> [I]n certain cases the actions of the parties create an implied agreement to share certain costs or risks. In the particular appeal here under consideration, we cannot conclude that [the contractor] must shoulder the entire risk of all extra expenses attributable to the lack of a certification procedure for its hydrostatic test equipment. [The contractor's] inability to use its equipment did not excuse its failure to perform, but it did place a burden on the Government to do more than blithely reiterate its insistence that the problem was entirely [the contractor's] to solve. Catch-22 ought not to be part of the Federal Procurement Regulations . . . . Neither party was in any way at fault here. And even though [the contractor] failed to go elsewhere and was subsequently defaulted, that does not mean that [the contractor] must absorb the entirety of the consequences including all excess procurement costs.

See also *Richard J. Wand*, AGBCA 83-215-3, 83-2 BCA ¶ 16,820, in which the board found both the government and the contractor responsible for the increased costs. The board stated at 83,675 that it was unable to find either party solely responsible for all of the increased costs. Therefore, the parties shared the costs equally.

Although this concept may be an attractive method to resolve difficult cases, it is not appropriate for use when the costs associated with each party's fault or negligence can be ascertained with an acceptable degree of accuracy. However, it was used in one such case, *T. Brown Constructors, Inc.*, DOTBCA 1986, 95-2 BCA ¶ 27,870, *aff'd*, 132 F.3d 724 (Fed. Cir. 1997). There the board found that the contractor had used unreasonable assumptions in bidding the work, and the government had ordered performance not required by the specifications. Rather than pricing the cost of the government's order, the board held that the parties should share the costs above the contractor's bid price except for costs of contractor mismanagement of the work.

A. Joint Fault

Proportional risk allocation is used in cases where the additional costs are a result of the fault of both parties. For example, in *Frank Briscoe Co.*, GSBCA 6169 (5145)-REIN, 81-2 BCA ¶ 15,456, the contractor sought delay costs relating to defective government-furnished specifications but had also incurred costs due to its own problems of coordination. In granting one-half of the additional costs, the board noted at 76,584:

> [Since the parties] have been unable to shed enough light on the delay period to permit us to assign the responsibility firmly to either party, we must have recourse to a jury verdict. . . . However, we see no reason why the Government should have to answer for the cost of more than half the total delay, even including the month it has already agreed to shoulder, and for lack of anything better to do we simply split the entire delay down the middle.

In *Bruce-Andersen Co.*, PSBCA 1000, 83-2 BCA ¶ 16,733, increased costs were divided in proportion to the parties' responsibility. The board found at 83,222 that the "design defect [bore] a substantially greater share of the responsibility . . . than the workmanship defects." The government was 65 percent liable and the contractor was 35 percent liable, and the damages were apportioned accordingly. See *Pacific W. Constr., Inc.*, DOTCAB 1084, 82-2 BCA ¶ 16,045, *recons. denied*, 83-1 BCA ¶ 16,337, where the government breached its duty to disclose pertinent information; however, the contractor should have detected the problem earlier. Under a theory of comparative responsibility, the board apportioned losses by holding the government liable for all costs incurred up to the time a reasonable contractor would have discovered the problem, and the contractor liable for all costs thereafter incurred. Similarly, in *Circle Elec. Contractors, Inc.*, DOTCAB 76-27, 77-1 BCA ¶ 12,339, the government provided defective specifications, and the contractor engaged in mismanagement during the contract performance. As a result, the board concluded that both parties jointly contributed to the delays and were equally responsible for the costs. Compare *ACS Constr. Co.*, ASBCA 28488, 84-1 BCA ¶ 17,179, where there were three causes that required the contractor to tear out and replace work: (1) erroneous government-furnished drawings, (2) subcontractor error in column fabrication, and (3) poor workmanship resulting in undulated concrete. The government was responsible for the first cause, but the contractor was responsible for the other two causes due to defective contractor performance. Unable to determine whether any of the three causes was predominantly responsible for the difficulties, and without any factual basis for apportionment of the costs involved among these causes, the board allocated the costs equally between the contractor and the government. In *Celesco Indus., Inc.*, ASBCA 21928, 81-2 BCA ¶ 15,260, the contractor recovered only 20 percent of additional testing costs when only one of the five possible causes of failure was attributed to the government. See also *Grumman Aerospace Corp. v. United States*, 213 Ct. Cl. 178, 549 F.2d 767 (1977), in which the court required the government to absorb half of the costs incurred by the contractor under a subcontract since neither the contractor nor the government sufficiently scrutinized the subcontractor's cost justifications.

Other types of government fault have also led to apportionment of losses. For example, in *Chronometrics, Inc.*, NASABCA 185-2, 90-3 BCA ¶ 22,992, the contractor was at fault in designing a product that did not comply with the contract specifications but, when the product was subjected to the government-required tests, the government did not test the product thoroughly and did not disclose all of the deficiencies. The contractor incurred additional costs attempting to correct the deficiencies with repeated testing and rework. Eventually, the government corrected the deficiencies and charged the costs of this work to the contractor. The board held that the government was not entitled to recover such costs and that the contractor was entitled to an equitable adjustment in the amount of 50 percent of the costs that had been incurred after the government's initial notification that the product had failed its tests—up to the original contract price. See also *William Fehn*, PSBCA 2302, 89-2 BCA ¶ 21,663, in which joint fault was found when the sewer lines on leased property were damaged. The board found that government employees were at fault in flushing improper materials down the toilets, and the contractor was at fault in providing a building with very old, badly designed sewer lines. Joint fault was also found in *Inversiones Aransu, S.A.*, ENGBCA PCC-77, 92-1 BCA ¶ 24,584, where the government left a trench open on the work site and the contractor was late in starting the work and failed to provide adequate drainage at the site, thus exacerbating the problem. The board concluded at 122,672 that each of the parties contributed to the material becoming unsuitable for use as backfill. In *Dickman Builders, Inc.*, ASBCA 32612, 91-2 BCA ¶ 23,989, the contractor failed to inquire about a patent ambiguity in the specifications. In addition, the government had received an inquiry from another bidder regarding the ambiguity, but failed to notify the other bidders about the ambiguity, and the board concluded that the government was equally at fault in permitting procurement to continue while knowing about the ambiguity in the drawings.

B. Joint Negligence

Proportional risk allocation is used where both parties perform inadequately or negligently. In *Environmental Growth Chambers, Inc.*, ASBCA 25845, 83-2 BCA ¶ 16,609, the contractor failed to follow the contract requirements, and the government failed to properly protect the work and respond to alarms. Both parties' negligence caused the damage; hence, each was liable under a comparative negligence theory. The board stated at 82,601 that "it was unable to determine that any party's actions or omissions were a greater cause of damage." Therefore, it apportioned one-half of the repair costs to each party. Relying on a theory of comparative negligence, the board stated at 82,600:

> The concept behind the doctrine of comparative negligence is consistent with the manner in which the Boards of Contract Appeals and the Court of Claims have apportioned damages under appropriate circumstances. See, e.g. *Hilltop Electric Construction, Inc.*, DOT CAB No. 78-6, 78-2 BCA ¶ 13,421; *M. Liodas*, ASBCA No. 12829, 71-2 BCA P9015, *reconsid. denied*, 71-2 BCA P9120; *Grumman Aerospace Corporation*, 213 Ct. Cl. 178, 549 F.2d 767. We note also that . . . the United States Supreme Court . . . opt[s] . . . for a rule of comparative negligence

> in which, in the case of property damage, liability for such damage is to be allocated among the parties proportionately to the comparative degree of their fault, and that liability for such damages is to be allocated equally only when the parties are equally at fault or when it is not possible fairly to measure the comparative degree of their fault. *United States v. Reliable Transfer Co.*, 421 U.S. 397 at 411, 44 L.Ed. 251 at 262 (1975).

Proportional risk allocation has also been used in cases where the government seeks to recover costs from the contractor. See *United States v. Seckinger*, 397 U.S. 203 (1970), in which the court interpreted a contract clause providing that the contractor "shall be responsible for all damages to persons or property that occur as a result of [its] fault or negligence" as premising liability on a comparative negligence theory. An employee of the contractor was injured because the government negligently failed to de-energize a wire at the work site or, in the alternative, negligently failed to inform the workers of the energized wire. In addition, the contractor was negligent in causing its employee's injury. As a result of the contractor's negligence, the government recovered one-half of its costs from the contractor. See also *Clovis Heimsath & Assocs.*, NASABCA 180-1, 83-1 BCA ¶ 16,133, where the contractor negligently designed a facility and the government was negligent in reviewing and approving the design, as it failed "to discover significant, readily recognizable omissions, inconsistencies or defects in the design package." With the negligence of both parties contributing to the collapse of the facility, the government recovered only one-half of the amount for which the contractor would have been liable due to its own negligence.

C. Improper Default Terminations

There are several cases sharing costs when a default termination has been found to be improper but the contractor has not totally fulfilled its obligations. See *Dynalectron Corp. v. United States*, 207 Ct. Cl. 349, 518 F.2d 594 (1975), in which a default termination was found to have been improper because the government had issued a contract that contained defective specifications and had failed to correct some of the specifications when notified of the defects by the contractor. However, the contractor had incurred a substantial amount of costs after it knew of some defects, but did not give the government notice of such defects. The court apparently felt that the lack of notice deprived the government of its rightful opportunity to mitigate those costs by taking some action to correct the defective specifications. The court also concluded that both parties had mismanaged the contract—causing the incurrence of additional costs. The court apportioned the costs of these actions by awarding the contractor 50 percent of its convenience termination costs, stating at 367-69:

> The contract we think does not provide a measure of damages and it has to be provided by common law or equitable principles. When, as here, the defaulted contractor is not without fault or negligence, but the default was wrongful because of the Government's previous fault or negligence, [the contract] may impose a

ceiling in that the damages perhaps may not exceed those that would be computed by the termination formula.

If [the contract] does not reduce the damages awardable to zero, we must go elsewhere to learn how to measure them. We find instruction in *National Presto Industries, Inc. v. United States*, 167 Ct. Cl. 749, 338 F.2d 99 (1964), *cert. denied*, 380 U.S. 962 (1965). There in a mutual fault situation we effected a reformation of the contract on the theory of a mutual mistake, sharing the losses equally. Since, unlike here, we there rejected the claim for breach liability and had therefore to find a remedy under the contract, this case would seem a fortiori eligible for a similar innovative approach. The equitable powers of this court in actions at law are not limited to instances of mutual mistake. . . . Here, since the convenience termination formula is ruled out, except as a ceiling, we think the formula of shared costs as in a joint venture is likewise applicable. The Government benefited from [the contractor's] flounderings at least to this extent: it tried out a number of false leads and learned what would not work at [the contractor's] cost.

* * *

Accordingly...the parties are to share equally the allowable and reasonable costs normally recoverable by [the contractor] in a convenience termination.

Several board decisions have followed this guidance of not awarding full termination settlement costs to the contractor after converting an improper default termination into a convenience termination. None of these decisions has called for an even sharing of the costs incurred in performing the contract prior to the termination. Rather, in each case the board fashioned an appropriate remedy based on the specific facts and circumstances. See, for example, *A.J.C.A. Constr. v. General Servs. Admin.*, GSBCA 11541, 94-2 BCA ¶ 26,949, holding that the government had improperly terminated the contract for default but concluding that the contractor was also at fault in not responding promptly to a request to price a contract change and in not telling the government it was leaving the job when no change order was issued. The board held that the contractor had already been paid for the work it had accomplished, and converted the default termination into a no-cost convenience termination, depriving the contractor of settlement costs and the government of excess reprocurement costs. A similar result was arrived at in *Insul-Glass, Inc.*, GSBCA 8223, 89-1 BCA ¶ 21,361, in which the board found that the parties' dispute over shop drawings was not a valid reason for a default termination. At the same time, the contractor had been at fault in participating, along with the government, in a "profound failure to communicate." The board therefore converted the default termination into one for the convenience of the government, but denied recovery of any of the administrative costs incurred by the contractor because the contract was "so badly administered."

This cost sharing has not been permitted when the government's only improper action is poor contract administration. In such cases, the default termination has been held to be proper. See *Olson Plumbing & Heating Co. v. United States*, 221 Ct. Cl. 197, 602 F.2d 950 (1979), stating at 209:

> Poor contract administration, standing alone, which does not amount to a breach, does not entitle a party to shift part of the cost of its own breach to the non-breaching party. [The contractor's] bare allegation, that the Government's poor administration of the contract contributed to the failure of the system and entitles it to have its losses split, fails to prove, as required by the decision in *Dynalectron*, that the parties were equally responsible for the delay in discovering the faulty specifications and/or the losses accompanying this delay. Furthermore, [the contractor's] request that we find that the Government's alleged poor contract administration contributed to [the contractor's] inability to complete the contract assumes there is causal connection between the alleged "fault" on the part of the Government and the losses sustained. This position is contradicted by the board's finding that the failure to perform was solely [the contractor's] fault. [Footnote omitted.]

The boards of contract appeals have followed this reasoning in a few cases. See *Independent Mfg. & Serv. Cos. of Am.*, ASBCA 47542, 95-2 BCA ¶ 27,915, upholding a default termination despite the contractor's assertions of poor contract administration by the government. The board found that the government's actions during contract administration were not the "substantial cause" of the contractor's lack of finances, which precipitated the default termination. See also *American Astro-Sys., Inc.*, ASBCA 9008, 66-1 BCA ¶ 5561, *aff'd. sub nom., Astro Science Corp. v. United States*, 200 Ct. Cl. 354, 471 F.2d 624 (1973) (upholding a default termination because the drawing deficiencies for which the government was responsible were "not inordinately large or disproportionate"), and *Sermor, Inc.*, ASBCA 29798, 94-1 BCA ¶ 26303 (denying a claim for delay damages when the contract had been validly terminated for default—commenting that although the government's contract administration had been "flawed" and it had contributed to the contractor's performance difficulties, the board could find no legal remedy).

D. Concurrent Delays

Costs are not generally allocated proportionally if they result from concurrent government-caused and contractor-caused delays. See *Sauer, Inc. v. Danzig*, 224 F.3d 1340 (Fed. Cir. 2000), stating at 1348:

> [T]o establish a compensable delay, a contractor must separate government-caused delays from its own delays. See, e.g., *T. Brown Constructors, Inc. v. Pena*, 132 F.3d 724, 734-35 (Fed. Cir. 1998); *Commerce Int'l Co. v. United States*, 167 Ct. Cl. 529, 338 F.2d 81, 89-90 (Ct. Cl. 1964) (applying "the rule that there can be no recovery where the [government's] delay is concurrent or intertwined with other delays").

See also *Singleton Contracting Corp.*, ASBCA 51692, 03-2 BCA ¶ 32,260, *rev'd on other grounds*, 395 F.3d 1353 (Fed. Cir. 2005), and *Wilner Constr. Co.*, ASBCA

26621, 84-2 BCA ¶ 17,411. In *Celesco Indus., Inc.*, ASBCA 21928, 81-2 BCA ¶ 15,260, the contractor was unable to recover costs attributable to any government delay. The board applied the well-established rule at 75,556:

> [T]hat when Government caused delays are concurrent or inter-twined with other delays for which the Government is not responsible, a contractor cannot recover delay damages if the delays for which the Government was not responsible cannot be separated from those for which it was. *Commerce International Company v. United States*, 167 Ct. Cl. 529, 338 F.2d 81 (1964); *Fishbach & Moore International Corp.*, ASBCA No. 18146, 77-1 BCA ¶ 12,300 at 59,224-25.

See also *Coffey Constr. Co.*, VABCA 3361, 93-2 BCA ¶ 25,788, in which neither the government nor the contractor could recover for delay costs. The board, quoting *William F. Klingensmith v. United States*, 731 F.2d 805, 809 (Fed. Cir. 1984), stated at 128,325:

> The general rule is that "[w]here both parties contribute to the delay neither can recover damage[s], unless there is in the proof a clear apportionment of the delay and expense attributable to each party." Courts will deny recovery where the delays are concurrent and the contractor has not established its delay apart from that attributable to the Government. *[Blinderman Construction Co., Inc. v. United States*, 695 F.2d 552, 559 (Fed. Cir. 1982), quoting *Coath & Goss, Inc. v. United States*, 101 Ct. Cl. 702, 714-715 (1944).]
>
> Hence, even if certain delay could be chargeable to the Government, the Contractor has neither established the proximate cause of its delay nor distinguished and separated the various causes of delay. *Clover Builders, Inc.*, VABCA Nos. 2033, 2034, 88-2 BCA ¶ 20,629.

The board then quoted *Kink Bros., Mech. Contractors, Inc.*, ASBCA 43788, 93-1 BCA ¶ 25,325, stating at 128,326:

> Where the delay is caused solely by the Government, it is compensable; where the delay is caused solely by the [contractor], [the contractor] is responsible . . . . Where the delay is prompted by inextricably intertwined concurrent Government and contractor causes, the delay is not compensable . . . .

Thus, with overlapping and concurrent delays "neither party [could] use them as the basis of a delay claim against the other." See also *Wexler Constr. Co.*, ASBCA 23782, 84-2 BCA ¶ 17,408 (since the parties were mutually at fault, neither party was able to recover for delays); *ADCO Constr. Co.*, PSBCA 2355, 90-3 BCA ¶ 22,944 (delays were concurrent and could not be segregated or apportioned); and *Skipper & Co.*, ASBCA 30327, 89-1 BCA ¶ 21,490 (contractor was also concurrently delayed by its lack of performance).

Before delays are found to be concurrent, the facts should be analyzed to ensure that they cannot be assigned to each party. See *Essex Electro Eng'rs, Inc. v. Danzig*,

224 F.3d 1283 (Fed. Cir. 2000), remanding the case to the board to apportion delays incurred by the contractor in submitting engineering change proposals in the wrong form and the government in not acting promptly when the proposals were properly submitted.

A contrary view was expressed regarding a single delay caused by both parties. In *E.H. Marhoefer, Jr. Co.*, DOTCAB 70-17, 70-1 BCA ¶ 8177, the board stated at 40,848:

> Here there is but a single period of delay, part of which was caused by the Government's dereliction and part of which was caused by the contractor's actions. Rather than two separable concurrent delays, there is CONCURRENT fault on the part of each party.

Since the contractor was at greater fault, it was liable for two-thirds of the delay costs, indicating that when both parties are jointly responsible for a single delay, damages will be apportioned according to the degree of fault.

CHAPTER 4

CHANGES

Most government contracts include a Changes clause, which gives the government the unilateral right to order changes in contract work during the course of performance. The contractor has no right to receive such change orders because the clause vests the ordering power solely in the government. See *Hunkin Conkey Constr. Co. v. United States*, 198 Ct. Cl. 638, 461 F.2d 1270 (1972), in which a contracting officer was permitted to buy changed work from another contractor after finding that the contractor's price for changed work was unacceptably high, and *Bridgewater Constr. Corp.*, VABCA 2936, 91-3 BCA ¶ 24,273, *recons. denied*, 92-1 BCA ¶ 24,446, where a contracting officer was allowed to buy items inadvertently omitted from the specifications from a vendor after obtaining an engineering change proposal from the contractor.

The FAR contains two basic Changes clauses for fixed-price contracts. The fixed-price supply contract clause is contained in FAR 52.243-1. Alternatives, with minor modifications, are provided for service contracts. A separate clause for fixed-price construction contracts is contained in FAR 52.243-4. The clauses contain procedures for the ordering of changes and describe the types of changes that may be made. They provide for an "equitable adjustment" if the change increases or decreases the cost or time of performance. They are also used to process claims where the cost of the work has been changed as a result of government actions or orders not identified as changes, under a theory of "constructive changes." Contracts for commercial items contain a unique changes provision greatly limiting the operation of the clause. See ¶ (c) of the Contract Terms and Conditions—Commercial Items clause, FAR 52.212-4, stating:

> *Changes*. Changes in the terms and conditions of this contract my be made only by written agreement of the parties.

The first section of this chapter considers the purposes served by the clauses and the types of changes which they cover. The second section discusses the procedures used by the government in ordering changes. The third section deals with the special problems related to value engineering where the contractor is encouraged to submit proposals for price reduction changes. The next section is a detailed analysis of the use of the Changes clause in processing claims under the constructive changes doctrine. The chapter concludes with a discussion of the notice provisions. The pricing of equitable adjustments is discussed in Chapter 8.

I. PURPOSE AND COVERAGE OF THE CHANGES CLAUSE

There are many reasons why the government may wish to order changes. However, although the Changes clause confers broad powers on the government to alter or adjust the work performed by the contractor, there are definite limits to such powers. This section considers the purposes served by and the limitations on the Changes clauses.

A. Purposes Served

The Changes clause serves four major purposes:

1. To provide operating flexibility by giving the government the unilateral right to order changes in the work to accommodate advances in technology and changes in the government's needs and requirements.

This flexibility is particularly advantageous to the government in a procurement environment where rapid advances in "state-of-the-art" and applicable technologies might make agreed-upon methods of performance unduly costly, time-consuming, or burdensome to the government. In addition, since government needs are very often defined well before a contract is issued or has been substantially performed, this flexibility helps ensure that the government's actual requirements are met.

The flexibility afforded by the clause can also operate to the benefit of the contractor, who will usually have an interest in keeping abreast of technological changes and utilizing them during contract performance. Furthermore, changes in the government's requirements will, in most instances, result in additional sales through increases in the contract price. Such sales may be particularly desirable price-wise since they are obtained outside the competitive procurement environment.

The government is deprived of this flexibility when procuring commercial items.

2. To provide the contractor a means of proposing changes to the work, thereby facilitating more efficient performance and improving the quality of contract end products.

This function of the clause is important to the government. In many instances the contractor is much more abreast of the technical aspects of the work than are the employees of the contracting agency. If the contractor knows that the change procedure will be used to order changes that it suggests, the contractor will be much more willing to suggest improvements than if it is unsure of the use the government will make of the suggestions. Here the clause serves to open communications between the parties.

The fact that the Changes clause provides for an equitable adjustment serves to encourage contractors to propose suggestions of changed methods of performance when the result will be an increase in costs. However, cost-saving suggestions are not encouraged because their adoption would result in a price reduction for the costs saved plus overhead and profit on those costs. To encourage such suggestions, Value Engineering clauses are used in most contracts.

3. To furnish procurement authority to the contracting officer to order additional work within the "general scope" of the contract without using the procedures required for "new procurement" or utilizing new funds.

The purchase of work under an existing contract permits the government to avoid the additional time and expense associated with a new procurement. This is permitted as long as such work meets the test of being within the general scope of the contract. Thus, the Changes clause serves as the basis for the authority to make such sole source purchases. Since such changes are within the scope of the original work on the contract, they may also be funded with the same funds that were used on that contract, 23 Comp. Gen. 943 (1944).

4. To provide the legal means by which the contractor may process claims against the government.

Prior to the Contract Disputes Act of 1978, 41 U.S.C. § 601 et seq., the boards of contract appeals devised the doctrine of "constructive changes" in order to take jurisdiction of contractor claims for a variety of communications and actions of the government that had increased their costs of performance. While this jurisdictional basis is no longer necessary, the boards as well as the Court of Federal Claims have continued to place this class of claims under the Changes clause in order to determine the amount due the contractor in accordance with the rules governing the computation of equitable adjustments.

B. Coverage

The Changes clauses describe the limits on their use in two ways. First, changes are permitted only "within the general scope of the contract." Second, the clauses contain descriptive words setting forth the types of changes that may be made. For a change to be obligatory on the contractor, it must meet both tests, that is, it must be within the general scope and be one of the types of changes described by the clause.

This section addresses the coverage of the Changes clause in defining the limits of the power it grants the government. It should be noted that this issue is not vigorously contested by the contractor receiving the change order because, in most cases, the contractor is completely willing to perform changed work for the extra compensation provided by the clause. Hence, the litigated cases tend to derive from two sources: (1) those rare instances in which the contractor is displeased with the equitable adjustment it receives and therefore seeks to obtain a new trial by persuading a court to rule that the change was not under the clause, and (2) the more common situation in which a competitor of the contractor protests the issuance of a change order as depriving it of the opportunity to compete for the work.

1. Meaning of "Within the General Scope"

Most decisions defining the coverage of the Changes clause are resolved on the basis of the interpretation of the contract limitation that changes must be "within the general scope of the contract." This phrase is somewhat vague and has been subject to considerable judicial and administrative interpretation. Because of the slightly different focus of the analysis, the following discussion of these cases separates the cases dealing with disputes between the contractor and the government from those cases dealing with protests of competitors. In the former type of litigation, the Court of Claims coined the term "cardinal change" to describe those changes that are beyond the scope of the contract.

a. Disputes Between Contractor and Government

Whether changes are beyond the general scope of the contract is usually determined by comparing the total work performed by the contractor to the work called for by the original contract. The tests used in making this comparison are stated in different ways. One test focuses on changes in the nature of the work to be performed. The other focuses on the amount of effort the contractor is required to perform. The distinction between these tests, however, is not always clear. In *Air-A-Plane Corp. v. United States*, 187 Ct. Cl. 269, 408 F.2d 1030 (1969), the court held that a contractor that has failed in its attempts to obtain satisfactory equitable adjustments under the Change clause may pursue a claim for damages based on the fact that the changes were outside of the scope of the contract. In that case the government had issued approximately a thousand changes, which had led to disruption of the work and had added a significant development element to a manufacturing contract.

The time of issuance of change orders has not been considered a factor in determining whether they were beyond the general scope of the contract. For example, in *J.D. Hedin Constr. Co. v. United States*, 171 Ct. Cl. 70, 347 F.2d 235 (1965), the contracting officer issued six changes after completion of the work and granted a time extension of 102 days plus an equitable adjustment for the extra work. The court held that these changes were within the general scope.

(1) Nature of Work

In *Freund v. United States*, 260 U.S. 60 (1922), the Court stated that the work performed falls within the general scope if it "should be regarded as having been fairly and reasonably within the contemplation of the parties when the contract was entered into." The Court of Claims usually stated the test as being whether the work performed was "essentially the same work as the parties bargained for when the contract was awarded," *Aragona Constr. Co. v. United States*, 165 Ct. Cl. 382 (1964). In *Air-A-Plane Corp. v. United States*, 187 Ct. Cl. 269, 408 F.2d 1030 (1969), the court stated that a cardinal change occurs if the ordered deviations alter the nature of the thing to be constructed. In *Allied Materials & Equip. Co. v. United States*, 215 Ct. Cl. 406, 569 F.2d 562 (1978), the court stated that the test was whether the government made alterations so drastic that the contractor was required to perform duties materially different from those originally called for. See *Airprep Tech., Inc. v. United States*, 30 Fed. Cl. 488 (1994), in which the court found that the government's order to a contractor was a cardinal change. The contract was for design and installation of a "bag house" (a structure to hold filter bags intended to extract pollutants from an air stream). The court held that the government's order would have required a cylindrical structure of much thicker steel requiring fabrication at the site rather than the sheet metal box that would have met contract requirements. See also *Information Sys. & Networks Corp.*, ASBCA 46119, 02-2 BCA ¶ 31,952, in which the government's order to provide a worldwide telecommunications system was found to be a cardinal change because the original contract was for a system in the Washington, D.C. area, and *Hughes-Groesch Constr. Corp.*, VABCA 5448, 00-1 BCA ¶ 30,912, in which requiring a construction contractor to redesign a part of a building was found to be a cardinal change because such design work was not within the scope of a construction contract.

It appears that, if the function or nature of the work as changed is generally the same as the work originally called for, the changes will be held to fall within the general scope. For example, in *Aragona*, no changes beyond the scope were found where there were numerous changes in the materials used to build a hospital but the size and layout of the building remained the same. See also *Keco Indus., Inc. v. United States*, 176 Ct. Cl. 983, 364 F.2d 838 (1966), *cert. denied*, 386 U.S. 958 (1967) (change from gas to electric refrigeration units within the scope because the units were basically the same with the exception of the power system), and *Wunderlich Contracting Co. v. United States*, 173 Ct. Cl. 180, 351 F.2d 956 (1965) (extensive changes to the details of a hospital requiring over 50 percent additional performance time within the scope because the resulting hospital was not substantially different from that contracted for). The same result was reached in *Contact Int'l, Inc. v. Widnall*, 106 F.3d 426 (Fed. Cir. 1997), in which the court rejected the argument that protests regarding the award of a contract amounted to a cardinal change because, although they altered the time of performance, they did not affect the work that was performed. See also *PCL Constr. Servs., Inc. v. United States*, 47 Fed. Cl. 745 (2000), *aff'd*, 96 Fed. Appx. 672 (Fed. Cir. 2004), holding that analyzing numerous problems encountered during performance was within the general scope of the contract, and *Contel Advanced Sys., Inc.*, ASBCA 49072, 02-1 BCA ¶ 31,808, holding that construction of a building at a different site was not a cardinal change.

(2) Cost and Disruption

The other test for determining whether a change is outside the general scope deals with the degree of work disruption and cost increases experienced by the contractor. Contractors have rarely been successful on these grounds. However, there are a few cases holding that the work was so much greater that it amounted to a cardinal change. In *Peter Kiewit Sons' Co. v. Summit Constr. Co.*, 422 F.2d 242 (8th Cir. 1969), a change requiring the subcontractor to place backfill simultaneously with the work of other subcontractors was held to be so disruptive as to be a change beyond the scope because it added over 200 percent to the cost of the backfill work. In *Atlantic Dry Dock Corp. v. United States*, 773 F. Supp. 335 (M.D. Fla. 1991), the court decided to hold a trial on the cardinal change issue where there had been 130 changes, the time of performance had been doubled, and costs of $4.6 million had been incurred above the contract price of $5.8 million. Compare *Axel Elecs., Inc.*, ASBCA 18990, 74-1 BCA ¶ 10,471, in which the board found no changes beyond the scope in a situation where the contractor was claiming equitable adjustments of 170 percent of the contract price because of alleged over-interpretation of the specifications. See also *Akcon, Inc.*, ENGBCA 5593, 90-3 BCA ¶ 23,250, stating that changes would not be outside the scope unless they made the work "wholly different" from the originally contracted work. In *Rumsfeld v. Freedom N.Y., Inc.*, 329 F.3d 1320, *reh'g denied*, 346 F.3d 1359 (Fed. Cir. 2003), *cert. denied*, 541 U.S. 987 (2004), no cardinal change was found even though the government (1) improperly denied, suspended, and delayed making progress payments; (2) improperly interfered with the contractor's ability to obtain financing; (3) diverted government-furnished material, (4) delayed delivery of government-furnished material it was contractually obligated to deliver; (5) imposed improper inspections; and (6) imposed improper testing requirements.

Changes have also been found to be outside the general scope of the contract when they resulted from defective government specifications and had a significant impact on the performance of the work. For example, in *Edward R. Marden Corp. v. United States*, 194 Ct. Cl. 799, 442 F.2d 364 (1971), the airplane hangar under construction collapsed because of defective specifications. The accident exposed the contractor to a number of claims by workers and led to significant costs to rebuild the project. The court concluded that the additional effort expended by the contractor was outside the general scope. Similarly, in *Luria Bros. & Co. v. United States*, 177 Ct. Cl. 676, 369 F.2d 701 (1966), the court found a change requiring extensive redesign of the work to be beyond the scope because it resulted from defective specifications. However, most defective specification claims have been treated as changes within the scope of the contract, and it has been stated that the impact of the defects would have to be "profound" in order to justify ruling that the changes were outside the scope of the contract, *Cannon Structures, Inc.*, AGBCA 90-207-1, 93-3 BCA ¶ 26,059. Compare *Big Chief Drilling Co. v. United States*, 26 Cl. Ct. 1276 (1992), with *American Line Builders, Inc. v. United States*, 26 Cl. Ct. 1155 (1992).

In the former case, the court found changes resulting from defective specifications to be outside the scope of the contract, while in the latter case, a similar number of changes was found to be within the scope. In neither case did the defective specifications cause a severe impact on the contractor.

The number of changes issued has not been considered to be a major factor in evaluating whether changes are beyond the scope of the contract. In *Coley Props. Corp.*, PSBCA 291, 75-2 BCA ¶ 11,514, *recons. denied*, 76-1 BCA ¶ 11,701, *rev'd on other grounds*, 219 Ct. Cl. 227, 593 F.2d 380 (1979), the board found that approximately 100 change orders were not beyond the general scope. Other cases finding a large number of changes to be within the scope include *Action Support Servs. Corp.*, ASBCA 46524, 00-1 BCA ¶ 30,701 (797 specification revisions); *Combined Arms Training Sys., Inc.*, ASBCA 44822, 96-2 BCA ¶ 28,617 (277 engineering change proposals); *Reliance Ins. Co. v. United States*, 20 Cl. Ct. 715 (1990), *aff'd*, 931 F.2d 863 (Fed. Cir. 1991) (200 changes); *Magoba Constr. Co. v. United States*, 99 Ct. Cl. 662 (1943) (62 change orders); and *In re Boston Shipyard Corp.*, 886 F.2d 451 (1st Cir. 1989) (86 changes). It seems apparent that an excessive number of changes might so alter the work that it would be beyond the scope, but the closest that a court or board has come to such a determination is in *Air-A-Plane*, in which a case involving 1,000 changes was sent back for trial.

In looking at the issue of the work contemplated by both parties at the time the contract was signed, the court has reasoned that contractors taking contracts for technologically sophisticated products should expect more changes than those taking contracts for relatively simple products, *General Dynamics Corp. v. United States*, 218 Ct. Cl. 40, 585 F.2d 457 (1978). In that case, a major series of changes that increased the price of the shipbuilding contract by approximately 165 percent and extended the time of performance by three years was held to be within the general scope of the contract, since the court believed that the contractor should have anticipated such changes in a contract for nuclear submarines. In this regard, the rule is similar to that discussed below for third-party protests—the broader the language of the contract, the greater the scope of the contract for purposes of ordering changes.

b. *Third-Party Protests*

When competitors protest the government's issuance of changes in lieu of using new procurement procedures, the test is whether the proposed change is within the scope of the competition. This is slightly different from the test used when the contractor questions a change. See *AT&T Communications, Inc. v. WilTel, Inc.*, 1 F.3d 1201 (Fed. Cir. 1993), stating at 1205:

> This case does not ask whether Government modifications breached a contract, but asks instead whether Government modifications changed the contract enough to circumvent the statutory requirement of competition. The cardinal change doc-

> trine asks whether a modification exceeds the scope of the contract's changes clause; this case asks whether the modification is within the scope of the competition conducted to achieve the original contract. In application these questions overlap. . . . A modification generally falls within the scope of the original procurement if potential bidders would have expected it to fall within the contract's changes clause.

The court appears to be saying that the "scope of the competition" test is essentially the same as the "scope of the contract" test (used in the breach cases) but that the focus is different. In the breach litigation, the focus is on what the contractor should have anticipated to be within the scope of the contract. In the protest litigation, the focus is on what the competitors should have anticipated to be within the scope of the competition. This requires analysis of the entire solicitation to determine what contract alterations might be called for. Thus, the court stated at 1205:

> This analysis . . . focuses on the scope of the entire original procurement in comparison to the scope of the contract as modified. Thus a broad original competition may validate a broader range of later modifications without further bid procedures.

The GAO gave a more precise description of the analysis used in making this determination in *Neil R. Gross & Co.*, 69 Comp. Gen. 247 (B-237434), 90-1 CPD ¶ 212:

> In weighing [whether a modification is beyond the scope of the competition], we look to whether there is a material difference between the modified contract and the prime contract that was originally competed. . . . In determining the materiality of a modification, we consider factors such as the extent of any changes in the type of work, performance period and costs between the contract as awarded and as modified. . . . We also consider whether the solicitation for the original contract adequately advised offerors of the potential for the type of changes during the course of the contract that in fact occurred . . . or whether the modification is of a nature which potential offerors would reasonably have anticipated under the changes clause.

The General Services Board of Contract Appeals used this same analysis when it had protest jurisdiction, *MCI Telecommunications Corp. v. General Servs. Admin.*, GSBCA 11963-P, 93-1 BCA ¶ 25,541.

The primary focus appears to be on whether the change could have been anticipated by the offerors. In this regard, the language of the solicitation is of great importance. For example, substantial changes have been permitted in data processing and telecommunications equipment contracts where the solicitation provided that equipment upgrades were anticipated during performance, *AT&T Communications, Inc. v. WilTel, Inc.*, 1 F.3d 1201 (Fed. Cir. 1993); *MCI Telecommunications Corp.*, GSBCA 10450-P, 90-2 BCA ¶ 22,735; *Engineering & Prof'l Servs., Inc.*, Comp. Gen. Dec. B-289331, 2002 CPD ¶ 24; *Hewlett Packard Co.*, Comp. Gen.

Dec. B-245293, 91-2 CPD ¶ 576. See also *National Data Corp.*, Comp. Gen. Dec. B-207340, 82-2 CPD ¶ 222, where one of two corporations sharing a teleprocessing contract was dropped and its share of the work was added to the other's contract. The GAO found that the substantial increase to the remaining contract was not a change beyond the scope of the competition because the bidders had been warned that such changes might occur. Similarly, in *Phoenix Air Group, Inc. v. United States*, 46 Fed. Cl. 90 (2000), a modification ordering additional work was held to be within the scope because the statement of work was broadly worded; in *Paragon Sys., Inc.*, Comp. Gen. Dec. B-284694.2, 2000 CPD ¶ 114, a modification adding higher-level engineers to a task order contract was held to be within the scope because the work they were assigned was contemplated by the original contract; and in *Astronautics Corp. of Am.*, 70 Comp. Gen. 554 (B-242782), 91-1 CPD ¶ 531, a major task order was held to be within the scope of an indefinite-quantity contract that described the work in very general terms. In contrast, in *Avtron Mfg., Inc.*, 67 Comp. Gen. 404 (B-229972), 88-1 CPD ¶ 458, a change expressly disallowed in the original solicitation was found to be outside the scope, and in *Sprint Communications Co.*, Comp. Gen. Dec. B-278407.2, 98-1 CPD ¶ 60, added services were found to be outside the scope because the contract stated that such services were not included in the contract effort. See also *MCI Communications Corp.*, Comp. Gen. Dec. B-276659.2, 97-2 CPD ¶ 90, in which a service that was intrinsically different from that covered by the contract was held to be beyond its scope.

If the change alters the type of work called for by the contract, it is very likely to be held to be outside the scope of the competition. See *American Air Filter Co.*, 57 Comp. Gen. 567 (B-188408), 78-1 CPD ¶ 443, in which a change substituting diesel for gasoline engines in heating units was held to be a change beyond the scope of an advertised manufacturing contract because it required significant development work, doubled the performance time, and increased the price by 29 percent. The GAO stated that "any modification is in our view to be determined by examining whether the alteration is within the scope of the competition which was originally conducted," and that this standard is based on "what potential offerors would have reasonably expected." Similarly, in *Makro Janitorial Servs., Inc.*, Comp. Gen. Dec. B-282690, 99-2 CPD ¶ 39, a task order for housekeeping work was found to be outside the scope of a contract for equipment maintenance, and in *Stoehner Sec. Servs., Inc.*, Comp. Gen. Dec. B-248077.3, 92-2 CPD ¶ 285, a change adding work calling for higher-skilled personnel was found to be outside the scope. Compare *Everpure, Inc.*, Comp. Gen. Dec. B-226395.4, 90-2 CPD ¶ 275, in which the change of the technical approach in a research and development contract was found to be within the scope, and *CESC Plaza Ltd. P'ship v. United States*, 52 Fed. Cl. 91 (2002), in which changes to the terms of a lease were held to be within the scope. See also *Northrop Grumman Corp. v. United States*, 50 Fed. Cl. 443 (2001), holding that major changes in technology during performance of a development contract did not constitute changes outside the scope requiring a recompetition of the follow-on production of the system.

Changes reducing the quality of the work have also been held to be outside the scope of the competition when such changes are seen as potentially enlarging the field of competition. See, for example, *Poly-Pac. Techs., Inc.*, Comp. Gen. Dec. B-296029, 2005 CPD ¶ 288, holding that a change deleting the requirement for the most difficult element of the work was outside the scope. See also *Marvin J. Perry & Assocs.*, Comp. Gen. Dec. B-277684, 97-2 CPD ¶ 128 (change allowing use of more available wood in furniture contract outside the scope), and *Avtron Mfg., Inc.*, 67 Comp. Gen. 404 (B-229972), 88-1 CPD ¶ 458, *recons. denied*, 67 Comp. Gen. 614 (B-229972.2), 88-2 CPD ¶ 273 (relaxed specification permitting method of performance prohibited by original contract outside the scope).

Major changes in the quantity of the work have been held to be outside the scope of the competition. Hence, large reductions in quantity are outside the scope, *PAI Corp.*, Comp. Gen. Dec. B-244287.7, 91-2 CPD ¶ 508; *Source AV, Inc.*, Comp. Gen. Dec. B-241155, 91-1 CPD ¶ 75. Similarly, a change adding quantities above the contractual maximums was found to be outside the scope, *Liebert Corp.*, 70 Comp. Gen. 448 (B-232234.5), 91-1 CPD ¶ 413.

Changes granting additional time to perform the work are generally within the scope of the competition. See, for example, *Saratoga Indus., Inc.*, Comp. Gen. Dec. B-247141, 92-1 CPD ¶ 397 (additional time to correct errors in the design), and *Ion Track Instruments, Inc.*, Comp. Gen. Dec. B-238893, 90-2 CPD ¶ 31. See, however, *CPT Corp.*, Comp. Gen. Dec. B-211464, 84-1 CPD ¶ 606, in which a significant modification to a contract adding requirements and extending the performance time was held to be outside the scope of the competition.

The focus on the competitive process can lead to a different result than would a focus on the work alone. For example, in *Webcraft Packaging, Div. of Beatrice Foods Co.*, Comp. Gen. Dec. B-194087, 79-2 CPD ¶ 120, a minor change permitting the use of a slightly different grade of paper in a printing contract was ruled beyond the scope of the original competition because the new grade of paper was readily available on the market, whereas the prior specified grade was very difficult to obtain. The GAO found that many potential competitors who were not able to bid because of the specified paper would have been able to bid if the new grade of paper had been specified. Similarly, in *Dynamac Corp.*, Comp. Gen. Dec. B-252800, 93-2 CPD ¶ 37, a task order adding slightly different engineering services was held to be outside the scope of the competition because the offerors would not have contemplated such services. See also *CCL, Inc. v. United States*, 39 Fed. Cl. 780 (1997), in which a small amount of services at more locations and for additional agencies was held to be outside the scope, and *Techplan Corp.*, Comp. Gen. Dec. B-232187, 88-2 CPD ¶ 580, in which services for a different component of the agency were held to be outside the scope. In *Memorex Corp.*, 61 Comp. Gen. 42 (B-200722), 81-2 CPD ¶ 334, *recons. denied*, 82-1 CPD ¶ 349, a change beyond the scope was found where an option to purchase disk drives was converted into a five-year lease-to-ownership plan that added an obligation to ensure continuous satisfactory performance of the disks. Although the end product remained unchanged, the burden and risk of nonperformance shifted from the government to the contractor, thus changing the obligations for which it originally competed. In an unusual case, a major change in the work, conceded to be beyond the scope, was allowed since compliance with statutory program deadlines required restricted competition, *Die Mesh Corp.*, Comp. Gen. Dec. B-190421, 78-2 CPD ¶ 36.

Concern about the use of the Changes clause to circumvent the statutory requirements for competition has led to a rule that a contracting officer may not award a contract when it is clear that changes would have to be made in the specifications and such changes were contemplated at the time of award, *A & J Mfg. Co.*, 53 Comp. Gen. 838 (B-178163), 74-1 CPD ¶ 240; *Midland Maint., Inc.*, Comp. Gen. Dec. B-184247, 76-2 CPD ¶ 127. See *NV Servs.*, Comp. Gen. Dec. B-284119.2, 2000 CPD ¶ 64, stating:

> The appropriate standard in reviewing these pre-contract actions is not whether the subsequent modification is within the scope of the original contract but whether the changed work could significantly affect the competitive positions of offerors such that the RFP should have been amended. *United Tel. Co. of Northwest*, [B-246977, Apr. 20, 1992, 92-1 CPD ¶ 374] at 10. Here it should have been apparent . . . that increasing the scope of the contract work by approximately 6 percent could affect the offerors' respective proposals.

Compare *RS Info. Sys., Inc.*, Comp. Gen. Dec. B-287185.2, 2001 CPD ¶ 98, in which the GAO stated that this rule would not be applied unless the change materially altered the work.

The GAO has also ordered the termination of a contract where the government improperly added another year's work to the contract and then attempted to comply with the law by writing a sole source justification for a new procurement after a protest had been lodged, *Kent Watkins & Assocs.*, Inc., Comp. Gen. Dec. B-191078, 78-1 CPD ¶ 377.

2. Descriptive Words

The clauses contain somewhat different statements of the types of changes that can be made. The supply clause at FAR 52.243-1 permits changes "in any one or more of the following":

> (1) Drawings, designs, or specifications when the supplies to be furnished are to be specially manufactured for the Government in accordance with the drawings, designs, or specifications.
>
> (2) Method of shipping or packing.
>
> (3) Place of delivery.

When the contract is for services, the changes may be made "in any one or more of the following":

(1) Description of services to be performed.

(2) Time of performance (i.e., hours of the day, days of the week, etc.).

(3) Place of performance of the services.

The construction contract clause at FAR 52.243-4(a) permits changes in the work within the general scope of the contract, "including" changes:

(1) In the specifications (including drawings and designs);

(2) In the method or manner of performance of the work;

(3) In the government-furnished facilities, equipment, materials, services, or site; or

(4) Directing acceleration in the performance of the work.

In considering whether the government is entitled to make a change not specifically listed in these clauses, the language of the clauses should be considered. By the use of the term "including," the construction clause would permit the government to order unlisted changes if they are of the kind and character of those specified. By contrast, the supply and services contract clauses do not indicate that unlisted changes are authorized since they use the term "in any one or more of the following." The following discussion deals with litigation over the types of changes permitted by the clauses.

a. *The Contract Work*

Every Changes clause provides for changes in the work called for by the contract, since this is the area where the government is primarily interested in having the right to direct changes. Generally, this is accomplished by providing for changes to the drawings or specifications. The clear intent of this term is to allow changes in the technical details of the end product or services called for by the contract. An exception to this rule is contained in supply contracts, which preclude such changes when the supplies are not specially manufactured.

The terms "drawings" and "specifications" may be given a broader meaning than the actual contractual documents, if necessary, to permit the government to keep control of the contract work. For example, prior to the issuance of the FAR, the civilian agencies of the government were using the supply contract Changes clause for service contracts. Although the language was imprecise when applied to such contracts, the boards attempted to give it meaning when possible, *JCM Corp.*,

DOTCAB 70-6, 70-2 BCA ¶ 8586; *D&D Aero Spraying, Inc.*, AGBCA 259, 70-1 BCA ¶ 8356; *Basys, Inc.*, GSBCA TD-7, 73-1 BCA ¶ 9798, *rev'd in part*, 74-1 BCA ¶ 10,565. Thus, in *Basys* the board reasoned that the government, having included the clause in a service contract, intended it to have a meaningful effect. The board broadly construed the term "specifications" as used in the clause to encompass changes in the amount of work to be done where that was described in the contract. Such interpretation will no longer be necessary under the FAR changes clauses for service contracts that contain a more precise description of the types of changes that can be made. However, these cases illustrate the breadth of interpretation that can be anticipated in this area.

b. Terms and Conditions

A literal reading of the Changes clause would not permit the government to change the terms and conditions of the contract. See *BMY Div. of Harsco Corp.*, ASBCA 36926, 91-1 BCA ¶ 23,565, in which the board ruled that a change could not be made to a warranty included in one of the standard contract clauses. The board reasoned that the warranty was not part of the drawings and specifications. Similar reasoning was followed in *E.L. Hamm & Assocs., Inc.*, ASBCA 43972, 94-2 BCA ¶ 26,724, holding that the government could not change the lease of a building to ownership of the building, and *B.F. Carvin Constr. Co.*, VABCA 3224, 92-1 BCA ¶ 24,481, holding that the government could not use the Changes clause to alter the payment terms of the contract. See also *TEM Assocs., Inc.*, DOTCAB 2556, 93-2 BCA ¶ 25,759, holding that the Changes clause did not permit the reduction of funding on a terminated cost-reimbursement contract; and *Cessna Aircraft Co.*, ASBCA 37726, 95-1 BCA ¶27,373, holding that the Changes clause did not permit deletion of contract line items (with commensurate deobligation of funds) when the contractor had begun work on the items. Similarly, in *Welbilt Constr., Inc.*, GSBCA 2530, 68-1 BCA ¶ 7031, the board held that the government had no right to unilaterally change one of the clauses in Standard Form 23-A. However, using a liberal definition of drawings and specifications, some boards have allowed the terms and conditions to be subject to the Changes clause. For example, in *Space Age Eng'g Inc.*, ASBCA 16588, 72-2 BCA ¶ 9636, the board apparently considered a minimum wage determination in a service contract to be part of the specifications and found a change when the government insisted on a different wage. Similarly, in *CompuDyne Corp.*, ASBCA 14556, 72-1 BCA ¶ 9218, the board apparently considered a technical data clause to be part of the specifications in its ruling on whether the government had violated the Changes clause. In *Melrose Waterproofing Co.*, ASBCA 9058, 1964 BCA ¶ 4119, the board held that the government could change the special conditions of the contract under the Changes clause because such provisions were listed as part of the contract specifications. See Spector, *An Analysis of the Standard "Changes" Clause,* 25 Fed. B. J. 177, 188 (1965), 2 YPA 1273. It therefore appears that the government may be able to greatly broaden the coverage of the Changes clause by arbitrarily calling all contract documents "specifications."

c. Changes in Quantity

Increases in the quantity of the major items to be furnished are generally thought not to be authorized by the Changes clause. For example, on a construction project separate buildings may not be added, 15 Comp. Gen. 573 (A-66501) (1935); 30 Comp. Gen. 34 (B-95069) (1950). A similar rule is applied to the addition of materials on a unit-price contract, *P.L. Saddler v. United States*, 152 Ct. Cl. 557, 287 F.2d 411 (1961). In that case, a change order almost doubling the amount of material required for an embankment was found to be beyond the scope of a contract to build a levee. Similar reasoning was used to hold that a major increase in the quantity of flags ordered under a requirements contract was outside of the scope of the Changes clause, *Valley Forge Flag Co.*, VABCA 4667, 97-2 BCA ¶ 29,246. Increases in the quantity of subsidiary items are generally authorized by the clause unless a variation is so large that it alters the entire bargain. See, for example, *Symbolic Displays, Inc.*, Comp. Gen. Dec. B-182847, 75-1 CPD ¶ 278, in which the addition of a quantity of new lights was held to be within the general scope of a contract for the manufacture of aircraft.

Deletions of major items or portions of the work are not authorized by the Changes clause. Buildings may not be deleted from construction contracts, *General Contracting & Constr. Co. v. United States*, 84 Ct. Cl. 570 (1937); *Nolan Bros., Inc.*, ASBCA 4378, 58-2 BCA ¶ 1910. The same rule is appropriate for application to supply contracts. For example, where a contract for radios was modified so that a reduced number of components was required, the board treated the modification as a partial termination for convenience rather than a change. The board considered the components to be the major contract item since the contractor was originally to deliver components, not assembled radios, *Doughboy Indus., Inc.*, FAACAP 67-3, 66-2 BCA ¶ 5712. One court stated that deletion of a portion of the work can be accomplished by change order unless it becomes so large as to alter the original bargain, *J.W. Bateson Co. v. United States*, 308 F.2d 510 (5th Cir. 1962). The court in *Bateson* suggested that "thinking in terms of major and minor variations in the plans" would help in determining how large a variation in quantity is permitted under the Changes clause. However, significant decreases in quantities have been held to be outside the Changes clause in a contract for drilling services, *Manis Drilling*, IBCA 2658, 93-3 BCA ¶ 25,931 (major deletions to two line items); construction work, *Kahaluu Constr. Co.*, ASBCA 33248, 90-2 BCA ¶ 22,663 (deletion of approximately one-half of work); cleaning services, *Toke Cleaners*, IBCA 1008-10-73, 74-1 BCA ¶ 10,633; and use of a computer facility, *Burroughs Corp.*, GSBCA 5019, 79-2 BCA ¶ 14,083, *recons. denied*, 80-2 BCA ¶ 14,487. In *Capital Elec. Co.*, GSBCA 5300, 81-2 BCA ¶ 15,281, deletion of more than 73 percent of unit-priced electrical and telephone outlets was outside the scope of the Changes clause and treated as partial termination for convenience. See *P.J. Dick, Inc. v. General Servs. Admin*, GSBCA 12215, 95-1 BCA ¶ 27,574, *modified on recons.*, 96-1 BCA ¶ 26,017 (deletion of part of building renovation treated as a change); *John N. Brophy*

Co., GSBCA 5122, 78-2 BCA ¶ 13,506 (deletion of instructional services permitted under Changes clause); and *Bromley Contracting Co.*, HUDBCA 75-8, 77-1 BCA ¶ 12,232 (minor change in amount of work considered a constructive change). If the parties negotiate an equitable adjustment for deleted work (in lieu of termination for convenience compensation), they may be bound by their bargain even though a major portion of the work is deleted, *Robinson Contracting Co. v. United States*, 16 Cl. Ct. 676 (1989), *aff'd*, 895 F.2d 1420 (Fed. Cir. 1990).

d. Changes in Time of Performance

Changes in the scheduled completion date of the work were traditionally thought to be outside the Changes clause because they were not enumerated as permissible types of changes. However, the boards altered this view with regard to constructive accelerations of performance, originally reasoning that such orders were changes to the specifications because the contract schedule was part of the specifications, Spector, *An Analysis of the Standard "Changes" Clause,* 25 Fed. B. J. 177 (1965), 2 YPA 1273. The construction contract Changes clause now lists accelerations as one of the permissible types of changes. In contracts not containing such specific language, one board has held that accelerations may not be ordered, *Coastal States Petroleum Co.*, ASBCA 31059, 88-1 BCA ¶ 20,468.

When the government delays the contractor, boards and courts focus primarily on whether the work has been changed or whether there has merely been an increase in the contractor's costs. Thus, decelerations of the schedule or delays have been held to be outside the coverage of the clause, *Simmel–Industrie Meccaniche Societa per Azioni*, ASBCA 6141, 61-1 BCA ¶ 2917; *Broome Constr., Inc.*, AGBCA 232, 71-2 BCA ¶ 9100, *aff'd*, 203 Ct. Cl. 521, 492 F.2d 829 (1974); *Cosmos Eng'rs, Inc.*, IBCA 979-12-72, 73-1 BCA ¶ 9972; *Freedom N.Y., Inc.*, ASBCA 43965, 02-1 BCA ¶ 31,676, *rev'd on other grounds*, 329 F.3d 1320, *reh'g denied*, 346 F.3d 1359 (Fed. Cir. 2003), *cert. denied*, 541 U.S. 987 (2004). See *Gunther & Shirley Co.*, ENGBCA 3691, 78-2 BCA ¶ 13,454, in which extra costs incurred as a result of a constructive deceleration order were treated under both the Suspension of Work clause and the Changes clause depending on whether the costs were in the nature of delay costs or costs of extra and changed work. When the construction contract Changes clause was issued, it was stated that this was the legal principle incorporated in the clause, 32 Fed. Reg. 16269 (1967). The logic of this principle is that such delays are in the nature of suspensions of work, which are covered by separate contract clauses. However, some decisions have refused to follow this rule on the theory that delays resulting in a change of sequence of the work are changes in the method or manner of performance of the work, *Commercial Contractors, Inc.*, ASBCA 30675, 88-3 BCA ¶ 20,877 (direction to work one building at a time is a change in sequence); *Pan Arctic Corp.*, ASBCA 20133, 77-1 BCA ¶ 12,514 (delay in issuance of notice to proceed added costs by depriving contractor of opportunity to perform two contracts simultaneously as had been understood by the parties before award); *Fred A.*

Arnold, Inc., ASBCA 18915, 75-2 BCA ¶ 11,496 (government delay in furnishing information forced contractor to do part of work out of sequence). Since these cases involve delays to only part of the work, making it possible to argue a change in sequence of performance, it is arguable that there have been no departures from the rule that "pure delay"—delay to the entire job under contract—is not a change. However, this theory will not be followed if the government action is a "pure delay," *McGaughan Co.*, PSBCA 2074, 90-1 BCA ¶ 22,411. For another theory making a delay a change, see *Kenyon Magnetics, Inc.*, GSBCA 4769, 77-2 BCA ¶ 12,786, in which the board held that government delay in testing a sample product was a constructive change in the nature of a defective specification because the contract did not contain a clause informing the contractor of the test requirement. See also *QES, Inc.*, ASBCA 22178, 78-2 BCA ¶ 13,512, *recons. denied*, 79-1 BCA ¶ 13,592, in which the board held delay in specifying whether renovation of office space was included in an Architect-Engineer contract to be compensable under the Changes clause, since it was in the nature of a defective specification.

The GAO has held that extensions of time to permit the contractor to complete the work called for by the original contract are within the scope of the competition, *Saratoga Indus., Inc.*, Comp. Gen. Dec. B-247141, 92-1 CPD ¶ 397 (additional time needed to overcome defective specifications); *Ion Track Instruments, Inc.*, Comp. Gen. Dec. B-238893, 90-2 CPD ¶ 31 (extension of research and development contract to a period more than five years in length). This more liberal interpretation merely holds that a contractor is not gaining an advantage over competitors by being permitted to complete the work. There is no implication in these decisions that the contractor was granted an equitable adjustment for the time extension.

If specific language is included in the Changes clause permitting changes to the schedule, it will be held that the clause has been broadened to include this category of change, *Spencer-Safford Loadcraft, Inc.*, ASBCA 6592, 1962 BCA ¶ 3315; *Ardell Marine Corp.*, ASBCA 7682, 1963 BCA ¶ 3991.

e. Method or Manner of Performance

Changes in the method or manner of performance were considered to be permissible changes at an early date, *Farnsworth & Chambers Co.*, ASBCA 5408, 59-2 BCA ¶ 2329; *Carpenter Constr. Co.*, NASABCA 18, 1964 BCA ¶ 4452. The logic was that such changes were changes to the work itself because they deprived the contractor of the opportunity of performing the contract in a way not prohibited by the specifications. The construction contract clause now lists such changes as an enumerated type of permissible change, and the cases have included a wide variety of types of changes in this category, *Melrose Waterproofing Co.*, ASBCA 9058, 1964 BCA ¶ 4119 (change in location of field office); *John McShain, Inc.*, GSBCA 3541, 73-1 BCA ¶ 9981 (change in storage area for materials to be used on job); *Liles Constr. Co. v. United States*, 197 Ct. Cl. 164, 455 F.2d 527 (1972) (improper disapproval of use of subcontractor); *Nichols Dynamics, Inc.*, ASBCA 17949, 75-2 BCA ¶ 11,556 (excessive noise adjacent to construction site); *M & H Constr. Co.*, ASBCA 21528, 79-1 BCA ¶ 13,688 (government entitled to deductive change where same individual performed function of quality control representative and superintendent); *Atlantic Dry Dock Corp.*, ASBCA 42609, 98-2 BCA ¶ 30,025, *recons. denied*, 99-1 BCA ¶ 30,208 (change to approved schedule for performing work). It is not necessary that there be specific contract language specifying a method of performance in order to find such a change if, in fact, the contractor has been ordered to use a method other than one that could properly have been used, *H.E. Johnson Co.*, ASBCA 48248, 97-1 BCA ¶ 28,921 (change in sequence of work contractor had planned to use); *Eagle Contracting, Inc.*, AGBCA 88-225-1, 92-3 BCA ¶ 25,018 (refusal to stake entire project to permit work as planned by contractor); *Thomas Elec., Inc.*, ASBCA 30832, 89-1 BCA ¶ 21,516 (refusal to permit performance method desired by contractor). But see *Continental Serv. Co.*, DOTCAB 73-27, 74-1 BCA ¶ 10,538, *recons. denied*, 74-1 BCA ¶ 10,631, in which the board found no change in the method of performance when the contracting officer revised the position descriptions of the contractor's employees but did not alter the statement of work to be performed.

f. Government-Furnished Property

Under the construction contract Changes clause, the government may make changes in "the Government-furnished facilities, equipment, materials, services, or site." This broad language makes it clear that this class of changes is within the coverage of the clause. The Court of Claims has indicated, however, that the government's failure to provide government-furnished property (GFP) might still be outside the coverage of the clause if it was beyond the scope of the contract, *Allied Materials & Equip. Co. v. United States*, 215 Ct. Cl. 406, 569 F.2d 562 (1978).

Other Changes clauses, such as the supply and service contract clauses and the pre-1968 construction contract clause, do not refer to GFP, raising a question as to whether it is covered by the clause. A few cases have held that it is covered on the theory that defective GFP is the equivalent of a defective specification, *Forest Dev., Inc.*, AGBCA 77-144, 79-1 BCA ¶ 13,626 (claim denied for failure to prove defects); *General Instrument Corp.*, NASABCA 268-3, 70-2 BCA ¶ 8460; *Wayne Constr., Inc.*, AGBCA 242, 70-2 BCA ¶ 8443. The opposite result was reached in *Computer Real Time Sys., Computer Usage Dev. Corp.*, NASABCA 570-8, 72-1 BCA ¶ 9250. In *Wayne*, the board distinguished between defective GFP, which it held was under the Changes clause, and late-delivered GFP, which it held was a delay that could only be administratively adjusted under the Suspension of Work clause. See also *Koppers/Clough, A Joint Venture v. United States*, 201 Ct. Cl. 344 (1973), in which the court commented that, had there been no separate Government-furnished Property clause in the contract, furnishing GFP late might have been a change in the manner of performance.

g. Place of Delivery

In the supply contract Changes clause, changes are permitted in the place of delivery. It has been held that this language permits the government to change the f.o.b. point from destination to origin, with the result that the supplies are shipped on commercial bills of lading, *L.B. Foster Co.*, ASBCA 12425, 69-1 BCA ¶ 7549.

C. Contractor's Acceptance of Change

If a contractor accepts a change and performs the changed work without reservation, it cannot subsequently claim that the change was beyond the scope of the contract for the purpose of claiming breach of contract, *Silberblatt & Lasker, Inc. v. United States*, 101 Ct. Cl. 54 (1944). Similarly, in *Amertex Enters., Ltd. v. United States*, 41 CCF ¶ 77,047 (Fed. Cl. 1995), *aff'd*, 108 F.3d 1392 (Fed. Cir. 1997), *cert. denied*, 522 U.S. 1075 (1998), the court rejected the contractor's argument that a cardinal change had occurred because it had entered into bilateral contract modifications revising the contract price to reflect the impact of over 100 changes. See also *International Tel. & Tel. v. United States*, 197 Ct. Cl. 11, 453 F.2d 1283 (1972), in which the court found a change where the contractor agreed to perform work on a multiyear contract but reserved the right to argue that the required notice of additional work had not been timely. The appeals boards have followed the principle that acquiescence by the contractor deprives it of the right to argue later that the change was beyond the scope of the contract, *Ashton-Mardian Co.*, ASBCA 7912, 1963 BCA ¶ 3836, *reh'g denied*, 1963 BCA ¶ 3928; *Edward E. Harwell*, ASBCA 9624, 66-1 BCA ¶ 5329. It has also been held that this reasoning requires the government to compensate the contractor for work ordered under the Changes clause, even though such work is beyond the scope of the contract, *Texas Trunk Co.*, ASBCA 3681, 57-2 BCA ¶ 1528. The board in *Texas Trunk* found that the government is bound once the contractor waives its right to object to a cardinal change. Accord, *Mac-Well Co.*, ASBCA 23097, 79-2 BCA ¶ 13,895. In these latter cases, the board did not address the issue of whether the contracting officer had authority to order such work without following the procedures required for new procurements.

II. FORMAL CHANGE ORDERS

The idea underlying a change can originate with either the government or the contractor, depending on the circumstances involved. In either case, the changes procedure will generally call for an interchange of documentation. Only in rare cases will the government issue a change without first coordinating with the contractor to obtain at least preliminary information as to the technical aspects of the change and its impact on the price and schedule of the contract. In some cases, formal procedures are provided to facilitate contractor-proposed changes in the work.

A. Contractor-Originated Changes

Under all government contracts, the contractor is free to suggest changes. In fact, it is widely believed that contractors propose changes as a means of increasing profits on their contracts. Those contractors with design cognizance and sizeable engineering staffs are best able to take advantage of this situation. Since the government is interested in improving the quality and performance of the supplies and services that it buys, it often encourages such suggestions.

The Department of Defense used an Engineering Change Proposals clause for many years to permit the contractor to propose changes. This clause was found in DFARS 252.243-7000 and called for such proposals to be submitted with a proposed "not to exceed" price. It was removed from the DFARS on October 1, 2001, 66 Fed. Reg. 49865, and the following guidance was added to DFARS 243.204-71:

> Engineering changes can originate with either the contractor or the Government. In either case, the Government will need detailed information from the contractor for evaluation of the technical, cost, and schedule effects of implementing the change.

The National Aeronautics and Space Administration still uses a clause of this type. See NFS 1852.243-70:

> Engineering Change Proposals (OCT 2001)
>
> (a) Definitions.
>
> "ECP" means an Engineering Change Proposal (ECP) which is a proposed engineering change and the documentation by which the change is described, justified, and submitted to the procuring activity for approval or disapproval.
>
> (b) Either party to the contract may originate ECPs. Implementation of an approved ECP may occur by either a supplemental agreement or, if appropriate, as a written change order to the contract.
>
> (c) Any ECP submitted to the Contracting Officer shall include a "not-to-exceed"—[price or estimated cost] increase or decrease adjustment amount, if any, and the required [time of delivery or period of performance] adjustment, if any, acceptable to the originator of the ECP. If the change is originated within the Government, the Contracting Officer shall obtain a written agreement with the Contractor regarding the "not-to-exceed"—[price or estimated cost] and [delivery or period of performance] adjustments, if any, prior to issuing an order for implementation of the change.
>
> (d) After submission of a Contractor initiated ECP, the Contracting Officer may require the Contractor to submit the following information:
>
>> (1) Cost or pricing data in accordance with FAR 15.403-5 if the proposed change meets the criteria for its submission under FAR 15.403-4; or

(2) Information other than cost or pricing data adequate for Contracting Officer determination of price reasonableness or cost realism. The Contracting Officer reserves the right to request additional information if that provided by the Contractor is considered inadequate for that purpose. If the Contractor claims applicability of one of the exceptions to submission of cost or pricing data, it shall cite the exception and provide rationale for its applicability.

(e) If the ECP is initiated by NASA, the Contracting Officer shall specify the cost information requirements, if any.

Prior to October 2001 these clauses required the submission of information in accordance with MIL-STD-973, which provided an elaborate system of configuration management and change control for all contractors. Under that standard, the contractor was expected to "fully document" the impact of any proposed change to engineering specifications. This standard was canceled by 66 Fed. Reg. 49865, October 1, 2001. However, contractors should still accompany ECPs with a complete submission in order to provide the government with full information upon which to make a sound decision as to whether the change should be adopted.

Contractor-suggested changes may be phrased in terms of offers that can be immediately accepted by the government, but more often they are invitations for the government to issue a change order that will then be priced under the Changes clause. See, however, *Bruce-Andersen Co.*, ASBCA 28125, 83-2 BCA ¶ 16,892, in which the board held that the government had accepted a contractor's proposal for a change and further held that the parties had impliedly agreed that the change would be at no increase in price. See also *L.J.C. Mech. Contractors, Inc.*, VABCA 3507, 94-1 BCA ¶ 26,266, in which the government was found to have accepted a proposed change when it issued a change order containing the language "per your proposal," and *General Ry. Signal Co.*, ENGBCA 6168, 96-1 BCA ¶ 27,981, finding no acceptance of a proposed change because the offer had been withdrawn prior to the government's acceptance. In view of these cases, contractors proposing changes for additional work should make it clear whether they are making offers to which they can be bound and, if so, how long the offer will remain open.

Contractors should also make it clear when suggesting a change when an equitable adjustment is expected if the change is approved. This will preclude the possibility that the government will claim that the change was being made voluntarily. See *S-TRON*, ASBCA 45893, 96-2 BCA ¶ 28,319, holding that a change improving a product was found to be voluntarily performed even though the contracting officer approved the change; *Jack Swedberg*, PSBCA 3876, 96-2 BCA ¶ 28,337, holding that a change improving the services rendered was voluntary even though the agency knew of the change; and *Lane Constr. Corp.*, ENGBCA 5834, 94-1 BCA ¶ 26,358, finding a "tacit agreement" that a change would be at no increase in price. See also *Nagy Enters.*, ASBCA 48815, 98-1 BCA ¶ 29,695, finding voluntary additional work where a contractor made changes to the material in order to obtain better compaction without obtaining the approval of the agency.

When a contractor proposes a change, it has no right to have the change adopted, and it must proceed with the work while the government is considering the change, *Exide Corp.*, ASBCA 43624, 92-3 BCA ¶ 25,154. However, if the changes are proposed as a means of correcting defective specifications, the government has an obligation to consider them in a reasonable time. If it does not, the contractor may be entitled to an excusable delay, *Umpqua Marine Ways, Inc. v. United States*, Civ. No. 91-282-FR (D. Ore. 1992) (holding that such delay could be a material breach overcoming a default termination); *DCX, Inc.*, ASBCA 37669, 92-3 BCA ¶ 25,125 (overturning a default termination because of the government's failure to act on proposed changes to correct defective specifications); or to compensation for the delay, *Perma-Cal Corp.*, ASBCA 42155, 91-2 BCA ¶ 24,034, *recons. denied*, 91-3 BCA ¶ 24,294.

B. Government Originated Changes

A significant number of changes originate because of changed government requirements or the identification of a problem by agency personnel. Engineering Change Proposals clauses permit the government to originate such changes in contracts for development or production of products. The clauses require contractors to prepare ECPs when the agency identifies the need for a change. However, the clauses are silent on the means of compensation to the contractor for the work of preparing such ECPs.

Most construction agencies originate changes with their own forces or through independent design agents. In such cases, the agency usually desires a pricing proposal from the contractor before issuance of a change order. This practice is used, for instance, by the Army Corps of Engineers and the Veterans Administration. For example, the Veterans Administration has used the following supplemental clause in construction contracts:

> When requested by the Contracting Officer, the Contractor shall submit proposals for changes in work to the Resident Engineer. Proposals, to be submitted within 30 calendar days after receipt of request, shall be in legible form, original and five copies, with an itemized breakdown that will include material, quantities, and unit prices, labor costs (separated into trades), construction equipment, etc. (Labor costs are to be identified with specific material placed or operation performed.) The Contractor must obtain and furnish with his proposal an itemized breakdown, as described above, signed by each subcontractor participating in the change regardless of tier.

This clause also is silent on the issue of compensation for the cost of preparing the change proposal.

When the government requests the contractor to prepare change proposals but later decides not to order the change, the contractor will not normally be entitled to compensation for the preparation costs, *Greenhut Constr. Co.*, ASBCA 14354, 70-1 BCA ¶ 8209; *Energy Eng'g Corp.*, PSBCA 319, 77-1 BCA ¶ 12,422, *recons. denied*, 77-2 BCA ¶ 12,578; *Fireman's Fund Ins. Co.*, ASBCA 35284, 89-1 BCA ¶ 21,343; *B.F. Carvin Constr. Co. v. General Servs. Admin.*, GSBCA 12770, 95-1 BCA ¶ 27,445; *BMT Servs.*, IBCA 3794A-97, 98-2 BCA ¶ 29,893; *Program & Constr. Mgmt. Group, Inc. v. General Servs. Admin.*, GSBCA 14178, 00-1 BCA ¶ 30,641. In some cases the reasoning is that these costs are considered to be included in the contractor's overhead, *Blake Constr. Co.*, VABCA 1725, 83-1 BCA ¶ 16,431. The rule has also been explained by the theory that the legal relationship between the contracting officer and the contractor is the same whether the contracting officer requests a change proposal or an original bid, *George E. Jensen Contractor, Inc.*, GSBCA 3260, 71-1 BCA ¶ 8850. This rule appears to be the same regardless of whether the contractor is compelled to submit the estimate or has submitted it voluntarily, *Bridgewater Constr. Corp.*, VABCA 2936, 91-3 BCA ¶ 24,273, *recons. denied*, 92-1 BCA ¶ 24,446 (estimate submitted under Veterans Administration contract clause set forth above). See also *Delco Indus. Textile Corp.*, ASBCA 21379, 78-1 BCA ¶ 12,912, applying the same rule to the costs of preparing a value engineering proposal.

A request for the preparation of an ECP has been considered a compensable change order where significant technical effort is required to prepare the ECP, *Cocoa Elec. Co.*, ASBCA 33921, 91-1 BCA ¶ 23,442, *recons. denied*, 91-2 BCA ¶ 23,780; *Bechtel Nat'l, Inc.*, NASABCA 1186-7, 90-1 BCA ¶ 22,549; *Discon Corp.*, ASBCA 15981, 71-2 BCA ¶ 9069; *Harman–B.J. Gladd Constr. Co.*, VACAB 1093, 75-1 BCA ¶ 11,262; where the work is done to correct errors in government specifications, *Acme Missiles & Constr. Corp.*, ASBCA 11786, 69-2 BCA ¶ 8057; where the government retains and uses the information in the ECP, *Campos Constr. Co.*, VABCA 3019, 90-3 BCA ¶ 23,108; and where the contracting officer was found to have ordered the preparation of the ECP, *Century Eng'g Corp.*, ASBCA 2932, 57-2 BCA ¶ 1419, *recons. denied*, 58-1 BCA ¶ 1625; *Mac-Well Co.*, ASBCA 23097, 79-2 BCA ¶ 13,895. See also *Bechtel Nat'l, Inc.*, ASBCA 51589, 02-1 BCA ¶ 31,673, *aff'd*, 65 Fed. Appx. 277 (Fed. Cir. 2002), and *Raytheon Co.*, ASBCA 50166, 01-1 BCA ¶ 31,245, *aff'd in part and remanded on other grounds*, 305 F.3d 1354 (Fed. Cir. 2002), awarding the cost of preparing ECPs documenting defects in the technical data package when that work was called for by the contract. In *Fire Sec. Sys., Inc. v. General Servs. Admin.*, GSBCA 12120, 97-1 BCA ¶ 28,994, *recons. denied*, 97-2 BCA ¶ 29,186, the board awarded the contractor the cost of travel to prepare the proposal, because it was a "substantial cost beyond that which would normally be contemplated for a change order," but denied the balance of the costs of preparing the proposal. The same result was reached in *Fire Sec. Sys., Inc. v. General Servs. Admin.*, GSBCA 12267, 97-2 BCA ¶ 28,992.

C. Unilateral versus Bilateral Change Orders

Although the major Changes clauses only discuss the possibility of unilateral orders from the contracting officer changing the work, most agencies favor the ordering of changes in the form of a bilateral modification to the contract. Thus, the general government policy is not covered by the language of the Changes clauses other than the clause used for commercial items.

1. Policy

The general government policy is set forth in FAR 43.102(b) as follows:

> Contract modifications, including changes that could be issued unilaterally, shall be priced before their execution if this can be done without adversely affecting the interest of the Government. If a significant cost increase could result from a contract modification and time does not permit negotiation of a price, at least a maximum price shall be negotiated unless impractical.

This policy is based on experience demonstrating that contractors' original estimates of the cost of changes are frequently low, causing the equitable adjustment following a unilateral change order to be higher than anticipated by the contracting officer. When that occurs, the agency has not set aside sufficient funds to cover the changed work and may find it difficult to obtain the funds at the time the work is finally priced. This result is precluded if the parties are able to negotiate the price of a proposed change at the time it is being considered and then to issue the change as a bilateral modification to the contract. The contractor is also benefited by the issuance of fully priced changes through bilateral modifications because payments for the costs of the changed work can then be obtained as soon as permitted by the normal payment procedures in the contract.

There are two major impediments to the use of bilateral changes. First, the parties may not know the point at which the change will become effective. They may need to do additional work, such as design or prototype manufacture and testing, to determine the specific nature of the change, and the time required for this work may be of indeterminate length. Second, the parties may not agree on the price of the change. In many cases, there is very little time available for the government to issue the change, and hence little time to estimate its cost and negotiate its price. For example, on construction projects, the need for changes is frequently perceived shortly before the contractor arrives at the point in the work where the change is required.

As a general proposition, forward pricing of changes is to the advantage of both parties. However, there are definite risks for both parties when the bilateral change order is used. The contractor runs the risk that it has not fully evaluated the impact of the change and has not included a sufficient amount in its price. This can be an especially troublesome problem when there are numerous changes because the impact costs may accumulate as the work progresses, and such costs probably are not adequately covered in early estimates of the cost of proposed changes. To avoid this risk, the contractor may include a contingency in its estimate. Therein lies the risk for the government. If the contingency is too large or the feared events do not occur, the government will have paid too much.

2. Modifying Language in Unilateral Change Orders

FAR 43.102(b) directs contracting officers to "negotiate" a "maximum price" when a firm price cannot be negotiated for change orders that could have a significant cost impact. To fully implement this regulation, the contracting officer would have to obtain the contractor's agreement to limiting language by issuing such changes as bilateral modifications to the contract. However, some agencies have attempted to obtain such maximum prices by including them in unilateral change orders. This practice has raised the question of whether such maximums are binding on the contractor—since it has not agreed to the amount in writing.

Agencies have also varied in the form of modifying language used to obtain maximum prices. The most common language is the "not to exceed" language called for by the Engineering Change Proposals clauses discussed above. Other agencies use language establishing a "ceiling price"—frequently based on the contractor's proposal. Whenever such language is used, a contractor should assume that it will be bound by it if it signs the contract modification. See *Contel Advanced Sys., Inc.*, ASBCA 49072, 02-1 BCA ¶ 31,808, and *City of Oxnard*, ASBCA 30344, 87-2 BCA ¶ 19,901, *aff'd*, 851 F.2d 344 (Fed. Cir. 1988), in which contractors were held bound to the "not to exceed" language in an original contract. In one case, a contractor was held to be bound by a ceiling price in a bilateral modification even though it did not sign the modification, *Samuel S. Barnett Co.*, GSBCA 4855, 80-1 BCA ¶ 14,355. Compare *General Ry. Signal Co.*, ENGBCA 6168, 96-1 BCA ¶ 27,981, holding that the contractor was not bound by the "not to exceed" price because its subsequent proposals for a higher price indicated that it had not agreed to be bound by the unilateral change order. See also *Decker & Co., GmbH*, ASBCA 33285, 88-3 BCA ¶ 20,925, *revised*, 89-1 BCA ¶ 21,399, in which the board held that the contractor was not bound by a "ceiling price" because it had not signed the change order. The change order was somewhat ambiguous in that it stated that the contractor should not exceed the ceiling "without prior approval of the contracting officer."

If a contractor wants to question a maximum price in a contract modification, it should do so when the change order is issued, not when the equitable adjustment is being negotiated. If the contractor has any reason to believe that the maximum amount may be insufficient, the contracting officer should be informed immediately and told that the contractor is reserving its right to request a greater amount. See *Accurtron Tool & Instrument Co.*, NASABCA 684-7, 85-3 BCA ¶ 18,340, in which the contractor was not bound to the ceiling because it objected to it at the time it signed the modification; *Delco Elec. Corp. v. United States*, 12 Cl. Ct. 367 (1987), *aff'd*, 909 F.2d 1595 (Fed. Cir. 1990), in which the contractor was not bound to a "not to exceed" price because it promptly objected; *Hemphill Contracting, Inc.*, ENGBCA 5698, 91-2 BCA ¶ 23,761, in which the contractor was not bound by the modification because it refused to sign it and immediately reserved its right to additional compensation; and *Hardrives, Inc.*, IBCA 2319, 94-1 BCA ¶ 26,267, where the contractor immediately objected to the "not to exceed" language only to be faced with another modification containing a ceiling price and a statement that commencement of work would constitute agreement with the ceiling. In the latter case, the board commented that these procedures were "atypical and unacceptable."

The most troublesome technique used to modify the change order when agreement cannot be reached on the price is the issuance of a unilateral change order with the notation that the price of the change is "not to exceed" a stated dollar amount. While the contractor might obtain some protection from the fact that it did not sign the change order, there is still a risk that it will be bound to the ceiling price by proceeding with the work. Some contractors have dealt with this type of form by adding clarifying language reserving their rights and returning the form to the contracting officer. Such a statement might read:

> The contractor's signature signifies only that receipt of this change order is acknowledged—not that the contractor is bound by the ceiling price. The contractor will proceed with the work as changed with the understanding that an equitable adjustment will be negotiated pursuant to the Changes clause of the contract.

The contractor should be protected by such a reservation of rights. See *Utley-James, Inc.*, GSBCA 5370, 85-1 BCA ¶ 17,816, *aff'd*,14 Cl. Ct. 804 (1988), in which such a reservation was enforced even though the contracting officer crossed it out before signing the contract modification ordering the change.

After returning the change order with the reservation, the contractor should proceed with the work. See *Discount Co. v. United States*, 213 Ct. Cl. 567, 554 F.2d 435, *cert. denied*, 434 U.S. 938 (1977), in which a contractor was held to have been properly default terminated for failing to proceed with work called for under a unilateral change order that provided for no increase in price. The court rejected the contractor's contention that the order constituted only a proposal upon which the contractor was not bound to proceed. The court stated at 574:

> In the circumstances here, it is immaterial whether the designation of the new borrow place was merely a government proposal or a fully operative and effective change order. Plaintiff knew that the designation of the alternate borrow site came to it in June 1969 on a form labeled "Contract Change Order or Data Sheet Covering Amendments" as "Change Order Number 3"; it also knew that the new site was available, that the Government was willing to have it used and wanted it used if it became the only suitable borrow open to the contractor. Moreover, plaintiff was aware, or should have known, that it could have protected its right to

> an equitable adjustment by simply saying so—that it would comply with Change Order Number 3 but would still pursue its alleged right to an increase in the contract price.

See also *Swiss Prods., Inc.*, ASBCA 40031, 93-3 BCA ¶ 26,163, in which a contractor was held to have been properly default terminated when it did not proceed with changed work ordered with a limitation of funds that was considerably less than the contractor believed was due for the work. The board commented that the contractor was protected by being able to assert its rights to a larger equitable adjustment under the disputes procedure in the contract. Compare *Wilner v. United States*, 26 Cl. Ct. 260 (1992), *rev'd on other grounds*, 24 F.3d 1397 (Fed. Cir. 1994), in which the court found that the contractor had acted properly in refusing to proceed with a change order that stated: "[Y]ou are hereby authorized to proceed with the following proposed change order. Cost of the work shall not exceed $90,000." Although the court did not discuss its reasoning, it may have read the change order language as not requiring the contractor to implement the change.

Another situation that occurs with some frequency is one in which the contractor is willing to agree to the direct costs of a change but requires that any delay or impact costs be reserved for future negotiation. Such a provision will be enforced if it is clearly written, *Bechtel Nat'l, Inc.*, NASABCA 1186-7, 90-1 BCA ¶ 22,549, *recons. denied*, 90-3 BCA ¶ 23,105 (reservation of costs of "cumulative effect of changes"). A reservation of such costs has also been found where the contracting officer specifically deleted such proposed costs when issuing the changes, *Freeman-Darling, Inc.*, GSBCA 7112, 89-2 BCA ¶ 21,882.

The parties can also reserve other types of costs when negotiating an equitable adjustment. See *CTA, Inc.*, ASBCA 47062, 00-2 BCA ¶ 30,946, where the parties negotiated the cost of altering the quantities of a production option but reserved the impact of changing subcontractors for a portion of the work.

3. Clause Permitting Only Bilateral Change Orders

Clauses stating that changes can be implemented only by bilateral agreement have rarely been used in government contracts. However, as discussed above, ¶ (c), of the commercial items clause, Contract Terms and Conditions—Commercial Items, in FAR 52.212-4 contains such a provision. Under such a clause, the government does not have the power to issue unilateral change orders. However, the boards have taken jurisdiction of claims that the government changed the work by its actions in *SAWADI Corp.*, ASBCA 53073, 01-1 BCA ¶ 31,357, and *Bradford E. Englander, Liquidating Tr. for Dulles Networking Assocs., Inc.*, VABCA 6473, 01-2 BCA ¶ 31,466. Prior to the Contract Disputes Act of 1978, it had been held that the boards and courts could not find communications or actions of the government to be constructive change orders under a bilateral changes clause, *Len Co. & Assocs. v. United States*, 181 Ct. Cl. 29, 385 F.2d 438 (1967); *Boise Cascade Corp.*, AGBCA

76-166, 78-1 BCA ¶ 12,957. See also *Zip-O-Log Mills*, Comp. Gen. Dec. B-188304, 78-2 CPD ¶ 178, suggesting that the agency use a standard unilateral Changes clause in order to facilitate the agency's ability to settle claims during performance.

D. Procedure for Ordering Changes

There has been considerable controversy over two issues regarding the ordering of changes: (1) whether such orders are effective only if in writing, and (2) whether they are effective only if ordered on Standard Form 30.

1. Requirement for Written Change Order

All Changes clauses require that change orders be in writing. The clauses, however, do not prevent a contractor from getting an equitable adjustment when the contracting officer orally orders a change and promises an equitable adjustment as soon as a fair amount can be determined, *W.H. Armstrong & Co. v. United States*, 98 Ct. Cl. 519 (1943). The appeals boards generally follow *Armstrong* in situations where the only government defense is the lack of a written change order, *C.A. Logeman Co.*, ASBCA 5692, 61-2 BCA ¶ 3232; *A.L. Harding, Inc.*, DCAB PR-44, 65-2 BCA ¶ 5261, *recons. denied*, 66-1 BCA ¶ 5463; *Lincoln Constr. Co.*, IBCA 438-5-64, 65-2 BCA ¶ 5234, *recons. denied*, 66-1 BCA ¶ 5343. See also *Len Co. & Assocs. v. United States*, 181 Ct. Cl. 29, 385 F.2d 438 (1967), in which the court stated at 38:

> The court has considered it to "be idle for the contractor to demand a written order from the contracting officer for an extra when the contracting officer was insisting that the work required was not additional . . ." and, therefore, has often dispensed, on these occasions, with the formality of issuing a written change order under the standard clause. *Fleisher Eng'r & Constr. Co. v. United States*, 98 Ct. Cl. 139, 158 (1942); *Fox Valley Eng'r, Inc. v. United States*, 151 Ct. Cl. 228, 238 (1960).

The construction contract Changes clause in FAR 52.243-4 recognized this rule by providing that constructive changes may occur through oral orders. This had been the rule prior to the adoption of the clause, *Holt Hauling & Warehousing Sys., Inc.*, ASBCA 19136, 76-2 BCA ¶ 12,185. Note that this clause continues to require that ordered changes be in writing, *Oren Childers Paint Contracting Co.*, ASBCA 13987, 70-2 BCA ¶ 8388. In *R/W Contracting*, ASBCA 17239, 73-2 BCA ¶ 10,130, the board found that a direct oral order to accelerate was not binding on the government because the parties had contemplated a written order in their negotiations.

The Court of Claims also held that the lack of a written change order does not bar recovery when the contracting officer and the appeals board consider the contractor's claim on the merits, *Centre Mfg. Co. v. United States*, 183 Ct. Cl. 115, 392 F.2d 229 (1968); *Kings Elecs. Co. v. United States*, 169 Ct. Cl. 433, 341 F.2d 632 (1965). See also *Del-Rio Drilling Programs, Inc. v. United States*, 46 Fed. Cl. 683 (2000), rejecting a government defense that there was no written order when the contract required the agency to issue a written confirmation of oral orders.

Another line of cases cites the lack of a written change order as a reason for denying a claim for price adjustment, *General Bronze Corp. v. United States*, 168 Ct. Cl. 176, 338 F.2d 117 (1964); *Instruments for Indus., Inc.*, DCAB NBS-16, 69-2 BCA ¶ 8025, *recons. denied*, 70-1 BCA ¶ 8169. These cases deny recovery on several grounds, and it can be argued that the lack of a written order is not dispositive. For example, in *Comspace Corp.*, GSBCA 3550, 72-2 BCA ¶ 9674, the board noted that, where a contractor's failure to get written approval had proven fatal, "the Contractor performed without the express or implied approval of the Contracting Officer or his authorized representative." The board also noted that the requirement for a written order "is an attempt to insure that there is evidence . . . of the change," and that while a written order is the best evidence, it is "not the only" evidence of a change order. There is a Supreme Court case denying recovery because of a lack of a written change order, *Plumley v. United States*, 226 U.S. 545 (1913).

In contrast to the rule regarding change orders, *Mil-Spec Contractors v. United States*, 835 F.2d 865 (Fed. Cir. 1987), appears to require bilateral contract modifications to be in writing. In that case, the contractor had orally agreed with a government contract negotiator to a modification subject to the approval of the contracting officer. The contracting officer prepared the modification, signed it, and sent it to the contractor. After the contractor refused to sign the modification, the government argued that the parties had a binding agreement. The court rejected this argument, stating at 867-69:

> Unless and until there was a binding modification to which both Mil-Spec and the contracting officer had agreed in writing, there could not be a binding modification of the contract. The oral agreement [between the contractor and the negotiator] could not and did not constitute a valid accord and satisfaction. The contracting officer's subsequent approval of the oral agreement, reflected in his signature of the written contract modification form he prepared, did not *nunc pro tunc* turn the prior oral agreement into a valid contractual commitment that bound the government.
>
> * * *
>
> In *SCM Corp. v. United States*, 219 Ct. Cl. 459, 595 F.2d 595, 598 (1979), the Court of Claims held that where the pertinent regulations required that contract modifications be written, an oral modification that had not been reduced to writing and signed by both parties was ineffective. The situation in *SCM* was analogous to that in the present case. . . . The court stated:
>
>> Oral understandings which contemplate the finalization of the legal obligations in a written form are not contracts in themselves. When legal obligations between the parties will be deferred until the time when a written document is executed, there will not be a contract until that time. Under the regulations, Government funds were not obligated until the execution

> of standard form 30. The parties were well aware of the fact that only the written contract modification could finalize their agreement. . . . We thus conclude that neither party was bound by its negotiations until standard form 30 was executed.

These cases have been interpreted as establishing a strict rule that alleged oral agreements to modify the terms of a contract are not valid, *Marshall Assoc. Contractors, Inc. & Columbia Excavating, Inc. (J.V.),* IBCA 1901, 98-1 BCA ¶ 29,565 (alleged agreement converting default to convenience termination and settling claims); *Cooper Realty Co. v. United States*, 36 Fed. Cl. 284 (1996) (alleged agreement by contracting officer that government would vacate premises earlier than term of lease); *Merrimac Mgmt. Inst., Inc.*, ASBCA 45291, 94-3 BCA ¶ 27,251 (alleged agreement that task order would fulfill government's minimum quantity ordering requirement on indefinite-delivery, indefinite-quantity contract); *Centennial Leasing v. General Servs. Admin.*, GSBCA 11451, 93-1 BCA ¶ 25,350, *aff'd*, 11 F.3d 1072 (Fed. Cir. 1993) (alleged agreement to extend term of contract); *Daly Constr., Inc.*, ASBCA 34322, 92-1 BCA ¶ 24,469, *aff'd*, 5 F.3d 520 (Fed. Cir. 1993) (alleged settlement agreement); *Edwards v. United States*, 22 Cl. Ct. 411 (1991) (alleged agreement to modify terms of lease); *Woodington Corp.*, ASBCA 37885, 91-1 BCA ¶ 23,579 (alleged bilateral changes); *C.M.P. Corp.*, ASBCA 36664, 89-1 BCA ¶ 21,317 (alleged option exercise). This rule has also precluded the government from enforcing oral modifications, *Staff, Inc.*, AGBCA 96-112-1, 97-2 BCA ¶ 29,285; *Knights' Piping, Inc.*, ASBCA 46986, 95-2 BCA ¶ 27,700. However, in *J.S. Alberici Constr. Co. v. General Servs. Admin.*, GSBCA 12386, 94-2 BCA ¶ 26,776, the board found the government liable on an oral agreement that was followed by a written contract modification that had been signed by the contractor but not signed by the government. The board cited *Essex Electro Eng'rs, Inc.*, ASBCA 30118, 88-1 BCA ¶ 20,440, holding the government liable in similar circumstances because, after reaching complete agreement on the modification, both parties "viewed the formal writing as a mere formality and not as a contingency." See *Johnson Mgmt. Group CFC, Inc.*, HUDBCA 96-C-132-C15, 00-2 BCA ¶ 31,116, *aff'd*, 308 F.3d 1245 (Fed. Cir. 2002), refusing to follow this reasoning in a case where a contract modification was prepared by the contracting officer but not signed by the contractor. In affirming, the Federal Circuit did not apply the *Mil-Spec* rule strictly but held that the *Alberici* exception did not apply because "there was not a sufficient meeting of the minds on the terms of the agreement to definitize it orally." See also *TRW, Inc.*, ASBCA 51003, 00-2 BCA ¶ 30,992, stating that the *Mil-Spec* rule is that, "The absence of a formal settlement agreement suggests the absence of a binding agreement."

Oral agreements have been held binding when they are not "contract modifications." See *Texas Instruments, Inc. v. United States*, 922 F.2d 810 (Fed. Cir. 1990), enforcing an oral agreement establishing the prices of unpriced contract line items, and *Montgomery Ross Fisher, Inc. & H.A. Lewis, Inc., A Joint Venture*, VABCA 3696, 94-1 BCA ¶ 26,527, enforcing an oral agreement settling a dispute. In the latter case, the board relied on *United States v. Bissett-Berman*

Corp., 481 F.2d 764 (9th Cir. 1973). Similarly, in *Tiburzi v. Department of Justice*, 269 F.3d 1346 (Fed. Cir. 2001), the court cited *Sargent v. Department of Health & Human Servs.*, 229 F.3d 1088 (Fed. Cir. 2000), for the proposition that "it is well-established that an oral settlement agreement is binding on the parties, particularly when the terms are memorialized into the record." See also *Adams Constr. Co.*, VABCA 4669, 97-1 BCA ¶ 28,801, in which the board concluded there were sufficient indications in writing to enforce an oral agreement that a contract completion date would be extended.

2. Standard Form 30

FAR 43.301 requires Standard Form 30 to be used in issuing either unilateral or bilateral change orders. Prior to the issuance of the FAR, the Federal Procurement Regulations were silent on whether use of the form was mandatory, whereas DAR 16-203 and DAR 16-405.4 required its use. In *SCM Corp. v. United States*, 219 Ct. Cl. 459, 595 F.2d 595 (1979), the court held that the contractor was responsible for knowing this regulatory requirement, with the result that the government was not bound by an oral agreement on the amount the government would add to the contract for changed work. The court found that the parties intended their agreement to be finalized by means of a supplemental agreement using Standard Form 30. Subsequently, *Mil-Spec Contractors, Inc. v. United States*, 835 F.2d 865 (Fed. Cir. 1987), and *Texas Instruments, Inc. v. United States*, 922 F.2d 810 (Fed. Cir. 1990), contained language that could be interpreted to impose the same requirement with regard to bilateral modifications.

Several cases have found the parties bound by written bilateral modifications not using Standard Form 30 by following the theory that neither party should be able to avoid a written contractual agreement because of a mechanical defect in the form of the agreement. See *Robinson Contracting Co. v. United States*, 16 Cl. Ct. 676 (1989), *aff'd*, 895 F.2d 1420 (Fed. Cir. 1990), and *Folk Constr. Co.*, ENGBCA 5839, 93-3 BCA ¶ 26,094. On the other hand, the lack of a Standard Form 30 was one element in a decision precluding the effectiveness of a written modification that had been signed by a government employee who was not a contracting officer, *Solar Turbines, Inc. v. United States*, 23 Cl. Ct. 142 (1991).

A contractor's insistence on the use of Standard Form 30 was held to be an unacceptable reason for a compensable delay, *P&M Indus., Inc.*, ASBCA 36625, 90-2 BCA ¶ 22,839. In the decision, the board did not discuss the FAR 43.301 requirement that this form be used to issue contract modifications.

Standard Form 30 is used for a number of purposes not related to the issuance of changes. Hence, the form does not necessarily signify that a change is being made, *Southwest Marine, Inc.*, DOTCAB 1497, 93-3 BCA ¶ 26,170.

3. Obtaining Proposal for Downward Adjustment

When the contracting officer has issued a unilateral change order that reduces the amount of work to be done, the contractor has little incentive to submit a proposal for a downward equitable adjustment. If such a proposal is not forthcoming, it has been held proper for the contracting officer to issue a unilateral modification reducing the price, *Metric Constructors, Inc.*, ASBCA 49343, 97-2 BCA ¶ 29,076; *Bruce-Andersen Co.*, ASBCA 29412, 89-2 BCA ¶ 21,872; or issue a final decision under the Disputes clause reducing the price, *Dawson Constr. Co.*, VABCA 3558, 94-1 BCA ¶ 26,362. When the parties cannot agree on the price reduction, after the contractor has submitted a proposal, the contracting officer has little choice but to issue a contract modification establishing the amount of the reduction. See, for example, *Connor Bros. Constr. Co.*, VABCA 2519, 95-1 BCA ¶ 27,409, *aff'd*, 113 F.3d 1256 (Fed. Cir. 1997). See also *Cottman Mech. Contractors, Inc.*, ASBCA 48882, 00-1 BCA ¶ 30,777, in which the board affirmed the propriety of the issuance of a unilateral modification, without asking for a contractor proposal, decreasing the price in an amount determined by using the Means estimating guide, and *Litton Sys., Inc.*, ASBCA 36976, 93-2 BCA ¶ 25,705, in which the board approved the issuance of a unilateral modification to the contract after the contractor refused to agree to the conversion of a letter contract into a firm contract. In *Blount, Inc.*, VABCA 3236, 93-1 BCA ¶ 25,474, the board commented that this was not a desirable manner for determining a downward equitable adjustment, indicating that it would have preferred to base the adjustment on a proposal from the contractor. However, some contractors may refuse to submit such a proposal in order to place the burden of proof of the amount of the adjustment on the government. See *State Mech. Corp.*, VABCA 2797, 91-2 BCA ¶ 23,830.

III. VALUE ENGINEERING

Contractors often can perform work in ways that are less expensive than the methods called for in the contract documents. However, since normal contract changes that reduce the cost of performance also reduce the contractor's profit, there is little incentive to propose such changes, even though the government could benefit from them. Value engineering is the procurement technique developed to encourage submission of cost-reducing change proposals by promising the contractor a share of the savings and no reduction in profit.

Value engineering regulations have undergone frequent revision since their first adoption by the Department of Defense in the early 1960s. The DoD regulations and clauses were periodically revised from 1964 to 1979, and in 1977 uniform regulations and clauses were adopted by the Department of Defense and the General Services Administration for use by all federal agencies. In 1984 these regulations and clauses were consolidated in Part 48 of the FAR. In 1988, after considerable congressional criticism of agencies that were not using value engineering, OMB Circular A-131 was promulgated to ensure that agencies were making full use of these procedures. The circular was reissued on May 21, 1993, and currently requires that senior management of agencies endeavor to make greater use of value engineering techniques.

One result of the constant revision of the standard Value Engineering clauses is that legal interpretation of one clause may not apply to another. Thus, it is essential to identify precisely the language relevant to a dispute in this area. In the following discussion references are to the FAR, unless otherwise indicated.

A. Standard Clauses

There are three Value Engineering clauses, FAR 48.201. The first has various provisions for supply and service contracts. The basic clause of this type, Value Engineering, in FAR 52.248-1, encourages contractors to voluntarily develop, prepare, and submit Value Engineering Change Proposals (VECPs) in return for a relatively large share of the savings and recovery of development and implementation costs if the VECP is accepted. This "incentive" clause is used primarily in contracts where the contractor is working to detailed specifications and is likely to recognize cost-saving measures. Alternate I to this Value Engineering clause requires a specific value engineering program effort as a part of the contract work. Under this type of clause, the contractor's share of the savings is smaller since its value engineering activities are priced into the contract. This "program requirement" clause is used primarily in contracts where contract specifications are less detailed and the government anticipates that considerable cost savings will be possible during performance. Alternate II to this Value Engineering clause can be used when the incentive will be placed on some contract line items and the program requirements on others.

The second clause, Value Engineering—Architect Engineer, in FAR 52.248-2, is a program requirements clause calling for specific value engineering efforts during the design of a project and precluding any share of the savings of such efforts.

The third clause, Value Engineering—Construction, FAR 52.248-3, is an incentive clause giving the contractor a share of the savings for adopted VECPs.

1. Types of Savings

Government savings that can be generated by a VECP are identified by FAR 48.001 as either "acquisition savings" or "collateral savings." Acquisition savings are those generated by contractors, while collateral savings are those of the government.

a. Acquisition Savings

Acquisition savings are defined differently in the clause for supply and service contracts and the clause for construction contracts. In the supply and service contract clause, these savings result from the application of a VECP to "contracts awarded by the same contracting office or its successor for essentially the same unit." Thus, there are no acquisition savings when the idea in the VECP is used by the government on in-house manufacturing work, *M. Bianchi of Cal.*, ASBCA 37029, 97-1 BCA ¶ 28,767, *aff'd but vacated on other grounds*, 178 F.3d 1310 (Fed. Cir. 1998). Neither are there acquisition savings if the contract is awarded by a different military service, *Ordnance Devices, Inc.*, ASBCA 42709, 93-2 BCA ¶ 25,794. There, the board ruled that the term "or its successor" required that there be a reorganization or a change of cognizance for the item being procured. See *Ordnance Devices, Inc.*, ASBCA 42709, 96-2 BCA ¶ 28,437, finding that, under the applicable regulations, the contractor was entitled to the savings if the head of the contracting activity had extended the coverage to the other service, but that no such extension had occurred. Similarly, the term "essentially the same unit" has been interpreted narrowly. See *M. Bianchi of Cal.*, ASBCA 36518, 93-2 BCA ¶ 25,801, *aff'd*, 19 F.3d 40 (Fed. Cir. 1994), in which the board rejected the contractor's contention that its VECP for a better way of stitching the clothing called for by the contract had been used in a large number of contracts for other types of clothing. The same result was reached in *M. Bianchi of Cal.*, ASBCA 37395, 94-1 BCA ¶ 26,417, *aff'd*, 61 F.3d 920 (Fed. Cir. 1995), *cert. denied*, 516 U.S. 1094 (1996), and *M. Bianchi of Cal.*, ASBCA 37029, 93-1 BCA ¶ 25,309, *aff'd but vacated on other grounds*, 31 F.3d 1163 (Fed. Cir. 1994). See also *Cosmos Eng'rs, Inc.*, ASBCA 24270, 88-2 BCA ¶ 20,795, holding that an item that did not meet the similarity test for the recovery of the costs of reprocurement after default termination did not meet the "essentially the same unit" test. Similarly, in *Johnny F. Smith Truck & Dragline Serv., Inc.*, ENGBCA 6261, 98-2 BCA ¶ 30,006, *aff'd*, 232 F.3d 915 (Fed. Cir. 2000), the board determined that no collateral savings had been justified because other service contracts awarded by the same contracting office were not for "essentially the same work" as the service contract on which the VECP had been submitted.

In supply and service contracts, acquisition savings are calculated on the basis of the cost reduction in the "unit cost" on the contract. As a result, there are no acquisition savings on such contracts if the contractor's VECP increases the life of an item with the result that the government buys fewer items, *Hayes Targets, PEMCO Aeroplex, Inc.*, ASBCA 44137, 93-3 BCA ¶ 25,999.

In contrast, the construction contract clause calls for the sharing of any cost reductions on the contract created by VECPs. Thus, acquisition savings occurred on such contracts when the VECPs suggested reducing the number of motors used on a hangar door, *W.R. Johnson, Inc.*, ASBCA 40251, 91-3 BCA ¶ 24,172, and reusing materials on the contract, *King Constr. Co.*, ASBCA 38303, 94-1 BCA ¶ 26,434, *recons. denied*, 94-2 BCA ¶ 26,630. However, no savings were generated on a contract where the element of the project to which the VECP pertained was deleted from the project by the government, *Dunn Constr. Co.*, ASBCA 48145, 97-2 BCA ¶ 29,103, *recons. denied*, 98-1 BCA ¶ 28,485.

The three types of savings that comprise acquisition savings are instant contract savings, concurrent contract savings, and future contract savings. See FAR 48.104-1. When all three types of savings are included in a contract, the normal procedure is to calculate each type of savings separately and to pay the total savings on the instant contract, as discussed below. However, FAR 48.104-3 permits the contracting officer to bypass this detailed calculation and to negotiate a "no cost settlement" where the parties agree to adopt the VECP without amending the contract price. This technique is appropriate when the government's share of savings on the instant contract is roughly commensurate with the contractor's share of savings on concurrent and future contracts.

(1) Instant Contract Savings

Instant contract savings are the net reductions generated by the application of a VECP to the instant contract. These savings are calculated by determining the cost reduction resulting from the VECP under the instant contract and subtracting allowable contractor costs of development and implementation. Any government costs (excluding the costs of processing the VECP) are then deducted, and sharing is based on the net result. In supply and service contracts, this calculation may result in negative instant contract savings—in which case concurrent and future contract savings are offset before the contractor is entitled to any sharing. If the end result is negative contract savings, the contract price is increased by that amount. See *Rig Masters, Inc.*, ASBCA 52891, 03-1 BCA ¶ 32,294, *aff'd*, 96 Fed. Appx. 683 (Fed. Cir. 2004), denying a claim for all development costs because the clause only called for payment of negative savings, comprising development costs minus instant savings.

In supply and service contracts, the term "instant contract" is defined narrowly to exclude "increases in quantities after acceptance of the VECP that are due to contract modifications, exercise of options, or additional orders." In multiyear contracts, the term does not include any quantities "funded after VECP acceptance." These limitations are omitted from the construction contract clause.

Instant contract savings must be savings incurred by the contractor, *Vemo Co.*, ASBCA 31911, 88-3 BCA ¶ 20,977, *aff'd*, 878 F.2d 1446 (Fed. Cir. 1989). Hence, government savings cannot be classified as instant contract savings.

(2) Concurrent Contract Savings

Concurrent contract savings are the "net reductions in the prices of other contracts that are definitized and ongoing at the time the VECP is accepted," FAR 48.001. Generally, these are the savings on supply or service contracts with other contractors for the same or similar units. Concurrent contract savings are calculated and shared in the same manner as instant contract savings, except that government costs are deducted only to the extent that they have not been fully recouped in the calculation of other savings.

(3) Future Contract Savings

Future contract savings are the net unit cost reduction multiplied by the number of units scheduled for delivery under a future contract during the "sharing period." The normal sharing period begins with acceptance of the first unit incorporating the VECP and ends at a date determined by the contracting officer, FAR 48.001. This date can be from 36 to 60 months after acceptance of the first unit in the discretion of the contracting officer and can be different for each VECP, FAR 48.104-1. Under the pre-2000 clauses the sharing period ended "the later of (a) three years after the first unit affected by the VECP is accepted or (b) the last scheduled delivery date of an item affected by the VECP under the instant contract delivery schedule in effect at the time the VECP is accepted." Under that prior regulation, the sharing period could be extended on contracts for items requiring an extended period of production, such as ships, to include any item that was essentially the same as the one for which the VECP was accepted and was produced under a contract awarded during what would otherwise be a normal sharing period.

Future contract savings are shared in the same proportions as concurrent contract savings and can be calculated in two ways. One way is to estimate purchases of items affected by the VECP under future contracts during the sharing period, in which case the contractor's share is paid in a lump sum. The second way is to calculate the savings as future contracts are awarded during the sharing period and to make royalty payments under the instant contract. In deciding between these two methods, the contracting officer should consider the accuracy of the estimate of future purchases, the availability of funds for making lump sum payments, and the expense of modifying the instant contract each time a royalty payment is made, FAR 48.104-1(a) and (b). When the lump sum method is used, the Value Engineering clause states that the payment "shall not be subject to subsequent adjustment." However, an appeals board agreed to review whether the lump sum amount was too low because the contracting officer materially misrepresented the anticipated future purchases of the item, *Sayco, Ltd.*, ASBCA 36534, 89-1 BCA ¶ 21,319.

It has been held that acceptance of a VECP (entitling a contractor to future contract savings resulting from future utilization of the VECP) did not obligate the government to utilize the VECP in future acquisitions, *Turco Prods.*, ASBCA 20290, 75-2 BCA ¶ 11,442.

Future contract savings provisions have generated a number of unique controversies. In *Applied Cos.*, ASBCA 50593, 99-2 BCA ¶ 30,554, the board denied a motion for summary judgment by the government contending that a modification disclaiming any "future contract sharing provisions" was an agreement to forego all future contract savings. In *Northeastern Mfg. & Sales, Inc.*, ASBCA 38307, 90-1 BCA ¶ 22,562, the cost of transportation was included in future contract savings because the later contracts called for delivery f.o.b. destination. The board rejected the argument that this was improper because the instant contract called for delivery f.o.b. origin, with the result that in that contract the savings in transportation cost were collateral savings. In *East-West Research, Inc.*, ASBCA 32367, 86-3 BCA ¶ 19,219, the government was held bound to a contract modification making royalty payments for future contract savings even though the government subsequently determined that the savings were not the result of the VECP. In *Honeywell, Inc.*, ASBCA 25553, 83-1 BCA ¶ 16,180, where a VECP changed a gasket from lead to cork and rubber, a second VECP changing the cork and rubber to fiber earned the contractor royalties in addition to those for the first VECP, notwithstanding the government's argument that the first VECP was no longer being "used." The precedential value of *Honeywell* is uncertain since the second VECP included a reservation providing that savings generated from the first VECP would be unaffected by the second. In *Antaya Bros.*, ASBCA 19390, 75-2 BCA ¶ 11,403, a contractor was not entitled to future savings awards on items originally scheduled for delivery within its future savings period where actual delivery occurred after expiration of the savings period. This decision dealt with a special clause basing future savings on the time of actual delivery rather than on the time of scheduled delivery under the standard clauses. It is therefore of little effect with regard to the proper interpretation of the standard clause. Under the standard clause it has been held that a contractor is not entitled to calculate the beginning of the future savings period based on options exercised under the instant contract since such orders are not within the definition of "originally scheduled," *Fermont Div., Dynamics Corp. of Am.*, ASBCA 22250, 79-2 BCA ¶ 14,086. In another case involving a special clause, it was held that a defaulted contractor's savings period began from the last scheduled delivery by that contractor, rather than the last scheduled delivery of the successor contractor after the default, *Guenther Sys., Inc.*, ASBCA 20363, 77-1 BCA ¶ 12,501. In *Raytheon Co. v. United States*, 2 Cl. Ct. 763 (1983), *aff'd*, 730 F.2d 1470 (Fed. Cir. 1984), the court held that there was no abuse of discretion in not including a longer future savings period in the clause. The court also literally interpreted the pre-1974 clause, which used different times for calculating future savings from the current clause. In *RCS Enters. v. United States*, 57 Fed. Cl. 590 (2003), the court denied future savings because they were to be paid from contract options that were held to be invalid because they violated the Anti-Deficiency Act, 31 U.S.C. § 1341(a).

b. Collateral Savings

Collateral savings are the net reductions in collateral costs incurred by the government (costs of operation, maintenance, logistic support, and government-furnished property) resulting from a VECP. The contractor's share of collateral savings is "20 to 100 percent of the estimated savings to be realized during a typical year of use but must not exceed the greater of—(1) the contract's firm fixed-price, target price, target cost, or estimated cost, at the time the VECP is accepted; or (2) $100,000," FAR 48.104-3. If the head of the contracting activity finds that the cost of measuring and tracking collateral savings exceeds the savings themselves, the collateral savings provisions can be excluded from the contract, FAR 48.201(e). However, collateral savings cannot be excluded from an individual VECP if the clause is in the contract, *Overstreet Elec. Co.*, ASBCA 52401, 00-2 BCA ¶ 30,981. In contrast, when a sharing provision is properly excluded from the Value Engineering clause of a contract, no award for the excluded type of savings is due the contractor, *Pathman Constr. Co.*, ASBCA 22002, 78-2 BCA ¶ 13,318 (deletion of future contract savings and collateral savings provisions); *Al Johnson Constr. Co.*, ENGBCA 3279, 73-2 BCA ¶ 10,295 (deletion of collateral savings provision); Comp. Gen. Dec. B-167932, Jan. 15, 1970, *Unpub.* (deletion of future contracts savings provision).

The limitation on collateral savings to the amount of the contract price "at the time the VECP is accepted" is interpreted to be the price *before* the contract is amended to reflect the impact of the VECP, *Sayco, Ltd.*, ASBCA 39366, 94-3 BCA ¶ 27,284, *aff'd*, 86 F.3d 1173 (Fed. Cir.), *cert. denied*, 519 U.S. 865 (1996).

Paragraph (j) of the Value Engineering clause in FAR 52.248-1 states that the amount of collateral savings generated by a VECP is determined solely by the contracting officer. However, if the contracting officer has incorrectly calculated the contractor's share of those savings, an appeal may be taken, *Banner Fabricators, Inc.*, ASBCA 25088, 81-2 BCA ¶ 15,215.

Collateral savings can be related to the work on the contract even though they are not part of the work directly. See, for example, *ICSD Corp.*, ASBCA 28028, 90-3 BCA ¶ 23,027, *aff'd*, 934 F.2d 313 (Fed. Cir. 1991), where collateral savings were found in a VECP suggesting a different type of battery for the equipment called for by the contract even though the contractor was not furnishing it.

2. Uses of the Value Engineering Clause

FAR 48.201 requires the use of Value Engineering clauses in all contracts of $100,000 or more except contracts for (1) research and development, (2) engineering services by nonprofit or not-for-profit organizations, (3) personal services, (4) product improvement, or (5) commercial products.

If a Value Engineering clause is erroneously included in a contract where it is prohibited, it will have no effect. See, for example, *Charles Beseler Co.*, ASBCA 22669, 78-2 BCA ¶ 13,483, where a military contract for commercial items included a Value Engineering clause without the necessary invocation of special military requirements and specifications required by DAR 1-1702.1(b) (July 1976). The board reasoned, following the *Christian* doctrine (*G.L. Christian & Assocs. v.*

United States, 160 Ct. Cl. 1, 312 F.2d 418, *reh'g denied*, 160 Ct. Cl. 58, 320 F.2d 345, *cert. denied*, 375 U.S. 954 (1963)), that the regulations precluding the use of such clauses on contracts for commercial items were binding on the parties.

a. Supply and Service Contracts

The Value Engineering clause used for supply and service contracts, FAR 52.248-1, may be written as an incentive or program requirement clause, or both. This is the only clause that provides for all four types of savings. The shares for instant, concurrent, and future savings are set at the rates called for by the following table in FAR 48.104-2(a)(1):

Government/Contractor Shares of Net Acquisition Savings

(Figures in percent)

	Incentive (voluntary)		Program requirement (mandatory)	
Contract Type	**Instant contract rate**	**Concurrent and future contract rate**	**Instant contract rate**	**Concurrent and future contract rate**
Fixed-price (other than incentive)	50/50*	50/50*	75/25	75/25
Incentive (fixed-price or cost)	**	50/50*	**	75/25
Cost-reimbursement (other than incentive)	75/25***	75/25***	85/15	85/15

* The contracting officer may increase the contractor's sharing rate to as high as 75 percent for each VECP. (See 48.102(g)(1) through (7).)

** Same sharing arrangement as the contract's profit or fee adjustment formula.

*** The contracting officer may increase the contractor's sharing rate to as high as 50 percent for each VECP. (See 48.102(g)(1) through (7).)

b. Construction Contracts

The Value Engineering clause used for construction contracts, FAR 52.248-3, is the incentive-type clause, but it cannot be used on incentive-type construction contracts. It provides for sharing instant savings, with the contractor getting 55 percent on fixed-price contracts and 25 percent on cost-reimbursement contracts. It also provides for collateral contract savings. The previous construction clause, DAR 7-602.50, did not allow sharing of collateral savings.

c. *Architect/Engineer Contracts*

The Value Engineering clause used for architect/engineer contracts, FAR 52.248-2, is used at the discretion of the agency. See FAR 48.201(f), stating that the clause will be used whenever such a contract "pays for a specific value engineering effort." The clause does not allow sharing of savings but compensates the contractor for its value engineering effort as a separately priced line item in the contract schedule. FAR 48.201(f) prohibits the use of the Value Engineering clause for supply and service contracts in architect/engineer contracts.

B. Interpretation

The length and complexity of the Value Engineering clauses has led to a large number of disputes regarding their application to specific situations encountered in processing and adopting VECPs. The major areas in which disputes have arisen are addressed below.

1. Liberal versus Literal Interpretation

In the early cases, the Court of Claims and the appeals boards frequently enunciated the policy that the provisions of the Value Engineering Incentive clause should be liberally interpreted in the contractor's favor, *Airmotive Eng'g Corp. v. United States*, 210 Ct. Cl. 7, 535 F.2d 8 (1976); *Dravo Corp. v. United States*, 202 Ct. Cl. 500, 480 F.2d 1331 (1973); *Mishara Constr. Co.*, ASBCA 17957, 75-1 BCA ¶ 11,206, *aff'd*, 230 Ct. Cl. 1008 (1982). In *Airmotive Eng'g Corp.*, ASBCA 17139, 74-1 BCA ¶ 10,517, *recons. denied*, 74-2 BCA ¶ 10,696, the board explained that, if the clause was not interpreted liberally, contractors would lose the incentive to propose money-saving devices and procedures. One board determined, however, that the normal rules of contract interpretation govern in construing value engineering clauses, *Umpqua River Navigation Co.*, ENGBCA 3881, 78-1 BCA ¶ 13,051. In addition, in *Raytheon Co.*, ASBCA 22711, 82-1 BCA ¶ 15,663, *aff'd*, 2 Cl. Ct. 763 (1983), *aff'd*, 730 F.2d 1470 (Fed. Cir. 1984), the board pointed out that a liberal interpretation still must be reasonable. The board denied Raytheon's claim for an extended royalty period, finding unreasonable the argument that acceptance of a VECP is not complete until the equitable adjustment is made.

More recent cases appear to apply a more literal interpretation to the Value Engineering clauses. See, for example, *Hayes Targets, PEMCO Aeroplex, Inc.*, ASBCA 44137, 93-3 BCA ¶ 25,999, holding that the clause did not apply to a change reducing the number of units because it did not reduce the unit price of the item being acquired on a supply contract; *M. Bianchi of Cal.*, ASBCA 37029, 93-1 BCA ¶ 25,309, *aff'd but vacated on other grounds*, 31 F.3d 1163 (Fed. Cir. 1994), holding that no collateral or future contract savings were earned when a packaging technique in a VECP was used for articles other than those bought on the instant contract; and

M. Bianchi of Cal., ASBCA 37395, 94-1 BCA ¶ 26,417, *aff'd*, 61 F.3d 920 (Fed. Cir. 1995), *cert. denied*, 516 U.S. 1094 (1996), holding that no future savings were earned when a sewing process in a VECP was used on articles other than those bought under the instant contract.

The liberal interpretation of the Value Engineering clause is illustrated by the decision in *Norair Eng'g Corp.*, ENGBCA 3730, 78-1 BCA ¶ 13,190. There, the contractor orally suggested that the government eliminate a part of a pending change order covering additional work that had been designed by the contractor. Although the change calling for the additional work was never formally issued, the board found that the contractor had been told to proceed with the work and, therefore, the later direction not to perform the work was an adoption of the VECP. Similarly, a contractor was found entitled to savings resulting from a VECP that was submitted to reduce the cost of a change order that has not yet been finalized, *Sentara Health Sys.*, ASBCA 51540, 00-2 BCA ¶ 31,122, *recons. denied*, 01-1 BCA ¶ 31,198. The board reasoned that the proposed change was an "implied contractual requirement." See also *McDonnell Douglas Corp.*, ASBCA No. 14314, 71-1 BCA ¶ 8859, finding a valid VECP to reduce the price of a change that had not yet been issued. Similarly, in *Morse Diesel Int'l., Inc. v. General Servs. Admin.*, GSBCA 13419, 97-1 BCA ¶ 28,634, the value engineering clause was applied when the contractor suggested a more efficient way of dealing with hazardous material after the government had selected the technique to be used when the material was discovered. Compare *J.S. Alberici Constr. Co. & Martin K. Eby Constr. Co. (A Joint Venture)*, ENGBCA 6178, 98-2 BCA ¶ 29,875, finding that no VECP had been submitted when the contractor suggested a different method but did not follow any of the procedures required for the submission of a VECP. Similarly, in *C.A. Rasmussen, Inc. v. United States*, 52 Fed. Cl. 345 (2002), the court held that no VECP had been submitted when the government adopted a contractor's oral cost-saving suggestion because the informational requirements in the clause had not been completely followed.

2. Applicability of the Value Engineering Clause

The Value Engineering clause generally applies to any contractor suggestion that reduces the cost of work called for by the contract. But the contractor is not entitled to compensation for VECPs affecting work outside the contract scope. See *John J. Kirlin, Inc. v. United States*, 11 Cl. Ct. 199 (1986), *aff'd on other grounds*, 827 F.2d 1538 (Fed. Cir. 1987), rejecting a contractor's claim on a VECP that affected adjacent work on a construction project; *Commonwealth Elec. Co.*, EBCA 108-12-79, 84-1 BCA ¶ 16,961, holding that a VECP correcting government information was not compensable because it did not affect contract work; and *Electra-Mech. of Am.*, GSBCA 6201, 83-2 BCA ¶ 16,806, holding that a VECP suggesting the use of different categories of government workers using the equipment was not within the scope of the contract. See also *Robin Indus., Inc. v. United States*, 29 Fed. Cl. 122 (1993), holding that a request for a deviation from the specifications was not a proper VECP because it did not result in the costs of performance being less than the contract price.

Other cases are more liberal in ruling that VECPs affect work within the scope of the contract. Thus, in *ICSD Corp.*, ASBCA 28028, 90-3 BCA ¶ 23,027, *aff'd*, 934 F.2d 313 (Fed. Cir. 1991), the board found that a VECP suggesting the use of a different type of battery to power the equipment being manufactured under the contract was within the scope of the contract even though the contractor was not responsible for furnishing the battery. Similarly, in *McDonnell Douglas Corp.*, ASBCA 14314, 71-1 BCA ¶ 8859, the board ruled that a VECP reducing the cost of maintenance work on a part of a building not covered by the maintenance contract was within the scope. The board reasoned that the maintenance could have been added to the contract by change order and hence was subject to the Value Engineering clause. See also *Sentara Health Sys.*, ASBCA 51540, 00-2 BCA ¶ 31,122, *recons. denied*, 01-1 BCA ¶ 28,767, finding valid a VECP that affected work that was not required by the contract but was later added to the contract by change order.

VECPs need not be related to major aspects of the work. They can be changes to minor contract items and corrections of errors in specifications. See *Cardan Co.*, ASBCA 25765, 82-1 BCA ¶ 15,628, where, under a contract for the construction of a rocket motor facility, the contractor corrected an error in the specified quantity of grass seed required for the grounds. The board stated at 77,199:

> While it may be true that it was contemplated by the Government that the greatest savings would result from proposals relating to complicated engineering problems, we know of nothing . . . which states that proposals must relate to such problems. As a matter of fact, the imposition of such a requirement would run counter to the entire value engineering incentive program.
>
> * * *
>
> [It] doesn't make any difference how the contractor discovers the problem. The entire concept is to save the Government money in its procurement activities. If a contractor through a "routine estimating exercise" achieves that goal it should not be denied participation in the savings just because it did not engage in some difficult engineering analysis.
>
> Likewise, we do not see any prohibition against paying a contractor if its suggestion results in the correction of an error as opposed to suggesting a new engineering concept.

3. *Origination of the Proposed Change*

To obtain compensation for a VECP, the contractor must demonstrate that it originated the change. This is so even though the current Value Engineering clauses merely require that contractors "develop, prepare, and submit" a VECP. Thus, if the government can demonstrate that its employees actually originated the change before receipt of the VECP, the contractor will obtain no compensation. See *Metric Constructors, Inc.*, NASABCA 76-0692, 93-2 BCA ¶ 25,780, *aff'd*, 14 F.3d 613 (Fed. Cir. 1993), where the government was processing the change internally at the time the VECP was submitted, and *Tennier Indus., Inc.*, ASBCA 29464, 86-3 BCA ¶ 19,046, where the government proved that its laboratory had completed work on the change before receipt of the VECP. In *Traylor Bros., Inc.*, ENGBCA 5305, 89-2 BCA ¶ 21,679, the contractor discussed a prospective change with the government but was told not to submit a VECP because the change was being processed. The board held that the contractor did not originate the idea because it was being processed within the agency. See also *Holloway Constr. Co.*, ENGBCA 3859, 79-1 BCA ¶ 13,551, where the government conceived an additional cost-savings measure based on a contractor's VECP. The contracting officer adopted the contractor's suggestion, giving the contractor a 50 percent share of the savings, and subsequently issued a separate change order covering the additional savings. The board ruled that the government was entitled to all of the savings on the second change because it was not a part of the contractor's original VECP.

The clauses require VECPs to contain detailed information on the saving technique proposed and the impact of its use. The lack of such information in a suggested method to improve performance has been held to indicate that no VECP was proposed, *C.A. Rasmussen, Inc. v. United States*, 52 Fed. Cl. 345 (2002); *J.S. Alberici Constr. Co. & Martin K. Eby Constr. Co. (A Joint Venture)*, ENGBCA 6178, 98-2 BCA ¶ 29,875.

Earlier clauses applied only to proposals "initiated and developed" by the contractor, yet the government's arguments that proposals were not "initiated" were almost uniformly rejected by the Court of Claims and the appeals boards, *B.F. Goodrich Co. v. United States*, 185 Ct. Cl. 14, 398 F.2d 843 (1968); *Airmotive Eng'g Corp.*, ASBCA 17139, 74-1 BCA ¶ 10,517, *recons. denied*, 74-2 BCA ¶ 10,696; *Xerox Corp.*, ASBCA 16374, 73-1 BCA ¶ 9784, *recons. denied*, 73-1 BCA ¶ 9881; *North Am. Rockwell Corp.*, ASBCA 14485, 71-1 BCA ¶ 8773; *Covington Indus., Inc.*, ASBCA 12426, 68-2 BCA ¶ 7286. In *Syro Steel Co.*, ASBCA 12530, 69-2 BCA ¶ 8046, the board explained that it "would serve neither justice nor the policy intended by the clause" to allow the Government to "escape sharing the resultant savings on the basis that it thought of the idea first, although not enough to use it until induced to do so by contractor action."

4. Origination by Two Contractors

Although the Value Engineering clauses used for supply and service contracts require that a contractor be given the specified share of savings on concurrent and future contracts with other contractors, the Federal Circuit has ruled that such savings must be shared when the VECP is submitted by two contractors working on concurrent contracts for the same item, *NI Indus., Inc. v. United States*, 841 F.2d 1104 (Fed. Cir. 1988). In subsequent litigation on the case, the Armed Services Board refused to give instructions on the precise method of sharing that should be used, *Chamberlain Mfg. Corp.*, ASBCA 33203, 88-2 BCA ¶ 20,724. However, in a later case, *Gulf Apparel Corp.*, ASBCA 27784, 89-2 BCA ¶ 21,735, the board held that the contractor that submitted the first VECP should be given "priority." Then in *ICSD Corp.*, ASBCA 28028, 90-3 BCA ¶ 23,027, *aff'd*, 934 F.2d 313 (Fed. Cir. 1991), the board agreed with the contracting officer's decision to give the first submitter 75 percent of the savings and the second submitter 25 percent on the grounds that one part of the second submitter's VECP was superior to that of the first proposer. These cases do not contain clear guidance on how the government should deal with VECPs that are submitted by two parallel contractors, but they do indicate that the government should not comply with the literal provisions of the clause in these circumstances. Compare *M. Bianchi of Cal.*, ASBCA 37029, 96-2 BCA ¶ 28,410, *recons. denied*, 97-1 BCA ¶ 28,767, and 01-1 BCA ¶ 31,237, *aff'd*, 26 Fed. Appx. 978 (Fed. Cir. 2002), in which the board awarded the contractor a 50 percent share of savings after another contractor had been awarded a 50 percent share on the same VECP.

5. *Finality of Contracting Officer Decisions*

The current Value Engineering clauses, which became effective on February 25, 2000 (see Federal Acquisition Circular 97-15, 64 Fed. Reg. 72414) provide that the decision to accept or reject a VECP "is a unilateral decision made solely at the discretion of the Contracting Officer." The prior clauses provided that "the Contracting Officer's decision to accept or reject all or part of any VECP and the decision as to which of the sharing rates applies shall be final and not subject to the Disputes clause or otherwise subject to litigation under the Contract Disputes Act." This language was given binding effect in *NI Indus., Inc. v. United States*, 841 F.2d 1104 (Fed. Cir. 1988), but similar language in an Award Fee clause was held to be void to divest the courts of jurisdiction because of the broad language in the Contract Disputes Act, *Burnside-Ott Aviation Training Ctr. v. Dalton*, 107 F.3d 854 (Fed. Cir. 1997). In *RCS Enters., Inc. v. United States*, 46 Fed. Cl. 509 (2000), the court refused to take jurisdiction of a decision to reject a VECP, holding that *Burnside-Ott* did not overrule *NI Industries*. Under the current clauses, this will no longer be an issue, and boards or courts will be able to review such decisions to determine whether rejection of a VECP by a contracting officer is arbitrary or capricious.

Substantially similar language in previous clauses has been held not to bar the board's jurisdiction over cases where government "constructive acceptance" of a proposal is alleged, *North Am. Rockwell Corp.*, ASBCA 14485, 71-1 BCA ¶ 8773. If the government rejected a proposal and did not use the contractor's idea, this decision was not appealable to a board, *Charles Beseler Co.*, ASBCA 22669, 78-2 BCA ¶ 13,483. In *McClain Int'l, Inc.*, ASBCA 23132, 80-1 BCA ¶ 14,365, the board found that no constructive acceptance of a contractor's VECP had occurred where the proposal was rejected on the merits and the government subsequently accepted a competitor's VECP making the same suggestion. The board found that the competitor had independently conceived the idea and the government had adopted the process as a result of that proposal rather than the first contractor's proposal.

Contractors have been unsuccessful in using VECPs as a means of curing defective specifications because, in such cases, the contracting officer can merely reject the proposal, *Dewey Elecs. Corp.*, ASBCA 33869, 91-1 BCA ¶ 23,443, *recons. denied*, 91-1 BCA ¶ 23,656; *DK's Precision Mach. & Mfg.*, ASBCA 39616, 90-2 BCA ¶ 22,830. See also *Rowe Indus., Inc.*, ASBCA 31875, 89-3 BCA ¶ 22,155, *aff'd*, 918 F.2d 186 (Fed. Cir. 1990), *cert denied*, 500 U.S. 952 (1991), in which the board held that the contractor could not avoid a default termination because it had delayed the work while awaiting a response to a VECP suggesting the correction of defective specifications. The board held that the contractor should have proceeded with the work pending action on the VECP.

Prior Value Engineering clauses stated that "the Contracting Officer shall be the sole determiner of the amount of collateral savings, and that amount shall not be subject to the Disputes clause or otherwise subject to litigation under 41 U.S.C. §§ 601-13 [Contract Disputes Act]." In *ICSD Corp.*, ASBCA 28028, 90-3 BCA ¶ 23,027, *aff'd* 934 F.2d 313 (Fed. Cir. 1991), the board held that this language did not preclude it from reviewing such a determination to find if it was arbitrary or capricious. See also *Whittaker Corp.*, ASBCA 18422, 81-1 BCA ¶ 15,055, in which a substantially similar provision was held to have no effect with respect to a particular VECP because the contracting officer had written a "right to appeal the Government's decision on collateral savings" into one of the modifications awarding royalty payments for the VECP. See also *Banner Fabricators, Inc.*, ASBCA 25088, 81-2 BCA ¶ 15,215, in which the board deferred to the contracting officer's decision on the amount of collateral savings generated by a VECP, but recalculated the contractor's share of those savings because the government had incorrectly calculated the share as zero. Under the current clauses boards or courts will be able to review determinations of the amount of collateral savings under an arbitrary or capricious standard.

6. Identification of Proposals Not Required

The current Value Engineering clauses do not require the identification of a VECP as a prerequisite to entitlement to an award. Prior to 1974, the clause did specifically require such identification, but failure to properly identify proposals was consistently held not to bar recovery, *B.F. Goodrich Co. v. United States*, 185 Ct. Cl. 14, 398 F.2d 843 (1968); *Covington Indus., Inc.*, ASBCA 12426, 68-2 BCA ¶ 7286 (equitable estoppel); *McDonnell Douglas Astronautics Co.*, ASBCA 19971, 76-2 BCA ¶ 12,117 (government not misled and board and court refused to undermine the enlightened objectives of value engineering by technicalities over the form of the value engineering submission).

If both parties change the contract without recognizing any VECP, they will not be permitted to later claim that a value engineering suggestion has been adopted. See *M.C. & D. Capital Corp.*, ASBCA 38181, 91-1 BCA ¶ 23,563, *aff'd*, 948 F.2d 1251 (Fed. Cir. 1991), where the parties discussed a value engineering idea but the contractor subsequently signed a contract modification containing a price adjustment deducting the full amount of the savings. The board held that the parties were bound by the modification. See also *Erickson Air Crane Co.*, EBCA 50-6-79, 83-1 BCA ¶ 16,145, *aff'd*, 731 F.2d 810 (Fed. Cir. 1984), in which the board denied a value engineering claim because the parties treated a modification of concrete footings as a normal change and neither party considered it to be value engineering until six months after the government accepted the change in writing. Although the Value Engineering clause in the contract did not require specific identification of a proposal as value engineering, the board focused on the lack of notice to the government and on the fact that the contractor did not originally intend to pursue a value engineering claim. In *U.S. Eng'g Co.*, ASBCA 28835, 83-2 BCA ¶ 16,902, *recons. denied*, 84-2 BCA ¶ 17,305, the government was foreclosed from claiming a credit under the Value Engineering clause where it had authorized a specification deviation without reference to that clause. See also *Fire Sec. Sys., Inc.*, ASBCA 53498, 02-1 BCA ¶ 31,806, *recons. denied*, 02-2 BCA ¶ 31,939, holding that the government was entitled to an equitable adjustment for all of the savings suggested by the contractor. Apparently, the contractor did not know it could treat its proposal as a VECP.

7. Acceptance of Proposals

A VECP is accepted when the contracting officer issues a contract modification incorporating the VECP, FAR 48.103(b). It is the order incorporating the VECP that controls when acceptance takes place, not the pricing of the VECP, which may take place much later, *Raytheon Co.*, ASBCA 22711, 82-1 BCA ¶ 15,663, *aff'd*, 2 Cl. Ct. 763 (1983), *aff'd*, 730 F.2d 1470 (Fed. Cir. 1984). If the government accepts the proposal contingent on test results, it will be bound by its acceptance if the test results prove that the VECP is successful, *Arden Eng'g Co.*, ASBCA 24829, 83-2 BCA ¶ 16,603.

The Value Engineering clauses permit acceptance of proposals either before or within a reasonable time after performance has been completed on the contract. In *Delco Indus. Textile Corp.*, ASBCA 21379, 78-1 BCA ¶ 12,912, the board permitted acceptance of a VECP 19 months after contract completion at a time when no compensation was due the contractor under the sharing provisions of the clause. The board rejected the contractor's arguments that it was entitled to compensation for this long delay in acceptance and that it was entitled to separate compensation for the costs of developing the VECP in these circumstances. The board commented that the protection against the late acceptance given the contractor by the Value Engineering clause is the right to withdraw the VECP if it is not accepted within a time specified in the proposal. In *Delco*, the contractor did not take advantage of this right, which has been preserved in all the FAR Value Engineering clauses for supply and service contracts and construction contracts. In *Tranco Indus., Inc.*, ASBCA 22379, 78-2 BCA ¶ 13,307, *recons. denied*, 78-2 BCA ¶ 13,522, the contractor orally withdrew a VECP and the government later issued a change using the ideas embodied in the proposal. The board held that this was permissible but that the government assumed the risk that the new performance method was practicable. In *Baltimore Contractors, Inc.*, ASBCA 17049, 74-1 BCA ¶ 10,442, the board commented that the contractor could have declined to proceed with the government's partial adoption of a VECP since it was not a full acceptance. This view seems questionable since the clauses provide for partial acceptance of proposals.

In an effort to assure contractors that the government will not delay in accepting value engineering proposals, the regulations provide that acceptance be made within 45 days of submission or that the contractor be notified of the estimated decision date and given the reasons for the delay, FAR 48.103(b). In *O.R. Ramstad*, ENGBCA 3722, 80-1 BCA ¶ 14,234, the board denied compensation for delay costs incurred while awaiting government action on a VECP for two months. The board noted that the clause provides that the government will not be liable for such delays and that the contractor remains liable for performance as originally specified until a VECP is adopted.

If the government rejects a VECP but subsequently uses the idea, it will be found to have "constructively accepted" the proposal. See *North Am. Rockwell Corp.*, ASBCA 14485, 71-1 BCA ¶ 8773, in which the contracting officer's decision that there was no acceptance of a VECP was reversed when it was found that the contract had been changed to include a requirement for the performance of a test "virtually identical" to that previously submitted as a VECP by the contractor. Similarly, in *Gulf Apparel Corp.*, ASBCA 27784, 89-2 BCA ¶ 21,735, the board found constructive acceptance when the contracting officer rejected a part of a contractor's VECP but later accepted the same idea from another contractor. Accord, *Thompson Aircraft Tire Corp.*, ASBCA 14432, 71-2 BCA ¶ 8981; *American Standard, Inc.*, DOTCAB 71-1, 72-1 BCA ¶ 9433; *McDonnell Douglas Astronautics Co.*, ASBCA 19971, 76-2 BCA ¶ 12,117.

In *John J. Kirlin Inc. v. United States*, 827 F.2d 1538 (Fed. Cir. 1987), the Federal Circuit ruled that no constructive acceptance could be found after the final completion of the contract. The court reached this conclusion on the questionable reasoning that the Value Engineering clause expired when the contract was closed out. This rule has been followed in *Amplitronics, Inc.*, ASBCA 44119, 94-1 BCA ¶ 26,520, and *M. Bianchi of Cal.*, ASBCA 37029, 93-1 BCA ¶ 25,309, *aff'd but vacated on other grounds*, 31 F.3d 1163 (Fed. Cir. 1994). This rule can be avoided by keeping the contract open by not submitting an invoice for the final work on the contract, *M. Bianchi of Cal.*, ASBCA 37029, 96-2 BCA ¶ 28,410, *recons. denied*, 97-1 BCA ¶ 23,7678. In *Vantage Assocs., Inc.*, ASBCA 51418, 00-2 BCA ¶ 31,141, the board rejected the contractor's argument that the contract was still open when a VECP was submitted four years after contract completion and only $5 for one spare part remained unbilled on the contract. The ruling was reversed in *Vantage Assocs., Inc. v. Secretary of the Navy*, 25 Fed. Appx. 859 (Fed. Cir. 2001).

8. Finality of Contract Modification

Price adjustments for VECPs are frequently based on estimated savings rather than actual costs. Nonetheless, once the adjustment has been finalized by the signing of a contract modification, neither party can claim a further adjustment to the price if the estimate is incorrect. See *Airmotive Eng'g. Corp.*, ASBCA 15235, 71-2 BCA ¶ 8988, rejecting the government's claim that the contracting officer that had negotiated the adjustment had participated in a mutual mistake. Contractors have also been denied repricing of the adjustment when the costs of performing the VECP were higher than estimated, *Guy F. Atkinson Const. Co.*, ENGBCA 6145, 98-1 BCA ¶ 29,582. In that case, the contractor was denied the costs of reinforcing a tunnel liner to ensure that it met the safety requirement called for by the VECP. The same result was reached in *G&P Constr. Co.*, ASBCA 49524, 98-1 BCA ¶ 29,457, and *H&S Corp.*, ASBCA 29156, 87-2 BCA ¶ 19,764. Similarly, the savings should not include price escalation on the work deleted from the contract by the VECP, *Dillon Constr., Inc.*, ENGBCA PCC-197, 99-2 BCA ¶ 30,576. If it is apparent that there will be no instant contract savings before the parties agree to a contract modification adopting the VECP, the contractor will be entitled to be paid the contract price for the work plus any collateral savings, *Johnny F. Smith Truck & Dragline Serv., Inc.*, ENGBCA 6261, 98-2 BCA ¶ 30,006, *aff'd*, 232 F.3d 915 (Fed. Cir. 2000).

C. Government Use of Data

The Value Engineering clauses for supply and service contracts and construction contracts provide that all data submitted by the contractor may be marked with a restrictive legend precluding the government from disclosing the information outside the government or using it for any purpose other than evaluation. Prior to 1977, the clause also provided that once the VECP was adopted the government was granted full rights to use, disclose, and duplicate the data in any manner and for any purpose whatsoever. Thus, by acceptance of a VECP the government acquired sweeping rights to the data contained in the proposal. See Comp. Gen. Dec. B-167932, Jan. 15, 1970, *Unpub.* The contractor's only protection against such loss of rights was withdrawal of the proposal before acceptance, in accordance with the provisions of the clause. In 1977, the regulations and clauses were modified to permit the contractor to submit technical data subject to continuing limited rights in the government to the extent that it could properly have been submitted as "limited rights technical data" in accordance with the clause of DAR 7-104.9(a). The current clauses state:

> If a VECP is accepted, the Contractor hereby grants the Government unlimited rights in the VECP and supporting data, except that, with respect to data qualifying and submitted as limited rights technical data, the Government shall have the rights specified in the contract modification implementing the VECP and shall appropriately mark the data.

It is not clear whether this provision permits a contracting officer to take unlimited rights in data by so stating in the contract modification, and the FAR contains no guidance on this issue.

D. Unsolicited Value Engineering Proposals

Under the current regulations there is no provision for accepting unsolicited value engineering proposals submitted without a contract containing a Value Engineering clause. The Court of Claims has held that, when a value engineering proposal is submitted without such a contract clause, there is no statutory authority to purchase "suggestions," *Grismac Corp. v. United States*, 214 Ct. Cl. 39, 556 F.2d 494 (1977). In this questionable decision, the court construed 10 U.S.C. § 2386, authorizing acquisition of "designs, processes, and manufacturing data," to be the only authority for acquisition of cost-saving proposals and held that Grismac's mere suggestion to use cheaper wood to make smaller pallets for stacking ammunition crates did not fall within the scope of this statute. In contrast to this reasoning, it would appear that every procuring agency has the authority to take necessary steps to reduce its costs.

The government can adopt regulations allowing the purchase of an unsolicited value engineering proposal that does not rise to the definition in 10 U.S.C. § 2386, *Alan Scott Indus.*, ASBCA 24729, 82-1 BCA ¶ 15,494. There the board held that the contractor was entitled to compensation for its idea, to heat-treat dental instruments in continuous belt furnaces instead of in batch furnaces, on the basis of a provision in ASPR 1-1708 from July 1974 to August 1977, which encouraged the submission of unsolicited value engineering proposals without a contract. The board reasoned that there was sufficient authority in ASPR 1-1708 to purchase the contractor's idea even it if did not rise to the definition of procurable items in 10 U.S.C. § 2386 since ASPR 1-1708 was based on the "statutory underpinning for the value engineering program long established for Department of Defense procurements." The GAO reached the opposite conclusion in *A Better Way, Inc.*, 58 Comp. Gen. 35 (B-191130), 78-2 CPD ¶ 298.

IV. CONSTRUCTIVE CHANGES

One of the major uses of the Changes clause has been to serve as the basis for administrative resolution of claims for price adjustment when the work performed during the course of a government contract is different from that called for. This section briefly discusses the basic theory underlying this use of the clause and reviews the different types of constructive changes that have been identified in the hundreds of litigated cases in this area. It concludes with a discussion of the procedures that should be used when constructive changes are encountered.

A. Basic Theory

A constructive change occurs when the contract work is actually changed but the procedures of the Changes clause have not been followed. In such cases, when the early appeals boards perceived that such changed work was informally ordered by the government or caused by government fault, they found that a change had "constructively" occurred. Similarly, if the different work reduced the contractor's costs, the boards held that the government could assert a claim for a constructive change. Under common law contractual analysis, such fact patterns would more likely be placed under theories of implied contract or breach of contract, but the administrative procedures developed for the resolution of disputes in federal contracts prior to the Contract Disputes Act of 1978 prevented the boards of contract appeals from using these theories. Hence, boards developed the alternate theory of constructive changes.

1. Continuing Vitality of the Doctrine

Although appeals boards can now resolve cases under breach of contract theory and thus use common law reasoning in disputes arising under the Contract Disputes Act, they have continued to deal with the type of conduct described in this section under the Changes clause in order to grant relief in the form of an equitable adjustment rather than in the form of contract damages. See *Johnson & Son Erectors*, ASBCA 24564, 81-1 BCA ¶ 15,082, *aff'd*, 231 Ct. Cl. 753, *cert. denied*, 459 U.S. 971 (1982), in which the board refused to permit a contractor to use breach of contract logic where the facts indicated that a constructive change had occurred. The board stated at 74,599:

> [A]ssuming that the evidence adduced is sufficient to establish entitlement we would find entitlement under the contract and not outside of it. It has long been the policy of this Board to seek a remedy under the contract. The constructive change doctrine is, perhaps, the foremost example of our commitment to providing relief under the contract whenever it is possible to do so.

See *Hardrives, Inc.*, IBCA 2319, 94-1 BCA ¶ 26,267, reanalyzing this issue and concluding that there are still valid reasons for treating most contract breaches as constructive changes. This reasoning permits the appeals boards to take advantage of the considerable amount of precedent covering the computation of equitable adjustments. The expansive definition of changes exemplified by the constructive changes doctrine is also likely to remain in use by government agencies in order to provide freedom of program implementation through use of the Changes clause rather than through new procurement procedures. Further reasons for continued adherence to the constructive changes doctrine are that the contractor will be held to the notice requirements in the clause and will be required to proceed with work pending resolution of disputes redressable under the contract. Thus, the concept of constructive changes appears to have become a fixture in the field of government contract law.

2. Elements of the Doctrine

Although the scope of constructive changes has become very broad, one board described the elements of such changes as being simple in their nature. See *Industrial Research Assocs., Inc.*, DCAB WB-5, 68-1 BCA ¶ 7069, at 32,685-86:

> As we see it, the constructive change doctrine is made up of two elements—the "change" element and the "order" element. To find the change element we must examine the actual performance to see whether it went beyond the minimum standards demanded by the terms of the contract. But, this is not the end of the matter.
>
> The "order" element also is a necessary ingredient in the constructive change concept. To be compensable under the changes clause, the change must be one that the government ordered the contractor to make. The government's representative, by his words or his deeds, must require the contractor to perform work that is not a necessary part of his contract. This differs from advice, comments, suggestions, or opinions ,which government engineering or technical personnel frequently offer to a contractor's employees.

Using this analysis, any government action or communication could be characterized as a constructive change order if it was found to have forced or induced the contractor to undertake extra work. However, the *Industrial Research* analysis is too narrow, since it is clear that government fault, either prior to or during contract performance, may meet the "order" requirement. Hence, it is more correct to state that a constructive change requires work beyond the contract requirements plus either an "order" or "fault" on the part of the government.

As the doctrine of constructive changes became established in case law, the government began to revise its contract language to reflect these new principles. The first instance of this was in the revised Changes clause for construction contracts contained in Standard Form 23-A, which became effective in 1968. This clause is now found in FAR 52.243-4. Its pertinent paragraphs state:

> (b) Any other written order or an oral order (which, as used in this paragraph (b), includes direction, instruction, interpretation, or determination) from the Contracting Officer that causes a change shall be treated as a change order under this clause; provided, that the Contractor gives the Contracting Officer written notice stating (1) the date, circumstances, and source of the order and (2) that the Contractor regards the order as a change order.

(c) Except as provided in this clause, no order, statement, or conduct of the Contracting Officer shall be treated as a change under this clause or entitle the Contractor to an equitable adjustment.

Note that these paragraphs set forth a somewhat limited definition of constructive changes—particularly with regard to action or inaction of the government. Apparently, this was an attempt to narrow the scope of the doctrine. The clause also requires in ¶ (b) that notice be given of all constructive changes, and in ¶ (d) provides a penalty for failure to give notice of certain constructive changes. A detailed analysis of the intent of the drafters of the clause is found in Hiestand, *A New Era in Government Construction Contracts,* 28 Fed. B.J. 165 (1968).

Although the supply and services contract clauses do not contain similar language dealing with constructive changes, the doctrine is applied to such contracts. Constructive changes are recognized in the Notification of Changes clause set forth in FAR 52.243-7 primarily for use in supply and research and development contracts for the acquisition of weapons systems and subsystems. It contains a broader definition of constructive changes than that in the construction clause and does not provide a penalty for failure to give notice. The key language of this clause defining constructive changes states:

Except for changes identified as such in writing and signed by the Contracting Officer, the Contractor shall notify the Administrative Contracting Officer in writing promptly, within . . . (to be negotiated) calendar days from the date that the Contractor identifies any Government conduct (including actions, inactions, and written or oral communications) that the Contractor regards as a change to the contract terms and conditions.

3. Government Claims for Price Decreases

The constructive changes doctrine can be used by the government to obtain deductive equitable adjustments in the contract price. Although such cases are a small minority of the constructive change cases, the principle was clearly established in *Varo, Inc.*, ASBCA 16087, 73-2 BCA ¶ 10,206, *rev'd on other grounds*, 212 Ct. Cl. 432, 548 F.2d 953 (1977). In that case the board stated at 48,144:

Constructive changes are not a one-way street. While parties involved in a constructive change are usually in the posture where a contractor is claiming increased costs, the Board sees no reason why the government cannot also claim a decrease in the contract price where a contractor is permitted to save costs through the authorized or unauthorized actions of its officers and employees.

Accord, *M & H Constr. Co.*, ASBCA 21528, 79-1 BCA ¶ 13,688. The apparent reasoning is that, since the government has the right to reject nonconforming work, it also has the right to issue an after-the-fact change order reducing the contract price to reflect the cost difference between the item specified and the item delivered. See *Farwell Co.*

v. United States, 137 Ct. Cl. 832, 148 F. Supp. 947 (1957) (court upheld contracting officer's change order reducing price after contractor used copper tube instead of specified copper pipe); *Porshia Alexander of Am.*, GSBCA 9604, 91-1 BCA ¶ 23,657 (board affirmed contracting officer's deduction from final payment to compensate government for work not performed at direction of government inspector); *Plaza Maya Ltd. P'ship*, GSBCA 9086, 91-1 BCA ¶ 23,425 (government credit for not complying with local building code, even though no amount had been included in price for compliance); *Arnold M. Diamond, Inc.*, ASBCA 38974, 92-2 BCA ¶ 24,869 (credit for fewer expansion joints than called for by specifications, even though contractor had design responsibility); *Santa Fe Eng'rs, Inc.*, ASBCA 44906, 93-1 BCA ¶ 25,298, *aff'd*, 19 F.3d 39 (Fed. Cir. 1994) (government credit for use of less expensive doors); *Marine Constr. & Dredging, Inc.*, ASBCA 38412, 95-1 BCA ¶ 27,286, *recons. denied*, 95-2 BCA ¶ 27,699 (credit for failure to perform required testing); *Environmental Data Consultants, Inc. v. General Servs. Admin.*, GSBCA 13244, 96-2 BCA ¶ 28,614 (credit for contractor-suggested redesign of excavation); *Fire Sec. Sys., Inc. v. General Servs. Admin.*, GSBCA 12120, 97-1 BCA ¶ 28,994 (credit for deleted work); *Jimenez, Inc.*, VABCA 6351, 02-2 BCA ¶ 32,019 (work not completed at end of contract); and *Taylor Constr. Co. v. General Servs. Admin.*, GSBCA 15421, 03-2 BCA ¶ 32,320 (credit for deleted work). Compare *Dawson Constr. Co.*, GSBCA 5672, 81-2 BCA ¶ 15,387, *recons. denied*, 82-2 BCA ¶ 15,914 (deduction denied since lower cost material was reflected in the bid price and deduction would have given government a windfall). If the government acts as a volunteer in curing a problem encountered by the contractor, there will be no recovery. See *Nationwide Postal Mgmt.*, PSBCA 3988, 98-1 BCA ¶ 29,364, denying recovery when the Postal Service paid a company to repair the air conditioning in a leased building when the owner of the building was asserting the right to have the work done without payment.

This theory has also been used when the government lost its right to correct defective work under the Inspection clause of the contract because it had not given the contractor the opportunity to correct it, as required by the clause. In that situation, when the government proceeded to correct the defects, the board concluded that the government had reduced the work of the contractor and was entitled to an equitable adjustment measured by the amount of the contractor's cost savings, *Techni Data Labs.*, ASBCA 21054, 77-2 BCA ¶ 12,667. The same theory was applied in *Worldwide Parts, Inc.*, ASBCA 38896, 91-2 BCA ¶ 23,717, but the price reduction was computed on the cost of correcting the work rather than the costs saved. Compare *Lionsgate Corp.*, ENGBCA 5809, 92-2 BCA ¶ 24,983, in which the government was denied relief in this situation—apparently because it asserted its claims under the Default and Inspection clauses, not the Changes clause.

B. Types of Constructive Changes

Constructive changes can be divided into four categories that represent the major uses of the constructive changes doctrine in administratively resolving claims against the government. In general, the substantive merits of these claims (the "change" element) are determined by the same rules that have been developed by the courts in dealing with contract interpretation disputes and breach of contract actions against the government, discussed in prior chapters. Thus, this section focuses on the different types of government actions that have been held to constitute orders or fault under the Changes clause (the "order/fault" element). However, with regard to acceleration claims, the change element is also covered because there has been no independent development of legal rules outside the constructive changes case law. The four categories of constructive changes follow:

Category	Change Element	Order/Fault Element
1. Disagreements between the parties over the contract requirements	Determined by application of rules of contract interpretation in Chapter 2	Part 1, below
2. Defective specifications and government nondisclosure of information	Determined in accordance with implied duties in Chapter 3	Part 2, below
3. Acceleration	Part 3, below	Part 3, below
4. Failure of the government to cooperate during performance	Determined in accordance with implied duties in Chapter 3	Part 4, below

Although categories 1 and 2 both relate to the specifications in the contract, they are very different in nature. In claims involving the interpretation of the specifications, the change results from a disagreement between the parties over the method of performance permitted by the contract (with the contractor arguing for a less expensive method), but there is no disagreement over the technical feasibility of either method. In contrast, in the defective specification and nondisclosure claims, the contractor has usually attempted to perform the work in accordance with the government's requirements but has encountered undue difficulties or has failed. Here there is no disagreement over the interpretation of the specifications—merely a claim that they did not lead to satisfactory results.

1. Disagreements Over Contract Requirements

The earliest type of constructive change found by the appeals boards involved a situation in which a contractor and the government disagreed on the work required to meet the contract specifications. Typically, the contractor proposes to perform the contract in a certain manner, and the contracting officer asserts that a more expensive method of performance is called for. Often, the ultimate result of this type of controversy is insistence by the government that the contractor perform in accordance with the government's interpretation of the contract requirements. As discussed in Chapter 10, the contractor is required to proceed with performance in accordance with directions of the contracting officer or suffer the risk of default termination, and hence it will normally utilize the method of performance that is required by the government. Only later, when the board of contract appeals or court rules on the issue of contract interpretation, will the parties know whether the contractor has been required to do work not called for by the contract.

The basic rule covering this type of constructive change is summarized in *Emerson-Sack-Warner Corp.*, ASBCA 6004, 61-2 BCA ¶ 3248, at 16,827:

> Where as a result of the Government's misinterpretation of contract provisions a contractor is required to perform more or different work, or to higher standards, not called for under its terms, the contractor is entitled to equitable adjustments pursuant to the Changes Article, including extensions of time. *Inca Metal Products Corp.*, ASBCA Nos. 4239, 4243, 58-1 BCA ¶ 1719; *James A. Dunbar d.b.a. Dunbar Roofing Co.*, ASBCA No. 3559, 57-2 BCA ¶ 1487; *White Star Heating & Supply, Inc.*, ASBCA No. 2815; *Taag Designs, Inc.*, ASBCA No. 2371; *Fansteel Metallurgical Corp.*, ASBCA No. 1689, and cases collected.

The rule was recognized by the Court of Claims in *W.H. Edwards Eng'g Corp. v. United States*, 161 Ct. Cl. 322 (1963). Two categories of constructive changes have occurred in these interpretation disputes: (1) those that fall clearly within the bounds of the Changes clause of the contract, and (2) those that could not normally be ordered under that clause.

a. Work That Could Have Been Ordered as a Change

Most instances of extra work required by contract interpretation involve work that clearly could have been ordered by the issuance of a change order. Such work is "within the general scope of the contract" and is within the limiting words of the Changes clause, as discussed earlier in this chapter. The government occasionally argues that, because there was no change order, the contractor has voluntarily performed the additional work. However, the usual understanding is that contractors do not, as a general rule, voluntarily perform work not called for by the contract, *Chris Berg, Inc. v. United States*, 197 Ct. Cl. 503, 455 F.2d 1037 (1972); *M.S.I. Corp.*, GSBCA 2428, 68-2 BCA ¶ 7262; *Brown Constr. Co.*, ASBCA 22648, 79-1 BCA ¶ 13,745; *Sigma Constr. Co.*, ASBCA 37040, 91-2 BCA ¶ 23,926; *North Star Alaska Hous. Corp. v. United States*, 30 Fed. Cl. 259 (1993); *Integrated Clinical Sys., Inc.*, VABCA 3745, 95-2 BCA ¶ 27,902; *Edsall Constr. Co.*, ASBCA 51787, 01-2 BCA ¶ 31,425, *aff'd*, 296 F.3d 1081 (Fed. Cir. 2002). Evidence of such voluntary effort has been required to be clear and convincing, *Driftwood of Ala.*, GSBCA 5429, 81-2 BCA ¶ 15,169, and the government has the burden of proving such voluntary effort, *Carl J. Bonidie, Inc.*, ASBCA 25769, 82-2 BCA ¶ 15,818. Compare *Quiller Constr. Co.*, ASBCA 14964, 72-1 BCA ¶ 9322 (voluntary performance found upon the preponderance of the evidence), with *Service Eng'g. Co.*, ASBCA 42126, 96-2 BCA ¶ 28,376 (no proof of voluntary performance when key government employees failed to testify at trial). However, when there is no indication of government direction to perform extra work, voluntary performance will frequently be found. See *Basic Marine, Inc.*, ASBCA 53256, 02-1 BCA ¶ 31,677 (services provided on

IDIQ contract with no order from government); *NavCom Def. Elec., Inc.*, ASBCA 50767, 01-2 BCA ¶ 31,546 (minor design changes to product after successful testing without government approval); *Inslaw, Inc. v. United States*, 40 Fed. Cl. 843 (1998) (delivery of enhanced version of software); *Nagy Enters.*, ASBCA 48815, 98-1 BCA ¶ 29,695 (change in construction method with no prior government approval); *S-TRON*, ASBCA 45893, 96-2 BCA ¶ 28,319 (contractor, with government permission, recalled product for rework exceeding specification requirement to ensure its safety); *Tempo, Inc.*, ASBCA 37589, 95-2 BCA ¶ 27,618 (rework voluntarily done to meet contractor's interpretation of specifications even though problem brought to contractor's attention by government personnel); *Knight Architects Eng'rs, Planners, Inc.*, PSBCA 3474, 94-3 BCA ¶ 27,178 (voluntary work in reviewing shop drawings in more detail than required by contract); *Jowett, Inc.*, ASBCA 47364, 94-3 BCA ¶ 27,110 (contractor voluntarily performed necessary survey work without telling government employees); *JEM Dev. Corp.*, ASBCA 42872, 92-1 BCA ¶ 24,709 (contractor voluntarily corrected problem with transformers on which work was to be done); and *Bay Decking Co.*, ASBCA 33868, 89-2 BCA ¶ 21,834 (contractor voluntarily performed desired work that was inadvertently omitted from specifications). In deciding whether a contractor has performed voluntarily or the government's actions have been sufficiently compelling to be a constructive change order, the courts and boards must balance the extent and directness of government pressure against the voluntary nature of the contractor's performance, taking the totality of circumstances into account.

The most common types of government action and inaction that have been held to be constructive change orders are discussed below.

(1) Direct Government Orders

The classic example of a constructive change occurs when the government directly orders the contractor to perform the work in a specified manner but simultaneously states that such order shall not be construed as a change order. For example, in *R.P. Farnsworth & Co.*, WDBCA 20, 1 CCF 32 (1943), an order to install benches, which the contract clearly did not require, was treated as a change order since the government "had the time, the opportunity, and the power" to issue a change order. Such orders are generally based on the mistaken belief that the work ordered was required by the specifications. See *Johnson Controls, Inc.*, ASBCA 26660, 82-2 BCA ¶ 15,909 (contractor required to do work not required by specifications); *Tecom, Inc.*, ASBCA 26022, 82-2 BCA ¶ 16,121, *recons. denied*, 83-1 BCA ¶ 16,372, *aff'd*, 732 F.2d 935 (Fed. Cir. 1984) (order to add off-base bus routes to a transportation contract not within the scope of other contract clauses permitting changes to routes); *Hudson Contracting, Inc.*, ASBCA 41023, 94-1 BCA ¶ 26,466 (order to cut trees one at a time when no contract provision so required); *Bay Ship & Yacht Co.*, DOTBCA 2913, 96-1 BCA ¶ 28,236 (order to remove asbestos not required by specifications); *Mertz Constr., Inc.*, AGBCA 94-165-1, 97-1 BCA ¶ 28,802, *recons.*

denied, 97-2 BCA ¶ 29,016 (order to paint doors with high-gloss paint not required by specifications); *Agro-Lawn Sys., Inc.*, ASBCA 49648, 98-1 BCA ¶ 29,635 (order to limit work during burials an unreasonable interpretation of contract language); *J&J Oilfield & Elec. Serv.*, ASBCA 46044, 98-2 BCA ¶ 29,965 (order to use separate people to manage different contracts not required by clause calling for management personnel); *Steele & Sons, Inc.*, ASBCA 49077, 00-1 BCA ¶ 30,837 (order to size heating system to provide for future expansion); and *Hensel Phelps Constr. Co. v. General Servs. Admin.*, GSBCA 14744, 01-1 BCA ¶ 31,249, *aff'd*, 36 Fed. Appx. 649 (Fed. Cir. 2002) (order to provide vibration isolation to plumbing).

In some cases the "order" is the result of a change in the government's operations. See, for example, *T&M Distribs., Inc.*, ASBCA 51405, 00-1 BCA ¶ 30,677, in which a constructive change was found when the closing of a government supply depot greatly altered the mix of bulk shipments versus single shipments for a contractor supplying parts to the agency. Compare *Cleveland Telecommunications Corp. v. United States*, 39 Fed. Cl. 649 (1997), rejecting a claim for a constructive change based on the contractor's payment of premium wages during the 1995–1996 government shutdown. The court reasoned that the contractor bore the risk that an arbitrator would order the payment of such wages.

(2) Government Suggestions

Suggestions by government personnel that the contractor perform work in a specified manner either can be treated as "orders" or can be seen as mere communications during the performance of the contract. This determination is made by ascertaining whether the suggestion was "coercive" in nature, *Watson, Rice & Co.*, HUDBCA 89-4468-C6, 90-1 BCA ¶ 22,499; *OFEGRO*, HUDBCA 88-3410-C7, 91-3 BCA ¶ 24,206; *Donald R. Stewart & Assocs.*, AGBCA 84-226-1, 92-1 BCA ¶ 24,705; *Valley Asphalt, Inc.*, AGBCA 97-118-1, 97-2 BCA ¶ 29,275. See also *A.D. & G.D. Fox*, AGBCA 76-139-4, 80-2 BCA ¶ 14,788, stating that "mere discussion of methods" is not sufficient to constitute a constructive change order "where the contractor is not directed or compelled to use a method other than by choice." Similarly, both *SAE/Americon-Mid-Atl., Inc. v. General Servs. Admin.*, GSBCA 12295, 97-1 BCA ¶ 28,912, *aff'd*, 178 F.3d 1312 (Fed. Cir. 1998), and *Quality Plus Equip., Inc.*, ASBCA 46932, 96-2 BCA ¶ 28,595, cite *Industrial Research Assocs., Inc.*, DCAB WB-5, 68-1 BCA ¶ 7069, for the proposition that there is a significant difference between ordered changes and the "advice, comments, suggestions, or opinions from Government engineering or technical personnel frequently offered to a contractors' employees." Earlier cases seem to have followed similar reasoning. For example, in *Lorentz Bruun Co.*, GSBCA 1023, 1964 BCA ¶ 4357, where the government gave the contractor a drawing calling for extra work without directly requiring compliance, the board found that it was logical to attribute the contractor's performance of the extra work to a belief that a change was being directed rather than that the government was making a suggestion that the contractor was free to reject. Similarly, a constructive change was found where there was a request for additional hours in *Environment Consultants, Inc.*, IBCA 1192-5-78, 79-2 BCA ¶ 13,937, and *Urban Pathfinders, Inc.*, ASBCA 23134, 79-1 BCA ¶ 13,709. In *Space Servs. of Ga., Inc.*, ASBCA 25793, 81-2 BCA ¶ 15,250, the government was held to have ordered extra labor hours through the issuance of memoranda marked in red ink and discussion with the contractor in which the Chief of Services stated that the alleged understaffing "makes me sick" and that he expected the problem to be corrected immediately. See also *S & M Traylor Bros. (JV)*, ENGBCA 3878, 82-1 BCA ¶ 15,484, in which the board reasoned that, since the contractor was not permitted to continue tunneling without an approved plan for protecting surface structures and had been informally advised that the government had decided that a grouting program was the best solution, its submission and execution of such a program could not have been voluntary given the alternative of remaining idle indefinitely. In contrast, mere suggestions followed without protest have been held not to constitute constructive change orders, *McElroy Mach. & Mfg. Co.*, ASBCA 46477, 99-1 BCA ¶ 30,185; *Hudson Contracting, Inc.*, ASBCA 41023, 94-1 BCA ¶ 24,466; *Lott Constructors, Inc.*, ENGBCA 5852, 93-1 BCA ¶ 25,449; *Singer Co., Librascope Div. v. United States*, 215 Ct. Cl. 281, 568 F.2d 695 (1977); *Iversen Constr. Co.*, IBCA 981-1-73, 76-1 BCA ¶ 11,644, *recons. denied*, 76-1 BCA ¶ 11,844; *Barbour Boat Works*, CGBCA T-4, 68-1 BCA ¶ 6790, *recons. denied*, 68-1 BCA ¶ 7009; *Twombly Tree Experts, Inc.*, ASBCA 6456, 61-1 BCA ¶ 3001. In addition, suggestions specifically identified as such have been held insufficiently compelling to be constructive change orders, *Labarge, Inc.*, ASBCA 19845, 78-2 BCA ¶ 13,376.

(3) Government Interpretation of Specifications

Government interpretation of the specifications has been held to be a constructive change even though the contractor was not explicitly ordered to follow the interpretation. In *Mifflinburg Body Works, Inc.*, ASBCA 427, 4 CCF ¶ 60,999 (1950), the board stated at 51,559:

> [S]ince the contractor had been called upon to produce under a more costly method by virtue of the government's interpretation of the ambiguous specifications, . . . such interpretation by the government amounted in reality to a change in the contract for which an equitable adjustment should be made.

Similarly, in *Triangle Elec. Mfg. Co.*, ASBCA 15995, 74-2 BCA ¶ 10,783, a constructive change was found where a contractor asked the government for assistance in devising a method of performing the work and the government included work beyond the contract requirements in the guidance given. See also *U.S. Fed. Eng'g & Mfg., Inc.*, ASBCA 19909, 75-2 BCA ¶ 11,578, finding a constructive change where the government responded to the contractor's request for an interpretation of the specifications by calling for work in addition to the minimum necessary to meet the contract. Similarly, a change was found in *Raytheon Serv. Co.*, ASBCA 36139, 92-1

BCA ¶ 24,696, where the government offered to accept a more expensive alternate mode of performance after the specified mode had failed because the government had not been able to furnish the property called for by the contract. Of course, if pressure is brought on the contractor to follow the government's interpretation, there is little question that a constructive change will be found, *Al Johnson Constr. Co. v. United States*, 20 Cl. Ct. 184 (1990).

Such interpretations can be communicated to the contractor indirectly as well as directly. For example, in *Unidynamics/St. Louis, Inc.*, ASBCA 17592, 73-2 BCA ¶ 10,360, the contractor told the government of its interpretation of the specifications, but the government permitted another contractor to perform the work in a way that precluded the contractor from following that interpretation. Finding the contractor's interpretation reasonable, the board held the government's action to be a constructive change. See also *Brown Constr. Co.*, ASBCA 22648, 79-1 BCA ¶ 13,745, in which a series of ambiguous communications from the government was held to communicate the government's interpretation requiring higher-priced material to the contractor.

Constructive changes may not be found in these interpretation situations if there is doubt whether the government employees knew that the contractor was asserting that a change had occurred. See *Green's Multi-Servs., Inc.*, EBCA C-9611207, 97-1 BCA ¶ 28,649, *recons. denied*, 97-1 BCA ¶ 28,811 (no proof of government direction to provide larger buses and no evidence that contractor questioned alleged order); *N & A Builders, Inc.*, VABCA 2610, 89-1 BCA ¶ 21,382 (no communication informing government that extra work being done was responsibility of government); and *Lloyd Moore Constr.*, AGBCA 87-151-3, 89-2 BCA ¶ 21,875 (no "persuasive" evidence of order and no notice that change had occurred). Similarly, in *Calfon Constr., Inc. v. United States*, 18 Cl. Ct. 426 (1989), *aff'd*, 923 F.2d 872 (Fed. Cir. 1990), the court found no constructive change where the parties had discussed two methods of performance and the contractor had adopted the more expensive method without making it clear to the government employees that this was considered a change.

Interpretations initially proffered by the contractor may not qualify as constructive changes under this theory. See, for example, *Rohr Indus., Inc.*, ENGBCA 4138, 83-1 BCA ¶ 16,509, in which the board concluded that government concurrence that certain work was required was not a constructive change because the contractor had decided earlier to include the work.

(4) Government Rejection of a Method Permitted by the Contract

Rejection of a method of performance selected or used by a contractor is clearly a constructive change if that method was permitted by the contract. For example, in *Grumman Aerospace Corp.*, ASBCA 50090, 01-1 BCA ¶ 31,316, *aff'd*, 34 Fed. Appx. 710 (Fed. Cir. 2002), a constructive change was found when the government imposed more stringent quality assurance procedures than had been used in the past 18 years. Similarly, in *J.B. Williams Co. v. United States*, 196 Ct. Cl. 491, 450 F.2d 1379 (1971), a constructive change was found where the government refused to approve a preproduction sample that performed as well as a government-furnished model, with the result that the contractor performed work beyond that required by the contract. In *Ocean Elec. Corp.*, NASABCA 371-8, 73-2 BCA ¶ 10,335, a constructive change resulted from the government's refusal to permit use of an item equal to a specified item where the contract contained an "or equal" clause. See also *Adventure Group, Inc.*, ASBCA 50188, 97-2 BCA ¶ 29,081, *recons. denied*, 98-1 BCA ¶ 29,362 (rejection of proposed model unit that met the specifications); *Max J. Kuney Co.*, DOTBCA 2759, 94-3 BCA ¶ 27,245 (prohibiting the use of local trade practice); *Abbott Prods., Inc.*, ASBCA 43054, 93-3 BCA ¶ 26,006 (rejection of first article); *ITT Gilfillan Div.*, ASBCA 37834, 92-1 BCA ¶ 24,490 (failure to conditionally accept work as required by contract); *CWC, Inc.*, ASBCA 28847, 84-2 BCA ¶ 17,282, *recons. denied*, 85-1 BCA ¶ 17,876 (rejection of alternate equipment permitted by specification); *Vi-Mil, Inc.*, ASBCA 25111, 82-2 BCA ¶ 15,840 (rejection of contractor's previously approved instruction plans); *Algernon Blair, Inc.*, ASBCA 23585, 81-2 BCA ¶ 15,375, *recons. denied*, 82-1 BCA ¶ 15,491 (rejection of contractor's previously approved construction plans); *John Murphy Constr. Co.*, AGBCA 418, 79-1 BCA ¶ 13,836 (prevention of planned sequence of performance); *John R. Hollingsworth Co.*, DOTCAB 69-15, 71-1 BCA ¶ 8760 (rejection of equipment); *Tecon-Green*, ENGBCA 2667, 67-1 BCA ¶ 6147, *aff'd*, 188 Ct. Cl. 15, 411 F.2d 1262 (1969) (rejection of method of performance); and *Gil-Brown Constructors, Inc.*, DOTCAB 67-21, 69-2 BCA ¶ 7804 (refusal to obtain fill from other borrow areas).

In these cases, the act of rejection is so clearly an adverse interpretation that the requirement of filing a protest is rarely raised or discussed. However, the lack of a clear rejection of the contractor's proposed method of performance has been used to support a holding that no constructive change order has occurred, *Blake Constr. Co.*, ASBCA 3406, 57-1 BCA ¶ 1281; *Ruscon Constr. Co.*, ASBCA 9371, 65-1 BCA ¶ 4599; *Avien, Inc.*, AECBCA 14-65, 67-2 BCA ¶ 6461, *recons. denied*, 67-2 BCA ¶ 6701.

(5) "Orders" of Authorized Representatives

In many instances the action or order resulting in extra work is made by a government inspector or other representative without formal contracting officer authority. See Chapter 9 for a discussion of the inspector cases. In such cases, the contractor must show not only that its interpretation was correct and that there was a constructive change order, but also that the inspector had the authority to act for the contracting officer or that the inspector's actions were ratified by a contracting officer. The rules used in determining authority of authorized representatives of the contracting officer are discussed in Chapter 1. See also *Urban Pathfinders, Inc.*, ASBCA 23134, 79-1 BCA ¶ 13,709, and *Randall H. Sharpe*, ASBCA 22800, 79-1 BCA ¶ 13,869. However, not all of the cases in this area specifically discuss the authority issue—in some instances the boards appear to assume that the government employee making the interpretation is closely enough associated with a contracting officer to circumvent the need for analysis.

b. Work Outside the Changes Clause

In some cases, the appeals boards and courts have stretched the constructive changes doctrine to cover situations that probably would not be held to be within the bounds of the Changes clause if the government attempted to use the clause to directly order such a change. These are cases in which the clause is used administratively to settle a controversy that could not have been resolved at that level because it was a breach of contract. With the advent of the Contract Disputes Act, all such claims can be resolved administratively without the use of this fiction. Hence, this use of the constructive change logic may not be as common in the future.

(1) Unauthorized Government Disclosure of Technical Data

In *Joanell Labs., Inc.*, ASBCA 15798, 72-1 BCA ¶ 9300, it was held that there was no appeals board jurisdiction over a claim for damages for unauthorized removal of proprietary legends and disclosure of proprietary data. In *CompuDyne Corp.*, ASBCA 14556, 72-1 BCA ¶ 9218, the same board treated such a claim as a constructive change. It does not appear logical to argue that this holding permits the government to directly order the contractor to give up proprietary rights under the Changes clause. Since such an order is not related to an alteration of the work being performed under the contract, it is not a change to the designs, drawings, or specifications included in the contract, and this relationship is one of the prerequisites to the issuance of a change order under one of the standard Changes clauses. Thus, this type of constructive change should be classified as one where an appeals board has used the doctrine to assume jurisdiction rather than as one based on an interpretation of the scope of the Changes clause.

The *CompuDyne* reasoning was followed in *General Elec. Automated Sys. Div.*, ASBCA 36214, 89-1 BCA ¶ 21,195. Compare *E.M. Scott & Assocs.*, ASBCA 45869, 94-1 BCA ¶ 26,258, in which the board took jurisdiction of a claim that the government had misused proprietary data under a breach of contract theory. In that case, the board could not use a constructive changes theory because there was no contract involved. The board took jurisdiction on the theory that there might be an implied contract not to misuse the data.

(2) Improper Exercise of Options

In several cases, constructive changes have been found where the government exercised an option after it had expired and the contractor proceeded to perform under protest. For example, in *International Tel. & Tel. v. United States*, 197 Ct. Cl. 11, 453 F.2d 1283 (1972), the contracting officer's failure to give required notice to the contractor that funds were available to continue the contract led to a constructive change when the contracting officer required the contractor to furnish equipment at option prices after the time for ordering the work had expired. Accord, *Keco Indus., Inc.*, ASBCA 16645, 73-2 BCA ¶ 10,056, *recons. denied*, 73-2 BCA ¶ 10,211; *Lear Siegler, Inc.*, ASBCA 12164, 69-1 BCA ¶ 7563. See also *Dynamics Corp. of Am. v. United States*, 182 Ct. Cl. 62; 389 F.2d 424 (1968), applying the same rule to an indefinite delivery/indefinite quantity contract calling for the issuance of orders before a specified date. It is clear that the Changes clause does not permit the ordering of large numbers of additional items, since such amounts would clearly constitute new procurement. In fact, in *Keco* the contracting officer commenced the purchase by issuing an IFB under the sealed bidding statute but later canceled it and exercised the contract option. In *General Dynamics Corp.*, ASBCA 20882, 77-1 BCA ¶ 12,504, the deciding judge noted that the Changes clause of the contract "limits itself specifically to modification affecting drawings, designs or specifications, methods of shipments and/or packing and places of delivery." Still, after acknowledging the lack of logic in the reasoning of *International Tel. & Tel.*, *Keco*, and *Lear Siegler*, the judge followed these cases and ruled that a constructive change resulted from the government's order of additional quantities.

The improper exercise of an option under a multiyear contract has also been found to be a constructive change, *Electrospace Corp.*, ASBCA 19742, 78-1 BCA ¶ 12,949. For another case involving the addition of work, see *Westinghouse Elec. Corp.*, DCAB NOAA-3-74, 78-1 BCA ¶ 13,133, where retaining a chartered vessel in standby status pending possible additional work was held to be a constructive change because government personnel knew of the situation. For other cases holding that option exercises were constructive changes, see *Holly Corp.*, ASBCA 24975, 83-1 BCA ¶ 16,327 (exercise of an option without adequate funds where contractor could not reasonably have known of the lack of funds); *New England Tank Indus. of N,H.*, ASBCA 26474, 88-1 BCA ¶ 20,395, *vacated and remanded*, 861 F.2d 685 (Fed. Cir. 1988), *decision on remand*, 90-2 BCA ¶ 22,892 (exercise of an option citing funds that could not be used for the work where contractor did not know of the unpublished regulation precluding the use of the funds); *Grumman Technical Servs., Inc.*, ASBCA 46040, 95-2 BCA ¶ 27,918 (changing terms of contract in option exercise); *Varo, Inc.*, ASBCA 47945, 96-1 BCA ¶ 28,161 (adding contract clauses to option quantities); and *Lockheed Martin IR Imaging Sys., Inc. v. West*, 108 F.3d 319 (Fed. Cir. 1997) (partial exercise of a "100 percent option"). In *Alliant Techsystems, Inc. v. United States*, 178 F.3d 1260, *reh'g denied*, 186 F.3d 1379 (Fed. Cir. 1999), the court expanded on these cases by holding that a contractor was properly terminated for default because it had a duty to proceed when it received such an improperly issued option.

(3) Improper Withholding of Progress Payments

Several cases have found improper withholdings of progress payments to be constructive changes and have ordered reimbursement to the contractor for interest costs of funds borrowed to finance the work in the interim. In the first such case, *Aerojet-Gen. Corp.*, ASBCA 13548, 70-1 BCA ¶ 8245, the board held that the government's erroneous interpretation of a Progress Payments clause, which deprived the contractor of substantial amounts of funds, was "an unauthorized and compensable unilateral change in the contract." Accord, *Ingalls Shipbuilding Div., Litton Sys., Inc.*, ASBCA 17717, 76-1 BCA ¶ 11,851; *Virginia Elecs. Co.*, ASBCA 18778, 77-1 BCA ¶ 12,393 (compensation granted for two-week delay resulting from improper rejection of progress payment request). See, however, *Lockheed Shipbuilding & Constr. Co.*, ASBCA 18460, 77-1 BCA ¶ 12,458, in which the board denied the contractor's motion to dismiss a government counterclaim based on the theory that a constructive change had occurred when the government allegedly made overpayments under a Progress Payments clause. In returning the matter for trial, the board commented that it doubted if such a claim was a valid constructive change even though *Aerojet-Gen.* had so held in the converse situation.

Since this type of constructive change is highly unusual and limited in nature, it is doubtful that it will be found in future cases. See *DMJM/Norman Eng'g Co.*, ASBCA 28154, 84-1 BCA ¶ 17,226, taking jurisdiction of a withholding case without reference to the Changes clause. See also *Systems Consultants, Inc.*, ASBCA 18487, 75-2 BCA ¶ 11,402, in which the board held that no such constructive change existed in a cost-reimbursement contract where the government had improperly withheld payments. This holding was based on the reasoning that *Aerojet-Gen.* could not be followed because the cost principles in DAR 15-205.17 precluded the payment of interest on cost-type contracts and interest on the withheld payments was the measure of the equitable adjustment under this type of constructive change.

In a similar situation, a constructive change was found where the government failed to make timely payment of Vietnamese currency with the result that the contractor was forced to acquire such currency at a higher exchange rate, *Daniel, Mann, Johnson & Mendenhall*, ASBCA 14360, 71-2 BCA ¶ 9003.

(4) Government Action Leading the Contractor to Increase Employee Wages

Constructive changes have also been found where government action induced or required the contractor to increase wages paid to employees. For example, in *Geronimo Serv. Co.*, ASBCA 14686, 70-2 BCA ¶ 8540, a constructive change was found where the government issued a new service contract wage determination containing higher minimum wages with the exercise of an option for additional work, and in *J.R. Cianchette*, ASBCA 4508, 60-2 BCA ¶ 2814, the board held that a constructive change had occurred when the contracting officer ruled that a labor classification with higher wages applied to the work under a contract subject to the Davis-Bacon Act. In two cases, constructive changes were found where contracts for work in Vietnam contained clauses stating that the contractor was required to pay the same wage rates as the Army and then the Army issued directives raising its wages, *Philco-Ford Corp.*, ASBCA 14623, 72-1 BCA ¶ 9390; *Pacific Architects & Eng'rs, Inc.*, ASBCA 16083, 74-2 BCA ¶ 10,755. See also *Thaihuat Eng'g Co.*, ASBCA 21906, 79-1 BCA ¶ 13,691, in which acquiescence to increases in severance pay required by Thai law was held to be a constructive change. Constructive changes were also found where the government applied pressure to the contractor to hire employees of a predecessor contractor at wage rates higher than required by the Service Contract Act wage determination, *Space Age Eng'g, Inc.*, ASBCA 16588, 72-2 BCA ¶ 9636, and where a new Service Contract Act wage determination was issued immediately after award, *C&H Reforesters, Inc.*, AGBCA 84-295-1, 88-3 BCA ¶ 21,067. The logic of these cases—that wage increases can be ordered under the Changes clause—was first enunciated by the Court of Claims in *Sunswick Corp. v. United States*, 109 Ct. Cl. 772, 75 F. Supp. 221, *cert. denied*, 334 U.S. 827 (1948), in which the court stated that a contracting officer should have issued a change order when the government forced the contractor to pay higher wages. However, since the wage rates are not part of the work under the contract, it is questionable if such an order is within the bounds of the Changes clause.

(5) Government-Ordered Change in Accounting System

In *Ford Aerospace & Communications Corp.*, ASBCA 23833, 83-2 BCA ¶ 16,813, a government order that the contractor use a total cost input base to allocate general and administrative expenses under Cost Accounting Standard 410 was held to be a constructive change. Similarly, in *Aydin Corp. v. Widnall*, 61 F.3d 1571 (Fed. Cir. 1995), an order to use a more precise accounting system not required by the contract was held to be a constructive change. It is unclear how such orders are within the bounds of the Changes clause.

2. Defective Specifications and Misleading Information

A second major category of constructive change occurs when the government misleads the contractor with the information it provides and the contractor incurs additional expense in attempting to perform in accordance with such information. In this situation, the government's breach of an implied duty is claimed to have caused the contractor to perform work beyond that originally contemplated. However, in many cases, there is nothing that can be characterized as a constructive change "order." Rather, to find a constructive change, the board or court focuses on the government fault—in effect satisfying the "order" element of this type of constructive change by finding that the government was at fault in breaching its implied duty. The cases fall within several categories discussed in Chapter 3—the implied warranty of specifications, impracticability of performance, misrepresentation, and nondisclosure.

a. Defective Specifications

In one of the first Court of Claims cases dealing with a constructive change for a defective specification, *Hol-Gar Mfg. Corp. v. United States*, 175 Ct. Cl. 518, 360 F.2d 634 (1966), the court accepted the doctrine by ruling that the costs of a change issued to overcome defective specifications should include costs incurred from the inception of the contract, since the contractor had incurred expenditures made useless by the faulty specifications. This logic effectively converts a government breach of its implied warranty of the specifications into a constructive change, thereby substituting the recovery of an equitable adjustment for breach of contract damages. The law evolved even further when constructive changes were found in situations where performance of the work was impossible or impracticable. The impracticability doctrine developed in the common law as a method of relieving contracting parties from liability for nonperformance, but it did not entitle one party to a damages claim against the other party. Yet in the government contracts field there exists a line of cases in which impracticability has been characterized as a constructive change, with the result that the contractor obtains an equitable adjustment compensating for the costs incurred in attempting to perform. In effect, a defense for nonperformance has been converted into an affirmative claim for compensation.

Although there are numerous decisions finding constructive changes based on defective government specifications or impracticability of performance, the "order" element of the change is not generally addressed by the appeals board. The early cases occasionally contained language pertaining to an order of the government, although it is questionable if an actual order had been given. For example, in *F.J. Stokes Corp.*, ASBCA 6532, 1963 BCA ¶ 3944, the board based its holding on the rule that "[a] direction to proceed under defective specifications imposing an unattainable requirement is itself a basis for price adjustment under the Changes clause." See also *Northeastern Eng'g, Inc.*, ASBCA 5732, 61-1 BCA ¶ 3026. In *Pastushin Indus., Inc.*, ASBCA 7663, 1963 BCA ¶ 3757, the order was found in the refusal of the government to recognize the defects and its insistence on performance in accordance with the specifications. However, some of the early cases contain no mention of an order but merely indicate that the use of defective specifications by the government is a constructive change, *Spencer Explosives, Inc.*, ASBCA 4800, 60-2 BCA ¶ 2795; *Unexcelled Chem. Corp.*, ASBCA 2399, 60-1 BCA ¶ 2587. In *Consolidated Diesel Elec. Corp.*, ASBCA 10486, 67-2 BCA ¶ 6669, the board stated at 30,952:

> [W]hen defective or impossible specifications cause frustration and "wheel-spinning" and increase the time and cost of performance until the specifications are corrected or relaxed, this also gives rise to a constructive change.

More recent cases rarely address the need for an order because they apparently accept as well established the rule that the change actually occurs when the contract is issued. Accordingly, these cases also accept the basic principle that the costs of this type of constructive change include all costs incurred in attempting to cope with the defective specification from the inception of the contract. This explains why no order in the form of an act or direction from the government is required, since issuance of the contract is the event that constitutes the constructive change. In effect, the government is liable for a constructive change in these circumstances because it was at fault when it issued a contract containing defective specifications or calling for work that was impracticable to perform.

In some cases, government fault is balanced against contractor responsibility to determine liability. Thus, no constructive change was found when the contractor participated in the drafting of the defective specification, *Bethlehem Corp. v. United States*, 199 Ct. Cl. 247, 462 F.2d 1400 (1972); *Johns-Manville Corp. v. United States*, 13 Cl. Ct. 72 (1987), *vacated for lack of jurisdiction*, 855 F.2d 1571 (Fed. Cir. 1988). Subsequent contractor fault can also determine the outcome of these types of constructive changes. For example, in *S. Head Painting Contractor, Inc.*, ASBCA 26249, 82-2 BCA ¶ 15,886, the board denied a contractor's claim for repainting necessitated by a defect in the specifications for primer because the contractor knew of the defect and failed to notify the government. Similarly, in *Oconto Elec., Inc.*, ASBCA 40421, 93-3 BCA ¶ 26,162, the contractor was denied relief for impracticability in part because it failed to give the government the opportunity to alter the specification to overcome the difficulty.

b. *Undisclosed or Incorrect Information*

Nondisclosure of information by the government is a later evolutionary step from the constructive change of furnishing defective specifications. As with defective specifications, such nondisclosure can result in extra work being done and is the breach of a duty that the government owes the contractor. Here, too, it is the fault of the government, rather than an act or communication, that constitutes the change "order." In recent years, the boards of contract appeals have ruled that constructive changes have occurred in a number of instances of nondisclosure. At the same time, the Court of Federal Claims treats nondisclosure as either breaches of contract or constructive changes, depending on how the case is pleaded by the contractor. Compare *J.F. Shea Co. v. United States*, 4 Cl. Ct. 46 (1983) (breach of contract) with *Granite Constr. Co. v. United States*, 24 Cl. Ct. 735 (1991) (constructive change). It is now accepted that nondisclosure of information is treated as essentially the same claim whether it is stated as a constructive change or a breach of contract, *Petrochem Servs., Inc. v. United States*, 837 F.2d 1076 (Fed. Cir. 1988). See *Ellett Constr.*

Co. v. United States, 93 F.3d 1537 (Fed. Cir. 1996), holding that this type of claim was properly submitted as a constructive change claim.

The constructive change cases based on misrepresentation or nondisclosure of information do not contain a clear rationale as to why such action is a change. Most of the cases seem to follow the logic that a specification that contains incorrect information or from which vital information is missing is defective, *Lear Siegler, Inc.*, ASBCA 16079, 73-1 BCA ¶ 10,004; *F.F. Slocomb Corp.*, ASBCA 16715, 73-2 BCA ¶ 10,209. Some of the cases, however, use the logic that nondisclosure of information is an indication of assumption of risk by the government, *Ortronix, Inc.*, ASBCA 12745, 72-2 BCA ¶ 9564. A third line of cases seems to treat nondisclosure as a constructive change of a distinct type, *General Precision, Inc.*, ASBCA 12078, 70-1 BCA ¶ 8144; *Walden Landscape Co.*, ENGBCA 3534, 75-2 BCA ¶ 11,538; *Beckman Constr. Co. v. General Servs. Admin.*, GSBCA 11796, 93-3 BCA ¶ 26,205; *Raytheon Co.*, ASBCA 50166, 01-1 BCA ¶ 31,245, *aff'd in part, vacated in part*, 305 F.3d 1354 (Fed. Cir. 2002). One case has also held nondisclosure to be a breach of the government's affirmative duty to cooperate with the contractor, *Automated Servs., Inc.*, GSBCA EEOC-2, 81-2 BCA ¶ 15,303.

Some constructive changes in this category are based on difficulties encountered during performance when the government enforced the specifications in a way that was unforeseen by the contractor at the time of bidding. In these cases, one basis for finding a constructive change is that the government knew of the difficulties inherent in its interpretation but did not disclose them to the contractor, *Koppers Co.*, ENGBCA 3033, 73-2 BCA ¶ 10,237; *Piracci Constr. Co.*, GSBCA 3715, 74-2 BCA ¶ 10,719, *recons. denied*, 74-2 BCA ¶ 10,767. Similarly, in *Elrich Constr. Co.*, GSBCA 3657, 73-2 BCA ¶ 10,187, a constructive change was found where the government ordered the contractor to comply literally with the specification, which required the contractor to buy a proprietary item at a high price. The board reasoned that a change had occurred because the government should have known, but did not disclose, that the item was proprietary. Cases in which the board would not follow this holding include *Arnold M. Diamond, Inc.*, ASBCA 22733, 78-2 BCA ¶ 13,447 (contractor had access to knowledge that item was patented because patents are published), and *Southwood Builders, Inc.*, ASBCA 43489, 93-3 BCA ¶ 26,072 (contractor could have determined that item was proprietary by making inquiry of prospective vendors). See also *Stanwick Corp.*, ASBCA 16113, 72-1 BCA ¶ 9285, where the government advised the contractor that correcting work of a prior contractor was part of its effort. The board found a constructive change based partially on the government's failure to reveal the state of the prior work in the solicitation. Accord, *NAB-Lord Assocs.*, PSBCA 318, 77-2 BCA ¶ 12,802; *Boland Mach. & Mfg. Co.*, ASBCA 13664, 70-2 BCA ¶ 8556.

Allocation of fault can be a key issue in nondisclosure cases. Where there is both government nondisclosure and contractor error in the bid preparation, the trend is to find the nondisclosure as the more egregious act. See *Commercial Mech. Contrac-*

tors, Inc., ASBCA 25695, 83-2 BCA ¶ 16,768, in which government nondisclosure was held to override contractor negligence in not investigating the conditions prior to bidding. In *Perini Corp.*, ENGBCA 3745, 78-1 BCA ¶ 13,191, the board stated that a contractor may rely on positive representations by the government about the amount of material to be used and need not make its own inspection to confirm the government's representations. Similarly, in *Logics, Inc.*, ASBCA 46914, 97-2 BCA ¶ 29,125, *recons. denied*, 98-1 BCA ¶ 29,483, a government misstatement that an item of needed test equipment was a stock item overcame the contractor's certification that it had determined the availability of all needed materials.

Nondisclosure of vital information by the government can also override a contractor's obligation to inquire about conflicts in the specifications. For example, in *Norair Eng'g Corp.*, ENGBCA 3787, 78-1 BCA ¶ 13,202, the board found that although the contractor normally must clarify conflicts in specifications or bear the risk of misinterpretation, the drawings indicated that the item in question was not in the contract, so the contractor was under no duty to inquire. Similarly, in *Record Elec., Inc.*, ASBCA 26385, 82-1 BCA ¶ 15,784, although the contractor was at fault for failing to inquire, the government committed the "more grievous fault" by failing to warn the contractor that it had to make an extraordinary modification to existing equipment (citing *Aerodex, Inc. v. United States*, 417 F.2d 1361 (Ct. Cl. 1969)). Compare *Dewey Elecs. Corp.*, ASBCA 33869, 91-1 BCA ¶ 23,443, *recons. denied*, 91-1 BCA ¶ 23,656, in which the government was absolved from liability for misrepresentation because the contractor had hired the designer of the equipment as a consultant and thus was fully capable of resolving problems with the specifications. The knowing inclusion of incorrect information in the specifications has also overcome the contractor's normal obligation to follow a manufacturer's installation instructions, *V&Z Heating Corp.*, DOTBCA 2953, 98-2 BCA ¶ 29,818. In *Pacific W. Constr., Inc.*, DOTCAB 1084, 82-2 BCA ¶ 16,045, *recons. denied*, 83-1 BCA ¶ 16,337, the board apportioned the costs of government nondisclosure coupled with contractor fault.

3. Acceleration

Acceleration of contract performance is another of the early types of constructive change recognized by the boards of contract appeals, *Sanders*, Army BCA 1468, 4 CCF ¶ 60,526 (1948); *Samuels et al., Exrs.*, Army BCA 1147, 4 CCF ¶ 60,703 (1949). The concept that accelerations were changes evolved rapidly, and acceleration was included as one of the enumerated changes in the expanded construction contract Changes clause that was issued in 1968.

An acceleration is a speeding up of the work in an attempt to complete performance earlier than otherwise anticipated. In some instances, a contractor may accelerate on its own initiative to ensure completion within the contract schedule or for some other purpose. The costs of such acceleration are, of course, not recoverable from the government. See, for example, *International Maint. Res., Inc.*, ASBCA 48157, 96-2 BCA ¶ 28,436 (contractor volunteered in meeting with contracting officer to acquire additional workers and equipment); *Atlantic Indus., Inc.*, ASBCA 46710, 95-2 BCA ¶ 27,610 (no acceleration where contractor accelerated for its own convenience but the government was unable to provide the necessary government-furnished property to permit delivery as early as intended); and *Robert H. O'Hair & O'Hare Constr. Co., a Joint Venture*, AGBCA 82-115-1, 89-1 BCA ¶ 21,384 (no acceleration where subcontractor worked overtime with extra equipment to finish prior to end of construction season). See also *SAWADI Corp.*, ASBCA 53073, 01-1 BCA ¶ 31,357, in which no acceleration was found when a contractor had to hire new employees and rent additional equipment because task orders were issued at the end of the contract. The board concluded that such actions were "the normal ongoing costs of doing business."

Compensable acceleration occurs when the government orders the effort. In almost all cases, such an order is found constructively where the government requires the contractor to speed up work to meet the current contract delivery schedule in the face of excusable delays—that is, since excusable delays give the contractor a theoretical entitlement to schedule extensions, an order to meet the unadjusted schedule is equivalent to an order to complete the work in advance of that extended schedule.

a. Elements of Constructive Acceleration

While the case law is not dogmatic in application, there appear to be five common elements of a constructive acceleration:

1. Excusable delay,

2. Knowledge by the government of such delay,

3. Some statement or act by the government that can be construed as an acceleration order,

4. Notice by the contractor that the order is a constructive change (required by the construction contract Changes clause), and

5. Incurring additional costs of accelerated effort in response to the order.

A more elaborate set of requirements for a constructive acceleration is set forth in *Fermont Div., Dynamics Corp. of Am.*, ASBCA 15806, 75-1 BCA ¶ 11,139, *aff'd*, 216 Ct. Cl. 448 (1978), at 52,999-53,000:

(1) existence of a given period of excusable delay; and

(2) contractor notice to the Government of the excusable delay, and request for extension of time together with supporting information sufficient to allow the Government to make a reasonable determination;

EXCEPTIONS:

(a) such notice, request and information are not necessary if the Government's order (see (3) below) directs compliance with a given schedule expressly without regard to the existence of any excusable delay,

(b) the supporting information is unnecessary if it is already reasonably available to the Government; and

(3) failure or refusal to grant the requested extension within a reasonable time; and

(4) a Government order, either express or implied from the circumstances, to (a) take steps to overcome the excusable delay, or (b) complete the work at the earliest possible date, or (c) complete the work by a given date earlier than that to which the contractor is entitled by reason of the excusable delay. Circumstances from which such an order may be implied include expressions of urgency by the Government, especially if coupled with (i) a threat of default or liquidated damages for not meeting a given accelerated schedule, or (ii) actual assessment of liquidated damages for not meeting a given accelerated schedule; and

(5) reasonable efforts by the contractor to accelerate the work, resulting in added costs, even if the efforts are not actually successful.

(1) Excusable Delay

The cornerstone of the constructive acceleration theory is an excusable delay. Thus, even under the Default (Fixed-Price Supply and Service) clause in FAR 52.249-8, which is silent as to the contractor's entitlement to a time extension, a constructive acceleration will be found if the contractor is required to accelerate to overcome an excusable delay. See, e.g., *Standard Store Equip. Co.*, ASBCA 4348, 58-2 BCA ¶ 1902. However, in no situation can there be a constructive acceleration without an excusable delay, *R. J. Lanthier Co.*, ASBCA 51636, 04-1 BCA ¶ 32,481; *National Radio Co.*, ASBCA 14707, 72-2 BCA ¶ 9486. See Chapter 6 for a full discussion of the legal rules on excusable delays.

(2) Knowledge of the Contracting Officer

For a constructive acceleration to occur, the contracting officer must have knowledge of the excusable delay at the time the acceleration is ordered. Apparently, it is reasoned that it is not logical to hold a contracting officer responsible for having issued a constructive acceleration order unless he or she knew of the contractor's entitlement to a time extension. In some cases, this element has been stated as a requirement that the contractor have actually submitted a request for a time extension, *Mechanical Utils., Inc.*, ASBCA 7466, 1962 BCA ¶ 3556; *California Shipbuilding & Dry Dock Co.*, ASBCA 21394, 78-1 BCA ¶ 13,168; *Commercial Contractors Equip., Inc.*, ASBCA 52930, 03-2 BCA ¶ 32,381. However, the key factor seems to be knowledge, as indicated in *Corbetta Constr. Co.*, PSBCA 299, 77-2 BCA ¶ 12,699, in which it was stated that the rule calling for a request for time extension "is flexible enough to be satisfied in the absence of a formal request but only where there is a very clear indication from the contracting officer that no delays in the schedule will be tolerated." See also *Sylvania Elec. Prods., Inc.*, ASBCA 11206, 67-2 BCA ¶ 6428, *recons. denied*, 67-2 BCA ¶ 6721. Hence, constructive accelerations were found without any notice of excusable delay or request for time extensions in *William Lagnion*, ENGBCA 3778, 78-2 BCA ¶ 13,260 (contracting officer closely monitored job and granted some time extensions without contractor request); *Fort Howard Paper Co.*, ASBCA 20284, 78-1 BCA ¶ 12,873, *recons. denied*, 78-1 BCA ¶ 13,027 (government-caused disruption was a direct cause of contractor acceleration effort without regard to excusable delay); *E.C. Morris & Son, Inc.*, ASBCA 20697, 77-2 BCA ¶ 12,622 (direct order to simultaneously perform work scheduled sequentially); *Greulich, Inc.*, ENGBCA 3832, 78-2 BCA ¶ 13,417 (requesting time extension a futile gesture where the government urged timely completion and maintained data showing the flood conditions that delayed the contractor); and *Hurst Excavating, Inc.*, ASBCA 37351, 93-3 BCA ¶ 25,935 (direct order to speed up work).

Where the government had neither actual nor constructive knowledge of the contractor's excusable delay, claims for constructive accelerations will be denied unless the contractor has given notice, requested a time extension, and furnished supporting information at the time of the delay, *Carney Gen. Contractors, Inc.*, NASABCA 375-4, 79-1 BCA ¶ 13,855, *recons. denied*, 80-1 BCA ¶ 14,243. See also *R. J. Lanthier Co.*, ASBCA 51636, 04-1 BCA ¶ 32,481 (no contemporaneous request for time extensions); *Gavosto Assocs., Inc.*, PSBCA 4058, 01-1 BCA ¶ 31,389 (no request for time extension submitted until two days before end of claimed acceleration period); *Hemphill Contracting Co.*, ENGBCA 5698, 94-1 BCA ¶ 26,491 (no notice of excusable delays or request for time extensions); *Allen L. Bender, Inc.*, PSBCA 2322, 91-2 BCA ¶ 23,828 (no requests for time extension before the contracting officer at the time of the alleged acceleration order); and *Nello L. Teer Co. v. Washington Metro. Area Transit Auth.*, 695 F. Supp. 583 (D.D.C. 1988) (no response to contracting officer's request for substantiating information to support claim of excusable delays).

(3) Orders to Accelerate

An essential element of a constructive acceleration is an act or a communication that can be reasonably construed as an order to accelerate. Thus, if a contractor accelerates to overcome job conditions without an order from the government, no constructive acceleration will be found. See, for example, *GBQC Architects v. Gen-*

eral Servs. Admin., GSBCA 15578, 02-1 BCA ¶ 31,846, in which no government liability for an acceleration was found where the architect was forced to speed up its contract administration work because the construction contractor worked to an earlier schedule than the contract schedule.

The deciding factor is the degree of compulsion to accelerate produced by a particular set of circumstances. A number of fact patterns have been dealt with by the boards and courts.

(A) Direct Orders

Most of the instances of direct orders to accelerate arose under the construction contract clause entitled Progress Charts and Requirements for Overtime Work, which was set forth in DAR 7-603.48. A slightly revised version of this provision is now contained in FAR 52.236-15, as follows:

> SCHEDULES FOR CONSTRUCTION CONTRACTS (APR 1984)
>
> (a) The Contractor shall, within five days after the work commences on the contract or another period of time determined by the Contracting Officer, prepare and submit to the Contracting Officer for approval three copies of a practicable schedule showing the order in which the Contractor proposes to perform the work, and the dates on which the Contractor contemplates starting and completing the several salient features of the work (including acquiring materials, plant, and equipment). The schedule shall be in the form of a progress chart of suitable scale to indicate appropriately the percentage of work scheduled for completion by any given date during the period. If the Contractor fails to submit a schedule within the time prescribed, the Contracting Officer may withhold approval of progress payments until the Contractor submits the required schedule.
>
> (b) The Contractor shall enter the actual progress on the chart as directed by the Contracting Officer, and upon doing so shall immediately deliver three copies of the annotated schedule to the Contracting Officer. If, in the opinion of the Contracting Officer, the Contractor falls behind the approved schedule, the Contractor shall take steps necessary to improve its progress, including those that may be required by the Contracting Officer, without additional cost to the Government. In this circumstance, the Contracting Officer may require the Contractor to increase the number of shifts, overtime operations, days of work, and/or the amount of construction plant, and to submit for approval any supplementary schedule or schedules in chart form as the Contracting Officer deems necessary to demonstrate how the approved rate of progress will be regained.
>
> (c) Failure of the Contractor to comply with the requirements of the Contracting Officer under this clause shall be grounds for a determination by the Contracting Officer that the Contractor is not prosecuting the work with sufficient diligence to ensure completion within the time specified in the contract. Upon making this determination, the Contracting Officer may terminate the Contractor's right to

> proceed with the work, or any separable part of it, in accordance with the default terms of this contract.

This clause gives the contracting officer the right to order accelerated efforts at no additional cost to the government if the contractor falls behind the contract schedule. Some of the earliest acceleration cases established the principle that an improper order under such a clause, when the contractor was entitled to excusable delay, was a constructive acceleration, *Farnsworth & Chambers Co.*, ASBCA 4945, 59-2 BCA ¶ 2433; *Hagstrom Constr. Co.*, ASBCA 5698, 61-1 BCA ¶ 3090. See also *Norair Eng'g Corp.*, ENGBCA 3804, 90-1 BCA ¶ 22,327, in which an order under this clause to accelerate work not on the critical path was found to be a constructive acceleration order. An order under this clause to accelerate performance to meet a noncontractual interim completion date was also found to be a constructive acceleration, *Hurst Excavating, Inc.*, ASBCA 37351, 93-3 BCA ¶ 25,935. Compare *Granite Constr. Co. v. United States*, 24 Cl. Ct. 735 (1991), in which an order under this clause to meet a contractual interim date was found to be a proper order. In *Yukon Constr. Co., Ltd.*, ASBCA 10859, 67-1 BCA ¶ 6334, the board stated that the substantial rights granted the contracting officer by this clause require that purported acts under the provision be closely scrutinized, and that the contracting officer was not justified in invoking the clause where the contractor's actual progress demonstrated a "close relationship" with the progress schedule under which the contractor was operating at the time of the order. See, however, *Robert Simmons Constr. Co.*, ASBCA 11019, 67-1 BCA ¶ 6279, for a less stringent view of the government's obligations. In *Carney Gen. Contractors, Inc.*, NASABCA 375-4, 80-1 BCA ¶ 14,243, the board noted that a notice to accelerate under this clause is "valid" if the contractor is behind schedule at the time of the order.

Other direct orders have been held to be constructive acceleration orders. For example, in *Alley-Cassetty Coal Co.*, ASBCA 33315, 89-3 BCA ¶ 21,964, *recons. denied*, 89-3 BCA ¶ 22,204, an order was found when the contracting officer directed the contractor to deliver coal in the face of an excusable delay, and in *Atlantic Dry Dock Corp.*, ASBCA 42609, 98-2 BCA ¶ 30,025, *recons. denied*, 99-1 BCA ¶ 30,208, an order was found when the government demanded a compressed schedule of work to make up for a late start that was not the fault of the contractor. Similarly, in *Maintenance Eng'rs*, ASBCA 23131, 81-2 BCA ¶ 15,168, *modified on recons.*, 83-1 BCA ¶ 16,411, the government constructively accelerated the contract when it ordered the contractor to continue mowing a field that had become soaked by heavy rains. The board emphasized that the contractor's costs for pulling its equipment out of the mud were compensable because the government refused to allow the time extension it was entitled to. Compare *Sherman R. Smoot Corp.*, ASBCA 52173, 03-1 BCA ¶ 32,212, finding no acceleration order when the contracting officer informed the contractor that it was required to meet a specified occupancy date but excepted from the direction a specific claim for a time extension. The board reasoned that the order was not "unconditional."

(b) Requests to Accelerate

In *Hyde Constr. Co.*, ASBCA 8393, 1963 BCA ¶ 3911, the board held that a request to accelerate was tantamount to an acceleration order, noting that in both a request and an order the initiative comes from the government for the government's convenience. In contrast, it has been held that urging a contractor to complete the work in accordance with the original schedule was not an acceleration order, *Kingston Bituminous Prods. Co.*, ASBCA 9964, 67-2 BCA ¶ 6638; *Guaranty Constr. Co.*, GSBCA 3109, 70-2 BCA ¶ 8483. In *A. Teichert & Son, Inc.*, ASBCA 10265, 68-2 BCA ¶ 7175, *recons. denied*, 68-2 BCA ¶ 7410, a request that the contractor submit a plan showing how lost time could be regained was held not to constitute an acceleration order. Similarly, giving advice to a contractor that more workers were needed was not an acceleration order, *Evergreen Forest Mgmt., Inc.*, AGBCA 84-299-1, 88-3 BCA ¶ 20,950.

(c) Threats to Terminate for Default

The consequences of a default termination are so serious that the boards have consistently ruled that a threat to terminate for default will constitute an acceleration order, *Lewis Constr. Co.*, ASBCA 5509, 60-2 BCA ¶ 2732; *Mechanical Utils., Inc.*, ASBCA 7345, 1962 BCA ¶ 3556; *William Lagnion*, ENGBCA 3778, 78-2 BCA ¶ 13,260. However, merely informing a contractor of the government's right to default terminate was held not to be an acceleration order in *Donald R. Stewart & Assocs.*, AGBCA 84-226-1, 92-1 BCA ¶ 24,705. Furthermore, issuing a cure notice when a contractor is behind schedule, mainly due to its own difficulties, is not the type of threat to default that will be construed as an acceleration order, *Consolidated Constr., Inc.*, ASBCA 46498, 99-1 BCA ¶ 30,148, *aff'd*, 230 F.3d 1378 (Fed. Cir. 2000). However, a constructive acceleration was found when the contracting officer issued a cure notice after failing to grant sufficient time extensions to cover the excusable delays that had been encountered, *Monterey Mech., Inc.*, ASBCA 51450, 01-1 BCA ¶ 31,380.

(d) Government Pressure to Complete on Schedule

Statements by government employees that a program is of high priority and delays cannot be tolerated will be construed as an acceleration order, *Electronic & Missile Facilities, Inc.*, ASBCA 9031, 1964 BCA ¶ 4338, *motion sustained in part, denied in part*, 1964 BCA ¶ 4474; *Gibbs Shipyard, Inc.*, ASBCA 9809, 67-2 BCA ¶ 6499; *Norair Eng'g Corp. v. United States*, 229 Ct. Cl. 160, 666 F.2d 546 (1981). In *Pathman Constr. Co.*, ASBCA 14285, 71-1 BCA ¶ 8905, a government statement of urgent need for completion coupled with a threat to assess liquidated damages was held to constitute an acceleration order. When the program for which the contract is issued is of lesser priority, it is more difficult to argue that government pressure is properly interpreted as an acceleration order. For example, continued expressions of concern about the progress of the contractor were held to be insufficient to constitute acceleration orders in *Gibson Co.*, ASBCA 13307, 70-1 BCA ¶ 8289. Other cases finding insufficient pressure to constitute an acceleration order include *Fermont Div., Dynamics Corp. of Am.*, ASBCA 15806, 75-1 BCA ¶ 11,139, *aff'd*, 216 Ct. Cl. 448 (1978) ("reasonable" pressure to complete on schedule); *Lamb Eng'g. & Constr. Co.*, EBCA C-9304172, 97-2 BCA ¶ 29,207, *recons. denied*, 98-1 BCA ¶ 29,359 (agency "continuously pressed" the contractor to complete on time); and *R. J. Lanthier Co.*, ASBCA 51636, 04-1 BCA ¶ 32,481 (single communication requesting that the project be completed on time).

(E) REFUSAL TO GRANT TIME EXTENSIONS PLUS LIQUIDATED DAMAGES

In one early case, the board ruled that the combination of a refusal to grant time extensions and assessment of heavy liquidated damages was sufficiently coercive to constitute an acceleration order, *Keco Indus., Inc.*, ASBCA 8900, 1963 BCA ¶ 3891. The Court of Claims in *Norair Eng'g Corp. v. United States*, 229 Ct. Cl. 160, 666 F.2d 546 (1981), stated at 165 that pressure to accelerate "even if it were merely implicit . . . is particularly strong where liquidated damages hover in the background" and that if the "Government refuses . . . to tell the contractor until the end of the project just what delay is excusable and what is not, the contractor [will be] under considerable additional pressure to accede to a request [to accelerate] because it does not know whether it will be found liable for liquidated damages." Similarly, in *Constructors-Pamco*, ENGBCA 3468, 76-2 BCA ¶ 11,950, an acceleration order was found where the contract contained a liquidated damages provision and the government refused to grant a time extension that was obviously due, refused to give instructions on how to proceed in face of problems, and insisted on maintaining the original schedule. In contrast, in *Robert A. Verrier Co.*, ASBCA 8693, 1964 BCA ¶ 4062, *recons. denied*, 65-1 BCA ¶ 4667, the board found that the failure to grant a time extension plus the mere presence of a liquidated damages clause did not result in constructive acceleration. In these cases, the board appeared to weigh the entire factual context in which the contractor found itself at the time the decision to accelerate was made to determine if it was reasonable to interpret the government's actions and communications as an order. Thus, in *Barrett Co.*, ENGBCA 3877, 78-1 BCA ¶ 13,075, the combination of liquidated damages plus a two-month delay in acting on a request for a time extension was found to be an acceleration order on a contract to be performed in 60 days. See *Larry Azure v. United States*, 129 F.3d 136 (Fed. Cir. 1997), affirming a Court of Federal Claims decision that failure to act on requests for time extensions until after contract completion, plus a reminder that the contractor was liable for liquidated damages, was held to be a government order to accelerate. See also *Unarco Material Handling*, PSBCA 4100, 00-1 BCA ¶ 30,682, finding an acceleration order when the contracting officer unilaterally imposed a contract completion date, refused to grant a time extension to overcome the improper data, and threatened liquidated damages.

(f) Refusal to Grant Time Extension and Insistence That Contractor Meet Original Schedule

If, in the course of refusing to grant time extensions, the contracting officer insists on contract completion as called for by the original schedule, an acceleration order will be found, *Earth Tech Indus., Ltd.*, ASBCA 46450, 99-1 BCA ¶ 30,341. Apparently, in this case the board concluded that the contracting officer was well aware of the impact of his actions. See also *P.J. Dick, Inc.*, VABCA 5597, 01-2 BCA ¶ 31,647, *rev'd on other grounds*, 324 F.3d 1364 (Fed. Cir. 2003), in which a constructive acceleration was found where the government continually pressed for completion in accordance with the schedule while it was granting short time extensions that did not reflect the excusable delays that had actually occurred. In this case, the contractor's claim was greatly enhanced because it continually notified the agency that it was being forced to accelerate by the government's inaction in dealing with the delays that were occurring during contract performance. Similarly, in *Hensel Phelps Constr. Co. v. General Servs. Admin.*, GSBCA 14744, 01-1 BCA ¶ 31,249, a constructive acceleration was found because the contractor made it clear to the contracting officer that it would have to accelerate if time extensions were not granted and the contracting officer continued to refuse to act on the requests for time extensions. In this instance, it appears that the board concluded that the contracting officer had unreasonably demanded more adequate documentation of the time extensions and had rejected some of them because they were not requested in a timely fashion. The Federal Circuit reached a similar result in *Fraser Constr. Co. v. United States*, 215 F.3d 1344 (Fed. Cir. 1999), in which it remanded a case to the Court of Federal Claims to determine if the government had, as alleged, refused to grant time extensions and pressed the contractor to complete the work in accordance with the contract schedule. On remand, 57 Fed. Cl. 56 (2003), *aff'd*, 384 F.3d 1359 (Fed. Cir. 2004), the court denied relief because, although agency personnel frequently expressed concern about the progress of the work, the contracting officer always timely acknowledged and granted the contractor's requests for weather-based time extensions.

(g) Failure to Grant Time Extension

A failure to grant a time extension, without more, has been held insufficiently compelling to constitute an order to accelerate, *Carroll Servs., Inc.*, ASBCA 8362, 1964 BCA ¶ 4365, *recons. denied*, 65-1 BCA ¶ 4613. While awaiting the contracting officer's response to its request for a time extension, the contractor has two alternatives: (1) continue performing at its current pace, thereby risking late completion, or (2) accelerate performance in order to complete according to the original schedule. In *Peter Kiewit Sons' Co.*, ASBCA 9921, 69-1 BCA ¶ 7510, the board stated that only if the contracting officer takes away the contractor's option of continuing performance at a normal pace will there be an order to accelerate. See also *Intermax, Ltd.*, ASBCA 41828, 93-2 BCA ¶ 25,699, *recons. denied*, 93-3 BCA ¶ 26,207, *aff'd*, 78 F.3d 604 (Fed. Cir. 1996), in which no acceleration order was found when the contracting officer refused to act on requests for time extensions because the contractor did not provide substantiating information with requests.

This can be a harsh rule, because if the contractor elects to continue at its current pace while assuming it will get an extension but then does not, it may find it more difficult to recoup lost time than it would have been had it accelerated earlier. If it assumes that it will not get the extension and accelerates, it will not be able to later prove the order element necessary for a constructive acceleration claim. According to the board in *Carroll*, this is simply the result of the contractor's duty to perform diligently during the resolution of a dispute, and the mere fact that a contractor that has not been granted an extension adjusts its schedule to complete the work on time does not show that the contractor was compelled to adjust its schedule. This situation can leave the contractor with a time extension that it cannot use since it was granted late in contract performance and acceleration costs that it cannot recover. Of course, if the contractor is certain that it has experienced an excusable delay, it should continue working at its current pace and can use the excusable delay as a defense to termination for default or assessment for liquidated damages. It is when the contractor is uncertain that this rule can work a hardship.

(h) Delays in Granting Extensions

The logic of the rule is stronger where the delay in granting the extension is reasonable in relation to the contractor's opportunity to adjust its schedule, *Peter Kiewit Sons' Co.*, ASBCA 9921, 69-1 BCA ¶ 7510. See, however, *Olin Mathieson Chem. Corp.*, ASBCA 7605, 1963 BCA ¶ 3983, *aff'd*, 179 Ct. Cl. 368 (1967), in which a three-to-four-month delay was found reasonable on a complex project even though the extensions were ultimately granted after contract completion. One board has commented with disapproval on the government technique of waiting to act on requests for time extensions until completion of the work, *Ashton Co.*, IBCA 1070-6-75, 76-2 BCA ¶ 11,934, noting that such practice can easily lead to a constructive acceleration. What the board seems to have said is that the compelling force of an unreasonable delay in granting a request for a time extension is greater than that of a reasonable delay, and therefore less additional compulsion will be required to constitute an order to accelerate. See also *Continental Consolidated Corp. v. United States*, 17 CCF ¶ 81,137 (Trial Judge Dec. 1972), *aff'd by order*, 200 Ct. Cl. 737 (1972), in which the court emphasized the importance of a timely response to requests for time extensions. In *Human Advancement, Inc.*, HUDBCA 77-215-C15, 81-2 BCA ¶ 15,317, delay in granting a time extension was held to have been a constructive acceleration since, by the time the extension was granted, the contractor had adjusted its work schedule to complete the added work without a time extension. See also *McKenzie Eng'g Co.*, ASBCA 53374, 02-2 BCA ¶ 31,972, denying a motion to dismiss because the contractor had offered proof that the government's substantial delay in acting on a request for a time extension had compelled it to accelerate the work.

Once the contracting officer knows of the delay and of the contractor's request for a time extension, the request should be acted on promptly, if at all possible. However, contracting officers frequently request contractors to substantiate their claims for time extensions. Such a request is somewhat questionable in construction contracts. The Default clause in FAR 52.249-10 contains the following provision regarding the responsibility of the contracting officer once notice of the causes of an excusable delay has been given:

> (b)(2) . . . The Contracting Officer shall ascertain the facts and the extent of delay. If, in the judgment of the Contracting Officer, the findings of fact warrant such action, the time for completing the work shall be extended. The findings of the Contracting Officer shall be final and conclusive on the parties, but subject to appeal under the Disputes clause.

In *Electronic & Missile Facilities, Inc.*, ASBCA 9031, 1964 BCA ¶ 4338, *motion sustained in part, denied in part*, 1964 BCA ¶ 4474, the board analyzed this clause and noted that, "while it is customary and proper for the contracting officer or his representative to request the contractor to submit a specific request for a stated number of days extension substantiated by supporting data, the contracting officer's authority to act under GP-5 is not conditional on any such submission by the contractor." The board went on to find that the government was not justified in delaying the granting of a time extension when information about the cause of the delay—unusually severe weather was readily available

In *Iversen Constr. Co.*, IBCA 981-1-73, 76-1 BCA ¶ 11,644, *aff'd*, 244 Ct. Cl. 692 (1980), the board agreed with the view that the contracting officer has an obligation to act on time extension requests but held that, once a contracting officer had refused to grant a time extension and had asked for more information, a reasonable contractor would furnish information in its possession. Similarly, in *Freeman Elec. Constr. Co.*, DOTCAB 74-23A, 77-1 BCA ¶ 12,258, *aff'd*, 221 Ct. Cl. 884 (1979), the board stated that the contract language obligated the contractor to submit sufficient information to at least make a prima facie showing that it was entitled to a time extension and to furnish information peculiarly within its knowledge. See also *Fermont Div., Dynamics Corp. of Am.*, ASBCA 15806, 75-1 BCA ¶ 11,139, *aff'd*, 216 Ct. Cl. 448 (1978), and *Intermax, Ltd.*, ASBCA 41828, 93-2 BCA ¶ 25,699, *recons. denied*, 93-3 BCA ¶ 26,207, *aff'd*, 78 F.3d 604 (Fed. Cir. 1996).

The length of the contract performance period may have a significant impact on what will be considered to be a reasonable amount of time to grant a time extension under this provision. For example, in *Barrett Co.*, ENGBCA 3877, 78-1 BCA ¶ 13,075, an acceleration was found when the contracting officer delayed for two months in acting on a request for a time extension to a contract with a 60-day performance period. Compare *Allen L. Bender, Inc.*, PSBCA 2322, 91-2 BCA ¶ 23,828, where the contracting officer was slow in acting on time extensions but, over the course of the contract, they were granted fairly. The board concluded that, in these circumstances, there was no reason for the contractor to believe that the government was desirous of acceleration to make up for excusable delays. See also *Riennes Constr. Co.*, IBCA 3572-96, 98-2 BCA ¶ 29,821, in which a time extension shortly before the end of contract completion was held sufficient to overcome any claim of an acceleration order.

(i) Denial of Request for Time Extension

Denial of a request for a time extension should be sufficiently compelling to constitute an order to accelerate. This had been recognized by the Court of Claims in *Norair Eng'g Corp. v. United States*, 229 Ct. Cl. 160, 666 F.2d 546 (1981), in which the court, in discussing the requirements for finding an acceleration order, noted that a requirement for a request for and a denial of a time extension is "in effect equivalent to the requirement of an order to accelerate." The court also noted that "mere failure to grant an extension at the time will not constitute a constructive order to accelerate." This is in recognition of the fact that, when the government affirmatively denies a time extension, it is in effect insisting on performance of the contract according to the original schedule subject to all the original contract provisions. See also *Fischbach & Moore Int'l Corp.*, ASBCA 18146, 77-1 BCA ¶ 12,300, *aff'd*, 223 Ct. Cl. 119, 617 F.2d 223 (1980), in which the board held that the contractor had been compelled to accelerate because denials and tardy approvals of time extensions coupled with government intransigence led the contractor to reasonably believe that the requested time extensions would not be granted and that it would be held to the original contract completion date. Applying the reasoning in *Fischbach* to a case of flat denial, it is clear that a denial leaves in force all the original contract provisions, including, for example, the completion date and any liquidated damages, and that a reasonable contractor will consider itself obligated to comply.

(4) Causation

The final element of a constructive acceleration is proof that the acceleration was in response to the "order." In most cases this is clear from the facts but, when there is doubt, the contractor must prove such causation. See, for example, *Solar Foam Insulation*, ASBCA 46278, 94-1 BCA ¶ 26,288, in which a claim was denied because the evidence showed that the contractor had increased its crew sizes prior to the alleged acceleration order and had taken no further steps to accelerate after the order was received. The board concluded that the accelerated effort had not resulted from the order of the government. Compare *Atlantic Dry Dock Corp.*, ASBCA 42609, 98-2 BCA ¶ 30,025, *recons. denied*, 99-1 BCA ¶ 30,208, in which the board found the government liable for acceleration because the contractor regularly informed government officials that it was accelerating to overcome government-caused delays and the officials did not object to this course of action.

b. Acceleration to Mitigate Delay

Acceleration costs are also recoverable against the government if they are incurred in mitigation of the effects of a government-caused delay, *Fischbach & Moore*

Int'l Corp., ASBCA 18146, 77-1 BCA ¶ 12,300, *aff'd*, 223 Ct. Cl. 119, 617 F.2d 223 (1980); *King Constr. Co.*, ASBCA 38303, 94-1 BCA ¶ 26,434, *recons. denied*, 94-2 BCA ¶ 26,630; *Canon Constr. Corp.*, ASBCA 16142, 72-1 BCA ¶ 9404. This type of acceleration is actually a claim for mitigation of delay costs pursued under the Suspension of Work clause rather than the Changes clause, *Day & Zimmermann-Madway*, ASBCA 13367, 71-1 BCA ¶ 8622. Thus, the normal elements of a constructive acceleration claim need not be present. In *Weaver Constr. Co.*, ASBCA 12577, 69-1 BCA ¶ 7455, it was held that such acceleration costs were not recoverable because the contractor was responsible for delays in addition to the government delays, and insufficient time had been recouped to prove that the acceleration costs had been incurred for the benefit of the government, since final performance was late a greater number of days than the amount of the government delay.

c. Post-Constructive Acceleration Time Extensions

A contracting officer can cut off the government's continuing liability for a constructive acceleration order by granting time extensions for excusable delays, *William Lagnion*, ENGBCA 3778, 78-2 BCA ¶ 13,260. After the granting of such extensions, the contractor is under no further pressure to meet an unenforceable schedule and hence has no claim against the government for subsequent acceleration costs.

d. Acceleration Orders Where There Are Both Excusable and Nonexcusable Delays

When an acceleration order has been given under a special clause granting the government the right to order acceleration without compensation to make up delays for which the contractor is responsible, it has been held that no acceleration costs are recoverable when the contractor did not make up such delays, even though there were also excusable delays, *Pan-Pac. Corp.*, ENGBCA 2479, 65-2 BCA ¶ 4984; *Joseph E. Bennett Co.*, GSBCA 2362, 72-1 BCA ¶ 9364. In both of these cases, the decision may have been influenced by the fact that the delay for which the contractor was responsible preceded the excusable delay. However, the theory of the cases seems to be that this special clause gives the government the right to specify which delays will be made up first. In *Electrical Enters., Inc.*, IBCA 971-8-72, 74-1 BCA ¶ 10,528, the board ruled that no compensable acceleration had occurred where there were both excusable and nonexcusable delays at the time of the acceleration order but no clause giving the government the right to order acceleration without compensation to make up nonexcusable delays. The board reasoned that the contractor would not have completed on time even if a time extension for excusable delays had been granted. This reasoning appears to be questionable since without the special clause, the contracting officer had no right to order acceleration without compensation. See also *Yukon Constr. Co.*, ASBCA 10859, 67-1 BCA ¶ 6334, in which the board found that costs should be apportioned when the government had the right to order acceleration for nonexcusable delays, both excusable delays and nonexcusable delays were present at the time of the acceleration order, and it was clear from the facts that all of the costs were not attributable to making up time lost through the excusable delays.

When there are both excusable delays and delays of the contractor, the contracting officer can ensure that the government is not liable for acceleration costs by granting time extensions for the excusable delays. This occurred in *Michael-Mark Ltd.*, IBCA 2697, 94-1 BCA ¶ 26,453, and *Donald R. Stewart & Assocs.*, AGBCA 84-226-1, 92-1 BCA ¶ 24,705. In *Lake Union Drydock Co. v. Department of Commerce*, GSBCA 10394-COM, 93-1 BCA ¶ 25,285, *recons. denied*, 93-2 BCA ¶ 25,838, the contracting officer avoided an acceleration claim by reducing the work and granting a time extension to overcome the entire excusable delay. The board ruled that there was no acceleration because all of the remaining delay was the fault of the contractor.

e. Recovery Not Dependent on Contractor's Recoupment of Lost Time

When the contractor accelerates the work at the direction of the government but cannot demonstrate that time lost through excusable delays was recouped, it is generally held that acceleration costs may be recovered since their reimbursement is not dependent on making up lost time. For example, in *Varo, Inc.*, ASBCA 15000, 72-2 BCA ¶ 9717, where the contracting officer had ordered completion ahead of the original contract schedule, the board permitted recovery of acceleration costs since the contractor had used its "best effort" to complete the work ahead of schedule. Accord, *M.S.I. Corp.*, GSBCA 2429, 68-2 BCA ¶ 7377. See also *Continental Consolidated Corp. v. United States*, 17 CCF ¶ 81,137 (Trial Judge Dec. 1972), *aff'd by order*, 200 Ct. Cl. 737 (1972), in which the trial judge found the contractor entitled to all of the acceleration costs incurred even though very little time had been made up in comparison with the amount of acceleration effort expended. The judge reasoned that, since the contractor was on schedule at the time the acceleration order was issued, the government had the burden of proving that the contractor was responsible for the failure to recoup much time.

4. Hindrance or Failure to Cooperate

The final major category of constructive change is the failure of the government to perform its obligation to cooperate with the contractor or not to hinder, interfere with, or delay its performance of the work. As discussed in Chapter 3, this duty is a part of the duty of good faith and fair dealing, which is imposed on both parties to the contract. The most common result of a breach of this duty is the performance of work beyond that called for by the contract — a result easily analyzed as a constructive change. However, because this was not a well-defined area of constructive change in 1978 when the Contract Disputes Act was enacted, contractors may be able to seek recovery either under the contract, on a constructive change theory, or under a breach of contract theory. Normally, the same legal standards are applied to ascertain government liability in noncooperation or hindrance of performance cases whether the claim is characterized as a breach of contract or constructive change. However, several older cases indicate that a contractor may recover from a board of contract appeals with a less egregious act of government interference than that necessary for a breach of contract claim. Compare *Banks Constr. Co. v. United States*, 176 Ct. Cl. 1302, 364 F.2d 357 (1966), with *A. Geris, Inc.*, ENGBCA 2869, 68-2 BCA ¶ 7320, and *John M. Bragg*, ASBCA 9515, 65-2 BCA ¶ 5050. Compare also *Bruno Law v. United States*, 195 Ct. Cl. 370 (1971), with *Carpenter Constr. Co.*, NASABCA 18, 1964 BCA ¶ 4452. Thus, it can be expected that such claims will be filed primarily as constructive change claims.

Whether the government has breached an implied duty to cooperate is determined by the reasonableness of its actions under the circumstances. Thus, in *Ben C. Gerwick, Inc. v. United States*, 152 Ct. Cl. 69, 285 F.2d 432 (1961), the contractor was denied relief where availability of the work site was delayed by another government contractor, not by an act or omission of the government. The officer in charge did all he could reasonably do to hasten the performance of the preceding contractor. See also *Asheville Contracting Co.*, DOTCAB 74-6, 76-2 BCA ¶ 12,027 (government "reasonably executed its duty to get timely completion" of other contract); *Tolis Cain Corp.*, DOTCAB 72-2, 76-2 BCA ¶ 11,954 (no government fault or negligence where government had no notice of any problems prior to shutdown and promptly had services restored upon receipt of notice); *Sun Oil Co. v. United States*, 215 Ct. Cl. 716, 572 F.2d 786 (1978) (contractor failed to establish that government acted unreasonably); *Zinco Gen. Contractor, Inc.*, GSBCA 6182, 82-2 BCA ¶ 15,917 (government acted with reasonable promptness in first rejecting contractor's proposal and then in negotiating a modification after reviving the proposal); *GLR Constructors, Inc.*, ENGBCA 6128, 96-1 BCA ¶ 28,218, *aff'd*, 114 F.3d 1206 (Fed. Cir. 1997) (government reasonably refused to revise specification to permit contractor to work more efficiently); *Commercial Prods. & Eng'g Co.*, ASBCA 40392, 96-2 BCA ¶ 28,411, *aff'd*, 155 F.3d 566 (Fed. Cir. 1998) (government action reasonable, although not completely responsive, in dealing with government-furnished material, first article approval and numerous changes); *Reflectone, Inc.*, ASBCA 42363, 98-2 BCA ¶ 29,869 (government administered contract strictly but responded to contractor with diligence); *Consolidated Constr., Inc.*, ASBCA 46498, 99-1 BCA ¶ 30,148, *aff'd*, 230 F.3d 1378 (Fed. Cir. 2000) (government direction to continue work in cold weather not interference because contractor was well behind schedule at time); *Tri Indus., Inc.*, ASBCA 47880, 99-2 BCA ¶ 30,529 (government failure to loan part or approve deviations not failure to cooperate because neither was necessary for performance); and *Centurion Elecs. Serv.*, ASBCA 48750, 00-1 BCA ¶ 30,642 (failure to make advance payments or accept partial deliveries not failure to cooperate because neither required by contract).

When courts and boards apply the logic of constructive change to breaches of this duty, they frequently grant relief without analyzing whether there has been an order to perform extra work. Rather, they look to whether the government's fault has compelled the contractor to perform extra work. Fault may arise from the mere fact that the government has breached its duty. More frequently, government fault results in a finding of constructive change where there has been a breach of duty, the contractor has put the government on notice that its failure to cooperate is costing the contractor money, and the government does not then move to correct the problem. Chapter 3 sets forth fully the nature of the government duty to cooperate or not hinder performance of the work and what constitutes a breach of that duty. A finding of breach will demonstrate that there has been a change to the contract. The additional element—an order or government fault required to prove constructive change—is discussed in the following subsections.

a. Direct Order

Where the government affirmatively insists that the contractor perform in a more expensive manner, a constructive change order is easily found. For example, in *Carpenter Constr. Co.*, NASABCA 18, 1964 BCA ¶ 4452, the government was informed that the contractor's pouring of concrete was being obstructed by other contractors on the project who were behind schedule. The government nevertheless directed the contractor to continue pouring rather than wait until the other work was completed. The board found the directive to be an order for additional work within the scope of the Changes clause. Similarly, in *Richerson Constr., Inc. v. General Servs. Admin.*, GSBCA 11161, 93-1 BCA ¶ 25,239, a direct order was found when the contracting officer ordered the contractor to obtain a different subcontractor.

b. Actions and Inactions

Direct or indirect actions or inactions that amount to a breach of the government's duty to cooperate or not hinder may also be held to be constructive changes. In these cases the key findings are that the government was at fault and had adequate notice, either actual or constructive, that its action or inaction was causing increased costs of performance to the contractor. In *Yarno & Assocs.*, ASBCA 10257, 67-1 BCA ¶ 6312, the government was informed in writing that it was allowing a second contractor to perform in such a way as to obstruct and ruin an on-site source of topsoil promised to Yarno. The board found "a change effected by the contracting officer in permitting the on-site contractor . . . [to prevent] . . . appellant from proceeding in the most efficient manner." Thus, government action, in the form of tacit permission to another contractor working on the same job, can constitute a constructive change order. Compare *Skip Kirchdorfer, Inc.*, ASBCA 40516, 00-1 BCA ¶ 30,625, in which no constructive change was found because the contractor did not request needed assistance in obtaining material from a supplier.

(1) Overzealous Inspection

Overzealous inspection is another type of government action that frequently results in a breach of implied duty to cooperate or not hinder. Although the government has the right to inspect work to ensure that it strictly complies with the specifications, *George Ledford Constr., Inc.*, ENGBCA 6218, 97-2 BCA ¶ 29,172, *recons. denied*, 98-2 BCA ¶ 29,335, *aff'd*, 178 F.3d 1308 (Fed. Cir. 1998); *Engineering Tech. Consultants, S.A.*, ASBCA 45065, 95-2 BCA ¶ 27,804, it may not exercise this right in a manner that unduly interferes with the contractor's performance. Such interference was recognized by the Court of Claims as a constructive change in *Adams v. United States*, 175 Ct. Cl. 288, 358 F.2d 986 (1966). Similarly, in *Murdock Constr. Co.*, IBCA 1050-12-74, 77-2 BCA ¶ 12,728, the project supervisor directed the contractor to perform in a specific way. This interference was immediately protested to the contracting officer, who refused to replace the supervisor. The contractor recovered the cost of redoing the work correctly under a constructive change theory. The same result occurs when the inspector completely takes over supervision of the work, instead of just inspecting, and requests additional work, *Stanley W. Wasco*, ASBCA 12288, 68-1 BCA ¶ 6986 (takeover of one part of the job requiring all-night work is a constructive change although no protest to higher authority). Overzealous inspection may also impact performance by changing the contractor's inspection system or significantly slowing progress, *Karnavas Painting Co.*, NASABCA 28, 1963 BCA ¶ 3633 (constructive change by directing contractor's employees on details of work—mild but ineffective protests by contractor sufficient to alert government to situation); *G.W. Galloway Co.*, ASBCA 16656, 73-2 BCA ¶ 10,270, *recons. denied*, 74-1 BCA ¶ 10,521 (constructive change by multiple inspections having disruptive effect that was known to contracting officer); *H.G. Reynolds Co.*, ASBCA 42351, 93-2 BCA ¶ 25,797 (constructive change when agency sent in project users and compiled a second punchlist containing a large number of minor items); *Centric/Jones Constructors*, IBCA 3139, 94-1 BCA ¶ 26,404 (constructive change when government rejected work without giving reason, demanded "novel test," and refused to pay for extra effort after the work passed the test); *Neal & Co. v. United States*, 36 Fed. Cl. 600 (1996), *aff'd*, 121 F.3d 683 (Fed. Cir. 1997) (a "nit-picking" punchlist); and *Grumman Aerospace Corp.*, ASBCA 50090, 01-1 BCA ¶ 31,316, *aff'd*, 34 Fed. Appx. 710 (Fed. Cir. 2002) (significantly more stringent inspection standards after 18-year use of more lenient procedures).

(2) Failure to Provide Assistance

Constructive changes through failure to cooperate with the contractor have been found when the government fails to provide assistance after a contractor has encountered problems during performance and has asked for assistance. For example, in *Hardrives, Inc.*, IBCA 2319, 94-1 BCA ¶ 26,267, the agency failed to respond to calls for assistance in resolving numerous problems encountered with the specifications and the site of the work. In lieu of obtaining resolution of the problems by the designing architect, the agency told the contractor to prepare change proposals containing solutions to the problems and refused to act without such proposals. The board held that this "misadministration" of the contract was a constructive change. Other cases of failure to provide assistance include *Environmental Safety Consultants, Inc.*, ASBCA 47498, 00-1 BCA ¶ 30,826 (failure to provide timely analysis of waste to be removed by contractor); *R.W. Jones Constr., Inc.*, IBCA 3656-96, 99-1 BCA ¶ 30,268 (continually refusing to help the contractor work with a utility that was operating the dam where the required work was being performed); *Turbine Aviation*, ASBCA 51323, 98-2 BCA ¶ 29,945 (failure to provide technical information in timely fashion); *Century Concrete Servs., Inc.*, ASBCA 48137, 97-1 BCA ¶ 28,889 (refusal to allow contractor's on-site batch plant to be added to government's environmental permit); *Celeron Gathering Corp. v. United States*, 34 Fed. Cl. 745 (1996) (failure to provide accurate information regarding ongoing problems with source of oil needed for contractor performance); *Midland Maint., Inc.*, ENGBCA 6085, 96-2 BCA ¶ 28,539 (failure to enforce rule that public could not build "fire rings" on camp site); *Keno & Sons Constr. Co.*, ENGBCA 5837, 95-2 BCA ¶ 27,687 (failure to provide reasons for refusing to permit contractor to use preferred method of performance); *Engineering Tech. Consultants, S.A.*, ASBCA 44912, 93-1 BCA ¶ 25,556, *recons. denied*, 93-2 BCA ¶ 25,732 (refusal to allow the contractor to use the existing utilities); *Eagle Contracting, Inc.*, AGBCA 88-225-1, 92-3 BCA ¶ 25,018 (failure to stake all culverts at beginning of road reconditioning contract so as to facilitate the contractor's efficiency); *James Lowe, Inc.*, ASBCA 42026, 92-2 BCA ¶ 24,835, *recons. denied*, 93-1 BCA ¶ 25,516 (failure to promptly reduce water pressure after break in water line); *Robert R. Marquis, Inc.*, ASBCA 38438, 92-1 BCA ¶ 24,692 (failure to resolve problems with another contractor on the site); *Old Dominion Sec.*, ASBCA 40062, 91-3 BCA ¶ 24,173, *recons. denied*, 92-1 BCA ¶ 24,374 (failure to issue a sufficient number of security clearances to permit contractor to perform guard service contract); *Harvey C. Jones, Inc.*, IBCA 2070, 90-2 BCA ¶ 22,762, *recons. denied*, 91-1 BCA ¶ 23,388 (failure to replace its inspection crew that was minimally competent and was rejecting work that had been correctly performed); and *Kahaluu Constr. Co.*, ASBCA 31187, 89-1 BCA ¶ 21,308, *recons. denied*, 89-1 BCA ¶ 21,525 (failure to tell contractor how to proceed after encountering differing site condition).

(3) Inaction or Silence

Government inaction or silence can also compel a contractor to perform work that goes beyond that called for in the contract. In *Altman Carpentry, Inc.*, HUDBCA 77-217-C16, 81-2 BCA ¶ 15,414, the board stated at 76,378:

> Earlier case law required that the Contracting Officer take some affirmative step to require performance in the face of a delay caused by another contractor in order to entitle the affected contractor to an equitable adjustment under the Changes clause rather than a pure cost adjustment under the Suspension of Work clause. See, Carpenter *Construction Company*, NASA BCA 18, 1964 BCA ¶ 4452. However,

> the Boards now recognize that inaction of a Contracting Officer to take steps to correct a delay by another contractor, after due notice and protest by the affected contractor, can constitute a constructive change.

In *Altman*, the board found a constructive change where the contractor notified the government that the site contained substantial amounts of pre-construction debris that was supposed to have been removed. The contractor received no response to its notification and then removed the debris itself in order to proceed with the work. The board remarked at 76,379:

> Corrective work that is done, as the only practical response to Government silence and inaction on a request for removal of a delay factor over which the Government has control, constitutes a change in the quantity of work under the contract.

See also *Midland Maint., Inc.*, ENGBCA 6085, 96-2 BCA ¶ 28,539, finding a constructive change where the government failed to enforce a rule that the public could not build "fire rings" on the campsite being maintained. Similarly, in *Hensel Phelps Constr. Co.*, ENGBCA 3368, 74-2 BCA ¶ 10,728, the board, though not directly addressing whether there was an order, found a constructive change where the contractor first notified the government that an access road had been damaged by a prior contractor, and then after an adverse response from the contracting officer, repaired the road. The board apparently reasoned that, because the road was essential to performance of the contract and the government was on notice of the damage, the government's failure to require the prior contractor to repair the damage or to otherwise have it fixed forced the contractor to do the repair work. Inaction also led to a constructive change in *Steele & Sons, Inc.*, ASBCA 49077, 00-1 BCA ¶ 30,837, where the government returned as-built drawings for correction without noting the precise information that was missing.

A constructive change has been found when the government observes the contractor performing extra work and intentionally does not inform the contractor of that fact. See *Chris Berg, Inc. v. United States*, 197 Ct. Cl. 503, 455 F.2d 1037 (1972), where a government project engineer who knew that certain areas were not to be painted by the contractor reprimanded the contractor's crew for not cleaning those areas as they were about to be painted. See also *Hydrospace Elecs. & Instrument Corp.*, ASBCA 17922, 74-2 BCA ¶ 10,682, in which the board found that a constructive change had occurred in these circumstances, stating at 50,806:

> [T]he Government was aware that [the contractor] was deviating from the contract requirement for stainless steel in a manner that was determined to be patently unacceptable. In our opinion the Government, under these circumstances, had a duty to inform [the contractor] of its erroneous course of action in a timely manner and the [contractor] is entitled to recovery for the consequences of the Government's failure to do so.

To recover on these grounds, the contractor must prove that government personnel "had actual knowledge of the nonconforming work and deliberately refrained from informing [the contractor] of its erroneous course of action," *G&C Enters., Inc.*, DOTBCA 1736, 89-1 BCA ¶ 21,556; *Hunter Ditch Lining*, AGBCA 87-391-1, 91-2 BCA ¶ 23,673. In spite of the difficult standard of proof, the appeals boards have found constructive changes in situations where the government employees watched the defective work being performed, *W. Southard Jones, Inc.*, ASBCA 6321, 61-2 BCA ¶ 3182, or where they did not inform the contractor that work was defective and thereby permitted the performance of a substantial amount of defective work after they knew of the defects, *Bromley Contracting Co.*, HUDBCA 75-8, 77-1 BCA ¶ 12,232, *aff'd*, 229 Ct. Cl. 750 (1982). See also *Maxwell Dynamometer Co. v. United States*, 181 Ct. Cl. 607, 386 F.2d 855 (1967), in which the court held that watching the contractor perform a test to more stringent standards than required by the specifications would bind the government to compensate for the extra work. Similarly, in *Altman Carpentry, Inc.*, HUDBCA 77-217-C16, 81-2 BCA ¶ 15,415, a constructive change was found where the government knew that the contractor was forced by government inaction to remove pre-construction debris that was not the contractor's responsibility, and in *BH Servs., Inc.*, ASBCA 39460, 93-3 BCA ¶ 26,082, the board found a constructive change where the authorized representative of the contracting officer observed the contractor performing extra work but did not inquire as to why it was being performed. See also *William F. Klingensmith, Inc.*, GSBCA 5451, 83-1 BCA ¶ 16,201, in which the board held the government liable when it did not reject defective work in a timely manner. There are some cases reaching the conclusion that government employees have no obligation to inform the contractors of defective performance, *Rosendin Elec., Inc.*, ASBCA 22996, 81-1 BCA ¶ 14,827; *Gene Fuller, Inc.*, ASBCA 21682, 79-2 BCA ¶ 14,039. In view of this disagreement in the decisions, the best course of action would be for government employees to inform the contractor when the work is clearly defective.

(4) Unreasonable Conduct

Failure to cooperate through unreasonable conduct can occur in a number of ways, including very late issuance of the notice to proceed and continual failure to respond when problems were raised, *Piedmont Painting Contractors*, IBCA 3772, 98-1 BCA ¶ 29,618; inducing an adjacent landowner not to enter into agreement to provide materials, *HK Contractors, Inc.*, DOTBCA 2766, 96-1 BCA ¶ 28,175; the failure to respond to a contractor's requests for information, *Hardie-Tynes Mfg. Co.*, ASBCA 20582, 76-2 BCA ¶ 11,972; approving contractor's proposed schedule of progress and billings knowing that "funds of this magnitude would not be appropriated because not requested," *S.A. Healy Co. v. United States*, 216 Ct. Cl. 172, 576 F.2d 299 (1978); failing to issue timely orders, *Raytheon Serv. Co.*, GSBCA 5695, 81-1 BCA ¶ 15,002; untimely furnishing of delivery orders needed for performance, *George A. Fuller Co. v. United States.*, 108 Ct. Cl. 70, 69 F. Supp. 409 (1947); late deliveries of materials and delayed acceptance of contractor's products, *Kehm Corp. v. United States*, 119 Ct. Cl. 454, 93 F. Supp. 620 (1950); untimely delivery of information on government-furnished property, *Ballenger Corp.*, DOTCAB 74-32, 84-1

BCA ¶ 16,973, *modified on other grounds*, 84-2 BCA ¶ 17,277; failing to provide plans and drawings when necessary, *Cedar Lumber, Inc. v. United States*, 5 Cl. Ct. 539 (1984); failing to provide access to work site, *Blinderman Constr. Co. v. United States*, 695 F.2d 552 (Fed. Cir. 1982); and failing to issue a notice to proceed at time specifically required by contract, *Abbett Elec. Corp. v. United States*, 142 Ct. Cl. 609, 162 F. Supp. 772 (1958).

There are a few cases finding a failure to cooperate because a government employee or agent has administered the contract in a manner intended to harm the contractor, *Libertatia Assocs., Inc. v. United States*, 46 Fed. Cl. 702 (2000) (personal animosity toward contractor); *Donohoe Constr. Co.*, ASBCA 47310, 98-2 BCA 30,076, *recons. denied*, 99-1 BCA ¶ 30,387 (withholding payments, delaying approvals, overinterpreting specifications, and rejecting satisfactory work).

(5) Other Actions

Other government actions that have been held to constitute constructive change by interference with a contractor's performance include incompetent management of shop drawing approval process, *Sterling Millwrights, Inc. v. United States*, 26 Cl. Ct. 49 (1992); failure to ensure that another contractor on the site performed in accordance with its contract, *Toombs & Co.*, ASBCA 34590, 91-1 BCA ¶ 23,403; refusal of permission to conduct preliminary test to determine whether work could be successfully accomplished, *Alonso & Carus Iron Works, Inc.*, ASBCA 38312, 90-3 BCA ¶ 23,147, *recons. denied*, 91-1 BCA ¶ 23,650; use of excessively high standard for approving welders, *Tom Shaw, Inc.*, DOTBCA 2108, 90-1 BCA ¶ 22,579; excessive noise from jet engines, *Nichols Dynamics Inc.*, ASBCA 17949, 75-2 BCA ¶ 11,556; diverting water into the construction site, *John M. Bragg*, ASBCA 9515, 65-2 BCA ¶ 5050; and preventing drainage from a site, *A. Geris, Inc.*, ENGBCA 2869, 68-2 BCA ¶ 7320, *recons. denied*, 71-1 BCA ¶ 8764. In each instance the government ordered continued performance despite the interference or failed to act to alleviate the problem.

c. *Abuse of Discretion*

The breach of the government's duty not to hinder, delay, or increase the costs of performance has frequently been found to be a constructive change when the government has been unreasonable in exercising its discretion. Discretion is granted to the government in a number of different areas of contract performance, including situations where the contract makes the precise manner of performance subject to the approval of the contracting officer and where the contracting officer may approve proposed subcontractors or make determinations of whether certain components meet the specifications. See Chapter 3 for a full discussion of abuse of discretion as a breach of the duty to cooperate. In almost all of these cases, a constructive change order is found in an overt act or communication that knowingly forces or induces the contractor to perform in a manner desired by the government, *Chris Berg, Inc. & Assocs.*, ASBCA 3466, 58-1 BCA ¶ 1792, *recons. denied*, 58-2 BCA ¶ 1894 (government rejection of plan for thawing permafrost and requirement that more expensive method be used); *S. Rosenthal & Son, Inc.*, ASBCA 6684, 1963 BCA ¶ 3791, *recons. denied*, 1964 BCA ¶ 4467 (contracting officer forced performance of the work in certain sequence by using his right to approve progress schedule); *Hensel Phelps Constr. Co.*, ENGBCA 3674, 77-1 BCA ¶ 12,475 (government order to cut off tops and leave bottoms of cofferdam pilings in place served no government purpose and contract reasonably gave right to contractor to salvage entire piling); *John C. Grimberg Co. v. United States*, 869 F.2d 1475 (Fed. Cir. 1989) (government rejection of request for waiver of Buy American Act when price differential was substantial); *Manning Elec. & Repair Co. v. United States*, 22 Cl. Ct. 240 (1991) (contracting officer disapproved an "equal" item); *Blount, Inc.*, VABCA 3719, 95-2 BCA ¶ 27,874 (refusal to approve an "equal" material handling system); *Environmental Safety Consultants, Inc.*, ASBCA 47498, 00-1 BCA ¶ 30,826 (refusal to approve competent subcontractors).

In the area of variable quantity contracts, the Armed Services Board has recognized constructive changes where the Court of Claims might not have found a breach of contract. In *Raby Hillside Drilling, Inc.*, ASBCA 20178, 76-2 BCA ¶ 11,982, *recons. denied*, 77-1 BCA ¶ 12,245, the government directed the contractor to drill a well deeper despite serious difficulties and in face of a vigorous protest from the contractor. The well collapsed, destroying the drilling equipment and requiring the contractor to start over. This request to drill deeper was held to be a constructive change order because of an unreasonable exercise of discretion. In an analogous case, *Brighton Sand & Gravel Co.*, ASBCA 11277, 66-2 BCA ¶ 5905, a constructive change was found when the contracting officer refused to order more excavation in a variable quantity contract, causing the contractor to expend extra sums in correcting the effects of an unstable subgrade. In both cases, decisions about quantity resulted in a constructive change.

C. Procedures for Resolving Constructive Changes

Almost all constructive changes result from problems that are encountered during the performance of a contract. Successful resolution of these problems requires prompt, cooperative effort by both parties to the contract. Initially, this calls for identification of the problem by the contractor and prompt communication with the government. The government then must investigate the situation, take prompt steps to resolve the problem, and communicate the solution to the contractor.

1. The Contractor's Obligations

In many constructive change situations, the government is at a significant disadvantage if it does not receive prompt notice of the problems being encountered by the contractor. Its main difficulty is that it cannot devise a solution to the problem if it does not know that it exists. This deprives the government of control of the work and of the amount of financial resources needed to complete it. The second difficulty is that the contracting officer—the government official charged with contract administration—is left out of the decision-making process. The contractual notice requirements, as discussed in the next section, have not proved to be effective in overcoming these difficulties, but the courts and boards have recognized them and have frequently denied constructive changes claims when they have concluded that the contractor has not been diligent in bringing problems to the government's attention.

a. *Loss of Control of Work*

In 1965 the Court of Claims recognized that the government is prejudiced by lack of notice of defective specifications and announced a rule denying a contractor compensation for costs that might have been avoided if the contractor had given timely notice, *Kings Elecs. Co. v. United States*, 169 Ct. Cl. 433, 341 F.2d 632 (1965). This rule was followed in other constructive changes cases where a contractor failed to give notice of a failure to cooperate, *Cameo Bronze, Inc.*, GSBCA 3646, 73-2 BCA ¶ 10,135, *recons. denied*, 73-2 BCA ¶ 10,365; of alleged impossibility of performance, *SMC Info. Sys., Inc. v. General Servs. Admin.*, GSBCA 9371, 93-1 BCA ¶ 25,485, *aff'd*, 16 F.3d 120 (Fed. Cir. 1993); *Sanders Assocs., Inc.*, ASBCA 17550, 74-1 BCA ¶ 10,536, *recons. denied*, 76-1 BCA ¶ 11,632; and of furnishing defective government-furnished special tooling, *Ferguson Propeller, Inc. v. United States*, 59 Fed. Cl. 51 (2003). See *Power Regulator Co.*, GSBCA 4668, 80-2 BCA ¶ 14,463, stating that this is basically a mitigation of damages rule—reasoning that failure to give notice is a failure to allow the government to reduce the financial impact of the problem.

The rule has been applied most widely in cases of defective specifications, *Dynalectron Corp. v. United States*, 207 Ct. Cl. 349, 518 F.2d 594 (1975) (failure to give notice of defective specifications prevents recovery of full costs of performance when improper default termination is converted to termination for convenience); *Canadian Commercial Corp.*, ASBCA 17187, 76-2 BCA ¶ 12,145, *recons. denied*, 77-2 BCA ¶ 12,758 (no recovery of costs because of failure to notify government of defective specifications); *Reese Mfg., Inc.*, ASBCA 35144, 88-1 BCA ¶ 20,358 (delay prior to notice of defective specification not chargeable to government); *Argo Tech., Inc.*, ASBCA 30522, 88-1 BCA ¶ 20,381, *recons. denied*, 89-1 BCA ¶ 21,395, *aff'd*, 889 F.2d 1099 (Fed. Cir. 1989) (defective specification claim denied because of lack of notice); *Signal Contracting, Inc.*, ASBCA 44963, 93-2 BCA ¶ 25,877, *recons. denied*, 93-3 BCA ¶ 26,058, *aff'd*, 17 F.3d 1442 (Fed. Cir. 1994) (failure to give notice of defective specifications precludes recovery of delay costs prior to notice); *Environmental Devices, Inc.*, ASBCA 37430, 93-3 BCA ¶ 26,138 (failure to give notice of defective specification precludes recovery for delay); *AIW - Alton, Inc.*, ASBCA 47921, 95-2 BCA ¶ 27,881 (contractor responsible for delays prior to notifying government that a key drawing was missing); *Precision Specialities, Inc.*, ASBCA 48717, 96-1 BCA ¶ 28,054; *McElroy Mach. & Mfg. Co.*, ASBCA 46477, 99-1 BCA ¶ 30,185 (alteration of design without notice deprives contractor of claim for defective specification).

The contractor will be given a reasonable time to determine the cause of problems being encountered before this notice requirement will be enforced. See *Tyger Constr. Co. v. United States*, 31 Fed. Cl. 177 (1994), concluding that the long time it took the contractor to identify the cause of its problems was understandable because of the complexity of the situation.

If the government is aware of defective specifications, the contractor will be relieved of its obligation to bring them to the government's attention. See *Metal Trades, Inc.*, ASBCA 41583, 94-2 BCA ¶ 26,611 (contractor promptly complained that the work conditions were different than represented); *Hoffman Constr Co.*, DOTBCA 2150, 93-2 BCA ¶ 25,803 (notice not required because government not prejudiced by lack of notice); and *Lloyd Kessler, Inc.*, AGBCA 88-170-3, 89-3 BCA ¶ 22,055 (notice defenses rejected, without discussing special rule for defective specifications, on basis that government was aware that contractor was performing extra work). The contractor can meet its obligation to inform the government of problems during performance by oral notice without the submission of any documented claim, *Pittsburgh-Des Moines Corp.*, EBCA 314-3-84, 89-2 BCA ¶ 21,739. See also *Casson Constr. Co.*, GSBCA 4884, 83-1 BCA ¶ 16,523, in which the rule was not applied because the contractor had told an employee of the government's construction manager about the defective specification.

If a problem makes it impossible for the contractor to proceed with some element of the work, with the result that delay costs will be incurred, the contractor should also notify the government of that fact. Otherwise, these delay costs will not be compensable as part of the equitable adjustment for the constructive changes, *Signal Contracting, Inc.*, ASBCA 44963, 93-2 BCA ¶ 25,877, *recons. denied*, 93-3 BCA ¶ 26,058, *aff'd*, 17 F.3d 1442 (Fed. Cir. 1994).

b. Informing the Contracting Officer

In situations where contractors have been directed or induced to perform extra work by a person without contracting officer authority, they have been held to have a "duty to protest" to the contracting officer in order to ensure that a person with authority knows that the contractor believes a constructive change has occurred. The Court of Claims enunciated this rule in the case of *J.A. Ross & Co. v. United States*, 126 Ct. Cl. 323, 115 F. Supp. 187 (1953), at 329:

> Whenever the [government] orders work done which the [contractor] thinks is in violation of the contract, or in addition to its requirements, [the contractor] is required to protest against doing it, or to secure an order in writing before doing it.

> It is basic in all Government contracts that the [contractor] cannot do work which it is not required to do by the contract, without registering a protest against being required to do it, or securing an order for extra work, and then later make a claim against the Government for additional compensation.
>
> If the [contractor] thought that an unforeseen condition had been encountered which necessitated revision of the contract, it was its duty to call that situation to the attention of the contracting officer, so that he could investigate the condition and make an equitable adjustment in the contract, in case the conditions warranted it. Or, if [the contractor] claimed that the contract had been changed in a way which increased the cost of doing the work, it was necessary for it to make claim therefor in order that the contracting officer might make an equitable adjustment.

This rule has been less strictly followed in recent years—probably because some government employee was aware of the problem and was expected to bring it to the attention of the contracting officer. See, for example, *A.R. Mack Constr. Co.*, ASBCA 50035, 01-2 BCA ¶ 31,593 (oral notice to project engineer and resident engineer sufficient to permit the agency to deal with the problem); *CEMS, Inc. v. United States*, 59 Fed. Cl. 168 (2003) (on-site project engineer knew of constructive changes); and *SIPCO Servs. & Marine, Inc. v. United States*, 41 Fed. Cl. 196 (1998) (contracting officer's technical representative was delegated broad responsibility to oversee the contract). However, it is still an important factor in deciding constructive change cases when it appears that a protest to the contracting officer could have altered the situation. For example, in *Singer Co., Librascope Div. v. United States*, 215 Ct. Cl. 281, 568 F.2d 695 (1977), the court held against a contractor who had failed to protest. The court explained that, although such failure was no longer an outright bar to a claim, it is "an evidentiary consideration" that can take on controlling significance when circumstances indicate that the government would not have known that the contractor considered the work to be "extra-contractual" absent a protest. Accord, *Kurz & Root Co.*, ASBCA 11436, 68-1 BCA ¶ 6916; *Astro Dynamics, Inc.*, NASABCA 1067-38, 74-1 BCA ¶ 10,634, reconsideration denied, 75-2 BCA ¶ 11,479; *Flinchbaugh Prods. Corp.*, ASBCA 19851, 78-2 BCA ¶ 13,375; *Wayne L. Grist, Inc.*, ENGBCA 5503, 90-2 BCA ¶ 22,915. Most of the recent cases have discussed this obligation in terms of "prejudice" to the government, and it is not always clear whether the courts and boards are enforcing a contractual notice requirement (as discussed in the next section) or this general obligation to protest. See, for example, *Northrop Grumman Corp. v. United States*, 47 Fed. Cl. 20 (2000) (constructive changes claims not presented to contracting officer after warnings that other employees had no authority); *Lamar Constr. Co.*, ASBCA 39593, 92-2 BCA ¶ 24,813, *aff'd*, 985 F.2d 583 (Fed. Cir. 1992) (claim for excessive preparation work on painting contract submitted after final painting—depriving the government of the opportunity to investigate claim); *Sol Flores Constr.*, ASBCA 32278, 89-3 BCA ¶ 22,154 (lack of notice to contracting officer of directions received from technical representative); *Calfon Constr., Inc. v. United States*, 18 Cl. Ct. 426 (1989), *aff'd*, 923 F.2d 872 (Fed. Cir. 1990) (no notice to contracting officer that direction of representative was causing extra work); *Southland Constr. Co.*, VABCA 2217,

89-1 BCA ¶ 21,548 (lack of notice impeded government's ability to defend against claim); *E.W. Jerdon, Inc.*, ASBCA 32957, 88-2 BCA ¶ 20,729 (lack of notice prevented government from correcting problem); and *Tompkins & Co.*, ENGBCA 4484, 85-1 BCA ¶ 17,853 (claim submitted after work had been completed deprived contracting officer of opportunity to countermand order of COR). Similarly, when a contractor asserts that a constructive change has occurred through failure of the government to approve substitute performance, the claim will fail if there has been no clear request for such approval. See *C. Sanchez & Son, Inc. v. United States*, 6 F.3d 1539 (Fed. Cir. 1993) (claim of abuse of discretion in granting a Buy American Act waiver denied because no clear request for the waiver). In *WRB Corp. v. United States*, 183 Ct. Cl. 409 (1968), the Court of Claims stated that overzealous inspection violating the duty not to impede, hinder, or interfere with the contractor's work imposes a lesser duty to protest to the contracting officer than a case of a "mere misinterpretation" of a specification by an inspector.

When a disagreement over contract requirements is clearly apparent and an order to proceed in a certain manner is given, a constructive change will almost always be found in spite of a lack of protest if the government's interpretation is later determined to call for work beyond the contract requirements, *Dunbar Roofing Co.*, ASBCA 3559, 57-2 BCA ¶ 1487; *George A. Fuller Co.*, ENGBCA 2875, 71-2 BCA ¶ 8973. The same result will occur if the government gives a direct order to proceed in a specified manner, the contractor protests that the order is a change, and the government permits performance to proceed in accordance with the order, *M.S.I. Corp.*, GSBCA 2428, 68-2 BCA ¶ 7262; *Eagle Paving*, AGBCA 75-156, 78-1 BCA ¶ 13,107; *Urban Pathfinders, Inc.*, ASBCA 23134, 79-1 BCA ¶ 13,709; *Granite Constr. Co.*, ENGBCA 4172, 89-2 BCA ¶ 21,683. In some cases the board finds a constructive change as a result of a direct order of the government without any indication that there was disagreement about the contract requirements at the time of the order, *Master Mfg. Co.*, ASBCA 12132, 68-1 BCA ¶ 6953; *COMPEC*, IBCA 573-6-66, 68-1 BCA ¶ 6776; *Goslin-Birmingham, Inc.*, ENGBCA 2800, 67-2 BCA ¶ 6402. The explanation for these decisions may be that they involve requirements that are rather obviously beyond the original contract specifications and that agency personnel, including the contracting officer, should have known that such requirements were constructive changes.

The requirement for identification of constructive changes has been incorporated into the construction contract Changes clause in FAR 52.243-4. See the discussion in the next section.

2. Government Resolution of Problem

Once the government is aware of a problem, it has the responsibility to arrive at a solution, *Hardrives, Inc.*, IBCA 2319, 94-1 BCA ¶ 26,267. Thus, it is improper to request that the contractor devise a solution and to defer action until the solution is proposed. See *Pilcher, Livingston & Wallace*, ASBCA 13391, 70-1 BCA ¶ 8331, *recons. denied*, 70-2 BCA ¶ 8488, stating at 38,764:

> Much of the delay and expense experienced by the contractor as a result of inadequate and defective specifications could have been avoided if the [government] representatives had recognized their responsibility for providing the contractor with correct and adequate specifications and taken prompt corrective action to correct deficiencies in the specifications promptly after they had been reported by [the contractor]. Instead, when [the contractor] reported a problem the general practice of the COR and his inspection staff was to impose on [the contractor] the burden of working out a proposed solution to the problem, submitting a shop drawing showing the proposed solution, and getting it approved by the COR, which was time consuming and was not the contractual responsibility of the contractor.

See also *Hughes-Groesch Constr. Corp.*, VABCA 5448, 00-1 BCA ¶ 30,912, holding that the government acted improperly in requiring a construction contractor to perform redesign work rather than obtaining the redesign from the cognizant architect/engineer.

The result of this rule is that the government is responsible for any costs of delay that occurred because the government ordered the contractor to solve the problem. See, for example, *Atlas Grinding & Mach. Corp.*, ASBCA 33011, 87-1 BCA ¶ 19,612, in which the government was held liable for the contractor's costs of wasted effort when it delayed dealing with a problem for 20 months after it learned that the contractor was interpreting a drawing in a way that made it impossible to complete the contract performance.

Once a solution has been devised, the government should issue a change order, priced or unpriced, directing the contractor to implement it. The contractor is not obligated to proceed until such a change order is issued, and any delay costs incurred while awaiting such a change order are compensable as a part of the change, *Wilner v. United States*, 26 Cl. Ct. 260 (1992), *aff'd*, 994 F.2d 783 (Fed. Cir. 1993). See also *Sterling Millwrights, Inc. v. United States*, 26 Cl. Ct. 49 (1992), holding that a default termination was improper because of government delays in responding to a contractor's requests for changes to correct defective drawings.

V. CONTRACTUAL NOTICE REQUIREMENTS

All of the standard Changes clauses contain notice requirements, but with the exception of the construction contract clause, these requirements are not well attuned to the needs of the government. As a result, the courts and boards have been reluctant to enforce the literal requirements of the clauses to deny claims in their entirety—understanding that this would amount to forfeiture of claims for which contractors should be paid. Thus, at the present time the notice requirements of the Changes clauses are enforced sporadically while the noncontractual obligation to give notice, which has been created by the courts and boards, as discussed above, is enforced when fairness demands. This has created the anomalous situation in which the notice requirements currently being imposed on contractors are those found in the decisional law rather than those found in the contract language.

A. Assertion of Right to Equitable Adjustment on Ordered Changes

When the contracting officer unilaterally orders a change, the contractor or the government is entitled to an equitable adjustment depending on the cost impact of the change. The supply contract clause requires the contractor to "assert its right" to an equitable adjustment as follows:

> (c) The Contractor must assert its right to an adjustment under this clause within 30 days from the date of receipt of the written order. However, if the Contracting Officer decides that the facts justify it, the Contracting Officer may receive and act upon a proposal submitted before final payment of the contract.

The construction contract clause contains more specific guidance on the nature of the required assertion, providing:

> (e) The Contractor must assert its right to an adjustment under this clause within 30 days after (1) receipt of a written change order under paragraph (a) of this clause . . . by submitting to the Contracting Officer a written statement describing the general nature and amount of proposal, unless this period is extended by the Government.

1. Contractor Claims

The requirement that the contractor give a form of notice within 30 days of the receipt of a change order is clearly intended to expedite the process of negotiation of equitable adjustments. A meaningful notice must include the contractor's estimate of the cost impact of the change, but this cannot always be done within a 30-day period. Furthermore, there is no significant harm to the government if this notice is late. As a result, this notice requirement has not been strictly enforced.

A technical reading of this notice provision also leads to the conclusion that it should not be strictly enforced. The current clauses in FAR 52.243 state that the contractor "must assert its right to an adjustment" within this time period. Prior to 1987 the clauses called for the submission of a "proposal for adjustment," and prior to 1980 they called for the assertion of a "claim for equitable adjustment." None of these formulations appears to have called for a fully documented proposal but, rather, for notice that the contractor believes that an equitable adjustment is called for by the change order. Thus, the notice does not appear to be a critical part of the contract administration process. It has been interpreted liberally in numerous holdings that failure to submit this notice will not bar a contractor's claim unless the government can show that the lack of notice was prejudicial in some way, *Golden W. Envtl. Servs.*, DOTBCA 2895, 00-2 BCA ¶ 30,990; *Valley Asphalt, Inc.*, AGBCA 97-118-1, 97-2 BCA ¶ 28,997; *Chimera Corp.*, ASBCA 18690, 76-1 BCA ¶ 11,901; *Weaver Constr. Co.*, ASBCA 12577, 69-1 BCA ¶ 7455; *Precision Tool & Eng'g Corp.*, ASBCA 14148, 71-1 BCA ¶ 8738. As noted in *Chimera*, an alternate way of dealing with this issue is to increase the contractor's burden of persuasion to compensate for the prejudice to the government when significant delay has occurred in the submission of the claim. See *Onsrud Mach. Works, Inc.*, ASBCA 14800, 71-2 BCA ¶ 9013; *Gardner Constr. Co.*, DOTCAB 70-18, 73-2 BCA ¶ 10,342. In *Progressive Enters., Inc.*, ASBCA 17360, 73-2 BCA ¶ 10,065, the board explained this version of the rule to mean that "[f]ailure to file such claims as soon as they have matured merely increases the burden of persuasion which rests upon the claimant." Some boards have also discussed the rule as involving the equitable doctrine of laches, drawing on court decisions in that area of the law to decide the case, *L. Rosenman Corp.*, GSBCA 4265, 77-2 BCA ¶ 12,843.

The Court of Claims affirmed a board finding of prejudice and barred a claim that was submitted five years after the date required by the contract in *Eggers & Higgins v. United States*, 185 Ct. Cl. 765, 403 F.2d 225 (1968). Board cases that have barred claims because of prejudice to the government include *Hawaiian Airmotive*, ASBCA 7892, 65-2 BCA ¶ 4946 (nearly three-year delay in submitting claim and government records lost in aircraft accident); *Industrial Research Assocs., Inc.*, DCAB WB-5, 67-1 BCA ¶ 6309 (claim submitted after completion of hearing before appeals board); and *L. Rosenman Corp.*, GSBCA 4265, 77-2 BCA ¶ 12,843 (12-year delay in submitting claim). See also *J.S. Alberici Constr. Co. & Martin K. Eby Constr. Co., A Joint Venture*, ENGBCA 6178, 98-2 BCA ¶ 29,875, barring a claim for defective government-furnished materials because the government was prejudiced when it did not receive timely notice, which would have permitted it to correct the materials.

In *B.L.I. Constr. Co.*, ASBCA 45560, 94-1 BCA ¶ 26,308, the government attempted to persuade the board to reverse the long line of cases that refused to strictly enforce the notice requirements, arguing that these cases were incorrectly decided because the government had never waived its sovereign immunity from suit when notice requirements were not complied with. The board rejected this argument, stating that it was "reluctant to depart from the well-established applications of the contract's notice requirements."

Claims asserted after final payment are specifically barred by the Changes clauses. Final payment is defined and discussed fully in Chapter 12. For this purpose the "assertion" requirement is quite liberal. In *Machinery Assocs., Inc.*, ASBCA 14510, 72-2 BCA ¶ 9476, the board gave guidance on the assertion of claims at 44,141:

> In asserting a claim a contractor need not cite a particular contract provision on which it relies or describe the substance or the claim of the amount, *Discon Cor-*

> *poration*, ASBCA No. 15981, 71-2 BCA ¶ 9069. It must, however, reasonably manifest to the Government its present intention to seek recovery of money based on a claim of legal right under the contract.

A casual statement expressing an indefinite intent to seek "additional compensation" made to a government employee authorized only to provide the contractor with technical assistance is not an assertion of a claim for purposes of the Changes clause, *Jo-Bar Mfg. Corp. v. United States*, 210 Ct. Cl. 149, 535 F.2d 62 (1976). However, if the contracting officer knows or is chargeable with knowledge that a claim either has been made or is outstanding prior to final payment, the fact of final payment will not bar consideration of that claim, *Missouri Research Labs., Inc.*, ASBCA 12355, 69-1 BCA ¶ 7762. Late assertion of a claim prior to final payment will not bar it from consideration by a board of contract appeals if the contracting officer has addressed the claim on its merits, *A.L. Harding, Inc.*, DCAB PR-44, 65-2 BCA ¶ 5261, *recons. denied*, 66-1 BCA ¶ 5463; *Proper Mfg. Co.*, GSBCA 3579, 73-2 BCA ¶ 10,029; *Monaco Builders, Inc.*, PSBCA 323, 78-1 BCA ¶ 12,924; *Human Advancement, Inc.*, HUDBCA 77-215-C15, 81-2 BCA ¶ 15,317; *West Land Builders*, VABCA 1664, 83-1 BCA ¶ 16,235, *recons. denied*, 83-1 BCA ¶ 16,430. The Court of Claims followed a similar rule, holding that late claims were not barred if they had been considered by the contracting officer and the appeals board on their merits, *Fox Valley Eng'g, Inc. v. United States*, 151 Ct. Cl. 228 (1960); *Dittmore-Freimuth Corp. v. United States*, 182 Ct. Cl. 507, 390 F.2d 664 (1968). However, if the claim is only addressed in a final decision of the contracting officer under the Disputes clause, final payment will still bar the claim, *Navales Enters., Inc.*, ASBCA 52202, 99-2 BCA ¶ 30,528.

2. Government Claims

Although the Changes clauses are silent as to notice by the government, claims by the government for a downward equitable adjustment will also be barred if not submitted to the contractor in a reasonable time. In *Joseph H. Roberts v. United States*, 174 Ct. Cl. 940, 357 F.2d 938 (1966), the court barred a government counterclaim asserting claims a number of years after completion of the contract. The court reasoned that the Changes clause "imposes upon the contracting officer the duty to make such an adjustment within a reasonable time, so as to afford the contractor an opportunity to appeal from an unreasonable or arbitrary decision while the facts supporting the claim are readily available and before the contractor's position is prejudiced by final settlement with his subcontractors, suppliers, and other creditors." After the *Roberts* decision a six-year statute of limitations on government claims was enacted, 28 U.S.C. § 2415. This statute, of course, applies only to assertion of claims in court and does not deal directly with claims asserted by the contracting officer under the Changes clause. Hence, the *Roberts* rule has been followed by the appeals boards in *Southwestern Eng'g Co.*, NASABCA 425-15, 68-1 BCA ¶ 6977, *recons. denied*, 68-2 BCA ¶ 7317 (more than two-year delay in asserting claim); *Futuronics, Inc.*, DOTCAB 67-15, 68-2 BCA ¶ 7079, *recons. denied*, 68-2 BCA ¶ 7235 (claim asserted more than one year after appeal process had commenced); and *Lindwall Constr. Co.*, ASBCA 23148, 79-1 BCA ¶ 13,822 (claim asserted as a counterclaim in a contract appeal proceeding 13 months after government knew of claim). In *Norcoast-Beck Aleutian*, ASBCA 26389, 83-1 BCA ¶ 16,152, the board stated that government claims for deductive changes under the Changes clause "must be made within a reasonable time after it becomes apparent that a change will cause a cost savings, and no later than final payment." See also *M&C Cumberland*, DOTBCA 3014, 00-1 BCA ¶ 30,700, in which the board rejected the government's claims for price reductions for reduced work because they were not asserted until after contract completion. The board concluded that the contractor had been prejudiced by the late notice because it had not taken steps to reduce its costs when it found that the government was not asking for the price reductions on a quarterly basis as called for by the contract. Compare *Olympiareinigung, GmbH*, ASBCA 53643, 04-1 BCA ¶ 32,458, permitting the government to assert a claim for a deductive change after payment for the work.

Oral notice to the contractor may meet the government's obligation. See *Porshia Alexander of Am.*, GSBCA 9604, 91-1 BCA ¶ 23,657, in which the contractor's defense that it had not been informed of a government claim was denied because it had been informally told during performance that the work should be reduced.

B. Constructive Changes Claims

Most government contracts contain no notice requirements that explicitly pertain to constructive changes. Thus, it is far more likely that the special requirements imposed by the courts and boards, as discussed earlier, will apply. This section discusses those instances when the government has alleged that a contractual provision applies to constructive changes.

1. *Applicability of 30-Day Notice Requirement*

The notice requirement that is common to all standard Changes clauses is the provision calling for assertion of a right to an adjustment within 30 days of the receipt of a change order. The appeals boards originally held that this requirement was not applicable to constructive changes since there was no written order that started the notice period running, *Burton-Rodgers, Inc.*, ASBCA 5438, 60-1 BCA ¶ 2558; *MECO, Inc.*, ASBCA 9849, 65-2 BCA ¶ 5132; *Carlin-Atlas*, GSBCA 2061, 66-2 BCA ¶ 5872; *ITT Commercial Servs., Inc.*, GSBCA 4210, 75-1 BCA ¶ 11,218; *Honeywell, Inc.*, VABCA 1166, 76-1 BCA ¶ 11,745. More recently, courts and boards have held that this type of notice requirement applies to constructive changes at least to the extent that the claim will be denied if the government is prejudiced by lack of notice, *R.R. Tyler*, AGBCA 381, 77-1 BCA ¶ 12,227; *JEMCO, Inc.*, ENGBCA 3879, 77-2 BCA ¶ 12,749; *Mingus Constructors, Inc. v. United* States, 812 F.2d 1387 (Fed. Cir. 1987); *Togaroli Corp.*, ASBCA 32995, 89-2 BCA ¶ 21,864, *recons. denied*, 89-3 BCA ¶ 22,102; *Watson, Rice & Co.*, HUDBCA 89-4468-C6, 90-1 BCA ¶ 22,499; *Max Blau & Sons, Inc.*, GSBCA 9827, 91-1 BCA ¶ 23,626; *Integrated Clinical Sys., Inc.*, VABCA 3745, 95-2 BCA ¶ 27,902; *SIPCO Servs. & Marine, Inc., v. United States*, 41 Fed. Cl. 196 (1998); *A.R. Mack Constr. Co.*, ASBCA 50035, 01-2 BCA ¶ 31,593. However, these cases hardly ever find that the government has been prejudiced. See, however, *Jo-Bar Mfg. Corp. v. United States*, 210 Ct. Cl. 149, 535 F.2d 62 (1976) (complaint dismissed because contractor's vague complaints to a technician were not sufficient to put government on notice); *John Murphy Constr. Co.*, AGBCA 418, 79-1 BCA ¶ 13,836 (claim denied because government had neither actual nor constructive notice under either ¶ (d) or (e) of the construction contract Changes clause and was prejudiced thereby); *Schouten Constr. Co.*, DOTCAB 78-14, 79-1 BCA ¶ 13,553 (board considered motion to dismiss for failure to give 30-day notice of constructive change but found waiver of notice requirement by government consideration of claim); and *T. Brown Constructors, Inc. v. Peña*, 132 F. 3d 724 (Fed. Cir. 1997) (claim denied because change in conditions of site kept government from investigating claim). In addition, some boards have adopted the position that, when prejudice is found, the result will be a higher burden of persuasion on the contractor rather than outright rejection of the claim, *Onsrud Mach. Works, Inc.*, ASBCA 14800, 71-2 BCA ¶ 9013; *M.M. Sundt Constr. Co.*, ASBCA 17475, 74-1 BCA ¶ 10,627. This result is based on the reasoning of the Court of Claims that was first stated in *B-W Constr. Co. v. United States*, 100 Ct. Cl. 227 (1943).

2. Construction Contract Notice Requirement

The construction contract Changes clause issued in 1968 and now contained in FAR 52.243-4 contains special notice provisions in paragraphs (b) and (d) pertaining to constructive change orders. Paragraph (b) requires that notice be given of all constructive changes but contains no time limitations on when the notice must be given. Paragraph (d) limits recovery for constructive changes to costs incurred no more than 20 days prior to the notice but excludes constructive changes based on defective specifications. Although the results of this 20-day notice provision are harsh, it was applied strictly by the appeals boards in most of the early cases interpreting the clause, *Preferred Contractors, Inc.*, ASBCA 15569, 72-1 BCA ¶ 9283 (letter giving notice dated 20 days after costs were incurred not timely absent proof that letter was mailed or received on twentieth day). The boards continue to apply the provision when there are no extenuating circumstances, such as actual knowledge of the government, *Northeastern Constr. Co.*, ENGBCA 3820, 78-1 BCA ¶ 13,052; *G.C. Indus., Inc.*, ASBCA 22890, 79-1 BCA ¶ 13,721; *Joseph Morton Co.*, GSBCA 4815, 81-1 BCA ¶ 14,980; *Hunt Bldg. Corp.*, ASBCA 31775, 89-1 BCA ¶ 21,196; *Pittsburgh-Des Moines Corp.*, EBCA 314-3-84, 89-2 BCA ¶ 21,739; *Lloyd Moore Constr.*, AGBCA 87-151-3, 89-2 BCA ¶ 21,875; *LaDuke Constr. & Krumdieck, Inc., J.V.*, AGBCA 83-177-1, 90-1 BCA ¶ 22,302; *Potomac Marine & Aviation, Inc.*, ASBCA 42417, 93-2 BCA ¶ 25,865. See also *Jimenez, Inc.*, LBCA 2001-BCA-

2, 02-2 BCA ¶ 31981, in which the board denied claims where no notice was given, without citing the paragraph of the clause that was applicable.

In 1972 the Court of Claims refused to apply a 20-day notice provision when the government actually knew of a situation that constituted a constructive suspension of work, *Hoel-Steffen Constr. Co. v. United States*, 197 Ct. Cl. 561, 456 F.2d 760 (1972). Thereafter, boards have generally followed a more liberal interpretation of this notice provision, finding that the requirement is met when the government has actual knowledge of the facts constituting the constructive change, *R.C. Hedreen Co.*, ASBCA 19439, 76-1 BCA ¶ 11,816 (request for clarification of specification by government field representative); *United Baeton Int'l*, VACAB 1209, 76-2 BCA ¶ 12,133 (discussion with resident government engineer and observation of extra work); *Hartford Accident & Indem. Co.*, IBCA 1139-1-77, 77-2 BCA ¶ 12,604 (discussion with government field inspector); *Corbell Constr. Co.*, AGBCA 77-129, 78-1 BCA ¶ 13,080 (government representatives directed performance of the work); *Building Maint. Corp.*, DOTCAB 76-42, 79-1 BCA ¶ 13,560 (oral and written notice that problems were being encountered); *J.W. Bateson Co.*, VACAB 1148, 79-1 BCA ¶ 13,573 (government aware of difficulties but left solution to contractor); *J.D. Abrams*, ENGBCA 4332, 89-1 BCA ¶ 21,379 (contractor told Resident Officer in Charge of Construction that it disagreed with interpretation); *Niko Contracting Co.*, IBCA 2368, 91-1 BCA ¶ 23,321 (problem raised with government representative on site); *Toland & Sons*, IBCA 2716, 91-3 BCA ¶ 24,263 (government showed no prejudice from lack of notice); *Dan Rice Constr. Co.*, ASBCA 52160, 04-1 BCA ¶ 32,595 (COTR had full knowledge of changes). For a case not following this type of reasoning, see *Piracci Constr. Co.*, GSBCA 3477, 74-1 BCA ¶ 10,647, *recons. denied*, 74-2 BCA ¶ 10,799 (notice to the government under the Suspension of Work clause insufficient to put the government on notice of problems under the Changes clause). In these cases, the boards frequently justify a liberal interpretation on the grounds that the government has not been prejudiced, but the critical factor appears to be the actual knowledge of a responsible government employee. However, a considerably broader view is expressed in *Mil-Pak Co.*, ASBCA 19733, 76-1 BCA ¶ 11,725, *recons. denied*, 76-1 BCA ¶ 11,836, in which the standard was whether the government would have acted differently had notice been given. Accord, *Imbus Roofing Co.*, GSBCA 10430, 91-2 BCA ¶ 23,820; *Atlantic Constr. Co.*, ASBCA 22647, 79-1 BCA ¶ 13,612. See also *Andy Int'l, Inc.*, ASBCA 20397, 76-2 BCA ¶ 12,046, in which the board noted at 57,815 that there is a "trend toward making the rule the same for both `mandatory' and `discretionary' notice provisions notwithstanding the contractual language and the published regulatory intent of the different clauses." Compare *R.R. Tyler*, AGBCA 381, 77-1 BCA ¶ 12,227, reaching the opposite conclusion.

Another basis for not enforcing the notice requirement is a finding by the board that the failure to give notice has been induced by actions or statements of the government, *Ionics, Inc.*, ASBCA 16094, 71-2 BCA ¶ 9030; *J.A. LaPorte, Inc.*, IBCA 1014-12-73, 75-2 BCA ¶ 11,486. See also *Universal Painting Corp.*, ASBCA

20536, 77-1 BCA ¶ 12,355. In *LaPorte*, the board also explained its nonenforcement of the 20-day notice provision on the grounds that there was no single, identifiable event upon which the claim was grounded that could be used to start the notice period running.

In *Powers Regulator Co.*, GSBCA 4668, 80-2 BCA ¶ 14,463, the board reviewed the decisions of all the boards of contract appeals and, at 71,320, stated the following instances in which the government's invocation of the 20-day notice provision will fail:

- Written notice is in fact given the contracting officer.
- The contracting officer has actual or imputed knowledge of the facts giving rise to the claim.
- Notice to the contracting officer would have been useless.
- The contracting officer frustrated the giving of the notice.
- The contracting officer considered the claim on the merits.

The 20-day notice requirement in the construction contract Changes clause specifically excludes claims for defective specifications. It can thus be argued that this contract language removes any requirement for notice of defective specifications, *H.M. Byars Constr. Co.*, IBCA 1098-2-76, 77-2 BCA ¶ 12,568. However, one board has reasoned that the same prejudice rule should apply under this clause because of the notice requirement in ¶ (b), *H.A. Anderson Co.*, ENGBCA 3724, 77-2 BCA ¶ 12,712. In that case, the board referred to the contractor's withholding of information about the defective specifications, to the government's prejudice, as a "failure to mitigate." A defective specification claim was denied on this basis in *Time Contractors, Joint Venture*, DOTBCA 1747, 1986 DOT BCA LEXIS 74.

3. Notification of Changes Clause

FAR 43.107 provides for the optional use of a Notification of Changes clause, FAR 52.243-7, in contracts for major weapon systems or subsystems. This clause contains the following notice requirement:

> (b) *Notice.* The primary purpose of this clause is to obtain prompt reporting of Government conduct that the Contractor considers to constitute a change to this contract. Except for changes identified as such in writing and signed by the Contracting Officer, the Contractor shall notify the Administrative Contracting Officer in writing promptly, within (to be negotiated) calendar days from the date that the Contractor identifies any Government conduct (including actions, inactions, and written or oral communications) that the Contractor regards as a change to the contract terms and conditions. On the basis of the most accurate information available to the Contractor, the notice shall state—
>
> > (1) The date, nature, and circumstances of the conduct regarded as a change;

> (2) The name, function, and activity of each Government individual and Contractor official or employee involved in or knowledgeable about such conduct;
>
> (3) The identification of any documents and the substance of any oral communication involved in such conduct;
>
> (4) In the instance of alleged acceleration of scheduled performance or delivery, the basis upon which it arose;
>
> (5) The particular elements of contract performance for which the Contractor may seek an equitable adjustment under this clause, including—
>
>> (i) What contract line items have been or may be affected by the alleged change;
>>
>> (ii) What labor or materials or both have been or may be added, deleted, or wasted by the alleged change;
>>
>> (iii) To the extent practicable, what delay and disruption in the manner and sequence of performance and effect on continued performance have been or may be caused by the alleged change;
>>
>> (iv) What adjustments to contract price, delivery schedule, and other provisions affected by the alleged change are estimated; and
>
> (6) The Contractor's estimate of the time by which the Government must respond to the Contractor's notice to minimize cost, delay or disruption of performance.

In *Grumman Aerospace Corp.*, ASBCA 46834, 03-1 BCA ¶ 32,203, *recons. denied*, 03-2 BCA ¶ 32,289, the board held that this notice requirement should be enforced in the same way that the 30-day notice requirements had been enforced—not "hypertechnically" but only if the government was prejudiced. It found no prejudice because the government officials administering the contract were well aware of the problems being encountered by the contractor. Compare *Ervin & Assocs., Inc. v. United States*, 59 Fed. Cl. 267 (2004), in which the court strictly enforced the 15-day notice requirement in the clause in denying a constructive changes claim. The court stated that the contracting officer should have been notified "directly." See also *MC II Generator & Elec.*, ASBCA 53389, 04-1 BCA ¶ 32,569, where the contracting officer denied a claim based on lack of notification as required by this clause but the board denied the claim because the government project manager did not direct a change and had no authority to do so.

4. Accelerations

The construction contract Changes clause requires written notice of constructive acceleration orders in ¶ (b) and denies recovery of costs incurred prior to 20 days before such notice is given in ¶ (d). In one case in which the government argued lack of notice as a defense to an acceleration claim, the board ruled that the requirement would not be enforced because the government had not been prejudiced by lack of notice, *E.C. Morris & Son, Inc.*, ASBCA 20697, 77-2 BCA ¶ 12,622. The facts indicated that the government knew of the acceleration order since it had directed the contractor to speed up. In addition, the board found that the government would not have been able to avoid the costs had it received notice. In contrast, acceleration claims have been barred for lack of notice, *Nello L. Teer Co. v. Washington Metro. Area Transit Auth.*, 695 F. Supp. 583 (D.D.C. 1988) (no notice for one year after excusable delay had occurred); *Girardeau Contractors, Inc.*, ENGBCA 5034, 88-1 BCA ¶ 20,391 (no proof of notice of acceleration). Compare *P.J. Dick, Inc.*, VABCA 5597, 01-2 BCA ¶ 31,647, where timely notice was given.

In a case involving an acceleration claim under the pre-1968 Standard Form 23-A Changes clause not containing the 20-day notice provision, the Court of Claims ruled that failure to give notice of an acceleration barred recovery because the government was prejudiced by lack of notice, *Eggers & Higgins v. United States*, 185 Ct. Cl. 765, 403 F.2d 225 (1968). The court concluded that the government could have altered the performance to avoid the acceleration costs if it had known that the contractor was construing the refusal to grant a time extension as an acceleration order.

5. Military Shipbuilding Contracts

In 1984 Congress enacted a special statute requiring timely notice of constructive changes claims on military shipbuilding contracts. 10 U.S.C. § 2405 read:

> (a) The Secretary of a military department may not adjust any price under a shipbuilding contract entered into after December 7, 1983, for an amount set forth in a claim, request for equitable adjustment, or demand for payment under the contract (or incurred due to the preparation, submission, or adjudication of any such claim, request, or demand) arising out of events occurring more than 18 months before the submission of the claim, request, or demand.
>
> (b) For the purposes of subsection (a), a claim, request, or demand shall be considered to have been submitted only when the contractor has provided the certification required by section 6(c)(1) of the Contract Disputes Act of 1978 (41 U.S.C. 605(c)(1)) and the supporting data for the claim, request, or demand.

This statute was repealed by § 810(a)(1) of Pub. L. No. 105-85, 111 Stat. 1839, Nov. 18, 1997. This repeal was "effective with respect to claims, requests for equitable adjustment, and demands for payment under shipbuilding contracts that have been or are submitted before, on, or after the date of the enactment of this Act." However, it was not effective with regard to claims that had been resolved with finality in the government's favor prior to the enactment of the statute.

The statute was interpreted to be in the nature of a notice requirement, not a statute of limitations, *Bath Iron Works Corp. v. United States*, 27 Fed. Cl. 114 (1992), *aff'd*, 20 F.3d 1567 (Fed. Cir. 1994). Thus, while it was binding on the military departments, it did not preclude the Court of Federal Claims from taking jurisdiction of cases where contractors were asserting constructive changes claims that had not been submitted to the government within the 18-month period. However, the court never stated what standard it would use in reviewing such claims—a strict rule or a prejudice rule. The Armed Services Board ruled that the statute should be interpreted strictly to bar untimely claims, *Bath Iron Works Corp.*, ASBCA 43303, 93-2 BCA ¶ 25,792, *recons. denied*, 93-3 BCA ¶ 25,992.

The "event" that began the running of this 18-month period was the beginning of work that is not called for by the contract, *Peterson Builders, Inc. v. United States*, 26 Cl. Ct. 1227 (1992), *aff'd*, 155 F.3d 566 (Fed. Cir. 1998). In that case, the court rejected the contractor's argument that the date should be the time when the contractor could fully quantify the claim. Thus, the contractor had 18 months to assemble all of the data necessary to submit a fully documented claim meeting the terms of ¶ (b) of the statute.

CHAPTER 5

DIFFERING SITE CONDITIONS

One of the major risks of a construction project is the type of subsurface or other latent physical conditions that may be encountered. If bidders were required to assume the full risk of these conditions, they would either have to make extensive examinations and analyses of the site or include contingencies in their bids to protect against potential unfavorable conditions. On the other hand, the government normally obtains information concerning site conditions during its design of the project prior to soliciting bids and wishes to avoid the disruption and bidding expense that would be involved if each bidder were to make borings or other extensive investigations. The government's response to this situation has been to allow bidders to have or examine the information it possesses concerning the site, to admonish bidders to make reasonable site investigations, and to relieve the contractor from the risk of certain types of unexpected unfavorable conditions while protecting itself if the conditions turn out to be more favorable than should have been expected. The major clause used in this risk allocation scheme is the Differing Site Conditions clause contained in FAR 52.236-2:

> DIFFERING SITE CONDITIONS (APR 1984)
>
> (a) The Contractor shall promptly, and before the conditions are disturbed, give a written notice to the Contracting Officer of (1) subsurface or latent physical conditions at the site which differ materially from those indicated in this contract, or (2) unknown physical conditions at the site, of an unusual nature, which differ materially from those ordinarily encountered and generally recognized as inhering in work of the character provided for in the contract.
>
> (b) The Contracting Officer shall investigate the site conditions promptly after receiving the notice. If the conditions do materially so differ and cause an increase or decrease in the Contractor's cost of, or the time required for, performing any part of the work under this contract, whether or not changed as a result of the conditions, an equitable adjustment shall be made under this clause and the contract modified in writing accordingly.
>
> (c) No request by the Contractor for an equitable adjustment to the contract under this clause shall be allowed, unless the Contractor has given the written notice required; *provided*, that the time prescribed in (a) above for giving written notice may be extended by the Contracting Officer.
>
> (d) No request by the Contractor for an equitable adjustment to the contract for differing site conditions shall be allowed if made after final payment under this contract.

The policy supporting this clause was described by the Court of Claims in *Foster Constr. C.A. & Williams Bros. Co. v. United States*, 193 Ct. Cl. 587, 435 F.2d 873 (1970), at 613-14:

> The purpose of the changed conditions clause is thus to take at least some of the gamble on subsurface conditions out of bidding. Bidders need not weigh the cost and ease of making their own borings against the risk of encountering an adverse subsurface, and they need not consider how large a contingency should be added to the bid to cover the risk. They will have no windfalls and no disasters. The Government benefits from more accurate bidding, without inflation for risks which may not eventuate. It pays for difficult subsurface work only when it is encountered and was not indicated in the logs.

This chapter examines the definitions of differing site conditions developed in the litigation that has flourished under this clause. It also considers the government's attempts to limit its liabilities under the clause through provisions providing for site investigation and exculpatory clauses.

While the Differing Site Conditions clause is written primarily for use in construction contracts, it can also be used in contracts for services when appropriate. See FAR 37.110(e), which requires contracting officers to include in services contracts provisions and clauses prescribed elsewhere in the FAR when they are applicable. Thus, some agencies use this or a similar clause when unknown conditions may impact the cost of performance of services contracts at government installations. See *Atlantic Dry Dock Corp.*, ASBCA 42609, 98-2 BCA ¶ 30,025 (renovation of a naval frigate). However, since the use of the clause in service contracts is optional, it will not be read in by operation of law. Thus, the clause was not, nor was it required to be, in a contract to paint a barge, *Marine Indus. Northwest, Inc.*, ASBCA 51942, 01-1 BCA ¶ 31,201.

I. GENERAL RULES GOVERNING APPLICATION OF THE CLAUSE

The clause separates differing site conditions into two categories:

> (1) Subsurface or latent physical conditions at the site that differ materially from those indicated in the contract (referred to as Category or Type I conditions).
>
> (2) Unknown physical conditions at the site, of an unusual nature, that differ materially from those ordinarily encountered and are generally recognized as inhering in work of the character provided for in the contract (referred to as Category or Type II conditions).

As can be seen from this language, there are some common and some unique aspects in each type of condition. This section explores the interpretative principles, as established by the courts and boards, that have common applicability to both types of differing site conditions. The following section analyzes the unique aspects of each type of differing site condition.

A. Condition Must Predate Contract

While a cursory reading of the Differing Site Conditions clause would indicate that it covers any condition encountered by the contractor during performance, regardless of the time of occurrence, the judicial and administrative interpretation of the contract language has not been that broad. It has generally been held that the clause covers only "a . . . condition existing at the time the contract was entered into and not one occurring thereafter," *John McShain, Inc. v. United States*, 179 Ct. Cl. 632, 375 F.2d 829 (1967). See also *Olympus Corp. v. United States*, 98 F.3d 1314 (Fed. Cir. 1996) (contamination of soil caused by co-contractor did not constitute differing site condition because it arose after the contract was signed). But see *Hoffman v. United States*, 166 Ct. Cl. 39, 340 F.2d 645 (1964), holding that the operative date is that of the issuance of the notice to proceed. The interpretation that events occurring during performance are not covered was first announced by the Court of Claims in *Arundel Corp. v. United States*, 96 Ct. Cl. 77 (1942), in which the court refused to allow recovery for a condition caused by a flood that occurred during contract performance, stating at 116:

> At the time cells 4, 5, 6, and 7 had been constructed the bed of the river was no different from what it was when the plans and specifications were drawn. The later change was brought about by an act of nature during the progress of the work. This provision of the contract refers to a latent condition existing at the time the contract was entered into, not to one occurring thereafter. The condition of the bed of the river until the flood was the same as that it had been represented to be before the contract was signed.

Unfortunately, the Court of Claims did not give its rationale for this legal conclusion. Since then, the courts and contract appeals boards have not been able to arrive at a clear statement of the precise time prior to which a condition must be created in order to be considered a differing site condition. In a later *Arundel* case, *Arundel Corp. v. United States*, 103 Ct. Cl. 688, *cert. denied*, 326 U.S. 752 (1945), relief was denied for a condition created by a hurricane that, from the reported facts, appeared to have occurred after award but before formal execution of the contract. In *Concrete Constr. Corp.*, IBCA 432-3-64, 65-1 BCA ¶ 4520, the board held that the controlling time was the initiation of the process of contract formation.

B. Force Creating Conditions

Physical conditions at the site may occur naturally or may be created by man. In either case, it is the time when the condition is created, not the force that creates the condition, that determines whether it will be covered by the clause.

1. Weather and Acts of God

Weather and acts of God that occur during contract performance are generally excluded from coverage of the Differing Site Conditions clause, *Turnkey Enters., Inc. v. United States*, 220 Ct. Cl. 179, 597 F.2d 750 (1979). In that case, the contractor contended that the weather creating the condition occurred prior to contract formation. The court found that there was no evidence to support such an assertion and denied the differing site condition claim. However, the court clouded the issue by stating that "[p]laintiff cites no authority in support of" its contention that weather occurring before award would constitute a differing site condition. This comment should be contrasted with an equally confusing statement in *Highland Reforestation Inc. v. United States*, 230 Ct. Cl. 1020 (1982). There, Mount St. Helens erupted during contract performance. The court denied the government's motion for summary judgment, stating at 1021:

> We are unable to state that interference with the work by a volcanic eruption is not and never can be compensable for added cost by an adjustment under the second changes clause quoted above. The contracting officer seems to have supposed that the Armed Services Board of Contract Appeals in *Hardeman-Monier-Hutcherson*, ASBCA No. 12392, 68-2 BCA ¶ 7220 held that severe weather and other "Acts of God" are outside the clause. But, in our review, affirming the result, we held we could not decide under so sweeping a rule of exclusion. *Hardeman-Monier-Hutcherson v. United States*, 198 Ct. Cl. 472, 486, 458 F.2d 1364, 1371 (1972).

Apparently, the confusion arises because the cases contain broad statements that conditions resulting from weather cannot be differing site conditions. However, conditions resulting from weather occurring before contract award would be covered if the resulting condition were unknown or latent and met the other requirements of the clause. Of course, if such weather is sufficient to put the contractor on notice of the conditions to be expected during performance, the condition will not be considered a differing site condition, *Tombigbee Constructors v. United States*, 190 Ct. Cl. 615, 420 F.2d 1037 (1970).

A variety of circumstances have been held to be caused by weather during performance and not covered by the clause. Thus, no changed condition was found as a result of frozen ground following unusually severe weather, *Overland Elec. Co.*, ASBCA 9096, 1964 BCA ¶ 4359; excess underground water caused by a hurricane, *E.W. Jackson Contracting Co.*, ASBCA 7267, 1962 BCA ¶ 3325; the washing out of roads as a result of a hurricane, *Lenry, Inc. v. United States*, 156 Ct. Cl. 46, 297 F.2d 550 (1962); severe sea conditions substantially reducing the number of available workdays for construction of a pier, *Hardeman-Monier-Hutcherson v. United States*, 198 Ct. Cl. 472, 458 F.2d 1364 (1972); flooding, *Security Nat'l Bank of Kansas City, Kan. v. United States*, 184 Ct. Cl. 741, 397 F.2d 984 (1968); unusually heavy snowfall causing collapse of warehouse roof, *Warren Painting Co.*, ASBCA 18456, 74-2 BCA ¶ 10,834; extra work needed to clear road after earthslide, *Jim Challinor*, AG-

BCA 75-133, 78-2 BCA ¶ 13,278; unusually high water, *Roen Salvage Co.*, ENGBCA 3670, 79-2 BCA ¶ 13,882; abnormally heavy rainfall overwhelming drainage system and damaging partially completed work, *Praxis-Assurance Venture*, ASBCA 24748, 81-1 BCA ¶ 15,028. See also *Cole's Constr. Co.,* ENGBCA 6158, 96-2 BCA ¶ 28,579 (no differing site condition based on unusually severe weather and unusually high river stages); *Toloff Constr.,* AGBCA 95-227-3, 96-1 BCA ¶ 28,156 (thawing of a frozen Alaskan marsh not a differing site condition); *Dennis T. Hardy Elec., Inc.*, ASBCA 47770, 97-1 BCA ¶ 28,840 (contractor could not recover for unanticipated dewatering effort because it was caused by unusually heavy rainfall); *HK Sys., Inc.*, PSBCA 3712, 97-2 BCA ¶ 29,079 (earthquake); *Luhr Brothers, Inc.,* ASBCA 52887, 01-2 BCA ¶ 31,443 (contractor failed to prove that the adverse sea conditions were anything other than unusually severe weather); *Kilgallon Constr. Co.*, ASBCA 51601, 01-2 BCA ¶ 31,621 (acts of God, standing alone, not a differing site condition); and *Jerry Dodds,* ASBCA 51682, 02-1 BCA ¶ 31,844 (rainwater runoff, not groundwater, not a differing site condition.).

2. Man-Made Conditions

Man-made conditions should also be analyzed in accordance with the time of their occurrence. The boards and courts appear to be quite consistent in this area. Thus, numerous conditions of this type existing at the time of contracting have been held to fall within the clause. For example, differing site conditions were found where underground reinforced concrete trenches were found at the site, *Boland & Martin, Inc.*, ASBCA 8503, 1963 BCA ¶ 3705; where underground debris was encountered, *Cosmo Constr. Co.*, ENGBCA 2785, 67-2 BCA ¶ 6516, *aff'd*, 196 Ct. Cl. 463, 451 F.2d 602 (1971); where the contractor encountered beer cans, live ammunition, and ladies' underwear in cleaning a duct system in a military barracks, *Community Power Suction Furnace Cleaning Co.*, ASBCA 13803, 69-2 BCA ¶ 7963; where the contractor encountered abnormally hard mortar, *George E. Jensen Contractor, Inc.*, ASBCA 20234, 76-1 BCA ¶ 11,741; where the contractor encountered double roofs, *Edgar M. Williams*, ASBCA 16058, 72-2 BCA ¶ 9734; and where asbestos was encountered at the site, *Frank Lill & Son, Inc.*, ASBCA 35774, 88-3 BCA ¶ 20,880.

On the other hand, man-made conditions occurring during contract performance have generally been held to fall outside the clause. For example, in *John McShain, Inc. v. United States*, 179 Ct. Cl. 632, 375 F.2d 829 (1967), the court held the contractor liable for the cost of repairing work damaged by a water main that broke during contract performance. The court quoted *Mittry v. United States*, 73 Ct. Cl. 341 (1931), at 642:

> The rule is well settled that where a contractor undertakes to erect a building, and during the process of construction the building is injured or destroyed without fault of either party to the contract, the contractor is still bound by his undertaking to complete the building, and is liable in damages if he fails to do so.

See also *Olympus Corp. v. United States,* 98 F.3d 1314 (Fed. Cir. 1996). Compare *Hoffman v. United States*, 166 Ct. Cl. 39, 340 F.2d 645 (1964), in which the court found a man-made condition created by another contractor to be a changed condition. The holding of *Hoffman* can be explained either on the theory that the condition was existing at the time of contracting or on the theory that the government created the condition since it had control over the other contractor. The latter theory was followed in *Frank W. Miller Constr. Co.*, ASBCA 22347, 78-1 BCA ¶ 13,039, in which the board found a changed condition when another contractor created an interfering condition during contract performance. The board stated at 63,704:

> [*Hoffman*] held that a changed condition can be man-made and that the Government has the duty to protect its contractors from man-made changed conditions created by other Government contractors working in the same general area.

In reaching its holding, the board also relied on *W.E. Callahan Constr. Co. v. United States*, 91 Ct. Cl. 538 (1940), which found the government liable for upstream work that increased the damage to the contractor's work caused by a flood. The reasoning of the court in *Callahan* that the government had breached its duty not to hinder the contractor is more appropriate than the conclusion of the court in *Hoffman* that a differing site condition had occurred. See also *Harding Equip. Co.*, ASBCA 2477, 6 CCF ¶ 61,853 (1955), holding the government liable under the Changes clause for additional work done because the government diverted the runoff of rainfall into the work site.

3. *Interaction of Site Conditions and Weather or Other Causes*

Relief may be allowed under the Differing Site Conditions clause where a condition not in itself compensable because it occurred during performance combines with physical factors at the site to change the contractor's work. The rationale of decisions granting such relief is that only one differing site condition is needed to qualify for relief. Thus, differing site conditions have been found where a contractor could not achieve the necessary soil compaction because of the combination of excessive rainfall and inadequate drainage, which was known to the government but was not revealed in the plans or specifications, *D.H. Dave & Gerben Contracting Co.*, ASBCA 6257, 1962 BCA ¶ 3493; where a road disintegrated due to the interaction of the spring thaw and the nature of the material in the road, *John A. Johnson Contracting Corp. v. United States*, 132 Ct. Cl. 645, 132 F. Supp. 698 (1955); where jet fuel was dumped into a sewage system containing blockages that prevented proper drainage, *Premier Elec. Constr. Co.*, FAACAP 66-10, 65-2 BCA ¶ 5080; and where a contractor had to perform extra work in painting a dock because of an unforeseeable condition that arose when ocean tides interacted with peculiar structural features of the dock known to the government but not disclosed, *Warren Painting Co.,* ASBCA 18456, 74-2 BCA ¶ 10,834. Boards have denied relief, however, when the contractor has pre-bid knowledge of the other factors, *F.D. Rich*

Co., ASBCA 6515, 1963 BCA ¶ 3710; *Welch Constr. Co.*, PSBCA 217, 77-1 BCA ¶ 12,322. In one case, the board denied the contractor's claim that a government-operated sprinkler system interacted with rainfall to cause drainage difficulties, finding that the sprinkler system was a minor and probably insignificant causative factor, *Monmouth Fund, Inc.*, ASBCA 20158, 77-1 BCA ¶ 12,305.

C. Physical Conditions

To fall within the scope of the clause, the condition encountered must be "physical." The term "physical" has generally been held to limit the clause to the condition of the site of the work. Thus, the term has not been construed to encompass physical force that increases the contractor's effort. This question most frequently arises in cases where interference by the government or its contractors is alleged to be a differing site condition. It has generally been held that such interference is not within the clause because it is not a "static physical condition," *Ames & Denning, Inc.*, ASBCA 6956, 1962 BCA ¶ 3406; *Yarno & Assocs.*, ASBCA 10257, 67-1 BCA ¶ 6312. Another rationale used in this area is contained in *Hallman v. United States*, 107 Ct. Cl. 555, 68 F. Supp. 204 (1946), in which the court stated that the clause had "no reference to changed governmental, political, or economic conditions."

In most cases, the outcome of this rule is quite straightforward. Thus, no differing site condition has been found where the government delayed in furnishing materials or equipment required for contract performance, *George A. Rutherford Co.*, NASABCA 12, 1962 BCA ¶ 3561; *Grenco Servs., Inc.*, NASABCA 867-27, 69-2 BCA ¶ 7789, *recons. denied*, 69-2 BCA ¶ 7916; where government failure to obtain a tree-cutting permit resulted in the contractor having to defend against a trespass suit, *Charney Constr. Corp.*, FAACAP 67-2, 66-1 BCA ¶ 5685; and where competing government contractors in the same area reduced a contractor's supply of workers or increased labor costs, *Bateson-Stolte, Inc. v. United States*, 145 Ct. Cl. 387, 172 F. Supp. 454 (1959), *Koppers Co., Malan Constr. Dept.*, ENGBCA 2699, 67-2 BCA ¶ 6532, and *Robert E. McKee, Gen. Contractor, Inc.*, ASBCA 5621, 60-1 BCA ¶ 2504. In these cases, the contractor may have a claim under some other clause of the contract or if there is sufficient government fault for breach of contract. See also the discussion of the *Hoffman* case above for a court decision that appears to classify a type of interference as a differing site condition.

There are two cases where the event was clearly "physical" but the appeals board held that the condition did not fall within the clause citing this line of cases. In *Keang Nam Enters., Ltd.*, ASBCA 13747, 69-1 BCA ¶ 7705, the board held that the Tet offensive during the Vietnam War was not a physical condition since it was not unknown but was a "potential extraneous event." Similarly, in *Cross Constr. Co.*, ENGBCA 3676, 79-1 BCA ¶ 13,707, the board held that no differing site condition had occurred when a breakdown in law enforcement permitted striking workers to attack the contractor's workforce. These cases could have been disposed of on the grounds that the event occurred during contract performance.

A myriad of conditions can qualify as physical conditions. *Hartford Cas. Ins. Co.*, VABCA 5262, 99-1 BCA ¶ 30,106 (bituthane waterproofing membrane on a concrete roof slab was a type I differing site condition); *David Boland, Inc.*, VABCA, 5858, 01-2 BCA ¶ 31,578 (artesian aquifer not indicated in the government's soil reports); *Donohoe Constr. Co.*, ASBCA 47310, 98-2 BCA ¶ 30,076 (steam lines buried inside a concrete tunnel and a concrete slab under asphalt paving constituted a differing site condition because the contract drawings showed only a layer of asphalt); *Triad Mech., Inc.*, IBCA 3393, 97-1 BCA ¶ 28,771 (government failed to disclose the existence of a clay liner in a canal bed that had been installed by the government and was reflected in government archives); *Southern Comfort Builders, Inc. v. United States*, 67 Fed. Cl. 124 (2005) (lead-based paint).

D. "At the Site"

The clause covers only conditions *at the site*. Though defining the scope of the term "site" would seem to be a crucial element in differing site condition claims regarding conditions at off-site areas such as access roads or quarries, surprisingly few decisions have faced this issue. In *L.G. Everist, Inc. v. United States*, 231 Ct. Cl. 1013 (1982), *cert. denied*, 461 U.S. 957 (1983), the court held that a quarry was not "at the site" for purposes of the clause because it "was not designated or even mentioned by the contract." The court noted, however, that conditions at quarries are sometimes compensable under the clause when the use of a particular authorized quarry is "necessarily so bound up with the contractor's performance that the Government should be responsible for conditions at the quarry," citing *Kaiser Indus. Corp. v. United States*, 169 Ct. Cl. 310, 340 F.2d 322 (1965) (government owned the only two quarries in the area and approved their use); *Tobin Quarries, Inc. v. United States*, 114 Ct. Cl. 286, 84 F. Supp. 1021 (1949); *Stock & Grove, Inc. v. United States*, 204 Ct. Cl. 103, 493 F.2d 629 (1974) (contract required contractor to use a particular quarry whose rock formations were incorrectly represented in the contract); *Morrison-Knudsen Co. v. United States*, 184 Ct. Cl. 661, 397 F.2d 826 (1968) (contract designated borrow pits and described them in great detail). However, the decision is unclear as to whether an area becomes a part of the site if it is "bound up with the contractor's performance" or whether a condition at such an area simply becomes compensable despite the fact that it is not a condition at the site. Note that none of the above cases cited by the court in *Everist* discussed the scope of the term "site." See *R.A. Heintz Constr. Co.*, ENGBCA 3380, 74-1 BCA ¶ 10,562, in which the board simply stated that, since the borrow pit "was a government-approved source . . . , we are of the view that the government must be held accountable [for conditions at the pit]." However, see *Blaze Constr. Co.*, IBCA 2863, 91-3 BCA ¶ 24,071, in which the contractor's claim for equitable adjustment because its leased yard and pit location was part of a secret, sacred Indian religious site was denied. The board held that government approval of the off-jobsite location was irrelevant and did not make the yard and pit a contract site where the contract did not specify yard and pit sites. For a case decided under the Site Investigation clause, in which the board held that the site consisted of the vicinity surrounding the work area as well as the work area itself, see *Praxis-Assurance Venture*, ASBCA 24748, 81-1 BCA ¶ 15,028. In *Pitt-Des Moines, Inc.*, ASBCA 42838, 96-1 BCA ¶ 27,941, a contractor successfully asserted a Type II claim based on the deterioration of a building adjacent to its building renovation, which forced it to alter the method of supporting the building.

E. Differing Materially

There is very little discussion in the cases of the requirement in the clause that to be compensable conditions must differ materially from those expected to be encountered. However, the courts and boards insist that to support recovery the contractor must present evidence of the difference that occurred. Such evidence may take the form of proof of a larger amount of work than originally contemplated or of the need to use a different method to accomplish the work. See, for example, *Wall Street Roofing*, VACAB 1373, 81-2 BCA ¶ 15,417, *recons. denied*, 83-2 BCA ¶ 16,568, where the contractor supported a differing site conditions claim for difficulties encountered in removing roofing by presenting evidence about the normal method for doing the work and the method used after the unusual conditions were encountered. The board found that the anticipated use of the normal method was reasonable and that the conditions encountered required use of the extraordinary methods. It thus found that the conditions differed materially. For a similar case, see *Southern Roofing & Petroleum Co.,* ASBCA 12841, 69-1 BCA ¶ 7599.

The Court of Claims has ruled that proof of increased cost is not essential to find that a condition differs materially, *Roscoe-Ajax Constr. Co. v. United States*, 198 Ct. Cl. 133, 458 F.2d 55 (1972). There, the contractor was required to use a different dewatering technique than originally planned because of the site conditions. The court ruled that this alone would be sufficient to prove that a differing site condition had occurred. The court went on to observe that, when the parties determined the amount of the equitable adjustment, the government would be free to prove that no costs had been incurred above those that would have been incurred without the differing site condition.

In most cases, the contractor will demonstrate that a condition was materially different by showing that increased effort was required to overcome the condition, *Dunbar & Sullivan Dredging Co.*, ENGBCA 3165, 73-2 BCA ¶ 10,285; *North Slope Tech. Ltd., Inc. v. United States*, 14 Cl. Ct. 242 (1988). In *J.A. Laporte, Inc.*, ENGBCA 5252, 88-3 BCA ¶ 20,953, the board found that a materially different condition existed where quantities of rock and "rock-like" materials substantially increased the difficulty and cost of the contractor's dredge operations.

To show that the condition encountered differed materially, the contractor must demonstrate the difference between the anticipated condition and the actual condition encountered. Failure of proof will result in rejection of the claim. See *Guy F. Atkinson Co.*, ENGBCA 4693, 87-3 BCA ¶ 19,971, in which the board found that no Category II condition existed where the contractor failed to establish the "normal" condition and hence could not prove that the condition actually encountered "differed materially." See also *Northwest Painting Serv., Inc.*, ASBCA 27854, 84-2 BCA ¶ 17,474, where the contractor failed to prove that the amount of chipping, spalling, and depressions caused by sandblasting exceeded the amount reasonably expected.

F. Burden of Proof

The cases uniformly hold that the contractor has the burden of proving a differing site condition by a preponderance of the evidence. See, for example, *Stuyvesant Dredging Co. v. United States*, 834 F.2d 1576 (Fed. Cir. 1987), and *Randa/Madison Joint Venture III v. Dahlberg*, 239 F.3d 1264 (Fed. Cir. 2001). Contractors often fail on one or more elements. For example, even potentially terrible problems are not recoverable unless the contractor can show they were not foreseeable. See *Bechtel Envtl., Inc.*, ENGBCA 6137, 97-1 BCA ¶ 28,640 (despite the possibility of buried explosive drums at the excavation site, there was no evidence that the actual conditions differed from those depicted in the contract). See also *Wright Dredging Co.*, ASBCA 52924, 01-2 BCA ¶ 31,583 (contractor failed to establish any of the elements of a Type I differing site condition); *SKR Constr. Corp.*, ASBCA 51980, 99-2 BCA ¶ 30,477 (insufficient proof because an affidavit offered by the contractor contained only a conclusory opinion by an affiant whose technical qualifications were not mentioned); *Resource Conservation Corp. v. General Servs. Admin.*, GSBCA 13399, 97-1 BCA ¶ 28,776 (contractor did not meet its burden of proving that the actual conditions encountered differed materially from its interpretation); and *Lamb Eng'g & Constr. Co.*, EBCA C-9304172, 97-2 BCA ¶ 29,207 (contractor did not establish that some groundwater might reasonably have been expected and failed to rule out the likelihood that some costs might have been mitigated by the hiring of a replacement drainage subcontractor). Claims have also failed when the contractor cannot prove that it substantially complied with the specifications. See *Queen City, Inc.*, ASBCA 45755, 96-1 BCA ¶ 28,229; *Phoenix Control Sys., Inc.*, IBCA 2844, 96-1 BCA ¶ 28,128. As in other areas, contemporaneous documentation is essential, *SKR Constr. Corp.*, ASBCA 51980, 99-2 BCA ¶ 30,477 (allegation of excessive dewatering first made eight months after the alleged events lacked any credibility in the absence of corroboration by the daily reports).

A contractor has a high burden of proof in establishing a claim for a Category II differing site condition. This has been called "a relatively heavy burden of proof," *Charles T. Parker Constr. Co. v. United States*, 193 Ct. Cl. 320, 433 F.2d 771 (1970); *Jack Walser v. United States*, 23 Cl. Ct. 591 (1991). Thus, it has been stated that "[a]s a general matter, it is more difficult to establish a Type II differing site condition," *CCI Contractors, Inc.*, AGBCA 84-314-1, 91-3 BCA ¶ 24,225, *aff'd*, 979 F.2d 216 (Fed. Cir. 1992). A contractor must establish the elements of a Category II condition by a preponderance of the evidence, *Youngdale & Sons Constr. Co. v. United States*, 27 Fed. Cl. 516 (1993). Because there is no government measurement with which to compare the conditions actually encountered, and because the contractor must show that the actual conditions differed from its general expectations, the basis of comparison is considerably “more amorphous” than for a Category I comparison, *Husman Bros., Inc.*, DOTCAB 71-15, 73-1 BCA ¶ 9889; *Snider/Chapman Constr. Co.*, EBCA 373-7-86, 87-1 BCA ¶ 19,629. See *Dennis T. Hardy Elec., Inc.*, ASBCA 47770, 97-1 BCA ¶ 28,840 (contractor’s allegations were not sufficient to prove a differing site condition, because there was no evidence as to the condition of the soil, the changes in the water table, or the time period during which those changes took place), and *V&W Constr. & Serv. Co.*, ASBCA 50812, 98-1 BCA ¶ 29,465 (contractor did not prove that the force of the subsurface water it encountered was materially different from the known or usual condition).

Contractors often fail to prove the conditions that were actually encountered. In *D.W. Sandau Dredging*, ENGBCA 5812, 96-1 BCA ¶ 28,064, *recons. denied*, 96-2 BCA ¶ 28,300, there was a lack of convincing evidence about what was encountered. The decision suggests that boring logs, measurements, samples, or photographs would be probative evidence of materials encountered. In *Resource Conservation Corp. v. General Servs. Admin.*, GSBCA 13399, 97-1 BCA ¶ 28,776, the contractor provided no contemporaneous measurements of actual depths of the asphalt or the quantities of asphalt that it removed. Without this evidence, it failed to prove that conditions it encountered differed materially from what was anticipated. It is also important that the contractor prove that the differing site condition occurred in the actual area where the work was performed. *Circle, Inc.*, ENGBCA 6048, 95-1 BCA ¶ 27,568, demonstrates that videotapes, photographs, and daily job logs can be effective evidence that the conditions encountered were materially different from those indicated in the contract documents.

The government has defended differing site conditions claims with the argument that the removal techniques for the differing materials were the same as those planned for the materials shown in the contract drawings. The argument is unpersuasive if the contractor can show that the conditions actually encountered were more difficult and more expensive to remove than expected. The issue in *Hartford Cas. Ins. Co.*, VABCA 5262, 99-1 BCA ¶ 30,106, for example, was whether bituthene roofing material was more difficult to remove than the liquid waterproofing membrane shown in the contract documents. Government experts testified that the removal techniques were “equally difficult,” but the contractor showed that areas with the bituthene material were more difficult and more expensive to remove than areas with the liquid membrane. The board explained: “This actual demonstrated difference in degree of difficulty is more persuasive than generalized testimony to the contrary from individuals denominated experts no matter how impressive their qualifications happen to be.”

II. UNIQUE ASPECTS OF THE TWO CATEGORIES OF CONDITIONS

During the design of a project, the government generally obtains considerable information concerning the site, such as drawings, core drillings, boring logs, geological reports, and similar data. Whether this information is disclosed to offerors and how it is disclosed can significantly affect the rights of the parties. If the information is included as a part of the contract documents, it may serve as a basis for a Category I differing site condition claim. At the same time, inclusion of the information in the contract gives offerors official notice of the indicated conditions and may preclude recovery of a claim under Category II. On the other hand, if the government withholds the information, it may be liable to the contractor for nondisclosure of a material fact if the data would have disclosed the existence of conditions not otherwise indicated or discoverable. Finally, the government may provide the information to offerors while indicating that the information is not part of the contract. This seeks to avoid responsibility for a Category I claim. In such cases, however, the government may have difficulty in charging the contractor with the responsibility for consulting such "non-contractual" information. These issues involving the furnishing of information are discussed in the various sections in the chapter where they arise. The contractual status of information is discussed in this section under the discussion of Category I conditions. The contractor's duty to consult the information is discussed in the sections covering site investigations and breach of contract claims related to differing site conditions.

In assessing claims for differing site conditions, the most common technique is to determine which category of condition is alleged and then determine whether the prerequisites for that category have been met. Emphasis is initially placed on distinguishing between the categories because each category focuses on different sources of information that the contractor is expected to use. The following discussion analyzes each type of condition separately.

A. Category I Conditions

Paragraph (a)(1) of the Differing Site Conditions clause, FAR 52.236-2, defines a Category I differing site conditions as "subsurface or latent physical conditions at the site which differ materially from those indicated in this contract." In *Weeks Dredging & Contracting, Inc. v. United States*, 13 Cl. Ct. 193 (1987), *aff'd*, 861 F.2d 728 (Fed. Cir. 1988), the court identified six indispensable elements to a successful Category I claim, at 218:

> (i) the contract documents must have affirmatively indicated or represented the subsurface conditions which form the basis of the plaintiff's claim;
>
> (ii) the contractor must have acted as a reasonably prudent contractor in interpreting the contract documents;

(iii) the contractor must have *reasonably* relied on the indications of subsurface conditions in the contract;

(iv) the subsurface conditions actually encountered, within the contract site area, must have differed *materially* from the subsurface conditions indicated in the same contract area;

(v) the actual subsurface conditions encountered must have been reasonably unforeseeable; and

(vi) the contractor's claimed excess costs must be shown to be solely attributable to the materially different subsurface conditions within the contract site.

See also *Stuyvesant Dredging Co. v. United States*, 834 F.2d 1576 (Fed. Cir. 1987).

The "materially different" requirement set forth in *Weeks* has been discussed in Section I. The other five elements are discussed below.

1. Contract Documents

The term "contract documents" has been given an expansive interpretation to include not only the solicitation documents (solicitations, drawings, specifications, and other documents physically furnished to offerors) but also documents and materials referred to in the solicitation documents, *Hunt & Willett, Inc. v. United States*, 168 Ct. Cl. 256, 351 F.2d 980 (1964) (geologic report referenced in a note on a contract drawing was a contract document). See *Randa/Madison Joint Venture III v. Dahlberg*, 239 F.3d 1264 (Fed Cir. 2001), holding that the term "contract indications," *includes* information that explicitly is "made available for inspection by the contract documents." See also *Neal & Co. v. United States*, 36 Fed. Cl. 600 (1996) *aff'd*, 121 F.3d 683 (Fed. Cir. 1997) (geotechnical information available for review); *Hoffman Constr. Co. of Or. v. United States*, 40 Fed. Cl. 184 (1998), *rev'd in part,* 178 F.3d 1313 (Fed. Cir. 1999) (information drawings available for review); *Billington Contracting, Inc.,* ASBCA 54147, 05-1 BCA ¶ 32,900 (referenced documents available in another location 750 miles away); *Felton Constr. Co.*, AGBCA 406-9, 81-1 BCA ¶ 14,932, *recons. denied*, 81-2 BCA ¶ 15,371 (soil survey referenced in plans and specifications); *Ballenger Corp.*, DOTCAB 74-32, 84-1 BCA ¶ 16,973, *modified on other grounds*, 84-2 BCA ¶ 17,277 (information on soil borings and test pits referenced in a note on a drawing); *A.S. McGaughan Co. v. United States*, 24 Cl. Ct. 659 (1991), *aff'd*, 980 F.2d 744 (Fed. Cir. 1992) (indications contained in soil test results referenced in the contract); and *Goss Fire Protection, Inc.*, DOTBCA 2782, 97-1 BCA ¶ 28,853 *recons. denied*, 97-2 BCA 28,991 (pre-bid conference summary). However, documents produced in the performance of the contract do not qualify, *McDevitt Mech. Contractors, Inc. v. United States*, 21 Cl. Ct. 616 (1990) (contractor's shop drawings, approved by the government, not contract indications because the contractor was contractually responsible for verification of the dimensions). Similarly, a contractor cannot rely on oral representations that horizontal pipes will be removed before work begins because the representations are not a contract document. *CM of N.D., Inc.*, VABCA 3986, 95-2 BCA ¶ 27,832.

FAR 52.236-4 contains the following mandatory clause to be used when physical data are to be furnished or made available to bidders:

> PHYSICAL DATA (APR 1984)
>
> Data and information furnished or referred to below is for the Contractor's information. The Government shall not be responsible for any interpretation of or conclusion drawn from the data or information by the Contractor.
>
> (a) The indications of physical conditions on the drawings and in the specifications are the result of site investigations by .... [*insert a description of investigational methods used, such as surveys, auger borings, core borings, test pits, probings, test tunnels*].
>
> (b) Weather conditions .... [*insert a summary of weather records and warnings*].
>
> (c) Transportation facilities .... [*insert a summary of transportation facilities providing access from the site, including information about their availability and limitations*].
>
> (d) .... [*insert other pertinent information*].

This clause is designed to disclaim *conclusions* and *interpretations* drawn by the contractor while making the government responsible for the data. Thus, everything enumerated in the Physical Data clause will be a contract document.

The government has sometimes attempted to avoid making a Category I indication by making information available but specifically excluding information from the contract documents. For example, a report was identified as "not part of the contract" in *Dravo Corp.*, ENGBCA 3901, 80-2 BCA ¶ 14,757. The board held at 72,850 that the contractor had no "contractual right to rely on that report." In *P.J. Maffei Bldg. Wrecking Corp. v. United States*, 732 F.2d 913 (Fed. Cir. 1984), the IFB stated that certain drawings were furnished "for information only and will not be part of the contract documents." Reversing a Claims Court decision holding that such language was ineffective to exclude specifically referenced documents from the contract, the Federal Circuit held that the contractor assumed the risk that the information was inaccurate when it based its bid on data contained in the drawings. The Circuit Court in *Maffei* also based its reversal on exculpatory language included in the contract and further stated in footnote 8 at 918:

> We do not decide that a contractual reference to data found within a document not incorporated in the contract may never constitute an "indication" upon which the contractor may properly rely. We hold that the contractual provision before us cannot be reasonably interpreted in that way.

In *Ashbach Constr. Co*, PSBCA 2718, 91-2 BCA ¶ 23,787, *aff'd*, 960 F.2d 155 (Fed. Cir. 1992), the board distinguished *Maffei* on the grounds that the contract did not contain a statement indicating that drawings made available for the contractor's inspection "were not part of the contract." The board stated, "we cannot say as a matter of law that the drawings were not part of the contract indications." Thus, it charged the offeror with knowledge of conditions specified in the drawings even though the government indicated that they were not guaranteeing the drawings for accuracy.

In view of the instructions in the Physical Data clause, it is arguable that the exclusion of information referenced in the bidding documents is inconsistent with the language of the clause. Thus, if the government wishes to identify data in the solicitation and except it from the contract documents, it would appear that a deviation would be required. In *A.S. McGaughan Co. v. United States*, 24 Cl. Ct. 659 (1991), *aff'd*, 980 F.2d 744 (Fed. Cir. 1992), the court distinguished, at note 8, a case such as *Maffei* which did not contain the Physical Data clause.

2. Indications

In order for a Category I condition to be found, there must be an express statement as to the conditions to be expected or there must be some statement from which the conditions can be fairly implied. Contract indications must be reasonably plain and reliable. If there is no indication of the conditions, there can be no Type 1 differing site condition. A contractor may not prevail if the contract documents do not provide sufficient detail concerning the existing conditions to induce the contractor's reliance. See *VECA Elec. Co.*, ASBCA 47733, 95-2 BCA ¶ 27,749, *recons. denied*, ASBCA 47733, 96-1 BCA ¶ 28,055 (diagrammatic drawings of conduit locations did not contain accurate details sufficient to create a differing site condition when actual locations of conduit differed); *Dailco Corp.*, ASBCA 50191, 00-2 ¶ BCA 31,048 (contract specification listing alternative methods for conducting field density tests did not constitute an implied warranty that subsurface conditions were free of rock); *Vega Roofing Co. v. International Boundary & Water Comm'n*, GSBCA 13576-IBWC, 97-2 BCA ¶ 28,990 (specifications required the removal of all existing roofing down to the wooden sheathing, but gave no indications regarding the number of layers of roofing); *Dennis T. Hardy Elec., Inc.*, ASBCA 47770, 97-1 BCA ¶ 28,840 (denying Type 1 differing site condition claim because the contract made no specific representation about the water-table level to be expected at the site); *Applied Constr. Tech., Inc.*, ASBCA 48365, 95-2 BCA ¶ 27,852 (no representation in the contract as to the conditions encountered); and *C&G Excavating, Inc.*, ENGBCA 6063, 95-1 BCA ¶ 27,289 (sunken vessel did not constitute a Type 1 differing site condition because contract made no indications as to its presence or absence). See also *Hardwick Bros. Co., II v. United States*, 36 Fed. Cl. 347 (1996), *aff'd*, 168 F.3d 1322 (Fed. Cir. 1998) (contract documents made no representation as to water levels because they "speak only as to the specific dates given for these data and do not represent an express or implied representation or guarantee that these water levels would stay the same"), and *Steele & Sons, Inc.*, ASBCA 49077, 00-1 BCA ¶ 30,837 (no Type I differing site condition because the contract made no representation at all with respect to subsurface conditions).

a. Express Indications

Contract indications may be express statements concerning a site condition. Thus, Category I claims existed in *Dunbar & Sullivan Dredging Co.*, ENGBCA 3165, 73-2 BCA ¶ 10,285 (rock encountered although contract documents said "sand and gravel"); *Dawco Constr., Inc. v. United States*, 18 Cl. Ct. 682 (1989), *aff'd in part and rev'd in part on other grounds*, 930 F.2d 872 (Fed. Cir. 1991) (cable, large root masses, rocks, concrete, and piping encountered although contract stated that the subsurface would be free from obstruction except for a lawn-watering system).

Contract indications may also be statements concerning general conditions that would lead a reasonable person to believe that *conditions not mentioned* are not present. See *Rottau Elec. Co.*, ASBCA 20283, 76-2 BCA ¶ 12,001 (contract drawings that failed to disclose concrete structures reasonably indicated to the contractor that no such obstructions existed), and *Shank-Artukovich v. United States*, 13 Cl. Ct. 346 (1987), *aff'd*, 848 F.2d 1245 (Fed. Cir. 1988) (specifications that described the types of ground expected without reference to "running ground" reasonably indicated that "running ground" would not be encountered). But see *Servidone Constr. Corp. v. United States*, 19 Cl. Ct. 346 (1990), *aff'd*, 931 F.2d 860 (Fed. Cir. 1991) (absence of an indication of soil toughness was not an implied assurance that the soil was not tough), and *Shumate Constructors, Inc.*, VABCA 2772, 90-3 BCA ¶ 22,946 (contract drawings indicating "major" piping containing asbestos could not be reasonably thought to indicate all the pipes containing asbestos).

Estimated quantities on bidding schedules can qualify as express contract indications even though qualifications such as "approximate" are included, *Dayton Constr. Co.*, HUDBCA 82-746-C34, 83-2 BCA ¶ 16,809; *Coastal Marine Constr.*, AGBCA 89-190-3, 90-2 BCA ¶ 22,895. In *J.F. Shea Co. v. United States*, 4 Cl. Ct. 46 (1983), *aff'd*, 754 F.2d 338 (Fed. Cir. 1985), the court stated that bidding schedules must be viewed in the light of exculpatory provisions and other indications to determine whether they qualify as Category I indications. The court made the following observations at 51-52:

> Bidding schedules can have legal significance as contract "indications" in the absence of express contract provisions disclaiming their significance. *Lord Brothers Contractors*, [59-1 BCA] ¶ 2069 at 8749; *Guy Atkinson Co.*, IBCA No. 385, 65 1 BCA ¶ 4642 at 22,176, n.16. In the instant case, [the contractor's] reliance on the bidding

> schedule estimates must be viewed against the government's express disclaimer of such estimates in the "Quantities and Prices" (approximate quantities) clause of the contract. This clause informed the bidder that bidding estimates provided in Schedule I were solely for bid comparison purposes. If an approximate quantities clause and its accompanying disclaimer were given full effect, a bidder would be precluded from relying on the bidding schedule estimates as a predicate for assertion of a changed conditions claim. Under such circumstances, estimates in the bidding schedule could not legally be "indications" in the contract documents which would support a claim for a Type I changed condition. *Guy Atkinson Co.*, ¶ 4642 at 22,174. [Footnote omitted.]
>
> However, this result should not automatically be applied to nullify the legal effect of a bidding schedule estimate. *Continental Drilling Co.*, ENGBCA No. 3455, 75-2 BCA ¶ 11,540 at 55,084-85. See *Peter Kiewit Sons' Co. v. United States*, 109 Ct. Cl. 517, 74 F. Supp. 165 (1947) (estimates in bid documents not rendered meaningless by approximate quantities clause). Rather, all specifications, drawings and other requirements of the contract must be examined to determine the nature of the work to be performed. The weight, if any, to be given to the information set forth in the bidding schedule estimate as an "indication" must depend upon the results obtained from the examination of all information provided or available. If such a study of drawings and specifications and available material indicated the actual situation encountered, a bidder could not rely on erroneous bidding schedule estimates as a contract indication supporting recovery for a Type I changed condition. *Otis Williams and Co.*, IBCA No. 324, 1962 BCA ¶ 3487 at 17,805, *Stock & Grove, Inc. v. United States*, 204 Ct. Cl. 103, 493 F.2d 629 (1974); *Perini Corporation*, ENGBCA No. 3745, 78-1 BCA ¶ 13,191 at 64,521-22 (presence or absence of an approximate quantities clause was not argued).

See also *Kent Nowlin Constr., Inc.*, ENGBCA 4681, 87-3 BCA ¶ 20,147, in which the board held that estimated grout ratio quantities contained in the bidding schedule were not contract indications due to exculpatory provisions in the specifications. Compare *Met-Pro Corp.,* ASBCA 49694, 98-2 BCA ¶ 29,776 (excavation and removal of over nine times the amount of contaminated soil estimated in the contract was a compensable Type I differing site condition when the geotechnical report indicated no contaminated soils requiring removal).

b. *Implied Indications*

Contract indications may also be implicit in the contract specifications or project design. In *Foster Constr. C.A. & William Bros. Co. v. United States*, 193 Ct. Cl. 587, 435 F.2d 873 (1970), the court held that indications need not be explicit or specific. As long as a reasonable contractor's reliance on indications of subsurface conditions is justified, the contract indications need not be explicit or specific, *Neal & Co. v. United States*, 36 Fed. Cl. 600, (1996), *aff'd*, 21 F.3d 683 (Fed. Cir. 1997). In *Pitt-Des Moines, Inc.*, ASBCA 42838, 96-1 BCA ¶ 27,941, the board granted the contractor's differing site conditions claim because the conditions encountered differed from those the contractor had inferred from "sketchy" drawings. See also *Amelco Elec.*, VABCA 3785, 96-2 BCA ¶ 28,381, in which the board stated:

> A bidder . . . is entitled to draw reasonable inferences about site conditions from information contained in the specifications or drawings . . . . [A] Type I DSC does not require an explicit representation of the conditions at the work site. The site conditions might just as well be implicitly represented so long as the implied condition are reasonably deduced by the bidder. [Citations omitted.]

The contractor is entitled to use "a simple logical process" in evaluating all of the information in the contract documents to determine the expected subsurface conditions, *Titan Atl. Constr. Corp.*, ASBCA 23588, 82-2 BCA ¶ 15,808. By requiring the material excavated for sewer installation be used for backfilling trenches, the government made implied indications that the excavation would yield a sufficient amount of backfill material, *Betancourt v. Gonzalez, S.E.*, DOTCAB 2785, 96-1 BCA ¶ 28,033.

Cases finding implied indications include *Stock & Grove, Inc. v. United States*, 204 Ct. Cl. 103, 493 F.2d 629 (1974) (designing an embankment requiring certain sizes and types of stone and designating a quarry constituted sufficient indications that the quarry would supply adequate quantities of rock); *J.E. Robertson Co. v. United States*, 194 Ct. Cl. 289, 437 F.2d 1360 (1971) (contract drawings implied that concrete was six to seven inches thick); *Bick-Com Corp.*, VACAB 1320, 80-1 BCA ¶ 14,285 (contract provision prohibiting blasting implied that no blasting would be required); *Mann Constr. Co.*, AGBCA 76-109, 80-2 BCA ¶ 14,674 (designation of specific borrow areas implied that the areas contained sufficient material for job); *S & M-Traylor Bros. (J.V.)*, ENGBCA 3878, 82-1 BCA ¶ 15,484 (specifications requiring the use of heavy equipment implied that silty soil was sufficiently stable to support the weight of the equipment); *GIIS Corp.*, DOTCAB 1534, 85-1 BCA ¶ 17,810 (description of the work implied that holes could be drilled without difficulty, that there would be a minimum of three feet of penetrable material, and that solid limestone would not be encountered); *Kinetic Builders, Inc.*, ASBCA 32627, 88-2 BCA ¶ 20,657 (specifications requiring "clearing" and "grubbing" with rakes implied that no muck would be encountered); *Minter Roofing Co.*, ASBCA 29387, 90-1 BCA ¶ 22,279 (manner in which contract drawings were drawn erroneously implied that the buildings were plumb); *CCM Corp. v. United States*, 20 Cl. Ct. 649 (1990) (contract indications impliedly represented that an asphalt-based waterproofing system would be encountered since the contract plans, specifications, and drawings did not reference the possibility of encountering a tar-based system, the contract contained a list of exclusively asphalt-based products, and the contract referred to "demolition" and not "decontamination"); *Caesar Constr., Inc.*, ASBCA 41059, 91-1 BCA ¶ 23,639, *recons. denied*, 91-2 BCA ¶ 23,953 (where there is an industry practice of identifying French drains in the contract plans, failure to identify drains as French impliedly represents that they are not French); *Cajun Contractors, Inc.*, ASBCA 49044, 98-2 BCA ¶ 30,062 (rock that required a ram hoe to remove was a Type I differing site condition because contract documents, specifically boring logs, indicated that only a hydraulic excavator would be necessary); and *W. R. Henderson Constr., Inc.*, ASBCA 52938, 02-1 BCA ¶ 31741 (Juniper "slash" constituted a Type 1 Differing Site Condition because the contract reasonably indicated the absence of logging debris).

In the following cases, it was held that there was not sufficient information to support the finding of an implied indication: *Sierra-Pac. Builders*, AGBCA 78-161, 80-2 BCA ¶ 14,609 (no "contract indications" where the drawings gave only performance-type information on the layout and location of a trail but contained no specific information on the physical conditions to be expected); *Aguirre Assocs.*, AGBCA 78-129, 80-2 BCA ¶ 14,648 (no indications of subsurface conditions where the drawings contained only a notation of numerous outcroppings); *L.G. Everist, Inc. v. United States*, 231 Ct. Cl. 1013 (1982), *cert. denied*, 461 U.S. 957 (1983) (mere authorization to use a quarry does not necessarily imply that material will be low in waste); *COVCO Haw. Corp.*, ASBCA 26901, 83-2 BCA ¶ 16,554 (denoting excavation as "unclassified" does not imply the existence or absence of any particular type of rock); *Raimonde Drilling Corp.*, ENGBCA 5107, 86-3 BCA ¶ 19,282 (enumeration of equipment in the specification did not reasonably imply that all equipment listed would be adequate under all weather conditions); *Hallmark Elec. Contractors, Inc.*, ASBCA 32595, 87-2 BCA ¶ 19,870, *recons. denied* 87-3 BCA ¶ 20,000 (absence of a "rock table" did not indicate that rock would not be encountered); *Gerald Miller Constr. Co.*, IBCA 2292, 91-2 BCA ¶ 23,829 (design estimate that rough and finish cut and fill would balance on the site did not mean that no off-site borrow would be required); *Jack L. Olsen, Inc*, AGBCA 87-345-1, 93-2 BCA ¶ 25,767, *rev'd in part,* 26 F.3d 141 (Fed. Cir. 1994) (government's designation of borrow sources did not imply that the sources were of reasonable quality); *James W. Collins Assocs., Inc.*, LBCA 92-BCA-8, 98-2 BCA ¶ 30,010 (statement that reasonable amount of electrical power would be available not an indication of specific voltage and amperage capacity available to contractor); *Dennis T. Hardy Elec., Inc.*, ASBCA 47770, 97-1 BCA ¶ 28,840 (no specific representations of water level at the site); *Vega Roofing Co. v. International Boundary & Water Comm.*, GSBCA 13576-IBWC, 97-2 BCA ¶ 28,990 (neither contract specifications nor contract drawings represented the number of layers of shingles to be removed.); *D.W. Sandau Dredging*, ENGBCA 5812, 96-1 BCA ¶ 28,064, *recons. denied*, 96-2 BCA ¶ 28,300 (contract's silence on trash and debris was not a "negative indication" that there was no trash or debris); and *Fire Sec. Sys., Inc. v. General Servs. Admin.*, GSBCA 12120, 97-2 BCA ¶ 28,994 (contract said nothing directly or indirectly concerning the condition of the ceiling tiles).

3. *Reasonably Unforeseeable*

The requirement that Category I conditions must be subsurface or latent is met when the contractor demonstrates that the conditions were reasonably unforeseeable. This does not necessarily mean that they must be hidden from view. Conditions that are not discoverable by a reasonable investigation of the contract documents and the site are considered reasonably unforeseeable. See *Dayton Constr. Co.*, HUDBCA

82-746-C34, 83-2 BCA ¶ 16,809, where the contractor was permitted to recover the costs of removing a greater quantity of asphalt than the approximate amount specified in the contract. The board held that it was not reasonable to expect the contractor to remeasure the asphalt under the circumstances. See also *JUD Constr. Co.*, ASBCA 36896, 90-3 BCA ¶ 22,954, *aff'd* 996 F.2d 1235 (Fed. Cir. 1993) (contractor not responsible for taking elevation measurements when it would have required clearing a heavily wooded site and performing a survey on it); *Gulf Constr. Group, Inc.*, ENGBCA 5850, 93-1 BCA ¶ 25,229 (underwater cleaning and visual inspection of hinge castings and bolts was not reasonably expected of a prospective contractor); and *Sergent Mech. Sys., Inc. v. United. States*, 34 Fed. Cl. 505 (1995) (contractor could not anticipate government's erroneous direction to protect vegetation that was not subject to environmental regulations). Compare *Randa/Madison Joint Venture III v. Dahlberg*, 239 F.3d 1264 (Fed. Cir. 2001), holding that the contractor was responsible for reviewing all of the information in the RFP, not just the boring logs. See also *Ruston Paving Co.*, VABCA 1950, 85-1 BCA ¶ 17,908 (no subsurface or latent condition where the contractor was contractually obligated to verify dimensions and quantities and the project was "simple and straightforward"); *RJS Constructors, Inc.*, ENGBCA 5975, 93-3 BCA ¶ 26,038 (no subsurface or latent condition where existing conditions were visible); *Cannon Structures, Inc.*, AGBCA 90-207-1, 93-3 BCA ¶ 26,059 (ground conditions and vegetation cannot be considered subsurface or latent); *Ivey's Constr., Inc.*, ASBCA 47855, 95-1 BCA ¶ 27,584 (large trees to be cleared were visible with a simple observation of the site); and *American Constr. & Energy, Inc.*, ASBCA 52031, 01-1 BCA ¶ 31,202 (although plumbing drawings might have misled the contractor, a site visit would have revealed the actual positioning of hot and cold water pipes).

In *Mojave Enters. v. United States*, 3 Cl. Ct. 353 (1983), the court stated a slightly different formulation of the requirement that the condition be subsurface or latent. The court held that a Category I condition must be "reasonably unforeseeable on the basis of all the information available to the contractor at the time of bidding." In *Stuyvesant Dredging Co. v. United States*, 834 F.2d 1576 (Fed. Cir. 1987), the court affirmed the Claims Court rationale that the court must view itself as a reasonable and prudent contractor and decide whether the site condition was reasonably unforeseeable at the time of the bidding in light of all then-available knowledge.

4. Reasonable Interpretation

The contractor must show that it reasonably interpreted the contract indications. A contractor cannot recover under a Category I claim if it misconstrues or misunderstands contract data. See *Meredith Constr. Co.*, DOTCAB 1548, 85-1 BCA ¶ 17,895, rejecting the contractor's argument that a contract drawing was intended to show the exact size and location of an oil tank where oil tanks come in a variety of configurations. See also *Spruce Constr., Inc.*, ASBCA 30679, 86-3 BCA ¶ 19,106 (contractor's argument that soft soil was indicated by a clause concerning the tendency of the deadman to sink was "contrived"), and *White & McNeil Excavating, Inc.*, IBCA 2448, 92-1 BCA ¶ 24,534 *aff'd* 996 F.2d 1235 (Fed. Cir. 1993) (contractor's interpretation that the waste yield would be "about" 50 percent was unreasonable where clause stated that the waste yield was "at least 50 percent "). A contractor's experience will be factored into the reasonableness of its interpretation of the contract documents. In *Shumate Constructors, Inc.*, VABCA 2772, 90-3 BCA ¶ 22,946, a contractor experienced in asbestos abatement unreasonably interpreted drawings as a positive representation that asbestos-containing-material piping would not be encountered. However, a contractor's inexperience is no excuse for misinterpreting the contract indications. See *Servidone Constr. Corp. v. United States*, 19 Cl. Ct. 346 (1990), *aff'd*, 931 F.2d 860 (Fed. Cir. 1991), where the contractor unreasonably interpreted the Liquid Limit Correlation Curve without understanding how it was generated or what it represented.

To arrive at a reasonable interpretation a contractor must consider all relevant documents in the solicitation. Thus, a contractor will be found to have interpreted the contract unreasonably where it can be shown that its interpretation is unsupported by the contract indications or that it is based on one contract indication to the exclusion of others. See *Guy F. Atkinson Co.*, ENGBCA 4693, 87-3 BCA ¶ 19,971 (contract references to sand did not infer that rock would not be encountered where there was no all-encompassing nomenclature for the classification of materials and there existed other objective descriptions of rock-like materials in the substrate); *Granite-Groves v. Washington Metro. Area Transit Auth.*, 845 F.2d 330 (D.C. Cir. 1988) (contract did not represent favorable mining conditions where "plain indications of the unfavorable mining conditions" existed in the pre-bid soil reports, boring logs, and profiles); *M.A. Mortenson Co.*, ASBCA 31903, 90-1 BCA ¶ 22,313 (contractor's estimation of the amount of hard rock to be removed by core boring unsupported by any reasonable interpretation of the contract); *Al Johnson Constr. Co. v. United States*, 20 Cl. Ct. 184 (1990) (contractor's dewatering design based on an unreasonable interpretation of the contract documents); *Great Lakes Dredge & Dock Co.*, ENGBCA 5606, 91-1 BCA ¶ 23,613 (presence of "hard" material did not constitute a differing site condition where the contractor "choose to ignore" contract indications that the material to be dredged was not just silt); *Wayne Constr.*, ENGBCA 4942, 91-1 BCA ¶ 23,535 (absence of the words "glacial till" in the contract documents did not reasonably imply that digging would not be difficult where there were objective and ascertainable indicia of difficult digging in the contract documents); *Fire Sec. Sys., Inc.*, VABCA 3086, 91-2 BCA ¶ 23,743 (contractor's interpretation of two sentences of the contract to mean that only outer doors of the building would be locked was unreasonable when a reading of the whole contract clearly implied that the building had extraordinary security throughout); *Gerald Miller Constr. Co.*, IBCA 2292, 91-2 BCA ¶ 23,829 (contractor's interpretation based on estimated quantities of total excavation contained in the solicitation was unreasonable because the contractor failed to consider other contract indications such as balance point and borrow information); and *Ilbau Constr., Inc.*, ENGBCA 5465, 92-1 BCA ¶ 24,476 (one paragraph of the geotechnical report did not indicate that conjugate joints would rarely be encountered, where numerous other indications of conjugate joints were contained in the contract documents).

Since contract borings are, of necessity, taken only at relatively few locations on most sites, the contractor must make a reasonable extrapolation of the conditions at the entire site. In *Weeks Dredging & Contracting, Inc. v. United States*, 13 Cl. Ct. 193 (1987), *aff'd*, 861 F.2d 728 (Fed. Cir. 1988), the court held that the contractor made an unreasonable assumption when it concluded that the quantity of each category of subsurface materials across the entire project site was precisely the same as indicated in the boring logs. See also *Erickson-Shaver Contracting Corp. v. United States*, 9 Cl. Ct. 302 (1985), in which the court held that a reasonable extrapolation from the auger hole data would have shown the condition that the contractor encountered on the site. This use of the boring logs has been accepted even when a disclaimer in the contract states that the logs represent conditions only at the exact location of the borings, *Luke Constr. Co.,* ASBCA 24889, 81-1 BCA ¶ 15,023.

A contractor cannot be said to have reasonably interpreted the contract documents if an examination of them would reveal patent ambiguities. *Hoffman Constr. Co. of Oregon v. United States*, 40 Fed. Cl. 184 (1998) *rev'd on other grounds,* 178 F.3d 1313 (Fed. Cir. 1999) (denying a subcontractor's differing site conditions claims because the contractor failed to inquire about a patent ambiguity in the bidding documents). See *Insul-Glass, Inc.*, ASBCA 33577, 89-3 BCA ¶ 22,033, concluding that the omission of window depth measurements in the contract plans was an obvious ambiguity and that the contractor could not reasonably interpret the omission to mean that there was only one window depth. Where ambiguities arise, the contractor has a duty to inquire, *Beacon Constr. Co. of Mass. v. United States*, 161 Ct. Cl. 1, 314 F.2d 501 (1963); *Wayne Insulation Co.,* VABCA 2024, 86-2 BCA ¶ 18,890. See also *State Mech. Corp.*, VABCA 2797, 91-2 BCA ¶ 23,830, rejecting the contractor's claim where its interpretation of contract instructions created a patent ambiguity that it did not raise at the pre-bid inquiry. In *Williams Supply Co.,* DOTBCA 2852, 96-2 BCA ¶ 28,269, "*PCB transformers*" in the specifications was an industry-related term and was defined by EPA regulations to mean a PCB concentration of greater than 500 m. Thus, it was unreasonable for the contractor to expect to encounter only PCB concentrations of lower than 500 m. But see *Stanger Indus. Inc.*, VABCA 2679, 90-1 BCA ¶ 22,300 (contractor not obligated to seek clarification because there was no obvious discrepancy in the contract provisions; contractor was not obligated to seek clarification), and *Lamb Eng'g & Constr. Co.*, EBCA C-9304172, 97-2 BCA ¶ 29,207 (contractor's interpretation of the solicitation logs was reasonable because the borehole logs were latently ambiguous and the contractor was not required to seek clarification).

Contract documents often offer conflicting information about the subsurface conditions. Although a patent ambiguity should be resolved during the bidding process, several decisions express a preference for the specific over the general in determining conflicting indications of subsurface materials. Boring logs taken at the site contain more specific information, for example, than a geotechnical report based on literature available for the region. To the extent there is an inconsistency, the boring logs should prevail. In *Gulf Coast Trailing Co.*, ENGBCA 6050, 96-1 BCA ¶ 28,217, the board explained the importance of boring logs to a Type 1 claim at 140,874:

> The contract borings are the most significant indication of the type of subsurface material a contractor can expect to encounter. A differing site condition occurs if the actual conditions encountered vary materially from the subsurface conditions for an area as indicated in the contract borings. [Citations omitted.]
>
> In this regard, in bidding for work, contractors are entitled to rely on the contract borings because they reasonably convey the specific, expected subsurface conditions at the site. [Citations omitted.] Thus, a differing site condition occurs if the borings reasonably represent small rocks (cobbles, rock fragments, gravel), but the contractor encounters boulders and large size pieces of rock.

Similarly, descriptions of materials at the elevations where work is to be done may prevail over descriptions of materials at other elevations, *Murray Walters, Inc.*, VABCA 1848, 87-2 BCA ¶ 19,947 (contractor need not anticipate limestone where boring logs indicate its presence only at elevations deeper than working area); *T. Brown Constructors, Inc. v. Peña*, 132 F.3d 724 (Fed. Cir. 1997) (the more specific test data trump the general test results).

5. Reliance

Not only must the contractor show that it examined the contract documents and reasonably interpreted them, but it must also show that it relied on its interpretation when calculating its bid, *Weeks Dredging & Contracting, Inc. v. United States*, 13 Cl. Ct. 193 (1987), *aff'd*, 861 F.2d 728 (Fed. Cir. 1988). The contract indications underlying a Category I differing site condition must be such as to induce "reasonable reliance by the successful bidder that subsurface conditions would be more favorable than those encountered," *Pacific Alaska Contractors, Inc. v. United States*, 193 Ct. Cl. 850, 436 F.2d 461 (1971); *PK Contractors, Inc.*, ENGBCA 4901, 92-1 BCA ¶ 24,583; *Framlau Corp.*, ASBCA 14205, 71-2 BCA ¶ 8989. The nature of the information and the government's description of the information will determine whether the contractor's reliance on the information is reasonable. See *Stuyvesant Dredging Co. v. United States*, 834 F.2d 1576 (Fed. Cir. 1987) (improper to rely on information identified as guide); *Peter Kiewit Sons' Co.*, ENGBCA 4861, 85-2 BCA ¶ 18,082 (unreasonable to rely on drawings without verifying them as specified in solicitation); and *John Massman Contracting Co. v. United States*, 23 Cl. Ct. 24 (1991) (not reasonable to rely on historical data that were identified as merely a guide).

The government's approval of the contractor's work plans can serve as a basis for the contractor's reasonable reliance on the indicated conditions. In *Triad Mech.,*

Inc., IBCA 3393, 97-1 BCA ¶ 28,771, the government had approved the contractor's stream diversion and foundation water removal plan. This was an indication of the amount of water the contractor could reasonably expect because the government found the plan would be sufficient to effectively dewater the site.

Although contractors are charged with knowledge of all unread contract documents, the converse is not true; that is, contractors cannot constructively rely on those documents without reviewing them. In *Comtrol, Inc. v. United States,* 294 F.3d 1357 (Fed. Cir. 2002), the court held that a contractor that had encountered soft sand in an area depicted by the contract documents as "hard material" could not demonstrate reliance because it admitted that it did not read the soils report before submitting its bid.

a. *No Reasonable Reliance*

Reasonable reliance will not be found where the contractor bid without having reviewed or considered all of the contract indications, *V&W Constr. & Serv. Co.,* ASBCA 50812, 98-1 BCA ¶ 29,465 (contractor testified that it did not rely on information from the boring logs and the monitoring wells and considered them insufficient to determine water levels); *L.B. Samford, Inc.*, DOTCAB 1457, 85-2 BCA ¶ 18,081 (no evidence that the contractor relied on the contract borings where the project manager testified, "[W]e had been working down there 10 years and we know exactly how hard that rock is"); *P & M Cedar Prods., Inc.*, AGBCA 89-167-1, 90-1 BCA ¶ 22,444 (contractor deliberately discounted provided data concerning traffic accommodation and control); *Wayne Constr.*, ENGBCA 4942, 91-1 BCA ¶ 23,535 (contractor did not reasonably rely on the contract indications where it failed to consider information available in sieve analyses and certain exploration logs); *Gerald Miller Constr. Co.*, IBCA 2292, 91-2 BCA ¶ 23,829 (no reasonable reliance where contractor bid "without paying a heck of a lot of attention" to the balance points on the plans); *White & McNeil Excavating, Inc.*, IBCA 2448, 92-1 BCA ¶ 24,534 (no reasonable reliance where contractor relied on language indicating waste yield only "[t]o a certain extent" and did not review drill core logs); *Donald R. Stewart & Assocs.*, AGBCA 84-226-1, 92-1 BCA ¶ 24,705 (no reasonable reliance where the contractor bid without reviewing the geologist's report); *Youngdale & Sons Constr. Co. v. United States*, 27 Fed. Cl. 516 (1993) (unreasonable and negligent to rely without reviewing boring logs that indicated the presence of subsurface rock); *One Way Constr., Inc.*, AGBCA 93-193-1, 94-3 BCA ¶ 27,275 (contractor ignored 12 borings that indicated conditions very similar to those actually encountered; reliance on 3 borings was improper). In *GIIS Corp.*, DOTCAB 1534, 85-1 BCA ¶ 17,810, the court found that a single boring situated approximately 1.35 miles from the site was not indicative of site conditions and that the contractor could not reasonably rely on it as such. The board articulated an analysis for determining the significance of test borings, stating at 89,001:

> Important factors in determining the reasonableness of a contractor's reliance on test borings include the proximity of the borings to excavation areas, terrain factors and general subsurface conditions in the vicinity of the site. [Citations omitted.]

The contractor will recover only upon a showing that it used the erroneous information when calculating its bid, *Dravo Corp.*, ENGBCA 3901, 80-2 BCA ¶ 14,757; *PK Contractors, Inc.*, ENGBCA 4901, 92-1 BCA ¶ 24,583. Thus, the contractor must produce sufficient evidence regarding its bidding assumptions, *Perini Corp.*, ENGBCA 4735, 86-1 BCA ¶ 18,524. In *Weeks Dredging & Contracting, Inc. v. United States*, 13 Cl. Ct. 193, *aff'd*, 861 F.2d 728 (Fed. Cir. 1988), the court found that the contractor did not reasonably rely on its interpretation at the time of bidding as it failed to recognize significant risks behind its assumptions and failed to calculate those risks into its bid. See also *Gulf Constr. Group, Inc.*, ENGBCA 5850, 93-1 BCA ¶ 25,229 (no proof that the contractor interpreted bolts in the contract drawings as monolithic before bidding); *Peter Kiewit Sons' Co.*, ENGBCA 4861, 85-2 BCA ¶ 18,082 (no reasonable reliance where there was no evidence that either the contractor or the subcontractor submitted their bids based on the contract drawing at issue); and *Mann Constr. Co.*, EBCA 361-6-86, 89-3 BCA ¶ 22,176 (refusing to find reasonable reliance where the contractor conducted an extensive site investigation but used its own data instead of government-supplied data in calculating its bid).

A contractor cannot be said to have reasonably relied on the contract indications if it has knowledge based on prior experience that the conditions are other than indicated. In *Wm. A. Smith Contracting Co. v. United States*, 188 Ct. Cl. 1062, 412 F.2d 1325 (1969), the court found that a contractor with previous experience in Alaska should have expected to encounter permafrost at locations other than those shown in the contract plans. In *John Massman Contracting Co. v. United States*, 23 Cl. Ct. 24 (1991), the court found that a contractor experienced in scour protection work unreasonably relied on approximate river flow averages when it "should have been aware that river flow is related directly to weather conditions." See also *Spirit Leveling Contractors v. United States*, 19 Cl. Ct. 84 (1989) (contractor could not recover where it knew of flooding conditions at the site regardless of what was or was not indicated in the contract), and *W.E. O'Neil Constr. Co. of Ariz.*, ASBCA 49040, 96-2 BCA ¶ 28,563 (although plans and specifications indicated the existence of a well, the contractor could not recover because it had actual knowledge that a well did not exist). Compare *Lamb Eng'g & Constr. Co.*, EBCA C-9304172, 97-2 BCA ¶ 29,207, holding that failing to obtain public documents concerning the geology of the site not referenced in the solicitation is not ordinarily required under the clause.

Reasonable reliance will not be found if the contractor's knowledge results from its own investigation, *American Int'l Contractors, Inc./Capitol Indus. Constr. Groups, Inc., A Joint Venture*, ASBCA 39544, 95-2 BCA ¶ 27,920 (test results of the contractor's own samples showed that material was not acceptable for backfill and fill). But see *Fred Benvenuti, Inc.*, DOTCAB 74-25, 75-2 BCA ¶ 11,482 (contractor not responsible for knowledge of conditions at site where it had done work 40 years earlier); *Corner Constr. Co.*, ASBCA 20156, 75-1 BCA ¶ 11,326 (contractor who built buildings on prior contract was not charged with knowledge of the actual location of conduits); and *Holloway Constr. Co. & Holloway Sand & Gravel Co.,* ENGBCA 4805, 89-2 BCA ¶ 21,713 (contractor's prior experience in the general area does not override clear contractual indications of contrary conditions).

b. Reasonable Reliance

Generally, a contractor has reasonably relied when it has used the erroneous contract indications in calculating its bid following an adequate site investigation that did not reveal any defect in the indications, *Reliance Enters.*, ASBCA 27638, 85-2 BCA ¶ 18,045, *recons. denied*, 85-3 BCA ¶ 18,357; *State Mech. Corp.*, VABCA 2797, 91-2 BCA ¶ 23,830; *Cherry Hill Constr., Inc. v. General Servs. Admin.*, GSBCA 11217, 92-3 BCA ¶ 25,179; *Praught Constr. Corp.*, ASBCA 39670, 92-3 BCA ¶ 25,896, *recons. denied*, 93-3 BCA ¶ 26,084; *Skyline Painting, Inc.*, ENGBCA 5810, 93-3 BCA ¶ 26,041; *Moon Constr. Co. v. General Servs. Admin.*, GSBCA 11766, 93-3 BCA ¶ 26,017. See also *T. Brown Constructors, Inc. v. Pena*, 132 F.3d 724 (Fed. Cir. 1997) (contractor's reliance on government-supplied results of a "washed sieve analysis" was reasonable when the government failed to include the note to the bidders, from the testing division, specifically alerting the bidders to the problem with the results); *Triad Mech., Inc.*, IBCA 3393, 97-1 BCA ¶ 28,771 (contractor's reliance on hydrograph included in contract documents was reasonable because "the government would not have placed the hydrograph into the contract documents if it had not believed it to be representative of the water conditions").

6. Costs Attributable to Condition

The contractor's claimed excess costs must be shown to be solely attributable to the differing subsurface conditions. Concurrent causes of excess cost, such as costs resulting from the contractor's own mistakes, must be carefully distinguished by the court, *Weeks Dredging & Contracting, Inc. v. United States,* 13 Cl. Ct. 193, aff'd, 861 F.2d 728 (Fed. Cir. 1988). See *All-State Constr., Inc.*, ASBCA 50513, 04-2 BCA ¶ 32,711 (contractor improperly stopped work because the debris did not obstruct operations). The contractor must establish this element of its claim via one of several methods, which are addressed in detail in Chapter 8. See *Hartford Cas. Ins. Co.,* VABCA 5262, 99-1 BCA ¶ 30,106 (cost incurred to mitigate damage was reasonable), and *SAE/Americon-Mid Atl., Inc. v. General Servs. Admin.,* GSBCA 12294, 98-2 BCA ¶ 30,084 (unexpected rock conditions reduced productivity from four or five caissons per day to one or two caissons per day).

B. Category II Conditions

The Differing Site Conditions clause describes Category II conditions as conditions "of an unusual nature, which differ materially from those ordinarily encountered and generally recognized as inhering in the work of the character provided for in the contract." In *Lathan Co. v. United States*, 20 Cl. Ct. 122 (1990), the court stated the requirements of this type of differing site condition claim at 128:

> A Type II claim requires [the contractor] to show three elements. First, [the contractor] must show that it did not know about the physical condition. Second, [the contractor] must show that it could not have anticipated the condition from inspection or general experience. Third, [the contractor] must show that the condition varied from the norm in similar contracting work. [Citations omitted.]

This requires that the contractor demonstrate that the condition was *unknown*, *unforeseeable*, and *unusual*. See *Kos Kam, Inc.*, ASBCA 34037, 88-3 BCA ¶ 21,100, in which the board required the contractor to prove that the condition was both unknown and unusual—denying recovery under Category II where the configuration of toilet waste lines was unknown but not unusual. Compare *Youngdale & Sons Constr. Co. v. United States*, 27 Fed. Cl. 516 (1993), in which the court stated that the contractor could recover if it could prove that the condition was *either* unknown or unusual. See also *S.T.G. Constr. Co. v. United States*, 157 Ct. Cl. 409 (1962), and *Perini Corp. v. United States*, 180 Ct. Cl. 768, 381 F.2d 403 (1967). However, reasonable anticipation of conditions does not require the contractor to "anticipate the worst," *Redman Serv., Inc.*, ASBCA 8853, 1963 BCA ¶ 3897; *Kinetic Builders, Inc.*, ASBCA 32627, 88-2 BCA ¶ 20,657. This section addresses the unknown, unforeseeable, and unusual status of conditions. The materially different requirement is not addressed here because it is the same as discussed above.

1. Unknown Condition

An unknown condition is one that could not have been reasonably anticipated from the contractor's study of the contract documents, its inspection of the site, and its general experience, *Youngdale & Sons Constr. Co. v. United States*, 27 Fed. Cl. 516 (1993); *Potomac Co.*, ASBCA 25371, 81-1 BCA ¶ 14,950. A condition cannot be "unknown" if it was described in the contract documents. If information regarding the condition is contained in the contract documents, failure to review them will preclude recovery. In *Youngdale*, the court refused to find that shale was an unknown condition because boring logs that indicated the presence of shale were made available to the contractor. See also *B&M Roofing & Painting Co.*, ASBCA 26998, 86-2 BCA ¶ 18,833, *recons. denied*, 86-3 BCA ¶ 19,306 (several layers of shingle were described in the contract drawings and the contractor was warned of their existence); *Titan Pac. Constr. Corp.*, ASBCA 24148, 87-1 BCA ¶ 19,626 (contractor had full knowledge of the condition of the soils at the site from the contract data); *Fire Sec. Sys., Inc.*, VABCA 3086, 91-2 BCA ¶ 23,743 (contractor was informed that it would encounter locked interior doors); and *George Ledford Constr., Inc.*, ENGBCA 6268, 98-2 BCA ¶ 30,016 (soft, wet sub-base material beneath the road in an otherwise rocky area constituted a differing site condition because neither party was aware of the existence of a leaky water valve causing the wet soil). A contractor who becomes or should become aware of conditions during the negotiation of contract price and terms will be precluded from recovery, *Gulf Constr. Group, Inc.*, ENG-BCA 5850, 93-1 BCA ¶ 25,229. Similarly, recovery will be denied if the contractor was aware of the actual volume of necessary excavation at the time of bidding, *J & D Servs. of Northern Minn., Inc.*, AGBCA 98-126-1, 99-2 ¶ BCA 30,478.

Whether a condition is unknown will also depend on the contractor's general knowledge and experience. For example, the presence of permafrost was not considered an unknown condition where a contractor had work experience in Alaska, *Fairbanks Builders, Inc.*, ASBCA 18288, 74-2 BCA ¶ 10,971. See also *Engineering Tech. Consultants, S.A.*, ASBCA 44912, 93-1 BCA ¶ 25,556, *recons. denied*, 93-2 BCA ¶ 25,732, finding that the flammability of a painted school deck was not an unknown condition because "[m]ost painted surfaces are flammable when intense heat is applied to them." In *Spirit Leveling Contractors*, 19 Cl. Ct. 84 (1989), the court found that the contractor had knowledge of excessive rainfall and flooding because it was forewarned of these conditions and had previous crisis experience. See also *N.L. Larsen & Son, Inc.*, AGBCA 85-201-3, 85-3 BCA ¶ 18,256 (condition not unknown where the contractor had encountered rock before); *M.A. Mortenson Co.*, ASBCA 31903, 90-1 BCA ¶ 22,313 (condition not unknown because the contractor had drilled in the area prior to the contract); *Wilson Constr., Inc.*, AGBCA 89-178-1, 92-2 BCA ¶ 24,798 (contractor's president was experienced, had lived in the area for many years, and should have anticipated that alders were dense and gnarled); *Cannon Structures, Inc.*, AGBCA 90-207-1, 93-3 BCA ¶ 26,059 (no evidence that seeps were not discoverable on the basis of the contractor's site visit or its general knowledge); and *Neal & Co. v. United States,* 36 Fed. C1. 600 (1996), *aff'd*, 121 F.3d 1683 (Fed. Cir. 1997) (contractor had experience working in area).

2. Unforeseeable Condition

A condition will not be considered unforeseeable if it was discoverable by a reasonable site investigation. See *Huntington Constr., Inc.*, ASBCA 33526, 89-3 BCA ¶ 22,150, *recons. denied*, 90-2 BCA ¶ 22,727. In *Betteroads Asphalt Corp.*, ASBCA 32417, 88-1 BCA ¶ 20,366, the board found that a contractor knew or should have known of the possibility of culverts being blocked by earth and debris where the drainage system was visible to the contractor during the site investigation. See also *C&L Constr. Co.,* ASBCA 22993, 81-1 BCA ¶ 14,943, *recons. denied*, 81-2 BCA ¶ 15,373 (boring samples should have alerted the contractor to loosely packed soil); *Sealtite Corp.*, ASBCA 26209, 83-2 BCA ¶ 16,792, *aff'd*, 739 F.2d 630 (Fed. Cir. 1984) (spalling and erosion of gypsum roof planks would have been ascertained by an adequate site investigation); *D.J. Barclay & Co.,* ASBCA 28908, 88-2 BCA ¶ 20,741 (deterioration of coatings not unforeseeable where the contractor did not perform a simple adhesion test common in the industry during its site investigation); *Fire Sec. Sys., Inc.*, VABCA 3086, 91-2 BCA ¶ 23,743 (simple site viewing would have revealed obstructions in attics); *Avisco, Inc.*, ENGBCA 5802, 93-3 BCA ¶ 26,172 (extent of vegetation growth was clearly observable); *D.W. Sandau*

Dredging, ENGBCA 5812, 96-1 BCA ¶ 28,064, *recons. denied*, 96-2 BCA ¶ 28,300 (contractor had failed to draw logical conclusions from pre-bid site visits as to the nature of trash and debris that ordinarily would be generated and encountered in an urban and commercial shipping area); *G&P Constr. Co.*, ASBCA 49524, 98-1 BCA ¶ 29,457 (reasonable site investigation would have revealed the condition actually encountered); *Lawrence M. Metzger*, ENGBCA 6426, 00-1 BCA 30,689 (contractor declined to conduct a pre-bid inspection, stating that it was intimately acquainted with the leased area from prior work there); *Moore Overseas Constr. Co.*, ENGBCA PCC-125, 98-1 BCA ¶ 29,682 (surface water flow from an underground source was a discoverable, physical condition that existed at the time bids were submitted); *Vega Roofing Co. v. Int'l Boundary & Water Comm'n*, GSBCA 13576-IBWC, 97-2 BCA ¶ 28,990 (the two layers of shingles could have easily been detected during the site inspection); *Lamb Eng' g & Constr. Co.*, EBCA C-9304172, 97-2 BCA ¶ 29,207 *recons. denied,* 98-1 BCA ¶ 29,369 (the probability of problematic soil was obvious under the circumstances of the known local rainfall and the soil materials, and a site investigation would have revealed the conditions); *American Constr. & Energy, Inc.*, ASBCA 52031, 01-1 BCA ¶ 31,202 (condition was visible on a site visit); *Orlosky, Inc. v. United States*, 64 Fed. Cl. 63 (2005) (contractor did not attend site visit so differing site condition claim denied, but defective specifications claim could be considered); and *Conner Bros. Constr. Co. v. United States,* 65 Fed. Cl. 657 (2005) (pre-bid inspection was deficient).

In some cases even an adequate site investigation will not discover the problem. See *R.A. Glancy & Sons, Inc.*, VABCA 2327, 87-3 BCA ¶ 20,068, in which the board found that a Category II condition existed because a reasonable site inspection of a flat, grassy area with a ball park would not reveal that buildings had previously been on the site and that debris was buried under it. See also *Yamas Constr. Co.*, ASBCA 27366, 86-3 BCA ¶ 19,090 (contractor could not have discovered that the concrete floor under the carpet was excessively uneven and laden with excess glue), and *Donald R. Stewart & Assocs.*, AGBCA 84-226-1, 92-1 BCA ¶ 24,705 (even if contractor had read the geological report, it would not have been alerted to the presence of sandstone).

A contractor cannot rely on the fact that it is a small, disadvantaged business in defending the reasonableness of its pre-bid analysis. See *H.B. Mac, Inc. v. United States*, 153 F.3d 1338 (Fed. Cir. 1998), rejecting the contractor's claim when groundwater at the site forced the installation of a sheet piling system, and holding the contractor to the same standard as any other contractor.

In determining whether a condition is unforeseeable, the contractor must make reasonable inquiries. Conditions discoverable by *reasonable inquiries* to local inhabitants are not considered unforeseeable under the clause, *Daymar, Inc.*, DOTBCA 77-13, 78-1 BCA ¶ 12,903. See *Servidone Constr. Corp. v. United States*, 19 Cl. Ct. 346, *aff'd*, 931 F.2d 860 (Fed. Cir. 1991), in which the court chastised the contractor for failing to inquire into local conditions where minimal inquiry would have put it on notice of difficult soil. See also *Steele & Sons, Inc.*, ASBCA 49077, 00-1 BCA ¶ 30,837 (common knowledge among "old timers" in the geographic area that certain roads had a concrete subsurface); *CCI Contractors, Inc.*, AGBCA 84-314-1, 91-3 BCA ¶ 24,225, *aff'd*, 979 F.2d 216 (Fed. Cir. 1992) (knowledgeable, experienced contractors in the area knew of the condition); and *Hardwick Bros. Co., II v. United States,* 36 Fed. Cl. 347 (1996), *aff'd*, 168 F.3d 1322 (Fed. Cir. 1998) (local residents knew of site conditions).

In assessing whether a condition was foreseeable, the contractor will be held to the standard of a reasonable contractor in its field, *Consolidated Constr. Inc.*, ASBCA 46498, 99-1 BCA ¶ 30,148 *aff'd* 230 F.3d 1378 (Fed. Cir. 2000) (no differing site condition because a reasonably prudent contractor would expect to find that the soil would be difficult to work and sensitive to moisture). Thus, a contractor doing "new work" dredging in a military port area should anticipate possibly dangerous debris, *Stuyvesant Dredging Co.*, ENGBCA 5558, 89-3 BCA ¶ 22,222.

A condition is not foreseeable merely because an expert would have foreseen it. See *Blake Constr. Co.,* ASBCA 20,747, 83-1 BCA ¶ 16,410, holding that the fact that an expert geologist could have predicted site conditions through available geological literature did not make the condition foreseeable to the contractor.

3. Unusual Condition

To be unusual, a condition need not be a geological freak, *Western Well Drilling Co. v. United States*, 96 F. Supp. 377 (D. Cal. 1951); *Conrad Weihnacht Constr. Inc.*, ASBCA 19666, 75-1 BCA ¶ 11,069, but it must differ from what is expected in that geographic area. See *Hardwick Bros. Co., II v. United States*, 36 Fed. Cl. 347 (1996), *aff'd*, 168 F.3d 1322 (Fed. Cir. 1998) (conditions in flood plain not unusual when contractor encountered excessive groundwater); *HK Sys., Inc.*, PSBCA 3712, 97-2 BCA ¶ 29,079 (subsurface conditions at site not unusual for construction in the project's hilly area); *Imbus Roofing Co.*, GSBCA 10430, 91-2 BCA ¶ 23,820 (contractor did not show that the adhesion of an existing vapor barrier was different from what was usual in the Cincinnati area or other areas where similar jobs were performed); *Kora & Williams Corp. v. General Servs. Admin.*, GSBCA 9270, 92-2 BCA ¶ 24,785 (presence of storm sewers not unusual given the highly urbanized character of the site); *Oconto Elec., Inc.*, ASBCA 40421, 93-3 BCA ¶ 26,162 (no evidence that soil encountered was unusual for the general area); *J.A. Laporte, Inc.*, ENGBCA 5252, 88-3 BCA ¶ 20,953 (bed of conch shells was not unusual for "new work" in the coastal areas of Georgia); and *Quality Servs. of N.C., Inc.*, ASBCA 34851, 89-2 BCA ¶ 21,836 (water highs not shown to be unequivocally unusual for the area). But see *Costello Indus,, Inc.,* ASBCA 49125, 00-2 BCA ¶ 31,098 (concrete was significantly harder than that ordinarily encountered in the geographic region).

To constitute an unusual condition, the condition must also significantly deviate from the norm for the type of work involved. In *Unitec, Inc.*, ASBCA 22025, 79-2 BCA ¶ 13,923, the board found that a concrete base under a runway was not so unusual as to render a limestone base "unusual." In *Hydro-Dredge Corp.*, ENGBCA 5303, 90-1 BCA ¶ 22,370, the board declined to find that sunken boat debris was unusual given the type of work involved. In *Walser v. United States*, 23 Cl. Ct. 591 (1991), the court found that increased debris caused by beavers and unauthorized people cutting down trees were conditions that could have been anticipated in the area. See *Goodwin Contractors, Inc.*, AGBCA 89-148-1, 92-2 BCA ¶ 24,931 (soil upheaval was a "well-known phenomenon"); *Lloyd Moore Constr.*, AGBCA 87-151-3, 89-2 BCA ¶ 21,875 (size of a bog was not deemed unusual where bogs were common in the type of work); *Union Roofing & Sheet Metal Co.,* PSBCA 2366, 90-1 BCA ¶ 22,505, *aff'd*, 909 F.2d 1496 (Fed. Cir. 1990) (use of wire mesh in lightweight insulating concrete was not uncommon in the roofing industry); *Fred A. Arnold, Inc.*, ASBCA 20150, 84-3 BCA ¶ 17,624 (muddy soil encountered near a reservoir not unusual); and *Giuliani Contracting Co.,* AGBCA 86-174-1, 91-2 BCA ¶ 23,827 (contractor constructing drop towers next to a swamp did not show that muck was unusual).

In the following cases, judges found the "unusual" test to be met: *Community Power Suction Furnace Cleaning Co.*, ASBCA 13803, 69-2 BCA ¶ 7963 (contractor encountered an unusual condition while cleaning air ducts when it came upon items ranging from "beer cans and jars of jam to gunpowder, live ammunition and ladies' underwear described as in a deplorable condition"); *Edgar M. Williams*, ASBCA 16058, 72-2 BCA ¶ 9734 (double roofs); *Baltimore Contractors, Inc. v. United States*, 12 Cl. Ct. 328 (1987) (encountering sewage during an excavation project); *Kahaluu Constr. Co.,* ASBCA 31187, 89-1 BCA ¶ 21,308, *recons. denied*, 89-1 BCA ¶ 21,525 (alkyd-type coating over bituminous coating on metal siding causing lack of adhesion); *Minter Roofing Co.,* ASBCA 29387, 90-1 BCA ¶ 22,279 (additional studding and blocked doorways); *Illinois Constructors Corp.*, ENGBCA 5678, 91-2 BCA ¶ 23,728 (extent and lack of deterioration of concrete); and *P-B Eng'g Co.*, ASBCA 39041, 90-2 BCA ¶ 22,686 (welded wire fabric reinforcement in basement floors because it normally occurs only where concrete is required to bear high loads); *Fire Sec. Sys., Inc. v. General Servs. Admin.*, GSBCA 12120, 97-2 BCA ¶ 28,994 (condition of tiles); and *R.B. Hazard, Inc.*, ASBCA 34289, 90-3 ¶ BCA 22,959 (rain caused excessive runoff and an elevated water table).

An unusual condition has been found where the condition is an obstruction that is in a strange location. See *Hercules Constr. Co.*, VABCA 2508, 88-2 BCA ¶ 20,527, in which the board granted recovery when the contractor encountered an interior brick wall. See also *W.S. Meadows Eng'g, Inc.*, ASBCA 32536, 88-2 BCA ¶ 20,616, in which the board granted recovery for jet fuel and steam in a subterranean culvert. However, conditions encountered in buildings constructed in a certain era will often not be considered unusual. See *J.J. Barnes Constr. Co.,* ASBCA 27876, 85-3 BCA ¶ 18,503 (condition of the building was to be expected given its era of construction); *Fred Burgos Constr. Co.,* ASBCA 41395, 91-2 BCA ¶ 23,706, *recons. denied*, 91-2 BCA ¶ 23,951 (two layers of shingle in an older building was not unusual); *Ben M. White Co.*, ASBCA 36422, 90-1 BCA ¶ 22,310, *recons. denied*, 90-1 BCA ¶ 22,384 (tile affixed to wallboard with an excessive amount of glue was not unusual given the age of the building); and *Shumate Constructors, Inc.*, VABCA 2772, 90-3 BCA ¶ 22,946 (asbestos-insulated domestic water lines were not unusual for building's vintage).

Conditions may be considered unusual when anticipated materials have appeared in higher proportions or degrees than reasonably anticipated, *R.J. Crowley, Inc.*, GSBCA 11080 (9521)-REIN, 92-1 BCA ¶ 24,499. In *Hydro-Dredge Corp.*, ENGBCA 5303, 90-1 BCA ¶ 22,370, the board found that encountering massive quantities of eelgrass was unusual and unforeseeable. See also *Blount Bros. Corp.*, ENGBCA 2803, 70-1 BCA ¶ 8256 (corrosive effect of subsurface water was greater than expected); *Marvaco, Inc.*, ENGBCA 3953, 79-2 BCA ¶ 14,015 (though both parties expected some unsuitable material of the kind experienced, neither expected the amount encountered); *Olson Constr. Co.*, ASBCA 23004, 81-1 BCA ¶ 14,985 (contractor encountered greater degree of water seepage than anticipated); and *Kinetic Builders, Inc.*, ASBCA 32627, 88-2 BCA ¶ 20,657 (existence of "tremendous" amount of muck was unusual).

Unusual conditions may also occur when materials react in an unanticipated manner, *J. Lawson Jones Constr. Co.,* ENGBCA 4363, 86-1 BCA ¶ 18,719. See *Paccon, Inc.*, ASBCA 7643, 1962 BCA ¶ 3546 (plasticity of clay was greater than anticipated); *R.A. Heintz Constr. Co.*, ENGBCA 3380, 74-1 BCA ¶ 10,562 (rock fractured differently than anticipated); *George E. Jensen Contractor, Inc.*, ASBCA 20234, 76-1 BCA ¶ 11,741 (mortar was abnormally hard); and *Wade Perrow Constr., Inc.*, ASBCA 50714, 97-2 BCA ¶ 29,250 (the tenacity of the bond required the use of a special "Terminator" machine).

III. BREACH OF CONTRACT CLAIMS RELATED TO DIFFERING SITE CONDITIONS

One of the major effects of the Differing Site Conditions clause has been to eliminate almost all related breach of contract claims. Claims that are fully redressable under contract clauses cannot be maintained under separate breach of contract actions, *Johnson & Sons Erectors Co. v. United States*, 231 Ct. Cl. 753, *cert. denied*, 459 U.S. 971 (1982); *Edward R. Marden Corp. v. United States*, 194 Ct. Cl. 799, 442 F.2d 364 (1971). Thus, to the extent that the Differing Site Conditions clause is applicable, breach of contract claims for misrepresentation or nondisclosure are precluded. While not applicable to Differing Site Conditions claims, breach of contract actions may be particularly useful to the contractor who encounters conditions not compensable under the Differing Site Conditions clause, such as unusual or severe weather, *Chris Berg, Inc. v. United States*, 186 Ct. Cl. 389, 404 F.2d 364

(1968) (government representation that work site was outside typhoon zone was incorrect); *Hardeman-Monier-Hutcherson v. United States*, 198 Ct. Cl. 472, 458 F.2d 1364 (1972) (government did not turn over weather and sea conditions reports even though the contractor asked for them), or a change in labor conditions, *J.A. Jones Constr. Co. v. United States*, 182 Ct. Cl. 615, 390 F.2d 886 (1968).

A. Misrepresentation and Category I Conditions

Misrepresentation is a common breach of contract claim that would be applicable to construction contracts not containing a Differing Site Conditions clause. See *Foster Constr. C.A. & Williams Bros. Co. v. United States*, 193 Ct. Cl. 587, 435 F.2d 873 (1970), stating that a claim for misrepresentation "is based on a breach of duty to disclose . . . though the contract contains no changed condition clause." The court explained that the Differing Site Conditions clause gives the contractor greater rights because, in a Category I changed conditions claim, the contractor need only prove "that actual conditions encountered 'materially differ' from those . . . indicated," while in order to prove a breach of duty to disclose, the contractor must show "Government culpability."

Under the current Differing Site Conditions clause, which provides compensation for costs "whether or not changed as a result of such [differing site] condition," the contractor can recover an amount at least equal to breach of contract damages, and recovery may actually be greater under the clause, *Kemmons-Wilson, Inc.*, ASBCA 16167, 72-2 BCA ¶ 9689. Thus, where conditions at the site are misrepresented in the contract documents, the Category I differing site condition claim is a better course of action for the contractor.

B. Government Nondisclosure and Category II Conditions

Failure by the government to disclose pertinent information in its possession regarding site conditions is a breach of contract, *Leal v. United States*, 149 Ct. Cl. 451, 276 F.2d 378 (1960); *Ragonese v. United States*, 128 Ct. Cl. 156, 120 F. Supp. 768 (1954). In a case where the information not disclosed relates to the type of conditions covered by the Differing Site Conditions clause, the contractor can present the claim as a Category II changed condition. If it is so presented, the contractor must, of course, demonstrate that the condition was unknown or unusual, whereas if it is presented as a nondisclosure claim, the contractor must show that the condition was material and that its presence could not have been readily determined.

Although application of these standards may be somewhat different in specific situations, there may be little practical difference between the two actions since appeals boards in Category II changed conditions actions have considered evidence that the government knew of the condition and did not disclose it, *Maryland Painting Co.*, ENGBCA 3337, 73-2 BCA ¶ 10,223; *Leonard Blinderman*

Constr. Co., ASBCA 18946, 75-1 BCA ¶ 11,018. See also *Unitec, Inc.*, ASBCA 22025, 79-2 BCA ¶ 13,923, in which the board discussed a Category II changed condition in terms of failure to disclose but refused to impute the knowledge held by the Army Corps of Engineers to contracting personnel at Fort Stewart. Judge Arons, concurring, recognized that the issue was one of materiality and the reasonableness of investigation and found that, regardless of imputed knowledge, the contractor should have discovered the condition. The significance of the government's nondisclosure of facts in Category II cases is illustrated by *Commercial Mech. Contractors, Inc.*, ASBCA 25695, 83-2 BCA ¶ 16,768, in which the board held that "any duty to inquire on [the contractor's] part is overcome by the Government's failure to alert bidders."

IV. INVESTIGATION OF DATA AND INSPECTION OF SITE

Bidding documents generally contain provisions requiring bidders to investigate data and inspect the work site prior to submitting their bids. The following clause is contained in FAR 52.236-3:

> SITE INVESTIGATION AND CONDITIONS AFFECTING THE WORK (APR 1984)
>
> (a) The Contractor acknowledges that it has taken steps reasonably necessary to ascertain the nature and location of the work, and that it has investigated and satisfied itself as to the general and local conditions which can affect the work or its cost, including but not limited to (1) conditions bearing upon transportation, disposal, handling, and storage of materials; (2) the availability of labor, water, electric power, and roads; (3) uncertainties of weather, river stages, tides, or similar physical conditions at the site; (4) the conformation and conditions of the ground; and (5) the character of equipment and facilities needed preliminary to and during work performance. The Contractor also acknowledges that it has satisfied itself as to the character, quality, and quantity of surface and subsurface materials or obstacles to be encountered insofar as this information is reasonably ascertainable from an inspection of the site, including all exploratory work done by the Government, as well as from the drawings and specifications made a part of this contract. Any failure of the Contractor to take the actions described and acknowledged in this paragraph will not relieve the contractor from responsibility for estimating properly the difficulty and cost of successfully performing the work, or for proceeding to successfully perform the work without additional expense to the Government.
>
> (b) The Government assumes no responsibility for any conclusions or interpretations made by the Contractor based on the information made available by the Government. Nor does the Government assume responsibility for any understanding reached or representation made concerning conditions which can affect the work by any of its officers or agents before the execution of this contract, unless that understanding or representation is expressly stated in this contract.

FAR 36.210 provides that the solicitation should notify bidders of the time and place for the site investigation and data examination. The Court of Claims has held that the site and data investigation requirement should not be viewed so expansively as to frustrate the policy of the clause, which is to relieve the contractor of the necessity of allowing for contingencies in bid computation, *Foster Constr. C.A. & Williams Bros. Co. v. United States*, 193 Ct. Cl. 587, 435 F.2d 873 (1970). See also *North Slope Tech. Ltd. v. United States*, 14 Cl. Ct. 242 (1988); *Harper Dev. & Assocs.*, ASBCA 34719, 90-1 BCA ¶ 22,534; *Cherry Hill Constr., Inc. v. General Servs. Admin.*, GSBCA 11217, 92-3 BCA ¶ 25,179. In *Foster*, the court held that contractors should be able to rely on contract indications unless "relatively simple inquiries might have revealed contrary conditions." This section reviews the data to be examined, the type of site investigation required of bidders, and the consequences of a failure to investigate the site.

A. Investigation of Data

In addition to deciding whether to physically inspect the work site, bidders must determine what data to examine. The extent to which the contractor will be charged with information contained in government-furnished data depends on the way in which the government has furnished the data.

Assumption of design responsibilities may also impose an elevated duty to investigate subsurface conditions. See *Pitt-Des Moines, Inc.*, ASBCA 42838, 96-1 BCA ¶ 27,941 (assumption of design responsibility imposes a greater duty on contractor to conduct a site investigation, but contractor met the duty by conducting an independent geotechnical study and inquiring specifically about the condition of the site).

1. Contract Documents

The contractor will be charged with information contained in data furnished as part of the documents or referred to in the documents and made available to bidders, *A.S. McGaughan Co. v. United States*, 24 Cl. Ct. 659 (1991), *aff'd*, 980 F.2d 744 (Fed. Cir. 1992). For example, the contractor must review the government geologic report if it is referred to in the contract, *Pleasant Excavating Co. v. United States*, 229 Ct. Cl. 654 (1981); *Hunt & Willett, Inc. v. United States*, 168 Ct. Cl. 256, 351 F.2d 980 (1964). See also *Randa/Madison Joint Venture III v. Dahlberg*, 239 F.3d 1264 (Fed. Cir. 2001) (contractor failed to review gradation curves and other information referred to in contract); *Ballenger Corp.*, DOTCAB 74-32, 84-1 BCA ¶ 16,973, *modified on other grounds*, 84-2 BCA ¶ 17,277 (contractor failed to examine site geological information clearly referenced in the specifications and available for inspection in the architect's office); and *Donald R. Stewart & Assocs.*, AGBCA 84-226-1, 92-1 BCA ¶ 24,705 (failure to review the geologist's report precludes recovery even if actual subsurface conditions differ). A contractor cannot rely solely on boring logs where other information is made available to it. In *Ashbach Constr. Co.*, PSBCA 2718, 91-2 BCA ¶ 23,787, *aff'd*, 960 F.2d 155 (Fed. Cir. 1992), the contractor could not recover where it failed to review drawings, which were referenced in the specifications, that contradicted the soil borings.

2. Data Not in Contract

Contractors are not required to inspect documents that are not a part of the contract. Thus, absent an express contract provision, the duty to inspect does not require examination of "as built" drawings that are not part of the contract, *Klefstad Eng'g Co.,* VACAB 602, 68-1 BCA ¶ 6965. Where some information is included in the contract and other information is available but specifically excluded from the contract, bidders have no duty to evaluate the excluded information, *American Structures, Inc.*, ENGBCA 3408, 75-1 BCA ¶ 11,283; *Holloway Constr. Co. & Holloway Sand & Gravel Co.,* ENGBCA 4805, 89-2 BCA ¶ 21,713. See also *American Structures, Inc.*, ENGBCA 3410, 76-1 BCA ¶ 11,683 (information contained in a soils report not binding on the contractor). In *Dravo Corp.*, ENGBCA 3901, 80-2 BCA ¶ 14,757, the board held that since there was no duty to evaluate data specifically excluded from the contract, the contractor had no right to rely on such information. See also *Cocoa Elec. Co.,* ASBCA 33921, 91-1 BCA ¶ 23,442, *recons. denied*, 91-2 BCA ¶ 23,780 (contractor relied at its own risk on as-built drawings that were not part of the contract).

3. Information Known to Competitors

Other contractors may have information concerning the conditions at the site that would be useful to a bidder in preparing its bid. However, the other contractors may be potential competitors and will probably be reluctant to share information, either because of concern that it would harm their competitive position or concerns of collusion or antitrust violations. A flavor of how such concerns might impact the bidding process can be seen in *Granite Constr. Co. v. United States*, 24 Cl. Ct. 735 (1991). In *Pacific W. Constr., Inc.*, DOTCAB 1084, 83-1 BCA ¶ 16,337, the board held that the contractor was not required to communicate with prior contractors who are competitors to ascertain what took place and what problems were encountered at the site. In contrast, *Hunt & Willett, Inc. v. United States*, 168 Ct. Cl. 256, 351 F.2d 980 (1964), held that the contractor's "representatives made an inadequate investigation of the site" because if the contractor had made inquiry of the contractor or personnel working at the site "it is reasonable to conclude that it would have then known" of the site condition. See also *Phyllis Wolf*, AGBCA 96-102-1, 96-2 BCA ¶ 28,504, holding that the knowledge of competitors indicated that a condition was known in the area where the work was to be performed. Thus, it would seem that bidders should address inquiries about the conditions to other contractors that have worked in the area.

4. Reasonableness of Investigation

The contractor will be held to a standard of a reasonable contractor in its investigation of the contract data. Thus, a contractor need not hire a geologist to assist in the analysis of contract documents, *E. Arthur Higgins*, AGBCA 76-128, 79-2 BCA ¶ 14,050. See *Shank-Artukovich v. United States*, 13 Cl. Ct. 346 (1987), *aff'd*, 848 F.2d 1245 (Fed. Cir. 1988), holding that the contractor could not have anticipated the likelihood of "running ground" or "caving ground" from language in the specifications that might have been construed by an expert to indicate that such ground could occur, and *Blake Constr. Co.,* ASBCA 20,747, 83-1 BCA ¶ 16,410, holding that the fact that an expert geologist could have predicted site conditions through available geological literature did not bar a differing site conditions claim. In *Coastal Marine Constr.*, AGBCA 89-190-3, 90-2 BCA ¶ 22,895, the board stated that, although a trained geologist might review the contract data and arrive at a different conclusion, "a reasonable contractor would rely heavily upon the repeated references to the freshness of the rock and the limited reference to weathering to conclude that the rock was for the most part fresh."

Contractors are, however, expected to understand the complexities of their undertakings. In *Pleasant Excavating Co. v. United States*, 229 Ct. Cl. 654 (1981), the government argued that, while core samples showed low water levels, other information in the bidding documents was sufficient to warn the contractor of possible moisture. The court held for the government, stating at 657-58:

> The core samples did indicate that, at the time of the tests, the water table level was below the elevation where Pleasant intended to excavate, leading [the contractor] (it says) to believe that the amount of soil moisture would be ideal for its purposes. But the descriptive notations accompanying the data significantly qualified any water level representation. The very frequent use of the term mottled indicated that the water could potentially reach higher elevations.
>
> * * *
>
> [The contractor] argues that the only evidence that it should have understood the term "mottles" comes from soil experts unqualified to testify as to what a reasonable contractor should have known.
>
> * * *
>
> What [the experts] alluded to was that the term was knowable by consulting with the Dictionary of Geologic Terms. It was reasonable and adequate for the Board to conclude from the evidence that contractors should be sufficiently aware to at least inquire into the meaning of the word once it is found in the test pit data.

See also *H.B. Mac, Inc. v. United States*, 153 F.3d 1338 (Fed. Cir. 1998), ruling that it was error to hold a small, disadvantaged business to a more lenient standard regarding the investigation and interpretation of site conditions, stating at 1345:

> The fact that a contract is a set aside for small-disadvantaged businesses does not change in any way the standard that a court applies in analyzing the contractor's pre-bid conduct. . . . [A]s a government contractor, an SDB has its conduct judged under the same standard as that of any other contractor.

The court ruled that a reasonable pre-bid inspection would have revealed widely varying surface conditions at a site near the ocean and intersected by streams. Given that information, the contractor's assumptions regarding the absence of surface water based on test borings taken 300 yards away was simply not reasonable.

The contractor will be held responsible for "patent indications plainly, to a layman, contradicting the contract documents," *Stock & Grove, Inc. v. United States*, 204 Ct. Cl. 103, 493 F.2d 629 (1974). If the contractor is on notice of inconsistencies in the information, further inquiries must be made. In *Parkland Design & Dev. Corp.*, IBCA 1442-3-81, 82-2 BCA ¶ 15,975, where five borings from the site indicated suitable material while one boring from the edge of the site indicated substantially decayed vegetation, the board stated at 79,231:

> Armed with a shovel and the knowledge that there was unsuitable material in the area, little effort would be required to open the surface at several nearby locations . . . [which] would have revealed the actual condition encountered. . . .

See also *Giuliani Contracting Co.,* ASBCA 33341, 87-2 BCA ¶ 19,743, *recons. denied*, 88-3 BCA ¶ 21,003 (contractor obligated to inquire where the contract indicated that asphalt and asphalt underlaid with concrete would be encountered, since the drawings failed to disclose the location where each condition could be expected). In *Weeks Dredging & Contracting, Inc. v. United States*, 13 Cl. Ct. 193 (1987), *aff'd*, 861 F.2d 728 (Fed. Cir. 1988), the court found that evidence of extensive commercial gravel operations in close proximity to the contractor's site should have put the contractor on notice that there may have been subsurface conditions different from those indicated in the boring logs. While the court agreed that the contractor need not hire a geotechnical engineer, it did find that the contractor acted unreasonably in failing to contact these commercial operators and make certain inquiries. However, if the contractor is not reasonably placed on notice of inconsistencies, further inquiry is not required. In *S & M-Traylor Bros.*, ENGBCA 3878, 82-1 BCA ¶ 15,484, where boring logs indicated silty material although the contract specified the use of heavy equipment, the contractor was justified in concluding that the silty material was stable enough to support the equipment. See also *W.D. McCullough Constr. Co.*, ENGBCA 4593, 87-1 BCA ¶ 19,515 (contractor "was not under a pre-bid duty . . . given the disclosed discrepancy between contour and profile data, skeptically to ferret out the latent conflict between the specification representations . . . and actual borrow requirements").

B. Inspection of Site

The adequacy of the site investigation is measured by what a reasonable, intelligent contractor, experienced in the particular field of work involved, could be expected to discover, not what a highly trained geologist might have found, *Stock & Grove, Inc. v. United States*, 204 Ct. Cl. 103, 493 F.2d 629 (1974); *Youngdale & Sons Constr. Co. v. United States*, 27 Fed. Cl. 516 (1993). In *Kaiser Indus. Corp. v. United States*, 169 Ct. Cl. 310, 340 F.2d 322 (1965), the government claimed that, because its test borings showed core cracks and fractures, the contractor was put on notice of possible unstable subsurface conditions. The court held for the contractor, stating at 324:

> Nor can [the contractor's] prebid examination of the core borings and the sites fairly be subjected to the harsh criticism [the Government] makes concerning the adequacy thereof. Both examinations were made with reasonable care. And [the contractor] was the only contractor to show up at a prebid conference arranged by [the Government]. Although trained geologists might debate interminably about the matter, insofar as an examination by a reasonably experienced and intelligent contractor-layman is concerned, there was no clear or obvious indication in the physical appearance of the Hover cores that the rock would act as it subsequently did.

See also *Baltimore Contractors, Inc. v. United States*, 12 Cl. Ct. 328 (1987) (reasonable bidder would have inspected the site without finding any evidence that the soil strength was other than indicated); *Holloway Constr. Co.& Williams Bros. Co.*, ENGBCA 4805, 89-2 BCA ¶ 21,713 (reasonable bidder would not be put on notice of large deposits of rock upon seeing a few scattered cobbles and boulders); and *Kinetic Builders, Inc.*, ASBCA 32627, 88-2 BCA ¶ 20,657 (presence of titi trees did not indicate the presence of muck, where "[the contractor] is a contractor, not a botanist").

If the government requires greater inspection expertise, it must specify it in the solicitation, *Darwin Constr. Co.*, ASBCA 27596, 86-1 BCA ¶ 18,645. Alternatively, it may add a standard "measurements" clause to the agreement, *Consolidated Constr., Inc.*, GSBCA 8871, 88-2 BCA ¶ 20,811, *aff'd*, 889 F.2d 1101 (Fed. Cir., 1989).

Where a reasonable site investigation reveals details that are omitted in the drawings, the contractor has a duty to inquire further before bidding, *Zinger Constr. Co.,* ASBCA 26331, 82-2 BCA ¶ 15,988, *aff'd*, 807 F.2d 979 (Fed. Cir. 1986). The contractor is also responsible for noting obvious discrepancies between the contract information and the site. In *Moon Constr. Co. v. General Servs. Admin.*, GSBCA 11766, 93-3 BCA ¶ 26,017, the board stated that during site investigation the contractor "must spot and consider glaring, patent discrepancies between the drawings and features found" (citing *Assurance Co.*, ASBCA 25254, 83-2 BCA ¶ 16,908, *aff'd*, 813 F.2d 1202 (Fed. Cir. 1987)). However, the contractor is not required to undertake extensive engineering efforts prior to bidding to verify the site conditions indicated in the contract, *Flores Drilling & Pump Co.*, AGBCA 82-204-3, 83-1 BCA ¶ 16,200, *recons. denied*, 83-1 BCA ¶ 16,336; *Richard P. Murray Co.*, AGBCA 77-152-4-A, 86-2 BCA ¶ 18,804; *Dawco Constr. Co. v. United States*, 18 Cl. Ct. 682 (1989), *aff'd in part and rev'd in part*, 930 F.2d 872 (Fed. Cir. 1991); *Minter Roofing Co.*, ASBCA 29387, 90-1 BCA ¶ 22,279; *Donald R. Stewart & Assocs.*, AGBCA 84-226-1, 92-1 BCA ¶ 24,705; *Jack L. Olsen, Inc.*, AGBCA 87-345-1, 93-2 BCA ¶ 25,767.

Some cases have imposed a relatively high requirement for a site investigation. See, for example, *Lamb Eng'g & Constr. Co.*, EBCA C-9304172, 97-2 BCA ¶ 29,207, holding that a reasonable contractor "would get out its shovel and explore near surface materials" by opening the surface at several locations to reveal the actual condition. See also *Vega Roofing Co. v. International Boundary & Water Comm'n*, GSBCA 13576-IBWC, 97-2 BCA ¶ 28,990, holding that an extra layer of shingles should have been apparent during the contractor's site inspection.

1. Category I Conditions

When Category I conditions are involved, the contractor will be held to what a relatively simple site viewing would have revealed. The site investigation clause "does not demand omniscience or Herculean measures to seek out possible adverse conditions," *Smith-Cothran, Inc.*, DOTBCA 1931, 89-1 BCA ¶ 21,554. See *Warren Beaves*, DOTCAB 1160, 84-1 BCA ¶ 17,198, stating at 85,634:

> The prospective bidder is entitled to rely on the accuracy of information included in the solicitation. He is under no obligation to conduct his own surveys, or go beyond what a simple site viewing might reveal. A simple site inspection would not normally include taking soundings of water depths. See *United States v. Atlantic Dredging Company*, 253 U.S. 1 (1920); *Morrison-Knudsen Company v. United States*, 170 Ct. Cl. 712 (1965); *Ragonese v. United States*, 128 Ct. Cl. 156 (1954); *Pacific Western Construction, Inc.*, [DOTCAB 1084, 82-2 BCA ¶ 16,045, *recons. denied*, 83-1 BCA ¶ 16,337].

See also *Quiller Constr. Co.*, ASBCA 8053, 1963 BCA ¶ 3815 (contractor not required to open walls of occupied houses to determine location of gas lines); *McKee v. United States*, 205 Ct. Cl. 303, 500 F.2d 525 (1974) (contractor not obligated to determine if trail was located on government property when drawings marked it as a government trail); *A.D. Herman Constr. Co.*, GSBCA 4823, 78-1 BCA ¶ 13,187 (demolition contractor not required to inspect a passenger elevator shaft for unusual steel framework); *Cottrell Eng'g Corp.*, ENGBCA 3964, 80-1 BCA ¶ 14,217 (contractor "not obligated to search the land records, locate monuments and do a survey" during site investigation in order to determine that government documents were incorrect in indicating size of disposal area); *Fermin O. Gonzalez*, ASBCA 21421, 80-1 BCA ¶ 14,254 (contractor need not "poke a hole through the roof" to discover pockets of water); *Fortec Constructors*, ASBCA 26453, 82-2 BCA ¶ 15,845 (contractor not obligated to verify the drawings with the actual site conditions); *Assurance Co.*, ASBCA 25254, 83-2 BCA ¶ 16,908, *aff'd*, 813 F.2d 1202 (Fed. Cir. 1987) (contractor not responsible for finding that crawl space was less than shown on drawings where the crawl space was not readily noticeable by simple viewing); *Central Mech., Inc.*, DOTCAB 1234, 83-2 BCA ¶ 16,642 (contractor not responsible for discovering the actual position of a duct when viewing the electrical vault); *Alart Plumbing Co.,* GSBCA 6487, 84-1 BCA ¶ 17,229 (contractor not required to poke holes in ceiling to discover beams obstructing crawl space); *GIIS Corp.*, DOTCAB 1534, 85-1 BCA ¶ 17,810 (contractor not required to conduct a "foot-by-foot" inspection of ground covered by tall grasses in order to discover a small outcropping nor perform subsurface probing to discover subsurface rock); *Darwin Constr. Co.*, ASBCA 27596, 86-1 BCA ¶ 18,645 (contractor had no duty to dislodge ceiling tiles to check for asbestos dust); *C.F.I. Constr. Co.*, DOTBCA 1782, 87-1 BCA ¶ 19,547 (contractor not required to excavate at the foot of the wall to determine the actual length of vertical connectors); *Southern Cal. Roofing Co.*, PSBCA 1737, 88-2 BCA ¶ 20,803 (contractor not required to cut into the roof to discover its composition); and *Minter Roofing Co.,* ASBCA 29387, 90-1 BCA ¶ 22,279 (contractor not responsible for discovering that buildings were not plumb where the buildings had corner boards). But see *Yamas Constr. Co.*, ASBCA 27366, 86-3 BCA ¶ 19,090 (contractor responsible for noting rubber-backed carpet where the contractor's agent saw it and reported it to the contractor).

2. Category II Conditions

A contractor asserting a Category II condition usually must show that it conducted a more thorough site investigation, *S.T.G. Constr. Co. v. United States*, 157 Ct. Cl. 409 (1962). In *Reid Contracting Co.,* IBCA 74, 58-2 BCA ¶ 2037, a case in which the contract contained no site investigation requirement, the board stated that "[a] contractor who asserts a changed condition in the second category is always charged with the duty of making a reasonably thorough site examination." In *Robert McMullan & Sons, Inc. v. United States*, 226 Ct. Cl. 565, 650 F.2d 292 (1980), the court implied that a reasonable site investigation might have required test borings where no borings or reports were provided by the government. This higher site investigation standard may require a contractor to familiarize itself as to local conditions. In *Servidone Constr. Corp. v. United States*, 19 Cl. Ct. 346 (1990), *aff'd*, 931 F.2d 860 (Fed. Cir. 1991), the court found that the contractor's site investigation was "desultory" and stated that the contractor should have acquainted itself with local conditions. See also *CCI Contractors, Inc.*, AGBCA 84-314-1, 91-3 BCA ¶ 24,225, *aff'd*, 979 F.2d 216 (Fed. Cir. 1992) (contractor's failure to inquire into conditions with experienced local contractors rendered its pre-bid inspection inadequate). In addition, the contractor may be required to conduct all tests that are standard practice during the pre-bid site investigation. In *D.J. Barclay & Co.,* ASBCA 28908, 88-2 BCA ¶ 20,741, no Category II differing site condition was found where the contractor did not follow industry practice and perform simple adhesion tests on the surfaces. Compare *Illinois Constructors Corp.*, ENGBCA 5678, 91-2 BCA ¶ 23,728, where the contractor's investigation was adequate where it did not conduct various tests to disclose concrete properties because such testing was not standard industry practice. In *Hercules Constr. Co.*, VABCA 2508, 88-2 BCA ¶ 20,527, the contractor's inspection was adequate where it visited the site four times, tapped on walls, and followed "normal trade practices and customs" for investigating. When the government specifies that a particular site is representative of others included in the contract, an investigation of that representative site will be sufficient, *Konoike Constr. Co., Ltd.*, ASBCA 36342, 91-1 BCA ¶ 23,440 (metal water heater supports in representative building and concrete support in other buildings).

This higher site investigation requirement with regard to Category II differing site conditions may be lessened if the government knows of the condition but does not reveal it to the bidders, *Commercial Mech. Contractors, Inc.*, ASBCA 25695, 83-2 BCA ¶ 16,768; *Leonard Blinderman Constr. Co.*, ASBCA 18946, 75-1 BCA ¶ 11,018; *Diversacon Indus., Inc.*, ENGBCA 3365, 75-1 BCA ¶ 11,059.

C. Failure to Investigate

Although the Site Investigation and Conditions Affecting the Work clause is worded to indicate that the contractor *has performed appropriate investigations*, failure to investigate or an inadequate investigation is not an absolute defense to a claim under the Differing Site Conditions clause, *Alps Constr. Corp.*, ASBCA 16966, 73-2 BCA ¶ 10,309; *R.J. Crowley, Inc.*, GSBCA 11080 (9521)-REIN, 92-1 BCA ¶ 24,499. Rather, the effect of the requirement is that a contractor who fails to inspect or who performs an inadequate inspection bears the risk of a condition that could have been discovered by a reasonable investigation of the site, *Vann v. United States*, 190 Ct. Cl. 546, 420 F.2d 968 (1970); *Mojave Enters.*, AGBCA 75-114, 77-1 BCA ¶ 12,337, *aff'd*, 3 Cl. Ct. 353 (1983); *Trans-Atl. Indus., Inc.*, GSBCA 10803, 91-3 BCA ¶ 24,320. Thus, a contractor who does not perform any investigation, or who performs an inadequate investigation, may recover for a differing site condition that would not have been discovered by a reasonable inspection, *Bernard McMenamy Contractor, Inc.*, ENGBCA 3413, 77-1 BCA ¶ 12,335; *Continental Drilling Co.*, ENGBCA 3455, 75-2 BCA ¶ 11,541. See *Darwin Constr. Co.*, ASBCA 27596, 86-1 BCA ¶ 18,645 (reasonable site investigation would not have revealed asbestos-contaminated tiles); *Daniel Mancini Constr. Co.*, ASBCA 30337, 87-1 BCA ¶ 19,379 (careful inspection of windows would not have revealed that flanges were nailed to the framing studs); *Smith-Cothran, Inc.*, DOTBCA 1931, 89-1 BCA ¶ 21,554 (site investigation would not have revealed that the contractor would be delayed by inmate work calls or the late arrival of the government escort into the prison, nor the need to padlock scaffold boards); *Servidone Constr. Corp. v. United States*, 19 Cl. Ct. 346 (1990), *aff'd*, 931 F.2d 860 (Fed. Cir. 1991) (reasonable inspection would not have revealed the actual conditions of the soils); *Gulf Constr. Group, Inc.*, ENGBCA 5850, 93-1 BCA ¶ 25,229 (underwater cleaning and visual inspection of castings and bolts would not have revealed information about embedded or covered castings and bolts and the difficulty of removing them); *Marty's Maid & Janitorial Serv. v. General Servs. Admin.*, GSBCA 10614, 93-1 BCA ¶ 25,284 (contractor could not have anticipated that previous contractor would stop cleaning the building upon learning that its contract was not renewed); *Skyline Painting, Inc.*, ENGBCA 5810, 93-3 BCA ¶ 26,041 (a more extensive site investigation was not required where nothing in a visual examination of the site contradicted the contract drawings and only a full-scale survey could have detected the condition of the spillway); and *Goss Fire Prot.*, DOTBCA 2782, 97-1 BCA ¶ 128,853, *recons. denied*, 97-2 BCA ¶ 28,991 (failure to investigate site did not preclude recovery because there was no evidence that a site investigation would have disclosed anything about the subsurface conditions).

Where a reasonable investigation would have disclosed the condition, failure to investigate or an inadequate investigation will preclude recovery. See *Continental Flooring Co.*, VABCA 2065, 85-2 BCA ¶ 18,130 (floor tiles with "bleeding of adhesives" would have been discovered by an inspection); *Bowie & K Enters., Inc.*, IBCA 1788, 87-1 BCA ¶ 19,338 (site investigation would have provided the contractor with a better perspective of terrain and aided in calculating bid); *Azerind, Inc.*, ASBCA 34294, 87-3 BCA ¶ 20,122 (site investigation would have revealed the amount of sandblasting that would be required); *Smith-Cothran, Inc.*, DOTBCA 1931, 89-1 BCA ¶ 21,554 (site investigation would have revealed certain security restrictions); *Winandy Greenhouse Co.*, AGBCA 88-239-3, 89-1 BCA ¶ 21,495 (site investigation would have revealed that structural parts needed removal before replacing); *J.S. Alberici Constr. Co.*, GSBCA 9897, 89-3 BCA ¶ 22,224 (contractor ignored data suggesting the presence of uneven angles of intersection and did not take measurements for the purposes of verification); *McCormick Constr. Co. v. United States*, 18 Cl. Ct. 259 (1989), *aff'd*, 907 F.2d 159 (Fed. Cir. 1990) (contractor would have seen large, nested boulders had it inspected the site); *Fred Burgos Constr. Co.*, ASBCA 41395, 91-2 BCA ¶ 23,706, *recons. denied*, 91-2 BCA ¶ 23,951 (inspection from the ground would have revealed the deteriorated condition of the roof); *Wayne Constr.*, ENGBCA 4942, 91-1 BCA ¶ 23,535 (pre-bid investigation would have revealed visible fracture planes that would make production of the requisite quantity of rock difficult); *RJS Constructors, Inc.*, ENGBCA 5975, 93-3 BCA ¶ 26,038 (reasonable site investigation would have revealed the actual conditions of the buildings); and *Orlosky, Inc. v. United States*, 64 Fed. Cl. 63 (2005) (reasonable site investigation would have revealed that there were no poles on which to install pole-mounted reclosers).

Where a reasonable investigation would have revealed the condition, a contractor may not defend its failure to inspect on the grounds that the inspection would have been rushed or difficult. See *M&M Enters., Inc.*, ENGBCA 5306, 89-2 BCA ¶ 21,641 (contractor not excused from investigating where inspection was hurried due to the illness of one of the contractor's officers); *Quality Servs. of N.C., Inc.*, ASBCA 34851, 89-2 BCA ¶ 21,836 (contractor not excused from investigating where it was afraid of snakes); and *Diamond Pac.*, NASABCA 45-0391, 92-1 BCA ¶ 24,615 (contractor not excused from investigating on the grounds that it would not have recognized any asbestos-indicating materials when the contractor's subcontractor inspected and recognized these materials).

A contractor who inspects the site but fails to comply with certain formalities, for example, arranging the inspection through the engineering officer, is not precluded from recovery if the inspection was reasonable and did not disclose the condition, *Tranco Contracting Co.*, VACAB 921, 71-2 BCA ¶ 9129; *Bromley Contracting Co.*, VACAB 1369, 81-1 BCA ¶ 14,920.

1. Prevention by Government

The contractor need not investigate the site if the government denies it access, *Pavement Specialists, Inc.*, ASBCA 17410, 73-2 BCA ¶ 10,082. See also *Hercules Constr. Co.*, VABCA 2508, 88-2 BCA ¶ 20,527, in which the board found that the contractor's site inspection was reasonable where it was not permitted to complete a more extensive examination. Compare *ECOS Mgmt. Criteria, Inc.*, VABCA 2058, 86-2 BCA ¶ 18,885, where the contractor conducted an inadequate investigation when it failed to investigate beyond the escorted tour and the government did not prevent a more thorough investigation. Similarly, a contractor need not investigate if the government has not allotted sufficient time to investigate, *Raymond Int'l of Del., Inc.*, ASBCA 13121, 70-1 BCA ¶ 8341; *J.D. Hedin Constr. Co. v. United States*, 171 Ct. Cl. 70, 347 F.2d 235 (1965). However, the contractor will be held responsible for data that would be disclosed under a reasonable inspection within the time available, *Tectonics, Inc.*, VACAB 1187, 77-1 BCA ¶ 12,228.

2. Impossibility

Absent government fault, impossibility of investigating the site is generally not an excuse, *Cal-Pac. Foresters*, AGBCA 230, 70-1 BCA ¶ 8087. There, the board found that a contractor who was prevented from investigating because of a snowstorm was under no obligation to bid and did so without full knowledge of the terrain, which was not specifically described in the contract documents. See also *Bo McAlister & Loyd Thompson*, IBCA 2144, 88-1 BCA ¶ 20,329, in which the board held that a densely wooded site infested with snakes could be investigated by riding or flying. However, in *Syblon-Reid Co.*, IBCA 1313-11-79, 82-2 BCA ¶ 16,015, the contractor recovered because it was not possible to verify the amount of sediment under water in the canal. See also *JUD Constr. Co.*, ASBCA 36896, 90-3 BCA ¶ 22,954, where inspection was impossible where the government's own architect-engineer freely admitted that the elevation information contained in the contract was incomplete because it was impossible to investigate a particular area of the site.

V. NOTICE

The Differing Site Conditions clause requires prompt written notice to the contracting officer before the different condition is disturbed. The purpose of such notice is to allow the government an opportunity to investigate and to exercise some control over the amount of cost and effort expended in resolving the problem, *Charles T. Parker Constr. Co*, DCAB PR-41, 65-1 BCA ¶ 4780. See *Resource Conservation Corp. v. General Servs. Admin.*, GSBCA 13399, 97-1 BCA ¶ 28,776 (the significance of the notice requirement is "not so much the lapse of time between discovery and notice, but whether the Government had an opportunity to observe the condition and suggest corrective measures"), and *David Boland, Inc.*, ASBCA 48715, 48716, 97-2 BCA ¶ 29,166 (contractor's failure to give any notice deprived the government of the ability to relax the compaction requirements and avoid the extra costs).

A. Nature of Notice

Notice need not follow any specific format but must merely show the existence of the condition, *T&B Builders, Inc.*, ENGBCA 3664, 77-2 BCA ¶ 12,663; *J.J. Welcome Constr. Co.*, ASBCA 19653, 75-1 BCA ¶ 10,997; *Piracci Constr. Co.*, GSBCA 2793, 70-1 BCA ¶ 8172. The requirement that the notice be in writing has been waived when the contractor has given oral notice, *M.M. Sundt Constr. Co.*, ASBCA 17475, 74-1 BCA ¶ 10,627 (oral notice given immediately after condition discovered); *Edgar M. Williams*, ASBCA 16058, 72-2 BCA ¶ 9734; *George A. Fuller Co.*, ASBCA 8524, 1962 BCA ¶ 3619. Oral notice may be given to an authorized representative of the contracting officer, *Shepherd v. United States*, 125 Ct. Cl. 724, 113 F. Supp. 648 (1953); *McCloskey & Co.*, PODBCA 497, 74-1 BCA ¶ 10,479. The burden of proving that oral notice was given is on the contractor. In cases of conflicting testimony, the determination will be based on the fact finder's view of the evidence, *Schnip Bldg. Co. v. United States*, 227 Ct. Cl. 148, 645 F.2d 950 (1981) (oral notice not found); *Leiden Corp.*, ASBCA 26136, 83-2 BCA ¶ 16,612, *recons. denied*, 84-1 BCA ¶ 16,947 (oral notice found). The Court of Claims has held that, once notice is given, no further notice is required when the same conditions recur on the job, *Allied Contractors, Inc. v. United States*, 149 Ct. Cl. 671, 277 F.2d 464 (1960). See also *Valco Constr. Co.*, ASBCA 47909, 96-2 BCA ¶ 28,344 (a contractor may supply adequate notice of the basis and amount of its claim without accounting for each cost component).

B. Actual or Constructive Government Notice

The notice requirement will not be enforced if the government has actual or constructive notice of the conditions encountered, *A.R. Mack Constr. Co.*, ASBCA 50035, 01-2 BCA ¶ 31,593 (contractor orally advised the government's project engineer and the resident engineers had knowledge of the contractor's alleged overexcavation two months before the claim was actually filed); *Eichberger Enters., Inc.*,

VABCA 3923, 95-2 BCA ¶ 27,693 (government project engineer had actual knowledge of condition); *C & L Constr. Co.*, ASBCA 22993, 81-1 BCA ¶ 14,943, *motion for new trial denied*, 83-2 BCA ¶ 16,785 (government daily reports showed that government on-site personnel knew of condition); *S. Kane & Sons, Inc.*, VACAB 1254, 78-1 BCA ¶ 13,100 (contracting officer's representative was aware of the changed condition when first encountered by the contractor). Compare *Schnip Bldg. Co. v. United States*, 227 Ct. Cl. 148, 645 F.2d 950 (1981), in which the court denied relief to a contractor for its failure to give timely notice to the contracting officer even though the contractor had received permission to use a different construction technique. The court reasoned that the different technique could have been required for reasons other than a differing site condition and that the government had no obligation to ferret out the reason. See also *Samkal Mines, Inc.*, DOTCAB 68-9, 71-1 BCA ¶ 8737 (mere observation of the condition by the government inspector did not in itself constitute notice), and *Piracci Constr. Co.*, GSBCA 2793, 70-1 BCA ¶ 8172 . In *Leiden Corp.*, ASBCA 26136, 83-2 BCA ¶ 16,612, *recons. denied*, 84-1 BCA ¶ 16,947, the board distinguished the *Schnip* case and found that the government's construction representative at the site had constructive notice of the condition based on his observation that the rock was breaking in unusual, large caps. This constructive notice was imputed to the contracting officer.

C. No Prejudice

Even if the government did not know of the condition in time to investigate, the contractor may still recover if the government is not prejudiced by the lack of notice, *R.C. Hedreen Co.*, GSBCA 4289, 77-1 BCA ¶ 12,521, *recons. denied*, 71-2 BCA ¶ 12,653; *William F. Klingensmith, Inc.*, GSBCA 3161, 71-2 BCA ¶ 9049. The government has the burden of showing that prejudice was caused by the contractor's failure to notify, *Parcoa, Inc.*, AGBCA 76-130, 77-2 BCA ¶ 12,658. This can be done by demonstrating (1) how the passage of time obscured the elements of proof or (2) how the contracting officer might have minimized extra costs if notice had been given, *R.R. Tyler*, AGBCA 381, 77-1 BCA ¶ 12,227. In *Schnip Bldg. Co. v. United States*, 227 Ct. Cl. 148, 645 F.2d 950 (1981), both these reasons were held to exist. The government contended that the lack of notice prohibited examination of the site and a possible redesign of the project. If the government is prejudiced to some extent because late notice increased the difficulty of defending against the claim, such prejudice may not entirely bar the claim but simply increase the amount of proof the contractor must produce to recover, *Peterson Sharpe Eng'g Corp.*, ASBCA 18780, 77-1 BCA ¶ 12,299; *C.H. Leavell & Co.*, ASBCA 16099, 72-2 BCA ¶ 9694, *recons. denied*, 73-1 BCA ¶ 9781. See, however, *DeMauro Constr. Corp.*, ASBCA 17029, 77-1 BCA ¶ 12,511, distinguishing *Leavell* because there the government had a means of verifying the contractor's data regarding the alleged changed condition. Boards are more likely to find prejudice from lack of notice in the case of a differing site condition than in the case of a change, since the differing site condition is usually hidden by later construction work and, therefore, the contracting officer has no opportunity to analyze the nature of the condition if notice is not given. See, for example, *Carson Linebaugh, Inc.*, ASBCA 11384, 67-2 BCA ¶ 6640; *Klefstad Eng'g Co.,* VACAB 522, 66-1 BCA ¶ 5678; *Guy R. Allen*, ASBCA 6896, 1962 BCA ¶ 3360; and *Coleman Elec. Co.*, ASBCA 4895, 58-2 BCA ¶ 1928.

VI. PROCEDURE

If the proper notice of the differing site condition is given, the procedures followed by the parties become critical. In a well-administered contract, this will be relatively simple—the parties will work together closely until the problem is solved. During this period, both parties should follow the terms of the contract.

A. Contractor's Duty to Proceed

Even though a contractor has encountered a differing site condition, it must "proceed diligently with performance" pending resolution of a claim. Its failure to do so may result in a proper default termination by the government, *Discount Co. v. United States*, 213 Ct. Cl. 567, 554 F.2d 435, *cert. denied*, 434 U.S. 938 (1977); *American Dredging Co.*, ENGBCA 2920, 72-1 BCA ¶ 9316, *aff'd*, 207 Ct. Cl. 1010 (1975). However, if the condition causes the contractor to be unable to proceed, the Court of Claims has held a default termination by the government to be improper, *Vann v. United States*, 190 Ct. Cl. 546, 420 F.2d 968 (1970).

B. Government's Procedure

After the contractor has given notice of a differing site condition, the government should take the initiative in devising the method to solve the problem encountered. In many cases, the solution is suggested by the contractor, but the government must determine the proper course of action. The new method is generally issued to the contractor by change order, and sometimes a stop-work order is issued while the problem is being studied. See *Foster Constr. C.A & Williams Bros. Co. v. United States*, 193 Ct. Cl. 587, 435 F.2d 873 (1970). If the new method involves work not called for by the contract, the work may be procured from another contractor even when it is within the general scope of the first contract, *Hunkin Conkey Constr. Co. v. United States*, 198 Ct. Cl. 638, 461 F.2d 1270 (1972). In that case, the government procured the work competitively after the contractor had submitted an unacceptably high estimate of its costs to perform it. For a case in which the government did not fulfill its obligations, see *Lamb Eng'g & Constr. Co.,* EBCA C-9304172, 97-2 BCA ¶ 29,207. There the contracting officer, in the face of strong contrary evidence, not only did not issue instructions on how to proceed in light of the enormous water problems encountered, but denied the existence of a differing site condition and then insisted upon less than optimal solutions (for which he refused responsibility), twice threatened default, and was dilatory in granting reasonable relief from contract requirements. The board held that the contractor had acted with reasonable prudence and diligence.

VII. EXCULPATORY CLAUSES

The general rules regarding exculpatory clauses are discussed in Chapter 3. These rules are applied even more strictly with regard to differing site conditions, where the government has adopted a policy of relieving the contractor of the risk of unknown and unforeseen conditions.

A. General Exculpatory Clauses

The Differing Site Conditions clause is held to override broad exculpatory clauses denying government liability for express or implied representations of condition, *United Contractors v. United States*, 177 Ct. Cl. 151, 368 F.2d 585 (1966). See *SAE/Americon-Mid Atl., Inc. v. General Servs. Admin.*, GSBCA 12294, 98-2 BCA ¶ 30,084 (allowing the government to exculpate test borings "would render the Differing Site Conditions clause meaningless as to 'Type I' claims"); *Whiting-Turner/A. L. Johnson, Joint Venture v. General Servs. Admin.*, GSBCA 15401, 02-1 BCA ¶ 31,708 (if government did not want potential contractors to rely on the boring logs and other information when preparing bids, it should not have performed the tests and provided the information). A number of different types of clauses have been held to fall within the scope of this rule:

(a) Clause stating that the government denies any responsibility for the accuracy of any subsurface data furnished and expects each bidder to satisfy itself as to the character, quantity, and quality of subsurface materials to be encountered, *Morrison-Knudsen Co. v. United States*, 184 Ct. Cl. 661, 397 F.2d 826 (1968);

(b) Clause stating that the government does not guarantee that data accurately depicts subsurface conditions and that bidders must make such investigations as to subsurface conditions as they consider necessary, *A.S. Horner Constr. Co.*, ASBCA 5334, 59-2 BCA ¶ 2321;

(c) Clause stating that data furnished gives only "general" information and that the contractor is responsible based on its investigation of the site, *Kaiser Indus. Corp. v. United States*, 169 Ct. Cl. 310, 340 F.2d 322 (1965);

(d) Clause stating that poor conditions "may" be encountered, *Bernard McMenamy Contractor, Inc.*, ENGBCA 3413, 77-1 BCA ¶ 12,335;

(e) Clause stating that no consideration would be given to the nature of materials encountered, *Zinger Constr. Co.*, Comp. Gen. Dec. B-203013, 81-2 CPD ¶ 217; and

(f) Clause stating that government will not provide data and expects the contractor to make its own determinations, *Syblon-Reid Co.*, IBCA 1313-11-79, 82-2 BCA ¶ 16,019.

B. Specific Exculpatory Clauses

It cannot be assumed that all exculpatory clauses or cautionary language will be ignored. Clear and unambiguous language that specifically limits the risk assumed by the government can qualify the provisions of the Differing Site Conditions clause, *United Contractors v. United States*, 177 Ct. Cl. 151, 368 F.2d 585 (1966). See *VECA Elec. Co.*, ASBCA 47733, 95-2 BCA ¶ 27,749, *recons. denied*, 96-1 BCA ¶ 28,055, where contract language stating that the drawings depicting the location of electrical conduits were general and did not attempt to show complete detail barred the contractor's claim; *Wm. A. Smith Contracting Co. v. United States*, 188 Ct. Cl. 1062, 412 F.2d 1325 (1969), in which the court, in denying the contractor's changed condition claim, considered contract warnings that the government made no representation concerning permafrost in areas other than those shown in contract drawings; and *Jefferson Constr. Co. of Fla. v. United States*, 176 Ct. Cl. 1363, 364 F.2d 420, *cert. denied*, 386 U.S. 914 (1966), where an express statement that a borrow pit was estimated to contain too little material to perform the entire contract barred the contractor's claim. See also *Hardwick Bros. Co., II v. United States*, 36 Fed. Cl. 347 (1996), giving the government the benefit of express language limiting the usefulness of data from which the contractor could infer the amount of water to be encountered. The court stated at 407:

> [A] contractor cannot ignore any data that is supplied even though a differing site condition clause is included in the contract. *Pacific Marine Constructors - Kodiac*, 68-1 B.C.A. P 6,979 (ENG BCA 1968). The contract documents contained several important disclaimers. Special Provision 5, for example, specifically stated that the information and data provided were for information only and that the government would not be responsible for any interpretation or conclusion drawn therefrom by the contractor. Subsection (5) specifically disclosed that the information provided between drill holes was inferred and that localized variations were anticipated. If such variations were encountered, this provision warned that such variations would not be a differing site condition. Subsection (c) also warned that the bidder should satisfy himself as to "hazards likely to arise from weather conditions." Subsection (e) informed bidders that Missouri River stages would fluctuate due to releases from upriver reservoirs and that operations should be scheduled to take advantage of favorable river stages. Subsection (e) also states that: "The contractor shall make his own assumptions relative to releases "from upstream reservoirs and [their effect upon] the work to be done under this contract. The government will not be responsible for any damage resulting from supplemental river stages."

C. Relation to Representation

The extent to which an exculpatory clause will relieve the government from liability for a condition may depend on whether the condition has been impliedly or expressly indicated by the government. See *P.J. Maffei Bldg. Wrecking Corp. v. United States*, 732 F.2d 913 (Fed. Cir. 1984), in which the court held that information furnished to the contractor but expressly stated to be "not included in the contract" was properly exculpatory. The court stated at 918:

> [The contractor's] recitation of precedents holding that the Government may not escape its responsibility by exculpatory clauses is not pertinent here. This is not a case where the Government has made an explicit or implicit representation of the particular condition (at issue in the particular case) in the contract or accompanying specifications, drawings (or other documents) but nevertheless seeks to avoid responsibility for that representation by the use of general exculpatory clauses. That was true of the decisions cited by Maffei. See, e.g., *Fehlhaber Corp. v. United States*, 138 Ct. Cl. 571, 151 F. Supp. 817, 810 (Ct. Cl.), *cert. denied*, 355 U.S. 877 (1957) (contract plans and specifications described subsurface materials inaccurately); *Morrison-Knudsen Co., Inc. v. United States*, 345 F.2d 535 (Ct. Cl. 1965) (data given by Government to prospective bidders along with IFB showed no permafrost in place where Government had indeed found permafrost); *Woodcrest Construction Co. Inc. v. United States*, 408 F.2d 406, 410 (Ct. Cl. 1969), *cert. denied*, 398 U.S. 958 (1970) (core boring logs furnished bidder by Government gave "inescapable impression" that there was no subsurface condition). In the current case, on the other hand, the contract provided no basis, either explicit or implicit, for any expectation regarding the amount of steel in the Pavilion. See our discussion, *supra*. The Government's caveats in IFB provision 1.2, *supra*, did not seek to nullify a representation as to a latent condition; rather, they are consistent with, and demonstrate, the absence of any indication that the structural drawings were accurate and should be relied upon for the amount of steel to be recovered. [Footnote omitted.]

VIII. VARIATION IN ESTIMATED QUANTITIES

In most construction contracts, items of work based on estimated quantities are now priced on the basis of unit prices rather than lump sum prices. This relieves the contractor of much of the risk of inaccurate quantity estimates. In addition, in these contracts the government frequently includes a special clause permitting adjustment of the unit prices if the actual quantities vary significantly from the estimates. The standard clause for this purpose is set forth in FAR 52.211-18:

> VARIATIONS IN ESTIMATED QUANTITY (APR 1984)
>
> If the quantity of a unit-priced item in this contract is an estimated quantity and the actual quantity of the unit-priced item varies more than 15 percent above or below the estimated quantity, an equitable adjustment in the contract price shall be made upon demand of either party. The equitable adjustment shall be based upon any increase or decrease in costs due solely to the variation above 115 percent or below 85 percent of the estimated quantity. If the quantity variation is such as to cause an increase in the time necessary for completion, the Contractor may request, in writing, an extension of time, to be received by the Contracting Officer before the date of final settlement of the contract. Upon receipt of a written request for an extension, the Contracting Officer shall ascertain the facts and make an adjustment for extending the completion date as, in the judgment of the Contracting Officer, is justified.

A substantially similar clause was included in DAR 7-603.27.

A. Absent a Variation in Quantity Clause

Material variations from the government estimates of the quantity of the work can be treated as Category I differing site conditions, *United Contractors v. United States*, 177 Ct. Cl. 151, 368 F.2d 585 (1966). See also *Triad Mech., Inc.*, IBCA 3393, 97-1 BCA ¶ 28,771, where relief was granted when the contractor encountered quantities of water unanticipated by either party that were considerably higher than the government estimate.

This rule was applied to a situation where the contractor was required to submit a lump sum bid for clearing timber on an estimated number of acres and the contract contained language warning that the estimate was based on aerial photographs and that the contractor would be required to do all work over the estimate, *Schutt Constr. Co., Genoa, Wis. v. United States*, 173 Ct. Cl. 836, 353 F.2d 1018 (1965). The court reasoned that to do otherwise "would negate one of the prime reasons for incorporating a 'changed condition' article into these contracts." In *AFGO Eng'g Corp.*, VACAB 1236, 79-2 BCA ¶ 13,900, *aff'd*, 227 Ct. Cl. 730 (1981), the board found a 62 percent under-run of the quantity of rock to be a differing site condition where the contractor had relied on the government's estimate in preparing its bid.

The rule applicable in these situations was summarized in *Perini Corp. v. United States*, 180 Ct. Cl. 768, 381 F.2d 403 (1967) at 780-81:

> The cases that have applied the Changed Conditions article to substantial variations from the quantity estimated in the contract have done so on the basis that such a material deviation was not reasonably foreseeable. They deal with special situations where (1) the contractor could not have verified the estimated quantities from the contract documents and his investigation of the site; (2) he had no opportunity to investigate the conditions at the site or for other reasons had the right to rely on the Government's estimate; or (3) both parties labored under a mutual mistake as to the accuracy of the Government's estimates.

In *Perini*, the court refused to grant a downward adjustment in the unit price for pumping water when the contractor encountered substantially greater quantities of water than the government had estimated but there were numerous indications in the contract and in the site that the estimate was inaccurate. The court reasoned that no changed condition had occurred because the clause applied only in cases where the parties could not reasonably anticipate the condition. The court found, further, that there was no mutual mistake as to the quantity of water because the contractor had anticipated larger quantities in preparing its bid. See also *Quintana Constr. Co.*, IBCA 1028-4-74, 75-2 BCA ¶ 11,391.

Variations that would not have been considered material if government figures had been estimates may be considered material when the figures "are not set forth as estimates or approximations indicating to the contractor that he will have to provide against a reasonable overrun in his bid," *Gregg, Gibson & Gregg, Inc.*, ENGBCA 3041, 71-1 BCA ¶ 8677.

B. Impact of Variation in Quantity Clause

Variation in Quantity clauses will not prevent the contractor from obtaining a price adjustment under the Differing Site Conditions clause when the variation in quantity occurs because of a condition that falls within the bounds of that clause, *United Contractors v. United States*, 177 Ct. Cl. 151, 368 F.2d 585 (1966). For example, in *Continental Drilling Co.*, ENGBCA 3455, 75-2 BCA ¶ 11,541, a differing site condition was found when the contractor had to use a substantially larger quantity of a drill hole casing than the estimated quantity. The board reasoned that the government estimate of a small amount of drill hole casing was an indication that a certain type of subsurface material would be encountered, whereas the need to use a large quantity of the casing indicated that a different type of material was actually present at the site. In *A.S. Horner, Inc.*, AGBCA 76-145, 79-1 BCA ¶ 13,561, a changed condition was found when the contractor had to use different methods to excavate a trench deeper than had been anticipated, and in *Brezina Constr., Inc.*, ENGBCA 3215, 75-1 BCA ¶ 10,989, a changed condition was found where the contractor was required to dispose of a large amount of material off-site although the parties had anticipated that there would be an approximate balance between the excavated material and the material used for fill. In *Brezina*, the board found a differing site condition rather than a variation in quantity because the contractor had encountered an "entirely different job" than anticipated. Similarly, in *Dunbar & Sullivan Dredging Co.*, ENGBCA 3165, 73-2 BCA ¶ 10,285, the board found a differing site condition where the contractor encountered an unforeseen rock ledge in the river being dredged even though the contract contained a unit price for dredging rock. The board reasoned that, since the unusual methods required to remove the rock ledge were not those included in the price of dredging loose rock, a differing site condition had been encountered although the amount of rock in the ledge was less than 1 percent of the estimated quantity of rock.

The Changes clause has also been held to override the Variations in Estimated Quantity clause in situations where the government orders the contractor to perform unit-priced work in excess of that contemplated when the quantity estimates were established. For example, in *Morrison-Knudsen Co. v. United States*, 184 Ct. Cl. 661, 397 F.2d 826 (1968), the court found the contractor entitled to a price adjustment under the Changes clause when the government overcame unforeseen conditions by ordering the contractor to perform the work in a different manner. See also *C.H. Leavell & Co.*, ENGBCA 3492, 75-2 BCA ¶ 11,596, where a contracting officer's order to change the concrete mixtures was held to be a change rather than a variation in quantity although there was a unit price in the contract for cement. The board reasoned that Variations in Estimated Quantity clauses "do not control when the cost of doing the work greatly differs from the stated unit price because of changes ordered by the government. In such event, the 'Changes' clause comes into play and overrides the special clause." Compare *Luedtke Eng'g Co.*, ASBCA 54226, 05-1 BCA ¶ 32,971, in which the board refused to agree that the Changes clause applied where the contractor had pursued the entire claim under the Variation in Estimated Quantity clause.

It has also been held that a variation in quantity clause will not apply if the original government estimate is negligently made, *Womack v. United States*, 182 Ct. Cl. 399, 389 F.2d 793 (1968). The court noted at 413:

> The clause does not require one party to bear the first 25 percent of the burden of the other party's negligence.

See also *John Murphy Constr. Co.*, AGBCA 418, 79-1 BCA ¶ 13,836. Neither will the contractor be given the benefit of the clause if it performs additional work because of its mismanagement of the project, *George Ledford Constr., Inc.*, ENGBCA 6218, 97-2 BCA ¶ 29,172.

In *Chemical Tech., Inc. v. United States*, 227 Ct. Cl. 120, 645 F.2d 934 (1981), a contract for mess attendant services priced at a fixed monthly rate contained a volume variation clause. Such a clause did not limit government liability where the government was unreasonable in computing its estimate of meals to be served. The government failed to disclose its superior knowledge regarding reserve training, which would increase monthly meals. The court noted at 145:

> In its dealings with contractors, the Government cannot provide inaccurate data in this manner and then be allowed to bar an equitable recovery by arguing that the resulting damages (in this case, a large increase in meals fed) fall within the 25 percent Volume Variation clause.

If a variation in quantity clause is used in an indefinite-delivery, indefinite-quantity contract, the government is liable for a price adjustment under the clause if it issues no orders for some of the work, *Westland Mech., Inc.*, ASBCA 48844, 96-2 BCA ¶ 28,419.

C. Interpretation of Variation in Quantity Clause

Variations in Estimated Quantity clauses provide that the unit prices set forth in the contract are to apply to all quantities of work within the range specified in the clause and that either party may demand repricing of the work that falls outside that range. In *N. Fiorito Co. v. United States*, 189 Ct. Cl. 215, 416 F.2d 1284 (1969), it was held that this type of clause binds the parties to the unit prices for quantities of work up to the full extent of the variation range (110 percent of the estimated quantity in the clause in question) with repricing to occur only as to the quantities in excess of the range. The standard clause at FAR 52.212-11 provides that any equitable adjustment under the clause will be based on increases or decreases in cost "due solely to the variation above 115 percent or below 85 percent of the estimated quantity." There have been a number of decisions containing conflicting interpretations of this language. The issue has been whether the unit prices for the quantities above 115 percent and below 85 percent of the estimated quantity should be (1) completely repriced or (2) adjusted only by the increased or decreased cost caused by the variation. In *Victory Constr. Co. v. United States*, 206 Ct. Cl. 274, 510 F.2d 1379 (1975), the court held that the party demanding the adjustment had the burden of proof that the costs had varied because of the difference in quantity and that the amount of the equitable adjustment was to be determined *solely* on the basis of the difference in cost because of the larger or smaller quantity rather than on a complete repricing of the work based on actual incurred costs for the excess quantity. In arriving at this conclusion, the court overruled the Corps of Engineers Board of Contract Appeals, which had held that the adjustment should be based on costs incurred for the added work, *Victory Constr. Co.,* ENGBCA 3009, 69-2 BCA ¶ 7920; *Dunbar & Sullivan Dredging Co.*, ENGBCA 3165, 73-2 BCA ¶ 10,285. However, see *Bean Dredging Co.*, ENGBCA 5507, 89-3 BCA ¶ 22,034, in which the board permitted the complete repricing of the quantity that exceeded 115 percent of the estimate. The board distinguished this decision from *Victory* on the grounds that in this case the actual unit costs for the nonadjustable quantities differed materially from the contract unit prices. In *Foley Co. v. United States*, 26 Cl. Ct. 936 (1992) *aff'd,* 11 F.3d 1032 (Fed. Cir. 1993), the Claims Court adopted the limited repricing interpretation and denied the government a reduction in the unit prices for the quantity exceeding 115 percent of the estimate because the government did not establish that the contractor's costs were reduced by the overrun. On appeal, the Court of Appeals for the Federal Circuit addressed the question of the interpretation of the language of the clause, with the majority of the court rejecting the complete repricing approach. In doing so, the court cited the binding precedent established by the Court of Claims in *Victory* and stated, "The express language of the VEQ clause precludes an equitable adjustment based on anything other than the contractor's costs."

It is difficult to prove that the higher or lower costs of increased quantities were solely the result of the increased quantity. See *S&T Enter.*, AGBCA 2002-159-1, 03-2 BCA ¶ 32,282 (denying the contractor's claim for an increase in unit price because it did not prove the higher costs resulted from the increased quantity), and *Ronald Adams Contractor, Inc.*, AGBCA 91-155-1, 94-3 BCA ¶ 27,018 (denying the government's claim for a reduction in the unit price of excess water used by the contractor because it did not prove that the lower costs incurred were the result of the higher quantity of water). However, in *Clement-Mtarri Cos.*, ASBCA 38,170, 92-3 BCA ¶ 25,192, *recons. denied*, 93-2 BCA ¶ 25,567, *aff'd*, 11 F.3d 1072 (Fed. Cir. 1993), the board granted an adjustment under the Variation in Estimated Quantity clause by computing the difference between the actual cost of the estimated quantity and the actual cost of the overrun quantity. Similarly, in *Gulf Constr. Group, Inc.*, ENGBCA 5944, 94-1 BCA ¶ 26,525, the board held that the adjustment for an underrun would be computed by comparing the cost of performing the actual work with the revenue that would have been derived at the contract unit prices. See also *NATCO Ltd. P'ship*, ENGBCA 6183, 96-1 BCA ¶ 28,062, holding that the computation of the costs of an under-run of the quantities can include both direct and indirect costs.

CHAPTER 6

DELAYS

Delays that neither party anticipated at the time they entered into the contract are some of the most frequent occurrences during the performance of government contracts. In determining the consequences of events that delay performance, general risk allocation principles have been supplemented by standard contract clauses. Under these clauses, the time and cost effects of delays are dealt with separately. Excusable delays provisions deal with the types of events that protect the contractor from sanctions for late performance. The Suspension of Work, Government Delay of Work, and Stop—Work Order clauses cover the circumstances that permit or prohibit the recovery of costs associated with delays. The interpretation of these clauses has resulted in a rather precise scheme of risk allocation for delays. The contractor bears the risk of both time and cost for delays that it causes or that are within its control. Generally, a contractor is excused from performance because of delays caused by factors for which neither it nor the government is responsible; however, the contractor must bear the cost impact of such delays. The government is responsible for both time and cost effects of delays that it causes, that are under its control, or for which it has agreed to compensate the contractor.

This system of risk allocation has been in use for a number of years and has resulted in an equitable distribution of risks in most cases. However, in recent years the risks of delay by events outside the control of either contracting party have increased significantly, with the result that the present risk allocation system sometimes places a great burden on the contractor. For example, environmental and energy problems have imposed substantially increased risks on contractors. Contractor responsibility for performance and the limitation of relief to additional time in cases of delays caused by outside factors can require the contractor to assume risks that may be difficult or impossible to price.

This risk allocation scheme is not completely precise in application. For example, the contractor may obtain some relief for the cost of delays through the doctrines of impossibility or commercial impracticability. In addition, interpretations of the Suspension of Work clause have held that the government assumes the risk of the cost as well as the time of certain unreasonable delays even though it did not cause the delay. Thus, the time-money distinctions appear to have become somewhat blurred in recent years.

I. EXCUSABLE DELAYS

Contract provisions dealing with excusable delays are found in a number of different standard clauses. The primary function of these provisions is to protect the contractor from sanctions for late performance. To the extent that the contractor has been excusably delayed, it is protected from default termination, liquidated damages, actual damages, or excess costs of reprocurement or completion. Excusable delays also may lead to recovery of additional compensation if the government constructively accelerates performance (as discussed in Chapter 4).

Most excusable delays involve temporary work interruptions. When the impediment is removed, the contractor is expected to resume performance, *Consolidated Molded Prods. Corp. v. United States*, 220 Ct. Cl. 594, 600 F.2d 793 (1979). *Restatement, Second, Contracts* § 269 contains a similar rule for temporary impracticability of performance but relieves the contractor of the obligation to resume performance if it is "materially more burdensome."

Whether or not a delay is viewed as excusable will depend on the language of the particular provision in question. Excusable delays in fixed-price supply and service contracts are governed by ¶¶ (c) and (d) of the Default clause contained in FAR 52.249-8, as follows:

> (c) Except for defaults of subcontractors at any tier, the Contractor shall not be liable for any excess costs if the failure to perform the contract arises from causes beyond the control and without the fault or negligence of the Contractor. Examples of such causes include (1) acts of God or of the public enemy, (2) acts of Government in either its sovereign or contractual capacity, (3) fires, (4) floods, (5) epidemics, (6) quarantine restrictions, (7) strikes, (8) freight embargoes, and (9) unusually severe weather. In each instance the failure to perform must be beyond the control and without the fault or negligence of the Contractor.
>
> (d) If the failure to perform is caused by the default of a subcontractor at any tier, and if the cause of the default is beyond the control of both the Contractor and subcontractor, and without the fault or negligence of either, the Contractor shall not be liable for any excess costs for failure to perform, unless the subcontracted supplies or services were obtainable from other sources in sufficient time for the Contractor to meet the required delivery schedule.

Excusable delays in fixed-price construction contracts are dealt with in ¶ (b) of the Default clause in FAR 52.249-10:

> (b) The Contractor's right to proceed shall not be terminated nor the Contractor charged with damages under this clause, if—
>
>> (1) The delay in completing the work arises from unforeseeable causes beyond the control and without the fault or negligence of the Contractor. Examples of such causes include (i) acts of God or of the public enemy, (ii) acts of the Government in either its sovereign or contractual capacity, (iii) acts of another Contractor in the performance of a contract with the Government, (iv) fires, (v) floods, (vi) epidemics, (vii) quarantine restrictions, (viii) strikes, (ix) freight embargoes, (x) unusually severe weather, or (xi) delays of subcontractors or suppliers at any tier arising from unfore-

> seeable causes beyond the control and without the fault or negligence of both the Contractor and the subcontractors or suppliers; and
>
> (2) The Contractor, within 10 days from the beginning of any delay (unless extended by the Contracting Officer), notifies the Contracting Officer in writing of the causes of delay. The Contracting Officer shall ascertain the facts and the extent of delay. If, in the judgment of the Contracting Officer, the findings of fact warrant such action, the time for completing the work shall be extended. The findings of the Contracting Officer shall be final and conclusive on the parties, but subject to appeal under the Disputes clause.

For contracts for commercial items, under FAR Part 12, ¶ (f) of the Contract Terms and Conditions—Commercial items clause in FAR 52.212-4 has a similar listing but adds another excusable delay basis, "delays of common carriers."

These clauses govern the parties' rights and obligations with respect to delays not covered by other contract provisions. The equitable adjustment to which the contractor is entitled under the Changes, Differing Site Conditions, and other contract clauses provides for time adjustments as well as money. Delays associated with actions under such clauses would not ordinarily be considered under the excusable delays provisions. However, the Suspension of Work clause does not provide for time adjustments. Thus, additional time for a suspension of work must be obtained under the excusable delays provisions.

A. General Requirements

The fact that a delay arises from one of the causes specifically referred to in the excusable delay provisions of the contract is, by itself, insufficient to justify the granting of an excusable delay. Not every fire, quarantine, strike, or freight embargo is an excuse for delay under the default clauses, *United States v. Brooks-Callaway Co.*, 318 U.S. 120 (1943). If such were the case, contractors could set fire to their own factories and successfully claim excusable delay. Thus, the general requirements of a clause are of paramount importance in determining whether an excusable delay has occurred. These general requirements apply to all excusable delays, whether or not the particular delay is specifically enumerated in the clause.

1. "Beyond the Control" of the Contractor

The first general requirement for excusability is that the event must be "beyond the control" of the contractor. The term has been applied in three ways. If an event is considered to be *foreseeable* at the time of contracting and the contractor enters into the contract without making provisions to protect itself, the event may be held not to be beyond its control because it assumed the risk. The second application deals with events that the contractor could *prevent* from occurring. Such events are literally within the contractor's control. Finally, events may not be beyond the contractor's control if it could have *overcome* the effects of the event.

When the event is considered foreseeable, the contractor may be held responsible for making alternative arrangements for performance or may be considered to have assumed the risk of the event. In *Hitemp Wires Co.*, ASBCA 11638, 67-1 BCA ¶ 6252, which involved a supply contract for copper wire, the board rejected the contractor's contention that the default was excusable because the copper market had been disrupted by military needs resulting from the Vietnam conflict. The board found that the escalation of the military effort in Vietnam was well underway at the time of contracting and its effect on the copper market was clear to the contractor as a fabricator and supplier of copper products. It was, therefore, not beyond the contractor's control. See also *E.L. David Constr. Co.*, ASBCA 29224, 90-3 BCA ¶ 23,025, involving a construction contract for the replacement of air conditioners on an Air Force base. The contractor claimed excusable delay due to difficulties encountered in processing the equipment through a foreign nation's customs and import procedures. The board found the delay foreseeable and denied relief, stating that it was the contractor's responsibility to assure itself before bidding that the specified equipment could be obtained on time to meet the contract's schedule. See also *Sierra Tahoe Mfg., Inc. v. General Servs. Admin.*, GSBCA 12679, 94-2 BCA ¶ 26,771 (delays in a supply contract due to a supplier's bankruptcy foreseeable where contractor had extended its bid with full knowledge of the supplier's bankruptcy), and *Earth Tech. Indus., Ltd.,* ASBCA 46450, 99-1 BCA ¶ 30,341 (foreseeable because contractor chose non-listed source to test aggregate).

If the contractor can prevent an event from occurring, it is not beyond its control. For example, in *Fox Constr., Inc. v. General Servs. Admin.*, GSBCA 11543, 93-3 BCA ¶ 26,193, a contractor was held responsible for freeze damage to air conditioning condenser units. The contractor argued that the damage was due to the government's breach of the implied warranty of the specifications and to delays in approving the switch gear, which resulted in a lack of electrical power at the site until February 1991. However, the board denied relief, holding that, although the contractor was technically correct, it failed to show that the damage was directly attributable to the design defect. The board found instead that the freeze damage to the coils was due to the contractor's failure to anticipate the need to perform pressure testing with a liquid other than water or with air. Similarly, in *American Constr. Co.*, ENGBCA 5728, 91-2 BCA ¶ 24,009, the board denied a contractor's claim of excusable delay, finding that the actual cause of delay was the concurrent performance of other contracts to which the contractor gave higher priority. See also *General Cutlery*, GSBCA 13154, 96-1 BCA ¶ 27,957 (time used to work on other contract does not justify or excuse a delay in performing a newly awarded contract because the timing of the contracts is foreseeable and within the contractor's control); *F.J.R. Builders, Inc.*, ASBCA 36293, 92-1 BCA ¶ 24,757 (delays caused by the contractor's problems with subcontractors, its allocation of resources, and its decision to perform contract tasks sequentially instead of concurrently were within the contractor's area of responsibility and unexcusable); and *Wellington House*, GSBCA 14665, 99-1 BCA ¶ 30,279 (failure to deliver due to subcontractor credit and pricing problems was the responsibility of the contractor and therefore did not constitute an excusable delay). However, compare *Ace Elecs. Assocs., Inc.*, ASBCA 13899, 69-2 BCA ¶ 7922, where a power surge damaged the contractor's testing equipment. In granting relief the board found that the contractor did all it could to bring such occurrences to the attention of the utility. It also found that there was no practical means by which the incoming power could be regulated to prevent such damage.

The most difficult application of the "beyond the control" rule is in cases where the government contends that the contractor should have overcome the delay. For some types of delays there are specific requirements. Under the supply contract excusable delays provisions, subcontractor delays are not excusable if the supplies can be obtained elsewhere. Similarly, FAR 22.101-2(b) provides that the contractor should be expected to take a number of actions to overcome the delays of strikes. See Section B.1.a. Whether covered by specific requirements or not, this application of the rule has not been uniform. In some cases, particularly those involving shortages of materials, relief may be denied unless the contractor demonstrates that it would be impossible or commercially impracticable to overcome the delay, *Jennie-O Foods, Inc. v. United States*, 217 Ct. Cl. 314, 580 F.2d 400 (1978).

Proving commercial impracticability can be difficult. In a fixed-price contract, demonstrating economic hardship alone does not constitute impossibility of performance—the contractor must establish the unavailability of alternative sources of supply that would have permitted it to meet the contract's delivery schedule, *Progressive Tool Corp.*, ASBCA 42809, 94-1 BCA ¶ 26,413. If there was an alternate source at a higher cost, the source will be considered available unless the cost was exorbitant. For example, in *C&M Mach. Prods., Inc.*, ASBCA 43348, 93-2 BCA ¶ 25,748, the board denied the contractor's claim of commercial impracticability, stating that "C&M has not shown that the plating cost was so exorbitant that no buyer would be willing to pay a price which included that cost." See also *RAPOCO, Inc.*, ASBCA 39371, 93-1 BCA ¶ 25,308 (increase of 31 percent of the bid price per room to repair wallboard was not an amount more than a reasonable buyer would have paid, nor was it an extreme and unreasonable expense), and *Gulf & Western Indus., Inc.*, ASBCA 21090, 87-2 BCA ¶ 19,881 (cost overrun of 50 percent to 70 percent not sufficient to constitute commercial impracticability).

However, it appears that proving complete impossibility is not necessary. In *Dessert Seed Co.*, GSBCA 5438, Feb. 29, 1980, *Unpub.*, heavy rain reduced the amount of the contractor's crop of grass seed by 85 percent. The government terminated for default, reprocured from another source, and argued that the contractor's refusal to supply the seed was not excusable since it could have been obtained from another source. The board held that the contractor had been excusably delayed because the unusually severe weather had destroyed most of the contractor's crops and those of other growers in the relatively small area where such seed is grown. The board observed that the contractor had made a good faith effort to obtain enough seed to fill as many government orders as possible. See also *Unicon Mgmt. Corp.*, ASBCA 10196, 65-1 BCA ¶ 4778, where a strike prevented the contractor from obtaining steel bar joists from its supplier. The board held that the contractor was not obligated to procure the joists "elsewhere at greatly excessive cost." A similar result was reached in *International Elecs. Corp. v. United States*, 227 Ct. Cl. 208, 646 F.2d 496 (1981), in which the contractor obtained relief after making "herculean," but unsuccessful, efforts to obtain necessary personnel.

These interpretations of the phrase "beyond the control," as well as unforeseeability, were discussed in *Automated Extruding & Packaging, Inc.*, GSBCA 4036, 74-2 BCA ¶ 10,949, *recons. denied*, 75-1 BCA ¶ 11,067, which held that the Arab oil embargo of 1973 was an event beyond the control of the contractor. The *Automated* case involved a supply contract for polyethylene plastic bags composed of petroleum-based resin. The contract was awarded before the embargo was imposed. The board stated, "We believe that the imposition of the embargo was unexpected and unforeseen by both parties," and it concluded that the embargo was "beyond the control . . . of either party." The contractor could not have prevented the embargo from occurring and, because it was unforeseeable, was unable to provide against it, and there was no alternative action that it could have taken once it occurred.

The inconsistency of the decisions in this area is illustrated by cases such as *Southern Flooring & Insulating Co.*, GSBCA 1360, 1964 BCA ¶ 4480, holding that the contractor had no duty to go to a two-shift operation to overcome the effects of unusually severe weather, and *Kevin Wells*, AGBCA 82-284-3, 83-1 BCA ¶ 16,507, *recons. denied*, 83-2 BCA ¶ 16,705, holding that the contractor was not obligated to have its crew walk one mile or drive another more circuitous route to overcome a blocked site access road.

2. Without Contractor's Fault or Negligence

In addition to being beyond the contractor's control, the event that caused the delay must be without the contractor's fault or negligence. "Fault or negligence" refers to acts or omissions of the contractor that cause delay. In *KARPAK Data & Design*, IBCA 2944, 93-1 BCA ¶ 25,360, the board denied relief to a drafting contractor who claimed that government-imposed excessive workloads excused the contractor's default. The contract established that the contractor need not honor orders that exceeded a certain number of drawings, but it imposed on the contractor the obligation to inform the government that it would not honor the excessive orders that it received. The board held that, because the delay was due to the contractor's failure to notify the government of its inability to perform all the work, the delay was not without the contractor's fault or negligence and, therefore, did not constitute an excusable delay. In *California Dredging Co.*, ENGBCA 5532, 92-1 BCA ¶ 24,475, relief was denied to a contractor who failed to establish the excusability of a performance delay that resulted from the sinking of its dredge. The board found that the sinking of the dredge was due to the negligence of the contractor because it had failed to overcome the maritime presumption that the dredge was unseaworthy. See also *J.R. Erickson*, AGBCA 333, 76-1 BCA ¶ 11,716 (denying relief for a delay due to damage to machinery caused by the contractor's negligence in unloading).

Some cases combine elements of fault or negligence with findings that the event causing the delay was within the control of the contractor. See *Akwa-Downey Constr. Co.*, ASBCA 14823, 75-1 BCA ¶ 11,254, *recons. denied*, 75-2 BCA ¶ 11,405, in which a contractor was denied relief for a delay caused by the embezzlement of funds by its secretary-treasurer. The board found that the contractor was negligent in not discovering the embezzlement and, further, that the embezzlement of funds by a corporate officer is an act within the control of the contractor. See also *C&M Mach. Prods., Inc.*, ASBCA 43348, 93-2 BCA ¶ 25,748, in which the board found that the failure of a contractor's chosen subcontractor to provide adequate plating for piston rods did not excuse the contractor's failure to deliver the rods, because the plating could have been provided by another subcontractor. Hence, the board held the default was not beyond the control or without the fault or negligence of the contractor.

3. Foreseeability

The excusable delays provision in construction contracts requires that excusable delays arise from unforeseeable causes. Foreseeability is generally equated with knowledge or reason to know prior to bidding, *Harriss & Covington Hosiery Mills, Inc.*, ASBCA 260, 4 CCF ¶ 60,806 (1949); *Arthur Venneri Co.*, GSBCA 847-851, 1964 BCA ¶ 4010; *Woodington Corp.*, ASBCA 37885, 91-1 BCA ¶ 23,579. A contractor is expected to know or have reason to know of those facts that are within the scope of its business operations pertaining to or possibly affecting its contract, *Diversified Marine Tech, Inc.*, DOTCAB 2455, 93-2 BCA ¶ 25,720. However, the mere possibility that an event might occur does not establish foreseeability, *J.D. Hedin Constr. Co. v. United States*, 187 Ct. Cl. 45, 408 F.2d 424 (1969). In *J.D. Hedin*, the Court of Claims reversed a Veterans Administration Board decision that had found a cement shortage to be foreseeable. The court found that the board had unrealistically viewed the foreseeability of the shortage and had imposed too high a standard of foresight upon the contractor, expecting it to have "prophetic insight and to take extraordinary preventive action which it is simply not reasonable to ask of the normal contractor."

The burden of proving an event unforeseeable falls on the contractor, *Orbas & Assocs.*, ASBCA 35832, 89-3 BCA ¶ 22,023. In discussing unforeseeability, the boards often consider whether the delay was caused by an existing or supervening event. Existing causes of delay are considered to be within the scope of the contractor's implied knowledge and not unforeseeable, *Chas. I. Cunningham*, IBCA 242, 60-2 BCA ¶ 2816. In *Cunningham*, the board stated the general rule that unforeseeable causes refer to future events, not existing ones. *Cunningham* involved a construction contract awarded during a steel strike. The board denied relief, holding that while the duration of the strike was unforeseeable, the strike itself was not. See also *Fraser Constr. Co. v. United States*, 384 F.3d 1354 (Fed. Cir. 2004) (occurrence of high water once every five years was foreseeable), and *J.H. Strain & Sons, Inc.*, ASBCA 34432, 90-2 BCA ¶ 22,770 (delay in delivery of pipe was foreseeable because the contractor knew that the specified pipe was unusual and that it was not one of its supplier's inventory items, and the supplier had informed the contractor that the specified pipe was made to order from noninventory materials).

Unforeseeability can be a high barrier to overcome. In *Electrical Enters., Inc.*, IBCA 972-9-72, 74-1 BCA ¶ 10,400, a construction contractor planned on obtaining supplies of crushed rock from a nearby quarry located next to railroad tracks. The quarry owner told the contractor that it had a right to cross the tracks whenever necessary and that other contractors had thus used the quarry with no problems. However, as soon as the contractor was ready to start transporting rock from the quarry, the owner of the track threatened to sue for trespass. After a two-month delay, a crossing agreement was negotiated. The board held that the delay was not unforeseeable since the contractor could reasonably be expected to foresee and expect some difficulties involving the crossing of a track owned by the railroad in the absence of an inquiry to the owner of the track. See also *S. Head Painting Contractor, Inc.*, ASBCA 26249, 82-1 BCA ¶ 15,629, *recons. denied*, 82-2 BCA ¶ 15,886 (Christmas holiday closing of a paint supplier not unforeseeable); *E.L. David Constr. Co.*, ASBCA 29224, 90-3 BCA ¶ 23,025 (annual vacation shutdown of supplier's plant not unforeseeable); and *Local Contractors, Inc.*, ASBCA 37108, 92-1 BCA ¶ 24,491, *recons. denied*, 92-1 BCA ¶ 24,693, *aff'd*, 988 F.2d 131 (Fed. Cir. 1993) (inadequacy of technical data package not unforeseeable because contractor knew of missing documentation before it signed contract).

The supply and services contract provisions do not state that events causing a delay must be "unforeseeable" in order for the delay to be excusable. In addition, with respect to construction contracts, FAR 52.249-10, Alternate II provides that contracts awarded during a period of national emergency may contain a revised clause that deletes the "unforeseeable" requirement and inserts the phrase "other than normal weather." However, 50 U.S.C. § 1601 et seq. terminates certain statutory powers based on the existence of a national emergency two years after it had begun.

The requirement that, to demonstrate excusability, an event causing a delay must be unforeseeable in a construction contract but not in a supply contract was expressly considered in 39 Comp. Gen. 478 (B-141269) (1959), which involved both supply and construction contracts awarded during a steel strike that continued during the performance of the contracts. The GAO held that, although the strike was beyond the control and without the fault or negligence of either contractor, because it was foreseeable, the delay was excusable only for the supply contract. An important consideration in the reasoning of these decisions was that in both instances the government had full knowledge of the strike prior to entering into the contract and did nothing to change the wording of the supply contract, which stated that a strike, beyond the control and without the fault or negligence of the contractor, would be an excusable delay. Similarly, in *Hagstrom Constr. Co.*, ASBCA 5698, 61-1 BCA ¶ 3090, the Armed Services Board employed this same reasoning to grant relief for a strike when the word "unforeseeable" had been deleted from the construction contract clause.

While the foreseeability of an event may not in itself defeat excusability in contracts that do not contain the "unforeseeable" requirement, the fact that the contractor knows or has reason to know of its probable occurrence may be pivotal in establishing that it could have taken alternative action. Thus, it may be concluded that the event was within its control or that it assumed the risk of its occurrence.

B. Causes of Delay

Examples of the types of events for which the contractor is entitled to an excusable delay are spelled out in the clauses. The first subsection discusses issues involving *specifically enumerated* causes of delay. The second subsection deals with the rationale of the courts in determining the excusability of delays resulting from events not specifically listed in the clauses.

1. Enumerated Causes of Delay

While the contract clauses contain slightly different lists of events that can be classified as excusable delays, they all contain a substantial number of common events. As discussed earlier, such events will lead to excusable delays only if the contractor meets the general requirements of the clauses.

a. Strikes

Delays caused by strikes are generally excusable. Strikes include job actions by a contractor's own employees, *Bill's Janitor Serv.*, ASBCA 10345, 65-2 BCA ¶ 4916, and by a subcontractor's employees, *Electronic & Missile Facilities, Inc.*, ASBCA 9325, 1964 BCA ¶ 4127. They also encompass other job actions that have the effect of a strike against the contractor, such as organizational strikes, *Fred A. Arnold, Inc.*, ASBCA 16506, 72-2 BCA ¶ 9608; jurisdictional strikes, *Manufacturers' Cas. Ins. Co. v. United States*, 105 Ct. Cl. 342, 63 F. Supp. 759 (1946); pickets protesting another contractor at the site, *Montgomery Ross Fisher, Inc.*, ASBCA 16843, 73-1 BCA ¶ 9799; a walkout in protest of contractor's accommodation, at government direction, of nonunion employees of another contractor, *Santa Fe Eng'rs, Inc.*, PSBCA 902, 84-2 BCA ¶ 17,377; and informational strikes, *Andrews Constr. Co.*, GSBCA 4364, 75-2 BCA ¶ 11,598. The boards have also granted relief for delays caused by impending strikes, *Products Eng'g Corp.*, GSBCA 3479, 72-2 BCA ¶ 9627; *Caskel Forge, Inc.*, ASBCA 6205, 60-2 BCA ¶ 2718, *recons. denied*,

61-1 BCA ¶ 2891. In *Capitol Coal Sales Corp.*, ASBCA 16551, 73-1 BCA ¶ 9779, a wildcat strike shutting down all mines in a six-state area entitled the contractor to an excusable delay.

In order to obtain an excusable delay for a strike, a contractor must prove that it acted reasonably by not wrongfully precipitating or prolonging the strike and took steps to avoid its effect. FAR 22.101-2(b) states:

> Labor disputes may cause work stoppages that delay the performance of government contracts. Contracting officers shall impress upon contractors that each contractor shall be held accountable for reasonably avoidable delays. Standard contract clauses dealing with default, excusable delays, etc., do not relieve contractors or subcontractors from the responsibility for delays that are within the contractors' or their subcontractors' control. A delay caused by a strike that the contractor or subcontractor could not reasonably prevent can be excused; however, it cannot be excused beyond the point at which a reasonably diligent contractor or subcontractor could have acted to end the strike by actions such as
>
> (1) Filing a charge with the National Labor Relations Board [NLRB] to permit the Board to seek injunctive relief in court;
>
> (2) Using other available government procedures; and
>
> (3) Using private boards or organizations to settle disputes.

In *Seaview Elec. Co.*, ASBCA 7189, 1962 BCA ¶ 3331, *rev'd on other grounds sub nom. D. Joseph DeVito v. United States*, 188 Ct. Cl. 979, 413 F.2d 1147 (1969), the board denied relief, finding that neither the contractor nor the subcontractor had acted reasonably in the face of a job slowdown. The subcontractor had tried to hide its labor difficulties, while the contractor was not diligent by failing to learn of them. In *Diversacon Indus., Inc.*, ENGBCA 3284, 76-1 BCA ¶ 11,875, the board, in denying the contractor's claim, accepted the NLRB's decision that the contractor's unfair labor practice had caused the disputed strike. A contractor's argument that a United Parcel Service strike excused late delivery, even though alternative carriers were available, was rejected, *Comspace Corp.,* DOTBCA 3095, 98-2 BCA ¶ 30,037.

b. Weather

Proper analysis of delays caused by unusually severe weather requires that the parties consider not only the severity of the weather but the type of work being performed and the effect of the weather on the work. Thus, for a determination that it is entitled to a time extension for unusually severe weather, the contractor must demonstrate (1) that the weather was unforeseeable, that is, unusually severe, and (2) that critical work was actually delayed by the weather.

(1) Unusually Severe

Generally, unusually severe weather is weather that is abnormal compared to the past weather at the same location for the same time of year, *Cape Ann Granite Co. v. United States*, 100 Ct. Cl. 53, *cert. denied*, 321 U.S. 790 (1943). In *Randolph & Co.*, ASBCA 52953, 03-1 BCA ¶ 32,080, *recons. denied*, 03-1 BCA ¶ 32,138, citing *Arundel Corp. v. United States,* 103 Ct. Cl. 688, *cert. denied*, 326 U.S. 752 (1945), the board held "When the actual adverse weather exceeds the historical average number of days to be expected within a given time, then time extensions will be allowed."

Since the weather causing the delay must be abnormal for that time of year and location, the fact that a contractor encounters extremely harsh weather that in fact prevents it from working is alone insufficient for finding an excusable delay if such weather is normal for the contract site. In *Cape Ann*, the contractor claimed that unusually severe weather delayed completion of a contract to repair jetties. In denying this claim, the court held that the contractor was on notice of the normally harsh weather conditions during the contract period and that the harsh weather was therefore foreseeable and, though severe, not unusually so. See also *Diversified Marine Tech, Inc.*, DOTBCA 2455, 93-2 BCA ¶ 25,720 (denying relief to a ship repair contractor for delay caused by frequent rain and high humidity because the weather conditions were foreseeable in the area of contract performance); *M. Zanis Contracting Corp.*, DOTBCA 2756, 96-2 BCA ¶ 28,439 (ice floes in the Connecticut River during winter months).

Weather statistics must relate to the place of performance. See *J&M Lumber, Inc.*, ASBCA 25951, 82-1 BCA ¶ 15,500, *recons. denied*, 82-1 BCA ¶ 15,617, where the government improperly rejected an excusable delay claim using weather data at the lumber supplier's location in northern Louisiana, which showed only normal precipitation during the period. The board found that the sawmill and the logging road that had been blocked as a result of heavy rains were in an area below sea level nearer to the Gulf of Mexico and that the weather over that general area of Louisiana was unusually severe.

Normally, proof that weather is unusually severe is accomplished through the comparison of United States weather statistics for past periods in the area with those recorded during the period of performance. Weather in the past is usually proved by using a five or ten-year record, *Allied Contractors, Inc.*, IBCA 265, 1962 BCA ¶ 3501, *recons. denied*, 1962 BCA ¶ 3591 (10-year period); *Skip Kirchdorfer, Inc.*, ASBCA 40515, 00-1 BCA ¶ 30,622 (five-year period); *Essential Constr. Co.*, ASBCA 18491, 78-2 BCA ¶ 13,314 (five-year period). However, in *D.F.K. Enter., Inc. d/b/a American Coatings v. United States,* 45 Fed. Cl. 280 (1999), the court concluded that a weather chart provided in the bid package could reasonably be relied upon by contractor as an affirmative representation of past weather conditions. Proof of weather conditions during performance is frequently done by using weather data but may also be accomplished by field logs, *Thomas J. Doyle*, ASBCA 13786, 72-2

BCA ¶ 9480. See *Commercial Union Ins. Co.*, PSBCA 258, 77-2 BCA ¶ 12,691, using both the number of rain days and the amount of precipitation in computing the adjustment. See also *Aulson Roofing, Inc.*, ASBCA 37677, 91-2 BCA ¶ 23,720, where a construction contractor experienced unusually severe weather that entitled it to an extension of time. However, the board held that the contractor was not entitled to an additional day's time for each day of rain because some rain delay was to be expected.

Some contracts contain a special clause which specifies the number of anticipated adverse weather days for the contract period and provides that no extension of time will be granted until the number of actual adverse days exceeds those anticipated. See *Cole's Constr. Co.*, ENGBCA 6158, 96-2 BCA ¶ 28,579, and *J.A. Jones Constr. Co.*, ENGBCA 6252, 97-1 BCA ¶ 28,918. Occasionally a contract will include clauses which shift the risk of adverse weather to a contractor. See *Con-Seal, Inc.*, ASBCA 41544, 97-1 BCA ¶ 28,819 (two clauses which required the contractor to assume the costs of hurricane preparation), and *J.C. Equip. Corp.*, ASBCA 42879, 97-2 BCA ¶ 29,197, *aff'd*, 360 F.3d 1311 (Fed. Cir. 2004) (contractor "responsible" for storm protection, dewatering, and for ensuring the trench was suitable for pipe laying under the contract).

(2) Impact of the Weather

An excusable delay should not be granted for unusually severe weather unless the contractor has shown that the weather actually had an *adverse impact* on critical work, *Skip Kirchdorfer, Inc.*, ASBCA 40515, 00-1 BCA ¶ 30,622 (excusable delay granted for only those days where unusual weather stopped work); *Fraya S. E.*, ASBCA 52222, 02-2 BCA ¶ 31,975 (contractor failed to prove how the hurricane delayed its selection of a qualified quality control manager for its administrative submittals). Thus, the mere comparison of past statistical averages with weather during the period of performance without considering the actual impact on the work has been criticized as an "unacceptable abstract basis," *Essential Constr. Co.*, ASBCA 18491, 78-2 BCA ¶ 13,314. In *Essential*, the Army used the so-called "Lellis formula" and denied relief for nine days of heavy rain during June on the basis of an eight and a half day average of time lost due to rain in the past five years. The board stated at 65,122:

> The key to time extensions for unusually severe weather is not the cause per se, i.e., the weather, but the effect of the unforeseen weather on the work being performed, *Montgomery Constr. Corp.*, ASBCA 5000, 59-1 BCA ¶ 2211; *Sunset Constr. Co., Inc.*, IBCA 454-9-64, 65-2 BCA ¶ 5188; *Gibbs Shipyard*, ASBCA 9809, 67-2 BCA ¶ 6499. For example, an exceptionally heavy one-day rain could have a serious adverse effect on a construction site highly subject to erosion. However, the same exceptionally heavy rain would cause less delay than a lighter rain continuously falling over a period of several days would cause on activities such as exterior painting. A light wind would normally have little if any effect on

> a construction project but if dust laden it could preclude activities such as painting or installation of sensitive electronic equipment. In construction work particularly sensitive to freezing, such as some paving and most masonry construction, a temperature of 10 degrees below zero probably would have no greater adverse effect than one of 10 degrees above.

Similarly, in *Commonwealth Elec. Co.*, EBCA 103-12-79, 84-1 BCA ¶ 16,961, the contractor demonstrated that the average rainfall during the period in question was approximately double the average for the previous five years (1.82" to .93"). However, after making a day-by-day analysis of weather conditions and job progress, the board denied relief, finding, among other things, that periods of unfavorable weather occurred either prior to the scheduled beginning of the work or on weekends. See also *Corry Bridge & Supply Co.*, AGBCA 81-149-1, 82-2 BCA ¶ 16,008 (proof of 55 days of rain without proof of effect on job insufficient for excusable delay); *Sauter Constr. Co.*, ASBCA 27050, 84-2 BCA ¶ 17,288 (unusually heavy rain proved but no proof of effect on job resulted in denial of excusable delay); *Sigma Constr. Co.*, ASBCA 37040, 91-2 BCA ¶ 23,926 (contractor failed to establish a correlation between the days when it rained and the days on which work was delayed); *N&P Constr. Co.*, VABCA 3283, 93-1 BCA ¶ 25,251 (construction contractor not entitled to an extension of time for winter weather delays because it failed to show that it could not perform meaningful work during the winter months); *Consolidated Constr., Inc.*, ASBCA 46498, 99-1 BCA ¶ 30,148 (contractor not entitled to recover because it failed to record the occurrence of adverse weather); *FruCon Constr. Corp. v. United States*, 43 Fed. Cl. 306, *modified in part on recons.,* 44 Fed. Cl. 298 (1999) (contractor denied recovery for its failure to contemporaneously document how the unusually severe weather affected its productivity); and *Standard Coating Servs., Inc.*, ASBCA 48611, 00-1 BCA ¶ 30,725 (contractor failed to show that meaningful work could not be performed during winter and delay was the contractor's own responsibility).

An excusable delay will be granted if the effect of unusually severe weekend weather impacts scheduled workdays, *Warwick Constr., Inc.*, GSBCA 5070, 82-2 BCA ¶ 16,091. There, the board granted an excusable delay for heavy weekend rain because the work site was particularly sensitive to runoff and the effect of weekend weather could last several days. See also *Alley-Cassetty Coal Co.*, ASBCA 33315, 89-3 BCA ¶ 21,964, *recons. denied*, 89-3 BCA ¶ 22,204, in which the board granted relief to a supply contractor because unusually severe weather prevented delivery. The contract provided that the coal was to be shipped by barge to a river port and then trucked the last eight miles to the delivery point. The board held that, although the contractor knew that during the winter the river would freeze and delivery by truck would be required, in this instance there was no reason for the contractor to anticipate the earliest winter weather in more than 20 years, and it reasonably expected to make delivery by barge on the scheduled date.

Even if the weather does not attain the requisite statistical level of severity, a contractor may succeed in its claim if it can prove that the impact on the work was unusually severe. In *R & R Constr. Co.*, VACAB 1101, 74-2 BCA ¶ 10,857, which dealt with a roofing contract containing specifications calling for the dry application of the roofing, the board stated at 51,636-37:

> Where weather conditions may not be totally abnormal from a statistical or average standpoint, but are abnormal and unusually severe in their effect on the particular type of contract work being performed, to an extent that they prevent undelayed progress in the work or create circumstances under which the Government has a contractual right to forbid performance because of a specification limitation, delays attributable thereto are excusable to the extent that they exceed the normal weather delays contemplated by the parties when they agreed upon the performance time of the contract.

See also *Wilmington Shipyard, Inc.*, ENGBCA 3378, 73-2 BCA ¶ 10,040; and *Fairbanks Builders, Inc.*, ENGBCA 2634, 66-2 BCA ¶ 5865. In *Fairbanks*, which dealt with a marine construction job in Nome, Alaska, the board stated at 27,241:

> While a contractor should not assume that he will encounter the most favorable weather conditions portended by weather data from previous years, neither must he assume for time purposes that he will encounter the worst conditions which might be deduced from such data. If the worst conditions do prevail he is penalized in having to suffer the increased costs occasioned thereby, but he is entitled to have his contract time extended.

In *Lambert Constr. Co.*, DOTCAB 77-9, 78-1 BCA ¶ 13,221, the contractor was granted an excusable delay for wet weather that was better than statistical averages because it was severe enough to make compaction to the specifications impossible. In some cases, weather may be so critical to the work that the parties adopt specific contract language to supplement the excusable delays provisions. See *Bryant Co.*, GSBCA 6299, 83-1 BCA ¶ 16,487, where the specifications for a reroofing contract provided that work would not be accomplished on any day that it rained or when the temperature was below 40° F and stated that the time would be extended in the event that "bad weather prevents . . . completion . . . in the allotted time." The board held that the term "bad weather" meant "something out of the ordinary but not as out of the ordinary" as unusually severe.

Often weather delays result when government delays push the contractor into periods of adverse weather, *Venetas De Equipo, S.A.*, ENGBCA PCC-135, 00-1 BCA ¶ 30,913 (government delays that push contractor's performance into periods of adverse weather not reasonably anticipated can be cause of additional compensatory delay if the delayed work is the activity controlling project completion); *Gavosto Assocs., Inc.,* PSBCA 4058, 01-1 BCA ¶ 31,389 (time extension justified because government-caused delays pushed the performance period into the rainy season in a tropical region). But see *J.A. Jones Constr. Co.*, ENGBCA ¶ 6348, 00-2 BCA ¶ 31,000 (contractor not entitled to compensation for work inefficiencies).

c. Government Acts

Acts of the government in either its sovereign or contractual capacity may be found to be excusable causes of delay. The distinction between contractual and sovereign acts is considered in detail in Chapter 3 and in the section in this chapter that deals with compensable delays.

(1) Contractual Acts

For a contractor to be excused by an act of the government in its contractual capacity, the contractor must prove that the government act causing the delay was *wrongful*. This distinction was recognized in *San Antonio Constr. Co.*, ASBCA 8110, 1964 BCA ¶ 4479, denying recovery absent government fault. The board stated at 21,533:

> With respect to [the contractor's] contention that its difficulties were occasioned by the Government's failure to pay for services performed, the Board recognizes that an improper failure of the Government to pay for work done may be a cause of later failure by a contractor to perform that is beyond the contractor's control and without its fault or negligence. *George E. Martin & Co.*, ASBCA 3117, 19 October 1956, 56-2 BCA ¶ 1150; *Q.V.S., Inc.*, ASBCA 3722, 17 November 1958, 58-2 BCA ¶ 1007; cf. *U.S. Servs. Corporation*, ASBCA 8291, 29 March 1963, 1963 BCA ¶ 3703.

Cases in which the government actions were considered reasonable include: *Warren Haddock*, ASBCA 7742, 1962 BCA ¶ 3470 (government actions not improper when security personnel escorted hay mowing contractor from air base after it violated base rules by crossing a runway); *Royal Elec., Inc.*, ASBCA 3481, 1962 BCA ¶ 3552 (investigation of possible wrongdoing not shown to be improper); *Max Jordan Bauunternehmung*, ASBCA 23055, 82-1 BCA ¶ 15,685, *aff'd,* 10 Cl. Ct. 672 (1986), 820 F.2d 1208 (Fed. Cir. 1987) (proposed subcontractors properly rejected for not meeting qualification/experience requirements); *Engineered Elec.*, ENGBCA 4944, 84-2 BCA ¶ 17,316 (refusal to give contractor key to building reasonable in view of availability of government personnel to admit contractor); *Thomas J. Aaron*, ASBCA 27361, 84-2 BCA ¶ 17,368 (contacting bonding company concerning possible Davis-Bacon Act violations not improper); *American Gen. Fabrication, Inc.*, ASBCA 43518, 92-2 BCA ¶ 24,955 (government did not take unreasonable time in issuing required approval); *Ordnance Parts & Eng'g Co.*, ASBCA 44327, 93-2 BCA ¶ 25,690 (delay in awarding contract did not excuse delay when material prices had increased because the government's acceptance fell within the extended acceptance period granted by the contractor); *Wilmer Mfg. Co.*, GSBCA 11705, 93-3 BCA ¶ 25,941 (contractor's failure to perform not excused by the government's insistence on compliance with all contract provisions); *SEPAC, Inc.*, ASBCA 39209, 94-3 BCA ¶ 27,052 (disapproval of first article reasonable in light of defects); *Old Dominion Security, Inc. v. General Servs. Admin.*, GSBCA 12974, 97-1 BCA ¶ 28,676 (contractor failed to establish that the shortage of guards and the resulting overtime hours were caused by GSA's alleged delays in determining suitability and in conducting written and firearms tests of potential guards); *Rowe, Inc. v. General Servs. Admin.*, GSBCA 14136, 00-1 BCA ¶ 30,668, *reh'g denied,* 00-1 BCA ¶ 30,797 (government followed reasonable procedures in responding to numerous contractor questions during performance of contract); and *NAVCOM Defense Elecs., Inc.*, ASBCA 50767, 01-2 BCA ¶ 31,546, *aff'd in part*, 53 Fed. App. 897 (Fed. Cir. 2002) (no delay from the government's delay in resolving conflict under a contract because the government explicitly informed the contractor it interpreted the contract as requiring the contractor to perform the analysis—any delay in production was caused by the contractor's refusal to accept the government's position).

It is not necessary that the government intend to harm the contractor in order for an act to be wrongful. See *George T. Johnson v. United States*, 223 Ct. Cl. 210, 618 F.2d 751 (1980), in which the court stated at 219:

> A well-intentioned but legally erroneous denial of essential funds by the Government meets the contractual requirements for relief as adequately as if the Government knew that the denial was legally impermissible at the time that it occurred. Attendant bad faith might well have other consequences but it would be superfluous to the contractor's rights under the exculpatory clause.

Wrongful acts result from the government's failure to perform its express or implied contractual duties. In *Tri-State Tool Co.*, ASBCA 16300, 73-1 BCA ¶ 9886, a contractor obtained an excusable delay when the board found that the contracting officer had failed to properly act on the contractor's request for a time extension. In *Michigan Standard Alloys, Inc.*, GSBCA 4407, 78-1 BCA ¶ 12,980, the board found that the government's failure to act in accord with its contractual duties and prior course of dealing was grounds for an excusable delay. Wrongful government actions entitling the contractor to additional time include improper inspection, *Argus Indus., Inc.*, ASBCA 9960, 66-2 BCA ¶ 5711; failure to disclose facts material to performance, *Hempstead Maint. Serv., Inc.*, GSBCA 3127, 71-1 BCA ¶ 8809; failure to respond to contractor's request for clarifications, *Henry Spen & Co.*, ASBCA 16296, 74-2 BCA ¶ 10,651; ordering contractor to stop work because gate was being locked, *Brand S. Roofing*, ASBCA 24688, 82-1 BCA ¶ 15,513; stopping work without cause, *Robert L. Rich*, DOTCAB 1026, 82-2 BCA ¶ 15,900; inordinate delay in solving construction problem, *Ascani Constr. & Realty Co.*, VABCA 1572, 83-2 BCA ¶ 16,635; insisting on completion of formal Critical Path Method (CPM) schedule before giving time extension when impact of delay was known to the government, *Continental Heller Corp.*, GSBCA 6929, 84-2 BCA ¶ 17,276; failure to act on change proposals requested from contractor, *Singleton Contracting Corp.*, GSBCA 8552, 90-1 BCA ¶ 22,298; delay in awarding contract, *Western States Mgmt. Servs., Inc.*, ASBCA 40212, 92-1 BCA ¶ 24,714; issuance of defective specifications, *DCX, Inc.*, ASBCA 37669, 92-3 BCA ¶ 25,125; failure to provide access to areas to be cleaned, *Marty's Maid & Janitorial Serv. v. General Servs. Admin.*, GSBCA 10614, 93-1 BCA ¶ 25,284; untimely supplying of government-furnished property, *Lear Astronics Corp.*, ASBCA 37228, 93-2 BCA ¶ 25,892; unduly strict inspection standards, *Zeller Zentralheizungsbau GmbH*, ASBCA 43109, 94-2 BCA ¶ 26,657; failure to approve reasonable alternatives to performing work, *U. A. Anderson Constr. Co.,* ASBCA 48087, 99-1 BCA ¶ 30,347; and failure to fix a drain back-up leaving "malodorous sanitary waste on the floors of the building," *Kinetic Builders, Inc.*, ASBCA 51012, 98-2 ¶ 29,899.

Such actions are often termed violations of the government's duty to cooperate or not to hinder or interfere with the contractor's performance. See *Piedmont Painting Contractors,* IBCA 3772, 98-1 BCA ¶ 29,618 (government inspector refused to monitor a contractor's performance over a long weekend but went hunting instead), and *R.W. Jones Constr., Inc.*, IBCA 3656-96, 99-1 BCA ¶ 30,268 (government refused to provide the contractor with a key to the worksite). When relief is granted under the Changes clause using the constructive change theory, there is no need to invoke the excusable delays clause. The same result would be achieved for constructive changes resulting from defective specifications or nondisclosure.

Government actions, while not causing the delay, may relieve the contractor from having to prove some element of an excusable delay. See *J.C. Hester Co.*, IBCA 1114-7-76, 77-1 BCA ¶ 12,292, in which a contractor claimed an excusable delay caused by the late delivery of supplies by two subcontractors with whom the government had communicated directly concerning their alleged delay. The board held that the government's communications with the subcontractors relieved the contractor of its burden of proving the subcontractor's lack of negligence, and, once free from this burden, the contractor was able to prove its own lack of fault and obtain relief. See also *CJP Contractors*, ASBCA 50076, 00-2 BCA ¶ 31,119, granting the contractor a one-week time extension because the building it was renovating was shut down and the government told the contractor it could take the week off. However, contractors must prove that the government action was the proximate cause of the delay. See *Brown Steel Contractors,* ASBCA 48172, 95-2 BCA ¶ 27,794 (although the delay was associated with a government proposal to change the method of demolition, the proximate cause of the delay was the contractor's failure to tell the government that the proposal was unacceptable); *Thomas A. Short Co.*, ASBCA 42248, 97-1 BCA ¶ 28,908 (government not responsible for delays incident to the issuance of quality deficiency reports, because the government had good reason to take all these actions).

(2) Sovereign Acts

Sovereign acts that delay the contractor's performance are grounds for excusable delays. In *D.D. Montague*, ASBCA 11837, 67-1 BCA ¶ 6217, a contractor was awarded a six-day delay as a result of its inability to secure normally available railroad cars for delivery of needed supplies. The board found that the unprecedented size of government demands for railroad cars arising from the

Vietnam conflict was a sovereign act of the government. Similarly, in *Southland Mfg. Corp.*, ASBCA 10519, 69-1 BCA ¶ 7714, *recons. denied*, 69-2 BCA ¶ 7968, the board held that the government's raising of the minimum wage "by a percentage much larger than could reasonably have been anticipated" and the Small Business Administration's "sudden and unanticipated" cancellation of a loan were excusable delays. See also *Gary Hegler*, AGBCA 89-145-1, 92-1 BCA ¶ 24,561 (fire closures are sovereign acts that entitle a contractor to additional time), and *Contractor's Northwest, Inc.*, AGBCA 97-101-1, 97-1 BCA ¶ 28,847 (government's issuance of a Suspend Work Order for the purpose of stopping contract due to a fire emergency a sovereign act entitling contractor to excusable delay but not price adjustment).

The occurrence of a sovereign act that merely increases the contractor's cost of performance will generally not entitle the contractor to an excusable delay because the contractor is responsible for overcoming such cost increases. See *Hydro-Space Sys. Corp.*, ASBCA 15275, 71-1 BCA ¶ 8739, and *Air-Speed, Inc.*, PSBCA 96, 75-1 BCA ¶ 11,113, in which the boards denied relief for claims arising from the government's fiscal policies causing a tight money supply. Similarly, in *Northern Va. Elec. Co.*, ASBCA 21446, 80-1 BCA ¶ 14,239, *aff'd*, 230 Ct. Cl. 722 (1982), the board held that the lifting of Phase II of the government's price control program did not entitle the contractor to an excusable delay when its planned supplier did not perform as expected. See also *Prestex, Inc. v. United States*, 3 Cl. Ct. 373 (1983), *aff'd,* 746 F.2d 1989 (Fed. Cir. 1989).

The operation of the government's priority system, 50 U.S.C. App. § 2071, can also qualify as a sovereign act excusing delay. Thus, if a contractor is unable to obtain materials because of subsequent priority orders, it will be entitled to an excusable delay, *Bromion, Inc. v. United States*, ASBCA 12075, 67-2 BCA ¶ 6543, *aff'd*, 188 Ct. Cl. 31, 411 F.2d 1020 (1969); *Kennedy Elec. Co.*, GSBCA 2135, 66-2 BCA ¶ 5877. However, a subcontractor is not entitled to an excusable delay for the impact of prior priority orders, *Crane Co.*, ASBCA 16999, 73-1 BCA ¶ 9961; and contractors will not be granted excusable delays if they have not made diligent efforts to use the priority system to obtain needed materials, *Hogan Mech., Inc.*, ASBCA 21612, 78-1 BCA ¶ 13,164; *McQuiston Assocs.*, ASBCA 24676, 83-1 BCA ¶ 16,187, *recons. denied*, 83-2 BCA ¶ 16,602. See *Angler's Co. v. United States*, 220 Ct. Cl. 727 (1979), in which the court held that the requirement for diligence did not require the contractor to perform useless acts when it was clear that use of the priority system would not have obtained the materials.

Excusable delays have also been granted for acts of other sovereigns. See *Thomas J. Papathomas,* ASBCA 49512, 97-2 BCA ¶ 29,317, recognizing that contractor was entitled to excusable delays due to a Greek security delay in processing access permits.

d. Subcontractor and Supplier Delays

When the delay is caused by problems encountered by a subcontractor or supplier, the contractor has an added burden in establishing excusability. Under the clauses currently in use, a delay by a subcontractor at any tier is not excusable to the contractor unless it is also excusable to the contractor and the subcontractors at each higher tier. Thus, before the contractor can be excused, it must be shown that the cause of delay was beyond the control and without the fault or negligence of the contractor and all intervening contractors including the delayed subcontractor. Previous versions of the clause did not contain the phrase "subcontractor at any tier." Thus, in *Schweigert, Inc. v. United States*, 181 Ct. Cl. 1184, 388 F.2d 697 (1967), the court interpreted the term "subcontractor" to mean first-tier subcontractor and granted relief for a delay caused by the fault of a second-tier subcontractor. Subsequently, the default clauses were modified to include the present language. Thus, if a subcontractor fails to deliver due to a dispute between it and the contractor, the resulting delay will not be excusable since it will be considered to be the fault of the parties, *Fairfield Scientific Corp.*, ASBCA 21152, 78-1 BCA ¶ 12,869, *aff'd*, 222 Ct. Cl. 167, 611 F.2d 854 (1979); *Empresas Electronicas Walser, Inc.*, DOTCAB 72-22, 72-2 BCA ¶ 9712, *recons. denied*, 73-1 BCA ¶ 9847. See also *General Ry. Signal Co.*, ENGBCA 6309, 97-2 BCA ¶ 29,170 (bankruptcy of a subcontractor not an excuse for a contractor's failure to perform or its delay in completion where there is no improper action by the government), and *Wescor Forest Prods Co.*, AGBCA 96-154-1, 97-2 BCA ¶ 29,242 (death of subcontractor no excuse).

(1) Subcontractors Designated by the Government

Delays caused by sole source subcontractors, even those designated by the government, do not qualify for excusable delays if the subcontractor is at fault, *Joseph J. Bonavire Co.*, GSBCA 4819, 78-1 BCA ¶ 12,877, *recons. denied*, 78-1 BCA ¶ 13,132; *Bromion, Inc.*, ASBCA 12075, 67-2 BCA ¶ 6543, *aff'd*, 188 Ct. Cl. 31, 411 F.2d 1020 (1969); *Federal Television Corp.*, ASBCA 9836, 1964 BCA ¶ 4392. See *Scale Elecs. Dev., Inc.*, ASBCA 21725, 77-2 BCA ¶ 12,615, in which the board stated at 61,153:

> Either way, whether [the contractor] was at fault or General Electrodynamics Corporation was at fault, it makes no difference that General Electrodynamics was a sole source. The RFP clearly stated that only the product of General Electrodynamics would be acceptable. [The contractor] knew in advance that it was proposing to deliver items which could only be obtained from one source. The following language from an earlier opinion sets forth our views on this point:
>
>> [The contractor] contracted with the Government to furnish all of the designated kit parts, some of which were sole source, others unrestricted source. [The contractor's] price included a charge for procuring sole source items just as for procuring unrestricted source items. [The contractor's] obligation to the Government to supply the sole source items

> was no different from its obligation to supply the remaining items. The limitation on the [contractor's] ability to select its suppliers because of the sole source designations was an inherent condition of the contract. [The contractor] agreed to this limitation when it entered into the contract; it was not imposed by the Government after the contract was made. The latter would present a wholly different problem. In making this type of contract [the contractor] was well aware that a sole source procurement might cause greater difficulties than an unrestricted source procurement. [The contractor] clearly assumed the risk that nonperformance by a sole source supplier entails. There is no basis on which [the contractor] can now be relieved of the contractual obligation which it assumed.
>
> *Aerokits, Inc.*, ASBCA 12324, 68-1 BCA ¶ 6917, *motion for recons. denied*, 68-2 BCA ¶ 7088. See also *Fuller—American, A Joint Venture*, ASBCA 19629, 75-2 BCA ¶ 11,438; *Federal Elec. Corp.*, ASBCA 20490, 76-2 BCA ¶ 12,035.

Of course, it hardly need be said that if [the contractor] considered the RFP unduly restrictive because it limited the scales to those manufactured by General Electrodynamics Corporation it should have challenged that before contract award in another forum.

Of course, the contractor will not recover if it causes the subcontractor's delay. See *Protech-Atlanta Inc.*, VABCA 6000, 02-1 BCA ¶ 31,736, in which the board ruled that although the government specified a sole source subcontractor, the contractor's problems with the subcontractor resulted from nonpayment.

See, however, *Electro-Nav, Inc.*, DCAB NOAA-1-74, 75-1 BCA ¶ 11,162, in which relief was granted on the grounds that no other source was available and the government implied that the item was available on the open market. Compare *Cascade Elec. Co.*, ASBCA 28674, 84-1 BCA ¶ 17,210, in which the board stated at 85,682-83:

> When the Government directs the installation of a sole source item, it represents only that the requirements of the contract can be met by using that item. However, such representation is predicated upon the assumptions that the item has been properly manufactured and timely delivered by the vendor and that it will be installed properly and timely by the contractor. See *Environmental Tectonics Corporation*, ASBCA 21657, 79-1 BCA ¶ 13,796, *recons. denied*, 79-1 BCA ¶ 13,876; *DeLaval Turbine, Inc.*, ASBCA 21797, 78-2 BCA ¶ 13,521.

See also Systems & Elecs., Inc., ASBCA 41113, 97-1 BCA ¶ 28,671 (despite the government's identification of a specific source, the government did not guarantee that the source would be on call and would timely provide the parts whenever the contractor felt like ordering them).

For a more liberal statement in a case dealing with a listing of "government-approved" sources, see the Trial Judge opinion in *Franklin E. Penny Co. v. United States*, 207 Ct. Cl. 842, 524 F.2d 668 (1975), stating at 853-55:

> Where the Government issues a contract drawing upon which are listed the names of Government-approved sources of supply, one could readily accept the proposition that such a listing constitutes a representation, *i.e.*, a warranty by the Government, that the listed suppliers have the *ability* to do the work contemplated by the contract. Indeed, the common sense of the situation could tolerate no less a construction of such contract statements. But it is quite another matter to say, as [the contractor] also does, that in addition to guaranteeing the abilities of the listed manufacturers to perform, the Government is also warranting their willingness to do so and within the time period contemplated by the contract.
>
> * * *
>
> To be sure, the rule would be otherwise if the delays resulted from circumstances with respect to which the Government bore the risk. Thus, for example, if it had been the case here that the Government had selected the subcontractor or had vouched for the competence of the one that was selected, then delays attributable to that subcontractor's technical problems (in doing the work) would remain within the Government's sphere of responsibility.

(2) Obtainable from Another Source

Even if the delay is otherwise excusable to both the contractor and subcontractor, it will not qualify as an excusable delay under the supply contract clause if "the supplies or services were obtainable from other sources in sufficient time to permit the Contractor to meet the required delivery schedule." The failure of the contractor to establish reasons for not obtaining the materials from other sources has resulted in a denial of excusability, *Cryer & Parker Elecs., Inc.*, ASBCA 15150, 71-2 BCA ¶ 8943; *ArBee Corp.*, ASBCA 46476, 95-2 BCA ¶ 27,646. See also *Smith Faison Military Sales Co.*, ASBCA 24229, 82-1 BCA ¶ 15,512 (delay not excusable because supplies were available from another source, albeit at a higher price); *Gatewood & Assocs., Ltd. v. General Servs. Admin.*, GSBCA 9182, 93-1 BCA ¶ 25,247 (denying relief to a contractor who failed to deliver artificial chamois cloth under an indefinite-quantities supply contract when the material was available elsewhere at a higher price); *C&M Mach. Prods., Inc.*, ASBCA 43348, 93-2 BCA ¶ 25,748 (relief denied where adequate plating could have been provided by another subcontractor but the contractor refused to pay the higher price demanded for the work); and *Progressive Tool Corp.*, ASBCA 42809, 94-1 BCA ¶ 26,413 (relief denied where contractor neglected to show that it made all reasonable attempts to locate an alternate supplier). The construction clause does not contain this language, but the boards appear to impose a similar requirement. See *Northern Va. Elec. Co. v. United States*, 230 Ct. Cl. 722 (1982) (no excusable delay absent evidence to support a finding that there was a shortage of "electrical equipment for a contractor willing to pay the increased prices"); *Signal Contracting, Inc.*, DOTCAB 1279, 83-1 BCA ¶ 16,424, *recons. denied*, 83-1 BCA ¶ 16,425, *aff'd*, 727 F.2d 1117 (Fed. Cir. 1983) (no excusable delay when contractor did not demonstrate that another source could not have timely delivered).

To deny recovery on these grounds, the supplies must be available elsewhere and in sufficient time. See *Southwest Eng'g Co.*, DOTCAB 70-26, 71-1 BCA ¶ 8818 (material could not be obtained elsewhere because the subcontractor was sole source); *Wiggins Elec. Co.*, ASBCA 14790, 72-1 BCA ¶ 9190 (ordering from another supplier would have increased rather than decreased the delivery time); and *Columbia Loose Leaf Corp.*, GSBCA 5805, 82-1 BCA ¶ 15,464 (insufficient time to secure deliveries from another supplier to permit timely manufacture makes delay excusable).

(3) Firms Classified as Subcontractors

Because of the significance attached to the delays of a subcontractor, it is important to determine what type of arrangement between a contractor and another party will be considered a subcontract for the purpose of the clause. The term has been extended to carriers, *Metro-Tel, Div. of Grow Corp.*, ASBCA 8471, 1964 BCA ¶ 4164. In *MPT Enters.*, ASBCA 25483, 83-2 BCA ¶ 16,767, *recons. denied*, 84-3 BCA ¶ 17,625, the board held that loss of the materials during shipment was not a sufficient excuse because a carrier is considered to be a subcontractor for purposes of excusable delays. The term does not, however, appear to be applied to utilities, *Ace Elecs. Assocs., Inc.*, ASBCA 13899, 69-2 BCA ¶ 7922.

In *Emerson-Sack-Warner Corp.*, FAACAP 66-2, 65-2 BCA ¶ 5003, the board ruled that, even though there was no enforceable contractual relationship between a contractor and a supplier, the term "subcontractor" applied to the supplier because "the prime contractor" and its supplier were dealing with each other on a regular and continuous basis in order to fill requirements under the contract. In *Herbach & Rademan, Inc.*, ASBCA 12323, 67-2 BCA ¶ 6639, the risk of refusal of a planned subcontractor to consummate the subcontract was treated as being within the contractor's basic performance responsibilities. See also *Scale Elecs. Dev., Inc.*, ASBCA 21725, 77-2 BCA ¶ 12,615, holding that a contractor will be found at fault if it does not obtain contractual commitments from necessary subcontractors.

e. Floods

In *Koppers Co.*, ENGBCA 2700, 67-2 BCA ¶ 6492, the board held that a "flood" must involve an overbank flow of water and that mere soaking or runoff was insufficient. See also *Potashnick Constr., Inc.*, ENGBCA 2865, 69-2 BCA ¶ 7817 (heavy rains and runoff not a flood). For a somewhat broader definition, see *Kakos Nursery, Inc.*, ASBCA 10989, 66-2 BCA ¶ 5733, *recons. denied*, 66-2 BCA ¶ 5909, interpreting flood as an overflow of water from any source. But see *Hensel Phelps Constr. Co.*, ENGBCA 3719, 77-2 BCA ¶ 12,853 (rejecting broader definition of flood and requiring overflow of stream banks).

In *Molony & Rubien Constr. Co.*, DOTBCA 2486, 93-1 BCA ¶ 25,384, *recons. denied*, 94-2 BCA ¶ 26,727, flooding in the basement of an air traffic control tower delayed the contractor from installing an elevator service. The board found that substantial rainfall entered a conduit system installed by another contractor doing work for the state of Rhode Island. The other contractor mistakenly connected the system to conduits that led into the basement, causing damage to the equipment stored there. The board held that the flooding was an excusable delay and granted the contractor a 17-day time extension.

f. Fires

Only a few cases have considered fires. See *Armstrong Featherweight Decoy Corp.*, WDBCA 354, 1 CCF ¶ 975 (1943) (contractor's plant and equipment destroyed by fire); and *Pat-Ric Corp.*, ASBCA 10581, 66-2 BCA ¶ 6026 (fire experienced by subcontractor excusable for contractor).

g. Epidemics

In *Big State Garment Co.*, ASBCA 337, 4 CCF ¶ 60,946 (1950), the contractor was excused for time needed by employees to overcome reactions to typhoid serum administered because of a flood. See also *Martin Mfg. Co.*, ASBCA 495, 5 CCF ¶ 61,096 (1950) (epidemic of measles and mumps slowed production of shirts). However, more recently it has been harder to prove that an epidemic was the sole cause of delay. In *Crawford Dev. & Mfg. Co.*, ASBCA 17565, 74-2 BCA ¶ 10,660, the board held that a flu epidemic did not involve a sufficient number of the contractor's employees to cause delay. See also *Tommy Nobis Ctr., Inc.*, GSBCA 8988-TD, 89-3 BCA ¶ 22,112 (no showing that the flu epidemic was of long duration or that it had an adverse effect on the volume of production).

h. Freight Embargoes

In *United States v. Meems Bros. & Ward*, 196 F. Supp. 188 (D.N.Y. 1961), a freight embargo on an ocean shipment of rhesus monkeys from India was found excusable even though air shipment was still possible at a greatly increased cost.

i. Acts of God

In 49 Comp. Gen. 733 (B-169473) (1970), an "act of God" was defined as a "singular, unexpected and irregular visitation of a force of nature." In *Nogler Tree Farm*, AGBCA 81-104-1, 81-2 BCA ¶ 15,315, the board characterized the eruption of Mount St. Helens as an act of God. *Nogler* was distinguished by *The Work Force*, AGBCA 80-175-1A, 84-2 BCA ¶ 17,322, holding that despite an act of God, the contractor must still show that the event affected contract performance. See also *Sach Sinha & Assoc., Inc.,* ASBCA 47594, 00-1 BCA ¶ 30,735 (delay allegedly due to earthquake damage did not excuse a contractor's default, because the contractor failed to prove that its facility sustained anything but cosmetic damage).

The illness or death of key contractor or subcontractor personnel is not a valid excuse justifying nonperformance, nor is it considered an act of God, as the contractor assumes the responsibility of employing and utilizing a competent work force, *Yankee Telecomm. Lab., Inc.*, ASBCA 25240, 85-1 BCA ¶ 17,786. See *M&T Constr. Co.*, ASBCA 42750, 93-1 BCA ¶ 25,223 (heart attack suffered by one of subcontractor's personnel not an "act of God" that should excuse contractor's nonperformance), and *Centennial Leasing v. General Servs. Admin.*, GSBCA 12037, 94-1 BCA ¶ 26,398 (death of subcontractor's chief operating officer is not a valid excuse justifying nonperformance). Loss of key employees is discussed in more detail in the next section.

2. Non-Enumerated Causes of Delay

The courts have taken a very restrictive view of the types of non-enumerated events that will be classified as excusable. In *Carnegie Steel Co. v. United States*, 240 U.S. 156 (1916), the Supreme Court enunciated the rule that the excusable delays provisions did not extend to delays due to "nonextraneous causes." In this case, the contractor claimed an excusable delay because it had encountered unforeseen technical problems in using a new manufacturing process. The Court held that such a problem was not the type of cause for delay covered by the excusable delays clause, stating at 165:

> Ability to perform a contract is of its very essence. It would have no sense or incentive, no assurance of fulfillment, otherwise; and a delay resulting from the absence of such ability is not of the same kind enumerated in the contract—is not a cause extraneous to it and independent of the engagements and exertions of the parties.

Thus, absent an underlying cause specifically enumerated in the contract, delays caused by a lack of or inability to obtain know-how, material, personnel, money, or machines are very difficult to establish as excusable. In almost all cases where such delays have been held excusable, the contractor has been able to demonstrate that performance was at least a practical impossibility and that it had not assumed the risk of the impossibility, a test not usually applied to delays arising out of causes specifically set forth in the clause. Whether this is so because the contractor is considered to have assumed the risk of the delay or because such matters are considered not beyond the control of the contractor is not readily apparent from the cases. One view of the matter is contained in *Austin Co. v. United States*, 161 Ct. Cl. 76, 314 F.2d 518, *cert. denied*, 375 U.S. 830 (1963), in which the court stated at 80:

> Notwithstanding this, because [the contractor] could not develop the system as planned, it claims that its failure to perform was due to causes beyond its control and thus is excused under the exculpatory provisions of the contract.
>
> The [government] disputes [the contractor's] claim that its failure of performance was covered by the exculpatory termination clause in the contract. [The

> government] contends that the clause in question was limited to excuse of non-performance solely due to occurrence of extraneous contingencies of the kind specifically enumerated thereunder. [The government] cites the rules of *ejusdem generis*, *i.e.*, general words in a contract are limited by particular words to things of the same *kind or class*, to support its contention that the words "causes beyond the control" refer solely to extraneous factors which might prevent performance, because only these kind of factors were enumerated in explanation of the causes to be considered.
>
> We agree with the [government] that the rule of *ejusdem generis* is applicable to interpretation of the nonperformance clause in this contract, and operates to restrict the clause to exculpation of nonperformance due to the kind or class of extraneous contingencies enumerated therein, *i.e.*, acts of God, etc. As we view the issue, if the [contractor's] failure of performance was due to the absolute impossibility of performance inherent in the subject matter of the contract itself, and which impossibility already existed at the time the contract was entered into, [the contractor's] failure would not be excused under the exculpatory clause of the contract. See *Carnegie Steel Company v. United States*, 240 U.S. 156.

See also *Consolidated Airborne Sys., Inc. v. United States*, 172 Ct. Cl. 588, 348 F.2d 941 (1965), applying the same rationale in denying relief to a contractor whose inability to perform was caused by lack of funds.

a. Financial Difficulties

The general rule is that the contractor assumes the risk of providing sufficient funds to perform the contract, *Southeastern Airways Corp. v. United States*, 673 F.2d 368 (Ct. Cl. 1982). Thus, neither undercapitalization, *Willems Indus., Inc. v. United States*, 155 Ct. Cl. 360, 295 F.2d 822 (1961), *cert. denied*, 370 U.S. 903 (1962), nor insolvency, *Medical Fabrics Co.*, ASBCA 11458, 66-2 BCA ¶ 5887, excuses a failure to perform. The fact that bankruptcy or financial ruin will result is apparently immaterial. In *Consolidated Airborne Sys., Inc. v. United States*, 172 Ct. Cl. 588, 348 F.2d 941 (1965), the contractor sought to be excused from performance because its financial condition was such that attempted performance of the contract would have rendered it hopelessly insolvent or even adjudicated bankrupt. The court held resulting delays not excusable, stating at 597:

> It must be deemed an implied term of every contract that the promisor will not permit himself, through insolvency or bankruptcy, much less the threat of the same, to be disabled from making performance and in this view, bankruptcy or insolvency is but the natural and legal consequence of something done or omitted to be done by the bankrupt or insolvent.

See also *Planned Sys. Int'l, Inc.*, GSBCA 4976, 78-2 BCA ¶ 13,264, stating that financial inability is no excuse regardless of severity. Such a result is more understandable if the contractor has not availed itself of possible avenues of relief. In *Magna Enters. Inc.*, ASBCA 51188, 02-1 BCA ¶ 31,660, inability to obtain anticipated funding was no excuse for nonperformance. The contractor, a small business, did not advise the government of its impaired financial condition nor seek assistance from the Small Business Administration.

The failure of expected loans to materialize will not, ordinarily, excuse performance, *Petrofuels Refining Co.*, ASBCA 9986, 1964 BCA ¶ 4341. See also *Centennial Leasing v. General Servs. Admin.*, GSBCA 12037, 94-1 BCA ¶ 26,398, in which a lender's failure to provide supplemental financing to the contractor to purchase vehicles necessary to fill contract delivery orders did not excuse delay. However, in some cases the failure may be held excusable. In *Security Signals, Inc.*, ASBCA 4634, 58-2 BCA ¶ 2045, the board implied that an excusable delay would be found if the contractor had made reasonable financial arrangements before award and subsequent events beyond its control had prevented such arrangements from coming to fruition. This case relied on *Paromel Elecs. Corp.*, ASBCA 4025, 57-2 BCA ¶ 1503, *recons. denied*, 58-2 BCA ¶ 1839, where the contractor's financial inability had been caused by suppliers repudiating their agreements and charging extremely high prices after award had been made to the contractor. For another rare case granting an excusable delay for lack of financing, see *Coastal Mfg. Co.*, ASBCA 11516, 67-1 BCA ¶ 6378, in which an excusable delay was granted to the estate of a deceased sole proprietor when the death occurred after bidding but prior to award and the complexities of probate prevented the estate from obtaining the necessary financing.

In contrast to the general rule denying relief for delays due to lack of financing, the contractor will be granted relief when the lack of financing is caused by wrongful government action. See *Brooklyn & Queens Screen Mfg. Co. v. United States*, 97 Ct. Cl. 532 (1942) (wrongful denial of progress payments); *Southland Mfg. Corp.*, ASBCA 10519, 69-1 BCA ¶ 7714, *recons. denied*, 69-2 BCA ¶ 7968 (wrongful cancellation of loan by Small Business Administration); *Shepard Div./Vogue Instrument Corp.*, ASBCA 15571, 74-1 BCA ¶ 10,498 (government incorrectly computed progress payments and defective government-furnished property caused financial difficulties); *Freedom NY, Inc.*, ASBCA 43965, 01-2 BCA ¶ 31,585, *recons. denied*, 02-1 BCA ¶ 31,676, *aff'd in part and rev'd in part on other grounds,* 329 F.3d 1320 (Fed. Cir. 2003), *cert. denied,* 541 U.S. 987 (2004) (government provided inaccurate information to the contractor's prospective sources of funding); *Discount Co.*, AGBCA 291, 74-1 BCA ¶ 10,511 (government delay in processing, considering, and paying contractor's rightful claims caused its financial distress); and *Texas Trinity Mfg. & Supply Co.*, ASBCA 10465, 75-1 BCA ¶ 11,151 (misapplication of inspection criteria by the government caused financial collapse).

The failure to make progress payments is the most often cited basis for excuse due to financial inability. See *George T. Johnson & Harvey Case v. United States*, 223 Ct. Cl. 210, 618 F.2d 751 (1980) (government's wrongful refusal to make progress payments rendered contractor financially unable to continue performance). Wrongful withholding or delay of payment excuses the contractor from performing other contracts that the contractor is unable to perform, as well as the contract under which the withholding or delay occurred, *R-D Mounts, Inc.*, ASBCA 14827, 71-1 BCA ¶ 8643, *recons. denied*, 71-1 BCA ¶ 8725. However, the withholding or delay must be wrongful. See *Pastushin Aviation Co.*, ASBCA 21243, 82-1 BCA ¶ 15,639 (no wrongful denial of progress payments in refusal to permit contractor to overbill); *Meyer Labs, Inc.*, ASBCA 18989, 83-2 BCA ¶ 16,598 (suspension of progress payments for failure to make progress not wrongful); and *Swiss Prods., Inc.*, ASBCA 40031, 93-3 BCA ¶ 26,163 (length of time government used to consider engineering change proposals not cause of contractor's financial problems).

In delayed payment or withholding cases, the contractor must establish that the government's action was the primary cause of the lack of funds, *Derrick Elec. Co.*, ASBCA 21246, 78-1 BCA ¶ 12,942; *Guenther Mfg. Co.*, ASBCA 15755, 73-2 BCA ¶ 10,327. Thus, government delay in making progress payments will not constitute the basis for an excusable delay where the delay is the result of the contractor's failure to timely provide requisite verifications of its claims, *E. Carron, Inc.*, ASBCA 19105, 76-1 BCA ¶ 11,727, *recons. denied,* 76-2 BCA ¶ 11,987. See also *J.C. Co.*, AGBCA 80-154-9, 82-1 BCA ¶ 15,542 (inability to perform did not result from underpayment); *J.G. Enters., Inc.*, ASBCA 27150, 83-2 BCA ¶ 16,808 (no showing that withholding caused financial difficulties); *Local Contractors, Inc.*, ASBCA 37108, 92-1 BCA ¶ 24,491, *recons. denied,* 92-1 BCA ¶ 24,693, *aff'd,* 988 F.2d 131 (Fed. Cir. 1993) (contractor's failure to provide first articles not excused by the government's failure to make progress payments); *El Greco Painting Co.*, ENGBCA 5693, 92-1 BCA ¶ 24,522 (contractor's inability to proceed not caused by wrongful actions of government where contract payments equaled or exceeded contractor's actual expenses); and *Durable Metal Prods., Inc.*, ASBCA 41446, 94-3 BCA ¶ 26,963 (contractor failed to establish that the government's actions—failure to make final 15 percent contract payment and placing the contractor on the "Contract Improvement Program" and the "Contractor Alert List"—were primary causes of financial difficulty).

b. Lack of Facilities and Equipment

A contractor assumes the risk of obtaining and maintaining the facilities and equipment necessary for performance, *Krauss v. Greenbarg*, 137 F.2d 569 (3d Cir.), *cert. denied*, 320 U.S. 791 (1943); *Vereinigte Osterreichische Eisen und Stahlwerke Aktiengesellschaft*, IBCA 327, 1962 BCA ¶ 3503; *Wescor Forest Prods., Co.,* AGBCA 96-154-1, 97-2 BCA ¶ 29,242. In *Ace Elecs. Assocs., Inc.*, ASBCA 13899, 69-2 BCA ¶ 7922, the board stated the general rule at 36,845:

> It is well settled that a contractor is responsible for providing plant, machinery, labor and finances required for the performance of a contract awarded to it. Accordingly, failure to have the necessary machinery or other such means for performance, whether at the time of contracting or subsequently, is under most circumstances not a valid excuse for failure of timely delivery. Thus, a breakdown

> of a contractor's machinery is not excusable per se unless such breakdown can be shown to have been caused by one or more of those causes listed in the Default Clause, or by a cause analogous thereto.

The board then went on to hold that a sudden power surge that was caused by a local utility company and that damaged a contractor's sensitive testing equipment was an excusable cause. The board found that a power surge was not a normal occurrence and that there was nothing practical that the contractor could have done to prevent the damage to its equipment. In *Park Moving & Storage Co.*, ASBCA 7798, 1962 BCA ¶ 3469, a warehousing contractor using a leased warehouse was excusably delayed when an independent contractor hired by the lessor of the warehouse to repair the warehouse roof caused goods stored by the contractor to be damaged by a rainstorm and rendered unsuitable the contractor's facilities. In finding the delay to have been beyond the contractor's control, the board stated that the contractor did not have reason to know of and prepare for the roofing repair contract, had no control over the roofer, and was not responsible for its performance. See also *Soletanche Rodio Nicholson (JV)*, ENGBCA 5796, 94-1 BCA ¶ 26,472, in which an excusable delay was found when the contractor encountered equipment problems caused by a differing site condition that made it practically impossible to continue performance.

c. Lack of Materials

A contractor assumes the risk of obtaining the materials necessary for performance, *Aargus Poly Bag*, GSBCA 4314, 76-2 BCA ¶ 11,927; *Environmental Devices, Inc.*, ASBCA 37430, 93-3 BCA ¶ 26,138. However, in *Automated Extruding & Packaging, Inc.*, GSBCA 4036, 74-2 BCA ¶ 10,949, *recons. denied*, 75-1 BCA ¶ 11,067, a plastic bag contractor was granted a delay when the 1973 Arab oil embargo caused unavailability of supplies of the petroleum-based resin necessary for performance. The board stressed that the oil embargo was unforeseeable causing "critical shortages" of necessary materials. Later cases, in distinguishing *Automated*, have stressed the practical unavailability of the supplies and repeated the general rule that mere shortages of costly yet available supplies are not excusable causes of delay, *Free-Flow Packaging Corp.*, GSBCA 3992, 75-1 BCA ¶ 11,105, *recons. denied*, 75-1 BCA ¶ 11,332; *C&M Mach. Prods., Inc.*, ASBCA 43348, 93-2 BCA ¶ 25,748. The board stated in *Betsy Ross Flag Co.*, ASBCA 12124, 67-2 BCA ¶ 6688, at 31,025:

> Market shortage is not an excusable cause for non-performance. The fact that supplies cannot be obtained except at a cost in excess of the contract price is no excuse. Unwillingness to perform, although at some loss, does not relieve [a contractor] from [its] contractual obligation.

See also *American Int'l Contractors, Inc./Capitol Indus. Constr. Groups, Inc., A Joint Venture*, ASBCA 39544, 95-2 BCA ¶ 27,920 (delay not excused by lack of adequate supply since government advised contractor of such at pre-proposal conference), and *SAI Indus. Corp.*, ASBCA 49149, 98-1 BCA ¶ 29,662 (supplier's refusal to supply materials in other than an unnecessarily large quantity not an excuse). In some circumstances, high costs of materials might sustain a claim of economic impracticability, *Brazier Lumber Co.*, ASBCA 18601, 76-2 BCA ¶ 12,207. However, a contractor that has bid in a time of volatile prices is deemed to have assumed the risks of increases in materials cost, *So Ros Sahakij, Ltd.*, ASBCA 19238, 75-1 BCA ¶ 11,028; *Aargus Poly Bag*, GSBCA 4314, 76-2 BCA ¶ 11,927.

d. Lack of Know-How

The rule of *Carnegie* is strongly followed in denying contractors' claims for delays due to lack of know-how or inability to perform, *Poloron Prods., Inc. v. United States*, 126 Ct. Cl. 816, 116 F. Supp. 588 (1953); *Richmond Eng'g Co.*, IBCA 426-2-64, 1964 BCA ¶ 4465; *Randolph Eng'g Co.*, ASBCA 5480, 1962 BCA ¶ 3502. In *Canfield Mach. & Tool Co.*, ASBCA 10390, 65-2 BCA ¶ 5018, the board stated that "the usage of materials and tools, as well as production methods and their coordination are all within a contractor's basic performance responsibility as aspects of know-how."

A contractor is expected to have the level of know-how of a qualified contractor for the same type of work involved, but it may be excused if the work is impossible and the risk was not assumed, *Utah-Manhattan-Sundt JV*, ASBCA 8991, 1963 BCA ¶ 3839, *recons. denied*, 1963 BCA ¶ 3854. In *Utah*, a contractor was excused for its subcontractor's delays due to production difficulties beyond the existing state of the art, which the board found to have been outside the contemplation of the parties at award. The board commented on the allocation of risk at 19,148-49:

> A contractor who undertakes to perform a contract is responsible for having the necessary "know-how" for the performance of the work specified. The rule is stated in *Golden City Hosiery Mills, Inc.*, ASBCA 244 (1950), as follows:
>
> > The "know-how" to produce specification supplies is something that contractors are assumed to possess when they enter into contracts with the Government. (Appeals of *Harcourt & Co., Inc.*, BCA No. 1199, 4 CCF ¶ 60,046—*Poloron Products, Inc.*, BCA No. 1277, 4 CCF ¶ 60,158) and delays in deliveries resulting from their lack of "know-how" are not excusable delays under their contracts. (Appeal of *Livingston Plastics Corp.*, BCA No. 1029, 3 CCF ¶ 976).
>
> The rule as to the responsibility of the contractor for having the requisite know-how has reference to the know-how to be expected of a qualified manufacturer of the type of product involved. Under a contract containing the standard "excusability" provision the contractor cannot be held responsible for delay or failure to perform caused by a production difficulty the solution of which is beyond the existing state of the art and which can be overcome only by a scientific or technological "break-through," unless there are special circumstances, such as where the contractor deliberately contracts to accomplish a result known to be beyond

> the existing state of the art. *Aerosonic Instrument Corp.*, ASBCA 4129, 59-1 BCA ¶ 2115; *The Austin Company*, ASBCA 4255, 61-1 BCA ¶ 2927. Production difficulties are not an excusable cause of delay when a contractor undertakes to produce an item by a specified time knowing that processes adequate for the production of the item have not yet been developed by itself or anyone else. Such a case was discussed by the Supreme Court in *Carnegie Steel Company v. United States*, 240 U.S. 156 (1915) . . . .
>
> Unlike the situation in the *Carnegie Steel* case, [this subcontractor] had no reasonable means of knowing that processes and welding materials previously used successfully in the fabrication of missile base pressure vessels from T-1 steel would not be satisfactory for vessels required to meet the requirements of the . . . specifications.

In *Stubnitz Greene Spring Corp.*, ASBCA 2608, 56-2 BCA ¶ 1034, a contractor was excused when delayed by its inability to overcome production difficulties caused by a government change order greatly increasing inspection standards. The board held that the change order, which was found to be within the scope of the contract, demanded a much higher degree of technical skill and expertise than normally would have been expected under the contract. In finding that the contractor had not represented its know-how as above average when accepting the contract, the board adopted the same analysis used in resolving impossibility claims, by determining that in this case the contractor had not impliedly assumed the risk of the production difficulties encountered.

e. Labor Problems

In the absence of a strike or other enumerated cause of delay, a contractor is generally not excused for labor difficulties. These difficulties usually involve either the loss of key personnel or an unexpected labor shortage. The boards have strictly adhered to the rule that the contractor assumes the risk of hiring and retaining a competent work force, *Telecommun. Lab., Inc.*, ASBCA 25240, 85-1 BCA ¶ 17,786. See *Electro-Magnetics, Inc.*, ASBCA 19830, 75-2 BCA ¶ 11,503, in which the board held that the fact that the contractor's president suffered a heart attack did not excuse the contractor's failure to complete its contract. The board reasoned that, in the president's absence, the vice president should be expected to step in and take over the president's responsibilities. See also *Centennial Leasing v. General Servs. Admin.*, GSBCA 12037, 94-1 BCA ¶ 26,398, where death of a subcontractor's chief operating officer was not an excusable cause of nonperformance. In *Stephen J. Yarling*, AGBCA 382, 75-2 BCA ¶ 11,540, the same rule was applied to a sole proprietorship when the owner's illness was alleged to have delayed the completion of the work. Since the contract did not require the personal services of the sole proprietor contractor, the board refused to grant an excusable delay.

Accidents that injure key personnel during the performance of the work do not excuse performance. See *Yumang, O'Connell & Assocs.*, AGBCA 83-171-1, 84-2

BCA ¶ 17,313 (excusable delay denied when the contractor's field supervisor fell on the job and sustained a concussion); *M&T Constr. Co.*, ASBCA 42750, 93-1 BCA ¶ 25,223 (heart attack suffered by one of subcontractor's personnel not an "act of God" that should excuse contractor's nonperformance); *Flight Refueling, Inc.*, ASBCA 46846, 97-2 BCA ¶ 29,000, *aff'd*, 168 F.3d 1318 (Fed. Cir. 1998) (the death of General Manager not an excuse because no evidence that the General Manager, who was lead project engineer, was a key employee or how his death affected the contractor's performance); *Ameritech Mfg. Co.,* ASBCA 49016, 96-2 BCA ¶ 28,397 (illness or deaths of relatives will not excuse a supplier's delay in delivering materials); and *Green Thumb Lawn Maint.*, ENGBCA 6249, 98-1 BCA ¶ 29,688 (no evidence that the government's pressure caused the plaintiff's poor health).

In *Space Sys. Lab., Inc.*, ASBCA 12162, 68-1 BCA ¶ 6859, which involved a contractor's inability to hire a skilled optician, the board stated that the scarcity of qualified opticians was a market condition prevailing at the time the contract was entered into and was thus a risk assumed by the contractor. See also *Sanitary Wiping Cloth & Burlap Co.*, GSBCA 2657, 68-2 BCA ¶ 7340. In *Wisconsin Mfg. Co.*, ASBCA 9040, 1964 BCA ¶ 4391, the board stated at 21,215:

> It is true that [the contractor] did not either cause or anticipate the labor shortage. It is, however, [the contractor's] responsibility to have available the means of performing its contract. In this case no excusable cause has contributed to the labor shortage. It was a market condition of which the [contractor] assumed the risk at the time of making the contract and the assumption of which was in his control.

Contractors have also been held to a high standard in overcoming delays due to loss of personnel. In *Alert Prods., Inc.*, ASBCA 5620, 59-2 BCA ¶ 2422, the board agreed that the unexpected resignation of a key engineer was originally beyond the control of and without the fault or negligence of the contractor. Stating that the contractor still had a duty to complete performance, however, the board found the contractor's subsequent conduct negligent in failing to overcome the labor problem.

An exception to the general rule regarding labor shortages is *Bannercraft Clothing Co.*, ASBCA 6247, 1963 BCA ¶ 3995, in which the board granted an excusable delay to a contractor whose qualified employees had been siphoned off by competitors and who had diligently tried to overcome this problem. However, *Bannercraft* has been narrowly construed as involving unique circumstances, *Weldon Farm Prods., Inc.*, AGBCA 200, 70-2 BCA ¶ 8454.

C. Time Extensions

A contractor is not entitled to relief upon the mere occurrence of an event that qualifies as an excusable delay. The contractor must show that the event caused delay to the *overall completion* of the contract and must establish the number of days of relief to which it is entitled.

The construction contract Default clause in FAR 52.249-10 specifically provides for a time extension while the Supply/Service clause does not. That clause provides for other relief. In addition, the Time Extensions clause in FAR 52.211-13, used in construction contracts, emphasizes the need for proof of delay.

1. Causation

The contractor must show that the delay that was incurred was caused by an excusable event. In *Fox-Sadler Co.*, ASBCA 8421, 1963 BCA ¶ 3768, the contractor's request for an excusable delay was denied even though greater than normal rain and cold temperatures were experienced, because there was no showing that such weather interfered with the installation of a boiler under the contract. In the same case, the contractor's late delivery of shop drawings could not be excused on the basis of an alleged inconsistency in government specifications discovered by the contractor approximately six months after the shop drawings were first due. The drawings had been previously submitted and rejected for other reasons. See also *Clark Field Bus Lines*, ASBCA 9281, 1964 BCA ¶ 4492 (no evidence that the strike affected bus service, nor was the strike in existence when the contractor defaulted), and *Pioneer Enters., Inc.*, ASBCA 43739, 93-1 BCA ¶ 25,395 (no evidence that delayed delivery of cement joists caused any slowdown of work). Similarly, the contractor will not be granted relief for unusually severe winter weather that would have prevented performance if it is shown that the contractor had not intended to work during that period, *Sunset Constr. Co.*, IBCA 454-9-64, 65-2 BCA ¶ 5188. See also *Murray J. Shiff Constr. Co.*, ASBCA 9029, 1964 BCA ¶ 4478 (government delay in approving shop drawings occurred after the contractor was so far behind schedule that the material was not needed for some time after the indicated date); *Jim Challinor*, AGBCA 76-185, 78-2 BCA ¶ 13,330 (unusually heavy rain did not delay work because soil in area drained well enough to work); and *Plandel, Inc.*, HUDBCA 92-7171-C1, 93-3 BCA ¶ 26,103 (relief denied for government delay in rejecting substitute products offered under a brand name or equal specification because the rejection was caused in substantial part by the contractor's incomplete submittal and failure to obtain sufficient information with respect to the product prior to submitting its offer).

2. Concurrent Delays

Another frequent causation problem stems from concurrent excusable delays and delays for which the contractor is responsible. S*ee* James, *Concurrency & Apportioning Liability & Damages in Public Contract Adjudications*, 20 Pub. Cont. L. J. 490 (1991). The preferred solution is to determine if one event is the controlling cause of the delay. See *Chas. I. Cunningham Co.*, IBCA 60, 57-2 BCA ¶ 1541, in which the board, citing *Robinson v. United States*, 261 U.S. 486 (1923) and *Sun Shipbuilding & Dry Dock Co. v. United States*, 76 Ct. Cl. 154 (1932), stated at 5,483:

> Accordingly, if an event that would constitute an excusable cause of delay in fact occurs, and if that event in fact delays the progress of the work as a whole, the contractor is entitled to an extension of time for so much of the ultimate delay in completion as was the result or consequence of that event, notwithstanding that the progress of the work may also have been slowed down or halted by a want of diligence, lack of planning, or some other inexcusable omission on the part of the contractor.

In *Morris Mech. Enters., Inc. v. United States*, 1 Cl. Ct. 50 (1982), the court held that the contractor was entitled to an excusable delay in completing testing even though its supplier had been late in delivering equipment to be installed in a government building. The court found that another government contractor's delay in making the building ready for installation of the equipment was the "proximate and effective" cause of the delay. However, in *Program & Constr. Mgmt. Group, Inc. v. General Servs. Admin.*, GSBCA 14178, 00-1 BCA ¶ 30,641, the government's failure to convene a preconstruction conference did not delay performance because the contract did not require a preconstruction conference. Although the contractor argued that the industry standard required the meeting before construction commenced, the contractor's failure to obtain security clearances and submit a safety plan caused a concurrent, non-reimbursable delay.

Concurrent delays occur when two or more causes have a simultaneous effect on contract performance. They must be distinguished from delays which occur sequentially. See *R. P. Wallace, Inc. v. United States*, 63 Fed. Cl. 402 (2004), stating at 409-10:

> Thornier issues are posed by concurrent or sequential delays—the first occurring where both parties are responsible for the same period of delay, the second where one party and then the other cause different delays *seriatim* or intermittently.

The court stated that where government and contractor delays are concurrent, while monetary recovery may be denied to the parties, "Concurrent delay is not fatal to a contractor's claim for additional time due to excusable delay." While the contractor may be relieved from the consequences of a default termination and may be excused from liability for government damages (actual or liquidated), it is not necessarily entitled to a time extension. Thus, the contractor could not recover on an acceleration claim if it was also the cause of the delay. There is a further discussion of concurrent delays in the following section on Compensable Delays and in Chapter 10 dealing with actual and liquidated damages.

In some concurrent delay cases, the consequences of the delay have been allocated to the parties based upon the degree of comparative responsibility. See *Raymond Constructors of Africa, Ltd. v. United States*, 188 Ct. Cl. 147, 411 F.2d 1227 (1969), stating at 164-65:

> Actually, there is no basis in the record on which a precise allocation of responsibility for the overall delay in completing the work under the contract can be made as between the defendant's delay in procuring equipment and delivering it to the Sudanese government at Port Sudan, the Sudanese government's delay in transporting equipment from Port Sudan to the job site, and the subcontractor's shortcomings. In such a situation, it seems that the only feasible thing to do is to make a finding in the nature of a jury verdict that the defendant's delay in procuring equipment and delivering it to the Sudanese government at Port Sudan was responsible for one-third of the overall delay in the completion of the work under the contract and, hence, for one-third of the extra indirect expenses that were incurred by the plaintiff because of such overall delay, or $7,440.

See also *Inversiones Aransu, S.A.*, ENGBCA CC-2-667, 92-1 BCA ¶ 24,584, finding the contractor entitled to a five-day time extension using the comparative responsibility theory.

In *Commerce Int'l Co. v. United States*, 167 Ct. Cl. 529, 338 F.2d 81 (1964), the court refused to consider allocating responsibility because the contractor did not separate its own delays from those charged to the government. While the term "apportionment" may connote the same meaning as "comparative responsibility," it has primarily been used in cases relieving the contractor from liability for liquidated damages involving sequential delays. See the discussion under Liquidated Damages in Chapter 10.

In *Essex Electro Engrs., Inc. v. Danzig*, 224 F.3d 1283 (Fed. Cir. 2000), the court used the term "apportionable" to refer to what it appeared to believe were sequential delays, stating at 1292:

> A finding that the government did not act reasonably in responding to Essex's ECP submissions may affect the Board's conclusion that most government-caused delays were concurrent with Essex-caused delays. As this court has stated, a contractor cannot recover "where the delays are 'concurrent or intertwined' and the contractor has not met its burden of separating its delays from those chargeable to the Government." *Blinderman Constr. Co. v. United States*, 695 F. 2d 552, 559 (Fed. Cir. 1982). Nevertheless, if "there is in the proof a clear apportionment of the delay and the expense attributable to each party," then the government will be liable for its delays. *Coath & Goss, Inc. v. United States*, 101 Ct. Cl. 702, 714-15, 1944 WL 3694 (1944). The sequential nature of Essex's submissions and the government's responses renders each party's delays inherently apportionable, at least in the case of ECP-related delays. A more definite attribution of ECP-related delays may affect the Board's overall conclusion of concurrency, as we discuss below.

3. Delay of Overall Completion Required

Even though a contractor can establish that an event or occurrence was unforeseeable, beyond its control, and occurred without its fault or negligence, it is not entitled to an excusable delay unless it can prove that the time lost delayed the completion of the job, *George A. Fuller Co.*, ASBCA 9590, 1964 BCA ¶ 4396. It is not sufficient to establish that some work was prevented; the work prevented must be work that will delay the overall completion of the job, *Sauer, Inc. v. Danzig,* 224 F.3d 1340 (Fed. Cir. 2000); *Essential Constr. Co.*, ASBCA 18491, 78-2 BCA ¶ 13,314. In *Powell's Gen. Contracting Co.*, DOTCAB 77-27, 79-1 BCA ¶ 13,694, *recons. denied,* 79-1 BCA ¶ 13,702, the board stated at 67,158 that "there must be identification of the work controlling the overall completion of the contract." The board also held that it is not necessary that work be completely prevented to establish excusability and granted the contractor an excusable delay because of loss of efficiency of 25 percent to 30 percent due to unusually severe weather. See also *D.J. Simons Constr. Co.*, ASBCA 41336, 93-1 BCA ¶ 25,306 (contractor failed to show that the government's alleged delay in approving its infrared heaters affected overall project completion), and *L.W. Schneider, Inc.*, ASBCA 44533, 95-2 BCA ¶ 27,774, *aff'd,* 98 F.3d 1359 (Fed. Cir. 1996) (despite the government's inattention to a problem raised by a contractor regarding the efficacy of a device for inspecting part of the contract work, the contractor was not entitled to compensation for alleged government-caused delay, because the inspection issue was minor and played no material role in preventing the discharge of the contractor's overall responsibility).

When the Critical Path Method of schedule control is used, it is held that the delay must be on the critical path, *Cimarron Constr. Co. v. United States,* 203 Ct. Cl. 742 (1974). This requirement does not mean that each event must delay the contractor past the scheduled completion date. As long as time is lost, the contractor is entitled to an excusable delay. However, in *Harrison Western/Franki-Denys (JV)*, ENGBCA 5506, 93-1 BCA ¶ 25,406, the board held that the fact that a particular project was on the critical path of a large construction contract did not automatically entitle a contractor to an extension of time because the contract specifically stated that, although placement on the critical path was a necessary condition to an extension of time, it was not by itself a sufficient condition. To obtain an extension of time, the contractor was required to show that the delay on the particular project resulted in delay in the overall contract.

The contractor will normally be entitled to an excusable delay even though the original contract delivery or completion schedule allows more time than is actually necessary to perform the work. In *Heat Exchangers, Inc.*, ASBCA 8705, 1963 BCA ¶ 3881, the board stated: "In respect to liquidated damages, the [contractor] is entitled to retain this cushion." See also *J.W. Merz*, IBCA 64, 59-1 BCA ¶ 2086, in which the contractor was held entitled to an excusable delay on account of unusually severe weather, even though it had been late in starting, because the weather caused actual delay and the contractor would have finished on time but for the weather. In *Lambert Constr. Co.*, DOTCAB 77-9, 78-1 BCA ¶ 13,221, the board held that the "contractor was free to allocate his time for the job subject to the contract delivery date." The contractor's freedom to allocate its time may be limited by contract provisions requiring it to begin performance within a certain period of time and to prosecute the work diligently. See, for example, the Commencement, Prosecution and

Completion of Work clause for construction contracts contained in FAR 52.211-10, which requires the contractor to commence work within a stipulated number of days after issuance of a notice to proceed and to prosecute the work diligently. A similar clause has been a requirement for DOD construction contracts since 1965. It might be argued that this clause should operate to deprive a contractor of an excusable delay arising from an event that might have been avoided had the contractor begun performance promptly. So construed, it might operate to deprive the contractor of its "cushion." In *Malor Constr. Corp.*, IBCA 1688-6-83, 84-1 BCA ¶ 17,023, a contractor was required to begin a roofing contract within 15 calendar days after receipt of a notice to proceed. The contract also prohibited work on days when the temperature was below 40° F or when moisture was present on the surface. The board denied an excusable delay on account of weather, finding that there would have been sufficient time to complete the job if the contractor had started within the required time.

In *Burgett Inv., Inc.*, AGBCA 81-108-1, 83-2 BCA ¶ 16,695, the contractor alleged that its starting of performance was delayed by late receipt of government-furnished property. During performance the contractor recovered and was making sufficient progress to complete on time, but subsequent unexcusable delays resulted in its failure to perform on time. The board denied an excusable delay, indicating that, even if the government had been at fault in the late delivery of the government-furnished property, the contractor could have performed within the contract schedule. This view appears to have been rejected in *J.W. Bateson Co.*, ASBCA 27491, 84-3 BCA ¶ 17,566, *recons. denied,* 85-1 BCA ¶ 17,927, *rev'd on other grounds,* 809 F.2d 787 (Fed. Cir. 1986), in which the board granted an excusable delay for a government-caused delay early in performance, stating at 87,539:

> [T]o say that it did not or should not add to the time available to complete the project would be, at least, unfair by forcing [the contractor] to make up the lost time by working overtime in the time remaining, or, at worst, would let the Government off scot-free despite having caused the problem to begin with.

Where the contractor is permitted to continue working past the scheduled completion date, it can take advantage of excusable delays that occur during this period to relieve it of the burden of liquidated damages, *C.R. Bagwell*, ASBCA 3514, 57-1 BCA ¶ 1322; *Tidewater Tennis Courts*, ASBCA 20059, 76-1 BCA ¶ 11,810. In *Optimum Designs, Inc.*, ASBCA 13370, 69-1 BCA ¶ 7681, the board stated at 35,640: "The protections of the excusability provisions of the Termination clause are not lost because the contractor is allowed to complete after the original completion date is passed."

4. Measuring Time Extensions

Once a contractor shows that it was actually delayed by an excusable cause, it still must establish the length of the time extension to which it is entitled. Generally, the duration of the time extension is governed by the extent to which the excusable cause of delay either increases the amount of time required for performance of the contract work as a whole, or defers the date by which the last of that work will be reasonably capable of completion, *Montgomery-Macri Co.*, IBCA 59, 1963 BCA ¶ 3819, *recons. denied*, 1964 BCA ¶ 4292.

A contractor "is entitled to only so much time extension as the excusable cause actually delayed performance," *Robert P. Jones Co.*, AGBCA 391, 76-1 BCA ¶ 11,824. See *CJP Contractors*, ASBCA 50076, 00-2 BCA ¶ 31,119 (appropriate time extension for delays encountered while waiting for government approval of a contract change was less than the total duration of the delay because the contractor continued to perform during part of the delay), and *Warbonnet Elec., Inc.*, VABCA 3771, 96-1 BCA ¶ 27,938 (contractor entitled to a time extension due to the government's delay in approving the contractor's initial submittals because it was unable to ship any materials to the project site absent government approval). The extension granted may be longer, shorter, or of the same duration as the delay period. In *Jones*, the contractor was awarded a 57-day period equal to the duration of the delaying event resulting from inadequate specifications. However, in *Blackhawk Heating & Plumbing Co.*, GSBCA 2432, 75-1 BCA ¶ 11,261, *recons. denied*, 76-1 BCA ¶ 11,649, the board disapproved of the "total time" method of computation, which involves awarding the contractor approximately the same amount of time as days delayed, reasoning that the "total time" method insufficiently correlated the delaying event with the amount of time the contract was actually delayed. In *Witzig Constr. Co.*, IBCA 92, 60-2 BCA ¶ 2700, a construction contractor erecting an electrical transmission line was allowed 16 days for an eight-day delay, since the excusable delay resulted in pushing the contract period into late autumn weather that was one-half as favorable as the summer contract period. See *Martin Constr. Co.*, ENG-BCA 3192, 75-2 BCA ¶ 11,384 (part of contractor's time extension included time awarded for a 25 percent reduction in productivity directly attributable to excessive precipitation), and *Skip Kirchdorfer, Inc.*, ASBCA 40516, 00-1 BCA ¶ 30,625 (contractor given one-half day time extension when it was ordered to secure the job site at 12:30 P.M.).

In *Ballenger Corp.*, DOTCAB 74-32, 84-2 BCA ¶ 17,277, the board held that the method of assessing delay and granting extension must be consistent with the contract performance schedule. Thus, it would not be appropriate to grant extension on a workday basis when the contract performance schedule is on a calendar basis. The board indicated that, if the delays are assessed on a workday basis, they can be adjusted to a calendar basis by multiplying the number of workdays by a factor of 7/5. See also *Coffey Constr. Co.*, VABCA 3361, 93-2 BCA ¶ 25,788 (a CPM schedule must reflect actual events if it is to be used to evaluate requests for time extensions), and *H.G. Reynolds Co.*, ASBCA 42351, 93-2 BCA ¶ 25,797 (contractor not entitled to time extension as the result of a fire in a subcontractor's site trailer because there was no evidence that the fire caused any delay in the completion of the work).

5. Burden of Proof

It is well settled that the contractor has the burden of proving the excusability of a delay, *Williamsburg Drapery Co.*, ASBCA 5484, 61-2 BCA ¶ 3111, *aff'd*, 177 Ct. Cl. 776, 369 F.2d 729 (1966); *Woodside Screw Mach. Co.*, ASBCA 6936, 1962 BCA ¶ 3308; *Beco, Inc.*, ASBCA 9702, 1964 BCA ¶ 4493. This burden must be established by a preponderance of the evidence, *Mil-Craft Mfg., Inc.*, ASBCA 19305, 74-2 BCA ¶ 10,840. However, the contractor will not be required to meet this burden when the government is in control of the evidence, *Meyer Labs, Inc.*, ASBCA 17061, 74-2 BCA ¶ 10,804. Even if the record does not support the contractor's proposed time extension, the board may make a jury verdict determination if there is sufficient basis, *Santa Fe Eng'rs, Inc.*, PSBCA 902, 84-2 BCA ¶ 17,377. In *Unitec, Inc.*, DOTCAB 77-29, 78-1 BCA ¶ 12,958, *recons. denied*, 78-2 BCA ¶ 13,222, the board relied on the resident engineer's weekly construction reports in calculating a time extension. See also *Intercontinental Mfg. Co.*, ASBCA 48506, 03-1 BCA ¶ 32,131 (delay claim denied because the contractor failed to show the government was the sole and proximate cause of tardy performance). Similarly, in *Hoffman Constr. Co. of Oregon v. United States*, 40 Fed. Cl. 184 (1998), *aff'd*, 178 F.3d 1313 (Fed. Cir. 1999), the court held that to prove that the government is the proximate cause of the delay, the contractor must demonstrate that no other cause delayed the contract, regardless of the government's actions.

The construction contract clause states that, once a contractor gives notice, the contracting officer "shall ascertain the facts and the extent of the delay." In *Manufacturers' Casualty Ins. Co. v. United States*, 105 Ct. Cl. 342, 63 F. Supp. 759 (1946), the court held the contracting officer to have a contractual duty to ascertain the facts upon the contractor's application for a time extension and failure to do so to be a breach of contract. In *Manufacturers'*, the court found for a surety attempting to obtain an excusable delay caused by a strike when the contracting officer never responded to the contractor's notice of delay. The scope of the contracting officer's duty was discussed in *Freeman Elec. Constr. Co.*, DOTCAB 74-23, 77-1 BCA ¶ 12,258, *aff'd*, 221 Ct. Cl. 884 (1979), which involved a weather delay. The board stated that a contractor is required to present a prima facie case of delay before the contracting officer's corresponding duty to ascertain the facts of delay arises. *Freeman* went on to note that, while the contracting officer is obligated to gather facts surrounding the delay, the contractor must produce all facts peculiarly within its own knowledge or control. *Freeman* was written in response to several board decisions involving weather delays that had found that the duty to gather weather data lay with the government and the board noted that this information was equally available to both parties. See *Paul A. Teegarden*, IBCA 382, 1963 BCA ¶ 3876.

To meet the burden of proof, contractors frequently use the Critical Path Method, particularly when concurrent delays are involved, *Basic Constr. Co.*, ASBCA 22582, 79-1 BCA ¶ 13,577; *Continental Consol. Corp.*, ENGBCA 2743, 68-1 BCA

¶ 7003, *modified*, 200 Ct. Cl. 737 (1972); Wickwire and Smith, *The Use of Critical Path Method Techniques in Contract Claims,* 7 Pub. Cont. L.J. 1 (1974). CPM is frequently required as part of the contract and is thus readily available to the parties, *Blackhawk Heating & Plumbing Co.*, GSBCA 2432, 75-1 BCA ¶ 11,261, *recons. denied*, 76-1 BCA ¶ 11,649; *Canon Constr. Corp.*, ASBCA 16142, 72-1 BCA ¶ 9404. However, even though not contractually required, CPM is often used by the parties to prove causation, *Blinderman Constr. Co.*, ASBCA 20725, 77-2 BCA ¶ 12,723; *Fischbach & Moore Int'l Corp.*, ASBCA 18146, 77-1 BCA ¶ 12,300, *aff'd*, 223 Ct. Cl. 119, 617 F.2d 223 (1980). Absent a formal CPM submittal, CPM-type analysis may still be applied in the determination of a cause of delay, *John Murphy Constr. Co.*, AGBCA 418, 79-1 BCA ¶ 13,836. When so used, the CPM analysis must be employed in an accurate manner and be consistent with events that actually occurred on the job. See *Ballenger Corp.*, DOTCAB 74-32, 84-1 BCA ¶ 16,973, *modified*, 84-2 BCA ¶ 17,277, in which the board found that the record established only five days of excusable delay rather than the 21 months indicated by the CPM submitted in litigation. See also *J.W. Bateson Co.*, ASBCA 27491, 84-3 BCA ¶ 17,566, in which the board refused to use the schedule portion of the CPM because it had no credibility.

Contractors are required to mitigate damages. Often this involves working around the problem. See *American Int'l Contractors, Inc./Capitol Indus. Constr. Groups, Inc., A Joint Venture*, ASBCA 39544, 95-2 BCA ¶ 27,920 (contractor's delay claims denied because excavation was possible in the work area in which there was no farming); *Hunter Mfg. Co.*, ASBCA 48693, 97-1 BCA ¶ 28,824 (contractor failed to show that the government's delay in resolving a conflict concerning the type of fuel caused a delay when the contractor resolved the conflict itself before the government formally resolved the conflict in the same manner); and *Elter S. A.*, ASBCA 52791, 02-1 BCA ¶ 31,672 (contractor's claim that government road closure delayed performance denied because evidence showed that detours permitted access without significant loss of productivity).

6. Notice and Schedule Extension

The construction contract Default clause in FAR 52.249-10 requires that the contractor notify the contracting officer in writing within 10 days from the beginning of any excusable delay and state the causes of the delay. The supply and services contract Default clause in FAR 52.249-8 does not contain a notice provision. Even when written notice is specified, oral notice is sufficient if the government is not prejudiced by the lack of written notice or has actual notice of the delay. In *Hoel-Steffen Constr. Co. v. United States*, 197 Ct. Cl. 561, 456 F.2d 760 (1972), involving a suspension of work claim, the Court of Claims stated at 573 that "notice provisions in contract-adjustment clauses [should] not be applied too technically and illiberally where the Government is quite aware of the operative facts." See also *Copco Steel & Eng'g Co. v. United States*, 169 Ct. Cl. 601, 341 F.2d 590 (1965), in which the court stated that written notice provisions "have frequently been held to be of no consequence where the conduct of the parties have made it clear that formal adherence would serve no useful purpose or that the parties have in fact waived it." Thus, even where the contractor has failed to give oral notice, the 10-day notice provision is usually waived, *Levelator Corp. of Am.*, VABCA 820, 71-1 BCA ¶ 8715, *recons. denied*, 71-2 BCA ¶ 9011. See *Southwest Marine, Inc.*, DOTBCA DTCG-31-83-10099, 94-2 BCA ¶ 26,641, in which the notice requirement was waived because the contracting officer's actions constituted clear evidence of his recognition that the contractor had encountered some delay.

On occasion, the boards have denied recovery in holding a contractor strictly to the 10-day notice provision, *Ardelt-Horn Constr. Co.*, ASBCA 14550, 73-1 BCA ¶ 9901, *aff'd*, 207 Ct. Cl. 995 (1975); *Volta Elec. Co.*, NASABCA 39, 1963 BCA ¶ 3871; *Emlyn T. Linkous*, GSBCA 3832, 74-1 BCA ¶ 10,473. However, these cases deal exclusively with contractors who failed to give any notice whatsoever, oral or written, and in circumstances indicating that the contractors were negligent in failing to do so.

The construction contract clause provides for a schedule extension, but the supply and services contract clause does not. Thus, schedule extensions during performance most commonly involve construction contracts.

II. COMPENSABLE DELAYS

Performance delays that have significant financial impact on contractors occur frequently in government contracts. A contractor's ability to recover increased costs resulting from delays will depend upon the cause of the delay, the nature of its impact on the contractor, and the contractual provisions dealing with compensation for delays.

The government's policy on compensating contractors for delays has changed over the years. At one time it was the government's policy to use contract clauses barring compensation for delays, even those that it caused; and such exculpatory clauses relieving it from liability were held to be enforceable, *Wells Bros. Co. v. United States*, 254 U.S. 83 (1920) (plain meaning of written contract containing clause is presumed valid); *Wood v. United States*, 258 U.S. 120 (1922) (clause enforceable despite lack of clause authorizing suspensions). However, such clauses have been used infrequently in recent years (see, e.g., *Broome Constr., Inc. v. United States*, 203 Ct. Cl. 521, 492 F.2d 829 (1974)); instead, the government has adopted a number of clauses granting the contractor compensation for delays caused by the government.

The delay compensation clause for fixed-price construction contracts is the Suspension of Work clause contained in FAR 52.242-14. FAR 42.1305(a) makes this clause mandatory in all fixed-price construction or architect-engineering contracts. A substantially similar clause has been in use by all government agencies since 1969.

These clauses, which provide for both ordered and constructive suspensions, evolved from the fixed-price contract Suspension of Work clause used by the Army Corps of Engineers during World War II. That clause gave the contracting officer the right to order the suspension of all or any part of the work, but it was silent with regard to the effect of acts of the government that delayed performance of the work by the contractor. However, the appeals boards soon developed the doctrine of constructive suspensions of work. See *Fire Sec. Sys., Inc.*, VABCA 3086, 91-2 BCA ¶ 23,743, and *John A. Johnson & Sons, Inc.*, ASBCA 4403, 59-1 BCA ¶ 2088, *aff'd*, 180 Ct. Cl. 969 (1967). By this rule the board treated the delaying act of the government as a de facto suspension order and granted a price adjustment under the provisions of the clause. The clause was modified in 1957 to incorporate the constructive suspension rule and again modified in 1968, when it was incorporated into Standard Form 23-A. In 1984, this clause was placed in the FAR without significant modification.

In supply and services contracts, ordered and constructive suspensions are covered by separate clauses. Ordered suspensions are covered by the Stop-Work Order clause contained in FAR 52.242-15, which is optional for use in negotiated supply, services, or research and development contracts (see FAR 12.1305(b)). Constructive suspensions in fixed-price contracts, other than for construction, are presently covered by the FAR 52.242-17, Government Delay of Work, clause. FAR 42.1305(d) makes this clause mandatory for fixed-price supply contracts involving noncommercial items and optional for fixed-price contracts for services and commercial or modified commercial items.

This section divides the discussion of the compensability of delays into three topics. The first is the situation where the contract does not contain a compensable delays clause or where the delay is caused by an event not covered by the clause incorporated into the contract. The second topic considers the clauses dealing with compensation for suspensions ordered by the contracting officer. The last topic is an analysis of constructive suspensions under the Suspension of Work and Government Delay of Work clauses.

A. No Applicable Clause

If a contract contains no clause giving the government the right to order a suspension of work, the contractor would not ordinarily be legally required to stop work when it received such an order. However, in *Robert A. & Sandra B. Moura*, PSBCA 3460, 96-1 BCA ¶ 27,956, the board held that the government had an inherent right to order a suspension because it had the contractual right to terminate for default on one day's notice, which necessarily encompassed the lesser right to suspend performance temporarily. The government suspended operation of the contract after a serious money shortage was discovered, first and second class mail was found in trash cans, and blank money orders and other accountable items were found unsecured.

In the absence of a clause dealing with suspensions of work, the contractor is not ordinarily entitled to compensation for delays unless they are the result of government fault, *Fritz-Rumer-Cooke v. United States*, 279 F.2d 200 (6th Cir. 1960). See also the discussion in *Consolidated Molded Prods. Corp. v. United States*, 220 Ct. Cl. 594, 600 F.2d 793 (1979). A major exception to this rule is present if the contract contains a representation that is held to be a warranty, in which case the government is liable even though it is without fault. Government fault will be found if the government breaches its implied duty not to hinder or interfere with the contractor's performance or its implied duty to cooperate with the contractor, *Cedar Lumber, Inc. v. United States*, 5 Cl. Ct. 539 (1984) (to be a breach, delay must be unreasonable; "[m]inor errors or minor hindrances" are not a breach); *Franklin L. Haney v. United States*, 230 Ct. Cl. 148, 676 F.2d 584 (1982). See Chapter 3 for a discussion of both the warranty without fault and the implied warranty cases.

B. Ordered Suspensions

Ordered suspensions are covered by the Suspension of Work clause and the Stop-Work Order clause. The Government Delay of Work clause does not provide for ordered suspensions, and FAR 42.1304(b) states that it shall not be used as the basis or justification of a stop-work order. Similarly, compensation under the Stop-Work Order clause will be available only when a written order has been issued. In *A.C.E.S., Inc.*, ASBCA 21417, 79-1 BCA ¶ 13,809, the contracting officer advised the contractor that government acceptance would be suspended pending clarification of the contract's technical data requirements but did not issue a written order. The contractor's subsequent work stoppage was therefore treated as a constructive suspension and compensated under the Government Delay of Work clause. In *Housatonic Valley Constr. Co.,* AGBCA 1999-181-1, 00-1 BCA ¶ 30,869, *recons. denied.,* 00-2 BCA ¶ 31,043, the contractor was not entitled to an price adjustment for a government suspension of work due to wet ground conditions, because the contract contained a secondary clause, "Suspension For Other Than the Convenience of the Government," which provided that the government would not be liable for suspensions ordered to prevent environmental damage.

Ordered suspensions covered by the Suspension of Work clause are compensable only if they result in unreasonable delay. The Stop-Work Order clause does not contain the unreasonable delay limitation contained in the Suspension of Work clause. Thus, the contractor should be entitled to recover for a stop-work order under that clause without being required to prove that the delay was unreasonable. In addition, the Stop-Work Order clause provides for "equitable adjustments," which include a reasonable profit, while mere "adjustments" under the Suspension of Work clause exclude profit from recovery. Both the reasonableness and unreasonableness of delays are discussed below.

Contractors will not be able to recover if the contracting officer is justified in suspending the work because of contractor fault. See, for example, *Eris Painting*

& Gen. Corp., ASBCA 27803, 84-1 BCA ¶ 17,148, *aff'd*, 765 F.2d 160 (Fed. Cir. 1985) (no recovery for suspension ordered because contractor could not do work to specifications); *Munck Sys., Inc.*, ASBCA 25600, 83-1 BCA ¶ 16,210, *aff'd*, 727 F.2d 1118 (Fed. Cir. 1983) ("do not ship" order fully justified because the contractor did not furnish detailed drawings as required so that government could check compliance with specifications); and *Mudsharks Co-op, Inc.*, AGBCA 81-238-3, 82-2 BCA ¶ 16,117 (suspension justified following noncooperation and verbal abuse of government representative by contractor). In such a case, the contractor was held not entitled to a cure notice prior to the issuance of a stop work order (suspending performance), *Green Int'l, Inc.*, ENGBCA 5706, 98-1 BCA ¶ 29,684. In *Toombs & Co. v. United States*, 4 Cl. Ct. 535 (1984), *aff'd*, 770 F.2d 183 (Fed. Cir. 1985), an ordered suspension was justified because of contractor fault, but failure to lift the suspension after the problems had been corrected was compensable.

C. Constructive Suspensions

In order for a constructive suspension to arise, work must be prevented, not voluntarily stopped by the contractor. Constructive suspensions occur when work is stopped absent an express order by the contracting officer and the government is found to be responsible for the work stoppage. Courts and boards have long held that, when the contractor's work is effectively suspended but the contracting officer does not issue an order of suspension, "the law considers that done which ought to have been done" and characterizes the circumstances as a constructive (or de facto) suspension, *Merritt-Chapman & Scott Corp. v. United States*, 192 Ct. Cl. 848, 429 F.2d 431 (1970). For a similar result under the Stop Work Order clause, see *Dynamics Research Corp.*, ASBCA 53788, 04-2 BCA ¶ 32,747, where the Program Manager directed contractor's employees be sent home because computers had crashed.

For the contractor to be compensated, the work must be prevented—voluntary work stoppages are not compensable, *CRF v. United States*, 224 Ct. Cl. 312, 624 F.2d 1054 (1980); *First Line Mfg., Inc.*, ASBCA 24443, 83-1 BCA ¶ 16,394, *recons. denied*, 83-2 BCA ¶ 16,601. This subsection considers the major circumstances that will constitute constructive suspensions.

1. Delays Not Attributable to Government Fault

It was originally thought that the Suspension of Work clause only covered those government acts that would otherwise have constituted a breach of contract. Thus, the clause was presented to, and approved by, the GAO on the theory that its sole function was to provide an administrative remedy for such acts, 36 Comp. Gen. 302 (B-127764) (1956). However, the Court of Claims interpreted the clause to require a price adjustment when the contractor is delayed for the "convenience" of the government for an undue length of time even though the government did not cause the delay by its actions or inactions in its administration of the contract (also called a "non-fault suspension"). Thus, although the principle of the delay for "convenience" language comes from the part of the clause providing for ordered suspensions, its logic was applied equally to constructive suspensions.

The original cases stating the "government convenience" rule were *John A. Johnson & Sons, Inc. v. United States*, 180 Ct. Cl. 969 (1967), where there was a delay of "almost a year" because the government gave priority to another contractor in accordance with a contract clause permitting such government action, and *Merritt-Chapman & Scott Corp. v. United States*, 192 Ct. Cl. 848, 429 F.2d 431 (1970), where there was a delay of 14 months to enable the government to determine how to cope with materially different subsurface conditions. In these instances, the court found that, despite lack of fault in the actions of the government, under the circumstances the contractor "cannot reasonably be expected to bear the risks and costs of the delay." Subsequently, the court followed this reasoning in *C.H. Leavell & Co. v. United States*, 208 Ct. Cl. 776, 530 F.2d 878 (1976), where there was a delay of five months awaiting a government appropriation to provide additional funding, and in *Fruehauf Corp. v. United States*, 218 Ct. Cl. 456, 587 F.2d 486 (1978), where there was a 15-month delay caused by a prior contractor at the work site who performed very poorly. See also *Henderson, Inc.*, DOTBCA 2423, 94-2 BCA ¶ 26,728, in which a suspension was found when the contractor was unable to perform dredging work during the entire five-month period specified in the contract because the state government was occupying the waters with a ferry service in response to a severe storm. In *International Builders of Fla., Inc.*, FAACAP 67-5, 71-1 BCA ¶ 8790, *aff'g*, 69-1 BCA ¶ 7706, the board recognized the principle articulated in *Merritt-Chapman* of suspension without government fault, but held that a 3½ -month delay because of breakage of dies at a subcontractor's plant was not so protracted as to require relief. Also, the contract had specifically allocated the risks of such performance difficulties to the contractor.

T.C. Bateson Constr. Co. v. United States, 162 Ct. Cl. 145, 319 F.2d 135 (1963), dealt with a slightly different situation. In *Bateson*, the government took possession of one building in a multi-building project in accordance with a contract provision allowing partial acceptance and staffed it with nonunion labor knowing that the contractor's labor union was threatening to strike in the face of such action. The court concluded that the ensuing strike was a constructive suspension since it was a gamble the government took at the expense of the contractor and was taken "for the convenience of the government." Subsequent decisions have applied this logic narrowly. See *Koppers Co.*, ENGBCA 2699, 67-2 BCA ¶ 6532 (no recovery where delay caused by loss of workers attracted to other government projects paying higher wages; government neither caused nor acted to precipitate a delay), and *Stolte-Santa Fe-Bing*, ASBCA 12920, 69-1 BCA ¶ 7637 (six-day strike called by union over grievance on another contract not compensable; unlike *T.C. Bateson*, strike here was not caused by government in administration of the contract; neither was it a major disruption, where it would be inequitable for contractor to absorb the cost).

2. Delay in Issuance of Notice to Proceed

These types of delays have been decided under the Suspension of Work clause using the same rationale that the Court of Claims used to decide such cases under breach of contract theory. In those cases, the court held that there was a breach of contract if a notice to proceed was not issued at the time promised in the contract if an express time was stated, *Abbett Elec. Corp. v. United States*, 142 Ct. Cl. 609, 162 F. Supp. 772 (1958), or within a reasonable time if no time was stated, *Ross Eng'g Co. v. United States*, 92 Ct. Cl. 253 (1940) (all time beyond 12 days unreasonable when there was no reason for delay and failure to issue notice to proceed forced contractor to work in winter); *A.S. Schulman Elec. Co. v. United States*, 145 Ct. Cl. 399 (1959) (suspension of work order accompanying notice to proceed constituted a breach of express provision of contract to give "effective notice to proceed"). See also *Alvarez & Assocs. Constr. Co.*, ASBCA 50185, 97-2 BCA ¶ 29,320 (there is an implied obligation to issue the notice to proceed within a reasonable time period). Compare *Stafford v. United States*, 109 Ct. Cl. 479, 74 F. Supp. 155 (1947), in which the court denied recovery for an 11-month delay in issuance of a notice to proceed, because the contract provided that the notice would be given after the prior contractor had completed its on-site work.

Similarly, compensable delays have been found under the Suspension of Work clause when the contract language set a date for issuance of the notice to proceed, *C.E.R., Inc.*, ASBCA 41767, 96-1 BCA ¶ 28,029 (when contract stated notice to proceed would be issued on or about 30 November, issuance in following March was compensable); *ABC Demolition Corp.*, GSBCA 2289, 68-2 BCA ¶ 7166 (contract stated notice to proceed would be issued upon submission of acceptable bonds); and when the government delayed issuance of the notice to proceed unreasonably, *Kraft Constr. Co.*, ASBCA 4976, 59-2 BCA ¶ 2347 (implied duty to give notice to proceed in a reasonable period of time and let contractor determine how to deal with other contractor on site); *L.O. Brayton & Co.*, IBCA 641-5-67, 70-2 BCA ¶ 8510 (facts indicated that government could have issued notice to proceed earlier had it been diligent). "The reasonable period runs from the date of the award of the contract, and the Government may not count the time it could have taken but did not in making the award," *Freeman Elec. Constr. Co.*, DOTBCA 74-23A, 77-1 BCA ¶ 12,258, *aff'd*, 221 Ct. Cl. 884 (1979). See also *Bechtel Envtl., Inc.*, ENGBCA 6137, 97-1 BCA ¶ 28,640, at 143,024-25 (even though contract was awarded earlier than planned, the government was still liable to issue notice to proceed within the time specified in the contract); *Goudreau Corp.*, DOTBCA 1895, 88-1 BCA ¶ 20,479 (delay of three months between furnishing of a performance bond and issuance of the notice to proceed to allow government to obtain a permit, was found unreasonable—even though the government could have taken 120 days under the contract to award but instead took 30 days to award and 90 days to issue the notice to proceed). See also *Strand Hunt Constr. v. General Servs. Admin.*, GSBCA 12859, 95-2 BCA ¶ 27,690 (government was obligated to cover costs imposed on contractor by virtue of delayed notice to proceed, but claim denied for lack of proof as to increased costs). In one unusual case, *Pan Arctic Corp.*, ASBCA 20739, 77-1 BCA ¶ 12,514, the board found that a delayed notice to proceed amounted to a constructive change in the method or manner of performance of the contract when the government had orally promised to issue the notice to proceed to permit concurrent work on two contracts held by the contractor. In *Welch Constr. Co.*, PSBCA 217, 77-1 BCA ¶ 12,322, the board held that a notice to proceed, issued in a timely manner but during a period of unusually severe weather, did not create a delay compensable under the Suspension of Work clause because there was no duty to issue the notice when the weather was accommodating.

There are a number of cases finding that the government delay in issuing the notice to proceed was reasonable. See *Commercial Contractors, Inc. v. United States*, 29 Fed. Cl. 654 (1993), in which a 40-day delay after receipt of performance and payment bonds was held to be reasonable. In *Manis Drilling*, IBCA 2658, 93-3 BCA ¶ 25,931, a 15-day delay was found to be reasonable when the contractor's delay in submitting payment and performance bonds contributed to delay in issuing the notice to proceed. See also *Marine Constr. & Dredging, Inc.*, ASBCA 38412, 90-1 BCA ¶ 22,573, in which the board denied a motion for summary judgment when the government did not issue the notice to proceed until six months after award. The board concluded that there were alleged reasons excusing this long delay that needed to be explored in a hearing on the issue.

The government is not bound by a statement in the solicitation that a notice to proceed is expected to be issued on a specified date, *M.A. Mortenson Co. v. United States*, 843 F.2d 1360 (Fed. Cir. 1988); *Bart Assoc., Inc.*, EBCA C-9406176, 97-2 BCA ¶ 29,206. These decisions reason that an "assumed date" is not a promise and does not bind the government to issue the notice to proceed to that particular date.

A delay in commencing work pending the outcome of a bid protest has been held to be reasonable under the Suspension of Work clause, *De Matteo Constr. Co. v. United States*, 220 Ct. Cl. 579, 600 F.2d 1384 (1979). There, the court affirmed a board decision finding that the contractor was on notice at the time of bidding that it was the government's policy to delay work when a bid protest occurred. Subsequently, the government adopted the Protest After Award clause, FAR 52.233-3, calling for the issuance of a stop-work order upon receipt of a protest. A delay in issuing a notice to proceed because of preaward delay caused by a bid protest was held compensable under this clause in *Hill Bros. Constr. Co.*, ENGBCA 5686, 90-3 BCA ¶ 23,276.

3. *Delays in Availability of Site*

Traditionally, the government was not liable for late site availability unless the contractor could show either government fault or an express government warranty that the site would be furnished at a specific time, *H.E. Crook Co. v. United States*, 270 U.S. 4 (1926); *United States v. Foley*, 329 U.S. 64 (1946). However, in both *Fruehauf Corp. v. United States*, 218 Ct. Cl. 456, 587 F.2d 486 (1978), and *John A. Johnson & Sons, Inc. v. United States*, 180 Ct. Cl. 969 (1967), the court found the government liable for nonavailability of a site under the "convenience" analysis.

Government fault has been found in several sets of circumstances. For example, in *P & A Constr. Co.*, ASBCA 29901, 86-3 BCA ¶ 19,101, government delay in making a site available caused the loss of a subcontractor and was compensable even though the contract was timely completed. Similarly, in *Peter Kiewit Sons' Co. v. United States*, 138 Ct. Cl. 668, 151 F. Supp. 726 (1957), government fault was found in the breach of the implied duty of cooperation where the government issued a notice to proceed knowing of difficulties being encountered by a prior contractor in the construction process and then caused further delay to that contractor. In *L.L. Hall Constr. Co. v. United States*, 177 Ct. Cl. 870, 379 F.2d 559 (1966), a similar breach was found where the government failed to furnish necessary material to a prior contractor and gave priority to less efficient contractors on the site without explanation for such actions. In *Wheatley Assocs.*, ASBCA 24629, 80-2 BCA ¶ 14,639, the government was held at fault where an eight-day delay in turning over a group of houses under a renovation contract that required successive groups to be completed in "approximately 21 calendar days" was found to be unreasonable. See also *Strand Hunt Constr. v. General Servs. Admin.*, GSBCA 12859, 95-2 BCA ¶ 27,690 (delay granted for late access to a building renovation site was limited to a four-day period during which the contractor had to be prepared to do the work, because there was no substantiation for the contractor's assertion that it had made preparations to begin work a month earlier and no evidence that such preparation was reasonably based on a government commitment); *Central Indus. Elec. Co.*, GSBCA 5607, 83-1 BCA ¶ 16,273 (suspension order issued 12 days after the notice to proceed and not rescinded until 101 days later, leaving only 67 days for completion, was unreasonable); *Human Advancement, Inc.*, HUDBCA 77-215-C15, 81-2 BCA ¶ 15,317 (six-day delay after award in designating which mobile home units were to be renovated under a 60-day contract, was unreasonable); and *Edward B. Friel*, GSBCA 5470, 80-2 BCA ¶ 14,651, *recons. denied*, 81-1 BCA ¶ 14,846 (preventing access to work site for 92 days to allow personnel and equipment to be moved from the site was unreasonable). Government fault was also found and compensation given in *Rivera Gen. Contracting*, GSBCA 5797, 81-2 BCA ¶ 15,288, where the contractor was refused access to the work site on a painting contract by a tenant agency that disapproved of the quality of the contractor's work, even though the contracting agency, not the tenant agency, was responsible for contract compliance. Similarly, in *Blinderman Constr. Co. v. United States*, 695 F.2d 552 (Fed. Cir. 1982), the court found that the government breached its implied duty to cooperate by failing to assist an electrical contractor in gaining entrance to family housing units when the contractor had done all it could to gain access on its own. See also *Green Thumb Lawn Maint.*, ENGBCA 6249, 98-1 BCA ¶ 29,688 (government delayed access and the suggestion that the contractor should have cut the locks securing the site was an unreasonable solution to the problem).

Generally, no government fault will be found where the government has been persistent in attempting to overcome extraneous causes of delayed site access. See *Arvid E. Benson*, ASBCA 11116, 67-2 BCA ¶ 6659 (government diligent in trying to get prior contractor to perform on time and in not terminating prior contractor when performance was delayed), and *Asheville Contracting Co.*, DOTCAB 74-6, 76-2 BCA ¶ 12,027 (government made reasonable efforts to induce prior contractor to perform its contract). In *J.W. Bateson Co.*, GSBCA 3441, 73-2 BCA ¶ 10,098, the government's exertion of its best efforts in getting a utility company to remove electric lines interfering with site access excused 30 days of delay, but the continued presence of the lines after the date by which the government had promised their removal was unreasonable and compensable under the Suspension of Work clause. See also *Ldek Constr. Co.*, VABCA 2037, 85-2 BCA ¶ 18,129, in which it was held that the government may properly delay the start of work if the contractor fails to meet administrative requirements.

Warranties of site availability have been difficult to establish. In cases involving contracts with no Suspension of Work clause, warranties would not be found unless the contract language was very specific. For example, in *Gilbane Bldg. Co. v. United States*, 166 Ct. Cl. 347, 352, 333 F.2d 867 (1964), the court found no warranty where the contract stated that the work "is being accomplished under another contract and will be completed and the site available to commence the work specified under this contract on November 22, 1954." The court held this to be merely a representation by the government, not a guarantee, and other provisions of the contract that excused delays caused by late site availability showed that compensation for such delays was not contemplated by the parties. However, in *Merritt-Chapman & Scott Corp. v. United States*, 194 Ct. Cl. 461, 439 F.2d 185 (1971), the court found a warranty in the sentence stating, "The Contractor is informed that no part of existing State Highway 7 shall be removed until the relocated highway is opened to traffic, *which will be about 1 December 1955*." The court treated this as an "unequivocal" assurance of availability by a date certain, and therefore a warranty. Subsequently, the appeals boards have been more liberal in finding warranties. In *Henderson, Inc.*, DOTCAB 2423, 94-2 BCA ¶ 26,728, the board found an "unqualified warranty" that dredging work could be performed before March 1 in a contract provision that stated that dredging work was not permitted between March 1 and September 30. The contractor was prevented from performance through the entire period during which the Coast Guard had represented that the work could be performed. The board stated at 132,994:

> We find that where, through no fault of its own, a contractor is prevented from performing a substantial portion of the contract work during the entire period during which the contract represented that such work was to be accomplished, such a delay is unreasonable and the contractor is entitled to an adjustment under the "Suspension of Work" clause.

See also *Renel Constr. Co.*, GSBCA 5175, 80-2 BCA ¶ 14,811, in which the board found a warranty through the government's approval of the contractor's construction schedule and issuance of a notice to proceed, and *Singleton Contracting Corp.*, GSBCA 9614, 90-3 BCA ¶ 23,125, *recons. denied*, 91-1 BCA ¶ 23,344, in which the board found a warranty that the site would be available when the contract language contained specific dates for performance, stating that the contractor "shall . . . commence installation under this contract by May 15, 1987" and "complete the entire work ready for use not later than June 30, 1987."

It has also been held that a promise to issue a notice to proceed at a specific time is a warranty of site availability so that the bare issuance of the notice to proceed in the face of nonavailability will not relieve the government of its obligation to compensate the contractor under the clause, *Head Constr. Co.*, ENGBCA 3537, 77-1 BCA ¶ 12,226 (since notice to proceed is equivalent to order to begin performance, government liable when it knew upon issuance that other contractor's work would delay site availability). See also *Abbett Elec. Corp. v. United States*, 142 Ct. Cl. 609, 162 F. Supp. 772 (1958) (contract language promising issuance of a notice to proceed within a specific time was express covenant; because no Suspension of Work clause was present, failure to comply with contract was compensable as a breach).

4. Delay Because of Interference with Contractor's Work

Interferences during performance are generally treated in the same manner as delays in site availability—relief is granted in cases where government fault is found or where there is a government warranty. Government fault has been found in a number of circumstances. For example, in *Premier Gear & Mach. Works, Inc.*, ASBCA 9978, 65-2 BCA ¶ 5182, failure of the government to issue a duty-free certificate when needed was found to be a compensable delay. See *American Household Storage Co.*, GSBCA 7511, 86-3 BCA ¶ 19,201, in which a contractor recovered increased costs for a period of delay caused by excessive rain because, had the government not changed the work schedule, the contractor would have finished before the rain started, and *Structural Painting Corp.*, ASBCA 36813, 89-2 BCA ¶ 21,605, *recons. denied*, 89-3 BCA ¶ 21,978, in which the contractor was granted extended overhead costs for a delay of one day caused by the government's order not to work because of fire risk when the order was based on an incorrect analysis of the situation.

Lack of diligence in administering the contract has led to a finding of compensable delay. In *CJP Contractors v. United States*, 45 Fed. Cl. 343 (1999), the delay was caused by improper government administration of the contract resulting from a suspension caused by unreasonably poor judgment. See *Sipco Servs. Marine Inc. v. United States*, 41 Fed. Cl. 196 (1998) (government delay because of "excessive supervision or control over the contractor," quoting *Lathan Co. v. United States*,

20 Cl. Ct. 122, 129 (1990)), and *Kaco Contracting Co.*, ASBCA 46346, 01-1 BCA ¶ 31,263 (contractor was entitled to a time extension beyond the actual number of days the government delayed in providing essential information because the contractor was delayed in ordering specially built equipment).

In most cases involving interference by other contractors, no compensable suspension of work will be found if the government has acted diligently, *Star Communications, Inc.*, ASBCA 8049, 1962 BCA ¶ 3538; *Asheville Contracting Co.*, DOTCAB 74-6, 76-2 BCA ¶ 12,027. However, if government fault is found, compensation will be granted. See *American Int'l Constructors, Inc.*, ENGBCA 3633, 77-2 BCA ¶ 12,606, granting relief for lack of government diligence in obtaining performance from another contractor in which the board found that the government had effective means to improve the other contractor's performance but refused to use such means. The government also has a duty to resolve conflicting work schedules and direct the order of the work when it has awarded two contracts that result in contractors being in the same place at the same time; failure to do so can result in a compensable delay, *Hudson Contracting, Inc.*, ASBCA 41023, 94-1 BCA ¶ 26,466. See also *Robert R. Marquis, Inc.*, ASBCA 38438, 92-1 BCA ¶ 24,692, in which the government was held to have breached its implied duty to cooperate by not resolving a conflict between two contractors performing electrical work at the same site.

When the interference is caused by a party outside the control of either party, the government will not be liable unless a warranty is found. Delays in cases finding warranties have been compensated for under the Changes clause, *Carl W. Linder Co.*, ENGBCA 3526, 78-1 BCA ¶ 13,114 (city closed streets giving access to site); *J.W. Bateson Co.*, GSBCA 4687, 80-2 BCA ¶ 14,608 (subway construction closed street adjacent to site); *Perini, Horn, Morrison-Knudsen (JV)*, ENGBCA 4621, 87-1 BCA ¶ 19,545 (reduced track outages from railroad adjacent to construction site). However, no warranty was found in a clause stating that the site was under federal jurisdiction, *Durocher Dock & Dredge, Inc.*, ENGBCA 5768, 91-3 BCA ¶ 24,145. In that case, the contractor was delayed for nine days when the local sheriff ordered the work stopped to permit a search for missing persons, but the board ruled that the contractual statement as to federal jurisdiction did not promise that no local authorities would exercise power on the site.

5. Government Delays of Approvals

When the contract provides that the contractor must obtain government approvals, a compensable suspension of work will occur if such approvals are not given within a reasonable time. See, for example, *Northeast Constr. Co.*, ASBCA 11109, 67-1 BCA ¶ 6282 (unreasonable delay in approving samples); *M.S.I. Corp.*, VACAB 503, 65-2 BCA ¶ 5203, *recons. denied,* 66-1 BCA ¶ 5340 (unreasonable delay in approving purchase of foreign product); *Sydney Constr. Co.*, ASBCA 21377, 77-2 BCA ¶ 12,719 (unreasonable delay in approving shop drawings); *G. Bliudzius*

Contractors, Inc., ASBCA 37707, 90-2 BCA ¶ 22,835 (compensation given for nine days when government took 19 days in approving a quality control plan on a contract with large liquidated damages); and *Altmayer v. Johnson*, 79 F.3d 1129 (Fed. Cir. 1996) (government's indecision in approving selection of materials which were on the critical path caused contractor to stand by for three months awaiting a decision). Compare *J.L. Malone & Assoc., Inc. v. United States*, 879 F.2d 841 (Fed. Cir. 1989), holding that four months to consider approval of new type of computer was not unreasonable when contractor's first two such proposals were not in compliance with the contract requirements.

To recover for such a delay, a contractor must establish the period it could reasonably have anticipated for approval time as to the particular work involved and the status of the project, *Law v. United States*, 195 Ct. Cl. 370 (1971); *R.J. Crowley, Inc.*, ASBCA 35679, 88-3 BCA ¶ 21,151. See *Hudson Contracting, Inc.*, ASBCA 41023, 94-1 BCA ¶ 26,466 (contractor's 24 hour advance notice requirement did not establish that a few hours' delay in government scheduling inspection was unreasonable because the purpose of advance notice was to schedule the inspector's time, not to establish a standard for reasonableness of delay). In one unusual case where the contract required approval of a first article test report within 30 days, the government's failure to provide the approval until nine days after the 30-day period had expired was treated under the Changes clause, allowing the contractor to recover profits for the delay period. The contract contained a clause stating that delay in approving the first article test would constitute a change, *Nordam, A Div. of R.H. Siegfried, Inc.*, ASBCA 22835, 79-2 BCA ¶ 13,948.

Contractors cannot recover for delays that result from failure to make a proper submittal. See *Sea Crest Constr. Corp. v. United States*, 59 Fed. Cl. 615 (2004) (rejection proper because drawing was deficient); *Carousel Dev., Inc.*, ASBCA 50719, 01-1 BCA ¶ 31,262 (delay in approving doors was the fault of contractor, not the government, because the contractor did not provide a certification from the manufacturer and did not demonstrate that the doors met the contract specifications); *Astro Pak Corp.*, ASBCA 49790, 97-1 BCA ¶ 28,657, *recons. denied,* 97-2 BCA ¶ 29,106 (contractor not entitled to delays because it failed to prove failure to present fully compliant hardware and documentation); *C.T. Lewis Indus., Inc.*, ENGBCA 6255, 99-1 BCA ¶ 30,334 (government's initial disapproval of a contractor's quality control manual did not constitute an actionable delay, because the control manual submitted was for work substantially different than that required under the contract); *U.S. Detention*, DOTBCA 2908, 99-1 BCA ¶ 30,305 (delays not attributable to a local government's failure to grant zoning and other approvals because the contractor failed to allow itself ample time to obtain the approvals, knew of a basic infirmity in its application, and gambled on its ability to circumvent the zoning process); *Aable Tank Servs., Inc.*, ASBCA 51407, 98-2 BCA ¶ 30,024, *recons. denied*, 00-1 BCA ¶ 30,836 (contractor delayed on submitting because it expected a submittal list in the specifications); *Donohoe Constr. Co.*, ASBCA 47310, 98-2 BCA ¶ 30,076, *recons. denied,* 99-1 BCA ¶ 30,387 (no relief for government's initial rejection and later acceptance of alternate materials because the contractor delayed in requesting permission to use the alternate material); *Fernavico, S.A.*, ENGBCA PCC-120, 95-2 BCA ¶ 27,665 (only two of 20 trusses were approved as being properly repaired and ready for sandblasting); and *Spiess Constr. Co.,* ASBCA 48247, 95-2 BCA ¶ 27,767, *recons. denied*, 96-1 BCA ¶ 27,952 (submittals delayed by contractor's fault).

A contractor will not recover when the government had to delay to fulfill its statutory or regulatory obligations, *Gaffny Corp.*, ASBCA 30345, 87-2 BCA ¶ 19,910 (no constructive suspension where government delayed in approving payment and performance bonds that bore incorrect date and address of contractor); *Max Jordan Bauunternehmung v. United States*, 10 Cl. Ct. 672 (1986), *aff'd*, 820 F.2d 1208 (Fed. Cir. 1987) (no recovery for refusal to approve proposed subcontractors who were not on the government-approved list and who had neither the experience nor the equipment to perform work with degree of care necessary).

Relief has been refused for government delays in approving shop drawings when the delays were caused by a shortage of government personnel, *Fullerton Constr. Co.*, ASBCA 12275, 69-2 BCA ¶ 7876, and when the contractor was also at fault by the late submission of the shop drawings, *C.H. Leavell & Co.*, PODBCA 168, 68-2 BCA ¶ 7082. In *Joseph Penner*, GSBCA 4647, 80-2 BCA ¶ 14,604, recovery was denied where late approval was attributable to the contractor's failure to submit data required for an informed evaluation of an elevator design. Compare *Specialty Assembling & Packing Co. v. United States*, 174 Ct. Cl. 153, 251 F.2d 554 (1966), in which the court found a suspension of work based on a breach of the government's implied duty of cooperation when the contractor had submitted preproduction samples five months late and the government had subsequently failed to approve them within the time called for by the contract.

A contractor cannot obtain relief for failure to grant approvals in a timely fashion if the lack of approval does not impede the work. Thus, relief was denied in *E.W. Eldridge, Inc.*, ENGBCA 5269, 89-3 BCA ¶ 21,899, where the government had directed that workers at a quarry site be paid wages under the Davis-Bacon Act, but the contractor had disagreed, stopping work to seek a determination from the Department of Labor. The board held that the contractor was not entitled to stop work over this difference in interpretation and the proper avenue of relief was a claim under the Disputes or Changes clause. See also *CJP Contractors,* ASBCA 50076, 00-2 BCA ¶ 31,119 (time extension less than total duration of approval delay because contractor continued to work).

6. Delay in Providing Funding

There are a number of contracts where the government does not provide sufficient funds to complete the entire job but provides that such funds will be provided intermittently as appropriations occur. The Court of Claims found no breach of the implied duty of cooperation if Congress failed to appropriate the funds, *Winston*

Bros. Co. v. United States, 131 Ct. Cl. 245, 130 F. Supp. 374 (1955). However, the court did find a breach if the contracting agency was at fault by not requesting sufficient funds or by not assisting the contractor by providing prompt information on the status of the funding, *S.A. Healy Co. v. United States*, 216 Ct. Cl. 172, 576 F.2d 299 (1978). Suspensions of work have also been found when the government unreasonably delays in providing the funds, *C.H. Leavell & Co. v. United States*, 208 Ct. Cl. 776, 530 F.2d 878 (1976) (5 1/2-month delay), and when preferential treatment is given to other contractors in providing funding, *Gunther & Shirley Co.*, ENGBCA 3691, 78-2 BCA ¶ 13,454. In most of these cases, there was a disclaimer of liability, which the court interpreted to be inapplicable to the facts of the case.

7. Delay in Inspection of the Work

Unreasonable delay in the inspection process has been held to be a breach of the government's implied duty of cooperation in instances where the contract contained no Suspension of Work clause, *Gardner Displays Co. v. United States*, 171 Ct. Cl. 497, 346 F.2d 585 (1965) ("dilatory and inconclusive" inspection); *Russell R. Gannon Co. v. United States*, 189 Ct. Cl. 328, 417 F.2d 1356 (1969) (unreasonable to require a 72-hour notice of acceptance tests to permit observation by government inspection); *Buck Indus., Inc.*, ASBCA 45321, 94-3 BCA ¶ 27,061 (delay in completion of drawing deficiencies because "there was never a clean definition of who would inspect"). In comparable situations suspensions of work have been found, *Maintenance Eng'rs*, ASBCA 17474, 74-2 BCA ¶ 10,760 (short work hours of government inspector caused unreasonable delay); *Caddell Constr. Co.*, VABCA 5068, 03-2 BCA ¶ 32,257 (government unreasonably protracted inspection). Compare *Southern Roofing & Petroleum Co.*, ASBCA 12841, 69-1 BCA ¶ 7599 (eight-day delay to test material for suspected defects reasonable even though no defects were found), and *Stamell Constr. Co.*, DOTCAB 68-27I, 75-1 BCA ¶ 11,087 (delay in reviewing corrective measures reasonable after contractor had submitted defective work).

8. Delay in Issuance of Changes

Delays preceding the issuance of a change order fall under the Suspension of Work clause rather than the Changes clause, *Weldfab, Inc.*, IBCA 268, 61-2 BCA ¶ 3121; *Model Eng'g & Mfg. Corp.*, ASBCA 7490, 1962 BCA ¶ 3363. See the explanatory comment to the former Standard Form 23-A Suspension of Work and Changes clauses in 32 Fed. Reg. 16269 (1967):

> Except for defective specifications, the Changes clause as revised will continue to have no application for any delay prior to the issuance of a change order. An adjustment for such type of delay, if appropriate, will be for consideration under the provisions of the Suspension of Work clause.

The government is entitled to order a suspension for a reasonable time in order to make changes but will be liable if it exceeds that time. See *Chaney & James Con-*

str. Co. v. United States, 190 Ct. Cl. 699, 421 F.2d 728 (1970), in which the court found 55 days reasonable and the remaining 55 days unreasonable. In *Decker & Co. GmbH*, ASBCA 35051, 88-3 BCA ¶ 20,871, the board analyzed an ordered partial suspension of 137 days to process significant changes to the contract drawings. It held that, since the contract performance period was only 160 days, the suspension was basically unreasonable. It therefore held that 30 days was a reasonable delay, 13 days were noncompensable due to contractor fault, and 94 days were compensable. See also *Timmons, Butt & Head, Inc.*, ASBCA 15948, 72-1 BCA ¶ 9247. Compare *Pathman Constr. Co.*, ASBCA 22003, 82-1 BCA ¶ 15,790, *modified on other grounds*, 82-2 BCA ¶ 16,019, where the government awarded the contract with knowledge that it would have to make changes and ordered a suspension until the revised drawings were available. The board considered this conduct unreasonable and compensated the contractor for the entire period of the delay.

The Suspension of Work clause has been used in a number of different circumstances to compensate contractors for unreasonable delays in issuing changes, *Triple "A" South*, ASBCA 43684, 94-2 BCA ¶ 26,609 (contractor asserted delay and disruption costs incurred as the result of more than 600 change orders under a contract to overhaul a naval warship); *Day & Zimmermann-Madway*, ASBCA 13367, 71-1 BCA ¶ 8622 (delay by government in acting on contractor's price change proposal submitted in response to government request; contractor justified in suspending work pending government decision because of magnitude of impact of change); *Utilities Contracting Co.*, ASBCA 9723, 65-1 BCA ¶ 4582 (contractor acted reasonably in stopping when government gave notice of intent to issue change orders); *George A. Fuller Co.*, ASBCA 8524, 1962 BCA ¶ 3619 (delay by government in issuing change after telling contractor it was in process; it would have been "irresponsible in the extreme" for the contractor to proceed with work to be changed); *Brand S. Roofing*, ASBCA 24688, 82-1 BCA ¶ 15,513 (government delay in formulating its position on a change was unreasonable where it was aware of the preexisting problem prior to the time that the contractor submitted a change proposal); *Noah Lewis, Contractor*, VACAB 1349, 81-2 BCA ¶ 15,209 *recons. denied*, 81-2 BCA ¶ 15,322 (government delayed contractor six hours while considering a changed method of installing partitions); *Fidelity Constr. Co.*, ASBCA 24882, 81-1 BCA ¶ 15,022 (delay was unreasonable where government first rejected contractor's change proposal for the repair of a collapsed wall and later accepted it); *U.A. Anderson Constr. Co.*, ASBCA 48087, 99-1 BCA ¶ 30,347 (work was suspended as a result of the government's failure to issue a change order required for the main gas connection. The contractor acted reasonably in waiting for the direction of the contracting officer).

When there is disagreement as to the need for changes and the contractor can reasonably proceed with the work, compensation under the Suspension of Work clause will be denied. See *Plandel, Inc.*, HUDBCA 92-7171-C1, 93-3 BCA ¶ 26,103 (no recovery for contractor who refused to proceed after claiming specifications were defective; government has right to have work proceed while dispute is pending; contractor not permitted to rely on own unreasonable interpretation of specifications), and *Leonhard Weiss, GmbH Co.*, ASBCA 37574, 93-1 BCA ¶ 25,443 (no recovery when government declined to issue changes; given previous 60 proposed changes, period of 17 days between proposal and decision meeting was not unreasonable). Under the Suspension of Work clause, a contractor must show that the government actually caused a delay. Thus, in *Atlas Contractors, Inc.*, ASBCA 34545, 88-1 BCA ¶ 20,225, no compensation was granted for government delay in providing information omitted from the specifications because the contractor did not have materials until after the omissions were corrected.

Contrast these cases granting relief under the Suspension of Work clause to older Court of Claims cases dealing more harshly with similar situations arising under contracts not containing such a clause. See *B-W Constr. Co. v. United States*, 97 Ct. Cl. 92 (1942), and *Vogt Bros. Mfg. Co. v. United States*, 160 Ct. Cl. 687 (1963). In both of these cases, the court denied recovery when the government delayed in acting on contractor requests for changes. In *Vogt*, the court stated at 709:

> [N]either the [contractor] nor the contracting officer was under any legal obligation to accept the other's proposal for a change in the requirements of the contract, or even to exercise due diligence in responding to such a proposal.

9. Miscellaneous Acts of the Government

Other types of government acts that have led to relief are pressure and threats to alter the sequence of the work, *Ingalls Shipbuilding Div., Litton Sys., Inc.*, ASBCA 17579, 78-1 BCA ¶ 13,038, *recons. denied*, 78-1 BCA ¶ 13,216; changing the work schedule and pushing the contractor into a period of excessive rain, *American Household Storage Co.*, GSBCA 7511, 86-3 BCA ¶ 19,201; delay in processing request for priority material, *M.D. Funk*, ASBCA 20287, 76-2 BCA ¶ 12,120; delay in furnishing government-furnished property, *S. Patti Constr. Co.*, ASBCA 8423, 1964 BCA ¶ 4225; delay in delivery of repair parts, *Teague Indus. & Technical Servs. Co.*, ASBCA 29230, 86-2 BCA ¶ 18,790; delay in securing labor certification and visas for temporary alien workers needed for renovation contract on the island of Guam, *Swinerton & Belvoir*, ASBCA 24022, 81-1 BCA ¶ 15,156; lack of government direction by waiting 15 days to tell a contractor whether an ordered suspension would be lifted when adverse weather conditions had abated or whether the contract would be terminated for convenience, *River Equip. Co.*, ENGBCA 5856, 93-2 BCA ¶ 25,654; and government delay by failing to resolve differing site condition; *Safeco Ins. Co. of America*, ASBCA 52107, 03-2 BCA ¶ 32,341.

D. Reasonableness of Delays

Recovery of costs under the Suspension of Work and government Delay of Work clauses is granted only for delays that are unreasonable in duration. This limitation of recovery to unreasonable delays is accomplished by determining whether the delay is the result of government fault or was incurred pursuant to a contractual right of the government. If fault is found, the courts and boards generally hold that the entire period of the delay is unreasonable, whereas in the case of delay due to exercise of a contractual right, the contractor is compensated for only the unreasonable portion of the delay. In *Davho Co.*, VACAB 1005, 72-2 BCA ¶ 9683, the board explained this process at 45,214:

> We cannot subscribe to the theory, that seems to be suggested by Government Counsel's argument, that the Government is permitted by the Suspension of Work clause to interfere with the contractor's performance, without incurring any obligation to pay the delay costs, in any situation where the suspension is for only a few days and no longer than necessary for the Government to make up its mind on some question that has arisen. The duration of the stoppage may of course be the decisive factor in determining whether the period of delay was unreasonable as where the Government holds up the work or a part thereof where it is necessary to consider an ordinary change of the usual type. But it also seems clear to us that the duration of the suspension is not the only factor to be considered but the relationship of what is unreasonable to all the other circumstances is also required to be considered, including the reason for the Government's interference and whether the act of interference was itself unreasonable. If the Government's stop order was itself unreasonable, as being capricious or as being the result of some error or fault of the Government that should not be attributed to the contractor, certainly the period of delay that is caused by the interference of that nature may also be unreasonable, whatever its duration may be. The distinction we have in mind is exemplified in *Chaney and James v. U.S.*, [190 Ct. Cl. 699, 421 F.2d 728 (1970)], where the Court held, with respect to delay incident to the making of certain changes in the lath and plaster finish of part of a building under construction, that only the excessive part of the time taken to consider the prospective change was unreasonable; but with respect to roof leader drain and roof washdown system changes which became necessary because of defective or erroneous specifications the government had included in the contract, all of the delay incident to making these changes was unreasonable per se.

1. Unreasonable Delays

Delays where the total delay period has been found unreasonable because of government fault include delays because of the inclusion of the wrong labor standards clause in the contract, *Davho Co.*, VACAB 1005, 72-2 BCA ¶ 9683; delay in obtaining a subdivision plan from a city government that could be obtained only by the federal agency, *Leonard Pevar Co.*, PSBCA 219, 77-2 BCA ¶ 12,690; delay in issuing notice to proceed beyond the date needed by the contractor to perform work efficiently, *L.O. Brayton & Co.*, IBCA 641-5-67, 70-2 BCA ¶ 8510; delays because of conflicting specifications, *Stamell Constr. Co.*, DOTCAB 68-27J, 75-1 BCA ¶ 11,334; and delays because of defective government specifications, *Chaney & James Constr. Co. v. United States*, 190 Ct. Cl. 699, 421 F.2d 728 (1970); *Minmar Builders, Inc.*, GSBCA 3430, 72-2 BCA ¶ 9599; *Sergent Mech. Sys., Inc. v. United States*, 34 Fed. Cl. 505 (1995).

In *White Buffalo Constr.*, IBCA 2166, 91-1 BCA ¶ 23,540, the work was suspended in winter on a road construction contract due to high moisture levels, but, in the spring, the government refusal to lift the suspension when moisture levels had abated resulted in an unreasonable delay. See also *Huff Sealing Corp.*, ASBCA 53587, 02-1 BCA ¶ 31,855 (suspension because of explosives at work site was unreasonable because of government prior knowledge), and *Central Indus. Elec. Co.*, GSBCA 5607, 83-1 BCA ¶ 16,273 (suspension over half of length of contract unreasonable).

With regard to defective specifications, the same result is achieved by including the delay costs in an equitable adjustment under the Changes clause, *La Crosse Garment Mfg. Co. v. United States*, 193 Ct. Cl. 168, 432 F.2d 1377 (1970). This is the normal analysis at the present time, *American Line Builders, Inc. v. United States*, 26 Cl. Ct. 1155 (1992). Use of the Changes clause does not affect the determination of reasonableness of the delay caused by defective specifications, but it does allow a contractor to recover profit as a part of the Changes clause equitable adjustment.

2. Reasonable Delays

Delays that have been found to be reasonable include delays in the award of the contract, *De Matteo Constr. Co. v. United States*, 220 Ct. Cl. 579, 600 F.2d 1384 (1979) (failure of government to award contract for the period required by the GAO regulations to process a bid protest was a reasonable delay because the prospective contractor was on notice of regulations); delays in issuing the notice to proceed, *Commercial Contractors, Inc. v. United States*, 29 Fed. Cl. 654 (1993) (40 days reasonable); delays in granting approvals, *R.J. Crowley, Inc.*, ASBCA 35679, 88-3 BCA ¶ 21,151 (one month reasonable to approve relatively complex shop drawings); and delays in issuing changes, *Chaney & James Constr. Co. v. United States*, 190 Ct. Cl. 699, 421 F.2d 728 (1970). The amount of time that is reasonable is highly dependent on the specific circumstances in each situation.

In *Gloe Constr., Inc.*, ASBCA 26434, 84-2 BCA ¶ 17,289, *recons. denied,* 84-3 BCA ¶ 17,516, the contractor was not entitled to recover for an ordered suspension because a temporary restraining order had been issued directing that the work be stopped. The board found that the delay was reasonable because the contracting officer had no choice but to stop the work. However, the contracting officer's continuation of the suspension after the court lifted the temporary restraining order was held to be an unreasonable delay, and the contractor recovered for that period of delay. See also *Commercial Contractors Equip.*, ASBCA 52930, 03-2 BCA ¶ 32,381 (no relief under the Suspension of Work clause because the contractor presented no proof that the suspension lasted an unreasonable time), and *Toloff Constr.*, AGBCA 95-227-3, 96-1 BCA ¶ 28, 156 (contractor not entitled to delay costs for an alleged two-hour suspension of work, because no evidence that two hours of suspension were unreasonable under the circumstances).

3. Measuring the Amount of Delay

The time that the government requires to take an action permitted by the contract is of material importance in determining the reasonableness of the delay and is generally balanced against the impact of the delay on the contract. The applicable legal test is whether the government acted reasonably under all the related circumstances, *Tenaya Constr.*, ASBCA 27799, 87-1 BCA ¶ 19,449. See *C & C Plumbing & Heating*, ASBCA 44270, 94-3 BCA ¶ 27,063, finding that the government actions in piecemeal release of workspace was unreasonable because of its severe impact on the contractor that was performing under a short-term contract. Compare *Tri-Cor, Inc. v. United States*, 198 Ct. Cl. 187, 458 F.2d 112 (1972), in which the court affirmed a board decision holding that no unreasonable delay had occurred because the contractor had worked around the delay. The court stated at 221:

> What is a reasonable period of time for the Government to do a particular act under the contract is entirely dependent upon the circumstances of the particular case. *Specialty Assembling & Packing Co. v. United States*, 174 Ct. Cl. 153, 170, 355 F.2d 554, 565 (1966).

In *F.H. McGraw & Co. v. United States*, 131 Ct. Cl. 501, 130 F. Supp. 394 (1955), where a government change order suspended all work on the changed portion of the contract and also on most other portions because they were dependent on the changed portions, the court scrutinized with care the time taken by the government and found a reasonable time to be quite brief. In other cases, however, where the contractor was able to mitigate the effects of delay by shifting to other portions of the contract work, quite lengthy delays have been found to be reasonable. See, for example,, *Continental Ill. Nat'l Bank & Trust Co. v. United States*, 121 Ct. Cl. 203, 242-43, 101 F. Supp. 755, 757, *cert. denied*, 343 U.S. 963 (1952).

See also *Craft Mach. Works, Inc.*, ASBCA 47227, 97-1 BCA ¶ 28,651 (contractor was entitled to an adjustment for 266 delay days because it proved that the delays were due solely to government acts, were not concurrent with contractor-caused delays, and that the overall completion of the contract was delayed by these many days), and *David Builders, Inc.*, ASBCA 51262, 98-2 BCA ¶ 30,021 (although the delivery of roofing material was 113 days later than provided in a government-approved schedule as the result of government delay, a contractor was not entitled to 113 days of compensable delay, because it did not show that the government-caused delay resulted in a 113-day delay to overall contract completion). In *RMR Constr. Co.*, DOTCAB 68-16, 69-2 BCA ¶ 7911, the board found two delays of one hour each and one delay of five hours to be unreasonable in a situation where close government cooperation was necessary to enable the contractor to perform the work. The board stated at 36,807-08:

> [I]t is not always easy to determine what constitutes a reasonable or an unreasonable delay for a particular contract. As one board noted:

> Much depends upon an evaluation of the total surrounding contract environment including the contract's allocation of risk, the contractor's particular needs at the time, the convenience to the Government's interest and the foreseeable consequences of the Government's action or failure to act.

See also *Conner Bros. Constr. Co.,* VABCA 2504, 95-2 BCA ¶ 27,910, *aff'd,* 113 F.3d 1256 (Fed. Cir. 1997) (government delay of three weeks in issuing a corrective redesign was excessive because only slightly more than four months remained on the contract), and *Robert L. Rich*, DOTCAB 1026, 82-2 BCA ¶ 15,900 (one day delay unreasonable when bad weather prevented the contracting officer from attending the pre-work meeting which the solicitation had stated would be held as soon as practicable after award). Compare *Sauer, Inc.*, ASBCA 37205, 90-2 BCA ¶ 22,784, in which a water shutoff for four hours due to an emergency in an industrial facility refit contract was found to be a reasonable delay.

In one unique case, the board found that both parties were at fault in delaying performance by taking an inordinately long time to determine the suitability of government-furnished property and determined the period of unreasonable delay by an analysis of comparative fault, *E.H. Marhoefer, Jr., Co.*, DOTCAB 70-17, 71-1 BCA ¶ 8791. The government was found at fault for not promptly investigating the problem, and the contractor was found at fault for conducting its own investigation in an unproductive manner. The board concluded that the contractor's fault was greater and granted recovery for the costs of 25 days of delay out of the total delay of 75 days.

4. Burden of Proving Unreasonableness

Ordinarily, the contractor has the burden of proving that a delay is unreasonable, but when the information concerning the cause of the delay is within the exclusive knowledge of the government, it has the burden of proof of reasonableness, *M.A. Santander Constr., Inc.*, ASBCA 15882, 76-1 BCA ¶ 11,798. In *Santander*, the entire period of delay was held unreasonable when the government ordered the contractor to vacate the work site and submitted no evidence of the reasonableness of such an order. The contractor also has the burden of proving the length of delay. In *Pathman Constr. Co. v. United States*, 227 Ct. Cl. 670, 652 F.2d 70 (1981), the court held that the contractor could not rely on the length of a time extension granted for completion of the contract to measure time-related delay costs but must independently demonstrate actual delay. The court reasoned that the purpose of the time extension was solely to abate the contractor's liability for liquidated damages and the contracting officer's agreement to the time extension could not be interpreted as a concession of actual delay for determining damages or an equitable adjustment. In sum, the contractor has the burden of demonstrating that (1) the specific delays were due to government-responsible causes, (2) the overall completion of the project was delayed as a result of its time-related extra costs, and (3) any government-caused delays were not concurrent with delays within the contractor's control, *Technical*

Mgmt. Servs. Corp., ASBCA 39999, 93-2 BCA ¶ 25,681, *aff'd*, 16 F.3d 420 (Fed. Cir. 1993). See also *The Wild Wood Assocs., Inc.*, AGBCA 96-150-3, 97-2 BCA ¶ 29,263, in which the government was not liable, even though the delays appeared to be caused by the government, because the contractor did not quantify the delays and the board would not guess at the possible length of the delays.

5. Proving the Delay

Network analysis techniques were first introduced into the construction field in the early 1960s. The government now requires network analysis on most, if not all, major construction projects and most such analyses are computer-generated. Even law review articles on the subject are replete with computer-generated graphs. See Wickwire, Hurlbut, and Lerman, *Use of Critical Path Method Techniques in Contract Claims: Issues and Developments, 1974–1988*, 18 Pub. Cont. L. J. 338 (1989).

Scheduled delay analysis typically involves

(1) Establishing the as-planned schedule;
(2) Establishing the as-built schedule;
(3) Identifying and analyzing the differences between the as-planned and as-built schedule; and
(4) Developing some types of entitlement schedules.

Building on that, to prove a delay, a contractor must, at a minimum,

(1) Identify a delay cause;
(2) Prove that this delay cause is either excusable or compensable;
(3) Identify the work delayed by the delay cause;
(4) Prove that the work was delayed by the delay cause;
(5) Prove that delayed work was on the project's critical path; and
(6) Reasonably quantify the delay.

Proving the fact and length of the delay would use similar techniques regardless of whether the allegations of an excusable or compensable delay. Excusable delays are discussed in Section I.

Lack of a sound analysis can lead to a failure to recover for delay. See, for example, *Thomas & Sons Bldg. Contractors, Inc.*, DOTBCA 3013, 01-1 BCA ¶ 31,386, where the contractor's proof consisted of its formal claim submission prepared by a subcontractor, and the testimony of its project manager who relied on the claim for his testimony. However, the record was devoid of documentation substantiating the contractor's alleged costs and the contractor failed to carry its burden of demonstrating that the allegedly delayed work was on the critical path. See also *Gavosto Assocs., Inc.*, PSBCA 4058, 01-1 BCA ¶ 31,389 (contractor did not show by contemporaneous records or any other evidence that "activities on the critical path to overall contract completion" were delayed by the actions of the government);

Galaxy Builders, Inc., ASBCA 50018, 00-2 BCA ¶ 31,040 (contractor's reliance on an as-built analysis to measure delays was improper when contractual provision provided that delays be established using a CPM analysis); and *Sunshine Constr. & Eng'g, Inc. v. United States*, 64 Fed. Cl. 346 (2005) (contractor's expert analysis did not present an accepted critical path methodology).

Contractors often fail in their burden of proof because of (1) the weakness of the fact witnesses, *Conner Bros. Const. Co.*, VABCA 2504, 95-2 BCA ¶ 27910 (contractor's case weakened by its failure to call its tile subcontractor to testify even though that subcontractor was the party most qualified to explain the alleged delay); or (2) the vagueness of their evidence, *Peter Bauwens Bauunternehmung GmbH & Co. KG*, ASBCA 44679, 98-1 BCA ¶ 29,551 (contractor pointed only to generalized and hypothetical testimony as to the causes of the delay and failed to prove through specific, detailed evidence that delay in fact impacted subcontractor work that was critical to completion of the project as a whole); *Hensel Phelps Constr. Co.*, ASBCA 49270, 99-2 BCA ¶ 30,531 (contractor failed to prove that defective specifications delayed any activities on the critical path and evidence indicated that the contractor's CPM schedule had been manipulated to conceal work that could not be completed in the time allowed); *Donohoe Constr. Co.*, ASBCA 47310, 98-2 BCA ¶ 30,076 (the numerical calculation of delays was rejected because the critical path analysis improperly assigned "leads and lags," and failed to assign necessary items to the critical path, resulting in an unreasonably short planned contract duration with the result that the underestimation of essential task time could not be used as a basis for the calculation of delay in substantial contract completion).

Updated CPM schedules do not, of themselves, constitute proof of the length of alleged delays. See *John T. Jones Constr. Co.*, ASBCA 48303, 98-2 BCA ¶ 29,892, *aff'd,* 178 F.3d 1307 (Fed. Cir. 1998), stating at 147,975:

> In *Titan Pacific Constr. Corp.* ASBCA Nos. 24148 et al., 87-1 BCA ¶ 19,626, the ASBCA properly disregarded a contractor's original, as-planned, CPM schedule and its periodic updates thereto, and relied instead upon the records reflecting actual field operations, to determine delays. The reviewing Court stated: "Analyses made after project completion . . . that make adjustments to attain new and revised *projected* scheduling . . . are of limited value" (emphasis in original). *Titan Pacific Constr. Corp. v. United States*, 17 Cl. Ct. 630, 637 (1989), aff'd, 899 F.2d 1227 (Fed. Cir. 1990) (Table). Similarly, the Boards gave little weight to updated, as-planned CPM schedules in isolation, and relied on as-built CPM schedule or other evidence of actual performance dates and durations to determine delays in *J.A. Jones Constr. Co.*, ENG BCA No. 6252, 97-1 BCA ¶ 28,918 at 144,164 (findings 13-14), 144,167-68; *Southwest Const. Corp.*, ENG BCA No. 5286, 94-3 BCA ¶ 27,120 at 135,208; and *Coffey Constr. Co., Inc.*, VABCA Nos. 3361 et al., 93-2 BCA ¶ 25,788 at 128,325. As stated in *Conner Bros. Constr. Co., Inc.*, VABCA Nos. 2504 et al., 95-2 BCA ¶ 27,910 at 139,269: "Additional activity days inserted in a CPM [schedule] do not necessarily equate to day-for-day extensions to the contract completion date."

The failure of a contractor to regularly update the CPM during performance to reflect changes as they occur will throw serious question into the usefulness of the contractor's CPM for establishing delay. See *Blinderman Constr. Co. v. United States*, 39 Fed. Cl. 529, 584-87 (1997), *aff'd*, 178 F.3d 1307 (Fed. Cir. 1998), denying the contractor's delay claims, even though the contractor established that the delays were unreasonable and were the fault of the government, because the contractor's CPM was absolutely useless in that the contractor (1) did not identify the critical path, (2) failed to update the schedule as changes occurred, and (3) failed to cross reference the CPM analysis with any of the contemporaneous daily activity reports. See also *F.G. Haggerty Plumbing*, VABCA 4482, 95-2 BCA ¶ 27,671 (contractor failed to introduce any evidence demonstrating the extent to which government caused delays extended contractor's performance period).

Delay experts are commonly used but will also be tested against the standard of whether their testimony is objective and logical. In *J.A. Jones Constr. Co.*, ENG-BCA 6348, 00-2 BCA ¶ 31,000, the schedule analysis performed by the contractor's expert witness was based on highly questionable assumptions and conclusions. In particular, the expert's allegation of a "logic tie" between separate work orders represented a wholly new theory "discovered" by the expert shortly before trial which was not proven by any contemporaneous records. The expert's conclusions represented little more than his own perception of a better way to build the project. See also *Gassman Corp.*, ASBCA 44975, 00-1 BCA ¶ 30,720 (contractor was not entitled to six "extra days" of delay, in accordance with a determination made by a government expert, because the expert did not have access to progress reports expressly noting six days of "slippage" in the delivery date by the contractor's steel supplier); *Jimenez, Inc.*, VABCA 6351, 02-2 BCA ¶ 32,019 (post-termination critical path analysis was rejected because it failed to reflect concurrent contractor caused delays). In *Jimenez* the board stated at 158,252:

> Appellant seeks to have us rely on its CPM expert, and its newly created CPM analysis, which was prepared during litigation. Not surprisingly, this CPM showed VA caused delays to the AHU accounting for the entire delay through 1999. Such self-serving analyses, created after project completion and which make adjustments to attain new and revised projected schedules, depending on theoretical contingencies, are of limited value.

The board in *Jimenez* cited *Bay Constr. Co.*, VABCA 5594, 02-1 BCA ¶ 31,795, in which the contractor's CPM consultant also attributed all of its time loss and extended performance time to government changes, delays and suspension. He ignored or casually dismissed any reference to the contractor's small crews and lack of progress, and did not appropriately consider any information that was unfavorable to the appellant. See also *Hensel Phelps Constr. Co.*, ASBCA 49270, 99-2 BCA ¶ 30,531 (although the contractor's expert stated that additional costs resulted from the large number of requests for information and government-issued change orders, other persuasive evidence suggested that the problems were due to the contractor's poor internal management). Compare *SAE/Americon-Mid Atl., Inc. v. General Servs. Admin.*, GSBCA 12294, 98-2 BCA ¶ 30,084, where the government did not present an independent analysis credibly identifying how concurrent delay from the contractor affected the critical path or quantifying these concurrent delay periods in terms of an impact on the critical path. In contrast, SAE's expert had credibly established that the delay attributable solely to the government was the major cause to the untimely performance of the contract.

Whether contractors rely on fact or expert witnesses, contemporaneous documents are essential. See *J.A. Jones Constr. Co.*, ENGBCA 6252, 97-1 BCA ¶ 28,918 (contemporaneous documents showing that delays allegedly caused by preconditions for approval of a two-flood procedure and changes in floor strut construction had no impact on the critical path were entitled to greater evidentiary weight than a contractor's mere allegations and after-the-fact consultant efforts), and *J.A. Jones Constr. Co.*, ENGBCA 6348, 00-2 BCA ¶ 31,000 (contractor did not prove a delay because there was no contemporaneous evidence demonstrating that the ordered work either delayed the completion or was on the critical path).

At one time, if the government granted a time extension, there was a rebuttable presumption that it was a compensable delay. See *Roberts, J. R. Corp.*, DOTBCA 2499, 98-1 BCA ¶ 29,680 (although a modification granting an extension of time for performance created a rebuttable presumption of compensable delays, a contractor was not entitled to the same number of days delay as provided in the modification, because the critical path analysis rebutted the presumption.); *Gavosto Assocs., Inc.*, PSBCA 4058, 01-1 BCA ¶ 31,389, 01-1 BCA ¶ 155,031 (contractor entitled to delay damages because after completion of the project, the government voluntarily granted a 14-day time extension for changes to the contract work); and *Gottfried Corp.*, ASBCA 51041, 98-2 BCA ¶ 30,063 (government's grant of a 16-day time extension amounted to a recognition that the overall project was delayed to that extent and was an administrative determination that the delay was not due to the fault or negligence of the contractor). However, the Federal Circuit eliminated that presumption in *England v. Sherman R. Smoot Corp.*, 388 F.3d 844 (Fed. Cir. 2004). Thus, contractors must now bear the burden of proving the compensability of a delay for which the government was willing to grant a time extension.

E. Limitations on Recovery

The contract clauses contain three limitations on recovery of compensation for delays.

1. Sovereign Acts

A number of cases have raised the issue of whether the effects of sovereign acts are compensable under the Suspension of Work clause. Paragraph (b) of the clause states that it is applicable to acts "of the contracting officer in the administration of this contract." Thus, although the government can agree by contract to pay for the effects of sovereign acts, *D & L Constr. Co.& Assoc. v. United States*, 185 Ct. Cl. 736, 402 F.2d 990 (1968), it is generally held that the Suspension of Work clause alone is not such an agreement to pay delay costs resulting from sovereign acts, *Amino Bros. Co. v. United States*, 178 Ct. Cl. 515, 372 F.2d 485, *cert. denied*, 389 U.S. 846 (1967); *E.V. Lane Corp.*, ASBCA 9741, 65-2 BCA ¶ 5076, *modified on other grounds on recons.,* 66-1 BCA ¶ 5472. Hence, a sovereign act will not be considered a constructive suspension of work. However, if the contracting officer orders a suspension in the face of a sovereign act, it has been held that the clause provides for compensation for the delay, *Henderson, Inc.*, DOTCAB 2423, 94-2 BCA ¶ 26,728 (sovereign act prevented contractor from performing the entire period during which the Coast Guard had represented that the work could be performed); *Empire Gas Eng'g Co.*, ASBCA 7190, 1962 BCA ¶ 3323 (contractor ordered to stay off air base during national emergency). In contrast, no suspension of work was found when work was suspended by an agency acting in its sovereign capacity, *Goodfellow Bros., Inc.*, AGBCA 75-140, 77-1 BCA ¶ 12,336, *modified on recons.,* 77-2 BCA ¶ 12,659, or by another agency performing its sovereign duties, *Mergentime Corp.*, ENGBCA 5765, 92-2 BCA ¶ 25,007 (work stopped by order of Secret Service); *Durocher Dock & Dredge, Inc.*, ENGBCA 5768, 91-3 BCA ¶ 24,145 (work stopped by local sheriff). See also *Borderland Spraying Serv.*, AGBCA 90-180-1, 93-3 BCA ¶ 26,214 (government determination that environmental impact statement was required in an herbicide contract was sovereign act), and *Tempo, Inc.*, ASBCA 38576, 95-2 BCA ¶ 27,618, *aff'd,* 108 F.3d 1391 (Fed. Cir. 1997), *cert. denied,* 522 U.S. 933 (1997) (denying contractor claim for delayed notice to proceed, because issuance of stop-work order (pursuant to the Competition in Contracting Act) was deemed a sovereign act, *citing Port Arthur Towing Co.*, ASBCA 37516, 90-2 BCA ¶ 22,857, *aff'd, Port Arthur Towing Co. v. Department of Defense*, Civ. No. 90-1889, D.D.C., order dated July 9, 1991).

A few cases have held that the government will be liable if it unduly interferes with a contract in the course of carrying out its sovereign powers. See *Weaver Constr. Co.*, DOTBCA 2034, 91-2 BCA ¶ 23,800 ("the government is not immune from contract damages for an act which implements national policy if the required implementation could have been achieved without disturbing contractual relationships"), and *Miller v. United States*, 135 Ct. Cl. 1 (1956) ("[t]here may be some authority for holding that government may be liable for its sovereign acts if it does not implement them in the least restrictive or least costly manner"). Compare *F2M, Inc.*, ASBCA 49719, 97-2 BCA ¶ 28,982, rejecting the government's argument that delayed issuance of notice to proceed, due to a pending protest, was a sovereign act for which no equitable adjustment could be awarded.

In some cases another contract clause is read in conjunction with the Suspension of Work clause to be a promise of compensation in the event of a sovereign act, *M.D. Funk*, ASBCA 20287, 76-2 BCA ¶ 12,120, *recons. denied,* 77-1 BCA ¶ 12,241 (clause requiring contractor to comply with the material priorities system combined with Suspension of Work clause to grant compensation when other government agency failed to process priority requests in timely manner); *L.S. Matusek*, ENGBCA 3080, 72-2 BCA ¶ 9625 (clause requiring contractor to close down operations for short fires read with Suspension of Work clause to provide for compensation for delays caused by long fires).

2. Concurrent Delays

The current Suspension of Work and government Delay of Work clauses preclude recovery for delays where there is a concurrent cause of the delay. This has been the rule when no contract clause was at issue and the suit was for breach of contract. In such cases, the courts have taken different positions on how harshly the rule would be interpreted. Some cases have held that a contractor could not recover damages unless it could show that the government delays were not "concurrent and intertwined" with other causes of delay, *Commerce Int'l Co. v. United States*, 167 Ct. Cl. 529, 338 F.2d 81 (1964) (no recovery when government delay in furnishing parts mixed with subcontractor delays and other delays for which the contractor was liable); *John McShain, Inc. v. United States*, 188 Ct. Cl. 830, 412 F.2d 1281 (1969) (no recovery when defective drawings were encountered during same period government issued almost 700 change orders, which it had a right to do with some delay). Another way of stating the rule is to preclude recovery when both parties contributed to the delay, *Vogt Bros. Mfg. Co. v. United States*, 160 Ct. Cl. 687 (1963) (court refused to apportion responsibility when the contractor delayed in replying to the government's counterproposal). In one case the court required proof that the government "directly caused" the delay, *Wunderlich Contracting Co. v. United States*, 173 Ct. Cl. 180, 351 F.2d 956 (1965) (defective specifications and government delay in ordering changes less responsible for delays than the impact of the Korean War). The Court of Claims, in an early interpretation of the current Suspension of Work clause, appeared to give a very restrictive interpretation to the current language. In *Merritt-Chapman & Scott Corp. v. United States*, 208 Ct. Cl. 639, 528 F.2d 1392 (1976), the court stated at 650:

> The 1960 Clause seems specifically to preclude recovery if the contractor would have been equally delayed by other concurrent causes regardless of the Government's action or inaction. The Clause prevents any allocation of damages because it in effect determines that a contractor is not *entitled* to any recovery. It should be noted that the Clause does not weigh whether the Government's action is of less importance than the concurrent cause or whether the concurrent factor is a superseding action. Under the 1960 Clause, a contractor would be entitled to recovery only if the Government's delay is the sole proximate cause of the contractor's additional loss and only if the contractor would not have been delayed for any other reason during that period.

The Federal Circuit clarified this language in *William F. Klingensmith, Inc. v. United States*, 731 F.2d 805 (Fed. Cir. 1984), in which it held that *Merritt-Chapman & Scott* "did not hold that a contractor could not prove the government's delay separate from that chargeable to the contractor." This case reasoned that denying relief for concurrent delay is based on one of two principles: (1) both parties are at fault, so neither should recover, or (2) the delay would have occurred due to some other cause, notwithstanding the delaying act. In *William Passalacqua Builders, Inc.*, GSBCA 4205, 77-1 BCA ¶ 12,406, *recons. denied,* 77-2 BCA ¶ 12,601, the board denied recovery based on the presence of a concurrent cause of delay, citing *Commerce Int'l* and *John McShain*. In *Passalacqua*, the "concurrent" delay was the contractor's delay in submitting change proposals while it stopped work pending government issuance of changes based on the proposals. It appears that the same result would have been reached using the *Merritt-Chapman & Scott* reasoning. See also *John Murphy Constr. Co.*, AGBCA 418, 79-1 BCA ¶ 13,836 (delays of contractor not separated from government delays); *Economy Mech. Indus., Inc.*, GSBCA 4683, 79-1 BCA ¶ 13,571, *modified*, 79-1 BCA ¶ 13,842 (strike); *Ferrell Constr. Co.*, AGBCA 78-134, 79-2 BCA ¶ 13,936 (weather); *RKM Indus., Inc.*, ASBCA 23441, 81-1 BCA ¶ 14,886 (contractor failed to submit test data); and *Welmetco, Ltd.*, ASBCA 22310, 82-1 BCA ¶ 15,492 (contractor failed to demonstrate ability and willingness to start work). See also *Pittman Constr. Co. v. United States*, 2 Cl. Ct. 211 (1983).

Concurrent delays are a broad subject encompassing situations not limited to those involving the Suspension of Work or government Delay of Work clauses. In *T. Brown Constructors, Inc. v. Secretary of Transp.*, 132 F.3d 724 (Fed. Cir. 1997), the Federal Circuit held that when both parties contribute to the delay, neither may recover the costs associated with the delay, unless there is a clear apportionment of the delay. Accord *Karchner Envtl. Inc.*, PSBCA 4085, 00-1 BCA ¶ 30,843 (the Postal Service could not assess liquidated damages and the contractor could not recover delay costs); *Fletcher Forest Prods., Inc.*, AGBCA 95-165-1, 97-1 BCA ¶ 28,809 (although each party argued that the other was obligated to act first, neither took the steps that they had stipulated must be completed before the contractor could begin operations); *Conner Bros. Constr. Co.*, VABCA 2504, 95-2 BCA ¶ 27,910; (contractor could not recover costs and government could not recover liquidated damages for concurrent delay); and *Hunter Mfg. Co.*, ASBCA 48693, 97-1 BCA ¶ 28,824 (contractor failed in its burden of separating the effect of the concurrent delays from the effect of the alleged government-caused delays). In *Singleton Contracting Corp. v. Harvey*, 395 F.3d 1353 (Fed. Cir. 2005), the court refused to apportion delays where the government could not furnish construction drawings for 10 months and the contractor did not furnish required insurance policies. The court reasoned that both delays blocked the initiation of the project although the contractor could have easily remedied its delay by merely furnishing the insurance policies.

Lack of timely notice compounds the problem. *See R. P. Richards Constr., Inc.*, DOTBCA 4019, 01-2 BCA ¶ 31,594 (by failing to inform the CO for 14 months after the contractor discovered the alleged ambiguity in the specifications, the government lost the opportunity to investigate the problem and take action to mitigate any claim for excess costs), and *Jimenez, Inc.*, LBCA 2001-BCA-2, 02-2 BCA ¶ 31,981 (contractor engaged in improper scheduling and failed to provide timely notice to the government of design and specification defects).

Critical path analysis has become the most commonly accepted method of proving that a government delay was the actual cause of the contractor's delay. The critical path of a project is the sequence of events demanding the most time to complete—with the result that any delay on that path will delay the entire project. The standard for determining if a change has delayed performance of a contract using the critical path method is whether overall construction was delayed, *Essential Constr. Co. & Himount Constructors Ltd., (JV)*, ASBCA 18706, 89-2 BCA ¶ 21,632. It is now accepted that, if government delay is on the critical path and non-government delay is on another path, the delay will not be found to be concurrent and compensation will be granted under the Suspension of Work clause, *G.M. Shupe, Inc. v. United States*, 5 Cl. Ct. 662 (1984) ("[t]he reason that the determination of the critical path is crucial to the calculation of delay damages is that only construction work on the critical path had an impact upon the time in which the project was completed"). Some cases have denied suspension of work claims because of the lack of critical path analysis—making the concurrency determination impossible, *Wilner v. United States*, 24 F.3d 1397 (Fed. Cir. 1994) ("[w]ithout a critical path analysis, the court cannot exclude the possibility that the contractor caused concurrent delay on the project"); *Moga Constr. Co. v. United States*, 29 Fed. Cl. 396 (1993) ("[t]he court cannot rely on assertions of a contractor, not supported by critical path analysis of the project, to award critical path delay costs"); *G. Bliudzius Contractors*, ASBCA 42366, 93-3 BCA ¶ 26,074 (critical path method or similar method of demonstrating causation required for recovery); *Youngdale & Sons Constr. Co. v. United States*, 27 Fed. Cl. 516 (1993) (contractor must quantify the number of days attributable to delay and provide proof that the said delays were in fact on the critical path); *Kelso v. Kirk Bros. Mech. Contractors, Inc.*, 16 F.3d 1173 (Fed. Cir. 1994) (determination of the critical path is crucial to the calculation of delay damages because only construction work on the critical path had an impact on the completion).

In some cases, the boards have apportioned the delays when it appeared that neither party should bear the entire burden of the delay. See *Fischbach & Moore Int'l Corp.*, ASBCA 18146, 77-1 BCA ¶ 12,300, *aff'd*, 223 Ct. Cl. 119, 617 F.2d 223 (1980) (a suspension of work case, in which the board approved the jury verdict method in allocating the proportion of a concurrent delay attributable to the government); *JRR Constr. Co.*., DOTCAB 1838, 88-3 BCA ¶ 20,905; *Xplo Corp.*, DOTCAB 1409, 86-3 BCA ¶ 19,280; *E.H. Marhoefer, Jr. Co.*, DOTCAB 70-17, 71-1 BCA ¶ 8791; *Circle Elec. Contractors, Inc.*, DOTCAB 76-27, 77-1 BCA ¶ 12,339. See also *Frank Briscoe Co.*, GSBCA 6169, 81-2 BCA ¶ 15,456, in which the board apportioned the delay where the parties were jointly responsible.

3. *Notice Requirement*

The Suspension of Work clause contains a stringent notice requirement stating that the contractor may not recover any costs incurred more than 20 days prior to the giving of notice of a constructive suspension. In *Hoel-Steffen Constr. Co. v. United States*, 197 Ct. Cl. 561, 456 F.2d 760 (1972), the Court of Claims gave a practical interpretation of this clause, holding that it should not be construed technically but that the requirement should be found to be met if the contractor conveyed actual knowledge of the event causing the delay to the government. The court stated at 570-73:

> [This notice provision] is not directed at the presentation of a monetary claim in connection with the suspension clause, but only at notification to the [government] "of the act or failure to act involved." That inquiry is simply whether the contractor put the Government on notice of the Government conduct complained about, so that the procurement officials could begin to collect data on the asserted increase in cost, and could also evaluate the desirability of continuing the delay-causing conduct.
>
> * * *
>
> The Board was too rigid in demanding that the [contractor] specifically accuse the Government of "unreasonable or unfair measures in attempting to resolve the problem." It is enough, under the suspension clause, that the proof demonstrate that the [government] knew or should have known that it was called upon to act.
>
> * * *
>
> To adopt the Board's severe and narrow application of the notice requirements, or the [government's] support of that ruling, would be out of tune with the language and purpose of the notice provisions, as well as with this court's wholesome concern that notice provisions in contract-adjustment clauses not be applied too technically and liberally where the Government is quite aware of the operative facts.

Prior to the *Hoel-Steffen* case, the boards had interpreted the 20-day notice rule strictly, *Louis J. Otremba, Inc.*, ASBCA 13083, 71-1 BCA ¶ 8714; *General Maint. & Eng'g Co.*, ASBCA 14643, 70-1 BCA ¶ 8243. See, however, *John F. Cleary Constr. Co.*, GSBCA 3158, 71-2 BCA ¶ 9127, in which the board held that the requirement did not apply to a constructive suspension of work resulting from defective specifications. There appears to be some relaxation of the strict interpretation of the rule since *Hoel-Steffen*. See *GMC Contractors, Inc.*, GSBCA 3730, 75-1 BCA ¶ 11,083, *recons. denied,* 75-1 BCA ¶ 11,200, in which the board held that notice had been given on the basis of evidence that was less than clear. However, in *Lane-Verdugo*, ASBCA 16327, 73-2 BCA ¶ 10,271, the board refused to waive the notice requirement when a general statement was made by the contractor that there was a delay claim. The board stated at 48,514:

> During most construction contracts delays are not unusual, some of which may be attributable to the Government, some of which may be attributable to the contractor, and some of which may be attributable to causes beyond the control of either party, such as weather delays. The mere fact the critical path networks and the associated print-outs showed that the contractor was estimating completion at a date later than that called for by the contract cannot reasonably be construed as complying with the requirements of the contract's Suspension of Work clause absent more specific and detailed supporting information.

See *F.G. Haggerty Plumbing Co.,* VABCA 4482, 95-2 BCA ¶ 27,671 (contractor could not recover for an alleged constructive suspension of work, because it did not discharge its duty, under the Suspension of Work clause, to inform the government that it was being delayed and that it would seek recompense).

When the government knows of operative facts that result in delay, it is normally not prejudiced by lack of formal notice, and under such circumstances, the notice requirement should not be construed strictly, *Decker & Co.*, ASBCA 35051, 88-3 BCA ¶ 20,871 (following *Hoel-Steffen*). Accord *Central Mech. Constr.*, ASBCA 29431, 85-2 BCA ¶ 18,061 (failure to give written notice not fatal to suspension claim; government knew of operative facts of delay). However, if the lack of notice prevents the agency from resolving a problem, the claim will be barred, *Dawson Constr. Co.*, VABCA 3306, 93-3 BCA ¶ 26,177, *aff'd*, 34 F.3d 1080 (Fed. Cir. 1994) (no notice that the government was withholding important information and was thus blocking progress on the critical path kept the government from evaluating "the desirability of continuing the delay-causing conduct").

In *Hoel-Steffen*, the court actually found that the contractor had in fact "given" the notice, but the case has since been expanded into the *Hoel-Steffen* principle that actual knowledge of government personnel should suffice in place of strict compliance with the notice requirement.

F. Applicability of Delay Clauses

Several issues have arisen regarding the applicability of the delay clause.

1. Other Clauses Granting Relief for Delays

Both the Suspension of Work and Government Delay of Work clauses state that they are not applicable if another clause of the contract provides for or excludes a price adjustment. Since all clauses providing for equitable adjustments include compensation for delays that occur as part of the event covered by that clause, the delay clauses are frequently superseded by the other clauses.

The Changes clause falls under this rule most frequently. In a number of cases, acts that would normally be constructive suspensions of work have been treated as constructive changes, *Carpenter Constr. Co.*, NASABCA 18, 1964 BCA ¶ 4452; *Mech-Con Corp.*, GSBCA 1373, 65-1 BCA ¶ 4574 (changes to the sequence of the work that delayed the contractor); *Burl Johnson & Assocs.*, ASBCA 11760, 68-2 BCA ¶ 7227 (delay in providing off-site utilities that forced the contractor to perform the work in a different way). This result has usually occurred in situations where the contract contains no Suspension of Work clause, but it can be argued that it is required by the language in the current clause providing for no price adjustment thereunder "for which an equitable adjustment is provided for or excluded under any other provision of the contract." Of course, it is to the benefit of the contractor to obtain relief under the Changes clause, where profit is part of the adjustment and compensation is granted for all delay whether reasonable or unreasonable. In one instance, the contractor had failed to give notice of its claim under the Changes clause and argued that recovery under the Suspension of Work clause was proper, *Piracci Constr. Co.*, GSBCA 3477, 74-2 BCA ¶ 10,800. The board ruled for the contractor, stating at 51,361:

> We also quote from the "legislative history" attending publication of the requirement that the Suspension of Work clause be included in Government contracts:
>
>> "For clarification, the second sentence of the clause as revised specifically indicates that an adjustment is not to be made under the clause in any instance where `an equitable adjustment is provided for or excluded under any other provision' of the contract. Accordingly, where a claim for delay expense is cognizable under the Changes clause or the Government-furnished Property clause, for example, an adjustment will be for consideration under these clauses in preference to the Suspension of Work clause" (Emphasis supplied) (41 Code of Federal Regulations 1-7, Appendix).
>
> In our opinion, the Government has misinterpreted the clause. The "history" makes it clear that, where a claim can be made under the Changes and the Suspension of Work clauses, use of the Changes clause is preferred to use of the Suspension clause. It does not, as the Government wants us to conclude, provide that availability of relief under the Changes clause precludes relief under the Suspension clause.

For a case in which the board ruled that a claim for deceleration of the work should be apportioned between the Changes and Suspension of Work clauses, see *Gunther & Shirley Co.*, ENGBCA 3691, 78-2 BCA ¶ 13,454.

Some confusion also exists with respect to the proper treatment of costs resulting from defective specifications. The Court of Claims held that contractors are entitled to an equitable adjustment under the Changes clause for costs resulting from attempts to conform to defective specifications from the inception of the contract, *Hol-Gar Mfg. Corp. v. United States*, 175 Ct. Cl. 518, 360 F.2d 634 (1966). The Court of Claims also held that, because the government impliedly warrants its specifications, delays resulting from defective specifications are per se unreasonable and therefore compensable under the Suspension of Work clause, *Chaney & James Constr. Co. v.*

United States, 190 Ct. Cl. 699, 421 F.2d 728 (1970). Despite the clear implication that alternative treatment is available, in *Minmar Builders, Inc.*, GSBCA 3430, 72-2 BCA ¶ 9599, the board held that delays resulting from defective specifications can be treated only under the Suspension of Work clause, stating at 44,857:

> The delay, being attributable to a deficiency in the Government specifications, is considered unreasonable per se. *Chaney and James Constr. Co. v. United States*, 190 Ct. Cl. 699, 421 F.2d 728 (1970). Appellant is therefore entitled to be compensated under the Suspension of Work clause for the extra costs attributable to the delay. The delay being unreasonable, however, is not compensable under the Changes clause.

This rationale was also followed in *John F. Cleary Constr. Co.*, GSBCA 3158, 71-2 BCA ¶ 9127. In *Pittman Constr. Co.*, GSBCA 4897, 81-1 BCA ¶ 14,847, *recon. denied*, 81-1 BCA ¶ 15,111, *aff'd*, 2 Cl. Ct. 211 (1983), the board noted that grounds for distinguishing between Changes and Suspension of Work clause recovery might be that Changes clause recovery would be appropriate where the predominant effect of the defective specifications is wasted effort.

Where defective specifications are at issue, the government's alleged unreasonable delays in issuing modifications were covered by the Suspension of Work clause, *Beauchamp Constr. v. United States*, 14 Cl. Ct. 430 (1988). See also *Reliance Enters.*, ASBCA 27638, 85-2 BCA ¶ 18,045, *recons. denied,* 85-3 BCA 18,357 (government's failure to correct inadequate drawings caused contractor to incur additional costs because of erosion and weed growth when the work was delayed until after the rainy season); *Big Chief Drilling Co. v. United States*, 26 Cl. Ct. 1276 (1992) (defective drilling specifications allowed contractor to recover damages); *Jordan & Nobles Constr. Co.*, GSBCA 8349, 91-1 BCA ¶ 23,659 (government responsible for delay caused by improper instructions to place defective brick on the building's exterior); *Hardrives, Inc.*, IBCA 2319, 94-1 BCA ¶ 26,267 (government liable for defective earthwork specifications in canal construction contract); and *Hill Aviation Logistics*, ASBCA 40817, 93-1 BCA ¶ 25,274 (contractor entitled to adjustments for additional time of performance caused by the misrepresentation of specification).

Unreasonable delays that occur after actual corrective actions caused by a differing site condition are compensable under the Differing Site Conditions clause, whereas delays preceding corrective action are covered by the Suspension of Work clause, *Berrios Constr. Co.*, VABCA 3152, 92-2 BCA ¶ 24,828. In that case, the board gave an adjustment under the Suspension of Work clause for delay caused by the discovery and removal of asbestos.

2. Completion Within Contract Schedule

The Suspension of Work and Government Delay of Work clauses are applicable even though the contract was completed within the scheduled completion time, *Met-*

ropolitan Paving Co. v. United States, 163 Ct. Cl. 420, 325 F.2d 241 (1963). In that case, the court formulated this rule in a situation where there was no Suspension of Work clause, stating at 423:

> While it is true that there is not an "obligation" or "duty" of [the government] to aid a contractor to complete prior to completion date, from this it does not follow that [the government] may hinder and prevent a contractor's early completion without incurring liability. It would seem to make little difference whether or not the parties contemplated an early completion, or even whether or not the contractor contemplated an early completion. Where [the government] is guilty of "deliberate harassment and dilatory tactics" and a contractor suffers damages as a result of such action, we think that [the government] is liable.

Accord, *Gary Constr. Co.*, ASBCA 19306, 77-1 BCA ¶ 12,461; *Sydney Constr. Co.*, ASBCA 21377, 77-2 BCA ¶ 12,719. See also *Owen L. Schwam Constr. Co.*, ASBCA 22407, 79-2 BCA ¶ 13,919, in which the contractor proved that it would have been able to finish early but was late because of government delay; and *CWC, Inc.*, ASBCA 26432, 82-2 BCA ¶ 15,907. In *Gardner Displays Co. v. United States*, 171 Ct. Cl. 497, 346 F.2d 585 (1965), the court applied the same rule to delays resulting from changes issued by the government. In *Barton & Sons Co.*, ASBCA 9477, 65-2 BCA ¶ 4874, the board first applied it to a delay under a contract containing a Suspension of Work clause. It has been held that the rule still applies where a contractor performs in accordance with a CPM schedule required to be submitted by contract clause but subsequently proves that it could have performed earlier had it not been for government delay, *Eickhof Constr. Co.*, ASBCA 20049, 77-1 BCA ¶ 12,398 (unreasonable delay compensable despite project completion on time; Suspension of Work clause states that, "if all or any part of the work is delayed," an adjustment shall be made of any increase in the cost of performance). See also *P & A Constr. Co.*, ASBCA 29901, 86-3 BCA ¶ 19,101 (government delay in making site available, which caused loss of subcontractor, compensable even though overall project was completed on time).

To take advantage of this rule, the contractor must present clear proof that it could have completed at an earlier time. For instance, in *Skyline Painting, Inc.*, ENGBCA 5810, 93-3 BCA ¶ 26,041, no recovery was granted to a contractor that could not reliably demonstrate that it intended to complete work before the contract completion time because no method of reasonable comparison existed to show that the contractor's rate of productivity in work performed after period of government-attributed delay expired would have been the same during previous period (different work force size, better site conditions, learning curve benefits). In *Interstate Gen. Gov't Contractors, Inc. v. West*, 12 F.3d 1053 (Fed. Cir. 1993), the court held that, in order to recover costs for government-caused delays despite the contractor's timely completion, the contractor must show that from the outset of the contract it intended to complete the contract early, had the capability to do so, and actually would have done so but for the government's action. See *Elrich Contracting, Inc. v. General*

Servs. Admin., GSBCA 10936, 93-1 BCA ¶ 25,316, and *Frazier-Fleming Co.*, ASBCA 34537, 91-1 BCA ¶ 23,378. See also *Libby Corp.*, ASBCA 40765, 96-1 BCA ¶ 28,255 (denying claim for unabsorbed overhead where contractor failed to meet the test set forth in *Interstate*); *Ronald Adams Contractor; Inc.*, AGBCA 91-155-1, 94-3 BCA ¶ 27,018, at 134,689 (denying claim for unabsorbed overhead because contractor failed to prove its "intent to finish early"); *Jim Smith Contracting Co.*, ENGBCA 5870, 94-2 BCA ¶ 26,879, at 133,791 (denying claim for work stoppage because the record did not show that the contractor contemporaneously intended to complete the contract early); and *Emerald Maint., Inc.*, ASBCA 43929, 98-2 BCA ¶ 29,903 (contractor failed to provide evidentiary support for underlying assumption that it could have realistically completed project early but for government delays).

In *Liles Constr. Co.*, ASBCA 11919, 68-1 BCA ¶ 7067, the contractor requested government assistance in attempting to complete ahead of schedule. After receipt of such assistance, the contractor filed a claim for compensation because of the inadequacy of the government assistance. The board ruled that there was no government liability for gratuitously attempting to assist the contractor to complete ahead of schedule. See also *Bell Coatings, Inc.*, ENGBCA 5787, 93-2 BCA ¶ 25,805, in which no recovery was permitted for a contractor who refused to perform during winter weather after a suspension was lifted. The board reasoned that this was an independent business decision animated by weather-related expectations and thus not solely attributable to the ordered suspension. See also *Craft Mach. Works, Inc.*, ASBCA 47227, 97-1 BCA ¶ 28,651 (contractor entitled to recover damages for 266 days of compensable delay because government-caused delays prevented contractor's planned early completion); *Maron Constr. Co.*, GSBCA 13,625, 98-1 BCA ¶ 29,685; and *U.A. Anderson Constr. Co.*, ASBCA 48087, 99-1 BCA ¶ 30,347.

Compensable delays can result even in cases of early completion. *See U.A. Anderson Constr. Co.*, ASBCA 48087, 99-1 BCA ¶ 30,347, holding that early completion was not a bar to recovery for increased costs associated with a government work stoppage because the contractor established that it was capable and intended to complete the project ahead of schedule. The board also held that there is no requirement that the government be notified of a planned early completion date. See also *Craft Mach. Works, Inc.*, ASBCA 47227, 97-1 BCA ¶ 28,651 (contractor entitled to recover costs resulting from government-caused delays, even though the contract was completed early, because the government was aware of the contractor's intention to deliver 16 to 21 months earlier than the contract required and did not object to the delivery dates), and *Maron Constr. Co.,* GSBCA 13625, 98-1 BCA ¶ 29,685 (contractor could be awarded early completion delay damages despite the existence of a contract clause that attempted to limit or eliminate the government's liability for such damages, because the government may have waived application of that provision by delaying the contractor's progress and by making it impossible for the contractor to prepare and update a critical path schedule). But see *J.A. Jones Constr. Co.*, ENGBCA 6348, 00-2 BCA ¶ 31,000 (contractor was not entitled to recovery for alleged government-caused delays, because it failed to show that its early completion schedule was reasonable or feasible and performed no analysis showing what work was resequenced or how any resequencing shortened completion of the project), and *Hensel Phelps Constr. Co.*, ASBCA 49270, 99-2 BCA ¶ 30,531 (even though the government approved the contractor's early completion schedule, its claim for early completion delay damages was denied because the contractor failed to show that it could have and would have finished early without the large number of changes and delays allegedly caused by the government).

The contractor must prove that early completion was achievable. See *Swanson Prods., Inc.*, ASBCA 48002, 96-2 BCA ¶ 28,289 (government not liable for delay because contractor responsible for preventing early completion), and *Hoffman Constr. Co. of Oregon v. United States*, 40 Fed. Cl. 184 (1998) (contractor did not prove its early completion date was feasible or attainable).

In one interesting case, *E.R. Mitchell Constr. Co. v. Secretary of the Navy*, 175 F.3d 1369 (Fed. Cir. 1999), the court reversed the decision of the ASBCA and ruled that the fact that the contractor completed a few weeks in advance of the completion date did not bar the subcontractor's unabsorbed home office overhead claim because of a delay suffered by the subcontractor because the work was suspended for 60 days while the Navy changed specifications. Compare *Fru-Con Constr. Corp.*, ASBCA 53544, 05-1 BCA ¶ 32,936, refusing to grant delay damages where a subcontractor was delayed beyond its early completion schedule because the subcontractor's schedule had neither been used nor approved by the contractor.

3. Delays Preceding Award

The Suspension of Work clause has been held not to apply to delays in making award of the contract, *M.A. Mortenson Co.*, ENGBCA 4780, 87-2 BCA ¶ 19,718, *aff'd*, 843 F.2d 1360 (Fed. Cir. 1988). In *K-W Constr., Inc. v. United States*, 229 Ct. Cl. 413, 671 F.2d 481 (1982), the contractor's bid was originally determined to be nonresponsive. On protest by the contractor, the GAO held that the rejection was improper and award was subsequently made. The contractor's claim for increased costs caused by the delay was denied because the Suspension of Work clause is not applicable to delays occurring "prior to administration of the contract." See also *Hoedad's, Inc.*, AGBCA 76-168-4, 83-1 BCA ¶ 16,288, and *Garcia Concrete, Inc.*, AGBCA 78-105-4, 82-2 BCA ¶ 16,046.

CHAPTER 7

GOVERNMENT PROPERTY

The government's policy is that contractors are ordinarily required to furnish all property necessary to perform a government contract, FAR 45.102. Nevertheless, government property, such as materials, production facilities, or test equipment, is often used by contractors during the performance of government contracts. Much of this property is in the nature of tooling or facilities furnished to assist contractors in performing the contractual work. Material to be incorporated into manufactured products is also furnished when the government decides that its interests will be served by furnishing the material rather than permitting the contractor to purchase it. When government property is used by a contractor in the performance of a government contract, the process of contract administration is more complex.

The term "government property" is broadly defined in the FAR to include not only property owned by the government and furnished to a contractor but also property that is acquired by the contractor during contract performance when title to such property vests in the government. The following definitions appear in FAR 45.101(a):

> "Government property," means all property owned by or leased to the Government or acquired by the Government under the terms of the contract. It includes both Government-furnished property and contractor-acquired property as defined in this section.
>
> "Contractor-acquired property," as used in this part, means property acquired or otherwise provided by the contractor for performing a contract and to which the Government has title.
>
> "Government-furnished property," as used in this part, means property in the possession of, or directly acquired by, the Government and subsequently made available to the contractor.

FAR Part 45 prescribes "policies and procedures for providing Government property to contractors, contractors' use and management of Government property, and reporting, redistributing, and disposing of contractor inventory," FAR 45.000. An initiative to rewrite this part of the FAR to reduce its administrative burdens was begun in 1994, and a proposed revision was promulgated for comment in 70 Fed. Reg. 54878 (September 19, 2005).

Clauses covering government property are required to be used in a wide variety of contracts. See FAR 45.106 for detailed instructions for use of these clauses. The two principal property clauses are Government Property (Fixed-Price Contracts),

FAR 52.245-2, and Government Property (Cost-Reimbursement, Time-and-Material, or Labor-Hour Contracts), FAR 52.245-5. A short-form Government-Furnished Property clause at FAR 52.245-4 may be used in solicitations and contracts when a fixed-price, time-and-material, or labor-hour contract is contemplated and the acquisition cost of all government-furnished property involved in the contract is $100,000 or less, unless the contract is with an educational or nonprofit organization, FAR 45.106(d). Alternate clauses are to be used for educational and nonprofit organizations.

The first section of this chapter reviews the procedures used when the contractor is to be furnished government property or is to acquire property under the terms of a contract. It also discusses procedures to be followed if a contractor desires to obtain government property during the performance of a contract. The second section covers defective or late government-furnished property (GFP). It focuses on the government's obligations to deliver GFP in a timely manner and to ensure that such property be suitable for its intended purpose. The section also deals with the contractor's duty to inspect GFP. The third section examines the contractor's obligations concerning government property, such as control, liability, and disposition.

I. OBTAINING PROPERTY FOR CONTRACT PERFORMANCE

Normally, before entering into a contract, the parties will have determined what property will be required to perform the contract and will have included contract language covering the procedures to be followed to obtain such property. In such cases, the effort during contract administration will be relatively routine unless one of the parties is unable to meet its commitments. In other instances, the contractor may find that it needs additional or different property than specified in the contract to perform the work. This entails greater effort during contract administration. This section discusses the procedures to be used in contract administration when property is to be obtained.

The FAR contains a variety of policies on a number of different types of government property. "Property" is defined broadly in FAR 45.101 as "all property, both real and personal. It includes facilities, material, special tooling, special test equipment, and agency-peculiar property." FAR Subpart 45.3 sets forth the policies on providing property to contractors. These policies are stated differently for each type of property—material (FAR 45.303), special tooling (FAR 45.306), special test equipment (FAR 45.307), facilities (FAR 45.302), and government production and research property (FAR 45.308).

A. Materials, Components, and Supplies

FAR 45.301 defines "material" as follows:

> "Material," as used in this subpart, means property that may be incorporated into or attached to a deliverable end item or that may be consumed or expended in per-

> forming a contract. It includes assemblies, components, parts, raw and processed materials, and small tools and supplies that may be consumed in normal use in performing a contract.

This definition does not include government property that is delivered to a contractor for repair or storage. Instead, it pertains to property that facilitates the manufacturing process, either by becoming a part of an end item or by being consumed. Note that small tools are included in this definition.

FAR 45.303-2 requires the government to specify in each solicitation any material that it will furnish to the contractor during performance. It is assumed that all other material necessary for performance will be furnished by the contractor and included in the contract price for the work. FAR 45.303-2 also requires the contracting officer to include the "appropriate" government property clause called for by FAR 45.106 in any contract where the government is going to provide any material. The two standard clauses in FAR 52.245-2 and FAR 52.245-5 contain relatively complete coverage of the rights of each party with regard to any such property. Paragraph (b) of these clauses permits the contracting officer to decrease the amount of property to be provided or substitute different property for any property that is to be provided by the government or acquired by the contractor. When this occurs, the contractor is entitled, under ¶ (h) of these clauses, to an equitable adjustment in the price "in accordance with the procedures of the Changes clause." The clauses are silent on the rights of the contractor to request alterations in the material to be furnished, but such requests normally are considered as part of the contract administration process as long as the government has access to the needed material and the contractor agrees to an appropriate equitable adjustment to the contract price.

Title to material is governed by ¶ (c) of the standard clauses. Under the Government Property (Fixed-Price Contracts) clause in FAR 52.245-2, the government will retain title to all material furnished to the contractor pursuant to ¶ (c)(1). In addition, it is given title to material if the contract contains a special provision, as follows:

> (c)(4) If this contract contains a provision directing the Contractor to purchase material for which the Government will reimburse the Contractor as a direct item of cost under this contract—
>
> > (i) Title to material purchased from a vendor shall pass to and vest in the Government upon the vendor's delivery of such material; and
> >
> > (ii) Title to all other material shall pass to and vest in the Government upon—
> >
> > > (A) Issuance of the material for use in contract performance;
> > >
> > > (B) Commencement of processing of the material or its use in contract performance; or

> (C) Reimbursement of the cost of the material by the Government, whichever occurs first.

If a fixed-price contract provides for progress payments based on costs, the Progress Payments clause in FAR 52.232-16 gives the government title to "property" as defined in ¶ (d):

> (2) "Property," as used in this clause, includes all of the below-described items acquired or produced by the Contractor that are or should be allocable or properly chargeable to this contract under sound and generally accepted accounting principles and practices.
>
> > (i) Parts, materials, inventories, and work in process.

The Government Property (Cost-Reimbursement, Time-and-Material, or Labor-Hour Contracts) clause in FAR 52.245-5 contains somewhat different provisions on title. It provides that the government will retain title to all material furnished to the contractor (¶ (c)(1)) and all material for which it is entitled to be reimbursed as a direct cost as soon as it is delivered to the contractor (¶ (c)(2)). In addition, it is given title to "other" material, as follows:

> (c)(3) Title to all other property, the cost of which is reimbursable to the Contractor, shall pass to and vest in the Government upon—
>
> > (i) Issuance of the property for use in contract performance;
> >
> > (ii) Commencement of processing of the property for use in contract performance; or
> >
> > (iii) Reimbursement of the cost of the property by the Government, whichever occurs first.

These provisions of the clauses in FAR 52.232-16 and FAR 52.245-5 have been held, for state tax purposes, to give the government title to material purchased for indirect cost accounts. See *Strayhorn v. Raytheon E-Sys., Inc.*, 101 S.W.3d 558 (Tex.App.-Austin), *petition for review denied*, Tex. S. Ct. 2003 (Unpub.); *Hughes Aircraft Co. v. County of Orange*, 117 Cal. Rptr. 2d 601 (Cal. Ct. App. 2002); *Motorola, Inc. v. Arizona Dep't of Revenue*, 993 P.2d 1101 (Ariz. Ct. App. 1999); *McDonnell Douglas Corp. v. Director of Rev.*, 945 S.W.2d 437 (Mo. 1997); and *Aerospace Corp. v. State Bd. of Equalization*, 267 Cal. Rptr. 685 (Ct. App. 1990). Compare *TRW Space & Def. Sector v. County of Los Angeles*, 58 Cal. Rptr. 2d 602 (Ct. App. 1996), reaching the opposite conclusion. These decisions permit contractors to avoid state taxes based on title to property to the extent that they have contracts containing these clauses. However, they are required to pay such taxes on a pro-rata share of the material purchased for indirect cost accounts that is allocated to fixed-price contracts that do not contain a progress payments clause and commercial contracts. It is not clear how this rule affects the contractor's obligations discussed in Section III.

B. Special Tooling and Special Test Equipment

Special tooling and special test equipment are subject to unique policies and procedures because they are not the types of items that a contractor would normally acquire for use in its general business.

1. Special Tooling

"Special tooling" is defined in FAR 45.101(a) as follows:

> [J]igs, dies, fixtures, molds, patterns, taps, gauges, other equipment and manufacturing aids, all components of these items, and replacement of these items, which are of such a specialized nature that without substantial modification or alteration their use is limited to the development or production of particular supplies or parts thereof or to the performance of particular services. It does not include material, special test equipment, facilities (except foundations and similar improvements necessary for installing special tooling), general or special machine tools, or similar capital items.

This category includes all types of personal property that are limited in use to producing or developing particular items or performing particular services, except for special test equipment. Tools and equipment that are not of a specialized nature are generally included within the definitions of facilities and plant equipment.

If the government has existing special tooling that can be used to perform a contract, FAR 45.306-1 requires the contracting officer to offer it to prospective contractors if "it will not disrupt programs of equal or higher priority, it is otherwise advantageous to the Government, and use of the special tooling is authorized under 45.402(a)." This latter requirement pertains to ensuring that there is no competitive advantage conferred when the government provides "Government production and research property," as discussed below. When the government furnishes existing special tooling, the contract must contain detailed coverage on what tooling will be provided and the obligations of the parties in placing the tooling in a condition that can be used to perform the contract, FAR 45.306-1(b). Further, if the contract is for a fixed price, it must contain the Special Tooling clause, FAR 52.245-17, in addition to the Government Property clause, FAR 45.306-5. Paragraph (d) of this clause places most of the risk for the suitability of the special tooling on the contractor:

> (d) *Special tooling furnished by the Government.* (1) Except as otherwise provided in this contract, all Government-furnished special tooling is provided "as is." The Government makes no warranty whatsoever with respect to special tooling furnished "as is," except that the property is in the same condition when placed at the f.o.b. point specified in the solicitation as when last available for inspection by the Contractor under the solicitation.
>
> (2) The Contractor may repair any special tooling made available on an "as is" basis. Such repair will be at the Contractor's expense, except as

> otherwise provided in this clause. Such property may be modified as necessary for use under this contract at the Contractor's expense, except as otherwise directed by the Contracting Officer. Any repair or modification of property furnished "as is" shall not affect the title of the Government.
>
> (3) If there is any change in the condition of special tooling furnished "as is" from the time inspected or last available for inspection under the solicitation to the time placed on board at the location specified in the solicitation or the Government directs a change in the quantity of special tooling furnished or to be furnished, and such change will adversely affect the Contractor, the Contractor shall, upon receipt of the property, notify the Contracting Officer detailing the facts, and, as directed by the Contracting Officer, either (i) return such items at the Government's expense or otherwise dispose of the property, or (ii) effect repair to return the property to its condition when inspected under the solicitation or, if not inspected, last available for inspection under the solicitation. After completing the directed action and upon written request of the Contractor, the Contracting Officer shall equitably adjust any contractual provisions affected by the return, disposition, or repair in accordance with procedures provided for in the Changes clause of this contract. The foregoing provisions for adjustment are the exclusive remedy available to the Contractor, and the Government shall not be otherwise liable for any delivery of special tooling in a condition or in quantities other than when originally offered.

Note that ¶ (3) of this clause permits equitable adjustments in certain circumstances.

In most cases where special tooling is needed to perform a contract, there is no existing tooling available, and the contractor has to manufacture it or acquire it in order to perform the contract. There is no guidance in the FAR as to the government's policy when contractors must acquire such special tooling to perform the contract, but generally the government will permit contractors to include the cost of such tooling in the contract price. In such cases, the government has an option to acquire title to the tooling under ¶ (b) of the Special Tooling clause. Paragraph (i) of the clause requires the contractor to submit lists of all such special tooling to the contracting officer, and FAR 45.306-3(a) contains guidance on when the government should exercise its option to acquire title. Paragraph (j) of the Special Tooling clause gives the contracting officer broad authority to control the disposition of the special tooling:

> (1) The Contracting Officer may identify specific items of special tooling to be retained or give the Contractor a list specifying the products, parts, or services including follow-on requirements for which the Government may require special tooling and request the Contractor to identify all usable items of special tooling on hand that were designed for or used in the production or performance of such products, parts, or services. Once items of usable special tooling required by the Government are identified, the Contracting Officer may—
>
> > (i) Direct the Contractor to transfer specified items of special tooling to follow-on contracts requiring their use. Those items shall be furnished for

use on the contract(s) as specified by the Contracting Officer and shall be subject to the provisions of the gaining contract(s); or

(ii) Request the Contractor to enter into an appropriate storage contract for special tooling specified to be retained by the Contractor for the Government. Tooling to be stored shall be stored pursuant to a storage contract between the Government and the Contractor; or

(iii) Direct the Contractor to transfer title to the Government (to the extent not previously transferred) and deliver to the Government those items of special tooling which are specified for removal from the Contractor's plant.

2. *Special Test Equipment*

FAR 45.101(a) defines "special test equipment" as follows:

> [E]ither single or multipurpose integrated test units engineered, designed, fabricated, or modified to accomplish special purpose testing in performing a contract. It consists of items or assemblies of equipment including standard or general purpose items or components that are interconnected and interdependent so as to become a new functional entity for special testing purposes. It does not include material, special tooling, facilities (except foundations and similar improvements necessary for installing special test equipment), and plant equipment items used for general plant testing purposes.

If the government has existing special test equipment that can be used to perform a contract, FAR 45.307-1 states that it should be offered to prospective contractors following the same procedures that pertain to special tooling. No special contract clause is provided by the FAR for use in these circumstances, but title to the equipment remains in the government pursuant to ¶ (c) of the standard government Property clauses, and the rights of the parties with regard to changes in the equipment provided, are governed by those clauses in the same manner as government-furnished material (as discussed above). See FAR 45.307-2(a), requiring the contract to separately identify each item of special test equipment to be furnished by the government.

If the contractor has to fabricate or acquire special test equipment during the performance of the contract, FAR 45.307-1(b) permits contracting officers to authorize the contractor to acquire such special test equipment. Presumably, the estimated cost of such equipment will be included in the contract price. If the parties know precisely what equipment is needed, FAR 45.307-2(a) calls for each item of such equipment to be separately identified. Again, no special contract clause is provided by the FAR for use in these circumstances, with the result that the parties' rights and obligations are governed by the Government Property clause in the contract. In contrast, if the parties know that special test equipment is required but do not know its "exact identification," FAR 45.307-3 requires that the contract contain the Special

Test Equipment clause in FAR 52.245-18, which includes notification and approval provisions, as follows:

> (b) The Contractor may either acquire or fabricate special test equipment at Government expense when the equipment is not otherwise itemized in this contract and the prior approval of the Contracting Officer has been obtained. The Contractor shall provide the Contracting Officer with a written notice, at least 30 days in advance, of the Contractor's intention to acquire or fabricate the special test equipment. As a minimum, the notice shall also include an estimated aggregate cost of all items and components of the equipment the individual cost of which is less than $5,000, and the following information on each item or component of equipment costing $5,000 or more:
>
>> (1) The end use application and function of each proposed special test unit, identifying special characteristics and the reasons for the classification of the test unit as special test equipment.
>>
>> (2) A complete description identifying the items to be acquired and the items to be fabricated by the Contractor.
>>
>> (3) The estimated cost of the item of special test equipment or component.
>>
>> (4) A statement that intra-plant screening of Contractor and Government-owned special test equipment and components has been accomplished and that none are available for use in performing this contract.
>
> (c) The Government may furnish any special test equipment or components rather than approve their acquisition or fabrication by the Contractor. Such Government-furnished items shall be subject to the Government Property clause, except that the Government shall not be obligated to deliver such items any sooner than the Contractor could have acquired or fabricated them after expiration of the 30-day notice period in paragraph (b) of this clause. However, unless the Government notifies the Contractor of its decision to furnish the items within the 30-day notice period, the Contractor may proceed to acquire or fabricate the equipment or components subject to any other applicable provision of this contract.

It is not clear what this clause means when it states that, with the approval of the contracting officer, the equipment can be acquired or fabricated "at Government expense." In a cost-type contract, it presumably means that the costs could be charged to the contract. In a fixed-price contract, perhaps it means that the costs can be properly allocated to the contract or that a contract line item for special test equipment can be adjusted to reflect the price of the equipment. In either event, title to the equipment vests in the government, and the other rights and liabilities of the parties regarding the "unknown" special test equipment are determined according to the standard Government Property clauses.

3. Accounting Rules

Expenditures made to acquire "special tooling" and "special test equipment" may be charged as an expense in a current accounting period rather than capitalized and recovered through depreciation. The Special Tooling & Special Test Equipment Costs cost principle, FAR 31.205-40, requires that such costs be allocated to the contract for which they were acquired, provided that the contract schedule does not prohibit acquisition of the items and that the items were not acquired prior to the effective date of the contract. The relative interests of the parties in having tooling costs designated as either special or general in nature was discussed in *Aerojet Gen. Corp.*, ASBCA 15703, 73-1 BCA ¶ 9932, in which the board stated at 46,594:

> All of the tooling in question was what was described in our record as "gray area" tooling. By that term is meant tooling which is not obviously either special or general purpose tooling. Aerojet has asserted and we believe that normally in negotiation of a cost type contract the contractor seeks to have this gray area tooling declared special tooling so that its costs may be recovered immediately out of that contract. On the other hand, Government negotiators customarily seek to have it declared general purpose tooling in order to spread out the costs over a greater period and reduce the price of the contract then being negotiated.

In *Aerojet* the board held that the government was bound by a contractual agreement that certain tooling would be treated as general purpose tooling and capitalized. See also *TV-R, Inc.*, ASBCA 17384, 75-1 BCA ¶ 11,144, holding that a contractor was not entitled to charge the government the entire cost of a videotape system purchased by the contractor to perform work called for under a change order, since it found that the decision to acquire the system was motivated in part by an expectation that the system could eventually be used on non-government work. Compare *Art Metal-U.S.A., Inc.*, GSBCA 5898(5245)-REIN, 83-2 BCA ¶ 16,881, holding that certain items could be expensed as special tooling based on the following analysis, at 83,989:

> The dispute over which of the new tooling and equipment appellant purchased to perform the contract as changed is general purpose tooling and equipment and which is special purpose tooling and equipment is centered upon the roll forming machines purchased to manufacture the tracks for the slide suspensions and the Durant measuring systems used on those roll formers. Appellant says that the evidence clearly demonstrates that the roll forming machines and the measuring systems used on them could be used by appellant only for production of slide suspension tracks and that the roll formers could not have been adapted to other uses without substantial and costly modifications. Appellant says that the definition of special purpose tooling and equipment in the applicable contract cost principles, specifically 41 C.F.R. 1-15.205-40(a) (1974), . . . mandates that we treat the roll formers and the Durant measuring systems as special purpose tooling and test equipment. The Government's rejoinder to that argument is based upon the testimony of one of BAH's analysts who said that the roll forming machines, if fitted with different rolls, could be used by appellant to produce many other parts and

> hypothesized that those machines would have value if sold as used equipment. We agree with appellant. The test of whether a particular item of tooling or equipment is general purpose or special purpose is subjective, not objective. *American Electric, Inc.*, ASBCA No. 16,635, 76-2 BCA ¶ 12,151, at 58,481-82, *modified on recons.*, 77-2 BCA ¶ 12,792. There is no evidence in this record that the roll formers and the Durant measuring systems attached to them could have been used by appellant for any purpose other than the manufacture of slide suspension tracks, at least not without changing the rolls themselves. That would have cost $24,000, while the acquisition cost of the machines and the measuring systems was $54,538. That the roll forming machines had a value as used equipment or that another contractor might have had a use for them is simply not relevant.

Costs of special tooling and special test equipment acquired prior to the effective date of a contract may be recovered only through depreciation or amortization charges, FAR 31.205-40(b). In *Rockwell Int'l Corp.*, ASBCA 20304, 76-2 BCA ¶ 12,131, deferred start-up costs consisting of special tooling and test equipment were allowable only as amortization during the period work was being performed using the tooling and test equipment. See also *R-D Mounts, Inc.*, ASBCA 17422, 75-1 BCA ¶ 11,077, *recons. denied*, 75-1 BCA ¶ 11,237.

In 1987, Congress sought to place additional risk and financing responsibility on defense contractors by requiring that not more than 50 percent of the cost of production special tooling and production special test equipment be reimbursed directly. In 1988, this was changed to provide that not *less* than 50 percent of the cost of such tooling and equipment *must* be paid under a contract if future contracts were contemplated. This change was codified in 10 U.S.C. § 2329. This statute was repealed effective October 13, 1994, with the result that this ill-advised policy is no longer in effect.

C. Facilities

"Facilities" is the generic term used by the government to describe capital equipment and land or buildings. FAR 45.301 defines "facilities" as follows:

> [P]roperty used for production, maintenance, research, development, or testing. It includes plant equipment and real property (see 45.101). It does not include material, special test equipment, special tooling, or agency-peculiar property.

It is the general policy of the government not to provide facilities to contractors, except in very limited circumstances, FAR 45.302-1. When facilities are provided, it is expected that the need for them will be determined during the formation of the production or research and development contract on which they will be used. Thus, the guidance in the FAR is written in terms of the actions that should be taken in conjunction with the negotiation of these contracts.

All facilities provided by a contracting activity for use by a contractor at any one plant or general location are to be governed by a single facilities contract, FAR

45.302-2, unless the exceptions in FAR 45.302-3 are applicable (in which case another type of contract containing a Government Property clause may be used). When a facilities contract is used, it must contain a series of clauses prescribed by FAR 45.302-6, including a broad Government Property (Consolidated Facilities) clause in FAR 52.245-7. This clause provides that title to facilities "shall pass to and vest in the Government upon delivery by the vendor of all such items purchased by the contractor for which it is entitled to be reimbursed as a direct item of cost under this contract." It also grants the government broad rights to alter the facilities and make a commensurate equitable adjustment to the price of any contract that is affected by the alteration. Both parties have broad termination rights under this clause. If the government exercises such rights, the contractor has the right to a price adjustment in affected contracts. Paragraph (m) states:

Termination of the use of the facilities. (1) The Contractor may at any time, upon written notice to the Contracting Officer, terminate its authority to use any or all of the facilities. Termination under this paragraph (m) shall not relieve the Contractor of any of its obligations or liabilities under any related contract or subcontract affected by the termination.

> (2) The Contracting Officer may at any time, upon written notice, terminate or limit the Contractor's authority to use any of the facilities. Except as otherwise provided in the Failure to Perform clause of this contract, an equitable adjustment may be made in any related contract of the Contractor that so provides and that is affected by such notice.

In *Dae Shin Enters., Inc.*, ASBCA 50533, 03-1 BCA ¶ 32,096, the government significantly reduced the funds being provided to maintain government facilities and notified the contractor that the facilities contract would be terminated in one year. These actions led the facilities contractor to conclude that it was impracticable to perform a production subcontract, with the result that the production contractor was terminated for default. The board rejected the defense that the default was caused by the government's actions on the facilities contract, concluding that these actions were not a material breach because the government was acting in good faith in reducing its obligations under that contract.

FAR 45.302-3 contains the following exceptions to the use of a separate facilities contract:

> (a) Facilities may be provided to a contractor under a contract other than a facilities contract when one of the following exceptions applies:
>
> > (1) The actual or estimated cumulative acquisition cost of the facilities provided by the contracting activity to the contractor at one plant or general location does not exceed $ 1,000,000;
> >
> > (2) The number of items of plant equipment provided is ten or fewer;

> (3) The contract performance period is twelve months or less;
>
> (4) The contract is for construction;
>
> (5) The contract is for services and the facilities are to be used in connection with the operation of a Government-owned plant or installation; or
>
> (6) The contract is for work within an establishment or installation operated by the Government.

> (b) When a facilities contract is not used, the Government's interest shall normally be protected by using the appropriate Government property clause or, in the case of subparagraph (a)(5) of this subsection, by appropriate portions of the facilities clauses.

When facilities are provided under a Government Property clause, the failure of the government to provide them will entitle the contractor to an equitable adjustment. See *E. L. Hamm & Assocs., Inc.*, ASBCA 51838, 03-1 BCA ¶ 32,243, *rev'd on other grounds*, 379 F.3d 1334 (Fed. Cir. 2004) (government obliged to deliver trailer "in sufficient time for it to be used in the ordinary and economical course of performance"). In *Rehabilitation Servs. of N. Cal.*, ASBCA 47085, 96-2 BCA ¶ 28,324, the board incorporated the Government Property clause into the contract by operation of law in order to validate a contract modification deleting an item of equipment that the government had agreed to furnish to the contractor. The board concluded that the clause expressed a significant procurement policy under *G.L. Christian & Assocs. v. United States*, 160 Ct. Cl. 1, 312 F.2d 418, *reh'g denied*, 160 Ct. Cl. 58, 320 F.2d 345, *cert. denied*, 375 U.S. 954 (1963), stating at 141,426:

> FAR 52.245-2 GOVERNMENT PROPERTY (DEC 1989), which was mandatory for this contract, was not included in the contract. The GFP clause expresses a significant strand of public procurement policy. At the end of fiscal year 1992, Department of Defense contractors possessed GFP costing over $ 83 billion. 142 Military Law Review 141 (Fall 1993). FAR 52.245-2 is a mandatory clause which expresses a significant and deeply engrained strand of public procurement policy and we have deemed the clause incorporated by operation of law. *Hart's Food Service, Inc.*, ASBCA Nos. 30756, 30757, 89-2 BCA ¶ 21,789; *Dayron Corp.*, ASBCA No. 24919, 84-1 BCA ¶ 17,213; but see, *Computing Application Software Technology, Inc.*, ASBCA No. 47554 (slip op. dated 14 February 1996) (more limited NASA clause not incorporated); *Chamberlin Manufacturing Corp.*, ASBCA No. 18103, 74-1 BCA ¶ 10,368 (dicta suggesting clause should not be incorporated). See also *General Engineering & Machine Works v. O'Keefe*, 991 F.2d 775 (Fed. Cir. 1993).

The procedures for obtaining facilities during contract performance are discussed below.

D. Special Rules for Government Production and Research Property

"Government production and research property" is not a separate category of government property but is a composite of several types of government property. FAR 45.301 states:

> "Government production and research property," as used in this subpart, means Government-owned facilities, Government-owned special test equipment, and special tooling to which the Government has title or the right to acquire title.

This category of property is treated as a separate block of government property for purposes of prescribing procedures for eliminating "competitive advantage" under FAR Subpart 45.2 and providing for the rental of property under FAR Subpart 45.4. This is based on the presumption that a significant number of major contractors have obtained this type of property in the course of performance of their contracts and will be able to reduce the costs of future contracts by continuing to use it. There is also the possibility that such property could be transferred to a successor contractor performing the same type of work.

If government production and research property is available for use in performing a production or research and development contract, such use is a reasonable means of minimizing the costs of performance. Thus, FAR 45.401 states that such "property in the possession of contractors or subcontractors shall be used to the greatest possible extent, provided that a competitive advantage is not conferred on the contractor or its subcontractors." This competitive advantage issue is addressed at the time of formation of a new production or research and development contract. See FAR 45.201, stating that competitive advantage must be eliminated "to the maximum practical extent." This is done either by "(1) adjusting the offers of [all contractors proposing to use such property] by applying, for evaluation purposes only, a rental equivalent evaluation factor or (2) when adjusting offers is not practical, by charging the contractor rent for using the property." See *Alliant Techsystems, Inc. v. Dalton*, 837 F. Supp. 730 (E.D. Va. 1993), denying a protest that the contracting officer had improperly followed this regulation to eliminate a perceived competitive advantage. Since elimination of competitive advantage is completed when the contract is awarded, the only contract administration issue that remains in this regard is the adjustment of rental charges that have been agreed to if the contractor requests alterations in the use of the property.

A contractor may request the use of government production and research property after award. FAR 45.203 specifically addresses such a request for the use of special tooling or special test equipment but is silent as to facilities. Under this provision, the administrative contracting officer must "obtain a fair rental or other adequate consideration if use is authorized." FAR Subpart 45.4 discusses the procedures concerning postaward use of government production and research property—focused primarily on requests for use during the contract formation process. However, it is clear that these same procedures must be followed if permission to use such property is granted after award. These procedures are divided into government use and non-government use. Non-government use is defined as all use other than on government contracts, including direct commercial sales to domestic and foreign customers. Generally, government use is on a rent-free basis, whereas non-government use is on a rental basis, FAR 45.401.

1. Use on Government Work

FAR 45.402 gives contracting officers on production or research and development contracts broad authority to permit their contractors to use existing government production and research property in the performance of their contracts when they "believe it to be in the Government's interest." Normally, such authority would not be granted without coordination with the contracting officer who has cognizance over the property, FAR 45.402(b). If the property is identified in the formation of a new production or research and development contract, the contracting officer would normally authorize such use on a rent-free basis if the contract was sole source or the use of a rental equivalent factor "would not affect the choice of contractors," FAR 45.201(a). Otherwise, the contracting officer must ensure that the competitive advantage is eliminated by using a rental equivalent factor or charging rent—both computed in accordance with the Use and Charges clause, FAR 52.245-9, in the facilities contract. If the property is identified during performance of the contract, rent-free use may be permitted if the contractor gives the government adequate consideration in the form of a price adjustment to the price of the production or research and development contract, FAR 45.404(c), or rent can be charged in accordance with the rental rate calculation in the Use and Charges clause. In the case of a cost-reimbursement contract, it would be expected that rent-free use would be authorized with an appropriate adjustment in the fee for the production or research and development contract on which the property is to be used.

Contractors must obtain permission to use government production and research property on a new production or research and development contract. See ¶ (a) of the Use and Charges clause in FAR 52.245-9 and ¶ (d) of the Government Property clauses in FAR 52.245-2 and FAR 52.245-5. If such property is used without authorization, the contractor can be charged rent for such use retroactively, *Astronautics Corp. of Am.*, ASBCA 48190, 97-1 BCA ¶ 28,978.

Rental rates and rental equivalent charges are calculated in accordance with the following paragraphs of the Use and Charges clause in FAR 52.245-9:

> (c) The following bases are or shall be established in writing for the rental computation prescribed in paragraphs (d) and (e) below in advance of any use of the facilities on a rental basis:

(1) The rental rates shall be those set forth in Table I.

(2) The acquisition cost of the facilities shall be the total cost to the Government, as determined by the Contracting Officer, and includes the cost of transportation and installation, if borne by the Government.

(i) When Government-owned special tooling or accessories are rented with any of the facilities, the acquisition cost of the facilities shall be increased by the total cost to the Government of such tooling or accessories, as determined by the Contracting Officer.

(ii) When any of the facilities are substantially improved at Government expense, the acquisition cost of the facilities shall be increased by the increase in value that the improvement represents, as determined by the Contracting Officer.

(iii) The determinations of the Contracting Officer under this subparagraph (c)(2) shall be final.

(3) For the purpose of determining the amount of rental due under paragraph (d), the rental period shall be not less than 1 month nor more than 6 months, as approved by the Contracting Officer.

(4) For the purpose of computing any credit under paragraph (e), the unit in determining the amount of use of the facilities shall be direct labor hours, sales, hours of use, or any other unit of measure that will result in an equitable apportionment of the rental charge, as approved by the Contracting Officer.

(d) The Contractor shall compute the amount of rentals to be paid for each rental period by applying the appropriate rental rates to the acquisition cost of such facilities as may have been authorized for use in advance for the rental period.

(e) The full rental charge for each period shall be reduced by a credit. The credit equals the rental amount that would otherwise be properly allocable to the work for which the facilities were used without charge under paragraph (a). The credit shall be computed by multiplying the full rental for the rental period by a fraction in which the numerator is the amount of use of the facilities by the Contractor without charge during the period, and the denominator is the total amount of use of the facilities by the Contractor during the period.

(f) Within 90 days after the close of each rental period, the Contractor shall submit to the Contracting Officer a written statement of the use made of the facilities by the Contractor and the rental due the Government. At the same time, the Contractor shall make available such records and data as are determined by the Contracting Officer to be necessary to verify the information contained in the statement.

(g) If the Contractor fails to submit the information as required in paragraph (f) of this clause, the Contractor shall be liable for the full rental for the period. However, if the Contractor's failure to submit was not the fault of the Contractor, the Contracting Officer shall grant to the Contractor in writing a reasonable extension of time to submit.

* * *

TABLE I

Rental Rates

(i) For real property and associated fixtures, a fair and reasonable rental shall be established, based on sound commercial practice.

(ii) For plant equipment of the types covered in Federal Supply classes 3405, 3408, 3410, and 3411 through 3419, machine tools; and in 3441 through 3449, secondary metal forming and cutting machines, the following monthly rates shall apply:

Age of Equipment	Monthly Rental Rates
Under 2 years old	3.0 percent
Over 2 to 3 years old	2.0 percent
Over 3 to 6 years old	1.5 percent
Over 6 to 10 years old	1.0 percent
Over 10 years old	0.75 percent

The age of each item of the equipment shall be based on the year in which it was manufactured, with a birthday on January 1 of each year thereafter. For example, an item of equipment manufactured on July 15, 1978, will be considered to be "over 1 year old" on and after January 1, 1979, and "over 2 years old" on and after January 1, 1980.

(iii) For personal property and equipment not covered in (i) or (ii) of this table, a rental shall be established at not less than the prevailing commercial rate, if any, or, in the absence of such rate, not less than 2 percent per month for electronic test equipment and automotive equipment and not less than 1 percent per month for all other property and equipment.

The formula in the Use and Charges clause does not account for potential government liabilities. For example, the lower rental rates for older property do not reflect the government's increased risk of having to repair or replace that property or pay the contractor an equitable adjustment for additional costs associated with using such property. The clause also does not provide for compensation of the contractor for costs incurred in using the property. See *Woodchips, Inc.*, AGBCA 82-147-3, 82-2 BCA ¶ 15,941, *aff'd*, 732 F.2d 166 (Fed. Cir. 1984), in which the board denied the contractor additional compensation for maintenance costs on rented government equipment, stating at 79,020:

> The Contractor admits it knew the machines were old, that they would need maintenance, and that maintenance was the Contractor's responsibility. If the maintenance became too onerous, his remedy was simply to return the machines to the Government and avoid the $4.00 per day charge.

In the rare situation where government production and research property is made available to all competitors, they are ordinarily required to assume all costs related to making it available for use, such as payment of transportation or rehabilitation costs, FAR 45.205(a).

2. Use on Non-Government Work

FAR 45.407 specifies that requirements for authorization and dollar thresholds for non-government use of specific types of plant equipment are matters to be dealt with by each agency. However, FAR 45.407(a) requires advance written approval of the contracting officer before any non-government use of active plant equipment and approval of the head of the agency that awarded the facilities contract, or designee, for any non-government use exceeding 25 percent. In the Department of Defense, such approval is granted by the Assistant Secretary of the military service responsible for acquisition, DFARS 245.407. If non-government use in excess of 25 percent is approved, the contracting officer may require the contractor to insure the property against loss or damage, FAR 45.407(c). FAR 45.407(b) provides that these approvals should be granted only when it is in the government's interest—

> (1) To keep the equipment in a high state of operational readiness through regular use;
>
> (2) Because substantial savings to the Government would accrue through overhead cost-sharing and receipt of rental; or
>
> (3) To avoid an inequity to a contractor who is required by the Government to retain the equipment in place.

A contractor may request the use of government production and research property for non-government use when the property is no longer needed "for performing Government contracts but is retained for spares or for mobilization and readiness requirements," FAR 45.402(c). Agencies may not "provide facilities to contractors solely for non-Government use, unless authorized by law," FAR 45.302-1(b)(3).

When non-government use is authorized, the contracting officer is required to charge contractors rent for using government production and research property. Rent is computed in accordance with the Use and Charges clause, FAR 52.245-9, as discussed above.

A contracting officer may authorize the use of government production and research property in the possession of a contractor on an independent research and development (IR&D) program, FAR 45.406. Such use may not conflict with the primary use of the property or enable the contractor to retain property that could otherwise be released. The contractor must agree not to include as a charge against the government the rental value of the property on the IR&D program. Any agreed-upon government share of the contractor's IR&D costs is to be reduced by a rental charge for the portion of the contractor's IR&D program cost allocated to commercial work.

E. Progress Payments Inventory

Paragraph (d)(1) of the FAR 52.232-16 Progress Payments clause for progress payments based on costs incurred under fixed-price contracts provides:

> Title to the property described in this paragraph (d) shall vest in the Government. Vestiture shall be immediately upon the date of this contract, for property acquired or produced before that date. Otherwise, vestiture shall occur when the property is or should have been allocable or properly chargeable to this contract.

The clause further states that the government has title to property such as inventory, special tools, and drawings, and to technical data that "are or should be allocable or properly chargeable" to the contract. However, once progress payments are liquidated, title to residual inventory vests in the contractor. See ¶ (d)(6) of the clause, which states:

> When the Contractor completes all of the obligations under this contract, including liquidation of all progress payments, title shall vest in the Contractor for all property (or the proceeds thereof) not -
>
> > (i) Delivered to, and accepted by, the Government under this contract; or
> >
> > (ii) Incorporated in supplies delivered to, and accepted by, the Government under this contract and to which title is vested in the Government under this clause.

The nature of the government's title under the Progress Payments clause has been subjected to differing interpretations. These cases have primarily focused on the rights of third parties, such as creditors, sureties, and subcontractors against the government. See, for example, *In re Double H Prods. Corp.*, 462 F.2d 52 (3d Cir. 1972), in which the court rejected the argument that the clause gives the government only a security title to protect cash advances. However, in *Marine Midland Bank v. United States*, 231 Ct. Cl. 496, 687 F.2d 395 (1982), *cert. denied*, 460 U.S. 1037 (1983), the Court of Claims held that the Progress Payments clause gives the government only a lien in the nature of a purchase money security interest. See also *Ralcon, Inc.*, ASBCA 43176, 94-2 BCA ¶ 26,935, in which the board, following *Marine Midland*, limited the government's entitlement to valve assembles to a security interest. Similarly, in *United States v. Hartec*, 967 F.2d 130 (5th Cir. 1992), and *United States v. Ribas Dominicci*, 899 F. Supp. 42 (D.P.R. 1995), the courts held that there could be no conviction of the crime of theft of government property under 18 U.S.C. § 641 because the government had only a security interest in property not yet delivered by the contractor. In some other jurisdictions the *Marine Midland* rule has been criticized or rejected. See *In re American Pouch Foods*, 769 F.2d 1190 (7th Cir. 1985), *cert. denied*, 475 U.S. 1082 (1986), and *In re Wincom Corp.*, 76 B.R. 1 (D. Mass. 1987). Thus, in *United States v. Lindberg Corp.*, 882 F.2d 1158 (7th Cir. 1988), the government's progress payments title enabled it to prevent an unpaid subcontractor from placing a lien on property in its possession and on which it had done work.

In *Marine Midland*, the court held that, even though the government had only a lien, it was entitled to priority over general creditors, stating at 511:

> The rule of decision we choose for this case is to make the government's security interest under its title vesting procedures paramount to the liens of general creditors. We believe that this merely follows the modern practice of giving priority to purchase money interests, as we consider purchase money to be closely analogous to the government's progress payments, and we lay down nothing new or unexpected. The government should be able to take out of the contractor the value that it has put in, if that value is identified with specific property, and it does not hurt a general creditor if this is done. We note also that giving the government an interest only to the extent of its progress payments prevents the government from taking possession to more value than it has put into the contractor.

Although the bank had filed under the U.C.C. claiming a security interest in the contract work, the government was given priority because the funds of the bank loan had been used to pay a debt unrelated to contract performance. See also *Welco Indus., Inc. v. United States*, 8 Cl. Ct. 303 (1985), *aff'd*, 790 F.2d 90 (Fed. Cir. 1986). In *First Nat'l Bank of Geneva v. United States*, 13 Cl. Ct. 385 (1987), the court held that a lender who financed a specific machine and filed a financing statement had priority over the government.

Progress payments under construction contracts, where the work is to be done on government-owned land or buildings, are covered by different rules. Paragraph (f) of the FAR 52.232-5 Payments Under Fixed-Price Construction Contracts clause provides:

> All material and work covered by progress payments made shall, at the time of payment, become the sole property of the Government.

Although this clause appears to give the government fewer rights than the Progress Payments clause in FAR 52.232-16, this is not so. Any construction work attached to the property owned by the government becomes the property of the government, and liens cannot be attached to the property regardless of whether or not the government has made payments for the work. With respect to work and materials not incorporated into the work, the government's rights depend on progress payments having been made.

II. GOVERNMENT OBLIGATIONS WHEN IT FURNISHES PROPERTY

When the government agrees to furnish property, the contracting officer is required to include the proper Government Property clause in the contract, FAR 45.106. Special clauses are provided for facilities contracts, FAR 45.302-6. All of these clauses specify the extent of the government's obligations with regard to the property to be furnished, covering two primary obligations: (1) to deliver the property in a timely manner, and (2) to furnish property suitable for its intended purpose. The property to be furnished is usually identified in the contract specifications or the schedule. Property that the government has agreed to furnish is referred to as GFP in this section, regardless of type.

The discussion that follows deals with these government obligations when it has agreed to furnish property. The major part of the discussion relates to the furnishing of material, documentation, or special tooling or test equipment. Thus, the primary focus is on the obligations under the Government Property clause in the contract. When facilities are to be furnished, they will normally be covered by a separate facilities contract if their value exceeds $1,000,000, unless they are provided under contracts for services or construction, FAR 45.302-3. There are also a few instances in which the government's obligations have been determined in the absence of one of the specified clauses.

The first subsection discusses the interpretation principles that are followed in government property disputes. The next two subsections address the government's obligation to timely deliver GFP and to furnish property suitable for its intended use. The fourth subsection reviews the notice requirements under the Government Property clauses. The last subsection addresses the government's use of a disclaimer clause for either late delivery or unsuitability of GFP.

A. Interpretation Principles

The courts and boards apply general principles of contract interpretation to determine whether property was intended to be furnished by the government. In *Norcoast-Beck Aleutian JV*, ASBCA 21900, 80-1 BCA ¶ 14,328, *recons. denied*, 80-2 BCA ¶ 14,592, the government was obligated under the terms of the contract to furnish coarse and fine aggregates for concrete. When the government did not satisfy that obligation, the contractor used aggregates that it had produced and stockpiled near the construction site. The government argued that the aggregate was produced from government-owned land and, therefore, was government property, and that the contractor was not entitled to compensation for its use. The board disagreed, stating that the government had acquiesced in the contractor's claim of ownership of the stockpiled aggregate for many years and there was no evidence indicating that the parties interpreted the government property provisions to be applicable to the stockpiles.

The government's absence of control over property may be a determinative factor in finding that such property was not intended to be furnished. In *Loral Corp.*, ASBCA 37627, 92-1 BCA ¶ 24,661, *aff'd*, 979 F.2d 215 (Fed. Cir. 1992), the government was not liable for defective government bearings that the contractor purchased from a government purchasing agent. The board based its decision on the lack of control by the contracting officer over the contractor's acquisition of the bearings and the absence of a contract provision identifying the bearings as material to be furnished by the government. Compare *American Mech., Inc.*, ASBCA 52033, 03-1 BCA ¶ 32,134, in which the government was held liable for not supplying calibration information on equipment that was not listed as GFP but had to be furnished to the contractor in order to permit performance. See also *South Pittsburgh Cable Co.*, ASBCA 40014, 91-3 BCA ¶ 24,125, in which the board held that, although ceiling channel lugs were not listed as GFP, these specialty items were part of the grid system of the suspended ceiling system that the government promised to furnish to the contractor.

B. Late or Not Delivered GFP

The Government Property clauses provide for timely delivery of GFP and provide remedies if the property is not delivered at the required time. See the clause at FAR 52.245-2, which states:

> (a) *Government-furnished property.* (1) The Government shall deliver to the Contractor, for use in connection with and under the terms of this contract, the Government-furnished property described in the Schedule or specifications together with any related data and information that the Contractor may request and is reasonably required for the intended use of the property (hereinafter referred to as "Government-furnished property").
>
> (2) The delivery or performance dates for this contract are based upon the expectation that Government-furnished property suitable for use (except for property furnished "as-is") will be delivered to the Contractor at the times stated in the Schedule or, if not so stated, in sufficient time to enable the Contractor to meet the contract's delivery or performance dates.
>
> * * *
>
> (4) If Government-furnished property is not delivered to the Contractor by the required time, the Contracting Officer shall, upon the Contractor's timely written request, make a determination of the delay, if any, caused the Contractor and shall make an equitable adjustment in accordance with paragraph (h) of this clause.

The clause at FAR 52.245-5 contains substantially the same language. The government's obligation to deliver GFP within these time constraints is not excused if, at the time of contract execution, the government does not possess the property or the property does not exist, *Koppers/Clough (JV) v. United States*, 201 Ct. Cl. 344 (1973).

This section covers both late delivery of and total failure to deliver property. The boards have consistently held that a contractor is entitled to recover increased costs of performance resulting from the government's failure or delay in delivering GFP as provided in the contract, *Fraass Survival Sys., Inc.*, ASBCA 22114, 78-2 BCA ¶ 13,445; *Ingalls Shipbuilding Div., Litton Sys., Inc.*, ASBCA 17717, 76-1 BCA ¶ 11,851. However, in order to recover, the contractor must prove that it was adversely affected by the government's failure to timely deliver GFP, *NavCom Def. Elecs., Inc.*, ASBCA 50767, 01-2 BCA ¶ 31,546 (costs of redesign of product attributed to faulty design not late delivery of GFP); *Leonhard Weiss GmbH & Co.*, ASBCA 37574, 93-1 BCA ¶ 25,443 (contractor failed to establish that it was delayed by the government's failure to furnish information or equipment). Thus, if the contractor is responsible for the delay in delivery, the contractor cannot fault the government for failing to meet the contract schedule, *Blaine Co. v. United States*, 157 Ct. Cl. 53 (1962).

If the contract specifies a delivery date and suitable GFP is not made available on or before that date, then delivery is late. See *So-Pak-Co.*, ASBCA 38906, 93-3 BCA ¶ 26,215, in which a meat packing contractor was held to be entitled to recover the costs of "downtime" resulting from government delays in furnishing materials such as beef, ham, and chicken à la king to be used in meals, ready-to-eat. See also *R-W Contracting, Inc.*, ASBCA 25459, 85-1 BCA ¶ 17,785, where GFP was delivered on the schedule date but considered late because it was in an unsuitable condition. When no delivery date is specified, it is required to be delivered in time to permit performance, *Grumman Aerospace Corp.*, ASBCA 46834, 03-1 BCA ¶ 32,203, *recons. denied*, 03-2 BCA ¶ 32,289. However, the GFP is considered late only if the contractor is unable to render timely performance as a result of such late delivery, *Peter Kiewit Sons' Co. v. United States*, 138 Ct. Cl. 668, 151 F. Supp. 726 (1957); *Thompson v. United States*, 130 Ct. Cl. 1, 124 F. Supp. 645 (1954). Note that, unlike the Changes clause, there is no requirement for the contractor to establish that the government issued an order, whether formally or informally, or that the government was at fault. Thus, under the Government Property clauses, the government will be strictly liable for late delivery of GFP. See *Finesilver Mfg. Co.*, ASBCA 28955, 86-3 BCA ¶ 19,243; *Sun Shipbuilding & Drydock Co.*, ASBCA 11300, 68-1 BCA ¶ 7054; *Bruno Law v. United States*, 195 Ct. Cl. 370 (1971); and *Torres v. United States*, 126 Ct. Cl. 76, 112 F. Supp. 363 (1953).

The Government Property (Consolidated Facilities) clause, FAR 52.245-7, used in facilities contracts, contains the following special provision covering late delivery or diversion of facilities:

(k) *Late delivery, diversion, and substitution.* (1) The Government shall not be liable for breach of contract for any delay in delivery or nondelivery of facilities to be furnished under this contract.

(2) The Government has the right, at its expense, to divert the facilities under this contract by directing the Contractor to—

(i) Deliver any of the facilities to locations other than those specified in the Schedule; or

(ii) Assign purchase orders or subcontracts for any of the facilities to the Government or third parties.

(3) The Government may furnish any facilities instead of having the Contractor acquire or construct them. In such event, the Contractor is entitled to reimbursement for the cost related to the acquisition or construction of the facilities, including the cost of terminating purchase orders and subcontracts.

(4) Appropriate equitable adjustment may be made in any related contract that so provides and that is affected by any nondelivery, delay, diversion, or substitution under this paragraph (k).

This clause relieves the government of liability for breach of contract but appears to call for an equitable adjustment if late delivery or nondelivery of facilities increases the cost of a production or research and development contract that was entered into based on use of the facilities. See *RMI Titanium Co.*, EBCA C-9304150, 02-2 BCA ¶ 32,012, denying a claim for breach of contract when the government shut down a facility that had been made available for commercial use. The board construed provisions similar to those above as follows, at 158,173:

In this case, apparently, the DOE did not want to enter into an agreement whereby it had to be concerned about the consequences of ending the contractor's use of the press, should the need to do so arise. Evidently, it was willing to let the contractor use the equipment on a non-interference basis as long as the DOE accepted no risk. Apparently, this was acceptable to RMI. With that in mind, they entered into the contract. This contract allowed RMI the use of the Government's press, with the understanding that that use could be withdrawn at any time. In other words, RMI was allowed access to the equipment for commercial purposes. However, in order to obtain this access, it had to agree that it would absorb any costs incurred if and when that use was withdrawn. The contract does not contain a requirement for notice before availability could be withdrawn. RMI freely accepted this risk.

C. Suitable for Intended Use

Government property must be given to the contractor in a condition suitable for its intended use under the contract. GFP is considered unsuitable if it is received in a damaged condition or has some design incompatibility. In either instance, the contractor has the burden of showing that the GFP was not received in a condition suitable for its intended purpose. To meet this burden the contractor must show that (1) the property in question was intended to be furnished as GFP, (2) the property was not suitable, (3) the unsuitability relates to its intended purpose, and (4) the unsuitability was the proximate cause of the contractor's injury for defective GFP. The Government Property clause in FAR 52.245-2 provides as follows:

> (a)(3) If Government-furnished property is received by the Contractor in a condition not suitable for the intended use, the Contractor shall, upon receipt of it, notify the Contracting Officer, detailing the facts, and, as directed by the Contracting Officer and at Government expense, either repair, modify, return, or otherwise dispose of the property. After completing the directed action and upon written request of the Contractor, the Contracting Officer shall make an equitable adjustment as provided in paragraph (h) of this clause.

The clause in FAR 52.245-5 contains substantially the same language.

The government has been found liable for inaccurate or misleading documents when they have been provided as GFP. See *E-Sys., Inc.*, ASBCA 46111, 97-1 BCA ¶ 28,975, in which the board found the government liable for a misleading report, stating at 144,305-06:

> Documentation that the Government describes in the contract and agrees to furnish a contractor regarding the contract work to be performed has been held to be GFP and required to be reasonably complete and accurate. *Lear Astronics Corporation*, ASBCA No. 37228, 93-2 BCA ¶ 25,892; *AAA Engineering and Drafting Company, Inc.*, ASBCA No. 21326, 77-1 BCA ¶ 12,454. We have found the Texas A & M Report was specifically identified in the contract as GFP and that the Government intended the study to be furnished as GFP. There was no disclaimer of being provided "for information only" in the contract. We find no basis for the Government to avoid the representation made in the GFP clause that the property would be suitable for its intended use. *Shepard Division/Vogue Instrument Corporation*, ASBCA No. 15571, 74-1 BCA ¶ 10,498 at 49,722-23.

1. *Intended Use*

Although government property may be specifically identified in the contract, the contract may state that the property is being furnished only for a limited purpose or may not specify any particular purpose at all. In these situations, it will be difficult for contractors to prove unsuitability for an intended purpose. The contractor's difficulty will be inversely proportional to the specificity of the property's stated purpose—the less specific the stated purpose, the more difficult the contractor's claim. In *Consol. Mktg. Network, Inc.*, DOTCAB 1680, 86-3 BCA ¶ 19,181, the specifications stated that the government would provide scooters for the contractor's use in performing building maintenance work under the contract but did not specify that they would be suitable for any particular purpose. The contractor attempted to use the scooters to transport lightbulbs to the buildings being maintained, but they proved to be unsuitable for this purpose. Consequently, the contractor purchased a suitable truck and sought reimbursement from the government, contending that the scooters were unsuitable GFP. The board noted that the specification required only that the government furnish scooters to the contractor within a certain time, which it did. Since it did not state that the government would provide vehicles suitable for transportation of lightbulbs, the board refused to read this requirement into the contract. See also *Ainslie Corp.*, ASBCA 29303, 89-2 BCA ¶ 21,811, in which the board denied the contractor's claim for additional costs incurred in copying a government-furnished model antenna. The board stated that the model was provided only for "the purpose of demonstrating the physical appearance of the units to be produced and to afford 'such information and assistance as it may provide the contractor in meeting the requirements of the contract.'" The board found that the government-furnished model accomplished this purpose.

Conversely, when the contract specifies suitability for a particular purpose, the contractor's burden of proof is eased. In *Grumman Aerospace Corp.,* ASBCA 46834, 03-1 BCA ¶ 32,203, *recons. denied*, 03-2 BCA ¶ 32,289, the government was held liable when the contractor was provided with defective drawings of a product that were required to achieve a proper interface. The board reasoned that accurate drawings were necessary for that purpose even though the contract contained a Total System Responsibility clause requiring the contractor to ensure the integration of all interfacing systems and to ensure the successful operation of the total integrated system. See also *Western States Mgmt. Servs., Inc.*, ASBCA 40546, 92-1 BCA ¶ 24,753, *recons. denied*, 93-1 BCA ¶ 25,273, where the government was obligated to furnish a custodial contractor with equipment and materials that were suitable to achieve a "uniform glossy finish" on the floors. The contractor's claim for the costs of equipment and materials purchased to replace defective GFP was granted because the board found that the GFP was not suitable to achieve that stated purpose.

In some instances, government property may be provided to contractors under circumstances that create no warranty of suitability for an intended purpose, either express or implied. The government often provides government property to contractors as an accommodation, without intending to incur liability for unsuitability. When this is the case, the contractor will generally not be able to recover an equitable adjustment. For example, in *Raytheon Serv. Co.*, ASBCA 36139, 92-1 BCA ¶ 24,696, the contractor was obligated to install an electronic monitoring system for the Army. Under a contract modification, the contractor proposed to use government telephone lines. The government provided the telephone lines with no consideration and no representation that the lines furnished under the modification would meet the standards of the lines the government was obligated to furnish under the original contract. Although the lines proved to be defective, the board denied the contractor's claim for repair costs, stating that "the availability of these lines to [Raytheon] was a gratuitous act for its benefit and, as such, creates no basis for liability on the part of the Government." The contractor, however, was successful in recovering its costs of correcting defects in the government lines furnished under the original contract. The board stated that this line was government-furnished material and the contract required them to be of a specified grade and suitable for computer data transmission.

The government may be held liable for unsuitable or defective government property that is not expressly identified in the contract as GFP if it is clear from the contract terms that it is to be furnished by the government. See *American Mech., Inc.*, ASBCA 52033, 03-1 BCA ¶ 32,134, in which the government was held liable for not supplying calibration information on equipment that was not listed as GFP but was listed in the contract as equipment that the contractor was to recalibrate and use in performance. See also *Tamarack Air*, IBCA 3526-95, 00-1 BCA ¶ 30,627 (government liable for defective fuel where contract provided that it would supply fuel but contract contained no Government Property clause); *South Pittsburgh Cable Co.*, ASBCA 40014, 91-3 BCA ¶ 24,125 (government obligated to provide ceiling channel lugs as part of the suspended ceiling system that the government promised to furnish in the contract); and *Hart's Food Serv., Inc.*, ASBCA 30756, 89-2 BCA ¶ 21,780 (government liable for unsuitability of some of the equipment and facility maintenance problems encountered even though items not listed as GFP and contract contained no Government Property clause).

2. Suitability

Once the "intended purpose" is identified, GFP will be considered suitable if it can be used in a manner that facilitates "expeditious and economical performance," *S.S. Mullen, Inc. v. United States*, 182 Ct. Cl. 1, 389 F.2d 390 (1968). These conditions will be satisfied if it performs as persons in the trade would reasonably expect and complies with any express representations in the contract. Government-furnished property will be considered suitable if it can be used by the contractor without unreasonable delay or expense, *Topkis Bros. Co. v. United States*, 155 Ct. Cl. 648, 297 F.2d 536 (1961); *Singer-Gen. Precision, Inc.*, ASBCA 15372, 72-2 BCA ¶ 9640. The property does not have to be 100 percent perfect, but it must allow the contractor to substantially use the property without undue hardship, *AAA Eng'g & Drafting Co.*, ASBCA 21326, 77-1 BCA ¶ 12,454. In *M. Rudolph Preuss v. United States*, 188 Ct. Cl. 469, 412 F.2d 1293 (1969), the court stated at 483:

> It is a question of fact to be determined in each case by considering the reasonable use that can be made of the property in manufacturing the end product as required by the contract as a whole and the results obtainable from such use at a reasonable cost, effort, and expense.

In *Preuss*, the court found that the microfilm was suitable because 66 percent of it was used to produce satisfactory results without undue costs. However, compare *Thompson Ramo Wooldridge, Inc. v. United States*, 175 Ct. Cl. 527, 361 F.2d 222 (1966), in which the court found government-furnished microfilm unsuitable because 75 percent of it was unusable. The court emphasized that there was no minimum usability percentage that must be achieved, but rather that usability must be examined on a case-by-case basis.

In *Wagner Awning & Mfg. Co.*, ASBCA 19986, 77-2 BCA ¶ 12,720, the contractor was entitled to an equitable adjustment when tent-making material furnished by the government tore easily. The board stated, "Material may be considered defective under a supply contract if it is known to be unsuitable for use in the customary setting for manufacturing the required supplies." In finding the material defective, the board stated at 61,830:

> [T]he condition of the cloth necessitated extensive patching and splicing never previously encountered and further necessitated the granting by [the Government] of a significant deviation from the repair criteria of the military specification; and . . . similar cutting and tearing problems with the GFM oxford cloth were encountered in manufacturing tent liner intermediate sections under contract 1548, to overcome which [the contractor] was again required to make significant changes to its customary manufacturing procedures. From the evidence in the record we have concluded that the 3.0 pound tearing strength GFM oxford cloth was unsuitable for the mass production manufacture of tent liner intermediate sections as contemplated by the contract.

See also *Propper Int'l, Inc.*, ASBCA 46334, 95-2 BCA ¶ 27,884, where fabric failed specified inspection criteria, and *Franklin Research Corp.*, ASBCA 6797, 61-2 BCA ¶ 3127, in which the board held that the GFP was received in a condition not suitable for its intended purpose because the GFP required the contractor to substitute manual labor for a mechanized process.

In some instances, GFP may not be suitable for its intended purpose even though it complies with the specifications of the contract. In *Topkis Bros. Co. v. United States*, 155 Ct. Cl. 648, 297 F.2d 536 (1961), the government provided cloth to a contractor for its use in manufacturing field jackets. Although the cloth complied with the specifications, it was too brittle for efficient production of the jackets. Thus, the contractor received an equitable adjustment for the increased costs of working with the difficult fabric. On the other hand, GFP may be deemed suitable for its intended purpose even though it does not comply with the specifications of the contract, *Universal Canvas, Inc.*, ASBCA 36141, 91-3 BCA ¶ 24,049, *rev'd on other grounds*, 975 F.2d 847 (Fed. Cir. 1992). In *Universal*, the board found that, although the cloth furnished to a tent contractor did not meet the tear-strength specifications of the contract, the cloth was suitable because it had sufficient tear strength for mass production purposes. However, see *Hollfelder Technische Dienste Ingenieurgesellschaft MBH*, ASBCA 28138, 88-1 BCA ¶ 20,471, in which the board found that the government breached the warranty of suitability by providing coal that did not meet specification standards even though the coal would burn.

3. *Cause of Contractor's Injury*

Even if the contractor establishes that the government-furnished property was unsuitable, it will not be entitled to an equitable adjustment unless it establishes that such unsuitability was the proximate cause of its injury, *Dynamic Sci., Inc.*, ASBCA 29510, 85-1 BCA ¶ 17,710. The contractor's injury may be increased costs to overcome the property's unsuitability, delay, or both. In *Dynamic Science*, the contractor was entitled to an equitable adjustment because the malfunctioning of government-furnished equipment prevented the contractor from performing. See also *Olsberg Excavating Corp.*, DOTCAB 1288, 84-1 BCA ¶ 16,931, in which the contractor was granted a time extension for delays caused by necessary repairs to government-furnished assembly materials. In some instances, the government may stipulate that the unsuitability of its property was the proximate cause of the contractor's injury, *Sterling Servs., Inc.*, ASBCA 42892, 92-1 BCA ¶ 24,541.

If a contractor fails to prove specifically how the unsuitable GFP caused its injuries, its claim for equitable adjustment will be denied. General allegations and innuendoes will not support a claim of unsuitability of GFP, *Metal-Tech Inc.*, ASBCA 14828, 72-2 BCA ¶ 9545. For example, recovery was denied in *Colo-Hydro, Inc.*, AGBCA 83-133-1, 86-1 BCA ¶ 18,599, because the contractor failed to prove that the spread of disease in government-furnished seedlings was caused by the unsuitability of the seedlings as opposed to the contractor's planting practices. In *Fairfield Mach. Co.*, ASBCA 22704, 85-2 BCA ¶ 17,969, the contractor sought an equitable adjustment for alleged delays and defects in government-furnished artillery breech rings for testing. The board denied the contractor's request because there was no showing of causation, stating at 90,081:

> [E]ven if the dates of promised delivery could be established and it could be found that the rings had been delivered later than such dates, there can be no recovery because there is no evidence as to the effect, if any, caused to [the contractor's] performance by such delay. Under the terms of the clause, equitable adjustment of price, performance time, and any other "affected provision" of the contract is not automatic upon showing of late delivery. It is due only "if the facts warrant such action."

See also *Tayag Bros. Enters., Inc.*, ASBCA 42097, 94-3 BCA ¶ 26,962, *recons. denied*, 95-1 BCA ¶ 27,599, in which the board found that the contractor did not show that the delay in wiring a fire alarm system was caused by defects in government-furnished material rather than by improper wiring and installation by the contractor.

The government will also be excused from liability for furnishing defective GFP if it can show that the contractor was responsible for its own injury. In *California Reforestation*, AGBCA 88-254-1, 91-3 BCA ¶ 24,306, a tree-planting contractor challenged the government's deductions for unacceptable trees, alleging that the problem was caused by defective government-furnished seedlings. The board upheld the price reductions, stating at 121,477:

> Given . . . that [the contractor's] method of digging prevented any determination as to whether the seedlings inspected for below-ground criteria were properly planted; and the unexplained discrepancy in planting quality between the two subitems, for which the same stock was provided, we conclude that [the contractor] has not met his burden of proof with regard to the quality of seedlings furnished. See *Forest Dev., Inc.*, AGBCA No. 78-186-4, 82-2 BCA ¶ 15,829; *Id.*, AGBCA No. 77-144, 79-1 BCA ¶ 13,626.

See also *Technadril, Inc.*, EBCA 186-12-81, 85-1 BCA ¶ 17,734 (contractor failed to establish that an allegedly defective government-furnished oil drill casing and not its own poor workmanship was responsible for its additional costs), and *Ainslie Corp.*, ASBCA 29303, 89-2 BCA ¶ 21,811 (contractor failed to show that the problems were with the model rather than inexperience of testing personnel, in-house problems, and lack of management). Compare *Essex Electro Eng'rs, Inc.*, ASBCA 49915, 99-1 BCA ¶ 30,229, *modified on recons.*, 99-2 BCA ¶ 30,418, *aff'd in part, vacated in part*, 224 F.3d 1283 (Fed. Cir. 2000), in which the government was found liable for the cost of attempting to repair defective test equipment even though the contractor eventually did not use the equipment. See also *Northwest Marine, Inc.*, ASBCA 43673, 95-2 BCA ¶ 27,888 (correcting defective drawings not inconsequential when government could not remedy defects), and *Marine Transport Lines, Inc.*, ASBCA 28962, 86-3 BCA ¶ 19,164 (defective work created by government-provided paint, not poor application by the contractor).

D. Notice Requirements

The Government Property clauses impose two different notice requirements on the contractor, depending on whether the contractor is alleging late delivery of GFP or unsuitability of GFP. In the former situation, the contractor must make a "timely written request" to the contracting officer, who then must determine if any part of the delay was caused by the contractor and, if appropriate, make an equitable adjustment. If the GFP is not suitable for its intended purpose, the contractor is required to "notify" the contracting officer, presumably by any means, and comply with the contracting officer's instructions regarding repairs, modifications, return, or disposal. See ¶ (a)(3) of the Government Property clause in FAR 52.245-2; and ¶ (a)(4) of the Government Property clause in FAR 52.245-5. After such action is taken, the contractor must make a written request to the contracting officer as a precondition to receiving an equitable adjustment. The Identification of Government-Furnished Property clause in FAR 52.245-3 also contains a requirement that the contractor verify the "quantity and condition" of GFP and report "any damage to or shortage of" the GFP "within 24 hours of delivery."

Recovery will be barred only if the government was prejudiced by the lack of adequate notice, *J.S. Alberici Constr. Co. & Martin K. Eby Constr. Co. (Joint Ven-*

ture), ENGBCA 6178, 98-2 BCA ¶ 29,875. In that case, the board found prejudice because the government was deprived of the opportunity to find a way to work around the lack of GFP. See also *Franklin Pavkov Constr. Co.*, ASBCA 50828, 00-2 BCA ¶ 31,100, *aff'd*, 279 F.3d 989 (Fed. Cir. 2002), denying a claim that an insufficient quantity of property had been furnished because late notice deprived the government of the opportunity of determining the extent of the shortfalls. Compare *W.F. Sigler & Assocs.*, IBCA 1159-7-77, 78-1 BCA ¶ 13,011, *recons. denied*, 78-1 BCA ¶ 13,137, where the government agreed to pay the contractor's costs of repairing GFP but refused to pay a fee for the repair. The board found that, by agreeing to pay the costs of repair, the government acknowledged that there was no prejudice from the failure to give prompt notice. For other cases where the lack of notice was found not to have prejudiced the government, see *Michael, Inc.*, ASBCA 35653, 92-1 BCA ¶ 24,412, and *Togaroli Corp.*, ASBCA 32995, 89-2 BCA ¶ 21,864, *recons. denied*, 89-3 BCA ¶ 22,102. See also *Grumman Aerospace Corp.,* ASBCA 46834, 03-1 BCA ¶ 32,203, *recons. denied*, 03-2 BCA ¶ 32,289, finding that the government waived lack of notice of unsuitable drawings when it considered the contractor's claim on the merits. In *E. L. Hamm & Assocs., Inc.*, ASBCA 48600, 01-1 BCA ¶ 31,247, the board denied a contractor's claim for replacing property because the notice implied that it would be at no cost to the government, depriving the agency of a choice of decisions on how to replace the property, but the Federal Circuit reversed, 26 Fed. Appx. 936 (Fed. Cir. 2002), because there was no evidence that the contractor had authorized such a statement in the notice.

Actual knowledge of the problem by responsible government employees will overcome any lack of formal notice. In *Oxwell, Inc.*, ASBCA 27523, 86-2 BCA ¶ 18,967, the government argued that the contractor failed to give proper notice to the administrative contracting officer. The board found that the contractor had given "adequate notice" and allowed recovery, stating at 95,777:

> This brings us to Government's argument that Oxwell's claims should fail because of lack of proper notice. The language of the notice requirement indicates the purpose of such notice. It was to assure that responsible Government personnel would be aware of any situation which might have an adverse impact on timely performance or affect the contract price. The evidence shows that not only did Oxwell constantly provide adequate notice to Government so as to permit an appropriate response but that Government's responsible officials knew, or ought to have known, of the potential claim. Government had previously been confronted with a claim for the very same kind of damages early in the performance of contract 2792 and had settled the claim by paying Oxwell in excess of $35,000. After settlement of such claim nothing changed. The parts shortages continued and the evidence shows that Government was fully aware of the situation. The record shows Government's responsible officials were regularly amending the contract to provide work-around, re-work, re-usage, substitution, etc., to keep Oxwell on the job. Certainly Government's officials were aware of the parts shortages or they would not have taken all the measures that appear in the record to keep the production of overhauls continuing. That an additional claim could be

> forthcoming under such circumstances should have been obvious. The purpose of the notice requirement was met amply well and Government cannot escape responsibility for its failings to provide proper GFP support by hiding behind an overly strict interpretation of the contract language in the light of the evidence in these appeals.

See also *Muncie Gear Works, Inc.*, ASBCA 15681, 72-1 BCA ¶ 9388, in which the board stated, "Technical compliance with the notice requirements of the clause is not an absolute essential to recovery thereunder." The board stated that, as long as the contractor notifies the government that the property is unsuitable, a subsequent claim for increased costs or other adjustment may be made prior to final payment.

The contractor's burden of establishing unsuitability will be considerably more difficult when it has been using the property over an extended period without complaint or apparent impact on performance. In *Space Age Eng'g, Inc.*, ASBCA 25761, 86-1 BCA ¶ 18,611, the board denied the contractor's claim for an equitable adjustment for costs incurred as a result of using allegedly unsuitable government-furnished forklifts, stating at 93,464:

> The closest evidence to support this contention is that after [the contractor] had used three heavy-duty forklifts for over a year it decided that they were too heavy. . . . We conclude that the most this shows is that after using these three forklifts for a year [the contractor] decided that smaller, more maneuverable forklifts would be better.

Even if unsuitability had been established in this case, the contractor probably would have been found to have waived the unsuitability by not informing the contracting officer as soon as practicable after receipt of the property. See also *C.M. Moore Div., K.S.H., Inc.*, PSBCA 1131, 85-2 BCA ¶ 18,110, *aff'd*, 818 F.2d 874 (Fed. Cir. 1987), in which the board denied recovery because the contractor did not complain about unsuitability until well into contract performance, and there was no evidence that the defects were latent.

E. Disclaimers

The government may attempt to limit its liability for late delivery or unsuitability of GFP by including the FAR Government Property Furnished "As Is" clause or a disclaimer clause.

1. Government Property Furnished "As Is"

The Government Property Furnished "As Is" clause, FAR 52.245-19, is commonly used in conjunction with government-furnished property to disclaim any warranty of suitability. This clause provides, in part:

> (a) The Government makes no warranty whatsoever with respect to Government property furnished "as is," except that the property is in the same condition when placed at the f.o.b. point specified in the solicitation as when inspected by the Contractor pursuant to the solicitation or, if not inspected by the Contractor, as when last available for inspection under the solicitation.
>
> (b) The Contractor may repair any property made available on an "as is" basis. Such repair will be at the Contractor's expense except as otherwise provided in this clause. Such property may be modified at the Contractor's expense, but only with the written permission of the Contracting Officer. Any repair or modification of property furnished "as is" shall not affect the title of the Government.

When this clause is used, the government has very limited liability. See *Arvin Indus., Inc.*, ASBCA 15215, 71-2 BCA ¶ 9143, in which the board held that the government-furnished drawings were "excluded from the operation of the warranty" under the GFP clause because they had clearly been furnished on an "as is" basis. See also *Baifield Indus., Div. of A-T-O, Inc. v. United States*, 29 CCF ¶ 82,237 (Ct. Cl. Trial Div. 1982) ("As Is" clauses are enforced unless vitiated by other contractual language or enforcement of the clause would be unconscionable). In *American Wyott Corp.*, ASBCA 42024, 94-2 BCA ¶ 26,758, the contractor asserted that the "suitable for intended use" provision in the Government Property clause made the government responsible for defective tools that it had furnished. The board disagreed, stating that the contract specifically and unambiguously made the tooling subject to the "As Is" clause. There are some cases where the standard FAR clause is not used but similar "As Is" language is contained in the contract. See, for example, *L.T. Indus., Inc.*, ASBCA 12832, 69-1 BCA ¶ 7534, *recons. denied*, 69-1 BCA, ¶ 7654, in which the board held that a disclaimer limited the scope of the GFP warranty. The clause read that "[n]otwithstanding any provisions to the contrary contained in the [GFP] clause . . . this tooling will, if required by the contractor, be furnished in its present condition 'as is' and 'where is' without warranty"

If the government makes an express general warranty and has superior knowledge that it fails to disclose, the "As Is" provision will not be enforced. In *Boland Mach. & Mfg. Co.*, ASBCA 13664, 70-2 BCA ¶ 8556, the government contracted to have a ship built following the default of another contractor. The government's failure to warn bidders of the limited nature of their inspection of the clean-up work from the previous contractor was deemed a breach of its duty to disclose superior knowledge. As a result, the contractor recovered costs relating to the clean-up despite the presence of the Government Property Furnished "As Is" clause. See also *G.W. Galloway Co.*, ASBCA 16656, 73-2 BCA ¶ 10,270, *recons. denied*, 74-1 BCA ¶ 10,521, in which an "as is" disclaimer on government-furnished property did not preclude recovery by the contractor. The contractor was entitled to additional expenses because the government knew that the tools it was providing to the contractor were defective and outdated. The board stated that "enforcement of thc 'as is' disclaimer of warranty provisions would . . . be unconscionable."

The boards and courts have held that the Government Property Furnished "As Is" clause and Government Property clause are not inconsistent with each other. In *C.M. Moore Div., K.S.H., Inc.*, PSBCA 1131, 85-2 BCA ¶ 18,110, *aff'd*, 818 F.2d 874 (Fed. Cir. 1987), the government was required to furnish molds for the production of plastic trays. The contract contained a standard property clause that obligated the government to provide property suitable for use "except for such property furnished 'as is.'" The contract also contained an "As Is" clause. The contractor argued that the molds were subject solely to the Government Property clause, which permitted compensation if the property was not suitable for its intended purpose. The board disagreed, holding that the molds were subject to the "As Is" clause because, even though not specifically referenced in that clause, they were described immediately following the boilerplate language of the clause in the same contract section. The boards and courts have been reluctant to enforce "As Is" clauses when GFP is provided for a specified purpose that is central to the procurement. See *Primex Techs.*, ASBCA 52000, 01-1 BCA ¶ 31,231, refusing to enforce the clause because there was no indication in the contract that the ammunition to be broken down and disassembled as the major task in performing the contract was subject to the clause. The board stated, at 154,147, that in the cases where the clause had been enforced the contract specifically and unambiguously provided that the property in issue was furnished "as is." The government pointed to no such provision in this contract.

Paragraph (c) of the Government Property Furnished "As Is" clause, FAR 52.245-19, provides for an equitable adjustment if there "is any change in the condition" of the property "from the time inspected or last available for inspection" to the time it is received by the contractor. See *McDonnell Douglas Corp.*, ASBCA 46266, 99-1 BCA ¶ 30,152, in which the board held the clause applicable to aircraft that had been designated as being furnished "as is" in a bilateral contract modification but found the contractor entitled to an equitable adjustment to the extent that it could identify defects not disclosed by inspection.

2. Government-Furnished Property Disclaimer Clause

As opposed to GFP furnished "as is," the boards and courts construe exculpatory clauses narrowly and restrictively, especially when the government attempts to avoid a remedy otherwise available under a contract clause, *Radionics Inc.*, ASBCA 22727, 81-1 BCA ¶ 15,011. In *Thompson Ramo Wooldridge, Inc. v. United States*, 175 Ct. Cl. 527, 361 F.2d 222 (1966), a contractual provision stated, "The Government does not . . . represent that the microfilm is legible in whole or in any particular part or that the drawings from which the microfilm was made, are complete and accurate in all respects or in any particular respect." The court construed this language in conjunction with the Government-furnished Property clause and concluded that this was not an exculpatory clause absolutely absolving the government from any liability. Instead, the contractor could reasonably expect the microfilm to be "substantially complete, accurate, and legible in most respects." In *Teledyne Lewisburg v. United States*, 699 F.2d 1336 (Fed. Cir. 1983), the contract contained a Government Property clause that obligated the government to provide drawings and a model for the manufacture of radios. The drawings proved to be outdated and the model was noncompliant with the specifications. The contractor claimed that it was entitled to the costs of reviewing the outdated, drawings and the costs of attempting to eliminate noncompliance with the specifications. At the board, ASBCA 20491, 79-2 BCA ¶ 14,165, the government contended that it was relieved of liability by a disclaimer clause, which provided, at 69,730:

> The following Government furnished items were accepted by the Government pursuant to the contract(s) under which they were originally procured by and delivered to, the Government, but the specifications and other requirements of said contract(s) may not be identical to the requirements of this contract; and the Government does not represent that the Government Furnished Radio Set, AN/PRC-75, and Manufacturing Drawings I.D. No. 06828 meet the requirements of this contract in every respect, nor does it represent that the Manufacturing drawings are complete or legible in whole or in any particular part or are complete and accurate and free from omissions, errors, inconsistencies or other defects and it does not represent that the equipments or repair parts made in accordance with the Government Furnished Radio Set AN/PRC-75 and Manufacturing Drawings, I.D. 06828 will meet the performance or other requirements of this contract including the specifications referenced directly or indirectly herein.

The board held that the disclaimer clause released the government from any liability resulting from the defective drawings and model. The Federal Circuit reversed, finding that the disclaimer clause did not apply to the major difficulties that the contractor encountered but rather only to minor errors and draftsmanship.

If the disclaimer is clear and unambiguous, it will be enforced. See *Arvin Indus., Inc.*, ASBCA 15215, 71-2 BCA ¶ 9143, in which the board held that a provision in the contract stating that the government would not be responsible "for the accuracy or completeness" of certain drawings furnished to the contractor was effective to "relieve the Government from responsibility to the contractor for errors or omissions" in the drawings, because the contract required the contractor to prepare and utilize its own drawings. See also *Drexel Dynamics Corp.*, ASBCA 9502, 66-2 BCA ¶ 5860, enforcing a provision stating, "[t]he contractor agrees that the contractor shall bear without recourse against the Government, the risk of whether or not such special tooling is IN A CONDITION SUITABLE FOR the contractor's INTENDED USE." The clause was sufficient to overcome the warranty of suitability for intended use under the GFP clause. The board stated, "The terms of the bargain . . . may have been harsh, in requiring [the contractor] to gamble on the suitability of the tooling, but it was clear and unambiguous."

If GFP is furnished for a specifically stated contractual purpose and is required to facilitate interchangeability, the disclaimer clause will not be enforced.

See *Thompson Ramo Wooldridge, Inc. v. United States*, 175 Ct. Cl. 527, 361 F.2d 222 (1966), in which the court held that, when a contractor is required to furnish a product that is "physically, mechanically and electrically interchangeable with corresponding parts and components of the Government-furnished sample transmitter," a disclaimer will not vitiate the representations regarding the purpose for which the drawings and model were furnished. In *Rixon Elecs., Inc. v. United States*, 210 Ct. Cl. 309, 536 F.2d 1345 (1976), there was a similar requirement for interchangeability, but the court enforced the disclaimer clause. The court distinguished *Thompson*, stating at 318-19:

> That case involved a claim for equitable adjustment, or alternatively, for breach of contract, by a contractor for radio transmission equipment who went through an experience much like the [contractor's] here, but signed no relevant release. There were equally bad, or worse microfilms, the same Government furnished property clause, with the same provision for equitable adjustment in case such property was not suitable for its intended use, and the same disclaimers of fitness expressly addressed to the microfilms. But there was an expressed statement that the microfilm would be of assistance in meeting the interchangeability requirement. This was essential to the [contractor's] case because it showed what the "intended use" was for which the warranty was given.

In *Lear Astronics Corp.*, ASBCA 37228, 93-2 BCA ¶ 25,892, the disclaimer associated with the government-furnished property was not enforced. The board, quoting from *Shepard Div./Vogue Instrument Corp.*, ASBCA 15571, 74-1 BCA ¶ 10,498, stated at 128,786:

> The language . . . relied on by the Government does not include the words "as is." The fact that property is furnished for such information and assistance as it may provide and that the Government makes no representations with respect to the property in the modification, does not, in our judgment, either implicitly or explicitly lead to the conclusion that the property is furnished on an "as is" basis. Had the Government desired to furnish the equipment "as is" it could have easily stated this intention.

F. Contractor Inspection

It has been stated that the obligation to notify the contracting officer "upon receipt" of unsuitable GFP "implicitly requires prompt inspection of the property upon receipt," *Logicon, Inc.*, ASBCA 39683, 90-2 BCA ¶ 22,786. In *Logicon*, the board held that disassembly of equipment to check for broken or missing parts fell within the realm of routine inspection, the cost of which is a part of contract performance. However, additional inspection was found to be more than routine, and the contractor was compensated for that effort. A contractor will not recover increased costs incurred as a result of defective GFP if defects would have been discovered by a reasonable inspection. In addition, when a defect is patent or the contractor inspects and discovers a defect, its use of the GFP without notifying the government will preclude recovery of defect-related costs, *Universal Canvas, Inc.*, ASBCA 36141, 91-3 BCA ¶ 24,049, *rev'd on other grounds*, 975 F.2d 847 (Fed. Cir. 1992). The reasonableness of the inspection will depend on the circumstances. In some instances, the contract will specify the method of inspection. In *Structural Sys. Tech., Inc.*, ASBCA 36950, 89-2 BCA ¶ 21,693, the contractor was not entitled to additional compensation for difficulties encountered with the length of guy wires furnished by the government because the contractor was required to inspect the property. The specifications required the contractor to "report any variation from job requirements to the Contracting Officer." The government asserted that "job requirements" required the contractor to verify the length of the government-furnished guy wires prior to installation. The contractor argued that its duty to inspect was limited to inspecting for damaged parts. The board found that "job requirements" included inspecting for variations in GFP and thus denied the contractor's claim for an equitable adjustment.

III. CONTRACTOR OBLIGATIONS

Contractors are directly responsible and accountable for all government property. They must establish a system to account for government property, which is subject to the approval of the contracting officer. Contractors must also maintain government property and can become liable to the government for its loss, damage, or destruction.

The first section below discusses the contractor's duty to establish a property control system and its obligation to account for government property and maintain records. The second section discusses contractor liability for risk of loss. The third section covers the disposition of government property.

A. Control of Property

The contracting agency must review and approve the contractor's property management system following the procedures set forth in FAR 45.104, as follows:

> (a) The review and approval of a contractor's property control system shall be accomplished by the agency responsible for contract administration at a contractor's plant or installation. The review and approval of a contractor's property control system by one agency shall be binding on all other departments and agencies based on interagency agreements.
>
> (b) The contracting officer or the representative assigned the responsibility as property administrator shall review contractors' property control systems to ensure compliance with the Government property clauses of the contract.
>
> (c) The property administrator shall notify the contractor in writing when its property control system does not comply with Subpart 45.5 or other contract require-

ments and shall request prompt correction of deficiencies. If the contractor does not correct the deficiencies within a reasonable period, the property administrator shall request action by the contracting officer administering the contract. The contracting officer shall—

(1) Notify the contractor in writing of any required corrections and establish a schedule for completion of actions;

(2) Caution the contractor that failure to take the required corrective actions within the time specified will result in withholding or withdrawing system approval; and

(3) Advise the contractor that its liability for loss of or damage to Government property may increase if approval is withheld or withdrawn.

The Government Property (Fixed-Price Contracts) clause, FAR 52.245-2, states:

(e) *Property administration.* (1) The Contractor shall be responsible and accountable for all Government property provided under this contract and shall comply with Federal Acquisition Regulation (FAR) subpart 45.5, as in effect on the date of this contract.

(2) The Contractor shall establish and maintain a program for the use, maintenance, repair, protection, and preservation of Government property in accordance with sound industrial practice and the applicable provisions of subpart 45.5 of the FAR.

The FAR 52.245-5 clause contains substantially the same language.

FAR 45.502 states the contractor's responsibility for having a property control system as follows:

(a) The contractor is directly responsible and accountable for all Government property in accordance with the requirements of the contract. This includes Government property in the possession or control of a subcontractor. The contractor shall establish and maintain a system in accordance with this subpart to control, protect, preserve, and maintain all Government property. This property control system shall be in writing unless the property administrator determines that maintaining a written system is unnecessary. The system shall be reviewed and, if satisfactory, approved in writing by the property administrator.

(b) The contractor shall maintain and make available the records required by this subpart and account for all Government property until relieved of that responsibility. The contractor shall furnish all necessary data to substantiate any request for relief from responsibility.

* * *

(e) If the property administrator finds any portion of the contractor's property control system to be inadequate, the contractor must take any necessary corrective action before the system can be approved. If the contractor and property administrator cannot agree regarding the adequacy of control and corrective action, the matter shall be referred to the contracting officer.

The purpose of this provision is broad and includes controlling, protecting, preserving, and maintaining government property. The contractor-maintained property record is the government's official record, and "[d]uplicate official records shall not be furnished to or maintained by Government personnel," FAR 45.105(a). See *Dennis Berlin*, ASBCA 51919, 02-1 BCA ¶ 31,675, *recons. denied*, 02-2 BCA ¶ 31,875, holding that the contractor was not entitled to a price adjustment for the cost of performing an inventory of contract material because the Progress Payments clause required the contractor to "maintain an accounting system and controls adequate for the proper administration of this clause"—a requirement similar to those in the Government Property clauses. See also *Griffin Servs., Inc. v. General Servs. Admin.*, GSBCA 14643, 99-2 BCA ¶ 30,556, holding a contractor liable for improper maintenance of equipment under a contract containing special clauses.

B. Risk of Loss

The contractor's liability for loss, damage, or destruction of government property will be determined by contract provisions or, in their absence, by bailment law.

1. Clauses Covering Risk of Loss

The general policy concerning liability for government property is set forth in FAR 45.103, as follows:

(a) Contractors are responsible and liable for Government property in their possession, unless otherwise provided by the contract.

(b) Generally, Government contracts do not hold contractors liable for loss of or damage to Government property when the property is provided under—

(1) Negotiated fixed-price contracts for which the contract price is not based upon an exception at 15.403-1;

(2) Cost-reimbursement contracts;

(3) Facilities contracts; or

(4) Negotiated or sealed bid service contracts performed on a Government installation where the contracting officer determines that the contractor has little direct control over the Government property because it is located on a Government installation and is subject to accessibility by personnel

> other than the contractor's employees and that by placing the risk on the contractor, the cost of the contract would be substantially increased.

Under this policy, contractors generally bear the risk of loss in sealed bid and competitive negotiated fixed-price contracts where certified cost or pricing data are not required. The extent of contractor liability is measured by the fair market value of the government property that was lost or destroyed, *Burgett Inv., Inc.*, AGBCA 81-108-1, 83-2 BCA ¶ 16,695. However, FAR 45.103(c) provides that a clause may be used imposing liability for loss or damage in an amount greater than contemplated by the Government Property clauses when government property is used primarily for commercial work.

This policy is implemented in ¶ (g) of the Government Property (Fixed-Price Contracts) clause, FAR 52.245-2, as follows:

> *Risk of loss.* Unless otherwise provided in this contract, the Contractor assumes the risk of, and shall be responsible for, any loss or destruction of, or damage to, Government property upon its delivery to the Contractor or upon passage of title to the Government under paragraph (c) of this clause. However, the Contractor is not responsible for reasonable wear and tear to Government property or for Government property properly consumed in performing this contract.

Under this clause, a contractor is strictly liable for loss, damage, or destruction of government property. See *Elizabeth Akoubian*, PSBCA 3813, 97-2 BCA ¶ 29,110 (theft of cash and postage stamps); *Clines Office Prods.*, PSBCA 3045, 92-1 BCA ¶ 24,725 (theft of postage stamps); *Wright's Auto Repair, Inc.*, ASBCA 30635, 86-3 BCA ¶ 19,154 (loss of vehicle destroyed by fire); *American Photographic Indus., Inc.*, ASBCA 29995, 86-1 BCA ¶ 18,738 (theft of photographic equipment); *Dynalectron Corp.*, ASBCA 29831, 85-3 BCA ¶ 18,320 (destruction of film during processing); *Chromalloy American Corp.*, ASBCA 19885, 76-2 BCA ¶ 11,997 (damage to turbine engine blades during overhaul); *B & W Constr. Corp.*, ASBCA 20502, 76-1 BCA ¶ 11,693 (weather damage to handball courts); and *WBW Servs., Inc.*, ASBCA 15269, 71-1 BCA ¶ 8747 (loss of truck through fire). See also *Braswell Shipyards, Inc.*, ASBCA 40610, 90-3 BCA ¶ 23,167, *aff'd*, 985 F.2d 553 (4th Cir. 1993), where the contract also contained a Liability and Insurance clause placing the "risk of loss of and damage to the vessels" on the government. The board held that the cost of retrieving the vessels after hurricane Hugo was not within this clause because the vessels were not lost, only washed away. The risk of loss was therefore placed on the contractor under the Government Property clause and "common law principles of bailment."

A contractor will not be liable either for normal wear and tear or for property consumed in performing the contract under the risk of loss clause, *Chromalloy Am. Corp.*, ASBCA 19885, 76-2 BCA ¶ 11,997. In *Chromalloy,* the board dealt with the issue of liability for damage to turbine engine blades under a contract for repair and overhaul of airplane engine components. The board examined the meaning and scope of the exceptions, stating at 57,559:

> "Reasonable wear and tear" is associated with the use of an item, ordinarily a tool or piece of production or test equipment, in performing a process such as the manufacture or fabricating of an end item. Where the Government-furnished equipment becomes worn through such use, paragraph (g) relieves the contractor from the risk of loss. Even without any Government Property clause, the contractor under a typical supply contract assumes the risk of loss for the end items being fabricated because he owns them and they do not become Government property until they have been delivered and accepted. See, e.g., *Allied Paint and Color Works, Inc.*, [ASBCA 2564, 57-1 BCA ¶ 1332, *aff'd*, 199 F. Supp. 285 (S.D.N.Y. 1961), *aff'd*, 309 F.2d 133 (2d Cir. 1962), *cert. denied*, 375 U.S. 813 (1963)]. Moreover, "wear and tear" would not apply to end items, whether under a supply or repair contract, because they are not subjected to "use" in the sense of being utilized to perform the function for which they are intended.
>
> "Consumed" is normally associated with expending or using up of materials in the course of performing a contract, or with causing an item of material or equipment to lose its character and identity by incorporating it into or attaching it to an end item, or by cannibalization. End items of supply contracts are not normally consumed. "Consumed" necessarily has only a narrowly-limited applicability to end items being repaired under a repair contract. The term might apply when several items, each consisting of divisible component parts, are not wholly reparable and the contractor salvages parts from some items in order to repair others. An end item being repaired would not otherwise be expected to be consumed by losing its identity, through incorporation in or attachment to another end item. Nor would an end item be expected to be expended or used up in the repair process. In a contract to repair an indivisible end item, such as a TF41 blade, the end item is expected to retain its identity throughout the process, from the time it goes in up to the time it comes out.

Relying on *Chromalloy*, the board in *Fairfield Mach. Co.*, ASBCA 22704, 85-2 BCA ¶ 17,969, found that the government was entitled to recover the cost of breech rings and tooling that were damaged as a result of machine malfunction. The board stated that the damage and destruction of the tooling resulted not from ordinary wear and tear but rather from machine malfunction for which the contractor was responsible. The board also found that the breech rings were not consumed, stating that "what occurred was not the removal of metal in the normal course of rough machining but rather the damaging of the rings beyond possibility of further use as the result of the aforesaid malfunctions." Finding that neither exception applied, the board held the contractor strictly liable for the loss. See also *Gillett Mach. Rebuilders, Inc.*, ASBCA 28341, 89-3 BCA ¶ 22,021, *recons. denied*, 90-1 BCA ¶ 22,428, holding that defectively repairing machine tools parts was neither reasonable wear and tear nor consumption. Similarly, in *Saudi Bldg. Technic Gen. Contracting Co., Ltd./Erectors, Inc. (JV)*, ENGBCA 5170, 86-2 BCA ¶ 18,761, the contractor failed to prove that shortages of government-furnished kitchen, bath, and toilet equipment and workers' housing furnishings were attributable to normal wear and tear. The board did recognize that loss of small personal items used over an extended period of time might appropriately be dealt with under the normal wear and tear exception. The government has the burden of proving that property was damaged beyond reasonable wear and tear and that its costs of repair were reasonable, *DWS, Inc.*, ASBCA 29866, 91-2 BCA ¶ 23,727.

For negotiated fixed-price contracts where cost or pricing data are furnished and for the other types of procurement exempted under FAR 45.103(b), a limited risk of loss provision is substituted for ¶ (g) of the clause. This alternate essentially relieves the contractor from loss unless resulting from (1) a risk required to be insured, (2) a risk that is in fact covered by insurance, or (3) willful misconduct or lack of good faith on the part of managerial personnel. This policy decision is based on the belief that it is more economical to act as a self-insurer than to reimburse the contractor for purchasing commercial insurance. See DOD 4161.2-M, DOD Manual for the Performance of Contract Property Administration. See *Computing Application Software Tech., Inc.*, ASBCA 47554, 96-1 BCA ¶ 28,204, in which the board refused to incorporate, by operation of law, a required clause, Liability for Government Property Furnished for Repair and Services, NFS 18-52.245-72, conflicting with this policy. The board concluded that *G.L. Christian & Assocs. v. United States*, 160 Ct. Cl. 1, 312 F.2d 418, *reh'g denied*, 160 Ct. Cl. 58, 320 F.2d 345, *cert. denied*, 375 U.S. 954 (1963), did not mandate incorporation of the clause because it did not "express a significant or deeply ingrained strand of public procurement policy."

The government may also assume the risk of loss over a specified dollar amount of government property in the hands of a contractor—in effect, becoming a self-insurer with a deductible amount. See, for example, ¶ (e) of the Ground and Flight Risk clause at DFARS 252.228-7001, which provides:

> With the exception of damage, loss, or destruction in flight, the Contractor assumes the risk and shall be responsible for the first $25,000 of loss or damage to aircraft in the open or during operation resulting from each separate event, except for reasonable wear and tear and to the extent the loss or damage is caused by negligence of Government personnel.

Note that this clause states that the contractor will be responsible for the first $25,000 of loss or damage resulting from "each separate event." In *Boeing Co.*, ASBCA 18916, 74-2 BCA ¶ 10,976, the board held that a hail storm was a single "event" regardless of the fact that six aircraft were damaged. The board stated at 52,232-33:

> An examination of the cases in this field discloses that the term "event" is considered as synonymous with "occurrence," "incident," or "accident," and is employed in insurance policies with the intent of limiting the liability of insurers to a specified sum on the basis of "each accident or occurrence" being further associated with the supplementary phrase "arising from one accident or occurrence." Such phraseology has generally been construed by the courts as relating solely

to cause, in this instance, the hail storm, rather than to the possible widespread effect resulting from a single incident. Thus it is held that where there is but one proximate, uninterrupted and continuing cause, constituting a single event, the consequent loss or damage will be considered in the aggregate as part of a single accident, occurrence or event. *Maurice Pincoffs Co. v. St. Paul Fire and Marine Insurance Co.*, 315 F. Supp. 964 (1970), *aff'd*, 447 F.2d 204 (CA 5, 1971); *Barrett v. Iowa National Mutual Insurance Co.*, 264 F.2d 224 (CA 9, 1959); *St. Paul-Mercury Indemnity Co. v. Rutland*, 225 F.2d 689 (CA 5, 1955); *Truck Insurance Exchange v. Rohde*, 49 Wash.2d 465, 303 P.2d 659 (1957); compare *Elston-Richards Storage Company v. Indemnity Insurance Co.*, 194 F. Supp. 673 (1960), *aff'd*, 291 F.2d 627 (CA 6, 1961). See discussion of these matters, Anno., 55 ALR2d 1300 et seq.

When the government relieves the contractor from the risk of loss of government property, the clause generally provides that the contractor shall reimburse the government if it is reimbursed or compensated for the loss. However, the contractor is not expected to carry insurance on the government property in this situation because the fixed-price contract clauses in which the government assumes the risk of loss contain a warranty that no such insurance is included in the contract price, and the cost principles used in cost-reimbursement contracts make premiums on such insurance an unallowable cost, FAR 31.205-19.

In clauses in which the government relieves the contractor of the risk of loss of government property, a major exception is loss due to the "willful misconduct or lack of good faith" of the contractor's managerial personnel. No case has found such willful misconduct. In *Fairchild Hiller Corp.*, ASBCA 14387, 72-1 BCA ¶ 9202, the board analyzed similar language in the Ground and Flight Risk clause, stating at 42,698-99:

There is little question that the record before us would sustain, if it would not compel, a finding that the burning of aircraft No. 62-1831 was due to the negligence of [the contractor's] employees at work on the aircraft on the day when the accident occurred. There is also sufficient evidence in the record to sustain a finding, if it were necessary or needful, that [the contractor's] administration of its safety program at the working level was less consistent, careful and effective than was necessary to insure an operation free of major accidents or of the risk that such accidents might occur. To the extent that the lack of enforcement or observation of safety rules contributed to the effective cause of the burning of aircraft No. 62-1831, [the contractor's] managerial personnel must bear a share of the responsibility for the accident. Its negligence in strictly enforcing safety rules and procedures cannot on the record made here be denied.

But even if such findings were made respondent would not be helped. For it must show that the criticized failure of [the contractor's] managerial personnel in regard to maintenance and administration of a program for the protection and preservation of aircraft in the open, as aircraft No. 62-1831 was here, or during operation, in accordance with sound industrial practice, amounted to "willful misconduct or lack of good faith" (ASPR 10-404(a), Cl., par. (d)(i)).

The authorities are unanimous in holding that proof of negligence does not establish willful misconduct or lack of good faith. See *Acker v. Schultz*, 74 F. Supp. 683 (S.D.N.Y. 1947); *Berry Bros. Buick, Inc. v. General Motors Corp.*, 257 F. Supp. 542 (E.D. Pa. 1966). Mere indifference to duty also is not enough. *Ibid.* What amounts to willful misconduct or lack of good faith is to be "recreant" to one's duty (*Tyler v. Grange Assurance Association*, 3 Wash. App. 167, 473 P.2d 193), to refuse deliberately to perform a plain, well-understood contractual or statutory obligation without just cause or excuse (*Brandoline v. Lindsay*, 269 Cal. App. 2d 319; *NLRB v. Knoxville Publishing Co.*, 124 F.2d 825 (6th Cir. 1942)). Willful misconduct has also been described as the conscious failure to use the necessary means to avoid peril and indifference to its consequences. *Holman v. Brady*, 241 Ala. 487, 3 So.2d 30; *Ridge v. Boulder Creek etc. School District*, 60 Cal. App. 2d 453, 140 P.2d 990; see also *Meadows v. Vaughn*, 81 Ga. App. 45, 57 SE2d 689; *Goepp v. American Overseas Airlines*, 281 App. Div. 105, 117 NYS 2d 276. When faced with this problem, the NASA Board has reached the same result. *McDonnell-Douglas Corporation*, NASABCA No. 865-28, 68-1 BCA ¶ 7021. Under contracts involving a similar managerial responsibility clause our predecessor, the War Department Board of Contract Appeals, has adopted a comparable approach. *Cf. Sweet Briar, Inc.*, BCA Nos. 986, 987 (1945).

We thus reach the final question: did the conduct of [the contractor's] managerial personnel evince a refusal to perform its duty, a conscious failure to use appropriate means to avoid industrial accidents and indifference to their consequences so that its performance of its job can be characterized as permeated with misconduct in safety matters and with that suggestion of duplicity or dishonesty which the law calls bad faith. See *Fenner v. American Insurance Co. of N.Y.*, 97 SW2d 741 (Tex. Civ. App.). We believe that on the record made here this question must clearly be answered in the negative.

[The contractor's] general manager and his deputy might be criticized for inadequate enforcement of their own or contractually-required safety programs at the working level. But at the higher management level they had instituted a program and a safety management which was clearly adequate compliance with [the contractor's] obligations and they had, even if often at Air Force suggestion or prodding, greatly improved the safety of [the contractor's] facility. Nothing in the record proves that they took their responsibility for aircraft safety lightly, that they were unmindful of it, or failed to give it substantial personal attention. Conflicting considerations of scheduling and performance may have at times counterbalanced their consideration of aircraft safety. But there is no evidence that they subordinated their responsibility for safety to other goals to such an extent that one could find willful misconduct or lack of good faith in regard to safety concerns.

See also *PAE Int'l*, ASBCA 45314, 98-1 BCA ¶ 29,347 (failure to detect theft scheme not willful misconduct); *LTV Aerospace & Def. Co.*, ASBCA 37571, 93-3 BCA ¶ 26,248 (investigative report of aircraft crash contained no indication of willful misconduct); and *Morton-Thiokol, Inc.*, ASBCA 32629, 90-3 BCA ¶ 23,207 (carelessness not willful misconduct). The burden of proof of willful misconduct is on the government, *Pacific Architects & Eng'rs, Inc.*, ASBCA 19513, 78-2 BCA ¶ 13,540.

Under the current FAR clauses limiting the contractor's risk of loss in this manner, there is a conclusive presumption of willful misconduct of managerial personnel if the government notifies the contractor of disapproval of its system of maintenance, repair, protection, or preservation of the property. None of the litigated cases has addressed clauses containing this language, but it appears to give the government some protection in this narrow fact situation.

2. Bailment Rules

If the government furnishes property to a contractor without specific contract language covering the risk of loss, a bailment will result. Although the degree of care to which a bailee is held varies with the circumstances, the government contractor will normally be held to be a mutual benefit bailee responsible for exercising due and reasonable care, *James Weston*, ASBCA 41624, 92-1 BCA ¶ 24,569; *Premier Elec. Constr. Co.*, FAACAP 66-10, 65-2 BCA ¶ 5080; *Nacirema Operating Co.*, ASBCA 3453, 56-2 BCA ¶ 1081. To recover under bailment law, the government must prove that the property was delivered to the contractor in good condition and was returned in a damaged condition (or not at all), *Meeks Transfer Co.*, ASBCA 11819, 67-2 BCA ¶ 6567, *recons. denied*, 68-1 BCA ¶ 7063. It may be difficult for the government to meet this burden if it has to rely on a contractor's accounting system found to be incomplete and inaccurate, *Gary Aircraft Corp.*, ASBCA 22018, 90-1 BCA ¶ 22,492. If the government establishes the necessary facts, and that the property was under the contractor's exclusive control, there will be a presumption that the contractor failed to exercise ordinary care over the property. The contractor/bailee then has the burden of proving that it exercised ordinary care, *Nilson Van & Storage*, ASBCA 29898, 85-1 BCA ¶ 17,937; *Tryon Moving & Storage, Inc.*, ASBCA 25358, 82-1 BCA ¶ 15,703; *Newport Ship Yard, Inc.*, DCAB NOAA-6-77, 79-2 BCA ¶ 14,182.

3. Subcontractor Risk of Loss

Paragraph (g) of the Government Property clause in FAR 52.245-2, requiring the contractor to bear the risk of loss of government property, is silent on property used by subcontractors, leaving that risk with the contractor. The alternate ¶ (g), which relieves the contractor of the risk of loss, contains explicit language requiring the contractor to require the subcontractor to bear the risk of loss. Special language relieving the subcontractor of such risk of loss may be used if the government property is furnished directly to the subcontractor, FAR 45.103(d), or with the specific approval of the contracting officer, FAR 45.103(e).

4. Risk of Loss for Incomplete Work

In fixed-price supply contracts, the government's title to progress payments inventory does not carry with it the risk of loss or damage to the contractor inventory.

See ¶ (e) of the Progress Payments clause at FAR 52.232-16, imposing the risk of loss on the contractor until delivery and acceptance of the work.

Although work under a construction contract becomes government property when attached to the realty, a government construction contractor usually bears the risk of loss of such work until completion and acceptance by the government. The standard Permits and Responsibilities clause, FAR 52.236-7, used in government construction contracts provides:

> The Contractor shall also be responsible for all damages to persons or property that occur as a result of the Contractor's fault or negligence. The Contractor shall also be responsible for all materials delivered and work performed until completion and acceptance of the entire work, except for any completed unit of work which may have been accepted under the contract.

See *De Armas v. United States*, 108 Ct. Cl. 436 (1947) (risk of damage to jetty caused by storm fell to contractor), and *Keyser Roofing Contractors, Inc.*, ASBCA 13380, 70-1 BCA ¶ 8141 (contractor liable under Permits and Responsibilities clause for cost of repairing wind damage occurring during a suspension of work). A contractor also bears the risk prior to acceptance of contract work of loss or damage caused by tortious conduct of third parties, *Mittry v. United States*, 73 Ct. Cl. 341 (1931); *Okano Elec. Contracting Corp.*, ASBCA 20978, 78-1 BCA ¶ 12,914. See also *Golder Constr. Co.*, ASBCA 4390, 58-1 BCA ¶ 1626; *Edward R. Marden Corp.*, ASBCA 13199, 69-2 BCA ¶ 7878, *recons. denied*, 70-1 BCA ¶ 8135; and *John McShain, Inc. v. United States*, 179 Ct. Cl. 632, 375 F.2d 829 (1967). Substantial completion of the work does not cause the risk of loss to shift to the government, *Construction Serv. Co.*, ASBCA 16434, 73-1 BCA ¶ 10,021. For more detailed analysis of risk of loss in construction contracting, see Bednar et al., *Construction Contracting* Chapter 18 (1991).

5. Faulty Government-Furnished Design Specifications

Risk of loss will not be shifted to a contractor if damage is attributable to faulty government-furnished design specifications, *Anthony P. Miller*, ASBCA 6383, 60-2 BCA ¶ 2836. In *Miller*, the board found that a construction contractor was not liable for damage to the work occurring prior to completion and acceptance because the damage, which resulted from freezing and bursting of pipes, was attributable to faulty government-furnished specifications. In *B.J. Lucarelli & Co.*, ASBCA 8768, 65-1 BCA ¶ 4655, *modified on recons.*, 65-1 BCA ¶ 4820, a construction contractor was entitled to recover the cost of additional work following substantial completion of the work necessitated by faulty government-furnished design specifications.

C. Disposal of Government Property

A contractor's management responsibilities for government property in its possession do not end when the property is no longer needed to meet contract obligations. Regulations setting forth the procedures for disposal of unused government property are contained in FAR Subpart 45.6. These regulations were completely rewritten in FAC 2001-22, 69 Fed. Reg. 17,741, April 5, 2004. Prior regulations contained somewhat more complex procedures.

At the completion of a contract, the contractor is required to initiate action to dispose of the property under the direction of the government's "Plant Clearance Officer." Paragraph (i)(2) of the Government Property (Fixed-Price Contracts), FAR 52.245-2, and the Government Property (Cost-Reimbursement, Time-and-Material, or Labor-Hour Contracts), FAR 52.245-5, clauses states:

> (2) *Pre-disposal requirements.* When the Contractor determines that a property item acquired or produced by the Contractor, to which the Government has obtained title under paragraph (c) of this clause, is no longer needed for performance of this contract, the Contractor, in the following order of priority:
>
> > (i) May purchase the property at the acquisition cost.
> >
> > (ii) Shall make reasonable efforts to return unused property to the appropriate supplier at fair market value (less, if applicable, a reasonable restocking fee that is consistent with the supplier's customary practices).
> >
> > (iii) Shall list, on Standard Form 1428, Inventory Disposal Schedule, property that was not purchased under paragraph (i)(2)(i) of this clause, could not be returned to a supplier, or could not be used in the performance of other Government contracts.

FAR 45.602-1 requires plant clearance officers to review, accept, or reject the Inventory Disposal Schedule within 10 days and to provide disposition instructions to the contractor within 120 days of receipt of a schedule that is properly filled out. This regulation points out that "failure to provide timely disposition instructions might entitle the contractor to an equitable adjustment."

The first step in the disposal process is for the contractor to "remove" property from the schedule by its own means. FAR 45.602-1(c) provides:

> (1) Plant clearance officers should approve removal when—
>
> > (i) The contractor wishes to purchase a contractor-acquired or contractor-produced item at acquisition cost and credit the contract;
> >
> > (ii) The contractor is able to return unused property to the supplier at fair

> market value and credit the contract (less, if applicable, a reasonable restocking fee that is consistent with the supplier's customary practices);
>
> (iii) The Government has authorized the contractor to use the property on another Government contract; or
>
> (iv) The contractor has requested continued use of Government property, and the plant clearance officer has consulted with the appropriate program and technical personnel.

Under the prior regulation, if the property was returned to the supplier, the government had to be given full credit for the price paid, and the restocking charge was not permitted to exceed 25 percent of the cost. See *Industrial Pump & Compressor, Inc.*, ASBCA 39003, 93-2 BCA ¶ 25,757, in which a contractor was entitled to recover the restocking charge of a returned steel plate but not the G&A markup on the plate's purchase price, which the board found to be part of the plate's cost.

Plant clearance officers are responsible for "screening" the property remaining on the schedule to determine if it can be reused. Screening procedures are set forth in FAR 45.602-3, and the following priorities are set forth in FAR 45.602-2:

> Authorized [reutilization] methods, listed in descending order from highest to lowest priority, are—
>
> (a) Reuse within the agency (see 45.603 for circumstances under which excess personal property may be abandoned, destroyed, or donated);
>
> (b) Transfer of educationally useful equipment, with GSA approval, to other Federal agencies that have expressed a need for the property;
>
> (c) Transfer of educationally useful equipment to schools and nonprofit organizations (see Executive Order 12999, Educational Technology: Ensuring Opportunity For All Children In The Next Century, April 17, 1996), and 15 U.S.C. 3710(i);
>
> (d) Reuse within the Federal Government; and
>
> (e) Donation to an eligible donee designated by GSA.

Guidance on the use of these reutilization methods is contained in FAR 45.602-4, 45.603, and 45.604. The plant clearance officer also has the contractual right to abandon any property without further liability to the contractor. See ¶ (j) of the Government Property (Fixed-Price Contracts), FAR 52.245-2, and the Government Property (Cost-Reimbursement, Time-and-Material, or Labor-Hour Contracts), FAR 52.245-5, clauses.

The disposition of special tooling provided under cost contracts is handled in the same manner as discussed above for other types of contract inventory. However, the Special Tooling clause, FAR 52.245-17, governs the disposition of special tooling furnished or acquired under a fixed-price contract. Under this clause, the contracting officer must provide the contractor with written disposition instructions within 180 days of receipt of the contractor's special tooling list and within 90 days of receipt of the contractor's list of excess special tooling. The contracting officer may then direct the contractor to transfer usable special tooling to another contract, put it in storage, or deliver it to the government. The contracting officer may also direct the contractor to sell or scrap the special tooling. In this case, the contractor may be entitled to an equitable adjustment for resulting costs, or the government may be entitled to a credit for net proceeds. As a final option, the contracting officer may give the contractor a letter disclaiming any further government interest or right in the special tooling. No matter how the government chooses to dispose of the special tooling in a fixed-price contract, it is under no obligation to restore or rehabilitate the contractor's premises unless otherwise provided in the contract.

CHAPTER 8

PRICING OF ADJUSTMENTS

This chapter deals with the techniques used to measure the amount of a price adjustment (quantum) once the right to the adjustment (entitlement) has been established. The vast majority of price adjustments arise under contract clauses that provide for an "equitable adjustment" if the contractor's cost of performance is increased or decreased by the event covered by the clause. These equitable adjustments cover many of the types of claims that would otherwise have been classified as damages for breach of contract. As a result, breach of contract claims and other price adjustments are relatively rare.

Since it is expected that price adjustments will be settled through negotiation, the initial task of the party claiming the adjustment is to submit sufficient data to convince the other party that the proposed adjustment is warranted. The price adjustment clauses give little guidance on the amount of substantiating data required to support a claim. For example, the supply contract Changes clause in FAR 52.243-1 merely states that the contractor must "assert its right to an adjustment," while the construction contract Changes clause in FAR 52.243-4 calls for the submission of "a written statement describing the general nature and amount of proposal." The major informational requirement applicable to contractor claims for equitable adjustments is for the submission of certified cost or pricing data on price adjustments over $550,000. FAR 15.403-4(a)(1)(iii) provides that, for the purpose of determining the applicability of the cost or pricing data requirement, the price of the change will be calculated by adding the cost of work added and the cost of work deleted by the change. Thus, a change adding $300,000 and deleting $260,000 would be a $560,000 change for which cost or pricing data would be required. FAR 15.403-4(a)(2) also permits heads of contracting activities to authorize contracting officers to obtain certified cost or pricing data for changes between $100,000 and $550,000, if they make a written finding that such data are "necessary to determine whether the price is fair and reasonable." Cost or pricing data may not be obtained for changes with a value of less than $100,000, FAR 15.403-1(a). Table 15-2, Instructions for Submitting Cost/Price Proposals When Cost or Pricing Data Are Required, in FAR 15.408, calls for a separate statement of the costs of the work added and the work deleted by the change order. There are similar requirements imposed on the government when it asserts claims for price adjustments.

It is general policy to finalize price adjustments as quickly as possible after the parties have identified a claim. See, for example, FAR 43.204(b)(1), calling for negotiation of an equitable adjustment "in the shortest practicable time" after issuance of a unilateral change order. However, there is no mechanism available to either party to ensure that timely pricing occurs. Either party may delay the pricing action as the work is performed and actual costs are incurred. In such a case, the correct basis for the pricing of adjustments will be the incurred costs rather than estimates of prospective costs that might have been prepared earlier, *Itek Corp., Applied Tech. Div.*, ASBCA 13528, 71-1 BCA ¶ 8906; *Bridgewater Constr. Corp.*, VABCA 2936, 91-3 BCA ¶ 24,273, *recons. denied*, 92-1 BCA ¶ 24,446; and, to meet the requirement that the data be "current," the contractor is required to submit supplemental cost or pricing data on contract changes as the additional costs are incurred, *Aerojet-Gen. Corp.*, ASBCA 16988, 73-2 BCA ¶ 10,242. See ¶ (b) of the Requirements for Cost or Pricing Data or Information Other Than Cost or Pricing Data—Modifications clause in FAR 52.215-21 requiring the submission of such data in accordance with Table 15-2 unless an exception is granted. Similar procedures are followed when the government desires pricing information in order to negotiate the equitable adjustment prior to the issuance of the change order. See, for example, the National Aeronautics & Space Administration Engineering Change Proposals (Oct 2001) (ECPs) clause, NFS 1852.243-70, permitting the contracting officer to require the contractor to provide cost or pricing data to support ECPs. Other requirements for substantiating data are imposed by various agencies.

When the parties cannot settle a claim for a price adjustment, it will be decided by an appeals board or a court using formal rules of evidence. The material in this chapter sets forth the elaborate rule structure that has been devised in the litigation process. These rules control the outcome of such litigation and therefore are of value in providing guidance to the negotiating parties. The chapter focuses primarily on equitable adjustments and other types of contractual price adjustments, but it also considers breach of contract damages and quantum meruit claims. The first section deals with the basic principles for recovery, addressing the rules for measuring the amount of compensation for the direct effect of the government act or order leading to extra costs. The second section covers the techniques used to prove the amount. The third section explores special problems involved in impact and delay costs as well as consequential damages. The fourth section focuses on the rules for recovery of overhead and profit. The fifth section addresses the special problems of pricing adjustments for government claims of defective pricing. Finally, the last section covers claims processing costs and the cost of financing the amount of the adjustment.

I. BASIC PRINCIPLES

There are three different bases for repricing government contracts. The first, and by far most common, is repricing under standard contract clauses. Occasionally, contract repricing occurs through the determination of damages for breach of contract. Finally, there are some actions where the pricing is computed by the value of the benefit received by the government (commonly called "quantum meruit"). The basic principles of each of these bases are discussed in this section.

A. Price Adjustments Under Contract Clauses

The overriding basic principle applicable to price adjustments under contract clauses is that they are almost always measured by the cost impact on the contractor. This is reflected in the standard clauses that call for an equitable adjustment, upward or downward, if the cited occurrence (change, differing site condition, defective or late government property, issuance of stop-work order, etc.) causes an increase or decrease in the contractor's cost of performance of the work. The term "equitable adjustment" has become a term of art that, wherever used in government contracts, is given the same interpretation. See *Pacific Architects & Eng'rs, Inc. v. United States*, 203 Ct. Cl. 499, 491 F.2d 734 (1974), and *General Builders Supply Co. v. United States*, 187 Ct. Cl. 477, 409 F.2d 246 (1969). The construction contract Suspension of Work clause and the supply contract government Delay of Work clause do not use the term "equitable" in describing the adjustment to which the contractor is entitled but do call for pricing based on cost increases. Paragraph (b) of the Suspension of Work clause at FAR 52.242-14 states:

> [A]n adjustment shall be made for any increase in the cost of performance of this contract (excluding profit) necessarily caused by the unreasonable suspension, delay, or interruption, and the contract modified in writing accordingly.

The Government Delay of Work clause at FAR 52.242-17 states:

> [A]n adjustment (excluding profit) shall be made for any increase in the cost of performance of this contract caused by the delay or interruption and the contract shall be modified in writing accordingly.

The primary focus of this subsection is on contractor money claims for increases in the price and the methods of establishing the amount of such claims. However, the basic principles discussed are equally applicable to government claims for reductions in price through the equitable adjustment process.

1. Basic Pricing Formula

Alterations to the work that result in price adjustments are of many types, but they can be described in a few clear-cut categories for purposes of stating pricing rules. Three major categories are apparent:

1. Actions that *add* work.

2. Actions that *delete* work.

3. Actions that *substitute* one item of work for another item of work.

It can be seen that the third category is actually a combination of the first two, with the result that all pricing actions can be dealt with if rules are formulated to provide techniques for pricing added work and deleted work. The cases that have established the basic pricing formula have conceptualized the matter in precisely these terms. Thus, the basic pricing formula for an equitable adjustment has been expressed as "the difference between what it would have reasonably cost to perform the work as originally required and what it reasonably cost to perform the work as changed," *Modern Foods, Inc.*, ASBCA 2090, 57-1 BCA ¶ 1229; *Jack Picoult*, VACAB 1221, 78-1 BCA ¶ 13,024. See also *Celesco Indus., Inc.*, ASBCA 22251, 79-1 BCA ¶ 13,604, in which the board stated at 66,683 that "[t]he measure of the equitable price adjustment is the difference between the reasonable cost of performing without the change or deletion and the reasonable cost of performing with the change or deletion."

The technique that is used to attain this result is to attempt to limit the repricing to the effect of the change alone without altering the basic profit or loss position of the contractor before the change occurred. See Duncan, *Equitable Adjustments Under Fixed-Price Contracts,* 22 Fed. B.J. 307 (1962), calling this the "leave them where you find them" approach. The Court of Claims explained this approach in *Pacific Architects & Eng'rs, Inc. v. United States*, 203 Ct. Cl. 499, 491 F.2d 734 (1974), stating at 508:

> It is well established that the equitable adjustment may not properly be used as an occasion for reducing or increasing the contractor's profit or loss, or for converting a loss to a profit or vice versa, for reasons unrelated to a change. A contractor who has underestimated his bid or encountered unanticipated expense or inefficiencies may not properly use a change order as an excuse to reform the contract or to shift his own risks or losses to the Government. *Nager Electric Co. v. United States*, 194 Ct. Cl. 835, 851-853, 442 F.2d 936, 945-946 (1971); *Keco Industries, Inc. v. United States*, 176 Ct. Cl. 983, 999-1002, 364 F.2d 838, 849-850 (1966), *cert. denied*, 386 U.S. 958 (1967); *S.N. Nielsen Co. v. United States*, 141 Ct. Cl. 793, 796-797 (1958).

a. *Pricing the Deleted Work*

As the above formula indicates, one element of the adjustment is the amount that it would have cost the contractor to perform the work without the change or other basis for a price adjustment. Here, the focus is on only work that will not be performed because of the alteration to the contract. All other work originally called for is expected to be performed at the original contract price (work made less efficient by the change will be addressed later in the chapter). To the extent that work that has already been completed is made obsolete by the contract change, there may be a surplus property problem, but there is no need for repricing of the contract, since that work will already have been included in the original contract price.

Where a credit is claimed for decreased work, the credit is measured by the net cost savings to the contractor, *Fordel Films W.*, ASBCA 23071, 79-2 BCA ¶ 13,913; *A. A. Beiro Constr. Co.*, GSBCA 3915, 74-2 BCA ¶ 10,860. Usually, there will be no price reduction if the contractor realizes no savings from a change. See *Temsco Helicopters, Inc.*, IBCA 2594-A, 89-2 BCA ¶ 21,796, where the contractor did not fire a mechanic that was no longer needed to perform the work as changed because it had employed two mechanics for the duration of the job and would be less able to hire mechanics in the future if it broke its commitment. The board held that there should be no downward price adjustment because the contractor had not saved any costs.

When the contractor has saved costs, deleted work is priced at the amount it would have cost the contractor had it not been deleted. It is often argued that this amount should be based on the contractor's original cost estimates at the time the parties established the contract price. The contractor usually uses this argument when the work in the contract is underpriced, and the government uses it when the work has been overpriced. However, the boards and courts, with rare exceptions, reject this argument when one of the parties presents better evidence of the cost that the contractor would have actually incurred had the work not been altered, *Skinker & Garrett, Inc.*, GSBCA 1150, 65-1 BCA ¶ 4521. Thus, if the contractor has a legitimate claim that an event has occurred that has increased its costs of performance, it will recover even though its contract price included greater costs than were necessary for performance of the changed work. See *B-E-C-K–Christensen Raber-Kief & Assocs.*, ASBCA 16467, 73-1 BCA ¶ 9884, in which the board held that the contractor was entitled to a price increase for improperly being required to comply with the Davis-Bacon Act for demolition work where it had included sufficient costs in its bid for such wages but had found a cheaper way to perform the work. The board stated at 46,203:

> The Government seems concerned that upholding of the contractor's claim would result in a "windfall" to it, since presumably it had already included in the contract price the cost of doing the demolition. We question whether a $6,000 saving on a $1.5 million contract constitutes a "windfall." Nor does it appear whether the contractor made or lost money on the contract as a whole. In any event, such considerations are irrelevant. This was a formally advertised firm fixed-price contract. Under such a contract, the contractor was entitled to the full benefit of any savings it could have made by entering into the demolition agreement with the Barrow residents, so long as it did not involve a change to the contract.

In this case, the board based the amount it would have cost the contractor to perform without the erroneous order on the wages it would have paid but for the order.

(1) Deductive Changes

The major application of the "would have cost" rule occurs in cases involving deductive changes or changes where one portion of the work is deleted and other work is added in substitution. See *Noblebrook Contractors, Inc.*, ASBCA 9736, 1964 BCA ¶ 4283, *recons. denied*, 1964 BCA ¶ 4408, and *Admiral Corp.*, ASBCA 8634, 1964 BCA ¶ 4161. In *Noblebrook*, although the government issued a change deleting a specification requirement for which the contractor neglected to include costs in its bid, the board held that the government was entitled to a price reduction based on the amount that the contractor would have spent to perform the deleted work. In *Admiral*, the government changed the specifications for a battery case from one that would have cost the contractor $7.52 to one that cost it $11.63. The contracting officer rejected the contractor's price increase proposal and contended that the government was entitled to a price reduction of $.85 since the contractor had included $12.48 for the battery case in its original price proposal. The board rejected this contention and granted the contractor a price increase of $4.11 ($11.63 – $7.52) plus general and administrative expense and profit. These decisions are based on an earlier court decision in *S.N. Nielsen Co. v. United States*, 141 Ct. Cl. 793 (1958), in which the government ordered a change from underground installation of electrical ducts and cable to an overhead distribution system. During negotiations for the equitable adjustment, it was discovered that it would have cost $60,800 to do the electrical work as originally specified, and that, as changed, the work would cost $19,180. The government therefore proposed to reduce the contract price by $41,620, the net difference. The contractor objected, since it had included only $34,800 for the deleted work when making up its original bid price. It contended that a reduction of $41,620 would have it do the work for nothing and pay $6,710 for doing so. The court rejected this argument, holding that the contractor's own improvident bid, not the change, caused the difficulties, and that to hold for it would be tantamount to reforming the contract for the contractor's unilateral mistake. The court thus used $60,800 as the proper amount of cost that should be deducted as part of the equitable adjustment process. See also *Bruce Andersen Co.*, ASBCA 29412, 89-2 BCA ¶ 21,872; *Jack Simpson Contractor, Inc.*, ENGBCA 3752, 79-1 BCA ¶ 13,766, and *Fordel Films W.*, ASBCA 23071, 79-2 BCA ¶ 13,913. Contrast *Dawson Constr. Co.*, GSBCA 5672, 81-2 BCA ¶ 15,387, *recons. denied*, 82-2 BCA ¶ 15,914, in which the board refused to grant a downward equitable adjustment because the contractor had already deducted the savings from its original bid price (assuming the change would be approved after award). In *Plaza Maya Ltd. P'ship*, GSBCA 9086, 91-1 BCA ¶ 23,425, the board refused to follow *Dawson* but followed the standard rule, stating that *Dawson* had been decided on the unique facts that had occurred. Similarly, in *Fire Sec. Sys., Inc.*, ASBCA 53498, 02-2 BCA ¶ 31,939, the board held that the government was entitled to reduce the price in the amount that deleted work would have cost even though the contractor had not included the work in its original bid price.

These cases do not hold that the amount included in the contractor's original estimate can never be used to determine the amount that the work would have cost, but that later evidence such as purchase order prices or vendor quotations is normally a better indicator of the costs that the contractor would have incurred. See, e.g., *Cottman Mech. Contractors, Inc.*, ASBCA 48882, 00-1 BCA ¶ 30,777 (estimate based on Means Guide better than original bid amount); *Westphal GmbH & Co. KG*, ASBCA 39401, 96-1 BCA ¶ 28,194, *recons. denied*, 96-2 BCA ¶ 28,466, *aff'd in part, remanded in part*, 135 F.3d 778 (Fed. Cir. 1998) (subcontract price better than government estimate based on costs charged to another customer); *J.S. Alberici Constr. Co.*, GSBCA 10306, 91-2 BCA ¶ 23,846 (quotation received from subcontractor before change order better than estimating manual); and *Atlantic Elec. Co.*, GSBCA 6016, 83-1 BCA ¶ 16,484 (invoice submitted by contractor for a part that was identical to deleted item under change order accurately reflected the contractor's actual costs). If there is no such evidence, however, the original estimate may be considered the best available evidence of this amount, *State Mech. Corp.*, VABCA 2797, 91-2 BCA ¶ 23,830 (original bid estimate preferred to new estimates of either party); *Select Contractors, Inc.*, ENGBCA 3919, 82-2 BCA ¶ 15,869 (original estimate of contractor used but adjusted to include overhead and profit that had been allocated in the bid to the mobilization item in order to recover the costs earlier); *Cecil Pruitt, Inc.*, ASBCA 18344, 73-2 BCA ¶ 10,213 (in the absence of more conclusive proof, the higher government estimate was used to find reasonable cost). It is more likely in such circumstances that one or both of the parties will present current estimates of the amount of costs that the contractor would have incurred, and the most persuasive of such estimates will be used. See, for example, *Globe Constr. Co.*, ASBCA 21069, 78-2 BCA ¶ 13,337, *recons. denied*, 80-1 BCA ¶ 14,354 (greater weight given to estimates offered by contractor; government estimates were predicated upon a manual that was more suited to pricing new construction than to pricing rehabilitation work); and *G & M Elec. Contractors Co.*, GSBCA 4771, 78-2 BCA ¶ 13,452, *recons. denied*, 79-1 BCA ¶ 13,791 (presumption of the reasonableness of the follow-on contractor's costs rebutted by the wide disparity between those costs and the government's estimate). In some cases, list prices of materials have been used as the best measure of what the work would have cost, *Koll Constr. Co. v. General Servs. Admin.*, GSBCA 12306, 94-1 BCA ¶ 26,501, *recons. denied*, 94-2 BCA ¶ 26,599 (board rejected contractor's claim that it would have received a significant discount); *Mit-Con, Inc.*, ASBCA 43021, 92-1 BCA ¶ 24,632 (board rejected government argument that work would have been obtainable only by special order).

In making this computation, the actual effect of the change on the contractor will be taken into account. For example, in *Harrison W./Franki-Denys (JV)*, ENGBCA 5506, 93-1 BCA ¶ 25,406, the board rejected the contractor's argument that the deleted work should be estimated using industry averages. The board favored the government's approach of using other costs of comparable work to arrive at the estimate of what the deleted work would have cost the contractor. The board stated at 126,585:

> This cost category is an estimate of what it would have cost *this* contractor—not an average contractor or some other contractor—to accomplish the work in question in the absence of [the change]. The estimate must thus reflect *this* contractor's actual performance on the job.

(2) Exceptions to General Rule

There are a number of exceptions to the "would have cost" rule. In some unique factual situations, the starting point of the equitable adjustment will be the amount included in the contract price.

(A) Complete Deletion of a Severable Item

If *severable* work is entirely deleted, its entire price, not what it would have cost, is the proper measure of the adjustment. In *Gregory & Reilly Assocs., Inc.*, FAACAP 65-30, 65-2 BCA ¶ 4918, the contracting officer canceled one of the four phases of work on the contract by change order and reduced the contract price by the amount shown for that phase. In upholding the contracting officer, the board stated at 23,253:

> We would agree with the Contractor that, where there is a change order reducing work under a lump sum contract, an appropriate equitable adjustment is the cost of performing that deleted work. In such a case, since no firm fixed prices have been agreed upon for separate items of work, it would be appropriate to consider what it would have cost the Contractor to accomplish the deleted work in arriving at an equitable adjustment for a deductive change. However, that is not the case here. The original Invitation for Bids is clear that the basis for bidding was on a firm fixed price for each phase of the work and in no way can be construed as proposing a lump sum contract. Contrary to the Contractor's understanding, Article II, Standard Form 22 of the Invitation for Bids expressly reserved to the Government right to make awards to different low bidders on the various phases of work or on a total aggregate price basis.
>
> * * *
>
> Nor does the fact that Contractor claims it submitted an unbalanced bid alter the above proposition. We recognize that the practice of submitting unbalanced bids in the construction industry is not uncommon. Where such bids do not involve collusion or fraudulent conduct by the bidder or some substantial irregularity affecting fair and competitive bidding, they are not objectionable.

In this case, the contractor had considerably overpriced the phase that had been deleted and had underpriced another phase of the work. See also *Holtzen Constr. Co.*, AGBCA 413, 75-2 BCA ¶ 11,378, *aff'd*, 212 Ct. Cl. 545 (1976).

Whether the items in a contract are severable will depend on the provisions of the solicitation, the nature of the work, and the intentions of the parties. Mere recitation of a separate unit price does not make the item severable. For example, in "all or none" bids the items would not be severable. In *Askenazy Constr. Co.*, HUDBCA 78-2, 78-2 BCA ¶ 13,402, the board held that it was reasonable to conclude that the items were not severable in an IFB that provided for "only one award." In *Griffin Servs., Inc. v. General Servs. Admin.*, GSBCA 10841, 92-2 BCA ¶ 24,945, a deleted item was found not severable because the items were bid on an aggregate basis. See also *American Imaging Servs., Inc.*, VABCA 4842, 97-2 BCA ¶ 29,270, stating that deletion of work at unit prices is proper only when those prices are "both separate and severable." In *CTA, Inc.*, ASBCA 47062, 00-2 BCA ¶ 30,946, the price of a production option was found not severable because the ceiling price of the fixed-price incentive contract covered all of the line items cumulatively. In contrast, in *Eugene Iovine, Inc.*, PSBCA 2867, 92-2 BCA ¶ 25,013, an item was deleted at its line-item price because the solicitation had permitted award of "any or all" line items. See also *Keco Indus., Inc. v. United States*, 176 Ct. Cl. 983, 364 F.2d 838 (1966), deleting items at their contract unit price when similar items were substituted by change order, and *Oneida Constr., Inc./David Boland, Inc., Joint Venture*, ASBCA 47914, 95-1 BCA ¶ 27,363, in which the board permitted deletion of work at its line-item price without discussing whether it was severable. In a questionable decision, *Bral Envtl. Servs., Inc.*, DOTBCA 2980, 97-1 BCA ¶ 28,762, the board applied the severability rule to delete work that was not separately priced at the cost reflected in the contractor's proposal. The board stated that the severability rule was applicable whenever there was an "agreed price" and that the contractor's submission of pricing data to the government in its best and final offer reflected such an agreement.

(b) Ambiguous Specifications

A contractor is entitled to an equitable adjustment if the specifications are ambiguous and it is required to follow a more expensive method of performance than it innocently and reasonably believed the specifications required. In such cases, the adjustment is considered to compensate the contractor for injuries received in reliance on the government's ambiguous specifications. If the contractor did not consider the less expensive method of performance in preparing its bid or proposal, it cannot be said that it relied on the ambiguous specification. In that case, the adjustment will be measured from the amount included in the proposed price, *Bern Kane Prods., Inc.*, ASBCA 8547, 1963 BCA ¶ 3823; *Olive Hill Mfg. Co.*, ASBCA 8365, 65-1 BCA ¶ 4863. This same rationale would also appear to be applicable to equitable adjustments for constructive changes caused by defective specifications, where relief is predicated on the contractor's reliance on the government's specifications. In *National Mfg., Inc.*, ASBCA 15816, 74-1 BCA ¶ 10,580, the board recognized the potential application of this exception but refused to apply it because the contractor had extremely limited bidding time and apparently used figures in the preparation of its bid that it knew it could better at the time of placing orders. Thus, the equitable adjustment was measured from the amount for which the items would have been purchased absent the ambiguous specifications.

(c) Special Contracting Agreements

At the time of contracting, the parties may, in anticipation of changes, agree on the basis for equitable adjustments. See *Batson-Cook Co.*, GSBCA 4069, 74-2 BCA ¶ 10,801, in which the board held that the parties had agreed that the equitable adjustment for deductive changes would be the unit prices included in the contract. See also *Military Servs., Inc.*, ASBCA 21595, 79-1 BCA ¶ 13,614, where a unit price for each meal outside the permissible range of variation was included in the contract as the basis for computation of the equitable adjustment. Although this method of computation was applied to one claim, the board remanded for further negotiations where costs of operating in new mess halls were higher than the original costs that had served as the basis for the specified rate. Further, in *Hayes Int'l Corp.*, ASBCA 21758, 79-1 BCA ¶ 13,596, the board refused to apply a clause providing for compensation at fixed hourly rates for "over and above" work. A separate clause in the contract provided that the claim for extra work was to be processed as a change.

Agencies sometimes include special clauses in their contracts to determine the estimated costs to be used as the basis for computation of equitable adjustments. The Naval Facilities Engineering Command had altered the general rule for pricing deleted work by including the following language in its general provisions:

> In making all equitable adjustments under Clause 3, compensation for additions will be based upon estimated costs at the time the work is performed and credit for deductions will be based upon estimated costs at the time the contract was made.

However, that clause was held not to guarantee the contractor that the amount of the deduction will be computed by the amount included in the bid estimate. Rather, the Armed Services Board of Contract Appeals has interpreted the provision to mean that the estimate at the time of the bid must be a reasonable estimate of the cost at that time. See *Williams & Burrows Contractors Inc.*, ASBCA 8415, 1963 BCA ¶ 3781, and *Koppers-Clough*, ASBCA 12364, 70-1 BCA ¶ 8150. This interpretation tends to confuse the method of computing the adjustment, since the parties must still obtain all available information to determine what is a reasonable cost.

(d) Deletion of Minor Items

In *Pacific Contractors, Inc.*, ENGBCA PCC-29, 79-2 BCA ¶ 13,998, the board recognized that it might be customary to use the contractor's bid price to delete relatively minor items, stating at 68,720:

> The Board is aware that it is customary to use the contractor's bid item price when deleting a relatively minor item of work as in the present case. No doubt it is usually an efficacious approach to the equitable adjustment due, since there will be no actual costs to serve as a guide and since otherwise estimating and negotiating an equitable adjustment may be costly and time consuming without promise of a better result. In this case, however, the Board finds that the best estimate of the equitable adjustment due the Company is the $300 that Mr. Coffey testified he intended to use for item B-15.

(e) Waiver of Buy American Act

Under certain circumstances, the government may waive the application of the Buy American Act, 41 U.S.C. § 10. Although such waivers should ordinarily occur before the contract is awarded, they are sometimes made after award. In such cases, the question has arisen as to whether the government is entitled to a price adjustment when the waiver is based on the cost of the domestic material being unreasonably higher than the foreign material. In some cases the government has been granted a reduction on the theory that without the waiver the contractor would have been obligated to furnish the higher priced domestic material. However, see *L.G. Lefler, Inc. v. United States*, 6 Cl. Ct. 514 (1984), *aff'd*, 801 F.2d 387 (Fed. Cir. 1986), in which the court denied an equitable adjustment decreasing the price by the difference between the domestic and foreign prices of materials. The court found that the contractor had used the foreign costs in its bid and had thus incurred no cost reductions from a government waiver of the Buy American Act. The reasoning of the court was based on the determination that the waiver would not have given the contractor a competitive advantage since it would have been the low bidder even without the waiver.

b. Pricing the Added Work

The other element of the basic pricing formula is the cost of the added work. Unless there is a cost increase, the contractor is not entitled to an equitable adjustment, *Lectro Magnetics, Inc.*, ASBCA 15971, 73-2 BCA ¶ 10,112. In *United States v. Callahan Walker Constr. Co.*, 317 U.S. 56 (1942), the Court stated at 61:

> An "equitable adjustment" of the [contractor's] additional payment for extra work involved merely the ascertainment of the cost of digging, moving, and placing earth, and the addition to that cost of a reasonable and customary allowance for profit.

This case established the principle that the goal of the parties is to establish the cost that the contractor has incurred if the work was completed or would incur if the work had not yet been performed at the time of pricing the adjustment. Thus, if the parties price the change before the work has been accomplished, estimates of the increased cost will form the basis of the adjustment. If the work has been performed, the additional cost will be based on the costs incurred for the added work, if they can be ascertained. If not, estimates will be used. In all cases, the incurred cost or estimated cost must meet the test of reasonableness, as discussed below.

2. Cost Impact on Contractor

The proper measure of an equitable adjustment is the reasonable cost impact on the contractor. Attempts to measure the adjustment by market value of the work or by the costs that would have been incurred by other contractors are generally rejected. See *Bruce Constr. Corp. v. United States*, 163 Ct. Cl. 97, 324 F.2d 516 (1963), stating at 100-01:

> [W]e are called upon only to decide the narrow question whether "cost" or "fair market value" controls in the award of an equitable adjustment.

> Equitable adjustments in this context are simply corrective measures utilized to keep a contractor whole when the Government modifies a contract. Since the purpose underlying such adjustments is to safeguard the contractor against increased costs engendered by the modification, it appears patent that the measure of damages cannot be the value received by the Government, but must be more closely related to and contingent upon the altered position in which the contractor finds himself by reason of the modification. We held this view in the early case of *James McFerran v. United States*, 39 Ct. Cl. 441 (1904).
>
> * * *
>
> Use of the "reasonable cost" measure does not constitute "an objective and universal procedure, involving the determination of the reasonable value (or reasonable cost of any contractor similarly situated) of the work involved"; but determination of reasonable cost requires, in and of itself, an objective test. The particular situation in which a contractor found himself at the time the cost was incurred, *Appeal of Wyman-Gordon Co.*, ASBCA 5100 (1959) and the exercise of the contractor's business judgment, *Appeal of Walsh Construction Co.*, ASBCA 4014 (1957), are but two of the elements that may be examined before ascertaining whether or not a cost was "reasonable."
>
> But the standard of reasonable cost "must be viewed in the light of a *particular* contractor's costs . . . ," and not the universal, objective determination of what the cost would have been to other contractors at large (emphasis added).

See also *Ensign-Bickford Co.*, ASBCA 6214, 60-2 BCA ¶ 2817, where a contractor's costs were used in pricing the equitable adjustment even though another contractor had implemented the same change at substantially lower costs, and *Mit-Con, Inc.*, ASBCA 43021, 92-1 BCA ¶ 24,632, where the cost paid to a vendor was included in an equitable adjustment even though the government submitted evidence that other vendors would have charged less.

a. *Incurrence of Costs*

By their very nature, estimates are based on predictions of the costs of events that might or might not occur. Thus, where price adjustments are based on estimates, the question of incurred costs does not arise. However, when the pricing takes place after the work has been performed, the issue of what constitutes an incurred cost arises. In most cases, it will be determined that a contractor's cost has been increased when it makes increased payments or incurs increased obligations as a result of the change. However, in cases where the contractor's liability is contingent, costs may not be considered to have been incurred. See, for example, *SAB Constr., Inc. v. United States*, 66 Fed. Cl. 77 (2005) ("cost" of self-insurance for potential asbestos liability in building renovation contract not incurred and too speculative), and *Akcon, Inc.*, ENGBCA 5593, 90-3 BCA ¶ 23,250 (agreement to pay employee contingent on settlement with the agency not cost incurred). In *Ed*

Goetz Painting Co., DOTCAB 1168, 83-1 BCA ¶ 16,134, *recons. denied*, 83-1 BCA ¶ 16,432, the board considered a case where a terminated contractor's surety arranged for completion of the work, made payments to a successor contractor, and then sued the contractor for indemnification under the bond. The board held that the contractor's liability was contingent on the surety's recovery in the lawsuit, and hence no cost had been incurred. That decision should be contrasted with *Wolfe Constr. Co.*, ENGBCA 5309, 89-3 BCA ¶ 21,122, *clarified*, 89-3 BCA ¶ 22,187, where the amount the contractor had agreed to indemnify the surety was included in the adjustment. The board noted that the obligation was clearly stated in the agreement between the contractor and the surety. The fact that the amount had not yet been paid was not critical. A somewhat similar rationale was used in *Cottrell Eng'g Corp.*, ENGBCA 3038, 70-2 BCA ¶ 8462, in which the board permitted a contingency factor for the contractor's potential liability resulting from the performance of hazardous work. By contrast, the board in *C.F. Bean Corp.*, ENGBCA 4537, 86-3 BCA ¶ 19,283, refused to include a contingency for weather in an adjustment being made after the work was accomplished. In addition to distinguishing *Cottrell*, the board indicated that it had "considerable doubt" whether it would reach the same conclusion if it were deciding *Cottrell*. See also *Historical Servs., Inc.*, DOTCAB 73-1, 72-2 BCA ¶ 9729, *recons. denied*, 73-1 BCA ¶ 9870, in which the board denied an equitable adjustment although a constructive change had been found where the government directed the contractor to furnish previously made movie masters that the contractor could use only with government approval. The board held that no equitable adjustment was called for since no cost had been incurred as a result of the government's action.

The "incurred cost" problem was also encountered in *Winston Bros. Co. v. United States*, 198 Ct. Cl. 37, 458 F.2d 49 (1972). There, the contractor sought recovery for equipment lost in a cave-in caused by a deficient government-designed bolt. The court refused to allow recovery, reasoning that, since the item was covered by insurance, the contractor need not be put in the same position as a contractor claiming unreimbursed "out of pocket" costs. The court concluded that the contractor had suffered no increase in costs, even though the insurer had only "loaned" the contractor the insurance proceeds from the lost equipment. The opposite result was reached in *North Slope Tech., Ltd. v. United States*, 27 Fed. Cl. 425 (1992), in which the court permitted the contractor to sue for the costs resulting from defective specifications, distinguishing *Winston* on the ground that there the contract had required the insurance, while in *North Slope* the contract contained no such requirement. In *North Slope*, the suit was brought on behalf of the insurance company that had paid for the loss. See *Sturm Craft Co.*, ASBCA 27477, 83-1 BCA ¶ 16,454, *recons. denied*, 83-2 BCA ¶ 16,683, in which the board refused to include a cost for "warranty exposure" in a contract modification—apparently because the estimated amount requested was not reasonable. Compare *Gilles & Cotting, Inc.*, GSBCA 5754, 83-1 BCA ¶ 16,480, permitting the inclusion of an amount for an unincurred warranty risk.

b. Value Measures

Under *Bruce*, it is firmly established that cost, not value, is the normal measure of an equitable adjustment. See, for example, *Montoya Constr. Co.*, ASBCA 34691, 89-1 BCA ¶ 21,575, in which the board limited an equitable adjustment to the actual costs incurred by the contractor, commenting that value to the government is not the proper measure. However, in some cases, a contractor's costs may be increased by a change even though it makes no additional expenditure or incurs no additional obligation. Costs are considered to be incurred when the contractor is deprived of something of value. In *Norcoast Constructors, Inc.*, ASBCA 12751, 72-2 BCA ¶ 9699, *aff'd*, 201 Ct. Cl. 695, 477 F.2d 929 (1973), the contractor was entitled to an equitable adjustment for the value of several storage tanks taken by the government. The government had argued that the contractor's costs were not increased by its actions. However, the board reasoned that if the contractor had been permitted to dispose of the tanks, it could have credited the proceeds to the contract, thereby reducing the contract costs. See also *Norcoast-Beck Aleutian (JV)*, ASBCA 21900, 80-1 BCA ¶ 14,328, *recons. denied*, 80-2 BCA ¶ 14,592, in which the board held that the contractor was entitled to recover the "reasonable value" of aggregate that it had stockpiled from previous contracts and used in performance of the current contract after the government failed to provide necessary material. Similarly, in *Xplo Corp.*, DOTCAB 1409, 86-3 BCA ¶ 19,280, the contractor recovered the decrease in value of scrap from demolition work under the contract that was attributable to government delay. Compare *SAE Am.*, PSBCA 3866, 00-1 BCA ¶ 30,867, denying recovery for the value of rock that could have been sold but for the change on the grounds that this was "too remote and speculative." In *S.W. Aircraft, Inc. v. United States*, 213 Ct. Cl. 206, 551 F.2d 1208 (1977), the court held that an insured contractor could recover the market value of destroyed property when the contract placed the risk of loss on the government and the government had not "paid" for the insurance. Compare *JEM Dev. Corp.*, DOTBCA 1961, 88-3 BCA ¶ 21,022, in which the board rejected the use of a value measurement when a contractor lost a sale of scrap when the government deleted demolition work from a contract. The board agreed that value was the theoretically correct measure but held that a more equitable adjustment was the lost sale price for the scrap where the contractor had negotiated the sale during the bidding process and had deducted that amount from its bid to the government.

While catalog or market prices of the items for which the adjustment is made would appear to be the appropriate measure in some instances, the *Bruce* case may appear to limit their use. In *Software Designs, Inc.*, ASBCA 23616, 82-2 BCA ¶ 16,073, *recons. denied*, 83-1 BCA ¶ 16,260, the board stated at 79,740:

> Catalog prices are an indication of fair market value of ordered supply items but the usually accepted method of determining an equitable adjustment is based on reasonable incurred cost, not fair market value. *Bruce Construction Corp. v. United States*, 163 Ct. Cl. 97, 324 F.2d 516 (1963).

> Absent a stipulation we cannot, at this juncture, determine that the Government is obligated to compensate [the contractor] at the stated catalog prices for the four additional accounting features. The catalog prices may ultimately be found acceptable as a basis for determining the compensation due but the Government is only obligated to compensate [the contractor] for the reasonable cost of producing and delivering these features plus a reasonable profit thereon. Accordingly, the Government is entitled to scrutinize the calculations relied upon by [the contractor] to arrive at the amounts claimed for the four accounting features for which [the contractor] is entitled to be compensated.

Compare *Koll Constr. Co. v. General Servs. Admin.*, GSBCA 12306, 94-1 BCA ¶ 26,501, *recons. denied,* 94-2 BCA ¶ 26,599, and *Mit-Con, Inc.*, ASBCA 43021, 92-1 BCA ¶ 24,632, in which list prices were held to be the best measure of the cost of deleted work.

Another case dealing with the use of a value measure is *Coley Props. Corp. v. United States*, 219 Ct. Cl. 227, 593 F.2d 380 (1979). There, the court held that the contractor was not entitled to an equitable adjustment for the rents that it did not receive during periods of delay because the Changes clause covered extra out-of-pocket expenses but not economic detriment such as production of income.

c. Allowable Costs

Costs used in determining equitable adjustments are generally required to meet the allowability standards of the Cost Principles. Prior to 1970, fixed-price contracts did not incorporate provisions governing allowability of costs. Thus, in equitable adjustments under fixed-price contracts, contractors were previously permitted to recover types of cost that were unallowable under the Cost Principles used for cost-reimbursement contracts. See, e.g., *Joseph Bell v. United States*, 186 Ct. Cl. 189, 404 F.2d 975 (1968) (interest), and *Luzon Stevedoring Corp.*, ASBCA 11650, 68-2 BCA ¶ 7193, *recons. denied*, 69-1 BCA ¶ 7545 (entertainment, contributions, advertising). However, in the early 1970s, the government adopted a Pricing of Adjustments clause making the Cost Principles applicable to fixed-price contracts. This clause was used by all agencies until 1984, when the FAR was issued without the prescription of this clause. Subsequently, some agencies included the clause in their FAR supplements. See DFARS 252.243-7001 (setting forth a mandatory Pricing of Contract Modifications clause for the Department of Defense); NFS 1852.231-70 (National Aeronautics & Space Administration); GSAR 552.243-70 (General Services Administration); HHSAR 352.270-4 (Department of Health and Human Services); and United States Postal Procurement Manual B.2.1. Other agencies may use the clause in selected contracts. See, for example, *Hardrives, Inc.*, IBCA 2319, 94-1 BCA ¶ 26,267 (clause used in contract of Bureau of Reclamation of Department of Interior). The clause used by the Department of Defense reads:

> Pricing of Contract Modifications
>
> When costs are a factor in any price adjustment pursuant under this contract, the contract cost principles and procedures in FAR Part 31 and DFARS Part 231, in effect on the date of this contract, apply.

Thus, some agencies expressly make the allowability of cost rules applicable to modifications of fixed-price contracts. FAR 31.201-2 provides that, to be allowable, a cost must meet all of the following tests:

> 1. Reasonableness.
>
> 2. Allocability.
>
> 3. Standards promulgated by the CAS Board, if applicable, otherwise, generally accepted accounting principles and practices appropriate to the circumstances.
>
> 4. Terms of the contract.
>
> 5. Any limitations set forth in this subpart.

When this type of clause is present, the Cost Principles will be applied to contractors. See *England v. Contel Advanced Sys., Inc.*, 384 F.3d 1372 (Fed. Cir. 2004) (interest); *Servidone Constr. Corp. v. United States*, 931 F.2d 860 (Fed. Cir. 1991) (interest on borrowed funds); and *Blount, Inc.*, ASBCA 41476, 94-2 BCA ¶ 26,807 (interest and claim preparation costs). See, however, *Automation Fabricators & Eng'g Co.*, PSBCA 2701, 90-3 BCA ¶ 22,943, in which the board granted interest following the *Bell* case because the Pricing of Adjustments clause stated that the Cost Principles would be "used as a guide" in pricing equitable adjustments.

Other agencies do not expressly include this allowability requirement in their contracts. However, FAR 31.102 provides:

> The applicable subparts of Part 31 [of the FAR] shall be used in the pricing of fixed-price contracts, subcontracts, and modifications to contracts and subcontracts whenever (a) cost analysis is performed, or (b) a fixed-price contract clause requires the determination or negotiation of costs. However, application of cost principles to fixed-price contracts shall not be construed as a requirement to negotiate agreements on individual elements of cost in arriving at agreement on the total price. The final price accepted by the parties reflects agreement only on the total price. Further, notwithstanding the mandatory use of cost principles, the objective will continue to be to negotiate prices that are fair and reasonable, cost and other factors considered.

It is not clear whether this provision of the regulations will bind contractors to the Cost Principles in pricing equitable adjustments in the absence of express contract language. See *AT&T Techs., Inc.*, DOTBCA 2007, 89-3 BCA ¶ 22,104, *recons.*

denied, 90-1 BCA ¶ 22,380, noting that the provision gives some flexibility but using a cost principle to award pre-contract costs to a contractor. A similar result was reached in *General Dynamics Corp., Pomona Div.*, ASBCA 39500, 92-1 BCA ¶ 24,657, in which the Cost Principles were used to define the allowable costs of defending claims that should be paid to a contractor on fixed-price contracts. See also *Balentine's S. Bay Caterers, Inc.*, DOTBCA 2319, 92-2 BCA ¶ 25,006 (Cost Principles applied to deny attorneys' fees in pricing an equitable adjustment); *Betancourt & Gonzalez, S.E.*, DOTBCA 2785, 96-1 BCA ¶ 28,033 (Cost Principles applied to determine which costs were the costs of prosecuting claims); and *Kelley Martinez*, IBCA 3140, 97-2 BCA ¶ 29,243 (stating that the FAR provision makes the Cost Principles applicable to fixed-price contracts).

3. Subcontract Problems

When a change affects a subcontractor, it is normally expected that the contractor will negotiate an equitable adjustment with the subcontractor and subsequently include that amount in its proposal for equitable adjustment to the government. If it follows reasonable procedures in this process, the government will be bound to accept the amount the contractor negotiated with the subcontractor, *Ensign-Bickford Co.*, ASBCA 6214, 60-2 BCA ¶ 2817 (pricing of added work); *Hammond Constr., Inc.*, NASABCA 06-0290, 93-1 BCA ¶ 25,288 (pricing of deleted work). However, if the procedures followed are not reasonable, the government will not be bound by the negotiation with the subcontractor, *Delco Elecs. Corp. v. United States*, 17 Cl. Ct. 302 (1989), *aff'd*, 909 F.2d 1495 (Fed. Cir. 1990) (only two-thirds of subcontract adjustment included because contractor failed to obtain required cost or pricing data—even though court found that contractor had engaged in "arm's length bargaining"); *Fireman's Fund Ins. Co.*, ASBCA 39666, 91-1 BCA ¶ 23,372 (unreasonable to accept, without analysis, subcontractor estimate of labor hours needed for change); *Sentry Ins., a Mut. Co.*, VABCA 2617, 91-3 BCA ¶ 24,094, *modified on recons.*, 92-3 BCA ¶ 25,147 (unreasonable to accept subcontractor estimate of labor rates that were higher than prevailing rates). Compare *Dawson Constr. Co.*, GSBCA 5364, 82-1 BCA ¶ 15,701, in which the board accepted the contractor's proposed credit based on estimates obtained from subcontractors rather than on government estimates. The board did not address the obligation of the contractor to negotiate these credits with the subcontractors but apparently assumed that they represented the correct price reduction for the deleted work.

The contractor is required to act with reasonable promptness in securing price reductions from subcontractors. In *CRF v. United States*, 224 Ct. Cl. 312, 624 F.2d 1054 (1980), the subcontractor proposed a price reduction of $96,389 for a deductive change, but the contractor took no apparent action until nine months later, on March 6, 1970, when the cost proposal was forwarded to the government with a request for an audit. The government completed the audit on May 27, 1970, and furnished it to the contractor on August 6, 1970. But on August 11, 1970, the subcontractor declared bankruptcy, and the contractor was unable to secure a reduction. The Court of Claims affirmed the Armed Services Board of Contract Appeals, holding that the contractor's failure to obtain the reduction was due to its own avoidable delay. Thus, the government was entitled to the price reduction.

There are two unique problems that arise when changes affect subcontractors. First, there are legal rules pertaining to the ability of the contractor to recover from the government on behalf of its subcontractors. Second, there are problems when the subcontract does not contain a clause calling for an equitable adjustment.

a. Claims by Subcontractors in Contractor's Name

Since subcontractors generally have no privity of contract with the government, their claims against the government must be brought in the name of the contractor. In such cases, the question often arises whether the suit can be maintained if the contractor is not obligated to the subcontractor. See *Severin v. United States*, 99 Ct. Cl. 435 (1943), *cert. denied*, 322 U.S. 744 (1944), in which the court denied recovery because the subcontract contained a provision exculpating the contractor from liability to the subcontractor for damages resulting from government actions. The precise meaning of the *Severin* doctrine has been difficult to ascertain. In *Severin* and in *Pearson, Dickerson, Inc. v. United States*, 115 Ct. Cl. 236 (1950), the decisional language appeared to clearly state a damages rule—that the contractor had to prove liability to the subcontractor as a prerequisite to recovery. This view was partially confirmed in *Gardner Displays Co. v. United States*, 171 Ct. Cl. 497, 346 F.2d 585 (1965), in which the court stated that "actual damage to the prime is a prerequisite to recovery either for himself or for those subordinate to him." However, in that case the court permitted recovery without proof of such damage where the subcontract did not negate liability but was silent on the subject. Later cases indicate that the doctrine will apply only when the government can prove that the subcontract contained a clause exculpating the contractor from liability, *Southern Constr. Co. v. United States*, 176 Ct. Cl. 1339, 364 F.2d 439 (1966); *Folk Constr. Co. v. United States*, 2 Cl. Ct. 681 (1983); *George Hyman Constr. Co. v. United States*., 30 Fed. Cl. 170 (1993), *aff'd*, 39 F.3d 1197 (Fed. Cir. 1994); *E.R. Mitchell Constr. Co. v. Danzig*, 175 F.3d 1369 (Fed. Cir. 1999).

The *Severin* doctrine does not apply to releases that provide that the contractor will only be liable to the subcontractor if the government is found liable for the claimed event. See *J.L. Simmons Co. v. United States*, 158 Ct. Cl. 393, 304 F.2d 886 (1962); *Kentucky Bridge & Dam, Inc. v. United States*, 42 Fed. Cl. 501 (1998); and *W.G. Yates & Sons Constr. Co. v. Caldera*, 192 F.3d 987 (Fed. Cir. 1999).

It has been held that the *Severin* doctrine does not apply to claims for equitable adjustments under the Changes clause, *Blount Bros. Constr. Co. v. United States*, 172 Ct. Cl. 1, 348 F.2d 471 (1965); *Morrison-Knudsen Co.*, ASBCA 4929, 60-2

BCA ¶ 2799, *remanded on other grounds*, 170 Ct. Cl. 712, 345 F.2d 535 (1965); *F.E. Constructors*, ASBCA 25784, 82-1 BCA ¶ 15,780; *Robert H. O'Hair & O'Hair Constr. Co. (JV)*, AGBCA 82-115-1, 89-1 BCA ¶ 21,384; *Jordan-DeLaurenti, Inc.*, ASBCA 45467, 94-3 BCA ¶ 27,031; or the Differing Site Conditions clause, *Ball, Ball & Brosamer, Inc.*, IBCA 2841, 97-1 BCA ¶ 28,897; *Turner Constr. Co.*, ASBCA 25602, 87-3 BCA ¶ 20,192; *Tutor-Saliba-Perini*, PSBCA 1201, 87-2 BCA ¶ 19,775, *aff'd*, 847 F.2d 842 (Fed. Cir. 1998). This rule also applies to claims under the Suspension of Work clause, *J.R. Roberts Corp.*, DOTBCA 2499, 98-1 BCA ¶ 29,680; *Atlantic States Constr., Inc. v. Hand*, 892 F.2d 1530 (11th Cir. 1990); *CWC, Inc.*, ASBCA 26432, 82-2 BCA ¶ 15,907. See, however, *George Hyman Constr. Co. v. United States*, 30 Fed. Cl. 170 (1993), *aff'd*, 39 F.3d 1197 (Fed. Cir. 1994), in which the court applied the *Severin* doctrine to a case that appeared to be a claim for constructive changes, without discussing this exception to the rule. See also *Metric Constructors, Inc. v. United States*, 314 F.3d 578 (Fed. Cir. 2002), limiting this rule if the subcontractor releases the contractor from liability in clear terms that include liability under contract clauses.

b. Lack of Equitable Adjustment Clause

Where the effect of a change is to reduce the costs of the subcontractor, the contractor may be liable to the government even though it is unable to obtain a price reduction from the subcontractor, *Edward R. Marden Corp.*, ASBCA 10725, 65-2 BCA ¶ 5204. It is the contractor's responsibility to include provisions in its subcontracts to protect itself in such cases, *A. Du Bois & Son, Inc.*, ASBCA 4063, 58-2 BCA ¶ 1879. On the other hand, if the contractor's inability to obtain a price reduction from the subcontractor occurs because of subcontract clauses that are reasonable in the circumstances, the contractor will not be liable to the government. In *Varo, Inc. v. United States*, 212 Ct. Cl. 432, 548 F.2d 953 (1977), the government eliminated certain tests on the lamps in the searchlights being procured and sought a price reduction from the contractor based on the costs of the eliminated tests. In reversing a board of contract appeals decision in favor of the government, the court, quoting from the trial judge's opinion, stated at 442-43:

> The evidence before the Board showed that the changes in the lamp specification previously mentioned did not have any effect on Varo's costs in performing its searchlight contract with the Army. Before the changes were made, Varo had entered into a subcontract with Hanovia under which the latter was to manufacture and supply to Varo, at a fixed price, xenon lamps that "qualified" under the lamp specification. The subcontract price was firm, and it covered the testing by Hanovia of lamps to ensure that they possessed the essential electrical characteristics. Thus, Varo's costs involved in procuring the lamps from Hanovia were not reduced by reason of the Army's action in reducing the number of lamps that had to be tested for electrical characteristics.
>
> On the other hand, since the original requirements that every lamp be tested for electrical characteristics was relaxed by the Army to the extent that only four

of the 270 lamps involved in the searchlight contract had to be tested by Hanovia, this change did reduce to some extent Hanovia's costs in testing lamps for electrical characteristics under the subcontract from Varo. On this point, the Board made a factual finding "that elimination of 266 tests resulted in a cost saving to Hanovia of $7,118.16 (266 x the $26.76 per lamp actual cost as performed by Hanovia)."

In discussing the problem of whether, under the circumstances, the Government was entitled to an equitable adjustment downward in the contract price, the Armed Services Board of Contract Appeals said:

> * * * Where work or material is deleted regardless of who is to perform the work or supply the material, there is a presumption that the prime contractor will benefit by the saving. If the prime contractor has made subcontracts which unreasonably frustrate the Government's right to obtain such savings via the contractual chain, this is a problem which the prime contractor must solve on his own. * * *

The Board concluded its consideration of ASBCA No. 16087 by deciding that the Government was entitled to a reduction of $7,118.16 in the contract price, this being the amount by which (according to the Board's finding) Hanovia's costs of performing its subcontract with Varo were reduced as a result of the Army's action in reducing the number of lamps to be tested for electrical characteristics from 270 to four.

However, the "presumption that the prime contractor will benefit by the saving" involved in a contractual change was overcome in this instance by evidence before the Board showing that Varo, the prime contractor, did not benefit from the reduction in Hanovia's costs of performing the subcontract.

B. Damages

There have been relatively few cases holding that the government has breached a procurement contract, because most contractor claims for additional compensation fall within contract clauses granting price adjustments, and the Termination for the Convenience of the Government clause is applicable to almost all instances where the government ends contract performance prior to completion (see Chapter 11). However, there is guidance on the computation and recoverability of damages in an increasing number of cases where the government has breached nonprocurement contracts.

1. *Similarity to Equitable Adjustment*

Virtually all procurement contracts contain clauses calling for equitable adjustment of the contract price if the government is responsible for performance that deviates from that originally called for. In most instances, the measure of damages for breach of contract would be essentially the same as that for a claim for a price adjustment under one of these clauses. See, for example, *William Green Constr. Co.*

v. United States, 201 Ct. Cl. 616, 477 F.2d 930, *cert. denied*, 417 U.S. 909 (1974), in which the court stated at 626-27:

> Lastly, we are told that an equitable adjustment of the convenience-termination type does not give full enough relief for the injuries suffered, and therefore [the contractors] should be allowed to seek, through this court, the part of the remedy which the administrative award cannot give them. The answer is that the premise is incorrect. "The only substantial difference between the sum calculated under" equitable adjustment or convenience-termination standards "and the amount recoverable in a common law action for contract breach is the non-inclusion in the former of anticipated but unearned profits." *Nolan Brothers, Inc. v. United States, supra*, 186 Ct. Cl. at 607, 405 F.2d at 1253. This exclusion from relief of unearned profits is a settled policy which has long been accepted and enforced. 186 Ct. Cl. at 608-09, 405 F.2d at 1254-55; *General Builders Supply Co. v. United States, supra*, 187 Ct. Cl. at 485-86, 409 F.2d at 251; *G.C. Casebolt Co. v. United States, supra*, 190 Ct. Cl. at 788, 421 F.2d at 713. And even in a common-law suit there would be no recovery for general loss of business, the claimed loss of the entire [contractor] net worth, and losses on the non-federal work—such damages are all deemed too remote and consequential. *See Ramsey v. United States*, 121 Ct. Cl. 426, 433-35, 101 F. Supp. 353, 357-58 (1951), *cert. denied*, 343 U.S. 977 (1952); *Dale Constr. Co. v. United States*, 168 Ct. Cl. 692, 738 (1964); *Specialty Assembly & Packing Co. v. United States*, 174 Ct. Cl. 153, 175, 355 F.2d 554, 567-68 (1966). The conclusion must be that the administrative remedy is, as we have already said, a full and permissible substitute for the award of damages under the former "breach" claim.

The same result would generally occur in defective specification situations. Most of these cases are treated as constructive changes resulting in equitable adjustment pricing. See, however, *Luria Bros. & Co. v. United States*, 177 Ct. Cl. 676, 369 F.2d 701 (1966), and *Big Chief Drilling Co. v. United States*, 26 Cl. Ct. 1276 (1992), in which the court treated a defective specification as a breach and computed damages incurred in the same manner that an equitable adjustment would be calculated. Compare *Edward R. Marden Corp. v. United States*, 194 Ct. Cl. 799, 442 F.2d 364 (1971), where the damages for a defective specification included the costs the contractor had incurred in paying for the injury and death of workers that occurred because of the defective specifications—a type of cost that might have been questionable under equitable adjustment theory. See also *Quality Diesel Engines, Inc. v. Department of Commerce*, GSBCA 11672-COM, 93-3 BCA ¶ 25,953, computing damages for extra work done pursuant to government direction in the way that an equitable adjustment would have been determined.

Damages that are similar to an equitable adjustment have also been awarded when the government breaches a requirements contract by providing a negligent estimate of the quantities of work. See *Rumsfeld v. Applied Cos.*, 325 F.3d 1328 (Fed. Cir.), *cert. denied*, 540 U.S. 981 (2003), in which the damages were computed by adjusting the prices of the work ordered to reflect the prices that would have been offered had the lesser quantities been used to do the original pricing. Compare

Hi-Shear Tech. Corp. v. United States, 356 F.3d 1372 (Fed. Cir. 2004), in which the court affirmed the lower court's award of fixed overhead plus G&A expenses on that overhead for the products that had not been ordered. The court agreed that the amount of work not ordered should be calculated based on a correct estimate of the requirements, not the faulty estimate in the contract. The court also stated that no profit should be added to the damages because under *Applied Cos.* lost profit is not a proper element of the damages.

The courts sometimes refer to "damages" when dealing with an adjustment under the contract. See *Joseph Pickard's Sons Co. v. United States*, 209 Ct. Cl. 643, 532 F.2d 739 (1976), and *Inland Container, Inc. v. United States*, 206 Ct. Cl. 478, 512 F.2d 1073 (1975).

The major distinction between a price adjustment under a contract clause and a suit for damages for a breach of contract is that the Cost Principles for determining allowable cost do not appear to be applicable to a suit for damages. See *Meva Corp. v. United States*, 206 Ct. Cl. 203, 511 F.2d 548 (1975), in which the court computed the overhead portion of a damages claim on the basis of a jury verdict determination rather than an accounting computation under the Cost Principles.

2. *Methods of Computing Damages*

There are three methods used to determine the damages a party has suffered when the other party breaches the contract. See *Restatement, Second, Contracts* § 344, stating:

> Judicial remedies under the rules stated in this Restatement serve to protect one or more of the following interests of a promisee:
>
> (a) his "expectation interest," which is his interest in having the benefit of his bargain by being put in as good a position as he would have been in had the contract been performed,
>
> (b) his "reliance interest," which is his interest in being reimbursed for loss caused by reliance on the contract by being put in as good a position as he would have been in had the contract not been made, or
>
> (c) his "restitution interest," which is his interest in having restored to him any benefit that he has conferred on the other party.

a. Expectancy Damages

The primary method of computing damages is to base them on the "expectancy interest." See Comment a. to *Restatement, Second, Contracts* § 344, stating:

> Ordinarily, when a court concludes that there has been a breach of contract, it enforces the broken promise by protecting the expectation that the injured party has when he made the contract. It does this by attempting to put him in as good a position as he would have been in had the contract been performed . . . The interest protected in this way is called the "expectation interest." It is sometimes said to give the injured party the "benefit of the bargain."

There are three requirements for the recovery of such damages: They must be unavoidable, foreseeable, and provable with a degree of certainty. As to *avoidability*, *Restatement, Second, Contracts* § 350 provides that damages are not recoverable if the injured party could have avoided incurring the damages "without undue risk, burden or humiliation." Thus, damages are not recoverable if the government can establish that a contractor could have stopped performing or could have otherwise taken steps to reduce the size of its loss. As to *foreseeability*, *Restatement, Second, Contracts* § 351 requires that damages must be foreseeable to the party in breach. It also provides for the limitation of damages to avoid "disproportionate compensation":

> (1) Damages are not recoverable for loss that the party in breach did not have reason to foresee as a probable result of the breach when the contract was made.
>
> (2) Loss may be foreseeable as a probable result of a breach because it follows from the breach
>
> > (a) in the ordinary course of events, or
> >
> > (b) as a result of special circumstances, beyond the ordinary course of events, that the party in breach had reason to know.
>
> (3) A court may limit damages for foreseeable loss by excluding recovery for loss of profits, by allowing recovery only for loss incurred in reliance, or otherwise if it concludes that in the circumstances justice so requires in order to avoid disproportionate compensation.

As to *certainty*, *Restatement, Second, Contracts* §352 states that "[d]amages are not recoverable for loss beyond an amount that the evidence permits to be established with reasonable certainty." Although this provision focuses on uncertainty of the amount of damages, uncertainty over whether the breach or other factors caused the loss can also defeat a claim.

The principal issue that has arisen with regard to expectancy damages is the recoverability of consequential damages. This is an issue when a contractor on a procurement contract claims that it would have entered into profitable collateral transactions but for the government breach and when a party on a nonprocurement contract claims that the government's breach has deprived it of the opportunity to make a profit on collateral transactions. With regard to breaches of procurement contracts, it has been very difficult to recover such consequential damages because the contractor has been unable to meet the foreseeability and certainty requirements. Lost profits have been denied in *CCM Corp. v. United States*, 15 Cl. Ct. 670 (1988); *H.H.O., Inc. v. United States*, 7 Cl. Ct. 703 (1985); and *Land Movers, Inc.*, ENGBCA 5656, 91-1 BCA ¶ 23,317. Loss of a business opportunity has been denied in *Olin Jones Sand Co. v. United States*, 225 Ct. Cl. 741 (1980); *Cox & Palmer*, ASBCA 37328, 89-3 BCA ¶ 22,197; and *Worsham Constr. Co.*, ASBCA 25907, 85-2 BCA ¶ 18,016. Compensation for the destruction of a business was denied in *Ramsey v. United States*, 121 Ct. Cl. 426, 101 F. Supp. 353 (1951). See also *Northern Helex Co. v. United States*, 207 Ct. Cl. 862, 524 F.2d 707 (1975), *cert. denied*, 429 U.S. 866 (1976), denying recovery of the costs of the operation of its plant after termination by the government to perform non-federal work with its related companies because such costs are too remote, speculative, and consequential. Compare *Data Enter. of the Northwest v. General Servs. Admin.*, GSBCA 15607, 04-1 BCA ¶ 32,539, awarding lost profit on sales that were lost because the government revealed the contractor's proprietary information and software to a competitor. The profit was computed at 70 percent of the lost revenue over the period that the competitor would not have been able to devise the software system but for its use of the proprietary information.

In nonprocurement contracts, there has been a minimal amount of recovery of consequential damages. Contrast *Wells Fargo Bank, N.A. v. United States*, 88 F.3d 1012 (Fed. Cir. 1996), *cert. denied*, 520 U.S. 1116 (1997), denying lost profits when the government breached a contract to guarantee loans, with *Energy Capital Corp. v. United States*, 47 Fed. Cl. 382 (2000), *aff'd*, 302 F.3d 1314 (Fed. Cir. 2002), awarding lost profits when the government breached a contract that permitted the contractor to originate up to $200 million in loans for energy-efficiency improvements for government-assisted housing. The court found in *Wells Fargo* that the profits were remote and uncertain, while it found in *Energy Capital* that the profits had been proved with the requisite certainty and that the foreseeability requirement was satisfied because the profits were an integral part of the undertaking. See also *Neely v. United States*, 152 Ct. Cl. 137, 285 F.2d 438 (1961), in which a lessee of land from the government was held entitled to recover lost profits when the government prohibited it from using the land in the most productive manner. The court concluded that the certainty requirement had been met because the land had later been used for the prohibited purpose. In the numerous cases involving the government's breach of its contracts with savings and loan banks to permit the use of goodwill as an asset (cases following *United States v. Winstar Corp.*, 518 U.S. 839 (1996)), there has been very little recovery of lost profits although *California Fed. Bank v. United States*, 245 F.3d 1342 (Fed. Cir. 2001), *cert. denied*, 534 U.S. 1113 (2002), held that lost profits were not speculative and could be recovered if the contractor could prove them with a reasonable degree of certainty. On remand, 54 Fed. Cl. 704 (2002), *aff'd*, 395 F.3d 1263 (Fed. Cir. 2005), lost profits were denied for lack of foreseeability, certainty, and proof of causation. See also *Bluebonnet Sav. Bank F.S.B. v. United States*, 266 F.3d 1348 (Fed. Cir. 2001), *on remand*, 52 Fed. Cl. 75 (2002), *vacated*, 339 F.3d 1341 (Fed. Cir. 2003), *on remand*, 67 Fed. Cl. 231 (2005), holding that expectancy damages are intrinsically recoverable in these cases, and *Lasalle Talman Bank, F.S.B. v. United States*, 64 Fed. Cl. 90 (2005), awarding a small amount of lost profits on investments that were divested because of the government breach.

In the *Winstar* cases, costs incurred by banks to mitigate the government's breach of the contracts have been awarded in a number of cases. See, for example, *Bluebonnet Sav. Bank, F.S.B. v. United States*, 52 Fed. Cl. 75 (2002), *vacated*, 339 F.3d 1341 (Fed. Cir. 2003), *on remand*, 67 Fed. Cl. 231 (2005) (post-breach actions to mitigate the impact of the breach); *California Fed. Bank v. United States*, 43 Fed. Cl. 445 (1999), *aff'd but rev'd on other issues*, 245 F.3d 1342 (Fed. Cir. 2001), *cert. denied*, 534 U.S. 1113 (2002), *on remand*, 54 Fed. Cl. 704 (2002), *aff'd*, 395 F.3d 1263 (Fed. Cir. 2005) (post-breach actions to replace goodwill taken away by government breach); *Lasalle Talman Bank F.S.B. v. United States*, 64 Fed. Cl. 90 (2005) (post-breach actions in replacing capital in response to government breach); and *Citizens Fed. Bank v. United States*, 66 Fed. Cl. 179 (2005) (transaction costs to restore bank's capital position).

b. Reliance Damages

Reliance damages compensate the injured party for "expenditures made in preparation for performance or in performance, less any loss that the party in breach can prove with reasonable certainty the injured party would have suffered had the contract been performed," *Restatement, Second, Contracts* § 349. Since this measure of damages does not include any profit that would have been derived from the breached contract, it has rarely been chosen by procurement contractors.

This measure of damages is also subject to the rule that the damages must be unavoidable, foreseeable, and provable with a degree of certainty. However, these requirements appear to be most easily met in the *Winstar* situation involving the breach of the government's contracts with savings and loan banks to permit the use of goodwill as an asset. See *Glendale Fed. Bank v. United States*, 239 F.3d 1374 (Fed. Cir. 2001), *on remand*, 54 Fed. Cl. 8 (2002), concluding that "reliance damages provide a firmer and more rational basis" than either expectancy or restitution. The court also concluded that reliance damages could be calculated based on amounts spent by the injured party both before and after the breach by the government. On remand, 54 Fed. Cl. 8 (2002), the court awarded $380,787,000 in reliance damages.

c. Restitutionary Damages

As discussed below, restitution is normally measured by the amount of benefit conferred on the other contracting party. However, when damages are computed using restitutionary theory, it has been stated that the amount of recovery can also be measured by the contractor's costs. See *Acme Process Equip. Co. v. United States*, 171 Ct. Cl. 324, 347 F.2d 509 (1965), *rev'd on other grounds*, 385 U.S. 138 (1966), in which the court of Claims reviewed the rules for recovery of restitution measured by a contractor's costs where the government breached the contract, stating at 359-60:

> The next argument is that [the contractor's] recovery must be limited to the reasonable value of the goods it actually delivered prior to cancellation. It is clear, however, that restitution is permitted as an alternative remedy for breach of contract in an effort to restore the innocent party to its precontract *status quo*, and not to prevent the unjust enrichment of the breaching party. "Judgment will be given for the value of service * * * rendered, even though the product created thereby has been lost or destroyed by the [government], and *even though there never was any product created by the service that added to the wealth of the [Government]*." Restatement, Contracts § 348, Comment "a" (emphasis added). It is when the [contractor] is the party in default that his recovery may be limited by the amount of the benefit to the [government]. See *Schwasnick v. Blandin*, 65 F.2d 354, 357 (C.A. 2, 1933). But "if the promisee has performed so far as he has gone, and the promisor breaks his promise, the promisee may abandon the contract and sue for restitution, in which he can recover the reasonable value of his services, measured by what he could have got for them in the market, and not by their benefit to the promisor." *Ibid.* See, also, Restatement, Contracts § 347, Comment "c." [The contractor's] recovery is not limited to the value of the goods received by the Government under the contract; rather, it can be based on the reasonable value of the entire performance.
>
> [The contractor's] position is that the reasonable value of its services is most accurately reflected by the actual costs it incurred in the performance of Contract 1213. As the best means of restoring the *status quo ante*, cost of performance is often used as the basis for determining the amount of *quantum meruit* recovery, in the absence of "any challenging evidence." *United States ex rel. Susi Contracting Co. v. Zara Contracting Co.*, 146 F.2d 606, 611 (C.A. 2, 1944); see, also, *United States ex rel. Arc & Gas Welder Associates, Inc. v. Blount*, 182 F. Supp 648, 665 (D. Md.), *aff'd*, 285 F.2d 863 (C.A. 4, 1960), *cert. denied*, 366 U.S. 919 (1961); *United States ex rel. Wander v. Brotherton*, 106 F. Supp. 353, 354-55 (S.D.N.Y. 1952). But if the [Government] is able to show that the costs incurred by the contractor were excessive (as a result, for example, of inefficiency or extravagance), the amount of recovery is commensurately reduced. *Cf. Barrett Co. v. United States*, 273 U.S. 227, 235 (1927); *United States v. Behan*, 110 U.S. 338, 345-46 (1884).

This measurement of restitutionary damages is essentially the same as the measurement of reliance damages. See *Restatement, Second, Contracts* § 373, stating that restitution encompasses "any benefit that he has conferred on the other party by way of part performance or reliance." See also *Lasalle Talman Bank F.S.B. v. United States*, 45 Fed. Cl. 64 (1999), *aff'd in part, vacated in part*, 317 F.3d 1363 (Fed. Cir. 2003), arguing that, in spite of *Acme*, restitution does not include reliance damages that do not confer a benefit on the breaching party.

The restitutionary measure of damages is rarely used in procurement contracts because no profit is included and benefit is difficult to prove. However, it has been argued in the *Winstar* situation involving the breach of the government's contracts with savings and loan banks to permit the use of goodwill as an asset. In *Glendale Fed. Bank v. United States*, 239 F.3d 1374 (Fed. Cir. 2001), *on remand*, 54 Fed. Cl. 8 (2002), and *California Fed. Bank v. United States*, 245 F.3d 1342 (Fed. Cir. 2001), *cert. denied*, 534 U.S. 1113 (2002), *on remand*, 54 Fed. Cl. 704 (2002), *aff'd*, 395 F.3d 1263 (Fed. Cir. 2005), the court rejected restitution measuring the amount of the benefit conferred on the government because it was too speculative. However, in *Landmark Land Co. v. Federal Deposit Ins. Corp.*, 256 F.3d 1365 (Fed. Cir. 2001), the court approved the award of the amount the bank had contributed when it entered into the contract with the government (assuming the obligations of a failed savings and loan bank). See *Hansen Bancorp, Inc. v. United States*, 367 F.3d 1297 (Fed. Cir. 2004), providing additional guidance on the computation of restitutionary damages. See also *Mobil Oil Exploration & Prod. Southeast, Inc. v. United States*, 530 U.S. 604 (2000), *on remand*, 236 F.3d 1313 (Fed. Cir. 2000), giving a lessee restitutionary damages in the amount of the payments it had made on the leases without regard to whether profits would have been earned, and *La Van v. United States*, 56 Fed. Cl. 580 (2003), giving investors that made required contributions to a savings and loan that had been taken over by a solvent bank restitutionary damages in the amount of their investment.

C. Quantum Meruit

If the contractor has conferred a benefit on the government, without the presence of an express contract, recovery can sometimes be had using the legal theory that there is an implied in fact contract. In such cases the measure of recovery is "quantum meruit."

1. Value Standard

In quantum meruit claims the goal is to compensate the contractor for the value of the benefit conferred on the government, *Restatement, Second, Contracts* § 370. Value can be measured in a number of different ways depending on the circumstances of the case and the information available to the court or board. See *Restatement, Second, Contracts* § 371, giving two primary means of measuring this value:

> (a) the reasonable value to the other party of what he received in terms of what it would have cost him to obtain it from a person in the claimant's position, or
>
> (b) the extent to which the other party's property has been increased in value or his other interest advanced.

See *Barrett Ref. Corp. v. United States*, 242 F.3d 1055 (Fed. Cir. 2001), *on remand*, 50 Fed. Cl. 567 (2001) (market value of oil when express contract was invalid); *United States v. Amdahl Corp.*, 786 F.2d 387 (Fed. Cir. 1986) (market value of the use government made of equipment obtained in invalid contract); *Urban Data Sys., Inc. v. United States*, 699 F.2d 1147 (1983) (market value of supplies and services obtained in invalid contract); and *Cities Serv. Gas Co. v. United States*, 205 Ct. Cl. 16, 500 F.2d 448 (1974) (market value of gas provided to government without a written contract).

2. Value Measured by Contractor's Costs

In spite of the preference for other measures of value, the costs incurred by the contractor are frequently the best indication of the value of the benefit conferred on the government. This can be so when there is no ready means of measuring market value and the costs appear to be reasonable. However, the costs incurred by the contractor are sometimes rejected as the best measure of value. See *Cities Serv. Gas Co. v. United States*, 205 Ct. Cl. 16, 500 F.2d 448 (1974), in which the court stated at 32:

> On the other hand, value determined on a *quantum meruit* basis under an implied in fact contract is not based on costs nor a reasonable return on investment of the seller, but on the reasonable value in the marketplace of the property sold. *See United States v. North American Trans. & Trading Co.*, 253 U.S. 330, 335 (1920); *Campbell v. Tennessee Valley Authority*, 421 F.2d 293, 295-96 (5th Cir. 1969); and *Buffalo & Fort Erie Public Bridge Authority v. United States*, 106 Ct. Cl. 731, 65 F. Supp. 476, 483 (1946); *National Savings & Trust Co. v. Kahn*, 300 F.2d 910 (D.C. Cir. 1962); Costigan, Implied in Fact Contracts and Mutual Assent, 33 Harv. L. Rev. 376 (1920); 3 Corbin, *Contracts*, Sec. 566 (1960).

See also *Chris Craft Indus., Inc. v. United States*, 209 Ct. Cl. 700 (1976). In *Yosemite Park & Curry Co. v. United States*, 217 Ct. Cl. 360, 582 F.2d 552 (1978), the court permitted a quantum meruit recovery for the benefit received by the government under an illegal contract, stating that the recovery was to be measured by the benefit received by the government but limited by the actual costs incurred by the contractor under the illegal contract. The court stated at 375:

> In determining the amount which [the contractor] is entitled to recover, the Trial Judge is instructed that we do not deem the Government to have assented to payment of more than 10 percent of the *total costs of [the contractor's] performance of the contract* nor to reimbursement of federal income taxes, since such assent would have been patently illegal, *see, e.g., W. Penn. Horological Inst., Inc. v. United States*, 146 Ct. Cl. 540 (1959). The amount of [the contractor's] recovery is to be limited accordingly. However, we do determine that [the contractor] is to recover the value of services rendered *both* in providing the equipment (*i.e.*, the costs of ownership, including a reasonable return on money invested in the equipment, fixed costs, etc.) and in operating that equipment (maintenance, fuel, wages, etc.), and that, to the extent the value of [the contractor's] service does not exceed the *entire, total, provable costs* [it] incurred in performance of the Agreement, plus 10 percent, [the contractor] should be able to recover the full reasonable value of these services rendered.

II. PROOF OF ADJUSTMENT

Much of the litigation on the pricing of adjustments focuses on the problems of proof of the amount of the adjustment. The major difficulty in this regard is that many contractors do not account separately for the costs attributable to adjustments—in spite of the fact that the basic pricing theory demands that price adjustments be limited to the effect of the change or delay. Thus, there is much contention about the various methods that can be used to estimate the impact of such changes and delays when precise cost information is not available.

A. Burden of Proof

In establishing the total amount of an equitable adjustment, the burden of proof is allocated to the party that is claiming the benefit of the adjustment. Thus, in *Globe Constr. Co.*, ASBCA 21069, 78-2 BCA ¶ 13,337, *recons. denied*, 80-1 BCA ¶ 14,354, the board stated that the government has the "burden of proving how much downward adjustment should be made for the deleted work and the contractor bears the burden of proving the amount of any upward adjustment to which it may be entitled. *Nager Electric Co. v. United States*, 194 Ct. Cl 835, 442 F.2d 936 (1971)." See also *Victory Constr. Co. v. United States*, 206 Ct. Cl. 274, 510 F.2d 1379 (1975). In fulfilling this burden of proof, the party must establish both the reasonableness of the costs claimed and their causal connection to the alleged event on which the claim is based, *S.W. Elecs. & Mfg. Corp.*, ASBCA 20698, 77-2 BCA ¶ 12,631, *recons. denied*, 77-2 BCA ¶ 12,785, *aff'd*, 228 Ct. Cl. 333, 655 F.2d 1078 (1981). The proper standard to be used in determining whether that burden has been met is the "preponderance of the evidence" test and not "beyond a reasonable doubt," *Teledyne McCormick Selph v. United States*, 214 Ct. Cl. 672, 558 F.2d 1000 (1977).

In *Wunderlich Contracting Co. v. United States*, 173 Ct. Cl. 180, 351 F.2d 956 (1965), the court held that the standard of proof is satisfied if a reasonable basis for computation of the amount is established, stating at 199:

> A claimant need not prove his damages with absolute certainty or mathematical exactitude. *Dale Construction Co. v. United States*, 168 Ct. Cl. 692 (1964); *Houston Ready-Cut House Co. v. United States*, 119 Ct. Cl. 120, 96 F. Supp. 629 (1951). It is sufficient if he furnishes the court with a reasonable basis for computation, even though the result is only approximate. *F.H. McGraw & Co. v. United States*, [131 Ct. Cl. 501, 130 F. Supp. 384 (1955)]; *Locke v. United States*, 151 Ct. Cl. 262, 283 F.2d 521 (1960). Yet this leniency as to the actual mechanics of computation does not relieve the contractor of his essential burden of establishing the fundamental facts of liability, causation and resultant injury. *River Construction Corp. v. United States*, [159 Ct. Cl. 254 (1962)]; *Addison Miller, Inc. v. United States*, 108 Ct. Cl. 513, 70 F. Supp. 893 (1947), *cert. denied*, 332 U.S. 836; *J.D. Hedin Construction Co., Inc. v. United States,* [171 Ct. Cl. at 86-7], 347 F.2d at 246-47. It was [the contractor's] obligation in the case at bar to prove with reasonable certainty the extent of unreasonable delay which resulted from [the Government's] actions and to provide a basis for making a reasonably correct approximation of the damages which arose therefrom. *Aragona Construction Co., Inc. v. United States,* [165 Ct. Cl. 382 (1964)]; *Laburnum Construction Corp. v. United States,* [163 Ct. Cl. 339, 325 F.2d 451 (1963)]. Broad generalities and inferences to the effect that [the Gov-

> ernment] must have caused some delay and damage because the contract took 318 days longer to complete than anticipated are not sufficient. *Commerce International Co., Inc. v. United States,* [167 Ct. Cl. 529, 338 F.2d 81 (1964)].

In ruling on the amount of a claim, boards of contract appeals will decide the matter "de novo"; their deliberations do not consist of a mere review of the contracting officer's final decision. See *Assurance Co. v. United States*, 813 F.2d 1202 (Fed. Cir. 1987), in which the court held that an appeals board can properly award an adjustment less than the amount stated in the decision of a contracting officer from which the appeal was taken. The contractor still bears the burden of proof for an affirmative claim and cannot carry that burden by bringing in "dollar figures bandied about in claim negotiations," since such figures are not normally admissible in quantum litigation, *Systems & Computer Info., Inc.*, ASBCA 18458, 78-1 BCA ¶ 12,946. In that case, the board further held that the mere fact that the contractor's records were unavailable (padlocked by the IRS) did not excuse it from the burden of proof. See also *Schleicher Cmty. Corrs. Ctr., Inc.*, DOTBCA 3046, 02-2 BCA ¶ 32,004, *recons. denied*, 03-1 BCA ¶ 32,136 (claim stated in terms of lost revenue but no proof of added costs). Despite these rules, a number of cases have granted a jury verdict at the amount in the contracting officer's decision, *Freeman Gen., Inc. v. United States*, 918 F.2d 188 (Fed. Cir. 1990), *on remand*, 02-1 BCA ¶ 31,758; *Togaroli Corp.*, ASBCA 32995, 89-2 BCA ¶ 21,864, *recons. denied*, 89-3 BCA ¶ 22,102; or the amount in a prior government estimate, *E. W. Eldridge, Inc.*, ENGBCA 5269, 90-3 BCA ¶ 23,080.

1. Causation

The cost increase or decrease must be caused by the event for which the adjustment is being granted. See, e.g., *Environment Consultants, Inc.*, IBCA 1192-5-78, 79-2 BCA ¶ 13,937, and *J. W. Bateson Co.*, VACAB 1148, 79-1 BCA ¶ 13,573, *recons. denied*, 81-1 BCA ¶ 14,869. In *Southeastern Servs., Inc.*, ASBCA 21278, 78-2 BCA ¶ 13,239, the board stated at 64,756:

> In addition to its essential burden of proving Government fault, the contractor has the burden of establishing the fundamental facts of causation and resultant injury. *Electronic & Missile Facilities, Inc. v. United States*, 189 Ct. Cl. 237, 416 F.2d 1345 (1969); *Wunderlich Contracting Co. v. United States*, 173 Ct. Cl. 180, 351 F.2d 956 (1965). *Cf United States v. Penn Foundry & Mfg. Co.*, 337 U.S. 198 (1949) (proof of lost profits); *Boeing Company v. United States*, 202 Ct. Cl. 315, 480 F.2d 854 (1973) (proof of method of cost allocation).

More recently, in *Delco Elecs. Corp. v. United States*, 17 Cl. Ct. 302 (1989), *aff'd*, 909 F.2d 1495 (Fed. Cir. 1990), the court analogized causation to the concept of allocability of costs, stating at 320:

> Within the legal lexicon of government procurement, the element of causation is, to a certain extent, conceptually akin to the concept of allocability Allowable costs associated with a change caused by government action may be said to be allocable.

There is very little discussion in the decisional law about the acceptable methods of proving causation. However, it appears that there are two aspects to the proof of causation. First, the costs must bear a time relationship to the event on which the adjustment is based. Normally, this is demonstrated by showing that the costs followed the event in a predictable sequence. Second, the costs must be connected logically with the event such that they can be seen to have resulted from its occurrence. If the event has caused the contractor to perform a different type of work than that called for by the original contract, this relationship will easily be established. If the additional work is of the same type as that called for in the original contract, it will be far more difficult to prove causation. See *PCL Constr. Servs., Inc. v. United States*, 47 Fed. Cl. 745 (2000), *aff'd*, 96 Fed. Appx. 672 (Fed. Cir. 2004) (no proof that delay and disruption were caused by government's defective drawings); *Sauer, Inc.*, ASBCA 39605, 01-2 BCA ¶ 31,525 (work allegedly impacted by change not connected to change); *Cooper Mech. Contractors & Continental Eng'g*, IBCA 2744, 92-2 BCA ¶ 24,821 (contractor failed to show that government caused delays); and *Santa Fe Eng'rs, Inc. v. United States*, 818 F.2d 856 (Fed. Cir. 1987) (lack of proof that additional labor hours incurred in contract performance were caused by government-ordered changes).

2. Reasonableness of Amount

In *Bruce Constr. Corp. v. United States*, 163 Ct. Cl. 97, 324 F.2d 516 (1963), it was held that actual ("historical") costs are presumed to be reasonable. See also *Cal Constructors*, ASBCA 21179, 78-1 BCA ¶ 12,992, and *Triple "A" Mach. Shop, Inc.*, ASBCA 21561, 78-1 BCA ¶ 13,065. This presumption was addressed in the Defense Procurement Improvement Act of 1985, Pub. L. No. 99-145, which stated in § 933:

> In a proceeding before the Armed Services Board of Contract Appeals, the United States Claims Court, or any other Federal court in which the reasonableness of indirect costs for which a contractor seeks reimbursement from the Department of Defense is in issue, the burden of proof shall be upon the contractor to establish that such costs are reasonable.

When this provision was implemented, it was applied to all costs. Thus, FAR 31.201-3(a) now states:

> No presumption of reasonableness shall be attached to the incurrence of costs by a contractor. If an initial review of the facts results in a challenge of a specific cost by the contracting officer or the contracting officer's representative, the burden of proof shall be upon the contractor to establish that such cost is reasonable.

This rule has not had any significant impact on the outcome of many cases because they are determined on the basis of the evidence submitted, not presumptions. However, if the contractor enters no evidence, it is likely that the costs will not be considered reasonable. See *Morrison Knudsen Corp. v. Fireman's Fund Ins. Co.*, 175 F.3d 1221 (10th Cir. 1999) (lack of evidence of reasonableness of attorneys' fees and causation of constructive change). Conversely, if the contractor enters evidence of the incurrence of costs and the government enters no evidence, it is likely that the contractor's actual costs will be found to be reasonable, *Green's Indus. Painting*, ASBCA 26569, 82-1 BCA ¶ 15,786.

In determining whether a particular expenditure is reasonable or unreasonable, the contractor's action or inaction in incurring the cost must be examined, *Stanley Aviation Corp.*, ASBCA 12292, 68-2 BCA ¶ 7081. Normally, a contractor has great discretion in performing the work, *Teledyne Indus., Geotech Div.*, ASBCA 18049,73-2 BCA ¶ 10,088; *Hirsch Tyler Co.*, ASBCA 20962, 76-2 BCA ¶ 12,075. Thus, costs will not be determined to be unreasonable unless the contractor has abused this discretion, *DeMauro Constr. Corp*, ASBCA 12514,73-1 BCA ¶ 9830; *Vare Indus.*, ASBCA 12126, 68-2 BCA ¶ 7120; *Canon Constr. Corp.*, ASBCA 15208, 71-1 BCA ¶ 8780. In *Bromley Contracting Co.*, ASBCA 20271, 77-2 BCA ¶ 12,715, the government attempted to establish that the contractor's expenditures were unreasonable. In holding for the contractor, the board stated at 61,749-50:

> The Government contends that [the contractor] could have avoided the overtime and premium wages by doubling its workcrews and renting more power tools and scaffolding. However, the procurement was a total set-aside for mall business companies. The Government usually conducts a preaward survey to ascertain the prospective contractor's ability to perform from the viewpoints of experience, financial capability, facilities and management. No such information was presented to the Board to show [the contractor's] ability so to extend itself in the manner suggested on short notice. At various times [the contractor] was working on one-half of the 13 elevations or sides to the building, using different workcrews, tools and scaffolding for cutting in the granite and limestone areas, which overlapped. [The contractor] had to exercise its best business judgment in organizing and performing the work and no evidence was presented that it did not. The Government made no complaint along these lines during performance.

There appears to be a relaxed standard of reasonableness if a contractor is required to implement changes that demand technical skill beyond that called for by the original contract. See *Delco Elecs. Corp. v. United States*, 17 Cl. Ct. 302 (1989), *aff'd*, 909 F.2d 1495 (Fed. Cir. 1990), stating at 322:

> It has been recognized that a contractor's costs will be considered reasonable in spite of production difficulties and delays where a government change order demands a much higher degree of technical skill and expertise than would have normally been expected under the original contract. This principle was acknowledged by the Supreme Court in the early case of *Carnegie Steel Co. v. United States*, 240 U.S. 156, 36 S. Ct. 342, 60 L. Ed. 576 (1916). There the Court ruled that a contractor delayed by production difficulties in manufacturing steel plate of a quality beyond the current state of the art was not excused, but only because it had specifically undertaken to manufacture such an advanced product, and the production difficulties encountered were foreseeable at the time of award. *Id.* at 164-65.

There are a number of cases finding costs unreasonable. For example, some management decisions have been held to be unreasonable. See *Stewart & Stevenson Servs., Inc.*, ASBCA 43631, 97-2 BCA ¶ 29,252, *recons. denied*, 98-1 BCA ¶ 29,653 (choosing poor suppliers and subcontractors and inefficient organization and management); *Condor Reliability Servs., Inc.*, ASBCA 40538, 90-3 BCA ¶ 23,254 (buying defective components unreasonable when preliminary analysis would have shown defects); and *Stewart Avionics, Inc.*, ASBCA 21361, 78-1 BCA ¶ 13,130 (contractor's decision to produce parts in its own plant was unreasonable because it knew that it could purchase them at a lower cost). Similarly, accepting a subcontractor's estimate without scrutiny has been held unreasonable, *Delco Elecs. Corp. v. United States*, 17 Cl. Ct. 302 (1989), *aff'd*, 909 F.2d 1495 (Fed. Cir. 1990); *Fireman's Fund Ins. Co.*, ASBCA 39666, 91-1 BCA ¶ 23,372. Inefficient methods of performance have also been held unreasonable in *Bruce-Andersen Co.*, ASBCA 31663, 89-3 BCA ¶ 22,013 (using more manpower than necessary); *Southwest Marine, Inc.*, ASBCA 33208, 88-3 BCA ¶ 20,982, *recons. denied*, 89-1 BCA ¶ 21,197 (using less efficient painting method); and *Pennsylvania Drilling Co.*, IBCA 1187-4-78, 82-1 BCA ¶ 15,697 (not using "readily available" industry practices to overcome a differing site condition unreasonable). In *Jets Boiler Servs. GmbH*, ASBCA 24168, 82-2 BCA ¶ 15,934, the board reduced the contractor's actual labor costs to reflect the amount of time that the employees had not properly performed the contract services. Similarly, in *Kelley Martinez*, IBCA 3140, 97-2 BCA ¶ 29,243, unsupported labor and material costs were held unreasonable. See also *Automation Fabricators & Eng'g Co.*, PSBCA 2701, 90-3 BCA ¶ 22,943, in which hiring a consultant to prepare a request for equitable adjustment was held to be unreasonable. Compare *Sage Constr. Co.*, ASBCA 34284, 90-1 BCA ¶ 22,576, *recons. denied*, 90-2 BCA ¶ 22,726, in which hiring a consultant to prove that the government had improperly rejected work was held to be reasonable. If the contractor fails to follow the direction of the contracting officer on the method to accomplish a change, the government may be better able to demonstrate unreasonableness. See *Norcoast-Beck Constructors, Inc.*, ASBCA 25261, 83-1 BCA ¶ 16,435.

B. Methods of Proof

Generally, the contractor is expected to prove its costs by submitting the best available evidence in the circumstances.

1. Actual Cost Data

The preferred method for establishing the amount of the adjustment is through the introduction of actual cost data for the additional work. The boards and courts have regularly underscored this preference, *American Line Builders, Inc. v. United States*, 26 Cl. Ct. 1155 (1992); *Cen-Vi-Ro of Tex. v. United States*, 210 Ct. Cl. 684 (1976); *Cherry Hill Constr., Inc. v. General Servs. Admin.*, GSBCA 12087-REIN, 93-2 BCA ¶ 25,810; *A.O.K. Builders, Inc.*, PSBCA 2389, 89-3 BCA ¶ 22,076; *Buck Brown Contracting Co.*, IBCA 1119-7-76, 78-2 BCA ¶ 13,360; *Engineered Sys., Inc.*, DOTCAB 75-5, 76-2 BCA ¶ 12,211. The preference for actual cost data is highlighted by the requirement that contractors submit "accurate, complete and current" cost or pricing data in support of contract modifications over $550,000.

In some cases, the contractor may be obligated to segregate the cost of changes. See FAR 42.205(f), permitting the use of the following clause set forth in FAR 52.243-6 in construction contracts and supply and research and development contracts of "significant technical complexity":

> CHANGE ORDER ACCOUNTING (APR 1984)
>
> The Contracting Officer may require change order accounting whenever the estimated cost of a change or series of related changes exceeds $100,000. The Contractor, for each change or series of related changes, shall maintain separate accounts, by job order or other suitable accounting procedure, of all incurred segregable, direct costs (less allocable credits) of work, both changed and not changed, allocable to the change. The Contractor shall maintain such accounts until the parties agree to an equitable adjustment for the changes ordered by the Contracting Officer or the matter is conclusively disposed of in accordance with the Disputes clause.

This clause requires a degree of cost accounting that may not be practicable if numerous changes occur. However, if used intelligently, it will assist the parties in determining the cost of a contract modification. See FAR 43.203(b), giving the following guidance on when segregation of costs is expected:

> The following categories of direct costs normally are segregable and accountable under the terms of the Change Order Accounting clause:
>
> (1) Nonrecurring costs (e.g., engineering costs and costs of obsolete or reperformed work).
>
> (2) Costs of added distinct work caused by the change order (e.g., new subcontract work, new prototypes, or new retrofit or backfit kits).
>
> (3) Costs of recurring work (e.g., labor and material costs).

Cost Accounting Standard 405, 48 C.F.R. § 9904.405-40(d), also requires accounting records that will provide "ready separation from the costs of authorized work projects" for the costs of those work projects that are not contractually authorized. Thus, it could be argued that, for contracts subject to Cost Accounting Standards, costs should be segregated for work added as a result of constructive changes and other claims that have not been specifically authorized by the contracting officer.

The Change Order Accounting clause contains no penalty for noncompliance, and it has been held that a contractor is entitled to an equitable adjustment even though it does not comply with the clause, *Harrison W./Franki-Denys,*

ENGBCA 5577, 90-3 BCA ¶ 22,991. The board reasoned that the contractor had conferred a benefit on the government by performing the extra work and that it was therefore entitled to be paid for the benefit. In such cases, it can be expected that the amount of the adjustment will be set at a low level to compensate for the lack of actual cost data.

If the contractor has segregated its costs and submitted them to the government, the costs should be considered in the negotiation, *Texas Instruments, Inc.*, ASBCA 27113, 90-1 BCA ¶ 22,537, *aff'd*, 922 F.2d 810 (Fed. Cir. 1990); *Ocean Tech., Inc.*, ASBCA 21363, 78-1 BCA ¶ 13,204. In *Ford Constr. Co. v. United States*, 202 Ct. Cl. 1133 (1973), the court stated that actual costs may not be thrust aside by calling them the bad name of "total cost approach." See also *R.N.G. Contracting, Inc.*, AGBCA 1999-170-1, 01-2 BCA ¶ 31,579, awarding a percentage of the segregated costs of rock excavation to reflect the rock encountered in a differing site condition; *J.E. Dunn Constr. Co. v. General Servs. Admin.*, GSBCA 14477, 00-1 BCA ¶ 30,806, subtracting the original design costs from its total design costs to compute the costs of redesign; and *South Ga. Cleaning Servs., Inc.*, ASBCA 38546, 93-2 BCA ¶ 25,800, rejecting the government's argument that the use of actual costs was pricing based on total costs. If the actual cost information is available, the contractor's failure to submit the information may preclude its recovery, *Charles D. Weaver v. United States*, 209 Ct. Cl. 714 (1976). See *River/Rd. Constr., Inc.*, ENGBCA 6256, 98-1 BCA ¶ 29,334 (no recovery of labor and equipment costs because contractor did not submit records of daily work performed), and *HOF Constr., Inc. v. General Servs. Admin.*, GSBCA 13317, 96-2 BCA ¶ 28,406 (no recovery when subcontractor submitted no actual cost data such as payroll records, material receipts, or time sheets). Compare *Ramar Co.*, ASBCA 16060, 74-2 BCA ¶ 10,874, where the contractor failed to produce its records but recovered on its claim because the government's estimate was unreasonably low.

In the absence of a contract provision requiring segregation of costs, the decisions are in conflict about whether a contractor is required to segregate its costs. Traditionally, it was generally held that the contractor should not be penalized if its accounting records were not kept in sufficient detail to permit the determination of the precise costs of a change, *Neal & Co. v. United States*, 17 Cl. Ct. 511 (1989); *Keco Indus., Inc.*, ASBCA 15061, 72-1 BCA ¶ 9450, *recons. denied*, 72-2 BCA ¶ 9575; *Central Mech., Inc.*, DOTCAB 1234, 83-2 BCA ¶ 16,642. When there were a large number of changes, the boards found that it was not practicable to segregate the costs of individual changes, *Parsons of Cal.*, ASBCA 20867, 82-1 BCA ¶ 15,659. See *Grumman Aerospace Corp.*, ASBCA 50090, 01-1 BCA ¶ 31,316, *aff'd*, 34 Fed. Appx. 710 (Fed. Cir. 2002), recognizing the difficulty of collecting the costs of a complex claim of a subcontractor and stating at 154,646:

> An early awareness of potential impact is not the same as the ability to collect separately the costs. Similarly, the early engagement of experienced professionals may not guarantee the result. On the other hand, the inability of an experienced

> professional to come up with the data might indicate that it could not reasonably be done. We are not prepared to fully subscribe to [the subcontractor's] claim that it would have had to assign a person to every . . . worker on the production floor and monitor the worker's activities each day. However, we do think there is merit to the view that any type of charging system would have required the individual . . . worker to know what was a change and what was not a change and to record accurately the impact of the [government] changes.

See also *Litton Sys., Inc., Applied Tech. Div.*, ASBCA 49787, 00-2 BCA ¶ 30,969, recognizing that costs are not normally segregated against each paragraph of a specification, and *Neal & Co. v. United States*, 19 Cl. Ct. 463 (1990), *aff'd*, 945 F.2d 385 (Fed. Cir. 1991), stating that it would have been "grossly unfair" for the contract to have required the contractor to keep separate invoices.

In contrast, the Court of Appeals for the Federal Circuit stated a more stringent requirement in *Dawco Constr., Inc. v. United States*, 930 F.2d 872 (Fed. Cir. 1991), in which the court denied an equitable adjustment because the contractor had not segregated the costs of a differing site condition. The court stated that the "issuance of a change order request should signal to the prudent contractor that it must maintain records detailing any additional work, just as should the encountering of differing site conditions." See also *Baifield Indus., Div. of A-T-0, Inc.*, ASBCA 13418, 77-1 BCA ¶ 12,308, *aff'd*, 706 F.2d 320 (Fed. Cir. 1983), stating at 59,455:

> The absence of records supports our findings on entitlement. We cannot conceive that a responsible contractor would knowingly incur losses of millions of dollars, for which it considered the Government to be responsible, without maintaining records of the costs claimed to be the Government's responsibility. (The contractor] kept extensive records but, in support of its quantum claim, has presented none identifying Government responsibility.

The *Dawco* segregation requirement has been followed in a few cases. See *Nav-Com Def. Elecs., Inc.*, ASBCA 50767, 01-2 BCA ¶ 31,546 (board denied claims because contractor did not issue charge numbers for "out-of-scope" costs); *Cavalier Clothes, Inc. v. United States*, 51 Fed. Cl. 399 (2001) (court denied recovery because contractor did not maintain records of changed work); and *River/Rd. Constr., Inc.*, ENGBCA 6256, 98-1 BCA ¶ 29,334 (labor and equipment costs of placing extra stone not placed in the board record). In *Romac, Inc.*, DOTBCA 4028, 01-2 BCA ¶ 31,552, the board denied the claim because the contractor did not segregate the costs of additional work but then, on reconsideration, 02-1 BCA ¶ 31,670, held that there was sufficient evidence to grant a jury verdict for some of the claimed costs.

Actual costs are normally proved through the introduction of the contractor's accounting records. They will be accepted by the boards of contract appeals if they have been audited by the government and are unrebutted, *Celesco Indus., Inc.*, ASBCA 22251, 79-1 BCA ¶ 13,604. However, mere notations on cost accounting records will not constitute proof of incurred costs in the absence of supporting detail, *Mar-Pak Corp.*,

ASBCA 14398, 71-2 BCA ¶ 9034, *aff'd*, 203 Ct. Cl. 718 (1973). Further, the contractor's account titles are not conclusive of the types of cost included in the account, *Todd Shipyards Corp.*, ASBCA 14409,71-2 BCA ¶ 9102. Actual costs may also be established by informal records, *Gary Constr. Co.*, ASBCA 19306, 77-1 BCA ¶ 12,461 (contractor instituted on-site system to record lost time and transcribed on-site notes into longhand), or they can be reconstructed on the basis of testimony of engineering and accounting experts, *Bailey Specialized Bldgs., Inc.*, ASBCA 10576, 71-1 BCA ¶ 8699.

2. Estimates

Estimates are used almost exclusively to establish the cost of deleted work and, in the absence of actual costs, to establish the cost of added work. If actual costs are available, estimates may not be used, *Delco Elec. Corp. v. United States*, 17 Cl. Ct. 302 (1989), *aff'd*, 909 F.2d 1495 (Fed. Cir. 1990); *Omni Contractors, Inc. v. General Servs. Admin.*, GSBCA 13270, 96-2 BCA ¶ 28,405.

Estimates should be supported by detailed, substantiating data. The type of substantiating data that will support an estimate was discussed in *Paccon, Inc.*, ASBCA 7890, 65-2 BCA ¶ 4996, *recons. denied*, 65-2 BCA ¶ 5227, in which the board stated at 23,575-76:

> [The contractor's] estimates were prepared by Mr. McPherson. His estimates were set forth in detailed schedules received in evidence and he testified at length concerning his estimates and was subjected to cross-examination thereon. He also produced at the hearing his work sheets of more than 100 pages.
>
> * * *
>
> [The contractor's] method of computing the increased labor costs was explained in elaborate detail at the hearing, and we are of the opinion that the method used was sound and proper for the intended purpose. The estimates were prepared with care by a competent engineer having adequate knowledge of the facts and circumstances. They are uncontroverted by any other estimates, and the Government was not shown any error in the estimates, except the misplaced decimal which has been corrected. The Government has not advanced any reason we deem valid for questioning the reasonable accuracy of [the contractor's] computation of the increased labor costs caused by the suspensions of work.

See also *Parsons of Cal.*, ASBCA 20867, 82-1 BCA ¶ 15,659, in which the board accepted the contractor's estimates because the estimators were highly competent and some of the estimates were verified by subsequent actual costs.

a. Vague Estimates

Proof requirements are not met by vague evidence, *C W. Stack & Assocs.*, DOT-CAB 72-4, 72-1 BCA ¶ 9313; uncorroborated estimates, *Maryland Painting Co.*,

ENGBCA 3337, 73-2 BCA ¶ 10,223; *Piracci Corp.*, GSBCA 6007, 82-2 BCA ¶ 16,047; or unpersuasive affidavits, *Rice v. United States*, 192 Ct. Cl. 903, 428 F.2d 1311 (1970). Similarly, the government's "ball park" estimate, *Industrial Textile Mills, Inc.*, ASBCA 18163, 73-2 BCA ¶ 10,232, or its unaudited negotiating figure, *Pavement Specialists, Inc.*, ASBCA 17410, 73-2 BCA ¶ 10,082, is generally not adequate. See, however, *Fidelity Constr. Co.*, DOTCAB 1113, 81-2 BCA ¶ 15,345, *aff'd*, 700 F.2d 1379 (Fed. Cir.), *cert. denied*, 464 U.S. 826 (1983), in which the board used a government estimate of what the work should have cost. Estimates are particularly vulnerable if they lack specific factual material concerning performance or are not supported by corroborating data, *Luria Bros. & Co. v. United States*, 177 Ct. Cl. 676, 369 F.2d 701 (1966); *Leopold Constr. Co.*, ASBCA 23705, 81-2 BCA ¶ 15,277; *Harvey-Wells Elecs., Inc.*, ASBCA 6507, 67-2 BCA ¶ 6603; *Algernon Blair, Inc.*, ASBCA 8496,1963 BCA ¶ 3862.

b. Expert Testimony

Expert testimony is often helpful in the presentation of estimates, *Sovereign Constr. Co.*, ASBCA 17792, 75-1 BCA ¶ 11,251; *Turnbull, Inc. v. United States*, 180 Ct. Cl. 1010, 389 F.2d 1007 (1967). However, even uncontradicted testimony of an expert may be rejected if it is unconvincing, *Petro-Chem Mktg. Co. v. United States*, 221 Ct. Cl. 211, 602 F.2d 959 (1979). The best use of expert testimony is to demonstrate the relationship of actual and estimated cost data to the circumstances giving rise to the adjustment. See *Larry Azure v. United States*, 129 F.3d 136 (Fed. Cir. 1997), reversing the Court of Federal Claims' denial of an equitable adjustment because the contractor's expert had made a detailed estimate of equipment and labor costs incurred because of an acceleration. Compare *Pittsburgh-Des Moines Corp.*, EBCA 314-3-84, 89-2 BCA ¶ 21,739, in which the board stated that the opinions of experts are "valid only to the extent that [their] sources are credible and the information relied upon is valid." Mere opinion testimony by experts is given much less weight, *Western Contracting Corp. v. United States*, 144 Ct. Cl. 318 (1958); *Luria Bros. & Co. v. United States*, 177 Ct. Cl. 676, 369 F.2d 701 (1966), and "unsubstantiated and conclusory assertions" of experts will be disregarded, *Roy D. Garren Corp.*, AGBCA 85-196-1, 91-1 BCA ¶ 23,306. See also *Sauer, Inc.*, ASBCA 39605, 01-2 BCA ¶ 31,525 (expert made no independent analysis based on facts); *Hensel Phelps Constr. Co.*, ASBCA 49270, 99-2 BCA ¶ 30,531, *recons. denied*, 00-1 BCA ¶ 30,733, *aff'd*, 13 Fed. Appx. 949 (Fed. Cir. 2001) (testimony of expert unpersuasive because it was not based on analysis of facts of case); *Hemphill Contracting Co.*, ENGBCA 5698, 94-1 BCA ¶ 26,491 (testimony of claims consultant disregarded because it did not tie into actual cost data and contained obvious errors); *Southwest Marine, Inc.*, DOTBCA 1497, 93-3 BCA ¶ 26,170 (computations of expert rejected because they were not based on "contemporaneous records"); and *Cosmic Constr. Co.*, ASBCA 24014, 88-2 BCA ¶ 20,623 (expert testimony disregarded because it was "pure conjecture" not matching the facts). Ordinarily, expert testimony is discounted if the expert is not familiar with the facts of performance. See *B.P.O.A.*,

ASBCA 25276, 82-2 BCA ¶ 15,816, *recons. denied*, 82-2 BCA ¶ 15,924. However, see *A&J Constr. Co.*, IBCA 1142-2-77, 79-1 BCA ¶ 13,621, where the expert had not even seen the site until seven months after the contract work was completed. In giving weight to the expert's testimony, the board cited the government's actions that prevented the expert from making an effective investigation of the work site.

Expert testimony in delay and disruption cases is most effective when the expert allocates the delay between the government and the contractor based on an unbiased assessment of government fault and contractor mismanagement. Thus, expert opinions have been found to be unpersuasive when the expert attributed all delay and disruption to the government when there were facts demonstrating that the contractor had been responsible for some of the problems, *Gulf Contracting, Inc.*, ASBCA 30195, 89-2 BCA ¶ 21,812, *recons. denied*, 90-1 BCA ¶ 22,393, *aff'd*, 23 Cl. Ct. 525 (1991), *aff'd*, 972 F.2d 1353 (Fed. Cir.), *cert. denied*, 506 U.S.999 (1992); *PCL Constr. Servs., Inc. v. United States*, 47 Fed. Cl. 745 (2000), *aff'd*, 96 Fed. Appx. 672 (Fed. Cir. 2004).

Expert testimony of employees of the contractor can be as convincing as testimony of outside experts. See *Illinois Constructors Corp.*, ENGBCA 5827, 94-1 BCA ¶ 26,470, stating at 131,754:

> Ultimately, it is the quality, logic and probativeness of the estimate that is determinative, whether it is prepared by an "outsider" or an "insider." In this case, [the contractor] generally has established the reasonableness of its own estimates as modified and adjusted herein. The fact that most subcontract accounts were impacted is simply a logical consequence of the nature of the subcontracted work and the scope of the [differing site condition]. We have considered the fact that the estimates were internally prepared . . . as an evidentiary matter in assigning weight. However, under the circumstances, it is as accurate a method as was reasonably possible to present. Evidence from knowledgeable, careful, analytical "in-house" estimators is in no way to be considered inferior to or degraded when compared with that from "outside" professional consultants. Sometimes the opposite is true. Individual circumstances stand alone.

However, uncorroborated opinions of the contractor or its employee will not be persuasive even though that person may have substantial experience and expertise. For example, in *Arthur Painting Co.*, ASBCA 20267, 76-1 BCA ¶ 11,894, the government refused to accept the contractor's foreman's estimate of the normal time required to prepare a house for repainting because it was substantially lower than the published estimate of the Painting and Decorating Contractors of America. In contrast, well-documented opinions of "in-house" experts have been accepted. See *Impresa C.E.S.I.C.A.*, ASBCA 25437, 82-1 BCA ¶ 15,656, *recons. denied*, 82-2 BCA ¶ 15,903, in which the board accepted the estimate of the government's "experienced cost estimator" when the contractor's evidence did not prove causation, and *Rohr Indus., Inc.*, ENGBCA 4094, 82-2 BCA ¶ 15,867, in which the board accepted the contractor's estimates as explained by two company cost estimators with "many years' experience" using the company's detailed estimating system. See also *Bath Iron Works Corp.*, ASBCA 44618, 96-2 BCA ¶ 28,475, *aff'd*, 113 F.2d 1256 (Fed. Cir. 1997), accepting the company's estimate of some labor hours caused by a change but rejecting other estimates for failure to prove causation. Similarly, in *Triad Mech., Inc.*, IBCA 3393, 97-1 BCA ¶ 28,771, the board accepted the opinion of the company's project manager and estimator that it had suffered a 25 percent loss of productivity during a period when it added a number of workers to a crowded work site to stay on schedule.

When statistical methods and estimating techniques are used, expert testimony may be required to verify their validity and to demonstrate that they are properly applied. See *Algernon Blair, Inc.*, GSBCA 4072, 76-2 BCA ¶ 12,073, in which the board refused to accept an estimate based on an article that discussed the 10 key factors affecting mechanical estimating because the author did not testify.

c. *Statistical Techniques*

Statistical estimating techniques are often used and are persuasive when based on available actual data and supported by expert testimony. See *Monroe Garment Co.*, ASBCA 14465, 75-2 BCA ¶ 11,569. The learning curve technique is often used, *Rohr Indus., Inc.*, ENGBCA 4094, 82-2 BCA ¶ 15,867; *Ortronix, Inc.*, ASBCA 12745, 72-2 BCA ¶ 9564; *E. W. Bliss Co.*, ASBCA 9489, 68-1 BCA ¶ 6906; *Fairchild Stratos Corp.*, ASBCA 9169, 67-1 BCA ¶ 6225, *recons. denied*, 68-1 BCA ¶ 7053; *Hicks Corp.*, ASBCA 10760, 66-1 BCA ¶ 5469; *M-K-0*, ASBCA 9740, 65-2 BCA ¶ 5288. However, in *Ets-Hokin Corp.*, AECBCA 70-5-70, 72-2 BCA ¶ 9606, it was rejected because it was (1) not applicable to the special situation, (2) not consistently used by the contractor, and (3) not made a part of the claim presentation until after the appeal was filed. See also *Mel Williamson Constr. Co.*, VACAB 1199, 76-2 BCA ¶ 12,168, in which the government demonstrated that the estimating formula was not applicable to the particular claim.

Trade association manuals are often used in establishing the reasonableness of an estimate or to calculate an adjustment, A. *Geris, Inc.*, DOTCAB 72-25, 72-2 BCA ¶ 9481; *Arthur Painting Co.*, ASBCA 20267, 76-1 BCA ¶ 11,894; *B.P.O.A.*, ASBCA 25276, 82-2 BCA ¶ 15,816, *recons. denied*, 82-2 BCA ¶ 15,924; *Ed Goetz Painting Co.*, DOTCAB 1168, 83-1 BCA ¶ 16,134, *recons. denied*, 83-1 BCA ¶ 16,432; *Spiros Vasilatos Painting*, ASBCA 37938, 89-3 BCA ¶ 22,244, *modified on recons.*, 90-1 BCA ¶ 22,618; *Fire Sec. Sys., Inc.*, VABCA 3086, 91-2 BCA ¶ 23,743. Sometimes the manual to be used is specified in procurement regulations, *Frank J. Comeau*, ASBCA 20361, 76-1 BCA ¶ 11,892. Manuals with inefficiency factors have also been used. See *Hensel Phelps Constr. Co. v. General Servs. Admin.*, GSBCA 14744, 01-1 BCA ¶ 31,249, *aff'd*, 36 Fed. Appx. 649 (Fed. Cir. 2002), and *Clark Constr. Group, Inc.*, VABCA 5674, 00-1 BCA ¶ 30,870, *recons. denied*, 00-2 BCA ¶ 30,997, using, with modifications, the loss of productivity factors in the Mechanical Contractors Association of America, Inc., manual.

C. Total Cost Method

The "total cost" method of establishing the amount of adjustment consists of subtracting the costs in the bid price from the actual costs of performance and adding a profit to the resulting amount. This can be done at the level of the entire contract price or for some segment of the contract work. In either case, it is an imprecise method of computing a price adjustment because it does not identify the specific extra costs that were caused by the changes, differing site conditions, or delays that were encountered in the performance of the contract.

1. Not Favored

The total cost method will not be used if there is another, more reliable method available to establish the adjustment, *Wunderlich Contracting Co. v. United States*, 173 Ct. Cl. 180, 351 F.2d 956 (1965). See *Ingalls Shipbuilding Div., Litton Sys., Inc.*, ASBCA 17579, 78-1 BCA ¶ 13,038, *recons. denied*, 78-1 BCA ¶ 13,216, in which the board commented at 63,667-68:

> The Government contends that [the contractor's] claim is based on a total cost/total time presentation which fails to fall within any of the exceptions established by the boards or the Court of Claims which permit the use of such approach. The use of a so-called total cost approach is not prohibited *per se. Boyajian v. United States*, 191 Ct. Cl. 233, 423 F.2d 1231 (1970). However, because of the dangers inherent in such approach, it is subject to careful scrutiny so as to satisfy the adjudicating body that the Government is not charged with the difference between actual cost incurred and the bid merely because the difference exists. Therefore, various tests or considerations have been developed to assure that there is some reasonable basis upon which to make a determination of quantum. Essentially, the courts and boards will permit recovery where convinced that proper safeguards exist, that there is no better method of proving costs, and that there is some basis of reaching a determination of a reasonable amount related to the entitlement found. See *H. John Homan Co. v. United States*, 189 Ct. Cl. 500, 418 F.2d 522 (1969); *WRB Corporation v. United States*, 183 Ct. Cl. 409 (1968); *Fermont Division, Dynamics Corporation of American*, ASBCA No. 15806, 75-1 BCA ¶ 11,139; *Ingalls Shipbuilding Division, Litton Systems, Inc.*, ASBCA No. 17717, [76-1 BCA ¶ 11,851].

The board then rejected the total cost approach of the contractor in favor of an attempt by the government to make a specific computation for each category of increased cost. The Court of Claims refused to apply the total cost method when expert opinions were offered concerning the cost impact, *Turnbull, Inc. v. United States*, 180 Ct. Cl. 1010, 389 F.2d 1007 (1967). The total cost method has also been rejected when there were fragmentary data available, *Consultores Profesionales de Ingenieria, S.A.*, ENGBCA PCC-78-Q, 97-2 BCA ¶ 29,011, *clarified on recons.*, 98-1 BCA ¶ 29,584; *Cen-Vi-Ro of Tex., Inc.*, IBCA 718-5-68, 73-1 BCA ¶ 9903, *aff'd in part, denied in part*, 80-2 BCA ¶ 14,536. See also *Raytheon Co.*, ASBCA 50166, 01-1

BCA ¶ 31,245, *rev'd on other grounds*, 305 F.3d 1354 (Fed. Cir. 2002), *on remand*, 03-2 BCA ¶ 32,359, rejecting a total cost computation in favor of a computation identifying the impact of a change on "discrete events." However, if a contractor is able to convince the board or court that its total cost estimate is the most logical and accurate approximation of the actual costs for which the government is responsible, it is unlikely that its estimate will be rejected merely because some other estimating method might be available. See *Sovereign Constr. Co.*, ASBCA 17792, 75-1 BCA ¶ 11,251, in which the board used the contractor's total cost proposal as a basis for arriving at a jury verdict for 90 percent of the amount computed using the total cost basis.

The total cost method is particularly inappropriate when some of the contractor's claims have been denied, *Great Lakes Dredge & Dock Co.*, ENGBCA 5606, 91-1 BCA ¶ 23,613; *Diversified Marine Tech, Inc.*, DOTBCA 2455, 93-2 BCA ¶ 25,720. However, when the government is responsible for all major factors contributing to the extra costs, it can be appropriately used to compute the labor hours attributable to changes, *S & E Contractors, Inc.*, AECBCA 97-12-72, 74-2 BCA ¶ 10,676. It is also appropriate when a major change completely alters the work to be done on the contract, *Delco Elecs. Corp. v. United States*, 17 Cl. Ct. 302 (1989), *aff'd*, 909 F.2d 1495 (Fed. Cir. 1990), and when the claim is for extra effort in performing the work with no new work added to the contract, *Jack L. Olsen, Inc.*, AGBCA 87-345-1, 93-2 BCA ¶ 25,767, *rev'd on other grounds*, 26 F.3d 141 (Fed. Cir. 1994).

2. Safeguards for Use

In *WRB Corp. v. United States*, 183 Ct. Cl. 409 (1968), the court laid down four safeguards for use of the total cost method, at 426:

> The acceptability of the method hinges on proof that (1) the nature of the particular losses make it impossible or highly impracticable to determine them with a reasonable degree of accuracy; (2) the [contractor's] bid or estimate was realistic; (3) its actual costs were reasonable; and (4) it was not responsible for the added expenses. See *J.D. Hedin Construction Co. v. United States, supra*, 171 Ct. Cl. at pages 86-87, 347 F.2d at pages 246-47; *Oliver-Finnie Co. v. United States, supra*, 150 Ct. Cl. at pages 197, 200, 279 F.2d at pages 505-06; *F.H. McGraw & Co. v. United States*, *supra*, 131 Ct. Cl. at page 511, 130 F. Supp. at page 400.

In some instances, this decision has been construed as requiring denial of a contractor's total cost claim if all four safeguards have not been proved. More frequently, a "modified total cost method" has been used, with adjustments being made to the total cost presentation to compensate for failure to meet one of the safeguards.

a. Other Methods of Proof Not Available

The first test appears to be little more than a restatement of the requirement that there not be a more reliable method of determining the amount of equitable adjustment available to the board or court. Often, attention is focused on the absence of cost records in support of the adjustment. If it is impossible to detail the cost impact of a change because the contractor failed to keep accurate records when they could have been kept, the total cost method will not be used, *S.W. Elecs. & Mfg. Corp.*, ASBCA 20698, 77-2 BCA ¶ 12,631, *recons. denied*, 77-2 BCA ¶ 12,785, *aff'd*, 228 Ct. Cl. 333, 655 F.2d 1078 (1981). Thus, when the contractor knew of the claim at the time the costs began to accumulate but did not segregate costs, the use of the method was rejected, *Youngdale & Sons Constr. Co. v. United States*, 27 Fed. Cl. 516 (1993). See also *Propellex Corp.*, ASBCA 50203, 02-1 BCA ¶ 31,721, *aff'd*, 342 F.3d 1335 (Fed. Cir. 2003) (contractor could have segregated costs of change); *Freedom N.Y., Inc.*, ASBCA 43965, 02-1 BCA ¶ 31,676, *rev'd on other grounds*, 329 F.3d 1320 (Fed. Cir. 2003), *cert. denied*, 541 U.S. 987 (2004) (no proof that costs could not be segregated); *Cavalier Clothes, Inc. v. United States*, 51 Fed. Cl. 399 (2001) (contractor did not maintain records of changed work); *Doninger Metal Prods. Corp. v. United States*, 50 Fed. Cl. 110 (2001) (contractor could not produce records documenting costs); *Defense Sys. Corp.*, ASBCA 44131R, 00-1 BCA ¶ 30,851 (fact that contractor incurred more costs than estimated not proof that costs could not have been collected); and *Sefco Constructors*, VABCA 2747, 93-1 BCA ¶ 25,458 (contractor encountered asbestos on first day of job but kept no separate accounts). See, however, *Salem Eng'g & Constr. Corp. v. United States*, 2 Cl. Ct. 803 (1983), in which the court excused the absence of accounting records that had been lost by another court. Generally, the nature of the changes or cost increases themselves must be such that it is impossible or impractical to segregate the particular costs that were increased by the change. Such a situation existed in *Robert McMullan & Sons, Inc.*, ASBCA 19129, 76-2 BCA ¶ 12,072, in which the board stated at 57,962:

> [The contractor's] claim is that the right to an equitable adjustment arose almost from the beginning of the contract and continued and enlarged itself in almost every day of contract operations to completion, all due to the fault of the Government. To that claim we agree. To attempt to segregate delay and lost time, set up and breakdown estimates, delay in transit from one location to another on site and loss of efficiency as opposed to normal time would be a wasteful exercise for, in the end, the result should approach the total cost actually experienced. Had we some period of performance free of the dispute we might be better able to judge the damages based on estimates. It is impractical if not impossible to determine with any real degree of accuracy the contract work from extra work.

See *Hewitt Contracting Co.*, ENGBCA 4596, 83-2 BCA ¶ 16,816, in which the method was used because there was no way of identifying the costs of numerous "intertwined, overlapping events." See also *Perini Corp.*, ENGBCA 3745, 78-1 BCA ¶ 13,191, and *Continental Drilling Co.*, ENGBCA 3455, 77-1 BCA ¶ 12,280.

b. *Realistic Contract Price*

The second element—that the contractor's cost estimate in the contract price be realistic—was discussed in *R. C. Hedreen Co.*, GSBCA 4841, 78-2 BCA ¶ 13,475, at 65,926:

> [The contractor's] claim is basically a total cost one, i.e., the difference between actual cost incurred and bid estimate. The total cost theory has been looked upon unfavorably. *Joseph Sternberger v. United States*, 185 Ct. Cl. 528, 401 F.2d 1012 (1968); *WRB Corporation v. United States*, 183 Ct. Cl. 409 (1968). One of the elements which [the contractor] must show in order for this Board to accept a total cost approach is the reasonableness of the original bid estimate. *WRB Corporation v. United States, supra*. No proof on this point was submitted, however. While [the subcontractor's] bid worksheets show $14,107 labor costs allocated for total ceiling installation, no supporting documentation or testimony was given as to that figure's reasonableness. We thus have no way of finding it a reasonable sum.

The contractor can prove that its original bid was a reasonable estimate of what the job would have cost if performed unchanged by offering expert testimony that the estimate was reasonable and arrived at by sound estimating techniques, or by showing that it was very close to other bids or the government's preaward estimate. These techniques were discussed in *Perini, Continental Drilling,* and *Robert McMullan & Sons*. See also *J.D. Hedin Constr. Co. v. United States*, 171 Ct. Cl. 70, 347 F.2d 235 (1965). However, if it is clear that the contractor's contract price was underestimated, the total cost method will not be used, *Centex Bateson Constr. Co.*, VABCA 4613, 99-1 BCA ¶ 30,153, *aff'd*, 250 F.3d 761 (Fed. Cir. 2000); *Hill Aviation Logistics*, ASBCA 40817, 93-1 BCA ¶ 25,274; *Arrow, Inc.*, ASBCA 39621, 90-3 BCA ¶ 23,217; *Umpqua Marine Ways, Inc.*, ASBCA 27790, 89-3 BCA ¶ 22,099; *Servidone Constr. Co.*, ENGBCA 4736, 88-1 BCA ¶ 20,390. The use of budget estimates as the base for the computation has also been rejected, *Bruce-Andersen Co.*, ASBCA 31663, 89-3 BCA ¶ 22,013.

c. *Reasonableness of Actual Costs*

The third safeguard is that the contractor's actual costs must be reasonable. Thus, failure by the contractor to demonstrate that actual costs were incurred in a reasonable manner will bar recovery based on a total cost approach, *Penn York Constr. Corp. v. United States*, 215 Ct. Cl. 899, 566 F.2d 1190 (1977). In that case, the trial judge held that the presumption of reasonableness of incurred costs did not apply to total cost claims. It is difficult to see the logic of this conclusion since this presumption was available in all other cases involving actual costs. The presumption was used in *Continental Drilling Co.*, ENGBCA 3455, 77-1 BCA ¶ 12,280. See *Teledyne McCormick-Selph v. United States*, 218 Ct. Cl. 513, 588 F.2d 808 (1978), in which the court stated at 516-17:

> [T]his case involves a very unique set of circumstances. The dollar amounts are not disputed; a previous Board determination has found that the Government was at fault and did provide defective specifications. [The contractor] is confronted with an accusation that some of its costs should be disallowed. However, no reason whatsoever has been given as to why these costs should be disallowed. Other than the defective specifications, all other possible reasons for these additional costs have been eliminated. In requiring [the contractor] to prove still more (more

> than it has already proven), in the absence of evidence by the Government as to why the costs should be disallowed, the Board, in effect, applied a standard of proof approaching "beyond a reasonable doubt."

The government has been able to prove unreasonable costs in only a few cases. See *Wackenhut Corp.*, IBCA 2311, 91-1 BCA ¶ 23,318 (inefficient performance and voluntary performance of work not required by contract), and *Wilbur Smith & Assocs., Inc.*, ASBCA 35301, 89-3 BCA ¶ 22,025 (government demonstrated that contractor had performed contract badly). However, some cases appear to require the contractor to prove that it performed the work efficiently. See, for example, *Cosmic Constr. Co.*, ASBCA 24014, 88-2 BCA ¶ 20,623, in which the board denied the use of a total cost computation, stating that the "assumption that there was no inefficiency in [the contractor's] performance finds no support in the record and is conjectural at best."

d. Contractor Not Responsible for Increases

The fourth and final requirement is that the contractor must not be responsible for the added expense. This is the requirement for proving causation. In other words, the contractor must prove that nothing other than the matter for which the government was responsible caused the increase in cost. It is probably this requirement that is most difficult for the contractor to overcome. For example, in *C-Ran Corp.*, ASBCA 37643, 90-3 BCA ¶ 23,201, *recons. denied*, 91-2 BCA ¶ 23,752, the board rejected the total cost method because many of the extra labor hours incurred on the job were caused by the receipt of defective components from a vendor.

3. Modified Total Cost Method

In most cases where the total cost method is used, the two elements of the computation—the original costs in the contract price and the total costs of performance—are adjusted to ensure that the resulting price adjustment does not contain amounts for which the government is not responsible. This "modified total cost" approach has been endorsed by the Court of Appeals for the Federal Circuit, *Servidone Constr. Corp. v. United States*, 931 F.2d 860 (Fed. Cir. 1991), in which the Claims Court had made such adjustments after taking extensive testimony on the level of the original contract price and the relative responsibility for extra costs, 19 Cl. Ct. 346 (1990). However, the method cannot be used when the contractor can prove its costs directly by segregating them from the costs of other work, *Propellex Corp. v. Brownlee*, 342 F.3d 1335 (Fed. Cir. 2003).

Adjustments to the contract price have been quite common. For example, in *Servidone*, the court used, as a basis for the computation, the higher price that a competing offeror had included for the item of work that was affected by the change. See also *Baldi Bros. Constructors v. United States*, 50 Fed. Cl. 74 (2001) (bid price adjusted to reflect contractor's overly optimistic rate of productivity); *Bechtel Nat'l, Inc.*, NASABCA 1186-7, 90-1 BCA ¶ 22,549, *recons. denied*, 90-3 BCA ¶ 23,105 ("realistic" contract price was average of all bids and government estimate—board called this approach a "jury verdict"); and *Ingalls Shipbuilding Div., Litton Sys., Inc.*, ASBCA 17579, 78-1 BCA ¶ 13,038, *recons. denied*, 78-1 BCA ¶ 13,216 (differences between the government's and contractor's re-estimates were reconciled by using a "jury verdict" approach that was then subtracted from the actual costs).

Most cases using the modified total cost approach also make adjustments to the total costs incurred. In some cases, the contractor makes a careful attempt to eliminate costs that are not the government's responsibility, and this persuades the board or court to adopt the modified total cost method, *Hardrives, Inc.*, IBCA 2319, 94-1 BCA ¶ 26,267; *J & T Constr. Co.*, DOTCAB 73-4, 75-2 BCA ¶ 11,398. See *Parsons of Cal.*, ASBCA 20867, 82-1 BCA ¶ 15,659, in which the board used a modified total cost method to compute delay and disruption costs. The board ascertained the labor hours attributable to delay and disruption caused by defective specifications by subtracting the contractor's estimates of labor hours for compensable changes and extra work for which the contractor was responsible from the total hours incurred over its bid estimate. The equitable adjustment was then computed on the basis of the pro rata share of the delay and disruption labor hours to the labor hours incurred on compensable changes. See also *Robert McMullan & Sons, Inc.*, ASBCA 19129, 76-2 BCA ¶ 12,072, and *Tri-Delta Corp.*, ASBCA 17456, 75-1 BCA ¶ 11,160, in which the board used a "jury verdict" based on the contractor's total cost claim.

D. Jury Verdict

The "jury verdict" technique is the method by which boards and courts resolve conflicting evidence of the amount or arrive at an amount of compensation when incomplete evidence has been submitted or when they are not persuaded by the evidence of either party.

1. Conditions for Use

The conditions for use of the jury verdict technique were originally stated in *WRB Corp. v. United States*, 183 Ct. Cl. 409 (1968), at 425:

> Before adopting the "jury verdict" method, the court must first determine three things: (1) that clear proof of injury exists; (2) that there is no more reliable method of computing damages; and (3) that the evidence is sufficient for a court to make a fair and reasonable approximation of the damages.

This method is not to be used as a substitute for proving the claim by the best evidence possible, whether by actual costs or estimates, unless the contractor demonstrates a justifiable inability to produce such evidence, *Joseph Pickard's Sons Co. v. United States*, 209 Ct. Cl. 643, 532 F.2d 739 (1976). It is also not to be used if the contractor unjustifiably failed to maintain cost records of the additional costs caused by a change, differing site condition, or delay, *Dawco Constr., Inc. v. United States*, 930 F.2d 872 (Fed. Cir. 1991).

A number of cases follow the *Dawco* rule that the jury verdict technique should not be used when the contractor could have collected data on the costs of a change. Most of them appear to be based on the fact that the evidence submitted was insufficient to make an approximation of the amount of the adjustment. See *Dawco Constr., Inc.*, ASBCA 42120, 92-2 BCA ¶ 24,915, and *Production Corp.*, DOTBCA 2424, 92-2 BCA ¶ 24,796, in which claims were denied because the contractor had not collected cost data and had not submitted evidence sufficient to approximate the adjustment. See also *Donahue Elec., Inc.*, VABCA 6618, 03-1 BCA ¶ 32,129 (insufficient evidence to support a jury verdict); *NavCom Def. Elecs., Inc.*, ASBCA 50767, 01-2 BCA ¶ 31,546 (board denied claims because contractor did not issue charge numbers for "out-of-scope" costs); *McTeague Constr. Co. v. General Servs. Admin.*, GSBCA 14765, 01-1 BCA ¶ 31,203 (board denied some claims because of lack of supporting data); *Cavalier Clothes, Inc. v. United States*, 51 Fed. Cl. 399 (2001) (court denied recovery because contractor did not maintain records of changed work); *Doninger Metal Prods. Corp. v. United States*, 50 Fed. Cl. 110 (2001) (court granted summary judgment against contractor that could not produce records documenting costs); *Deval Corp.*, ASBCA 47132, 99-1 BCA ¶ 30,182, *recons. denied*, 99-2 BCA ¶ 30,522 (board denied recovery because of lack of data on labor costs before and after termination); *Emerald Maint., Inc.*, ASBCA 43929, 98-2 BCA ¶ 29,903 (board denied recovery for impact claim for lack of "direct proof" of loss of productivity because of government changes); *Datalect Computer Servs., Ltd. v. United States*, 41 Fed. Cl. 720 (1998), *rev'd on other grounds*, 215 F.3d 1344 (Fed. Cir. 1999), *cert. denied*, 529 U.S. 1037 (2000), *on remand*, 56 Fed. Cl. 178 (2003) (court denied recovery because evidence was incomplete and unconvincing); *J.R. Roberts Corp.*, DOTBCA 2499, 98-1 BCA ¶ 29,680 (board denied recovery when expert testified that all loss of productivity was based on change but gave no data to support apportionment to other causes); and *Engineering Tech. Consultants, S.A.*, ASBCA 44912, 93-1 BCA ¶ 25,556, *recons. denied*, 93-2 BCA ¶ 25,732 (board denied most elements of the claim for failure to keep cost records but awarded a small adjustment where there was sufficient evidence). In *Roy D. Garren Corp.*, AGBCA 85-196-1, 91-1 BCA ¶ 23,306, a case decided before *Dawco*, the board denied a claim where the contractor had not collected data on costs of a change after the contracting officer had acknowledged government liability. See also *Green Int'l, Inc.*, ENGBCA 5706, 98-1 BCA ¶ 29,684, granting recovery at a very small percentage of the amount claimed and criticizing the contractor for not presenting better evidence. In *Romac, Inc.*, DOTBCA 4028, 01-2 BCA ¶ 31,552, the board denied the claim because the contractor did not segregate the costs of additional work but then, on reconsideration, 02-1 BCA ¶ 31,670, held that there was sufficient evidence to grant a jury verdict for some of the claimed costs. Similarly, in *Fanning, Phillips & Molnar*, VABCA 3856, 96-1 BCA ¶ 28,214, the board denied relief based on the fact that the timesheets of the engineer performing extra work did not identify time spent on that work and then reversed itself in 96-2 BCA ¶ 28,427, holding that the timesheets contained sufficient detail to estimate that 40 percent of the time was spent on the extra work.

There may also be situations where it is impracticable to collect detailed cost data on changes. See *Service Eng'g Co.*, ASBCA 40274, 93-1 BCA ¶ 25,520, *re-*

cons. denied, 93-2 BCA ¶ 25,885, in which the board held that it was impracticable to collect segregated cost data in a complex change. In reaching this conclusion, the board commented that, had the government felt the data necessary, it could have included the Change Order Accounting clause.

The jury verdict technique has been used to estimate the amount of a government claim for a downward adjustment, *Karcher Envtl., Inc.*, PSBCA 4085, 00-1 BCA ¶ 30,843, *aff'd*, 15 Fed. Appx. 863 (Fed. Cir. 2001). See, however, *Trailboss Enters., Inc.*, VABCA 5454, 99-2 BCA ¶ 30,555, denying a downward adjustment for performing punchlist work because the government submitted no credible evidence of the costs of the work.

2. Purposes Served

Fundamentally, the jury verdict technique is a method of resolving disputes on the amount of a price adjustment. In accomplishing this result, several purposes can be served.

a. Resolving Conflicting Evidence

If competent but conflicting evidence is introduced, the courts or boards will use a jury verdict to arrive at the amount of the adjustment. Thus, the jury verdict technique is often viewed as a means for resolving a case in which there has been conflicting testimony, rather than as a method of proof of quantum. See *Delco Elecs. Corp. v. United States*, 17 Cl. Ct. 302 (1989), *aff'd*, 909 F.2d 1495 (1990), in which the court stated at 323-24:

> The conceptual touchstone for the use of the jury verdict approach is the existence of conflicting competent evidence calling into question the accuracy and reliability of the [contractor's] computations. As the name implies, the technique by necessity requires the application of the fair, equitable and informed discretion of the trial judge. The court believes that the use of the approach is especially appropriate here, where the sole source of guidance is the nebulous concept of "reasonableness."

See also *Johnson, Drake & Piper, Inc.*, ASBCA 9824, 65-2 BCA ¶ 4868, in which the board made the following observations concerning this aspect of the jury verdict technique, at 23,073:

> There is neither a single nor a precise method of arriving at the dollar amount of an equitable adjustment. In general we seek to reach a figure as an equitable adjustment which represents the cost to a reasonably efficient contractor of performing the changed work under his contract. Evidence of this amount may be found in the actual costs of the particular contract, to the extent that those costs are not shown to be other than reasonable, and in engineering estimates of reasonable cost made by experts who bring into play their experience and knowledge to attempt to visual-

> ize the price at which that reasonably efficient contractor could perform. Neither estimating nor accounting are such exact arts that either can produce figures which will be agreed to by all parties without legitimate argument. We recognize that often, despite protestations to the contrary, extreme positions on monetary entitlement are taken during litigation. We think that this case is no exception.
>
> Even though presented with wildly divergent monetary positions by the parties before us, we cannot escape the necessity of bringing an end to the matter and determining a figure as the amount of an equitable adjustment. This ordinarily is a figure some place between the amount contended for by each party to the litigation. Sometimes the courts have referred to such a conclusion as an amount in the nature of a "jury verdict." This is a figure which in the view of the trier of the facts is fair in the light of all of the facts of the case, or, put another way, is supported by consideration of the entire record.

See also *Environment Consultants, Inc.*, IBCA 1192-5-78, 79-2 BCA ¶ 13,937; *William P. Bergan, Inc.*, IBCA 1130-11-76, 79-1 BCA ¶ 13,671; and *J.F. Shea Co.*, IBCA 1191-4-78, 82-1 BCA ¶ 15,705. In some cases, the jury verdict approach is used when the evidence of the contractor is not convincing but it is clear that extra costs were incurred, *Lawrence D. Krause*, AGBCA 76-118-4, 82-2 BCA ¶ 16,129. In *J.W. Bateson Co.*, VACAB 1148, 79-1 BCA ¶ 13,573, *recons. denied*, 81-1 BCA ¶ 14,869, the board used a modified jury verdict and modified total cost method. The jury verdict technique has also been used to benefit the government, *Dawson Constr. Co.*, PSBCA 439, 79-2 BCA ¶ 13,881.

b. Evidence Not Available

The jury verdict technique is also used to determine the amount of an adjustment when there are gaps in the evidence or the evidence is not completely persuasive. In such cases, the court or board must use its discretion because the jury verdict approach is not properly used unless there is "sufficient evidence" to arrive at a fair result. However, there is a hesitancy to completely deny recovery in cases where it is reasonably certain what injury did, in fact, occur. Thus, many decisions find that even if the evidence is sparse, it is sufficient to fashion a jury verdict. See, for example, *Freeman Gen., Inc. v. United States*, 918 F.2d 188 (Fed. Cir. 1990), in which the court reversed a board decision that had denied any recovery because of lack of evidence from the contractor proving the amount of the adjustment. The court concluded that it was an error not to award a jury verdict in the amount of the government's estimate of the value of the claim—which was in the evidence presented to the board. See also *Clark Constr. Group, Inc.*, VABCA 5674, 00-1 BCA ¶ 30,870, *recons. denied*, 00-2 BCA ¶ 30,997, in which the board granted a jury verdict for lost productivity, recognizing that precise evidence was not possible. Similarly, in *Harold Benson*, AGBCA 384, 77-1 BCA ¶ 12,490, the evidence did not support the amount claimed by the contractor but did indicate that the amount allowed by the contracting officer was too low. In *Custom Roofing Co.*, ASBCA 19164, 74-2 BCA ¶ 10,925, the board granted a jury verdict recovery based on "rough estimates," and in *Rocky Mountain Constr. Co.*, IBCA 1091-12-75, 77-2 BCA ¶ 12,692, the board applied the jury verdict technique to an item whose cost was "totally unclear." See also *Central Colo. Contractors, Inc.*, IBCA 1203-8-78, 83-1 BCA ¶ 16,405, in which the board criticized the contractor for not segregating costs of changes but used a jury verdict to determine the adjustment. In *Meva Corp. v. United States*, 206 Ct. Cl. 203, 511 F.2d 548 (1975), the court rejected the contractor's total cost calculations but applied the jury verdict technique. The jury verdict technique has also been used to award the government for retrofit work when detailed cost records had not been maintained, *Norair Eng'g. Corp.*, ENGBCA 5244-Q, 98-2 BCA ¶ 29,967. Compare *Geo-Con, Inc.*, ENGBCA 5749-Q, 96-1 BCA ¶ 28,112, denying a modified total cost claim and awarding the amount of the government estimate with a small profit adjustment, and *Diversified Marine Tech., Inc.*, DOTBCA 2455, 93-2 BCA ¶ 25,720, denying a number of total cost claims in their entirety because there was insufficient evidence to permit the board to arrive at a jury verdict.

As discussed earlier, *Dawco* appears to preclude the use of partial evidence when the contractor could have collected cost data on the change. However, shortly after that decision, the court affirmed a General Services Board jury verdict award based on clear findings that the contractor had been forced to incur additional costs and that there was sufficient evidence to arrive at an amount that did not overcompensate the contractor, *Tele-Sentry Sec., Inc.*, GSBCA 10945(7703)-REIN, 91-2 BCA ¶ 23,880, *aff'd*, 950 F.2d 730 (Fed. Cir. 1991). This decision gives little weight to the question of whether the contractor could have collected detailed cost data supporting the adjustment. Board decisions shortly after *Dawco* followed this reasoning and continued to grant jury verdicts on the basis of partial evidence deemed sufficient to fashion a fair result, *Tayag Bros. Enters., Inc.*, ASBCA 42097, 94-3 BCA ¶ 26,962, *recons. denied*, 95-1 BCA ¶ 27,599; *Service Eng'g. Co.*, ASBCA 40275, 94-1 BCA ¶ 26,382; *Michael-Mark, Ltd.*, IBCA 2697, 94-1 BCA ¶ 26,453; *MJW Enters., Inc.*, ENGBCA 5813, 93-1 BCA ¶ 25,405; *Marty's Maid & Janitorial Serv. v. General Servs. Admin.*, GSBCA 10614, 93-1 BCA ¶ 25,284; *Fletcher & Sons, Inc.*, VABCA 3248, 92-1 BCA ¶ 24,726. Some later cases also follow this approach. See, for example, *Kumin Assocs., Inc.*, LBCA 94-BCA-3, 98-2 BCA ¶ 30,007 (board awarded architect for extra drawings at average number of hours per page where no records of actual hours were kept). This approach has also been used to award price reductions to the government when no precise data are available, *Gladwynne Constr. Co.*, VABCA 6594, 02-1 BCA ¶ 31,848, *recons. denied*, 02-2 BCA ¶ 31,948.

c. Adjusting for Lack of Proof of Causation

The boards have also used the jury verdict approach to reduce the amount claimed by the contractor when causation is not fully demonstrated. For example, in *Steve P. Rados, Inc.*, AGBCA 77-130-4, 82-1 BCA ¶ 15,624, the board made its own computations of the amount of claimed costs that were attributable to government action. These calculations were possible because the contractor had provided detailed evidence of the events that had occurred and of the costs that had been incurred. See, however, *Joseph Pickard's Sons Co. v. United States*, 209 Ct. Cl. 643, 532 F.2d 739 (1976), in which the court refused to use the jury verdict approach to prove causation.

3. Techniques Used

The jury verdict technique is highly flexible, permitting the board or court to fashion a price adjustment that best compensates the contractor yet does not force the government to pay an amount that is unfair in the circumstances. A number of different techniques have been identified.

a. Computing a "Round" Number

In virtually every case involving the jury verdict technique, the court or board awards an amount between the positions of the two parties. In some cases, the amount selected is clearly a "round" number or a "round" percentage of the contractor's claim, which the judge arrives at without any detailed explanation. See, for example, *Delco Elecs. Corp. v. United States*, 17 Cl. Ct. 302 (1989), *aff'd*, 909 F.2d 1495 (Fed. Cir. 1990), in which the court granted an award in the amount of two-thirds of the claim because the contractor had not collected cost data on the changes. See also *Federal Ins. Co.*, IBCA 3236, 96-2 BCA ¶ 28,415 ($300,000 award on delay claim of $1,855,352); *Environmental Protection Inspection & Consulting, Inc.*, ASBCA 41264, 91-1 BCA ¶ 23,637 (adjustment for 3,500 cubic yards of earth moving when contractor had claimed 5,300 cubic yards); *Wackenhut Corp.*, IBCA 2311, 91-1 BCA ¶ 23,318 ($550,000 award when contractor had claimed $777,318); *Andersen Constr. Co.*, IBCA 2346, 90-3 BCA ¶ 23,135 ($78,000 award on total cost claim of $175,297); and *Harvey C. Jones, Inc.*, IBCA 2070, 90-2 BCA ¶ 22,762, *recons. denied*, 91-1 BCA ¶ 23,388 ($250,000 award on total cost claim of $866,484).

b. Awarding an Amount Based on the Government Estimate

In most cases, the parties will have attempted to negotiate a settlement for which the government will have made an estimate of the correct amount of the price adjustment. When this estimate is before the court or board, it is competent evidence on which a jury verdict can be based—even if the contractor's evidence is rejected, *Freeman Gen., Inc. v. United States*, 918 F.2d 188 (Fed. Cir. 1990). In that case, the court ruled that it was error for the appeals board to disregard this evidence and deny the claim in its entirety. The government estimate was also used as the basis for a jury verdict in *Cocoa Elec. Co.*, ASBCA 33921R, 94-1 BCA ¶ 26,298. See also *Northrop Grumman Corp. v. United States*, 47 Fed. Cl. 20 (2000) (court awarded amount of government estimate); *Cyrus Contracting, Inc.*, IBCA 3233, 98-2 BCA ¶ 29,755, *award adjusted on recons.*, 98-2 BCA ¶ 30,036 (board awarded amount less than had been offered by the contracting officer's technical representative); *Mark A. Carroll & Sons, Inc.*, IBCA 3427, 96-1 BCA ¶ 28,224 (board awarded one-half of government estimate of maximum amount reasonable); *Michael, Inc.*, ASBCA 35653, 92-1 BCA ¶ 24,412 (board used government estimate of amount of work done); *E.W. Eldridge, Inc.*, ENGBCA 5269, 90-3 BCA ¶ 23,080 (board used the highest of a number of government estimates based on a total cost approach); and *J.D. Abrams*, ENGBCA 4332, 89-1 BCA ¶ 21,379 (board used government estimate of extra work done). There are also a number of cases in which the board granted a jury verdict at the amount named in the decision of the contracting officer, *B&M Roofing & Painting Co.*, ASBCA 44323, 93-1 BCA ¶ 25,504, *recons. denied*, 93-2 BCA ¶ 25,691; *Togaroli Corp.*, ASBCA 32995, 89-2 BCA ¶ 21,864, *recons. denied*, 89-3 BCA ¶ 22,102; *Cosmic Constr. Co.*, ASBCA 24014, 88-2 BCA ¶ 20,623.

c. Making an Independent Calculation

The most common jury verdict technique is for the court or board to make its own detailed computation of the adjustment, based on all of the data provided by the parties. This, of course, can only be done when there are sufficient data available to allow the judge to manipulate the figures and arrive at a final amount to be awarded to the contractor. However, in most cases these data are before the board and available for use. See, for example, *Midwest Envtl. Control, Inc.*, LBCA 93-BCA-12, 98-2 BCA ¶ 30,058 (board made numerous adjustments to contractor's estimates); *Staff, Inc.*, AGBCA 96-112-1, 97-2 BCA ¶ 29,285 (board used estimates of cost of original work and changed work); *Taylor Constr. Co. v. General Servs. Admin.*, GSBCA 12915, 96-2 BCA ¶ 28,547 (board used both contractor and government estimates with accompanying data); *Betancourt & Gonzalez, S.E.*, DOTBCA 2785, 96-1 BCA ¶ 28,033 (board calculated excavation costs and awarded 80.31 percent of them, reflecting the government responsibility for extra excavation work); *O.K. Johnson Elec. Co.*, VABCA 3464, 94-1 BCA ¶ 26,505 (board used government estimate with addition of 20 percent inefficiency factor); *Michael-Mark, Ltd.*, IBCA 2697, 94-1 BCA ¶ 26,453 (board used audited data); *Service Eng'g Co.*, ASBCA 40274, 93-1 BCA ¶ 25,520, *recons. denied*, 93-2 BCA ¶ 25,885 (board estimated hours required for extra work); *Batteast Constr. Co.*, ASBCA 35818, 92-1 BCA ¶ 24,697 (board made detailed calculations of extra material and loss of efficiency of laborers); *Fire Sec. Sys., Inc.*, VABCA 3086, 91-2 BCA ¶ 23,743 (board calculated of loss of efficiency factors); *Great Lakes Dredge & Dock Co.*, ENGBCA 5606, 91-1 BCA ¶ 23,613 (board used data in contractor's claim); *Shumate Constructors, Inc.*, VABCA 2772, 90-3 BCA ¶ 22,946 (board made extensive adjustments to contractor's claims); *Atlas Constr. Co.*, GSBCA 7903, 90-2 BCA ¶ 22,812 (board used audit adjustments to contractor's claim); *Spiros Vasilatos Painting*, ASBCA 37938, 89-3 BCA ¶ 22,244, *modified on recons.*, 90-1 BCA ¶ 22,618 (board used estimating-manual averages for labor and material quantities and actual costs for labor and material rates); and *Pittsburgh-Des Moines Corp.*, EBCA 314-3-84, 89-2 BCA ¶ 21,739 (board made major adjustments to contractor's claim).

d. *Awarding a Percentage of the Total Extra Costs Incurred*

In some cases the boards have fashioned a jury verdict by separating the parts of the claim for which the government is clearly responsible and computing the extra costs as a portion of the total extra costs incurred. See, for example, *Akcon, Inc.*, ENGBCA 5593, 90-3 BCA ¶ 23,250 (contractor awarded cost increases for specific elements of work); *Industrial Constructors Corp.*, AGBCA 84-348-1, 90-2 BCA ¶ 22,767 (contractor awarded a percentage of the total extra costs equivalent to the percentage of the work where the government was responsible for extra effort); and *David J. Tierney Jr., Inc.*, GSBCA 7107, 88-2 BCA ¶ 20,806, *recons. denied*, 88-3 BCA ¶ 20,906 (contractor awarded 40 percent of total extra costs because 40 percent of claims had been granted).

III. IMPACT AND DELAY

The recovery of impact and delay costs has been the subject of considerable controversy and confusion. Part of the problem stems from the terminology used in this area. Impact and delay costs are those that result from a lack of productivity. Requests for recovery of such costs are sometimes referred to as "delay," "disruption," or "ripple effect" claims. The costs may be caused by the contractor being required to perform otherwise unnecessary work, alter the sequence of its operations, use inefficient methods of performance, work in later time periods, perform during periods of interference, or stop work. The other source of confusion has been disagreement over the contractor's right to recover such costs. Numerous legal issues have arisen based on the intermingling or overlapping of common law and contract remedies, the interpretation of contract language, and the limitations on the recovery of consequential damages. While many of these issues have been resolved in favor of the contractor's right to recover, major problems are still encountered by contractors in proving causation and amount. The greatest difficulty involves claims for costs incurred during periods when no work is being performed and claims for increased costs of unchanged work. When the contractor's claim is for additional or changed work, lack of productivity is usually recovered as an integral part of the actual or estimated cost of such work and is not considered separately in the negotiations.

This section considers the types of costs recoverable, the techniques used for measuring the amounts, and the circumstances under which they may be recovered.

A. Theory of Recovery

The extent to which delay and impact costs are recoverable depends on the nature of the government action and the theory under which the contractor presents its claim. If the government action merely results in a delay, with no physical changes in the work to be accomplished, recovery is not permitted under the Changes clause.

Recovery must be through a breach of contract action or under the Suspension of Work or government Delay of Work clauses. Under either the suspension or breach theory, both delay and impact costs may be recovered. Where, however, the government's action results in more than mere delay and is thus considered to be a change under the Changes clause, or the claim comes under the Differing Site Conditions clause, the matter becomes very complex. Depending on the language of the specific clause involved, the nature of the government action, and the time when a delay occurs, delay or impact costs may be recoverable under the equitable adjustment for the change or differing site condition, under a breach of contract action or suspension theory, or not at all.

1. Delays Preceding a Change

With the exception of delays resulting from defective specifications, delays preceding the issuance of a change order are not compensable under the Changes clause. The theory advanced for this interpretation of the Changes clause is that "delays antecedent to a change order and not resulting from it are not justifiable under the Changes article," *Model Eng'g & Mfg. Corp.*, ASBCA 7490,1962 BCA ¶ 3363. See also *Weldfab, Inc.*, IBCA 268, 61-2 BCA ¶ 3121. Equitable adjustments for constructive changes based on defective specifications may include such pre-change delay costs, *J. W. Hurst & Son Awnings, Inc.*, ASBCA 4167, 59-1 BCA ¶ 2095. When the present construction contract Changes clause was adopted, the regulations issuing the clause adopted this rule and the defective specifications exception. See 32 Fed. Reg. 16269 (1967), stating:

> Except for defective specifications, the Changes clause as revised will continue to have no application to any delay prior to the issuance of a change order. An adjustment for such type of delay, if appropriate, will be for consideration under the provisions of the Suspension of Work clause.

Thus, the cost of delays that precede a change must be recovered either under a breach of contract theory or under the Suspension of Work clause. See *Luria Bros. & Co. v. United States*, 177 Ct. Cl. 676, 369 F.2d 701 (1966), in which, in a breach of contract action, the contractor recovered both delay costs (costs incurred while no work was being accomplished) and impact costs (increased costs of performing work).

This rule has been followed quite consistently by the courts and boards. See, for example, *Leonhard Weiss GmbH & Co.*, ASBCA 37574, 93-1 BCA ¶ 25,443 (no compensation under Suspension of Work clause for 17-day delay in issuing change order because that amount of time was reasonable); *Berrios Constr. Co.*, VABCA 3152, 92-2 BCA ¶ 24,828 (entire delay in determining how to overcome a differing site condition compensable under Suspension of Work clause); and *Beauchamp Constr. Co. v. United States*, 14 Cl. Ct. 430 (1988) (entire delay in ordering new technique to overcome differing site condition compensable under Suspension of Work clause). Compare *Rex Sys., Inc.*, ASBCA 45874, 94-1 BCA ¶ 26,370, *recons.*

denied, 94-2 BCA ¶ 26,637, in which the board apparently gave an equitable adjustment under the Changes clause for a 54-day delay in processing a request for a deviation from the specifications.

2. Delays Resulting from a Change or Differing Site Condition

After a change order is issued, delay and impact costs may involve both changed work and unchanged work. Current Changes clauses provide for recovery of costs of unchanged work, and this language is construed as covering delay cost after issuance of the change. See the explanatory language in 32 Fed. Reg. 16269 (1967), stating that under this language "an equitable adjustment clearly encompasses the effect of a change order upon any part of the work, including delay expense; provided, of course, that such effect was the necessary, reasonable, and foreseeable result of the change."

The equitable adjustment language in early Changes clauses did not specifically refer to unchanged work. The recovery of delay and impact costs of unchanged work was denied in *Chouteau v. United States*, 95 U.S. 61 (1877), where the contractor claimed a substantial adjustment in price as the result of numerous changes that had been ordered by the contracting officer. The Court found that the increase in price was due to delayed performance, during which time the costs of labor and material increased, stating at 68:

> It is very clear that both parties contemplated the probability that the work would not be completed at the precise period of eight months from the date of the contract. They also contemplated that changes would be made in construction of the battery. They made such provision for these matters as they deemed necessary for the protection of each party. For the reasonable cost and expenses of the changes made in the construction, payment was to be made; but for any increase in the cost of the work not changed, no provision was made. . . . [W]e are very clear that without any such provision [the contractor] must be held to have taken the risk of the prices of the labor and materials which he was bound to furnish, as every other contractor does who agrees to do a specified job at a fixed price.

In *United States v. Rice*, 317 U.S. 61 (1942), the government delayed the commencement of the work for a number of months while revising the specifications to compensate for an unsuitable soil condition. The Court found that the contractor was entitled to an equitable adjustment for the changed work but not for the effect of the long delay, stating at 67:

> It seems wholly reasonable that "an increase or decrease in the amount due" should be met with an alteration of price, and that "an increase or decrease in the time required" should be met with alteration of the time allowed; for "increase or decrease of cost" plainly applies to the changes in cost due to the structural changes required by the altered specification and not to consequential damages which might flow from delay taken care of in the "difference in time" provision.

These decisions were known as the "Rice Doctrine," which many believed precluded the recovery of such costs even if the costs were a direct result of the change. See, however, Shedd, *The Rice Doctrine and the Ripple Effect of Changes,* 32 Geo. Wash. L. Rev. 62 (1963), analyzing the application of this rule and pointing out that numerous board decisions allowed equitable adjustments in unchanged work when the increased costs were the direct result of the change, citing *Northeastern Eng'g, Inc.*, ASBCA 5732, 61-1 BCA ¶ 3026. In *Power Equip. Corp.*, ASBCA 5904, 1964 BCA ¶ 4025, *recons. denied*, 1964 BCA ¶ 4228, the board stated at 19,815:

> Where costs on a work item are increased as a direct result of a change in that item, the increased costs are compensable, including costs of delays in performance in the change order issued pursuant to the Changes clause.

In *Paul Hardeman, Inc. v. United States*, 186 Ct. Cl. 743, 406 F.2d 1357 (1969), the court further construed *Rice* and *Chouteau* as not precluding recovery of impact costs that would have resulted from the change whether or not a delay occurred. The court stated at 749-50:

> The term "delay" implies a stopping or hindrance for some period; "delay damages" are obviously those which flow from that increment in time. In this context, standby equipment expense, additional overhead, increased labor costs—typical delay damage items—are not incurred unless there is a prolongation of performance beyond the anticipated date of completion.
>
> In contrast, the costs sought by [the contractor] would have been incurred even had the contract been performed as soon as physically possible. An interruption in one phase of the work under a contract does not always result in an increase in the time necessary for total performance. In such a case, the absence of any delay would obviously preclude recovery therefor. Had there in fact been no delay in the completion of the instant contract, [the contractor's] restricted pouring operations would still have caused the increased costs alleged. [The contractor's] damages accordingly could not have been the result of any delay in performance, and the board erred in concluding otherwise.
>
> There remains the further question concerning the relation of the "Rice doctrine" to increased costs in the performance of work which is required by the contract, but which is not changed in scope by the changed condition. It is our opinion that the Supreme Court cases relied upon by defendant are not applicable to the instant situation.

See also the concurring opinion of Judge Davis at 752:

> I join in the court's opinion because I understand it to lay down and apply the same standard as has been used by the Boards of Contract Appeals in cases such as *Ivey Bros. Construction Co., Inc.*, Eng. BCA No. 1764 (1960) (unreported decision); *Gust K. Newberg Construction Co.*, Eng. BCA No. 2754, 67-2 BCA ¶ 6490, at 30,116-18; *I.K. Construction Co.*, Eng. BCA No. 10987, 67-1 BCA ¶

6271, at 29,027; *Eastridge Excavating Contractors, Inc.*, Eng. BCA No. 2683, 67-1 BCA ¶ 6379, at 29,534-35; *A.L Harding, Inc.*, DCAB No. PR-44, 65-2 BCA ¶ 5261, at 24,777, *aff'd on recons.*, 66-1 BCA ¶ 5463, at 25,590-91, and *Power City Construction & Equipment, Inc.*, IBCA No. 490-4-65, 68-1 BCA ¶ 7126, at 33,024-26. That rule permits an equitable adjustment to cover increased costs which were the direct and necessary result of the change or changed conditions, where the condition or the change directly leads to disruption, extra work, or new procedures. The record makes it very clear that such is the situation here and that the Engineers Board could not properly find the [contractor's] added costs to be merely "consequential."

The trial judge's opinion, adopted by the court in *Frank Briscoe Co v. United States*, 214 Ct. Cl. 801, 566 F.2d 1189 (1977), indicates that delay costs are still not recoverable under the pre-1967 version of the construction contract Changes clause. However, *Coley Props. Corp. v. United States*, 219 Ct. Cl. 227, 593 F.2d 380 (1979), dealt with a Changes clause remarkably similar to the pre-1967 construction clause and permitted the contractor to recover impact costs resulting from delays in the unchanged portion of the contract caused by issuance of change orders.

Some cases have identified "cumulative impact," which may be claimed separately from specific changes, *Pittman Constr. Co.*, GSBCA 4897, 81-1 BCA ¶ 14,847, *recons. denied*, 81-1 BCA ¶ 15,111, *aff'd*, 2 Cl. Ct. 211 (1983). This case relied on the reasoning in *Ingalls Shipbuilding Div., Litton Sys., Inc.*, ASBCA 17579, 78-1 BCA ¶ 13,038, *recons. denied*, 78-1 BCA ¶ 13,216, granting a substantial recovery where several thousand changes occurred. In *Pittman*, recovery for cumulative impact was denied because the contractor had incurred concurrent delay and disruption for which it was responsible and had been unable to prove that the government changes had been the cause of the impact costs. See *Freeman-Darling, Inc.*, GSBCA 7112, 89-2 BCA ¶ 21,882, stating at 110,101:

> We have recognized that contract changes may result in two types of impact costs, direct and cumulative, and have defined these two as follows:
>
> > The term "direct impact" refers to costs that are, more or less, the direct consequences of a change. Such costs are readily foreseeable, and a contractor is expected to recognize them in forward pricing a change. . . .
> >
> > "Cumulative impact" costs . . . are cost associated with impact on distant work, and are not readily foreseeable or, if foreseeable, are not readily computable as direct impact costs. The source of such costs are the sheer number and scope of the changes to the contract. The result is an unanticipated loss of efficiency and productivity which increases the contractor's performance costs and usually extends his stay on the job.
>
> *Haas & Haynie Corp.*, GSBCA Nos. 5530, 6244, 6638, 6919, 6920, 84-2 BCA ¶ 17,446, at 86,897.

This distinction has not influenced the compensability of these costs but has been used as a means of permitting recovery of cumulative impact costs when a contractor has signed a release of claims for the changes causing the impact. See, for example, *Hensel Phelps Constr. Co. v. General Servs. Admin.*, GSBCA 14744, 01-1 BCA ¶ 31,249, *aff'd*, 36 Fed. Appx. 649 (Fed. Cir. 2002) (finding that tacit agreement to price cumulative impacts costs separately overrode releases), and *Hercules Constr. Corp.*, ASBCA 51296, 99-2 BCA ¶ 30,406 (summary judgment denied because contractor alleged government agreed to deal with cumulative impact separately). However, there have been very few recoveries of cumulative impact costs because of lack of convincing proof of the amount of costs attributable to the impact, *J.A. Jones Constr. Co.*, ENGBCA 6348, 00-2 BCA ¶ 31,000; *Centex Bateson Constr. Co.*, VABCA 4613, 99-1 BCA ¶ 30,153, *aff'd*, 250 F.3d 761 (Fed. Cir. 2000); or lack of proof that a significant number of changes actually caused such impact, *Hensel Phelps Constr. Co.*, ASBCA 49270, 99-2 BCA ¶ 30,531, *recons. denied*, 00-1 BCA ¶ 30,733, *aff'd*, 13 Fed. Appx. 949 (Fed. Cir. 2001); *Coates Indus. Piping, Inc.*, VABCA 5412, 99-2 BCA ¶ 30,479; *Southwest Marine, Inc.*, ASBCA 36854, 95-1 BCA ¶ 27,601, *recons. denied*, 95-2 BCA ¶ 27,861; *Southwest Marine, Inc.*, DOT-BCA 1663, 94-3 BCA ¶ 27,102; *McMillin Bros. Constructors, Inc.*, EBCA 328-10-84, 91-1 BCA ¶ 23,351, *aff'd*, 949 F.2d 403 (Fed. Cir. 1991); *Bechtel Nat'l, Inc.*, NASABCA 1186-7, 90-1 BCA ¶ 22,549, *recons. denied*, 90-3 BCA ¶ 23,105; *Saudi Tarmac Co.*, ENGBCA 4841, 89-3 BCA ¶ 22,132. Compare *Clark Constr. Group, Inc.*, VABCA 5674, 00-1 BCA ¶ 30,870, *recons. denied*, 00-2 BCA ¶ 30,997, in which a contractor recovered for both direct and cumulative impact.

B. Impact on Other Work

Although the contractor now appears to be entitled to recover impact and delay costs on the unchanged portion of a contract in an equitable adjustment under the Changes or Differing Site Conditions clauses, an adjustment under the Suspension of Work clause, or a breach of contract action, it is a different matter when the impact costs are incurred on other contracts or private work. Generally, recovery of these costs is not permitted under the contract in which the change, suspension, or breach occurred. Such damages are usually considered to be too remote or too speculative and subject to the rule that consequential damages are not recoverable under government contracts. See *Northern Helex Co. v. United States*, 207 Ct. Cl. 862, 524 F.2d 707 (1975), *cert. denied*, 429 U.S. 866 (1976), in which the court stated at 886-87:

> Furthermore, remote and consequential damages are not recoverable in a common-law suit for breach of contract. See *Globe Refining Co. v. Landa Cotton Oil Co.*, 190 U.S. 540, 543 (1903). This is especially true in suits against the United States for the recovery of common-law damages, such as the instant case. See *Ramsey v. United States*, 121 Ct. Cl. 426, 101 F. Supp. 353 (1951), *cert. denied*, 343 U.S. 977 (1952); *Dale Constr. Co. v. United States*, 168 Ct. Cl. 692, 738 (1964); *Specialty Assembling & Packing Co. v. United States*, 174 Ct. Cl. 153, 175, 355 F.2d 554,

> 567-68 (1966); *William Green Constr. Co. v. United States*, 201 Ct. Cl. 616, 626-27, 477 F.2d 930, 936-37 (1973), *cert. denied*, 417 U.S. 909 (1974).

Additional guidance was given in *General Dynamics Corp. v. United States*, 218 Ct. Cl. 40, 585 F.2d 457 (1978), where the contractor had acquired a shipyard at Quincy, Massachusetts and, with the government's approval, had been assigned two submarine construction contracts that had been awarded to the previous owner. Later, also with the government's approval, the contractor moved two submarines that it had been constructing at another shipyard in Groton, Connecticut, to its newly acquired Quincy yard. The purpose of the move was to relieve congestion at the Groton facility and to take advantage of skilled personnel at the Quincy yard. Claiming that changes to the submarines that had been moved to Quincy caused increased costs on the other contracts, the contractor sought an equitable adjustment for those impact costs. In denying recovery, the court stated at 54-55:

> Where the extra costs result from the "impact" of one contract on another, the situation appears to be different.
>
> * * *
>
> The cases [*J.A. Jones Construction Co. v. United States*, 182 Ct. Cl. 615, 390 F.2d 886 (1968), *Allied Paint Mfg. Co. v. United States*, 200 Ct. Cl. 313, 470 F.2d 556 (1972); *Specialty Assembling & Packing Co. v. United States*, 174 Ct. Cl. 153, 355 F.2d 554 (1966)] seem to lead to the conclusion that only in exceptional circumstances can an equitable adjustment be made for extra cost in performing one contract, caused by the government doing things it has a right to do, respecting other contracts. Such rare cases will be those of concealment from the [contractor], when it bids, of already formulated plans and intentions respecting other contracts, which plans and intentions the [contractor] needs to know to estimate its costs, possibly some instances of intentionally and knowingly hindering the [contractor] in doing the contract work, and perhaps other instances where some degree of government culpability and "proximate cause" exist.

An exception to the general rule was found in *Ingalls Shipbuilding Div., Litton Sys., Inc.*, ASBCA 17579, 78-1 BCA ¶ 13,038, *recons. denied*, 78-1 BCA ¶ 13,216, in which a contractor who was suspended on one contract was permitted to recover on that contract for delay and disruption costs incurred on other contracts because of the suspension. The board emphasized that such recovery was permitted only because of the specific language contained in the unique Suspension of Work clause used in shipbuilding contracts, stating at 63,659:

> A very major distinction between the Suspension clause language in these contracts and language in the standard or usual Suspension clause is that the clause here present allows for "such adjustment in the contract price as will equitably compensate the Contractor for the increased costs incurred by it arising out of such suspension. . . ." The Suspension of Work (Feb. 1968) clause set forth at ASPR 7-602.46 provides that "an adjustment shall be made for any increase in

> the cost of performance of this contract (excluding profit. . . ." We need not and do not consider the question of whether the language of the usual Suspension of Work clause would permit recovery of costs such as here claimed. That is a more difficult question which will be reserved until such time as actually before us. The language of the clause we deal with is, as noted previously, much broader. In our opinion it is sufficiently broad to permit recovery for all foreseeable impact costs including those for other work in the shipyard if such impact and costs arising therefrom are proved.

The board also emphasized that, even in these special circumstances, such costs would not be recoverable unless they were foreseeable by the government, stating at 63,659-61:

> If a causal relationship is established between the impacting and impacted contracts so that the increased costs which were incurred did in fact arise out of the suspension, they must be paid in order for a contractor to be equitably compensated for such increased costs as required by the contract. To hold otherwise would negate the clear words of the contract. See *Bruce Construction Co. v. United States*, 163 Ct. Cl. 97, 324 F.2d 516 (1963).
>
> The legal question of whether an equitable adjustment can include adverse financial impact or ripple effects on other contracts is one of first impression.
>
> * * *
>
> The closest case on point is *Cornell Wrecking Company, Inc. v. United States*, 184 Ct. Cl. 289 (1968). In that case the Government failed to make a building available to the contractor for scheduled demolition. The contractor was forced to keep equipment idle at the work site pending the Government release of the buildings. The contractor was eventually able to demolish the Government building but was forced to rent equipment from a commercial source for performance of a non-Government contract. Noting the absence of a Suspension of Work clause in the Government contract which would have permitted an equitable adjustment, the court allowed the cost of renting equipment under the non-Government contract as damages for breach of the Government contract.
>
> * * *
>
> [The government] argues that recovery is not available since the "impact" costs were not direct and reasonable costs of the submarines relying, *inter alia*, on the "Rice doctrine" and the leading case of *Hadley v. Baxendale*, 9 Ex. 341 (1854) which propounded the rule of foreseeability . . . .
>
> * * *
>
> [W]e conclude that the likelihood that, in the event of a suspension, submarine construction would be pushed into a period for which [the contractor] had other shipbuilding responsibilities was foreseeable.

The contractor was a commercial shipbuilder and, as previously discussed, sought to maintain a level work force by "shingling" its various contracts. This was known to the government when the three submarine contracts involved in this dispute were executed. See also *Alabama Dry Dock & Shipbuilding Corp.*, ASBCA 36839, 90-2 BCA ¶ 22,758, permitting a claim for extra work on a contract caused by government action on an adjacent contract. Compare *Smith v. United States*, 34 Fed. Cl. 313 (1995) (denying ripple effect claim on three other contracts because such costs remote and speculative); *Sermor, Inc.*, ASBCA 30576, 94-1 BCA ¶ 26,302, *recons. denied*, 94-3 BCA ¶ 27,244 (denying impact costs resulting from events on other contracts because there were no "exceptional circumstances"); and *Flores Drilling & Pump Co.*, AGBCA 82-204-3, 83-1 BCA ¶ 16,200, *recons. denied*, 83-1 BCA ¶ 16,336 (denying impact costs on other contracts because the contract contained no special provision).

C. Consequential Damages

There has been almost no recovery against the government for consequential damages. This may be because of a very difficult rule requiring a contractor to prove both foreseeability and direct causation of the damages. This requirement is derived from the following statement in *Myerle v. United States*, 33 Ct. Cl. 1 (1897), at 27:

> We hold that the [contractor] can only recover those items of damage which are the proximate result of the acts of the Government. What those items are is somewhat difficult to determine. For a damage to be direct there must appear no intervening incident (not caused by the defaulting party) to complicate or confuse the certainty of the result between the cause and the damage; the cause must produce the effect inevitably and naturally, not possibly nor even probably. The damage must be such as was to have been foreseen by the parties, who are assumed to have considered the situation, the contract, and the usual course of events; but eliminated from this consideration must be any condition of affairs peculiar to the contractor individually in the particular case and not of general application under similar conditions. There must not be two steps between cause and damage.

See *CCM Corp. v. United States*, 15 Cl. Ct. 670 (1988), and *Land Movers, Inc.*, ENGBCA 5656, 91-1 BCA ¶ 23,317, interpreting this statement to require proof that the damages are both foreseeable and the natural and probable consequence of the government's actions.

Contractors have been unable to meet these requirements when they have submitted claims for destruction of their business. See, for example, *Ramsey v. United States*, 121 Ct. Cl. 426, 101 F. Supp. 353 (1951), *cert. denied*, 343 U.S. 977 (1952), and *David J. Tierney, Jr., Inc.*, GSBCA 7107, 88-2 BCA ¶ 20,806, *recons. denied*, 88-3 BCA ¶ 20,906. They have also failed to recover for lost business opportunities, *Wells Fargo Bank, N.A. v. United States*, 88 F.3d 1012 (Fed. Cir. 1996), *cert. denied*, 520 U.S. 1116 (1997); *Olin Jones Sand Co. v. United States*, 225 Ct. Cl. 741 (1980); *H.H.O., Inc. v. United States*, 7 Cl. Ct. 703 (1985); *Cox & Palmer*, ASBCA 37328,

89-3 BCA ¶ 22,197; *Nevada Skylines, Inc.*, AGBCA 92-167-1, 92-3 BCA ¶ 25,089, *recons. denied*, 93-1 BCA ¶ 25,352. Similarly, relief has been denied for lost profits on other contracts that were not obtained because of government action, *Rumsfeld v. Freedom N.Y., Inc.*, 329 F.3d 1320 (Fed. Cir. 2003), *cert. denied*, 541 U.S. 987 (2004); *CCM Corp. v. United States*, 15 Cl. Ct. 670 (1988); *Land Movers, Inc.*, ENGBCA 5656, 91-1 BCA ¶ 23,317; *A-1 Garbage Disposal & Trash Serv., Inc.*, ASBCA 43006, 93-1 BCA ¶ 25,465. Claims for financial injury to the owner of the contractor have also been denied, *Tele-Sentry Sec., Inc. v. General Servs. Admin.*, GSBCA 8950, 92-3 BCA ¶ 25,088.

D. Unabsorbed Overhead

Contractors have been permitted to recover additional overhead for delays either on the theory that additional overhead costs are incurred when the contract period is extended or on the theory that the contract has not absorbed its share of overhead during the period when no work, or a lesser amount than planned, has been accomplished. Such overhead has been called "unabsorbed overhead" or "extended overhead." In cases using the unabsorbed overhead theory, it is assumed that extending the performance period will increase the overhead costs allocable to the contract. The seminal case, *Eichleay Corp.*, ASBCA 5183, 60-2 BCA ¶ 2688, *recons. denied*, 61-1 BCA ¶ 2894, used this theory to grant recovery of home office overhead on a construction contract on the basis of a pro rata amount per day without regard to whether any actual costs were incurred. The "Eichleay formula" consists of the following three steps:

$$1.\ \frac{\text{Contract billings}}{\text{Total billings for actual contract period}} \times \text{Total overhead incurred during contract} = \text{Overhead allocable to the contract}$$

$$2.\ \frac{\text{Allocable overhead}}{\text{Actual days of contract performance}} = \text{Overhead allocable to contract per day}$$

$$3.\ \text{Daily overhead} \times \text{Number of days of delay} = \text{Unabsorbed overhead}$$

In the 1980s there was concern as to whether the Eichleay formula could lead to over-recovery because little additional overhead was actually incurred, the delay period was short, or some of the overhead costs were variable costs. However, in *Capital Elec. Co. v. United States*, 729 F.2d 743 (Fed. Cir. 1984), the court held that the formula was properly used in such circumstances, stating at 745-46:

> Although these points have some degree of validity, we are not persuaded that they correctly reflect the concept of the Eichleay formula, at least as far as [the contractor] is concerned. In this case, *compensable* delay was stipulated before the board. More-

> over, [the contractor] introduced unrebutted evidence that it could not have taken on any large construction jobs during the various delay periods due to the uncertainty of the delays and (except after the original contract period, when a major portion of the project had been completed and accepted) due to the limitation on its bonding capacity. Thus, [the contractor] has not actually used an *ipso facto* approach. Indeed, as stated in *Eichleay*, 61-1 BCA ¶ 2894 at 15,117: "The mere showing of these facts is sufficient to transfer to the Government the burden of going forward with proof that [the contractor] suffered no loss or should have suffered no loss."

Subsequently, in a long series of cases, the Federal Circuit established the critical test for application of the formula as the contractor's proof that it was on "standby" during a period of government-caused delay. If this is proved, the government can then overcome application of the formula by proving that the contractor could have taken on additional work during the standby period. This formulation was summarized in *P.J. Dick, Inc. v. Principi*, 324 F.3d 1364 (Fed. Cir. 2003), at 1370:

> To show entitlement to . . . Eichleay damages, the contractor must first prove there was a government-caused delay to contract performance (as originally planned) that was not concurrent with a delay caused by the contractor or some other reason. *Sauer Inc. v. Danzig*, 224 F.3d 1340, 1347-48 (Fed. Cir. 2000). The contractor must also show that the original time for performance of the contract was thereby extended, or that he finished the contract on time or early but nonetheless incurred additional, unabsorbed overhead expenses because he had planned to finish even sooner. *Interstate Gen. Gov't Contractors, Inc. v. West*, 12 F.3d 1053, 1058-59 (Fed. Cir. 1993). Once the contractor has proven the above elements, it must then prove that it was required to remain on standby during that delay. *Id.* If the contractor proves these three elements it has made a prima facie case of entitlement and a burden of production shifts to the government to show that it was not impractical for the contractor to take on replacement work and thereby mitigate its damages. *Melka* [*Marine, Inc. v. United States*], 187 F.3d [1370] at 1376 [(Fed. Cir. 1999)]. If the government meets its burden of production, however, the contractor bears the burden of persuasion that it was impractical for it to obtain sufficient replacement work. Id.

Recognizing that the standby requirement was the most difficult to understand and apply, the court summarized its prior holdings on this issue at 1371-73:

> A review of the pertinent case law shows that the standby inquiry is multifaceted. In making that inquiry, the court should first determine whether the CO has issued a written order that suspends all the work on the contract for an uncertain duration and requires the contractor to remain ready to resume work immediately or on short notice. See *Interstate*, 12 F.3d at 1055, 1057 n.4. In such a case, the contractor need not offer further proof of standby. In the cases where the CO does not issue such a written order, the contractor must then prove standby by indirect evidence. See *id.* To do so, the contractor must show three things.
>
> First, the contractor must show that the government-caused delay was not only substantial but was of an indefinite duration. See *id.* at 1058. For example,

where the government suspends all work on the contract, but tells the contractor work will begin again on a date certain, the contractor cannot be on standby. See *Melka*, 187 F.3d at 1376.

Second, the contractor must show that during that delay it was required to be ready to resume work on the contract, at full speed as well as immediately. See *id.* Our case law has not elaborated on this requirement, but it is clear that once the suspension period is over, the contractor must be required to be ready to "resume full work immediately." E.g., *id.* at 1375; [*West v. All State Boiler, Inc.*], 146 F.3d [1368] at 1373 [(Fed. Cir. 1998)]. Thus, where the government gives the contractor a reasonable amount of time to remobilize its work force once the suspension is lifted, the contractor cannot be on standby. *Mech-Con Corp. v. West*, 61 F.3d 883, 887 (Fed. Cir. 1995) (holding the contractor could not be on standby where the government gave the contractor three months to remobilize its work force on site). Presumably, the same result would follow if the government required immediate resumption of the work, but only with a reduced work force and allowed the contractor to gradually increase its work force over some reasonable amount of time. See, e.g., *Melka*, 187 F.3d at 1375. In addition, satisfaction of this element of standby clearly requires something more than an uncertain delay as this is a separate requirement of the case law; the implication is that the contractor must be required to keep at least some of its workers and necessary equipment at the site, even if idle, ready to resume work on the contract (i.e., doing nothing or working on something elsewhere that allows them to get back to the contract site on short notice). See, e.g., *Sergent Mech. Sys. v. United States*, 54 Fed. Cl. 47, 49-50, 54 Fed. Cl. 636 (Fed. Cl. 2002).

Third, the contractor must show effective suspension of much, if not all, of the work on the contract. *Cf. Melka*, 187 F.3d at 1375. Our early decisions do contain some statements that arguably support the notion that suspension of the work and idleness are not prerequisites to a determination that the contractor is on standby. E.g., *Altmayer v. Johnson*, 79 F.3d 1129, 1134 (Fed. Cir. 1996) ("There is no requirement that a contract be suspended before a contractor is entitled to recover under Eichleay."); *Interstate*, 12 F.3d at 1057 n.4 ("Although idleness of workers is evidence that a contractor is on standby, i.e., performance has been suspended, it is neither conclusive nor required."). At no time, however, has this court *held* that a contractor has been placed on standby merely because a government-caused delay of uncertain duration occurred, at the end of which the contractor must be ready to resume work. *Altmayer*, oft cited for that proposition, held no such thing. *Altmayer* merely held that a contractor's performance of "minor tasks" during a suspension does not prevent it from recovering Eichleay damages. *Altmayer*, 79 F.3d at 1134. Nor does *Interstate's* statement that idleness is not a prerequisite to standby support the idea that a contractor can be deemed on standby where there is no delay or suspension of the work. 12 F.3d at 1057 n.4. A closer reading of *Interstate* indicates that its reference to "idleness" simply means the workers need not be "physically standing by idly." *Id.* at 1057 n.5 (referencing a quote in a previous opinion and stating "these two phrases ["stand by idly and suspend its work"] clearly refer to standing by in the sense that no work is being performed on the contract, not that there must be workers physically standing by idly"); see also *id.* at 1057 n.4 ("If the test were whether the contractor's work force assigned to the contract in issue was standing by, the contractor would be penalized for, and thus deterred from, mitigating its damages for direct costs by reassigning its employees to other jobs or laying them off during the period of delay."). Indeed, every case where this court has held a contractor to be placed on standby has involved a complete suspension or delay of all the work or at most continued performance of only insubstantial work on the contract. *See, e.g., E.R. Mitchell Constr. Co. v. Danzig*, 175 F.3d 1369, 1372, 1374 (Fed. Cir. 1999) (holding subcontractor was entitled to Eichleay damages where it performed "some work" on the contract, but where most "work could not proceed until the faults [causing the suspension] were cured"); *All State Boiler, Inc.*, 146 F.3d at 1370, 1373 (holding contractor was entitled to Eichleay damages where the government suspended all work on the contract); *Satellite Elec. Co. v. Dalton*, 105 F.3d 1418, 1421 (Fed. Cir. 1997) (holding contractor was on standby where all the work on the contract was stopped, but denying recovery of Eichleay damages for other reasons); *Altmayer*, 79 F.3d at 1134; *Mech-Con*, 61 F.3d at 887 (holding contractor was entitled to Eichleay damages where work on the contract was completely suspended); *see also Interstate*, 12 F.3d at 1058 (noting that the record "could support" a conclusion that a contractor was on standby where all work on the contract was suspended).

In addition to being implicit in our early cases, our later decisions explicitly state that such a suspension or delay of the work on the contract is a prerequisite to a finding that the government placed the contractor on standby. *Melka*, 187 F.3d at 1375-76; *see also Interstate*, 12 F.3d at 1057 (discussing standby as requiring "suspension of work on the contract"). In *Melka*, we held that a contractor was not on standby where it "was working on the contract and the government had not suspended all contract work." 187 F.3d at 1375. There, the government stopped work on one type of work, but, by resequencing the work under the contract, the contractor was able to perform substantial work on another type of work with comparable direct cost billings. *Id.* at 1375-76. . . . Thus, even though it is the typical scenario, formal suspension is not an absolute prerequisite. Contract performance also could be stopped or significantly slowed by government inaction, such as failure to vacate spaces in which the contract was to be performed.

It can be seen that contractors will have great difficulty in meeting this stringent standby test since it will be difficult to prove the "indefinite duration" element and the "immediate resumption" element. See *Williams Constr., Inc. v. White*, 326 F.3d 1376 (Fed. Cir. 2003), rejecting an Eichleay claim because the contractor did not prove the "immediate resumption" requirement or that there were any days when it could do no work. However, if the test is met, the government then has the burden of demonstrating that it was not impractical for the contractor to take on replacement work. This burden was extensively discussed in *West v. All State Boiler, Inc.*, 146 F.3d 1368 (Fed. Cir. 1998), in which the court discussed the concept of a "replacement contract" as follows, at 1377:

[A] contractor is injured only when it cannot reallocate that portion of its indirect costs to an alternative or substitutional contract, and thereby those costs are unabsorbed. When a contractor is able to reallocate its indirect expenses to a contract it

> obtains beyond the work it performs in the ordinary course of business, however, it sustains no injury and therefore compensation under the Eichleay formula is not justified. This alternative or substitutional work we will hereafter call a "replacement" contract. Such a replacement contract might be a contract different in size or duration from a contractor's ordinary type of work (for example, a $ 100,000 contract by a contractor who normally obtains multi-million dollar contracts), or a contract for a different type of work (for example, a repair contract rather than new construction). The critical factor, then, is not whether the contractor was able to obtain or to continue work on other or additional projects but rather its ability to obtain a replacement contract to absorb the indirect costs that would otherwise be unabsorbed solely as a result of a government suspension on one contract.

The Federal Circuit has held that the Eichleay formula is the exclusive way of computing extended or unabsorbed overhead, *Wickham Contracting Co. v. Fischer*, 12 F.3d 1574 (Fed. Cir. 1994). However, since this was stated in the context of a construction contract, it is not clear whether it applies to other types of contracts. The Armed Services Board stated that the Eichleay formula is the exclusive method of computing this compensation on supply contracts, *Libby Corp.*, ASBCA 40765, 96-1 BCA ¶ 28,255, *aff'd*, 106 F.3d 427 (Fed. Cir. 1997). See also *Genisco Tech. Corp.*, ASBCA 49664, 99-1 BCA ¶ 30,145, *recons. denied*, 99-1 BCA ¶ 30,324, *aff'd*, 250 F.3d 757 (Fed. Cir. 2000), denying recovery because the contractor did not furnish the data necessary to apply the formula. A few earlier board cases used the Eichleay formula on supply contracts. See *So-Pak-Co, Inc.*, ASBCA 38906, 93-3 BCA ¶ 26,215; *Bristol Elecs. Corp.*, ASBCA 24792, 84-3 BCA ¶ 17,543, *recons. denied*, 85-1 BCA ¶ 17,821; *Kestrel Corp.*, ASBCA 17968, 74-1 BCA ¶ 10,555 (formula used with modifications); and *Therm-Air Mfg. Co.*, ASBCA 16453, 73-1 BCA ¶ 9983. One case rejected the use of the formula, *Do-Well Mach. Shop*, ASBCA 35867, 92-2 BCA ¶ 24,843, while another case computed unabsorbed manufacturing overhead and unabsorbed G&A expense by calculating the amount of these indirect costs that would have been allocated to the contract if no delay had occurred and the amount that was actually allocated to the contract, *Industrial Pump & Compressor, Inc.*, ASBCA 39003, 93-2 BCA ¶ 25,757. The Federal Circuit relaxed the exclusivity rule in *Nicon, Inc. v. United States*, 331 F.3d 878 (Fed. Cir. 2003), ruling that the contractor could deviate from the Eichleay formula in the situation where it had remained on standby prior to the issuance of a notice to proceed and had then been terminated for convenience.

The contractor can recover extended or unabsorbed overhead expenses even if it finishes the work within the contract period if it can show that it could have completed early. In *Interstate Gen. Gov't Contractors, Inc. v. West*, 12 F.3d 1053 (Fed. Cir. 1993), the court stated the test as follows, at 1058-59:

> Where a contractor is able to meet the original contract deadline or, as here, to finish early despite a government-caused delay, the originally bargained for time period for absorbing home office overhead through contract performance payments has not been extended. Therefore, in order to show that any portion of

> the overhead was unabsorbed, such a contractor must prove that the bargained for ratio of performance revenue to fixed overhead costs during the stipulated performance period, not just the delay period, . . . has been adversely affected by the delay. This can only be established if such a contractor shows that from the outset of the contract it (1) intended to complete the contract early; (2) had the capability to do so; and (3) actually would have completed early, but for the government's actions.

In that case, the court did not award any unabsorbed overhead because the contractor did not meet these tests. The contractor also failed to prove that it could have completed the work ahead of schedule in *Skyline Painting, Inc.*, ENGBCA 5810, 93-3 BCA ¶ 26,041, and *Bell Coatings, Inc.*, ENGBCA 5787, 93-2 BCA ¶ 25,805.

Contract clauses imposing a ceiling on the amount of overhead that can be recovered in pricing equitable adjustments under the Changes clause limit the recovery of home office overhead using the Eichleay formula, *Reliance Ins. Co. v. United States*, 932 F.2d 981 (Fed. Cir. 1991); *Santa Fe Eng'rs, Inc. v. United States*, 801 F.2d 379 (Fed. Cir. 1986). These cases applied a special clause used by the Department of Veterans Affairs to limit the recovery of unabsorbed overhead. The clause did not apply to suspensions of work, with the result that unabsorbed overhead incurred through a delay caused by a suspension would have been compensable using the Eichleay computation if the tests were met.

There were two other formulas used for supply contracts. In *Carteret Work Uniforms*, ASBCA 1647, 6 CCF ¶ 61,561 (1954), the board used the following two steps:

1. Incurred overhead rate during delay period	–	Normal overhead rate	=	Excess rate of overhead
2. Excess rate of overhead	x	Total base cost during delay	=	Unabsorbed overhead

In *Allegheny Sportswear Co.*, ASBCA 4163, 58-1 BCA ¶ 1684, a similar formula was used:

1. Incurred overhead rate during actual period	–	Incurred overhead rate for projected performance period	=	Excess rate of overhead
2. Excess rate of overhead	x	Base costs of contract	=	Unabsorbed overhead

The recovery of field overhead for extended periods of performance on construction contracts must be distinguished from that of home office overhead. In field overhead cases, the costs may actually have been increased by the delay because the contractor must continue on site for an additional period of time and incur costs that would not have been incurred but for the delay. The contractor is clearly entitled to recover such costs, *Pathman Constr. Co.*, ASBCA 22003, 82-1 BCA ¶ 15,790, *modified on other grounds*, 82-2 BCA ¶ 16,019; *Armada/Hoffler Constr. Co.*, DOT-BCA 2437, 93-1 BCA ¶ 25,446. However, the Eichleay formula should not be used without considering what costs should have been mitigated. See *Kemmons-Wilson, Inc.*, ASBCA 16167, 72-2 BCA ¶ 9689, recognizing the right to recovery but limiting the amount to fixed costs. See also *K.L. Conwell Corp.*, ASBCA 35489, 90-1 BCA ¶ 22,487.

E. Idle Labor and Equipment

In some cases, good business judgment will indicate that a contractor should keep labor or equipment available to continue performance of the work once the delay or disruption has ended. The costs of such idle labor or unused equipment are compensable subject to the normal analysis of the contractor's mitigation of damages. See *Hardeman-Monier-Hutcherson (JV)*, ASBCA 11785, 67-1 BCA ¶ 6210, in which the board stated at 28,748-49:

> A contractor has the duty to minimize its costs in the execution of a change order in the same manner as he must mitigate his damages after a breach. Normally he would be required to transfer or discharge idle men, and find uses for his equipment pending the time that work can commence. The remote location of this site, fully described in Finding No. 1, and the difficulties of mobilization, demobilization and remobilization at such a site, made this impracticable while [the contractor] was waiting for the bracing steel. Most of the skilled workmen had been recruited in eastern Australia 3,500 miles away, and in the United States, half-way around the earth from the site. Equipment and materials had been shipped great distances. Men could not be discharged with any hope of later availability, and there were no projects to which they and equipment could be temporarily assigned. As the result [the contractor] and its subcontractors incurred standby costs from idle men and equipment.

1. Labor

As indicated in *Hardeman*, the contractor is normally expected to discharge or reassign workers when they cannot be productively used on a job. However, each case must be analyzed based on the circumstances faced by the contractor at the time the delay or disruption occurred. See *Melka Marine, Inc. v. United States*, 41 Fed. Cl. 122 (1998), *aff'd*, 187 F.3d 1370 (Fed. Cir. 1999), *cert. denied*, 529 U.S. 1053 (2000), where the contractor was unable to prove that "core" workers were idle when they performed "shop work" during the delay, *Signal Contracting, Inc.*, ASBCA 44963, 93-2 BCA ¶ 25,877, *recons. denied*, 93-3 BCA ¶ 26,058, *aff'd*, 17 F.3d 1442 (Fed. Cir. 1994), where the contractor could have used the idle workers on other parts of the work, and *Boublis Elec., Inc.*, ASBCA 34056, 89-3 BCA ¶

22,094, in which the contractor was unable to demonstrate that it had been necessary to keep an electrician on the payroll during a 305-day delay. Compare *Edwards Mfg. Co.*, ASBCA 26936, 84-1 BCA ¶ 17,205, in which the contractor's continued employment of personnel doing productive work was not held to be a failure to mitigate because of the government's frequent advice that the delivery of GFP was imminent. See also *Caddell Constr. Co.*, VABCA 5608, 03-2 BCA ¶ 32,257 (idle and unproductive labor in shifts barred from site by contamination included in claim); *Raytheon STX Corp. v. Department of Commerce*, GSBCA 14296-COM, 00-1 BCA ¶ 30,632 (key employees retained during indefinite delay period); *Stroh Corp. v. General Servs. Admin.*, GSBCA 11029, 96-1 BCA ¶ 28,265 (pay differential for job foreman assigned to small project during delay); *Tayag Bros. Enters., Inc.*, ASBCA 42097, 94-3 BCA ¶ 26,962, *recons. denied*, 95-1 BCA ¶ 27,599 (electricians and an air conditioning technicians awaiting government direction—idle labor during long delay denied); *OC-W&M (JV)*, GSBCA 4694, 83-2 BCA ¶ 16,667 (construction manager's supervisory staff salaries were fully included in a delay claim that covered a longer construction period than originally anticipated). No compensation will be granted for the owners of a company that were not on the payroll during contract performance, *Hoyer Constr. Co.*, ASBCA 32178, 87-3 BCA ¶ 20,184.

The contractor's recovery of labor costs will be reduced by the amount of productive work, if any, accomplished during the delay period, *Laburnum Constr. Corp. v. United States*, 163 Ct. Cl. 339, 325 F.2d 451 (1963). Further, recovery will be denied if the contractor fails to present evidence by which the amount of idle or unproductive time can be ascertained, *Oxwell, Inc.*, ASBCA 27119, 83-2 BCA ¶ 16,762, *recons. denied*, 84-2 BCA ¶ 17,412.

Severance pay to idled employees could be included in a delay claim if it is paid pursuant to "law, agreement or policy," *Edward K. Dilworth*, PSBCA 1205, 84-2 BCA ¶ 17,346. There, voluntary payments to idled employees were held not allowable.

2. Contractor-Owned Equipment

The cost of contractor-owned equipment that is made idle by a delay or disruption is compensated at either actual costs or rates derived from equipment rate manuals. FAR 31.105(d)(2) provides the following guidance regarding construction equipment:

> (i) Allowable ownership and operating costs shall be determined as follows:
>
> > (A) Actual cost data shall be used when such data can be determined for both ownership and operations costs for each piece of equipment, or groups of similar serial or series equipment, from the contractor's accounting records. When such costs cannot be so determined, the contracting agency may specify the use of a particular schedule of predetermined rates

> or any part thereof to determine ownership and operating costs of construction equipment. . . .
>
> (B) Predetermined schedules of construction equipment use rates (e.g., the Construction Equipment Ownership and Operating Expense Schedule published by the U.S. Army Corps of Engineers, industry sponsored construction equipment cost guides, or commercially published schedules of equipment use cost) provide average ownership and operating rates for construction equipment. . . .

Under this guidance, each agency must determine whether to include a reference to a rate schedule in its contracts or to use actual costs. If no contract clause or regulation is applicable, actual costs are the preferred method of calculating these costs, *Charles D. Weaver v. United States*, 209 Ct. Cl. 714, 538 F.2d 346 (1976). However, rates called for by the contract will control. See *Servidone Constr. Corp. v. United States*, 19 Cl. Ct. 346 (1990), *aff'd*, 931 F.2d 860 (Fed. Cir. 1991) (AGC rates); *C.L. Fairley Constr. Co.*, ASBCA 32581, 90-2 BCA ¶ 22,665, *recons. denied*, 90-3 BCA ¶ 23,005 (Corps of Engineers rates); *Sanders Constr. Co.*, IBCA 2309, 90-1 BCA ¶ 22,412 (AGC rates); and *Granite-Groves (JV)*, ENGBCA 5674, 93-1 BCA ¶ 25,475 (State of California manual for equipment listed and AGC rates for unlisted equipment). See also *Capital Elec. Co.*, GSBCA 5316(5059)-REIN, 83-2 BCA ¶ 16,548, *aff'd in part and rev'd in part on other grounds*, 729 F.2d 743 (Fed. Cir. 1984), in which the board used the AGC rates in preference to a schedule published by the National Electrical Contractors Association.

It is common practice to reduce the rates called for in the rate manuals by one-half when computing the cost of contractor-owned idle equipment during periods of delay, *Luria Bros. & Co. v. United States*, 177 Ct. Cl. 676, 369 F.2d 701 (1966). In *Tom Shaw, Inc.*, DOTBCA 2106, 90-1 BCA ¶ 22,580, the board used this technique even though the equipment was fully depreciated. See also *Winston Bros. Co. v. United States*, 131 Ct. Cl. 245, 130 F. Supp. 374 (1955); *L.L. Hall Constr. Co. v. United States*, 177 Ct. Cl. 870, 379 F.2d 559 (1966); *Gallup Constr. Co.*, AGBCA 283, 72-2 BCA ¶ 9522; and *Tom Shaw, Inc.*, ASBCA 28596, 95-1 BCA ¶ 27,457. In *Taylor Constr. Co. v. General Servs. Admin.*, GSBCA 12915, 96-2 BCA ¶ 28,547, *recons. denied*, 97-2 BCA ¶ 29,127, the board used 50 percent of the rental rates for the equipment, while in *Manson-Osberg*, ENGBCA 4069, 82-1 BCA ¶ 15,543, the board applied the 1974 AGC Schedule calling for 50 percent of depreciation plus "all other annual equipment ownership expenses," which exclude all operating expenses. The FAR is silent on this 50 percent calculation. However, DAR 15-402.1(c) specifically provided for reduction of the rates for idle equipment, stating:

> In periods of suspension of work for the convenience of the Government under an appropriate contract clause, the allowance for equipment ownership expense shall not exceed 50% of the amount computed as herein indicated.

Some decisions have held that there is a special rule applicable to contractor-owned equipment. Recovery is denied unless the equipment was required to remain at the site when it could have been productively used elsewhere. See *J.D. Shotwell Co.*, ASBCA 8961, 65-2 BCA ¶ 5243, in which the board stated at 24,687:

> An allowance of standby ownership expense must be supported by a showing that the equipment for which compensation is claimed was reasonably and necessarily set aside and awaiting use in performing the contract. Stated differently, we must be able to conclude that a contractor would prudently have held the equipment for which claim is made in readiness to perform the Government contract rather than making some other disposition of it, in order to find that the Government should pay the charges for that equipment. We cannot reach such a conclusion as to Watts' equipment. Rather, we conclude that Watts left the equipment for which it now makes claim at McChord for its own convenience, having no other place to use it at the time, rather than for the Government's and because of the suspension of work, and that it neither employed, nor had reasonable expectation of employing, the equipment on the contract under which this claim has been filed during the period for which claim is made. We are convinced that had there been some other use for its equipment, the subcontractor could and would prudently have moved it off the Base to that use, returning it as needed for the work of this contract.

See also *Wardroup & Assocs., Inc.*, ASBCA 23433, 79-1 BCA ¶ 13,693; *Excavation-Construction, Inc.*, ENGBCA 3858, 82-1 BCA ¶ 15,770, *recons. denied*, 83-1 BCA ¶ 16,338; *Lionsgate Corp.*, ENGBCA 5388, 91-2 BCA ¶ 24,008; and *Melka Marine, Inc. v. United States*, 41 Fed. Cl. 122 (1998), *aff'd*, 187 F.3d 1370 (Fed. Cir. 1999), *cert. denied*, 529 U.S. 1053 (2000). See *Dillon Constr., Inc.*, ENGBCA PCC-101, 96-1 BCA ¶ 28,113, explaining *Shotwell* at 140,353:

> The [Government] incorrectly limits *Shotwell* to require that the contractor must show that the equipment could have been used elsewhere. Use on another contract is but one indication that the equipment possessed economic value beyond the government contract. The board in *Shotwell* understood that there may be circumstances imposed by the conditions of the government contract which may prevent reasonable use elsewhere.

Based on this reasoning, the board granted recovery because the equipment was not readily transportable and the delay was relatively short. Similarly, in *Anderson Constr. Co.*, ASBCA 48087, 99-1 BCA ¶ 30,347, *recons. denied*, 99-2 BCA ¶ 30,565, the board stated that recovery was permitted when the equipment was required to perform the work and the contractor "could not reasonably remove its equipment and use it elsewhere and did not leave the equipment idle on site merely for its own convenience." See *Safeco Ins. Co. of Am.*, ASBCA 52107, 03-2 BCA ¶ 32,341, granting recovery for specialized equipment left at the site when the government could give no indication of the length of the delay. See also *C.L. Fairley Constr. Co.*, ASBCA 32581, 90-2 BCA ¶ 22,665, *recons. denied*, 90-3 BCA ¶ 23,005 (contractor recovered by proving that the equipment was needed as soon as the delay was lifted); *Tom Shaw, Inc.*, DOTBCA 2111, 90-3 BCA ¶ 22,963, *recons. denied*, 90-3 BCA ¶ 23,157 (reasonable for the contractor to keep the equipment available until final tests were completed).

For a case denying recovery for contractor-owned equipment because it appeared that the contractor had been fully reimbursed for its costs in its original bid price plus negotiated modifications, see *Community Heating & Plumbing Co.*, ASBCA 37981, 92-2 BCA ¶ 24,870, *aff'd*, 987 F.2d 1575 (Fed. Cir. 1993). This case appears to deviate from the normal theory of pricing adjustments separately by including the costs in the original price in the computation.

3. Rented Equipment

When the contractor rents equipment from others, usually referred to as "third-party rental," the full rental payment is recovered if the contractor is unable to mitigate by using the equipment elsewhere, *Isaac Degenaars Co.*, ASBCA 11045, 72-2 BCA ¶ 9764; *Folk Constr. Co. v. United States*, 2 Cl. Ct. 681 (1983). If the contractor obtains the equipment from a source under common control with the contractor, ownership rates—not rental rates—should be used, *Degenaars Co. v. United States*, 2 Cl. Ct. 482 (1983) (AGC rates used when rental was from principal owners of contractor). However, when the government cannot prove common control, rental rates are proper if the contractor can demonstrate that the rent was paid, *Weaver-Bailey Contractors, Inc. v. United States*, 19 Cl. Ct. 474, *recons. denied*, 20 Cl. Ct. 158 (1990).

F. Loss of Efficiency

A contractor may recover for loss of efficiency if it can establish both that a loss of efficiency has resulted in increased costs and that the loss was caused by factors for which the government was responsible, *Luria Bros. & Co. v. United States*, 177 Ct. Cl. 676, 369 F.2d 701 (1966). Thus, in *Joseph Pickard's Sons Co.*, ASBCA 13585, 73-1 BCA ¶ 10,026, *aff'd*, 209 Ct. Cl. 643, 532 F.2d 739 (1976), the contractor was denied recovery because it did not establish that its increased costs were caused by the government's issuance of a change order. See also *Fermont Div., Dynamics Corp. of Am.*, ASBCA 15806, 75-1 BCA ¶ 11,139, *aff'd*, 216 Ct. Cl. 448 (1978). Similarly, recovery has been denied because the contractor could not establish that it incurred increased costs, *Metro Eng'g*, AGBCA 77-121-4, 83-1 BCA ¶ 16,143; *Harvey-Wells Elecs., Inc.*, ASBCA 6507, 67-2 BCA ¶ 6603, *aff'd*, 195 Ct. Cl. 453 (1971); *Hicks Corp.*, ASBCA 10760, 66-1 BCA ¶ 5469; *Rainier Co.*, ASBCA 3565, 59-2 BCA ¶ 2413.

Loss of efficiency has been recognized as resulting from various conditions causing lower than normal or expected productivity. One of the most commonly accepted causes of loss of efficiency has been the disruption of the contractor's work sequence. See *Youngdale & Sons Constr. Co. v. United States*, 27 Fed. Cl.

516 (1993) (work out of planned sequence and in bad weather); *Fire Sec. Sys., Inc.*, VABCA 3086, 91-2 BCA ¶ 23,743 (government unable to give sole occupancy of job site); *Louis M. McMaster*, AGBCA 76-156, 79-1 BCA ¶ 13,701 (disruption made planned simultaneous work impossible); *Fischbach & Moore Int'l Corp.*, ASBCA 18146, 77-1 BCA ¶ 12,300, *aff'd*, 223 Ct. Cl. 119, 617 F.2d 223 (1980) (forced abandonment of orderly work sequence); *Sun Shipbuilding & Drydock Co.*, ASBCA 11300, 68-1 BCA ¶ 7054 (work sequence disrupted and compressed); and *International Aircraft Servs., Inc.*, ASBCA 8389, 65-1 BCA ¶ 4793 (production disrupted and numerous work stoppages). The effect of extended work has also been recognized as a cause of loss of efficiency. See *Casson Constr. Co.*, GSBCA 4884, 83-1 BCA ¶ 16,523 (overtime); *Maryland Sanitary Mfg. Corp. v. United States*, 119 Ct. Cl. 100 (1951) (judicial recognition that efficiency would be impaired by working 12-hour days and seven-day weeks); *Continental Consol. Corp.*, ENGBCA 2743, 68-1 BCA ¶ 7003, *modified*, 200 Ct. Cl. 737 (1972) (60-hour work week); and *Lew F. Stilwell, Inc.*, ASBCA 9423, 1964 BCA ¶ 4128 (overtime). Other generally accepted causes of loss of efficiency include working under less favorable weather conditions, *Warwick Constr., Inc.*, GSBCA 5070, 82-2 BCA ¶ 16,091; *Baltimore Contractors, Inc.*, ASBCA 14819, 72-2 BCA ¶ 9554; *Tyee Constr. Co.*, IBCA 692-1-68, 69-1 BCA ¶ 7748; the necessity of hiring untrained or less-qualified workers, *Algernon-Blair, Inc.*, GSBCA 4072, 76-2 BCA ¶ 12,073; *Ortronix, Inc.*, ASBCA 12745, 72-2 BCA ¶ 9564; *Gibbs Shipyard, Inc.*, ASBCA 9809, 67-2 BCA ¶ 6499; and working in crowded areas, *Lew F. Stilwell* and *Gibbs Shipyard*.

A contractor is not expected to keep accounting records from which loss of efficiency can be ascertained by audit, *Paccon, Inc.*, ASBCA 7890, 1963 BCA ¶ 3659, *recons. denied*, 1963 BCA ¶ 3730. In a later decision in the *Paccon* case, 65-2 BCA ¶ 4996, the board granted an adjustment for loss of efficiency based on an uncontroverted estimate that had been prepared in great detail. See also *Coastal Dry Dock & Repair Corp.*, ASBCA 36754, 91-1 BCA ¶ 23,324, and *International Aircraft Servs., Inc.*, ASBCA 8389, 65-1 BCA ¶ 4793. One of the most common techniques used in estimating loss of efficiency is the "measured mile" technique comparing the period when loss of efficiency occurred with a period during which normal efficiency was experienced. The normal period must be similar in terms of working conditions but for the causes of inefficiency and should be as close in time as possible to the impacted period, *International Terminal Operating Co.*, ASBCA 18118, 75-2 BCA ¶ 11,470. See *Clark Concrete Contractors, Inc. v. General Servs. Admin.*, GSBCA 14340, 99-1 BCA ¶ 30,280, stating at 149,747 that the board would "accept a comparison if it is between kinds of work which are reasonably alike, such that the approximations it involves will be meaningful." A comparison of similar work was accepted as a "measured mile" in *P.J. Dick, Inc.*, VABCA 5597, 01-2 BCA ¶ 31,647, *aff'd in part, rev'd in part*, 324 F.3d 1364 (Fed. Cir. 2003). This technique has been used in a number of cases. See *W.G. Yates & Sons Constr. Co.*, ASBCA 49398, 01-2 BCA ¶ 31,428 (comparison of labor for steel erection before and after problem); *Lamb Eng'g & Constr. Co.*, EBCA 9304172, 97-2 BCA ¶ 29,207, *recons. denied*, 98-1 BCA ¶ 29,359 (comparison of productivity of earthwork before and after differing site condition); *DANAC, Inc.*, ASBCA 33394, 97-2 BCA ¶ 29,184, *recons. denied*, 98-1 BCA ¶ 29,454 (comparison of productivity in renovating and upgrading housing units where productive period occurred at the end of contract performance); *Flex-Y-Plan Indus., Inc.*, GSBCA 4117, 76-1 BCA ¶ 11,713 (comparisons between working in occupied and unoccupied barracks); *E.W. Bliss Co.*, ASBCA 9489, 68-1 BCA ¶ 6906 (experience of working on one torpedo tube compared with that on three others); and *Elliott Constr. Co.*, ASBCA 23483, 81-2 BCA ¶ 15,222, *recons. denied*, 82-1 BCA ¶ 15,625 (renovation work on one wing of a building compared with prior work on another wing). The costs of the normal period may be established by estimates, *Batteast Constr. Co.*, ASBCA 35818, 92-1 BCA ¶ 24,697 (46.43 percent loss of efficiency); *Southwest Marine, Inc.*, ASBCA 33208, 88-3 BCA ¶ 20,982, *recons. denied*, 89-1 BCA ¶ 21,197; *Coley Props. Corp.*, PSBCA 276, 77-1 BCA ¶ 12,442, *rev'd on other grounds*, 219 Ct. Cl. 227, 593 F.2d 380 (1979). However, the failure to corroborate the estimate can lead to denial of the claim, *Continental Consol. Corp.*, ASBCA 14372, 71-1 BCA ¶ 8742; *Dravo Corp.*, ENGBCA 3800, 79-1 BCA ¶ 13,575. The difference in costs between the normal and inefficient periods may also be established by actual cost records, *Therm-Air Mfg. Co.*, ASBCA 15842, 74-2 BCA ¶ 10,818. However, a mere comparison of costs without adequate detail and explanation may be rejected as a "total cost" claim, *Southwest Marine, Inc.*, ASBCA 39472, 93-2 BCA ¶ 25,682; *Joseph Pickard's Sons Co. v. United States*, 209 Ct. Cl. 643, 532 F.2d 739 (1976). See also *Bay Constr. Co.*, VABCA 5594, 02-1 BCA ¶ 31,795, and *J.A. Jones Constr. Co.*, ENGBCA 6348, 00-2 BCA ¶ 31,000, denying claims in their entirety because the contractor did not submit convincing evidence tying inefficient work to government actions. See also *Emerald Maint., Inc.*, ASBCA 43929, 98-2 BCA ¶ 29,903, rejecting a hypothetical "measured mile" estimate because it was not based on recorded costs for a base period and did not take contractor problems into account, and *Kit-San-Azusa, J.V. v. United States*, 32 Fed. Cl. 647 (1995), *aff'd*, 86 F.3d 1175 (Fed. Cir. 1996), awarding 20 percent of the claimed loss of productivity costs to account for simultaneous contractor inefficiency and government issuance of numerous disruptive changes. In some cases, the appeals boards have granted awards for loss of efficiency based on total costs incurred during the impacted period with adjustments based on the evidence, *Ingalls Shipbuilding Div., Litton Sys., Inc.*, ASBCA 17579, 78-1 BCA ¶ 13,038, *recons. denied*, 78-1 BCA ¶ 13,216; *Sovereign Constr. Co.*, ASBCA 17792, 75-1 BCA ¶ 11,251. See *Capital Elec. Co.*, GSBCA 5316(5059)-REIN, 83-2 BCA ¶ 16,548, *aff'd in part and rev'd in part on other grounds*, 729 F.2d 743 (Fed. Cir. 1984), in which the board rejected the contractor's estimate of the impact of efficiency loss and adopted the government's approach of apportioning all labor hours in excess of hours bid to delays for which the government and the contractor were liable.

Inefficiency factors in manuals of contractor associations have also been used to estimate the percentage loss of efficiency from specified events. See *Fire Sec. Sys., Inc.*, VABCA 5559, 02-2 BCA ¶ 31,977; *Hensel Phelps Constr. Co. v. General Servs. Admin.*, GSBCA 14744, 01-1 BCA ¶ 31,249, *aff'd*, 36 Fed. Appx. 649 (Fed.

Cir. 2002); and *Clark Constr. Group, Inc.*, VABCA 5674, 00-1 BCA ¶ 30,870, *recons. denied*, 00-2 BCA ¶ 30,997, using, with modifications, the loss of productivity factors in the Mechanical Contractors Association of America, Inc., manual.

In some cases, the appeals boards have approved loss of efficiency claims with relatively little evidence or explanation, *Warwick Constr., Inc.*, GSBCA 5070, 82-2 BCA ¶ 16,091 (loss of efficiency of 40 percent and 60 percent based on testimony of contractor and subcontractors on effect of weather); *California Shipbuilding & Dry Dock Co.*, ASBCA 21394, 78-1 BCA ¶ 13,168 ($60,000 awarded for loss of efficiency based on "jury verdict"); *Algernon-Blair, Inc.*, GSBCA 4072, 76-2 BCA ¶ 12,073 (8 percent loss of efficiency awarded based on board's appraisal of contractor's claim for 30 percent); *Baltimore Contractors, Inc.*, ASBCA 14819, 72-2 BCA ¶ 9554 (loss of efficiency for effect of working in winter). In other cases, however, the claim has been denied in its entirety because the contractor has not submitted adequate proof, *Roy D. Garren Corp.*, AGBCA 85-196-1, 91-1 BCA ¶ 23,306; *Gulf Contracting, Inc.*, ASBCA 30195, 89-2 BCA ¶ 21,812, *recons. denied*, 90-1 BCA ¶ 22,393, *aff'd*, 972 F.2d 1353 (Fed. Cir.), *cert. denied*, 506 U.S. 999 (1992); *Pittsburgh-Des Moines Corp.*, EBCA 314-3-84, 89-2 BCA ¶ 21,739.

G. Escalation of Labor Rates and Material Prices

In cases involving delay, the contractor is entitled to include in the adjustment the impact of higher wages or material prices. See *Excavation-Constr., Inc.*, ENGBCA 3858, 82-1 BCA ¶ 15,770, *recons. denied*, 83-1 BCA ¶ 16,338, in which escalation was given at the rate of 1 percent per month on all labor, material, and subcontract costs, and *Garcia Concrete, Inc.*, AGBCA 78-105-4, 82-2 BCA ¶ 16,046, in which a $.55 wage increase was awarded on work that would have been done before the effective date of the increase but for the delay. See also *Stroh Corp. v. General Servs. Admin.*, GSBCA 11029, 96-1 BCA ¶ 28,265; *Sydney Constr. Co.*, ASBCA 21377, 77-2 BCA ¶ 12,719; and *International Builders of Fla., Inc.*, FAACAP 67-5, 69-1 BCA ¶ 7706, *recons. denied*, 71-1 BCA ¶ 8790. In *Berkeley Constr. Co.*, VABCA 1962, 88-1 BCA ¶ 20,259, the board calculated the labor and material escalation that had occurred over the 1,462 days of total contract delay and assessed the government its pro rata share for the 813 days for which it was found responsible.

H. Miscellaneous Costs

There have been a variety of other types of costs included in delay and impact claims. In delay claims the contractor has been held entitled to the cost of remobilization and demobilization of its workforce, *Marlin Assocs., Inc.*, GSBCA 5663, 82-1 BCA ¶ 15,739; additional bond premium, *Proserv, Inc.*, ASBCA 20768, 78-1 BCA ¶ 13,066; and state and local taxes, *Folk Constr. Co. v. United States*, 2 Cl. Ct. 681 (1983). The board denied a claim for the lost value of equipment sold to finance the work during a delay because it was not a "direct and foreseeable consequence of the delay," *Sermor, Inc.*, ASBCA 32824, 94-1 BCA ¶ 26,301, *recons. denied*, 94-3 BCA ¶ 27,244.

IV. OVERHEAD AND PROFIT

Overhead represents the contractor's indirect costs allocable to the job, and profit is the contractor's reward for performing the work. The amount of these items to be recovered in price adjustments is usually determined by applying percentage rates to the cost of the work. The rates for overhead are determined by using allocability and allowability rules contained in the government's Cost Principles. The rates for profit are determined in accordance with the principles set out in FAR 15.404-4 as implemented by DFARS 215.404-4 and other regulations supplementing the FAR.

The allowance for overhead compensates the contractor for costs not included in direct material or labor. Contractor expenditures that do not meet the tests for allowability will be subject to disallowance under the Pricing of Adjustments clause. In such a case, they must be recovered, if at all, through the allowance for profit. This section addresses the rules covering the inclusion of overhead and profit in the adjustment. Note that this section deals with the overhead allocable to the increased or decreased direct costs of the price adjustment, not unabsorbed or extended overhead, which has been discussed previously.

A. Overhead

The normal cost allocability rules will determine the method of computing the overhead rate and the types and amounts of costs included in the overhead. However, one problem associated with overhead in price adjustments is the treatment of fixed costs in overhead. Since such costs by definition do not vary with changes in the volume of work, they will be neither increased nor decreased by a change that can be accomplished with the same facilities and within the same time period as the initial contract work. Thus, should an allocation for such fixed costs be included in the adjustment, the amount would not be for costs, since such expenditures would be neither increased nor decreased by the adjustment. This problem has not been resolved through litigation. In most cases, the contractor's full overhead rate for the period in which the work was done is applied, *Raytheon Co.*, ASBCA 50166, 03-2 BCA ¶ 32,410; *Advanced Eng'g & Planning Corp.*, ASBCA 53366, 03-1 BCA ¶ 32,157, *aff'd*, 292 F. Supp. 2d 846 (E.D. Va. 2003); *Norair Eng'g. Corp.*, ENGBCA 5244-Q, 98-2 BCA ¶ 29,967; *Keco Indus., Inc.*, ASBCA 15131, 72-1 BCA ¶ 9262. See *Ordnance Materials, Inc.*, ASBCA 32371, 88-3 BCA ¶ 20,910, stating that indirect costs "need not be proven to have been the direct result of a change" because a contractor "is entitled to his overhead, computed in accordance with the applicable regulations and generally accepted accounting principles." However, in order to recover normal overhead rates, the contractor must present some evidence of the rates that were incurred, *Spiros Vasilatos Painting*, ASBCA 37938, 90-1 BCA ¶ 22,618. In a few cases, the fixed-cost issue has been raised. See *B.J. Lucarelli & Co.*, ASBCA 8768, 65-1 BCA ¶ 4655, holding that no amount for overhead should be included because the contractor could not demonstrate that its overhead expenditures were increased by the change, and *J.G. Watts Constr. Co.*, ASBCA 9454, 1964 BCA ¶ 4171, holding otherwise. See also *Natco Ltd. P'ship*, ENGBCA 6183, 96-1 BCA ¶ 28,062, permitting the assessment of the impact on overhead of a reduction in the quantity of work, and *Lionsgate Corp.*, ENGBCA 5425, 90-2 BCA ¶ 22,730, using a lower overhead rate for work that was deleted at the end of the contract because most of the overhead had already been incurred at that time. Possibly, the best solution would be to require recomputation of the overhead rate for major dollar changes but to apply the contractor's "normal" overhead rates for minor dollar changes.

Field office expenses on construction contracts that are not incurred in the direct performance of the work can be treated either as direct costs or overhead, FAR 31.105(d)(3). If the contractor chooses to treat such expenses as overhead, it must use a single distribution base to allocate these expenses. See *M.A. Mortenson Co.*, ASBCA 40750, 98-1 BCA ¶ 29,658, where a contractor had charged such costs as a percentage of direct costs when a change did not extend the time of performance and on a per diem basis when the change extended the time. The senior deciding group of the board interpreted FAR 31.203 to require only one distribution base and held that the contractor could choose either base (cost or time) but could not alternate between bases on one contract. It also stated that if a contractor chose the cost base, the government could not challenge the payment of overhead costs on the grounds that they were all fixed costs that did not vary because the time of performance was not extended. In an earlier decision, a panel of the board had decided, in 97-1 BCA ¶ 28,623, that fixed costs should be excluded from field office overhead if a change did not extend the time of performance. See *Caddell Constr. Co.*, ASBCA 53144, 02-1 BCA ¶ 31,850, denying the government's motion for summary judgment when the contractor retroactively claimed that it was entitled under *Mortenson* to charge all of its field overhead costs as a percentage of direct costs because that case had made its prior dual charging technique impermissible. The board held that a trial was necessary to determine if special circumstances permitted this change in accounting practice.

B. Profit

Profit has generally been included as an integral part of the term "equitable adjustment," *United States v. Callahan Walker Constr. Co.*, 317 U.S. 56 (1942) (contractor entitled to "reasonable and customary allowance for profit" on extra work). See *General Builders Supply Co. v. United States*, 187 Ct. Cl. 477, 409 F.2d 246 (1969); *George Bennett v. United States*, 178 Ct. Cl. 61, 371 F.2d 859 (1967); and *United States v. Pickett's Food Serv.*, 360 F.2d 338 (5th Cir. 1966). The rationale for inclusion of profit was explained in *New York Shipbuilding Co.*, ASBCA 16164, 76-2 BCA ¶ 11,979, *recons. denied*, 83-1 BCA ¶ 16,534, at 57,427:

> Without the payment of a profit which is fair under the circumstances, the Government would be getting something for nothing and the contractor would not truly be made whole.

However, this logic will not be applied to adjustments under the Suspension of Work clause at FAR 52.242-14, which specifically excludes recovery of profit. See *Dravo Corp.*, ENGBCA 3915, 79-1 BCA ¶ 13,603, and *Big 4 Constr. Co.*, DOTCAB 75-18, 76-2 BCA ¶ 12,029. Similarly, profit is not allowed under the Government Delay of Work clause at FAR 52.242-17. But see the Stop-Work Order clause at FAR 52.242-15, which includes profit for government-ordered delays by providing for an "equitable adjustment."

Whenever equitable adjustments are made under other contract provisions, profit is included. See *BellSouth Communications Sys., Inc.*, ASBCA 45955, 94-3 BCA ¶ 27,231, in which the board included profit (as well as costs) when the Davis-Bacon Act was added to a contract during performance. The board noted that the regulations permitted such addition by change order, which necessarily required an equitable adjustment. The same result was reached in *Professional Servs. Unified, Inc.*, ASBCA 45799, 94-1 BCA ¶ 26,580, in which the board added profit to an adjustment required when the government corrected a Service Contract Act wage determination. In the latter case, however, the board noted that no profit was to be included when wage determinations for option years increased the contractor's costs because the Price Adjustment clause specifically precluded profit (and indirect costs) when such adjustment occurred.

1. Intermingled Changes and Suspensions

When changes and suspension are intermingled, the claim may be divided between the two clauses, with one carrying profit and the other excluding it. See *Gunther & Shirley Co.*, ENGBCA 3691, 78-2 BCA ¶ 13,454, in which the board stated at 65,757-58:

> [S]ome of the extra costs incurred by the contractor were in the nature of delay costs and should be treated under the Suspension of Work clause while others were in the nature of costs incurred in the performance of extra and changed work and should be treated under the Changes clause.

Another view of such intermingled claims is that the entire pricing action can be accomplished under the Changes clause or the Differing Site Conditions clause. This result would appear to be required by the provision in the Suspension of Work clause that states that no adjustment will be made thereunder when it is provided for by another clause. See *Steve P. Rados, Inc.*, AGBCA 77-130-4, 82-1 BCA ¶ 15,624, holding that profit should be included on delay costs resulting from lack of cooperation of another contractor since the claim fell under the Changes clause; *Folk Constr. Co. v. United States*, 2 Cl. Ct. 681 (1983), and *Bruce-Anderson Co.*,

ASBCA 28099, 83-2 BCA ¶ 16,832, *recons. denied*, 84-1 BCA ¶ 17,177, in which profit was included in the cost of delays resulting from changes; and *Roy McGinnis & Co.*, ASBCA 49867, 01-2 BCA ¶ 31,622, *recons. denied*, 02-1 BCA ¶ 31,720, and *Youngdale & Sons Constr. Co. v. United States*, 27 Fed. Cl. 516 (1993), in which profit was included on delay and impact costs occurring because of differing site conditions. See also *D.H. Dave, Inc.*, ASBCA 13005, 73-2 BCA ¶ 10,191, in which the board stated at 47,999:

> [T]he Board has concluded that it is not necessary to decide which of the three articles is relied upon in making the adjustments. The Board recognizes that suspension of work articles and Board decisions thereunder have varied as to whether profit is to be allowed on increased costs, and the Government, as to certain claims, has raised the question as to whether profit should be allowed. Under changes articles and changed conditions articles profit, based on the amount of increased or decreased costs, has almost always been allowed as a part of the upward or downward equitable adjustment. The Board concludes that in this case when increased costs are found to be allowable some profit allowance is proper in the equitable adjustment because the increased costs are costs that would not have been incurred had the changed condition not been encountered.

Where costs arose from the government's failure to make timely deliveries of government furnished property, the board held that the Government-Furnished Property clause rather than the Government Delay of Work clause governed and that profits should be permitted, *E.V. Lane Corp.*, ASBCA 9741, 66-1 BCA ¶ 5472. Compare *Wilner v. United States*, 23 Cl. Ct. 241 (1991), and *Richerson Constr., Inc. v. General Servs. Admin.*, GSBCA 11161-R, 93-3 BCA ¶ 26,206, in which profit was denied on claims that had elements of constructive changes. The denial was based on the reasoning that the delays were properly compensable under the Suspension of Work clause.

2. Deductive Changes

A reasonable allowance for overhead and profit will also be made where there is a deductive change order, *G & M Elec. Contractors Co.*, GSBCA 4771-R, 79-1 BCA ¶ 13,791; *Hensel Phelps Constr. Co.*, ASBCA 15142, 71-1 BCA ¶ 8796. However, where deleted work would have been performed at a loss, the Armed Services Board has refused to allow the government to deduct profit since such action would constitute an inequitable addition to the contractor's losses, *CRF*, ASBCA 17340, 76-1 BCA ¶ 11,857. See also *G.M. Co. Mfg., Inc.*, ASBCA 2883, 57-2 BCA ¶ 1505, *recons. denied*, 57-2 BCA ¶ 1574. Comptroller General Report B-118623, Nov. 23, 1976, criticized the GSA policy of not obtaining credits for profit on deductive changes in construction contracts. This GSA policy was changed, and the March 1980 edition of the GSA Modification of General Conditions stated, "Equitable adjustments for deleted work shall include credits for Overhead, Profit and Commission." In *Koll Constr. Co. v. General Servs. Admin.*, GSBCA 12306, 94-1 BCA ¶ 26,501, *recons. denied*, 94-2 BCA ¶ 26,599, and *Santa Fe Eng'rs, Inc.*, AS-

BCA 31762, 91-1 BCA ¶ 23,571, the board used the same overhead and profit rates for deductive changes that the parties had previously used for additive changes. In *Gladwynne Constr. Co.*, VABCA 6594, 02-1 BCA ¶ 31,848, *recons. denied*, 02-2 BCA ¶ 31,948, the board used the rates called for in the contract clause applying to additive changes.

Profit will not be subtracted from the adjustment for a deductive change covered by the Value Engineering Incentive clause. See *Dravo Corp. v. United States*, 202 Ct. Cl. 500, 480 F.2d 1331 (1973), stating at 512:

> It is of course obvious when one thinks about it that it is inimical to the achievement of contractor economy and efficiency to allow the idea to dominate, that his profit must be in some fixed ratio to his cost, whether the latter be great or small. We are dealing with a contract clause which on its face indicates that profit should not be reduced because the contractor discovers how to make the job less costly. The policy which underlies the regulations promulgated in connection with the clause demonstrates an intent to induce the cooperation of the contractor by making such cooperation economically attractive. And we are shown that the authors of these regulations were aware that contractors might retain expected profit under the regulations and specifically accepted such practice. By all approaches to contract interpretation it would appear that the plaintiff is in a strong position on the question of retention of expected profits.

3. Breach of Contract Claims

The rule for recovery of profit on breach of contract claims is somewhat uncertain. Where the contractor seeks to recover delay costs and has not performed extra work, profit is not allowed, *Laburnum Constr. Corp. v. United States*, 163 Ct. Cl. 339, 325 F.2d 451 (1963). See also *Meva Corp. v. United States*, 206 Ct. Cl. 203, 511 F.2d 548 (1975), in which the court without discussion refused to grant profit on the contractor's costs incurred as a result of the government's breach of contract, and *J.D. Hedin Constr. Co. v. United States*, 171 Ct. Cl. 70, 347 F.2d 235 (1965). However, where the government breach has forced the contractor to perform extra work, the contractor is entitled to the profit that could have been earned but for the breach, *Big Chief Drilling Co. v. United States*, 26 Cl. Ct. 1276 (1992). There, the contractor's damages included 15 percent profit based on the rate that it normally charged for drilling work.

Where the breach of contract action involves a claim that is cognizable under a contract clause, profit will be allowed, *George Bennett v. United States*, 178 Ct. Cl. 61, 371 F.2d 859 (1967). But see *Chaney & James Constr. Co. v. United States*, 190 Ct. Cl. 699, 421 F.2d 728 (1970), in which no profit was allowed for delays treated under the Suspension of Work clause.

4. Amount of Profit

The rate of profit included in an equitable adjustment should fairly reflect the nature of the work and the risks involved. If the change requires work that is more difficult or involves a higher degree of risk than the original work under the contract, the contractor is entitled to a higher rate of profit than that included in the original contract price, *American Pipe & Steel Corp.*, ASBCA 7899, 1964 BCA ¶ 4058. Similarly, when a repricing action involved pricing added quantities under a Variation in Quantities clause in a contract that had been awarded through formal advertising, the board used a higher profit rate since the costs were reduced, *Carvel Walker*, ENGBCA 3744, 78-1 BCA ¶ 13,005. Conversely, if the change requires work that is less demanding or risky than originally required, the rate of profit should be lower than the contract rate, *Varo, Inc.*, ASBCA 15000, 72-2 BCA ¶ 9717. In many cases, however, the rates are not separately negotiated. When small changes are involved, the parties often agree to use the same profit rate for the change that was applied to the original contract work, FAR 15.404-4(c)(6). Further, a rate of 10 percent is often treated as more or less standard, *Carvel Walker*, ENGBCA 3744, 78-1 BCA ¶ 13,005. See also *Campbell Indus.*, ASBCA 40436, 94-2 BCA ¶ 26,760; *J & T Constr. Co.*, DOTCAB 73-4, 75-2 BCA ¶ 11,398; and *Larco-Indus. Painting Corp.*, ASBCA 14647, 73-2 BCA ¶ 10,073.

FAR 15.404-4(b)(1) requires use of a "structured profit approach" for pricing actions of major contracting agencies based on cost analysis. This would include almost all contract modifications involving a significant change in dollar amount. FAR 15.404-4(c)(6) permits the use of the profit rate used in the basic contract when a modification is "for essentially the same type and mix of work as the basic contract" or is "of a small dollar value." Agencies have implemented the requirement for a structured profit approach by adopting "weighted guidelines" profit formulas, and these have been used in the computation of equitable adjustments. See, for example, *Bechtel Nat'l, Inc.*, ASBCA 51589, 02-1 BCA ¶ 31,673, *aff'd*, 65 Fed. Appx. 277 (Fed. Cir. 2003) (8.92 percent used for subcontractor); *Harrison W./Franki-Denys*, ENGBCA 5577, 90-3 BCA ¶ 22,991 (8.4 percent profit where contract clause called for use of formula); and *Texas Instruments, Inc.*, ASBCA 27113, 90-1 BCA ¶ 22,537, *aff'd*, 922 F.2d 810 (Fed. Cir. 1990) (weighted guidelines used although board "not bound to use" them). Compare *Hardrive, Inc.*, IBCA 2319, 94-1 BCA ¶ 26,267, in which the board refused to use the weighted guidelines because it was not bound by them. Cases applying the prior DAR on this subject include *Ingalls Shipbuilding Div., Litton Sys., Inc.*, ASBCA 17579, 78-1 BCA ¶ 13,038, *recons. denied*, 78-1 BCA ¶ 13,216; *Elliott Mach. Works, Inc.*, ASBCA 16135, 72-2 BCA ¶ 9501; and *Kurz & Root Co.*, ASBCA 11436, 68-1 BCA ¶ 6916. For discussion of the weight to be given to the contractor's assumption of cost risk, see *Aerojet-Gen. Corp.*, ASBCA 17171, 74-2 BCA ¶ 10,863. The board affirmed the contracting officer's usage of the weighted guidelines method in *Fred A. Arnold, Inc.*, ASBCA 27151, 83-2 BCA ¶ 16,795, *modified on other grounds*, 84-3 BCA ¶ 17,517. The weighted guidelines approach will be irrelevant where a percentage limitation on profit is included in a contract clause, *R.C. Hedreen Co.*, ASBCA 20004, 76-2 BCA ¶ 12,202, *modified on other grounds*, 78-1 BCA ¶ 12,991.

Where pricing occurs after the costs of the change have been incurred, some boards have held that a lower risk exists and have, therefore, granted a lower rate of profit. The computation of the rate has not been at all uniform in these circumstances. See *Texas Instruments, Inc.*, ASBCA 27113, 90-1 BCA ¶ 22,537, *aff'd*, 922 F.2d 810 (Fed. Cir. 1990) (8.24 percent based on weighted guidelines calculation—dissent argued for 14.8 percent); *Armada/Hoffler Constr. Co.*, DOTBCA 2437, 93-1 BCA ¶ 25,446 (8.3 percent derived from rounding dollar amount); *I. Alper Co. v. General Servs. Admin.*, GSBCA 11335, 92-3 BCA ¶ 25,038 (7 percent derived from weighted guidelines); and *Coastal Dry Dock & Repair Corp.*, ASBCA 36754, 91-1 BCA ¶ 23,324 (10 percent based on weighted guidelines). In some cases, the boards have not discussed the fact that the equitable adjustment was priced after the work was completed, *Sanders Constr. Co.*, IBCA 2309, 90-1 BCA ¶ 22,412. In *Keco Indus., Inc.*, ASBCA 18730, 74-2 BCA ¶ 10,711, the board, citing *Newport News Shipbuilding and Dry Dock Co. v. United States*, 179 Ct. Cl. 97, 374 F.2d 516 (1967), reasoned that the weighted guidelines risk factor was to be applied prospectively and not with the benefit of hindsight. The board, however, in apparent error, stated that the risk factor is not applicable on a prospective basis. See also *Gilles & Cotting, Inc.*, GSBCA 5754, 83-1 BCA ¶ 16,480, in which the board refused to reduce the profit rate because the work had been completed, reasoning that the contractor had incurred a large risk since the government had denied responsibility for the change. Compare *Doyle Constr. Co.*, ASBCA 44883, 94-2 BCA ¶ 26,832, in which the board apparently rejected the government use of a reduced risk factor for late pricing but awarded only 6 percent profit because a subcontractor—not the general contractor—had taken the major risk of performing in a remote area.

The contractor may recover profit on indirect costs for extra work it performed, *Kemmons-Wilson, Inc.*, ASBCA 16167, 72-2 BCA ¶ 9689, or for extra work performed by a subcontractor, *Foster Constr. Co.*, DOTCAB 71-16, 73-1 BCA ¶ 9869. Profit is also allowed on rental rates, *Contractors Equip. Rental Co.*, ASBCA 15737, 72-1 BCA ¶ 9193.

A contractor who bids a job at no profit will still be entitled to recover a fair profit on additional work, *Keco Indus., Inc.*, ASBCA 15184, 72-2 BCA ¶ 9576, *recons. denied*, 72-2 BCA ¶ 9633 (5 percent in this case). Contrast *BH Servs., Inc.*, ASBCA 39460, 93-3 BCA ¶ 26,082, denying any profit because the original contract was bid at a loss—apparently under the theory that it would afford the contractor an opportunity to convert a loss to a profit. Later cases have affirmed the contractor's entitlement to recover a reasonable profit as part of equitable adjustments even though the contract is being performed at a loss. See *Stewart & Stevenson Servs., Inc.*, ASBCA 43631, 97-2 BCA ¶ 29,252, *recons. denied*, 98-1 BCA ¶ 29,653, and *Grumman Aerospace Corp.*, ASBCA 50090, 01-1 BCA ¶ 31,316.

5. *Construction Contract Clauses*

Most construction agencies include clauses in their contracts that limit the amount of the equitable adjustment pertaining to overhead, profit, and commission. Generally, these clauses describe the elements that can be recovered by contractors or subcontractors and establish maximum percentages for recovery. For example, the General Services Administration Equitable Adjustments clause in GSAAR 552.243-71 Form 1139 states:

> Overhead, Profit and Commission
>
> (2) The allowable overhead shall be determined in accordance with the contract cost principles and procedures in Part 31 of the Federal Acquisition Regulation (48 CFR Part 31) in effect on the date of this contract. The percentages for profit and commission shall be negotiated and may vary according to the nature, extent and complexity of the work involved, but in no case shall exceed the following unless the Contractor demonstrates entitlement to a higher percentage:

	Overhead	Profit	Commission
To contractor on work performed by other than his own forces	—	—	10%
To first tier subcontractor on work performed by his subcontractors	—	—	10%
To contractor and/or the subcontractors for the portion of the work performed with their respective forces	To be negotiated	10%	—

> Not more than four percentages will be allowed regardless of the number of tier subcontractors. The Contractor shall not be allowed a commission on the commission received by a first tier subcontractor. Equitable adjustments for deleted work shall include credits for overhead, profit and commission. On proposals covering both increases and decreases in the amount of the contract, the application of overhead and profit shall be on the net change in direct costs for the Contractor or subcontractor performing the work.

The Veterans Administration clause, 48 C.F.R. § 852.236-88, also allows up to four percentages but uses a declining scale to determine the percentage limits for overhead and profit:

> 10 percent overhead and 10 percent profit on first $20,000; 7½ percent overhead and 7½ percent profit on next $30,000; five percent overhead and five percent profit on balance over $50,000.

This clause explicitly provides that any portion of a change involving credit items must be deducted prior to adding overhead and profit for the party performing the work, and that overhead, profit, and fee will be excluded where a change involves only credit items. This clause has been interpreted to preclude recovery of extended job-site overhead in excess of the prescribed rate, *Reliance Ins. Co. v. United States*, 20 Cl. Ct. 715 (1990), *aff'd*, 932 F.2d 981 (Fed. Cir. 1991); *Santa Fe Eng'rs, Inc. v. United States*, 801 F.2d 379 (Fed. Cir. 1986); *Amelco Elec.*, VABCA 3785, 96-2 BCA ¶ 28,381. It has also been held that the percentages are maximums that are not applicable when subcontract work was done on a cost-reimbursement basis, *Sentry Ins., a Mut. Co.*, VABCA 2617, 91-3 BCA ¶ 24,094 (15 percent given in lieu of 20 percent maximum in clause). See also *Lecher Constr. Co.*, Comp. Gen. Dec. B-224357, 86-2 CPD ¶ 369, in which the GAO held that this clause was inconsistent with FAR 15.901(c) (now 15.404-4), prohibiting "administrative ceilings" on profits.

The clause used by the National Park Service permits recovery of a fixed fee for general supervisory and office expenses and profit of up to 15 percent, but limits this percentage to the actual necessary costs as determined by the contracting officer. It does not mention commission.

The Naval Facilities Engineering Command Changes Board and Estimates clause sets rates of 6 percent for profit, 10 percent for field overhead, and 3 percent for home office overhead, but these rates have been held to be "merely . . . a beginning point for negotiation between the parties," *Community Heating & Plumbing Co.*, ASBCA 37981, 92-2 BCA ¶ 24,870, *aff'd*, 987 F.2d 1575 (Fed. Cir. 1993). In *Bruce-Andersen Co.*, ASBCA 35791, 89-2 BCA ¶ 21,871, the board rejected the contractor's argument that this clause violated the DAR.

One of the major issues addressed by a number of the clauses is the question of who may recover an equitable adjustment for overhead, profit, and commission. An earlier version of the GSA clause provided for only three percentages and was heavily litigated. When a contractor sought to recover commission on work performed by a second-tier subcontractor, for which the first-tier subcontractor claimed 10 percent overhead and 10 percent profit, the board denied both the first-tier subcontractor's claim of entitlement to a 10 percent markup and the contractor's claimed entitlement to commission on that markup, *Lawrence Constr. Co.*, GSBCA 1450, 65-2 BCA ¶ 4963. In *Norair Eng'g Corp.*, GSBCA 1178, 66-1 BCA ¶ 5312, *recons. denied*, 66-1 BCA ¶ 5702, the board upheld the percentage limitation in denying the contractor's claim. See also *Blake Constr. Co.*, GSBCA 1834, 66-2 BCA ¶ 5741, in which the board refused to allow additional adjustments for profit, overhead, and commission on work performed by the second-tier subcontractor.

Strict readings of the limiting clauses have been challenged on several theories. In *Jack Picoult v. United States*, 207 Ct. Cl. 1052, 529 F.2d 532 (1975), the contractor argued that the first-tier subcontractor was entitled to additional recovery for the direct labor costs of administering changed work actually performed by the second-tier subcontractor. In addition, the subcontractor claimed 10 percent of these costs for profit and 10 percent as overhead. The court stated at 1053:

> The issue here is one of contract interpretation. The contract specifically provided, in Section 1-23 ("Changes") that "allowable overhead, profit and commission percentages [i.e., a maximum of 10 percent on each] . . . shall include . . . field and office supervisors and assistants." The personnel provided by [the subcontractor] were of that type. Hence, the costs involved in paying them are "overhead," and not direct costs, which would be reimbursable under the "Changes" article. There is no ambiguity in the contract; the cited portions clearly cover the dispute here. The contract did not provide for any supervisory compensation beyond the "3 10's" which have already been paid.

The court affirmed the board's denial of an adjustment for work performed by the subcontractor, *Jack Picoult*, GSBCA 3516, 72-2 BCA ¶ 9621, *recons. denied*, 73-1 BCA ¶ 9971. Similarly, despite a contractor's claim that its field supervisor's work was included as a direct cost rather than as part of its overhead under its cost accounting system, the board held that the contractor was not entitled to an adjustment for 10 percent of the subcontractor's price for overhead or 10 percent for profit, *Pyramid Constr. Co.*, GSBCA 4882, 78-1 BCA ¶ 13,215, *recons. denied*, 78-2 BCA ¶ 13,422.

A supplemental clause that was occasionally used by the Public Buildings Service allowed higher percentages for overhead "[i]f established by practice of the trade." A contractor was allowed a 14 percent adjustment for overhead claimed by the excavation subcontractor after it submitted evidence of a local survey showing the average overhead charged to be either exact costs or 15 percent. Other evidence included a letter from the subcontractor's CPA showing the subcontractor's overhead rate to be 18.19 percent for the previous year and letters from competitors stating their policy of placing a 15 percent overhead charge on all their work, *Blake Constr. Co.*, GSBCA 1724, 66-1 BCA ¶ 5336. However, in *Chaney & James Constr. Co.*, GSBCA 1307, 68-2 BCA ¶ 7164, *recons. denied*, 69-1 BCA ¶ 7504, the board rejected a similar claim for a 38.5 percent overhead allowance on the grounds that the contractor, as the moving party, did not meet its burden of establishing entitlement to overhead in excess of 10 percent. The board found the contractor's evidence that the usual rate of overhead charged ranged between 25 and 33 percent to be unconvincing, since the witnesses also testified that the contractors had never claimed more than the standard 10 percent overhead allowance in their dealings with the GSA. See also *E.E. Steinlicht*, IBCA 834-4-70, 71-1 BCA ¶ 8767 (argument that it was customary practice in Oregon to add 10 percent for the price above the 15 percent charged by the subcontractor was rejected as contrary to the contract).

Contractors have unsuccessfully challenged these limitations on adjustments on grounds of duress, *E.E. Steinlicht*, IBCA 834-4-70, 71-1 BCA ¶ 8767, or that the clause does not accord with federal procurement policy, *Gulf-Tex Constr., Inc.*, VACAB 1341, 83-1 BCA ¶ 16,355. In *Paragon Mech.*, VACAB 1324, 79-2 BCA ¶ 13,889, the board held that it had no authority to modify the clause in response to the contractor's claim that the rates were badly in need of updating. One board has also held that a contractor cannot avoid the overhead percentage limits by claiming that additional overhead costs incurred through time extensions due solely to work authorized under the Changes clause are covered by the Suspension of Work clause, *C.A. Fielland, Inc.*, GSBCA 2903, 70-2 BCA ¶ 8566, *recons. denied*, 71-1 BCA ¶ 8734.

The Postal Service Board permitted recovery of an equitable adjustment for overhead in excess of the 10 percent limitation where the contractor had previously recovered adjustments for similar costs in contracts using the nearly identical Public Buildings Service clause and where the government had failed to advise the contractor of its misinterpretation of the clause when it had the opportunity, *Jervis B. Webb Co.*, PSBCA 420, 78-2 BCA ¶ 13,544. The board distinguished the case from other cases involving challenges to the percentage limitations, stating at 66,353:

> Those cases are not germane or controlling in this appeal, however, because (1) some of them relate to situations in which sub- or sub-subcontractors are involved, (2) some of them turn on the issue of trade practices—a question not present in this appeal, and (3) more importantly, not one of them relates to a situation, like the present one, in which there was a long history of prior contracts disclosing the parties' interpretations of the same or similar provisions. Also in this case, unlike the cited cases, there is evidence of detrimental reliance which could have been avoided by prompt action on the part of [the Government].

6. Cost-Plus-Percentage-of-Cost Relationship

It is sometimes claimed that an allowance for profit on a price adjustment after the costs are incurred would violate the statutory restriction against cost-plus-percentage-of-cost contracting. In *Laburnum Constr. Corp. v. United States*, 163 Ct. Cl. 339, 325 F.2d 451 (1963), the court reiterated its long-standing position against the allowance of profit on delay claims and then added the following statement at 353:

> The allowance of so-called profit on the costs incurred during the delay would violate the statutory prohibition against cost-plus-percentage-of-cost procurement (10 U.S.C. § 2306) and would be manifestly unfair to [the Government].

This view that profit on delay costs would violate the rule prohibiting cost-plus-percentage-of-cost procurement would appear to be highly questionable. Of course, if compensation for a delay is granted under a Suspension of Work or Government Delay of Work clause, the clause itself precludes profit. But, if compensation for the delay is granted under a Changes or Differing Site Condition clause, the equitable adjustment would normally include profit on all costs. See *Rex Sys., Inc.*, ASBCA 49065, 98-2 BCA ¶ 29,926, *recons. denied*, 98-2 BCA ¶ 29,926, stating at 148,096:

> Laburnum . . . involved a breach of contract claim. The instant claim arises under the Changes clause of the contract. Under established principles of law, profit is allowable on equitable adjustment claims, including claims for unabsorbed

overhead, unless expressly prohibited by some pertinent contract provision. *BEI Defense Systems Co.*, ASBCA No. 46399, 95-1 BCA ¶ 27,328; *BellSouth Communications Systems, Inc.*, ASBCA No. 45955, 94-3 BCA ¶ 27,231; *Professional Services Unified, Inc.*, ASBCA No. 45799, 94-1 BCA ¶ 26,580; *Bennett Construction Company v. United States*, 178 Ct. Cl. 61, 371 F.2d 859 (1967).

Compare *Altmayer v. General Servs. Admin.*, GSBCA 12639, 95-1 BCA ¶ 27,515, *aff'd in part, rev'd in part*, 79 F.3d 1129 (Fed. Ci. 1996), citing *Laburnum* for the proposition that no profit is allowed on delay costs whether compensation is granted under the Changes clause or on a breach of contract theory.

Regardless of the proper rule on delay claims, profit has been allowed as an element of an equitable adjustment for extra work priced after completion, *E.V. Lane Corp.*, ASBCA 9741, 65-2 BCA ¶ 5076, *recons. denied*, 66-1 BCA ¶ 5472; *Kemmons-Wilson, Inc.*, ASBCA 16167, 72-2 BCA ¶ 9689. See also *Allison Div., Gen. Motors Corp.*, ASBCA 15528, 72-1 BCA ¶ 9343, in which the board stated at 43,383:

> The granting of additional profit in connection with increased work under change orders has never been considered, to our knowledge, a violation of the cost-plus-a-percentage-of-cost system of contracting. The changed work, in effect, constitutes a new procurement under which a contractor is entitled to profit

An additional rationale for the proposition that the inclusion of profit does not violate the statutory proscription is that the contractor is not assured of any specific rate of profit and in some cases may not even receive all of its expenditures. However, if a contract were to state that the contractor is to be paid a fixed rate of profit on its costs, there might be a violation. Such a clause was used in *Sun Shipbuilding & Dry Dock Co. v. United States*, 183 Ct. Cl. 358, 393 F.2d 807 (1968). It provided that the contractor was to be paid "110% of the net increase in estimated cost." The issue of cost-plus-percentage-of-cost was not raised in that case. The construction contract clauses discussed above avoid this problem by stating the percentages as maximums.

V. GOVERNMENT CLAIMS FOR DEFECTIVE PRICING

The Truth in Negotiations Act, 10 U.S.C. § 2306a and 41 U.S.C. § 254A, calling for the submission of certified cost or pricing data on most noncompetitive pricing actions over $550,000, requires that contracts subject to the Act contain a clause calling for price reduction if the required data are defective. The statutes contain elaborate guidance on the computation of price reductions, as follows:

> *Price reductions for defective cost or pricing data.* (1)(A) A prime contract (or change or modification to a prime contract) under which a certificate under subsection (a)(2) is required shall contain a provision that the price of the contract to the United States, including profit or fee, shall be adjusted to exclude any significant amount by which it may be determined by the head of the agency that such

price was increased because the contractor (or any subcontractor required to make available such a certificate) submitted defective cost or pricing data.

(B) For the purposes of this section, defective cost or pricing data are cost or pricing data which, as of the date of agreement on the price of the contract (or another date agreed upon between the parties), were inaccurate, incomplete, or noncurrent. If for the purposes of the preceding sentence the parties agree upon a date other than the date of agreement on the price of the contract, the date agreed upon by the parties shall be as close to the date of agreement on the price of the contract as is practicable.

(2) In determining for purposes of a contract price adjustment under a contract provision required by paragraph (1) whether, and to what extent, a contract price was increased because the contractor (or a subcontractor) submitted defective cost or pricing data, it shall be a defense that the United States did not rely on the defective data submitted by the contractor or subcontractor.

(3) It is not a defense to an adjustment of the price of a contract under a contract provision required by paragraph (1) that—

(A) the price of the contract would not have been modified even if accurate, complete, and current cost or pricing data had been submitted by the contractor or subcontractor because the contractor or subcontractor—

(i) was the sole source of the property or services procured; or

(ii) otherwise was in a superior bargaining position with respect to the property or services procured;

(B) the contracting officer should have known that the cost or pricing data in issue were defective even though the contractor or subcontractor took no affirmative action to bring the character of the data to the attention of the contracting officer;

(C) the contract was based on an agreement between the contractor and the United States about the total cost of the contract and there was no agreement about the cost of each item procured under such contract; or

(D) the prime contractor or subcontractor did not submit a certification of cost and pricing data relating to the contract as required under subsection (a)(2).

The statutory provisions are implemented, with almost no additional guidance, in FAR 15.407-1(b) and two mandatory contract clauses, Price Reduction for Defective Cost or Pricing Data in FAR 52.215-10 and Price Reduction for Defective Cost or Pricing Data—Modifications in FAR 52.215-11.

A. When the Government Is Entitled to a Reduction

Although the statutes provide for price reduction only when the effect of the defective data is to increase the contract price by a "significant amount," the government has been permitted to recover any amount that the price has been increased by a defect. See, for example, *Conrac Corp. v. United States*, 214 Ct. Cl. 561, 558 F.2d 994 (1977), in which the court interpreted the statutory language as relieving agencies from having to pursue trivial claims but permitted claims in any amount that an agency considered to be meaningful. In that case, the claim was for an overpricing of $8,050 on a $548,100 contract. In *American Bosch Arma Corp.*, ASBCA 10305, 65-2 BCA ¶ 5280, the board held that a claim for $20,746 on a contract over $15 million was significant. In *Kaiser Aerospace & Elecs. Corp.*, ASBCA 32098, 90-1 BCA ¶ 22,489, *recons. denied*, 90-2 BCA ¶ 22,695, the board awarded a price reduction of $5,527.82 on orders, under a basic ordering agreement, of $2,754,581, holding that even if this might "appear to be insignificant," it was bound to award that amount by *Conrac Corporation*.

B. Government Reliance on the Defective Data

In order to obtain a price reduction, the government must demonstrate that the contract price negotiated by the parties was increased because of government reliance on the defective data. The government is aided in this task by the "natural and probable consequence" rule developed by the Armed Services Board in *Lambert Eng'g Co.*, ASBCA 13338, 69-1 BCA ¶ 7663; *McDonnell Douglas Corp.*, ASBCA 12786, 69-2 BCA ¶ 7897. This rule holds that the natural and probable consequence of the furnishing of defective data is a dollar-for-dollar increase in the negotiated price. This rule has been termed a "rebuttable presumption," *American Mach. & Foundry Co.*, ASBCA 15037, 74-1 BCA ¶ 10,409. However, it has the effect of requiring the contractor, in order to avoid a price reduction, to demonstrate that the price was not impacted by the defective data, *Sylvania Elec. Prods., Inc. v. United States*, 202 Ct. Cl. 16, 479 F.2d 1342 (1973). See *EDO Corp.*, ASBCA 41448, 93-3 BCA ¶ 26,135, in which the price was reduced by the full amount of the reduced price that a supplier gave a subcontractor, because the contractor could not furnish evidence to overcome the presumption that the contract price had been impacted by this amount. Compare *Black River Ltd. Partnership*, ASBCA 51754, 02-1 BCA ¶ 31,839, *recons. denied*, 02-2 BCA ¶ 31,885, in which the contractor persuaded the board that the government was not misled by missing data.

The natural and probable consequence rule has led to a number of rulings that the contractor was responsible for a dollar-for-dollar price increase. See *Hughes Aircraft Co.*, ASBCA 46321, 97-1 BCA ¶ 28,972; *P.A.L. Sys. Co.*, GSBCA 10858, 91-3 BCA ¶ 24,259; *Millipore Corp.*, GSBCA 9453, 91-1 BCA ¶ 23,345; *Kaiser Aerospace & Elecs. Corp.*, ASBCA 32098, 90-1 BCA ¶ 22,489, *recons. denied*, 90-2 BCA ¶ 22,695; *Etowah Mfg. Co.*, ASBCA 27267, 88-3 BCA ¶ 21,054; *Boeing*

Military Airplane Co., ASBCA 33168, 87-2 BCA ¶ 19,714; *Sylvania Elec. Prods., Inc.*, ASBCA 13622, 70-2 BCA ¶ 8387, *aff'd*, 202 Ct. Cl. 16, 479 F.2d 1342 (1973); and *Aerojet-Gen. Corp.*, ASBCA 12264, 69-1 BCA ¶ 7664. Prior to October 1998, this result was called for in DFARS 215.804-7(b)(2), which stated:

> Unless there is clear evidence to the contrary, the contracting officer may presume the defective data were relied on and resulted in a contract price increase equal to the amount of the defect plus related overhead and profit or fee. The contracting officer is not expected to reconstruct the negotiation by speculating as to what would have been the mental attitudes of the negotiating parties if the nondefective data had been known.

This guidance was deleted when the FAR Part 15 Rewrite was implemented in the DFARS, 63 Fed. Reg. 55040, October 14, 1998.

Contractors have been successful in demonstrating lack of reliance in several cases. See, for example, *United Tech. Corp.*, ASBCA 51410, 05-1 BCA ¶ 32,860, finding no reliance when neither the contracting officer, the government auditor, nor the government pricing personnel reviewed the data that had been submitted as part of the contractor's best and final offer. Similarly, in *Texas Instruments, Inc.*, ASBCA 30836, 89-1 BCA ¶ 21,489, and *Hughes Aircraft Co.*, ASBCA 30144, 90-2 BCA ¶ 22,847, the board found that the government would not have used current prices of materials because the contract price had been negotiated using average prices of materials based on accumulated costs after the materials went through the manufacturing process. Thus, the board concluded that no price reduction was called for because the government would not have used the data had it been disclosed. See also *Levinson Steel Co.*, ASBCA 16520, 73-2 BCA ¶ 10,116 (contracting officer testified he would not have used data); *Muncie Gear Works, Inc.*, ASBCA 18184, 75-2 BCA ¶ 11,380 (auditor would not have used data because he rejected similar data as inaccurate); and *Rose, Beaton & Rose*, PSBCA 459, 80-1 BCA ¶ 14,242 (government would not have reduced its offer because it contained far less overhead than indicated by undisclosed data).

Several defenses demonstrating that the government did not rely on the defective data have been barred by the language in 10 U.S.C. § 2306a(3) and 41 U.S.C. § 254A(3). Thus, it may no longer be possible to argue that there was no reliance because the contractor would not have accepted a lower price. This argument had been used successfully in *Universal Restoration, Inc. v. United States*, 798 F.2d 1400 (Fed. Cir. 1986). See also *Luzon Stevedoring Corp.*, ASBCA 14851, 71-1 BCA ¶ 8745 (contractor made take-it-or-leave-it offer), and *American Mach. & Foundry Co.*, ASBCA 15037, 74-1 BCA ¶ 10,409 (contractor in strong bargaining position). Similarly, in *J.S. Latsis Group of COs./Petrola Eng'g Int'l & RET-SER Eng'g Agency*, ENGBCA 4276, 86-2 BCA ¶ 18,853, the board denied any price reduction for nondisclosure of detailed information on overhead because the contracting officer had negotiated overhead rates on a gross basis without regard to the contents of the overhead pool.

C. Computing the Price Reduction

In computing the amount of the price reduction, the court or board must determine the dollar amount that would have been included in the price had the data been disclosed and the dollar amount that was included in the contract price because of the nondisclosure. The determination of the latter amount has led to significant controversy. In *Sperry Corp. Computer Sys.*, ASBCA 29525, 88-3 BCA ¶ 20,975, *aff'd sub nom. Unisys Corp. v. United States*, 888 F.2d 841 (Fed. Cir. 1989), the board used the labor dollars that the government's documents indicated had been included in the contract price. The board rejected the contractor's argument that a lower amount should be used because the parties had arrived at the price through a "bottom line" settlement. In *Grumman Aerospace Corp.*, ASBCA 35188, 90-2 BCA ¶ 22,842, the board used the labor rates agreed to by the parties in the negotiation of the contract price rather than the labor rate originally proposed by the contractor because "a contractor is not liable for overstated costs that were eliminated during the price negotiation process." In that case, the board rejected the government's argument that the labor hours in the contract price would have been derived from labor hours on a prior contract projected down a learning curve. The board found that the parties had concluded during the price negotiation that difficulties in performing the work would prevent learning and had therefore used the same number of hours for the new contract as had been incurred on the previous contract. Similarly, in *Aerojet Ordnance Tenn.*, ASBCA 36089, 95-2 BCA ¶ 27,922, the board rejected the use of a learning curve because the evidence indicated that both parties did not believe it would yield accurate results. In that case, the board also concluded that the parties would have included lower material costs in the price even though the agreed amount was lower than the government estimate—because the government estimate was based on lower quantities and the nondisclosed data indicated lower material quantities. See also *Rosemount, Inc.*, ASBCA 37520, 95-2 BCA ¶ 27,770, rejecting the use of a learning curve because the government did not prove it would use this technique. In *Etowah Mfg. Co.*, ASBCA 27267, 88-3 BCA ¶ 21,054, the board used the government estimate prior to the negotiation rather than the considerably higher amount included in the contract price. The board apparently concluded that the contractor's nondisclosure of relevant data was not the cause of the government's willingness to include a higher amount in the price and, therefore, that the contractor was not responsible for any amount greater than the difference between the government estimate and the amount derived from the undisclosed data.

The dollar amount that would have been included in the contract price had the data been disclosed has also created controversy. In *Sperry Corp. Computer Sys.*, the board used the undisclosed labor dollars incurred in manufacturing the product 18 months before the negotiations even though there was evidence that the parties had agreed in the negotiations that a higher figure would be required for the instant contract because of decreases in volume. The precise amount in the undisclosed data was also used in *Etowah Manufacturing*. In earlier cases, the boards had been more willing to base the computation of this figure on the record of the actual negotiations. For example, in *Aerojet-Gen. Corp.*, ASBCA 12873, 69-1 BCA ¶ 7585, the board noted that the parties had arrived at the contract price by splitting the difference in their final negotiation positions. The board therefore assumed that the defective data would have decreased the government's negotiation position by the amount of the defect and that the parties would have split the difference—resulting in a price reduction of one-half of the amount of the defective data. Similarly, in *Bell & Howell Co.*, ASBCA 11999, 68-1 BCA ¶ 6993, the board concluded that, had the data been disclosed, the parties would not have been able to negotiate a firm fixed-price contract. It therefore assumed that they would have negotiated an incentive contract with a 60/40 share and awarded a price reduction in the amount of 60 percent of the defect.

In order to make a full computation of the impact of the price reduction on the contract price, the price must be reconstructed using the pricing structure that the parties used in the original negotiation. Thus, the computation must also include all elements of the contractor's costs that would normally be added to the cost item that is adjusted because of the defective data. See, for example, *Grumman Aerospace Corp.*, ASBCA 35188, 90-2 BCA ¶ 22,842, in which the board computed the price reduction for defective data on labor dollars by adding all categories of work that were estimated as percentages of labor dollars (manufacturing engineering, sustaining engineering, program management, and foreign sales) plus all applicable overheads, general and administrative expense, and profit. Similarly, in *Kaiser Aerospace & Elecs. Corp.*, ASBCA 32098, 90-1 BCA ¶ 22,489, *recons. denied*, 90-2 BCA ¶ 22,695, the price reduction for defective data on labor rates was computed by adding overhead, general and administrative expense, warranty, and profit.

If there has been a statutory violation because a contractor or subcontractor refuses to submit any cost or pricing data and no exemption applies, the contractor is paid the reasonable value of the work, *Beech Aircraft Corp.*, ASBCA 25388, 83-1 BCA ¶ 16.532. In *Dewey Elec. Corp.*, ASBCA 17696, 76-2 BCA ¶ 12,146, this was determined by adding a reasonable profit to the actual costs incurred. In *Grumman Aerospace Corp.*, ASBCA 48282, 98-2 BCA ¶ 29,943, the board rejected the government's claim for noncompliance with the statute because its repricing after the fact indicated that the reasonable value was greater than the agreed contract price.

D. Offset

Early in the litigation of price reductions for defective cost or pricing data, it was determined that a contractor was entitled, up to the amount of any price reduction, to offset any amount due to underpricing that had occurred because of defective data in the same pricing action, *Cutler-Hammer, Inc. v. United States*, 189 Ct. Cl. 76, 416 F.2d 1306 (1969); *Lockheed Aircraft Corp. v. United States*, 193 Ct. Cl. 86, 432 F.2d 801 (1970). This rule was incorporated in the statutes in 10 U.S.C. § 2306a(e) and 41 U.S.C. § 254A(e), as follows:

(4)(A) A contractor shall be allowed to offset an amount against the amount of a contract price adjustment under a contract provision required by paragraph (1) if—

(i) the contractor certifies to the contracting officer (or to a designated representative of the contracting officer) that, to the best of the contractor's knowledge and belief, the contractor is entitled to the offset; and

(ii) the contractor proves that the cost or pricing data were available before the date of agreement on the price of the contract (or price of the modification) or, if applicable consistent with paragraph (1)(B), another date agreed upon between the parties, and that the data were not submitted as specified in subsection (a)(3) before such date.

(B) A contractor shall not be allowed to offset an amount otherwise authorized to be offset under subparagraph (A) if—

(i) the certification under subsection (a)(2) with respect to the cost or pricing data involved was known to be false when signed; or

(ii) the United States proves that, had the cost or pricing data referred to in subparagraph (A)(ii) been submitted to the United States before the date of agreement on the price of the contract (or price of the modification), the submission of such cost or pricing data would not have resulted in an increase in that price in the amount to be offset.

Offsets are permitted only when the contractor proves that there was an understatement of "factual pricing data," *J.S. Latsis Group of Cos./Petrola Eng'g Int'l & RETSER Eng'g Agency*, ENGBCA 4276, 86-2 BCA ¶ 18,853. In that case, the board found that the evidence was very unclear but, if there were any errors to which a low price could be attributed, they were errors of judgment, not errors in cost or pricing data. See also *GKS, Inc.*, ASBCA 47692, 00-1 BCA ¶ 30,914 (no offset for intentionally understated G & A rate); *AM Gen. Corp.*, ASBCA 48476, 99-1 BCA ¶ 30,130 (no offset for management decision to amortize costs because that was a judgmental decision); and *Lockheed Corp.*, ASBCA 36420, 95-2 BCA ¶ 27,722 (no offset when contractor disclosed certain concessions it was making in agreeing to the price).

Offsets may not be made between different contracts, *Norris Indus., Inc.*, ASBCA 15442, 74-1 BCA ¶ 10,482; *Minnesota Mining & Mfg. Co.*, ASBCA 20266, 77-2 BCA ¶ 12,823, or between unrelated contract modifications, *Muncie Gear Works, Inc.*, ASBCA 18184, 75-2 BCA ¶ 11,380. Neither can offsets lead to a price increase by the contractor, *Baldwin Elecs., Inc.*, ASBCA 19683, 76-2 BCA ¶ 12,199 (offsets exceeding the claimed price reduction led to sustaining of contractor's appeal). However, offsets are proper even when the contractor has intentionally understated the dollar amounts in the data, *Rogerson Aircraft Controls*, ASBCA 27954, 85-1 BCA ¶ 17,725, *aff'd*, 785 F.2d 296 (Fed. Cir. 1986) (government knew of understatements and was not "hindered or deceived" by them). Compare *United*

Tech. Corp., ASBCA 43645, 98-1 BCA ¶ 29,577, in which an offset of data found in a "sweep" was not permitted because the contractor had not disclosed the data to the government prior to signing the certificate. The board distinguished *Rogerson* on the grounds that in this case the government negotiators were "deprived of the opportunity" to use the data in determining their course of action. This decision was affirmed with regard to data discovered before certification but reversed as to data discovered after certification, *United Tech./Pratt & Whitney v. Peters*, 215 F.3d 1343 (Fed Cir. 1999). In *Hughes Aircraft Co.*, ASBCA 46321, 97-1 BCA ¶ 28,972, offset was permitted when a contractor failed to disclose increases in its material rates and other direct costs. A contractor has also been permitted to offset an amount that was mistakenly omitted from the price when the contractor deleted the wrong item of material in adjusting its proposed price, *United Tech. Corp.*, ASBCA 51410, 04-1 BCA ¶ 32,556, and to offset its omitted in-house costs of completing work from an overstated subcontract price for the same work, *TGS Int'l, Inc.*, ASBCA 31120, 87-2 BCA ¶ 19,683, *recons. denied*, 87-3 BCA ¶ 19,989. However, offset was denied in *Aerojet Ordnance Tenn.*, ASBCA 36089, 95-2 BCA ¶ 27,922, because the contractor had recovered the cost of an undisclosed management decision through a separate agreement, and the board concluded that permitting offset would give the contractor double recovery of the amount claimed.

E. Defective Subcontractor Data

If subcontractor cost or pricing data have been submitted to the government before the negotiation of the contract price of a firm-fixed-price contract, the contractor is liable for defects in those data, *Lockheed Aircraft Corp. v. United States*, 193 Ct. Cl. 86, 432 F.2d 801 (1970). In that case, the court held the contractor liable even though the subcontractor data had been submitted directly to the government—not to the contractor. The court reasoned that the contractor's liability was dictated by the contract clause requiring price reductions. See also *McDonnell Aircraft Co.*, ASBCA 44504, 97-1 BCA ¶ 28,977, holding a contractor liable when its subcontractor failed to disclose its analysis of a subsubcontractor's proposal. If subcontractor cost or pricing data are not submitted to the contractor until after the negotiation of the price, there is no contractor liability for a price reduction because there could be no government reliance on those data. See *Motorola, Inc.*, ASBCA 51789, 03-1 BCA ¶ 32,195, holding that the government was not entitled to a price reduction on a subcontract that was negotiated one month after the agreement on the contract price but finding that a price reduction should be factored into the finally redetermined price of the fixed-price incentive contract.

FAR 15.404-3 imposes additional requirements on contractors and subcontractors as follows:

> (b) The prime contractor or subcontractor shall—
>
> > (1) Conduct appropriate cost or price analyses to establish the reasonableness of proposed subcontract prices;

(2) Include the results of these analyses in the price proposal; and

(3) When required by paragraph (c) of this subsection, submit subcontractor cost or pricing data to the Government as part of its own cost or pricing data.

(c) Any contractor or subcontractor that is required to submit cost or pricing data also shall obtain and analyze cost or pricing data before awarding any subcontract, purchase order, or modification expected to exceed the cost or pricing data threshold, unless an exception in 15.403-1(b) applies to that action.

(1) The contractor shall submit, or cause to be submitted by the subcontractor(s), cost or pricing data to the Government for subcontracts that are the lower of either—

(i) $ 10,000,000 or more; or

(ii) Both more than the pertinent cost or pricing data threshold and more than 10 percent of the prime contractor's proposed price, unless the contracting officer believes such submission is unnecessary.

The requirement for submission of analyses of subcontract prices was applied in *McDonnell Aircraft Co.*, ASBCA 44504, 03-1 BCA ¶ 32,154. There the board held that the contractor was liable for nonsubmission of an analysis that a prospective subcontractor had conducted of its sub-subcontractor's price proposal. The board rejected the contractor's arguments that it did not know of the analysis and could not have reasonably obtained it from a company with which it had no contract.

The contractor is expected to include price reduction clauses in all subcontracts under cost-reimbursement or fixed-price-incentive or redeterminable contracts, and price reductions obtained through such clauses are expected to be credited to the costs billed to the government, FAR 15.407-1(f)(2). This applies even though the subcontractor's cost or pricing data were never submitted to the government or used as the basis for the original contract price.

F. Interest and Penalties

The statutes require the addition of interest and penalties in certain cases where the government has overpaid the contractor as a result of defective cost or pricing data. 10 U.S.C. § 2306a and 41 U.S.C. § 254A state:

(f) *Interest and penalties for certain overpayments.* (1) If the United States makes an overpayment to a contractor under a contract subject to this section and the overpayment was due to the submission by the contractor of defective cost or pricing data, the contractor shall be liable to the United States—

(A) for interest on the amount of such overpayment, to be computed—

(i) for the period beginning on the date the overpayment was made to the contractor and ending on the date the contractor repays the amount of such overpayment to the United States; and

(ii) at the current rate prescribed by the Secretary of the Treasury under section 6621 of the Internal Revenue Code of 1986; and

(B) if the submission of such defective data was a knowing submission, for an additional amount equal to the amount of the overpayment.

(2) Any liability under this subsection of a contractor that submits cost or pricing data but refuses to submit the certification required by subsection (a)(2) with respect to the cost or pricing data shall not be affected by the refusal to submit such certification.

Statutory interest applies only to contracts and contract modifications awarded after the dates specified in the 1985 and 1986 statutes adopting this provision. In *Motorola, Inc.*, ASBCA 51789, 01-1 BCA ¶ 31,233, the board ruled that the statute did not apply to a 1984 contract modification because the date specified for such modifications was November 7, 1985. As a result, interest did not begin to run until the date of the first government demand. In *United States v. United Tech. Corp., Sikorsky Aircraft Div.*, 51 F. Supp. 2d 167 (D. Conn. 1999), the court found the statute applicable because, although the contractor had signed a modification before November 7, 1985, the government did not sign it until January 1986. The court, however, tolled the running of interest during the time that the government held a check that had been submitted by the contractor to settle the claim.

VI. COSTS OF PREPARING AND FINANCING ADJUSTMENTS

Some of the costs incurred by contractors in preparing and presenting proposals and claims for contract price adjustments are recoverable from the government. However, there are special rules covering both the costs of preparing and negotiating such adjustments and the imputed interest that a contractor can recover on claims under the Contract Disputes Act. This section covers this special problem area.

A. Preparation and Negotiation Costs

FAR 31.205-47(f)(1) provides that costs are unallowable if they are incurred in connection with:

(1) Defense against Federal Government claims or appeals or the prosecution of claims or appeals against the Federal Government (see 2.101).

This broad rule barring the recovery of costs of prosecution or defense of claims is consistent with the traditional rule that attorneys' fees are not allowed in suits against the government in the absence of an express statutory provision permitting recovery, *Piggly Wiggly Corp. v. United States*, 112 Ct. Cl. 391, 81 F. Supp. 819 (1949). See also *Texas Instruments Inc. v. United States*, 991 F.2d 760 (Fed. Cir. 1993), in which the court rejected the theory that a large contractor could recover legal fees because the government breached its obligation to deal with the contractor in good faith. The court refused to depart from the rule that legal fees are not recoverable unless there is an express statute calling for their payment.

In contrast, the costs of normal contract administration are allowable costs, which can be included in the costs of a claim to the extent that the contractor's accounting system permits their inclusion as a direct cost, or otherwise can be included in the contractor's appropriate indirect cost account. Thus, the recovery of the cost of preparing and negotiating contract price adjustments is dependent on the distinction between claim prosecution and contract administration.

1. Distinction Between Claim Prosecution and Contract Administration

FAR 31.205-47(f)(1) cross references FAR 2.101, which contains the definition of the term "claim" that is applicable to the Contract Disputes Act of 1978. See Chapter 13 for a full discussion of this term. This confirms the long-standing rule that a suit in a court or an appeal to a board of contract appeals would constitute such a claim, *Grumman Aerospace Corp. v. United States*, 217 Ct. Cl. 285, 579 F.2d 586 (1978); *Lew F. Stilwell, Inc.*, ASBCA 9423, 1964 BCA ¶ 4128. Thus, it is clear that costs incurred in such litigation are not recoverable. Prior to 1964, it was considered that this prohibition did not apply to costs incurred in presenting the claim to a contracting officer before a final decision, *Lake Union Drydock Co.*, ASBCA 3073, 59-1 BCA ¶ 2229. Then, in *Power Equip. Corp.*, ASBCA 5904, 1964 BCA ¶ 4025, *recons. denied*, 1964 BCA ¶ 4228, the board denied recovery of $22,903.21 in attorneys' fees incurred in presenting claims to the contracting officer under the Changes clause of the contract. It is not clear from the decision whether the board was objecting to the allowability of such costs on the basis of DAR 15-205.31 or whether it was objecting to the attempt at recovery as a direct charge against the change order rather than through an allowance for overhead. However, subsequent decisions citing *Power Equipment* disallowed costs of preparing change order proposals on the theory that they were not incurred in the prosecution of the work under the change, *Coastal Dry Dock & Repair Corp.*, ASBCA 36754, 91-1 BCA ¶ 23,324; *Erickson Air Crane Co.*, EBCA 50-6-79, 83-1 BCA ¶ 16,145, *aff'd*, 731 F.2d 810 (Fed. Cir. 1984). See also *Excavation-Constr., Inc.*, ENGBCA 3858, 82-1 BCA ¶ 15,770, *recons. denied*, 83-1 BCA ¶ 16,338, not allowing the cost of preparing a proposal for delay costs. The board did allow the recovery of such costs as direct charges in *Allied Materials & Equip. Co.*, ASBCA 17318, 75-1 BCA ¶ 11,150, stating that "the request for an equitable adjustment was on its face meritorious" and that the matter never became "so disputatious as to reach the level of a claim against the Government." In *Singer Co., Librascope Div. v. United States*, 215 Ct. Cl. 281, 568 F.2d 695 (1977), the court distinguished *Allied Materials*, stating at 327-28:

> Plainly, the situation presented in the instant matter differs significantly from that encountered in the *Allied* case. Here, the claims for equitable adjustment were not presented to the contracting officer until all work had been completed, they addressed no situation in which Government liability was clear or apparent and, in content, they offered nothing that could reasonably be considered as benefitting the contract purpose. Judged both from the standpoint of the time of their submission and the purpose of their submission, Librascope's requests for equitable adjustment were not performance-related; they bore no beneficial nexus either to contract production or to contract administration. Accordingly, the attorneys' fees are not recoverable. As to the other claim preparation costs which plaintiff also seeks, these too are not allowable and for the same reason—they bear no relation to contract performance.

Additional guidance on this distinction was given in *Bill Strong Enters., Inc. v. Shannon*, 49 F.3d 1541 (Fed. Cir. 1995). There the contractor had submitted a request for equitable adjustment to the contracting officer and had subsequently hired a consultant to provide documentation of the merits of the claim. The parties then settled the claim, but the contracting officer would not include the costs of the consultant in the settlement. In the suit for such costs, the court held that the fact that a Contract Disputes Act claim was not filed led to *a strong presumption* that the consultant costs were for contract administration. It also held that contract administration can, and often does, continue after completion of work. Third, it held that the mere presence of disagreement during negotiations did not move the costs into the unallowable category of claim prosecution costs, stating at 1549-50:

> In the practical environment of government contracts, the contractor and the CO usually enter a negotiation stage after the parties recognize a problem regarding the contract. The contractor and the CO labor to settle the problem and avoid litigation. Although there is sometimes an air of adversity in the relationship between the CO and the contractor, their efforts to resolve their differences amicably reflect a mutual desire to achieve a result acceptable to both. This negotiation process often involves requests for information by the CO or Government auditors or both, and, inevitably, this exchange of information involves costs for the contractor. These costs are contract administration costs, which should be allowable since this negotiation process benefits the Government, regardless of whether a settlement is finally reached or whether litigation eventually occurs because the availability of the process increases the likelihood of settlement without litigation. See 48 C.F.R. § 33.204 (1987). ("It is the Government's policy to try to resolve all contractual issues by mutual agreement at the contracting officer's level, without litigation.") Additionally, contractors would have a greater incentive to negotiate rather than litigate if these costs of contract administration were recoverable. See 7 Nash & Cibinic Report ¶ 48, at 134-35.

> In classifying a particular cost as either a contract administration cost or a cost incidental to the prosecution of a claim, contracting officers, the Board, and courts should examine the objective reason why the contractor incurred the cost. See [*Singer Co. v. United States*], 568 F.2d at 721 (judging the "purpose" of the contractor's submission). If a contractor incurred the cost for the genuine purpose of materially furthering the negotiation process, such cost should normally be a contract administration cost allowable under FAR 31.205-33, even if negotiation eventually fails and a CDA claim is later submitted. See [*Armada, Inc.*], 84-3 BCA ¶ 17,694, at 88,242-43. On the other hand, if a contractor's underlying purpose for incurring a cost is to promote the prosecution of a CDA claim against the Government, then such cost is unallowable under FAR 31.205-33.

Thus, there is a strong presumption that, if a contractor chooses to present a request for equitable adjustment rather than a Contract Disputes Act claim, it is for the purpose of "materially furthering the negotiation process" with the result that the costs incurred will be allowable. See *Advanced Eng'g & Planning Corp.*, ASBCA 53366, 03-1 BCA ¶ 32,157, where the parties negotiated for a year after the work was completed attempting to resolve all of the problems that had arisen in the performance of a job order. When they could not agree, the contractor submitted a claim under the Contract Disputes Act. The board held that the costs up to the time when the negotiation failed were allowable contract administration costs, while the costs of "updating the REA and converting the REA into a CDA claim" were unallowable claim prosecution costs. See also *American Mech., Inc.*, ASBCA 52033, 03-1 BCA ¶ 32,134 (board awarded the costs of a subcontractor's employees that had prepared requests for equitable adjustment during and after contract performance to obtain compensation for design changes and deficiencies and provided information to resolve the issues without litigation); *Information Sys. & Networks Corp.*, ASBCA 42659, 00-1 BCA ¶ 30,665, *recons. denied*, 00-1 BCA ¶ 30,866 (board awarded cost of accounting consultant that prepared termination settlement proposal but denied award of cost of attorney that protested contractor's exclusion from reprocurement contract); *Unarco Material Handling*, PSBCA 4100, 00-1 BCA ¶ 30,682 (boarded awarded profit on the costs that were incurred in preparing a proposal for an equitable adjustment); *Taylor Constr. Co. v. General Servs. Admin.*, GSBCA 12915, 96-2 BCA ¶ 28,547, *recons. denied*, 97-2 BCA ¶ 29,127 (board awarded cost of consultant whose effort used in furthering negotiations); and *Federal Ins. Co.*, IBCA 3236, 96-2 BCA ¶ 28,415 (board awarded cost of consultant hired during contract performance whose efforts were used in negotiations). Compare *Brero Constr., Inc.*, LBCA 1997-BCA-4, 99-2 BCA ¶ 30,578, in which the costs were denied because the negotiation of the alleged changes were conducted after the completion of the contract work. The most unique case is *Propellex Corp.*, ASBCA 50203, 02-1 BCA ¶ 31,721, *aff'd*, 342 F.3d 1335 (Fed. Cir. 2003), in which the contractor submitted an improperly certified claim on December 27, 1993, and a CDA claim on September 16, 1994. The board awarded attorneys' fees of $25,497 for work performed from January 1994 until September 16, 1994, on the theory that because the contracting officer made the contractor a settlement offer in 1996, the work must have been "for the purpose of materially furthering the negotiation process."

A number of cases have found that costs were unallowable because they were incurred in the prosecution of a claim. This result is most likely when the contractor appears to have been preparing for litigation from the outset. See *Grumman Aerospace Corp.*, ASBCA 50090, 01-1 BCA ¶ 31,316, *aff'd*, 34 Fed. Appx. 710 (Fed. Cir. 2002), in which the board denied a subcontractor's (Rohr) costs of preparing a proposal/claim appealed in the contractor's name on behalf of the subcontractor. The board reasoned that the subcontractor had assumed a "litigation posture" from the outset, stating at 154,675:

> The record that is before us discloses a litigation posture from the outset. The initial focus was on Grumman, for its own actions and those of the Government as Grumman's "agent," in the event Grumman would not sponsor an appeal. The 14 July 1988 letter to Grumman from Rohr's vice president, commercial business, made clear that if Grumman did not protect Rohr's "right to appeal to the appropriate board or court," Rohr would be required to bring an action against Grumman. Subsequently, by letter dated 22 August 1988, Rohr promised Grumman that it would "provide full support for its claim" and would "certify that claim as required by the Contract Disputes Act."

See also *Bechtel Nat'l, Inc.*, ASBCA 51589, 02-1 BCA ¶ 31,673, *aff'd*, 65 Fed. Appx. 277 (Fed. Cir. 2003) (board found legal fees of a subcontractor unallowable when subcontractor certified initial presentation and threatened litigation if claim was not paid); *Innovative Refrigeration Concepts*, ASBCA 48625, 01-1 BCA ¶ 31,250 (contractor did not offer evidence showing that expenses relating to a criminal investigation were "related to either contract performance or administration"); *Stewart & Stevenson Servs., Inc.*, ASBCA 43631, 97-2 BCA ¶ 29,252 (legal expenses were incurred after negotiations had concluded); and *Systems & Elec., Inc.*, ASBCA 41113, 97-1 BCA ¶ 28,671 (parties already before the board when revised claim prepared). In two instances, costs of a consultant were disallowed because the board concluded that the consultant had impeded rather than furthered settlement of the claims with the contracting officer, *Fire Sec. Sys., Inc.*, VABCA 5559, 02-2 BCA ¶ 31,977 (consultant antagonized contracting officer by making derogatory comments about her competence); *Fire Sec. Sys., Inc. v. General Servs. Admin.*, GSBCA 12267, 97-2 BCA ¶ 28,992 (consultant did not further negotiations and "appear[ed] to have aided and abetted appellant in refusing to provide any cost or pricing data"). The most difficult decision to understand is *Plano Builders Corp. v. United States*, 40 Fed. Cl. 635 (1998), in which the court denied all consultant costs even though the consultant had assisted in explaining the proposals for equitable adjustment to the contracting officer. The decision can be explained by a statement by the court that it did not believe that *Bill Strong* was the controlling law.

If a contractor has not carefully segregated its costs to clearly identify those costs that were incurred in the contract administration process, it risks denial of all of the costs. This was an element of the reasoning in both *Grumman* and *Bechtel National*. In *Bechtel* the board found at 156,527:

> A "big hunk" of [subcontractor's] "REA" preparation cost claim was for legal fees for the counsel who ultimately tried this appeal. The evidence does not indicate how much this "big hunk" was, or what part if any of the total "REA" preparation cost was for the genuine purpose of materially furthering negotiation of a price adjustment as a matter of contract administration, as distinct from preparation for prosecution of a claim.

See also *Atherton Constr., Inc.*, ASBCA 48527, 00-2 BCA ¶ 30,968 (board showed a willingness to allow some of the contractor's claim preparation costs but was unable to do so because the contractor had "not attempted to segregate" any of the costs that would have been allowable); *Lamb Eng'g & Constr. Co.*, EBCA C-9304172, 97-2 ¶ 29,207, *recons. denied*, 98-1 BCA ¶ 29,359 (not enough evidence to allocate consultant costs); and *Ball, Ball & Brosamer, Inc.*, IBCA 2841, 97-2 BCA ¶ 29,072 (consultant provided no specific information concerning any settlement attempts and no breakdown of its claimed costs as to purpose and time period covered).

Costs of contract administration can be charged as a direct cost or an indirect cost depending on the contractor's accounting system. *Allied Materials & Equip. Co.*, ASBCA 17318, 75-1 BCA ¶ 11,150, held that costs of preparing proposals to the contracting officer were properly charged as direct costs because "to regard the expenses as indirect costs would . . . unfairly and inequitably burden other contracts." The same rule is set forth in Interpretation No. 1 to Cost Accounting Standard 402, 41 Fed. Reg. 24,691 (1976), which recognizes that costs of preparing proposals specifically required by a provision of an existing contract may be charged directly even though other proposal costs are charged indirectly. The comments accompanying this interpretation indicate that proposals for equitable adjustments are specifically included in this interpretation. See *FMC Corp.*, ASBCA 30130, 87-2 BCA ¶ 19,791, *aff'd*, 853 F.2d 882 (Fed. Cir. 1998), interpreting this cost accounting standard and the Cost Principles to prohibit the treatment of such costs as indirect costs. The board's decision in *Owen L. Schwam Constr. Co.*, ASBCA 22407, 79-2 BCA ¶ 13,919, seems to indicate that the costs disallowed as direct charges may be recoverable through G&A expense. See also *Lear Siegler, Inc.*, ASBCA 20040, 79-1 BCA ¶ 13,687. Compare *Propellex Corp.*, ASBCA 50203, 02-1 BCA ¶ 31,721, *aff'd*, 342 F.3d 1335 (Fed. Cir. 2003, in which the board refused to pay the costs of a contractor's employees because it concluded that they were already included in the contractor's indirect costs.

2. Costs Covered

Prior to 1989, FAR 31.205-33 dealt with "costs of legal, accounting, and consultant services and directly associated costs." This coverage appeared to be subject to the interpretation that the disallowance did not cover costs of employees of the contractor. The definition was broadened to cover all costs—both external and in-house—in 1989, when the following definition was included in FAR 31.205-47:

> *Costs* include, but are not limited to, administrative and clerical expenses; the costs of legal services, whether performed by in-house or private counsel; the

costs of the services of accountants, consultants, or others retained by the contractor to assist it; costs of employees, officers, and directors; and any similar costs incurred before, during, and after commencement of a judicial or administrative proceeding which bears a direct relationship to the proceedings.

3. Recovery by Small Contractors

Small contractors can recover some claims presentation costs under the Equal Access to Justice Act (EAJA). 5 U.S.C. § 504(a)(1) states:

> An agency that conducts an adversary adjudication shall award, to a prevailing party other than the United States, fees and other expenses incurred by that party in connection with that proceeding, unless the adjudicative officer of the agency finds that the position of the agency was substantially justified or that special circumstances make an award unjust. Whether or not the position of the agency was substantially justified shall be determined on the basis of the administrative record, as a whole, which is made in the adversary adjudication for which fees and other expenses are sought.

28 U.S.C. § 2412(d)(1) contains substantially the same provision dealing with the recovery of fees and expenses in litigation in federal courts, such as the Court of Federal Claims. Claims for fees and expenses must be filed within 30 days after final disposition of a case in court or by an appeals board. Fees and expenses incurred prior to a final decision of a contracting officer are not includable in awards under the Act, *Levernier Constr., Inc. v. United States*, 947 F.2d 497 (Fed. Cir. 1991).

a. Eligibility Requirements

The Act is applicable to individuals having a net worth not exceeding $2 million or the sole owner of an unincorporated business, or a partnership, corporation, association, or organization whose net worth did not exceed $5 million at the time the case was filed or who did not have more than 500 employees at the time the case was filed. Size and net worth limitations may be waived for certain tax exempt organizations or cooperative associations.

When a claim is brought by a contractor in the name of and for the benefit of a subcontractor, it is the net worth and size of the contractor, not the subcontractor, that determines eligibility, *Teton Constr.*, ASBCA 27700, 87-2 BCA ¶ 19,766. This rule has been followed in *SCL Materials & Equip. Co.*, IBCA 3866-97F, 98-2 BCA ¶ 30,000; *General Ins. Co. of Am.*, ASBCA 46368, 95-2 BCA ¶ 27,856; and *Southwest Marine, Inc.*, ASBCA 36287, 93-1 BCA ¶ 25,225, *aff'd*, 43 F.3d 420 (9th Cir. 1994). It has also been applied to a surety that has entered into a takeover agreement with the government, *Sentry Ins. Co.*, VABCA 2617E, 93-3 BCA ¶ 26,124. These cases reject a "real party in interest" analysis, and the board in *SCL Materials* speculates as to whether that test might apply to court litigation because the definition of "party" is broader in 28 U.S.C. § 2412 than in 5 U.S.C. § 504.

There is disagreement on whether a contractor can recover legal fees and expenses incurred by a subcontractor when the contractor brings the suit and both the contractor and subcontractor meet the eligibility requirements. In *R.C. Constr. Co. v. United States*, 42 Fed. Cl. 57 (1998), the court denied such a claim, reasoning that the subcontractor was not the party bringing the suit and only the fees and expenses incurred by that party were covered by the Act. However, the boards have reached the opposite result. See *T.H. Taylor, Inc.*, ASBCA 26494-0(R), 86-3 BCA ¶ 19,257, reasoning that fees incurred by the subcontractor were also incurred by the contractor. The same result was reached in *Jordan & Nobles Constr. Co. v. General Servs. Admin.*, GSBCA 11278-C-R(8576), 93-2 BCA ¶ 25,741, and *Sentry Ins. Co.*, VABCA 2617E, 93-3 BCA ¶ 26,124. See also *Ed A. Wilson, Inc. v. United States*, 126 F.3d 1406 (Fed. Cir. 1997), awarding fees incurred by an insurance company that provided legal representation for the contractor.

Using a "totality of facts" basis, in *Design & Prod., Inc. v. United States*, 20 Cl. Ct. 207 (1990), *recons. denied*, 21 Cl. Ct. 145 (1990), the court held that a wholly owned subsidiary of another corporation was eligible for attorneys' fees and costs because it was the real party of interest. In making this holding, the court looked at the physical, administrative, and managerial connections between the subsidiary and the parent. This "totality of facts" test was extended in *United States v. Paisley*, 957 F.2d 1161 (4th Cir. 1992), *cert. denied*, 506 U.S. 822 (1992), to include an inquiry into who bears the legal expense.

b. Prevailing Parties

Only "prevailing parties" are entitled to recover under the Act, but the definition of this term is very liberal. Thus, a contractor is considered to be "prevailing" if it is successful on any substantial issue in the case. However, if the contractor wins on only a portion of the claims filed, it will generally be given only a portion of its fees and expenses. See *Hensley v. Eckhart*, 461 U.S. 424 (1984), in which the Court gave the following guidance at 432-34:

> [P]laintiffs may be considered "prevailing parties" for attorney's fee purposes if they succeed on any significant issue in litigation which achieves some of the benefit the parties sought in bringing suit. . . . This is a generous formulation that brings the plaintiff only across the statutory threshold. It remains for the . . . court to determine what fee is "reasonable."
>
> * * *
>
> There remain other considerations that may lead the . . . court to adjust the fee upward or downward, including the important factor of the "results obtained." This factor is particularly crucial where a plaintiff is deemed "prevailing" even though he succeeded on only some of his claims for relief. In this situation two questions must be addressed. First, did the plaintiff fail to prevail on claims that were unrelated to the claims on which he succeeded? Second, did the plaintiff achieve

> a level of success that makes the hours reasonably expended a satisfactory basis for making a fee award?
>
> In some cases a plaintiff may present in one lawsuit distinctly different claims for relief that are based on different facts and legal theories. In such a suit, even where the claims are brought against the same defendants . . . counsel's work on one claim will be unrelated to his work on another claim. Accordingly, work on an unsuccessful claim cannot be deemed to have been "expended in pursuit of the ultimate result achieved." . . . The congressional intent to limit awards to prevailing parties requires that these unrelated claims be treated as if they had been raised in separate lawsuits, and therefore no fee may be awarded for services on the unsuccessful claim.

Parties have been held to be "prevailing" when they have recovered on only a small portion of their claims, *Summit Contractors*, AGBCA 86-259-10, 87-1 BCA ¶ 19,604 (contractor won one out of 11 claims); *N&P Constr. Co.*, VABCA 3283E, 93-3 BCA ¶ 26,257 (contractor won less than 2 percent of claimed amount); *On Time Postal Servs., Inc.*, PSBCA 2528, 91-2 BCA ¶ 23,770 (contractor awarded only $776). However, a litigant is not a prevailing party if it wins on a procedural issue, *Jarman v. Department of the Navy*, 144 F.3d 794 (Fed. Cir. 1998) (court reversed a ruling that a board lacked jurisdiction); *A. Hirsh, Inc. v. United States*, 948 F.2d 1240 (Fed. Cir. 1991) (remand requiring explanation of decision). Neither is a contractor a prevailing party if it wins a case on entitlement but subsequently is unable to prove any monetary injury, *Freeman Gen., Inc.*, ASBCA 34611, 90-2 BCA ¶ 22,660.

If the parties settle the claim without the aid of a board or court, the contractor cannot recover EAJA fees, *Brickwood Contractors, Inc. v. United States*, 288 F.3d 1371 (Fed. Cir. 2002), *cert. denied*, 537 U.S. 1106 (2003). This rule is predicated on the Supreme Court's decision in *Buckhannon Board & Care Home, Inc. v. West Virginia Dep't of Health & Human Res.*, 532 U.S. 598 (2001), holding that there could be a "prevailing party" only when there was a "judicially sanctioned change in the legal relationship of the parties." In so holding, the Court rejected the "catalyst theory" that had been in wide use—allowing a party to be the prevailing party if the litigation was a significant cause of the settlement. Under the new rule, a dismissal of a claim by an appeals board will deprive the contractor of attorneys' fees because it is not a judicially sanctioned change in relationship, *Elrich Contracting, Inc.*, ASBCA 50867, 02-2 BCA ¶ 31,950; *Poly Design, Inc.*, ASBCA 48591, 01-2 BCA ¶ 31,644. However, if a board issues a judgment consenting to the settlement, attorneys' fees will be available if the party meets the other EAJA requirements, *Centron Indus., Inc.*, ASBCA 52581, 02-2 BCA ¶ 32,022. In both *Elrich* and *Centron* the government had agreed to convert a default termination into a termination for convenience, but in *Elrich* the board granted a motion to dismiss, while in *Centron*, in a 3–2 decision, the board refused to dismiss and granted judgment for the contractor. The dissent explained the impact of such a consent judgment at 158,262:

> In Board proceedings, a decision sustaining an appeal is the equivalent of an enforceable judgment on the merits. Such a decision results in a Board-ordered change in the legal relationship of the parties. That is why in our consent judgments, we sustain the appeal.

In a subsequent decision, 04-1 BCA ¶ 32,531, Centron was denied fees because the government's position in the appeal was substantially justified.

If a contractor wins an amount less than a rejected settlement offer, the facts will be carefully analyzed to determine if it is a prevailing party. In *Tom Shaw, Inc.*, DOTBCA 2105-E, 90-3 BCA ¶ 23,247, the board concluded that the contractor was not a prevailing party where, during negotiation of an equitable adjustment, it had rejected a higher offer of the contracting officer. The board reasoned that the entire appeal would have been avoided had the offer been accepted. In *McTeague Constr. Co. v. General Servs. Admin.*, GSBCA 15479-C, 01-2 BCA ¶ 31,462, fees were denied because the contractor rejected a settlement offer that included all of the amount awarded, interest on that amount, and significant legal fees. In contrast, in *AST Anlagen-und Sanierungstechnik GmbH*, ASBCA 42118, 93-3 BCA ¶ 25,979, a contractor was found to be a prevailing party when it rejected a settlement offer made immediately before the hearing. The board reasoned that the contractor had acted reasonably in going forward at that time. A middle ground was found in *N&P Constr. Co.*, VABCA 3283E, 93-3 BCA ¶ 26,257, in which the board found that the contractor was the prevailing party but excluded all fees incurred after the settlement offer was rejected. In *Donahue Elec., Inc.*, VABCA 6618E, 03-2 BCA ¶ 32,370, the board refused to consider a settlement offer made in an ADR proceeding because it was not part of the record before the board.

When a contractor has won only a portion of its claims, the fees and expenses are usually apportioned in accordance with the time spent on the winning claims. See *Community Heating & Plumbing Co. v. Garrett*, 2 F.3d 1143 (Fed. Cir. 1993), in which the contractor recovered 30 percent of its legal fees when it won on only one of seven claims. The contractor was able to present documentation showing that its attorneys had spent this amount of time on the winning claim. See also *Lamb Eng'g. & Constr. Co.*, EBCA E-9803274, 98-2 BCA ¶ 30,075, in which the board did its own analysis of the amount of time the attorneys worked on claims that did not succeed. Another method of apportionment, necessary when attorneys do not keep detailed records by claim, is to use the percentage of the amount awarded against the amount claimed, *Geiler Co.*, VABCA 5137E, 99-1 BCA ¶ 30,183 (85 percent fee commensurate with losing one claim); *Tele-Sentry Sec., Inc. v. General Servs. Admin.*, GSBCA 11639-C, 93-2 BCA ¶ 25,816, *recons. denied*, 94-1 BCA ¶ 26,565 (75 percent of fee because contractor proved government responsible for 75 percent of delay); *Servidone Constr. Corp. v. United States*, 20 Cl. Ct. 725 (1990) (2.5 percent of fee where contractor won on one claim valued at 1.3 percent of total amount claimed); *White & McNeill Excavating, Inc.*, IBCA 3108-F, 94-1 BCA ¶ 26,360 (10 percent of fee because contractor won 10 percent of claimed amount).

Apportionment is not appropriate if a contractor is awarded only a portion of the compensation requested, *Baldi Bros. Constructors v. United States*, 52 Fed. Cl. 78 (2002) In some cases, the court or board has refused to apportion the fees, determining that the contractor had submitted a single claim, *Design & Prod., Inc. v. United States*, 20 Cl. Ct. 207 (1990), *recons. denied*, 21 Cl. Ct. 145 (1990). In contrast, no fee award has been granted in some situations where the claim amount awarded was small and the contractor had no records to apportion its fees, *MJW Enters., Inc.*, ENGBCA 5813-F, 93-3 BCA ¶ 26,045.

c. *Substantially Justified*

If a contractor is a prevailing party on an issue, the government can escape liability for fees or expenses under the Act by demonstrating that its position on that issue was "substantially justified." In *Pierce v. Underwood*, 487 U.S. 552 (1988), the Court ruled that the term "substantial" meant "in substance or in the main" rather than "considerable in amount or degree." Based on this interpretation, it concluded that the term "substantially justified" meant "justified in substance or in the main," and that this was the same as the interpretation of the circuit courts—that the government's position had to have had "a reasonable basis both in law and fact." The government has the burden of proving substantial justification, *Community Heating & Plumbing Co. v. Garrett*, 2 F.3d 1143 (Fed. Cir. 1993).

The position of the government that is evaluated is the position during the litigation as well as the record of the agency's action or failure to act that preceded the litigation, *Gavette v. OPM*, 808 F.2d 1456 (Fed. Cir. 1986). Thus, no substantial justification will be found if the government has been unreasonable in its actions prior to the appeal, *Beta Eng'g., Inc.*, ASBCA 53570, 03-1 BCA ¶ 32,213 ("poor contract administration" in default terminating after waiver of delivery schedule); *Carousel Dev., Inc.*, ASBCA 50719, 01-2 BCA ¶ 31,590 ("ill-conceived business decision" to hold back work because of alleged unsatisfactory performance); *R&R Enters.*, IBCA 2664-F, 90-3 BCA ¶ 23,039 (contracting officer offered small compensation for major problem); *Bogue Elec. Mfg. Co.*, ASBCA 25184, 89-3 BCA ¶ 21,951 (termination for default because contractor would not work with defective government-furnished material); *Dean Kurtz Constr. Co.*, ASBCA 35483, 89-3 BCA ¶ 22,001 (contracting officer offered $2,000 to settle defective specification claim); *Tempo, Inc.*, ASBCA 35659, 89-1 BCA ¶ 21,439 (contracting officer made no offer to settle claim that was conceded to be valid). The government may not assert a new justification for its position after the original litigation is concluded, *Design & Prod., Inc. v. United States*, 20 Cl. Ct. 207 (1990), *recons. denied*, 21 Cl. Ct. 145 (1990); *Western Avionics, Inc.*, ASBCA 33158, 90-2 BCA ¶ 22,664.

Denial of any recovery when there is merit to the claims precludes a finding of substantial justification, *Logics, Inc.*, ASBCA 46914, 01-2 BCA ¶ 31,482 (refusal to give equitable adjustment for defective specification); *McTeague Constr. Co. v.*

General Servs. Admin., GSBCA 15479-C, 01-2 BCA ¶ 31,462 (refusal to pay any amount on multiple claims under construction delivery orders).

The government's position will be found to be substantially justified if the case requires substantial legal analysis to arrive at the correct result, *United States v. Paisley*, 957 F.2d 1161 (4th Cir. 1992) (substantial justification even though government had lost the substantive case on 9–0 decision in Supreme Court, *Crandon v. United States*, 494 U.S. 152 (1990)). See also *ROI Invs. v. General Servs. Admin.*, GSBCA 15488-C, 01-1 BCA ¶ 31,352, *recons. denied*, 01-2 BCA ¶ 31,523, and *DRC Corp. v. Department of Commerce*, GSBCA 15172-C, 00-1 BCA ¶ 30,841, in which substantial justification was found when the contractor won on a different legal theory than that asserted. Substantial justification has also been found where there is no clear legal rule on the issue in dispute, *ACE Servs., Inc. v. General Servs. Admin.*, GSBCA 12067-C, 93-2 BCA ¶ 25,727 (issue decided against government by GAO but no prior decision in appeals boards); *Delfour, Inc.*, VABCA 2049E, 90-3 BCA ¶ 23,066 (no prior decisions on issue). Compare *Healthcare Practice Enhancement Network, Inc.*, VABCA 6854E, 02-1 BCA ¶ 31,770, in which the board found no substantial justification when the government argued that a contracting officer had not ratified an unauthorized action when he attended a meeting at which it was discussed. See also *Community Heating & Plumbing Co. v. Garrett*, 2 F.3d 1143 (Fed. Cir. 1993), in which the government's position was found to be unjustified even when it won the case before an appeals board.

Substantial justification has been found when the government reasonably relies on its witnesses, *Infotec Dev., Inc.*, ASBCA 31809, 92-2 BCA ¶ 24,817 (fact witness); *United Constr. Co. v. United States*, 11 Cl. Ct. 597 (1987) (expert witness), or when the contractor does not present a coherent view of the case at the outset, *Hurlen Constr. Co.*, ASBCA 31069, 86-3 BCA ¶ 19,153; *Stephen J. Kenney*, IBCA 2132-F, 87-3 BCA ¶ 20,197. However, lack of substantial justification has been found in cases where there was a "close question," *Francis Paine Logging*, AGBCA 91-156-10, 92-3 BCA ¶ 25,043.

Substantial justification has been found when the contractor has failed to present credible documentation to support its claims, *Mediax Interactive Tech., Inc.*, ASBCA 43961, 01-1 BCA ¶ 31,239 (lack of accounting records to support claimed costs); *Aislamientos y Construcciones Apache S.A.*, ASBCA 45437, 98-1 BCA ¶ 29,373 (failure to retain critical records supporting large portion of claim).

The most difficult cases appear to be those involving issues of contract interpretation. The government interpretation has been substantially justified if it is reasonable, *Cox Constr. Co. v. United States*, 17 Cl. Ct. 29 (1989) (government interpretation based on expert opinion); *Jen-Beck Assocs., Inc.*, ASBCA 29844, 89-3 BCA ¶ 22,157 (government reasonable in expecting offerors to request clarification of specifications). However, strained interpretations will not meet the substantial justification test, *Design & Prod., Inc. v. United States*, 20 Cl. Ct. 207 (1990), *recons.*

denied, 21 Cl. Ct. 145 (1990) (government "glaringly misrepresented" contract requirements); *Kunz Constr. Co. v. United States*, 16 Cl. Ct. 431 (1989), *aff'd*, 899 F.2d 1227 (Fed. Cir. 1990) (government relied on vague contract language); *Kos Kam, Inc.*, ASBCA 34684, 88-3 BCA ¶ 21,049 (government relied on trade practice not related to issue). The government's position on the interpretation of an ambiguous regulation was held to be substantially justified because no case had previously interpreted the regulation, *Rex Sys., Inc.*, ASBCA 52247, 02-1 BCA ¶ 31,760. In *A.A. Conte & Son, Inc.*, ENGBCA 6104-F, 00-1 BCA ¶ 30,770, the board rejected the government's argument that it was substantially justified because it relied on a specification that had been used over a long period without challenge.

d. Amount Recovered

The fees and expenses that may be recovered under the Act are defined in 5 U.S.C. § 504(b)(1) as follows:

> (A) "[F]ees and other expenses" includes the reasonable expenses of expert witnesses, the reasonable cost of any study, analysis, engineering report, test or project which is found by the agency to be necessary for the preparation of the party's case, and reasonable attorney or agent fees. (The amount of fees awarded under this section shall be based upon prevailing market rates for the kind and quality of the services furnished, except that (i) no expert witness shall be compensated at a rate in excess of the highest rate of compensation for expert witnesses paid by the agency involved, and (ii) attorney or agent fees shall not be awarded in excess of $125 per hour unless the agency determines by regulation that an increase in the cost of living or a special factor, such as the limited availability of qualified attorneys or agents for the proceedings involved, justifies a higher fee.)

Prior to Pub. L. 104-121, March 29, 1996, the rate for attorneys and agents was $75 per hour. The $125 rate applies to all action commenced after that date of enactment. Substantially the same language covering the Court of Federal Claims is found in 28 U.S.C. § 2412(d)(2)(A), except that the limitation on expert witness fees is the amount paid by the entire government, and the power to award attorneys' and agents' fees in excess of $125 per hour is granted to the courts.

The Court of Federal Claims adjusted the earlier $75 per hour ceiling on attorneys' fees in accordance with increases in the Consumer Price Index applicable to the area in which the services were rendered, *Kunz Constr. Co. v. United States*, 16 Cl. Ct. 431 (1989), *aff'd*, 899 F.2d 1227 (Fed. Cir. 1990). Increases were measured from October 1, 1981 (the date of enactment of the Act) to the date when the legal services were performed, *Hong-Yee Chiu v. United States*, 948 F.2d 711 (Fed. Cir. 1991). In that case, the court commented that it had no objection to the use of a midpoint of the rendering of services to calculate a single ceiling. For cases filed after March 29,1996, the rate of $125 is adjusted for cost of living increases from March 1996 until the date the services were rendered, *Lion Raisins, Inc. v. United States*, 57 Fed. Cl. 505 (2003); *California Marine Cleaning, Inc. v. United States*, 43 Fed.

Cl. 724 (1999). Once the ceiling rate is determined, the contractor is entitled to attorneys' fees at the prevailing market rate or the ceiling rate, whichever is lower, *Levernier Constr., Inc. v. United States*, 947 F.2d 497 (Fed. Cir. 1991). In that case, the court also determined that there should be no ceiling adjustment for fees paid to paralegals. The prevailing market rate will normally be established at the rate that the attorney was actually paid for the services, *Devine v. National Treasury Employees Union*, 805 F.2d 384 (Fed. Cir. 1986), *cert. denied*, 484 U.S. 815 (1987). For a full discussion of the use of market rates, see *Raney v. Federal Bureau of Prisons*, 222 F.3d 927 (Fed. Cir. 2000) (en banc). This frequently results in the payment of lower fees when attorneys are employees of the litigant.

The $125 per hour ceiling on attorneys' fees has not been adjusted by any agency regulations. Therefore, the appeals boards are bound by that rate, *Granco Indus., Inc. v. General Servs. Admin.*, GSBCA 15572-C, 01-2 BCA ¶ 31,628 (rejecting contention that expertise in construction and government contract law is a "special factor" justifying a higher rate); *Carousel Dev., Inc.*, ASBCA 50719, 01-2 BCA ¶ 31,590; *Trailboss Enters., Inc.*, VABCA 5454E, 00-1 BCA ¶ 30,800. Prior to 1996, they had held that they were bound by the $75 rate, *Community Plumbing & Heating Co.*, ASBCA 33839, 90-3 BCA ¶ 23,022; *Cotton & Co.*, EBCA 441-2-90(E), 91-1 BCA ¶ 23,507; *Better Enters., Inc.*, GSBCA 10122-C, 91-1 BCA ¶ 23,420; *Gracon Corp.*, IBCA 2582-F, 90-1 BCA ¶ 22,550. One board raised the ceiling on the basis of a "special factor," *Operative Plasters & Cement Masons Int'l Ass'n*, LBCA 89-BCA-6, 91-2 BCA ¶ 23,782 (rate of $220 per hour paid because of large amount at stake and complexity of issues). Compare *Kumin Assocs., Inc.*, LBCA 94-BCA-3, 98-2 BCA ¶ 30,008, denying a higher fee based on special circumstances when a senior partner litigated the case. The statutory rate has been applied to accountants because they are considered "agents," *Logics, Inc.*, ASBCA 46914, 01-2 BCA ¶ 31,482.

The Armed Services Board has paid fees at the "prevailing market rate" when there was no agreement to pay an attorney at a fixed rate, *Consolidated Tech., Inc.*, ASBCA 33560R, 90-1 BCA ¶ 22,603 (market rate above statutory ceiling, so contractor entitled to be paid fee at ceiling rate of $75 when agreement with attorney was for contingent fee—resulting compensation far greater than contingent fee); *Margaret Howard*, ASBCA 28648, 88-3 BCA ¶ 21,040, 89-3 BCA ¶ 21,936 (attorneys' fees awarded although insurer paid for losses and suit was brought by insurance company as subrogee). Other boards have required that there be payment of fees to meet the requirement that they be "incurred." Thus, compensation has been denied for hours not billed to the contractor, *Ed. A. Wilson, Inc. v. General Servs. Admin.*, GSBCA 13532-C, 96-2 BCA ¶ 28,545, *aff'd in part, rev'd in part*, 126 F.3d 1406 (Fed. Cir. 1997); *American Fed. Contractors, Inc.*, PSBCA 1359, 88-2 BCA ¶ 20,526; *Input Output Computer Servs., Inc.*, GSBCA 8435, 87-3 BCA ¶ 20,073, *recons. denied*, 88-3 BCA ¶ 20,851. In *Alamo Navajo Sch. Bd., Inc.*, IBCA 2578-F, 90-1 BCA ¶ 22,523, the board stated that this test was met if the contractor was "legally obligated" to the attorney. Some appeals boards refuse to pay for work of paralegals at the billing rate of the law firm and pay only at the rate of their salaries, *E.W. Eldridge, Inc.*, ENGBCA 5269-F, 92-1 BCA ¶ 24,626; *Walsky Constr. Co.*, ASBCA 36940, 92-1 BCA ¶ 24,694; *Francis Paine Logging*, AGBCA 91-156-10, 92-3 BCA ¶ 25,043. Compare *Spectrum Leasing Corp. v. General Servs. Admin.*, GSBCA 10902-C, 93-1 BCA ¶ 25,317, following the practice of the Court of Federal Claims and awarding paralegal fees at the rates they were billed to the contractor.

The Court of Federal Claims will normally accept the number of hours billed by attorneys. See *Florida Rock Indus., Inc. v. United States*, 9 Cl. Ct. 285 (1985), *rev'd on other grounds*, 791 F.2d 893 (Fed. Cir. 1986), *cert. denied*, 479 U.S. 1003 (1987), *on remand*, 23 Fed. Cl. 653 (1991), *vacated*, 18 F.3d 1560 (Fed. Cir. 1994), *cert. denied*, 513 U.S. 1109 (1995), *on remand*, 45 Fed. Cl. 21 (1999), stating at 289:

> In a case such as this, the risk of abuse is minimal because plaintiff has no assurance of recovering and must assume it will bear the full cost of the litigation. Plaintiff can therefore be expected to exercise control over the time spent and the rates charged. Absent some specific showing of abuse, the court will not disapprove counsel's decision [on the amount of effort expended].

This reasoning was adopted in *Lion Raisins, Inc. v. United States*, 57 Fed. Cl. 505 (2003).

The Act permits compensation for expert witnesses but limits the rate to that paid by the government. This has been a significant limitation on the rates, *H.E. Johnson Co.*, ASBCA 48248, 99-1 BCA ¶ 30,264 (rate limited to top rate for a GS-15 employee in accordance with DFARS 237.104(f)); *Keno & Sons Constr. Co.*, ENGBCA 5837-F, 99-1 BCA ¶ 30,273 (rate limited to rate paid the government's employee-expert on the case); *C & C Plumbing & Heating*, ASBCA 44270, 96-1 BCA ¶ 28,100 (rate limited to DFARS rate). See *Techplan Corp.*, ASBCA 41470, 98-2 BCA ¶ 29,954, in which the DFARS 137.104(f) rate was found not binding because the government paid its expert a higher rate.

The appeals boards have held that the costs of employees are not reimbursable under the Act because such costs are not "fees or expenses," *American Power, Inc.*, GSBCA 10558-C, 91-2 BCA ¶ 23,766; *M. Bianchi of Cal.*, ASBCA 26362, 90-1 BCA ¶ 22,369; *James W. Sprayberry Constr.*, IBCA 2298-F, 89-2 BCA ¶ 21,797. This precludes recovery if the contractor argues a case without an attorney ("pro se"), *Naekel v. Department of Transp.*, 845 F.2d 976 (Fed. Cir. 1988); *The Writing Co. v. Department of the Treasury*, GSBCA 15097-TD, 00-1 BCA ¶ 30,840, *recons. denied*, 00-1 BCA ¶ 30,863. The General Services Board has also used this rule to deny recovery of the costs of an attorney employed by the contractor, *Giancola & Assocs. v. General Servs. Admin.*, GSBCA 12305-C, 93-3 BCA ¶ 26,146.

Other normal costs incurred by attorneys in litigation are recoverable, *Oliveira v. United States*, 827 F.2d 735 (Fed. Cir. 1987). Thus, the costs of consultants are reimbursable under the Act, *Hughes Moving & Storage, Inc.*, ASBCA 45346, 00-1 BCA ¶ 30,776; *Spectrum Leasing Corp. v. General Servs. Admin.*, GSBCA 10902-C, 93-1 BCA ¶ 25,317. However, the contractor will not be reimbursed for a consultant that is not a lawyer but performs legal services, *Union Precision & Eng'g*, ASBCA 37549, 93-1 BCA ¶ 25,337. Other reimbursable costs include translators and hearing transcripts, *Staff, Inc.*, AGBCA 98-152-10, 99-1 BCA ¶ 30,260; long distance phone calls and photocopying, *Arapaho Communications, Inc./Steele & Sons, Inc., Joint Venture*, ASBCA 48235, 98-1 BCA ¶ 29,563; and facsimile, couriers and express mail, *Walsky Constr. Co.*, ASBCA 41541, 95-2 BCA ¶ 27,889. However, costs incurred by pro se litigants have been denied by most boards, *Simpson Contracting Corp.*, EBCA E-9602190, 96-2 BCA ¶ 28,471; *Gaffney Corp.*, ASBCA 39740, 96-1 BCA ¶ 28,138, *rev'd on other grounds*, 108 F.3d 1391 (Fed. Cir. 1997); *Danrenke Corp.*, VABCA 3601E, 94-1 BCA ¶ 26,504; *P-B Eng'g. Co.*, ASBCA 39041, 91-3 BCA ¶ 24,361; *J.V. Bailey Co.*, ENGBCA 5348-F, 91-3 BCA ¶ 24,350. Other boards have awarded such expenses, *American Power, Inc.*, GSBCA 10558-C, 91-2 BCA ¶ 23,766 (allowing travel expenses of a litigant); *Preston-Brady Co.*, VABCA 1992E, 88-1 BCA ¶ 20,446 (allowing "minor" corporate expenses).

B. Costs of Financing Adjustments

The recovery of the cost of financing adjustments depends on the time period to which the cost applies, on applicable contract provisions, and on whether the adjustment is based on a claim under the Disputes clause. Under the Contract Disputes Act of 1978, 41 U.S.C. § 611, and the Disputes clause, FAR 52.233-1, the contractor is entitled to recover interest from the date the claim is received. The Cost Principles, in FAR 31.205-20, make all interest not given by statute or contract clause an unallowable cost. Thus, where the Cost Principles are applicable, adjustment financing costs are not recoverable if incurred prior to the submission of a claim.

The term "interest" is often used to refer to the cost of borrowings, the use of equity capital ("imputed" interest), or a combination of both. In some cases, loans may be made specifically to finance the contract or change order. In other cases, the contractor's loans become so commingled with other contractor funds that it is impossible to associate specific loans with contracts or change orders. The funds, whether coming from equity or borrowed capital, are a necessary part of the effort involved in performing the work and have a cost to the contractor in paid interest on a loan or lost interest on equity capital. After the work is performed and payment is due from the government, any interest involved is considered interest on a delay in payment. See Chapter 12.

1. Interest on Claims

The Contract Disputes Act, 41 U.S.C. § 611, provides for the payment of *imputed* interest on claims as follows:

> Interest on amounts found due contractors on claims shall be paid to the contractor from the date the contracting officer receives the claim pursuant to section 605(a) of this title from the contractor until payment thereof. The interest provided for in this section shall be paid at the rate established by the Secretary of the Treasury pursuant to Public Law 92-41 . . . .

To recover interest under the Act, the contractor must have filed a "claim" that met the requirements of the Act. See Chapter 13, discussing the detailed rules on this topic. Prior to 1992, one of these requirements was that, if a claim over $50,000 was not properly certified, no interest was due on that claim. This rule was changed by Pub. L. 102-572, which changed the rule with regard to all claims that were not subject to an appeal or a suit filed before October 29, 1992. This amendment to the Act gave the following guidance:

> (3) If any interest is due under [41 U.S.C. § 611] of the Contract Disputes Act of 1978 on a claim for which the certification under section 6(c)(1) is, on or after [October 29, 1992], found to be defective [such interest] shall be paid from the later of the date on which the contracting officer initially received the claim or [October 29, 1992].

Under this provision, interest will run on claims where the certificate does not contain the required statements or where it is signed by an official without authority. However, shortly after passage of the statute, this rule was held not to apply if no certificate of any kind was submitted, *Hamza v. United States*, 31 Fed. Cl. 315 (1994); *Applied Sci. Assocs., Inc.*, EBCA 9301146, 93-3 BCA ¶ 26,051; *Eurostyle, Inc.*, ASBCA 45934, 94-1 BCA ¶ 26,458; *Paroscientific, Inc.*, IBCA 3230, 95-1 BCA ¶ 27,318; *Dunlap Enters.*, AGBCA 94-126-1, 96-1 BCA ¶ 28,024. The appeals boards have also ruled that interest will not run if the contractor's claim reflects "an intentional or negligent disregard" of the CDA certification requirements, *Walashek Indus. & Marine, Inc.*, ASBCA 52166, 00-1 BCA ¶ 30,728 (contractor failed to include correct language after being explicitly told of the requirement); *Keydata Sys., Inc. v. Department of the Treasury*, GSBCA 14281-TD, 97-2 BCA ¶ 29,330 (contractor took no action to submit a proper certificate after being told of the specific requirement).

The requirement for some type of certificate to ensure that interest begins to run has been interpreted liberally in some cases. See *Ellett Constr. Co. v. United States*, 93 F.3d 1537 (Fed. Cir. 1996), holding that the termination settlement proposal certificate in Standard Form 1436 met the requirement. See also *SAE/Americon–Mid-Atl., Inc. v. General Servs. Admin.*, GSBCA 12294, 94-2 BCA ¶ 26,890 (interest runs when the claim was accompanied by the "Certificate of Current Cost or Pricing Data" required by the Truth in Negotiations Act, 10 U.S.C. § 2306a; 41 U.S.C. § 254b). Compare *Scan-Tech Sec., L.P. v. United States*, 46 Fed. Cl. 326 (2000), holding that neither the Standard Form 1411 nor a cover letter contained sufficient language to be a defective certificate. The SF 1411 stated: "This proposal . . . reflects our best estimates and/or actual costs as of this date and conforms with the instructions in FAR

15.804-6(b)(1) and Table 15-2," while the letter stated: "I have spent considerable time accumulating and checking the various invoices and related material and trust that this is as complete an assembly as possible." See also *AT&T Communications v. General Servs. Admin.*, GSBCA 14932, 99-2 BCA ¶ 30,415, holding that the submission of an unsigned and undated CDA certification did not rise to the level of a defective certification that could be corrected, and *Lockheed Martin Tactical Def. Sys. v. Department of Commerce*, GSBCA 14450-COM, 98-1 BCA ¶ 29,717, holding that the submission of a subcontractor's CDA certificate with a statement that the claim was certifiable was not a correctable defective certification.

In accordance with the Act, interest begins to run upon "receipt" of the claim by the contracting officer. The Disputes clause adds a requirement stating:

> (h) The Government shall pay interest on the amount found due and unpaid from (1) the date the Contracting Officer receives the claim (properly certified if required); or (2) the date that payment otherwise would be due, if that date is later, until the date of payment.

In *Servidone Constr. Corp. v. United States*, 931 F.2d 860 (Fed. Cir. 1991), the court disregarded the second provision of this paragraph and held that the Act required payment of interest from the date of receipt of the claim even if the costs had not been incurred at that time. The court concluded that the clear language of the Act as well as its legislative history established a "single, red-letter date for interest on all amounts found due by a court without regard to when the contractor incurred the costs." See also *J.S. Alberici Constr. Co. & Martin K. Eby Constr. Co. (Joint Venture)*, ENGBCA 6179, 97-1 BCA ¶ 28,639, *recons. denied*, 97-1 BCA ¶ 28,919, *aff'd*, 153 F.3d 1381 (Fed. Cir. 1998), rejecting the government's argument that the *Servidone* court had misinterpreted the Disputes clause. This rule makes it clear that interest under the Act is imputed interest that is to be paid without regard to whether the contractor paid any interest on borrowed funds. It has also been held that interest must be paid at the statutory rate even if the contractor requests payment at a lower rate in its claim before an appeals board, *Gebrueder Kruse GmbH*, AGBCA 87-338-1, 89-3 BCA ¶ 22,179.

Interest is not due if the contractor does not actually pay its employees the amount awarded by an appeals board, *Richlin Security Serv. Co. v. Chertoff*, No. 05-1085 (Fed. Cir. 2006). In Richlin the contractor won an appeal for back wages owed its employees but was financially unable to pay the employees before receipt of the funds from the government. After the government refused to pay on this basis, the parties agreed to place the funds in escrow and have the escrow agency pay the employees. The court ruled that, in these circumstances, no amount had been "found due" to the contractor. See also *Raytheon Co. v. White*, 305 F. 3d 1354 (Fed Cir. 2002), holding that a contractor was not entitled to interest on an amount found to be a proper price adjustment to a contract to be used in the computation of the amount of a termination settlement. The court concluded that no interest was due on because the amount was not a computation of incurred costs. It stated, however, that interest would be due on the amount of the termination settlement that was arrived at using this price adjustment.

Interest does not stop running until actual payment of the adjustment. Thus, the issuance of a contract modification does not stop the running of interest, *Oxwell, Inc.*, ASBCA 27119, 83-2 BCA ¶ 16,762, *recons. denied*, 84-2 BCA ¶ 17,412. When the parties settle a claim, the settlement agreement should clearly state whether interest has been included in the settlement and whether it will continue to run if the government does not pay the claim in a timely fashion. See, for example, *Blake Constr. Co.*, GSBCA 8376, 89-3 BCA ¶ 22,082, *recons. denied*, 90-1 BCA ¶ 22,408, where the agreement stated that the issue of interest was reserved for decision in accordance with an appeal. See also *River City Contractors*, DOTBCA 2073, 91-1 BCA ¶ 23,531, in which a broad release in a contract modification embodying a settlement was held to bar the running of interest on a claim.

2. *Interest on Borrowings*

A contractor can recover interest paid on borrowed funds as part of a price adjustment if its contract is not subject to the Cost Principles, *Joseph Bell v. United States*, 186 Ct. Cl. 189, 404 F.2d 975 (1968). There the court held that interest costs incurred as a result of borrowing to finance a constructive change could be included in an equitable adjustment even though interest on delays in payment could not be recovered due to the court's jurisdictional statute and the long-standing rule against recovery of interest from the government absent a statute or contract clause. In *Bell*, the contractor was permitted to recover the cost of interest on borrowings that were necessary for the performance of a change order. The *Bell* rule had limited applicability after 1970 because the Cost Principles in FPR 1-15.205-17 and DAR 15.205-17, making interest unallowable, were incorporated into almost all contracts by the mandatory Pricing of Adjustments clause, *J.W. Bateson Co.*, ASBCA 22337, 78-2 BCA ¶ 13,523, *recons. denied*, 79-1 BCA ¶ 13,658. However, as discussed earlier in this chapter, since the FAR omits the Pricing of Adjustments clause and only a few agencies have included it in their FAR supplements, it is possible that the *Bell* rule will be applicable to some contracts issued after April 1, 1984. No case has yet granted such interest. See, however, *Automation Fabricators & Eng'g Co.*, PSBCA 2701, 90-3 BCA ¶ 22,943, in which the Postal Service board paid interest on borrowings where the contract contained a unique Pricing of Adjustments clause that stated that the Cost Principles would "serve as a guide" for pricing adjustments.

a. *Recovery When Cost Principles Not Applicable*

If the Cost Principles are not applicable to the adjustment, interest on borrowings is properly included in the adjustment. However, cases following this rule have held that the interest must be actually paid to an outside entity, and no allowance is made for the use of equity capital, *Oxford Corp.*, ASBCA 12298, 69-2 BCA ¶ 7871. See also *Lorentz Bruun Co.*, GSBCA 8504, 88-2 BCA ¶ 20,719 (no evidence of borrowed funds); *Gevyn Constr. Corp.*, ENGBCA 3031, 83-1 BCA ¶ 16,428, *aff'd*, 11 Cl. Ct. 203 (1986), *aff'd*, 827 F.2d 752 (Fed. Cir. 1987) (higher borrowings of subcontractor caused by withholdings of contractor not changes); *LTV Electrosystems, Inc.*, ASBCA 14832, 74-2 BCA ¶ 10,870, *recons. denied*, 75-1 BCA ¶ 11,310 (no proof of borrowed funds); *Amecom Div., Litton Sys., Inc.*, ASBCA 15554, 73-2 BCA ¶ 10,155 (no proof of relationship between advance from parent corporation and contract performance); and *Excavation-Constr., Inc.*, ENGBCA 3858, 82-1 BCA ¶ 15,770, *recons. denied*, 83-1 BCA ¶ 16,338 (no proof of borrowing). But compare *Space Dynamics Corp.*, ASBCA 19118, 78-1 BCA ¶ 12,885 (interest on loans from officers). In cases following *Bell*, the contractor has established that borrowed funds were used on the change through proof of general business borrowings and a showing of clear necessity for borrowing to finance the change, *S.S. Silberblatt, Inc. v. United States*, 228 Ct. Cl. 729 (1981); *Singer Co., Librascope Div.*, ASBCA 13241, 73-2 BCA ¶ 10,258, *aff'd*, 215 Ct. Cl. 281, 568 F.2d 695 (1977); *Keco Indus., Inc.*, ASBCA 15131, 72-1 BCA ¶ 9262. However, in *Framlau Corp. v. United States*, 215 Ct. Cl. 185, 568 F.2d 687 (1977), and *Dravo Corp. v. United States*, 219 Ct. Cl. 416, 594 F.2d 842 (1979), the court stated that the contractor must show what part of its borrowings were necessitated by the change order.

b. Recovery When Cost Principles Applicable

In contracts where interest was not recoverable, whether because the Cost Principles making it unallowable were incorporated into the contract or the contractor used equity capital or could not sufficiently trace its borrowings to the change, the boards of contract appeals began to include an additional amount for "imputed interest" in their profit determinations, *New York Shipbuilding Co.*, ASBCA 16164, 76-2 BCA ¶ 11,979, *recons. denied*, 83-1 BCA ¶ 16,534 (concept of equitable adjustment demands that contractor be compensated for equity capital used in changes); *Fischbach & Moore Int'l Corp.*, ASBCA 18146, 77-1 BCA ¶ 12,300, *aff'd*, 223 Ct. Cl. 119, 617 F.2d 223 (1980) (pre-Pricing of Adjustments clause, but contractor could not trace borrowings); *Ingalls Shipbuilding Div., Litton Sys., Inc.*, ASBCA 17579, 78-1 BCA ¶ 13,038, *recons. denied*, 78-1 BCA ¶ 13,216; *Systems & Computer Info., Inc.*, ASBCA 18458, 78-1 BCA ¶ 12,946 (12 percent profit because of "financing effort" of contractor); *R.L. Spencer Constr. Co.*, ASBCA 18450, 75-2 BCA ¶ 11,604 (16 percent profit because of heavy borrowing). This was based on the theory that the basic premise supporting the disallowance of interest was that, in order to equalize the situation between contractors that financed work with borrowed or equity capital, contractors should recover interest through profit made in performing contracts. However, the Court of Claims refused to endorse this principle in *Dravo Corp. v. United States*, 219 Ct. Cl. 416, 594 F.2d 842 (1979). The ASBCA followed *Dravo* in *Owen L. Schwam Constr. Co.*, ASBCA 22407, 79-2 BCA ¶ 13,919; *Washington Patrol Serv.*, ASBCA 26470, 82-2 BCA ¶ 15,846; and

Tomahawk Constr. Co., ASBCA 45071, 94-1 BCA ¶ 26,312. Accord, *Technology, Inc.*, DCAB NBS-1-78, 79-1 BCA ¶ 13,752; *Marlin Assocs., Inc.*, GSBCA 5663, 82-1 BCA ¶ 15,739; *Fletcher & Sons, Inc.*, VABCA 3248, 92-1 BCA ¶ 24,726. See also *Servidone Constr. Corp. v. United States*, 19 Cl. Ct. 346 (1990), *aff'd*, 931 F.2d 860 (Fed. Cir. 1991) (no inclusion of interest in the computation of profit because the Cost Principles in FAR 31.205-20 disallow "[i]nterest on borrowings (however represented)"), and *Environmental Tectonics Corp.*, ASBCA 42540, 92-2 BCA ¶ 24,902 (no inclusion of "opportunity cost of money" in damages because that is just another way of characterizing disallowed interest).

See also *Creative Elec., Inc.*, ASBCA 26368, 83-1 BCA ¶ 16,363, *recons. denied*, 83-2 BCA ¶ 16,680, in which interest as an element of profit was foreclosed because the contractor had previously agreed to an equitable adjustment including profit, reserving only a claim for interest, and *International Equip. Servs., Inc.*, ASBCA 21104, 83-2 BCA ¶ 16,675, *recons. denied*, 84-1 BCA ¶ 17,025, in which the board refused to follow the cases providing a higher profit rate.

CHAPTER 9

INSPECTION, ACCEPTANCE, AND WARRANTIES

When the Federal government enters into a contract for construction, supplies, or services, its primary goal is to obtain timely performance in accordance with the contract specifications. A secondary goal is to preserve the integrity of the competitive procurement system. To ensure that these goals are achieved, various clauses are included in the contract giving the government substantial rights to monitor performance and to take appropriate steps when performance is unsatisfactory. Generally, performance problems fall into two broad categories—those dealing with timely performance under the threat of default, and those dealing with compliance with the specifications. This chapter discusses the clauses and procedures used by the government to ensure such specification compliance.

Government policies dealing with quality assurance and specification compliance are set forth in FAR Part 46, Quality Assurance. FAR 46.102 contains brief general policy guidance on quality assurance requirements, as follows:

> Agencies shall ensure that—
>
> (a) Contracts include inspection and other quality requirements, including warranty clauses when appropriate, that are determined necessary to protect the Government's interest;
>
> (b) Supplies or services tendered by contractors meet contract requirements;
>
> (c) Government contract quality assurance is conducted before acceptance (except as otherwise provided in this part), by or under the direction of Government personnel;
>
> (d) No contract precludes the Government from performing inspection;
>
> (e) Nonconforming supplies or services are rejected, except as otherwise provided in 46.407;
>
> (f) Contracts for commercial items shall rely on a contractor's existing quality assurance system as a substitute for compliance with Government inspection and testing before tender for acceptance unless customary market practices for the commercial item being acquired permit in-process inspection (Section 8002 of Public Law 103-355). Any in-process inspection by the Government shall be conducted in a manner consistent with commercial practice; and

> (g) The quality assurance and acceptance services of other agencies are used when this will be effective, economical, or otherwise in the Government's interest (see Subpart 42.1).

The basic clauses that contain the fundamental rules and procedures for government quality assurance and acceptance of the work are the various inspection clauses. The primary fixed price inspection clauses are contained in FAR 52.246-1 (simplified acquisition for supplies and services); FAR 52.246-2 (supply); FAR 52.246-4 (services); FAR 52.246-6 (time and material and labor hour contracts); and FAR 52.246-7 (research and development contracts). The standard inspection clause for fixed-price construction contracts is at FAR 52.246-12. When this clause was adopted in 1984, it included a requirement that the contractor maintain an inspection system. Previously, a separate clause was required for the contractor to have such responsibility. For contracts for commercial items under FAR Part 12, ¶ (a) of the Contract Terms and Conditions—Commercial Items clause in FAR 52.212-4 details the inspection rights. Supplemental clauses and warranty clauses are frequently used to give the government additional rights during the inspection process as well as after acceptance and provide for increased levels of contractor inspection and quality control. Many of these clauses are specifically tailored to suit particular types of procurements.

This chapter explores the relationships among inspection, acceptance, and warranty, and how the corresponding rights and obligations of both the government and the contractor are interpreted by the boards and courts.

I. INSPECTION

Inspection, by either the government or the contractor, is the primary means of ensuring that the government receives the quality of work for which it bargained. Since the government may have limited rights after acceptance, careful scrutiny of the work prior to acceptance is essential. Moreover, inspection during performance allows early discovery of defects, thus enabling timely corrective action.

This section considers the broad as well as specific rights that the contract clauses give the government to inspect work and the obligations that the clauses impose on the contractor to fulfill contract specifications and facilitate government inspection. It also discusses the contractor's responsibility to maintain inspection and quality control systems and the effects this responsibility has on the rights and obligations of both the government and the contractor.

A. Government Inspection

The government carries out its inspection process either by inspecting the work or by conducting surveillance of the contractor's inspection system. The trend in government procurement has increasingly been to place the responsibility for detailed inspection of the work on the contractor. This, however, does not preclude the government from conducting its own independent inspections and tests for verification purposes. Inspection or tests may be performed by government personnel or by third parties under the direction or supervision of the government. Inspections or tests for which the contractor is responsible are typically performed by the contractor itself or by subcontractors or third parties acceptable to the government.

The standard inspection clauses provide the government with broad and comprehensive rights to inspect the contractor's work. Paragraph (c) of the Inspection of Supplies—Fixed-Price clause at FAR 52.246-2 provides:

> The Government has the right to inspect and test all supplies called for by the contract, to the extent practicable, at all places and times, including the period of manufacture, and in any event before acceptance. The Government shall perform inspections and tests in a manner that will not unduly delay the work. The Government assumes no contractual obligation to perform any inspection and test for the benefit of the Contractor unless specifically set forth elsewhere in this contract.

Paragraph (b) of the Inspection of Construction clause at FAR 52.246-12 provides, in part:

> All work shall be conducted under the general direction of the Contracting Officer and is subject to Government inspection and test at all places and at all reasonable times before acceptance to ensure strict compliance with the terms of the contract.

Finally, ¶ (c) of the Inspection of Services clause at FAR 52.246-4 provides:

> The Government has the right to inspect and test all services called for by the contract, to the extent practicable at all times and places during the term of the contract. The Government shall perform inspections and tests in a manner that will not unduly delay the work.

These rights have generally been held to be for the benefit of the government and create no government duty to inspect, except under very special circumstances. See *Kaminer Constr. Corp. v. United States*, 203 Ct. Cl. 182, 488 F.2d 980 (1973), in which the court held that the Inspection clause was "meant merely to outline the Government's right to inspect and did not impose upon the Government a duty to inspect." See also *Penguin Indus., Inc. v. United States*, 209 Ct. Cl. 121, 530 F.2d 934 (1976), in which the court held that the government was not required to inspect every "routine task" in the manufacturing process. This rule has been reinforced in the supply contract clause in FAR 52.246-2 by the addition of the following sentence to ¶ (c):

> The Government assumes no contractual obligation to perform any inspection and test for the benefit of the Contractor unless specifically set forth elsewhere in this contract.

See also ¶ (c) of the construction contract clause at FAR 52.246-12, stating:

> Government inspections and tests are for the sole benefit of the Government and do not—
>
> > (1) Relieve the Contractor of responsibility for providing adequate quality control measures . . . .

Even special clauses imposing greater inspection obligations on the government do not relieve the contractor of its obligation to perform in accordance with the specifications. See *Kenneth Reed Constr. Corp. v. United States*, 201 Ct. Cl. 282, 475 F.2d 583 (1973), in which the court found that a special construction contract clause calling for work to be done "in the presence of a Government inspector" could be waived by the government and did not relieve the contractor of the responsibility to provide work meeting the specification. See also *United States v. Franklin Steel Prods., Inc.*, 482 F.2d 400 (9th Cir. 1973), *cert. denied,* 415 U.S. 918 (1979) (special "100% Government inspection" clause creates no government duty to inspect and provides no defense to breach of warranty), and *Granite Constr. Co. v. United States*, 962 F.2d 998 (Fed. Cir. 1992), *cert. denied,* 506 U.S. 1048 (1993) (government right to inspect did not relieve the contractor of the responsibility to ensure that waterstop material complied with contract specifications).

One recurring inspection issue involves the government's liability for delays and additional costs resulting from actions of its inspectors. While government inspectors typically do not have the authority to order contract changes or waive contract requirements, they do have the responsibility to interpret contract specifications and make evaluations as to whether the contractor has complied with them. If the inspector's erroneous interpretation or evaluation causes the contractor to perform to a higher standard, a constructive change or other basis for price adjustment may be found. For a discussion of the issue of contractual authority of government officials, including inspectors, see Chapter 1, Section III. This section analyzes the scope of the government's broad right to inspect the work and the contractual impact arising out of this right.

1. Type of Inspection or Test

The government has great latitude in choosing the type of inspection or test it will use in determining whether the work conforms to the contract requirements. FAR 46.101 contains the following definition:

> "Testing," means that element of inspection that determines the properties or elements, including functional operation of supplies or their components, by the application of established scientific principles and procedures..

a. Contractually Specified Test

Contracts sometimes specify tests to be conducted by the government as a basis for accepting or rejecting the work. The contractor cannot complain that the specified tests are too severe if they are clearly required by the contract, *General Time Corp.*, ASBCA 22306, 80-1 BCA ¶ 14,393. The presence in the contract of a specified test to evaluate one element of the specifications does not preclude the government from conducting unspecified tests that are "reasonable and necessary" to determine compliance with other specification elements, *Crown Coat Front Co. v. United States*, 154 Ct. Cl. 613, 292 F.2d 290 (1961).

If a specified test has established the standard of performance that the contractor must meet, it is improper to use a different test that establishes a higher standard of performance. In *Astro Dynamics, Inc.*, ASBCA 28381, 88-3 BCA ¶ 20,832, the board found that the government's inspection method used a more stringent test for the threads on the tendered rocket motor tubes. The initial government inspection test damaged the threads and rendered them unable to pass further testing procedures. Upon discovery of the defect in the government's inspection gauge, the government refused to accept the tubes solely on the basis of the (accurate) contractor tests. Rather, the government chose to submit the tube threads to a more stringent optical comparator test. The board held that this was tantamount to a constructive change and thus the default termination should be converted into a termination for convenience. Similarly, in *Process Equip. Co.*, NASABCA 166-3, 67-1 BCA ¶ 6142, *recons. denied*, 67-2 BCA ¶ 6563, the contract required that nitrogen-cooled shrouds in a space simulator heat up to ambient temperature within 30 minutes. The government and the contractor, in a formal modification, agreed to a specific test utilizing thermocouples at specified points to determine compliance with this specification. The space simulator was found to have fully satisfied the agreed test procedure. However, a subsequent visual inspection, along with a thermometer reading by government representatives, indicated that the shroud was not at ambient temperature. Due to this deficiency, the work was rejected. The board held that the rejection was improper because the contractor was led to believe, and subsequently relied upon its belief, that a specific test procedure would be used to verify compliance with the specification. See also *United Tech. Corp. v. United States*, 27 Fed. Cl. 393 (1992), *recons. denied*, 31 Fed. Cl. 698 (1994), holding that the contractor had met the contract metallurgical fatigue requirements when its product passed the test that the contractor had developed and the government had accepted.

An acceptance test performed by the government must also be compatible with the government-specified test required of the contractor, *G.W. Galloway Co.*, ASBCA 17407, 75-2 BCA ¶ 11,472 (rejection of warheads held improper when government gauges supplied to the contractor for in-house inspection were incompatible with those used by government at destination). However, see *Ralbo, Inc.*, ASBCA 43548, 93-2 BCA ¶ 25,624, *denied*, 93-3 BCA ¶ 25,965 (contractor claim that rejection of supplies by the government was wrongful for lack of proper inspection equipment at origin was denied because the evidence showed the tendered supplies would have failed to meet inspection criteria, equipment deficiencies notwithstanding).

b. Use of Unspecified Tests

The government may use an unspecified test as a basis for rejection if such a test determines that the work does not, in fact, comply with the contract requirements. An unspecified test is acceptable as a basis for rejection if it is "accurate and reasonably calculated to determine compliance with the specifications," *Lowell Monument Co.*, VACAB 1191, 77-1 BCA ¶ 12,439. In *Ball, Ball & Brosamer, Inc.*, IBCA 2103-N, 93-1 BCA ¶ 25,287, the board found that testing of sealant by a simple test using uncomplicated machinery was reasonable. Thus, the government's rejection of the tendered work was not wrongful. See also *Mutual Maint. Co.,* GSBCA 7637, 91-1 BCA ¶ 23,287, in which the board held that there was no evidence that inspectors, who routinely carry flashlights, used them to conduct improperly strict inspections for dust.

The government may use tests in lieu of those specified in the contract as a basis for rejection if they do not impose a more stringent standard of performance, *Circle Constr. Group*, ASBCA 38844, 90-3 BCA ¶ 22,999 (government's use of visual inspection instead of the technical laboratory methods enumerated in the contract did not render the rejection of the 90 percent deficient roadway construction improper because it was not a higher standard); *Donald C. Hubbs, Inc.*, DOTBCA 2012, 90-1 BCA ¶ 22,379 (use of a rolling straightedge instead of the hand-held straightedge to test excavation was valid because it still complied with the contract tolerance specifications); *Stewart & Stevenson Servs., Inc.,* ASBCA 52140, 00-2 BCA ¶ 31,041 (summary judgment for the contractor denied in order to determine factually whether additional government tests imposed more stringent standards). Thus, an unspecified test may be used if it reasonably and accurately determines compliance or noncompliance, *Solar Labs., Inc.*, ASBCA 19269, 74-2 BCA ¶ 10,897, *recons. denied*, 75-1 BCA ¶ 11,049 (rejection was proper since thermocouples used in place of contractually specified thermometers to measure temperature achieved "comparable" results in similar applications); *Kilgore Corp.*, ASBCA 31899, 90-3 BCA ¶ 23,226 (although the government did not contractually specify all of the variations of the battery capacity temperature tests that it used, the test results were not invalid because the procedures did not materially affect the outcome). In *Gibbs Shipyard, Inc.*, ASBCA 9809, 67-2 BCA ¶ 6,499, the specifications required that the welds have no "open root" conditions. The contract contemplated visual inspection of the welds to determine compliance. However, the government used ultrasonic tests and found open root welds. The board found that rejection of these welds was proper because the open roots clearly violated the contract specifications. The fact that such defects would also have been discovered by visual inspection was further proof that the unspecified ultrasonic test imposed no greater standard of performance. See also

Kan-Du Tool & Instrument Corp., ASBCA 37636, 89-2 BCA ¶ 21,822, in which the board upheld the government's rejection of tendered transmitter covers even though the government could not prove that its inspection testing conformed to the contractually specified procedures and tolerances. The board stated that, since it was readily apparent that the supplies were nonconforming, the government's test was a reasonable means of determining contract compliance and did not impose a more stringent standard.

If the unspecified tests do not reasonably measure contract compliance, they are improper, *Tester Corp.*, ASBCA 21312, 78-2 BCA ¶ 13,373, *recons. denied*, 79-1 BCA ¶ 13,725, *aff'd*, 227 Ct. Cl. 648 (1981) (default termination could not be based on contractor's failure to satisfy a different soil compaction test when contracting officer did not answer the contractor's request for a new measurement). See also *Technical Ordnance, Inc.*, ASBCA 34748, 89-2 BCA ¶ 21,818, in which the board sustained the contractor's appeal of a default termination because the government had added a "built pulse generator" and a "counter to test apparatus" to the specifications and used faulty equipment to test the supplied torpedo bolts. In *Tucker & Assocs. Contracting, Inc.*, IBCA 1468-6-81, 83-1 BCA ¶ 16,140, the board held that rejection of concrete was improper because the government made untimely use of a testing device not agreed to in the contract rather than the one specified and recommended by the industry. An industry paper pointed out that an alcohol gauge "is not a substitute . . . for the more accurate pressure and volumetric methods." The board stated: "[W]e cannot presume that a prompt test with an approved gauge would have shown an improper air content." By using an unreliable test at an inappropriate time, the government failed to meet its burden of proof that the cement did not comply with the contract specifications.

(1) Increased Costs

The contractor may recover increased costs resulting from unspecified government tests if such inspection was not reasonably foreseeable at the time of contracting. In *Kenyon Magnetics, Inc.*, GSBCA 4769, 77-2 BCA ¶ 12,786, the government delayed shipment of the contractor's completed production lot of 600 units for eight weeks pending testing of two sample units in a government laboratory. The board found that this delay was unreasonable and that the government had, in effect, issued a change order when it issued the contract without the standard Preproduction Sample clause and later acted as if the clause had been included. See also *Grumman Aerospace Corp.*, ASBCA 50090, 01-1 BCA ¶ 31,316, *aff'd*, 34 Fed. Appx. 710 (Fed. Cir. 2002) (equitable adjustment granted where systematic changes in the inspection procedure unreasonably disrupted performance).

Additional costs are not recoverable if the unspecified inspection is necessitated by contractor fault, *Chronometrics, Inc.*, NASABCA 185-2, 90-3 BCA ¶ 22,992, *recons. denied*, 91-1 BCA ¶ 23,479 (repeated acceptance testing of electronic equipment was the result of contractor's design deficiency); *Coliseum Constr. Inc.*, ASBCA 36642, 89-1 BCA ¶ 21,428 (delay caused, in part, by contractor's order of improper equipment); *O'Neal Constr. Co.*, ENGBCA 5038, 87-2 BCA ¶ 19,935 (deficient work justified a higher inspection standard, so the construction contractor was not entitled to an equitable adjustment); *Keyser Roofing Contractors, Inc.*, ASBCA 32069, 90-3 BCA ¶ 23,024 (contractor not entitled to extra costs of making and repairing cuts in completed roof in order to inspect because initial inspection of work showed poor quality).

Similarly, there will be no recovery if the unspecified tests do not unreasonably delay or interfere with the contractor, *Eagle Contracting Inc.*, AGBCA 88-225-1, 92-3 BCA ¶ 25,018, *recons. denied,* 93-1 BCA ¶ 25,320 (the board rejected the contractor's claim for 10 percent impact costs due to the absence of an inspector because this "relaxation" of the contract specification did not unduly delay the work); *Washington Constr. Co.*, ENGBCA 5318, 89-3 BCA ¶ 22,077, *aff'd,* 907 F.2d 158 (Fed. Cir. 1990) (no unreasonable delay in Corps' decision to conduct a survey of excavation work although there was a two-month lapse between the time when the Corps obtained knowledge of the deficiency and the survey). In *Allied Paint Mfg. Co. v. United States*, 200 Ct. Cl. 313, 470 F.2d 556 (1972), new testing procedures implemented by the government delayed the shipment of paint from the contractor's plant by as much as four months. Under the old testing procedure, the contractor inspected the paint, subject to government verification testing, thus permitting shipments to be made within 24 to 48 hours. The court upheld the board's conclusion that, despite the adverse impact of the delay on the contractor's manufacturing and warehouse capacity, the purchase orders were properly terminated for default after the contractor failed to make delivery. The board and the court determined that the contractor had failed to present sufficient evidence to establish that the changed inspection procedures interfered with or prevented performance of the terminated purchase orders. See also *William F. Klingensmith, Inc.*, GSBCA 5520-REM, 85-2 BCA ¶ 18,030, in which the board held that the contractor was not entitled to added costs from changed cement specifications because the delay was the contractor's fault.

(2) Notice

If the government changes the test method, it must inform the contractor of what test results are to be met under the new test if the contractor so requests, *Tester Corp.*, ASBCA 21312, 78-2 BCA ¶ 13,373, *recons. denied*, 79-1 BCA ¶ 13,725, *aff'd*, 227 Ct. Cl. 648 (1981). See also *Pinay Flooring Prods., Inc.*, GSBCA 9286, 91-2 BCA ¶ 23,682, in which the board held that, after years of allowing testing to be done in small samples, the government was not entitled to change the test method, without notice to the contractor, to include testing of all tendered floor covering. In one case, a default termination was converted into a termination for convenience after the contractor abandoned performance because the government did not state firm objective requirements after changing the testing method and procedure, *Puma Chem. Co.*, GSBCA 5254, 81-1 BCA ¶ 14,844.

c. Subjective Standards

As long as the test method is reasonable, the test may involve some degree of subjectivity. For example, in *Interstate Reforesters, Dale Whitley*, AGBCA 87-374-3, 89-1 BCA ¶ 21,375, the board upheld a finger-press test for evaluation of the firmness of soil for planting trees. The board reasoned that when the subjective nature of the test was balanced against the vast experience of the inspector, the test was not unreasonable. Such subjective standards can impose problems, however, as goods and services acceptable to one inspector may be rejected by another. For that reason, in its emphasis on performance-based contracting, the government stresses objective, measurable criteria. See FAR 37.602-2, dealing with performance-based services contracting specifications. There is no comparable provision in FAR dealing with supply contracts. However, the preference for performance based contracting applies to both services and supply contracts.

Tests that conform to generally accepted industry practice are considered reasonable. See *MJW Enters., Inc.*, ENGBCA 5813, 93-1 BCA ¶ 25,405, in which the government's request for the contractor to trim seven extra feet of growth was held to be unreasonable because an industry standard for trimming new growth in hedges should have been applied. See also *DiCecco, Inc.*, ASBCA 11944, 69-2 BCA ¶ 7,821 (rejecting canned mushrooms on the basis of color according to USDA standards), and *A & D Fire Prot. Inc.*, ASBCA 53103, 02-2 BCA ¶ 32,053 (government inspector's rejection of material based solely on its appearance was an unreasonably strict, subjective judgment).

d. Tests Imposing Higher Standards

A test or inspection conducted by the government may not be used as a basis for rejection if it imposes a higher standard of performance than that established in the contract, *General Motors Corp.*, ASBCA 10418, 65-2 BCA ¶ 4,885 (improper to subject containers to a "rough handling" test when specifications only required them to withstand damage or movement in ordinary handling); *E.W. Eldridge, Inc.*, ENGBCA 5269, 89-3 BCA ¶ 21,899 (government standard defining "sound" jetty stone as "free from cracks, joints, and chunks" was more stringent than the permissible imperfections the contractor had a right to expect, rendering the government's rejection wrongful); *Al Johnson Constr. Co.*, ENGBCA 4170, 87-2 BCA ¶ 19,952 (contractor was entitled to costs incurred due to a two-week work suspension that occurred because of the government's use of a two-point soil compaction test as opposed to the standard five-point test); *A-Nam Cong-Ty*, ASBCA 14200, 70-1 BCA ¶ 8,106 (barges were improperly rejected after being tested in rough, open sea because contract called for barges to be used in coastal waters); *Teems, Inc. v. General Servs. Admin.*, GSBCA 14090, 98-1 BCA ¶ 29,357 (rejection improper because the retest was conducted with uncalibrated equipment and utilized an incorrect standard).

If the contractor performs to the higher standard, a constructive change may be found, entitling the contractor to an equitable adjustment. See *Xplo Corp.*, DOTCAB 1246, 86-2 BCA ¶ 18,871 (contractor was entitled to costs for extra time and money spent complying with a more stringent waterway surveillance standard); *Allstate Leisure Prods., Inc.*, ASBCA 35614, 89-3 BCA ¶ 22,003 (contractor was entitled to an equitable adjustment for costs of complying with the government's stricter interpretation of the seam size requirements, especially because the government knew of the contractor's adherence to a different standard); and *Dan Rice Constr. Co.*, ASBCA 52160, 04-1 BCA ¶ 32,595 (inspector's mis-identification of a problem, deficiency, or nonconformity constructively changed the contract).

When the government requires the contractor to perform at a higher inspection standard than is common to the industry, the contractor may be entitled to an equitable adjustment. In *D.E.W., Inc.*, ASBCA 37232, 93-1 BCA ¶ 25,444, the board sustained the contractor's appeal of the Army Corps of Engineers' rejection of tendered panels. The board held that when blisters appeared on panels, the applicable industry standard was repair, not rejection. The board also held that a government offer to accept panels if they passed a bake test was inappropriate because such test was not the industry standard. See *Forsberg & Gregory, Inc.*, ASBCA 17598, 75-1 BCA ¶ 11,176 (allowing compensation for forced adherence to the contract specification that framing "fit closely" when the relevant trade usage required "reasonable tolerance" due to the imperfect nature of carpentry), and *Vi-Mil, Inc.*, ASBCA 25111, 82-2 BCA ¶ 15,840 (clothing contractor entitled to an equitable adjustment for added work caused by the inspector's improper use of the military standard as opposed to the less stringent commercial standard). In *Marvin Eng'g Co.*, ASBCA 25460, 82-2 BCA ¶ 16,021, the board held that the contractor was entitled to an extension of time for complying with a more stringent "out of roundness" standard for ejector rack housings. The board stated that it would consume more time to ensure that each hole was perfectly round than to apply the industry standard of some tolerance. But see *Kos Kam, Inc.*, ASBCA 34682, 92-1 BCA ¶ 24,546, in which the board found that the contractor, under the painting clause of a housing renovation contract, was not entitled to an equitable adjustment for multiple coating costs since it was not inconsistent with the contract specification of "complete hiding of the surface."

Requiring a contractor to meet a higher standard by imposing a more stringent set of test criteria than required by the contract can invalidate a default termination, *Nomura Enters., Inc.*, ASBCA 50959, 01-1 BCA ¶ 31,168.

e. *Inspection Standards Established by Conduct*

The actions of the parties can also establish the inspection standard. Thus, where the specifications are not precise, the government's inspection standards used early in performance can establish the contract's quality requirements. Similarly, under certain circumstances, lax inspection standards may result in a waiver of specifications. See *J.R. Cheshier Janitorial*, ENGBCA 5487, 91-3 BCA ¶ 24,351, stating at 121,651:

> [A] change occurs because of over-inspection if during the latter stages of performance an inspector interprets specification requirements more strictly than at earlier stages with the result that the contractor has to change its procedures at added cost to meet the increased requirements. *Stanley W. Wasco*, ASBCA No. 12288, 68-1 BCA ¶ 6986; *see John H. Roberts v. United States*, 174 Ct. Cl. 940, 357 F.2d 938 (1966); *WRB Corp. v. United States*, [183 Ct. Cl. 409 (Ct. Cl. 1968)]; *Gonzales Custom Painting, Inc.*, ASBCA No. 39527, *et. seq.*, 90-3 BCA ¶ 22,950; *Tripod, Inc.*, ASBCA No. 25104, 89-1 BCA ¶ 21,305. *Cf. W.F. Kilbride Constr., Inc.*, ASBCA No. 19484, 76-1 BCA ¶ 11,726; *Chelan Packing Co.*, ASBCA No. 14419, 72-1 BCA ¶ 9290; *Lasker-Goldman Corp.*, ASBCA No. 9110, 1964 BCA ¶ 4200. Related to this point, Government actions may result in a waiver of a contract requirement if it continuously accepts deficient work as conforming to the contract's requirements over an extended period of time during performance, and the Contracting Officer is aware that this is being done. *Gresham & Co. v. United States*, 200 Ct. Cl. 97, 470 F.2d 542 (1972); *B&L Constr. Co.*, [ENGBCA 5708, 91-2 BCA ¶ 23,840]; *Walsky Constr. Co.*, [ASBCA 36940, 90-2 BCA ¶ 22,934]; *see also L.W. Foster Sportswear Co. v. United States*, 186 Ct. Cl. 499, 405 F.2d 1285 (1969); *Emily Malone*, ASBCA No. 30383, 87-2 BCA ¶ 19,758; *Wilkinson & Jenkins Constr. Co.*, ENG BCA No. 5176, 87-2 BCA ¶ 19,950; *Moving Services, Ltd.*, IBCA No. 1540-12-81, 84-2 BCA ¶ 17,267; *Mann Construction Co., Inc.*, AGBCA No. 76-111-4, 81-1 BCA ¶ 15,087.

In *Towne Realty, Inc. v. United States*, 1 Cl. Ct. 264 (1982), the court found that acceptance by the government of a prototype housing unit "enlarged the standards of acceptable finish work" by establishing "an in-the-field standard pursuant to which minor cosmetic deficiencies . . . were to be regarded as acceptable so long as their cumulative visual effect . . . was no more severe than the finish appearance shown in the prototype." In *Gonzales Custom Painting, Inc.*, ASBCA 39527, 90-3 BCA ¶ 22,950, the parties intended the paint merely to be sealed of all imperfections and began performance under this standard. The dispute arose when the second inspector interpreted the contract quality assurance provision as requiring the removal of all the existing paint. The inspector, acting under the authority of the contracting officer, ordered the contractor to do this substantial amount of extra work. The board held that the contractor was entitled to additional compensation for costs incurred from the new inspector's misinterpretation of the inspection standard. See also *Tripod, Inc.*, ASBCA 25104, 89-1 BCA ¶ 21,305 (contractor was entitled to costs incurred while complying with cleaning requests by inspectors in excess of previous requirements and the contract specifications), and *Gary Aircraft Corp.*, ASBCA 21731, 91-3 BCA ¶ 24,122 (government change from initial lax inspections to an overly rigid use of a 50-person inspection team that no longer permitted minor deviations entitled the contractor to an equitable adjustment for added costs of compliance).

2. Place of Inspection

The government has great latitude in choosing where it will conduct inspections. The Inspection of Supplies—Fixed Price clause at FAR 52.246-2 permits the government to inspect and test supplies "to the extent practicable, at all places." Similarly, the Inspection of Construction clause at FAR 52.246-12 provides that all construction work, including "materials, workmanship, and manufacture and fabrication of components . . . is subject to Government inspection and test at all places." The Inspection of Services—Fixed-Price clause at FAR 52.246-4 gives the government "the right to inspect and test all services . . . to the extent practicable at all . . . places during the term of the contract." Through their use of DD Form 250, DFARS 252.246-7000, NFS 18-52.246-72, GSAR 552.246-72, and other civilian agency regulations incorporate substantially similar language.

While the clauses give the government the right to inspect at all places, FAR 46.402 gives guidance on when the government should inspect at source, and 46.403 gives guidance on when the government should inspect at destination.

The fact that a contract specifies where inspection will take place does not deprive the government of the right to conduct inspection at other places. The Material Inspection and Receiving Report (MIRR), implemented by most of the agencies, provides one subsection for origin inspection and a second for inspection at destination. See, for example, *Ralbo, Inc.*, ASBCA 43548, 93-2 BCA ¶ 25,624, *recons. denied,* 93-3 BCA ¶ 25,965. In *Washington Tech. Assocs., Inc.*, ASBCA 10048, 65-2 BCA ¶ 4892, the board held that a special provision stating that inspection would be at the contractor's plant with "final acceptance on delivery" did not prevent the government from inspection at destination. The board stated that general provisions "are to be read conjunctively with any implementing contract Schedule provisions." Such special provisions would alter or limit the general provisions "only to the extent of a clear supersedure by a substituted inspection article in the Schedule or of clear inconsistency or conflict." The contractor should have known that the government could exercise its right to inspect and test before acceptance at the point of delivery and had no right to rely on any prior government inspection at the contractor's plant. A similar decision would result under ¶ (k) of the Inspection of Supplies clause at FAR 52.246-2, which states that "inspections and tests by the Government do not relieve the contractor of responsibility for defects or other failures to meet contract requirements discovered before acceptance." Accord, *Allied Specialties Co.*, ASBCA 10335, 67-2 BCA ¶ 6657. See also *Red Circle Corp. v. United States*, 185 Ct. Cl. 1, 398 F.2d 836 (1968), in which the court found that government inspections conducted at a place other than the one specified in the contract for the convenience of the contractor did not constitute a permanent election precluding the government from later conducting inspections at the specified place (contractor's plant). Thus, the contractor was not entitled to additional compensation for extra performance costs resulting from the on-premises inspections since it knew of this requirement prior to bidding and could have adjusted its bid accordingly.

Although the government may generally conduct inspections at places other than those specified in the contract, the contractor may be entitled to additional compensation if a change in location increases its costs. In *Boeing-Vertol Co.*, ASBCA 18838, 78-2 BCA ¶ 13,377, the government changed the location of its final inspection, increasing the need for support by the contractor's personnel over the previous level when the inspection took place at the contractor's plant as specified in the contract. The board held that the contractor was entitled to rely on the government inspection taking place as it had in the past (at the specified location) and was thus entitled to compensation for the additional costs resulting from the change in location. See also *Gordon H. Ball, Inc.*, ASBCA 8316, 1963 BCA ¶ 3925, and *J.A. Jones Constr. Co.*, ENGBCA 2728, 69-2 BCA ¶ 7814, in which the contractors were entitled to equitable adjustments for increased costs incurred when the government changed the place of inspection from the fabricators' plants to points of acceptance.

3. Time of Inspection

The inspection clauses in the FAR give the government broad rights as to when inspection may occur, providing that it may occur "at all . . . times. . . ." with the requirement that it does not unduly or unnecessarily interfere with or delay the work. The government may inspect during the performance of the work or after the work has been completed. The time of inspection can be critical in determining the government's right to reject nonconforming work. It may also affect the government's right to terminate the contract for default. When the government specifies a delivery date and then chooses to inspect after this date has passed, it risks the possibility that a waiver of the contractually specified date may be found. See *Multi Elec. Mfg., Inc.*, ASBCA 30055, 85-1 BCA ¶ 17,878, in which the board found that the government waived the delivery date when the late government inspection suggested corrective action that would increase the contractor's costs. For further discussion of limitations on the government's right to reject work with minor nonconformities, see Chapter 10.

a. Inspection During the Work

Government inspection during contractor performance must not be conducted in a manner that causes unreasonable delay or be at times that are unreasonable. In *Tripod Inc.*, ASBCA 25104, 89-1 BCA ¶ 21,305, the contractor was entitled to costs incurred in complying with inspections implemented during work hours when the contract specified that they should take place after work was done. See also *Ebonex, Inc.*, ASBCA 38205, 94-2 BCA ¶ 26,640, in which the board denied a contractor's claim for equitable adjustment for delay allegedly caused by the government's inspection practices. The board held that the government did not act unreasonably when it provided overtime inspection coverage instead of assigning a full-time inspector.

b. Acceptance Inspection

Acceptance inspection must occur within a reasonable time after the government knows or should know that the work is completed, *Martell Constr. Co.*, ASBCA 23679, 80-1 BCA ¶ 14,429 (nine-day delay in inspection under a construction contract was unreasonable because the government was in possession of the rooms and had knowledge of their completion). In *Woodchips, Inc.*, AGBCA 82-147-3, 82-2 BCA ¶ 15,941, a one-day delay was excused due to the unforeseeable illness of the contracting officer's representative, who was to conduct the inspection. In denying the contractor's claim, the board noted that the government had acted reasonably and promptly in rescheduling inspection for the following day. See also *Toombs & Co.*, ASBCA 34590, 91-1 BCA ¶ 23,403 (government did not begin inspection until 23 days after notice, as opposed to the 20-day period that it was entitled to).

c. Time of Inspection Affecting Validity

The time during which inspections and tests are conducted may also affect their validity or accuracy in determining compliance or noncompliance with the contract specifications. See *Tucker & Assocs. Contracting, Inc.*, IBCA 1468-6-81, 83-1 BCA ¶ 16,140 (test to determine the air content of concrete found invalid, in part, because it was not administered promptly as recommended by the industry), and *Jesco Res., Inc.*, GSBCA 6857, 84-1 BCA ¶ 16,927 (unreasonable for government inspectors to expect paper towel dispensers, which were required to be filled at noon, to remain full in late evening because the building was in constant use by many employees). The contractor was unsuccessful in *Mutual Maint., Inc.*, GSBCA 7637, 91-1 BCA ¶ 23,287 (rejecting the contractor's argument that government inspection of cleaning during work hours was unreasonable because it resulted in the government's use of the clean rooms before completion of the contract), and *Independent Mfg. & Serv. Cos. of Am., Inc., by Tr. in Bankr.*, ASBCA 47542, 95-2 BCA ¶ 27,915 (contract did not restrict the government's times for random inspections and did not require the dusting-buffing sequence used by the contractor).

4. Number of Inspections

The government may conduct multiple inspections provided that they are conducted at reasonable times and places and do not unnecessarily or unduly delay the work, *Cosmechem Co. v. General Servs. Admin.*, GSBCA 12147, 93-3 BCA ¶ 26,057 (government could inspect a cleaning compound both before and after the original delivery date because it was proven necessary for determining compliance). See also *Servidone Constr. Corp. v. United States*, 19 Cl. Ct. 346 (1990), *aff'd,* 931 F.2d 860 (Fed. Cir. 1991) (multiple testing of construction was valid because the contract permitted testing that was "deemed necessary in the Government's discretion" and the tests did not delay or hinder performance or increase costs), and *Jet Flight Transport, Inc.*, ASBCA 38823, 93-1 BCA ¶ 25,336 (multiple daily inspections were not improper because they were not imposed for harassment purposes but were a function of the random sampling technique specified in the contract). In *A.B.G. Instrument & Eng'g, Inc. v. United States*, 219 Ct. Cl. 381, 593 F.2d 394 (1979), the court stated that the government's right to reject goods before acceptance "necessarily implies that the Government should also have the right to reinspect those supplies at any time." In this case, the government had conducted only spot checks prior to transport of the goods for which deliveries were to be "F.O.B. Destination." See also *Lox Equip. Co.*, ASBCA 8518, 1964 BCA ¶ 4469 (government had the right to inspect vessels at point of manufacture and at delivery site). Prior to the FAR, the boards were unsure as to the proper scope of the government's broad right to reject nonconforming goods upon reinspection at destination subsequent to their approval in an inspection at origin. Compare *Apco Mossberg Co.*, GSBCA 3440, 72-1 BCA ¶ 9403 (government reinspection at destination was prohibited by prior approval) with *Trevco Eng'g & Sales*, VACAB 1021, 73-2 BCA ¶ 10,096 (government not estopped from reinspecting at destination). The *Trevco* rationale apparently has prevailed because the overriding spirit of the FAR emphasizes a broad government right to inspect.

FAR 46.401(d) provides that "[i]f a contract provides for delivery and acceptance at destination and the Government inspects the supplies at a place other than destination, the supplies shall not ordinarily be reinspected at destination." Thus, unlike its predecessor (the FPR), which precluded reinspection at destination outright, the FAR does not categorically reject the notion that reinspection can occur at a different location than anticipated at the time of contracting. However, FAR 46.503 does preclude reinspection "at destination for acceptance purposes" if the supplies were "accepted at a place other than destination."

If multiple inspections are used, they must be consistent with each other, *W.F. Kilbride Constr., Inc.*, ASBCA 19484, 76-1 BCA ¶ 11,726 (contractor entitled to equitable adjustment for increased costs caused by "multiple inspections to differing standards by different officials"); *Hull-Hazard, Inc.*, ASBCA 34645, 90-3 BCA ¶ 23,173 (contractor entitled to an equitable adjustment for delay costs incurred from the repeated use of ad hoc punchlists by various government inspectors); *WRB Corp. v. United States*, 183 Ct. Cl. 409 (1968) (inconsistent, multiple inspections).

5. Manner of Inspection

The government has been held liable if it exercises its inspection rights in a manner that unreasonably interferes with the contractor's performance or that increases the cost or amount of work required of the contractor, *Mutual Maint. Co.*, GSBCA 7637, 91-1 BCA ¶ 23,287 (overzealous enforcement of acceptance specifications for grout); *Xplo Corp.*, DOTCAB 1247, 86-2 BCA ¶ 18,872 (excessive resurvey testing amounted to an unreasonable delay of acceptance); *California Reforestation*, AGBCA 87-226-1, 89-1 BCA ¶ 21,301 (inconsistent and arbitrary definition of the word "quadrant" as opposed to the clear and unambiguous definition set out in the contract); *Hull-Hazard Inc.*, ASBCA 34645, 90-3 BCA ¶ 23,173 (imposition of an ad-hoc, individualized inspection system instead of the contractually required joint inspection system); *W.F. Kilbride Constr., Inc.*, ASBCA 19484, 76-1 BCA ¶ 11,726 (confusing and vacillating inspection procedures, multiple inspections to differing standards by different officials, and arbitrary refusal to perform inspections of completed work); *North Am. Maint. Co.*, ASBCA 21986, 78-2 BCA ¶ 13,316 (40 untrained inspectors caused a proliferation of acceptance standards in janitorial services contract). In *R.J. Crowley, Inc.*, ASBCA 35679, 88-3 BCA ¶ 21,151, the government abused its inspection rights by requiring the contractor to furnish a copy of its entire asbestos removal plan before allowing it to begin removing asbestos from an old building. This requirement was deemed an unnecessary hindrance, especially considering the health and safety needs of the contractor's employees and the lack of any contract specification requiring the submission of an approved plan. The board awarded the contractor an equitable adjustment and a time extension for the undue delay created by this action.

Faulty inspection testing by the government has also led to a finding of improper rejection of the item, *Rohr-Plessey Corp.*, PSBCA 36, 76-2 BCA ¶ 11,995 (tests of mail handling machine by inexperienced operators using poor quality, oversized mail were invalid); or additional government liability if the contractor consequently performs to a higher standard, *Zundel Bros.*, AGBCA 83-212-1, 85-3 BCA ¶ 18,451 (government inspector's failure to count "bait sets" outside specific plots led the gopher control contractor to do extra work to meet quality assurance standards); *Santa Fe Eng'rs, Inc.*, PSBCA 902, 84-2 BCA ¶ 17,377 (government failure to space mail-handling trays when placing them on a conveyor belt entitled contractor to additional costs for the resulting operational difficulties).

6. Government Inspection Not for Contractor Benefit

The mere fact that the government has inspected the work and has not indicated that the work is defective does not relieve the contractor of its primary responsibility of ensuring compliance with contract requirements. The supplies and construction inspection clauses provide that the government's inspection of the work is for its benefit. Paragraph (k) of the Inspection of Supplies—Fixed-Price clause at FAR 52.246-2 provides:

> Inspections and tests by the Government do not relieve the Contractor of responsibility for defects or other failures to meet contract requirements discovered before acceptance.

Paragraph (c) of the Inspection of Construction clause at FAR 52.246-12 provides:

> Government inspections and tests are for the sole benefit of the Government and do not—

(1) Relieve the Contractor of responsibility for providing adequate quality control measures;

(2) Relieve the Contractor of responsibility for damage to or loss of the material before acceptance;

(3) Constitute or imply acceptance; or

(4) Affect the continuing rights of the Government after acceptance of the completed work under paragraph (i) of this section.

The Inspection of Services clause at FAR 52.246-4 does not include a similar provision.

a. No Waiver or Acceptance from Inspection

The mere fact that an inspector has observed a contractor's performance that is in fact defective does not result in either acceptance of the work or waiver of the contract requirements. See *Fire Sec. Sys., Inc. v. General Servs. Admin.*, GSBCA 12120, 97-2 BCA ¶ 28,994, *recons. denied,* 97-2 BCA ¶ 29,186 (failure of on-site government inspector to mention any problem with the class B wiring a contractor was providing was not an implied repudiation of the requirement for class A wiring); *Twigg Corp. v. General Servs. Admin.*, GSBCA 14386, 00-1 BCA ¶ 30,722 (failure of government inspectors to inform a contractor that it was installing non-comforming wire was not an implied repudiation of the specifications); and *George Ledford Constr., Inc.*, ENGBCA 6218, 96-2 BCA ¶ 29,172 (the board rejected a contractor's contention that its noncomplying roadwork resulted from government inspectors' failure to take early corrective action when asphalt thickness and density requirements were not being met, because the government's inspection did not excuse the contractor's own responsibility).

One reason for this rule is that the government inspector may not have realized that the work did not conform. Further, even though the inspector may have actual knowledge of the defect, the failure to call attention to it may be due to inadvertence. See *Kelley Control Sys., Inc.*, VABCA 2337, 87-3 BCA ¶ 20,064, in which the board stated that, "To the extent the VA inspections missed pointing out the defect, we can only surmise that it was unwitting and without knowledge of the deviation." In *Bruce-Andersen Co.*, ASBCA 31663, 89-3 BCA ¶ 22,013, the board rejected the contractor's argument that the government impliedly accepted its installation of dowels because there was no evidence that the inspectors actually saw the contractor performing this work. In *Atterton Painting & Constr., Inc.*, ASBCA 31471, 88-1 BCA ¶ 20,478, *aff'd,* 865 F.2d 268 (Fed. Cir. 1988), the board held that there was no need for the government inspector to call defects to the contractor's attention because the contractor's workmen were also knowledgeable of the defects. Further, lack of familiarity with contract requirements by the inspector does not relieve the contractor of the contract requirements, *Mayfair Constr. Co.*, NASABCA 478-6, 80-2 BCA ¶ 14,772.

When approving "shop drawings" under construction contracts, the government's failure to object to nonconformities not specifically identified by the contractor has also been held not to constitute waiver or acceptance of the nonconformity, *Ulibarri Constr. Co.*, VABCA 1780, 87-3 BCA ¶ 20,169, *aff'd*, 861 F.2d 729 (Fed. Cir. 1988). In *Ralph Larsen & Son, Inc.*, PSBCA 2164, 89-1 BCA ¶ 21,228, the board held that the government's erroneous approval of shop drawings did not entitle the contractor to additional compensation. The contractor argued that the government should be held responsible for this defect because of its oversight in approving the drawings. In summarily rejecting this argument, the board stated at 107,074:

> To adopt such a contention would negate [the contractor's] responsibility to perform its contract in accordance with the designated plans and specifications and shift the risk of incurring added costs for defective performance from [the contractor] to [the Government]. The contract's Inspection and Acceptance provision requires [the Government] to inspect only at reasonable times, and it places all risk for deviation from the contract requirements on [the contractor].

See also *Price/CIRI Constr., J.V.*, ASBCA 37001, 89-2 BCA ¶ 21,697.

b. Basis for Government Liability

A number of cases have suggested that the government would be responsible for the costs of correcting a nonconformity if the contractor could prove (1) that the government had actual knowledge of the defect but deliberately allowed the work to continue uncorrected, or (2) there was evidence of either express acquiescence or a deliberate decision by the government not to point out the defect. See *Kelley Control Sys., Inc.*, VABCA 2337, 87-3 BCA ¶ 20,064. In *G & C Enters., Inc.*, DOTBCA 1736, 89-1 BCA ¶ 21,556, the board stated in dicta at 108,541:

> [A]pplicable precedents . . . hold that government inspections are designed to benefit the government only, and go further to state that it is only where the evidence shows a government inspector has knowledge the work is noncomplying and deliberately refrains, without reason, from pointing out the defects to the contractor, that the contractor is entitled to recover costs resulting from repairing the defects.
>
> * * *
>
> [The contractor] must demonstrate that the government inspectors had actual knowledge of the nonconforming work and deliberately refrained from informing [the contractor] of its erroneous course of action.

The rationale underlying this view is that it would be unfair and economically wasteful for an unknowing contractor to perform defective work when the government could easily inform it of the defect. However, the contractor will have a difficult time proving these facts. See *Robert McMullan & Son, Inc.*, ASBCA 21159, 77-1

BCA ¶ 12,453, in which the board found that "at most there is some basis for an inference that the Government inspector knew the facts but did not say anything until the job was almost completed." However, the board refused to grant relief because the mere lack of protest or comment could be explained away, stating at 60,373:

> We note that because of the CQC provisions of the contract it was not the Government inspector's primary responsibility to inspect the work for compliance with the contract terms. The possibility that the inspector might have noticed the absence of tops during shower stall installation does not mean that he would have been aware that [the contractor] or its subcontractor, B&W, did not intend to install tops at some time during performance. Presumably the Government inspector was aware of the B&W catalog cut which could reasonably be interpreted to indicate that B&W intended to install shower stalls with tops and thus he would not necessarily have been aware that B&W, and presumably [the contractor], interpreted the contract not to require tops. Recognition of this intent would only have become obvious after B&W, or other subcontractors, had "dressed out" the stalls in the old building.

An additional rationale for some of the cases refusing to relieve the contractor of responsibility based on an *inspector's* failure to notify the contractor of defects has been the fact that inspectors are not authorized to accept work or waive or change specifications. Where, however, the contracting officer has actual or constructive knowledge of the nonconformity and does not object, a waiver will be found, *Walsky Constr. Co.*, ASBCA 36940, 90-2 BCA ¶ 22,934 (board awarded an equitable adjustment because the inspector and the contracting officer knew that the work was proceeding and did nothing to stop it, thereby waiving the temperature requirement).

Although the inspector may not have authority to waive or modify specifications or accept performance, the inspector's failure to note nonconformities may have other implications. It may make the government's burden of proving that the work was defective much more difficult. See *Tidewater Contractors, Inc.*, AGBCA 90-195-1, 93-3 BCA ¶ 26,050, *recons. denied*, 93-3 BCA ¶ 26,151, in which the board stated at 129,500:

> While the presence or observance of an inspector does not shift responsibility for the acceptability of the work, the Government has the burden of showing the work is nonconforming. Where detailed diaries and testimony establish that the inspectors and the COR were frequently present to observe and measure the contractor's performance, and no nonconformities were noted, the CO's *post hoc* contention the work was nonconforming must overcome a heavy burden. *White Buffalo Constr.*, IBCA Nos. 2166, 2173, 91-1 BCA ¶ 23,540. Indeed, in the present case, with the exception of the first 2.6 miles of paving, there simply is no credible evidence that [the contractor's] paving was nonconforming.

The inspector's failure to object may also be used in support of the contractor's interpretation of ambiguous specifications, *Sentell Bros., Inc.*, DOTCAB 1824, 89-3 BCA ¶ 21,904, *recons. denied,* 89-3 BCA ¶ 22,219. For further discussion of contract interpretation, see Chapter 2.

7. Reinspection

Generally, the contractor will be liable for costs of government reinspection resulting from contractor fault. The supply contract inspection clause at FAR 52.246-2 provides that the contractor may be held liable for reinspection costs incurred by the government "[w]hen supplies are not ready at the time specified by the Contractor for inspection or test" or "when prior rejection makes a reinspection or retest necessary." The construction and service contract clauses are silent on this subject, but contractors have been held to have substantially similar liability. See *GEM Eng'g Co. v. Department of Commerce*, GSBCA 12826-COM, 94-3 BCA ¶ 27,152, in which the board allowed a setoff to be made against the contractor to cover the cost of an engineer's duplicate trip to inspect work that was not ready on the first trip because the contractor asked for an inspection on a certain date and should have been ready. In arguing that the government was not justified in assessing this charge, the contractor stated that the contract did not specify the length of the inspection period and that the inspector should have stayed on site longer until it was ready for inspection. The board disagreed, stating that the contractor's "view that an inspector must stay on the job until the contractor is prepared for him to check the work defies common sense." But see *John Blood,* AGBCA 2000-102-1, 02-1 BCA ¶ 31,726, where the record did not demonstrate "that the Government incurred sufficient unanticipated re-inspection costs as to be recoverable absent an explicit provision."

In *Okland Constr. Co.,* GSBCA 3557, 72-2 BCA ¶ 9675, the contractor was found liable for the cost of four additional reinspections when numerous omissions and defects were repeatedly found in work that the contractor in effect represented as being ready for final inspection. In *Minnesota Mining & Mfg. Co.*, GSBCA 4054, 75-1 BCA ¶ 11,065, the board held that the contractor's liability for reinspection costs, resulting from prior rejection, included the cost of transporting items to and from a testing facility even though the government usually bears this expense for initial inspection. The government may deduct such cost of reinspection from the contract price as an equitable adjustment. See *Coastal Structures, Inc.*, DOTBCA 1787, 88-3 BCA ¶ 21,016, in which the board found that the government was entitled to a downward adjustment in the contract price for costs incurred during the reinspection of bolt fastenings on an underwater construction. The initial inspection showed the bolts to be in gross noncompliance due to the negligence of the contractor. Thus, the parties were bound by the Inspection of Construction clause in the contract, which required the contractor to pay expenses that reasonably result from its errors.

If there is no formal rejection or an agreement that the contractor will bear the cost of further testing, the government's reinspection will be regarded as a continuation of an initial inspection consisting of one long series of tests, and it may not recover the incurred costs from the contractor, *Vare Indus., Div. of Audiger, Inc.*, ASBCA 10097, 67-2 BCA ¶ 6653 (although contractor made repairs in between three testing periods, there had been no formal rejection but only suspensions of the testing period).

The government must give the contractor a reasonable time to correct deficiencies discovered by the original inspection, and the contractor must be notified in advance before the government can conduct a reinspection at the contractor's expense, *Okland Constr. Co.,* GSBCA 3557, 72-2 BCA ¶ 9675 (contact between the contractor's representatives and the government inspector indicated that the contractor knew of the deficiencies and had time to correct them). In *Wimsco, Inc.*, ASBCA 51844, 99-1 BCA ¶ 30,378, the government's rejection of work and use of another contractor to make repairs was improper because the government did not furnish the contractor with a list of deficient items as required by the Inspection of Services clause, which also requires that the contractor be given prompt opportunity to correct deficiencies. See also *Winfield Mfg. Co.*, ASBCA 34901, 88-1 BCA ¶ 20,353, in which the government had to bear the cost of reinspection of clothing because the first rejection was based on easily correctable defects.

B. Contractor Inspection

The trend in government contracts has been to place greater responsibility for conducting inspections on the contractor. This is especially true in contracts for commercial items under FAR Part 12. Thus, although the government retains broad rights to conduct its own inspections and tests, an increasingly stronger focus is on government approval and surveillance of contract inspection systems and contractor-conducted tests. This places greater importance on determining the extent of the contractor's inspection obligations. The contractor's inspection responsibility varies, depending on whether the contract contains supplements to the standard inspection clauses with provisions calling for higher-level inspection systems or specific tests. Often contracts will require the contractor to submit a quality assurance plan prior to the government's giving approval to start work. *See Cape Romain Contractors,* ASBCA 50557, 00-1 BCA ¶ 30,697. The criteria for determining the appropriate contract quality assurance requirements are discussed in FAR 46.201 to .203. Some of these criteria are the complexity of the item, the critical nature of the work or service, and the necessity of discovering and correcting defects during performance. In contrast, in small purchases, no inspection clause is used unless the contracting officer determines that it is necessary "to ensure an explicit understanding of the contractor's inspection responsibilities," FAR 46.301. In such a case, the Contractor Inspection Requirements clause at FAR 52.246-1 is included in the purchase order.

The following subsection discusses the contractor's obligations when the government relies only on the standard inspection clauses. The subsection after that considers the situation in which the government supplements the standard clauses with detailed requirements for inspection systems or specific tests.

1. General Inspection Clauses

The standard FAR inspection clauses impose greater inspection responsibilities on the contractor than did the prior clauses. Some of these responsibilities were included in supplemental clauses used by the Department of Defense. Paragraph (b) of the revised Inspection of Supplies—Fixed-Price clause at FAR 52.246-2 now requires the contractor to provide and maintain an inspection system, as follows:

> The Contractor shall provide and maintain an inspection system acceptable to the Government covering supplies under this contract and shall tender to the Government for acceptance only supplies that have been inspected in accordance with the inspection system and have been found by the Contractor to be in conformity with contract requirements. As part of the system, the Contractor shall prepare records evidencing all inspections made under the system and the outcome. These records shall be kept complete and made available to the Government during contract performance and for as long afterwards as the contract requires. The Government may perform reviews and evaluations as reasonably necessary to ascertain compliance with this paragraph. These reviews and evaluations shall be conducted in a manner that will not unduly delay the contract work. The right of review, whether exercised or not, does not relieve the Contractor of the obligations under the contract.

The Inspection of Construction clause provides at ¶ (b):

> The Contractor shall maintain an adequate inspection system and perform such inspections as will ensure that the work performed under the contract conforms to contract requirements. The Contractor shall maintain complete inspection records and make them available to the Government.

The Inspection of Services—Fixed-Price clause provides at ¶ (b):

> The Contractor shall provide and maintain an inspection system acceptable to the Government covering the services under this contract. Complete records of all inspection work performed by the Contractor shall be maintained and made available to the Government during contract performance and for as long afterwards as the contract requires.

Since the prior clauses did not specifically require the contractor to maintain an inspection system, the contractor could only be required to use inspection procedures normal to the industry, *Lamb Rubber Corp.*, ASBCA 7928, 65-1 BCA ¶ 4614. The government could also demand that the contractor perform inspections that were reasonably necessary to ensure that the units complied with the contract requirements, *Mel Williamson, Inc.*, ASBCA 22983, 80-2 BCA ¶ 14,631, *aff'd*, 229 Ct. Cl. 846 (1982) (requirement that contractor test 100 percent of smoke detectors was reasonable).

Under the present FAR clauses, the contractor's inspection must demonstrate compliance with contract requirements. See, for example, *Coastal Structures, Inc.*, DOTBCA 1693, 88-3 BCA ¶ 20,943, in which the board found that the contractor could not recover costs incurred from misinterpreting the shop drawing specifications, because the contractor would have found the error if it had established its own inspection system, as it was required to do by the inspection clause. The board examined the parties' responsibilities under the clause, stating at 105,823:

> The contractor is responsible for assuring that he complies with contract requirements, and if upon completion of work it is found that he has produced nonconforming work, due to a failure to check his own work, the contractor will bear prime responsibility for the consequences. [citing *Pacific W. Constr., Inc.*, DOTCAB 1084, 82-2 BCA ¶ 16,045 at 79,514]

The board rejected the contractor's argument that the government inspector should have noticed the error. The board stated that the contractor had failed to provide an inspection system and that this omission was the controlling factor contributing to the accrual of extra costs. In *Windsor & Myatt Mech. Contractors, Inc.*, ASBCA 35370, 88-1 BCA ¶ 20,477, the board held that the government was not required to pay the contractor's costs incurred when correcting defective fittings. Under the Inspection of Construction clause incorporated into the contract, performing in compliance with the specifications was deemed to be the contractor's responsibility. Although a government inspection would have discovered the defect, the government was not obligated to do so. Thus, the government was not negligent in failing to notify the contractor of the nonconforming product.

For service contracts, FAR 37.602-2 provided the following guidance until 2006:

> Agencies shall develop quality assurance surveillance plans when acquiring services (see 46.103 and 46.401(a)). These plans shall recognize the responsibility of the contractor (see 46.105) to carry out its quality control obligations and shall contain measurable inspection and acceptance criteria corresponding to the performance standards contained in the statement of work. The quality assurance surveillance plans shall focus on the level of performance required by the statement of work, rather than the methodology used by the contractor to achieve that level of performance.

In 71 Fed. Reg. 211, Jan. 3, 2006, this requirement was made less stringent by substituting the following provision in FAR 37.604:

> Requirements for quality assurance and quality assurance surveillance plans are in Subpart 46.4. The Government may either prepare the quality assurance surveillance plan or require the offerors to submit a proposed quality assurance surveillance plan for the Government's consideration in development of the Government's plan.

For contracts for commercial items, FAR 12.208 states:

> Contracts for commercial items shall rely on contractors' existing quality assurance systems as a substitute for Government inspection and testing before tender for acceptance unless customary market practices for the commercial item being acquired include in-process inspection. Any in-process inspection by the Government shall be conducted in a manner consistent with commercial practice.

2. *Higher-Level Quality Control Requirement*

In order to ensure that contractors provide adequate inspection, contracts frequently contain supplemental clauses specifying details of the inspection system that the contractor must use. The Department of Defense achieved this result for a number of years by imposing MIL-I-45208 and MIL-Q-9858, which have been canceled, requiring a documented contractor inspection system. The former specification provided:

> These requirements pertain to the inspections and tests necessary to substantiate product conformance to drawings, specifications, and contract requirements and to all inspections and tests required by the contract. These requirements are in addition to those inspections and tests set forth in applicable specifications and other contract documents. . . . The inspection system requirements set forth in this specification shall be satisfied in addition to all detail requirements contained in the statement of work or other parts of the contract. The contractor is responsible for compliance with all the provisions of the contract and for furnishing specified articles which meet all requirements of the contract.

Effective February 16, 1999, the FAR was amended to replace preferences for government specifications with preferences for commercial quality standards as examples of higher-level contract quality requirements, 63 Fed. Reg. 70264, Dec. 19, 1998. See FAR 46.202-4, stating:

> (a) Requiring compliance with higher-level quality standards is appropriate in solicitations and contracts for complex or critical items (see 46.203(b) and (c)) or when the technical requirements of the contract require-
>
>> (1) Control of such things as work operations, in-process controls, and inspection; or
>>
>> (2) Attention to such factors as organization, planning, work instructions, documentation control, and advanced metrology.
>
> (b) When the contracting officer, in consultation with technical personnel, finds it is in the Government's interest to require that higher-level quality standards be maintained, the contracting officer shall use the clause prescribed at 46.311. The contracting officer shall indicate in the clause which higher-level quality standards will satisfy the Government's requirement. Examples of higher-level quality standards are ISO 9001, 9002, or 9003; ANSI/ISO/ASQ Q9001-2000; ANSI/ASQC Q9001, Q9002, or Q9003; QS-9000; AS-9000; ANSI/ASQC E4; and ANSI/ASME NQA-1.

This regulation seems to indicate that the invocation of "higher-level quality standards" incorporates a requirement for higher-quality contract management. Moreover, FAR 52.246-11 requires that a higher-level quality assurance standard be identified.

Some civilian agencies incorporate the General Services Administration's Federal Standard 368 to employ a stricter, higher-level quality control system than is required by the FAR. This standard provides:

> The contractor shall provide and maintain a documented quality control system which will ensure that the end products (services or supplies) and associated spare parts, manuals, packaging, marking, and any other contract requirements offered to the Government, conform to the contract requirements whether manufactured or processed by the contractor or procured from subcontractors or vendors. It shall be available for review by the Government prior to the start of production and during the life of the contract. It shall provide control over all phases of production from the initiation of design through manufacture and preparation for delivery.

See *Wilmer Mfg. Co. v. General Servs. Admin.*, GSBCA 11706, 93-3 BCA ¶ 25,942. The GSA has determined that contractor inspection systems that meet ISO standards for quality management are acceptable alternatives to Federal Standard 368. See also the Source Inspection by Quality Approved Manufacturer clause at GSAR 552.246-70 for further guidance as to the scope of Federal Standard 368A and the additional inspection requirements employed by the General Services Administration.

A common requirement of government-specified systems is that the contractor must obtain government approval of its method of compliance with the specification. The government may refuse to inspect tendered supplies until the contractor's inspection system is approved. For example, in *AGH Indus., Inc.*, ASBCA 25848, 85-1 BCA ¶ 17,784, the government would not inspect the supplied helicopter skid shoes because the inspection gauge used by the contractor would not have provided the government with an accurate basis for adjudging conformity with the specifications. The board stated that the contractor was responsible for choosing its method of inspection, and the government could continually reject the goods until the contractor established an inspection system that was satisfactory to the government. Moreover, this did not amount to a constructive change in the contract terms, so the contractor was not entitled to the additional costs of creating a reasonable quality control system.

The government may also choose to reject tendered supplies until the contractor provides an acceptable quality control system. In *Lamptek Co., Div. of Lamps, Inc.*, GSBCA 8378, 89-1 BCA ¶ 21,452, the board upheld the government's rejection of a sample of tendered lamps based on the contractor's failure to implement an adequate inspection system. The contract clearly and unambiguously incorporated Federal Standard 368A, which required the contractor to maintain a documented quality control system at no cost to the government. Thus, the board denied the contractor's claim for the costs incurred when the lamps were rejected. Even if the contractor's quality control plan is accepted, the government retains the right to reject products if it can be shown that the contractor deviated from the accepted plan. See *David B. Lilly Co.,* ASBCA 34678, 92-2 BCA ¶ 24,973 (government's approval of a contractor bomb suspension lug testing plan did not bar rejection of the inspection results when product deficiencies indicated systemic failures due, in part, to contractor deviations from the approved plan).

The government may also evaluate a contractor's quality control system as part of its own pre-acceptance inspection. If the existing contractor quality control does not satisfactorily comply with the government's requirements, the government may, after notification and a reasonable time to cure the deficiency, terminate the contract for default, *St. Angelo Furniture Serv., Inc.*, GSBCA 8454, 89-3 BCA ¶ 22,083 (default termination was valid due to the contractor's failure to establish an inspection system even after the government sent a cure notice).

In *Big 4 Mech. Contractors, Inc.*, ASBCA 20897, 77-2 BCA ¶ 12,716, the board held that numerous inspection clauses (including the Responsibility for Inspection clause) were consistent and that the government had acted properly in insisting that the contractor fully implement the inspection procedures called for by MIL-I-45208. The board reasoned that the government had a right to full compliance with these detailed contractor inspection requirements. The board also found, however, that a constructive change had occurred when the government ordered the contractor to hire an additional full-time inspector when there was no showing that the contractor's quality control obligations would not have been met without a second inspector. In *Alco Mach. Co.*, ASBCA 38183, 90-2 BCA ¶ 22,856, *recons. denied,* 90-3 BCA ¶ 23,149, the board rejected a contractor's claim for reformation or rescission of the contract for its failure to realize that it had to comply with the strict inspection standards of MIL-I-45208A. The contractor argued that it had made an error in submitting its bid and that the government should have inquired when the contractor made an unreasonably low bid. The board found, however, that the military standard was unambiguously referenced in the contract and that the government was entitled to strict compliance with the requisites of MIL-I-45208A. In *H&R Machinists Co.*, ASBCA 39655, 90-3 BCA ¶ 22,948, a default termination was upheld against a contractor's argument that the testing equipment supplied by the government was defective. The board's rationale was that the contractor had failed to establish adequate inspection and calibration procedures as required by MIL-I-45208A. Further support was lent to the board's decision by the government's issuance of a cure notice specifying the need for compliance with the military standard and by the fact that the completion date had already been extended more than eight months.

Government approval of a contractor's inspection system can establish the extent of the contractor's obligation. Thus, subsequent government-ordered changes in contractor quality control or inspection procedures can result in a constructive change, *Lehigh Chem. Co.*, ASBCA 8427, 1963 BCA ¶ 3749, *recons. denied*, 1963 BCA ¶ 3822. See also *Munck Sys., Inc.*, ASBCA 25600, 83-1 BCA ¶ 16,210, *aff'd*, 727 F.2d 1118 (Fed. Cir. 1983) (under paragraph 3.5 of MIL-I-45208, contractor could rely on government's expression of approval of its quality control procedures for the remainder of the contract). In *Maizel Labs., Inc.*, ASBCA 8597, 1963 BCA ¶

3898, the government was found to have waived objections it might have otherwise raised to the contractor's quality control procedure. By permitting the contractor to perform under the procedure without raising any objections, the government in effect approved the procedure as in compliance with the quality control requirements or as an authorized deviation from them. Compare *David B. Lilly Co.,* ASBCA 34678, 92-2 BCA ¶ 24,973, in which the board found that the government's tightened requirements for gauge calibration for the inspection of bomb suspension lugs under MIL-I-45208A was not a constructive change in the contract although the government had already accepted the lower tolerances. The board found that the decision to change the gauge calibration was the result of consensus between the government and the contractor rather than a unilateral government demand.

3. Specified Tests

When the contract requires specific tests to be conducted by the contractor, this may establish the scope of the contractor's inspection obligation, *P.B. Lynn Co.*, ASBCA 28819, 84-2 BCA ¶ 17,334 (tendered aircraft parts were properly rejected because the contractor had agreed to perform contractually specified tests rendering the government's prior approval of the parts irrelevant). Such decisions are made on a case-by-case basis, considering all contract provisions. See *Santa Fe Eng'rs, Inc.*, PSBCA 902, 84-2 BCA ¶ 17,377, in which the contractor was compensated for conducting tests in addition to those specified in the contract. See also *AGH Indus., Inc.*, ASBCA 27960, 89-2 BCA ¶ 21,637, in which the board found that the contractor was entitled to an equitable adjustment for complying with the government's demand to tighten tolerances on its inspection gauge. Compare *Modern Constr., Inc.*, ASBCA 24218, 81-1 BCA ¶ 14,832, in which the contractor was found obligated to perform an operating test needed to determine whether a swimming pool met contract specifications. Although the contract failed to specify who would perform the test, it did contain provisions that required the contractor to perform all tests, except those specifically noted to be performed by the government, and to turn over a pool "ready for use." Based on these provisions, the board concluded that the pool was not "ready for use" until it had been filled with water and tested under normal operating conditions. The contractor, however, was entitled to recover the cost of chemicals used in the test. The board stated that "[s]ince the contract was silent on the matter, it was not unreasonable for [the contractor] to assume that these materials [chemicals] would be furnished by the Government which would need them to operate the pool." But see *Fairfield Mach. Co.,* ASBCA 22704, 85-2 BCA ¶ 17,969, in which it was held that the contractor was not entitled to an equitable adjustment for conducting performance testing of tools beyond the extent envisioned in the contract because the tests were implemented to correct defects for which the contractor was responsible. Moreover, the contractor was not entitled to recover the costs of the tools needed to conduct this further testing. The board distinguished this case from *Modern Construction* on the grounds that industry practice required the contractor to pay for all tools necessary for this testing and that there was adequate evidence that the contractor had knowledge of this practice. Thus, the intent of the parties could be determined although the contract was silent as to which party should pay for inspection and testing equipment.

A contractor may not, however, recover the costs of performing voluntary inspections or tests not required by either the contract or the government, *SanColMar Indus., Inc.*, ASBCA 16193, 74-1 BCA ¶ 10,426 (government approved barrels for shipment despite contractor's assertion that contract-specified inspection procedures were defective). A contractor also cannot recover the cost of a second test ordered by the government when the first test did not meet the contract requirements, *Kencom, Inc.*, GSBCA 6037, 83-2 BCA ¶ 16,583; *Timberland Paving & Constr. Co. v. United States*, 18 Cl. Ct. 129 (1989) (contractor's claim for an equitable adjustment for the costs of complying with safety standards and industry practice was denied because correction of nonconforming construction was its responsibility).

The government is entitled to a price reduction in the amount of the contractor's cost savings if the contractor is relieved of the obligation of performing required tests, *Platt & Sons*, ASBCA 20349, 75-2 BCA ¶ 11,511. In *Hamilton Tech., Inc.*, ASBCA 22959, 79-1 BCA ¶ 13,584, the board held that when the government elects to exercise its contractual right to reduce the testing requirements and the number of test samples to be provided by the contractor, the government is entitled to an equitable adjustment reducing the price based on the cost of the deleted work even though the contractor claimed it had not included any amount in its price for the total possible number of test samples. The board reasoned that the contractor assumed the risk of the government exercising this right and should have included the cost of the test samples in the unit price. In any event, there was no doubt that the deletion would result in some savings to the contractor. Compare *Varo, Inc. v. United States*, 212 Ct. Cl. 432, 548 F.2d 953 (1977), in which a change relieving a subcontractor of performing certain electrical tests was held to not entitle the government to a reduction in price because the contractor did not financially benefit as a result. Alternatively, the government could choose to correct the defective work itself and receive an equitable adjustment for its incurred costs. See *El-ABD Eng'g*, ASBCA 32023, 88-2 BCA ¶ 20,555 (government was entitled to the costs of correcting work after the contract was terminated for default for defective work, but was not entitled to the costs for upgraded or additional work).

As in the case of government-conducted inspections or tests, a constructive change will also be found if the government requires contractor testing that increases the standard of performance, *Baifield Indus., Div. of A-T-O, Inc.*, ASBCA 14582, 72-2 BCA ¶ 9676 (waterproofing test that was more stringent than the one used in first article testing imposed additional work requirements). In *B.B. Andersen Constr. Co.,* VABCA 2265, 88-2 BCA ¶ 20,630, the contractor's claim for additional compensation for a constructive change was sustained because the government required the contractor to perform additional testing of concrete slabs at a higher ⅝ inch deflection standard. The government's acting on the erroneous belief that the contractor's tendered work was nonconforming provided further support for this holding. See also *P & M Indus. Inc.*, ASBCA 38759, 93-1 BCA ¶ 25,471, in which the board found that a contractor was entitled to an equitable adjustment for costs incurred in resolving a dispute involving the government's unanticipated interpretation that magnetic particle inspection should occur both at the casting stage and after machining. In *R.P.M. Constr. Co.*, ASBCA 36965, 90-3 BCA ¶ 23,051, the contractor was entitled to costs for added leakage testing caused by the government's failure to disconnect a deficient gasoline tank from the system. In *Industrial Consultants, Inc.*, VABCA 3249, 91-3 BCA ¶ 24,326, the board rejected the contractor's argument that it was entitled to costs incurred due to an unreasonable delay in conducting a revised inspection of the work. The board held that the contractor had failed to prove unreasonable delay even though the government had taken over six months to order revised tests and subsequently canceled the new test.

C. Cost of Inspection

The general rule is that each party bears the cost of the inspections and tests it conducts. However, the contractor is required to provide assistance to the government's inspectors. In addition, the contractor will be required to provide reasonable facilities for the inspection. Finally, the contractor is liable for the government's reinspection costs if the reinspection is due to contractor fault.

1. *Contractor Duty to Facilitate Government Inspection*

The standard inspection clauses require the contractor to bear those costs reasonably necessary to facilitate government inspection. Paragraph (d) of the supply contract clause at FAR 52.246-2 provides:

> If the Government performs inspection or test on the premises of the Contractor or a subcontractor, the Contractor shall furnish, and shall require subcontractors to furnish, at no increase in contract price, all reasonable facilities and assistance for the safe and convenient performance of these duties. Except as otherwise provided in the contract, the Government shall bear the expense of Government inspections or tests made at other than the Contractor's or subcontractor's premises; *provided*, that in case of rejection, the Government shall not be liable for any reduction in the value of inspection or test samples.

Paragraph (e) of the construction contract clause at FAR 52.246-12 provides, in part:

> The Contractor shall promptly furnish, at no increase in contract price, all facilities, labor, and material reasonably needed for performing such safe and convenient inspections and tests as may be required by the Contracting Officer.

The contractor will be required to pay normal costs incurred in furthering government inspection. See *Tecon Corp. v. United States*, 188 Ct. Cl. 15, 411 F.2d 1262

(1969), in which the court held that the contractor was required to pay the costs of labor and equipment needed to take soil samples to determine the strength of the material when placed and compacted. However, the contractor is protected from improper and disproportionate demands by the reasonableness qualification in these clauses. See *J.L. Ewell Constr. Co.*, ASBCA 37746, 90-1 BCA ¶ 22,485, in which the board suggested that additional testing costs incurred due to government-caused delays would not have to be paid by the contractor due to the reasonableness criteria. In *Corbetta Constr. Co.,* ASBCA 5045, 60-1 BCA ¶ 2613, the board held that the contractor was entitled to recover the cost of shallow observation wells that the government required the contractor to excavate. The board stated that the wells were, in purpose and effect, special inspection devices, compensable under a "testing foundations" article and were not "reasonable facilities" to be furnished without additional charge under the Inspection and Testing article.

The reasonableness standard under the clause is determined by what the contractor can be expected to have foreseen at the time of entering into the contract. For example, in *Gordon H. Ball, Inc.*, ASBCA 8316, 1963 BCA ¶ 3925, the contract stated that the government would inspect welds at the steel fabricator's plant. The board held that the government could waive this right without liability but could not impose on the contractor the financial burden of government inspection at the point of acceptance. The board reasoned that the contractor had relied on in-plant inspection in pricing the contract and was entitled to an equitable adjustment in the price for the additional costs of complying with the government's order to provide facilities for x-ray inspection at the construction site. See also *Aulson Roofing, Inc.*, ASBCA 37677, 91-2 BCA ¶ 23,720, in which the board held it reasonable for the contractor to pay fees for the government representative it had hired to reinspect its tendered shingles after the government had issued a deficiency notice. The board rejected the contractor's argument that the government should be held liable for these costs because the consultant approved the work. The board reasoned that the contractor's decision to hire the representative was a unilateral one and that, as such, the government should not have to pay for it. In *Moro, Inc.*, AGBCA 85-307-1, 87-2 BCA ¶ 19,832, the board rejected the contractor's claim for the costs of purchasing equipment needed to restore land to better condition so as to prepare it for inspection. Inspection would have otherwise been impossible because the land was flooded with water. The board concluded that it was reasonable for the government to insist that the water be pumped from the land. The Inspection and Acceptance clause placed the responsibility for repairing damage prior to acceptance on the contractor. In *Fernavico, S.A.*, ENGBCA PCC-106, 94-2 BCA ¶ 26,922, the contractor was required to reposition work for inspection even though a clause in the specification provided that certain inspections be "conducted without expense to the contractor" because the repositioning of work was necessary for the contractor to perform repairs to the work. Compare *Boeing-Vertol Co.*, ASBCA 18838, 78-2 BCA ¶ 13,377, in which the board held that the contractor was entitled to additional personnel costs incurred when the government relocated its test site from that specified in the contract.

2. Cost of Tearing Out Completed Work

Paragraph (h) of the construction contract clause at FAR 52.246-12 contains a unique provision that gives the government the right to remove or tear out completed work in order to examine it for defects and requires the contractor to assist in this effort. This provision provides:

> If, before acceptance of the entire work, the Government decides to examine already completed work by removing it or tearing it out, the Contractor, on request, shall promptly furnish all necessary facilities, labor, and material. If the work is found to be defective or nonconforming in any material respect due to the fault of the Contractor or its subcontractors, the Contractor shall defray the expenses of the examination and of satisfactory reconstruction. However, if the work is found to meet contract requirements, the Contracting Officer shall make an equitable adjustment for the additional services involved in the examination and reconstruction, including, if completion of the work was thereby delayed, an extension of time.

In *Santa Fe Eng'rs, Inc.*, ASBCA 48409, 95-1 BCA ¶ 27,526, the cutting of grooves in liquid glazed wall coatings to test thickness was destructive testing that entitled the contractor to an equitable adjustment for the costs of testing and recoating those walls whose coatings met the contract's thickness requirements. The contract's Inspection and Acceptance clause specifically obligated the government, when testing involved the "removing or tearing out" of a portion of the work (i.e., destructive testing), to bear the costs of examination and reconstruction of work found to conform to the contract requirements. The board found the contract's Contractor Inspection System clause, which required the contractor to perform testing, applied only to nondestructive testing. Compare *The Little Susitna Co.*, PSBCA 1576, 88-1 BCA ¶ 20,240, in which the government was absolved of any liability for reconstruction when the tearing out of a leaking roof demonstrated that the defects were the contractor's fault. However, the contractor was entitled to an equitable adjustment for costs incurred correcting the second destructive leakage inspection because there was no evidence that the cuts in the rubber membrane of the roof (the cause of the leak) were the fault of the contractor or one of its subcontractors. Compare *MK+ABD+FM*, ASBCA 27760, 83-2 BCA ¶ 16,729, in which the contractor was held liable for reinspection costs under this provision of a prior clause and another contract clause when the contractor-caused defect consisted of an uncertainty as to the integrity of welds even though the welds proved to be free of defects upon later reinspection. In *Ben M. White Co.*, ASBCA 36643, 90-1 BCA ¶ 22,420, the board held that the contractor was entitled to its expense in tearing out a completed section of its construction at the behest of the government to determine the cause of a leak. When it was proved that the leak was not the contractor's fault, consistent with the contract provisions, the contractor was entitled to its costs.

A pre-acceptance failure to implement destructive testing (tearing out of completed work) can be used as evidence against government recovery upon a post-acceptance discovery of a defect. See *Ahern Painting Contractors, Inc.*, GSBCA 7912, 90-1 BCA ¶ 22,291, in which the board rejected the government's claim for the costs of repairing defects discovered during destructive testing when it had only used simple, periodic testing before acceptance. The board concluded that the government could have discovered the defect before acceptance by employing destructive testing but had failed to do so. As such, it was unreasonable for the government to argue that the contractor should compensate it for the costs of correcting the work. The government's refusal to submit the tendered performance to destructive testing may also be seen as evidence against its argument that the construction is nonconforming. See *Richerson Constr., Inc. v. General Servs. Admin.*, GSBCA 11161, 93-1 BCA ¶ 25,239, in which the board sustained the contractor's appeal because of the government's unwillingness to employ destructive testing. The contractor argued that the columns it built were properly constructed and conformed to the specifications. The board held that this argument had more support than the government's claim that destructive testing would have imposed a safety hazard. Hence, the government's rejection of the construction was improper. To avoid this type of dispute, the parties to a contract may choose to specify that destructive testing is discouraged, *Hoboken Shipyards, Inc.*, DOTBCA 1920, 90-2 BCA ¶ 22,752, or may preclude it altogether, *Gebr. Kittlelberger GmbH & Co.*, ASBCA 36596, 89-1 BCA ¶ 21,306.

D. Special Inspection Techniques and Issues

There are a number of situations in which quality and inspection problems have resulted in the development of special inspection techniques or unique inspection issues have arisen. One of these issues relates to preaward testing to establish Qualified Bidders, Manufacturers or Products Lists when the nature of the work is critical and postaward testing alone will not adequately protect the government's interests. This subject is dealt with in *Formation of Government Contracts* (3d ed. 1998). This section deals with postaward inspections, which are inspection by sampling, first article testing, and safety inspection.

1. Inspection by Sampling

Inspection by sampling is commonly used when the procurement involves large quantities that can be divided into lots or when destructive testing is required. Sampling may be specified contractually or may be used by the government, in some circumstances, as a basis for rejecting all the work without the necessity of 100 percent testing or inspection.

a. Contractually Specified Sampling

Contractual sampling agreements generally provide that entire lots may be rejected if defects in excess of the number specified are present in the sample. Conversely, the entire lot may not be rejected if less than the number of specified defects are present. In the latter case, the government retains the right to inspect any individual unit and reject any nonconforming unit regardless of whether it was within the sample.

There may be a number of different techniques for establishing the sampling procedure. However, the most commonly used method by both defense and civilian agencies is MIL-STD 105. This specification establishes standard mathematical formulas for determining sample and lot sizes and frequency of testing. It incorporates instructions for the division of supplies into sample lots or sublots and provides guidance on the type of sampling to be used as well as the level of testing to be performed.

Contractually imposed sampling procedures are strictly construed. Thus, the government must make a prima facie showing that such procedures were followed when it rejects tendered supplies, *Roda Enters., Inc.*, ASBCA 22323, 81-2 BCA ¶ 15,419. Specified lot sizes may not be varied to the contractor's detriment, nor may lots be commingled. In *Associate-Aircraft-Tool & Mfg., Inc.*, ASBCA 7255, 1963 BCA ¶ 3739, only the smaller of two commingled lots was found to be properly rejected when it could not be determined from which lot the defective units came. See also *Columbia Prods., Inc.*, ASBCA 21172, 78-1 BCA ¶ 13,089, in which the contractor was entitled to an equitable adjustment when the government failed to reduce its verification inspection, as required by the contract, but imposition of a lot-by-lot verification inspection instead of a reduced level was proper when a specified level of nonconformity was found, and *W.C. Fore Trucking, Inc.*, ASBCA 32156, 89-2 BCA ¶ 21,869, in which the government did not follow the sampling procedure set out in the contract. The contractor proved that the sample was too small and was not representative of the complete performance. The government had obtained all of the sample lots from a selected portion of the work. As a result, the contractor was entitled to its costs for additional testing. However, once the specified number of defects is found, the entire agreed-upon sample need not be tested in order to justify rejection of the lot, *A.B.G. Instrument & Eng'g, Inc. v. United States*, 219 Ct. Cl. 381, 593 F.2d 394 (1979). The government, however, may choose to take a reduction in the contract price for individual defective samples so long as the amount subtracted reasonably reflects the reduced value of services performed or products tendered.

Contracts providing for inspection by sampling may not specify all of the details or specific procedures for sample testing. In such cases, reasonable procedures may be used. See *Capital Servs., Inc.*, ASBCA 40510, 91-1 BCA ¶ 23,310, in which the government was held entitled to use a reasonable lot size. In *Pinay Flooring Prods., Inc.*, GSBCA 9286, 91-2 BCA ¶ 23,682, the sampling procedures on prior contracts were held to establish standards under the ambiguous contract requirements. In *Tri-States Serv. Co.*, ASBCA 31139, 90-3 BCA ¶ 23,059, the contract provided for random sampling of job orders but did not specify that random sampling be used to inspect the items produced under the selected job orders. Thus, the board held that the government had properly inspected 100 percent of the services performed in the sample job orders to ascertain whether the contract's quality and timeliness requirements had been met.

Although the government is not prohibited from reinspecting work under the standard inspection clauses, MIL-STD 105 calls for mandatory acceptance of a lot that passes the sampling inspection. Thus, it is improper for the government to resample such a lot, but it may reinspect and reject individual units found to be defective. See *H & H Enters., Inc.*, ASBCA 26864, 86-2 BCA ¶ 18,794, in which the board stated at 94,711:

> [T]he more explicit mandate of MIL-STD 105D for acceptance if a lot passes inspection by sampling controls over any authority that is otherwise implicit in the Inspection article for reinspection of supplies. We emphasize that reinspection of individual units before acceptance, and rejection of defective individual units, is always permissible, but not reinspection of an entire lot by sampling once it has passed inspection.

The board also considered the circumstances under which MIL-STD 105 permits the government to impose tighter sampling inspection standards when "2 out of 5 consecutive lots or batches have been rejected on original inspection" (¶ 8.3.1) or when "lots or batches found unacceptable are resubmitted for reinspection" (¶ 6.4). It found that the government's requirement for the use of stricter testing was improper because an earlier sample lot was found to be improper.

b. Sampling Not Specified

Even if the contract is silent on sampling, sampling may be used to reject all tendered items. The validity of the rejection will depend on the government's using a statistically representative sample plus a rejection rate that adequately indicates significant defects in all the work. See *Mason's Inc. & Mason Lazarus t/a Mason's Inc.*, ASBCA 27326, 86-3 BCA ¶ 19,250 (sample of 13 out of 34 airplane parts was found to be reasonable so as to justify rejection of all 34, although the contract required "100% inspection at origin"), and *Ball, Ball, & Brosamer*, IBCA 2103-N, 93-1 BCA ¶ 25,287 (representative samples that showed bubbling of sealant justified rejection although the contract was silent as to testing).

In *Kingston Constructors Inc.*, ENGBCA 6006, 95-2 BCA ¶ 27,841, *aff'd in part,* 930 F. Supp. 651 (D.D.C. 1996), rejection of an entire lot of 22 transformers was justified because 48 percent of them had failed performance tests. The government could not tolerate a possible failure rate anywhere near that magnitude, because transformer failure would immobilize the rapid transit system in which the transformers were to be used. Compare *Puma Chem. Co.*, GSBCA 5254, 81-1 BCA ¶ 14,844 (government testing of topmost particles of granular drain cleaner instead of well-mixed samples did not "accurately and uniformly" predict the physical characteristics of the entire lot), and *Pams Prods., Inc.*, ASBCA 15847, 72-1 BCA ¶

9401 (inspection samples representing less than three square yards were inadequate to evaluate a 725,000-square-foot surface).

2. First Article Testing

First article testing (sometimes referred to as preproduction testing) is often used when (1) the contract contains performance specifications, (2) the contractor has not previously furnished the items, (3) the contractor has previously furnished the items but there has been some occurrence such as a change or break in production, or (4) "when it is essential to have an approved first article to serve as a manufacturing standard," FAR 9.303. A primary reason for requiring first article testing is to give the government assurance that subsequent production will be acceptable. Thus, the government has no duty to test a first article that has been produced in a plant other than the plant where the production units are to be made, *Yankee Telecommuns. Labs., Inc.*, ASBCA 35403, 89-2 BCA ¶ 21,726. In the absence of a specific contract clause, the government has no right to require first article testing, *Kenyon Magnetics, Inc.*, GSBCA 4769, 77-2 BCA ¶ 12,786. In *Vision Blocks, Inc.*, B-281246, 99-1 CPD ¶ 20, the government properly waived first article testing because the awardee had previously passed first article testing on the same military specifications as in the current contract.

FAR 52.209-3 and FAR 52.209-4 provide standard clauses for first articles with contractor or government testing. Theses clauses clearly state each party's responsibilities. However, if the contract language does not clearly state which party is to conduct the tests, the ambiguity will be construed against the government as the drafter of the document. For example, in *Varo, Inc. v. United States*, 212 Ct. Cl. 432, 548 F.2d 953 (1977), the court held that, although the contract did not expressly state who was to perform the first article tests, the statement that the supplier would "furnish" three lamps for testing implied that the testing would be done by the government. The government may avoid application of this interpretive concept by specifically providing for contractor first article testing in the contract. When a contract clause specifies that a contractor is to conduct the test, the contractor is responsible for selecting the testing conditions and cannot later complain that test results should be disregarded because the conditions were deficient, *Idaho Norland Corp.*, ASBCA 33487, 90-2 BCA ¶ 22,858.

The clauses provide that the government's approval of the first article does not relieve the contractor from "complying with all requirements of specifications and all other conditions of the contract." Approval of the first article merely permits the contractor to proceed with production. Thus, in the case of a convenience termination following the approval of the first article, the contractor would be entitled to recover the reasonable costs of manufacturing production units. When the contractor proceeds with production without approval, the clauses provide that those costs are not recoverable in a termination. See *Basic Tool Co.*, ASBCA 29683, 88-2 BCA

¶ 20,638, in which the board rejected the contractor's claim, after a convenience termination, for costs incurred in manufacturing production units because it had failed to obtain government approval of the work as specified in the contract. The board held that the plain language of the contract clause overrode the fact that the contractor had received a copy of a memorandum from a government quality control representative recommending approval of the first article and that it had received no timely disapproval of the first article. Where the government is negligent in failing to provide first article approval, however, the risk of loss will shift to the government. See *West Point Research, Inc.*, ASBCA 25511, 83-1 BCA ¶ 16,443, in which the contractor was held to be entitled to compensation for the government's delay in testing, but recovery for production costs incurred before first article approval was barred under ¶ (h) of the first article approval clause.

In contrast, the contractor is entitled to recover reasonable costs in producing and testing first articles in the event of a convenience termination, *Seiler Instrument & Mfg. Co.,* ASBCA 44380, 93-1 BCA ¶ 25,436, *recons. denied,* 93-1 BCA ¶ 25,551. See also *Aerospace Swaging & Mfg., Inc.*, ASBCA 38534, 90-2 BCA ¶ 22,834, which also held that while the contractor is entitled to receive the reasonable cost of producing and testing the first article, the government is not liable for costs incurred in attempting to become a "qualified producer."

The test procedure accepted by the government also sets the standard for performance tests, *Baifield Indus., Div. of A-T-O, Inc.*, ASBCA 14582, 72-2 BCA ¶ 9676. See also *Process Equip. Co.*, NASABCA 166-3, 67-1 BCA ¶ 6142, *recons. denied,* 67-2 BCA ¶ 6563 (government approval of a specific test procedure was, in effect, a recognition that such a test was the appropriate method to verify compliance with the specifications of the contract).

The government will be liable if it uses improper testing procedures or delays in conducting a test or notifying a contractor of test results. In *Creative Elec., Inc.*, ASBCA 21498, 79-1 BCA ¶ 13,615, the board held that the government improperly rejected the first article and delayed the contractor's performance for almost eight months when the defects in the first article were correctable and minor. The government's requirement of a higher level of quality than prescribed by the specifications entitled the contractor to an equitable adjustment. Similarly, if the government requires contractor testing prior to government testing, it will be liable if it does not cooperate with the contractor's tests, *Allomatic Indus., Inc.*, ASBCA 30301, 87-1 BCA ¶ 19,380. In *Astro Pak Corp.*, ASBCA 49790, 97-1 BCA ¶ 28,657, *vacated in part on recons.,* 97-2 BCA ¶ 29,106, the government did not unreasonably delay in providing a contractor with a list of deficiencies from a first article test, because the delay was caused by the contractor's failure to provide a test report.

When the contract calls for contractor testing of the first article, the contractor will normally be required to devise the required tests. However, where a test is not feasible because of specific requirements of the specifications, the contractor has no obligation to devise a feasible test, *Sonora Mfg., Inc.*, ASBCA 31587, 91-1 BCA ¶ 23,444 (steering valve assembly on aircraft landing gear had so many different parts capable of leakage that it would be impossible to perform accurate leakage testing on the contract part after installation). In order to establish the "unfeasible test" defense to a default termination, however, the contractor must demonstrate that to satisfy the test requirements would be objectively impossible. When the contractor has the testing responsibility, the government is not liable for delays resulting from justifiable rejection of procedures or facilities, *Telectro Sys. Corp.*, ASBCA 26648, 86-1 BCA ¶ 18,646.

3. Safety Inspections

Contractors are required to comply with general statutory and regulatory safety requirements. In addition, the Accident Prevention clause in FAR 52.236-13, used for construction contracts, requires:

> (a) The contractor shall provide and maintain work environments and procedures which will (1) safeguard the public and Government personnel, property, materials, supplies, and equipment exposed to Contractor operations and activities; (2) avoid interruptions of Government operations and delays in project completion dates; and (3) control costs in the performance of this contract.

This clause was changed in 1991. Previously, the contractor had the obligation to protect the lives and health of "employees and other persons." The term "employees" was taken out and replaced with "Government personnel, property, materials, supplies, and equipment." The litigation surrounding the government inspection of safety requirement is concerned with (1) whether the government was obligated to conduct such inspections, and (2) whether the government is liable for negligence in the conduct of inspections.

a. Responsibility for Safety Inspections

Although the government has a broad right to inspect, it is generally held that that does not impose upon it a duty to inspect. The Inspection of Supplies clause (FAR 52.246-2), the Inspection of Services clause (FAR 52.246-4), and the Inspection of Construction clause (FAR 52.246-12) all provide for "the safe and convenient performance of [inspection] duties." See *Zocco v. Department of the Army*, 791 F. Supp. 595 (E.D.N.C. 1992) (government's right to inspect for employees' safety did not obligate it to do so). In *Murdock v. United States*, 951 F.2d 907 (8th Cir. 1991), *cert. denied,* 505 U. S. 1206 (1992), the court rejected the contractor's argument that the government's right to inspect established a mandatory duty to make safety inspections and that the failure to do this was tantamount to negligence. The court reasoned that, although the government had a right to inspect, it had delegated most of the responsibilities for ensuring safety to the contractor. Thus, the government did not maintain sufficient control over the safety issue to be held accountable for injuries at the excavation site.

The government's exercise of its right to make safety inspections does not relieve the contractor of its responsibilities, *Larsen v. Empresas El Yunque, Inc.*, 812 F.2d 14 (1st Cir. 1986); *Williams v. United States*, 50 F.3d 299 (4th Cir. 1993). See also *Hall v. General Servs. Admin.*, 825 F. Supp. 427 (D.N.H. 1993) (government supervisory inspections did not render it liable for a worker's injuries at construction site).

The nature and scope of government safety inspections is a discretionary matter, *Layton v. United States*, 984 F.2d 1496 (8th Cir. 1993) (delegation of safety inspection to contractor with government spot checks discretionary act). In *Duff v. United States*, 999 F.2d 1280 (8th Cir. 1993), the court held that the decision to select a particular contractor also falls within the discretionary act exception. See also *Irving v. United States*, 162 F.3d 154 (1st Cir. 1998), *cert. denied,* 528 U. S. 812 (1999); *Feyers v. United States*, 749 F.2d 1222 (6th Cir. 1984), *cert. denied*, 471 U.S. 1125 (1985); and *Judy v. United States Dep't of Labor*, 864 F.2d 83 (8th Cir. 1988). These cases should be contrasted with *Phillips v. United States*, 956 F.2d 1071 (11th Cir. 1992), in which the court found the Army Corps of Engineers accountable for the employee's injuries. In this case, the Army did not delegate its mandated safety responsibilities to the contractor, nor did it have merely a limited supervisory inspection obligation. The government inspectors had mandatory inspection duties and were at fault for failing to ensure the inspection of scaffolds.

b. Government Liability for Negligence

Although the government is generally not obligated to conduct safety inspections, it may be liable if it actually conducts inspections and does so in a negligent manner. Since any negligence suit would be brought under the Federal Tort Claims Act (FTCA), 28 U.S.C. § 2680(a), the government will not be liable for negligence if the inspection is classified as a discretionary inspection. See 28 U.S.C. § 2680(a), providing that the government is not liable for

> [a]ny claim based upon an act or omission of an employee of the Government, exercising due care, in the execution of a statute or regulation, whether or not such statute or regulation be valid, or based upon the exercise or performance or the failure to exercise or perform a discretionary function or duty on the part of a federal agency or an employee of the Government, whether or not the discretion involved be abused.

In *United States v. Gaubert*, 499 U.S. 315 (1991), the Supreme Court established a two-prong test for determining whether a government employee's actions or omissions were discretionary. First, the courts must decide whether any statute, regulation, or public policy permits any discretion to the employee as to how to do his or her job. If not, then the government could be held liable for damages. If so, then the inquiry turns to whether the discretion involves policy choices. In deciding what constitutes a policy choice, the Court stated at 324:

> When established governmental policy, as expressed or implied by statute, regulation, or agency guidelines, allows a Government agent to exercise discretion, it must be presumed that the agent's acts are grounded in policy when exercising that discretion. For a complaint to survive a motion to dismiss, it must allege facts which would support a finding that the challenged actions are not the kind of conduct that can be said to be grounded in the policy of the regulatory regime. The focus of the inquiry is not on the agent's subjective intent in exercising the discretion conferred by statute or regulation, but on the nature of the actions taken and on whether they are susceptible to policy analysis.

In *Gaubert*, the Court held that the discretionary function exception does not apply where a federal regulation "specifically prescribes a course of action for an employee to follow [because] the employee has no rightful option but to adhere to the directive" quoting *Berkovitz v. United States*, 486 U. S. 531 (1988). See also *McMichael v. United States*, 856 F.2d 1026 (8th Cir. 1988), in which the court held the government responsible under the FTCA for injuries and deaths resulting from an accident because the contract incorporated a 51-step checklist to ensure that the safety of the workers was maintained. One of these specifications required the government inspector to shut down the manufacturing plant during an electrical storm. The inspector's primary responsibility was to ensure compliance with the specifications, but safety concerns were also an important aspect of his duties. The court held that the government was responsible when the inspector failed to shut down the plant as required by the contract. See also *Appley Bros. v. United States*, 164 F.3d 1164 (8th Cir. 1999). Compare *Tracor/MBA, Inc. v. United States*, 933 F.2d 663 (8th Cir. 1991), in which the court upheld a summary judgment for lack of subject matter jurisdiction because the injuries were caused by discretionary activity driven by policy considerations. A DoD employee filed suit for injuries incurred in a fire allegedly caused by the quality assurance representative's failure to follow the 47-part safety procedure incorporated into the contract. See ¶¶ (b) and (d) of the Safety Precautions for Ammunition and Explosives clause in DFARS 252.223-7002. In holding that the government was not responsible, the court distinguished this case from *McMichael* on the grounds that the 47-step checklist did not mandate any specific procedures but merely outlined a "very general course of conduct for the inspectors to follow." *See also Kirchmann v. United States*, 8 F.3d 1273 (8th Cir. 1993) (government did not exercise type of day-to-day control that would allow contractor personnel to be considered government employees for purposes of FTCA).

Under the *Gaubert* analysis, the courts are split as to whether the word "shall" in ¶(d) of the Accident Prevention clause at FAR 52.236-13 renders actions taken by the contracting officer's representative mandatory. This paragraph states in part:

> Whenever the Contracting Officer becomes aware of any noncompliance with these requirements or any condition which poses a serious or imminent danger to the health or safety of the public or Government personnel, the Contracting Officer shall notify the Contractor orally, with written confirmation, and request immediate initiation of corrective action.

It should be noted that FAR 2.101, Definitions, states: "Shall means the imperative."

In *Routh v. United States*, 941 F.2d 853 (9th Cir. 1991), the court held that the word "shall" in this paragraph was not specific enough to provide a policy justification, such as concern over costs of safety or risk of loss. Therefore, the government could be held liable for damages incurred due to the resulting injuries. However, in *Doud v. United States*, 797 F. Supp. 138 (N.D.N.Y. 1992), the court rejected an injured worker's argument that FAR 52.236-13 imposed mandatory language, stating at 144:

> FAR Section 52.236-13, as it is incorporated in the contract does not impose any mandatory obligation on the United States with respect to the method the Government's employees use to detect noncompliance nor does it specify any particular course of action, other than notification, once such non-compliance is found. Rather, it leaves such determinations entirely to the discretion of the Government's employees . . . . [E]ven if the Government's employees negligently performed their inspections as plaintiff alleges, this fact alone would not remove the challenged conduct from the protection of the discretionary function exception.

See also *Ayer v. United States*, 902 F.2d 1038 (1st Cir. 1990) (Air Force decision not to conduct adequate safety inspections and use caution was a policy choice and thus the government was not liable for injuries). *Noel v. United States*, 893 F. Supp. 1410 (N.D. Cal. 1995), distinguished *Ayer* because *Ayer* was based on a regulation, but no similar regulation applied to *Noel*. In *Clark v. United States*, 805 F. Supp. 84 (D.N.H. 1992), the court held that the government had no affirmative duty to issue a stop-work order for safety deficiencies because ¶ (d) of the Accident Prevention clause stating that the contracting officer "may" issue a stop-work order is discretionary language. On the other hand, where the government orders a work stoppage as a reasonable safety precaution under the Accident Prevention clause, the contractor will not be entitled to an equitable adjustment. See *HVAC Constr. Co., v. United States*, 28 Fed. Cl. 690 (1993), in which the contractor's claim for the costs of a work stoppage to remove and reinstall a barrier that contained asbestos was denied because the order was a reasonable safety precaution within the government's rights under the contract.

II. REJECTION, ACCEPTANCE, AND REMEDIES FOR DEFECTS

Rejection and acceptance are key points in the government's enforcement of the contract's quality requirements. The contractor is not entitled to be paid the contract price if the work has been properly rejected. In addition, a proper rejection can form the basis for a default termination. The government's rights to obtain correction of defects or reductions in the contract price for defective work are also triggered by rejection of the work. Similarly, acceptance of the work affects a number of legal relationships. Once the work has been accepted, the contractor is entitled to payment of the price. Title to supplies passes to the government upon acceptance and, with certain exceptions, the work may not be rejected once it has been accepted. In addition, warranty periods may begin with acceptance. Therefore it is essential to determine whether work has been properly rejected or has been accepted. This section first explores the legal rules applicable to rejection and acceptance and concludes with the government's remedies for defective work discovered prior to acceptance.

A. Rejection

Rejection is the means by which the government officially notifies the contractor that the work is defective and that it is not being accepted. FAR 46.407 spells out the government's policy concerning rejection of the work and states that the contracting officer "should" reject nonconforming work but specifies additional circumstances where acceptance may be allowed. The following material first analyzes the types of defects which permit rejection. The issues related to proving that defects exist are then considered. Next, the procedures for giving notice of rejection are treated. Finally, the conditions which limit the government's right to reject are examined.

1. Rejection Standards

Whether the government has the right to reject work depends on the type of defect, the nature of the specification, and when the defect is discovered. This subsection first considers the concept of strict compliance. It then deals with the impact of the specifications on the government's right of rejection. The subsection concludes with the limited circumstances in which substantial performance precludes rejection of the entire item.

a. Strict Compliance

The government is generally entitled to enforce strict compliance with contract requirements. This rule serves to ensure that the contractor's performance will satisfy the government's needs, that public funds will not be improperly expended, and that the integrity of the public bidding system will not be compromised. In *Ideal Rest. Supply Co.,* VACAB 570, 67-1 BCA ¶ 6237, the board implied that one purpose of strict compliance is to discourage a contractor from submitting a low bid while intending to use less-expensive materials than those required by the contract. In *Carothers Constr. Co.*, ASBCA 41268, 93-2 BCA ¶ 25,628, the board stated, "The Government is entitled to insist on strict compliance with its specifications, and has no obligation to accept substitutes, even if the substitutes are equivalent or superior to that which is specified." It has also been held that a contractor "may not substitute its judgment" in complying with contract requirements, "regardless of the quality of its substituted product," *J.L. Malone & Assocs.*, VABCA 2335, 88-3 BCA ¶ 20,894, *aff'd*, 879 F.2d 841 (Fed. Cir. 1989); *Bhandari-Davis-Eckert, J.V.,* VABCA 3475, 93-1 BCA ¶ 25,456. Similarly, a contractor cannot use an alternative method of performance that has not been disclosed to or approved by the government, *4-D & Chizoma, Inc.*, ASBCA 49550, 00-1 BCA ¶ 30,782; *The Davis Group, Inc.*, ASBCA 51832, 00-2 BCA ¶ 30,985 (doors proposed by contractor were properly rejected by the government because contractor failed to obtain a required notarized certification from an officer of the company manufacturing the doors stating that the doors met specifications). In *Agro-Lawn Sys., Inc.*, ASBCA 49648, 98-1 BCA ¶ 29,635, sod at a national cemetery not watered until approximately 28 hours after placement was correctly rejected as not meeting specifications because watering "immediately" after placement was deemed a design specification that must be strictly construed, otherwise there could be long-term adverse effects.

Strict compliance has been upheld even though the requirements "are difficult, redundant, exceed what is required for a satisfactory result, or differ from common practice," *White & McNeil Excavating, Inc.*, IBCA 2448, 92-1 BCA ¶ 24,534, *appeal after remand*, 93-1 BCA ¶ 25,286, *aff'd*, 996 F.2d 1235 (Fed. Cir. 1993). See also *R.B. Wright Constr. Co. v. United States*, 919 F.2d 1569 (Fed. Cir. 1990); *Leonard Pevar Co.*, VABCA 1308, 78-2 BCA ¶ 13,468; and *ETA Tech. Corp.*, ASBCA 48417, 97- 1 BCA ¶ 28,666 (failure to comply with contractually specified college degrees even though employee had technical experience).

Rejection of work not in strict compliance with the specifications does not require the government to prove that it will suffer harm from the defects. For example, rejection was sustained where meat was frozen more slowly than specified in *Newark Boneless Meat Prods., Inc.*, ASBCA 22132, 78-2 BCA ¶ 13,229. The board in *Newark* stated that "[w]hether not achieving compliance with the specifications did or did not have a 'major' effect on serviceability is immaterial." In *Arrow Lacquer Corp.*, ASBCA 4667, 58-2 BCA ¶ 2003, the board condoned rejection of paint that was slightly different from the specified color even though it was to be used as an undercoat. The logic behind these cases is that "the Government is ordinarily entitled to get the features it has specified and it is not within the province of a contractor to substitute its judgment by determining that something different is suitable and will be furnished," *D.E.W., Inc.*, ASBCA 17030, 72-2 BCA ¶ 9494. See *BECO Corp.*, ASBCA 27296, 83-2 BCA ¶ 16,724 (neither the contractor's unilateral declaration that the work was substantially completed nor the fact that defects were minor in nature affects the government's right to enforce strict compliance), and *C.H. Hyperbarics, Inc.*, ASBCA 49375, 04-1 BCA ¶ 32,561 (government has right to strict compliance with provision requiring valves to be of the same manufacturer as other parts of the product—even though valves furnished were arguably superior).

b. Nature of Specifications

The government's right to reject work for failure to strictly comply with a contract requirement is dependent on the requirement being (1) specifically called out in the contract and (2) susceptible to some form of precise measurement. Where either of these requirements are not present, the government may only reject if the work will not be suitable for its intended purpose. Thus, the strict compliance rule will be enforced where the contract contains precise design (dimensions, tolerances, materials, etc.) or performance (weight, speed, etc.) requirements. Although it has been stated that performance specifications are not as strictly enforced as design requirements, *Falcon Jet Corp.*, DOTBCA 78-32, 82-1 BCA ¶ 15,447, it is the nature of the requirement as opposed to the specification type that determines the right to reject for failure to strictly comply.

(1) Specifications Not Suited to Strict Compliance

In general, specifications are not suited for application of the strict compliance doctrine if they state a requirement in either absolute or imprecise terms. Specifications containing absolute requirements are usually enforced using subjective standards because the absolute requirement cannot literally be attained. See, for example, *Mid-American Eng'g & Mfg.*, ASBCA 20939, 78-1 BCA ¶ 12,870, where the specifications required the contractor to provide a "bubble free" compound. The board recognized that absolute compliance with the government specifications was impossible and relied on industry standards to determine the level of performance. Compare *Carmon Constr., Inc. v. General Servs Admin.*, GSBCA 11227, 92-2 BCA ¶ 25,001, sustaining the rejection of castings where the contract for the repair and renovation of a historic staircase stated that "all new castings shall exactly match existing castings."

Imprecisely stated requirements are also interpreted subjectively because they cannot be strictly construed. In *Dirigo Compass & Instrument Co.*, ASBCA 9162, 65-2 BCA ¶ 4938, the board found the standard of performance from a list of "subjective" deficiencies compiled by the government and agreed to by the contractor. The government admitted that the specification was "loosely written" and the board concluded that rejection of the second preproduction sample was permissible only on the basis of defects that were on the prior list of defects or found explicitly in the contract specifications. In *Bonny Prods., Inc.*, GSBCA 4577, 76-2 BCA ¶ 12,158, the board felt the handles of can openers to determine whether or not they met the level of performance, which required that the handles have "rounded surfaces, free of sharp edges, for comfortable operation." Since the handles did not meet this level of performance, the contractor's appeal was denied.

(2) Brand Name or Equal Specifications

A brand name or equal specification is one where a specific brand name is called for but the contractor is given the option of furnishing an equal item. See FAR 52.211-6 for the Brand Name or Equal clause. Such specifications are required to indicate the features of the brand name item that are important to the government—often designated as salient characteristics. See FAR 11.104 stating:

> (a) While the use of performance specifications is preferred to encourage offerors to propose innovative solutions, the use of brand name or equal purchase descriptions may be advantageous under certain circumstances.
>
> (b) Brand name or equal purchase descriptions must include, in addition to the brand name, a general description of those salient physical, functional, or performance characteristics of the brand name item that an "equal" item must meet to be acceptable for award. Use brand name or equal descriptions when the salient characteristics are firm requirements.

Thus, the nature of brand name or equal specifications is such that the government will have the right to reject a proposed substitution if it does not meet the salient characteristics or is not an equal. The strict compliance rule applies to precise design or performance requirements specifically designated as salient characteristics, *J.K. Richardson Co.*, ASBCA 46309, 94-2 BCA ¶ 26,900; *EZ Constr. Co.*, ASBCA 31510, 87-3 BCA ¶ 20,186; *Central Mech., Inc.*, ASBCA 29360, 84-3 BCA ¶ 17,674. If the contractor offers an item without specifying its characteristics and then substitutes an allegedly equal item, the substituted item need only be of the same standard of quality and the functional equivalent of the offered brand name item, *Jack Stone Co. v. United States*, 170 Ct. Cl. 281, 344 F. 2d 370 (1965). In that case, it has been held that the salient characteristics can be "inferred," *Overstreet Elec. Co.*, ASBCA 52401, 00-2 BCA ¶ 30,981 at 152,910, *aff'd*, 20 Fed. Appx. 878 (Fed. Cir. 2001). See *Sherman R. Smoot Corp.*, ASBCA 52150, 03-1 BCA ¶ 32,073, where a substituted item was rejected because it did not meet the product's inferred salient characteristics. The *Jack Stone* rule would also appear to be applicable when the brand name or equal specification fails to enumerate salient characteristics, whether or not specifically identified as such. However, in one unusual case it was held that even though salient characteristics were not specified, a contractor should have known that a particular characteristic of a brand name was important and, therefore, failure to meet it was grounds for rejection of the proffered substitute, *Bay West Elec. Co.*, NASABCA 287-4, 88-3 BCA ¶ 20,598.

(3) Brand Name and Proprietary Specifications

A brand name specification is one where a brand name item is specified and the words "or equal" or their equivalent are not included. A proprietary specification is one where a brand name is not specified but the specifications can only be met by a specific brand name product. In both cases, the question arises as to whether the strict compliance rule will require the contractor to furnish the brand name product specified or described or furnish an equal item. FAR 11.105 limits the use of brand name or proprietary specifications as follows:

> Agency requirements shall not be written so as to require a particular brand name, product, or a feature of a product, peculiar to one manufacturer, thereby precluding consideration of a product manufactured by another company, unless—

> (a) The particular brand name, product, or feature is essential to the Government's requirements, and market research indicates other companies' similar products, or products lacking the particular feature, do not meet, or cannot be modified to meet, the agency's needs;
>
> (b) The authority to contract without providing for full and open competition is supported by the required justifications and approvals (see 6.302-1); and
>
> (c) The basis for not providing for maximum practicable competition is documented in the file when the acquisition is awarded using simplified acquisition procedures.

In construction contracts, this issue is addressed directly by ¶ (a) of the Material and Workmanship clause at FAR 52.236-5, which provides:

> References in the specifications to equipment, material, articles, or patented processes by trade name, make or catalog number, shall be regarded as establishing a standard of quality and shall not be construed as limiting competition. The Contractor may, at its option, use any equipment, material, article, or process that, in the judgment of the Contracting Officer, is equal to that named in the specifications, unless otherwise specifically provided in this contract.

The reach of this clause was extended to proprietary specifications in *William R. Sherwin v. United States*, 193 Ct. Cl. 962, 436 F.2d 992 (1971). The court reasoned that there was a "long-established policy against drafting specifications in ways which would tend to eliminate competition for the furnishing of items to be used in the performance of public construction contracts." In *Sherwin*, the contract included the standard Material and Workmanship clause. The court held that the government erred in not permitting the use of a functionally equivalent item. In *Harvey Constr. Co.*, ASBCA 39310, 92-3 BCA ¶ 25,162, the board stated at 125,414:

> The fact that a brand name is not called out in the specification does not prevent us from enforcing the Government's admission that [the specification] was proprietary. As correctly argued by [the contractor], when there is a detailed description of the characteristics of an item that is manufactured by only one source, the courts and the boards will consider the specification to have called out the brand name.

In order to take advantage of the *Sherwin* rule, the contractor is required to show that (1) the specification was proprietary, (2) information was submitted to the government indicating the features of the substitute product, and (3) the substitute product was the same standard of quality as the specified or described product, *Blount Bros. Corp.*, ASBCA 31202, 88-3 BCA ¶ 20,878. A specification is considered to be proprietary if only one product can meet its requirements, *Manning Elec. & Repair Co. v. United States*, 22 Cl. Ct. 240 (1991). It has been held that a specification drafted around a specific product is not a proprietary specification if, at the time it was drafted, another product could have met its requirements, *C&D Constr., Inc.*, ASBCA 48590, 97-2 BCA ¶ 29,283; *R&M Mech. Contractors, Inc.*, DOTCAB 75-51, 76-2

BCA ¶ 12,084. See also *J.R. Youngdale Constr. Co.*, ASBCA 27793, 88-3 BCA ¶ 21,009, in which the board indicated that it did not believe the specification was proprietary but decided the case on the assumption that it was. There, another product that met all the requirements was available when the specification was drafted but was not available at the time of performance.

Rejection of a proposed substitute is not proper merely because it does not meet one of the specified characteristics or one of the features of an identified product. In *Eslin Co.*, AGBCA 90-222-1, 93-1 BCA ¶ 25,321, the specification for windows was written around a specific product. One of the requirements was that the frames were to be aluminum. The board held that it was improper to reject the non-aluminum substitute, which met all the "essential performance criteria" and was a "functional equivalent" of the described product. However, where the contract clearly indicated that a specific feature would not be accepted, rejection of a substitute containing that feature was upheld, *Baker & Co.*, ASBCA 21896, 78-1 BCA ¶ 13,116. In *Youngdale*, the board refused to permit substitution of a similar product that deviated in some respects because all of the listed characteristics were considered by the user of the product to be essential. See also *Overstreet Elec. Co.,* ASBCA 52401, 00-2 BCA ¶ 30,981, *aff'd*, 20 Fed. Appx. 878 (Fed. Cir. 2001) (government's rejection of substituted military airfield beacons was proper because the beacons were not the functional equivalent of the beacon type identified in the specifications, which were essential for guiding pilots to the airfield at night and in low visibility conditions).

The contractor has the burden of proving that the proposed substitute is of the same standard of quality and is the functional equivalent of the specified or described product. In *R.D. Lowman Gen. Contractor, Inc.*, ASBCA 36961, 91-1 BCA ¶ 23,456, the substitute was properly rejected because it did not meet the strength and durability attributes of the specified brand name. Compare *D.E.W., Inc.,* ASBCA 36698, 89-1 BCA ¶ 21,312, involving the same products, where the substitute was permitted on the basis that it was the functional equivalent. In *Lowman*, the board distinguished its holdings on the basis of requirements in the specifications in that case, which differed from the earlier *D.E.W.* specification. The contractor carried the burden in *R.R. Mongeau Eng'rs, Inc.,* ASBCA 29341, 87-2 BCA ¶ 19,809 (substitute differing from specified characteristics was functional equivalent), and *Santa Fe Eng'rs, Inc.*, ASBCA 33510, 88-3 BCA ¶ 20,933 (substitute found to be the same standard of quality as described product).

Other contract provisions have also been held to have established a standard of quality, with the result that only functional requirements must be met. In *Page Constr. Co.*, AGBCA 92-191-1, 93-3 BCA ¶ 26,060, references to material by brand name in a contract that permitted substitution of approved equal equipment were found to establish a standard of quality. See also *Consolidated Diesel Elec. Co. v. United States,* 209 Ct. Cl. 521, 533 F.2d 556 (1976), where acceptance of a contractor's technical proposal that included four possible engine combinations allowed the contractor to substitute one combination for another since they were functionally equivalent and both engines were included in the government's qualified products list, and *Wismer & Becker Contracting Eng'rs,* DOTCAB 76-24, 78-1 BCA ¶ 13,199, *recons. denied,* 78-2 BCA ¶ 13,395, in which a special clause in a supply contract providing for "equal" items was held to establish a standard of quality requiring acceptance of functionally equivalent items. However, see *American Elec. Contracting Corp. v. United States*, 217 Ct. Cl. 338, 579 F.2d 602 (1978), in which the court held that a special standard of quality clause in a supply contract describing the item by proprietary characteristics was limited by another special clause permitting the use of only qualified products that had passed tests prior to bid opening. The court held that the government was entitled to reject a functionally equivalent item that had not been qualified because this latter requirement was a clear limitation on the standard of quality clause.

c. Limitations on Strict Compliance

Limitations on the strict compliance rule have been adopted in two situations. Under certain circumstances, the government may not reject work under construction contracts if the work has been substantially performed. A similar rule has been applied to the rejection of first articles.

(1) Construction Contracts

The strict compliance rule is applicable to construction contracts. In *Troup Bros., Inc. v. United States*, 224 Ct. Cl. 594, 643 F.2d 719 (1980), the court implied that because the government was entitled to strict compliance, the contractor's argument that work required by the specifications was not necessary was irrelevant. However, the government's remedies for failure to strictly comply may depend on when the contractor is notified and the relationship of the cost of correcting the defects to the government's damage.

When a potential noncompliance is discovered before performance, the government has broad latitude. It has been held proper for the government to reject shop drawings proposing work not strictly in accordance with the specifications, *Robert McMullan & Son, Inc.*, ASBCA 21159, 77-1 BCA ¶ 12,453. See also *Stallings & McCorvey, Inc.*, ASBCA 22668, 78-2 BCA ¶ 13,339 (contractor must comply with government requirements regardless of their technical soundness), and *Allen M. Campbell Co.*, ASBCA 16934, 72-2 BCA ¶ 9639 (a method specified by the government must be followed even though the contractor's proposed method would have met the government's needs). Rejection of proposed materials not in strict compliance has also been approved, *Tectonics, Inc. of Fla.*, ASBCA 28609, 84-1 BCA ¶ 17,153 (face brick was properly rejected for color discrepancy even though conforming in function and quality); *Delta Lines Constr. Co.*, ASBCA 21485, 79-1 BCA ¶ 13,599 (government was entitled to strict compliance even though a less-expensive substitute was available). The government is also entitled to order the contractor to perform rehabilitation work in a sequence that is convenient to the government when the specifications call for minimum interference, *Wil-Freds, Inc.*, DOTCAB 74-10, 74-2 BCA ¶ 10,948, and to refuse a contractor's request that a substitute material be used, *Polyphase Contracting Corp.*, ASBCA 11787, 68-1 BCA ¶ 6759.

After the work has been performed, application of the strict compliance rule to require correction is permitted when the cost of correction does not involve economic waste, *Eller Constr., Inc.*, AGBCA 77-171-4, 83-2 BCA ¶ 16,560. Nevertheless, contractors have been required to tear out and replace work not complying with specifications without discussion of this factor. See *Haas & Haynie Corp.*, GSBCA 5530, 84-2 BCA ¶ 17,446 (air conditioning components); *Castle Constr. Co.*, ASBCA 28401, 84-1 BCA ¶ 17,041 (plumbing fixtures); *Beutt Constr. Co.*, ASBCA 20000, 75-1 BCA ¶ 11,208 (concrete footings); *Stamell Constr. Co.*, DOTCAB 68-27I, 75-1 BCA ¶ 11,087 (concrete work); and *K & M Constr.*, ENGBCA 3060, 72-1 BCA ¶ 9195 (hinges). Similarly, the strict compliance rule has been used to justify requiring substantial repairs to work not meeting the specifications, *COAC, Inc.*, IBCA 1004-9-73, 74-2 BCA ¶ 10,982, *recons. denied,* 75-1 BCA ¶ 11,104 (government is entitled to specify reasonable method of repair in order to attain contract compliance). In *S.S. Silberblatt, Inc. v. United States*, 193 Ct. Cl. 269, 433 F.2d 1314 (1970), the court rejected the argument that "the Government should have permitted [the contractor] to proceed according to its own dictates and then settled the matter by a downward adjustment in the contract price; this in the spirit of conformity with alleged trade practice," reasoning that the contract contained clear grade requirements and that the trade practice in the building industry could not override the contractor's obligation to strictly comply. The court rejected the argument that a constructive change occurred when the contracting officer insisted on strict compliance with the specifications rather than allowing the contractor to meet a substantial performance test, *H.L.C. & Assocs. Constr. Co. v. United States*, 176 Ct. Cl. 285, 367 F.2d 586 (1966). The court reasoned that two requisite elements for the test of substantial performance, forfeiture and economic waste, were not present, because the contractor had been paid in full.

The concept of economic waste has been applied by the court when the repair or replacement is economically wasteful and the government receives work that substantially complies with the specifications. In such a case, the government's remedy is limited to a price adjustment based on loss of value or savings to the contractor. In *Granite Constr. Co. v. United States*, 962 F.2d 998 (Fed. Cir. 1992), *cert. denied,* 506 U.S. 1048 (1993), the court stated at 1006-07:

> We recognize that the government generally has the right to insist on performance in strict compliance with the contract specifications and may require a contractor to correct nonconforming work. *S.S. Silberblatt, Inc. v. United States,* [193 Ct. Cl. 269] 433 F.2d 1314 (1970). However, there is ample authority for holding that the government should not be permitted to direct the replacement of work in situations where the cost of correction is economically wasteful and the work is otherwise adequate for its intended purpose. In such cases, the government is only

> entitled to a downward adjustment in the contract price. *Toombs & Co.*, ASBCA 34590, 91-1 BCA ¶ 23,403.

This reversed the prior decision of the board, which required Granite to remove and replace the waterstop. Since Granite had already removed and replaced the waterstop, the court held it was entitled to an adjustment for this expense. In *Ball, Ball & Brosamer, Inc.*, IBCA 2103-N, 93-1 BCA ¶ 25,287, the board stated that although the "Government is entitled to insist upon strict compliance . . . it cannot direct replacement of work when the cost of correction is economically wasteful and the work is adequate for its intended purpose. Instead its remedy is a contract price adjustment." See *Valley Asphalt Corp.*, ASBCA 17595, 74-2 BCA ¶ 10,680, in which the government was awarded nominal damages because no loss of value was established and there was no indication that the government would attempt correction. See also *Toombs & Co.*, ASBCA 34590, 91-1 BCA ¶ 23,403, in which the "rule of economic waste" was held to limit the right of the government to require replacement of nonconforming work. The remedies to which the government was entitled in *Toombs* were either damages for diminished value of the nonconforming work or a reduction of the contract price for the cost saved by the contractor. Similarly, in *George Ledford Constr., Inc.*, ENGBCA 6268, 98-2 ¶ 30,016, rejection of concrete slabs and planters and demands for replacement of the slabs and planters in strict compliance with specifications were found to be unreasonable because the government failed to consider whether the defects could be repaired or were non-obvious and minor, and whether replacement instead of repair constituted economic waste. See also *Donohoe Constr. Co.*, ASBCA 47310, 98-2 ¶ 30,076, *recons. denied,* 99-1 BCA ¶ 30,387 (requirement that the contractor reinstall concrete wall panels so that the beveled edges all pointed north and were essentially smooth were unreasonable and constituted economic waste because the overall quality met contract specifications, the changes were aesthetic, and the majority of the panels would be obscured from sight), and *Jimenez, Inc.*, VABCA 6351, 02-2 BCA ¶ 32,019, (rejection denied because the deficiencies were relatively minor and might have been repaired or corrected). These cases should be contrasted with *Fire Sec. Sys., Inc. v. General Servs. Admin.*, GSBCA 12120, 97-2 BCA ¶ 28,994, *recons. denied,* 97-2 BCA ¶ 29,186, which held it was not economically wasteful for the government to insist that a contractor replace class B wiring to initiating devices in a fire protection system with class A wiring as required under the contract, because the contractor did not prove that the class B wiring provided the requisite degree of reliability called for in the contract specification.

(2) First Articles

In contracts requiring the submission of a first article, the first article may not be disapproved because it is not in strict compliance with the specifications. Rather, the proper standard is whether the defects in the first article are so serious as to demonstrate that the contractor cannot produce an item meeting the specifications. The reason for this rule is ¶ (d) of the first article clause at FAR 52.209-4, which provides:

> If the Contractor fails to deliver any first article on time, or the Contracting Officer disapproves any first article, the Contractor shall be deemed to have failed to make delivery within the meaning of the Default clause of this contract.

In *National Aviation Elecs., Inc.*, ASBCA 18256, 74-2 BCA ¶ 10,677, a default termination was found improper due, in part, to the government's rejection of a first article with easily correctable defects. The board stated at 50,752:

> The first article approval clause does not give the government the right to disapprove a first article for any noncompliance with specifications that would be a valid reason for rejection of supplies tendered for delivery under the contract. Ordinarily the primary purpose for requiring first article submission is to prove the capability of the contractor to produce end products that will meet the contract requirements. . . . Deficiencies in a first article that are correctable in production are not a valid basis for an outright disapproval of a first article, and, in recognition of this, the first article approval clause expressly provides for conditional approval. The contract does not provide for subjecting the contractor to such a severe forfeiture as a default termination without any opportunity to correct defects when the only defects in the first article are of such a nature as to be correctable in production.

The First Article Approval clause litigated in this case was similar to the FAR 52.209-4 clause, which provides the procedures for the approval of first articles.

In *Advanced Precision Indus., Inc.*, ASBCA 34676, 89-2 BCA ¶ 21,597, the board held a default termination improper because the problems with the first articles were easily correctable or were the result of Army-drafted defective specifications. See also *Defense Tech. Corp.*, ASBCA 39551, 91-3 BCA ¶ 24,189, in which the board held that first articles may not be rejected if the defects are easily correctable. In *Bailey Specialized Bldgs., Inc. v. United States*, 186 Ct. Cl. 71, 404 F.2d 355 (1968), the court reached a similar result by reasoning that a preproduction model was not a deliverable end item under the contract and, therefore, could not be the basis of a default termination for failing to comply with the delivery schedule. However, this contract did not contain a First Article Approval clause, which in some situations would justify immediate termination for default if the contractor either fails to deliver any first article on time or delivers an unacceptable first article.

The contractor must prove that the defects in the first article were easily correctable in order to show that termination was improper, *Marvin Eng'g Co.*, ASBCA 27016, 84-2 BCA ¶ 17,401. See also *James Elecs., Inc.*, ASBCA 43505, 93-2 BCA ¶ 25,677, in which the board held that the contractor did not meet its burden of proving that the defects in the first articles could be easily corrected in production. Where the contractor delivers first articles with "critical and significant deficiencies . . . termination for default has been held to be proper," *West Point Research, Inc.*, ASBCA 25511, 83-1 BCA ¶ 16,443.

2. *Proving Noncompliance*

When the government rejects the work, it has the burden of going forward with evidence that the contract requirements have not been met, *Hardeman-Monier-Hutcherson (J.V.)*, ASBCA 11785, 67-1 BCA ¶ 6210 (contractor was entitled to an equitable adjustment for extra costs resulting from rejection of steel that the government failed to prove did not meet contract requirements). In *Inter-West, Ltd.*, DOTBCA 2238, 92-1 BCA ¶ 24,601, *opinion withdrawn on other grounds*, 92-3 BCA ¶ 25,073, *aff'd,* 996 F.2d 1235 (Fed Cir. 1993), the board stated that "where the Government holds the contractor responsible for nonconforming work, the Government bears the burden of persuasion that the rejected work was not in compliance with the contract requirements." In *Ben M. White Co.*, ASBCA 36643, 90-1 BCA ¶ 22,420, the board found that the government did not prove that a leaking patio was caused by "flashing" incorrectly installed by the contractor. In fact, the government's evidence was weak, while the contractor presented substantial evidence in its favor. In *Fraton, Inc.*, ASBCA 32935, 87-1 BCA ¶ 19,613, the board stated that the government "bears the burden of proving that the work which it rejected and required the [contractor] to correct did not conform to the contract requirements." In *Sigma Constr. Co.*, ASBCA 37040, 91-2 BCA ¶ 23,926, the contract required the contractor to have protective covering for concrete, which it did not have. The board held that the government, in rejecting the concrete as damaged, had the burden of proving that the rain caused the concrete not to conform to the contract requirements. See also *Ramar Co.*, ASBCA 16060, 72-2 BCA ¶ 9644 (the government failed to establish that leaks from manhole covers were the result of poor workmanship by the contractor rather than poor design or fabrication by the government); *Donohoe Constr. Co.,* ASBCA 47310, 98-2 BCA ¶ 30,076, *recons. denied,* 99-1 BCA ¶ 30,387 (deduction from contractor's payment for work performed by a follow-on contractor improper, because government failed to prove that contractor was responsible for damage or had performed work that did not comply with the specifications); *Duran Constr., Co.*, AGBCA 1999-171-2, 00-1 BCA ¶ 30,758 (contractor entitled to additional compensation for re-excavating a sewer line at government's direction because the contention of nonconformance was inconsistent with the government's actions and contemporaneous reports); and *Ellis-Don Constr., Inc.*, ASBCA 51029, 99-2 BCA ¶ 30,408 (record contained no convincing proof that the original soils work did not comply with contract specifications). Compare *Independent Mfg. & Serv. Cos. of America, Inc.,* ASBCA 47542, 95- 2 BCA ¶ 27,915 (government proved that its inspection was proper and work was defective).

The government may be relieved of its burden if the contractor prevents it from performing tests. See *Gooch Pkn. Co.*, VACAB 1387, 80-2 BCA ¶ 14,559, in which the contractor was found to have waived its right to challenge the propriety of the government's rejection of meat. The board noted that, because the contractor retook possession of the meat and for a protracted period of time did not object to the rejection or request testing, it "effectively denied the VA an opportunity to demonstrate the condition of the steak and the cause of its deterioration."

The government frequently meets its burden by submitting the results of the tests it has conducted. This shifts the burden to the contractor to establish the invalidity of such tests, *C.W. Roen Constr. Co.*, DOTCAB 75-43, 76-2 BCA ¶ 12,215 ("scant evidence" presented by the contractor did not fulfill the "heavy burden" required to prove invalidity of the government's tests). See also *Continental Chem. Corp.*, GSBCA 4483, 76-2 BCA ¶ 11,948, in which the board stated that "there is a presumption that the method of testing followed by a Government laboratory is proper" and that "such presumption must be overcome by concrete evidence to the contrary." However, boards have held that the government has the burden of proving that its tests and inspections are accurate, *Continental Chem. Corp.*, GSBCA 3037, 70-1 BCA ¶ 8334. In *E.W. Eldridge, Inc.*, ENGBCA 5269, 89-3 BCA ¶ 21,899, the board found that the government did not meet its burden of proving that the test performed on the jetty stone was valid. See also *Puma Chem. Co.*, GSBCA 5254, 81-1 BCA ¶ 14,844, in which the board stated that the government must prove that the testing it performed fully complied with the test procedures detailed in the contract specifications. If testing is not in accordance with the contract requirements or no test is specified in the contract, the government must show that the test used is comparable or achieves the same results as the contractually prescribed method, *Solar Labs., Inc.*, ASBCA 19269, 74-2 BCA ¶ 10,897, *recons. denied*, 75-1 BCA ¶ 11,049, or that the test used does not impose an increased standard of performance, *Interstate Reforesters*, AGBCA 87-374-3, 89-1 BCA ¶ 21,375. See also *Circle Constr. Group*, ASBCA 38844, 90-3 BCA ¶ 22,999 (government met its burden of proving that the inspection method used was reasonable), and *Kan-Du Tool & Instrument Corp.*, ASBCA 37636 89-2 BCA ¶ 21,822, *recons. denied*, 91-1 BCA ¶ 23,611 (government did not impose a more stringent requirement in the testing of transmitter covers). In *General Elec. Co.,* ASBCA 45936, 95-1 BCA ¶ 27541, the government's rejection of all parts on the basis of noncompliance with specification requirements was upheld because the evidence indicated the cause of the deficiency was a manufacturing process flaw, and all of the parts were manufactured using the same process.

When the contractor has submitted its own evidence that the work conformed to the specifications, the boards will weigh the evidence of each party, *National Aviation Elecs., Inc.*, ASBCA 18256, 74-2 BCA ¶ 10,677 (contractor's initial showing of compliance with the contract specifications based on its own tests was not overcome by the government's showing of noncompliance based on its mere test results without further evidence of the test conditions or equipment employed by government technicians). See *Reliance Enters., Inc.*, ASBCA 25618, 83-1 BCA ¶ 16,167, *recons. denied*, 83-1 BCA ¶ 16,329, in which the government failed to establish that pipe samples did not meet specifications after the contractor made a prima facie showing of compliance. See also *Arden Eng'g Co.,* ASBCA 24829, 83-2 BCA ¶ 16,603 (government failed to demonstrate noncompliance when contractor presented "equally persuasive conflicting testimony"), and *Air-O-Plastik Corp.*, GSBCA 4802, 81-2 BCA ¶ 15,338 ("once both sides have submitted evidence . . . the board awards the decision to the party prevailing upon the preponderance of the evidence.") In one instance, the board itself examined the product furnished by the contractor to determine whether it complied with the contract requirements when neither the contractor nor the government produced any persuasive expert opinion on the subject, *Bonny Prods., Inc.*, GSBCA 4577, 76-2 BCA ¶ 12,158.

Although the government typically bears the risk of nonpersuasion in establishing noncompliance when rejecting work, the burden of persuasion that tendered work complies with the contract requirements is sometimes shifted to the contractor through the use of contractor inspection and testing requirements. In *MK + ABD + FM*, ASBCA 27760, 83-2 BCA ¶ 16,729, the contractor bore the burden of persuasion that the work met the contract requirements when radiographs of welds it was required to take for determining compliance were inconclusive due to extraneous material that obscured the image of the welds. The board stated at 83,209:

> From examination of radiograph View 9-10 in light of the evidence and arguments submitted by parties, we conclude that a defect existed in the weld as we interpret the term defect within the contract provisions. A defect at least by contract definition existed as long as the radiographs did not convincingly establish the integrity of the weld within contract standards. The contract terms make any uncertainty as to the integrity of the weld a defect if the uncertainty cannot be resolved with assurance without resorting to destructive testing. Under the terms of the contract it is of no consequence for this appeal that the weld was found on reinspection to be free of defects.

3. Notice of Rejection

Giving a proper and timely notice of rejection is necessary to protect the government's interests. An untimely notice can result in a finding of implied acceptance or limit the government's remedies for defects. However, the government's rights under the Default clause are not limited by the Inspection clause. Thus, a contracting officer's failure to comply with the requirement under the Inspection clause to provide the contractor written notice of performance deficiencies did not invalidate a default termination because the contractor had actual notice of the violations, took no corrective action during the one-month period it was on notice of these violations, and failed to show any prejudice by the lack of written notice, *Fantastique Ultimatique Nautique*', PSBCA 3652, 96-1 BCA ¶ 28,150. Similarly, rejection for an improper reason can also limit the government's remedies.

a. Content

Although the standard inspection clauses contain no requirement that a rejection notice provide reasons for rejection, FAR 46.407(g) requires that the reasons be stated:

> (g) Notices of rejection must include the reasons for rejection and be furnished promptly to the contractor. Promptness in giving this notice is essential because,

> if timely nature of rejection is not furnished, acceptance may in certain cases be implied as a matter of law. The notice must be in writing if—
>
> (1) The supplies or services have been rejected at a place other than the contractor's plant;
>
> (2) The contractor persists in offering nonconforming supplies or services for acceptance; or
>
> (3) Delivery or performance was late without excusable cause.

If the government neglects to provide the reasons for rejection and there is adequate time to correct defects within the contract delivery schedule, rejection and a subsequent default termination are improper, *Space Dynamics Corp.*, ASBCA 12085, 69-1 BCA ¶ 7662 (improvement or repairs could not be made without adequate information). In such cases, the contractor may be entitled to an equitable adjustment for extra work done because of the failure to state the reasons, *Chula Vista Elec. Co.*, ASBCA 9830, 65-1 BCA ¶ 4745, *recons. denied*, 65-2 BCA ¶ 4900. In *Chula Vista*, the board distinguished cases where the rejection notice provided the wrong reasons and the contractor had a reasonable time to make the corrections from a similar scenario in which the contractor had no time left to correct. In the latter scenario, "if a valid ground existed to support the rejection, it can be successfully interposed even though not expressed at the time of rejection." In *Merando, Inc.*, ASBCA 41402, 92-3 BCA ¶ 25,158, *vacated on other grounds*, 996 F.2d 1236 (Fed. Cir. 1993), the board expressed agreement with *Chula Vista* that even though the government "was not aware of the [particular] deviation at the time it rejected the piles, the rejection may nevertheless be sustained on that ground." In *General Time Corp.*, ASBCA 22306, 80-1 BCA ¶ 14,393, *recons. denied,* 85-1 BCA ¶ 17,842, the board dismissed a contractor's contention that the government advanced an incorrect basis for rejecting a lot of defective fuses by stating, "The fact that the Government was proved to be wrong did not shift the risk of performance back to the Government."

The government's responsibility is not limited to providing notice of deficiencies but includes taking all steps reasonably necessary to ensure that the contractor will have adequate knowledge of the deficiencies, thereby making accurate notice possible. In *Chronometrics, Inc.*, NASABCA 185-2, 90-3 BCA ¶ 22,992, *recons. denied*, 91-1 BCA ¶ 23,479, the board stated that the government "was at fault for not fully testing the [console] during the [factory inspection test] so that [the contractor] could be notified of basic deficiencies when correction was still possible within the contract delivery schedule and price, or when damages could have been mitigated significantly." In *Craig Enters.*, AGBCA 92-183-1, 95-2 BCA ¶ 27,766, the government's notice of rejection was found inadequate because it did not indicate how the work did not reasonably comply with a dimensional description in the specifications.

The rule requiring accurate notice will not be applied if the rejection notice erroneously states the reason for rejection but the contractor is not misled, *Manhattan Lighting Equip. Co.*, ASBCA 6533, 61-2 BCA ¶ 3140 (use of the word "louvers" rather than "reflector" did not mislead the contractor). If the contractor is aware of the defects, the rule will also not apply, *Standard Elecs. Corp.*, ASBCA 14753, 73-2 BCA ¶ 10,137. In *Standard*, the board sustained the rejection despite the government's failure to inform the contractor of specific failures until after termination. Further, notice of the reasons for rejection will not be required if the contractor knowingly tenders nonconforming supplies, *Premiere Bldg. Servs., Inc. v. General Servs. Admin.*, GSBCA 11741, 93-1 BCA ¶ 25,476 (contemporaneous notice of deficiency to the contractor's on-site representative held to impute knowledge of nonconformity to the contractor). See also *Government Contractors, Inc.*, GSBCA 6776, 84-1 BCA ¶ 16,934 (government's failure to notify the contractor of nonperformance of work was not prejudicial because the contractor must have known of the government's dissatisfaction from prior dealings on contract), and *Nova Commercial Co.*, GSBCA 9111, 88-3 BCA ¶ 21,088 (detailed inspection reports coupled with the contract specifications supplied adequate notice to the contractor so that deductions for nonconformity were proper).

b. Time

Paragraph (j) of the supply contract clause in FAR 52.246-2 states, "The Government shall accept or reject supplies as promptly as practicable after delivery, unless otherwise provided in the contract." Paragraph (i) of the construction contract clause in FAR 52.246-12 requires the government to "accept, as promptly as practicable after completion and inspection, all work required by the contract" unless otherwise specified. Similarly, FAR 46.407(g) requires that notice of rejection "be furnished promptly to the contractor . . . because, if timely notice of rejection is not furnished, acceptance may in certain cases be implied as a matter of law."

The length of time that is reasonable depends on the nature of work, the difficulty of inspection, and the impact of delay on the contractor. Accordingly, this issue of fact must be determined on a case-by-case basis. For example, in *Max Bauer Meat Packer, Inc. v. United States*, 198 Ct. Cl. 97, 458 F.2d 88 (1972), a three-hour delay in rejection of pork roasts for excessive fat was held unreasonable when the contractor had the right to return and resubmit the roasts for acceptance if they were initially rejected. The court reasoned that the delay had deprived the contractor of its rights because the roasts had become too frozen for retrimming at the time of rejection. Therefore, the government was deemed to have accepted the roasts. In *Snowbird Indus. Inc.*, ASBCA 31368, 88-2 BCA ¶ 20,618, the board found that the contractor was prejudiced by a seven-month delay in rejection of ice flake machines. See *Utley-James, Inc.*, GSBCA 6831, 88-1 BCA ¶ 20,518, in which the board held that an unexplained two-and-a-half-year delay between discovery of the cause of a defect in pavement and the government's decision to seek repairs was unreasonable, and the delay amounted to a constructive acceptance. In *Tranco Indus., Inc.*, ASBCA 26305, 83-1 BCA ¶ 16,414, *recons. denied*, 83-2 BCA ¶ 16,679, the government's four-month delay in rejecting the work after completion was unreasonable and therefore constituted implied acceptance. The board pointed out that the contractor "was prejudiced by this delay by being deprived of the opportunity to correct the defects within a reasonable time of leaving the job site, and by the additional deterioration that would occur to the paint exposed to the weather during the period of delay." See also *Mazur Bros. & Jaffe Fish Co.*, VACAB 512, 65-2 BCA ¶ 4932 (five days was an unreasonable delay in notification of rejection of perishable shrimp); *Cone Bros. Contracting Co.*, ASBCA 16078, 72-1 BCA ¶ 9444 (delay longer than one day unreasonable in rejection of concrete poured daily); *Wholesome Dairy, Inc.*, ASBCA 11058, 66-2 BCA ¶ 5824 (two-month delay in rejection of milk declared unreasonable); *Norwood Precision Prods.*, ASBCA 24083, 80-1 BCA ¶ 14,405 (government lost right to rescind "questionable" acceptance of items from default terminated contractor because of delay in taking action); and *Ordnance Parts & Eng'g Co.*, ASBCA 40293, 90-3 BCA ¶ 23,141 (although concerning claim of rejection based on latent defect, government took an unreasonably lengthy period to test the vehicular towing eyes). In *West Point Research, Inc.*, ASBCA 25511, 83-1 BCA ¶ 16,443, acceptance was implied by delay in testing and rejecting first articles since a remedy was provided by the First Article Approval clause.

The cases finding no unreasonable delay focus on the lack of prejudice to the contractor. See *William F. Klingensmith, Inc.*, GSBCA 5451, 83-1 BCA ¶ 16,201, in which the board stated at 80,491:

> We conclude that where the Government has information concerning the nonconformity of the contractor's product, it has a duty to reject the product within a reasonable time. If the length of the delay prevents the contractor from intelligently deciding whether or not the Government's rejection is correct, or prevents re-work or repair, or causes the contractor unnecessary work or expense, then it may be unreasonable.

The board found, however, that the three-week delay in notifying the contractor of the defects was not unreasonable and did not prejudice the contractor because the understrength columns were not repairable, even if earlier notice had been given. In *Basic Marine, Inc.*, ENGBCA 5299, 87-1 BCA ¶ 19,426, the board held a 14-day delay in notifying the contractor reasonable where there was no evidence of detrimental reliance by the contractor. In *Washington Constr. Co.*, ENGBCA 5318, 89-3 BCA ¶ 22,077, the board held that a five-month delay in notifying the contractor was not unreasonable and, therefore, the government did not constructively accept the excavation work. The board considered the contractor's own delay in remobilization as part of its reasonableness determination. See also *Granite Constr. Co.*, ENGBCA 4642, 89-3 BCA ¶ 21,946, in which a six-week delay between inspection and notice of defect to the contractor was found reasonable because the contractor's welding foreman was notified upon discovery of the defect and failed to act on this knowledge.

Lengthy delays in rejection have been held reasonable in circumstances where the delay is necessary and no undue prejudice to the contractor has occurred. See *Mann Chem. Labs., Inc. v. United States*, 182 F. Supp. 40 (D. Mass. 1960), in which a seven-month delay was found reasonable for rejection of water purification tablets when the laboratory test took that amount of time and the tablets would have endangered lives if defective. See also *Hy-Cal Eng'g Corp.*, NASABCA 871-18, 75-2 BCA ¶ 11,399, in which the board held a 50-day delay in rejecting reference junctions clearly unreasonable but awarded no recovery because of lack of prejudice to the contractor. In *Granite Constr. Co.*, ENGBCA 4642, 89-3 BCA ¶ 21,946, the board found that the contractor's representatives had knowledge of the defects, thereby precluding a finding of unreasonableness despite a six-week interval between inspection and written notice of defects. A late rejection of lumber (more than 90 days from receipt) has been found to be a contract change rather than an implied acceptance of the goods, *Wyatt Lumber Co.*, ASBCA 21604, 77-1 BCA ¶ 12,481. See also ¶ (e) of the supply contract clause to be used in cost-reimbursement contracts in FAR 52.246-3, which provides for implied acceptance 60 days after delivery (assuming the government neither accepts nor rejects beforehand).

4. Previous Action Limiting Rejection

Ordinarily, the government is not precluded from rejecting work merely because it has accepted work with the same or similar characteristics in the past. However, where the specifications are susceptible to two or more reasonable interpretations, the previous acceptance of the same or similar work could establish the meaning of the specifications. See Chapter 2. Under some circumstances, the acceptance of work that does not meet the specifications might be considered a waiver of the specifications requirement. Thus, previous approval of defective work may prevent rejection in circumstances in which the courts or boards conclude that it would be unfair to permit the government to enforce its rights after the contractor has relied on the approval. However, see *WorldwideParts, Inc.*, ASBCA 38896, 91-2 BCA ¶ 23,717 (when pricing a follow-on contract with no knowledge of failure to comply with specifications of prior contract, no reliance shown.) The principles of estoppel are applied in such cases. *See* Pitou, *Equitable Estoppel: Its Genesis, Development and Applications in Government Contracting,* 19 Pub. Cont. L.J. 606 (1990). In *Automated Datatron, Inc.*, GPOBCA 25-87, Apr. 12, 1989, Westlaw Cite 1989 WL 384974 (G.P.O. BCA), the board enumerated the following requirements for holding the government estopped from rejecting based on its prior action:

> The Government may be estopped from strictly enforcing Program B-154-S length specification for diazo duplicate microfiche if [the contractor] proves, by a preponderance of substantial evidence, that the CO, as the responsible officer having actual authority to waive contract specifications under the contract, had actual or imputed knowledge of the nonconformance of the microfiche as to its length, and did waive the diazo microfiche length limitation provisions of such specification by actual or implied acceptance of such microfiche, and did commu-

> nicate such acceptance to [the contractor] such a clear and unambiguous manner as to convey the sense of waiver to [the contractor] in order to induce continued performance in accordance with such waiver; and that [the contractor], in reliance upon such communication, did in fact continue its performance and will be injured by the Government's action if estoppel is not granted.

In *Gresham & Co. v. United States*, 200 Ct. Cl. 97, 470 F.2d 542 (1972), because government quality assurance representatives had accepted supplies not in compliance with the specifications on 21 prior contracts and the contracting officer had knowledge of such noncompliance, the board deemed that the government had waived nonconformity. The court stated that "[t]here can be no doubt that a contract requirement for the benefit of a party becomes dead if that party knowingly fails to exact its performance, over such an extended period, that the other side reasonably believes the requirement to be dead." The court also noted that a waiver of specifications "requires a decision by a responsible officer assigned the function of overseeing the essentials of contract performance" and that "[s]uch a waiver by one with such authority will estop the Government [from later requiring strict compliance with the specifications]." See *H. Bendzulla Contracting*, ASBCA 51869, 01-2 BCA ¶ 31,665 (*Gresham* distinguished because specifications in the two contracts were different); *Parris v. General Servs. Admin.*, ASBCA 15512, 01-2 BCA ¶ 31,629 (*Gresham* distinguished because a single incident in which the government failed to insert mutual compliance "did not constitute an expense or implied waiver"); *R & R Marine & Industrial Repair*, ASBCA 34279, 88-2 BCA ¶ 20,747 (no waiver when interchangeable use of two substitute products had been permitted on prior contracts); *American Transparents Plastics Corp.*, GSBCA 7006, 91-1 BCA ¶ 23,349 (no waiver when only evidence of prior conduct is government actions under one previous contract that was still potentially subject to a retroactive price adjustment); and *W.S. Jenks & Son*, GSBCA 10513, 92-1 BCA ¶ 24,502 (no waiver of nonconforming multimeter even though same multimeter had been accepted on other contracts, because no indication that contracting officer knew of nonconformity). There must be a course of conduct that indicates that the government will continue to accept the same defects. See *United Computer Supplies, Inc. v. United States*, 43 Fed. Cl. 351 (1999) (no evidence of waiver by someone with authority). In *L.W. Foster Sportswear Co. v. United States*, 186 Ct. Cl. 499, 405 F.2d 1285 (1969), waiver was found because the government had allowed deviations from defective specifications under every prior contract, thereby establishing a consistent practice.

Acceptance of initial deliveries of nonconforming supplies will not, in itself, constitute a waiver. In *Doyle Shirt Mfg. Corp. v. United States*, 199 Ct. Cl. 150, 462 F.2d 1150 (1972), the court permitted the government to require strict compliance in subsequent deliveries of shirts despite the fact that it had granted a waiver of a shade requirement on an early portion of the contract. The court pointed out that the shade defect did not affect serviceability or appearance, unlike the defects upon which later rejection was based, and that the government in granting the initial waiver expressly warned the contractor that it was not thereby waiving its right to reject future deliveries for nonconformance. See also *Santa Fe Eng'rs, Inc.*, ASBCA 23897, 92-1 BCA ¶ 24,495 (isolated government compensation of contractor for cutting piping sleeve not a waiver).

The government was estopped from rejecting work as noncomplying in *Inet Power*, NASABCA 566-23, 68-1 BCA ¶ 7020. There, the contractor, at an early stage of performance, had informed the government that it was extremely doubtful that the specifications could be met. The board held that the government's exhortations to the contractor to continue performance, with knowledge of this imputed to the contracting officer, estopped it from rejecting the items as noncomplying. See also *General Motors Corp.*, ASBCA 15807, 72-1 BCA ¶ 9405 (government's instructions to continue production of units so that delivery schedules could be met were reasonably interpreted by the contractor as authorization to continue regardless of the known reliability deviations), and *Joseph Morton Co.*, ASBCA 19793, 78-1 BCA ¶ 13,173, *recons. denied*, 80-2 BCA ¶ 14,502 (government estopped from rescinding its approval of the installation of a sizable number of shower stalls that clearly deviated from the specifications). However, government approval will not estop the government from requiring strict compliance if the contractor has certified its compliance with the specifications. See *Panhandle Grading & Paving, Inc.*, ASBCA 38539, 90-1 BCA ¶ 22,561 (approval of nonconforming item by the project engineer and the contracting officer did not estop the government from relying on the contractor's signed certification that the goods complied).

B. Acceptance

Acceptance plays a number of crucial roles in contract administration. In addition to limiting the government's rights relating to patent defects, acceptance entitles the contractor to payment of the contract price and usually transfers the risk of loss of the work from the contractor to the government.

This subsection discusses how and when acceptance occurs. It also deals with the legal rights of the parties when the government uses the work prior to acceptance and when the government has followed a pattern of accepting nonconforming work.

1. Authority to Accept

The Inspection clauses do not specifically identify the government official authorized to accept the work; FAR 46.502 states:

> Acceptance of supplies or services is the responsibility of the contracting officer. When this responsibility is assigned to a cognizant contract administration office or to another agency (see 42.202(g)), acceptance by that office or agency is binding on the Government.

In addition, contracts often contain provisions identifying the persons or organizations authorized to accept the work on behalf of the government. See, for example,

W.S. Jenks & Son, GSBCA 10513, 92-1 BCA ¶ 24,502 (inspector not authorized to accept where the contract expressly delegated such authority to another organization). In some cases, the contract may contain express provisions limiting an official's authority to accept. See *Design & Prod., Inc. v. United States*, 18 Cl. Ct. 168 (1989) (COTR did not have authority to accept or reject but could only "notify the contractor and the Contracting Officer of any deficiencies observed"). Further, contractors are usually provided with specific statements of authority and limitations on authority of government officials, including inspectors involved in contract administration. Thus, the government will not be bound by the erroneous signing of an acceptance form by an unauthorized person, *Wolverine Diesel Power Co.*, ASBCA 5079, 59-2 BCA ¶ 2327. In *A&D Fire Prot., Inc.*, ASBCA 53103, 02-2 BCA ¶ 32,053, the actions of the contracting officer were held to constitute a constructive change because of the contracting officer's authority to inspect or accept.

In *Trevco Eng'g & Sales*, VACAB 1021, 73-2 BCA ¶ 10,096, a statement by the contracting officer that the inspector would provide notice to ship the goods upon "acceptance by the inspector" did not constitute a delegation of acceptance authority. The language merely conditioned shipment of the items upon approval of the inspector. Compare *Wisconsin Mach. Corp.*, ASBCA 18500, 74-1 BCA ¶ 10,397, where a Defense Contract Administration Service (DCAS) inspector apparently had the authority to accept a press brake by virtue of language in the contract schedule specifying that inspection and acceptance of the press brake were to take place at the subcontractor's plant and were to be accomplished by representatives of the DCAS. Similarly, in *Henry Angelo & Co.*, ASBCA 30502, 87-1 BCA ¶ 19,619, the board found that where the contract expressly assigned acceptance authority to the "Base Civil Engineer or his designated representative," it was improper for the contracting officer to require execution of a final acceptance certificate. See also *Vern W. Johnson & Sons, Inc.*, ENGBCA 5554, 90-1 BCA ¶ 22,571, *recons. denied*, 90-2 BCA ¶ 22,914, in which it was found that a government inspector's statement to the contractor that the tendered work was satisfactory did not amount to an acceptance. Although few cases require clear delegation of acceptance authority from the contracting officer, *Gonzales Custom Painting, Inc.*, ASBCA 39527, 90-3 BCA ¶ 22,950, some decisions suggest that acceptance by an unauthorized government employee would also be "final and conclusive" if the contracting officer knew or should have known of the situation and by some act (or failure to act) ratified the unauthorized acceptance. See *Norwood Precision Prods.*, ASBCA 24083, 80-1 BCA ¶ 14,405, and *Allstate Leisure Prods., Inc.*, ASBCA 35614, 89-3 BCA ¶ 22,003.

2. Time and Place of Acceptance

Guidance as to when and where acceptance should take place is contained in various sections of the FAR. For example, FAR 46.102(c) states that agencies shall ensure that "Government contract quality assurance is conducted before acceptance (except as otherwise provided in this part) by or under the direction of Government personnel." FAR 46.501 permits acceptance at any time depending upon the specific contract provisions but cautions that "ordinarily" it should not occur before completion of government quality assurance. FAR 46.503 states the government policy with respect to place of acceptance:

> Each contract shall specify the place of acceptance. Contracts that provide for Government contract quality assurance at source shall ordinarily provide for acceptance at source. Contracts that provide for Government contract quality assurance at destination shall ordinarily provide for acceptance at destination. (For transportation terms, see Subpart 47.3.) Supplies accepted at a place other than destination shall not be reinspected at destination for acceptance purposes, but should be examined at destination for quantity, damage in transit, and possible substitution or fraud.

The contract clauses themselves contain guidance as to when acceptance shall take place. Paragraph (i) of the construction contract clause at FAR 52.246-12 states, "Unless otherwise specified in the contract, the Government shall accept, as promptly as practicable after completion and inspection, all work required by the contract or that portion of the work the contracting officer determines can be accepted separately." Paragraph (j) of the supply contract clause at FAR 52.246-2 similarly states, "The Government shall accept or reject supplies as promptly as practicable after delivery, unless otherwise provided in the contract." Although FAR 52.246-2 seems to require prompt acceptance after delivery and FAR 46-501 permits acceptance before, during, or after delivery, both permit acceptance to take place according to the particular terms and conditions of the contract. In *Electro Plastic Fabrics, Inc.*, ASBCA 14762, 71-2 BCA ¶ 8996, the board found that the government improperly withheld acceptance of ponchos pending verification testing of the basic material when the contract provisions only permitted withholding of acceptance pending verification testing of the end items. However, in *ETA Tech. Corp.*, ASBCA 48417, 97-1 BCA ¶ 28,666, a substantial completion certificate did not establish the time of final acceptance, because while the certificate indicated that substantial work was being "accepted," it also indicated that considerable work remained. The certificate also anticipated the possibility of final acceptance in the future.

3. *Methods of Acceptance*

Neither the standard inspection clauses nor the regulations require that acceptance be made in any specific manner. Normally, acceptance is expected to occur through the execution of a formal written document, but in some cases it has been implied from acts of the government.

a. *Formal Acceptance*

FAR 46.101 contains the following definition:

> "Acceptance," means the act of an authorized representative of the Government by which the Government, for itself or as agent of another, assumes ownership

> of existing identified supplies tendered or approves specific services rendered as partial or complete performance of the contract.

FAR 46.501 adds the following guidance:

> Acceptance constitutes acknowledgment that the supplies or services conform with applicable contract quality and quantity requirements, except as provided in this subpart and subject to other terms and conditions of the contract. Acceptance may take place before delivery, at the time of delivery, or after delivery, depending on the provisions of the terms and conditions of the contract. Supplies or services shall ordinarily not be accepted before completion of Government contract quality assurance actions (however, see 46.504). Acceptance shall ordinarily be evidenced by execution of an acceptance certificate on an inspection or receiving report form or commercial shipping document/packing list.

FAR Part 12 has specific rules regarding inspection and acceptance in contracts for commercial items. The standard clause for such items, Contract Terms and Conditions—Commercial Items, in FAR 52.212-4, contains the following paragraph:

> (a) *Inspection/Acceptance.* The Contractor shall only tender for acceptance those items that conform to the requirements of this contract. The Government reserves the right to inspect or test any supplies or services that have been tendered for acceptance. The Government may require repair or replacement of nonconforming supplies or reperformance of nonconforming services at no increase in contract price. The Government must exercise its postacceptance rights (1) within a reasonable time after the defect was discovered or should have been discovered; and (2) before any substantial change occurs in the condition of the item, unless the change is due to the defect in the item.

FAR 12.402 provides the following guidance on the use of this provision:

> (a) The acceptance paragraph in 52.212-4 is based upon the assumption that the Government will rely on the contractor's assurances that the commercial item tendered for acceptance conforms to the contract requirements. The Government inspection of commercial items will not prejudice its other rights under the acceptance paragraph. Additionally, although the paragraph does not address the issue of rejection, the Government always has the right to refuse acceptance of nonconforming items. This paragraph is generally appropriate when the Government is acquiring noncomplex commercial items.
>
> (b) Other acceptance procedures may be more appropriate for the acquisition of complex commercial items or commercial items used in critical applications. In such cases, the contracting officer shall include alternative inspection procedure(s) in an addendum and ensure these procedures and the postaward remedies adequately protect the interests of the Government. The contracting officer must carefully examine the terms and conditions of any express warranty with regard to the effect it may have on the Government's available postaward remedies (see 12.404).

> (c) The acquisition of commercial items under other circumstances such as on an "as is" basis may also require acceptance procedures different from those contained in 52.212-4. The contracting officer should consider the effect the specific circumstances will have on the acceptance paragraph as well as other paragraphs of the clause.

FAR Subpart 46.6 requires agencies to "prescribe procedures and instructions for the use, preparation, and distribution of material inspection and receiving reports and commercial shipping document/packing lists to evidence Government inspection (see 46.401) and acceptance (see 46.501)." The Department of Defense has implemented this requirement in DFARS Subpart 246.6. The DD Form 250, Material Inspection and Receiving Report, is used to evidence inspection and acceptance. This form can be found in DFARS 253.303-250.

DD Form 250 may signify both inspection and acceptance. See *Sperry Corp. v. United States*, 845 F.2d 965 (Fed. Cir. 1988), *cert. denied*, 488 U.S. 986 (1988) (date DD Form 250 was signed constituted acceptance). In some instances, the form has been used to evidence inspection only, *Boga Forge & Mach. Works, Inc.*, ASBCA 9370, 65-1 BCA ¶ 4727 (DD Form 250 not binding when acceptance language deleted and contractor did not rely on it); *Lox Equip. Co.*, ASBCA 8518, 1964 BCA ¶ 4469 (acceptance language in DD Form 250 deleted and contractor "was not legally entitled at that time to an unqualified acceptance that was conclusive except as regards latent defects, fraud, [etc.]"); *Gillen Mach. Rebuilders, Inc.*, ASBCA 28341, 89-3 BCA ¶ 22,021, *recons. granted in part, on other grounds*, 90-1 BCA ¶ 22,428 (signing of DD Form 250 including conditional language that the supplies must pass certain operational tests not an acceptance). For contracts for commercial items, SF 1499 can also be used as an acceptance document.

b. Implied Acceptance

Implied acceptance has been found in several situations where the government does not formally accept the work.

(1) Late Rejection

One form of implied acceptance has been discussed earlier—late rejection. Thus, prompt notice that the goods are nonconforming will normally preclude a finding of implied acceptance. In *Cooper Mech. Contractors*, IBCA 2744, 92-2 BCA ¶ 24,821, the board rejected the contractor's argument that the government had impliedly accepted its tendered transformers when the project officer had "promptly notified [the contractor] that the transformer was being wired improperly." See also *Granite Constr. Co.*, ENGBCA 4642, 89-3 BCA ¶ 21,946, where notice of defects was given to the contractor contemporaneous with their discovery such that a finding of implied acceptance was precluded. Compare *Fischer Imaging Corp.*, VABCA 6125, 02-2 BCA ¶ 32,003, in which, relying on a specific clause, the board ruled that the government accepted the contractor's medical equipment because the agency failed to inspect the equipment within the time allotted by the contract.

The Prompt Payment clause in FAR 52.232-25 contains a special provision on the time of acceptance. Subparagraph (a)(5)(i) of the clause states:

> (i) For the sole purpose of computing an interest penalty that might be due the Contractor, Government acceptance is deemed to occur constructively on the 7th day (unless otherwise specified in this contract) after the Contractor delivers the supplies or performs the services in accordance with the terms and conditions of the contract, unless there is a disagreement over quantity, quality, or Contractor compliance with a contract provision. If actual acceptance occurs within the constructive acceptance period, the Government will base the determination of an interest penalty on the actual date of acceptance. The constructive acceptance requirement does not, however, compel Government officials to accept supplies or services, perform contract administration functions, or make payment prior to fulfilling their responsibilities.

This provision appears to be of limited application, and it is unlikely that it will affect any rights other than the right to assert late payment.

(2) Government Acts Inconsistent with Contractor Ownership

The other major type of implied acceptance is a government act inconsistent with the contractor's ownership of the contract items. The rule governing this type of implied acceptance was discussed in *John C. Kohler Co. v. United States*, 204 Ct. Cl. 777, 498 F.2d 1360 (1974), in which the court cited U.C.C. § 2-606(1)(c), which declares that acceptance of goods occurs when the buyer does any act inconsistent with the seller's ownership. The court stated that "[t]he most common act which falls under this provision is the retention and use of the goods by the buyer." The court then reasoned that the government's "custody of the boiler, its operation of the boiler for its own purpose for over 80 days, its selection of the employees to operate the boiler, its control over when the boiler was operated and for what periods, its determination of the load the boiler was to carry, and the selection of fuel, air and steam rations to use" were factors that must be held inconsistent with the contractor's ownership. Following this logic, implied acceptance has been found in supply contracts when the government lost items that had been delivered to it, *Replac Corp.*, ASBCA 7275, 1962 BCA ¶ 3527; and when it altered the nature of the supplies prior to rejection, *Frosty Morn Meats, Inc.*, ASBCA 4221, 58-1 BCA ¶ 1746 (government may alter only that quantity of supplies "fairly and reasonably necessary to determine its quality"); *Waterbury Cos., Inc.*, ASBCA 6634, 61-2 BCA ¶ 3158 (delivered items on which the government performed work were deemed accepted). In addition, government use of supplies without destruction or alteration has been held to constitute implied acceptance, *Flight Test Eng'g Co.*, ASBCA 7661, 1962 BCA ¶ 3606 (government required to pay the contractor for parts used by the government after delivery); *Trio-Tech, Inc.*, VACAB 598, 68-1 BCA ¶ 6828 (government's general use of the equipment was "inconsistent with continuation of [contractor's] ownership or lack of finality in the property transfer"). However, concurrent government use coupled with the initiation of payment procedures by the government did not rise to the level of implied acceptance, *Jack L. Hartman & Co.,* AGBCA 84-126-1, 91-1 BCA ¶ 23,546.

In many cases, the determination of whether an implied acceptance has taken place is based on a consideration of all the facts and circumstances surrounding the alleged acceptance. Thus, no implied acceptance was found in *K-Square Corp.*, NASABCA 1271-23, 76-1 BCA ¶ 11,867, *recons. denied*, 76-2 BCA ¶ 12,093, in which government use concurrent with the contractor's continuing attempts to correct major defects was held not to constitute implied acceptance; and *King Mgmt. Corp.*, ASBCA 21422, 77-1 BCA ¶ 12,412, where the government had placed rejected items in a separate area and thereby had avoided implied acceptance by use. See also *Hasco Elec. Corp.*, GSBCA 7921, 89-2 BCA ¶ 21,878, in which the board held that inspector silence while observing nonconforming work by itself did not amount to an implied acceptance. Similarly, in *Better Rds. of Lake Placid, Inc.*, ASBCA 39133, 93-2 BCA ¶ 25,580, *aff'd*, 11 F.3d 1074 (Fed. Cir. 1993), the board rejected the contractor's argument that daily inspections by the government amounted to acceptances, which limited the government's right to seek correction of subsequently discovered defects. The board determined that such daily inspections were for the benefit of the government and did not alter its rights under the contract. In *A.B.G. Instrument & Eng'g, Inc. v. United States*, 219 Ct. Cl. 381, 593 F.2d 394 (1979), the court found no implied acceptance where the government rightfully rejected defective supplies, requested disposition instructions, and used the items after more than a year had passed without disposition instructions being received from the contractor. Such action by the government was in accordance with the purpose and intent of U.C.C. § 2-604, which provides that "if the seller gives no instructions within a reasonable time after notification of rejection the buyer may store the rejected goods for the seller's account or reship them to him or resell them for the seller's account" and that "[s]uch action is not acceptance or conversion."

In *Ateron Corp.,* ASBCA 46867, 96-1 BCA ¶ 28,165, the government's failure to reject and use of certain delivered items in planning, performing, and documenting preliminary and critical design reviews constituted implied acceptance of those items, thereby liquidating progress payments for them. The board noted that although the contractor had not submitted invoices for the items and the government had not signed receiving report forms, the FAR prescribes that acceptance shall "ordinarily," rather than invariably, be evidenced by execution of an acceptance certificate on an inspection or receiving report or commercial shipping document/packing list.

c. *Payment Alone Not Acceptance*

Payment itself has not constituted an implied acceptance, *Industrial Data Link Corp.*, ASBCA 31570, 91-1 BCA ¶ 23,382, *recons. denied*, 91-1 BCA ¶ 23,570 (internal government "acceptance" for "progress payments only" is not a final acceptance under the Inspection and Acceptance clause); *G.M. Co. Mfg., Inc.*, AS-

BCA 5345, 60-2 BCA ¶ 2759 (payment action initiated by person without authority to accept or reject work); *Sovereign Constr. Co.*, GSBCA 913, 1964 BCA ¶ 4468 (progress payments did not constitute implied acceptance). See also *Keyser Roofing Contractors, Inc.*, ASBCA 13380, 70-1 BCA ¶ 8141, in which the board found that a roof that had been inspected and certified for payment under the Progress Payments clause was not sufficiently used by the government to constitute implied acceptance.

Payment does not estop the government from taking remedial actions for deficient work, *ETA Tech. Corp.,* ASBCA 48417, 97-1 BCA ¶ 28,666 (government not estopped from demanding the recovery of money erroneously paid for nonperformance of services); *Benju Corp.,* ASBCA 43648, 97-2 BCA ¶ 29,274 (payment in full for first article test procedures with notice of deficiencies did not mislead contractor into believing that payment constituted acceptance).

d. Acceptance for a Limited Purpose

Not all actions purporting to be acceptances are acceptances for finality purposes under the standard clauses. See *Spectrum Leasing Corp.*, GSBCA 7347, 90-3 BCA ¶ 22,984 (execution of DD Form 250 not a final acceptance where the contract required formal acceptance testing before final acceptance), and *Rosendin Elec., Inc.*, ASBCA 22996, 81-1 BCA ¶ 14,827 ("acceptance" constituting inspector's approval under the contract specifications not acceptance under Inspection clause). In *Rosendin*, the board stated that the acceptance contemplated by the Inspection clause was acceptance of the entire project. For a different approach to such cases, see *Harold Bailey Painting Co.*, ASBCA 28443, 84-1 BCA ¶ 17,043, holding that partial acceptances were permitted. See also *Henry Angelo & Co.*, ASBCA 30502, 87-1 BCA ¶ 19,619, in which the board implied the need for partial acceptance from the specification requirement for incremental sequencing or scheduling of painting operations for separate housing units and incremental inspections thereof.

Inspection and approval of items by government inspectors at the contractor's plant is generally not an acceptance, *Mack Equip. & Machine Co.*, ASBCA 12532, 68-2 BCA ¶ 7140. In *Lox Equip. Co.*, ASBCA 8518, 1964 BCA ¶ 4469, the board found that the government had not "finally accepted" items at the contractor's plant so as to be barred from making any subsequent claim against the contractor for noncompliance. Although the contract provided for "acceptance for shipment" at the contractor's plant and "acceptance of delivery" at the delivery point, the board found that other language, which clearly indicated that the vessels would be tested at the site and subjected to rejection for noncompliance, was incompatible with the idea that finality would attach to the government's factory "acceptance." See also *Trevco Eng'g & Sales*, VACAB 1021, 73-2 BCA ¶ 10,096, in which the board held that no acceptance had occurred during a source inspection when the contracting officer's shipping instructions to the contractor contained the notation that "upon acceptance of the item by the inspector he will give notice to ship." The board found this language insufficient to change the place of acceptance, which, according to the standard inspection clause in the contract, was to occur "after delivery" or, in this case, at destination.

e. Use and Possession Under Construction Contracts

Implied acceptance by acts inconsistent with the contractor's ownership is somewhat more complex in construction contracts because of the presence of additional clauses bearing on the issue. The clause at FAR 52.236-11 permits the government to take possession of construction without accepting the work. It reads as follows:

> USE AND POSSESSION PRIOR TO COMPLETION (APR 1984)
>
> (a) The Government shall have the right to take possession of or use any completed or partially completed part of the work. Before taking possession of or using any work, the Contracting Officer shall furnish the Contractor a list of items of work remaining to be performed or corrected on those portions of the work that the Government intends to take possession of or use. However, failure of the Contracting Officer to list any item of work shall not relieve the Contractor of responsibility for complying with the terms of the contract. The Government's possession or use shall not be deemed an acceptance of any work under the contract.
>
> (b) While the Government has such possession or use, the Contractor shall be relieved of the responsibility for the loss of or damage to the work resulting from the Government's possession or use, notwithstanding the terms of the clause in this contract entitled "Permits and Responsibilities." If prior possession or use by the Government delays the progress of the work or causes additional expense to the Contractor, an equitable adjustment shall be made in the contract price or the time of completion, and the contract shall be modified in writing accordingly.

In addition, the Permits and Responsibilities clause at FAR 52.236-7 contains the following sentence relating to contractor liability for work prior to acceptance:

> The Contractor shall also be responsible for all materials delivered and work performed until completion and acceptance of the entire work, except for any completed unit of work which may have been accepted under the contract.

The pre-FAR version of the Use and Possession Prior to Completion clause stated that "such possession or use shall not be deemed an acceptance of any work not completed in accordance with the contract." It was held that this language implied that the government's use or possession of *conforming* work should be deemed an implied acceptance. See *Mike Bradford & Co.,* ASBCA 11196, 66-2 BCA ¶ 5831 (government held liable for hurricane damage), and *Bell & Flynn, Inc.*, ASBCA 11038, 66-2 BCA ¶ 5855 (government held liable for defects discovered subsequent to its use and possession). The FAR clause provides that "the Government's possession or use shall not be deemed an acceptance of *any* work *under the contract*" (emphasis added).

Under this clause, the *Bradford* rule is not applicable. Thus, unless it accepts the work, the government is liable only if damage to the work results from its use or possession. If the contractor can establish government use or possession, the government must demonstrate that something or someone other than the government caused the damage to the contractor's work. See *Fraser Eng'g Co.,* VABCA 3265, 91-3 BCA ¶ 24,223 (government in possession of work liable for damage to fan motors because it could not meet its burden of proof that the damage was caused by an act of God or some other third party). See also *Labco Constr., Inc.*, ASBCA 39995, 92-1 BCA ¶ 24,543 (board concluded that there had been neither a final acceptance nor an implied acceptance and, thus, the contractor was liable for damages caused by a hail storm under the FAR Use and Possession Prior to Completion clause).

It is uniformly held that, under the FAR clause, government use or possession does not constitute implied acceptance, *Firma Tiefbau Meier*, ASBCA 46951, 95-1 BCA ¶ 27,593 (government's partial occupancy of a hall constructed by a contractor did not constitute acceptance of the work precluding a default termination); *Hudson Contracting, Inc.*, ASBCA 41023, 94-1 BCA ¶ 26,466 (government's possession for beneficial occupancy, in and of itself, insufficient to be an implied acceptance under the clause); *Kimmins Contracting Corp.*, ASBCA 43305, 93-1 BCA ¶ 25,463 (no implied acceptance when punchlist defects remaining to be corrected); *M.C. & D. Capital Corp. v. United States*, 948 F.2d 1251 (Fed. Cir. 1991) (difficult to understand how contractor can argue implied acceptance in view of Use and Possession Prior to Completion clause); *Stable Constr. Co.*, ASBCA 38138, 89-3 BCA ¶ 22,241 (no implied acceptance when government took possession prior to completion and subsequently did not correct the defective work); *PCL Constr. Servs., Inc v. United States,* 47 Fed. Cl. 745 (2000) (government's occupation of substantially completed building did not constitute constructive acceptance of the uncompleted work, nor did it preclude termination of any severable portion of the work); *Elter S. A.*, ASBCA 52791, 02-1 BCA ¶ 31,667 (government's beneficial occupancy of buildings does not relieve contractor of performance requirements.) But see *Conner Bros. Constr. Co.,* VABCA 2504, 95-2 BCA ¶ 27,910, *aff'd,* 113 F.3d 1256 (Fed. Cir. 1997) (for purposes of calculating liquidated damages, the government's decision to drop a renovated building from its inspection requirements was tantamount to acceptance of that portion of the project).

f. Conditional Acceptance

In a 1997 report, *Defense Acquisition: Guidance Is Needed on Payments for Conditionally Accepted Items,* GAO/NSIAD-98-20, Dec. 12, 1997, the GAO criticized the government's conditionally accepting incomplete work from contractors without withholding sufficient funds to cover the estimated costs of completing the work. The GAO noted the absence of guidance for withholding payment for work to be performed after delivery. Accordingly, in 1999 FAR 46.101 was amended to add the following definition of conditional acceptance:

> "Conditional acceptance" means acceptance of supplies or services that do not conform to contract quality requirements, or are otherwise incomplete, that the contractor is required to correct or otherwise complete by a specified date.

FAR 46.407(f) was also modified to provide direction on conditional acceptance:

> (f) When supplies or services are accepted with critical or major nonconformances as authorized in paragraph (c) of this section, the contracting officer must modify the contract to provide for an equitable price reduction or other consideration. In the case of conditional acceptance, amounts withheld from payments generally should be at least sufficient to cover the estimated cost and related profit to correct deficiencies and complete unfinished work. The contracting officer must document in the contract file the basis for the amounts withheld. For services, the contracting officer can consider identifying the value of the individual work requirements or tasks (subdivisions) that may be subject to price or fee reduction. This value may be used to determine an equitable adjustment for nonconforming services. However, when supplies or services involving minor nonconformances are accepted, the contract need not be modified unless it appears that the savings to the contractor in fabricating the nonconforming supplies or performing the nonconforming services will exceed the cost to the Government of processing the modification.

There have been no reported decisions under this language. However, earlier decisions recognized the concept of conditional acceptance. See *Northrop Grumman Corp.*, ASBCA 48282, 98-2 BCA ¶ 29,443 (parties entered into conditional acceptance agreement, which spelled out in detail the deficiencies to be corrected and modifications to be made), and *BMY-Contract Sys. Div. of Harsco Corp.*, ASBCA 39495, 98-1 BCA ¶ 29,575 (conditional acceptance of sample vehicles with list of deficiencies). See also *Firma Tiefbau Meier*, ASBCA 46951, 95-1 BCA ¶ 27,593, in which the government's payment and certification of a partial invoice for roof construction work did not constitute acceptance of the work precluding a default termination because any acceptance was conditioned on the results of a subsequent inspection, at which the work was specifically rejected.

C. Remedies

The government's remedies under the Inspection clause are (1) to require contractor correction; (2) to correct the defects itself or have them corrected by another contractor, charging the contractor for the expense; or (3) to obtain a price reduction.

1. Contractor Correction

The present standard inspection clauses deal with correction of defective work by the contractor. Paragraph (f) of the construction contract clause in FAR 52.246-12 requires the contractor to "without charge, replace or correct work found by the Government not to conform to contract requirements, unless in the public interest the Government consents to accept the work with an appropriate adjustment in contract price." Paragraph (f) of the supply contract clause in FAR 52.246-2 permits the government "either to reject or require correction of nonconforming supplies."

The government's notice of rejection may be accompanied by directions for correction of the work, or may merely indicate that the work has been rejected. If the delivery date has passed, the contract is subject to being terminated for default. However, the contractor must be given the opportunity to correct the supplies if such correction can be accomplished within the contract delivery schedule, 45 Comp. Gen. 823 (B-157319) (1966) (the GAO rejected the contractor's assertion that it was entitled to 10 days for correction when delivery was to be in fewer days). In *Filtron Co.*, DCAB ESSA-3, 69-2 BCA ¶ 8039, the contract was found to have been properly terminated for default when correction required complete redesign and reinstallation, which could not have been accomplished in a reasonable time. FAR 46.407(b) states that "the contracting officer ordinarily must give the contractor an opportunity to correct or replace nonconforming supplies or services when this can be accomplished within the required delivery schedule." In addition, the contractor is entitled to a reasonable time beyond the contract delivery schedule to correct minor defects in supplies delivered within the contract date if the contractor had reasonable grounds to believe the supplies would be accepted, *Radiation Tech., Inc. v. United States*, 177 Ct. Cl. 227, 366 F.2d 1003 (1966). See Chapter 10 for a discussion of this rule.

It is the government's right to require correction, *Better Rds. of Lake Placid, Inc.*, ASBCA 39133, 93-2 BCA ¶ 25,580, *aff'd*, 11 F.3d 1074 (Fed. Cir. 1993) ("Government had full authority and right under the contract terms to insist upon correction of the defective work"). In *Cooper Mech. Contractors*, IBCA 2744, 92-2 BCA ¶ 24,821, the board stated that "[a]s long as the cost of correction of completed work . . . is not economically wasteful, the Government may properly require repair or replacement of nonconforming work." See also *Eller Constr., Inc.*, AGBCA 77-171-4, 83-2 BCA ¶ 16,560, which discusses the government's right to require replacement of defective work, as opposed to repair, along with the concept of economic waste. The limit imposed upon correction by the doctrine of economic waste was fully discussed in Section II.A.1.c.

When the government orders correction, the contractor is entitled to a reasonable period of time to perform the corrective work without regard to the original delivery schedule, *Baifield Indus., Div. of A-T-O, Inc.*, ASBCA 14582, 72-2 BCA ¶ 9676 (government, by urging corrective action despite clear inability of contractor to meet original delivery schedule, waived right to default terminate on original schedule and was obligated to give contractor a reasonable time extension in which to correct deficiencies). In *Nanofast, Inc.*, ASBCA 12545, 69-1 BCA ¶ 7566, the board ruled that the government had a duty to cooperate with the contractor during the period that corrective work was being performed. Although the contract clauses are silent on this point, one appeals board has held that the government is entitled to require the contractor to submit the proposed corrective measures for approval before proceeding to correct the defective work, *Stamell Constr. Co.*, DOTCAB 68-27I, 75-1 BCA ¶ 11,087 (government desire to consider corrective measures was reasonable where contractor's initial assessment of the problem had been incorrect).

Service contracts have frequently provided for notice to the contractor of defective work. It has been held that such provision "requires that the contractor be given a fair chance" to correct unsatisfactory work or to furnish omitted work, *Jesco Resources, Inc.*, GSBCA 6857, 84-1 BCA ¶ 16,927. In *Mutual Maint. Co.*, GSBCA 7492, 85-2 BCA ¶ 17,944, the board stated that the "[d]efault provision in this custodial services contract requires written notice and a fair chance to correct unsatisfactory cyclic work or to complete omitted cyclic work before a deduction may be taken." See also *Moustafa Mohamed*, GSBCA 5760, 83-1 BCA ¶ 16,162, *recons. denied*, 83-2 BCA ¶ 16,805, in which the board concluded that a lesser period for correction of deficiencies than to perform the original work was not justified. The standard service contract clause in FAR 52.246-4 contains no such notice provision, but states that "the Government may require" the contractor to reperform services that do not comply with the specifications. It is likely that the contractor will be held to have a reasonable opportunity to correct defective work under this clause. See *Exquisite Serv. Co.*, ASBCA 21058, 77-2 BCA ¶ 12,799, in which the board so held under the prior DoD clause, which was similar to the present FAR clause.

2. Government Correction

The standard inspection clauses provide that if the contractor fails to promptly replace or correct rejected work or supplies or to reperform rejected services, the government may by contract or otherwise replace or correct the work or perform the services and charge the costs to the contractor.

First, the government must prove the original work was defective. See *Walk, Haydel & Assocs. v. General Servs. Admin.*, GSBCA 13233, 96-1 BCA ¶ 28,121, holding that the government was not entitled to recover because it did not prove that the contractor's work did not conform to contract requirements. The government placed letters and affidavits into the record that were written years after performance to show that the project was prematurely accepted as complete on the contractor's advice. However, the statements were not supported by the contemporaneous documents, which showed that the contractor had warned the government that there were deficiencies in the project and said nothing about substantial completion. The government must then prove the work was necessary and within the scope of the original contract, *Mark A. Carroll & Sons, Inc.*, IBCA 3427, 96-1 BCA ¶ 28,224 (electrical contractor liable for the cost of punchlist corrections demanded by the government and performed by another electrician, because the correcting electrician's testimony, as well as photographs, established that the work was necessary and within the scope of the original contract).

Second, the government may charge the contractor for the cost of correction only if the contractor was first given the opportunity to correct the work and failed to do so within a reasonable time, *E.R. Smith Constr. Co.,* DOTCAB 1077, 80-1 BCA ¶ 14,386. In *Pearl Props.,* HUDBCA 95-C-118-C4, 96-1 BCA ¶ 28,219, the government could not deduct the cost of correcting a contractor's work, because the government chose not to ask the contractor to reperform the deficient work and did not even notify the contractor that it considered any of the performance unacceptable until after an interim contractor had corrected it. Thus, the government waived any right that it may have had to reduce its payment to the original contractor. See also *Donohoe Constr. Co.*, ASBCA 47310, 98-2 BCA ¶ 30,076, *recons. denied,* 99-1 BCA ¶ 30,387 (deduction from a contractor's payment for work performed by a follow-on contractor not proper, because the government did not give the contractor the opportunity to inspect or make repairs itself); *Lionsgate Corp.*, ENGBCA 5809, 92-2 BCA ¶ 24,983 (government not entitled to reprocurement costs because the contractor was not given a reasonable opportunity to correct or replace the defective work); and *Abbott Power Corp.*, VACAB 1133, 77-1 BCA ¶ 12,427 (contractor not required to pay for government corrective work because, although the government notified the contractor of the deficiencies, it failed to make demand for corrections to the contractor before engaging another contractor). In *Lyons Lumber Mill*, AGBCA 90-136-3, 90-3 BCA ¶ 23,136, the board stated at 116,173:

> There is ample precedent for a holding that the Government's decision to take over uncompleted work must be preceded by notice to the contractor; a reasonable time for response; a lack of response; and a contract provision that allows the Government to perform unfinished work and charge the contractor with the costs of same.

For cases holding that the government appropriately charged the contractor for correction work, see *Lenoir Contractors, Inc.*, DOTCAB 78-7, 80-2 BCA ¶ 14,459 (government's election to perform corrective work was proper after contractor was given reasonable notice and opportunity to correct defects but failed to respond), and *Singleton Contracting Corp.*, DOTBCA 1470, 84-3 BCA ¶ 17,526 (the contractor had been properly notified by the government but had failed to make the repairs within a reasonable time).

3. Price Reduction

The Court of Claims addressed the government's right to obtain a price reduction in *Farwell Co. v. United States*, 137 Ct. Cl. 832, 148 F. Supp. 947 (1957). In *Farwell*, the government reduced the price when the contractor used tubing rather than contract-specified pipe. The court permitted the price reduction, noting that allowing the contractor to be paid as if it had adhered to contract requirements would put it in a more advantageous bidding position than the other bidders, who calculated their bids based on pipe. In *Stable Constr. Co.*, ASBCA 38138, 89-3 BCA ¶ 22,241, the board stated that "the Government was, by circumstance, forced to accept nonconforming work. Its resort to a unilateral price reduction and withholding is justified and clearly supported by precedent." See also *Alta Constr. Co.*, PSBCA 1334, 87-1 BCA ¶ 19,491, *recons. denied,* 87-1 BCA ¶ 19,655 (a price reduction may be claimed when the government accepts nonconforming work); *M & H Con-*

str. Co., ASBCA 21528, 79-1 BCA ¶ 13,688 (price reduction was proper when contractor failed to furnish separate quality control person under Contractor Quality Control clause); and *T. Brown Constructors, Inc.,* DOTBCA 1986, 95-2 BCA ¶ 27,870 (government entitled to accept, at a reduced price, a highway construction contractor's nonconforming asphalt, because the parties had not agreed to use alternative procedures for acceptance of asphalt on the basis of a supplier's certification of quality).

To determine the measure of an equitable adjustment, the boards have primarily looked to "[t]he change in cost of performance to [the contractor] and not damages to the Government," *Davis Constructors, Inc.*, ASBCA 40630, 91-1 BCA ¶ 23,394. There, the board stated that "[w]hen the contractor performs in a manner less costly than the manner the contract requires, the Government is entitled to the cost savings realized by the contractor." See also *Cameo Bronze, Inc.*, GSBCA 3646, 73-2 BCA ¶ 10,135, *recons. denied*, 73-2 BCA ¶ 10,365 (price reduction for savings of contractor in not following design-type specifications was appropriate). However, the government must be prepared to prove the amount of the contractor's savings. In *California Shipbuilding & Dry Dock Co.*, ASBCA 21394, 78-1 BCA ¶ 13,168, the board refused to grant such a deductive equitable adjustment because the government failed to prove the amount saved by the contractor. The government must also prove the work did not meet the specifications, *Laboratory Sys. Servs., Inc.*, ASBCA 47901, 95-1 BCA ¶ 27,527, and that the specification could have been followed, *Donat Gerg Haustechnik*, ASBCA 41197, 97-2 BCA ¶ 29,272, *aff'd,* 194 F.3d 1336 (Fed. Cir. 1999) (government had the right to accept the nonconforming work with a reduction in the contract price but no entitlement to a price reduction when a specified product did not exist, rendering the basis of the claim too speculative).

The government's remedies are not constrained by the clauses. For example, ¶ (e) of the Inspection of Services clause at FAR 52.246-4, provides only partial relief for defects in services and does not preclude a claim for breach of contract seeking relief for other damages caused by the theft of fuel, *PAE Int'l.*, ASBCA 45314, 98-1 BCA ¶ 29,347.

If the government has lost its right to obtain the cost of correction, it may still be able to obtain the contractor's savings. In *Techni Data Labs.*, ASBCA 21054, 77-2 BCA ¶ 12,667, the board held that the government could not charge the contractor its cost of correcting defects because the contractor had not been given the opportunity to correct them, but that the government was entitled to make a downward equitable adjustment in price, deducting the cost the contractor saved by not having to correct the defects. See also *John Lembesis Co.*, ASBCA 24100, 80-2 BCA ¶ 14,571, in which the board held that deductions for defective work should be based on contractor savings rather than government costs, unless government personnel actually perform corrections. See also FAR 46.407(f), which provides in part:

> However, when supplies or services involving minor nonconformances are accepted, the contract need not be modified unless it appears that the savings to the contractor in fabricating the nonconforming supplies or performing the nonconforming services will exceed the cost to the Government of processing the modification.

The doctrine of substantial performance may also limit the amount of the price reduction to which the government is entitled. In *Valley Asphalt Corp.*, ASBCA 17595, 74-2 BCA ¶ 10,680, a completed runway did not have elevations conforming precisely to the contract. The court discussed possible damages—cost of replacement or the difference in value between the construction as completed and the construction as it would have been had all contract terms been followed. Since the value of the runway was, "insofar as elevations are concerned, not measurably less than the value of the completed runway as promised," the board concluded that the government was entitled "to little more than the equivalent of nominal damages." The board determined that greater damages would have imposed economic waste. In *Donald C. Hubbs, Inc.*, DOTBCA 2012, 90-1 BCA ¶ 22,379, *aff'd*, 918 F.2d 185 (Fed. Cir. 1990), the board stated at 112,459:

> Under the doctrine of substantial performance, one or two minor aberrations in the pavement over the length of the project would not justify the FHWA in requiring a complete overlaying of the highway. Under the common law doctrine of substantial performance, it might not even justify an FHWA withholding of a portion of the contract price. However, the parties have agreed to specific terms in their contract, applicable to this situation. By paragraph (f) of the Inspection of Construction clause, . . . [the contractor] has assumed the obligation to either correct all work not conforming to the contract specifications or accept an "appropriate" contract price reduction.

However, because the area in question in *Hubbs* was flood damaged, which made it impossible or impracticable to repair, the board found that the proper remedy was reduction in contract price.

III. POST-ACCEPTANCE RIGHTS

Acceptance by the government imposes a major limitation on its rights. The standard clauses contain a unique provision making acceptance final, with the result that the government has no rights against the contractor for patent defects absent fraud, gross mistake, or a warranty clause. Paragraph (i) of the inspection clause for construction contracts at FAR 52.246-12 states:

> Acceptance shall be final and conclusive, except for latent defects, fraud, gross mistakes amounting to fraud, or the Government's rights under any warranty or guarantee.

Paragraph (k) of the inspection clause for supply contracts at FAR 52.246-2 states:

> Acceptance shall be conclusive, except for latent defects, fraud, gross mistakes amounting to fraud, or as otherwise provided in the contract.

These contractual provisions are significantly different from the Uniform Commercial Code. Under the U.C.C., acceptance of goods containing patent defects generally precludes the buyer from subsequently rejecting the goods but does not preclude recovery of damages. Under these standard government contract inspection clauses, acceptance of work containing patent defects precludes all remedies. In contrast, neither the inspection clause for service contracts at FAR 52.246-4 nor the standard clause for contracts for commercial items at FAR 52.212-4 contains any finality of acceptance language. Similarly, the small purchase forms, SF 347 in FAR 53.302-347 and DD Form 1155 in DFARS 253.303-155, contain no provision relating to the finality of acceptance. In *Peters Mach. Co.*, ASBCA 21857, 79-1 BCA ¶ 13,649, the board found that, absent a governing provision in the purchase order, a dispute concerning revocation of acceptance must be resolved by reference to U.C.C. § 2-608. However, where the contract incorporates any clause that requires the contractor to repair the defective work after final acceptance, the U.C.C. analysis will not be necessary, *Loral Corp., Def. Sys. Div.-Akron*, ASBCA 37627, 92-1 BCA ¶ 24,661, *aff'd,* 979 F.2d 215 (Fed. Cir. 1992).

Finality applies to work accepted with patent defects whether or not the government has knowledge of the defects. In *McQuagge v. United States*, 197 F. Supp. 460 (W.D. La. 1961), government officials accepted work with knowledge of patent defects, and the accepted work was accorded finality. The same result was obtained in *California Power Sys., Inc.*, GSBCA 7462, 86-1 BCA ¶ 18,598, in which the board rejected the government's argument that defects in the tendered cabinets were latent. There, the government had argued that the defects were concealed by the shipping crates that surrounded the cabinets during inspection. The board concluded, however, that the defects were obviously patent and that the government was bound by its acceptance. See also *Genuine Motor Parts of Pa., Inc.*, ASBCA 19063, 76-1 BCA ¶ 11,860, in which the government was bound by acceptance based on an inadequate inspection. The importance of the language providing for finality and conclusiveness of acceptance can be seen in *United States v. Hamden Co-op. Creamery Co.*, 185 F. Supp. 541 (E.D.N.Y. 1960), *aff'd*, 297 F.2d 130 (2d Cir. 1961), where the contract did not contain such provisions and the court relied on the Uniform Sales Act (New York) to enable the government to reject and recover for defective powdered milk.

This unique role of acceptance in government contracts has several important ramifications, which are addressed in this section. The first subsection analyzes the exceptions to finality of acceptance: (1) latent defects, (2) fraud, and (3) gross mistakes amounting to fraud. Since the most common means available to the government to avoid the finality of acceptance is to demonstrate that a defect falls within one of these exceptions, there has been substantial litigation on this issue. This area is also important because the clauses have no time limitations restricting the government's rights when one of these exceptions is proved. The second subsection deals with the use of warranty provisions—the other major technique for preserving government rights after acceptance. Such provisions are explicitly recognized in the construction clause and implicitly recognized in the supply contract clause.

A. Latent Defects, Fraud, and Gross Mistakes

Latent defects, fraud, and gross mistakes are exceptions to finality of acceptance that give the government broad rights, including the right to retract acceptance. See, for example, *Munson Hammerhead Boats*, ASBCA 51377, 00-2 BCA ¶ 31,143, stating at 253,806:

> It is settled that, upon discovery of latent defects, respondent is entitled to set aside its earlier acceptance and to terminate the contract. E.g., *Cross Aero Corporation*, ASBCA No. 14801, 71-2 BCA ¶ 9075 at 42,086. Such "action may be taken within a reasonable time after the latent defects have become known." *Bar Ray Products, Inc. v. United States*, 162 Ct. Cl. 836, 838 (1963).

This section considers when such rights may be invoked and the remedies that they afford.

1. Latent Defects

Latent defects are defects that existed at the time of acceptance but could not have been "discovered by observation or inspection made with ordinary care," *ABM/Ansley Bus. Materials v. General Servs. Admin.*, GSBCA 9367, 93-1 BCA ¶ 25,246; *H.B. Zachry Co.*, ASBCA 42266, 95-2 BCA ¶ 27616. In *Herley Indus., Inc.*, ASBCA 13727, 71-1 BCA ¶ 8888, the board set out the essential elements of latent defects at 41,309:

> Under the first of these exceptions by which the Government seeks to avoid the conclusive effect of final acceptance, it must establish the existence of defects at the time of final acceptance which were hidden from knowledge as well as sight and could not be discovered by the exercise of reasonable care. It is further well established that defects which can be discovered readily by an ordinary examination or test are not latent and a failure to make the examination or test does not make them so; the finality of acceptance is not diminished by such failure. *Polan Industries, Inc.*, ASBCA Nos. 3996 et al., 58-2 BCA ¶ 1982, p. 8172; *Hercules Engineering & Manufacturing Company*, ASBCA No. 4979, 59-2 BCA ¶ 2426.

FAR 2.101 has essentially adopted this definition, providing that "latent defect" is "a defect that exists at the time of acceptance but cannot be discovered by a reasonable inspection." FAR 46.101 states: "'Patent defect' means any defect which exists at the time of acceptance and is not a latent defect."

Latent defects disputes are fact-intensive and difficult to resolve on summary judgment, *Stewart & Stevenson,* ASBCA 52140, 00-2 BCA ¶ 31,041. The government must prove that (1) a defect existed in the contractor's work based on the specification, (2) the defect existed when the government accepted the work, (3) a reasonable inspection would not have revealed the defect, and (4) the defect caused injury to the government. To establish the defect, the government cannot apply a more severe inspection procedure or acceptance standard than the contract imposed, *Southwest Welding & Mfg. Co. v. United States*, 188 Ct. Cl. 925, 413 F.2d 1167, 1185 (1969). See also *Peter Kiewit Sons' Co.,* IBCA 3535-95, 1999 WL 373384, distinguishing *Southwest.*

a. Known Defects

If the defects were actually known to the government at the time of acceptance, they are patent, *Southwest Welding & Mfg. Co. v. United States*, 188 Ct. Cl. 925, 413 F.2d 1167 (1969). This is true even if such defects might not have been discoverable by a reasonable inspection. See *United Techs. Corp., Sikorsky Aircraft Div. v. United States*, 27 Fed. Cl. 393 (1992), *recons. denied*, 31 Fed. Cl. 698 (1994) (limited fatigue life of helicopter spindles was known to the government prior to acceptance, so any such defect was patent although not discernible through the contractually specified inspection procedures). The pre-acceptance knowledge obtained by the government must be sufficient to determine the risks involved in using defective materials. In *Norair Eng'g Corp.*, ENGBCA 5244, 92-2 BCA ¶ 25,009, the board found the contractor's use of polyester as a substitute material to be a latent defect despite the fact that the government knew it was substitute material. The board reasoned that it was not clear to the government prior to acceptance that polyester suffered rapid deterioration when exposed to water and lime. Hence, it was not the substitute nature of the material that was the latent defect but the risks involved in using the product that rendered the product defective. See also *Shea-Ball (JV)*, ENGBCA 5608, 99-1 BCA ¶ 30,277 (defects were not latent because there had been multiple approvals by the government with knowledge of the defects).

b. Reliance on Contractor Testing or Assurances

One of the factors to be considered in deciding whether the government should have performed an inspection or test is whether the government is entitled to rely on a contractor's testing obligations. In *Utley-James, Inc.*, GSBCA 6831, 88-1 BCA ¶ 20,518, defects were held to be latent even though discoverable through a thorough government inspection because the contract specified that the contractor would be responsible for inspection and testing. See also *General Elec. Co.*, ASBCA 36005, 91-3 BCA ¶ 24,353, in which readily discoverable defects were found to be latent because the contractor was responsible for testing. *Tricon-Triangle Contractors*, ENGBCA 5553, 92-1 BCA ¶ 24,667 involved two defects. One was latent because the government was entitled to expect that an experienced contractor would perform a test that would discover the defect. The other was patent because the government failed to insist that the contractor perform contractually required tests that would have disclosed the defect. See also *Jung Ah Indus. Co.*, ASBCA 22632, 79-1 BCA ¶ 13,643, *recons. denied*, 79-2 BCA ¶ 13,916; *Wickham Contracting Co.,* ASBCA 32392, 88-2 BCA ¶ 20,559; and *Norair Eng'g Corp.*, ENGBCA 5244, 92-2 BCA ¶ 25,009. See *Munson Hammerhead Boats*, ASBCA 51377, 00-2 BCA ¶ 31,143, stating that since the contract required the contractor to maintain an inspection system, visual observation was all that was required to constitute a reasonable government inspection. Government reliance has also been found when the contractor is required to provide a certificate of conformance. See Subsection 4 for a discussion of this issue.

c. Nature of the Specification

The more critical the item or the more specific or detailed its description in the contract specification, the greater the likelihood the government will be expected to test it. In *Geranco Mfg. Corp.*, ASBCA 12376, 68-1 BCA ¶ 6898, it was held that the contractor's failure to use a noncorroding pump in a steam cleaner constituted a patent defect. The board stated at 31,860:

> The contracting officer states that normal inspection does not require the dismantling or teardown of the cleaner and an analysis of the materials used. This would seem to be true if one were buying one, or a small quantity of, "off the shelf" cleaners. But we are here concerned with contracts for 456 cleaners, at a total price of $347,268.89, to be designed and produced to conform to Government specifications. The specifications contain requirements to be met by materials and components. When the Government specifies that materials and components are to have certain properties and meet certain requirements it presumably has some way of inspecting or testing to see if the specifications are met.

Accord, *Sentell Bros., Inc.*, DOTBCA 1824, 89-3 BCA ¶ 21,904, *recons. denied*, 89-3 BCA ¶ 22,219 (use of nonconforming paint in full view of the government inspector not a latent defect). In *USA Petroleum Corp. v. United States*, 821 F.2d 622 (Fed. Cir. 1987), the court discussed the question of whether the Inspection clause applied to the quantity of items as opposed to their quality. However, it did not decide the issue, finding that even if the clause applied to quantity, the government would be entitled to a remedy because the deficient quantity of crude oil was not discoverable by a reasonable inspection.

d. Ease of Government Inspection

The degree of difficulty and expense of conducting tests are important factors in determining the reasonableness of a government test. For example, dimensional defects, discoverable by measurement, are commonly held not latent, *Jo-Bar Mfg. Corp.*, ASBCA 18292, 73-2 BCA ¶ 10,353, *recons. denied*, 74-1 BCA ¶ 10,392 (cylinder assemblies did not conform to specified dimensions). See also *Ahern Painting Contractors, Inc.*, GSBCA 7912, 90-1 BCA ¶ 22,291 (mortar defects were patent because discoverable through simple test). The fact that the test was not specified is not relevant to the determination that it was a reasonable inspection procedure, *Bart Assocs., Inc.,* EBCA C-9211144, 96-2 BCA ¶ 28,479.

Even an easy inspection may not be required to meet the reasonableness standard if the circumstances make that inspection impracticable. In *Kaminer Constr. Corp. v. United States*, 203 Ct. Cl. 182, 488 F.2d 980 (1973), the court upheld the board's finding that 16 undersized bolts in a 11,967-bolt structure constituted a latent defect. Although the defects could have been easily discovered by a torque wrench inspection, which was specified in the contract, the board determined that a simple visual inspection was reasonable under the circumstances and that the undersized bolts could not have been discovered thereby. See also *Globe Seed & Feed Co.,* AGBCA 90-164-1, 91-2 BCA ¶ 23,968 (precluding a finding of patency where noxious seeds were not discernible by visual inspection), and *Wickham Contracting Co.,* ASBCA 32392, 88-2 BCA ¶ 20,559 (because defects were not discernible through visual inspection and the contractor was liable for all inspection and testing, the defects were latent). Compare *Harold Bailey Painting Co.*, ASBCA 28443, 84-1 BCA ¶ 17,043 (loose boards, lack of featheredging, and improperly driven nails were readily discoverable and therefore not latent defects).

The availability of test facilities has also been considered in determining whether a test could reasonably have been made. See *Herley Indus., Inc.*, ASBCA 13727, 71-1 BCA ¶ 8888, in which a defect in the composition of metal was found patent because the government had a readily available laboratory that conducted metal analyses. Compare *Jung Ah Indus. Co.*, ASBCA 22632, 79-1 BCA ¶ 13,643, *recons. denied*, 79-2 BCA ¶ 13,916, in which the board found a defect to be latent despite the fact that there was a testing facility available to determine whether wall paneling was "incombustible treated." The board concluded that the government had acted reasonably in not submitting the material to this testing facility because the contractor had stated on the invoice and had provided oral assurances that the material met the requirement.

If a defect can be discovered only by operating the item for a period of time, it may be considered latent. See *Keco Indus., Inc.*, ASBCA 13271, 71-1 BCA ¶ 8727, in which the board found defects in sealed clutch assemblies latent because in many instances they could have been discovered only by continual operation beyond the required 500-hour service life before the failures occurred. Because the imposition of such a test would have amounted to "a requirement for destruction of the component, and a frustration of the purposes of the operational warranty," the board concluded that the test was not reasonable and the defects were therefore latent. Similarly, in *Triple "A" Mach. Shop, Inc.*, ASBCA 16844, 73-1 BCA ¶ 9826, the board found that a defect that went undetected after the units were tested for one-and-a-half to two hours was latent because this appeared to be a reasonable test. See also *Tricon-Triangle Contractors*, ENGBCA 5553, 92-1 BCA ¶ 24,667 (defective assembly of pipes was latent because government was entitled to assume that an experienced contractor would have performed an inspection that would have disclosed the defect), and *Wickham Contracting Co.*, ASBCA 32392, 88-2 BCA ¶ 20,559 (fact that tendered cables were in operation for more than a year before discovery of the defect was evidence of latency).

e. Past Experience

The degree of the contractor's past experience with the items, the past performance of the contractor, and representations made by the contractor have all been considered in determining whether it would have been reasonable for the government to conduct a test that would have disclosed the defect. The experience of the contractor has been considered in determining what constitutes a reasonable inspection, *Triple "A" Mach. Shop, Inc.*, ASBCA 16844, 73-1 BCA ¶ 9826 (one hour per day of government inspection was reasonable for work that was not difficult for such an experienced contractor); *Norair Eng'g Corp.*, ENGBCA 5244, 92-2 BCA ¶ 25,009 (assurances by experienced contractor and its consultant sufficient to excuse government from conducting independent analysis). Conversely, where the contractor has had no previous experience in performing the work, a higher degree of government inspection is required, *T.M. Indus.*, ASBCA 19068, 75-1 BCA ¶ 11,056.

2. Fraud

The criteria for revoking acceptance based on fraud were stated by the board in *Dale Ingram, Inc.*, ASBCA 12152, 74-1 BCA ¶ 10,436 at 49,331:

> In order for the Government to have a legal right to revoke its final acceptance on the ground of fraud, it has the burden of proving (1) that its acceptance was induced by its reliance on (2) a misrepresentation of fact, actual or implied, or the concealment of a material fact, (3) made with knowledge of its falsity or in reckless or wanton disregard of the facts, (4) with intent to mislead the Government into relying on the misrepresentation, (5) as a consequence of which the Government has suffered injury, 12 Williston, *Contracts*, (3rd Ed.), Section 1487A. All of these elements must be present in order for the Government to have a legal right to rescind its final acceptance on the ground of fraud.

The board denied the government's claim on the grounds that it had failed to prove either that the contractor knew of the error or that the government relied on the misrepresentation. In *Umpqua Excavation & Paving Co.*, AGBCA 84-185-1, 91-1 BCA ¶ 23,452, the board found that acceptance could be revoked even though the government (through its contracting officer) had knowledge of the contractor's use of false weight certificates at the time of acceptance. The board reasoned that the contractor's vice president, who was responsible for the fraud, had not yet been convicted at the time of acceptance. The board also held that the fraud constituted a material breach of the contract and that, therefore, the contractor had no right to rely on the finality provisions in the contract's Inspection clause.

Performance of nonconforming work, in and of itself, does not constitute fraud and overcome final acceptance, *Henry Angelo & Co.,* ASBCA 30502, 87-1 BCA ¶ 19,619. However, fraud was found in *BMY-Combat Sys.Div. of Harsco Corp. v. United States,* 38 Fed. Cl. 109 (1997), in which the court found misrepresentation when the contractor did not disclose that it had not conducted contract-required tests on the DD 250 forms, and intent to deceive when the contractor neither corrected the problem nor requested a waiver of the test requirement after it found out that the tests were not being conducted. See also *United States ex rel. Roby v. Boeing Co.*, 302 F.3d 637 (6th Cir. 2002), and *Varljen v. Cleveland Gear Co.*, 250 F.3d 426 (6th Cir. 2001), which discuss the effect of certification and failure to notify the purchaser, as required by the contract, that a change in manufacturing process took place.

The government's statutory civil and criminal remedies under the False Claims Act, 18 U.S.C. § 287; 31 U.S.C. § 3729, and the False Statements Act, 18 U.S.C. § 1001, are much more favorable than those under the inspection clauses. See *Carrier Corp. v. United States*, 164 Ct. Cl. 666, 328 F.2d 328 (1964), where the government first suspended and later canceled the contract after discovering contractor fraud. The court upheld the government's action and denied the contractor any claims arising under the fraudulently performed contract. In *United States v. Aerodex, Inc.*, 469 F.2d 1003 (5th Cir. 1972), the government avoided the finality of acceptance and recovered penalties under 31 U.S.C. § 3729 when the contractor deliberately mislabeled parts. As a result, the government infrequently relies on the inspection clause remedies when its acceptance was induced by fraud. These fraud remedies have become even easier to obtain since the 1986 Amendment to the False Claims Act, 31 U.S.C. § 3729(b), eliminated the need for specific intent to defraud in order to satisfy the Act's knowledge requirement. See *United States v. TDC Mgmt. Corp.*, 24 F.3d 292 (D.C. Cir. 1994). In *United States v. Hercules, Inc.*, 929 F. Supp. 1418 (D. Utah 1996), the court stated a different view of the pre-1986 statute but held that the statutory change eased the government's burden of proving intent to defraud. See also *Varljen v. Cleveland Gear Co.,* 250 F.3d 426 (6th Cir. 2001).

3. Gross Mistake Amounting to Fraud

In *Bar Ray Prods., Inc. v. United States*, 167 Ct. Cl. 839, 340 F.2d 343 (1964), the court commented that the elements of gross mistake amounting to fraud are the same as those of fraud, except that there is no requirement to prove intent to mislead. In *Catalytic Eng'g & Mfg. Corp.*, ASBCA 15257, 72-1 BCA ¶ 9342, *recons. denied*, 72-2 BCA ¶ 9518, the board further distinguished between fraud and gross mistake, stating that "fraud" has the connotation of deliberate misstatement, while mistake "connotes an unintentional misstatement." Thus, the board described a "gross mistake amounting to fraud" as being a major mistake "so serious or uncalled for as not to be reasonably expected, or justifiable, in the case of a responsible contractor" or a mistake that "cannot be reconciled with good faith." Such a mistaken representation as to a material fact (i.e., a misleading statement, act, or admission), which induces acceptance by the government in reliance on the misrepresentation and thereby causes injury to the government, overcomes finality of acceptance.

a. Nature of Misrepresentation

Not all mistaken representations rise to the level of gross mistakes amounting to fraud. The degree of recklessness or lack of good faith of the contractor will be determined by considering all aspects of the transaction. In *Catalytic Eng'g & Mfg.*, the gross mistake leading to acceptance of nonconforming items consisted of the contractor's failure to inform the government that changes had been made in the drawings and that, as a result, polystyrene instead of polyvinyl chloride would be used in end pieces. The board found that there was no basis for the contractor to reasonably believe that the government either knew about the substitution or would have agreed to it. Similar logic was followed in *Jo-Bar Mfg. Corp.*, ASBCA 17774, 73-2 BCA ¶ 10,311, where the contractor made gross mistakes both in determining that aircraft bolts did not have to be heat treated and in not treating them. In light of the apparent need for such heat treatment based on the specifications, the board concluded at 48,684:

> No responsible supplier who holds himself out as qualified to produce this type of bolt could reasonably be expected to make such gross mistakes. These gross mistakes, coupled with [the contractor's] misrepresentation [to the Government] as to the requirement for heat treatment, caused the acceptance of items not conforming to the contract requirements.

See also *D & H Constr. Co.*, ASBCA 37482, 89-3 BCA ¶ 22,070, in which the contractor was held liable for gross mistake amounting to fraud when a subcontractor used counterfeit certification labels on tendered equipment. Similarly, in *Chilstead Bldg. Co.,* ASBCA 49548, 00-2 BCA ¶ 31,097, a gross mistake amounting to fraud was found where the contractor told the contracting officer it was performing the work in accordance with the contract drawings when it was actually deviating from them. A misrepresentation can also occur where facts are not disclosed to the government, *Mason's, Inc. & Mason's Lazarus t/a Mason's Inc.*, ASBCA 27326, 86-3 BCA ¶ 19,250 (failure to notify the government that tendered supplies had not been tested as required by the specifications was "at the least" a gross mistake amounting to fraud).

The mere fact that the contractor tenders defective work does not constitute a gross mistake amounting to fraud. The actions of the contractor may indicate that it was merely an innocent mistake. In *Mit-Con, Inc.*, ASBCA 39377, 90-2 BCA ¶ 22,707, the board stated: "This is not a case where the contractor . . . attempted to avoid a contract requirement. To the contrary, it incurred a substantial expense for labor to modify the dishwasher in a timely fashion once it discovered [the defect]." In addition, government knowledge of the facts will preclude a finding that the contractor misrepresented them, *Sentell Bros., Inc.*, DOTBCA 1824, 89-3 BCA

¶ 21,904, *recons. denied*, 89-3 BCA ¶ 22,219 (no misrepresentation of a material fact since government had full knowledge of contractor's performance).

The facts and circumstances surrounding the contractor's performance and the government's indifference to the existence of defects will be considered. In *Peters Mach. Co.*, ASBCA 21857, 79-1 BCA ¶ 13,649, the contractor had intentionally deviated from the specifications yet certified on the invoice that the articles conformed. The articles were subsequently accepted by the government based on this certification. The board stated that this set of facts would ordinarily justify a finding of gross mistake amounting to fraud. However, government acceptance of the articles, with full knowledge of the deviation under a prior contract, the contractor's disclosure of its fabrication method, and its reliance on the actions of unauthorized government personnel who apparently "granted" a deviation from the specifications, precluded a finding that the contractor's actions were so "reckless or so uncalled for as to constitute gross mistake amounting to fraud."

In *Gavco Corp.*, ASBCA 29763, 88-3 BCA ¶ 21,095, disclosure of the defects to the government at the time of final acceptance precluded a finding of gross mistake amounting to fraud. There, a contractor used a nonconforming latex mix in repairing the government's drydock. Several workmanship defects were also present, and the combination of these factors might well have amounted to a gross mistake. However, the defects were subjected to an extensive inspection by the contractually specified architect-engineer and his consultants. The consultants even advised the government that the shoddy workmanship "would cause debonding within a relatively short period of time." A contractor's failure to comply with source qualification requirements was found not to be a gross mistake when it appeared that the government did not attach any importance to the requirements and the items "fully complied with all the technical requirements of the contract," *Ordnance Parts & Eng'g Co.*, ASBCA 18841, 74-2 BCA ¶ 10,717. In *Southern Pipe & Supply Co., Div. of Hajoca Corp.*, NASABCA 570-7, 72-2 BCA ¶ 9512, the board held that even assuming that the contractor knew that the pipe stock from which the end item and tubing was made was of foreign origin, the furnishing of the end item tubing as a domestic product would not amount to a gross mistake amounting to fraud. That case could be justified based on the confusion surrounding what constitutes a domestic product under the Buy American Act. However, confusion did not prevent the contractor from being liable under the False Claims Act for submitting hacksaw blades made from Swedish steel as domestic products in *United States v. Rule Indus., Inc.*, 878 F.2d 535 (1st Cir. 1989).

b. Reliance

An essential element in the government's case is reliance. In *Hydro Fitting Mfg. Corp.*, ASBCA 16394, 73-2 BCA ¶ 10,081, the board stated at 47,368:

> In order to substantiate a claim of gross mistake amounting to fraud, it is essential also to demonstrate that the gross mistake complained of actually induced the final acceptance which is sought to be set aside.

See also *Boston Pneumatics, Inc.*, GSBCA 3122, 72-2 BCA ¶ 9682, in which the board found that acceptance of defective items was induced by a gross mistake when the contractor furnished a certification that the items were identical to those previously tested and approved. However, where the contractor made a full disclosure to the government of the materials and procedures it intended to use, which differed from those required by the contract, and government inspectors observed the work without objecting, the board refused to find the reliance necessary to demonstrate a gross mistake amounting to fraud, *H. Bendzulla Contracting, Inc.*, ASBCA 18588, 74-2 BCA ¶ 10,690. See also *Stewart Avionics, Inc.*, ASBCA 15512, 75-1 BCA ¶ 11,253, in which the presence of three government inspectors on duty at the contractor's plant imputed knowledge of the nonconformance to the government so as to exclude the possibility of reliance. Compare *Chilstead Bldg. Co.,* ASBCA 49548, 00-2 BCA ¶ 31,097, finding that the government inspector had reasonably relied on the contractor's statement that it was performing the work in accordance with the contract drawings when he did not himself inspect the work.

c. Injury

To succeed in retracting acceptance on the grounds of gross mistake amounting to fraud, the government must prove that it was harmed by the mistake, that is, that the completed work was of inferior quality or otherwise noncomplying with the contract requirements. In *Massman Constr. Co.*, ENGBCA 3443, 81-2 BCA ¶ 15,212, acceptance was held not final when many welds, which the contractor represented as meeting contract standards, were seriously flawed and had to be repaired. See also *Catalytic Eng'g & Mfg. Corp.*, ASBCA 15257, 72-1 BCA ¶ 9342, *recons. denied*, 72-2 BCA ¶ 9518 (substitute material used by the contractor rendered items unsuitable for their intended use and substantially impaired their value to the government), and *D & H Constr. Co.*, ASBCA 37482, 89-3 BCA ¶ 22,070 (lack of proper certification for freezers and coolers due to counterfeiting lowered the value of those supplies to the government). In *H. Bendzulla Contracting, Inc.*, ASBCA 18588, 74-2 BCA ¶ 10,690, the board found no injury to the government where the contractor met the performance requirements by using a procedure different from that specified. Compare *United States v. Aerodex, Inc.*, 469 F.2d 1003 (5th Cir. 1972), in which the court held that the mere fact that mismarked parts were as good as those contracted for was no defense to a charge of civil fraud.

4. Effect of Contractor Certification

FAR 46.504 permits the use of a certificate of conformance executed by the contractor, as follows:

A certificate of conformance (see 46.315) may be used in certain instances instead of source inspection (whether the contract calls for acceptance at source or destination) at the discretion of the contracting officer if the following conditions apply:

> (a) Acceptance on the basis of a contractor's certificate of conformance is in the Government's interest.
>
> (b)(1) Small losses would be incurred in the event of a defect; or
>
> > (2) Because of the contractor's reputation or past performance, it is likely that the supplies or services furnished will be acceptable and any defective work would be replaced, corrected, or repaired without contest. In no case shall the Government's right to inspect supplies under the inspection provisions of the contract be prejudiced.

The certificate contained in the Certificate of Conformance clause at FAR 52.246-15 states:

> I certify that on .... [insert date], the .... [insert Contractor's name] furnished the supplies or services called for by Contract No. .... via .... [Carrier] on .... [identify the bill of lading or shipping document] in accordance with all applicable requirements. I further certify that the supplies or services are of the quality specified and conform in all respects with the contract requirements, including specifications, drawings, preservation, packaging, packing, marking requirements, and physical item identification (part number), and are in the quantity shown on this or on the attached acceptance document.
>
> Date of Execution:
>
> Signature:
>
> Title:

Since neither the clause nor the certificate specifies how the certificate affects the rights of the parties, the boards have expressed varying views on its impact when performance is not as certified. In *Boston Pneumatics, Inc.*, GSBCA 3122, 72-2 BCA ¶ 9682, the board held that acceptance was not final because of gross mistake amounting to fraud. The board appears to have to concluded that the incorrect certification was part of the conduct comprising the gross mistake, stating at 45,212:

> [T]he furnishing of the certification by the [contractor] affords the Government a greater degree of protection than would be the case if the Government relied solely on the provision of the specifications in seeking any redress from the Contractor. The certification, in effect, survives acceptance by the Government and is a material provision to be relied on by Contracting Officer.

The Armed Services Board followed similar reasoning in *Jo-Bar Mfg. Corp.*, ASBCA 17774, 73-2 BCA ¶ 10,311, stating at 48,685:

> Under the contract, technical responsibility for final inspection and test rested on [the contractor] and, even though the Government retained the right to verify such inspection and test results, the procedure of relying on the contractor's certification of the compliance of its product with the specifications was a reasonable one.

A few cases have dealt with this situation under the "latent defects" exception rather than the "gross mistakes amounting to fraud" exception. The boards have held that it is reasonable for the government to conduct a more limited inspection in reliance on a certificate of conformance. If the defect is not discoverable by such a "reasonable" limited inspection, it is latent, *Harrington & Richardson, Inc.*, ASBCA 9839, 72-2 BCA ¶ 9507 ("[t]he existence of the contractually-specified procedure, requiring the use of certificates of compliance tends to negate an understanding that such a defect is patent"); *Jung Ah Indus. Co.*, ASBCA 22632, 79-1 BCA ¶ 13,643, *recons. denied*, 79-2 BCA ¶ 13,916. In *Jung Ah*, the contractor was not required to submit a certificate of conformance, but was required to assure that wall paneling had been "incombustible treated." This contractual obligation, coupled with the contractor's voluntary statement on the delivery invoices and its oral assurances that the wall paneling had been "incombustible treated," led the board to conclude that the government's limited inspection was reasonable and that the lack of such treatment was a latent defect. The government did not argue that there had been a gross mistake amounting to fraud, and the board did not discuss whether such a gross mistake had occurred.

These statements by the boards might be interpreted as indicating that contractor certificates are, in themselves, an independent ground for overcoming the finality of acceptance. However, no board has so stated. In *Peters Mach. Co.*, ASBCA 21857, 79-1 BCA ¶ 13,649, the board expressly held that certificates are not warranties with lives of their own and that the "contract provision authorizing shipments upon certificates of compliance limits the Government's rights to those afforded by the Inspection clause." The board concluded that the contractor had not committed a gross mistake amounting to fraud. Although DAR 7-104.100 contained no specific language that afforded the government additional post-acceptance rights, FAR 52.246-15(c) may provide such additional rights by allowing the government to reject supplies within a reasonable time after "delivery" depending on when acceptance is deemed to have taken place.

Perhaps much of the confusion surrounding the issue of whether to proceed under a theory of gross mistake or latent defects has finally been resolved by the board's discussion in *ABM/Ansley Bus. Materials v. GSA*, GSBCA 9367, 93-1 BCA ¶ 25,246. The board concluded that the existence of an inspection certification amounted to probative evidence of the latency of the defects. This did not, however, alleviate the government's normal burden of establishing that the defect was not discoverable and could not have been detected through reasonable means at the time of final acceptance, but was merely probative evidence thereof. The board concluded that the defects were patent. In a footnote, the board addressed the conflicting theories used to decide such cases, stating at 125,749:

> Some cases have dealt with the existence of defects despite a certification under the "gross mistakes amounting to fraud exception." See *Boston Pneumatics, Inc.*, GSBCA 3122, 72-2 BCA ¶ 9682. In this case, however, there is a genuine conflict in the evidence as to whether the [tendered] pads were defective. Moreover, the evidence shows that the goods were satisfactory to the Government for an initial period. Even the ACO conceded that she was unable . . . to verify complaints before December, 1986. With this room for dispute, it seems unlikely that the [contractor's] certification could fairly be termed a "gross mistake amounting to fraud."

Accordingly, it appears that the courts and boards will look at the weight of the evidence of latency in determining whether a contractor's certification amounts to a gross mistake. If this is the case, then successful claims under this theory of recovery will be rare.

5. Notice and Proof of Defects

Essential to government claims are proof of a defect and timely notice to the contractor.

a. Proof of Defect

When the government seeks to overcome the finality of acceptance, it bears the burden of proving that a defect existed at the time of acceptance, *Hydro Fitting Mfg. Corp.*, ASBCA 16394, 73-2 BCA ¶ 10,081; *M.A. Mortenson Co. v. United States*, 29 Fed. Cl. 82 (1993); *Sentell Bros., Inc.*, DOTBCA 1824, 89-3 BCA ¶ 21,904, *denied*, 89-3 BCA ¶ 22,219; *General Elec. Co.*, ASBCA 36005, 91-3 BCA ¶ 24,353; *D.L. Kaufman, Inc.*, PSBCA 4159, 00-1 BCA ¶ 30,846. The government must prove that the work did not comply with the specifications, *United Techs. Corp., Sikorsky Aircraft Div. v. United States*, 27 Fed. Cl. 393 (1992). Performance failures caused by events after acceptance do not establish contractor liability, *Marmon-Herrington Co.*, ASBCA 10889, 67-2 BCA ¶ 6523 (evidence showed that the probable cause of compressors' failures was their excessive movement over rough roads by the government). It must also be shown that the failure was caused by the defect, *Jo-Bar Mfg. Corp.*, ASBCA 18292, 73-2 BCA ¶ 10,353, *recons. denied*, 74-1 BCA ¶ 10,392; *Ordnance Parts & Eng'g Co.*, ASBCA 40277, 90-3 BCA ¶ 23,142 (government latent defect argument rejected because of conflicting evidence as to which party caused the defects). Existence of a defect and its causal connection to the alleged failure must be established by direct proof and not by inference, *Datamark, Inc.*, ASBCA 12767, 69-1 BCA ¶ 7464; *Santa Barbara Research Ctr.*, ASBCA

27831, 88-3 BCA ¶ 21,098, *recons. denied*, 89-3 BCA ¶ 22,020 (government's argument that "something happened in the vendor's manufacturing process that led to some defective devices being delivered," without any evidence as to what actually happened, was too speculative).

The government has the burden of proving these elements by a "preponderance of the evidence," *M.A. Mortenson Co. v. United States*, 40 Fed. Cl. 389 (1998) (citing *Southwest Welding & Mfg. Co. v. United States,* 188 Ct. Cl. 925, 413 F.2d 1167 (1969), among others). See also *Northrop Grumman Corp.,* ASBCA 52178, 04-2 BCA ¶ 32,804, *recons. denied*, 05-2 BCA ¶ 32,992, and *Bart Assocs., Inc.*, EBCA C-211144, 96-2 BCA ¶ 28,479. The mere fact that an item fails to function does not establish that a defect existed at the time of acceptance, *Professional Printing of Kan., Inc.,* GPOBCA 28-93, 1997 WL 742498 GPO BCA 02-93 (May 19, 1995).

In *Roberts v. United States*, 174 Ct. Cl. 940, 357 F.2d 938 (1966), where deficiencies were due to both patent and latent defects as well as to faulty design, the court refused to award the cost of repair to the government absent specific proof of the portion of the costs attributable to latent defects. The court stated at 957:

> There is no way to approximate the amount of the claimed replacement costs that are due to [the contractor's] failure to observe the contract provisions separately from replacement costs that are required because of patent defects and defendant's faulty design.

b. Notice of Defect

Government claims must be timely asserted. In *Catalytic Eng'g & Mfg. Corp.*, ASBCA 15257, 72-1 BCA ¶ 9342, *recons. denied*, 72-2 BCA ¶ 9518, the board stated the general rule that the time for revocation of acceptance is "within a reasonable time after the [government] discovered or should have discovered" the defect. See also *Perkin-Elmer Corp. v. United States,* 47 Fed. Cl. 672 (2000), stating at 675:

> Where latent defects in manufactured articles are found, the government has a "reasonable time" to take action and assert a claim. *Bar Ray Prods., Inc. v. United States*, 162 Ct. Cl. 836, 837-38 (1963). "In order to revoke acceptance of the supply, the government must assert its claim in a timely manner, and prove by a preponderance of the evidence that a latent defect existed at the time of final acceptance which was hidden from knowledge as well as sight, and could not be discovered by the exercise of reasonable care." *Spandome Corp. v. United States*, 32 Fed. Cl. 626, 630 (1995) (citing *United Techs. Corp. v. United States*, 27 Fed. Cl. 393, 398 (1992)). Although the government must assert its claim in a timely matter, the government acts reasonably when it delays revocation of acceptance in order to determine conclusively that supplies do not comply with contractual specifications, or the Government works with a contractor to solve the problem. See *Jung Ah Indus. Co.*, ASBCA No. 22632, 79-1 B.C.A. (CCH) ¶ 13,643, at 66,929 (1979).

In *ETA Tech. Corp.*, ASBCA 48417, 97-1 BCA ¶ 28,666, the government could not revoke its acceptance because it had failed to take prompt action after learning of the defects. Although the government knew of the defect in 1981, it took no action to make a claim or revoke acceptance until the contracting officer's final decision in 1991. See also *Fischer Imaging Corp.*, VABCA 6125, 02-2 BCA ¶ 32,003 (government waived its right to revoke its acceptance because it used the allegedly nonconforming equipment for 12 months after it discovered the alleged defects), and *Traylor Bros., Inc. & S & M Constructors (JV)*, ENGBCA 5884, 99-1 ¶ 30,136 (contractor not liable for a latent defect because the government's three year delay in providing notice of the defect to the contractor was unreasonable as a matter of law). Contractors were assumed to have been prejudiced and the revocation of acceptance was not permitted where the assertion of latent defects was not made until three years and nine years after acceptance, *Ball Healy (JV),* ENGBCA 5892, 96-2 BCA ¶ 28,429; *Granite Groves (JV),* ENGBCA 5896, 97-1 BCA ¶ 28,673.

Essentially the same standard is contained in U.C.C. § 2-608(2), which states "Revocation of acceptance must occur within a reasonable time after the buyer discovers or should have discovered the ground for it and before any substantial change in condition of the goods which is not caused by their own defects." The discovery of a defect can occur a number of years after the beginning of use of the item by the government. See *General Elec. Co.*, IBCA 442-6-64, 65-2 BCA ¶ 4974, in which timely assertion was found when a latent defect caused an explosion four years after electrical equipment was put in service. In *Jung Ah Indus. Co.*, ASBCA 22632, 79-1 BCA ¶ 13,643, *recons. denied*, 79-2 BCA ¶ 13,916, the contractor argued that the government should not be allowed to recover because of an unreasonable delay in asserting its claim of latent defect. The board found that because the government was conducting tests to determine conclusively that the items did not comply and was working with the contractor to resolve the problem, the 10-month time lapse between acceptance and retraction of acceptance was not unreasonable. By contrast, in *Ordnance Parts & Eng'g Co.*, ASBCA 40293, 90-3 BCA ¶ 23,141, the government could not revoke its acceptance of 300 towing eyes for either latent defects or gross mistake because of a government-caused 10-month delay in the hiring of an independent testing company after the government knew the goods were failing. The laboratory company completed its report in just two weeks. Therefore, the board concluded that the delay was unreasonable. Accord, *Utley-James, Inc.*, GSBCA 6831, 88-1 BCA ¶ 20,518, in which an unexplained two-and-a-half-year delay between discovery of the defect and the revocation of acceptance was held unreasonable.

6. *Government Rights After Retraction of Acceptance*

Although neither the pre-FAR supply contract inspection clause nor the construction contract inspection clause specified remedies in this area, the generally accepted principle was that when the government retracted acceptance it could avail itself of all the protection of the original contract, *Jo-Bar Mfg. Corp.*, ASBCA 17774, 73-2 BCA ¶ 10,311. Paragraph (l) of the current supply contract inspection clause in FAR 52.246-2 explicitly gives the government the option of ordering the contractor to correct the defect or seeking an equitable price adjustment. The construction contract clause in FAR 52.246-12 contains no similar provision explicitly dealing with the government's rights after retraction of acceptance. However, it contains the following broad provision:

> (f) The Contractor shall, without charge, replace or correct work found by the Government not to conform to contract requirements, unless in the public interest the Government consents to accept the work with an appropriate adjustment in contract price.

Normally, the government seeks to have the contractor repair or replace the defective work at the contractor's expense, *Kaminer Constr. Corp. v. United States*, 203 Ct. Cl. 182, 488 F.2d 980 (1973); *Tricon-Triangle Contractors*, ENGBCA 5553, 92-1 BCA ¶ 24,667.

If the contractor refuses to correct the defect, the government may do so and recover any reasonable costs incurred, *Corporate Diesel, Inc.*, ASBCA 17134, 74-1 BCA ¶ 10,612 (government could reduce contract price by the amount spent to recalibrate fuel pumps that contractor had defectively overhauled); *Mallory Eng'g, Inc.*, DCAB NOAA-10-77, 77-2 BCA ¶ 12,745 (contractor liable for additional costs incurred when the government contracted for local repair services to correct defects that the contractor had refused to correct unless the government paid transportation and service costs). In *Jung Ah Indus. Co.*, ASBCA 22632, 79-1 BCA ¶ 13,643, *recons. denied*, 79-2 BCA ¶ 13,916, the board awarded the government the costs incurred in installing and removing defective supplies. The board counted these costs as "real damages" resulting from the contractor's failure to comply with the contract terms. Accord, *General Elec. Co.*, ASBCA 36005, 91-3 BCA ¶ 24,353 (cracks in redesigned afterburner lining in tendered aircraft held to be a latent condition, thus requiring the contractor to incur all expenses necessary to correct this condition); *Federal Pac. Elec. Co.*, IBCA 334, 1964 BCA ¶ 4494 (government awarded all costs attributable to the defect). If the existence of latent defects necessitates a more thorough government inspection than anticipated, the contractor must bear the additional costs occasioned thereby, *Harrington & Richardson, Inc.*, ASBCA 9839, 72-2 BCA ¶ 9507.

Another alternative, which is specifically provided for in the current supply contract clause, is an equitable reduction in price where the government decides not to have the defect corrected. Although not explicitly related to post-acceptance cases, this same alternative also appears to be available under both the past and present construction contract clauses in view of the language, which states that the contractor shall correct or replace defects "unless in the public interest the Government consents to accept such material or workmanship with an appropriate adjustment in price." The pre-FAR supply contract clause also permitted the government to accept work with a reduction in price if the contractor could not correct the defect within the delivery schedule. Since post-acceptance defects claims are most often asserted after the delivery date, the government would have this alternative. If the government is not successful in obtaining a price reduction under one of these theories, it may be able to obtain an equitable adjustment for a deductive construction change measured by the cost saved by the contractor in performing defective work, *Techni Data Labs.*, ASBCA 21054, 77-2 BCA ¶ 12,667.

Upon proper revocation of acceptance, the government also has the right to return the items to the contractor and demand the return of the purchase price, *Catalytic Eng'g & Mfg. Corp.*, ASBCA 15257, 72-1 BCA ¶ 9342, *recons. denied*, 72-2 BCA ¶ 9518. The work must be returned to the contractor unless it is utterly worthless, *Teltron, Inc.*, ASBCA 14894, 72-2 BCA ¶ 9502. Even if items are worthless, the contractor is to be credited with their scrap value, *Atlantic Hardware & Supply Corp.*, ASBCA 10450, 66-1 BCA ¶ 5378. Return of the contract price was permitted without the institution of termination for default procedures in *Trio Chem. Works, Inc.*, GSBCA 2572, 70-1 BCA ¶ 8156, and *Jung Ah Indus. Co.*, ASBCA 22632, 79-1 BCA ¶ 13,643, *recons. denied*, 79-2 BCA ¶ 13,916.

Regardless of the remedy selected by the government, the contractor should be credited with the benefit, if any, that the government obtained from the use or retention of the defective work. Thus, when the government has had the use of the product for a long period of time, the contractor's liability may be decreased in proportion to the benefit, *Norair Eng'g Corp.*, ENGBCA 5244, 92-2 BCA ¶ 25,009. See also *Midwest Indus. Painting of Fla., Inc. v. United States*, 4 Cl. Ct. 124 (1983), in which the government was denied damages when the contractor's defective performance destroyed government items that had been in use longer than their useful life. The government must credit the contractor with the benefit that the government has obtained from the use or retention of defective items and must credit the contractor with the reasonable value (even scrap value) of any material that is not returned, *Spandome Corp. v. United States*, 32 Fed. Cl. 626 (1995).

In order to claim any damages, the government must segregate and prove its damages. *M.A. Mortenson Co. v. United States*, 40 Fed. Cl. 389 (1998) (government not entitled to recover on a counterclaim for latent defects in a dispute over a construction contract that contains both latent and patent defects along with faulty specifications unless the government distinguishes the damages resulting from the latent defects from the costs incurred due to patent defects and defective specifications).

The contractor's failure to correct or replace the items promptly subjects it to termination for default. In *Jo-Bar Mfg. Corp.*, ASBCA 17774, 73-2 BCA ¶ 10,311, the board upheld the contracting officer's final decision terminating the contract for default and demanding that the contractor repay the contract price. See also *Aerometals, Inc.*, ASBCA 53688, 03-2 BCA ¶ 32,295, holding that default termination is a proper remedy because the supply contract inspection clause in FAR 52.246-2 provides in ¶ (l) that the government will have any other remedies provided by law. It was also held proper to partially terminate the contract for default after the contractor refused to agree to a downward price adjustment, *Munson Hammerhead Boats,* ASBCA 51377, 00-2 BCA ¶ 31,143. In *Sentell Bros., Inc.*, DOTBCA 1824, 89-3 BCA ¶ 21,904, *recons. denied*, 89-3 BCA ¶ 22,219, the board reversed a termination for default because there was no evidence of a proper ground for avoiding finality of acceptance. The board did concede, however, that had such a ground existed, default termination would have been an appropriate remedy.

Not every provision of the original contract will carry over to the post-acceptance period in every case. In *Standard Transformer Co. v. United States*, 108 Ct. Cl. 214, 69 F. Supp. 1019 (1947), the court refused to allow liquidated damages for delay to cover the time during which the contractor was repairing latent defects at the government's election of repair over rejection.

The government may also be equitably estopped from asserting these remedies. See *Merchants Nat'l Bank of Mobile v. United States*, 231 Ct. Cl. 563, 689 F.2d 181 (1982), in which the government was estopped from asserting a latent defect claim against an assignee bank because funds were provided by the bank in reliance on government acceptance.

B. Warranties

Some performance requirements are too important to be left to the vagaries of inspection. As noted by the Defense Systems Management College, *Warranty Handbook* (October 1992), clearly identified essential performance requirements transcend the normal acceptance process.

The term "warranty" has been the subject of considerable confusion in government contracting. In some cases, the term refers to a specific clause (infrequently referred to as a Guaranty clause), which gives the government a remedy for defects (latent or patent) discovered after acceptance. The clause is included in contracts to overcome the finality of acceptance of the Inspection clauses. A second meaning, adapted from commercial contracting, describes a "warranty" as a promise by the seller assuring the quality of the goods. FAR 2.101 adopts this meaning by defining "warranty" as a "promise or affirmation given by a contractor to the Government regarding the nature, usefulness, or condition of the supplies or performance of services furnished under the contract." This definition describes the product or service that the contractor is to furnish, while the primary purpose of Warranty clauses is to permit the government to obtain remedies after acceptance. However, the distinction between the two uses is sometimes blurred by language in the Warranty clauses and cases.

The FAR contains an elaborate set of Warranty clauses. See the Warranty of Supplies of a Noncomplex Nature (FAR 52.246-17), Warranty of Supplies of a Complex Nature (FAR 52.246-18), Warranty of Construction (FAR 52.246-21), Warranty of Systems and Equipment under Performance Specifications or Design Criteria (FAR 52.246-19), and Warranty of Services (FAR 52.246-20) clauses. The use of the FAR warranty clauses is optional. Until repealed by the FY 1998 Defense Authorization Act, Pub. L. No. 105-85, 10 U.S.C. § 2403 and its implementing regulation in DFARS 246.770-2 provided that departments and agencies were not permitted to contract for the production of a weapon system with a unit cost of $100,000 or an estimated total procurement cost in excess of $10 million unless the contractor provided a written warranty. The implementing clause has now been deleted.

In determining whether a warranty is appropriate for a specific acquisition, FAR 46.703 requires the contracting officer to consider several factors:

(a) *Nature and use of the supplies or services*. This includes such factors as —

(1) Complexity and function;

(2) Degree of development;

(3) State of the art;

(4) End use;

(5) Difficulty in detecting defects before acceptance; and

(6) Potential harm to the Government if the item is defective.

(b) *Cost*. Warranty costs arise from—

(1) The contractor's charge for accepting the deferred liability created by the warranty; and

(2) Government administration and enforcement of the warranty (see paragraph (c) of this section).

(c) *Administration and enforcement*. The Government's ability to enforce the warranty is essential to the effectiveness of any warranty. There must be some assurance that an adequate administrative system for reporting defects exists or can be established. The adequacy of a reporting system may depend upon such factors as the—

(1) Nature and complexity of the item;

(2) Location and proposed use of the item;

(3) Storage time for the item;

(4) Distance of the using activity from the source of the item;

(5) Difficulty in establishing existence of defects; and

(6) Difficulty in tracing responsibility for defects.

(d) *Trade practice*. In many instances an item is customarily warranted in the trade, and, as a result of that practice, the cost of an item to the Government will be the same whether or not a warranty is included. In those instances, it would be in the Government's interest to include such a warranty.

(e) *Reduced requirements*. The contractor's charge for assumption of added liability may be partially or completely offset by reducing the Government's contract quality assurance requirements where the warranty provides adequate assurance of a satisfactory product.

Consideration of additional criteria may depend on agency requirements. For example, NFS 1846.703-70 states that the following criteria must be considered in determining whether to use a warranty clause:

(a) Cost of correction or replacement, either by the contractor or by another source, in the absence of a warranty.

(b) The warranty as a deterrent against the furnishing of defective or nonconforming supplies.

(c) Whether the contractor's quality program is reliable enough to provide adequate protection without a warranty, or, if not, whether a warranty would cause the contractor to institute an effective quality program.

(d) Reliance on "brand-name" integrity.

(e) Whether a warranty is regularly given for a commercial component of a more complex end item.

FAR Part 12 expands the rules on warranties—both express and implied. FAR 12.404 states, regarding express warranties in contracts for commercial items:

(b) *Express warranties*. The Federal Acquisition Streamlining Act of 1994 (41 U.S.C. 264 note) requires contracting officers to take advantage of commercial warranties. To the maximum extent practicable, solicitations for commercial items shall require offerors to offer the Government at least the same warranty terms, including offers of extended warranties, offered to the general public in customary commercial practice. Solicitations may specify minimum warranty terms, such as minimum duration, appropriate for the Government's intended use of the item.

> (1) Any express warranty the Government intends to rely upon must meet the needs of the Government. The contracting officer should analyze any commercial warranty to determine if—
>
> > (i) The warranty is adequate to protect the needs of the Government, *e.g.*, items covered by the warranty and length of warranty;
> >
> > (ii) The terms allow the Government effective postaward administration of the warranty to include the identification of warranted items, procedures for the return of warranted items to the contractor for repair or replacement, and collection of product performance information; and
> >
> > (iii) The warranty is cost-effective.
>
> (2) In some markets, it may be customary commercial practice for contractors to exclude or limit the implied warranties contained in 52.212-4 in the provisions of an express warranty. In such cases, the contracting officer shall ensure that the express warranty provides for the repair or replacement of defective items discovered within a reasonable period of time after acceptance.
>
> (3) Express warranties shall be included in the contract by addendum (see 12.302).

This subsection includes a discussion of the legal problems related to warranty clauses. The discussion encompasses the scope of warranty clauses, implied warranties in government contracts, notification and burden of proof requirements, and remedies available to the government.

1. Scope of Warranty Clauses

The types of defects covered by warranty clauses differ from clause to clause. The language of warranty clauses is strictly construed against the government, excluding defects not specifically enumerated in the warranty clause, *Joseph Penner*, GSBCA 4647, 80-2 BCA ¶ 14,604. Thus, under prior warranty or guaranty clauses in construction contracts the government received limited coverage. In *H.P. Carney*, ASBCA 8222, 1964 BCA ¶ 4149, a clause covering defects in material, workmanship, or design was held not to cover improper installation of floor tiles. The board subsequently held that there was no authorization for the government to require correction or obtain replacement at the contractor's cost. See also *Norla Gen. Contractors Corp.*, ASBCA 6497, 61-2 BCA ¶ 3183 (check valve and steam ladder were not included on a list of five components specified in the guaranty clause), and *J.S. Brown-E.F Olds Plumbing & Heating Corp.*, ASBCA 4973, 59-2 BCA ¶ 2282 (Guaranty clause specifying defects in manufacture did not cover poor workmanship during installation). The effect of such limitations is avoided by the expansive language of the Warranty of Construction clause at FAR 52.246-21, which covers defects of "equipment, material or design furnished, or workmanship" as well as any failure to conform to the contract requirements. See *Mid E. Builders, Inc.*, ASBCA 39882, 93-3 BCA ¶ 25,920, in which the contractor was required to fix defective floor coverings. Similar coverage is contained in the Warranty of Supplies of a Noncomplex Nature clause at FAR 52.246-17, which provides that "all supplies furnished under this contract will be free from defects in material or workmanship and will conform with all requirements of this contract."

Two of the clauses do not contain explicit statements on the scope of the warranty. Paragraph (b) of the clause for noncomplex supplies at FAR 52.246-17 does not explicitly state that it covers only defects at the time of acceptance, but it can have the same effect by providing that

> The Contractor warrants that for . . . . [*Contracting Officer shall state specific period of time after delivery, or the specified event whose occurrence will terminate the warranty period; e.g., the number of miles or hours of use, or combinations of any applicable events or periods of time*]—(i) All supplies furnished under this contract will be free from defects in material or workmanship and will conform with all requirements of this contract . . .

Similarly, ¶ (a) of the clause at FAR 52.246-21 for construction contracts provides:

> [T]he Contractor warrants . . . that work performed under this contract conforms to the contract requirements and is free of any defect in equipment, material, or design furnished, or workmanship performed by the Contractor or any subcontractor or supplier at any tier.

Another potentially broad warranty is found in the Warranty of Systems and Equipment Under Performance Specifications or Design Criteria clause, FAR 52.246-19, which defines "defect" as "any condition or characteristic in any supplies or services . . . that is not in compliance with the requirements of the contract." The weapon systems statute, 10 U.S.C. § 2403, repealed by Pub. L. No. 105-85, required written guarantees that the item "conforms to the design and manufacturing requirements and essential performance requirements, as specifically delineated in the production contract" and that "at the time it was delivered to the United States was free from all defects in materials and workmanship." If these provisions were to be given their broadest possible interpretation, the contractor would be promising failure-free performance for the expected life of the item. This view was rejected in *Araco Co.*, VACAB 532, 67-2 BCA ¶ 6440. The board considered Guaranty clauses that did not limit their application to defects in materials or workmanship or to defects that existed at the time the guaranty period began. The board concluded that "these distinctive provisions . . . sufficiently broad in scope to cover repair of breakdowns [resulting from] design characteristics" are not limited to defects in materials and workmanship. However, the board noted that this did not mean the clauses were unlimited in scope. They would not, for example, cover conditions caused by the government or by an extraneous event beyond the contractor's control.

The warranty period does not begin to run until acceptance. Prior to that, the government's remedy is the Inspection clause. In *Donat CERG Haustechnik*, ASBCA 41197, 97-2 BCA ¶ 29,272, *aff'd*, 194 F. 3d 1336 (Fed. Cir. 1999), the board held that the government's remedy lay with the Inspection of Construction clause rather than the Warranty of Construction clause because the government had repeatedly noted that the system did not conform to the contract and demanded correction during a two-year period after the work was completed.

If both the Inspection clause and Warranty clause are operable, the government can select either one as its remedy. In *Hogan Constr. Inc.*, ASBCA 38801, 95-1 BCA ¶ 27,396, *recons. denied*, 95-2 BCA ¶ 27,688, the fact that the government cited both the Inspection of Construction and the Warranty of Construction clauses in rejecting a contractor's work did not preclude enforcement of only the express warranty under the Warranty of Construction clause. Thus, the government did not have to prove a latent defect, fraud, or gross mistake amounting to fraud under the Inspection of Construction clause.

Some clauses, such as Warranty of Construction, FAR 52.246-21, Alternate I, require the contractor to have the warranty executed by the supplier, manufacturer, or subcontractor directly to the government. This is common where the item is a brand name. In *Lee Lewis Constr., Inc. v. United States*, 54 Fed. Cl. 88 (2002), the court held that a contractor was not liable under a warranty because the contract merely required the "roofing contractor" to provide the warranty and did not make the contractor liable. Because the contract required that "The roofing contractor shall furnish to the Owner the Manufacturer's . . . guarantee . . . [and] warranty," the court found that this relieved the contractor of any warranty responsibility because a subcontractor was the "roofing contractor." Although the contractor was liable for the acts and omissions of its subcontractors, there were no acts or omissions complained of here. The roofing subcontractor furnished the manufacturer's warranty to the government.

2. Specification Provisions and Implied Warranties

Contract requirements contained in specifications and drawings (referred to under the U.C.C. as express warranties) and implied warranties operate to describe the quality level of the contractor's performance. In the absence of a warranty clause, specification provisions do not survive acceptance, *T.M. Indus.*, ASBCA 19068, 75-1 BCA ¶ 11,056. Compare *Keco Indus., Inc.*, ASBCA 13271, 71-1 BCA ¶ 8727, in which the board apparently believed that a specification requirement that the contract item "shall be capable of operating for 500 hours at design capacity without failure of any major part" was a warranty that survived acceptance. Failures that occurred after 500 hours were held to be latent defects.

The implied warranties of merchantability, U.C.C. § 2-314, and fitness for a particular purpose, U.C.C. § 2-315, may be applicable to describe the quality requirements in government contracts in appropriate circumstances, *General Elec. Co.*, IBCA 451-8-64, 66-1 BCA ¶ 5507. In *Pyronauts, Inc.*, ENGBCA 4070, 82-1 BCA ¶ 15,645, the board found that the government properly rejected fire extinguishers since they were neither merchantable nor fit for their intended purpose.

Since U.C.C. § 2-316 permits the exclusion of these warranties by clear language, the finality language of the inspection clauses would seem to preclude them from surviving final acceptance. This is particularly the case in supply contracts, where the inspection clause makes acceptance conclusive unless "otherwise provided in the contract except as regards latent defects, fraud, or such gross mistakes as amount to fraud," *Republic Aviation Corp.*, ASBCA 9934, 66-1 BCA ¶ 5482. In *Trio-Tech, Inc.*, VACAB 598, 68-1 BCA ¶ 6828, the board held that acceptance bars claims based on implied warranties unless latent defects, fraud, or gross mistakes could be shown. See *Newport News Shipbuilding & Drydock Co.*, ENGBCA 3117, 72-1 BCA ¶ 9210, in which a finding that excessive vibration in turbines was a latent defect would have resulted in the defect being covered by an implied warranty of fitness for the intended use. But see *Transit Prods. Co.,* ENGBCA 4796, 88-2 BCA ¶ 20,673, in which the board stated that neither *Republic Aviation* nor *Trio-Tech* involved implied warranties, nor did it hold that implied warranties survive acceptance when latent defects, fraud, or gross mistakes are shown. There is some debate, therefore, as to whether implied warranties would survive acceptance if the defects claimed fell within the scope of latent defects.

The applicability of implied warranties is somewhat clarified under the warranty clauses for supplies and systems in FAR 52.246-17, -18, and -19, by the inclusion of the following language:

> All implied warranties of merchantability and "fitness for a particular purpose" are excluded from any obligation contained in this contract.

This language goes beyond dealing with finality; it would also appear to preclude the government from rejecting goods prior to acceptance when not covered by express specification requirements. If commercial items are to be acquired, the above language is omitted, and the paragraph stating that the supplies will be "free from defects in material or workmanship and will conform with all requirements" is replaced with what is, in effect, an express warranty of merchantability that operates notwithstanding the conclusiveness of acceptance. See Alternate I in FAR 52.246-17 and FAR 52.246-18. Thus, implied warranties may either be expressly excluded or, in the case of the implied warranty of merchantability with respect to commercial items, be made express, thereby eliminating much of the confusion in this area. By contrast, ¶ (g) of the construction contract Warranty clause at FAR 52.246-21 attempts to preserve, for the benefit of the government, any implied warranties from subcontractors.

There appears to be little doubt that the U.C.C. implied warranties will survive acceptance in government supply contracts that do not contain the language of the standard inspection clauses making acceptance final and conclusive. For example, in *Reeves Soundcraft Corp.*, ASBCA 9030, 1964 BCA ¶ 4317, the board found an implied warranty of fitness for a particular purpose in a contract that did not contain the standard Inspection clause and thus did not include the finality of acceptance language. The board concluded, however, that no implied warranty remained since the government had inspected the goods and the defects in question were patent. See also *United States v. Hamden Co-op. Creamery Co.*, 185 F. Supp. 541 (E.D.N.Y. 1960), *aff'd*, 297 F.2d 130 (2d Cir. 1961) (government right of rejection for latent defects not lost upon acceptance), and *Whitin Mach. Works v. United States*, 175 F.2d 504 (1st Cir. 1949) (applying the Uniform Sales Act in determining that an implied warranty had not been breached). In these cases concerning contracts containing short inspection clauses, the board and courts accepted the principle that government purchases of goods are governed by commercial law. Compare *Cooper-Bessemer Corp.*, ASBCA 12878, 69-1 BCA ¶ 7623, in which a contractor's obligation under a Guaranty provision to "correct or replace the defective or nonconforming article" included all labor necessary to repair entire generating units and was not limited to mere replacement of defective parts.

FAR 12.404(a) states that it is the government's policy to include the implied warranties of merchantability and fitness for a particular purpose in contracts for commercial items. This policy is implemented in the Contract Terms and Conditions—Commercial Items clause in FAR 52.212-4, stating:

> (o) *Warranty*. The Contractor warrants and implies that the items delivered hereunder are merchantable and fit for use for the particular purpose described in this contract.

If an express warranty clause is to be included in the contract, FAR 12.404(b)(3) requires it to be added by Addendum.

3. Notice and Burden of Proof

In order to recover under a warranty clause, the government must give appropriate notice to the contractor and prove the existence of a defect.

a. Government Notice of Nonconformance

In order to invoke the protection of a warranty, the government must give the contractor "reasonably prompt notice, in the particular circumstance," *Instruments for Indus., Inc. v. United States*, 496 F.2d 1157 (2d Cir. 1974). See *J.R. Simplot Co.*, ASBCA 3952, 59-2 BCA ¶ 2306, in which the board found that "notice within a reasonable time was required but was not given" since the government waited more than five months to effectively inform the supplier that onions did not meet specifications. The date on which the reasonable period began to run was the day on which the government knew or should have known of the defects. See also *Globe Corp.*,

ASBCA 45131, 93-3 BCA ¶ 25,968 (nonstandard warranty clause provided for notice within 13 months from receipt of supplies at destination); *Land O'Frost*, ASBCA 55012, 03-2 BCA ¶ 32,395 (seven-month notice requirement). In *ABM/Ansley Bus. Materials*, GSBCA 9367, 93-1 BCA ¶ 25,246, the warranty clause required notification of defects within 12 months after acceptance. Because some items were accepted more than 12 months prior to notice and the government could not show the time of acceptance of the defective items, the notice was untimely. Although written notice is preferable, oral notification has been held to be sufficient, *Harwell Constr. Co.*, ENGBCA PCC-30, 79-2 BCA ¶ 14,061 (oral notification within warranty period to contractor's representative on day that defects were discovered was adequate). Where the warranty period is stated in terms of operation such as miles or hours of operation, the warranty period could extend for several calendar years or more.

b. Government's Burden of Proof

When the government asserts that the contractor has breached a warranty, it "assumes the burden of proving all elements of its claim," *Globe Corp.*, ASBCA 45131, 93-3 BCA ¶ 25,968; *Vi-Mil, Inc.*, ASBCA 16820, 75-2 BCA ¶ 11,435, *recons. denied*, 75-2 BCA ¶ 11,618. There are three elements that the government must prove in a warranty claim. The government must show that (1) timely notice was given, (2) "furnishing the defective materials or workmanship was the responsibility of the contractor," and (3) it did not cause or contribute to the failures or the defects, *Joseph Penner*, GSBCA 4647, 80-2 BCA ¶ 14,604.

The government does not need to be explicit but must "show by a preponderance of the evidence, that the defective material or workmanship was the most probable cause of the failure when considered with any other possible cause," *ABM/Ansley Bus. Materials*, GSBCA 9367, 93-1 BCA ¶ 25,246. In *Inter-West, Ltd.*, DOTBCA 2238, 92-3 BCA ¶ 25,073, *aff'd*, 99 F. 2d 1235 (Fed. Cir. 1993), the board (quoting from *George E. Jensen Contractor, Inc.*, ASBCA 23284, 81-2 BCA ¶ 15,207) stated that "it is sufficient to show that the most likely or probable cause of the failures, considered with other possible causes, were defects attributable to the contractor's design, material, or workmanship." See *Caesar Constr., Inc.*, ASBCA 36547, 93-1 BCA ¶ 25,226 (government fulfilled burden of proof by showing that "most probable cause" was contractor's defective work); *A.L.S. Elecs. Corp.*, ASBCA 23128, 82-2 BCA ¶ 15,835 (most probable cause of failure was electromagnetic interference at naval shipyard); *Great Valley Constr. Co.,* ASBCA 24449, 81-2 BCA ¶ 15,308 (mere existence of a failure does not satisfy the government's burden of proof); *Abney Constr. Co.,* ASBCA 23686, 80-2 BCA ¶ 14,506 (government failed to prove that contractor's alleged failure to comply with specifications was the most probable cause of the system's failure when considered with the other possible causes); and *Genco Co., Constructors*, DOTCAB 75-22, 76-1 BCA ¶ 11,823 (burden of proof test is "whether the preponderance of evidence indicates that the probable cause of the defect is attributable to the appellant").

Once it is established that the most likely cause of the failure was the contractor's design, material, or workmanship, the burden of proof shifts to the contractor, *Inter-West, Ltd.*, DOTBCA 2238, 92-3 BCA ¶ 25,073, *aff'd*, 99 F 2d 1235 (Fed. Cir. 1995). The contractor must come forward with evidence that it was not responsible for the defects under the contract or that such defects did not exist, *Cochran Constr. Co.*, ASBCA 40294, 90-3 BCA ¶ 23,239, *aff'd*, 937 F.2d 624 (Fed. Cir. 1991). In *George E. Jensen Contractor, Inc.*, ASBCA 23284, 81-2 BCA ¶ 15,207, the board concluded that door failures were caused by heavy and careless usage by transient troops and not by any fault of the contractor. Thus, the contractor was able to have a final opportunity to prove that the defect was beyond its scope of responsibility or liability.

In the following cases the government failed to fulfill its burden of proof: *Philadelphia Biologics Ctr.*, ASBCA 32597, 88-3 BCA ¶ 21,147 (government testing failed to show that alleged defects would occur with proper use of the product); *Ed Dickson Contracting Co.,* ASBCA 27205, 84-1 BCA ¶ 16,950 (government failed to prove that the contractor was responsible for defective sealant); and *Camrex Reliance Paint Co.,* GSBCA 6166, 83-1 BCA ¶ 16,485 (government failed to prove breach of warranty since the contract required paint to be shaken before testing). See also *Lucerne Constr. Corp.*, VACAB 1494, 82-2 BCA ¶ 16,101 (proof of defective workmanship or materials may not be inferred from the failure of the product); *Armstrong & Armstrong, Inc.*, IBCA 1311-10-79, 82-1 BCA ¶ 15,622 (valve failures resulting from negligence in operation not a failure to meet contract requirements); *Joseph Penner*, GSBCA 4647, 80-2 BCA ¶ 14,604 (government failed to prove that collapsed ceiling was the result of defective installation); *Julian A. McDermott Corp.*, ASBCA 23435, 80-1 BCA ¶ 14,210 (government testing that did not comply with Warranty clause requirements failed to establish contractor responsibility for defects); *Harwell Constr. Co.*, ENGBCA PCC-30, 79-2 BCA ¶ 14,061 (government presentation of "plausible theories" as to the cause of the failure was insufficient); *Klefstad Eng'g Co.,* VACAB 705, 69-1 BCA ¶ 7675 (defects attributable to normal wear and tear not chargeable to contractor); and *R.E. Lee Elec. Co.,* GSBCA 1040, 1964 BCA ¶ 4401 (government testimony as to theories of possible failure and ultimate reliance on *res ipsa loquitur* did not carry burden of proof). In *International Data Prods. Corp. v. United States,* 64 Fed. Cl. 642 (2005), a termination for convenience was held to have extinguished the government's warranty rights.

In the following cases the government fulfilled its burden of proof: *Inter-West, Ltd.*, DOTBCA 2238, 92-3 BCA ¶ 25,073, *aff'd*, 99 F 2d 1235 (Fed. Cir. 1995) (a cable failure was due to improper installation or defective materials, which were the responsibility of the contractor); *Meredith Constr. Co.,* ASBCA 40481, 91-1 BCA ¶ 23,643, *recons. denied*, 91-2 BCA ¶ 23,902 (government established by a preponderance of the evidence that the most probable cause of a failure of an underground cable was defective installation by the contractor); *Verne Eng'g Corp.*, ASBCA 25348, 83-1 BCA ¶ 16,240 (contractor's overall responsibility for the design of a crane made it liable under warranty for performance failure); *Robert Builders, Inc.*,

ASBCA 24762, 81-1 BCA ¶ 15,115 (contractor's acquiescence to responsibility for repairs during performance led to board's conclusion of contractor's ultimate liability); and *Jefferson Constr. Co.*, ASBCA 7008, 61-2 BCA ¶ 3222, *recons. denied*, 1962 BCA ¶ 3409 (a "most probable" causal connection between defect and failure confirmed by an independent laboratory's finding of noncompliance with specification). Once the government has met its burden of proof and the contractor is unable to contradict the evidence, the board looks for the appropriate remedies available to the government.

4. Remedies Under Warranty Clauses

Although government remedies under the standard warranty clauses are somewhat similar to those under the standard inspection clauses, remedies for breach of warranty are generally more specific and often strictly construed. FAR 46.706(b)(2) sets forth guidelines as to the nature and extent of government remedies that should be provided in warranties:

> (i) Normally, a warranty shall provide as a minimum that the Government may—
>
> > (A) Obtain an equitable adjustment of the contract, or
> >
> > (B) Direct the contractor to repair or replace the defective items at the contractor's expense.
>
> (ii) If it is not practical to direct the contractor to make the repair or replacement, or, because of the nature of the item, the repair or replacement does not afford an appropriate remedy to the Government, the warranty should provide alternate remedies, such as authorizing the Government to—
>
> > (A) Retain the defective item and reduce the contract price by an amount equitable under the circumstances; or
> >
> > (B) Arrange for the repair or replacement of the defective item, by the Government or by another source, at the contractor's expense.
>
> (iii) If it can be foreseen that it will not be practical to return an item to the contractor for repair, to remove it to an alternate source for repair, or to replace the defective item, the warranty should provide that the Government may repair, or require the contractor to repair, the item in place at the contractor's expense. The contract shall provide that in the circumstance where the Government is to accomplish the repair, the contractor will furnish at the place of delivery the material or parts, and the installation instructions required to successfully accomplish the repair.
>
> (iv) Unless provided otherwise in the warranty, the contractor's obligation to repair or replace the defective item, or to agree to an equitable adjustment of the contract, shall include responsibility for the costs of furnishing all labor and material to—

(A) Reinspect items that the Government reasonably expected to be defective,

(B) Accomplish the required repair or replacement of defective items, and

(C) Test, inspect, package, pack, and mark repaired or replaced items.

(v) If repair or replacement of defective items is required, the contractor shall generally be required by the warranty to bear the expense of transportation for returning the defective item from the place of delivery specified in the contract (irrespective of the f.o.b. point or the point of acceptance) to the contractor's plant and subsequent return. When defective items are returned to the contractor from other than the place of delivery specified in the contract, or when the Government exercises alternate remedies, the contractor's liability for transportation charges incurred shall not exceed an amount equal to the cost of transportation by the usual commercial method of shipment between the place of delivery specified in the contract and the contractor's plant and subsequent return.

When remedies are specified in a warranty clause, the government is limited to those remedies listed when a defect is covered by the clause, *Kordick & Son, Inc. v. United States*, 12 Cl. Ct. 662 (1987); *Tracor Data Sys.*, GSBCA 4662, 78-1 BCA ¶ 13,143. The government's remedies are also subject to the conditions stated in the clause. See *Schouten Constr. Co.*, DOTCAB 78-14, 79-1 BCA ¶ 13,553, in which the government could not charge the contractor the cost of repair when it failed to give the contractor the opportunity to correct defects as required by the warranty clause. In *Kulcor Coatings Co.*, GSBCA 4135, 75-2 BCA ¶ 11,422, requiring a refund of the purchase price from the contractor while keeping defective goods was not permitted because the warranty clause gave the government the right to either correction, replacement, or disposal of defective goods for the contractor's account.

The alternative remedies available to the government under warranty clauses are comparable to those under the latent defect provisions of the Inspection clause, *General Elec. Co.*, ASBCA 36005, 91-2 BCA ¶ 23,958, *aff'd*, 987 F 2d 747 (Fed. Cir. 1993). Where the contract provides for alternative remedies, the government has the authority to choose the remedy, *Cross Aero Corp.*, ASBCA 15092, 71-2 BCA ¶ 9076. In *Gavco Corp.*, ASBCA 29763, 88-3 BCA ¶ 21,095, the "other remedies" provision of the Warranty of Construction clause allowed the government to suspend further work and reduce the contract price for the remaining deficiencies. In *White Packing Co.,* ASBCA 23274, 80-1 BCA ¶ 14,201, the Warranty of Supplies clause permitted the government to change from the replacement option to the refund option after determination was made that supplies were no longer needed. In *Vi-Mil, Inc.*, ASBCA 16820, 75-2 BCA ¶ 11,435, *recons. denied*, 75-2 BCA ¶ 11,618, the board held that the government could change its election of remedies under a supply warranty clause after notifying the contractor of a breach of warranty. The government chose equitable adjustment rather than contractor correction or replacement of nonconforming supplies.

Early cases found default termination to be an improper remedy for breach of warranty when the warranty clause did not include this remedy, *Astubeco, Inc.*, ASBCA 8727, 1963 BCA ¶ 3941. This rule was followed even in instances where the contractor refused to correct or replace defective work as required by the warranty clause, *Ganary Bros.*, ASBCA 7779, 1963 BCA ¶ 3721, *recons. denied*, 1963 BCA ¶ 3875. More recently, boards have found termination to be a proper remedy in certain circumstances. In *Sentell Bros., Inc.*, DOTBCA 1824, 89-3 BCA ¶ 21,904, *recons. denied*, 89-3 BCA ¶ 22,219, the board stated that "where the Government has a right to recover for defective work under another contract provision, termination is an appropriate remedy." In *M-Pax, Inc.*, HUDBCA 80-529-C11, 81-2 BCA ¶ 15,410, the board suggested that the phrase "the Government shall have the right to . . . otherwise remedy such failure, defect, or damage, at the contractor's expense" in ¶ (f) of the Warranty of Construction clause is broad enough to include the default remedy under the Inspection and Acceptance clause. In *Cross Aero Corp.*, ASBCA 15092, 71-2 BCA ¶ 9076, the board found default termination a proper remedy for breach of warranty where the defects were latent.

When the remedy specified in the warranty clause is an equitable adjustment in the price, recovery of the entire price of the item has been held proper when the defective item is of no value, *Mercury Chem. Co.*, ASBCA 12882, 69-1 BCA ¶ 7769. The contractor is still entitled to reimbursement for scrap value of the defective material, *ABM/Ansley Bus. Materials*, GSBCA 9367, 93-1 BCA ¶ 25,246. In *Atlantic Hardware & Supply Corp.*, ASBCA 10450, 66-1 BCA ¶ 5378, the government was entitled to the full purchase price less scrap value, if any, of nonconforming socket head blades. In *Aero Prods. Research, Inc.*, ASBCA 25956, 87-1 BCA ¶ 19,425, *mot. to vac. denied*, 87-3 BCA ¶ 20,061, the board adopted the "reasonable cost to correct the supplies" as a measure of the government's recovery for defective clipboards.

As with most remedies at law for breach of contract, the government may not recover under a warranty clause for damages that it could reasonably have mitigated. See *Oklahoma Aerotronics, Inc.*, ASBCA 25605, 87-2 BCA ¶ 19,917, *aff'd*, 852 F.2d 1293 (Fed. Cir. 1988), in which the board found that the government could not recover reprocurement costs from the contractor when the government did not attempt to mitigate damages or obtain a reasonable reprocurement price. Similarly, in *Verne Eng'g Corp.*, ASBCA 25348, 83-1 BCA ¶ 16,240, the cost of an additional gearbox purchased when correcting a performance failure was not recoverable from the contractor since the government overlooked the fact that the gearbox had already been replaced.

The contractor may also be liable for consequential damages to the government if it can be shown that the damages were caused by the defect and that the other requirements for consequential damages, such as foreseeability, have been met. However, the government may relieve the contractor from such liability. See, for example, the policy set forth in FAR 46.803(b) relieving contractors with contracts for high value items from the risk of loss or damage to those items, and the Limitation of Liability clauses contained in FAR 52.246-23 and 52.246-24, relieving the contractor from liability for loss or damage to government property in certain circumstances. This policy has been adopted for acquisition of commercial items. Thus, ¶ (p) of the FAR 52.212-4, Limitation of Liability provision states:

> Except as otherwise provided by an express warranty, the Contractor will not be liable to the Government for consequential damages resulting from any defect or deficiencies in accepted items.

The inclusion of a Limitation of Liability clause in the contract may not excuse the contractor from liability for consequential damages if such damages are included in the contractor's insurance coverage. In *Luster-On Prods., Inc.*, ASBCA 23367, 80-2 BCA ¶ 14,777, the contractor was found liable for damage caused by a subcontractor, resulting from improper repair during the warranty period, despite the presence of a Limitation of Liability clause (DAR 7-104.45) in the contract. The board stated that the clause provided that the contractor will be liable for damages and losses suffered by the government to the extent that contractor insurance covers the loss. Paragraph (c) of the clause in FAR 52.246-23 contains similar language.

In other cases, the decision of whether the contractor is liable for consequential damages turns on the issue of whether the remedy in the warranty provision or the remedy in the Inspection clause applies. In *United States v. Aerodex, Inc.*, 469 F.2d 1003 (5th Cir. 1972), the court held the contractor responsible for the cost of removing and replacing noncomplying engine bearings. Although the government's remedies under the warranty provision in the contract were exclusive and did not specifically include consequential damages, any breach involving latent defects, fraud, or gross mistakes amounting to fraud was held to constitute an exception to this exclusivity of remedies. Since the noncomplying bearings were delivered fraudulently, the exception applied and there was nothing left in the contract precluding the recovery of these damages. See also *United States v. Franklin Steel Prods., Inc.*, 482 F.2d 400 (9th Cir. 1973), *cert. denied*, 415 U.S. 918 (1974), in which the board reached a similar result with similar damages but on the basis of latent defects instead of fraud. The board stated that consequential damages may include replacement of the defective goods or damages for injuries caused by the defective goods. The strength of the holdings in these cases, however, is questionable since the damages sought in both situations were arguably direct rather than consequential and could easily be construed to come under the remedy of "correction or replacement" specified in the warranty.

In *Norfolk Shipbuilding. & Drydock Corp.*, ASBCA 21560, 80-2 BCA ¶ 14,613, *recons. denied*, 81-1 BCA ¶ 15,056, the board held the contractor responsible for damage to a fuel tank resulting from the contractor's faulty overhaul work. Although the guarantee clause in the contract provided that the contractor's liability did not extend beyond correction of defects or deficiencies or payments of costs thereof, it did not relieve the contractor of liability for consequential damages arising under another contract clause that made it liable for "loss or damage of whatsoever nature . . . arising or growing out of performance of the work."

C. Cumulative Remedies

Government remedies under various warranty provisions are generally construed to be cumulative with each other and with government remedies under the Inspection clauses relating to latent defects, fraud, and gross mistakes amounting to fraud. As a result, government rights with respect to latent defects will continue after the expiration of an applicable warranty provision since such rights are not limited to a specific period, *Federal Pac. Elec. Co.*, IBCA 334, 1964 BCA ¶ 4494. In this case, the board relied on § 15(b) of the Uniform Sales Act, which stated that "[a]n express warranty or condition does not negate a warranty or condition implied under this act unless inconsistent therewith" and § 2-317 of the Uniform Commercial Code, which provides that "[w]arranties whether express or implied shall be construed as consistent with each other and as cumulative, but if such construction is unreasonable the intention of the parties shall determine which warranty is dominant." A similar result was reached in an early case involving latent defects in which the board construed Guaranty and Inspection clauses to be complementary when the Guaranty clause specifically limited treatment of latent defects to the Inspection clause "to make it clear that the 'Guaranty' clause does not reduce the Government's rights as to latent defects," *F.W. Lang Co.*, ASBCA 2677, 57-1 BCA ¶ 1334. See also *Keco Indus., Inc.*, ASBCA 13271, 71-1 BCA ¶ 8727 (contractor's liability under Inspection clause for latent defects "survives a time limitation" in a separate warranty provision); *Charles G. Williams Constr., Inc.*, ASBCA 24967, 81-1 BCA ¶ 14,893 (warranty requiring that work be performed in a "skillful and workmanlike manner" cumulative with other provisions); *General Elec. Co.*, IBCA 442-6-64, 65-2 BCA ¶ 4974 (warranty that all materials "shall be 'free from defects' . . . indicative of a purpose to enlarge rather than limit the rights of the government under the Inspection clause"). In *Mallory Eng'g, Inc.*, DCAB NOAA-10-77, 77-2 BCA ¶ 12,745, the board held that remedies under a warranty clause and the Inspection clause were both available during the warranty period, with the result that the contractor was liable for the full cost of repairing latent defects under the Inspection clause even though its obligation under the Guaranty clause was limited to furnishing replacement parts.

The most commonly used warranty clauses contain language stating that they override the finality of acceptance under the Inspection clause. See, for example, FAR 52.246-17(c)(5), which states: "The rights and remedies of the Government provided in this clause are in addition to and do not limit any rights afforded to the Government by any other clause of this contract." In *Gresham & Co.,* ASBCA 13812, 70-1 BCA ¶ 8318, *rev'd on other grounds*, 200 Ct. Cl. 97, 470 F.2d 542 (1972), it was held that patent as well as latent defects come under the Warranty clause. The court stated that "[o]ne purpose of this type of warranty clause is to exempt the Government from the necessity of exercising extreme diligence in its inspections." See also *M-Pax, Inc.*, HUDBCA 80-529-C11, 81-2 BCA ¶ 15,410 (Warranty of Construction clause survives inspection and acceptance); *Vi-Mil, Inc.*,

ASBCA 16820, 75-2 BCA ¶ 11,435, *recons. denied*, 75-2 BCA ¶ 11,618 (Warranty of Supplies clause survived final acceptance); and *United States v. Franklin Steel Prods., Inc.*, 482 F.2d 400 (9th Cir. 1973), *cert. denied*, 415 U.S. 918 (1974) (warranty supersedes the Inspection clause). In the past the specific language of certain clauses was found to be insufficient to overcome acceptance. But see *Miller Elevator v. United States*, 30 Fed. Cl. 662 (1994) (oral instruction of authorized official sufficient to waive certain contract requirements). In *Instruments for Indus., Inc. v. United States*, 496 F.2d 1157 (2d Cir. 1974), unlike *Gresham*, the Guaranty clause purported to cover patent defects without making specific reference to acceptance under the Inspection clause. While the Inspection clause for supply contracts did contain language stating acceptance was final "except as otherwise provided in this contract," the court concluded that a "more direct and specific caveat" was needed to overcome the finality of acceptance accomplished under that clause—especially in light of the absence of any explicit indication in the Guaranty clause that it would have effect notwithstanding acceptance or operate as an exception to the conclusiveness of acceptance. See also *Bergen Expo Sys., Inc.*, IBCA 1348-4-80, 82-2 BCA ¶ 16,010, in which patent defects were not excluded from the Inspection clause, making acceptance conclusive. Compare *Abney Constr. Co.*, ASBCA 23686, 80-2 BCA ¶ 14,506, in which the government's rights under a Warranty of Construction clause were found to survive acceptance even though the clause contained no language excepting its operation from the conclusiveness of acceptance. The difference in *Abney*, however, was in the more specific language of the Inspection and Acceptance clause for construction contracts, which provided that "[a]cceptance shall be final and conclusive except as regards . . . the Government's rights under any warranty or guarantee."

The FAR warranty provisions have generally taken this problem into account by including language that overcomes the finality of acceptance. FAR 46.705(c) provides:

> Except for warranty clauses in construction contracts [presumably, due to the more specific language in the Inspection clause for construction mentioned above, see FAR 52.246-12], warranty clauses shall provide that the warranty applies notwithstanding inspection and acceptance or other clauses or terms of the contract.

Although most of the standard warranty clauses in the FAR contain such language, the basic complex supplies warranty clause in FAR 52.246-18 does not. Under this provision, the government may face a problem similar to the one in *Instruments for Industry* in securing post-acceptance warranty rights.

The Warranty of Systems and Equipment under Performance Specifications or Design Criteria clause, FAR 52.246-19, does not contain the same explicit language as the other warranty clauses but does state that the rights and remedies of the government under the clause are not "affected in any way by any terms or conditions of this contract concerning the conclusiveness of inspection and acceptance." However, both of these provisions state that "[t]he rights and remedies of the Government provided in this clause are in addition to . . . any rights afforded to the Government by any other clause" and this language alone may be sufficient to overcome the finality of acceptance.

CHAPTER 10

DEFAULT TERMINATION, DAMAGES, AND LIQUIDATED DAMAGES

Default termination is the ultimate method of dealing with a contractor's unexcused present or prospective failure to perform in accordance with the contract specifications and schedule. By exercising its right to terminate for default, the government effectively notifies the contractor that its performance failure discharges government duties under the contract while exposing the contractor to potential liability for the consequences of its breach.

The FAR contains two basic clauses covering default termination. The default clause in FAR 52.249-8 is used for both fixed-price supply and service contracts. The clause for fixed-price construction contracts is contained in FAR 52.249-10. The government's policies with respect to termination for default are contained in FAR Subpart 49.4. The termination for cause of contracts for commercial items is covered in FAR 12.403 and the applicable clause is ¶ (m) of FAR 52.212-4.

With the exception of the relatively new FAR 52 212-4, the government's rights and obligations under these clauses have been litigated extensively. (For one case dealing with terminations under FAR 52.212-4, see *Southeast Tech. Servs.,* ASBCA 52319, 02-1 BCA ¶ 31,727.) This litigation has developed a number of legal rules, which are the subject of this chapter. The first section examines the consequences of a default termination. The second section reviews the types of performance failures that entitle the government to terminate for default and the circumstances under which it can waive these rights. The third section discusses the termination decision. The fourth section covers procedures for termination. The fifth section discusses excess costs of reprocurement. The chapter concludes with a discussion of liquidated damages. Much of the litigation that arises regarding default terminations focuses on whether the failure to perform on time is "excused" as being attributable to causes beyond the control or without the fault or negligence of the contractor. These issues are discussed in detail in Chapter 6.

I. CONSEQUENCES OF DEFAULT TERMINATION

A default termination is a traumatic event for both parties. The contractor and the government are both likely to suffer severe economic and time consequences.

A. Impact on Contractor

The impact of a default termination under a fixed-price supply contract is usually quite severe. A default termination may have the following effects on the relationship between the parties:

- The government is not liable for the costs of unaccepted work—the contractor is entitled to receive payment only for work accepted by the government;
- The government is entitled to the return of progress, partial, or advance payments;
- The government has the right but not the duty to appropriate the contractor's material, inventory, construction plant and equipment at the site, and, under supply contracts, drawings and plans—with the price for the appropriated items to be negotiated;
- The contractor is liable for excess costs of reprocurement or completion;
- The contractor is liable for actual or liquidated damages; and
- The contractor may be subject to debarment.

See FAR 9.406-2(b)(1)

A default termination may also adversely affect the contractor's eligibility for award of other government contracts since past performance is considered in determining responsibility and is evaluated in negotiated contracts. Because of these consequences and since a default termination not infrequently leads to the contractor's financial ruin, the Court of Claims has branded default termination a species of forfeiture, *De Vito v. United States*, 188 Ct. Cl. 979, 413 F.2d 1147 (1969). Although some of these consequences are also applicable to construction and service contracts, a contractor who has been properly terminated for default under those contracts is nevertheless entitled to payment for work that was properly performed prior to the default termination, *J.G. Enters., Inc.*, ASBCA 27150, 83-2 BCA ¶ 16,808; *Ventilation Cleaning Eng'rs, Inc.*, ASBCA 18580, 74-2 BCA ¶ 10,873; *Mercury Co.*, ASBCA 14926, 70-2 BCA ¶ 8419. However, it is not entitled to recover the contract amount minus the cost of completion of the work, *Century Marine, Inc. v. United States*, 153 F.3d 225 (5th Cir. 1998) (reasoning that such recovery would permit the recovery of anticipatory profit). In contrast, under supply contracts, the contractor generally has no right following proper default termination to recover costs incurred in producing supplies not accepted by the government, *Valley Sand & Gravel*, AGBCA 385, 75-1 BCA ¶ 10,986. The logic underlying this different treatment is that in the case of service and construction contracts the government has benefited from the contractor's partial performance in the form of services rendered or permanent improvement of government-owned property. In the case of supply contracts, however, the government is not benefited by the contractor's performance efforts unless it has accepted the supplies.

Even if the contractor is successful in overturning the termination, the relief obtainable may well be limited. The default clauses provide that if the termination is improper the "rights and obligations" of the parties will be "the same as if the termination had been issued for the convenience of the Government." The Termination for the Convenience of the Government clause permits recovery of costs incurred but does not permit the recovery of anticipated profit (see Chapter 11). Furthermore, it contains a provision reducing the recovery by the rate of anticipated loss. Thus, recovery of anticipatory profits will occur only in those rare cases where the contractor can prove that the government terminated in bad faith. See *Apex Int'l Mgmt. Servs. Inc.*, ASBCA 38087, 94-2 BCA ¶ 26,842; *Carter Indus.*, DOTBCA 4108, 02-1 BCA ¶ 31,738.

In addition, the contractor may not recover more than it would have been entitled to if the government had exercised all of the rights available to it. Thus, in *A/S Dampshibssetshabet Torm v. United States*, 64 F. Supp. 2d 298 (S.D.N.Y. 1999), even though the court found that the agency improperly terminated for default, the court denied the contractor's request to convert the termination into one for convenience when the agency proved that it could have canceled the contract under the "Inspection" clause.

Even extra costs resulting from government-directed changes in the work may not be recoverable following a valid default termination of a fixed-price supply contract where the product of the extra effort has not been accepted by, or has not resulted in a benefit to, the government. In *A.C. Hoyle Co.*, ASBCA 15363, 71-2 BCA ¶ 9137, the board stated that a "valid termination for default negates the Government's liability for . . . any equitable increase for extra work performed in producing rejected winches." See also *Jules Teitelbaum, Tr. in Bank. for Victory Elecs., Inc.*, ASBCA 12885, 70-1 BCA ¶ 8210, in which the board rejected the contention that the contractor was entitled to recover costs of performing "additional testing." The board reasoned that, since the testing was incomplete at the time of the default and no test data had ever been delivered, "no benefit accrued to the Government." See, however, *Laka Tool & Stamping Co. v. United States*, 226 Ct. Cl. 83, 639 F.2d 738 (1980), *reh'g denied*, 227 Ct. Cl. 468, 650 F.2d 270, *cert. denied*, 454 U.S. 1086 (1981), in which the Court of Claims held that a fixed-price contractor was entitled to recover the "excess costs" it incurred in trying to comply with defective government specifications despite its eventual default for reasons unrelated to the defective specifications. In concluding that the government's proper default termination action did not serve as an absolute bar to recovery of the contractor's "out-of-pocket loss in the form of expenditures for efforts wasted because of the impossible specifications," the court emphasized that the costs resulted from acts that the government "had no right to do under the contract," stating at 472:

> This last factor distinguishes the case where a contractor terminated for default would seek to recover for a mere change. The Government does have the right under the contract to issue change orders. If, instead of supplying impossible specifications, the Government had simply increased the amount of magazines required under the contract by change order and [the contractor] had completed the contract, it would have been entitled to the contract price for the originally required work plus an equitable adjustment for the additional work. However, should [the

> contractor] be properly terminated for default without making any acceptable deliveries in such a case, it would get nothing for the original work. Furthermore, our opinion today should not be read as allowing a recovery for work covered by a change order, even though the change order might have caused a [contractor] to do extra work just as the impossible specifications did here. A crucial distinction is that the Government does have the right to issue change orders.

See *Harent, Inc.*, ASBCA 16206, 73-2 BCA ¶ 10,074, in which the board held that a ship repair contractor could recover for extras following a valid default termination where the government had "received the benefit" of the extra work. See also *Robert B. Joy*, PSBCA 938, Sept. 30, 1981, *Unpub.*, allowing the contractor to rely on an "adjustment in compensation" provision despite a valid default termination.

B. Impact on Government

Even if the government is successful in litigating the propriety of a default termination, it will also most likely suffer severe consequences. The impact of a default termination on the government was discussed in *Clay Bernard Sys. Int'l, Ltd v. United States*, 22 Cl. Ct. 804 (1991), as follows at 810:

> Termination for default, however, is a drastic adjustment of the contractual relationship and the Government is held to strict accountability in using this sanction. *J.D. Hedin Constr. Co. v. United States*, 408 F.2d 424, 431, 187 Ct. Cl. 45 (1969); *Schlesinger v. United States*, 390 F.2d 702, 709, 182 Ct. Cl. 571 (1968). A termination for default generally results in lost time to the Government in obtaining the services or goods it sought; it always penalizes the contractor, and frequently the Government is exposed to substantial additional costs, particularly if the action subsequently is found to be one for convenience of the Government. Further, a default termination is an acknowledgment that previous procedural safeguards—i.e., bidding and negotiation procedures to select a contractor, examinations to determine contractor competence and qualifications, and review and approval of contractor competence and qualifications, and review and approval of subcontract and subcontractors—have failed to realize their purposes.

For these reasons, if the government still needs the work, it will usually not terminate the contract unless it is convinced that the contractor is incapable of performing the work or another contractor will be able to satisfy its needs in a significantly shorter period of time than the defaulting contractor.

C. Fixed-Price Supply Termination Inventory

Paragraph (e) of the FAR default clause for supply and service contracts provides that, following default termination, the government may direct the contractor to "transfer title and deliver to the Government . . . any (1) completed supplies, and (2) partially completed supplies and materials, parts, tools, dies, jigs, fixtures, plans, drawings, information, and contract rights (collectively referred to as `manufacturing materials' in this clause)." Paragraph (f) states that payment for "completed supplies delivered and accepted" will be at the "contract price." In contrast, payment for "manufacturing materials" delivered to and accepted by the government will be in an amount agreed to by the parties. In *Metadure Corp.*, ASBCA 24533, 83-1 BCA ¶ 16,325, the board upheld the government's use of a "percentage of completion" method for valuing termination inventory. This technique was described by the board at 81,136:

> Using the inventory obtained by the Government through its replevin suit, the team determined the material and component parts that were not included in the inventory delivered and had yet to be procured by [the contractor] to complete the contract. These missing items were priced and that amount subtracted from the total contract price to arrive at a cost basis for determining the percentage of contract completion.
>
> Based upon a Defense Contract Audit Agency (DCAA) audit report and the contract, the team determined the value of the missing material and component parts using [the contractor's] available purchase orders for those items. The team used this process throughout their evaluation. Based upon the available purchase orders the team applied a value to each item. The team concerned itself only with the high cost items. It did not include peripheral parts to complete the contract. Based upon its evaluation, the team made its determination as to the percentage of contract completion. Based upon an evaluation of material and component part costs, the percentage of contract completion was determined to be 78 percent. This percentage figure did not include the labor necessary to complete the contract. The team determined that the requisite labor constituted 9 percent of the estimate to complete the contract. The 9 percent for labor was deducted from the 78 percent, resulting in a percentage of 69.

Note that this approach, by using the original contract price as the basis for determining the percentage of completion, will for the most part preserve the contractor's profit or loss position relative to the partially completed items.

In *Jules Teitelbaum, Tr. in Bankr. for Victory Elecs., Inc.*, ASBCA 12885, 70-1 BCA ¶ 8210, the board rejected the proposition that the total cost incurred by the contractor in producing "manufacturing materials" was conclusive of the true value of such termination inventory, essentially objecting to this approach as a form of total cost valuation long disfavored by the boards and courts. In addition, the board recognized that costs incurred in producing termination inventory that were attributable to causes for which an equitable adjustment was available under the contract would be recoverable, but it found no proof supporting such entitlement in that case. The board also acknowledged that the costs the contractor incurred in "converting components into assemblies" should be considered in arriving at a "fair and reasonable value" for this termination inventory. As to valuation of termination inventory taken from subcontractors, the board did accept as conclusive the costs set forth in the purchase orders under which the materials had been furnished by the contractor to the subcontractors. See also *Munck Sys., Inc.*, ASBCA 25600, 83-1

BCA ¶ 16,210, *aff'd*, 727 F.2d 1118 (Fed. Cir. 1983), holding that the contractor was entitled to recover additional amounts for components taken by the government following default where the government had directed changes in the contractor's previously approved quality control procedures and had directed the contractor to use a particular control device not specifically required by the contract.

In *Meyer Labs, Inc.*, ASBCA 18989, 83-2 BCA ¶ 16,598, the board held that in computing excess costs the government could not charge the contractor for expenses it incurred in removing termination inventory. The board also concluded that there was no need to determine the value of the inventory since the government had turned it over to the reprocurement contractor, thus making its value a "cost of reprocurement" and resulting in a "wash" transaction. For cases relating to a contractor's post-termination costs relating to the inventory, compare *Dennis Berlin d/b/a Spectro Sort & as Spectro Sort Mfg. Co.*, ASBCA 51919, 02-1 BCA ¶ 31,675 (contractor not entitled to the costs of performing an inventory of material after the termination for default because the contract obligated the contractor to do so), with *C.T. Genvis Indus., Inc.,* ENGBCA 6255, 99-1 BCA ¶ 30,334 (contractor's claimed costs relating to the government's efforts to take delivery of partially completed work after the default termination "could constitute a separate claim under the changes provision of the contract").

II. RIGHT TO TERMINATE

The common law right to follow a course of action equivalent to default termination is said to arise when there is an "uncured material failure" to perform, *Restatement, Second, Contracts* § 237. In describing these material failures, the courts have used terms such as "material breach" or "failure of consideration." These terms have been invoked when the failure to perform on time involves a very significant portion of the contract work. They may also be used when it appears that completion of performance will be delayed long beyond the specified completion date. When termination is considered to be justified for relatively short delays, the courts often state that "time is of the essence." Thus, when such a termination is considered improper, the judicial response is usually that the parties did not make time of the essence in their contract.

The presence of the default clauses in government contracts has raised the question of whether these common law concepts are applicable to federal contracts. Consequently, this section first deals with the types of performance failures or contractor conduct that will justify default termination by the government. It then considers the matter of when a failure to perform a portion of the stated contract work justifies termination of the entire contract. The section concludes with a discussion of the concept of waiver through which the government, by conduct inconsistent with the exercise of its default rights, loses the right to terminate. This discussion includes an examination of the rights of the parties once a waiver has occurred.

A. Grounds for Termination

The standard default clauses identify three different grounds for termination: (1) failure to deliver the product or complete the work or service within the stated time, (2) failure to make progress in prosecuting the work and thereby endangering timely completion, and (3) breach of "other provisions" of the contract.

In addition to these specifically enumerated grounds for default termination, two additional types of contractor conduct have frequently served as the basis for default termination. The first—failure to proceed—arises when the contractor fails or refuses to go forward with the work according to the contracting officer's directions. The second—anticipatory repudiation—occurs when the contractor clearly expresses through words or conduct an intention not to complete the contract work on time. This subsection discusses in detail each of these bases for default termination.

1. Failure to Perform or Deliver

The supply and service contracts default clause provides that the government may terminate for default if the contractor "fails to deliver the supplies or to perform the services within the time specified." The construction contract default provision states that the government may terminate for default when the contractor "fails to complete" the work within the "time specified in this contract." Similar language is set forth in the other FAR default clauses.

Although these clauses explicitly make untimely performance the basis for the default action, it is important to recognize that nearly every government contract spells out the contractor's required performance in terms of the nature of the product or service that is to be delivered or performed as well as the time by which this performance is to be completed. Thus, in order for the contractor to render "timely performance," two basic requirements must be satisfied: (1) the product, service, or construction work must conform to the required contract design/performance specifications, and (2) the product must be delivered or the work completed by the specified due date. See *Radiation Tech., Inc. v. United States*, 177 Ct. Cl. 227, 366 F.2d 1003 (1966); *Air, Inc.*, GSBCA 8847, 91-1 BCA ¶ 23,352; and *Nash Metalware Co.*, GSBCA 11951, 94-2 BCA ¶ 26,780.

a. Slight Delays in Performance

The government rarely terminates contracts for slight delays. Thus, there are relatively few decisions in which the issue to be decided is whether "time is of the essence." It has been argued that the presence of default clauses gives the contractor sufficient notice that time is of the essence in all government contracts, Coons & Whelan, *Default Termination of Defense Department Fixed Price Supply Contracts,* 32 Notre Dame L. Rev. 189, 191 (1957). For the contrary view, see Risik, *Defaults in Federal Government Contracts,* 14 Fed. B.J. 339, 348 (1954).

The Court of Claims never squarely decided the question of whether a termination for a slight delay is appropriate, and neither has the Court of Appeals for the Federal Circuit. However, there is language in Court of Claims decisions supporting both views. One view is expressed in *De Vito v. United States*, 188 Ct. Cl. 979, 413 F.2d 1147 (1969), in which the court stated that "[t]ime is of the essence in any contract containing fixed dates for performance." This view was taken in *National Farm Equip. Co.*, GSBCA 4921, 78-1 BCA ¶ 13,195 (contract's default clause grants the government the right to terminate the contract when delivery is not made on the contractually specified date and does not require the government to wait one day more); and *Thomas C. Wilson, Inc.*, ASBCA 26035, 83-1 BCA ¶ 16,149 (time became of the essence where the contract specified the delivery date and included the default clause; time remained an essence of the contract even though the government did not need the supplies at the time of the delivery date).

De Vito was apparently followed by the Armed Services Board of Contract Appeals in *Nuclear Research Assocs., Inc.*, ASBCA 13563, 70-1 BCA ¶ 8237, where a contractor tendered specially manufactured supplies on the first working day after the due date, but the government issued a default termination notice 30 minutes after delivery. In upholding the termination, the ASBCA Senior Deciding Group stated that, once a contractor "has failed to deliver on time, the Government, absent excusable cause of delay, has an indefeasible right to terminate the contract, unless its own conduct deprives it of that right." The board also noted that it did not matter that the late delivery was made before the sending of the default termination telegram. However, in a dissenting opinion, three judges stated that the substantial performance doctrine was applicable because time was not of the essence in the contract. (Much of *Nuclear Research* was later overruled by *Darwin Constr. Co. v. United States*, 811 F.2d 593 (Fed. Cir. 1987), but the requirement that "time is of the essence" remained intact.)

For other cases, involving both standard and specially manufactured goods, expressing the view that the default clause in supply contracts gives the government the immediate right to terminate once the due date has arrived, see *M.H. Colvin & Co.*, GSBCA 5209, 79-2 BCA ¶ 13,981 (screw driver bits and adapters not delivered on scheduled inspection dates); *National Farm Equip. Co.*, GSBCA 4921, 78-1 BCA ¶ 13,195 (pruning shears and garden spades available for delivery one day after scheduled date); *Fairfield Scientific Corp.*, ASBCA 21152, 78-1 BCA ¶ 12,869, *aff'd*, 228 Ct. Cl. 264, 655 F.2d 1062 (1981) (termination five days after contractor failed to deliver impulse cartridges on scheduled date); *H.N. Bailey & Assocs.*, ASBCA 21300, 77-2 BCA ¶ 12,681 (link assemblies for RC-135 C/M aircraft not timely delivered for first article testing despite two time extensions); and *R & O Indus., Inc.*, GSBCA 4804, 80-1 BCA ¶ 14,196 (cooking knives not delivered despite five time extensions). See also *Riggs Eng'g Co.*, ASBCA 26509, 82-2 BCA ¶ 15,955, in which the board recognized a right to immediately terminate because the contractor failed to deliver a first article on the specified date.

Time has also been held to be of the essence in construction contracts. For example, in *Ajax Co.*, ENGBCA 3377, 76-1 BCA ¶ 11,645, the board noted that, despite the absence of monetary damages, the contractor's delays could interfere with the discharge of governmental functions. Note that in *Ajax* the original contract contained a provision requiring the contractor to work as many shifts as were necessary to ensure completion within the specified time period. Further, a contract amendment extending the delivery date contained a specific provision reserving the government's right to terminate for untimely performance. The government terminated the day following the extended delivery date.

The contrary view that time may not necessarily be of the essence is supported by the trial judge's opinion as adopted by the court in *Franklin E. Penny Co. v. United States*, 207 Ct. Cl. 842, 524 F.2d 668 (1975). There, the issue of whether time is of the essence was said to depend on the nature of the contract and the particular circumstances of the case. See also *Clay Bernard Sys. Int'l, Ltd. v. United States*, 22 Cl. Ct. 804 (1991), which involved the design, development, and delivery of a material handling system. The court observed that this was not the "normal" supply contract. *Franklin E. Penny* was cited with approval in *West Coast Research Corp.*, ASBCA 21087, 77-1 BCA ¶ 12,510, stating that failure to deliver goods strictly "on time" was not, under the circumstances, sufficient of itself to authorize termination for default. The board observed that time was certainly not of the essence in a contract where delivery due on Friday was actually made on Sunday, although the goods remained unopened for 16 or 17 days after delivery. Nevertheless, the default was upheld because the delivered items did not substantially comply with contract requirements.

Service contracts are covered by the FAR 52.249-8 clause, which permits termination for failure "to perform the services within the time specified." A predecessor clause with this language for use only on service contracts was included in DAR 7-1902.8. Since service contracts often contemplate performance according to detailed work schedules, it has been stated that time is of the essence, *Riteway Sanitation Serv.*, ASBCA 14304, 70-2 BCA ¶ 8553 (contractor failed to comply with collection schedules of a sanitation services contract). In *Michigan Bldg. Maint., Inc.*, IBCA 1945, 87-1 BCA ¶ 19,461, the board stated at 98,368:

> The law on service contracts is relatively well settled . . . . Appeals boards have recognized that cleaning services are a vital function that the contractor must perform satisfactorily, or else the contractor must be replaced. If properly documented, termination can be accomplished very quickly.

Failure to perform services on time and in accordance with specifications has been held to justify an immediate termination for default only when there has been a "substantial failure of performance." See *Suburban Indus. Maint. Co.*, ASBCA 23570, 85-2 BCA ¶18,148, stating that for a service contract to be terminated for specific failures to perform on time, "a sufficient number of such failures must accumulate such that it could be said that there had been a substantial failure of performance." This rule was followed in *Plum Run, Inc.*, ASBCA 46091, 05-1 BCA ¶ 32,977 (recurring lack of performance a substantial failure); *Swanson Group, Inc.,* ASBCA 44664, 98-2 BCA ¶ 29,896 (government failed to prove substantial failures); *William Howard Wilson,* ASBCA 47831, 97-1 BCA ¶ 28,911 (failure to work for two weeks clearly a substantial failure); *CardioMetrix v. Department of the Treasury,* GSBCA 13462-TD, 97-1 BCA ¶ 28,775 (substantial failure when contractor failed to secure the status of the physicians as its employees as proposed, failed to notify the government of subcontracting relationships, and failed to provide proof of adequate insurance coverage); and *Handyman Bldg. Maint. Co.*, IBCA 1335-3-80, 83-2 BCA ¶ 16,646 (no substantial failure in specific omissions of janitorial services). Earlier decisions had stated a stricter rule permitting default termination upon a single failure of performance. See *Utah Waste Paper Co.*, VACAB 1104, 75-1 BCA ¶ 11,058 (some garbage pickups were made late and some were not made at all). In *Ortec Sys., Inc.*, ASBCA 43467, 92-2 BCA ¶ 24,859, the board sustained a termination where the asbestos abatement project was to be completed. The board noted the importance of timely completion to the government and that time was "of the essence." The contractor had left the site seven days earlier and the government was unable to reach the contractor prior to the termination. See also *Decatur Realty Sales*, HUDBCA 75-26, 77-2 BCA ¶ 12,567, in which the board held that the government had the right to "summarily" terminate for failure to provide management brokerage services according to the contract schedule. Even where only a portion of the required services are not performed on time, it has been held that the entire contract may be terminated, *Al's Enters., Ltd.*, ASBCA 13576, 70-1 BCA ¶ 8080 (less than one-half of the containers emptied). The right to terminate immediately may also be limited by specific contract provisions, *Mr.'s Landscaping & Nursery*, HUDBCA 75-6, 76-2 BCA ¶ 11,968 (default overturned where government failed to observe provision entitling the contractor to notice of deficiencies and an opportunity to correct). In *Itra Coop Ass'n*, GSBCA 7974, 90-1 BCA ¶ 22,410, the board found a default termination improper because the contractor's performance was within the terms of an informal "side agreement" with the agency receiving the service. Although the contractor failed to perform a number of typewriter repair services within the 10-hour period specified by the contract, it did meet the requirements of the side agreement requiring a technician to be present for repairs only two days a week. The board held that the side agreement established a course of dealing upon which the contractor relied and that the government was not free to find the contractor in default for proceeding in accordance with established practice. In addition, the board noted that it was not appropriate to terminate the entire contact since the majority of documented complaints occurred at only one of approximately 50 service locations. The board stated at 112,564:

> In general, it is not appropriate to terminate an entire contract for default where it is possible to terminate only a severable portion of the work as to which an actual default has been demonstrated.

b. Timely Delivery of Defective Supplies

In *Radiation Tech., Inc. v. United States*, 177 Ct. Cl. 227, 366 F.2d 1003 (1966), the court invoked the doctrine of "substantial compliance" as a limitation of the government's broad termination rights under a supply contract. Under this doctrine, summary default termination may be prevented when supplies have been delivered on time and substantially comply with the contract requirements.

The substantial compliance doctrine is similar to U.C.C. § 2-508(2), which gives a seller reasonable time to cure a defective shipment of goods provided that it had reasonable grounds to believe that the goods would be accepted, *Environmental Tectonics Corp.*, ASBCA 20340, 76-2 BCA ¶ 12,134. Substantial compliance differs from the concept of substantial completion (as discussed in detail below) in two respects. First, under the *Radiation Technology* rule of substantial compliance, the right to terminate the entire contract will revive unless the defect in the goods is cured within a reasonable time, *Levelator Corp. of Am.*, VACAB 738, 71-1 BCA ¶ 8721, while substantial completion bars termination of the completed work. Second, the supply contractor's state of mind is relevant to application of the *Radiation Technology* rule, whereas state of mind is not a factor in assessing a contractor's substantial completion. Despite these differences, the *Radiation Technology* rule has occasionally been cited in evaluating a construction contractor's substantial completion, *R.M. Crum Constr. Co.*, VABCA 2143, 85-2 BCA ¶ 18,132; *Samuel Quarno & Co.*, HUDBCA 76-21, 77-2 BCA ¶ 12,599; *Corway, Inc.*, ASBCA 20683, 77-1 BCA ¶ 12,357; *Capitol City Constr. Co.*, DOTCAB 74-29, 75-1 BCA ¶ 11,012; *K & M Constr.*, ENGBCA 2998, 73-2 BCA ¶ 10,034.

The *Radiation Technology* rule has also been applied to service contracts that require, in part, the delivery of goods, *Metzger Towing, Inc.*, ENGBCA 5862, 94-2 BCA ¶ 26,651 (substantial compliance doctrine made default termination improper where the deficiencies were remedied quickly and the dredge plant substantially complied with the contract requirements); *Itra Coop Ass'n*, GSBCA 7974, 90-1 BCA ¶ 22,410 (board stated that "[t]he principle of 'substantial compliance' places a considerable limitation upon an agency's exercise of its right to terminate for default a service contract"); *Palmetto Enters., Inc.*, ASBCA 19588, 76-2 BCA ¶ 12,139 (default termination of a contract to provide refueling services held proper due to numerous, complex deficiencies; no substantial compliance with requirements found). In addition, the substantial compliance doctrine has been applied to limit the government's right to default terminate for submission of a defective "first article" or "preproduction" model.

(1) Timely Tender

In order to take advantage of the substantial compliance rule, the contract articles must be received by the due date, *SCM Corp.*, ASBCA 19941, 75-2 BCA ¶

11,508. Thus, the doctrine does not apply where there has been no delivery. See *Nash Metalware Co.*, GSBCA 11951, 94-2 BCA ¶ 26,780 (default termination proper because contractor failed to tender goods that conformed to the specifications, failed to propose corrective action, and ultimately failed to deliver by the due date); *Norwood Precision Prods., Textron Inc.*, ASBCA 38095, 90-3 BCA ¶ 23,200 (government justified in terminating contract for default if the contractor fails to deliver supplies within the time specified); *Hedlund Lumber Sales, Inc.*, ASBCA 14815, 71-1 BCA ¶ 8782 (default termination for failure to make timely delivery proper despite failure of government to notify contractor of its intent to deny request for time extension); and *Fitzgerald Labs., Inc.*, ASBCA 15205, 71-2 BCA ¶ 9029 (no persuasive evidence that strikes caused contractor's failure to deliver). It also does not apply when there is a late delivery of less than the required quantity, *Forest Scientific, Inc.*, ASBCA 17822, 74-1 BCA ¶ 10,447 (contractor had 96 of the required 98 items ready for one delivery deadline but had already missed two prior deadlines). It has been stated, but not held, that *Radiation Technology* might apply even where goods are tendered after the due date, *Franklin E. Penny Co. v. United States*, 207 Ct. Cl. 842, 524 F.2d 668 (1975). However, to date, the only clear exception to the requirement for delivery by the due date is where waiver of the due date has rendered time no longer of the essence. See *Astro Dynamics, Inc.*, ASBCA 28381, 88-3 BCA ¶ 20,832, in which the board stated at 105,366:

> When a due date has passed and the contract has not been terminated for default within a reasonable time, the inference is created that time is no longer of the essence so long as the constructive election not to terminate continues and the contractor proceeds with performance.

In such cases, the *Radiation Technology* rule has been relied on to reverse a default, *Video Research Corp.*, ASBCA 14684, 71-2 BCA ¶ 9006 (due-date extensions had been given to allow for correction of defects).

(2) Reasonable Belief That the Goods Conform

Another prerequisite for use of the substantial compliance doctrine is that the contractor must have had a reasonable belief that the tendered goods conformed to the stated requirements, *Hannon Elec. Co. v. United States*, 31 Fed. Cl. 135 (1994) (contractor knew goods did not conform to specifications); *Kurz-Kasch, Inc.*, ASBCA 32486, 88-3 BCA ¶ 21,053 (substantial compliance not applicable where the contractor submitted the units knowing that they did not comply with the contract specifications); *Environmental Tectonics Corp.*, ASBCA 20340, 76-2 BCA ¶ 12,134 (no substantial compliance where the contractor knowingly shipped defective sterilizers with the expectation that it would be permitted additional time to rework the units and correct defects at the delivery site). Thus, the *Radiation Technology* rule will not apply if the contractor knows that the goods do not comply or if the contractor's belief that the goods comply is unreasonable. For example, knowledge of noncompliance defeats application of the doctrine, *Meyer Labs, Inc.*, ASBCA

18347, 77-1 BCA ¶ 12,539 (tendered bomb release units contained various components that had previously been rejected as nonconforming); and *Century Hone Div. of Desert Labs., Inc.*, ASBCA 18360, 78-1 BCA ¶ 12,990, *recons. denied*, 78-2 BCA ¶ 13,343 (delivery of metal honing device with knowledge of 90 percent failure of metal removal tests). Similarly, an unreasonable belief that the goods conformed also defeats application of the doctrine, *Gillett Mach. Rebuilders, Inc.*, ASBCA 28341, 89-3 BCA ¶ 22,021 (where three of four spindles did not meet spindle runout tests, contractor could not reasonably conclude that the spindles conformed to the contract requirements or that the defects were minor or readily correctable); *Vanbar*, ASBCA 20762, 77-2 BCA ¶ 12,798 (breach of requirement to notify government prior to conducting first article test upon which nonconforming test report was based); *Filcon Corp.*, ASBCA 19578, 75-1 BCA ¶ 11,303, *recons. denied*, 75-2 BCA ¶ 11,527 (quantity of defects supported inference of no reasonable belief that the goods would conform); *Solar Labs., Inc.*, ASBCA 19269, 74-2 BCA ¶ 10,897, *recons. denied*, 75-1 BCA ¶ 11,049 (failure to conduct testing of articles even though not required by contract); *Kain Cattle Co.*, ASBCA 17124, 73-1 BCA ¶ 9999 (failure to inspect at origin as required by contract); *Frank A. Pellicia v. United States*, 208 Ct. Cl. 278, 525 F.2d 1035 (1975) (shipment of noncomplying goods under erroneous belief that specifications had been waived). Contrast *Products Eng'g Corp. v. General Servs. Admin.*, GSBCA 12503, 98-2 BCA ¶ 29,851, where the contractor did not know of the tests used by the government to establish the defects, and *Argent Indus., Inc.*, ASBCA 15207, 71-2 BCA ¶ 9172, where reasonable belief was found because assembly was made by very experienced workers and testing performed at all production stages.

(3) Defects Minor in Nature and Readily Correctable

In order to take advantage of the additional time to correct under the substantial compliance doctrine, the contractor must demonstrate that the defects are minor and readily correctable. Whether a defect is minor is a question of fact, based on a consideration of (1) whether the items are usable, (2) the nature of the product, (3) the urgency of the government's needs, and (4) the extent of repair and adjustment necessary to produce a fully conforming product, *Kain Cattle Co.*, ASBCA 17124, 73-1 BCA ¶ 9999.

Defects were found to be minor in *Radar Devices, Inc.*, ASBCA 43912, 99-1 BCA ¶ 30,223, *recons. denied*, 99-2 BCA ¶ 30,396 (items repaired in less than one hour); *Trident Indus. Prods. Corp.*, DOTBCA 2807, 98-1 BCA ¶ 29,619 (slightly less than specified quantity of cloth); *Metzger Towing, Inc.*, ENGBCA 5862, 94-2 BCA ¶ 26,651 (remaining dredge plant deficiencies were remedied within a few days); *Cosmos Eng'g, Inc.*, ASBCA 19780, 77-2 BCA ¶ 12,713 (only 10 days needed to correct minor work on complex audiovisual); *Orion Elecs. Corp.*, ASBCA 18010, 75-1 BCA ¶ 11,006 (packing and packaging defects could be corrected in one day); *National Aviation Elecs., Inc.*, ASBCA 18256, 74-2 BCA ¶ 10,677 (instruments could easily be packaged to meet dimensional requirements); *Video Research Corp.*, ASBCA 14684, 71-2 BCA ¶ 9006 (one hour of work and $10.00 per unit would allow tape recorders to pass "drift" test); and *Argent Indus., Inc.*, ASBCA 15207, 71-2 BCA ¶ 9172 (even the most serious defect could have been corrected in 10 minutes).

In *Defense Tech. Corp.*, ASBCA 39551, 91-3 BCA ¶ 24,189, the board found a default termination unjustified because defects in first articles were easily correctable and enough time remained in the first article schedule to allow timely correction. The board stated at 120,988:

> We have consistently held that the Government may not demand strict compliance with the [first article] specifications as with supplies tendered for final delivery. The purpose of a First Article is to discover defects. Therefore, if defects are discovered and are easily correctable in production the Government may not reject the [first article].

See *National Aviation Elecs., Inc.*, ASBCA 18256, 74-2 BCA ¶ 10,677, in which the board noted that the substantial compliance doctrine of *Radiation Technology* applied "a fortiori" to a first article submission and overturned the default where the only defects were "correctable in production." See also *Advanced Precision Indus., Inc.*, ASBCA 34676, 89-2 BCA ¶ 21,597; *Acudata Sys., Inc.*, DOTCAB 1198, 84-1 BCA ¶ 17,046; and *Argent Indus., Inc.*, ASBCA 15207, 71-2 BCA ¶ 9172. The Court of Claims also held that the validity of termination for submission of a defective preproduction model that was to become the first production item upon approval following "acceptance testing" would be judged according to the *Radiation Technology* standard, *Astro Sci. Corp. v. United States*, 200 Ct. Cl. 354, 471 F.2d 624 (1973). Compare *Flight Refueling, Inc.*, ASBCA 46846, 97-2 BCA ¶ 29,000, holding that the doctrine does not apply when the contractor delivers only one of two required prototypes.

Defects are not minor when they affect the "efficiency" and "inherent functioning" of an item, *Technical Sys. Assocs., Inc. v. Department of Commerce*, GSBCA 13277-COM, 00-1 BCA ¶ 30,684. See also *Integrated Sys. Group, Inc.*, ASBCA 46918, 97-2 BCA ¶ 29,316, finding no substantial compliance when the defects went to the functioning and servicability of the computers being procured. For other cases finding that defects were not minor or readily correctable, see *Halifax Eng'g, Inc. v. United States*, 915 F.2d 689 (Fed. Cir. 1990) (contractor could not show that guard services deficiencies could be remedied within a short time); *Shiffer Indus., Inc.*, ASBCA 30919, 91-3 BCA ¶ 24,316; *Introl Corp.*, ASBCA 27610, 85-2 BCA ¶ 18,044 (modification of rotor shaft assembly to reduce its height would be a costly operation requiring 18 to 20 weeks to complete); *Astro Sci. Corp. v. United States*, 200 Ct. Cl. 354, 471 F.2d 624 (1973) (numerous minor defects when considered together were major nonconformity); *Reach Elecs., Inc.*, VACAB 1375, 79-2 BCA ¶ 14,048 (proposed corrections would not have complied); *Environmental Tecton-*

ics Corp., ASBCA 20340, 76-2 BCA ¶ 12,134 (sterilizers had major problems with doors and locking devices as well as numerous minor defects in workmanship that, taken together, were major); *Sperry-Vision Corp.*, ENGBCA 3489, 76-2 BCA ¶ 12,055 (television monitors failed eight different tests); *K-Square Corp.*, NASABCA 1271-23, 76-1 BCA ¶ 11,867, *recons. denied*, 76-2 BCA ¶ 12,093 (electron microscope failed intermittently and daily performance was essential); *Inforex, Inc.*, GSBCA 3859, 76-1 BCA ¶ 11,679 (contractor asked for two months to cure); *Frequency Elecs, Inc.*, ASBCA 17917, 74-2 BCA ¶ 10,792 (previous nonconforming cesium beam clocks with similar defects had taken several months to correct); *Levelator Corp.*, VACAB 1069, 74-2 BCA ¶ 10,763 (seven weeks needed to correct defects, and hospital was scheduled to open in one week); *Kain Cattle Co.*, ASBCA 17124, 73-1 BCA ¶ 9999 (excess fat rendered shipment of beef significantly defective); *Nuclear Equip. Corp.*, NASABCA 1170-18, 73-1 BCA ¶ 9815 (after two-day investigation, contractor could not propose a solution to various complex technical problems); *Echo Sci. Corp.*, NASABCA 671-9, 72-2 BCA ¶ 9755 (contractor needed one week to determine why tape recorder failed vibration test); *Renwin Metal Prods., Inc.*, ASBCA 15413, 72-1 BCA ¶ 9233, *recons. denied*, 72-1 BCA ¶ 9329 (powder separators deviated from dimensional tolerances to such a degree that equipment was not compatible with equipment manufactured by others); *Consolidated Mach. Corp.*, ASBCA 14176, 72-1 BCA ¶ 9212 (sterilizers were wired to operate on wrong voltage, had improperly placed controls, and contained exposed wiring); *Bardeen Mfg. Co.*, ASBCA 14381, 71-2 BCA ¶ 9007 (aircraft link assemblies could have failed at high temperatures since tensile strength requirements were not met and copper brazing was not performed); and *Filtron Co.*, DCAB ESSA-3, 70-1 BCA ¶ 8086 (electromagnetically shielded enclosure contained numerous defects including defective doors that required redesign, refabrication, and reinstallation).

(4) The Cure Period

When the contractor meets the above requirements, the *Radiation Technology* rule entitles it to cure the defect within a reasonable period of time, which may extend beyond the contract delivery schedule. The length of the cure period may vary depending on the nature of the defects and urgency of the government's needs. There is no right to any specific cure period, although at least one board has indicated that a 10-day cure period would apply, *Inforex, Inc.*, GSBCA 3859, 76-1 BCA ¶ 11,679 (default termination proper where the contractor asked for an "inordinate" time extension). A contractor that has already been afforded a reasonable opportunity to cure the defects may not later invoke the *Radiation Technology* rule, *Technics EMS, Inc.*, GSBCA 6679-COM, 84-1 BCA ¶ 17,060 (contractor failed to meet performance specifications for dual chamber ion mill after three opportunities to cure defects); *Electro-Neutronics, Inc.*, ASBCA 12947, 71-2 BCA ¶ 8961 (contractor was given four chances to correct the goods). There is no requirement for the contracting officer to direct that goods be corrected, and the absence of a contractor's expression of willingness to cure may defeat application of the doctrine,

Frequency Elecs., Inc., ASBCA 17917, 74-2 BCA ¶ 10,792 (contractor "never undertook to make the corrections"). See also *Donald C. Hubbs, Inc.*, DOTBCA 2012, 90-1 BCA ¶ 22,379 (contractor failed to take corrective action to remedy the defect); *Appli Tronics*, ASBCA 31540, 89-1 BCA ¶ 21,555 (contractor neither offered nor undertook corrective action with respect to substantiated defects); and *Kain Cattle Co.*, ASBCA 17124, 73-1 BCA ¶ 9999 (absence of willingness to cure defective meat was one factor in denying application of the doctrine).

c. *Limitations on Termination of All Work*

The right of the government to terminate all the work when only a part is in default is limited in certain situations.

(1) Accepted Work

The right to terminate for default is limited to the executory portion of a contract. Thus, acceptance of work bars default termination of that work in construction contracts, *Sentell Bros., Inc.*, DOTBCA 1824, 89-3 BCA ¶ 21,904; *Building Contractors, Inc.*, ASBCA 14840, 71-1 BCA ¶ 8884; *Hogan Constr., Inc.*, ASBCA 39014, 95-1 BCA ¶ 27,398; and in supply contracts, *K Square Corp.*, IBCA 959-3-72, 73-2 BCA ¶ 10,363. In *Donat Gerg Haustechnick*, ASBCA 41197, 97-2 BCA ¶ 29,272, termination for default was not available for a contractor's refusal to provide records for examination and audit, because no contract work remained to be performed nor any outstanding demand by the government for performance of work. Under those circumstances, the contract could fairly be said to have been complete. Compare *Aerometals, Inc.,* ASBCA 53688, 03-2 BCA ¶ 32,295, stating that a termination would be proper after the delivery schedule had been waived if the contractor delivered items that were substantially nonconforming, citing *Louisiana Lamps & Shades*, ASBCA 45294, 95-1 BCA ¶ 27,577; *Northeastern Mfg. & Sales,* ASBCA 35493, 89-3 BCA ¶ 22,093; and *Appli Tronics*, ASBCA 31540, 89-1 BCA ¶ 21,555.

Likewise, acceptance precludes imposition of other default remedies, such as excess costs of reprocurement on the accepted portion of the work, *Onus Co.*, ASBCA 16706, 72-2 BCA ¶ 9722. However, proper revocation of acceptance may revive the government's right to terminate for default, *Cross Aero Corp.*, ASBCA 14801, 71-2 BCA ¶ 9075 (discovery of latent defects allowed revocation of acceptance and subsequent termination for default); *Spandome Corp. v. United States,* 32 Fed. Cl. 626 (1995) (termination for default upheld when acceptance revoked more than one year after final acceptance); *Chilstead Bldg. Co.*, ASBCA 49548, 00-2 BCA ¶ 31,097 (termination effected without a cure notice upon discovery of contractor's gross mistake amounting to fraud). See Chapter 9 for a discussion of revocation of acceptance.

(2) Substantial Completion

The principle of "substantial completion" is often applied when the contractor has substantially but not completely performed the contract requirements. The term "substantial completion" is used synonymously with the term "substantial performance" to mean performance that is in good faith and in compliance with the contract but that falls short of complete performance due to minor and relatively unimportant deviations. The doctrine of substantial completion prevents the government from assessing liquidated damages or terminating the contract without giving the contractor reasonable time to correct deficiencies. However, it does not prevent the government from demanding strict compliance and full completion of the work, or from obtaining an equitable adjustment in the contract price if strict compliance is not attained.

Contractors bear the burden of proving substantial completion. If the contractor's assertions at trial conflict with its contemporaneous documents (daily reports), it is more difficult to sustain this burden, *Dixon Contracting, Inc.*, AGBCA 98-191-1, 00-1 BCA ¶ 30,766.

(A) Construction Contracts

Occasionally, government construction contractors who have undertaken considerable efforts but have failed to complete all of the specified work by the due date have successfully invoked the doctrine of "substantial completion" to avoid the consequences of default termination. Although the boards have sometimes indicated that the government has no right to terminate for default where the work has been substantially completed, it is clear that the government retains full rights to terminate the contractor's right to proceed with that portion of the work that has not been completed by the due date. See *G.A. Karnavas Painting Co.*, VACAB 992, 72-1 BCA ¶ 9369; *Southland Constr. Co.*, VABCA 2217, 89-1 BCA ¶ 21,548, and *Environmental Data Consultants, Inc. v. General Servs. Admin.*, GSBCA 13244, 96-2 BCA ¶ 28,614. This rule was explained in *PCL Constr. Servs. Inc. v. United States*, 47 Fed. Cl. 745 (2000), *aff'd*, 96 Fed. Appx. 672 (Fed. Cir. 2004), as follows at 810:

> PCL's second argument regarding the propriety of the termination for default asks the court to adopt a rule that a construction contractor cannot be terminated for default after in fact substantially completing the contract. It is true that some cases in the Board of Contract Appeals have allowed a construction contractor to avoid a termination for default because it had substantially performed the contract. See *Metzger Towing, Inc.*, E.N.G.B.C.A. No. 5862, 94-2 B.C.A. (CCH) ¶ 26,651 (1994); *Wolfe Constr. Co.*, E.N.G.B.C.A. Nos. 3607-3611, 3853, 4752, 84-3 B.C.A. (CCH) ¶ 17,701 at 88,329 (1984); *Cosmos Eng'rs, Inc.*, A.S.B.C.A. No. 19780, 77-2 B.C.A. (CCH) ¶ 12,713 at 61,710-11 (1977); *Edward S. Good, Jr.*, A.S.B.C.A. No. 10514, 66-1 B.C.A. (CCH) ¶ 5362 at 25,157 (1966). The doctrine of substantial performance, however:

> should not be carried to the point where the non-defaulting party is compelled to accept a measure of performance substantially less than had been bargained for. Substantial performance "is never properly invoked unless the promisee has obtained to all intents and purposes all benefits which he reasonably anticipated receiving under the contract."
>
> *Blinderman Constr. Co. Inc. v. United States*, 39 Fed. Cl. 529, 572 (citing *Franklin E. Penny Co. v. United States*, 207 Ct. Cl. 842, 857-58, 524 F.2d 668, 677 (quoting *In re Kinney Aluminum Co.*, 78 F. Supp. 565, 568 (S.D. Cal. 1948)), *aff'd*, 178 F.3d 1307 (Fed. Cir. 1998) (table)); see also *M.C. & D. Capital Corp. v. United States*, 948 F.2d at 1256.
>
> In the instant case, the legally supportable and sensible approach appears to be to simply follow the language of the FAR and the contract and to allow the government to terminate the "separable portion" of the contract, the separable portion being the uncompleted work. See 48 CFR § 52.249-10(a) (1990). The result is to prevent the government from avoiding its obligation to pay provable monies owed on the contract, while allowing an appropriate reduction for the uncompleted work and any consequences normally associated with a default termination on that portion of the contract the plaintiff refused to perform.

Thus, the better-reasoned decisions recognize that the true effect of substantial completion is to prevent the government from avoiding the obligation to pay the contract price for the substantially completed work, less an appropriate reduction for uncompleted work, *Edward S. Good, Jr.*, ASBCA 10514, 66-1 BCA ¶ 5362.

The basic rationale for invoking the "substantial completion" doctrine in construction contracts has been to avoid a forfeiture where the contractor has made permanent improvements on government property. See *H.L.C. & Assocs. Constr. Co. v. United States*, 176 Ct. Cl. 285, 367 F.2d 586 (1966), and *Cosmos Eng'g, Inc.*, ASBCA 19780, 77-2 BCA ¶ 12,713. In *R.M. Crum Constr. Co.*, VABCA 2143, 85-2 BCA ¶ 18,132, the board stated the reasoning behind the "substantial completion" doctrine at 91,009:

> We agree that often construction contracts are not fully completed to perfection by the due date, often having minor discrepancies and problems needing correction. The existence of those incomplete items or deviations often do not necessarily deprive the Government of what it contracted for and anticipated as a complete project. When that is the case, those deficiencies should not be available to sustain the harsh remedy of termination. While forfeiture is an element to be considered in analyzing a default, we do not consider it an essential element if the project has otherwise been substantially performed.

Such reasoning has occasionally been questioned, however, because construction contractors have consistently recovered at least the fair value of work performed prior to the time of default, *G.A. Karnavas Painting Co.*, VACAB 992, 72-1 BCA ¶ 9369. See *Keyser Roofing Contractors, Inc.*, ASBCA 32069, 90-3 BCA ¶ 23,024 (substantial completion doctrine not applicable where contractor was paid 86 percent of the contract price, which was the percentage of work done), and *Cosmic Constr. Co.*, ASBCA 24014, 88-2 BCA ¶ 20,623 (substantial completion doctrine not applicable where contractor had been paid or credited for the work it performed on percentage of completion basis and the termination for default affected only the uncompleted or remaining work). In *General Ship & Engine Works, Inc.*, ASBCA 19243, 79-1 BCA ¶ 13,657, which involved a ship repair contract having attributes of both a construction and a supply contract, the board stated at 67,022:

> [W]here a contractor has been paid or given credit for all work properly performed or corrected, there is less likelihood that a showing of forfeiture may be made so as to call for the application of the doctrine of substantial performance and to upset an otherwise proper termination for default.

See also *Mark Smith Constr. Co.*, ASBCA 25058, 81-2 BCA ¶ 15,306, in which the board concluded that the substantial completion doctrine was "not for application" since the contractor had been paid for the work performed on a "percentage of completion" basis and the default termination affected only the "uncompleted or remaining work."

The basic test for substantial completion is generally stated to be whether the product is capable of being occupied or used by the government for its intended purpose, *Dimarco Corp.*, ASBCA 28529, 85-2 BCA ¶ 18,002. In *Barton & Sons Co.*, ASBCA 14097, 70-2 BCA ¶ 8429, substantial completion warranted reversal of a default termination where airport runways being repaired were operational despite the need to perform minor capping of approximately 3 percent of total runway joints. In *Corway, Inc.*, ASBCA 20683, 77-1 BCA ¶ 12,357, the board found substantial completion where deficiencies in tennis courts were "primarily of a cosmetic nature" and were "mostly outside of the playing area" of the courts. However, see *M.C. & D. Capital Corp. v. United States*, 948 F.2d 1251 (Fed. Cir. 1991), finding no substantial completion where the roofing was not installed by a certified roofer and was not warranted as required by the contract. See also *Joseph Morton Co.*, GSBCA 4876, 82-2 BCA ¶ 15,839, where various defects in a courthouse heating and cooling system denied the government beneficial occupancy of the building and thereby precluded a determination of substantial completion. Accord, *Nagy Enters.*, ASBCA 48815, 98-1 BCA ¶ 29,695 (facility could not be used for its intended purpose because the filtration system was not operational when the contractor stopped working).

In *Two State Constr. Co.*, DOTCAB 78-31, 81-1 BCA ¶ 15,149, involving a contract to construct an airport control tower, the government terminated because of the contractor's failure to diligently correct "punchlist" items. The contractor contended that the project had been substantially completed at the time of the termination, noting that the government had entered the building to begin installation of air traffic control equipment. In upholding the termination, the board emphasized that the listed deficiencies "in their totality" constituted a significant amount of work that "impaired" and rendered "hazardous" the FAA's use of the facility, stating at 74,939:

> We cannot equate the entry of FAA personnel to commence installation with substantial completion. That an owner is willing to risk hazards to expedite ultimate availability of a project for the intended use does not mean the project is capable of intended use.

Although the boards have occasionally looked to the "percentage of completion" of total contract work as an indication of substantial completion, *Highland Constr. Corp.*, GSBCA 2470, 68-1 BCA ¶ 6966; *Edward S. Good, Jr.*, ASBCA 10514, 66-1 BCA ¶ 5362, it has also been stated that application of a "rigid percentage of completion test" is not appropriate, *Two State Constr. Co.*, DOTCAB 78-31, 81-1 BCA ¶ 15,149.

The substantial completion doctrine has been applied to contracts that represent a hybrid between supply and construction, *Cosmos Eng'rs, Inc.*, ASBCA 19780, 77-2 BCA ¶ 12,713 (contract for design, fabrication, and installation of an audiovisual system apparently using a supply contract clause); *Pacific Coast Refrigeration, Inc.*, ASBCA 14546, 71-2 BCA ¶ 9146 (contract to furnish and install refrigerated display cases contained both supply and construction default clauses). See also *General Ship & Engine Works, Inc.*, ASBCA 19243, 79-1 BCA ¶ 13,657, in which the board indicated that the substantial completion doctrine has some limited applicability to supply contracts but qualified its potential impact by stating at 67,021:

> How often [the doctrine of substantial completion] may properly be applied in view of the competing rules that time is of the essence in any case where fixed dates for performance are specified, and that the government is entitled to require strict compliance with its specifications, is another question.

(b) Service Contracts

Although the boards have occasionally stated that a contractor's failure to perform all specified services in a timely fashion establishes a government right to immediately terminate for default, *Marble & Chance*, HUDBCA 85-908-C2, 87-1 BCA ¶ 19,337; *Utah Waste Paper Co.*, VACAB 1104, 75-1 BCA ¶ 11,058, the doctrine of "substantial completion" has become a significant limitation on this right. See *Reliable Maint. Serv.*, ASBCA 10487, 66-1 BCA ¶ 5331, *recons. denied*, 67-1 BCA ¶ 6194, in which the board stated at 25,044:

> The failure to perform a daily task is not cured by the performance of a similar task which is also required on a following day. Each individual failure is technically a default, though not necessarily the basis for a default termination, and when a sufficient number of individual defaults accumulate then it can be said the contract has not been substantially performed, the contract is then terminable under subparagraph [(a)(1)(i)] of the Default clause.

See *Contract Maint., Inc.*, ASBCA 18528, 75-1 BCA ¶ 11,247, in which the board invoked the "substantial completion" doctrine to overturn a default termination where the number of omitted tasks was "inconsequential" compared to the total number of janitorial tasks called for under the contract. In reaching this conclusion, the board found it significant that the contract provided the remedy of deductions from contract billings for "insubstantial elements of nonperformance and uncorrected substandard tasks." Similarly, in *Handyman Bldg. Maint. Co.*, IBCA 1335-3-80, 83-2 BCA ¶ 16,646, the board overturned a default termination based on repeated nonperformance of various janitorial tasks, stating at 82,775:

> The presence of the inspection clause and the accompanying schedule of deductions in the contract indicate a recognition on the part of the Government that janitorial service is not likely to be the one perfect aspect of an otherwise imperfect world. The clause provides a mechanism, short of default, for dealing with anticipated omissions of services.

See *C.S. Smith Training, Inc.*, DOTCAB 1273, 83-1 BCA ¶ 16,304, where a contractor's failure to promptly pay subjects being furnished for biomedical experiments was found not to be of sufficient magnitude to justify summary termination. The board stated at 81,016:

> Elementary fairness dictates that when a contractor is actually performing, and is actually performing a substantial portion of the required services, as was the case here, he is entitled to receive formal notification if the Contracting Officer considers the work to be substandard and a termination for default to be a real possibility.

See also *W.M. Grace, Inc.*, ASBCA 23076, 80-1 BCA ¶ 14,256, overturning a default in similar circumstances, holding that the government, by taking deductions for performance deficiencies, "effectively waived the performance failures . . . as a basis for default termination, while still preserving its right to terminate the contract for default if these failures were not cured in the future."

However, see *Cervetto Bldg. Maint. Co. v. United States*, 2 Cl. Ct. 299 (1983), rejecting the contractor's contention that the government was precluded from relying on, as grounds for default, any deficiencies for which deductions had been taken, stating at 301:

> Despite its elegance, [the contractor's] argument must be rejected as leading to an absurd result. The contract plainly contemplates that minor deficiencies in performance will be addressed through remedies short of termination for default. Equally plainly, it was intended that minor deficiencies be the exception and that performance be satisfactory on most days. When deficiencies become the rule, as they did in this case, necessitating corrections or deductions virtually every day, overall performance under the contract can be deemed unsatisfactory even though individual problems are resolved. See *Pride Unlimited*, 75-2 BCA at 54,500. In such a case, the repeated need for correction may itself serve as the default, making termination an appropriate remedy.

(3) Severability

The concept of severability, sometimes referred to as divisibility, is that there are, in reality, two or more contractual agreements in a single document. When it is concluded that the document is severable or divisible, the government's right to terminate for default is limited to those severable or divisible parts that are in default, *Murphy v. United States*, 164 Ct. Cl. 332 (1964). There, the language in the construction contract clause was held not to permit the government to terminate the entire contract when only a separable part of the work is in default. The case involved a lump sum contract for construction of the Fort Sumner Diversion Dam on the Pecos River. The contract specified a completion date for the entire project and interim dates for the release of irrigation waters. A series of financial and supervisory difficulties led the contracting officer to terminate for failure to prosecute the work "with such diligence as will insure its completion within the time specified in Article I," which required overall completion within 450 days from the date of notice to proceed. However, the evidence did not indicate that the contractor could not meet the final deadline, but only that it would be unable to release the irrigation waters on time. The court concluded that the contract terms made the release of irrigation waters separate from and incidental to the construction of the dam. The contracting officer was permitted to terminate the right to proceed on that portion of the contract but not on the entire contract. See *Brett Arnold, P. C. v. United States*, 98 Fed. Appx. 854 (Fed. Cir. 2004), which distinguished *Murphy* on the grounds that the deficiency was a critical function of the contract. See also *Plum Run, Inc.*, ASBCA 46091, 05-1 BCA ¶ 32,977 (one CLIN in maintenance contract severable from 21 other CLINs); *Itra Coop Ass'n*, GSBCA 7974, 90-1 BCA ¶ 22,410 (default termination of entire contract for typewriter maintenance not warranted since most of documented complaints took place at only one of approximately 50 service locations); and *Overhead Elec. Co.*, ASBCA 25656, 85-2 BCA ¶ 18,026 (default termination of entire contract containing three work items—two involving electrical work and one requiring chemical disposal services—on the basis of the contractor's failure to perform the chemical removal was improper because the work items were separable).

Determining whether portions of the work are severable or the contract is entire is often difficult. The presence or absence of separate item numbers, prices, and delivery dates is not conclusive. See *Pennsylvania Exch. Bank v. United States*, 145 Ct. Cl. 216, 170 F. Supp. 629 (1959), finding a contract with four items of work an entire contract because the separately priced items were incidental to the ultimate aim of volume production. The fact that a contract contained a single bid item and a lump sum price was considered significant in holding a telephone engineering study not to be severable even though some work could be done independently, *Telecommunication Consultants*, ASBCA 13801, 69-2 BCA ¶ 7925. In *Spartan Aircraft Co. v. United States*, 120 Ct. Cl. 327, 100 F. Supp. 171 (1951), the contractor was required to perform 14 items of inspection, repair, and maintenance of government aircraft, including a 100-hour inspection. There was no total contract price stipulated, and of the 14 items, three were at a fixed hourly rate, 10 had a net cost specified, and one flight testing was to be free. The court reasoned that the payment provisions could be apportioned, which was evidence of divisibility. However, the court also found that the government would not have entered into the contract without the 100-hour inspection and concluded that this was evidence of indivisibility. Based on this latter finding, the court held that the contract was probably entire. With considerable candor, the court stated that severability is "a very vexing problem. . . . The authorities hold that the question is essentially one of the intention of the parties; examination of some of the many cases on the point suggests rather that resolution of the question has more commonly been a matter of the intention of the court." See also *Capitol City Constr. Co.*, DOTCAB 74-29, 75-1 BCA ¶ 11,012 (government could not terminate entire building repair contract for contractor's refusal to provide "chillers," which were unrelated to the other work and had been added by a change order). However, in *Phillip Bradley & Sons*, AGBCA 314, 71-2 BCA ¶ 9002, where a contractor leasing earth-moving equipment was unable to provide the specified multi-use equipment, the board found the contract not to be severable even though a portion of the work could have been completed on time using substitute equipment offered by the contractor, emphasizing that the contractor's obligation was to provide "all of the equipment required for performance."

The board may find the contract severable to prevent forfeiture. See *Nestos Painting Co.*, GSBCA 6945, 86-2 BCA ¶ 18,993, where an entire painting contract was terminated for default because of the contractor's failure to comply with the specified method in preparing 65 percent of the surfaces to be painted. The board converted the default termination to a termination for convenience for the 35 percent of the surfaces that were acceptably prepared and painted, stating at 95,916:

> Termination of the entire contract for default would enable GSA to benefit from the acceptable portion of [the contractor's] work without any payment and would result in a forfeiture. . . . Such a result is not favored.

(4) Installment Contracts Excepted

Although many government contracts call for delivery in installments, the individual installments are not necessarily treated as severable contracts. Thus, when one due date has been missed, the right to terminate extends to both the delinquent quantity and all future installments if the future installments are not severable, *Guenther Sys., Inc.*, ASBCA 14032, 72-1 BCA ¶ 9443 (failure to make first delivery as specified endangered performance of the entire contract). The right to terminate accrues each time an installment due date is missed, *Raytheon Serv. Co.*, ASBCA 14746, 70-2 BCA ¶ 8390 (government permitted to delay issuance of a partial default termination until the final delivery date, although the contractor failed to meet several prior delivery dates). Even where late deliveries of installments have been accepted, the government retains the right to terminate for subsequent delinquencies, *Lapp Insulator Co.*, ASBCA 13303, 70-1 BCA ¶ 8219, *recons. denied*, 70-2 BCA ¶ 8471 (government had accepted late deliveries on the first two installments before terminating for default). See also *Container Sys. Corp.*, ASBCA 40611, 94-1 BCA ¶ 26,354 (despite government acceptance of late deliveries of installments under a contract for missile containers, termination for failure to deliver was proper because each successive increment represented a severable obligation to deliver on the contract delivery date); *Papco Tool Corp.*, GSBCA 5679, 81-1 BCA ¶ 15,077 (despite waiver of delinquency in delivery of past increments, the government retains the right to terminate for delinquencies on subsequent increments); and *Phoenix Petroleum Co.,* ASBCA 42763, 96-2 BCA ¶ 28,284 (termination proper for late delivery even though prior delinquencies under an incremental delivery contract were waived). However, when a contractor catches up on past due installments, it is no longer in default, and the right to terminate is extinguished until another due date is missed, *Gibraltar Fabrics, Inc.*, ASBCA 15709, 73-1 BCA ¶ 9905. In *Consumers Oil Co.*, ASBCA 24172, 86-1 BCA ¶ 18,647, the board found that an indefinite delivery, indefinite quantity contract calling for delivery in installments was a separable contract using the "agreed equivalents" reasoning of *Restatemen, Second, Contracts* § 240, Part Performance of Agreed Equivalents.

The federal contract rule permitting termination of the entire contract for a missed installment differs from commercial contract principles, which permit termination only when the missed installment constitutes a substantial impairment of the whole contract, in accordance with U.C.C. § 2-612. The federal contract rule was defended in *Artisan Elecs. Corp. v. United States*, 205 Ct. Cl. 126, 499 F.2d 606 (1974), in which the court stated that "the plain language of the contract," which incorporated the standard default clause, obviated the need to consider the application of U.C.C. principles.

d. Preproduction Items

FAR 52.209-3 and -4 provide special clauses to be used when government or contractor first article testing and approval are required. Paragraph (d) of these clauses provides:

> If the contractor fails to deliver any first article on time, or the Contracting Officer disapproves any first article, the Contractor shall be deemed to have failed to make delivery within the meaning of the "Default" clause of this contract.

Similar clauses were called for by DAR 1-1903. In *Electro-Neutronics, Inc.*, ASBCA 12947, 71-2 BCA ¶ 8961, such a clause was found to have the effect of making the "make delivery" language in subparagraph (a)(i) of the default clause applicable in situations where first articles were properly disapproved by the contracting officer. See also *FJW Optical Sys., Inc.*, ASBCA 33885, 87-2 ¶ 19,905 (default termination justified where contract included a First Article Approval–Government Testing clause, and the contractor failed to timely deliver the first article for inspection).

Thus, when such a clause is used, failure to deliver the first article justifies summary termination without the 10-day cure period set out by ¶ (a)(2) of the default clause, *H.N. Bailey & Assocs.*, ASBCA 21300, 77-2 BCA ¶ 12,681 (contract terminated for default when contractor failed to deliver first article because of a subcontracting complication for which contractor was responsible); *Kit Pack Co.*, ASBCA 33135, 89-3 BCA ¶ 22,151 (contract properly terminated for default without government providing cure notice after contractor failed to timely deliver first article because of financial difficulties in acquiring materials and components). Even without a first article clause, the conduct of the parties may impliedly modify the contract to provide that failure to deliver acceptable preproduction quantities will justify summary termination under paragraph (a)(1)(i). In *Monitor Sys.*, ASBCA 14261, 71-1 BCA ¶ 8885, the contractor induced the government to extend the date for preproduction testing by repeatedly promising that a conforming article would be tendered, and the government repeatedly asserted that a nonconforming item would result in default rather than another extension. A first article clause will not justify termination for nondelivery of required first article test procedures, *AAR Corp.*, ASBCA 16486, 74-2 BCA ¶ 10,653 (board specifically stated that termination was allowed because of a lack of progress rather than the failure to submit test procedures). However, the definition of first article was more broadly construed in *Inforex, Inc.*, GSBCA 3859, 76-1 BCA ¶ 11,679, where a preproduction demonstration was considered a first article.

However, absent such a clause, failure to deliver acceptable preproduction items (e.g., first articles and prototypes) is not a failure to deliver "supplies" within the meaning of ¶ (a)(1)(i) of the supply contract default clause, since "supplies" refers to the end items required by the contract, *Bailey Specialized Bldgs., Inc. v. United States*, 186 Ct. Cl. 71, 404 F.2d 355 (1968) (preproduction tower that was required to be ready for inspection on a certain date, but was not required to be ready for delivery until four weeks later, was not an end item). See also *System Dev. Corp.*, VABCA 1976, 87-2 BCA ¶ 19,946 (failure to deliver computer unit for acceptance testing was not a failure to deliver an end item under ¶ (a)(1)(i) of the default clause, even though the unit would ultimately be used as a functioning item). Likewise, such failures do not constitute a failure to deliver "services," since ¶ a(1)(i) refers to "services" as an end item, *Dubrow Elec. Indus., Inc.*, ASBCA 8464, 65-1 BCA ¶ 4859. Thus, absent a special clause, such terminations can only be supported under a theory of failure to make progress or failure to perform some "other provision" of the contract, *Lorch Elecs. Corp.*, ASBCA 21496, 78-1 BCA ¶ 12,911 (termination for default was improper where the government did not show that the contractor had failed to make progress in any aspect of performance other than making a preproduction item ready for inspection). See *System Dev. Corp.*, VABCA 1976, 87-2 BCA ¶ 19,946, in which the board stated at 100,951:

> In the absence of a first article approval clause, it is well established that failure to deliver a timely preproduction or test unit is a failure "to make progress" under paragraph (a)(ii) of the disputes clause and not a breach of contract under (a)(i).

As discussed earlier, the "substantial compliance" doctrine of *Radiation Technology* may operate to limit the government's right to default terminate for timely delivery of a slightly nonconforming first article or preproduction item, *National Aviation Elecs., Inc.*, ASBCA 18256, 74-2 BCA ¶ 10,677. For example, a default termination was not upheld where first article defects were easily correctable, in *International Foods Retort Co.*, ASBCA 34954, 92-2 BCA ¶ 24,994 (blandness of packaged chicken à la king was a minor defect easily remediable by the addition of salt); *Penjaska Tool Co.*, ASBCA 31836, 89-2 BCA ¶ 21,700 (excessive discoloration of rifle firing pins was easily correctable by use of special devices for production runs). However, the board did not find the defects minor or readily correctable in *Sonora Mfg. Co.*, ASBCA 31587, 91-1 BCA ¶ 23,444 (discrepancies in dimensions of actuator piston not a minor defect because part was crucial to the safe operation of aircraft); *Idaho Norland Corp.*, ASBCA 33487, 90-2 BCA ¶ 22,858 (failure of a first article snow-removal machine to meet the contract requirements in three separate tests was not minor in nature or easily correctable).

2. Progress Failures

The standard clauses contain somewhat different language concerning default termination for failure to make progress. The supply and service contract clause permits termination if the contractor fails to "[m]ake progress, so as to endanger performance of this contract." The construction contract clause permits termination if the contractor "refuses or fails to prosecute the work or any separable part, with the diligence that will insure its completion within the time specified in this contract." Most litigation has occurred under the supply and service contract language.

a. Basic Principle

The necessity for and impact of a reservation of the right to terminate before the due date was discussed in *United States v. O'Brien*, 220 U.S. 321 (1911), in which Justice Holmes stated at 327:

> The sole material express promise of the contractors was to complete the work by July 1, 1902. If the work was done at that date that promise was performed, no matter how irregularly or with what delays in the earlier months. Under its terms the United States was not concerned with the stages of performance, but only with the completed result. See *Bacon v. Parker*, 137 Massachusetts, 309, 311. Its interest in the result, however, made it reasonable to reserve the right to employ someone else if, when time enough had gone by to show what was likely to happen, it saw that it probably would not get what it bargained for from the present hands. But it would be a very severe construction of the contract, a contract, too, framed by the United States, to read the reservation of a right to annul, for want of a diligence not otherwise promised, as importing a promise to use such diligence as should satisfy the judgment of the engineer in charge. It is one thing to make the right to continue work under the contract depend upon his approval, another to make his dissatisfaction with progress conclusive of a breach. In this case it

> was admitted that there was time enough left to finish the work under the contract when the [contractors] were turned off. It would be a very harsh measure to pronounce the contract broken when but for the prohibition of the United States the [contractors] might have done the work in time.

b. *Evaluating Progress Failures*

Early default cases did not clearly enunciate a test for evaluating the propriety of progress failure terminations. See Speidel, Default for Failure to Make Progress, Government Contractor Briefing Paper No. 64-5, October 1964. Although the supply contract default clause uses the phrase "endanger performance," a test requiring the government to prove that it was impossible for the contractor to complete by the due date was used in early cases.

(1) The "Impossible" Test

Initially, in order to justify termination for progress failures, the government was required to prove that it was not possible for the contractor to complete the contract work within the schedule. See *Emsco Screen Pipe Co. of Tex., Inc.*, ASBCA 11917, 69-1 BCA ¶ 7710 (government has burden of establishing that contractor was in fact incapable of performing the contract); *Midwest Eng'g & Constr. Co.*, ASBCA 5801, 1962 BCA ¶ 3289 (cure notice affords the contractor "an opportunity to demonstrate that timely completion was possible"); *Northeastern Eng'g, Inc.*, ASBCA 6504, 61-2 BCA ¶ 3108 (termination improper "when delivery is not shown to have been beyond [the contractor's] power"); and *Manhattan Lighting Equip. Co.*, ASBCA 5113, 60-1 BCA ¶ 2646 (default improper unless the contractor "had deprived itself of power to make enough progress . . . to permit performance" by the due date). Impossibility was found in *Samuel M. Wagner*, GSBCA 2722, 69-2 BCA ¶ 7776 (over 60 percent of the time for performance had passed but only 10 percent of the work was complete, no second shift was added, and contractor expressly stated performance was impossible unless time extensions were granted); *Isolation Prods., Inc.*, AECBCA 19-11-65, 66-1 BCA ¶ 5505 (state court enjoined contractor from using manufacturing process essential to performance); *General Prods. Co.*, ASBCA 6522, 61-1 BCA ¶ 3003 (even assuming maximum productivity, timely completion was unattainable, and it was "highly unlikely" that another supplier could be found).

(2) The "No Reasonable Likelihood" Test

The Court of Claims apparently rejected the impossibility test in favor of a demonstrated lack of diligence test. In *Universal Fiberglass Corp. v. United States*, 210 Ct. Cl. 206, 537 F.2d 393 (1976), the court upheld a default termination after waiver of the right to default terminate when no schedule existed, based on the lack of progress, without evidence of impossibility, stating at 217:

> [The contractor] was making no progress at all, had never manufactured a vehicle under the new specifications it had agreed to, did not have the necessary parts and could not obtain them and had allowed its labor force to wither away. If this situation is not what this failure to make progress clause is about and is not the exact case for which it was written, we are at a loss to understand why it was put in the contract at all.

In *Globe Eng'g Co.*, ASBCA 23934, 83-1 BCA ¶ 16,370, *recons. denied*, 84-1 BCA ¶ 16,941, the board expressly rejected the impossibility test, citing *Universal Fiberglass* as representing the "correct rule" in progress failure cases. See also *RFI Shield-Rooms*, ASBCA 17374, 77-2 BCA ¶ 12,714, concluding that the test was that "there was no reasonable likelihood that appellant could perform the entire contract effort within the time remaining for contract performance." Later cases have upheld progress failure terminations without a specific finding that timely performance was impossible, *California Dredging Co.*, ENGBCA 5532, 92-1 BCA ¶ 24,475; *Stephen-Leedom Carpet Co.*, GSBCA 4835, 79-1 BCA ¶ 13,570; *John F. Lehnertz*, AGBCA 77-132, 78-1 BCA ¶ 12,895. See also *Ranco Constr., Inc. v. General Servs. Admin.*, GSBCA 11923, 94-2 BCA ¶ 26,678, in which the board overturned the default termination on other grounds, stating at 132,703:

> GSA is not required to establish that timely performance by Ranco was impossible. Rather, GSA is required to establish that, at the time of the termination, there was a reasonable, valid basis for concluding that there was no reasonable likelihood that Ranco could perform within the time remaining for performance.

In *Santee Dock Builders,* AGBCA 96-161-1, 99-1 BCA ¶ 30,190, the board held that to terminate for lack of diligent prosecution of work, the government need not prove impossibility but must show that the contractor's performance was so lacking as to establish either an intention not to complete the work or lack of ability to timely complete the work. In *Morganti Nat'l, Inc. v. United States*, 49 Fed. Cl. 110 (2001), *aff'd*, 36 Fed. Appx. 452, (Fed. Cir. 2002), the court upheld the default termination although the contractor was entitled to additional time because schedule analyses made it clear that contract completion would not be achieved by the modified completion date. Evidence indicated that at the time of default, when approximately 75 percent of the contract was complete, the contractor was progressing at 1 percent per month, hardly sufficient to complete the project in the remaining eight months. See also *Bender GmbH v. Brownlee*, 106 Fed. Appx. 728 (Fed. Cir. 2004) (repeated delays and contractor's inability to prove it could meet the completion schedule), and *R. F. Lusa & Sons Sheet Metal, Inc.*, LBCA 2000-BCA-00002, 04-2 BCA ¶ 32,780 (contractor had completed only 45 percent of the work by the substantial completion date—termination upheld).

(3) Failure to Comply with the Contract Quality and Other Requirements

Factual considerations supporting termination for failure to make progress include consistent failure to meet industry standards, *Engineering Serv. Sys.*, PSBCA

2933, 92-3 BCA ¶ 25,146; failure to provide quality work consistent with the acceptable skill and workmanship standards of the contract, *Dozie I. Rienne*, ENGBCA 5711, 91-1 BCA ¶ 23,432; failure to give a meaningful response to a cure notice, *Midwest Eng'g & Constr. Co.*, ASBCA 6171, 61-2 BCA ¶ 3125; failure to submit data and drawings for approval, *C.C. Galbraith & Son, Inc.*, ASBCA 10769, 67-2 BCA ¶ 6488; failure to deliver preproduction model and procurement of only 3 percent of components although over half the performance period had passed, *Telecomputing Corp.*, ASBCA 7154, 1962 BCA ¶ 3620, *recons. denied*, 65-2 BCA ¶ 5223; and failure to timely initiate preproduction testing, *Midwest Eng'g & Constr. Co.*, ASBCA 5390, 1962 BCA ¶ 3460. In *Santee Dock Builders,* AGBCA 96-161-1, 99-1 BCA ¶30,190, the failure was demonstrated by showing failure to meet acceptable standards of skill and workmanship. Throughout the project, the contractor's progress was less than diligent, and the contractor had inadequate workers, inadequate equipment, failed to comply with contract provisions, and had inadequate supervision.

Work can be so defective that a termination will be upheld even if a suspension of work order has been issued. In *Pipeline Constr., Inc.*, ASBCA 50744, 98-2 BCA ¶ 29,991, the board held that such a default termination would be invalid only "when the suspension is not lifted so as to permit a contractor to make simple corrections by the contract completion date." Where the contractor's work is so "gravely deficient" that it could not be performed by the completion date, the default termination is proper and the suspension justified. Similarly, in *Zimcon Prof'ls,* ASBCA 49346, 00-1 BCA ¶ 30,839, the government, after a show cause notice, directed the contractor to perform no further work on the project. Twelve days later the government default terminated for failure to complete by the completion date. The board upheld the termination based in part on the amount of outstanding work (43 percent) and the contractor's past performance.

c. Proof of Endangered Performance

Although the government is not required to show that contractor performance was impossible, it must reasonably believe that the contractor could not perform the entire contract within the time remaining for performance, *Lisbon Contractors, Inc. v. United States*, 828 F.2d 759 (Fed. Cir. 1987); *McDonnell Douglas Corp. v. United States*, 182 F.3d 1319 (Fed. Cir. 1999), *cert denied*, 529 U.S. 1097 (2000), 50 Fed. Cl. 311 (2001), *aff'd in part & rev'd in part,* 323 F.3d 1006 (Fed. Cir. 2003). The government may reasonably find performance to be endangered when the contractor's monthly progress reports indicate that delivery will be late and a time extension is sought, *Fitzgerald Labs., Inc.,* ASBCA 15205, 71-2 BCA ¶ 9029. Likewise, actual on-site inspection of the contractor's efforts may indicate that performance is endangered, *Ubique, Ltd.*, DOTCAB 71-28, 72-1 BCA ¶ 9340 (virtually no work was done in the 30 days following first cure notice). See also *Sach Sinha & Assocs., Inc.*, ASBCA 47594, 00-1 ¶ 30,735 (failure to make progress justified a default termination because it was clear that the contractor was not making progress and had all but abandoned the contract).

Another indication of endangered performance is inconsistent contractor representations as to the time that delivery will be made, *Guenther Sys., Inc.*, ASBCA 14032, 72-1 BCA ¶ 9443 (following oral discussion of potential revised delivery schedule, contractor's written request the next day recommended a different schedule that further delayed deliveries). However, in *T.C. & Sarah C. Bell,* ENGBCA 5872, 92-3 BCA ¶ 25,076, poor attitude, uncooperativeness, and failure to interpret contract policies did not endanger the performance, because these deficiencies were "readily remediable."

In determining that the rate of progress is "endangering" timely performance, all circumstances should be considered, *Michigan Joint Sealing, Inc.*, ASBCA 41477, 93-3 BCA ¶ 26,011. In *Omni Dev. Corp.,* AGBCA 97-203-1, 01-2 BCA ¶ 31,487, the board described the factors to consider when reviewing a default decision: "the status of the project at the time [of default], how much time remained to complete [the project], the resources available to the contractor, the ability of the contractor to execute steps needed to perform the work and the materiality of any interim failures to meet milestones." See *Arrowhead Starr Co.*, AGBCA 81-236-1, 83-1 BCA ¶ 16,320 (contractor had completed only 42 percent of tree planting work in 66 percent of allotted time and could offer no plan for timely completion). A contractor's failure to make business arrangements vital to performance may also be grounds for a progress failure termination. In *ABC Knitwear Corp.*, ASBCA 22575, 81-1 BCA ¶ 14,826, a termination was upheld where the contractor failed to secure financing for acquisition of raw materials.

In the following cases, the government failed to sustain its burden: *SAE/Americon-Mid Atl., Inc. v. General Servs. Admin.,* GSBCA 12294, 98-2 BCA ¶ 30,084 (contractor had sufficient resources to complete performance without the schedule as extended to compensate for government-caused delays); *CJP Contractors, Inc. v. United States*, 45 Fed. Cl. 343 (1999) (contractor could meet the contract completion date as extended by 47 days for excusable delays); *Haselrig Constr. Co.*, PSBCA 4148, 00-1 BCA ¶ 30,674 (although the contractor was clearly behind schedule and failed to meet an interim milestone, it could still have accelerated its performance and finished the project on time, especially in view of the government's failure to cooperate in resolving a latent subsurface design problem, which contributed to the delays); *Hillebrand Constr. of the Midwest, Inc.*, ASBCA 45853, 95-1 BCA ¶ 27,464 (contractor's failure to submit shop drawings within the required 30 days after award not proof that the contractor was unable or unwilling to perform the contract within the remaining period of completion); *American Sheet Metal Corp. v. General Servs. Admin.,* GSBCA 14066, 99-1 BCA ¶ 30,329 (agency prematurely terminated before calculating the extended completion date). Curiously, in *American Sheet Metal Corp v. General Servs. Admin.*, GSBCA 15165-C, 00-2 BCA ¶ 31,126, requesting recovery of attorneys' fees, the board nevertheless held that the government's position in defaulting the contractor was substantially justified, precluding recovery under the EAJA, because of a "lack [of] confidence in the ability of [the] contractor to complete the job on time . . . numerous time extensions, performance problems, [and] insufficient progress in a time which should have been a time of considerable acceleration."

Failure to meet pre-due-date milestones or interim submission requirements is often significant, *Dubrow Elec. Indus., Inc.,* ASBCA 8464, 65-1 BCA ¶ 4859; *Melcor Elecs. Corp.,* ASBCA 17211, 73-1 BCA ¶ 10,015 (contractor repeatedly failed to meet performance milestones that it had suggested to the government). Such milestones may be the requirement to submit test plans, *Allied Tech., Inc.,* ASBCA 18101, 74-1 BCA ¶ 10,621 (default proper since nonconforming test plan was not corrected); *AAR Corp.,* ASBCA 16486, 74-2 BCA ¶ 10,653; a preproduction model, *Fitzgerald Lab., Inc.,* ASBCA 15205, 71-2 BCA ¶ 9029; or a first article, *Ubique, Ltd.*, DOTCAB 71-28, 72-1 BCA ¶ 9340.

Even though the government allows a progress milestone to pass without taking action to terminate for progress failure, the missed milestone may be relied on at a later date if performance has in fact become endangered, *AAR Corp.,* ASBCA 16486, 74-2 BCA ¶ 10,653 (date for submission of test procedures had passed and government delayed seven months before issuing a cure notice; termination was proper since, absent the test procedures, the pending first article due date was endangered). When the government has a reasonable basis to expect that a progress milestone will be missed, it is proper to issue the cure notice for progress failure in advance of the milestone date, *Melcor Elecs. Corp.,* ASBCA 17211, 73-1 BCA ¶ 10,015. However, although progress milestones may indicate that performance is endangered, the right to terminate does not necessarily arise from a missed milestone, *Ubique, Ltd.*, DOTCAB 71-28, 72-1 BCA ¶ 9340. See *McDonnell Douglas Corp. v. United States*, 182 F.3d 1319 (Fed. Cir. 1999), *cert denied*, 529 U.S. 1097 (2000), 50 Fed. Cl. 311 (2001), *aff'd in part & rev'd in part,* 323 F.3d 1006 (Fed. Cir. 2003), finding termination for failure to make progress improper when it was based on the contractor's prospective inability to deliver the initial prototype on a contract calling for delivery of a number of aircraft.

d. Construction Contracts

In *Discount Co. v. United States*, 213 Ct. Cl. 567, 554 F.2d 435, *cert. denied,* 434 U.S. 938 (1977), the court expressly rejected the argument that the construction contract clause requires a showing that timely performance is impossible in order to justify a pre-due-date termination. Rather, the court noted that the overall evidence of dilatory performance made the government "justifiably insecure" and that default was proper upon a finding that a "demonstrated lack of diligence indicated that the Government could not be assured of timely completion." See *Lisbon Contractors, Inc. v. United States*, 828 F.2d 759 (Fed. Cir. 1987), holding that the standard is whether the contracting officer had a "reasonable belief" that the contractor could not complete performance within the remaining time.

In assessing the construction contractor's diligence and evaluating the reasonableness of the government's insecurity, the boards frequently have compared the percentage of completion with the percentage of time remaining for performance. Where the resulting comparison showed that the contractor was ahead of schedule, default termination was found improper, *Mishara Constr. Co.*, ASBCA 8604, 1964 BCA ¶ 4345 (over half the time for performance remained and over 60 percent of the work was complete). Similarly, where the time remaining approximated the amount of work to be done, default was found improper even though the board itself had some doubt whether the contractor would have completed on time, *G.A. Karnavas Painting Co.*, ASBCA 19569, 76-1 BCA ¶ 11,837.

Direct comparison of percentage of time remaining may not be solely determinative where remaining work is likely to be done at a faster rate. In a situation similar to construction, the board found that remaining tree planting was to take place in soil conducive to a better rate of progress, *Robert Hart*, IBCA 659-8-67, 68-1 BCA ¶ 6984.

Most decisions upholding progress failure terminations consider all the circumstances, including percentage of completion, time remaining, and other pertinent factors. See *Bender GmbH*, ASBCA 52052, 03-2 BCA ¶ 32,292, *aff'd*, 106 Fed. Appx. 728 (Fed. Cir. 2004) (repeated delays, inability to protect work site from flooding, and unwillingness to work after partial suspension); *Cox & Palmer Constr. Corp.*, ASBCA 38739, 92-1 BCA ¶ 24,756 (contractor lost some key personnel, returned part of the required materials, failed to provide a revised schedule and management plan, and was only 58 percent complete instead of 80.8 percent); *Dozie I. Rienne*, ENGBCA 5711, 91-1 BCA ¶ 23,432 (contractor failed to acquire professional masons and masonry tools); *TMI, Inc.*, ENGBCA 5524, 89-3 BCA ¶ 22,029 (contractor had completed only 4 percent of the project when 70 percent of the time for performance had passed); *W.B. Branin Constr. Co.*, AGBCA 313, 73-1 BCA ¶ 9887 (only 15 percent of the work was completed in 60 percent of the time for performance, and the contractor was behind in payments to employees and materialmen); *J.E. DeKalb Co.*, VACAB 1317, 79-2 BCA ¶ 13,939 (job only 75 percent complete, superintendent but no workforce on job, and no performance for several weeks); *Community Window Shade Co.*, ASBCA 13675, 72-2 BCA ¶ 9587 (contractor failed to furnish data to indicate that storm windows would meet specifications, thus precluding the government from ordering fabrication and installation to commence); *Olympic Painting Contractors*, ASBCA 15773, 72-2 BCA ¶ 9549 (more than one-third of the time for performance had passed but only 7 percent of the work was done, and there were many discrepancies); and *Airco Eng'rs*, AGBCA 245, 72-1 BCA ¶ 9215 (contractor had been granted an extended date to complete in return for an agreement to average $2,760 worth of work per day but averaged only $1,650). Compare, however, *Western Contracting Corp.*, ENGBCA 3835, 82-1 BCA ¶ 15,486, overturning a default termination of a dam construction contract for failure to make progress where the contractor was only 5 percent behind schedule and had increased its efforts, and the dam was already providing the intended protection.

Failure to submit a proposed progress schedule can also be a significant factor in evaluating the contractor's lack of diligence, *Discount Co. v. United States*, 213 Ct. Cl. 567, 554 F.2d 435, *cert. denied*, 434 U.S. 938 (1977) (failure to furnish revised work schedule coupled with prior unsatisfactory performance showed that contractor was not "ready, willing and able to make progress"); *K & M Constr.*, ENGBCA 2998, 72-1 BCA ¶ 9366, *recons. granted*, 73-2 BCA ¶ 10,034 (no submission of revised progress schedule and failure to comply with speed-up orders).

3. Failure to Comply with Other Provisions

Government contracts impose many duties on contractors that are in addition to the contract requirements for the delivery of supplies, performance of services, or completion of construction. Failure to comply with a contract's "other provisions" may result in the contract being terminated for default even though the contractor is complying with the contract requirements for delivery or performance of the supplies, services, or construction.

a. Scope of Right

The FAR Default (Fixed-Price Supply and Service) clause specifically provides that the government may terminate for default based on the contractor's failure to comply with "other provisions of this contract." The construction contract clause is silent on this matter. The significance of the "other provisions" language in the default clause is to give the government the right to terminate prior to the delivery date without the necessity of establishing a progress failure. However, the provision does require a 10-day cure notice before termination. Thus, the government cannot summarily terminate a supply or service contract for failure to comply with another provision.

Generally, in order to sustain a default termination for failure to perform some other provision of the contract, that provision must represent a "material requirement" of the contract, *Brandywine Prosthetic-Orthotic Serv., Ltd.*, VABCA 3441, 93-1 BCA ¶ 25,250. In *Brandywine*, the board stated, at 125,765:

> To sustain a default for failure to perform other provisions of the contract, the Government must establish that the Contractor breached a material provision of the contract and that the Contractor has been given the opportunity to rectify or cure its breach. *Corban Industries, Inc.*, VABCA Nos. 2181, 2559T, 88-3 BCA ¶ 20,843.

In *Precision Prods.*, ASBCA 25280, 82-2 BCA ¶ 15,981, the board held that the contractor's violation of a clause requiring production items to be produced at the same facility as a first article did not justify default termination, stating at 79,247:

> However, to sustain a default termination, the Government must demonstrate that the breach of other provisions, not pertaining to accomplishment of the contract work itself, constituted a material breach. See *Universal Fiberglass Corp. v. Unit-*

ed States, 210 Ct. Cl. 206, 537 F.2d 393 (1976); *Conway Electric Co.*, ASBCA 6256, 61-1 BCA 2991.

> In our opinion, [the contractor's] contract non-compliance did not constitute a material breach of the contract.

The board relied heavily on the following facts: (1) government officials administering the contract "knew or should have known" that the contractor intended to subcontract for production units, (2) the contracting officer admitted that it would have accepted units that were produced by the subcontractor and that were exactly like the first article, and (3) the production units did in fact duplicate the first article.

b. Application of Rule

Examples of failures to perform other material provisions include *Kelso v. Kirk Bros. Mech. Contractors, Inc.*, 16 F.3d 1173 (Fed. Cir. 1994) (failure to maintain pay records); *Ann Riley & Assocs., Ltd.*, DOTBCA 2418, 93-3 BCA ¶ 25,963 (failure to provide records); *Old Dominion Sec., Inc.*, GSBCA 8563, 88-2 BCA ¶ 20,785 (failure to provide a state security contractor license); *Johnson & Gordon Sec., Inc.*, GSBCA 7804, 87-3 BCA ¶ 20,074 (failure to obtain a state license); *P.A. Arrietta,* GSBCA 4650, 77-1 BCA ¶ 12,334 (failure to provide performance bonds required by ash removal services contract); *Airport Indus. Park, Inc. d/b/a P. E. C. Contracting Eng'rs v. United States,* 59 Fed. Cl. 332 (2004) (inadequate bond); *Denny Furniture*, GSBCA 4502, 76-2 BCA ¶ 12,095 (required brochure not furnished); *Conncor, Inc.*, GSBCA 3932, 74-1 BCA ¶ 10,563 (failure to furnish preproduction sample); *K Square Corp.*, IBCA 959-3-72, 73-2 BCA ¶ 10,363 (failure to perform duties under Warranty clause); *White Lines, Inc.*, ASBCA 17756, 73-2 BCA ¶ 10,126 (bus transport contractor failed to furnish ICC certificate); *Genisco Tech. Corp.*, NASABCA 1068-18, 69-2 BCA ¶ 7802, *recons. denied*, 69-2 BCA ¶ 7999 (failure to deliver property under termination for convenience clause); *Inter-Continental Equip., Inc.,* ASBCA 37422, 96-1 BCA ¶ 28,048 (failure to demonstrate compliance with the "Cargo Preference" clause (U.S.-flag vessels)); *Airtronics, Inc.*, ASBCA 12608, 69-1 BCA ¶ 7757 (tender of nonconforming sample); *Samuel A. Moore*, PSBCA 1063, 83-1 BCA ¶ 16,376 (plea of nolo contendere to embezzlement charge where contract clause authorized agency to terminate for "conviction of a crime"); *American Bus. Sys.*, GSBCA 5140, 80-2 BCA ¶ 14,461 (failure to maintain adequate records as required by the Examination of Records clause); and *Christina Corp.*, PSBCA 762, Dec. 24, 1980, *Unpub.* (failure to provide required insurance certificates).

In some cases, the failure to perform in accordance with specifications has been characterized as a failure to perform other provisions. See, for example, *Nash Metalware Co.*, GSBCA 11951, 94-2 BCA ¶ 26,780 (contractor failed to respond to cure notice and to deliver conforming ladles); *Maywood Cab Serv., Inc.*, VACAB 1210, 77-2 BCA ¶ 12,751 (contractor's drivers lacked proper licenses); *Vaqueria Tres Monjitas, Inc.*, VACAB 1120, 75-1 BCA ¶ 11,308 (milk failed to meet sanitary standards); and *Long Island Nuclear Serv. Corp.*, ASBCA 12454, 69-1 BCA ¶ 7492 (spilling radioactive waste violated specifications requiring caution during performance). In *Space Dynamics Corp.*, ASBCA 13376, 71-1 BCA ¶ 8853, the failure to timely deliver conforming end items was apparently treated as a breach of another provision. The classification in these cases is questionable. Failures to meet specifications in end items should be treated as delivery failures if they occur after the scheduled delivery date or as progress failures if they occur before the scheduled delivery date.

Since the construction contract default clause does not specifically refer to "other provisions," there are relatively few decisions dealing with the government's right to terminate for such failures in such contracts. However, the failure to furnish bonds required by the Invitation for Bid has been held to be a sufficient basis for default termination, *Gupta Carpet Prof'ls*, GSBCA 5229, 79-1 BCA ¶ 13,834; *Walsh Constr. Co. of Ill.*, ASBCA 52952, 02-2 BCA ¶ 32,004.

Various other contract clauses provide independent bases for terminating a contractor's right to proceed with the work when the provisions of such clauses are breached. For example, the Covenant Against Contingent Fees clause, FAR 52.203-5, permits the government to "annul" the contract. Likewise, the Equal Opportunity clause, FAR 52.222-26, provides that a contract may be "cancelled, terminated, or suspended." In addition, there are other statutes and regulations that provide similar sanctions for improper conduct. See FAR 52.203-3 (anti-gratuities clause) and 41 U.S.C. §§ 51-54 (Anti-Kickback Act, prohibiting any subcontractor from making a gift to a contractor or higher-tier subcontractor as inducement for the award of a subcontract). When the violation of such provisions is at issue, the government's right to terminate may be derived from the particular clause or statute concerned. Thus, there is apparently no need to rely on the provisions of a default clause to justify such a termination. However, as a practical matter, the government may issue a default termination as the procedural mechanism for effectuating the substantive rights created by such clauses or statutes. For example, in *Joseph Morton Co. v. United States*, 757 F.2d 1273 (Fed. Cir. 1985), the Federal Circuit held that fraud in connection with one change order in a very large contract enabled the government to terminate the contract for default.

Default terminations have been used to enforce the right to terminate for violations of the Buy American Act, *H&R Machinists Co.*, ASBCA 38440, 91-1 BCA ¶ 23,373; *Ballantine Labs., Inc.*, ASBCA 35138, 88-2 BCA ¶ 20,660; *Integrated Sys. Group, Inc. v. Social Sec. Admin.*, GSBCA 14054-SSA, 98-2 BCA ¶ 29,848; the Walsh-Healey Act, *SanColMar Indus., Inc.*, ASBCA 15339, 73-2 BCA ¶ 10,086; the Service Contract Act, *Giltron Assocs., Inc.*, ASBCA 14561, 70-1 BCA ¶ 8316; and the Davis-Bacon and Contract Work Hours Standards Acts, *Edgar M. Williams*, ASBCA 16058, 72-2 BCA ¶ 9734. However, in *Herman B. Taylor Constr. Co. v. Barram*, 203 F.3d 808 (Fed. Cir. 2000), the court held that a contractor's consent decree with the Department of Labor was not a final adjudication of Davis-Bacon

Act violations and could not be the basis for a default termination since neither party admitted or determined anything about the alleged violation.

Although difficult to categorize, terminations are sometimes justified on the basis of outrageous conduct by the contractor. In *Tom Kime*, PSBCA 3480, 95-1 BCA ¶ 27,490, a contractor was properly terminated because of his abusive behavior toward a postal clerk and the postmaster as well as a failure to obey the postmaster's instructions. Other contracts were terminated after the contractor assaulted the postmaster and a postal clerk. In *Larry J. Miller,* PSBCA 3632, 95-1 BCA ¶ 27,448, a postal delivery contractor's intentional disposal of extra advertising mail in a trash bin was a serious enough violation of the contract requirements to merit a default termination.

False certifications also justify a default termination. In *National Med. Staffing Inc.*, DOTBCA 2568, 95-1 BCA ¶ 27,341, the contractor's knowingly false certification that it had not been terminated for default in the prior three years by any federal agencies was sufficient basis for default termination of a contract. See also *Spread Info. Sciences, Inc.,* ASBCA 48438, 96-1 BCA ¶ 27,996. In *Ricmar Eng'g, Inc.*, ASBCA 44260, 97-2 BCA ¶ 29,084, the contract was terminated because the contractor and its president had been convicted of conspiring to submit a fraudulent progress payment request. Compare *Technical Sys. Assocs., Inc. v. Department of Commerce,* GSBCA 13277-COM, 97-2 BCA ¶ 30,684 (government's motion for summary judgment to uphold the default termination based on the contractor's false certification regarding previous default terminations denied because the contractor alleged that the government knew of the prior terminations for default before the contract was awarded).

4. *Failure to Proceed*

The Contract Disputes Act of 1978, 41 U.S.C. § 605(b), authorizes agencies to include clauses requiring contractors to proceed with performance pending "final decision of an appeal, action or final settlement." The standard Disputes clause set forth at FAR 52.233-1 for contracts subject to the Disputes Act implements this authority in ¶ (i), as follows:

> The Contractor shall proceed diligently with performance of this contract, pending final resolution of any request for relief, claim, appeal, or action arising under the contract, and comply with any decision of the Contracting Officer.

Language requiring the contractor to proceed with performance during pendency of disputes was also included in the standard pre-Act Disputes clauses:

> Pending final decision of a dispute hereunder, the Contractor shall proceed diligently with the performance of the contract and in accordance with the Contracting Officer's decision.

The basic rationale for imposing such a "duty to proceed" was articulated by the Armed Services Board in *Detroit Designing & Eng'g Co.*, ASBCA 8807, 1964 BCA ¶ 4214, at 20,452:

> Regardless of the merits of a [contractor's] dispute, the plain provisions of the contract and the public interest do not for a moment permit us to countenance possible hampering of operations which might involve the lives of servicemen or the political position of the country in its myriad world-wide commitments and responsibilities. Yet, this might be the precise effect of prolonged suspension of contract performance even in connection with the most commonplace item of supply.

The contractor's rights are in theory protected by permitting the contractor to subsequently assert a claim and challenge a contracting officer's adverse decision through an appeal to a board of contract appeals or suit in the U.S. Court of Federal Claims. See *Dyanamics Corp. of Am. v. United States*, 182 Ct. Cl. 62, 389 F.2d 424 (1968).

The contractor's duty to proceed in the standard Disputes clause is applicable only to disputes "arising under the contract." This phrase means that there must be a remedy-granting clause in the contract applicable to the matter in dispute for the duty to proceed to be binding. Thus, if there is no remedy-granting clause applicable, the contractor would be entitled to abandon the work upon a material breach by the government. However, the wide class of government breaches, such as many constructive changes, which are covered by remedy-granting clauses, has severely narrowed the universe of government misconduct that can be characterized as a material breach and upon which a contractor rescission or abandonment of performance could therefore properly be based.

An even greater limit on the contractor's right to abandon the work on the government's breach is contained in the alternate version of the Disputes clause provided in FAR 52.233-1, which calls for the contractor to proceed diligently with performance "pending final resolution of any request for relief, claim, appeal, or action arising under or relating to the contract." DFARS 233.013 requires this alternate to be used in Department of Defense contracts for aircraft, ships, and major defense systems. This language may also be included in DOD contracts where performance is vital to national security or public health or welfare. NFS 1833.104 authorizes inclusion of this alternate provision "where continued performance is vital to national security, the public health and welfare, critical/major agency programs, or other essential supplies or services whose timely procurement from other sources would be impracticable." Note that FAR 33.213(b) states that the agency should consider providing financial assistance to contractors being instructed to proceed pending resolution of claims not arising under, but related to, the contract. Under this alternate provision, arguably, the contractor would have a duty to proceed even in the event of a "material breach" that would otherwise constitute grounds for rescission or abandonment under contracts containing either the pre-Act or standard Disputes Act disputes clauses. See the discussion of "material breach" that follows.

The requirement to proceed pending resolution of a dispute is also stated in the supply contract Changes clause at FAR 52.243-1, which states in part, "nothing in this clause shall excuse the contractor from proceeding with the contract as changed." Similar language appeared in earlier versions of the construction contract Changes clause, but it was removed in 1968 as unnecessary, Hiestand, *A New Era in Government Construction Contracts,* 28 Fed. B.J. 165, 180-81 (1968). The Changes clause requirement to proceed has been relied on in whole or in part to uphold defaults in *Nasco Prods. Co.*, VACAB 974, 72-2 BCA ¶ 9556 (contractor's failure to proceed pursuant to "a clear and unambiguous contract requirement" resulted in default), and *Telecommunication Consultants*, ASBCA 13801, 69-2 BCA ¶ 7925 (contractor failed to continue performance when it felt that certain drawings were not required by specifications despite the contracting officer's directions). The duty to proceed in accordance with the Changes clause has been infrequently cited as the specific ground for upholding a default.

While neither the Disputes clauses nor the standard default clauses specify the contractor's failure to proceed as a grounds for default termination by the government, a contractor's failure to proceed has occasionally been cited as proper grounds for default termination. While it has been suggested that, under the supply contract default clause, a contractor's failure to proceed provides a grounds for default as a failure to perform another provision of the contract, it would seem that a failure to proceed with the work in accordance with contracting officer's directions should properly provide a basis for default termination only where default would otherwise be justified based on failure to make progress or anticipatory repudiation.

The failure to proceed pending resolution of a dispute has sometimes been equated with anticipatory repudiation. See, for example, *Ortec Sys., Inc.*, ASBCA 43467, 92-2 BCA ¶ 24,859 (contractor abandonment is actual repudiation); *Aero Prods. Co.*, ASBCA 44030, 93-2 BCA ¶ 25,868 (contractor refusal to perform according to directions constituted a material breach); *Twigg Corp.*, NASABCA 62-0192, 93-1 BCA ¶ 25,318 (contractor refusal to remove and replace concrete slabs supported a termination for anticipatory breach); and *Kirk Casavan*, AGBCA 76-192, 78-2 BCA ¶ 13,459 (contractor, by refusing to perform during a dispute, "exhibited no inclination, and in fact refused, to prosecute the work with such diligence as to insure its completion within the contract time," thereby repudiating the contract).

Contractors often condition their continued performance upon the granting of other relief such as the payment of money or changes of technical requirements. Agencies properly terminated contracts for default on the grounds of anticipatory breach when the contractor conditioned the continuation of its performance on the authorization of a price adjustment, and the agency had not required work beyond the scope of the contract. See *Starghill Alternative Energy Corp.*, ASBCA 49612, 98-1 BCA ¶ 29,708; *Brenner Metal Prods. Corp.*, ASBCA 25294, 82-1 BCA ¶ 15,462 (contractor refused to proceed with work unless it was granted a price increase for alleged government-caused delays); and *Howell Tool & Fabricating, Inc.*,

ASBCA 47939, 96-1 BCA ¶ 28,225. However, although failure to proceed pending resolution of a dispute is analogous to repudiation, there are some distinctions. Failure to proceed pending resolution of a dispute does not necessarily involve abandonment or repudiation but may involve merely work stoppage that the contractor believes to be justified.

a. *Notification to Proceed*

The contractor's duty to proceed under the Disputes clause requires an indication from the contracting officer that the government expects continued performance. This most clearly exists where the contracting officer has issued an appealable final decision concerning a matter in dispute, *RFI Shield-Rooms*, ASBCA 19005, 77-1 BCA ¶ 12,237. Although it has been argued that absent a contracting officer's final decision pursuant to the Disputes clause the duty to proceed does not attach, the contractor's duty has not been so narrowly construed. Thus, the duty to proceed also "embraces the period when the dispute is in the `embryonic stage' before the contracting officer's formal decision," *Winder Aircraft Corp.*, ASBCA 4364, 59-1 BCA ¶ 2257 (contractor complained of inadequacy of specification drawings); *Stoeckert v. United States*, 183 Ct. Cl. 152, 391 F.2d 639 (1968) (contractor's refusal to follow contracting officer's directions in a stop-work order to remove and replace previously laid tile).

The direction from the contracting officer may take the form of a unilateral order directing the contractor to proceed with stated contract work, *Eriez Constr., Inc.*, VACAB 1273, 78-2 BCA ¶ 13,547; *Aero Prods. Co.*, ASBCA 44030, 93-2 BCA ¶ 25,868 (clear direction to provide plotting board carrying cases that added 20 percent to cost of performance, pending resolution of interpretation dispute); or a notice directing some specific action, *RFI Shield-Rooms*, ASBCA 19005, 77-1 BCA ¶ 12,237 (explicit direction that full-load test plan be submitted); *Colangelo Constr. Co.*, ENGBCA 3313, 74-2 BCA ¶ 10,853 (specific order to correct defective asphalt in accordance with the construction contract inspection clause); *Sanders Assocs., Inc.*, ASBCA 17653, 75-1 BCA ¶ 11,043 (cure notice required contractor to correct numerous technical discrepancies). Specific notice would appear to be required if the requirement to proceed is questionable, *Seven Sciences, Inc.*, ASBCA 21079, 77-2 BCA ¶ 12,730 (default termination without specific notice improper where the government failed to supply all the drawings needed for fabrication of battery chargers).

However, where the facts and circumstances clearly indicate that the contractor should proceed, a formal unilateral order is unnecessary. See *American Dredging Co.*, ENGBCA 2920, 72-1 BCA ¶ 9316, where, following the contracting officer's denial of a channel-dredging contractor's claim for adjustment due to differing site conditions, the contractor became aware that only blasting and drilling would accomplish the required results but did not proceed with the work.

In addition to explicit orders or the existence of a clear requirement to proceed, other factors may place the contractor on notice that continued performance is expected. Such factors include issuance of a cure notice for failure to make progress, *APCO Mossberg Co.*, GSBCA 3440, 72-1 BCA ¶ 9403; explicit notification that the delivery schedule remains in effect, *Geophysical Instrument & Supply Co.*, IBCA 996-6-73, 74-1 BCA ¶ 10,404; and clear statements as to the government's interpretation of contract language, *Charles Bainbridge, Inc.*, ASBCA 15843, 72-1 BCA ¶ 9351. The government's indication that work should proceed may also be found where the contracting officer has made statements of intended future actions that are consistent only with continued performance, *Campbell Keypunch Serv.*, GSBCA 3123, 71-1 BCA ¶ 8800 (contractor required to proceed when, following overpayment on a requirements contract, contracting officer expressed intent to set off against amounts payable on future orders).

b. Scope and Nature of Obligation

The nature of the duty to proceed is broad. See *Essex Electro Eng'rs, Inc.*, ASBCA 49115, 02-1 BCA ¶ 31,714, stating at 156,699:

> After the Contracting Officer has given an interpretation of the contract requirements, the contractor must perform as directed and may not stop work. If the contractor believes the interpretation erroneous, the determination may be appealed in the claims procedure. *Benju Corporation,* ASBCA 43648, et al. 97-2 BCA 29274 at 145, 654-55. In *Benju* we made clear that even if the Government's interpretation were wrong, the contractor is not justified in refusing to do as directed since the merits of the controversy have no effect on the requirement that a contractor continue performance. A contractor may disagree with the Government's representative as to how the work is to be completed, but nevertheless is under a duty to proceed diligently with performance. *Advanced Mechanical Services, Inc.* ASBCA 38832, 94-3 BCA 26964.

The contractor must proceed even where the government erroneously advises that no relief for its claim is possible, *Accu-Met Prods., Inc.*, ASBCA 19704, 75-1 BCA ¶ 11,123 (following clarification of a defective specification, the government denied responsibility for delays and cost increases due to the defect); *Mai Huu An Co.*, ASBCA 14953, 71-1 BCA ¶ 8874 (default upheld where a Vietnamese contractor, who was "apparently" able to read and write English, was initially advised that there would be no price adjustment to compensate for adverse impact of an austerity tax, although the contracting officer later stated "relief might be granted" and the form contract in use contained an explicit right to an adjustment).

The contractor must also proceed even though it believes the government's action to be wrong. If the contractor refuses to proceed, it risks termination even if its belief concerning the dispute is correct, *Schmid Plumbing & Heating Co. v. United States*, 173 Ct. Cl. 302, 351 F.2d 651 (1965) (contractor had the duty to install more expensive boilers erroneously demanded by the contracting officer even though the department head later ruled in the contractor's favor); *Scientific Book Serv., Inc.*, GSBCA 3096, 70-1 BCA ¶ 8357 (contractor refused to deliver publications, although it was able to do so, because of a disagreement over the meaning of a list price provision); *Benju Corp.*, ASBCA 43648, 97-2 BCA ¶ 29,274, *aff'd,* 178 F.3d 1312 (Fed. Cir. 1999) (refusal to furnish test procedures that contractor believed were not required); *Protech Atlanta*, ASBCA 52217, 01-2 BCA ¶ 31,434 (refusal to continue when contracting officer refused to consider deviation requests); *George F. Marshall & Gordon L. Blackwell,* ENGBCA 6066, 00-1 BCA ¶ 30,730 (refusal of takeover contractor to continue, in belief that additional payments were due).

The Disputes clause duty to proceed provision also precludes a contractor from stopping work on one contract because of a pending dispute on another contract, *Kirk Casavan*, AGBCA 76-192, 78-2 BCA ¶ 13,459 (tree-thinning contractor improperly refused to perform until "positive action" was taken on claims under other contract); *Clinical Supply Corp.*, ASBCA 15466, 72-1 BCA ¶ 9452 (contractor required to continue performance despite improper government claim under the warranty provisions of other contracts ultimately adjudicated in the contractor's favor).

Default terminations for breach of the duty to proceed have been found proper regardless of the time at which the refusal to proceed occurs. See, for example, *Skip Kirchdorfer, Inc.*, ASBCA 32637, 91-1 BCA ¶ 23,380 (undue lapse of time between default and actual termination did not affect valid termination); *Campbell Keypunch Serv.*, GSBCA 3123, 71-1 BCA ¶ 8800 (requirements contractor refused to accept job orders that were, in effect, notices to proceed); *Hackett Corp.*, GSBCA 3942, 75-1 BCA ¶ 11,060 (after award but prior to the due date); *Accu-Met Prods., Inc.*, ASBCA 19704, 75-1 BCA ¶ 11,123 (the due date was apparently uncertain since a defective specification had delayed performance for some time and no revised date had been established); and *Kirk Casavan*, AGBCA 76-192, 78-2 BCA ¶ 13,459 (prior to due date). Where the due date has passed prior to termination, defaults have been upheld in part because of the contractor's failure to proceed pending resolution of a dispute. See *Eriez Constr., Inc.*, VACAB 1273, 78-2 BCA ¶ 13,547 (contractor's refusal to install casework classified as a failure to proceed pending resolution of a dispute even though the date for completion had passed). In finding defaults proper in such cases, the boards have implicitly held that the contractor's untimely performance, which is an independent basis for default, cannot be excusable merely because there was a dispute during the period of performance. The nonexcusability of such delays was explicitly recognized in *Pennsylvania Testing Lab.*, ASBCA 6185, 61-2 BCA ¶ 3234 (contractor's allegations of deficient government preliminary drawings were not an excusable cause for delay).

In one case, the court held that the contractor was required to proceed to perform an option that had been invalidly exercised by the contracting officer by specifying a rate of delivery not required by the contract, *Alliant Techsystems, Inc. v. United States,* 178 F.3d 1260 (Fed. Cir. 1999). There the court upheld a termination for default for failure to perform the option at a rate that had been specified by the Court of Federal Claims in a declaratory judgment, stating at 1276:

> Alliant's obligations under the Disputes clause are independent of its obligations under the Option clause. Because we have determined that the Disputes clause requires Alliant to perform the option as directed pending resolution of its challenge to the Contracting Officer's order, we hold that Alliant was obligated to deliver the option quantities until and unless it obtained a court order excusing it from its performance obligations. The Court of Federal Claims issued its declaratory judgment prior to the first delivery of option quantities required by the contracting officer's decision. Alliant was therefore not obligated to perform at the contracting officer's rate, but absent reversal or interim relief from this court, Alliant was required by the disputes clause to perform at the rate specified by the Court of Federal Claims.

Although the Disputes clause in the contract required the contractor to proceed only when claims met the "arising under" standard, the decision contains no reference to any remedy-granting clause that applied to improperly exercised options. However, the decision does reject the contractor's contention that the option exercise was a "cardinal change"—perhaps indicating that the court believed that the Changes clause was the applicable remedy-granting clause.

In *Dae Shinn Enters., Inc., d/b/a Dayron*, ASBCA 50533, 03-1 BCA ¶ 32,096, the board ruled that even in the face of its allegation of commercial impracticability, Dae Shinn should have proceeded with performance while pursuing extra compensation under the Changes and Government Property clause.

c. *Exceptions to the Duty to Proceed*

The courts and boards have excused the contractor from its duty to proceed where it would be unfair or illogical to require it to continue contract performance. A failure to proceed may be excused where government actions materially breach the contract or make performance impractical or impossible, or where the government does not provide the contractor with clear direction necessary to perform the contract.

(1) Government Material Breach

Under a well-established common law principle, a contracting party is under no duty to continue rendering required performance in the face of an "uncured material failure" or "material breach" by the other party, *Restatement, Second, Contracts* § 237. The standard pre-CDA and post-CDA clause would appear to severely limit a contractor's ability to rely on this doctrine by making many kinds of government misconduct subject to resolution under the disputes procedures and specifically directing the contractor to proceed with the work pending resolution of such disputes. Nevertheless, the doctrine of "material breach" remains applicable to government contracts and serves as an important exception to the duty to proceed.

Since the government's major obligation in its contracts is to pay the contractor, most material breaches occur when timely payment in accordance with the contract provisions is not made. In *General Dynamics Corp.*, DOTCAB 1232, 83-1 BCA ¶ 16,386, the board held that the government's failure to pay five invoices under a cost-reimbursement contract, based on the contractor's alleged failure to make progress, constituted a material breach justifying the contractor's suspension of performance. In reaching this conclusion, the board relied on a contract provision stating that the contractor was entitled to be paid its incurred costs up to a certain ceiling without regard to its success in performing. In *Drain-A-Way Sys.*, GSBCA 6473, 83-1 BCA ¶ 16,202, the board explicitly recognized that, while the government's failure to pay for services performed was "clearly a dispute of fact arising under the contract," the contractor was nevertheless under no duty to continue with performance, stating that "where the Government has itself committed a material breach, it may not compel its contractor to continue performance under the Disputes clause." In *Seven Sciences, Inc.*, ASBCA 21079, 77-2 BCA ¶ 12,730, the board stated that the discharge of a contractor's duty to perform "depends on the seriousness of the Government's breach, both the nature of the breach and the impact on the contractor's ability to perform." A serious breach was found in *Northern Helex Co. v. United States*, 197 Ct. Cl. 118, 455 F.2d 546 (1972), in which the court stated at 124:

> [M]ere delay in payment, for a while, would not be a material breach but there is a clear distinction between delay of that kind and a total failure to pay over many months. Our jurisprudence strongly suggests that the latter sort of breach by the Government is material, just as it would be in the case of a private party.

Where government failure to make payments justifies a contractor's failure to proceed, default termination is improper. See *U.S. Servs. Corp.*, ASBCA 8291, 1963 BCA ¶ 3703, in which the board stated at 18,509:

> Under the circumstances, the Government's attempt to terminate the contract for default was ineffective because the [contractor] had already exercised its right to rescind the contract.

In *H.E. & C.F. Blinne Contracting Co.*, ENGBCA 4174, 83-1 BCA ¶ 16,388, the board overturned a default termination, holding that the government's failure to remit the proper amount of progress payments constituted a "Government breach." In *Building Maint. Specialist, Inc.*, ENGBCA 4115, 83-2 BCA ¶ 16,629, the board held that unauthorized deductions from payments for services performed justified abandonment of work even though the underpayment did not render the contractor financially incapable of performing. The contractor's right to stop performance for payment failures was also upheld in *Contract Maint., Inc.*, ASBCA 19409, 75-1 BCA ¶ 11,207 (four-month failure to pay amounts admittedly due); *Robert O. Redding*, AGBCA 272, 69-2 BCA ¶ 7888 (withholding one month's progress payment); *R. H. J. Corp.,* ASBCA 9922, 66-1 BCA ¶ 5361, *recons. denied*, 66-1 BCA ¶ 5625 (progress payments were to be calculated on the basis of incurred costs, but government suspended payments pending submission of an acceptable first article); *Valley Contractors*, ASBCA 9397, 1964 BCA ¶ 4071 (failure to pay janitorial services contractor where at least 51 percent of monthly fee was admittedly due); and *U.S. Servs. Corp.*, ASBCA 8291, 1963 BCA ¶ 3703 (one month's progress payment wrongfully withheld). Following work stoppage, the contractor may have no obligation to return to work even where the government subsequently offers to make the payments, *Suburban Contracting Co. v. United States*, 76 Ct. Cl. 533 (1932). However, the government's withholding of payment excuses the contractor's default only where it is both improper and the primary or controlling cause of default, and not where the contractor has repudiated its contractual obligations, *Graham Int'l*, ASBCA 50360, 01-1 BCA ¶ 31,222. Moreover, a wrongful withholding may still be reasonable under the circumstances. In *Bill J. Copeland,* AGBCA 1999-182-1, 02-2 BCA ¶ 32,049, *aff'd,* 350 F.2d 1230 (Fed. Cir. 2003), the agency properly withheld progress payments based on a Department of Labor investigator's recommendation even though a subsequent DOL decision found the withholding to be grossly excessive. The board found that since the agency's reliance on the investigator's recommendation was both reasonable and in accordance with applicable law, the default termination was proper.

Another type of material breach that may justify refusal to proceed is action by the government in excess of that authorized by the contract, *United States v. Spearin*, 248 U.S. 132 (1918). For example, it has been held that a "cardinal change"—defined as a change that fundamentally alters the contractual undertaking—constitutes a material breach and that in such circumstances "there is no contractual duty on the part of the contractor to comply with the change or continue performance," *Kakos Nursery, Inc.*, ASBCA 10989, 66-2 BCA ¶ 5733, *recons. denied*, 66-2 BCA ¶ 5909. Unreasonable and untimely inspections by the government may also justify a failure or refusal to proceed, *Wayne Welding Equip. Co.*, GSBCA 4560, 77-1 BCA ¶ 12,532. In *Brand S. Roofing,* ASBCA 24688, 82-1 BCA ¶ 15,513, a three-month government delay in informing the contractor of defects in performance greatly increased costs of correction and constituted a material breach that justified refusal to perform as directed. Furthermore, government failure to follow the procedures required by the Disputes clause was found to be so egregious that refusal to perform was justified, *Penker Constr. Co. v. United States*, 96 Ct. Cl. 1 (1942) (perfunctory administrative review of the contractor's claim so denied the contractor's right to an effective hearing that the court characterized the process as a "travesty of justice").

The contractor may elect to waive a material breach by the government and continue performance, but in such situations the contractor should notify the government of this election and reserve the right to seek redress for the breach, *Ling-Temco-Vought, Inc. v. United States*, 201 Ct. Cl. 135, 475 F.2d 630 (1973). See also *Empire Energy Mgmt. Sys., Inc.*, ASBCA 46741, 03-1 BCA ¶ 32,079; *aff'd,* 362 F.3d 1343 (Fed. Cir. 2004), holding that the government retained the right to terminate a utility construction contract for default because, although the contractor ceased work for a year citing alleged site contamination, it resumed work after the performance period had lapsed. The board reasoned that although the contractor alleged that the government breached the contract, the rights and obligations of the parties remained in effect for as long as the contractor continued performance.

The alternate Disputes clause, requiring the contractor to proceed in the event of disputes "relating to" as well as those "arising under" the contract, may compel the contractor to continue with performance even in the face of a "material breach" by the government. See *Metric Sys. v. McDonnell Douglas Corp.*, 850 F.Supp. 1568 (N.D. Florida 1994), in which the judge upheld a termination based on the failure to proceed because, inter alia, the contract clause was modeled after the Disputes clause, Alternate 1, and required performance even in the face of a breach.

(2) Impractical to Proceed

Government acts may excuse a contractor from the duty to proceed even though the disputes process provides administrative relief for the effects of such actions if the contractor is unable to perform or is delayed by the government's conduct. See *E.L. Cournand & Co.*, ASBCA 2955, 60-2 BCA ¶ 2840, in which the board stated that the clauses requiring the contractor to proceed must be read "together with the words in the 'Default' article which in effect excuse a failure to perform any provision of the contract if the failure arises out of causes beyond the control and without the fault or negligence of the contractor. Acts of the Government are included in such causes." Thus, a wrongful failure to pay may excuse a subsequent default if the failure to pay caused the default, *Pilcher, Livingston & Wallace, Inc.*, ASBCA 13391, 70-1 BCA ¶ 8331, *recons. denied*, 70-2 BCA ¶ 8488 (default excused since failure to make progress payments deprived contractor of funds essential to pay subcontractors, and subsequent failure to complete work was due to subcontractors' failure to proceed absent payment); *Q.V.S., Inc.*, ASBCA 3722, 58-2 BCA ¶ 2007 (default excused since government failure to make payments precluded timely performance).

When the government requires a contractor to follow detailed plans and specifications, it impliedly warrants that if the specifications are followed the results will be adequate, *United States v. Spearin*, 248 U.S. 132 (1918). Defects in government design or specifications may excuse the contractor from its duty to proceed. See *D.E.W., Inc.*, ASBCA 35896, 94-3 BCA ¶ 27,182, in which the board found that defects in a bearing bolt design made it impossible for the contractor to proceed with hanger construction in accordance with the government's plans and specifications. Thus, the termination for default was converted to a termination for the convenience of the government. Impossibility of performance may also be found if the contractor can establish that performance of the contract could not be accomplished without commercially unacceptable costs and time input far beyond that contemplated in the contract, *Foster Wheeler Corp. v. United States*, 206 Ct. Cl. 533, 513 F.2d 588 (1975). See *Soletanche Rodio Nicholson (JV),* ENGBCA 5796, 94-1 BCA ¶ 26,472, in which a contractor's failure to complete its excavation contract was excusable because a differing site condition "made it legally, commercially, and practically impossible to continue performance." The contractor proposed the use of a rock mill as a performance method based on an assumption that it would encounter normal ground stress. However, the contractor encountered unusual ground stress at the site, and the excavation could not be performed with a rock mill. In converting the default termination to a termination for the convenience of the government, the board stated that the evidence established "the classic case for legal, practical and commercial impossibility." See *Defense Sys. Corp. & Hi-Shear Tech. Corp.*, ASBCA 42939, 95-2 BCA ¶ 27,721, holding that the government improperly terminated a contract for default when the contractor stopped work because an inadequate technical data package coupled, with unrealistic acceptance criteria, combined to make performance of an ammunition production contract commercially impracticable.

Even if continued performance is possible and the contractor has a clear idea of what the government desires in the way of performance, there may be no duty to proceed if the circumstances make continued performance impractical, *Ned C. Hardy*, AGBCA 74-111, 77-2 BCA ¶ 12,848 (denial of permission for workers to camp at worksite rendered national forest site preparation contractor's performance impractical since unattended equipment was subject to vandalism and contractor reasonably suspected that a single night watchman would be in personal danger from ecology activists); *Hempstead Maint. Serv., Inc.,* GSBCA 3127, 71-1 BCA ¶ 8809 (cleaning services contractor encountered severe difficulty in opening numerous windows, and employees' union advised workers not to push pivot windows for fear of falling from the fifth floor).

It is also considered impractical to proceed with performance where the contractor knows that the resulting work will be defective or useless, *Seven Sciences, Inc.*, ASBCA 21079, 77-2 BCA ¶ 12,730; *Ascani Constr. & Realty Co.*, VABCA 1572, 83-2 BCA ¶ 16,635. In *Puma Chem. Co.,* GSBCA 5254, 81-1 BCA ¶ 14,844, the contractor's refusal to proceed was justified where government imposition of improper inspection methods and test procedures was likely to lead to rejection of finished supplies. See also *Astro Dynamics, Inc.*, ASBCA 28320, 83-2 BCA ¶ 16,900, where a high rate of rejections resulting from demanding tolerance specifications made it reasonable for the contractor to seek a solution rather than proceed with work in the hope that the government would grant "waivers" as to definitive items. Moreover, it has been stated that a contractor may not proceed with performance when it knows the resulting work will be defective. In *J.D. Hedin Constr. Co. v. United States*, 171 Ct. Cl. 70, 347 F.2d 235 (1965), the court stated at 77:

> [A]n experienced contractor cannot rely on government-prepared specifications where, on the basis of the government furnished data, he knows or should have known that the prepared specifications could not produce the desired result for ". . . he has no right to make a useless thing and charge the customer for it." *R.M. Hollingshead Corp. v. United States*, 124 Ct. Cl. 681, 683, 111 F. Supp. 285, 286 (1953).

However, in *Switlik Parachute Co. v. United States*, 216 Ct. Cl. 362, 573 F.2d 1228 (1978), the court indicated that recovery was appropriate when the contractor proceeded with the work even though the government failed to take corrective action after being notified of the alleged defect, stating at 374:

> Even if it be assumed that [the government's] design specifications were deficient, [the contractor] in notifying the defendant on May 3, 1973 of the alleged design deficiencies, had discharged its duty not to knowingly produce defective items without first contacting [the government]. *See Blount Brothers Construction Co. v. United States*, 171 Ct. Cl. 478, 495-97, 346 F.2d 962, 972-73 (1965). Thereafter, given the absence of either an order by [the government] immediately to suspend production or of a change order modifying the design specifications, it was [the contractor's] right to go forward with production, even though in so doing [the government] might incur liability for defective products. After all, it is the [government] who warrants that compliance with its design specifications will result in an acceptable product. *United States v. Spearin*, 248 U.S. 132 (1918). *See*, also, *R.E.D.M. Corp. v. United States*, 192 Ct. Cl. 891, 901-02, 428 F.2d 1304, 1309-10 (1970).

In *S.W. Elecs. & Mfg. Corp. v. United States*, 228 Ct. Cl. 333, 655 F.2d 1078 (1981), a contractor was denied an equitable adjustment for increased costs attributable to defective work after the contracting officer had issued instructions to substitute a workable switch for the inadequate switch identified in the specifications. The court rejected the contractor's attempt to rely on *Switlick*, stating at 345:

> Nor does this court's opinion in *Switlik Parachute Co. v. United States*, 216 Ct. Cl. 362, 573 F.2d 1228 (1978), support the [contractor's] position. Rather, that case tends to support the position that a contractor would be entitled to continue production of what the contractor believed were defective units, once the contractor had advised the Government of the problem and the Government had failed to take corrective action. In *Switlik* the Government believed that the vests which [the contractor] was producing met the contract requirements and concluded that corrective action was not necessary. *Switlik* stated that under those circumstances the contractor had a right to continue production. In this case, everyone agreed that the radios which incorporated the Ledex switch did not function. More importantly, the contracting officer instructed the [contractor] on the appropriate action to take, *i.e.*, use the Oak switch. It is clear that the reasoning in *Switlik* would not justify [the contractor's] continued production using the Ledex switch on the facts of this case. [The contractor's] reliance on *Switlik* assumes that [the contractor] was following the Government's instructions in producing all of the defective radios, whereas [the contractor] clearly was not.

The risk of stopping performance to avoid producing defective work is illustrated by *Martin & Turner Supply Co.*, ASBCA 16809, 72-2 BCA ¶ 9610, in which the board upheld a default termination, stating at 44,936:

> [The contractor's] position was simply that it could have provided an item that would conform to specifications but that it refused to do so since it knew that the item was not what the Government intended to acquire. However praiseworthy [the contractor's] motives may have been, it had the duty to perform under the contract just as the Government had the duty to accept the item if it conformed to specifications even were the item different from what it desired. On failure to perform, the Government had no choice but to terminate for default and quite properly so.

See also *Al-Cal Painting Co.*, GSBCA 2806, 70-1 BCA ¶ 8319 (total abandonment of job was not justified by allegation that government specifications calling for a single coat of white paint over green paint would not produce satisfactory results).

Even where performance is impossible, a contractor generally may not abandon performance and repudiate the contract unless the government has been adequately informed of the problem and afforded an opportunity to relax the specifications, *Wise Instrumentation & Control, Inc.*, NASABCA 1072-12, 75-2 BCA ¶ 11,478, *recons. denied*, 76-1 BCA ¶ 11,641; *Suffolk Envtl. Magnetics, Inc.*, ASBCA 17593, 74-2 BCA ¶ 10,771; or to assist the contractor by providing special equipment, *Thermovac Indus. Corp.*, AECBCA 64-11-69, 70-1 BCA ¶ 8157.

Once performance is again practicable, the duty to proceed revives, *D.H. Dave & Gerben Contracting Co.*, ASBCA 6257, 1962 BCA ¶ 3493. Likewise, contractors must proceed with severable portions of the work that are not impracticable, *James G. Henderson*, ASBCA 15353, 72-2 BCA ¶ 9567. However, the contractor does not have to proceed if the government has specifically indicated that it will not accept performance of the severable work absent completion of the impracticable work, *Stamell Constr. Co.*, DOTCAB 68-27J, 75-1 BCA ¶ 11,334.

(3) Lack of Clear Direction

Lack of clear direction necessary for performance can justify a failure to proceed in accordance with the Disputes clause, *Industrial-Denver Co.*, ASBCA 13735, 70-1 BCA ¶ 8118 (failure to provide design criteria to meet government's interpretation of specification); *Foremost Mech. Sys., Inc. v. General Servs. Admin.*, GSBCA 12335, 95-1 BCA ¶ 27,382 (failure to give timely response to requests to resolve numerous technical issues); *Turbine Aviation*, ASBCA 51323, 98-2 BCA ¶ 29,945 (failure to provide crucial technical information in a timely manner); *Alsace Indus., Inc.*, ASBCA 50720, 98-1 BCA ¶ 29,576 (government failed to answer an unnecessary but good faith query on technical requirements); *SAE/Americon-Mid Atl., Inc. v. General Servs. Admin.*, GSBCA 12294, 98-2 BCA ¶ 30,084 (failure of government's architect to answer technical inquiries). Whether directions are so unclear that the contractor need not continue is a factual question. Thus, contractors must be certain that there is a significant uncertainty and must make some attempt to resolve the problem, *Florida Sys. Corp.*, ASBCA 12443, 69-2 BCA ¶ 8028 (contractor requested no information despite the contracting officer's express willingness to clarify disputed items). In *Robert R. Marquis, Inc.*, ASBCA 38438, 92-1 BCA ¶ 24,692, the government failed to tell a contractor how to proceed in the face of a potential conflict with another contractor's work despite repeated requests. Thus, the contractor was unable to proceed in the absence of direction.

Requests for clarification must be reasonable. See *Electromagnetic Indus., Inc.*, ASBCA 11485, 67-2 BCA ¶ 6545, in which the board stated at 30,410:

> It is true that [the contractor] cannot, by continually writing letters requesting information and clarification, impose an obligation on the Government to answer every letter thereby postponing indefinitely the "day of reckoning"—default termination.

In *Pennsylvania Testing Lab., Inc.*, ASBCA 6185, 61-2 BCA ¶ 3234, the board discussed the reasonableness of the contractor's requests for clarification, stating at 16,765-66:

> [The contractor] could have obtained the information claimed to be indispensable to performance at any time by resort to published industry data of general circulation. He chose instead to compel the Government to assemble such information for him, losing many months in the process. When [the contractor] received the essential data he was so entrenched in contumacy that he declined to use them on the pretext that the data came into his possession indirectly. Rather than proceed he insisted upon contract amendments for the avowed objective of vindicating his opinions on the questions of interpretation. [The contractor] did not want information; he wanted change orders.

See also *Dynatran Elecs. Corp.*, ASBCA 8371, 1963 BCA ¶ 4006 (board found that the contractor "did not want a solution to the problems of manufacture but change orders vindicating its point of view"); *Fraya, S.E.*, ASBCA 52222, 02-2 BCA ¶ 31,975 ("the duty to cooperate is a duty not to hinder or interfere with the contractor's performance. It 'is not a duty to do whatever a contractor demands,'" citing *Tri-Indus., Inc.*, ASBCA 47880, 99-2 BCA ¶ 30,529 at 150,765). However, in *Bison Trucking & Equip. Co.*, ASBCA 53390, 0l-2 BCA ¶ 31,654, the board held that the contractor was justified in stopping performance when the government failed to respond to its request for testing locations.

Where a reasonable request for clarification has been made, the contractor need not inform the government that work has stopped so long as such stoppage could reasonably be anticipated, *Milwaukee Transformer Co.*, ASBCA 10814, 66-1 BCA ¶ 5570. Likewise, performance may be stopped even where the government has not issued a stop-work order, so long as there has been a reasonable request for clarification, *Pacific Devices, Inc.*, ASBCA 19379, 76-2 BCA ¶ 12,179. Obviously, where a stop-work order has been issued, the contractor need not proceed, *Delta Eng'g & Sales, Inc.*, ASBCA 16326, 72-1 BCA ¶ 9373 (default improper where termination was issued while stop-work order was still in effect). A request for clarification may justify stopping work even though the specifications are not in fact defective, *Monitor Plastics Co.*, ASBCA 11187, 67-2 BCA ¶ 6408. Once lack of clear direction is proven, a default may be excused whether it was based on a missed due date, *Stockwell Rubber Co.*, ASBCA 20952, 76-2 BCA ¶ 12,130; *Henry Spen & Co.*, ASBCA 16296, 74-2 BCA ¶ 10,651; or failure to make progress, *CML-Macarr, Inc.*, ASBCA 19950, 76-2 BCA ¶ 12,047; *Avco Corp.*, NASABCA 869-18, 76-1 BCA ¶ 11,736. Likewise, a default based on nonconforming goods will be overturned where lack of clear direction precluded the contractor from correcting alleged discrepancies, *Remm Co.*, ASBCA 18430, 74-2 BCA ¶ 10,876.

5. *Anticipatory Repudiation*

An additional ground for default termination of a government contract arises where a contractor "repudiates" its obligations under the contract. The well-settled rule for invoking the doctrine of "anticipatory repudiation" is that there must be a "definite and unequivocal manifestation of intention on the part of the repudiator that he will not render the promised performance when the time fixed for it in the contract arrives," *Corbin on Contracts* § 973. Although standard default clauses do not specifically enumerate anticipatory repudiation as a basis for default termination, the right to terminate in such cases is an established common law remedy that the government retains.

Generally, the government may treat the contractor's repudiation as a total breach of contract, *Restatement, Second, Contracts* § 253. If the government elects to terminate the contract because of the repudiation, the common law right of rescission may be used. However, the government normally exercises this common law right by issuance of a notice of "default termination." The anticipatory repudiation must be expressed clearly, absolutely, and unequivocally, *Western States Mgmt. Serv. Inc.*, ASBCA 40212, 92-1 BCA ¶ 24,714; *Scott Aviation*, ASBCA 40776, 91-3 BCA ¶ 24,123. The repudiation must manifest either the contractor's clear refusal to perform or an unequivocal expression of its inability to perform the contract, *Beeston, Inc.*, ASBCA 38969, 91-3 BCA ¶ 24,241; *Premier Microwave Corp.*, ASBCA 36546, 88-3 BCA ¶ 20,984. Since repudiation must be "definite and unequivocal," there is no anticipatory breach where the professed inability to perform can be overcome and the contractor "expresses a willingness to continue performance," *Fairfield Scientific Corp.*, ASBCA 21151, 78-1 BCA ¶ 13,082, *recons. denied*, 78-2 BCA ¶ 13,429, *aff'd*, 228 Ct. Cl. 264, 655 F.2d 1062 (1981). There, the board also noted that such manifestation may be expressed either orally or through action. The contractor's refusal to perform in the presence of a government material breach is not an anticipatory repudiation, *Murdoch Mach. & Eng'g Co. of Utah v. United States*, 873 F.2d 1410 (Fed. Cir. 1989). See also *Marine Constr. & Dredging, Inc.*, ASBCA 39246, 95-1 BCA ¶ 27,286. However, see *United States v. DeKonty Corp.*, 922 F.2d 826 (Fed. Cir. 1991), reversing a board decision holding that a contractor was justified in stopping work based on the government's withholding of a greater amount than permitted by the contract's payment clause. The court found that the government's actions were not an unequivocal refusal to make payments.

a. *Timing of the Remedy*

Default termination is an available remedy for anticipatory repudiation regardless of the stage of contract performance. Thus, anticipatory repudiation has justified default termination before issuance of a notice to proceed, *Aireborne Sec., Inc.*, GSBCA 3333, 71-1 BCA ¶ 8872 (determined a progress failure, but since no cure notice apparently was sent, repudiation was implicitly found); prior to the date services were to begin, *What Mac Contractors, Inc.*, GSBCA 4766, 78-2 BCA ¶ 13,279; prior to execution of the written contract, *Urban Indus. Corp.*, GSBCA 3050, 72-2 BCA ¶ 9604; before any attempted performance had begun, *Central Fire Truck Corp.*, ASBCA 12715, 72-1 BCA ¶ 8946; after the due date where no "waiver of due date" had occurred, *Drillmation Co.*, ASBCA 12501, 69-1 BCA ¶ 7632; *Transdyne Corp.*, ASBCA 12834, 69-1 BCA ¶ 7615; where the delivery date was disestablished but the contractor insisted on a change order and payment as conditions to resuming work, *Polyurethane Prods. Corp.*, ASBCA 42251, 96-1 BCA ¶ 28,154; where nine months passed after the due date had been "waived," *Giannini-Voltex*, ASBCA 15077, 72-1 BCA ¶ 9199; *Simplex Mfg. Co.*, ASBCA 13897, 71-1 BCA ¶ 8814; where the due date had been "waived" but no new due date had been set, *B.F. Goodrich Co.*, ASBCA 19960, 76-2 BCA ¶ 12,105; *Menches Tool & Die, Inc.*, ASBCA 21469, 78-1 BCA ¶ 13,167; and where the government had expressly allowed a delinquent contractor to continue after the due date, *Bobco Mfg. Co.*, ASBCA 13430, 69-1 BCA ¶ 7537. When the due date has passed, the contractor's present failure alone would apparently support a default termination. However, if the due date has been "waived," there is no right to default terminate unless there is some independent ground to support the termination. Repudiation, being such a ground, will thus defeat the contractor's claim of "waiver."

The government's flexibility in the timing of an anticipatory repudiation default reflects the fact that a contractor's words or acts may amount to repudiation at any stage of performance. When repudiation has occurred, a notice of termination is not required, *Imperial Van & Storage Co.*, ASBCA 11462, 67-2 BCA ¶ 6621 (notification of the termination would have constituted a "vain and futile act"). Rather, the government may take immediate action to safeguard its interests, *James E. Kennedy v. United States*, 164 Ct. Cl. 507 (1964) (government promptly relet the contract to another contractor after repossessing the government-furnished material from the defaulting contractor). However, good contract administration would seem to call for the sending of a termination notice to the contractor to avoid subsequent misunderstandings.

b. Evidence Considered

Generally, the contracting officer may consider any acts or words of the contractor in evaluating whether a repudiation has occurred. However, in order to find repudiation, the acts and words of the contractor must indicate at the time of termination an "unequivocal manifestation of the contractor's intention not to perform." See *Fairfield Scientific Corp.*, ASBCA 21151, 78-1 BCA ¶ 13,082, *recons. denied*, 78-2 BCA ¶ 13,429, *aff'd*, 228 Ct. Cl. 264, 655 F.2d 1062 (1981), in which the board stated that the government "is not permitted the luxury of establishing through hindsight that the cure notice may have been useless. To permit this would effectively nullify the contractual requirement for a cure notice." In *Fairfield*, the board held that, since the government reestablished the due date, only subsequent contractor actions or words should be considered. The boards may always weigh the words and actions of both parties to determine whether a clear repudiation was present, *Mountain State Constr. Co.*, ENGBCA 3549, 76-2 BCA ¶ 12,197 (the contracting officer's "defensive approach" in evaluating work accomplished was considered in deciding that the contract was improperly terminated); *Hubbard Trucking, Inc.*, PSBCA 3701, 04-2 BCA ¶ 32,667 (default termination for abandonment was upheld because the contractor failed to apply for a medical release, which was required under the contract).

c. *Examples of Anticipatory Repudiation*

Anticipatory repudiation is commonly found when a contractor clearly expresses its intention not to perform the contract or unequivocally states that it is unable to perform the work. It can also be found in actions indicating that the contractor is unable to perform.

(1) Express Refusal to Perform

The classic example of anticipatory repudiation occurs when a contractor expressly refuses to perform the work. Such an express repudiation has been found in *Betakut USA, Inc. v. General Servs. Admin.*, GSBCA 12512, 94-2 BCA ¶ 26,945 (refusal to supply items in excess of estimated quantity as required by contract); *Gerald M. Davy,* PSBCA 3270, 94-2 BCA ¶ 26,690 (refusal to perform followed by failure to appear on job); *Twigg Corp.*, NASABCA 62-0192, 93-1 BCA ¶ 25,318 (contractor refused to remove and replace concrete); *Cox & Palmer Constr. Corp.,* ASBCA 38739, 92-1 BCA ¶ 24,756 (contractor sent letter to its surety, with copies to the government, stating that it would leave the project and allow the surety to take over performance); *Interstate Indus., Inc.,* GSBCA 5252, 79-2 BCA ¶ 13,954 (repeated refusal to accept orders under requirements contract); *North Am., Ltd.*, ASBCA 22718, 79-2 BCA ¶ 13,894 (contractor abandoned work and telegraphed government "to take any action you deem necessary for operation of mess facilities"); *Big 3 Contracting Corp.*, ASBCA 20929, 79-1 BCA ¶ 13,601 (contractor left job, removed equipment, and stated it would resume performance only upon a condition contrary to contract requirements); *Sharjon, Inc.*, ASBCA 22954, 79-1 BCA ¶ 13,585 (contractor's contract manager, who had "full authority," stated that the work was being abandoned, equipment was removed, and no personnel were at the site); *Rex Conklin Reforestation,* AGBCA 76-155, 78-1 BCA ¶ 13,070 (following a unilateral bid mistake, contractor advised the COR that it would not perform and sent a mailgram stating, "We rejected the contract by phone and reassigned our crews"); *TS Reforestation Co.,* AGBCA 414, 76-1 BCA ¶ 11,780 (contractor's letter to contracting officer stated, "I have terminated the . . . contract"); *Wear Ever Shower Curtain Corp.,* GSBCA 4360, 76-1 BCA ¶ 11,636 (express refusal to perform following government refusal to increase contract price to compensate for the lifting of price controls); *Video Eng'g Co.*, DOTCAB 72-5, 72-1 BCA ¶ 9432 (contractor failed to qualify the bid "all or none," refused to accept single-item award, returned the purchase order, and denied the authority of the agent who signed the bid); *LTD Indus. Corp.*, ASBCA 16565, 72-1 BCA ¶ 9332, *recons. denied,* 72-2 BCA ¶ 9499 (refusal to perform following denial of relief under Pub. L. No. 85-804); and *Hawaii Fence & Iron Works,* ASBCA 15242, 71-1 BCA ¶ 8690 (contractor used abusive language to a government official, agreed that the contract should be cancelled, and stated it neither cared about nor wanted the work).

Anticipatory repudiation may be found if the contractor mistakenly believes it does not have to perform. See *EFG Assocs., Inc.,* ASBCA 50546, 01-1 BCA ¶ 31,324, in which a § 8(a) contractor's misinterpretation of a regulation, leading it to believe that its contract ended when the contractor was sold, was considered an anticipatory repudiation.

Anticipatory repudiation is commonly found when a contractor clearly expresses that it is not required to do the work, either by arguing that the contract was never formed or that it has ended. In *Integrated Sys. Group, Inc. v. Social Sec. Admin.*, GSBCA 14056-SSA, 98-2 BCA ¶ 29,848, the contractor asserted that it did not have to proceed because the contract was voidable because of a mistake in bid. The board disagreed and concluded that that did not justify failure to proceed. Such an express repudiation believing that the contractual obligations had ended has been found in *Betakut USA, Inc. v. General Servs. Admin.*, GSBCA 12512, 94-2 BCA ¶ 26,945 (refusal to supply items in excess of estimated quantity as required by contract).

Lack of an unequivocal refusal to perform was found in *McKenzie Marine Constr. Co.*, ENGBCA 3245, 74-2 BCA ¶ 10,673 (contractor's letter stated, "I have no moral or contractual obligation . . . to pursue . . . such an insane project," but the board found that government actions gave the contractor "reason to vent his frustrations"); *Michael J. Gotskind,* GSBCA 4999R, 78-1 BCA ¶ 13,144 (high bidder on surplus sale requested to withdraw bid but later asked to discuss the matter with the contracting officer); *Martin Suchan*, ASBCA 22521, 83-1 BCA ¶ 16,323 (statement that difficulty with suppliers would render contractor unable to "honor" prices in its bid). In *HBS Nat'l Corp. v. General Servs. Admin.*, GSBCA 14302, 98-2 BCA ¶ 29,935, the board held that a copy the contractor sent to the contracting officer of a draft letter required under the Worker Adjustment and Retraining Notification Act notifying its employees that it planned to discontinue performance and that the employees would be terminated, and a second letter the contractor sent to the contract administrator indicating that the contractor would soon request a "no cost" termination but would not leave the government without services or supplies, did not establish a positive, definite, unconditional, and unequivocal intent not to perform necessary to justify the default termination.

(2) Failure to Give Adequate Assurances

Failure to give adequate assurances after the government has issued a cure notice indicating that it has grounds to believe that the contractor will not complete the work as required can provide grounds for a default termination. See *Danzig v. AEC Corp.*, 224 F.3d 1333 (Fed. Cir. 2000), *cert. denied,* 532 U.S. 995 (2001), sustaining a default termination based on lack of adequate assurances and stating at 1337:

> The law applicable to a contractor's failure to provide assurances of timely completion is a branch of the law of anticipatory repudiation. See, e.g., *Discount Co.*, 554 F.2d at 441 (when the government was not assured of timely completion, the court could properly "rely upon cases involving abandoned or repudiated contracts"). At common law, anticipatory repudiation of a contract required an unambiguous and unequivocal statement that the obligor would not or could not perform the contract. See *Dingley v. Oler*, 117 U.S. 490, 503, 29 L. Ed. 984, 6 S. Ct. 850 (1886); *Cascade Pac. Int'l v. United States*, 773 F.2d 287, 293 (Fed. Cir. 1985). As the Restatement of Contracts has recognized, however, modern decisions do not limit anticipatory repudiation to cases of express and unequivocal repudiation of a contract. Instead, anticipatory repudiation includes cases in which reasonable grounds support the obligee's belief that the obligor will breach the contract. In that setting, the obligee "may demand adequate assurance of due performance" and if the obligor does not give such assurances, the obligee may treat the failure to do so as a repudiation of the contract. *Restatement, Second, Contracts* § 251 (1981). The Uniform Commercial Code has adopted a similar rule for contracts involving the sale of goods. See U.C.C. § 2-609.
>
> The law of government contracts has adopted that doctrine, expressing it as a requirement that the contractor give reasonable assurances of performance in response to a validly issued cure notice. See *Tubular Aircraft Prods., Inc. v. United States*, 23 Cont. Cas. Fed. (CCH) ¶ 81,327, at 86,619 (Ct. Cl. Trial Div. Nov. 29, 1976) (recommended decision) (citing the Restatement and stating that "parties are entitled to ask for reassurances when persons with whom they have contracted have by word or deed created uncertainty about their ability or intent to perform and they are entitled to treat the failure to provide such assurances as a repudiation of the contract"), *approved and op. adopted by court, id.* at 86,610, 213 Ct. Cl. 749 (1977); *National Union Fire Ins.*, 90-1 B.C.A. (CCH) P22,266, at 111,855, ASBCA No. 34744 (Aug. 23, 1989); *Salzburg Enters.*, 87-2 B.C.A. (CCH) ¶ 19,761, at 99,994, ASBCA No. 29509 (Mar. 30, 1987). That rule, as the Restatement explains, rests "on the principle that the parties to a contract look to actual performance 'and that a continuing sense of reliance and security that the promised performance will be forthcoming when due, is an important feature of the bargain.'" *Restatement, Second, Contracts* § 251 cmt. a (quoting U.C.C. § 2-609 cmt. 1).

See also *L&M Thomas Concrete Co.*, ASBCA 49198, 03-1 BCA ¶ 32,194, finding a valid termination for default because the contractor failed to provide adequate assurances, but not characterizing this as an anticipatory repudiation, and *NECCO, Inc.*, GSBCA 16354, 05-1 BCA ¶ 32,902, finding a valid termination for default when the contractor failed to provide adequate assurances, characterizing it as a failure to make progress. Compare *Omni Dev. Corp.*, AGBCA 97-203-1, 05-1 BCA ¶ 32,982, in which the board refused to find an anticipatory repudiation where the contractor's assurances were somewhat equivocal but stated that it would complete the contract on time.

(3) Express Statement of Inability to Perform

Anticipatory repudiation is also commonly found where a contractor has unequivocally stated that it cannot perform, *Nation-wide Reporting & Convention Coverage*, GSBCA 8309, 88-2 BCA ¶ 20,521. Often such statements of inability are coupled with other factors that further substantiate the finding of a repudiation. Some common examples of such factors are acts of abandonment, *Ortec Sys., Inc.*, ASBCA 43467, 92-2 BCA ¶ 20,521; or nonperformance and claims for payments or relief from matters as to which the contractor had assumed the risk. For cases finding anticipatory repudiation for stated inability to perform, see *Bendix Corp.*, GSBCA 4352, 77-2 BCA ¶ 12,656 (stated inability to meet accuracy requirements for oceanographic data system and request for specification waiver indicated inability to cure); *Comdata Sys., Inc.*, ASBCA 19893, 77-1 BCA ¶ 12,463 (inability to perform following explosion in plant unless extraordinary financial assistance was provided); *J.W. Bibb, Inc.*, ASBCA 19589, 76-2 BCA ¶ 12,135 (road construction contractor admitted performance could not be completed on time, requested the balance of contract work be deleted, and advised the government to send future communications to a law firm); *L & W Contracting*, AGBCA 416, 76-2 BCA ¶ 12,023, *recons. denied*, 76-2 BCA ¶ 12,165 (contractor's letters stated essential equipment was unobtainable absent government guarantee of payment to subcontractors); *B.F. Goodrich Co.*, ASBCA 19960, 76-2 BCA ¶ 12,105 (contractor claimed that the specifications for coated fabric tanks were beyond the state of the art and requested a convenience termination); *Jesse W. Wayne*, AGBCA 410, 75-2 BCA ¶ 11,394 (contractor letter stated in part, "I am not qualified to complete the job. I'm sorry it has to be this way."); *SRM Mfg. Co.*, IBCA 1032-4-74, 75-1 BCA ¶ 11,279 (due to rising materials costs, contractor stated performance was impossible absent 33 percent price increase); *R & O Indus., Inc.*, GSBCA 4094, 75-1 BCA ¶ 11,061 (two contractor letters requested immediate termination since no qualified supplier could be found); *National Cleaners & Laundry, Inc.*, ASBCA 16186, 74-2 BCA ¶ 10,978, *recons. denied*, 75-1 BCA ¶ 11,035 (stated inability to perform since IRS had seized plant and equipment); *National Farm Equip. Co.*, GSBCA 3833, 73-2 BCA ¶ 10,300 (stated inability to manufacture goods absent specification waiver); *Amexicana Corp.*, ASBCA 14417, 71-1 BCA ¶ 8886, *recons. denied*, 71-2 BCA ¶ 8990 (contractor advised that production facility would close absent progress payments that were specifically precluded by the IFB); *Hellmuth, Obata & Kassabaum, Inc.*, PSBCA 524, 73-1 BCA ¶ 9894 (contractor admitted inability to design a building that could be constructed within the cost limitations set by the contract); *Pacific Electro Dynamics, Inc.*, ASBCA 16805, 72-1 BCA ¶ 9380 (contractor admitted financial incapacity and sought no-cost termination); *Giannini-Voltex*, ASBCA 15077, 72-1 BCA ¶ 9199 (contractor admitted financial incapacity, stated intention to sell product line to another company, and failed to commit to a new delivery schedule); *Aireborne Sec., Inc.*, GSBCA 3333, 71-1 BCA ¶ 8872 (guard services contractor failed to provide performance bonds and insurance and to obtain security clearances, stated inability to perform, and returned contract documents to the government); *Sparkadyne, Inc.*, ASBCA 15162, 71-1 BCA ¶ 8854 (contractor admitted going out of business and gave the status of outstanding orders in order to assist the government to reprocure); *Hydro-Space Sys. Corp.*, ASBCA 15275, 71-1 BCA ¶ 8739 (contractor admitted it could not perform because of the government's "tight money" policy); *Clean Sweep, Inc.*, ENGBCA 2967, 71-1 BCA ¶ 8701 (contractor stopped work, removed equipment, and wrote a letter to the contracting officer expressly admitting inability to complete performance); *Mission Valve & Pump Co.*, ASBCA 13552, 69-2 BCA ¶ 8010 (contractor letter stated in part, "We regret we will be unable to furnish the valves on subject contract"); *Ringer Co.*, ASBCA 13654, 69-2 BCA ¶ 7938 (shirt manufacturer claimed inability to find a satisfactory subcontractor, stopped production, made a final shipment, returned necessary cloth to the government, and admitted being on the verge of bankruptcy); *Drillmation Co.*, ASBCA 12501, 69-1 BCA ¶ 7632 (stated inability to continue manufacture following denial of Pub. L. 85-804 relief for "grave error" in cost estimate); and *Bobco Mfg. Co.*, ASBCA 13430, 69-1 BCA ¶ 7537 (refusal to sign modification reflecting price increase granted under Pub. L. 85-804, refusal of no-cost settlement, and stated inability to continue).

Stated inability to perform may constitute a repudiation even where the statement is made by someone other than the contractor. See *Menches Tool & Die, Inc.*, ASBCA 21469, 78-1 BCA ¶ 13,167, where in response to the government's unilateral reestablishment of the due date, the contractor's attorney sent a letter stating, "this corporation is unable to produce the contract item." A carbon copy of the letter was sent to the contractor, who did not deny the attorney's authority until after a default termination was issued. Furthermore, repudiation by stated inability to perform may be found where the statements originate from a successor in interest to the contractor, *Aerospace Support Equip., Inc.*, ASBCA 13579, 71-1 BCA ¶ 8904 (stated inability to perform coupled with request for convenience termination or no-cost settlement).

No clear indication of inability to perform was found in *Production Serv. & Tech., Inc.*, ASBCA 53353, 02-2 BCA ¶ 32,026 (letter addressed difficulties being encountered but implied that contractor would continue performing); *Talano Transp.*, PSBCA 3812, 97-1 BCA ¶ 28,898 (contractor threatened to cease performance, but continued to perform); *Paul E. McCollum, Sr.*, ASBCA 20120, 77-1 BCA ¶ 12,271 (stated intent to file a claim under the Changes clause or an appeal under the Disputes clause); *Norfolk Air Conditioning Serv. & Equip. Corp.*, ASBCA 14080, 71-1 BCA ¶ 8617 (contractor data submission indicated nonspecification equipment would be provided and contractor requested an unwarranted equitable adjustment); *C.T.M. Co.*, ASBCA 7332, 65-1 BCA ¶ 4757, *recons. denied*, 65-2 BCA ¶ 5219 (contractor characterized "catch up" order as impossible but continued trying to perform); and *Denison Research Found.*, ASBCA 7653, 1963 BCA ¶ 3651 (contractor's statement that proceeding with a specification modification would be useless amounted to an "honest professional opinion expressed in an effort to obtain reconsideration").

(4) Actions Indicating Inability to Perform

There have been a number of cases indicating that a contractor may demonstrate, even unintentionally, that it is unable to perform and that such a demonstrated likelihood of inability to perform may amount to a repudiation. See, for example, *Pennsylvania Exch. Bank v. United States*, 145 Ct. Cl. 216, 170 F. Supp. 629 (1959) (contractor's assignment for the benefit of creditors constituted a total breach, since the contractor was disabled from performing); *Hampton Business Forms, Inc.*, GSBCA 4026, 75-2 BCA ¶ 11,532 (contractor required to supply 74,174 boxes of paper within one year, but by seventh month only 2,561 boxes were delivered, the facility was abandoned, and contractor failed to secure necessary machinery or supplies); *Wyodak Enters., Inc., dba Healthmart*, VABCA 3678, 95-1 BCA ¶ 27,493, (with eight months remaining on the contract, the contractor's president repudiated it by stating that he could not be in compliance even if the government gave him a year); *Atronix, Inc.*, ASBCA 16644, 72-2 BCA ¶ 9763 (contracting officer became aware that, in addition to passage of the due date without a conforming delivery, the contractor's plant had been padlocked due to an IRS lien); *Protective Coating Co.*, ENGBCA 3205, 72-1 BCA ¶ 9431 (contractor returned rented equipment that was essential to performance and walked off the job); *Simplex Mfg. Co.*, ASBCA 13897, 71-1 BCA ¶ 8814 (following a conference concerning failure to make progress, contractor reduced the work force and cut labor and material expenditures); *Transdyne Corp.*, ASBCA 12834, 69-1 BCA ¶ 7615 (following waiver of due date and a government request for a revised delivery schedule, contractor responded that performance would resume four months after approval of its request for relief under Pub. L. 85-804). However, a contrary result was reached in *Reliable Bay Ridge Car Serv., Inc.*, VACAB 1127, 75-1 BCA ¶ 11,276 (even though only two days remained until performance was to commence, there was conflicting evidence whether the contractor could clear its vehicles through local licensing officials); *Donald R. Schlueter*, GSBCA 3232, 71-1 BCA ¶ 8700 (contractor filed bankruptcy petition and failed to commence work as promised, but bankruptcy trustee stated that contractor had necessary equipment and capability to perform); *Therm-Air Mfg. Co.*, NASABCA 180-2, 82-2 BCA ¶ 15,881 (letter informing contracting officer of suspension of manufacturing operations did not constitute grounds for default where contractor was "actively trying to resolve its financial problems . . . so that it could resume normal manufacturing operations"); and *Milo Werner Co.*, IBCA 1202-7-78, 82-1 BCA ¶ 15,698 (contractor repeatedly expressed intention to complete work, left some equipment at the work site, and sought to obtain additional funding).

d. Retraction of Repudiation

Under *Restatement, Second, Contracts* § 256 and U.C.C. § 2-611, a repudiation may be retracted before the injured party materially changes its position or makes it known that it considers the repudiation to be final. In *Nation-wide Reporting & Convention Coverage*, GSBCA 8309, 88-2 BCA ¶ 20,521, the contractor's unequivocal repudiation could not later be retracted, since the government considered the repudiation to be final. Thus, if the contracting officer has issued a termination notice following the repudiation, it may not be retracted, *What Mac Contractors, Inc.*, GSBCA 4766, 78-2 BCA ¶ 13,279. In *Gerald M. Davy*, PSBCA 3270, 94-2 BCA ¶ 26,690, the contractor's attempted retraction was too late because the government had already contracted with an emergency replacement.

6. *Subcontractor Termination*

A contractor is responsible for contract performance and thus is subject to default termination if its subcontractor fails to perform or deliver or fails to proceed and endangers timely performance. If a subcontractor is in default, the government and contractor can agree to substitute alternative performance in lieu of terminating the contractor for default. In *McLain Plumbing & Elec. Serv. v. United States*, 30 Fed. Cl. 70 (1993), the contractor claimed that the government improperly ordered the default termination of a subcontractor during the performance of a contract. This claim arose after the defaulted subcontractor prevailed against the contractor in a contract arbitration proceeding for improper default termination. The court held that the contractor's claim was barred by accord and satisfaction and that there was no basis for economic duress, stating at 82:

> [T]he [contractor] contends that it had no choice but to accept the terms of the proposed alternative to default termination. The result, the [contractor] states, constituted economic duress.
>
> In contrast, the [government] contends that the United States sought no remedies other than those conferred under the terms of the contract. Thus, upon untimely performance, the [government] cites the right to terminate under the Default clause of the contract. The [government] points out: "At worst, the VA merely insisted upon its rights under the contract and reminded [the contractor] of the consequences of nonperformance. Such conduct is neither offensive not illegal." As such, the [government] argues that the offer to consider an alternative performance, in the form of a recovery schedule and upon the replacement of the subcontractor, constituted nothing more than an attempt at settlement. Further, as the [contractor] purportedly presents no evidence of coercion, the [government] denies any showing of economic duress. Based on the evidence presented, this Court finds the [government's] arguments persuasive.

B. Waiver of the Right to Terminate

If the government does not exercise its right to terminate for default within a reasonable time, and the contractor relies to its detriment on such forbearance by continuing with performance, the government will be held to have waived the right to terminate, *De Vito v. United States*, 188 Ct. Cl. 979, 413 F.2d 1147 (1969); *S.T. Research Corp.*, ASBCA 39600, 92-2 BCA ¶ 24,838; *Motorola Computer Sys., Inc.*, ASBCA 26794, 87-3 BCA ¶ 20,032. In *De Vito*, the court explained this rule at 990-91:

> The Government is habitually lenient in granting reasonable extensions of time for contract performance, for it is more interested in production than in litigation. Moreover, default terminations—as a species of forfeiture—are strictly construed. *Murphy, et al., v. United States*, 164 Ct. Cl. 332 (1964); *J.D. Hedin Construction Co. v. United States*, 187 Ct. Cl. 45, 57, 408 F.2d 424, 431 (1969).
>
> Where the Government elects to permit a delinquent contractor to continue performance past a due date, it surrenders its alternative and inconsistent right under the Default clause to terminate, assuming the contractor has not abandoned performance and a reasonable time has expired for a termination notice to be given. This is popularly if inaccurately referred to as a "waiver" of the right to terminate. 5 Williston, *Contracts, Third Ed.*, § 683. The election is sometimes express, but more often is to be inferred from the conduct of the non-defaulting party. McBride and Wachtel, *Government Contracts*, § 31.170. The determination of what conduct constitutes such an election is more conjectural than to prescribe the proper method of effecting a valid termination once the election has occurred.
>
> * * *
>
> The necessary elements of an election by the non-defaulting party to waive default in delivery under a contract are (1) failure to terminate within a reasonable time after the default under circumstances indicating forbearance, and (2) reliance by the contractor on the failure to terminate and continued performance by him under the contract, with the government's knowledge and implied or express consent.

No waiver was found were the government terminated the contractor when it failed to perform and subsequently terminated the surety when it failed to perform in a timely manner with a replacement contractor, *Florida Dep't of Ins. v. United States,* 81 F.3d 1093 (Fed. Cir. 1996). The court found no waiver because the Government had continually reminded the surety that time was of the essence by pointing out that liquidated damages were continuing to accrue

The government may forbear for a reasonable period of time after the default occurs before taking action, *Eraklis Eraklidis,* ASBCA 40110, 91-3 BCA ¶ 24,188; *Kit Pack Co.*, ASBCA 33135, 89-3 BCA ¶ 22,151.

1. The Basic Concept

Use of the term "waiver" to describe the facts that operate to divest the government of its right to terminate creates some confusion. Waiver suggests the voluntary relinquishment of a vested right, which government officials are prohibited from doing, 47 Comp. Gen. 170 (B-160886) (1967). In *General Equip. Co.*, ASBCA 6415, 1964 BCA ¶ 4166, *recons. denied*, 1964 BCA ¶ 4307, the board stated at 20,273:

> There was no waiver of the extended delivery schedule in this case because there was no voluntary and intentional relinquishment by the Government of the right to terminate for the failure to deliver and there was no consideration for any such

relinquishment. Such matters are necessary to find waiver. *U.S. v. Chichester*, 312 F.2d 275 (1963) upon review of *The Aircraftsmen Company*, ASBCA 3592 et al., 26 March 1958, 58-1 BCA ¶ 1667.

Contrast this view with U.C.C. § 1-107, which permits waiver without consideration if evidenced by a signed writing delivered to the other party.

In *De Vito*, the court preferred to use the term "election." In addition, the court found that contractor reliance on government action or inaction was an indispensable element of the "waiver" or "election" theory. Thus, the government's waiver or election is binding, not because of consideration, but on principles of fair dealing or estoppel. See U.C.C. § 2-209 for a similar rule.

Waiver has been a more significant issue in supply contracts than in construction contracts, since the supply contractor that continues performance while in default frequently incurs costs that will not be recovered if the government later properly terminates for default. See *Acme Process Equip. Co. v. United States*, 171 Ct. Cl. 324, 347 F.2d 509 (1965), *rev'd on other grounds*, 385 U.S. 138 (1966), in which the court observed that the government "cannot allow an unwary contractor to continue performance and thus incur large expenses, all of which the Government will refuse to reimburse if and when it decides to cancel the contract on the ground of the violation." However, in construction contracts the contractor will be reimbursed for acceptable work performed at the site even if the contract is terminated. For this reason, continued performance of a construction contract will not ordinarily support a claim of waiver or election.

a. *Construction Contracts*

The inapplicability of the waiver rule to construction contracts was explained in *Brent L. Sellick*, ASBCA 21869, 78-2 BCA ¶ 13,510, as follows at 66,194-95:

> The essence of the waiver of the delivery date doctrine as explained in *DeVito*, *supra*, is that through Government actions or inactions, and contractor reliance thereon, the Government is estopped from enforcing a specified contractual delivery date. However, as explained by this Board in recent cases, this estoppel rationale is not normally applicable where the contract contains the usual provisions applicable to construction contracts entitling the contractor to payment for work performed subsequent to the specified completion date but also entitling the Government to recover liquidated damages for late completion. With such provisions in the contract, detrimental reliance on the contractor's part cannot be found merely from a period of Government forbearance coupled with continued contractor performance in reliance thereon. *Olson Plumbing & Heating Co.*, ASBCA Nos. 17965, 18411, 75-1 BCA ¶ 11,203; *Fraenkische Parkettverlegung R.*, ASBCA 18453, 75-2 BCA ¶ 11,388; *Joseph Morton Company, Inc.*, ASBCA 19793, 78-1 BCA ¶ 13,173. Moreover, with these provisions in the contract Government encouragement to expedite completion during a forbearance period should not be

> interpreted as a disestablishment of the contractually-prescribed completion date absent further manifestation by the Government that it no longer considered that date to be enforceable. Such a disestablishment was indeed found in *Corway, Inc.*, ASBCA 20683, 77-1 BCA ¶ 12,357, where the Government neither mentioned nor assessed liquidated damages and otherwise manifested lack of concern with the contractor's late completion. Under those circumstances, the *DeVito* doctrine was invoked with recognition that the case was unusual.

See also *Arens Corp.,* ASBCA 50289, 02-1 BCA ¶ 31,671, rejecting the application of the doctrine of waiver to a construction contract where there had been a 102-day delay in terminating the contract because the contract was for construction work and the government notified the contractor it was not waiving its rights.

There are a few construction cases that accept the waiver rationale. See, for example, *Nisei Constr. Co.*, ASBCA 51464, 99-2 BCA ¶ 30,448, in which the board accepted the limited application of *De Vito* in construction cases. It noted that a construction case would have to be "so unusual" to fall within *De Vito.* One such unusual case is *B. V. Constr., Inc.,* ASBCA 47766, 04-1 BCA ¶ 32,604, finding a waiver when the government allowed the contractor to perform for 20 months after the completion date without expressing concern. See also *Jess Howard Elec. Co.*, ASBCA 44437, 96-2 BCA 28,345, finding an actual waiver when the government offered a later schedule if the contractor met specified conditions. In *American Sheet Metal Corp. v. General Servs. Admin.*, GSBCA 14068, 99-1 BCA ¶ 30,329, the government nullified a prior completion date and failed to establish a new one. The board considered this to be "tantamount to a waiver." See also *AFV Enters., Inc.*, PSBCA 2691, 01-1 BCA ¶ 31,388 (board analyzed a construction case as though the doctrine were applicable, but did not find waiver).

A number of cases have held that there can be no waiver in a construction contract if the contractor is told that the government will continue to assess liquidated damages, *Olson Plumbing & Heating Co. v. United States*, 221 Ct. Cl. 197, 602 F.2d 950 (1979); *Indemnity Ins. Co. of N. Am. v. United States,* 14 Cl. Ct. 219 (1988); *LaCoste Builders, Inc.*, ASBCA 29884, 88-1 BCA ¶ 20,360; *Delta Constr. Co.,* ASBCA 42453, 96-1 BCA ¶ 28, *recons. granted in part & denied in part*, 96-1 BCA P28,251, *aff'd*, 114 F.3d 1206 (Fed. Cir. 1997); *Nagy Enters*., ASBCA 48815, 98-1 BCA ¶ 29,695. In *Olson Plumbing & Heating* the court stated at 204:

> Where the right to terminate has been expressly reserved or when liquidated damages have been imposed by the [government], the [contractor] has a heavier burden of proving that the right to terminate for failure to deliver on time has been waived.

In contrast, waiver of the completion date has been found based on the failure of the contracting officer to either mention or assess liquidated damages, *Overhead Elec. Co.*, ASBCA 25656, 85-2 BCA ¶ 18,026.

The default termination of a contract to construct and lease a post office was overturned even though the contractor had admittedly failed to submit required bonds. Although the contract called for the submission of bonds within 20 days of acceptance of the lease, the Postal Service did not demand the bonds until more than a year later and never informed the contractor of the penal amount it would require on the bonds, *Upwest Corp.,* PSBCA 4281, 01-2 BCA ¶ 31,474.

b. Waiver Prior to a Due Date

Although most cases of waiver involve government actions after the delivery date has passed, a waiver may result from government action prior to the due date evidencing that time is not of the essence. See *Delta Marine, Inc.*, ASBCA 39649, 93-3 BCA ¶ 26,164, where a default based on the contractor's failure to complete work items within the time specified in a cure notice was not proper, because the contracting officer had required the contractor to perform work before the contractually required date; *Lanzen Fabricating, Inc.*, ASBCA 40328, 93-3 BCA ¶ 26,079, in which default termination was improper because there was no schedule against which to measure progress; and *Baifield Indus., Div. of A-T-O, Inc.*, ASBCA 14582, 72-2 BCA ¶ 9676, where government waiver of certain performance requirements, which had resulted in production delays five days prior to the due date, was found to have "manifested a Government lack of concern" with the original delivery schedule. See also *Acudata Sys., Inc.*, DOTCAB 1198, 84-1 BCA ¶ 17,046, where the Government's waiver of the due date for presentation of the preproduction prototype also constituted waiver of the production schedule. Accord, *Heat Exchangers, Inc.*, ASBCA 9349, 1964 BCA ¶ 4381; *American Sheet Metal Corp. v. General Servs. Admin.*, GSBCA 14066, 99-1 BCA ¶ 30,329.

In *Polyurethane Prods. Corp.*, ASBCA 42251, 96-1 BCA ¶ 28,154, the board stated at 140,544:

> It is undisputed that the delivery schedule set by Modification A000001 was disestablished and no new delivery schedule was ever established, thereby foreclosing this default termination resting on either of those subparagraphs [(a)(1)(i) and (a)(1)(ii)]. See *Lanzen Fabricating, Inc.*, ASBCA No. 40328, 93-3 BCA ¶ 26,079 at 129,609; *Motorola Computer Systems, Inc.,* ASBCA No. 26794, 87-3 BCA ¶ 20,032 at 101,416; *Electronics of Austin*, ASBCA No. 24912, 86-3 BCA ¶ 19,307 at 97,631.

Similarly, in *Freedom, NY, Inc.*, ASBCA 35671, 96-2 BCA ¶ 28,328, *decision corrected*, 96-2 BCA ¶ 28,502, the board overturned the termination for default for failure to make progress because of waiver, stating at 141,478:

> [T]he Government's right to terminate for a contractor's "fail[ure] to make progress" requires the existence of a valid delivery schedule against which the contractor's progress can properly be measured.

2. Reasonable Forbearance

Failure to terminate immediately when the right to terminate accrues does not constitute a waiver, *Frank A. Pelliccia v. United States*, 208 Ct. Cl. 278, 525 F.2d 1035 (1975). The contracting officer has a reasonable period to investigate the facts and determine what course of action will be in the best interests of the government, *Eraklis Eraklidis*, ASBCA 40110, 91-3 BCA ¶ 24,188. During this period, which is called the forbearance period, the government may terminate at any time, without prior notice, *Raytheon Serv. Co.*, ASBCA 14746, 70-2 BCA ¶ 8390; *Lapp Insulator Co.*, ASBCA 13303, 70-1 BCA ¶ 8219, *recons. denied*, 70-2 BCA ¶ 8471. The determination of what length of time constitutes a reasonable forbearance period depends on the facts and circumstances of each case, *H.N. Bailey & Assocs. v. United States*, 196 Ct. Cl. 156, 449 F.2d 387 (1971). In *Westinghouse Elec. Corp.*, ASBCA 20306, 76-1 BCA ¶ 11,883, it was observed that there is no clear demarcation between reasonable forbearance and waiver.

If the contractor is incurring costs in continued efforts to perform, the government has an obligation to act expeditiously in making a decision. In contrast, if the contractor has ceased performance, the need for rapid action is not as great since the contractor is not prejudiced by the delay. Cases that have found the delay to be a reasonable forbearance period include *Scandia Mfg. Co.*, ASBCA 20888, 76-2 BCA ¶ 11,949 (seven-day delay between due date and termination); *Aargus Poly Bag*, GSBCA 4314, 76-2 BCA ¶ 11,927 (delays of 25 and 35 days between due date and termination); *Cosmos Eng'g, Inc.*, ASBCA 19780, 77-2 BCA ¶ 12,713 (three-day delay between due date and termination); *Fairfield Scientific Corp.*, ASBCA 21152, 78-1 BCA ¶ 12,869, *aff'd*, 228 Ct. Cl. 264, 655 F.2d 1062 (1981) (five-day delay "patently reasonable"); and *Honig Indus. Diamond Wheel, Inc.*, ASBCA 46875, 96-1 BCA ¶ 28,028, *aff'd*, 116 F.3d 1496 (Fed. Cir. 1997) (government reasonably took 19 days to issue show cause letter and two months to terminate).

In *Amecom Div., Litton Sys., Inc.*, ASBCA 19687, 77-1 BCA ¶ 12,329, *recons. denied*, 77-2 BCA ¶ 12,554, a 50-day delay was found unreasonable. The board stated that the reasonable forbearance period was confined to the single day on which the right to terminate accrued because "[at] that point in time, the Navy had all the information necessary to make the decision." Also, there were prior government actions indicating that time was no longer of the essence. On reconsideration, and in response to the government's argument that the board's decision would have "detrimental impact on the procurement community because it eliminates the normal forbearance period," the board responded that decisions on forbearance turn on their own facts and are precedent only when applied to similar fact situations.

In *Precision Dynamics, Inc.*, ASBCA 41360, 97-1 BCA ¶ 28,722, a waiver was found when the contracting officer left the contract "in a delinquent status" and delayed for more than 70 days before terminating the contract while the contractor expended time and money continuing to perform the contract. See also *Ralbo, Inc.,* ASBCA 49541, 99-2 BCA ¶ 30,438, denying summary judgment for the government because the contractor alleged that it had been allowed to perform for three years after the government had knowledge of the erroneous certification on which the termination was based. Compare *A.R. Sales Co. v. United States,* 51 Fed. Cl. 370 (2002), where, despite a failure to terminate the contract until five months after the contract completion date, and not establishing a new completion date, no indications of waiver were found because the government repeatedly asked for a revised completion date to determine when or if the project could be completed and the contractor could not show any reliance on the government's forbearance.

3. Government Election to Continue Performance

One indispensable element of waiver is that the government indicates a willingness to have the contractor continue performance. This willingness, also often referred to as an election to continue, can be manifested in a number of ways, ranging from unreasonable delay in terminating to express statements or acts of the government.

a. Unreasonable Delay

Unreasonable delay in terminating is a frequent basis for finding an election, *H.N. Bailey & Assocs. v. United States*, 196 Ct. Cl. 166, 449 F.2d 376 (1971). In *Westinghouse Elec. Corp.*, ASBCA 20306, 76-1 BCA ¶ 11,883, the board found that the government's silence for a 57-day period following receipt of the contractor's letter indicating that it was continuing performance constituted an election, stating at 59,964:

> Insofar as the record shows, [the government] did nothing for another 57 days from the date of the [contractor's] letters. [The government's] delay, for which it has furnished no explanation, deprived [the contractor] of the opportunity to stop work and to reduce the loss which it will sustain if the termination for default is permitted to stand. The unexplained delay was unreasonably long. Absent an acceptable explanation for its silence and inaction during the 57-day period, [the government] may not, in light of [the contractor's] continued efforts to perform, be heard to argue that such silence and inaction does not constitute an election to permit continued performance.

See also *Prestex, Inc.*, ASBCA 21284, 81-1 BCA ¶ 14,882, *recons. denied*, 81-2 BCA ¶ 15,397 (waiver based on 60-day delay in taking action following show cause letter); *Beta Eng'g, Inc.,* ASBCA 53570, 02-2 BCA ¶ 31,879, *recons. denied,* 02-2 BCA ¶ 31,970 (inaction following time extension request waives government's right to default terminate supply contract).

b. Acts of the Government

For cases finding an election to continue based on the words or actions of the government, see *S.T. Research Corp.*, ASBCA 39600, 92-2 BCA ¶ 24,838 (government waived right to terminate where the contracting officer told the contractor to continue and proposed a new delivery schedule); *Marci Enters., Inc.*, GSBCA 12197, 94-1 BCA ¶ 26,563 (government waived delivery date by telling the contractor to delay shipment for inspection and continuing to encourage the contractor to correct deficiencies); *Vista Scientific Corp.*, ASBCA 25974, 87-1 BCA ¶ 19,603 (waiver by supporting contractor's efforts to fulfill contract after due date); *Sidney G. Kornegay & Florence Kornegay*, ASBCA 18454, 76-1 BCA ¶ 11,744 (issuance of speed-up orders); *Aargus Poly Bag*, GSBCA 4314, 76-2 BCA ¶ 11,927 (acceptance of late partial delivery); *Automated Servs., Inc.*, GSBCA EEOC-2, 81-2 BCA ¶ 15,303 (acceptance of deliverable items after due date and meetings with contractor to discuss establishing revised delivery schedule); *Menches Tool & Die, Inc.*, ASBCA 19255, 74-2 BCA ¶ 10,969 (failure to respond to contractor's excuses for delay and government assistance in expediting delivery); *Acorn Specialty & Supply Co.*, GSBCA 4367, 76-2 BCA ¶ 12,086 (conduct implying late deliveries would be permitted combined with partial acceptance); *Flexonics Div., Universal Oil Prods. Co.*, ASBCA 18485, 74-1 BCA ¶ 10,525 (acceptance of late deliveries); *Baifield Indus., Div. of A-T-O, Inc.*, ASBCA 14582, 72-2 BCA ¶ 9676 (urging corrective action to meet specifications); *Lowell Monument Co.*, VACAB 1111, 75-1 BCA ¶ 11,341, *recons. denied*, 75-2 BCA ¶ 11,460 (late deliveries continually accepted); *Clavier Corp.*, ASBCA 19144, 75-1 BCA ¶ 11,241 (government letters encouraged continued performance but disclaimed any intent to waive); *Wayne Group*, HUDBCA 75-24, 77-2 BCA ¶ 12,727 (encouragement of continued performance); *Corway, Inc.*, ASBCA 20683, 77-1 BCA ¶ 12,357 (encouragement of continued performance); *Milo Werner Co.*, IBCA 1202-7-78, 82-1 BCA ¶ 15,698 (letter encouraging "early resumption and completion of remaining work"); *Cecile Indus., Inc.*, ASBCA 24600, 83-2 BCA ¶ 16,842 (two-month delay where there was history of government acceptance of late deliveries); and *Divecon Servs., LP v. Department of Commerce*, GSBCA 15997, 04-2 BCA ¶ 32,656 (encouraging contractor to make expensive repairs and keep its personnel on stand-by).

In *Action Support Servs. Corp.*, ASBCA 46524, 00-1 BCA ¶ 30,701, the board found that the government had waived delivery dates by allowing the contractor to work through several missed deadlines and continuing to pay progress payments. Although the government reserved its right to terminate for default in a show cause letter, the government also gave signals that it would not insist on the contractor's meeting the delivery dates and knew the contractor was continuing to work and incur costs. In *SITCO Servs. & Marine, Inc. v. United States,* 41 Fed. Cl. 196 (1998), the government waived its rights after working with the contractor for over seven months after the contract completion date. In *Radar Devices, Inc.,* ASBCA 43912, 99-1 BCA ¶ 30,223, waiver was found when, although a show cause notice stated that any acceptance of delinquent goods would be solely to mitigate damages, the contracting officer orally advised the contractor that delivery would not be considered delinquent if the goods were delivered within the 10-day period covered by the notice, and informal departures from contract terms were commonplace between the parties. See also *Ming C. Phua,* PSBCA 4180, 00-1 BCA ¶

30,872, where the contracting officer informed the contractor that if he did not provide a satisfactory vehicle by January 16, 1998, his contract would be suspended until he did so. On January 20, 1998, in reliance on this notice, the contractor was en route to present a vehicle for inspection when it was terminated. The board found that the government waived its right to default terminate until the contracting officer imposed a new deadline. Compare *Nisei Constr. Co.*, ASBCA 51464, 99-2 BCA ¶ 30,448, holding that the government did not waive its right to terminate for default by encouraging the contractor to continue performance past the scheduled completion date because there was no indication that the government considered the completion date unenforceable.

For cases finding that acts of contract administration did not amount to an election, see *Fairfield Scientific Corp.*, ASBCA 21152, 78-1 BCA ¶ 12,869, *aff'd,* 228 Ct. Cl. 264, 655 F.2d 1062 (1981) (willingness to consider revised delivery schedule for $500 price reduction); *Allied Paint Mfg. Co.*, GSBCA 1488, 67-1 BCA ¶ 6387 (conference to establish present status and future production plans); and *Precision Prods., Inc.,* ASBCA 14284, 70-2 BCA ¶ 8447 (inspection of late delivery was only to determine conformity; conforming goods would have been accepted only to mitigate contractor damages). In *H.N. Bailey & Assocs. v. United States,* 196 Ct. Cl. 166, 449 F.2d 376 (1971), the court explained that acts of assistance and encouragement do not always indicate an election to continue, stating at 181-82:

> In sum, we find ample support in the record for the conclusion of the ASBCA that [the government's] actions, quite obviously influenced by [the contractor's] optimistic projections, did not amount to encouragement or inducement to the defaulting contractor to continue production efforts beyond default. In light of [the government's] extensive experience in Government procuring and in the absence of convincing evidence, it cannot be presumed that [the government] waived its right to terminate for default, even impliedly, in a situation where the procured item is urgently needed as part of a vital and high integrity national program, and the contractor has yet to demonstrate satisfactorily that it is capable of successfully producing the article. If we are to penalize [the government] for displaying a benevolent attitude toward the defaulting contractor (a posture, incidentally, which the Government does not frequently assume), we must be prepared for the predictable and undesirable consequence of discouraging [the government] from again rendering any assistance, voluntary or otherwise, beyond that specifically required by the contract, for fear of waiving an essential contractual right.

4. *Contractor Reliance*

Contractor reliance is an indispensable element for the waiver or election to be binding on the government. See *A.B.G. Instrument & Eng'g, Inc. v. United States*, 219 Ct. Cl. 381, 593 F.2d 394 (1979), stating at 398:

> The *De Vito* decision has no application to the facts of this case. That decision addresses itself only to the situation where the Government's forbearance from pressing its right to demand timely delivery is coupled with continued perfor-

> mance on the contractor's part. In these so-called "waiver-after-breach" situations, it is the contractor's reliance that counts rather than the Government's failure to have insisted upon strict adherence to the terms of the delivery schedule. There was no reliance in this case. The Government's final show cause letter was issued on September 17, 1969; as of October 6, 1969, the contractor's production had ceased altogether and was never thereafter revived.

Further, the contractor's reliance must be induced by the government. See the trial judge's recommended decision, adopted by the court in *Northrop Carolina, Inc. v. United States*, 213 Ct. Cl. 670, 553 F.2d 105 (1977), finding no inducement by the government since the contractor made a "management decision" to continue the work. There was no showing that the contractor was acting under any governmental influence in deciding to continue production.

The reliance must also be reasonable, *General Prods. Corp.*, ASBCA 16658, 72-2 BCA ¶ 9629. In that case, the contractor's reliance was unreasonable and not justified since the contractor knew that the administrative contracting officer, who had agreed to recommend acceptance of its schedule revision proposal, was not authorized to accept the proposal. See also *Meyer Labs., Inc.*, ASBCA 17169, 73-1 BCA ¶ 9841 (reliance not reasonable since performance after due date was premised on obtaining a specification waiver), and *Chester Morton Elecs.*, ASBCA 14904, 72-1 BCA ¶ 9185 (experienced contractor with knowledge that all other extensions had been formally approved through established procedure not justified in proceeding). Compare, however, *ITT Def. Communications Div.*, ASBCA 12964, 69-1 BCA ¶ 7720, finding the contractor's reliance reasonable where the government's show cause letter indicating that a time extension was pending was considered by the board to be an invitation to negotiate.

Merely incurring additional costs will not constitute reliance unless they are incurred in connection with continued performance or some other activity caused by the government's action. See *Olson Plumbing & Heating Co. v. United States*, 221 Ct. Cl. 197, 602 F.2d 950 (1979), in which the court stated at 205:

> After January 11, 1972, [the contractor] never resumed performance under the contract with the exception of minor housekeeping activities and the joint testing project which ended on May 5, 1972. In *Acme*, the court held it would be unfair to permit the contractor to continue incurring performance costs for which the Government would not make reimbursement. Housekeeping costs which merely attempt to preserve the status quo and are unrelated to continued performance, and which are not caused by the Government's failure or by a condition excusing the delay, are properly placed on [the contractor]. In order to have the costs, incurred after the passage of the due date, considered as a factor weighing in favor of a finding of a waiver, it must be shown that the expenses contributed to performance.

For cases finding sufficient justifiable reliance to support a waiver or election, see *Park Indus., Inc.*, ASBCA 13218, 69-1 BCA ¶ 7508 (contractor leased new machines, hired new employees, and built a new plant); *Nanofast, Inc.*, ASBCA 12545, 69-1 BCA ¶ 7566 (attempts to correct defects); *Legion Utensils Co.*, GSBCA 2732, 69-1 BCA ¶ 7745, *recons. denied*, 69-2 BCA ¶ 7896 (continued production albeit at lower rate); *Alton Iron Works, Inc.*, GSBCA 2596, 69-2 BCA ¶ 7841, *recons. denied*, 70-1 BCA ¶ 8202 (continued performance); *Al Greene, Inc.*, ASBCA 15225, 71-1 BCA ¶ 8789 (contractor made commitments for labor and material); *ISC/Phonplex Corp., Instrument Sys. Corp.*, ASBCA 16668, 73-2 BCA ¶ 10,361 (continued performance); *Menches Tool & Die, Inc.*, ASBCA 19255, 74-2 BCA ¶ 10,969 (production continued); *Hamill Mfg. Co.*, ASBCA 20926, 78-1 BCA ¶ 13,088 (continued production, negotiation with suppliers, and receipt of material); *American Trans-Coil Corp.*, ASBCA 22233, 78-1 BCA ¶ 13,157 (production continued after due date); *Prestex, Inc.*, ASBCA 21284, 81-2 BCA ¶ 15,397 (continued production efforts by subcontractors); and *Pacific Coast Welding & Mach., Inc.*, ASBCA 26105, 83-1 BCA ¶ 16,398 (subcontractor performance).

The best evidence of reliance is complete or substantial performance. In *Trident Indus. Prods. Corp.,* DOTBCA 2807, 98-1 BCA ¶ 29,619, the contractor failed to ship fabrics by the contract deadline but tendered substantially all of the items months later, and the government failed to terminate the contract and establish a new delivery schedule, thereby waiving the original delivery schedule. See also *Cadillac Gage Co.*, ASBCA 18416, 75-1 BCA ¶ 11,210 (completed most of work following due date).

Insufficient evidence of justifiable reliance was found in *Doyle Shirt Mfg. Corp. v. United States*, 199 Ct. Cl. 150, 462 F.2d 1150 (1972) (all work was complete and contractor was just seeking specification waiver); *Lieco., Inc.*, ASBCA 13681, 69-1 BCA ¶ 7489 (contractor was out of business); *Temco, Inc.*, ASBCA 13907, 71-1 BCA ¶ 8683 (increased production was in contractor's own best interest to amortize costs and avoid loss on follow-on contract); *Ace Elecs. Assocs., Inc.*, ASBCA 14245, 71-1 BCA ¶ 8729 (only contractor efforts occurred after default termination); *KDI Precision Prods., Inc.*, ASBCA 17382, 73-2 BCA ¶ 10,231 (only action involved seeking Pub. L. No. 85-804 relief or no-cost settlement); *Crawford Dev. & Mfg. Co.*, ASBCA 17565, 74-2 BCA ¶ 10,660 (no reliance because contractor recouped its continuing expenditures on unterminated portion of partially terminated contract); *Westholt Mfg., Inc.*, ASBCA 19519, 75-1 BCA ¶ 11,196 (production stopped before due date and not resumed); *CTS Knights, Inc.*, ASBCA 20028, 75-1 BCA ¶ 11,259 (no expenditures during 86-day period following due date); *Belmont Instrument Corp.*, ASBCA 18861, 77-1 BCA ¶ 12,332 (expenditure of $1,168.80 did not reach level of detriment amounting to reliance); *Electro-Methods, Inc.*, ASBCA 50215, 99-1 BCA ¶ 30,230 (absent clear proof that the government knew of the contractor's continuing performance, 7 percent progress during forbearance period "not sufficiently material" to establish detrimental reliance); *E.O. Mfg. Co.*, ASBCA 52120, 01-2 BCA ¶ 31,587 (total lack of action by contractor during the government's eight-month silence concerning the contractor's failure to meet delivery date); and *Comspace Corp.,* DOTBCA 4011, 02-1 BCA ¶ 31,792 (no evidence of continued performance after delivery date).

5. *Reservation of Right to Terminate After Completion Date*

The government often attempts to preclude a finding of waiver or election by expressly reserving its right to terminate during the period of reasonable forbearance. See, for example, the show cause letter in FAR 49.607, which includes a provision stating:

> Any assistance given to you on this contract or any acceptance by the Government of delinquent goods or services will be solely for the purpose of mitigating damages, and it is not the intention of the Government to condone any delinquency or to waive any rights the Government has under the contract.

Such a reservation will be considered with all the other facts and circumstances of the case to determine whether a waiver has occurred, *Olson Plumbing & Heating Co. v. United States*, 221 Ct. Cl. 197, 602 F.2d 950 (1979); *Engineering Design & Dev.*, ASBCA 22067, 77-2 BCA ¶ 12,774; *Belmont Instrument Corp.*, ASBCA 18861, 77-1 BCA ¶ 12,332; *Obrisco Elecs., Inc.*, ASBCA 18533, 76-2 BCA ¶ 12,049; *Echo Science Corp.*, NASABCA 671-9, 72-2 BCA ¶ 9755. See *Roberts Supply Co.*, ASBCA 14775, 70-2 BCA ¶ 8522, in which the board found that the government made it "unmistakably clear" that it did not wish to waive its right to terminate. See also *Camel Mfg. Co.*, ASBCA 41231, 93-1 BCA ¶ 25,470, in which the board found that the government had reserved its right to terminate for default while attempting to negotiate a revised schedule after giving a cure notice. However, if the government's actions indicate an election to continue, the mere presence of a reservation will not preclude a finding of election or waiver. In *Flintkote Co.*, GSBCA 4223, 76-2 BCA ¶ 12,031, the contract contained a supplemental clause to the Default clause. This clause, prescribed for use with General Services Administration contracts, stated:

> (b) Waiver of Delivery Schedule
>
> None of the following shall be regarded as an extension, waiver, or abandonment of the delivery schedule or a waiver of the Government's right to terminate for default: (i) the delay by the Government in terminating for default; (ii) acceptance of delinquent deliveries; and (iii) acceptance or approval of samples submitted either after default in delivery or in insufficient time for the contractor to meet the delivery schedule.
>
> Any assistance rendered to the Contractor on this contract or acceptance by the Government of delinquent goods or services hereunder will be solely for the purpose of mitigating damages, and is not to be construed as an intention of the Government to condone any delinquency, or as a waiver of any rights the Government may have under subject contract.

The board concluded that this provision did not preclude it from finding a waiver, stating at 57,746:

> Government counsel points out on brief that this Board has not heretofore interpreted the Non-waiver clause. However, it argues that since the contract contains an "*express* statement of an intent to forbear, as long as the Government's right to terminate for default was exercised within a *reasonable* period of time, it should be sustained." He further argues that where there is an "express intent to forbear, the delivery schedules can only be waived by an *express* waiver," and that in the absence of such waiver, "the conduct of the parties alone is insufficient to overcome the specific language of a contract clause."
>
> In arguing for a "reasonable period of time" to decide upon a course of action following delivery failure, we think that counsel for the Government recognizes the broad implication of this provision and the Government's failure to define a reasonable period of delay within this provision. Taken literally, the provision permits the Government to extend the forbearance period in perpetuity. It eliminates the doctrine of waiver and renders meaningless a long-standing line of Board and Court decisions which charge the Government with the inherent obligation to exercise its discretionary right to terminate or not to terminate, within a reasonable time. It discourages contractors from continuing performance and incurring costs, for there is no way to determine the course which the Government might eventually settle upon. The delay in termination would delay reprocurement, resulting in almost certain increased repurchase costs. It is an attempt to contract away nonfeasance. Thus, notwithstanding the language of clause 11(b)(i) we find that the Government does not have the right to forbear for an indeterminable period.

Accord, *Flexonics Div., Universal Oil Prods. Co.*, ASBCA 18485, 74-1 BCA ¶ 10,525, dealing with similar language in a show cause letter.

In *Abcon Assocs., Inc. v. United States*, 44 Fed. Cl. 625 (1999), the court upheld the government's avoidance of a waiver when the government notified the contractor, after there had been a failure of performance, that nothing the government does may be construed as a waiver of its rights to terminate for default because it was exercising its rights of forbearance. Thus, the 70-month delay between issuance of the show cause notice and actual termination and the contractor's continued work in reliance on the government's forbearance did not amount to waiver; the court noting that in construction contracts continued performance alone will not ordinarily support a claim of waiver.

6. Reestablishment of the Right to Terminate After Waiver

Following waiver, the right to terminate may be reestablished either by giving the contractor notice of a new date or through a bilateral agreement, *Lumen, Inc.*, ASBCA 6431, 61-2 BCA ¶ 3210; *Aviation Tech., Inc.*, ASBCA 48063, 00-2 BCA ¶ 31,046. A new delivery date established by the parties is presumed to be reasonable, *Trans World Optics, Inc.*, ASBCA 35976, 89-3 BCA ¶ 21,895. However, in order to hold the contractor to the new bilaterally established date, it must be shown that there has in fact been such an agreement. For example, in *Bailey Specialized Bldgs., Inc. v. United States*, 186 Ct. Cl. 71, 404 F.2d 355 (1968), the contractor's revised delivery schedule was accepted by the government. The schedule included a date when a preproduction model would be available for inspection and also listed later dates for delivery. The inspection revealed defects, and the government terminated for default. In reversing the termination, the court held that the only mutually agreed-upon dates in the revised schedule were those relating to final products and that the setting of inspection dates did not mean that the contractor had agreed to deliver goods without defect on those occasions.

In reaching a new schedule by agreement, the government is apparently entitled to use hard bargaining, short of duress. In S*immonds Precision Prods., Inc. v. United States*, 212 Ct. Cl. 305, 546 F.2d 886 (1976), the contractor agreed to a new date and the insertion of a liquidated damages clause into the contract after the contracting officer had threatened a default termination following what the contractor claimed was a waiver. The court stated at 313:

> [I]n his negotiations, the PCO was not seeking to re-impose the original delivery schedules which, [the contractor] says, the Government had previously "waived." Rather, the PCO sought only to establish a specific new schedule for deliveries. From the facts known to him, a two to three-month time extension seemed adequate and reasonable, and he threatened default if some such reasonable schedule were not forthwith submitted to him by the contractor. In so doing, the contracting officer appears merely to have followed the guidelines developed by this court concerning waiver by the Government of its right to terminate a contract where the contractor has failed to meet the contract delivery date.

When the government unilaterally attempts to reestablish the due date after waiver, it must establish a specific date, *International Tel. & Tel. Corp. v. United States*, 206 Ct. Cl. 37, 509 F.2d 541 (1975); *Sun Cal., Inc. v. United States*, 21 Cl. Ct. 31 (1990). In *International*, following waiver of initial delivery dates, the government attempted to obtain a bilateral agreement setting the new delivery date as February 9, 1968, but because of performance problems the contractor declined to accept. Upon learning of the government's decision to terminate for default, the contractor arranged a meeting on February 15 and informed the government that the system was ready for shipment. At that time the government presented the contractor with a letter containing a blank space for inserting a final test date in February. The contractor refused to sign this letter, but the parties agreed to resume tests on February 19. When the February 19 tests failed, the government terminated for default, contending that February 19 had been unilaterally set as the final delivery date. The court ruled that the February 15 letter containing a blank space for the final test date did not constitute an appropriate notice of a unilateral new delivery date because it failed to set a specific time for performance as required by *De Vito*. The court also found that the agreement to resume testing on February 19 did not establish that as the date upon which the government could default terminate for failure to make delivery. The issuance of a cure notice or a show cause notice is not sufficient, *Lanzen Fabrication, Inc.*, ASBCA 40328, 93-3 BCA ¶ 26,079 (issuance of a show cause letter is "practically useless" where the delivery schedule has been "disestablished").

The reestablished date must be reasonable in view of the performance capabilities of the contractor at the time the notice is given, *McDonnell Douglas Corp. v. United States*, 182 F.3d 1319 (Fed. Cir. 1999), *cert denied*, 529 U.S. 1097 (2000), *on remand*, 50 Fed. Cl. 311 (2001), *aff'd in part & rev'd in part,* 323 F.3d 1006 (Fed. Cir. 2003). In the latter decision, the Federal Circuit rejected the contractor's contention that the standard for reasonableness was objective, ruling that the date would be reasonable if the contracting officer subjectively believed it was reasonable based on the available evidence at the time it was reestablished. The court stated at 1019:

> If the government opts to act unilaterally, the new date that it sets must be "both reasonable and specific from the standpoint of the performance capabilities of the contractor at the time the notice is given." [*DeVito v. United States*, 413 F.2d 1147, 1154-55, 188 Ct. Cl. 979 (Ct. Cl. 1969)], at 1154. The reasonableness of the action turns on what the government "knew or should have known" at the time it imposed the new schedule. *ITT Corp. v. United States*, 509 F.2d 541, 549-50, 206 Ct. Cl. 37 (Ct. Cl. 1975).
>
> Beyond this standard of reasonableness, our precedent does not impose the additional burdens that the Contractors would impose on the government when the United States unilaterally imposes a new completion date. Contrary to what [the contractor] contends, our precedent neither requires a determination of "what work remained to be completed as of the date the unilateral schedule was issued," nor does it necessitate an inquiry into "how long it likely would have taken the contractor to complete the remaining work, given its actual production capabilities as of the date the schedule was issued." Although those inquiries may be appropriate in certain situations, they are not requisite underpinnings for the DeVito reasonableness determination. Similarly, we reject the "objective achievability" paradigm suggested by the Contractors as not rooted in our precedent. Were we to adopt this new criterion, we would depart from our case law by requiring more than reasonableness; we would compel the government to have perfect prescience and be infallible in its decision. Because such an expectation is unachievable, the touchstone of this inquiry must remain grounded on reasonableness based on what the government knew or should have known when it adopted the unilateral schedule.

Earlier cases had appeared to require that the reestablished date be objectively reasonable, *Oklahoma Aerotronics, Inc.*, ASBCA 25605, 87-2 BCA ¶ 19,917; *Vista Scientific Corp.*, ASBCA 25974, 87-1 BCA ¶ 19,603; *Spasors Elecs. Corp.*, ASBCA 12877, 70-1 BCA ¶ 8119, *recons. denied*, 70-1 BCA ¶ 8346. A revised delivery schedule suggested by the contractor will probably be considered prima facie evidence of reasonableness, *Mark Assocs., Inc.*, ASBCA 12272, 67-1 BCA ¶ 6313, no matter how ill-considered the schedule may have been, *Tampa Brass & Aluminum Corp.*, ASBCA 41314, 92-2 BCA ¶ 24,865. See *National Bag Corp.*, GSBCA 4331, 77-2 BCA ¶ 12,664 (new time reasonable since performance problems had been solved, the date was based on contractor's estimate, and it allowed one-half the original performance time to complete one-third of the work); *Sidney G. Kornegay & Florence Kornegay*, ASBCA 18454, 76-1 BCA ¶ 11,744 (unilaterally imposed date, although based on prior estimates by the contractor, was unreasonable where it failed to take account of intervening severe weather); and *Aargus Poly Bag*, GSBCA 4314, 76-2 BCA ¶ 11,927 (new dates were reasonable because they were based on contractor's estimates and contractor did not complain when new dates were set). See also *Rowe, Inc. v. General Servs. Admin.,* GSBCA 14211, 01-2 BCA ¶ 31,630 (although the government overlooked the contractor's failure to meet two previously established delivery dates, the contracting officer reasonably established a new delivery date by allowing the extra 15 days requested by the contractor, and adding another 12 days to ensure flexibility in the schedule).

Termination following waiver without a reestablished delivery date will not be improper in the case of an anticipatory repudiation by the contractor. See *Herlo Corp.*, ASBCA 19198, 77-2 BCA ¶ 12,820, in which the board stated at 62,409:

> An extended examination of the waiver issue would avail the [contractor] nothing because, even if we were to conclude there had been a waiver of delivery schedule, no reestablishment of a reasonable delivery date, and consequently that the Government lost its right to terminate for failure to delivery on time, it would not affect the Government's right to terminate the contract for "anticipatory breach." The contractor's inability to perform, amounting to an anticipatory breach, is a separate basis for terminating a contract for default.

The tender of delivery following a waiver of the contract delivery date establishes a new and enforceable delivery date. In *Louisiana Lamps & Shades*, ASBCA 45294, 95-1 BCA ¶ 27,577, even if the government had waived the completion date of a contract for floor lights, it was justified in terminating the contract for default because the lights delivered did not substantially comply with the contract specifications.

III. THE TERMINATION DECISION

The fact that the government has the legal right to terminate is only one factor considered in making the business decision to terminate. In determining whether to terminate for default, the contracting officer must first decide if the contractor is in a default status without excuse, and second, whether it is in the government's interest to terminate the contract despite the contractor's being in default. The crucial issue is how best to complete the work called for by the contract. In many instances, evaluation of the situation indicates that working with the delinquent contractor is the most promising means of completing the work. In other instances, an immediate default termination followed by a quick selection of a new contractor may appear to be the most expedient course of action. The government never has to terminate for default, even if the contractor has been placed on the debarment list, FAR 9.405-

1(a). But see *Ohio Casualty Ins. Co. v. United States,* 12 Cl. Ct. 590 (1987), where the government was found liable because it had waited too long to terminate a contractor and in so doing had failed in its equitable obligations to the surety.

Default termination may also be improper if the government has already exercised other contractual rights that solve the problem. For example, the agency improperly terminated a lease for failure to maintain the property in accordance with the lease when the agency already had exercised its right to make repairs at the lessor's expense, *Oscar Narvaez Venegas*, ASBCA 49291, 98-1 BCA ¶ 29,690.

It is well established that "A default termination is a drastic sanction . . . which should be imposed (or sustained) only for good grounds and on solid evidence," *J. D. Hedin Constr. Co. v. United States*, 187 Ct. Cl. 45, 408 F.2d 424 (1969). The government bears the burden to prove a default termination justified. The contracting officer's default decision must not be arbitrary or capricious or an abuse of discretion, *Darwin Constr. Co. v. United States,* 811 F. 2d 593 (Fed. Cir. 1987). The default clause does not require the government to terminate a contract for default but merely gives it the discretion to do so, *Schlesinger v. United States,* 182 Ct. Cl. 571, 390 F.2d 702 (1968). That discretion must be exercised reasonably. In order to prevail, the government must show that the termination for default was correct procedurally, that it was not an abuse of discretion, and that it was proper substantively.

A. Discretionary Decision

This decision is highly discretionary, based on the business judgment of the contracting officer and any advisors in the procuring agency, *Mega Constr. Co. v. United States*, 29 Fed. Cl. 396 (1993). In *Schlesinger v. United States,* 182 Ct. Cl. 571, 390 F.2d 702 (1968), the Court of Claims found a default termination invalid because the government had not exercised discretion in making the decision to terminate. The Navy had terminated in response to pressure from a congressional committee without considering the impact on the contractor or the government. The court found that the contractor was technically in default at the time of the termination, but stated at 581-84:

> Our difficulty is that the default article does not *require* the Government to terminate on finding a bare default but merely gives the procuring agency discretion to do so, and that discretion was not exercised here by the Navy. The existence of discretion is undeniable. The clause says that "the Government *may* . . . terminate" (emphasis added), not "shall" or "must". We have recognized that a decision to terminate for convenience is rooted in discretion (*Commercial Cable Co. v. United States*, 170 Ct. Cl. 813, 821 (1965); *John Reiner & Co. v. United States*, 163 Ct. Cl. 381, 390, 325 F.2d 438, 442-43 (1963), *cert. denied*, 377 U.S. 931 (1964)), and though the factors the Government will wish to consider may be different when a default is involved there is no reason to read the default article, contrary to its literal terms and the accepted practice, as compelling termination. We are certain that there have been a great many instances in which the Government has not termi-

> nated a contractor in technical default, but has granted an extension or waived the noncompliance. In this very case the [government], as the Board found, excused the earlier non-delivery on May 31st which was, of course, also a default. Our ruling today is not new. More than ten years ago, the court specified that procurement officials had to exercise judgment in terminating an agreement for default and were not automatons. *John A. Johnson Contracting Corp. v. United States*, 132 Ct. Cl. 645, 658-60, 132 F. Supp. 698, 704-05 (1955).
>
> We hold, too, that this discretion was never exercised but the Navy simply surrendered its power of choice. This is so clear from the Board's record that we are warranted in reaching the conclusion despite the Board's failure to consider the point. Although the Congressional communication does not appear to have suggested that the [contractor's] contract be canceled without consideration of [its] rights or situation, or even that it be terminated for default rather than for convenience (which would give the contractor [its] reasonable expenses to date), the Navy acted as if it had no option but to terminate for default (barring all compensation) once the mere fact of non-delivery was found. The Navy did not consider whether an extension should be granted or the June 30th default waived (as that of May 31st had been) so as to allow delivery in July. The guillotine was dropped immediately after the non-delivery of June 30th, and was strongly contemplated even before that day had been reached or passed.

The court in *Schlesinger* restated the rule that in terminating a contract for default, government procurement officials shall not act as "automatons." Rather, the party with default-termination power shall make a "judgment as to the merits of the case before terminating a contract for default."

The *Schlesinger* rule was limited in *McDonnell Douglas Corp. v. United States,* 182 F.3d 1319 (Fed. Cir. 1999), *cert denied,* 529 U.S. 1097 (2000), *on remand*, 50 Fed. Cl. 311 (2001), *aff'd in part & rev'd in part,* 323 F.3d 1006 (Fed. Cir. 2003), where the contracting officer had terminated for default shortly after the Secretary of Defense refused to continue funding of a major weapon system. The court, in its 1999 decision, reversed the decision of the Court of Federal Claims that no discretion had been exercised, stating at 1326:

> Properly understood, then, *Schlesinger* and its progeny merely stand for the proposition that a termination for default that is unrelated to contract performance is arbitrary and capricious, and thus an abuse of the contracting officer's discretion. This proposition itself is but part of the well established law governing abuse of discretion by a contracting official. See, e.g., *United States Fidelity & Guaranty Co. v. United States*, 230 Ct. Cl. 355, 676 F.2d 622, 630 (Ct. Cl. 1982) (listing four factors to be used in determining if conduct by a government official is arbitrary and capricious: (1) evidence of subjective bad faith on the part of the government official, (2) whether there is a reasonable, contract-related basis for the official's decision, (3) the amount of discretion given to the official, and (4) whether the official violated an applicable statute or regulation).

1. Person Exercising Discretion

The court in *Schlesinger* indicated that the person exercising discretion to terminate did not necessarily have to be the contracting officer, stating at 584:

> We do not put our decision on the failure of the contracting officer to exercise his own judgment. This agreement gave the default-termination power to "the Government" and did not single out the contracting officer as the official to decide that particular question. But the record affirmatively shows that nobody in the Navy, neither the contracting officer nor his superiors, exercised the discretion they possessed under the article. [The contractor's] status of technical default served only as a useful pretext for the taking of action felt to be necessary on other grounds unrelated to the [contractor's] performance or the propriety of an extension of time.

However, since the termination notice is described as a final decision under the Disputes clause, FAR 49.402-3(g)(5) and (7), it is generally assumed that discretion must be exercised by the contracting officer issuing the termination notice. See *Fairfield Scientific Corp. v. United States*, 222 Ct. Cl. 167, 611 F.2d 854 (1979), stating at 181-82:

> The default clause does not say that the Government "shall" or "must" terminate the contract in the event of default, only that the Government "may" terminate it. Not only is the contracting officer to consider whether or not the default is excusable, but the regulations require him to consider at least seven factors in addition to the default in deciding whether or not to terminate the contract. "The existence of discretion is undeniable." *Schlesinger v. United States*, 182 Ct. Cl. 571, 581, 390 F.2d 702, 707 (1968). If the contracting officer was improperly influenced by [the contractor's] competitor or by anyone else to terminate the contract for default rather than to exercise his own independent judgment in the light of the factors set out in the regulations, it would represent an abdication rather than an exercise of his discretion.

Fairfield Scientific appears to assume that a contracting officer is required to make the decision to terminate. This question has not been authoritatively decided. One decision has held that the decision to terminate for default need not be a "personal decision" of the contracting officer so long as there was not a complete abdication of discretion, *Square Constr. Co. & LaFera Contracting Co.*, ENGBCA 3494, 76-1 BCA ¶ 11,747. In *Novelty Prods. Co.*, ASBCA 21077, 78-1 BCA ¶ 12,989, a termination decision was made despite a recommendation from the administrative contracting officer to negotiate a new delivery schedule based on the contractor's progress. The board found that the contracting officer who terminated the contract did not give any weight to this recommendation and did not bring it to the attention of the Director of the Defense Logistics Agency, who approved the termination. Nevertheless, the board upheld the default, stating that there is "no requirement that the contracting officer must adopt the ACO's recommendations favorable to the contractor." In any event, the contracting officer is entitled to receive advice from others. See the trial judge's recommended decision, 22 CCF ¶ 80,535, adopted by the court in *Northrop Carolina, Inc. v. United States*, 213 Ct. Cl. 670, 553 F.2d 105 (1977), stating at 85,756:

> The contracting officer (J.C. Darcy) responsible for [the contractor's] default termination testified at the Board hearing. His testimony establishes that the decision to terminate [the contractor's] contract for default was his independent decision based on the failure of [the contractor] to deliver the badly needed flares in a timely fashion. His judgment in this regard involved a review of pertinent documentation and receipt of advice from his subordinate supportive personnel, as well as from a Contract Review Board. He recognized that termination of a contract for default required a high degree of judgment and maturity, and the tenor of his testimony reflected an awareness that a default termination was a drastic sanction. See *J.D. Hedin Constr. Co. v. United States*, 187 Ct. Cl. 45, 57, 408 F.2d 424, 431 (1969). On this record, there is no question but that the contracting officer exercised his independent discretion in terminating [the contractor's] contract for default.
>
> [The contractor's] claim of lack of discretion on the part of the contracting officer rests primarily on the following assertion. [The contractor] argues that Darcy had not conferred with a representative of [the contractor] for a period of almost 2 months prior to default. This is immaterial since representatives of Darcy, including William C. Schreffler, a management and administrative contracting officer on [the contractor's] contract and a subordinate of Darcy, had conferred with [the contractor's] representatives during the pertinent period. Plaintiff complains because Darcy did not participate in the deliberations of the Contract Review Board. This, too, is immaterial. More importantly, Darcy was not a member of this Board. This Board submitted recommendations to Darcy relative to proposed default actions, which recommendations could be accepted or rejected by him. Finally, [the contractor] points to the fact that Darcy was not present at the December 17, 1970, meeting. While [the contractor] alleges that it requested that he be at this conference, it cites no record reference in support thereof. In any event, Schreffler was present at this meeting and [the contractor's] position was fully set forth in writing by [the contractor's] president and made available to and reviewed by Darcy before he reached his decision on the matter. As a result, his unavailability at this meeting was of no importance. In sum, these contentions do not establish in any way that the terminating contracting officer's decision failed to rest on the exercise by him of his discretion.

See also *McDonald Welding & Mach. Co.*, ASBCA 36284, 94-3 BCA ¶ 27,181 (procurement contracting officer made the decision which was "concurred in" by a board of review). However, in *Dulles Networking Assocs., Inc.,* VABCA 6077, 00-1 BCA ¶ 30,775, the termination notice was issued by someone other than the contracting officer. Rather than overturn the termination, the board held it had no jurisdiction absent a contracting officer decision.

In *PLB Grain Storage Corp. v. Glickman*, 113 F.3d 1257 (Fed. Cir. 1997), in a nonprecedential decision, the court held that, even though other government officials had instructed the contracting officer to terminate the contract for default, the contracting officer was the final decision maker and had exercised independent, personal judgment. The court did not discuss *Nuclear Research Corp. v. United States*, 814 F.2d 647 (Fed. Cir. 1987), in which the court stated that the contractor had failed to show that the contracting officer's superiors had directed him to terminate, implying that such a direction would have made the termination improper. In *Larry J. Miller*, PSBCA 3632, 95-1 BCA ¶ 27,448, any representations by postal inspectors to a contractor that he would not be fired if he cooperated and told the truth did not preclude a default termination, because the contract authorized termination for mistreatment of mail and the postal inspectors lacked authority to commit the contracting officer to refrain from acting on information of a contract violation. See also *Fraya, S.E.*, ASBCA 52222, 02-2 BCA ¶ 31,975.

In *Industrial Design Labs., Inc.*, ASBCA 20369, 78-1 BCA ¶ 12,945, the termination was found proper since there was no evidence that the termination was due to any influence outside the procuring agency or that the termination was based on grounds other than the contractor's default.

2. Factors to Be Considered

There is considerable guidance, both in the FAR and the case law, on the factors that must be considered in making the decision to terminate for default.

a. FAR Factors

FAR 49.402-3 states:

> (f) The contracting officer shall consider the following factors in determining whether to terminate a contract for default:
>
> > (1) The terms of the contract and applicable laws and regulations.
> >
> > (2) The specific failure of the contractor and the excuses for the failure.
> >
> > (3) The availability of the supplies or services from other sources.
> >
> > (4) The urgency of the need for the supplies or services and the period of time required to obtain them from other sources, as compared with the time delivery could be obtained from the delinquent contractor.
> >
> > (5) The degree of essentiality of the contractor in the Government acquisition program and the effect of a termination for default upon the contractor's capability as a supplier under other contracts.
> >
> > (6) The effect of a termination for default on the ability of the contractor to liquidate guaranteed loans, progress payments, or advance payments.
> >
> > (7) Any other pertinent facts and circumstances.

* * *

> (j) If the contracting officer determines before issuing the termination notice that the failure to perform is excusable, the contract shall not be terminated for default. If termination is in the Government's interest, the contracting officer may terminate the contract for the convenience of the Government.
>
> (k) If the contracting officer has not been able to determine, before issuance of the notice of termination whether the contractor's failure to perform is excusable, the contracting officer shall make a written decision on that point as soon as practicable after issuance of the notice of termination. The decision shall be delivered promptly to the contractor with a notification that the contractor has the right to appeal as specified in the Disputes clause.

In *DCX, Inc. v. Perry,* 79 F.3d 132 (Fed. Cir. 1996), the court held that while compliance or noncompliance with FAR 49.402-3(f) may aid a board or court in determining whether a contracting officer has abused his discretion in terminating a contract for default, the factors "are not prerequisites to a valid termination," and do not confer rights on a contractor. See also *International Elecs. Corp.*, ASBCA 18934, 76-1 BCA ¶ 11,817, *recons. denied*, 76-2 BCA ¶ 11,943, *rev'd on other grounds*, 227 Ct. Cl. 208, 646 F.2d 496 (1981), in which the board stated that there was no requirement for the government to prove that each and every factor in DAR 8-602.3 (the predecessor to FAR 49.402-3(f)) was considered before terminating. Thus, there is doubt as to what evidence is necessary to establish discretion or lack thereof. Not every provision must be cited in the default termination, *White Buffalo Constr. Co.*, AGBCA 90-133-1, 93-3 BCA ¶ 26,236. In *Phoenix Petroleum Co.*, ASBCA 42763, 94-1 BCA ¶ 26,537, the board stated that failure to consider one or more of the factors stated in FAR 49.402-3(f) does not render the default improper. Accord, *Walsky Constr. Co.*, ASBCA 41541, 94-2 BCA ¶ 26,698; *AIW-Alton, Inc.*, ASBCA 45032, 96-1 BCA ¶ 28,232. In *LaFayatte Coal Co.*, ASBCA 32174, 89-3 BCA ¶ 21,963, the board stated that the failure to consider one or more of these factors was "not an automatic admission to a termination for convenience." Therefore, despite the mandatory terms of FAR 49.402-3(f), the government's failure to comply with the FAR requirement does not automatically invalidate a termination for default.

After *DCX v. Perry,* challenges to default terminations based on claims of abuse of discretion by the contracting officer by failing to consider all of the factors in FAR 49.402-3(b) have had little success. See *Double B Enters., Inc.,* ASBCA 52010, 01-1 BCA ¶ 31,396; *Imperial Props. Constr., Inc.,* ASBCA 49899, 01-1 BCA ¶ 31,382; *Morganti Nat'l, Inc. v. United States*, 49 Fed. Cl. 110 (2001), *aff'd*, 36 Fed. Appx. 452 (Fed. Cir. 2002); *Nisei Constr. Co.*, ASBCA 51464, 99-2 BCA ¶ 30,448; and *Imperial Properties/Constr., Inc.,* ASBCA 49899, 01-1 BCA ¶ 31,382.

b. Other Relevant Considerations

The FAR factors in no way limit the contracting officer. The contracting officer can move beyond the FAR and focus on the totality of the circumstances, *Jamco Constructors, Inc.*, VABCA 3271, 94-1 BCA ¶ 26,405, *recons. denied*, 94-2 BCA ¶ 26,792. In *Jamco*, the board stated at 131,361:

> The exercise of discretion involves more that a *pro forma* check off of factors drawn from FAR 49.402-3(f). It presupposes an active and reasoned consideration of available and sometimes contradictory information. Various factors must be evaluated and the totality of circumstances weighed by the Contracting Officer in arriving at a decision which "has the most serious consequences for a contractor." *Executive Elevator Service*, VABCA 2152, 87-2 BCA ¶ 19,849 at 100,438.

The board concluded that a contracting officer abused his discretion in terminating a contract for default when he failed to analyze independently the input of others. See *L & H Constr. Co.*, ASBCA 43833, 97-1 BCA ¶ 28,766 (termination decision was based on materially erroneous information regarding the contractor's culpability for delay and the labor and time required to complete the work); *CJP Contractors, Inc. v. United States,* 45 Fed. Cl. 343 (1999) (termination decision based on incorrect understanding of the remaining work and the time left for completion). Compare *Philadelphia Regent Builders, Inc.*, VACAB 1179, 79-1 BCA ¶ 13,856 (termination of "8(a) minority contractor" proper since decision made only after contractor was irretrievably in default and Veterans Administration and Small Business Administration had made every proper effort to assist contractor with financial problems); and *SCM Corp.*, ASBCA 19941, 75-2 BCA ¶ 11,508 (termination proper since contracting officer considered that convenience termination would be costly, contractor was in default, and government no longer needed supplies).

Default terminations are improper and, therefore overturned, when contractors demonstrate that, for example, the government had not adequately considered schedule extensions and concurrent delays, *SAE/Americon-Mid Atl., Inc. v. General Servs. Admin.,* GSBCA 12294, 98-2 BCA ¶ 30,084; and when the government's specifications were defective, *ABS Baumashinenvertieb GmbH,* ASBCA 48207, 00-2 BCA ¶ 31,090. In *SAE/Americon-Mid Atl.,* the board noted that the termination notice was "terse and gives short shrift to the many pending claims filed by SAE for delay and extra work." In the circumstances, where the contracting officer only visited the site a few times each month, the board was not persuaded that the termination was a "product of the careful assessment of the facts and circumstances contemplated by applicable regulation and the guidance of [applicable case law]." In *American Sheet Metal Corp. v. General Servs. Admin.*, GSBCA 14066, 99-1 BCA ¶ 30,329, the default termination was also wrongful because the government terminated in the absence of a clear overall completion date before the time expired in the cure notice. Given that the contractor had significantly accelerated its efforts and the potential costs and disruption of bringing on a reprocurement contractor to complete a roof that was almost finished were substantial, the board held that the government should at least have waited until the end of the cure period before terminating.

c. *Alternatives*

FAR 49.402-4 specifies alternative courses of action that may be followed by the contracting officer in lieu of terminating for default:

> Procedure in lieu of termination for default.
>
> The following courses of action, among others, are available to the contracting officer in lieu of termination for default when in the Government's interest:
>
> > (a) Permit the contractor, the surety, or the guarantor, to continue performance of the contract under a revised delivery schedule.
> >
> > (b) Permit the contractor to continue performance of the contract by means of a subcontract or other business arrangement with an acceptable third party, provided the rights of the Government are adequately preserved.
> >
> > (c) If the requirement for the supplies and services in the contract no longer exists, and the contractor is not liable to the Government for damages as provided in 49.402-7, execute a no-cost termination settlement agreement using the formats in 49.603-6 and 49.603-7 as a guide.

(1) Convenience Termination

Although termination for convenience is neither expressly authorized nor proscribed by the regulations or standard default clauses as an alternative to a termination for default, the previously quoted language of the Court of Claims in *Schlesinger v. United States*, 182 Ct. Cl. 571, 390 F.2d 702 (1968), stressing the discretionary nature of the decision to default terminate, arguably authorizes the contracting officer to terminate for convenience instead of default where a contractor is inexcusably in default. However, the Armed Services Board has stated that the regulations prohibit the contracting officer from terminating for convenience where the right to terminate for default exists. In *Artisan Elecs. Corp.*, ASBCA 14154, 73-1 BCA ¶ 9807, *aff'd*, 205 Ct. Cl. 126, 449 F.2d 606 (1974), the board stated at 45,824:

> Except for no cost cancellations, where the right to terminate for default exists, the contracting officer not only may, but, under the cited regulations of his agency, must terminate for default if he is to terminate at all. Under such circumstances he may not terminate for the convenience of the Government. This has not always been the policy.
>
> * * *

> But, as the current regulations show, . . . while individual viewpoints on the merits of the policy may differ, neither a contracting officer nor this Board may, in accordance with those regulations, relieve a contractor in default by means of a convenience termination.

Accord, *Bendix Corp.*, ASBCA 23081, 79-1 BCA ¶ 13,717; *Trinity Resources*, AGBCA 80-187-1, 83-1 BCA ¶ 16,505.

On the other hand, it has been held that if the contracting officer does in fact issue a termination for convenience, the government may not change it to a termination for default, even though circumstances justifying default termination are present. See *Roged Inc.*, ASBCA 20702, 76-2 BCA ¶ 12,018, in which the board stated at 57,653-54:

> Presumably to rectify its procedural misstep, [the government] subsequently issued a notice of termination conversion whereby the initial convenience termination would be converted to a default termination. [The government] argued the original termination constituted a waiver of the Government's rights without legal consideration, thus it was an act beyond the scope of the contracting officer's authority and not binding on the Government. However, in those cases where the propriety of attempted conversions of prior terminations for convenience to default terminations have been judicially or administratively reviewed, it has been held the Government may not change a convenience termination to one for default. (*Richardson Camera Co., Inc.*, ASBCA 11930, 68-1 BCA ¶ 6990; *Line Construction Co. v. United States*, 109 Ct. Cl. 154 (1947); *American Kal Enterprises*, GSBCA 4460, 76-1 BCA ¶ 11,749.) We see no reason in this appeal to depart from those holdings, particularly since it is not even alleged the PCO did not intend to issue the termination for convenience in the form and at the time she did, nor has it been suggested the [contractor] in any way misled the PCO into issuing the convenience termination.

(2) Negotiating a Schedule Extension

If continued performance by the defaulting contractor is desired, a revised delivery schedule should be negotiated with the contractor to clearly establish the contractor's obligation and to avoid the complications that would arise if a waiver was subsequently found. The preferred method of establishing a new schedule would be the negotiation of a time extension supported by consideration from the contractor, *Comp-Con Tech. & Mfg., Inc.*, ASBCA 21150, 78-1 BCA ¶ 13,152. However, the government takes the risk that its expression of willingness to extend the delivery schedule for consideration could be construed as an election to continue, *Traders Distrib. Co.*, GSBCA 2718, 69-1 BCA ¶ 7463, *recons. denied*, 69-1 BCA ¶ 7677. Further, the demand for consideration, coupled with a threat of default termination, could be grounds for a finding of duress if the government does not in fact have the right to terminate. See *Urban Plumbing & Heating Co. v. United States*, 187 Ct. Cl. 15, 408 F.2d 382 (1969), *cert. denied*, 398 U.S. 958 (1970).

If the contractor refuses to furnish consideration for a delivery extension, the contracting officer apparently can establish a new delivery schedule without consideration. See *Free-Flow Packaging Corp.*, GSBCA 3992, 75-1 BCA ¶ 11,332, stating at 53,960:

> It is a well-established principle in Government contract law that while the Default clause gives the Government the absolute right to terminate the contract upon failure of the contractor to make timely delivery of the procurement item, the clause permits the Contracting Officer to exercise his right to use discretion in deciding whether to immediately terminate the contract, or any part thereof, or, among other things, to allow the contractor to continue performance under a new delivery schedule. No new consideration is necessary to support what the Default clause already permits the Contracting Officer to do. It is also a principle of law that a waiver of delivery date can be inferred from the Government's behavior after the contractor fails to make delivery as promised. Acceptance of a new delivery date can be established by agreement of the parties or by acts of the Government. Here again, acceptance by the Government can be implied from the circumstances.

See also *Gillet Mach. Rebuilders, Inc.*, ASBCA 28341, 89-3 BCA ¶ 22,021. Care should be taken to protect the government's rights to damages if the contracting officer grants a schedule extension without consideration.

3. *Improper Decision Making*

Exercise of discretion appears to require that the decision must not be arbitrary, must be based on a judgment on the merits, must demonstrate a consideration of available alternatives, and must be free from outside influence. In *Switlik Parachute Co. v. United States*, 216 Ct. Cl. 362, 573 F.2d 1228 (1978), the court held that the decision to terminate was fully justified and in no way arbitrary or capricious where the government had offered to extend the delivery schedule for consideration and terminated when the contractor did not accept the offer. Judge Nichols, dissenting, felt that there was no exercise of discretion and stated that a contractor has a right to an "informed and deliberate exercise of discretion." The court has indicated, however, that it may be difficult to find the exercise of discretion if a termination was based on "a few deficiencies of the kind every construction contractor experiences on every job," *J.D. Hedin Constr. Co. v. United States*, 187 Ct. Cl. 45, 408 F.2d 424 (1969).

In *McDonnell Douglas Corp. v. United States*, 182 F.3d 1319 (Fed. Cir. 1999), *cert denied*, 529 U.S. 1097 (2000), *on remand*, 50 Fed. Cl. 311 (2001), *aff'd in part & rev'd in part,* 323 F.3d 1006 (Fed. Cir. 2003), the court referred to the following four factors that should be considered in determining whether there had been an abuse of discretion: "(1) evidence of subjective bad faith on the part of the government official, (2) whether there is a reasonable, contract-related basis for the official's decision, (3) the amount of discretion given to the official, and (4) whether the official violated an applicable statute or regulation." In *Empire Energy Mgmt. Sys., Inc.,* ASBCA 46741, 03-1 BCA ¶ 32,079, *aff'd*, 362 F.3d 1343 (Fed Cir. 2004), the board analyzed the termination decision following these four factors and found no abuse of discretion. With regard to the issue of "subjective bad faith" the board reasoned that it should follow *Am-Pro Protective Agency, Inc. v. United States*, 281 F.3d 1234 (Fed. Cir. 2002), requiring the contractor to establish bad faith by "something stronger than a 'preponderance of evidence' . . . to overcome the presumption [of] good faith." The board found no bad faith because the contractor did not show with "convincing clarity a high probability that [the contracting officer] acted from personal animus with specific intent to injure Empire." See also *Quality Env't Sys., Inc.*, ASBCA 22178, 87-3 BCA ¶ 20,060, using the same factors. Compare *Tecom, Inc. v. United States,* 66 Fed. Cl. 736 (2005), concluding, after a detailed analysis, that the presumption of good faith on the part of government officials was not applicable to cases not involving allegations of criminal activity.

Regardless of the category (abuse of discretion, bad faith, arbitrary and capricious) the judges select, default terminations are found to be improper if 1) they are infected with informational deficiencies, i.e., either the contracting officer did not consider all relevant information or considered erroneous data; 2) an improper motive was present; or 3) other objectionable government conduct is present.

a. *Informational Deficiencies*

Abuse of discretion will be found where there is an indication that relevant information has not been considered or evaluated. See *Monaco Enters. v. United States*, 907 F.2d 159 (Fed. Cir. 1990), in which the court in a non-precedential opinion reversed a board decision. The court stated that failure to consider the lack of urgency, the contractor's willingness to perform, and the fact that a substitute contractor would not likely perform any earlier constituted an abuse of discretion. See also *Jamco Constructors, Inc.*, VABCA 3271, 94-1 BCA ¶ 26,405 (failure to evaluate conflicting information on the time needed for contractor to complete performance). However, the failure to consider a factor will not be an abuse of discretion where other factors indicate a termination to be warranted, *Hannon Elec. Co. v. United States*, 31 Fed. Cl. 135 (1994).

In *Marshall Associated Contractors, Inc.–Columbia Excavating, Inc. (J.V),* IBCA 1901, 01-1 BCA ¶ 31,248, the board found that the contracting officer had abused his discretion in terminating for default because he had not reviewed the claim material presented by the contractor and had relied entirely on the advice of technical personnel, who had performed an inadequate analysis. Moreover, the termination was suspect because the government was not prejudiced by the contractor's delay. See also *Ryan Co.*, ASBCA 48151, 00-2 BCA ¶ 31,094, *recons. denied*, 01-1 BCA ¶ 31,151, finding an abuse of discretion when the contracting officer had inaccurate information on which to base the termination decision because other government personnel intentionally withheld crucial information. However, in *Dinah Wolverton Perkins*, PSBCA 3691, 95-2 BCA ¶ 27,670, the board upheld the termination for default and ruled that a contracting officer is not obligated to investigate numerous complaints against the contractor before terminating for default. Although there might be such a duty if the termination relied on only one or two major irregularities, the significant number of complaints about similar problems justified the termination.

b. Improper Motive

In *Darwin Constr. Co. v. United States*, 811 F.2d 593 (Fed. Cir. 1987), the court overturned a default termination because of an abuse of discretion—based on the board's finding that the government's reason for the termination was solely to rid itself of the contractor. The court rejected the government's argument that motive could not be considered in determining whether a default termination was an abuse of discretion. See also *Libertatia Assocs., Inc. v. United States,* 46 Fed. Cl. 702 (2000), ruling that a default termination was improper because of the contracting officer's representative's personal animosity toward the contractor. The court characterized this as "bad faith." See also *ABS Baumaschinenvertrieb GmbH*, ASBCA 48207, 00-2 BCA ¶ 31,090, in which the board concluded that the termination for default was an abuse of discretion because the government's specifications were defective, a machine built to the IFB's specifications would not have met the performance requirements specified, and the government had engaged in improper conduct by meeting with the contractor's competitor after contract award in a "conflict of interest so patent that the Government cannot be assured of getting unbiased advice as to the content of the specifications." The contracting officer relied on information that "taint[edl the decision process leading to the [default]" such as the advice of technical advisors in determining whether the proposed machine, as submitted by the contractor, met the design specifications. Indicative of this "subjective bad faith" was the advisors' withholding from the contracting officer the fact that the machine was no longer required.

Earlier board cases based on the allegation that the termination was motivated by animosity toward the contractor generally rejected such arguments on the grounds that, if the government has a right to terminate and followed the proper procedures, its motive is irrelevant, *Walsky Constr. Co.*, ASBCA 41541, 94-2 BCA ¶ 26,698. See *Standard Mfg. Co.*, ASBCA 13624, 72-1 BCA ¶ 9371, in which the board stated at 43,508-09:

> The [contractor's] final argument is that the termination of the [contractor's] order should be for convenience because the Government terminated the appellant's order for reasons unrelated to [the contractor's] performance thereunder. [The contractor] alleges that the order was terminated because of certain prejudices toward the [contractor's] proprietary designs and because of the fact that the need for [the contractor's] items had been extinguished prior to default termination by the Government's procurement of substitute items from an alternate source of supply. It contended that *Schlesinger v. United States*, 182 Ct. Cl. 571, 390 F.2d 702 (1968) stands for the proposition that termination for

reasons unrelated to the contractor's performance can only be the basis for a termination for convenience.

We find nothing in the *Schlesinger* opinion to support a conclusion so broad as that urged by the [contractor]. In that case the court held that the Navy was required to exercise the discretion which the Default clause gives it, and could not terminate for default, although the contractor was in technical default, upon the dictates of a Senate Subcommittee, without the exercise of that discretion. There was no abdication of that responsibility by the Air Force in the present case.

The record indicates that the Air Force representatives were unhappy at being forced to purchase a proprietary product from this [contractor] in view of its recalcitrance in complying with the Truth in Negotiations Act and implementing regulations. The fact that by the time of the [contractor's] default a substitute item was available elsewhere was one of the factors considered in arriving at the decision to terminate.

* * *

The [contractor] defaulted in its delivery requirements, without excusable cause. The Air Force considered the factors specified in ASPR before deciding to terminate for default. Among these were the facts that the [contractor] failed to offer a substitute delivery schedule which indicated any attempt at urgency, and the Air Force could secure the quantity it needed elsewhere at a lower price. The termination for default was proper.

See also *Sach Sinha & Assoc., Inc.,* ASBCA 47594, 00-1 ¶ 30,735, where allegations of bad faith in the form of conspiracy, prejudice, incompetence, and vindictiveness were unproven because the evidence offered, if any, fell short of "well-nigh irrefragable proof;" *George H. Robertson*, HUDBCA 76-31, 78-1 BCA ¶ 13,035, in which the board held that, even if the government had been motivated by bias against the contractor, termination was not improper because the contractor was actually in default and proper procedures were followed; and *Nuclear Research Assocs., Inc.*, ASBCA 13563, 70-1 BCA ¶ 8237, in which the board stated, "[D]efault termination is a matter of right, not motive. If the right clearly exists, the board does not examine into the contracting officer's 'motives' or judgment leading to its exercise."

In *Bob Brottmiller*, AGBCA 94-196-3, 95-1 BCA ¶ 27,468, default was not excused by the government's alleged failure to afford the contractor the same treatment as other contractors because whether other contractors were guilty of violations of their contracts had no bearing on whether the contract at issue was properly terminated. See also *Adelaide Blomfield Mgmt. Co. v. General Servs. Admin.*, GSBCA 12851, 95-1 BCA ¶ 27,514, in which a lessor of a building failed to overcome the presumption of governmental good faith in terminating the lease because the government entered the lease with the intention of honoring it but later needed more space to house its tenant agencies. The board concluded that it was not evidence of bad faith that the government did not follow the lessor's suggestion to move one agency out and backfill the vacated space with a smaller agency.

c. Other Objectionable Conduct by the Government

Often bases for overturning a default termination do not conveniently fit into any category. In *Riyste & Ricas, Inc.*, ASBCA 51841, 02-2 BCA ¶ 31,883, the board ruled that the contracting officer's failure to promptly rule on requests for a time extension, coupled with the contracting officer's failure to tell the contractor that the government disagreed with it, constituted an abuse of discretion that warranted converting a default termination into a termination for convenience.

The fact that the government no longer needs the items has been frequently rejected as a basis for overturning an otherwise proper default termination. See *Artisan Elecs. Corp.*, ASBCA 14154, 73-1 BCA ¶ 9807, *aff'd*, 205 Ct. Cl. 126, 449 F.2d 606 (1974), in which the ASBCA Senior Deciding Group held that the government's need for the supplies and services is irrelevant to its right to terminate for default. In affirming, the Court of Claims noted that the government's requirements were reduced but did not comment on this specific finding of the board. From the decision, it does not appear that the contractor raised the discretion issue to the court. See also *Precision Standard, Inc.*, ASBCA 41375, 96-2 BCA ¶ 28,461; *American Gen. Fabrication, Inc.*, ASBCA 43518, 92-2 BCA ¶ 24,955; *Scandia Mfg. Co.*, ASBCA 20888, 76-2 BCA ¶ 11,949; *Hydraulic Sys. Co.*, ASBCA 16856, 72-2 BCA ¶ 9742; *Standard Mfg. Co.*, ASBCA 13624, 72-1 BCA ¶ 9371; *Interspace Eng'g & Support,* ASBCA 14459, 70-1 BCA ¶ 8263; and *Rowe, Inc. v. General Servs. Admin.*, GSBCA 14211, 01-2 ¶ 31,630.

B. Reconsideration of Default Termination

FAR 49.102(d) provides that a contract terminated for default "may be reinstated by mutual agreement where the contracting officer determines that such reinstatement is advantageous to the Government." The GAO has held that agencies have "inherent authority" to reinstate a default-terminated fixed-price contract "wherever they determine in good faith that the basis for the default no longer exists and that it is reasonable to expect satisfactory completion of contract performance upon reinstatement," *Stancil- Hoffman Corp.*, Comp. Gen. Dec. B-193001.2, 80-2 CPD ¶ 226. See *Ohnstad Constr., Inc.*, AGBCA 81-160-1, 83-1 BCA ¶ 16,144, *recons. denied*, 83-1 BCA ¶ 16,319, where the contracting officer reinstated a portion of the terminated work and also indicated that the termination of the balance would be "reconsidered" based on contractor progress on the reinstated portion.

In *Ra-Nav Labs., Inc. v. Widnall,* 137 F.3d 1344 (Fed. Cir. 1998), nearly 10 years after being terminated for default, Ra-Nav Laboratories filed an appeal alleging an invalid default termination and breach of contract, claiming that the contract had been reinstated. The court rejected this argument because all of the communications of the government subsequent to the termination had indicated that any further work by the contractor would be only for the purpose of mitigating damages.

IV. TERMINATION PROCEDURES

The mere fact that harsh results may accompany a default termination cannot be used as a basis to deny the government this contractual right. However, the boards and courts have not been hesitant to hold terminations improper when the government has failed to strictly observe rules established to protect the contractor's rights. The contracting officer must follow specific procedures if contemplating a default termination, *Lionsgate Corp.*, ENGBCA 5809, 92-2 BCA ¶ 24,983. The doctrines of waiver and failure to exercise discretion, discussed in previous sections, are techniques used to limit the government's rights. Excusable delays also operate to limit the government's right to terminate. This section examines the required procedures for default termination and the impact of the government's failure to comply with these procedures.

A. Delinquency Notices

The Default clause for supply and service contracts in FAR 52.249-8 requires that a cure notice be sent to the contractor prior to termination based on a failure to make progress or a failure to perform any other provision of the contract. A pre-default termination cure notice is also required by the termination clause at FAR 52.249-6 for cost-reimbursement contracts. In addition, the regulations provide for an optional show cause notice, which may be used to obtain information from the contractor prior to default termination, FAR 49.607(b).

1. Cure Notices

Paragraph (a)(2) of the FAR Default clause for supply and service contracts, FAR 52.249-8, provides:

> The Government's right to terminate this contract under subdivisions (1)(ii) and (1)(iii) above, may be exercised if the Contractor does not cure such failure within 10 days (or more if authorized in writing by the Contracting Officer) after receipt of the notice from the Contracting Officer specifying the failure.

FAR 49.607(a) gives the following guidance concerning the use and form of such cure notices:

> *Cure notice.* If a contract is to be terminated for default before the delivery date, a "Cure Notice" is required by the Default clause. Before using this notice, it must be ascertained that an amount of time equal to or greater than the period of "cure" remains in the contract delivery schedule or any extension to it. If the time remaining in the contract delivery schedule is not sufficient to permit a realistic "cure" period of 10 days or more, the "Cure Notice" should not be issued. The "Cure Notice" may be in the following format:

CURE NOTICE

> You are notified that the Government considers your . . . [*specify the contractor's failure or failures*] a condition that is endangering performance of the contract. Therefore, unless this condition is cured within 10 days after receipt of this notice [*or insert any longer time that the Contracting Officer may consider reasonably necessary*], the Government may terminate for default under the terms and conditions of the . . . [*insert clause title*] clause of this contract.

Failure to give a cure notice, when required, will result in an improper termination, *T.C. & Sarah C. Bell*, ENGBCA 5872, 92-3 BCA ¶ 25,076. There, a park attendant's deficiencies in performance did not amount to a failure of performance, so a cure notice was required. Because the contracting officer gave no cure notice, the termination was overturned. In *Cross Petroleum, Inc. v. United States,* 54 Fed. Cl. 317 (2002), the court overturned a termination for default, finding that the required cure notice was not issued. In *Griffin Servs., Inc.,* ASBCA 53802, 03-1 BCA ¶ 32,200, the default termination was overturned because the government had rescinded its cure notice and then terminated on grounds not mentioned in the cure notice.

A notice in the nature of a cure notice is required in the Postal Service's Inspection of Work clause. See *Green Shack Marketplace,* PSBCA 4557, 01-2 BCA ¶ 31,595, holding that a postal inspectors' unilateral action in closing down a postal unit with no prior notice as required by this clause was not justified despite later ratification by the contracting officer. However, a contracting officer's failure to comply with this notice requirement to provide the contractor written notice of performance deficiencies did not invalidate a default termination because the contractor had actual notice of the contract violations, took no corrective action during the one-month period it was on notice of these violations, and failed to show any prejudice by the lack of written notice, *Fantastique Ultimatique Nautique*', PSBCA 3652, 96-1 BCA ¶ 28,150.

a. Circumstances for Use

A 10-day cure notice is to be used only when the delivery (or performance) schedule has not yet expired. Thus, a cure notice is not required when a contract is being terminated under (a)(1)(i) of the Default clause for failure to deliver supplies, *Lafayette Coal Co.*, ASBCA 32174, 89-3 BCA ¶ 21,963; *Comspace Corp.*, DOTBCA 4011, 02-1 BCA ¶ 31,792, or to perform services, *Chambers-Thompson Moving & Storage, Inc.*, ASBCA 43260, 93-3 BCA ¶ 26,033; *NDJ Restoration, Inc. v. General Servs. Admin.,* GSBCA 14487, 98-2 BCA ¶ 29,987.

A cure notice is not required if there is a repudiation prior to a completion date, since there is no need for the contracting officer to do a "futile act," *Bendix Corp.*, GSBCA 4352, 77-2 BCA ¶ 12,656. See also *Cox & Palmer Constr. Corp.*, ASBCA 38739, 92-1 BCA ¶ 24,756; *Fairfield Scientific Corp.*, ASBCA 21151, 78-1 BCA ¶ 13,082, *recons. denied*, 78-2 BCA ¶ 13,429, *aff'd*, 228 Ct.

Cl. 264, 655 F.2d 1062 (1981); and *De-Luxe Vans, Inc.*, ASBCA 23708, 81-2 BCA ¶ 15,421.

Another situation in which the 10-day cure notice is not required is when fewer than 10 days remain before the due date, FAR 49.607(a); *Century Hone Div. of Desert Labs., Inc.*, ASBCA 18360, 78-1 BCA ¶ 12,990, *recons. denied*, 78-2 BCA ¶ 13,343. In *McQuiston Assocs.*, ASBCA 24676, 83-1 BCA ¶ 16,187, *recons. denied*, 83-2 BCA ¶ 16,602, the board held that the government's failure to provide the Small Business Administration with a copy of a cure notice prior to default termination of a small business concern, as specifically called for by DAR 8-602.3(b)(4), was not grounds for overturning the termination where the notice was to be provided to the SBA "as a matter of information," with no response from the SBA required, and where the contractor could not demonstrate how failure to abide by this provision prejudiced its position.

Construction contracts do not require cure notices. In *Professional Servs. Supplier, Inc. v. United States*, 45 Fed. Cl. 808 (2000), the court refused to imply a cure notice requirement in a construction contract and rejected the contractor's argument that common law required a cure notice. However, if the government chooses to issue a cure notice, it should fully evaluate the contractor's response before deciding to terminate for default. See *Omni Dev. Corp.*, AGBCA 97-203-1, 01-2 BCA ¶ 31,487. In *Empire Energy Mgmt. Sys., Inc.*, ASBCA 46741, 03-1 BCA ¶ 32,079, *aff'd*, 362 F.3d 1343 (Fed. Cir. 2004), the board determined that a hybrid contract that contained elements of both the supply contract and the construction contract Default clauses did not contain a requirement for a cure notice because the contract was more in the nature of a construction contract.

b. Form of Cure Notice

The 10-day cure notice must be in writing, *Electromagnetic Refinishers, Inc.*, GSBCA 5035, 79-1 BCA ¶ 13,697; and must be specific, *American Marine Upholstery Co. v. United States*, 170 Ct. Cl. 564, 345 F.2d 577 (1965). The mere inclusion of a 10-day provision in a letter will not satisfy the requirements for the notice if the clear intention of the letter is to inform the contractor that the government will await further developments, *Long Island Nuclear Serv. Corp.*, ASBCA 12454, 69-1 BCA ¶ 7492.

The adequacy of a cure notice must be judged in light of correspondence and conversations preceding the notice, and, accordingly, the failure to specify all performance deficiencies does not necessarily invalidate the termination, *RFI Shield-Rooms*, ASBCA 17374, 77-2 BCA ¶ 12,714. See *Composite Laminates, Inc. v. United States*, 27 Fed. Cl. 310 (1992), in which the court stated at 318:

> Standards by which to determine the adequacy of a cure notice include the following:

> The notice required by the default clause is intended to inform the contractor that it has failed to meet one or more terms of the contract, except for the delivery clause, as perceived by the government at the time. It need not cite each and every failure, but it must list with enough particularity the performance failures which have placed the contractor in danger of termination for default. Where the [contractor] has received prior notice of its failures, whether by telephone, letter, or word of mouth, that information will be considered properly in conjunction with the cure notice.

Int'l Verbatim Reporters, Inc. v. United States, 9 Cl. Ct. 710, 721 (1986) (citing *Finast Metal Products, Inc.*, 77-1 BCA (CCH) ¶ 12,331 (1977).

In *Integrated Sys. Group, Inc.*, ASBCA 46918, 97-2 BCA ¶ 29,316, the board rejected the contractor's claim that the notice did not adequately inform it of the deficiencies, because the cure notice was followed by discussions between the contractor and the government, the contractor itself had seen the same deficiencies in its own testing, and no evidence had been presented by the contractor that it had been misled by the notice. However, if the contractor is not made aware of the defects, the cure notice is improper and may not be relied on.

c. *Effect of Denial of Cure Period*

Where the 10-day cure notice is required, failure to give proper notice will invalidate the termination, *Composite Laminates, Inc. v. United States*, 27 Fed. Cl. 310 (1992); *Kovatch Truck Ctr.*, GSBCA 5864, 82-2 BCA ¶ 15,855; *Mr.'s Landscaping & Nursery*, HUDBCA 75-6, 76-2 BCA ¶ 11,968; *River City Mfg. & Distrib. Co.*, AGBCA 92-157-1, 93-2 BCA ¶ 25,881.

Termination prior to the expiration of the 10-day period is also improper, *Swanson Group, Inc.*, ASBCA 44664, 98-2 BCA ¶ 29,896; *River City Mfg. & Distrib. Co.*, AGBCA 92-157-1, 93-2 BCA ¶ 25,881; *Introl Corp.*, DOTCAB 1030, 80-1 BCA ¶ 14,380; *B & C Janitorial Servs.*, ASBCA 11084, 66-1 BCA ¶ 5355. In *Cervetto Bldg. Maint. Co. v. United States*, 2 Cl. Ct. 299 (1983), the court invalidated a default termination issued on the final day of the 10-day cure period, concluding that the actual "decision" to terminate had been arrived at prior to expiration of the 10-day cure period and that the contracting officer had failed to consider a letter from the contractor responding to cited performance deficiencies apparently received on the final day of the cure period and had also failed to consider the contractor's performance of janitorial services on the last day. However, wrongful conduct or repudiation by the contractor during the cure period may relieve the government of the requirement to wait until the end of the period. See *Lee Maint. Co.*, PSBCA 522, 79-2 BCA ¶ 14,067, in which the board stated at 69,127:

> Prior decisions have held that once a cure notice is issued, even though a right to terminate a contract may have previously existed, the contract cannot be terminated until expiration of the period afforded the contractor to cure its unacceptable

> performance. *San Antonio Construction Company*, ASBCA 8110, 1964 BCA ¶ 4479; *B&C Janitorial Service*, ASBCA 11084, 66-1 BCA ¶ 5355. However, exceptions to this position have been made. *Soledad Enterprises*, ASBCA 20376, 77-2 BCA ¶ 12,552.
>
> In this appeal, the period afforded the [contractor] to cure its defective performance was preempted because of the [contractor's] threats to do physical harm to Postal Service personnel. The *Restatement of The Law of Contracts* (1932), § 315 states in part:
>
> "Sec. 315. Breach By Preventing or Hindering Performance By The Other Party.
>
> "(1) Prevention or hindrance by a party to a contract of any occurrence or performance requisite under the contract for the creation or continuance of a right in favor of the other party, or the discharge of a duty by him, is a breach of contract, unless
>
> "(a) the prevention or hindrance is caused or justified by the conduct of the other party."
>
> * * *
>
> (Also see § 295 "Excuse of Condition by Prevention or Hindrance" and *Williston on Contracts*, 3rd edition, §§ 1601 et seq.) We conclude that any obligation the Postal Service had to afford the [contractor] the ten day period indicated in the cure notice was terminated by the [contractor's] wrongful conduct.

See also *Ohnstad Constr., Inc.*, AGBCA 81-160-1, 83-1 BCA ¶ 16,144, *recons. denied*, 83-1 BCA ¶ 16,319, in which the board upheld a default termination issued prior to the expiration of the designated cure period because the contract did not actually require a cure notice and the contractor had not shown any substantial reliance on the cure notice, and *Contract Auto. Repair & Mgmt.*, ASBCA 45316, 94-1 BCA ¶ 26,516, in which the board held that a partial default termination during the 10-day cure period was proper because the contractor did not show that it could have or would have cured the deficiencies before the end of the cure period.

d. Adequate Assurances

Once a valid 10-day cure notice has been issued, the contractor's failure to advise the government during the period that corrective action will be taken justifies a default termination, *Composite Laminates, Inc. v. United States*, 27 Fed. Cl. 310 (1992). Conversely, if the contractor timely cured its deficiency by providing proof that it had obtained proper insurance coverage, termination was improper, *Hughes Moving & Storage, Inc.*, ASBCA 45346, 98-1 BCA ¶ 29,693.

The government is entitled to "adequate assurances" of performance similar to those required under U.C.C. § 2-209 and *Restatement, Second, Contracts* § 251. The applicability of these common law and commercial law concepts to the resolution of government contracts progress failure cases was implicitly recognized in *Supertechnology Corp.*, NASABCA 570-9, 72-2 BCA ¶ 9619, in which the board described the government as an "insecure buyer" and upheld the progress failure termination since the contractor had failed to give "assurances." See *Danzig v. AEC Corp.*, 224 F.3d 1333 (Fed. Cir. 2000), in which the board had overturned the default termination of a construction contract on the basis that the government failed to present evidence that the contractor could not have completed the contract on time and that it had not expressed "unequivocal unwillingness" to perform, where the contractor stated it could not predict when it would finish the job only two months before the scheduled completion date. On appeal, the Federal Circuit reversed, holding that, although the government did not have sufficient cause to terminate the contract for failure to make progress, the contractor's response to the cure notice did not satisfy its obligation to provide assurances to the agency that it could timely complete the contract where the contractor did not dispute that it would be unable to complete the contract by the completion date, removed contract files and office equipment from the worksite. and disconnected telephones at the worksite office. Thus, the agency was entitled to regard the contractor's failure as a breach justifying termination of the contract for default. The court thus enhanced the importance of the U.C.C.'s "adequate assurances," by reasoning that failure to provide adequate assurance was an anticipatory repudiation and reversing the board's decision that no anticipatory repudiation had occurred because there was no "unequivocal statement" that the contractor could not or would not perform. See also *Twigg Corp.*, NASABCA 62-0192, 93-1 BCA ¶ 25,318 and *National Union Fire Ins. Co.*, ASBCA 34744, 90-1 BCA ¶ 22,266.

Even though the assurances do not provide a clear indication that the contractor will complete on time, the contracting officer should make an independent analysis before concluding that default termination is proper. See *Omni Dev. Corp.*, AGBCA 97-203-1, 01-2 BCA ¶ 31,487, in which the board found that shortcomings in the contractor's response to a cure notice did not excuse the contracting officer from performing the detailed analysis of the contractor's ability to complete work in the time remaining, before terminating for failure to make progress. Accord, *Bison Trucking & Equip. Co.,* ASBCA 53390, 01-2 BCA ¶ 31,654; *Beacon Cyberport,* AGBCA 2002-102-1, 03-1 BCA ¶ 32,105. Compare *Thomas & Sons, Inc.,* ASBCA 51874, 01-1 BCA ¶ 31,166, finding a proper default termination where, after the contractor responded to the cure notice by requesting an additional 60 to 90 days to complete the work, the government performed its own independent analysis of the updated schedule and concluded that the contractor could not perform within the time remaining for performance. See also *Automated Power Sys., Inc.,* DOTBCA 2678, 01-1 BCA ¶ 31,259, in which the board relied in part on the contractor's failure to provide assurances in response to a cure notice in upholding a default termination. Accord, *L&M Thomas Concrete Co.*, ASBCA 49198, 03-1 BCA ¶ 32,194.

Assurances generally involve both contractor acts (e.g., hiring additional employees, performing additional work) and words (e.g., submission of proposed work schedules or requests for excusable delays). For a discussion of the adequacy of assurances, see *RFI Shield-Rooms*, ASBCA 17374, 77-2 BCA ¶ 12,714. Assurances were found inadequate in *John F. Lehnertz*, AGBCA 77-132, 78-1 BCA ¶ 12,895 (90 percent of tree thinning not completed with 10 percent of contract time remaining, and contractor failed to respond to a request for a progress schedule specifying how it intended to finish the work within the contract time); *Building Maint. Specialists, Inc.*, ENGBCA 3540, 77-2 BCA ¶ 12,810 (contractor failed to commence grounds maintenance and cleaning services on time and was unable to hire employees or secure needed equipment); *Dozie I. Rienne*, ENGBCA 5711, 91-1 BCA ¶ 23,432 (mere promise to improve insufficient); *John E. Faucett*, AGBCA 396, 76-2 BCA ¶ 11,946 (failure to provide revised progress schedule); *J.W. Bibb, Inc.*, ASBCA 19589, 76-2 BCA ¶ 12,135 (contractor's response to cure notice was that further inquiries should be addressed to a law firm); *R.C. Hudson & Assocs., Inc.*, ASBCA 20711, 76-2 BCA ¶ 12,201 (proposed completion schedule included subcontractor commitments that were contingent on receiving back payments totaling $109,000, pending contractor claims for progress payments were uncertain and amounted to only $85,000, and prior contractor performance was erratic); and *Comdata Sys., Inc.*, ASBCA 19893, 77-1 BCA ¶ 12,463 (continued performance dependent on relief under Pub. L. No. 85-804, to which contractor was not entitled). In *Lorch Elecs. Corp.*, ASBCA 21496, 78-1 BCA ¶ 12,911, the progress failure was found to be cured when a breadboard model was successfully demonstrated to the government inspector, who did not report the success to the contracting officer.

2. The Show Cause Notice

FAR 49.402-3 contains the following guidance on the use of show cause notices:

> (e)(1) If termination for default appears appropriate, the contracting officer should, if practicable, notify the contractor in writing of the possibility of the termination. This notice shall call the contractor's attention to the contractual liabilities if the contract is terminated for default, and request the contractor to show cause why the contract should not be terminated for default. The notice may further state that failure of the contractor to present an explanation may be taken as an admission that no valid explanation exists. When appropriate, the notice may invite the contractor to discuss the matter at a conference. A format for a show cause notice is in 49.607.
>
> (2) When a termination for default appears imminent, the contracting officer shall provide a written notification to the surety. If the contractor is subsequently terminated for default, a copy of the notice of default shall be sent to the surety.
>
> (3) If requested by the surety, and agreed to by the contractor and any assignees, arrangements may be made to have future checks mailed to the contractor in care of the surety. In this case, the contractor must forward a written request to the designated disbursing officer specifically directing a change in address for mailing checks.

(4) If the contractor is a small business firm, the contracting officer shall immediately provide a copy of any cure notice or show cause notice to the contracting office's small business specialist and the Small Business Administration Regional Office nearest the contractor. The contracting officer should, whenever practicable, consult with the small business specialist before proceeding with a default termination (see also 49.402-4).

FAR 49.607(b) provides the following form of notice and states that "it should be sent immediately upon expiration of the delivery period":

SHOW CAUSE NOTICE

Since you have failed to ______ [*insert* "perform Contract No. ___ within the time required by its terms", *or* "cure the conditions endangering performance under Contract No. ___ as described to you in the Government's letter of _______ (date)"], the Government is considering terminating the contract under the provisions for default of this contract. Pending a final decision in this matter, it will be necessary to determine whether your failure to perform arose from causes beyond your control and without fault or negligence on your part. Accordingly, you are given the opportunity to present, in writing, any facts bearing on the question to _____ [*insert the name and complete address of the contracting officer*], within 10 days after receipt of this notice. Your failure to present any excuses within this time may be considered as an admission that none exist. Your attention is invited to the respective rights of the Contractor and the Government and the liabilities that may be invoked if a decision is made to terminate for default.

Any assistance given to you on this contract or any acceptance by the Government of delinquent goods or services will be solely for the purpose of mitigating damages, and it is not the intention of the Government to condone any delinquency or to waive any rights the Government has under the contract.

The use of a show cause notice is not mandatory, *Sandia Die & Cartridge*, AGBCA 89-176-1, 94-2 BCA ¶ 26,927. In *Nisei Constr. Co.*, ASBCA 51464, 99-2 BCA ¶ 30,448 the board rejected the contractor's argument that FAR 49.607(b) required a 10-day response period to a show cause notice rather than the six days the government actually gave. The board noted that FAR 49.607(b) was merely precatory and did not mandate that the government literally follow it. Moreover, there is no need for a show cause notice in a supply contract after the delivery date has passed. See *Connecttec, Inc.*, ASBCA 51579, 02-2 BCA ¶ 32,021(issuance of a show cause notice was non-mandatory and was not required because the contractor failed to meet the revised delivery date).

The legal effect of a show cause notice issued after the due date was discussed in *Aargus Poly Bag*, GSBCA 4314, 76-2 BCA ¶ 11,927, in which the board stated at 57,184:

The Default clause permits the Government to immediately terminate the whole or any part of a contract where the contractor fails to deliver the supplies within

> the time specified in the contract. However, it is to the mutual benefit of the parties for the Government to forbear where the contractor appears capable of performance and the Government might be willing to accept late deliveries. Thus, in the administration of supply contracts, it has become almost routine practice for the Government to issue a show-cause notice prior to termination; not so much, in our opinion, to determine excusability, but rather, to gain information relative to the contractor's performance capability. However, the Government is not legally obligated to issue such notice. The notices issued under this contract do not state, nor suggest, that the 10 days constitute an isolated period of immunity from termination. Thus, we conclude that the Government, whatever its motive, may see fit, at any time, to terminate and permit [the contractor] to show excusability at a later date under 11(e) of the Default clause.

Such a notice does not grant the contractor an automatic 10-day extension, *Kan-Du Tool & Instrument Corp.*, ASBCA 23466, 79-2 BCA ¶ 13,907; *Churchill Chem. Corp.*, GSBCA 4321, 77-1 BCA ¶ 12,318. The government can, therefore, terminate before the end of the period specified in the notice unless the contractor can show prejudice from an earlier termination, and prejudice will not normally be present when the government has the right to terminate without the notice, *Mission Paint Mfg. Co.*, GSBCA 4914, 78-2 BCA ¶ 13,389. These show cause rules also appear to apply to extended cure periods, *Litcom Div., Litton Sys.*, ASBCA 13413, 78-1 BCA ¶ 13,022.

Nor does a show cause waive a prior delivery date. In *Flight Refueling, Inc.*, ASBCA 46846, 97-2 BCA ¶ 29,000, a contractor's contention that the government's transmission of a show cause letter requesting information on excusable delay constituted a waiver of a prior delivery date was rejected. On the other hand, a contractor's failure to respond to a show cause notice does not waive a contractor's claims, *Roxco, Ltd. v. United States*, 60 Fed. Cl. 39 (2004).

FAR 49.402-3(e)(4) requires that show cause notices and cure notices be immediately provided to the Small Business Administration when they affect a small business. However, in *Baltimoy Mfg. Co.*, ASBCA 47140, 98-2 BCA ¶ 30,017, the board held that the agency's failure to follow this regulation did not preclude an otherwise proper default termination when the contractor was not prejudiced by the omission because the contract administrator had orally notified the SBA. Accord, *S&W Assocs.*, DOTBCA 2633, 96-2 BCA ¶ 28,326 (notice is for informational purposes only); *Rowe, Inc. v. General Servs. Admin.*, GSBCA 14211, 01-2 BCA ¶ 31,630 (government's failure to consult with an SBA specialist prior to terminating a contract for default did not render the termination procedurally defective, because the government put SBA on notice it was considering the action, and consultation with SBA is not a mandatory requirement).

B. Termination Notice

FAR 49.402-3(g) provides the following guidance as to the form of a default termination notice:

If, after compliance with the procedures in paragraphs (a) through (f) of this 49.402-3, the contracting officer determines that a termination for default is proper, the contracting officer shall issue a notice of termination stating —

(1) The contract number and date;

(2) The acts or omissions constituting the default;

(3) That the contractor's right to proceed further under the contract (or a specified portion of the contract) is terminated;

(4) That the supplies or services terminated may be purchased against the contractor's account, and that the contractor will be held liable for any excess costs;

(5) If the contracting officer has determined that the failure to perform is not excusable, that the notice of termination constitutes such decision, and that the contractor has the right to appeal such decision under the Disputes clause;

(6) That the Government reserves all rights and remedies provided by law or under the contract, in addition to charging excess costs; and

(7) That the notice constitutes a decision that the contractor is in default as specified and that the contractor has the right to appeal under the Disputes clause.

DAR 8-602(d) and FPR 1-8.602.3(d) contained similar guidance. The Court of Claims held that government failure to strictly observe these formalities in issuing a default termination notice will not necessarily provide grounds for overturning a default termination where the contractor has not been prejudiced by such failures. In *Philadelphia Regent Builders, Inc. v. United States*, 225 Ct. Cl. 234, 634 F.2d 569 (1980), the court upheld the default despite several "formal defects" in the default termination notice, including lack of citation to the proper contract number, lack of statement that it constituted a final decision, and failure of the contracting officer to sign the notice, where the contractor failed to show that it was "harmed in any way by the admitted defects in the notice." Compare *Kisco Co. v. United States*, 221 Ct. Cl. 806, 610 F.2d 742 (1979), in which the court overturned a partial default termination, relying on both the lack of a "cure notice" and the absence of "final decision" notification in the termination notice. The termination notice will be ineffective if it does not clearly indicate that the contract is being terminated for default, *Stroud Realty*, HUDBCA 75-13, 76-1 BCA ¶ 11,770. In that case, since the "cancellation" notice referred to both the convenience and default clauses, the board declined to hold that the contract had been terminated for default.

A default termination notice, as a contracting officer's final decision, must include information for the contractor on how to appeal the decision. In *George Ledford Constr., Inc.*, VABCA 6630, 02-1 BCA ¶ 31,662, the contracting officer's failure to put this information in a September 1996 notice of termination caused the board to refuse to dismiss the contractor's notice of appeal filed in May 2001, nearly five years later. Defective notice of appeal rights will not trigger the 90-day appeal period to the board, *Atlantis Constr. Corp.*, ASBCA 44044, 96-1 BCA ¶ 28,045; *Delta Constr. Co.*, ASBCA 42453, 96-1 BCA ¶ 28,106. However, in *State of Fla., Dep't of Ins. v. United States*, 81 F.3d 1093 (Fed. Cir. 1996), the court stated that relief may only be granted for the omission of the statement of appeal rights required by the Contract Disputes Act of 1978 if the absence of the notification prejudiced the party. There, the appellant could not show prejudice because it had actual notice of its appeal rights from other documents. See also *Decker & Co. v. West,* 76 F.3d 1573 (Fed. Cir. 1996) (a defect in an otherwise proper termination of default notice will justify relief only when accompanied by detrimental reliance). A contracting officer's final decision is not required for default grounds discovered after termination, *Glazer Constr. Co. v. United States,* 52 Fed. Cl. 513 (2002).

Terminations for present failures have been upheld, even though the reasons cited in the termination notice would not support default termination, so long as proper grounds for default termination did in fact exist at the time of termination, *Shields Enters., Inc. v. United States,* 28 Fed. Cl. 615 (1993); *Joseph Morton Co. v. United States*, 757 F.2d 1273 (Fed. Cir. 1985); *Pots Unlimited, Ltd. v. United States*, 220 Ct. Cl. 405, 600 F.2d 790 (1979); *American Photographic Indus., Inc.,* ASBCA 29272, 90-1 BCA ¶ 22,491; *Tester Corp.,* ASBCA 21312, 78-2 BCA ¶ 13,373, *recons. denied*, 79-1 BCA ¶ 13,725, *aff'd*, 227 Ct. Cl. 648 (1981); *Ralbo, Inc.*, ASBCA 49541, 99-2 BCA ¶ 30,438. Accord, *Cogefar-Impresit U.S.A., Inc.,* DOTBCA 2721, 97-2 BCA ¶ 29,188; *CJP Contractors, Inc. v. United States,* 45 Fed. Cl. 343, 379 (1999). The government may rely on other grounds for default unless the government's error in incorrectly specifying the basis for the default action has prejudiced the contractor, *United Detection Sys., Inc.,* ASBCA 46603, 98-1 BCA ¶ 29,368, *recons. denied,* 98-1 BCA ¶ 29,369. The government can so rely even if the other ground was known to the contracting officer at the time of termination, *Empire Energy Mgmt. Sys., Inc. v. Roche*, 362 F.3d 1343 (Fed. Cir. 2004). While the government can rely on other factors to justify the termination for default, it cannot do so if it was aware of all of the alleged instances and encouraged and demanded continued performance notwithstanding, *Aptus Co. v. United States,* 61 Fed. Cl. 638 (2004).

This rule has not been applied to progress failure terminations. In *Cross Aero Corp.*, ASBCA 14801, 71-2 BCA ¶ 9075, the board discussed the different rules, stating at 42,085:

> [The contractor] argues that the dimensional deficiencies of the pins, discovered after termination, may not be used as a basis to justify the TCO's antecedent decision to terminate. This Board held in *Marmac Industries, Inc.*, ASBCA 11861, 69-2 BCA ¶ 8067, that where default termination is sought for failure to make progress, the subsequent termination action can be based only on those failures of which the contractor had been given notice and which it had an opportunity to

> cure or validly excuse. Where default termination is, however, based on default in delivery, the Board has held as long ago as 1955 that assertion of an invalid reason in the termination notice does not void it provided that at the time of termination a valid ground does in fact exist. *Royal Lumber Co., Inc.*, ASBCA 2847 (1955). Both the Court of Claims and this Board have ever since followed the rule laid down in *Royal Lumber*. *Nesbitt v. United States*, 170 Ct. Cl. 666 (1965); *Telecommunication Consultants*, ASBCA 13801, 69-2 BCA ¶ 7925; *Logan Electronic Corporation*, ASBCA 13054, 70-1 BCA ¶ 8083. Accordingly, the default termination, if otherwise permissible, is supported both on the ground that the pins cannot be considered to be the new pins of designated manufacturers and that they were dimensionally defective.

The default termination notice is effective when delivered to the contractor's place of business even if the person who signs the receipt for the notice is not empowered to bind the contractor, *Fred Schwartz*, ASBCA 20724, 76-1 BCA ¶ 11,916, *recons. denied*, 76-2 BCA ¶ 11,976. In *National Rag & Waste Co. v. United States*, 237 F.2d 846 (5th Cir. 1956), the court upheld the validity of a termination notice that was issued three weeks ahead of the completion date that clearly and unequivocally stated that the contract was terminated if the date was not met.

V. EXCESS COSTS OF REPROCUREMENT

Excess costs of reprocurement or completion are the unique remedies given to the government upon a valid default termination. The standard default clauses for fixed-price supply, service, and construction contracts state that the right to assess excess costs is "in addition to any other rights and remedies provided by law or under this contract." Thus, if the government loses its right to assess excess costs, it still retains the right to collect actual damages if they can be proved. The ease of proving excess costs, however, makes it a far more desirable remedy in most cases than attempting to prove actual damages.

The specific language giving the government the right to recover excess costs is contained in the Default clause at FAR 52.249-8 for supply and service contracts, which provides:

> If the Government terminates this contract in whole or in part, it may acquire, under the terms and in the manner the Contracting Officer considers appropriate, supplies or services similar to those terminated, and the Contractor will be liable to the Government for any excess costs for those supplies or services. However, the Contractor shall continue the work not terminated.

The Default clause at FAR 52.249-10 for construction contracts provides rights after termination as follows:

> In this event, the Government may take over the work and complete it by contract or otherwise, and may take possession of and use any materials, appliances, and

> plant on the work site necessary for completing the work. The Contractor and its sureties shall be liable for any damage to the Government resulting from the Contractor's refusal or failure to complete the work within the specified time, whether or not the Contractor's right to proceed with the work is terminated. This liability includes any increased costs incurred by the Government in completing the work.

FAR 49.402-6 contains the following procedures to be followed by the contracting officer in making repurchases against the contractor's account:

> (a) When the supplies or services are still required after termination, the contracting officer shall repurchase the same or similar supplies or services against the contractor's account as soon as practicable. The contracting officer shall repurchase at as reasonable a price as practicable, considering the quality and delivery requirements. The contracting officer may repurchase a quantity in excess of the undelivered quantity terminated for default when the excess quantity is needed, but excess cost may not be charged against the defaulting contractor for more than the undelivered quantity terminated for default (including variations in quantity permitted by the terminated contract). Generally, the contracting officer will make a decision whether or not to repurchase before issuing the termination notice.
>
> (b) If the repurchase is for a quantity not over the undelivered quantity terminated for default, the statutory requirements for formal advertising are inapplicable. However, the contracting officer shall use formal advertising procedures unless there is a good reason to negotiate. If the contracting officer decides to negotiate the repurchase contract, any appropriate negotiation authority in Subpart 15.2 may be used. If none of the negotiation authorities is used, the contracting officer shall cite the Default clause as the authority. If the repurchase is for a quantity over the undelivered quantity terminated for default, the contracting officer shall treat the entire quantity as a new acquisition.
>
> (c) If repurchase is made at a price over the price of the supplies or services terminated, the contracting officer shall, after completion and final payment of the repurchase contract, make a written demand on the contractor for the total amount of the excess, giving consideration to any increases or decreases in other costs such as transportation, discounts, etc. If the contractor fails to make payment, the contracting officer shall follow the procedures in Subpart 32.6 for collecting contract debts due the Government.

A. The Fulford Doctrine

Because the assessment of excess costs does not ordinarily occur at the time of the default termination, a contractor may sometimes choose not to contest the default termination because it does not anticipate any monetary liability. In other instances, a contractor may have simply failed, through inadvertence or otherwise, to make a timely challenge to the default action. In *Fulford Mfg. Co.*, ASBCA 2144, 6 CCF ¶ 61,815, the board announced the rule that ultimately became known as the "Fulford doctrine." The *Fulford* case allowed the defaulted contractor to challenge the underlying termination on the government's assessment of excess costs of reprocurement only in cases involving excusable delay. Prior to the enactment of the Contract Disputes Act, however, the boards broadened the scope of this doctrine "beyond the issue of excusable delays" so as to "permit the consideration of any challenge to the original [unappealed] default termination," *Fairfield Scientific Corp.*, ASBCA 21151, 78-1 BCA ¶ 13,082, *recons. denied*, 78-2 BCA ¶ 13,429, *aff'd*, 228 Ct. Cl. 264, 655 F.2d 1062 (1981). In that case, the board held that a contractor, on timely appeal of the assessment of excess costs, may contest the propriety of any default termination even though there had been no timely appeal of the default action. If the subsequent challenge to the default termination is successful, the improper default termination will be converted into a termination for the convenience of the government, and the contractor may use proof of the impropriety of the default as a basis for defeating an excess cost assessment. Thus, the decision by the government to assess excess costs may present some considerable risk to the government where no timely challenge to the default termination has been made, where the partial liability under termination for convenience is substantial, and where excess costs are not very large. Subsequently, the Fulford doctrine has been held applicable to appeals under the Contract Disputes Act, *Kellner Equip., Inc.*, ASBCA 26006, 82-2 BCA ¶ 16,077; and "direct access" suits under the Act, *D. Moody & Co. v. United States*, 5 Cl. Ct. 70 (1984). See *Z.A.N. Co. v. United States*, 6 Cl. Ct. 298 (1984), holding that this doctrine permits a contractor to challenge the default termination on the grounds that there was an excusable delay but not to challenge the fact of default or the government's right not to pay the contract price. There is, however, an apparent conflict between the 90-day jurisdictional requirements of the Contract Disputes Act and the Fulford doctrine, which allows issues to be litigated well beyond 90 days following the termination decision by a contracting officer.

Despite this apparent conflict, most of the boards continue to apply the Fulford doctrine to all situations in which the government seeks excess reprocurement costs. See, for example, *Parkway Distrib. & Bldg. Servs., Inc.*, ASBCA 36190, 89-3 BCA ¶ 22,199; *Primepak Co.*, GSBCA 10514, 90-3 BCA ¶ 22,280; and *High Tech Group, Inc.*, ENGBCA 5685, 90-2 BCA ¶ 22,822. In fact, the IBCA has even extended the doctrine to the "reverse Fulford" cases, where the underlying termination for default is timely challenged but the assessment of reprocurement costs is not challenged until more than 90 days after the contracting officer's imposition of those costs, *Tom Warr*, IBCA 2360, 88-1 BCA ¶ 20,231 (allowing a contractor to bootstrap its otherwise untimely challenge to the government's claim for excess costs to its timely challenge of the merits of the underlying default termination).

However, a broad construction of the doctrine is not employed by the boards uniformly. One board has implied that problems exist with the current state of the law in this area, while another has rejected the Fulford doctrine outright. In *Petroleum Constr., Inc.*, DOTBCA 2533, 93-2 BCA ¶ 25,760, the board recognized the conflict but did not address the issue because the claim was not one for excess costs of reprocurement. The Agriculture board, however, has employed a stricter interpretation of the Fulford doctrine. The board distinguishes the *Fulford* case, and hence the doctrine that takes its name, on the ground that the Default clause involved there did not require the contracting officer to consider the excusability of the default prior to the termination. Accordingly, the board has determined that, where the Default clause at issue requires an inquiry into excusability prior to the termination, board review of that issue is precluded 90 days after the contracting officer's decision to terminate, *Ace Reforestation, Inc.*, AGBCA 84-272-1, 87-3 BCA ¶ 20,218 (Default clause akin to FAR 52.249-10 found to require an excusability determination prior to the default decision). See also *Interstate Forestry, Inc.*, AGBCA 89-114-1, 91-1 BCA ¶ 23,660, and *In Re Bloodgood*, AGBCA 97-178-2, 98-2 BCA ¶ 29,770. Where the contract does not incorporate this particular FAR clause, the language of the Default clause at issue will be scrutinized to determine whether excusability is a prerequisite to the default decision. In *Mike Horstman*, AGBCA 87-388-1, 89-2 BCA ¶ 21,752, the board converted a termination for default into a termination for the convenience of the government after ascertaining the merits of the underlying default decision because the language of the clause incorporated into the contract (FAR 52.249-8) did not require an excusability analysis prior to the decision. See also *Paul Evans Co.*, AGBCA 90-198-1, 91-3 BCA ¶ 24,062. Moreover, if the contracting officer's final decision issuing the termination is not properly worded, the AGBCA will apply the Fulford doctrine regardless of the wording of the Default clause because the contractor is not placed on adequate notice that the jurisdictional clock has begun to run, *B & M Constr., Inc.*, AGBCA 91-132-1, 91-2 BCA ¶ 23,670; *Theodore R. Korotie*, AGBCA 86-245-1, 89-3 BCA ¶ 22,214. In sum, while the other boards will apply the Fulford doctrine in all cases regardless of the language of the incorporated Default clause, the AGBCA will carefully analyze the language and, in the process, will strictly construe the application of the doctrine due to its belief that the doctrine is inconsistent with the Contract Disputes Act. The Court of Appeals for the Federal Circuit has yet to hear a case addressing this conflict.

In the post-CDA era, virtually all of the boards of contract appeals have been unwilling to extend the doctrine beyond the situation in which the government subsequently seeks to recover excess reprocurement costs. Thus, the merits of the default termination will not be permitted to be placed at issue where the government later brings a claim for the return of unliquidated progress payments, *Mactek Indus. Corp.*, ASBCA 33277, 87-1 BCA ¶ 19,345; where the termination for default is timely appealed but not adjudicated on the merits (dismissed with prejudice), *Bulloch Int'l, Inc.*, ASBCA 44210, 93-2 BCA ¶ 25,692; or where the government attempts to recover for contractor-caused damage to government property under the Permits and Responsibilities clause, *Dailing Roofing, Inc.*, ASBCA 34739, 89-1 BCA ¶ 21,311; *Smith & Smith Aircraft Co.*, ASBCA 37793, 92-2 BCA ¶ 24,871. These cases specifically rejected a pre-CDA case that had referred to a "Fulford analogy." See *Pantronics, Inc.*, ASBCA 20982, 78-2 BCA ¶ 13,285, in which the board stated at 64,984:

> There appears to be no practical difference whether an assessment of costs is made by the Government under paragraph (b) or paragraph (f) of the Default clause, the

> net effect on the contractor involved is to assess damages against it for allegedly defaulting under [a] Government contract containing a Default clause.

In *Dailing Roofing*, the board specifically confined the reasoning of *Pantronics* to its facts. The board stated at 107,475-76:

> The "*Fulford* analogy" announced in *Pantronics* equated a Government claim for damages under the preservation of all rights (whether common law or contract created) provision in paragraph (f) of the standard supply contract Default clause (and in paragraph (d) of the Default clause in the captioned construction contract) with the assessment of excess reprocurement costs under paragraph (b) of the supply Default clause.
>
> Despite the foregoing sweeping equation, claims for various types of damages arising from deficient contractor performance may be asserted by the Government without necessitating the termination of the contract for default. For example, under a construction contract a contractor may be liable, *inter alia*, for damages under the permits and responsibilities clause, as asserted here, or for liquidated damages for late completion of the work. In neither situation does the contractor's right to proceed need to be terminated. By contrast, termination of the work, in whole or in part, is a prerequisite for asserting a claim for excess completion or reprocurement costs.
>
> * * *
>
> However, rather than dismiss the "*Fulford* analogy" announced in *Pantronics* as mere dictum, we confine its application to the factual setting in which it arose. Judgment on the viability of the *Pantronics* "*Fulford* analogy" can await such time as we are confronted with a "timely" appeal predating the damages claim to which it relates.

Thus, the boards are extremely reluctant to extend the Fulford doctrine any farther than the situations to which it has already been applied. See *Carter Indus., Inc.*, DOTBCA 2995, 98-1 BCA ¶ 29,625, in which the board refused to apply the Fulford doctrine when excess costs were collected through a proof of claim in a bankruptcy proceeding rather than by a contracting officer decision assessing excess costs. The board also rejected the contractor's contention that it had justifiably waited to appeal the decision because of the contracting officer's stated intention to demand reprocurement—noting that, while the FAR requires that a demand for repayment be made if a contracting officer's final decision results in a finding that the contractor is indebted to the government, a contracting officer has no legal obligation to issue a final decision.

The Fulford doctrine does not permit a contractor to relitigate the propriety of a default termination. See *Premiere Bldg. Servs., Inc.,* ASBCA 51804, 00-1 BCA ¶30,696, granting summary judgment against the contractor when it attempted to question the default termination after the government sought excess reprocurement costs because the contractor had taken the question of the propriety of the default to the Court of Federal Claims prior to the reprocurement cost assessment.

The Fulford doctrine allows a contractor to litigate the propriety of the initial termination for default; it does not afford a contractor the right to recover costs upon showing that the underlying default termination was improper, *American Telecom Corp. v. United States*, 59 Fed. Cl. 467 (2004).

B. Reasonableness of Government Action

In *Cascade Pac. Int'l v. United States*, 773 F.2d 287 (Fed. Cir. 1985), the court established what has now become the general test for determining whether the government's assessment of excess reprocurement costs is reasonable. It stated at 293-94:

> [E]xcess reprocurement costs may be imposed only when the Government meets its burden of persuasion that the following conditions (factual determinations) are met: (1) the reprocured supplies are the same as or similar to those involved in the termination; (2) the Government actually incurred excess costs; and (3) the Government acted reasonably to minimize the excess costs resulting from the default. The first condition is demonstrated by comparing the item reprocured with the item specified in the original contract. *Environmental Tectonics Corp.*, 78-1 BCA at 63,308. The second condition requires the Government to show what it spent in reprocurement. *Fairfield Scientific Corp. v. United States*, [222 Ct. Cl. 167,] 611 F.2d 854, 863-66 (1979). The third condition requires that the Government act within a reasonable time of the default, use the most efficient method of reprocurement, obtain a reasonable price, and mitigate its losses.

Judges typically test whether the contracting officer acted within a reasonable time after the default, obtained a reasonable repurchase price, used a reasonable manner of repurchase, and tried to mitigate the damages caused by the default, *Bertot Indus., Inc.*, ASBCA 41262, 96-1 BCA ¶ 28,230. Reasonableness is the critical criterion for the recovery of reprocurement costs as well as other expenses incurred that were reasonably foreseeable and the proximate result of the default, *Reddy-Buffaloes Pump, Inc.*, ENGBCA 6049, 96-1 BCA ¶ 28,111. See *M.D.R.-RIC,* PSBCA 4472, 01-1 BCA ¶ 31,302, finding a replacement contract reasonable, even though it was awarded at an annual rate nearly double that of the defaulted contractor, because it had to be awarded quickly in light of the emergency nature of the service contract and the government solicited a reasonable number of potential contractors and awarded the contract to the lowest offeror. Conversely, in *ARCO Eng'g, Inc.,* ASBCA 52450, 01-1 BCA ¶ 31,218, the board found considerable deficiencies, such as the inability to determine whether the reprocurement contract contained provisions impacting price, the absence of evidence indicating whether the reprocurement contract had been analyzed, the absence of evidence of whether the reprocurement contract had been negotiated, and the failure to justify the accelerated nature of the reprocurement contract.

1. Similarity

The determination of similarity is the threshold issue in deciding whether to uphold the assessment of excess costs, *Environmental Tectonics Corp.*, ASBCA 21204, 78-1 BCA ¶ 12,986; *Old Dominion Sec., Inc.*, GSBCA 9126, 90-2 BCA ¶ 22,745. The Default clause for supply and service contracts, FAR 52.249-8, contains language explicitly requiring the repurchased supplies and services to be "similar" to the terminated items. The construction contract clause does not contain the word "similar." Instead, it merely provides that the government may take over the work and prosecute it to completion. The boards have held, however, that a similarity determination under the construction contract clause is "largely analogous" to that under the service and supply contract clause, *Rayco, Inc.*, ENGBCA 4792, 88-2 BCA ¶ 20,671. In this case, the boards noted that in determining similarity, boards have refused to award reprocurement costs where fragmentation of the work in the reprocurement "materially altered the terms and conditions . . . of the original contract" or resulted in "substantial increase in the reprocurement contract price." See *Alfred L. Scevers, Jr.*, IBCA 1358-5-80, 83-2 BCA ¶ 16,579 (excess reprocurement costs not awarded where government reprocurement for tree-thinning contract materially altered the terms and conditions of the contract by dividing the remaining acres into two tracts, extending the time of performance, and awarding two separate contracts), and *G. O'Connor*, AGBCA 75-154, 78-1 BCA ¶ 12,981 (excess reprocurement costs not awarded because the reprocurement contract was almost three times the original price and material differences existed between the services in the original contract and the reprocurement agreement). It has been held that, under the construction contract provisions, the government is not entitled to make "material changes" in the reprocurement specifications resulting in "substantial alterations" in the work, *United States v. Axman*, 234 U.S. 36 (1914); *California Bridge & Constr. Co. v. United States*, 50 Ct. Cl. 40 (1915), *aff'd*, 245 U.S. 337 (1917).

The reprocured supplies or services must meet the similarity test, even though they do not have to be identical to the terminated work, or else the government loses its right to recover excess costs and must recover, if at all, under its common law right to damages. The effect of this rule is that, when a reprocured item is not "similar," the excess costs may not be adjusted to account for dissimilarities. In contrast, when the similarity test is met, but the reprocured item is not identical, the excess costs are adjusted to account for the differences in the items. The rationale for this dichotomy is that when the changes in the reprocured item are substantial and make the work more "onerous," the reprocurement price does not serve as a valid basis for comparison, *Octagon Process, Inc.*, ASBCA 3981, 58-1 BCA ¶ 1773. See *Romeo P. Yusi & Co.*, ASBCA 19810, 76-1 BCA ¶ 11,835, holding that the items were "not sufficiently comparable" and that the difference rendered it "impossible to make a rational comparison of the work." In *Cosmos Eng'rs, Inc.*, ASBCA 24270, 88-2 BCA ¶ 20,795, the board concluded that the differences between the defaulted contract specifications and the reprocurement contract specifications were so substantial that "to require [the contractor] to pay excess reprocurement costs would be patently unfair."

When determining the amount of excess reprocurement costs, the effect contract changes have on the contract price properly may be a fact issue and should not be decided on a motion for summary judgment, *Seaboard Lumber Co. v. United States*, 41 Fed. Cl. 401 (1998), *aff'd*, 308 F.3d 1283 (Fed. Cir. 2002).

a. Changes Reducing Cost of Work

While the lack-of-similarity argument appears to be a sufficient basis for denying excess costs when the effect of changes in the specifications is to make the reprocured article more expensive to produce than the defaulted item, its application would seem not to be called for in cases where the effect of specification changes is to make the reprocured item easier and less expensive to produce than the terminated item. Thus, the relaxation of specifications on reprocurement would appear to cause no harm to the defaulted contractor, would appear to be consistent with the government's requirement to mitigate its damages, and ought to be encouraged if it can clearly be shown that the changed reprocurement was less expensive than reprocurement of identical items would have been. Nevertheless, in some cases involving relaxed specifications, excess costs have been denied on the basis of dissimilarity. In *Hofman Indus., Inc.*, ASBCA 3435, 57-2 BCA ¶ 1468, the board stated that the specification changes on reprocurement, even though making the item less expensive to produce, showed that the government did not want the original item, never got it, and therefore should not be able to collect damages for not obtaining it on the original contract. In *Lome Elecs., Inc.*, ASBCA 8642, 1963 BCA ¶ 3833, the board recognized the mitigation argument but rejected it, stating at 19,102:

> The Government contends the change in specifications simplified the item, made it less costly and in effect rendered it an off the shelf item for the reprocurement contractor and therefore saved the defaulted contractor money. That the Government in its repurchase received nothing more than it was entitled to under the [contractor's] contract and received a similar item which it vitally needed, and its effort to simplify the specifications as to the computer, can only be interpreted as an honest effort to obtain the items needed as soon as possible, and at the lowest possible price.
>
> The board is impressed with the Government's contention and argument with respect to mitigating the amount of the excess cost. However, the board, although it recognizes the laudability of the Government's efforts to minimize the cost of reprocurement, does not believe that the reprocurement of a cheaper type of item is of itself determinative of this appeal.

The board in *B & M Constr., Inc.*, AGBCA 90-165-1, 93-1 BCA ¶ 25,431, reaffirmed this general rule, stating at 126,669:

> We have little sympathy for a contractor who abandons performance. Given the CO's clear rejection of [the contractor's] proposed design change, [the contractor] had a duty to proceed diligently with performance and file a claim for changed or additional work. [The contractor] did not so do.
>
> Nevertheless, we find that there were material differences between the project to be constructed under [the contractor's] contract and that ultimately delivered on reprocurement. The Government no longer wanted the access ramp removed or the area returned to its pristine pre-construction state. Nor did the Government want a field stone headwall or off-site disposal of construction debris. The terms and conditions of reprocurement differed materially from those under the defaulted contract, and SCS's treatment of [the contractor] and the reprocurement contractor was indeed disparate. We conclude that these factors alone are sufficient to support denial of the Government's claim for excess costs.

The fact that the differences in contracts reduced the difficulty and cost of the project was considered irrelevant in the board's determination of similarity. However, this logic will be inapposite where the relaxation of the contract requirements is found to be immaterial to the "quality, function, or manufacture" of the product. See *Meyer Labs., Inc.*, ASBCA 19525, 87-2 BCA ¶ 19,810 (allowing recovery of excess reprocurement costs where the relaxation of testing requirements did not relate to the causes of the default termination).

b. Test for Determining Similarity

One aspect of the determination of similarity involves comparing the end item delivered on the reprocurement contract with the item specified in the original contract at the time of default. It is generally stated that similarity requires that the item be similar in "physical and mechanical characteristics as well as functional purpose," *Lome Elecs., Inc.*, ASBCA 8642, 1963 BCA ¶ 3833. See *AGH Indus., Inc.*, ASBCA 27960, 89-2 BCA ¶ 21,637, in which the board determined that changes in testing requirements for helicopter skid tube assemblies were significant, stating at 108,863:

> The test to be applied in determining similarity is a comparison of end items delivered under the reprocurement contract with the item specified in the original contract at the time of default. It is well settled that the word "similar" need not be treated as meaning "identical."
>
> Therefore, while it is true that minor variations in the repurchased items will not relieve a contractor of its liability under the DEFAULT clause for excess reprocurement costs, substantial and material differences between the end items in the original contract and reprocurement contract will completely relieve the contractor of its liability for excess costs. [citation omitted]
>
> Moreover, changes in the specifications after the default of [the contractor's] contract do not invalidate the excess reprocurement cost assessment where the changes are corrections of errors or omissions, normal updating of specifica-

> tions as more production experience leads to simplifying manufacture or product improvement as long as the specification changes do not go to the heart of the procurement by affecting function of the product or by affecting the repurchase price. However, a difference in the reprocurement contract requiring or omitting a stringent test may invalidate the assessment of excess reprocurement costs. Thus, if the difference in testing would cause greater acceptance or rejection of one product over another, the difference would be significant. *Marmac Industries, Inc.*, ASBCA 12158, 72-1 BCA ¶ 9249.

See also *B & M Constr., Inc.*, AGBCA 90-165-1, 93-1 BCA ¶ 25,431, in which the board denied the government's claim for excess costs of reprocurement because the government's deletion of a contract requirement to remove an access ramp amounted to a substantial change in the desired end item.

One apparently broader test suggested for determining similarity is whether the changes in specifications would have fallen within the scope of the Changes clause of the defaulted contract. In *Skiatron Elecs. & Television Corp.*, ASBCA 9564, 65-2 BCA ¶ 5098, the board held that variations in reprocured resistance bridges were similar because they could have been made under the Changes clause, stating at 24,016:

> To hold otherwise would defeat the very purpose of the reprocurement privilege the Default clause allows or it would place the Government in the dilemma of reprocuring obsolete items in order to effect an assessment of excess costs. Obviously, this was never intended. No where in the record do we find any basis for vitiating the entire assessment or working a specific downward adjustment in the amount.

See also *Angler's Co.*, GSBCA 4390, 76-2 BCA ¶ 12,065, *recons. denied*, 77-1 BCA ¶ 12,319, *rev'd on other grounds*, 220 Ct. Cl. 727 (1979), in which the board held that the use of commercial rather than specification vinyl did not render the procured portfolios so different that they could not have been ordered under the Changes clause of the original contract. In *Dave's Aluminum Siding, Inc.*, ASBCA 34092, 90-3 BCA ¶ 23,053, the board found that changes in the degree of painting required under the reprocurement contract did not establish dissimilarity because such a revision fell within the scope of the Changes clause under the original contract. In view of the broad rights given to the government under the Changes clause, it is doubtful that this test is usable in all cases. In practice, the boards rarely even mention this approach as a viable standard for determining similarity.

Where there is no proof that the change caused an increase in the reprocurement price, similarity normally will be found. See *Arjay Mach. Co.*, ASBCA 16535, 73-2 BCA ¶ 10,179 (slight modifications of the drawings were not material); *Meyer Labs, Inc.*, ASBCA 19525, 87-2 BCA ¶ 19,810 (substitution of materials and modes of measurement did not preclude a similarity finding as they were minor variations); and *Solar Labs., Inc.*, ASBCA 19957, 76-2 BCA ¶ 12,115 (revised purchase description neither increased costs nor created substantial or material changes in functional purpose or physical and mechanical characteristics of the pads). Even where there is an increase in cost, similarity may be found where "the material, essential configuration and purpose of the reprocured articles [are] the same" as those that were to be furnished by the defaulted contractor, *H.N. Bailey & Assocs. v. United States*, 196 Ct. Cl. 166, 449 F.2d 376 (1971).

The reprocured work was found to be similar in *Associated Traders, Inc. v. United States*, 144 Ct. Cl. 744, 169 F. Supp. 502 (1959) (although reprocurement contractor furnished a different quality adhesive than defaulted contractor, both items met the same specifications); *Guenther Sys., Inc.*, ASBCA 18343, 77-1 BCA ¶ 12,501 (reprocured components found functionally, physically, and mechanically similar although manufactured from bar stock rather than from castings); *UMM, Inc.*, ENGBCA 5330, 87-2 BCA ¶ 19,893 (new contract for lawn mowing work incorporated essentially "the same services . . . on virtually identical terms" as the defaulted contract); *Sequal, Inc.*, ASBCA 30838, 88-1 BCA ¶ 20,382 (minor dimensional differences in specifications insufficient to find dissimilarity); *Predator Sys., Inc.*, NASABCA 43-0291, 92-2 BCA ¶ 24,903 (reprocurement modification changing the pounds per square inch on the calibration system did not render the new contract dissimilar); and *Arctic Corner, Inc.*, ASBCA 38075, 94-1 BCA ¶ 26,317 (similarity found where the reprocurement involved the same specifications and basically the same drawings as the defaulted contract). In *MPT Enters.*, ASBCA 25483, 83-2 BCA ¶ 16,767, the board upheld an excess cost assessment based on repurchase of "newly manufactured items" following default under a contract that permitted the contractor to provide "surplus" items, even though the repurchase price was three times the original contract price, because "it does not appear unreasonable in the light of the price history and the risk appellant assumed under the Default clause that the respondent might reprocure the more expensive manufactured units in lieu of surplus."

The reprocurement was found dissimilar in *American Sheet Metal Corp., v. General Servs. Admin.*, GSBCA 14066, 99-1 BCA ¶ 30,329 (reprocurement contractor certified only to install a completely different roof system, with a different number of membranes and a different application process); *Ace Reforestation, Inc.*, AGBCA 84-272-1, 87-3 BCA ¶ 20,218 (deletion of hand-scalping requirement and clearer indication of the degree of work to be completed under the reprocurement contract rendered it dissimilar to the defaulted contract); *Tenney Eng'g, Inc.*, ASBCA 19289, 75-1 BCA ¶ 11,249 (added floor support "significantly additional" to that required by specifications); *Suffolk Envtl. Magnetics, Inc.*, ASBCA 17593, 74-2 BCA ¶ 10,771 (waiver of tolerance specifications rendered reprocured items dissimilar in physical and mechanical characteristics); *Cosmos Eng'rs, Inc.*, ASBCA 24270, 88-2 BCA ¶ 20,795 (substantial relaxation of specifications on reprocurement of radio transmitters precluded award of excess reprocurement costs); *Star Food Processing, Inc.*, ASBCA 34161, 90-1 BCA ¶ 22,390 (lack of similarity between reprocured diced beef and terminated ham slices prevented recovery); *G. O'Connor*, AGBCA 75-154, 78-1 BCA ¶ 12,981 (extension of work area resulting in a price more than twice that of the original contract); *NEH Logging*, AGBCA 76-187, 77-2 BCA ¶

12,850 (reduction in work area and government's inability to allow salvage rights to timber on reprocurement constituted material variations); *Aerosonic Corp.*, ASBCA 11718, 72-1 BCA ¶ 9241 (repurchase contract was "essentially a research and development rather than a production effort"); and *Accutherm, Inc.*, ASBCA 25474, 83-1 BCA ¶ 16,307 (repurchase specifications called for heat-treat furnaces "more modern in material and design").

The "physical and mechanical characteristics" test has been held not to be applicable to a reprocurement under a terminated two-step formally advertised contract, *Steelship Corp.*, ENGBCA 3830, 78-2 BCA ¶ 13,478. There, the second low bidder on the two-step procurement was awarded the reprocurement contract for an item that was significantly better and more expensive than the one that was to have been provided under the defaulted contract. The board determined that a two-step procurement differs from the normal procedure in that the competition is on performance specifications. It further noted that, if the physical and mechanical characteristics test for similarity were applied, the government would be unable to recover any excess costs despite its efforts to "cover," stating at 65,943:

> In this situation, we believe that it is sufficient that the replacement item is similar in function and utility, and that variations in physical characteristics need not (subject to the duty of mitigation) bar the Government from recovering reasonable excess costs.

Note, however, that the board did hold the contractor entitled to a $140,000 reduction in the excess cost assessment to account for this "betterment" in design.

c. *Changes in Inspection and Testing*

The changes do not have to be in the end item specifications for dissimilarity to be found. The addition or deletion of an inspection or test can result in the excess cost assessment being invalidated. In *AGH Indus., Inc.*, ASBCA 27960, 89-2 BCA ¶ 21,637, the tightening of tolerance specifications on a helicopter assembly contract rendered the reprocurement dissimilar because it would have an effect on the rejection rate of the reprocurement as well as the repurchase price. Similarly, in *Luis Martinez*, AGBCA 86-148-1, 87-3 BCA ¶ 20,219, the board found the reprocurement dissimilar because the resolicited contract had relaxed the degree of compliance necessary to satisfy the standard for acceptability of grubbing work, which amounted to substantially disparate treatment. However, not all changes in tests or inspections result in dissimilarity. In *Puroflow Corp.*, ASBCA 36058, 93-3 BCA ¶ 26,191, the board held that the addition in their entirety of several military specifications that had only been referenced in the defaulted contract did not render the reprocurement contract dissimilar. The board found it compelling that the variations were shown neither to have caused any unreasonable expense to the reprocurement contractor nor to have created a different, more expensive product. Likewise, in *Churchill Chem. Corp.*, GSBCA 4353, 77-1 BCA ¶ 12,318, *aff'd*, 221 Ct. Cl.

284, 602 F.2d 358 (1979), the reprocurement was similar despite the addition of a test for adhesive quality of a sealing compound because there was no evidence that the addition induced increases in the pricing data utilized on reprocurement, and in *Meyer Labs, Inc.*, ASBCA 19525, 87-2 BCA ¶ 19,810, no dissimilarity was found because the addition of several tests did not affect the function or manufacture of the end items.

d. Changes in Terms and Conditions

The GAO has concluded that there is no regulatory requirement that a reprocurement be conducted using precisely the same terms as the original procurement, *Vereinigte Gebaudereinigungsgesellschaft*, Comp. Gen. Dec. B-280805, 98-2 CPD ¶ 117. Dissimilarity may be found, however, if the terms and conditions of the reprocurement contract differ materially from those of the defaulted contract, *Seay's Moving & Storage Co.*, ASBCA 12806, 69-1 BCA ¶ 7639 (reprocurement of moving services through purchase orders given by oral quotations held to be "a clean break" from the original contract); *Allied Sales Co.*, ASBCA 12650, 68-2 BCA ¶ 7257 (omission of a price warranty clause); *B & M Constr., Inc.*, AGBCA 90-165-1, 93-1 BCA ¶ 25,431 (deletion of access ramp requirement found to be a material change in terms and conditions). The focus in such cases is usually on whether the different terms and conditions would increase the reprocurement contractor's cost of performance or result in higher bids. Thus, in *Skiatron Elecs. & Television Corp.*, ASBCA 9564, 65-2 BCA ¶ 5098, the insertion of a liquidated damage clause in the reprocurement contract was held not to make the reprocurement dissimilar because it did not increase the cost of performance and the price was unchanged in alternate bidding—with or without the liquidated damages clause. In *Rhocon Constructors*, AGBCA 86-125-1, 91-1 BCA ¶ 23,308, the board noted that, despite evidence of similarity, a 25 percent increase in reprocurement price coupled with a lack of evidence addressing the terms and conditions of the reprocurement contract precluded an assessment of excess reprocurement costs.

In *James A. Connor,* ASBCA 10356, 68-2 BCA ¶ 7409, the government terminated a negotiated fixed-price contract for tracking antennas and awarded a cost-plus-incentive-fee contract on reprocurement. In response to the defaulted contractor's arguments that this change in pricing arrangement should invalidate the excess costs assessment, the board stated at 34,451:

> Further, it does not appear that the use of the cost-plus incentive fee method of contracting enlarged the damages. In fact, based upon the Radiation two-phase proposal, the first phase alone would have been, according to its 26 October 1964 proposal, $187,309 and, as indicated in its 6 October 1964 proposal, the second phase had a "ball park estimate" of $500,000. If this is any indication of what its contingency planning would be, a fixed-price bid may have been considerably higher than the actual cost-plus incentive fee contract turned out to be. It is fairly clear from the record that there were many uncertainties once the Air Force made

> the decision to take and use the ASI items in their condition at the time of termination. If the solutions were not clear and simple, it is because the problems left with the Air Force as a result of the ASI default were not clear and simple.

Contrast *Matthews Co.*, AGBCA 459, 76-2 BCA ¶ 12,164, *recons. denied*, 77-1 BCA ¶ 12,434, in which the board found that a reprocurement contractor working on a cost-reimbursement contract had incurred costs that were "clearly excessive."

Similarity has been found despite a difference in terms and conditions, *Lester Phillips, Inc.*, ASBCA 20735, 77-1 BCA ¶ 12,447 (although clauses specifying the date for container removal and limiting the number of refuse collection containers were not included in reprocurement contracts, the number actually used did not exceed the original limits, and the reprocurement contractor's bid was slightly lower than its bid on the original contract); *Schmalz Constr. Ltd.*, AGBCA 92-177-1, 94-1 BCA ¶ 26,423 (modification to reprocurement contract deleting the last 836 feet of road construction found not to be a material change in terms and conditions); *George E. Marshall & Gordon L. Blackwell,* ENGBCA 6066, 00-1 BCA ¶ 30,730 (reprocurement contract differed from the terminated contract due to "conditions on the ground after [the contractor] abandoned the work and by minor, required updating of the specifications and clauses that have not been shown to have increased the costs to complete").

e. Changes in Method of Procurement

A change in procurement technique is not, in and of itself, a sufficient reason to find dissimilarity in the reprocurement. The courts and boards have held that "[i]n reprocuring items on a defaulted contract, the contracting officer has very broad discretionary powers," and the choice of procurement methods falls within that discretion, *Astro-Space Labs., Inc. v. United States*, 200 Ct. Cl. 282, 470 F.2d 1003 (1972). See *Old Dominion Sec., Inc.*, GSBCA 9126, 90-2 BCA ¶ 22,745, where reprocurement of a security services contract by negotiation rather than sealed bidding was found to be within the contracting officer's discretion. The board dismissed as speculation the contractor's argument that the use of negotiation rather than sealed bidding drove up reprocurement prices. See also *Orlotronics Corp.*, ASBCA 23287, 79-2 BCA ¶ 13,912, in which the board rejected as speculative and unsupported a contractor's contention that reprocurement of aircraft barrel assemblies through negotiation rather than formal advertising had resulted in increases in previously submitted offers. In *Rayco, Inc.*, ENGBCA 4792, 88-2 BCA ¶ 20,671, the fragmentation of a construction contract reprocurement into 13 purchase orders and two solicitations for bids was upheld because, in the circumstances, the fragmentation was reasonable and within the contracting officer's discretion. However, see *Mathews Co.*, AGBCA 459, 76-2 BCA ¶ 12,164, *recons. denied*, 77-1 BCA ¶ 12,434, in which the board found that the government had failed to mitigate damages and obtain a reasonable price in reprocuring a fixed-price construction contract on a cost-reimbursement basis. In denying the government's claim for excess reprocurement costs, the board held that the reprocurement contract was inadequately supervised and that the contractor incurred costs that were clearly excessive.

Generally, the statutes and regulations governing federal procurements are not strictly applicable to reprocurement of defaulted contracts. *E. Huttenbauer & Son, Inc.*, Comp. Gen. Dec. B-239142.2, 90-2 CPD ¶ 140. Rather, the contracting officer may use any terms and acquisition method deemed appropriate under the circumstances that result in a reasonable price and maximum practicable competition. For example, the contracting officer may also choose to reprocure the items by placing an order under an existing Federal Supply Schedule contract rather than conduct a new competition under which the defaulted contractor might have participated, *ATA Def. Indus., Inc.*, Comp. Gen. Dec. B-275303, 97-1 CPD ¶ 161.

2. *Effect of Relaxed Specifications That Contractor Could Have Met*

Some boards of contract appeals are reluctant to assess excess costs based on relaxed specifications that the defaulted contractor could have met, even though the default termination is held to be proper. See *Blake Constr. Co.*, GSBCA 4013, 75-2 BCA ¶ 11,487, stating at 54,806:

> It is an established principle in the law of Government contracts that the contractor will not be liable for the excess costs of reprocurement where the contract requirements are relaxed on reprocurement and where the facts indicate that the contractor could have performed given the same relaxation in requirements. *Appeal of Federal Identification Co.*, ASBCA 9117, 1964 BCA ¶ 4191.

See also *Luis Martinez*, AGBCA 86-148-1, 87-3 BCA ¶ 20,219, in which the board further established this principle, stating at 102,407:

> [T]he burden [is] on the [contractor] to show performance could have been accomplished under the relaxed standard. . . . Mere allegations without more are not acceptable as proof. [The contractor] has, however, shown a relaxed standard was applied. We conclude such showing, coupled with the change in contract specifications, evidences so material a difference between the original and reprocurement contracts as written and administered as to preclude assessment of reprocurement costs.

Accord, *Sterling Tool, Inc.*, ASBCA 19790, 75-2 BCA ¶ 11,577. See *F.R. Schultz Constr. Co.*, AGBCA 455, 79-2 BCA ¶ 13,890, overturning an excess costs assessment where the government failed to place any time limitation on completion of the work in the reprocurement contract; and *Pervo Paint Co.*, GSBCA 8220, 87-1 BCA ¶ 19,409, finding that where the reprocurement contractor also failed to maintain proper testing controls that had led to the default of the original contractor, excess reprocurement costs were improper. Compare, however, *Rio Hondo Containers*, GS-

BCA 3494, 72-2 BCA ¶ 9514 (no indication that elimination of a sidewall thickness requirement from the reprocurement contract for plastic caps would have prevented the performance difficulties encountered by the defaulted contractor); *Russ Leadabrand*, AGBCA 75-126, 77-2 BCA ¶ 12,765 (no evidence that the defaulted contractor could have properly written and prepared Forest Service leaflets had it been granted the same time extension); and *Birken Mfg. Co.*, ASBCA 32590, 90-2 BCA ¶ 22,845 (no evidence that the defaulted contractor could have delivered spacers had first article deliveries not been required). Generally, the contractor bears the burden of proving that it could have performed under the specifications incorporated in the reprocurement contract, *T.M. Indus.*, ASBCA 21025, 77-1 BCA ¶ 12,400, *recons. denied*, 77-1 BCA ¶ 12,545; *Butler Enters.*, AGBCA 74-106, 76-2 BCA ¶ 12,094.

There is authority that the contractor's ability to perform to the reprocurement specifications is not relevant to the issue of excess costs, *American Sur.y Co. of N.Y. v. United States*, 317 F.2d 652 (8th Cir. 1963) (substitution permitted to reprocurement contractor but denied to original contractor); *United States v. McMullen*, 222 U.S. 460 (1912) (government denying permission to defaulted contractor to dump spoil in deep water and granting permission to completing contractor did not preclude assessment of cost since diminished cost was the only change).

3. Variations in Quantity Reprocured

The contracting officer has broad discretion to vary the quantity reprocured, and if increased costs result, the reprocurement cost will be adjusted rather than totally disallowed, *Consolidated Airborne Sys., Inc. v. United States*, 172 Ct. Cl. 588, 348 F.2d 941 (1965). For example, in *M.S.I. Corp.*, VACAB 599, 67-2 BCA ¶ 6643, where the government contracted for completion of repair of 600 feet of footwalk but the original contractor had been obliged to repair only 400 feet, the board reduced the government's assessment of costs against the contractor by one-third. In many cases, the purchase of a larger quantity tends to reduce the unit price of the items. Thus, the defaulted contractor is often benefited by an increased quantity because the excess costs are measured by the unit price paid on reprocurement for the number of units that were to have been provided under the terminated contract, *Charles Nugent*, AGBCA 92-195-1, 93-3 BCA ¶ 26,213 (deduction for variation of quantity of acres to be scalped led to reduction of excess cost recovery); *F.P. Pla Tool & Mfg. Co.*, ASBCA 19073, 75-1 BCA ¶ 11,091 (increase did not prejudice the defaulted contractor).

On the other hand, the impact of purchasing fewer items may be to increase the unit cost. In such cases, the increased unit cost should be offset against the lower number of units. Thus, a case-by-case price comparison must be made. When there is a determination that the reduction in quantities has no impact on the price, the full amount of the excess cost assessment will generally be upheld, *Consolidated Mach. Corp.*, ASBCA 14366, 73-1 BCA ¶ 9942 (a quantity discount for the original quantity was apportioned equally among those units and subtracted from the total of the reprocurement to arrive at the excess cost assessment); *Bardeen Mfg. Co.*, ASBCA 19128, 75-1 BCA ¶ 11,036 (no impact on price through repurchase of reduced quantity except for minor errors in computation that were adjusted by the board). However, where the reduction does increase the cost of the reprocurement, a downward adjustment in the excess cost assessment normally will be made, *Agni Eng'g Co.*, ASBCA 10885, 67-1 BCA ¶ 6250 (reprocurement contractor's quotation for the same quantity reflected a 19 percent increase in unit price but indicated a 43 percent price increase on the reduced quantity); *R & O Indus., Inc.*, GSBCA 4917, 79-1 BCA ¶ 13,832 (increased price not linked solely to reduction in quantity but also to inflationary market conditions); *Rayco, Inc.*, ENGBCA 4792, 88-2 BCA ¶ 20,671 (reduction of quantity by a factor of 10 or greater found to be the logical cause of increased prices on reprocurement and did not reduce recovery).

When comparison of unit prices of the original contract items and the reduced quantity of reprocured items is impossible, the excess cost assessment may be completely denied, *Management Servs., Inc.*, ASBCA 11190, 67-1 BCA ¶ 6103 (price adjustment mechanism in the reprocurement contract indicated that the price of meals varied inversely with the quantity). In *Alfred L. Scevers, Jr.*, IBCA 1358-5-80, 83-2 BCA ¶ 16,579, the board disallowed an excess cost assessment where terminated work under a tree-thinning contract was divided into two tracts and reprocured under two separate contracts, causing fixed costs to be allocated over a smaller number of acres and resulting in a higher price per acre. See also *B & M Constr., Inc.*, AGBCA 90-165-1, 93-1 BCA ¶ 25,431, in which the board found that neither the unreasonably low government estimate nor the unreasonably high reprocurement contract price provided a reasonable basis for calculating excess costs. Therefore, the costs were denied completely.

When a requirements contract is terminated, the government is entitled to assess costs not only on the items actually ordered but not delivered under the defaulted contract, but also on items that could have been ordered under the defaulted contract, *Interroyal Corp.*, GSBCA 5439, 83-1 BCA ¶ 16,339; *Zan Mach. Co.*, ASBCA 39462, 91-3 BCA ¶ 24,085.

4. *Mitigation*

In pricing and awarding the reprocurement contract, the government must endeavor to mitigate its damages, *Cascade Pac. Int'l v. United States*, 773 F.2d 287 (Fed. Cir. 1985), and make the reprocurement award at a reasonable price, FAR 49.402-6. Both these requirements will be satisfied if the government acts reasonably in selecting the reprocurement contractor and in establishing the reprocurement price. In *Barrett Ref. Corp.*, ASBCA 36590, 91-1 BCA ¶ 23,566, the board stated at 118,145:

> The duty the Government owes the defaulted contractor in reprocuring for its account is not one of perfection, but one of reasonableness and prudence under the

> circumstances. [citations omitted] This duty is to be carried out within the confines of Federal procurement statutes, regulations, policies and directives and the Government is not required to change such policies to secure a better reprocurement price for a defaulted contractor. *X-Tyal International Corp.*, ASBCA Nos. 24353, 26495, 84-2 BCA ¶ 17,251. Further, it is not the contracting officer's obligation to do everything that he or she might to secure a lower price for a defaulted contractor, and in the process subordinate the Government's own best interests.

In making this determination, the board will consider both the government's actions and the relationship between the reprocurement price and that of the defaulted contract. In *Solar Labs., Inc.*, ASBCA 19957, 76-2 BCA ¶ 12,115, the board identified a number of the factors to be considered, stating at 58,196:

> Specifically, in numerous cases upholding assessments of excess costs incurred in a sole-source reprocurement, this Board and others, in determining reasonableness of the reprocurement price and whether the Government had made reasonable efforts to mitigate damages, have considered whether give-and-take negotiations were conducted, whether a cost breakdown was obtained, whether the Government performed any cost or price analysis, and whether the Government obtained a satisfactory explanation for any substantial increase over the reprocurement contractor's bid on the original contract. See, for example, *Consolidated Airborne Systems, Inc.*, ASBCA 5498, 61-1 BCA ¶ 2933, in which the Board, relying on the facts that the Government obtained cost data and negotiated a price reduction, upheld the assessment of excess costs, in the face of a substantial increase over the original contract price. The decision was sustained by the Court of Claims. *Consolidated Airborne Systems, Inc. v. United States*, [*supra*], 172 Ct. Cl. 588, 348 F.2d 941 (1965). In upholding the reasonableness of the reprocurement price as a basis for measuring excess costs, the Board has also relied on the fact that vigorous, arm's-length negotiations were conducted, even though no price reduction resulted. *Kollsman Instrument Corp.*, ASBCA 10667, 66-1 BCA ¶ 5696. A similar result was reached in *Applied Scientific Production and Research*, ASBCA 17245, 74-2 BCA ¶ 10,877, in which the Board noted that the contracting officer had obtained an explanation for the difference between the reprocurement contractor's price as compared with his original bid.
>
> On the other hand, the amount of the Government's excess cost recovery has frequently been reduced where the Government did not show adequate efforts to obtain the lowest reasonable price on the reprocurement, especially where the reprocurement contractor was a sole source. In some cases the Board has relied simply on the absence of an explanation for increases in the reprocurement contractor's price over his bid on the defaulted contract or other earlier contracts. *Standard Engineering & Manufacturing Co.*, ASBCA 3733, 57-2 BCA ¶ 1477 at p. 5067, *reconsid. denied*, 57-2 BCA ¶ 1568 (10.1 and 25.9 percent higher, respectively, than two of his previous contract prices); *Dakota Process Equipment Co.*, ASBCA 4435, 58-2 BCA ¶ 1981 (55 percent increase over original bid one year before); *Agni Engineering Co.*, ASBCA Nos. 10885 and 11535, 67-1 BCA ¶ 6250 at p. 28,951 (net unexplained increase of 24 percent over original bid 21 months before).

In other cases the Board has emphasized specific actions that the Government could or should have taken, but did not, to assure price reasonableness or mitigate excess costs—sometimes in the face of substantial increases over previous prices, but other times even without mention of such increases. In these cases the Board has emphasized variously the absence of give- and-take negotiations to obtain a lower price or an explanation of price increases; the absence of inquiry as to catalog or market prices; the absence of showing of prices established in earlier Government contracts; the failure to obtain a cost breakdown; the omission of a most-favored customer warranty included in the defaulted contract; the failure to perform price analysis; and the inconsistency of an explanation of a price increase even where a cost breakdown was obtained. *De Lisser Manufacturing Corp.*, ASBCA 1002, 22 September 1952, *reconsid. denied*, 9 January 1953 (reprocurement price 91 percent higher than defaulted contract price and 16 1/3 percent higher than his bid thereon one year before); *General Electronic Laboratories, Inc.*, ASBCA Nos. 8918 and 8926, 1964 BCA ¶ 4326 at p. 20,932 (25 percent increase over original bid five months before); *Goldhaber*, ASBCA Nos. 8277 and 8370, 65-2 BCA ¶ 5083 at p. 23,955; *Lutz Company*, GSBCA 2173, 68-1 BCA ¶ 6762 (10 percent increase over original bid five months before); *Reliable Maintenance Service*, ASBCA 11010, 68-1 BCA ¶ 6853 (24 percent increase over original bid five months before); *Atlas Manufacturing Co., Inc.*, ASBCA 15177, 71-2 BCA ¶ 9026 at 41,929; *Fitzgerald Laboratories, Inc.*, ASBCA Nos. 15205 and 15594, 71-2 BCA ¶ 9029 (40 percent increase over original bid); *Empresas Electronicas Walser, Inc.*, ASBCA 17524, 74-2 BCA ¶ 10,664 at p. 50,639; *Century Tool Co.*, GSBCA 4000, 76-1 BCA ¶ 11,855; *Marine Engine Specialties Corp.*, ASBCA Nos. 20418, 20521 and 20522, 76-1 BCA ¶ 11,891 (in ASBCA 20521, 25 percent increase over original bid); *Marine Engine Specialties Corp.*, ASBCA 21053, 76-2 BCA ¶ 12,034 (23 July 1976) (19 percent increase over original bid).

The board found that the government had failed to mitigate because, despite a 41 percent increase in cost, it had not demanded cost data, conducted a price analysis, checked catalog prices, negotiated for a lower price, or sought a quantity discount.

a. Lack of Negotiation or Price Analysis

The government must follow reasonable business practices to ensure that the reprocurement price is not inflated. In *Century Tool Co.*, GSBCA 4000, 76-1 BCA ¶ 11,855, the board found no mitigation where the contracting officer had neither negotiated for a lower price nor attempted to obtain an explanation, despite the fact that the reprocurement unit price was $.03 greater than a bid by the same contractor two weeks earlier. See also *A.L.S. Elec. Corp.*, ASBCA 18417, 74-1 BCA ¶ 10,589 (failure to investigate reprocurement contractor's much lower bids on previous contracts resulted in a repurchase price that was "grossly excessive and completely out of line"); *Wise Instrumentation & Control, Inc.*, NASABCA 1072-12, 75-2 BCA ¶ 11,478, *recons. denied*, 76-1 BCA ¶ 11,641 (no give-and-take negotiations or price analysis though procurement price was 37 percent over the original price); *Associated Cleaning, Inc.*, GSBCA 8360, 91-1 BCA ¶ 23,360 (use of flawed price estimate found unreasonable where the reprocurement contract price amounted to 30 percent more than the original contract price and was higher than the bids of all those who responded to the original solicitation); *T.M. Indus.*, ASBCA 21026, 77-1 BCA ¶ 12,451 (no price analysis when reprocurement contractor's bid was 35 percent higher than the price of the defaulted contract); *Birken Mfg. Co.*, ASBCA 32590, 90-2 BCA ¶ 22,845 (lack of price analysis and negotiation with the reprocurement contractor when price was 67 percent higher than that of the defaulted contractor found unreasonable); *Rhocon Constructors*, AGBCA 86-125-1, 91-1 BCA ¶ 23,308 (25 percent increase in price with no evidence of efforts by the government to mitigate held unreasonable); *Puroflow Corp.*, ASBCA 36058, 93-3 BCA ¶ 26,191 (excess costs reduced due to the lack of negotiations with the reprocurement contractor, whose bid was 12.5 percent higher than it had been for the original solicitation); and *Acorn Specialty & Supply Co.*, ASBCA 22710, 79-1 BCA ¶ 13,820 (failure to adequately explore the technical acceptability of another manufacturer's product that was known to be much lower in price).

For cases finding the reprocurement price to be reasonable because of adequate negotiation, see *Airosal Co.*, GSBCA 4374, 76-1 BCA ¶ 11,781 (government researched increased performance costs and conducted bona fide negotiations to award contract for accelerated delivery costing 32 percent more on one item and at least 97 percent more on another); *Pinel Tool Co.*, GSBCA 4380, 76-2 BCA ¶ 12,009 (price analysis conducted and found to justify award where only one offer received); *American Kal Enters., Inc.*, GSBCA 4449, 76-2 BCA ¶ 11,929 (negotiations for lower price unsuccessful, but the closeness of the three offered prices indicated reasonable market price); *Mattatuck Mfg. Co.*, GSBCA 4847, 80-1 BCA ¶ 14,349 (reprocurement price 87 percent higher found reasonable based on general increase in steel prices, accelerated delivery requirement, and original contract price that was 32 percent low); *Barrett Ref. Corp.*, ASBCA 36590, 91-1 BCA ¶ 23,566 (temporary shifting of oil from different suppliers already under contract when other contractors were available at a lower price found reasonable because this was the prior government practice); and *Great Northern Forestry Serv.*, AGBCA 85-260-1, 90-2 BCA ¶ 22,668 (8 percent increase in price for immediate reprocurement found reasonable given that the reprocurement contractor had been the second low bidder on the original procurement and a substantial amount of rework needed to be done).

b. Lack of Competition

The extent of competition on reprocurement is also important to a determination of reasonableness. See FAR 49.402-6(b), stating that "the contracting officer shall obtain competition to the maximum extent practicable for the repurchase." Nonetheless, each reprocurement is evaluated in terms of the circumstances faced by the government at the time of the reprocurement. See *Old Dominion Sec., Inc.*, GSBCA 9126, 90-2 BCA ¶ 22,745, in which the board concluded that the method of reprocurement is within the "very broad discretionary powers" of the contracting officer and is not, by itself, sufficient to overcome a claim for excess costs of reprocurement;

and *Interstate Forestry, Inc.*, AGBCA 89-114-1, 91-1 BCA ¶ 23,660, in which the board cited FAR 49.402-6 for the proposition that, for reprocurement, the contracting officer may use "any terms and acquisition method deemed appropriate" as long as it is completed promptly and competition is obtained to the "maximum extent practicable." See also *H & H Mfg. Co. v. United States*, 168 Ct. Cl. 873 (1964), holding that a sole source, negotiated reprocurement was justified by the urgent need although the unit price was nearly 60 percent above that of the original contract. The importance of competition as a factor in determining whether the government acted reasonably may diminish when there is an urgent need for the supplies or services or when other special circumstances preclude full competition, *Erickson Enters.*, AGBCA 77-168, 79-1 BCA ¶ 13,628 (government efforts to locate contractor sufficient in view of limited time to perform work); *Ross & McDonald Contracting, GmbH*, ASBCA 38154, 94-1 BCA ¶ 26,316 (contacting firms from original solicitation rather than resoliciting found reasonable given the urgent need for janitorial services on two military bases); *Luther Benjamin Constr. Co.*, ASBCA 40401, 93-1 BCA ¶ 25,459 (use of sole source negotiations found reasonable given the urgency involved in a contract for an administrative building and the fact that the government had complied with the justification and approval requirements for the establishment of compelling urgency under FAR 6.302-2). In *Ronald L. Collier*, ASBCA 26972, 89-1 BCA ¶ 21,328, award to a contractor doing similar work in the same region as the defaulted contractor was found reasonable due to the urgent need for the performance of such services at 550 naval bases. The board placed great emphasis on the fact that the prices paid to the reprocurement contractor were the same as those the government would have paid for the same services on a competitive basis.

The standard for determining the adequacy of the solicitation for the reprocurement was set forth in *Camrex Reliance Paint Co.*, GSBCA 6870, 85-3 BCA ¶ 18,376, at 92,179-80:

> To obtain adequate competition in the reprocurement, offers must be solicited from a sufficient number of competent potential sources to ensure adequate competition. The Government is not required, however, to solicit every known source of supply; nor is it required to solicit all who bid on the original solicitation. Where there is no reason to believe that solicitation of a greater number of potential contractors would have resulted in lower prices, the Government will be found to have fulfilled its duty to mitigate damages.

See *San Antonio Constr. Co.*, ASBCA 8110, 1964 BCA ¶ 4479 (no indication that costs would have been lower had negotiations been conducted with more than one firm); *Marmac Indus., Inc.*, ASBCA 12158, 72-1 BCA ¶ 9249 (only 14 of the original 57 bidders were solicited, but no evidence was presented of resultant cost increase or of other firms being qualified); *Brazier Lumber Co.*, ASBCA 18601, 76-2 BCA ¶ 12,207 (government solicited bids from five regular lumber suppliers on reprocurement of six contracts, and 18 of 23 line item prices were less than those quoted in a trade publication); *Star Food Processing, Inc.*, ASBCA 34161, 90-1 BCA ¶ 22,390 (solicitation of 10 offerors found reasonable); and *John L. Hartsoe*, AGBCA 88-116-1, 93-2 BCA ¶ 25,614 (award to lowest of four bidders found reasonable even though the price was 300 percent greater than that of the defaulted contractor, in part because the price was still lower than the government's in-house estimate).

In *A.L.S. Elec. Corp.*, ASBCA 18417, 74-1 BCA ¶ 10,589, the reprocurement was found deficient where, in addition to other problems, only three firms were orally solicited despite the existence of at least 26 other qualified manufacturers. Similarly, in *Disan Corp.*, ASBCA 21297, 79-1 BCA ¶ 13,677, the board overturned an excess cost assessment because only one source had been solicited and its price was approximately 200 percent higher than the defaulted contract price. In *JR & Assocs.*, ASBCA 41377, 92-1 BCA ¶ 24,654, the board substantially reduced a claim for excess costs where the reprocurement contract had been awarded on a sole source basis and there existed neither an urgent need for new windows nor a reasonable basis in the record for the higher price. Failure to publish the repurchase solicitation may also indicate a failure to mitigate costs, *Continental Chem. Corp.*, GSBCA 4483, 76-2 BCA ¶ 11,948.

Sole source reprocurement will be permitted if required by the circumstances, *Consolidated Airborne Sys., Inc. v. United States*, 172 Ct. Cl. 588, 348 F.2d 941 (1965) (urgent need); *Agni Eng'g Co.*, ASBCA 10885, 67-1 BCA ¶ 6250 (no evidence that other qualified producers were interested in bidding); *AAR Corp.*, ASBCA 17194, 74-1 BCA ¶ 10,607 (reprocurement contractor was the only supplier of the items other than the defaulted contractor and another who had been unable to perform a previous contract, the only one on the qualified products list, and the only one who could ensure timely delivery); *EDI Corp.*, ASBCA 21705, 79-1 BCA ¶ 13,650 (only other firm to respond to original solicitation). However, where evidence exists that other sources are capable of doing the work and are reasonably obtainable, sole source awards are improper, *John L. Hartsoe*, AGBCA 88-116-1, 93-2 BCA ¶ 25,614 (lack of evidence of adequate competition precluded assessment of excess costs of reprocurement, despite price equal to the defaulted contractor's, in part because the reprocurement contractor had not been included in the original procurement).

In *Pastushin Aviation Co.*, ASBCA 21243, 82-1 BCA ¶ 15,639, the board held that the government could not recover the costs incurred by the reprocurement contractor in completing units using the defaulted contractor's termination inventory where it had never solicited "competing proposals" from other sources. The board did, however, allow the government to recover the difference between the contract price and the fair market value of the uncompleted items at the time of the default. In *Donahines Inv. Co.*, ASBCA 23825, 82-1 BCA ¶ 15,791, a geographical restriction in the repurchase solicitation was not grounds for upsetting an excess cost assessment where no out-of-state firms had submitted bids on the original contract and there was a question whether the government's "urgent needs" could be met by non-local firms.

c. Soliciting Original Bidders

It is a common practice on reprocurement for the government to solicit those firms that bid on the original procurement. See *Ross & McDonald Contracting, GmbH*, ASBCA 38154, 94-1 BCA ¶ 26,316. Recovery has been allowed where only the original small business bidders were contacted for reprocurement, *American Marine Upholstery Co. v. United States*, 170 Ct. Cl. 564, 345 F.2d 577 (1965). However, when a small business is granted the reprocurement contract award while the other participants are not solicited, the award has been found improper, *Associated Cleaning, Inc.*, GSBCA 8360, 91-1 BCA ¶ 23,360 (unreasonable to make the reprocurement contract a set-aside and award for a 30 percent higher price when the original solicitation had been an open procurement). Further, failure to make a reasonable effort at contacting the original offerors may result in denial or reduction of the excess costs assessment. See *AAA Janitorial Serv.*, ASBCA 9603, 67-1 BCA ¶ 6091, in which the board noted at 28,184:

> In effect a presumption has been applied that the repurchase could have been completed at the price previously quoted by a lower bidder if an effort had been made to do so. Such a presumption would clearly be rebuttable since prior bid prices—or bidders for that matter—are not always available on repurchase. But in the absence of any rebuttal evidence [the contractor's] burden of showing a failure to mitigate can be met, prima facie, by showing a failure by the Government to make any effort to reprocure from sources whose prices on the original procurement were lower than those of the repurchase contractor.

See also *Dillon Total Maint., Inc. v. United States*, 218 Ct. Cl. 732 (1978), where the government failed to solicit six of the original bidders, three of whom had submitted bids in the original procurement that were lower than the reprocurement price, which was 68 percent higher than the defaulted contract price; and *American Photographic Indus., Inc.*, ASBCA 29272, 90-1 BCA ¶ 22,491, *recons. denied*, 90-2 BCA ¶ 22,728, where the government failed to solicit the second low bidder because it was located out of state and would have further delayed completion. However, the board noted that probable delay "does not excuse the Government's failure to mitigate its damages." In part for this reason, the board denied the government's request for excess reprocurement costs.

The government often attempts to reprocure by approaching the second low bidder on the original contract. However, there is no necessity to do this, particularly when the second low bidder is experiencing difficulties on another procurement, *Zoda v. United States*, 148 Ct. Cl. 49, 180 F. Supp. 419 (1960); *United Microwave Co.*, ASBCA 7947, 1963 BCA ¶ 3701. Furthermore, absent a showing that the government solicited additional offers, award of a reprocurement contract to the second low bidder on the original contract for a high price may not support a conclusion that the government acted reasonably to mitigate excess costs, *Marine Engine Specialties Corp.*, ASBCA 20521, 76-1 BCA ¶ 11,891 (reduction of excess cost assessment where repurchase unit price was 25 percent greater than that of the original contract and no effort was made to contact three other contractors who had submitted offers on the original procurement). Compare *Wisconsin Lift Truck Corp.*, AGBCA 82-288-1, 87-2 BCA ¶ 19,736 (soliciting next best bidder held reasonable because the bid was merely 1 percent greater than the defaulted bid price and lower than the government estimate).

d. Delayed Award of Reprocurement Contract

Failure to mitigate also occurs when the government unreasonably delays in awarding a reprocurement contract. The determination of what is a reasonable time is based on the circumstances of each procurement but focuses on any government explanation for the delay and any prejudice suffered by the defaulted contractor. Timeliness is measured as the time between the default termination and the date of award of the reprocurement contract, *Arctic Corner, Inc.*, ASBCA 38075, 94-1 BCA ¶ 26,317 (6½-month delay did not prejudice defaulted contractor). The mere existence of a long period of time between default and reprocurement, absent evidence that the price increased due to the delay, is not sufficient to show a failure to mitigate, *Conn-cor, Inc.*, GSBCA 4654, 77-2 BCA ¶ 12,857 (4½-month delay in repurchase); *Lee Mfg. & Eng'g Co.*, ASBCA 22866, 79-1 BCA ¶ 13,814 (eight-month delay); *Jimm Worthington*, AGBCA 77-175, 79-1 BCA ¶ 13,710 (eight-month delay in issuing first request for proposals was justified because work was not normally performed during that period, and an additional three-month delay in awarding final contract was reasonable); *B.R. Servs., Inc.*, ASBCA 47673, 99-2 BCA ¶ 30,397 (eleven-month delay but cost was close to government estimate). The excess cost assessment may also be upheld when the defaulted contractor contributes to the delay, *Astro-Space Labs., Inc. v. United States*, 200 Ct. Cl. 282, 470 F.2d 1003 (1972) (default created shortages of urgently needed ring fittings). In *Grimco Pneumatic Corp.*, ASBCA 50977, 00-1 BCA ¶ 30,727, the board found that the government acted reasonably in soliciting offers within two months following its default termination.

A defaulted contractor bears the burden of proving that the delay prejudiced it in terms of price. See *Standard Eng'g & Mfg. Co.*, ASBCA 3733, 57-2 BCA ¶ 1477, *recons. denied*, 57-2 BCA ¶ 1568, in which the board stated that an assessment of excess costs could not be barred by a delay of four months from the time of default when the delay did not increase the amount of the assessment. Similarly, in *Comspace Corp.*, ASBCA 37202, 89-3 BCA ¶ 22,027, a delay of three months was found reasonable because the record contained no evidence that the delay increased the cost of the end items. However, the ultimate burden of persuasion to establish mitigation is on the government, *Carlyle Rubber Co.*, ASBCA 23070, 79-2 BCA ¶ 14,117.

For cases in which delays have been found unreasonable, see *Continental Chem. Corp.*, GSBCA 4483, 76-2 BCA ¶ 11,948 (government delayed four months, failed to rebut the contractor's allegations that the delay increased the reprocurement contract prices by 47.5 percent, and failed to obtain necessary competition); *Disan Corp.*, ASBCA 21297, 79-1 BCA ¶ 13,677 (unexplained delay of seven months in reprocurement of radar power supplies despite statement in the reprocurement contract concerning the urgency of the need); *AGH Indus., Inc.*, ASBCA 27960, 89-2 BCA ¶ 21,637 (unexplained 17-month delay in reprocurement); *Sonico, Inc.*, ASBCA 31110, 89-2 BCA ¶ 21,611 (eight-month delay found unreasonable); and *AAA Eng'g & Drafting, Inc.,*. ASBCA 44605, 96-1 BCA ¶ 28,182 (unexplained delay of two years in repurchasing a computer software program). An excess cost assessment may be invalidated when the delay in reprocurement encompasses a period of severe inflation. In *American Packers Supply*, ASBCA 20024, 75-2 BCA ¶ 11,451, the board denied excess costs for the repurchase, which had been "delayed over 10 months during a period of raging inflation." See also *B & M Constr., Inc.*, AGBCA 90-165-1, 93-1 BCA ¶ 25,431, in which the board denied an excess cost claim, in part because of a government-caused delay between bid opening and award of the reprocurement contract. Due to 100 percent inflation, both bid prices were deemed unacceptable and the government unsuccessfully sought to renegotiate with other contractors.

The actions of the government during the delay are also pertinent to determining whether the government failed to mitigate. See *Consolidated Airborne Sys., Inc.*, ASBCA 5498, 61-1 BCA ¶ 2933, *aff'd*, 172 Ct. Cl. 588, 348 F.2d 941 (1965) (five-month delay while the government negotiated with the reprocurement contractor for lower prices was reasonable); *AAR Allen Aircraft Corp.*, ASBCA 32702, 88-2 BCA ¶ 20,581 (four-month delay reasonable because the government needed the time to develop a list of potential offerors and to arrange the new solicitation); and *Mega Constr. Co. v. United States*, 29 Fed. Cl. 396 (1993) (five-month delay found reasonable because the government, rather than sitting idly by, consulted with an architect-engineering firm to set up the resolicitation and negotiated lower prices with potential offerors). Compare *Old Dominion Sec., Inc.*, GSBCA 9126, 90-2 BCA ¶ 22,745 (delay caused by the government's post-default misinterpretation of labor standards found unreasonable). However, when the procuring agency's internal funding and other problems caused a delay, these problems were not permitted to be "visited upon" the defaulted contractor through an excess cost assessment, *Maitland Bros. Co.*, ASBCA 30089, 90-1 BCA ¶ 22,367. See also *ASC Sys. Corp.*, DOTCAB 73-37, 78-1 BCA ¶ 13,119, *aff'd*, 223 Ct. Cl. 672 (1980), where, despite a critical need for the equipment, a 13-month delay in the repurchase was caused by the government's internal procedures for determining the form of purchasing and obtaining approval, and the unit price was nearly twice that under the terminated contract.

Even if it reprocures within a reasonable time after termination, the government may lose the right to assess excess costs if the termination has been delayed for an unreasonable time, *Allied Tech., Inc.*, ASBCA 18101, 74-1 BCA ¶ 10,621 (the government's urgent need to enter into a sole source negotiated contract and the resultant cost increases had been created by the government's own action in delaying termination of the original contract for default); *Wolverine Diesel Power Co.*, AS-

BCA 20609, 77-2 BCA ¶ 12,551 (price rose 51 percent when the contracting officer delayed termination until six months after contract repudiation, delayed solicitation of the reprocurement for three months after termination, and delayed award for three months after solicitation).

In an unusual case, *Ketchikan Pulp Co. v. United States*, 20 Cl. Ct. 164 (1990), the court rejected the contractor's argument that the government should have waited several extra months to resell so that two major companies would be able to take part in the bidding. The court stated at 167:

> [The contractor] seeks to hold the Forest Service to an impossibly high standard for mitigation. Although the agency is charged with administering timber sales, it cannot be expected to predict with perfect accuracy the state of the future market. Carried to its logical extreme, the [contractor's] argument would prevent the Forest Service from ever collecting damages resulting from a defaulted timber sales contract because it might always be able to resell the timber at a higher price some time in the future.

Thus, because any future delay in resale might result in a finding of unreasonableness, the court concluded that the government had acted reasonably in not delaying resale until the two major companies would be available to bid.

e. Effect of Failure to Mitigate

There is a conflict of authority on whether the reprocurement cost can be adjusted to compensate for failure to mitigate and obtain a reasonable price on reprocurement. In *Francis M. Marley v. United States*, 191 Ct. Cl. 205, 423 F.2d 324 (1970), the court held that the failure to mitigate completely prohibits recovery of excess costs, even in reduced amount, stating at 221:

> Such phrases as "failure to minimize excess costs" or "failure to mitigate damages" do not make applicable, to questions of excess costs, the law of breach of contract damages, in which failure to mitigate damages need not prevent an award but only affect its amount. A proceeding to pass on excess costs is far different from the trial of an issue of breach-of-contract damages. An award of excess costs is by the terms of the contract clause based on a single reprocurement. A proper reprocurement relieves the Government of the burden of proving market value in a suit for damages for breach of contract. The contractor's pocket must, however, be protected from the consequences of an extravagant or improper reprocurement. The award is therefore conditioned upon proof of a reprocurement action reasonably designed to minimize the excess costs. When the reprocurement relied upon by the Government is found, for a sufficient reason, not to have been so designed, it may not be a basis for an award, and the right to excess costs is lost. *Rumley v. United States*, 152 Ct. Cl. 166, 285 F.2d 773 (1961) (reprocurement too late); *Alabama Shirt & Trouser Co. v. United States*, 121 Ct. Cl. 313 (1952) (insufficient solicitation of bids). See Paul, *United States Government Contracts & Subcontracts*, 481-485 (1964). This is what occurred in this case.

The court also held, however, that the government retained its right to seek a common law remedy of damages for breach of contract despite loss of the express contractual right to excess costs. Accord, *Rumley v. United States*, 152 Ct. Cl. 166, 285 F.2d 773 (1961); *Hideca Trading, Inc.*, ASBCA 24161, 87-3 BCA ¶ 20,040; *ERG Consultants, Inc.*, VABCA 3223, 92-2 BCA ¶ 24,905.

The boards never strictly adhered to the *Marley* rule. Where evidence has permitted determination of a fair and reasonable excess cost assessment, the boards have regularly awarded the government reduced excess costs of reprocurement. This rationale was explained in *Cable Sys. & Assembly Co.*, ASBCA 17844, 73-2 BCA ¶ 10,172, at 47,892-93:

> The amount of excess costs actually incurred by the Government is not necessarily the amount of excess costs for which the [contractor] is liable because, in the event of an improper reprocurement, such amount may include costs which would not have been incurred had a proper reprocurement been made. Questions as to whether the reprocurement was improper and, if so, the amount of excess costs reasonably occasioned thereby are principally factual in nature.
>
> It is, and as shown by the cases cited below for sometime has been, the practice of the Board in excess cost cases to determine whether the evidence shows that the amount claimed is correct and, when the evidence does not so show, to determine the correct amount of excess costs if the evidence permits such a determination. We do not read *Marley* as holding that this established practice of the Board is improper and should be discontinued.
>
> * * *
>
> We find that the term "excess costs" as used in subparagraph (b) of the contract's Default provisions includes any costs that the Government may have incurred in the reprocurement of similar supplies or services. If the reprocurement action was proper in all respects, the Government need not establish a "fair market value" of the similar supplies or services at the time of default. However, if the reprocurement action is defective, the Government then has the burden of establishing that the costs claimed represent what the reprocurement cost reasonably should have been which is sometimes stated as "fair market value" at the time of default or a reasonable period thereafter, such period being that amount of time which may be justified for effecting a reprocurement.

See also *Rayco, Inc.*, ENGBCA 4792, 88-2 BCA ¶ 20,671 (reductions for rework not included in the first contract price and for significant inflation between contracts found reasonable where evidence of such increased costs was fairly based in the record and the costs were not caused by the default). Moreover, where excess costs are improperly computed, the government does not lose its rights to recover those costs as long as there is a firm basis in the record for their recovery, *Ronald L. Collier*, ASBCA 26972, 89-1 BCA ¶ 21,328.

In cases where evidence does not permit determination of what a fair excess cost assessment would have been had the government fulfilled its duty to mitigate, the boards have denied the government the right to assess excess costs, *Matthews Co.*, AGBCA 459, 76-2 BCA ¶ 12,164, *recons. denied*, 77-1 BCA ¶ 12,434 (cost of completing road construction was clearly excessive); *Barrett Chem. Co.*, GSBCA 4544, 77-2 BCA ¶ 12,625 (failure to conduct give-and-take negotiations); *ASC Sys. Corp.*, DOTCAB 73-37, 78-1 BCA ¶ 13,119, *aff'd*, 223 Ct. Cl. 672 (1980) (extended delay and negotiated sole source procurement made prices obtained not reflective of fair market value); *B & M Constr., Inc.*, AGBCA 90-165-1, 93-1 BCA ¶ 25,431 (100 percent inflation and a five-month delay, coupled with substantial modifications to the specifications, left no basis in the record for determining reasonable costs).

A variety of methods have been used to calculate the reduced excess costs assessment. One frequently used method is to base the assessment on the difference between the original contract price and the second low bid on the original contract, *Fitzgerald Labs., Inc.*, ASBCA 15205, 71-2 BCA ¶ 9029; *Atlas Mfg. Co.*, ASBCA 15177, 71-2 BCA ¶ 9026; *Marine Engine Specialties Corp.*, ASBCA 21053, 76-2 BCA ¶ 12,034; *Wolverine Diesel Power Co.*, ASBCA 20609, 77-2 BCA ¶ 12,551; *Jefferson Constr. & Demolition Co.*, ASBCA 22787, 79-1 BCA ¶ 13,606; *American Photographic Indus., Inc.*, ASBCA 29272, 90-1 BCA ¶ 22,491, *recons. denied*, 90-2 BCA ¶ 22,728. However, a second low bid will not be used as a basis for computing the excess costs where it appears unreasonable. Thus, in *Solar Labs., Inc.*, ASBCA 19957, 76-2 BCA ¶ 12,115, the board measured excess costs by the difference between the original contract price and the price at which the reprocurement contractor had accepted a concurrent contract for the same items. See also *Birken Mfg. Co.*, ASBCA 32590, 90-2 BCA ¶ 22,845, in which the board used the reprocurement contractor's price on a similar contract as the basis for the valuation of excess costs of reprocurement because the government had not provided any evidence that this amount was inappropriately low and it was a fairer basis for measurement.

Other measures used include the difference between the defaulted contract price and what it would have cost the defaulted contractor to produce the items, *R.C. Allen Bus. Machs., Inc.*, ASBCA 12932, 72-1 BCA ¶ 9325; deduction of a specific amount, *Irvin Fisher*, HUDBCA 77-198-C10, 79-2 BCA ¶ 14,076 (assessment reduced by that portion of reprocurement price caused by a different manner of contract administration); *Old Dominion Sec., Inc.*, GSBCA 9126, 90-2 BCA ¶ 22,745 (deduction of costs incurred due to the unreasonable portion of the delay); and a jury verdict method, *Belmont Instrument Corp.*, ASBCA 18861, 77-1 BCA ¶ 12,332 (determination of what price would have been had the items been repurchased through one rather than two contracts), and *William A. Hulett*, AGBCA 91-230-3, 93-1 BCA ¶ 25,389, *recons. denied*, 93-2 BCA ¶ 25,888 (determination of value of work already done by the defaulted contractor).

Some of the confusion surrounding the appropriate measure of damages for a failure to mitigate costs of reprocurement may have been resolved by the Federal

Circuit's decision in *Cascade Pac. Int'l v. United States*, 773 F.2d 287 (Fed. Cir. 1985), in which the court concluded that the proper measure of damages should be the "reasonable reprocurement price less the original contract price." In *Interstate Forestry, Inc.*, AGBCA 89-114-1, 91-1 BCA ¶ 23,660, the board provided further explanation of the appropriateness of this remedy at 118,521:

> This analysis is consistent not only with the recent board decisions reducing excess costs, but also with the Court of Claims' earlier statement that contractual excess cost provisions merely take the common law rule for determining damages and say that if the Government repurchases within a reasonable time, the repurchase price will be accepted as the reasonable cost of obtaining performance without further proof. *Rumley v. United States*, *supra* at 777.
>
> In the case at bar, it makes little difference whether we consider the Government's claim as one for common law damages or as one for excess costs which should be reduced because of failure to mitigate. In either case, we will look to the reasonableness of the first reprocurement contract price. The price of the second reprocurement contractor, used by the CO, is not a proper measure of damages because, as indicated above, the additional cost did not reasonably flow from [the contractor's] default. In common law terms, it was not a foreseeable, direct, natural or proximate result of [the contractor's] breach of contract. See *Birken Mfg. Co.*, ASBCA 32651, 88-1 BCA ¶ 20,385, citing *Hadley v. Baxendale*, 9 Exch. 341, 156 Eng. Rep. 145 (1854).

The board concluded that the appropriate method of measuring damages was to subtract the original contract price from the reasonable reprocurement costs or price. See also *Mega Constr. Co. v. United States*, 29 Fed. Cl. 396 (1993), in which the court employed this standard in finding the government entitled to recover as excess reprocurement costs the cost of repairing defective workmanship and consultant's fees as well as the difference in price between the original and reprocurement contracts. Similarly, in *Associated Cleaning, Inc.*, GSBCA 8360, 91-1 BCA ¶ 23,360, the board found that, where the government had not made a reasonable effort to mitigate damages, excess costs could be recomputed by evaluating the difference between the original contract price and the price of a potential offeror on reprocurement.

f. Refusal to Deal with Original Contractor

There is considerable controversy over whether the government loses the right to excess costs by refusing to deal with the defaulting contractor. In seeking to resist the assessment of excess costs, the contractor often argues that it would be able to perform more quickly and less expensively than other firms. FAR 49.102(d) authorizes the contracting officer, with the contractor's agreement, to reinstate the contract if doing so would be advantageous to the government. However, the government is not required to do so, *Churchill Chem. Corp. v. United States*, 221 Ct. Cl. 284, 602 F.2d 358 (1979); *Lafayette Coal Co.*, ASBCA 32174, 89-3 BCA ¶ 21,963.

Although the government may not be obligated to deal with a defaulted contractor, failure to do so may be considered a failure to mitigate damages and may result in a loss of the right to assess reprocurement costs. At a minimum, the government must accept completed supplies that meet specifications rather than include such quantities in a reprocurement. See *Guenther Sys., Inc.*, ASBCA 18343, 77-1 BCA ¶ 12,501, in which the board stated at 60,592:

> After termination the Government accepted 95 completed firing lock assemblies. Since these were all that had been completed at that time, respondent discharged its obligation to mitigate damages in this respect. Once the contract had been terminated, [the Government] was under no obligation to accept further assemblies that [the contractor] offered to complete. Also, neither the default termination nor the reprocurement are tainted, if otherwise proper, by the prospect that it would have been more advantageous for the Government to stay with the terminated contractor and to obtain from him earlier deliveries than obtainable on reprocurement. *C.W. Wood Mfg., Inc.*, ASBCA 9640, 65-2 BCA ¶ 4972.

Failure to take completed items can lead to a refusal to allow an excess cost assessment, *United Microwave Co.*, ASBCA 9420, 65-1 BCA ¶ 4641, *recons. denied*, 65-2 BCA ¶ 5244 (items repurchased from another firm had no time or price advantage over those that were available from the defaulted contractor subsequent to the default termination and prior to the reprocurement); *Junkunc Bros., American Lock Co.*, ASBCA 12042, 68-1 BCA ¶ 7059 (items had been completed but not packaged for shipment on the termination date but became available for shipment prior to reprocurement), or to a reduction in excess costs of reprocurement by an estimate of the value of the services already rendered, *William A. Hulett*, AGBCA 91-230-3, 93-1 BCA ¶ 25,389, *recons. denied*, 93-2 BCA ¶ 25,888 (employing a jury verdict approach to establish the value of the benefit conferred on the reprocurement contractor by the pre-default work). The government is not required to take such work if doing so would result in a waiver of the government's rights, *Hyland Elec. Supply Co.*, ASBCA 19270, 75-2 BCA ¶ 11,466 (defaulted contractor's offer to supply additional items was properly rejected since the offer was contingent on a waiver of the excess cost assessment for the remaining defaulted quantity). In *R & O Indus., Inc.*, GSBCA 4804, 80-1 BCA ¶ 14,196, the board found that the government's failure to use completed items was excused because the contractor did not make a timely tender of the items. Excess costs will also not be reduced when the pre-default work is found to be defective in some way. In *Flooring Co.*, GSBCA 8297, 89-3 BCA ¶ 22,167, the value of carpeting work done prior to the default did not reduce the amount of recovery because the work did not comply with the specifications.

When a decision to reprocure has been made, the question has been raised as to whether the defaulted contractor should be given an opportunity to participate in the competition. Although the Armed Services Board has asserted that the government may have a contractual right to exclude a defaulted contractor from the reprocurement action, *TYCO Air Spec Div.*, ASBCA 16534, 73-1 BCA ¶ 9951, the GAO had previously stated that there can be no per se rule excluding the defaulted contractor.

Such an exclusion would, in effect, constitute a predetermination of lack of responsibility and would improperly preclude a consideration of all the facts surrounding the default, *Ikard Mfg. Co.*, Comp. Gen. Dec. B-192316, 78-2 CPD ¶ 315 (contracting officer may not automatically exclude defaulted contractor from reprocurement, but urgent need for parts justified limiting reprocurement competition to prior producers); *Master Sec., Inc.*, Comp. Gen. Dec. B-235711, 89-2 CPD ¶ 303 (noncompetitive reprocurement improper for option years). The continued vitality of *Ikard* is now questionable since in *Montage, Inc.* Comp. Gen. Dec. B-277923.2, 97-2 CPD ¶ 176, the GAO ruled that the contracting officer may exclude the defaulted contractor from the competition for reprocurement and overruled previous contrary decisions, stating "To the extent that *PRB Uniforms, Inc.*, [56 Comp. Gen. 976 (1977), 77-2 CPD ¶ 213], and other decisions citing that case state that a defaulted contractor may not be automatically excluded from the competition for the reprocurement of the requirement as to which it defaulted, those cases will not be followed." Generally, the boards and courts hold that the government is neither required to solicit an offer from nor make an award to a defaulted contractor. However, it may do so. See *Churchill Chem. Corp. v. United States*, 221 Ct. Cl. 284, 602 F.2d 358 (1979), in which the court upheld the government's refusal to award the repurchase contract to a defaulted contractor who had given no indication of interest prior to reprocurement, stating at 293:

> While the Government need not, in all cases, consider a defaulted contractor for reprocurement, the contractor may be permitted to bid on the repurchase solicitation. If the defaulted contractor is found to be responsible and capable of performance, is *responsive* to the solicitation, and is the lowest bidder, it may receive the repurchase contract; on reprocurement, the defaulted contractor, notwithstanding its submission of the lowest bid, may not receive more than the initial contract price for its reprocurement performance. (See, e.g., Opinion of Comptroller General, B-182323, 54 Comp. Gen. 853.)

The contracting officer's refusal to deal with the defaulted contractor has been upheld, *United States v. Thompson*, 168 F. Supp. 281 (N.D. W. Va. 1958), *aff'd*, 268 F.2d 426 (4th Cir. 1959) (defaulted contractor rejected as nonresponsible); *Marmac Indus., Inc.*, ASBCA 12158, 72-1 BCA ¶ 9249 (defaulted contractor nonresponsible); *Wear Ever Shower Curtain Corp.*, GSBCA 4360, 76-1 BCA ¶ 11,636 (reliability of defaulted contractor in question); *Ketchikan Pulp Co. v. United States*, 20 Cl. Ct. 164 (1990) (no requirement that the government delay reletting the contract until the defaulted contractor was free to enter); *Birken Mfg. Co.*, ASBCA 32590, 90-2 BCA ¶ 22,845 (defaulted contractor nonresponsible); *Morton Mfg., Inc.*, ASBCA 30716, 89-1 BCA ¶ 21,326 (no obligation to solicit the defaulted contractor because its noncompliance caused the need to reprocure in the first place). However, where it appears that the defaulted contractor is clearly a responsible contractor, the failure to deal has resulted in loss of reprocurement costs, *World-Wide Dev. Co.*, ASBCA 16608, 73-2 BCA ¶ 10,140 (temporary inability cured at time of reprocurement). See also *Tom W. Kaufman Co.*, GSBCA 4623, 78-2 BCA ¶ 13,288, in which the board held that the government had failed to mitigate costs through its failure to solicit a clearly responsible defaulted contractor who had the greatest ability to deliver promptly, and *Walsh Constr. Go.*, ENGBCA 6325, 98-1 BCA ¶ 29,683, in which the board denied the government's motion for summary judgment because the agency's refusal to allow a contractor to compete in the reprocurement may have been unreasonable when the agency assumed that the contractor's bid would have been the sum of its original bid plus the amount of its alleged error.

Considerations advanced to justify permitting a defaulted contractor to participate include (1) providing other offerors with notice that the award might go to the defaulted contractor, (2) obtaining an offer lower than the original contract price, and (3) assessing changes in price due to any changes made in the specifications. In *R.H. Pines Corp.*, Comp. Gen. Dec. B-182323, 75-1 CPD ¶ 224, the defaulted contractor was found to be the "lowest responsive, responsible bidder under the reprocurements" and was properly awarded the contracts. However, the GAO has stated that a repurchase contract may not be awarded to the defaulted contractor at a price greater than that of the original contract because doing so would be tantamount to modifying an existing contract without consideration, *Aerospace Am., Inc.*, Comp. Gen. Dec. B-181553, 74-2 CPD ¶ 130; *Air, Inc.*, Comp. Gen. Dec. B-233501, 88-2 CPD ¶ 505. Compare *Western Filament, Inc.*, Comp. Gen. Dec. B-181558, 74-2 CPD ¶ 320, stating that the government may award a subsequent contract that is not a reprocurement to the defaulted contractor at a price higher than that of the terminated contract if the defaulted contractor is the low bidder on the new contract for similar supplies or services. The GAO has found it reasonable for the contracting officer to take specification changes into account when determining whether the award is actually for a greater price than the defaulted contract, *A.R.E. Mfg. Co.*, Comp. Gen. Dec. B-246161, 92-1 CPD ¶ 210 (specification alterations between the defaulted contract and the reprocurement solicitation accounted for an almost $6,000 increase in the defaulted contractor's price and thus allowed award to be made to the defaulted contractor). However, the defaulted contractor may not reduce its offer in order to qualify for the reprocurement contract when its offer is not otherwise acceptable and responsible, *F&H Mfg. Co.*, Comp. Gen. Dec. B-184172, 76-1 CPD ¶ 297. Finally, the GAO has determined that a defaulted contractor may not recover the costs of preparing its offer when it is properly rejected, *Aerospace Am., Inc.*, Comp. Gen. Dec. B-181553, 74-2 CPD ¶ 130.

The government also has a right to acquire the contractor's inventory but is not required to do so, *Thermodyne Int'l, Ltd.*, ASBCA 21997, 80-1 BCA ¶ 14,333 (government acted correctly in not taking inventory that contained defective materials). With respect to the use of the contractor's inventory by a reprocurement contractor, it appears that the government satisfies its responsibilities if it makes the reprocurement contractor aware of the inventory and does not impede its use by the reprocurement contractor, *C.W. Wood Mfg., Inc.*, ASBCA 9640, 65-2 BCA ¶ 4972; *Vanbar*, ASBCA 18488, 76-2 BCA ¶ 11,924 (no need to use the defaulted contractor's tooling where the reprocurement contractor had existing tooling that could be used and did not increase the repurchase price); *Meyer Labs, Inc.*, ASBCA 19525, 87-2 BCA ¶ 19,810 (no violation of duty to mitigate when the government disposed of the defaulted contractor's inventory, tools, and materials when the reprocurement contractor implemented different manufacturing and testing techniques that rendered the tools only minimally valuable).

C. The Reprocurement Contract

In order to obtain excess costs of reprocurement, the government must also prove that the reprocurement contract was issued and administered in a way that did not increase the costs assessed.

1. *Intent to Reprocure*

In order to assess excess costs, the government must show that the contract on which such costs were incurred was intended to be a reprocurement. As long as this intent is shown, it is not necessary that the reprocurement contract be awarded after the termination. See *Olean Case Corp.*, GSBCA 4673, 78-1 BCA ¶ 12,905, in which the board stated at 62,860:

> Neither the issuance of the invitation for bids for the reprocurement prior to termination of all the purchase orders, nor award of the reprocurement contract five days prior to termination of the last delivery under [the contractor's] contract affects our holding. See *Allied Paint Mfg. Co., Inc.*, ENGBCA 3043, 71-1 BCA ¶ 8765 (issuance of solicitation prior to default); *Tilton Machine & Tool Co.*, GSBCA Nos. 4198, 4199, 76-1 BCA ¶ 11,750 (repurchase from an existing term contract). In the *Tilton Machine & Tool Co.* opinion, it was stated that ". . . there is nothing sacred in the date of award of the contract under which the Government repurchases supplies against the account of a defaulted contractor." In that case, it was held to be in the [contractor's] best interest to effect the purchase from the existing term contract, as reprocurement costs were clearly mitigated. Here the Contracting Officer issued the solicitation at the earliest possible time. The firm bid was obtained on August 31, 1976, and when it became apparent on September 10, 1976, that [the contractor] was 100 percent in default of its contract, and would probably never perform, the repurchase contract was awarded. The Government clearly acted reasonably and promptly in an effort to mitigate excess costs.

In *Foster Refrigerator Corp.*, ASBCA 32059, 88-1 BCA ¶ 20,398, the board allowed excess reprocurement cost recovery even though the reprocurement contract had been initiated three months before the prior contract had been terminated. In fact, this added time had enabled the government agency to solicit 59 competitors for the reprocurement, thus improving competition substantially, consistent with its duty to mitigate damages.

Excess costs were also permitted where the reprocurement was effected through exercise of an option that had been included in another procurement in anticipation of the terminated contractor's default, *AAR Corp.*, ASBCA 16486, 74-2 BCA ¶ 10,653. The exercise of an option under an existing contract may also be appropriate. In *Southwest Safety Prods. Mfg. Co.*, ASBCA 22902, 79-1 BCA ¶ 13,617, the board found that the government reasonably mitigated its costs by canceling a solicitation that had resulted in high bids and by electing to exercise an option under two existing contracts at lower unit prices. In *Ronald L. Collier*, ASBCA 26972, 89-1 BCA ¶ 21,328, the board held that the contracting officer had not breached its duty to mitigate damages by reprocuring through the addition of options to the contract of a contractor performing similar services in the same geographic area because (1) there was an urgent need for maintenance services, (2) the completion contract was for services identical to those in the defaulted contract, (3) the contracting officer acted as promptly as practicable to obtain the reprocurement contractor, and (4) the contract price would be equal to that of the defaulted contract. However, in *General Optical, Ltd.*, ASBCA 23835, 84-1 BCA ¶ 17,026, the board found a failure to mitigate where the government reprocured through exercise of an option under another contract without having solicited offers to determine whether competitive prices would be lower than the option prices. Accordingly, the excess costs were based on a lower price that had been obtained in a related competitive procurement for similar items.

In *Fairfield Scientific Corp. v. United States*, 222 Ct. Cl. 167, 611 F.2d 854 (1979), the court held that it was not necessary to use the same appropriation in the repurchase. So long as it acts reasonably and in a manner designed to mitigate damages, the government may repurchase by placing orders at reasonable prices under existing indefinite quantity or requirements contracts, *Tilton Mach. & Tool Co.*, GSBCA 4198, 76-1 BCA ¶ 11,750 (expressly overruling previous case disallowing the excess cost assessment for a reprocurement through orders under an existing contract). Thus, where the government shows that an existing requirements contract provides the best price available, an excess cost assessment based on orders under that contract will be upheld, *Woodford Hardware Co.*, ASBCA 16062, 72-1 BCA ¶ 9445; *Hyland Elec. Supply Co.*, ASBCA 19270, 75-2 BCA ¶ 11,466; *Barrett Ref. Corp.*, ASBCA 36590, 91-1 BCA ¶ 23,566.

There is some question as to whether the government has a duty or merely an option to utilize existing contracts for reprocurement. See *American Air Prods. Corp.*, ASBCA 4754, 60-1 BCA ¶ 2514 (excess costs assessment upheld despite government's failure to attempt placing orders with an existing contractor). But compare *Century Tool Co.*, GSBCA 4006, 76-2 BCA ¶ 12,030 (government failed to mitigate excess costs by not evaluating prospects for delivery under an existing requirements contract). Excess cost assessments have also been upheld, *American Kal Enters., Inc.*, GSBCA 4449, 76-2 BCA ¶ 11,929 (government failed to order quantities from an existing term contractor that was having difficulties meeting delivery schedules); *Palmetto Indus., Inc.*, ASBCA 21955, 79-1 BCA ¶ 13,594 (government failed to exercise an option extended by a prior contractor).

2. *Proof of Cost Incurrence*

Since reprocurement costs are based on the amount paid to the reprocurement contractor, the government must demonstrate that the costs were in fact incurred by showing that the reprocurement contract has been completed and the contractor paid, *Whitlock Corp. v. United States*, 141 Ct. Cl. 758, 159 F. Supp. 602, *cert. denied*, 358 U.S. 815 (1958). See FAR 49.402-6(c), which states that the demand for excess costs shall be made "after completion and final payment of the repurchase contract." See *Hunt's Janitor Serv.*, ASBCA 27719, 83-1 BCA ¶ 16,455 (government could not properly withhold amounts due contractor for completed services to cover potential excess costs); *Pyramid Packing, Inc.*, AGBCA 86-128-1, 92-2 BCA ¶ 24,831 (rejecting claim for excess reprocurement costs because the government had presented no evidence that the contract had been awarded, completed, and paid); *Patty Armfield*, AGBCA 91-185-1, 93-1 BCA ¶ 25,235 (denying recovery where excess costs were assessed prior to payment of reprocurement price); *Scalf Eng'g Co. & Pike County Constr., J.V.*, IBCA 2328, 89-3 BCA ¶ 21,950 (lack of evidence of payment precluded excess cost recovery); and *American Photographic Indus., Inc.*, ASBCA 29272, 90-1 BCA ¶ 22,491 (recovery of excess costs reduced to only those incurred and paid at the time of the assessment—four months). Accord, *What Mac Contractors, Inc.*, GSBCA 5015, 79-2 BCA ¶ 14,179. Compare *Servicemaster of W. Cent. Ga.*, DOTCAB 1096, 80-2 BCA ¶ 14,676, upholding a decision to withhold funds to "offset the contractor's potential liability for the excess costs of reprocurement." A demand for payment of excess costs prior to completion of the reprocurement contract is premature and will not be effective as a "final decision" under the CDA, *United Aero, Inc.*, ASBCA 26967, 83-1 BCA ¶ 16,268.

The government was denied recovery of excess reprocurement costs because the only evidence it put on to support recovery was the first two pages of the reprocurement contract. The board found this inadequate to determine if the government had met its obligation to act reasonably to minimize costs, *ARCO Eng'g, Inc.*, ASBCA 52450, 01-1 BCA ¶ 31,218.

In *C. Howdy Smith*, AGBCA 90-154-1, 92-2 BCA ¶ 24,884, the board expressed displeasure at the seemingly harsh and inefficient results created by the implementation of this doctrine, stating at 124,107:

> To deny recovery for excess reprocurement costs simply because the contract had yet to run its natural course to completion may seem anomalous and an impediment to the CO's giving prompt attention to claim presentation. That, nevertheless, appears to be well established law.

Accordingly, the board concluded that the reprocurement costs should be returned to the defaulted contractor because they had been assessed seven months prior to the completion of the reprocurement contract.

3. Poor Administration of Reprocurement Contract

The defaulted contractor may also be able to show that the government's administration of the reprocurement contract was sufficiently different to invalidate the assessment of excess costs, *Irvin Fisher*, HUDBCA 77-198-C10, 79-2 BCA ¶ 14,076. There, the board found some reprocurement costs to be improper because the contracting officer administered the initial services provision of a lawn maintenance contract differently by allowing the new contractor rather than the agency to determine the need for the services, as had been the case for the defaulted contractor. In order to obtain sufficient information to present such arguments, the defaulted contractor often attempts to inspect the reprocurement contractor's work. However, it has consistently been held that the defaulted contractor has no right to demand such an inspection. In *Industrial Elecs. Hardware Corp.*, ASBCA 10201, 68-2 BCA ¶ 7174, the board stated at 33,283:

> [T]he Board is aware of no case holding that in order for a buyer to collect excess costs from a defaulting seller the buyer must permit the seller to witness the inspection of the repurchase contractor's tenders. Nor is the Board aware of any case holding that in order to collect excess costs from a defaulting seller the buyer must turn over to the seller for inspection a representative sample of the repurchased items, or permit a joint inspection, so that the seller can satisfy himself that the repurchased items met specifications.

Likewise, in *Betsy Ross Flag Co.*, GSBCA 2786, 69-1 BCA ¶ 7692, the defaulted contractor "made repeated demands that the Government furnish it with a flag of another manufacturer for its inspection, contending that it had a right to inspect a flag made by another company to substantiate its claim that no other company could produce a better flag." The board affirmed the denial of the demand.

In *Boyd Tools, Inc.*, GSBCA 3469, 73-1 BCA ¶ 9874, the defaulted contractor's motion for discovery by having samples of the reprocured articles submitted for its inspection was denied. Similarly, in *Ranger Constr. Co.*, DOTCAB 74-32B, 75-2 BCA ¶ 11,524, the defaulted contractor's efforts to obtain discovery by having its own inspectors observe the conduct of a major cost-reimbursement construction reprocurement were unsuccessful. The government asserted that the facts sought by the defaulted contractor were more discoverable by government supervision, evaluation, and control, that the responsibility for site control was placed on the reprocurement contractor, and therefore the surety could monitor the validity of the completion costs. The board upheld the government's assertions and added that the government's obligation not to impede or interfere with the reprocurement contractor's performance was also a factor. Thus, the board concluded that "good cause" had not been shown for discovery by on-site inspection.

In *Western Contracting Corp.*, ENGBCA 3920, 78-1 BCA ¶ 12,922, discovery by use of an on-site inspector was allowed. However, the purpose of the inspection was to gather evidence to support the defaulted contractor's claim of changed site conditions as an excuse for default, rather than to observe the performance of the reprocurement contractor.

Where the reprocurement contractor also defaults on the contract, the original contractor will not have to pay excess costs for the administration of the second contract. See *Interstate Forestry, Inc.*, AGBCA 89-114-1, 91-1 BCA ¶ 23,660, holding that the added costs of the second reprocurement contract did not directly result from the initial default and therefore should not be assessed to the first defaulted contractor. The board limited recovery of reprocurement costs from the original contractor to the reasonable difference in costs between the first and second contracts. The first reprocurement contractor, if anyone, should be held liable for excess costs involved with the second reprocurement contract.

4. Use of Government Personnel

The government may also satisfy its requirements and preserve its rights through the use of government personnel to complete the work. The construction contract clause provides that the government "may take over the work and complete it by contract or otherwise." This language allows the government to use its employees to complete the work and deduct the resulting costs from the contract price. However, the government must act reasonably and incur reasonable costs. Although the standard supply and services contract clause does not specifically permit completion of the contract by the government's own forces as a proper method of reprocurement, the Armed Services Board has apparently recognized that a reprocurement could be effected by the government's in-house completion of the work. In fact, where it is clear that the government has the in-house capability to complete the defaulted contract, the failure at least to explore this alternative will be deemed a breach of the duty to mitigate, *ERG Consultants, Inc.*, VABCA 3223, 92-2 BCA ¶ 24,905 (rejecting claim for excess costs where the government had on staff professional engineers and industrial hygienists capable of completing the remaining 5 percent of the design contract although this option was not even considered).

In-house performance has been permitted when the need for the defaulted items is urgent and other forms of repurchasing are impractical, *R.A. Miller Indus., Inc.*, ASBCA 16433, 72-1 BCA ¶ 9409 (critical need for firing cases and lack of evidence that supplies could have been procured in time to obtain a lower price); *Guenther Sys., Inc.*, ASBCA 18343, 77-1 BCA ¶ 12,501 (urgent need for reliable production); *Star Contracting Co.*, ASBCA 27848, 89-2 BCA ¶ 21,587 (interim use of on-base personnel for emergency requests for services upheld as reasonable and consistent with the duty to mitigate damages).

The government may not complete the work with its own forces at a cost higher than available elsewhere unless circumstances require such action. See *Brent L. Sellick*, ASBCA 21869, 78-2 BCA ¶ 13,510, in which the board stated at 66,196:

> Turning to the Government's assessment of excess completion costs, the principal issue raised is whether the Government was justified in using an in-house public works crew without soliciting any bids from potential contractors. In undertaking the completion effort the Government had a duty to mitigate the damages chargeable to [the contractor] and the burden of persuasion is on the Government to establish that it acted reasonably to minimize the damages occasioned by [the contractor's] default. *Environmental Tectonics Corporation*, ASBCA 21204, 78-1 BCA ¶ 12,986. In prior cases we have upheld Government claims for excess completion costs, based on use of Government employees without prior solicitation of bids or proposals, where there was an urgent need to complete the work and the circumstances allowed no other reasonable alternative. See *Collins Electronics, Inc.*, ASBCA 16956, 72-2 BCA ¶ 9542; *Superior Disposal*, ASBCA 19910, 75-2 BCA ¶ 11,464; *Superior Disposal*, ASBCA Nos. 19350, 19816 and 20016, 75-2 BCA ¶ 11,523; *P&B Catering Service, Inc.*, ASBCA Nos. 20726 & 21722, 77-2 BCA ¶ 12,770. The *Superior Disposal* appeals and *P&B Catering Service, supra*, involved threats to base or mess hall sanitation occasioned by the default of refuse disposal and mess attendant service contractors respectively.
>
> In the instant appeal the Government would have us conclude that the existence of the safety hazard at [the contractor's] work site justified the use of a Government public works crew on a non-competitive basis. However, the facts of record do not support the conclusion that, from an objective standpoint, the need to remove the debris was as urgent as the Government contends. A safety hazard at the site had persisted at the site from 7 September, if not earlier, and once the walls came down in October, the hazard was qualitatively and quantitatively the same until [the contractor's] contract was terminated for default. If the threat to safety was as great as the Government maintains, it was unreasonable for the Government to wait as long as it did to terminate the contract for default. The decision to use public works forces on a non-competitive basis stemmed in large part from pressure exerted by the base commander to remove the debris as quickly as possible. The base commander's perception of an urgent need to eliminate immediately a long persistent safety hazard and eyesore does not support the conclusion that use of public works forces was the only reasonable alternative.

Thus, the government remains obligated to act reasonably and to mitigate excess costs when completing the work with government personnel. In *Elton E. Widdifield & Excavating Unlimited*, AGBCA 81-115-1, 83-2 BCA ¶ 16,639, the board found a failure to mitigate where the government had the work completed in part by government employees and in part through use of a reprocurement contractor, since the total costs of performing the work in this manner were substantially higher than they would have been had the reprocurement contractor performed the entire job. See *Surf Cleaners, Inc.*, ASBCA 20197, 77-2 BCA ¶ 12,687 (government failed to solicit another contractor who might have been able to perform defaulted janitorial services immediately); *Made-Rite Tool Co.*, ASBCA 22127, 79-2 BCA ¶ 13,975 (no proof of reasonableness by government); and *Datronics Eng'rs, Inc. v. United States*, 190 Ct. Cl. 196, 418 F.2d 1371 (1969) (reducing excess cost assessment by travel costs incurred in bringing government personnel from distant location to perform unskilled labor tasks).

As long as the costs incurred by the government employees are those that would not have been incurred in their normal work, they will be recoverable. In *Landmark Interior Builders, Inc.*, GSBCA 8382, 91-1 BCA ¶ 23,386, the board allowed recovery of excess costs incurred by government employees who worked overtime because overtime was necessary since the straight-time work day was devoted to their normal tasks. In *Sam's Elec. Co.*, GSBCA 9359, 90-3 BCA ¶ 23,128, the board allowed full recovery because there was no evidence that the government's use of in-house employees to complete the contract had increased the costs of performance.

Taking items out of existing stock and charging the contractor the price the government paid for the stock will not satisfy the requirement for a reprocurement, *Naples Food Prods. Co.*, ASBCA 8191, 1963 BCA ¶ 3932. However, if the government borrows from stock to satisfy immediate needs and then contracts for items to replenish the stock, such a contract would be a reprocurement, *Rockingham Poultry Mktg. Corp.*, ASBCA 1319 (1953).

D. Computation of Excess Costs

The computation of recoverable excess costs is based on the difference in price between the defaulted contract and the reprocurement contract as adjusted for all increases in the original contract price to which the defaulted contractor is entitled, and for any cost increases resulting from changes in the work or government misconduct under the reprocurement contract.

1. Price Adjustments Under Defaulted Contract

In computing excess costs of reprocurement, the price of the defaulted contract must be adjusted to account for all price increases to which the defaulted contractor is entitled. In *Big Star Testing Co.*, GSBCA 5793, 81-2 BCA ¶ 15,335, *recons. denied*, 82-1 BCA ¶ 15,635, the adjustment in price due because of the contractor's "justified" inability to obtain third-party testing services specified in the contract eliminated the entire excess cost assessment. See also *D.H. Dave & Gerben Contracting Co.*, ASBCA 6257, 1962 BCA ¶ 3493 (assessment reduced to account for price increases due for changes, suspensions, and changed conditions encountered); *Iran B. Tech Enter., Ltd.*, ASBCA 24820, 81-2 BCA ¶ 15,424 (assessment reduced to account for constructive changes); *American Dredging Co.*, ENGBCA 2920, 78-2 BCA ¶ 13,494 (assessment reduced to account for differing site condition); *B.R. Servs., Inc.*, ASBCA 47673, 99-2 BCA ¶ 30,397 (assessment reduced for constructive changes); and *Walsh Constr. Co. of Ill.*, ASBCA 52952, 02-2 BCA ¶ 32,004 (assessment reduced for increased labor costs attributable to updated wage rate determinations). In *American Kal Enters., Inc.*, GSBCA 4987, 80-2 BCA ¶ 14,522, the board refused to adjust the defaulted contract price to reflect that it had been evaluated as a foreign bid. By contrast, if the costs are a reasonably foreseeable result of the defaulted contractor's failure to complete the work, the costs will be recoverable,

Milner Constr. Co., DOTBCA 2043, 91-3 BCA ¶ 24,195 (allowing recovery of temporary storage of hazardous waste materials during the resolicitation period as a reasonably foreseeable result of the default); *Sealtite Corp.*, ASBCA 34156, 90-2 BCA ¶ 22,844 (cost of performance of architect-engineering firm found foreseeable).

2. Adjustments in Reprocurement Contract Costs

If the costs eventually paid by the government under the reprocurement contract increase due to government misconduct during administration of the reprocurement contract, an appropriate downward adjustment in the excess cost assessment should be made. In addition, if the government calls for effort under the reprocurement contract that was not required under the defaulted contract, but the reprocurement constitutes a valid reprocurement of "similar" work, costs attributable to the extra work required under the reprocurement contract must be excluded from any excess cost assessment. See *Datronics Eng'rs, Inc. v. United States*, 190 Ct. Cl. 196, 418 F.2d 1371 (1969) (excluding costs of repairing damage to transmission lines for which the defaulted contractor was not responsible); *Lee Mfg. & Eng'g Co.*, ASBCA 22866, 79-1 BCA ¶ 13,814 (reprocurement price adjusted to eliminate costs of additional testing); *Steelship Corp.*, ENGBCA 3830, 78-2 BCA ¶ 13,478 (reprocurement price reduced by $140,627 to account for improvement over defaulted contractor's ship design); *Gardner Constr. Co.*, DOTCAB 70-18, 73-2 BCA ¶ 10,342 (reprocurement price reduced to reflect work added to reprocurement contract); *Foster Refrigerator Corp.*, ASBCA 32059, 88-1 BCA ¶ 20,398 (reprocurement price reduced to reflect deletion of first article testing requirement); and *Schmalz Constr. Ltd.*, AGBCA 92-177-1, 94-1 BCA ¶ 26,423 (deletion of right-of-way timber purchase requirement entitled contractor to a reduction in price).

The price must also be adjusted for specification waivers granted to the reprocurement contractor without price reductions or for the government's failure to obtain consideration for the reprocurement contractor's schedule extensions, *Specialty Wood Prods.*, ASBCA 22324, 79-1 BCA ¶ 13,815; *RFI Shield-Rooms*, ASBCA 17991, 77-2 BCA ¶ 12,714 (reduction for schedule extension given without requiring consideration). In *Iran B. Tech Enter., Ltd.*, ASBCA 24820, 81-2 BCA ¶ 15,424, where a reprocurement contractor performing work in Iran was able to complete only 78 percent of the work because of the Iranian revolution, the excess cost assessment was based on only 78 percent of the reprocurement price even though the government had actually paid the reprocurement contractor 96 percent of the price.

In *Guenther Sys., Inc.*, ASBCA 18343, 77-1 BCA ¶ 12,501, the board refused to credit the defaulted contractor for its value engineering incentive earnings on the reprocured items. Reasoning that such a credit, if allowed, would only "add to the Government's procurement costs" and thus would increase the liability of the defaulted contractor, the board concluded that reducing the assessment in such circumstances would be inconsistent with the government's rights under the Default clause. In contrast, in *Fairfield Scientific Corp.*, ASBCA 21152, 78-1 BCA ¶ 12,869, *aff'd*, 222 Ct. Cl. 167, 611 F.2d 854 (1979), the board used the reprocurement price without reductions reflecting value engineering incentives earned by the reprocurement contractor. There, the board also reduced the defaulted contractor's price by an amount for prompt payment discounts that the government would have earned.

3. Time Period Covered

The government is also entitled to recover costs incurred during the entire reprocurement period, including additional option years, as long as the original contractor had agreed to perform for that duration, *Lewis Mgmt. & Serv. Co.*, ASBCA 24802, 85-3 BCA ¶ 18,416. The government must still comply, however, with the basic option requirements of FAR 17.207 that (1) funds are available; (2) the requirement covered by the option fulfills a government need; and (3) the exercise of the option is the most advantageous method of fulfilling the government's need, price, and other factors considered. In the reprocurement context, this provision has been interpreted to require the contracting officer to meet the mandates of similarity and mitigation before the option costs will be made allowable aspects of excess reprocurement costs. Thus, in *Ross & McDonald Contracting, GmbH*, ASBCA 38154, 94-1 BCA ¶ 26,316, the board, acting consistently with this general rule, allowed recovery of excess costs associated with the exercise of an option on the reprocurement contract because the identical option had been included in the defaulted contract and the requirements of FAR 17.207 had been satisfied. However, the board mitigated the recovery by the value of certain options that had been added to the reprocurement contract but not included in the original contract, as these costs had not directly resulted from the default.

E. Right to Other Damages

As noted previously, the standard default clauses for fixed-price contracts state that the government's right to assess excess costs of reprocurement following default termination is "in addition to any other rights and remedies provided by law or under this contract." Thus, in cases where the government loses its right to assess excess costs, such as where the reprocured work is found to be "dissimilar," the government may fall back on its right to common law damages. Common law damages are measured as the reasonable excess costs of completing the work in compliance with the contract regardless of whether or not the work has been completed by the government, *M.C. & D. Capital Corp.*, ASBCA 40159, 91-3 BCA ¶ 24,084. The government cannot, of course, recover actual damages that have been already recovered through an excess cost assessment. In addition, the government's right to recover actual damages not covered by an excess cost assessment may be limited to the extent that the contract contains a liquidated damages clause covering such damages, *Sorensen v. United States*, 51 Ct. Cl. 69 (1916). But see *Hideca Trading, Inc.*, ASBCA 24161, 87-3 BCA ¶ 20,080 (the board allowed the government, the aggrieved buyer, the traditional common law or U.C.C. damages, i.e., the difference between the contract price at date of contract delivery and the market price, even though the government did not reprocure.) In *Kirk Bros. Mech. Contractors, Inc.*, ASBCA 47801, 96-2 BCA ¶ 28,291, the board held that the inspection clause did not limit the government's default clause right to reprocure the defective work and charge the contractor.

The government must credit the contractor for work accepted. A properly defaulted contractor may recover for changed work incorporated into end items delivered to and accepted by the government and also recover for "wasted work" attempting to comply with impossible specifications even though no end items were delivered and the government otherwise received no benefit from the work. In *Dennis Berlin d/b/a Spectro Sort,* ASBCA 53549, 03-1 BCA ¶ 32,075, a contractor unsuccessfully sought a 20 percent profit added on to the cost of acquisition in determining the correct value of the manufacturing materials accepted by the government after the termination. The board noted that in the past it has approximated the value by adjusting the contractor's cost by the indicated rate of loss on delivered end items or by applying the percentage of completion method and subtracting the price of delivered items or by using the jury verdict valuation. A fixed-profit percentage, however, has no relationship to the market value of the material.

The other remedies mentioned in the clause have been held by the Court of Claims to include the right to collect certain "administrative costs" incurred by the agency in connection with the reprocurement contract, *Southeastern Airways Corp. v. United States*, 230 Ct. Cl. 47, 673 F.2d 368 (1982). Accord, *Tester Corp. v. United States*, 1 Cl. Ct. 370 (1982) (expenses for government inspection, testing, and travel); *Futura Sys., Inc.*, ENGBCA 6037, 95-2 BCA ¶ 27,654 (costs of observing a reprocurement contractor's contractually required testing and costs of a supervisor who traveled to the reprocurement contractor's facility to ensure that problems experienced in the original procurement would not recur). See also FAR 49.402-7 recognizing the government's right to recover "any other ascertainable damages" resulting from the default; *Birken Mfg. Co.*, ASBCA 32590, 90-2 BCA ¶ 22,845 (costs of issuing reprocurement purchasing request found to be reasonable administrative costs); *Sealtite Corp.*, ASBCA 34156, 90-2 BCA ¶ 22,844 (costs of administering funds due to labor violations found recoverable). Such costs can be proven by reasonable and reliable estimates, *Walsh Constr. Co. of Ill.*, ASBCA 52952, 02-2 BCA ¶ 32,004; *ARCO Eng'g, Inc.*, ASBCA 52450, 01-1 BCA ¶ 31,218.

In *Sach Sinha & Assocs., Inc.,* ASBCA 50640, 00-2 BCA ¶ 31,111, the government's recoupment claim for unliquidated progress payments was reduced because the per-item contract price was the proper measure for calculating the amount the contractor was entitled to retain. The government accepted the first two of three equal lots, but terminated for default after the contractor failed to deliver the third lot. The government argued that the contractor only delivered two-thirds of the required quantity and was entitled to retain only two-thirds of the progress payments.

However, the Default clause required the government to pay the contract price for items delivered and accepted. Therefore, the proper method of calculating the amount due was to multiply the number of items accepted by the contract's per-item price and to deduct that from the amount of the progress payments.

F. Administrative Requirements for Reprocurement

A reprocurement is technically a purchase for the contractor's account and not a new purchase by the government. See FAR 49.402-6. Thus, reprocurement following a termination for default does not require justification under one of the exceptions to the statutory preference for full and open competition, *Old Dominion Sec., Inc.*, GS-BCA 9126, 90-2 BCA ¶ 22,745; *Conti v. United States*, 158 F.2d 581 (1st Cir. 1946); *American Smelting & Ref. Co. v. United States*, 259 U.S. 75 (1922). FAR 49.402-6(b) limits this exemption from the full and open competition requirement to cases where the repurchased quantity does not exceed the quantity of the defaulted contract. If the repurchased quantity is greater, the regulation requires that the procurement be treated as a new procurement. Analogously, where an original contract is restricted to small businesses, there is no requirement that the reprocurement contract must be so restricted, *Bud Mahas Constr., Inc.*, Comp. Gen. Dec. B-235261, 89-2 CPD ¶ 160.

The GAO has continued to review protests over the propriety of the reprocurement even though the reasonableness of the reprocurement remains for the board's determination. See *Hemet Valley Flying Serv., Inc.*, Comp. Gen. Dec. B-191922, 78-2 CPD ¶ 117, upholding the award of a negotiated reprocurement contract on a sole source basis to the third low bidder on the original contract because the normal procurement regulations are not strictly applicable to the reprocurement and the need for the airplanes was urgent. The GAO also found that, because the award of a repurchase contract to the second low bidder is a recognized method of reprocurement, the award to the third low bidder was reasonable where the second low bidder was unable to perform. In determining whether award to the second low bidder is proper, the GAO will examine the time between the original award and the default, the time available after the default to undertake a new solicitation, and the difference between the price of the defaulted contractor and the second low bidder, *DCX, Inc.*, Comp. Gen. Dec. B-232692, 89-1 CPD ¶ 55. See *International Tech. Corp.*, Comp. Gen. Dec. B-250377.5, 93-2 CPD ¶ 102, in which award to the second low bidder was upheld as proper due, in part, to the fact that only 80 days had passed between award and default. If, however, the repurchase exceeds the quantity under the defaulted contract, the GAO will treat it as a new procurement, *Euclid Designs & Dev. Co.*, Comp. Gen. Dec. B-186679, 76-2 CPD ¶ 321.

A reprocurement contract issued in a subsequent fiscal year may be charged to an annual appropriation used for the original contract, *Funding of Replacement Contracts*, Comp. Gen. Dec. B-232616, 88-2 CPD ¶ 602, citing 34 Comp. Gen. 239 (B-121248) (1954). The requirement that the funds be initially obligated within the appropriate year for bona fide needs occurring during that year still applies. See 32 Comp. Gen. 565 (B-114334) (1953), where a reprocurement contract could not be funded from a prior year's appropriations because the original contract did not reflect bona fide needs when obligated.

The GAO had long held that excess costs recovered following default termination had to be deposited in the Treasury as "miscellaneous receipts" rather than credited to the appropriation out of which the contract had been funded. As a result, the excess cost proceeds were unavailable to the agency for funding the reprocurement work, 14 Comp. Gen. 729 (A-60541) (1935); 52 Comp. Gen. 45 (B-173735) (1972). The GAO has partially reversed this line of cases, stating in *Bureau of Prisons*, Comp. Gen. Dec. B-210160, 84-1 CPD ¶ 91:

> We therefore decide that to the extent necessary to cover the full costs of a replacement contract, excess reprocurement costs recovered by an agency from a breaching contractor need not be deposited in the Treasury as miscellaneous receipts, but rather may be applied to the costs of the replacement contract. The replacement contract must be coextensive with the original contract; that is, it may procure only those goods or services which would have been provided under the breached contract. Any recovered excess reprocurement costs which are not necessary or used for such a replacement contract must still be deposited into the Treasury as miscellaneous receipts.

VI. LIQUIDATED DAMAGES

Like many other buyers of goods and services, the federal government has made substantial use of liquidated damages—primarily as a method of motivating contractors to perform on time. Such damages are spelled out in a contract clause in specific dollar amounts rather than leaving the parties to determine actual damages if a breach occurs. Liquidated damages clauses are regularly used in construction contracts and occasionally in supply and service contracts. DFARS 211.503 makes their use mandatory in fixed-price construction contracts over $500,000, except for cost-plus-fixed-fee contracts where the contractor cannot "control the pace of the work." The use of liquidated damages leads to substantial judicial intervention because federal contracts are subject to the normal common law rule that liquidated damages will not be enforced if they are a penalty, *Priebe & Sons, Inc. v. United States*, 332 U.S. 407 (1947). However, the contractor has the burden of proof that a liquidated damages clause has been improperly used, *DJ Mfg. Corp. v. United States,* 86 F.3d 1130 (Fed. Cir. 1996).

Since liquidated damages clauses infrequently assess damages that are penal, they are generally enforced. However, the government is required to strictly adhere to the provisions of the clause. See, for example, *Abcon Assocs., Inc. v. United States,* 49 Fed. Cl. 678 (2001), in which an assessment of liquidated damages earlier than the time permitted by the clause was held to constitute a breach by the government that invalidated a default termination. See also *William F. Klingensmith, Inc.*, ASBCA 52028, 01-2 BCA ¶ 32,072 (liquidated damages only assessable for phases 1-5 of contract, not "final phase).

A. General Policy

FAR Subpart 11.5 provides guidance on when and how liquidated damages clauses are to be used. FAR 11.501 contains the general policy on the use of such clauses:

> (a) The contracting officer must consider the potential impact on pricing, competition, and contract administration before using a liquidated damages clause. Use liquidated damages clauses only when –
>
> > (1) The time of delivery or timely performance is so important that the Government may reasonably expect to suffer damage if the delivery or performance is delinquent; and
> >
> > (2) The extent or amount of such damage would be difficult or impossible to estimate accurately or prove.
>
> (b) Liquidated damages are not punitive and are not negative performance incentives (see 16.402-2). Liquidated damages are used to compensate the Government for probable damages. Therefore, the liquidated damages rate must be a reasonable forecast of just compensation for the harm that is caused by late delivery or untimely performance of the particular contract. Use a maximum amount or a maximum period for assessing liquidated damages if these limits reflect the maximum probable damage to the Government. Also, the contracting officer may use more than one liquidated damages rate when the contracting officer expects the probable damage to the Government to change over the contract period of performance.
>
> (c) The contracting officer must take all reasonable steps to mitigate liquidated damages. If the contract contains a liquidated damages clause and the contracting officer is considering terminating the contract for default, the contracting officer should seek expeditiously to obtain performance by the contractor or terminate the contract and repurchase (see subpart 49.4). Prompt contracting officer action will prevent excessive loss to defaulting contractors and protect the interests of the Government.
>
> (d) The head of the agency may reduce or waive the amount of liquidated damages assessed under a contract, if the Commissioner, Financial Management Service, or designee approves (see Treasury Order 145-10).

This policy deals only with liquidated damages as a substitute for actual damages for *late delivery or completion of the work*. As a result, the standard contract clauses provide for the concurrent assessment of both liquidated damages and the excess costs of reprocurement that are called for by the default clauses. The only guidance for establishing the rate of liquidated damages pertains to construction contracts. See FAR 11.502, which states:

> (b) Construction contracts with liquidated damages provisions must describe the rate(s) of liquidated damages assessed per day of delay. The rate(s) should include the estimated daily cost of Government inspection and superintendence. The rate(s) should also include an amount for other expected expenses associated with delayed completion such as –
>
> (1) Renting substitute property; or
>
> (2) Paying additional allowance for living quarters.

There are two standard liquidated damages clauses. The clause for construction contracts in FAR 52.211-12 provides:

> Liquidated Damages—Construction (Sept 2000)
>
> (a) If the Contractor fails to complete the work within the time specified in the contract, the Contractor shall pay liquidated damages to the Government in the amount of ____________ [*Contracting Officer insert amount*] for each calendar day of delay until the work is completed or accepted.
>
> (b) If the Government terminates the Contractor's right to proceed, liquidated damages will continue to accrue until the work is completed. These liquidated damages are in addition to excess costs of repurchase under the Termination clause.

The standard clause for other types of contracts in FAR 52.211-11 provides:

> Liquidated Damages-Supplies, Services, or Research and Development (Sept 2000)
>
> (a) If the Contractor fails to deliver the supplies or perform the services within the time specified in this contract, the Contractor shall, in place of actual damages, pay to the Government liquidated damages of $__________ per calendar day of delay [*Contracting Officer insert amount*].
>
> (b) If the Government terminates this contract in whole or in part under the Default-Fixed-Price Supply and Service clause, the Contractor is liable for liquidated damages accruing until the Government reasonably obtains delivery or performance of similar supplies or services. These liquidated damages are in addition to excess costs of repurchase under the Termination clause.
>
> (c) The Contractor will not be charged with liquidated damages when the delay in delivery or performance is beyond the control and without the fault or negligence of the Contractor as defined in the Default-Fixed-Price Supply and Service clause in this contract.

B. Enforceability of Liquidated Damages Clause

The general rule as to whether liquidated damages are enforceable was stated in the first *Restatement of Contracts* § 339 as follows:

> An agreement, made in advance of breach, fixing the damages therefor, is not enforceable as a contract and does not affect the damages recoverable for the breach, unless
>
> (a) the amount so fixed is a reasonable forecast of just compensation for the harm that is caused by the breach, and
>
> (b) the harm that is caused by the breach is one that is incapable or very difficult of accurate estimation.

This two-part test is stated in FAR 11.501(a) and is cited in most government contract cases, *Southwest Eng'g Co. v. United States*, 341 F.2d 998 (8th Cir.), *cert. denied*, 382 U.S. 819 (1965).

To overcome the imposition of liquidated damages, it is usually stated that the contractor has the burden of proving that the amount is an unenforceable penalty, *Mega Constr. Co. v. United States*, 29 Fed. Cl. 396 (1993); *JEM Dev. Corp.*, ASBCA 45912, 94-1 BCA ¶ 26,407. However, see *Clifford La Tourelle*, AGBCA 93-132-1, 94-1 BCA ¶ 26,509, stating that the government is obligated to show that the amount is reasonable. See also *DJ Mfg. Corp. v. United States,* 86 F.3d 1130 (Fed. Cir. 1996), indicating that the courts are reluctant to overturn liquidated damages clauses. The court stated at 133-34:

> When damages are uncertain or difficult to measure, a liquidated damages clause will be enforced as long as "the amount stipulated for is not so extravagant, or disproportionate to the amount of property loss, as to show that compensation was not the object aimed at or as to imply fraud, mistake, circumvention or oppression." *Wise v. United States*, 249 U.S. 361, 365, 63 L. Ed. 647, 39 S. Ct. 303 (1919); see *United States v. Bethlehem Steel Co.*, 205 U.S. at 121 ("The amount is not so extraordinarily disproportionate to the damage which might result from the [breach], as to show that the parties must have intended a penalty and could not have meant liquidated damages."). With that narrow exception, "there is no sound reason why persons competent and free to contract may not agree upon this subject as fully as upon any other, or why their agreement, when fairly and understandingly entered into with a view to just compensation for the anticipated loss, should not be enforced." *Wise v. United States*, 249 U.S. at 365; see also *Sun Printing & Publishing Ass'n v. Moore*, 183 U.S. 642, 674, 22 S. Ct. 240, 46 L. Ed. 366 (1902) (except where "the sum fixed is greatly disproportionate to the presumed actual damages," a court "has no right to erroneously construe the intention of the parties, when clearly expressed, in the endeavor to make better contracts for them than they have made for themselves").

Liquidated damages clauses are enforceable so long as the government, at contract formation, reasonably could have anticipated harm flowing from a breach of the contract, and the stipulated amount was a reasonable estimate of the anticipated harm. Whether the stipulated amount represents a penalty instead of compensation is highly fact-specific. Liquidated damages are a creature of contract and must be assessed in accordance with the contract.

The government's motive in using a liquidated damages provision is not relevant to determining the enforceability of the provision. See *DJ Mfg. Corp. v. United States*, 86 F.3d 1130 (Fed. Cir. 1996), in which the court provided one of its more extensive discussions of liquidated damages. The court rejected the contractor's argument that the contracting officer's statement about needing to get the items to the troops quickly showed that the liquidated damages clause was designed to "spur performance" and not for just compensation. The court ruled that a liquidated damages clause is not unenforceable simply because the government hopes that it will encourage the contractor's prompt performance.

1. Reasonableness of the Forecast

At the time the contract is made, a forecast of liquidated damages must be based on a reasonable possibility that the government will sustain damages if the contract is breached, and the stipulated liquidated amount must be a reasonable estimate of the anticipated harm to the government. In *FBS Generalbau GmbH*, ASBCA 44743, 95-1 BCA ¶ 27,504, liquidated damages were proper because they were based on the German economy.

a. Time of the Forecast

The government contract rule is that the reasonableness of the forecast of liquidated damages is evaluated by looking at the situation at the time the contract is made rather than at the time of breach, *Sunflower Landscaping & Garden Ctr.*, AGBCA 87-342-1, 91-3 BCA ¶ 24,182; *Downing Elec., Inc.*, ASBCA 37851, 90-3 BCA ¶ 23,001; *Coliseum Constr., Inc.*, ASBCA 36642, 89-1 BCA ¶ 21,428; *Rivera-Cotty Corp.*, ASBCA 32291, 86-3 BCA ¶ 19,148. In several instances, this analysis has led to the enforcement of a liquidated damages clause in a situation where no actual damages were incurred by the government, *William F. Klingensmith, Inc.*, ASBCA 52028, 01-2 BCA ¶ 31,589 ("the focus of an inquiry concerning the propriety of an LDs rate is at the time of contract award, not LDs assessment"); *Southwest Marine, Inc.*, DOTBCA 1577A, 95-1 BCA ¶ 27,519 (whether the government suffered actual damage was immaterial); *Mit-Con, Inc.*, ASBCA 42884, 92-1 BCA ¶ 24,634 (liquidated damages based on the daily costs for one inspector found reasonable even though there was no evidence that the government had been damaged by any delay in awarding the follow-on contract); *Central Ohio Bldg. Co.*, PSBCA 2742, 92-1 BCA ¶ 24,399 ($250 per day was a reasonable rate at the time of contracting, so it is valid even though the government did not incur actual damages); *American Constr. Co.*, ENGBCA 5728, 91-2 BCA ¶ 24,009. Likewise, on various occasions, liquidated damages awards have been upheld despite being substantially greater than actual damages, *Connell Rice & Sugar Co.*, AGBCA 85-483-1, 87-1 BCA ¶ 19,489, *rev'd on other grounds,* 837 F.2d 1068 (Fed. Cir. 1988) (liquidated damages award of $289,549 upheld even though the government's actual out-of-pocket expenses were only $27,645); *First Interstate Bank of Denver, N.A.*, GSBCA 9484, 89-1 BCA ¶ 21,453 (upholding $67,600 in liquidated damages due to a one-year delay in making land ready for lease to the government even though the contractor had not been receiving the government's rent income during the delay).

In *Triad, Inc.*, VABCA 1774, 89-2 BCA ¶ 21,661, the contractor argued that the not only had the government failed to incur damages as a result of the contractor's delay, the government had profited from the delay. Accordingly, the contractor argued that the incorporation of the liquidated damages provision in the contract had been improper because any liquidated damages the government could recover would be less than the government's savings in terms of interest payments. More specifically, the contractor asserted that the government was saving 10 percent of the contract price in interest payments for each year of delay, while the liquidated damages payment of $50 per day would yield a substantially lower yearly total. The board rejected this argument on the grounds that it would require the government to take the time value of money into account for every contract and would not be consistent with prior precedent that liquidated damages are to be judged from the time of contracting rather than from the time of assessment. See also *Conner Bros. Constr. Co.*, VABCA 2504, 95-2 BCA ¶ 27,910, where the government made significant alterations to the project but still assessed liquidated damages at the original rate. The board affirmed the assessment, finding no evidence that the rate was "disproportionately high to the reasonably anticipated damages").

The boards have refused to assess such damages where the government did not incur and should not have anticipated incurring any actual damages, *Sunflower Landscaping & Garden Ctr.*, AGBCA 87-342-1, 91-3 BCA ¶ 24,182 (rejecting assessment of liquidated damages for failure to make progress default with 130 days left before the completion date because the government reprocured immediately thereafter with a 50-day performance period); *Ford Constr. Co.,* AGBCA 241, 72-1 BCA ¶ 9275 (liquidated damages could not be collected to cover a period where there was no chance of damage to the government by the contractor's delay); *Garden State Painting Co.,* ASBCA 22248, 78-2 BCA ¶ 13,499 (liquidated damages of $100 per calendar day a penalty because the government knew that there would be no daily inspection or supervision costs). Compare *Hogan Mech., Inc.*, ASBCA 21612, 78-1 BCA ¶ 13,164, where the assessment of liquidated damages on a calendar-day basis was upheld even though the personnel who generated the bulk of the administrative costs upon which the assessment was based worked only a five-day week. In *Kingston Constructors Inc.*, ENGBCA 6006, 95-2 BCA ¶ 27,841, the board found the liquidated damages unreasonable because the facts on which the rate had been determined had changed prior to award of the contract. However, the board reduced the assessment from $1,000 to $500 per day. On appeal the court held that if the liquidated damages amount is not a reasonable forecast, it must be stricken as an unreasonable penalty, *Kingston Constructors, Inc., v. WMATA,* 930 F. Supp. 651 (D.D.C. 1996).

Restatement, Second, Contracts § 356 appears to indicate that the presence or absence of actual damages should also be considered in determining the reasonableness of liquidated damages:

> (1) Damages for breach by either party may be liquidated in the agreement but only at an amount that is reasonable in the light of the anticipated or actual harm caused by the breach and the difficulties of proof of loss. A term fixing unreasonably large liquidated damages is unenforceable on grounds of public policy as a penalty.

However, this statement has had no impact on government contract litigation.

b. Accuracy of Measurement of Forecast Damages

In general, a forecast of damages will be held unreasonable if the contractor can demonstrate that the deductions taken by the government are not reasonably related to the government's anticipated loss or injury such that the damages amount to an unwarranted penalty. The decision of whether or not an award amounts to a penalty depends on the facts and circumstances of each case. Most often, this issue will arise when the liquidated damages assessment is contractually specified as a percentage of the contract price. See *Tommy Nobis Ctr., Inc.*, GSBCA 8988-TD, 89-3 BCA ¶ 22,112 (40 to 60 percent reduction in contract price rejected as unreasonable); *JEM Dev. Corp.*, ASBCA 42645, 92-1 BCA ¶ 24,428 (47 percent of contract price found to be based on disproportionate estimates of government expense caused by delays); and *W.H. Smith Hardware Co.*, ASBCA 34532, 89-2 BCA ¶ 21,606 (assessment of 15 percent of contract price was unreasonable because there was no connection made between that figure and the damages that the government incurred as a result of the contractor's improper use of an other than small supplier). Compare *Winfield Mfg. Co.*, ASBCA 35743, 89-2 BCA ¶ 21,837 (liquidated damages of 8 percent of the contract price with a mandated cap at 25 percent found reasonable).

If the contractor had substantial involvement in negotiating the liquidated damages rate, a finding of reasonableness will be more likely, *Tricon-Triangle Contractors*, ENGBCA 5553, 92-1 BCA ¶ 24,667 (because the contractor had negotiated a change in the liquidated damages provision in the contract, a finding of penalty was precluded); *Downing Elec., Inc.,* ASBCA 37851, 90-3 BCA ¶ 23,001 (contractor's unquestioned knowledge of the formula for the daily rate of liquidated damages rendered assessment proper). However, there is no requirement that a liquidated damages clause must be negotiated for it to have the desired effect, *JEM Dev. Corp.,*

ASBCA 45912, 94-1 BCA ¶ 26,407 (lack of negotiation of liquidated damages rate did not necessitate a finding of penalty).

(1) Proportional Application

Liquidated damages will be held to be a reasonable forecast if the amount assessed varies in proportion to the anticipated harm to the government. Conversely, a liquidated damages rate may well be considered a penalty if it is an "all or nothing" rate; that is, the full rate is applied even though significant portions of the work are complete. In *Charley O. Estes.*, IBCA 1198-7-78, 84-1 BCA ¶ 17,073, a clause in a tree-planting contract, which provided for no payment when tree-planting efforts were deemed to be below the 85 percent level of performance, was held to be unenforceable as a penalty since it made no allowance for the value of timber in a partially planted unit. Accord, *JMNI, Inc. v. United States*, 4 Cl. Ct. 310 (1984). See also *Green Int'l, Inc.*, ENGBCA 5706, 98-1 BCA ¶ 29,684 (liquidated damages clause was void as a penalty because the clause required the payment of damages for the entire amount of work due under contract milestones even though significant portions of the work toward the milestones had been completed early). In *Conner Bros. Constr. Co.*, VABCA 2504, 95-2 BCA ¶ 27,910, the government's decision to drop a renovated building from its inspection requirements under a hospital construction project was tantamount to acceptance of that portion of the project. Thus, the contractor was entitled to a pro rata reduction of liquidated damages.

(2) Fixed Daily Rates

Since almost all liquidated damages clauses cover only delay damages (for an exception, see FAR 19.705-7), they are usually assessed at a fixed rate of dollars per day. On construction contracts, where the government does not usually accept the work until it is substantially completed, the use of such daily rates has generally been held reasonable, *Wise v. United States*, 249 U.S. 361 (1919) (liquidated damages of $200 per day for each day of delay in completion of two laboratories were permissible); *Mitchell Eng'g & Constr. Co.*, ENGBCA 3785, 89-2 BCA ¶ 21,753 ($85 per day partially based on cost of daily site inspections not unreasonable even though daily inspections did not occur due to the contractor's frequent, unjustified absences from the job site); *Browne-Morse Co.*, IBCA 390, 65-2 BCA ¶ 5037, *recons. denied*, 65-2 BCA ¶ 5096 (liquidated damages of $75 per day for each day of delay in completion reasonable); *Triad, Inc.*, VABCA 1774, 89-2 BCA ¶ 21,661 ($50 per day reasonable despite the contractor's claim that flat liquidated damage rates are per se penalties). But see *Coliseum Constr. Inc.*, ASBCA 36642, 89-1 BCA ¶ 21,428 (liquidated damages of greater than $1,800 per day found unreasonable).

Liquidated damages assessed at a fixed rate per day are not necessarily reasonable when multiple quantities are to be delivered on supply contracts, *Graybar Elec. Co.*, IBCA 773-4-69, 70-1 BCA ¶ 8121 (flat rate of $50 per day unreasonable where

10 of 18 items were delivered on time, six items two days late, and two items five days late); *Southern Mapping & Eng'g Co.*, AGBCA 224, 71-2 BCA ¶ 9040 ($25 per day flat rate for failure to deliver any portion of required photographic prints unreasonable because the government failed to prove that partial deliveries were not of value when received). Accord, *Standard Coil Prods., Inc.*, ASBCA 4878, 59-1 BCA ¶ 2105; *Marathon Battery Co.*, ASBCA 9464, 1964 BCA ¶ 4337. In *Southern Mapping*, the board recognized that a liquidated damages rate may remain the same until a construction project is substantially complete and available for use but refused to assume that the parties meant to stipulate the same damages for both total and partial failure to deliver items. See also *Northwestern Terra Cotta Co. v. Caldwell*, 234 F.2d 491 (8th Cir.), *cert. denied*, 242 U.S. 643 (1916). However, one board has specifically rejected a contractor's claim that fixed liquidated damages rates are penalties as a matter of law for multiple quantity contracts. See *Triad, Inc.*, VABCA 1774, 89-2 BCA ¶ 21,661, in which the board stated at 108,964:

> There is no evidence that the Government's administrative and inspection costs did not continue until completion of the contract. Some degree of reduction of this activity may have been experienced in the later stages of the contract but the extent of the reduction, if any, is not disclosed—the matter is simply not addressed. Furthermore, it is well established that the legality of a liquidated damage provision is to be determined on facts and estimates extant at the outset of the contract, and the actual damages experienced thereafter are generally considered not material.

Accordingly, the board concluded that it was irrelevant whether the contractor had installed only one window or almost all of them prior to the termination. The contractor was charged the $50-per-day rate for the full 186-day delay.

Assessment of liquidated damages at a per-unit per-day rate is generally upheld. In *Henry Angelo & Co.*, ASBCA 44648, 93-3 BCA ¶ 26,131, the board held that a liquidated damages assessment of $10 per day for each house not renovated was reasonable because the contractor had provided no evidence tending to demonstrate that this figure was not a "reasonable forecast of damages" or that it bore "no reasonable relation to damages for delay." Accord, *Bayou Culvert Mfg., Inc.*, AGBCA 400, 76-1 BCA ¶ 11,796. In *Simmonds Precision Prods., Inc. v. United States*, 212 Ct. Cl. 305, 546 F.2d 886 (1976), liquidated damages were upheld because the parties had negotiated a per-item per-day rate even though the contract mistakenly included a clause calling for such damages on a per-day rate. However, in *Pre-Con, Inc.*, IBCA 986-3-73, 74-2 BCA ¶ 10,957, a liquidated damages provision of $3 per unit per day was held unreasonable because the effect of the delayed deliveries was to require special installation of the units at an approximate cost of $50 per unit, regardless of the extent of the delay. In *Lauhoff Grain Co.*, AGBCA 75-120, 80-1 BCA ¶ 14,192, liquidated damages at a fixed rate per unit per day were held unreasonable because a GAO study stated that they were too high and the government submitted no evidence of either estimated or actual damages.

(3) Inclusion of Administrative Expenses

In accordance with FAR 11.502(b) most contracts set the liquidated damages rate based on anticipated administrative expenses. The courts and boards generally uphold such liquidated damages because such administrative expenses—that is, inspection, superintendence, or engineering costs—can be reasonably anticipated if a delay is encountered, *Downing Elec., Inc.,* ASBCA 37851, 90-3 BCA ¶ 23,001 (liquidated damages of $265 per day reasonable because they were measured as one-half the daily cost of a typical inspector plus administrative and overhead expenses); *Southland Constr. Co.,* VABCA 2217, 89-1 BCA ¶ 21,548 ($45 per day upheld because the contracting officer had warned the contractor at a pre-construction conference that liquidated damages would include storage costs); *Robert E. McKee, Inc.,* ASBCA 33643, 90-1 BCA ¶ 22,391 (liquidated damages assessment based upon delay in only one of 15 construction items not a penalty because such a delay would foreseeably disrupt the inspector's capability to work and the liquidated damages formula was based upon these perceived costs); *FBS Generalbau GmbH*, ASBCA 44743, 95-1 BCA ¶ 27,504 (liquidated damages properly included increased costs for inspector and for the contracting officer's representative.); *Young Assocs., Inc. v. United States*, 200 Ct. Cl. 438, 471 F.2d 618 (1973) (liquidated damages of $100 per day not unreasonable because they were based on an approximation of administrative and engineering costs that would be incurred by such a delay). Such reasonableness has been found even though the daily rate is established by regulation and based on a sliding scale that lists the dollars of liquidated damages to be used for various contract prices. In *Young,* the court stated at 445:

> Citing the liquidated damages policy section of the Federal Procurement Regulations, 41 CFR § 1-1.315-2(c) (1972), [the contractor] says that the incorporation of FP-61 (promulgated in 1961 by the Commerce Department) into this Interior Department 1964 contract shows that no "case-by-case" consideration was given to the rate of liquidated damages. The answer is, we think, that the regulation does not require a liquidated-damage schedule to be tailor-made for each individual contract. It is enough if the amount stipulated is reasonable for the particular agreement at the time it is made. We have no reason to doubt that that was so here, and [the contractor] suggests none. The court can take judicial notice that costs did not generally decrease from 1961 to 1964, and the [Government] points out that other procuring agencies were using the same charge of $100 per day for a contract of this magnitude. We cannot say, therefore, that in June 1964 it was unreasonable to adopt that amount as daily liquidated damages for delay on this road-building project.

See also *Lane Co.*, ASBCA 21691, 79-1 BCA ¶ 13,651. In *George F. Marshall & Gordon L. Blackwell,* ENGBCA 6066, 00-1 BCA ¶ 30,780, the board expressed doubt about the propriety of an "interest" component in the liquidated damages clause. Although it did not determine whether this rendered the clause a penalty per se, it did state that to the extent the government recovers under such a liquidated damages provision, it would be recovering interest on interest. The board called such an "interest" methodology "highly dubious."

(4) Maximum Assessment

Merely because a liquidated damages clause does not contain a time limit or maximum amount of liquidated damages, does not make it unreasonable and a penalty. In *Hughes Bros. v. United States*, 133 Ct. Cl. 108, 134 F. Supp. 471 (1955), the court approved a liquidated damages clause that could have allowed assessed damages on a per-day basis for an indefinite period. Accord, *Bayou Culvert Mfg., Inc.*, AGBCA 400, 76-1 BCA ¶ 11,796; *Southland Constr. Co.*, VABCA 2217, 89-1 BCA ¶ 21,548; *Weldon Farm Prods., Inc. v. Commodity Credit Corp.*, 214 F. Supp. 678 (D. Minn. 1963); *Jennie-O Foods, Inc. v. United States*, 217 Ct. Cl. 314, 580 F.2d 400 (1978); 35 Comp. Gen. 484 (B-126434) (1956). This has led to the assessment of liquidated damages in excess of the contract price, *Parker-Schram*, IBCA 96, 59-1 BCA ¶ 2127; *Ivy H. Smith Co. v. United States*, 154 Ct. Cl. 74 (1961). Contrast *Operational Serv. Corp.*, ASBCA 37059, 93-3 BCA ¶ 26,190, in which the board, in concluding that the assessment amounted to a penalty, gave substantial weight to the fact that the liquidated damages assessment was greater than the contractor's bid price.

(5) Use of Standard Formulae

The use of certain standard formulas for measuring has not only been upheld as reasonable but has also been accepted by the courts and boards as prima facie evidence of the reasonableness of the liquidated damages assessment. For example, the 20 percent liquidated damages provision incorporated into the SF 114C Default clause used in all government sales of property has been ruled presumptively reasonable and not a penalty, *Baltazar Torres v. General Servs. Admin.,* GSBCA 11472, 92-3 BCA ¶ 25,178 (no evidence that the failure to pay for four automobiles precluded an assessment of 20 percent of the contract price where the figure represented a reasonable estimate of anticipated damages); *Mike Casey v. General Servs. Admin.*, GSBCA 11570, 92-2 BCA ¶ 24,882 (20 percent upheld where the bidder failed to demonstrate grounds to void the sale of a truck); *Harry W. Griffith v. General Servs. Admin.*, GSBCA 11571, 93-1 BCA ¶ 25,421 (20 percent is a reasonable estimation of the government's administrative costs for sales of property); *Spiess Constr. Co.,* ASBCA 48247, 95-2 BCA ¶ 27,767 (assessment of liquidated damages was enforceable because the daily rate for the assessment was arrived at by using a standard government manual); *Orbas & Assocs.*, ASBCA 48260, 97-2 BCA ¶ 29,281 (liquidated damages rate of $50 per day was enforceable because the rate in the contract was significantly less than the rate of $200 a day prescribed by the regulation governing the calculation of liquidated damages rates for government contracts of this value); *Valenzuela Eng'g, Inc.,* ASBCA 53936, 04-1 BCA ¶ 32,517 (daily rate for liquidated damages presumed reasonable because it came from a government contracting manual).

Similarly, the use of tables such as those in the NAVFAC P-68 manual is presumed reasonable because the purpose of these tables is to establish a reasonable estimate of government expense in case of a delay. In *Fred A. Arnold, Inc. v. United States,* 18 Cl. Ct. 1 (1989), *recon.*, 24 Cl. Ct. 6 (1991), *rev'd on other grounds,* 979 F.2d 217 (Fed. Cir. 1992), the court reversed the conclusion that $1,728 per day based on the NAVFAC formula incorporated into the contract was a penalty and upheld that award, stating at 13:

> [T]o hold that the regulation was unreasonable, or in need of substantiation by independent proof, is tantamount to requiring the Government to "reinvent the wheel" each time it enters into a contract for the construction of military housing that is to include a liquidated damages provision. By the Board's reasoning, the Government would be obliged to re-calculate the per diem damage rate for each and every contract. Such a result is impractical, inefficient, and, indeed, unwise because it robs the Government of the more informed decision-making that enters into the development and promulgation of a service-wide regulatory standard. We must presume, therefore, that this regulation, like federal regulations in general, is reasonable absent evidence to the contrary. Here there was no such evidence.

One board followed this decision in *Brooks Lumber Co.*, ASBCA 40743, 91-2 BCA ¶ 23,984, in which it noted that the utilization of these tables is prima facie evidence that the liquidated damages assessment is reasonable. Accord, *JEM Dev. Corp.*, ASBCA 45912, 94-1 BCA ¶ 26,407 ($100 per day upheld, though determined by a formula, because the formula was based on properly recoverable administrative costs); *Skip Kirchdorfer, Inc.,* ASBCA 40515, 00-1 BCA ¶ 30,622 (upholding rates less than those prescribed by Naval Facilities Engineering Command manual). Thus, formulas will generally be upheld unless, of course, doing so would be unreasonable or unconscionable. See *Operational Serv. Corp.*, ASBCA 37059, 93-3 BCA ¶ 26,190 (penalty found where the use of a contractually mandated formula—hourly rate multiplied by period of delay—led to an assessment greater than the original bid price). If the standard formula is wrongly applied, however, the rate may be rejected. In *George F. Marshall & Gordon L. Blackwell*, ENGBCA 6066, 00-1 BCA ¶ 30,780, the agency erroneously applied its own internal guidelines, resulting in a liquidated damages rate that grossly exceeded the per diem amount that was computable pursuant to the regulations.

In *Young Assocs., Inc. v. United States*, 200 Ct. Cl. 438, 471 F.2d 618 (1973), the court noted that a liquidated damages schedule is not required to be tailor-made for each individual contract. Similarly, in *DJ Mfg. Corp. v. United States*, 86 F.3d 1130 (Fed. Cir. 1996), the court approved a liquidated damages clause even though the amount was not calculated specifically for the contract. The court rejected the contractor's argument that the regulations in effect at the time, FAR 12.202(b), required the contracting officer specifically to tailor the liquidated damages clause to the particular contract in advance, holding that the regulation provided advice and "internal guidance rather than [creating] rights in contracting parties." In addition, the court found nothing "inherently unreasonable" in the rate reducing the price by 1/15 of 1 percent per day.

2. *Difficulty of Accurate Estimation*

It is generally stated that liquidated damages will not be enforced unless the harm is difficult to determine, *Robert E. Dineen v. United States*, 109 Ct. Cl. 18, 71 F. Supp. 742 (1947), *cert. denied*, 333 U.S. 842, *reh'g denied*, 334 U.S. 816 (1948); *Broderick Wood Prods. Co. v. United States*, 195 F.2d 433 (10th Cir. 1952); *First Interstate Bank of Denver, N.A.*, GSBCA 9484, 89-1 BCA ¶ 21,453; *Downing Elec., Inc.*, ASBCA 37851, 90-3 BCA ¶ 23,001; *Work Force Reforestation, Inc.*, AGBCA 90-131-3, 90-3 BCA ¶ 23,138; *Jennie-O Foods, Inc. v. United States*, 217 Ct. Cl. 314, 580 F.2d 400 (1978). However, this requirement has rarely been dispositive, and testimony by a government witness to the effect that the government cannot accurately estimate the amount of damages due to delay is usually adequate proof of difficulty. See *Green Int'l, Inc.*, ENGBCA 5706, 98-1 BCA ¶ 29,684, accepting the government's argument that it was difficult to assess the damage when dealing with a public project such as the construction of a subway station.

C. Relief from Liquidated Damages

Liquidated damages will not be assessed during any period in which the contractor experienced an excusable delay, or after the date on which the contractor substantially completed the work.

1. *Excusable Delays*

The standard clause used to include liquidated damages in supply, service, or research and development contracts contains a provision relieving the contractor from the assessment of such damages during any period of excusable delay, FAR 52.211-11. The construction contract default termination clause in FAR 52.249-10 accomplishes the same result by granting the contractor schedule extensions for excusable delays. For a detailed discussion of the types of excusable delays, see Chapter 6.

Even if liquidated damages are included in a contract without cross-reference to excusable delays, it is likely that no assessment would be allowed for an excusable delay period. See *North Am. Aviation, Inc.*, ASBCA 11603, 68-1 BCA ¶ 6998 (target delivery date adjusted for excusable delays in incentive contract with delivery bonus that did not cross-reference excusable delays provision); *General Precision, Inc.*, ASBCA 11071, 66-2 BCA ¶ 5904 (neither delivery bonus nor penalty assessable in incentive contract without cross-reference to excusable delays provisions where both government delays and excusable delays were concurrent); and *Morganti Nat'l Inc. v. United States,* 49 Fed. Cl. 110 (2001), *aff'd,* 36 Fed. Appx. 452 (Fed Cir. 2002) (because the contractor was entitled to a time extension, which extended beyond the date of the default termination, the court directed the return of the liquidated damages.)

Contractors have the burden of proving that the delay was excusable under the Default clause of the contract, *Sauer Inc. v. Danzig,* 224 F.3d 1340 (Fed. Cir. 2000). Compare *Fire Sec. Sys., Inc. v. General Servs. Admin.,* GSBCA 12120, 97-2 BCA ¶ 28,994, stating that the government has the "initial burden of establishing the facts upon which the assessment of liquidated damages is based."

Where a contractor is delayed by a series of nonconcurrent causes, liquidated damages will be assessed after the excusable delays are accounted for, *Southwest Eng'g Co. v. United States,* 341 F.2d 998 (8th Cir.), *cert. denied*, 382 U.S. 819 (1965). However, when both excusable and inexcusable causes of delay would have prevented work from being accomplished on a given day, liquidated damages have generally not been assessed, *Vogt Bros. Mfg. Co. v. United States*, 160 Ct. Cl. 687 (1963) (where both parties are responsible for contract delays, neither party has a claim against the other); *Brooks Lumber Co.,* ASBCA 40743, 91-2 BCA ¶ 23,984 (government changes and delays running concurrently with subcontractor delays in restarting performance precluded recovery for that period). See also *Arrow, Inc.*, ASBCA 39621, 90-3 BCA ¶ 23,217; *Spectrum Leasing Corp.*, GSBCA 7347, 90-3 BCA ¶ 22,984, and *ADCO Constr., Inc.*, PSBCA 2355, 90-3 BCA ¶ 22,944. Thus, concurrent delays will invalidate an assessment of liquidated damages, *Conner Bros. Constr. Co.*, VABCA 2504, 95-2 BCA ¶ 27,910 (contractor entitled to reimbursement for periods of concurrent government-caused and contractor-caused delay); *Tempo, Inc.*, ASBCA 37589, 95-2 BCA ¶ 27,618 (liquidated damages reduced because the government failed to meet its burden of proving that any part of the delay period was not concurrent with government-caused delay).

In some cases, it has been stated that concurrent delays will lead to "annulment" of the liquidated damages provision. See *Schmoll v. United States,* 91 Ct. Cl. 1 (1940), in which the court stated at 28:

> In *Levering & Garrigues Co. v. United States*, 73 C. Cls. 566, 578, this court stated that "where a contractor is prevented from executing his contract according to its terms, he is relieved from the obligations of the contract (as to time of completion) and from paying liquidated damages." In several cases we have held that where delays are caused by both parties to the contract the court will not attempt to apportion them, but will simply hold that the provisions of the contract with reference to liquidated damages will be annulled.

See also *Acme Process Equip. Co. v. United States*, 171 Ct. Cl. 324, 347 F.2d 509 (1965), *rev'd on other grounds*, 385 U.S. 138 (1966).

Cases indicate that an effort will be made to avoid annulment by seeking to ascertain the controlling cause of the delay, *Industrial Design Labs., Inc.*, ASBCA 21603, 80-1 BCA ¶ 14,269. Thus, if the government can prove that the total project delay was caused by contractor fault, concurrent excusable delays not delaying the total project will not be used to relieve the contractor of liquidated damages, *G. Bliudzius Contractors, Inc.*, ASBCA 42366, 93-3 BCA ¶ 26,074 (despite the lack of a critical path method schedule in the contract, several government-caused delays were found not to require remission of all damages because those delays did not affect final completion); *Central Ohio Bldg. Co.*, PSBCA 2742, 92-1 BCA ¶ 24,399 (government delay in approval of an additive ruled irrelevant because the contract precluded the use of this additive and the contractor had been responsible for a 41-day delay after receiving the notice to proceed); *Harold J. Younger, Inc.*, ASBCA 38922, 91-1 BCA ¶ 23,436 (inclusion of alleged extra and unnecessary items on a punch list by the government held not critical to the completion of the overall project); *G.Q. Carmichael Surveyors & Eng'rs, Inc.*, AGBCA 86-186-1, 92-1 BCA ¶ 24,743 (government's refusal to provide plans and specifications found not the central cause of delay; the contractor's failure to provide a supervisor at the work site was so found). See also Wickwire and Smith, *The Use of Critical Path Method Techniques in Contract Claims,* 7 Pub. Cont. L.J. 1, 43-45 (1974). In each of these cases, the critical path method (CPM) was used to apportion concurrent delays, with the board holding that the delay on the critical path was the causative delay. As this type of accurate evidence of the impact of various delays becomes more widely available, it is likely that there will be more apportionment of delays for purposes of assessing liquidated damages. Without such evidence, however, the boards continue to refuse to assess liquidated damages where concurrent delays have occurred, *H.G. Reynolds Co.*, ASBCA 42351, 93-2 BCA ¶ 25,797 (conflicting punchlists issued by the government precluded a liquidated damages assessment even though the contractor had also been responsible for the delay). Accord, *Jordan & Nobles Constr. Co.*, GSBCA 8349, 91-1 BCA ¶ 23,659; *ADCO Constr. Inc.*, PSBCA 2355, 90-3 BCA ¶ 22,944. See, however, *Lawrence D. Krause*, AGBCA 76-118-4, 82-2 BCA ¶ 16,129, holding that the contractor has the burden of proof that its delay was not the cause of the late delivery.

In one unique case, the Department of Transportation Board of Contract Appeals apportioned concurrent delays on the basis of comparative fault rather than proof of causation, *Hilltop Elec. Constr., Inc.*, DOTCAB 78-6, 78-2 BCA ¶ 13,421. The board granted time extensions for one-half the delay period on the theory that the parties were equally at fault. The effect of such time extensions was that the contractor was assessed one-half the liquidated damages.

In recent decisions, seeking the casue of delays has been called "apportionment." Apportionment was allowed in *Sauer, Inc. v. Danzig,* 224 F.3d 1340 (Fed. Cir. 2000), because of clear fault on both sides. See also *R. P. Wallace, Inc. v. United States*, 63 Fed. Cl. 402 (2004) (reviewing decisions and apportioning "sequential delays"), and *Sunshine Constr. & Eng'g, Inc. v. United States*, 64 Fed. Cl. 346 (2005) (agreeing with *Wallace*). In *PCL Constr. Servs., Inc. v. United States,* 53 Fed. Cl. 479 (2002), however, the court continued to adhere to the rule against apportionment, finding that *Sauer* had not overruled *Acme Process Equipment.*

Where apportionment is considered inappropriate, contractors have been relieved from liability for liquidated damages, *Wexler Constr. Co.*, ASBCA 23782,

84-2 BCA ¶ 17,408; *Powell's Gen. Contracting Co.*, DOTCAB 77-27, 79-1 BCA ¶ 13,694, *recons. denied*, 79-1 BCA ¶ 13,702; *Myers-Laine Corp.*, ASBCA 18234, 74-1 BCA ¶ 10,467; *ICA Southeast, Inc.*, AGBCA 331, 73-1 BCA ¶ 9969. In *Kirk Bros. Mechanical Contractors, Inc.*, ASBCA 43738, 93-1 BCA ¶ 25,325, the board relieved a contractor of 37 days of liquidated damages—seven days for government-caused delays and 30 days for concurrent delays. However, in *Acme Process Equip. Co. v. United States*, 171 Ct. Cl. 324, 347 F.2d 509 (1965), *rev'd on other grounds*, 385 U.S. 138 (1966), the court indicated that, even though the contractor is relieved from liquidated damages, it would still be liable for actual damages suffered by the government as a result of a concurrent delay.

2. Substantial Completion

Liquidated damages will not be assessed after the date on which the work is substantially completed. Substantial completion has been defined as the moment when the construction sites or the tendered supplies are capable of being used for their intended purposes, *Theon v. United States*, 765 F.2d 1110 (Fed. Cir. 1985); *Central Ohio Bldg. Co.*, PSBCA 2742, 92-1 BCA ¶ 24,399. This rule is applied primarily on construction contracts where substantial completion is held to have occurred when a high percentage of the work is completed and the project is available for its intended use, *Lindwall Constr. Co.*, ASBCA 23148, 79-1 BCA ¶ 13,822 (because building was available for beneficial occupancy, it was substantially complete); *Vern W. Johnson & Sons, Inc.*, ENGBCA 5554, 90-1 BCA ¶ 22,571 (government had beneficial occupancy of a pumping station for a fish hatchery and could not demonstrate that it was not working as intended); *Long Elevator & Mach. Co.*, VABCA 2246, 90-2 BCA ¶ 22,637 (substantial completion found where one elevator was returned to service, even though minor punch list items remained to be completed); *Matthew Andrew Kalosinakis*, ASBCA 41337, 91-2 BCA ¶ 23,744 (substantial completion occurred where the only remaining work was the permanent installation of a receptacle in the bathroom of a house and some minor clean-up items); *R.J. Crowley, Inc.*, GSBCA 11080 (9521)-REIN, 92-1 BCA ¶ 24,499 (substantial completion found despite lack of installation of a fire alarm); *Batson-Cook of Atlanta, Inc.*, ASBCA 44902, 97-1 BCA ¶ 28,754 (government failed to prove that deficiencies in the contractor's work precluded use of that phase of the project); *Orbas & Assocs.*, ASBCA 48260, 97-2 BCA ¶ 29,281 (record strongly suggested that the system was substantially completed when government began withholding only $1,920 as retainage). Conversely, if a building is not available for its intended use, no substantial completion will be found, *Randolph & Co.*, ASBCA 52953, 03-1 BCA ¶ 32,080, *recons. denied,* ASBCA 52957, 03-1 BCA ¶ 32,138 (government had not accepted the work and it was not suitable for its intended purpose); *Gassman Corp.,* ASBCA 44975, 00-1 BCA ¶ 30,720 (building not available for follow-on contractor to perform the interior finish work necessary for the facility to be used as a research laboratory).

While the contractor must show that performance is near completion, there is no set percentage that establishes substantial completion. However, when a significant percentage of the work remains unperformed, substantial completion will not be found, *Wilton Corp.*, ASBCA 39876, 93-2 BCA ¶ 25,897 (substantial completion rejected where price of unperformed lintel work was 11 percent of total price); *Toombs & Co.*, ASBCA 34590, 91-1 BCA ¶ 23,403 (government occupation of two buildings did not demonstrate substantial completion because work on the roofs of the buildings had yet to pass the contract testing requirements); *Foremost Mgmt. Sys., Inc.*, ENGBCA-PCC-145, 99-1 BCA ¶ 30,137 (completion of 9 out of 10 phases was not substantial completion because the parties had planned for each phase to be of equivalent importance). This is true even though the government may be able to derive some benefit from the uncompleted project, *J&A Pollin Constr. Co.*, GSBCA 2780, 70-2 BCA ¶ 8562 (although classes were held for nine days before heat was provided, building was not substantially complete until heat was provided). See also *Capitol City Constr. Co.*, DOTCAB 74-29, 75-1 BCA ¶ 11,012, and *Lambert Constr. Co.*, DOTCAB 77-9, 78-1 BCA ¶ 13,221. The board will determine the percentage of completion from the contractor's progress reports unless evidence exists that they overstate the actual percentage of completion of the project, *Electronic & Missile Facilities, Inc.*, GSBCA 2787, 71-1 BCA ¶ 8785.

Board decisions place more emphasis on the availability of the work for its intended use than the application of any rigid formula as to the percentage of work that has been accomplished, *Electrical Enters., Inc.*, IBCA 972-9-72, 74-1 BCA ¶ 10,400. If the product cannot be used as intended, liquidated damages generally are assessed. See *Mit-Con, Inc.*, ASBCA 44509, 93-2 BCA ¶ 25,570, holding that a building was not substantially complete when the contractor had yet to complete wire mesh cages for safe storage of equipment and had yet to remove nonconforming pavement. The board concluded that, although most of the work had been completed, without these essential components the building could not be used for its intended purpose. See also *Pathman Constr. Co.*, ASBCA 16781, 74-2 BCA ¶ 10,785, holding that a mess hall was not substantially complete where performance of remaining work would have interfered with food preparation, and *Fisher Constr. Co.*, ASBCA 7264, 1962 BCA ¶ 3497, finding a facility not substantially complete where deficiencies rendered it unsafe for use. Accord, *Fred Loffredo*, ASBCA 22218, 82-1 BCA ¶ 15,509 (hangar not fit for intended purpose even though only minor effort was required to correct out-of-line door aperture); *Martell Constr. Co.*, ASBCA 23679, 80-1 BCA ¶ 14,429 (even though government was able to occupy building, no substantial completion found because building could not be used for its intended purpose as an audiovisual center); *Lane Co.*, ASBCA 21691, 79-1 BCA ¶ 13,651 (no substantial completion of building where toilets had been installed and used but sewage treatment system not fully operational); *Hof Constr. Co.*, ASBCA 22136, 78-1 BCA ¶ 13,062 (automatic data processing center not substantially complete without functioning air conditioning system since ADP equipment required a cool temperature to function properly); *Electronic & Missile Facilities, Inc.*, GSBCA 2787, 71-1 BCA ¶ 8785 (no substantial completion where punchlist totaling 1,200 defects, many of them minor, made building unsuitable for normal business functions); *George A. Grant, Inc.*, IBCA 100-7-

73, 74-2 BCA ¶ 10,851 (defective drain pipes representing only 3.35 percent of the drain line interfered with farming operations in the area).

The doctrine of substantial completion will not be applied in cases where delivery of the item complete and intact is required in order for it to be used at all, *Southwest Welding & Mfg. Div., Yuba Consolidated Indus., Inc.*, IBCA 281, 1962 BCA ¶ 3564; *Bayou Culvert Mfg., Inc.*, AGBCA 400, 76-1 BCA ¶ 11,796.

Substantial completion will not be found where the government does not have notice that the work has been substantially completed and beneficial occupancy can take place, *Seaboard Surety Co.*, ASBCA 43281, 93-1 BCA ¶ 25,510.

D. Relationship with Default Termination

The termination for default of a contract containing a liquidated damages provision may result in the assessment against the contractor of liquidated damages that are in addition to the excess costs of reprocurement or other actual damages not covered by the provision.

1. Concurrent Running of Liquidated Damages and Excess Costs of Reprocurement

When a contract containing a liquidated damages provision is terminated for default, the standard clauses provide that the government may assess liquidated damages until it obtains completion of the work. The time period used to compute such damages begins at the contract completion date, as adjusted for excusable delays, and ends when the work would have been completed had the government acted reasonably in reprocuring the work, *Racine Screw Co. v. United States*, 156 Ct. Cl. 256 (1962). See *Biehler Painting Co.*, ASBCA 18855, 76-1 BCA ¶ 11,729, in which the government argued that liquidated damages should be assessed starting at the date the contractor abandoned the contract, but the board held that the proper date to begin the running of liquidated damages was the original contract completion date. See also *Frontier Contracting Co.*, ASBCA 33658, 89-2 BCA ¶ 21,595, in which the board remitted liquidated damages that had been assessed against the contractor for the period between the original completion date and the actual completion date because a time extension had been granted due to government insistence that the contractor fix leaks in the roof.

The contractor is not necessarily liable for the entire time necessary for completion. The reasonableness of the government's reprocurement will be closely scrutinized, and liquidated damages will not be assessed for any period of delay caused by the government, *Arctic Corner, Inc.*, ASBCA 38075, 94-1 BCA ¶ 26,317 (cost of 6½-month delay in awarding the reprocurement contract must be excluded from liquidated damages assessment); *Biehler Painting Co.*, ASBCA 18855, 76-1 BCA ¶ 11,729 (liquidated damages would not run to the actual completion date of the reprocurement contract where it was found that "but for unreasonable delay in awarding the reprocurement contract, work thereunder would have been completed one month earlier"). See *Nichols Dynamics, Inc.*, ASBCA 17610, 74-2 BCA ¶ 10,820, in which liquidated damages were reduced because the government had allowed the contractor to continue to perform for 25 days following termination for default before issuing a solicitation for completion of the work. The board disallowed liquidated damages for the full 25-day period and also denied the contractor payment for work performed during that period. See also FAR 11.501(c), noting that efficient administration of reprocurements is imperative to avoid the loss of liquidated damages.

Liquidated damages may not be assessed unless work is completed or the supplies are reprocured, *Manart Textile Co. v. United States*, 111 Ct. Cl. 540, 77 F. Supp. 924 (1948). The government cannot recover liquidated damages for the period of an attempted but incomplete procurement, *Standard Coating Serv., Inc.*, ASBCA 48611, 00-1 BCA ¶ 30,725. Here, the government canceled the reprocurement after issuing its solicitation but before award. Thus the contractor was not liable for liquidated damages after the date of termination. See also *Designatronics, Inc.*, ASBCA 10149, 65-1 BCA ¶ 4812, and *Hydro Flex Inc.*, ASBCA 20352, 77-1 BCA ¶ 12,353. Accordingly, where the government did not reprocure but instead proposed, as the amount of a liquidated damages assessment, a hypothetical minimum amount that the reprocurement would cost, the board rejected it as improper, *Dave's Aluminum Siding, Inc.*, ASBCA 34092, 90-3 BCA ¶ 23,053 (no evidence presented establishing the reasonableness of the minimum). Similarly, liquidated damages will be denied where the reprocured items were not similar to those purchased under the original contract, *Milro Controls Co.*, ASBCA 11550, 68-2 BCA ¶ 7372.

The contractor is not liable for delays encountered by the reprocurement contractor, *Mega Constr. Co. v. United States*, 29 Fed. Cl. 396 (1993); *Matthews Co.*, AGBCA 459, 76-2 BCA ¶ 12,164, *recons. denied*, 77-1 BCA ¶ 12,434. See *Olympic Painting Contractors*, ASBCA 15773, 72-2 BCA ¶ 9549, in which the board held that liquidated damages could be assessed only through the scheduled completion date of the reprocurement contract and not for the 30 days of excusable delay encountered by the reprocurement contractor. If the reprocurement contractor fails to perform and a second reprocurement is awarded, liquidated damages may be assessed against the original contractor only through the scheduled completion date of the first reprocurement contract, *Interstate Forestry, Inc.*, AGBCA 89-114-1, 91-1 BCA ¶ 23,660. In a questionable decision, the GAO allowed the government to assess liquidated damages for a period beyond the scheduled completion date of the reprocurement contract where the original contract stated that liquidated damages could be assessed up to a "45 day maximum," *California Meat Co.*, Comp. Gen. Dec. B-190150, 78-2 CPD ¶ 250. When the reprocurement contractor failed to complete the work by the reprocurement scheduled completion date, or within 45 days of the completion date of the original contract, the contracting officer assessed liquidated damages for 45 days. The GAO upheld the contracting officer's decision, stating:

> The fact that the terminated contractor had no control over the replacement contractor's efforts to deliver the goods, required that there be established a maximum period for which liquidated damages could be assessed, but provides no further equitable basis for remitting damages within the agreed maximum period. Equity is implicit in the maximum 45 day period.

2. *Effect of Waiver*

Waiver of the original completion date by forbearance from default action does not preclude assessment of liquidated damages beginning on the original completion date, *Southland Constr. Co.*, VABCA 2279, 89-1 BCA ¶ 21,271; *Clifford La Tourelle*, AGBCA 93-132-1, 94-1 BCA ¶ 26,509; *Robert E. Moore Constr.*, AGBCA 85-262-1, 90-2 BCA ¶ 22,803; *Instruments for Indus., Inc.*, ASBCA 10543, 65-2 BCA ¶ 5097, *recons. denied*, 70-1 BCA ¶ 8246. In the last case, the board reasoned that the liquidated damages provision specifically imposed damages where the government elected to permit the contractor to continue work after the original completion date. In *JEM Dev. Corp.*, ASBCA 42872, 92-1 BCA ¶ 24,709, the board rejected an assessment of liquidated damages against a construction contractor because the government had knowledge of the causes of the contractor's delay and had acquiesced in the result. In general, however, waiver of delivery date will rarely be found in construction contracts. Similarly, issuance of a change order after the completion date of the contract does not bar the imposition of liquidated damages for any period of inexcusable delay prior to the date of issuance of the order, *Thomas E. Schroyer & Co.*, GSBCA 3465, 72-1 BCA ¶ 9181; *M.S.I. Corp.*, VACAB 626, 68-1 BCA ¶ 6773; *Norfolk Shipbuilding & Drydock Corp.*, ENGBCA 3225, 73-1 BCA ¶ 9950. Contra, *Jan R. Smith, Contractor*, FAACAP 66-21, 65-2 BCA ¶ 5306. However, where both parties negotiate the time extensions for changes and the date for overall completion of the contract is not affected as a result, liquidated damages will be upheld, *Eurostyle Inc.*, GSBCA 10037, 91-1 BCA ¶ 23,595.

E. Computation of Time Covered by Liquidated Damages

Under the standard clauses, liquidated damages are assessed for each calendar day of delay. Holidays are included in the computation, *Pressed Steel Car Co. v. Eastern Ry. Co. of Minn.*, 121 F. 609 (8th Cir. 1903); *Hogan Mech., Inc.*, ASBCA 21612, 78-1 BCA ¶ 13,164; *Winslow Tele-Tronics, Inc.*, ASBCA 15036, 72-1 BCA ¶ 9234. In *J.H. Strain & Sons, Inc.*, ASBCA 34432, 90-2 BCA ¶ 22,770, the board denied the contractor's argument that liquidated damages could not be assessed for weekends and holidays, stating at 114,298:

> The fact that the Government assessed liquidated damages for week-ends and holidays does not invalidate the liquidated damages assessment. Both contract performance and liquidated damages were measured in terms of calendar days, not weekdays.

In *Diane Assocs., Inc.*, ASBCA 23836, 80-1 BCA ¶ 14,453, the board rejected the contractor's argument that because work was permitted only on weekdays, the period of assessment should include only weekdays. In *Steele Contractors, Inc.*, ENGBCA 6043, 95-2 BCA ¶ 27,653, the government improperly withheld liquidated damages for the final day of the original contract performance period, because the record did not reveal the government's rationale for including that day in its assessment.

In *Fa. Kammerdiener Gmb H & Co. (KG)*, ASBCA 45248, 95-1 BCA ¶ 27,295, the board rejected the contractor's argument that the word "days" in a contract clause providing for a specific amount of liquidated damages meant working days because the board had held otherwise in *Hogan Mech.* However, in *Monaco Enters., Inc.*, ASBCA 19725, 75-1 BCA ¶ 11,122, the board limited the assessment of liquidated damages to working days, reasoning that the nature of the contractor's obligations required that it be available for work during weekdays. In *Custom Roofing Co.*, ASBCA 19164, 74-2 BCA ¶ 10,925, the board avoided the imposition of liquidated damages by computing the contract completion date using working days rather than calendar days.

F. Government Right to Actual Damages

When a contract contains a liquidated damages provision, the damages specified by the provision will generally serve as a substitute for any actual damages that the government may suffer. When such a clause is present, the government may collect only liquidated damages unless the contract specifically authorizes the assessment of actual damages as an alternative or as a supplement. The government does, however, have the right to assess actual damages for any harm not covered by the Liquidated Damages clause.

1. Damages Covered by the Clause

The government gives up the right to obtain actual damages for any harm covered by a liquidated damages provision. In *Sorensen v. United States*, 51 Ct. Cl. 69 (1916), the court held that government inspection costs during the delay period were not recoverable since they were included in liquidated damages, stating at 83-84:

> When they liquidated in advance the amount of the damages they fixed the amount which the one could be required to pay or the other be entitled to recover in case of breach, and the clause as much limits the [Government's] right to recover as it affects the [contractor's] obligation to pay. Both are bound by the liquidated damage clause.

See *Desert Sun Eng'g Corp.*, IBCA 725-8-68, 69-1 BCA ¶ 7431, where delay damages paid to another contractor because of a contractor's delay were not recoverable because they were included in liquidated damages for delay in performance. See also *Simmonds Precision Prods., Inc. v. United States*, 212 Ct. Cl. 305, 546 F.2d 886 (1976), and *Nichols Dynamics, Inc.*, ASBCA 17610, 74-2 BCA ¶ 10,820.

The standard clauses used with liquidated damages do not describe what types of damages they cover. In *Cargill, Inc.*, AGBCA 84-164-1, 88-3 BCA ¶ 21,064, the board discussed the difficulty of determining what damages are covered by liquidated damages at 106,368:

> It is a long established principle that actual damages cannot be recovered when they are also included in liquidated damages. *Sorenson v. United States*, 51 Ct. Cl. 69 (1916). However, the Government generally retains the right to obtain actual damages for any harm not covered by the liquidated damages clause [citations omitted].
>
> We therefore, turn to the liquidated damages clause (VII C.) to determine what damages are covered by the clause. The clause does not give any indication as to what damages are, or are not, covered in the provision for liquidated damages, in addition to actual damages. The clause could easily state in unequivocal language that liquidated damages, in addition to actual damages, are for impairment to the price support program and to the Government's credibility with warehousemen, or any other intangible elements difficult to quantify as argued in the Government's brief. The clause does not, however, contain any such language. [The government] contends that the clause provides for both liquidated damages and actual damages. [The contractor] contends that the clause is an either or situation, where, if [the government] does not terminate the contract, actual damages cannot be claimed.
>
> We find that the clause is capable of being read both ways, and [the contractor's] contention is reasonable. Under the clause [the government] had an option to either allow continued performance with the imposition of liquidated damages or, if the delivery is not completed within 30 days beyond the last day of the specified period, to default the contractor and exercise its right to resell the quantity undelivered and claim actual damages.

The board concluded that because the government had neither defaulted the contractor nor exercised the right to resell, actual damages could not be recovered and the contractor's interpretation prevailed.

If a liquidated damages provision is held to be unenforceable as a penalty, the government will be entitled to seek common law breach of contract damages, *United States v. Reisman*, 611 F.2d 325 (9th Cir. 1980).

In *ROI Invs. v. General Servs. Admin.,* GSBCA 14402, 99-1 ¶ 30,353, the government had a right to withhold rent and to assess liquidated damages on the same rental space at the same time because there was no law prohibiting parties from agreeing to a lease that allowed both actions. The withholding of the rent was to ensure that the government paid only for space it occupied, whereas the liquidated damages were intended to compensate the government for administrative costs incurred by the government in inspecting construction progress, communicating with the lessor and local building inspectors, and having to work in overcrowded space while revising plans for its move into new block space.

2. *Damages Outside the Clause*

The government generally retains the right to obtain actual damages for any harm not covered by a liquidated damages clause. The clause is carefully analyzed to determine what harm is covered, *United States v. American Sur. Co.*, 322 U.S. 96 (1944) (no liquidated damages after default when clause limited their recovery to situation in which contractor was permitted to complete). The present standard clauses provide that a defaulted contractor will be liable for both excess costs of completion or reprocurement and liquidated damages, but they are silent as to what other damages are excluded from liquidated damages. In *Wells Constr.*, IBCA 737-10-68, 69-2 BCA ¶ 7866, costs of restoring uncompleted work and excess costs of completion were recovered because they were not included in liquidated damages for delay. See *Casson Constr. Co.*, GSBCA 4884, 78-1 BCA ¶ 13,032, holding that the government's rights under a special clause authorizing recovery of acceleration payments to a follow-on contractor following the first contractor's unexcused delay were not limited by a liquidated damages provision. In *Timberland Paving & Constr. Co. v. United States*, 18 Cl. Ct. 129 (1989), the court allowed the recovery of liquidated damages for untimely performance at the same time as recovery of an offset of the contractor's claims. The court concluded that both recoveries "served a different, non-overlapping function."

In addition to reprocurement costs and liquidated damages, the government is also "entitled to damages, including reasonable administrative expenses," *Grimco Pneumatic Corp.,* ASBCA 50977, 00-1 BCA ¶ 30,727.

G. Remission of Liquidated Damages

A unique aspect of the use of liquidated damages in government contracts is the statutory authority of the Secretary of the Treasury (formerly the Comptroller General) to remit such damages in accordance with 41 U.S.C. § 256a:

> Whenever any contract made on behalf of the Government by the head of any Federal Agency, or by officers authorized by him so to do, includes a provision for liquidated damages for delay, the Secretary of the Treasury upon recommendation of such head is authorized and empowered to remit the whole or any part of such damages as in his discretion may be just and equitable.

Substantially similar language is contained in 10 U.S.C. § 2312.

The Secretary of the Treasury, as the Comptroller General previously, will not exercise this power except upon receipt of a recommendation from the head of the agency involved, *J. Murray Co.*, Comp. Gen. Dec. B-236673, 90-1 CPD ¶ 55; *American Constr. & Energy, Inc.*, Comp. Gen. Dec. B-227253, 87-2 CPD ¶ 186. In addition, before the GAO would provide such relief, the contractor must have exhausted all administrative remedies, *Pine Belt Helicopters, Inc.*, Comp. Gen. Dec

B-181787, 74-2 CPD ¶ 115; Comp. Gen. Dec. B-152201, Sept. 26, 1963, *Unpub.* See, however, Comp. Gen. Dec. B-155678, Aug. 18, 1966, *Unpub.*, holding that a previous decision by the GAO denying remission would not prevent the contractor from appealing under the Disputes clause or preclude the contracting officer or appeals board from granting a time extension for changed work conditions, thereby eliminating any liquidated damages due.

The remitting official may also condition remission on the actions of the contractor. See Comp. Gen. Dec. B-174147, Mar. 12, 1973, *Unpub.*, in which the contractor's claim for $20,200 was reduced to $4,500 provided it accepted that amount as full settlement of the claim.

The merit of a contractor's claim is "dependent upon a showing as to his ability to have prevented the situation in which he finds himself," 34 Comp. Gen. 251 (B-120656) (1954). Strong and persuasive equities must favor the contractor before GAO remission is likely, 36 Comp. Gen. 143 (B-128218) (1956), and remission will not be allowed to rescue the contractor from the consequences of its own negligence and carelessness, 46 Comp. Gen. 252 (B-159546) (1966). The contractor bears the burden of persuading the Comptroller that the reasons for delay merit remission. The GAO has refused remission where there were conflicting facts as to the cause of the delay, Comp. Gen. Dec. B-149899, Oct. 25, 1962, *Unpub.*, and where the contractor was careless in preparing its bid, *Construction Elec. Co.*, Comp. Gen. Dec. B-187820, 77-1 CPD ¶ 403. The fact that the government suffered little actual damage is not alone sufficient to obtain remission, Comp. Gen. Dec. B-156765, July 7, 1965, *Unpub.*

However, where liquidated damages include damages that are an unforeseeable consequence of a delay, remission will be appropriate. This result has been applied where the liquidated damages assessment included actual damages, *Panama Canal Comm'n*, Comp. Gen. Dec. B-242980, Sept. 20, 1991, *Unpub.*, or where the government had played a substantial role in the delay, *Preston's Legal Support & Court Reporting Serv.*, Comp. Gen. Dec. B-254610, Apr. 20, 1994, *Unpub.* For a discussion of the GAO's previous power to remit liquidated damages, see Preston, *The Role of the Comptroller General in Remitting Liquidated Damages,* 30 Fed. B.J. 144 (1971).

CHAPTER 11

TERMINATION FOR CONVENIENCE

The Termination for Convenience of the Government clause is one of the most unique provisions contained in government contracts. In no other area of contract law has one party been given such complete authority to escape from contractual obligations. This clause gives the government the broad right to terminate without cause and limits the contractor's recovery to costs incurred, profit on work done, and costs of preparing the termination settlement proposal. Recovery of anticipated profit is precluded. Thus, this mandatory provision confers a major contract right on the government with no commensurate advantage to the contractor.

The courts have also fashioned a constructive termination doctrine that applies the clause to prevent recovery of anticipated profit where government acts would otherwise have been material breaches of the contract. In these cases, the contracting officer elects not to use the clause but is still given the benefit of the clause in limiting the contractor's recovery. This is an additional broad limitation on a government contractor's rights.

This chapter addresses the scope of both actual and constructive termination for convenience of the government. It then reviews the rules governing termination settlements.

I. BACKGROUND

The concept of termination for convenience of the government was developed principally as a means to end the massive procurement efforts that accompanied major wars. Although the government had always had the power to terminate its contracts, such action constituted a breach of contract. Questions developed concerning the authority to settle such breach of contract claims and the procedures to be used in negotiating a settlement. These questions have persisted even though the Supreme Court, in *United States v. Corliss Steam Engine Co.*, 91 U.S. 321 (1875), clearly indicated that contracting officials were authorized to settle termination claims. A more important question concerned the contractor's remedy for termination. There were many objections to paying a contractor profits on unperformed work, and yet the contractor was entitled to such a remedy if the government did not have a right to terminate the contract. See *G.L. Christian & Assocs. v. United States*, 160 Ct. Cl. 1, 312 F.2d 418, *reh'g denied* 160 Ct. Cl. 58, 320 F.2d 345, *cert. denied*, 375 U.S. 954 (1963).

A number of regulatory and statutory provisions were developed to resolve these questions concerning settlement authority and the compensation due the terminated contractor. As early as 1863, Rule 1179 of the Army Regulations provided that contracts for subsistence stores "shall expressly provide for their termination at such time as the Commissary-General may direct." See *United States v. Speed*, 75 U.S. (8 Wall.) 77 (1868), for a discussion of this provision. However, it was not until World War I that contracts were terminated in large numbers. Some agencies had already developed termination clauses, but the majority of claims were settled under statutory authority—the most important of which was the Dent Act, 40 Stat. 1272 (1919). During World War II, further statutory and regulatory provisions were developed, including the Contract Settlement Act of 1944, 58 Stat. 649.

After the war, regulatory provisions began to require termination clauses in contracts. The 1950 edition of the Armed Services Procurement Regulation (ASPR) contained mandatory Termination for Convenience clauses to be used in the majority of DoD contracts over $1,000, DAR 8-701-705. In 1964 the first edition of the Federal Procurement Regulations (FPR) contained optional termination for convenience clauses to be used "whenever an agency considered it necessary or desirable . . . ," FPR 1-8.700-2. In June 1967, the FPR was revised to make the Termination for Convenience clauses mandatory, with limited exceptions, in fixed-price supply contracts over $2,500 and fixed-price construction contracts over $100,000, 32 Fed. Reg. 9683 (1967). FAR 49.502 continues to require broad use of Termination for Convenience clauses, with the result that the broad rights developed for war contracts have come to be applied to all types of contracts, civilian as well as military, in times of both peace and war.

II. THE RIGHT TO TERMINATE

Termination for convenience is a government right to be exercised in the best interests of the government. In cases where a contractor is performing at a loss, a termination might be beneficial to the contractor. However, the government has no duty to terminate for convenience to benefit the contractor, *Rotair Indus., Inc.*, ASBCA 27571, 84-2 BCA ¶ 17,417.

A. Termination Clauses

There are three basic types of convenience termination clauses currently in use in standard federal contracts. For most fixed-price contracts there are "long form" clauses for contracts over $100,000, FAR 52.249-2, and "short form" clauses for contracts that do not exceed $100,000, FAR 52.249-1. The FAR includes specialized versions of these clauses for research and development, services, construction, architect and engineer, dismantling, and nonprofit institution contracts. There is also a "short form" clause for service contracts in FAR 52.249-4. Cost-reimbursement contract clauses are of the "long form" variety, but they differ from fixed-price contract clauses in that they cover both convenience and default terminations, FAR 52.249-6. Prior to the FAR there were suggested clauses for fixed-price subcontracts, DAR 8-706 and FPR 1-8.706, and for cost-reimbursement subcontracts,

DAR 8-703. FAR 49.502(e) contains guidance on appropriate modification of the standard clauses for use in subcontracts.

FAR 49.502 prescribes when these clauses are to be used. In general, the "long form" clauses are required to be used in all contracts over $ 100,000, except that the "short form" clause in FAR 52.249-4 is prescribed for use in service contracts over $ 100,000 by FAR 49.502(c) as follows:

> The contracting officer shall insert the clause at 52.249-4, Termination for Convenience of the Government (Services) (Short Form), in solicitations and contracts for services, regardless of value, when a fixed-price contract is contemplated and the contracting officer determines that because of the kind of services required, the successful offeror will not incur substantial charges in preparation for and in carrying out the contract, and would, if terminated for the convenience of the Government, limit termination settlement charges to services rendered before the date of termination. Examples of services where this clause may be appropriate are contracts for rental of unreserved parking space, laundry and drycleaning, etc.

The service contract "short form" clause is very restrictive, providing only for payment "for services rendered before the effective date of the termination." Thus, its use has been challenged in a number of cases and has been held to be an abuse of discretion, *DWS, Debtor in Possession*, ASBCA 29742, 90-2 BCA ¶ 22,696 ($11.4 million contract requiring extensive construction, repairs, training, parts, and supply purchases); *Carrier Corp.*, GSBCA 8516, 90-1 BCA ¶ 22,409 (significant start-up costs that could not be recovered in payments for preventative maintenance services on a monthly basis); *Guard-All of Am.*, ASBCA 22167, 80-2 BCA ¶ 14,462 (use of clause unfair when government knew that termination of guard services might happen shortly after award of contract). Compare *Mid-Atl. Sec. Servs., Inc.*, ENGBCA 6302, 97-2 BCA ¶ 29,012, finding no abuse of discretion, stating at 144,539-40:

> Factors relevant to our inquiry include: the nature of the services; unusual and substantial "start-up" type costs and other requirements that are not separately priced and are not "common items" which can be reallocated to other work; the nature of the pricing provisions of the solicitation and any elements of "unfairness" in those mechanisms if the contract is terminated early; how the contractor actually priced its offer; Government, pre-award knowledge of the likelihood of early termination; the existence of any protest or concerns expressed to contracting officials during the solicitation process concerning use of the "short form" clause; and the overall fairness of judicially rewriting the contract and, thereby reallocating the termination cost risks to the Government given all the facts and circumstances.

In contracts for commercial items, the Contract Terms and Conditions—Commercial Items clause at FAR 52.212-4 also limits the contractor's recovery, as follows:

> (l) *Termination for the government's convenience.* The government reserves the right to terminate this contract, or any part hereof, for its sole convenience. In the event of such termination, the Contractor shall immediately stop all work

> hereunder and shall immediately cause any and all of its suppliers and subcontractors to cease work. Subject to the terms of this contract, the Contractor shall be paid a percentage of the contract price reflecting the percentage of the work performed prior to the notice of termination, plus reasonable charges the Contractor can demonstrate to the satisfaction of the government using its standard record keeping system, have resulted from the termination. The Contractor shall not be required to comply with the cost accounting standards or contract cost principles for this purpose. This paragraph does not give the Government any right to audit the Contractor's records. The Contractor shall not be paid for any work performed or costs incurred which reasonably could have been avoided.

FAR 12.403 provides the following general guidance on termination of commercial contracts:

> (a) *General.* The clause at 52.212-4 permits the Government to terminate a contract for commercial items either for the convenience of the Government or for cause. However, the paragraphs in 52.212-4 entitled "Termination for the Government's Convenience" and "Termination for Cause" contain concepts which differ from those contained in the termination clauses prescribed in Part 49. Consequently, the requirements of Part 49 do not apply when terminating contracts for commercial items and contracting officers shall follow the procedures in this section. Contracting officers may continue to use Part 49 as guidance to the extent that Part 49 does not conflict with this section and the language of the termination paragraphs in 52.212-4.
>
> (b) *Policy.* The contracting officer should exercise the Government's right to terminate a contract for commercial items either for convenience or for cause only when such a termination would be in the best interests of the Government. The contracting officer should consult with counsel prior to terminating for cause.

For a case involving termination for convenience of a contract for a commercial item, see *Individual Dev. Assocs., Inc.*, ASBCA 53910, 04-2 BCA ¶ 32,740.

Periodically, especially in Non-Appropriated Fund Instrumentality contracts, non-standard termination clauses are used. In *Home Entm't, Inc.,* ASBCA 50791, 99-2 BCA ¶ 30,550, the contract with the Army and Air Force Exchange Service to operate a video rental concession at military installations in Panama did not contain the standard Termination for Convenience clause but provided that the contract could be terminated "without cause" on 30 days' written notice. In *Dart Advantage Warehousing, Inc. v. United States,* 52 Fed. Cl. 694 (2002), the warehousing contract contained both a standard Termination for Convenience clause and a Termination on Notice clause permitting either party to terminate the contract on 180 days' notice. The contractor contended that the Termination on Notice provision modified the Termination for Convenience clause, making an improper termination for default a breach, entitling it to 180 days of anticipated profits. The court held that the two clauses served different purposes and that the contractor would be limited to recovery under the Termination for Convenience clause. In *Poston Logging*, AGBCA

99-143-R, 00-1 BCA ¶ 30,829, *motion to vacate denied*, 00-2 BCA ¶ 30,973, rather than the standard Termination for Convenience clause, the timber contract included a special clause providing for termination based on a Forest Service determination that continued performance would damage the environment.

B. Exercising the Right to Terminate

The courts and boards have placed few limitations on the ability of the government to exercise its right to terminate a contract for convenience. This subsection first discusses the factors a contracting officer should consider in deciding whether to terminate a contract for the convenience of the government and then discusses the limitations that have been placed on the contracting officer when making such a decision.

1. The Decision to Terminate

The language giving the government the right to terminate is brief and very broad. For example, the termination clause contained in FAR 52.249-2 states:

> (a) The government may terminate performance of work under this contract in whole or, from time to time, in part if the Contracting Officer determines that a termination is in the government's interest.

If the contracting officer decides to terminate for convenience, the government's liability will be admitted, and the contractor will recover its incurred allowable costs and profit on work done. If another means of severing the relationship is used, litigation over the obligations of the parties is likely. However, even if the contractor wins such litigation, the application of the constructive termination for convenience doctrine will limit its recovery to that permitted under the Termination for Convenience clause. Thus, the government takes little risk, other than the cost of litigation, in choosing some other means of severing the relationship. If such action is upheld, the contractor's recovery may be limited. If it is not, the government pays nothing more than it would have paid had it initially elected to terminate for convenience. It is therefore possible that in many such cases contracting officers "decide" that to terminate for convenience is not in the interest of the government. Thus, it is unlikely that the Termination for Convenience clause will be used if there is a more favorable method of severing the relationship. Whether this is an appropriate policy is another question.

a. "The Government's Interest"

The regulations contain no guidance on the factors to be considered in determining "the government's interest." However, FAR 49.101(b) provides that a negotiated no-cost settlement shall be used in lieu of a convenience termination if the contractor will accept such a settlement; if no government property has been furnished to the contractor; and if there are no outstanding payments, debts, or other contractor obligations due the government. If the undelivered balance of the contract is less than $5,000, the contract should normally be allowed to run to completion, FAR 49.101(c).

Termination for convenience is most common when the government no longer needs the contract work, but it often occurs in other situations. For example, if the contractor is in default but has raised potential defenses, the contracting officer must decide whether to terminate for default or convenience. See FAR 49.402-3(j). A contractor's refusal to accept a modification supports a termination for convenience, *Saltwater, Inc.*, Comp. Gen. Dec. B-293335.3, 2004 CPD ¶ 106. If there are questions concerning the propriety of an award or its continued performance, the award may be canceled or a termination for convenience may be ordered. In *Landmark Constr. Corp.,* Comp. Gen. Dec. B-281957.3, 99-2 CPD ¶ 75, the GAO held that the immediate termination of an 8(a) set-aside contract (improperly awarded to an ineligible offeror) was permissible but was not required. The agency could allow the contract to remain in place to meet its ongoing requirements until a new contract is awarded. Sometimes a convenience termination may be required if, for example, an 8(a) firm is sold to a large business, *International Data Prods. Corp. v. United States,* 64 Fed. Cl. 642 (2005).

A contract may be terminated for the convenience of the government based on the deterioration of the business relationship between a contractor and the agency, *Embrey v. United States*, 17 Cl. Ct. 617 (1989). In *Bryan D. Highfill*, HUDBCA 96-C-118-C7, 99-1 BCA ¶ 30,316, among the factors the board considered in upholding the agency's termination for convenience were the contractor's statements to the contract specialist that "he was about ready to kill a man" and that he would like to hire someone to do it, which the contract specialist interpreted as a reference to another agency employee.

Convenience termination may also be used to restructure multiple contractual arrangements. Northrop-Grumman was one of four contractors on the space station. Subsequently, the program experienced substantial cost overruns and NASA feared that the entire project would be lost if the contractors' management structure and contractual relationships were not adjusted. NASA's administrator met with the CEOs of the four contractors and proposed that one of the contractors would become the single contractor and that the other three would be "novated" as subcontractors to the single contractor. The four contracts were terminated for convenience and Boeing was selected as the contractor. After Northrop-Grumman was awarded a new subcontract with substantially less work, it sued alleging that its contract had been terminated in "bad faith." The court disagreed, noting that the government had acted with the sole intent of saving the space station program, not to acquire a better bargain from another source even if that was the final result. Even if NASA knew that Northrop-Grumman's scope of work would be reduced under the single contract, such knowledge did not establish any intent to injure Northrop-Grumman, *Northrop Grumman Corp. v. United States*, 46 Fed. Cl. 622 (2000).

b. Special Situations

One requirement is that there must be a contract to terminate. If a contract has not been awarded or has legitimately expired, for example, when an option is not exercised, a termination for convenience is inappropriate. In *Sierra Rock v. Regents of Univ. of Cal.*, EBCA C-9705223, 99-2 BCA ¶ 30,507, the board held that where a contractor cannot show even an implied-in-fact contract with the government, it cannot establish a bad faith termination for convenience. The board also noted that the remedy for bad faith actions by the government is limited to anticipatory profits rather than punitive damages. The latter are unavailable unless the contract allows the same or provides that a particular state law applies that clearly allows the imposition of punitive damages

Neither is there any obligation to terminate an indefinite delivery/indefinite quantity contract after ordering the specified minimum quantity, *J. Cooper & Assocs., Inc. v. United States*, 53 Fed. Cl. 8 (2002), *aff'd,* 65 Fed. Appx. 731 (Fed. Cir. 2003). There the government allowed a letter contract for an ID/IQ contract to expire rather than definitize it or issue a termination for convenience. The court found that since the government's sole obligation in an ID/IQ contract is to order the minimum amount, the government was under no obligation to terminate the contract for convenience, nor was there a constructive termination or bad faith. The contractor was limited to payment for task orders issued, and it could not recover for items such as preparing proposals for anticipated future orders.

Blanket purchase agreements, by themselves, generally need not be terminated formally because the government can simply elect not to issue orders under the agreement. In *BSG Constr. Servs., Inc.*, ENGBCA 6127, 95-1 BCA ¶ 27,520, the board concluded that the government improperly included a Termination clause in a blanket purchase agreement and then attempted to invoke that clause. The government's errors, however, did not create any rights in the contractor. The government's invocation of the clause gave the contractor notice that it would receive no additional orders under the agreement, which was more notice than the contractor would have been entitled to had the termination clause not been present.

c. Terminations in Support of Competition

One particular justification for a termination for convenience is to uphold the statutory preference for full and open competition by terminating a potentially improper award. While the Competition in Contracting Act (CICA) does not deal with terminations for convenience, correcting a flawed procurement can certainly be considered an appropriate means to further full and open competition. The majority of the cases cited in *Torncello v. United States,* 231 Ct. Cl. 20, 681 F.2d 756 (1982), the leading case limiting the right to terminate for convenience, as demonstrating changed circumstances, were flawed contract awards. Flawed awards might be an irregularity in the award process, such as improper nonresponsibility determinations or specifications not reflecting the government's needs, or cases where the competition was not procedurally flawed but the government later decides that an unwise decision was made. The court in *Torncello* stated at 37:

> The history of cases in this court demonstrates [the use of the clause in changed circumstances]. *John Reiner & Co. v. United States*, 163 Ct. Cl. 381, 325 F.2d 438 (1963), *cert. denied*, 377 U.S. 931 (1964) (irregularity in the bid award); *Brown & Son Elec. Co. v. United States,* 163 Ct. Cl. 465, 325 F.2d 446 (1963) (irregularity in bid award); *Nesbitt v. United States,* 170 Ct. Cl. 666, 345 F.2d 583 (1965), *cert. denied,* 383 U.S. 926 (1966) (refusal of contractor to meet requirements); *Warren Bros. Roads Co. v. United States,* 173 Ct. Cl. 714, 355 F.2d 612 (1965) (irregularity in the bid award); *Coastal Cargo Co. v. United States*, 173 Ct. Cl. 259, 351 F.2d 1004 (1965) (irregularity in bid award); *Schlesinger v. United States*, 182 Ct. Cl. 571, 390 F.2d 702 (1968) (plaintiff under investigation by Senate for procurement irregularities, and in technical default); *Nolan Bros. v. United States,* 186 Ct. Cl. 602, 405 F.2d 1250 (1969) (physical changes at site made performance impossible); *G.C. Casebolt Co. v. United States,* 190 Ct. Cl. 783, 421 F.2d 710 (1970) (irregularity in the bid award).

In *Krygoski Constr. Co v. United States*, 94 F.3d 1357 (Fed. Cir. 1996), the court explained that when faced with an allegation that a contracting officer abused his or her discretion in terminating a contract for the convenience of the government, "this court will avoid a finding of abused discretion when the facts support a reasonable inference that the contracting officer terminated for convenience in furtherance of statutory requirements for full and open competition." *Krygoski* found that one indication that termination was necessary to further competition is whether, if the government had retained the contract, it would have imposed a cardinal change in the scope of the contract to meet its requirements.

In *T&M Distribs., Inc. v. United States,* 185 F.3d 1279 (Fed Cir. 1999), the Federal Circuit determined that CICA, which compels the promulgation of regulations and procedures to ensure full and open competition in contracting, sufficiently addressed the concerns of earlier decisions regarding the government's shopping for lower prices after the contract award. CICA's competitive fairness requirement provides the additional restraint on a contracting officer's contract administration, under which contracting officers have no incentive to terminate a contract for convenience except to maintain full and open competition under CICA. Thus, the court found that the contracting officer did not act in bad faith or abuse his discretion because he had a reasonable basis for terminating the contract and conducting a competitive reprocurement—the increased asbestos removal constituted a cardinal change. See also *EROS Div. of Res. Recycling Int'l., Inc.*, ASBCA 48355, 99-1 BCA ¶ 30,207 (bad faith or abuse of discretion not present when the contracting officer terminated for convenience because the improper award of the contract, without a synopsis and concurrence of the government's competition advocate, were reasonable grounds for the termination).

A termination for convenience may also be used to get the government out of a lawfully awarded contract that the government realizes contains unbalanced line item prices. In *Custom Printing Co. v. United States,* 51 Fed. Cl. 729 (2002), the government awarded a contract for printing services that included a high-priced line item, then found that it required a high volume of that type work. After failing to negotiate a contract modification lowering the line item price, the contracting officer terminated the contract for convenience. The court held that the circumstances justified the termination and there was an absence of bad faith on the part of the government. See also *Kellie W. Tipton Constr. Co.,* Comp. Gen. Dec. B-281331.3, 99-1 CPD ¶ 73 (termination for convenience upheld when shortly after award agency determined its award had been based on a mistaken evaluation of another bidder's past performance).

2. Limitations on the Right to Terminate

The Termination for the Convenience of the Government clauses state that the contract can be terminated when it is determined to be "in the Government's interest," with no stated limits on that right. The judicial interpretation of the government's rights under this clause has led some commentators to conclude that there are "virtually no limitations on the Government's right to terminate," Pearlman and Goodrich, *Termination for Convenience Settlements,* 10 Pub. Cont. L.J. 1 (1978). However, an unlimited government right of termination raises serious questions as to whether the government furnishes consideration in a contract containing a termination clause. *Restatement, Second, Contracts* § 77 states:

> A promise or apparent promise is not consideration if by its terms the promisor or purported promisor reserves a choice of alternative performance unless (a) each of the alternative performances would have been consideration if it alone had been bargained for; or (b) one of the alternative performances would have been consideration and there is or appears to the parties to be a substantial possibility that before the promisor exercises his choice events may eliminate the alternatives which would not have been consideration.

See also 1 *Williston, Contracts* § 105 (3d ed. 1957 and Supp. 1979), which states at 418: "[a]n agreement wherein one party reserves the right to cancel at his pleasure cannot create a contract."

Surprisingly, this issue has rarely been raised in relation to current convenience termination clauses. An early government contract case dealing with the question of lack of consideration in a contract containing a termination clause is *Sylvan Crest Sand & Gravel Co. v. United States*, 150 F.2d 642 (2d Cir. 1945). In that case the clause stated: "Cancellation by the Procurement Division may be effected at any time." The appellate court held that the contract was based on consideration and hence was not illusory because it contained an implied promise by the government to give notice of cancellation within a reasonable time if it did not want to accept the goods. In *Torncello v. United States*, 231 Ct. Cl. 20, 681 F.2d 756 (1982), the court discussed the consideration issue extensively and concluded that the scope of termination rights had to be limited to prevent a finding of lack of consideration. The court also indicated that it disagreed with the reasoning in *Sylvan Crest* that the bare requirement to give notice constituted consideration. The Court of Claims concluded, in a plurality opinion, that "a party may not reserve to itself a method of unlimited exculpation without rendering its promises illusory and the contract void."

In *Montana Ref. Co.,* ASBCA 50515, 00-1 BCA ¶ 30,694, the board rejected the argument that the government's attempt to terminate an IDIQ contract before it had purchased the guaranteed minimum quantity was improper because it would render the contract illusory due to lack of consideration. The board held that the compensation available under the Termination for Convenience clause provides adequate consideration to the contractor.

So, courts and boards are still searching for meaningful limitations that will accommodate the government's legitimate needs and leave the contractor with some rights under this clause. Prior to 1982, the view was that terminations for convenience would be overturned only in the event of bad faith or an abuse of discretion on the part of the government, *Kalvar Corp. v. United States*, 211 Ct. Cl. 192, 543 F.2d 1298 (1976), *cert. denied*, 434 U.S. 830 (1977). However, in 1982, the court in *Torncello v. United States,* 231 Ct. Cl. 20, 681 F.2d 756 (1982), determined that bad faith, as articulated by *Kalvar*, was not a meaningful limitation on the government's right to terminate. The three-judge plurality concluded that the scope of the termination power had to be narrowed so that public contracts would not be illusory for lack of consideration on the part of the government. Accordingly, the plurality opinion held that a convenience termination could only be justified where there was a "change in circumstances" after the contract was awarded from those in existence when the contract was formed. The impact of *Torncello* was undercut in *Krygoski Constr. Co. v. United States*, 94 F.3d 1537 (Fed. Cir. 1996), *cert. denied*, 520 U.S. 1210 (1997). These three decisions, *Kalvar, Torncello,* and *Krygoski*, are basic to understanding the limitations on the government's right to terminate for convenience.

a. *The Kalvar Test—Government Bad Faith or Abuse of Discretion*

The convenience termination cases give little guidance on abuse of discretion or bad faith. The bad faith and abuse of discretion standards have been, at best, only superficially examined in the opinions, and many inconsistencies exist between the facts of the cases and the language of the decisions. But other areas of government contracting provide guidance. For example, the government may not arbitrarily refuse to grant approval where a clause provides that approval must be obtained by the contractor, e.g., *Hoel-Steffen Constr. Co. v. United States*, 231 Ct. Cl. 128, 684 F.2d 843 (1982). This is one aspect of the implied duty of good faith and fair dealing that all contracting parties are required to observe. In addition, the government is required to exercise discretion in deciding whether to terminate a contract for default, *Schlesinger v. United States,* 182 Ct. Cl. 571, 390 F.2d 702 (1968). It would be appropriate to apply the abuse of discretion standards developed under these other areas to convenience terminations.

Because the plaintiff failed to distinguish between bad faith and abuse of discretion, the *Kalvar* court treated them the same "only for purposes of the decision." The contractor's burden of proving governmental bad faith, however, is quite heavy, *Kalvar Corp. v. United States*, 211 Ct. Cl. 192, 543 F.2d 1298 (1976), *cert. denied*, 434 U.S. 830 (1977). There, the court indicated that "specific intent to injure" the contractor must be demonstrated. An oft-repeated statement indicates that to prove bad faith a contractor must (1) prove specific intent to harm the plaintiff and (2) prove this intent with well-nigh irrefragable proof. But upon analysis, it is unclear whether proof of specific intent to harm the plaintiff is really a requirement. The following statement from *Kalvar* at 198-99 is usually credited with announcing the proposition:

> Any analysis of a question of Governmental bad faith must begin with the presumption that public officials act "conscientiously in the discharge of their duties." *Librach v. United States,* 147 Ct. Cl. 605, 612 (1959). The court has always been "loath to find to the contrary," and it requires "well- nigh irrefragable proof" to induce the court to abandon the presumption of good faith dealing. *Knotts v. United States,* 128 Ct. Cl. 489, 492, 121 F. Supp. 630, 631 (1954).
>
> In the cases in which the court has considered allegations of bad faith, the necessary "irrefragable proof" has been equated with evidence of some specific intent to injure the plaintiff. Thus, in *Gadsden v. United States,* 111 Ct. Cl. 487, 489-90, 78 F. Supp. 126, 127 (1948), the court compared bad faith to actions which are "motivated alone by malice." In *Knotts, supra,* at 128 Ct. Cl. 500, 121 F. Supp. 636, the court found bad faith in a civilian pay suit only in view of a proven "conspiracy . . . to get rid of plaintiff." Similarly, the court in *Struck Constr. Co. v. United States,* 96 Ct. Cl. 186, 222 (1942) found bad faith when confronted by a course of Governmental conduct which was "designedly oppressive." But in *Librach, supra,* at 147 Ct. Cl. 614, the court found no bad faith because the officials involved were not "actuated by animus toward the plaintiff."

This specific intent statement in *Kalvar* apparently motivated the *Torncello* plurality to adopt the changed circumstances concept. By contrast, Judge Davis did not believe that proof of specific intent to harm was a necessary ingredient to a finding of bad faith and that *Kalvar* did not necessarily so hold. His concurring opinion in *Torncello* stated at 50-51:

> Third, I do not agree that "bad faith" is as narrow as Judge Bennett says it is. In *Kalvar, supra*—the case he cites—this court said, without in any way seeking to modify our prior holdings: ". . .many of our prior decisions seem implicitly to accept the equivalence of bad faith, abuse of discretion, and gross error." 211 Ct. Cl. at 198, note 1, 543 F.2d at 1301, note 1. *Kalvar* expressly held that that contractor had failed to show either bad faith or abuse of discretion. . .and the limited definition of bad faith quoted in the opinion gave merely one aspect of the concept of "bad faith." Here, too, I would be ready to hold that a contracting officer acted in bad faith when he terminated a contract for convenience to get a better price of which he had full knowledge (and which was available) at the time when he deliberately entered into the contract with plaintiff.

In footnote 3, *Krygoski* cites *Keco Indus., Inc. v. United States*, 203 Ct. Cl. 566, 492 F.2d 1200 (1974), for the proposition that four factors are listed for determining whether discretion has been abused. The first of these is bad faith, followed by "the reasonableness of the decision, the amount of discretion delegated to the procurement official," and finally, whether violations of an applicable regulation or statute alone are arbitrary.

It has been virtually impossible for terminated contractors to demonstrate government bad faith. See *McFadden, Inc. v. United States,* 215 Ct. Cl. 918 (1977) (even if contracting officer followed directions of superiors in canceling award, bad faith not present); *Kalvar Corp. v. United States*, 211 Ct. Cl. 192, 543 F.2d 1298 (1976), *cert. denied,* 434 U.S. 830 (1977) (bad faith not established by failure to disclose information making determinations favorable to another contractor concerning coverage of requirements contracts, or by taking the other contractor's word concerning specifications and evaluating bids based on a different thickness of material); *Gould, Inc. v. Chafee,* 450 F.2d 667 (D.C. Cir. 1971) (termination based on agreement with GAO decision or on acquiescence to avoid conflict unlikely to be found arbitrary and capricious); and *Librach v. United States,* 147 Ct. Cl. 605 (1959) (miscalculation of requirement not bad faith). In *Allied Materials & Equip. Co. v. United States,* 215 Ct. Cl. 902 (1977), the court stated that the contractor "should harbor no illusions that the task of overcoming the presumption that Government officials perform their duty in good faith is less than burdensome." In the absence of bad faith or a clear abuse of discretion, the contracting officer's decision to terminate a contract for convenience is conclusive. Because contracting officers are presumed to act in good faith when performing their procurement functions, a contractor must present virtually irrefutable proof of bad faith before the court will overturn the decision to terminate for convenience, *T&M Distribs., Inc. v. United States*, 185 F.3d 1279 (Fed. Cir. 1999). See also *Melvin R. Kessler,* PSBCA 2820, 92-2 BCA ¶ 24,857, *recons. denied,* 92-3 BCA ¶ 25,092 (relying on presumption that public officials discharge their duties conscientiously, board found no bad faith in termination of mail delivery contract resulting from conflict between contractor and postmaster over proposed schedule change). Compare *Benjamin P. Garcia,* ASBCA 18035, 73-2 BCA ¶ 10,196, in which the board stated that a termination based on discrimination would be improper, but because of discrimination proceedings in another tribunal, dismissed the case pending substantiation of the charges; and *Apex Int'l Mgmt. Servs., Inc.*, ASBCA 38087, 94-2 BCA ¶ 26,842, *recons. denied,* 94-2 BCA ¶ 26,852, in which the board found bad faith based on numerous actions designed to injure the contractor.

In a number of cases, it has been stated that a "clear abuse of discretion" would also invalidate a termination for convenience, *A-Transport Northwest Co. v. United States*, 36 F.3d 1576 (Fed. Cir. 1994). However, although this appears to be a lesser standard of proof, it has also been difficult to establish. In *TLT Constr. Corp.*, ASBCA 40501, 93-3 BCA ¶ 25,978, the government attempted to negotiate a no-cost termination, and when it was unsuccessful, ordered the contractor to perform, then terminated the contract for convenience. The board held that there was no abuse of discretion, even though the government still needed the work.

The ability to show either bad faith or an abuse of discretion is virtually impossible if the contracting officer can show an alternative reason for the termination, *"Quazar,"* ASBCA 23504, 79-1 BCA ¶ 13,828 (not bad faith to terminate contract for band performance because of poor reception given to band at high school dance). In *Stan Harris dba Harris & Co.*, ASBCA 47771, 95-1 BCA ¶ 27,585, the government did not act in bad faith in canceling for convenience, a week before the event, a contract for a dance band performance, because the sole reason for the cancellation was disappointing potential audience response. The government held the event but substituted other entertainment that it believed would generate greater revenue for its officers' club. See also *Northrop Grumman Corp v. United States,* 46 Fed. Cl. 622 (2000) (government had acted with the sole intent of saving the space station program, not to acquire a better bargain from another source even if that was the final result.)

Nevertheless, despite the difficulty of proof, the contractor is entitled to present evidence of bad faith, as indicated in *Allied Materials* and *National Factors, Inc. v. United States*, 204 Ct. Cl. 98, 492 F.2d 1383 (1974). But there is a very low likelihood of meeting this standard. For example, the court applied the "well nigh irrefragable proof" standard in refusing to overturn a termination for convenience where the contracting officer determined there was a gross misestimate of quantities in the solicitation, *Custom Printing Co. v. United States,* 51 Fed. Cl. 729 (2002). Accord, *Fields v. United States,* 53 Fed. Cl. 412 (2002).

In 2002, the Federal Circuit attempted once more to clarify its past cases on bad faith. In *Am-Pro Protective Agency, Inc. v. United States,* 281 F.3d 1234 (Fed. Cir. 2002), the contractor alleged that it had signed a release under duress and threats from the contracting officer that its contract would be canceled and options not exercised if it pursued its claim for contract changes. Although the contractor's case was weak on the facts under any standard, the court took the occasion to "clarify" the standard of proof for showing government bad faith. The court held that "clear and convincing" evidence was closest to "well nigh irrefragable proof," and it stated that in the future it would apply the clear and convincing standard, but would include within that standard a requirement that the contracting officer was motivated by malice toward the contractor. See also *Tecom, Inc. v. United States*, 66 Fed. Cl. 736 (2005), concluding that there was no presumption of regularity of government action.

b. The Torncello Test—No Change in Circumstances

In 1982 the Court of Claims added a new limitation on the government's right to terminate. In *Torncello v. United States*, 231 Ct. Cl. 20, 681 F.2d 756 (1982), the court held that the government could not terminate for convenience unless there had been a change in circumstances. Although the "changed circumstances" test has been severely weakened after some cases in the late 1990s, it was used for over a decade.

Torncello arose out of a requirements contract for janitorial and other services awarded by the Navy to Soledad Industries, Inc., for multiple items, with bids solicited and award made on an "all or none" basis. During performance, the Navy never issued any calls to Soledad for even one item, but had all of the work performed by an in-house Navy organization. The contract was terminated for default, and one of the defenses raised by Soledad was the government's failure to order the work. The Armed Services Board of Contract Appeals held that even in a requirements contract, the government could have terminated the contract for its convenience and that, therefore, the government's failure to order work would not be a breach of contract, *Soledad Enters., Inc.*, ASBCA 20376, 77-2 BCA ¶ 12,552. Since the contract included a short form Termination for Convenience clause that permitted recovery only for services performed, this gave Soledad no recovery. The appeal was decided by the full court "because of the exceptional importance of the legal issues involved." Three judges joined in a "plurality opinion." The other three judges wrote individual concurring opinions, each disagreeing to some extent with the opinion of the three judges who had joined together. However, the end result was a determination that the Navy had breached the contract, and the case was remanded to the Trial Division to determine the amount of damages.

In *Torncello,* the court ruled that the Termination for Convenience clause could not be used to avoid paying anticipated profits unless there had been some change in circumstances between the time of award of the contract and the time of termination. The court found that no changed circumstances had occurred and overruled *Colonial Metals Co. v. United States,* 204 Ct. Cl. 320, 494 F.2d 1355 (1974), which had held that a termination for convenience was proper when the government awarded a contract knowing of a lower price and subsequently terminated the contract to obtain that price. The plurality opinion reasoned that this limitation on the use of the clause was necessary to avoid the creation of an illusory bargain where the government had no obligation to the contractor, stating at 26:

> We note as one of the most elementary propositions of contract law that a party may not reserve to itself a method of unlimited exculpation without rendering

> its promises illusory and the contract void, and we question if the government's termination for convenience clause should be construed that broadly.

It then traced the development of the concept of termination for convenience, finding that it was a device to get the government out of a contract when circumstances changed after the contract was awarded. The opinion declared that the "history of cases in this court demonstrates this" concept, stating further at 36-37:

> The response in this court was to rely on the risk allocation nature of the concept and to allow termination for convenience only when the expectations of the parties had been subjected to a substantial change. The contractor risked losing the full benefit of his performance if something occurred, apart from the bargain and the expectations of the parties, that made continuance of the contract clearly inadvisable.

It rejected the government's contention that not permitting convenience terminations when motivated by "bad faith" or as a result of an "abuse of discretion" would satisfy the consideration requirement and held that a termination for convenience could only be justified in situations where there was a "change in circumstances" from the time the contract was awarded.

The three concurring opinions assist in understanding *Torncello*. Judge Davis thought it unnecessary to invoke a changed circumstances doctrine because in this case the contracting officer acted in bad faith. In addition, he stated that he "would have no difficulty in holding that it was an abuse of discretion to use the clause to end the contract because lower prices could be obtained elsewhere when the contracting officer already knew that very fact before he consummated the contract with plaintiff."

Judge Nichols went further in his concurring opinion, recognizing the "all or none" basis of the contract award, and would have found an abuse of discretion under the circumstances. He stated at 52 that the government:

> would be estopped to eliminate from the award by termination any items just because, separately considered, they were at unfavorable prices, while retaining all those bid at favorable prices. The administration of the contract must be consistent with the rules used in evaluating the bids, to which the bidders conformed in bidding.

Chief Judge Friedman concurred on the understanding that the decision was limited to the specific facts of the case, stating at 49:

> As I understand the court's opinion, the court holds only that when the government enters into a requirements contract, knowing that it can obtain an item the contract covers for less than the contract price and intending to do so, there cannot be a constructive termination for convenience of the government when the government follows that course. On that basis, I join in the opinion.

This view adds the requirement of government intent to buy at the lower price at the time of contracting. See *David R. Brown, Jr.*, IBCA 1600-7-82, 83-1 BCA ¶ 16,423; *Tamp Corp.*, ASBCA 25692, 84-2 BCA ¶ 17,460; and the concurring opinion of Administrative Judge Lieblich in *Drain-A-Way Sys.*, GSBCA 7022, 84-1 BCA ¶ 16,929. This view appears to be unduly restrictive in that the basic purpose of requiring changed circumstances is to ensure that the government has entered into a real, not illusory, obligation at the time of contract award. See also the discussion in *Federal Data Corp.*, DOTCAB 2389, 91-3 BCA ¶ 24,063, construing *Torncello* narrowly.

Torncello has been cited numerous times by the boards of contract appeals, Claims Court, Court of Federal Claims, and Court of Appeals for the Federal Circuit, but the focus has generally been solely on the plurality opinion. The scope of the *Torncello* rule has been viewed somewhat restrictively by later decisions. In *Automated Servs., Inc.*, DOTBCA 1753, 87-1 BCA ¶ 19,459, the board interpreted *Torncello* narrowly, stating that, absent the same fact pattern, invocation of the Termination for Convenience clause is just as valid and enforceable in indefinite-quantity type contracts as it is in other types of supply contracts, even in situations where the goods or services contracted for have not yet been delivered. Compare *S & W Tire Servs., Inc.,* GSBCA 6376, 82-2 BCA ¶ 16,048, in which the board found that the Termination for Convenience clause did not overcome the government's obligation to pay anticipated profits when it failed to order requirements because of a subsequent decision to contract out the entire government operation that had previously had the requirements. The board reasoned that the government knew of the decision to contract out at the time of the award of the requirements contract and, hence, that there was no change in circumstances between award and termination. See also *Adams Mfg. Co.,* GSBCA 5747, 82-1 BCA ¶ 15,740, *aff'd,* 714 F.2d 161 (Fed. Cir. 1983), in which the board found that the Termination for Convenience clause precluded anticipated profits where no work had been ordered on a requirements contract because of a moratorium on the further purchase of office furniture, which was imposed after award of the contract with no evidence that officials had known or conceived of it before award. The Federal Circuit decision in *Adams Manufacturing,* however, was unpublished and is not citable as precedent. For additional discussion of the scope of the rule, see *Drain-A-Way Sys.*, GSBCA 7022, 84-1 BCA ¶ 16,929.

In the years since *Torncello*, the courts and boards have had difficulty deciding whether there is a "changed circumstance" rule, and if so, what constitutes such a change. In *Maxima Corp. v. United States*, 847 F.2d 1549 (Fed. Cir. 1988), the court seemed to adopt the changed circumstance rule. In holding that the government may not use a termination for convenience to avoid obligation on a contract already performed, the court quoted from *Municipal Leasing Corp. v. United States,* 7 Cl. Ct. 43 (1984), saying that the government's right to terminate arises "only in the event of some kind of change from the circumstances of the bargain or in the expectations of the parties." Subsequently, in *Salsbury Indus. v. United States*, 905 F.2d 1518 (Fed. Cir. 1990), *cert. denied*, 498 U.S. 1024 (1991), the court seemed to retreat from such a broad application of *Torncello* and return to the bad faith or abuse of discretion standards as the only limitations on the government's right to terminate. In that case, the government had entered into the contract after determining that another offeror was not responsible. However, the contracting officer had not advised that offeror that the determination was based on allegations that government employees had received kickbacks from that offeror under previous contracts. The contract was terminated to comply with a district court injunction. The court stated at 1521:

> Salsbury's second argument is that under *Torncello v. United States*, 231 Ct. Cl. 20, 681 F.2d 756 (1982), the termination of its contract was improper because it was the foreseeable victim of the Postal Service's illegal conduct . . . in disqualifying Doninger before it awarded the contract to Salsbury, the *Doninger* injunction does not justify allocating the burden of changed circumstances to Salsbury.
>
> *Torncello* has nothing to do with this case. It stands for the unremarkable proposition that when the government contracts with a party knowing full well that it will not honor the contract, it cannot avoid a breach claim by adverting to the convenience termination clause.

Thus, the court essentially imposed an additional intent requirement on contractors seeking to rely on *Torncello*—not only must they establish "changed circumstances," they must also show that the government entered into the contract with the intent to breach it. This "explanation" of *Torncello* was cited with approval in *Caldwell & Santmyer, Inc. v. Glickman*, 55 F.3d 1578 (Fed. Cir. 1995)—another case concerning termination for convenience following a flawed award. The court unequivocally stated that "bad faith . . . is a prerequisite for a *Torncello* claim." Thus, in order to invoke *Torncello*, the contractor faces a formidable burden—that is, it must be able to establish that, before award, the government specifically intended to terminate the contract. In *Caldwell*, the Federal Circuit refused to extend *Torncello* to the situation in which the government contracts in good faith but, at the same time, has knowledge of facts supposedly putting it on notice that, at some future date, it may be appropriate to terminate the contract for convenience. The court declined to apply *Torncello* to limit the government's termination for convenience rights in such circumstances. Accord, *Advanced Materials, Inc. v. United States*, 34 Fed. Cl. 480 (1995). See *Bryan D. Highfill,* HUDBCA 96-C-118-C7, 99-1 BCA ¶ 30,316 (government's right to terminate a contract for convenience is unlimited unless the termination is motivated by bad faith, the contracting officer abused his discretion in terminating the contract, or the government entered into the contract with no intention of allowing it to be completed); and *C.F.S. Air Cargo, Inc.*, ASBCA 36113, 91-1 BCA ¶ 23,583 (the *Torncello* rule did not apply to a termination where the government learned of better prices half-a-year after the award).

For a case applying the principles of *Torncello*, see *Operational Serv. Corp.*, ASBCA 37059, 93-3 BCA ¶ 26,190, holding that a grass mowing requirements contract was improperly terminated for convenience because the government knew at the time of contract formation that it intended to terminate the contract when either the government or a commercial activity contractor took over the work. The contractor was not informed of the government's intentions, nor was it given the opportunity to revise its prices. Relying on *Torncello*, the board held that the termination was an abuse of discretion and breach of contract. See also *Cray Research, Inc. v. United States*, 41 Fed. Cl. 427 (1998) (government may terminate for convenience only in the event of a change in the circumstances or in the parties' expectations).

c. The Krygoski Test—No Intention to Fulfill Promise

In *Krygoski Constr. Co. v. United States*, 94 F.3d 1537 (Fed. Cir. 1996), *cert. denied*, 520 U.S. 1210 (1997), the Federal Circuit again rejected an attempt to challenge a termination for convenience based on the *Torncello* changed circumstances doctrine and held that, when there was no bad faith or abuse of discretion, the government could terminate for convenience unless it had entered into the contract with no intention of fulfilling its promises.

In *Krygoski* the contracting officer decided to terminate for convenience in order to obtain new competition when it was discovered that there was a requirement for far more extensive asbestos removal than anticipated when the contract was awarded. The contracting officer believed that such termination was required because the new work was a "cardinal change" in the contract. The Court of Federal Claims concluded that this was not a changed circumstance with the result that the termination for convenience was improper and a breach of contract. As an alternative basis for overturning the termination, the court found that the government had abused its discretion, presumably because the contracting officer failed to justify the determination that the expansion of the contract work constituted a cardinal change. Accordingly, the court awarded Krygoski $1,456,851.20 in damages, which included anticipatory profits.

The Federal Circuit reversed, holding that, absent bad faith or abuse of discretion, a contracting officer's decision to terminate a contract for the convenience of the government is conclusive and will not be disturbed by the courts. The court concluded that *Torncello* stands only for the narrow proposition that the government may not invoke the Termination for Convenience clause, and thereby avoid breach of contract liability for anticipatory profits, when it enters a contract that it does not intend to honor. The Federal Circuit panel stated: "Although arguably the Government's circumstances had sufficiently changed to meet even the *Torncello* plurality standard, this court declines to reach this issue because *Torncello* applies only when the Government enters a contract with no intention of fulfilling its promises." The panel in *Krygoski* found that the changed circumstances test was merely an application of the *Kalvar* bad faith test and concluded that in *Torncello* the changed circumstances test had been "articulated in dicta."

The *Krygoski* decision appears to be based on the reasoning that with the advent of CICA, the "changed circumstances" test is no longer necessary to protect contractors against improper terminations for convenience. The court viewed a "lenient convenience termination" standard as consistent with the goal of full and open competition. The role of convenience terminations in the "CICA regime" is therefore seen as distinct from pre-CICA cases such as *Torncello*. The court stated at 1544:

> In sum, on two recent occasions after enactment of CICA, this court has expressly repeated the narrow applicability of *Torncello*. [*Caldwell*, 55 F.3d] at 1582; *Salsbury*, 905 F.2d at 1521. Indeed this court's recent pronouncements are fully consistent with the policy goals of CICA and other Government procurement statutes. Under these policies, contracting officers have no incentive to terminate a contract for convenience except to maintain full and open competition under CICA. With an adequate contractor in place, the contracting officer has no interest to reprocure. Moreover, where an officer must choose between modifying or terminating a contract, ease of administration usually imparts a bias in favor of modification. Thus *Salsbury* and *Caldwell* suggest that this court will avoid a finding of abused discretion when the facts support a reasonable inference that the contracting officer terminated for convenience in furtherance of statutory requirements for full and open competition.

A contractor is therefore essentially left with only the theories of bad faith and abuse of discretion to try to support such a challenge. As recognized by the Federal Circuit in *Krygoski,* a contractor's burden of proof in such cases is a heavy one, and "contractors have rarely succeeded in demonstrating the Government's bad faith."

The *Krygoski* court did not have the authority to explicitly overrule *Torncello*, since a panel of the Federal Circuit decided the former and the latter was decided en banc by the Court of Claims. See, for example, *South Corp. v. United States*, 690 F.2d 1368, (Fed. Cir. 1982).

Since *Krygoski*, courts and boards have been reluctant to convert terminations for convenience into breach of contract claims in the absence of strong evidence of bad faith or abuse of discretion in the termination decision. See *T&M Distribs., Inc. v. United States*, 185 F.3d 1279 (Fed. Cir. 1999) (no evidence that government did not intend to fulfill its promise when it terminated after large increase in requirements); *Charles G. Williams Constr., Inc.*, ASBCA 49775, 00-2 BCA ¶ 31,047, *vacated and remanded on other grounds,* 271 F.3d 1055 (Fed. Cir. 2001) (no bad faith because there was no evidence that the government intended to terminate the contract at the time of the award); and *Max S. Castle*, AGBCA 97-137-1, 00-1 BCA ¶ 30,871, *recons. denied,* 03-2 BCA ¶ 32,270 (contractor not entitled to recover costs incurred in remodeling a building for rental to the government because there was no evidence that the government had misled the lessor regarding the length of the lease term).

d. Violation of Paramount Government Policies

The courts have enjoined convenience terminations on the grounds that they violate or avoid other government policies of paramount importance. See *National Helium Corp. v. Morton*, 455 F.2d 650 (10th Cir. 1971), upholding an injunction against termination based on the government's failure to file an environmental impact statement as required by law. The court noted that the action was otherwise "within the discretion of the secretary." In *Art-Metal-USA, Inc. v. Solomon*, 473 F. Supp. 1 (D.D.C. 1978), the contractor was granted a preliminary injunction against a convenience termination on the grounds that the termination, along with actions the government was contemplating on other contracts, would constitute a constructive debarment without required procedural safeguards. The contractor was under investigation for alleged improper dealings but had not been officially accused of wrongdoing. The court found that the termination was based on unfavorable publicity and fear of political pressure. The injunction was made permanent, 25 CCF ¶ 82,962 (D.D.C. 1979). The case was voluntarily dismissed by both parties on appeal, No. 79-1296 (D.C. Cir. 1979). A termination for convenience was also enjoined when it was based on arbitrary and capricious action during the source selection process, *Vibra-Tech Eng'rs, Inc. v. United States*, 567 F. Supp. 484 (D. Colo. 1983). There, three months after the contracting officer had awarded a contract based on a clearly superior technical proposal, the contract was terminated for convenience and an award was made to an offeror with a lower price. The court found no rational basis for this action and enjoined the termination. Similarly, in *Law Eng'g Testing Co. v. Lee*, 25 Gov't Ctr. ¶ 26 (D. La. 1982), a termination was enjoined because the contracting officer had based the decision on an arbitrary and capricious recommendation of the GAO in response to a protest from a competitor. In *Gould, Inc. v. Chafee*, 450 F.2d 667 (D.C. Cir. 1971), the court stated that if the contractor could substantiate its claim that the termination was arbitrary and capricious it would be entitled to an injunction against the termination.

C. Partial Terminations

The termination clauses specifically entitle the government to make partial terminations and require the contractor to complete the unterminated work. Although a contracting officer, absent a deviation from the FAR, may not restrict the government's right to partially terminate, other clauses in the contract may control the financial results of a termination, *Raytheon Co.*, DOTCAB 1363, 84-1 BCA ¶ 16,969, *recons. denied in part, aff'd in part*, 84-2 BCA ¶17,459 (overhead ceiling applicable as long as work varied no more than 15 percent from estimate, but not applicable after partial termination reduced work more than 15 percent). There appear to be no limitations on the extent of a partial termination, which can run to the great majority of the contract work. See *Memheth, Ltd.*, ASBCA 21395, 77-1 BCA ¶ 12,274, where the government's failure to provide work resulted in a constructive partial termination of 118 units out of 181 units of heat exchangers being overhauled. Further, the character of the work can change drastically as a result of a partial termination. In *Lieb Bros., Inc.,* ASBCA 10007, 73-2 BCA ¶ 10,131, *recons. denied,* 74-1 BCA ¶ 10,509, the board upheld a partial termination that removed the major and most attractive portion of the job, explaining that "the Government was simply exercising its contractual rights." Thus, while the termination clauses call for an equitable adjustment in the unterminated portion of the work, the contractor bears a substantial risk of loss if the most profitable portion of the work is terminated.

D. Procedural Requirements

There are relatively few procedural requirements for a termination for convenience.

1. Notice of Termination

In addition to the provisions in the termination clause, FAR 49.102(a) contains the following guidance with respect to the notice of termination:

> The contracting officer shall terminate contracts for convenience or default only by a written notice to the contractor (see 49.601). When the notice is mailed, it shall be sent by certified mail, return receipt requested. When the contracting office arranges for hand delivery of the notice, a written acknowledgement shall be obtained from the contractor. The notice shall state—
>
>> (1) That the contract is being terminated for the convenience of the Government (or for default) under the contract clause authorizing the termination;
>>
>> (2) The effective date of termination;
>>
>> (3) The extent of termination;
>>
>> (4) Any special instructions; and
>>
>> (5) The steps the contractor should take to minimize the impact on personnel if the termination, together with all other outstanding terminations, will result in a significant reduction in the contractor's work force (see paragraph (g) of the notice in 49.601-2). If the termination notice is by telegram, include these "steps" in the confirming letter or modification.

FAR 49.601 provides model forms to be used for both telegraphic and letter notices of termination. The letter notice contains detailed guidance to the contractor on the procedures to be followed. DFARS 249.102 requires the use of Standard Form 30 for such notices.

A contracting officer's oral statements that he intended to convert a default termination into a convenience termination were not binding on the government because the contract terms and the regulations required notice of a convenience termination to be in writing, *Marshall Assoc. Contractors, Inc.*, IBCA 1901, 98-2 BCA ¶ 29,756.

Based on the language of the termination clause, in *Okinawa Climate Control Corp.*, ASBCA 19753, 77-2 BCA ¶ 12,669, the board refused to consider allegations that acts of the contracting officer's superior resulted in a termination for convenience, holding that it is the contracting officer who makes the decision to terminate the contract for convenience.

2. Termination for Default versus Termination for Convenience

In some cases, there has been confusion about whether a contract was being terminated for the contractor's default or the government's convenience. In *Richardson Camera Co.*, ASBCA 11930, 68-1 BCA ¶ 6990, the board held that if the contractor reasonably believes the notice of termination to be for convenience it will be treated as a termination for convenience even though it lacks the technical language normally found in such notices. Conversely, where the contractor knows that the termination is for default, the mere fact that the notice describes it as a convenience termination will not permit the contractor to treat it as such. See *Hadden v. United States*, 131 Ct. Cl. 326, 130 F. Supp. 610 (1955), where, in order to "save face" for the contractor, the contracting officer agreed to cancel the contract for convenience with the understanding that the contractor's recovery would be limited by the Default clause. When the termination notice was issued, reference to the Default clause limitations was inadvertently omitted. The court refused to permit the contractor to recover under the convenience clause because both parties knew that the termination was really for default. However, where there was genuine uncertainty over the type of termination, the board treated the termination as one for convenience, *Stroud Realty*, HUDBCA 75-13, 76-1 BCA ¶ 11,770. There, the contractor requested to be informed of the basis for the "cancellation," and the contracting officer replied by referring to both the default and the convenience termination provisions. The board stated that the government had a clear obligation to specify the exact method by which it was terminating the contract and ruled that it would be construed as a termination for convenience.

E. Finality of Termination for Convenience

Once a contract has been terminated for convenience, the act is treated as final, and the contractor's obligations to complete the terminated work are considered to be at an end. Thus, even though grounds for a default termination existed at the time the convenience notice was given, conversion to a default termination is not permitted, *Roged, Inc.*, ASBCA 20702, 76-2 BCA ¶ 12,018. See also *ITT Def. Communications Div.*, ASBCA 11858, 70-2 BCA ¶ 8415. Similarly, the contractor is not obligated to correct defective work in the terminated portion of the contract and is entitled to be paid the cost of the defective work, *New York Shipbuilding Co.*, ASBCA 15443, 73-1 BCA ¶ 9852. In that case, the board stated that "by terminating the contract for convenience the Government deprives the contractor of the opportunity to overcome deficiencies by better performance as the contract is nearing completion." The board also noted that to hold otherwise "would be inconsistent with the nature of a termination for convenience which is not based upon any fault or negligence on the part of the contractor." Finally, the board stated that its holding did not prevent the estimated costs of the contractor for correcting the deficiencies from being considered when reaching a termination settlement. Consideration of such costs would be important in determining whether a loss adjustment was required.

In *Cross Petroleum, Inc. v. United States*, 51 Fed. Cl. 549 (2002), the court held that the termination for default was improper in the absence of a 10-day cure notice. However, the court rejected the contractor's claim that, because the improper termination for default would be converted to a termination for convenience, it had no further liability for the remediation. The court distinguished the usual situation in which an improper termination for default went to the subject matter of the contract from the present case, in which the remediation obligation was ancillary. The court ruled that the damages should be determined under standard contract law, under which the contractor has the burden to show that government-incurred costs were unreasonable.

FAR 49.102(d) states that a terminated contract may be reinstated with the written consent of the contractor. In *Richardson Camera Co.*, ASBCA 11930, 68-1 BCA ¶ 6990, the government unsuccessfully attempted to change a termination from convenience to a termination for default. Thereafter, the contractor accepted the return of a prototype and attempted corrective action. In holding that such action did not reinstate the contract, the board stated that "performance cannot be construed as agreement to complete the contract."

F. Deletion of Work Through Termination for Convenience, Changes, or Other Clauses

Both the Termination for Convenience of the Government clause and the Changes clause provide mechanisms for deleting work. However, the pricing formulas, claims processing, cost recovery, settlement procedures, and inventory disposition methods may be substantially different depending on which method is selected. FAR 49.002(c) permits the use of termination principles in determining equitable adjustments under the Changes clause—but there is no means for imposing such adjustments on a contractor when they result in less compensation than is available through use of normal equitable adjustment principles. Thus, the basic rights of the parties will be determined by the clause used by the contracting officer to delete the work. The Termination for the Convenience of the Government clause must be used when major portions of the work are deleted and no additional work is substituted. Otherwise, either clause may be used, *Nager Elec. Co. v. United States*, 194 Ct. Cl. 835, 442 F.2d 936 (1971).

J.W. Bateson Co. v. United States, 308 F.2d 510 (5th Cir. 1962) is the leading case for the rule that major deletions may not be accomplished under the Changes clause. The court cited with approval the trial judge's statement that "the proper yardstick in judging between a change and a termination in projects of this magnitude would best be found by thinking in terms of major and minor variations in the plans." See also *John N. Brophy Co.,* GSBCA 5122, 78-2 BCA ¶ 13,506 (deletion of small amount of instructional services permitted under Changes clause), and *Bromley Contracting Co.*, HUDBCA 75-8, 77-1 BCA ¶ 12,232 (minor change in amount of work to be considered a constructive change). In *Celesco Indus., Inc.*, ASBCA 22251, 79-1 BCA ¶ 13,604, the board stated that termination for convenience was more appropriate for eliminating units of work or identifiable work items or tasks, whereas changes were normally used to delete work by changing the specifications. In that case a partial termination was treated as a change. Contrast *G.L. Cory, Inc.,* GSBCA 4383, 77-2 BCA ¶ 12,824, *recons. denied,* 78-2 BCA ¶ 13,356, in which a deletion of defective work under the Changes clause was treated as a termination for convenience.

In cases where the contracting officer initially orders the deletion under the Changes clause, it has been held that he or she can subsequently proceed under the termination clause if a binding agreement on the equitable adjustment has not been consummated, *Frederick Constr. Co.,* ASBCA 12241, 68-1 BCA ¶ 6832; *Gyrodyne Co. of America,* ASBCA 17415, 73-2 BCA ¶ 10,208. However, in view of the degree of finality accorded a notice of termination, the reverse would not appear to be true.

How the parties treated the deletion at the time is often outcome determinative. In *Honeycomb Co. of Am., Inc.*, ASBCA 44612, 02-1 BCA ¶ 31,703, the board held that reduction from 116 to 21 units was not a partial termination for convenience because the contractor voluntarily entered into bilateral modification designating the reduction as a change. In *P.J. Dick, Inc. v. General Servs. Admin.,* GSBCA 12215, 95-1 BCA ¶ 27,574, *modified on recons.,* 96-1 BCA ¶ 28,017, although the government purported to partially terminate for convenience a building renovation contract, the pricing of the government's credit was based on the cost of the deleted work under the Changes clause rather than under the Termination for Convenience clause because both parties had analyzed the matter and treated it as a deductive change. The board stated that it would not disturb the parties' treatment of the matter in the absence of a compelling reason to do so.

The government may delete work under other clauses. In *Jiminez, Inc.,* VABCA 6351, 02-2 BCA ¶ 32,019, the government relied on the Inspection of Construction clause to have unsatisfactory work completed by another contractor. The board rejected the contractor's assertion that the work should have been deleted from the contract as a termination for convenience. The use of a particular clause depends on the extent of work being deleted, rather than on which clause provides the greatest benefit to the contractor. Here, since only 2 percent of work was not completed, it was appropriate to use the Inspection of Construction clause.

III. CONSTRUCTIVE TERMINATION

There are significant differences between an express termination and a constructive termination. Express terminations occur when the clause is specifically invoked. Constructive terminations and constructive changes are both judicial constructs in situations when a breach might otherwise result. Constructive changes, however, were designed to provide contractors with an administrative remedy, while a constructive termination insulates the government from breach damages, including anticipated profits.

In *John Reiner & Co. v. United States,* 163 Ct. Cl. 381, 325 F.2d 438 (1963), *cert. denied,* 377 U.S. 931 (1964), the Court of Claims enunciated the principle that any government action preventing a contractor from continuing performance would be adjusted for under the Termination for Convenience clause if the contracting officer could have used the clause at the time of the action. This principle has prevented contractors from recovering anticipated profits in a number of situations where the government elected not to terminate for convenience but rather to end the contractual relationship in some other way. This result might also be obtained even if the clause was omitted from the contract documents but was required by the regulations to be included, under the rationale of *G.L. Christian & Assocs. v. United States,* 160 Ct. Cl. 1, 312 F.2d 418, *cert. denied,* 375 U.S. 954 (1963).

In *Diversified Energy, Inc. v. TVA*, 223 F.3d 328 (6th Cir. 2000), the court refused to apply the constructive termination logic to benefit the contractor. The contractor had argued that the government's exercise of a "reopening" provision, which permitted the parties to reopen the contract at its midway point to renegotiate the contract terms, was a "constructive" termination, thus triggering the Unilateral Termination provision, which permitted the TVA to terminate the contract upon 60 day' notice but imposed a penalty requiring payment of $14 for each ton scheduled for delivery under the remainder of the contract. The court concluded that the purpose of the constructive termination rule was to retroactively justify the government's actions, avoiding breach and limiting liability. See also *Contact Int'l, Inc. v. Widnall,* 106 F.3d 426 (Fed. Cir. 1997), rejecting a contractor's claim that a constructive termination for convenience occurred based on uncertainty created by the government about whether it was going to terminate the contract for convenience.

In *United Techs. Corp.*, ASBCA 46880, 97-1 BCA ¶ 28,818, the board held that the constructive termination rule does not apply to promises to buy more products in the future. It therefore rejected the government's argument that its breach of an Investment Incentive clause calling for the future award of jet engines should be treated as a convenience termination.

A. Wrongful Default Terminations

For a number of years the government has, by contract clause, provided for the application of the convenience termination provisions to wrongful default terminations. Paragraph (g) of the present fixed-price supply contract Default clause contained in FAR 52.249-8 states:

> If, after termination, it is determined that the Contractor was not in default, or that the default was excusable, the rights and obligations of the parties shall be the same as if the termination had been issued for the convenience of the Government.

Similar provisions are contained in ¶ (c) of the fixed-price construction contract Default clause in FAR 52.249-10 and in ¶ (g) of the fixed-price research and development contract Default clause in FAR 52.249-9. The default termination will be converted to a convenience termination if the contractor was not in default or if its failure is excusable. Thus, there is little likelihood of a contractor recovering anticipated profits when a contract is improperly terminated for default.

The conversion of default to convenience terminations by boards and courts is a very common practice and has been extended to practically any reason for wrongful default termination. See *Specialty Constr. Co.*, ASBCA 21132, 78-2 BCA ¶ 13,348 (waiver of right to terminate for default); *Electro-Magnetic Refinishers, Inc.*, GSBCA 5035, 79-1 BCA ¶ 13,697 (failure to follow procedures—no written cure notice); *Sayers Custom Mowing*, ENGBCA 3950, 79-1 BCA ¶ 13,695 (contractor excusably delayed); *Mr.'s Landscaping & Nursery*, HUDBCA 75-6, 76-2 BCA ¶ 11,968 (contracts substantially performed); *A.W. Burton*, AGBCA 431, 77-1 BCA ¶ 12,307 (contractor not in default); and *Whittaker Corp.*, ASBCA 14740, 79-1 BCA ¶ 13,805 (contract impossible to perform). See also *Carter Indus.*, DOTBCA 4108, 02-1 BCA ¶ 31,738, applying the Termination for Convenience clause when the government breached the contract by requiring the bankrupt contractor (acting as a debtor in possession) to either accept or reject the contract in the bankruptcy proceedings. For a case considering but rejecting application of the *Torncello* rule to an improper default termination, see *Drain-A-Way Sys.*, GSBCA 7022, 84-1 BCA ¶ 16,929.

In *Apex Int'l Mgmt. Servs., Inc.,* ASBCA 38087, 94-2 BCA ¶ 26,842, *recons. denied,* 94-2 BCA ¶ 26,852, the board refused to convert an improper default termination into a termination for convenience. It found that the government's actions satisfied all the requirements of bad faith. The government employees, unhappy with the contracting-out involved, attempted to block the award and then "declared war" on the contractor, making false statements and committing numerous acts designed to harass and injure the contractor.

B. Government's Failure to Perform Under an Indefinite Delivery Contract

The government's failure to perform its obligations under a requirements contract has been alternatively treated as a constructive change or a breach of contract. If the government action is considered a breach, the *Reiner* rule has been applied to limit recovery on the theory that a convenience termination was possible and could have been used by the contracting officer, *Nesbitt v. United States*, 170 Ct. Cl. 666, 345 F.2d 583 (1965), *cert. denied,* 383 U. S. 926 (1966). See *Inland Container, Inc. v. United States*, 206 Ct. Cl. 478, 512 F.2d 1073 (1975), and *Kalvar Corp. v. United States*, 211 Ct. Cl. 192, 543 F.2d 1298 (1976), *cert. denied*, 434 U.S. 830 (1977). A constructive termination for convenience has also been found where the government failed to order work under a multiyear contract when funds were available, *Varo, Inc.*, ASBCA 13739, 70-1 BCA ¶ 8099.

In two cases, the *Reiner* rule has been rejected when the government breached a requirements contract. In *Torncello v. United States*, 231 Ct. Cl. 20, 681 F.2d 756 (1982), and *S & W Tire Servs., Inc.*, GSBCA 6376, 82-2 BCA ¶ 16,048, anticipated profits were included in the contractor's damages because there had been no change in circumstances leading to the government decision to buy its requirements from another contractor. Compare *Adams Mfg. Co.*, GSBCA 5747, 82-1 BCA ¶ 15,740, *aff'd*, 714 F.2d 161 (Fed. Cir. 1983), in which the *Reiner* rule was applied when the government had breached a requirements contract by not informing the contractor of a moratorium on its requirements. See also *Atlantic Garages, Inc.*, GSBCA 5891, 82-1 BCA ¶ 15,479, in which the board held that failure to inform the contractor of reduced requirements was a breach rather than a constructive termination for convenience but did not discuss the measure of damages.

Constructive termination is not available for a completed contract. In *Maxima Corp v. United States*, 847 F.2d 1549 (Fed. Cir. 1988), the court held that the government cannot retroactively terminate a completed contract to avoid a breach. In *Ace-Fed. Reporters, Inc. v. Barram,* 226 F.3d 1329 (Fed. Cir. 2000), the court held that, by ordering services from other vendors in violation of requirements-like contracts, the GSA breached the contracts and was liable for lost profits. The court rejected the GSA's constructive termination argument since the contracts were completed and the contractors stood ready to perform throughout, stating that the "concept is a fiction to begin with, but there has to be some limit to its elasticity." See also *Mid Eastern Indus., Inc.*, ASBCA 53016, 02-1 BCA ¶ 31,657 (government's failure to order the minimum quantity on an ID/IQ contract not a constructive termination for convenience because contractor maintained its capability until completion of contract period); *T&M Distribs., Inc.*, ASBCA 51279, 01-2 BCA ¶ 31,442 (applying *Ace-Federal Reporters* to hold that the government's diversion of purchases from a requirements contract constituted a breach that could not be recast by the government as a partial constructive termination for convenience); and *Carroll Autom.*, ASBCA 50993, 98-2 BCA ¶ 29,864 (denying the government's argument that purchase of some supplies from other sources was a constructive partial termination for convenience because the government first invoked its constructive partial convenience termination theory two years after the contract had been performed, and the contract's termination provisions required an equitable adjustment of the nonterminated portion of the contract in the event of a partial termination). Compare *Hermes Consol., Inc.,* ASBCA 52308, 02-1 BCA ¶ 31,767, holding that the government's partial termination for convenience reducing the minimum quantity under an IDIQ contract was a permissible termination for convenience even though the termination notice was issued only eight days before the end of one contract.

C. Cancellation of Award

The convenience termination clause has been consistently applied to limit the contractor's recovery when the government wrongfully cancels as a result of an award controversy. In *G.C. Casebolt Co. v. United States*, 190 Ct. Cl. 783, 421 F.2d 710 (1970), the government contended that an award had not been made because the notice of award had been retrieved from the mail and the award canceled. The court held that, even if the award had been consummated, the contractor's recovery would be limited by the convenience termination clause. See also *Albano Cleaners, Inc. v. United States*, 197 Ct. Cl. 450, 455 F.2d 556 (1972) (award canceled on erroneous belief that bid was nonresponsive); *McFadden v. United States,* 215 Ct. Cl. 918 (1977) (all bids rejected because government estimate exceeded but award had already been made to plaintiff); and *Dairy Sales Corp. v. United States,* 219 Ct. Cl. 431, 593 F.2d 1002 (1979) (partial cancellation because award for one item should have gone to another bidder—converted to partial termination).

IV. TERMINATION SETTLEMENTS

Contracts terminated for the convenience of the government may be settled by negotiated agreement, determination of the Termination Contracting Officer (TCO) (only when settlement cannot be reached by agreement), costing out in cost-reimbursement contracts, or a combination of these methods, FAR 49.103. If agreement on a settlement cannot be reached, the "long form" clauses require the government to pay the contractor the costs incurred in performing the terminated work, the costs of settling and paying settlement proposals under terminated subcontracts, and a fair and reasonable profit on work performed. The "short form" clauses and the clause for contracts for commercial items provide for minimal compensation to the contractor.

The terms of a convenience termination recovery are governed by U.S. public contract law, not the law of the country in which the contract is performed. See *Empresa de Viacao Terceirense,* ASBCA 49827, 00-2 BCA ¶ 31,120, *recons. denied,* 01-1 BCA ¶ 31,243, rejecting the contractor's argument that Portuguese law should govern whether severance pay costs are allowable and reimbursable as part of the termination settlement.

A. Procedures

After a contract has been terminated for the convenience of the government, the parties are faced with the problem of stopping the work to the extent terminated, disposing of the termination inventory, and adjusting the contract price. These matters are covered in detail in the "long form" termination clauses, and FAR Part 49 contains detailed procedures covering terminations.

1. Obligations of the Parties

The contractor's and contracting officer's duties are summarized at FAR 49.104 and FAR 49.105, as follows:

> 49.104 Duties of prime contractor after receipt of notice of termination.
>
> After receipt of the notice of termination, the contractor shall comply with the notice and the termination clause of the contract, except as otherwise directed by the TCO. The notice and clause applicable to convenience terminations generally require that the contractor—
>
> > (a) Stop work immediately on the terminated portion of the contract and stop placing subcontracts thereunder;
> >
> > (b) Terminate all subcontracts related to the terminated portion of the prime contract;
> >
> > (c) Immediately advise the TCO of any special circumstances precluding the stoppage of work;
> >
> > (d) Perform the continued portion of the contract and submit promptly any request for an equitable adjustment of price for the continued portion, supported by evidence of any increase in the cost, if the termination is partial;
> >
> > (e) Take necessary or directed action to protect and preserve property in the contractor's possession in which the Government has or may acquire an interest and, as directed by the TCO, deliver the property to the Government;
> >
> > (f) Promptly notify the TCO in writing of any legal proceedings growing out of any subcontract or other commitment related to the terminated portion of the contract;
> >
> > (g) Settle outstanding liabilities and proposals arising out of termination of subcontracts, obtaining any approvals or ratifications required by the TCO;
> >
> > (h) Promptly submit the contractor's own settlement proposal, supported by appropriate schedules; and

(i) Dispose of termination inventory as directed or authorized by the TCO.

49.105 Duties of termination contracting officer after issuance of notice of termination.

(a) Consistent with the termination clause and the notice of termination, the TCO shall—

(1) Direct the action required of the prime contractor;

(2) Examine the settlement proposal of the prime contractor and, when appropriate, the settlement proposals of subcontractors;

(3) Promptly negotiate settlement with the contractor and enter into a settlement agreement; and

(4) Promptly settle the contractor's settlement proposal by determination for the elements that cannot be agreed on, if unable to negotiate a complete settlement.

(b) To expedite settlement, the TCO may request specially qualified personnel to—

(1) Assist in dealings with the contractor;

(2) Advise on legal and contractual matters;

(3) Conduct accounting reviews and advise and assist on accounting matters; and

(4) Perform the following functions regarding termination inventory (see Subpart 45.6);

(i) Verify its existence.

(ii) Determine qualitative and quantitative allocability.

(iii) Make recommendations concerning serviceability.

(iv) Undertake necessary screening and redistribution.

(v) Assist the contractor in accomplishing other disposition.

(c) The TCO should promptly hold a conference with the contractor to develop a definite program for effecting the settlement. When appropriate in the judgment of the TCO, after consulting with the contractor, principal subcontractors should be requested to attend. Topics that should be discussed at the conference and documented include—

(1) General principles relating to the settlement of any settlement proposal, including obligations of the contractor under the termination clause of the contract;

(2) Extent of the termination, point at which work is stopped, and status of any plans, drawings, and information that would have been delivered had the contract been completed;

(3) Status of any continuing work;

(4) Obligation of the contractor to terminate subcontracts and general principles to be followed in settling subcontractor settlement proposals;

(5) Names of subcontractors involved and the dates termination notices were issued to them;

(6) Contractor personnel handling review and settlement of subcontractor settlement proposals and the methods being used;

(7) Arrangements for transfer of title and delivery to the Government of any material required by the Government;

(8) General principles and procedures to be followed in the protection, preservation, and disposition of the contractor's and subcontractor's termination inventories, including the preparation of termination inventory schedules;

(9) Contractor accounting practices and preparation of SF 1439 (Schedule of Accounting Information (49.602-3));

(10) Form in which to submit settlement proposals;

(11) Accounting review of settlement proposals;

(12) Any requirement for interim financing in the nature of partial payments;

(13) Tentative time schedule for negotiation of the settlement, including submission by the contractor and subcontractors of settlement proposals, termination inventory schedules, and accounting information schedules (see 49.206-3 and 49.303-2);

(14) Actions taken by the contractor to minimize impact upon employees affected adversely by the termination (see paragraph (g) of the letter notice in 49.601-2); and

(15) Obligation of the contractor to furnish accurate, complete, and current cost or pricing data, and to certify to that effect in accordance with

> 15.403-4(a)(1) when the amount of a termination settlement agreement, or a partial termination settlement agreement plus the estimate to complete the continued portion of the contract exceeds the threshold in 15.403-4.

2. Basis for Settlement Proposals

Two fundamental approaches are available for use in the submission of settlement proposals: (1) an "inventory" basis, which FAR 49.206-2 states is the "preferred" method; and (2) a "total cost" basis. Under both methods for submission of settlement proposals, the contractor is paid the contract price for items completed and accepted, FAR 49.205, but the accounting treatment of the work in process is quite different.

Under the inventory method the contractor must separately itemize charges to be allocated to the settlement proposal. FAR 49.206-2(a)(1) requires the separation of the following costs:

> (i) Metals, raw materials, purchased parts, work in process, finished parts, components, dies, jigs, fixtures, and tooling, at purchase or manufacturing cost;
>
> (ii) Charges such as engineering costs, initial costs, and general administrative costs;
>
> (iii) Costs of settlements with subcontractors;
>
> (iv) Settlement expenses; and
>
> (v) Other proper charges.

Use of the inventory method requires the contractor to have an accounting system that is capable of accurately segregating costs of the partially performed work. If the contractor's accounting system is not sufficiently well developed for this purpose, the total cost basis for submission of settlement proposals will generally be approved for use.

Under the total cost basis for submission of settlement proposals, the contractor itemizes all costs incurred in performance of the contract work. Costs are not segregated between the completed and partially performed portions of the work. FAR 49.206-2(b) provides for use of the total cost approach as follows:

> (1) When use of the inventory basis is not practicable or will unduly delay settlement, the total-cost basis (SF-1436) may be used if approved in advance by the TCO as in the following examples:
>
> > (i) If production has not commenced and the accumulated costs represent planning and preproduction or "get ready" expenses.

(ii) If, under the contractor's accounting system, unit costs for work in process and finished products cannot readily be established.

(iii) If the contract does not specify unit prices.

(iv) If the termination is complete and involves a letter contract.

FAR 49.206-2(b) also contains the following guidance concerning use of the total cost method in both complete and partial termination situations:

(2) When the total-cost basis is used under a complete termination, the contractor must itemize costs incurred under the contract up to the effective date of termination. The costs of settlements with subcontractors and applicable settlement expenses must also be added. An allowance for profit (49.202) or adjustment for loss (49.203(c)) must be made. The contract price for all end items delivered or to be delivered and accepted must be deducted. All unliquidated advance and progress payments and disposal and other credits known when the proposal is submitted must also be deducted.

(3) When the total-cost basis is used under a partial termination, the settlement proposal shall not be submitted until completion of the continued portion of the contract. The settlement proposal must be prepared as in [subparagraph (2) above], except that all costs incurred to the date of completion of the continued portion of the contract must be included.

When the inventory approach is used, the contractor must pay careful attention to those costs that were to have been recovered or amortized over all contract work—completed units as well as partially completed and terminated work—especially costs such as engineering and development expenses, preproduction, and starting load costs. Unless the contractor separates and allocates an appropriate portion of such costs to the termination claim, the inventory approach may unfairly limit the contractor's recovery.

For commercial contracts, FAR 12.403 states:

(d) Termination for the Government's convenience.

(1) When the contracting officer terminates a contract for commercial items for the Government's convenience, the contractor shall be paid—

(i) The percentage of the contract price reflecting the percentage of the work performed prior to the notice of the termination, and

(ii) Any charges the contractor can demonstrate directly resulted from the termination. The contractor may demonstrate such charges using its standard record keeping system and is not required to comply with the cost accounting standards or the con-

> tract cost principles in Part 31. The Government does not have any right to audit the contractor's records solely because of the termination for convenience.

(2) Generally, the parties should mutually agree upon the requirements of the termination proposal. The parties must balance the Government's need to obtain sufficient documentation to support payment to the contractor against the goal of having a simple and expeditious settlement.

3. *Time of Submission of Proposals*

Paragraph (d) of the "long form" termination clause in FAR 52.249-2 requires that the contractor submit its settlement proposal within "1 year from the effective date of termination" unless the period is extended in writing by the contracting officer. If the contractor fails to do so, the contracting officer may make a unilateral determination of the amount due the contractor, although contracting officers do have discretion to act upon late settlement proposals, FAR 52.249-2. Paragraph (j) of the "long form" clause provides that contractors lose their right to appeal a unilateral termination determination of a contracting officer if they have neither submitted their settlement proposal within one year nor requested a time extension. See *England v. Swanson Group, Inc.*, 353 F.3d 1375 (Fed. Cir. 2004), holding that the board had no jurisdiction to consider an appeal of a contracting officer's award of settlement costs after the contractor had failed to submit a settlement proposal within one year. The court reached this conclusion even though the board had found that the contractor had requested an extension of time to submit the proposal within the one-year period. The court reasoned that the Contract Disputes Act did not provide for an appeal of the contracting officer's determination because it was not an appeal from a final decision on a claim that Swanson had submitted. See also *Industrial Data Link Corp.,* ASBCA 49348, 98-1 BCA ¶ 29,634, *recons. denied,* 98-2 BCA ¶ 29,775, *aff'd,* 194 F.3d 1337 (Fed. Cir. 1999), and *Rivera Tech. Prods., Inc.,* ASBCA 48171, 96-2 BCA ¶ 28,564, holding that the contractors had lost the right to appeal the contracting officer's determination of the amount due on their late termination settlement proposals. None of these cases addresses the issue of whether the contractor could challenge the settlement proposal as being arbitrary and capricious. See also *United Elecs. Co.,* ASBCA 21686, 78-1 BCA ¶ 13,091.

In *Do-Well Mach. Shop, Inc. v. United States*, 870 F.2d 637 (Fed. Cir. 1989), the court held that the requirement that the settlement proposal be submitted no later than one year after the termination was not inconsistent with the Contract Disputes Act. Thus, the failure to file within the time limit was a valid defense that could be raised by the government. See *Dynatech Bldg. Sys. Corp.*, ASBCA 47462, 95-1 BCA ¶ 27,325, in which the contractor's failure to file a termination for convenience claim within the required one-year period was not excused by a hurricane because the contractor failed to request a time extension from the contracting officer. The purpose in requiring the contractor to present a prompt settlement proposal is to permit the government to close out the terminated contract within a reasonable time, to budget its funds, and to enable it to gather evidence concerning the pricing of the contractor's claims, if necessary.

The one-year period begins to run when the contractor is given notice of the termination. In *Swanson Group, Inc.*, ASBCA 52109, 01-1 BCA ¶ 31164, the board held that the one-year period for the submission of the proposal or request for extension began when the contractor received notice of the conversion of the default termination to one for convenience. In *Space Dynamics Corp.*, ASBCA 25106, 81-2 BCA ¶ 15205, the board rejected the argument that the one-year period began with the contractor's receipt of the notice of the default termination. In *Voices R Us, Inc.,* ASBCA 51565, 99-1 BCA ¶ 30,213, the termination notice specified the effective date as April 15, 1997, and a Federal Express air bill established that the contractor received a hard copy of the notice on April 16, 1997. The board rejected the government's argument that the proposal was untimely because the government had sent the contractor a facsimile of the termination notice on April 14, 1997, finding that the contractor's records for the period showed no facsimile received on April 14, 1997, and the government offered no record of the alleged facsimile.

4. Imperfect Proposals

The primary function of a termination settlement proposal is to foster negotiations between the parties. Therefore, a proposal that is initiated within the one-year period for submission, but that contains flaws, may be valid if the flaws are not so severe as to render the proposal meaningless for purposes of negotiation and are remediable within a reasonable time, *Astor Bolden Enters., Inc.*, ASBCA 52377, 00-2 BCA ¶ 31,115. In *Marine Instrument Co.,* ASBCA 41370, 97-2 BCA ¶ 29,082, the government, alleging that the contractor had failed to submit a proper settlement proposal within one year, was denied summary judgment because it failed to show that the contractor's timely submissions "were so deficient as to be meaningless for the purposes of negotiation." In *Consolidated Def. Corp.*, ASBCA 52315, 01-2 BCA ¶ 31,484, the government was not entitled to summary judgment that a termination settlement proposal not submitted within one year from the termination for convenience was untimely where (a) the contractor's initial proposal, submitted five months after the termination for convenience, was not so flawed as to be meaningless for resolution of the termination for convenience; (b) the contractor had requested additional time to submit a corrected proposal before the one year expired; (c) the contractor did submit a final proposal within 14 months of the termination for convenience; (d) a succession of termination contracting officers made partial payments and negotiated with the contractor on the submittals; and (e) the government waited five years before asserting that the proposal was untimely.

A related issue involves whether claims separate from the termination are waived if they are not presented within one year with the termination settlement proposal. In *Ellett Constr. Co. v. United States,* 93 F.3d 1537 (Fed. Cir. 1996), the court held that a termination for convenience does not subsume within the termination settlement proposal all claims a contractor might have against the government. Therefore, terminating the contract does not eliminate valid contractor claims. Relying on *Ellett*, the Department of Agriculture Board of Contract Appeals vacated part of its prior decision dismissing a terminated contractor's equitable adjustment claims when it denied jurisdiction of the appeal of the contracting officer's determination after a late settlement proposal, *RBW Assocs,* AGBCA 95-208-1, 96-2 BCA ¶ 28,416, *recons. granted*, AGBCA 96-205R, 96-2 BCA ¶ 28,616. *Ellett* also appears to have overruled *M-Pax, Inc.*, HUDBCA 81-570-C10, 81-2 BCA ¶ 15,409, barring appeal of a denial of a constructive changes claim submitted by the contractor after failure to submit a settlement proposal within one year.

5. Terminations for Convenience Settlement Proposals Under a Termination for Default

Contractors often submit a termination settlement proposal even when the contract has been terminated for default in case the default is overturned. One purpose for this course of action is to begin the running of interest. In *Kit Pack Co.*, ASBCA 53155, 01-2 BCA ¶ 31,479, a contractor whose contract had been terminated for default filed a CDA-certified termination for convenience settlement proposal. The board noted that the date of the submission of the proposal would establish the date on which interest would begin to run in the event the default termination were converted to a convenience termination, but it held that it could not consider the convenience termination claim until it ruled on the propriety of the termination for default. In *Foremost Mech. Sys., Inc. v. General Servs. Admin.*, GSBCA 12335, 95-1 BCA ¶ 27,382, although the board had denied a default termination, the board was not free to decide the amount of the contractor's recovery and conversion of the action to a convenience termination because the certified convenience termination claim had to be presented to the contracting officer before the board could take jurisdiction.

6. Negotiation of Final Settlement

Following submission of the contractor's termination settlement proposal, ¶ (e) of the "long form" clause calls for the contractor and the contracting officer to seek to negotiate a final settlement. See also FAR 49.103, which states:

> When possible, the TCO should negotiate a fair and prompt settlement with the contractor. The TCO shall settle a settlement proposal by determination only when it cannot be settled by agreement.

There is great latitude given to the parties in negotiating the settlement agreement. Paragraph (f) of the "long form" clause in FAR 52.249-2 states:

> Subject to paragraph (e) of this clause, the Contractor and the Contracting Officer may agree upon the whole or any part of the amount to be paid or remaining to be paid because of the termination. The amount may include a reasonable allowance for profit on work done. However, the agreed amount, whether under this paragraph (f) or paragraph (g) of this clause, exclusive of costs shown in paragraph (g)(3) of this clause, may not exceed the total contract price as reduced by (1) the amount of payments previously made and (2) the contract price of work not terminated. The contract shall be modified, and the Contractor paid the agreed amount. Paragraph (g) of this clause shall not limit, restrict, or affect the amount that may be agreed upon to be paid under this paragraph.

FAR 49.107(a) requires the TCO to "refer each prime contractor settlement proposal of $100,000 or more to the appropriate audit agency for review and recommendations." However, FAR 49.107(d) states that the "audit report is advisory only, and is for the TCO to use in negotiating a settlement or issuing a unilateral determination." Formerly, FPR 1-8.211-2(a) required that proposed termination settlements involving $50,000 or more be approved by a settlement review board before a settlement agreement was executed. The DAR at one time also required such review. Air Force DAR Supplement 8-210.1 also required settlement review board approvals for settlements over $100,000. Failure to obtain mandated settlement review board approval has been held to invalidate a settlement agreement, *Atlantic Gulf & Pac. Co. of Manila, Inc. v. United States,* 207 Ct. Cl. 995 (1975). See also *Bromley Contracting Co.,* DOTCAB 1284, 84-2 BCA ¶ 17,233, *aff'd,* 14 Cl. Ct. 69 (1987), *aff'd,* 861 F.2d 729 (Fed. Cir. 1988), where failure to obtain audit review required by regulations prior to execution of a modification in excess of $100,000 provided the government with grounds for voiding the agreement.

Termination settlement agreements must cover any setoffs that the government has against the contractor, FAR 49.109-1. This provision does not require the termination contracting officer to include setoffs arising from different contracts between the same contractor and the government, although the contractor may negotiate to bar the government from exercising its setoff right against the proceeds of the termination settlement agreement, *Applied Cos. v. United States,* 144 F.3d 1470 (Fed. Cir. 1998).

A contractor's appeal was untimely when it waited 33 months before claiming duress in entering into a no-cost termination for convenience. The board held that the contractor could not challenge the termination for convenience when the government accepted the terms the contractor proposed after refusing to perform in accordance with the contracting officer's direction, *Inca Contracting Co.*, ASBCA 52697, 01-1 BCA ¶ 31,255.

Where a construction contractor had entered into agreement providing for "no cost settlement (Termination for Convenience)" while stating that all claims related to the contract "remain in force," the board held that claims submitted shortly after the agreement was made were not precluded because the government did not obtain the release for a no-cost termination settlement provided in FAR 49.603-6. The board considered the contractor's claims but denied them on the merits, *Bay Constr. Co.*, VABCA 5594, 02-1 BCA ¶ 31,795.

Since no finality attaches to an unallowable payment, the government may recover the illegal or improper payment of anticipatory profits and likewise may recover overpayment of a partial payment on a termination proposal before full settlement is achieved. In *Arbor 111 Realty Co.,* HUDBCA 96-C-114-C5, 98-2 BCA ¶ 29,344, *aff'd*, 914 F.3d 1335 (Fed. Cir. 1999), the board held that a 7 percent commission for sales that occurred after a termination for convenience was an impermissible anticipatory profit even though the contracting officer and a real estate broker providing management and listing services had orally agreed to it.

A contractor was not entitled to collect Contract Disputes Act interest on its termination settlement proposal following a settlement, because the resulting settlement agreement was conclusive evidence that negotiations had not reached an impasse. A settlement agreement is not a final decision by the TCO, but rather, a mutually agreed-upon resolution of termination rights, *Rex Sys., Inc. v. Cohen,* 224 F.3d 1367 (Fed. Cir. 2000).

7. Unilateral Determination

If the contracting officer and the contractor cannot agree, ¶ (f) of the "long form" clause requires the contracting officer to make a unilateral determination of the amounts due the contractor. This determination may then be challenged by the contractor pursuant to the Contract Disputes Act procedures. Paragraph (g) provides that such determinations shall include:

> (1) The contract price for completed supplies or services accepted by the Government (or sold or acquired under paragraph (b)(9) of this clause) not previously paid for, adjusted for any saving of freight and other charges.
>
> (2) The total of—
>
> > (i) The costs incurred in the performance of the work terminated, including initial costs and preparatory expense allocable thereto, but excluding any costs attributable to supplies or services paid or to be paid under paragraph (g)(1) of this clause;
> >
> > (ii) The cost of settling and paying termination settlement proposals under terminated subcontracts that are properly chargeable to the terminated portion of the contract if not included in subdivision (g)(2)(i)of this clause; and
> >
> > (iii) A sum, as profit on subdivision (g)(2)(i) of this clause, determined by the Contracting Officer under 49.202 of the Federal Acquisition Regulation, in effect on the date of this contract, to be fair and reasonable; how-

ever, if it appears that the Contractor would have sustained a loss on the entire contract had it been completed, the Contracting Officer shall allow no profit under this subdivision (g)(2)(iii) and shall reduce the settlement to reflect the indicated rate of loss.

(3) The reasonable costs of settlement of the work terminated, including—

(i) Accounting, legal, clerical, and other expenses reasonably necessary for the preparation of termination settlement proposals and supporting data;

(ii) The termination and settlement of subcontracts (excluding the amounts of such settlements); and

(iii) Storage, transportation, and other costs incurred, reasonably necessary for the preservation, protection, or disposition of the termination inventory.

8. Appeal of Convenience Terminations

To appeal a contracting officer decision under the Contract Disputes Act, the contractor must submit a "claim." In *Reflectone, Inc. v. Dalton*, 60 F.3d 1572 (Fed. Cir. 1995), the court held that "routine" requests for payment had to be in dispute to constitute a CDA claim, but that "nonroutine" requests could be appealed immediately. Subsequently, in *Ellett Constr. Co. v. United States*, 93 F.3d 1537 (Fed Cir. 1996), the court held that the appeal of a contracting officer's unilateral determination of the settlement amount met the definition of a "claim" because it was a nonroutine request for payment. The court stated at 1542:

> [I]t is difficult to conceive of a less routine demand for payment than one which is submitted when the government terminates a contract for its convenience. Such a demand, which occurs only in a fraction of government contracts is certainly less routine than a request for an equitable adjustment, several of which a contractor might submit on any one contract. Indeed, in concluding that a request for an equitable adjustment is not routine in *Reflectone*, we pointed to Supreme Court precedent equating a request for an equitable adjustment with an assertion of a breach of contract. That analogue is even more appropriate here, where, but for the convenience termination clause, the government's action would be a breach of contract, and it would be liable for resulting damages.

The court reasoned, however, that nonroutine requests for payment must also be submitted to the contracting officer for a decision to constitute a claim. It concluded that Ellett's termination for convenience proposal, although nonroutine, was not a claim when it was initially submitted for negotiation, but "ripened " into a claim when the parties reached an impasse, requiring the contracting officer to issue a decision. Thus, in *Ellett* the Federal Circuit held that termination settlement proposals are nonroutine submissions that constitute "claims" for the purposes of the CDA, if they (1) make a written demand (2) seeking as a matter of right (3) a sum certain. A settlement proposal must be submitted to the contracting officer for a decision in order to "ripen" into a claim. However, there need not be a preexisting dispute or impasse for the government to issue a final decision on a claim arising out of a termination for convenience, *Eurasia Heavy Indus., Inc.,* ASBCA 52878, 01-2 BCA ¶ 31,574.

In *Metric Constructors, Inc.,* ASBCA 50843, 98-2 BCA ¶ 30,088, the board held that a contractor's certified termination settlement proposal became a CDA claim when the parties reached an impasse before the contracting officer's issuance of a unilateral contract modification. The board held that the standard certification contained in the termination settlement proposal is correctable to comply with the certification language required by the CDA. The board acknowledged that it was rejecting its previous decision in *Chan Computer Corp.*, ASBCA 46763, 96-1 BCA ¶ 28,005, which held that the termination settlement proposal certification language could not be corrected to meet CDA certification requirements. In *Airo Servs., Inc. v. General Servs. Admin.*, GSBCA 14301, 98-2 BCA ¶ 29,909, the contractor submitted a termination settlement proposal and later asked the contracting officer to consider the proposal as a claim for an equitable adjustment and issue a final decision. The board held that the termination settlement proposal was an equitable adjustment claim for uncompensated costs under a modification, even though it did not include an express demand, because all the facts relevant to the equitable adjustment were incorporated within the facts of the termination claim.

Contract claims are not extinguished by the termination. A contractor whose work has been terminated for convenience may still submit a breach or other claim for costs independent of its termination settlement with the government as long as it follows the applicable jurisdictional requirements for submitting such a claim, such as requesting a final decision. See *Advanced Materials, Inc. v. United States*, 46 Fed. Cl. 697 (2000), holding, however, that the contractor's failure to submit its breach of contract claim to the contracting officer for a final decision meant that the court did not have jurisdiction over the breach claim. See also *Raytheon Co.,* ASBCA 50166, 01-1 BCA ¶ 31,245, *aff'd in part & remanded in part,* 305 F.3d 1354 (Fed. Cir. 2002), holding that, after a termination for convenience, the contractor was entitled to an equitable adjustment for the government's misrepresentation of the condition of the technical data package and for its failure to disclose its superior knowledge with respect to that condition.

Pursuant to 28 U.S.C. § 1491(b), the Court of Federal Claims possesses jurisdiction over claims relating to the government's obligations in the contract formation process. However, this jurisdiction does not extend to decisions to terminate for convenience in order to comply with these obligations, *Davis/HRGM Joint Venture v. United States*, 50 Fed. Cl. 539 (2001). The court held that such claims are more appropriately brought under the Contract Disputes Act. See also *Writing Co. v. Department of the Treasury*, GSBCA 15097-TD, 00-1 BCA ¶ 30,840, *recons. denied,* 00-1 BCA ¶ 30,863, denying jurisdiction of a contractor's letter seeking broad relief including relief from a convenience termination. The board reasoned that a termination for convenience decision "is not in and of itself an appealable contracting officer's decision."

B. Nature and Amount of Settlements

FAR 49.201(a) makes "fair compensation" the guiding principle for termination settlements for fixed-price contracts. The concept of fair compensation and the inconsistent FAR provisions implementing it has resulted in considerable confusion concerning the application of the cost principles to termination settlements. This subsection discusses the principles involved in fairly compensating the terminated contractor and analyzes the applicability of the termination cost principle, FAR 31.205-42.

1. Basic Principles

Perhaps the major impact of the termination for convenience procedure is that it relieves the government of the obligation of paying anticipated profits for unperformed work if it terminates the contractor's performance of the work, *Dairy Sales Corp. v. United States,* 219 Ct. Cl. 431, 593 F.2d 1002 (1979). The result is that the contractor's recovery under a convenience termination is based on incurred costs plus some reasonable amount of profit on those incurred costs. In fact, it has been stated that the effect of a termination for convenience is to convert a fixed-price contract into a cost-reimbursement contract as to the work performed up to the effective date of the termination, *Southland Mfg. Corp.*, ASBCA 16830, 75-1 BCA ¶ 10,994, *recons. denied,* 75-1 BCA ¶ 11,272; *International Space Corp.*, ASBCA 13883, 70-2 BCA ¶ 8519. If the contractor has incurred no cost, there is no recovery. Allowable costs incurred, plus profit, will be recovered, subject to the overall limitation of the contract price and the possible application of the loss adjustment provisions. The contractor's recovery is thus measured by the costs recovered rather than the value of the performance to the government. See *Fil-Coil Co.*, ASBCA 23137, 79-1 BCA ¶ 13,618, *recons. denied*, 79-1 BCA ¶ 13,683, where the amounts the contractor paid its employees, rather than the value of the services they rendered, were the proper measure of recovery. Conversely, the government may not use the value of the work completed to avoid reimbursing the contractor's allowable costs, *Scope Elecs., Inc.,* ASBCA 20359, 77-1 BCA ¶ 12,404, *recons. denied,* 77-2 BCA ¶ 12,586; *Arnold H. Leibowitz,* GSBCA CCR-1, 76-2 BCA ¶ 11,930.

The termination for convenience clauses have been held to preclude recovery of "consequential damages." See *Aerdco, Inc.*, GSBCA 3776, 77-2 BCA ¶ 12,775, *recons. denied,* 78-1 BCA ¶ 12,926, in which the board stated that "contractual limitations on cost recovery" prevent a contractor from recovering for the cost of bankruptcy, the loss of existing business to the company, and its loss of future profits. In *H & J Constr. Co.*, ASBCA 18521, 75-1 BCA ¶ 11,171, *recons. denied,* 76-1 BCA ¶ 11,903, the board also refused to grant recovery to the contractor for any of its damage claims, which included an alleged loss of 13 future contracts, damages to the company's standing and reputation, impairment of the company's credit, and loss of production. See also *William Green Constr. Co. v. United States*, 201 Ct. Cl. 616, 477 F.2d 930, *cert. denied*, 417 U.S. 909 (1973).

2. Recoverable Costs

The Termination for Convenience clauses state that all costs claimed or agreed to shall be in accordance with the applicable contract cost principles in Part 31 of the FAR. The cost principles determine which costs are allowable and which are not. They contain extensive allowability rules as well as specific rules for costs likely to be involved in termination claims. The general allowability rules are discussed here only to the extent that recurring termination cost problems are involved. The specific termination cost principle, FAR 31.205-42, is analyzed in detail. See Cibinic and Nash, *Cost-Reimbursement Contracting* (3d ed. 2004) for a discussion of the cost principles and general applicability. Cost principles substantially identical to those in the FAR were contained in FPR, Part 1-15 and DAR, Section XV.

Proceedings before the board to determine the amount of the settlement following a convenience termination are wholly de novo (i.e., the findings in the contracting officer's final decision are given no weight), *Stanley Aviation, Inc.*, ASBCA 49932, 97-1 BCA ¶ 28,764. The contractor has the burden of establishing the amount of incurred costs, and, in the absence of evidence to the contrary, the contracting officer's termination allowance will be accepted, *Roberts Int'l Corp.,* ASBCA 15118, 71-1 BCA ¶ 8869. See also *Delaware Tool & Die Works, Inc.,* ASBCA 14033, 71-1 BCA ¶ 8860, *recons. denied,* 72-1 BCA ¶ 9206, where the contractor had no proof of the costs incurred in the terminated portion of the work. It is preferable to establish incurred costs from accounting records.

Although a contractor generally may recover the costs incurred in the performance of terminated work, including initial costs and preparatory work allocable thereto, the contractor bears the burden of establishing the claimed cost with sufficient certainty so that the determination of liability will be more than mere speculation. In *James Greer,* ENGBCA 6283, 97-2 BCA ¶ 29,013, a terminated contractor was unable to convince the board that it was entitled to additional recovery where there was no support for its claims. In *Nomura Enter., Inc.*, ASBCA 51456, 99-2 BCA ¶ 30,441, the contractor contended that damages should be determined according to the formula set forth in *C.F.S. Air Cargo, Inc.*, ASBCA 36113, 91-1 BCA ¶ 23,583, which relied on estimated annual costs for the deleted work. However, because specific cost information was available, it was not necessary to rely on estimates to determine the amount recoverable. On the other hand, if accounting records are not available, due to no fault of the contractor, the costs may be established on the basis of estimates, FAR 49.206-1(c); *Bailey Specialized Bldgs., Inc.*, ASBCA 10576, 71-1 BCA ¶ 8699.

Even if estimates are used, the contractor still has the burden of proof. See *Clary Corp.,* ASBCA 19274, 74-2 BCA ¶ 10,947, in which the board stated that, although the burden need not be met through the use of accounting records, it cannot be carried by unsupported allegations. See also *R.G. Robbins & Co.,* ASBCA 27516, 83-1 BCA ¶ 16,420 (disallowing claim for G&A recovery not supported by cost data or accounting testimony). In *Mediax Interactive Techs., Inc.*, ASBCA 43961, 99-1 BCA ¶ 30,318, *recons. denied,* 99-2 BCA ¶ 30,453, the contract was terminated in 1983, and the contractor relied on computer-generated listings of costs to support its claim. When the claimed costs were audited in 1996, the contractor was out of business and the controls on its former computer system could not be validated. The board found that, to the extent the contractor relied on computerized reports and after-the-fact narratives, its proof was insufficient. A contractor that expended time and money in obtaining a requirements contract, preparing its business to fulfill the contract, and completing compliant first articles was entitled to recover its initial costs following the convenience termination of a contract because the amount of time the contractor expended was within the range of reasonableness. Although the hours could seem excessive for particular efforts, the contractor met its burden of establishing that its president, chief financial officer, and general manager expended the time indicated. The government's determinations to reduce the claimed hours were not reasonably supported by the record, *Teems, Inc. v. General Servs. Admin.*, GSBCA 14090, 98-1 BCA ¶ 29,357.

The application of the cost principles to termination settlement claims is the subject of confusing FAR provisions. FAR 49.113 states that cost principles in Part 31 are to be used in determining termination settlement costs "subject to the general principles in 49.201." However, FAR 49.201 indicates that strict application of the cost principles is not necessary, stating:

> (a) A settlement should compensate the contractor fairly for the work done and the preparations made for the terminated portions of the contract, including a reasonable allowance for profit. Fair compensation is a matter of judgment and cannot be measured exactly. In a given case, various methods may be equally appropriate for arriving at fair compensation. The use of business judgment, as distinguished from strict accounting principles, is the heart of a settlement.
>
> (b) The primary objective is to negotiate a settlement by agreement. The parties may agree upon a total amount to be paid the contractor without agreeing on or segregating the particular elements of costs or profit comprising this amount.
>
> (c) Cost and accounting data may provide guides, but are not rigid measures, for ascertaining fair compensation. In appropriate cases, costs may be estimated, differences compromised, and doubtful questions settled by agreement. Other types of data, criteria, or standards may furnish equally reliable guides to fair compensation. The amount of recordkeeping, reporting, and accounting related to the settlement of terminated contracts should be kept to a minimum compatible with the reasonable protection of the public interest.

Additional uncertainty is created by FAR 49.303-5(d), which states:

> If an overall settlement of costs is agreed upon, agreement on each element of cost is not necessary. If appropriate, differences may be compromised and doubtful questions settled by agreement. An overall settlement shall not include costs that are clearly not allowable under the terms of the contract.

The cases are not very helpful in clarifying these confusing provisions. In *Codex Corp.*, ASBCA 17983, 74-2 BCA ¶ 10,827, *recons. denied*, 75-2 BCA ¶ 11,554, *remanded*, 226 Ct. Cl. 693 (1981), which involved essentially the same language in predecessor regulations, the contractor had argued that the cost principles should not be applied in a termination settlement to disallow costs. In this case, the contract was awarded March 25, 1971, with an effective date of April 2, 1971. It was terminated on April 15, 1971, before any deliveries were made. Practically all costs claimed by the contractor were incurred between September 1968 and February 1970 in developing and producing the items that were the subject of the contract. In denying the costs, the board found that they did not come within allowable pre-contract costs under DAR 15-205.30 since they were not incurred directly pursuant to the negotiation of the contract and there was no evidence that they were necessary in order to meet the proposed delivery schedule. The board also held that the costs did not qualify under the initial costs and preparatory expense provisions of DAR 15-205.42. On appeal, the Court of Claims trial judge reversed, concluding that ASPR 8-301 (similar to FAR 49.201) "identifies fundamental fairness as the overriding criterion in the formulation of appropriate terms for the settlement of a convenience termination of a fixed-price contract." The Court of Claims refused to adopt the trial judge's holding but did remand the case to the Armed Services Board, stating at 698-99:

> The proper reconciliation of the strict standard of allowable costs in section 15.205-30 and the fairness concept in section 8.301 is a matter primarily within the discretion of the Board of Contract Appeals. The Board did not decide the question. In its opinion on reconsideration, it stated that it "expresses no opinion as to whether the disputed costs concerned in this appeal would or would not be allowable as a part of the termination settlement if allowability were to be governed by paragraph 8.301." 75-2 BCA ¶ 11,554, pp. 55,149-50. Our holding is not that section 8.301 governs the [contractor's] claim for the field case costs, but that the application of the cost principles in part 2 of section 15 to that claim must be made "subject to the general policies set forth" in section 8.301.
>
> Accordingly, we shall remand the case to the Board of Contract Appeals to make that determination.

There was no decision on remand because the case was settled.

See, however, *Bennie J. Meeks,* GSBCA 6605-REM, 85-2 BCA ¶ 17,947, which involved costs of training employees to perform planting services undertaken prior to receipt of notice of award. The board initially found that it was unreasonable for the contractor to have trained its employees before receiving a notice to proceed since there would have been sufficient time to conduct the training after receipt of the notice. On remand, however, the board allowed the training costs, finding the contractor's actions in hiring and training employees reasonable under the circumstances. The board stated at 89,923:

> After bid opening, when [the contractor] knew that he was low bidder and would be awarded the contract, he was "on the hook." The Government could accept his offer at any time, and he could not withdraw it. . . . The costs he incurred in hiring, training, and keeping a group of workmen on a standby basis were legitimately a part of his gearing-up effort, and he would not have incurred them except in anticipation of performing the subject contract.

The board noted that its conclusion was consistent with the Termination for Convenience clause in the contract and with FPR 1-8.301(a), which provided (in language similar to FAR 49.201(a)) that "[a] settlement should compensate the contractor fairly for . . . the preparations made for the terminated portions of the contract."

In *General Elec. Co.*, ASBCA 24111, 82-1 BCA ¶ 15,725, *recons. denied*, 83-1 BCA ¶ 16,207, the board relied on *Codex* in holding that the contractor could recover certain post-termination costs, including employee retraining expenses and depreciation on idle equipment, that were subject to question under a strict application of the cost principles. In *Kasler Elec. Co.*, DOTCAB 1425, 84-2 BCA ¶ 17,374, the board went even further, permitting the contractor to recover clearly unallowable bid and proposal costs in a termination settlement because it was deprived of the opportunity of amortizing them out of "expected overhead and profit recovery." In including the costs in the settlement, the board stated at 86,566:

> [W]hen applied to a termination for convenience settlement, the cost principles of Part 1-15 are general principles only, not of mandatory application in all cases to the extent they would be in administering an ongoing cost reimbursement contract.
>
> The gist of § 1-8.301 is clear: a fair compensation is the goal, within the *general* parameters of the cost guidelines.

See also *General Dynamics Land Sys., Inc.*, ASBCA 52283, 02-1 BCA ¶ 31,659, holding that a termination settlement between a contractor and its subcontractor should be recognized because (1) in a termination for convenience, the board has discretion to reconcile basic fairness with the strict application of accounting principles (citing *Codex*); (2) recovery for loss of useful value of STE is not limited to the amount that was included in the price (citing *American Elec.*, ASBCA 16635, 76-2 BCA ¶ 12,151, *modified in part on recons.*, 77-2 BCA ¶ 12,792); and (3) the subcontractor settlement was competently entered into at arm's length at an amount significantly less than the subcontractor might have obtained in litigation (citing *General Elec. Co.*, ASBCA 24111, 82-1 BCA ¶ 15,725, *recons. denied,* 83-1 BCA ¶ 16,207). Thus, while the cases do not provide clear guidance on the applicability of the cost principles in termination settlements, it is clear that FAR 49.201 grants latitude to contracting officers and tribunals in this area, and this latitude should be used appropriately.

One major limitation on costs recoverable in a termination settlement is that the costs must be incurred in performing work authorized by the contract. Thus, in *Derrick Elec. Co.*, ASBCA 21246, 77-2 BCA ¶ 12,643, *motion for new hearing denied*, 78-1 BCA ¶ 12,942, the contractor was denied recovery for costs incurred in performing work in accordance with an unapproved value engineering proposal under a Value Engineering Incentive clause. A similar result is obtained where the work is covered by the contract but the contractor has not been authorized to proceed with the work. Construction contracts often provide that a contractor shall not proceed with on-site work until a notice to proceed has been given by the contracting officer. In such cases, on-site costs incurred prior to the notice are not recoverable in the termination settlement, *Sherkade Constr. Corp.*, DOTCAB 68-29, 68-2 BCA ¶ 7365.

Work authorization problems also occur frequently in contracts containing first article approval clauses. The clauses contained at FAR 52.209-3 and -4 specifically provide that the costs of proceeding with production incurred before first article approval "shall not be allocable to this contract for . . . termination settlements." Identical language was contained in the clauses at DAR 7-104.55. This provision was enforced in *Semco, Inc. v. United States*, 6 Cl. Ct. 81 (1984). However, for an exception to this rule, see *Switlik Parachute Co.*, ASBCA 18024, 75-2 BCA ¶ 11,434, in which the board acknowledged that "a contractor is not bound by this risk provision when it would be impossible to wait until first article approval before ordering production materials, and still to meet the delivery schedule."

Following a convenience termination, compensation for completed work pursuant to a work order was not to be calculated using the full dollar amount of the work order because the contractor previously received a $50,000 progress payment for that work. The contractor was only entitled to the amount sought in its second progress payment request, which had never been paid. The government was entitled to receive a credit for work left incomplete. *D.L. Kaufman, Inc.*, PSBCA 4159, 00-1 BCA ¶ 30,846.

a. Common Items

FAR 31.205-42(a) provides as follows:

> *Common items.* The costs of items reasonably usable on the contractor's other work shall not be allowable unless the contractor submits evidence that the items could not be retained at cost without sustaining a loss. The contracting officer should consider the contractor's plans and orders for current and planned production when determining if items can reasonably be used on other work of the contractor. Contemporaneous purchases of common items by the contractor shall

> be regarded as evidence that such items are reasonably usable on the contractor's other work. Any acceptance of common items as allocable to the terminated portion of the contract should be limited to the extent that the quantities of such items on hand, in transit, and on order are in excess of the reasonable quantitative requirements of other work.

This cost principle requires that the costs of common items—those that are reasonably usable on the contractor's other work—be excluded from the settlement. The common item exclusion applies only to items that are usable by the contractor on other work, not to items that simply are commonly used in the industry. See *American Packers, Inc.*, ASBCA 14275, 71-1 BCA ¶ 8846, rejecting applicability of this principle where the terminated contract was the contractor's only use for the material and the only realizable value of the inventory was resale at secondhand prices. In *Essex Electro Eng'rs, Inc.*, DOTCAB 1025, 81-1 BCA ¶ 14,838, *recons. denied*, 81-1 BCA ¶ 15,109, *aff'd*, 702 F.2d 998 (Fed. Cir. 1983), assorted motor generators and electric parts of the same type needed to perform ongoing government contracts were held not to be "common items" since the contractor had already purchased other materials for use in connection with this ongoing work. In *Fiesta Leasing & Sales, Inc.*, ASBCA 29311, 87-1 BCA ¶ 19,622, the board stated at 73,250:

> The respective burdens placed upon the parties relative to establishing the proper classification of residual equipment is very clearly laid out above in FPR 1-15.205-42(a). As an initial proposition, the contractor must go forward with evidence to demonstrate it could not retain the equipment at cost for use on other work without sustaining a loss. Once this is done, the burden shifts to the Contracting Officer to show that there has been an evaluation of the contractor's current and scheduled work plans, orders and supplies to determine if such residual equipment is in fact reasonably usable by the contractor or in excess of the latter's reasonable needs. The extent to which these requirements are met determines the proper classification of residual equipment.

DCAAM (Defense Contract Audit Agency Manual) 12-304.5(b) suggests that an auditor can determine whether inventory items are properly classified as common items:

> In determining whether common items are reasonably usable by the contractor on other work, review the contractor's plans and orders for current/scheduled production and for current purchases of common items. Also determine whether the contractor properly classified inventory items as common items. Do this by reviewing stock records to see if the items are being used for other work and by reviewing bills of material and procurement scheduled for products similar to those included in the termination inventory. Limit acceptance of common items as part of termination inventory to the quantities on hand, in transit, and on order which exceed reasonable quantities required by the contractor for work on other than the terminated contract. In determining whether the inventory contains common items, the contractor should first assign total available quantity (inventory on-hand, in transit, and on order) to continuing or anticipated government or commercial production and assign the remainder, if any, to the terminated contract.

> The contractor, therefore, should assign to the terminated contract (1) the least processed inventory, and (2) those purchase commitments that result in the least cost when terminated.

The auditor may also examine "nonstandard" stock items. DCAAM 12-304.5(c) provides that, under certain circumstances, even "complex or specialized items may qualify as common items." For instance, the DCAAM states that "the compressor unit of a military jet engine might qualify as a common item if the contractor also uses the unit in commercial jet engine production."

The boards have also applied the common items analysis to productive assets used in contract work. These costs would more properly be dealt with under the principle covering loss of value of assets. See *Fiesta Leasing & Sales, Inc.,* ASBCA 29311, 87-1 BCA ¶ 19,622, *modified as recons., (decision as to quantum modified),* 88-1 BCA ¶ 20,499 (buses usable in contractor's daily rental business); *Metered Laundry Servs.,* ASBCA 21573, 78-1 BCA ¶ 13,206, *modified on recons.*, 78-2 BCA ¶ 13,451 (washers and dryers used in contract to provide automatic laundry); *Globe Air, Inc.*, AGBCA 76-119, 78-1 BCA ¶ 13,079 (helicopter provided under helicopter rental contract); and *American Packers, Inc.*, ASBCA 14275, 71-1 BCA ¶ 8846 (pickup trucks usable under contract for packing and hauling household goods).

In *Symetrics Indus., Inc.,* ASBCA 48529, 96-2 BCA ¶ 28,285, the contractor could not recover for common items when it failed to prove that the items would be retained at a loss.

b. Costs Continuing After Termination

FAR 31.205-42(b) provides the following broad guidance on costs that continue after termination:

> *Costs continuing after termination.* Despite all reasonable efforts by the contractor, costs which cannot be discontinued immediately after the effective date of termination are generally allowable. However, any costs continuing after the effective date of the termination due to the negligent or willful failure of the contractor to discontinue the costs shall be unallowable.

DCAAM 12-305.7(a)(1) provides the following coverage concerning costs continuing after termination:

> Reasonable costs associated with termination activities are allowable. FAR 31.205-42(b) recognizes there may be instances where costs incurred after termination may be allowable. For example, the contractor may have contract personnel at a remote or foreign location or there may be personnel in transit to or from these sites. The cost of their salaries or wages would be allocable to the terminated contract for a reasonable period required to transfer the personnel to sites for termination or used on the contractor's other work. In another example,

> components or end items may be in a heat-treating or electroplating process when termination occurs and the contractor may elect to complete rather than disrupt the process and risk complete loss of the items.

Costs continuing after termination are often associated with a contractor's facilities, such as contractor-owned and contractor-leased buildings, machinery, and equipment. Recovery for the loss of useful value of facilities is covered in FAR 31.205-42(d), and rental costs under unexpired leases are dealt with in FAR 31.205-42(e).

To be recovered, costs continuing after the termination must have been incurred as a result of performing the terminated work or must flow from the termination, *Aviation Specialists, Inc.*, DOTBCA 1967, 91-1 BCA ¶ 23,534. There, the government terminated for convenience a requirements contract involving the use of one aircraft by the Federal Aviation Administration. After the termination, the contractor made efforts to sell the plane but was unable to dispose of it for 18 months. As a result, the contractor incurred additional costs in retaining the aircraft. In its settlement proposal, the contractor sought reimbursement for the following costs continuing after termination: depreciation, insurance, maintenance costs, cost of facilities capital, overhead, advertising, general and administrative expenses, and profit. In the settlement proposal the contractor also included a credit for profit earned on commercial leasing of the plane during that period. The board held for the contractor, stating that these incurred costs could not be reasonably discontinued immediately following the termination. The contractor could recover such costs up to the estimated contract price. This case is distinguished from *Chamberlain Mfg. Corp.*, ASBCA 16877, 73-2 BCA ¶ 10,139, in that the costs claimed in *Aviation Specialists* were incurred as a direct result of obligations the contractor undertook to perform the contract, whereas in *Chamberlain,* which involved a manufacturing contract, the claimed post-termination overhead costs were neither incurred as a result of the work performed on the contract nor generated directly by the termination action.

Many of the costs continuing after a termination are normally charged as indirect expenses by the contractor. In a termination, such charges may be allowable as direct costs if separately identified and properly justified. This does not violate CAS 402, which requires consistency in treatment of like costs incurred for like purposes. Reclassified costs, however, must be withdrawn from their former indirect cost pools to avoid double billing.

A contractor bears the cost of employees retained subsequent to a termination if they are not required to wind up work on the terminated contract. In *Engineered Sys., Inc.,* ASBCA 18241, 74-1 BCA ¶ 10,492, the board found that costs resulting from a decision to retain key employees were not incurred incidental to the work but related to future work of the contractor. The contractor must also demonstrate a reasonable effort to discontinue the costs. In this respect, salaries for retained employees are not recoverable if the contractor has no binding agreement with the employees and they are available for other work of the contractor, *Globe Air, Inc.*,

AGBCA 76-119, 78-1 BCA ¶ 13,079. Further, a contractor's "moral obligation" to retain employees has been held insufficient to support recovery for their retention, *Kay & Assocs., Inc.,* GSBCA TD-17, 76-2 BCA ¶ 12,127. Severance payments to employees terminated as the result of a convenience termination may be recoverable provided the contractor makes the payment as part of an established company policy or an employer-employee agreement in existence at the time of the termination, *Columbia Univ.*, ASBCA 15578, 73-1 BCA ¶ 9777. See also *System Dev. Corp.,* ASBCA 16947, 73-1 BCA ¶ 9788, in which the board found mass severance costs supported by company policy and therefore allowable.

The contractor's reasonable business judgment will be the criterion used to determine the length of the period for reimbursement after termination. In *Baifield Indus. Div. of A-T-O, Inc.*, ASBCA 20006, 76-2 BCA ¶ 12,096, *recons. denied*, 76-2 BCA ¶ 12,203, the contractor was permitted to recover continuing costs, despite having passed up earlier opportunities to dispose of the items, because its attempts to get higher prices for the items were reasonable. The board stated at 58,092 that, in determining allowability of continuing costs, there must be "a clear connection between the costs claimed and the terminated contract and, further, that those costs could not have been reasonably shut off upon the termination." In some cases, the continuing costs may be the subject of express agreements between the parties. See *ITT Fed. Support Servs., Inc. v. United States,* 209 Ct. Cl. 157, 531 F.2d 522 (1976), dealing with post-termination management of a pension fund.

c. Initial Costs

FAR 31.205-42 contains the following guidance concerning recovery of initial costs:

> (c) *Initial Costs*. Initial costs [see 15.804-6(f)], including starting load and preparatory costs, are allowable as follows:
>
> > (1) Starting load costs not fully absorbed because of termination are nonrecurring labor, material, and related overhead costs incurred in the early part of production and result from factors such as—
> >
> > > (i) Excessive spoilage due to inexperienced labor;
> > >
> > > (ii) Idle time and subnormal production due to testing and changing production methods;
> > >
> > > (iii) Training; and
> > >
> > > (iv) Lack of familiarity or experience with the product, materials, or manufacturing processes.
> >
> > (2) Preparatory costs incurred in preparing to perform the terminated contract include such costs as those incurred for initial plant rearrangement

> and alterations, management and personnel organization, and production planning. They do not include special machinery and equipment and starting load costs.
>
> (3) When initial costs are included in the settlement proposal as a direct charge, such costs shall not also be included in overhead. Initial costs attributable to only one contract shall not be allocated to other contracts.
>
> (4) If initial costs are claimed and have not been segregated on the contractor's books, they shall be segregated for settlement purposes from cost reports and schedules reflecting that high unit cost incurred during the early stages of the contract.
>
> (5) If the settlement proposal is on the inventory basis, initial costs should normally be allocated on the basis of total end items called for by the contract immediately before termination; however, if the contract includes end items of a diverse nature, some other equitable basis may be used, such as machine or labor hours.

The consideration of initial and preparatory costs in termination settlements has caused considerable confusion. The termination clauses provide that the contractor is to be paid the contract price for "completed supplies or services accepted by the Government." This creates a problem where the contractor has allocated nonrecurring costs to both accepted and terminated items or where the accepted and terminated items are priced the same even though the accepted items may actually have cost more to produce than the terminated items would have cost. This problem is dealt with in either of two ways. When the termination is considered a partial termination, the clause provides that the price of the unterminated items may be equitably adjusted. If the termination is not considered a partial termination, a fair result may be achieved by allocating initial and preparatory costs to the termination settlement. Both of these methods appear to yield the same result, and it appears that they are sometimes used interchangeably. See *Dunbar Kapple, Inc.,* ASBCA 3631, 57-2 BCA ¶ 1448. But compare *Sternberger v. United States,* 185 Ct. Cl. 528, 401 F.2d 1012 (1968). Care must be taken that double recovery does not result when both methods are applied to the same termination, *Elastic Stop Nut Co. v. United States,* 126 Ct. Cl. 100 (1953).

There is not much conceptual difficulty in allowing the contractor to recover such nonrecurring costs as engineering, tooling, employee training, and plant rearrangement, as it is obvious that these expenditures were made for both the terminated and unterminated work. The contractor has even been permitted to recover these expenses as direct charges to the termination settlement although they were initially treated as overhead expense, *Condec Corp.,* ASBCA 14234, 73-1 BCA ¶ 9808. There is greater difficulty when the actual costs recorded for producing the unterminated items include labor charges that are higher than those that would have been incurred in producing the terminated items. In allocating such costs to the termination settlement, contractors often use learning curves to establish the average unit cost of the total contract quantity and then request, as initial costs, the difference between that amount and the average unit cost of completed units. This has led to objections by the government on the basis that labor inefficiencies and other factors that result in higher costs of producing earlier units are not "nonrecurring" costs as stated in the termination cost principle for initial costs. Further, the government has argued that, since the costs were incurred in actually producing the accepted items, they cannot be properly considered costs allocable to the terminated items. In *Lockley Mfg. Co.,* ASBCA 21231, 78-1 BCA ¶ 12,987, the board granted the contractor recovery and explained at 63,319:

> A contractor bidding a fixed price per unit of work for a number of units must include in that fixed unit price all the costs of all the units knowing all the while that the cost experienced during the manufacture of the earlier units will be greater than on the later units. Therefore, lest the contractor is to lose the portion of such costs as yet unrecovered through the price paid for delivered items, it must be permitted to recover it as part of the cost of terminated work.

In *Celesco Indus., Inc.*, ASBCA 21928, 81-2 BCA ¶ 15,260, the contractor was permitted to recover "unamortized labor costs" on the unterminated portion of the production work through application of a learning curve approach, but the board excluded from such recovery an amount attributable to a "prolonged 'abnormal' production phase" experienced by the contractor. The board reached this result without specifically indicating that the costs attributable to the abnormal production phase were "unreasonable." In *VHC, Inc. v. Peters*, 179 F.3d 1363 (Fed. Cir. 1999), the court held that recovery of unamortized labor learning costs is not "automatically prohibited where the original contract pricing was not level." Equitable adjustments for unamortized labor learning costs are a legitimate form of recovery after a partial termination for convenience where the contractor loses the opportunity to amortize the increased early labor costs over the original life of the contract.

Pre-contract costs, except bid and proposal costs, are recoverable when incurred in anticipation of award to meet the contract delivery schedule, *Orbas & Assocs.*, ASBCA 50467, 97-2 BCA ¶ 29,107, but such costs are not recoverable if they are not needed to meet the delivery schedule, *Aislamientos y Construcciones Apache S. A.,* ASBCA 45437, 97-1 BCA ¶ 28,632. Start-up costs excluding bid and proposal preparation costs incurred prior to the formal contract award have been awarded a contractor following a termination for convenience where the contractor showed that it reasonably believed the project was urgent, *Barsh Co.*, PSBCA 4481, 00-2 BCA ¶ 30,917.

A contractor was entitled to a portion of its costs to move to a larger facility in order to perform a contract because the contractor established that the larger facilities required by the contract precipitated the move. The contractor, however, did not justify its allocation rate, so a percentage based on burden rates calculated by the contractor was utilized to determine the amount allocable, *Teems, Inc. v. General Servs. Admin.*, GSBCA 14090, 98-1 BCA ¶ 29,357. The termination cost principle for initial costs has also been used to award the costs of setting up a plant to perform the terminated contract. See *Inland Container, Inc. v. United States*, 206 Ct. Cl. 478, 512 F.2d 1073 (1975). It is questionable whether this was a proper application of this cost principle because, since the entire contract was terminated before any work was ordered or performed, there was no need to allocate costs between completed and terminated work.

d. Loss of Value of Assets

FAR 31.205-42 contains the following provision on loss of useful value of assets:

> (d) *Loss of useful value.* Loss of useful value of special tooling, and special machinery and equipment is generally allowable, provided—
>
> > (1) The special tooling, or special machinery and equipment is not reasonably capable of use in the other work of the contractor;
> >
> > (2) The Government's interest is protected by transfer of title or by other means deemed appropriate by the contracting officer; and
> >
> > (3) The loss of useful value for any one terminated contract is limited to that portion of the acquisition cost which bears the same ratio to the total acquisition cost as the terminated portion of the contract bears to the entire terminated contract and other Government contracts for which the special tooling, or special machinery and equipment was acquired.

FPR 1-8.101(t) and DAR 8-101.21 contained a definition of special machinery and equipment that included the requirement that the asset be acquired "solely" for the performance of the terminated contract. This definition is omitted from the FAR, with the result that there is less guidance in this area in the current regulation.

Contractors often acquire productive assets for the performance of a specific contract or group of contracts in anticipation of receiving sufficient revenue from the performance of the contracts to cover the cost of the assets. So long as the contract is a fixed-price contract and its performance is completed, the contractor's expectation will be realized. Whether this expectation will be met where the contract is terminated for convenience depends on the cost allowability rules. If the asset meets the tests for special tooling and special test equipment in FAR 45.101, it is clear that the entire cost of the asset must be charged to the contract or contracts and will be recovered as a part of the termination settlement. If the asset does not meet the FAR 45.101 definition of special tooling or special test equipment, a portion of its costs may still be recovered if it can be classified as "special machinery and equipment." If, on the other hand, the asset is considered to be a general purpose asset for which the contractor has other uses, the only appropriate charge to the termination settlement is depreciation on the asset for the period during which it was used on the terminated contract, *Dairy Sales Corp. v. United States*, 219 Ct. Cl. 431, 593 F.2d 1002 (1979).

In *American Elec., Inc.*, ASBCA 16635, 76-2 BCA ¶ 12,151, *modified on other grounds*, 77-2 BCA ¶ 12,792, the board determined that equipment that could not be used by the contractor on other work was properly characterized as "special machinery and equipment" even though other contractors could have used the machinery for other purposes. See also *Southland Mfg. Corp.*, ASBCA 16830, 75-1 BCA ¶ 10,994, *recons. denied*, 75-1 BCA ¶ 11,272. In *Tubergen & Assocs., Inc.*, ASBCA 34106, 90-3 BCA ¶ 23,058, the board determined that a braiding machine was special machinery where it was acquired solely for the performance of the contract and was not used after termination. The board concluded that the contractor was entitled to the loss of the useful value of the braiding machine but because there was no evidence as to its useful value, remanded the issue for determination in accordance with DAR 15-205.42(d). See *Celesco Indus., Inc.*, ASBCA 22460, 84-2 BCA ¶ 17,295, where specially adapted equipment was treated as general purpose equipment because the contractor had capitalized it, intending to use it for other work, and *General Dynamics Land Sys., Inc.* ASBCA 52283, 02-1 BCA ¶ 31,659, where a subcontractor's special test equipment fabrication costs were allowable because the subcontract specifically contemplated the fabrication. Although the record did not support a conclusion that a lathe was special tooling under regulatory definitions, a contractor was entitled to fair and reasonable recovery of lathe costs because it would have recouped some of the lathe costs incurred to perform the contract had the contract not been terminated, *Teems, Inc. v. General Servs. Admin.*, GSBCA 14090, 98-1 BCA ¶ 29,357.

The contractor's intention when the equipment was acquired may operate to deny recovery. In *Contract Maint., Inc.*, ASBCA 20689, 77-1 BCA ¶ 12,446, there was no recovery since the items were standard equipment used or made available for use in another contract and were written off in full. See also *Metered Laundry Servs.*, ASBCA 21573, 78-1 BCA ¶ 13,206, *modified on recons.*, 78-2 BCA ¶ 13,451, in which the contractor recovered the loss of value on some equipment but was denied recovery on other equipment because the sale price was not unreasonably low and the loss was less than depreciation for the period that the items were used. In *Manual M. Liodas*, ASBCA 12829, 71-2 BCA ¶ 9015, *recons. denied*, 71-2 BCA ¶ 9120, the board reduced the contractor's allowance by 50 percent because the government's interest had not been sufficiently protected. The contractor had obtained only an exclusive right to use the tooling; title was retained by a subcontractor.

Costs of special equipment to be used for developing microwave technology in anticipation of the government's exercise of an option, but not necessary in performance of the existing contract, were unallowable in a termination settlement, as were the costs of renting and adapting rental premises to accommodate the equipment, *Energy Compression Research Corp.*, ASBCA 46560, 99-2 BCA ¶ 30,564.

A contractor may recover reasonable standby or idle equipment costs following a termination for convenience, *Walsky Constr. Co.*, ASBCA 52772, 01-2 BCA ¶ 31,557.

e. Rental Costs

Rental costs under unexpired leases, less the residual value of such leases, are generally allowable when shown to have been reasonably necessary for the performance of the terminated contract, FAR 31.205-42(e). The amount of rental costs claimed, however, must not exceed the "reasonable use value of the property leased for the period of the contract and such further period as may be reasonable." The contractor must also make "all reasonable efforts to terminate, assign, settle, or otherwise reduce the cost of such lease." In determining whether the rental was reasonably necessary for performance of the contract, as required by the cost principle, the facts and circumstances existing at the time of the decision to lease will be examined, *American Elec., Inc.*, ASBCA 16635, 76-2 BCA ¶ 12,151, *modified on other grounds*, 77-2 BCA ¶ 12,792. Although the cost principle does not require that the lease be made solely for the performance of the contract, it has been held that rent under leases entered into prior to the date of the contract and available for other uses of the contractor is not reimbursable, *Legislative Res., Inc.*, DCABOMBE-16-74, 76-2 BCA ¶ 11,951.

American Electric holds that what is a reasonable period of time is a question of fact and is based on the reasonable efforts of the contractor to reduce the lease costs. See also *Southland Mfg. Corp.*, ASBCA 16830, 75-1 BCA ¶ 10,994, *recons. denied*, 75-1 BCA ¶ 11,272, holding a period of 29 months following a default termination to be reasonable in view of the contractor's efforts and the existing circumstances. The period may extend beyond the contract completion date if reasonable, *Sundstrand Turbo v. United States*, 182 Ct. Cl. 31, 389 F.2d 406 (1968). Compare *Max S. Castle,* AGBCA 97-137-1, 00-1 BCA ¶ 30,871, *recons. denied,* 03-2 BCA ¶ 32,270 (contractor not entitled to recover costs incurred in remodeling a building for rental to the government because there was no evidence that the government had misled the lessor regarding the length of the lease term). See also *Information Sys. & Networks Corp.*, ASBCA 46119, 02-2 BCA ¶ 31,952 (continuing costs after a termination for convenience were allowable because one-year leases for communication circuits were not unreasonable and gave the government significant cost savings over a monthly lease), and *Aviation Specialists Inc.*, DOTBCA 1967, 02-1 BCA ¶ 31,788 (costs of maintaining a leased aircraft after a convenience termination were recoverable because they were incurred as a direct result of obligations undertaken to perform the contract).

In *Manuel M. Liodas*, ASBCA 12829, 71-2 BCA ¶ 9015, *recons. denied*, 71-2 BCA ¶ 9120, the premises had been used for both the contract work and other work. Therefore, the board allowed the contractor to recover only a portion of the unexpired lease costs, measured by the ratio that the allowable G&A costs allocable to the terminated contract had to the total allowable G&A costs. In *American Electric*, the board deducted a credit for the use of facilities on other work after the termination.

The court limited rental costs for a facility owned by key employee's mother to ownership costs of facility transferred between entities under common control, *Advanced Materials, Inc. v. United States,* 54 Fed. Cl. 207 (2002).

In *Qualex Corp.*, ASBCA 41962, 93-1 BCA ¶ 25,517, the contractor had made the decision to lease space and equipment based on its expectations that the contract would be extended. The government subsequently terminated the contract for convenience. The contractor sought reimbursement of rental costs associated with the facility until its obligations under the lease were discharged or, alternatively, the amount allegedly saved because of the advantageous five-year lease it had obtained. The board rejected the contractor's first basis for reimbursement, stating that the contractor bore the risk, even if the risk was reasonable, for the augmented period. The board, however, found at 127,089:

> We conclude that the reasonable use value for the space during the contract period was the rental prescribed by the lease for that period, which was less than the amount incurred by [the contractor] over the life of the lease which resulted in the concessions. The Government enjoyed the benefit of the longer lease period by reimbursing [the contractor] only $6,421.50 monthly to reflect a credit for the rent-free 11 months granted by the lessor in consideration of the longer lease. Accordingly, we believe that fairness requires that [the contractor] receive the $45,277.14 it would have incurred and charged the Government for leasehold and parking facilities for the contract period in excess of the lower charges enjoyed under the longer lease—less any sublease payments which it received during that period.

The cost of alterations to leased property, when necessary for the performance of a contract, and the reasonable restoration required by the provisions of the lease are also allowable, FAR 31.205.42(f). However, unexpired lease costs should be adjusted by any residual value of the lease resulting from the termination, assignment, or settlement of the lease agreement, DCAAM 12-305.5(b).

f. Subcontract Claims

Detailed procedures for settling subcontractor termination claims are contained in FAR 49.108. FAR 31.205-42(h) gives the following guidance with regard to allowability of the costs of subcontractor claims:

> *Subcontractor claims.* Subcontractor claims, including the allocable portion of the claims common to the contract and to other work of the contractor, are generally allowable. An appropriate share of the contractor's indirect expense may be allocated to the amount of settlements with subcontractors; provided, that the amount allocated is reasonably proportionate to the relative benefits received and

> is otherwise consistent with 31.201-4 and 31.203(d). The indirect expense so allocated shall exclude the same and similar costs claimed directly or indirectly as settlement expenses.

The primary standard for allowability of the costs of settling subcontractor claims is reasonableness, *Bos'n Towing & Salvage Co.*, ASBCA 41357, 92-2 BCA ¶ 24,864. In deciding the reasonableness and prudence of such costs, the boards and courts will consider whether a contractor's settlement with its subcontractor was reached through an "arm's-length" transaction. In *General Elec. Co.*, ASBCA 24111, 82-1 BCA ¶ 15,725, *recons. denied*, 83-1 BCA ¶ 16,207, the board found reasonable a bottom-line subcontract termination settlement amount. The board stated at 77,806:

> [The] amount . . . was considered by the parties to be a fair and reasonable compromise price. We have found that the settlement amount was arrived at after arm's length bargaining, without collusion, and reflected a sound exercise of prudent judgment by [the prime contractor].

In *Bos'n Towing*, however, the board disallowed the contractor's claim for costs of terminating the charter of two tugs because it appeared that the contractor's settlement with the subcontractor was not an arm's-length transaction. The board stated that the contractor did not appear to be truly independent in its dealings with its subcontractor.

In *Information Sys. & Network Corp.*, ASBCA 42659, 00-1 BCA ¶ 30,665, *recons. denied,* 00-1 BCA ¶ 30,866, the board allowed recovery of legal fees in defense of a subcontractor claim in the convenience termination. In *Spectrum Leasing Corp. v. General Servs. Admin.*, GSBCA 12189, 95-1 BCA ¶ 27,317, the contractor was not allowed to recover the amount it had paid in settlement of the subcontractor's claim because the contractor's claim was barred by its agreement with the government on a modification that resulted in the termination of the subcontractor. The contractor should have anticipated the possibility that a claim might arise in the termination of the subcontractor and reserved its rights to recover costs it might incur under the subcontract as a result of the modification.

The termination clauses provide that a settlement proposal may include "the cost of settling and paying termination settlement proposals under terminated subcontracts." Substantially identical language in the DAR and FPR termination clauses had been interpreted to mean that the contractor must either have paid the subcontractor the amount of its claim or have reached a binding settlement agreement with the subcontractor, before the contractor can recover the amount of the subcontractor's claim, *Atlantic, Gulf & Pac. Co. of Manila, Inc.*, ASBCA 13533, 72-1 BCA ¶ 9415, *recons. denied*, 72-2 BCA ¶ 9698. However, the mere fact that the contractor and subcontractor have reached an agreement does not make the government liable to reimburse the contractor for the amount of the agreement. See *Aerojet Gen. Corp. v. United States*, 209 Ct. Cl. 750 (1976), in which the court refused to accept the contractor's allocation of the costs of three subcontracts to one subcontract and submission of the settlement of that subcontract termination under its contract settlement proposal. The trial judge's opinion, adopted by the court and contained in 22 CCF ¶ 80,022 (1976), notes that the government's obligation to reimburse for subcontractor settlements is dependent upon privity of contract, such that "the considerations between [the subcontractor and contractor] which justified their reconciliation of accounts on a single program basis would have to apply with equal force to the contractual relationship between [the contractor] and the Government in order to warrant imposition upon the Government."

Similarly, a judgment holding the contractor liable to the subcontractor does not entitle the contractor to recover the cost from the government unless the cost is allowable, *McDonnell Douglas Corp.*, NASABCA 467-13, 68-2 BCA ¶ 7316 (cost of subcontractor judgment for termination unallowable because contractor had not obtained approval of initial subcontract and price was unreasonable). However, where the contractor's actions in dealing with the subcontractor are reasonable, the subcontractor's judgment will support allowability, *Nolan Bros, Inc. v. United States*, 194 Ct. Cl. 1, 437 F.2d 1371 (1971). FAR 49.108-5 contains the following provisions directing the contracting officer to recognize judgments and arbitration awards:

> (a) When a subcontractor obtains a final judgment against a prime contractor, the TCO shall, for the purposes of settling the prime contract, treat the amount of the judgment as a cost of settling with the contractor, to the extent the judgment is properly allocable to the terminated portion of the prime contract, if—
>
> > (1) The prime contractor has made reasonable efforts to include in the subcontract a termination clause described in 49.502(e), 49.503(c), or a similar clause excluding payment of anticipatory profits or consequential damages;
> >
> > (2) The provisions of the subcontract relating to the rights of the parties upon its termination are fair and reasonable and do not unreasonably increase the common law rights of the subcontractor;
> >
> > (3) The contractor made reasonable efforts to settle the settlement proposal of the subcontractor;
> >
> > (4) The contractor gave prompt notice to the contracting officer of the initiation of the proceedings in which the judgment was rendered and did not refuse to give the Government control of the defense of the proceedings; and
> >
> > (5) The contractor diligently defended the suit or, if the Government assumed control of the defense of the proceedings, rendered reasonable assistance requested by the Government.
>
> (b) If the conditions in subparagraphs (a)(1) through (5) of this Section are not all met, the TCO may allow the contractor the part of the judgment considered fair

for settling the subcontract settlement proposal, giving due regard to the policies in this part for settlement of proposals.

(c) When a contractor and a subcontractor submit the subcontractor's settlement proposal to arbitration under any applicable law or contract provision, the TCO shall recognize the arbitration award as the cost of settling the proposal of the contractor to the same extent and under the same conditions as in paragraph (a) and (b) of this Section.

The amount of the subcontractor's recovery from the contractor will depend on the terms of the termination clause, if any, contained in the subcontract, *Dayton T. Brown, Inc. v. Republic Aviation Corp.*, 7 CCF ¶ 71,176 (D.C.N.Y. 1959); *General Steel Tank Co.*, ASBCA 7254, 61-2 BCA ¶ 3098. In this regard, FAR 49.108-2 suggests that for their own protection contractors should include termination clauses similar to those contained in FAR 52.249 in their subcontracts. See also FAR 49.502(e) and FAR 49.503(c). These clauses essentially give the subcontractor the same type of recovery that the contractor would receive from the government, most significantly excluding anticipated profits and consequential damages. FAR 49.108-5 further provides that reimbursement greater than the amount allowed under the contract clauses will be allowed only in unusual cases when the contracting officer is satisfied that "the terms of the subcontract did not unreasonably increase the rights of the subcontractor." These provisions are obviously aimed at preventing a contractor from assuming liability for anticipated profits on the theory that it would be able to pass on the subcontractor's claims to the government. However, if the subcontractor refuses to accept the termination clause and the contractor has made a good faith effort to include it, the subcontractor would be permitted to recover anticipated profits from the contractor, and apparently the contractor could include that amount in its termination claim.

While FAR 49.108-1 emphasizes the lack of privity between the government and the subcontractor, the government does retain the right to approve or ratify subcontract settlements, FAR 49.108-3, unless the contractor has been authorized to settle claims ($100,000 or less) without approval or ratification under FAR 49.108-4. In rare cases, however, the contract may contain a clause giving the subcontractor a right directly against the government where the subcontract termination is based upon the government's termination of the contract, *Compudyne Corp. v. Maxon Constr. Co.*, 248 F. Supp. 83 (D.C. Pa. 1965). In addition, the government could create a contractual relationship by dealing directly with the subcontractor. See, for example, *United States v. Georgia Marble Co.*, 106 F.2d 955 (5th Cir. 1939). In *Steel Improvement & Forge Co. v. United States*, 174 Ct. Cl. 24, 355 F.2d 627 (1966), a subcontractor alleged that the government had entered into such an arrangement by directing it to ship the termination inventory directly to the government and by agreeing to settle the claim directly. The court avoided reaching these issues, holding that, even if valid, any such claim would have been barred by the statute of limitations.

52 Comp. Gen. 377 (B-176596) (1972) demonstrates the kinds of problems a subcontractor can encounter under the no-privity rule. The GAO stated that the subcontractor could not expect the government to enforce the subcontractor's rights by conditioning government payment on contractor payment of subcontractor claims. The termination clauses give the government the right, but not the obligation, to settle subcontractor's claims directly. FAR 49.108-8 provides that this right will be exercised only when in the best interests of the government. In *Universal Fiberglass Corp. v. United States*, 210 Ct. Cl. 220, 537 F.2d 400 (1976), the court held that the government's receipt of a subcontractor claim and rejection "largely on the grounds of lack of privity" did not constitute an election to settle the claim directly with the subcontractor. The court further held that the amounts included in the contractor's settlement claim for subcontract settlements were subject to setoff for contractor debts to the government.

g. Termination Inventory

The costs of producing termination inventory are generally recoverable subject to the overall allowability requirements of the cost principles. See FAR 31.205-26(e) (limitations on allowability for intra-company transfer of materials). A contractor is, however, entitled to recover its incurred costs for work in process inventory in a termination for convenience settlement, even where that inventory was thrown away as scrap, *Industrial Tectonics Bearings Corp. v. United States*, 44 Fed. Cl. 115 (1999). Allowable costs include those costs incurred in producing defective material as well as those incurred for material complying with contract requirements, as long as the amount of defective material is not unreasonable. See *Best Lumber Sales*, ASBCA 16737, 72-2 BCA ¶ 9661, in which the board stated that costs of defective material may be recoverable if they are "reasonable, allocable and allowable," *Caskel Forge, Inc.*, ASBCA 7638, 1962 BCA ¶ 3318. In *Best Foam Fabricators, Inc. v. United States,* 38 Fed. Cl. 627 (1997), the court held that the contractor on a constructively terminated contract was entitled to recover its costs for termination inventory—even if that inventory did not comply in all respects with the specification requirements—absent proof that the defects resulted from the contractor's gross disregard of its contractual obligations. See also *New York Shipbuilding Co.*, ASBCA 15443, 73-1 BCA ¶ 9852, holding that a terminated contractor has no obligation to correct defective work.

The termination clauses provide that the contractor is responsible for preservation of the termination inventory and must tender the inventory to the government. Thus, they provide that the value of property that is "destroyed, lost or stolen" is to be excluded from the termination settlement. In *Best Lumber Sales*, the contractor was held liable for stolen lumber because the board was not convinced "that some reasonable means was not available to [the contractor] to protect the lumber from theft." Disposal of the inventory is subject to the instructions of the government's plant clearance officer. In *Thiokol Chem. Corp.*, ASBCA 17544, 76-1 BCA ¶ 11,731, the board found that the government was "bound by the plant clearance officer's determination that the residual inventory was allocable to the terminated contract and should be scrapped."

The contractor, however, need not retain the inventory for an unreasonable time. See *Southland Mfg. Corp.*, ASBCA 16830, 75-1 BCA ¶ 10,994, *recons. denied*, 75-1 BCA ¶ 11,272, where the contractor was relieved from tendering inventory that had been sold at public auction during the five years that had elapsed before a wrongful default termination was changed to a convenience termination. Where the government first made a claim for the value of inventory seven years after the termination for convenience, the contractor's defenses of laches and estoppel were legally viable and raised triable issues of material fact, so that neither party was entitled to summary judgment, *Eurasia Heavy Indus., Inc.*, ASBCA 52878, 01-2 BCA ¶ 31,574.

3. Settlement Expenses

FAR 31.205-42 compensates the contractor for expenses caused by the termination. This cost principle provides as follows:

> (g) *Settlement expenses.* (1) Settlement expenses, including the following, are generally allowable:
>
> > (i) Accounting, legal, clerical, and similar costs reasonably necessary for—
> >
> > > (A) The preparation and presentation, including supporting data, of settlement claims to the contracting officer; and
> > >
> > > (B) The termination and settlement of subcontracts.
> >
> > (ii) Reasonable costs for the storage, transportation, protection, and disposition of property acquired or produced for the contract.
> >
> > (iii) Indirect costs related to salary and wages incurred as settlement expenses in (i) and (ii); normally, such indirect costs shall be limited to payroll taxes, fringe benefits, occupancy costs, and immediate supervision costs.
>
> (2) If settlement expenses are significant, a cost account or work order shall be established to separately identify and accumulate them.

Accounting, legal, and clerical costs may be recovered if they are accurately documented and reasonable, *Unified Eng'g, Inc.*, ASBCA 21565, 81-1 BCA ¶ 14,940. Contractors often fail to recover total legal fees claimed in connection with termination settlements because of faulty record keeping. For instance, in *Nolan Bros., Inc.*

v. United States, 194 Ct. Cl. 1, 437 F.2d 1371 (1971), the court denied the contractor's claim for 2,400 hours of work, stating that the record did not contain evidence showing "either the exact or the approximate time" devoted to the claim by any of the attorneys who worked on it. Instead, the court awarded the contractor expenses for 400 hours of legal work. See also *H & J Constr. Co.*, ASBCA 18521, 76-1 BCA ¶ 11,903 (contractor awarded only $500 rather than claimed $48,000 in legal fees), and *Air-Cool, Inc.*, ASBCA 32838, 88-1 BCA ¶ 20,399 ($1.700 of claimed $2.000 fee sustained). Conclusory testimony that legal work was necessary for the preparation and presentation of the settlement claim will be insufficient. In *G.E. Boggs & Assocs.*, ASBCA 34841, 91-1 BCA ¶ 23,515, the board (using FPR 1-15.205-42(f)) denied the contractor's claim for legal fees where the contractor failed to submit time records or estimates, stating that conclusory testimony that the legal work was necessary was insufficient to carry the burden. Rather, the board concluded that a showing of the "exact or the approximate amount of time" that was devoted to the preparation of the termination claim through "records, estimates or otherwise" was required. This reasoning was affirmed in *Industrial Refrigeration Servs. Corp.*, VABCA 2532, 91-3 BCA ¶ 24,093, in which the government successfully argued that the contractor's invoices for legal services lacked specificity and there was no corroboration of the contractor's explanation of the context of the services. Settlement expenses may be proven by contemporary records; memoranda; and diary entries maintained by the attorneys, employees, and accountants, *Foremost Mech. Sys., Inc.*, GSBCA 13250, 98-1 BCA ¶ 29,652.

The number of hours expended in working on the termination claim and the rate charged must be reasonable. The hours and rates are analyzed on a case-by-case basis. See *American Packers, Inc.*, ASBCA 14275, 71-1 BCA ¶ 8846 (unreasonable for attorney to spend so many hours on small claim); *Bailey Specialized Bldgs., Inc.*, ASBCA 10576, 71-1 BCA ¶ 8699 (matters not legally complex but effort warranted in view of evidentiary effort required); *Cryo-Sonics, Inc.*, ASBCA 13219, 70-1 BCA ¶ 8313 ($100 per hour attorney fee reasonable for the practitioner's locality and the work involved); *Transcendental Aircraft Corp.*, ASBCA 5823, 61-1 BCA ¶ 2952 (accountant's rate accepted based on his testimony that charges were normal); and *Acme Coppersmithing & Mach. Co.*, ASBCA 4473, 59-1 BCA ¶ 2136, *recons. denied*, 59-2 BCA ¶ 2314 (accountant's rate accepted but number of days reduced).

Termination settlement costs are allowable whether incurred by the contractor's own employees or by outside personnel, *Douglas Corp.*, ASBCA 8566, 69-1 BCA ¶ 7578, *recons. denied*, 69-1 BCA ¶ 7699; *H & J Constr. Co.*, ASBCA 18521, 75-1 BCA ¶ 11,171, *recons. denied*, 76-1 BCA ¶ 11,903. However, the contractor cannot bill separately for the "value" of services furnished by a salaried employee, *Fil-Coil Co.*, ASBCA 23137, 79-1 BCA ¶ 13,618, *recons. denied*, 79-1 BCA ¶ 13,683. Settlement expenses for work performed by in-house personnel are computed on the basis of salary as an employee rather than as an hourly billing rate, *TRC Mariah Assoc., Inc.*, ASBCA 51811, 99-1 BCA ¶ 30,386. If the board determines that the contractor's rates are not credible, it may apply "reasonable" hourly rates in determining the appropriate recovery, *Teems, Inc. v. General Servs. Admin.,* GSBCA 14090, 98-1 BCA ¶ 29,357.

One of the government's arguments has been that it is improper to have settlement costs related to claims that are ultimately disallowed. Generally, this position has been rejected by the boards on the theory that the validity is not determined until after the claim has been submitted. See, for example, *Engineered Sys., Inc.*, ASBCA 18241, 74-1 BCA ¶ 10,492, and *Contract Maint., Inc.*, ASBCA 20689, 77-1 BCA ¶ 12,446. However, where the contractor's claim is for anticipated profits—made expressly unallowable by the regulations—the attorneys' fees associated with that claim are unallowable, *Dairy Sales Corp. v. United States*, 219 Ct. Cl. 431, 593 F.2d 1002 (1979); *Topeka Janitor Serv.*, ASBCA 9989, 65-2 BCA ¶ 4911.

In order to be allowable, professional service costs must also meet the requirements of FAR 31.205-33. Among other restrictions, this regulation, and its predecessors at FPR 1-15.205-31 and DAR 15-205.31, prohibits reimbursement of fees that are contingent upon recovery from the government and fees incurred in the prosecution of claims against the government. The contingent fee limitation was applied in *Manuel M. Liodas*, ASBCA 12829, 71-2 BCA ¶ 9015, *recons. denied*, 71-2 BCA ¶ 9120. See also *Hugo Auchter GmbH*, ASBCA 39642, 91-1 BCA ¶ 23,645, *recons. denied*, 91-2 BCA ¶ 23,777, in which the board disallowed a claim for legal expenses that the contractor was obligated to pay "only after the case was settled" on the basis that it was a contingent fee. In *Fiesta Leasing & Sales, Inc.*, ASBCA 29311, 87-1 BCA ¶ 19,622, *modified on recons. (on other grounds),* 88-1 BCA ¶ 20,499, the government attempted to prevent recovery of attorneys' fees because they were charged under a deferred billing arrangement, not actually paid. The fees, extensively documented, left no question that they were related to settlement expenses. While noting the prohibition against contingent fees, the board allowed recovery, stating that the government had not rebutted evidence establishing that the fees were deferred rather than contingent. *Hugo Auchter* and *Fiesta Leasing* can be distinguished on the basis of when the obligation to pay the attorneys' fees arose. In *Hugo*, there apparently was no obligation to pay until and unless the settlement claim had been paid by the government. In *Fiesta Leasing*, the obligation arose at the time services were rendered and were, therefore, recoverable. See also *R-D Mounts, Inc.*, ASBCA 17422, 75-1 BCA ¶ 11,077, *recons. denied,* 75-1 BCA ¶ 11,237; *Southland Mfg. Corp.*, ASBCA 16830, 75-1 BCA ¶ 10,994, *recons. denied*, 75-1 BCA ¶ 11,272; and *Atlantic, Gulf & Pac. Co. of Manila, Inc.*, ASBCA 13533, 72-1 BCA ¶ 9415, *recons. denied*, 72-2 BCA ¶ 9698.

The costs of processing board and court actions against the government clearly come within the unallowable category of processing claims against the government, *Robertson Co. v. United States*, 194 Ct. Cl. 289, 437 F.2d 1360 (1971). FAR 31.207-47(f) specifically provides that the cost of prosecuting claims or appeals against the government is clearly unallowable. See *A.T. Kearney, Inc.*, DOTCAB 1580, 86-1 BCA ¶ 18,613. If an attorneys' fee relates to any other portion of the contract action, it is unallowable as part of the convenience termination settlement.

In determining whether legal fees claimed by a contractor are allowable in the termination settlement, the courts and boards will look at the nature of the work rather than the time at which the work was performed, *Alta Constr. Co.*, PSBCA 1463, 92-2 BCA ¶ 24,824, *recons. denied*, 92-3 BCA ¶ 25,128. There, the contractor claimed attorneys' fees incurred in 1985. The contract was terminated for default in 1985 and converted to a termination for convenience in 1990. The government defended against the settlement claim on three grounds. First, it asserted that attorneys' fees incurred before the termination should have been included in the company's general overhead cost rather than attributed to the convenience termination. Second, it argued that the fees should not be allowed because they were incurred before actual termination. Third, it asserted that the fees were actually incurred as part of a claim against the government and were, therefore, unallowable. The board stated that the record did not support the government's third argument. In discussing the timing of the legal work, the board concluded at 123,835:

> It is the nature of the work and not the time at which it was performed which controls whether the associated costs may be recovered as part of a termination for convenience claim. *Kalvar Corp., Inc. v. United States* [22 CCF ¶ 80,737], 543 F.2d 1298 (Ct. Cl. 1976); *Industrial Refrigeration Services Corp.*, VABCA No. 2532, 91-3 BCA ¶ 24,093; *Baifield Industries, Division of A-T-O, Inc.*, 76-2 BCA ¶ 12,096, *recons. denied* 76-2 BCA ¶ 12,203.

See also *Richerson Constr., Inc. v. General Servs. Admin.*, GSBCA 11161, 93-1 BCA ¶ 25,239, *modified on recons.*, 93-3 BCA ¶ 26,206, where the government asserted that the certification of the proposal, coupled with a request for a final decision, followed by a prompt filing of a notice of appeal, demonstrated the contractor's litigation posture. The board disagreed, stating at 125,713:

> The fact that [the contractor] was not unduly optimistic about the prospects for reaching a mutually satisfactory settlement, and thus sought to protect its right to recover interest in the event litigation was ultimately necessary, does not change the nature of the activities for which expenses were incurred. [The contractor's] settlement proposal was just that. Indeed, the Government treated it thus, requesting the customary audit of [the contractor's] proposal, so as to enable it to negotiate with [the contractor]. Accordingly, we are not persuaded by the argument that the running of CDA interest, started by the filing of a certified claim, precludes the recovery of legal expenses incurred in preparing the termination settlement proposal and negotiating with the Government in an effort to settle the matter.

Generally, the end of negotiations with the contracting officer and the issuance of a final decision are considered to be the cutoff point for allowable settlement costs, *Western States Painting Co.*, ASBCA 13843, 69-1 BCA ¶ 7616. However, it has been recognized that settlement negotiations can continue past the filing of an appeal and that costs legitimately incurred in negotiating a settlement can be allowed even though a hearing on the case is in process, *ACME Process Equip. Co. v. United States*, 171 Ct. Cl. 251, 347 F.2d 538 (1965); *Frigitemp Corp.*, VACAB 646, 68-1

BCA ¶ 6766. In *Vincent Ogonnaya Ofor,* PSBCA 3965, 99-1 BCA ¶ 30,317, the board rejected the agency's assertions that the contractor's legal and accounting costs, incurred after a termination settlement proposal was converted to a claim, were unallowable costs associated with the prosecution of a claim against the government. The board noted that the nature and form of legal activities are more objective standards for determining if the costs may be reimbursed than is their relationship in time to the filing of an appeal to the board. Thus, the board allowed the contractor to recover the costs of direct labor for preparation of the proposal, as well as costs for legal and accounting time.

When a contractor sues the government for breach of contract and the government action is found to have been a constructive termination and the amount of recovery is determined, it has been stated that "it is only fair to allow the contractor the equivalent of legal expenses he would have incurred in preparing a settlement claim after termination," *Kalvar Corp., Inc. v. United States*, 211 Ct. Cl. 192, 543 F.2d 1298 (1976), *cert. denied*, 434 U.S. 830 (1977). However, in that case the court limited recovery to the costs incurred in responding to a court order for a supplemental brief to determine whether the contractor had incurred costs recoverable under a termination settlement. Subsequently, the court concluded that the contractor had incurred no expenses in connection with the brief because its attorney had not billed it for the preparation of the brief and it had not paid him, *Kalvar Corp. v. United States*, 218 Ct. Cl. 433, 587 F.2d 49 (1978). Expenses incurred in dealing with the contracting officer as part of a genuine attempt to negotiate a settlement are allowable even though the efforts may benefit the subsequent legal prosecution of the claim, *Baifield Indus., Div. of A-T-O, Inc.*, ASBCA 20006, 76-2 BCA ¶ 12,096, *recons. denied*, 76-2 BCA ¶ 12,203. However, if the board is convinced that the amount and nature of the settlement efforts are influenced by the likelihood of their being useful in subsequent litigation, they may be disallowed, *Power Equip. Corp.*, ASBCA 5904, 1964 BCA ¶ 4228.

If the settlement effort is performed by the contractor's own employees, the contractor is entitled to charge overhead to direct labor employees performing the effort in accordance with its normal accounting system, *Worsham Constr. Co.*, ASBCA 25907, 85-2 BCA ¶ 18,016; *Thiokol Chem. Corp.*, ASBCA 17544, 76-1 BCA ¶ 11,731; *The Boeing Co.*, ASBCA 12685, 69-2 BCA ¶ 7795. If the effort is performed by personnel normally charged indirectly, there is authority for the contractor to charge those efforts directly to the termination settlement, *Aydin Corp.*, EBCA 355-5-86, 89-3 BCA ¶ 22,044; *A.T. Kearney, Inc.*, DOTBCA 1580, 86-1 BCA ¶ 18,613; *Celesco Indus., Inc.*, ASBCA 22460, 84-2 BCA ¶ 17,295; *Bermite Div. of Tasker Indus.*, ASBCA 18280, 77-1 BCA ¶ 12,349, *modified on recons.*, 77-2 BCA ¶ 12,731. This reclassification on its face appears to violate CAS 402. Settlement costs, however, do not trigger the requisite circumstances of "in like manner" or "for the same purpose" as referenced in CAS 402 because the functions performed by the contractor in settling terminated contracts are different from those required for normal business operations. When reclassifying, the contractor must make appropriate adjustments to overhead to prevent double counting, and the board must be assured that the contractor has not already recovered the costs through overhead allocations.

4. Overhead, Profit, and Loss Contracts

Termination settlements are subject to special rules for post-termination overhead, profit, and loss contracts.

a. Post-Termination Overhead

Except to the extent that it is allocable to direct settlement expenses, recovery of post-termination overhead has been prohibited in termination claims for completely terminated contracts. See *Nolan Bros., Inc. v. United States*, 194 Ct. Cl. 1, 437 F.2d 1371 (1971); *Chamberlain Mfg. Corp.*, ASBCA 16877, 73-2 BCA ¶ 10,139; *Pioneer Recovery Sys., Inc.*, ASBCA 24658, 81-1 BCA ¶ 15,059; *Celesco Indus., Inc.*, ASBCA 22460, 84-2 BCA ¶ 17,295; and *Foremost Mech. Sys., Inc. v. General Servs. Admin.*, GSBCA 13250-C(12335), 98-1 BCA ¶ 29,652. In *Technology, Inc.*, ASBCA 14083, 71-2 BCA ¶ 8956, *recons. denied*, 72-1 BCA ¶ 9281, the board held that such a recovery would be similar to anticipated profits and would not be recoverable as continuing costs. However, in *Southland Mfg. Corp.*, ASBCA 16830, 75-1 BCA ¶ 10,994, *recons. denied*, 75-1 BCA ¶ 11,272, the board permitted the contractor to recover unabsorbed overhead for a reasonable time after an improper default termination that directly resulted in the contractor going out of business. Substantially similar results were obtained in *American Elec., Inc.*, ASBCA 16635, 76-2 BCA ¶ 12,151, *modified on other grounds*, 77-2 BCA ¶ 12,792, where the contractor was able to recover the costs of facilities established solely for the contract. See also *Baifield Indus., Div. of A-T-O, Inc.*, ASBCA 20006, 76-2 BCA ¶ 12,096, *recons. denied*, 76-2 BCA ¶ 12,203, in which the board allowed the contractor to recover continuing costs for a manufacturing plant that, although not been acquired solely for the performance of the contract, "was necessary from the standpoint of maximizing efficiency of production and minimizing plant alteration costs." Following termination, the contractor had no further need for the plant. The proper conclusion may have been reached in the *Baifield* case because some of the costs allowed by the board as continuing costs were rental, depreciation, and other costs that would appear to be allowable under the cost principle dealing with continuing rental costs and loss of useful life.

An increased allocation of fixed indirect costs to the continued portion of the contract based on an allocation to all of the contractor's ongoing work and not solely to the continued work on the contract was held to be allowable in *Cal-Tron Sys, Inc.*, ASBCA 49279, 97-2 BCA ¶ 28,986.

b. Profit or Loss Adjustment

The "long form" termination clauses for fixed-price contracts provide that the termination settlement is to include either a "reasonable allowance for profit on work done" or a loss adjustment in the event that the contractor would have sustained a loss on the entire contract had it been completed.

(1) Profit

The clause for fixed-price supply contracts in FAR 52.249-2 calls for the contracting officer to pay a "fair and reasonable" sum of profit on "costs incurred in the performance of the work terminated, including initial costs and preparatory expense allocable thereto." Alternate I of that clause for fixed-price construction contracts is slightly different, stating that a "fair and reasonable" sum of profit is to be paid on the costs of contract work "performed before the effective date of termination." This difference is most likely not significant, however, since both clauses incorporate FAR 49.202 which expressly states that profit shall be allowed on "preparations made and work done by the contractor for the terminated portion of the contract." Thus, under both types of contracts, the contractor would appear to be entitled to a profit on costs incurred under the contract even though no physical work had been accomplished. The wording of the specific termination clause may, however, restrict the profit. See *Advance Window Sys., Inc.*, VACAB 1276, 78-1 BCA ¶ 13,126, where the termination clause provided for profit only "on work done." The board allowed the contractor to recover its out-of-pocket costs but refused to allow any profits.

If the contractor has incurred no costs, it is clear that no profit recovery is allowed, *Shin Enters., Inc.*, ASBCA 16542, 72-1 BCA ¶ 9391. FAR 49.202(a) states that "[p]rofit shall not be allowed the contractor for material or services that as of the effective date of the termination have not been delivered by a subcontractor, regardless of the percentage of completion." Following a partial convenience termination, in *TRW, Inc.*, ASBCA 51003, 00-2 BCA ¶ 30,992, the board found that a contract's "ship in place" provisions would have allowed materials delivered under its provisions to have been eligible for profit, but that mere completion of a milestone was not synonymous with delivery. The board held, however, that the contractor was entitled to recover profit on data delivered by the subcontractor but not separately priced in the subcontract, provided a reasonable value could be placed on the data. See also *Lockheed Martin Corp.*, ASBCA 53032, 03-2 BCA ¶ 32,408 (fee not allowed on subcontractor effort even in Leader Company contracting).

FAR 49.202 states that the contracting officer may "use any reasonable method to arrive at a fair profit" and provides the following guidance:

(b) In negotiating or determining profit, factors to be considered include—

(1) Extent and difficulty of the work done by the contractor as compared with the total work required by the contract (engineering estimates of the percentage of completion ordinarily should not be required, but if available should be considered);

(2) Engineering work, production scheduling, planning, technical study and supervision, and other necessary services;

(3) Efficiency of the contractor, with particular regard to—

(i) Attainment of quantity and quality production;

(ii) Reduction of costs;

(iii) Economic use of materials, facilities, and manpower; and

(iv) Disposition of termination inventory;

(4) Amount and source of capital and extent of risk assumed;

(5) Inventive and developmental contributions, and cooperation with the Government and other contractors in supplying technical assistance;

(6) Character of the business, including the source and nature of materials and the complexity of manufacturing techniques;

(7) The rate of profit that the contractor would have earned had the contract been completed;

(8) The rate of profit both parties contemplated at the time the contract was negotiated; and

(9) Character and difficulty of subcontracting, including selection, placement, and management of subcontracts, and effort in negotiating settlements of terminated subcontracts.

(c) When computing profit on the terminated portion of a construction contract, the contracting officer shall—

(1) Comply with paragraphs (a) and (b) of this Section;

(2) Allow profit on the prime contractor's settlements with construction subcontractors for actual work in place at the job site; and

(3) Exclude profit on the prime contractor's settlements with construction subcontractors for materials on hand and for preparations made to complete the work.

No profit is allowed on settlement expenses. FAR 49.202(a) states that, although the contractor's efforts in settling subcontractor proposals will be considered in determining the overall rate of profit, profit for such efforts is not to be based on the "dollar amount" of the settlements.

The contractor has the burden of proving both the estimated cost to complete the contract, *Clary Corp.,* ASBCA 19274, 74-2 BCA ¶ 10,947, and the rate of profit, *John M. Brown,* AGBCA 77-105, 78-1 BCA ¶ 12,892. Note, however, that when a cost-reimbursement contract is terminated the government has the burden of proof as to the amount of reduction of the fee, *Emerson Elec. Co.,* ASBCA 15591, 72-1 BCA ¶ 9440. Determination of the rate of profit is done on a case-by-case basis, and the application of the regulatory guidelines is considered a matter of judgment, *Metered Laundry Servs.,* ASBCA 21573, 78-1 BCA ¶ 13,206, *modified on recons.*, 78-2 BCA ¶ 13,451. The rates of profit have varied widely. See *Fil-Coil Co.*, ASBCA 23137, 79-1 BCA ¶ 13,618, *recons. denied*, 79-1 BCA ¶ 13,683 (20 percent more than fair where contractor had claimed 70 percent of anticipated profit, which amounted to 65 percent of cost incurred); *Lockley Mfg. Co.*, ASBCA 21231, 78-1 BCA ¶ 12,987 (contractor requested 10 percent but board awarded 4.93 percent, the actual experienced rate calculated by the government); *Metered Laundry Servs.,* ASBCA 21573, 78-1 BCA ¶ 13,206, *modified on recons.*, 78-2 BCA ¶ 13,451 (contractor claimed 35 percent but board found 20 percent more than reasonable); *Amplitronics, Inc.*, ASBCA 20545, 76-1 BCA ¶ 11,760 (contractor's investment, expertise, and actions supported 5 percent rate rather than 4.6 percent suggested by government); and *Switlik Parachute Co.,* ASBCA 18024, 75-2 BCA ¶ 11,434 (contractor claimed 12 percent as its normal bidding rate, government offered 6 percent, and board balanced risk and job difficulty to award 9 percent). In *E.W. Eldridge, Inc.*, ENGBCA 4879, 93-1 BCA ¶ 25,355, the contractor claimed 20 percent based on its assertion that the deleted work would have been the most profitable under the contract and that the deceased president of the company always bid on the basis of high profit rates. The board, while noting it "seldom" used a rate higher than 10 percent, found that the contracting officer's earlier estimate of 14 percent was the best estimate of the rate of profit the contractor would have earned had the contract been completed and therefore awarded that amount. In *Marshall Associated Contractors Inc. & Columbia Excavating Inc. (J. V.),* IBCA 1901, 02-1 BCA ¶ 31,797, a 30 percent profit was allowed under a terminated contract in light of the "[contractor's] truly remarkable production rate . . . under the most difficult and adverse of situations," especially as compared with the re-procurement contractor's production. The board awarded the contractor $17.5 million, plus 18 years of CDA interest, on a $6.6 million contract. Clearly influenced by the severity of the government's conduct, the board allowed (1) cost of facilities capital on the initial value of special equipment, rather than the value as depreciated during performance; (2) rental rates on pre-owned equipment based on "Blue Book" rates, enhanced by 39 percent to reflect the ultra-harsh performance conditions; and (3) "unabsorbed overhead" at contractor's historical overhead percentage in normal periods (10 percent), rather than the lower 5 percent rate actually incurred during performance caused by increases in the direct base due to the cost of the project. The board rejected application of the loss formula, since the government contributed to the contractor's loss.

When a contract fee is determined at the inception of a cost contract, a contractor has a reasonable expectation of receiving some portion of the fee if the contract is terminated for convenience. In that case, the adjusted fee generally will be computed by measuring the percentage-of-completion at the time of termination. But, when a fee has not been fixed at the beginning of the contract and is subject to periodic discretionary adjustment by the government such as an award fee, percentage-of-completion is not the appropriate formula to determine the fee to be paid upon termination of the contract. In *Textron Def. Sys. v. Widnall,* 143 F.3d 1465 (Fed. Cir. 1998), the court affirmed the board's rejection of Textron's attempt to collect 77.4 percent of its award fee based on the percentage-of-completion formula, when the government terminated the contract for convenience. The court opined that the "plain language of the contract" made the Termination clause inapplicable to award fees. Even if the Termination clause did apply to award fees, "a contractor in a cost-plus-award-fee contract is not entitled to a specific share of an award fee."

(2) Loss Adjustment

The "long form" termination clauses state that, if it appears that the contractor would have incurred a loss had the entire contract been completed, an appropriate adjustment shall be made to reduce the amount of the settlement to reflect the indicated rate of loss. FAR 49.203 provides that the formula for applying the loss adjustment is to multiply the incurred costs of the terminated portion of the contract by the ratio of the contract price to the total of the incurred costs plus the estimate to complete the work. In some cases, such as *G.A. Karnavas Painting Co.*, ASBCA 22281, 78-2 BCA ¶ 13,312, the board applied this percentage directly to the incurred costs to obtain the cost allowance for settlement. In others, the reciprocal of this ratio is applied to the incurred costs to get an amount to be subtracted from the incurred cost to obtain the cost allowance for settlement. See *Henry Spen & Co.*, ASBCA 20766, 77-2 BCA ¶ 12,784. These are merely different ways of presenting the figures, and the end results are the same.

In *Boeing Def. & Space Group,* ASBCA 50048, 98-2 BCA ¶ 29,927, the board applied the Christian doctrine to incorporate the FAR loss adjustment provision under FAR 49.203 into a fixed-price incentive fee contract for use as guidance in interpreting the contract's Termination for Convenience clause. The board held that, although the contract required separate contract item costs for purposes of incentive price revisions, incremental funding, and progress payments, it did not prohibit the use of a combined loss ratio to determine the termination settlement amount.

When a contractor submits a termination settlement proposal on an inventory basis, the percentage of loss ("loss formula") is calculated on the entire contract, but is applied only to the terminated portion. By contrast, where the settlement proposal is on the cost basis, the loss formula is applied to the entire contract, *Voices R Us, Inc.,* ASBCA 51565, 01-1 BCA ¶ 31,328.

The loss adjustment will not be made if the government is responsible for the cost increase, *R.H.J. Corp.*, ASBCA 12404, 69-1 BCA ¶ 7587; or if the contractor is excused from performing because of impossibility, *Scope Elecs., Inc.*, ASBCA 20359, 77-1 BCA ¶ 12,404, *recons. denied*, 77-2 BCA ¶ 12,586; *D.E.W, Inc.,* ASBCA 50796, 00-2 BCA ¶ 31,104, *modified on recons.,* 01-1 BCA ¶ 31,150. The adjustment also will not be made where the contractor is entitled to an equitable adjustment that takes the contract out of the loss position, *Douglas Corp.*, ASBCA 8566, 69-1 BCA ¶ 7578, *recons. denied*, 69-1 BCA ¶ 7699.

It is not appropriate to apply the loss adjustment factor or to limit the settlement to the contract price without giving consideration to unpriced changes or other modifications. The most straightforward method of accomplishing this is for the parties to negotiate the appropriate price increase or decrease and amend the contract accordingly. If the parties fail to do so, the board may determine the amount of the adjustment, *Pilcher, Livingston & Wallace, Inc.*, ASBCA 13391, 70-1 BCA ¶ 8331, *recons. denied*, 70-2 BCA ¶ 8488. However, in some cases the boards will merely ignore the loss adjustment if the contractor is entitled to price adjustments. See *Scope Elecs., Inc.*, ASBCA 20359, 77-1 BCA ¶ 12,404, *recons. denied*, 77-2 BCA ¶ 12,586 (contractor entitled to recover all reasonable costs under terminated loss contracts in view of objective impossibility), and *Douglas Corp.*, ASBCA 8566, 69-1 BCA ¶ 7578, *recons. denied*, 69-1 BCA ¶ 7699 (loss adjustment factor held inapplicable due to defective government-furnished specifications). In asserting the right to such adjustments, contractors still must prove their claims. In *Defense Sys. Corp.*, ASBCA 44131R, 00-1 BCA ¶ 30,851, the board held that a contractor whose default termination had been converted to a termination for convenience due to defective specifications and impossibility of performance was not entitled to recover costs in excess of the adjusted contract price because the contractor failed to demonstrate that the government was responsible for the specified costs. Although the contract price ceiling was adjusted for the increased costs caused by the impossibility, the contractor was denied recovery for costs above the adjusted contract price for which the contractor had shown no government-responsible causation.

The regulations do not contain guidance on adjusting the contract price except in FAR 49.114, which indicates the appropriate contracting officer to negotiate unadjusted changes:

> (a) Before settlement of a completely terminated contract, the TCO shall obtain from the contracting office a list of all related unsettled contract changes. The TCO shall settle, as part of final settlement, all unsettled contract changes after obtaining the recommendations of the contracting office concerning the changes.

(b) When the contract has been partially terminated, any outstanding unsettled contract changes will usually be handled by the contracting officer. However, the contracting officer may delegate this function to the TCO.

In *David Boland, Inc.,* VABCA 5931, 01-2 BCA ¶ 31,578, the board held that because a termination for convenience converts a fixed-price contract into a cost-reimbursement contract, the contractor's quantum claims for the site condition and other matters would be merged into the termination settlement provisions "insofar as they do not, in the aggregate amount, exceed the contract price." By this language, the board appeared to ignore the fact that, if the claims were recognized, the contract price would be increased, resulting in a potentially greater recovery by the contractor. See *Freedom NY, Inc.,* ASBCA 43965, 01-2 BCA ¶ 31,585, *recons. denied,* 02-1 BCA ¶ 31,676, *aff'd in part & rev'd in part,* 329 F.3d 1320 (Fed. Cir. 2003), *cert. denied,* 541 U. S. 987 (2004) (contractor's breach claim, to the extent sustained, constituted an adjustment to the contract price for affecting both the total recovery and application of the termination for convenience loss formula).

The government has the burden of proving that the contractor would have been in a loss position at completion since it is seeking to reduce the contractor's recovery, *Systems & Computer Info., Inc.*, ASBCA 18458, 78-1 BCA ¶ 12,946. In that case, the board resorted to a "jury verdict" determination and favored the contractor in computing the amount of anticipated loss because the government had not fully met its burden. For another case basing the estimate to complete on a "jury verdict" determination, see *Supreme Equip. & Sys. Corp.*, ASBCA 20079, 76-1 BCA ¶ 11,858. In determining the estimate to complete, all expected costs are considered, including the costs the contractor would have had to expend to correct defective performance had the contract not been terminated, *Power Generators, Inc.*, ASBCA 7607, 1962 BCA ¶ 3358.

5. Variable Quantity Contracts and Cost Limitation Clauses

With most types of contract the parties can determine the contract price from the terms of the contract. However, when variable quantity contracts are involved, a number of questions arise. If a requirements contract is terminated for convenience, the contractor's recovery is not limited by the ordered amount or by a nominal minimum quantity, *Albano Cleaners, Inc. v. United States*, 197 Ct. Cl. 450, 455 F.2d 556 (1972). If the contract is an indefinite delivery/indefinite quantity (IDIQ) contract and the government is not bound to place orders, the termination settlement will be limited to the ordered amount or the minimum quantity, whichever is greater. These problems were present in *Okaw Indus., Inc.*, ASBCA 17863, 77-2 BCA ¶ 12,793, in which the board held that the contract price was to be calculated according to the ordered services, so long as the amount ordered exceeded the contract minimum. It did not matter that the amount ordered was less than the "estimated amount," since there was adequate consideration to bind both parties. In *Unified Eng'g, Inc.*, ASBCA 21565, 81-1 BCA ¶ 14,940, the agency had failed to order the minimum quantities on four items and had exceeded the minimum on the balance on others. The board allowed the contractor to recover in excess of the price corresponding to the price of the minimum quantities under each category, reasoning that "the contract price would not be reached . . . until an amount equivalent to the value of the under-ordered minimums had been established as due" the contractor.

When an IDIQ contract was allowed to expire without reaching the minimum quantity, the contractor was awarded the entire price of the minimum quantity, *Maxima Corp. v. United States*, 847 F.2d 1549 (Fed. Cir 1988). The court reasoned that a constructive termination had not occurred and that the contractor had fully performed the contract by being available to perform. However, other cases have awarded not the full price for the unordered IDIQ work, but rather the amount the contractor lost as the result of the government's failure to order the minimum quantity, *PHP Healthcare Corp.*, ASBCA 39209, 91-1 BCA ¶ 23,647; *Apex Int'l Mgmt. Servs. Inc.*, ASBCA 38087, 94-2 BCA ¶ 26,842. In *Delta Constr. Int'l, Inc.*, ASBCA 52162, 01-1 BCA ¶ 31,195, *recons. granted,* 01-1 BCA ¶ 31,242, the board had followed *Maxima* in awarding the difference between the dollar amount of work the government actually ordered and the total minimum dollar amount the contract obligated the government to order. On appeal, *White v. Delta Constr. Int'l, Inc.*, 285 F.3d 1040 (Fed. Cir 2002), the court reversed, concluding that the board's method was an impermissible basis for calculating damages because it would put the contractor in a more favorable position than it would have been in if the government had performed rather than breached its contractual commitment. Instead, the court stated that the proper basis for damages was the loss the contractor suffered as a result of the government's breach, not the total amount it would have received without the breach.

Where a letter contract is terminated for convenience, the Limitation of Government Liability clause would appear to be applied in the same way as the Limitation of Cost clause in cost-reimbursement contracts. In such a termination claim, the contractor can recover costs in excess of the estimated cost only in cases where it was impossible for the contractor to give the required notice of overrun or where the contracting officer had agreed to fund the overrun, *Frederick Burk Found.*, ASBCA 15728, 73-1 BCA ¶ 9959. In *Breed Corp.*, ASBCA 14523, 72-1 BCA ¶ 9304, *rev'd*, 223 Ct. Cl. 702 (1980), the board held that the revised clause precluded a contractor from recovering termination settlement costs in excess of the estimated cost. On appeal, the Court of Claims held that termination costs were included under the Limitation of Cost clause as performance costs but reversed the board's decision, reasoning that the government had "waived" the benefit of the clause by requesting the contractor to take specific termination actions with full knowledge that the contract funds had been exhausted, thereby leading the contractor to reasonably conclude that the government would fund its termination costs. The same result was reached in *General Am. Research Div.*, PSBCA 91, 77-1 BCA ¶ 12,372. See, however, *American Elec., Inc.*, ASBCA 16635, 76-2 BCA ¶ 12,151, *modified on other grounds*, 77-2 BCA ¶ 12,792, in which the limitation was held to have been waived by the contracting officer's settlement offers in excess of the limitation.

If a contract is a cost-sharing one, the contractor will only be entitled to its contractual share of the termination costs, *Jacobs Eng'g Group, Inc. v. United States*, 63 Fed. Cl. 451 (2005). The court reached this conclusion based on the language in the cost-reimbursement termination clause in FAR 52.249-6 calling for payment of "all costs reimbursable under this contract." The court reasoned that the cost-sharing provision survived termination and that the no fee arrangement also survived termination.

6. *Partial Termination*

A partial termination is defined in FAR 49.001 as "the termination of a part, but not all, of the work which has not been completed and accepted under the contract." This definition envisions that some work will continue after the issuance of the notice of termination. However, in practice, the term also has been applied to cases where a part of the work has already been completed and accepted and the balance terminated. The wrongful failure by the government to place all its orders under a requirements contract has also been referred to as a "constructive partial termination," *Wheeler Bros., Inc.,* ASBCA 20465, 79-1 BCA ¶ 13,642. Determining whether a termination is partial is important since it affects the method of pricing the termination settlement. The termination clauses provide for an equitable adjustment of the prices of the unterminated work when a partial termination is involved. Paragraph (l) of the termination clause contained in FAR 52.249-2 states:

> If the termination is partial, the Contractor may file a proposal with the Contracting Officer for an equitable adjustment of the price(s) of the continued portion of the contract. The Contracting Officer shall make any equitable adjustment agreed upon. Any proposal by the Contractor for an equitable adjustment under this clause shall be requested within 90 days from the effective date of termination unless extended in writing by the Contracting Officer.

If the termination is not considered a partial termination, the contractor's remedies for the effect of the reduced volume of work must be obtained under the termination cost principle for initial costs.

The equitable adjustment is computed by increasing the price of the unterminated work by the amount of costs that would have been recovered in the prices of the terminated work. In *Wheeler Bros.*, the board permitted the contractor to recover fixed overhead that would have been allocated to the terminated portion of the work, even though the contractor would have made a profit at the unadjusted prices notwithstanding the termination. The board specifically distinguished fixed overhead from anticipatory profit. In *Celesco Indus., Inc.*, ASBCA 22460, 84-2 BCA ¶ 17,295, the board refused to apply higher overhead rates caused by the termination to the equitable adjustment for the unterminated units on the questionable theory that this amounted to compensation for unabsorbed overhead. See also *Contract Maint., Inc.*, ASBCA 18595, 74-2 BCA ¶ 10,963, and *Space Age Eng'g, Inc.*, ASBCA 16525, 73-1 BCA ¶ 9921, where the government terminated lower cost work that the contractor had anticipated using to recoup expenses of the higher cost work, which was not terminated. In these cases, the contractors' offers had been conditioned on being awarded both parts of the work. However, where the government completely terminates a severable item, there is no equitable adjustment to the remaining items, *Gregory & Reilly Assocs., Inc.*, FAACAP 65-30, 65-2 BCA ¶ 4918. The contractor has the burden of proof that costs have been "increased by the termination," *Askenazy Constr. Co.*, HUDBCA 78-2, 78-2 BCA ¶ 13,402.

An equitable adjustment for partial contract termination can raise issues of the amount of unrecovered fixed overhead costs associated with the terminated portion of the work. In *Jay Auto. Specialties, Inc.*, ASBCA 50036, 99-1 BCA ¶ 30,186, the board held that the contractor was entitled to recover fixed overhead costs based on a rate that accounted for the difference between the contractor's actual revenues and the revenues that would have resulted in the absence of the partially terminated work.

The equitable adjustment arising out of partial termination is for the increased cost of continued work due to the partial termination and not for claimed increased cost that would have been incurred in the absence of the termination, *Aeronca, Inc.*, ASBCA 51927, 01-1 BCA ¶ 31,230. In that case, a contractor's claim for additional indirect costs allocated to the unterminated portion of a contract was unproven. The contractor's calculation included both fixed and variable costs and indirect costs properly allocable to all of its remaining work. Although the contractor was entitled to recover any increased allocation of fixed costs to the unterminated portion of the contract, it could not recover the increased allocation to other work resulting from the termination, *Hunter Mfg. Co.*, ASBCA 48693, 97-1 BCA ¶ 28,924.

C. Short Form Termination Settlements

FAR 52.249-1 sets forth a "short form" termination clause to be used in fixed-price contracts of $100,000 or less:

TERMINATION FOR CONVENIENCE OF THE GOVERNMENT (FIXED-PRICE) (SHORT FORM) (APR 1984)

The Contracting Officer, by written notice, may terminate this contract, in whole or in part, when it is in the Government's interest. If this contract is terminated, the rights, duties, and obligations of the parties including compensation to the Contractor, shall be in accordance with Part 49 of the Federal Acquisition Regulation in effect on the date of this contract.

Another "short form" termination clause is available for use in fixed-price service contracts of any amount where the contracting officer determines that "the successful offeror will not incur substantial charges in preparation for and in carrying out the contract." This clause, set forth in FAR 52.249-4, provides as follows:

TERMINATION FOR CONVENIENCE OF THE GOVERNMENT (SERVICES) (SHORT FORM) (APR 1984)

> The Contracting Officer, by written notice, may terminate this contract, in whole or in part, when it is in the Government's interest. If this contract is terminated, the Government shall be liable only for payment under the payment provisions of this contract for services rendered before the effective date of termination.

As long as the contracting officer makes the prescribed determination, the use of this "short form" clause is appropriate regardless of contract value when a fixed-price service contract is contemplated, *Arrow, Inc.*, ASBCA 41330, 94-1 BCA ¶ 26,353. In that case, the contractor's claim for the useful value of special machinery and equipment was denied because the short form clause, which limits settlement charges to services rendered before the date of termination, was included in the contract. The contractor unsuccessfully argued that the long form clause (FAR 52.249-2) should have been used because the contract for grounds maintenance exceeded $100,000 in value.

Clauses substantially identical to FAR 52.249-4, which were set forth in DAR 7-1902.16 and FPR 1-8.705-1, had consistently been interpreted as precluding recovery of start-up and post-termination costs. See *Trans-Student Lines, Inc.*, ASBCA 20230, 75-1 BCA ¶ 11,343, *recons. denied*, 75-2 BCA ¶ 11,419, in which the board stated at 54,348:

> [T]he Termination for Convenience clause provides for no recovery except for payment in accordance with the payment provisions of the contract for services rendered prior to the effective date of termination. In other words, [the contractor] agreed to a contract that permitted the Government to terminate at any time and pay only for the bus service tendered at the stipulated price with no payment to be made for start-up costs or other costs normally paid pursuant to a termination for convenience.

See *Tefft, Kelly & Motley, Inc.*, GSBCA 6562, 83-1 BCA ¶ 16,177, *recons. denied*, 83-1 BCA ¶ 16,279, and *Maibens, Inc.*, ASBCA 25915, 82-1 BCA ¶ 15,668, *recons. denied*, 82-1 BCA ¶ 15,796. But see *Grover Contracting Corp.*, GSBCA 4115, 75-2 BCA ¶ 11,550, *recons. denied*, 76-1 BCA ¶ 11,906, involving a contract to unload copper ore where, after it was able to make available only one-third of the amount of ore stated in the contract, the government terminated the contract for convenience. The contractor was entitled to recover for the work actually performed at a higher unit price than that stated in the contract, based on the government's negligent failure to accurately approximate its unloading requirements. See also *Steelcare, Inc.*, GSBCA 5491, 81-1 BCA ¶ 15,143.

CHAPTER 12

PAYMENT AND DISCHARGE

Payment is the government's principal contractual obligation, and many disputes occur over whether that obligation has been properly met. Payments during performance provide a flow of funds to contractors to assist them in financing the work under the contract. Delays or interruptions in this flow of funds can seriously impact the performance of the work. "Withholding" and "setoff" are the terms used to describe the government's refusal to pay all the costs included in a contractor's invoice. Final payment may signify that the performance obligations of both parties to the contract have been discharged. This chapter discusses these aspects of the payment process. It also considers other discharge devices such as release and accord and satisfaction. The first section discusses the types of payment used in government contracts and when payment is due. The second section examines payment procedures, including withholding. The third section covers setoff. The fourth section addresses contractor remedies for delayed payment and government remedies for overpayment and improper claims. The last section deals with the question of when contractual obligations are discharged through final payment, release, or accord and satisfaction.

I. TYPES OF PAYMENT

The three major types of payment under government contracts are payment of the contract price for completed items of work, progress payments based on costs incurred or a percentage of completion of the work, and payments based on the performance of the work. Another method, used only in extraordinary situations, is payment in advance of performing the work. The first subsection discusses payment of the contract price for accepted work. The second discusses various types of progress payments that are made prior to the completion of the work. The third subsection discusses less frequently used techniques—advance payments and provisional payments.

A. Payment of the Price

In government contracts, as in private contracts, payment of the contract price is due upon the completion of the work and submission of appropriate invoices, unless otherwise agreed to by the parties. The Payments clause for supply and service contracts in FAR 52.232-1 provides in part:

> The Government shall pay the Contractor, upon the submission of proper invoices or vouchers, the prices stipulated in this contract for supplies delivered and accepted or services rendered and accepted, less any deductions provided in this contract.

Paragraph (h) of the FAR 52.232-5 construction contracts Payments clause contains the following provision:

> The Government shall pay the amount due the Contractor under this contract after—
>
> > (1) Completion and acceptance of all work;
> >
> > (2) Presentation of a properly executed voucher; and
> >
> > (3) Presentation of release of all claims against the Government arising by virtue of this contract, other than claims, in stated amounts, that the Contractor has specifically excepted from the operation of the release. A release may also be required of the assignee if the Contractor's claim to amounts payable under this contract has been assigned under the Assignment of Claims Act of 1940 (31 U.S.C. 3727 and 41 U.S.C. 15).

The Payments clause for time-and-materials and labor-hour contracts at FAR 52.232-7 states:

> The Government will pay the Contractor as follows upon the submission of invoices or vouchers approved by the Contracting Officer:
>
> > (a) Hourly rate. (1) The amounts shall be computed by multiplying the appropriate hourly rates prescribed in the Schedule by the number of direct labor hours performed. The rates shall include wages, indirect costs, general and administrative expense, and profit. Fractional parts of an hour shall be payable on a prorated basis. Vouchers may be submitted once each month (or at more frequent intervals, if approved by the Contracting Officer), to the Contracting Officer or designee. The Contractor shall substantiate vouchers by evidence of actual payment and by individual daily job timecards, or other substantiation approved by the Contracting Officer. Promptly after receipt of each substantiated voucher, the Government shall, except as otherwise provided in this contract, and subject to the terms of (e) below, pay the voucher as approved by the Contracting Officer.
> >
> > > (2) Unless otherwise prescribed in the Schedule, the Contracting Officer shall withhold 5 percent of the amounts due under this paragraph (a), but the total amount withheld shall not exceed $ 50,000. The amounts withheld shall be retained until the execution and delivery of a release by the Contractor as provided in paragraph (f) below.
> > >
> > > (3) Unless the Schedule prescribes otherwise, the hourly rates in the Schedule shall not be varied by virtue of the Contractor having performed work on an overtime basis. If no overtime rates are provided in the Schedule and overtime work is approved in advance by the Contracting Officer, overtime rates shall be

negotiated. Failure to agree upon these overtime rates shall be treated as a dispute under the Disputes clause of this contract. If the Schedule provides rates for overtime, the premium portion of those rates will be reimbursable only to the extent the overtime is approved by the Contracting Officer.

(b) Materials and subcontracts. (1) The Contracting Officer will determine allowable costs of direct materials in accordance with Subpart 31.2 of the Federal Acquisition Regulation (FAR) in effect on the date of this contract. Direct materials, as used in this clause, are those materials that enter directly into the end product, or that are used or consumed directly in connection with the furnishing of the end product.

(2) The Contractor may include reasonable and allocable material handling costs in the charge for material to the extent they are clearly excluded from the hourly rate. Material handling costs are comprised of indirect costs, including, when appropriate, general and administrative expense allocated to direct materials in accordance with the Contractor's usual accounting practices consistent with Subpart 31.2 of the FAR.

(3) The Government will reimburse the Contractor for supplies and services purchased directly for the contract when the Contractor—

(i) Has made payments of cash, checks, or other forms of payment for these purchased supplies or services; or

(ii) Will make these payments determined due—

(A) In accordance with the terms and conditions of a subcontract or invoice; and

(B) Ordinarily within 30 days of the submission of the Contractor's payment request to the Government.

(4)(i) The Government will reimburse the Contractor for costs of subcontracts that are authorized under the subcontracts clause of this contract, provided that the costs are consistent with paragraph (b)(5) of this clause.

(ii) The Government will limit reimbursable costs in connection with subcontracts to the amounts paid for supplies and services purchased directly for the contract when the Contractor has made or will make payments determined due of cash, checks, or other forms of payment to the subcontractor—

(A) In accordance with the terms and conditions of a subcontract or invoice; and

(B) Ordinarily within 30 days of the submission of the Contractor's payment request to the Government.

(iii) The Government will not reimburse the Contractor for any costs arising from the letting, administration, or supervision of performance of the subcontract, if the costs are included in the hourly rates payable under paragraph (a)(1) of this clause.

Absent special contract provisions, this clause would appear to require the contractor to bill for subcontractor work on the contract at the amount paid to the subcontractor with no markups by the contractor. See *Compliance Corp.*, ASBCA 35317, 89-2 BCA ¶ 21832, in which the board held that no markups were appropriate under a clause permitting the subcontractor's hours to be billed at the hourly rates in ¶ (a) of the Payment clause. See also *Software Research Assocs.*, ASBCA 33578, 88-3 BCA ¶ 21046, permitting consultants to be billed at the rates referred to in ¶ (a). Some contractors have contended that these cases permit all subcontractor effort in performing the work to be billed as direct labor under ¶ (a), but both cases interpret contracts containing a special provision in addition to the Payments clause.

For contracts for commercial items, the Contract Terms and Conditions—Commercial Items clause at FAR 52.212-4 states:

(i) *Payment.* Payment shall be made for items accepted by the Government that have been delivered to the delivery destinations set forth in this contract. The Government will make payment in accordance with the Prompt Payment Act (31 U.S.C. 3903) and OMB prompt payment regulations at 5 CFR part 1315. In connection with any discount offered for early payment, time shall be computed from the date of the invoice. For the purpose of computing the discount earned, payment shall be considered to have been made on the date which appears on the payment check or the specified payment date if an electronic funds transfer payment is made.

1. Partial Payments

When delivery or performance is authorized in installments, or when a number of items of work are called for by the contract, payment of a portion of the price may be made before the entire contract work is completed. Such payment is an important means of providing funds for performance but is not considered a financing technique. Such payments are considered to be partial payments. FAR 32.102(d) encourages the use of partial payments for supplies or services, as follows:

> Partial payments for accepted supplies and services that are only a part of the contract requirements are authorized under section 305 of the Federal Property and Administrative Services Act (41 U.S.C. 255). Although partial payments are generally treated as a method of payment and not as a method of contract financing, using partial payments can assist contractors to participate in Government contracts without, or with minimal, contract financing. When appropriate, agencies shall use this payment method.

The following provisions for partial payments are contained in the FAR 52.232-1 Payments clause for fixed-price supply and service contracts:

> Unless otherwise specified in this contract, payment shall be made on partial deliveries accepted by the Government if—
>
> (a) The amount due on the deliveries warrants it; or
>
> (b) The Contractor requests it and the amount due on the deliveries is at least $1,000 or 50 percent of the total contract price.

Although the Payments Under Fixed Price Construction Contracts clause at FAR 52.232-5 does not specifically use the term partial payments, ¶ (g) requires payment for each separately priced item, stating, "on completion and acceptance of each separate building, public work, or other division of the contract, for which the price is stated separately in the contract, payment shall be made for the completed work without retention of a percentage."

2. Billing Prices

A significant number of fixed-price contracts do not contain firm prices at the outset but are subject to redetermination of the price during or after performance. The most common contracts of this type are fixed-price incentive contracts and price redetermination contracts. In these types of contracts, the target prices are used as billing prices for the purpose of making payment before the determination of the final contract prices. See the standard clauses in FAR 52.216-5 (Price Redetermination—Prospective); FAR 52.216-6 (Price Redetermination—Retroactive), FAR 52.216-16 (Incentive Price Revision—Firm Target), and FAR 52.216-17 (Incentive Price Revision—Successive Targets). These clauses make it clear that such payments are provisional in nature and provide for adjustment of the billing prices if circumstances change. A typical paragraph outlining the use of such billing prices is contained in the FAR 52.216-5 clause:

> (g) *Adjusting billing prices.* Pending execution of the contract modification (see paragraph (f) above), the Contractor shall submit invoices or vouchers in accordance with the billing prices stated in this contract. If at any time it appears that the then-current billing prices will be substantially greater than the estimated final prices, or if the Contractor submits data showing that the redetermined price will

be substantially greater than the current billing price, the parties shall negotiate an appropriate decrease or increase in billing prices. Any billing price adjustment shall be reflected in a contract modification and shall not affect the redetermination of prices under this clause. After the contract modification for price redetermination is executed, the total amount paid or to be paid on all invoices or vouchers shall be adjusted to reflect the agreed-upon prices, and any requested additional payments, refunds, or credits shall be made promptly.

B. Progress Payments

There are two major types of progress payments—those based on costs and those based on completion of work. Progress payments based on costs are considered financing methods, while those based on completion of the work are not, FAR 32.102(b). Nevertheless, here both types of progress payments are considered as types of payments.

1. Progress Payments Based on Costs

The government's policies with respect to progress payments based on costs are set forth in FAR Subpart 32.5. Provision for progress payments is made by the inclusion of the Progress Payments clause at FAR 52.232-16 in the contract. This clause has Alternates for small businesses, letter contracts, and indefinite-delivery contracts or basic ordering agreements. FAC 2001-13, 68 Fed. Reg. 4047, Jan. 27, 2003, amended the FAR to add a ¶ (m) to these clauses, providing that the contractor is to treat progress payment requests in indefinite-delivery contracts as if each delivery order or task order were a separate contract. This is to ensure that progress payments are segregated by orders, because orders may be funded and accounted for differently.

Normally, progress payments are only included in contracts over $1,000,000 in value ($100,000 for small businesses) that require a substantial amount of time (six months for large businesses and four months for small businesses) between the beginning of performance and the time for deliveries to begin, FAR 32.502-1. Progress payments may be added to contracts when circumstances warrant. FAR 32.501-4(b) indicates that a contract may be amended to provide for progress payments where "unanticipated circumstances arise during contract performance" so long as "adequate new consideration" is provided. Criteria for testing the adequacy of consideration are set forth at FAR 32.501-4(d). See also the Attachment to 5 CFR § 1315, which requires consideration for more favorable progress payments terms.

Determining the amount of progress payments based on costs is quite complex. The contractor is entitled to recover a stipulated percentage of its own costs plus the amount of progress payments made to subcontractors. The percentage of the contractor's costs that may be included in progress payments can change from time to time to time. Thus, the contract clause must be consulted to determine the rate.

The rates for "customary" progress payments are currently 85 percent of costs for small businesses and 80 percent for others. Under limited circumstances, a higher rate, called "unusual" progress payments, may be included, FAR 32.501-2.

The costs upon which progress payments are based will include costs for which the contractor has already made payment or "that are determined due and will be paid to subcontractors [as required by] the terms and conditions of a subcontract or invoice; and [o]rdinarily within 30 days." Previously this ability to include costs incurred but not yet paid in progress payments requests was afforded only to small businesses. It was amended to cover large businesses by FAC 2001-10, 67 Fed. Reg. 70520, Nov. 22, 2002.

Subparagraph (a)(4) of the clause specifically precludes inclusion of the following costs in progress payments for both large and small businesses:

> (4) The Contractor shall not include the following in total costs for progress payment purposes in subparagraph (a)(1)(i) above:
>
> > (i) Costs that are not reasonable, allocable to this contract, and consistent with sound and generally accepted accounting principles and practices.
> >
> > (ii) Costs incurred by subcontractors or suppliers.
> >
> > (iii) Costs ordinarily capitalized and subject to depreciation or amortization except for the properly depreciated or amortized portion of such costs.
> >
> > (iv) Payments made or amounts payable to subcontractors or suppliers, except for—
> >
> > > (A) Completed work, including partial deliveries, to which the Contractor has acquired title; and
> > >
> > > (B) Work under cost-reimbursement or time-and-material subcontracts to which the Contractor has acquired title.

Although the clause does not specifically refer to the Cost Principles in FAR 31.205, contractors under fixed-price incentive and redeterminable contracts would be required to exclude unallowable costs from their billings. This would also be required for contracts covered by Cost Accounting Standards and contracts for which the certification of allowability of overhead costs is required.

2. Progress Payments Based on Percentage of Completion

FAR 32.102(e) provides that progress payments based on a percentage or stage of completion "may be used as a payment method under agency procedures." DFARS 232.102 states that use of progress payments based on percentage or stage of completion will be confined to contracts for construction; shipbuilding; and ship conversion, alteration, or repair. This type of progress payment is standard for construction contracts for all agencies. *See Imperial Props./Constr., Inc.*, ASBCA 49899, 01-1 BCA ¶ 31,382 (the contracting officer's recommendations of the percentages of completion were reasonable and provided a valid basis for the amounts of progress payments). The Payments Under Fixed-Price Construction Contracts clause at FAR 52.232-5 states:

> (b) The Government shall make progress payments monthly as the work proceeds, or at more frequent intervals as determined by the Contracting Officer, on estimates of work accomplished which meets the standards of quality established under the contract, as approved by the Contracting Officer. The Contractor shall furnish a breakdown of the total contract price showing the amount included therein for each principal category of the work, which shall substantiate the payment amount requested in order to provide a basis for determining progress payments, in such detail as requested by the Contracting Officer. In the preparation of estimates the Contracting Officer may authorize material delivered on the site and preparatory work done to be taken into consideration. Material delivered to the Contractor at locations other than the site may also be taken into consideration if—
>
> > (1) Consideration is specifically authorized by this contract; and
> >
> > (2) The Contractor furnishes satisfactory evidence that it has acquired title to such material and that the material will be used to perform this contract.

Since the percentage of completion is applied to the contract price, profit (presuming that the contract is profitable) will be included in the computation of each billing.

This type of payment is also used for fixed-price architect/engineer contracts. See the clause at FAR 52.232-10.

Construction contracts contain special provisions to ensure that (1) timely payment is made to subcontractors and (2) payment is made only for "work accomplished which meets the standards of quality established under the contract." These provisions, required by the Prompt Payment Act, are contained in the certification in ¶ (c) of the clause:

> Along with each request for progress payments, the contractor shall furnish the following certification, or payment shall not be made: (However, it the Contractor elects to delete paragraph (c)(4) from the certification, the certification is still acceptable.)
>
> I hereby certify, to the best of my knowledge and belief, that—
>
> > (1) the amounts requested are only for performance in accordance with the specifications, terms, and conditions of the contract;

(2) Payments to subcontractors and suppliers have been made from previous payments received under the contract, and timely payments will be made from the proceeds of the payment covered by this certification, in accordance with subcontract agreements and the requirements of chapter 39 of Title 31, United States Code; and

(3) This request for progress payments does not include any amounts which the prime contractor intends to withhold or retain from a subcontractor or supplier in accordance with the terms and conditions of the subcontract.

(4) This certification is not to be construed as final acceptance of a subcontractor's performance.

____

(Name)

____

(Title)

____

(Date)

3. Performance-Based Payments

Another type of progress payment based on completion of segments of work is "performance-based" payment. Such payments were adopted by the Federal Acquisition Streamlining Act of 1994, Pub. L. 103-355, amending 10 U.S.C. § 2307(b) and 41 U.S.C. § 255(b). These provisions require "performance-based" payments "whenever practicable" using any of the following bases:

(1) Performance measured by objective, quantifiable methods such as delivery of acceptable items, work measurement, or statistical process controls.

(2) Accomplishment of events defined in the program management plan.

(3) Other quantifiable measures of results.

FAR Subpart 32.10 provides policy and procedures for performance-based payments under noncommercial purchases pursuant to Subpart 32.1.

FAR 32.1001 states:

(a) Performance-based payments are the preferred Government financing method when the contracting officer finds them practical, and the contractor agrees to their use.

(b) Performance-based payments are contract financing payments that are not payment for accepted items.

As discussed below, because performance-based payments are contract financing payments, they are not subject to the interest-penalty provisions of prompt payment.

Performance-based payments may be made on any of the following bases: (a) performance measured by objective, quantifiable methods; (b) accomplishment of defined events; or (c) other quantifiable measures of results, FAR 32.1002. But FAR 32.1003 adds that performance-based payments shall be used only if the following conditions are met:

(a) The contracting officer and offeror are able to agree on the performance-based payment terms;

(b) The contract is a definitized fixed-price type contract; and

(c) The contract does not provide for other methods of contract financing, except that advance payments in accordance with Subpart 32.4, or guaranteed loans in accordance with Subpart 32.3 may be used.

The FAR was amended effective March 27, 2000, to permit the use of performance-based payments in contracts for research and development and contracts awarded through competitive negotiation procedures, as well as to expand the use of subcontractor performance-based payments and commercial financing payments. 59 Fed. Reg. 16276, Mar. 27, 2000.

The applicable clause is Performance-Based Payments in FAR 52.232-32. The solicitation provision Invitation to Propose Performance-Based Payments at FAR 52.232-28 is used in negotiated solicitations that invite offerors to propose performance-based payments.

C. Other Financing Techniques

In some instances, the government will provide payments to a contractor that are not related to completion or delivery of any separately priced or identified portion of the contract work in order to assist the contractor in financing the performance of the contract as a whole. The major type of financing is progress payments, discussed above. While "partial payments" and "billing prices," discussed above, serve to assist the contractor in financing performance of the work, they differ from the payment techniques discussed in this subsection in that they also represent payment of a separately stated price for completed work or delivered items. The payments discussed in this subsection are less frequently used to assist contractors in financing the work.

1. Advance Payments

The most restricted and infrequently used method of financing is advance payment. Advance payments are made prior to a contractor's incurrence of costs to enable it to perform. Thus, they differ from progress and partial payments, which are based on the contractor's completion of work, measured performance, or cost of performance. The general policy of the government authorizing and limiting the use of advance payments is stated in 31 U.S.C. § 3324. Other statutes expressly permit the use of advance payments. For example, 10 U.S.C. § 2307 permits advance payments by the head of the defense agencies up to the unpaid contract price if the contractor gives adequate security and the head of the agency determines that to make advance payment would be in the public interest. A comparable statute, 41 U.S.C. § 255, permits advance payments by the civilian agencies. In 31 U.S.C. § 3324(d), advance payments are expressly permitted for all types of publications. The Federal Acquisition Streamlining Act of 1994, Pub. L. 103-355, added a provision in 10 U.S.C. § 2307 providing for advance payments for commercial items, not to exceed 15 percent of the contract price. It also permits advance payments for salvage contracts. See FAR 32.202. FAR 32.403 outlines the appropriate uses of advance payments.

If advance payments are not expressly permitted by statute, they are usually held to be invalid. See *Johnson Mgmt. Group CFC, Inc. v. Martinez*, 308 F.3d 1245 (Fed. Cir. 2002) (modification to the advance payment provisions of the contract was void as beyond the authority of the contracting officer); *Advance Payment for Maint. of Equip.*, 64 Comp. Gen. 710 (B-219074), 85-2 CPD ¶ 97 (payments to cover maintenance services to be performed in the future were unauthorized advance payments because "agents of the Government are strictly prohibited by statute from compensating contractors for any service or goods which have not been received"). See also *United States v. Amdahl Corp.*, 786 F.2d 387 (Fed. Cir. 1986), in which the court held that a $1.2 million advance payment for equipment was not permitted by any statutory exceptions.

In determining whether a payment is prohibited, the GAO has taken the view that payments are not prohibited if the government will not suffer a loss should the recipient of the payment refuse or fail to perform in the future. Thus, the inclusion of a separately priced warranty in a contract has been distinguished from pre-paid maintenance agreements. In *United States Dep't of Interior—Purchase of Warranties in Advance*, Comp. Gen. Dec. B-249006 (1993), the GAO held that such a warranty does not violate the prohibition against advance payments, stating:

> The purpose of 31 U.S.C. § 3324 is to preclude the possibility of loss to the Government in the event that a contractor, after receipt of payment, should fail to perform his contract or refuse or fail to refund moneys advanced.

The GAO went on to hold that warranties, which ensure the quality of goods purchased and which are bought contemporaneously with those goods, cannot bring about loss to the government. See also *Air Force Request for Advance Decision*, 57 Comp. Gen. 399 (B-191300), 78-1 CPD ¶ 260, holding that the advance payment of rent on an annual basis for the lease of land from a state would not violate the statutory limitation on advance payments because the statute was designed to prevent monetary loss to the government, and since a state was to be the recipient of the advance payment and the lease required no active performance by the state, risk of loss to the government would be remote. But see *National Guard Bureau—Request for Advance Decision*, 58 Comp. Gen. 29 (B-193052), 78-2 CPD ¶ 291, in which the GAO disallowed advance payments to the state because the services to be provided were generally and commercially available in the marketplace.

In *Reimbursements of Total Performance or Payment Bond Premiums to Contractor in First Progress Payment*, 57 Comp. Gen. 25 (B-189402), 77-2 CPD ¶ 319, the GAO held that the reimbursement to contractors of the full amount paid for performance and payment bond premiums in the first progress payment does not contravene the statutory mandate against advance payments. However, the statute was found to have been violated when the District of Columbia paid the full contract price on a computer services contract prior to system installation and delivery of a software package, *Computer Election Sys., Inc.*, Comp. Gen. Dec. (B-195595), 79-2 CPD ¶ 413.

Problems have also arisen in interpreting the statute permitting advance payments for periodicals. For example, in *Advance Payment for Lease/Rental of Microfilm Library to Info. Handling Servs.*, 57 Comp. Gen. 583 (B-192093), 78-2 CPD ¶ 4, the GAO stated that the legislative history of the statute permitting advance payments for subscriptions or other charges for newspapers, magazines, and periodicals indicates that advance payments could be used for the rental as well as purchase of microfilm libraries. On the other hand, in *Advance Payments for Equip. Rental*, Comp. Gen. Dec. B-188166, 77-1 CPD ¶ 391, the GAO stated that 31 U.S.C. § 3324 does not permit advance payment for items of equipment necessary for use in conjunction with these publications. Thus, advance payment could not be made for the rental of microphotographic equipment.

2. Commercial Item Financing

10 U.S.C. § 2307(f) and 41 U.S.C. § 255(f) allow the government to provide financing in the procurement of commercial items if such financing is customary in the commercial marketplace. FAR Subpart 32.2 provides guidance on providing financing in contracts for commercial items. FAR 32.202-1 states:

> (a) *Use of financing in contracts.* It is the responsibility of the contractor to provide all resources needed for performance of the contract. Thus, for purchases of commercial items, financing of the contract is normally the contractor's responsibility. However, in some markets the provision of financing by the buyer is a commercial practice. In these circumstances, the contracting officer may include

appropriate financing terms in contracts for commercial purchases when doing so will be in the best interest of the Government.

(b) *Authorization.* Commercial interim payments and commercial advance payments may be made under the following circumstances—

(1) The contract item financed is a commercial supply or service;

(2) The contract price exceeds the simplified acquisition threshold;

(3) The contracting officer determines that it is appropriate or customary in the commercial marketplace to make financing payments for the item;

(4) Authorizing this form of contract financing is in the best interest of the Government (see paragraph (e) of this subsection);

(5) Adequate security is obtained (see 32.202-4);

(6) Prior to any performance of work under the contract, the aggregate of commercial advance payments shall not exceed 15 percent of the contract price;

(7) The contract is awarded on the basis of competitive procedures or, if only one offer is solicited, adequate consideration is obtained (based on the time value of the additional financing to be provided) if the financing is expected to be substantially more advantageous to the offeror than the offeror's normal method of customer financing; and

(8) The contracting officer obtains concurrence from the payment office concerning liquidation provisions when required by 32.206(e).

FAR 32.202-3 contemplates that contracting officers will determine whether contract financing is customary in the commercial market for the product of service. If it is customary, FAR 32.204 calls for the financing terms to be included in the solicitation. If no such determination is made, FAR 32.205 calls for the use of the Terms for Financing of Purchase of Commercial Items clause, FAR 52.231-29 in the solicitation. The provision allows offerors to propose financing terms that meet the requirements of the FAR. FAR 32.205(c) requires the contracting officer to factor the varying amounts of financing into the best value assessment to determine the most favorable price.

3. Provisional Payments

If final prices have not been established, the government may nevertheless make a provisional payment covering a part or all of the work that has been accomplished. Such a payment is subject to a condition subsequent, that is, final establishment of the price as evidenced by a contract action. Such provisional payments are a financing technique not provided for by the FAR, and their use is restricted to unusual circumstances where they are necessary to enable the contractor to continue performance. See DFARS 232.102-70, stating:

> (a) The contracting officer may establish provisional delivery payments to pay contractors for the costs of supplies and services delivered to and accepted by the Government under the following contract actions if undefinitized:
>
> > (1) Letter contracts contemplating a fixed-price contract.
> >
> > (2) Orders under basic ordering agreements.
> >
> > (3) Spares provisioning documents annexed to contracts.
> >
> > (4) Unpriced equitable adjustments on fixed-price contracts.
> >
> > (5) Orders under indefinite-delivery contracts.
>
> (b) Provisional delivery payments shall be—
>
> > (1) Used sparingly;
> >
> > (2) Priced conservatively; and
> >
> > (3) Reduced by liquidating previous progress payments in accordance with the Progress Payments clause.
>
> (c) Provisional delivery payments shall not—
>
> > (1) Include profit;
> >
> > (2) Exceed funds obligated for the undefinitized contract action; or
> >
> > (3) Influence the definitized contract price.

Provisional payments have also been used where the contractor has asserted a right to price adjustments when no work has been delivered or accepted and no final determinations as to quantum or government liability have been made. Generally, when the government issues a unilateral change order under the Changes clause, the contractor is required to perform the changed work as ordered but cannot bill for that work until the contract is modified to add the negotiated equitable adjustment to the contract price. A problem often arises when the government rejects an invoice that includes the value of changed work and the contractor claims interest under the Prompt Payment Act, 31 U.S.C. § 3901, et seq. As discussed below, no payment is due under the Act because it only applies to proper invoices, and an invoice, to be proper, can only include billings against the contract price. However, in *Bruce-An-*

derson Co., ASBCA 34489, 88-1 BCA ¶ 20,355, the board held that changed work could be properly added to an invoice before the contract modification was executed, relying on a special contract clause entitled Contractor-Prepared Network Analysis System, which modified the standard Payments clause. There, the contracting officer issued provisional payment modifications of $750,000, $750,000, and $400,000. Although the FAR is silent regarding provisional payments on undefinitized change orders, contractors performing a significant amount of work on unilateral change orders that cannot be priced in a timely manner may request contract modifications permitting provisional payments for such work.

DFARS 216.405-2 addresses the use of provisional award fee payments under cost-plus-award-fee contracts. The rule provides for successfully performing contractors to receive a portion of award fees within an evaluation period prior to a final evaluation for that period. This provision was added by DFARS Case 2001-D013, 68 Fed. Reg. 64561, Nov. 14, 2003.

Provisional payments are also allowed on undefinitized contracts, such as letter contracts. FAR 16.603-2 provides that "[a] letter contract may be used when (1) the Government's interests demand that the contractor be given a binding commitment so that work can start immediately and (2) negotiating a definitive contract is not possible in sufficient time to meet the requirement." A negotiating schedule must be included in undefinitized contracts calling for definitized payment terms within 180 days after the date of the letter contract, but this requirement can be waived by the contracting officer, FAR 16.603-2(c). See *Sanders Assocs., Inc. v. United States*, 191 Ct. Cl. 157, 423 F.2d 291 (1970), where the time period for definitization was extended past 180 days. Once work on an undefinitized contract has been performed, provisional payments are allowed as a form of financing. FAR 32.102(e)(2) provides that payments "may not exceed 80 percent of the eligible costs of work accomplished on undefinitized contract actions." 10 U.S.C. § 2326 also sets forth a limitation on the expenditure of funds. Under this provision, the contracting officer for an undefinitized contract action "may not expend with respect to such contractual action an amount that is equal to more than 50 percent of the negotiated overall ceiling price until the contractual terms, specifications, and price are definitized for such contractual action." The amount may be increased to no more than 75 percent if a contractor submits a qualifying proposal before 50 percent of the not-to-exceed price has been expended by the government. This statute is implemented in DFARS 217.7404-4. The government has the option to lower the ceiling, *Litton Sys., Inc., Applied Tech. Div.*, ASBCA 36976, 93-2 BCA ¶ 25,705.

II. PAYMENT PROCEDURES

The subject of payment procedures is complicated by the fact that the regulations do not address the subject in a coherent fashion. Part 32 of the FAR, entitled Contract Financing, covers all types of payment, FAR 32.000. However, the procedures for payment are scattered through its various sections and the contract clauses dealing with payments. Many of the procedures are required by the Prompt Payment Act, 31 U.S.C. § 3901, et seq. This statute requires the government to pay an interest penalty for undisputed "invoice" payments for "each completed item of property or service." Invoice payments are defined as payments for partial deliveries and construction progress payments but excluding financing payments, FAR 32.902. Thus, progress payments based on costs are not covered.

This section deals with all types of payments, whether or not covered by the Prompt Payment Act. It first considers matters important to all types of payments, including the requirements for submission of invoices and vouchers, the personnel involved in the payment process, and the documentation necessary for payment. It then covers the procedures unique to the different types of payment and concludes with an examination of the government's right to withhold payments.

A. Documentation and Authority

The payment process begins with the contractor's submission of a request for payment. This is then reviewed by the government and payment is made if warranted.

1. *Invoices and Vouchers*

The terms "invoice" and "voucher" are used in varying contexts in the statutes and regulations. In some cases they are used synonymously to refer to contractors' billings. In other cases, they may have distinctly different meanings. Vouchers are regularly submitted for payments under cost-reimbursement contracts. However, they are also used under fixed-price contracts. For example, upon completion of a construction contract, the contractor is to present "a properly executed voucher," FAR 52.232-5(h)(2). Vouchers are also used by government officials for approving and recording payments.

The accuracy and completeness of an invoice or voucher becomes critical when the issue arises as to whether a contractor's request for payment subjects the government to the payment of interest if the payment is not made on a timely basis. As noted above, under the Prompt Payment Act the contractor is entitled to interest for delayed payments when proper invoices are submitted for each "complete delivered item of property or service." This is implemented by the Payments clause at FAR 52.232-1, prescribed for fixed-price supply and service contracts, stating that the government's obligation to make payment is conditioned upon the submission by the contractor of a "proper invoice or voucher." The Prompt Payment Act does not apply, however, when there is a bona fide disagreement about the quantity or quality of the work performed or when the contractor's invoices are confusing, *Fanning, Phillips & Molnar*, VABCA 3856, 96-1 BCA ¶ 28,214. Thus, the contractor must submit a "proper invoice" to obtain interest for a delayed payment.

The Prompt Payment Act, 31 U.S.C. § 3901(a)(3), states that a "'proper invoice' is an invoice containing or accompanied by substantiating documentation the Director of the Office of Management and Budget may require by regulation and the head of the appropriate agency may require by regulation or contract." 5 CFR § 1315.9(b) contains detailed guidance concerning the required content of contractor invoices. To constitute a proper invoice, the billing must include the following information:

> (b)(1) Except for interim payment requests under cost-reimbursement service contracts, which are covered by paragraph (b)(2) of this section, the following correct information constitutes a proper invoice and is required as payment documentation:
>
> > (i) Name of vendor;
> >
> > (ii) Invoice date;
> >
> > (iii) Government contract number, or other authorization for delivery of goods or services;
> >
> > (iv) Vendor invoice number, account number, and/or any other identifying number agreed to by contract;
> >
> > (v) Description (including, for example, contract line/subline number), price, and quantity of goods and services rendered;
> >
> > (vi) Shipping and payment terms (unless mutually agreed that this information is only required in the contract);
> >
> > (vii) Taxpayer Identifying Number (TIN), unless agency procedures provide otherwise;
> >
> > (viii) Banking information, unless agency procedures provide otherwise, or except in situations where the EFT requirement is waived under 31 CFR 208.4;
> >
> > (ix) Contact name (where practicable), title and telephone number;
> >
> > (x) Other substantiating documentation or information required by the contract.
>
> (2) An interim payment request under a cost-reimbursement service contract constitutes a proper invoice for purposes of this part if it correctly includes all the information required by the contract or by agency procedures.

In addition to these requirements, FAR 32.905(b)(1)(vii) requires the "name (where practicable), title, phone number, and mailing address of person to be notified in event of a defective invoice." The voucher must also include an accounting classification, the amount to be disbursed, method of disbursement, and payee, Department of Defense Financial Management Regulation, DOD 7000.14-R (DOD FMR), Vol. 5, ¶ 110102. In *General Constr. Co.*, DOTBCA 4137, 03-1 BCA ¶ 32,102, the board ruled that Prompt Payment Act interest accrues on submission of the original invoice, not a facsimile, because a facsimile was not a "proper" invoice.

An invoice will not be proper if it fails to include the required documentation. For instance, in *Radcliffe Constr. Co.*, ASBCA 39252, 90-2 BCA ¶ 22,651, several contract clauses relating to labor standards required the submission of payrolls along with the invoices. The contractor failed to submit its subcontractor's payrolls, and therefore the invoice was found to be improper. In *Ross Plumbing & Heating Co.*, HUDBCA 85-932-C7, 85-3 BCA ¶ 18,478, the board found that, in the absence of documented purchase order authorizations as well as the absence of documented approval recorded in required property inspection reports, the contractor's invoices did not qualify as "proper invoices." See also *Hardrives, Inc.*, IBCA 2319, 94-1 BCA ¶ 26,267, in which the board found that a contractor's invoice was improper because it did not include the requested substantiating documentation, that is, lien waivers for unincorporated on-site materials. Invoices or vouchers with minor spelling or grammatical errors will not be improper, *Tyger-Sayler, (JV)*, ASBCA 33922, 91-2 BCA ¶ 23,726.

Invoices containing amounts for change orders or contractor proposals for an upward adjustment before the execution of a contract modification are not proper invoices. In *Ricway, Inc.*, ASBCA 30205, 86-1 BCA ¶ 18,539, the contractor completed the portion of the work required by a change order and submitted an invoice for progress payments. At the time the invoice was submitted, the total contract price had not yet been adjusted upward to include the value of the changed work. Since progress payments are based on the total contract price and the percentage of work complete, the board ruled that the invoice was not a proper invoice for the value of the changed work. However, the board held that a second invoice, which was submitted after the price adjustment modification, was a proper invoice. In *Columbia Eng'g Corp.*, IBCA 2322, 89-2 BCA ¶ 21,762, the contractor argued that the invoice was proper merely because it had satisfied all the regulatory requirements prescribed by OMB and the FAR. The board rejected this argument, stating at 109,509-10:

> There is an obvious problem with this position in that it presupposes that the amount claimed by [the contractor] for the added or changed work is correct and therefore promptly payable. This position does not allow for the exercise of any judgment by Government personnel in evaluating the claimed compensation and determining it to be in error or excessive. Acceptance of this position would be tantamount to saying that amounts claimed by contractors for changes become immediately due and payable without negotiation, evaluation for merit or error, or other considerations of validity; all on the principle that the Prompt Payment Act places accrual of interest over the determination of merit of the claimed compensation.
>
> The documentation submitted by [the contractor] for each of the modifications were simply proposals for adjustments of the contract price to pay the

> changed work. Prior to incorporation into the contract, the proposed price is subject to change by reason of various reviews by Government personnel and by reason of negotiation with [the contractor]. Until a proposal is accepted by the Government and incorporated into the contract, there exists no sum certain owing to the contractor. Therefore, there cannot be a proper invoice against the contractor's proposed price adjustment prior to incorporation of the agreed amount into the contract.

While this rationale seems fair in cases where the government is diligently trying to negotiate a fair price, it appears harsh in cases where the government cannot explain a lengthy delay in approving a modification. See *Hunter Constr. Co.*, ASBCA 32193, 89-3 BCA ¶ 21,970, in which the board noted that the record did not explain why the government delayed approving the modification for six months. Although the board criticized the government's action as a "failure to act in an appropriate and business-like manner," the board nevertheless applied the *Ricway* rule and found that the invoice was not proper. See also *Sociedade De Construcoes*, ASBCA 37949, 89-3 BCA ¶ 22,028 (10-month delay between negotiation of price and execution of modification).

Upon receipt of an invoice the government agency is given seven days to notify the contractor if it is not a proper invoice. If the agency takes longer than seven days, the excess time is subtracted from the 30-day payment period for the corrected invoice, FAR 32.907(b). Lack of notification has also resulted in a reduction of available time to pay under 5 CFR § 1315, *Bruce-Anderson Co.*, ASBCA 34489, 88-1 BCA ¶ 20,355. The fact that an agency failed to notify a contractor of claimed deficiencies within the required time was also considered strong evidence that the invoice was proper, *EMS, Inc.*, GSBCA 9588, 90-2 BCA ¶ 22,876.

A valid request for payment may also need to include a release if the contract requires it, *United Pac. Ins. Co.*, ASBCA 53051, 03-2 BCA ¶ 32,267 (surety not entitled to payment because it did not provide the release required by FAR 52.232-5(h)(3)).

2. Documentation of Acceptance

Documentation of the completion of work or receipt of supplies is generally accomplished on written "receiving reports." These receiving reports and the contractor's invoices form the documentation for payment. 5 CFR § 1315.9(c) contains the following guidance concerning receiving reports:

> (c) Except for interim payment requests under cost-reimbursement service contracts, the following information from receiving reports, delivery tickets, and evaluated receipts is required as payment documentation:
>
> (1) Name of vendor;

(2) Contract or other authorization number;

(3) Description of goods or services;

(4) Quantities received, if applicable;

(5) Date(s) goods were delivered or services were provided;

(6) Date(s) goods or services were accepted;

(7) Signature (or electronic alternative when supported by appropriate internal controls), printed name, telephone number, mailing address of the receiving official, and any additional information required by the agency.

Because of the importance of the delivery or completion date in determining the payment due date, agencies are required to ensure that receipt and acceptance are executed as promptly as possible. Receiving reports must be forwarded in time to be received by the designated payment office by the fifth business day after acceptance, unless other arrangements are made. Designated payment offices are required to stamp receiving reports and invoices with the date received in that office.

In the Department of Defense, DD Form 250, Material Inspection and Receiving Report, has long been used for this purpose. This form is now set forth at DFARS 253.303-250c and is also specified for use by NFS 18-53.303. The General Services Administration has included GSA Form 3025, Receiving Report, at GSAR 553.370-3025. The FAR does not contain a form designed to function as a receiving report. In commercial contracting under FAR Part 12, SF 1449 also can be used as an acceptance document.

3. Assignment of Payment

The Assignment of Claims Act of 1940, 31 U.S.C. §3727, 41 U.S.C. § 15, permits contractors to assign the right to payment to "financing institutions." FAR 32.802 implements this Act as follows:

> Under the Assignment of Claims Act, a contractor may assign moneys due or to become due under a contract if all the following conditions are met:
>
> (a) The contract specifies payments aggregating $ 1,000 or more.
>
> (b) The assignment is made to a bank, trust company, or other financing institution, including any Federal lending agency.
>
> (c) The contract does not prohibit the assignment.
>
> (d) Unless otherwise expressly permitted in the contract, the assignment–

(1) Covers all unpaid amounts payable under the contract;

(2) Is made only to one party, except that any assignment may be made to one party as agent or trustee for two or more parties participating in the financing of the contract; and

(3) Is not subject to further assignment.

(e) The assignee sends a written notice of assignment together with a true copy of the assignment instrument to the–

(1) Contracting officer or the agency head;

(2) Surety on any bond applicable to the contract; and

(3) Disbursing officer designated in the contract to make payment.

If the government pays the contractor after a valid assignment of payment, it will be liable to pay the assignee the amount of the payment, *Produce Factors Corp. v. United States*, 199 Ct. Cl. 572, 467 F.2d 1343 (1972); *Central Nat'l Bank v. United States*, 117 Ct. Cl. 389, 91 F. Supp. 738 (1950). Generally the assignee must ensure that the formal requirements for valid assignments are strictly complied with, but in a few cases it has been held that the government waived such requirements. See *Riviera Fin. of Tex., Inc. v. United States,* 58 Fed. Cl. 528 (2003) (government recognized assignment by modifying contract to substitute the assignee's address and made payments to the assignee), and *Norwest Bank Ariz. v. United States*, 37 Fed. Cl. 605 (1997) (government modified contract to recognize assignment). Compare *Banco Bilbao Vizcaya-Puerto Rico v. United States*, 48 Fed. Cl. 29 (2000), rejecting the assignee's contention that the government had waived the formalities because it took no steps that indicated that it had accepted the assignment.

Generally, the government is not bound to pay an assignee that is not a financing institution. However, in *D & H Distrib. Co. v. United States,* 102 F.3d 542 (Fed. Cir. 1996), the contracting officer had modified the contract to make the contractor and the subcontractor joint payees. Despite the statutory prohibition on the assignment of rights in government contracts, the court found that the contract modification could be viewed as making the subcontractor a third party beneficiary of the right of payment under the contract. The court stated at 546-47:

> In the case of a contract in which the promisee provides goods or services to the promisor, it has long been settled that a clause providing for the promisor to pay the proceeds of the contract to a third party is enforceable by the third party where the payment is intended to satisfy a present or future liability of the promisee to the third party. The third party beneficiary in that situation has traditionally been referred to as a "creditor beneficiary" and has been accorded full rights to sue under the original contract. See 4 Arthur Linton Corbin, Corbin on Contracts § 787

(1951); 3 E. Allan Farnsworth, Farnsworth on Contracts § 10.2 (1990); 2 Samuel Williston, A Treatise on the Law of Contracts §§ 361-64, 381 (Walter H.E. Jaeger ed., 3d ed. 1959); Restatement of Contracts § 133(1)(b) (1932); see also *Restatement, Second, Contracts* § 302 (1981) (extending third party beneficiary status to the broader category of "intended" beneficiaries).

The same principle would apply if the payment clause provided that a portion of the proceeds would be paid to the promisee and a portion to the third party. Indeed, the government has often successfully invoked that rule in seeking to enforce a contract between private parties that included an undertaking by the promisor to pay a debt owed by the promisee to the government. See, e.g., *United States v. Wood*, 877 F.2d 453, 457-58 (6th Cir. 1989); *Karpe v. United States*, 167 Ct. Cl. 280, 335 F.2d 454, 463 (Ct. Cl. 1964); *United States v. Phoenix Indem. Co.*, 231 F.2d 573, 575 (4th Cir. 1956); and *United States v. Scott*, 167 F.2d 301, 302-03 (8th Cir. 1948); see also *Fireman's Fund Ins. Co. v. United States*, 909 F.2d 495, 499 n. (Fed. Cir. 1990) (identifying government as intended third-party beneficiary of performance bond contract between contractor and surety).

We see no reason to adopt a different rule in the case of a joint payment provision, such as the one in this case, where the only difference is that the respective shares of the two parties is not specified in the contract. Consistent with this analysis, court decisions involving such joint payment agreements have characterized them as making the joint payee a third-party beneficiary of the contract with the right to sue the promisor for breach. See, e.g., *United States ex rel. Youngstown Welding & Eng'g Co. v. Travelers Indem. Co.*, 802 F.2d 1164, 1167-68 (9th Cir. 1986); *Merco Mfg., Inc. v. J.P. McMichael Constr. Co.*, 372 F. Supp. 967, 971-72 (W.D. La. 1974); *cf. Maccaferri Gardens, Inc. v. Dynateria, Inc.*, 91 F.3d 1431, 1441 (11th Cir. 1996) (assuming arguendo that joint payment provision in contract created a third-party beneficiary arrangement under Florida law).

4. Payment Authority

Although contracting officers have authority to enter into contracts that obligate the government to pay for goods and services provided by contractors, generally only officers and employees designated as "disbursing officials" of the Department of the Treasury may disburse public monies available for expenditure by an "executive agency," 31 U.S.C. § 3321. The Secretary of the Treasury also designates personnel in other executive agencies to disburse public monies. In addition, 31 U.S.C. § 3321(c) specifically authorizes the "heads of the military departments of the Department of Defense" to designate personnel to disburse public monies.

The responsibilities and authority of disbursing officers are set forth in agency regulations and federal statutes. 31 U.S.C. § 3325 provides as follows:

(a) A disbursing official in the executive branch of the United States Government shall—

(1) disburse money only as provided by a voucher certified by—

(A) the head of the executive agency concerned; or

(B) an officer or employee of the executive agency having written authorization from the head of the agency to certify vouchers;

(2) examine a voucher if necessary to decide if it is—

(A) in proper form;

(B) certified and approved; and

(C) computed correctly on the facts certified; and

(3) except for the correctness of computations on a voucher, be held accountable for carrying out clauses (1) and (2) of this subsection.

(b) Subsection (a) of this section does not apply to disbursements of a military department of the Department of Defense, except for disbursements for departmental pay and expenses in the District of Columbia.

(c) On request, the Secretary of the Treasury may provide to the appropriate officer or employee of the United States Government a list of persons receiving periodic payments from the Government. When certified and in proper form, the list may be used as a voucher on which the Secretary may disburse money.

For detailed guidance on the appointment, authority, and responsibility of disbursing and certifying officers, see the Treasury Financial Manual, and if a DoD contract is involved, the DOD Financial Management Regulation.

Certifying and disbursing officials may be held liable for improper payments, 31 U.S.C. § 3322 and § 3541. The Department of Defense provides specific procedures to investigate any lost funds or improprieties by the officials, DOD FMR, Vol. 5, Chapter 6. The person accountable may be relieved of liability by the GAO, 31 U.S.C. § 3527 and § 3528. If not, 31 U.S.C. § 3542 provides for the seizure of the accountable official's property and imprisonment until the debt is discharged. In addition, 31 U.S.C. § 3545 requires a civil action to be brought by the Justice Department for the amount due. Disbursing or certifying officials who are in doubt concerning the propriety of a payment are entitled to an advance decision from the GAO, 31 U.S.C. § 3529.

5. *Overpayments*

Prior to 2001 contractors had no obligation to notify the government if they were paid amounts that they were not owed. However, FAC 2001-02, 66 Fed. Reg.

65347, Dec. 18, 2001, added a new paragraph to the Prompt Payment clause, FAR 52.232-25, the Prompt Payment for Fixed-Price Architect-Engineer Contracts clause, FAR 52.232-26, and the Prompt Payment for Construction Contracts clause, FAR 52.232-27, requiring the reporting of overpayments. This paragraph reads:

> *Overpayments*. If the Contractor becomes aware of a duplicate payment or that the Government has otherwise overpaid on an invoice payment, the Contractor shall immediately notify the Contracting Officer and request instructions for disposition of the overpayment.

There is no such obligation if one of these clauses is not in the contract, but contractors should report such payments nonetheless.

The government has a clear legal right to recover overpayments. See *ETA Tech. Corp.*, ASBCA 48417, 97-1 BCA ¶ 28,666 (government's failure to get the services of a computer scientist having the credentials specified in a service contract was sufficient proof of damages, entitling the government to the recovery of its overpayment for the employee's services).

6. Discounts

The government must insert the Discounts for Prompt Payment clause, FAR 52.232-8, in solicitations and contracts when a fixed-price supply contract or fixed-price service contract is contemplated, FAR 32.111(c)(1). This clause provides as follows:

> (a) Discounts for prompt payment will not be considered in the evaluation of offers. However, any offered discount will form a part of the award, and will be taken if payment is made within the discount period indicated in the offer by the offeror. As an alternative to offering a prompt payment discount in conjunction with the offer, offerors awarded contracts may include prompt payment discounts on individual invoices.
>
> (b) In connection with any discount offered for prompt payment, time shall be computed from the date of the invoice. For the purpose of computing the discount earned, payment shall be considered to have been made on the date which appears on the payment check or the date on which an electronic funds transfer was made.

Although prompt payment discount clauses are mandatory for fixed-price supply and services contracts, there is nothing to preclude their use in other types of contracts, such as cost-reimbursement contracts, *Jerry Fairbanks Prods.*, Comp. Gen. Dec. B-181811, 75-1 CPD ¶ 154; interim payments under a cost-reimbursement contract, *Technology for Communications Int'l*, ASBCA 36265, 93-3 BCA ¶ 26,139; and construction contracts, Comp. Gen. Dec., B-177811, Apr. 9, 1973, *Unpub*. Prompt payment discounts may also be taken on progress payments, *Jay Dee Militarywear, Inc.*, ASBCA 46539, 94-2 BCA ¶ 26,829. In *Jay Dee*, the contractor submitted five separate claims based on allegedly improper early payment discounts taken in liquidation of progress payments on invoices not paid within the discount period. In finding that the government was entitled to take prompt payment discounts, the board stated at 133,453:

> Once deliveries have commenced, under the "Payments" clause the contractor is entitled to receive payment for the items delivered, usually based on the invoices submitted in connection with shipments, as was the case here. As long as the contractor is credited with the payments, it is immaterial for prompt payment purposes that a portion of payment is allocated to the liquidation of progress payments and another portion is paid in the form of a check or electronic transfer. This is in conformance with FAR 32.503-8 (Liquidation rates—ordinary method) which states that progress payments "are recouped by the Government through the deduction of liquidations from payments that would otherwise be due to the contractor for completed items."
>
> The provisions of the contract entitled the government to compute a discount when payment was made (mailing a check or electronic transfer) within a specified period from "the date of delivery" or from "the date a proper invoice or voucher is received . . . by the Government," whichever was later.
>
> As stated by the Board and the Comptroller General in their opinions, progress payments are made in advance of delivery and thus prior to the beginning of the discount period. "Certainly the progress payment has been a prompt payment within the terms of the discount clause . . . . The contractor has had the use of these funds and the finance officer is entitled to take a prompt payment discount on them at the time they are recouped." 46 Comp. Gen. 430, 433 (1966).

See also *Metadure Corp.*, ASBCA 21327, 77-1 BCA ¶ 12,477, in which the board held that the government was entitled to a prompt payment discount on progress payments remitted to the contractor after the discount period but prior to delivery of the items.

5 CFR § 1315.7 states that prompt payment discounts offered by contractors are to be taken whenever "economically justified," but only after acceptance has occurred. In such circumstances, the regulation provides that payment will be made "as close as possible" to the discount date. The burden of accomplishing acceptance and making timely payment in order to qualify for a discount is on the agency.

B. Electronic Payment

31 U.S.C. § 3332(f) requires "all federal payments" after January 1, 1999, to be made by electronic funds transfer (EFT) unless waived by the Secretary of the Treasury. Waivers are set forth in 31 CFR § 208.4. These requirements are implemented in FAR 32.1103 as follows:

> The Government shall provide all contract payments through EFT except if—

(a) The office making payment under a contract that requires payment by EFT, loses the ability to release payment by EFT. To the extent authorized by 31 CFR part 208, the payment office shall make necessary payments pursuant to paragraph (a)(2) of the clause at either 52.232-33 or 52.232-34 until such time as it can make EFT payments;

(b) The payment is to be received by or on behalf of the contractor outside the United States and Puerto Rico (but see 32.1106(b));

(c) A contract is paid in other than United States currency (but see 32.1106(b));

(d) Payment by EFT under a classified contract could compromise the safeguarding of classified information or national security, or arrangements for appropriate EFT payments would be impractical due to security considerations;

(e) A contract is awarded by a deployed contracting officer in the course of military operations, including, but not limited to, contingency operations as defined in 2.101, or a contract is awarded by any contracting officer in the conduct of emergency operations, such as responses to natural disasters or national or civil emergencies, if—

(1) EFT is not known to be possible; or

(2) EFT payment would not support the objectives of the operation;

(f) The agency does not expect to make more than one payment to the same recipient within a one-year period;

(g) An agency's need for supplies and services is of such unusual and compelling urgency that the Government would be seriously injured unless payment is made by a method other than EFT;

(h) There is only one source for supplies and services and the Government would be seriously injured unless payment is made by a method other than EFT; or

(i) Otherwise authorized by Department of the Treasury Regulations at 31 CFR Part 208.

The requirement for payment by EFT is included in contracts by the use of either the Payment by Electronic Funds Transfer—Central Contractor Registration clause in FAR 52.232-33 or the Payment by Electronic Funds Transfer—Other Than Central Contractor Registration clause in FAR 52.232-34. FAR 32.1110 contains instructions on the use of these clauses as well as accompanying solicitation provisions. This procedure is not a substitution for an assignment of claims to a financial institution, FAR 32.1105.

The government can also make electronic payments by using a government-wide commercial purchase card, FAR 32.1108. When this is intended, the Payment by Third Party clause in FAR 52.232-36 is to be included in the contract or purchase order.

When a contractor enters information into the central contractor registration system, its EFT account is required to be included. This will automatically direct contract payments to that account unless the contractor changes the information for a specific contract. See *JGB Enters., Inc. v. United States*, 63 Fed. Cl. 319 (2004), for a case describing the difficulties that a contractor may encounter in making such a change. There a subcontractor recovered as a third-party beneficiary when such a change was made by a contract modification but did not recover when a different payee was included in a purchase order. See also *FloorPro, Inc.*, ASBCA 54143, 04-1 BCA ¶ 32,571, holding that nothing in the FAR 52.232-33 clause barred the contracting officer from modifying the contract to require the government to pay by checks made out jointly to the contractor and a subcontractor. The board held that this arrangement made the subcontractor a third-party beneficiary in accordance with *D & H Distrib. Co. v. United States*, 102 F.3d 542 (Fed. Cir. 1996). This allowed the subcontractor to recover against the government when a payment was made solely to the contractor. Compare *Flexfab, L.L.C. v. United States*, 62 Fed. Cl. 139 (2004), *aff'd*, 424 F.3d 1254 (Fed. Cir. 2005), finding no third-party beneficiary arrangement when the contracting officer modified the contract to require payment to a subcontractor's escrow agent without knowledge of that person's status. The court ruled that the lack of knowledge precluded a finding that the contracting officer intended to benefit the subcontractor. The result was that the subcontractor could not recover against the government when it made an EFT to the contractor's central contractor registration account instead of the subcontractor's escrow agent as required by the modification.

C. Time for Payment of the Price

The Prompt Payment Act's requirement for the payment of interest on late payments makes it essential to determine when payment is due. This is considered in the first section that follows. The next section considers an optional "fast payment" procedure, which may be used for purchases within the simplified acquisition threshold.

1. Other Than Simplified Acquisitions

The government's due date for making payment is generally either (1) on the date(s) specified in the contract or (2) if a payment date is not specified in the contract, 30 days after the government receives a proper invoice for the amount due, 31 U.S.C. § 3903(a)(1); 5 CFR § 1315. This period is shortened for the acquisition of certain food products and perishable agricultural commodities. Specifically, the 1988 Amendments to the Prompt Payment Act set the due date for meat products at seven days after delivery. This statutory time period cannot be altered by contract. The

Amendments left it to OMB to set the due date for perishables, which the Circular established at 10 days unless otherwise specified by contract. The Amendments also expanded the definition of meat products to include poultry and eggs, 31 U.S.C. § 3903(a)(2), and added a new section requiring payment within 10 days of receipt of a proper invoice for dairy products and edible fats and oils, which cannot be varied by contract, 31 U.S.C. § 3903(a)(4). Payment due dates are important because they trigger the running of interest on those payments covered by the Prompt Payment Act.

The FAR implementation of the 1988 Amendments largely repeats the statute but makes some significant selections concerning payment due dates. FAR 32.903 states the following policy with respect to payment due dates:

> All solicitations and contracts subject to this subpart shall specify payment procedures, payment due dates, and interest penalties for late invoice payment. Invoice payments and contract financing payments will be made by the Government as close as possible to (or earlier as determined by the Agency head to be necessary on a case-by-case basis), but not later than the due dates specified in the contract by incorporation of the clauses at 52.232-25, Prompt Payment, 52.232-26, Prompt Payment for Fixed-Price Architect-Engineer Contracts, or 52.232-27, Prompt Payment for Construction Contracts. Payment will be based on receipt of a proper invoice or contract financing request and satisfactory contract performance. Agency procedures shall ensure that, when specifying due dates, full consideration is given to the time reasonably required by Government officials to fulfill their administrative responsibilities under the contract.

Thus, the FAR mandates that all solicitations and contracts subject to the Prompt Payment Act specify payment due dates. Moreover, FAR 32.905(a)(1) requires due dates that are generally the later of 30 days after receipt of a proper invoice or 30 days after acceptance of the supplies delivered or services performed. Paragraph (i)(2) of the Contract Terms and Conditions—Commercial Items clause, FAR 52.212-4, making contracts for commercial items subject to the Prompt Payment Act, contains no guidance on due dates.

The first step in calculating the payment due date is to determine when an invoice or voucher was received. 31 U.S.C. § 3901(a)(4) provides:

> (4) for the purposes of determining a payment due date and the date upon which any late payment interest penalty shall begin to accrue, the head of the agency is deemed to receive an invoice—
>
> > (A) on the later of—
> >
> > > (i) the date on which the place or person designated by the agency to first receive such invoice actually receives a proper invoice; or
> > >
> > > (ii) on the 7th day after the date on which, in accordance with the terms and conditions of the contract, the property is actually

delivered or performance of the services is actually completed, as the case may be, unless—

(I) the agency has actually accepted such property or services before such 7th day; or

(II) the contract (except in the case of a contract for the procurement of a brand-name commercial item for authorized resale) specifies a longer acceptance period, as determined by the contracting officer to be required to afford the agency a practicable opportunity to inspect and test the property furnished or evaluate the services performed; or

(B) on the date of the invoice, if the agency has failed to annotate the invoice with the date of receipt at the time of actual receipt by the place or person designated by the agency to first receive such invoice.

OMB Circular A-125 was succeeded and replaced by the Prompt Pay Regulation of 5 CFR Part 1315. This Regulation also includes a controversial provision covering timely payment, which provides:

> 4.1. Timely payment. An agency shall make payments no more than seven days prior to the payment due date, but as close to the due date as possible, unless the agency head or designee of such officer has determined, on a case-by-case basis for specific payments, that earlier payment is necessary. This authority must be used cautiously, weighing the benefit of making an early payment against the good stewardship inherent in effective cash management practices.

This provision has in some instances resulted in slower processing of payment requests than was normal prior to passage of the Prompt Payment Act.

Under the Prompt Payment Act, payment is deemed to occur not upon the contractor's receipt of a government check, but rather "on the date a check for payment is dated or an electronic fund transfer is made," 31 U.S.C. § 3901(a)(5). Payments made by electronic fund transfer (EFT) are made on the "settlement date," which means the date on which an EFT payment is credited to the contractor's financial institution, FAR 32.903. Payment by EFT is mandated in most situations, FAR 32.1103.

2. Fast Payment

FAR 13.4 establishes a "fast payment" procedure, which allows for expedited payment for small purchases. FAR 13.402 states that "the fast payment procedures may be used, provided that use of the procedure is consistent with the other conditions of the purchase." The conditions for use of the fast payment procedure are as follows:

(a) Individual purchasing instruments do not exceed $25,000 except that executive agencies may permit higher dollar limitations for specified activities or items on a case-by-case basis.

(b) Deliveries of supplies are to occur at locations where there is both a geographical separation and a lack of adequate communications facilities between Government receiving and disbursing activities that will make it impractical to make timely payment based on evidence of Government acceptance.

(c) Title to the supplies passes to the Government—

(1) Upon delivery to a post office or common carrier for mailing or shipment to destination; or

(2) Upon receipt by the Government if the shipment is by means other than Postal Service or common carrier.

(d) The supplier agrees to replace, repair, or correct supplies not received at destination, damaged in transit, or not conforming to purchase requirements.

(e) The purchasing instrument is a firm-fixed price contract, a purchase order, or a delivery order for supplies.

(f) A system is in place to ensure—

(1) Documentation of evidence of contractor performance under fast payment purchases;

(2) Timely feedback to the contracting officer in case of contractor deficiencies; and

(3) Identification of suppliers who have a current history of abusing the fast payment procedure (also see subpart 9.1).

Under this procedure, payment is processed upon the agency's receipt of the invoice without the need to wait for inspection and formal acceptance of the goods. In return, the contractor is required to represent that it has delivered the goods and will replace, repair, or correct any damaged or nonconforming items. The Prompt Payment clause requires government payment to contractors within 15 days after receipt of a proper invoice, FAR 52.232-25(c). DFARS 213.402 allows the use of these procedures for orders above the simplified acquisition threshold for (1) brand name commissary resale subsistence and (2) medical supplies for direct shipment overseas. Purchase orders incorporating the fast payment procedure will ordinarily be issued on Optional Form 347, Order for Supplies or Services, or the agency's authorized Purchase Order form. Fast payment procedures may also be used under Blanket Purchase Agreements. The clause to be included in solicitations and contracts under which fast payment procedures are intended for use is set forth at FAR 52.213-1.

D. Progress Payment Procedures

The billing procedures and timing are radically different for the different types of progress payments. One reason for this difference is that cost-based progress payments are considered to be financing techniques not subject to the Prompt Payment Act's interest penalties. In addition, the Prompt Payment Act contains a number of specific requirements applicable to construction contract progress payments.

1. Cost-Based Progress Payments

Cost-based progress payments are made on the basis of contractor requests for payment, which are subject to audit by the government, FAR 52.232-16(g). This section considers the time when payment is to be made and the government's rights to suspend or reduce payments.

a. Time for Payment

The Progress Payments clause at FAR 52.232-16 provides that payment shall be made when requested by the contractor "as the work progresses, but not more frequently than monthly." The length of time that the government has to make the payment depends on agency policy. FAR 32.906 states that agencies should not generally set the time for payment earlier than 7 days.

The Department of Defense guidance is set forth in DFARS 232.906, as follows:

> (a)(i) DoD policy is to make contract financing payments as quickly as possible. Generally, the contracting officer shall insert the standard due dates of 7 days for progress payments and 14 days for interim payments on cost type contracts in subparagraphs (b)(1) of the Prompt Payment clauses at FAR 52.232-25, 52.232-26, and 52.232-27.

b. Delays in Payment

Unjustified delays in making progress payments may entitle the contractor to excusable delays. In *Shepard Div., Vogue Instrument Corp.*, ASBCA 15571, 74-1 BCA ¶ 10,498, a default termination was held improper because of excusable delays that included government refusal to pay progress payments based on a misinterpretation of a funding limitation in the progress payments provisions of the contract. Similarly, in *Lea County Constr. Co.*, ASBCA 10093, 67-1 BCA ¶ 6243, an excusable delay was recognized for government delays in making progress payments. However, the delay must be the government's responsibility and must be the cause of the contractor's inability to perform on time, *MVI Precision Mach., Ltd.*, ASBCA 37393, 91-2 BCA ¶ 23,898.

It has been held proper to "delay" the initiation of progress payments pending the conclusion of a satisfactory audit, *Finast Metal Prods., Inc.*, ASBCA 19860, 77-1 BCA ¶ 12,331; *Midwest Metal Stamping Co.*, ASBCA 11543, 67-2 BCA ¶ 6605. However, the refusal to pay progress payments to force the contractor into complying with contract terms could be improper, depending on the nature of the term and the potential injury to the government. See *Martin Marietta Corp.*, ASBCA 31248, 87-2 BCA ¶ 19,875, *recons. denied*, 88-1 BCA ¶ 20,422 (refusal to make payments on cost-reimbursement contracts to "club" contractor into making internal audit reports available not proper).

A "delay" in paying the entire payment request is not actionable if the government estimate of how much work was done is reasonable. See *Delta Constr. Co.*, ASBCA 42453, 96-1 BCA ¶ 28,106, holding that the contractor was not entitled to an equitable adjustment for an alleged government misestimate of progress payments. The parties' progress estimates differed to a maximum of 13.85 percent, and the parties came to substantial agreement on the percentage of progress, differing by only 0.67 percent by the time of the twenty-seventh invoice.

c. Suspension or Reduction of Progress Payments

The Progress Payments clause at FAR 52.232-16 contains the following paragraph giving the contracting officer the right to reduce or suspend progress payments:

> (c) *Reduction or suspension.* The Contracting Officer may reduce or suspend progress payments, increase the rate of liquidation, or take a combination of these actions, after finding on substantial evidence any of the following conditions:
>
> > (1) The Contractor failed to comply with any material requirement of this contract (which includes paragraphs (f) and (g) in this clause).
> >
> > (2) Performance of this contract is endangered by the Contractor's (i) failure to make progress or (ii) unsatisfactory financial condition.
> >
> > (3) Inventory allocated to this contract substantially exceeds reasonable requirements.
> >
> > (4) The Contractor is delinquent in payment of the costs of performing this contract in the ordinary course of business.
> >
> > (5) The unliquidated progress payments exceed the fair value of the work accomplished on the undelivered portion of this contract.
> >
> > (6) The Contractor is realizing less profit than that reflected in the establishment of any alternate liquidation rate in paragraph (b) above, and that rate is less than the progress payment rate stated in subparagraph (a)(1) above.

This paragraph contains the requirement that the contracting officer's decision be based on "substantial evidence." FAR 32.503-6 instructs the contracting officer on the use of and prerequisites for this authority, such as notifying the contractor of the intended action, providing an opportunity for discussion, and "considering the general equities of the particular situation." Progress payment suspensions have been upheld when the contracting officer has followed this guidance, *Davis v. United States*, 180 Ct. Cl. 20 (1967) (commenting on the substantial evidence issue); *National E. Corp. v. United States*, 201 Ct. Cl. 776, 477 F.2d 1347 (1973). For other cases upholding the suspension of progress payments, see *Dennis Berlin d/b/a Spectro Sort and as Spectro Sort Mfg. Co.*, ASBCA 51919, 02-1 BCA ¶ 31,675 (government properly suspended progress payments because the contractor was delinquent in delivery, had no accounting system to properly administer progress payments and could not support an audit of the incurred costs); *Sach Sinha & Assoc., Inc.,* ASBCA 47594, 00-1 BCA ¶ 30,735 (suspension of progress payments justified because the contracting officer had reason to conclude that contractor's accounting system was inadequate, as its indirect costs were unidentifiable); *Flight Refueling, Inc.*, ASBCA 46846, 97-2 BCA ¶ 29,000 (refusal to make progress payments proper because the contractor's accounting system and controls were inadequate for progress payment purposes); *Sermor, Inc.*, ASBCA 30576, 94-1 BCA ¶ 26,302 (reasonable to suspend a progress payment while considering whether a contract should be default terminated); *Murdock Mach. & Eng'g Co. of Utah*, ASBCA 20409, 88-1 BCA ¶ 20,354, *rev'd on other grounds*, 873 F.2d 1410 (Fed. Cir. 1989) (suspension reasonable because of contractor's lack of progress and poor financial condition); *Sermor, Inc.*, ASBCA 29046, 87-1 BCA ¶ 19,568 (progress payment suspension proper because contractor failed to comply with the delivery schedule and was in an unsatisfactory financial condition); and *Electro Optical Mechanisms, Inc.*, ASBCA 20704, 79-2 BCA ¶ 14,135 (progress payment suspension proper where it became clear that the contractor's financial ability to fulfill the contract was in jeopardy).

Where the contracting officer has not fully investigated the contractor's financial situation or has not properly interpreted the clause, relief for suspension of progress payments has been granted. For example, in *National Radio Co.*, ASBCA 14707, 72-2 BCA ¶ 9486, the board held that liquidated damages should not be assessed when the contractor had been delayed by a suspension of progress payments without discussion with the contractor or written findings by the contracting officer. Further, progress payments may not be withheld or suspended for failure to comply with equal employment opportunity requirements without a prior hearing in accordance with 41 CFR § 60-1.26, 52 Comp. Gen. 476 (B-167015) (1973).

The statutes call for reduction or suspension of contract payments when there is "substantial evidence" of fraud. See 10 U.S.C. § 2307, stating:

> (i) *Action in case of fraud.* (1) In any case in which the remedy coordination official of an agency finds that there is substantial evidence that the request of a contractor for advance, partial, or progress payment under a contract awarded by that

agency is based on fraud, the remedy coordination official shall recommend that the head of the agency reduce or suspend further payments to such contractor.

The same language is used in 41 U.S.C. § 255(g). These statutes are implemented in FAR 32.006-4, which contains the following procedures:

(a) In any case in which an agency's remedy coordination official finds substantial evidence that a contractor's request for advance, partial, or progress payments under a contract awarded by that agency is based on fraud, the remedy coordination official shall recommend that the agency head reduce or suspend further payments to the contractor. The remedy coordination official shall submit to the agency head a written report setting forth the remedy coordination official's findings that support each recommendation.

(b) Upon receiving a recommendation from the remedy coordination official under paragraph (a) of this subsection, the agency head shall determine whether substantial evidence exists that the request for payment under a contract is based on fraud.

(c) If the agency head determines that substantial evidence exists, the agency head may reduce or suspend further payments to the contractor under the affected contract(s). Such reduction or suspension shall be reasonably commensurate with the anticipated loss to the Government resulting from the fraud.

(d) In determining whether to reduce or suspend further payment(s), as a minimum, the agency head shall consider—

(1) A recommendation from investigating officers that disclosure of the allegations of fraud to the contractor may compromise an ongoing investigation;

(2) The anticipated loss to the Government as a result of the fraud;

(3) The contractor's overall financial condition and ability to continue performance if payments are reduced or suspended;

(4) The contractor's essentiality to the national defense, or to the execution of the agency's official business; and

(5) Assessment of all documentation concerning the alleged fraud, including documentation submitted by the contractor in its response to the notice required by paragraph (e) of this subsection.

(e) Before making a decision to reduce or suspend further payments, the agency head shall, in accordance with agency procedures—

(1) Notify the contractor in writing of the action proposed by the remedy coordination official and the reasons therefor[e] (such notice must be suf-

ficiently specific to permit the contractor to collect and present evidence addressing the aforesaid reasons); and

(2) Provide the contractor an opportunity to submit information within a reasonable time, in response to the action proposed by the remedy coordination official.

(f) When more than one agency has contracts affected by the fraud, the agencies shall consider designating one agency as the lead agency for making the determination and decision.

(g) The agency shall retain in its files the written justification for each—

(1) Decision of the agency head whether to reduce or suspend further payments; and

(2) Recommendation received by an agency head in connection with such decision.

(h) Not later than 180 calendar days after the date of the reduction or suspension action, the remedy coordination official shall—

(1) Review the agency head's determination on which the reduction or suspension decision is based; and

(2) Transmit a recommendation to the agency head as to whether the reduction or suspension should continue.

When a request for a progress payment is made, the contractor must submit an estimate of the cost of completion of the contract. If the cost of the already completed work, taken together with the cost of completion estimate, exceeds the contract price, the contracting officer can modify progress payments to avoid a loss to the government, FAR 32.503-6(g). However, the contracting officer cannot modify progress payments if a subcontractor, not the contractor, is operating at a loss, *Aydin Corp. (West)*, ASBCA 42760, 94-2 BCA ¶ 26,899 *rev'd on other grounds,* 61 F.3d 1571 (Fed. Cir. 1995). The government can also reduce or suspend progress payments if the contractor's estimate to complete is fraudulent, 10 U.S.C. § 2307(e)(2) and 41 U.S.C. § 255(g).

d. Liquidation of Progress Payments

Progress payments are recovered or "recouped" by the government through application of a "liquidation rate" to the contract price for items delivered and accepted, and deduction of the resulting amount from sums otherwise due the contractor for the completed work. FAR 32.503-8 provides that the "ordinary method" is for the liquidation rate to be "the same as the progress payment rate." Since progress payments are based on costs only, while liquidation is based on price (including profit), use of the same rate will not permit the contractor to recover full profit on work delivered and accepted. However, FAR 32.503-9 permits the contracting officer in certain circumstances to employ an "alternate" liquidation rate, thereby permitting the contractor to retain the "earned profit element of the contract prices for completed items." *See Freedom N.Y., Inc.*, ASBCA 43965, 01-2 BCA ¶ 31,585, *aff'd,* 02-1 BCA ¶ 31,676, *aff'd in part & rev'd in part,* 329 F.3d 1320 (Fed. Cir. 2003), *recons. denied*, 346 F.3d 1359 (Fed. Cir. 2003) (government properly liquidated progress payments at a rate of 100 percent where the contractor failed to make progress, or was in such unsatisfactory financial condition as to endanger performance of the contract).

Liquidation does not equate with acceptance, *Sach Sinha & Assocs., Inc.,* ASBCA 50640, BCA ¶ 31,111 (after a default termination, contractor not entitled to offset manufacturing costs for undelivered items against repayment of unliquidated progress payments, because the items were never accepted by the government).

2. *Construction Progress Payments*

5 CFR § 1315 states that a construction progress payment includes "a monthly percentage of completion progress payment or milestone payments for completed phases, increments, or segments of any project." Where unit prices are included in the contract, progress payments will be made as units of work are completed. Where lump sum payments are involved, payment is based on estimates of the percentage of completion of the item of work. In accordance with ¶ (b) of the Payments Under Fixed-Price Construction Contracts clause in FAR 52.232-5, progress payments are based on "estimates of work accomplished which meets the standards of quality established under the contract, as approved by the Contracting Officer." To determine the amount of work accomplished, the parties negotiate percentages for each of the principal categories of work and then multiply the contract price by the percentage. The following subsections deal with the time for payment, the certifications required to be made by the contractor, and payments to subcontractors.

a. *Time for Payment*

The Prompt Payment Act, 31 U.S.C. § 3903(a)(6)(A), requires the payment of interest on construction progress payments if they are unpaid for:

> (i) a period of more than 14 days after receipt of the payment request by the place or person designated by the agency to first receive such requests,; or
>
> (ii) a longer period, specified in the solicitation, if required to afford the Government a practicable opportunity to adequately inspect the work and to determine the adequacy of the contractor's performance under the contract.

b. Certification

Special documentation is required to constitute a proper request for a progress payment. The amount requested must be substantiated and the contractor must furnish a certificate indicating substantiation of amount requested and a certificate. 31 U.S.C. § 3903(b)(1) provides:

> A payment request may not be approved under subsection (a)(6)(A) [construction progress payments] unless the application for such payment includes—
>
> (A) substantiation of the amounts requested; and
>
> (B) a certification by the prime contractor, to the best of the contractor's knowledge and belief, that—
>
> (i) the amounts requested are only for performance in accordance with the specifications, terms, and conditions of the contract;
>
> (ii) payments to subcontractors and suppliers have been made from previous payments received under the contract, and timely payments will be made from the proceeds of the payment covered by the certification, in accordance with their subcontract agreements and the requirements of this chapter; and
>
> (iii) the application does not include any amounts which the prime contractor intends to withhold or retain from a subcontractor or supplier in accordance with the terms and conditions of their subcontract.

The form of the certificate is set forth in ¶ (c) of the Payments under Fixed-Price Construction Contracts clause at FAR 52.232-5.

Paragraph (b) of the FAR 52.232-5 clause requires the contractor to furnish the following information with each request for a progress payment:

> (1) The Contractor's request for progress payments shall include the following substantiation:
>
> (i) An itemization of the amounts requested, related to the various elements of work required by the contract covered by the payment requested.
>
> (ii) A listing of the amount included for work performed by each subcontractor under the contract.
>
> (iii) A listing of the total amount of each subcontract under the contract.
>
> (iv) A listing of the amounts previously paid to each such subcontractor under the contract.

(v) Additional supporting data in a form and detail required by the Contracting Officer.

c. Subcontract Payments

In order to ensure timely payment to subcontractors in construction contracts, Congress amended the Prompt Payment Act in 1988 to require contractors to pay subcontractors within seven days of receiving payment from the government. This requirement is contained in 31 U.S.C. § 3905, which provides:

> (b) Each construction contract awarded by an agency shall include a clause that requires the prime contractor to include in each subcontract for property or services entered into by the prime contractor and a subcontractor (including a material supplier) for the purpose of performing such construction contract—
>
> (1) a payment clause which obligates the prime contractor to pay the subcontractor for satisfactory performance under its subcontract within 7 days out of such amounts as are paid to the prime contractor by the agency under such contract; and
>
> (2) an interest penalty clause which obligates the prime contractor to pay to the subcontractor an interest penalty on amounts due in the case of each payment not made in accordance with the payment clause included in the subcontract pursuant to paragraph (1) of this subsection—
>
> (A) for the period beginning on the day after the required payment date and ending on the date on which payment of the amount due is made; and
>
> (B) computed at the rate specified by section 3902(a) of this title.

Subcontractors are required to flow clauses to the same effect to each lower-tier subcontractor. The subcontract may contain a provision entitling the contractor or higher tier subcontractor to "retain (without cause) a specified percentage of each progress payment otherwise due to a subcontractor for satisfactory performance under the subcontract," 31 U.S.C. § 3905(d)(1). Withholding is also proper for defective work if notice has been given to both the subcontractor and the government, 31 U.S.C. § 3905(e). See *JP, Inc.*, ASBCA 38426, 90-1 BCA ¶ 22,348, in which the board found that withholding a retainage of slightly more than 10 percent was justified when the contractor did not submit certification of payment to the subcontractor.

This provision left unclear how contracting officers were to deal with complaints from subcontractors that they were not being paid within the seven-day period. Consequently, Congress included a provision in the DOD Authorization Act for Fiscal Years 1992 and 1993, Pub. L. 102-190, § 806, requiring that subcontractors be given information about payment requests by contractors. This provision was amended by the Federal Acquisition Streamlining Act, Pub. L. 103-355. It is applicable to all DoD subcontractors, not just subcontractors under construction contracts. It has been implemented in FAR 32.112 as follows:

> 32.112-1 *Subcontractor assertions of nonpayment.*
>
> (a) In accordance with Section 806(a)(4) of Pub. L. 102-190, as amended by Sections 2091 and 8105 of Pub. L. 103-355, upon the assertion by a subcontractor or supplier of a Federal contractor that the subcontractor or supplier has not been paid in accordance with the payment terms of the subcontract, purchase order, or other agreement with the prime contractor, the contracting officer may determine—
>
> (1) For a construction contract, whether the contractor has made—
>
> (i) Progress payments to the subcontractor or supplier in compliance with Chapter 39 of Title 31, United States Code (Prompt Payment Act); or
>
> (ii) Final payment to the subcontractor or supplier in compliance with the terms of the subcontract, purchase order, or other agreement with the prime contractor;
>
> (2) For a contract other than construction, whether the contractor has made progress payments, final payments, or other payments to the subcontractor or supplier in compliance with the terms of the subcontract, purchase order, or other agreement with the prime contractor; or
>
> (3) For any contract, whether the contractor's certification of payment of a subcontractor or supplier accompanying its payment request to the Government is accurate.
>
> (b) If, in making the determination in paragraphs (a)(1) and (2) of this section, the contracting officer finds the prime contractor is not in compliance, the contracting officer may—
>
> (1) Encourage the contractor to make timely payment to the subcontractor or supplier; or
>
> (2) If authorized by the applicable payment clauses, reduce or suspend progress payments to the contractor.
>
> (c) If the contracting officer determines that a certification referred to in paragraph (a)(3) of this section is inaccurate in any material respect, the contracting officer shall initiate administrative or other remedial action.
>
> 32.112-2 *Subcontractor requests for information.*

(a) In accordance with Section 806(a)(1) of Pub. L. 102-190, as amended by Sections 2091 and 8105 of Pub. L. 103-355, upon the request of a subcontractor or supplier under a Federal contract for a non-commercial item, the contracting officer shall promptly advise the subcontractor or supplier as to—

(1) Whether the prime contractor has submitted requests for progress payments or other payments to the Federal Government under the contract; and

(2) Whether final payment under the contract has been made by the Federal Government to the prime contractor.

(b) In accordance with 5 U.S.C. 552(b)(1), this subsection does not apply to matters that are—

(1) Specifically authorized under criteria established by an Executive order to be kept classified in the interest of national defense or foreign policy; and

(2) Properly classified pursuant to such Executive order.

To further enhance a subcontractor's right to be paid, the FAR also now allows subcontractors, upon a written or oral request, to obtain the name and address of the payment bond surety, the penal amount of the bond, and a copy of the bond itself, FAR 28.106-6(d).

d. Retainage

The Payments Under Fixed-Price Construction Contracts clause at FAR 52.232-5 authorizes the contracting officer to retain a portion of the payment in accordance with the following paragraph:

(e) If the Contracting Officer finds that satisfactory progress was achieved during any period for which a progress payment is to be made, the Contracting Officer shall authorize payment to be made in full. However, if satisfactory progress has not been made, the Contracting Officer may retain a maximum of 10 percent of the amount of the payment until satisfactory progress is achieved. When the work is substantially complete, the Contracting Officer may retain from previously withheld funds and future progress payments that amount the Contracting Officer considers adequate for protection of the Government and shall release to the Contractor all the remaining withheld funds. Also, on completion and acceptance of each separate building, public work, or other division of the contract, for which the price is stated separately in the contract, payment shall be made for the completed work without retention of a percentage.

While the pre-FAR Payments to Contractor clause formerly provided for release of payments in full only after the project had been 50 percent completed, the contracting officer now has discretion to forego retainages at any time.

OFPP Policy Letter 83-1 announced that contracting officers should not withhold funds from construction contract progress payments without cause. FAR 32.103 adopts this policy, stating:

> When satisfactory progress has not been achieved by a contractor during any period for which a progress payment is to be made, a percentage of the progress payment may be retained. Retainage should not be used as a substitute for good contract management, and the contracting officer should not withhold funds without cause. Determinations to retain and the specific amount to be withheld shall be made by the contracting officer on a case-by-case basis. Such decisions will be based on the contracting officer's assessment of past performance and the likelihood that such performance will continue. The amount of retainage withheld shall not exceed 10 percent of the approved estimated amount in accordance with the terms of the contract and may be adjusted as the contract approaches completion to recognize better than expected performance, the ability to rely on alternative safeguards, and other factors. Upon completion of all contract requirements, retained amounts shall be paid promptly.

The purpose of retainage "is to protect the interests of the Government in the event of unsatisfactory performance," *U.S. Fid. & Guar. Co. v. United States*, 201 Ct. Cl. 1, 475 F.2d 1377 (1973). A contracting officer has broad discretion in deciding to withhold a progress payment because the contractor has not made satisfactory progress, *U.S. Fid. & Guar. Co. v. United States*, 201 Ct. Cl. 1, 475 F.2d 1377 (1973); *Argonaut Ins. Co. v. United States*, 193 Ct. Cl. 483, 434 F.2d 1362 (1970); *Atlas Constr. Co.*, GSBCA 7903, 90-2 BCA ¶ 22,812. See *Westphal GmbH & Co. KG*, ASBCA 38439, 91-3 BCA ¶ 24,175, in which the contractor alleged that the contracting officer abused his discretion by refusing to release the 10 percent retainage. The board denied the contractor's claim, stating that the record showed that the contractor had not completed its work and had failed to submit as-built drawings. See also *Plandel, Inc.*, HUDBCA 92-7171-C1, 93-3 BCA ¶ 26,103 (retainage reasonable to ensure completion of the contract); *M.C.&D. Capital Corp.*, ASBCA 38181, 91-1 BCA ¶ 23,563 (retainage of 2.5 percent of progress payments proper in light of warranty defects); *Decker & Co., GmbH*, ASBCA 33285, 88-3 BCA ¶ 20,925, *recons. denied,* 89-1 BCA ¶ 21,399 (retainage proper because building control system did not perform properly and several elements of system had not been installed); *Fortec Constructors*, ASBCA 27480, 83-2 BCA ¶ 16,727 (contracting officer obliged to make findings as to satisfactory progress but not an abuse of discretion to give the government the "benefit of the doubt"); and *Jefferson Constr. Co.*, ASBCA 14544, 70-1 BCA ¶ 8336 (retainage may be maintained on bond premiums since they are not a "division" of the contract). The contractor has the burden to show abuse of discretion in retaining progress payments, *Fortec Constructors*, ASBCA 27480, 83-2 BCA ¶ 16,727. Although the purpose of retainage in construction contracts is to ensure that a project is completed satisfactorily, retained progress payments may also be used to offset government claims, *Leonhard Weiss GmbH & Co. & Huebsch Industrieanlagen Spezialbau GmbH, (JV)*, ASBCA 37574, 93-1 BCA ¶ 25,443; *Orbas & Assocs.*, ASBCA 3222, 87-3 BCA ¶ 20,051. In *NAGY Enters.*, ASBCA

48815, 98-1 BCA ¶ 29,695, the government withheld funds for failure to submit basic payroll records and failure to make satisfactory progress. The contractor agreed to modify the regular progress payment schedule by agreeing to hold the withheld amount in dispute in exchange for receiving the next scheduled payment.

In some instances improper retainage has been found. See *Atlas Constr. Co.*, GSBCA 7903, 90-2 BCA ¶ 22,812, in which the board found that retainage on one of the progress payments was unreasonable because the contractor's progress was hindered by changes and hidden conditions. In *Orbas & Assocs.*, ASBCA 32922, 87-3 BCA ¶ 20,051, the board stated that "[a]lthough the contract confers discretion on the contracting officer . . . in making and withholding payments, such discretion is not unfettered." In that case, it was unreasonable for the contracting officer to retain payments when there remained no unsatisfactory performance by the contractor to be corrected. In *Revere Elec. Supply Co.,* ASBCA 46413, 95-1 BCA ¶ 27,385, a nonstandard payments clause permitting the government to retain 20 percent of the price of certain delivered equipment pending completion of field testing of the installed system was unenforceable because it was inconsistent with the standard payments clause requiring payment as promptly as practicable after delivery.

E. Payment Under Incrementally Funded Contracts

The Limitation of Government's Obligation clause, DFARS 252.232-7007, is used in incrementally funded fixed-priced contracts. The clause sets out how much money is allotted to the contractor and provides that the government will not be obligated to pay any amount exceeding the allotment. Thus, during the period that the allotment is lower than the total contract price, the government is only obligated to pay up to that allotment, and progress payments may not exceed the government's obligation, *Progress Payments Pursuant to Raytheon Co. Contract*, 59 Comp. Gen. 526 (B-198257), 80-1 CPD ¶ 414. In *Raytheon*, the Progress Payments clause stated that the contractor could be paid up to 80 percent of the total contract price. The GAO held that the contractor could collect up to the full amount of the allotment and was not limited to 80 percent of the allotted funds.

F. Withholding

"Withholding" and "setoff" are the terms used to describe the government's refusal to pay all or part of a contractor's invoice. The courts, boards, and GAO have sometimes used these terms interchangeably, which has led to some confusion over the differences between the two concepts. Given the imprecise use of terms, it is necessary to examine the particular circumstance under which a nonpayment arises rather than the term used in a decision. The discussion of withholding does not involve the recovery of money owed to the United States under another contract or pursuant to some other contractor obligation such as taxation. Deductions from money owed to the contractor for such claims are covered in the discussion of "setoff." This section reviews the government's right to withhold, then considers limitations on withholding. Procedures to be followed by the government in withholding are discussed along with setoff procedures in Section III.

Our use of the term *withholding* refers to an intra-contractual right that allows the government to refuse payment to which the contractor is not entitled. It generally arises under one of three circumstances. First, it may involve the government's refusal to pay all, or a part, of an invoice because of overpayment on past invoices, *Allied Signal, Inc. v. United States*, 941 F.2d 1194 (Fed. Cir. 1991), or because work covered by an invoice has not been properly accomplished, *AVCO Corp. v. United States*, 10 Cl. Ct. 665 (1986). In these situations, the government will withhold part or all of the contract price or progress payment. Second, a withholding may involve a deduction from an invoice because of damages incurred to government property or excess costs of reprocurement because of improper work under the contract, *Servicemaster of W. Cent. Ga.*, DOTCAB 1096, 80-2 BCA ¶ 14,676 (estimated amount withheld pending an assessment of excess costs of reprocurement and resolution of a disputed default termination). Withholdings also occur because of defective cost or pricing data, *Fairchild Republic Co.*, ASBCA 29385, 85-2 BCA ¶ 18,047, *recons. denied*, 86-1 BCA ¶ 18,608.

The government bears the burden of proof on a withholding. See *Program & Constr. Mgmt. Group, Inc. v. General Servs. Admin.*, GSBCA 14178, 00-1 BCA ¶ 30,641 (government not justified in withholding the cost of asbestos abatement from a contractor's final payment because the government failed to prove that the material released from old pipes was asbestos or that the contractor should have known that asbestos was present).

1. Government Right to Withhold

A number of contract provisions expressly authorize withholding. For example, the Patent Rights clause in FAR 52.227-12 and the Technical Data—Withholding of Payment clause in DFARS 252.227-7030 both permit significant amounts of withholding if the contracting officer determines that the contractor has not complied with contract requirements. Other contract clauses authorize the government to withhold when the contractor is failing to meet its obligations under various labor statutes such as the Davis-Bacon Act, 40 U.S.C. § 276a *et seq.*; the Service Contract Act, 41 U.S.C. § 351 *et seq.*; and the Contract Work Hours and Safety Standards Act, 40 U.S.C. § 327 *et seq.* See *Cascade Reforestation, Inc.*, 56 Comp. Gen. 499 (B-187997), 77-1 CPD ¶ 250, holding that the government could withhold funds in order to satisfy wage underpayment claims because the contract was covered by the Service Contract Act. See also *Green Thumb Lawn Maint.*, ENGBCA 6249, 98-1 BCA ¶ 29,688, denying recovery of funds withheld at the direction of the Department of Labor because the government was required to withhold the funds pending completion of a DOL investigation and the funds could not be dispensed until a ruling was issued. In *Overstreet Elec. Co.*, ASBCA 51653, 01-2 BCA ¶ 31,646, a contracting officer properly withheld contract payments for alleged labor violations without first referring the matter to the DOL.

Bill J. Copeland v. Veneman, 350 F.3d 1230 (Fed. Cir. 2003), was an extreme situation. There the court affirmed a board decision upholding a default termination and rejecting the contractor's argument that the contracting officer's withholding of funds from progress payments for alleged Davis-Bacon Act violations was improper and the cause of the delay. Although a DOL administrative law judge had eventually dismissed the violations and ordered that withheld funds be returned, the court found that the determination by the contracting officer was reasonable and in accordance with the contract provisions. The court also noted that because the contractor had the burden of showing that the delay was excusable, it also had the burden of showing that the withholding was excessive.

Contractors facing such labor payment deductions may not be able to use the Contract Dispute Act for relief. In *Active Fire Sprinkler Corp. v. General Servs. Admin.*, GSBCA 15318, 01-2 BCA ¶ 31,521, a claim for interest on withholdings in excess of the amount needed to cover Davis-Bacon Act violations was not redressable. Such a claim would require the boards to examine the reasonableness of a DOL investigation and of the DOL's backpay and overtime calculations, none of which the boards have jurisdiction to do. See also *Thomas & Sons Bldg. Contractors, Inc.*, ASBCA 51590, 01-1 BCA ¶ 31,246, *recons. denied*, 0l-1 BCA ¶ 31,295 (contractor's claim that the agency had improperly withheld payment was really a disguised attack on a wage determination, over which the board has no jurisdiction).

The government also has an implied right to withhold payment. For example, amounts may be withheld as a result of downward price adjustments resulting from such actions as price reductions for defective cost or pricing data, *Fairchild Republic Co.*, ASBCA 29385, 85-2 BCA ¶ 18,047, *recons. denied*, 86-1 BCA ¶ 18,608; deductive changes, *Atlantic States Constr., Inc.*, ASBCA 27681, 85-3 BCA ¶ 18,501; or to assess liquidated damages, *Information Consultants, Inc.*, GSBCA 8130-COM, 86-3 BCA ¶ 19,198.

2. Limitations on Withholding

A contracting officer may withhold the payment only for that portion of work that is unsatisfactory, and a reasonable relationship must be shown between the suspended payment and that work, *Eastern Mass. Prof'll Standards Review Organization, Inc.*, ASBCA 33639, 91-3 BCA ¶ 24,301. The amount withheld must constitute a reasonable estimate of the contractor's potential liability, *Norair Eng'g Corp.*, GSBCA 3539, 75-1 BCA ¶ 11,062. Thus, the appeals boards have carefully scrutinized withholdings for unperformed work to ensure that the withholdings represent an amount commensurate with the reasonable value of such work, *Wright's Auto Repair, Inc.*, ASBCA 31372, 88-1 BCA ¶ 20,449; *Harrell- Patterson Contracting, Inc.*, ASBCA 30803, 87-2 BCA ¶

19,805. In addition, the amount should not be so excessive as to impair the ability of a contractor to perform, *Bailey v. Secretary of Labor*, 810 F. Supp. 261 (D. Alaska 1993). Similarly, a withholding under the labor provisions of a contract was found unreasonable when it was almost 10 times the amount of the incorrect payment made by the contractor to its employees, *Columbia Eng'g Corp.*, IBCA 2351, 88-2 BCA ¶ 20,595. In *Clarkies, Inc.*, ASBCA 22784, 81-2 BCA ¶ 15,313, the government had withheld contract payments for defective cleaning services. The board held that such withholding was unreasonable because the government inspected on an "all or none" inspection procedure and failed to credit the contractor on a pro rata basis for work properly performed. But see *Avco Corp. v. United States*, 10 Cl. Ct. 665 (1986), holding that the procuring agency could properly withhold payments beyond the 10 percent retainage if there was delay and deficient performance by the contractor.

While the government has the right to conduct an audit before making a payment, it may not withhold final payment beyond a reasonable time, *TEM Assocs., Inc.*, DOT-BCA 2024, 89-1 BCA ¶ 21,266. In *TEM*, the board found that six months was not a reasonable time and therefore payment was due. In *Grumman Aircraft Eng'g Corp.*, ASBCA 10309, 66-2 BCA ¶ 5846, the board held that the government may rightfully withhold payment in order to gain access to audit information. In *Grumman*, the board reasoned that, when the government is determining the allowability of overhead or indirect costs, it may be necessary for the government to examine records other than those for labor, material, and equipment used directly in performance of a contract. The board stated, however, that the government must show the reasonableness of its demand for such records. See *SCM Corp. v. United States*, 227 Ct. Cl. 12, 645 F.2d 893 (1981), in which the court stated that a contractor is entitled to payment of asserted costs only if the government is allowed an unrestricted audit. Compare *Martin Marietta Corp.*, ASBCA 31248, 87-2 BCA ¶ 19,875, holding that it was improper to withhold payments as a means of forcing the contractor to give the government access to internal audit reports. The board stated that it was not necessary for the government to have access to the requested documents to make a determination on the allowability of costs.

FAR 52.232-9 calls for the inclusion of the following clause in all service and supply contracts that contain two or more clauses "authorizing the temporary withholding of amounts otherwise payable to the contractors":

LIMITATION ON WITHHOLDING OF PAYMENTS

If more than one clause or Schedule term of this contract authorizes the temporary withholding of amounts otherwise payable to the Contractor for supplies delivered or services performed, the total of the amounts withheld at any one time shall not exceed the greatest amount that may be withheld under any one clause or Schedule term at that time; provided, that this limitation shall not apply to—

(a) Withholdings pursuant to any clause relating to wages or hours of employees;

(b) Withholdings not specifically provided for by this contract;

(c) The recovery of overpayments; and

(d) Any other withholding for which the Contracting Officer determines that this limitation is inappropriate.

It should be noted that this clause does not apply to withholdings that are not specifically provided for by contract clauses.

If the contractor suffers no prejudice, the failure to strictly follow procedures for informing the contractor of defective performance will not deprive the government of the right to withhold. In *Custodial Guidance Sys., Inc.*, GSBCA 6952, 83-2 BCA ¶ 16,749, the government was permitted to take deductions for the contractor's deficient performance of services, first assessed 133 days after contract completion, despite the fact that the contract required the government to assess deductions "within 45 calendar days following expiration of the contract." The board emphasized that the contractor had been informed of the deficiencies throughout performance and had not been prejudiced by the government's delay in assessing the deductions. See also *Harbert Int'l Servs.*, ASBCA 36983, 90-1 BCA ¶ 22,449, in which the board cited *Custodial* to support the view that "a contracting officer's late issuance of a notice concerning assessed deductions [is] of no legal significance without a showing of any resulting prejudice or injury to the contractor." But see *Maintenance Eng'rs*, GSBCA 10364, 91-1 BCA ¶ 23,527, in which the board held that a contracting officer cannot withhold payment for unsatisfactory performance when it does not inform the contractor of the proposed deductions in a timely fashion, as required by the contract.

As a general rule, the government is not required to issue a final decision or make any formal determination prior to withholding payment of the contract price or progress payments for such matters as the contractor's failure to perform or to recover previous overpayments under the contract. For instance, in *Allied Signal*, the government simply withheld payment on a present invoice due to overpayment on prior invoices. In cases where a government claim is involved, such as when there is a downward equitable adjustment under the Changes clause or defective cost or pricing data, the government sometimes withholds money without issuing a final decision. In either case, the contractor may not appeal the withholding without first asserting a claim for the withheld money, *e.g.*, *H.B. Zachary Co.*, ASBCA 39202, 90-1 BCA ¶ 22,342 *overruled by* 91-2 BCA ¶ 23,958. See Chapter 13 for a discussion of disputes.

3. Discretionary Actions

Withholding such payments is discretionary. In *Davis Group, Inc.,* ASBCA 48431, 95-2 BCA ¶ 27,702, the contracting officer did not abuse his discretion in withholding progress payments. The contractor was required to show the materials as a percentage of the work and include them on a progress schedule. The contractor's progress schedule did not show acquisition of materials as a step in the construction or as a percentage of the work. See *Riennes Constr. Co.*, IBCA 3572-96, 98-2 BCA ¶ 29,821, in which a construction contractor was not entitled to a progress payment for materials on-site but not yet used in the dwelling to be constructed. The contractor later acknowledged that he boxed up rock, contending that it was expensive mechanical equipment, in order to secure a progress payment. Under these circumstances, the contracting officer did not abuse her discretion. See also *Kingston Constructors Inc.*, ENGBCA 6006, 95-2 BCA ¶ 27,841, *recons. granted in part*, 97-1 BCA ¶ 28,646 (failure of a contractor's transformers to pass required tests and to function after installation justified the government's withholding of progress payments), and *Defense Sys. Co.*, ASBCA 50918, 00-2 BCA ¶ 30,991 (government justified in withholding progress payments under a rocket supply contract because the rockets were non-conforming and the contractor had failed to make adequate progress in correcting the deficiency). In *Keith Crawford & Assocs.*, ASBCA 46893, 95-1 BCA ¶ 27,388, the government's withholding of the remaining balance of construction contract funds was reasonable in view of the contractor's inexcusable refusal to timely complete performance and daily accrual of liquidated damages owed by the contractor. Compare *Sundstrand Corp.*, ASBCA 51572, 01-1 BCA ¶ 31,167, finding it improper to refuse to make commercial contract installment payments unless the contractor provided a lien when the FAR authorized the agency to make such payments while relying on only the company's financial condition as security.

In *Johnson v. All-State Constr., Inc.*, 329 F.3d 848 (Fed. Cir. 2003), the contractor submitted an invoice for progress payments, which the contracting officer denied, stating that the government's pending liquidated damages exceeded the amount of the progress payment. The contract was then terminated for default. Upon appeal, the board found that the government had breached the contract by retaining the progress payment, and changed the termination for default into one for convenience. The court reversed and held that the government is entitled to withhold progress payments pursuant to its common law right of setoff. The court did, however, reject the argument that the government is entitled to withhold progress payments when a default termination is imminent.

III. SETOFF

"Setoff" (or "administrative offset") arises when the government refuses to pay amounts due under a contract as a means of collecting sums improperly paid to the contractor on another contract or unrelated transaction. Common law has long recognized the right of a creditor to collect a debt by applying monies, otherwise owed to the debtor, toward satisfaction of the debt. The government also enjoys this right of setoff, *United States v. Munsey Trust Co.*, 332 U.S. 234 (1947). Because of its multiple relationships with most contractors, the government frequently finds itself in a position where it may choose to exercise its setoff rights. For instance, a setoff occurred when the government withheld payment on several contracts because disallowed overhead costs had been paid in full under previous contracts, *IBM Corp.*, ASBCA 28821, 84-3 BCA ¶ 17,689. Other examples of setoffs include losses sustained by the government through the contractor's default on a prior contract, *Filtron Co.*, DCAB ESSA-5, 70-1 BCA ¶ 8086; excess costs of reprocurement, *Crystal Soap & Chem. Co. v. United States*, 103 Ct. Cl. 166 (1945); and unpaid taxes due and owing the government, *General Cas. Co. v. United States*, 130 Ct. Cl. 520 (1955); *UNIDEV, Inc.*, Comp. Gen. Dec. (B-184067), 75-1 CPD ¶ 375.

A. Right to Setoff

Generally, the government has the right to set off any claim it has against a contractor by refusing payment of funds that are otherwise due the contractor. The GAO stated at Comp. Gen. Dec. B-176791, Sept. 8, 1972, *Unpub.*:

> The right of set off has been held to be inherent in the United States and to be grounded in the common law right of every creditor to apply the monies of his debtor in his hands to the extinguishment of the amounts due him from the debtor. *Gratiot v. United States*, 40 U.S. 336 (1841); *McKnight v. United States*, 98 U.S. 176 (1878); *Barry v. United States*, 229 U.S. 47 (1913). Thus, where a person is both a debtor and creditor to the Government in any form, the accounting officers are required by law to consider both the debts and credits and to set off one indebtedness against the other, and certify only the balance. *Taggert v. United States*, 17 Ct. Cl. 322 (1881). Furthermore, the Government's right to set off a contractor's debts against contract proceeds extends to debts owed by the contractor as a result of separate and independent transactions. *United States v. Munsey Trust Co.*, 332 U.S. 234 (1947). Additionally, where the amount due the Government had not been finalized under the procedures provided by the contract, we sanctioned the unilateral deduction of the amount estimated by the Government to be due.

In *Project Map, Inc. v. United States*, 203 Ct. Cl. 52, 486 F.2d 1375 (1973), the contractor sued to recover a sum of money that was admittedly owed to the contractor under a particular contract. The government refused to pay on this contract because it had overpaid on two previous contracts. At the time of the setoff, appeals against the contracting officer's findings of overpayment on the two previous contracts were pending before the board of contract appeals. The contractor argued that since no dispute existed in connection with the contract for which it was suing, it was entitled to payment in full under that agreement. While the government admitted the lack of dispute on the current contract, it asserted its right to set off an amount equal to that which it claimed was due under the other two contracts. Both sides moved for summary judgment. The court ruled for the government, stating at 53-54:

> Part III of *Dale Ingram, Inc. v. United States*, 201 Ct. Cl. 56, 76, 475 F.2d 1177, 1188 (March 1973), dealt with precisely the same problem. In that instance, too, the [Government] withheld payment of a sum awarded by the Board of Contract Appeals on one contract because there was then pending before the Board a dispute as to another of the contractor's agreements under which the contracting

> officer had held the contractor indebted to the Government in a larger sum. That [contractor], just like Project Map, Inc., argued that the failure to pay the conceded sum was a breach of contract entitling the claimant to immediate judgment. The court squarely rejected this contention "because the Government has a right of off-set with respect to the decision of the contracting officer [on the other contract] now pending before the Board in which he held that the plaintiff is indebted to the Government in the sum of [a figure greater than that withheld]. The decision of the contracting officer in this regard is final and binding until and unless it is reversed or changed by the Board or by this court should the case be appealed here from the Board. Consequently, the Government has the right to withhold the [sum withheld] awarded to the [contractor] in this case until [the other appeal] has been finally decided."

Accord, *Jung Ah Indus. Co.*, ASBCA 22632, 79-1 BCA ¶ 13,643. See also *Bonneville Power Admin.*, Comp. Gen. Dec. (B-188473), 77-2 CPD ¶ 74 (setoff is proper even if liability and the amount of the debt are in dispute), and *Ray E. Buhl*, ASBCA 45818, 94-2 BCA ¶ 26,805.

The government's right to setoff can be waived unless action is taken in Bankruptcy court. See *VER-VAL Enters., Inc.*, ASBCA 49892, 01-2 BCA ¶ 31,513, and *Englander*, VABCA 6475, 01-2 BCA ¶ 31,544.

B. Limitations on Setoff

The limitations on the government's broad rights of setoff derive from either statute or rules fashioned by the courts.

1. *Rights to Payment Assigned to Financing Institutions*

The Assignment of Claims Act of 1940, 31 U.S.C. § 3727(d), permits the inclusion of "no setoff" provisions during periods of national emergency, in contracts with the Department of Defense, the General Services Administration, the Department of Energy and other agencies designated by the president. See FAR 32.801 and 32.803. Such "no setoff" provisions, become effective if a contractor obtains a loan from a financing institution to fund contract performance and secures that loan by assigning to the institution the contractor's right to payment under the contract. By allowing such an assignment of contract payments, the government seeks to encourage the private financing of that contract.

The "no setoff" provision prevents the government from setting off any claim that is "independent of the contract," 31 U.S.C. § 3727(d)(1). In addition, the statute specifically lists renegotiation claims, fines, penalties (other than penalties relating to contract performance), taxes, and Social Security contributions as claims not subject to setoff. This provision has been interpreted broadly by the Supreme Court to preclude, during performance, the setoff of unpaid taxes against monies due the assignee. In *Central Bank v. United States*, 345 U.S. 639 (1953), the Court stated at 643, 646-47:

> The Assignment of Claims Act of 1940 was evidently designed to assist in the national defense program through facilitating the financing of defense contracts by limiting the Government's power to reduce properly assigned payments. Borrowers were not to be penalized in security because one contracting party was the Government. Contractors might well have obligations to the United States not imposed by the contract from which the payments flowed, as for example the contractor's income tax for prior earnings under the contract.
>
> * * *
>
> To grant the Government its sought-for rights of set-off under the circumstances of this case, would be to defeat the purpose of Congress. It would require the assignee to police the assignor's accounting and payment system. It would increase the risk to the assignee, the difficulty of the assignor in financing the performance, and the ultimate cost to the Government.

"No setoff" provisions have been held applicable only to an assignee lender whose loan was used, or available for use, in financing the particular government contract for which setoff-free payment is sought, *First Nat'l City Bank v. United States*, 212 Ct. Cl. 357, 548 F.2d 928 (1977) (loan made subsequent to contract completion subject to setoff); *Manufacturers Hanover Trust Co. v. United States*, 218 Ct. Cl. 563, 590 F.2d 893 (1978); and *Bamco Mach., Inc.*, 55 Comp. Gen. 155 (B-181246), 75-2 CPD ¶ 111 (assignments made after contractor ceased operations subject to setoff). See also *Applied Cos. v. United States*, 37 Fed. Cl. 749 (1997), *aff'd,* 144 F.3d 1470 (Fed. Cir. 1998).

2. Performance-Bond Surety

Although a payment-bond surety is not entitled to protection against setoff, *United States v. Munsey Trust Co.*, 332 U.S. 234 (1947); *Sentry Ins. v. United States*, 12 Cl. Ct. 320 (1987), a performance-bond surety who completes the contract work is entitled to setoff protection, *Aetna Cas. & Sur. Co. v. United States*, 435 F.2d 1082 (5th Cir. 1970). See *Morrison Assurance Co. v. United States*, 3 Cl. Ct. 626 (1983), holding that the government is not entitled to set off the amount of a contractor's tax deficiency from contract proceeds payable to a performance-bond surety that undertakes completion work. In addition, when a performance-bond surety and the government enter into a formal takeover agreement, the government is not permitted to set off funds for debts owed by the contractor, since the surety's claim under the performance bond takes precedence over the government's claim, *Security Ins. Co. of Hartford v. United States*, 192 Ct. Cl. 754, 428 F.2d 838 (1970); *Capitol Indem. Corp.*, Comp. Gen. Dec. (B-186206), 76-2 CPD ¶ 4.

3. Separate Debts of Partners or Joint Venturers

Claims arising against an individual partner or joint venturer may not, as a general rule, be set off against payments due the partnership or joint venture, *Economy Plumbing & Heating Co. v. United States*, 197 Ct. Cl. 839, 456 F.2d 713 (1972); 39 Comp. Gen. 438 (B-141063) (1959).

4. Bid Deposits

Bid deposits given in lieu of bid bonds may not be used by the government for setoff purposes, 33 Comp. Gen. 262 (B-116430) (1953). However, deposits given in government property sales are considered part of the contract price and, as such, may be set off against payments due the contractor, 45 Comp. Gen. 504 (B-157957) (1966).

IV. DEBT COLLECTION PROCEDURES

The process of debt collection by withholding and setoff has been complicated by a number of statutes and regulations that are not well coordinated and contain diverse provisions. Thus, the Federal Claims Collection Act of 1966, 31 U.S.C. § 3701 *et seq.*; the Debt Collection Act of 1982, 31 U.S.C. § 3701 *et seq.* (which amended the 1966 Act); the Contract Disputes Act of 1978, 41 U.S.C. § 601 *et seq.*; and the Federal Acquisition Regulation all establish procedures to be followed by government agencies in collecting debts. The Federal Claims Collection Standards, issued jointly by the Department of the Treasury and the Department of Justice, implement the Claims Collection and Debt Collection Acts, 31 CFR Chapter IX, Part 901.

These statutes and regulations have caused a great deal of debt-collection confusion, probably because two different issues are involved in a debt-collection action, each requiring the use of a significantly different procedure. The first issue is whether the contractor is in fact indebted to the government. The second issue is whether, after the debt is ascertained, collection should be undertaken by setoff or some other technique before the liability for the debt has been established. This section first examines FAR procedures for withholding and setoff. It then considers the applicability of the Debt Collection Act and the Contract Disputes Act.

A. FAR Debt Collection Procedures

FAR Subpart 32.6, prescribes "policies and procedures for the government's actions in ascertaining and collecting *contract* debts. . ." (emphasis supplied), FAR 32.600. The procedures appear to be applicable to both withholding and offset. They are discussed in the following sections.

1. Debt Determination

FAR 32.606 contains the following guidance on determination of the debt:

(a) If any indication of a contract debt arises, the responsible official shall determine promptly whether an actual debt is due the Government and the amount. Any unwarranted delay may contribute to—

(1) Loss of timely availability of the funds to the program for which the funds were initially provided;

(2) Increased difficulty in collecting the debt; or

(3) Actual monetary loss to the Government.

(b) In determining the amount of any contract debt, the responsible official shall fairly consider both the Government's claim and any contract claims by the contractor against the Government. This determination does not constitute a settlement of such claims, nor is it a contracting officer's final determination under the Contract Disputes Act of 1978.

This will also serve as the first step in establishing a government claim under the Contract Disputes Act.

2. Negotiation and Demand

FAR 32.608 does not *require* that a debt be negotiated with the contractor, but negotiation requirements are implied in the FAR language:

(a) The responsible official shall ensure that any negotiations concerning debt determinations are completed expeditiously. If consistent with the contract, the official shall make a unilateral determination promptly if the contractor is delinquent in any of the following actions:

(1) Furnishing pertinent information.

(2) Negotiating expeditiously.

(3) Entering into an agreement on a fair and reasonable price revision.

(4) Signing an interim memorandum evidencing a negotiated pricing agreement involving refund.

(5) Executing an appropriate contract modification reflecting the result of negotiations.

(b) The amount of indebtedness determined unilaterally shall be an amount that—

> (1) Is proper based on the merits of the case;
>
> (2) Does not exceed an amount that would have been considered acceptable in a negotiated agreement; and
>
> (3) Is consistent with the contract terms.
>
> (c) For unilateral debt determinations, the contracting officer shall issue a decision as required by the clause at 52.233-1, Disputes. Such decision shall include a demand for payment (see 33.211(a)(4)(vi)). No demand for payment under 32.610 shall be issued prior to a contracting officer's final decision. A copy of the final decision shall be sent to the appropriate finance office.

FAR 32.610 is confusing in that it appears to place the demand for repayment ahead of the need for negotiation. It states in part:

> (a) A demand for payment shall be made as soon as the responsible official has computed the amount of refund due. If the debt arises from excess costs for a default termination, the demand shall be made without delay, as explained in 49.402-6.
>
> (b) The demand shall include the following:
>
> (1) A description of the debt, including the debt amount.
>
> (2) Notification that any amounts not paid within 30 days from the date of the demand will bear interest from the date of the demand, or from any earlier date specified in the contract and that the interest rate shall be the rate established by the Secretary of the Treasury, for the period affected, under Public Law 92-41. . . .
>
> (3) A notification that the contractor may submit a proposal for deferment of collection if immediate payment is not practicable or if the amount is disputed.
>
> (4) Identification of the responsible official designated for determining the amount of the debt and for its collection.

The most sensible interpretation of these provisions is that they require the contracting officer to (1) notify the contractor of a debt, (2) enter quickly into negotiations if the contractor is cooperative, and (3) issue a contracting officer's decision under the Contract Disputes Act if settlement cannot be achieved. These steps meet the procedural requirements of the Contract Disputes Act and also the requirements of the Debt Collection Act that limit the government's right to offset if the notice to the contractor offers all of the rights listed in the Act.

The confusing requirement in FAR 32.610, which appears to require the issuance of a demand letter before negotiation, is probably included in the regulation because of the provision in the Federal Claims Collection Standards stating that "demand letters are normally the first step in the debt collection process." 31 CFR § 901.2(b) requires that the initial demand letter inform the debtor of:

> (1) The basis for the indebtedness and rights, if any, the debtor may have to seek review within the agency;
>
> (2) The applicable standards for imposing interest, penalties, or administrative costs;
>
> (3) The date by which payment is to be made to avoid late charges (i.e., interest, penalties and administrative costs) and enforced collection, which generally should be not more than 30 days from the date that the demand letter is mailed or hand-delivered; and
>
> (4) The name, address, and phone number of a contact person or office within the agency.

The standards state that "generally one demand letter should suffice," 31 CFR § 901.2(a). Such demands are inappropriate for dealing with a contractor that furnishes goods or services to the government. In such cases, negotiation and settlement of the problem are a more efficient way to handle the matter.

3. Deferment Agreement

FAR 32.610 requires that, at the time of the demand, the contractor be given notification of the opportunity to submit a "proposal for deferment of collection" if immediate payment is not practicable or the amount is in dispute. Detailed guidance concerning deferment of collection actions is set forth at FAR 32.613. These regulations provide that when the contractor has appealed the debt or filed an action under the Disputes clause of the contract, the responsible government official may, pending resolution of the matter, arrange for deferment or installment payments to (1) "avoid possible over collection," and, (2) in the case of small business concerns and financially weak contractors, balance the "need for Government security against loss and undue hardship on the contractor." Where no Disputes clause action or appeal is pending, a deferment agreement or installment payments may be authorized if the contractor is "unable to pay at once in full or the contractor's operations under national defense contracts would be seriously impaired," FAR 32.613(f).

In *Lockheed Corp. v. Garrett*, 1991 WL 317041 (C.D. Cal. 1991), the court held that the Navy could not collect by offset $124 million from Lockheed until after it reconsidered the contractor's deferment request. The court found that the Navy had failed to comply with the Defense Contracting Financing Regulations and had also neglected to consider the possibility of over collection in its consideration of Lockheed's deferment request.

4. Contracting Officer Decision

If negotiations fail, FAR 32.608(c) requires that the contracting officer issue a decision under the Disputes clause demanding payment of the debt. FAR 32.612 calls for "withholding" contract payments if the contractor does not pay the amount demanded within 30 days or does not request a deferment. Once the contracting officer has issued this final decision, the procedures of the Contract Disputes Act, as discussed in Chapter 13, come into effect.

In *Applied Cos. v. United States*, 144 F.3d 1470 (Fed. Cir. 1998), the contractor had notified the government that it had paid the contractor more than the amounts invoiced and proposed that the amount be repaid by setting off the overpayment against obligations the government owed the contractor on other contracts. The government did not agree to such offsets but unilaterally set off the contractor's debts against an amount the government had agreed to pay the contractor under a termination settlement on another contract. In the ensuing litigation, the contractor argued that the government had no right to exercise its setoff rights without the contracting officer's final decision The court rejected this argument because the government setoff could not be characterized as "relating to a contract." The overpayment occurred simply from a computer error (the insertion of an extra digit in the checks the government sent). "The Government may recover erroneous payments of that kind without recourse to the procedures of the Contract Disputes Act."

In *Kearfott Guidance & Navigation Corp.*, ASBCA 49263, 99-2 BCA ¶ 30,518, the government asserted a claim for "billing errors and progress payments exceeding 90% of the total contract price." Even thought the board admitted that the government claim was "related to" a contract, it permitted the offset without regard to the procedures in the Contract Disputes Act or FAR 32.608(c), stating at 150,696:

> [I]n view of the time honored nature of the Government's common law right of setoff, . . . [and] since neither the CDA nor FAR 32.608(c) explicitly bars the Government's exercise of its common law right of setoff, the contracting officer was not required to issue a final decision under the CDA before collecting the amount due.

But see *D.L. Kaufman, Inc.*, PSBCA 4159, 00-1 BCA ¶ 30,846 (no jurisdiction on issue of whether government was entitled to set off against possible recovery in a counterclaim in a separate lawsuit, because the government never issued a final decision asserting its counterclaim.)

5. Withholding or Setoff

The FAR requires that withholding or setoff take place if the contractor does not satisfy the debt following the government's demand. The FAR does not make the issuance of a final decision under the Disputes clause a requirement before these actions are taken. The decision to withhold is a discretionary decision of the contracting officer based on the status of contract performance and the financial needs of the contractor. See FAR 32.612, which states:

> During the 30 days following the issuance of a demand, the advisability of withholding payments otherwise due to the contractor shall be considered based on the circumstances of the individual cases. If payment is not completed within 30 days, and deferment is not requested, withholding of principal and interest shall be initiated immediately. In the event the contract is assigned under the Assignment of Claims Act of 1940 (31 U.S.C. 3727 and 41 U.S.C. 15), the rights of the assignee will be scrupulously respected and withholding of payments shall be consistent with those rights.

The Federal Claims Collection Standards at 31 CFR § 900.1(c) encourage agencies to "use all authorized remedies, including alternative dispute resolution and arbitration, to collect civil claims." FAR Subpart 32.6 implements this requirement by prescribing procedures for the collection of contract debts. FAR 32.605 requires cooperation within the government in effecting setoff:

> (a) To protect the Government's interests, contracting officers, contract financing offices, disbursing officials, and auditors shall cooperate fully with each other to—
>
> (1) Discover promptly when a contract debt arises;
>
> (2) Ascertain the correct amount of the debt;
>
> (3) Act promptly and effectively to collect the debt;
>
> (4) Administer deferment of collection agreements; and
>
> (5) Provide up-to-date information on the status of the debt.
>
> (b) For most kinds of contract debts, the contracting officer has the primary responsibility for determining the amounts of and collecting contract debt. Under some agency procedures, however, the individual who is responsible for payment under the contract; e.g., the disbursing officer, may have this primary responsibility.

This regulation deals only with *contract debts* for which contracting officers are responsible. However, a contractor can owe the government many other kinds of debts, such as unpaid taxes or judgments. These debts may also be set off against contract payments, but the regulations provide little guidance on cooperative arrangements regarding such debts other than a statement in 31 CFR § 901.1(c) that agencies "shall cooperate with one another." See, however, 31 CFR § 901.3(c), providing the following general guidance:

> Generally, non-centralized administrative offsets are ad hoc case-by-case offsets that an agency conducts, at the agency's discretion, internally or in cooperation with the agency certifying or authorizing payments to the debtor. Unless otherwise prohibited by law, when centralized administrative offset is not available or appropriate, past due, legally enforceable nontax delinquent debts may be collected through non-centralized administrative offset. In these cases, a creditor agency may make a request directly to a payment authorizing agency to offset a payment due a debtor to collect a delinquent debt.

If the contracting officer unilaterally determines the amount of a debt in accordance with FAR 32.608, the amount of debt collected through setoff shall "not exceed an amount that would have been considered acceptable in a negotiated agreement," FAR 32.608(b)(2). In *Newton Constr.*, AGBCA 236, 71-2 BCA ¶ 9093, the board found improper a setoff of funds, due under a Forest Service contract, to collect for tort damages arising out of a previous contract. The contracting officer made a determination to set off, without having a request from the contracting officer who had jurisdiction over the previous contract. If an agency decides to exercise its discretion to seek collection through setoff, the so-called demand cycles may be discontinued, 31 CFR § 901.2(f).

B. The Debt Collection Act

The Debt Collection Act (DCA) of 1982, with revisions, was adopted primarily to facilitate recovery of outstanding amounts under federal student loan programs. As a result, there has been some question as to whether the Act applies to any attempt by the government to use contract funds to satisfy a government demand against the contractor. There are three types of government collection actions. First there is the collection, which is based on a government demand arising out of the same contract under which collection is sought (intra-contract collection). This is the type of action we characterize as a withholding. The second type of collection is where the government demand arises out of a different government contract than the one under which collection is sought (inter-contract collection), which we characterize as one type of setoff. The third type of collection is where the government demand has a non-contractual basis, such as income tax or other contractor debt, another type of setoff. The early cases held that the DCA did not apply to the first type, e.g., *AVCO Corp. v. United States*, 10 Cl. Ct. 665 (1986), but did apply to the second type, for example, *DMJM/Norman Eng'g Co.*, ASBCA 28154, 84-1 BCA ¶ 17,226, and *IBM Corp.*, ASBCA 28821, 84-3 BCA ¶ 17,689. However, in *Cecile Indus. Inc. v. United States*, 995 F.2d 1052 (Fed. Cir. 1993), the court held that the DCA does not apply to the first two categories. In holding that the DCA does not apply to either intra- or inter-contractual debts, the court stated at 1056:

> Because the Debt Collection Act does not govern the Government's common law right to offset contractual debts, the Board correctly determined that the Center possessed an independent common law right to offset Cecile's debts under contract 2851 against payments due to Cecile under contract 2851. However, the

> Center also possessed the same right to offset Cecile's debt against payments due to Cecile under contracts 2414 and 4247. The Center did not need to avail itself of section 3716 for any of the offsets. Thus, the Center did not need to satisfy the notice and opportunity requirements of section 3716. Accordingly, the Board erred in holding that the Center needed to comply with section 3716 for the GFM offsets affecting contracts 2414 and 4247. That error was harmless, however, because the Board provided the Center with an opportunity to cure the noncompliance. Otherwise, this court affirms the Board's decision.

The *Cecile* court did not rule on the question of whether the DCA applies to the setoff of non-contractual debts (our third category) against contract proceeds. However, to the extent that it does, the procedures that it requires are quite similar to those contained in the FAR Subpart 32.6. See 31 U.S.C. § 3716, which states:

> (a) After trying to collect a claim from a person under section 3711(a) of this title [31 USCS § 3711(a)], the head of an executive or legislative agency may collect the claim by administrative offset. The head of the agency may collect by administrative offset only after giving the debtor—
>
> > (1) written notice of the type and amount of the claim, the intention of the head of the agency to collect the claim by administrative offset, and an explanation of the rights of the debtor under this section;
> >
> > (2) an opportunity to inspect and copy the records of the agency related to the claim;
> >
> > (3) an opportunity for a review within the agency of the decision of the agency related to the claim; and
> >
> > (4) an opportunity to make a written agreement with the head of the agency to repay the amount of the claim.

Thus, it could be argued that satisfaction of the FAR would satisfy the DCA.

C. The Contract Disputes Act

The relationship between government debt collection and the Contract Disputes Act of 1978, 41 U.S.C. § 601 *et seq.*, is another area where confusion exists. When the government seeks to collect a contract debt, it is making a claim under the contract where the alleged debt arose. Section 605(a) states that "[a]ll claims by the government against a contractor relating to a contract shall be the subject of a decision by the contracting officer." If the contractor has been given notice of the alleged debt, the contracting officer may then issue a final decision, *Keystone Coat & Apron Mfg. Corp. v. United States*, 150 Ct. Cl. 277 (1960). The contractor can then appeal the final decision and is not required to certify the claim, but if the government has withheld or set off the money, the contractor will not be able to recover interest, *Blosam*

Contractors, Inc., VABCA 2305, 88-1 BCA ¶ 20,370. As an alternative, the contractor can attempt to convert the government claim into its claim which, if successful, will entitle it to interest but will require certification if over the threshold, *Security Assocs. Int'l, Inc.*, DOTCAB 1340, 84-2 BCA ¶ 17,444. When the government withholds money without making a final decision, the contractor may make a claim for the money, *Boeing Co.*, ASBCA 36612, 89-1 BCA ¶ 21,421. There is also authority that the withholding or setoff in itself constitutes a final decision from which the contractor can appeal, *Placeway Constr. Corp. v. United States*, 920 F.2d 903 (Fed. Cir. 1990); *KAL M.E.I. Mfg. & Trade, Ltd.*, ASBCA 44367, 94-1 BCA ¶ 26,582.

The government may set off claims against money due the contractor even though the claims have not been finally determined under the contract from which they arose, *California Inflatables Co.*, ASBCA 45859, 94-2 BCA ¶ 26,877. In addition, claims under other contracts of the same agency will be considered as a defense against a contractor's appeal, *Roy E. Buhl*, ASBCA 45818, 94-2 BCA ¶ 26,805. However, claims arising out of contracts of another agency were not permitted as a defense against the contractor's appeal in *Heptacon Commercial Constr. & Design, Inc.*, DOTBCA, 2764, 95-1 BCA ¶ 27,307. In addition, government claims will not be considered either as a counterclaim or a defense in the Court of Federal Claims unless they are the subject of a final decision, *Foley Co. v. United States*, 26 Cl. Ct. 936 (1992), *aff'd*, 11 F.3d 1032 (Fed. Cir. 1993).

V. REMEDIES

This section covers the contractor's and government's remedies associated with the payment process. The first section considers the contractor's remedies. Government remedies for overpayment and improper contractor claims are dealt with in the second section.

A. Contractor Remedies for Delayed Payment

Delays in payments to contractors can occur in a number of ways. The government may have no arguable defense for nonpayment, but simply fail to process the contractor's invoice in a timely fashion. In addition, the government may refuse payment of a contractor's invoice or voucher on the grounds that the work is defective, that payment is not yet due, or that the costs being sought are unallowable charges. Payment delays may result from the government's refusal to recognize, or the government's delay in recognizing, the contractor's right to recover additional compensation, such as through a constructive change in the work. Further, delay in payment can occur when the government, in order to satisfy a government claim against the contractor or alleged debt of the contractor to the government (as discussed in the prior section), makes use of, or sets off, funds admittedly due the contractor. The reasons for the government's failure to pay and the contractor's response to the failure can significantly affect the relief available to the contractor.

The first subsection discusses the contractor's ability to recover interest for late payment pursuant to statute or contract clause. The second subsection then considers the availability of injunctions and other forms of contractor relief for delayed payment.

1. Interest

The traditional common law remedy for delayed payment has been interest, *Ramsey v. United States*, 121 Ct. Cl. 426, 101 F. Supp. 353 (1951). It is sometimes stated that interest is the sole remedy. See *Loudon v. Taxing Dist.*, 104 U.S. 771 (1881), in which the Court stated at 774:

> [A]ll damages for delay in the payment of money owing upon contract are provided for in the allowance of interest, which is in the nature of damages for withholding money that is due. The law assumes that interest is the measure of all such damages.

See also *ReCon Paving, Inc. v. United States*, 745 F.2d 34 (Fed. Cir. 1984) (payment of interest is remedial in nature, meant to compensate a contractor for costs of money associated with financing additional or disputed work while pursuing an administrative remedy, and is also designed to encourage prompt consideration by contracting officer of contractor's request for payment).

The long-standing rule in government contracts has been that interest is not assessed against the government unless expressly permitted either by statute or contract provision, *United States v. Thayer-West Point Hotel Co.*, 329 U.S. 585 (1947); *Davis Group, Inc.*, ASBCA 48431, 95-2 BCA ¶ 27,702 (absent other authority, the FAR cost principle barring interest on borrowings precluded a contractor from recovering interest on progress payments withheld by the government). In certain limited circumstances, however, interest has been allowed as part of an equitable adjustment, without any express authorization for the recovery of interest. Two principal statutes serve as a basis for contractor recovery of interest for government delays in payment on fixed-price contracts: (1) the Prompt Payment Act of 1982, 31 U.S.C. § 3901 *et seq.*, covering undisputed delays in payment, and (2) the Contract Disputes Act of 1978, 41 U.S.C. § 611, providing for interest on contractor claims.

a. Prompt Payment Act

In the past, contractors have traditionally been unable to recover interest for so-called pure delays in payment—where the government simply fails to make timely payment of an amount that is not in dispute. To remedy this situation, Congress enacted the Prompt Payment Act (PPA), 31 U.S.C. § 3901 *et seq.*, which is effective for contracts entered into on or after October 1, 1982. The Act was amended in 1988 by Pub. L. No. 100-496. Section 3902 of the Act requires each federal agency that fails to make payment for each "delivered item of property or service by the required payment date" to pay an interest penalty. The Act is implemented by FAR Subpart

32.9. The Office of Management and Budget has also implemented the Act through 5 CFR § 1315. DFARS 232.905 contains guidance for the Department of Defense.

To determine whether the liability for interest due on late payment falls on the program office or on the defense finance accounting service, see *Liability for Prompt Payment Interest Payments Under Interagency Agreements*, 65 Comp. Gen. 795 (B-219474) (1986). The PPA states that when the government is liable for interest on late payments, the Act "does not authorize the appropriation of additional amounts to pay an interest penalty. The head of an agency shall pay a penalty under this section out of amounts made available to carry out the program for which the penalty is incurred," 31 U.S.C. § 3902(f).

Contractors must act to preserve their rights. See *Freedom N.Y., Inc.*, ASBCA 43965, 01-2 BCA ¶ 31,585, *recons. denied,* 02-1 BCA ¶ 31,676, *aff'd in part and rev'd in part,* 329 F.3d 1320 (Fed. Cir. 2003), *recons. denied*, 346 F.3d 1359 (Fed. Cir. 2003), denying jurisdiction over a claim for Prompt Payment Act interest on a settlement received after a default termination was converted into a termination for the convenience of the government because the contractor's original settlement claim did not allege any right to PPA interest.

(1) Coverage

All federal agencies including certain nonappropriated fund activities are covered by the Act. Although Tennessee Valley Authority is covered, the 5 CFR § 1315 provisions do not apply to it. All contracts for the acquisition of property or services are covered, including leases. The Act applies overseas, *Held & Baukitjengesellschaft*, ASBCA 42463, 92-1 BCA ¶ 24,712. See FAC 90-39, 61 Fed. Reg. 31658, June 20, 1996, amending the FAR to change the clauses and regulations that had stated that the Act did not apply to foreign purchase. The Act does not apply to a claim for attorneys' fees under the Equal Access to Justice Act (EAJA). In *FDL Techs., Inc. v. United States*, 26 Cl. Ct. 484, *aff'd,* 967 F.2d 1578 (Fed. Cir 1992), the court stated that attorneys' fees are not within the contemplation of a contract as a complete delivered item, property, or service. Thus, the court stated that a contractor who was awarded EAJA attorneys' fees was not entitled to prompt payment interest. Neither does the Act apply to invalid contract actions. See *Production Packing,* ASBCA 53662, 03-2 BCA ¶ 32,338, holding that the Act did not apply to orders issued on a Basic Ordering Agreement that were above the dollar limits of the agreement and the authority of the ordering officer.

The Act calls for payment of an interest penalty where the government fails to make timely payment for each "complete delivered item of property or service." The 1988 Amendments to the Act provide for the payment of interest on progress payments in construction contracts, 31 U.S.C. § 3903(a)(6)(A), as well as interest on retainage, 31 U.S.C. § 3903(a)(6)(B). This provision provides for the payment of interest on a progress payment that remains unpaid for a period of more than 14 days after receipt of the payment request or a longer period, as specified in the contract to allow time to inspect the work. These payments subject to interest are called "invoice payments," FAR 32.902. They exclude financing payments, including progress payments based on costs.

Originally the Act did not specify whether it applied to interest payments under a cost reimbursement contract, but the boards were split. In *Northrop Worldwide Aircraft Servs., Inc. v. Department of the Treasury*, GSBCA 11162-TD, 92-2 BCA ¶ 24,765, the board had held that under regulations in effect prior to the 1998 amendments to the PPA, interest was due for late payment of interim payments of costs when the service was being performed or completed at the time of the invoice. However, the ASBCA, in *Johnson Controls World Servs., Inc.*, ASBCA 51640, 01-2 BCA ¶ 31,531, held that the revised regulations precluded the recovery of PPA interest for late payment of interim invoices on cost reimbursement contracts for services.

Section 1010 of the National Defense Authorization Act for Fiscal Year 2001, Pub. L. 106-398, requires agencies to pay an interest penalty whenever they make interim payments under cost-reimbursement services contracts more than 30 days after receipt of a proper invoice. The FAR was amended to change FAR 32.001 to include the following as a definition of "contract financing payments."

> (vi) Interim payments under a cost reimbursement contract, except for cost reimbursement contract for services when Alternate I of the Clause at 52.232-25, Prompt Payment, is used.

In addition, "invoice payments" are now defined to include:

> (iv) Interim payments under cost reimbursement contact for services when Alternate I of the Clause at 52.232-25, Prompt Payment is used. Since FAR 32.908(c)(3) calls for the use of Alternate I in all cost reimbursement contracts for services, these definitions are operative on all such contracts.

Since FAR 32.908(c)(3) calls for the use of Alternate I in all cost-reimbursement contracts for services, contractors will be entitled to interest on late payments of invoices for completed services if the contract specifies a procedure for invoicing costs for specific services. See the following guidance in FAR 32.102 making it mandatory that cost-reimbursement contracts for services contain such a procedure:

> (d) Payments for accepted supplies and services that are only a part of the contract requirements (i.e., partial deliveries) are authorized under 41 U.S.C. 255 and 10 U.S.C. 2307. In accordance with 5 CFR 1315.4(k), agencies must pay for partial delivery of supplies or partial performance of services unless specifically prohibited by the contract. Although payments for partial deliveries generally are treated as a method of payment and not as a method of contract financing, using partial

delivery payments can assist contractors to participate in contracts without, or with minimal, contract financing. When appropriate, contract statements of work and pricing arrangements must permit acceptance and payment for discrete portions of the work, as soon as accepted (see 32.906(c)).

See also FAR 32.906, stating:

(c) *Partial deliveries.* (1) Contracting officers must, where the nature of the work permits, write contract statements of work and pricing arrangements that allow contractors to deliver and receive invoice payments for discrete portions of the work as soon as completed and found acceptable by the Government (see 32.102(d)).

(2) Unless specifically prohibited by the contract, the clause at 52.232-1, Payments, provides that the contractor is entitled to payment for accepted partial deliveries of supplies or partial performance of services that comply with all applicable contract requirements and for which prices can be calculated from the contract terms.

(2) Interest Penalty

The Prompt Payment Act provides for the payment of interest on contract payments at 31 U.S.C. § 3902(a):

Under regulations prescribed under section 3903 of this title, the head of an agency acquiring property or service from a business concern, who does not pay the concern for each complete delivered item of property or service by the required payment date, shall pay an interest penalty to the concern on the amount of the payment due. The interest shall be computed at the rate of interest established by the Secretary of the Treasury, and published in the Federal Register, for interest payments under section 12 of the Contract Disputes Act of 1978 (41 U.S.C. 611), which is in effect at the time the agency accrues the obligation to pay a late payment interest penalty.

Interest is paid at the rate prescribed by the Secretary of the Treasury beginning the day after payment was due and ending on the day payment was made, 31 U.S.C. § 3902. The rate used is the rate in effect on the first day interest is due, 31 U.S.C. § 3902(a). The amount is compounded monthly, 31 U.S.C. § 3902(e) and FAR 32.907-1(d). The interest is to be paid automatically, and the contractor is not required to make a claim for interest. Under the Act, interest begins to accrue for most supply and service contracts 30 days after receipt of a proper invoice and runs for a maximum of one year. For construction contracts the period is 14 days and for perishable commodities, the times vary, being as short as 7 days. After the one-year period, a contractor can keep interest running by converting the government obligation into a claim under the Contract Disputes Act, as discussed below. If the government does not pay a required interest penalty within 10 days after it is due, and the contractor makes a written demand not later than 40 days after receiving a payment that excludes interest, the contractor is entitled to an additional interest penalty, FAR 32.907(g).

(3) Procedures

Prompt Payment Act interest begins to accrue upon receipt of a "proper invoice." Paragraph (a)(4) of the Prompt Payment clause in FAR 52.232-25 lists the minimum requirements for information that must be included with a proper invoice, the most important information being (1) a description of the work for which the payment is due and (2) documentation required by the contract. A contractor should ascertain early in contract performance precisely what documentation is needed by the government and include that documentation with all invoices submitted under the contract. It is clear that a proper invoice cannot be submitted for work covered by a contract modification until the modification is signed by both parties, *Columbia Eng'g Corp.*, IBCA 2322, 89-2 BCA ¶ 21,762; *D.H. Blattner & Sons, Inc.*, IBCA 2589, 89-3 BCA ¶ 22,230 *rev'd* 909 F.2d 1495; *Ricway, Inc.*, ASBCA 30204, 86-3 BCA ¶ 19,234. Further, no interest accrues during the period of delay in preparing or processing a contract modification, *Sociedade De Construcoes Soares Da Costa*, ASBCA 37875, 90-2 BCA ¶ 22,691. Contractors who submit invoices that they know are defective or incorrect risk losing their entitlement to interest, *MASCO, Inc.*, HUDBCA 95-G-147-C16, 96-2 BCA ¶ 28,364. Compare *Atherton Constr., Inc.,* ASBCA 48527, 00-2 BCA ¶ 30,968, in which a contractor was entitled to PPA interest on an unpaid invoice because the government's only objection to the invoice was that it was not reduced for alleged liquidated damages. The government twice returned the invoice with a request for information as to whether the contractor had defenses to the liquidated damages, but never asserted any improprieties in the invoices. Because the government did not pay the undisputed amount within 14 days of receiving the invoices, it was required to pay interest on that amount. For further discussion of what constitutes a "proper invoice," as well as notification procedures for improper invoices, see Section II.A.

The interest penalty accrues only for one year or until the submission of a claim, whichever occurs first, 31 U.S.C. § 3906; *Morgan Mgmt. Sys., Inc.*, ASBCA 49169, 96-2 BCA ¶ 28,491. Interest ceases to accrue on the date a contractor files a claim for interest under the Contract Disputes Act. See *Technocratica*, ASBCA 44347, 94-1 BCA ¶ 26,584, where the government failed to make payment within 14 days of submission of a proper invoice on a construction contract. The government paid the principal but refused to pay the interest. The contractor then filed a claim for the interest. The board held that the contractor was entitled to interest from the time payment was due until the principal was paid; to this was added a penalty and the amount was compounded until the date that the contractor filed its claim for interest. In addition, the contractor was entitled to recover CDA interest from the date it filed its claim until it was paid. In *Marine Constr. & Dredging, Inc.*, ASBCA 38412, 95-1 BCA ¶ 27,286, the contractor was entitled to Prompt Payment Act interest penalty on a request for payment due 30 days after the government received a request for payment and was entitled to Contract Disputes Act interest thereon from the date of the government's receipt of the contractor's claim for PPA interest penalties. The board rejected the government's contention that the contractor was not entitled to interest under the PPA because the payment request was made prior to the government's issuance of the notice of proceed. The board ruled that part of the payment request concerned bond premiums, which are included within the scope of progress payment requests.

PPA interest applies only if the Act and the contract are complied with. In *Videotronics, Inc.*, ASBCA 47690, 95-1 BCA ¶ 27,558, PPA interest did not accrue on an amount allegedly owed to a contractor because final payment became due only on the contractor's submission of a proper voucher, rather than on physical completion of the contract work. The government disputed the amount invoiced in the contractor's final voucher, and the dispute was genuine, not frivolous. See *Marut Testing & Inspection Servs., Inc. v. General Servs. Admin.,* GSBCA 15412, 02-2 BCA ¶ 31,945 (contractor not entitled to interest under the PPA because the contract provided that the government would not owe PPA interest if a disbursement delay resulted from a disagreement over the payment amount), and *Southern Comfort Builders, Inc. v. United States*, 67 Fed. Cl. 124 (2005) (PPA interest does not apply when payment in question is disputed).

b. The Contract Disputes Act

Where a contractor's request for payment has been "disputed" because the government believes either the contractor has not properly performed, the identified costs are unallowable, or the contractor is not entitled to additional compensation, no interest penalty under the Prompt Payment Act may be recovered for the resulting delay in payment. The Prompt Payment Act specifically disclaims its applicability to payments delayed by reason of a "dispute" between the parties, 31 U.S.C. § 3907(c). Thus, if interest is to be recovered in such circumstances, the contractor must rely on the Contract Disputes Act.

The Contract Disputes Act provides for the payment of interest on claims at 41 U.S.C. § 611:

> Interest on amounts found due contractors on claims shall be paid to the contractor from the date the contracting officer receives the claim pursuant to section 6(a) [41 USCS § 605(a)] from the contractor until payment thereof. The interest provided for in this section shall be paid at the rate established by the Secretary of the Treasury pursuant to Public Law 92-41 (85 Stat. 97) for the Renegotiation Board.

(1) Time of Accrual of Interest

The Act is clear that interest begins to accrue on the date that the contracting officer received a "claim." An appeal to a board of contract appeals or the Court of Federal Claims is not required to entitle the contractor to interest on a claim. The contractor is entitled to interest from the time that it files a claim until payment is made, whether or not litigation ensues, *Newport News Shipbuilding & Drydock Co.*, ASBCA 32289, 90-2 BCA ¶ 22,859. There, the government withheld a payment but paid it after the contractor filed a claim contesting the withholding. The board held that interest accrued from the date of the claim to the date of payment. See also *The Swanson Group, Inc.*, ASBCA 53254, 02-1 BCA ¶ 31,838 (CDA interest computed from the date the contracting officer receives a claim, not from the date of the entitlement ruling).

Interest on termination settlement proposals accrues at the time an impasse occurred, *Ellett Constr. Co. v. United States*, 93 F.3d 1537 (Fed. Cir. 1996). See *Rex Sys., Inc. v. Cohen*, 224 F.3d 1367 (Fed. Cir. 2000), in which a contractor was not entitled to collect interest on its termination settlement proposal because the resulting settlement agreement was conclusive evidence that negotiations had not reached an impasse.

Interest begins to accrue on costs before the contractor incurs them, *Caldera v. J.S. Alberici Constr. Co.*, 153 F.3d 1381 (Fed. Cir. 1998). There the court held that even if certain regulations prohibit claims for future costs, the statute overrides conflicting regulations. Interest will also accrue on all costs of the claim even if they were not included in the original claim, *Sprint Communications Co., L.P. v. General Servs. Admin.*, GSBCA 15139, 01-2 BCA ¶ 31,464. There the contractor submitted a certified claim for approximately $500,000, but later revised this amount to nearly $1.5 million. After finding for the contractor on entitlement, the board determined that the contractor's claim for CDA interest began to run on the first claim from the original submission date, notwithstanding the subsequent claim revision, because the revised claim did not include any new elements.

(2) Rate of Interest

Interest under the Act should be calculated on a simple rather than compound basis using whichever six-month Treasury Department rates are in effect during the period from claim submission until the date of payment, *Brookfield Constr. Co. v. United States*, 228 Ct. Cl. 551, 661 F.2d 159 (1981); *Industrial Contractors, Inc.*, ASBCA 31270, 91-3 BCA ¶ 24,053; *EMS, Inc.*, GSBCA 9588, 90-2 BCA ¶ 22,876; *Isadore Klein*, GSBCA 9269, 89-1 BCA ¶ 21,222; *The Swanson Group, Inc.*, ASBCA 53254, 02-1 BCA¶ 31,838 (not bank interest rate). The interest provision in the standard Disputes clause was amended to reflect the *Brookfield* decision. See also FAR 33.208. Note that CDA interest accrues on the combined total of both principal and PPA interest that remains unpaid on the date of the CDA claim, *Columbia Eng'g Corp.*, IBCA 2351, 88-2 BCA ¶ 20,595. See also *Ronald Adams, Contractor, Inc.*, AGBCA 91-155-1, 94-3 BCA ¶ 27,018, holding that a contractor was entitled to interest in accordance with the PPA prior to filing the claim as well as CDA interest thereafter. A variable rather than a fixed rate of interest is used in order to protect contractors against the losses of borrowing money, *Honeywell, Inc.*, GSBCA 5458, 81-2 BCA ¶ 15,383.

(3) Delay in Payment

The CDA does not provide for interest for a mere delay by the government in making a payment. Interest accrues only upon the contracting officer's receipt of a "claim" from the contractor. Initial, undisputed requests for payments do not constitute "claims" upon which interest may accrue. See *Esprit Corp. v. United States*, 6 Cl. Ct. 546 (1984), in which the contractor was not entitled to interest for delayed payments on a contract modification since this undisputed request did not constitute a claim. The current Disputes clause at FAR 52.233-1 specifically provides:

> A voucher, invoice, or other routine request for payment that is not in dispute when submitted is not a claim under the Act.

See *Dombrowski & Holmes*, GSBCA 6328, 83-1 BCA ¶ 16,300. See also the FAR 33.001 definition of "claim," which contains this same statement. Moreover, if a claim for money has not been filed, a request for interest is not by itself a "claim," *Lee Roofing Co.*, IBCA 1506-8-81, 82-1 BCA ¶ 15,789; *Dawson Constr. Co.*, VABCA 2005, 84-3 BCA ¶ 17,587 (Contract Disputes Act is meant to address "interest on claims, as opposed to interest as claims"); *Erickson Air Crane Co. of Wash., Inc.*, 731 F.2d 810 (Fed. Cir. 1984), *aff'g*, EBCA 50-6-79, 83-1 BCA ¶ 16,145 (Contract Disputes Act does not apply to interest arising from cost of performing extra work).

Interest cannot be recovered by a contractor whose own actions cause the delay. See *Mil-Pak Co.*, GSBCA 7332, 84-3 BCA ¶ 17,555 (contractor failed to execute release of claims and certify payment to subcontractors), and *Fidelity Constr. Co.*, DOTCAB 1113, 82-1 BCA ¶ 15,633, *aff'd,* 700 F.2d 1379 (Fed. Cir. 1983) (contractor delayed recovery by precluding settlement and grossly overstating claim). Compare *Tom Shaw, Inc.*, ENGBCA 5541, 89-3 BCA ¶ 21,961, in which the board reasoned that mere overstatement of a claim should not deprive the contractor of the remedial aspect to the CDA. It stated that the government would not be harmed by the payment of interest on the amount recovered because the award is based on the "amount found due," not on the amount claimed. It found that the actions of the contractor had not delayed the recovery.

(4) Conversion into a Claim

While a contractor's invoice or request for an equitable adjustment may not constitute a claim upon which interest accrues when first submitted, it may be "converted into" a demand for payment in the form of a proper "claim" following the advent of a dispute or after an unreasonable delay in payment, *Sol Flores Constr., A Div. of Floresol & Co.*, ASBCA 32278, 89-3 BCA ¶ 22,154; *Falcon Research & Dev. Co.*, ASBCA 27002, 82-2 BCA ¶ 16,049. In some early cases, it was found that an unreasonable delay by the government in paying invoices "converted" the invoices into "claims" against the government entitling the contractor to interest,

Capital Sec. Servs., Inc., GSBCA 5722, 81-1 BCA ¶ 14,923. However, later cases have required the contractor to take some affirmative action after the delay to convert the initial request into a claim, *Falcon Research & Dev. Co.*, ASBCA 27002, 82-2 BCA ¶ 16,049. The current Disputes clause contains language that expressly provides for the conversion of a contractor's "routine request for payment" into a claim, stating:

> The submission may be converted to a claim under the Act, by complying with the submission and certification requirements of this clause, if it is disputed either as to liability or amount or is not acted upon in a reasonable time.

(5) Settlement

When the parties negotiate a settlement agreement, they should consider the question of interest and incorporate language into the agreement either including interest in the settled amount or excluding it. Such agreements will be enforced, *Blake Constr. Co.*, GSBCA 8376, 89-3 BCA ¶ 22,082 (settlement agreement expressly reserved the contractor's right to seek interest). A contractor may also discharge its legal right to CDA interest on a claim by expressly waiving that right as part of the negotiation and settlement of the claim, *Central Intelligence Agency*, Comp. Gen. Dec. B-211737, 83-2 CPD ¶ 475. However, where the settlement agreement does not contain express language concerning interest, the board or court must decide whether the parties agreed to include or exclude it. This involves interpretation of the settlement agreement. Matters to be considered are the nature of the settlement agreement and the communications of the parties prior to and at the time of agreement.

Where the parties enter into a settlement containing broad release language and no express reservation for recovery is included, it is likely that it will be concluded that interest has been included in the settled amount. See *Gulf Coast Trailing Co.*, ENGBCA 6072, 94-2 BCA ¶ 26,646, in which the board stated at 132,564-65:

> Thus, full and complete settlement of a claim for a lump sum amount based on the contractor's execution of a contract modification with a release and payment of the underlying claim constitutes an accord and satisfaction extinguishing the claim and any right to pre-settlement interest inherent in the underlying claim. *Spickard Enterprises, Inc.*, ENG BCA No. 4583, 91-3 BCA ¶ 24,348; *River City Contractors, Inc., supra*. Compare *Progressive Brothers Construction Co., Inc.*, ENG BCA No. 5550, 89-2 BCA ¶ 21,644. In this regard, a claim for CDA interest cannot stand alone without an underlying claim. *Spickard Enterprises, Inc., supra*.
>
> The language of Mod 5's release of "all costs" sufficiently defines the parties' express intent to resolve "all costs," including the direct and indirect costs, related to Gulf Coast Trailing's rock claim. The release is broad enough to construe it as capturing CDA interest as the cost, or damage, to Gulf Coast Trailing for its "pre-settlement" direct and indirect costs, particularly where neither party mentioned the application of CDA interest during the course of negotiations lead-

> ing to the lump sum settlement. See *Beaty Electric Co., Inc.*, EBCA No. 408-3-88, 90-2 BCA ¶ 22,829.
>
> Further, Gulf Coast Trailing executed Mod 5 without reserving its right to CDA interest. It neither excepted CDA interest from the release language which covered all direct and indirect costs for its rock claim, nor otherwise notified the Corps that it did not consider CDA interest to be covered in its direct and indirect costs included in the full and complete settlement of its rock claim.
>
> In this regard, Gulf Coast Trailing contends that the parties did not intend the release to cover CDA interest, since CDA interest was not a direct or indirect "cost" of the contractor's performance of the rock claim work but a payment mandated by statute. We disagree. The term "interest" generally is understood, and referred to, as a "cost for the use of money." See *Federal Electric Corp., supra*. When used in contract litigation, interest commonly is referred to by the term "interest cost." See *Dawson Construction Co., Inc.*, GSBCA No. 5777, 80-2 BCA ¶ 14,817. Thus, the release of all costs in Mod 5 applied to pre-settlement CDA interest giving the term, "costs," its ordinarily understood meaning under normal rules of contract interpretation.

See also *Amplitronics, Inc.*, ASBCA 46249, 94-2 BCA ¶ 26,856 (general release and discussions in settlement negotiations considered to determine interest included in the absence of express reservation).

Where, however, a settlement is incorporated into a price adjustment without broad release language, it is less likely that interest will be considered to be included in the settled amount. See *Central Mech., Inc.*, ASBCA 29193, 85-2 BCA ¶ 18,005, holding that in such an agreement, interest would be considered to be included in the settlement only if expressly stated to be included. Another factor to be considered would be whether the parties discussed the inclusion or exclusion.

The inclusion of interest in the settlement agreement does not preclude the recovery of interest if the settlement agreement is not paid, *Elkhorn Constr. Co.*, VABCA 1493, 83-2 BCA ¶ 16,864. In *Elkhorn* the board concluded that while the lump-sum settlement agreement should be construed to encompass "pre-settlement interest," there was nothing in the settlement agreement to prevent the running of interest from the date of the settlement through the date of payment. Likewise in *Federal Elec. Corp.*, ASBCA 24002, 82-2 BCA ¶ 15,862, *aff'd,* 2 FPD ¶ 9 (Fed. Cir. 1983), the board disallowed interest under the Act from the date of the claim until the date of a comprehensive written settlement agreement, pointing to the absence of any express reservation of such interest in the settlement agreement and the contractor's awareness of the government's position that no such interest would be allowed. However, the board did allow recovery of interest from the date of settlement until payment, stating at 78,672:

> But it is equally clear that this consideration of interest covered only a limited possible delay in obtaining payment on these claims, certainly not extending beyond the 23 April 1979 execution date of the settlement agreement. Neither can

> we find any intention to toll the running of interest by the execution of the settlement agreement nor interpret the agreement as producing such result.

It would seem that post-settlement interest should be paid under the Prompt Payment Act if there is merely a delay in making the payment.

(6) Government Claims

If the government asserts a claim against a contractor and recovers funds as a result, the contractor can only recover interest under the Act if a "contractor claim" has been asserted, because the Act does not provide for interest on government claims, *Ruhnau-Evans-Ruhnau Assocs. v. United States*, 3 Cl. Ct. 217 (1983); *Southwest Marine Inc.*, DOTBCA 1666, 96-1 BCA ¶ 28212. In *Ruhnau*, the contracting officer issued a final decision, finding that an architect-engineering firm had provided the government with defective drawings and specifications for renovation work. The contracting officer demanded payment of damages. The contractor paid the amount demanded and brought a direct access suit in the Claims Court challenging the final decision. The court found that the contractor was not liable for the full amount assessed by the contracting officer but held that the contractor was not entitled to interest on the amount due since the claim was deemed a government claim rather than a contractor claim. The court also stated that a "letter of protest" accompanying the contractor's payment was not a "predecisional" contractor claim. Similarly, in *Martin Marietta Corp.*, ASBCA 25828, 84-1 BCA ¶ 17,119, the government made a DCAA Form 1 cost disallowance of a "token amount" submitted on a contractor's voucher to account for allegedly unallowable insurance charges that had been paid to the contractor over several years. While the contractor was successful in challenging the cost disallowance, the board did not allow the contractor to recover interest under the Contract Disputes Act on the amount that had been improperly withheld. The board concluded that since the contractor "had never submitted to the contracting officer a demand or 'claim' for payment of the amounts disallowed and withheld," no interest recovery could be had. These cases demonstrate that interest may not be recovered unless the contractor fully complies with the procedures of the Contract Disputes Act. Had the contractor submitted claims for the money held by the government, rather than litigating the merits of the government's claim, interest would have been recoverable. Thus, if the government has asserted a claim against the contractor in excess of $ 100,000, and if that claim has been satisfied through either voluntary payment by the contractor or government withholding, the contractor is required to make a certified claim for payment in order to initiate the running of interest under the Act, even though the contractor is entitled to litigate the merits of the government's claim before the boards and courts without providing certification, *Perkins & Will*, ASBCA 28335, 84-1 BCA ¶ 16,953; *General Dynamics Corp., Elec. Boat Div.*, ASBCA 25919, 82-1 BCA ¶ 15,616. See *Fortec Constructors*, ASBCA 27601, 83-1 BCA ¶ 16,402, in which the contractor was permitted to recover interest, on an amount improperly withheld by the government to cover "potential liquidated damages," from the date that the contractor submitted a certified claim for payment of the amount withheld.

Interest recovery in the situations presented in *Ruhnau* and *Martin Marietta* may now be mandated under FAR 32.613(l), which provides:

> Any amount collected by the Government in excess of the amount found to be due on appeal under the Disputes clause of the contract shall be refunded to the contractor with interest thereon from the date of collection by the Government at the annual rate established by the Secretary of Treasury under Public Law 92-41.

2. Injunctions and Other Remedies

Injunctive or mandamus type relief is generally not available to compel a government agency to make payment. Contractor attempts to obtain such relief have generally been dismissed for lack of jurisdiction. In *Warner v. Cox*, 487 F.2d 1301 (5th Cir. 1974), the district court, pending resolution of an appeal before the ASBCA, had issued an injunction under the Administrative Procedures Act (APA) to compel the Navy to continue payment on the contractor's weekly vouchers. The fifth circuit reversed, holding that the Tucker Act provided the contractor an "adequate remedy at law" in the form of money damages and thereby precluded injunctive relief under the APA. See also *Hamilton Sec. Advisory Servs.., Inc. v. United States*, 60 Fed. Cl. 111 (2004), denying a request for a declaratory judgment that the government had improperly withheld payment on a contract. The court reasoned that, while it had the authority to rule on the issue as a matter of contract interpretation (which would have been in the nature of a declaratory judgment), there was no need for an early resolution of the matter because the contract had been completed. At 60 Fed. Cl. 296 (2004) the court held that the government had breached the contract by withholding funds based on an erroneous interpretation of the contract. Compare *Hangar One, Inc.*, ASBCA 19460, 76-1 BCA ¶ 11,830, *recons. denied*, 76-1 BCA ¶ 11,899, in which the board urged the government to release withheld payments after a district court ruled that a government claim had no merit even though an appeal to the circuit court was pending. See also *Boston Pneumatics, Inc.*, GSBCA 4203, 75-1 BCA ¶ 11,014. In *IBM Corp.*, ASBCA 28821, 84-3 BCA ¶ 17,689, the board ordered the government to refund amounts that had been set off without following the procedures of the Debt Collection Act, 31 U.S.C. § 3716.

Improper withholding may also serve as a defense against government claims. Thus, improper withholding has prevented the government from recovering (1) damages for the contractor's failure to perform and (2) property created through contract performance, *United States v. Lennox Metal Mfg. Co.*, 225 F.2d 302 (2d Cir. 1955). Further, the government's failure to make timely payment may serve to excuse the contractor's subsequent default, *Contract Maint., Inc.*, ASBCA 19409, 75-1 BCA ¶ 11,207. While it has been held that government failure to make payment will not excuse contractor default if the controlling cause of the default is other than nonpayment, *TGC Contracting Corp. v. United States*, 736 F.2d 1512 (Fed. Cir. 1984); *Mercury Data Sys. Corp.*, ASBCA 18837, 75-2 BCA ¶ 11,495, it has also been held that a failure to pay may constitute a "material breach" by the government, justifying the contractor's abandonment of performance even where the contractor could have completed the work, *Building Maint. Specialist, Inc.*, ENGBCA 4115, 83-2 BCA ¶ 16,629; *R.H.J. Corp.*, ASBCA 9922, 66-1 BCA ¶ 5361, *recons. denied*, 66-1 BCA ¶ 5625.

To the extent that the government's delay in making payment causes an unreasonable delay, the contractor may also have grounds for recovery of delay damages under a breach of contract theory or under the Suspension of Work or Government Delay of Work clauses. In *Virginia Elecs. Co.*, ASBCA 18778, 77-1 BCA ¶ 12,393, a contractor was awarded an equitable adjustment for a delay found to have been caused by the government's wrongful late payment of progress payments, although the decision neither specifies the contract clause on which relief was based nor acknowledges any departure from the common law rule limiting payment delay damages to interest. The board stated at 60,018:

> The rejection of the initial progress payment request was arbitrary and unreasonable. The total contract amount entry was immaterial to the contractor's entitlement to the payment requested. Certainly the bureaucratic passion for dotted "i's" and crossed "t's" should not be allowed to deprive a contractor of monies required to pay for supplies needed to perform the contract. The Government knew the tight financial condition of the contractor and audited each progress payment request because of that condition. It should have known that appellant probably needed the progress payment to pay its suppliers and get on with performance. Therefore, it was obligated to act reasonably in paying progress payment requests.

B. Government Remedies for Overpayment and Improper Claims

Government remedies for overpayment on a contract depend on when the government makes a demand for repayment and whether the contractor's billing was fraudulent. In addition, there may be a government remedy if the contractor fails to disclose that an overpayment has occurred. See the overpayments provisions in the Prompt Payment clauses in FAR 52.232-25 (¶ (d)), FAR 52.232-26 (¶ (c)), and FAR 52.232-27 (¶ (l)). These provisions impose an affirmative duty on the contractor to disclose an overpayment.

1. Interest on Overpayments

In the absence of express statutory or contractual authorization to the contrary, the government is generally entitled to collect interest on contractor debts, *Swartzbaugh Mfg. Co. v. United States*, 289 F.2d 81 (6th Cir. 1961); *Harrisville Heights, Inc.*, ASBCA 20707, 77-1 BCA ¶ 12,358; *Read Plastics, Inc.*, GSBCA 4159, 77-2 BCA ¶ 12,859. The awarding of interest is discretionary in such circumstances, however, and will be denied if not clearly warranted by the facts of the case, *Stoeckert v. United States*, 183 Ct. Cl. 152, 391 F.2d 639 (1968); *Astro-Space Labs., Inc. v.*

United States, 200 Ct. Cl. 282, 470 F.2d 1003 (1972). In denying interest in *Stoeckert*, the court stated at 167:

> Finally, consideration must be given to the [Government's] contention that, under its counterclaim, it is entitled to interest on the excess cost assessment allowed by the CEBCA [Corps of Engineers Board of Contract Appeals]. The [Government] admits that the award of interest is discretionary and, in the exercise of discretion, the court declines to make such an award in this case. We take into account the [contractor's] apparent financial condition, the long time it has taken to bring this case to final judgment, the [contractor's] good faith though he acted erroneously, and the fact that contractors prevailing over the Government do not normally collect interest on their awards.

See *Flag Real Estate, Inc.*, HUDBCA 84-899-C14, 88-3 BCA ¶ 20,866, in which the government's claim for interest was denied because the government "egregiously mismanaged the contract by failing to respond directly to [the contractor's] request for a contract amendment, failing to properly check invoices, negligently certifying to incorrect invoices, losing and confusing contract amendments, and compromising the independence of the contracting officer."

a. Statutory Requirement

The Debt Collection Act, 31 U.S.C. § 3717, sets forth detailed requirements for the government concerning the recovery of interest on debts. The Federal Claims Collection Standards, 49 Fed. Reg. 8889 (1984), implement the Act's requirements at 4 CFR § 102.13. Under the statute, the head of an executive or legislative agency is required to charge a "minimum annual rate of interest on an outstanding debt on a United States Government claim" equal to the "average investment rate for the Treasury tax and loan accounts for the 12-month period ending on September 30 of each year." The regulations specifically state that the agency may assess a higher rate if such action is "necessary to protect the interests of the United States." The rate initially assessed will generally "remain fixed for the duration of the indebtedness," 4 CFR § 102.13(c); 31 U.S.C. § 3717(c)(2).

The statute provides for a mandatory 30-day "grace period" and states that no interest may be charged if "the amount due on the claim is paid within 30 days after the date from which interest accrues." The agency head is also authorized to extend the 30-day grace period, 31 U.S.C. § 3717(d).

The statute also mandates that the agency assess a "charge to cover the cost of processing and handling a delinquent claim" and a "penalty charge of not more than 6 percent a year for failure to pay a part of a debt more than 90 days past due," 31 U.S.C. § 3717(e). For contracts containing the interest clause set forth below, 4 CFR § 102.13(i) provides that, "The provisions of 31 U.S.C. § 3717 do not apply . . . to debts where [a] contract either prohibits such charges or explicitly fixes the charges that apply to the debts involved."

b. Contract Clause

FAR 32.617(a) requires that the following clause, set forth at FAR 52.232-17, be included in most contracts:

INTEREST (JUNE 1996)

(a) Except as otherwise provided in this contract under a Price Reduction for Defective Cost or Pricing Data clause or a Cost Accounting Standards clause,, all amounts that become payable by the Contractor to the Government under this contract (net of any applicable tax credit under the Internal Revenue Code (26 U.S.C. 1481)) shall bear simple interest from the date due until paid unless paid within 30 days of becoming due. The interest rate shall be the interest rate established by the Secretary of the Treasury as provided in Section 12 of the Contract Disputes Act of 1978 (Public Law 95-563), which is applicable to the period in which the amount becomes due, as provided in paragraph (b) of this clause, and then at the rate applicable for each six-month period as fixed by the Secretary until the amount is paid.

(b) Amounts shall be due at the earliest of the following dates:

(1) The date fixed under this contract.

(2) The date of the first written demand for payment consistent with this contract, including any demand resulting from a default termination.

(3) The date the Government transmits to the Contractor a proposed supplemental agreement to confirm completed negotiations establishing the amount of debt.

(4) If this contract provides for revision of prices, the date of written notice to the Contractor stating the amount of refund payable in connection with a pricing proposal or a negotiated pricing agreement not confirmed by contract modification.

(c) The interest charge made under this clause may be reduced under the procedures prescribed in 32.614-2 of the Federal Acquisition Regulation in effect on the date of this contract.

FAR 32.614-1(c) provides that interest shall run until (1) the date payment is received from the contractor, (2) the date of issuance of a check to the contractor from which an amount otherwise due the contractor has been withheld as a credit against the contract debt, or (3) the date on which an amount withheld and applied to the contract debt would otherwise have become payable to the contractor.

FAR 32.614-2, referred to in the Interest clause, requires that, when the amount of a contractor's liability is being established, equitable consideration be given to government delays in payment, provided that no interest penalty has been paid for such delay. The boards have reduced the amount of interest owed by a contractor in accordance with a comparable provision in the DAR, *Univac Div., Sperry Rand Corp.*, ASBCA 12855, 68-1 BCA ¶ 6938; *Atlantic Terminal Co.*, ASBCA 13699, 71-1 BCA ¶ 8866. The GAO has held that this equitable-consideration requirement does not apply to government delays in payment on unrelated transactions, *Land-Air, Inc.*, Comp. Gen. Dec. B-174899, 74-2 CPD ¶ 53.

While the Interest clause indicates that interest generally begins to accrue on the date of the government's "first written demand for payment consistent with this contract," it is clear that interest does not begin to run on the demand date unless the amount sought is actually due at that time. Thus, in cases involving government demands for payment of the excess costs of reprocurement, where the long-standing rule has been that the contractor is not liable for excess costs until payment has been made to the reprocurement contractor, interest does not begin to accrue until at least the date of such payments, *American Supply Co.*, ASBCA 13668, 69-1 BCA ¶ 7700. See also *Telectro Sys. Corp.*, ASBCA 21976, 78-2 BCA ¶ 13,480, *recons. denied*, 79-1 BCA ¶ 13,593, where interest did not begin to accrue until 30 days after the payment.

2. Fraudulent Claims for Payment

The submission of a fraudulent invoice for payment may subject the contractor to liability under the False Claims Act. Originally enacted in 1863, this Act is now divided into a civil provision in 31 U.S.C. § 3729 and a criminal provision in 18 U.S.C. § 287.

a. Civil Fraud

For many years, the civil provision of the False Claims Act was set forth in 31 U.S.C. § 231. In 1982, it was codified in 31 U.S.C. § 3729 and amended by the False Claims Amendments Act of 1986 to read as follows:

> (a) Liability for certain acts. Any person who—
>
> > (1) knowingly presents, or causes to be presented, to an officer or employee of the United States Government or a member of the Armed Forces of the United States a false or fraudulent claim for payment or approval;
> >
> > (2) knowingly makes, uses, or causes to be made or used, a false record or statement to get a false or fraudulent claim paid or approved by the Government;
> >
> > (3) conspires to defraud the Government by getting a false or fraudulent claim allowed or paid;

(4) has possession, custody, or control of property or money used, or to be used, by the Government and, intending to defraud the Government or willfully to conceal the property, delivers, or causes to be delivered, less property than the amount for which the person receives a certificate or receipt;

(5) authorized to make or deliver a document certifying receipt of property used, or to be used, by the Government and, intending to defraud the Government, makes or delivers the receipt without completely knowing that the information on the receipt is true;

(6) knowingly buys, or receives as a pledge of an obligation or debt, public property from an officer or employee of the Government, or a member of the Armed Forces, who lawfully may not sell or pledge the property; or

(7) knowingly makes, uses, or causes to be made or used, a false record or statement to conceal, avoid, or decrease an obligation to pay or transmit money or property to the Government, is liable to the United States Government for a civil penalty of not less than $5,000 and not more than $10,000, plus 3 times the amount of damages which the Government sustains because of the act of that person, except that if the court finds that—

(A) the person committing the violation of this subsection furnished officials of the United States responsible for investigating false claims violations with all information known to such person about the violation within 30 days after the date on which the defendant first obtained the information;

(B) such person fully cooperated with any Government investigation of such violation; and

(C) at the time such person furnished the United States with the information about the violation, no criminal prosecution, civil action, or administrative action had commenced under this title with respect to such violation, and the person did not have actual knowledge of the existence of an investigation into such violation;

The court may assess not less than 2 times the amount of damages which the Government sustains because of the act of the person. A person violating this subsection shall also be liable to the United States Government for the costs of a civil action brought to recover any such penalty or damages.

The 1986 amendments enable the government to prove a case of fraud more easily. Under the Act, the government can establish liability without showing that the contractor had a specific intent to defraud. "Knowing," which was not defined in the original Act, is now defined as (1) actual knowledge of the information, (2) deliberate ignorance of the truth or falsity of the information, or (3) reckless disregard of the truth or falsity of the information. The government is allowed to prove its civil claims by a "preponderance of the evidence," 31 U.S.C. § 3731(c). In addition, the "qui tam" provision, which permits individuals with evidence of fraud to file suit for the benefit of the government and keep part of the government's recovery, has been changed to give the government greater control over the litigation, 31 U.S.C. § 3730(b). The amendments also reflect the intent of Congress to improve the Act's deterrent effect. For instance, the potential liability was increased to a fixed statutory penalty of not less than $5,000 and not more than $10,000 plus treble damages.

"Knowingly has been held to include 'an aggravated form of gross negligence' or 'gross negligence plus,'" *United States v. Krizek,* 111 F.3d 934 (D. C. Cir. 1997). Innocent mistakes or negligence are not offenses under the Civil False Claims Act, *United States v. United Techs. Corp., Sikorsky Aircraft Div.,* 51 F. Supp. 2d 167 (D. Conn. 1999). Even a factually correct voucher can constitute a false claim if the work which it identifies has not been completely performed, *Shaw v. AAA Eng'g & Drafting, Inc.*, 213 F.3d 519 (10th Cir. 2000). The issue of whether a claim is false can also be determined by whether a contractor's representations were accurate in light of applicable law. See *United States ex rel. Oliver v. Parsons Co.,* 195 F.3d 457 (9th Cir. 1999). False claims can also include claims made to the government for payment under a subcontract that was approved by the government based on false statements of the contractor, thereby making the claims for payment "false" under the Act, *Harrison v. Westinghouse Savannah River Co.*, 176 F.3d 776 (4th Cir. 1999).

In 1986, Congress also enacted the Program Fraud Civil Remedies Act, 31 U.S.C. § 3801 *et seq.*, as part of the Omnibus Budget Reconciliation Act of 1986. The Act provides the government with an administrative remedy for collecting civil judgments in cases that otherwise would be economically impractical to litigate. The Act provides for an administrative hearing, an agency appeal, and limited judicial review. This remedy applies only to claims of less than $150,000, and the maximum penalty is $5,000 plus double the amount falsely claimed.

10 U.S.C. § 2324(i) and 41 U.S.C. § 256(i) provide that both the civil and criminal provisions of the False Claims Act, 31 U.S.C. § 3729 and 18 U.S.C. § 287, are applicable to a "proposal for settlement of costs for any period after such costs have been accrued that includes a cost that is expressly specified by statute or regulation as being unallowable, with the knowledge that such cost is unallowable."

b. Criminal Fraud

18 U.S.C. § 287, as amended by the False Claims Amendments Act of 1986, provides:

> Whoever makes or presents to any person or officer in the civil, military, or naval service of the United States, or to any department or agency thereof, any claim upon or against the United States, or any department or agency thereof, knowing

> such claim to be false, fictitious, or fraudulent, shall be imprisoned not more than five years and shall be subject to a fine in the amount provided in this title.

Generally, this statute subjects a person convicted of false billings to a fine of $10,000 per billing. See, however, 18 U.S.C. § 1031, which greatly increases such fines in the case of "major fraud." Under that provision, fines up to $1,000,000 may be imposed for false claims in contracts or subcontracts over $1,000,000.

VI. DISCHARGE

The final phase of the payment process involves the "discharge" or extinguishment of all or part of the continuing rights and obligations of the parties under the contract. Discharge is frequently accomplished by the government making "final payment" following the contractor's completion of performance and the government's acceptance of the work. As discussed below, final payment may have far-reaching legal effects on the ability of the contractor and the government to pursue claims against each other. In some instances, the government seeks at the time of final payment to extend the scope of the discharge of its potential obligations by requiring the contractor to provide a "release of claims" as a precondition to final payment. Discharge can also occur where the parties mutually agree to release each other from unperformed or "executory" obligations under the contract. In addition, discharge of rights and obligations of the parties may be accomplished through the execution of a contract modification in the form of an "accord and satisfaction." Mutual "releases" are often executed by the parties in connection with negotiation of settlement agreements in order to precisely define the scope of potential rights and obligations to be discharged through the negotiated agreement. Each of these forms of discharge is discussed below.

A. Final Payment

Final payment is made, upon completion and acceptance of all work required under a contract, after the contractor presents a properly executed and duly certified voucher or invoice to the disbursing officer showing the amount agreed upon, less any amounts previously paid.

1. Delay in Contract Closeout

In some instances, although work on a contract is complete, closeout procedures are not, often because of a delay in finalizing negotiated overhead rates. A delay may also occur because of a failure to submit reports and perform other administrative requirements of a contract. A contractor cannot bill for final payment if contract closeout is incomplete. Prior to the passage of § 1405 of the Department of Defense Authorization Act for 1991, Pub. L. 101-510, and § 8080 of the DOD Appropriations Act for 1991, Pub. L. 101-511, funds would expire for obligational purposes at the end of one, two, or three years, depending on the type of appropriation, but remained available for payment indefinitely. After two years, such expired funds were folded into merged "M" accounts for accounting convenience. The government used these "expired" funds to make final payment, fund overruns, settle claims, or take other action that was not considered a new procurement. In some cases, these actions occurred many years after normal contract closeout would have been anticipated.

Pub. L. 101-510, § 1405 amended 31 U.S.C. § 1552 to provide that:

> (a) On September 30th of the 5th fiscal year after the period of availability for obligation of a fixed appropriation account ends, the account shall be closed and any remaining balance (whether obligated or unobligated) in the account shall be canceled and thereafter shall not be available for obligation or expenditure for any purpose.

This means that expired funds previously used to fund contract closeout, claims, overruns, or other such actions are no longer available after five years. Furthermore, any uninvoiced contract funds are also canceled after five years. At that time, the contracting officer has to obtain new funds, from current or supplemental appropriations, to pay the contractor any amounts due on the contract. No clauses or FAR provisions have been issued stating the procedures to be followed if this occurs.

2. *Legal Effect of Final Payment*

Final payment is of ultimate importance to both the contractor and the government, since it may have far-reaching legal effects on each party's ability to pursue claims against the other. Final payment also represents an allowability determination regarding costs under the contract.

a. The Contractor's Release of Claims

Paragraph (h) of the Allowable Cost and Payment clause in cost-reimbursement contracts requires the contractor to submit a release within one year after completion of the work under contract before final payment of any remaining allowable costs or fees will be made. This release must

> discharg[e] the Government, its officers, agents, and employees from all liabilities, obligations, and claims arising out of or under this contract, except—
>
> > (A) Specified claims stated in exact amounts, or in estimated amounts when the exact amounts are not known;
> >
> > (B) Claims (including reasonable incidental expenses) based upon liabilities of the Contractor to third parties arising out of the performance of this

> contract; provided, that the claims are not known to the Contractor on the date of the execution of the release, and that the Contractor gives notice of the claims in writing to the Contracting Officer within 6 years following the release date or notice of final payment date, whichever is earlier; and
>
> (C) Claims for reimbursement of costs, including reasonable incidental expenses, incurred by the Contractor under the patent clauses of this contract, excluding, however, any expenses arising from the Contractor's indemnification of the Government against patent liability.

In addition, payment clauses in fixed-price contracts may mandate releases prior to final payment. See ¶ (h)(3) of the Payment Under Fixed-Price Construction Contracts, FAR 52.232-5, and ¶ (d) of the Payments Under Fixed-Price Architect-Engineer Contracts, FAR 52.232-10, clauses. There is no particular form for the final payment release required by these clauses, *Siska Constr. Co.*, VABCA 3470, 92-1 BCA ¶ 24,578.

b. Effect of Release

An unconditional general release by the contractor operates to bar all existing contractor claims, including pending claims and all known and unknown claims. See *B.D. Click Co. v. United States*, 222 Ct. Cl. 290, 614 F.2d 748 (1980), in which the court stated at 305:

> It is well settled that a contractor who executes a general release is thereafter barred from maintaining a suit for damages or for additional compensation under the contract based upon events that occurred prior to the execution of the release.

See also *Environmental Devices, Inc.*, ASBCA 37430, 93-3 BCA ¶ 26,138 (claim arose prior to execution of modification and was barred by general release provision). General releases signed at the time of final payment are given more weight by boards and courts than releases in individual modifications to a contract, *Middlesex Contractors & Riggers, Inc.*, IBCA 1964, 89-1 BCA ¶ 21,557.

Final payment on a contract generally bars subsequent submission of claims under the same contract because the government usually demands the release of all but expressly reserved claims at the time of final payment. However, in *Chronometrics, Inc.*, ASBCA 46581, 95-1 BCA ¶ 27,476, where final payment allegedly had been made without a release of claims, the contractor was free to pursue claims that it "asserted" within the life of the contract. "Assertion" of a right to a contract adjustment is less formal than submission of a claim; the assertion need not mention the Changes clause nor demand a specific amount of money but must be a demand as of right notifying the government of the contractor's belief that it is entitled to an adjustment.

Some clauses provide that the contractor may preserve its right to specific claims by expressly excepting those claims "in exact amounts, or in estimated amounts" at the time the release is executed. See ¶ (f) of the Payments under Time-And-Materials and Labor-Hour Contracts clause, FAR 52.232-7, ¶ (h)(3) of the Payments under Fixed-Price Construction Contracts clause, FAR 52.232-5, and ¶ (h)(2)(ii)(A) of the Allowable Cost and Payment clause, FAR 52.216-7. Similarly, the Payments Under Fixed-Price Architect-Engineer Contracts clause, FAR 52.232-10, releases all claims "other than any claims that are specifically excepted by the Contractor." The contractor is entitled to final payment no matter how many exceptions are listed in the release. Thus, the government may not insist upon an unconditional release as a prerequisite to final payment, *Winn-Senter Constr. Co. v. United States*, 110 Ct. Cl. 34, 75 F. Supp. 255 (1948). See *Joseph Fusco Constr. Co.*, GSBCA 5717, 81-1 BCA ¶ 14,837, holding that the government improperly withheld final payment in order to coerce the contractor into releasing a disputed liquidated damages claim.

A claim need not be final and certified under the Contract Disputes Act to survive a general release and final payment, but the contractor must, at a minimum, describe the substance of the claim and the amount demanded. See *Mingus Constructors, Inc. v. United States*, 812 F.2d 1387 (Fed. Cir. 1987), holding that a vague "blunderbuss" exception stating nothing more than an intent to file a claim failed to inform the government of the source, scope, or substance of the contractor's specific contentions and was, therefore, an invalid exception to the required release. In that case, the contractor's release listed two claims that it was preparing for subsequent submission. The court found, however, that the claims were not described with sufficient specificity. See also *N&P Constr. Co.*, VABCA 2578, 92-1 BCA ¶ 24,447, *aff'd*, 979 F.2d 217 (Fed. Cir. 1992) ("generalized complaints with vaguely stated intentions to make claim at some undisclosed future date are not such 'claims' as would survive the release"), and *Pan-Alaska Constr., Inc.*, ASBCA 38525, 90-3 BCA ¶ 23,050 (release that merely excepted an overhead claim without any other identification or quantification was not preserved after final payment). Compare *Resource Conservation Corp. v. General Servs. Admin.*, GSBCA 13399, 97-1 BCA ¶ 28,776, in which a contractor's price adjustment claim was not barred by final payment because the contractor indicated its present intent was to seek recovery when it reserved the claim in the release of claims submitted with its request for final payment.

In *S & J Contractors*, VABCA 3743, 93-3 BCA ¶ 26,022, the board found a lack of specificity of claims in a release, and in the exceptions set forth in a referenced letter, at 129,365-66:

> The release specifically stated:
>
>> For and in consideration of the payments heretofore made, and payment of the above recited sum now due by reason of performance of the above contract, the undersigned contractor hereby releases and discharges the United

> States of America of and from all liab[il]ities, obligations and claims whatsoever under or arising out of said contract except the following:
>
> 1. Other specific claims:
>
> SEE ATTACHED LETTER DATED DECEMBER 21, 1989
> FROM S&J CONTRACTORS, INC.
>
> All other items and conditions of the above mentioned contract remain in full force and effect.

The attached December 21, 1989 letter from S&J's President, Sherman Tibbs, stated:

> S&J hereby charges the Veterans Administration with the following regarding the above referenced contract:
>
> (1) Breach of Contract
>
> (2) Tortious Interference
>
> (3) Violation of the Civil Rights Act
>
> (4) Loss of Business
>
> (5) Liquidated Damages
>
> Please be advised that actions of the Veterans Administration have damaged S&J Contractors as outlined above. S&J Contractors in no way intends to release VA from liability for these charges and all losses resulting from same. S&J Contractors intends to recoup these losses by means of a claim under the Contract Disputes Act. (emphasis added)

In denying the contractor's appeal, the board stated that the release and letter did not put the government on notice of any specific claims. The letter "manifestly asserts broad complaints rather than specific claims with stated amounts as required by FAR 52.232-5(f)(3)."

In an earlier case, the Armed Services Board held that even in the absence of a specific reservation, a contractor's claim for unliquidated damages was not barred by the contractor's release when the contracting officer indicated that he would continue to process the contractor's unliquidated damages claim after final payment was made, *Able Prods., Co.*, ASBCA 24221, 80-2 BCA ¶ 14,733. Similarly, the GAO has indicated that only final payment gives effect to the release and that the release under some circumstances may be withdrawn or modified prior to payment. For example, in *DNH Dev. Corp.*, 57 Comp. Gen. 407 (B-191140), 78-1 CPD ¶ 270, a contractor that executed a general release while its claim was pending was not precluded from pursuing the claim since the contracting officer was notified prior to final payment that the release was not intended to extinguish the outstanding claim. The GAO stated at 409:

> In 46 Comp. Gen. 414 (1966), we held, consistent with court decisions, that a general release executed without reserving claims against the Government was a valid defense to a contractor's claim for unliquidated damages. See, e.g., *United States v. Wm. Cramp & Sons Co.*, 206 U.S. 118 (1907); *J. G. Watts Construction Company v. United States*, 161 Ct. Cl. 801 (1963). However, we also found in that case that the attendant circumstances did not place the contracting officer on notice of possible error. We reach a different conclusion here.
>
> * * *
>
> We believe that where the contracting officer has been actually notified of a mistake in the execution of a release before final payment effectuating the release has been made, subsequent payment with such knowledge by the contracting officer does not extinguish the Government's liability under the contract.

c. Government Claims

Although the release executed by the contractor does not deal with government claims, and the government signs no such release in return, final payment may bar any subsequent government claim. A line of decisions beginning with the Court of Claims decision in *Poole Eng'g & Mach. Co. v. United States*, 57 Ct. Cl. 232 (1922), states that there is a "general presumption" that all rights and obligations of the parties are extinguished upon final payment. See, for example, *Lester B. Knight & Assocs., Inc.*, GSBCA 4913, 78-2 BCA ¶ 13,327, in which the board held that a government claim to recover for damages caused by the construction contractor during contract work was barred by final payment. The damage was done to work unrelated to the contract under which damages were sought. Even where this "general presumption" has been invoked, however, claims first asserted after final payment have survived under certain "exceptions," including those situations in which the basis for the claim was "latent" and not discoverable until after final payment, and situations in which misrepresentations amounting to fraud were made, *Bar Ray Prods., Inc. v. United States*, 162 Ct. Cl. 836 (1963); or situations in which the contract specifically provided for particular claims to survive final payment, *Baifield Indus., Div. of A-T-O, Inc.*, ASBCA 19025, 75-1 BCA ¶ 11,245.

A few cases adopt the opposite reasoning, holding, as a general rule, that final payment does not bar a government claim. See, for example, *Berkeley Constr. Co.*, PSBCA 1153, 84-1 BCA ¶ 17,047, holding, that a government claim for liquidated damages for delayed completion was not barred by final payment. See also *American Western Corp. v. United States*, 730 F.2d 1486 (Fed. Cir. 1984), in which the court stated that the final payment rule was inapplicable since the contract contained an Economic Price Adjustment provision "allowing the government to make a unilateral price adjustment, with no express time limit." The court ruled that the government merely had to act within a reasonable time in seeking its refund.

d. Clauses Barring Claims After Final Payment

Although the scope of a release submitted by the contractor with its invoice for final payment generally controls the rights of the contractor with regard to future claims, not all contracts have a requirement for such a release. However, there are several specific clauses that deal with the effects of final payment. The standard Changes, Suspension of Work, and Government Delay of Work clauses expressly bar claims not asserted prior to final payment, and such contract requirements are generally enforced, *Adamation, Inc.*, ASBCA 22495, 80-1 BCA ¶ 14,385. Thus, in *Toyad Corp.*, ASBCA 26785, 84-1 BCA ¶ 17,030, a contractor claim for an adjustment relating to government-furnished material was barred where language in the Government-Furnished Material clause stated that the GFM account would be "adjusted prior to final payment" and where the contractor failed to "express a present intention to seek recovery under a claim of right" prior to final payment. See also *Automated Power Sys., Inc.*, DOTBCA 2930, 98-1 BCA ¶ 29,638, barring a claim under the Changes clause because it was submitted after final payment. A contrary result was reached in *Powerine Oil Co.*, EBCA 278-2-83, 84-2 BCA ¶ 17,363, in which, because an express contractual agreement allowed contractors to take unilateral action and because no time limitation was specified, it was held that final payment was not an automatic bar to subsequent claims. See also *American Transparents Plastics Corp.*, GSBCA 7006, 85-1 BCA ¶ 17,819.

If a claim is pending before the contracting officer at the time of final payment, it is likely that the clauses mentioned above will not bar the continued negotiation or litigation of that or other claims. This result is based on the reasoning that "final payment" cannot occur if the contracting officer is working on a claim. See *Gulf & Western Indus., Inc. v. United States*, 6 Cl. Ct. 742 (1984), in which the court held that it was unrealistic to think that the government would have made final payment when the contracting officer knew or should have known that the contractor had asserted a legal claim for additional money under the contract. The court stated at 755:

> Final payment should not be found as a matter of surprise. *Northrop Carolina, Inc.*, ASBCA No. 13958, 71-2 BCA ¶ 8970. Rather, it is the "payment which can reasonably and logically be considered the 'final payment' under the contract that marks [the] cut-off point for the contractor." *Historical Services, Inc.*, DOT CAB Nos. 72-8, 72-8A, 72-2 BCA ¶ 9592 at 44,839. Consequently . . . the facts and circumstances here, inescapably compel the conclusion that the contract balance payment of October 19, 1972, was not the "final payment" under the contract.

Thus, a court or board will look at the "totality of the facts and circumstances of a particular case" to determine whether final payment occurs for purposes of these clauses, *SEI Computer Servs.*, VABCA 1478, 81-2 BCA ¶ 15,399. In *SEI*, the board found that no final payment had occurred where neither the contractor's invoice nor the payment documents contained any indication that final payment was intended.

A formal certified claim is not necessary to establish an intent to seek recovery, *Marvin Eng'g Co.*, ASBCA 28470, 85-3 BCA ¶ 18,305. See also *Coastal Indus., Inc. v. United States*, 32 Fed. Cl. 368 (1994), in which the court found that the contracting officer had notice of one claim, which resulted in it surviving final payment, but did not have notice of another claim, which was barred by final payment. While oral notice might be sufficient to satisfy the requirement of notice, proof of notice will be less of a problem if written notice is given.

B. Mutual Agreement and Rescission

Parties to a contract may effectively discharge the contract, in whole or in part, releasing each other from executory obligations under the contract, by mutual agreement. The Supreme Court, in *Savage Arms Corp. v. United States*, 266 U.S. 217 (1924), held that a proposal by the contractor to reduce the number of units to be covered by a partial termination contemplated by the government resulted in a valid release of mutual obligations upon acceptance by the government. In rejecting the contractor's argument that the release of obligations was without valid consideration, the court stated at 220-21:

> The bare recital of the facts practically disposes of the case. From them, it appears that appellant not only acceded to the elimination of 142,000 magazines from the obligations of the contract but made persistent and repeated efforts to secure from the Ordnance Office a change in the original notice so as to include that number instead of 298,000, expressly agreeing that if this were done it would abandon and settle all claims, controversies and disputed points growing out of the contract. The Government, through its authorized officials, accepted this proposal and the arrangement became fixed and binding. A good deal is said by appellant to the effect that this agreement was without consideration; but we need not stop to review the contention. It is enough to say that the parties to a contract may release themselves, in whole or in part, from its obligations so far as they remain executory, by mutual agreement without fresh consideration. The release of one is sufficient consideration for the release of the other. If authority for a rule so elementary be required, see, for example: *Hanson & Parker v. Wittenberg*, 205 Mass. 319, 326; *Collyer & Co. v. Moulton*, 9 R.I. 90, 92; *McCreery v. Day*, 119 N.Y. 1, 7; *Dreifus, Block & Co. v. Salvage Co.*, 194 Pa. St. 475, 486.

See also *Folk Constr. Co.*, ENGBCA 5839, 93-3 BCA ¶ 26,094, where the government accepted the contractor's offer to release the government from its claims if it would end the contract. The government later attempted to get out of the agreement, claiming, among other things, that the agreement lacked consideration. Although *Savage* would have supported the agreement, the board did not rely on *Savage*, holding that the contractor's release of claims would be sufficient even if they were without merit.

C. Contract Modifications

Discharge by contract modification embodies the concept of accord and satisfaction. The agreements of the parties or the performances that they have agreed to make serves as consideration for the discharge. The parties often include specific release language in their contract modifications, but sometimes such language is omitted. The Court of Federal Claims in *McLain Plumbing & Elec. Serv., Inc. v. United States*, 30 Fed. Cl. 70 (1993), distinguished between general releases and releases included in contract modifications, stating at 78-79:

> Albeit commonly confused, discharge by release and discharge by accord and satisfaction implicate different theories. The discharge of a claim by accord and satisfaction involves an accord by bilateral agreement among the contracting parties, and discharge occurs only after the satisfaction of an additional or alternative performance. *Valcon II, Inc. v. United States*, 26 Cl. Ct. 393, 397 (1992). In contrast, the discharge of a claim by release generally involves a unilateral act, whereby a party immediately disclaims a contract right or obligation. *Adler Constr. Co. v. United States*, 191 Ct. Cl. 607, 613, 423 F.2d 1362, 1365 (1970), *cert. denied*, 400 U.S. 993, 91 S.Ct. 461, 27 L.Ed.2d 441 (1971). Despite the distinction, when contracting parties execute an accord and satisfaction which also contains an express release, courts frequently recognize the discharge by release and ignore any issue of discharge by accord and satisfaction; in other more limited situations, courts have even used the words discharge and release interchangeably. Unfortunately, the resulting confusion has led some to believe, as does the [contractor] here, that a release constitutes a prerequisite of a valid discharge by accord and satisfaction. To the contrary, while an accord and satisfaction may contain an express release for the immediate discharge of a contractual right or obligation, a release constitutes no condition precedent to discharge by accord and satisfaction.

The first subsection below discusses the concept of accord and satisfaction. The second subsection deals with contract modifications not containing specific release language. The last subsection examines cases where the modification included such specific language.

1. *Accord and Satisfaction*

Accord and satisfaction may be the most complex and, as such, the most disputed method of discharge. An accord is usually regarded as a bilateral agreement requiring some specified additional performance to satisfy a disputed claim, *Spirit Leveling Contractors v. United States*, 19 Cl. Ct. 84 (1989). Satisfaction is accomplished upon completion of the specified performance, *Restatement, Second, Contracts* § 281. Accords and satisfactions commonly concern price changes due to events such as changes or differing site conditions. The accord and satisfaction can occur in two ways. When the agreement itself discharges the claim, the agreement is both the accord and satisfaction. Such an agreement is often referred to as a "substituted contract." See *Kuehne & Nagel, Inc. v. United States*, 17 Cl. Ct.

11 (1989). When the claim is not to be discharged until performance of the agreement (usually payment by the government), the agreement is called an "executory accord." The subsequent payment constitutes the "satisfaction," and the claim is discharged at that point. The difference between the two is that if the agreement is a substituted contract, suit may only be brought on that new contract. However, if the agreement is an executory accord, the failure to perform the agreement revives the original claim. For example, if the parties had agreed that the equitable adjustment for a change order was $100,000, the government's failure to pay that amount would permit the contractor to sue only for the $100,000 if the agreement was considered to be a substituted contract. If the agreement were to be considered an executory accord, the contractor would be able to reopen the original claim and recover any higher amount that could be established. This is what occurred in *P.J. Dick Contracting, Inc.*, PSBCA 992, 84-1 BCA ¶ 16,992, where the contractor and the government reached an understanding that changed work would be performed for a $1,500,000 price increase. However, the government later refused to sign the modification and subsequently issued a unilateral order increasing the price to only $1,136,100, which was then paid to the contractor. The government argued that the contractor's subsequent attempt to recover in excess of $1,500,000 was barred by the initial agreement, and that the contractor's only remedy was for breach of that agreement. The board rejected the government's position, stating at 84,637:

> [The government] cites *Robert J. DiDomenico*, GSBCA No. 5539, 82-2 BCA ¶ 16,093, for the proposition that [the contractor's] proper remedy is to pursue damages for breach of the alleged agreement. However, that case is distinguishable. In *DiDomenico*, the Board had before it executed bilateral modifications fully performed by one party and allegedly not performed by the other. The Board found no lack of consideration, as, in effect, a promise had been exchanged for a promise, and that [the contractor] "[chose] not to repudiate the agreement but accept it and claim . . . damages for breach." *Id.* at 79,889. Here, [the contractor] has chosen to repudiate the agreement instead of pursuing a breach claim, and [the government] not only failed to perform but repudiated its promise to pay $1,500,000 by issuing a unilateral modification for $1,136,100. Therefore, [the government] did not satisfy the consideration requirement.

See, however, *Singleton Contracting Corp.*, DOTCAB 1449, 84-1 BCA ¶ 17,072, in which rescission on the grounds that the government did not pay the amount promised in a settlement for two months was refused.

Whether an accord and satisfaction occurs depends on the intention of the parties, *Todd-Grace, Inc.*, ASBCA 34469, 92-1 BCA ¶ 24,742. The existence of the accord and satisfaction, its nature, and the claims included are determined by the facts of each case. In *McLain Plumbing & Elec. Serv., Inc. v. United States*, 30 Fed. Cl. 70 (1993), the contractor argued that its claim should not be barred by accord and satisfaction because there was no meeting of the minds and no consideration. The court disagreed, stating that the contractor's recovery schedule, which was adopted in the contract modification, recited the consideration. The court also found that the contract modification evidenced that there was a meeting of the minds between the parties. The court stated that the recovery schedule clearly defined the intentions of the parties in submitting a proposal for alternative performance, which the contractor accepted without modification or reservation. See also *Busby Sch. Bd. of the N. Cheyenne Tribe*, IBCA 3007, 94-1 BCA ¶ 26,327. However, in *CYR Constr. Co. v. United States*, 27 Fed. Cl. 153 (1992), the court stated that there was no showing as to what the contractor was to negotiate as to time and cost in the various modifications, contractor's responses, and the content of the relevant negotiations. Thus, the court found that the materials in the record were not adequate to show the intent of the parties or a meeting of the minds on disputed matters. For other cases in which the courts and boards have found that there was no meeting of the minds, see *XXX Constr. Co. v. United States*, 16 Cl. Ct. 491 (1989) (contractor understood the modification to require only remeasure of the acreage covered by the windrows, not the entire acreage of the project), and *American Tel. & Tel. Co., Fed. Sys. Advanced Techs*, DOTBCA 2479, 93-3 BCA ¶ 26,250 (modification did not resolve anything with finality, but rather only constituted an agreement to revise the statement of work, with the details and terms and conditions, including price, to be worked out later). Negotiation of a settlement and payment operates as an accord and satisfaction only as to the claims considered during the settlement process, *Tri-O, Inc. v. United States*, 28 Fed. Cl. 463 (1993).

2. Modifications Without Specific Release Language

Absent clear release language, price adjustment modifications are narrowly construed if there is any question that the claimed costs were not considered when the adjustment was negotiated, *Wright Assocs., Inc.*, ASBCA 33721, 87-3 BCA ¶ 20,056. See *Ryco Constr., Inc. v. United States*, 55 Fed. Cl. 184 (2002), denying a government motion for summary judgment because of the need to interpret the modification. See also *Crawford Tech. Servs., Inc.*, ASBCA 40388, 93-3 BCA ¶ 26,136, in which the bilateral modification did not constitute an accord and satisfaction for a price adjustment to compensate for certain vacation costs. The board stated that the government's price negotiation memorandum concerning a wage increase for one employee's vacation pay did not establish that the parties discussed remuneration for vacation pay for employees who became eligible during the extended period. In *Richards Constr. Co.*, AGBCA 88-156-1, 94-1 BCA ¶ 26,384, the board held that a modification did not act as a bar to a contractor's claim for costs associated with the delay and wasted costs for work performed prior to the issuance of new plans. The board stated that the terms of the modification covered new plans and associated costs but did not identify work that the contractor performed under the original plan. The board noted that a strong indication of the parties' intent was reflected in the fact that the contractor continued to press the claim and the Forest Service continued to consider it after the execution of the modification. See also *Western Commerce Corp.*, AGBCA 85-146-1, 87-2 BCA ¶ 19,914 (continued discussion of claim after contract modification indicated that claim was not intended to be included in modification). Similarly, in *Metric Constructors, Inc.*, ASBCA 46279, 94-1 BCA ¶ 26,532, the board held that a modification did not include a price adjustment claim which was currently on appeal because the contractor was pursuing its claim before the board at the time the modification was signed. Thus, the board stated that this indicated that the parties never understood the modification as an abandonment of the contractor's earlier claim. In *Teledyne Lewisburg v. United States*, 699 F.2d 1336 (Fed. Cir. 1983), the court held that a contract modification "waiving" the contractor's duties to perform EMI testing in return for its performance of "new unrelated work" did not bar contractor claims for costs previously incurred in attempting to solve EMI-related difficulties. The court relied on the fact that the contractor had successfully resisted a government attempt to have language precluding recovery of such costs included in the modification.

In *Laka Tool & Stamping Co. v. United States*, 226 Ct. Cl. 83, 639 F.2d 738 (1980), the parties executed a contract modification which constituted a compromise as to the proper interpretation of a "flatness" requirement in the specifications after the contractor had experienced difficulty performing according to the government's interpretation. The contract was eventually terminated for default when the contractor was unable to perform according to the modified specification. While the court upheld the default termination, it concluded that the contractor was entitled to recover expenses it had incurred in attempting to work to the "impossible" specification as reflected by the government's initial interpretation. The court rejected the government's argument that the contract modification operated as an accord and satisfaction as to this defective specification claim, since the "claim" concerning the expenses incurred in attempting to meet the original specification was not being disputed at the time of the modification. The court also held that language in the modification providing that it would "in no way affect contract price or delivery schedule" did not operate as a "waiver" of the defective specification claim.

Absent a release, neither party is foreclosed from raising other issues. In *Alvarez & Assocs. Constr. Co.*, ASBCA 49341, 98-1 BCA ¶ 29,559, the board held that extending a completion date without referring to liquidated damages being assessed is not an automatic waiver of such damages. The government had extended performance by letter, but the board said that to constitute a waiver there must be an "intentional relinquishment or abandonment of a known right or privilege."

A modification providing an equitable adjustment for a change has also been held not to bar a later claim for the costs of a partial termination although the change affected the same work as the termination, *Stewart Avionics, Inc.*, ASBCA 10226, 65-2 BCA ¶ 5111, *recons. denied*, 65-2 BCA ¶ 5173; *Aircraft Armaments, Inc.*, ASBCA 9049, 1963 BCA ¶ 3934. In *Nielsons, Inc.*, IBCA 1126-9-76, 79-1 BCA ¶ 13,729, the board held that a settlement agreement adjusting the contract price for increased energy costs bound the contractor only for the period up to the time of the agreement, since there had been no clear meeting of the minds as to the length of time covered by the agreement.

In many instances, contract modifications increasing contract time, but not contract price, have been held not to bar subsequent claims based on the same circumstances for price adjustments under the Suspension of Work clause. This result has been reached when there was uncertainty as to whether the parties considered the additional compensation claims when negotiating the time extension amendments, *Kurz & Root Co.*, ASBCA 17146, 74-1 BCA ¶ 10,543; *Pilcher, Livingston & Wallace, Inc.*, ASBCA 13391, 70-1 BCA ¶ 8331, *recons. denied*, 70-2 BCA ¶ 8488; *Ferri Elec. Co.*, ASBCA 13110, 69-1 BCA ¶ 7527. See, however, *Leonhard Weiss GmbH & Co. and Huebsch Industrieanlagen Spezialbau GmbH (JV)*, ASBCA 37574, 93-1 BCA ¶ 25,443, in which the board barred a claim for an extension of time on the basis of defective specifications for a ventilating system. The board stated that the modification afforded full compensation for all delays relating to changes in the ventilating system, including time.

3. *Modifications with Release Language*

It is customary for the government to include release language in contract modifications. FAR 43.204(c) states that a contracting officer should include a release similar to the following in supplemental agreements finalizing equitable adjustments:

CONTRACTOR'S STATEMENT OF RELEASE

> In consideration of the modification(s) agreed to herein as complete equitable adjustments for the Contractor's ______(describe)_______ "proposal(s) for adjustment," The Contractor hereby releases the Government from any and all liability under this contract for further equitable adjustments attributable to such facts or circumstances giving rise to the "proposal(s) for adjustment" (except for ________).

When this language is used, the contractor is not barred from pursuing claims under the contract which are not connected with the particular equitable adjustment but is barred from claims that are connected. See *Moore Overseas Constr. Co.*, ENGBCA PCC-125, 98-1 BCA ¶ 29,682, when under a contract modification containing a general release, the contractor was paid for extra work and granted an extension of time for a differing site condition. Subsequently, the board rejected the contractor's defective specification claim for the cost of using more complex and expensive methods to deal with the work, concluding that parties' resolution of the differing site condition claims necessarily encompassed the defective specification claim because both issues arose from the same set of facts. Similarly, in *Spectrum Leasing Corp. v. General Servs. Admin.*, GSBCA 12189, 95-1 BCA ¶ 23,317, the contractor was not allowed to recover the amount it had paid in settlement of the subcontractor's claim because the contractor's claim was barred by its agreement with the government on a modification that resulted in the termination of the subcontractor. Although it is not clear if a formal release was used, the board concluded that the contractor should have anticipated the possibility that a claim might arise, yet did not reserve its rights. See also *R.P. Richards Constr. Co. v. United States*, 51 Fed. Cl. 116 (2001) (evidence indicated that release in modification covered later claims); *Starflight Boats v. United States*, 48 Fed. Cl. 592 (2001) (broad release language barred additional claims); *Kaco Contracting Co.*, ASBCA 44939, 01-2 BCA ¶ 31,584 (claim barred because the contractor signed a contract modification relieving the government of any liability associated with the work); *Peter Bauwens Bauunternehmung GmbH & Co. KG,* ASBCA 48209, 99-2 BCA ¶ 30,547 (claim denied because the contractor executed a broad release and the claim did not fall within the single reservation of claim); *Coates Indus. Piping, Inc.*, VABCA 5412, 99-2 BCA ¶ 30,479 (absent a showing of "well-nigh-irrefragable" evidence of government misconduct, a contractor's claim for equitable adjustment was barred by a series of bilateral supplemental agreements); *Larson Constr. Servs., Inc.*, ASBCA 53443, 02-1 BCA ¶ 31,730 (general release in a modification precluded contractor's claim for lost labor and productivity incurred when government-caused delay pushed the work into a period of adverse weather); and *Industrial Consultants, Inc.*, ASBCA 45205, 97-1 BCA ¶ 28,806 (contractor's claims denied because the costs had been discussed, negotiated, and included in comprehensive release language).

However, in *Atlantic Dry Dock Corp.*, ASBCA 42679, 99-1 BCA ¶ 30,208, *recons. denied,* 98-2 BCA ¶ 13,0025, the board rejected the agency's argument that release language in various contract modifications for extra work resulted in a waiver of the contractor's right to recover under the Changes clause for the cumulative disruption caused by additional work. The agency had a long-standing policy that such impact costs as delay and disruption, acceleration, and lost time would not be addressed in the change order but would be addressed upon completion of contract performance. The board held that the agency could not "have it both ways" by forcing the contractor to defer its impact costs and to accept a modification with a release clause and later denying the contractor the right to assert an impact claim because of the release.

In *Consolidated Indus., Inc. v. United States*, 195 F.3d 1341 (Fed. Cir. 1999), the contractor had failed to meet several contract deadlines. The parties executed a "no cost" modification that included the contractor's unconditional waiver of any other charges against the government, and constituted a "full and final settlement, satisfaction and accord of any and all claims." The contracting officer then issued a termination for default when the contractor subsequently failed to make scheduled deliveries. Although the contractor argued that defective specifications and the government's failure to assist contributed to the delivery delays, the court concluded that such defenses were barred by the modification.

In *Balimoy Mfg. Co. of Venice, Inc.*, ASBCA 47140, 98-2 BCA ¶ 30,017, *aff'd,* 243 F.3d 561 (Fed. Cir. 2000), the government terminated a contract for default, and then partially reinstated the contract by a contract modification stating that it was a "full release" of all claims "arising under or related to" the termination. After additional modifications, the contractor defaulted again, but negotiated a conversion to a convenience termination. The board held that the modification precluded claims for equitable adjustments to cover expenses associated with the terminated portion of the contract.

The government sometimes includes a clause in its contracts providing that the contractor will submit complete claims requiring a waiver and release of any additional costs once a claim has been settled. See *Molony & Rubien Constr. Co.*, ASBCA 20652, 76-2 BCA ¶ 11,977, *aff'd,* 219 Ct. Cl. 616 (1979), holding that the contractor had released the government from liability for additional overhead costs not requested in its equitable adjustment proposal, relying on the following clause:

> Equitable Adjustments: Waiver and Release of Claims
>
> (a) Whenever the Contractor, after receipt of notification of a change made pursuant to the clause of this contract entitled 'Changes' or after affirmation of a constructive change thereunder, submits any claim for equitable adjustment under that clause, such claim shall include all types of adjustments in the total amounts to which that clause entitles the Contractor, including but not limited to adjustments arising out of delays or disruptions or both caused by such change. Except as the parties may otherwise expressly agree, the Contractor shall be deemed to have waived (i) any adjustments to which it otherwise might be entitled under the aforesaid clause where such claim fails to request such adjustment, and (ii) any increase in the amount of equitable adjustments additional to those requested in its claim.
>
> (b) Further, the Contractor agrees that, if required by the Contracting Officer, he will execute a release, in form and substance satisfactory to the Contracting Officer, as part of the supplemental agreement setting forth the aforesaid adjustment, and that such release shall discharge the Government, its officers, agents and employees, from any further claims, including but not limited to further claims arising out of delays or disruptions or both, caused by the aforesaid change.

This clause was also enforced in *J. C. Equip. Corp. v. England*, 360 F.3d 1311 (Fed. Cir. 2004) (delay claims waived when differing site conditions modification included money and time extension and contained no exceptions); *H.Z. & Co., Ltd.*, ASBCA 31055, 86-2 BCA ¶ 18,976 (claim for interest and damages resulting from delayed payment waived by clause); *CCC Constr. Co.*, ASBCA 20530, 76-1 BCA ¶ 11,805 (failure to raise claims based on foreseeable impact constituted a waiver); and *Dyson & Co.*, ASBCA 21673, 78-2 BCA ¶ 13,482, *recons. denied*, 79-1 BCA ¶ 13,661 (foreseeable impact costs waived even though no release required by the government pursuant to ¶ (b) of clause). In *R.C. Hedreen Co.*, ASBCA 20599, 77-1 BCA ¶ 12,328, this clause was held not to preclude an extended overhead claim because the contractor orally reserved the claim during negotiations and the language of the contract modification was not broad enough to cover the claim. Accord, *Arntz Bros.*, ASBCA 19183, 79-2 BCA ¶ 14,038 (letter reserving right to adjustment for extended overhead on all changes claims bars application of clause absent clear language to the contrary in contract modification). In *Braselton Constr. Co.*, ASBCA 18654, 76-2 BCA ¶ 12,113, the board refused to apply the clause to claims not covered by the Changes clause.

The majority of cases find that price adjustment modifications constitute accord and satisfaction agreements barring subsequently asserted contract claims because of the clarity of the contractual language. See *John Massman Contracting Co. v. United States*, 23 Cl. Ct. 24 (1991) (modifications plainly and unambiguously provided that the government would extend the contract completion date with no modification to the contract price); *King Fisher Marine Serv., Inc. v. United States*, 16 Cl. Ct. 231 (1989) (clear language of agreement released all of contractor's claims regarding the work performed under the change order); and *NAGY Enters.*, ASBCA 48815, 98-1 BCA ¶ 29,695 (bilateral contract modifications containing releases of "all other claims" concerning the specified additional or changed work barred later claims because no work different than that compensated by the modifications was shown and acceptance of the modification amounted to accord and satisfaction).

It is especially difficult for contractors to overcome modifications containing language releasing claims when they are executed after completion of the work. In this situation, the contractor is generally aware of its potential claims and has been put on notice by the release language that it must either reserve such claims or loose them. In *Adler Constr. Co. v. United States*, 191 Ct. Cl. 607, 423 F.2d 1362 (1970), the court held that large and meritorious claims which the contractor did not reserve were barred, stating at 612:

> The time to have reserved such claims was upon execution of the release. . . . [The contractor's] contentions now urged that he lacked sufficient information at the time of the release to frame proper exceptions to reserve his present claims . . . do not excuse his failure to state his exceptions covering his present claims in general terms which would have sufficed the purpose of preserving his right to pursue them.

In *D.W. Young Constr. Co.*, ASBCA 29388, 87-2 BCA ¶ 19,762, the board barred a contractor's claims for differing site conditions because the contractor executed a valid release without reservation or exception. In reaching this decision, the board stated at 99,998:

> Especially where, as here, the contract contains the Equitable Adjustments, Waiver and Release of claims clause, a contractor cannot successfully maintain a suit based upon events which occurred prior to the execution of the release when the contractor has the right to reserve claims from the operation of the general release but fails to do so.

For other cases barring claims because the events occurred prior to the execution of the release, see *Urbanizadora Santa Clara, S.A. v. United States*, 207 Ct. Cl. 297, 518 F.2d 574 (1975) (claim for additional rent); *Langoma Indus., Inc. v. United*

States, 133 Ct. Cl. 248, 135 F. Supp. 282 (1955) (claims based on deletion of part of the work settled by appeals board decision); *Saturn Constr. Co.*, VABCA 3229, 91-3 BCA ¶ 24,151 (claim for increased performance costs); *Bridgewater Constr. Corp.*, VABCA 2796, 91-3 BCA ¶ 24,365 (claim for delay costs incurred as a result of defective plans and specifications); *Paul Pent Landscape Co.*, ASBCA 28637, 84-1 BCA ¶ 17,181 (claim for recoupment of liquidated damages); *Roy I. Strate*, ASBCA 19914, 78-1 BCA ¶ 13,128 (claim for additional time); *Graham Contracting, Inc.*, ASBCA 11800, 69-1 BCA ¶ 7596 (claims for acceleration costs); and *Columbus Jack Corp.*, ASBCA 7249, 1962 BCA ¶ 3288 (claims for extra work).

In some instances, a contractor will seek recovery of impact and delay costs resulting from the performance of various changes to a contract modification. For example, in *Chantilly Constr. Corp.*, ASBCA 24138, 81-1 BCA ¶ 14,863, language in a modification to the effect that the amount stated represented "full and complete price adjustment . . . for all work" required by the modification did not bar a subsequent claim for impact and delay claims where it was found that the parties had not discussed such costs in negotiations leading up to the modification. See also *Dawson Constr. Co.*, GSBCA 5910, 83-1 BCA ¶ 16,160, *recons. denied*, 83-1 BCA ¶ 16,275, in which the board found that there was no discharge of a subcontractor's claim for delay costs where the parties had specifically agreed to exclude that claim from their negotiations and where the contracting officer had not "adequately expressed" an intention to have the time extension that was allowed the contractor serve as "full compensation" for the claim. Compare *Commercial Contractors, Inc. v. United States*, 29 Fed Cl.. 654 (1993), in which the court held that the contractor was barred by accord and satisfaction from recovering alleged delay costs resulting from additional testing of asphalt concrete. The parties had negotiated a reduction in the contract price in return for the acceptance of nonconforming asphalt. The modification, reproduced at 668, provided as follows:

> It is understood and agreed that this adjustment constitutes compensation in full on behalf of the contractor and its subcontractors and suppliers for all costs and markup directly or indirectly attributable to the change ordered, for all delays related thereto, and for performance of the change within the time frame stated.

The court found that the modification plus the negotiations leading up to the modification covered impact and delay costs. The court noted that the contracting officer specifically requested information from the contractor concerning costs for "all work involved in the modification, whether such work is deleted, added or changed, and shall also include the effects of the changes on unchanged work (impact) if any." Thus, the court barred the contractor's testing delay claim. See also *Valcon II, Inc. v. United States,* 26 Cl. Ct. 393 (1992), in which the court held that a modification that released the government from "any and all liabilities" barred a delay claim.

Continued consideration of a claim by the government is compelling evidence that a release did not cover a future claim. See *Community Heating & Plumbing Co., Inc. v. Kelso,* 987 F.2d 1575 (Fed. Cir. 1993), stating at 1581:

> [C]ourts may refuse to bar a claim based upon the defense of accord and satisfaction where the parties continue to consider the claim after execution of a release. *Winn-Senter Constr. Co. v. United States*, 110 Ct. Cl. 34, 75 F. Supp. 255 (Ct. Cl. 1948). "Such conduct manifests an intent that the parties never construed the release as an abandonment of plaintiff's earlier claim." *A & K Plumbing & Mechanical, Inc. v. United States*, 1 Cl. Ct. 716, 723 (1983). Here, the evidence in the record indicates that the Navy continued to negotiate and audit Community's claims years after they were submitted. Accordingly, Community's claims were not barred by an accord and satisfaction, and each claim must therefore be addressed individually.

See also *John T. Jones Constr. Co.*, ASBCA 48303, 98-2 BCA ¶ 29,892 (contract modification accompanied by an unqualified release of claims did not result in accord and satisfaction barring future claims because the government continued to consider a contractor claim after executing the release).

D. General Releases

A release is generally defined as a written instrument terminating rights under a contract. Releases included in contract modifications were considered above. This section deals with general releases. General releases may be required under contract clauses or may be demanded by the government in return for some action. If the government's action constitutes consideration the latter type of release will be binding. Contractually required releases need no additional consideration to be effective, *Detroit Testing Lab., Inc.*, EBCA 153-1-81, 83-1 BCA ¶ 16,458.

A general release relieves the government from either (1) all claims without reference to any particular grounds, or (2) claims in addition to specifically stated ones. One example of a general release is set forth in ¶ (h) of the Payments under Fixed-Price Construction Contracts clause, FAR 52.232-5. This clause states that the government shall pay the amount due after:

> (3) Presentation of release of all claims against the Government arising by virtue of this contract, other than claims, in stated amounts, that the Contractor has specifically excepted from the operation of the release. A release may also be required of the assignee if the Contractor's claim to amounts payable under this contract has been assigned under the Assignment of Claims Act of 1940 (31 U.S.C. 3727 and 41 U.S.C. 15).

Another example of a general release is contained in ¶ (d) of the Payments under Fixed-Price Architect-Engineer Contracts clause, FAR 52.232-10. This clause provides:

> Before final payment under the contract, or before settlement upon termination of the contract, and as a condition precedent thereto, the Contractor shall execute and deliver to the Contracting Officer a release of all claims against the Government arising under or by virtue of this contract, other than any claims that are spe-

> cifically excepted by the Contractor from the operation of the release in amounts stated in the release.

A similar general release clause is found in the Payments Under Time-And-Materials and Labor-Hour Contracts clause, FAR 52.232-7, and the Allowable Cost and Payment clause, FAR 52.216-7, used in cost-reimbursement contracts. The FAR payment clauses for fixed-price supply, services, and research and development contracts do not include a provision for general releases.

Agencies sometimes use ad hoc general releases. For instance, the following general release was used in *Progressive Bros. Constr. Co. v. United States*, 16 Cl. Ct. 549 (1989):

> For and in consideration of the payments heretofore made, and payment of the above recited sum now due by reason of performance of the above contract, the undersigned contractor hereby releases and discharges the United States of America of and from all liabilities, obligations and claims whatsoever under or arising out of said contract, except the following: [list of specific claims].

The contractor signed the release without specifically enumerating any excepted claims. The court found that the contractor was precluded from maintaining a suit based on events which occurred prior to the execution of the release. The court stated that "[i]t is well settled that the execution of a release discharges the Government of all claims and demands arising out of a contract."

When a contractor, pursuant to a contract, has executed a general release upon contract completion, it is usually barred from later asserting any claims not excepted from the release, *Watts Constr. Co. v. United States*, 161 Ct. Cl. 801 (1963); *Inland Empire Builders, Inc. v. United States*, 191 Ct. Cl. 742, 424 F.2d 1370 (1970). In *Kadin Corp*., DOTCAB 1229, 82-2 BCA ¶ 16,114, the contractor was barred from pursuing relief on a claim that was pending before the contracting officer at the time the contractor executed a release which failed to except that claim. In *Clark Mech. Contractors, Inc. v. United States*, 5 Cl. Ct. 84 (1984), an appeal of a contracting officer's final decision on a dispute was barred when the contractor signed a general release one month after receipt of the decision. Reasons for this rule include: the government's need for finality, the fact that the parties are usually aware of any claims they may have under the completed contract, and the clear and forceful language of the general release that clearly notifies the contractor that his signing will release the government from all claims not specifically reserved.

Most disputes involving general releases center on the interpretation of the release. It has been said that releases are interpreted with liberality. In *Southeastern, Inc.*, ASBCA 7677, 1963 BCA ¶ 3904, the board commented on this statement at 19,362:

> A reading of the cases cited in support of the rule of liberality will disclose that the scope of inquiry itself is confined by various principles intended to determine the intent of the parties at the time the release is executed such as, words employed in a release should be interpreted in the light of the situation attending its execution;—the intent of the parties should be sought from the whole and every part of the instrument itself, etc. *Thorn Wire Hedge Co. v. Washburn & M. Mfg. Co.*, 159 U.S. 423, 40 L. Ed. 205; *Moore v. Maryland Casualty Co.*, 150 NC 153, 63 N.E. 675; *Westinghouse Electric Supply Co. v. Burgess*, 223 N.C. 97, 25 S.E. 2nd 390, citing 23 R.C.L. 389, Sec. 26.

The intent of the parties is of vital importance in release interpretation. Examination of the parties' conduct subsequent to release has often been relied upon to discern the intent of the parties. Thus, it has been found that government consideration of the merits of a claim following the execution of a release indicates that the parties did not intend the release to extinguish that claim, *Mecon Co.*, ASBCA 13620, 69-2 BCA ¶ 7786; *Haines, Lundberg & Waehler*, GSBCA 3124, 72-1 BCA ¶ 9460; *Harold Benson*, AGBCA 384, 75-1 BCA ¶ 11,087; *Addison Constr. Co.*, IBCA 1064-3-75, 76-2 BCA ¶ 12,118; *A & K Plumbing & Mech., Inc. v. United States*, 1 Cl. Ct. 716 (1983). See also *Campbell Indus.*, ASBCA 38688, 93-3 BCA ¶ 26,165, in which a ship repair contractor's claim for the costs of rescheduling dry-docking for a vessel was not barred by a release. The board stated that it was clear from the conduct of the parties that the release covered only the costs of the change of location of the dry-docking, not the costs of the change in scheduling the dry-docking. The board noted that if the release resolved all claims associated with the modification, then the government's allowance of a time extension in performance of the modification would have made no sense. In *Steven E. Austin*, AGBCA 83-193-1, 84-1 BCA ¶ 17,017, a contractor was not barred from recovering in excess of an amount stated in a general release where the contracting officer issued a final decision denying the claims without making reference to the release. Similarly, in *Gavosto Assocs., Inc.*, PSBCA 4058, 00-1 BCA ¶ 30,913, the board dismissed the applicability of a "general release" because it was vague and ambiguous, stated claims would be submitted to the contracting officer at a later date, and was not relied on by the contracting officer.

A routinely sent general release, signed through inadvertence rather than with the intent to release all claims, has sometimes been held not to bar assertion of unexpected claims, *Petroleum Contractors, Inc.*, ASBCA 21985, 78-2 BCA ¶ 13,340; *Gene Fuller, Inc.*, ASBCA 19813, 76-1 BCA ¶ 11,898; *Arnold M. Diamond, Inc.*, ASBCA 19080, 75-2 BCA ¶ 11,605. Compare *Dawson Constr. Co.*, GSBCA 5910, 83-1 BCA ¶ 16,160, *recons. denied*, 83-1 BCA ¶ 16,275, in which the board held that the contractor was barred from asserting a "comprehensive claim" on behalf of its subcontractor which had not been specifically excepted from a general release, stating that while the contractor may not have been certain about the "amount or scope" of the subcontractor's claim at the time of the release, it did possess "sufficient knowledge, in general terms, to identify the claim and except it from the release."

E. Techniques for Avoiding Releases

There are a number of theories used by contractors seeking to avoid a general release or a release that has been included in a contract modification. This section discusses those theories.

1. Lack of Consideration

Supplemental agreements must generally be supported by consideration if they are to be binding. The adequacy of such consideration will not, however, be examined by the boards and courts, *United States v. American Trading Co. of San Francisco*, 138 F. Supp. 536 (N.D. Calif. 1956); *Woodroffe Corp. v. United States*, 122 Ct. Cl. 723, 104 F. Supp. 984 (1952); *United States v. Newport News Shipbuilding & Dry Dock Co.*, CA 75-88-NN (E.D. Va. 1977).

Lack of consideration is usually found where the parties have signed a supplemental agreement embodying an equitable adjustment increasing the price and it is later determined that the work for which the price adjustment was actually given was required by the original contract, *Wheeler Bros., Inc.*, ASBCA 16112, 73-1 BCA ¶ 9916; *A.O. Smith Corp.*, ASBCA 16788, 72-2 BCA ¶ 9688. See *Edward Hines Lumber Co.*, AGBCA 75-125, 76-1 BCA ¶ 11,854, refusing to enforce a contract amendment increasing the contract price to account for a faulty government estimate of the amount of crushed rock required to construct a road. The board reasoned that there was no consideration flowing to the government since the contract expressly stated that the estimates were for informational purposes only and that the contractor was responsible for completing the road according to the specifications. In *G. Issaias & Co. (Kenya), Ltd.*, ASBCA 30359, 88-1 BCA ¶ 20,441, a modification which changed the contract from Kenya shillings to U.S. dollars was invalid because there was no new consideration provided. The board stated that "performance of a preexisting obligation does not constitute legal consideration to alter the terms of a contract where the sole bargain is to accord only one party a benefit; e.g., additional money." See also *Beavers Constr. Co.*, AGBCA 83-125-1, 84-1 BCA ¶ 17,067, where a modification allowing the contractor additional compensation for repair of floodwater damage was not binding since the contractor bore responsibility for such repair work under the Permits and Responsibilities clause. In *Tempo, Inc.*, ASBCA 35659, 88-2 BCA ¶ 20,705, the board held that the contractor was not entitled to an equitable adjustment for the installation of cap flashing. The board interpreted the flashing specification to be a functional specification, thereby requiring flashing wherever necessary to make the work watertight. Since the contract already required cap flashing, the change order, without more, did not authorize compensation for the installation of flashing.

A subsequent finding that work for which a price adjustment has been given was actually required by the contract as written will not prevent enforcement of the modification, however, where the parties have reached a "bargain" following a legitimate dispute over their respective rights and obligations, *Airmotive Eng'g Corp.*, ASBCA 15235, 71-2 BCA ¶ 8988. See also *Russell & Assocs.–Fresno, Ltd.*, GSBCA 3976, 76-2 BCA ¶ 12,066, *rev'd*, 219 Ct. Cl. 663; 618 F.2d 120 (1979), in which the board held that the contracting officer could rescind a modification agreeing to pay for work because the belief that the government was responsible was "erroneous" but the court reversed finding that the government was bound to its interpretation at the time it signed the modification.

Lack of consideration flowing to the contractor has also been used to prevent enforcement of contract modifications, *Paccon, Inc. v. United States*, 185 Ct. Cl. 24, 399 F.2d 162 (1968) (refusing to enforce a release "inserted gratuitously" by the contractor). Accord, *Universal Painting Corp.*, ASBCA 20536, 77-1 BCA ¶ 12,355; *Bootz Mfg. Co.*, ASBCA 18787, 76-1 BCA ¶ 11,799 (modification that merely confirmed the contractor's "pre-existing rights" to a time extension lacking consideration); *Roy A. Araujo, D.D.S.*, ASBCA 15588, 71-2 BCA ¶ 9014 (payment of an amount on one claim that was not disputed by the government could not serve as consideration to support an accord and satisfaction on a separate disputed claim); *Tamarack Constr.*, AGBCA 99-108-1, 00-1 BCA ¶ 30,629 (release agreement did not bar a contractor's differing site condition claim, because the record contained no evidence showing that the government had paid the consideration required by the agreement).

2. Mistake

A mutual mistake of the parties will usually serve as a basis for invalidating a contract amendment or release. However, the cases have applied this rule with varying results. In *Packard & Co. v. United States*, 66 Ct. Cl. 184 (1928), the court found that there had been a mutual mistake where the contractor appeared to release a particular claim following a verbal understanding with the government that this claim was to be excluded from the release. The court concluded at 192:

> It is perfectly clear from the record that the parties to the settlement contract did not intend to include within its terms the claim here sued on. To include it within the general release relied upon by the [government] involves giving effect to the settlement of an item which was never within the contemplation of the parties in making it, which was not under consideration by them when the settlement was made, and was mutually understood to be aside from the matters closed up by the settlement. If it was included by the terms of the settlement it is clearly a mutual mistake, and the settlement contract may be reformed.

For cases arriving at similar results, see *United States Cartridge Co. v. United States*, 62 Ct. Cl. 214 (1926); *H.A. Ekelin & Assocs.*, ASBCA 31694, 88-3 BCA ¶ 21,033; and *Blinderman Constr. Co.*, ASBCA 18946, 74-2 BCA ¶ 10,811. In *Pacific Alaska Contractors, Inc.*, DCAB PR-46, 66-1 BCA ¶ 5532, *recons. denied*, 66-2 BCA ¶ 6043, the board found a mutual mistake when the work required under a change order was greatly increased but the contractor had previously accepted the change order at no increase in price and had signed an amendment to that effect.

A contract modification cannot be avoided on the basis of a unilateral mistake of which the other party neither knew nor had reason to know. In *Bubsy Sch. Bd. of the N. Cheyenne Tribe*, IBCA 3007, 94-1 BCA ¶ 26,327, the board held that a contracting officer could not reverse a settlement simply because someone decided he had made a mistake. The board stated at 130,969:

> [W]hen a valid and binding settlement agreement has been created, neither party can cast it aside without the most compelling of reasons, including proof of invalidity, either by fraud or mutual mistake. A unilateral mistake is not sufficient to limit or avoid the effect of an otherwise valid settlement agreement. *Cheyenne-Arapaho*, 671 F.2d at 1309, 1311.

See *H.L.C. & Assocs. Constr. Co. v. United States*, 176 Ct. Cl. 285, 367 F.2d 586 (1966), holding that the inadvertent execution of a general release by the contractor's vice president was a "unilateral mistake or omission," which was therefore enforceable as written. Accord, *Watts Constr. Co. v. United States*, 161 Ct. Cl. 801 (1963); *Detroit Testing Lab., Inc.*, EBCA 153-1-81, 83-1 BCA ¶ 16,458; *Rocky River Co. v. United States*, 169 Ct. Cl. 203 (1965). See also *Canadian Commercial Corp.*, ASBCA 37528, 89-1 BCA ¶ 21,462, in which the board found that there was no reason to believe that the government knew or should have known that the contractor had a mistaken interpretation as to the scope of the modification. In some instances, it is the government that makes the unilateral mistake. In *Essex Electro Eng'rs, Inc.*, ASBCA 20716, 76-2 BCA ¶ 11,936, the board held the government bound by an amendment it signed due to unilateral mistake on its part.

If the government knows or has reason to know of the contractor's unilateral mistake, avoidance will be permitted. In *Edward R. Marden Corp.*, ASBCA 22906, 79-1 BCA ¶ 13,821, the board found that the contractor was not bound by an equitable adjustment agreement based in part on work to be done by a subcontractor where the subcontractor had made a mistake in estimating the amount of work and the government knew of the mistake at the time the adjustment was negotiated. Compare *Merritt-Chapman & Scott Corp.*, VACAB 540, 66-2 BCA ¶ 5990, *aff'd,* 198 Ct. Cl. 223, 458 F.2d 42 (1972), where the contractor was unable to recover for the subcontractor because of a signed release, notwithstanding the fact that the subcontractor's claim had been grossly under priced.

In *DMS*, ASBCA 45723, 95-1 BCA ¶ 27,367, a German contractor's possibly mistranslated oral statement that it was signing the final payment release "in reviso" raised the possibility of a mutual or obvious unilateral mistake that would prevent the release from barring the contractor's claim before additional compensation; but in *American Int'l Contractors, Inc./Capitol Indus. Constr. Groups, Inc., A Joint Venture,* ASBCA 39544, 95-2 BCA ¶ 27,920, a modification barred claims for delays, despite the contractor's assertion that the parties were mutually mistaken about the delay impact when they signed the modification, because the assertion of mutual mistake was not supported by any factual evidence, just an unpersuasive expert.

3. Economic Duress

Use of unfair tactics by the government in persuading a contractor to sign a contract amendment or release may provide a basis for overturning the agreement. The Court of Claims stated the general rules of duress in *Fruhauf Southwest Garment Co. v. United States*, 126 Ct. Cl. 51, 111 F. Supp. 945 (1953), as follows at 62:

> The law of duress has broadened somewhat during recent years making it virtually impossible to arrive at any clear-cut definition, and the courts have stated that its application must of necessity depend upon the circumstances of each individual case. *Morrill v. Amoskeag Sav. Bank*, 9 Atl.2d (N.H.) 519, 524. An examination of the cases, however, makes it clear that three elements are common to all situations where duress has been found to exist. These are: (1) that one side involuntarily accepted the terms of another; (2) that circumstances permitted no other alternative; and (3) that said circumstances were the result of coercive acts of the opposite party. *United States v. Bethlehem Steel Corp.*, 315 U.S. 289, 301; *French v. Schoemaker*, 14 Wall. (US) 314, 332. In order to substantiate the allegation of economic duress or business compulsion, the [contractor] must go beyond the mere showing of a reluctance to accept and of financial embarrassment. There must be a showing of acts on the part of the [government] which produced these two factors. The assertion of duress must be proven to have been the result of the [government's] conduct and not by the [contractor's] necessities. In *DuPuy v. United States*, 67 C. Cls. 348, 381, this court stated:
>
>> In order to successfully defend on the ground of force or duress, it must be shown that the party benefited thereby constrained or forced the action of the injured party, and even threatened financial disaster is not sufficient.
>
> It has become settled law that the mere stress of business conditions will not constitute duress where the [government] was not responsible for those circumstances.

Agreements obtained after the contracting officer has threatened to deny payment on one claim unless the contractor releases a different claim have been voided for economic duress, *Paccon, Inc.*, ASBCA 7890, 1963 BCA ¶ 3659, *recons. denied*, 1963 BCA ¶ 3730. However, merely delaying payment without any threats will generally not constitute duress, *Inland Empire Builders, Inc. v. United States*, 191 Ct. Cl. 742, 424 F.2d 1370 (1970); *E.E. Steinlicht*, IBCA 834-4-70, 71-1 BCA ¶ 8767. In *Progressive Bros. Constr. Co. v. United States*, 16 Cl. Ct. 549 (1989), the contractor asserted that, based on a conversation with the contracting officer, it believed that a final progress payment would not be paid unless it signed the release. The contractor stated that the contracting officer "insisted" that it sign the release, which caused duress. The court found that the contractor failed to show any coercive behavior on the part of the government.

Improper threats to default terminate a contract have been held to constitute duress. In *Universal Sportswear, Inc. v. United States*, 145 Ct. Cl. 209, 180 F. Supp. 391 (1959), threats by the contracting officer to default terminate unless the contractor signed a change order at no price increase were held to be economic duress. Similarly, the contracting officer's threat to default terminate was held to constitute duress where the contractor was behind schedule because of government-caused delays, *Urban Plumbing & Heating Co. v. United States*, 187 Ct. Cl. 15, 408 F.2d 382 (1969), *cert. denied*, 398 U.S. 958 (1970). Note, however, that where the contractor's own delays cause the contracting officer to threaten default, duress will generally not be found, *Harvey-Whipple, Inc. v. United States*, 169 Ct. Cl. 689, 342 F.2d 48 (1965); *River Assocs., Inc.*, CGBCA T-166, 66-1 BCA ¶ 5448.

Merely insisting upon its rights under the contract or stating the consequences of nonperformance will not constitute duress by a contracting officer, *McLain Plumbing & Elec. Serv., Inc.*, 30 Fed. Cl. 70 (1993); *Liebherr Crane Corp. v. United States*, 810 F.2d 1153 (Fed. Cir. 1987). See also *Robinson Contracting Co. v. United States*, 16 Cl. Ct. 676 (1989), in which the court stated at 687 that "[a]t worst, the record indicates that the Corps merely insisted on its rights under the contract and reminded [the contractor] and its counsel of the severe consequences of default." Similarly, a contracting officer's statement that if the bilateral agreements were not signed, the contractor would be in default was not in and of itself coercive, but rather was a statement of fact, *Bridgewater Constr. Corp.*, VABCA 2796, 91-3 BCA ¶ 24,365. Telling a contractor that if it accepted the amount agreed upon, the contractor would be paid with greater speed than if it held out for a greater sum because funds were not immediately available to pay the greater amount, was not duress, *D.W. Young Constr. Co.*, ASBCA 29388, 87-2 BCA ¶ 19,762. In *Tolis Cain Corp.*, DOTCAB 72-2, 76-2 BCA ¶ 11,954, the board held that hard bargaining after the government had failed to pay an invoice did not constitute duress because the contracting officer had a legitimate fear that payment would exceed the contract ceiling. In *Johnson, Drake & Piper, Inc. v. United States*, 209 Ct. Cl. 313, 531 F.2d 1037 (1976), the court held that a threat to terminate for default was not wrongful because the contracting officer's sincerity was not challenged nor was it shown that his position was ill-grounded. In *Singleton Contracting Corp.*, DOTCAB 1449, 84-1 BCA ¶ 17,072, the board found no duress because pressure from government had been withdrawn at the time of execution of the settlement agreement. See also *Custom Blending & Packaging, Inc.*, ASBCA 49819, 00-2 BCA ¶ 31,083 (even if government withheld knowledge that a contract specification was unrealistic, this knowledge, even if true, did not rise to the level of duress).

In *Allied Materials & Equip. Co.*, ASBCA 17318, 75-1 BCA ¶ 11,150, the board found that a contracting officer's bad faith in threatening to consider a contract terminated for convenience a loss contract constituted duress, thereby indicating that the government's motivation for an act or threat might be more important to a finding of duress than the strict legality or illegality of the act. This reasoning, which comports with the more liberal common law decisions holding that duress may be present where, even though a threatened act is "perfectly legal," it is made as a result of malicious or unconscionable motives, was adopted by the Court of Claims in *David Nassif Assocs. v. United States*, 226 Ct. Cl. 372, 644 F.2d 4 (1981), stating at 385:

> To render an agreement voidable on grounds of duress it must be shown that the party's manifestation of assent was induced by an improper threat which left the recipient with no reasonable alternative save to agree. *RESTATEMENT, SECOND, CONTRACTS* § 317 (Tent. Draft No. 11, April 1976). Contemporary case law has expanded the concept of improper threat beyond the categories first recognized, namely, threats to commit a crime or a tort; now also included are threats that would accomplish economic harm. *RESTATEMENT, SECOND, CONTRACTS* § 318, Comment a (Tent. Draft No. 11, April 1976); *Johnson, Drake & Piper, Inc. v. United States*, 209 Ct. Cl. 313, 531 F.2d 1037 (1976); *Aircraft Associates & Mfg. Co. v. United States*, 174 Ct. Cl. 886, 357 F.2d 373 (1966). Such forms of economic duress, or, as it is sometimes also called, business compulsion, include threats that would breach a duty of good faith and fair dealing under a contract as well as threats which, though lawful in themselves, are enhanced in their effectiveness in inducing assent to unfair terms because they exploit prior unfair dealing on the part of the party making the threat.

Addressing the merits, the court concluded that the government's threatened refusal to take occupancy of a building until the contractor agreed to commit itself to maintaining food service facilities, thereby inducing the contractor to enter into a supplemental agreement under which it was ultimately responsible for liquidated damages for late completion, did not constitute economic duress. The court relied primarily upon the fact that the supplemental agreement did not "irretrievably bind" the contractor, but left it free to litigate the correctness of the government contention that the contractor was required under the contract to provide food service facilities. The court also pointed to the reasonableness of the government's position in threatening to postpone its own performance in the face of the contractor's repudiation of a "material part" of their bargain. The bad faith rule was also accepted in *Systems Tech. Assocs., Inc. v. United States*, 699 F.2d 1383 (Fed. Cir. 1983), in which the court stated that "[a]n act the Government is empowered to take under law, regulation, or contract may nonetheless support a claim of duress if the act violates notions of fair dealing by virtue of its coercive effect," and also stated that the standard for duress now "looks more closely at the defeat of will of the party coerced" than the "fine metaphysical analysis of illegality." However, the court rejected the contractor's contention that government delay in reaching a settlement allegedly to take advantage of the contractor's deteriorating financial condition constituted duress, where the government was at most responsible for a delay of six weeks. *See also WRB Corp., et al, a Joint Venture d/b/a Robertson Constr. Co. v. United States*, 183 Ct. Cl. 409 (1968), where the government said nothing of a defect until the contract work was deemed complete and demanded a price reduction. The court branded this an "ambush" and unallowable.

In *Rumsfeld v. Freedom N.Y., Inc.*, 329 F.3d 1320 (Fed. Cir. 2003), *cert. denied*, 541 U.S. 987 (2004), the agency's insistence that the contractor agree to a modification before a progress payment would be made was an improper act of duress that vitiated the modification.

Acts of third parties are unlikely to be found to be duress. For example, in *Riennes Constr. Co.*, IBCA 3572-96, 98-2 BCA ¶ 29,821, a contractor was bound by a general release because it failed to show it signed the release as a result of duress. During the course of the contract, the contractor made payments to its suppliers and workers on a closed bank account. The state district attorney contacted the contractor and advised the principal that he might be liable for fines and imprisonment if he failed to make the bad checks good. The board held that such communication from the state was not coercive action by the government. See also *Tri-Star Def., Inc.*, ASBCA 46650, 98-1 BCA ¶ 29,482 (contractor that alleged it was threatened with default termination if it did not sign a modification did not have its default excused by government actions, because the contracting office denied ever raising the termination issue with the contractor and was no longer with the tank command when the threat was alleged to have taken place).

4. Fraud and Misrepresentation

A showing of fraud, particularly in the negotiation of contract amendments and releases, will, of course, usually allow the parties to avoid the agreement, *Watts Constr. Co. v. United States*, 161 Ct. Cl. 801 (1963). An important exception may occur, however, if the government has knowledge of the fraud in the original transaction and still enters into a settlement agreement. In such a case, the Court of Claims has held that the government will be bound by the agreement, *Carrier Corp. v. United States*, 164 Ct. Cl. 666, 328 F.2d 328 (1964).

Misrepresentation was found to be grounds for avoiding releases in *C & H Commercial Contractors, Inc. v. United States*, 35 Fed. Cl. 246 (1996). There, the contracting officer had told the contractor that clear release language in modifications would not bar additional claims. In denying the government's motion for summary judgment, the court stated at 256-57:

> For the purpose of resolving this motion, we assume that the government's position in this litigation (i.e., that C & H's execution of the modifications containing comprehensive release language constitutes a bar to claims for delay/impact costs) is consistent with its real position at the time each modification was executed. Based on this assumption, and further assuming plaintiff's version of the facts to be true, the government is guilty of material misrepresentations on which plaintiff reasonably relied. *RESTATEMENT, SECOND, CONTRACTS* describes when misrepresentation makes a contract voidable: "If a party's manifestation of assent is induced by either a fraudulent or a material misrepresentation by the other party upon which the recipient is justified in relying, the contract is voidable by the recipient." *RESTATEMENT, SECOND, CONTRACTS* § 164(1) (1979). Ex-

> trinsic evidence is admissible to prove that a plaintiff entered a contract based on a misrepresentation by defendant. *T.L. Roof & Assocs. Constr. Co. v. United States*, 28 Fed. Cl. 572 (1993).
>
> It is generally understood that four conditions must be met before a contract may be voided for misrepresentation: (1) a misrepresentation was made; (2) the misrepresentation was either fraudulent or material; (3) reliance; and (4) justification in reliance. *RESTATEMENT, SECOND, CONTRACTS* § 164; *Barrer v. Women's Nat'l Bank*, 245 U.S. App. D.C. 349, 761 F.2d 752, 758 (D.C.Cir. 1985).
>
> It is reasonable to infer from the deposition testimony of C & H's officers and from [the contracting officer's] memorandum and trial testimony that (1) Air Force personnel made repeated misrepresentations to plaintiff; (2) these misrepresentations were material; (3) plaintiff relied on these representations in assenting to the agreements; and (4) its reliance upon assurances by professional contracting officers who would be reviewing subsequent delay claims was justified.

Compare *Jackson Constr. Co. v. United States*, 62 Fed. Cl. 84 (2004), finding no compelling evidence of misrepresentation and enforcing release language in contract modifications.

5. Lack of Authority

The government has been allowed to disavow alleged settlements that were beyond the actual authority of the executing official, *Atlantic Gulf & Pac. Co. of Manila v. United States*, 207 Ct. Cl. 995 (1975). In *Bromley Contracting Co.*, DOT-CAB 1284, 84-2 BCA ¶ 17,233, the government was able to avoid a settlement where the contracting officer failed to follow the mandate of the Federal Procurement Regulations for performance of an audit prior to any contract modification in excess of $100,000. See *SCM Corp. v. United States*, 219 Ct. Cl. 459, 595 F.2d 595 (1979), in which the Court of Claims found that the contracting officer's failure to follow certain mandated procedures was persuasive evidence that the parties had not intended to be bound to an alleged settlement.

CHAPTER 13

DISPUTES

Disputes between a contractor and the government are resolved under the procedures prescribed by the Contract Disputes Act of 1978 (CDA), 41 U.S.C. § 601 *et seq.*, which codified and broadened existing disputes procedures. In the early part of the 20th century, prior to the adoption of contract disputes procedures, contractors could assert claims against the government under the Tucker Act, 28 U.S.C. § 1346(a) and § 1491, which waived sovereign immunity for "any claim against the United States, founded either upon the Constitution, or any Act of Congress, or any regulation of an executive department, or upon any express or implied contract with the United States."

As procurement became a significant factor in the operations of the government in the twentieth century, contractors' rights to use the waiver of sovereign immunity through suits in court were significantly limited by the incorporation of disputes provisions into contracts with the government. These clauses required that the contracting officer make the initial decision on a dispute. The contractor could then appeal this decision to the head of the agency or a board designated by the agency head. Contractors were required to exhaust these administrative remedies before bringing suit on any case within the purview of the disputes clauses, *United States v. Holpuch Co.*, 328 U.S. 234 (1946). Under the Wunderlich Act, 41 U.S.C. §§ 321 and 322, such clauses were prohibited from making agency decisions final on questions of law but were permitted to limit judicial review by making agency decisions final on questions of fact, as long as those decisions were supported by substantial evidence and were not "fraudulent or arbitrary or capricious or so grossly erroneous as to necessarily imply bad faith." Considerable litigation arose under these disputes clauses concerning the types of claims covered and the jurisdiction of agency boards of contract appeals and the courts.

The disputes procedure was restructured and made statutory by the CDA, which introduced two major changes. First, the Act broadens the scope of the disputes procedure by removing the need for a "remedy granting clause" as a prerequisite for jurisdiction. Second, it gives the contractor the right to appeal a contracting officer's decision to either an agency board of contract appeals or the Court of Federal Claims, but not U.S. District Courts, *Campanella v. Commerce Exch. Bank*, 137 F.3d 885 (6th Cir. 1998).

To have a viable contract claim under the Tucker Act, a plaintiff must establish privity of contract with the government or a contractual relationship with the government as a third-party beneficiary. To determine whether plaintiff is an intended third-party beneficiary under a contract, the court will examine the entire contractual relationship and determine whether the beneficiary would be reasonable in relying on the promise as intending to confer a right on him, *Sallee v. United States*, 41 Fed. Cl. 509 (1998).

This chapter provides an overview of the disputes process and discusses in detail the types of controversies subject to the CDA, the procedures for asserting claims, the role of the contracting officer in the disputes process, the contractor's options of litigating before the boards of contract appeals or the Court of Federal Claims, alternative dispute resolutions, and judicial review of board or court decisions by the United States Court of Appeals for the Federal Circuit. The last section briefly reviews several types of relief outside the scope of the CDA.

The Disputes process is resorted to when the parties cannot settle their problems by agreement. It can be initiated by either the contractor or the government and involves a number of steps from the initial presentation of a matter to the possible (but rare) review by the Supreme Court. However, once the parties begin the process they are not obligated to continue. Either party can capitulate by abandoning the process at any stage. Hopefully they will be able to resolve the matter through negotiation. Figure 13-1 illustrates the procedures followed in the presentation, request, or litigation of claims. As will be noted, the parties have the choice at each stage of the process to conclude the matter through negotiation.

I. COVERAGE OF DISPUTES PROCESS

Although Congress, in passing the CDA, broadened the coverage of the Disputes clause, the Act does not make all disagreements between the government and a contractor subject to the process. The language delineating the scope of the Disputes clause is the phrase *relating to the contract*. This section deals with the criteria for determining whether a claim is one relating to the contract and thus subject to the disputes process.

Some, but not all, of the coverage issues are discussed in the following Chapter. To aid in determining coverage of specific issues, a summary of the Act's coverage is in Figure 13-2.

Figure 13-1

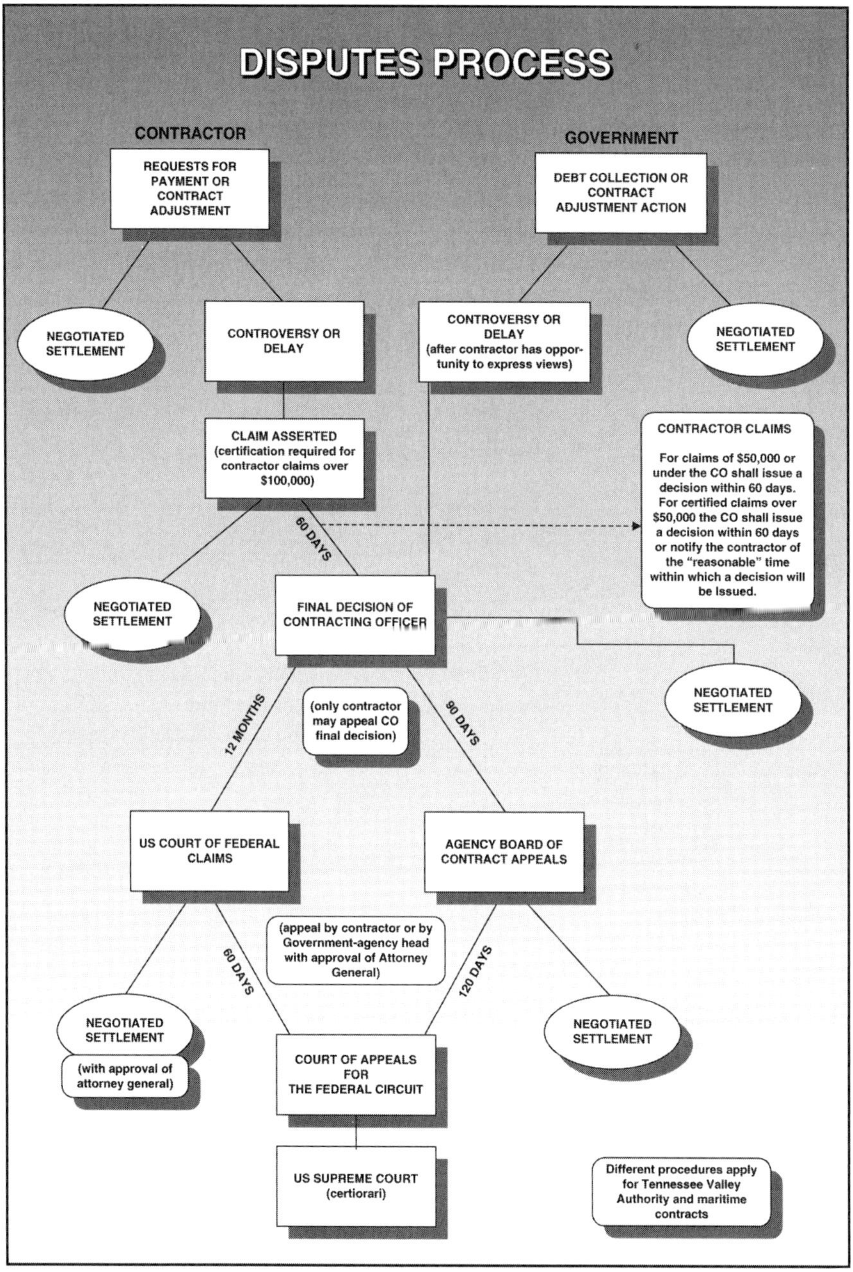
DISPUTES PROCESS
CONTRACTOR
GOVERNMENT
REQUESTS FOR PAYMENT OR CONTRACT ADJUSTMENT
DEBT COLLECTION OR CONTRACT ADJUSTMENT ACTION
NEGOTIATED SETTLEMENT
CONTROVERSY OR DELAY
CONTROVERSY OR DELAY (after contractor has opportunity to express views)
NEGOTIATED SETTLEMENT
CLAIM ASSERTED (certification required for contractor claims over $100,000)
CONTRACTOR CLAIMS
For claims of $50,000 or under the CO shall issue a decision within 60 days. For certified claims over $50,000 the CO shall issue a decision within 60 days or notify the contractor of the "reasonable" time within which a decision will be issued.
60 DAYS
NEGOTIATED SETTLEMENT
FINAL DECISION OF CONTRACTING OFFICER
NEGOTIATED SETTLEMENT
12 MONTHS
(only contractor may appeal CO final decision)
90 DAYS
US COURT OF FEDERAL CLAIMS
AGENCY BOARD OF CONTRACT APPEALS
(appeal by contractor or by Government-agency head with approval of Attorney General)
60 DAYS
120 DAYS
NEGOTIATED SETTLEMENT
(with approval of attorney general)
COURT OF APPEALS FOR THE FEDERAL CIRCUIT
NEGOTIATED SETTLEMENT
US SUPREME COURT (certiorari)
Different procedures apply for Tennessee Valley Authority and maritime contracts

Figure 13-2

CDA Coverage	Mandatory Coverage	Coverage Excluded or Optional
Date of Contract	Contracts entered into after March 1, 1979[1]	Contracts entered into prior to March 1, 1979 excluded unless contractor elects coverage on final decisions issued after March 1, 1979[2]
Government Organization	Executive agencies[3] and exchange services[4]	Nonappropriated fund activities[5] other than exchange services[6]
Nature of Transaction	Procurement of property;[7] services;[8] construction, alteration, repair or maintenance of real property.[9] Disposal of personal property.[10] Leases of real property.[11] Maritime contracts involving procurement of property or services.[12]	Procurement of real property in being,[13] contracts with foreign governments or agencies[14]
Type of Agreement	Express or implied-in-fact contracts[15]	Implied-in-law contracts and implied contracts to consider bids or proposals fairly[16]
Type of Claim	Arising under or relating to a contract[17]	Restitution (quasi-contract)[18] claims not related to contract,[19] claims involving fraud,[20] claims involving statutory penalties or forfeitures under specific jurisdiction of another federal agency[21]
Nature of Relief	Money in a sum certain, adjustment or interpretation of contract terms, or other relief[22]	Injunctive relief[23] and declaratory judgment[24]

1 92 Stat. 2391.

2 92 Stat. 2391.

3 41 U.S.C. § 602(a). Executive agencies include independent establishments, military departments, wholly owned government corporations, the United States Postal Service and the Postal Rate Commission, 41 U.S.C. § 601(2). An entity's receipt of federal funds does not make it a federal agency for CDA purposes, *Morgan v. United States*, 55 Fed. Cl. 706 (2003). An agency selecting and buying for exchanges is an exchange, *McDonald's Corp. v. United States*, 926 F.2d 1126 (Fed. Cir. 1991).

4 28 U.S.C. § 1491.

5 Contracts of nonappropriated fund activities other than exchange services are not subject to 28 U.S.C. § 1491, *Research Triangle Inst. v. Board of Governors of the Fed. Reserve Sys.*, 132 F.3d 985 (4th Cir. 1997) (Federal Reserve Board); *Kyer v. United States*, 177 Ct. Cl. 747, 369 F.2d 714 (1966), *cert. denied*, 387 U.S. 929 (1967) (agricultural marketing committee using no appropriated funds). For other nonappropriated fund activities not covered, see *Furash & Co. v. United States*, 252 F.3d 1336 (Fed. Cir. 2001) (Federal Housing Finance Board); *AINS, Inc. v. United States*, 56 Fed. Cl. 522 (2003), *aff'd*, 365 F.3d 1333 (Fed. Cir. 2004) (United States Mint); *Core Concepts of Fla., Inc. v. United*

States, 327 F.3d 1331 (Fed. Cir. 2003) (Federal Prison Industries); and *Trent Jones, Inc.,* AGBCA 98-104-1, 99-1 BCA ¶ 30,196 (United Soybean Board). But see *MDB Communications, Inc. v. United States*, 53 Fed. Cl. 245 (2002), holding that the Public Enterprise Fund of the United States Mint was an appropriated fund activity because it was a revolving fund.

6 41 U.S.C. § 602(b) (TVA may use CDA for contracts except those for sale of power or fertilizer).

7 41 U.S.C. § 602(a)(1). See *City of Adelanlo,* ASBCA 48202, 96-2 BCA ¶ 28,422 (procurement of water rights, because water is severable from real estate without material harm and, therefore, is personalty).

8 41 U.S.C. § 602(a)(2). See *Enrique (Hank) Hernandez*, ASBCA 53011, 01-1 BCA ¶ 31,220 (commissary agreement for grocery bagging services, even though the baggers were to be compensated solely by tips from shoppers at the commissary, is procurement of services).

9 41 U.S.C. § 602(a)(3).

10 41 U.S.C. § 602(a)(4). A dispute arising from a lease was subject to CDA jurisdiction because a lease involved the disposal of personal property rather than the sale of real property, *William P. Schnaetzel*, ENGBCA 6365, 98-2 BCA ¶ 29,937. Data used in exchange for services qualified the contract as a disposal of personal property contract so the CDA applied, *Marketing & Mgmt. Info., Inc.* v. *United States*, 57 Fed. Cl. 665 (2004).

11 *6800* Corp., GSBCA 5880, 81-2 BCA ¶ 15,388; *George Ungar*, PSBCA 935, 82-1 BCA ¶ 15,549. See *Up State Fed. Credit Union v. Walker, 1*98 F.3d 372 (2d Cir. 1999) (contract to build and operate a facility under a one-year land lease is a lease of real property giving CDA jurisdiction)

12 *Marine Logistics, Inc. v. England*, 265 F.3d 1322 (Fed. Cir. 2001) (appeals from boards of contract appeals decisions are to U.S. district courts, not the Federal Circuit, 41 U.S.C. § 603). Maritime contracts subject to admiralty jurisdiction are not under the CDA, 41 U.S.C. § 609. See *Thrustmaster of Tex., Inc. v. United States*, 59 Fed. Cl. 672 (2004) (ship repair contract).

13 41 U.S.C. § 602(a)(1).

14 41 U.S.C. § 602(c).

15 41 U.S.C. § 602(a). See *Roy v. United States*, 38 Fed. Cl. 184 (1997); *National Micrographics Sys., Inc. v. United States*, 38 Fed. Cl. 46 (1997); *Charles Hartlerode*, ASBCA 52634, 02-1 BCA ¶ 31,716 (appeal from a re-offer of an auction item was dismissed for lack of jurisdiction because there was no binding contract with the government); and *D&N Bank v. United States,* 331 F.3d 1374 (Fed. Cir. 2003) (no proof of mutuality of intent to contract and therefore no jurisdiction). In *Gould, Inc. v. United States*, 67 F.3d 925 (Fed. Cir. 1995), the court stated that, even when an express contract is illegal, a contractor may recover under an implied-in-fact contract in some circumstances.

16 *Coastal Corp. v. United States,* 713 F.2d 728 (Fed. Cir. 1983). In *Barrett Ref. Corp. v. United States*, 242 F.3d 1055 (Fed. Cir. 2001), the Federal Circuit held that the COFC had jurisdiction over the government's implied-in-law claim because the Tucker Act's prohibition on implied-in-law claims does not extend to counterclaims. See 28 U.S.C. §§ 1503, 2508.

17 41 U.S.C. § 605.

18 *Dean Prosser & Crew*, IBCA 1471681, 81-2 BCA ¶ 15,294; *Rowdybush*, ASBCA 24955, 83-1 BCA ¶ 16,188, *recons. denied,* 83-1 BCA ¶ 16,442, *recons. denied*, 83-2 BCA ¶ 16,549.

19 *Western Pine Indus. Inc. v. United States,* 231 Ct. Cl. 885 (1982).

20 41 U.S.C. § 605(a).

[21] 41 U.S.C. § 605(a). The Interstate Commerce Act, 31 U.S.C. § 3726, preempts the CDA regarding a contract for transportation of perishable foods, *Inter-Coastal Xpress, Inc. v. United States*. 49 Fed. Cl. 531 (2001).

[22] Pub. L. 102-572, § 907.

[23] *Ulrich McMillan*, GSBCA 7029COM, 83-2 BCA ¶ 16,595; *Maria Manges*, ASBCA 25350, 81-2 BCA ¶ 15,398, *recons. denied,* 82-1 BCA ¶ 15,665; *Applied Ordnance Tech., Inc.*, ASBCA 51297, 98-2 BCA ¶ 30,023. See *Western Aviation Maint., Inc. v. General Servs. Admin.*, GSBCA 14165, 98-2 BCA ¶ 29,816 (no jurisdiction over claims for specific performance). See also *Veda, Inc. v. Department of the Air Force*, 111 F.3d 37 (6th Cir. 1997) (District Court, not the Court of Federal Claims, had jurisdiction over the declaratory and injunctive relief sought by the contractor).

[24] A provision granting the Court of Claims jurisdiction under the Declaratory Judgments Act was deleted during the floor debate on the Contract Disputes Act, 124 Cong. Rec. S18,63941 (daily ed. Oct. 12, 1978). See *Alaska Pulp Corp. v. United States*, 38 Fed. Cl. 141 (1997) (contractor's claim for declaratory relief was not encompassed by the contractor's claims for monetary relief). Relief in the nature of declaratory relief is available through contract interpretation, *Alliant Techsystems, Inc. v. United States*, 178 F.3d 1260 (Fed. Cir. 1999). When the real issue is money and not the contract's terms, however, the board will refuse such declaratory relief, *McDonnell Douglas Corp.*, ASBCA 50592, 97-2 BCA ¶ 29,199, *recons. denied,* 98-1 BCA ¶ 29,504. See also *SUFI Network Servs., Inc.*, ASBCA 54503, 04-1 BCA ¶ 32,606. A contractor was not entitled to seek an advance determination of its liability before performing disputed work in *Valley View Enters., Inc. v. United States,* 35 Fed. Cl. 378 (1996).

A. Claims Relating to the Contract

Prior to the CDA, the Disputes clause stated that disputes procedures would apply to any dispute "concerning a question of fact arising under the contract." This was interpreted to mean that the court and boards had jurisdiction over a dispute only when the contract contained a "remedy granting" clause providing for the remedy requested by the contractor, *United States v. Utah Constr. & Mining Co.*, 384 U.S. 394 (1966).

The CDA, 41 U.S.C. § 605, broadened this coverage to all disputes "relating to the contract," providing:

> (a) All claims by a contractor against the Government relating to a contract shall be in writing and shall be submitted to the contracting officer for a decision. All claims by the Government against a contractor relating to a contract shall be the subject of a decision by the contracting officer . . ..

This "all-disputes" language encompasses both contract claims covered by remedy granting clauses and claims not covered by specific clauses in the contract. The Disputes clause at FAR 52.2331 incorporates both types of claims as follows:

> (b) Except as provided in the Act, all disputes arising under or relating to this contract shall be resolved under this clause.

The sweep of this language is pervasive. In *Burnside-Ott Aviation Training Ctr. v. Dalton,* 107 F. 3d 854 (Fed. Cir. 1997), the court held that a contract provision stating that the agency's award fee determination was not subject to the CDA was invalid. The court said that, by enacting the CDA, Congress, in effect, prohibited the use of such provisions. In *Rig Masters, Inc. v. United States*, 42 Fed. Cl. 369 (1998), a contracting officer's value engineering decision as to the contractor's share of savings was subject to the Contract Disputes Act and was therefore disputable despite the fact that the Value Engineering clause, FAR 52.248-1, states that such determinations are subjective and not subject to the Disputes Act. Compare *NI Indus., Inc. v. United States*, 841 F.2d 1104 (Fed. Cir. 1988) (holding that rejection of a value engineering proposal was an abuse of discretion), with *RCS Enters., Inc. v. United States,* 46 Fed. Cl. 509 (2000) (holding that rejection of a value engineering proposal was not subject to the CDA). See also *D&R Mach. Co.,* ASBCA 50730, 98-1 BCA ¶ 29,462, taking jurisdiction over an appeal from a contracting officer's decision to deny a contractor's claim for attorneys' fees and costs incurred in defending a trade misappropriation lawsuit in a U.S. District Court, notwithstanding the contractor's agreement in a previous District Court settlement waiving its right to appeal to the board. The board held that the parties could not, by agreement, override the plain dictates of Congress.

1. Remedy Granting Clauses

Most contracts contain a number of standard clauses granting remedies to either the government or contractor. For example, a contractor may be granted compensation or other remedies if the government orders additional work (Changes—Cost-Reimbursement, FAR 52.2432; Changes—Fixed-Price, FAR 52.2431), or if the government delays the contractor (Suspension of Work, FAR 52.21212). In addition, construction contracts contain a clause calling for an equitable adjustment if the contractor encounters unforeseen physical conditions (Differing Site Conditions, FAR 52.2362). Other clauses granting remedies include the Termination for the Convenience of the Government, FAR 52.2496 (applicable to both fixed-price and cost-reimbursement type contracts); Government Property (Fixed-Price Contracts), FAR 52.2452; Government Property (Cost-Reimbursement, Time-and-Material, or Labor-Hour Contracts), FAR 52.2455; Price Reduction for Defective Cost or Pricing Data, FAR 52.21522; Inspection of Services—Fixed-Price, FAR 52.2464 and Inspection of Services—Cost-Reimbursement, FAR 52.2465. The result is that most events leading to a claim are covered by contract clauses providing for the remedy sought.

2. Breach of Contract Claims

Under the pre-CDA procedure, "breach of contract" was a term of art used to refer to contractor claims alleging that the government failed to perform an express or implied duty for which no relief was available under the terms of the contract and which thus fell outside the scope of the pre-Act disputes process, *Globe Eng'g Co.*, ASBCA 23934, 83-1 BCA ¶ 16,370, *recons. denied*, 84-1 BCA ¶ 16,941. Since such breach of contract claims are related to the contract, they are within the scope of the statutory disputes process, *Essex Electro Eng'rs, Inc. v. United States*, 702 F.2d 998 (Fed. Cir. 1983); *Mega Constr. Co. v. United States*, 29 Fed. Cl. 396 (1993); *Stephens Assocs.*, PSBCA 1049, 84-1 BCA ¶ 16,921; *Tefft, Kelly & Motley, Inc.*, GSBCA 6562, 83-1 BCA ¶ 16,177, *recons. denied*, 83-1 BCA ¶ 16,279.

3. Mistakes Alleged After Award

Prior to the CDA, the appeals boards consistently held that they lacked jurisdiction over mistake allegations, other than as a basis for excusing a default. Such claims, however, are clearly related to the contract. Thus, FAR 33.205(b) now specifically provides that for postaward mistakes "[a] contractor's allegation that it is entitled to rescission or reformation of its contract in order to correct or mitigate the effect of a mistake shall be treated as a claim under the [Contract Disputes] Act." See *Paragon Energy Corp. v. United States*, 227 Ct. Cl. 176, 645 F.2d 966 (1981), *relief denied,* 230 Ct. Cl. 884 (1982), in which the court held that procuring agencies have authority under the CDA to reform contracts and award monetary relief to mitigate the effect of a unilateral bid mistake of which the government knew or had reason to know. See also *Gentex Corp.*, ASBCA 24040, 80-2 BCA ¶ 14,732. In *John J. Eufemio, M.D.*, ASBCA 26625, 82-2 BCA ¶ 15,990, *aff'd*, 702 F.2d 998 (Fed. Cir. 1983), the board held that, in spite of the fact that the contractor previously sought relief from the agency under Pub. L. 85-804, the board's jurisdiction to reform or rescind a contract after award (due to a bid mistake) was not affected. The board stated at 79,287:

> Since our consideration of all appeals is de novo, the fact that [the contractor] may have pursued his claim before the agency under a different theory than that now presented does not defeat his rights to have his appeal considered by us under a proper theory of recovery.

B. Government–Contractor Controversies Not Subject to Disputes Process

Although the coverage of the CDA has sometimes been referred to as an "all disputes" process, the Act does not extend to all controversies between the government and the contractor. Further, not all government instrumentalities are covered under the Act, and certain types of agreements are excluded. For instance, the Act does not cover nonappropriated fund activities other than exchange services; Tennessee Valley Authority (TVA) contracts, 41 U.S.C. § 602(b); the sale of real property, 41 U.S.C. § 602(a); or contracts with foreign governments or agencies, 41 U.S.C. § 602(c).

1. Independent Torts

The Court of Federal Claims and the boards have no jurisdiction to hear tort cases that are not also breaches of contract. The CDA did not expand the court's jurisdiction, which is limited by the Tucker Act, 28 U.S.C. § 1491, to "any claim against the United States founded . . . upon any express or implied contract with the United States . . . in cases not sounding in tort," *Allbritton v. United States*, 178 F.3d 1307 (Fed. Cir.1998); *H.H.O., Inc. v. United States*, 7 Cl. Ct. 703 (1985). The boards' jurisdiction is similarly limited, *Asfaltos Panamenos, S.A.*, ASBCA 39425, 91-1 BCA ¶ 23,315; *Aulson Roofing, Inc.*, ASBCA 37677, 91-2 BCA ¶ 23,720.

If, however, the purported tort relates to or arises out of an express or implied contractual obligation, the disputes process applies. See *Chain Belt v. United States*, 127 Ct. Cl. 38, 115 F. Supp. 701 (1953), in which the court stated at 54:

> Inasmuch as we found that [the government's] removal methods resulted in unnecessary and excessive damage to the floors, we discuss briefly [the government's] contention that this claim is beyond the court's jurisdiction because it sounds in tort. While it is true that this court does not have jurisdiction over claims sounding primarily in tort, an action may be maintained in this court which arises primarily from a contractual undertaking regardless of the fact that the loss resulted from the negligent manner in which [the government] performed its contract. *Chippewa Indians of Minnesota v. United States*, 91 Ct. Cl. 97, 130, 131. A tortious breach of contract is not a tort independent of the contract so as to preclude an action under the Tucker Act. *United States v. Huff*, 165 F.2d 720, 723.

See also *Awad v. United States*, 301 F.3d 1367 (Fed. Cir. 2002), stating "where a tort claim stems from a breach of contract, the cause of action is ultimately one arising in contract, and thus is properly within the exclusive jurisdiction of the Court of Federal Claims"; *Wood v. United States*, 961 F.2d 195 (Fed. Cir. 1992) (quoting *San Carlos Irrigation & Drainage Dist. v. United States*, 877 F.2d 957, 960 (Fed. Cir. 1989) "If an action arises 'primarily from a contractual undertaking,' jurisdiction lies in the Claims Court 'regardless of the fact that the loss resulted from the negligent manner in which defendant performed its contract.'").

Thus, even though a contractor alleges that a government employee has engaged in tortious conduct, the key question is whether that conduct was related to a contract. See, for example, *Thomas S. Rhoades & Stephen L. Schluneger*, ENGBCA 6097, 95-1 BCA ¶ 27,375, in which the board refused to dismiss as a tort claim a claim of a subcontractor that government employees were responsible for sinking a barge. The board construed the claim as a violation of the contractual duty to cooperate. Similarly, in *Richard T. Gannon,* ASBCA 47332, 95-1 BCA ¶ 27,422, the board held that the contractor's allegation that "a safe working environment is understood under the contract" sufficiently alleged an implied contractual obligation, which gave the board jurisdiction to decide the claim. See also *Maron Constr. Co. v. General Servs. Admin.*, GSBCA 13625, 98-1 BCA ¶ 29,497 (claim for fraud and deceit during contract formation a contract claim for nondisclosure of information and failure to cooperate); *L&M Thomas Concrete Co.*, ASBCA 49198, 98-1 BCA ¶ 29,560 (claims that government improperly assessed liquidated damages, improperly withheld payments, and improperly collected reprocurement costs not tort claims but had a contractual nexus to the defaulted contract); *Polaris Travel, Inc.*, EBCA C-9401166, 96-2 BCA ¶ 28,518 (subcontractor claims that contractor on behalf of the government converted drafts and misused proprietary information are both based on contract provisions); *Morris v. United States,* 33 Fed. Cl. 733 (1995) (misrepresentation during sale a contract claim); *Kolar, Inc.,* ASBCA 28482, 84-1 BCA ¶ 17,044 (contractor's allegation of fraudulent inducement, although containing elements of a tort action, was based on the contract); *Act IV Constr. Co.*, ASBCA 26378, 82-1 BCA ¶ 15,621 (government claim for damages for fire loss not a tort claim but under the Permits and Responsibilities clause); *Sierra Pac. Airlines,* AGBCA 821121, 82-1 BCA ¶ 15,710 (alleged tortious conduct of government employees who instructed the contractor to park its aircraft in an area covered with volcanic ash was contract claim under clause that allocated risk between the parties and placed the contractor under the government's control during performance); and *Electrospace Corp*. ASBCA 19742, 78-1 BCA ¶ 12,949 (claim that government and bank financing the contractor's performance had conspired to compel the contractor to accept settlement of a claim far below its fair value not a claim sounding in tort but a contract claim based on economic duress).

Although the court and boards have no jurisdiction under the CDA to hear pure tort claims, a contractor can resubmit a petition to "conform with the requirements of a contract claim," *Western Pine Indus., Inc. v. United States*, 231 Ct. Cl. 885 (1982). Merely alleging, however, that the tort relates in some general sense to the contractual relationship is not sufficient to confer jurisdiction on the court or board: "Contractors must demonstrate a direct nexus between the Government's alleged tortious conduct and its obligations under the contract," *Asfaltos Panamenos, S.A.*, ASBCA 39425, 91-1 BCA ¶ 23,315. See also *H.H.O., Inc. v. United States*, 7 Cl. Ct. 703 (1985), and *L'Enfant Plaza Props., Inc. v. United States*, 227 Ct. Cl. 1, 645 F.2d 886 (1981).

The Court of Appeals for the Fourth Circuit held that U.S. District Courts lack jurisdiction over government tort claims against a contractor where the tort claims require examination and resolution of issues under the contract itself, *United States v. J&E Salvage Co.,* 55 F.3d 985 (4th Cir. 1995).

2. Fraud

The CDA provides that agency heads are not authorized to "settle, compromise, pay or otherwise adjust any claim involving fraud," 41 U.S.C. § 605(a). The Federal Circuit has held that this provision precludes the issue of fraud from being litigated under the CDA because fraud is assigned to the Department of Justice, *Martin J. Simko Constr. Co. v. United States*, 852 F.2d 540 (Fed. Cir. 1988). Similarly, the Court of Federal Claims lacks jurisdiction over a contractor's appeal from a contracting officer's decision that was based on his belief that the contractor had submitted fraudulent invoices for payment, *Medina Constr., Ltd. v. United States*, 43 Fed.

Cl. 537 (1999). Boards also refuse to litigate contentions of fraud in the formation of a contract, *Thomas S. Rhoades,* ENGBCA 6025, 97-1 BCA ¶ 28,672.

The Act also provides at 41 U.S.C. § 604 that:

> If a contractor is unable to support any part of his claim and it is determined that such inability is attributable to misrepresentation of fact or fraud on the part of the contractor, he shall be liable to the Government for an amount equal to such unsupported part of the claim in addition to all costs to the Government attributable to the cost of reviewing said part of his claim. Liability under this subsection shall be determined within six years of the commission of such misrepresentation of fact or fraud.

Under both pre-Act and post-Act procedures, the boards have refused to litigate directly the issue of fraud but have frequently continued to process claims by severing the fraud element from the contract claim, *Time Contractors, (JV)*, DOTCAB 1669, 86-2 BCA ¶ 19,003. In determining whether to stay proceedings, the boards balance the contractor's right to an expeditious resolution of its dispute, 41 U.S.C. § 607(e), against the harm to the parties of trying fraud issues in a CDA case rather than in a civil or criminal fraud case. The current rule is summarized as follows in *Hardrives, Inc.*, IBCA 2319, 91-2 BCA ¶ 23,769, at 119,064:

> Traditionally, Boards have identified at least four situations in which they "should give consideration to suspending proceedings. . .balancing the estimated duration of the suspension against each party's right to a timely resolution." *Fidelity Construction Co.,* DOTCAB Nos. 1113, 1123, 80-2 BCA ¶ 14,819 at 73,142. They are: (1) when a criminal or civil action has been filed in a competent court involving issues directly relevant to the claims before the Board; (2) when [the Department of Justice] or other authorized investigatory authority formally has requested suspension to protect a civil action or to avoid conflict with a criminal investigation; (3) when the Government can demonstrate that a real possibility of fraud exists of such a nature effectively to preclude a Board from ascertaining the facts and circumstances surrounding a claim; and (4) when [a contractor] requests a suspension to avoid compromising rights in a potential or actual criminal proceeding.

In *Hardrives*, the government alleged fraud in every element of the claim and filed suit under the Civil False Claims Act, 31 U.S.C. § 3729, in a federal district court. Weighing the facts of the case, the board suspended the CDA proceedings. In contrast, the DOTBCA held it would not suspend proceedings on a mere allegation of fraud but would consider the particular circumstances presented in deciding whether to do so, *American Constr. Servs., Inc.*, DOTBCA 2993, 97-1 BCA ¶ 28,641. See also *Mayfair Constr. Co.*, NASABCA 4786, 80-1 BCA ¶ 14,261, in which the board suspended the case pending a court action. In *Northrop Corp., Northrop Elecs. Sys. Div. v. United States*, 27 Fed. Cl. 795 (1993), the contractor sought to have a Court of Federal Claims stay lifted for the limited purpose of allowing discovery on the contractor's CDA claims. Previously, the district court had issued an order staying a related case involving an allegation of false claims initiated by qui tam plaintiffs against Northrop Corporation. The district court subsequently lifted the stay. In the Court of Federal Claims case, the government argued that comity and judicial economy required continuance of the court's stay until the resolution of the district court proceeding. The court agreed with the government stating that the "close bond between the two litigations favors deferral of the instant proceeding." The court also stated that judicial economy "demanded" resolution of the district court action prior to continuance of the CDA claim.

Stays have been denied even though a fraud case is pending in a district court. In *Meridith Relocation Corp.*, GSBCA 9124, 90-2 BCA ¶ 22,677, *recons. denied,* 90-3 BCA ¶ 23,129, the board denied a stay even though a civil fraud case had recently been filed in a district court. The board reasoned that the issues were not identical and that the contractor had a right to an expeditious resolution of its appeal of a default termination. Similarly, in *TDC Mgmt. Corp.*, DOTBCA 1802, 90-1 BCA ¶ 22,627, the board declined to suspend an appeal, pending resolution of a concurrent civil action under the False Claims Act, noting that the issues on appeal were separate from those under the False Claims Act proceeding. The board stated that the False Claims Act proceeding involved falsified progress reports whereas the appeal before the board involved a claim for reimbursement of a cost overrun.

Stays are more likely to be denied if the government has not filed a criminal or civil fraud case in court. See, for example, *Triax Co.*, ASBCA 33899, 88-3 BCA ¶ 20,830, in which the board refused to grant a stay upon the "mere allegation" of fraud by the government, and *Fleischzentrale Sudwest GmbH*, ASBCA 37273, 89-3 BCA ¶ 21,956, in which the board refused to stay the proceedings even though the government had submitted an affidavit stating that a criminal investigation was underway. In *Fleischzentrale*, the board stated a stringent test for the government at 110,444:

> [T]he Government . . . is obliged to show a compelling "need in terms of protecting the criminal litigation" which "overrides the injury to the parties being stayed" and that "there are `substantially similar' issues, facts and witnesses in both proceedings," *E-Systems, Inc.*, [ASBCA 32033, 88-2 BCA ¶ 20,753] at 104,868. "[T]he supplicant for a stay must make out a clear case of hardship or inequity in being required to go forward, *if there is even a fair possibility* that the stay for which he prays will work damage to someone else," [emphasis added] *Landis v. North American Company*, 229 U.S. 248, 255 (1936).

The ASBCA has been the most aggressive board in determining that fraud does not totally deprive it of jurisdiction. In *Nexus Constr. Co.,* ASBCA 51004, 98-1 BCA ¶ 29,375, the board held that an allegation that the contractor submitted a fraudulent claim does not deprive the board of jurisdiction under the CDA. In *Donat Gerg Haustechnik,* ASBCA 41197, 96-2 BCA ¶ 28,333, the board held that it is not prohibited from considering assertions of fraud in a counterclaim against a contractor because the prohibition against consideration of issues involving fraud in the CDA,

41 USC § 605(a), applies to agency heads, not boards. Similarly, the government was permitted to raise fraud as an affirmative defense to the contractor's claim even though the board would not have jurisdiction over a counterclaim of fraud unless it had been set forth in the contracting officer's final decision, *ORC, Inc.*, ASBCA 49693, 96-2 BCA ¶ 28,371; *Westphal GmbH & Co.*, ASBCA 39401, 96-1 BCA ¶ 28,194, *recons. denied,* 96-2 BCA ¶ 28,466, *aff'd in part, remanded in part, 1*35 F.3d 778 (Fed. Cir. 1998) (case remanded so board could consider unpriced work claims*)*. In *TRW, Inc.*, ASBCA 51172, 99-2 BCA ¶ 30,407, the board held that it had jurisdiction over a contractor's contract interpretation claim although the underlying facts were also the subject of two parallel U.S. District Court qui tam lawsuits under the False Claims Act.

If a board decides a case in which the government contends that fraud is present, the contractor probably will not collect on the decision until the fraud allegation is resolved, *TDC Mgmt. Corp.*, DOTBCA 1802, 88-1 BCA ¶ 20,242. In *TDC*, the board stated at 102,466 that:

> Government agencies have legal authority to withhold payment from a contractor of amounts which a Board determines to be due that contractor on a claim, in the nature of set-off, until issues of fraud have been disposed of by a court having jurisdiction over Government claims for civil or criminal penalties

In *United States v. Marovic*, 69 F.Supp. 2d 1190 (N.D. Cal. 1999), the government argued that its breach of contract and unjust enrichment claims were properly before the District Court because the CDA's exclusive jurisdiction does not apply to any claim "involving fraud," 41 USC § 605(a). Noting that the CDA was established to foster administrative resolution of government contract disputes, the District Court adopted a narrow reading of the "involving fraud" exception to CDA jurisdiction and held that the exception did not apply in this case because the government could prove its contract claims against the contractor without proving that the contractor itself committed fraud.

Although in most cases the contract and fraud claims are heard in separate forums, the Court of Federal Claims can take jurisdiction over both civil fraud and contract claims when the contractor asserts a contract claim and the government subsequently asserts the civil fraud as a counterclaim, *Young-Montenay, Inc. v. United States*, 15 F.3d 1040 (Fed. Cir. 1994). In this situation, the decision of whether to merge the claims in a single court is in the hands of the Department of Justice. For cases in which both civil fraud and contract claims were merged in the Court of Federal Claims, see *Godley v. United States*, 26 Cl. Ct. 1075 (1992), *vacated and remanded on other grounds*, 5 F.3d 1473 (Fed. Cir. 1993), and *Sterling Millwrights, Inc. v. United States*, 26 Cl. Ct. 49 (1992). In these cases, although the court heard the government's fraud counterclaims, it dismissed all of the charges as either late or insufficiently supported by the evidence. Fraud counterclaims also may be filed by the government without first obtaining a contracting officer decision on the counterclaims, *Martin J. Simko Constr., Inc. v. United States*, 852 F.2d 540 (Fed. Cir. 1988). This rule is premised on the fact that a contracting officer has no authority under the CDA to handle fraud claims. One of the outcomes of this procedure is that the contractor gives up its right to a jury trial on the fraud claim, which has been held to be a consequence of the contractor's election to file its contract claim in the Court of Federal Claims, *BMY-Combat Sys. Div. of Harsco Corp. v. United States*, 26 Cl. Ct. 846 (1992). See also *Daff v. United States*, 78 F.3d 1566 (Fed. Cir. 1996), in which the court ruled that the Court of Federal Claims had jurisdiction of a default termination even though the contracting officer's decision referred to contractor fraud because there were other grounds for the termination. Having such jurisdiction also gave the court jurisdiction over the government's counterclaim under the False Claims Act even though there had been no contracting officer decision on that issue.

Section 2354 of the Federal Acquisition Streamlining Act of 1994, Pub. L. 103-355, amended the CDA to give U.S. District Court judges authority to obtain advisory opinions from boards of contract appeals by adding the following to 41 U.S.C. § 609:

> (f)(1) Whenever an action involving an issue described in paragraph (2) is pending in a district court of the United States, the district court may request a board of contract appeals to provide the court with an advisory opinion on the matters of contract interpretation at issue.
>
> (2) An issue referred to in paragraph (1) is any issue that could be the proper subject of a final decision of a contracting officer appealable under this Act.
>
> (3) A district court shall direct any request under paragraph (1) to the board of contract appeals having jurisdiction under this Act to adjudicate appeals of contract claims under the contract or contracts being interpreted by the court.
>
> (4) After receiving a request for an advisory opinion under paragraph (1), a board of contract appeals shall provide the advisory opinion in a timely manner to the district court making the request.

This authority could be used to obtain advisory opinions on contract issues involved in fraud cases.

3. *Penalties or Forfeitures Administered by Other Agencies*

41 U.S.C. § 605(a) provides:

> The authority of this subsection shall not extend to a claim or dispute for penalties or forfeitures prescribed by statute or regulation which another federal agency is specifically authorized to administer, settle or determine.

The legislative history is silent on the meaning of this statutory language, the primary effect of which has been to exclude certain labor-related disputes from the scope of the disputes process. Historically, the boards have refused to exercise jurisdiction over matters that involve determining the contractor's obligations under a variety of statutes prescribing labor standards for contractors. These statutes include the Davis-Bacon Act, 40 U.S.C. § 276; the Service Contract Act, 41 U.S.C. § 351; and the Contract Work Hours and Safety Standards Act, 40 U.S.C. § 327. See *Imperator Carpet & Interiors, Inc.*, GSBCA 6167, 81-2 BCA ¶ 15,266; *Wickham Contracting Co.*, GSBCA 6579, 82-2 BCA ¶ 15,883; and *James B. Nolan Investigative & Protective Co.*, GSBCA 5905, 82-2 BCA ¶ 15,943. In addition, boards held that they lacked jurisdiction to consider a maritime subcontractor's claim, despite District Court precedent to the contrary, *Southwest Marine, Inc.,* ASBCA 49617, 96-2 BCA ¶ 28,347.

In *Dalton v. Sherwood Van Lines, Inc.*, 50 F.3d 1014 (Fed. Cir. 1995), the court concluded that the CDA provided no jurisdictional basis for disputes concerning transportation services obtained from common carriers through government bills of lading. See *Merchants Moving & Storage, Inc.,* ASBCA 48308, 95-2 BCA ¶ 27,789, which relied on *Dalton* and held the board had no jurisdiction. This undercuts the validity of *Merchants Moving & Storage Inc.*, ASBCA 47370, 95-1 BCA ¶ 27,298, which held the board had subject matter jurisdiction over a dispute arising out of a contract to transport household goods because the CDA contains broad language in covering contracts for vehicular services and does not specifically exempt agreements that might also be covered by the Interstate Commerce Act or the Transportation Act of 1940. See also *Stapp Touring Co.*, ASBCA 48375, 96-2 BCA ¶ 28,293 (a dispute under a bulk fuel transportation contract was governed by the Interstate Commerce Act and deprived the board of jurisdiction). See *Custom Blending & Packaging, Inc.,* ASBCA 49819, 00-2 BCA ¶ 31,083, holding that the board had no authority to consider a claim that Department of Agriculture inspectors had delayed performance because they were functioning under a separate statute calling for inspection of plants processing food products.

The matters that other agencies have cognizance over are usually issues in the Labor Department. Service contracts subject to the Service Contract Act contain the following provision in the Service Contract Act of 1965, As Amended clause, FAR 52.222-41:

> (t) *Disputes Concerning Labor Standards*. The U.S. Department of Labor has set forth in 29 CFR parts 4, 6, and 8 procedures for resolving disputes concerning labor standards requirements. Such disputes shall be resolved in accordance with those procedures and not the Disputes clause of this contract. Disputes within the meaning of this clause include disputes between the Contractor (or any of its subcontractors) and the contracting agency, the U.S. Department of Labor, or the employees or their representatives.

See *J.R. Cheshier Janitorial*, ENGBCA 5487-Q, 95-1 BCA ¶ 27,376 no board jurisdiction over dispute on requirement to pay overtime); *Ball, Ball & Brosamerr Inc.*,

IBCA 3542-95, 98-1 BCA ¶ 29,637 (no board jurisdiction over a dispute involving the proper classification of laborers for wage purposes); and *Midland Maint., Ins.*, ENGBCA 6080, 96-2 BCA ¶ 28,302 (no board jurisdiction over a dispute involving wage classification). Compare *Inter-Con Sec. Sys., Inc.*, ASBCA 46251, 95-1 BCA ¶ 27,424, in which the board took jurisdiction to decide whether a modification of a collective bargaining agreement was part of a wage determination by the Department of Labor because the board's decision was neither the making of a wage determination nor a ruling on the propriety of a wage determination.

Construction contracts contain the following Disputes Concerning Labor Standards clause, FAR 52.222-14:

> The United States Department of Labor has set forth in 29 CFR parts 5, 6, and 7 procedures for resolving disputes concerning labor standards requirements. Such disputes shall be resolved in accordance with those procedures and not the Disputes clause of this contract. Disputes within the meaning of this clause include disputes between the Contractor (or any of its subcontractors) and the contracting agency, the U.S. Department of Labor, or the employees or their representatives.

See *Emerald Maint., Inc. v. United States*, 925 F.2d 1425 (Fed. Cir. 1991) (no board jurisdiction over application of wage determination). Compare *MMC Constr. Inc.*, ASBCA 50863, 99-1 BCA ¶ 30,322, taking jurisdiction to decide a contractor's breach of contract claim against the government based on excessive withholding of Davis-Bacon Act wages because the Department of Labor had completed its investigation of the alleged wage underpayments and the government had withheld those amounts from contract progress payments due the contractor. The board concluded that, although DOL wage determinations generally may be disputed only through DOL's administrative process, where that process is completed and a contractor "claims a price adjustment for the effects of the DOL wage determination," the boards (or Court of Federal Claims) have jurisdiction of the claim under the CDA. The GSBCA reached the same conclusion in *Twigg Corp. v. General Servs. Admin.*, GSBCA 14639, 99-1 BCA ¶ 30,217.

4. Contract Award Controversies and Mistakes Alleged Prior to Award

Challenges to procurement contract award procedures are not subject to the CDA. The Act covers disputes between the contractor and the government that arise during or after the performance of a contract but does not cover contract award controversies that result when an offeror or prospective contractor contests the award of the contract or the conduct of the solicitation process itself, *Coastal Corp. v. United States*, 713 F.2d 728 (Fed. Cir. 1983). The Competition in Contracting Act (CICA) establishes protest procedures for challenging the conduct of an agency procurement process. For a discussion of these protest procedures, see *Formation of Government Contracts* (3d ed. 1998), Chapter 11. See also *Meyers Co.*, ENGBCA 6360, 98-1

BCA ¶ 29,473 (board lacked jurisdiction over a bid protest involving a solicitation for outleases because the Secretary of the Army had delegated authority to consider only appeals concerning leases and lessees, not protests by disappointed bidders); *Integrated Sys. Group Inc.*, GSBCA 11336-C (11214-P), 95-1 BCA ¶ 27,308 (board had no jurisdiction over intervenor's motion to recover costs of defending a protest brought in bad faith because it lacked authority to adjudicate rights between private parties); *Ammon Circuits Research*, ASBCA 50885, 97-2 BCA ¶ 29,318 (no jurisdiction over agency's failure to award contract); and *RC 27th Ave. Corp.*, ASBCA 49176, 97-1 BCA ¶ 28,658 (no jurisdiction of claim for lost profits because of failure to award contract).

Preaward mistakes also are not covered by the CDA. Suspected mistakes in contractors' proposals are dealt with either as clarifications or discussions, depending on the circumstances. For a discussion of this process, see *Formation of Government Contracts* (3d ed. 1998), Chapter 6, and *Cost-Reimbursement Contracting* (3d ed. 2004), Chapter 5.

5. Violation of Statutory or Constitutional Rights

The boards lack jurisdiction to consider claims of racial discrimination under the Fifth Amendment or any federal statute, *Sturghill Alternative Energy Corp.*, ASBCA 49612, 98-1 BCA ¶ 29,708; *Duran Constr. Co.*, AGBCA 19991712, 00-1 BCA ¶ 30,758 (no jurisdiction over contractor's claim for "racial prejudice"); *Northeast Air Group, Inc.*, ASBCA 46350, 95-2 BCA ¶ 27,679 (no jurisdiction over alleged violation of contractor's civil rights). The boards have also held that they have no jurisdiction over claims under other statutes. See *McKirch & Co.*, ASBCA 51824, 99-2 BCA ¶ 30,468 (no jurisdiction over alleged violations of the Constitution, the Trade Secrets Act, the Copyright Act, state Trade Secrets Acts, and the common law), and *Data Enters. of the Northwest v. General Servs. Admin.*, GSBCA 15607, 04-1 BCA ¶ 32,539 (no jurisdiction over alleged violations of the Copyright Act or Fifth Amendment takings). Compare *Ervin & Assocs., Inc. v. United States*, 59 Fed. Cl. 267 (2004), in which the Court of Federal Claims ruled on a claim for copyright infringement.

Although the Court of Federal Claims has jurisdiction over "taking" claims under the Fifth Amendment pursuant to the Tucker Act, the boards of contract appeals have no such jurisdiction under the CDA, *United Techs. Corp.*, ASBCA 46880, 95-1 BCA ¶ 27,456, *recons. denied,* 95-2 BCA ¶ 27,698; *Sermor, Inc.*, ASBCA 46956, 95-2 BCA ¶ 27,748.

C. Subcontractor Controversies

Generally, subcontractors have no right to use the disputes process in their own name. See *Lockheed Martin Corp. v. United States*, 50 Fed. Cl. 550 (2001), *aff'd,*

48 Fed. Appx. 752 (Fed. Cir. 2002); *Detroit Broach Cutting Tools, Inc.*, ASBCA 49277, 96-2 BCA ¶ 28,493; *Southwest Marine, Inc.*, ASBCA 49617, 96-2 BCA ¶ 28,347; and *Department of Army v. Blue Fox*, 525 U.S. 255 (1999). However, in the rare case where a subcontractor is in privity of contract with the government, it may file a claim directly against the government. If there is no privity, the subcontractor's claim must be sponsored by the contractor.

1. Direct Subcontractor Claims

It is against the government's policy to deal directly with subcontractors. See FAR 44.203(b)(3), which prohibits contracting officers from giving their consent to "subcontracts obligating the contracting officer to deal directly with the subcontractor." As a result, direct subcontractor claims are very rare.

There are several possible—but not often successful—ways for a subcontractor to establish privity. In some cases, the government has entered into a direct contractual relationship with a subcontractor. See *United States v. Georgia Marble Co.*, 106 F.2d 955 (5th Cir. 1939), in which the court found that the government entered into an implied contract to pay the subcontractor for material the government took from the subcontractor. Such cases are extremely rare. In addition, direct subcontractor claims have been permitted if the contractor is an agent of the government, *Kern-Limerick v. Scurlock*, 347 U.S. 110 (1954). Here, too, the likelihood of a contractor being considered an agent of the government is remote. In *United States v. Johnson Controls, Inc.*, 713 F.2d 1541 (Fed. Cir. 1983), *aff'd,* 827 F.2d 1554 (Fed. Cir. 1987), the court held that a contractor that served as a construction manager was not, for that reason, an agent of the government. The court stated that the contractor was not a purchasing agent, that there was no contractual designation of an agency relationship with the government, and that the government was not bound to pay the subcontractor directly. See also *United States v. New Mexico*, 455 U.S. 720 (1982), in which the Court stated that contractors operating government facilities had a substantially independent role in making purchases, were not agents of the government, and, therefore, were not immune from taxation. Similarly, in *Parsons Brinckerhoff Quade & Douglas, Inc.*, DOTCAB 1299, 84-2 BCA ¶ 17,309, the board denied a subcontractor's claim, holding that the subcontractor had no privity with the government. The board stated at 86,266:

> It is a general rule that, under the Tucker Act, a subcontractor cannot recover directly from the Government as there is no contractual relationship. *Merritt v. United States*, 267 U.S. 338 (1925). However, if some type of contract can be found to exist between a subcontractor and the Government, an action may be directly brought. *United States v. Munsey Trust Co.* [4 CCF ¶ 60,304], 332 U.S. 234, 241 (1947). In *Kern-Limerick Inc. v. Scurlock* [6 CCF ¶ 61,498], 347 U.S. 110 (1954) and *Western Union Telegraph Co. v. United States*, 66 Ct. Cl. 38 (1938), the courts permitted a subcontractor to bring an action directly against the United States since the prime contractor was simply acting as the Government's

> agent. Both of these cases have carved out narrow exceptions to the general rule that waivers of sovereign immunity are to be strictly construed. *United States v. Mitchell*, 445 U.S. 535 (1980).

The board found that the government had made it clear that it could not deal directly with Parsons and that Parsons assented to this relationship by executing its contract with the contractor and by requesting payment from the contractor. Thus, the board found that there was no contractual relationship between the government and the subcontractor. For a discussion of agency relationship between the government and a contractor, see Chapter 1.

The most feasible way of establishing privity is for the subcontractor to make its claim as a third-party beneficiary of the government's agreement with a contractor. See *Maneely v. United States*, 68 Ct. Cl. 623 (1929). See also *D & H Distrib. Co. v. United States*, 102 F.3d 542 (Fed. Cir. 1996), in which the court found that a subcontractor had a third-party beneficiary relationship with the government when the contracting officer had modified the contract to make the contractor and the subcontractor joint payees. In addition, despite the statutory prohibition on the assignment of rights in government contracts, the court found that the contract modification at issue could be viewed as a valid assignment of payment rights from the contractor to the subcontractor because the contracting officer assented to the assignment. The government's subsequent failure to make payments according to the modified contract was a breach entitling the subcontractor to damages. See also *FloorPro, Inc.*, ASBCA 54143, 04-1 BCA 32571 (board has jurisdiction of subcontractor appeal as third-party beneficiary). But see *JGB Enters., Inc. v. United States,* 63 Fed. Cl. 319 (2004), stating that the Federal Circuit in D&H had only allowed third-party jurisdiction on the basis of the Tucker Act, not the CDA but granting relief as a third-party beneficiary on one contract. See also *Flexfab, L.L.C. v. United States,* 62 Fed. Cl. 139 (2004), *aff'd*, 424 F.3d 1254 (Fed. Cir. 2005), denying recovery as third-party beneficiary because the government employee that authorized the payment to an agent of the subcontractor had no contracting officer authority.

Contracts administered through the Small Business Administration (SBA) 8(a) Program are technically contracts between the procuring agency and the SBA; the SBA then subcontracts out to preferred 8(a) contractors. However, the boards have uniformly held that such SBA subcontractors are in privity with the government and, therefore, able to bring claims directly against the government under the Disputes Act, *Decorama Painting, Inc.*, ASBCA 25299, 81-1 BCA ¶ 14,992, *modified on other grounds*, 82-1 BCA ¶ 15,746. Some Department of Energy Management and Operations (M&O) contracts contained provisions authorizing subcontractors to obtain decisions by contracting officers and to take appeals to the Department's board of contract appeals. See, e.g., *Lafollette Coal Co.*, EBCA 336585, 87-3 BCA ¶ 20,099. Where the M&O contract does not contain such a provision, the board will not take the subcontractor's appeal, *Johnson Tank & Tower Co.*, EBCA 9302148, 93-3 BCA ¶ 26,251.

2. Indirect (Sponsored) Subcontractor Claims

Sponsored claims are permitted only if the contractor can charge the cost of the subcontractor's claim to the government contract or make a claim against the government based on the subcontractor's recovery. This practice, developed under the pre-statutory process, has been continued under the CDA. The contractor sponsors the subcontractor's claim by bringing an appeal on the subcontractor's behalf or by permitting the subcontractor to bring an appeal in the contractor's name. FAR 44.203(c) explicitly allows indirect subcontractor appeals and provides that:

> Contracting officers should not refuse consent to a subcontract merely because it contains a clause giving the subcontractor the right of indirect appeal to an agency board of contract appeals if the subcontractor is affected by a dispute between the Government and the prime contractor. Indirect appeal means assertion by the subcontractor of the prime contractor's right to appeal or the prosecution of an appeal by the prime contractor on the subcontractor's behalf. The clause may also provide that the prime contractor and subcontractor shall be equally bound by the contracting officer's or board's decision. The clause may not attempt to obligate the contracting officer or the appeals board to decide questions that do not arise between the Government and the prime contractor or that are not cognizable under the clause at 52.2331, Disputes.

The Severin Doctrine limits a subcontractor's right to have its claim sponsored by the contractor. It is based upon the theory that if the contractor has not paid the subcontractor and has no possible liability to the subcontractor, the contractor has suffered no harm at the hands of the government. See *Severin v. United States*, 99 Ct. Cl. 435 (1943), *cert. denied*, 322 U.S. 733 (1944), holding that, if the subcontract contains a clause exculpating the contractor from liability for damages to the subcontractor, the contractor may sue on behalf of its subcontractor only if the contractor has reimbursed its subcontractor for the latter's damages or remains liable for such reimbursement in the future. Later cases have limited the application of the *Severin* doctrine by interpreting exculpatory clauses as applying only to breach of contract claims. Thus, the doctrine has been held inapplicable to claims covered by contract clauses, such as those for constructive changes, for equitable adjustment under the Changes clause. See *F.E. Constructors*, ASBCA 25784, 82-1 BCA ¶ 15,780, and *Aydin Corp.*, EBCA 355586, 89-3 BCA ¶ 22,044. Similarly, see *CWC, Inc.*, ASBCA 26432, 82-2 BCA ¶ 15,907, in which the board held that the *Severin* Doctrine was inapplicable to a contractor's sponsorship of a claim for a price adjustment because the claim was redressable under the contract's Suspension of Work clause. The same result has been reached for claims based on the Differing Site Conditions clause, *Turner Constr. Co.*, ASBCA 25602, 87-3 BCA ¶ 20,192; *Tutor-Saliba-Parini*, PSBCA 1201, 87-2 BCA ¶ 19,775, *aff'd*, 847 F.2d 842 (Fed. Cir. 1988). If the exculpatory clause does not completely free the contractor from liability, sponsorship will be permitted. Thus, when the subcontract provides that the contractor will pass subcontractor claims through to the government but will have no further liability, it has been held that the *Severin* doctrine does not bar the claim, *Castagna & Son,*

Inc., GSBCA 6906, 84-3 BCA ¶ 17,612. See also *Folk Constr. Co. v. United States*, 2 Cl. Ct. 681 (1983), and *Pan Arctic Corp. v. United States*, 8 Cl. Ct. 546 (1985). A clause that relieves the contractor from responsibility to the subcontractor for price increases, damages, and additional compensation as a consequence of delay does not necessarily preclude the contractor from recovering against the government on behalf of its subcontractor; *Roberts, JR. Corp.*, DOTBCA 2499, 98-1 BCA ¶ 29,680. In *Ball, Ball & Brasamer, Inc.,* IBCA 2841, 97-1 BCA ¶ 28,897, the board held that the doctrine did not apply because the contractor was liable to the subcontractor for any payment the contractor received from the government, and the subcontractor had not released its claim against the contractor.

The Severin Doctrine will not apply if the agreement between the parties conditions the contractor's liability to the subcontractor on recovery from the government, *J.L. Simmons Co. v. United States*, 158 Ct. Cl. 393, 304 F.2d 886 (1962). In *W.G. Yates & Sons Constr. Co. v. Caldera,* 192 F.3d 987 (Fed. Cir. 1999), both the contractor and a subcontractor pursued their claim against the government pursuant to a "Liquidation and Consolidation Claim Agreement" where the contractor agreed to sponsor the claims and pay the subcontractor the amount it recovered. In exchange, the contractor received a promise to pay the contractor's reprocurement costs regardless of the board's decision. The court determined that this agreement making the contractor "conditionally liable" to the subcontractor avoided the application of the Severin Doctrine.

Although the Severin Doctrine has infrequently precluded sponsored claims, it still has vitality in those cases in which the contractor has paid the subcontractor no money and is not even conditionally liable. See *James Reeves Contractor, Inc. v. United States*, 31 Fed. Cl. 712 (1994), in which an arbitration binding under state law denied the subcontractor's claim against the contractor without reservation. In *George Hyman Constr. Co. v. United States*, 30 Fed. Cl. 170 (1993), *aff'd,* 39 F.3d 1197 (Fed. Cl. 1994), the subcontractor executed a general release in favor of the contractor. The court held that this release was unconditional and that sponsorship was not permitted. The court rejected the contractor's argument that the parties had not intended to include the particular claim in the release. It also rejected a later release excepting the claim. The court held that even if the later release were binding under state law, sponsorship would not be permitted because it depended on "continuing" not "revived" liability.

The right of a subcontractor to appeal in the name of a contractor has been affirmed, even when the contractor has neither paid the claim nor admitted liability, as long as the claim is made in good faith, *TRW, Inc.*, ASBCA 11373, 66-2 BCA ¶ 5882, and the contractor intends to be held liable for any possible fraud attributable to assertion of the claim, *Transamerica Ins. Corp., Inc. v. United States*, 973 F.2d 1572 (Fed. Cir. 1992); *Blake Constr. Co. v. United States*, 28 Fed. Cl. 672 (1993), *aff'd,* 29 F.3d 645 (Fed. Cir. 1994). However, the fact that the contractor does not agree with the subcontractor may be used as evidence of the reasonableness of the government's position, *Willard-Brent Co.*, GSBCA 3651, 73-2 BCA ¶ 10,134. Sponsorship is considered an evidentiary rather than a jurisdictional matter. Thus, it is sufficient if sponsorship is alleged by statements in the complaint. Proof of sponsorship is not necessary at the time of filing the notice of appeal, although a complete failure to plead sponsorship would give rise to the jurisdictional question, *Dawson Constr. Co.*, EBCA 155281, 81-2 BCA ¶ 15,162. See *Coastal Drilling, Inc.*, ASBCA 54023, 03-1 BCA ¶ 32,241 (board refused to take jurisdiction of an unsponsored claim of a subcontractor even where fraud on the part of the contractor is alleged); *Malaspina Invs., Inc. (Sampson Steel Co., Subcontractor),* AGBCA 2003-180-1, 04-1 BCA ¶ 32,418 (board took jurisdiction based on letter from contractor's president, sent after 90-day appeal period had expired, stating that contractor's project coordinator had requested subcontractor to send appeal directly to the board); and *J. E. McAmis, Inc.* ASBCA 54455, 04-2 BCA ¶ 32,746 (appeal was proper when contractor certified and forwarded subcontractor's Notice of Appeal and requested that it be sent a Rule 4 file even though contractor did not specifically state that it was appealing the contracting officer's decision).

Although a contractor may sponsor the claim of a subcontractor, the subcontractor has no privity of contract with the government and is not a proper party before a board of contract appeals. See *Zenith Data Sys.*, ASBCA 49611, 98-1 BCA ¶ 29,721, in which the board denied a contractor's request to add its subcontractor as a "co-appellant." See also *McPherson Contractors, Inc.*, ASBCA 50830, 98-1 BCA ¶ 29,349 (board has no jurisdiction over an appeal by a contractor on behalf of its subcontractor after the contractor withdrew its sponsorship). After a termination for default, a surety took over and entered into a subcontract with the original contractor to complete the job. On appeal, the default termination was overturned and converted to a termination for convenience. The board held it did not have jurisdiction over that part of the termination settlement proposal covering costs incurred while contractor was acting as subcontractor to the surety because the claim was not sponsored by the surety, *Walsky Constr. Co.,* ASBCA 52772, 01-2 BCA ¶ 31,557.

II. ASSERTION OF CLAIMS

The submission of a claim initiates the disputes process. The contractor's claim triggers the contracting officer's obligation to make a timely decision, 41 U.S.C. § 605(c), and begins the running of interest, 41 U.S.C. § 611. The CDA contains no definition of the word *claim*. It does, however, at 41 U.S.C. § 605(a), specify two requirements for a claim: "All claims by a contractor against the Government relating to a contract shall be in writing and shall be submitted to the contracting officer for a decision." The Disputes clause at FAR 52.233-1 provides additional guidance on the definition of *claim*, as follows:

> Claim, as used in this clause, means a written demand or written assertion by one of the contracting parties seeking, as a matter of right, the payment of money in a sum certain, the adjustment or interpretation of contract terms, or other relief

> arising under or relating to this contract. . . . A voucher, invoice, or other routine request for payment that is not in dispute when submitted is not a claim under the Act. The submission may be converted into a claim under the Act, by complying with the submission and certification requirements of this clause, if it is disputed either as to liability or amount or is not acted upon in a reasonable time.

The following discussion considers the essential elements of a claim by examining the requirement that a claim be a nonroutine request for payment; the assertion of nonmonetary claims; the elements of a contractor claim; the assertion of a government claim; and the time for submittal of claims.

A. Nonroutine Requests for Price Adjustment

The early interpretation of the term "claim" had treated the first two sentences of the FAR definition as establishing the full requirements governing whether a contractor had properly asserted a claim under the CDA. However, in *Dawco Constr., Inc. v. United States*, 930 F.2d 872 (Fed. Cir. 1991), the Federal Circuit read the entire definition to require that no contractor claim (not just undisputed requests for payment) could be properly asserted unless there had been a "preexisting dispute." Since there was virtually no support for this interpretation in the history of the drafting of the CDA or its implementation in the FAR, the issue was reconsidered by the court in *Reflectone, Inc. v. Dalton*, 60 F.3d 1572 (Fed. Cir. 1995). That decision overruled *Dawco* and held that only claims for routine requests for payment had to be based on preexisting disputes. Thus, a contractor submitting a "nonroutine" request for additional compensation or other action under the Disputes clause is not required to bring the matter to "dispute" between the parties before it can submit a valid claim under the CDA.

1. *Distinguishing Routine and Nonroutine Requests for Payment*

All requests for price adjustment called for by contract clauses constitute nonroutine requests—including a request for equitable adjustment for a constructive change, *AAA Eng'g & Drafting, Inc.*, ASBCA 47940, 99-2 BCA ¶ 30,443; *McDonnell Douglas Corp.*, ASBCA 46582, 96-2 BCA ¶ 28,377; a request for equitable adjustment for ordered changes, *Triad Microsystems, Inc.*, ASBCA 39478, 99-1 BCA ¶ 30,234; a request for an equitable adjustment for a recognized differing site condition, *J.S. Alberici Constr. Co.*, ENGBCA 6179, 97-1 BCA ¶ 28,639; a claim for lost revenue, *Schleicher Cmty. Corrections Ctr., Inc.*, DOTBCA 3046, 98-2 BCA ¶ 29,941; a request for a contract rate adjustment to reflect wage and fringe benefit changes made by a contractor in accordance with a wage determination issued by the Department of Labor, *Keydata Sys., Inc. v. Department of the Treasury*, GSBCA 14281-TD, 97-2 BCA ¶ 29,330. In such cases, the contractor has the choice of submitting a request for equitable adjustment ("REA") to the contracting officer—calling for a negotiated settlement—or of submitting a CDA claim requesting a contracting officer decision and starting the running of interest. See *Twigg Corp. v. General Servs. Admin.*, GSBCA 13345, 97-2 BCA ¶ 29,088, where the board held that the contractor was not entitled to CDA interest because it had submitted a proposal for pricing a contract modification rather than a CDA claim.

Claims for damages for breach of contract or a cardinal change are nonroutine requests for payment, *Kentucky Bridge & Dam, Inc. v. United States*, 42 Fed. Cl. 501 (1998). A request for interpretation of the cost principles to determine the allowability of designated costs (unquantified) is also a nonroutine request, *TRW, Inc.*, ASBCA 51172, 99-2 BCA ¶ 30,407.

Routine requests for payment include billing of the contract price for articles delivered or services rendered, billing for progress payments, *American Serv. & Supply, Inc.*, ASBCA 50606, 00-1 BCA ¶ 30,858, and submitting a voucher for allowable costs or fee under a cost-reimbursement contract, *Moshman Assocs., Inc.*, ASBCA 52320, 00-1 BCA ¶ 30,906 (final voucher). However, invoices sent requesting payment for modifications that had not been negotiated were not routine requests but were claims, *MDP Constr., Inc.*, ASBCA 52769, 01-1 BCA ¶ 31,359.

2. Routine Request Converted Into a Claim

A routine request for payment may be "converted" into a claim. However, it will not be converted automatically, *Martin Marietta Corp.*, ASBCA 25828, 84-1 BCA ¶ 17,119 ("transformation of a routine voucher into a claim does not take place automatically, as if by osmosis, or upon the mere passage of time"). For a conversion to take place, the contractor must make a formal demand subsequent to an unreasonable delay in payment or disagreement with the Government, *JWA Emadel Enters., Inc.*, ASBCA 51016, 98-2 BCA ¶ 29,765, *recons. denied*, 98-2 BCA ¶ 29,960 (*resubmission* of a voucher which had previously been submitted and denied will be considered a nonroutine request for payment); *TRS Research*, ASBCA 50086, 98-2 BCA ¶ 29,780 (claim filed after nonpayment of legitimate invoices a valid CDA claim); *Falcon Research & Dev. Co.*, ASBCA 27002, 82-2 BCA ¶ 16,049 (invoice converted to claim only after contractor made formal demand subsequent to an unreasonable delay in payment). But see *Sprint Communications Co. v. General Servs. Admin.*, GSBCA 15139, 01-2 BCA ¶ 31,464 (no claim for Prompt Payment Act interest submitted to contracting officer); *A.T. Kearney, Inc.*, DOTCAB 1263, 83-2 BCA ¶ 16,835, *recons. denied*, 84-1 BCA ¶ 17,052 (invoice never converted into a claim by a request for a written decision); and *Granite Constr. Co.*, ASBCA 26023, 83-2 BCA ¶ 16,843 (long Government delay in payment of undisputed amounts not converted without further action by the contractor).

3. REA Submissions Converted Into Claim

Many contractors submit their initial request as a proposal rather than a claim to facilitate a negotiated settlement. The primary reason for proceeding in this manner is that costs incurred during the negotiation process generally will be considered administration costs and will most likely be allowable costs. By proceeding in this manner contractors forgo the commencement of interest on a claim. However, costs incurred during the negotiation process will most likely exceed what the contractor would have received in interest on the claim. Another reason for submitting a proposal such as an REA rather than a claim is that the submission of a claim may chill negotiations. If the contracting officer does not act on the proposal or there is a breakdown in negotiations, then the contractor can submit a claim. Generally the necessary steps to covert the REA proposal into a claim is requesting a contracting officer's final decision and certifying the claim, if it is over the $100,000 threshold. See *AAA Eng'g & Drafting, Inc.*, ASBCA 47940, 99-2 BCA ¶ 30,443 (proposal subsequently converted into claim when contractor requested final decision and certified claim).

4. Convenience Termination Settlement Proposals

The Federal Circuit has held, in *James M. Ellett Constr. Co. v. United States*, 93 F.3d 1537 (Fed. Cir. 1996), that a convenience termination settlement proposal is a nonroutine request for payment and that, if the proposal is not submitted as a claim, it will be automatically converted into a claim if the parties reach an impasse in attempting to reach a settlement. The court stated at 1543–44:

> When a contractor submits a termination settlement proposal, it is for the purpose of negotiation, not for a contracting officer's decision. A settlement proposal is just that: a proposal. *See* 48 C.F.R. § 49.001 (1995) ("a proposal for effecting settlement of a contract terminated in whole or in part, submitted by a contractor or subcontractor in the form, and supported by the data, required by this part"). Indeed, it is a proposal that Ellett contractually agreed to submit in the event of a convenience termination. The parties agreed that they would try to reach a mutually agreeable settlement. If they were unable to do so, however, it was agreed, consonant with the FAR's requirements, that the contracting officer would issue a final decision, *see id.* §§ 52.249-2(f) (Alternate I), 49.103, 49.105(a)(4), which Ellett could appeal to the court or to the Department of Agriculture Board of Contract Appeals, *id.* § 52.249-2(i). Consequently, while Ellett's termination settlement proposal met the FAR's definition of a claim, at the time of submission it was not a claim because it was not submitted to the contracting officer for a decision.
>
> Once negotiations reached an impasse, the proposal, by the terms of the FAR and the contract, was submitted for decision; it became a claim. In other words, in accordance with the contract's prescribed method of compensating Ellett for a convenience termination, a request that the contracting officer issue a decision in the event the parties were unable to agree on a settlement was implicit in Ellett's proposal. After ten months of fruitless negotiations, Ellett explicitly requested

> that the contracting officer settle its claim. This demand is tantamount to an express request for a contracting officer's decision.

See *Rapid Movers & Forwarders Co.*, ASBCA 48194, 98-2 BCA ¶ 29,339, where the board, following *Ellett*, held that a certified settlement proposal ripened into a CDA claim when the settlement negotiations reached an impasse. See also *Advanced Materials, Inc. v. United States*, 46 Fed. Cl. 697 (2000), finding a valid CDA claim when the contractor submitted a second termination settlement proposal labeled a "claim" and meeting all of the requirements for a claim.

Some appeals boards have construed this language to require that the parties reach an impasse in negotiations before there can be a CDA claim for termination for convenience settlement costs. For example, in *Central Envtl., Inc.*, ASBCA 51086, 98-2 BCA ¶ 29,912, the contractor filed a termination for convenience settlement proposal on April 29, 1997. A week later, on May 6, 1997, the contractor submitted a letter advising the contracting officer that it considered the matter "in dispute," requesting the contracting officer's final decision on its "claim" and providing a CDA certification. The contractor also stated that it would not appeal its "claim" so long as the parties were negotiating a termination settlement. The board ruled that the letter was not a CDA claim because no impasse had been reached, stating at 148,080:

> When a contractor submits a termination for convenience settlement proposal to the Government, the proposal first must ripen into a claim before we have jurisdiction to review that submission. *James M. Ellett Construction Company, Inc. v. United States*, 93 F.3d 1537, 1444 (Fed. Cir. 1996). A termination settlement proposal is not a CDA claim when it is first submitted to the contracting officer even though it otherwise meets the requirements of the CDA because the proposal is not submitted to the contracting officer for a final decision. *Id.*, 93 F.3d 1537 (Fed. Cir. 1996). Instead, the proposal represents an instrument of negotiation. *Id.*, 93 F.3d at 1543-1544; *Mid-America Eng'g and Mfg.*, ASBCA No. 48831, 96-2 BCA ¶ 28,558 at 142,585. Only after the negotiations reach an impasse, at a point when the contractor demands a final decision, does the termination proposal convert to a CDA claim. *Ellett*, 93 F.3d at 1544; *National Interior Contractors, Inc.*, ASBCA No. 46012, 96-2 BCA ¶ 28,560 at 142,588 (finding no jurisdiction without evidence of an impasse).

See also *Voices R Us, Inc*, ASBCA 51565, 01-1 BCA ¶ 31,328 ("Notwithstanding its submission . . . as a certified claim, the proposal did not become a claim until there was an impasse in negotiation"). In *Rex Sys., Inc.*, ASBCA 49502, 99-1 BCA ¶ 30,179, *recons. denied*, 99-1 BCA ¶ 30,377, *aff'd*, 224 F.3d 1367 (Fed. Cir. 2000), and *Mediax Interactive Techs., Inc.*, ASBCA 43961, 99-1 BCA ¶ 30,318, *recons. denied*, 99-2 BCA ¶ 30,453, the board discussed the impasse requirement but found that the contractor had not submitted a claim because it had not requested a contracting officer's decision when it submitted the settlement proposal. In contrast, in *Mid-America Eng'g & Mfg.*, ASBCA 48831, 96-2 BCA ¶ 28,558, the board found that a claim had been filed when the contractor, after submitting a settlement proposal, specifically requested a contracting officer's decision after the contracting officer failed to respond to a request for a meeting to negotiate a settlement. See also *McDonnell Douglas Corp. v. United States*, 37 Fed. Cl. 285 (1997), *rev'd on other grounds*, 182 F.3d 1319 (Fed. Cir. 1999), where the court found that an impasse had been reached immediately when the contractor demanded a termination for convenience settlement after its contract had been terminated for default. See also *Kit Pack Co.*, ASBCA 53155, 01-2 BCA ¶ 31,479, where the board stated that interest would begin to run from the date of the termination settlement proposal submitted as a CDA claim shortly after a termination for default. The board also held that it would not rule on the termination claim until it had determined whether the contract had been improperly default terminated.

In *Ellett*, the court held that requests for equitable adjustment submitted as CDA claims after the contract had been terminated for convenience were valid claims without regard to the requirements pertaining to termination settlement proposals. This same result was reached in *Kentucky Bridge & Dam, Inc. v. United States*, 42 Fed. Cl. 501 (1998).

5. Continued Negotiations

Contractors and the government need not cease talking to each other after submission of a claim because they disagree on its merits. In fact, the continuation of negotiations benefits both parties and is in the spirit of the CDA. Continued offers to negotiate a settlement do not impair an existing CDA claim, *Transamerica Ins. Corp. v. United States*, 973 F.2d 1572 (Fed. Cir. 1992). See also *AAA Eng'g & Drafting, Inc.*, ASBCA 47940, 99-2 BCA ¶ 30,443; and *Holmes & Narver Servs., Inc.*, ASBCA 40111, 92-3 BCA ¶ 25,052.

B. Nonmonetary Claims versus Declaratory Relief

Under certain circumstances, claims can also be nonmonetary in nature. However, there has been considerable confusion over the distinction between nonmonetary claims and requests for declaratory relief. A declaratory judgment is a court ruling that declares the rights and other legal relations of the parties without awarding any further relief. The Declaratory Judgment Act, 28 U.S.C. § 2201, confers jurisdiction upon federal courts to hear and decide such cases. But the United States Court of Claims and its successor, the Court of Federal Claims, were never granted jurisdiction over declaratory judgments. See *United States v. King*, 395 U.S. 1 (1969).

Nonetheless, both the Court of Federal Claims and the boards of contract appeals can take jurisdiction over nonmonetary claims. The appeals boards traditionally ruled on such claims and the CDA does not restrict the practice, *Malone v. United States*, 849 F.2d 1441 (Fed. Cir. 1988). The Court of Federal Claims was given this jurisdiction in 1992 when § 907 of the Federal Courts Administration Act, Pub. L. 102-572, amended 28 U.S.C. § 1491(a)(2) to provide for jurisdiction over disputes

> concerning termination of a contract, rights in tangible or intangible property, compliance with Cost Accounting Standards, and other nonmonetary disputes on which a decision of the contracting officer has been issued under the [CDA].

See *Information Sys. & Networks Corp. v. United States*, 48 Fed. Cl. 265 (2000), exercising this jurisdiction and stating that, "A complaint for declaratory judgment appealing a denial of claims by a final decision of a contracting officer falls within the jurisdiction of the Court of Federal Claims over nonmonetary claims." The jurisdiction to rule on nonmonetary claims is recognized in FAR 33.201 and the definition of "claim" in the Disputes clause which included a demand for "the adjustment or interpretation of contract terms, or other relief arising under or relating to the contract."

The exercise of this jurisdiction is discretionary. In *Alliant Techsystems, Inc. v. United States,* 178 F.3d 1260 (Fed. Cir. 1999), *reh'g denied*, 186 F.3d 1379 (Fed. Cir. 1999), the court stated at 1271:

> [Neither] the Court of Federal Claims (or an agency board of contract appeals) is required to issue a declaration of rights whenever a contractor raises a question of contract interpretation during the course of contract performance. In responding to such a request, the court or board is free to consider the appropriateness of declaratory relief, including whether the claim involves a live dispute between the parties, whether a declaration will resolve that dispute, and whether the legal remedies available to the parties would be adequate to protect the parties' interests.
>
> While a contractor may want to know ahead of time how a contract issue will be resolved—such as whether the contractor will be entitled to additional compensation under the changes clause for a particular item of work directed by the contracting officer—such cases do not ordinarily put into question whether the contractor is obligated to perform at all. In such a case, the dispute typically concerns whether the government will be obligated to grant an equitable adjustment after the ordered performance is completed. It would normally be appropriate in such cases for the court or board to decline to issue a declaratory judgment and to await a later equitable adjustment claim by the contractor. In refusing a request for declaratory relief in the absence of a need for an early declaration of the parties' rights, the court or board would be applying a principle analogous to the traditional rule that courts will not grant equitable relief when money damages are adequate.
>
> The discretion to grant declaratory relief only in limited circumstances allows the court or board to restrict the occasions for intervention during contract performance to those involving a fundamental question of contract interpretation or a special need for early resolution of a legal issue.

In *Alliant* the court took jurisdiction of the question of whether the contractor was required to perform an invalidly exercised option. In *Garrett v. General Elec. Co.*, 987 F.2d 747 (Fed. Cir. 1993), the court agreed that the appeals board properly took jurisdiction over the contracting officer's revocation of acceptance of purportedly, latently defective goods and direction to the contractor to replace the goods at no additional cost. See also *CW Gov't Travel, Inc. v. United States*, 63 Fed. Cl. 369 (2004), taking jurisdiction but denying summary judgment on the issue of whether special contract language required the government to exercise an "option," and *Tiger Natural Gas, Inc. v. United States*, 61 Fed. Cl. 287 (2004), taking jurisdiction but denying summary judgment on issue of whether the contract guaranteed a saving when furnishing natural gas.

The most common nonmonetary claim, over which the boards have always taken jurisdiction, is the validity of a default termination. See *Sharman Co. v. United States*, 30 Fed. Cl. 231 (1994), *aff'd,* 41 F.3d 1520 (Fed. Cir. 1994), in which the Court of Federal Claims took jurisdiction, retroactively, to decide this issue after the statutory change in 1992.

Another common situation where jurisdiction has been granted is claims involving the proper accounting of costs. See *Information Sys. & Networks Corp. v. United States*, 48 Fed. Cl. 265 (2000), ruling that state income taxes on the corporate income of a S corporation are reimbursable under the FAR. See also *TRW, Inc.*, ASBCA 51172, 99-2 BCA ¶ 30,407, in which the board took jurisdiction of the contractor's request for interpretation of several provisions of the cost principles, and *Robert Orr–SYSCO Food Serv. Co.*, ASBCA 51430, 97-1 BCA ¶ 28,903, interpreting the contract's Rebate clause. Compare *McDonnell Douglas Co.*, ASBCA 50592, 97-2 BCA ¶ 29,199, in which the board denied jurisdiction of the contractor's appeal of the contracting officer's disallowance of costs because the contractor did not explicitly "seek the adjustment or interpretation of contract terms." The boards have also taken jurisdiction of disputes concerning the interpretation of the Cost Accounting Standards, *Litton Sys., Inc.*, ASBCA 45400, 94-2 BCA ¶ 26,895 (CAS 405 & 410); *Litton Sys., Inc.*, ASBCA 37131, 94-2 BCA ¶ 26,731 (CAS 418); *Martin Marietta Corp.*, ASBCA 38920, 90-1 BCA ¶ 22,418 (change in accounting practice).

The court and boards have frequently denied jurisdiction when a request for contract interpretation can be readily resolved by the submission of a monetary claim. See *Westinghouse Elec. Corp.*, ASBCA 47868, 95-1 BCA ¶ 27,364, and cases cited therein. See also *Westar Eng'g, Inc.*, ASBCA 52484, 02-1 BCA ¶ 31,759, refusing to rule on whether the contractor had properly priced its equitable adjustment. The contractor had asked for this ruling as a means of overcoming a fraud investigation. See *Hamilton Secs. Advisory Servs., Inc. v. United States*, 60 Fed. Cl. 144 (2004) (refusing to rule on issue of whether government had right to withhold funds when case was scheduled for trial on contractor's monetary claim and government counterclaim), and *Aeronca, Inc.*, ASBCA 51927, 01-1 BCA ¶ 31,230 (refusing to declare whether an equitable adjustment was due because of a partial termination and whether contract modifications were binding). Compare *William D. Euille & Assocs., Inc. v. General Servs. Admin.*, GSBCA 15261, 00-1 BCA ¶ 30,910, in which the board ruled that a letter disputing the contracting officer's directive to replace conduit constituted a "claim" because it sought an adjustment or interpretation of the contract terms, even though the contractor also estimated the cost of the change to be "somewhere between $ 1 and $ 99,999.

The jurisdiction to rule on nonmonetary claims does not extend to the granting of specific performance, *Sabbia Corp.*, VABCA 5557, 99-2 BCA ¶ 30,394; *Western Aviation Maint. Inc. v. General Servs. Admin.*, GSBCA 14165, 98-2 BCA ¶ 29,816.

C. Assertion of Contractor Claim

A claim does not arise upon the mere occurrence of a dispute or controversy. The party asserting the claim must make a "demand" or "assertion" to the other party. The Disputes clause provides in ¶ (c) that a claim is a "written demand or written assertion by one of the contracting parties." Paragraph (d)(1) of the clause further provides that a claim by the contractor "shall be made in writing and submitted to the contracting officer for a written decision." Because it is the contractor's claim that triggers the running of interest and starts the time running for the contracting officer's final decision, the primary focus has been on determining what type of contractor demand or assertion constitutes a claim. The following discussion examines what parties can assert claims and what information must be included in such claims.

1. Party Entitled to Assert Claim

Appeals often involve threshold issues of 1) whether the dissolved contractor can file a suit; 2) whether a separate entity is entitled to sue on behalf of the contractor; or 3) who can speak for the contractor.

a. Dissolved Contractors

State law determines whether an individual is authorized to act on behalf of an otherwise incapacitated business entity and, therefore, has standing to file an appeal under the CDA. See *RMS Tech., Inc.,* ASBCA 50954, 00-1 BCA ¶ 30,763 (former manager of a terminated corporation lacked standing to file appeal because only directors were authorized to file suit in the corporate name under Virginia law); *Frénce Mfg. Co.*, ASBCA 46233, 95-2 BCA ¶ 27,802 (involuntarily dissolved contractor that was reinstated under Illinois law can file appeal); and *Microtool Eng'g, Inc.*, ASBCA 31136, 86-1 BCA ¶ 18,680 (dissolved corporation could not sue under New York law). In *Weststar, Inc.,* ASBCA 52837, 03-1 BCA ¶ 32,248, the board held an assignee is not a real party in interest to prosecute an appeal where the contractor has become insolvent and been liquidated under state law. On reconsideration, 04-1 BCA ¶ 32,501, the board reinstated the appeal based on California law which allowed the contractor to recover its corporate status.

Administrative dissolution does not necessarily preclude the dissolved corporation from proceeding with a claim. State law often provides that a dissolved corporation may continue its corporate existence and may wind up and liquidate its business, including the collecting of its assets and discharging its liabilities. See

DCO Constr, Inc., ASBCA 52701, 02-1 BCA ¶ 31,851 (an administrative dissolution at the time appeal notices were filed did not deprive a contractor of capacity to sue because Florida law allows a defunct entity to continue certain dealings), and *International Crane Co.*, ASBCA 49604, 00-1 BCA ¶ 30,624, *recons. denied,* 00-2 BCA ¶ 31,085 (trustee of dissolved corporation had standing to file appeal because he was entitled to bring suit in the corporate name under Maryland law).

A contractor undergoing liquidation under Chapter 7 of the Bankruptcy Code has no right to conduct business, including the prosecution or defense of claims, outside the bankruptcy estate, *Microscience, Inc.*, ASBCA 45264, 98-1 BCA ¶ 29,480 (holding that president and sole shareholder of a defunct corporation did not have the capacity to prosecute an appeal); *Terrace Apartments, Ltd.*, ASBCA 40125R, 95-1 BCA ¶ 27,458. For various views on whether bankrupt corporations are subject to state law or bankruptcy law with regard to their corporate status, see *Caesar Constr. Co.*, ASBCA 46023, 97-1 BCA ¶ 28,665.

b. Separate Entities

There are a number of separate entities that have been denied the right to assert a claim for the contractor. The inability to assert such contractor claims does not necessarily preclude them from asserting claims on their own behalf such as claims of an assignee for payment of contract funds to the contractor.

(1) Assignees

Assignees of the right to receive payment under the Assignment of Claims Act, 31 USC § 3727, may not assert contract claims because an assignee is not a "contractor" within the meaning of the CDA, *Produce Factors Corp. v. United States*, 199 Ct. Cl. 572, 467 F.2d 1343 (1972; *Thomas Funding Corp. v. United States*, 15 Cl. Ct. 495 (1988); *Innovative Tech. Sys., Inc. v. Department of the Treasury*, GSBCA 13474-TD, 97-1 BCA ¶ 28,971, *recons. denied,* 97-2 BCA ¶ 29,086; *Barnes, Inc.*, AGBCA 97-111-1, 97-2 BCA ¶ 29,237; *Banco Disa, SA*, ASBCA 49167, 96-2 BCA ¶ 28,728; *First Commercial Funding, L.L.C.,* ENGBCA 6447, 00-1 BCA ¶ 30,769. One board has held, in *John E. Gallno*, AGBCA , 97-146-1, 98-1 BCA ¶ 29,616, that a contractor may file an appeal after making an assignment, because the appellant's status as a "contractor" under the CDA at the time the claim arose was not changed by the assignment agreement. The board also noted that the question whether the contractor waived its rights against the government when it assigned the contract was related to the merits of the case rather than the contractor's status or the board's jurisdiction. The board found that the assignment agreement was not a release of claims because the transfer did not clearly and specifically set out a release, and the government, as a party to the assignment agreement, could not receive the benefit of inferences or ambiguous language.

(2) Sureties

Performance bond sureties can sue for the unpaid balance on a contract if they assume responsibility for the work and incur costs in that amount, *Aetna Cas. & Sur. Co. v. United States*, 845 F.2d 971 (Fed. Cir. 1988). The theory of such suits is equitable subrogation, *Balboa Ins. Co. v. United States*, 775 F.2d 1158 (Fed. Cir. 1985), and the basis for such suits is the Tucker Act, not the CDA, *Fireman's Fund Ins. Co. v. England*, 313 F.3d 1344 (Fed. Cir. 2002). The impact of *Fireman's Fund* is that the boards have no jurisdiction over such claims. Further, such suits may not encompass claims for additional compensation on the contract.

If such a surety enters into a takeover agreement with the government, it will become a contractor and will be able to assert claims in the Court of Federal Claims to the extent that the terms of the agreement permit such claims. This would allow recovery on post-takeover claims and pre-takeover claims to the extent allowed by the agreement. See *Employers Ins. of Wausau v. United States*, 23 Cl. Ct. 579 (pre-takeover claims are viable if "the takeover agreement . . . encompass[es] the prior contract's rights and obligations), and *Reliance Ins. Co. v. United States*, 27 Fed. Cl. 815 (1993) (considering pre-takeover claims). See also *Roxco, Ltd. v. United States*, 60 Fed. Cl. 39 (2004), taking jurisdiction of a suit by a contractor for claims based on events before its default termination when a surety had completed the project without entering into a takeover agreement.

Boards of contract appeals do not have this broad authority. See *United Pac. Ins. Co. v. Roche*, 380 F.3d 1352 (Fed. Cir. 2004), holding that under the CDA the boards have no authority to grant relief on pre-takeover claims even when the take-over agreement is broadly worded. The court stated at 1356-57:

> United contends that it has a "contractual right" to assert its overpayment claim before the Board because the takeover agreement states that the "SURETY expressly reserves all prior rights including but not limited to the Government's overpayment to" Castle. *United Pac. Ins. Co.*, 03-2 B.C.A. ¶ 32,267 at 159,613. Contrary to United's argument, however, this provision did not give the Board jurisdiction over the claim. The Board's jurisdiction is defined by the Contract Disputes Act. Parties cannot, by agreement, confer upon a tribunal jurisdiction that it otherwise would not have. See *Fla. Power & Light Co. v. United States*, 307 F.3d 1364, 1370 (Fed. Cir. 2002) ("Contractual language . . . cannot confer jurisdiction" under the Contract Disputes Act.) Thus, a "reference to the [Contract Disputes Act] in the contract" could not vest the Board with "jurisdiction over the . . . claim[] if it was not otherwise authorized" to adjudicate it. *Id.* at 1371. The provision of the takeover agreement upon which United relies reserves only its "prior" rights, i.e., those that existed before the takeover agreement. Under *Fireman's Fund*, the Board had no jurisdiction over claims based upon those rights.
>
> United also cites the following language of the takeover agreement as a basis for Board jurisdiction: the "SURETY shall be entitled to exercise such rights as are afforded by the . . . Contract Disputes Act." *United Pac. Ins. Co.*, 03-2 B.C.A.

> ¶ 32,267 at 159,613. That contractual provision merely recognized that United retained whatever rights it otherwise had under the Contract Disputes Act. As we have explained, United had no right under that Act to maintain before the Board a claim based on pre-takeover agreement events.

No jurisdiction attaches to an appeal of a surety that had paid the penal sum of its payment bond but had not assumed contract performance or made any payments under its performance bond. See *Admiralty Constr., Inc.*, ASBCA 48627, 96-2 BCA ¶ 28,280, *aff'd,* 156 F.3d 1217 (Fed. Cir. 1998). See also *Brent M. Davies*, ASBCA 51938, 00-1 BCA ¶ 30,678 (where a surety pays out under its payment bond to the defaulted contractor's creditors but neither enters into a takeover agreement with the government nor finances the contract's completion, it lacks privity as a "contractor" and cannot rely on subrogation to support its standing before the board to appeal excessive reprocurement costs and liquidated damages).

A surety also has no rights to recover where the contractor agrees to a no-cost settlement to convert a default termination to a termination for convenience, *Intercargo Ins. Co. v. United States,* 41 Fed. Cl. 449 (1998), *aff'd,* 215 F.3d 1348 (Fed. Cir. 1999).

(3) Merged Contractors

Although a surviving company that has succeeded to a contract by a valid merger may assert contract claims, a company that has purchased a contractor's assets may have no such rights. In *Siracua Moving & Storage*, ASBCA 51433, 99-2 BCA ¶ 30,447, the board held that it lacked jurisdiction of a claim asserted by a company that had purchased a contractor's assets because the company was not a "contractor" as defined by the CDA. The board reached this conclusion because the transfer of the contractor's assets violated the Anti-Assignment Act and there was no valid, completed novation agreement. In contrast, the same board held in *Omega Envtl., Inc.*, ASBCA 51639, 99-1 BCA ¶ 30,253, that the transfer of rights in connection with mergers gives the status of "contractor" within the CDA and is not precluded by the anti-assignment statutes. Thus, a successor by merger has standing to appeal an adverse contracting officer's decision.

A company that the government had agreed (in a novation agreement) to look upon as a contractor's successor for all purposes had the right to pursue claims for events that predated the novation, *Vought Aircraft Co.*, ASBCA 47357, 95-1 BCA ¶ 27,421. See also *General Dynamics Corp. v. United States*, 47 Fed. Cl. 514 (2000), holding that a corporation, rather than its wholly owned subsidiary, was the real party in interest and therefore entitled to bring suit on a contract claim.

(4) Agents of a Contractor

Agents of a contractor with power of attorney may assert claims, *Rudolf Bieraeugel, Stahl-und Metallbau, Gesellschaft mit beschraenkter Haftung*, ASBCA

47145, 95-1 BCA ¶ 27,536, *aff'd,* 91 F.3d 167 (Fed. Cir. 1996). Compare *Blakely Crop Hall, Inc. & Farmer Alliance Mut. Ins. Co.*, AGBCA 2001-153-F, 02-1 BCA ¶ 31,796, holding that a crop insurer's managing general agent did not have standing to assert the claim to the board. See also *Hubsch Industrieanlagen Spezialbau GmbH*, ASBCA 51937, 02-1 BCA ¶ 31,740 (contractor could not recover an affiliate's lost profits or costs relating to a foreclosure on its director's home, because neither the affiliate nor the director were parties to the contract).

2. Claim Content

A valid CDA money claim must contain (1) a written demand (2) seeking as a matter of right (3) the payment of money in a sum certain, *Scientific Mgmt. Assocs., Inc.*, ASBCA 50956, 98-1 BCA ¶ 29,656. Although the CDA prescribes no particular format, a claim must contain sufficient detail to permit the contracting officer to give meaningful, reasoned consideration to the claim, and the sufficiency of claims will be determined on a case-by-case basis, *Metric Constr. Co. v. United States*, 1 Cl. Ct. 383 (1983). In *Marine Constr. & Dredging, Inc.*, ASBCA 38412, 90-1 BCA ¶ 22,573, the board stated that the claim "must contain sufficient detail to notify the contracting officer of the factual allegations upon which the claim is premised." In *Tecom, Inc. v. United States*, 732 F.2d 935 (Fed. Cir. 1984), a claim was found to have been filed by a letter asserting that the government's order was beyond the contract's requirements and specifically asking "compensation of $11,000.04 per year, to be billed at $916.67 per month." See *Blake Constr. Co.*, ASBCA 34480, 88-2 BCA ¶ 20,552, in which the board stated that "the statement of claim must provide a basis for meaningful dialogue between the parties aimed toward settlement or negotiated resolution of the claim if possible, or for adequate identification of the issues to facilitate litigation should that become necessary." See also *ECC Int'l Corp. v. United States*, 43 Fed. Cl. 359 (1999) (the submission of a valid claim requires the contractor to specify its bases for relief, although there is no requirement that a claim be submitted in any particular form or use any particular verbiage), and *Clearwater Constructors, Inc. v. United States,* 56 Fed. Cl. 303 (2003) (a contractor and subcontractor's letters combined constituted a valid, non-monetary claim because the subcontractor's letter clearly outlined its position that the government's demand for "explosion-proof" doors constituted extra work while the contractor's letter sought a contracting officer's final decision concerning the contract's meaning).

As long as the contractor's assertion contains the minimum information necessary to inform the contracting officer of what is being claimed and the grounds of the claim, the contracting officer must act on the claim and deny it if the information is insufficient to approve it, *Fred A. Arnold, Inc.*, ASBCA 27151, 83-2 BCA ¶ 16,795, *modified on other grounds*, 84-3 BCA ¶ 17,517.

Claims should have adequate supporting documentation. In *Aerojet Gen. Corp.*, ASBCA 48136, 95-1 BCA ¶ 27,470, the contracting officer requested full cost or pricing data approximately a month and a half after a claim had been submitted. Rather than providing the data, the contractor appealed to the board arguing that it should take jurisdiction under 41 U.S.C. § 605(c)(5) which states that failure of a contracting officer to provide a timely decision will be "deemed" to be a decision denying the claim (a "deemed" denial). The board found that the contractor had failed to comply and in fact violated both the letter and the spirit of the statute. See *Environmental Chem. Corp.*, ASBCA 53958, 03-1 BCA ¶ 32,254 (no jurisdiction where appellant had not identified the contract in its claim and there was no indication that contracting officer had prior or concurrent information of the contract(s) affected); *Holk Dev., Inc.*, ASBCA 40579, 90-3 BCA ¶ 23,086 (no claim because the supporting data were general cost information not connected to the contract in question); and *I.B.A. Co.*, ASBCA 37182, 89-1 BCA ¶ 21,576 (no claim where the contractor claimed that the government had not made proper payment in the amount of $25,000 and refused to furnish any documentation in support of its claim). However, compare *Bridgewater Constr. Corp.*, VABCA 2866, 90-2 BCA ¶ 22,764, and *Marshall Constr., Ltd.*, ASBCA 37014, 90-1 BCA ¶ 22,597, in which proper claims were found even though the contractor submitted almost no supporting data. In *H.G. Smith, Inc. v. Dalton,* 49 F.3d 1563 (Fed. Cir. 1995), the court rejected any requirement for a contractor to submit substantiation for the dollar amount requested in a claim at the time of claim submission. See also *John T. Jones Constr. Co.,* ASBCA 48303, 96-1 BCA ¶ 27,997, holding that if the claim is sufficient, the contracting officer's desire for more information does not change the "claim" status of the contractor's submission.

In *Bio-Temp Scientific, Inc.*, ASBCA 41388, 91-1 BCA ¶ 23,548, the board held that a letter by the contractor's attorney that he had been retained "to prosecute . . . a dispute with respect to the full contract amount" failed to constitute "a clear and unequivocal statement that gives the contracting officer adequate notice of the basis and amount of the claim." In *Natural Landscape Contractors, Inc.*, GSBCA 9187, 91-2 BCA ¶ 23,886, *recons. denied*, 93-1 BCA ¶ 25,422, the government asserted that the contractor had never filed a claim for a differing site condition. The contractor argued that "the general site condition claim was included in its more general certified claim for 'GSA's failure to properly and timely administer the contracts.'" The board disagreed with the contractor, stating at 119,656:

> The specifics of the claim concerned alleged wrongful reductions for work performed under the contract with payment subsequently disallowed, not for extra work that had to be performed because of a differing site condition or constructive change. The equitable adjustment claimed as a result of the alleged differing site condition is not mentioned in the claim letter. As the differing site condition claim was not presented to the contracting officer for decision, we lack jurisdiction to decide it. 41 U.S.C. § 605(a) (1988); *Modular Devices Inc.*, ASBCA No. 24198, 82-1 BCA ¶ 15,536.

See, however, *General Constr. Co.*, ASBCA 39983, 91-1 BCA ¶ 23,314, *recons. denied*, 93-1 BCA ¶ 25,275, in which the board held that the contractor's claims stating that its increased costs were due to either a differing site condition or defective specifications provided sufficient facts to permit the contracting officer to render a final decision. Similarly, in *R&R Enters.*, ASBCA 41382, 91-2 BCA ¶ 23,707, the contractor's letter seeking compensation for additional staffing of a mess hall constituted a claim because it provided sufficient information for the contracting officer to give the claim meaningful review. In *Mendenhall v. United States*, 20 Cl. Ct. 78 (1990), the court found that the contractor's letter making a claim for "changed conditions" qualified as a claim. The court stated that the submission was a clear, unequivocal notice of the basis for the claim since the contracting officer understood what was referred to as a result of earlier discussions with the contractor.

3. Request for Sum Certain

A contractor must state a sum certain if that is possible at the time the claim is filed, *RCS Enters., Inc. v. United States,* 46 Fed. Cl. 509 (2000); *Writing Co. v. Department of Treasury,* GSBCA 15097, 00-1 BCA ¶ 30,840, *recons. denied,* 00-1 BCA ¶ 30,910; *Colon v. United States* 35 Fed. Cl. 337 (1996); *Harris Mgmt. Co.*, ASBCA 27291, 84-2 BCA ¶ 17,378; *Logus Mfg. Co.*, ASBCA 26436, 82-2 BCA ¶ 16,025; *Harnischfeger Corp.*, ASBCA 23918, 80-2 BCA ¶ 14,541. Failure to quantify a claim will render the claim ineffectual if the essence of the dispute is increased costs, *Winding Specialists Co.*, ASBCA 37765, 89-2 BCA ¶ 21,737; *Endless Gutter & Sheetmetal Co.*, ASBCA 39369, 90-1 BCA ¶ 22,474. Thus, if a monetary amount can be determined, that amount must be stated. See *Liberty Painting Co.*, ASBCA 39562, 91-1 BCA ¶ 23,561 (no claim found where contractor filed a claim for extra compensation for painting but made no estimate of the amount of the claim), and *Rixie Iron & Metal Co.*, ASBCA 40835, 90-3 BCA ¶ 23,238, *recons. denied*, 91-1 BCA ¶ 23,453 (no claim found where contractor gave some monetary information but did not clearly state the amount it was requesting). See also *Metric Constr. Co. v. United States*, 14 Cl. Ct. 177 (1988) (a claim "exceeding" a specified dollar amount did not meet the test); *Godwin Equip. Inc.*, ASBCA 53462, 02-1 BCA ¶ 31,674 (claim "in excess of" $5 million did not constitute a sum certain). In *SEA CON Corp.*, AGBCA 812041, 81-2 BCA ¶ 15,316, the board dismissed without prejudice a claim alleging mistake in bid because the contractor had submitted no specific dollar claim and had provided no certification. Similarly, a contractor was required to clarify language requesting "more or less than $50,000" before proceeding with an uncertified claim, *Ernest Zapanta*, ASBCA 27633, 83-1 BCA ¶ 16,259, *recons. denied*, 83-2 BCA ¶ 16,622.

A claim in which the amount can be easily determined by simple mathematical calculation or from the contractor's submission to the contracting officer is sufficient for purposes of the CDA, *Mendenhall v. United States*, 20 Cl. Ct. 78 (1990) (claim requested return of all the money paid to government under timber sale contract); *Metric Constr. Co. v. United States*, 1 Cl. Ct. 383 (1983) (amount of request for 7.5 percent for bond premium on all changes ordered easily determinable by contracting officer since amount of change orders were known); *Dillingham Shipyard*, ASBCA 27458, 84-1 BCA ¶ 16,984 (sum determinable by simple arithmetic since government knew both the number of hours and the rate). See *Automated Power Sys., Inc.*, DOTBCA 2925, 98-1 BCA ¶ 29,568, stating that this requirement will be met if the claim states either the exact amount or a description that would enable the contracting officer to determine the specific amount through the use of simple arithmetic. Thus, the sum certain requirement can be met by setting forth a finite amount but also with data that allow for reasonable determination of the recovery available at the time the claim is presented or decided by the contracting officer, such as at a fixed rate, *Mulunesh Berhe,* ASBCA 49681, 96-2 BCA ¶ 28,339.

A claim will meet the sum certain requirement even if it demands two different sums if the sums are clearly stated as alternatives and each is based upon a different legal theory but the same factual circumstances, *Heyl & Patterson, Inc. v. O'Keefe*, 986 F.2d 480 (Fed. Cir. 1993), *overruled on other grounds*, *Reflectone, Inc. v. Dalton*, 60 F.3d 1572 (Fed. Cir. 1995). Similarly, the requirement will be met if the claim seeks different sum certain amounts under alternative theories of recovery, *United Techs. Corp.,* ASBCA 46880, 96-1 BCA ¶ 28,226.

The sum certain need not be the total claim of a contractor. In *MDP Constr., Inc.*, ASBCA 52769, 01-1 BCA ¶ 31,359, each of several invoices qualified as a "claim" under the CDA, even though the contractor also expressed an intent to submit at some future time a claim for unabsorbed home office overhead expenses. Because each invoice stated a specific monetary amount, the invoices represented a sum certain. The fact that a contractor has not completed all work under a particular contract modification or change does not mean that the contractor is prohibited from submitting one or more claims for the portions of the work that have been completed. See *J.S. Alberici Constr. Co.*, ENGBCA 6179, 97-1 BCA ¶ 28,639, *recons. denied,* 97-1 BCA ¶ 28,919, *aff'd,* 153 F.3d 1381 (Fed. Cir. 1998), where the contractor's submission of estimated costs was a valid claim even though it represented a demand for payment for work not yet performed and of costs not yet incurred, and *Fairchild Indus. Inc.,* ASBCA 46197, 95-1 BCA ¶ 27,594, in which the board held that the decision in *Servidone Constr. Corp. v. United States,* 931 F.2d 860 (Fed. Cir. 1991), implied that a claim that included amounts for not-yet-incurred costs could be properly filed under the CDA. See also *Sentara Health Sys.*, ASBCA 51540, 99-1 BCA ¶ 30,323, *recons. denied,* 99-2 BCA ¶ 30,454, (although a valid contractor's claim must include a demand for the "payment of money in a sum certain," the reservation of a right to seek additional "acquisition savings" does not render an existing claim in a specified amount uncertain), and *Writing Co. v. Department of the Treasury,* GSBCA 15117-TD, 00-2 BCA ¶ 31,076 (submittal of invoice partially disputed by the DCAA constitutes a CDA claim for disputed amount).

4. Request for Contracting Officer Decision

The requirement that the contractor request a contracting officer decision is in neither the CDA nor the FAR but rather derives from case law. See *Mingus Con-*

structors, Inc. v. United States, 812 F.2d 1387 (Fed. Cir. 1987). In *Mingus*, the court held that the contractor's letters did not constitute a claim because they did not request a decision from the contracting officer. See also *Robert Irsay Co. v. United States Postal Serv.*, 21 Cl. Ct. 502 (1990), in which the court held that there was no claim because the letter lacked a request for a contracting officer decision on the contractor's request for equitable adjustment.

The request for a decision may be either explicit or implied. In *James M. Ellett Constr. Co. v. United States*, 93 F.3d 1537 (Fed. Cir. 1996), the court clarified that a contractor need not explicitly request a final decision "'as long as what the contractor desires by its submissions is a final decision . . . .'" citing *Transamerica Ins. Corp. v. United States,* 973 F.2d 1572 (Fed. Cir. 1992). The court recognized that "'a request for a final decision can be implied from the context of the submission." See *CleanServ Executive Servs., Inc.*, ASBCA 47781, 96-1 BCA ¶ 28,027; *Rex Sys., Inc.,* ASBCA 49065, 96-1 BCA ¶ 27,967. In *Mendenhall v. United States*, 20 Cl. Ct. 78 (1990), the court found an implied request when the contractor requested in a letter that the contracting officer take action on specific issues that had arisen between the parties. An implied request was also found in a series of letters between the contractor and the contracting officer followed by a meeting on the "claim" at which the parties could not agree on a resolution of the issues, *Mitchco, Inc.*, ASBCA 41847, 91-2 BCA ¶ 23,860. See also *Cable Antenna Sys.*, ASBCA 36184, 90-3 BCA ¶ 23,203, in which the board found an implied request for a contracting officer decision in a demand that the contracting officer promptly respond to the asserted claims and in a statement that the claim was being submitted "pursuant to Disputes clause." In *Transamerica Ins. Corp. v. United States*, 973 F.2d 1572 (Fed. Cir. 1992), the court stated that, although the contractor did not use the explicit words "we request a final decision from the contracting officer," it was obvious that the contractor wanted a final decision on its equitable adjustment claim. Similarly, in *Atlas Elevator Co. v. General Servs. Admin.*, GSBCA 11655, 93-1 BCA ¶ 25,216, the board held that a letter seeking payment for a contractor's elevator repairs constituted a claim, even though the contractor did not explicitly demand payment as a matter of right or explicitly request final payment. The board stated that a "common sense analysis should be applied to ascertain whether a particular submission" constitutes a request for a final decision. See also *Intercontinental Mfg Co.,* ASBCA 51005, 98-1 ¶ 29,459, finding an implied request when the contractor submitted a request for equitable adjustment but called it a "claim" and included the CDA certification.

A request for contract interpretation also is a demand for a final decision (even though it is not a request for a sum certain) because nonmonetary claims are within the jurisdiction of the board, *Procontrols Corp.*, VABCA 5477, 98-1 BCA ¶ 29,622. However, the court will not find an implied request for a contracting officer decision if the contractor requests a meeting to discuss the matter, *Sun Eagle Corp. v. United States*, 23 Cl. Ct. 465 (1991), or requests continued discussions, *M.A. Mortenson Co. v. General Servs. Admin.*, GSBCA 13570, 96-2 BCA ¶ 28,451. Compare *Kevin J. LeMay*, GSBCA 16093, 03-2 BCA ¶ 32,345, holding that a request that the contracting officer order an agency to perform was a request for a decision.

Mere precatory language will not suffice, *Jones, Inc.*, VACAB 1708, 84-2 BCA ¶ 17,382 (letter stating "your prompt payment will be appreciated" in response to government rejection of progress-payment request was insufficient). See also *Robert Irsay Co. v. United States Postal Serv.*, 21 Cl. Ct. 502 (1990) (request that an equitable adjustment be made to the contract did not constitute a request for a final decision), and *Wayne R. Hilf*, PSBCA 2800, 91-1 BCA ¶ 23,628 (letter appealing an implicit contracting officer decision was held not to be a claim because the letter did not request a contracting officer decision). See *Fisherman's Boat Shop, Inc.*, ASBCA 50324, 97-2 BCA ¶ 29,257 (no final decision possible if contractor's letter explicitly states it is not seeking a final decision). In *Heyl & Patterson, Inc. v. O'Keefe*, 986 F.2d 480 (Fed. Cir. 1993), *overruled on other grounds*, *Reflectone, Inc. v. Dalton*, 60 F.3d 1572 (Fed. Cir. 1995), the Federal Circuit upheld a board decision that a contractor had not manifested an intent to bring a claim under the CDA. The court seemed to rely on the fact that there was no request for a final decision in reaching this conclusion. The court stated at 485:

> Each of the three earlier submissions, November 3, 1987, January 28, 1988, and March 23, 1988, suggests in one way or another that *Heyl & Patterson* and the government were still negotiating. In the November 3, 1987 submission, *Heyl & Patterson* indicated that it awaited the government's "preliminary position." In the January 28, 1988 submission, *Heyl & Patterson* indicated that it would submit a "formal request" at a later date. In the March 23, 1988 submission, *Heyl & Patterson* indicated that it was "anxious to proceed with the settlement." None of the submissions requested a final decision, explicitly or implicitly. The third submission, though styled a "claim," merely continued the dialogue of the first two. Indeed, as late as the March 23, 1988 submission, *Heyl & Patterson* inquired whether "any other information [was] needed before the Audit [could] begin." While we agree that "[t]here is no necessary inconsistency between the existence of a valid CDA claim and an expressed desire to continue to mutually work toward a claim's resolution," *Transamerica*, 973 F.2d at 1579, where, as here, "there is no implication that the [contractor] desired a final decision," *id.* at 157778, no claim exists under the CDA as implemented by the FAR.

This case demonstrates the difficulty of discerning the precise element that the contractor failed to establish in bringing a "claim" under the CDA.

5. *Submittal to the Contracting Officer*

Under 41 U.S.C. § 605(a) "all claims by a contractor against the Government relating to a contract shall be in writing and shall be submitted to the contracting officer for a decision." Thus, claims submitted to other government officials will not qualify as claims. See *White Sands Corp.*, ASBCA 53056, 01-1 BCA ¶ 31,348 (submission to government lawyer not a claim); *D.L. Braughler Co., Inc. v. West*, 127 F.3d 1476 (Fed. Cir. 1997) (submission to Resident Engineer not seeking contracting officer decision not a claim); and *J&F Salvage Co.*, 37 Fed. Cl. 256 (1997), *aff'd*, 152 F.3d 945 (Fed. Cir. 1998), *cert. denied*, 525 U. S. 827 (1998) (letter to Department of Justice rather than contracting agency not a claim).

Some cases have held that submittal to a person that can be expected to send the claim to the contracting officer will meet the submittal requirement. See *Gardner Zemke Co.,* ASBCA 51499, 98-2 BCA ¶ 29,997, in which the board held that the contractor's submission of its claim to a private company acting as the primary contact of the government satisfied the requirements of the CDA because the contractor reasonably expected that the private company would forward the claim to the contracting officer. Similarly, in *CACI, Inc.-Fed. v. General Servs. Admin.,* GSBCA 15588, 02-1 BCA ¶ 31,712, the contractor had filed a claim on an Federal Supply Shedule contract with the ordering agency, with a copy to the GSA contracting officer. After the ordering agency and the contractor reached an impasse, and having received no response from the GSA contracting officer, the contractor filed an appeal. The board held that submitting the claim both to the ordering agency and the GSA "is consonant with the operational realities of FSS contracting, under which the ordering agencies and contractors are expected to make initial attempts to resolve disputes." See also *United Partitions Sys., Inc. v. United States.,* 59 Fed. Cl. 627 (2004), in which the Court of Federal Claims ruled that both the Air Force and GSA's contracting officers had partial authority on FSS contracts.

After a default termination has been converted to a termination for convenience, the contractor must submit a new claim to the contracting officer before the board can take jurisdiction, *Foremost Mech. Sys., Inc. v. General Servs. Admin.*, GSBCA 12335, 95-1 BCA ¶ 27,382.

6. Certification

A number of certifications may be required of a contractor seeking money from the government. The determination of whether a certification is required and the time when it is to be submitted depends upon the agency involved, whether the request is a claim under the CDA, and whether the matter is settled through negotiation. The most prominent certificate requirements are contained in the CDA, 41 U.S.C. § 605(c), and the Truth in Negotiations Act, 10 U.S.C. § 2306a(a)(2), and 41 U.S.C. § 254b(a)(2). DOD's Contract Claims Certification, 10 U.S.C. § 2410e, was repealed by The Federal Acquisition Streamlining Act of 1994, Pub. L. No. 103-355. As amended, 10 U.S.C. § 2410 applies only to requests for equitable adjustment and relief under Pub. L. 85-804. The new legislation makes clear that provisions of the CDA regarding the certification of claims governs claims on a government-wide basis. Figure 13-3 summarizes the dollar threshold and the timing of these certificates.

Figure 13-3

Statute	Threshold	Time of Certificate	Material Certified
Contract Disputes Act	Over $100,000	Submission of claim	Good faith, supporting data, accuracy, and authority of signer
Truth in Negotiations Act	Over $550,000	Conclusion of negotiation arriving at settlement of dispute	Cost or pricing data current, accurate and complete
10 U.S.C. § 2410	Over Simplified Acquisition threshold	Submission of request for Equitable Adjustment or relief under Pub. L. 85-804	Good faith and supporting data

Certifications are also required by the standard forms for termination settlement proposals, Standard Forms 1435, 1436, 1437, and 1438 in FAR 53.301-1435 though -1438 respectively.

In *Paul E. Lehman, Inc. v. United States*, 230 Ct. Cl. 11, 673 F.2d 352 (1982), the court held that the CDA certification requirement was jurisdictional. Thus, in the absence of the required certificate, the court stated that "there is simply no claim that this court may review." The result was hundreds of cases in which a technical defect in the certification required the contractor to begin the disputes process all over again no matter what stage the proceedings were in. In these cases, the contractor was deprived of interest, which did not begin to accrue until a proper claim was filed. The Federal Courts Administration Act of 1992, Pub. L. 102-572, § 907, corrected this unfair procedure by amending 41 U.S.C. § 605(c) so that the contracting officer and a board or court are no longer required to start over because of a technical defect in the certification. As amended, 41 U.S.C. § 605(c) provides:

> (1) A contracting officer shall issue a decision on any submitted claim of $100,000 or less within sixty days from his receipt of a written request from the contractor that a decision be rendered within that period. For claims of more than $100,000, the contractor shall certify that the claim is made in good faith, that the supporting data are accurate and complete to the best of his knowledge and belief, that the amount requested accurately reflects the contract adjustment for which the contractor believes the government is liable, and that the certifier is duly authorized to certify the claim on behalf of the contractor.
>
> * * *
>
> (6) The contracting officer shall have no obligation to render a final decision on any claim of more than $100,000 that is not certified in accordance with paragraph (1) if, within 60 days after receipt of the claim, the contracting officer notifies the contractor in writing of the reasons why any attempted certification was found to be defective. A defect in the certification of a claim shall not deprive a court or an agency board of contract appeals of jurisdiction over that claim. Prior to the entry of a final judgment by a court or a decision by an agency board of

> contract appeals, the court or agency board shall require a defective certification to be corrected.

Paragraph (6) of the statute makes it clear that the contracting officer can permit correction of any certification problems when a claim is initially submitted. Thus, contracting officer should review claims for proper certification and immediately notify the contractor if the certification does not fully comply with the statutory requirement. See FAR 33.211(e) stating:

> The contracting officer shall have no obligation to render a final decision on any claim exceeding $ 100,000 which contains a defective certification, if within 60 days after receipt of the claim, the contracting officer notifies the contractor, in writing, of the reasons why any attempted certification was found to be defective.

This new procedure is retroactively effective for all claims submitted before the amendment, except those claims that have been appealed to an agency board or filed in court before the date of enactment of the amendment. These claims are still subject to the old certification rules. See *Blake Constr. Co. v. United States*, 28 Fed. Cl. 672 (1993), *aff'd,* 29 F.3d 645 (Fed. Cir. 1994) (litigation filed prior to date of legislative enactment and, therefore, strict certification rules applied to determine that contractor met prior certification requirements), and *McDonnell Douglas Corp.*, ASBCA 46582, 96-2 BCA ¶ 28,377 (claim filed prior to legislative enactment but new certification rules applied because appeal filed after enactment).

a. *Threshold*

When enacted, the CDA required certification of all contractor claims over $50,000. In 1994, Pub. L. 103-355 changed this threshold to $100,000. In determining the dollar amount of a claim, the increased and decreased costs involved in the claim must be aggregated, FAR 33.207(d). Thus, a contract of $70,000 with a change involving $60,000 of added work and $45,000 of deleted work would be required to be certified since the combined amount of the addition and deletion ($105,000) exceeded the $100,000 threshold. A contractor cannot avoid the certification requirement by splitting what is, in fact, one claim into several sub$100,000 claims. See, for example, *Warchol Constr. Co. v. United States*, 2 Cl. Ct. 384 (1983), and *Walsky Constr. Co. v. United States*, 3 Cl. Ct. 615 (1983).

Whether there is one "claim" that exceeds $100,000 and, therefore, must be certified, or multiple claims, each for less than $100,000 that need not be certified, depends on whether the claims or demands arise out of essentially interrelated conduct or services and the same or closely connected operative facts, in which case they comprise a unitary claim. Thus, multiple contract administrative claims involving separate and distinct facts and circumstances are not a unitary claim, *Dunlap Enters.*, AGBCA 94-126-1, 96-1 BCA ¶ 28,024, but they are unitary when they arise out of virtually identical facts, *Columbia Constr. Co.,* ASBCA 48536, 96-1 BCA ¶

27,970. See also *D & K Painting Co.*, DOTBCA 4014, 98-2 BCA ¶ 30,064, in which the contractor improperly fragmented claims that amounted to less than $100,000 individually but more than $100,000 together. The claims were not "separate and independent," as the contractor argued, but rather a "single unitary claim." Hence the claims were dismissed because the contractor did not certify them as required by the Contract Disputes Act. In *Velia Flying Horse v. United States,* 49 Fed. Cl. 419 (2001), several members of an Indian tribe filed collective claims totaling more than $100,000. Because the claim letter stated, "we are filing individual contract claims with you, as the contracting officer," the contracting officer considered each contract dispute as a separate claim and each plaintiff as a separate contractor. The court thus found that no individual claim was for more than $100,000 and that separate certification was not required.

b. *Significance of Defective Certification or Absence of Certification*

Under the new CDA certificate requirements, a defective certification will not deprive the court or board of jurisdiction. FAR 33.201 contains the following definition:

> Defective certification means a certificate which alters or otherwise deviates from the language in 33.207(c) or which is not executed by a person duly authorized to bind the contractor with respect to the claim. Failure to certify shall not be deemed to be a defective certification.

This distinction between a defective certification and failure to certify is a key distinction because defective certifications can be corrected without adverse consequences to the contractor, such as loss of interest, whereas failure to submit a certification deprives the court or board of jurisdiction.

(1) Correctable Defective Certifications

If a contractor submits a certification that meets most of the four CDA requirements it is likely that it will be found to be a defective certification that is subject to correction. See *JSA Health Care Corp.*, ASBCA 48262, 97-2 BCA ¶ 29,126, stating that a certification that omits "some, but not all, of the required statements" must be corrected before the board issues a decision. See *also Rosinka Joint Venture*, ASBCA 48143, 97-1 BCA ¶ 28,653 (only one of the four required CDA statements missing); *Sprint Communications Co. v. General Servs. Admin.*, GSBCA 15139, 01-2 BCA ¶ 31,464 (substantial increase in amount certified to); and *Thomas Creek Lumber & Log Co.*, IBCA 4020-1999, 00-2 BCA ¶ 31,077 (statement that signer had authority missing). However, a certification that contains almost none of the required statements will not be subject to correction. See *Sam Gray Enters., Inc. v. United States*, 32 Fed. Cl. 526, 529 (1995) (statement that included "I acted in good faith" did not remotely resemble required CDA certification so as to permit correction).

There were a few important cases prior to the CDA amendments in 1993 that held that certifications with minor defects met the prior strict certification requirement. See *W.H. Moseley Co. v. United States*, 230 Ct. Cl. 405, 677 F.2d 850, *cert. denied*, 459 U.S. 836 (1982) (specific statutory words need not be used as long as the certification and documents referenced by it contain the essence of the required statements); *United States v. General Elec. Corp.*, 727 F.2d 1567 (Fed. Cir. 1984) (certification met statutory requirement even though it did not state that "the amount requested accurately reflects the contract adjustment for which the contractor believes the government is liable") *Fischbach & Moore Int'l Corp. v. Secretary of State*, 987 F.2d 759 (Fed. Cir. 1993) (certification stating that the supporting data were accurate and complete to the best of the contractor's "understanding and belief" rather than "knowledge and belief" substantially complied with the CDA); and *Heyl & Patterson, Inc. v. O'Keefe*, 986 F.2d 480 (Fed. Cir. 1993), *overruled on other grounds*, *Reflectone, Inc. v. Dalton*, 60 F.3d 1572 (Fed. Cir. 1995) (certification omitting the word "supporting" was in substantial compliance with CDA). Compare *Aeronetics Div., AAR Brooks & Perkins Corp. v. United States*, 12 Cl. Ct. 132 (1987), in which the court found that the certification did not comply with the requirements of the CDA because it substituted the words "without fraud or misrepresentation" for the required good-faith assertion, omitted the assertion regarding the accuracy of data, and for the third assertion stated that the "amount fairly reflects what the Government owes."

The submission of only the certification on one of the termination settlement forms has been held to be a correctable CDA certification. See *James M. Ellett Constr. Co. v. United States*, 93 F.3d 1537 (Fed. Cir. 1996), holding that only a technical defect was present when the contractor submitted the termination settlement proposal certification in Standard Form 1436 in lieu of the required CDA certification. Because many elements of the CDA certificate are missing from the Standard Form 1436 certification, *Ellett* effectively reversed prior decisions holding that the Standard Form 1436 certificate was an inadequate substitute for CDA certification. The *Ellett* rule has been followed in *Metric Constructors, Inc.*, ASBCA 50843, 98-2 BCA ¶ 30,088, and *J&E Salvage Co. v. United States*, 37 Fed. Cl. 256 (1997), *aff'd*, 152 F.3d 945 (Fed. Cir.), *cert. denied,* 525 U. S. 827 (1998). In *Medina Constr., Ltd. v. United States*, 43 Fed. Cl. 537 (1999), the court reached the same conclusion in a situation where the contractor had asserted that it had never submitted a valid CDA claim in an effort to avoid a fraud counterclaim by the government. The court held that it was bound by the *Ellett* ruling even though the contractor had refused to correct the certificate so that it contained the CDA language.

The Standard Form 1411, the form previously used for certified cost or pricing data, is not a correctable CDA certificate. See *Scan-Tech Sec. L.P. v. United States*, 46 Fed. Cl. 326 (2000), holding that the statement on this form did "not contain language that remotely corresponds to that of the CDA."

An unsigned certificate is not a defective certification subject to correction. See *Hawaii CyberSpace*, ASBCA 54065, 04-1 BCA ¶ 32,455; *AT&T Communications v. General Servs. Admin.*, GSBCA 14932, 99-2 BCA ¶ 30,415; *Eurostyle Inc.*, ASBCA 45934, 94-1 BCA ¶ 26,458.

(2) Intentional or Negligent Disregard

Correction is not permitted if the contractor's claim reflects "an intentional or negligent disregard" of the CDA certification requirements. Thus, no correction was permitted in *Walashek Indus. & Marine, Inc.*, ASBCA 52166, 00-1 BCA ¶ 30,728, where the contractor failed with "knowing and intentional disregard of the applicable certification requirements" to include only two prongs of the CDA language after being explicitly told of the requirement by the contracting officer. See also *Keydata Sys. Inc. v. Department of Treasury*, GSBCA 14281-TD, 97-2 BCA ¶ 29,330 (correction not permitted when there was "negligent disregard" of the CDA certification requirements and the contractor took no action to submit a proper certificate after being told of the specific requirements by the contracting officer); *Production Corp.*, ASBCA 49122-812, 96-1 BCA ¶ 28,053 (affidavit that was intentionally and deliberately drafted to avoid all of the essential requirements of a CDA certification).

(3) Absence of Certificate

The lack of any certification deprives the court or board of jurisdiction even if the contracting officer has issued a decision on the "claim," *Hemmer—IRS Ltd. Partnership v. General Servs. Admin.*, GSBCA 16134, 04-1 BCA ¶ 32,509; *AMR Group, Inc. t/a Landmark Allied,* ASBCA 51330, 01-1 BCA ¶ 31,361; *Golub-Wegco Kansas City 1, LLC v. General Servs. Admin.*, GSBCA 15387, 01-2 BCA ¶ 31,553; *Hamilton Sec. Advisory Servs., Inc. v. United States*, 43 Fed. Cl. 566 (1999), *vacated*, 46 Fed. Cl. 718 (2000); *Vanalco, Inc. v. United States*, 48 Fed. Cl. 68 (2000); *Twigg Corp. v. General Servs. Admin.*, GSBCA 13345, 97-2 BCA ¶ 29,088; *Denro Inc.*, DOTBCA 3070, 97-2 BCA ¶ 29,099; *TGMI Contractors, Inc. v. General Servs. Admin.*, GSBCA 14488, 98-2 BCA ¶ 29,890; *D&K Painting Co.*, DOTBCA 4014, 98-2 BCA ¶ 30,064; *CDM Int'l Inc.*, ASBCA 52123, 99-2 BCA ¶ 30,467; *Hamza v. United States*, 31 Fed. Cl. 315 (1994).

The absence of a contractor's certification when submitting a claim on behalf of a subcontractor is also not correctable. See *Lockheed Martin Tactical Defense Sys. v. Department of Commerce*, GSBCA 14450-COM, 98-1 BCA ¶ 29,717 (the submission of a subcontractor's CDA certificate with a statement that the claim was certifiable was not a correctable defective certification).

The rule barring correction when there is no certificate does not apply if the absence of the certificate is attributable to the fact that the original claim was under the $100,000 threshold for certification and the claim is later amended to exceed $100,000, *William P. Schaetzel,* ENGBCA 6365, 98-2 BCA ¶ 29,937; *Pevar Co. v. United States,* 32 Fed. Cl. 822 (1995).

(4) Certification by Combination

The certificate does not have to be signed on the same date as the claim if it is, in fact, certifying the elements of the claim as well as its supporting data. In *D.L. Braughler Co. v. West,* 127 F.3d 1476 (Fed. Cir. 1997), the Federal Circuit held that a submission from a contractor may be a CDA "claim" even if it is not certified where an earlier "letter claim" submitted by the contractor (to an engineer rather than the contracting officer) had been certified and the two submissions were substantially identical and based on the same supporting data. See also *P.I.O. GmgH Bau und Ingenieurplanung v. International Broadcasting Bureau*, GSBCA 15934-IBB, 04-1 BCA ¶ 32,592 (certificate signed several months before claim but covered essentially same facts and supporting data). Compare *Loral Fairchild Corp.*, ASBCA 45719, 95-1 BCA ¶ 27,425, where the contractor submitted a claim and certification in 1992 bearing a certification date of 1990 (the date of a previous claim submission). The board rejected application of the certification to the first claim, which had been the subject of an appeal before the revisions to the CDA. The board considered the 1992 submission to be a new claim, however, and permitted the contractor to correct the certification to reflect the 1992 submission date.

c. *Revision of Claim*

It is generally accepted by the courts and boards that a contractor can increase the amount of its claim on appeal after certifying the claim for a lesser amount to the contracting officer, so long as the revised claim involves no new claim, *J.F. Shea Co. v. United States*, 4 Cl. Ct. 46 (1983) (there is no bar to the court's jurisdiction over increased damages flowing from a factual claim that has been submitted to the contracting officer and certified by the contractor); *Rocky Mountain Constructors, Inc.,* AGBCA 82-256-1, 83-2 BCA ¶ 16,704; *Central Indus. Elec. Co.*, GSBCA 5607, 83-1 BCA ¶ 16,273. In *Tom Shaw, Inc.*, ASBCA 28596, 95-1 BCA ¶ 27,457, *recons. denied,* 96-1 BCA ¶ 28,007, a contractor's revisions over an extended period of time of the amount of some of its multiple claims did not constitute new claims requiring new certifications because the underlying claim allegations remain the same. The revisions were simply attempts at accuracy with the dollars claimed for specific items both increasing and decreasing.

In *Newell Clothing Co.*, ASBCA 24482, 80-2 BCA ¶ 14,774, the board stated at 72,916:

> Even after a certification has been submitted, a contractor is not precluded from changing the amount of the claim or producing additional data. The only requirements are that the contractor certify to the amount he then honestly believes is due and that the data furnished at the time are accurate and complete to the best of his knowledge and belief.

Newell was followed in *Computer Sciences Corp.*, ASBCA 27275, 83-1 BCA ¶ 16,452, in which the board stated that "certification under the CDA does not preclude subsequent proof of a higher amount." Compare *Fort Vancouver Plywood Co.*, AGBCA 83-139-1, 84-1 BCA ¶ 16,982, the board held that the Act requires certification of any increase in the amount of a contractor's claim. The board declined to follow *Computer Sciences*, although the facts were similar, and noted that, although *Newell* held that certification does not bar subsequent proof of higher damages, it also holds that such an increase needs to be certified to be recovered. The prevalent view is that recertification is not required, *Essex Electro Eng'rs., Inc.*, ASBCA 40553, 91-2 BCA ¶ 23,712 (increase from $881,569 to $1,065,932 did not require recertification); and *Miya Bros. Constr. Co. v. United States*, 12 Cl. Ct. 142 (1987). See *Modeer v. United States*, 68 Fed. Cl. 131 (2005), stating at 137:

> [I]f the dollar value of a claim increases based on new information available only after the claim was submitted to the contracting officer, it is the same claim, not a new claim, as long as it arises from the same operative facts as the original claim and claims the same categories of relief. See, e.g., *Cerberonics, Inc. v. United States*, 13 Cl. Ct. 415, 418 (1987) (testing for new claims by determining whether a claim "is based on a different set of operative facts or seeks different categories of relief"); *Miya Bros. Constr. Co. v. United States*, 12 Cl. Ct. 142, 146 (1987) (holding that "the increased amount of plaintiff's claim that was not submitted to the contracting officer for decision does not represent a new 'claim' . . . [because] the factual basis for the [increased] claims are identical to the claims that were . . . certified to the contracting officer") (citing *Curley, Inc. v. United States*, 6 Cl. Ct. 274, 276-78 (1984); *Spradlin Corp.*, ASBCA No. 23,974, 81-2 BCA ¶ 15,423 (Sept. 30, 1981)); *Kunz [Constr. Co. v. United States*], 12 Cl. Ct. [74 (1987)] at 79 (stating that increased claim amounts in this court are permitted if the operative facts are the same as those presented to the contracting officer and "the court finds that the contractor neither knew nor reasonably should have known, at the time when the claim was presented to the contracting officer, of the factors justifying an increase in the amount of the claim" (citations omitted)); *J.F. Shea Co. v. United States*, 4 Cl. Ct. 46, 55 (1983) (finding jurisdiction over a claim when "the factual basis of the claim before this court is identical to the claim which was certified to the contracting officer").

A claim that does not require certification because it is under the threshold when submitted to the contracting officer, need not be certified if it increases to over the threshold during the disputes process but still is not a new claim, *Tecom, Inc. v. United States*, 732 F.2d 935 (Fed. Cir. 1984). In that case, the claim grew in amount when the government exercised an option after appeal of the contracting officer's decision. The court pointed out that this rule would not cover claims deliberately or carelessly uncertified. The same result was reached in *Burgett Inv., Inc.*, AGBCA 811081, 83-2 BCA ¶ 16,695. But compare *The Vemo Co.*, ASBCA 27048, 83-1 BCA ¶ 16,194, in which the board, when the additional amount of a claim resulted in an amount exceeding the threshold, permitted interest to run on the additional claim only from the time the government received a certificate.

d. Claims Not Involving Quantum

The boards have concluded that claims for nonmonetary relief are not required to be certified. See *Summit Contractors*, AGBCA 811361, 81-1 BCA ¶ 14,872, and *Sims Paving Corp.*, DOTCAB 1822, 87-2 BCA ¶ 19,928. Apparently, this same conclusion was reached by the Court of Federal Claims in an unpublished decision. See *Alliant Techsystems, Inc. v. United States*, 178 F.3d 1260 (Fed. Cir. 1999), *reh'g denied*, 186 F.3d 1379 (Fed. Cir. 1999), stating at 1267:

> The CDA requires certification for claims that exceed $ 100,000. See 41 U.S.C. § 605(c)(1) (1994). The government argued before the Court of Federal Claims that Alliant's claim required certification. The court decided otherwise, and the government has not challenged that aspect of the court's decision. For purposes of this case, we therefore take as correct the trial court's ruling that certification was not necessary and that the contracting officer's conclusion on the issue of finality, which was based on the absence of certification, was accordingly in error.

Claims seeking to overturn a default termination or asserting rights under the contract's Patent Rights clause are examples of claims that might be found not to involve quantum. Note, however, that if the contractor subsequently seeks to recover over $ 100,000 from the government as a result of a holding against the government, it would then be required to submit a certified claim to the contracting officer.

The certification requirement cannot be avoided however, by failing to seek a determination of quantum when the claim is essentially a monetary claim, *Newell Clothing Co.*, ASBCA 24482, 80-2 BCA ¶ 14,774; *Woodington Corp.*, ASBCA 37272, 89-2 BCA ¶ 21,602; *Eaton Contract Servs., Inc.*, ASBCA 52888, 02-2 BCA ¶ 32,023.

e. Authorized Signature

Paragraph (7) of amended 41 U.S.C. § 605(c) provides a simple rule on authorized signatures, stating that "[t]he certification required by paragraph (1) may be executed by any person duly authorized to bind the contractor with respect to the claim." See also FAR 33.207(e). Although simplified, the new provisions state that an individual who certifies a claim or request must be authorized to bind the contractor and must have *knowledge* of the basis for the claim or request, *knowledge* of the accuracy and completeness of the supporting data, and *knowledge* of the claim or request. See *Metric Constructors, Inc.*, ASBCA 50843, 98-2 BCA ¶ 30,088 (senior project manager authorized to sign certification); *Home Entm't , Inc.*, ASBCA 50791, 98-1 BCA ¶ 29,641 (contractor's attorney authorized to sign certification); and *Donat Gerg Haustechnik*, ASBCA 41197, 97-2 BCA ¶ 29,272 (general manager of individual proprietorship authorized to sign certification in place of owner because he had a power of attorney). In *Stradedile/Aegis Joint Venture*, ASBCA 39318, 95-1 BCA ¶ 27,397, the presidents of two companies in a joint venture had authority, together, to certify the venture's claim, even though the venture agreement did not expressly authorize them to represent the venture. Compare *I.J. Chung Assocs.*, LBCA 89-BCA -1, 98-2 BCA ¶ 30,014, holding that a certification was fatally flawed because it was signed by only one member of a joint venture. In contrast, in *McDonnell Douglas Corp.*, ASBCA 46582, 96-2 BCA ¶ 28,377, the board held that the execution of a CDA certification by an improper person is a correctable defect.

7. Conversion into a Claim

If a contractor's initial request for relief does not constitute a claim when submitted, it may be "converted" into a claim. This occurs most frequently when the contractor initially submits a routine request for payment which is not honored by the government. In such case, for a conversion to take place, the contractor must make a formal demand subsequent to an unreasonable delay in payment or disagreement with the government, *Falcon Research & Dev. Co.*, ASBCA 27002, 82-2 BCA ¶ 16,049. See also *Martin Marietta Corp.*, ASBCA 25828, 84-1 BCA ¶ 17,119 ("transformation of a routine voucher into a claim does not take place automatically, as if by osmosis, or upon the mere passage of time"); *Raimonde Drilling Corp.*, IBCA 1359-5-80, 83-1 BCA ¶ 16,294; *Fred A. Arnold, Inc.*, ASBCA 27151, 83-2 BCA ¶ 16,795, *modified on other grounds*, 84-3 BCA ¶ 17,517 (both delay and a written demand for a decision essential); *A.T. Kearney, Inc.*, DOTCAB 1263, 83-2 BCA ¶ 16,835, *recons. denied*, 84-1 BCA ¶ 17,052 (invoice never converted into a claim by a request for a written decision); and *Granite Constr. Co.*, ASBCA 26023, 83-2 BCA ¶ 16,843 (long government delay in payment of undisputed amounts not converted without further action by the contractor).

In several cases, the General Services Board of Contract Appeals indicated that conversion would take place automatically. See *Dawson Constr. Co.*, GSBCA 5777, 80-2 BCA ¶ 14,817; *Joseph Fusco Constr. Co.*, GSBCA 5717, 81-1 BCA ¶ 14,837; and *Capital Sec. Servs., Inc.*, GSBCA 5722, 81-1 BCA ¶ 14,923. However, in *Safeguard Maint. Corp.*, GSBCA 6054, 83-1 BCA ¶ 16,276, the board refused to acknowledge a dispute because of the mere nonpayment of an invoice and distinguished *Safeguard* from its decision in the *Dawson* case. The basis for the distinction was that, in *Dawson*, the invoice was based upon an oral agreement on the settlement of an equitable adjustment that was the subject of the claim. In *Federal Elec. Corp.*, ASBCA 24002, 82-2 BCA ¶ 15,862, *aff'd*, 2 FPD ¶ 9 (Fed. Cir. 1983), an invoice submitted following the negotiation of a settlement agreement demanded payment within 60 days and a decision of the contracting officer if payment was not forthcoming. The board found that the invoice was sufficient to constitute a claim of nonpayment, without additional action by the contractor. See also *Kirk Bros. Mech. Contractors, Inc.*, ASBCA 43347, 93-1 BCA ¶ 25,372, in which the board found that, although the contractor's original submissions were not CDA claims, a later request by the contractor for a final decision converted an earlier submission into a claim.

The concept of "automatic conversion" has also been applied to termination for convenience settlement proposals. See *James M. Ellett Constr. Co. v. United States*, 93 F.3d 1537 (Fed. Cir. 1996), holding that the proposal was a nonroutine request for payment that was not a claim because it did not ask for a contracting officer's decision but which was converted into a claim when the contracting officer had completed review of the proposal and reached a conclusion on the amount due. The court stated at 1543-44:

> When a contractor submits a termination settlement proposal, it is for the purpose of negotiation, not for a contracting officer's decision. A settlement proposal is just that: a proposal. See 48 CFR § 49.001 (1995) ("a proposal for effecting settlement of a contract terminated in whole or in part, submitted by a contractor or subcontractor in the form, and supported by the data, required by this part"). Indeed, it is a proposal that Ellett contractually agreed to submit in the event of a convenience termination. The parties agreed that they would try to reach a mutually agreeable settlement. If they were unable to do so, however, it was agreed, consonant with the FAR's requirements, that the contracting officer would issue a final decision, see *id.* §§ 52.249-2(f) (Alternate I), 49.103, 49.105(a)(4), which Ellett could appeal to the court or to the Department of Agriculture Board of Contract Appeals, *id.* § 52.249-2(i). Consequently, while Ellett's termination settlement proposal met the FAR's definition of a claim, at the time of submission it was not a claim because it was not submitted to the contracting officer for a decision.
>
> Once negotiations reached an impasse, the proposal, by the terms of the FAR and the contract, was submitted for decision; it became a claim. In other words, in accordance with the contract's prescribed method of compensating Ellett for a convenience termination, a request that the contracting officer issue a decision in the event the parties were unable to agree on a settlement was implicit in Ellett's proposal. After ten months of fruitless negotiations, Ellett explicitly requested that the contracting officer settle its claim. This demand is tantamount to an express request for a contracting officer's decision.

D. Assertion of Government Claims

Prior to the CDA, the government followed a variety of methods for asserting and adjudicating claims against its contractors. It issued final decisions under the Disputes clause, *United States v. A.L. Ulvedal*, 372 F.2d 31 (8th Cir. 1967); *A. Padilla Lighterage*, ASBCA 17288, 75-2 BCA ¶ 11,406; sued in state courts, *Cotton v. United States*, 52 U.S. (11 How.) 229 (1850); *United States v. Bank of New York & Trust Co.*, 296 U.S. 463 (1936); sued in federal courts under 28 U.S.C. § 1345, *United States v. Franklin Steel Prods., Inc.*, 482 F.2d 400 (9th Cir. 1973), *cert. denied,* 415 U. S. 918 (1974); *United States v. Systron-Donner Corp.*, 486 F.2d 249 (9th Cir. 1973); asserted counterclaims to contractor suits, *Horton J. Brown v. United States*, 207 Ct. Cl. 768, 524 F.2d 693 (1975); and set off its claims against payments due the contractor, thereby forcing the contractor to bring suit, *Project Map, Inc. v. United States*, 203 Ct. Cl. 52, 486 F.2d 1375 (1975). The CDA now limits the government's options by requiring that "all claims by the Government against a contractor relating to a contract shall be the subject of a decision of the contracting officer," 41 U.S.C. § 605(a). Thus, the adjudication of entitlement on government claims relating to a contract must now occur under the disputes procedure.

The major question that has arisen with regard to the application of the CDA to government claims is whether the government is now deprived of the common law right of setoff without the issuance of a contracting officer's decision under the CDA. *Cecile Indus., Inc. v. Cheney*, 995 F.2d 1052 (Fed. Cir. 1993), appears to hold that setoffs relating to the contract must be accomplished under the CDA procedures. However, *Kearfott Guidance & Navigation Corp.*, ASBCA 49263, 99-2 BCA ¶ 30,518, reached the opposite conclusion, permitting an agency finance officer to setoff overpayments on the instant contracts as well as other contracts without obtaining a contracting officer's decision. See also *Applied Cos. v. United States*, 144 F. 3d 1470 (Fed. Cir. 1988), permitting a setoff without following CDA procedures because a government claim for erroneous payment was not a claim relating to the contract. The court reasoned that, to be related to a contract, a claim has to have "some relationship to the terms or performance of a government contract." There are also a number of cases in which contracting officers have reduced the contract price without issuing a final decision under the CDA and the board has taken jurisdiction of the case based on an appeal of the contractor. See *Sea-Land Serv., Inc.*, ASBCA 47200, 94-3 BCA ¶ 27,226 (deduction from invoices for allegedly improper billings); *General Motors Corp.*, ASBCA 35634, 92-3 BCA ¶ 25,149 (unilateral modification reducing price to reflect allegedly inapplicable state tax); *Triasco Corp.*, ASBCA 42465, 91-2 BCA ¶ 23,969 (deduction in payments to reflect alleged overpayment for materials not used); and *Blosam Contractors, Inc.*, VABCA 2305, 88-1 BCA ¶ 20,370 (unilateral modification reducing price to reflect alleged deductive change orders). See *A.J. Fowler Corp.*, ASBCA 28965, 86-2 BCA ¶ 18,970, explaining that such actions by the government are not government claims, as such, but are merely the proper refusal to pay amounts considered not due and, therefore, can be taken without issuing a contracting officer's decision under the CDA.

Government claims subject to the CDA procedures include those for reimbursement of costs of reprocurement, *Defense Techs., Inc.*, GSBCA 9570, 90-1 BCA ¶ 22,406; excess costs due to defects in performance, *Ruhnau-Evans-Ruhnau Assocs. v. United States*, 3 Cl. Ct. 217 (1983); *Chandler Mfg. & Supply*, ASBCA 27030, 82-2 BCA ¶ 15,997; recovery of overpayments provisionally paid to a contractor, *American Mfg. Co. of Texas*, ASBCA 25816, 83-2 BCA ¶ 16,608 (goods); *Dodd Frazier & Co.*, IBCA 1591-6-82, 83-1 BCA ¶ 16,231 (services); recovery of payments made on undelivered goods, *Unimatic Mfg., Co.*, ASBCA 25212, 81-1 BCA ¶ 15,095, *recons. denied*, 84-1 BCA ¶ 17,099; setoff against provisionally paid costs later claimed to be unallowable, *General Dynamics Corp., Elec. Boat Div.*, ASBCA 25919, 82-1 BCA ¶ 15,616; *Martin Marietta Corp.*, ASBCA 25828, 84-1 BCA ¶ 17,119; setoff for unauthorized contract adjustment, *Space Age Eng'g, Inc.*, ASBCA 26028, 82-1 BCA ¶ 15,766; claims for defective pricing, *Honeywell Fed. Sys., Inc.*, ASBCA 39974, 92-2 BCA ¶ 24,966; failure to comply with cost accounting standards, *Aydin Corp.*, ASBCA 50301, 97-2 BCA ¶ 29,260; *Brunswick Corp.*, ASBCA 26691, 83-2 BCA ¶ 16,794; *International Tel. & Tel. Corp.*, ASBCA 27802, 83-2 BCA ¶ 16,773; assessment of liquidated damages, *R.F. Lusa & Sons Sheetmetal, Inc.*, LBCA 2000, 04-2 BCA ¶ 32,780; *Evergreen Int'l Aviation, Inc.*, PSBCA 2468, 89-2 BCA ¶ 21,712; demands for warranty work, *Outdoor Venture Corp.*, ASBCA 49756, 96-2 BCA ¶ 28,490; and a request for remission of alleged overpayments for work not required by the contract, *Bean Horizon-Weeks Marine (J.V.)*, ENGBCA 6398, 99-1 BCA ¶ 30,134.

A few cases have held that there no jurisdiction over an alleged government claim because the contracting officer had not issued a final decision. See *Computer Network Sys., Inc. v. General Servs. Admin.*, GSBCA 11368, 93-1 BCA ¶ 25,260; *Diamond Envelope Corp.*, GSBCA 10752, 91-3 BCA ¶ 24,138; and *Iowa-Illinois Cleaning Co. v. General Servs. Admin.*, GSBCA 12595, 95-2 BCA ¶ 27,628. In the latter case, a dissenting opinion commented that it was unfair for the contracting officer to avoid adjudication by merely making the demand without characterizing it as a final decision.

The court in *J&E Salvage, Co. v. United States*, 37 Fed. Cl. 256 (1997), *aff'd,* 152 F.3d 945 (Fed. Cir. 1999), *cert. denied*, 525 U.S. 827 (1998), held that a government claim against a contractor need not be documented in a writing separate from the contracting officer's final decision. In *McDonnell Douglas Corp.*, ASBCA 50592, 98-1 BCA ¶ 29,504, the board declined to reconsider its previous ruling that a contracting officer's premature final decision disallowing a claim for overhead costs did not constitute a government claim because the decision did not seek payment of money (as required by the FAR definition of a claim), and it did not request interpretation of contract terms.

In some cases it is difficult to distinguish between government and contractor claims. See *Fortec Constructors,* ASBCA 27601, 83-1 BCA ¶ 16,402, where, when the government withheld "potential liquidated damages" from final payment, the contractor's claim for this amount was held to be a contractor claim. In *Fullerton Ctr. Ltd. P'ship,* GSBCA 6833, 83-1 BCA ¶ 16,348, the government's withholding of payment for liquidated damages was characterized as a government claim, but when the contractor later brought a claim to recover the withheld amount and interest, the board apparently considered it to be a contractor claim. See also *Security Assocs. Int'l, Inc.*, DOTCAB 1340, 84-2 BCA ¶ 17,444, in which the withholding of payment was characterized as a government claim that was converted to a contractor claim through the issuance of a formal demand for payment. In *Martin Marietta Corp.,* ASBCA 25828, 84-1 BCA ¶ 17,119, the contractor's failure to submit a formal demand following the government's disallowance of cost prohibited the claim from being characterized as a contractor claim.

As with contractor claims, there must be a properly asserted claim in order for the court and boards to have jurisdiction over the matter. A request for a payment that was not in dispute did not constitute a government claim within the meaning of 41 U.S.C. § 605(a), *A.E. Finley & Assoc., Inc. v. United States*, 898 F.2d 1165 (1990). Similarly, a letter from a contracting officer, stating that if repairs were not completed in a specified time the government would take remedial action, did not constitute a claim, *RSH Constructors, Inc. v. United States*, 14 Cl. Ct. 655 (1988). The government is required to give the contractor prior notice before and an opportunity to respond before issuing a final decision. In *Instruments & Controls Serv. Co.*, ASBCA 38332, 89-3 BCA ¶ 22,237, the contracting officer issued a decision demanding payment of $144,300 to compensate for defective work. The board dismissed for lack of jurisdiction because the contracting officer had made no attempt to negotiate a settlement or even discuss the problem with the contractor. It is not necessary for the government to make a money claim. It is sufficient if it directs the contractor to perform a contractual obligation. See *Secretary of the Navy v. General Elec. Co.*, 987 F.2d 747 (Fed. Cir. 1993), in which the court held that a demand for the contractor to repair or replace defective engines constituted a government claim. This decision apparently overrules decisions such as *H.B. Zachry Co.*, ASBCA 39202, 90-1 BCA ¶ 22,342, in which the board held that a demand that a contractor repair defective work was not a government claim because the government did not demand payment for the defective work but merely sought performance of the contract as specified.

Generally, nonmonetary claims deal with instances where the contracting officer has asserted a government right and the contractor is contesting the contracting officer's legal theory. See *McDonnell Douglas Corp.*, ASBCA 26747, 83-1 BCA ¶ 16,377, *aff'd in part & rev'd on other grounds*, 754 F.2d 365 (Fed. Cir. 1985) (government right to examine records); *Systron Donner, Inertial Div.*, ASBCA 31148, 87-3 BCA ¶ 20,066 (compliance with cost accounting standards); and *General Elec. Automated Sys. Div.*, ASBCA 36214, 89-1 BCA ¶ 21,195 (government assertion of unlimited rights in technical data).

The certification requirement does not apply to government claims. See *Brunswick Corp.*, ASBCA 26691, 83-2 BCA ¶ 16,794; *General Dynamics Corp., Elec. Boat Div.*, ASBCA 25919, 82-1 BCA ¶ 15,616; *Fruit Growers Express Co.*, ASBCA 28951, 84-1 BCA ¶ 17,158; and *Martin Marietta Corp.*, ASBCA 25828, 84-1 BCA ¶ 17,119. A contractor cannot recover interest on a government claim, *Ruhnau-Evans-Ruhnau Assocs. v. United States*, 3Cl. Ct. 217 (1983), because 41 U.S.C. § 611 does not authorize payment of interest on a contractor award stemming from an underlying government claim. Thus, to recover interest the contractor must convert the government claim to a contractor claim and certify the claim if it exceeds $100,000, *Security Assocs. Int'l, Inc.*, DOTCAB 1340, 84-2 BCA ¶ 17,444. In *TEM Assocs., Inc.*, NASABCA 330990, 91-2 BCA ¶ 23,730, the board held that a contracting officer's letter disallowing certain salary costs and notifying the contractor that the government would deduct the unreasonable amounts from future contract payments constituted a final decision even though the contractor did not certify the claim. The board found that the letter pertained to a government claim and therefore did not require certification.

E. Time for Submittal

41 U.S.C. § 605(a) includes the following time limitations on the submission of both contractor and government claims:

> Each claim by a contractor against the government relating to a contract and each claim by the government relating to a contract and each claim by the government against a contractor relating to a contract shall be submitted within 6 years after the accrual of the claim. The preceding sentence does not apply to a claim by the government against a contractor that is based on a claim by the contractor involving fraud.

The six-year requirement for contractor claims is included in ¶ (d)(1) of the Disputes clause in FAR 52.233-1 and in FAR 33.206(a), which also notes that the rule does not apply to claims relating to contracts awarded prior to October 1, 1995. See *Walsh Constr. Co.,* ENGBCA 6325, 98-1 BCA ¶ 29,683. The clause does not implement the statutory requirement that the six-year rule also applies to government claims but this rule is stated in FAR 33.206(b).

The Act does not define what constitutes "accrual" of a claim. However, FAR 33.201 contains the following definition:

> Accrual of a claim means the date when all events, that fix the alleged liability of either the Government or the contractor and permit assertion of the claim, were known or should have been known. For liability to be fixed, some injury must have occurred. However, monetary damages need not have been incurred.

The CDA's statute of limitations, not the two-year statute of limitations in the Suits in Admiralty Act, governs disputes involving maritime contracts subject to the CDA, *Dalton v. Southwest Marine, Inc., 1*20 F.3d 1249 (Fed. Cir.1997).

Under the antifraud provision of the CDA, 41 U.S.C. § 604, a contractor's liability to the government for a fraudulent claim and the government's costs of reviewing the claim must be determined "within six years of the commission of such misrepresentation of fact or fraud." In *UMC Elecs. Co. v. United States*, 45 Fed. Cl. 507 (2000), the court concluded that the government's claim for costs attributable to the review of a claim pursuant to the CDA's antifraud provision was not time barred. The contractor argued that because more than six years had elapsed since the contracting officer denied its fraudulent equitable adjustment claim, the claim was barred by the six-year statutory limitation period. The court indicated that Congress did not intend to allow a contractor to engage in lengthy pretrial and trial procedures to escape liability when a court eventually finds that the contractor committed fraud. Furthermore, the court found that the fraud was ongoing and repeated in submissions presented by contractor to the bankruptcy court and the Court of Federal Claims as well as through the testimony of the contractor's witnesses.

Other time limitations involve different statutes or circumstances. The Supreme Court held a contract claim under the Tucker Act timely even though the suit was filed more than six years after legislation repudiated plaintiff's contract because the claim did not accrue until the government dishonored a prepayment, *Franconia Assocs. v. United States,* 536 U.S. 129 (2002). See also *Rocky Mountain Log Homes, Inc.,* AGBCA 97125-1, 98-1 BCA ¶ 29,716 (claim not precluded by provision in a timber sales contract imposing a 60-day time limit for filing a road construction claim with the contracting officer because the contractor's claim also related to other contract provisions), and *United States v. American States Ins. Co.,* 252 F.3d 1268 (11th Cir. 2001) (demand that surety pay reprocurement costs on a defaulted bonded contract subject to six-year statute of limitations in 28 U.S.C. § 2415(a) not the CDA because the government was not a party to the defaulted contractor's performance bond).

Claims can also be time-barred under the doctrine of laches. See *LaForge & Budd Constr. Co. v. United States*, 48 Fed. Cl. 566 (2001), stating at 570:

> Fundamental to laches is the maxim that equity aids the vigilant, not those who slumber on their rights. *Cornetta v. United States*, 851 F.2d 1372, 1375 (Fed. Cir. 1988). Laches is a fairness doctrine that implements the public policy of discouraging stale claims by barring recovery when a plaintiff's delay prejudices the proponent of laches by jeopardizing the court's ability "to arrive at safe conclusions as to the truth." *Deering v. United States*, 223 Ct. Cl. 342, 347, 620 F.2d 242, 244 (1980).
>
> To invoke laches a party must show (1) that the delay from the time the claimant knew or reasonably should have known of its claim against the party was unreasonable and inexcusable; and (2) that the delay caused either economic prejudice or injury to the party's ability to mount a defense. *A.C. Aukerman Co. v. R.L. Chaides Constr. Co.*, 960 F.2d 1020, 1032 (Fed. Cir. 1992) (en banc); accord *Cornetta*, 851 F.2d at 1377-78. The proponent of a laches defense has the burden of proving both elements, and the failure to do so will prevent the application of laches. *Costello v. United States*, 365 U.S. 265, 282, 5 L. Ed. 2d 551, 81 S. Ct. 534 (1961). The application of laches is within the discretion of the court and should not be made by application of "mechanical rules." *Aukerman*, 960 F.2d at 1032 (citing *Holmberg v. Armbrecht*, 327 U.S. 392, 396, 90 L. Ed. 743, 66 S. Ct. 582 (1946)). Thus, the court must examine the facts against the well-established laches standards to determine if defendant has met its burden of proving both delay and prejudice.

See also *Staff, Inc.*, AGBCA 99-138-1, 00-1 BCA ¶ 30,617, in which a claim submitted five years after contract completion was not barred by laches, because the government's contract file remained open during the period, the government was aware that the file remained open, and the government was not prejudiced by any unavailability of witnesses. The government did nothing during the five-year period to finalize the contract after performance. Moreover, all necessary government personnel were available as witnesses. But in *Perkin-Elmer Corp. v. United States*, 47 Fed. Cl. 672 (2000), the court granted summary judgment for a contractor, holding "as a matter of law, that the Air Force did not assert its claim against [the contractor] within a reasonable time when it waited over six years between discovering the alleged latent defect and finally revoking acceptance."

III. CONTRACTING OFFICER'S ROLE

One of the major duties of a contracting officer is to deal with disagreements between the government and contractors. In performing this function, a contracting officer should first attempt to dispose of such matters through negotiated settlement agreements that bind the parties involved. If such an agreement cannot be reached and the contractor submits a claim, the contracting officer must issue a final decision from which the contractor is entitled to appeal to a board of contract appeals or the Court of Federal Claims. A contracting officer's final decision becomes binding on both parties (finality attaches) unless a timely appeal is taken from the decision. In *United States v. Holpuch Co.*, 328 U.S. 234 (1946), the court held that a contractor's claim was "outlawed" by reason of the contractor's failure to appeal to the board of contract appeals within the time period prescribed in the Disputes clause. Under the CDA, a contracting officer's final decision becomes "final and conclusive and not subject to review by any forum, tribunal or Government agency," 41 U.S.C. § 605(b), unless appeal is taken to a board of contract appeals within ninety days after receipt of the contracting officer's decision, 41 U.S.C. § 606, or to the Court of Federal Claims within 12 months following receipt of the decision, 41 U.S.C. § 609(a).

Thus, the contracting officer functions in a dual capacity—acting as (1)the government's advocate while conducting negotiations with the contractor and (2) a quasi-judicial official when rendering a final decision under the Disputes clause. A contracting officer's final decision serves a dual function—it is the final settlement offer of the government and a prerequisite to the contractor's use of the adjudicatory proceedings called for by the CDA.

This section explores these dual roles of the contracting officer. First, the extent of the contracting officer's negotiation responsibilities and authority are considered. The section then focuses on the final decision process.

A. Negotiated Settlement

Negotiations between the contractor and the contracting officer may take place at various times during the administration of the contract. Settlement of routine requests for contract adjustment by mutual agreement will dispose of such matters before a claim ever arises. The vast majority of contract administration issues are settled in this manner. Negotiated settlements also frequently take place following assertion of the claim and prior to the formal rendering of a final decision. Once a final decision is issued, negotiated settlements may still be accomplished unless the contractor has allowed the appeal time on the final decision to run out. Finally, settlement can also occur during the various stages of litigation. Following is a discussion of the government's policy favoring negotiated settlement and an examination of the scope of the contracting officer's settlement authority.

1. Policy Favoring Settlement

It has generally been understood that the contracting officer's initial obligation with regard to claims by or against the government is to attempt to negotiate a settlement with the contractor. Hence, a final decision under the Disputes clause has always been regarded as a last resort. The legislative history of the CDA contains the following statement at 124 Cong. Rec. H10,725 (1978):

> It is still the policy of Congress that contractor claims should be resolved by mutual agreement, in lieu of litigation, to the maximum extent possible.

The policy favoring settlements without litigation was furthered by the Administrative Dispute Resolution Act of 1996 (ADRA), 5 U.S.C. §§ 571-584. In an effort to increase the use of ADR, the Federal Acquisition Streamlining Act of 1994, Pub. L. 103-355, amended the Contract Disputes Act, 41 U.S.C. § 605 by adding the following ¶ (e):

> In any case in which the contracting officer rejects a contractor's request for alternative dispute resolution proceedings, the contracting officer shall provide the contractor with a written explanation, citing one or more of the conditions in section 572(b) of title 5, United States Code, or such other specific reasons that alternative dispute resolution procedures are inappropriate for the resolution of the dispute. In any case in which a contractor rejects a request of an agency for alternative dispute resolution proceedings, the contractor shall inform the agency in writing of the contractor's specific reasons for rejecting the request.

FAR 33.214 implements this policy. In addition, FAR 33.204 states:

> The Government's policy is to try to resolve all contractual issues in controversy by mutual agreement at the contracting officer's level. Reasonable efforts should be made to resolve controversies prior to the submission of a claim. Agencies are encouraged to use ADR procedures to the maximum extent practicable.

The ADRA defines "alternative means of resolving disputes" to include but not be limited to such procedures as settlement negotiations, conciliation, facilitation, mediation, fact-finding, mini-trials, and arbitration, 5 U.S.C. § 571(3). With the exception of binding arbitration, all of those ADR techniques are methods of facilitating settlement which can be used by contracting officers or higher level officials to carry out the government's settlement policy without recourse to the authority conferred by the ADRA. See Executive Order 12988, 61 Fed. Reg. 4729, Feb. 7, 1996, on Civil Justice Reform, stating at § 1(c):

> (1) Whenever feasible, claims should be resolved through informal discussions, negotiations, and settlements rather than through utilization of any formal court proceeding. Where the benefits of Alternative Dispute Resolution ("ADR") may be derived, and after consultation with the agency referring the matter, litigation counsel should suggest the use of an appropriate ADR technique to the parties.
>
> (2) It is appropriate to use ADR techniques or processes to resolve claims of or against the United States or its agencies, after litigation counsel determines that the use of a particular technique is warranted in the context of a particular claim or claims, and that such use will materially contribute to the prompt, fair, and efficient resolution of the claims.

The new ADR method for government contracting—binding arbitration—has limited application. However, it is permitted by 5 U.S.C. § 575 after the head of an agency, in consultation with the Attorney General, issues "guidance on [its] appropriate use." Prior to the ADRA, such binding arbitration was believed to be impermissible, *Tenaska Wash. Partners II, L.P. v. United States*, 34 Fed. Cl. 434 (1995); *Dames & Moore*, IBCA 1308-10-79, 81-2 BCA ¶ 15,418. However, an opinion of the Office of Legal Counsel of the Department of Justice on September 7, 1995 ruled that there are no constitutional impediments to the use of binding arbitration and the ADRA provides positive authority for its use. The opinion concludes that an agency can consent to binding arbitration as long as an Article III court can review constitutional issues and can review the arbitration decisions for fraud, misconduct, or misrepresentations.

The Interior Board of Contract Appeals has held that the government may not agree to settle a dispute by binding arbitration and then challenge the arbitrator's decision, *Lac Courte Oreilles Band of Lake Superior Chippewa Indians*, IBCA 4102-99, 00-1 BCA ¶ 30,774 ("ADR is not a trial balloon or a means of gaining a better grasp of the other party's position, or merely an opportunity to practice arguments on a neutral third party prior to the real contest").

2. Settlement Authority

The authority to enter into contracts carries with it the implied authority to agree to contract modifications, *Gene Peters v. United States*, 694 F.2d 687 (Fed. Cir. 1982); *LDG Timber Enters. v. Glickman*, 114 F.3d 1140 (Fed. Cir. 1997). Thus, courts have recognized that contracting officers have authority to reach binding mutual agreements with contractors, conclusively disposing of claims for unliquidated damages, *Cannon Constr. Co. v. United States*, 162 Ct. Cl. 94, 319 F.2d 173 (1963). At one time, the GAO took the position that the contracting officer's settlement authority was limited to claims "arising under" the contract, 44 Comp. Gen. 353 (B-155343) (1964). But in *Perez & Assocs., Inc.*, Comp. Gen. Dec. B-187003, 77-1 CPD ¶ 48, the GAO specifically reversed prior decisions and recognized the authority of the procuring agencies to settle "breach of contract" claims.

The initial drafts of the CDA contained language that would have expressly authorized each agency to "settle, compromise, pay or adjust any claim by or against, or dispute with, a contractor relating to a contract," H.R. 11,002, 124 Cong. Rec. H10725 (1978). This section was deleted from the Act by the Senate, with the following statement at 124 Cong. Rec. S18,641 (1978):

> Executive agency compromise and settlement authority is not addressed in this Act as this is a matter considered to be included in their existing procurement/acquisition authority under the established precedents.

FAR 33.210 contains the following broad settlement authority language:

> Except as provided in this section, contracting officers are authorized, within any specific limitations of their warrants, to decide or resolve all claims arising under or relating to a contract subject to the Act. In accordance with agency policies and 33.214, contracting officers are authorized to use ADR procedures to resolve claims. The authority to decide or resolve claims does not extend to—
>
>> (a) A claim or dispute for penalties or forfeitures prescribed by statute or regulation that another Federal agency is specifically authorized to administer, settle, or determine; or
>>
>> (b) The settlement, compromise, payment or adjustment of any claim involving fraud.

The limitations incorporated into FAR 33.210(a) and (b), above, derive from the statutory limitations contained in § 6(a) of the CDA, 41 U.S.C. § 605(a). Requests for relief that have been held to be outside the contracting officer's jurisdiction because they are "penalties or forfeitures" include disputes concerning Davis-Bacon Act wage classifications, *Prime Roofing, Inc.*, ASBCA 25836, 81-2 BCA ¶ 15,203, *recons. denied*, 84-2 BCA ¶ 17,253; *Emerald Maint., Inc. v. United States*, 925 F.2d 1425 (Fed. Cir. 1991); Service Contract Act violations, *Imperator Carpet & Interiors, Inc.*, GSBCA 6167, 81-2 BCA ¶ 15,266; *Kass Mgmt. Servs., Inc.*, GSBCA 8819, 88-3 BCA ¶ 20,891; and Contract Work Hours and Safety Standards Act violations, *Nolan Investigative & Protective Co.*, GSBCA 5905, 82-2 BCA ¶ 15,943; *Wickham Contracting Co.*, GSBCA 6579, 82-2 BCA ¶ 15,883; *Mobile Calibration Serv., Inc.*, GSBCA 6217, 82-1 BCA ¶ 15,532.

The CDA states at 41 U.S.C. § 605(a) that the Act "shall not authorize any agency head to settle, compromise, pay, or otherwise adjust any claim involving fraud." FAR 33.210(b) interprets this provision as barring contracting officers from negotiating settlements on any claim where fraud is alleged.

a. Negotiation after Issuance of Final Decision

The issuance of a final decision and the filing of an appeal before an agency board of contract appeals by the contractor do not deprive the contracting officer of authority to negotiate and execute an agreement settling the claim, *Purvis Constr. Co.*, GSBCA 905, 69-1 BCA ¶ 7723. However, if a contracting officer enters into settlement negotiations after issuing a proper final decision, but before the time for appeal has expired, the decision may lose its finality. In such cases, a board may reason that the contracting officer is inviting further discussion or otherwise indicating that the matter "decided" is still an open question. In *Continental Chem. Corp.*, GSBCA 2986, 69-2 BCA ¶ 7926, a contracting officer's agreement to submit samples of rejected soap for retesting prevented finality from subsequently attaching to the contracting officer's letter to the contractor informing it of the termination of the contract. Similarly, in *Precision Tool & Eng'g Corp.*, ASBCA 16652, 73-1 BCA ¶ 9878, the board held that no finality attached to a default termination notice where the contractor subsequently tendered items for delivery before the appeal period expired and was informed by the contracting officer that the termination would be rescinded if the items were satisfactory. In *Sach Sinha & Assocs., Inc.*, ASBCA 46916, 95-1 BCA ¶ 27, 499, the board held that the finality of a contracting officer's decision to terminate the contract for default was vitiated by his discussion of the termination and his request that the contractor submit, in writing, settlement alternatives proposed during the parties' meeting. The board held that this result could occur if the contractor could have reasonably concluded that the contracting officer was reconsidering his prior final decision, stating at 137,042:

> We have determined repeatedly that the issue to be resolved with respect to vitiation of "finality" is whether the contractor presented evidence showing it reasonably or objectively could have concluded the CO's decision was being reconsidered. E.g., *Royal International Builders Co.*, ASBCA No. 42637, 92-1 BCA ¶ 24,684 (finality vitiated where CO actions created sufficient uncertainty that contractor could reasonably believe decision not final); *Birken Manufacturing Co.*, ASBCA No. 36587, 89-2 BCA ¶ 21,581 (finality attached where contractor not reasonably led to believe decision being reconsidered); *Johnson Controls, Inc.*, ASBCA No. 28340, 83-2 BCA ¶ 16,915 (finality vitiated where CO granted contractor audience to discuss decision and did not "make it very clear" that original appeal period was running); *Precision Tool & Engineering Corp.*, ASBCA No. 16652, 73-1 BCA ¶ 9878 (use of word "reconsider" not "a sine qua non"; issue is whether contractor "reasonably concluded" CO was "reconsidering his final decision").
>
> Other tribunals have determined likewise. *Edward R. Ester and Lorraine Ester*, PSBCA No. 3051, 92-2 BCA ¶ 24,822 (reasonable interpretation of letter was CO willing to reconsider; contractor led to believe decision would be reconsidered); *Summit Contractors v. United States*, 15 Cl. Ct. 806 (1988) (post-decision review of same record vitiated finality); *Jen-Beck Associates*, VABCA No. 1988, 85-2 BCA ¶ 18,086 ("test is not limited to the subjective state of the [contractor's] mind but is an objective one considering all the facts"; finality not

vitiated where meetings were to discuss matters other than decision); *Riverside General Constr. Co.*, IBCA No. 1603-7-82, 82-2 BCA ¶ 16,127 at 80,049 (issue is what CO caused contractor to believe after issuance; finality vitiated because CO "held out the prospect . . . that what was described as a 'final decision' would be subject to further discussion and possibly reconsideration").

In *Sach Sinha* the board also concluded that once a final decision has been vitiated, the appeal period can only be reinstated by the issuance of a new final decision complying fully with the CDA. This result was originally reached in *Roscoe-Ajax Constr. Co. v. United States*, 198 Ct. Cl. 133, 458 F.2d 55 (1972), in which the court reversed an appeals board's ruling that contracting officer's agreement to discuss the matter after a final decision had been issued merely "tolled" the running of the appeal period. See also *Summit Contractors v. United States*, 15 Cl. Ct. 806 (1988), holding that the operative decision after reconsideration was the new decision. In *Arono, Inc. v. United States,* 49 Fed. Cl. 544 (2001), the contracting officer's letter advising contractor that the government would continue to pay rent pending resolution of the contractor's breach of lease claim implied that the contracting officer was reconsidering the final decision terminating the lease for default. Therefore the contractor's appeal, filed 19 months after the contracting officer's initial final decision but nine months after the contracting officer's letter affirming that decision was timely. Similarly, in *DK&R Co.*, ASBCA 53451, 02-1 BCA ¶ 31,769, the contracting officer's willingness to meet with the contractor was evidence of reconsideration of the final decision. Compare *Ra-Nav Labs., Inc. v. Widnall*, 137 F.3d 1344 (Fed. Cir. 1998), rejecting the contractor's contention that the contracting officer's correspondence after a termination for default had indicated that he was reconsidering the termination decision. The court held that the latter correspondence was only for the purpose of allowing the contractor to mitigate the damages flowing from the termination and that the correspondence clearly so indicated.

Various types of conduct have led to the conclusion that the contracting officer has decided to reconsider a final decision. See *Nationwide Postal Mgmt.*, PSBCA 5043, 04-1 BCA ¶ 32,492 (discussion with "Manager" led contractor to believe that decision was being reconsidered even though contracting officer did not participate); *DK&R Co.*, ASBCA 53451, 02-1 BCA ¶ 31,769 (after decision parties met and contractor furnished additional documentation at the request of the contracting officer). However, requests for additional efforts at settlement by the contractor with no response from the contracting officer will not demonstrate that the contracting officer is reconsidering the decision, *D'Tel Communications,* ASBCA 50093, 97-2 BCA ¶ 29,251; *Propulsion Controls Eng'g*, ASBCA 53307, 01-2 BCA ¶ 31,494.

b. Settlement During Litigation

The contracting officer retains settlement authority during litigation before the boards of contract appeals. For example, a bilateral settlement agreement entered into after a decision by the Armed Services Board but prior to the expiration of time for a motion for reconsideration was held to constitute an accord and satisfaction binding both parties, *American Bosch Arma Corp.*, ASBCA 10305, 67-2 BCA ¶ 6564. See also *E-Systems, Inc.*, ASBCA 21091, 79-1 BCA ¶ 13,806, in which the board stated at 67,702:

> The cases cited by the [contractor] confirm the authority of the contracting officer to settle and compromise a claim in dispute even while an appeal is *pending before a board.* However, in all of these cases, the boards considered that the matter was still pending before a board while, at the same time, permitting the Government through its contracting officer to settle and compromise the claims under dispute, either in part or in whole, and then dismissed such claims and, in an appropriate situation, vacated a decision as barred by an accord and satisfaction. [emphasis added]

An agency may be bound by a settlement agreement executed by its attorneys during litigation of an appeal before the agency board, *United States v. Bissett-Berman Corp.*, 481 F.2d 764 (9th Cir. 1973). See, however, *Defoe Shipbuilding Co.*, ASBCA 17095, 74-1 BCA ¶ 10,537, in which the board, in view of an agency regulation that precluded any final settlement agreement without the written approval of the contracting officer, held the government not bound to a stipulation of liability in the nature of a settlement signed only by the Navy trial attorney. See also *Marino Constr. Co.*, VABCA 2752, 90-1 BCA ¶ 22,553, in which the board rejected the validity of a settlement agreement negotiated by the government's attorney. The board ruled that the contracting officer had not approved the settlement and that the attorney did not have the authority to bind the government to the settlement. Boards may not reject a settlement that has been agreed to by a contracting officer, *Federal Data Corp. v. SMS Data Prods. Group*, 819 F.2d 277 (Fed. Cir. 1987).

The contracting officer's authority to settle claims does not extend to cases in which litigation has commenced in a court. In *United States v. Newport News Shipbuilding & Dry Dock Co.*, 571 F.2d 1283 (4th Cir.), *cert. denied*, 439 U.S. 875 (1978), the court held that the government was not bound by a settlement entered into by a contracting officer, because the matter was pending in the courts. The court noted that 28 U.S.C. § 516 and § 519 and Executive Order 6166 gave the Attorney General sole authority to settle cases being litigated in the courts. However, this authority has been narrowly construed, *Hughes Aircraft Co. v. United States*, 209 Ct. Cl. 466, 534 F.2d 859 (1976) (authorization to infringe a patent in future given after suit filed); *PBI Elec. Corp. v. United States*, 17 Cl. Ct. 128 (1989) (progress payment made by government after suit filed).

B. Final Decision of the Contracting Officer

If the parties are unable to dispose of a dispute through settlement, the issuance of a contracting officer's final decision is the first step in the litigation process. Once a contractor asserts a claim, the CDA requires the issuance of a final decision, 41

U.S.C. § 605(a). However, no final decision may be issued on a matter that is already in litigation. See *Sharman Co. v. United States*, 2 F.3d 1564 (Fed. Cir. 1993), *overruled in part, Reflectone, Inc. v. Dalton*, 60 F.3d 1572 (Fed. Cir. 1995), in which a final decision demanding the return of progress payments after a default termination was held invalid because the contractor had already filed suit contesting the default termination. Compare *Case, Inc. v. United States*, 88 F.3d 1004 (Fed,. Cir. 1996), in which a final decision denying a contractor's claim for equitable adjustments for constructive changes was found valid even though suit was pending on the validity of the default termination of the same contract. The court reasoned that the second decision concerned different matters than those involved in the pending suit.

A contracting officer's decision is a jurisdictional requirement for the court or board to hear an appeal. This is generally not a problem with contractor claims because contractors can appeal the lack of a contracting officer's decision as a "deemed denied" decision, as discussed below. However, contractors are not permitted to bring new claims into an appeal when they have not be subject to a contracting officer's decision. See *J. Cooper & Assocs., Inc. v. United States,* 47 Fed. Cl. 280 (2000), in which the contractor filed an appeal of a contracting officer's decision denying a constructive termination claim. The contractor's suit included a breach of contract claim. The court dismissed the breach claim because the termination and breach claims did not involve the same operative facts, legal theories, or damage demands. Jurisdiction has also been denied when a purported decision was issued by a person without the proper contracting officer authority, *United Partition Sys., Inc.*, ASBCA 53915, 03-2 BCA ¶ 32,264 (decision to default terminate order on Federal Supply Service contract issued by contracting officer in ordering agency when regulations required it to be issued by GSA contracting officer); *Dulles Networking Assocs., Inc.* VABCA 6077, 00-1 BCA ¶ 30,775 (default termination by government employee without authority); *John C. Grimburg, Co.*, AGBCA 96141-1, 96-2 BCA ¶ 28,503 (decision issued by administrative contracting officer); *Diversified Energy, Inc. v. TVA*, 223 F.3d 328 (6th Cir. 2000) (letter purporting to terminate the parties' business relations issued by official with no contracting officer authority).

The jurisdictional bar because of lack of a contracting officer's decision has posed greater problems with regard to government claims. See *Blinderman Constr. Co. v. United States*, 39 Fed. Cl. 529 (1997), *aff'd, 1*78 F.3d 1307 (Fed. Cir. 1998), in which the court ruled it had no jurisdiction of a government counterclaim that had not been the subject of a decision by the contracting officer. The court distinguished *Placeway Constr. Corp. v. United States*, 920 F.2d 903 (Fed. Cir. 1990), which had held that there was jurisdiction over a counterclaim for a setoff because the contracting officer's decision on the contractor's claim had necessarily considered the setoff because the contracting officer had denied the claim based on the agency's intention to make a setoff. See also *Kit-San-Azusa, JV v. United States*, 32 Fed. Cl. 647 (1995), in which the court took jurisdiction of a case where the contracting officer failed to issue any decision on the contractor's claim, and the contractor appealed on the basis of a deemed denial. The court held that the contracting officer's constructive denial of the contractor's claim for a release of a retainage was logically equivalent to a decision to grant a government claim to keep the retainage. The court, therefore, permitted the government to assert a setoff up to the amount of the retainage based on a liquidated damages provision of the contract. But see *Volmar Constr., Inc. v. United States*, 32 Fed. Cl. 746 (1995), denying jurisdiction over several government counterclaims because of a lack of a contracting officer's decision dealing with the issues involved and extensively analyzing the confusing rules on government counterclaims. See also *D.L. Kaufman, Inc.*, PSBCA 4159, 00-1 BCA ¶ 30,846, (no jurisdiction over a government counterclaim for anticipated recoveries in a False Claim Act suit because the contracting officer had not issued a final decision asserting that claim); *Larry J Miller,* PSBCA 3632, 95-1 BCA ¶ 27,448 (government's asserted counterclaim for reprocurement costs had not been the subject of a final decision and, thus, was not appropriate for litigation during the contractor's appeal of a termination for default decision); and *Frankstown Fish Co.,* AGBCA 94-188-1, 95-1 BCA ¶ 27,579, (no jurisdiction because the contracting officer's memorandum to the contracting agency asserting government claims, with a copy to the contractor, was not designated as a final decision and did not include advice as to appeal rights). Compare *Kearfott Guidance & Navigation Corp.*, ASBCA 49263, 99-2 BCA ¶ 30,518, holding that a final decision was not required to assert a government setoff because the government could rely on a common-law right of setoff without complying with the CDA requirement for a contracting officer's final decision.

The following material deals with the time for making final decisions and the criteria for a valid decision.

1. *Time for Issuance of Decision*

Prior to the CDA, the timing of the issuance of a final decision was within the discretion of the contracting officer, subject only to the broad requirement that a decision be issued within a reasonable time following submission of a claim. The CDA deals with this topic variously, based upon the dollar value of a claim.

41 U.S.C. § 605(c) requires a contracting officer to issue a decision "on any submitted claim of $100,000 or less within sixty days from his receipt of a written request from the contractor that a decision be rendered within that period." Since the running of the 60-day period is triggered by the submission of a claim, the contractor has the ability to defer the start of the 60-day period while settlement negotiations are being undertaken, H.R. 1556, 95th Cong., 2d Sess. (1978) at 18.

41 U.S.C. § 605(c)(2) contains different procedures for claims exceeding $ 100,000:

> A contracting officer shall, within sixty days of receipt of a submitted certified claim over $100,000—

(A) issue a decision; or

(B) notify the contractor of the time within which a decision will be issued.

A further requirement at 41 U.S.C. § 605(c)(3) states:

> The decision of a contracting officer on submitted claims shall be issued within a reasonable time, in accordance with regulations promulgated by the agency, taking into account such factors as the size and complexity of the claim and the adequacy of the information in support of the claim provided by the contractor.

FAR 33.211(d) implements this statute.

The court and boards have ruled that the specified time for issuing a decision must be a date certain. Thus, in *Obras & Assocs. v. United States*, 26 Cl. Ct. 647 (1992), the court held that a contracting officer's statement in a letter to the contractor that it should not expect a final decision prior to June 30 failed to satisfy the notification provision of § 605(c)(2) and, thus, the claim was "deemed denied." See also *Boeing Co. v. United States,* 26 Cl. Ct. 257 (1992), finding inadequate the contracting officer's statement that he would "endeavor to respond" to the claims by a stated date but if unable "I will advise you . . . when I will respond." In *Northrop Grumman Corp.,* ASBCA 52263, 00-1 BCA ¶ 30,676, the specific date requirement was not met when the contracting officer stated that a final decision would be issued "no later than 90 days after termination of the ADR if the ADR process does not result in resolution of all issues." Similarly, in *Aerojet Gen. Corp.,* ASBCA 48136, 95-1 BCA ¶ 27,470, a notice stating that the contracting officer did not anticipate issuing a final decision until the early March time frame and that his ability to meet that date was contingent on the claimant's cooperation in supplying cost and pricing data was deemed to be subjective, indefinite, and a conditional response which did not satisfy the CDA's requirements. See also *McDonnell Douglas Corp.,* ASBCA 48432, 96-1 BCA ¶ 28,166, in which the contracting officer's statement that the agency would issue a final decision promptly if and when the board dismissed the contractor's pending appeal was found deficient. Compare *Defense Sys. Co.,* ASBCA 50534, 97-2 BCA ¶ 28,971, in which the board held adequate a contracting officer's statement that a decision would be issued "on or before" a date nine months after the date of the claim.

The "reasonable time" requirement for claims over $ 100,000 will be assessed by considering the complexity of the issues in the claim. See *Defense Sys. Co.,* ASBCA 50534, 97-2 BCA ¶ 28,971, reasoning that nine months was not an undue amount of time to review a $ 71 million claim for breach of contract. In *Suburban Middlesex Insulation, Inc.,* VABCA 4896, 96-2 BCA ¶ 28,481, the board found that it was reasonable to set a decision time seven months after submission of a claim because it had been referred to the agency inspector general for criminal investigation. The board ruled, however, that it was unreasonable to extend the decision date by over three more months because the investigation was not yet completed. Compare *Dillingham/ABB-SUSA, J.V.,* ASBCA 51195, 98-2 BCA ¶ 29,778, finding 14 months far too long for deciding "a relatively small, straightforward construction claim." See also *Fru-Con Constr. Corp.*, ASBCA 53544, 02-1 BCA ¶ 31,729 (13 months an unreasonable time). In *Adventure Group, Inc.,* ASBCA 52687, 00-2 BCA ¶ 30,994, the board held that it was improper for the contracting officer to postpone indefinitely the issuance of a contracting officer's decision while waiting for the Department of Labor to issue a wage determination. The board concluded that if the absence of a wage determination precluded the issuance of a decision on the merits, the contracting officer should deny the claim for lack of information.

The fact that a claim submission may be inadequate will not relieve the contracting officer from his or her statutory duty to choose between issuing a timely decision or forecasting the date for a decision, and failure to do so is an appealable decision properly before a board, *Westlox Military Prods.,* ASBCA 25592, 81-2 BCA ¶ 15,270. If a contracting officer considers information submitted by a contractor to be insufficient, the contracting officer's proper course is to deny the claim for lack of proof, not to decline to issue a decision, *Scott Timber Co.,* IBCA 3771-97, 99-1 BCA ¶ 30,184; *MK-Ferguson Co.,* ASBCA 42435, 91-3 BCA ¶ 24,308. See, however, *Gauntt Constr. Co.,* ASBCA 33323, 87-3 BCA ¶ 20,221, in which the board focused on the contractor's requirement to submit a claim in sufficient detail to allow the contracting officer to form a reasoned position. In that case, the board established a standard that, in order to at least support an appeal from a contacting officer's failure to issue a timely decision, the claim must contain sufficient information to allow the contracting officer to make a meaningful review of the claim. Subsequently, in *Blake Constr. Co.,* ASBCA 34480, 88-2 BCA ¶ 20,552, the board attempted to balance the appeals burden between contractor and contracting officer by establishing a predictable policy for dealing with allegedly inadequate claim submissions. The board stated at 103,891:

> When a contractor's claim submission fails to contain the requisite specificity, the contractor may appeal, in the absence of a decision, when it can be shown that the CO not only failed to render the decision but also failed to take other responsible action such as properly advising the contractor that the submittal was inadequate and required additional information before a decision could be made

See also *Dewey Elecs. Corp.,* DOTCAB 1224, 82-2 BCA ¶ 15,828 in which the board directed the contracting officer to issue a final decision 10 months after submission of the claim since the government had not challenged the adequacy of the contractor's submissions.

The contracting officer may decide distinct parts of a claim when they are susceptible of separate consideration and may reserve other portions of a claim for different or later treatment, In *Omni Abstract, Inc.,* ENGBCA 6254, 96-2 BCA ¶

28,367, the board ruled that, as to those separate matters decided by the contracting officer, the contractor's time to appeal the matters decided begins to run even though other distinct parts were not decided. As to the latter, the contractor may appeal these portions when decided or deemed denied.

In *Logicvision, Inc. v. United States*, 54 Fed. Cl. 549 (2002), the court ruled that the CDA 60-day time limit for extending the final decision deadline was satisfied when the contracting officer mailed the notice within the 60-day period informing the contractor that a final decision would be issued later, not when the contractor received the letter, which was two days after the 60-day deadline expired.

2. Failure to Issue a Timely Decision

If a contractor is not willing to wait for a decision of the contracting officer, it has two alternatives when faced with a contracting officer's failure to issue a decision. The contractor may request that the board or the Court of Federal Claims order the contracting officer to make a decision, 41 U.S.C. § 605(c)(4), or process the case as an appeal of a "deemed denied" decision, 41 U.S.C. § 605(c)(5). Prior to the Federal Acquisition Streamlining Act, Pub. L. 103-355, this authority was vested only in the boards. Section 2351 of the Act extended the authority to a "tribunal concerned," thereby including the Court of Federal Claims.

These provisions only apply to decisions on contractor claims. The court or board cannot direct issuance of a final decision on a government claim, *McDonnell Douglas Corp. v. United States*, 754 F.2d 365 (Fed. Cir. 1985); *Carter Indus., Inc.*, DOTBCA 2997, 96-2 BCA ¶ 28,548; *MGM Contracting Co.*, ASBCA 26895, 83-1 BCA ¶ 16,191.

a. An Order to Issue a Decision

41 U.S.C. § 605(c)(4) states:

> A contractor may request the tribunal concerned to direct a contracting officer to issue a decision in a specified period of time, as determined by the tribunal concerned, in the event of undue delay on the part of the contracting officer.

If a contractor proceeds under this section, the case is not regarded as an appeal on the merits but merely the request for an order to issue a decision, *Dewey Elecs. Corp.*, DOTCAB 1224, 82-2 BCA ¶ 15,828. Therefore, once a contracting officer's decision is issued, the contractor must file a new appeal if it wants to challenge the decision, *Dillon Constr., Inc*, ENGBCA PCC-195, 99-2 BCA ¶ 30,471.

If the claim is for $100,000 or less, it would appear that the court or board has no authority to give the contracting officer more than the required 60 days to issue the decision. Nonetheless, in *DHR, Inc.*, EBCA 4011287, 88-1 BCA ¶ 20,451, the board directed a contracting officer to issue a decision within four weeks of its decision even though the claim was submitted four months prior to the issuance of the board decision. The board stated at 103,430:

> We are . . loath to take actions which diminish]the] role [of the contracting officer in resolving claims] or which may result in an appeal without the Contracting Officer having first considered and decided the claim and without the Contractor having thereafter reviewed the decision and concluded that it is wrong. Such interplay delineates the issues and fosters responsible deliberation and careful assessment by each party of its own position. It requires each party to take affirmative actions based upon carefully made determinations. Most importantly, it provides a last clear chance to avoid litigation. We recognize that when we issue an order directing a Contracting Officer to issue a decision we set the stage for an appeal without the benefit of this last clear chance, since one consequence of a failure to comply would be to obviate the jurisdictional requirement for a Contracting Officer's decision.

If the claim is for over $ 100,000, the board will assess the facts and give the contracting officer a reasonable time to issue a decision. See *VECO, Inc.,* DOTBCA 2961, 96-1 BCA ¶ 28,108, in which the board directed a contracting officer to issue a final decision by a date that was approximately one year after the contractor's initial request for an equitable adjustment. The contractor had submitted 23 volumes of documentation in support of its claim for $ 5.7 million. In *Washington Constr. Co.*, DOTBCA 3026, 96-2 BCA ¶ 28,582, the board directed a contracting officer to issue a decision on an equitable adjustments claim on a date approximately eight months after the submission of a claim, in contrast to the ten months requested by the contracting officer.

Section 605(c)(4), however, does not entitle a contractor to obtain a board directive requiring a more detailed decision than the one already issued, *Sentry Ins.*, VABCA 2617, 88-1 BCA ¶ 20,236; *A.D. Roe Co.*, ASBCA 26078, 81-2 BCA ¶ 15,231.

b. Appeal of "Deemed Denied" Decisions

Alternatively, when the contracting officer does not issue a timely decision, a contractor may appeal a "deemed denied" decision under 41 U.S.C. § 605(c)(5) which states:

> Any failure by the contracting officer to issue a decision on a contract claim within the period required will be deemed to be a decision by the contracting officer denying the claim and will authorize the commencement of the appeal or suit on the claim as otherwise provided in this Chapter. However, in the event an appeal or suit is so commenced in the absence of a prior decision by the contracting officer, the tribunal concerned may, at its option, stay the proceedings to obtain a decision on the claim by the contracting officer.

For claims of $100,000 or less, a contractor may immediately appeal once the contracting officer has failed to issue a decision by the end of the 60-day period, *GPA-I, LP v. United States*, 46 Fed. Cl. 762 (2000). Although the boards will take jurisdiction of such cases, they have noted that the contracting officer may still issue a decision after the appeal has been filed, *Gardner Zemke Co.*, ASBCA 51499, 98-2 BCA ¶ 29,997; *Sayco, Ltd.*, ASBCA 39366, 92-1 BCA ¶ 24,573.

The 60-day time limit is a statutory requirement. In *Voices R Us, Inc.*, ASBCA 50373, 97-1 BCA ¶ 28,768, the contracting officer neither paid nor denied claims within the 60-day period. The board denied the government's motion to dismiss without prejudice for the purpose of "allowing the contracting officer to issue a meaningful final decision or negotiate resolution of the claims," holding that the failure to issue a decision within the 60-day period was a deemed denial from which the contractor was entitled to appeal. Moreover, the board stated that the fact that the decision was delayed because of a lack of cooperation between the contracting personnel and the government's legal department did not excuse the government's delay. See also *Viktoria Schaefer Internationale Spedition,* ASBCA 47792, 97-1 BCA ¶ 28,805, *aff'd,* 168 F.3d 1316 (Fed. Cir. 1998), in which the board refused to dismiss an appeal after a deemed denial on the basis that the contractor's failure to provide supporting data had precluded any meaningful review of the claim by the contracting officer. Instead, the board stated that all that is required for a claim is a clear and unequivocal written statement that gives adequate notice of the basis and amount of the claim, without accounting for each cost component. In *Landmark Constr. Corp.*, ASBCA 53139, 01-1 BCA ¶ 31,372, the government claimed that the contracting officer was not obligated to issue a decision on a claim because the claim was replaced and superseded by amended claims and thus that the board had no jurisdiction over the claim. The board found, however, that the contractor expressly included the claim in the amended claims and sought a final decision. Where the contracting officer neither issued a decision nor informed the contractor when a decision would be issued, the contractor was entitled to take a "deemed denial" appeal.

For claims exceeding $100,000, a claim will not be deemed denied until a reasonable time to issue a decision has expired, *Defense Sys. Co.*, ASBCA 50534, 97-2 BCA ¶ 28,981. However, a claim will be deemed denied if the contracting officer fails to specify a time in which a decision will be issued, *McDonnell Douglas Corp.*, ASBCA 48432, 96-1 BCA ¶ 28,166; fails to issue a timely decision, *Steve P. Rados, Inc.*, ENGBCA 6130, 96-1 BCA ¶ 27,982; or specifies an unreasonable time, *Cessna Aircraft Co.*, ASBCA 43196, 92-1 BCA ¶ 24,425. In *Briggs Eng'g & Testing Co. v. United States*, 230 Ct. Cl. 828 (1982), the court refused to dismiss a direct access suit filed 14 months after the claim was submitted to the contracting officer and ordered a stay of proceedings until the contracting officer rendered a decision. Compare *Fru-Con Constr. Corp.*, ASBCA 53544, 02-1 BCA ¶ 31,729, in which the board considered a decision "deemed denied" after the contracting officer had been considering the claim for 7½ months and had stated that a decision would not be issued for another six months. See also *Macsons, Inc.*, DOTBCA 4049, 00-2 BCA ¶

31,037, in which a decision was deemed denied because the contracting officer had issued no decision after settlement negotiations broke down.

The boards have also considered nonmonetary claims to be deemed denied when the contracting officer failed to issue a decision within a reasonable time, *Holmes & Narver, Inc.*, ASBCA 51430, 99-1 BCA ¶ 30,131; *Martin Marietta Corp.*, ASBCA 38920, 90-1 BCA ¶ 22,418.

In some cases in which the contractor has appealed in the absence of a final decision, it is not always clear whether the contractor had properly submitted a claim or whether the contracting officer had a reasonable opportunity to decide the claim. In such cases, the proceedings will be stayed to obtain a decision, *Gentex Corp.*, ASBCA 24040, 79-2 BCA ¶ 14,007, *recons. denied*, 79-2 BCA ¶ 14,139. See also *6800 Corp.*, GSBCA 5880, 81-2 BCA ¶ 15,388, in which the board ordered a stay of proceedings for a reasonable period to allow a contracting officer to consider the claim because it was not clear whether the contractor's tort/contract claim had been submitted to a contracting officer. Compare, however, *Boeing Co.*, ASBCA 27396, 83-1 BCA ¶ 16,256, in which the board dismissed a contractor's appeal as premature because the contractor had never submitted either a claim or the requisite certifications to a contracting officer for final decision. See also *Data Sys. Div. of Litton Sys., Inc.*, ASBCA 27684, 83-1 BCA ¶ 16,334, in which the board dismissed the appeal rather than staying proceedings because the contractor failed to certify its claim to the contracting officer.

Although "deemed denied" decisions give jurisdiction to the court or boards, they do not start the twelve-month limitation period for filing direct access suits under the CDA or the 90-day limitation period for filing appeals in the agency board. See *Pathman Constr. Co. v. United States*, 817 F.2d 1573 (Fed. Cir. 1987), holding that this period does not begin to run "until the contracting officer renders an actual written decision on the contractor's claim." The court stated at 1578:

> In view of the detailed specification Congress provided for the content and furnishing of the contracting officer's decision to the contractor, it is most unlikely Congress intended the twelve-month limitation period to start running on the 'deemed denial' of the claim, which by definition the contracting officer never furnished to the contractor and which the contractor therefore never received.

For cases applying this rule, see *Information Handling Servs., Inc. v. General Servs. Admin.*, GSBCA 14318, 98-1 BCA ¶ 29,620; *Carter Indus., Inc.*, DOTBCA 2995, 98-1 BCA ¶ 29,625; *Omni Abstract, Inc.*, ENGBCA 6254, 96-2 BCA ¶ 28,367; and *Bravo Mfg., Inc.*, ASBCA 45293, 94-3 BCA ¶ 27,236.

3. Form and Content of Decision

Since the failure to appeal from a contracting officer's decision within the time required can result in the loss of all the contractor's rights, the boards and courts have paid particular attention to the form and content of the decision to see that the contractor has been sufficiently protected.

a. Written Decision

The CDA requires that final decisions be made in writing, 41 U.S.C. § 605(a). Oral notification by a contracting officer of a decision on a contractor's claim will generally not constitute a proper final decision for purposes of starting the appeal period, *Brookfield Constr. Co. v. United States*, 228 Ct. Cl. 551, 661 F.2d 159 (1981). A telegraphic message will satisfy the requirement for a written decision, *Avondale Shipyards, Inc.*, DOTCAB 6718B, 68-1 BCA ¶ 7030, *recons. denied,* 68-2 BCA ¶ 7196. Similarly, in *Tyger Constr. Co.*, ASBCA 36100, 88-3 BCA ¶ 21,149, the board ruled that a facsimile copy sent by telecopier served as effective notice of the contracting officer's decision.

The boards of contract appeals have occasionally accepted jurisdiction of contractor appeals from oral notification of denial of a claim, *Bay Hardware*, ASBCA 7119, 61-2 BCA ¶ 3114. In *Ray & Ray's Carpet & Linoleum, Inc.*, GSBCA 5666, 83-1 BCA ¶ 16,184, the board took jurisdiction of a contractor's request for contract reformation even though there had been no written claim and no contracting officer's decision on the issue. The board found that the parties had in effect waived the statutory requirements for a written claim and decision and held that "even under the CDA there are situations in which the statutory formalities need not be observed." The board stressed, however, that there had been both a written claim and a contracting officer's decision on other aspects of the case and the government had characterized referral of the reformation issue to a contracting officer as a "useless act." See also *Cosmic Constr. Co.*, VACAB 1504, 82-1 BCA ¶ 15,696, and *Mid-America Prot., Inc.*, GSBCA 5476, 83-1 BCA ¶ 16,341.

The decision may be sent only to the contractor. See *F.E. Constructors, JV,* ASBCA 24488, 80-2 BCA ¶ 14,505, rejecting a contractor's contention that the government's failure to send a copy of the final decision to the contractor's lawyer excused an untimely filing of appeal.

b. Notification

For many years the regulations have required that final decisions contain language expressly notifying the contractor that the communication constitutes a final decision within the disputes procedures and stating the contractor's appeal rights. FAR 33.211(a)(4)(v) provides that a paragraph substantially similar to the following must be included in the decision:

> This is the final decision of the Contracting Officer. You may appeal this decision to the agency board of contract appeals. If you decide to appeal, you must, within 90 days from the date you receive this decision, mail or otherwise furnish

> written notice to the agency board of contract appeals and provide a copy to the Contracting Officer from whose decision this appeal is taken. The notice shall indicate that an appeal is intended, reference this decision, and identify the contract by number. With regard to appeals to the agency board of contract appeals, you may, solely at your election, proceed under the board's small claim procedure fix claims at $50,000 or less or its accelerated procedure for claims of $100,000 or less. Instead of appealing to the agency board of contract appeals, you may bring an action directly in the United States Court of Federal Claims [now the Court of Federal Claims] (except as provided in the Contract Disputes Act of 1978, 41 U.S.C. 603, regarding Maritime Contracts) within 12 months of the date you receive this decision.

Following the guidance of *Pathman Constr. Co. v. United States*, 817 F.2d 1573 (Fed. Cir. 1987), the boards consistently held that a contracting officer's decision that does not contain language substantially similar to that above was procedurally defective with the result that the time limitations on appeals did not apply. However, in *Decker & Co. v. West*, 76 F.3d 1573 (Fed. Cir. 1996), the court held that an incorrect notification of appeal rights would not excuse an untimely appeal unless the contractor could demonstrate "detrimental reliance on that defect." In that case, the court held that the agency appeals board had no jurisdiction to hear an appeal filed two years after the contracting officer's decision even though the notification was incorrect in stating that a default termination could be challenged in the Court of Federal Claims.

Detrimental reliance has been found in several cases. See *Eastern Computers, Inc.*, ASBCA 49185, 96-2 BCA ¶ 28,343 (board, citing *Decker*, stated that the appeal was timely because the contractor was misled as to whether the copy of the final decision sent by facsimile or the copy sent by mail started the appeal time running); *SRM Mfg. Co.*, ASBCA 44750, 96-2 BCA ¶ 28,487, *recons. granted*, 98-1 BCA ¶ 29,471, *recons. denied*, 00-1 BCA ¶ 30,618 (contractor's counsel had advised it that contracting officer's defective notification permitted deferral of appeal); and *TPI Int'l Airways, Inc.*, ASBCA 46462, 96-2 BCA ¶ 28,373, *recons. denied,* 96-2 BCA ¶ 28,602, *aff'd,* 135 F.3d 776 (Fed. Cir. 1998), *cert. denied*, 525 U. S. 874 (1998) (testimony of a contractor's president that he did not appeal within 90 days of receiving the final decision because of the erroneous advice in the notice that he had one year to appeal to the Claims Court).

Some boards have concluded that if the contracting officer's decision lacks "critical" or "essential" information, there will be no need to prove detrimental reliance. See *George Ledford Constr., Inc.*, VABCA 6630, 02-1 BCA ¶ 31,662 (decision provided no information as to when, where or how an appeal could be taken), and *Lawrence Harris Constr., Inc.,* VABCA 7219, 05-1 BCA ¶ 32,830 (decision did not inform the contractor of the critical 90-day time limit). In *Harris* the board stated that since the small disadvantaged business had indicated that it did not realize there was a 90-day appeal period, it would find detrimental reliance if that were necessary.

Following *Decker*, there have been some decisions dismissing late appeals because of the lack of detrimental reliance. See *State of Fa., Dep't of Ins. v. United States*, 81 F.3d 1093 (Fed. Cir. 1996) (surety had actual notice of appeal rights); *Carter Indus., Inc.*, DOTBCA 2995, 98-1 BCA ¶ 29,625 (contractor did not prove that it relied on the decision's failure to state to which agency board an appeal should be sent); *Medina Contracting Co.*, ASBCA 52783, 02-2 BCA ¶ 31,979 (contractor's statement that it would appeal default termination indicated lack of reliance on missing information in contracting officer's decision); and *American Renovation & Constr. Co.*, ASBCA 54039, 03-2 BCA ¶ 32,296 (contractor had actual knowledge of its appeal rights). See also *Int'l Air Response v. United States*, 49 Fed. Cl. 509 (2001), in which the court dismissed the contractor's complaint for failure to appeal the contracting officer's final decision within one year. The contractor argued that the U.S. District Court of Arizona had stayed all deadlines relevant to its claims under the CDA. The court held, however, that a district court has no power, inherently or statutorily, to derogate the jurisdiction of the court or to toll the CDA's limitations provisions. Moreover, because the district court lifted its stay six weeks before the original CDA 12-month filing deadline. the court found that the contractor had ample time to file its complaint at the court. The Federal Circuit reversed, holding that the stay order tolled the running of the appeal period because the government did not appeal the order, but did not decide whether the district court had jurisdiction to issue it, *Int'l Air Response v. United States*, 302 F.3d 1363 (Fed. Cir. 2002).

Since the notification is for the contractor's benefit, it will be permitted to appeal the decision even if it contains a defective notification. See *J. Fiorito Leasing, Ltd.*, PSBCA 1102, 83-1 BCA ¶ 16,546, in which the board held that a contractor who received a procedurally defective contracting officer's decision could either continue the board appeal, choose to appeal to the Claims Court, or request a new final decision. See also *Outdoor Venture Corp.*, ASBCA 49756, 96-2 BCA ¶ 28,490 (contractor entitled to appeal government demand that the contractor proceed with warranty work even though the demand was defective); *Sprint Communications Co. v. General Servs. Admin.*, GSBCA 13182, 96-1 BCA ¶ 28,068 (contractor entitled to appeal from letter detailing contractor's deficiencies and the amount of deductions the agency would take, even though it did not expressly state that it was a final decision, because it unequivocally informed the contractor that payment was due); and *Midwest Props., LLC v. General Servs. Admin.*, GSBCA 15822, 03-2 BCA ¶ 32,344 (contractor entitled to appeal government claim because contracting officer's letter was tantamount to a final decision). Similarly, a contracting officer's letter rejecting the entire amount claimed by the contractor constituted a final decision sufficient to trigger an appeal even though the contracting officer's letter did not state that it was a final decision, *The Writing Co. v. Department of the Treasury,* GSBCA 15117-TD, 00-2 BCA ¶ 31,076.

Procedurally defective decisions returned by the boards to the contracting officers with orders to issue a new decision include *Lucerne Constr. Corp.*, VACAB 1494, 82-2 BCA ¶ 16,101 (contracting officer's decision held invalid because it did not inform contractor of its right to proceed under the CDA), and *Imperator Carpet*

& Interiors, Inc., GSBCA 6156, 81-2 BCA ¶ 15,248 (contracting officer's letter was not a final decision because it did not inform the contractor of its appeal rights).

In some cases boards have rendered decisions on timely appeals from procedurally defective contracting officer's decisions, *Daiei Denki Co., Ltd.*, ASBCA 28499, 84-1 BCA ¶ 16,954; *Vepco, Inc.*, ASBCA 26993, 82-2 BCA ¶ 15,824; *Habitech, Inc.*, ASBCA 26388, 82-1 BCA ¶ 15,794.

c. Responsive to the Claim

Although the Act is silent on the matter, it has long been held that a contracting officer's decision must be responsive to the contractor's claim. In other words, the decision must contain an unequivocal expression dealing with the matter in dispute, *AVANTE Int'l Sys. Corp.*, ASBCA 26649, 83-1 BCA ¶ 16,416. In *Fred A. Arnold*, ASBCA 10886, 65-2 BCA ¶ 5151, a decision that confused the location of disputed items in a construction plan was not a proper final decision from which timely appeal had to be taken. The board stated at 24,248:

> The Board observes initially that in large part the confusion in this case is attributable to [the contractor] because [the contractor's] claim letters were obscure as to the location of the conduit with which appellant was concerned. It would also appear that the contracting officer made no investigation with respect to the claim, at least insofar as any contacts with [the contractor] were concerned. As a result there has been no meeting of the minds on the alleged factual basis for the claim.

An ambiguous decision by a contracting officer will not be afforded finality. In *Lakeview Lumber Prods. Co. v. United States*, 215 Ct. Cl. 914 (1977), a contracting officer's decision that granted the contractor's claim for direct costs but was entirely silent on the contractor's claim for indirect costs was not a final decision as to the latter types of costs. See also *E.P. Cline*, PSBCA 2926, 91-2 BCA ¶ 23,992, where the contracting officer's letter was not a final decision because it did not clearly communicate the government's intentions concerning costs associated with the proposed modification of the perimeter wall of a leased facility.

If a decision covers only part of the claims submitted, it will not be effective as to the omitted claims, *Omni Abstract, Inc.*, ENGBCS 6254, 96-2 BCA ¶ 28,367. See also *JWA Emadel Enters., Inc.*, ASBCA 51016, 98-2 BCA ¶ 29,765, *recons. denied*, 98-2 BCA ¶ 29,960, in which the board rejected the government's argument that denial of a claim for a cost overrun should be read as a denial of subsequent overrun claims based on different facts. Although a partial decision constitutes a valid final decision for those matters that are clearly decided, substantial confusion may result from such "piecemeal" decisionmaking and lead to the conclusion that an otherwise proper final decision is ambiguous, *Skyline Constr. Co.*, DOTCAB 7417, 75-1 BCA ¶ 11,147.

d. Reasons for the Decision

41 U.S.C. § 605(a) provides that a final decision "shall state the reasons for the decision reached" and that "specific findings of fact are not required." FAR 33.211(a)(4) amplifies these provisions by requiring supporting rationale and a statement of factual areas of agreement and disagreement. However, boards have been reluctant to find that decisions contained too little reasoning. See *RMTC Sys., Inc.*, ASBCA 46496, 94-2 BCA ¶ 26,743 (contracting officer's decision adequate even though tersely worded and sparse in detail). In *Inca Contracting Co.*, ASBCA 52171, 00-1 BCA ¶ 30,672, the board stated that the decision was sufficient if its "analysis is sufficient to place the dispute in its appropriate contractual context."

Where a contractor disputes the content of the contracting officer's decision rather than its sufficiency, the board will not issue a directive requiring a more detailed decision. In *A.D. Roe Co.*, ASBCA 26078, 81-2 BCA ¶ 15,231, the board refused a contractor's request to issue a directive requiring a more detailed contracting officer's final decision because the statute only authorized a direction to issue a final decision when there had been undue delay, which was not the case there. The board reasoned that where the contracting officer had actually issued a final decision, a request for more information went to the merits of the claim and could be properly resolved as part of the appeals process.

A contracting officer may amend a final decision on a CDA claim even after the contractor has appealed the decision to an appellate board, *Space Age Eng'g, Inc.*, ASBCA 26028, 82-1 BCA ¶ 15,766.

e. Decision in Wrong Form May Bind the Government

Although a contracting officer decision that fails to satisfy these formal requirements will not normally result in a forfeiture of a contractor's rights under the Disputes clause, it may bind the government. In *Bell Helicopter Co.*, ASBCA 17776, 74-1 BCA ¶ 10,411, a contracting officer sent a letter informing the contractor of his determination that certain defective pricing allegations made by the DCAA were "unfounded." A successor contracting officer sought to "withdraw" this decision, arguing that the government was not bound by the letter since it failed to contain the terminal language required in final decisions. The board responded at 49,192:

> This statement clearly and unequivocally is a decision intended to resolve a dispute between the parties.

In *General Elec. Co. v. United States*, 188 Ct. Cl. 620, 416 F.2d 1215, *recons. denied,* 189 Ct. Cl. 116 (1969), a contracting officer's endorsement of a recommendation from the chief legal officer of the procurement activity that a contractor's cost overrun be funded was held to be a binding final decision. See *Texas Instruments, Inc. v. United States*, 922 F.2d 810 (Fed. Cir. 1990), in which an administrative contracting officer's signature on a Price Negotiation Memorandum (PNM) was found to constitute a final binding decision to approve the negotiated price. Following *General Electric*, the court concluded that by signing the PNM, the contracting officer had decided to express a definite opinion on the merits of the claim and in the absence of contrary testimony or evidence had in fact made a decision. Likewise, in *Sperry Gyroscope Co.*, ASBCA 9700, 1964 BCA ¶ 4514, a letter informing a contractor of the contracting officer's decision to allow reimbursement for certain cost items bound the government even though the letter was not intended to constitute a "final and binding determination" on the allowability of the cost items. The board stated that since the contracting officer's intention—not to have the letter interpreted as a determination—"had not been communicated to Sperry, it can have no effect upon the parties' agreement."

4. Quality of the Decisional Process

The courts and various boards of contract appeals have construed the standard Disputes clause as requiring a contracting officer to make a "personal and independent" judgment on the merits of a contractor's claim, *Climatic Rainwear Co. v. United States*, 115 Ct. Cl. 520, 88 F. Supp. 415 (1950); *Byrd Foods, Inc.*, VACAB 1679, 83-1 BCA ¶ 16,313. See also *Dravo-Groves*, ENGBCA 4801, 83-1 BCA ¶ 16,158, in which the board dismissed government counterclaims raised in a contractor's appeal because the counterclaims had not been subject to a decision of a contracting officer exercising independent judgment.

a. Replacement of Contracting Officer

The requirement for a personal and independent decision generally does not prevent the government agency from replacing the original contracting officer. However, a proper final decision of a contracting officer cannot be reversed by a successor contracting officer. See *General Elec. Co. v. United States*, 188 Ct. Cl. 620, 416 F.2d 1215 (1969), *reh'g denied,* 189 Ct. Cl. 116, 416 F.2d 1320 (1969); *Liberty Coat Co.*, ASBCA 4119, 57-2 BCA ¶ 1576; and *Airmotive Eng'g Corp.*, ASBCA 15235, 71-2 BCA ¶ 8988. See also *Bell Helicopter Co.*, ASBCA 17776, 74-1 BCA ¶ 10,411, in which the board held that a valid settlement agreement cannot be reversed by a successor contracting officer issuing a "final decision." Compare *Kirschner Assocs.*, ASBCA 25824, 81-2 BCA ¶ 15,304, holding that a successor contracting officer is not bound by a modification agreement drafted by a predecessor contracting officer once the original agreement has been rejected by the parties. In *Kirschner*, the successor contracting officer was permitted to reassess the contractor's claim for payment of a cost overrun, determine that the contractor had failed to comply with the contract's Limitation of Cost clause, and deny the claim based upon the reassessment.

Replacement of the contracting officer may be improper if the contract designates a particular government official (either by name or office) to make the decision. In *New York Shipbuilding Corp. v. United States*, 180 Ct. Cl. 446, 385 F.2d 427 (1967), the contract designated a particular government official, the Nuclear Projects Officer, as the person who would initially decide contract disputes. The government subsequently abolished that post and transferred its functions to a newly created research and development office whose chief had responsibility over all types of merchant vessels as well as nuclear ships. The Court of Claims declared that a decision on a contractor's claim made by the chief of the R&D office was without legal effect as a final decision.

b. Advice from Other Officials

The courts and boards have also recognized that the contracting officer is entitled to rely upon the opinions and conclusions of technical and legal advisors in arriving at a final decision under the Disputes article. See *Barringer & Botke*, IBCA 428364, 65-1 BCA ¶ 4797, *modified on other grounds*, 66-1 BCA ¶ 5458, in which the board stated at 22,775:

> While it is well settled that a decision of a contracting officer must represent his own judgment and not that of another, it is also recognized that a contracting officer may, for the purpose of forming his independent judgment, obtain information and advice from his staff officers and advisors, particularly in the areas of law, accounting and engineering, in which fields he may have little or no expertise. We consider that it would be poor judgment on his part if he did not do so.

In *Pacific Architects & Eng'rs, Inc. v. United States*, 203 Ct. Cl. 499, 491 F.2d 734 (1974), the contracting officer was found to have made a personal and independent judgment in exercising his discretion even though his decision was based principally upon legal advice given by government attorneys. The court stated at 517:

> On the other hand, it is unreasonable to construe the requirement for decision by the contracting officer to preclude the obtaining of legal advice, and particularly where the contracting officer is not a lawyer. Even if an overly liberal grant by a contracting officer would not be reviewable on the government's appeal, it would have to be assumed that the contracting officer like any other officer of the United States would do his best to follow the requirements of law. It was contemplated that after receiving recommendations, legal opinions and advice, "in the end he put his own mind to the problems and render his own decisions." *New York Shipbuilding Co. v. United States*, . . . , 385 F.2d at 435. But there was no implied prohibition against his first obtaining or even agreeing with the views of others.

See also *Nuclear Research Corp. v. United States*, 814 F.2d 647 (Fed. Cir. 1987), finding a valid decision where the contracting officer initially argued against a termination for default, but changed his mind after discussions with personnel in the affected agency. Similarly, in *AirOPlastik Corp.*, GSBCA 4802, 81-2 BCA ¶ 15,338, a contracting officer's reliance on secondhand information, a recommended course of action, and preparation of correspondence by a subordinate reflected no more than routine government procedure and did not provide grounds for overturning a final decision on the basis that the contracting officer has not exercised independent judgment. In *American Transparents Plastics Corp.*, GSBCA 7006, 91-1 BCA ¶ 23,349, three contracting officers administering separate contracts for plastic bags sought reimbursement for payments made under identical price adjustment clauses found in each contract. The contractor contended that the contracting officers did not exercise independent judgment because they were intimidated by a strong recommendation made by the agency Inspector General or, in one case, because the contracting officer relied on the opinion of a subordinate. In denying the contractor's contention, the board stated at 117,086:

> In this case, the Inspector General provided advice, and that advice the Contracting Officer is required to consider as an important aspect of the litany of advice provided, viz., legal advice, accounting advice, and advice from subordinates and colleagues.

In *Mike Gibson & Mike Bearden, Co-Trs. in Dissolution of Delta Prods. Co.*, AGBCA 88-139-1, 93-2 BCA ¶ 25,615, the board considered the extent of personal involvement required of the contracting officer when rendering decisions. In that case, a decision issued by a contracting officer but written by others was held to be a properly rendered decision. The board stated at 127,509:

> [I]t is clear that while the CO was not the primary decision maker and had little or no role in actually preparing the decision, he read it in detail, consulted with others within the agency, and agreed with the decision before signing it. . . . The fact that the CO did not know who prepared the initial draft of the decision, or that he was not made aware of a relevant fact at the time he signed the decision, is irrelevant. . . . The CO need only make the decision.

The same conclusion was reached in *PLB Grain Storage Corp.*, AGBCA 89-152-1, 92-1 BCA ¶ 24,731, where the decision was written by the agency's counsel but signed by the contracting officer. See also *Kearfott Guidance & Navigation Corp.*, ASBCA 49271, 04-2 BCA ¶ 32,757 (reliance on DCAA in cost matters permissible).

Although a contracting officer is entitled to rely upon the recommendations of advisors in formulating a final decision, the contracting officer may not substitute the judgments and conclusions of those advisors for his or her own independent consideration of the merits of a claim. See *J.E. Peters, Inc.*, ASBCA 4198, 57-2 BCA ¶ 1375. In *Beals Plumbing & Heating, Inc.*, GSBCA 1163, 1964 BCA ¶ 4358, the board held that a personal and independent decision had not been rendered where a construction engineer, acting as an authorized representative of the contracting officer, had "acquiesced completely" in an interpretation of the specifications urged upon him by a third party. Similarly, in *CEMS, Inc. v. United States*, 65 Fed. Cl. 473 (2005), the court found that the contracting officer "failed to conduct an independent review and take ownership" of his decision when he relied almost entirely on a consultant that had been hired by the agency to work on the matter. See also *Digital Simulation Sys., Inc.*, NASABCA 1751, 75-1 BCA ¶ 11,336, in which the board held that no finality would attach to a contracting officer's decision where the record indicated that the decision had been based upon a "down the line" adoption of recommendations by the Defense Contract Audit Agency without determinable input by the contracting officer or any other NASA official. Similarly, in *Edmund Leising Bldg. Contractor, Inc.*, VACAB 1428, 81-1 BCA ¶ 14,925, the board invalidated a contracting officer's final decision, which had been imposed upon the contracting officer by the Veterans Administration's central office staff. See also *Equitable Constr. Co.*, GSBCA 2642, 70-1 BCA ¶ 8196, *recons. denied,* 70-1 BCA ¶ 8327, in which the decision issued by the contracting officer was denied finality because a project engineer testified that all letters and the final decision regarding the dispute were written by him personally or under his direction.

In a split decision of the ASBCA, the panel majority held that a contracting officer is entitled to rely on his subordinates in reaching a final decision and is not required to investigate independently the facts of a claim. Instead, the contracting officer need only exercise independent discretion in deciding the claims before him, which the majority considered to have been satisfied by the contracting officer's testimony that the decision represented his independent judgment. The board member who presided over the appeal dissented on the basis that the decision neither resulted from the contracting officer's personal and independent consideration of the issues and records nor reflected his own independent judgment, *Prism Constr. Co.*, ASBCA 44682, 97-1 BCA ¶ 28,909, *recons. denied,* 97-2 BCA ¶ 29,004.

c. *Orders of Superior*

A decision by a contracting officer who follows the command direction of a superior without making a personal and independent judgment on the merits of a contractor's claim will not be a valid final decision under the Disputes clause. In *John A. Johnson Contracting Corp. v. United States*, 132 Ct. Cl. 645, 132 F. Supp. 698 (1955), the court denied legal effect to a decision of a contracting officer denying a contractor's claims for time extensions and terminating the contract for default. The court found that the contracting officer had initially intended to grant the time extensions but instead abdicated his contractual responsibility to the commanding officer of the base where the work was being performed by complying with the commander's demand that the contract be terminated and the work redesigned. See also *International Builders of Fla., Inc.*, FAACAP 675, 69-1 BCA ¶ 7706, *recons. denied*, 71-1 BCA ¶ 8790, in which the board stated that "[d]ecisions by contracting officers under the Disputes clause must be their own independent determinations, subject to advice by others, but not subject to command direction." The board went on to deny a motion to require the contracting officer to issue an independent decision, however, because it found that the direction to the contracting officer from a superior concerned a proposed settlement agreement rather than the final decision eventually issued. Compare *Jack Graham Co.*, ASBCA 4585, 58-2 BCA ¶ 1998, where a letter signed by the contracting officer that informed the contractor of a decision of "Headquarters, First United States Army" was deemed a proper final decision since both parties to the dispute "accepted the decision as that of the contracting officer." Similarly, in *Kilgore v. United States*, 121 Ct. Cl. 340 (1952), a decision by a district engineer who was himself a contracting officer and a superior of the contracting officer of record was afforded finality under the Disputes clause. The court concluded that although the contractor would have had the right to insist upon a decision from the contracting officer of record, its failure to object to the decision of the district engineer amounted to a waiver of its right to have that decision declared a nullity.

d. Review of Decisions

Certain agency regulations require contracting officers to refer proposed final decisions to superiors for review. It has been held that a contracting officer's decision submitted to a superior for "approval" will constitute a valid final decision. In *Jacob Schlesinger, Inc. v. United States*, 94 Ct. Cl. 289 (1941), the court stated at 307:

> [The contractor] now complains that the contracting officer did not, individually and without consulting his superiors, decide the question. In fact he did, although he did not communicate his decision until he had submitted it to his superior officer in the form of a recommendation, as was the usual practice. His letter to [the contractor] did attribute his decision to the War Department which, perhaps, gave it an air of finality which would discourage an appeal. . . . As to his consulting his superior, we see no objection to that, if the contracting officer, in fact, put his mind on the problem as it existed at the place where the contract was being carried out, and if, as here, the decision which he communicated to the contractor was his own, although it also had the approval of his superior. The question had not, in fact, been submitted to the head of the department, as [the contractor] could have learned if it had inquired or shown any desire to appeal as provided in the contract.

See *Systems Tech. Assocs., Inc.*, IBCA 1108476, 81-1 BCA ¶ 14,934, *recons. denied*, 81-1 BCA ¶ 15,084, *aff'd*, 699 F.2d 1383 (Fed. Cir. 1983) (agency procedure mandating review by superiors of contracting officer's decisions involving substantial amounts of money does not destroy the independence of a decision so long as the contracting officer independently determined the amount of settlement offered).

e. Unbiased and Impartial Decision

The contracting officer is required to make an unbiased and impartial judgment of the merits of the contractor's claim. In *Penner Installation Corp. v. United States*, 116 Ct. Cl. 550, 89 F. Supp. 545, *aff'd*, 340 U.S. 898 (1950), the court stated at 56364:

> In other words, the contracting officer must act impartially in settling disputes. He must not act as a representative of one of the contracting parties, but as an impartial, unbiased judge. If the evidence shows he has failed so to act, there can be no doubt that we have jurisdiction to set aside his decision. *Northern Pacific Railway Co. v. Twohy Bros. Co.*, 86 F.2d 220, 225; *Anderson v. Imhoff, et. al.*, 34 Neb. 335, 51 N.W. 854, 856. The duty to act impartially was imposed upon him by the contract. If we are convinced he has failed to discharge this contractual obligation, then his decision cannot have that finality provided for in the contract, and we are free to decide the case as we see it.
>
> Some contracting officers regard themselves as representatives of the [government], charged with the duty of protecting its interests and of exacting of the contractor everything that may be in the interest of the Government, even though no reasonable basis therefor can be found in the contract documents; but the Supreme Court has said that in settling disputes this is not his function; his function, on the other hand, is to act impartially, weighing with an even hand the rights of the parties.

IV. LITIGATION OF DISPUTES ACT CLAIMS

The CDA permits contractors to litigate disputes in either the agency board of contract appeals or the Court of Federal Claims. This election applies to both contractor claims and government claims with the result that the government has no right to determine the forum in which its claims will be litigated. This section focuses on the factors that contractors should consider when litigating claims. The first section discusses the decision to contest the contracting officer's findings. Next, the choice of forum is covered followed by a discussion of the time constraints for filing appeals or bringing suit. The chapter concludes with a summary of the organization and roles of the boards and courts involved in the Disputes process.

A. The Decision to Appeal or Bring Suit

As with any litigation, CDA appeals or suits should be undertaken only after full consideration of such factors as chance of success, cost of litigation, impact on customer relations, possible disruptive influence on operations, and desirability of creating precedent. In addition, the scope of any appeal or suit should be carefully analyzed because the boards and the court judges will analyze whether the operative facts are the same. If, in an appeal, the claims described in the pleadings arise from operative facts different from those that form the basis of the claim presented to the contracting officer, or if the claims are not contained within the scope of the claim previously presented to the contracting officer, the board lacks jurisdiction to consider them, *Wilson v. General Servs. Admin.*, GSBCA 13152, 96-1 BCA ¶ 28,266. However, the court or board will carefully scrutinize the operative facts to determine if they are the same as a seemingly new appeal. See *William L. Crow Constr. Co.*, ASBCA 41508, 97-2 BCA ¶ 29,124 (contractor permitted to raise new legal theories on appeal arising from the same operative facts as its certified claim); *Scott Timber*

Co. v. United States, 333 F.3d 1358 (Fed. Cir. 2003) (although plaintiff presented different legal theories to the court than it had to the contracting officer, the underlying operative facts and remedies requested were the same); and *Peter Bauwens Bauunternehmung GmbH & Co. KG,* ASBCA 44679, 98-1 BCA ¶ 29,551, *aff'd,* 194 F.3d 1338 (Fed. Cir. 1999) (changing the amount demanded and revising the number of days of alleged government-caused delay based on further information not reasonably available when the initial claim was submitted, and not the result of any deliberate understatement or careless initial appraisal of the claim, are properly before the board on appeal). If the scope of the appeal is less than the issues covered by the final decision of the contracting officer, the portions of the final decision not covered in the notice of appeal will be dismissed, *Cafritz Co. v. General Servs. Admin.*, GSBCA 13525, 97-1 BCA ¶ 28,969 (rule applied even though contractor attached the contracting officer's entire decision to its notice of appeal).

The findings of fact and legal conclusions in final decisions of contracting officers will play virtually no role in the subsequent litigation. Under 41 U.S.C. § 605(a), specific findings of fact made by the contracting officer "shall not be binding in any subsequent proceeding." The CDA also provides that suits in the Court of Federal Claims shall proceed de novo, 41 U.S.C. § 609(a)(3). Thus, the contracting officer's decisions will be affirmed or reversed based upon the evidence introduced in the proceedings before the agency board or the Court of Federal Claims and the law as interpreted by the forum involved. In the past, findings of fact and legal conclusions adverse to the contractor were not entitled to any presumption of validity in proceedings before a board of contract appeals. See *Southwest Welding & Mfg. Co. v. United States*, 188 Ct. Cl. 925, 413 F.2d 1167 (1969). In contrast, decisions in favor of the contractor have in the past been held to constitute an "evidentiary admission" of liability entitled to presumptive validity, *Norair Eng'g Corp.*, GSBCA 3473, 73-2 BCA ¶ 10,288. The Court of Claims had apparently endorsed this view, *Dean Constr. Co. v. United States*, 188 Ct. Cl. 62, 411 F.2d 1238 (1969); *George A. Fuller Co. v. United States*, 108 Ct. Cl. 70, 69 F. Supp. 409 (1947); *J.D. Hedin Constr. Co. v. United States*, 171 Ct. Cl. 70, 347 F.2d 235 (1965). However, in *Wilner Constr. Co. v. United States*, 24 F.3d 1397 (Fed. Cir. 1994), the court, in an in banc decision, overruled this line of decisions stating that "once an action is brought following a contracting officer's decision, the parties start in court or before the board with a clean slate." See *Heyl & Patterson, Inc.*, ASBCA 43307, 96-2 BCA ¶ 28,515, in which the board followed the *Wilner* decision, stating that it could weigh the evidence anew, without regard to the contracting officer's decision. Similarly, in *Airo Servs., Inc. v. General Servs. Admin.*, GSBCA 14301, 98-2 BCA ¶ 29,909, the board held that a contracting officer's concession in her deposition testimony that a contractor was entitled to compensation under a termination settlement proposal did not presumptively impute liability to the government. The board reasoned that, although the contracting officer's stance was a factor to consider in resolving the case, it was not controlling because, if the contracting officer's final decision does not constitute an evidentiary admission, neither can statements of lesser importance, such as those given in a deposition. See also *White v. Delta Constr. Int'l, Inc.*, 285 F.3d 1040 (Fed.

Cir. 2002) (contractor cannot rely on contracting officer's interpretation of amount due in the event of a government breach); *Kinetic Builders, Inc. v. Peters*, 226 F.3d 1307 (Fed. Cir. 2000) (contracting officer's findings of fact entitled to no deference); *Conner Bros. Constr. Co. v. United States*, 65 Fed. Cl. 657 (2005) (contracting officer's findings of fact are not evidence); and *C.F. Electronics Inc.*, ASBCA 43212, 95-1 BCA ¶ 27,394, *recons. denied,* 95-2 BCA ¶ 27,719 (contracting officer's decision granting partial recovery to a contractor entitled to no presumptive evidentiary weight). See also *Roxco, Ltd. v. United States*, 60 Fed. Cl. 39 (2004), holding that the contractor is not bound by an unappealed default termination in asserting claims that could have been asserted as a defense to the termination.

The *Wilner* reasoning was followed in *England v. Sherman R. Smoot Corp.*, 388 F.3d 844 (Fed. Cir. 2004), holding that the so-called "McMullen presumption," that if the government grants time extensions for delays, it is presumed to be at fault for the delays, was "at odds" with the CDA. Thus, this presumption will no longer be available to contractors appealing contracting officer decisions.

B. Choice of Forums

Numerous consequences can result from the contractor's election of a forum, including the degree of formality of the proceedings, availability of accelerated procedures, possibility of recovery of Equal Access to Justice Act attorneys' fees, scope of review by the Court of Appeals for the Federal Circuit, and presence or absence of precedent or recent decisions on similar issues. Thus, the selection of a forum is an important decision. This section discusses the binding nature of the contractor's election.

1. Election of Forum Binding

After filing an appeal or bringing suit with notice of the available options, the contractor is precluded from changing forums. This rule is known as the Election Doctrine. See *Tuttle/White Constructors, Inc. v. United States*, 228 Ct. Cl. 354, 656 F.2d 644 (1981), where a contractor appealed a contracting officer's final decision to the Armed Services Board of Contract Appeals and was precluded from appealing the adverse decision directly to the court. See also *Diamond Mfg. Co. v. United States*, 3 Cl. Ct. 424 (1983); *Whited Co.*, VABCA 1776, 83-1 BCA ¶ 16,295, *recons. denied,* 83-2 BCA ¶ 16,734; and *Stewart-Thomas Indus., Inc.*, ASBCA 38773, 90-1 BCA ¶ 22,481. Compare *National Elec. Coil v. United States*, 227 Ct. Cl. 595 (1981), holding an election of the appeals board not binding because the final decision had not notified the contractor of the right to elect.

Contractors should carefully consider the Election Doctrine before choosing a forum. In one case a contractor filed a timely appeal to the GSA Board of Contract Appeals but then decided that the case was more properly lodged in the Claims Court (now the Court of Federal Claims). Although the board dismissed the contractor's appeal without prejudice, the court dismissed the appeal because the case had been originally filed in the board and that decision was affirmed on appeal, *Bonneville Assocs. v. United States*, 43 F.3d 649 (Fed. Cir. 1994). The contractor's subsequent request to the board to reinstate its voluntarily dismissed appeal was denied on the grounds that this new appeal was untimely, *Bonneville Assoc. v. General Servs. Admin.*, GSBCA 13134, 96-1 BCA ¶ 28,122, *aff'd, 1*65 F.3d 1360 (Fed. Cir. 1999), *cert. denied,* 528 U.S. 809 (1999).

The Election Doctrine does not apply if the forum that is originally chosen does not have jurisdiction at the time the appeal or suit is filed, *National Neighbors, Inc. v. United States*, 839 F.2d 1539 (Fed Cir. 1988). See *Ball & Brosamer, Inc.*, IBCA 3542-95, 98-1 BCA ¶ 29,637, holding that the Election Doctrine did not preclude a contractor from timely appealing to the board after first electing the Court of Federal Claims because that court dismissed the case for lack of jurisdiction. The contractor consented to dismissal of the case on the basis that the court lacked jurisdiction to consider wage matters within the purview of the Department of Labor. See also *Hettich GmbH*, ASBCA 42602, 93-3 BCA ¶ 26,035 (board took appeal after Claims Court had dismissed prior suit for lack of jurisdiction), and *Warchol Constr. Co. v. United States*, 2 Cl. Ct. 384 (1983) (court took suit after board dismissed case for lack of certification of claim).

The untimely appeal to a board of contract appeals does not preclude the contractor from filing a timely suit in the Court of Federal Claims, *Olsberg Excavating Co. v. United States*, 3 Cl. Ct. 249 (1983).

2. Fragmentation and Consolidation of Claims

A contractor may appeal different claims, even those under a single contract, to different forums. See *American Nucleonics Corp.*, ASBCA 27894, 83-1 BCA ¶ 16,520, where the contractor appealed a default termination to the Claims Court and appealed an excess reprocurement cost assessment claim under the same contract to the board. However, a contractor's attempt to fragment such claims can be defeated by exercise of the Court of Federal Claims' consolidation powers. 41 U.S.C. § 609(d) provides:

> If two or more suits arising from one contract are filed in the United States Court of Federal Claims and one or more agency boards, for the convenience of parties or witnesses or in the interest of justice, the United States Court of Federal Claims may order the consolidation of such suits in that court or transfer any suits to or among the agency boards involved.

The decision to consolidate or transfer is solely within the court's discretion, *Marshall Associated Contractors, Inc. v. United States*, 31 Fed. Cl. 809 (1994). Moreover, an agency board cannot decline to accept a transfer, *Technical Servs.*

GmbH, ASBCA 44457, 96-2 BCA ¶ 28,338. The Court of Federal Claims weighs the positions of both parties and refuses to give controlling weight to the contractor's preference in deciding which forum shall hear a consolidated appeal, *E.D.S. Fed. Corp. v. United States*, 1 Cl. Ct. 212 (1983).

3. Bankrupt Contractors

If a contractor becomes bankrupt, its claims under the CDA can be lodged with a bankruptcy court, *Quality Tooling, Inc. v. United States*, 47 F.3d 1569 (Fed. Cir. 1995). However, the court in *Quality Tooling* held that the district court with cognizance of the bankruptcy proceeding had discretion to transfer the CDA claim to the Court of Federal Claims for resolution, acknowledging that "prudence will often counsel such a transfer." See also *United States v. Bagley*, 990 F.2d 567 (10th Cir. 1993), agreeing that the decision of the district court to retain jurisdiction of the claims against the government or transfer them to the Court of Federal Claims was a discretionary one. Compare *Gary Aircraft Corp. v. United States*, 698 F.2d 775 (5th Cir.), *cert. denied*, 464 U.S. 820 (1983), holding that the court should have allowed the board of contract appeals before which the case was pending to resolve the appeal because it was a forum with specialized competence.

C. Timely Appeal or Suit

The CDA provides that a "contracting officer's decision on the claim shall be final and conclusive and not subject to review by any forum, tribunal, or Government agency, unless an appeal or suit is timely commenced," 41 U.S.C. § 605(b). This is a codification of the rule that was developed under the contractual disputes procedure. See *United States v. Holpuch*, 328 U.S. 234 (1946), holding that a contractor's claim was "outlawed" by reason of the contractor's failure to appeal within the prescribed time.

There are different times for filing an appeal before a board of contract appeals and for bringing suit in the Court of Federal Claims. However, both times begin on the same date—the date the contractor receives the final decision of the contracting officer. The contractor is given 90 days from the receipt of the decision to "appeal such decision to an agency board," 41 U.S.C. § 606, while 41 U.S.C. § 609(a) provides that an action in the Court of Federal Claims "shall be filed within twelve months from the date of the receipt."

The time provisions are considered to be jurisdictional and the boards and the Court of Federal Claims do not have authority to waive them. See *Cosmic Constr. Co. v. United States*, 697 F.2d 1389 (Fed. Cir. 1982. In *Gregory Lumber Co. v. United States*, 229 Ct. Cl. 762 (1982), the court stated at 763:

> Congress has set the twelve-months limit, and this court cannot and should not read into it exceptions and tolling provisions Congress did not contemplate or authorize.

See also *Construcciones Electromecanicas*, ENGBCA PCC65, 90-2 BCA ¶ 22,864, in which the board dismissed a Panamanian contractor's appeal because the 90-day filing period was jurisdictional and could not be waived even though the contractor claimed the notice of appeal was mailed late due to the United States' military invasion of Panama. The boards will not consider personal circumstances or equitable considerations or in any other way exercise discretion as to acceptance of an appeal filed later that the statutory deadline, *D.L. Woods Constr., Inc. v. General Servs. Admin.*, GSBCA 13882, 97-2 BCA ¶ 29,009. See also *Devcomm Sys., Inc.*, ASBCA 50127, 98-1 BCA ¶ (no jurisdiction of appeal filed on 91st day afer receipt of decision); *Gateway El Paso Bus. Ctr. Assocs. v. General Servs. Admin.*, GSBCA 13883, 97-1 BCA ¶ 28,777 (no jurisdiction of appeal filed three day late); and *Glenna Romero*, PSBCA 5137, 04-2 BCA ¶ 32,790 (mental disability not an excuse for failure to meet 90-day filing period). See also *L&D Servs., Inc. v. United States,* 34 Fed. Cl. 673 (1996), finding no jurisdiction and rejecting the contractor's argument that it did not file within one year because it received the contracting officer's decision very quickly after it submitted the claim.

If a contractor files an appeal before the expiration of 60 days after its claim was submitted and there has been no contracting officer's decision, it will be found to be premature, *Max Castle*, AGBCA 97-128-1, 97-1 BCA ¶ 28,833; *Procontrols Corp.*, VABCA 5477, 98-1 BCA ¶ 29,622; *Zbigniew Ostaszewski & Ryszard Grabowski v. Department of State,* GSBCA 16319-ST, 04-2 BCA ¶ 32,640. However, if a contractor's appeal is premature when filed but the contracting officer subsequently fails to comply with the 60-day requirement for issuing either a decision or a notice of decision date, the appeal will not be dismissed but will be treated as an appeal of a "deemed denied" decision, *La Belle Indus., Inc.*, ASBCA 49307, 96-1 BCA ¶ 28,158; *Dennis Anderson Constr. Corp.*, ASBCA 48780, 96-1 BCA ¶ 28,075.

1. Receipt of Decision

Oral notification of a contracting officer's decision does not start the appeal period, *Lone Star Multinational Dev. Corp.*, ASBCA 20126, 75-2 BCA ¶ 11,530; *Gonzalez Constr. Co.*, NASABCA 67816, 79-1 BCA ¶ 13,663. The government bears the burden of proving when the contractor actually received the final decision. The government must prove "actual physical receipt of [the] decision by the contractor [or his representative]," *Pathman Constr. v. United States*, 817 F.2d 1573 (Fed. Cir. 1987); *Borough of Alpine v. United States*, 923 F.2d 170 (Fed. Cir. 1991)

Proof of receipt is generally accomplished by sending the final decision by certified mail. Furthermore, the boards have generally engaged in a presumption that mail properly addressed and bearing necessary postage is received by the addressee in due course, *SanColMar Indus., Inc.*, ASBCA 16879, 73-1 BCA ¶ 9812. See also *Hawkins v. United States*, 1 Cl. Ct. 221 (1983), in which the court relied on affidavits of a postal service official and provisions of the Domestic Mail Manual Regulations to conclude that the contractor received the decision on a specified date. The board also took note of the fact that the duties of the secretary who signed the postal receipts included receiving incoming mail. In *SAI Indus. Corp.*, ASBCA 51575, 98-2 BCA ¶ 29,913, the government presented return receipts to verify the delivery date and the contractor did not present any evidence in response. Similarly, in *Nielsen Dillingham Builders, Inc.*, VABCA 5255, 97-2 BCA ¶ 29,005, the government met it burden by establishing that it had properly addressed the final decision to the contractor's principal place of business, mailed it by certified mail, and that it had been subsequently signed for by a mail delivery service company. See *Omni Abstract, Inc.*, ENGBCA 6254, 96-2 BCA ¶ 28,367, holding that a government attorney's affidavit was sufficient to show the date of receipt. Compare *National Interior Contractors, Inc.*, VABCA 4561, 95-2 BCA ¶ 27,695, holding that the government did not meet its burden when the decision had been sent by a private mail service. The Department of Veterans Affairs regulations specifically provide that the 90-day period for appealing a final decision does not begin to run until a contractor's receipt of the final decision transmitted by U.S. Postal Service certified mail, *Kimberly Constr., Inc.*, VABCA 4542, 96-1 BCA ¶ 28,136.

Proof of transmission of a facsimile of a final decision is not adequate evidence of receipt. See *Riley & Ephriam Constr. Co. v. United States,* 408 F.3d 1369 (Fed. Cir. 2005), stating at 1372-73:

> [W]e cannot infer receipt from evidence of transmission. Proof of message exit from a transmitting machine cannot serve as a proxy for proof of actual receipt of the sent message by a remote receiving terminal. Simply put, the evidence offered by the government is not the type of "objective indicia of receipt" that the CDA requires to begin the limitations period. The fax cover sheet is only evidence that the fax was prepared. The phone records and contracting officer's statement indicate a fax was transmitted but do not evidence receipt of the fax by the contractor's attorney. The Boards of Contract Appeal have similarly found that a fax transmission sheet is insufficient to show receipt by the contractor stating "we have held that a 'successful' transmission report for a fax transmission was not reliable evidence of receipt of the final decision where the Government did not otherwise confirm receipt." *Pub. Serv. Cellular, Inc.*, ASBCA No. 52,489, 2000-1 BCA (CCH) ¶ 30,832. Fax receipt was usually confirmed in these cases by calling the intended recipient of the decision. See, e.g., *Tyger Constr. Co.*, ASBCA Nos. 36,100, 36,101, 88-3 B.C.A. (CCH) ¶ 21,149 (Aug. 25, 1988). The Boards of Contract Appeal have also been reluctant to "make the quantum leap and infer from the Government's transmission report's statement 'Transmission OK' that the final decision was received by [the contractor]." *Pub. Serv.*, ASBCA No. 52,489. We correspondingly find that receipt by the contractor cannot be inferred from the contracting officer's statement that the machine indicated a successful transmission. In essence, the government has not offered any evidence that the fax was actually received by the contractor's attorney.

In *Mid-Eastern Indus., Inc.*, ASBCA 51287, 98-2 BCA ¶ 29,907, sufficient proof of receipt was found when the contractor had requested that the final decision be sent by facsimile and there was evidence showing successful transmission to contractor's facsimile number. See also *Leixab, S.A.*, ASBCA 51581, 98-2 BCA ¶ 29,962, in which the government presented unrebutted evidence that the facsimile was received and the contractor acknowledged receipt of the decision. However, see *David Grimaldi Co.*, ASBCA 49795, 97-2 BCA ¶ 29,201, in which the board held that proof of the facsimile transmission was inadequate to establish the date of the contractor's receipt of the decision. The board rejected the contention that a "circled x" appearing on each page of the transmitted decision proved receipt.

Although the usual destination for a final decision is the place of business through which the contract was made, delivery to places other than the contractor's place of business has sometimes been considered sufficient to commence the running of the appeal period. In *Pleasant Logging & Milling Co.*, AGBCA 79-172 CDA, 80-2 BCA ¶ 14,605, the board held that time began to run when an agency employee hand delivered a final decision to the home of the president of the contractor even though the president was on vacation at the time. The board took note that the president did not object to such delivery when notified by telephone and that this was the past practice between the parties in the small town involved. See also *M.D. Willner*, DOTCAB 739, 75-1 BCA ¶ 11,011, in which delivery to a contractor's wife was held to be proper. In *Fred Schwartz*, ASBCA 20724, 76-1 BCA ¶ 11,916, *recons. denied*, 76-2 BCA ¶ 11,976, the board stated at 57,121:

> It is not a prerequisite to the effectiveness of a notification sent to an unincorporated business concern that the notification be received only by an official of the concern authorized to bind the company contractually.

Compare *Idela Constr. Co.*, ASBCA 50222, 97-2 BCA ¶ 29,256, in which the board held that the government did not meet its burden of proof when the decision was sent to the contractor's attorney as a previous address and it was rerouted to the wrong forwarding address by the Postal Service. See also *Riley & Ephriam Constr. Co. v. United States,* 408 F.3d 1369 (Fed. Cir. 2005), finding inadequate proof of receipt the fact that the certified contracting officer's decision was delivered to the post office where the contractor maintained a box. The Post Office had returned the letter to the government and there was no evidence that the contractor had consented to its receipt of certified mail.

A contractor's refusal to accept a hand delivered final decision cannot preclude its "receipt" of the decision within the meaning of the CDA, *CWU Consultants & Servs. v. General Servs. Admin.*, GSBCA 13889, 98-1 BCA ¶ 29,343.

If there is more than one final decision related to a single claim, the 90-day appeal period will run from the later final decision. See *William P. DeLacy*, AGBCA 82-213-1, 82-2 BCA ¶ 15,810, where, although the decision to terminate a contract for default was received by the contractor on July 27, 1981, a letter of April 3, 1982 appealing the default was timely; on February 8, 1982 there had been a subsequent final decision issued with respect to excess reprocurement costs, and the appeal on April 3 was made within 90 days from receipt of the second decision. Compare *Gregory Lumber Co.*, IBCA 1237-12-78, 80-1 BCA ¶ 14,322 (the contracting officer's response to a contractor's letter does not "toll" the 90-day appeal period where the response was an informal reiteration of the original final decision, rather than a reconsideration of the original decision).

2. Date of Appeal or Suit

In addition to the difference in the time periods, the method of determining compliance with the filing date differs among the boards of contract appeals and the Court of Federal Claims.

a. Boards of Contract Appeals

Rule 1 of the Uniform Rules of Procedure for boards of contract appeals requires that written notice of an appeal be mailed or delivered to the board within 90 days following a contracting officer's decision. A copy of the appeal notice must also be furnished to the contracting officer from whose decision the appeal is taken. Oral notice to the contracting officer of an intent to appeal will not satisfy the requirement, *Lows Enter., Inc.*, ASBCA 51585, 99-1 BCA ¶ 30,623.

Some boards have embraced a liberal policy regarding misdirected appeal notices. Constructive notice has been upheld when the contractor has sent a timely notice of intent to appeal to the Secretary of the Air Force through the contracting officer, *ContravesGoerz Corp.*, ASBCA 26317, 83-1 BCA ¶ 16,309, or directly to the contracting officer, *Thompson Aerospace, Inc.*, ASBCA 51548, 99-1 BCA ¶ 30,232; *Rex Sys., Inc.*, ASBCA 50456, 98-2 BCA ¶ 29,956; *Sharp Constr. Co.*, DOTBCA 3094, 98-1 BCA ¶ 29,567; *Yankee Telecomm. Lab., Inc.*, ASBCA 25240, 82-1 BCA ¶ 15,515; *Dawson Constr. Co.*, EBCA 155-2-81, 81-2 BCA ¶ 15,162. A timely appeal was also found when the contractor's letter of intent to appeal was delivered to the contracting officer prior to the final decision, *Richard A. Guthrie*, GSBCA 5721, 80-2 BCA ¶ 14,612. See also *P&L Mgmt. & Consulting, Inc.,* DOTBCA 4086, 00-1 BCA ¶ 30,759, in which the board found a contractor's appeal timely notwithstanding the fact that it was not received by the board until 94 days after receipt of the final decision. The board noted that the contracting officer's failure to respond to the contractor's misdirected notice of appeal to that office, the inaccurate information given by the agency as to the proper place to send the appeal, and the dilatory action of the agency's chief of procurement in waiting until after the 90-day period had elapsed to inform the contractor that his office was the wrong place to send the appeal all violated the "spirit" of the CDA and were themselves sufficient to hold the 90-day limitation period in abeyance.

The Agriculture Board does not follow this liberal policy. See *American Agrisurance, Inc.*, AGBCA 98-169-F, 99-1 BCA ¶ 30,237, in which the board dismissed an appeal as untimely because it was sent to the agency not the board. See also *Dan Nelson*, AGBCA 97-130-1, 97-1 BCA ¶ 28,967, dismissing an appeal that had been received by the contracting officer, but not the board, within the 90-day period. The board distinguished an earlier case, *Frank Dufour*, AGBCA 95-170-1, 96-1 BCA ¶ 27,964, in which it had followed the precedent of the other boards. Compare *Malaspina Invs., Inc.*, AGBCA 2003-180-1, 04-1 BCA ¶ 32,418, in which the board took jurisdiction of an appeal timely filed by subcontractor where a letter from contractor sent after the 90-day appeal period had expired stated that it had requested the subcontractor to send the appeal directly to the board. The board reasoned that the subcontractor could appeal directly with the permission of the contractor and that the contractor's letter indicated that it had granted permission at the time of the subcontractor's appeal.

Unless the contracting officer withdraws the decision, extensions of the appeal period cannot be granted. See *Lamb Enters.*, ASBCA 48314, 95-1 BCA ¶ 27,559, holding that a request for an extension did not excuse an untimely filing of an appeal. See also *JWA Emadel Enters., Inc.*, ASBCA 51016, 98-2 BCA ¶ 29,765, *recons. denied*, 98-2 BCA ¶ 29,960, holding that a letter to a contracting officer attempting to keep the contractor's options open to elect to appeal to the board or file suit in the Court of Federal Claims was ineffective.

If Federal Express or another delivery service is used, the notice of appeal must actually be received by the board within the 90-day period, *Leixab, S.A.*, ASBCA 51581, 98-2 BCA ¶ 29,962; *Elaine Dunn Realty*, HUDBCA 98-C-101-C1, 98-1 BCA ¶ 29,581; *CWI Consultants & Srevs. v. General Servs. Admin.*, GSBCA 13889, 98-1 BCA ¶ 29,343; *C & S Managing Serv.*, AGBCA 96-184-1, 97-1 BCA ¶ 28,625; *Innovative Refrigeration Concepts*, ASBCA 48869, 96-1 BCA ¶ 28,231. In *Tiger Nat'l Gas, Inc.*, GSBCA 16039, 03-2 BCA ¶ 32,321, the fact that a Federal Express courier could not find the offices of the board did not excuse late delivery.

In computing this time limitation, the boards exclude the date on which the contractor received the contracting officer's final decision and include the date on which the contractor mailed or delivered its appeal, *Lincoln Gage Co.*, ASBCA 3781, 57-1 BCA ¶ 1261. Thus, the date of dispatch determines the timeliness of a notice of appeal to a board, *Western Adhesives*, GSBCA 6868, 83-1 BCA ¶ 16,182, *recons. denied*, 83-1 BCA ¶ 16,493. An appeal mailed on the first working day following the 90th day after the contractor received the contracting officer's final decision is timely, *Pacific Steel Bldg. Sys., Inc.*, ASBCA 26346, 83-1 BCA ¶ 16,362. An appeal is also timely when filed on the 91st day from receipt of the final decision when the ninetieth day is a Sunday, *Interstate Constr., Inc.*, ASBCA 43261, 91-3 BCA ¶ 24,338; *Vappi & Co.*, PSBCA 924, 81-1 BCA ¶ 15,080, or a federal holiday, *Bushman Constr. Co.*, IBCA 193, 59-1 BCA ¶ 2148 (construing the pre-CDA 30-day appeal period), and perhaps if it is a Saturday. Most board rules state that Saturday, Sunday, and legal holidays are not included in the calculation of the last day of the filing period. Thus, in *Peninsula Marine, Inc.*, ENGBCA 3219, 75-1 BCA ¶ 11,130, the board, in construing the pre-CDA 30-day appeal period, held that when the 30th day falls on a Saturday, an appeal is timely if it is mailed on the next succeeding business day. Compare *Wyman P. Guye*, ASBCA 4756, 59-1 BCA ¶ 2060, holding, in construing the pre-CDA 30day appeal period, that when the 30th day is a Saturday, the appeal must be mailed on that date or it is too late.

Evidence of mailing is established by the postmark on the envelope, *SMS Agoura Sys., Inc.*, ASBCA 50926, 97-2 BCA ¶ 29,325 (board rejected argument that computer records established that drafts of the appeal notices were created over the weekend prior to the deadline and office procedures were such that notices would have been signed and placed in the company mail for postmarking before the deadline); *Bradley Constr., Inc.*, ENGBCA 6004, 93-2 BCA ¶ 25,631 (board rejected contractor's counsel's statement that he believed appeal notice was mailed on the date it was prepared).

Under the "Fulford Doctrine," a contractor may dispute an underlying default termination as part of a timely appeal from a government demand for excess improvement cost, even though the contractor failed to appeal the underlying default termination in a timely manner, *Fulford Mfg. Co.*, ASBCA 2143, 6 CCF 61,815 (May 20, 1955); *Deep Joint Venture*, GSBCA 14511, 02-2 BCA ¶ 31,914; *Delta Constr. Co.*, ASBCA 42453, 96-1 BCA ¶ 28,106; *Southwest Marine, Inc.*, DOTBCA 1891, 96-1 BCA ¶ 27,985. But see *Phoenix Petroleum Co.,* ASBCA 45414, 02-1 BCA ¶ 31,835 (Fulford Doctrine did not apply to an attempt to reinstate an appeal from a contracting officer's decision assessing excess reprocurement costs because the doctrine permits an untimely default appeal only if the contractor appealed the excess costs claim in a timely manner). The Fulford Doctrine allows one to litigate the propriety of the initial termination of a default; it does not afford a contractor the right to recover costs upon showing that the underlying default termination was improper, *American Telecom Corp. v. United States*, 59 Fed. Cl. 467 (2004).

If a contractor declares bankruptcy during the appeal period, the trustee may extend the appeal period pursuant to 11 USC § 108(a). See *Carter Indus., Inc.*, DOTBCA 2995, 98-1 BCA ¶ 29,625, analyzing the statute and concluding that it did not apply to the situation where the contractor filed for bankruptcy prior to the contracting officer's decision to terminate the contract for default because no appeal was pending at the time of the bankruptcy petition.

After an appeal is filed, the contracting officer cannot divest the board of jurisdiction by unilateral decision, such as attempting to withdraw his final decision, *Holmes & Narver, Inc.*, ASBCA 51430, 99-1 BCA ¶ 30,131; *West State, Inc.*, DOTBCA 2817, 96-1 BCA ¶ 28,268; *Triad Microsystems, Inc.*, ASBCA 48763, 96-1 BCA ¶ 28,078. See also *World Computer Sys., Inc.*, DOTBCA 2802, 95-1 BCA ¶ 27,399, stating that "parties may not by negotiation, agreement, or stipulation bestow or withhold Board jurisdiction." In *General Eng'g Corp.*, ENGBCA 6369, 98-2 BCA ¶ 29,948, the board rejected the government's argument that it lacked jurisdiction because the contracting officer would allow entitlement on another basis than that claimed by the contractor. The board characterized the government's position as an "affirmative defense" and ruled that affirmative defenses defeat claims and appeals, if at all, on substantive, not jurisdictional grounds.

b. Court of Federal Claims

The Court of Federal Claims does not follow the liberal policy of the boards regarding receipt of an appeal by the agency. Hence, suit in the court is only timely if a complaint is received within the statutory one-year period. Rule 3 of the court provides that a civil action "shall be commenced by filing a complaint with the clerk of the court," whose records are final and conclusive evidence of the date of filing subject to a corrective order by the court. Rule 3(b)(C) permits consideration of complaints mailed by certified or registered mail in sufficient time to be received before the due date if the sender exercised no control over the complaint after mailing. In *B.D. Click Co. v. United States*, 1 Ct. Cl. 239 (1982), the contractor's counsel was not permitted to file a complaint because it did not conform to court rules. Since the subsequent corrected complaint was not mailed in sufficient time to be received by the due date, it was untimely.

D. Organization and Function of Forums

The trial forums, the agency board of contract appeals or the Court of Federal Claims, have unique organizations and function in different ways. Appeals for decisions of these forums are heard by the United States Court of Appeals for the Federal Circuit, which is a specialized circuit court functioning within the federal judicial establishment. This section contains a brief overview of the organization and function of these forums.

1. Boards of Contract Appeals

Prior to the CDA, the boards of contract appeals were established by the heads of agencies for the purpose of carrying out their function of reviewing contracting officers' final decisions. Under 41 U.S.C. § 607, however, the boards acquired independent statutory status, with their jurisdictions determined by the CDA. This statute gives the agency head the right either to appoint a board consisting of at least three members if sufficient workload is anticipated or to have appeals decided by the board of another agency.

The 2004 composition of the 10 boards of contract appeals was as follows:

Board	Number of Members
Armed Services Board of Contract Appeals (ASBCA)	30
Department of Energy Board of Contract Appeals (EBCA)	3
Department of Agriculture Board of Contract Appeals (AGBCA)	3
Department of Interior Board of Contract Appeals (IBCA)	2
Department of Transportation Board of Contract Appeals (DOTBCA)	3
General Services Administration Board of Contract Appeals (GSBCA)	8
Postal Service Board of Contract Appeals (PSBCA)	4
Department of Veterans Affairs Board of Contract Appeals (VABCA)	6
Department of Labor Board of Contract Appeals (LBCA)	3
Department of Housing and Urban Development Board of Contract Appeals (HUDBCA)	3

Effective January 6, 2007, the boards of contract appeals for the Departments of Agriculture, Energy, Housing and Urban Development, Labor, Transportation, and Veterans Affairs will be combined with the General Services Board of Contract Appeals to create a single Civilian Board of Contract Appeals. This change is the result of a provision in the 2006 Department of Defense Appropriations Act, Pub. L. No. 109-163, § 847.

The appeals boards conduct trials at locations most convenient to the parties. The general procedure is for the hearing to be conducted by a single administrative judge who normally writes the decision. Subsequently, this decision is adopted by a panel of judges as the decision of the full board. These procedures are an attempt to maintain uniformity of decision within each board. From their inception, the agency boards of contract appeals have been thought of as administrative bodies that should hear and decide contractor appeals quickly and inexpensively. See 41 U.S.C. § 607(3) stating that boards "shall provide, to the fullest extent practicable, informal, expeditious, and inexpensive resolution of disputes." However, this goal has been thwarted, in considerable measure, because the boards give full due process including discovery and trial-type hearings. The ability of the boards to give full due process is enhanced by 41 U.S.C. § 610, which allows boards the quasi-judicial power to "administer oaths to witnesses, authorize depositions and discovery proceedings, and require by subpoena the attendance of witnesses and production of books and papers."

Efficiency in resolution of disputes is promoted by mandating an "accelerated" procedure for handling claims of $100,000 or less, 41 U.S.C. § 607(f), and an "expedited" procedure for claims of $50,000 or less, 41 U.S.C. § 608(a). Both procedures are available solely at the election of the contractor. Under the accelerated procedure, the board is required to make a decision, "whenever possible, within

180 days from the date the contractor elects to utilize such procedure," and "appeals under the small claims procedure shall be resolved, whenever possible, within 120 days from the date the contractor elects to utilize such procedure." The boards have also adopted alternative dispute resolution procedures in an effort to enhance the efficiency of the appeals process. The ADR procedures most commonly available are settlement judges, mini-trials, and summary trials with binding decisions.

The Act also formalizes the appointment process for board members by requiring that they be "selected and appointed to serve in the same manner as administrative law judges appointed pursuant to section 3501 of Title 5 of the United States Code," 41 U.S.C. § 607(b)(1). This section also provides that board members must have a minimum of five years' public contract law experience and specifies that compensation for board chairmen, vice chairmen, and members "shall be determined under section 5372a of Title 5 of the United States Code."

The boards of contracts appeals are not bound by decisions of the GAO. However, the ASBCA noted that it is appropriate for the board to look to GAO opinions for guidance and that the GAO's decisions are helpful in matters involving the award of a contract, *Dante Calcagni,* ASBCA 49903, 98-1 BCA ¶ 29,554.

2. *Court of Federal Claims*

The Federal Courts Improvement Act of 1982, Pub. L. 97-164, created the U.S. Claims Court pursuant to Article I of the Constitution. The court was renamed the Court of Federal Claims by the Federal Courts Administration Act of 1992, Pub. L. 102-572. The Court of Federal Claims is composed of sixteen judges, appointed for fifteen-year terms by the President, and fourteen "senior judges" whose fifteen-year term has expired, 28 U.S.C. Chapter 7. As Article I judges, the Court of Federal Claims judges are vested with authority to "enter dispositive judgments," including orders on dispositive motions. Pursuant to 28 U.S.C. § 2503(b) the proceedings of the Court of Federal Claims are conducted according to the Federal Rules of Evidence. The court is not bound by the Federal Rules of Civil Procedure, but it has incorporated them "to the extent that they appropriately can be applied to the proceedings in this court," U.S.C.C. Rule 1(b).

The Court of Federal Claims sits in Washington, D.C. and may hold a trial at any location depending upon the convenience of the parties and witnesses, 28 U.S.C. § 173. Cases before the Court of Federal Claims are heard and decided by one judge, 28 U.S.C. § 174(a). The Court of Federal Claims judges have not hesitated in refusing to follow each other's decisions. Compare *Big Bud Tractors, Inc. v. United States*, 2 Cl. Ct. 195 (1983), with *Dean Forwarding Co. v. United States*, 2 Cl. Ct. 559 (1983). Conflicts between the decisions of individual judges on the court are resolved by the Court of Appeals for the Federal Circuit.

Congress may refer cases to the Court of Federal Claims for a report, 28 U.S.C. § 1492. The procedures for these "Congressional reference" cases are set forth in 28 U.S.C. § 2509. These cases are heard first by a Court of Federal Claims judge sitting as a hearing officer. After the hearing officer's decision, the parties may bring any exceptions to a review panel consisting of three judges. The review panel is authorized by statute to review the findings and conclusions of the hearing officer and the record in the case. The hearing officer's findings of fact are not reviewed de novo and may not be set aside unless clearly erroneous. See *INSLAW, Inc. v. United States,* 40 Fed. Cl. 843 (1998), for a discussion of this procedure.

3. Court of Appeals for the Federal Circuit

The Court of Appeals for the Federal Circuit hears appeals directly from both board decisions and Court of Federal Claims decisions, pursuant to their respective CDA jurisdictions. The Federal Courts Improvement Act amended 41 U.S.C. § 609(c) to require that if the trial record is insufficient for court review, the case must be remanded to the trial forum. Prior to these amendments, the Court of Claims could, in its discretion and in lieu of remand, retain the case and take such additional evidence or action as necessary for final disposition of the case.

a. Review of Board Decisions

The CDA was amended by the Federal Courts Improvement Act to give the Federal Circuit exclusive jurisdiction to hear government or contractor appeals filed with the court within 120 days of a board of contract appeals decision. This authority is stated in 41 U.S.C. § 607(g)(1) (see also 28 U.S.C. § 1295(a)(10) and § 1295(b)):

> The decision of an agency board of contract appeals shall be final, except that—
>
> (A) a contractor may appeal such a decision to the United States Court of Appeals for the Federal Circuit within one hundred twenty days after the date of receipt of a copy of such decision, or
>
> (B) the agency head, if he determines that an appeal should be taken, and with the prior approval of the Attorney General, transmits the decision of the board of contract appeals to the Court of Appeals for the Federal Circuit for judicial review under section 1295 of Title 28, within one hundred and twenty days from the date of the agency's receipt of a copy of the board's decision.

The 120-day appeal period runs from the date on which an appeals board denies a contractor's timely petition for reconsideration, not from the date of the board's initial decision, *Precision Piping, Inc. v. United States*, 230 Ct. Cl. 741 (1982). This rule is consistent with the predominant rule prior to the Federal Courts Improvement

Act which stated that the old 90-day period for appealing an adverse board decision to the Court of Claims ran from the board's denial of a timely request for reconsideration, *B. D. Click Co. v. United States*, 222 Ct. Cl. 290, 614 F.2d 748 (1980). In order to be timely, an appeal must be received by the clerk for the Federal Circuit within the 120-day statutory period, *Placeway Constr. Corp. v. United States*, 713 F.2d 726 (Fed. Cir. 1983). Note that this receipt rule is contrary to the rule generally adopted by the boards, that an appeal from a contracting officer's final decision is considered filed in a board of contract appeals for purposes of the 90-day statutory period when the contractor mails its appeal notice, 41 U.S.C. § 606. In small claims appeals, the court's jurisdiction is limited to board decisions tainted by fraud, 41 U.S.C. § 608(d). See *Palmer v. Barram*, 184 F.3d 1373 (Fed. Cir. 1999).

Appeals to the court are only proper when the appeals board has rendered a "final" decision. The court has ruled that board decisions are not final when they decide only entitlement and remand to the parties to allow them to negotiate quantum, *AAA Eng'g & Drafting Inc. v. Widnall*, 129 F.3d 602 (Fed. Cir. 1997); *United Pac. Ins. Co. v. Roche*, 294 F.3d 1367 (Fed. Cir. 2002). Thus, the court will not accept appeals of entitlement decisions when quantum has not yet been determined. The result of this procedure is that when quantum has been decided and the appeal is filed, the party will have the right to challenge entitlement as well as quantum, *Brownlee v. Dyncorp*, 349 F.3d 1343 (Fed. Cir. 2003) (government appeal); *J. C. Equip. Corp. v. England*, 360 F.3d 1311 (Fed. Cir. 2004) (contractor appeal). See *Kinetic Builders, Inc. v. Peters,* 226 F.3d 1307 (Fed. Cir. 2000), holding that some claims in which the board has decided both entitlement and quantum can be appealed even though other claims have been remanded to negotiation of quantum. See also *Dewey Elecs. Corp. v. United States*, 803 F.2d 650 (Fed. Cir. 1986), permitting appeal of a board decision denying some claims even though the board had ruled favorably on other claims and remanded them for negotiation of entitlement.

Review of board decisions by the Federal Circuit on questions of law is "de novo" with the result that the court can overturn any ruling with which it disagrees. Review of questions of fact is conducted pursuant to the "substantial evidence" standard which was previously contained in the Wunderlich Act, 41 U.S.C. §§ 321, 322. See *Systems Tech. Assocs., Inc. v. United States*, 699 F.2d 1383 (Fed. Cir. 1983). This standard of review is stated in 41 U.S.C. § 609(b) (see also 28 U.S.C. § 1295(c)), which provides:

> In the event of an appeal by a contractor or the Government from a decision of any agency board pursuant to section 607 of this title, notwithstanding any contract provision, regulation, or rules of law to the contrary, the decision of the agency board on any question of law shall not be final or conclusive, but the decision on any question of fact shall be final and conclusive and shall not be set aside unless the decision is fraudulent, or arbitrary, or capricious, or so grossly erroneous as to necessarily imply bad faith, or if such decision is not supported by substantial evidence.

See *Phoenix Control Sys., Inc. v. Babbitt,* 113 F.3d 1255 (Fed. Cir. 1997), and *Conner Bros. Constr. Co. v. Brown,* 113 F.3d 1256 (Fed. Cir. 1997), in which the court concluded that the contractor challenging the board's findings had failed to meet this heavy burden and noted that the mere fact that the record contains conflicting evidence does not mean that the board's findings are unsupported by substantial evidence.

b. Review of Court of Federal Claims Decisions

The Federal Circuit has exclusive jurisdiction to hear appeals from final decisions of the Court of Federal Claims, 28 U.S.C. § 1295(a)(3). These appeals must be received by the clerk of the court within 60 days of entry of the Court of Federal Claims' judgment, 28 U.S.C. § 2107. See *Sofarelli Assocs., Inc. v. United States*, 716 F.2d 1395 (Fed. Cir. 1983). The Court of Federal Claims' findings of fact will only be set aside if "clearly erroneous," § 52(a), Federal Rules of Civil Procedure. In *United States v. United States Gypsum Co.*, 333 U.S. 364 (1948), the Court stated that "A finding is 'clearly erroneous' when although there is evidence to support it, the reviewing court on the entire evidence is left with the definite and firm conviction that a mistake has been committed."

STANDARD FAR CLAUSES QUICK INDEX

Standard FAR Supply Contract Clauses

FAR 52.232-1 Payments 1234
FAR 52.243-1 Changes—Fixed-Price 1234
FAR 52.243-7 Notification of Changes 1234
FAR 52.246-2 Inspection of Supplies—Fixed-Price 1234
FAR 52.249-8 Default (Fixed-Price Supply and Service) 1234

Standard FAR Service Contract Clauses

FAR 52.243-1 Changes—Fixed-Price 1234
FAR 52.246-4 Inspection of Services—Fixed-Price 1234
FAR 52.249-8 Default (Fixed-Price Supply and Service) 1234

Standard FAR Construction Contract Clauses

FAR 52.232-5 Payments Under Fixed-Price Construction Contracts. 1234
FAR 52.236-1 Performance of Work by the Contractor 1234
FAR 52.236-2 Differing Site Conditions. 1234
FAR 52.236-3 Site Investigation and Conditions Affecting the Work. 1234
FAR 52.336.4 Physical Data 1234
FAR 52.236-5 Material and Workmanship 1234
FAR 52.236-6 Superintendence by the Contractor 1234
FAR 52.236-7 Permits and Responsibilities 1234
FAR 52.236-8 Other Contracts 1234
FAR 52.236-9 Protection of Existing Vegetation, Structures, Equipment, Utilities, and Improvements 1234
FAR 52.236-10 Operations and Storage Areas 1234

Standard FAR Construction Contract Clauses (continued)

FAR 52.236-11 Use and Possession Prior to Completion 1234
FAR 52.236-12 Cleaning Up 1234
FAR 52.236-13 Accident Prevention 1234
FAR 52.236-21 Specifications and Drawings for Construction 1234
FAR 52.246-12 Inspection of Construction 1234
FAR 52.249-10 Default (Fixed-Price Construction) 1234

Standard FAR Research and Development Contract Clauses

FAR 52.232-2 Payment Under Fixed-Price Research and Development Contracts 1234
FAR 52.243-1 Changes—Fixed-Price 1234
FAR 52.246-7 Inspection of Research and Development—Fixed-Price 1234
FAR 52.249-9 Default (Fixed-Price Research and Development) 1234

Standard FAR Clauses Applicable to All Types of Contracts

FAR 52.202-1 Definitions 1234
FAR 52.232-25 Prompt Payment 1234
FAR 52.233-1 Disputes 1234
FAR 52.233-2 Service of Protest 1234
FAR 52.233-3 Protest After Award 1234
FAR 52.245-2 Government Property (Fixed-Price Contracts) 1234
FAR 52.249-2 Termination for Convenience of the Government (Fixed-Price) 1234

STANDARD FAR CLAUSES

The following standard FAR clauses are current through FAC 2005-08, January 5, 2006. The clauses are grouped according to type of contract as follows: supply, service, construction, and research and development. Clauses that are applicable to all four types of contracts are listed together in the last section of the Appendix.

STANDARD FAR SUPPLY CONTRACT CLAUSES

FAR 52.232-1 Payments

PAYMENTS (APR 1984)

The Government shall pay the Contractor, upon the submission of proper invoices or vouchers, the prices stipulated in this contract for supplies delivered and accepted or services rendered and accepted, less any deductions provided in this contract. Unless otherwise specified in this contract, payment shall be made on partial deliveries accepted by the Government if—

(a) The amount due on the deliveries warrants it; or

(b) The Contractor requests it and the amount due on the deliveries is at least $1,000 or 50 percent of the total contract price.

FAR 52.243-1 Changes—Fixed-Price

CHANGES—FIXED-PRICE (AUG 1987)

(a) The Contracting Officer may at any time, by written order, and without notice to the sureties, if any, make changes within the general scope of this contract in any one or more of the following:

(1) Drawings, designs, or specifications when the supplies to be furnished are to be specially manufactured for the Government in accordance with the drawings, designs, or specifications.

(2) Method of shipment or packing.

(3) Place of delivery.

(b) If any such change causes an increase or decrease in the cost of, or the time required for, performance of any part of the work under this contract, whether or not changed by the order, the Contracting Officer shall make an equitable adjustment in the contract price, the delivery schedule, or both, and shall modify the contract.

(c) The Contractor must assert its right to an adjustment under this clause within 30 days from the date of receipt of the written order. However, if the Contracting Officer decides that the facts justify it, the Contracting Officer may receive and act upon a proposal submitted before final payment of the contract.

(d) If the Contractor's proposal includes the cost of property made obsolete or excess by the change, the Contracting Officer shall have the right to prescribe the manner of the disposition of the property

(e) Failure to agree to any adjustment shall be a dispute under the Disputes clause. However, nothing in this clause shall excuse the Contractor from proceeding with the contract as changed.

FAR 52.243-7 Notification of Changes

NOTIFICATION OF CHANGES (APR 1984)

(a) Definitions. "Contracting Officer," as used in this clause, does not include any representative of the Contracting Officer. "Specifically Authorized Representative (SAR)," as used in this clause, means any person the Contracting Officer has so designated by written notice (a copy of which shall be provided to the Contractor) which shall refer to this subparagraph and shall be issued to the designated representative before the SAR exercises such authority.

(b) Notice. The primary purpose of this clause is to obtain prompt reporting of Government conduct that the Contractor considers to constitute a change to this contract. Except for changes identified as such in writing and signed by the Contracting Officer, the Contractor shall notify the Administrative Contracting Officer in writing promptly, within .....(to be negotiated) calendar days from the date that the Contractor identifies any Government conduct (including actions, inactions, and written or oral communications) that the Contractor regards as a change to the contract terms and conditions. On the basis of the most accurate information available to the Contractor, the notice shall state —

(1) The date, nature, and circumstances of the conduct regarded as a change;

(2) The name, function, and activity of each Government individual and Contractor official or employee involved in or knowledgeable about such conduct;

(3) The identification of any documents and the substance of any oral communication involved in such conduct;

(4) In the instance of alleged acceleration of scheduled performance or delivery, the basis upon which it arose;

(5) The particular elements of contract performance for which the Contractor may seek an equitable adjustment under this clause, including—

(i) What contract line items have been or may be affected by the alleged change;

(ii) What labor or materials or both have been or may be added, deleted, or wasted by the alleged change;

(iii) To the extent practicable, what delay and disruption in the manner and sequence of performance and effect on continued performance have been or may be caused by the alleged change;

(iv) What adjustments to contract price, delivery schedule, and other provisions affected by the alleged change are estimated, and

(6) The Contractor's estimate of the time by which the Government must respond to the Contractor's notice to minimize cost, delay or disruption of performance.

(c) Continued performance. Following submission of the notice required by paragraph (b) of this clause, the Contractor shall diligently continue performance of this contract to the maximum extent possible in accordance with its terms and conditions as construed by the Contractor, unless the notice reports a direction of the Contracting Officer or a communication from a SAR of the Contracting Officer, in either of which events the Contractor shall continue performance; provided, however, that if the Contractor regards the direction or communication as a change as described in paragraph (b) of this clause, notice shall be given in the manner provided. All directions, communications, interpretations, orders and similar actions of the SAR shall be reduced to writing promptly and copies furnished to the Contractor and to the Contracting Officer. The Contracting Officer shall promptly countermand any action which exceeds the authority of the SAR.

(d) Government response. The Contracting Officer shall promptly, within ..... (to be negotiated) calendar days after receipt of notice, respond to the notice in writing. In responding, the Contracting Officer shall either—

(1) Confirm that the conduct of which the Contractor gave notice constitutes a change and when necessary direct the mode of further performance;

(2) Countermand any communication regarded as a change;

(3) Deny that the conduct of which the Contractor gave notice constitutes a change and when necessary direct the mode of further performance; or

(4) In the event the Contractor's notice information is inadequate to make a decision under paragraphs (d)(1), (2), or (3) of this clause, advise the Contractor what additional information is required, and establish the date by which it should be furnished and the date thereafter by which the Government will respond.

(e) Equitable adjustments. (1) If the Contracting Officer confirms that Government conduct effected a change as alleged by the Contractor, and the conduct causes an increase or decrease in the Contractor's cost of, or the time required for, performance of any part of the work under this contract, whether changed or not changed by such conduct, an equitable adjustment shall be made —

(i) In the contract price or delivery schedule or both; and

(ii) In such other provisions of the contract as may be affected.

(2) The contract shall be modified in writing accordingly. In the case of drawings, designs or specifications which are defective and for which the Government is responsible, the equitable adjustment shall include the cost and time extension for delay reasonably incurred by the Contractor in attempting to comply with the defective drawings, designs or specifications before the Contractor identified, or reasonably should have identified, such defect. When the cost of property made obsolete or excess as a result of a change confirmed by the Contracting Officer under this clause is included in the equitable adjustment, the Contracting Officer shall have the right to prescribe the manner of disposition of the property. The equitable adjustment shall not include increased costs or time extensions for delay resulting from the Contractor's failure to provide notice or to continue performance as provided, respectively, in paragraphs (b) and (c) above. NOTE: The phrases "contract price" and "cost" wherever they appear in the clause, may be appropriately modified to apply to cost-reimbursement or incentive contracts, or to combinations thereof.

FAR 52.246-2 Inspection of Supplies—Fixed-Price

INSPECTION OF SUPPLIES—FIXED-PRICE (AUG 1996)

(a) Definition. "Supplies," as used in this clause, includes but is not limited to raw materials, components, intermediate assemblies, end products, and lots of supplies.

(b) The Contractor shall provide and maintain an inspection system acceptable to the Government covering supplies under this contract and shall tender to the Government for acceptance only supplies that have been inspected in accordance with the inspection system and have been found by the Contractor to be in conformity with contract requirements. As part of the system, the Contractor shall prepare records evidencing all inspections made under the system and the outcome. These records shall be kept complete and made available to the Government during contract performance and for as long afterwards as the contract requires. The Government may perform reviews and evaluations as reasonably necessary to ascertain compliance with this paragraph. These reviews and evaluations shall be conducted in a manner that will not unduly delay the contract work. The right of review, whether exercised or not, does not relieve the Contractor of the obligations under the contract.

(c) The Government has the right to inspect and test all supplies called for by the contract, to the extent practicable, at all places and times, including the period of manufacture, and in any event before acceptance. The Government shall perform inspections and tests in a manner that will not unduly delay the work. The Government assumes no contractual obligation to perform any inspection and test for the benefit of the Contractor unless specifically set forth elsewhere in this contract.

(d) If the Government performs inspection or test on the premises of the Contractor or a subcontractor, the Contractor shall furnish, and shall require subcontractors to furnish, at no increase in contract price, all reasonable facilities and assistance for the safe and convenient performance of these duties. Except as otherwise provided in the contract, the Government shall bear the expense of Government inspections or tests made at other than the Contractor's or subcontractor's premises; provided, that in case of rejection, the Government shall not be liable for any reduction in the value of inspection or test samples.

(e) (1) When supplies are not ready at the time specified by the Contractor for inspection or test, the Contracting Officer may charge to the Contractor the additional cost of inspection or test.

(2) The Contracting Officer may also charge the Contractor for any additional cost of inspection or test when prior rejection makes reinspection or retest necessary.

(f) The Government has the right either to reject or to require correction of nonconforming supplies. Supplies are nonconforming when they are defective in material or workmanship or are otherwise not in conformity with contract requirements. The Government may reject nonconforming supplies with or without disposition instructions.

(g) The Contractor shall remove supplies rejected or required to be corrected. However, the Contracting Officer may require or permit correction in place, promptly after notice, by and at the expense of the Contractor. The Contractor shall not tender for acceptance corrected or rejected supplies without disclosing the former rejection or requirement for correction, and, when required, shall disclose the corrective action taken.

(h) If the Contractor fails to promptly remove, replace, or correct rejected supplies that are required to be removed or to be replaced or corrected, the Government may either (1) by contract or otherwise, remove, replace, or correct the supplies and charge the cost to the Contractor or (2) terminate the contract for default. Unless the Contractor corrects or replaces the supplies within the delivery schedule, the Contracting Officer may require their delivery and make an equitable price reduction. Failure to agree to a price reduction shall be a dispute.

(i) (1) If this contract provides for the performance of Government quality assurance at source, and if requested by the Government, the Contractor shall furnish advance notification of the time (i) when Contractor inspection or tests will be performed in accordance with the terms and conditions of the contract and (ii) when the supplies will be ready for Government inspection.

(2) The Government's request shall specify the period and method of the advance notification and the Government representative to whom it shall be furnished. Requests shall not require more than 2 workdays of advance notification if the Government representative is in residence in the Contractor's plant, nor more than 7 workdays in other instances.

(j) The Government shall accept or reject supplies as promptly as practicable after delivery, unless otherwise provided in the contract. Government failure to inspect and accept or reject the supplies shall not relieve the Contractor from responsibility, nor impose liability on the Government, for nonconforming supplies.

(k) Inspections and tests by the Government do not relieve the Contractor of responsibility for defects or other failures to meet contract requirements discovered before acceptance. Acceptance shall be conclusive, except for latent defects, fraud, gross mistakes amounting to fraud, or as otherwise provided in the contract.

(l) If acceptance is not conclusive for any of the reasons in paragraph (k) hereof, the Government, in addition to any other rights and remedies provided by law, or under other provisions of this contract, shall have the right to require the Contractor (1) at no increase in contract price, to correct or replace the defective or nonconforming supplies at the original point of delivery or at the Contractor's plant at the Contracting Officer's election, and in accordance with a reasonable delivery schedule as may be agreed upon between the Contractor and the Contracting Officer; provided, that the Contracting Officer may require a reduction in contract price if the Contractor fails to meet such delivery schedule, or (2) within a reasonable time after receipt by the Contractor of notice of defects or nonconformance, to repay such portion of the contract as is equitable under the circumstances if the Contracting Officer elects not to require correction or replacement. When supplies are returned to the Contractor, the Contractor shall bear the transportation cost from the original point of delivery to the Contractor's plant and return to the original point when that point is not the Contractor's plant. If the Contractor fails to perform or act as required in (1) or (2) above and does not cure such failure within a period of 10 days (or such longer period as the Contracting Officer may authorize in writing) after receipt of notice from the Contracting Officer specifying such failure, the Government shall have the right by contract or otherwise to replace or correct such supplies and charge to the Contractor the cost occasioned the Government thereby.

Alternate I (JUL 1985). If a fixed-price incentive contract is contemplated, substitute paragraphs (g), (h), and (l) below for paragraphs (g), (h), and (l) of the basic clause.

(g) The Contractor shall remove supplies rejected or required to be corrected. However, the Contracting Officer may require or permit correction in place, promptly after notice. The Contractor shall not tender for acceptance corrected or rejected supplies without disclosing the former rejection or requirement for correction, and when required shall disclose the corrective action taken. Cost of removal, replacement, or correction shall be considered a cost incurred, or to be incurred, in the total final negotiated cost fixed under the incentive price revision clause. However, replacements or corrections by the Contractor after the establishment of the total final price shall be at no increase in the total final price.

(h) If the Contractor fails to promptly remove, replace, or correct rejected supplies that are required to be removed or to be replaced or corrected, the Government may either (1) by contract or otherwise, remove, replace, or correct the supplies and equitably reduce the target price or, if established, the total final price or (2) may terminate the contract for default. Unless the Contractor corrects or replaces the nonconforming supplies within the delivery schedule, the Contracting Officer may require their delivery and equitably reduce any target price or, if it is established, the total final contract price. Failure to agree upon an equitable price reduction shall be a dispute.

(l) If acceptance is not conclusive for any of the reasons in paragraph (k) hereof, the Government, in addition to any other rights and remedies provided by law, or under other provisions of this contract, shall have the right to require the Contractor (1) at no increase in any target price or, if it is established, the total final price of this contract, to correct or replace the defective or nonconforming supplies at the original point of delivery or at the Contractor's plant at the Contracting Officer's election, and in accordance with a reasonable delivery schedule as may be agreed upon between the Contractor and the Contracting Officer; provided, that the Contracting Officer may require a reduction in any target price, or, if it is established, the total final price of this contract, if the Contractor fails to meet such delivery schedule; or (2) within a reasonable time after receipt by the Contractor of notice of defects or nonconformance, to repay such portion of the total final price as is equitable under the circumstances if the Contracting Officer elects not to require correction or replacement. When supplies are returned to the Contractor, the Contractor shall bear the transportation costs from the original point of delivery to the Contractor's plant and return to the original point when that point is not the Contractor's plant. If the Contractor fails to perform or act as required in (1) or (2) above and does not cure such failure within a period of 10 days (or such longer period as the Contracting Officer may authorize in writing) after receipt of notice from the Contracting Officer specifying such failure, the Government shall have the right by contract or otherwise to replace or correct such supplies and equitably reduce any target price or, if it is established, the total final price of this contract.

Alternate II (JUL 1985). If a fixed-ceiling-price contract with retroactive price redetermination is contemplated, substitute paragraphs (g), (h), and (l) below for paragraphs (g), (h), and (l) of the basic clause:

(g) The Contractor shall remove supplies rejected or required to be corrected. However, the Contracting Officer may require or permit correction in place, promptly after notice. The Contractor shall not tender for acceptance corrected or rejected supplies without disclosing the former rejection or requirement for correction, and when required shall disclose the corrective action taken. Cost of removal, replacement, or correction shall be considered a cost incurred, or to be incurred, when redetermining the prices under the price redetermination clause. However, replacements or corrections by the Contractor after the establishment of the redetermined prices shall be at no increase in the redetermined price.

(h) If the Contractor fails to promptly remove, replace, or correct rejected supplies that are required to be removed or to be replaced or corrected, the Government may either (1) by contract or otherwise, remove, replace, or correct the supplies and equitably reduce the initial contract prices or, if established, the redetermined contract prices or (2) terminate the contract for default. Unless the Contractor corrects or replaces the nonconforming supplies within the delivery schedule, the Contracting Officer may require their delivery and equitably reduce the initial contract price or, if it is established, the redetermined contract prices. Failure to agree upon an equitable price reduction shall be a dispute.

(l) If acceptance is not conclusive for any of the reasons in paragraph (k) hereof, the Government, in addition to any other rights and remedies provided by law, or under other provisions of this contract, shall have the right to require the Contractor (1) at no increase in the initial contract prices, or, if it is established, the redetermined prices of this contract, to correct or replace the defective or nonconforming supplies at the original point of delivery or at the Contractor's plant at the Contracting Officer's election, and in accordance with a reasonable delivery schedule as may be agreed upon between the Contractor and the Contracting Officer; provided, that the Contracting Officer may require a reduction in the initial contract prices, or, if it is established, the redetermined prices of this contract, if the Contractor fails to meet such delivery schedule; or (2) within a reasonable time after receipt by the Contractor of notice of defects or nonconformance, to repay such portion of the initial contract prices, or, if it is established, the redetermined prices of this contract, as is equitable under the circumstances if the Contracting Officer elects not to require correction or replacement. When supplies are returned to the Contractor, the Contractor shall bear the transportation costs from the original point of delivery to the Contractor's plant and return to the original point when that point is not the Contractor's plant. If the Contractor fails to perform or act as required in (1) or (2) above and does not cure such failure within a period of 10 days (or such longer period as the Contracting Officer may authorize in writing) after receipt of notice from the Contracting Officer specifying such failure, the Government shall have the right by contract or otherwise to replace or correct such supplies and equitably reduce the initial contract prices, or, if it is established, the redetermined prices of this contract.

FAR 52.249-8 Default (Fixed-Price Supply and Services)

DEFAULT (FIXED-PRICE SUPPLY AND SERVICE) (APR 1984)

(a)(1) The Government may, subject to paragraphs (c) and (d) of this clause, by written notice of default to the Contractor, terminate this contract in whole or in part if the Contractor fails to —

(i) Deliver the supplies or to perform the services within the time specified in this contract or any extension;

(ii) Make progress, so as to endanger performance of this contract (but see subparagraph (a)(2) of this clause); or

(iii) Perform any of the other provisions of this contract (but see subparagraph (a)(2) of this clause).

(2) The Government's right to terminate this contract under subdivisions (a)(1)(ii) and (1)(iii) above, may be exercised if the Contractor does not cure such failure within 10 days (or more if authorized in writing by the Contracting Officer) after receipt of the notice from the Contracting Officer specifying the failure.

(b) If the Government terminates this contract in whole or in part, it may acquire, under the terms and in the manner the Contracting Officer considers appropriate, supplies or services similar to those terminated, and the Contractor will be liable to the Government for any excess costs for those supplies or services. However, the Contractor shall continue the work not terminated.

(c) Except for defaults of subcontractors at any tier, the Contractor shall not be liable for any excess costs if the failure to perform the contract arises from causes beyond the control and without the fault or negligence of the Contractor. Examples of such causes include (1) acts of God or of the public enemy, (2) acts of the Government in either its sovereign or contractual capacity, (3) fires, (4) floods, (5) epidemics, (6) quarantine restrictions, (7) strikes, (8) freight embargoes, and (9) unusually severe weather. In each instance the failure to perform must be beyond the control and without the fault or negligence of the Contractor.

(d) If the failure to perform is caused by the default of a subcontractor at any tier, and if the cause of the default is beyond the control of both the Contractor and subcontractor, and without the fault or negligence of either, the Contractor shall not be liable for any excess costs for failure to perform, unless the subcontracted supplies or services were obtainable from other sources in sufficient time for the Contractor to meet the required delivery schedule.

(e) If this contract is terminated for default, the Government may require the Contractor to transfer title and deliver to the Government, as directed by the Contracting Officer, any (1) completed supplies, and (2) partially completed supplies and materials, parts, tools, dies, jigs, fixtures, plans, drawings, information, and contract rights (collectively referred to as "manufacturing materials" in this clause) that the Contractor has specifically produced or acquired for the terminated portion of this contract. Upon direction of the Contracting Officer, the Contractor shall also protect and preserve property in its possession in which the Government has an interest.

(f) The Government shall pay contract price for completed supplies delivered and accepted. The Contractor and Contracting Officer shall agree on the amount of payment for manufacturing materials delivered and accepted and for the protection and preservation of the property. Failure to agree will be a dispute under the Disputes clause. The Government may withhold from these amounts any sum the Contracting Officer determines to be necessary to protect the Government against loss because of outstanding liens or claims of former lien holders.

(g) If, after termination, it is determined that the Contractor was not in default, or that the default was excusable, the rights and obligations of the parties shall be the same as if the termination had been issued for the convenience of the Government.

(h) The rights and remedies of the Government in this clause are in addition to any other rights and remedies provided by law or under this contract.

Alternate I (APR 1984). If the contract is for transportation or transportation-related services, delete paragraph (f) of the basic clause, redesignate the remaining paragraphs accordingly, and substitute the following paragraphs (a) and (e) for paragraphs (a) and (e) of the basic clause:

(a)(1) The Government may, subject to paragraphs (c) and (d) of this clause, by written notice of default to the Contractor, terminate this contract in whole or in part if the Contractor fails to —

(i) Pick up the commodities or to perform the services, including delivery services, within the time specified in this contract or any extension;

(ii) Make progress, so as to endanger performance of this contract (but see subparagraph (a)(2) of this clause); or

(iii) Perform any of the other provisions of this contract (but see subparagraph (a)(2) of this clause).

(2) The Government's right to terminate this contract under subdivisions (a)(1)(ii) and (iii) of this clause, may be exercised if the Contractor does not cure such failure within 10 days (or more if authorized in writing by the Contracting Officer) after receipt of the notice from the Contracting Officer specifying the failure.

(e) If this contract is terminated while the Contractor has possession of Government goods, the Contractor shall, upon direction of the Contracting Officer, protect and preserve the goods until surrendered to the Government or its agent. The Contractor and Contracting Officer shall agree on payment for the preservation and protection of goods. Failure to agree on an amount will be a dispute under the Disputes clause.

STANDARD FAR SERVICE CONTRACT CLAUSES

FAR 52.243-1 Changes—Fixed Price

CHANGES—FIXED-PRICE (AUG 1987)

(a) The Contracting Officer may at any time, by written order, and without notice to the sureties, if any, make changes within the general scope of this contract in any one or more of the following:

(1) Drawings, designs, or specifications when the supplies to be furnished are to be specially manufactured for the Government in accordance with the drawings, designs, or specifications.

(2) Method of shipment or packing.

(3) Place of delivery.

(b) If any such change causes an increase or decrease in the cost of, or the time required for, performance of any part of the work under this contract, whether or not changed by the order, the Contracting Officer shall make an equitable adjustment in the contract price, the delivery schedule, or both, and shall modify the contract.

(c) The Contractor must assert its right to an adjustment under this clause within 30 days from the date of receipt of the written order. However, if the Contracting Officer decides that the facts justify it, the Contracting Officer may receive and act upon a proposal submitted before final payment of the contract.

(d) If the Contractor's proposal includes the cost of property made obsolete or excess by the change, the Contracting Officer shall have the right to prescribe the manner of the disposition of the property.

(e) Failure to agree to any adjustment shall be a dispute under the Disputes clause. However, nothing in this clause shall excuse the Contractor from proceeding with the contract as changed.

FAR 52.246-4 Inspection of Services—Fixed-Price

INSPECTION OF SERVICES—FIXED-PRICE (AUG 1996)

(a) Definitions. "Services," as used in this clause, includes services performed, workmanship, and material furnished or utilized in the performance of services.

(b) The Contractor shall provide and maintain an inspection system acceptable to the Government covering the services under this contract. Complete records of all inspection work performed by the Contractor shall be maintained and made available to the Government during contract performance and for as long afterwards as the contract requires.

(c) The Government has the right to inspect and test all services called for by the contract, to the extent practicable at all times and places during the term of the contract. The Government shall perform inspections and tests in a manner that will not unduly delay the work.

(d) If the Government performs inspections or tests on the premises of the Contractor or a subcontractor, the Contractor shall furnish, and shall require subcontractors to furnish, at no increase in contract price, all reasonable facilities and assistance for the safe and convenient performance of these duties.

(e) If any of the services do not conform with contract requirements, the Government may require the Contractor to perform the services again in conformity with contract requirements, at no increase in contract amount. When the defects in services cannot be corrected by reperformance, the Government may (1) require the Contractor to take necessary action to ensure that future performance conforms to contract requirements and (2) reduce the contract price to reflect the reduced value of the services performed.

(f) If the Contractor fails to promptly perform the services again or to take the necessary action to ensure future performance in conformity with contract requirements, the Government may (1) by contract or otherwise, perform the services and charge to the Contractor any cost incurred by the Government that is directly related to the performance of such service or (2) terminate the contract for default.

FAR 52.249-8 Default (Fixed-Price Supply and Services)

DEFAULT (FIXED-PRICE SUPPLY AND SERVICE) (APR 1984)

(a)(1) The Government may, subject to paragraphs (c) and (d) of this clause, by written notice of default to the Contractor, terminate this contract in whole or in part if the Contractor fails to —

(i) Deliver the supplies or to perform the services within the time specified in this contract or any extension;

(ii) Make progress, so as to endanger performance of this contract (but see subparagraph (a)(2) of this clause); or

(iii) Perform any of the other provisions of this contract (but see subparagraph (a)(2) of this clause).

(2) The Government's right to terminate this contract under subdivisions (a)(1)(ii) and (1)(iii) above, may be exercised if the Contractor does not cure such failure within 10 days (or more if authorized in writing by the Contracting Officer) after receipt of the notice from the Contracting Officer specifying the failure.

(b) If the Government terminates this contract in whole or in part, it may acquire, under the terms and in the manner the Contracting Officer considers appropriate, supplies or services similar to those terminated, and the Contractor will be liable to the Government for any excess costs for those supplies or services. However, the Contractor shall continue the work not terminated.

(c) Except for defaults of subcontractors at any tier, the Contractor shall not be liable for any excess costs if the failure to perform the contract arises from causes beyond the control and without the fault or negligence of the Contractor. Examples of such causes include (1) acts of God or of the public enemy, (2) acts of the Government in either its sovereign or contractual capacity, (3) fires, (4) floods, (5) epidemics, (6) quarantine restrictions, (7) strikes, (8) freight embargoes, and (9) unusually severe weather. In each instance the failure to perform must be beyond the control and without the fault or negligence of the Contractor.

(d) If the failure to perform is caused by the default of a subcontractor at any tier, and if the cause of the default is beyond the control of both the Contractor and subcontractor, and without the fault or negligence of either, the Contractor shall not be liable for any excess costs for failure to perform, unless the subcontracted supplies or services were obtainable from other sources in sufficient time for the Contractor to meet the required delivery schedule.

(e) If this contract is terminated for default, the Government may require the Contractor to transfer title and deliver to the Government, as directed by the Contracting Officer, any (1) completed supplies, and (2) partially completed supplies and materials, parts, tools, dies, jigs, fixtures, plans, drawings, information, and contract rights (collectively referred to as "manufacturing materials" in this clause) that the Contractor has specifically produced or acquired for the terminated portion of this contract. Upon direction of the Contracting Officer, the Contractor shall also protect and preserve property in its possession in which the Government has an interest.

(f) The Government shall pay contract price for completed supplies delivered and accepted. The Contractor and Contracting Officer shall agree on the amount of payment for manufacturing materials delivered and accepted and for the protection and preservation of the property. Failure to agree will be a dispute under the Disputes clause. The Government may withhold from these amounts any sum the Contracting Officer determines to be necessary to protect the Government against loss because of outstanding liens or claims of former lien holders.

(g) If, after termination, it is determined that the Contractor was not in default, or that the default was excusable, the rights and obligations of the parties shall be the same as if the termination had been issued for the convenience of the Government.

(h) The rights and remedies of the Government in this clause are in addition to any other rights and remedies provided by law or under this contract.

Alternate I (APR 1984). If the contract is for transportation or transportation-related services, delete paragraph (f) of the basic clause, redesignate the remaining paragraphs accordingly, and substitute the following paragraphs (a) and (e) for paragraphs (a) and (e) of the basic clause:

(a)(1) The Government may, subject to paragraphs (c) and (d) of this clause, by written notice of default to the Contractor, terminate this contract in whole or in part if the Contractor fails to —

(i) Pick up the commodities or to perform the services, including delivery services, within the time specified in this contract or any extension;

(ii) Make progress, so as to endanger performance of this contract (but see subparagraph (a)(2) of this clause); or

(iii) Perform any of the other provisions of this contract (but see subparagraph (a)(2) of this clause)

(2) The Government's right to terminate this contract under subdivisions (a)(1)(ii) and (iii) of this clause, may be exercised if the Contractor does not cure such failure within 10 days (or more if authorized in writing by the Contracting Officer) after receipt of the notice from the Contracting Officer specifying the failure.

(e) If this contract is terminated while the Contractor has possession of Government goods, the Contractor shall, upon direction of the Contracting Officer, protect and preserve the goods until surrendered to the Government or its agent. The Contractor and Contracting Officer shall agree on payment for the preservation and protection of goods. Failure to agree on an amount will be a dispute under the Disputes clause.

STANDARD FAR CONSTRUCTION CONTRACT CLAUSES

FAR 52.232-5 Payments Under Fixed-Price Construction Contracts

PAYMENTS UNDER FIXED-PRICE CONSTRUCTION CONTRACTS (SEP 2002)

(a) Payment of price. The Government shall pay the Contractor the contract price as provided in this contract.

(b) Progress payments. The Government shall make progress payments monthly as the work proceeds, or at more frequent intervals as determined by the Contracting Officer, on estimates of work accomplished which meets the standards of quality established under the contract, as approved by the Contracting Officer.

(1) The Contractor's request for progress payments shall include the following substantiation:

(i) An itemization of the amounts requested, related to the various elements of work required by the contract covered by the payment requested.

(ii) A listing of the amount included for work performed by each subcontractor under the contract.

(iii) A listing of the total amount of each subcontract under the contract.

(iv) A listing of the amounts previously paid to each such subcontractor under the contract.

(v) Additional supporting data in a form and detail required by the Contracting Officer.

(2) In the preparation of estimates, the Contracting Officer may authorize material delivered on the site and preparatory work done to be taken into consideration. Material delivered to the Contractor at locations other than the site also may be taken into consideration if

(i) Consideration is specifically authorized by this contract; and

(ii) The Contractor furnishes satisfactory evidence that it has acquired title to such material and that the material will be used to perform this contract.

(c) Contractor certification. Along with each request for progress payments, the Contractor shall furnish the following certification, or payment shall not be made: (However, if the Contractor elects to delete paragraph (c)(4) from the certification, the certification is still acceptable.)

I hereby certify, to the best of my knowledge and belief, that—

(1) The amounts requested are only for performance in accordance with the specifications, terms, and conditions of the contract;

(2) All payments due to subcontractors and suppliers from previous payments received under the contract have been made, and timely payments will be made from the proceeds of the payment covered by this certification, in accordance with subcontract agreements and the requirements of chapter 39 of Title 31, United States Code;

(3) This request for progress payments does not include any amounts which the prime contractor intends to withhold or retain from a subcontractor or supplier in accordance with the terms and conditions of the subcontract; and

(4) This certification is not to be construed as final acceptance of a subcontractor's performance.

____

(Name)

____

(Title)

____

(Date)

(d) Refund of unearned amounts. If the Contractor, after making a certified request for progress payments, discovers that a portion or all of such request constitutes a payment for performance by the Contractor that fails to conform to the specifications, terms, and conditions of this contract (hereinafter referred to as the "unearned amount"), the Contractor shall —

(1) Notify the Contracting Officer of such performance deficiency; and

(2) Be obligated to pay the Government an amount (computed by the Contracting Officer in the manner provided in paragraph (j) of this clause) equal to interest on the unearned amount from the 8th day after the date of receipt of the unearned amount until —

(i) The date the Contractor notifies the Contracting Officer that the performance deficiency has been corrected; or

(ii) The date the Contractor reduces the amount of any subsequent certified request for progress payments by an amount equal to the unearned amount.

(e) Retainage. If the Contracting Officer finds that satisfactory progress was achieved during any period for which a progress payment is to be made, the Contracting Officer shall authorize payment to be made in full. However, if satisfactory progress has not been made, the Contracting Officer may retain a maximum of 10 percent of the amount of the payment until satisfactory progress is achieved. When the work is substantially complete, the Contracting Officer may retain from previously withheld funds and future progress payments that amount the Contracting Officer considers adequate for protection of the Government and shall release to the Contractor all the remaining withheld funds. Also, on completion and acceptance of each separate building, public work, or other division of the contract, for which the price is stated separately in the contract, payment shall be made for the completed work without retention of a percentage.

(f) Title, liability, and reservation of rights. All material and work covered by progress payments made shall, at the time of payment, become the sole property of the Government, but this shall not be construed as —

(1) Relieving the Contractor from the sole responsibility for all material and work upon which payments have been made or the restoration of any damaged work; or

(2) Waiving the right of the Government to require the fulfillment of all of the terms of the contract.

(g) Reimbursement for bond premiums. In making these progress payments, the Government shall, upon request, reimburse the Contractor for the amount of premiums paid for performance and payment bonds (including coinsurance and reinsurance agreements, when applicable) after the Contractor has furnished evidence of full payment to the surety. The retainage provisions in paragraph (e) of this clause shall not apply to that portion of progress payments attributable to bond premiums.

(h) Final payment. The Government shall pay the amount due the Contractor under this contract after —

(1) Completion and acceptance of all work;

(2) Presentation of a properly executed voucher; and

(3) Presentation of release of all claims against the Government arising by virtue of this contract, other than claims, in stated amounts, that the Contractor has specifically excepted from the operation of the release. A release may also be required of the assignee if the Contractor's claim to amounts payable under this contract has been assigned under the Assignment of Claims Act of 1940 (31 U.S.C. 3727 and 41 U.S.C. 15).

(i) Limitation because of undefinitized work. Notwithstanding any provision of this contract, progress payments shall not exceed 80 percent on work accomplished on undefinitized contract actions. A "contract action" is any action resulting in a contract, as defined in FAR Subpart 2.1, including contract modifications for additional supplies or services, but not including contract modifications that are within the scope and under the terms of the contract, such as contract modifications issued pursuant to the Changes clause, or funding and other administrative changes.

(j) Interest computation on unearned amounts. In accordance with 31 U.S.C. 3903(c)(1), the amount payable under subparagraph (d)(2) of this clause shall be —

(1) Computed at the rate of average bond equivalent rates of 91-day Treasury bills auctioned at the most recent auction of such bills prior to the date the Contractor receives the unearned amount; and

(2) Deducted from the next available payment to the Contractor.

FAR 52.236-1 Performance of Work by the Contractor

PERFORMANCE OF WORK BY THE CONTRACTOR (APR 1984)

The Contractor shall perform on the site, and with its own organization, work equivalent to at least __________ [insert the appropriate number in words followed by numerals in parentheses] percent of the total amount of work to be performed under the contract. This percentage may be reduced by a supplemental agreement to this contract if, during performing the work, the Contractor requests a reduction and the Contracting Officer determines that the reduction would be to the advantage of the Government.

FAR 52.236-2 Differing Site Conditions

DIFFERING SITE CONDITIONS (APR 1984)

(a) The Contractor shall promptly, and before the conditions are disturbed, give a written notice to the Contracting Officer of (1) subsurface or latent physical conditions at the site which differ materially from those indicated in this contract, or (2) unknown physical conditions at the site, of an unusual nature, which differ materially from those ordinarily encountered and generally recognized as inhering in work of the character provided for in the contract.

(b) The Contracting Officer shall investigate the site conditions promptly after receiving the notice. If the conditions do materially so differ and cause an increase or decrease in the Contractor's cost of, or the time required for, performing any part of the work under this contract, whether or not changed as a result of the conditions, an equitable adjustment shall be made under this clause and the contract modified in writing accordingly.

(c) No request by the Contractor for an equitable adjustment to the contract under this clause shall be allowed, unless the Contractor has given the written notice required; provided, that the time prescribed in (a) above for giving written notice may be extended by the Contracting Officer.

(d) No request by the Contractor for an equitable adjustment to the contract for differing site conditions shall be allowed if made after final payment under this contract.

FAR 52.236-3 Site Investigation and Conditions Affecting the Work

SITE INVESTIGATION AND CONDITIONS AFFECTING THE WORK (APR 1984)

(a) The Contractor acknowledges that it has taken steps reasonably necessary to ascertain the nature and location of the work, and that it has investigated and satisfied itself as to the general and local conditions which can affect the work or its cost, including but not limited to (1) conditions bearing upon transportation, disposal, handling, and storage of materials; (2) the availability of labor, water, electric power, and roads; (3) uncertainties of weather, river stages, tides, or similar physical conditions at the site; (4) the conformation and conditions of the ground; and (5) the character of equipment and facilities needed preliminary to and during work performance. The Contractor also acknowledges that it has satisfied itself as to the character, quality, and quantity of surface and subsurface materials or obstacles to be encountered insofar as this information is reasonably ascertainable from an inspection of the site, including all exploratory work done by the Government, as well as from the drawings and specifications made a part of this contract. Any failure of the Contractor to take the actions described and acknowledged in this paragraph will not relieve the Contractor from responsibility for estimating properly the difficulty and cost of successfully performing the work, or for proceeding to successfully perform the work without additional expense to the Government.

(b) The Government assumes no responsibility for any conclusions or interpretations made by the Contractor based on the information made available by the Government. Nor does the Government assume responsibility for any understanding reached or representation made concerning conditions which can affect the work by any of its officers or agents before the execution of this contract, unless that understanding or representation is expressly stated in this contract.

FAR 52.336.4 Physical Data

PHYSICAL DATA (APR 1984)

Data and information furnished or referred to below is for the Contractor's information. The Government shall not be responsible for any interpretation of or conclusion drawn from the data or information by the Contractor.

(a) The indications of physical conditions on the drawings and in the specifications are the result of site investigations by ________ [insert a description of investigational methods used, such as surveys, auger borings, core borings, test pits, probings, test tunnels].

(b) Weather conditions ________ [insert a summary of weather records and warnings].

(c) Transportation facilities _______ [insert a summary of transportation facilities providing access from the site, including information about their availability and limitations].

(d) ________ [insert other pertinent information].

FAR 52.236-5 Material and Workmanship

MATERIAL AND WORKMANSHIP (APR 1984)

(a) All equipment, material, and articles incorporated into the work covered by this contract shall be new and of the most suitable grade for the purpose intended, unless otherwise specifically provided in this contract. References in the specifications to equipment, material, articles, or patented processes by trade name, make, or catalog number, shall be regarded as establishing a standard of quality and shall not be construed as limiting competition. The Contractor may, at its option, use any equipment, material, article, or process that, in the judgment of the Contracting Officer, is equal to that named in the specifications, unless otherwise specifically provided in this contract.

(b) The Contractor shall obtain the Contracting Officer's approval of the machinery and mechanical and other equipment to be incorporated into the work. When requesting approval, the Contractor shall furnish to the Contracting Officer the name of the manufacturer, the model number, and other information concerning the performance, capacity, nature, and rating of the machinery and mechanical and other equipment. When required by this contract or by the Contracting Officer, the Contractor shall also obtain the Contracting Officer's approval of the material or articles which the Contractor contemplates incorporating into the work. When requesting approval, the Contractor shall provide full information concerning the material or articles. When directed to do so, the Contractor shall submit samples for approval at the Contractor's expense, with all shipping charges prepaid. Machinery, equipment, material, and articles that do not have the required approval shall be installed or used at the risk of subsequent rejection.

(c) All work under this contract shall be performed in a skillful and workmanlike manner. The Contracting Officer may require, in writing, that the Contractor remove from the work any employee the Contracting Officer deems incompetent, careless, or otherwise objectionable.

FAR 52.236-6 Superintendence by the Contractor

SUPERINTENDENCE BY THE CONTRACTOR (APR 1984)

At all times during performance of this contract and until the work is completed and accepted, the Contractor shall directly superintend the work or assign and have on the worksite a competent superintendent who is satisfactory to the Contracting Officer and has authority to act for the Contractor.

FAR 52.236-7 Permits and Responsibilities

PERMITS AND RESPONSIBILITIES (NOV 1991)

The Contractor shall, without additional expense to the Government, be responsible for obtaining any necessary licenses and permits, and for complying with any Federal, State, and municipal laws, codes, and regulations applicable to the performance of the work. The Contractor shall also be responsible for all damages to persons or property that occur as a result of the Contractor's fault or negligence. The Contractor shall also be responsible for all materials delivered and work performed until completion and acceptance of the entire work, except for any completed unit of work which may have been accepted under the contract.

FAR 52.236-8 Other Contracts

OTHER CONTRACTS (APR 1984)

The Government may undertake or award other contracts for additional work at or near the site of the work under this contract. The Contractor shall fully cooperate with the other contractors and with Government employees and shall carefully adapt scheduling and performing the work under this contract to accommodate the additional work, heeding any direction that may be provided by the Contracting Officer. The Contractor shall not commit or permit any act that will interfere with the performance of work by any other contractor or by Government employees.

FAR 52.236-9 Protection of Existing Vegetation, Structures, Equipment, Utilities, and Improvements

PROTECTION OF EXISTING VEGETATION, STRUCTURES, EQUIPMENT, UTILITIES, AND IMPROVEMENTS (APR 1984)

(a) The Contractor shall preserve and protect all structures, equipment, and vegetation (such as trees, shrubs, and grass) on or adjacent to the work site, which are not to be removed and which do not unreasonably interfere with the work required under this contract. The Contractor shall only remove trees when specifically authorized to do so, and shall avoid damaging vegetation that will remain in place. If any limbs or branches of trees are broken during contract performance, or by the careless operation of equipment, or by workmen, the Contractor shall trim those limbs or branches with a clean cut and paint the cut with a tree-pruning compound as directed by the Contracting Officer.

(b) The Contractor shall protect from damage all existing improvements and utilities (1) at or near the work site, and (2) on adjacent property of a third party, the locations of which are made known to or should be known by the Contractor. The Contractor shall repair any damage to those facilities, including those that are the property of a third party, resulting from failure to comply with the requirements of this contract or failure to exercise reasonable care in performing the work. If the Contractor fails or refuses to repair the damage promptly, the Contracting Officer may have the necessary work performed and charge the cost to the Contractor.

FAR 52.236-10 Operations and Storage Areas

OPERATIONS AND STORAGE AREAS (APR 1984)

(a) The Contractor shall confine all operations (including storage of materials) on Government premises to areas authorized or approved by the Contracting Officer. The Contractor shall hold and save the Government, its officers and agents, free and harmless from liability of any nature occasioned by the Contractor's performance.

(b) Temporary buildings (e.g., storage sheds, shops, offices) and utilities may be erected by the Contractor only with the approval of the Contracting Officer and shall be built with labor and materials furnished by the Contractor without expense to the Government. The temporary buildings and utilities shall remain the property of the Contractor and shall be removed by the Contractor at its expense upon completion of the work. With the written consent of the Contracting Officer, the buildings and utilities may be abandoned and need not be removed.

(c) The Contractor shall, under regulations prescribed by the Contracting Officer, use only established roadways, or use temporary roadways constructed by the Contractor when and as authorized by the Contracting Officer. When materials are transported in prosecuting the work, vehicles shall not be loaded beyond the loading capacity recommended by the manufacturer of the vehicle or prescribed by any Federal, State, or local law or regulation. When it is necessary to cross curbs or sidewalks, the Contractor shall protect them from damage. The Contractor shall repair or pay for the repair of any damaged curbs, sidewalks, or roads.

FAR 52.236-11 Use and Possession Prior to Completion

USE AND POSSESSION PRIOR TO COMPLETION (APR 1984)

(a) The Government shall have the right to take possession of or use any completed or partially completed part of the work. Before taking possession of or using any work, the Contracting Officer shall furnish the Contractor a list of items of work remaining to be performed or corrected on those portions of the work that the Government intends to take possession of or use. However, failure of the Contracting Officer to list any item of work shall not relieve the Contractor of responsibility for complying with the terms of the contract. The Government's possession or use shall not be deemed an acceptance of any work under the contract.

(b) While the Government has such possession or use, the Contractor shall be relieved of the responsibility for the loss of or damage to the work resulting from the Government's possession or use, notwithstanding the terms of the clause in this contract entitled "Permits and Responsibilities." If prior possession or use by the Government delays the progress of the work or causes additional expense to the Contractor, an equitable adjustment shall be made in the contract price or the time of completion, and the contract shall be modified in writing accordingly.

FAR 52.236-12 Cleaning Up

CLEANING UP (APR 1984)

The Contractor shall at all times keep the work area, including storage areas, free from accumulations of waste materials. Before completing the work, the Contractor shall remove from the work and premises any rubbish, tools, scaffolding, equipment, and materials that are not the property of the Government. Upon completing the work, the Contractor shall leave the work area in a clean, neat, and orderly condition satisfactory to the Contracting Officer.

FAR 52.236-13 Accident Prevention

ACCIDENT PREVENTION (NOV 1991)

(a) The Contractor shall provide and maintain work environments and procedures which will (1) safeguard the public and Government personnel, property, materials, supplies, and equipment exposed to Contractor operations and activities; (2) avoid interruptions of Government operations and delays in project completion dates; and (3) control costs in the performance of this contract.

(b) For these purposes on contracts for construction or dismantling, demolition, or removal of improvements, the Contractor shall —

(1) Provide appropriate safety barricades, signs, and signal lights;

(2) Comply with the standards issued by the Secretary of Labor at 29 CFR part 1926 and 29 CFR part 1910; and

(3) Ensure that any additional measures the Contracting Officer determines to be reasonably necessary for the purposes are taken.

(c) If this contract is for construction or dismantling, demolition or removal of improvements with any Department of Defense agency or component, the Contractor shall comply with all pertinent provisions of the latest version of U.S. Army Corps of Engineers Safety and Health Requirements Manual, EM 385-1-1, in effect on the date of the solicitation.

(d) Whenever the Contracting Officer becomes aware of any noncompliance with these requirements or any condition which poses a serious or imminent danger to the health or safety of the public or Government personnel, the Contracting Officer shall notify the Contractor orally, with written confirmation, and request immediate initiation of corrective action. This notice, when delivered to the Contractor or the Contractor's representative at the work site, shall be deemed sufficient notice of the noncompliance and that corrective action is required. After receiving the notice, the Contractor shall immediately take corrective action. If the Contractor fails or refuses to promptly take corrective action, the Contracting Officer may issue an order stopping all or part of the work until satisfactory corrective action has been taken. The Contractor shall not be entitled to any equitable adjustment of the contract price or extension of the performance schedule on any stop work order issued under this clause.

(e) The Contractor shall insert this clause, including this paragraph (e), with appropriate changes in the designation of the parties, in subcontracts.

Alternate I (Nov 1991). If the contract will involve (a) work of a long duration or hazardous nature, or (b) performance on a Government facility that on the advice of technical representatives involves hazardous materials or operations that might endanger the safety of the public and/or Government personnel or property, add the following paragraph (f) to the basic clause:

(f) Before commencing the work, the Contractor shall —

> (1) Submit a written proposed plan for implementing this clause. The plan shall include an analysis of the significant hazards to life, limb, and property inherent in contract work performance and a plan for controlling these hazards; and
>
> (2) Meet with representatives of the Contracting Officer to discuss and develop a mutual understanding relative to administration of the overall safety program.

FAR 52.236-21 Specifications and Drawings for Construction

SPECIFICATIONS AND DRAWINGS FOR CONSTRUCTION
(FEB 1997)

(a) The Contractor shall keep on the work site a copy of the drawings and specifications and shall at all times give the Contracting Officer access thereto. Anything mentioned in the specifications and not shown on the drawings, or shown on the drawings and not mentioned in the specifications, shall be of like effect as if shown or mentioned in both. In case of difference between drawings and specifications, the specifications shall govern. In case of discrepancy in the figures, in the drawings, or in the specifications, the matter shall be promptly submitted to the Contracting

Officer, who shall promptly make a determination in writing. Any adjustment by the Contractor without such a determination shall be at its own risk and expense. The Contracting Officer shall furnish from time to time such detailed drawings and other information as considered necessary, unless otherwise provided.

(b) Wherever in the specifications or upon the drawings the words “directed”, “required”, “ordered”, “designated”, “prescribed”, or words of like import are used, it shall be understood that the “direction”, “requirement”, “order”, “designation”, or “prescription”, of the Contracting Officer is intended and similarly the words “approved”, “acceptable”, “satisfactory”, or words of like import shall mean “approved by”, or “acceptable to”, or “satisfactory to” the Contracting Officer, unless otherwise expressly stated.

(c) Where “as shown”, “as indicated”, “as detailed”, or words of similar import are used, it shall be understood that the reference is made to the drawings accompanying this contract unless stated otherwise. The word “provided” as used herein shall be understood to mean “provide complete in place”, that is “furnished and installed”.

(d) Shop drawings means drawings, submitted to the Government by the Contractor, subcontractor, or any lower tier subcontractor pursuant to a construction contract, showing in detail (1) the proposed fabrication and assembly of structural elements and (2) the installation (i.e., form, fit, and attachment details) of materials of equipment. It includes drawings, diagrams, layouts, schematics, descriptive literature, illustrations, schedules, performance and test data, and similar materials furnished by the contractor to explain in detail specific portions of the work required by the contract. The Government may duplicate, use, and disclose in any manner and for any purpose shop drawings delivered under this contract.

(e) If this contract requires shop drawings, the Contractor shall coordinate all such drawings, and review them for accuracy, completeness, and compliance with contract requirements and shall indicate its approval thereon as evidence of such coordination and review. Shop drawings submitted to the Contracting Officer without evidence of the Contractor’s approval may be returned for resubmission. The Contracting Officer will indicate an approval or disapproval of the shop drawings and if not approved as submitted shall indicate the Government’s reasons therefor. Any work done before such approval shall be at the Contractor’s risk. Approval by the Contracting Officer shall not relieve the Contractor from responsibility for any errors or omissions in such drawings, nor from responsibility for complying with the requirements of this contract, except with respect to variations described and approved in accordance with (f) below.

(f) If shop drawings show variations from the contract requirements, the Contractor shall describe such variations in writing, separate from the drawings, at the time of submission. If the Contracting Officer approves any such variation, the Contracting

Officer shall issue an appropriate contract modification, except that, if the variation is minor or does not involve a change in price or in time of performance, a modification need not be issued.

(g) The Contractor shall submit to the Contracting Officer for approval four copies (unless otherwise indicated) of all shop drawings as called for under the various headings of these specifications. Three sets (unless otherwise indicated) of all shop drawings, will be retained by the Contracting Officer and one set will be returned to the Contractor.

Alternate I (APR 1984). When record shop drawings are required and reproducible shop drawings are needed, add the following sentences to paragraph (g) of the basic clause:

Upon completing the work under this contract, the Contractor shall furnish a complete set of all shop drawings as finally approved. These drawings shall show all changes and revisions made up to the time the equipment is completed and accepted.

Alternate II (APR 1984). When record shop drawings are required and reproducible shop drawings are not needed, the following sentences shall be added to paragraph (g) of the basic clause:

> Upon completing the work under this contract, the Contractor shall furnish .... [Contracting Officer complete by inserting desired amount] sets of prints of all shop drawings as finally approved. These drawings shall show changes and revisions made up to the time the equipment is completed and accepted.

FAR 52.246-12 Inspection of Construction

INSPECTION OF CONSTRUCTION (AUG 1996)

(a) Definition. "Work" includes, but is not limited to, materials, workmanship, and manufacture and fabrication of components.

(b) The Contractor shall maintain an adequate inspection system and perform such inspections as will ensure that the work performed under the contract conforms to contract requirements. The Contractor shall maintain complete inspection records and make them available to the Government. All work shall be conducted under the general direction of the Contracting Officer and is subject to Government inspection and test at all places and at all reasonable times before acceptance to ensure strict compliance with the terms of the contract.

(c) Government inspections and tests are for the sole benefit of the Government and do not —

(1) Relieve the Contractor of responsibility for providing adequate quality control measures;

(2) Relieve the Contractor of responsibility for damage to or loss of the material before acceptance;

(3) Constitute or imply acceptance; or

(4) Affect the continuing rights of the Government after acceptance of the completed work under paragraph (i) below.

(d) The presence or absence of a Government inspector does not relieve the Contractor from any contract requirement, nor is the inspector authorized to change any term or condition of the specification without the Contracting Officer's written authorization.

(e) The Contractor shall promptly furnish, at no increase in contract price, all facilities, labor, and material reasonably needed for performing such safe and convenient inspections and tests as may be required by the Contracting Officer. The Government may charge to the Contractor any additional cost of inspection or test when work is not ready at the time specified by the Contractor for inspection or test, or when prior rejection makes reinspection or retest necessary. The Government shall perform all inspections and tests in a manner that will not unnecessarily delay the work. Special, full size, and performance tests shall be performed as described in the contract.

(f) The Contractor shall, without charge, replace or correct work found by the Government not to conform to contract requirements, unless in the public interest the Government consents to accept the work with an appropriate adjustment in contract price. The Contractor shall promptly segregate and remove rejected material from the premises.

(g) If the Contractor does not promptly replace or correct rejected work, the Government may (1) by contract or otherwise, replace or correct the work and charge the cost to the Contractor or (2) terminate for default the Contractor's right to proceed.

(h) If, before acceptance of the entire work, the Government decides to examine already completed work by removing it or tearing it out, the Contractor, on request, shall promptly furnish all necessary facilities, labor, and material. If the work is found to be defective or nonconforming in any material respect due to the fault of the Contractor or its subcontractors, the Contractor shall defray the expenses of the examination and of satisfactory reconstruction. However, if the work is found to meet contract requirements, the Contracting Officer shall make an equitable adjustment for the additional services involved in the examination and reconstruction, including, if completion of the work was thereby delayed, an extension of time.

(i) Unless otherwise specified in the contract, the Government shall accept, as promptly as practicable after completion and inspection, all work required by the contract or that portion of the work the Contracting Officer determines can be accepted separately. Acceptance shall be final and conclusive except for latent defects, fraud, gross mistakes amounting to fraud, or the Government's rights under any warranty or guarantee.

FAR 52.249-10 Default (Fixed-Price Construction)

DEFAULT (FIXED-PRICE CONSTRUCTION) (APR 1984)

(a) If the Contractor refuses or fails to prosecute the work or any separable part, with the diligence that will insure its completion within the time specified in this contract including any extension, or fails to complete the work within this time, the Government may, by written notice to the Contractor, terminate the right to proceed with the work (or the separable part of the work) that has been delayed. In this event, the Government may take over the work and complete it by contract or otherwise, and may take possession of and use any materials, appliances, and plant on the work site necessary for completing the work. The Contractor and its sureties shall be liable for any damage to the Government resulting from the Contractor's refusal or failure to complete the work within the specified time, whether or not the Contractor's right to proceed with the work is terminated. This liability includes any increased costs incurred by the Government in completing the work.

(b) The Contractor's right to proceed shall not be terminated nor the Contractor charged with damages under this clause, if—

(1) The delay in completing the work arises from unforeseeable causes beyond the control and without the fault or negligence of the Contractor. Examples of such causes include —

(i) Acts of God or of the public enemy,

(ii) Acts of the Government in either its sovereign or contractual capacity,

(iii) Acts of another Contractor in the performance of a contract with the Government,

(iv) Fires,

(v) Floods,

(vi) Epidemics,

(vii) Quarantine restrictions,

(viii) Strikes,

(ix) Freight embargoes,

(x) Unusually severe weather, or

(xi) Delays of subcontractors or suppliers at any tier arising from unforeseeable causes beyond the control and without the fault or negligence of both the Contractor and the subcontractors or suppliers; and

(2) The Contractor, within 10 days from the beginning of any delay (unless extended by the Contracting Officer), notifies the Contracting Officer in writing of the causes of delay. The Contracting Officer shall ascertain the facts and the extent of delay. If, in the judgment of the Contracting Officer, the findings of fact warrant such action, the time for completing the work shall be extended. The findings of the Contracting Officer shall be final and conclusive on the parties, but subject to appeal under the Disputes clause.

(c) If, after termination of the Contractor's right to proceed, it is determined that the Contractor was not in default, or that the delay was excusable, the rights and obligations of the parties will be the same as if the termination had been issued for the convenience of the Government.

(d) The rights and remedies of the Government in this clause are in addition to any other rights and remedies provided by law or under this contract.

STANDARD FAR RESEARCH AND DEVELOPMENT CONTRACT CLAUSES

FAR 52.232-2 Payment Under Fixed-Price Research and Development Contracts

PAYMENTS UNDER FIXED-PRICE RESEARCH AND DEVELOPMENT CONTRACTS (APR 1984)

The Government shall pay the Contractor, upon submission of proper invoices or vouchers, the prices stipulated in this contract for work delivered or rendered and accepted, less any deductions provided in this contract. Unless otherwise specified, payment shall be made upon acceptance of any portion of the work delivered or rendered for which a price is separately stated in the contract.

FAR 52.243-1 Changes—Fixed-Price

CHANGES—FIXED-PRICE (AUG 1987)

(a) The Contracting Officer may at any time, by written order, and without notice to the sureties, if any, make changes within the general scope of this contract in any one or more of the following:

(1) Drawings, designs, or specifications when the supplies to be furnished are to be specially manufactured for the Government in accordance with the drawings, designs, or specifications.

(2) Method of shipment or packing.

(3) Place of delivery.

(b) If any such change causes an increase or decrease in the cost of, or the time required for, performance of any part of the work under this contract, whether or not changed by the order, the Contracting Officer shall make an equitable adjustment in the contract price, the delivery schedule, or both, and shall modify the contract.

(c) The Contractor must assert its right to an adjustment under this clause within 30 days from the date of receipt of the written order. However, if the Contracting Officer decides that the facts justify it, the Contracting Officer may receive and act upon a proposal submitted before final payment of the contract.

(d) If the Contractor's proposal includes the cost of property made obsolete or excess by the change, the Contracting Officer shall have the right to prescribe the manner of the disposition of the property.

(e) Failure to agree to any adjustment shall be a dispute under the Disputes clause. However, nothing in this clause shall excuse the Contractor from proceeding with the contract as changed.

FAR 52.246-7 Inspection of Research and Development—Fixed-Price

INSPECTION OF RESEARCH AND DEVELOPMENT—
FIXED-PRICE (AUG 1996)

(a) The Contractor shall provide and maintain an inspection system acceptable to the Government covering the work under this contract. Complete records of all inspection work performed by the Contractor shall be maintained and made available to the Government during contract performance and for as long afterwards as the contract requires.

(b) The Government has the right to inspect and test all work called for by the contract, to the extent practicable at all places and times, including the period of performance, and in any event before acceptance. The Government may also inspect the premises of the Contractor or any subcontractor engaged in contract performance. The Government shall perform inspections and tests in a manner that will not unduly delay the work.

(c) If the Government performs any inspection or test on the premises of the Contractor or a subcontractor, the Contractor shall furnish and shall require subcontractors to furnish, at no increase in contract price, all reasonable facilities and assistance for the safe and convenient performance of these duties. Except as otherwise provided in the contract, the Government shall bear the expense of Government inspections or tests made at other than the Contractor's or subcontractor's premises.

(d) The Government shall accept or reject the work as promptly as practicable after delivery, unless otherwise specified in the contract. Government failure to inspect and accept or reject the work shall not relieve the Contractor from responsibility, nor impose liability on the Government, for nonconforming work. Work is nonconforming when it is defective in material or workmanship or is otherwise not in conformity with contract requirements.

(e) The Government has the right to reject nonconforming work. If the Contractor fails or is unable to correct or to replace nonconforming work within the delivery schedule (or such later time as the Contracting Officer may authorize), the Contracting Officer may accept the work and make an equitable price reduction. Failure to agree on a price reduction shall be a dispute.

(f) Inspection and test by the Government does not relieve the Contractor from responsibility for defects or other failures to meet the contract requirements that may be discovered before acceptance. Acceptance shall be conclusive, except for latent defects, fraud, gross mistakes amounting to fraud, or as otherwise specified in the contract. If acceptance is not conclusive for any of these causes, the Government, in addition to any other rights and remedies provided by law, or under other provisions of this contract, shall have the right to require the Contractor (1) at no increase in contract price, to correct or replace the defective or nonconforming supplies (work) at the original point of delivery or at the Contractor's plant at the Contracting Officer's election, and in accordance with a reasonable delivery schedule as may be agreed upon between the Contractor and the Contracting Officer; provided, the Contracting Officer may require a reduction in contract price if the Contractor fails to meet such delivery schedule; or (2) within a reasonable time after the Contractor's receipt of notice of defects or nonconformance, to repayment of such portion of the contract price as is equitable under the circumstances if the Government elects not to require correction or replacement. When supplies (work) are (is) returned to the Contractor, the Contractor shall bear transportation costs from the original point of delivery to the Contractor's plant and return to the original point of delivery when that point is not the Contractor's plant.

FAR 52.249-9 Default (Fixed-Price Research and Development)

DEFAULT (FIXED-PRICE RESEARCH AND DEVELOPMENT) (APR 1984)

(a)(1) The Government may, subject to paragraphs (c) and (d) of this clause, by written Notice of Default to the Contractor, terminate this contract in whole or in part if the Contractor fails to —

(i) Perform the work under the contract within the time specified in this contract or any extension;

(ii) Prosecute the work so as to endanger performance of this contract (but see subparagraph (a)(2) of this clause); or

(iii) Perform any of the other provisions of this contract (but see subparagraph (a)(2) below)

(2) The Government's right to terminate this contract under subdivisions (a)(1)(ii) and (iii) of this paragraph may be exercised if the Contractor does not cure such failure within 10 days (or more, if authorized in writing by the Contracting Officer) after receipt of the notice from the Contracting Officer specifying the failure.

(b) If the Government terminates this contract in whole or in part, it may acquire, under the terms and in the manner the Contracting Officer considers appropriate, work similar to the work terminated, and the Contractor will be liable to the Government for any excess costs for the similar work. However, the Contractor shall continue the work not terminated.

(c) Except for defaults of subcontractors at any tier, the Contractor shall not be liable for any excess costs if the failure to perform the contract arises from causes beyond the control and without the fault or negligence of the Contractor. Examples of such causes include (1) acts of God or of the public enemy, (2) acts of the Government in either its sovereign or contractual capacity, (3) fires, (4) floods, (5) epidemics, (6) quarantine restrictions, (7) strikes, (8) freight embargoes, and (9) unusually severe weather. In each instance the failure to perform must be beyond the control and without the fault or negligence of the Contractor.

(d) If the failure to perform is caused by the default of a subcontractor at any tier, and if the cause of the default is beyond the control of both the Contractor and subcontractor, and without the fault or negligence of either, the Contractor shall not be liable for any excess costs for failure to perform, unless the subcontracted supplies or services were obtainable from other sources in sufficient time for the Contractor to meet the required delivery schedule or other performance requirements.

(e) If this contract is terminated for default, the Government may require the Contractor to transfer title and deliver to the Government, as directed by the Contracting Officer, any (1) completed or partially completed work not previously delivered to, and accepted by, the Government and (2) other property, including contract rights, specifically produced or acquired for the terminated portion of this contract. Upon direction of the Contracting Officer, the Contractor shall also protect and preserve property in its possession in which the Government has an interest.

(f) The Government shall pay the contract price, if separately stated, for completed work it has accepted and the amount agreed upon by the Contractor and the Contracting Officer for (1) completed work for which no separate price is stated, (2) partially completed work, (3) other property described above that it accepts, and (4) the protection and preservation of the property. Failure to agree will be a dispute under the Disputes clause. The Government may withhold from these amounts any sum the Contracting Officer determines to be necessary to protect the Government against loss from outstanding liens or claims of former lien holders.

(g) If, after termination, it is determined that the Contractor was not in default, or that the default was excusable, the rights and obligations of the parties shall be the same as if the termination had been issued for the convenience of the Government.

(h) The rights and remedies of the Government in this clause are in addition to any other rights and remedies provided by law or under this contract.

STANDARD FAR CLAUSES APPLICABLE TO ALL TYPES OF CONTRACTS

FAR 52.202-1 Definitions

DEFINITIONS (JUL 2004)

(a) When a solicitation provision or contract clause uses a word or term that is defined in the Federal Acquisition Regulation (FAR), the word or term has the same meaning as the definition in FAR 2.101 in effect at the time the solicitation was issued, unless —

(1) The solicitation, or amended solicitation, provides a different definition;

(2) The contracting parties agree to a different definition;

(3) The part, subpart, or section of the FAR where the provision or clause is prescribed provides a different meaning; or

(4) The word or term is defined in FAR Part 31, for use in the cost principles and procedures.

(b) The FAR Index is a guide to words and terms the FAR defines and shows where each definition is located. The FAR Index is available via the Internet at http://www.acqnet.gov at the end of the FAR, after the FAR Appendix.

FAR 52.232-25 Prompt Payment

PROMPT PAYMENT (OCT 2003)

Notwithstanding any other payment clause in this contract, the Government will make invoice payments under the terms and conditions specified in this clause. The Government considers payment as being made on the day a check is dated or the date of an electronic funds transfer (EFT). Definitions of pertinent terms are set forth in sections 2.101, 32.001, and 32.902 of the Federal Acquisition Regulation. All days referred to in this clause are calendar days, unless otherwise specified. (However, see paragraph (a)(4) of this clause concerning payments due on Saturdays, Sundays, and legal holidays.)

(a) Invoice payments —(1) Due date. (i) Except as indicated in paragraphs (a)(2) and (c) of this clause, the due date for making invoice payments by the designated payment office is the later of the following two events:

(A) The 30th day after the designated billing office receives a proper invoice from the Contractor (except as provided in paragraph (a)(1)(ii) of this clause).

(B) The 30th day after Government acceptance of supplies delivered or services performed. For a final invoice, when the payment amount is subject to contract settlement actions, acceptance is deemed to occur on the effective date of the contract settlement.

(ii) If the designated billing office fails to annotate the invoice with the actual date of receipt at the time of receipt, the invoice payment due date is the 30th day after the date of the Contractor's invoice, provided the designated billing office receives a proper invoice and there is no disagreement over quantity, quality, or Contractor compliance with contract requirements.

(2) Certain food products and other payments. (i) Due dates on Contractor invoices for meat, meat food products, or fish; perishable agricultural commodities; and dairy products, edible fats or oils, and food products prepared from edible fats or oils are —

(A) For meat or meat food products, as defined in section 2(a)(3) of the Packers and Stockyard Act of 1921 (7 U.S.C. 182(3)), and as further defined in Pub. L. 98-181, including any edible fresh or frozen poultry meat, any perishable poultry meat food product, fresh eggs, and any perishable egg product, as close as possible to, but not later than, the 7th day after product delivery.

(B) For fresh or frozen fish, as defined in section 204(3) of the Fish and Seafood Promotion Act of 1986 (16 U.S.C. 4003(3)), as close as possible to, but not later than, the 7th day after product delivery.

(C) For perishable agricultural commodities, as defined in section 1(4) of the Perishable Agricultural Commodities Act of 1930 (7 U.S.C. 499a(4)), as close as possible to, but not later than, the 10th day after product delivery, unless another date is specified in the contract.

(D) For dairy products, as defined in section 111(e) of the Dairy Production Stabilization Act of 1983 (7 U.S.C. 4502(e)), edible fats or oils, and food products prepared from edible fats or oils, as close as possible to, but not later than, the 10th day after the date on which a proper invoice has been received. Liquid milk, cheese, certain processed cheese products, butter, yogurt, ice cream, mayonnaise, salad dressings, and other similar products, fall within this classification. Nothing in the Act limits this classification to refrigerated products. When questions arise regarding the proper classification of a specific product, prevailing industry practices will be followed in specifying a contract payment due date. The burden of proof that a classification of a specific product is, in fact, prevailing industry practice is upon the Contractor making the representation.

(ii) If the contract does not require submission of an invoice for payment (e.g., periodic lease payments), the due date will be as specified in the contract.

(3) Contractor's invoice. The Contractor shall prepare and submit invoices to the designated billing office specified in the contract. A proper invoice must include the items listed in paragraphs (a)(3)(i) through (a)(3)(x) of this clause. If the invoice does not comply with these requirements, the designated billing office will return it within 7 days after receipt (3 days for meat, meat food products, or fish; 5 days for perishable agricultural commodities, dairy products, edible fats or oils, and food products prepared from edible fats or oils), with the reasons why it is not a proper invoice. The Government will take into account untimely notification when computing any interest penalty owed the Contractor.

(i) Name and address of the Contractor.

(ii) Invoice date and invoice number. (The Contractor should date invoices as close as possible to the date of the mailing or transmission.)

(iii) Contract number or other authorization for supplies delivered or services performed (including order number and contract line item number).

(iv) Description, quantity, unit of measure, unit price, and extended price of supplies delivered or services performed.

(v) Shipping and payment terms (e.g., shipment number and date of shipment, discount for prompt payment terms). Bill of lading number and weight of shipment will be shown for shipments on Government bills of lading.

(vi) Name and address of Contractor official to whom payment is to be sent (must be the same as that in the contract or in a proper notice of assignment).

(vii) Name (where practicable), title, phone number, and mailing address of person to notify in the event of a defective invoice.

(viii) Taxpayer Identification Number (TIN). The Contractor shall include its TIN on the invoice only if required elsewhere in this contract.

(ix) Electronic funds transfer (EFT) banking information.

(A) The Contractor shall include EFT banking information on the invoice only if required elsewhere in this contract.

(B) If EFT banking information is not required to be on the invoice, in order for the invoice to be a proper invoice, the Contractor shall have submitted correct EFT banking information in accordance with the applicable solicitation provision (e.g., 52.232-38, Submission of Electronic Funds Transfer Information with Offer), contract clause (e.g., 52.232-33, Payment by Electronic Funds Transfer —Central Contractor Registration, or 52.232-34, Payment by Electronic Funds Transfer —Other Than Central Contractor Registration), or applicable agency procedures.

(C) EFT banking information is not required if the Government waived the requirement to pay by EFT.

(x) Any other information or documentation required by the contract (e.g., evidence of shipment).

(4) Interest penalty. The designated payment office will pay an interest penalty automatically, without request from the Contractor, if payment is not made by the due date and the conditions listed in paragraphs (a)(4)(i) through (a)(4)(iii) of this clause are met, if applicable. However, when the due date falls on a Saturday, Sunday, or legal holiday, the designated payment office may make payment on the following working day without incurring a late payment interest penalty.

(i) The designated billing office received a proper invoice.

(ii) The Government processed a receiving report or other Government documentation authorizing payment, and there was no disagreement over quantity, quality, or Contractor compliance with any contract term or condition.

(iii) In the case of a final invoice for any balance of funds due the Contractor for supplies delivered or services performed, the amount was not subject to further contract settlement actions between the Government and the Contractor.

(5) Computing penalty amount. The Government will compute the interest penalty in accordance with the Office of Management and Budget prompt payment regulations at 5 CFR part 1315.

(i) For the sole purpose of computing an interest penalty that might be due the Contractor, Government acceptance is deemed to occur constructively on the 7th day (unless otherwise specified in this contract) after the Contractor delivers the supplies or performs the services in accordance with the terms and conditions of the contract, unless there is a disagreement over quantity, quality, or Contractor compliance with a contract provision. If actual acceptance occurs within the constructive acceptance period, the Government will base the determination of an interest penalty on the actual date of acceptance. The constructive acceptance requirement does not, however, compel Government officials to accept supplies or services, perform contract administration functions, or make payment prior to fulfilling their responsibilities.

(ii) The prompt payment regulations at 5 CFR 1315.10(c) do not require the Government to pay interest penalties if payment delays are due to disagreement between the Government and the Contractor over the payment amount or other issues involving contract compliance, or on amounts temporarily withheld or retained in accordance with the terms of the contract. The Government and the Contractor shall resolve claims involving disputes and any interest that may be payable in accordance with the clause at FAR 52.233-1, Disputes.

(6) Discounts for prompt payment. The designated payment office will pay an interest penalty automatically, without request from the Contractor, if the Government takes a discount for prompt payment improperly. The Government will calculate the interest penalty in accordance with the prompt payment regulations at 5 CFR part 1315.

(7) Additional interest penalty. (i) The designated payment office will pay a penalty amount, calculated in accordance with the prompt payment regulations at 5 CFR part 1315 in addition to the interest penalty amount only if—

(A) The Government owes an interest penalty of $1 or more;

(B) The designated payment office does not pay the interest penalty within 10 days after the date the invoice amount is paid; and

(C) The Contractor makes a written demand to the designated payment office for additional penalty payment, in accordance with paragraph (a)(7)(ii) of this clause, postmarked not later than 40 days after the invoice amount is paid.

(ii)(A) The Contractor shall support written demands for additional penalty payments with the following data. The Government will not request any additional data. The Contractor shall—

(1) Specifically assert that late payment interest is due under a specific invoice, and request payment of all overdue late payment interest penalty and such additional penalty as may be required;

(2) Attach a copy of the invoice on which the unpaid late payment interest is due; and

(3) State that payment of the principal has been received, including the date of receipt.

(B) If there is no postmark or the postmark is illegible—

(1) The designated payment office that receives the demand will annotate it with the date of receipt, provided the demand is received on or before the 40th day after payment was made; or

(2) If the designated payment office fails to make the required annotation, the Government will determine the demand's validity based on the date the Contractor has placed on the demand, provided such date is no later than the 40th day after payment was made.

(iii) The additional penalty does not apply to payments regulated by other Government regulations (e.g., payments under utility contracts subject to tariffs and regulation).

(b) Contract financing payment. If this contract provides for contract financing, the Government will make contract financing payments in accordance with the applicable contract financing clause.

(c) Fast payment procedure due dates. If this contract contains the clause at 52.213-1, Fast Payment Procedure, payments will be made within 15 days after the date of receipt of the invoice.

(d) Overpayments. If the Contractor becomes aware of a duplicate contract financing or invoice payment or that the Government has otherwise overpaid on a contract financing or invoice payment, the Contractor shall immediately notify the Contracting Officer and request instructions for disposition of the overpayment.

Alternate I (Feb 2002). As prescribed in 32.908(c)(3), add the following paragraph (e) to the basic clause:

(e) Invoices for interim payments. For interim payments under this cost-reimbursement contract for services —

(1) Paragraphs (a)(2), (a)(3), (a)(4)(ii), (a)(4)(iii), and (a)(5)(i) do not apply;

(2) For purposes of computing late payment interest penalties that may apply, the due date for payment is the 30th day after the designated billing office receives a proper invoice; and

(3) The contractor shall submit invoices for interim payments in accordance with paragraph (a) of FAR 52.216-7, Allowable Cost and Payment. If the invoice does not comply with contract requirements, it will be returned within 7 days after the date the designated billing office received the invoice.

FAR 52.233-1 Disputes

DISPUTES (JUL 2002)

(a) This contract is subject to the Contract Disputes Act of 1978, as amended (41 U.S.C. 601-613).

(b) Except as provided in the Act, all disputes arising under or relating to this contract shall be resolved under this clause.

(c) Claim, as used in this clause, means a written demand or written assertion by one of the contracting parties seeking, as a matter of right, the payment of money in a sum certain, the adjustment or interpretation of contract terms, or other relief arising under or relating to this contract. However, a written demand or written assertion by the Contractor seeking the payment of money exceeding $100,000 is not a claim under the Act until certified. A voucher, invoice, or other routine request for payment that is not in dispute when submitted is not a claim under the Act. The submission may be converted to a claim under the Act, by complying with the submission and certification requirements of this clause, if it is disputed either as to liability or amount or is not acted upon in a reasonable time.

(d)(1) A claim by the Contractor shall be made in writing and, unless otherwise stated in this contract, submitted within 6 years after accrual of the claim to the Contracting Officer for a written decision. A claim by the Government against the Contractor shall be subject to a written decision by the Contracting Officer.

(2)(i) Contractors shall provide the certification specified in subparagraph (d)(2)(iii) of this clause when submitting any claim exceeding $100,000.

(ii) The certification requirement does not apply to issues in controversy that have not been submitted as all or part of a claim.

(iii) The certification shall state as follows: "I certify that the claim is made in good faith; that the supporting data are accurate and complete to the best of my knowledge and belief; that the amount requested accurately reflects the contract adjustment for which the Contractor believes the Government is liable; and that I am duly authorized to certify the claim on behalf of the Contractor."

(3) The certification may be executed by any person duly authorized to bind the Contractor with respect to the claim.

(e) For Contractor claims of $100,000 or less, the Contracting Officer must, if requested in writing by the Contractor, render a decision within 60 days of the request. For Contractor-certified claims over $100,000, the Contracting Officer must, within 60 days, decide the claim or notify the Contractor of the date by which the decision will be made.

(f) The Contracting Officer's decision shall be final unless the Contractor appeals or files a suit as provided in the Act.

(g) If the claim by the Contractor is submitted to the Contracting Officer or a claim by the Government is presented to the Contractor, the parties, by mutual consent, may agree to use alternative dispute resolution (ADR). If the Contractor refuses an offer for ADR, the Contractor shall inform the Contracting Officer, in writing, of the Contractor's specific reasons for rejecting the offer.

(h) The government shall pay interest on the amount found due and unpaid from (1) the date that the Contracting Officer receives the claim (certified, if required); or (2) the date that payment otherwise would be due, if that date is later, until the date of payment. With regard to claims having defective certifications, as defined in (FAR) 48 CFR 33.201, interest shall be paid from the date that the Contracting Officer initially receives the claim. Simple interest on claim shall be paid at the rate, fixed by the Secretary of the Treasury as provided in the Act, which is applicable to the period during which the Contracting Officer receives the claim and then at the rate applicable for each 6-month period as fixed by the Treasury Secretary during the pendency of the claim.

(i) The Contractor shall proceed diligently with performance of this contract, pending final resolution of any request for relief, claim, appeal, or action arising under the contract, and comply with any decision of the Contracting Officer.

Alternate I (DEC 1991). As prescribed in 33.215, substitute the following paragraph (i) for paragraph (i) of the basic clause:

> (i) The Contractor shall proceed diligently with performance of this contract, pending final resolution of any request for relief, claim, appeal, or action arising under or relating to the contract, and comply with any decision of the Contracting Officer.

FAR 52.233-2 Service of Protest

SERVICE OF PROTEST (AUG 1996)

(a) Protests, as defined in section 33.101 of the Federal Acquisition Regulation, that are filed directly with an agency, and copies of any protests that are filed with the General Accounting Office (GAO), shall be served on the Contracting Officer (addressed as follows) by obtaining written and dated acknowledgment of receipt from ___________ [Contracting Officer designate the official or location where a protest may be served on the Contracting Officer.]

(b) The copy of any protest shall be received in the office designated above within one day of filing a protest with the GAO.

FAR 52.233-3 Protest After Award

PROTEST AFTER AWARD (AUG 1996)

(a) Upon receipt of a notice of protest (as defined in FAR 33.101) or a determination that a protest is likely (see FAR 33.102(d)), the Contracting Officer may, by written order to the Contractor, direct the Contractor to stop performance of the work called for by this contract. The order shall be specifically identified as a stop-work order issued under this clause. Upon receipt of the order, the Contractor shall immediately comply with its terms and take all reasonable steps to minimize the incurrence of costs allocable to the work covered by the order during the period of work stoppage. Upon receipt of the final decision in the protest, the Contracting Officer shall either—

(1) Cancel the stop-work order; or

(2) Terminate the work covered by the order as provided in the Default, or the Termination for Convenience of the Government, clause of this contract.

(b) If a stop-work order issued under this clause is canceled either before or after a final decision in the protest, the Contractor shall resume work. The Contracting Officer shall make an equitable adjustment in the delivery schedule or contract price, or both, and the contract shall be modified, in writing, accordingly, if—

(1) The stop-work order results in an increase in the time required for, or in the Contractor's cost properly allocable to, the performance of any part of this contract; and

(2) The Contractor asserts its right to an adjustment within 30 days after the end of the period of work stoppage; provided, that if the Contracting Officer decides the facts justify the action, the Contracting Officer may receive and act upon a proposal submitted at any time before final payment under this contract.

(c) If a stop-work order is not canceled and the work covered by the order is terminated for the convenience of the Government, the Contracting Officer shall allow reasonable costs resulting from the stop-work order in arriving at the termination settlement.

(d) If a stop-work order is not canceled and the work covered by the order is terminated for default, the Contracting Officer shall allow, by equitable adjustment or otherwise, reasonable costs resulting from the stop-work order.

(e) The Government's rights to terminate this contract at any time are not affected by action taken under this clause.

(f) If, as the result of the Contractor's intentional or negligent misstatement, misrepresentation, or miscertification, a protest related to this contract is sustained, and the Government pays costs, as provided in FAR 33.102(b)(2) or 33.104(h)(1), the Government may require the Contractor to reimburse the Government the amount of such costs. In addition to any other remedy available, and pursuant to the requirements of Subpart 32.6, the Government may collect this debt by offsetting the amount against any payment due the Contractor under any contract between the Contractor and the Government.

Alternate I (JUN 1985). As prescribed in 33.106(b), substitute in paragraph (a)(2) the words "the Termination clause of this contract" for the words "the Default, or the Termination for Convenience of the Government clause of this contract." In paragraph (b) substitute the words "an equitable adjustment in the delivery schedule, the estimated cost, the fee, or a combination thereof, and in any other terms of the contract that may be affected" for the words "an equitable adjustment in the delivery schedule or contract price, or both."

FAR 52.245-2 Government Property (Fixed-Price Contracts)

GOVERNMENT PROPERTY (FIXED-PRICE CONTRACTS)
(MAY 2004)

(a) Government-furnished property.

(1) The Government shall deliver to the Contractor, for use in connection with and under the terms of this contract, the Government-furnished property described in the Schedule or specifications together with any related data and information that the Contractor may request and is reasonable required for the intended use of the property (hereinafter referred to as "Government-furnished property").

(2) The delivery or performance dates for this contract are based upon the expectation that Government-furnished property suitable for use (except for property furnished "as-is") will be delivered to the Contractor at the times stated in the Schedule or, if not so stated, in sufficient time to enable the Contractor to meet the contract's delivery or performance dates.

(3) If Government-furnished property is received by the Contractor in a condition not suitable for the intended use, the Contractor shall, upon receipt of it, notify the Contracting Officer, detailing the facts, and, as directed by the Contracting Officer and at Government expense, either repair, modify, return, or otherwise dispose of the property. After completing the directed action and upon written request of the Contractor, the Contracting Officer shall make an equitable adjustment as provided in paragraph (h) of this clause.

(4) If Government-furnished property is not delivered to the Contractor by the required time, the Contracting Officer shall, upon the Contractor's timely written request, make a determination of the delay, if any, caused the Contractor and shall make an equitable adjustment in accordance with paragraph (h) of this clause.

(b) Changes in Government-furnished property. (1) The Contracting Officer may, by written notice, (i) decrease the Government-furnished property provided or to be provided under this contract, or (ii) substitute other Government-furnished property for the property to be provided by the Government, or to be acquired by the Contractor for the Government, under this contract. The Contractor shall promptly take such action as the Contracting Officer may direct regarding the removal, shipment, or disposal of the property covered by such notice.

(2) Upon the Contractor's written request, the Contracting Officer shall make an equitable adjustment to the contract in accordance with paragraph (h) of this clause, if the Government has agreed in the Schedule to make the property available for performing this contract and there is any —

(i) Decrease or substitution in this property pursuant to subparagraph (b)(1) above; or

(ii) Withdrawal of authority to use this property, if provided under any other contract or lease.

(c) Title in Government property. (1) The Government shall retain title to all Government-furnished property.

(2) All Government-furnished property and all property acquired by the Contractor, title to which vests in the Government under this paragraph (collectively referred to as "Government property"), are subject to the provisions of this clause. However, special tooling accountable to this contract is subject to the provisions of the Special Tooling clause and is not subject to the provisions of this clause. Title to Government property shall not be affected by its incorporation into or attachment to any property not owned by the Government, nor shall Government property be-

come a fixture or lose its identity as personal property by being attached to any real property.

(3) Title to each item of facilities and special test equipment acquired by the Contractor for the Government under this contract shall pass to and vest in the Government when its use in performing this contract commences or when the Government has paid for it, whichever is earlier, whether or not title previously vested in the Government.

(4) If this contract contains a provision directing the Contractor to purchase material for which the Government will reimburse the Contractor as a direct item of cost under this contract —

(i) Title to material purchased from a vendor shall pass to and vest in the Government upon the vendor's delivery of such material; and

(ii) Title to all other material shall pass to and vest in the Government upon —

(A) Issuance of the material for use in contract performance;

(B) Commencement of processing of the material or its use in contract performance; or

(C) Reimbursement of the cost of the material by the Government, whichever occurs first.

(d) Use of Government property. The Government property shall be used only for performing this contract, unless otherwise provided in this contract or approved by the Contracting Officer.

(e) Property administration. (1) The Contractor shall be responsible and accountable for all Government property provided under this contract and shall comply with Federal Acquisition Regulation (FAR) Subpart 45.5, as in effect on the date of this contract.

(2) The Contractor shall establish and maintain a program for the use, maintenance, repair, protection, and preservation of Government property in accordance with sound industrial practice and the applicable provisions of Subpart 45.5 of the FAR.

(3) If damage occurs to Government property, the risk of which has been assumed by the Government under this contract, the Government shall replace the items or the Contractor shall make such repairs as the Govern-

ment directs. However, if the Contractor cannot effect such repairs within the time required, the Contractor shall dispose of the property as directed by the Contracting Officer. When any property for which the Government is responsible is replaced or repaired, the Contracting Officer shall make an equitable adjustment in accordance with paragraph (h) of this clause.

(4) The Contractor represents that the contract price does not include any amount for repairs or replacement for which the Government is responsible. Repair or replacement of property for which the Contractor is responsible shall be accomplished by the Contractor at its own expense.

(f) Access. The Government and all its designees shall have access at all reasonable times to the premises in which any Government property is located for the purpose of inspecting the Government property.

(g) Risk of loss. Unless otherwise provided in this contract, the Contractor assumes the risk of, and shall be responsible for, any loss or destruction of, or damage to, Government property upon its delivery to the Contractor or upon passage of title to the Government under paragraph (c) of this clause. However, the Contractor is not responsible for reasonable wear and tear to Government property or for Government property properly consumed in performing this contract.

(h) Equitable adjustment. When this clause specifies an equitable adjustment, it shall be made to any affected contract provision in accordance with the procedures of the Changes clause. When appropriate, the Contracting Officer may initiate an equitable adjustment in favor of the Government. The right to an equitable adjustment shall be the Contractor's exclusive remedy. The Government shall not be liable to suit for breach of contract for —

(1) Any delay in delivery of Government-furnished property;

(2) Delivery of Government-furnished property in a condition not suitable for its intended use;

(3) A decrease in or substitution of Government-furnished property; or

(4) Failure to repair or replace Government property for which the Government is responsible.

(i) Government property disposal. Except as provided in paragraphs (i)(1)(i), (i)(2), and (i)(8)(i) of this clause, the Contractor shall not dispose of Government property until authorized to do so by the Plant Clearance Officer.

(1) Scrap (to which the Government has obtained title under paragraph (c) of this clause). (i) Contractor with an approved scrap procedure.

(A) The Contractor may dispose of scrap resulting from production or testing under this contract without Government approval. However, if the scrap requires demilitarization or is sensitive property, the Contractor shall submit the scrap on an inventory disposal schedule.

(B) For scrap from other than production or testing the Contractor may prepare scrap lists in lieu of inventory disposal schedules (provided such lists are consistent with the approved scrap procedures), except that inventory disposal schedules shall be submitted for scrap aircraft or aircraft parts and scrap that—

(1) Requires demilitarization;

(2) Is a classified item;

(3) Is generated from classified items;

(4) Contains hazardous materials or hazardous wastes;

(5) Contains precious metals; or

(6) Is dangerous to the public health, safety, or welfare.

(ii) Contractor without an approved scrap procedure. The Contractor shall submit an inventory disposal schedule for all scrap.

(2) Pre-disposal requirements. When the Contractor determines that a property item acquired or produced by the Contractor, to which the Government has obtained title under paragraph (c) of this clause, is no longer needed for performance of this contract, the Contractor, in the following order of priority:

(i) May purchase the property at the acquisition cost.

(ii) Shall make reasonable efforts to return unused property to the appropriate supplier at fair market value (less, if applicable, a reasonable restocking fee that is consistent with the supplier's customary practices).

(iii) Shall list, on Standard Form 1428, Inventory Disposal Schedule, property that was not purchased under paragraph (i)(2)(i) of this clause, could not be returned to a supplier, or could not be used in the performance of other Government contracts.

(3) Inventory disposal schedules. —(i) The Contractor shall use Standard Form 1428, Inventory Disposal Schedule, to identify —

(A) Government-furnished property that is no longer required for performance of this contract, provided the terms of another Government contract do not require the Government to furnish that property for performance of that contract; and

(B) Property acquired or produced by the Contractor, to which the Government has obtained title under paragraph (c) of this clause, that is no longer required for performance of that contract.

(ii) The Contractor may annotate inventory disposal schedules to identify property the Contractor wishes to purchase from the Government.

(iii) Unless the Plant Clearance Officer has agreed otherwise, or the contract requires electronic submission of inventory disposal schedules, the Contractor shall prepare separate inventory disposal schedules for -

(A) Special test equipment with commercial components;

(B) Special test equipment without commercial components;

(C) Printing equipment;

(D) Computers, components thereof, peripheral equipment, and related equipment;

(E) Precious Metals;

(F) Nonnuclear hazardous materials or hazardous wastes; or

(G) Nuclear materials or nuclear wastes.

(iv) Property with the same description, condition code, and reporting location may be grouped in a single line item. The Contractor shall describe special test equipment in sufficient detail to permit an understanding of the special test equipment's intended use.

(4) Submission requirements. The Contractor shall submit inventory disposal schedules to the Plant Clearance Officer no later than —

(i) Thirty days following the Contractor's determination that a Government property item is no longer required for performance of the contract;

(ii) Sixty days, or such longer period as may be approved by the Plant Clearance Officer, following completion of contract deliveries or performance; or

(iii) One hundred twenty days, or such longer period as may be approved by the Plant Clearance Officer, following contract termination in whole or in part.

(5) Corrections. The Plant Clearance Officer may require the Contractor to correct an inventory disposal schedule or may reject a schedule if the property identified on the schedule is not accountable under this contract or is not in the quantity or condition indicated.

(6) Postsubmission adjustments. The Contractor shall provide the Plant Clearance Officer at least 10 working days advance written notice of its intent to remove a property item from an approved inventory disposal schedule. Unless the Plant Clearance Officer objects to the intended schedule adjustment within the notice period, the Contractor may make the adjustment upon expiration of the notice period.

(7) Storage. —(i) The Contractor shall store the property identified on an inventory disposal schedule pending receipt of disposal instructions. The Government's failure to provide disposal instructions within 120 days following acceptance of an inventory disposal schedule might entitle the Contractor to an equitable adjustment for costs incurred to store such property on or after the 121st day.

(ii) The Contractor shall obtain the Plant Clearance Officer's approval to remove Government property from the premises at which the property is currently located prior to receipt of final disposition instructions. If approval is granted, any costs incurred by the Contractor to transport or store the property shall not increase the price or fee of any Government contract. The storage facility shall be appropriate for assuring the property's physical safety and suitability for use. Approval does not relieve the Contractor of any liability under this contract for such property.

(8) Disposition instructions. —(i) If the Government does not provide disposition instructions to the Contractor within 45 days following ac-

ceptance of a scrap list, the Contractor may dispose of the listed scrap in accordance with the Contractor's approved scrap procedures.

(ii) The Contractor shall prepare for shipment, deliver f.o.b. origin, or dispose of Government property as directed by the Plant Clearance Officer. The Contractor shall remove and destroy any markings identifying the property as Government property prior to disposing of the property.

(iii) The Contracting Officer may require the Contractor to demilitarize the property prior to shipment or disposal. Any equitable adjustment incident to the Contracting Officer's direction to demilitarize Government property shall be made in accordance with paragraph (h) of this clause.

(9) Disposal proceeds. The Contractor shall credit the net proceeds from the disposal of Government property to the price or cost of work covered by this contract or to the Government as the Contracting Officer directs.

(10) Subcontractor inventory disposal schedules. The Contractor shall require a subcontractor that is using property accountable under this contract at a subcontractor-managed site to submit inventory disposal schedules to the Contractor in sufficient time for the Contractor to comply with the requirements of paragraph (i)(4) of this clause.

(j) Abandonment of Government property.—(1) The Government will not abandon sensitive Government property without the Contractor's written consent.

(2) The Government, upon notice to the Contractor, may abandon any nonsensitive Government property in place at which time all obligations of the Government regarding such abandoned property shall cease.

(3) The Government has no obligation to restore or rehabilitate the Contractor's premises under any circumstances; however, if Government-furnished property is withdrawn or is unsuitable for the intended use, or if other Government property is substituted, then the equitable adjustment under paragraph (h) of this clause may properly include restoration or rehabilitation costs.

(k) Communications. All communications under this clause shall be in writing.

(l) Overseas contracts. If this contract is to be performed outside of the United States of America, its territories, or possessions, the words "Government" and "Government-furnished" (wherever they appear in this clause) shall be construed as "United States Government" and "United States Government-furnished," respectively.

Alternate I (APR 1984). As prescribed in 45.106(b)(2), substitute the following paragraph (g) for paragraph (g) of the basic clause:

(g) Limited risk of loss. (1) The term "Contractor's managerial personnel," as used in this paragraph (g), means the Contractor's directors, officers, and any of the Contractor's managers, superintendents, or equivalent representatives who have supervision or direction of—

(i) All or substantially all of the Contractor's business;

(ii) All or substantially all of the Contractor's operation at any one plant or separate location at which the contract is being performed; or

(iii) A separate and complete major industrial operation connected with performing this contract.

(2) The Contractor shall not be liable for loss or destruction of, or damage to, the Government property provided under this contract (or, if an educational or nonprofit organization, for expenses incidental to such loss, destruction, or damage), except as provided in subparagraphs (3) and (4) below.

(3) The Contractor shall be responsible for loss or destruction of, or damage to, the Government property provided under this contract (including expenses incidental to such loss, destruction, or damage)—

(i) That results from a risk expressly required to be insured under this contract, but only to the extent of the insurance required to be purchased and maintained, or to the extent of insurance actually purchased and maintained, whichever is greater;

(ii) That results from a risk that is in fact covered by insurance or for which the Contractor is otherwise reimbursed, but only to the extent of such insurance or reimbursement;

(iii) For which the Contractor is otherwise responsible under the express terms of this contract;

(iv) That results from willful misconduct or lack of good faith on the part of the Contractor's managerial personnel; or

(v) That results from a failure on the part of the Contractor, due to willful misconduct or lack of good faith on the part of the Contractor's managerial personnel, to establish and administer a program or system for the control, use, protection, preservation, maintenance, and repair of Government property as required by paragraph (e) of this clause.

(4) (i) If the Contractor fails to act as provided in subdivision (g)(3)(v) above, after being notified (by certified mail addressed to one of the Contractor's managerial personnel) of the Government's disapproval, withdrawal of approval, or nonacceptance of the system or program, it shall be conclusively presumed that such failure was due to willful misconduct or lack of good faith on the part of the Contractor's managerial personnel.

(ii) In such event, any loss or destruction of, or damage to, the Government property shall be presumed to have resulted from such failure unless the Contractor can establish by clear and convincing evidence that such loss, destruction, or damage —

(A) Did not result from the Contractor's failure to maintain an approved program or system; or

(B) Occurred while an approved program or system was maintained by the Contractor.

(5) If the Contractor transfers Government property to the possession and control of a subcontractor, the transfer shall not affect the liability of the Contractor for loss or destruction of, or damage to, the property as set forth above. However, the Contractor shall require the subcontractor to assume the risk of, and be responsible for, any loss or destruction of, or damage to, the property while in the subcontractor's possession or control, except to the extent that the subcontract, with the advance approval of the Contracting Officer, relieves the subcontractor from such liability. In the absence of such approval, the subcontract shall contain appropriate provisions requiring the return of all Government property in as good condition as when received, except for reasonable wear and tear or for its use in accordance with the provisions of the prime contract.

(6) Upon loss or destruction of, or damage to, Government property provided under this contract, the Contractor shall so notify the Contracting Officer and shall communicate with the loss and salvage organization, if any, designated by the Contracting Officer. With the assistance of any such organization, the Contractor shall take all reasonable action to pro-

tect the Government property from further damage, separate the damaged and undamaged Government property, put all the affected Government property in the best possible order, and furnish to the Contracting Officer a statement of—

(i) The lost, destroyed, or damaged Government property;

(ii) The time and origin of the loss, destruction, or damage;

(iii) All known interests in commingled property of which the Government property is a part; and

(iv) The insurance, if any, covering any part of or interest in such commingled property.

(7) The Contractor shall repair, renovate, and take such other action with respect to damaged Government property as the Contracting Officer directs. If the Government property is destroyed or damaged beyond practical repair, or is damaged and so commingled or combined with property of others (including the Contractor's) that separation is impractical, the Contractor may, with the approval of and subject to any conditions imposed by the Contracting Officer, sell such property for the account of the Government. Such sales may be made in order to minimize the loss to the Government, to permit the resumption of business, or to accomplish a similar purpose. The Contractor shall be entitled to an equitable adjustment in the contract price for the expenditures made in performing the obligations under this subparagraph (g)(7) in accordance with paragraph (h) of this clause. However, the Government may directly reimburse the loss and salvage organization for any of their charges. The Contracting Officer shall give due regard to the Contractor's liability under this paragraph (g) when making any such equitable adjustment.

(8) The Contractor represents that it is not including in the price and agrees it will not hereafter include in any price to the Government any charge or reserve for insurance (including any self- insurance fund or reserve) covering loss or destruction of, or damage to, Government property, except to the extent that the Government may have expressly required the Contractor to carry such insurance under another provision of this contract.

(9) In the event the Contractor is reimbursed or otherwise compensated for any loss or destruction of, or damage to, Government property, the Contractor shall use the proceeds to repair, renovate, or replace the lost, destroyed, or damaged Government property or shall otherwise credit the proceeds to or equitably reimburse the Government, as directed by the Contracting Officer.

(10) The Contractor shall do nothing to prejudice the Government's rights to recover against third parties for any loss or destruction of, or damage to, Government property. Upon the request of the Contracting Officer, the Contractor shall, at the Government's expense, furnish to the Government all reasonable assistance and cooperation (including the prosecution of suit and the execution of instruments of assignment in favor of the Government) in obtaining recovery. In addition, where a subcontractor has not been relieved from liability for any loss or destruction of, or damage to, Government property, the Contractor shall enforce for the benefit of the Government the liability of the subcontractor for such loss, destruction, or damage.

Alternate II (JUN 2003). As prescribed in 45.106(b)(3) substitute the following paragraphs (c) and (g) for paragraphs (c) and (g) of the basic clause:

(c) Title in Government property. (1) The Government shall retain title to all Government-furnished property.

(2) All Government-furnished property and all property acquired by the Contractor, title to which vests in the Government under this paragraph (collectively referred to as "Government property"), are subject to the provisions of this clause. Title to Government property shall not be affected by its incorporation into or attachment to any property not owned by the Government, nor shall Government property become a fixture or lose its identity as personal property by being attached to any real property.

(3) Title to each item of facilities, special test equipment, and special tooling (other than that subject to a special tooling clause) acquired by the Contractor for the Government under this contract shall pass to and vest in the Government when its use in performing this contract commences, or when the Government has paid for it, whichever is earlier, whether or not title previously vested in the Government.

(4) Title to equipment (and other tangible personal property) purchased with funds available for research and having an acquisition cost of less than $5,000 shall vest in the Contractor upon acquisition or as soon thereafter as feasible; provided, that the Contractor obtained the Contracting Officer's approval before each acquisition. Title to equipment purchased with funds available for research and having an acquisition cost of $5,000 or more shall vest as set forth in the contract. If title to equipment vests in the Contractor under this subparagraph (c)(4), the Contractor agrees that no charge will be made to the Government for any depreciation, amortization, or use under any existing or future Government contract or subcontract thereunder. The Contractor shall furnish the Contracting Officer

a list of all equipment to which title is vested in the Contractor under this subparagraph (c)(4) within 10 days following the end of the calendar quarter during which it was received.

(5) Vesting title under this paragraph (c) is subject to civil rights legislation, 42 U.S.C. 2000d. Before title is vested and by signing this contract, the Contractor accepts and agrees that—

"No person in the United States or its outlying areas shall, on the ground of race, color, or national origin, be excluded from participation in, be denied the benefits of, or be otherwise subjected to discrimination under this contemplated financial assistance (title to equipment)."

(g) Limited risk of loss. (1) The term "Contractor's managerial personnel," as used in this paragraph (g), means the Contractor's directors, officers, and any of the Contractor's managers, superintendents, or equivalent representatives who have supervision or direction of—

(i) All or substantially all of the Contractor's business;

(ii) All or substantially all of the Contractor's operation at any one plant, laboratory, or separate location at which the contract is being performed; or

(iii) A separate and complete major industrial operation connected with performing this contract.

(2) The Contractor shall not be liable for loss or destruction of, or damage to, the Government property provided under this contract (or, if an educational or nonprofit organization, for expenses incidental to such loss, destruction, or damage), except as provided in subparagraphs (3) and (4) below.

(3) The Contractor shall be responsible for loss or destruction of, or damage to, the Government property provided under this contract (including expenses incidental to such loss, destruction, or damage)—

(i) That results from a risk expressly required to be insured under this contract, but only to the extent of the insurance required to be purchased and maintained, or to the extent of insurance actually purchased and maintained, whichever is greater;

(ii) That results from a risk which is in fact covered by insurance or for which the Contractor is otherwise reimbursed, but only to the extent of such insurance or reimbursement;

(iii) For which the Contractor is otherwise responsible under the express terms of this contract;

(iv) That results from willful misconduct or lack of good faith on the part of the Contractor's managerial personnel; or

(v) That results from a failure on the part of the Contractor, due to willful misconduct or lack of good faith on the part of the Contractor's managerial personnel, to establish and administer a program or system for the control, use, protection, preservation, maintenance, and repair of Government property as required by paragraph (e) of this clause.

(4)(i) If the Contractor fails to act as provided in subdivision (g)(3)(v) above, after being notified (by certified mail addressed to one of the Contractor's managerial personnel) of the Government's disapproval, withdrawal of approval, or nonacceptance of the system or program, it shall be conclusively presumed that such failure was due to willful misconduct or lack of good faith on the part of the Contractor's managerial personnel.

(ii) Furthermore, any loss or destruction of, or damage to, the Government property shall be presumed to have resulted from such failure unless the Contractor can establish by clear and convincing evidence that such loss, destruction, or damage —

(A) Did not result from the Contractor's failure to maintain an approved program or system; or

(B) Occurred while an approved program or system was maintained by the Contractor.

(5) If the Contractor transfers Government property to the possession and control of a subcontractor, the transfer shall not affect the liability of the Contractor for loss or destruction of, or damage to, the property as set forth above. However, the Contractor shall require the subcontractor to assume the risk of, and be responsible for, any loss or destruction of, or damage to, the property while in the subcontractor's possession or control, except to the extent that the subcontract, with the advance approval of the Contracting Officer, relieves the subcontractor from such liability. In the absence of such approval, the subcontract shall contain appropriate provisions requiring the return of all Government property in as good condition as when received, except for reasonable wear and tear or for its use in accordance with the provisions of the prime contract.

(6) Upon loss or destruction of, or damage to, Government property provided under this contract, the Contractor shall so notify the Contracting Officer and shall communicate with the loss and salvage organization, if any, designated by the Contracting Officer. With the assistance of any such organization, the Contractor shall take all reasonable action to protect the Government property from further damage, separate the damaged and undamaged Government property, put all the affected Government property in the best possible order, and furnish to the Contracting Officer a statement of—

(i) The lost, destroyed, or damaged Government property;

(ii) The time and origin of the loss, destruction, or damage;

(iii) All known interests in commingled property of which the Government property is a part; and

(iv) The insurance, if any, covering any part of or interest in such commingled property.

(7) The Contractor shall repair, renovate, and take such other action with respect to damaged Government property as the Contracting Officer directs. If the Government property is destroyed or damaged beyond practical repair, or is damaged and so commingled or combined with property of others (including the Contractor's) that separation is impractical, the Contractor may, with the approval of and subject to any conditions imposed by the Contracting Officer, sell such property for the account of the Government. Such sales may be made in order to minimize the loss to the Government, to permit the resumption of business, or to accomplish a similar purpose. The Contractor shall be entitled to an equitable adjustment in the contract price for the expenditures made in performing the obligations under this subparagraph (g)(7) in accordance with paragraph (h) of this clause. However, the Government may directly reimburse the loss and salvage organization for any of their charges. The Contracting Officer shall give due regard to the Contractor's liability under this paragraph (g) when making any such equitable adjustment.

(8) The Contractor represents that it is not including in the price, and agrees it will not here after include in any price to the Government, any charge or reserve for insurance (including any self-insurance fund or reserve) covering loss or destruction of, or damage to, Government property, except to the extent that the Government may have expressly required the Contractor to carry such insurance under another provision of this contract.

(9) In the event the Contractor is reimbursed or otherwise compensated for any loss or destruction of, or damage to, the Government property, the Contractor shall use the proceeds to repair, renovate, or replace the lost, destroyed, or damaged Government property or shall otherwise credit the proceeds to or equitably reimburse the Government, as directed by the Contracting Officer.

(10) The Contractor shall do nothing to prejudice the Government's rights to recover against third parties for any loss or destruction of, or damage to, Government property. Upon the request of the Contracting Officer, the Contractor shall, at the Government's expense, furnish to the Government all reasonable assistance and cooperation (including the prosecution of suit and the execution of instruments of assignment in favor of the Government) in obtaining recovery. In addition, where a subcontractor has not been relieved from liability for any loss or destruction of, or damage to, Government property, the Contractor shall enforce for the benefit of the Government the liability of the subcontractor for such loss, destruction, or damage.

FAR 52.249-2 Termination for Convenience of the Government (Fixed-Price)

TERMINATION FOR CONVENIENCE OF THE GOVERNMENT (FIXED-PRICE) (MAY 2004)

(a) The Government may terminate performance of work under this contract in whole or, from time to time, in part if the Contracting Officer determines that a termination is in the Government's interest. The Contracting Officer shall terminate by delivering to the Contractor a Notice of Termination specifying the extent of termination and the effective date.

(b) After receipt of a Notice of Termination, and except as directed by the Contracting Officer, the Contractor shall immediately proceed with the following obligations, regardless of any delay in determining or adjusting any amounts due under this clause:

(1) Stop work as specified in the notice.

(2) Place no further subcontracts or orders (referred to as subcontracts in this clause) for materials, services, or facilities, except as necessary to complete the continued portion of the contract.

(3) Terminate all subcontracts to the extent they relate to the work terminated.

(4) Assign to the Government, as directed by the Contracting Officer, all right, title, and interest of the Contractor under the subcontracts terminated, in which case the Government shall have the right to settle or to pay any termination settlement proposal arising out of those terminations.

(5) With approval or ratification to the extent required by the Contracting Officer, settle all outstanding liabilities and termination settlement proposals arising from the termination of subcontracts; the approval or ratification will be final for purposes of this clause.

(6) As directed by the Contracting Officer, transfer title and deliver to the Government —

(i) The fabricated or unfabricated parts, work in process, completed work, supplies, and other material produced or acquired for the work terminated; and

(ii) The completed or partially completed plans, drawings, information, and other property that, if the contract had been completed, would be required to be furnished to the Government.

(7) Complete performance of the work not terminated.

(8) Take any action that may be necessary, or that the Contracting Officer may direct, for the protection and preservation of the property related to this contract that is in the possession of the Contractor and in which the Government has or may acquire an interest.

(9) Use its best efforts to sell, as directed or authorized by the Contracting Officer, any property of the types referred to in subparagraph (b)(6) of this clause; provided, however, that the Contractor (i) is not required to extend credit to any purchaser and (ii) may acquire the property under the conditions prescribed by, and at prices approved by, the Contracting Officer. The proceeds of any transfer or disposition will be applied to reduce any payments to be made by the Government under this contract, credited to the price or cost of the work, or paid in any other manner directed by the Contracting Officer.

(c) The Contractor shall submit complete termination inventory schedules no later than 120 days from the effective date of termination, unless extended in writing by the Contracting Officer upon written request of the Contractor within this 120-day period.

(d) After expiration of the plant clearance period as defined in Subpart 49.001 of the Federal Acquisition Regulation, the Contractor may submit to the Contracting Officer a list, certified as to quantity and quality, of termination inventory not previously disposed of, excluding items authorized for disposition by the Contracting Officer. The Contractor may request the Government to remove those items or enter into an agreement for their storage. Within 15 days, the Government will accept title to those items and remove them or enter into a storage agreement. The Contracting Officer may verify the list upon removal of the items, or if stored, within 45 days from submission of the list, and shall correct the list, as necessary, before final settlement.

(e) After termination, the Contractor shall submit a final termination settlement proposal to the Contracting Officer in the form and with the certification prescribed by the Contracting Officer. The Contractor shall submit the proposal promptly, but no later than 1 year from the effective date of termination, unless extended in writing by the Contracting Officer upon written request of the Contractor within this 1-year period. However, if the Contracting Officer determines that the facts justify it, a termination settlement proposal may be received and acted on after 1 year or any extension. If the Contractor fails to submit the proposal within the time allowed, the Contracting Officer may determine, on the basis of information available, the amount, if any, due the Contractor because of the termination and shall pay the amount determined.

(f) Subject to paragraph (e) of this clause, the Contractor and the Contracting Officer may agree upon the whole or any part of the amount to be paid or remaining to be paid because of the termination. The amount may include a reasonable allowance for profit on work done. However, the agreed amount, whether under this paragraph (f) or paragraph (g) of this clause, exclusive of costs shown in subparagraph (g)(3) of this clause, may not exceed the total contract price as reduced by (1) the amount of payments previously made and (2) the contract price of work not terminated. The contract shall be modified, and the Contractor paid the agreed amount. Paragraph (g) of this clause shall not limit, restrict, or affect the amount that may be agreed upon to be paid under this paragraph.

(g) If the Contractor and the Contracting Officer fail to agree on the whole amount to be paid because of the termination of work, the Contracting Officer shall pay the Contractor the amounts determined by the Contracting Officer as follows, but without duplication of any amounts agreed on under paragraph (f) of this clause:

(1) The contract price for completed supplies or services accepted by the Government (or sold or acquired under subparagraph (b)(9) of this clause) not previously paid for, adjusted for any saving of freight and other charges.

(2) The total of—

(i) The costs incurred in the performance of the work terminated, including initial costs and preparatory expense allocable thereto, but excluding any costs attributable to supplies or services paid or to be paid under subparagraph (g)(1) of this clause;

(ii) The cost of settling and paying termination settlement proposals under terminated subcontracts that are properly chargeable to the terminated portion of the contract if not included in subdivision (g)(2)(i) of this clause; and

(iii) A sum, as profit on subdivision (g)(2)(i) of this clause, determined by the Contracting Officer under 49.202 of the Federal Acquisition Regulation, in effect on the date of this contract, to be fair and reasonable; however, if it appears that the Contractor would have sustained a loss on the entire contract had it been completed, the Contracting Officer shall allow no profit under this subdivision (g)(2)(iii) and shall reduce the settlement to reflect the indicated rate of loss.

(3) The reasonable costs of settlement of the work terminated, including—

(i) Accounting, legal, clerical, and other expenses reasonably necessary for the preparation of termination settlement proposals and supporting data;

(ii) The termination and settlement of subcontracts (excluding the amounts of such settlements); and

(iii) Storage, transportation, and other costs incurred, reasonably necessary for the preservation, protection, or disposition of the termination inventory.

(h) Except for normal spoilage, and except to the extent that the Government expressly assumed the risk of loss, the Contracting Officer shall exclude from the amounts payable to the Contractor under paragraph (g) of this clause, the fair value, as determined by the Contracting Officer, of property that is destroyed, lost, stolen, or damaged so as to become undeliverable to the Government or to a buyer.

(i) The cost principles and procedures of Part 31 of the Federal Acquisition Regulation, in effect on the date of this contract, shall govern all costs claimed, agreed to, or determined under this clause.

(j) The Contractor shall have the right of appeal, under the Disputes clause, from any determination made by the Contracting Officer under paragraph (e), (g), or (l) of this clause, except that if the Contractor failed to submit the termination settlement proposal or request for equitable adjustment within the time provided in paragraph (e) or (l), respectively, and failed to request a time extension, there is no right of appeal.

(k) In arriving at the amount due the Contractor under this clause, there shall be deducted —

(1) All unliquidated advance or other payments to the Contractor under the terminated portion of this contract;

(2) Any claim which the Government has against the Contractor under this contract; and

(3) The agreed price for, or the proceeds of sale of, materials, supplies, or other things acquired by the Contractor or sold under the provisions of this clause and not recovered by or credited to the Government.

(l) If the termination is partial, the Contractor may file a proposal with the Contracting Officer for an equitable adjustment of the price(s) of the continued portion of the contract. The Contracting Officer shall make any equitable adjustment agreed upon. Any proposal by the Contractor for an equitable adjustment under this clause shall be requested within 90 days from the effective date of termination unless extended in writing by the Contracting Officer.

(m)(1) The Government may, under the terms and conditions it prescribes, make partial payments and payments against costs incurred by the Contractor for the terminated portion of the contract, if the Contracting Officer believes the total of these payments will not exceed the amount to which the Contractor will be entitled.

(2) If the total payments exceed the amount finally determined to be due, the Contractor shall repay the excess to the Government upon demand, together with interest computed at the rate established by the Secretary of the Treasury under 50 U.S.C. App. 1215(b)(2). Interest shall be computed for the period from the date the excess payment is received by the Contractor to the date the excess is repaid. Interest shall not be charged on any excess payment due to a reduction in the Contractor's termination settlement proposal because of retention or other disposition of termination inventory until 10 days after the date of the retention or disposition, or a later date determined by the Contracting Officer because of the circumstances.

(n) Unless otherwise provided in this contract or by statute, the Contractor shall maintain all records and documents relating to the terminated portion of this contract for 3 years after final settlement. This includes all books and other evidence bearing on the Contractor's costs and expenses under this contract. The Contractor shall make these records and documents available to the Government, at the Contractor's office, at all reasonable times, without any direct charge. If approved by the Contracting Officer, photographs, microphotographs, or other authentic reproductions may be maintained instead of original records and documents.

Alternate I (SEP 1996). If the contract is for construction, substitute the following paragraph (g) for paragraph (g) of the basic clause:

(g) If the Contractor and Contracting Officer fail to agree on the whole amount to be paid the Contractor because of the termination of work, the Contracting Officer shall pay the Contractor the amounts determined as follows, but without duplication of any amounts agreed upon under paragraph (f) of this clause:

> (1) For contract work performed before the effective date of termination, the total (without duplication of any items) of—
>
> > (i) The cost of this work;
> >
> > (ii) The cost of settling and paying termination settlement proposals under terminated subcontracts that are properly chargeable to the terminated portion of the contract if not included in subdivision (g)(1)(i) of this clause; and
> >
> > (iii) A sum, as profit on subdivision (g)(1)(i) of this clause, determined by the Contracting Officer under 49.202 of the Federal Acquisition Regulation, in effect on the date of this contract, to be fair and reasonable; however, if it appears that the Contractor would have sustained a loss on the entire contract had it been completed, the Contracting Officer shall allow no profit under this subdivision (g)(1)(iii) and shall reduce the settlement to reflect the indicated rate of loss.
>
> (2) The reasonable costs of settlement of the work terminated, including—
>
> > (i) Accounting, legal, clerical, and other expenses reasonably necessary for the preparation of termination settlement proposals and supporting data;
> >
> > (ii) The termination and settlement of subcontracts (excluding the amounts of such settlements); and
> >
> > (iii) Storage, transportation, and other costs incurred, reasonably necessary for the preservation, protection, or disposition of the termination inventory.

Alternate II (SEP 1996). If the contract is with an agency of the U.S. Government or with State, local, or foreign governments or their agencies, and if the Contracting

Officer determines that the requirement to pay interest on excess partial payments is inappropriate, delete subparagraph (m)(2) of the basic clause.

Alternate III (SEP 1996). If the contract is for construction and with an agency of the U.S. Government or with State, local, or foreign governments or their agencies, substitute the following paragraph (g) for paragraph (g) of the basic clause. Subparagraph (m)(2) may be deleted from the basic clause if the Contracting Officer determines that the requirement to pay interest on excess partial payments is inappropriate.

(g) If the Contractor and Contracting Officer fail to agree on the whole amount to be paid the Contractor because of the termination of work, the Contracting Officer shall pay the Contractor the amounts determined as follows, but without duplication of any amounts agreed upon under paragraph (f) of this clause:

(1) For contract work performed before the effective date of termination, the total (without duplication of any items) of—

(i) The cost of this work;

(ii) The cost of settling and paying termination settlement proposals under terminated subcontracts that are properly chargeable to the terminated portion of the contract if not included in subdivision (g)(1)(i) of this clause; and

(iii) A sum, as profit on subdivision (g)(1)(i) of this clause, determined by the Contracting Officer under 49.202 of the Federal Acquisition Regulation, in effect on the date of this contract, to be fair and reasonable; however, if it appears that the Contractor would have sustained a loss on the entire contract had it been completed, the Contracting Officer shall allow no profit under this subdivision (iii) and shall reduce the settlement to reflect the indicated rate of loss.

(2) The reasonable costs of settlement of the work terminated, including —(i) Accounting, legal, clerical, and other expenses reasonably necessary for the preparation of termination settlement proposals and supporting data;

(ii) The termination and settlement of subcontracts (excluding the amounts of such settlements); and

(iii) Storage, transportation, and other costs incurred, reasonably necessary for the preservation, protection, or disposition of the termination inventory.

ACRONYMS AND ABBREVIATIONS

ABND	American Bank Notes Development Corporation
ACO	Administrative Contracting Officer
ACSN	Advance Change Supply Notice
Admin.	Administration
ADPE	Automatic data processing equipment
ADR	Alternative Dispute Resolution
AFARS	Army Federal Acquisition Regulation Supplement
AFFARS	Air Force Federal Acquisition Regulation Supplement
aff'd	Affirmed
AISC	American Institute of Steel Construction
APA	Administrative Procedures Act
ASPM	Armed Services Pricing Manual
ASPR	Armed Services Procurement Regulation
Ass'n	Association
Assoc.(s)	Associate(s)
AWS	American Welding Society
BAFO(s)	Best and final offer(s)
BCA	Board of Contract Appeals Reports (CCH)
CACO	Corporate Administrative Contracting Officer
CAFC	Court of Appeals for the Federal Circuit
CAS	Cost Accounting Standards
CBD	Commerce Business Daily
CCF	Contract Cases Federal (CCH)
CCH	Commerce Clearing House (Publisher)
CDA	Contract Disputes Act
Cert. denied	Certiorari denied
C.F.I.	Chief Flight Instructor
CICA	Competition in Contracting Act
Civ. No.	Civil Number (docket number)
C.O.	Contracting Officer
COR	Contracting Officer Representative
COTR	Contracting Officer Technical Representative
Comp. Gen.	Comptroller General (GAO)
Cong. Rec.	Congressional Record
Constr.	Construction
Corp.	Corporation
CPD	Comptroller procurement decisions
CPM	Critical Path Method

Ct. Cl.	Court of Claims
Ctr.	Center
DAR	Defense Acquisition Regulation
DCA	Defense Contract Audit
DCAA	Defense Contract Audit Agency
DCAAM	Defense Contract Audit Agency Manual
DCAS	Defense Contract Administration Service
D.C. Cir.	Court of Appeals for the District of Columbia Circuit
DEA	Drug Enforcement Administration
Dev.	Development
DFARS	Defense Federal Acquisition Regulation Supplement
DLAR	Defense Logistic Acquisition Regulation
DOD	Department of Defense
DOD FMR	Department of Defense Financial Management Regulation
DOE	Department of Energy
DOJ	Department of Justice
DOT	Department of Transportation
EAJA	Equal Access to Justice Act
ECP	Engineering Change Proposal
E.D.N.Y.	District Court, Eastern District of New York
EDAR	Education Acquisition Regulation
Educ.	Education
Elec.	Electric; electronic
Eng'g	Engineering
Enters.	Enterprises
Envtl.	Environmental
E.O.	Executive Order
EPA	Environmental Protection Agency
Equip.	Equipment
ESLH	Estimated standard labor hours
F.2d	Federal Reporter, Second Series
F.3d	Federal Reporter, Third Series
FAR	Federal Acquisition Regulation
FBI	Federal Bureau of Investigation
Fed. Cir.	Court of Appeals for the Federal Circuit
Fed. Cl.	Court of Federal Claims
Fed'n	Federation
Fed. Reg.	Federal Register
FIRREA	Federal Insurance Reform, Recovery and Enforcement Act
FOIA	Freedom of Information Act
Found.	Foundation
FPM	Federal Personnel Manual
FPR	Federal Procurement Regulations
F. Supp.	Federal Supplement
FTCA	Federal Tort Claims Act

G&A	General and administrative
GAO	Government Accountability Office
GFM	Government-furnished material
GFP	Government-furnished property
Gov't	Government
GPO	Government Printing Office
GSA	General Services Administration
GSAR	General Services Acquisition Regulation
GTE	Government Technical Evaluator
GTR	Government Technical Representative
H.R.	House Report
IFB	Invitation for bids
Inc.	Incorporated
Indus.	Industry
Info.	Information
Int'l	International
Inv.	Investment
IR&D	Independent Research and Development
ISSG	Information Systems Support Group
J.V.	Joint Venture
Lab.	Laboratory(ies)
LOC	Limitation of Cost
LOF	Limitation of Funds
Ltd.	Limited
Mach.	Machinery
MECOM	Mobility Equipment Command
Mfg.	Manufacturing
MILSRAP	Military Standard Contract Administration Procedures
MIL-STD	Military Standard
MIRR	Material Inspection and Receiving Report
Mktg.	Marketing
NAPS	Navy Acquisition Procedures Supplement
NARSUP	Navy Acquisition Regulation Supplement
NASA	National Aeronautics and Space Administration
NASA PR	National Aeronautics and Space Administration Procurement Regulation
NFS	NASA FAR Supplement
NHB	NASA Handbook
NRLB	National Labor Relations Board
NPR	NASA Procurement Regulation
OFPP	Office of Federal Procurement Policy
OMB	Office of Management and Budget
PCO	Procuring Contracting Officer
P.L.	Public Law
PPA	Prompt Payment Act

Prods.	Products
Pub. Cont. L.J.	Public Contract Law Journal
QAE	Quality Assurance Evaluator
R&D	Research and Development
REA	Request for Equitable Adjustment
Recons. denied	Reconsideration denied
Rev.	Revised
RFP	Request for proposals
RFQ	Request for quotations
S.	Senate Bill
SBA	Small Business Administration
SCN	Specification Change Notice
Serv.(s)	Service(s)
SF	Standard Form
S. Rep.	Senate Report
Sys.	System(s)
TCO	Termination Contracting Officer
TFM	Treasury Financial Manual
TINA	Truth In Negotiations Act
TVA	Tennessee Valley Authority
U.C.C.	Uniform Commercial Code
Univ.	University
U.S.C.	United States Code
VAAR	Veterans Administration Acquisition Regulation
VECP	Value Engineering Change Proposal

SUBJECT INDEX

A

Acceleration of Contract Performance ... 445
  Both Excusable and Non-Excusable Delays ... 457
  Constructive Changes Claims ... 475
  Elements of ... 446
    Causation ... 456
    Excusable Delay ... 447
    Knowledge of Contracting Officer ... 447
    Orders to Accelerate ... 448
  Mitigation of Delay ... 456
  Post-Constructive Time Extensions ... 457
  Recovery Not Dependent on Contractor's Recoupment of Lost Time ... 458
Acceptance and Rejection ... 814
  Acceptance ... 833
    Authority to ... 833
    Methods of ... 835
    Time and Place of ... 834
  Estoppel ... 831
    Notice of Rejection ... 827
    Content of ... 827
    Time of ... 829
  Strict Compliance Standard ... 815
    Brand Name and Proprietary ... 818
    Brand Name or Equal ... 817
    Construction Contracts ... 821
    First Articles ... 823
    Limitations on ... 821
    Specifications Not Suited to Strict Compliance ... 817
  See also Inspection; Post-Acceptance Rights; Warranties
Acquisition Savings ... 410
Acts of God
  As Cause of Excusable Delay ... 559
  Differing Site Conditions ... 486
Adjustments. *See* Pricing of Adjustments
Apparent Authority ... 58
Authority. *See* Government Personnel Authority; Contractor Personnel Authority
Authorized Representatives ... 34, 38
  Formally Designated ... 39
  Other ... 41

B

Boards of Contract Appeals ... 1322
  Review of Board Decision ... 1325
Brand Name or Equal ... 817
Bribery ... 82
  Corrupt Intent ... 84
  Public Official ... 85
  Thing of Value ... 83
Burden of Proof ... 687
  Causation ... 688
  Reasonableness of Amount ... 689
Buy-In, Definition ... 12

C

Category I Conditions ... 494
  Contract Documents ... 495
    Express Indications ... 498
    Implied Indications ... 499
  Costs Attributable to Condition ... 508
  Reasonable Interpretation ... 502
  Reliance ... 505
    No Reasonable Reliance ... 506
    Reasonable Reliance ... 508
  Reasonably Unforeseeable ... 501
  Site Inspection ... 522
Category II Conditions ... 508
  Site Inspection ... 523
  Unforeseeable Condition ... 510
  Unknown Condition ... 509
  Unusual Condition ... 512
Changes ... 379
  Constructive Changes ... 426
    Basic theory ... 427
    Claims ... 475

Resolution Procedures 466
Types of 430
Contractual Notice Requirements 471
Assertion of Claim for Equitable Adjustment ... 472
Constructive Changes Claims 475
Formal Change Orders 397
Contractor Originated Changes 397
Government Originated Changes 399
Procedure for Ordering Changes 405
Unilateral vs. Bilateral Change Orders 401
Purpose and Coverage of Clause 380
Contractor's Acceptance of Change 396
Coverage 381
Purpose 380
Value Engineering 409
Government Use of Data 425
Interpretation 417
Standard Clauses 410
Unsolicited Proposals 426
Collateral Savings 414
Compensable Delays 576
Applicability of Delay Clauses 605
Completion Within Contract Schedule 607
Delays Preceding Award 610
Other Clauses Granting Relief 605
Constructive Suspensions 579
Availability of Site 582
Inspection of Work 589
Interference with Contractor's Work 585
Issuance of Changes 589
Issuance of Notice to Proceed 581
Miscellaneous Acts of Government 591
Not Attributable to Government Fault 579
Government Delays of Approvals 586
Providing Funding 588
Limitations on Recovery 599
Concurrent Delays 601
Notice Requirement 604
Sovereign Acts 599
No Applicable Clause 577
Ordered Suspensions 578
Unreasonable Delays 592
Burden of Proving Unreasonableness 595
Measuring Reasonable Amount of Delay 594
Proving the Delay 596
Reasonable 593
Concurrent Actions. *See* Discussions and Concurrent Actions
Constructive Changes 426
Basic Theory 427
Continuing Vitality of Doctrine 427
Elements of Doctrine 428
Government Claims for Price Decreases 429
Claims 475
Accelerations 480
Construction Contract Notice Requirement 476
Military Shipbuilding Contracts 480
Notification of Clause 478
Thirty-Day Notice Requirement 475
Resolution Procedures 466
Contractor's Obligations 466
Government Responsibilities . 470
Types of 430
Acceleration 445
Defective Specifications/ Misleading Information 441
Disagreements Over Contract Requirements 431
Hindrance/Failure to Cooperate 458
See also Changes

Conspiracy 153
Contingent Fees, Covenant Against 108
Contract Interpretation 155
Contract Document Language
Analysis 167
Enumerated Items 180
Order of Precedence 176
Writings Read as a Whole 169
Definition of Terms 159
Dictionary/Common
Usage Definitions 159
Document Definitions 159
Technical Terms 163
Extrinsic Evidence 183
Custom and Trade Usage 218
Discussions/Concurrent
Actions 184
Prior Course of Dealing 210
Objective 157
Post-Interpretation
Ambiguities 226
Duty to Seek Clarification 235
Finding Ambiguous Terms ... 227
Interpretation Against
Drafter 228
Contracting Officer
Authorized Representatives 38
Formally Designated 39
Other 41
Designation of 35
Responsibilities 11
Role in Contract Disputes 1286
Final Decision 1292
Negotiated Settlement 1286
Contractor Claim 1260
Certification 1270
Authorized Signature 1278
Claims Not Involving
Quantum 1278
Defective/Absent
Certificate 1273
Revision of Claim 1276
Threshold 1272
Claim Content 1264
Conversion into a Claim 1279
Party Entitled to Assert 1260
Request for Contracting
Officer Decision 1267
Request for Sum Certain 1266
Contractor Obligations for
Government Property 646
Control of Property 646
Disposal of Government Property 656
Risk of Loss 648
Bailment Rules 654
Clauses Covering 648
Faulty Government-Furnished
Design Specifications 655
Incomplete Work 654
Subcontractor 654
Contractor Personnel Authority 58
Apparent Authority 58
Delegation 58
Ratification and Estoppel 59
Cost or Pricing Data 130
Costs of Preparing and Financing
Adjustments 754
Costs of Financing
Adjustments 769
Interest on Borrowings 772
Interest on Claims 769
Preparation and Negotiation
Costs 754
Distinction Between Claim
Prosecution and Contract
Administration 755
Costs Covered 759
Court of Appeals for the
Federal Circuit 1325
Review of Board Decisions 1325
Review of Court of Federal
Claims Decisions 1327
Court of Federal Claims 1324
Decisions Review by Court
of Appeals for the
Federal Circuit 1327
Cure Notices 970
Adequate Assurances 974
Circumstances for Use 971
Effect of Denial of Cure
Period 973
Form of 972
Custom and Trade Usage 218
Ambiguous Language
Not Required 220
Clear Language Superior
to Trade Custom 221
Interpreting Vague Language 218

Proof of Trade Practice.................. 224
Supplying Missing Terms............. 226

D

Damages.. 678
Methods of Computing.................. 680
Similarity to Equitable
Adjustment................................ 678
See also Liquidated Damaged
Data. *See* Investigation of Data
Debt Collection Procedures 1175
Contract Disputes Act................. 1182
Debt Collection Act..................... 1181
FAR Procedures.......................... 1175
Contracting Officer
Decision......................... 1179
Debt Determination 1176
Deferment Agreement......... 1178
Negotiation and Demand........ 1176
Withholding/Setoff 1179
Default Termination 883
Consequences of........................... 883
Impact on Contractor............ 883
Impact on Government 886
Fixed-Price Supply
Termination Inventory......... 886
Decision to.................................... 955
Alternatives to....................... 963
Exercise of Discretion 956
Reconsideration of................ 969
Excess Costs of
Reprocurement........................... 981
Administrative
Requirements.................. 1023
Computation of Excess
Costs 1019
Fulford Doctrine 982
Other Damages Right 1021
Reasonableness
of Action 986
Reprocurement Contract.........1013
Liquidated Damages.................... 1024
Computation of Time
Covered.......................... 1043
Enforceability of Clause........ 1027
General Policy 1025
Government Right to
Actual Damages.............. 1044
Relationship with
Default Termination...........1041
Relief from.......................... 1036
Remission of....................... 1046
Procedures 970
Delinquency Notices............. 970
Termination Notice 978
Relationship with
Liquidated Damages 1041
Concurrent Time Periods.... 1041
Effect of Waiver................. 1043
Right to Terminate......................... 888
Grounds for........................... 889
Waiver of.............................. 940
See also Excess Costs of
Reprocurement; Liquidated
Damages; Right to Terminate
Delays 537
Compensable 576
Applicability of Delay
Clauses............................. 605
Constructive Suspensions........ 579
Limitations on Recovery 599
No Applicable Clause 577
Ordered Suspensions 578
Reasonableness
of Delays........................... 591
Excusable...................................... 537
Causes of.............................. 545
General Requirements 539
Time Extensions 567
Delinquency Notices............................. 970
Cure Notices 970
Adequate Assurances............ 974
Circumstances for Use.......... 971
Effect of Denial of
Cure Period....................... 973
Form of 972
Show Cause Notice........................ 976
Design Specifications............................ 279
Differing Site Conditions....................... 483
Breach of Contract Claims 514
Government Nondisclosure
and Category II Conditions .. 515
Misrepresentation and
Category I Conditions........ 515
Exculpatory Clauses 530
General................................. 530
Relation to
Representation 531
Specific 531
General Rules 484

At the Site 490
Burden of Proof 492
Condition Must Predate Contract 485
Differing Materially............. 491
Force Creating Conditions 485
Physical Conditions 489
Inspection of Site/ Investigation of Data.................. 516
Failure to Investigate 524
Investigation of Data............ 517
Inspection of Site.................. 521
Notice 527
Actual or Constructive Government Notice........... 527
Nature of.............................. 527
No Prejudice 528
Procedure..................................... 529
Contractor's Duty to Proceed 529
Government's Procedure......... 529
Unique Aspects.......................... 494
Category I Conditions........... 494
Category II Conditions 508
Variation in Estimated Quantities.................................. 532
Absent Variation in Quantity Clause 533
Impact in Quantity Clause 534
Interpretation in Quantity Clause 535
Discharge 1202
Contract Modifications 1210
Accord/Satisfaction 1210
With Release Language......... 1214
Without Specific Release Language 1212
Final Payment............................. 1202
Delay in Contract Closeout.... 1202
Legal Effect 1203
General Releases 1219
Mutual Agreement and Rescission.......................... 1209
Techniques for Avoiding Releases.................................. 1222
Economic Duress................ 1225
Fraud and Misrepresentation 1228
Lack of Authority................ 1229
Lack of Consideration 1222
Mistake 1223
Disclaimer and Exculpatory Clauses 344
Clear Disclaimers 348
Commonly Used Clauses 352
Coordination 358
Omissions and Misdescriptions................. 352
Preproduction Evaluation of Technical Data............. 355
Production Drawing Changes 354
Shop Drawings 357
Verification............................ 356
Differing Site Conditions 530
General................................. 530
Relation to Representation.... 531
Specific 531
Effect on Other Clauses................ 351
Interpretation 346
Misleading Statements and Nondisclosure...................... 349
Public Policy................................. 345
Discussions and Concurrent Actions 184
Clarification Requests................... 184
Limitations on Use of Discussions/ Concurrent Actions 196
Authority.............................. 196
Parol Evidence Rule 199
Post-Dispute Conduct/ Discussions Excluded 198
Pre-Bid and Post-Bid Conferences.... 187
Pre-Dispute Actions Evidencing Interpretation............................. 190
Pre-Dispute Interpretations............ 189
Made Known to Other Party.... 194
Disputes.. 1231
Assertion of Claims 1252
Contractor Claim 1260
Government Claim.............. 1280
Nonmonetary vs. Declaratory Relief........... 1257
Nonroutine Requests for Price Adjustment....... 1253
Time for Submittal.............. 1284
Contracting Officer's Role........... 1286
Final Decision..................... 1292
Negotiated Settlement......... 1286
Coverage..................................... 1232

Claims Relating to Contract... 1236
Government-Contractor Controversies Not Subject to 1238
Subcontractor Controversies........ 1247
Litigation of Disputes Act Claims... 1311
Choice of Forums 1313
Decision to Appeal/Bring Suit........ 1311
Organization/Function of Forums........ 1322
Timely Appeal/Suit........ 1315

E

Eichleay Formula 720
Enumerated Causes of Excusable Delay 545
Acts of God........ 559
Epidemics 559
Fires 559
Floods 558
Freight Embargoes........ 559
Government Acts 551
Subcontractor/Supplier Delays...... 555
Strikes 545
Weather........ 546
Estoppel
Acceptance and Rejection 831
Contractor Personnel Authority....... 59
Government Bound by Authorized Agents' Conduct........ 60
Government Not Estopped by Unauthorized Actions 67
Improper Use of........ 71
Injury 70
Reliance 69
Sovereign Capacity Exception........ 68
Waiver........ 70
Excess Costs of Reprocurement........ 981
Administrative Requirements...... 1023
Computation of Excess Costs...... 1019
Adjustments in Reprocurement Contract Costs 1019
Price Adjustments Under Defaulted Contract........ 1020
Time Period Covered........ 1021
Fulford Doctrine 982
Reasonableness of Action........ 986
Effect of Relaxed Specifications Contractor Could Have Met........ 995
Mitigation 997
Similarity 987
Variations in Quantity Reprocured........ 996
Other Damages Right 1021
Reprocurement Contract........ 1013
Intent to Reprocure 1013
Poor Administration of Reprocurement Contract ... 1016
Proof of Cost Incurrence..... 1015
Use of Government Personnel 1017
Exculpatory Clauses. *See* Disclaimer and Exculpatory Clauses
Excusable Delays 537
Causes of 545
Enumerated........ 545
Non-Enumerated........ 560
General Requirements 539
"Beyond the Control" of Contractor 539
Foreseeability........ 543
Without Contractor's Fault or Negligence 542
Time Extensions 567
Burden of Proof 574
Causation 568
Delay of Overall Completion Required........ 570
Measuring 572
Notice/Schedule Extension... 575

F

"Facilities," Definition 620
False
Claims........ 111
Statements 122
Formal Change Orders........ 397
Contractor Originated Changes 397
Government Originated Changes .. 399
Procedure for Ordering Changes ... 405
Downward Adjustment Proposal 409
Standard Form 30 408

Written Requirement 405
Unilateral vs. Bilateral Change Orders 401
Clause Permitting Only Bilateral 404
Modifying Language in Unilateral 402
Policy 401

G

Government Accountability Office (GAO) Role in Contract Administration...... 17
GFP. *See* Government-Furnished Property
"Gift," Definition 87
"Good Faith," Definition 4
Good Faith in Enforcement 5
Good Faith Performance 5
Government. *See* Government Bound by Authorized Agents' Conduct; Government Personnel Authority; Government Procurement Standards of Conduct; Suits Against Government Employees
Government Bound by Authorized Agents' Conduct 60
Estoppel 65
Government Not Estopped by Unauthorized Actions 67
Improper Use of 71
Injury 70
Reliance 69
Sovereign Capacity Exception ... 68
Waiver 70
Finality 60
Authority Required 63
Prejudicial Decisions 63
Sources of 61
Government Claims
Disputes 1280
For Defective Pricing 745
Computing Price Reduction 749
Defective Subcontractor Data ... 752
Government Entitled to Reduction 747
Government Reliance on Defective Data 747
Interest and Penalties 753
Offset 750
Government-Furnished Property (GFP)..... 611
See also Government Property; Late or Defective Government-Furnished Property
Government Personnel Authority 31
Actual Authority Required 31
Delegation of Authority 33
Authorized Representatives 38
Designated Contracting Officers 35
Personnel Lacking Specifically Delegated Contractual Authority 43
Implied Authority 43
Ratification 46
See also Suits Against Government Employees
Government Procurement Standards of Conduct 76
Conspiracy 153
Honesty in Dealing 110
Statutory Requirements 110
Types of Illegal Conduct 142
Improper Influence of Government Decisions 82
Anti-Kickback Act 107
Bribery 82
Covenant Against Contingent Fees 108
Current Employees' Conduct 98
Former Employees' Conduct 91
Gratuities 85
Sanctions 76
Debarment 78
Forfeiture and Cancellation 76
Suspension or Dismissal of Government Employees 81
Government Property 611
Contractor Obligations 646
Control of Property 646
Disposal of Government Property 656
Risk of Loss 648
Government Obligations 630
Contractor Inspection 645
Disclaimer Clause 641
Interpretation Principles 630
Late or Not Delivered Property 631
Notice Requirement 639

Suitable for Intended Use 633
Obtaining Property for Contract Performance 612
Facilities 620
Materials, Components, and Supplies 612
Progress Payments Inventory ... 628
Special Rules for Government Production/Research Property 623
Special Tooling/Test Equipment 615
Gratuities 85
Purpose of 88
Thing of Value 86
Grounds for Termination 889
Anticipatory Repudiation 932
Evidence Considered 933
Examples of 934
Retraction of 939
Timing of Remedy 932
Failure to Comply with Other Provisions 915
Application of Rule 916
Scope of Right 915
Failure to Perform or Deliver 889
Limit on Termination of All Work 898
Preproduction Items 906
Slight Delays in Performance 889
Timely Delivery of Defective Supplies 893
Failure to Proceed 918
Exceptions to Duty to Proceed 924
Notification to Proceed 921
Scope/Nature of Obligation 922
Progress Failures 908
Basic Principle 908
Construction Contracts 913
Evaluation of 909
Proof of Endangered Performance 911
Subcontractor Termination 940

I

Immunity 72
Impact and Delay 711
Consequential Damages 719
Escalation of Labor Rates and Material Prices 733
Idle Labor and Equipment 726
Contractor-Owned Equipment 727
Labor 726
Rented Equipment 730
Impact on Other Work 716
Loss of Efficiency 730
Miscellaneous Costs 733
Theory of Recovery 711
Delays Preceding Change 712
Delays Resulting from Change/Differing Site Condition 713
Unabsorbed Overhead 720
Implied Authority 43
Implied Duty of Good Faith and Fair Dealing 296
Breach by the Contractor 312
Deliberate Inaction in Asserting a Claim 313
Lack of Diligence 313
Breach by the Government 298
Duty to Cooperate/Not Hinder Performance 299
Improper Contract Administration 308
Lack of Good Faith in Negotiating Modifications 310
Implied Warranty of Specifications 272
Causation and Reliance 290
Contract Formation 290
Performance 294
Government Responsibility Basis ... 273
Scope 275
Commercial Availability 287
Degree of Accuracy Required 289
Specified Alternatives 286
Type of Specification Language 276
Impracticability of Performance 314
Increased Costs 320
Competence of Contractor 315
Unforeseen Technological Problems 317

Incorrect Statements ... 256
  Estimates ... 258
  Factual Statements ... 256
  Laws and Regulations ... 257
Inspection ... 776
  Contractor ... 795
    General Clauses ... 795
    Higher-Level Quality Control Requirement ... 798
    Specified Tests ... 801
  Cost of ... 803
    Contractor Duty to Facilitate Government ... 803
    Tearing Out Completed Work ... 805
  Government ... 776
    Manner of ... 789
    Not for Contractor Benefit ... 790
    Number of ... 788
    Place of ... 786
    Reinspection ... 794
    Time of ... 787
    Type of ... 778
  Of Site ... 521
    Category I Conditions ... 522
    Category II Conditions ... 523
  Special Techniques and Issues ... 806
    First Article Testing ... 809
    Safety Inspections ... 811
    Sampling ... 806
  See also Acceptance; Warranty
Investigation of Data ... 517
  Contract Documents ... 517
  Data Not in Contract ... 518
  Information Known to Competitors ... 518
  Reasonableness of Investigation ... 519

K

"Kickback," Definition ... 107

L

Late or Not Delivered Government-Furnished Property ... 631
  Government Obligations ... 630
    Contractor Inspection ... 645
    Disclaimers ... 641
    GFP Suitable for Intended Use ... 633
    Interpretation Principles ... 630
    Late/Not Delivered GFP ... 631
    Notice Requirements ... 639
Liquidated Damages ... 1024
  Computation of Time Covered ... 1043
  Enforceability of Clause ... 1027
    Accurate Estimation Difficulty ... 1036
    Reasonableness of Forecast ... 1028
  General Policy ... 1025
  Government Right to Actual Damages ... 1044
    Damages Covered by Clause ... 1044
    Damages Outside Clause ... 1046
  Remission of ... 1046
  Relationship with Default Termination ... 1041
    Concurrent Time Periods ... 1041
    Effect of Waiver ... 1043
  Relief from ... 1036
    Excusable Delays ... 1036
    Substantial Completion ... 1039

M

"Material," Definition ... 612
Mischarging ... 143
Misrepresentation of Fact ... 140
Mistake ... 322
  Mutual Mistake ... 322
    Basic Assumption ... 322
    Integration ... 329
  Remedies ... 341
  Unconscionability ... 339
  Unilateral Mistake ... 330

N

Nature and Purpose of Contract Administration ... 1
  Nature of Contract Administration ... 2
    Partnering ... 10
    Problem Identification and Resolution ... 8
    Working Relationship ... 3
  Protection of Public Interest ... 11
    Competitors' Complaints ... 13
    Consideration Required ... 12
See also Nature of Contract Administration; Purpose of Contract Administration
Nature of Contract Administration ... 2
  Partnering ... 10

Problem Identification and Resolution ... 8
Working Relationship ... 3
Cooperation and Good Faith ... 3
Mutual Confidence and Respect ... 6
Nondisclosures ... 261
Contractor Knowledge/Reason to Know ... 266
Government Knowledge of Vital Information ... 262
Government Knowledge/Reason to Know of Contractor Ignorance ... 270
Non-Enumerated Causes of Excusable Delay ... 560
Financial Difficulties ... 561
Labor Problems ... 566
Lack of Facilities/Equipment ... 563
Lack of Know-How ... 565
Lack of Materials ... 564

O

Order of Precedence ... 176
Clauses ... 176
Common Law Rule ... 179
Overhead ... 734

P

Parol Evidence Rule ... 199
Complete/Partial Integration ... 201
Contradiction vs. Ambiguity Resolution ... 206
Establishing an Ambiguity ... 207
Integrated Agreements ... 200
"Partnering" ... 10
Payment ... 1125
Procedures ... 1139
Documentation/Authority ... 1140
Incrementally Funded Contracts ... 1166
Progress Payment ... 1155
Time for Payment of the Price ... 1151
Withholding ... 1166
Types ... 1125
Financing Techniques ... 1134
Payment of the Price ... 1125
Progress Payments ... 1130
Payment of the Price ... 1125
Billing Prices ... 1129
Partial ... 1128
Time for ... 1151
Fast Payment ... 1153
Other Than Simplified Acquisitions ... 1151
Performance Specifications ... 285
Post-Acceptance Rights ... 848
Cumulative Remedies ... 880
Latent Defects, Fraud, and Gross Mistakes ... 850
Contractor Certification Effect ... 858
Fraud ... 854
Government Rights After Retraction of Acceptance ... 863
Gross Mistakes Amounting to Fraud ... 855
Latent Defects ... 850
Notice/Proof of Defects ... 860
Warranties ... 866
Implied ... 871
Notice and Burden of Proof ... 873
Remedies Under Clauses ... 876
Scope of Clauses ... 869
Specifications Provisions ... 871
Prevailing Parties ... 761
Price Adjustments Under Contract Clauses ... 661
Basic Pricing Formula ... 661
Pricing Added Work ... 669
Pricing Deleted Work ... 662
Cost Impact on Contractor ... 669
Allowable Costs ... 673
Incurrence of Costs ... 670
Value Measures ... 672
Subcontract Problems ... 675
Claims by Subcontractors in Contractor's Name ... 676
Lack of Equitable Adjustment Clause ... 677
Pricing of Adjustments ... 659
Costs of Preparing and Financing Adjustments ... 754
Costs of Financing Adjustments ... 769

Preparation and Negotiation Cost 754
Government Claims for Defective Pricing 745
Computing Price Reduction 749
Defective Subcontractor Data 752
Government Entitled to Reduction 747
Government Reliance on Defective Data 747
Interest and Penalties 753
Offset 750
Impact and Delay 711
Consequential Damages 719
Escalation of Labor Rates and Material Prices 733
Idle Labor and Equipment 726
Impact on Other Work 716
Loss of Efficiency 730
Miscellaneous Costs 733
Theory of Recovery 711
Unabsorbed Overhead 720
Overhead and Profit 734
Overhead 734
Profit 735
Principles 660
Damages 678
Price Adjustments Under Contract Clauses 661
Quantum Meruit 685
Proof of Adjustment 686
Burden of Proof 687
Jury Verdict 704
Methods of Proof 691
Total Cost Method 699
Prior Course of Dealing 210
Interpretation 211
Actual Knowledge Required 212
Application to Changed Language 214
Waiver of Legal Rights 215
Procurement Regulations, Sources Of
Executive Branch 18
Legislative Branch 16
Profit 735
Amount of Profit 739
Breach of Contract Claims 738
Construction Contract Clauses 741
Cost-Plus-Percentage-of-Cost Relationship 744
Deductive Changes 737
Intermingled Changes and Suspensions 736
Progress Payments 1130
Based on Costs 1130
Based on Percentage of Completion 1131
Based on Performance 1133
Procedures 1155
Construction 1160
Cost-Based 1155
Proof of Adjustment
Burden of Proof 686
Causation 688
Reasonableness of Amount 689
Jury Verdict 704
Conditions for Use 704
Purposes Served 706
Techniques Used 709
Methods of Proof 691
Actual Cost Data 691
Estimates 695
Total Cost Method 699
Modified Method 703
Not Favored 699
Safeguards for Use 700
Public Official 85

Q

Quantum Meruit 685
Value Measured by Contractor's Costs 686
Value Standard 685

R

Ratification
Contractor Personnel Authority 46
Government Personnel Authority 46
Adoption of Unauthorized Acts 51
Authority to Perform/ Authorize Acts Being Ratified 48
Authority to Ratify 46
Knowledge of Unauthorized Acts 49
Ratification and Quantum

Meruit 52
Rejection. *See* Acceptance and Rejection
Remedies
Contractor Remedies for Delayed
Payment.................................. 1183
Injunctions/Other Remedies 1195
Interest 1184
Defects.. 814
Contractor Correction 843
Government Correction 845
Price Reduction..................... 846
Government Remedies for
Overpayment and Improper
Claims 1196
Fraudulent Claims for
Payment 1199
Interest 1196
Reprocurement. *See* Excess Costs of
Reprocurement
Right to Terminate 888
Grounds for................................... 889
Anticipatory Repudiation 932
Failure to Comply with
Other Provisions 915
Failure to Perform or Deliver ... 889
Failure to Proceed 918
Progress Failures.................. 908
Subcontractor Termination ... 940
Termination for Convenience 1050
Clauses............................... 1050
Deletion of Work 1071
Exercising Right 1053
Finality of 1070
Partial................................. 1068
Procedural Requirements.... 1069
Waiver of 940
Basic Concept...................... 941
Contractor Reliance 948
Government Election to
Continue Performance 946
Reasonable Forbearance....... 945
Reestablishment of Right
After Waiver..................... 952
Reservation of Right After
Completion Date.............. 951
Risk Allocation 245
Government Defenses.................... 344
Disclaimer and Exculpatory
Clauses............................. 344
Duty of Coordination............ 359
Sovereign Acts Doctrine 361
Government Promises
(Warranties) of Future Events
or Conditions............................. 246
Access to Site........................ 250
Notice to Proceed.................. 254
Utilities Availability.............. 253
Work Site Availability........... 247
Implied Duty of Good Faith
and Fair Dealing......................... 296
Breach by the Contractor...... 312
Breach by the Government ... 298
Implied Warranty of Specifications ... 272
Causation and Reliance 290
Government Responsibility
Basis 273
Warranty Scope..................... 275
Impracticability of Performance
and Mistake............................... 314
Impracticability..................... 314
Mistake 322
Incorrect Statements and
Nondisclosures........................... 255
Incorrect Statements 256
Nondisclosures...................... 261
Proportional Risk Allocation 369
Concurrent Delays 375
Improper Default Termination....
373
Joint Fault 370
Joint Negligence 372
Rules and Sources of Contract
Administration 16
Deviations and Waivers 28
Deviations 28
Waivers 29
Executive Branch............................ 18
Procurement Regulations........ 18
Publication 22
Regulations' Legal Effect 19
Judicial and Quasi-Judicial
Decisions.................................... 23
Legislative Branch........................... 16
Appropriations and
Authorizations 16
Government Accountability
Office 17
Oversight Function 17

Procurement Legislation......... 17
Statutes and Regulations with
Force and Effect of Law 24
Contract Avoidance................ 24
Exclusion/Inclusion of Clause 26
Government Bound................ 27

S

Setoff.. 1171
Right to 1172
Limitations.................................. 1173
Bid Deposits 1175
Performance-Bond Surety .. 1174
Rights to Payment
Assigned to Financing
Institutions 1173
Separate Debts of Partners
or Joint Venturers 1175
Settlements.. 1076
Nature and Amount...................... 1089
Basic Principles 1089
Overhead, Profit, and Loss
Contracts 1114
Partial Termination 1122
Recoverable Costs 1090
Settlement Expenses........... 1109
Variable Quantity
Contracts/Cost Limitation
Clauses 1120
Procedures 1077
Basis for Proposals 1080
Final Settlement
Negotiation 1084
Obligations of Parties 1077
Time of Proposal
Submission 1082
Unilateral Determination 1086
Short Form 1123
Show Cause Notice 976
Site Conditions. *See* Differing Site
Conditions
Sovereign Acts Doctrine 361
Contract Language Impact 367
Contractual Acts 365
Implementation of Act.................. 365
Public and General Acts 362
"Special Test Equipment," Definition 617
"Special Tooling," Definition 615
Specifications
Defective....................................... 441
Design... 279
Nature of....................................... 816
Brand Name and Proprietary ... 818
Brand Name or Equal 817
Specifications Not Suited
to Strict Compliance 817
Performance.................................. 285
Standard Form 30................................. 405
Strict Compliance Standard 815
Brand Name and Proprietary 818
Brand Name or Equal 817
Construction Contracts 821
First Articles 823
Limitations on............................... 821
Specifications Not Suited to Strict
Compliance 817
Strikes as Cause of Excusable Delay 545
"Substantive Rules" 22
Suits Against Government Employees..... 72

T

Termination. *See* Default Termination;
Right to Terminate; Termination for
Convenience
Termination for Convenience............... 1049
Background................................. 1049
Constructive................................ 1073
Cancellation of Award 1076
Government's Failure
to Perform 1075
Wrongful Default................ 1074
Right to Terminate 1050
Clauses............................... 1050
Deletion of Work 1071
Exercising Right 1053
Finality of 1070
Partial................................. 1068
Procedural Requirements.... 1069
Settlements 1076
Nature and Amount............ 1089
Procedures 1077
Short Form 1123

V

Value Engineering................................ 409
Government Use of Data 425

Interpretation 417
Acceptance of Proposals 423
Applicability of 418
Finality of Contract
Modification 425
Finality of Contracting
Officer's Decision 421
Identification of Proposals
Not Required 422
Liberal v. Literal 417
Origination of Proposed
Change 419
Origination by Two
Contractors 420
Standard Clauses 410
Types of Savings 410
Uses of 415
Unsolicited Proposals 426

W

Waiver 70
Warranty
Government Promises of Future
Events or Conditions 246
Access to Site 250
Notice to Proceed 254
Utilities Availability 253
Work Site Availability 247
Implied Warranty of Specifications ... 272
Causation and Reliance 290
Government Responsibility
Basis 273
Warranty Scope 275
See also Acceptance; Inspection; Post-Acceptance Rights
Weather
As Cause of Excusable Delay 546
Differing Site Conditions 486, 488
Withholding 1166
Government Right 1167
Limitations 1168
"Within the General Scope" 382
Contractor/Government Disputes .. 382
Third-Party Protests 385